A DICTIONARY,
HINDUSTANI & ENGLISH

A DICTIONARY, HINDUSTANI & ENGLISH

ACCOMPANIED BY

A REVERSED DICTIONARY

ENGLISH AND HINDUSTANI.

THE SECOND EDITION

GREATLY ENLARGED, AND MUCH IMPROVED

BY DUNCAN FORBES, LL.D.

PROFESSOR OF ORIENTAL LANGUAGES AND LITERATURE IN KING'S COLLEGE, LONDON; MEMBER OF THE ROYAL ASIATIC SOCIETY OF GREAT BRITAIN AND IRELAND AND AUTHOR OF SEVERAL WORKS TENDING TO FACILITATE THE ACQUISITION OF THE HINDUSTANI AND PERSIAN LANGUAGES

PART I—HINDUSTANI AND ENGLISH.

GYAN

Published by

Gyan Publishing House
5, Ansari Road
Daryaganj, New Delhi-110002
Phone: 011-47034999, 9811692060
E-mail: books@gyanbooks.com

Distribution Network
gyanbooks.com
India, USA, Canada, UK, Australia, France

ISBN : 978-81-212-4423-7 (PB)
First Published, 1866

2nd Impression 2020

Printed at: Gyan Press, Delhi.

A Dictionary, Hindustani & English
Author: Duncan Forbes

A

DICTIONARY,

HINDUSTANI & ENGLISH:

ACCOMPANIED BY

A REVERSED DICTIONARY,

ENGLISH AND HINDUSTANI.

The Second Edition,

GREATLY ENLARGED, AND MUCH IMPROVED.

By DUNCAN FORBES, LL.D.

PROFESSOR OF ORIENTAL LANGUAGES AND LITERATURE IN KING'S COLLEGE, LONDON;
MEMBER OF THE ROYAL ASIATIC SOCIETY OF GREAT BRITAIN AND IRELAND.
AND AUTHOR OF SEVERAL WORKS TENDING TO FACILITATE THE ACQUISITION OF THE HINDUSTANI AND PERSIAN LANGUAGES.

PART I.—HINDUSTANI AND ENGLISH.

LONDON:
WM. H. ALLEN & CO., 13, WATERLOO PLACE. S.W.
PUBLISHERS TO THE INDIA OFFICE.

1866.

PREFACE.

A Dictionary, Hindūstānī and English, accompanied by a reverse part, English and Hindūstānī, has hitherto been a desideratum in this country. It must be obvious to every one that the student of a foreign language, desirous of speaking and writing, as well as reading it, should have not only the words of such foreign language explained in his own, but also the words of his own tongue rendered into that foreign language; and that any Dictionary confined merely to one department is essentially defective.

Thirty years' experience in teaching the Hindūstānī language has convinced me that this deficiency, added to the exorbitant prices charged for Hindūstānī Dictionaries, has greatly impeded learners. I have therefore endeavoured to remove this impediment by compiling a Dictionary of the principal colloquial language of India at once copious, portable, and of a moderate price. These objects have been attained by using a small but clear and distinct letter-press; by employing the Roman character wherever it answered the purpose better than the Oriental; and by excluding every thing not practically useful. By these means I have been enabled in the following work to comprise in a single volume, of convenient dimensions, both parts of a complete Hindūstānī and Hindī Dictionary, including, at the same time, not only more words, but more information really useful to the student, than will be found in any Dictionary of the language hitherto published.

"It is proper that I should here give a brief account of the sources to which I am indebted for the materials of this Dictionary, and of the mode in which I have compiled both its parts. The basis of the first part is the '*Dictionary, Hindoostanee and English,*' in 2 vols. 4to., published by William Hunter, M.D., Calcutta, 1808. Upon this foundation I have superadded at least fifteen thousand words and phrases from the following sources: 1st. A vast number of useful words, both Urdū and Hindī, from the eccentric, but copious vocabulary appended to Dr. Gilchrist's '*Hindee Moral Preceptor,*' 8vo. London, 1821. 2ndly, All the useful words and phrases occurring in Gladwin's '*Dictionary of Mahomedan Law and Bengal Revenue Terms,*' 4to., Calcutta, 1797. 3rdly, A great number of new words from '*A Glossary of Indian Terms,*' 8vo., Agra, 1845, by H. M. Elliot, Esq., Bengal Civil Service. 4thly, Many Persian and Arabic words (which occur in Hindūstānī), from Professor Johnson's last edition of Richardson's '*Persian and Arabic Dictionary.*' 5thly, Several thousands of Hindī words from Dr. Adam's '*Hindī Dictionary,*' 2nd edition, 8vo., Calcutta. 6thly, From the Vocabulary accompanying the '*Prem Sāgar,*' 4to., Calcutta, 1825, I have extracted all such words as were not found in Hunter's Dictionary.

7thly, From Thompson's '*Hindī and English Dictionary*,' royal 8vo., Delhī, 1846, I have culled many pure Hindī or Sanskrit words not to be found in any of the sources above mentioned. 8thly, I have inserted in their proper places all the words occurring in the Appendix to the '*Dukhnee Unwari Soheilee*,' printed at Madras, 1824; also many words from the '*Qanoon e islam*,' by Dr. Herklots, London, 1832. To the materials collected from all the foregoing sources I have added numerous words, phrases, and significations that I have met with in the course of my experience in teaching the language."*

In preparing this Second Edition, neither toil nor expense has been spared on the part of the author and publishers, in order to render it the most complete work of the kind ever offered to the public. The improvements and enlargements now effected are the following—

First. All the words contained in the Hindī Dictionaries of Dr. Adam and Mr. Thomson have, in this edition, been incorporated each in its proper place. By this means the student is now enabled, for the first time, to read by the aid of one single Dictionary, any production that may fall in his way, whether Urdū or Hindī.

Secondly. All Sanskrit and Hindī words are given both in the Persian and Devanāgarī characters; while words from the Arabic and Persian, together with those peculiar to the Dakhan, are given in the Persian character only. This enables the student at a glance to distinguish the words which are purely Indian or Hindū, from those which are Exotic or Musalmān.

Thirdly. I have inserted all the words contained in the Persian text of the Gulistān of Sa'dī, so as to enable the learner, by the aid of my Persian Grammar and this Dictionary alone, to qualify himself for passing the requisite examination in Persian.

Fourthly. To my friend and quondam pupil, Robert B. M. Binning, Esq., of the Madras Civil Service, I am indebted for numerous words and phrases peculiar to the corrupt dialect of the Dakhan, or South India; besides many interesting explanations and definitions of words purely Hindūstānī, that have never before appeared in any Dictionary of the language. These, when of some length, I have, in justice to Mr. Binning, marked with his name or initials; and I feel both pride and pleasure in thus publicly acknowledging how much I have been benefited by that gentleman's kind and disinterested services. At his own request an interleaved copy of the first edition was, some years ago, forwarded to him in India; and the result has been that the same was in due time returned to me, well filled with sound and valuable information.

Fifthly. I have also to express my sincere thanks to Dr. Charles Rieu, of the British Museum, for his able and hearty co-operation throughout, both in preparing the work for the press, and also in correcting the proof sheets as they were issued in the course of printing. Dr. Rieu, with a view to improve, or, more correctly speaking, to complete, his knowledge of the language, has, within the last four or five years, read the following important works; viz. in Urdū—the "*Akhlāqi Hindī*," the "*Khirad-Afroz*," the "*Guli Bakāwalī*," the "*Arā,ishi Maḥfil*," and the "*Ikhwānu-ṣ-Ṣafā*; and in Hindī—the "*Baitāl Pachīsī*," the "*Singhāsan Battīsī*," and the "*Prem Sāgar*." He used an interleaved copy of the first edition of this Dictionary; and marked down in its proper place every word not already included in that work, by which means a multitude of words and phrases has been collected that had hitherto escaped the notice of lexicographers, myself among the number.

* Preface to the First Edition, 1848.

Lastly. I have to acknowledge my obligations to the valuable work recently published by Professor H. H. Wilson, Librarian to the East-India Company, &c. &c., entitled *"A Glossary of Judicial and Revenue Terms, and of useful words occurring in Official Documents relating to the Administration of the Government of British India."* From that work I have here inserted all such words as are Arabic, Persian, Hindūstānī, Sanskrit, or Hindī. Many of them never before appeared in any Dictionary, and a vast number of others may be met with in Dictionaries that have not attached to them the significations they bear in official documents. All such significations I have carefully added where they were wanted; and when the explanations were too long for insertion in full, I have referred the student to Professor Wilson's work for further information.

I have been enabled to save a vast deal of space by making a free and legitimate use of the Roman character, according to a fixed system—that of Sir William Jones. The economy of this plan will be seen at once by a reference to the words آنکھ *āṅkh*, "the eye;" دل *dil*, "the heart;" گل *gul*, "a rose," or to the numerous compounds under the particles بي *be*, نا *nā*, and لا *lā*, &c.; where I have, in one column, given as much matter as the great quarto Dictionaries furnish in four or five. This has been effected by rejecting the Oriental type, which has enabled me to use a much smaller Roman type after the first line of every article. The use of the Roman character in all phrases and compounds, &c. originating from the leading word, as, for example, under آنکھ *āṅkh*, &c., is just as unerring as if the Persian and Devanāgarī characters accompanied it throughout. Every Roman letter has its corresponding symbol in either of the Oriental characters; hence there can be no difficulty or uncertainty in converting any word written in the former into either of the latter. If the reader has the least doubt on this score, he has merely to cast his eye over the following tables.

1st. A Table shewing the correspondence of the vowels in the Persian, Roman, and Devanāgarī characters:—

VOWELS.			INITIAL.			NON-INITIAL.		
Persian.	Roman.	Devanāgarī.	Persian.	Roman.	Devanāgarī.	Persian.	Roman.	Devanāgarī.
ا	*a*	अ	اب	*ab*	अब	بد	*bad*	बद
اِ	*i*	इ	اِس	*is*	इस	دِن	*din*	दिन
اُ	*u*	उ	اُس	*us*	उस	بُت	*but*	बुत
آ	*ā*	आ	آس	*ās*	आस	بات	*bāt*	बात
او	*o*	ओ	اوک	*ok*	ओक	سو	*so*	सो
اُو	*ū*	ऊ	اُود	*ūd*	ऊद	تُو	*tū*	तू
اَو	*au*	औ	اَور	*aur*	और	نَو	*nau*	नौ
اي	*e*	ए	ايک	*ek*	एक	بي	*be*	बे
اِي	*ī*	ई	اِيکھ	*īkh*	ईख	سِي	*sī*	सी
اَي	*ai*	ऐ	اَيسا	*aisā*	ऐसा	هَي	*hai*	है

Let it be remembered, that in all Oriental words *a* is to be sounded short, as in "happy," "America;"—*i*, short, as in "fit," "fin;"—*u*, short, as in "put," "push;"—*ā*, long, as in "war," "water;"—*o*, long, as in "pole," "mole;"—*ū*, long, as in "rule;"—*au*, like our *ou* in "sound," or the German *au* in "haus," a house:—*e*, like our *ea* in "bear," or the French *é* in *dé*, only longer in quantity;—*ī*, long, as in the words "police," "machine;" and—*ai*, like our *i* in fire," "fine," or the German *ai* in "Kaiser," a Cæsar or emperor. The anomalous Sanskrit vowel ऋ *ṛi* is expressed in the Persian character merely by ر (*re* with a *kasra*) and in the Roman character by *ṛi*, sounded as *ri* in "rill," "rip," &c. The Arabic termination ﻪ is represented in the Roman character by *ạ* or *ā̤*, according as its sound is short or long.

2ndly, A Table shewing the agreement of the consonants, Persian, Roman, and Devanagarī—

CONSONANTS.

Persian.	Roman.	Devanāgarī.	Persian.	Roman.	Devanāgarī.	Persian.	Roman.	Devanāgarī.
ب	*b*	ब	د	*d*	द	ظ	*ẓ*	ज़
بھ	*bh*	भ	دھ	*dh*	ध	ع	'	अ &c.
پ	*p*	प	ڈ	*ḍ*	ड	غ	*g͟h*	ग़
پھ	*ph*	फ	ڈھ	*ḍh*	ढ	ف	*f*	फ़
ت	*t*	त	ذ	*ẕ*	ज़	ق	*ḳ*	क़
تھ	*th*	थ	ر	*r*	र	ک	*k*	क
ٹ	*ṭ*	ट	ڑ	*ṛ*	ड़	کھ	*kh*	ख
ٹھ	*ṭh*	ठ	ڑھ	*ṛh*	ढ़	گ	*g*	ग
ث	*s̤*	स़	ز	*z*	ज़	گھ	*gh*	घ
ج	*j*	ज	ژ	*zh*	झ़	ل	*l*	ल
جھ	*jh*	झ	س	*s*	स	م	*m*	म
چ	*ch*	च	ش	*sh*	श	ن	*n*	न
چھ	*chh*	छ	ص	*ṣ*	स़	و	*w*	व
ح	*ḥ*	ह़	ض	*ẓ*	ज़	ه	*h*	ह
خ	*k͟h*	ख़	ط	*t̤*	त़	ي	*y*	य

The Arabic consonant ع is represented in the Roman character by an apostrophe, thus, بعد *ba'd*. This can never lead into error, as the apostrophe is never used (in the Oriental words) for any other purpose. The symbol *hamza* ء of the Persian character is indicated by a similar mark (,) at the bottom of the line, and the imperceptible ه *h* at the end of Persian words is represented by the short vowel *a*, as may be seen in the word فائدہ *fā,ida* "gain or advantage." The nasal sound of the letter ن is indicated in the Roman character by ṅ, and in Devanāgarī by the mark ˙ above the letter with which it is connected: thus, وهاں wahāṅ वहाँ "there;" هنسنا haṅsnā हँसना "to laugh." The terminations an̲, in̲, un̲, denote the Arabic nūnation, and the w̤ denotes the Persian و which in some words is not sounded, as in kẖw̤āh, خواه. Lastly, the u̥ indicates the short sound of و in a few Persian words, as خود kẖu̥d.

3rd. A Table for converting the Devanāgarī characters into the corresponding Persian and Roman characters:—

1st.—INITIAL VOWELS.

अ	आ	इ	ई	उ	ऊ	ऋ	ए	ऐ	ओ	औ
ا	آ	اِ	اِي	اُ	اُو	رِ	اي	اَي	او	اَو
a	ā	i	ī	u	ū	ṛi	e	ai	o	au

2nd.—CONSONANTS.

क	ख	ग	घ	ङ	च	छ	ज	झ	ञ	ट	ठ	ड	ढ
ک	کھ	گ	گھ	ن	چ	چھ	ج	جھ	ن	ٹ	ٹھ	ڈ	ڈھ
k	kh	g	gh	n	ch	chh	j	jh	n	ṭ	ṭh	ḍ	ḍh

ण	त	थ	द	ध	न	प	फ	ब	भ	म	य	र	ल
ن	ت	تھ	د	دھ	ن	پ	پھ	ب	بھ	م	ي	ر	ل
ṇ	t	th	d	dh	n	p	ph	b	bh	m	y	r	l

व	श	ष	स	ह
و	ش	ش or کھ	س	ه
w	sh	sh̤	kh̤	s	h

3rd.—VOWELS FOLLOWING A CONSONANT.

बद	बाद	बिद	बीद	बुद	बूद
بد	باد	بِد	بِيد	بُد	بُود
bad	bād	bid	bīd	bud	būd
बृद	बेद	बैद	बोद	बौद	बः
بِرد	بيد	بَيد	بود	بَود	به
bṛid	bed	baid	bod	baud	ba

It may be observed, that the Devanāgarī letter ड has sometimes the sound of a cerebral ṛ; in which case it is marked with a dot beneath, thus ड़, and corresponds with ڑ or ڙ in the Persian character; as, बड़ा baṛā, "great," بڑا; and in like manner ढ ḍh with a dot beneath becomes ڑھ ṛh, as in बुढ़ापा "old age," بڑھاپا buṛhāpā. The various nasals of the Devanāgarī are represented in the Persian character by the letter ں, which will be found sufficient for all useful purposes. The letter श is generally represented by ش; but sometimes by س; and the letter ष is more frequently کھ than ش. The compound क्ष is generally represented by چھ *chh* or کھ *kh*, more rarely by کش *ksh*, its proper sound. The compound ज्ञ is represented by گی; as, आज्ञा *āgyā* (*ājnā*), آگیا: its real sound is that of *gn* in the French words *champagne*, *ligne*, &c.

It appears, then, that the Devanāgarī alphabet may be represented with tolerable exactness in the Persian character; but the converse does not hold, as the Persi-Arabic alphabet has fourteen letters which have no exact counterpart in the Devanāgarī. The plan adopted in this case is to represent the letters in question by such Nāgarī letters as approximate nearest to them in sound, which in printed books are generally distinguished with a dot underneath; thus,

ق	ف	غ	ع	ظ	ط	ض	ص	ژ	ز	ذ	خ	ح	ث
क़	फ़	ग़	अ़ &c.	ज़	त़	ज़	स़	ज़	ज़	ज़	ख़	ह़	स़

In some printed books, for instance in Dr. Gilchrist's "*Hindee Story-teller*," an attempt has been made to form distinct Devanāgarī letters for the various forms of the Persian and Arabic *z*, which, it will be observed, are all represented by ज़; but in reality the object is not worth the labour. In the first place, the Hindūs, who alone use the Devanāgarī character, are sparing in the use of Persian or Arabic words, to one or other of which the various forms of the letter *z* belong; and secondly, such words as they have in the course of centuries adopted have become naturalized, or rather corrupted, so as to suit the elements of the Nāgarī; thus, حاضری is generally written and sounded हाजिरी *hājirī*. The letter ع is generally represented in Nāgarī by employing the vowel with which it is connected, in the initial form, with a dot under it: as, بعد अ़बद *ba'd*; عِلم इ़लम *'ilm*; عُمر उ़मर *'umr*. This method is sufficient for practical use; but it is by no means satisfactory, as may be seen in the monosyllable बअ़द, which in Persian and Arabic is sounded *ba'd* (the *a* uttered from the bottom of the throat); but according to the rules of the Devanāgarī alphabet it makes *bă'ăd*. In fact, the Hindūs seem to view the letter ع as a vowel, and not as a consonant, which it really is.

In the compilation of the Second Part, my principal authority is Dr. Gilchrist's "*Dictionary, English and Hindoostanee*," 2 vols. 4to. with Appendices, Calcutta, 1798, reprinted, &c. Edinburgh, 1810, in one volume, 4to. The merits of this work have been amply appreciated by Hindūstānī scholars for more than half a century. The first orientalist of the present day speaks of it as "a work of great merit and labour: the collection of Hindūstānī synonyma for every word is singularly full, and peculiarly adapted to a language which, varying in the use of words though not in structure, in every province abounds with synonymous terms, each of local and restricted employment. The whole (edition 1810) is in the Roman character, a singularity in its compilation which alone is indicative of no ordinary industry and perseverance." Such being the case, I have, as a general rule, availed myself of all the words occurring in Dr. Gilchrist's Dictionary, subject, however, to a strict course of correction. In Dr. Gilchrist's early days, the Hindūstānī language was in a manner unformed, and its orthography unsettled: hence, in a multitude of words he gives the long *ū* (oo) instead of the short *u*, and *vice versâ*. I have throughout endeavoured to follow as my guides on this head the standard writers of the language, such as Mīr Amman, in the "*Bāgh o Bahār*;" Ikrām 'Alī, in the "*Ikhwānu-ṣ-ṣafa*," &c. &c. To the very copious collection furnished by Dr. Gilchrist, I have added several thousands of Persian and Arabic words (known to be used in Urdū) from the "*Dictionary, English, Persian, and Arabic*," by Dr. Wilkins, London, 1810, 4to. From Adam's "*Dictionary, English and Hinduwee*," I have extracted many pure Hindī words which escaped the notice of Dr. Gilchrist. I have also found many useful words and phrases in the "*Dictionary, English, Bangālī, and Hindūstānī*," of P. S. D'Rozario, Calcutta, 1837, 8vo. Lastly, I have added numerous synonymous and expressive words and phrases which my own experience has supplied.

It will probably be thought that the Second Part of this Dictionary errs on the side of excess; but I have deemed it the safer course to run the risk of inserting a superfluous or even a *vulgar* word, rather than omit one that could by possibility occur in writing or conversation. It must be recollected that the Hindūstānī is, in more senses than one, a *vulgar tongue*, and that it abounds in a class of words, for the eschewing of which the great Dr. Johnson is said to have been once complimented by some elderly lady, to whom the polite lexicographer replied, "Yes, Madam, I have omitted all such words, but I find that you have been looking for them."

In Part First, compound words are generally to be found under the first or leading member of the compound; at the same time, it is proper to observe that the Hindūstānī language is capable of admitting or forming thousands of compounds not to be found in any dictionary: hence, the learner should bear in mind the more general rules of composition, as laid down in any good grammar of the language. The same remark applies with regard to the rules for derivation, particularly those relating to the formation of causal verbs and abstract nouns.

The few contractions used throughout the work are the following: The letters *a*, *p*, *s*, at the end of many definitions, denote that the word is from the Arabic, Persian, or Sanskrit respectively; the letter *h* distinguishes such words as are aboriginal or purely Indian; and *d* such as are peculiar to the Deccan (dakhan): the few words marked *t* and *g* are of Tartarian and Greek origin respectively. The other contractions are, m. denoting the masculine gender; f. feminine; a. an active or transitive verb; and n. a verb neuter. The letter v. imports vide, and pl. the plural number.

In Part Second, and occasionally in Part First, the following contractions are used in the formation of compound verbs: *k*, for *karnā* (or the Persian *kardan*), "to make;" *h*, for *honā*, "to be, to become;" *j*, for *jānā*, "to go, to be;" *r*, for *rakhnā*, "to keep, to have;" *d*, for *denā*, "to give;" *l*, for *lenā*, "to take;" *ḍ*, for *ḍālnā*, "to throw;" and *b*, for *bāndhnā*, "to bind." These, with the exception of the first two, are chiefly used in the formation of intensives, and consequently they have then laid aside their own primitive signification. As a general rule, compound words have their parts or members separated by a hyphen, thus, *dil-nishīn*, *tan-durust*, *sar-gardān*, &c. Such compounds, when transferred into the Oriental characters, are optionally written entire as one word, or distinct as two. The short *i*, denoting the Persian *iẓāfat*, is indifferently written either as the last letter of the governing word, or separately between the two words, as *dardi sar* or *dard i sar*, the sense being abundantly obvious either way, as no Persian word ends in the short *i* except it be in a state of construction with the substantive or adjective following.

I have avoided cross references, which are very embarrassing to the learner, retaining only those in which the word referred to is either close at hand, or is attended by a long explanation which it would be needless to repeat.

Some good-natured friends have occasionally expressed to me their regret that the Second Part of the work had not been given in the Persian character. Had it been so, I must either, in the first place, have added the pronunciation in Roman characters to each word (otherwise the work would be utterly useless), and this would have increased its size to at least six times what it now is; or, in the second place, omitting the Roman character, I must have given all the vowel marks and other orthographical symbols, which would have extended it to at least ten times its actual bulk, without possessing one single advantage over what it now has.*

In conclusion, I have only to add, that amidst such a mass of small letters, it will not seem surprising that an occasional error of the press should occur. I trust, however, that the number of such errors is small; and I am confident that the generous, the learned, and the experienced (and it is only *their* good opinion I am ambitious to obtain) will not deny me their kind indulgence.

---

* Two lines of even the smallest Oriental types in this country would occupy at least as much space as five lines of the Roman character used in Part II. of this work. If the vowel-points, &c. be used, the spaces between the lines must be nearly doubled: hence the truth of the above remark will be obvious to those at all conversant with Oriental typography.

DUNCAN FORBES.

58, BURTON CRESCENT,
January, 1857.

A DICTIONARY,

HINDŪSTĀNĪ AND ENGLISH.

ا

ا *alif*, the first letter of the Arabic alphabet; in numeration it counts one. अ *a* or *a-kāra*, the first elementary sound in the Sanskrit alphabet; it is a name of God, or *Vishnu*. As an inseparable particle prefixed to a word, it signifies negation or privation; as, *a-dharm*, injustice, or irreligion, from *dharm*, justice, &c. It is akin to the *alpha privativum* of the Greek, the *in* of the Latin, or the *un* of the German and English. As in Greek, it becomes *an* before a vowel, as *an-anta*, endless, or without end.

اب अब *ab*, now, presently, just now, a little while ago; by adding *kā, ke, kī*, it forms an adjective, as *ab-kā zamānā*, the present time. *h.*

اب इब *ib*, thus, as, in like manner. *s.*

اب *ab* (contract. from ابو), a father. In Hindūstānī, the plural is of most frequent occurrence, as in *ābā o ajdād*, fathers and grandfathers, ancestors. *a.*

آب *āb*, m. water, splendour, elegance, dignity, lustre (in gems), temper (of steel, &c.), edge, sharpness (of a sword, &c.). The word *āb* in Persian is used in a great many metaphoric and idiomatic expressions. *p.*

ابا *ibā*, m. denial; *ibā-k*, to refuse, deny. *a.*

آبا *ābā*, fathers (pl. of اب or ابو, q. v.). *a.*

ابابيل *abābīl*, m, a swallow. *a.*

اباحت *ibāḥat*, f. permitting, giving liberty. *a.*

آباد *ābād*, cultivated, peopled, pleasant; full of buildings and inhabitants; used in composition in the sense of city or *ville*, as *akbar-ābād*, the city of Akbar, or (as the Americans would say) *Akbar-ville*, the city of Agra. *p.*

آبادان *ābādān*, synonymous with *ābād*. *p.*

آباداني *ābādānī*, f. a habitation, a cultivated, populous, pleasant place; population, cultivation, abundance. In Hindūstānī it is seldom used except in poetry, *ābādī* being the common expression. *p.*

آباد بيشي *ābād-beshī*, f. first assessment of newly-settled or cultivated land. *p.*

آبادكار *ābād-kār*, the original or first settler on waste land. *p.*

آباد كرنا *ābād karnā*, a. to build, cultivate, make a place habitable and populous. *p.*

آبادها आबाधा *ābādhā*, f. segment of the base of a triangle. *s.*

آبادي *ābādī*, synonymous with *ābādānī*. *p.*

ابت

ابارنا उबारना *ubārnā*, a. to set at liberty. *s.*

ابارنا उबारना *ubārnā*, a. to keep in reserve. *h.*

اباك अबाक *a-bāk*, dumb, speechless. *s.*

اباكنا उबाकना *ubāknā*, a. to vomit, reject. *h.*

ابالنا उबालना *ubālnā*, a. to boil, to make boil. *h.*

آبان *ābān*, m. the eighth month of the Persian year. *p.*

ابانا उबाना *ubānā*, a. to sow, to plant. *h.*

آبائی *ābā,ī*, belonging to or descending from one's ancestors, paternal. *a.*

آب باران *āb i bārān*, m. rain-water. *p.*

آب بازي *āb-bāzī*, f. play or sport in water; swimming. *p.*

آب بسته *ābi basta*, m. ice, glass. *p.*

اببيك अबिबेक *a-bibek*, m. want of discrimination; *abibekī*, indiscreet; *abibekatā*, folly. *s.*

آب پاشي *āb-pāshī*, f. sprinkling water on fields, &c. *p.*

آبتاب *āb-tāb*, f. splendour; also *āb o tāb*. *p.*

ابتب *ab-tab*, presently; *ab-tab h.* to be in a dying state, to be all over with one. *h.*

آبتابه *ābtāba*, m. an ewer; generally written *āftāba*, and sometimes *āftāwa*. *p.*

ابتدا *ibtidā*, f. beginning, commencement, exordium. *a.*

ابتداءً *ibtidā,an*, in the beginning, at first, in the first place. *a.*

ابتذال *ibtiẕāl*, m. vileness, meanness, servitude; carelessness in preserving any thing. *a.*

ابتر *abtar*, worthless, spoiled, wanton, dissolute; *abtarī*, worthlessness. *a.*

ابتسام *ibtisām*, m. cheerfulness, a smile. *a.*

ابتك *ab-tak*,
ابتلك *ab-talak*,
ابتلگ *ab-talag*,
ابتوري *ab-torī*,
ابتوڑي *ab-toṛī*,
} till now, hitherto, yet, up to the present time, as yet, still, notwithstanding. *h.*

ابتلا *ibtilā*, m. suffering, misfortune. *a.*

ابتهاج *ibtihāj*, m. gladness, alacrity, cheerfulness. *a.*

ابتئں अबतईं *ab-ta,īṅ*, till now, till this time. *h.*

ابتیں अबतें *ab-teṅ*, from this time, hence. *h.*

ابٹن उबटन *ubṭan*, m. a detergent substance for rubbing on the body; a cosmetic: also *ubaṭ*, or *ubṭi*, or *ubṭanā*, same as *upṭan*, q. v. *h.*

ابٹنا *ubaṭnā*, a. to rub on the body the cosmetic *ubṭan* or *upṭan*. *h.*

ابج अब्ज *abja*, m. the nymphæa or lotus; the moon; a conch; a species of tree. *s.*

آب جاري *ābi-jārī*, m. running water, a stream, rivulet, tears flowing. *p. a.*

ابجد *abjad*, m. the alphabet; a mode of reckoning numbers by the letters of the alphabet; the first letter counting one, the second two, &c., according to their ancient arrangement.—Vide Persian Grammar, p. 23, or Hindūstānī Grammar, p. 20. *a.*

ابجدخوان *abjad-khwān*, m. one who is learning his alphabet. *a. p.*

آبجو *āb-jo*, f. a rivulet or streamlet. *p.*

آب جوش *āb-josh*, m. gravy, soup. *p.*

آب جوي *ābi jo,e*, f. the water of a rivulet. *p.*

ابچ अबच *a-bach*, that which has not escaped. *h.*

ابچار अबिचार *a-bichār*, m. want of consideration, injustice. *s.*

ابچاري *a-bichārī*, m. *a-bichārin*, f. an unjust man or woman, or a man or woman destitute of consideration or reflection. *s.*

آب چڑھانا *āb-chaṛhānā*, a. to whet or polish one's sword, &c. *p. h.*

آب چشم *ābi chashm*, m. water of the eye, tears. *p.*

آب چشي *āb-chashī*, f. giving drink to a child for the first time (generally about six months of age) preparatory to weaning him. *p.*

ابچل अबिचल *a-bichal*, motionless, unmoved, unshaken, resolute, firm. *s.*

ابچھرا अबछरा *abchharā*, f. a female dancer in the court of Indra; also *apchharā* and *apsarā*, q.v. *s*

آب حرام *ābi ḥarām*, forbidden water, *i. e.* wine; insincere or hypocritical tears. *p. a.*

آب حسرت *ābi ḥasrat*, m. water of desire, wish, appetite, longing. *p. a.*

آب حيات *ābi ḥayāt*, m. the water of life, immortality. *p. a.*

آب حيوان *ābi ḥaiwān*, m. water of life; a fabulous fountain so called. *p. a.*

آب خانه *āb-khāna*, m. a repository of water, a reservoir; a cellar. *p.*

ابخره *abkhira* (pl. of بخار), m. vapours, exhalations. *a.*

آب خست *āb-khast*, a water melon or cucumber. *p.*

آب خضر *ābi khiẓr*, water of immortality; inspired knowledge. *p. a.*

ابخل *abkhal*, very or more avaricious. *a.*

آب خور *āb-khur*, } m. victuals, food and
آب خورد *āb-khurd*, } drink; fortune. *p.*

آب خوره *āb-khura*, m. a narrow-mouthed vessel for drinking out of, a cup for drinking water. *p.*

ابد *abad*, m. eternity, without end. *a.*

ابدًا *abadan*, eternally, for ever; never. *a.*

آبدار *āb-dār*, m. the person intrusted with the charge of water for drinking. adj. polished, of a good water (as gems), well tempered (as steel). *p.*

آبدارخانه *āb-dār-khāna*, m. a repository of drinking-water. *p.*

آبداري *āb-dārī*, f. sharpness (of a sword, &c.); polish (of gems); office of *ābdār*. *p.*

ابداع *ibdā'*, m. the production of something new. *a.*

ابدال *ibdāl*, m. change, exchange, substituting one thing for another. *a.*

ابدال *abdāl*, m. a religious person, devotee, enthusiast. *abdālī*, of or relating to a devotee; an epithet assumed by *Aḥmad*, the founder of the late Afghān dynasty. *a.*

آب‌دانه *āb-dāna*, m. food and drink: also *āb o dāna*. *p.*

آب‌دست *āb-dast*, m. washing the hands (particularly after any unclean action). *p.*

آب‌دندان *ābi dandān*, m. sharpness and polish of the teeth; debility. *p.*

ابده अबध *a-badh*, sacred, inviolable. *s.*

ابده अबुध or अबुद्धि *a-budh* or *a-buddhi*, stupid, ignorant; also s. f. ignorance. *s.*

ابدها अबधा *abdhā*, f. a segment of the base of a triangle. *s.*

ابدهمان अबुद्धिमान *a-buddhimān*, stupid, unintelligent. *s*

ابدهوت अबधूत *abdhūt*, m. a kind of *faḳīr* or devotee. This class are worshippers of Shiva. fem. *abdhūtnī*. *s.*

ابدهي अबध्य *a-badhya*, not deserving death, not to be slain, inviolable. *s.*

ابدي *abadī*, eternal, without end. *a.*

ابديا अबिद्या *a-bidyā*, f. ignorance. *s.*

آبديده هونا *āb-dīda honā*, to shed tears. *p. h.*

ابر *abr*, m. a cloud. *abri siyāh*, a black cloud. *abri ghalīẓ*, a thick cloud. *abri āẕur*, a cloud without rain. *p.*

ابر अबर *abar*, now, at present. *h.*

ابرا अबरा *abrā*, m. the outer fold of a double garment; distinguished from *astar*, the lining. Written also *abrā*, q. v. *h.*

ابرار *abrār* (pl. of برّ), just men, holy, pious, dutiful (to parents). *ibrār*, victory superiority. *a.*

ابرانا *ubrānā*, a. to keep in reserve. (same as *ubārnā*). *h.*

ابراهيم *Ibrāhīm*, the patriarch Abraham. *Ibrāhīm Adham*, name of a pious sovereign that formerly reigned at *Balkh*. *a.*

ابرد *abrad*, colder, most or very cold. *a.*

ابرص *abraṣ*, leprous. *a.*

ابرق *abraḳ* or ابرك *abrak*, m. talc, mica. *a.*

ابرنا उबरना *ubarnā*, n. to be kept in reserve, to remain over. *h.*

آبشار *āb-shār*, m. f. a waterfall, cascade, cataract. *p.*

آب شناس *āb-shinās*, the lead-man, or person who takes the soundings in a ship, a pilot. *p.*

آب شور *āb i shor*, m. brackish or salt water. *p.*

آب شوره *āb-shora* or *ābi-shora*, m. water cooled artificially by means of a solution of saltpetre; iced sherbet. *p.*

آبشولا *ābsholā* (Dakh.), same as *ābshora*. *p.*

ابشیك *a-bishek* or ابکهیك *abikhek*, m. sprinkling-water, which the Hindūs (after pronouncing certain prayers over it) use for cleansing their persons, and other utensils used in sacrifice, holy water; accession to a throne, inauguration. v. *abhishek*. *s.*

ابصار *abṣār* (pl. of بصر), views, looks; perception, understanding. *a.*

ابطال *ibṭāl*, m. abolition, act of destroying or annihilating, refuting. *a.*

ابطل *abṭal*, comp. more vain or fruitless, very vain, &c. *a.*

ابعاد *ab'ād* (pl. of بعد), distances, divarications. *a.*

ابعد *ab'ad*, more distant, very far. *a.*

آب عشرت *ābi 'ashrat*, wine, *semen genitale*. *p.a.*

ابقا *ibḳā*, m. confirmation, establishment, preservation, rendering permanent. *a.*

ابکا *ab-kā*, *ab-ke*, and *ab-kī*, of or belonging to the present time, from *ab*. *h.*

آبکار *āb-kār*, m. a distiller (particularly of spirituous liquors); a water-carrier, a sprinkler; a wine-merchant, or seller of spirituous liquors; a drinker of wine. *p.*

آبکاري *āb-kārī*, f. the business of a distiller; revenue derived from a duty levied on distilleries, also on houses for the sale of spirituous liquors, eating-houses, houses of entertainment, &c.

ابکانا उबकाना *ubkānā*, a. to cause one to vomit. *h.*

ابکائي उबकाई *ubkā,ī*, f. the act of vomiting. *h.*

ابکت अविक्त *a-bikt*, hidden, unintelligible. *s.*

ابکت گنت अविक्तगणित *a-bikt ganit*, f. arithmetic of unknown quantities; algebra. *s.*

آب کش *āb-kash*, a drawer of water; *āb-kashī*, act of drawing or carrying water. *p.*

ابکنا उबकना *ubaknā*, n. to vomit. *h.*

آب کوثر *ābi-kausar*, m. nectar. *p. a.*

ابکیشي अबकेशी *abkeshī*, without fruit, barren (tree). *s.*

آبگذار *āb-guzār*, a ford, a ferry; an express. *p.*

آبگذر *āb-guzar*, a canal or channel for water. *p.*

آب گرم *ābi garm*, warm water, a hot-bath. *p.*

آب گوشت *ābi gosht*, soup, gravy, broth. *p.*

آب گوهر *ābi gohar*, water of pearls, pure limpid water. *p.*

آب گیر *āb-gīr*, a receptacle for water, a pool, pond, ditch; a weaver's brush. *p.*

ابرنجن *abranjan*, ابرنجین *abranjīn*, a bracelet, an ankle ornament of gold or silver. *p.*

ابرو *abrū*, f. the eye-brow. *abrū par girih mārnī*, a. to frown. *p.*

آبرو *ābrū*, f. honour, character, renown, elegance; the name of a poet. *ābrū-utārnā*, a. to dishonour, disgrace. *ābrū-bar-bād-denā*, a. to lose one's own character, or destroy that of another. *ābrū-denī*, a. to bestow honour or reputation on any one, or to surrender or lose one's own. *ābrū-rez*, a calumniator. *ābrū-rezī*, f. slander, calumny. *ābrū-karnī*, a. to treat with respect. *ābrū-lenī*, a. to take away one's character or reputation. *p.*

آبروان *āb-rawān*, m. a very fine kind of muslin or gauze, which when spread out on the grass is said to have been scarcely visible. The art of manufacturing this stuff is now lost. *p.*

ابرودھ *a-birodh*, m. quietness, tranquillity. *s.*

ابرودھني अविरोधिनी *a-birodhinī*, ابرودھي अविरोधी *a-birodhī*, quiet, tranquil. *s.*

ابره *abra*, m. the outside of a garment; same as *abrā*. *p.*

آبرهن *ābarhan* (*vide* آبهرن), m. ornaments, jewels, &c. *s.*

ابري *abrī*, clouded, variegated. *abrī kāghaz*, a kind of thick and shining paper clouded, (from Cashmir). *p.*

آبریز *āb-rez*, a pot for sprinkling water, such as a gardener's; used also in baths for pouring water over the body. *p.*

آبریشم *ābresham* (also *abresham*), m. sewing silk. *p.*

آبریشمي *ābreshmī*, silken, made of silk. *p.*

ابریق *ibrīḳ*, m. an ewer, a water-pot. *a.*

ابڑدھبڑ *abaṛ-dhabaṛ*, coarse, rough, common. *h.*

آب زر *ābi-zar*, water of gold; white wine. *p.*

آب زلال *ābi zulāl*, m. pure limpid water. *p.a.*

ابس अवश *a-bas*, powerless, without choice. *s.*

آبسال *ābsāl*, m. a vineyard, a garden. *p.*

آبسته *ābista*, pregnant (a woman), with young (an animal), new-born (a child). The forms *ābist*, *ābistan*, and *ābistān* are given in Gilchrist. *p.*

آبستگي *ābistagī*, also *ābistanī*, &c. f. pregnancy. *p.*

ابسن अवसन *a-basan*, naked, without clothes. *s.*

ابسن अविसन *a-bisan*, without desire, indifferent. *s.*

ابسنا उबसना *ubasnā*, n. to rot, putrefy. *h.*

ابسواس अविस्वास or अविश्वास *a-biswās*, m. want of confidence, distrustfulness. *s.*

ابسواسي *a-biswāsī*, *abiswāsin*, *abiswāsinī*, distrustful. *s.*

ابسانا *ubsānā*, a. to cause to rot. *h.*

اب سون *ab-soṅ*, اب سي *ab-se*, from this time. *h.*

ابسي دور *ab-se dūr*, is an expression of those who, after describing a past misfortune, pray to be preserved from a repetition of it; q.d. Far be it from us! *h. p.*

آبگينه *ābgina*, m. a mirror, looking-glass, a drinking-glass; wine; a diamond. *p.*

ابل अबल *a-bal*, weak, without strength or power *s.*

ابلا अबला *a-balā*, f. weak, powerless; a woman. *s.*

ابلاپا अबलापा *a-balāpā*, m. weakness, frailty. *s.*

ابلاغ *iblāgh*, m. conveying, sending, causing to arrive. *a.*

ابلانا उबलाना *ublānā*, a. to cause to boil, (by the hands of another); to boil any thing so as to be fit to eat; to cook. *h.*

ابلاي अबलाई *a-balā,ī*, f. weakness, debility. *s.*

ابلق *ablaḳ*, piebald, black and white, party-coloured. *a.*

ابلقا *ablaḳā*, m. a bird of the maina kind, a starling. *a.*

ابلمب अबिलम्ब *a-bilamb*, m. quickness, diligence. *s.*

ابلنا उबलना *ubalnā*, n. to boil or bubble up. *h.*

آبلوج *ablūj* (also *ablūch*), sugar-candy. *p.*

آبله *ābila*, m. a blister. *p.*

آبلهٔ فرنگ *ābila,i farang*, m. the French pox, a bubo. *p.*

ابله *ablah*, foolish, silly, ignorant, bashful. *a.*

ابلهي *ablahī*, f. folly, silliness. *a.*

ابلي अबली *abalī*, f. a row, a range, a continuous line. *s.*

ابلي अबली *a-balī*, weak, powerless. *s.*

ابليس *iblīs*, the devil, Satan. *a.*

ابن *ibn*, m. a son, a child; *ibnu-s-sabīl*, a son of the road, a traveller; *ibnu-l-gharaz*, a selfish person; *ibnu-l-ghaib*, one of whom little is known, a parvenu. *a.*

ابنا *abnā*, (pl. of ابن) sons; people; tribes. *a.*

ابناس अबिनास *a-bināas*, m. safety. s.

ابناسي *a-bināsī*, safe, entire, free from loss. *s.*

ابن الوقت *ibn-ul-waḳt*, a time-server. *a.*

ابناء جنس *abnā,i jins*, pl. companions, comrades, equals; those of the same rank, quality, or species. *n.* *abnā,e dahr*, or *abnā,e rozgār*, sons of the time, contemporaries. *a. p.*

ابندو अबिन्दु *a-bindu*, without point or dot. *s.*

آب نقره *ābi nuḳra*, m. quicksilver. *p. a.*

آبنوس *ābnūs*, m. ebony. *p.*

آبنوسي *ābnūsī*, made of ebony. *p.*

ابني अबनी *abnī*, f. the earth, world. *s.*

آب ني *āb-nai*, m. the straight tube of a *ḥuḳḳa*, on which the chillam is fixed. *p.*

ابني अबिनय *a-binai*, m. wantonness, pertness. *s.*

ابنيت अबिनीत *a-binīt*, wanton, pert, petulant. *s.*

ابو *abū*, m. father; the word is frequently used as the first member of a man's name or epithet, thus, *abū-l-bashar*, the father of the human race, Adam. *abū-bakr*, the father-in-law and first successor to Muhammad. *abū-turāb*, 'Alī, the son-in-law of Muhammad. *abū-l-fazl*, the name of the secretary to the Emperor Akbar, *abū-jahl*, the name of an uncle of Muhammad, noted for his stubbornness. *abū huraira*, one of the companions of Muhammad, *abū-'alī sinā*, a celebrated sage and physician, commonly known in Christendom as Avicenna. *abū -fawāris*, the ass, lit. the father of horsemen. *abū-bakr*, the name of an *atābak* prince to whom *Sa'dī* dedicated his Gulistan. *abū-naṣr*, the name of the minister of the last mentioned prince. *a.*

ابواب *abwāb* (pl. of باب), doors, gates, chapters, sections; in the revenue language of India the word means almost any kind of cesses, imposts, and charges levied by the officials of government. *a.*

ابوجه अबूझ *a-būjh*, stupid, without understanding. *s.*

ابوجها अबूझा *a-būjhā*, not understood, incomprehensible. *h.*

ابوده अबोध *a-bodh*, m. ignorance, stupidity. adj. ignorant, stupid; puzzled, perplexed. *s.*

ابودهگميه अबोधगम्य *a-bodh-gamya*,
ابودهنيه अबोधनीय *a-bodhanīya*, } incomprehensible, unintelligible. *s.*

ابول अबोल *a-bol*, silent. *h.*

ابولا अबोला *a-bolā*, disposed or accustomed to silence. *h.*

آب ودانه *āb o dāna*, water and grain, food and drink. *p.*

آب وهوا *āb o hawā*, f. atmosphere, air, climate. *p. a.*

ابه अभि *abhi*, a particle denoting priority in time or place, prefixed to Sanskrit words. *s.*

ابه इभ *ibh* or *ibha*, m. an elephant. *ibha-pālak*, the keeper of an elephant. *s.*

آبها आभा *ābhā*, f. light, splendour, beauty. *s.*

ابهار अभार *a-bhār*, light, of little weight. *s.*

ابهار उभार *ubhār*, m. swelling, tumefaction, plumpness. *h.*

ابهارنا उभारना *ubhārnā*, a. to raise up, to excite, to persuade, to plump up. *h.*

ابهاڑنا उभाड़ना *ubhāṛnā*, a. to take away, to steal. *h.*

آبهاس आभास *ābhās*,
آبهاش आभाष *ābhāsh*, } m. a preface, a preamble, an introduction, &c. *s.*

ابهاگ अभाग *a-bhāg*, also *a-bhāgya*, m. misfortune, ill-luck. *s.*

ابهاگا अभागा *a-bhāgā*, also *a-bhāginī* and *a-bhāgī*, unfortunate, destitute. *s.*

ابهال अभाल *abhāl*, m. a cloud. *h.*

ابهام *ibhām*, m. the thumb; suspicion, ambiguity; covered, concealed, unknown. *a.*

ابهانا उभाना *ubhānā*, a. to alarm, disturb. *h.*

ابهاو अभाव *a-bhā,o*, m. absence, non-existence, want; as in this proverb, *rājā ke ghar men, kyā motiyon kā abhā,o?* Is there a want of pearls in the raja's house? *s.*

ابهباد अभिबाद *abhibād*, m. act of kissing the feet or of worshipping, an obeisance; also an insult. *s.* [as *abhibād*. *s.*

ابهبادن अभिबादन, *abhibādan*, m. the same

ابهبهوت अभिभूत *abhibhūta*, subdued, domineered over. *s.*

ابهپراي अभिप्राय *abhiprāy*, m. sentiment, intention, opinion, design, wish, purpose; the main purport of a book, &c. *s.*

ابهجت अभिजित *abhijit*, m. the 21st *nakshatra*, or lunar asterism; the 8th *muhūrt*, or division of the day. *s.* [spell causing death or disease. *s.*

ابهچار अभिचार *abhichār*, m. a charm or

ابهدهان अभिधान *abhidhān*, m. a dictionary. Strictly speaking, it denotes a list of the substantives of the Sanskrit language, such as the "Amara Kosha," &c. *s.*

ابهر अभ्र *abhra*, m. the sky, a cloud. *s.*

ابهرا उभरा *ubhrā*, unladen (as a cart or boat). *h.* [till it run over. *h.*

ابهرانا उभराना *ubhrānā*, a. to fill a vessel

ابهرك अभ्रक *abhrak*, m. talc, mica. *s.*

ابهركي *abhrakī*, made of talc or mica. *s.*

ابهرم अभरम *a-bharam*, without respect. *s.*

آبهرن आभरन *ābharan*, m. jewels, ornaments, decoration; also *abharan*, with the initial vowel short. *s.*

ابهرنا उभरना *ubharnā*, n. to overflow. *h.*

آبهس आभस *ābhas*, little, few. *s.*

ابهساركا अभिसारिका *abhisārikā*, also *abhisārī* and *abhisārinī*, f. (a woman) going to an assignation with her lover, a lewd woman. *s.*

ابهشكت अभिषिक्त *abhishikta*, installed, baptized, anointed to office, enthroned. *s.*

ابهشيك अभिषेक *abhishek*, m. bathing, anointing, royal unction; a religious ceremony consisting in sprinkling a person with the water of the Ganges. *s.*

ابهك उभक *ubhak*, m. a bear. *h.*

ابهكت अभक्ति *a-bhakti*, f. disregard, want of desire, indifference, unbelief. *s.*

ابهكتمان *a-bhaktimān*, unbelieving, indifferent to. *s.*

ابهلاش अभिलाष *abhilāsh*, m. and *abhilāshā*, f. wish, desire; (generally written *abhilākh*). *s.*

ابهلاشي अभिलाषी *abhilāshī*, wishing, desiring, longing for. *s.* [sire. *s.*

ابهلاكه *abhilākh* or *abhilākhā*, m. wish, de-

ابهمان अभिमान *abhimān*, m. pride, haughtiness, self-conceit. *s.*

ابهمان پتر अभिमानपुत्र *abhimāna-putra*, m. a foster-son. *s.* [arrogance. *s.*

ابهمانتا अभिमानता *abhimānatā*, f. pride,

ابهماني *abhimānī* or *abhimānya*, proud, conceited. *s.*

ابهمت अभिमत *abhimat*, consented to, approved of, chosen, agreed, accepted. *s.*

ابهمتتا अभिमतता *abhimatatā* or *abhimattā*, f. desire, love. *s.*

ابهمكه अभिमुख *abhimukh*, present, before. *s.*

ابهمكهتا अभिमुखता *abhimukhatā*, f. presence, proximity. *s.*

ابهنو अभिनव *abhinav*, new, quite new. *s.*

ابهواد अभिवाद *abhivād*, m. abusive language. *s.* [stration. *s.*

ابهوادن अभिवादन *abhivādan*, m. bow, pro-

ابهوت अभूत *a-bhūt*, non-existent. *s.*

ابهوج अभोज *a-bhoj*, also *a-bhojya*, unfit to eat, not eatable. *s.* [fasting. *s.*

ابهوجي अभोजी *a-bhojī*, not having eaten,

آبهوشن आभूषन *ābhūshan*, m. ornaments, jewellery, finery. *s.* (Commonly written in the Persian characters as follows):

آبهوكهن *ābhūkhan*, m. jewels, ornaments. *s.*

ابهوگ अभोग *a-bhog*, unfit for use, unpossessed. *s.*

ابهون अभूं *ab-hūn*, hitherto, yet. *h.*

ابهي अभी *ab-hī*, even now, just now. *h.*

ابهي अभय *a-bhay*, without fear, fearless. *s.*

ابهي उभय *ubhaya*, both (used in Sanskrit phrases.) [yellow myrobalan. *s.*

ابهيا अभया *abhayā*, f. name of a flower, the

ابهياس अभ्यास *abhyās*, m. practice, meditation, study, the frequent repetition of a thing in order to fix it on the memory. *s.*

ابهياسي अभ्यासी *abhyāsī*, studious, practising, repeating. *s.*

ابهياگت अभ्यागत *abhyāgat*, m. a guest, a visitor; arrived. *s.*

ابهيپتر अभयपत्र *abhaya-patra*, } m. assurance
ابهيدان अभयदान *abhaya-dān*, } of safety or
ابهيواك अभयवाक् *abhaya-vāk*, } protection,
an amnesty. *s.* [unalarmed. *s.*

ابهيت अभीत *a-bhīta*, fearless, undaunted,

ابهيت अभीति *a-bhīti*, f. fearlessness. *s.*

ابهيپست अभीप्सित *abhīpsit*, } loved, wish-
ابهيشٹ अभीष्ट *abhīshṭa*, } ed for. *s.*

ابهيچ *abhīch* (dakh.), same as *abhī*, now, just now

ابهيد अभेद *a-bhed*, } united, fastened toge-
ابهيو अभेव *a-bhew*, } ther, known, celebrated. *s.*

آبهير आभीर *ābhīr*, m. a cow-herd. *s.*

آبي *ābī*, of or belonging to water, aquatic, watery, moist, humid. *p.*

ابي अबे *abe*, an interjection of vocation expressive of scorn, as Sirrah! *h.*

ابي abī, now (sometimes used for ab-hī). h.

ابيات abyāt (plur. of بيت), houses, (and more usual) distichs, verses. a.

آبيار āb-yār, m. a waterer, a sprinkler. p.

آبياري āb-yārī, f. irrigation; a kind of thin linen cloth; a species of dove. p.

ابيج अबीज a-bīj, grain that does not germinate. s.

ابير अबेर a-ber, f. delay; late, unseasonable. s.

ابير अबीर abīr, m. red powder used at the holī Saturnalia. s.

ابيض abyaz, white, very splendid or shining. s

اپ अप apa, a Sanskrit particle; prefixed to words it denotes inferiority, privation, separation. It is much used in compound words from the Sanskrit, as apādān, m. taking away, the ablative case in grammar; apāng, m. the outer corner of the eye; apabhāshā, f. the vulgar tongue; also applied to the language of foreigners; apabhansh, f. ungrammatical language; apachay, m. loss, diminution; apashabd, m. vulgarisms, slang; apakrisht, worthless, little, vile; apakarma, m. a bad action, misconduct; apamrityu, f. sudden death, dying without any disease; apavād, m. censure, blame; apavādī, censorious; apahartā, m. a robber, a thief; apaharan, m. seizing forcibly, carrying off; apahnav, m. concealment. s.

اپ उप upa, a Sanskrit particle, denoting vicinity, or resemblance in an inferior degree, as upaveda, the sub-veda or minor veda.

آپ आप āp, pron. self, yourself, used instead of the personal pronoun of the second person by an inferior when addressing his superior. h.

آپ आप āp, m. water. s.

آپا आपा āpā, f. an elder sister; self. h.

اپاپ अपाप a-pāp, guiltless, without crime. s.

آپ آپ āp-āp, m. selfishness, egotism. h.

اپاتر अपात्र a-pātr, unfit, unworthy. s.

اپادان अपादान apādān, m. taking away; the ablative case in grammar. s.

اپادان उपादान upādān, m. cause, motive. s.

اپادھ उपाध upādh, f. violence, injury, injustice. s.

اپادھ उपाधि upādhi, m. a virtuous reflection; deception, disguise; a nickname. s.

اپادهي उपाधी upādhī, violent, unjust. s.

اپادهياي उपाध्याय upādhyāy, m. a spiritual preceptor. s.

اپادهيايا उपाध्याया upādhyāyā,
اپادهيايي उपाध्यायी upādhyāyī,
اپادهياني उपाध्यानी upādhyānī, } f. an instructress, the wife of a spiritual preceptor. s.

اپار अपार a-pār, boundless, excessive. s.

اپار ipār, thyme, wild marjoram. p.

اپارجت उपार्जित upārjit, acquired, gained. s.

اپارجن उपार्जन upārjan, m. acquiring, gaining. s.

اپاڑنا उपाड़ना upāṛnā, a. to root up, extirpate, eradicate. s.

اپاس उपास upās, m. a fast, hunger. s.

اپاسا उपासा upāsā, hungry, one who fasts. s.

اپاسك उपासक upāsak, a worshipper, a servant. s.

اپاسنا उपासना upāsanā, f. reverence, worship, attendance; v. to reverence. s.

اپاسي उपासी upāsī, serving, worshipping. s.

اپاسيه उपास्य upāsya, worthy of reverence. s.

اپاشريه अपाश्रय apāshraya, helpless, destitute, without shelter. s.

اپاك अपाक a-pāk, raw, unripe, undressed. s.

اپاكهيان उपाख्यान upākhyān, m. an old story, a legend. s.

اپالنبھ उपालम्भ upālambh, m. abuse; delaying. s.

اپان अपान apān, m. emission of wind (backwards). s.

اپانا उपाना upānā, a. to create, produce, earn, adopt, contrive. h.

اپانگ अपाङ्ग apāng, m. the outer corner of the eye, a sectarial mark on the forehead; adj. maimed, crippled. apāng-darshan, m. a side glance, a leer, a wink. s.

اپاو उपाव upā,o, m. remedy, redress. s.

اپاون अपावन a-pāvan, defiling, polluting. s.

اپاهج अपाहज apāhaj, lazy, cripple; a person who never visits any one. s.

اپاي उपाय upāe, m. remedy, plan, scheme, preparation. s.

اپاي अपाय apāya, injurious, destructive. s.

اپايي उपायी upāyī, contriving, remedying. s.

اپباد अपवाद apabād, m. complaint, accusation. s.

اپبادي अपवादी apabādī, m. a complainant, an accuser. s.

اپبتر अपवित्र a-pabitr or a-pavitr, impure, unclean. s.

اپبترتا अपवित्रता a-pabitrata, f. uncleanness, impurity. s.

اپبس अपवस apabas, also अपवश्य apabashya, absolute, independent. s.

اپبن उपवन upaban, m. a grove, an artificially planted wood or garden. s.

اپبهاشا अपभाषा apabhāshā, f. low, vulgar, or obscene language. s.

اپبهرنش अपभ्रंश apabhransh,
اپبهنش अपभंश apabhansh, } m. common or vulgar language, ungrammatical speech. s.

اپپاتك उपपातक upapātak, m. a great crime, such as the killing of a cow, atheism, &c. s.

اپپت उपपति upapati, m. a gallant, one who keeps a woman to whom he is not married. s.

آپت आपत or आपत्ति) āpat and āpatti, f. calamity, misfortune. āpat-kāl, m. time of distress. s.

آپت आप्त *āpta*, true, trustworthy. *s.*

اپت अपति *apati*, f. disgrace, dishonour. *s.*

آپتا आप्ता *āptā*, f. quotient, an equation of a degree. *s.*

اپتاپ उपताप *upatāp*, m. sickness, pain, heat. *s.* [spring, childless. *s.*

اپتر अपुत्र also अपुत्रक *a-putr*, without off-

اپتورتا अपतिव्रता *a-pativratā*, an unchaste woman, a courtesan. *s.*

اپتھ अपथ *a-path*, m. a wrong path, error. *s.*

اپتھي अपथ्य *a-pathya*, indigestible. *s.*

اپتي अपत्य *a-patya*, m. offspring, race. *s.*

اپتيا अपतिया *a-patiyā*, } faithless, trea-
اپتيارا अपतियारा *a-patiyārā*, } cherous. *s.*

اپٹ अपटु *a-paṭu*, awkward, uncouth. *s.*

اپٹک अपटक *a-paṭak*, one whose hands and feet are become useless, paralytic. *h.*

اپٹن उपटन *upṭan*, } m. a paste for scour-
اپٹنا उपटना *upṭanā*, } ing the skin when bathing. *h.*

اپٹھنا उपठना *upaṭhnā*, n. to be tired, or to be sick of a business. *h.* [the chorus. *h.*

اپج उपज *upaj*, f. the burthen of a song,

اپجانا उपजाना *upjānā*, a. to produce, to make to grow. *h.*

اپجاو उपजाऊ *upjā,ū*, fertile, productive. *h.*

اپجت उपजित *upajit*, produced, propagated. *s.* [exertion. *s.*

اپجتن उपजतन *upajatan*, m. preparation,

اپجس अपजस *apajas*, m. infamy, disgrace. *s.*

اپجسي अपजसी *apajasī*, infamous, unfortunate. *s.*

اپجنا उपजना *upajnā*, n. to spring up, to grow, to proceed. *h.*

اپجيوكا उपजीविका *upajīvikā*, also उपजीवन *upajīvan*, f. livelihood, means of living. *s.*

اپجيوي उपजीवी *upajīvī*, dependent, living by or on. *s.*

اپچار उपचार *upachār*, m. service, remedy, practice of physic, usage. *s.*

اپچھ अपुच्छ *a-puchh*, without a tail. *s.*

اپچھا अपुच्छा *a-puchhā*, f. name of a species of tree. *s.* [waste. *s.*

اپچي अपचय *apachaya*, m. loss, detriment,

آپد आपद *āpad*, or آپدا आपदा *āpadā*, f. misfortune, calamity. *āpad-grasta*, involved in calamity. *s.*

اپدا उपदा *upadā*, f. a meeting, a present made at an interview. *s.*

اپدرو उपद्रव *upadrav*, m. a portent; violence, injury. *s.* [vour. *s.*

اپدنش उपदंश *upadaṅsh*, m relish, fla-

اپدھات उपधातु *upadhātu*, m. a sort of inferior mineral. *s.*

اپديس उपदेश *upades*, m. advice, counsel, exhortation, admonition. *s.* [adviser. *s.*

اپديسن उपदेशिन *upadesin*, advising, an

اپديسي उपदेशी *upadesī* and *upadesak*, m. an adviser. *s.*

اپر अपर *apar*, another, a second, opposite. *s.*

اپر उपर *upar* (also उपरि *upari*), over, above. *s.* [non-acquisition. *s.*

اپراپت अप्राप्ति *a-prāpti*, f. non-attainment,

اپراٹا उप्राटा *uprāṭā*, m. the west. *d.*

اپراجت अपराजित *a-parājit*, unerring, invincible. *s.*

اپراجتا अपराजिता *a-parājitā*, f. the name of a twining shrub; called also *koyal*, or *kawwā-ṭhenṭī*, crow's-beak. Clitoria ternatea. *s.*

اپراجي अपराजय *a-parājay*, m. victory. *s.*

اپراچين अपराचीन *a-parāchīn*, modern, recent. *s.*

اپرادھ अपराध *aparādh*, m. crime, fault. *s.*

اپرادھن अपराधिन *aparādhin*, } a criminal,
اپرادھي अपराधी *aparādhī*, } a sinner, an offender. *s.*

اپرال उप्राल *uprāl*, over, above. *d.*

اپرالا उप्राला *uprālā*, m. aid, assistance. *uprālā karnā*, a. to take one's part, to protect, stickle for. *h.* [wards. *h.*

اپرانت उप्रान्त *uprānt*, after which, or after-

اپراوري उप्रावरी *uprāwarī*, quarrelsome, wrangling. *h.*

اپراهن अपराह्ण *aparāhna*, m. the third pahar; afternoon. *s.*

اپربھا अप्रभा *a-prabhā*, f. darkness, dulness, want of splendour. *s.*

اپرپاٹي अपरिपाटी *a-paripāṭī*, f. deviation from established custom. *s.*

اپرتاپ अप्रताप *a-pratāp*, m. want of acuteness, of power, or of fortune. *s.*

اپرتاپي अप्रतापी *a-pratāpī*, blunt, powerless, unfortunate. *s.*

اپرتبندھا अप्रतिबंधा *a-pratibandhā*, m. an undisputed inheritance. *s.*

اپرتشٹھا अप्रतिष्ठा *a-pratishṭhā*, f. want of respectability. *s.* [*a-pratyaksh*, q. v.) *s.*

اپرتکش अप्रतक्ष *a-pratakṣh*, secret (properly

اپرتھا अप्रथा *a-prathā*, f. deviation from custom; secrecy. *s.*

اپرتيت अप्रतीत *a-pratīt*, without credit. *s.*

اپرتيتي अप्रतीति *a-pratīti*, f. want of confidence or of credit, mistrust. *s.*

اپرتيکش अप्रत्यक्ष *a-pratyaksha*, invisible, not obvious to the eye. *s*

اپرتيي अप्रत्यय *a-pratyay*, m. distrust, unbelief. *s.*

[trustful. *s.*

اپرتييي अप्रत्ययी *a-pratyayī*, doubtful, mis-

اپرچنڈ अप्रचण्ड *a-prachanḍ*, without dignity, not strong. *s.*

[trial or proof. *s.*

اپرچها अपरिच्छा *a-parichchhā*, f. want of

اپردهان अप्रधान *a-pradhān*, little, mean, powerless, subordinate, not chief. *s.*

اپرس अपर्श *apars*, m. the state of a Hindū after bathing previous to worship or to eating, during which it is unlawful for him to touch any one. Leprosy, from Arab. *abraṣ*. *uparas*, m. a kind of red chalk; bitumen; a subordinate flavour.

اپرساد अप्रसाद *a-prasād*, m. disapprobation, disfavour. *s.*

اپرسادي अप्रसादी *a-prasādī*, that which is not presented to the Deity. *s.*

اپرسده अप्रसिद्ध *a-prasiddh*, unknown, hidden, not celebrated. *s.*

اپرسن अप्रसन्न *a-prasanna*, disagreeable, dissatisfied. *s.*

[nate. *s.*

اپرش अपुरुष *a-purush*, impotent, effemi-

اپركاش अप्रकाश *a-prakāsh*, m. that which is hidden or obscure. *s.*

اپركٹ अप्रकट *a-prakaṭ*, unmanifested, not apparent. *s.*

اپرلا उपरला *uparlā*, superficial, the outside of a cloth or raiment (opposed to the lining). *h.*

اپرمان अप्रमान *a-pramān*, without proof, untrue. *s.*

[tic, without authority. *s.*

اپرمانك अप्रमाणिक *a-pramānik*, unauthen-

اپرمانيه अप्रमाण्य *a-pramānya*, want of proof or of authority. *s.*

[finite. *s.*

اپرم‌پار अपरंपार *a-param-pār*, boundless, in-

اپرمت अपरिमित *a-parimit*, unmeasured, unlimited. *s.*

اپرنا उपरना *uparnā*, m. a scarf, a covering. *h.*

اپروائي تروائي उपरवाई तरवाई *uparwā,ī tarwā,ī*, f. surfeit, mort de chien, cholera morbus. *h.*

آپروپ आपरूप *āp-rūp*, m. self, self-formed, the Deity. Dakh. strange, wonderful, rare. *h.*

اپروده उपरोध *uparodh*, m. partiality, support, favour, kindness. *s.*

اپرونچها उपरौंचा *upraunchā*, m. a towel or cloth for wiping the body. adj. superficial. *h.*

اپروين अप्रवीन *a-pravīn*, unskilful; *apravīnatā*, f. want of skill or of experience. *s.*

اپري अप्रिय *a-priy*, hated, disliked, unfriendly. *s.*

[dislike. *s.*

اپريت अप्रीति *a-prīti*, f. enmity, hatred,

اپريكش अपरीक्षा *a-parīkshā*, f. want of trial or proof, an insufficient trial of any thing. *s.*

اپريم अप्रेम *a-prem*, m. want of love, enmity, hatred. *s.*

اپڑنا उपड़ना *upaṛnā*, n. to be rooted out, to be pulled out; to be skinned. *h.*

اپڑنا अपड़ना *apaṛnā*, n. to come to hand. *d.*

آپس आपस *āpas*, pron. recip. themselves, one another; hence kindred, brotherhood, fellowship. *āpas meṅ rahnā* is applied to signify adultery, &c. *h.*

اپس उपस *upas*, f. stink, staleness, putrefaction, rottenness. *h.*

اپستري उपस्त्री *upastrī*, f. a concubine. *s.*

اپستھ उपस्थ *upasth*, m. f. the organ of generation of males or females. *s.*

اپستهت उपस्थित *upasthit*, ready, present, at hand, arrived. *s.*

اپسرا अप्सरा *apsarā*, f. a female dancer in the court of Indra. *s.*

اپسرگ उपसर्ग *upasarga*, m. a particle or preposition; a portent or natural phenomenon. *s.*

اپسمار अपस्मार *apasmār*, m. the epilepsy. *s.*

اپسنا उपसना *upasnā*, n. to become musty, to rot. *h.*

اپسوید अपसव्य *apasavya*, m. the right side (or half) of the body; adj. opposite, contrary. *s.*

اپشاستر उपशास्त्र *upashāstra*, m. sciences connected with or derived from the shāstra. *s.*

اپشانت उपशान्त *upashānta*, calm, pacified, appeased. *s.*

[or tranquil. *s.*

اپشانتي उपशान्ती *upashāntī*, one who is calm

اپشبد अपशब्द *apashabd*, m. wind broken backwards; a disagreeable sound. *s.*

اپشپت अपुष्पित *a-pushpit*, without flowers (a tree or plant), that does not bear flowers, not in flower. *s.*

[lean. *s.*

اپشٹ अपष्ट *apashṭ*, hidden, secret; *a-pushṭ*,

اپشکن अपशकुन *apashakun*, m. any unlucky omen or portent, also *apasakun*. *s.*

اپشم उपशम *upasham*, m. patience, calmness. *s.*

اپك अपक *a-pak*, or अपक्क *a-pakk*, unripe. *s.*

آپ كاج आपकाज *āp-kāj*, }
آپ كاجي आपकाजी *āp-kājī*, } attending to one's own business, attending to one's own affairs. *s.*

اپكار अपकार *apakār*, m. a hindrance, detriment, injury. *s.*

اپكار उपकार *upakār*, m, favour, kindness, protection. *s.*

[ing. *s.*

اپكاري उपकारी *upakārī*, beneficent, aid-

اپكارك उपकारक *upakārak*, m. a friend, a protector. *s.*

اپكتا अपक्वता *a-paktā*, f. immaturity. *s.*

اپكرشٹ अपकृष्ट *apakrishṭa*, bad, inferior, deteriorated. *s.*

اپكرم उपक्रम *upakram*, m. deliberate commencement of an undertaking; a stratagem. *s.*

اپكرم अपकर्म *apakarm*, m. a mean or unworthy action. *s.*

اپکرن उपकरण *upakaran*, m. the insignia of royalty; means, materials. *s.*

اپکش अपक्ष *a-paksh*, without wings, without assistance or protection. *s.*

اپکلنگ अपकलंक *apakalang*, m. an indelible disgrace. *s.*

اپگت उपगत *upagat*, promised, agreed. *s.*

اپگره उपग्रह *upagrah*, m. a prisoner, a man or animal in confinement. *s.*

اپگم उपगम *upagam*, m. agreement, promise, approach. *s.* [cious stone, a jewel. *s.*

اپل उपल *upal*, m. a rock, a stone; a pre-

اپلا उपला *uplā*, m. a cake of dried cowdung. *h.*

آپلاو आप्लाव *āplāv*, m. bathing, ablution. *s.*

اپلپت उपलिप्त *upalipta*, plastered, smeared over. *s.*

آپلت आप्लुत *āplut*, bathed, sprinkled (upon); m. an initiated householder. *s.*

اپلج अपलज्ज *apalajj*, }
اپلجي अपलज्जी *apalajjī*, } impudent, immodest, shameless. *s.*

اپلجا अपलज्जा *apalajjā*, f. impudence, shamelessness. *s.* [omen or bad sign. *s.*

اپلچهن अपलक्षण *apalachchhan*, m. a bad

اپلچهن उपलक्षण *upalachhan* (properly *upalakshan*), m. a figure of speech, an elliptical expression, a synecdoche. *s.*

اپلچهنا अपलक्षणा *apalachchhanā*, }
اپلچهني अपलक्षणी *apalachchhanī*, } of a bad omen, or of suspicious appearance, unlucky. *s.*

اپلو अप्लव *aplav*, m. bathing, ablution. *s.*

اپلي उपली *uplī*, f. smaller kind of cakes of cow-dung. *h.*

اپليپ उपलेप *upalep*, m. smearing, plastering. *s.*

اپليپن उपलेपन *upalepan*, m. act of smearing, plastering with cow-dung. *s.*

اپما उपमा *upamā*, f. comparison, simile, that thing to which another is likened. *s.* [last. *s.*

اپمان उपमां *upamāṅ*, m. simile, &c. as the

اپمان अपमान *apamān*, m. disgrace, an affront. *s.* [graced. *s*

اپمانت अपमानित *apamānit*, degraded, dis-

اپماني अपमानी *apamānī*, or अपमान्य *apamānya*, disgraced, abased. *s.* [likeness. *s.*

اپمت उपमिति *upamiti*, f. resemblance,

اپمرتي अपमृत्यु *apamrityu*, f. an unnatural or untimely death. *s.*

آپن आपन *āpan*, pron. recip. self. *h.*

آپن आपन्न *āpanna*, afflicted, gained or acquired; one who comes to another for shelter. *s.*

اپنا अपना *apnā*, m. }
اپني अपनी *apnī*, f. } pron. of or belonging to self. *apnī gā,onā*, to sing one's own praises, to egotize. *h.*

اپنانا अपनाना *apnānā*, a. to make a thing one's own, to convert to one's own use. *h.* [kindred. *h.*

اپنايت अपनायत *apnāyat*, f. family relations,

اپنپا अपंपा *apaṅpā* or *apampā*, m. one's self. Used only in the accusative, as *apaṅpā bachānā*, to guard or protect one's self. *h.*

اپنتهه अपंथ *a-paṅth*, m. a wrong road, or bad road, a devious track; heresy. *s.*

اپنتهي अपंथी *a-paṅthī*, one who has lost his way, devious, heretical, a heretic.

اپنشد उपनिषद *upanishad*, m. sacred texts or extracts from the Vedas. *s.*

آپنک आपनिक *āpanik*, m. an emerald. *s.*

اپنگ उपंग *upang*, m. a kind of musical instrument. *s.* [adj. wicked, void of merit. *s.*

اپني अपुण्य *apunya*, m. uncharitableness;

اپني उपनय *upanaya*, }
اپنين उपनयन *upanayan*, } m. the initiation of the three first classes of Hindūs; investiture with a peculiar thread or cord worn over the left shoulder. Vide Wilson. *s.*

اپنيتر उपनेत्र *upanetra*, m. spectacles, glasses for the eye. *s.*

اپنيه अपुण्य *apunya*, m. uncharitableness. *s.*

اپواد अपवाद *apavād*, m. complaint, reproach, accusation. *s.* [accuser. *s.*

اپوادي अपवादी *apavādī*, m. a complainer,

اپواس उपवास *upavās*, m. fasting, a fast. *s.*

اپواسي उपवासी *upavāsī*, m. one who fasts. *s.*

اپوت अपूत *a-pūt*, childless; undutiful (child). *s.*

اپوتر अपवित्र *a-pavitra*, unclean, defiled. *s.*

اپوترتا अपवित्रता *a-pavitratā*, f. uncleanness, filth. *s.*

اپوٹ *apūt*, pure, unadulterated. *d.*

اپوجك अपूजक *apūjak*, ungodly, irreligious. *s.*

اپوجيه अपूज्य *apūjya*, that which is not worshipped, or not a proper object of worship. *s.*

اپوديا उपविद्या *upavidyā*, f. profane science, (opposed to sacred). *s.*

اپورب अपूरब *a-pūrb*, new, unheard of, admirable, uncommon, remarkable. *s.* [ardly. *s.*

اپورش अपौरुष *a-paurush*, unmanly, cow-

اپورگ अपवर्ग *apavarg*, m. liberation, deliverance, emancipation. *s.*

اپورن अपूर्ण *a-pūrn*, m. a fraction; adj. not full, incomplete. *apūrn-kāl*, premature, untimely. *s.*

اپورنتا अपूर्णता *a-pūrnatā*, f. incompleteness. *s.*

اپورنن उपवर्णन *upavarnan*, m. a minute description. *s.* [ralleled, eminent, unheard of. *s.*

اپوروه अपूर्व *a-pūrva*, unprecedented, unpa-

اپوش उपविष *upavish*, m. a narcotic. *s.*

اپون उपवन *upavan*, m. a grove, an artificially-planted wood. *s.*

اپویت उपवीत *upavīt*, m. the brahminical thread. *s.*

اپوید उपवेद *upaved*, m. the Purānas, &c. q.d. depending on, or derived (springing from) the Veda. *s.*

اپہاس उपहास *upahās*, m. laughter, fun, sport. *s.*

اپھرانا अफराना *aphrānā*, a. to feed one so that his belly swell; met. to give one (money, &c.) to the utmost extent of his desire. Also used in a neuter sense. *h.*

اپھرائي अफराई *aphrā,ī*, f. gluttony, a surfeit. *h.*

اپہرتا अपहर्ता *apahartā*, m. a robber, a plunderer. *s.*

اپہرن अपहरण *apaharan*, m. act of plundering, purloining.

اپھرنا अफरना *apharnā*, n. to swell out (the belly); to gormandize, to eat to satiety; to become very rich. *h.*

اپھریا अफरिया *aphariyā*, f. a subdivision of the caste or tribe called *ābhīr* or *ahīr*, q.v. *h.*

اپھل अफल *a-phal*, fruitless, barren. *s.*

اپھلت अफलित *a-phalit*, not in fruit. *s.*

اپھلتا अफलिता *a-phalitā*, f. barrenness, unproductiveness. *s.*

اپھننا उफन्ना *uphannā*, n. to boil over. *h.*

اپہنو अपह्नव *apahnav*, m. denial, concealment. *s.*

آپھو आफू *āphū*, } f. opium. *h.*
آپھیم आफीम *āphīm*, }

اپھین अफेन *a-phen*, without foam. *s.*

اپھینڈا अफेंडा *aphendā*, self-conceited, obstinate. *s.*

اپي अपे *ape*, same as *āp*, self. *ape son ape*, of one's own accord, spontaneously. *h*

اپیر अपीर *a-pīr*, without pain. *s.*

اپیش अपयश *apayash*, m. infamy, disgrace. *s.*

اپیشي अपयशी *apayashī*, infamous, unfortunate. *s.*

اپیکت उपयुक्त *upayukta*, worthy, fit, proper, qualified. *s.*

اپیکشا अपेक्षा *apekshā*, f. expectation, hope. *s.*

اپیکشت *apekshit*, expected, waited for, hoped for. *s.*

اپیکشك अपेक्षक *apekshak*, m. an expectant; adj. expecting, waiting for.

اپیکشي अपेक्षी *apekshī*, expecting, hoping; an expectant.

اپیکھ अपेख *apekh*, invisible, unseen. *s.*

اپیکھا उपेखा उपेक्षा *upekhā*, or *upekshā*, f. trick, fraud, stratagem. *s.*

اپین अपीन *apīn*, light, lean. *s.*

اپینس अपीनस *apīnas*, m. dryness of the nose, want of smell, a cold. *s.*

اپیوگي उपयोगी *upayogī*, useful, suitable. *s.*

اپیي अपेय *a-peya*, unfit to drink, forbidden liquor. *s.*

ات अति *ati*, a particle denoting excess, used in compounds, as *ati-pān*, m. a drunkard, or one who drinks to excess; *ati-parākram*, very powerful. *s.*

ات इत *it*, or *ita*, here, hither, उत *ut*, or *uta*, there, thither. इति *iti*, a word usually written at the end of books, letters, &c., denoting that it is finished, like the Persian expressions, *tamām shud, ziyāda chi*, &c. *s.*

آت आत *āt*, m. custard apple. Annona squamosa. *h.*

آتا आता *ātā*, or अता *atā*, m. father; a custard apple. Annona squamosa. *p. h.*

اتا or اتال इता *itā*, or इताल *itāl*, now, at present. *d.*

اتا इत्ता *ittā*, this much or many. *h.*

اتا उत्ता *uttā*, that much or many. *h.*

اتابك *atābak*, m. (q. d. *ātābeg*, the lord father), a master, teacher, a title given to kings or prime-ministers; name of a family who occupied the throne of Persia from A.D. 1148 to 1264; *Sa'dī* dedicates his Gulistān to a prince of this family. *p.*

اتار उतार *utār*, m. descent. *utār-denā*, to bring down; met. to disgrace, dishonour. *h.*

اتارا उतारा *utārā*, m. answer; ransom, self-devotion; cast-off or second-hand. *h.*

اتارن उतारन *utāran*, f. a fragment descent, disgrace. *h.*

اتارنا उतारना *utārnā*, a. to bring down; to tear off, cut off, or break off (a portion of any thing). *utāre hūe*, pl. engaged with desperate resolution in any enterprise (metaphor taken from cavalry, who dismount to fight on foot, with a determination to conquer or die). *h.*

اتارنا *utārnā*, a. to act according to circumstances. *d.*

اتالیق *atālīk*, m. a private tutor. *atālīkī*, private tuition, education. *t.*

اتان उतान *utān* (also *uttān*), supine, lying on the back. *h*

اتانا उताना *utānā*, proud, conceited; also supine. See *chit*. *d.*

اتاول उतावल *utāval*, f. quickness, speed, despatch. *h.*

اتاولا उतावला *utāwlā*, m. } swift, quick,
اتاولي उतावली *utāwlī*, f. } speedy. *h.*

اتاي अताई *atā,ī*, m. one who sings and dances gratis. *h.*

آتاین आत्तायिन *āttāyin*, } m. a felon, thief,
اتایي आत्तायी *āttāyī*, } murderer, incendiary. *s*

اتبار अतिबार *atibār*, very frequent. *s.*

اتباع *atbā'* (pl. of تبع or تابع) followers, dependants. *itbā'* and *ittibā'*, following, obeying, obedience. *a.*

اتبکتا अतिबक्ता *atibaktā*, m. a great talker, a babbler. *s.*

اتبل अतिबल *atibal*, very powerful. *s.*

اتبھار अतिभार *atibhār*, m. a very great or excessive burden. *s.*

اتبیل अतिबेल *atibel*, frequently, very often. *s.*

آتپ आतप *ātap*, m. sunshine, sunbeams. *s.*

اتپات उत्पात *utpat*, m. violence, injustice, injury. *s.*

اتپاتک अतिपातक *atipātak*, m. a heinous sin. *s.*

اتپاتکي अतिपातकी *atipātakī*, one who commits a very great or heinous sin. *s.*

اتپاٹن उत्पाटन *utpāṭan*, m. plucking out, eradicating. *s.*

اتپادن उत्पादन *utpādan*, m. producing. *s.*

اتپان अतिपान *atipān*, m. a drunkard; excessive drinking, inebriety. *s.*

اتپت उत्पत्ति *utpatti*, *utpatt*, f. birth, origin. *s.*

اتپت उत्तप्त *uttapta*, anxious, excited. *s.*

اتپریکشا उत्प्रेक्षा *utpreksha*, f. indifference, carelessness; illustration (in poetry, &c.). *s.*

اتپل उत्पल *utpal*, m. a species of the lotus flower. *s.*

اتپن उत्पन्न *utpann*, produced, gained; s. m. produce. *s.* [a guest. *s.*

اتتھ अतिथि *atitha* or *atithi*, m. a stranger,

اتتھا अतथा *a-tathā*, powerless, without authority. *s.*

آتتھیہ आतिथ्य *ātithya*, } hospitable, attentive to a guest. *s.*
آتتھییہ आतिथेय *ātitheya*, } [acrid; very pungent. *s.*

اتتیکشن अतितीक्ष्ण *atitīkshna*, sharp, hot, or

اتجاگر अतिजागर *atijāgar*, m. the black curlew; adj. very wakeful, restless. *s.*

اتجوگ अतिजोग *atijog*, very worthy. *s.*

اتجیرن अतिजीर्ण *atijirna*, very old, decayed. *s.*

اتچار अतिचार *atichār*, m. the rapid motion of a planet from one sign to another. *s.*

اتحاد *ittiḥād*, m. union, concord, intimate friendship. *a.* [berality. *s.*

اتدان अतिदान *atidān*, m. munificence, li-

اتداہ अतिदाह *atidāh*, m. great heat, violent inflammation. *s.* [culty or distress. *s.*

اتدرگت अतिदुर्गत *atidurgat*, f. great diffi-

اتدشکر अतिदुष्कर *atidushkar*, very difficult. *s.*

اتدور अतिदूर *atidūr*, m. a great distance, afar off. *s*

اتدوش अतिदोष *atidosh*, m. a great fault. *s.*

اتر उत्तर *uttar*, m. an answer; the north. Adj. posterior, subsequent. *s.*

اتر अत्र *atra*, here, in this place. *s.*

اتر इतर *itar*, affected, giving one's self airs; playful, wanton, coquettish, gay; other, different, low, vile. *itar-lok*, people of low caste. *s.*

آتر आतुर *ātur*, grieved, sick, perplexed. *s.*

اترا उत्तरा *uttarā*, northern, northerly; f. north-wind. *s.*

اترادھکار उत्तराधिकार *uttarādhikār*, m. an inheritance. *s.* [an heir. *s.*

اترادھکاري उत्तराधिकारी *uttarādhikārī*, m.

اترآردھ उत्तरार्ध *uttar-ārdh*, the second or last half (of a book, &c.) *s.*

اتراشاڑھا उत्तराषाढ़ा *uttarāshāṛhā*, f. the twenty-first lunar mansion. *s.*

اتراك *Atrāk* (plur. of ترك), a Tartar or Turcoman. *a.*

اترانا उतराना *utrānā*, a. to boil over; to take down, to pull down (by the hands of a third person: to do it one's self is *utārnā*). *h.*

اترانا इतराना *itrānā*, a. to give one's self airs, to act with affectation; to act in an unnatural or unusual manner. *h.*

اتراون उत्तरावन *uttarāwan*, m. a place where fish throng to. *h.*

اتراها उत्तराहा *uttarāhā*, of or belonging to the north. *s.* [wanton. *h.*

اترايا इतराया *itrāyā*, affected, playful,

اترائي هونا उतराई होना *utrā,ī-hona*, to be thankful or grateful. *d.*

اتراين उत्तरायन *uttarāyan*, m. northing; the six months from *Māgh*, when the sun is north of the equator. *s.*

اتربھادرپد उत्तरभाद्रपद *uttar-bhādrapad*, m. a mansion of the moon (the twenty-seventh). *s.*

اترپال अतरपाल *atarpāl*, m. land that is left uncultivated. *s.*

اترپت अतर्पित *a-tarpit*, dissatisfied. *s.*

اترپت अतृप्त *a-tripta*, restless, uneasy. *s.*

اترپھلگني उत्तरफल्गुनी *uttar-phalgunī*, f. the twelfth lunar mansion. *s.*

اترن अत्रन *atran*, m. name of a climbing plant used in medicine, (Cynanitum extensum). *d.*

اترن उतरन *utran*, f. a fragment, any thing taken off from the body; cast clothes. *rin se utran-honā*, to be freed from debt. *h.*

اترنا उतरना *utarnā*, n. to come down from a height; to pass over; to go off; to become insipid; to fall in value or in dignity. *nashā utrā*, his intoxication is gone off. *h.*

اتروانا उतरवाना *utarwānā*, a. to cause to be brought down, or lowered. *h.*

اتروتر उत्तरोत्तर *uttarottar*, m. further and further; a rejoinder to a reply in law. *s.*

اتروگ अतिरोग *atirog*, m. consumption. *s.*

اتري پھل इत्रीफल *itrī-phal*, m. an electuary composed of myrobalan with coriander-seed and honey. *d.* [another. *d.*

اتڑ उत्तड़ *uttaṛ*, placing one thing over

اتسار अतिसार *atisār*, m. dysentery, diarrhoea. *atisārakī* and *atisārī*, dysenteric, afflicted with dysentery. *s*

اتساه उत्साह *utsāh*, m. joy, gladness, pleasure; perseverance. *s.*

اتسرگ उत्सर्ग *utsarg*, abandoning, consecrating; a rule or precept. *s.*

اتسانچیه अतिसंचय *atisanchaya*, m. a hoard, great accumulation. *s.*

اتسو उत्सव *utsav*, m. rejoicing, public demonstrations of joy. *s.*

اتسي अतसी *atsī*, f. flax (*linum usitatissimum*. *s.*

آتش *ātish* or *ātash*, f. fire, flame. *p.*

آتش افرازه *ātish-afrāza*, m. a rocket. *p.*

آتش افروز *ātish-afroz*, kindling fire, fuel. *p.*

آتش افگن *ātish-afgan*, casting or throwing fire. *s.*

آتش انداز *ātish-andāz*, casting out fire. *p.*

آتش انگیز *ātish-angez*, kindling, spreading or stirring fire; an incendiary, a seditious man. *p.*

آتش بار *ātish-bār*, flaming, fiery, raining fire; a fire-lock, tinder-box. *p.*

آتش باز *ātish-bāz*, m. a maker of fireworks; *ātish-bāzī*, f. a display of fireworks. *p.*

آتش پاره *ātish-pāra*, m. a spark, a lighted coal; a beautiful person; an exciter of quarrels, quarrelsome. *p.*

آتش پرست *ātish-parast*, m. a worshipper of fire, a guebre, of the sect of the magi; *ātish-parastī*, fire-worshipping. *p.*

آتش خانه *ātish-khāna*, m. a fire-temple; park of artillery. *p.*

آتش خوار *ātish-khwār*, m. a fire-eater, a bird so called (in Hind. Chakor). A variety of *Tetrao rufus*, Linn., a salamander. *p.*

آتش دان *ātish-dān*, m. a hearth, a fire-place, a chafing-dish. *p.*

آتش ریز *ātish-rez*, pouring out fire; an incendiary or exciter of quarrels. *p.*

آتش زدگي *ātish-zadagī*, f. a fire (i.e. houses, &c. on fire, accidentally or by design). *p.*

آتش زن *ātish-zan*, or آتش زنه *ātish-zana*, m. tinder, touchwood, any thing combustible; a tinder-box, with flint and steel; *ātish-zanī*, or *ātish-zanagī*, the act of striking fire. *p.*

آتشستان *ātishistān*, f. the region of fire, a place where fire abounds (hence applied to a hot fire of cannon or small-arms in battle); a large fire; a funeral pile. *p.*

آتش طبع *ātish-tab'*, of a fierce or fiery disposition. *p. a.*

آتشفشان *ātish-fishān*, scattering fire, a volcano. *p.*

آتش فگن *ātish-figan*, fire-dispersing. *p.*

آتشك *ātishak*, f. the venereal disease. *p.*

اتشکت अतिशक्त *atishakta*, very powerful. *atishakti*, f. great power. *atishaktatā*, f. heroic valour, prowess. *s*

آتش کده *ātish-kada*, m. a furnace, grate, chimney; the temple of fire-worshippers; name of a recent biographical work in the Persian language. *p*

آتش مزاج *ātish-mizāj*, fiery-tempered. *p. a.*

آتش ناك *ātish-nāk*, fiery, hot. *p.*

اتشي अतिशय *atishay*, excessively, very much. *s.*

آتشي *ātishī*, } fiery, hot, irascible, chole-
آتشین *ātishīn*, } ric. *ātishī ā,īna*, a burning lens. *ātishīn āb*, red wine; hot tears. *ātishīn golā*, a bomb-shell. *p.*

اتشیت अतिशीत *atishīt*, excessively cold. *s.*

اتصاف *ittiṣāf*, m. description, qualification, excellence, praise. *a.*

اتصال *ittiṣāl*, m. conjunction, adhesion, union, attachment, neighbourhood, contiguity. *a.*

اتفاق *ittifāk*, m. equality; friendship, union, concord, similarity of disposition; chance, fortune, accident, lot, success, incident, opportunity; probability. *ittifāk-k*, to unite. *ittifāk-h*, to happen, to be agreed. *ittifāk-se*, accidentally, jointly, conjunctly. *a.*

اتفاقا *ittifākan*, accidentally, by chance. *a.*

اتفاقات *ittifākāt* (pl. of اتفاق), accidents; successes, occurrences, events *a.*

اتفاق حسنه *ittifāki ḥasana*, m. unexpected good fortune; agreeable accidents. *a.*

اتفاقي *ittifākī*, accidental, concurring. *a.*

اتقا *ittikā*, m. avoiding, shunning, abstaining (from vice); piety, abstinence. *a.*

اتقاف *ittikāf*, restraining one's senses; praying and fasting, as in the month of Ramazān. *a.*

اتقیا *atkiyā* (pl. of تقي), religious men, devotees; the abstemious; those who fear God. *a.*

اتك इतक *itak*, so much, this much. *h.*

اتکا अतिका *atikā*, much, excessively. *h.*

آتکاري *ātkārī*, a caste of silkweavers in the Dakhan. *d.*

اتکال अतिकाल *ati-kāl*, m. delay, a long time. *s.*

اتکرشت उत्कृष्ट *utkrishṭa*, good, excellent. *utkrishṭa-bhūm*, m. a good soil. *s.*

اتکل उत्कल *utkal*, a name of the province of *Urisā*, vulgarly called Orissa. *s.*

اتکنٹها उत्कण्ठा *uthanṭhā*, f. regretting, longing for any thing. *s.*

اتگت अतिगति *atigati*, very much, very great. *s.*

اتل अतुल *a-tul*, unweighed; that cannot be weighed. *s.*

اتل अतल *a-tal*, the name of one of the seven patālas or infernal regions; literally, bottomless. *s.*

اتلا उतला *utlā* (v. *utāwalā*), swift, quick. *h.*

اتم उत्तम *uttam*, great, principal, first chief, the best. *uttam-purush*, an excellent man. *s.*

آتم आत्म *ātma*, m. self, soul, life, body; much used in the composition of Hindūī words, as *ātma-nāmī*, self-evident; *ātma-pālak*, self-cherishing, selfish; *ātma-ghāt*, self-murder. *s.*

اتم *atamm*, more or most perfect (from *tāmm*, perfect, complete). *a.*

آتما आत्मा *ātmā*, f. the soul; the body; the heart; the understanding. *s.*

اتمام *itmām*, perfection, accomplishment, completion. *a.*

آتمبدهه आत्मबुद्धि *ātma-buddhi*, f. self-knowledge. *s.*

آتمبندهه आत्मबन्धु *ātma-bandhu*, m. one's own kinsman. *s.*

آتمبوده आत्मबोध *ātma-bodh*, m. spiritual instruction. *s.*

آتمپالك *ātma-pālak*, self-cherisher, selfish. *s.*

آتمج आत्मज *ātmaj*, springing from one's self; m. a son. *s.*

آتمجا आत्मजा *ātma-jā*, f. a daughter. *s.*

اتمسنديه आत्मसंदेह *ātma-sandeh*, m. internal doubt. *s.*

آتمسنيم आत्मसंयम *ātma-sañyam*, m. self-restraint. *s.*

آتمشكت आत्मशक्ति *ātma-shakti*, f. inherent power. *s.*

آتمشلاگها आत्मश्लाघा *ātma-shlāghā*, f. self-praise. *s.*

آتمك आत्मिक *ātmik*, belonging to self, own. *s.*

آتمكتا आत्मिकता *ātmikatā*, f. identity, sameness. *s.*

آتمگهات आत्मघात *ātma-ghāt*, m. self-murder. *ātmaghātak* and *ātmaghātī*, one who commits suicide. *s.*

آتمگیان आत्मज्ञान *ātma-gyān*, m. self-knowledge. *s.*

آتمنامي आत्मनामी *ātma-nāmī*, self-evident. *s.*

آتمودیا आत्मविद्या *ātma-vidyā*, f. spiritual knowledge. *s.*

آتموكري आत्मविक्रयी *ātma-vikrayī*, one who sells himself as a slave. *s.*

آتمهت आत्महित *ātma-hit*, beneficial to one's self. *s.*

آتمهتیا आत्महत्या *ātma-hatyā*, f. self-destruction, suicide. *s.*

آتمیه आत्मिय or आत्मीय *ātmiya* or *ātmīya*, own, selfish. *s.*

اتن अतन *a-tan*, Kāmdev, the god of love among the Hindūs. *s.*

اتنا इतना *itnā*, as much as this, this much; *itne-men*, in the mean time. *h.*

اتنا उतना *utnā*, as much as that, that much. *h.*

اتنت अतन्त *atant* (properly *atyanta*), very much, exceeding. *s.*

آتنك आतंक *ātank*, } m. fear, pain, affliction;
آتنگ आतंग *ātang*, } pomp, dignity, show. *s.*

اتنگ उत्तुंग *uttung*, high, lofty. *s.*

اتو उत्तू *uttū*, m. plaits of cloth; *mār-kar uttū banāyā uske ta,īn*, he beat him to a mummy; lit. that his body was marked like the plaits in cloth. *h.*

اتو इतौ *itau*, same as *itnā*, this much. *h.*

آتو आतू *ātū*, f. a female teacher, a governess. *h.*

اتوار इतवार *itwār*, m. Sunday. *s.*

اتواس अतिवास *ativās*, m. a rigid fast observed on certain occasions. *s.*

اتوش अतिविष *ativish*, m. an antidote to poison. *s.*

اتوشا अतिविषा *ativishā*, f. a tree whose bark is used in dyeing. *s.*

اتول अतोल *a-tol*, unweighed. *h.*

آتون आतू *ātūn*, } f. a female teacher, a
آتونجي आतूंजी *ātūnjī*, } governess. *h.*

اتهه अथ *ath*, m. the beginning, commencement, an indeclinable particle, denoting now, here goes, &c. *s.*

اتها अथा *athā* (for *a-thāh*), deep, unfathomable, out of man's depth. *s.*

اتهاپن उथापन *uthāpan*, m. act of raising a thing up. *s.*

اتهاس इतिहास *itihās*, m. a story, fable; history, tradition. *atihās*, m. excessive laughter. *s.*

اتهام *ittihām*, m. suspicion, censure; in law, a charge, an imputation. *a.*

اتهان उत्थान *utthān*, m. rising up, awaking from sleep; effort, exertion. *utthān ekādashī*, or *devothān*, the 11th of the *shukl-paksh* of *kārtik*, when Vishnu awakes from sleep; during the months that he sleeps it is unlawful to marry. *s.*

اتهاه अथाह *a-thāh*, m. an abyss, unfathomable. *s.*

اتهاين अथाईं *athā,īn*, f. a place where people meet to converse and amuse themselves. *s.*

اتهت अथित *a-thit*, unstable, unsteady. *s.*

اتهربن अथरबन (properly अथर्वेण), *atharban*, name of one of the Vedas. *s.*

آتهرون आथर्वण *ātharvvan*, m. a Brahman versed in the Atharvan Veda. *s.*

اتهك अथक *a-thak*, unwearied, insensible of fatigue. *h.*

اتهل अथल *a-thal*, unstable, unsteady, wavering; land farmed or rented. *s.*

اتهلا उथला *uthlā*, shallow, shelving. *s.*

اتهلانا (उथलाना) *uthlānā*, a. to cause to turn over, or to be overset. *s.*

اتهل پتهل उथल पुथल *uthal-puthal*, overturned, upset, topsy-turvy. *h.*

اتهلنا उथलना *uthalnā*, m. to turn over, to upset (of itself); *uthalnā puthalnā*, to be overset. *h.*

اتهمنا अथमना *athmanā*, sunset, the west. *s*

اتهوا अथवा *athavā*, or, or even. *s.*

اتي इति *iti* (vide ات *iti*), a word usually written at the end of a letter, book, &c., signifying that it is finished; as the Latin *Finis*, &c. *s.*

اتي अती *atī*, much, very. *s.*

اتياد इत्यादि *ityādi*, et cætera, and so forth. *s.*

اتيبار (अतीबार) *atībār*, frequently, very often. *s.*

اتيبكتا अतिबक्ता *atibaktā*, a great talker, a babbler. *s.*

آتي پاتي आतीपाती *ātīpātī*, f. name of a kind of game. *h.*

اتيت अतीत *atīt*, m. an ascetic, or devotee among Hindūs. *s.*

اتيت अतीत *atīt*, gone by, elapsed, expired. *atīt-kāl*, m. (in gram.) the past or preterite tense. *s.*

اتيركت अतीरिक्त *atīrikta*, much, excessive. *s.*

اتيرن उतीरन *utīran*, worn, cast off (clothes, jewels, &c.). *s.*

اتيرن उत्तीर्ण *uttīrna*, arrived, rescued. *s.*

اتيس अतीस *atīs*, m. the name of a root used in medicine. *s.*

اتيك इतेक *itek*, so much, this much. *h.*

اتيهاس *itīhās* (same as *itihās*), m. a history, story, fable. *s.*

آٹ *āṭ* (dakh.), eight. Properly آٹھ, q.v.

آٹا आटा *āṭā*, m. flour, meal, any ground grain; when sifted, the finer flour, called *maida*, is separated from the coarser meal, called *sūjī*. *h.*

اٹا अटा *aṭā*, m. an upper room, or story. *h.*

آٹ اٹھارا आटअठारा *āṭ-aṭhārā*, perplexed, distressed. *d.*

اٹاري अटारी *aṭārī*, f. a thatched upper room. *h.*

اٹال अटाल *a-ṭāl*, f. a stack, a rick (of grass, corn, &c.), a heap (of baggage, &c.), q. d. immoveable. *h.*

اٹالا अटाला *aṭālā*, m. a heap, furniture. *h.*

اٹالكا अट्टालिका *aṭṭālikā*, an upper chamber. *h.*

آٹاماٹي هونا आटामाटी होना *āṭāmāṭī honā*, to be utterly destroyed, or undone. *h.*

اٹپٹانگ अटपटांग *aṭpaṭāng*, poor, wicked, disorderly. *h.*

اٹپٹانگي अटपटांगी *aṭpaṭāngī*, wickedness, absurdity. *h.*

اٹپٹهي अटपठी *aṭpaṭhī*, } اٹپٹي अटपटी *aṭpaṭī*, } thoughtless, inconsiderate, irregular, unstudied. *h.*

اٹٹ अटट *aṭaṭ*, coarse, strong cloth. *h.*

اٹك अटक *aṭak*, f. prevention, bar, obstacle, name of a river, the Attock. *h.*

اٹكا अटका *aṭkā*, m. a vessel for performing ablution; also the pot in which victuals are dressed for the public, at the door of the temple of Jagannāth; part. aground, stopped, hindered. *h.*

اٹكانا अटकाना *aṭkānā*, a. to prevent, to hinder, to stop, to restrain, to detain, to challenge as a sentry. *h.*

اٹكاو अटकाव *aṭkāw*, or *aṭkā,o*, } اٹكاونا अटकावना *aṭkāwanā*, } m. prevention, arrest, stop, a challenge. *h.*

اٹكرليس उटक्करलैस *uṭakkarlais*, precipitate, rash, acting without consideration. *h.*

اٹكل अटकल *aṭkal*, f. guess, conjecture, judgment, opinion; quantity, size. *aṭkal-bāz*, a good guesser, an appraiser. *aṭkal-pachchū*, m. one who guesses at a venture, or without the slightest grounds; adv. by guess, at random. *aṭkal-maṭkal*, name of a kind of play among children something like our "guess if you can." *h.*

اٹكلنا अटकलना *aṭkalnā*, a. to guess, to conjecture, to judge, to think. *h.*

اٹك مٹك अटकमटक *aṭak-maṭak*, amorous dalliance, fond tricks and gestures. *d.*

اٹكنا अटकना *aṭaknā*, n. to be stopped, to be restrained, to be prevented, to adhere, cease, rest, remain. *h.*

اٹكهيل अटखेल *aṭkhel*, wanton, playful. *h.*

اٹكهيلي अटखेली *aṭkhelī*, f. wantonness, an affected (also a graceful) pace or mode of walking. *h.*

اٹل अटल *a-ṭal*, immoveable, fixed, of determined resolution. *h.*

اٹم अटम *aṭam*, m. a heap, pile, or mass. *h.*

اٹمبر अटंबर *aṭambar*, a crowd of people, a tribe. *d.*

اٹن अटन *aṭan*, a balcony, an upper room; (plur. of *aṭā*). *h.*

اٹنا अटना *aṭnā*, n. to be contained, to be filled; as, *kūā aṭ-gayā*, the well is filled up; also to fill up (actively). *h.*

اٹنگن उटंगन *uṭangan*, the name of a river near Go,āliār, the name of a plant. *h.*

اٹني अटनी *aṭnī*, f. the horn of a bow. *s.*

آٹو *āṭo* (for *āṭhoṅ*), the eight, the entire eight. *d.*

اٹوات كهٹوات अटवाटखटवाट *aṭwāṭ-khaṭwāṭ*, f. the state of a person who in great affliction remains bedridden. *aṭhwāṭī-khaṭwāṭī lenā*, to be confined to bed by severe sickness. *h.*

آٹوان *āṭwān* (for *āṭhwān*), the eighth. *d.*

اٹوب अटोब *aṭob*, m. nature, constitution, essence, power. *d.*

اٹوٹ अटूट *a-ṭūṭ*, not liable to be broken, inexhaustible. *s.*

اٹوٹي كهٹوٹي *aṭhwaṭī-khaṭwāṭī*, f. being bedridden, (v. *aṭwāṭ*, &c).

اٹوك अटोक *a-ṭok*, unrestrained, uninterrupted, without hindrance, unquestioned. *h.*

اٹول अटोल *a-ṭol*, unpolished (stones or jewels), and hence when applied to persons it denotes rude, unmannerly. "A rough diamond." *h.*

اٹوي अटवी *aṭvī*, f. forest, wilderness. *s.*

آٹھ आठ *āṭh*, eight; *āṭh āṭh āṅsū ronā*, to shed floods of tears, to weep exceedingly. *āṭh pahar*, perpetually; lit. during the whole eight watches of day and night. *āṭh-paharī*, one who is constantly on duty, an eight-watch man. *āṭh-khambā*, a canopy supported by eight posts. *h.*

اٹھا *aṭṭhā*, the eight at cards. *d.*

اٹھا بٹھانا उठाबिठाना *uṭhā-biṭhānā*, a. to lead into error, cause to err. *d.*

اٹھابیٹھی उठाबैठी *uṭhā-baiṭhī*, f. act of frequently rising and sitting down, inconstancy, restlessness. *h.*

اٹھارہ अठारह *aṭhārah*, eighteen. *aṭhārahwāṅ*, also *aṭhārwāṅ*, the eighteenth. *h.*

اٹھاسی अठासी *aṭhāsī*, eighty-eight. *h.*

اٹھان उठान *uṭhān*, m. an area, or court; f. act of appearing, arising. *h.*

اٹھانا उठाना *uṭhānā*, a. to lift or raise up; to contract debts or purchase on credit, to drive away, to exhibit. *uṭhā-d*, to abolish, to do away with. *h.*

اٹھانوے अठानवे *aṭhānawwe*, or *aṭhānwe*, ninety-eight. *h.*

اٹھاون अठावन *aṭhāwan*, fifty-eight. *h.*

اٹھائیس अठाईस *aṭhā,is*, (also *aṭhāwis*) twenty-eight. *h.*

اٹھائی گیرا उठाईगीरा *uṭhā,ī-gīrā*, m. a plunderer, one who pilfers. *h. p.*

اٹھ بیٹھ उठबैठ *uṭh-baiṭh*, f. restlessness; a kind of exercise. *uṭh-baiṭh lagnā*, n. to be uneasy in mind. *h.*

اٹھتالیس अठतालीस *aṭhtālīs*, forty-eight. *h.*

اٹھتر अठत्तर *aṭhattar*, seventy-eight. *h.*

اٹھتیس अठतीस *aṭhtīs*, thirty-eight. *h.*

اٹھسٹھ अठसठ *aṭhsaṭh*, sixty-eight. *h.*

آٹھکونی आठकोनी *āṭh-konī*, eight-cornered, octangular. *s.* [tonness. *s.*

اٹھکیلی अठकेली *aṭhkelī*, f. playfulness, wan-

اٹھل अठल *aṭhal*, m. bathing (of the bride and bridegroom together, the third day after marriage). *h.*

اٹھلانا इठलाना *iṭhlānā*, a. to walk affectedly or coquettishly, to express tenderness or kindness by gestures. *h.*

اٹھماس अठमास *aṭhmās*, m. land constantly ploughed (for sugar-cane) from the month of *asāṛh* to the month *māgh*, both inclusive. *s.*

آٹھمنا आठमना *āṭhmanā*, the west, in opposition to *agmanā* the east. *s.*

اٹھنا उठना *uṭhnā*, n. to rise up; to go away. *h.*

اٹھنگل उठंगल *uṭhangal*, out of order, without manner, dull, heavy, stupid. *d.*

اٹھنگن उठंगन *uṭhangan*, m. a prop, or support. *h.* [ness, &c. *h.*

اٹھواٹی अठवाटी *aṭhwāṭī*, (vide *aṭwāṭ*), sick-

اٹھوارہ अठवार *aṭhwāra*, m. the eighth day after any other, a week. *h.*

آٹھواں आठवां *āṭhwāṅ*, the eighth; (from *aṭh*). *h.*

اٹھوانا उठवाना *uṭhwānā*, a. to cause to be raised up. *s.* [dred and eight. *h.*

اٹھوترسو अठोतरसौ *aṭhotar-sau*, one hun-

اٹھویا उठवैया *uṭhwaiyā*, that which rises or goes away. *s.*

اٹھہتر अठहत्तर *aṭhhattar*, seventy-eight. *h.*

اٹھیاسی अठेआस्सी *aṭhe,āssī*, (for *aṭhāsī*), eighty-eight. *h.*

اٹھیانو *aṭheānaw*, **اٹھیانوے** *aṭheānawe*, } (for *aṭhānawe*) ninety-eight. *h.* [pushed. *s.*

اٹھیل अठेल *a-ṭhel*, immoveable, not to be

اٹھیہتر *aṭhehattar*, (for *aṭhhattar*), seventy-eight.

اٹی अट्टी *aṭṭī*, f. a hank or bundle of thread; a cant word for a turban. *h.*

اٹیر अटेर *aṭer*, f. the name of a town. *h.*

اٹیرن अटेरन *aṭeran*, m. a skein or bundle of thread, a reel; the lounge or circle in the manege. *h.*

اٹیرنا अटेरना *aṭernā*, a. to make up thread into skeins, to reel; to lounge a horse *h.*

اٹیک अटेक *a-ṭek*, without support. *h.*

اثاث *as̤ās̤*, household furniture, wealth, goods, money, slaves, cattle, &c. *a.*

اثاث البیت *as̤ās̤-ul-bait*, **اثاثہ** *as̤ās̤a*, } household furniture. *a.*

آثار *ās̤ār*, (pl. of اثر), signs, marks, traces, vestiges; histories, traditions, memorable events, the traditions of Muhammad; a weight of one *sīr*, nearly two pounds avoirdupois. *a.*

اثامی *as̤āmī*, m. a defendant in a lawsuit; a culprit, a criminal *a.*

اثبات *is̤bāt*, m. f. confirmation, affirmation, proof, certain knowledge; Dr. Hunter says that its gender in Hindī (when used in composition) depends on that of the object (or word following), as, *is̤bāti mudda,ā kiyā*; *is̤bāti taḳrīr kī*; but this is a well-known rule in the language.—Vide Hind. Gram. gender of comp. words. *a.*

اثر *as̤ar*, m. a mark, sign, effect, impression. *as̤ar-pazīr* susceptive of impression, effective. *a.*

اثقل *as̤qal*, very heavy, heavier. *h.*

اثنا *as̤nā*, m. the middle, interstice, interval; as *as̤nā-i-rāh*, in the middle of the road, *i. e.* during the journey; a fold or plait. *a.*

اثناعشر *is̤nā-'ashar*, the twelve, in reference to the twelve Imāms. *a.*

اثیر *as̤īr*, m. æther; adj. marked, chosen. *a.*

اثیم *as̤īm*, m. a liar, sinner, criminal. *a.*

اج अज *aj*, m. a goat; (also the same as *aj*) to-day, now *s.*

آج आज *āj*, to-day. *āj-kal*, to-day or to-morrow, soon, in a few days. *āj kal-k.*, or *āj kal batānā*, to procrastinate. *h.*

آجا आजा *ājā*, m. a paternal grandfather. *h.*

اجا अजा *ajā*, f. a she-goat. *s.*

اجاب *ijāb*, m. (in law) the first proposal made in a contract &c. by one of the contracting parties. *a.*

اجابت *ijābat*, f. consent, approbation. *a.*

اجات अजात *a-jāt*, expelled from one's caste. *s.*

اجاتي अजाती *a-jātī*, m. a man who has lost his caste. *s.*

اجاره *ijāra*, (also اجار *ijār*), m. a farm; a privilege, or income of variable amount sold or let for a fixed sum. *ijāra-dār*, m. a farmer of land or of revenue, one that has purchased the labour of another; the holder of a monopoly. *ijāra-dārī*, farming or contracting for rent or revenue. *ijārdārī-paṭṭā*, *ijār-paṭṭā* and *ijār-nāma*, a lease, any document under which a lease or farm is held. *a.*

اجاڑ अजाड़ *ajāṛ*, m. canvas, cloth made of hemp. *h.*

اجاڑ उजाड़ *ujāṛ*, deserted, desolate, abandoned. *ujāṛ-k*, a. to raze to the ground. *h.*

اجاڑنا उजाड़ना *ujāṛnā*, a. to lay waste, to desolate; to injure, to expose to loss, as *maiṅ ne terā kyā ujāṛā*, in what respect have I injured you? *h.*

اجاڑو उजाडू *ujāṛū*, m. a spoiler, destroyer. *h.*

اجازت *ijāzat*, f. commands, orders, permission, leave, dispensation, sanction. *ijāzat-khwāh*, a petitioner, one who asks leave or permission. *ijāzat-nāma*, m. any written order or permission. *a.*

اجاگر उजागर *ujāgar*, splendid, gaudy; celebrated. *h.*

اجالا उजाला *ujālā*, m. light, splendour. *ujāle ka tārā*, the planet Venus. *h.*

اجالنا उजालना *ujālnā*, a. to cleanse, to polish (metals or jewels). *h.*

اجالي उजाली *ujālī*, f. light, splendour, glare, brightness. *h.*

اجامل अजामिल *ajāmil*, the name of a great sinner and penitent. *s.*

اجان अजान *a-jān*, ignorant, simple, innocent. *h.*

اجان उजान *ujān*, m. the direction, or part, of a river which is opposite to the course of the stream; up the river. *h.*

آجانا आजाना *ā-jānā*, n. to come suddenly; to befall, to happen, to come. *h.*

اجاني अजानी *a-jānī*, f. ignorance, simplicity. *s.*

اجت अजित *a-jit*, unsubdued, unconquered, invincible. ;

اجتماع *ijtimā'*, m. act of assembling or gathering together; conjunction (in astronomy). *a.*

اجتناب *ijtināb*, m. abstinence, continence *a.*

اجتهاد *ijtihād*, m. care, effort, diligence; carrying on war against infidels. *a.*

اجداد *ajdād*, (pl. of جد) ancestors, forefathers.

آجدھ आजुध *ājudh* (properly *āyudh*), m. a weapon. *s.*

اجڈ उजड्ड *ujaḍḍ*, inconsiderate, rash, ignorant, clownish. *h.*

اجر *ajr*, m. retribution, reward of good or bad actions, hire, fare. *a.*

اجر अजर *a-jar*, ever young, not liable to decay or old age. *s.*

اجر अजिर *ajir*, m. an area or court. *s.*

اجرا *ijrā*, m. performance, execution. *ijrā-k*, to perform, to put in practice. *a.*

اجرام *ajrām*, (pl. of جرم) bodies. *a.*

اجرت *ujrat*, f. reward, wages, hire. *a.*

اجڑنا उजड़ना *ujaṛnā*, n. to become desolate. *h.*

اجڑوانا उजड़वाना *ujaṛwānā*, a. to cause to be laid waste (by the hands of a third person). *h.*

اجزا *ajzā* (pl. of جزء q. v.), parts, portions sections of the *ḳurān*, of which there are thirty. *a.*

اجس अजस *a-jas*, infamous, disreputable. *s.*

اجساد *ajsād* (pl. of جسد) bodies. *a.*

اجسام *ajsām* (pl. of جسم) bodies. *a.*

اجکت अजुक्त *a-jukt*, f. violence, oppression, compulsion: adj. unfit. *s.*

اجگت अजुगत *a-jugat*, f. violence, oppression, compulsion: adj. unfit. *s.*

اجگت अजगुत *ajgut*, surprising, wonderful. *s.*

اجگر अजगर *ajgar*, m. a dragon, a kind of large snake, the boa-constrictor; lit. the goat-eater. *s.*

اجل *ajal*, f. death, delay, a stated time, respite, period for the payment of a debt. *ajal-rasīda* or *ajal-girifta*, seized by fate, on the point of death, in a situation that leaves no hopes of life. *ājil*, (in law) procrastination, or suffering such an interval to elapse as to render complaint inadmissible, like our statute of limitations. *a.*

اجل *ajall*, comp. more glorious. *a.*

اجل उज्जल *ujjal*, clean, pure, shining; blown, expanded. *s.*

اجلا उजला *ujlā*, clear, bright, white, light. *s.*

اجلاس *ijlās*, f. act of sitting, especially of a court of justice like our word sessions. *ijlāsi kāmil*, a full court. *a.*

اجلاف *ajlāf*, (pl. of جلف) wretches, tyrants, mean people. *a.*

اجلال *ijlāl*, m. the bestowing or acknowledging of greatness, respect. *a.*

اجلانا उजलाना *ujlānā*, a. to cause to cleanse to brighten. *s.*

اجلت उज्ज्वलित *ujjalit*, pure, clean, clear. *s.*

اجلنا उजलना *ujalnā*, n. to become clean, to shine, to be bright. *s.*

اجله *ajilla*, (pl. of جليل) glorious, illustrious. *a.*

اجماع *ijmā'*, m. act of assembling, an assembly, senate, council, court of justice, a crowd, a collection, amount, the whole. *ijmā'-i ummat*, m. general assembly of the people, unanimous consent. *ijmā'i ṣaḥābat*, the unanimous authority of the companions of the prophet on a point of law. *a.*

اجمال *ijmāl*, m. an abstract, abridgement, compendious account, synopsis, summary; also applied to joint occupancy or possession.

اجمالي *ijmālī*, abridged, compendious; in law it denotes what is held in common (as an estate) undivided, unpartitioned. *ijmālī mahall*, an undivided estate. *a.*

اجمعين *ajma'īn*, (pl. of اجمع) the whole. *a.*

اجمل *ajmal*, comp. more beautiful, perfect. *a.*

اجمود अजमूद *ajmūd*, } m. parsley. (*Apium*
اجمودا अजमोदा *ajmodā*, } *involucratum*, *Roxb.*), common carraway (*Carum Carui*), a kind of lovage (*Ligusticum Ajowan*). *p. s.*

اجن (अजिन) *ajin*, m. the hide of an antelope, lion, tiger, &c., on which the religious students sit or sleep. *s.*

اجناس *ajnās*, (pl. of جنس) goods and chattels, kinds, sorts, species. *a.*

اجنب *ajnab*, } foreign, strange, unknown
اجنبي *ajnabī*, } person. *a.*

اجنبيت *ajnabīyat*, f. strangeness, the circumstance or state of being a foreigner. *a.*

اجنم अजन्म *a-janma*, unborn, and unbegotten. *s.*

اجنه *ajinna* or *ajinnat*, (pl. of جنين), embryos. *a.*

اجوان अजवान *ajwān*, seed of the Ajowan ligusticum &c. (v. *ajwāyan*). *h.*

اجوانا उजवाना *ujwānā*, a. to order a person to pour from one vessel into another. *h.*

اجواين अजवायन *ajwāyan*, f. the seed of a plant of the dill kind (*Ligusticum Ajowan*). A kind of aniseed. *ajwāyani khurāsānī*, henbane. *h.*

اجوائني अजवाइनी *ajwā,inī*, f. a kind of candle. *d.*

اجوت अजोत *a-jot*, without splendour, dull. *s.*

اجوتها अजूठा *a-jūṭhā*, untouched, untasted (victuals). *h.*

اجوره *ajūra*, m. hire, wages, fare. *ajūra-dār*, m. a labourer for hire (whether paid by the day, or for completing a given work). *a.*

اجوري *ajaurī*, f. advances, particularly to agricultural labourers. *h.*

اجوڙ अजोड़ *a-joṛ*, without joining, matchless, rare. *h.*

اجول उज्ज्वल *ujjwal*, clean, bright; blown, expanded. *s.*

اجولت उज्ज्वलित *ujjwalit*, pure, clean, clear. *s.*

اجولتا उज्ज्वलता *ujjwaltā*, f. splendour, radiance. *s.*

اجولي *ajaulī*, f. perquisite of the lower castes from the threshing-floor. *h.*

اجون अजों *ajoṅ*, hithertho, as yet, to this day. *h.*

اجهالنا उझालना *ujhālnā*, a. to pour from one vessel into another. *h.*

اجهڙ (उज्झड़ or उजड़) *ujjhaṛ*, ignorant, illiterate, clownish. *h.*

اجهكنا उझकना *ujhaknā*, a. to observe, to spy. *h.*

اجهل *ajhal*, more ignorant, very ignorant. *a.*

اجهلنا उझलना *ujhalnā*, n. to flow, or be poured from one vessel into another. It is also used in a transitive sense, like *ujhālnā*, q. v. *h.*

اجهو अजहू *ajhū*, to-day even, presently. *h.*

اجهول अझोल *a-jhol*, of steady pace (epithet of an elephant). *h.*

اجهون अजहूं *aj-hūṅ*, yet, hitherto, even yet, this very day. *h.*

اجي अजी *ajī*, an interjection to call, or bespeak attention. In Bengal it is always addressed to an inferior, or in cases of great intimacy; but in the western provinces, often to a superior as a term of respect. *h.*

اجي अजय *a-jai* or *ajaya*, unsuccessful, subdued, not victorious. m. defeat. *s.*

آجيبكا आजीविका *ājībikā*, f. livelihood, subsistence, means or mode of living. *s.*

اجيت अजीत *a-jīt*, invincible, unsubdued. *s.*

اجيت برن अजीतवर्ण *a-jīt-barna*, m. leprosy (of a bad kind). *s.*

اجيتن *ajīṭan*, m. a corruption of our word adjutant.

اجيد *ajyad*, very best, good, excellent. *a.*

اجير *ajīr*, m. a slave. *ajīr-i-mushtarik*, a general or common hireling. *a.*

اجيرن अजीर्ण *a-jīrna*, m. indigestion, surfeit, flatulence. adj. undecayed, unimpaired. *s.*

اجين उज्जैन *ujjain*, m. the name of a city and province, of old the residence of *Vikramāditya* or *Bikramājit*. *s.*

اجيو अजीव *a-jīw*, lifeless, deprived of life. *s.*

آجيو आजीव *ājīw*, m. livelihood, profession, subsistence. *s.*

آجيوكا आजीविका *ājīvikā*, f. subsistence, means of supporting life (v. *ājībikā*). *s.*

اچ उच्च *uchcha*, high, lofty, (for *ūṅchā*). *s.*

اچا अचा *achā* (for *achchhā*), good, excellent. *h.*

اچاپٹ उचापट *uchāpaṭ*, m. taking up goods on credit; also, the goods so taken up; money borrowed. *h.*

اچاٹ उचाट *uchāṭ*, sorrowful, dejected, separate. *uchāṭ-h*, to be tired, to be disgusted. *h.*

اچاٹن उचाटन *uchchāṭan*, m. the act of vexing, or rendering sorrowful. *s.*

اچاٹنا उचाटना *uchāṭnā* (act. of *uchaṭnā*), to separate, &c. *h.*

اچاٹي उचाटी *uchāṭī*, f. sorrow, vexation, separation. *h.*

اچار उच्चार *uchchār*, m. pronunciation, utterance. *s.*

آچار आचार *āchār* or अचार *achār*, m. manner of life, common practice, rule of conduct, religious observance. *āchār-varjit*, irregular, out of rule, out of caste. *s.*

اچار अचार, आचार *achār*, also *āchār*, m. pickles. *h.*

اچارت उच्चारित *uchchārit*, pronounced, uttered. *s.*

اچارج *achāraj* (for आचार्य *āchārya*), m. an instructor in matters of religion; a learned *paṇḍit*. *s.*

آچارن आचारण *āchāran*, m. manner of life, religious observance. *s.*

اچارن उच्चारन *uchchāran*, m. pronunciation, utterance. *s.*

اچارنا उच्चारना *uchchārnā*, a. to pronounce, to utter. *s.*

آچاري आचारी *āchārī*, a strict observer of religious ceremonies. *s.*

آچاريا आचार्या *āchāryā*, f. a spiritual preceptress. *s.*

آچارياني आचार्यानी *āchāryānī*, f. the wife of an āchārya or religious instructor. *s.*

آچاريه आचार्य *āchārya*, m. an instructor (especially in matters of religion), the founder of a religious sect. *s.*

اچان उच्चान *uchchān*, f. height, elevation. *s.*

اچانا अचाना *achānā*, a. to wash the mouth after eating, to drink. *h.*

اچانا उचाना *uchānā*, a. to lift up a burden, to raise, elevate, exalt, hoist up. *h.*

اچانچك अचानचक *achānchak*, اچانك अचानक *achānak*, } suddenly, unawares, unexpectedly. *h.*

اچاوا उचावा *uchāwā*, m. raving or talking incoherently, as in one's sleep; the night mare. *h.*

اچپل अचपल *achpal*, com. اچپلا अचपला *achpalā*, m. اچپلي अचपली *achpali*, f. } restless, playful, inconstant, wanton, brisk; obstinate, unruly. *h.*

اچپلاهٹ अचपलाहट *achpalāhaṭ*, اچپلي अचपली *achpalī*, } f. restlessness, playfulness, vivacity, inconstancy. *h.*

اچت उचित *uchit*, proper, becoming. *s.*

اچت अच्युत *a-chchut*, m. a name of Vishnu or of God, (q. d. which breaketh not); incorruptible, immortal. *s.*

اچتا उच्चता *uchchtā*, f. height. *s.*

اچتانا अचताना *achtānā* or *achtānā-pachtānā*, (v. *achhtānā*), to regret, to repent. *h. s.*

اچتر अचतुर *a-chatur*, stupid, inactive. *s.*

اچٹنا उचटना *uchaṭnā*, n. to separate, or be separated (as plaster from a wall); to slip, slide, rebound (as a sword striking obliquely a hard body), to be broken or interrupted (sleep). *h.*

اچر अचर *a-char*, immoveable, inanimate. *s.*

اچرج or اچرچ अचरज or अचरच *acharj* or *acharch*, m. wonder, admiration, astonishment. adj. astonishing. *h.*

آچرن आचरण *ācharan*, m. manner of life, conduct, custom, practice, institute, religious observance. *s.*

اچرنا उचरना or उच्चरना *ucharnā* or *uchcharnā*. n. to separate (as the skin from the flesh, &c.); to speak, to pronounce; to be uttered, pronounced. *h.*

اچرنگ उचरंग *uchrang*, m. a moth. *h.*

اچکا उचक्का *uchakkā*, m. a thief, a pick-pocket, a swindler; (in Western India) swindling, theft. *uchakkā-panā*, m. robbery, theft. *h.*

اچکانا उचकाना *uchkānā*, a. to lift, or raise up. *h.*

اچکري अचकरी *achkarī*, f. wantonness, lasciviousness, wickedness. *h.*

اچکش अचक्षु *a-chakshu*, blind. f. spectacles. *s.*

اچکن अचिक्कन *a-chikkan*, rough, unpolished. *s.*

اچکنا उचकना *uchaknā*, n. to rise, be raised, or lifted; to leap, bound, spring up. *ichaknā*, to grin, to shew the teeth, as a dog. *h.*

اچکي उचक्की *uchakkī*, f. a female thief or pick-pocket. *h.*

اچل अचल *a-chal*, immoveable (either from strength or weakness); an aged person; m. a mountain. *nīl-achal*, the blue mountain near Balasore. *s.*

اچلا अचला *a-chalā*, f. the earth, supposed to be immoveable as the centre of the universe. *s.*

اچلانا उचलाना *uchlānā*, a. to order a person to separate (one thing from another). *h.*

اچلنا उचलना *uchalnā*, n. to separate or be separated. *h.*

اچمبها अचंभा *achambhā*, also *achambā*, m. a wonderful thing, astonishment, cause of astonishment. adj. rare, wonderful. *h.*

آچمن आचमन *āchaman*, m. act of rincing the mouth, sipping a little water out of the hand and spitting it out again; a ceremony performed before eating. *s.*

اچن अचिन *a-chin*, without note or consequence. *s.*

اچنبها अचंभा *achambhā*, or *achambā*, m. a wonder, marvel; adj. strange, wonderful. *h.*

اچنت अचिन्त *a-chint*, thoughtless, rash. *s.*

اچنتا अचिन्ता *a-chintā*, f. disregard, absence of thought.

اچنچل अचंचल *a-chanchal*, fixed, unmoved, firm, inactive. *s.*

اچنڈ अचंड *a-chaṇḍ*, gentle, not passionate. *s.*

اچواني अचवानी *achwānī*, f. caudle (v. *achhwānī*). *h.*

اچوك अचूक *a-chūk*, unerring; hence, a good marksman, a dead shot. *h.*

اچھ अछ *achh*, m. a die, cubic or oblong; the spots on dice. *achhi*, m. the eye. *s.*

اچھ इछु *ichhu*, f. sugar-cane. *s.*

اچھا अच्छा *achchhā*, good, excellent, righteous, healthy. *achchhā honā*, to recover. *achchhā-k*, to cure. *achchhā-lagnā*, to become, beseem, to be pleasing. *achchhe se achchhā*, best of all. *s.*

اچھا इच्छा *ichchhā*, f. will, wish, desire. *ichchhā-bhojan*, food agreeable and abundant to the utmost desire. *s.*

آچھادن आच्छादन *āchchhādan*, m. cloth, garments; a covering, cloak, &c. *s.*

اچهالنا उछालना *uchhālnā*, a. to throw up a thing (as a ball, &c.) and catch it in the hand. *h.*

اچهان अछान *achhān*, not strained, impure. *h.*

اچهانش अक्षांश *achhānsh*, m. a degree of latitude or longitude. *s.*

اچهاه उच्छाह *uchchhāh*, m. joy, gladness. *h.*

اچهبهاگ अक्षभाग *achh-bhāg*, m. a degree of latitude. *s.*

اچهت अच्छत or अक्षत *achhat*, or *akshat*, f. infallible, indelible; m. whole or unbroken rice used in oblations. *achhat tilak*, f. the ceremony of putting a few grains of rice on the forehead of an image when addressed, or of a Brahman when invited to an entertainment. *s.*

اچهت अच्छत *achhat*, remaining, existing. *h.*

اچهتارا अक्षितारा *achhi-tārā*, f. the pupil of the eye. *s.*

اچهتانا پچهتانا अछताना पछताना *achhtānā pachhtānā*, m. to repent, regret. *s. h.*

اچهر छाहिर *achhir*, m. the thrush, a complaint to which children are liable. *h.*

اچهر अच्छर or अक्षर *achchhar* or *akshar*, m. a letter of the alphabet. *s.*

اچهرس इक्षुरस *ichhu-ras*, m. the juice of the sugar-cane. *s.*

اچهرنا उछरना *uchharnā*, to leap or bound, to spring (a fountain), to fly up. *h.*

اچهروٹي अछरौटी *achhrauṭī*, f. orthography; a mode of playing on a stringed instrument so as to express the words of a song. *h.*

اچهري अक्षरी or अच्छरी *achchharī*, scientific; writing an elegant hand; lettered. *s.*

اچهڑنا *uchharnā*, same as اکهڑنا to be rooted up. *d.*

اچهسار इक्षुसार *ichhu-sār*, m. molasses, raw sugar. *s.*

اچهشٹ उच्छिष्ट *uchchhishṭ*, m. the remainder of victuals; leavings. *s.*

اچهك इच्छक,इक्षुक *ichchhak* or *ichchuk*, wishing, desirous. *s.*

اچهكانڈ इक्षुकाण्ड *ichhu-kāṇḍ*, m. a species of sugar-cane (*Saccharum munja*). *s.*

اچهل پڑنا *uchhal-parnā*, n. to become enraged. *d.*

اچهلانا उछलाना *uchhlānā*, a. to order another to throw up any thing. *h.*

اچهلنا उछलना *uchhalnā*, n. to leap or bound, to spring up (as water in a fountain). *h.*

اچهمتي इक्षुमती *ichhu-matī*, f. the name of a river in Bengal, the Issamutty.

اچهميهي इक्षुमेही *ichhumehī*, adj. diabetic. *s.*

اچهن इच्छन *ichchhan*, m. seeing, sight. *s.*

اچهن उच्छिन्न *uchchhinn*, ruined, laid waste, destroyed. *h.*

اچهنا अछना *achhnā*, also *āchhnā*, n. to be, to remain. *d.*

اچهواس उच्छ्वास *uchchhwās*, m. breath, breathing; hope, expectation; division of a book. *s.*

اچهواني अछवानी *achhwānī*, f. caudle. *h.*

اچهوتا अछूता *a-chhūtā*, intangible (victuals dressed for saints, &c.), inviolable *h.*

اچهودن अच्छोदन *achchhodan*, m. the chase, hunting. *s.*

اچهوهني अक्षौहिणी or अच्छौहिणी *achchhauhinī*, (properly *akshauhinī*), f. a complete army of 109,350 foot, 65,610 horse, 21,870 chariots, and 21,870 elephants. *s.*

اچهي अक्षय or अच्छय *achhai*, imperishable. *achhai briksh*, an undecayable tree. *achhai-lok*, m. heaven, the imperishable world. *s.*

آچهيپ आक्षेप *āchhep*, m. reproof, sarcasm, abuse. *s.*

اچهيتا अक्षयता *achhaitā*, f. durability, imperishableness. *s.*

اچهين आछें *āchhen*, adj. plur. good, excellent. *h.*

اچيت अचेत *a-chet*, out of mind or senses, senseless, thoughtless. *s.*

اچيت अच्युत *a-chyut*, firm, fixed, steady; imperishable, eternal; m. a name of Vishnu or God. *s.*

اچيتا अचीता *a-chītā*, unwished for; not painted (paper, &c.) *h.*

اچيلنا उचेलना *uchelnā*, a. to separate one thing from another. *h.*

اچين अचैन *a-chain*, uneasy, uncomfortable. *s.*

اح *uh*, an exclamation expressing pain: it is often reiterated, *uh, uh*. *a.*

آحاد *āhād* (pl. of احد), cardinal numbers; singly. *a.*

احاديث *ahādis* (pl. of حديث), f. traditions, particularly traditions or sayings of *Muhammad*, as constituting the basis of the *sunnat* or traditional law; lit. news. *a.*

احاطه *ihāta*, f. surrounding, inclosure; besieging (generally means the thing surrounded or inclosed, as a park, &c.) *a.*

احب *ahabb*, adj. comp. more beloved, a friend, most lovely, amiable. *a.*

احباب *ahbāb* (pl. of حبيب), friends. *a.*

احتراز *ihtirāz*, m. abstinence, regimen; abstaining from improper actions of any kind; forbearance, controlling the passions. *a.*

احتراق *ihtirāk*, m. strong desire, burning. *a.*

احترام *ihtirām*, m. act of honouring, paying attention, treating with respect. *a.*

احتساب *ihtisāb*, m. making up accounts; superintendence of police, censorship; superintendence of weights and measures in a city or market. *a.*

احتسابي *ihtisābī*, m. the superintendant or clerk of the market. *a.*

احتشام *ihtishām*, m. having many followers, &c.; pomp, retinue, magnificence. *a.*

احتكار *ihtikār*, in its literal sense signifies the laying up of any thing; and in the language of the law, the purchasing of grain, or other necessaries of life, and keeping them up, with a view of enhancing the price. *a.*

احتلام *ihtilām*, m. nocturnal pollution. *a.*

احتمال *iḥtimāl*, m. act of bearing or supporting; doubt, uncertainty; probability. *iḥtimāl-h*, to be probable. *iḥtimāl-k*, to doubt, to impute. *a.*

احتمالاً *iḥtimālan*, probably, very likely. *a.*

احتمالي *iḥtimālī*, probable, conjectural. *a.*

احتياج *iḥtiyāj*, m. necessity, want, occasion, need; plur. *iḥtiyājāt*, requisite things, wants. *a.*

احتياط *iḥtiyāṭ*, caution, circumspection, foresight, scrupulousness; *iḥtiyāt se* or *iḥtiyāṭan*, carefully, cautiously. *a.* [mares. *a.*

احجار *aḥjār* (plur. of حجر), stones; brood

احد *aḥad*, unity, one, an individual. *aḥadu-t-ṭarafain* or *aḥadu-l-mutakhāṣimain*, in law, denotes one of the two parties concerned in a suit.

احداث *iḥdāṣ*, m. act of making or producing any thing new; a novelty, a rare invention. *a.*

احدي *aḥadī*, a species of military corps (in India). *a.*

احديت *aḥadīyat*, f. unity, concord, alliance. *a.*

احرار *aḥrār* (pl. of حرّ), the noble, the free born. *a.* [fire. *a.*

احراق *iḥrāḳ*, m. act of burning, or setting on

احرام *iḥrām*, m. act of forbidding or interdicting; determination or resolution. At a certain distance from Mecca the pilgrims interdict themselves from all worldly enjoyments, &c.: here their resolution is fixed to complete the pilgrimage, and hence the word means the resolution or intention then formed. It also signifies a mean dress, worn by pilgrims on visiting Mecca or Medina; also, the act of putting on such a dress; also the period of the pilgrimage. *iḥram bāndhnā*, to make one's vows as a pilgrim. *a.*

احزان *aḥzān* (pl. of حزن), grievances, sorrows. *a.*

احسان *iḥsān*, m. benevolence, benevolent actions, beneficence, benefits, favour, courtesy, kindness. *iḥsān-k*, to oblige. *a.* [*mandī*, gratitude. *a.*

احسانمند *iḥsān-mand*, obliged, grateful. *iḥsān-*

احسن *aḥsan*, better, more beautiful, more excellent, more agreeable. *aḥsan-allāhu*, may God be gracious. *aḥsanta*, bravo, well done. *a.*

احشا *aḥshā* (pl. of حشا), the contents of the thorax or chest. *a.*

احشام *aḥshām* (pl. of حشم), servants, retinue; a kind of militia or armed police. *aḥshām daftar*, the muster-roll of militia, &c. *aḥshām-daftar-dār*, the militia accountant. *aḥshām-jā,egīr*, an assignment of revenue for the support of irregular troops or local militia. *a.*

احصا *iḥṣā*, numbering, reckoning. *lā-iḥṣā*, innumerable, beyond calculation. *a.*

احصان *iḥṣān*, restraining, circumscribing. *a.*

احضار *iḥẓār*, m. act of making to appear, or of calling, a summons. *a.* [serving. *a.*

احق *aḥaḳḳ*, comp. more proper, more de-

احقاق *iḥḳāḳ*, m. act of proving or establishing the truth of a doctrine, restoring to rights, administration of justice. *a.*

احقر *aḥḳar*, more or most contemptible (a self-humiliatory expression). *a.*

احكام *aḥkām* (pl. of حكم), orders, commands, decrees or decisions (of the government or of a judge). *aḥkām-nāma*, written orders. *a.*

احكامي *aḥkāmī*, one who is ordered or appointed by the ruling powers: such is the *aḥkāmī zamīndār* *a.*

احكم *aḥkam*, stronger, firmer, more stable. *a.*

احمد *aḥmad*, comp. more or most commendable, or praiseworthy; the name of *Muḥammad* and others. *aḥmad-maḥmūd*, a term applied in law to two persons who have combined to defraud a third. *a.*

احمدي *aḥmadī*, of or belonging to *Aḥmad*; name of a gold coin. *a.*

احمداباد *aḥmadābād*, name of a city in Gujrāt, and of another in the *Dakkhan*; the latter called also *aḥmad-nagar*. *a. p.*

احمر *aḥmar*, red, gold, barbarous. *a.*

احمق *aḥmaḳ*, a blockhead, most foolish. *aḥmaḳ kī dum* (*d.*), a fool. *a.*

احمقاپن *aḥmaḳāpan*, m. folly, stupidity. *a.h.*

احمقانه *aḥmaḳāna*, foolishly, stupidly; figuratively, it is applied to money which an *'āmil* is obliged to pay, to make good the deficiency of the revenue. *a. p.*

احمق پن *aḥmaḳ-pan*, folly, stupidity (same as *aḥmaḳāpan*). *a. h.*

احمقي *aḥmaḳī*, f. folly, stupidity. *a.*

احوال *aḥwāl*, m. condition, circumstances, events, occurrences, state, account; a report of the particulars of an affair, or of the condition of a thing or person. *aḥwāl batlānā*, to state one's condition. *aḥwāl-purs* or *-pursān*, one who inquires after another's health. *aḥwāl-pursī*, inquiry after health, circumstances, &c. *a.* [double. *a.*

احول *aḥwal*, squinting, one who sees objects

احيا *aḥyā* (pl. of حي), living things. *iḥyā*, m. act of giving life, saving, preserving. *iḥyā-l-mawāt*, lit. reviving of the dead, applied to the process of bringing waste land into cultivation. *a.*

احيانا *aḥyānan*, sometimes, now and then, from time to time; in the event, in case, should. *a.*

اخ *akh*, a brother; *ukh*, inter. sound of coughing; *akh-akh*, an exclamation of joy. *a.*

اخا *akhkhā*, an exclamation of surprise. *a.*

اخبار *akhbār* (pl. of خبر), news, a newspaper. *akhbār-nawīs*, a writer of news, an appointed intelligencer, such as "our own correspondent." *ikhbār*, m. act of giving intelligence or information. *a.*

اخبث *akhbas*, very impure or contemptible. *a.*

اخپخ *akhpakh*, m. understanding, wisdom, intelligence. *p.*

اخت *ukht*, f. a sister; adj. similar, congenial. *a.*

اختتام *ikhtitām*, m. completion, fulfilment, finishing. *a.*

اختر *akhtar*, m. a star, constellation; good fortune, good omen, horoscope. *akhtar-shumār*, an astrologer. *akhtar-shumārī*, the calculation of one's horoscope. *p.*

اختراع *i<u>kh</u>tirā'*, m. invention, inventing, discovering, fancying. *a.*

اختصار *i<u>kh</u>tiṣār*, m. abridgment, act of contracting, reducing, curtailing. *a.*

اختصاص *i<u>kh</u>tiṣāṣ*, m. peculiarity, appropriation. *a.*

اختفا *i<u>kh</u>tifā*, m. act of hiding, concealing, covering. *a.*

اختلاط *i<u>kh</u>tilāṭ*, m. friendship, intercourse, conversation; act of mixing; mixture, confusion. *a.*

اختلاف *i<u>kh</u>tilāf*, m. difference of opinion, opposition, discord, disagreement, misunderstanding between friends, coolness; pl. *i<u>kh</u>tilāfāt*. *a.*

اختلال *i<u>kh</u>tilāl*, m. interruption, obstacle. *a.*

آختة *ā<u>kh</u>ta*, also *a<u>kh</u>ta*, (literally, castrated) a gelding. *a<u>kh</u>ta-murgh*. a capon. *p.*

اختيار *i<u>kh</u>tiyār*, m. authority, power, will, choice, option, election. *i<u>kh</u>tiyār meṅ honā*, to be in the power of, or dependant on. *i<u>kh</u>tiyār-k*, to approve of, to adopt, to choose. *i<u>kh</u>tiyār-nāma* m. a power of attorney. *a.*

اختياري *i<u>kh</u>tiyārī*, f. approbation, choice, authority, power; adj. in one's power; subject to election, at one's disposal. *i<u>kh</u>tiyārī ṣulḥ*, in law, an optional compromise. *i<u>kh</u>tiyārī-zabḥ*, the killing of an animal for food by cutting its throat, as is done by Jews and Moslems. *a.*

اخذ *a<u>kh</u>z*, f. objection, cavil, hostility; taking, seizing, intercepting. *a<u>kh</u>z-k*, to seize, assume, accept. *a.*

آخر *ā<u>kh</u>ir*, the last; m. the end, issue; adv. at last, finally. *ā<u>kh</u>ir-ul-amr* or *ā<u>kh</u>iri kār*, at the end, finally, at last. *ā<u>kh</u>iri shab*, the end of the night, before dawn. *ā<u>kh</u>iri sāl*. the end of the revenue year. *a.*

اخراج *i<u>kh</u>rāj*, m. expulsion, turning out of possession, eviction; expense or disbursement; pl. *i<u>kh</u>rājāt* (corrupted *a<u>kh</u>arjāt*), expenses, disbursements; allowance for expenses. *i<u>kh</u>rājāti aurang*, expenses incurred in the manufacture, storing, and transporting of salt and other goods. *a.*

آخرت *ā<u>kh</u>irat*, f. futurity, a future state; the world to come, in opposition to *dunyā*, the present world. *a.*

آخرش *ā<u>kh</u>irash*, at last, finally, after all. *a. p.*

اخروٹ अखरोट *a<u>kh</u>roṭ*, m. a walnut. (The fruit of the *Aleurites triloba* is also so called.) *h.*

آخري *ā<u>kh</u>irī*, last, late, of or belonging to the end, final or ultimate. *ā<u>kh</u>irī ḥisāb <u>kh</u>arch*, adjustment of revenue at the end of the year. *ā<u>kh</u>irī nikās*, final settlement of an account. *a.*

آخرين *ā<u>kh</u>irīn*, last or latest comers; posterity. *ā<u>kh</u>irīn ḥarf*, a decree of fate. *ā<u>kh</u>irīn dam*, the last breath. *a.*

اخس *a<u>kh</u>ass*, more avaricious, meaner, or very mean. *a.*

اخص *a<u>kh</u>aṣṣ*, more especial, more excellent. *a.*

اخفا *i<u>kh</u>fā*, concealment. *'ilmi i<u>kh</u>fā*, the art of rendering one's self invisible, like Jack the giant-killer, or Æneas at Carthage. *a.*

اخفش *a<u>kh</u>fash*, one who has weak eyes, one who sees better by night than by day. *a.*

اخگر *a<u>kh</u>gar*, m. live ashes; a spark of fire. *p.*

اخلاص *i<u>kh</u>lāṣ*, m. affection, friendship, love. *i<u>kh</u>lāṣ-k* or *rakhnā*, to esteem, &c. *i<u>kh</u>lāṣ-mand*, affectionate, friendly, a friend. *i<u>kh</u>lāṣmandī*, friendliness, affection, sincerity. *a.*

اخلاط *a<u>kh</u>lāṭ* (pl. of خلط), the humours of the body of man and animals. *a<u>kh</u>lāṭi arba'a*, the four temperaments. *a.*

اخلاق *a<u>kh</u>lāḳ*, m. (pl. of خلق), disposition, the good properties of mankind; ethics, morals. *a.*

اخني پلاو *a<u>kh</u>nī-pulāo*, a kind of stew. *d.*

اخوان *i<u>kh</u>wān*, | اخوت *i<u>kh</u>wat*, } (plur. of اخ), brothers, friends, companions. *i<u>kh</u>wāni zamān*, cotemporaries. *a.*

آخور *ā<u>kh</u>or* or *ā<u>kh</u>ur*, f. refuse, offals; a stable; waste grass of the stable. *p.*

آخوں *ā<u>kh</u>oṅ*, master, lord, preceptor. *d.*

آخون *ā<u>kh</u>ūn*, | آخوند *ā<u>kh</u>ūnd*, } m. tutor, preceptor. *p.*

اخوي *a<u>kh</u>awī*, brotherly, fraternal. *a.*

اخيا *a<u>kh</u>yā* (for أُخَيّ), m. a little brother. *a.*

اخيار *a<u>kh</u>yār* (pl. of خير), the good, the excellent. *a.*

اخيافي *a<u>kh</u>yāfī*, a brother or sister, by the same mother but different fathers. *a.*

اخير *a<u>kh</u>īr*, last; m. the end, accomplishment, completion. *a<u>kh</u>yar*, better, best. *a.*

اخيرًا *a<u>kh</u>īran*, at last, in the end. *a.*

اُد उद *ud* (same as उत *ut*), above, over. *s.*

اد अद *ad* (same as *ādh* or *adh*), half. *s.*

آد आद *ād*, or आदि *ādi*, m. beginning; the first, originally: as a termination to a Sanskrit word it denotes "et cetera." *s.*

ادا *adā*, f. blandishments, coquetry; discharge, payment, performance; voice. *adā-k*, to liquidate, to pay. *adā-bandī*, the fixing a period for the performance of a contract, or payment by instalments. *adā-fahm*, one who understands by signs. *a. p.*

آدا आदा *ādā*, m. ginger in the undried state. *s.*

آداب *ādāb*, m. (pl. of ادب) etiquette, devoirs, ceremonies, politeness, forms of address in writing and speaking, salutation, respects. *a.*

ادات *adāt*, f. a particle, in grammar; a tool or utensil. *a.*

ادات उदात्त *udātta*, m. the acute accent, a high sharp tone; gift, donation, a kind of musical instrument, a large drum. *s.*

اداتا उदात्ता *udāttā*, liberal, generous, dearly beloved. *s.*

اداتا अदाता *a-dātā*, also *a-dānī*, avaricious, stingy. *s.*

ادار उदार *udār*, liberal, generous, munificent. *s.*

اادارتا उदारता *udārtā*, f. liberality, generosity, munificence. *s.*

اداس उदास *udās*, dejected, indifferent, sorrowful; m. loneliness; (in agriculture) a sickly crop. *s.*

اداسا उदासा *udāsā*, m. a cord worn as a shoulder belt. *d.*

اداسي उदासी *udāsī*, f. dejection, sorrow, solitude, loneliness; m. a class of *faķīrs* or devotees; adj. lonely, retired, dejected. *s.*

اداسين उदासीन *udāsīn*, m. one who is completely detached from the world, whose family is unknown, and who has neither friend nor foe; a class of mendicants of the Panjāb, an hermit, a misanthrope, a stoical, indifferent person, an umpire. *s.*

ادام الله *adāma-llāh*, may God preserve (him &c.) *a.*

ادان उदान *udān*, m. one of the five vital airs, that which rises up the throat and passes into the head. *s.*

آدان आदान *ādān*, m. taking, receipt, acceptance. *ādān-pradān* m. giving and taking. *s.*

آدانت आद्यंत *ād-ant*, adj. from first to last, from beginning to end; m. the beginning and the end. *s.*

اداني अदानी *a-dānī*, avaricious, stingy. *s.*

اداني *adānī*, (pl. of ادني) low, mean, or contemptible people. *a.*

اداهٹ उदाहट *udāhaṭ*, } f. brown colour,
ادائي उदाई *udā,ī* } brownness. *s.*

اداهرن उदाहरण *udāharan*, m. an example, a simile, a comparison, an opposite argument; one of the five modes of logical reasoning. *s.*

اداي دين *adā,e dain* m. payment of debt. *a.*

ادب *adab*, m. act of preserving the boundaries of every thing; good-breeding, politeness, respect, urbanity, polite literature. *adab-k*, to respect, to behave politely. *a.* [ruin. *a.*

ادبار *idbār*, f. misfortune, ill-luck, adversity,

ادبودھ उद्बोध *udbodh*, m. recollection the recognising of any thing. *s.*

ادبچ *adbich*, among, in the midst. *d.*

ادبهت अद्भुत *adbhut*, wonderful, admirable; m. surprise, astonishment. *s.*

ادبهو उद्भव *udbhav*, m. act of being born, of springing up (as plants from seed), birth, production. *s.* [names of Vishnu. *s.*

آدپرش आदिपुरुष *ādi-purush*, m. one of the

ادت अदिति *aditi*, f. the proper name of the mother of the gods. *s.*

آدت *ādit* (for आदित्य *āditya*), m. a deity in general; a deity of a particular class. The ādityas are 12 in number, and are forms of the sun as distinct in each month; the sun. *āditya-bār*, Sunday. *ādit* is also met with in the same sense as *ādik*, et cætera. *s.*

ادت उदित *udit*, risen (as the sun), distinguished, shining (as valour, &c.). *s.*

ادت अदत्त *a-datta*, not given. In Hindu law it is applied to an illegal donation, consequently void and resumable. *s.*

ادتا अदत्ता *a-dattā*, not given in marriage (a female). *s.*

ادتري *adatrī*, hanging; infirm. *d.*

ادتنندن अदितिनन्दन *aditi-nandan*, m. a deity, i. e. a son of *aditi*. *s.*

آدتو आदित्व *āditwa*, m. priority, precedence. *s.* [same as *ādityabār*. *s.*

آدتيوار आदित्यवार *āditya-wār*, m. Sunday,

آدتيه आदित्य *āditya*, m the sun, etc. See *ādit*. *s.*

ادخال *idkhāl*, m. entering, introducing. *a.*

اددھ उदधि *udadhi*, m. the ocean. *s.*

آدر आदर *ādar*, m. respect, regard, act of treating with attention and deference, politeness. *ādar-mān*, reverence and honour. *s.*

ادر उदर *udar*, m. the belly. उद्र *udra*, m. an offer. (dakh) *udar*, that way; *adar*, this way.

آدرا आद्रा *ādrā*, f. the name of the sixth lunar mansion (probably *a Orionis*); the beginning of the rainy season. *s.* [in another. *a.*

ادراج *idrāj*, m. act of inserting one thing

ادرار *idrār*, m. involuntary discharge of urine; hard rain, liberality. *a.*

ادرازي *idrārī*, a pension, allowance. *a.*

ادراك *idrāk*, m. understanding comprehension. *a.*

ادرامي उदरामय *udarāmay*, m. diarrhœa, dysentery. *s.* [worm. *s.*

ادراويشٹ उदरावेष्ट *udarāveshṭ*, m. the tape-

ادرپساچ उदरपिशाच *udar-pisāch*, glutton, voracious, one who devours every thing, one who has the devil for his belly. *s.*

ادرس *a-dris* for अदृश्य *a-drishya*, } invi-
ادرسن अदर्शन *a-darsan* or *a-darshan*, } sible, unseen. *s.*

ادرسا अदरसा *adarsā*, m. a kind of very fine muslin; a kind of sweetmeat. *h.*

ادرش अदर्श *a-darsh*, } invisible, unseen;
ادرشٹ अदृष्ट *a-drishṭ*, } m. unforeseen danger, fortune, fate. *s.*

آدرش आदर्श m. a mirror; a commentary, original manuscript; a copy, a sign. *s.*

ادرشن अदर्शन *a-darshan*, m. disappearance; adj. invisible. *s.*

ادرك अद्रक *adrak*, m. ginger in an undried state (*Amomum-zinziber*). *s.*

ادركي अद्रकी *adrakī*, f. a kind of sweetmeat. *h.*

ادرل उदरिल *udaril* }
ادرن उदरिन *udarin* } pot-bellied, fat, corpulent. *s.*
ادري उदरी *udarī* } [honour. *s.*

آدرمان आदरमान *ādar-mān*, m. respect and

ادرنی उदरिणी *udariṇī*, f. a pregnant woman. *s.*

ادروه अद्रोह *a-droh*, m. mildness, moderation, the absence of tyranny. *s.*

ادروهي अद्रोही *a-drohī*, innocuous, mild. *s.*

ادري उदरी *udarī*, f. enlargement of the abdomen from dropsy or flatulency. adj. abdominal. *s.*

ادريس *idrīs*, the Arabian name for the prophet Enoch. *a*

ادشت अदिष्ट *a-disht*, m. misfortune, fate. *s.*

ادعا *iddi'ā*, m. the act of demanding one's right or just claims. *a.*

ادعيه *ad'iya* (pl. of ادعا), salutations, congratulations, compliments, prayers, blessings. *a.*

ادغام *idghām*, m. duplication of a letter by tashdīd; coalescence of letters (in Arabic construction). *a.*

ادق *adakk*, more or very subtle, abstruse or difficult. *a.*

ادقچه *adakcha*, m. a cover, a wrapper. *p.*

ادك उदक *udak*, m. water. *s.*

ادك *adik*, (for अधिक *adhik*), more, much. *d.*

آدك आदिक *ādik*, relating to the beginning; (in comp.) and all the rest, et cætera. *s.*

آدكارن आदिकारण *ādikāran*, m. a primary cause. *s.*

ادكچا अदकचा *adakchā*, m. a cloth for carrying things in; a covering. See *adakcha*.

ادكهلا अदखिला *ad-khilā*, } half open, half
ادكهولا अदखोला *ad-kholā*, } blown (flower, &c.). *h.*

ادگار उद्गार *udgār*, m. vomiting; sound. *s.*

ادگت उद्गत *udgat*, vomited, cast up. *s.*

ادگدرا *adgadrā*, m. fruit fully formed, but unripe. *d.*

ادگڑها अदगड़हा *ad-garhā*, half driven (as a stake). *h.*

ادگهاٹت उद्घाटित *udghātit*, done with effort, exerted; opened. *s.*

ادگهاٹن उद्घाटन *udghātan*, m. the rope and bucket of a well, a leathern bucket for drawing water; an instrument for opening, a key, etc. *s.*

ادل بدل अदलबदल *adl-badl*, } exchange,
ادلابدلا अदलाबदला *adlāb-adlā*, } alteration.
ادلي بدلي अदलीबदली *adlī-badlī*, } *adl-badlī-k*, to exchange, to swop or barter; to confuse, displace; also *adlā-badlī-k* and *adl kā badl-k*. *h.*

ادله *adilla*, (pl. of دليل) proofs, indications. *a.*

آدم *ādam*, Adam, the first man; also, a man in the abstract. *a.*

ادم उद्दिम *uddim*, m. endeavour, exertion, profession, trade, calling, employment. *s.*

ادماد उदमाद *udmād*, m. lewdness, wantonness. *s.*

ادمادي उदमादी *udmādī* f. a paroxysm of lust; adj. wanton, lewd. *s.*

ادمبر उदुंबर *udumbar*, m. the glomerous fig-tree, or gūlar-tree (*Ficus glomerata*). *s.* sect of brāhmans *s.*

آدم خور *ādam-khur*, or خوار *khwār*, man-devouring, a cannibal. *a. p.*

ادمرا अदमरा *ad-marā*, m. } half dead. *h.*
ادمري अदमरी *ad-marī*, f. }

ادمڑا अदमड़ा *adamrā*, breathless, dead. *d.*

آدم زاد *ādam-zād* or *ādam-zāda*, descended of Adam; a man, mankind. *p.*

آدم گر *ādam-gar*, humane, benevolent. *p.*

آدم گري *ādam-garī*, f. humanity, benevolence. *p.*

ادموا अदमूआ *ad-mū,ā*, m. half-dead. *h.*

ادمي *ādmī*, a descendant of Adam; a human being (man or woman), individual, people. *a.*

آدميت *ādmīyat*, f. humanity, civility; *ādmīyat-k*, to behave with humanity. *ādmīyat pakarnā*, to become civilized. *ādmīyat sikhlānā* or *ādmīyat meṅ lānā*, to civilize. *ādmīyat uth-jānā*, to become savage, ferocious, and frantic. *a.*

ادن अदिन *a-din*, m. an unlucky day. *s.*

ادنا *adnā*, inferior, little, low, mean, a person of no consequence. *a.*

ادنتر *adantar*, also *adantarī* (same as *adurī*), pendulous, &c. *d.*

ادند अदंद *a-dand* or अद्वंद *a-dwand*, quiet, tranquil, free from strife. *s.*

ادنڈ अदंड *adand*, unpunished, m. impunity. *s.*

ادني *adnā*, see *adnā*, little, &c. *a.*

آدو आदौ *ādau*, at first, in the beginning. *s.*

ادوات *adawāt* (pl. of ادات), particles in grammar. *a.*

ادوار *adwār* (pl. of دور), revolutions; *idwār*, act of revolving. *a.*

ادوان अदवान *adwān*, } f. braces for
ادواين अदवायन *adwāyan*, } tightening the tape of a bedstead. *h.*

ادواه उद्वाह *udvāha*, m. marriage. *s.*

ادوت अद्योत *adot*, without splendour. *s.*

ادوتيه अद्वितीय *a-dwitiya*, peerless, matchless, unequalled; only, without a second. *s*

ادوري अदौरी *adaurī*, f. a kind of food eaten by Hindūs. *h.*

ادوكهل उदूखल *udūkhal*, m. a gum resin, bdellium. *s.*

ادوگن उद्विग्न *udvigna*, perplexed, dejected, anxious, troubled. *s.*

ادون *adwan*, very mean, or wretched. *a.*

ادوند अद्वन्द *a-dwand*, quiet, tranquil, free from strife. *s.*

ادويت अद्वैत *a-dwait*, peerless, matchless, unequalled. *s.*

ادويش अद्वेष *a-dwesh*, } harmless, not ma-
ادويشي अद्वेषी *a-dweshī*, } licious. *s.*

ادویگ उद्वेग *udveg*, m. perturbation (especially from pain), consternation, anxiety, perplexity, exertion, care; the fruit of the Areca catechu, betel-nut. *s.*

ادویگي उद्वेगी *udvegī*, perplexed, anxious, perturbed, agitated.

ادویه *adwiya* (pl. of دوا), medicines. *a.*

ادهِ अधि *adhi*, a particle denoting superiority; upon, over, above (the reverse of the particle *apa*). *s.*

ادهَ अध *adha*, down, downwards (the reverse of the particle *ut*). *s.*

ادهـ अध *adh*, in composition denotes half; as, *adh-mū,ā*, half dead. *s.*

آدهِ आधि *ādhi*, m. mental agony, anxiety; expectation, calamity; a pledge, pawn; location, fixing, site, &c.; engagement. *s.*

آدها आधा *ādhā*, half (in comp. *ādh, adh, ad*). *s.*

آدهار आधार *ādhār*, } m. food, aliment, victuals, nourishment. *h.*
ادهار अधार *adhār*,

ادهار उद्धार or उधार *uddhār* or *udhār*, m. debt (especially not bearing interest), loan, trust; deduction, discharge, deliverance, raising up from any place or state. *s.*

آدهار आधार *ādhār*, m. a patron, supporter, one on whom dependence is placed for assistance; comprehension, location; a dike, a canal; a basin round the foot of a tree. *s.*

ادهارمك अधार्मिक *adhārmik*, } unjust, unrighteous, wicked. *s.*
آدهارمك आधार्मिक *ādhārmik*,

ادهارنا उधारना or उद्धारना *udhārnā*, a. to liberate, to discharge. *s.*

آدهاري आधारी *ādhārī* (in compos.), an eater; as, *dūdh-ādhārī*, one who lives on milk. *h.*

ادهاسيسي अधासीसी *adhā-sīsī*, } f. pain affecting the half of the head, *hemicrania*. *s.*
آدهاسيسي आधासीसी *ādhā-sīsī*,

ادهان अधान *adhān*, m. oils, unguents. *h.*

آدهان आधान *ādhān*, m. pregnancy, conception; a ceremony performed previous to conception as conducive to it; a pledge, a deposit, a surety. *s.*

آدهانك आधानिक *ādhānik*, m. a ceremony performed after cohabitation to procure or favour conception. *s.*

ادهبٹائي अधबटाई *adh-baṭā,ī*, f. division of produce in equal shares. *s.*

ادهبر अधबर *adh-bar*, in the middle. *h.*

آدهبگڑا *ādh-bagṛā*, half cleaned (as rice from the husks). *d.*

ادهبنا अधबना *adh-banā*, half-made, half-prepared. *h.*

ادهبيچ अधबीच *adh-bīch*, in the middle. *h.*

ادهپ अधिप *adhipa*, m. king, master, or ruler. *s.*

ادهپاو अधपाव *adh-pā,o*, half a quarter. *h.*

ادهپت अधपत *adhpat*, properly अधिपति *adhipati*, m. prince, commander, *rājā*. *s.*

آدهپتيه आधिपत्य *ādhipatya*, m. sovereignty, government; lordship. *s.*

ادهپکا अधपक्का *adh-pakkā*, half ripe. *s.*

ادهت उद्धत *uddhat*, rude, arrogant, ill-behaved; m. a king's wrestler. *s.*

ادهتري *adhatrī* (v. *adatrī*), pendulous, &c.

ادهر अधर *adhar*, low, inferior, vile, m. the lip, the lower lip; pudendum muliebre. *s.*

ادهر अधर *adhar*, m. empty space, the space between heaven and earth; adj. suspended, separate, at a distance; in the middle. *h.*

ادهر इधर *idhar*, here, hither, this way. *idhar udhar*, about, around, up and down, here and there. *h.*

ادهر उधर *udhar*, there, thither, that way. *h.*

ادهرا उधरा *udhrā*, opened, undone, unrolled (as the seam in a garment, or thread which was rolled up in a clue). *h.*

ادهراج अधिराज *adhi-rāj*, supreme ruler. *s.*

آدهرجيه आधिराज्य *ādhirājya*, m. empire, supreme sway. *s.*

ادهرادهر इधरउधर *idhar-udhar*, this way and that, on all sides, all around. *h.*

ادهرامرت अधरामृत *adharāmrit*, m. the moisture or nectar of the lips. *s.*

ادهرپنا *adharpanā*, m. (for *adheṛ-panā*) middle age, manhood. *d.*

ادهرسا अधरसा *adharsā*, m. a half-piece of cloth, a sort of cloth. *h.*

ادهرم अधर्म *a-dharm*, m. injustice, impiety; sin, crime; adj. unjust, impious. *adharm-chārī*, unrighteous, wicked. *s.*

ادهرمپنا अधर्मपना *adharm-panā*, m. injustice, crime. *h.*

ادهرمتا अधर्मता *adharmatā*, f. unrighteousness. *s.*

ادهرمشٹه अधर्मिष्ठ *adharmishṭh*, very wicked. *s.*

ادهرمي अधर्मी *a-dharmī*, unjust, sinful, criminal. *s.*

ادهرےادهر *adhare-adhar*, separate, aside. *d.*

ادهڑنا *udharnā* (see *udheṛnā*), to undo, unravel. *d.*

ادهك अधिक *adhik*, more, greater, abundant, excessive, additional, augmented. *adhak*, a half, a part (less in use than *ādhā* or *ādh*). *s.*

ادهك उद्धक *uddhak*, m. asthma; act of gasping or panting; plethora in the vessels of the head; headache, indigestion. *s.*

ادهكار अधिकार *adhikār*, m. possession, extent of dominion, a kingdom; the bearing of royal insignia, authority, rule, privilege, inheritance. *s.*

ادهكاري अधिकारी *adhikārī*, m. a proprietor, sovereign ruler, autocrat, an owner, one possessing authority (absolute or derived), right, title, or privilege; one empowered. *s.*

ادهكانا अधिकाना *adhikānā*, a. to augment, to increase. *s.*

ادهكائي अधिकाई *adhikā,ī*, f. increase, augmentation, abundance, supremacy. *s.*

ادهكپالي अधकपाली *adh-kapālī*, f. a pain affecting half the head; a nut of Areca, shaped like a hemisphere (probably from two kernels being contained in one shell); to such a nut the virtue is ascribed of curing the disease of the same name. *s.*

ادهكتا अधिकता *adhiktā*, f. excess, addition. *s.*

ادهكچا अधकचा *adh-hachchā*, m. *adh-hachchī*, f. half ripe; a kind of soil in Sahāranpūr. *h.*

ادهكچرا अधकचरा *adh-kachrā*, m. *adh-kachrī*, f. half dressed (victuals). *h.*

ادهكر अधकर *adh-har*, m. half the tax, or duty of any kind, the other half being remitted. *adh-karī*, f. an instalment of eight ānas in the rupee. *s.*

ادهكرت अधिकृत *adhikṛit*, m. a superintendant, an inspector of receipts and disbursements, an auditor of public accounts. *s.*

ادهكرم अधिकर्म *adhikarma*, m. superintendence, supervision, government. *adhikarma-krit*, m. a supervisor. *s.* [title, right. *s.*

ادهكرن अधिकरण *adhikaraṇ*, m. superiority,

ادهكري अधकरी *adh-karī*, f. an instalment of eight ānās in the rupee, or half the government impost. *h.* [pronounced. *h.*

ادهكها अधकहा *adh-kahā*, half spoken, half

آدهكيه आधिक्य *ādhikya*, m. excess, an overplus, abundance. *s.*

ادهگدرا *adh-gadrā*, half ripe (fruit, &c.). *d.*

ادهم *adham*, a dark or dusky horse. *a.*

ادهم अधम *adham*, mean, vile, wretched, contemptible. *s.*

ادهمادهم अधमाधम *adhamādham*, extremely mean or base. *s.*

ادهماس अधिमास *adhimās*, m. an intercalary month, which happens once in three years, when two lunations occur within one solar month. *s.*—Hind. Gram.

ادهمانس अधिमांस *adhimāṅs*, m. fleshy excrescence of the eye, cancer of the eye. *s.*

ادهمرا अधमरा *adh-marā*,
ادهمرن अधमरन *adh-maran*, } half dead. *s.*
ادهموا अधमूआ *adh-mū,ā*,

ادهن अदहन *adhan*, m. water set to boil for the dressing of victuals. *h.*

ادهن अधन *a-dhan*, poor, destitute. *s.*

آدهنك आधुनिक *ādhunik*, recent, modern, belonging to the present time. *s.*

آدهنكتا आधुनिकता *ādhuniktā*, f. recentness, the being modern novelty. *s.*

ادهنگ अधंग *adhang*, m. palsy affecting half the body, *hemiplegia*. *s.*

ادهنگي अधंगी *adhangī*, palsied, paralytic. *s.*

ادهني अधनी *a-dhanī*, poor, indigent. *s.*

ادهواڑ अधवाड़ *adh-wār*, half (generally applied to pieces of cloth); a half-web. *h.*

ادهوتر अधोतर *adhotar*, f. a fine kind of cloth. *h.*

ادهورا अधूरा *adhūrā*, half ready, unfinished, half dressed; immature (a fœtus). *adhūrā-jānā*, to miscarry (a female). *h.*

ادهوڑي अधोड़ी *adhauṛī*, f. half a hide (of a thick strong kind). *h.*

ادهومكه अधोमुख *adho-mukh*, with the head downwards (a posture used in the *tapasyā* or austere devotion of the Hindūs); drooping the head (from grief or shame), headlong, inverted, turned upside down. *s.*

ادهون अधवन *adhwan*, half of any thing. *h.*

ادهونا अधिविन्ना *adhivinnā*, f. a superseded wife. *s.*

ادهوناد *adhonād*, half and half, *nisfā-nisfī*. *d.*

ادهويدانك अधिवेदनिक *adhivedanik*, m. dowry or alimony given to a wife who is superseded by a second marriage. *s.*

ادهي अड्ढी *addhī*, f. half of a *damṛī* (a small coin); half a piece of cloth. *h.*

آدهيا आध्या *ādhyā*, division of produce between two parties in equal shares, one furnishing the seed and the other the labour. *h.*

ادهيابك अध्यापक or आध्यापक *adhyāpak* or *ādhyāpak*, m. a teacher, one who instructs in the sacred books. *s.*

ادهياپن अध्यापन *adhyāpan*, m. instructing, teaching the sacred books. *s.*

ادهيار अधियार *adhiyār*, m. a man who passes half his time in one village and half in another: of such a one it is said, *adhiyār kartā hai*, "he acts as adhiyār." *h.*

ادهياري अधियारी *adhiyārī*, f. a half-share. *h.*

ادهيانا अध्याना or अधियाना *adhyānā* or *adhiyānā*, a. to halve, to divide. *h.*

ادهياي अध्याय *adhyāya*, m. section, chapter. *s.*

ادهيچه *adhyachh*, for अध्यक्ष *adhyaksh*, m. a master, superintendant, &c.; a man of rank. *s.*

ادهير अधीर *a-dhīr*, confused, perplexed, hasty, precipitate, irresolute, impatient, unsteady. *s.*

ادهيرتا अधीरता *a-dhīratā*, f. impatience, perplexity, haste, precipitation, fickleness, unsteadiness, confusion. *s.*

ادهيرج अधीरज *a-dhīraj*, m. perplexity, distraction, unsteadiness; adj. perplexed, distracted, unsteady, impatient, feeble, irresolute; also *a-dhairj*. *s.*

ادهيرجا अधीरजा *a-dhīrjā*, } perplexed, dis-
ادهيرجي अधीरजी *a-dhīrjī*, } tracted. अधैर्या *a-dhairjā*, m. instability, want of firmness. *s.*

ادهيرنا उधेरना *udhernā*, to undo. See *udheṛnā*.

ادهيڑ अधेड़ *adheṛ*, middle-aged; just past the prime of life (applied most frequently to women). *h.*

ادهيڑ उधेड़ *udheṛ*, m. unravelling, unweaving. *udheṛ-bun*, perplexity. *h.*

ادهيڑپنا अधेड़पना *adheṛ-panā*, m. the middle period of life, manhood, mature age. *h.*

ادهيڑنا उधेड़ना, *udheṛnā*, } to undo, un-
ادهيڑنون उधेड़नौं, *udheṛnauṅ*, } ravel. *h.*

ادهيشور अधीश्वर *adhīshwar*, m. an emperor, a king paramount. *s.*

ادهيكش अध्यक्ष *adhyaksh* m. a master, lord, governor, superintendant. *s.*

ادهيگن अध्यग्नि *adhyagni*, property or settlement given to a wife when superseded by a new marriage on the part of the husband: it is given during the marriage ceremony, over the nuptial fire. *s.*

ادهيلا अधेला *adhelā*, m. half a *paisā* (a small coin), amounting to 12½ *dāms* or 4 *damrīs*. *h.*

ادهيلي अधेली *adhelī*, f. half a *rupī*; also a kind of measure used for corn; also half a gold mohur. *h.* [half-share. *h.*

ادهيليا अधेलिया *adheliyā*, a proprietor of a

ادهين or آدهين अधीन or आधीन *adhīn* or *ādhīn*, submissive, obedient, obsequious, humble, docile, dependent. *s.*

ادهين अध्यन *adhyan* (for *adhyayan*) m. study, application, especially of the sacred books. *s.*

ادهينتا अधीनता or आधीनता *adhīnatā*, } f. sub-
آدهينتائی आधीनताई *ādhīnatā,ī*, } mission, obedience, obsequiousness, servility, dependence, slavery. *s.*

ادهيني अधीनी *adhīnī*, f. obsequiousness, servility, submission; petition. *s.*

ادي उदय *uday* or *udaya*, m. dawn, sunrise, ascent; the east, in opposition to *asta*, the west, the eastern mountain from behind which the sun is supposed to rise; light, splendour; prosperity. *uday-h.* to rise (as the sun). *uday-asta tak tumhārā rāj ho*, may your sway extend from the east to the west. *s.*

آدي आद्य *ādya*, first initial. *s.* [pity. *s.*

اديا अदया *a-dayā*, unfeeling, destitute of

ادياست उदयास्त *udayāsta*, from sun-rise to sun-set, from east to west. *s.*

اديان *adyān*, (pl. of دين), religions, religious rites or ceremonies. *a.*

اديان उद्यान *udyān*, m. a royal pleasure-ground. *s.*

اديب *adīb*, m. a teacher; adj. courteous. *a.*

اديپت उद्दीप्त *uddīpta*, illuminated. *s.*

اديپن उद्दीपन *uddīpan*, adj. exciting, inflaming, as passion; m. blazing, glowing, of a luminous body. *s.*

اديت उद्यत *udyat*, m. a section, a chapter; adj. raised, held up; active, persevering, labouring diligently and incessantly. *s.* [trace. *s.*

اديش उद्देश *uddesh*, m. a scope, a vestige, a

آديش आदेश *ādesh*, m. an order, a command; a salutation of Jogīs; in grammar, a substitute. *s.*

اديك *adīk*, (same as *adik* or *adhik*), more. *d.*

اديم उद्यम *udyam*, m. strenuous exertion, perseverance, labour; calling, trade. *s.*

اديم *adīm*, goats' leather perfumed, which they bring from Arabia. Pers. the face. *a.*

آدينت आद्यन्त *ādyant*, first and last, beginning and end; adj. from first to last, from beginning to end. *s.*

آدينه *ādīna*, Friday. *p.*

اديوت अद्योत *a-dyot*, without splendour. *udyot*, m. light, lustre.

ادي ودي *ade-wade*, m. procrastination. *ade-wade-k*, to put off, to evade, to shuffle. *d.*

اديوگ उद्योग *udyog*, m. exertion, perseverance, continued endeavour. *s.* [severing. *s.*

اديوگي उद्योगी *udyogī*, active, laborious, per-

اديي उदयी *udayī*, prosperous, flourishing. *s.*

آڈا आड्डा *āḍḍā*, m. a stand or station where porters &c. wait to be hired; a stall, booth, shop. &c. *āḍḍā-dār*, a palkī bearer or ḍāk runner. *v.* Wilson. *h.*

اڈراڈر अडरउडर *aḍar-uḍar*, m. a ditch and the mound of earth thrown up from it, forming the boundary of a field. *h.*

آڈمبر आडम्बर *āḍambar*, m. charge sounded by musical instruments; commencement; pride, arrogance; anger, passion; happiness, pleasure. *s.*

اڈوپ उडूप *uḍūp*, m. a raft, a float. *s.*

اڈول अडोल *a-ḍol*, immoveable, unshaken. *h.*

آڈهك आढक *āḍhak*, m. a measure of capacity (for dry measure), about 750 of our cubic inches. *h.*

اذ *iz̤* or اذا *iz̤ā*, when, lo, behold. *az̤ā*, vexation, injury. *a.*

اذار *az̤ār* or *āz̤ār*, name of one of the Chaldean months, nearly corresponding to our March; *āz̤ārī*, vernal. *a.*

اذان *az̤ān*, f. the summons to prayers, generally proclaimed from the minars or towers of a mosque. *a.*

اذبك *uz̤bak* (fem. *uz̤baknī*), an Uzbek, or one of the Tartar tribe so called. *p.*

آذر *āz̤ur*, m. fire; the name of Abraham's father (Terah); the ninth solar month. *p.*

اذرين *āz̤arīn* m. camomile flower, ox-eye. *p.*

اذعان *iz̤'ān*, m. obedience, submission; confidence, belief. *a.*

اذقه *az̤uḳa*, or *āz̤uḳa*, m. food, nourishment. *p.*

اذكار *az̤kār*, (pl. of ذكر) praises of God. *iz̤kār*, remembering, praising (God). *a.*

اذكيا *az̤kiyā*, (pl. of ذكي) people of penetration and understanding; the acute, the ingenious. *a.*

اذل *az̤all*, base, most vile, abject. *a.*

اذن *iz̤n* or *az̤n*, m. permission; dismission. *az̤in*, chanting the ḳur,ān; hearing. *a.*

اذوقه *az̤ūḳa* or *āz̤ūḳa*, m. food. *p.*

اذهان *az̤,hān* (pl. of ذهن), geniuses, intellects, capacities. *a.*

اذيت *aẕīyat*, f. wanton injury, oppression, distress, vexation. *a.*

آر *ār*, (r. of *āwardan*) bring thou; used in comp.; as, *bar-ār*, fruit-bringing, fertile. *p.*

آر आर *ār*, f. a goad, a kind of ladle; the artificial spur of a game cock. *h.*

ار *ar*, if; (contraction for اگر *agar*). *p.*

ار उर *ur*, m. the breast. *ur-l.* to embrace, to caress. उरु *uru*, f. the upper part of the thigh; adj. large, great, ample. अरि *ari*, a foe. *s.*

ار अरु *aru*, (same as اور), and, more, again. *h.*

آرا आरा *ārā*, m. a saw; a shoemaker's knife or awl; the name of a district, Arrah in Shāhābād. *h.*

آرا *ārā*, or *ārā,e*, in composition, denotes adorning; as, *jahān-ārā*, world-adorning. *p.*

ارابه *arāba*, m. a wheeled carriage, gun-carriage, &c., a cart. *p.*

آرات आराति *ārāti*, m. an enemy. *s.*

ارّاٹا अर्राटा *arrāṭā*, m. a loud and prolonged sound (as from the discharge of artillery, or the fall of a building). *h.*

آراجاري *ārā-jārī*, f. (for *ānā-jānā*), coming and going. *d.* [(a country). *s.*

اراجك अराजक *a-rājak*, destitute of a king,

ارادت *irādat*, } m. desire, inclination, wish, pur-
اراده *irāda*, } pose, design, plan, intention. *a.*

آرادهن आराधन *ārādhan*, m. worship, adoration, supplication; accomplishment, gratifying. *s.*

آرادهنا आराधना (or अराधना) *ārādhnā*, a. to worship, to adore, to serve, to accomplish; f. service, worship, adoration. *s.*

آرادهيه आराध्य *ārādhya*, worshipful, venerable; name of a class of brāhmans. *s.* [base. *a.*

اراذل *arāẕil* (pl. of ارذل), lowest, meanest, most

ارارا अरारा *arārā*, m. marks of nails left after scratching. *h.* [going. *d.*

آرازاري *ārāzārī*, f. thoroughfare, coming and

ارازل *arāzil*, lowest. See *arāẕil*. *a.*

آراستگي *ārāstagī*, f. dressing, preparation, getting into order, regularity, ornament. *p.*

آراستن *ārāstan* (r. *ārā* or *ārāy*), to adorn. *p.*

آراسته *ārāsta*, prepared, dressed, adorned, embellished, regular, decked out. *p.* [tions of land. *a.*

اراضي *arāẓī*, (pl. of ارض) lands, detached por-

اراقت *irāḳat*, f. spilling, pouring forth, pissing. *a.* [grove. *s.*

آرام आराम *ārām*, m. a pleasure-garden, a

آرام *ārām*, m. ease, rest, health, relief, repose. *ārām-k*, to rest, to repose. *ārām-pānā*, to recover. *ārām-ṭalab*, idle, slothful, a lover of ease. *ārām-giriftan*, to become quiet, to take it easy. *p.*

آرامگاه *ārām-gāh*, also *āram-gāh*, f. a resting-place, a bedchamber. *firdaus-ārāmgāh*, resting in paradise, an epithet applied to *Muḥammad Shāh* of Delhi. *p*

ارامل *arāmil*, (pl. of ارملة), widows; distressed, poor, in want of victuals (females). *a.*

آرامي *ārāmī*, a lover of ease, idle, slothful. *p.*

آراميده *ārāmīda*, (also *āramīda*), at ease, tranquil. *p.*

ارانا अर्राना *arrānā*, n. to produce a continued sound, as a mill (imitated from the sound). *h.*

آرايش *ārāyish*, f. embellishment, ornament, equipage, preparation, dressing; in dakh. artificial flowers, trees. &c., made of talk and tinsel. *d.*

ارب अर्ब *arb*, one hundred millions. *arb-kharb*, innumerable. *s.*

ارباب *arbāb* (pl. of رب), possessors, lords, masters. *arbābi jāh*, possessed of dignity. *arbābi-sukhan*, eloquent persons, poets. *arbābi-nishāṭ*, dancers and musicians. *arbābi-himmat*, men of high spirit. *arbābi-māl*, officers of the treasury. *arbābi shar'*, law-officers. *arbābi ma'nī*, spiritual persons. *h.*

ارباك अर्वाक *arbāk*, low, vile; adv. at first, formerly. *s.*

اربد अर्बुद *arbud*, one hundred millions. *s.*

اربرا उरबरा *urbarā*, f. fertile land or soil. *s.*

اربرانا अरबराना *arbarānā*, n. to hurry, to be confused, perplexed, agitated. *h.*

اربسي उर्वसी *urbasī*, name of an *apsarā*, or female dancer in the court of Indra; an ornament worn on the breast. *s.*

اربع *arba'*, four, (also *arba'a*). *a.*

اربعون *arba'ūn* and اربعين *arba,īn*, forty. *a.*

آربل आर्बल *ārbal*, f. age, duration of life. *s.*

اربند अरविन्द *arbind*, m. the lotus (*nymphæa nelumbo*). *s.*

اربهك अर्भक *arbhak*, m. a son, a child, a pupil. *s.*

ارپن अर्पण *arpan*, m. an offering, the making an offering; delivering, entrusting. *arpan-k*, to present an offering, to deliver, entrust. *arpan-nāma*, m. a deed of gift, especially to a temple or idol. *s.* [*s.*

ارپنا अरपना *arapnā*, a. to present an offering.

ارت *arat*, (corruption for *arth*, q. v.). *d.*

آرت आरत or आर्त्त *ārat* and *ārta*, grieved, afflicted, disturbed, confounded. *ārti*, f. pain, distress. *s.*

آرتا आरता *ārtā*, m. a ceremony attending marriage. When the bridegroom first comes to the house of the bride he is received by her relations, who present to him, and move circularly round his head, a platter, painted and divided into several compartments: in the middle of it is a lamp made of flour, filled with ghī, and having several wicks lighted. *h.*

ارتباط *irtibāṭ*, m. friendship, connection. *a.*

ارتحال *irtiḥāl*, m. death; act of marching or travelling. *a.*

ارتداد *irtidād*, m. apostasy, recantation; refusing, opposing. *a.* [a distinguishing mark. *a.*

ارتسام *irtisām*, m. plan, painting, writing;

ارتشا *irtishā*, accepting a bribe, (a judge); bribery, corruption. *a.*

ارتعاس *irti'ās*, } m. tremor, trembling, trepidation. *a.*
ارتعاش *irti'āsh*, }

ارتفاع *irtifā'*, m. elevation, exaltation, ascent, height, grandeur prosperity. *a.*

ارتكاب *irtikāb*, m. perpetration or commission (of a crime); commencement or undertaking of an enterprise. *a.*

ارتلا अर्तला *artalā*, m. a patron, protector. *h.*

ارتو उरटू *urtū*, m. crimpling, plaits (as of clothes). *urtū-gar*, a crimpler or plaiter. *h.*

ارتھ अर्थ *arth*, m. interpretation, definition, meaning, signification, sense, acceptation; intention, design; request, begging; riches; cause, sake. *tapasyārth*, for devotion's sake, for devotional purposes. *s.*

ارتھات अर्थात *arthāt*, videlicet, namely. *s.*

ارتهان *irtihān*, m. act of receiving any article as a pledge; a hostage. *a.* [ing. *s.*

ارتھانتر अर्थान्तर *arthāntar*, m. another mean-

ارتھ سدھ अर्थसिद्धि *artha-siddhi*, f. success. *s.*

ارتھ شاستر अर्थशास्त्र *artha-shāstra*, m. the science which teaches how to obtain things, as friends, money, or any other object. *s.*

ارتھي अर्थी *arthī*, supplicating, desirous, having an object to accomplish, self-interested, designing; m. a petitioner. *s.*

ارتھي अर्थी *arthī*, f. a bier. *h.*

ارتھيا अर्थीया *arthīyā*, m. a protégé, client, person recommended; a client, agent, broker. *h.*

آرتي आरती *ārtī*, f. a ceremony performed in adoration of the gods, by moving circularly round the head of the image a platter containing a burning lamp with several wicks. *s.*

ارث *irs*, heritage, inheritance. *a.*

ارج *arj*, worth, respect, honour. *p.*

آرج आरज or आर्य *āraj*, *ārj*, respectable, reverential, honourable. *s.* [tuting. *a.*

ارجاع *irjā'*, changing, returning, or substi-

ارجل *arjal*, a horse with one white fore foot; a large or tall man. *a.* [py, blessed. *p.*

ارجمند *arj-mand*, beloved, dear, noble; hap-

ارجن अर्जन *arjan*, m. act of gathering together; acquisition. *s.*

ارجن अर्जुन *arjun*, m. the name of a hero in the *Mahābhārat*, the third son of Pandu; the name of a tree (*Terminalia alata glabra*). *s.*

ارجنا अर्जना *arjanā*, to gain, gather, to acquire. *s.*

ارجھنا अरझना *arajhna*, *n.* to be ravelled or entangled (as thread or hair; met. the heart); to be bound (as in fetters); a. to quarrel without a cause, or unreasonably. *h.*

ارچ अरुचि *aruchi*, f. sickness at stomach; nausea; aversion, dislike, want of appetite, disgust.

अर्चि *archi*, m. flame, light, splendour. *s.*

ارچا अर्चा *archā*, } f. devotion, adoration; an image. *s.*
آرچا आर्चा *ārchā*, }

ارچت अर्चित *archit*, worshipped, adored. *s.*

ارچك अर्चक *archak*, adj. worshipping; m. a worshipper, an adorer. *s.*

ارچنا अर्चना *archanā*, a. to worship, to adore, to honour, to treat with ceremony; f. worship, homage. *s.*

ارحام *arḥām* (pl. of رحم), wombs, matrices; relations by the mother's side, uterine kindred. *a.*

ارحم *arḥam*, more or very merciful. *arḥam-ur-rāḥimīn*, the most merciful of the merciful, an attribute of God. *a.*

ارخاي عنان *ir<u>kh</u>ā,e 'inān*, m. act of loosening the reins; unruliness. *a.*

ارد उर्द *urd*, } m. a kind of vetch (*dolichos pilosus*). *h.*
اردھ उर्ध *urdh*, }

آرد *ārd*, m. flour, meal. *ard*, anger, rage. *p.*

اردابيگني उर्दाबेगनी *urdābegnī*, f. an armed female for attending the ladies of a royal harem. *h.*

ارداس अर्दास *ardās*, f. representation, offering to a deity. *h.* [meal. *h.*

اردادا अर्दावा *ardāwā*, m. coarsely-ground

اردبهشت *urdibihisht*, name of one of the Persian months, April. *p.*

اردر उद्र *urdra*, m. an otter. *s.*

آردر आर्द्र *ārdra*, wet, moist, damp. *s.*

آردرا आर्द्रा *ārdrā*, f. name of the sixth lunar mansion; same as *ādrā*. *s.*

آردرك आर्द्रक *ārdrak*, m. ginger in the undried state. *s.*

اردشير *ardshīr*, name of several of the Persian kings; Artaxerxes. *p.*

اردو *urdū*, m. an army, a camp; a market. *urdū,i mu'allā*, the royal camp or army (generally means the city of *Dihlī* or *Shāhjahānābād*; and *urdū,i mu'allā kī zabān*, the court language). This term is very commonly applied to the Hindūstānī language as spoken by the Musalman population of India proper. *t.*

اردھ अर्द्ध *arddha*, the half of any thing. *s.*

اردھ उरध *urdh*, m. (the same as *urd*), a kind of vetch. *h.*

اردھ بھاگ अर्द्धभाग *ardha-bhāg*, m. a half.

اردھ چندر अर्द्धचन्द्र *ardha-chandra*, m. a crescent, a half-moon, a semi-circle. *s.*

اردهانگ अर्द्धाङ्ग *ardhāng*, m. half the body, palsy affecting one side, or half the body, upper or lower, *hemiplegia*. *s.*

اردهانگي अर्द्धाङ्गी *ardhāngī*, a person afflicted with the above disease; f. a wife. *s.*

اردهچندر अर्द्धचंद्र *arddha-chandra*, m. a crescent, a half moon. *s.*

اردهراتر अर्द्धरात्र *ardha-rātra*, f. midnight. *s.*

اردهنگ ऊर्द्धंग *urdhang* (also *urdhag*), m. a disease occasioned by the mounting of wind upwards; flatulency. *s.*

اردي *urdī*, f. the first month in autumn. *p.*

ارذال *arẕāl* (pl. of رذل), little, mean (people); the vulgar (properly the refuse of any thing). *a.*

ارذل *arẕal*, most mean, vile, ignoble. *a.*

ارڑانا *araṛānā*, n. to scream out. *d.*

ارز *arz*, m. price, value; quantity; esteem, veneration; honour. *arz-i-bāzār*, price current, market price. *arz-i-irsāl*, invoice, particulars of the despatch of treasure, &c. *p.*

ارز *aruz* or *aruzz*, also *urz*, m. rice. *a.*

ارزاق *arzāḳ* (pl. of رزق), riches, possessions. *a.*

ارزان *arzān*, cheap, abundant. *p.*

ارزاني *arzānī*, f. cheapness; abundance of provisions. *arzānī-rakhnā*, or (*p.*) *arzānī dāshtan*, to present, give gratuitously. *p.*

ارزق *arzaḳ* (corruptly for *azraḳ*), blue, azure, cerulean; having cat's eyes. *arzaḳ-chashm*, blue-eyed, cat-eyed. *a.*

ارزن *arzan*, m. millet-seed; (Hind. *chīnā*). *p.*

آرزو *ārzū*, f. wish, desire; hope, want, distress. *p.* [longing. *p.*

آرزومند *ārzū-mand*, also *ārzū-kash*, desirous,

آرزومندي *ārzūmandī* or *ārzū-kashī*, f. eager desire, wishing, anxiety. *p.*

ارزيدن *arzīdan*, to be worth; to suit. *p.*

ارزيز *arzīz*, f. tin, base or light money. *p.*

ارژنگ *arzhang*, m. the house and gallery of *Mānī*, a celebrated painter. *p.*

ارس अरस *a-ras*, without juice, sapless, tasteless, dull, flat (as a composition). *s.*

ارس अरुस *arus*, m. name of a medicinal plant or tree (*justicia adhatoda* and *gandarussa*). *s.*

آرس आरस *āras*, m. weakness, laziness, inactivity. *s.*

ارس *iris* or *irs* (v. *irsī*), an axletree. *d.*

ارسال *irsāl*, m. mission; act of sending, especially a writing, letter, &c.: in revenue language it denotes monthly collections of rents, &c., forwarded to head-quarters by the subordinate revenue authorities. *irsāl-nāma*, m. an invoice of goods or rents, &c., forwarded as above. *a.*

ارس‌پرس अर्शपर्श *ars-pars*, m. partial bathing (throwing a very little water on the head with one's hand, instead of bathing), sprinkling or aspersion; act of touching. *s.*

ارسٹا अरसट्टा *arsaṭṭā*, m. guess, conjecture, valuation, appraisement; a mediator, a broker; a monthly treasury account of receipts and disbursements made up from the daily entries. *arsaṭṭā-navīs*, the clerk who keeps the monthly accounts. *h.*

ارسٹھ *arsaṭh*, m. a monthly account (of revenue). *h.*

ارسطاليس *arisṭaṭālīs*, } the Grecian philo-
ارسطو *arisṭū*, } sopher Aristotle. *g.*

ارسلان *arslān*, a lion; a man's surname; name or epithet of several Persian kings. *t.*

ارسي *irsī*, f. the axle of a wheel. *d.*

آرسي आरसी *ārasī*, weak, lazy, indolent, inactive. *s.*

آرسي आर्सी or आरसी *ārsī*, f. a mirror (but particularly applied to a mirror on the thumb). *h.*

ارسيلي نينا अरसीलेनैना *arsīle-nainā*, with weak eyes; with eyes as if just awake. *h.*

آرسيه आरस्य *ārasya*, m. insipidity, want of flavour or spirit. *s.*

ارشاد *irshād*, m. command, order. It is frequently used by an inferior as a respectful interrogation, in the sense of "What is your will or pleasure?" *a.*

ارش‌پرش अर्शपर्श *arsh-parsh*, m. partial bathing (throwing a little water on the head with one's hand), sprinkling, aspersion; act of touching. *s.*

ارشٹ अरिष्ट *arishṭ*, m. garlick, the nīmb tree (*melia azad-dirachta*); a crow; good fortune; misfortune, sign of death. *s.*

ارشد *arshad*, more or most upright, most tenacious of the right way; a person who explains orders, commands, &c., particularly of the deity. *a.*

ارض *arẓ*, f. the earth; a portion of land; pl. *arāẓī*, lands. *a.*

ارضي *arẓī*, terrestrial, earthly, mundane. *a.*

ارطال *arṭāl* (pl. of رطل *raṭl*), m. a measure of weight so called (about a pound). *a.*

ارغنون *arghanūn* (Οργανον), m. an organ. *g.*

ارغوان *arghavān*, m. a plant whose flowers and fruit are of a beautiful red (*arbor Judææ*); a red colour. *p.*

ارغواني *arghavānī*, of a red colour. *p.*

ارفاه *irfāh*, m. enjoyment of peace and the pleasures of tranquillity; bestowing affluence, comforting, cherishing. *a.*

ارفض *arfaẓ*, an obstinate heretic, particularly a bigoted *Shī'a*. *a.*

ارفع *arfa'*, more or most high, sublime. *a.*

ارقام *irḳām*, m. act of writing. *a.*

ارقان *arḳān*, m. jaundice; mildew. *a.*

ارك अर्क *ark*, m. the sun; name of a plant (*calatropus gigantea*) swallow-wort. *s.*

آرك आरुक *āruk*, m. a drug brought from the hills, of cooling properties. *s.*

اركاٹ अरकाट *arkāṭ*, name of a city in the *Dakkhan*; Arcot. *h.*

اركاتي अरकाटी *arkāṭī*, m. a pilot. It is supposed they got this name from the only pilots formerly, in this part of the world, being in the service of the *Nawwāb* of *Arkāṭ*, which seems very probable (Gilchrist's Naval Vocabulary); adj. belonging to *Arkāṭ*. *arkāṭī rupīya*, an Arcot rupee. *h.*

اركاشمن अर्काश्मन *arkāshman*, m. a crystal lens, a ruby. *s.*

اركان *arkān*, (pl. of ركن), pillars. *arkāni daulat*, nobles, grandees; lit. pillars of state. *a.*

اركانس अर्कांश *arkāns*, m. a digit or twelfth of the sun's disc. *m.*

آركت आरक्त *ārakta*, red, blood-red. *s.*

اركٹ अरकट *arkaṭ*, f. vigilance, activity, cleverness, ingenuity. *h.*

اركدن अर्कदिन *ark-din*, m. a solar day. *s.*

اركشت अरक्षित *a-rakshit*, unprotected, undefended. *s.* [of the sun. *s.*

ارك منڈل अर्कमण्डल *ark-manḍal*, m. the disc

اركوپل अर्कोपल *arkopal*, m. the sun-stone, a ruby; a crystal lens. *s.*

ارك ورش अर्कवर्ष *ark-varsh*, m. a solar year. *s.*

ارگ उरग *urag*, m. a snake. *urag-sthān*, m. the infernal regions. *s.*

ارگا अरगा *argā*, separate, apart, on one side. *s.*

ارگانا अरगाना *argānā*, a. to separate, to put on one side; n. to be separated. *s.*

ارگائي अरगाई *argā,ī*, f. being silent. *s.*

ارگجا अरगजा *argajā*, m. the name of a perfume, of a yellowish colour, compounded of several ingredients. *h.* [garments, &c.) *h.*

ارگجي अरगजी *argajī*, dyed with *argajā*, (as

ارگني अर्गनी *arganī*, m. a rope stretched for drying clothes or similar purposes; a wooden rod, or bamboo, stretched horizontally, has the same name. *h.*

ارگهـ अर्घ *argha*, m. libation, an oblation of eight ingredients offered to a god or a brāhman; act of pouring out water in honour of a deity, the sun, moon, &c., while performing their worship. *s.*

ارگها अर्घा *arghā*, m. a vessel shaped like a boat, used by the *Hindūs* in their devotions, for performing libation. *s.*

ارلا उरला *urlā*, adj. hithermost, of this side. *h.*

ارم *iram*, m. name of a fabulous garden in Arabia, paradise. *a.* [inclination. *p.*

ارمان *armān*, m. desire, wish, longing, hope,

ارماني *armānī*, desirous, hopeful. *p.*

آرمبهه आरम्भ *ārambh*, m. beginning, prologue. *s.*

ارمزاد *aramzād*, desirous, without resource. *d.*

ارمغان *armaghān*, m. rarity, curiosity, present; a piece of money. *p.*

ارمن *arman* or *irman*, Armenia. *armanī*, also *irmanī* or *armanīya*, an Armenian. *h.*

آرميدگان *ārāmīdagān*, (pl.) those at rest; the dead. *p.*

آرميدن *ārāmīdan*, to be at rest, to repose. *p.*

آرميده *ārāmīda*, quiet, at ease. *p.*

ارن अरुण *arun*, m. the sun; the dawn of day; a dark red colour. *s.*

ارنا अरणा *arnā*, or *arnā bhainsā*, m. a wild buffalo; cow-dung found spontaneously dried in the forests (used as fuel by the native apothecaries in the preparation of medicines). *h.*

ارنا अरना *arnā*, } n. to stop, hesitate. *h.*
آرنا आरना *ārnā*, }

ارنائي अरुणाई *arunā,ī*, f. the dawn, colour of the dawn, a dark red colour. *s.*

ارنب *arnab*, m. a hare, a rabbit. *a.*

آرنده *ārinda* or *āranda*, m. a porter, carrier. *p.*

ارنڈ अरण्ड *aranḍ*, m. the tree from which castor-oil is made (*Ricinus vulgaris* or *Palma Christi*). *s.*

ارنڈي अरण्डी *aranḍī*, f. the fruit of the *Ricinus vulgaris* or *Palma Christi*; a sort of fire-work. *s.*

ارنو अर्णव *arṇav*, m. the sea, the ocean. *s.*

ارنوپل अरुणोपल *arunopal*, m. a ruby. *s.*

ارنودي अरुणोदय *arunoday*, m. the first appearance of the dawn. *s.*

ارني अरणी *arnī*, f. a female wild buffalo. *h.*

آرنيه आरण्य *āraṇya*, m. a forest, a wilderness. *āranya-sabhā*, f. a forest court, a court for a community of hermits. *āranya-shashṭhī*, f. a religious ceremony observed by women. *s.*

ارواح *arwāḥ* (pl. of روح), souls, spirits. *a.*

آروپ आरोप *ārop*, m. a transmutation, a change. *s.*

آروپت आरोपित *āropit*, deposited, intrusted; transformed, changed into, feigned. *s.*

آروپن आरोपण *āropan*, m. planting. *s.*

اروا उर्वरा *urwarā*, f. fertile soil, yielding every kind of crop; land in general. *s.*

آروڑهه आरूढ़ *ārūṛh*, mounted on a horse or any thing else, elevated. *megh-ārūṛh*, seated on a cloud. *s.*

اروغ *arogh*, m. belch, eructation. *p.*

اروگ अरोग *a-rog*, } healthy, free from sickness. *s.*
اروگي अरोगी *a-rogī*, }

آروگيه आरोग्य *ārogya*, m. health, freedom from sickness; adj. healthy, (prop. *a-rogya* or *a-rogitā*). *s.*

ارون अरवन *arwan*, m. the first cuttings of corn, presented to the household gods. *h.* [*nelumbo*). *s.*

اروند अरविन्द *arwind*, m. lotus (*nymphæa*

آروندهنا आरूंधना *ārūndhnā*, a. to strangle. *kanṭh-ārūndhan*, m. strangulation. *h.*

آروهن आरोहण *ārohan*, m. rising, the growing of new shoots; ascent, staircase, ladder. *s.*

أروي अरवी *arwī*, f. a species of *arum*, the root of which is used in food (called also *ghoyan* or *ghūyan*, and in Bengal, *kachū*. *Arum colocasia*). *h.*

اروئ अरुई *arū,ī*, f. (corruptly for *aruchi*), sickness at stomach, arising from pregnancy. *h.*

اره *arra*, f. a saw. *arra-kash*, a sawyer. *arra sir par chalānā*, to oppress any one, to commit violence. *sir par arre chal gaye tau bhī madār madār*, he has incurred punishment and disgrace, yet has not reformed his manners. *p.*

آره आर: *āra* (for *ārā*), m. a saw, &c. *h.*

ارهٹ अरहट *arhaṭ*, m. an engine for raising water; the same as *rahaṭ*. *h.*

ارهر अरहर *arhar*, f. a species of pulse (*Cytisus cajan*); called also *tū,ar*. *h.*

ارهنا उरिहना *urihnā*, m. reproach, reproof. *h.*

ارهنت अर्हन्त *arhant*, m. a *sugat*, or follower of the doctrines of Buddh. *s.*

اريْ अरई *ara,ī*, f. the root of *Arum colocasia*; a goad at the end of a whip. *h.* [an awl. *h.*

آري आरी *ārī*, f. a small saw, a hand saw,

اري अरे *are*, a disrespectful mode of calling or address; fem. *arī*. *s.*

آري *ārī*, yes, yea verily. *p.* [kind. *h.*

آريا आरीया *ārīyā*, m. a plant of the gourd

اريب उरेब or अरेब *ureb* or *areb*, f. complication, deception. m. guilt. *h.*

اريبلي *arebale*, stratagem, deception. *d.*

اريت अरीति *a-rīti*, f. ill-manners, impoliteness, incivility, ill-breeding. *s.*

اري ري *are-re*, alas, woe's me. *d.*

آريه आर्य्य *ārya*, of a good family, respectable, venerable. *s.*

آڑ आड़ *āṛ*, f. a screen, shelter; a kind of ladle used in sugar manufactories; protection; a protector; an horizontal line drawn across the forehead; prevention, stop, hindrance. *h.*

آڑ *āṛ*, m. stop, hindrance; hence the boundary of a field &c. *āṛ-gīr*, a strip of sward encompassing a field. *h.*

اڑ *aṛ*, f. contention, objection, fault, contrariety, obstinacy. *aṛ-k*, to stop, to be obstinate (as a horse. *h.*

آڑ आड़ि *āṛi*, m. a bird, the Sarali (*turdus ginginianus*). *s.*

آڑا *āṛā*, oblique, crooked, across, transverse; m. a prop, a shelter; a large saw, a shoemaker's knife. *h.*

اڑادينا *aṛā-denā*, to abandon, give up. *d.*

اڑاڑ *aṛāṛ*, (also *uṛāṛ*) m. outhouses for cattle, harvest floor for the blossoms of the *māhwa*; also the steep bank of a pond or river. *h.*

اڑاڑا अड़ाड़ा *aṛāṛā*, m. high steep banks, of a river or tank. *h.*

اڑاڑي *aṛāṛī*, f. the measure of a field originally established in a lease or grant to which the occupant appeals in preference to an actual measurement or adjustment. *h.*

اڑاك उड़ाक *uṛāk*, capable of flying, fledged. *h.*

اڑامارنا *uṛā-mārnā*, to rob, to steal. *d.*

اڑان उड़ान *uṛān*, f. act of flying. *h.*

اڑانا उड़ाना *uṛānā*, a. to cause to fly; to spend extravagantly, dissipate, blow away, disperse, filch, entice. *uṛānā puṛānā*, to squander. *h.*

اڑانا अड़ाना *aṛānā*, a. to make to stop; to fasten one thing to another; m. the name of a tune. *h.*

اڑانچهو उड़ांछू *uṛānchhū*, m. flying away, disappearing; fraud, deceit, a deceitful stratagem; engine. *h.* [rasol. *h.*

اڑاني अड़ानी *aṛānī*, f. a large fan or pa-

اڑاؤ उड़ाऊ *uṛā,ū*, m. a spendthrift, an extravagant person. From *uṛānā*. *h.*

اڑائي *aṛā,ī* (for اڑهائي) two and a half. *d.*

اڑبال *aṛbāl*, a very distant relative, a pretended relative. *d.*

اڑبڑ अड़बड़ *aṛbaṛ*, m. words without meaning; adj. uneven, rugged. *aṛbaṛ baknā*, a. to speak inconsiderately, or without meaning; to rave, to talk absurdly. *h.* [tions. *h.*

اڑبڑنگ अड़बड़ग *aṛbaṛang*, m. foolish ac-

اڑبڑنگي अड़बड़गी *aṛbaṛangī*, inconsiderate. *h.*

اڑبند अड़बन्द *aṛband*, m. a cloth worn by Hindūs, passing from the waist, between the thighs, and fastened behind. *h.*

اڑبنگا अड़बंगा *aṛbangā*, crooked, uneven. *h.*

اڑپ उड़प *uṛap*, m. a raft, a float. *s.*

اڑپ بهڑپ अड़प झड़प *aṛap-jhaṛap*, need, necessity. *aṛap-jhaṛap meṅ honā*, to be hard up. *h.*

اڑتاليس *aṛtālīs*, forty-eight (for *aṭhtālīs*). *h.*

اڑتك *uṛtak*, m. housing of a saddle. *d.*

اڑتلا अड़तला *aṛtalā*, m. protection, shelter. *h.*

اڑتوك *aṛtūk*, m. hindrance; adj. erring, astray. *d.*

اڑتيس *aṛtīs*, (for *aṭh-tīs*) thirty-eight. *h.*

اڑتهي अड़ठी *aṛṭhī* } m. a broker, agent,
اڑتهيا अड़ठया *aṛṭhyā* } or salesman; one who conducts business on commission for a principal at a distance; a banker who grants and accepts bills on other bankers or correspondents. *h.*

اڑچك *uṛchak*, a thief, robber. *d.*

اڑچلنا उड़चलना *uṛ-chalnā*, n. to walk with a stately or affected gait. *h.*

اڑچن *aṛchan* or *aṛchin*, light, uneasy. *aṛchanī*, f. lightness. *d.*

اڑد *uṛud*, black grain, a kind of pulse. *d.*

اڑدابیگنی *urdābeganī* (for *urdabeganī*), f. an armed female. *d.*

اڑداوا *ardāwā*, mashed grain mixed with a little oil and water given to horses. *d.*

اڑدنڈا *ardandā*, m. stop, impediment; a bolt, a bar (of a door &c.); a yoke for oxen; adj. athwart, awry. *d.* [horses. *d.*

اڑدنگ *ardang*, m. the rheumatism in

اڑدو *urdū*, (for *urdū*) a camp, &c. *d.*

اڑذات *arzāt*, a villain; base-born. *d.*

اڑڑانا *ararānā*, m. to lament aloud, to shriek. *d.*

اڑس उड़स *ūras*, m. the common bug. *h.*

اڑسٹا *arsatā*, and اڑسٹگی, *arsatagī* f. laziness, sloth. *d.*

اڑسٹھ *arsath* (for *ath-sath*) sixty-eight. *d.*

اڑضامنی *ar-zāminī*, a counter security, or a surety for a surety, mutual responsibility. *h. a.*

اڑفاختہ *ur-fākhta*, a fool, a simpleton. *d.*

اڑك *arah*, a surname, epithet, title. *d.*

اڑکا *arkā*, a small brass coin, the eight part of a Madras fanam. *d.*

اڑکرنا *ar-karnā*, n. to stop, to hinder. *h.*

اڑکسب *ar-kasb*, m. following a trade (a Hindū) different from that of one's ancestors. *d. a.*

اڑگس بڑگس *argas-bargas*, m. lumber, worthless things. *d.* [firmament. *s.*

اڑگن उड़गण *urgan*, pl. the stars; the stary

اڑماپ *armāp*, m. measure more than the standard. *d.*

اڑمان *armān*, m. deposit, pledge, security. *d.*

اڑمٹیال *armattyāl*, silly, indiscreet, foolish. *d.*

اڑن उड़न adj. flying, on the wing. *s.*

اڑنا उड़ना *urnā*, n. to fly; to soar. *h.*

اڑنا *urnā*, (same as *urhna*), to cover one's self; to be clad. *d.*

اڑنا अड़ना *arnā*, n. to stop, to hesitate, to be restive (a horse). *h.*

آڑنا आड़ना *ārnā*, to afford shelter, to prop, to support. *h.*

اڑناگن उड़नागन *ur-nāgan*, f. a flying serpent or dragon. *s.*

اڑنگ अड़ंग *arang*, f. a manufacturing town; a warehouse where goods are sold wholesale; the place or dépôt where goods of any kind are manufactured, whether a town or not. *nīl kī arang*, an indigo factory.

اڑنگا अड़ंगा *urangā*, m. a mode of wrestling with feet; an obstacle. *h.*

آڑو आड़ू *ārū*, m. a peach. *urū*, much given to venery (a male animal), as a stallion &c. kept for procreation. *d.*

اڑوا अड़ूआ *arū,ā*, obstinate, perverse, mulish. *h.*

آڑواڑ अड़वाड़ *ār-wār*, f. a prop; obstacle; shelter. adj. stopping. *h.*

اڑود *urūd*, m. a kind of vetch, black grain. *d.*

اڑوسا अड़ूसा *arūsā*, m. a medicinal plant (*Justicia adhenatoda* and *gandarussa*).

اڑوس پڑوس अड़ोसपड़ोस *aros-paros*, m. neighbourhood. *h.*

آڑھ आढ़ *arh*, f. a kind of fish. *h.*

اڑھ *ārh*, in the dakhanī dialect this word denotes alternate, or an interval of a unit between two measures of time or space; as *yak roz ārh*, every alternate day. *yak kos ārh*, every alternate kos. *d.*

اڑھانا उढ़ाना *urhānā*, a. to put on clothes, to cause to clothe. *s.*

اڑھاي۔ अढ़ाई *arhā,ī*, two and a half; when used with a noun of number, twice and a half the aggregate number; f. a full gallop. *h.*

آڑھت आढ़त or अढ़त *ārhat*, *arhat*, f. agency, commission, sale by commission, brokerage. *h.*

اڑھکپر उढ़कपर *urhak-par*, a broach, a tilt. *h.*

اڑھك کرنا उढ़ककरना *urhak-k*, n. to seek, or cry for an absent person (applied only to a child). *h.*

اڑھکنا उढ़कना *urhaknā*, n. to be overset. *urhak-par*, overset, a tilt. *h.*

اڑھنا उढ़ना *urhnā*, n. to put on clothes, to be clad or covered. *s.*

اڑھنگن उढ़गन *urhangan*, m. any thing placed under a vessel to prevent it from upsetting; a prop, support. *h.*

اڑھول अढ़वल *arhwal*, m. a day-labourer. *h.*

اڑھونا उढ़ौना *urhaunā*, m. clothing. *h.*

آڑھي आढ्य *ārhya*, wealthy, rich, opulent. *s.*

اڑھیا उढ़ैया *urhaiyā*, a wearer or putter on of any dress. *h.*

اڑھیا अढ़ैया *arhaiyā*, m. a weight of two and a half sers; also a measure of the same capacity. *h.*

آڑي आड़ी *ārī*, m. a protector, supporter, a small saw or knife. *h.* [mode. *h.*

آڑي आड़ी *ārī*, f. a tune, a kind of musical

آڑي آنا आड़े or अड़ेआना *āre-ānā*, or *are-ānā*, to screen or shelter; to be protected. *h.* [lish. *h.*

اڑیل अड़यल *aryal*, obstinate, perverse, mul-

اڑینچ अड़ेंच *arench* or अड़ैंच *arainch*, also *arainsh*, f. enmity. *h.*

از *az*, from, by, than, with, out of. *p.*

آز *āz*, f. avarice. *p.*

آزاد *āzād*, free, solitary; a kind of *fakīr*, who shaves his beard, eyelashes, and eyebrows, and vows chastity, but considers himself exempt from all the ceremonial observances of his religion. *āzād karnā*, a. to manumit; set at liberty. *p.*

آزادگان *āzādagān* (pl. of *āzāda*), those free from worldly cares, religious men. *p.*

آزادگي *āzādagī*, } f. independence, release,
آزادي *āzādī*, } manumission, freedom. *p.*

ازاده *āzāda*, free, &c. v. *āzād*. *p.*

آزار *āzār*, m. sickness, disorder, disease; trouble, affliction, outrage, injury; used in composition as *dil-āzār*, injuring or outraging the heart. *p.*

ازار *izār*, f. drawers, trousers. *izār-band*, m. the string with which drawers are tied. *izār-bandī rishta*, connection through a wife; petticoat interest. *p.*

آزارده *āzār-dih*, one who gives trouble or injury. *āzār-dihī*, f. the act of troubling. *p.*

آزاري *āzārī*, a sick person, a patient. *p.*

ازاله *izāla*, m. removal, abolition; (in grammar) the elision of a letter or vowel-point from a word. *a.*

از ان *az-ān*, thence, therefore. *az-āni*, belonging to. *az-ān-jā ki*, for as much as. *p.*

ازبر *az-bar*, by rote, by heart, by memory. *p.*

ازبراي *az-barā,e* } on account of, for the sake
ازبهر *az-bahri* } of. *p.*

ازپا *az-pā*, lit. from on one's feet. *az-pā dar āmadan*, to fall into distress or trouble. *p.*

ازدحام *izdiḥām*, m. a crowd, a concourse. *a.*

ازدر *azdar*, worthy, proper, suitable; sometimes improperly used for *azhdar*, a dragon, q. v. *p.*

ازدري *azdarī*, f. worthiness, fitness. *p.*

ازدياد *izdiyād*, m. increase, addition. *a.*

آزردگي *āzurdagī*, f. vexation, affliction, displeasure, sorrow, grief. *p.*

آزردن *āzurdan* (r. *āzār*), to vex, to grieve. *p.*

آزرده *āzurda*, afflicted, sad, dispirited, sorrowful, vexed, displeased, weary. *āzurda-k͟hāṭir*, or *āzurda-dil*, grieved in heart; vexed, offended, disgusted. *p.*

ازرق *azraḳ*, blue, blue-eyed; pure, limpid; [beryl. *a.*

آزرم *āzarm*, modesty, mildness. *p.*

ازروي *az-rū,e*, by reason of, in consequence of. *p.*

ازقه *azuḳa* or *āzuḳa*, m. food, nourishment. *p.*

ازك توزك *uzak-tūzak*, m. pomp, splendour; the habits or fashions of a king; the king's seal. *t.*

ازل *azal*, f. eternity without beginning. *a.*

ازلت *azallat*, f. injustice, injury (suffered without power of redress), oppression; straits, famine, scarcity.—Hunter. N.B. This word not in any Persian or Arabic Dictionary to which we have had access. *a.*

ازلي *azalī*, eternal without beginning, or from all eternity. *a* [nity. *a.*

ازليت *azalīyat*, f. existence from all eter-

آزما *āzmā*, trying, trial (used in comp.). *p.*

ازمان *azmān* (pl. of زمان), times, seasons. *a.*

آزمانا *āzmānā*, a. to try, to prove, to examine to touch gold, &c. on the touchstone. *h.*

آزمايش *āzmāyish*, } f. trial, proof, exami-
آزمودگي *āzmūdagī*, } nation: in revenue language, it denotes an estimate of the crop while in the field by an officer of government. *āzmāyish-gumāshta* or *-mutaṣaddī*, the officer who estimates the crop. *p.*

ازمنه *azmina* (pl. of زمان), times, seasons. *a.*

آزمودن *āzmūdan* (r. *āzmā*), to try, test. *p.*

آزموده *āzmūda*, tried, proved, examined; *āzmūda-kār*, experienced in business. *p.*

ازواج *azwāj* (pl. of زوج or زوجه), spouses, wives. *a.*

آزو بازو *āzū-bāzū* (for *ās-pās*), all around, on all four sides. *d.*

ازوقه *azūḳa* or *āzūḳa*, m. food. *p.*

ازهردري *az-har-dare*, of all sorts and kinds. *p.*

اژدر *azhdar*, } m. a large serpent, a dra-
اژدرها *azhdarhā*, } gon. *p.*
اژدها *azhdahā*, }

اژدهات *azhdhāt*, m. bell-metal. *azhdhātī*, of or relating to bell-metal. *s.*

اس *is* and *us*, inflections of *yih* and *wuh*, q.v. *h.*

اس असि *asi*, m. a sword, a scimitar. *s.*

اس असु *asu*, m. life, breath; the five vital breaths or airs of the body; reflection, thought, or the heart as the seat of it; affection. *s.*

آس आस *ās*, or آسا आसा *āsā*, f. hope, dependence, confidence, trust, reliance. *ās*, added to words, signifies inclination, and *āsā*, possessed of that inclination, as from the root *pī*, drink, *piyās*, thirst, and *piyāsā*, thirsty. *s.*

آسا *āsā* (in composition), like, resembling; soothing, tranquillizing. *p.*

اسابيع *asābī'* (pl. of اسبوع), weeks. *a*

اساتذه *asātiza* (pl. of استاذ), teachers. *a*

اساته असाथ *a-sāth*, addicted to evil company. *s.* [an unknown person. *s.*

اساتهي असाथी *a-sāthī*, an upstart, a stranger,

اسادھ असाध or असाद्ध *a-sādh*, evil-minded, thievish; lazy, without desire or energy. *s.*

اسادھ असाधु *a-sādhu*, unrighteous, immoral, wicked. *s.*

اسادهتا असाधुता *a-sādhutā*, f. wickedness. *s.*

اسادهيه असाध्य *a-sādhya*, weak, powerless; impossible, incurable. *s.*

اسار असार *a-sār*, sapless, pithless; vain, unprofitable; hollow (like a reed); foolish, weak of understanding. *s.*

اسارا उसारा *usārā*, m. a porch, portico, peristyle, vestibule. *h.*

اسارنا उसारना *usārnā*, a. to remove, put out of place. *h.*

اساڑھ असाढ़ *asāṛh*, m. the name of a Hindū solar month, during which the sun is in Gemini; the first month of the rainy season, and consequently of cultivation. *s.*

اساڑھي असाढ़ी *asāṛhī*, f. the full moon in *asāṛh*, also the harvest of *asāṛh*. *s.*

اساس *asās*, f. foundation; a pedestal. *a.*

اساس उसास *usās*, m. breath, breathing. *h.*

اساسنا उसासना *usāsnā*, n. to breathe. *h.*

اساعت *a-sā'at*, f. an unlucky moment. *h. a.*

اساکھ असाख *a-sākh*, without credit or reputation. *h.*

اساکھات / اساکشات असाक्षात् *a-sākhāt*, *a-sākshāt*, in the absence of. *s.*

اساکهي असाखी or **असाक्षी** *a-sākhī*, m. a false witness, one whose evidence or testimony is inadmissible. *s.* *asākhya*, m. a want of testimony; adj. without credit or reputation. *s.*

آسام *āsām*, name of a province, Assam. *h.*

اسامرتھ असामर्थ *a-sāmarth*, weak, powerless. *s.*

اسامي *asāmī* (pl. of اسم), names; (for اثامي) a defendant (in a lawsuit); a tenant, renter, client; a person, or individual; f. office, place, appointment, substitution of one person to do the duty of another; ex. *ham apnī asāmī par fulāne ko rakh jāte hain*, I leave such a one in charge of my duty. *a.*

اسامي وار *asāmī-wār*, including all the names applied to revenue settlements made with the proprietors in detail. *a.*

آسان *āsān*, easy, convenient, commodious. *p*

اسانا उसाना *usānā*, a. to winnow. *h.*

اسانا उसान्ना *usānnā*, a. to boil, to cause to boil. *h.*

آساني *āsānī*, **آسانيت** *āsāniyat*, f. facility, easiness; *ba-āsānī*, easily. *p.*

اساودھان असावधान *a-sāvadhān*, careless, inadvertent. *s.*

اساوري असावरी or **आसावरी** *asāwarī*, *āsāwarī*, f. name of a *rāginī* or musical mode; a kind of pigeon; a kind of cotton cloth. *s.*

اساول *isāwal*, m. a pursuivant. *t.*

آساونت आसावन्त *āsāwant*, expectant, dependent. *s.*

اساونت असावन्त *a-sāwant*, fearful, unquiet, pitiful. *h.*

آسايش *āsāyish*, f. rest, ease, tranquillity, repose, quiet, indulgence, enjoyment. *p.*

اسب *asb*, m. a horse (properly اسپ, q.v.). *p.*

اسباب *asbāb*, m. (pl. of سبب) causes; goods and chattels, furniture, tools, apparatus, baggage. *a.*

اسباط *asbāṭ* (pl. of سبط), the tribes of Israel. *a.*

اسبق *asbaḳ*, past times, days of yore; most excellent, surpassing. *a.*

اسبوع *usbū'*, m. a week (from سبع seven). *a.*

اسبھيه असभ्य *a-sabhya*, rude, unfit for society, unpolite. *s.*

اسپ *asp*, a horse. *p.*

اسپات *ispāt*, m. steel of a tough kind. *h.*

آس پاس आसपास *ās-pās*, m. vicinity, circumference; adv. all around, on all sides. *h.*

آسپد आस्पद *āspad*, m. place, footing, rank. *s.*

اس پر *is-par*, upon this, hereupon. *us-par*, thereupon. *h.*

اسپرسي अस्पर्सी *asparsī*, palpable, tangible. The word is properly *sparsī*, to which the *alif* (*a*) is prefixed, to avoid the meeting of two quiescent consonants in the beginning of a word, which cannot be pronounced by the Persians and Arabs; *a-sparsī*, intangible (by prefixing the priv. *a* to *sparsī*). *s.*

اسپرشنييه अस्पर्शनीय *ā-sparshanīya*, **اسپرشيه अस्पृश्य** *a-sprishya*, impure, not to be touched. *s.*

اسپرمول *isparmūl*, m. name of a plant said to be an antidote to the bite of a snake (*Aristolochia Indica*). *h.*

اسپرھا इस्पृहा *isprihā*, f. inclination, desire. *s.*

اسپشٹ अस्पष्ट *a-spashṭa*, indistinct. *s.*

اسپغول *ispaghūl*, m. seed of fleawort or plantain (*Plantago psyllium?*). *p.*

اسپك *aspak*, f. bridge of a musical instrument; a little horse. *p.*

اسپند *ispand*, m. a seed of the henna plant, burnt at marriages, to drive away evil spirits. In like manner it is burnt some days after a child is born, particularly at the door, to prevent demons, &c., from entering. It is often mixed on these occasions with mustard-seed, and hence has been confounded with it. *p.*

اسپهان *ispahān*, or **اسفهان** *isfahān*, the capital of Persia (till very recently). *p.*

آس پيس *ās-pīs* (v. *ās-pās*), all around. *d.*

است असत *a-sat* (for *asatya*, q.v.), unholy, ungodly, non-existent, untrue, false. *s.*

است अस्त *ast* or *asta*, setting (as the sun, &c.). *ast-h.* to set (the sun). *s.*

استا उस्ता *ustā*, m. a barber. *h.*

استاچل अस्ताचल *astāchal*, the name of a mountain in the west, behind which the sun is supposed to set. *s.*

استاد *istād*, standing, erect. *p.*

استاد *ustād*, m. a teacher, a preceptor, a chief in a department; adj. skilful, competent. *a.*

استادگي *istādagī*, f. firmness; resistance. *p.*

استاده *istāda*, standing, set up, erected; hence, a pole, ensign-staff, &c., particularly a prop for supporting the door of a tent, not the tent-pole. *p.*

استادي *ustādī*, f. teaching; adj. masterly (as workmanship, &c.). *p.*

استاذ *ustāz* (the same as *ustād*), master, &c. *p.*

استار *istār*, a weight of 4½ miskāls or 6½ drams. *a.*

استامبول *istāmbol*, also *istānbol* and *islāmbol*, the city of Constantinople. *p.*

آستان *āstān*, آستانه *āstāna*, } m. a threshold; a *fakīr's* residence. *āstān-bos*, one who pays a visit to a superior. *āstān-bosī*, f. paying a respectful visit. *p.*

استبداد *istibdād*, m. absolute dominion, despotism; insisting upon a thing being done. *a.*

استبرا *istibrā*, m. cleansing; washing one's hands of a business, or desiring to be freed from it; a woman after being divorced from her husband, waiting a certain time (three months according to Muhammadan law), to ascertain whether she is pregnant or not, before she can contract another marriage. *a.*

استبرق *istabrak*, m. green colour; silk, cloth, or satin, whose colour seems to change agreeably to the light it is seen in (particularly green silk). *a.*

استبيست अस्तब्यस्त *astabyast*, dispersed, scattered, confused, perplexed. *s.*

استت अस्तुत *astut* (for *stuti*), f. praise; an anthem, a hymn. *s.*

استتار *istitār*, m. act of concealing. *a.*

استثقال *istisķāl*, m. heaviness, trouble, importunity. *a.*

استثنا *istisnā*, m. exception, distinction. *a.*

استجابت *istijābat*, f. accepting, consenting; hearing or receiving a petition. *a.*

استحاضه *istihāza*, m. immoderate flux of the menses. *a.*

استحاله *istihāla*, undergoing a change; being impossible or absurd. *a.*

استحباب *istihbāb*, m. contracting friendship; an action, the performance of which is meritorious, but the omission of which is not criminal; work of supererogation. *a.*

استجازت *istijāzat*, f. asking leave, begging permission. *a.*

استحسان *istihsān*, m. approving, praising, taking or considering as a favour. *a.*

استحضار *istihzār*, m. calling, citing to appear, summoning before. *a.*

استحقار *istihkār*, m. despising, vilifying, scorning, treating with contempt. *a.*

استحقاق *istihkāk*, m. demanding justice; merit; ability in law it denotes a claim of right preferred by others, to the subject of a sale. *a.*

استحكام *istihkām*, m. confirmation, firmness, strength. *a.*

استحلاف *istihlāf*, causing to swear, exacting an oath. *a.*

استخاره *istikhāra*, m. judging from omens; augury. *a.*

استخدام *istikhdām*, m. employing, making use of the labour of another; asking or getting employment. *a.*

استخراج *istikhrāj*, m. expulsion; drawing forth, extracting. *a.*

استخفاف *istikhfāf*, m. despising, holding in contempt or in small esteem. *a.*

استخلاص *istikhlāṣ*, m. desiring to liberate; liberty; freedom. *a.*

استخوان *ustukhwān*, m. a bone, kernel of the date fruit, &c. *ustukhwān-band*, a splint or fillet for tying up a broken bone. *p.*

استدامت *istidāmat*, f. assiduity; wishing to be quiet, permanent, steady, eternal, perpetual, everlasting. *a.*

استدانت *istidānat*, desiring to borrow: in its common acceptation, it signifies contracting debt in behalf either of one's self or of another. *a.*

استدراك *istidrāk*, m. comprehending, understanding; reaching, overtaking, obtaining. *a.*

استدعا *istid'ā*, f. request, desire, invitation, supplication, petition. *a.*

استدلال *istidlāl*, m. asking proofs, arguments, or reasons; demonstration. *a.*

استر अस्त्र *astra*, m. a missile weapon, a weapon in general. *astra-vidyā* or *astra-ved*, the military science. *astra-hīn*, unarmed. *s.*

استر *astar*, m. a mule. *istar*, a harrow. *p.*

استر *astar*, m. lining. *astar-kārī*, plastering. *p.*

استرا *usturā*, m. a razor (for استره q. v.). *p.*

استرا उस्तरा *ustarā*, m. a barber. *h.*

استراحت *istirāhat*, f. ease, rest; sleep; repose; tranquillity. *a.*

استران उस्तरां *ustarān*, gratis, free, for nothing. *h.*

استرجاع *istirjā'*, m. returning (to God), having recourse to God during affliction; repeating the sentence (from the *kur'ān*), "Verily we are of God, and to Him we return." *a.*

استرداد *istirdād*, m. demanding restitution of any thing, whether given, deposited in trust, or taken without consent; repelling, driving, forcing back. *istirdādi nīlām*, reversal of a public sale. *a.*

استرضا *istirzā*, f. desire to please, willingness, alacrity. *a.*

استرك *astarak*, m. storax. *g.*

استره *ustura*, m. a razor. This is one of the numerous old Persian words still preserved in Hindūstānī, although they have become obsolete in the original. The modern name in Persian for a razor is "*tighi dallākī*" (note by Binning). *p.*

استري इस्त्री *istrī* or *istirī* (for *strī*), f. a woman. *s.*

استري इस्त्री *istrī*, m. smoothing-iron. *istrī-karnā*, a. to iron; to smooth with an iron. *istrī-wālā* one who irons linen. *h.*

استسعاد *istis'ād*, m. desiring happiness; being fortunate; considering any thing as a happy presage; conceiving well of any thing. *a.*

استسقا *istisḳā*, m. the dropsy; *istisḳā,i-ziḳḳī*, the anasarca; *istisḳā,i-ṭablī*, tympany. *a.*

استشهاد *istishhād*, m. taking evidence; summoning witnesses; bringing testimony or proof; falling a martyr to religion. *a.*

استصناع *istiṣnā'*, m. a requisition of workmanship, forced labour, pressing into service. *a.*

استصواب *istiṣwāb*, m. approving; consultation. *a.*

استطاعت *istiṭā'at*, f. power, possibility; dependence, submitting to. *a.*

استظهار *istiẓhār*, m. imploring assistance; remembering, calling to memory. *a.*

استعاره *isti'āra*, m. borrowing; using a word metaphorically; a metaphor. *isti'āra-karnā*, a. to beseech, to beg earnestly. *a.*

استعانت *isti'ānat*, f. asking assistance, imploring help; assistance, protection. *a.*

استعجال *isti'jāl*, m. hastening, accelerating, ordering one to make haste, despatching any business soon; wishing to make haste. *a.*

استعداد *isti'dād*, f. ability, means, capacity, merit, readiness. *a.*

استعفا *isti'fā*, m. asking forgiveness; deprecating. *a.* [siring promotion. *a.*

استعلا *isti'lā*, m. superiority, exaltation; de-

استعمال *isti'māl*, m. custom, daily practice, use. *isti'māl-k.*, to use. *a.*

استعمالي *isti'mālī*, fit for practical use, used; m. fine rice. *a.*

استغاثه *istighāsa*, m. asking for help; demanding justice, complaining. *a.*

اسغراب *istighrāb*, m. great admiration, amazement, wonder. *a.*

استغراق *istighrāḳ*, being drowned, immerged in thought, drowned in sleep, engrossed, wholly employed, &c. *a.*

استغفار *istighfār*, m. begging mercy, craving grace, deprecating. *a.*

استغفرالله *astaghfirullāh*, I entreat forgiveness of God (or God forgive me! an expression signifying negation). *a.*

استغنا *istighnā*, independent (in point of fortune), contented; m. content, independence. *a.*

استفاده *istifāda*, m. seeking for gain; profit, advantage. *a.* [learned man. *a.*

استفتا *istiftā*, m. consulting (a lawyer or

استفراغ *istifrāgh*, m. vomiting, belching. *a.*

استفسار *istifsār*, m. asking an explanation; searching for information, inquiry, interrogation. *istifsār-karnā*, a. to inquire, to interrogate, to demand an explanation. *a.*

استفساري *istifsārī*, f. the statement of a prosecutor subject to investigation. *a.*

استفهام *istifhām*, m. inquiring, inquisitiveness; asking for explanation, desiring information. *ḥarfi istifhām*, an interrogative particle. *a.*

استفهامي *istifhāmī*, استفهاميه *istifhāmīya*, } interrogative (a term used in grammar). *a*

استقاله *istiḳāla*, m. requiring one to cancel an agreement. *a.*

استقامت *istiḳāmat*, f. rectitude, integrity; residence; firmness, constancy. *a.*

استقبال *istiḳbāl*, m. futurity; the ceremony of receiving a visitor in the open air by advancing to meet him; encountering, meeting. *a.*

استقرا *istiḳrā*, m. reasoning from induction. *a.*

استقرار *istiḳrār*, confirming, ratifying. *a.*

استقصا *istiḳṣā*, curiosity, strict investigation. *a.*

استقلال *istiḳlāl*, m. intrepidity, resolution, perseverance, vigour; absolute power, perpetuity. *a.*

استقلالي *istiḳlālī*, f. confirming in possession. *a.*

آستك आस्तिक *āstik*, a believer, pious, faithful. *s.*

استكبار *istikbār*, m. pride, presumption. *a.*

استكراه *istikrāh*, f. aversion, reluctance. *a.*

استكشاف *istikshāf*, wishing any thing to be made manifest or laid open. *a.*

استكمال *istikmāl*, completion, bringing to perfection; wishing any thing finished, or completed. *a.*

استلزام *istilzām*, m. necessity, rendering necessary. *a.*

استماع *istimā'*, m. hearing, listening (to music, &c., particularly); tidings, report, rumour, that which is heard; in law it denotes hearsay evidence, or indirect testimony, receivable only in particular cases and under certain restrictions. *a.*

استمالت *istimālat*, f. encouragement; comfort, consolation. *a.*

استمبه अस्तम्भ or इस्तम्भ *astambh* or *istambh*, m. the trunk of a tree; column, pile, post, pillar. *s.*

استمتاع *istimtā'*, m. enjoying, reaping the fruits of, being delighted; celebrating the solemnities of the festival of Mecca; enjoyment of a woman. *a.*

استمداد *istimdād*, f. begging assistance. *a.*

استمرار *istimrār*, perseverance, continuation; in law it signifies a rent not liable to alteration. *istimrār-dār*, the holder of a perpetual lease. *a.*

استمراري *istimrārī*, perpetual, permanent. *istimrārī jam'*, fixed or perpetual assessment of rent. *istimrārī jot*, a fixed or permanent tenure. *istimrārī māl-guzārī*, permanent or perpetual revenue. *istimrārī paṭṭā*, a perpetual lease of a farm. *istimrārī paṭṭā-dār*, the holder of a lease of lands at a permanent rent. *a.*

استمزاج *istimzāj*, asking an opinion; searching out one's purpose or intentions. *a.*

استناد *istinād*, leaning or resting upon. *a.*

استنباط *istimbāṭ*, m. deducting, extracting, inference. *a.*

استنجا *istinjā*, m. pissing; purification after a natural evacuation. *a.*

استنشاق *istinshāḳ*, m. throwing water into the nostrils, when performing the *Wazū*; snuffing up the air or odours, &c. *a.*

استوا *istiwā*, parallel, equal; *khaṭṭi-istiwā*, the equator. *a.*

استوار *ustuwār*, powerful, strong, firm; brave, resolute, solid. *p.*

استواري *ustuwārī*, f. strength; resolution, firmness, stability. *p.*

استويست अस्तव्यस्त *astavyast*, dispersed, confused, scattered. *s.*

استهي अस्थि *asthi*, m. a bone. *asthi-bhang*, a fracture; a plant of supposed efficacy in fractures (*cissus quadrangularis*). *asthi-bhed*, fracturing a bone. *asthi-panjar*, m. a skeleton. *asthi-shokh*, m. dryness and decay of the bones. *asthi-sandhi*, f. uniting of a broken bone. *s.*

آستها आस्था *āsthā*, f. prop, stay, place or means of abiding; effort, pains, care. *s.*

استهان अस्थान *asthān* (for *sthān*), m. place, abode, residence. *s.*

استهاور अस्थावर *a-sthāvar*, moveable, moving, not fixed. *s.*

استهر अस्थिर *a-sthir*, restless, unsteady, unstable, uncertain. *s.*

استهر इस्थिर *isthir* (for *sthir*), steady, firm. *s.*

استهرتا अस्थिरता *a-sthiratā*, f. unsteadiness, instability, fickleness. *s.*

استهرتا इस्थिरता *isthiratā*, f. rest, tranquillity, steadiness. *s.*

استهزا *istihzā*, m. derision, laughing at, a joke, jest, scorn. *a.*

استهل अस्थल *asthal* (for *sthal*), m. place, home, fixed residence, dry or firm ground. *isthal*, a place or stand of a *faḳīr*. *s.*

استهلاك *istihlāk*, m. ruining, destroying, consuming; wishing death or ruin to any one. *a.*

استهلال *istihlāl*, m. appearing of the new moon; the noise made by a child at its birth. *a.*

استهوت अस्थिवत *asthiwat*, bony, osseous. *s.*

است هونا *ast-honā*, n. to set (as the sun, &c.). *a.*

استهي *asthī*, m. a bone. (See *asthi*). *s.*

استهيرج अस्थैर्य *a-sthairj*, m. instability, unsteadiness. *s.*

استي असत्यी *a-satyī*, untrue, a liar. *s.*

آستي *āste*, (for آهسته) easy, gently, softly. *p.*

استي असती *a-satī*, a bad or unchaste woman. *a-satya*, untrue, false; m. untruth. *s.*

استيبادي असत्यबादी *a-satya-bādī*, a teller of lies, a liar. *s.*

استيصال *istīṣāl*, m. destroying, eradicating, pulling up by the roots, extirpating. *a.*

استيعاب *istī'āb*, m. asking in a present, taking (the whole). *a.*

استيفا *istīfā*, m. satisfying completely; paying or receiving the whole of what is due; renouncing, relinquishing; retiring from business or official duties, vacating or resigning a situation. *a.*

استيلا *istīlā*, m. predominance, conquest. *a*

استيلاد *istīlād*, in law, signifies a claim made by a man having a child born to him of a female slave, which child he acknowledges, as of his own begetting. *a.*

آستين *āstīn*, f. a sleeve; *āstīn kā sāmp*, a domestic enemy, an enemy who wears the mask of friendship. *p.*

استيناس *istīnās*, m. familiarity, intimacy, sympathy. *a.*

استيه असत्य *a-satya*, false; *a-satya-bādī*, one who speaks falsehood. *s.*

اسجن असज्जन *a-sajjun*, unfit, untrue, improper; not respectable, or of good family. *s.*

اسجنا उसिजना *usijnā*, n. to boil, to simmer. *h.*

اسچ असुच *a-such*, foul, impure. *a-suchi*, f. impurity, pollution. *s.*

اسحاق *is,ḥāḳ*, m. (a man's name) Isaac. *a.*

اسد *asad*, m. a lion, the sign or constellation Leo (in astronomy). *a.*

اسدم *is-dam*, directly, this moment. *h. p.*

اسدھ असिद्ध *a-siddha*, not effected, invalid, false, unripe, incomplete. *s.*

اسدھ असुद्ध *a-suddha*, wrong, impure, inaccurate, mistaken. *s.*

اسر असुर *asur*, and आसुर *āsur*, a demon; the *āsurs* reside at the south pole: they are considered demons of the first order, and in constant hostility with the Gods. *āsur*, a form of marriage in which the bridegroom gives to the bride, her father, and paternal kinsmen, as much as he can afford. *s.*

اسر अस्र *asra*, m. a corner; hair; blood; a tear. *asri*, f. ten millions. *s.*

آسرا आसरा *āsrā*, m. hope, dependence, defence, reliance, retreat, shelter, abode, house; ambush, concealment, shade, hiding-place. *s.*

اسرار *asrār*, (pl. of سرّ), secrets, confidential concerns. *isrār*, act of concealing; also, divulging or communicating a secret. *a.*

اسراف *isrāf*, m. prodigality, dissipation, abuse of wealth; ruin, extravagance. *a.*

اسرافيل *isrāfīl*, m. the name of an angel who will sound the last trumpet at the resurrection: a seraph. *a.*

اسرائيل *isrā,īl*, Israel. *banī isrā,īl*, the Israelites, or children of Israel. *a.*

آسرباد आसिर्बाद *āsirbād*, m. blessing, benediction.

آسرت आश्रित *āsrit*, } one who relies on an-
اسرتو आसर्तु *āsartū*, } other; a protégé. *s.*

اسردھا अश्रद्धा *a-sraddhā*, f. want of faith or confidence, unbelief. *s.*

آسرم आश्रम *āsram*, m. abode, residence; class of mankind, or religious order, whereof the *Hindūs* reckon four, viz. the *Brahmachārī*, who devotes his life to religious exercises, austerity, and celibacy. 2nd. *Grihi*, who lives in the world, and rears a family. 3rd. *Vānaprastha*, who retires from the world with his family, and passes his life in devotion in the forest 4th *Bhikshu*, or *Bhichchhu*, who lives on alms. *s.*

اسرميل *asarmel*, اسرويل *asarvel*, } m. the *Aristolachia Indica*, a plant supposed to be of great efficacy in curing snake bites. v. *isparmul*. *d.*

اسرن असरण or अशरण *a-saran*, helpless, unprotected. *s.*

اسرنا उसरना *usarnā*, n. to retreat, shrink from, recede. *h.*

اسرنج *isrinj*, m. minium, cinnabar. *p.*

اسرو अस्रू *asrū* (or *asru*), m. a tear. *s.*

آسري आसुरी *āsurī*, belonging to the *āsurs*, demoniacal, diabolical; a division of medicine, surgery; curing by cutting with instruments, applying the cautery, &c. *s.*

آسريمايا आसुरीमाया *āsurī-māyā*, f. deception of demons. *s.*

آسريت आश्रैत *āsrait*, hopeful, trusting, confident.

اسريه आश्रय *āsraya*, m. a refuge, asylum. *s.*

اسشت अशिष्ट *a-sishṭa*, rude, indecent, ill-behaved; profligate, irregular. *s.*

اسطبل *istabal*, m. a stable. *a.*

اسطرح *is-ṭaraḥ* or *is-ṭaraḥ-se*, in this manner, thus. *us-ṭaraḥ*, in that manner. *h. a.*

اسطرلاب *usṭurlāb*, m. an astrolabe. *g.*

اسطقسات *usṭuḳusāt*, (pl. of *usṭuḳus*) elements, principles. *usṭuḳusāti uḳlīdus*, Euclid's Elements of Geometry. *g.*

اسطوخودوس *usṭūkhūdūs*, French lavender. *g.*

اسعد *as'ad*, more happy, most happy. *a.*

اسفار *asfār* (pl. of سفر) books, volumes; (pl. of *safar*) voyages or travels, adventures. *a.*

اسفاناج *isfānāj*, m. spinach. *p.*

اسفل *asfal*, inferior, the lowest. *a.*

اسفنج *isfanj*, m. a sponge; a yeast dumpling. *g.*

اسفنديار *isfandiyār*, the son of *Gishtāsb*, of the first dynasty of Persian kings. *p.*

اسفهان *isfahān*, *Ispahān*, the capital of Persian *'Irāḳ* (the ancient Parthia). *a.*

اسقاط *isḳāṭ*, m. causing one to fall; miscarrying; taking away; dying (cattle); procuring an abortion. *a.*

اسقدر *is-ḳadar*, this much, to this extent. *h. a.*

اسقيل *isḳīl*, m. a squill, a wild onion. *g.*

اسكات *iskāt*, f. pacifying, soothing, silencing. *a.*

اسكانا उसकाना *uskānā*, a. to light a fire or candle; to excite, to instigate. *h.*

آسكت आस्कत or अस्कत, *āskat* or *askat*, f. drowsiness, laziness, tardiness. *s.*

آسكت आसक्त *āsakta*, addicted, devoted to; intent upon; fascinated, enamoured, diligent, zealously active; trusting to, confiding in; eternal. *s.*

آسكت आसक्ति *āsakti*, f. attachment to one object or pursuit, diligence, application. *s.*

آسكتانا आस्कताना *āskatānā*, or *askatānā*, n to be lazy. *h.*

آسكتي आस्कती or अस्कती, *āskatī* or *askatī* drowsy, lazy, remiss. *h.*

اسكندر *iskandar*, Alexander. *iskandar i rūmī*, Alexander of Greece, or Alexander the Great. *a.*

اسكندري *iskandarī*, of or relating to Alexander. *a.*

اسكندريه *iskandarīya*, Alexandria in Egypt. *a.*

اسكندھ *iskandh* (for *skandh*, q.v.), a section or portion of a poem, a division of a book. *s.*

اسكھ असुख *a-sukh*, m. sorrow, pain, restlessness, uneasiness, affliction. *s.*

آسكھ आसिख *āsikh*, m. benediction, admonition, instruction. *s.*

اسكھي असुखी *a-sukhī*, restless, uneasy, afflicted, unhappy. *s.*

اسگن असुगन *a-sugan*, m. bad omen. *h.*

اسگندھ असगन्ध *asgandh* or *isgandh*, m. the name of a plant used medicinally (*physalis flexuosa*). *s.*

اسل उसल *usal*, form, figure. *usal pasal jānā*, to be agitated, tossed, to get into confusion. *h.*

اسلا *islā*, consolation, comforting; causing to forget. *a.*

اسلاف *aslāf* (pl. of سلف), ancestors, forefathers. *a.*

اسلام *islām*, m. the religion of Muḥammad, orthodoxy (according to Muḥammadans). *a.*

اسلام‌بول *islām-bol* (for *istāmbol*), the city of Constantinople. *t.*

اسلامي *islāmī*, اسلاميه *islāmīya*, } faithful, orthodox, a follower of the Muhammadan religion. *a.*

اسل‌پسل‌جانا उसलपसलजाना *usal-pasal-jānā*, n. to be agitatated, to be tossed, to get into confusion. *h.*

اسلوب *uslūb* or *aslūb*, m. manner, mode, method, order, arrangement. *uslūb-dār*, symmetrical, of fair proportions. *a.*

اسم *ism*, m. name; a noun or substantive in grammar. *ismi istifhām*, an interrogative pronoun. *ismi ishāra*, a demonstrative pronoun. *ismi tankīr*, an indefinite pronoun. *ismi jāmid*, a primitive noun. *ismi a'ẓam*, the Almighty name, one of the ninety-nine attributes of the Divinity, the utterance of which is an irresistible spell over demons. *ismi jalālī*, the glorious name (of God). *ismi jins*, a generic name. *ismi ḥāliya*, present participle. *ismi 'adad*, a numeral adjective. *ismi fā'il*, a noun of agency, the nominative case. *ismi maf'ūl*, the past or passive participle. *ismi ṣifat*, a noun of quality, an adjective. *a.*

اسما *asmā* (pl. of اسم) names. *asmā,e ḥusnā* or *asmā,e 'usmā*, the ninety-nine names or epithets of God. *a.*

آسما *āsumā* or *āsmā*, heaven; adj. high. *p.*

اساپت असमाप्त *a-samāpta*, unfinished, incomplete. *a-samāpti*, f. incompleteness. *s.*

اسمار *usmār* (pl. of سمر), stories, evening entertainments. *a.*

اسماعيل *ismā'īl*, the name of a prophet; Ishmael, son of Abraham. *a.*

اسمان असमान *a-samān*, different, unlike, unequal. *s.*

اسمان असम्मान *a-sammān*, m. disrespect, disgrace. *s.*

آسمان *āsmān*, m. the sky, the firmament, heaven, the celestial orb. *āsmān par ḳadam rakhnā*, to give one's self airs, to aspire, to be vain. *āsmān par khainchnā*, to be proud, to affect greatness. *āsman se girnā*, to fall from the clouds, is applied, particularly by women, to signify an acquisition that has been made suddenly and unexpectedly, without labour or care, and the value of which is inconsiderable. *p.*

آسمانگيري *āsmān-girī*, f. a canopy or awning. *p.*

آسماني *āsmānī*, heavenly, celestial; azure, cerulean, sky-coloured. *āsmānī tīr*, &c., an arrow, &c. shot in the air. *āsmānī farmānī*, provision against injuries arising from calamitous seasons, &c. on the part of a *zamīn-dār*. *p.*

اسم با مسمي *ism bā musammā*, worthy of the name (it bears), whose name is expressive of its qualities. *a. p.*

اسمبدھ असंबद्ध *a-sambaddh*, not joined, unconnected. *s.*

اسمبھو असंभव *a-sambhav*, uncommon, inconsistent, unlikely. *s.* [perfect. *s.*

اسمپورن असंपूर्ण *a-sampūrna*, incomplete, im-

اسمت असम्मत *a-sammat*, dissentient, averse, contrary. *a-sammati*, f. dissent, dislike. *s.*

اسمرت *ismṛiti* (see *smṛiti*), f. the Hindū law. *s.* अस्मृति *a-smriti*, f. want of memory, forgetfulness. *s.*

اسمرتھ असमर्थ *a-samarth*, weak, powerless, unable, incompetent. *s.*

اسمرن अस्मरण *a-smaran*, m. forgetfulness, oblivion. *s.*

اسمعيل *isma'īl*, Ishmael, from whom the Arabs claim descent. (Same as *Ismā'īl*.) *a.*

آسمنتات आसमन्तात *āsamantāt*, adv. all round, on every side, wholly, altogether. *s.*

اسمنجس असमञ्जस *a-samanjas*, m. doubt, suspense, suspicion; unconformity, disparity, difference. *s.*

اسم وار *ism-wār*, entry in statements according to the order of persons' names. *a. p.*

اسمي असमय *a-samay*, unseasonable, out of time; m. a time of misfortune, distress, an improper time. *s.*

آسن आसन *āsan*, m. the inside or under part of the thigh; a stool, a seat; a small sarpet on which the Hindūs sit at prayer; seat, posture, attitude, sitting (particularly the attitudes used by Jogīs in their devotional exercises, of which they enumerate eighty-four); the withers of an elephant, the part where the driver sits. *āsan tale ānā*, to come under subjection. *āsan joṛnā*, to sit on the hams. *āsan ḍolnā*, spoken of a holy man, who, perceiving by supernatural intelligence that some one in distress has called on him, interposes in his behalf. *āsan se āsan joṛnā*, to sit close in contact with another person. *āsan lagānā*, to sit obstinately in a given posture, till one's request be obtained. *āsan mārnā*, to sit (particularly in an attitude practised by the Jogīs); to retain one's seat firmly on horseback. *s.*

آسن आसिन *āsin*, m. the sixth Hindū month, in which the moon is full near the stars in the head of Aries (September—October). *s.*

آسن आसन *āsan*, also *asan*, m. the name of a tree on which the tasar silkworm feeds. (*Terminalia alata tormentosa*). *s.* [named tree. *s.*

اسن असन *asan*, m. eating: also the last-

اسنا उसना *usnā*, boiled (from *usannā*, q.v.). *h.*

اسناد *asnād* (pl. of سند), grants, and law-papers in general, documents. *isnād*, an allegation on the authority of another. *a.*

اسناف *isnāf*, m. a snipe, apparently a corruption of the English word. *d.*

اسنان *asnān*, m. bathing (see *ashnān*). *s.*

اسنانا उसनाना *usnānā*, a. to cause to boil. *h.*

اسنتشٹ असंतुष्ट *a-santushṭa*, discontented, displeased, dissatisfied. *s.*

اسنتوکھ असंतोख *a-santokh*, or असंतोष *a-santosh*, m. discontent, displeasure. *s.*

اسنجوگ असंयोग *a-sanjog* (or *a-sañyog*), m. want of opportunity. *s.*

اسنشي असंशय *a-sañshaya*, undoubted. *s.*

اسنکھيه असंख्य *a-sanhhya*, countless, innumerable. *s.* [bad. *s.*

اسنگت असंगत *a-sangat*, absurd, improper,

اسنمان असंमान *a-sañmān*, m. disrespect. *s.*

اسنمت असम्मत *a-sammat*, dissentient, differing from, averse, contrary. *s.*

اسننا उसन्ना *usannā*, n. to boil, to simmer. *h.*

اسني आसनी *āsanī*, f. a small carpet, &c. on which the Hindūs sit at prayer. *s.* [tunity. *s.*

اسنيوگ असंयोग *a-sañyog*, m. want of oppor-

اسنيه अस्नेह *a-sneh*, harsh, unkind; m. unkindness, want of affection. *s.*

اسو अश्व *aswa*, m. a horse. *s.*

آسو आसव *āsav*, m. a kind of intoxicating liquor, distilled from sugar or molasses, rum. *s.*

آسواد आस्वाद *āswād*, m. savour, relish. *s.*

اسوار *aswār*, m. cavalry, a horseman; mounted, riding on any thing, as a horse, a carriage, a ship, &c. *p*

اسوارُوڑھ अश्वारूढ़ *aswārūṛh*, mounted on horse-back. *s.*

اسواري *aswārī*, f. riding; a mode of warfare [with battle-axes. *p.*

آسواس आश्वास *āswās*, m. completion, cessation; comfort, encouragement, consolation. *s.*

اسواسطي *is-wāste*, on this account. *us-wāste*, on that account. *h. a.*

اسوبھا असोभा *a-sobhā*, shapeless, ill-made, [ugly. *s.*

اسوپت अश्वपति *aswa-pati*, m. master of horses, a title used by some of the Hindū rājās. *s.*

اسوتھ अश्वत्थ *aswatth*, m. the sacred fig-tree; (*Ficus religiosa*). *s.*

اسوج असोज *asoj*, m. the sixth solar month. *s.*

اسوجھ असूझ *a-sūjh*, invisible, incorporeal. *h.*

اسوچ असोच *a-soch*, not contrivable, that which cannot be effected by reflection or study; not to be regretted. *h.*

اسوچه अशौचः *a-saucha*, m. social or legal uncleanness, as from the death of a relation, &c. *s.*

اسوچي असोची *a-sochī*, careless, indifferent, unconcerned. *h.*

اسود *aswad*, black, or blackest, powerful. *a.*

آسودگي *āsūdagī*, f. quiet, peace, content. *p.*

آسودن *āsūdan*, (r. *āsā*), to be at rest. *p.*

آسوده *āsūda*, full, glutted, satiated, saturated; quiet, satisfied, tranquil, at ease, contented. *āsūda-khāṭir*, or *āsūda-dil*, or *āsūda-ḥāl*, full, replete; contented, in easy circumstances. *āsūda*, in a figurative sense means dead and buried, hence plur. *āsūdagān*, the tranquil ones, *i. e.* the dead. *p.*

آسودھ आसौधः *āsaudha*, m. legal arrest. *s.*

اسوسالا अश्वशाला *aswa-sālā*, f. a stable. *s.*

اسوقت *is-waḳt*, now, at present. *us-waḳt*, then, at that time. *h. a.*

اسوک असोक *a-sok*, (for *askoka*), m. ease, tranquillity, cherfulness; a kind of tree (*Jonesia asoca*). *s.*

اسوگ असोग *a-sog*, m. ease, tranquillity; a tree called also *Deva-dāru* (*Uvaria longifolia*). *s.*

اسوگندھا अश्वगन्धा *aswa-gandhā*, m. the name of a plant (*physalis flexuosa*). *s.*

اسوگي असोगी *a-sogī*, at ease, unmolested. *s.*

اسون असौं *asoṅ*, this year. *h.*

اسوني अश्विनी *aswinī*, f. the name of the first lunar mansion, of the form of a horse's head (the three stars in the head of Aries). *s.*

اسويا असूया *asūyā*, f. detraction, malice, slan-[der. *s.*

اسهال *is,hāl*, m. loosening, opening, purging, flux. *a.*

اسهج असह्य *a-sahajj* or *a-sahij*, insufferable, [intolerable. *s.*

اسهل *as,hal*, more or most easy. *a.*

اسهن असहन *a-sahan*, impatient, not bearing with, unable to endure. *s.*

اسهنيه असहनीय *a-sahanīya*, } intolerable, un-
اسهيه असह्य *asahya*, } bearable. *s.*

اسي अस्सी *assī*, eighty. *h.*

اسي उसे *use*, him, that, &c. इसे *ise*, this, to this, or him, &c. *h.*

اسي *asī* (for असि *asi*), m. a sword, scimetar. *s.*

آسي आसय *āsai*, m. meaning, intention, aim; scope, theme, subject; an asylum, abode, or retreat. *s.*

آسيا *āsiyā*, f. a mill. *āsiyā-sang*, a mill-stone. *p.*

آسيانه *āsiyāna*, m. a whetstone. *p.*

آسيب *āseb*, (or *āsīb*), m. a misfortune (generally means such misfortunes as are the consequence of the shadow of a demon having fallen on one, and so forth), trouble, calamity, damage. *p.*

اسيجنا उसीजना *usījnā*, } a. to boil (food,
اسيجھنا उसीझना *usījhnā*, } &c.). *h.*

اسيچا *a-sīchā*, unirrigated (same as *a-sīṅchā*). *s.*

اسير *asīr*, m. a prisoner, a captive. *asīr i āb o gil*, attached to one's native soil. *a.*

اسير उसीर *usīr*, f. a grass, the root whereof is sweet-scented, and used for making *ṭaṭṭīs* (*andropogon muricatum*). *s.*

اسيرباد असीर्बाद or आसीर्बाद *asīrbād* or *āsīrbād*, m. blessing, benediction, salutation. *s.*

اسيري *asīrī*, f. imprisonment, captivity. *a.*

آسيس आसीस or असीस *āsīs* or *asīs*, f. blessing; return of compliment from a (Hindū) superior. *s.*

اسيسا उसीसा *usīsā*, m. a pillow, a cushion, head of a bed. *h.*

اسيش अशेष *a-sesh*, without remainder, entire. *s.*

اسيما असीमा *a-sīmā*, unbounded, unlimited. *s.*

آسيمه *āsīma*, amazed, astonished. *sar-āsīma*, bewildered in the head, astounded. *p.*

آسين आसीन *āsīn*, seated, sitting. *s.*

اسينچا असींचा *a-sīṅchā*, not watered, not irrigated (a field, &c.). *s.*

اسيوا असेवा *a-sevā*, } m. disobedience, inat-
اسيون असेवन *a-sevan*, } tention. *s.*

اسيونا उसेवना *usewnā*, a. to throw out the water from boiled rice. *h.*

اش *ush*, interj. fie, &c. (vide *uf*). *d.*

آش *āsh*, f. meat, victuals, viands, soup, broth, gruel, pottage. *āshi-jau*, barley-water or water-gruel. *āsh-pakānā*, a. to combine in any design; to conspire or contrive any thing against another. *āsh-māl*, a porridge-stick, a pestle. *p.*

آشا आशा *āshā*, f. hope, desire; dependence, reliance, trust. *āshā-prāpta*, successful, possessing the desired object. *āshā-bandh*, m. confidence, trust, expectation. *āshā-bhang*, disappointment. *āshā-want*, expectant, hopeful. *āshā-hīn*, desponding, despairing. *s.*

اشا उषा *ushā*, m. early morning, dawn, daybreak (also *ushā kāl*), f. the wife of Anirudha. *s.*

اشارت *ishārat*, } f. a sign, command, signal,
اشارة *ishāra*, } hint. *ism-i-ishāra*, a demonstrative pronoun. *a.*

اشاستر अशास्त्र *a-shāstra*, unlawful, illegal, irregular. *a-shāstriya*, contrary to law, inconsistent with the rules of science. *s.*

اشاڑھ असाढ़ or आषाढ़, *ashāṛh* or *āshāṛh*, m. the third solar month, (see أساڑھ). *s.*

اشاڑهي असाढ़ी *ashāṛhī*, f. day of the full moon in *Ashāṛh*. *s.*

آشام *āshām*, drink, (in comp.) drinking, as *sharāb-āshām*, wine-drinker. *p.*

آشاميدن *āshāmīdan*, to drink, to quaff. *p.*

اشانت अशान्त *a-shānt*, restless, anxious, unresigned. *a-shānti*, f. anxiety, restlessness. *s.*

اشاوري अशावरी *ashāwarī*, f. a *rāginī* or musical mode; a kind of pigeon; a sort of cotton cloth. *s.*

اشاونت अशावन्त *ashāwant*, fearful, unquiet, pitiful. *s.*

اشباح *ashbāḥ*, (pl. of شبح) bodies, objects. *a.*

اشبه अशुभ *a-shubh*, unfavourable, unpleasant, inauspicious, evil; m. misfortune, distress. *s.*

آشتاوا *āshtāwā*, } m. an ewer &c., same as
آشتاوه *āshtāwa*, } *āftāba* or *ābtāba*, q. v. *p.*

اشتباه *ishtibāh*, m. doubt, ambiguity, scruple. *a.*

اشتباهي *ishtibāhī*, suspicious, doubtful. *a.*

اشتداد *ishtidād*, m. confirming, strengthening, increasing in violence. *a.*

اشتر *ushtur*, m. a camel. *p.*

اشترا *ishtirā*, m. buying, selling, commerce. *a.*

اشتراك *ishtirāk*, m. partnership. *a.*

اشتعال *ishtiʿāl*, m. burning, inflaming, lighting a fire or candle; fomenting, instigating a quarrel. *a.*

اشتعالك *ishtiʿālak*, (dimin. of last word). *ishtiʿālak denā*, to foment (quarrels), to encourage to bad actions, to abet. *a.*

اشتغال *ishtighāl*, m. occupation, employment, study. *a.*

اشتقاق *ishtiḳāḳ*, m. derivation of one name from another. *a.*

اشتلم *ushtulum*, celerity, violence, injustice; firm. *p.*

اشتمال *ishtimāl*, m. comprehension, containing. *a.*

اشتها *ishtihā*, f. hunger, appetite. *a.*

اشتهار *ishtihār*, m. publication, divulging, fame, rumour, report, renown. *ishtihār-nāma*, a written or printed proclamation or public notice. *a.*

آشتي *āshtī*, f. peace, concord, reconciliation, agreement, convention, confederacy; amour, intrigue. *p.*

اشتياق *ishtiyāḳ*, m. wish, desire, strong inclination. *a.*

اشٹ इष्ट *ishṭa*, desired, wished, approved; worshipped, reverenced; cherished, beloved; m. a god, a deity, whatever is worshipped; an object, the thing wished for; a beloved person. *s.*

اشٹ अष्ट *ashṭ* or *ashṭa*, eight. *ashṭa-prahar*, incessant, the whole day and night. *ashṭa-mangal*, m. a horse with a white face, tail, breast, and hoofs; a collection of eight lucky things to be assembled on certain occasions, as a lion, a bull, an elephant, a water-jar, a fan, a flag, a trumpet, and a lamp. *s.*

اشٹادش अष्टादश *ashṭā-dash*, eighteen. *s.*

اشٹاشيت अष्टाशीति *ashṭāshīti*, eighty-eight. *s.*

اشٹانگ अष्टाङ्ग *ashṭāng*, m. eight parts of man; adj. of, or with eight members. *ashṭāng pranām*, prostration in salutation or adoration, so as to touch the ground with the eight principal parts of man, viz. with the hands, feet, thighs, breast, eyes, head, words, and mind. *s.*

اشٹاونشت अष्टाविंशति *ashṭā-vinshati*, twenty-eight. *s.*

اشٹ پنچاشت अष्टपञ्चाशत *ashṭa-panchāshat*, fifty-eight. *s.*

اشٹتا इष्टता *ishṭatā*, f. desirableness, reverence. *s.*

اشٹتر इष्टतर *ishṭatar*, dearer, more desired. *s.*

اشٹ ترن شت अष्टत्रिंशत् *ashṭa-trinshat*, thirty-eight. *s.*

اشٹتم इष्टतम *ishṭatam*, best beloved, dearest, most desired. *s.*

اشٹ چتوارن شت अष्टचत्वारिंशत् *ashṭa-chatwārinshat*, forty-eight. *s.*

اشٹدهات अष्टधातु *ashṭadhātu*, m. the eight metals, said to be gold, silver, copper, brass, tin, bell-metal, lead, and iron. *asht-dhātī*, f. a mixed metal, a compound of eight metals. *s.*

اشٹر उष्ट्र *ushṭra*, m. a camel. *s.*

اشٹ سپتتي अष्टसप्तति *ashṭa-saptati*, seventy-eight. *s.*

اشٹسدھ अष्टसिद्धि *ashṭa-siddhi*, m. the eight *siddhis*, the name of a superior order of beings, a personification of the powers and laws of nature; when they are subjected to the will by holiness and austerities, whatever the fancy desires, may, it is said, be obtained; universal sovereignty may be acquired, and implicit obedience to any command enforced; the magnitude, weight, or levity of the body may be increased or diminished at will, and the body be transported in an instant to any part of the universe. *s.*

اشٹ ششٹھ अष्टषष्टि *ashṭa-shashṭhi*, sixty-eight. *s.*

اشٹم अष्टम *ashṭam*, the eighth. *s.*

اشٹمي अष्टमी *ashṭamī*, f. the eighth day of the moon. *janmāshṭamī*, the eighth of *Bhādra Krishna paksh*, the birthday of *Krishna*. *s.*

اشٹنوت अष्टनवति *ashṭa-nawati*, ninety-eight. *s.*

اشجار *ashjār* (pl. of شجر), trees. *a.*

اشچ अशुचि *a-shuchi*, impure, unclean (ceremonially); f. impurity. *s.*

آشچرج आश्चर्य *āshcharj* (for *āshcharya*), m. amazement, astonishment, surprise; adj. astonishing, wonderful. *āshcharjyatā*, f. wonderfulness, astonishment. *s.*

اشخاص *ashkhās* (pl. of شخص), persons, people. *a.*

اشد *ashadd*, more or most vehement, severe, strong, violent, excessive. *a.*

اشدھ अशुद्ध *a-shuddh*, impure, inaccurate, wrong. *a-shuddhatā*, f. inaccuracy, impurity. *s.*

اشدھیا अशुद्धिया *a-shuddhiyā*, one who speaks or reads wrong. *s.*

اشر *asharr*, vicious, malignant, atrocious (or more vicious, &c.). *a.*

اشر अश्र *ashra*, m. a tear. *s.*

آشرا आश्रा *āshrā*,
آشري आश्रय *āshray*, } m. cheating, fraud, circumvention; proximity; a retreat, abode, a house; a means of defence; having recourse to protection or refuge; trust, reliance, hope; a patron, a protector. *s.*

اشرابات *ashrābāt*, drinks prohibited by the Muhammadan law, such as wines, &c. *a.*

اشرار *ashrār* (pl. of شرير), wicked, wretched, criminal, seditious (people). *a.*

اشراف *ashrāf* (pl. of شريف), nobles, grandees, gentlemen, men of high extraction. In Rohilkund, Oude, and Benares, the term is applied to a class of cultivators who claim certain privileges. *a.*

اشراق *ishrāḳ*, m. splendour, beauty, lustre, lit. the rising of the sun. *a.*

اشراقي *ishrāḳi*, eastern, oriental. *ishrāḳi-namāz*, morning prayer. *a.*

اشراك *ishrāk*, m. participating, entering into partnership. *a.*

آشرت आश्रित *āshrit* (see *āsrit*), a person protected, &c. *s.*

اشردھ अश्रद्धा *a-shraddhā*, f. aversion, contempt, disgust, loathing, distrust, disbelief. *s.*

اشرف *ashraf*, more noble; m. a gentleman, a person of noble or genteel birth, a nobleman. *ashraf-ul makhlūḳāt*, the most excellent of created beings, mankind. *ashraf-ul bilād*, the finest of regions. *a.*

اشرفي *ashrafī*, f. a gold coin so called. The Calcutta *ashrafī*, is about 1*l.* 11*s.* 8*d.*, and the gold of it is better than English standard gold, by five shillings in the ounce, or about one-sixteenth. By the Regulations of May 1793, it should weigh 190·894 grains troy weight, generally called by Europeans, "a gold more" (vide *muhr*). The gold more of Bengal is worth 16 rupees, that of Madras and Bombay 15 rupees. *p.*

آشرم आश्रम *āshram*, m. (same as *āsram*), abode, &c. &c. (v. *āsram*). *s.*

اشرن अशरण *a-sharan*, without shelter, helpless. *s.*

آشري आश्रय *āshray*, m. same as *āshrā*, q. v.

آشريت आश्रैत *āshrait*, hopeful, trusting, confident. *s.*

اشريري अशरीरी *a-sharīrī*, incorporeal. *s.*

آشس आशिस *āshis*, f. blessing, benediction. *s.*

اشِشٹ अशिष्ट *a-shishṭa*, unpolite, undisciplined, ungoverned; under the dominion of evil habits arising from a neglected education; rude, barbarous. *s.*

اشعار *ash'ār* (pl. of شعر), verses, poems. *a.*

اشغال *ashghāl* (pl. of شغل), employments, occupations, cares. *ishghāl*, being employed. *a.*

اشفاق *ashfāḳ* (pl. of شفق), kindnesses, favours. *ishfāḳ*, compassion, tenderness. *a.*

آشفته *āshufta*, wretched, miserable, distressed, distracted, uneasy, disturbed. *āshufta-ḥāl*, distressed in condition. *āshufta-khāṭir* or *āshufta-dil*, afflicted in mind. *āshufta-mū*, with dishevelled hair. *āshufta-sar*, or, *-dimāgh*, or, *-ṭab'*, distracted in head or brain. *p.*

آشفتگي *āshuftagī*, f. misery, distraction, uneasiness. *p.*

آشفتن *āshuftan*, to disturb, to be confounded. *p.*

اشق *ashuḳ*, gum-ammoniac. *p.*

اشقيا *ashḳiyā* (pl. of شقي), thieves, malefactors. *a.*

اشك *ashk*, m. a tear, tears. *ashk-bār*, mourning, shedding tears. *ashk-bārī*, f. weeping. *p.*

آشكار *āshkār*,
آشكارا *āshkārā*, } apparent, clear, public, known, revealed. *p.*
آشكاره *āshkāra*,

اشكال *ashkāl* (pl. of شكل), appearances, figures, shapes, semblances, forms. *a.*

اشكال *ishkāl*, m. difficulty, ambiguity, suspicion, painfulness. *a.*

اشكالنا *ishkālnā*, to deceive, to tempt, to delude, to wheedle. *d.*

اشكالي *ishkālī*, one who excites doubts or difficulties. *a.*

آشكت आशक्त *āshakta*, fond, attached, addicted; able, powerful. *āshakti*, f. attachment, fondness; power, might. *s.*

اشكت अशक्त *a-shakta*, powerless, unable. *a-shakti*, f. impotence, weakness. *s.*

اشكشت अशिक्षित *a-shikshit*, untaught, ignorant. *s.*

اشكن अशकुन *a-shakun*,
اشگن अशुगुण *a-shugun*, } m. portent, evil omen. *ashakunī* or *a-shugūnī*,
اشگون अशुगून *a-shugūn*, portentous, boding evil luck. *s.*

اشكيه अशक्य *a-shakya*, impossible. *s.*

اشل *ashall*, having a disjointed, withered, or paralytic hand. *a.*

اشلوك अश्लोक *ashlok* or *ishlok*, m. verse, distich. *s.*

اشليكها अश्लेषा *ashlekhā* or *ashleshā*, m. the name of the ninth lunar mansion (five stars near the southern claw of Cancer). *s.*

اشما ऊष्मा *ushmā*, f. warmth; wrath. *s.*

اشمام *ishmām*, m. diffusing odour, shedding perfume; giving to a quiescent consonant a slight sound of *ẓamma* or *kasra*, but so as not to lengthen the syllable, or make one syllable more. *a.*

اشمتا उष्मता *ushmatā*, f. heat, warmth. *s.*

اشمري अश्मरी *ashmarī*, f. the stone or gravel (the disease); strangury. *s.*

اشمل *ashmal*, more or most perfect, complete, surpassing, transcendant. *a.*

اشن उष्ण *ushṇa*, hot, warm, pungent, acrid; m. heat, warmth. *s.*

اشن अशन *ashan*, m. eating food; also आशन *āshan*, the *āsan* tree, on which the *tasar* silk-worm feeds (*Terminalia alata tomentosa*). *s.*

آشنا *āshnā*, an acquaintance, lover, friend; *āshnā-parast*, friendly. *p.*

اشنا उष्णा *ushannā*, n. to boil. *h.*

اشنان अश्नान *ashnān*, m. bathing. *s.*

آشنائي *āshnā,ī*, f. friendship, acquaintance. *āshnā,ī-k*, a. to unite, to associate. *āshnā,ī lagnā*. n. to become intimate, to be united in friendship. *p.*

آشنايانه *āshnāyāna*, in a friendly manner. *p.*

اشنتا उष्णता *ushnatā*, f. heat, warmth. *s.*

اشنك अशङ्क *a-shanka*, fearless, undaunted, secure. *s.*

آشنكا आशङ्का *āshankā*, f. fear, apprehension, awe, danger; doubt, uncertainty. *s.*

اشنيش उष्णीष *ushnīsh*, m. a turban, a diadem. *s.*

اشو अश्व *ashwa*, m. a horse. *s.*

اشواروڑھ अश्वारूढ़ *ashwārūṛh*, mounted on a horse; m. a horseman. *s.*

آشواس आश्वास *āshwās*, m. completion, cessation, comfort. *s.*

آشوب *āshob* or *āshūb*, m. tumult, clamour; inflammation of the eyes; terror; misfortune; storm, tempest; an impostor; in comp. exciting. *p.*

اشوبها अशोभा *ā-shobhā*, f. ugliness; adj. shapeless, ugly. *s.*

اشوپت अश्वपति *ashwa-pati*, m. a person of rank, attended by horsemen; a horseman. *s.*

اشوتھ अश्वत्थ *ashwattha*, m. the holy fig-tree (*Ficus religiosa*). *s.*

اشوچ अशोच *a-shoch*, m. content, tranquillity, absence of care. *a-shauch*, m. impurity; mourning. *s.*

اشوشالا अश्वशाला *ashwa-shālā*, f. a stable. *s.*

اشوك अशोक *a-shok*, at ease, unmolested; m. ease, tranquillity; a plant (*Jonesia asoka*). *s.*

اشوگندها अश्वगन्धा *ashwa-gandhā*, f. a plant (*Physalis flexuosa*). *s.*

اشوميدھ अश्वमेध *ashwa-medh*, m. the actual or emblematic sacrifice of a horse, an ancient religious ceremony among the Hindūs. This sacrifice is one of the highest order, and, when performed a hundred times, entitles the sacrificer to the dominion of *swarga* or paradise. It appears to have been originally typical; the horse and other animals being simply bound during the performance of certain ceremonies: the actual sacrifice is an introduction of a later period. *s.*

آشون आश्विन *āshwin*, m. the sixth Hindū month (September—October). *s.*

اشوني अश्विनी *ashwinī*, f. the name of the first lunar mansion (see *aswinī*). *s.*

اشوار अश्ववार *ashwa-vār*, m. a horseman. *s.*

اشويج अश्वयुज *ashwa-yuj*, f. the first lunar mansion. *s.*

اشهاد *ishhād*, m. taking to witness, bringing proof. *a.*

اشهاد *ushhād* (pl. of شاهد), witnesses (such as have been present); cye-witnesses. *a.*

اشهب *ashhab*, white, ash-coloured. *a.*

اشهد *ashhadu*, I testify, I declare. *a.*

اشهر *ashhar*, more or most celebrated; known. *a.*

آشي आशय *āshaya*, m. meaning, intention, aim; an object of desire; theme, subject; shelter; the mind. *s.*

اشيا *ashyā* (pl. of شيٌّ), things, effects. *a.*

آشيان *āshiyān*, } m. a bird's nest. *p.*
آشيانه *āshiyāna*, }

آشيت आशीति *āshīti*, eighty. *s.*

اشير उशीर *ushīr*, f. a fragrant root of grass, called in Persian *khas* (*Andropogon muricatum*). *s.*

آشيرباد आशीर्वाद *āshīr-bād*, } m. blessing, benediction. *s.*
آشيروچن आशीर्वचन *āshīr-vachan*, }

اشيش अशेष *a-shesh*, boundless, endless, all. *s.*

آشيش आशीस आशीश *āshīsh*, f. blessing, benediction. *s.*

اصاغر *aṣāghir* (pl. of اصغر), little, mean, contemptible, low, poor (people). *a.*

اصالت *iṣālat* or *aṣālat*, firmness, integrity, solidity of judgment; genuineness. *a.*

اصالتاً *aṣālatan*, radically, originally, altogether, absolutely, in proper person. *a.*

اصحاب *aṣḥāb*, (pl. of صاحب), grandees, lords, masters, companions, apostles, friends. In composition, it signifies possessed of; as, *aṣḥābi 'ilm*, learned men, &c. *aṣḥābi kibār* and *aṣḥābi guzīn*, the select friends and companions of Muḥammad. *aṣḥābi kahf*, the (seven) sleepers of the cave, famed in oriental romance. *a.*

اصدار *iṣdār*, m. producing, appearing, issuing. *a.*

اصرار *iṣrār*, persevering, obstinacy. *a.*

اصراف *iṣrāf*, m. expenditure, waste, prodigality. *iṣrāf-k*, a. to squander, &c. *a.*

اصطباغ *iṣṭibāgh*, m. dipping, baptism. *a.*

اصطباغي *iṣṭibāghī*, one who baptizes. *Yaḥyā Iṣṭibāghī*, John the Baptist. *a.*

اصطبل *iṣṭabil* (vulgarly *aṣṭabal*), m. a stable. *a.*

اصطخر *iṣṭakhar*, the ancient name of Persepolis. *p.*

اصطرلاب *uṣṭurlāb*, f. an astrolabe. *g.*

اصطلاح *iṣṭilāḥ*, f. a phrase, idiom, general acceptation; a figure in rhetoric. *a.*

اصطلاحات *iṣṭilāḥāt* (pl.), idioms, phrases, forms of speech. *a.*

اصطلاحي *iṣṭilāḥī*, technical, metaphorical, conventional. *a.*

اصغر *aṣg͟har*, less, least, smallest; the minor term in a logical proposition. *a.*

اصف *aṣaf*, m. the caper tree (*Capparis spinosa*). *a.*

آصف *āṣaf*, the name of a man, considered to have been Solomon's *wazīr*. *āṣaf-rā,e*, prudent as *āṣaf*. *āṣaf-ud-daula*, the *āsaf* of the state; a title generally applied to a *wazīr*. *a.*

اصفار *aṣfār* (pl. of صفر), ciphers. *a.*

اصفر *aṣfar*, yellow, saffron-coloured. *a.*

اصفهان *iṣfahān*, m. Ispahān, till recently the capital of Persia. *p.*

اصل *aṣl*, f. lineage; origin, root; foundation; a capital, principal sum, stock in trade. *aṣl-us-sūs*, m. liquorice. *a.*

اصلا *aṣlan* or *aṣlā*, by no means, never, not at all. *aṣlan muṭlaḳan*, absolutely never, by no manner of means. *a.*

اصلاح *iṣlāḥ*, f. amendment, cure, correction. *a.*

اصلح *aṣlaḥ*, best, most correct. *a.*

اصلي *aṣlī*, pure, of a noble family, noble, essential, radical, original; a registered village. *a.*

اصم *aṣamm*, deaf; a surd number in arithmetic, opposite of *munṭiḳ*. *jazr-i aṣamm*, the square root of a surd. *a.*

اصناف *aṣnāf* (pl. of صنف), sorts, kinds, varieties. *a.*

اصوات *aṣwāt*, (pl. of صوت) voices, sounds, reputations. *a.*

اصول *uṣūl*, (pl. of اصل) causes, roots; a mood or tone. *a.*

اصهار *aṣ,hār* (pl. of صهر), near relations, a general term for all relations by marriage within the degree in which marriage is prohibited. *a.*

اصيل *aṣīl*, well-born, noble, genuine; f. a maid-servant who is free, in opposition to *launḍī*, a female purchased slave. *a.*

اضافت *iẓāfat*, f. addition, an adjunct, an epithet; it is in grammar applied to the short vowel *kasra*, between two Persian nouns in the formation of the genitive case, or on the addition of an adjective. *ḥālati iẓāfat*, the genitive case. *a.*

اضافه *iẓāfa*, m. addition, junction, augmentation, attribute. *a.*

اضطراب *iẓṭirāb*, m. agitation, perturbation, restlessness, anguish, trouble, chagrin. *a.*

اضطرابي *iẓṭirābī*, f. haste, impatience. *a.*

اضطرار *iẓṭirār*, m. } violence, constraint, agi-
اضطراري *iẓṭirārī*, f. } tation. *a.*

اضعاف *aẓ'āf*, double. *iẓ'āf*, act of doubling, duplication. *a.*

اضعف *aẓ'af*, very helpless or weak, most impotent. *a.*

اضلاع *aẓla'*, (pl. of ضلع) districts; sides (of a square, &c.); ribs; convexities; arches. *a.*

اطاعت *iṭā'at*, f. subjection, obsequiousness, reverence, worshipping, obedience, submission. *a.*

اطاليق *aṭālīḳ*, m. preceptor, a guardian or governor. *aṭālīḳī*, instruction. *p.*

اطبا *aṭibbā*, (pl. of طبيب), physicians. *a.*

اطراف *aṭrāf* (pl. of طرف), sides, environs, confines, skirts, districts; all around. *a.*

اطري پهل *iṭrī-phal*, } m. a kind of electuary;
اطريفل *iṭrī-fal*, } vide *iṭrī-phal*.

اطفا *iṭfā*, extinction, putting out (a fire). *a.*

اطفال *aṭfāl*, (pl. of طفل), children, family. *a.*

اطلاع *iṭṭilā'*, f. manifesting, informing, declaring, investigating, knowledge, information. *iṭṭilā'-k.*, to acquaint, inform. *iṭṭilā'-nāma*, a written declaration, or notice in writing; a summons or citation. *iṭṭilā'-mand*, informed, acquainted. *a.*

اطلاق *iṭlāḳ*, m. setting at liberty; divorcing; freedom, disengagedness; in law, the office and records of summonses, also fees thereon. *a.*

اطلاق نويس *iṭlāḳ-navīs*, m. the officer who keeps the register of summonses and of the fees thereupon. *a. p.*

اطلس *aṭlas*, m. satin. *aṭlasī*, of or resembling satin, made of satin. *a.*

اطماع *iṭmā*, strong desire, longing for. *a.*

اطمئنان *iṭmīnān*, m. tranquillity, content, security, repose, rest, quiet. *iṭmīnāni k͟hāṭir*, peace of mind. *a.*

اطناب *aṭnāb* (pl. of طنب) tent ropes. *a.*

اطوار *aṭwār*, (pl. of طور) manners, behaviour, devoirs. *k͟hush-aṭwār*, well bred. *a.*

اطول *aṭwal*, very long or tall, prolix. *a.*

اطهار *aṭhār* (pl. of طاهر), the pure. *iṭhār*, purifying, purification. *a.*

اظلم *aẓlam*, more or most oppressive. *a.*

اظهار *iẓhār*, m. demonstration; revealing, publication, evincing. *a.*

اظهر *aẓhar*, very clear, more apparent. *aẓharu min ash-shamsi*, clearer than the sun. *a.*

اعادت *i'ādat*, (also *i'āda*), f. repetition, revising; visiting the sick. *a.*

اعتاق *i'tāḳ*, liberation, manumission. *a.*

اعانت *i'ānat*, f. help, aid, succour, favour, assistance. *a.*

اعتبار *i'tibār*, m. belief, faith, confidence; respect, esteem, veneration, reliance. *i'tibār rakhnā*, or *i'tibār-k.*, to give credit to, to believe. *a.*

اعتباري *i'tibārī*, trusty, confidential. *a.*

اعتدال *i'tidāl*, m. evenness, equilibrium; temperateness; rectitude, temperature, moderation. *a.*

اعتذار *i'tiẕār*, m. an excuse, apology. *i'tiẕār-nāma*, m. a letter of apology. *a.*

اعتذاري *i'tiẕārī*, one who apologizes. *a.*

اعتراض *i'tirāẓ*, f. refusing assent, objecting, discussion; criticism, animadversion, displeasure, opposition. *a.*

اعتراضي *i'tirāẓī*, f. displeasure, anger; one who objects. *a.*

اعتراف *i'tirāf*, m. confession, acknowledgment, avowal. *a.*

اعتزاز *i'tizāz*, excelling, overcoming. *a.*

اعتزال *i'tizāl*, secession, dissent; abdicating or withdrawing from office. *a.*

اعتصام *i'tiṣām*, preserving one's self from sin. *a.*

اعتقاد *i'tiḳād*, m. confidence, faith, trust, belief. *a.*

اعتقادي *i'tiḳādī*, one who has faith &c., or in whom faith is placed. *a.*

اعتكاف *i'tikāf*, m. restraining, curbing one's passion from religious motives, as in Lent; continuing in the mosque (particularly at Mecca). *a.*

اعتماد *i'timād*, m. faith, confidence; hope, dependence, reliance. *a.*

اعتمادي *i'timādī*, one in whom confidence is placed, a trustworthy person. *a.*

اعتنا *i'tinā*, taking pains, anxiety, care. *a.*

اعجاز *i'jāz*, m. disappointment; a miracle; wonder, amazement, astonishment, surprise. *i'jāzi masīḥā,ī*, miraculous cure, equalling the wonderful cures of the Messiah. *a.*

اعجم *a'jam*, a barbarian, a rustic: the term is strictly employed to one who does not speak pure Arabic, but it generally denotes a Persian. *a.*

اعدا *a'dā* (pl. of عدو), foes, enemies. *a.*

اعراب *i'rāb*, m. a vowel, the using of the vowel-points. *A'rāb*, the wandering Arabs of the desert. *a.*

اعرابي *a'rābī*, an Arab of the desert. *a.*

اعراج *i'rāj*, crippling, or making lame. *a.*

اعراض *i'rāẓ*, flying from, aversion. *i'rāẓ-k.*, to turn away from any thing with abhorrence. *a.*

اعراف *a'rāf*, m. purgatory: according to the Musalmāns it is a kind of neutral space between heaven and hell. The poet Sa'dī says that "to those in heaven A'rāf would seem hell, but the hellites would call A'rāf paradise."

اعرج *a'raj*, cripple from birth. *a.*

اعزاز *i'zāz*, m. respect, attention. *a.*

اعزه *a'izza* (pl. of عزيز), very excellent, worthy, or dear (persons or people). *a.*

اعصاب *a'ṣāb*, (pl. of عصب) nerves, tendons, sinews. *a.*

اعضا *a'ẓa*, (pl. of عضو) members of the body. *a'ẓā,e tanāsul*, organs of generation. *a'ẓā,e ra,isa*, the vital parts, as the heart, brain, &c. *a.*

اعظم *a'ẓam*, greatest, or very great. *a.*

اعلا *a'lā*, / اعلي *a'lā*, } supreme, high, the Most High. *a.*

اعلام *i'lām*, m. proclaiming, indicating, announcing; a warrant, notification. *a.*

اعلان *i'lān*, m. publishing, divulging. *a.*

اعلم *a'lam*, most knowing or wise. *a.*

اعما *a'mā*, for اعمي, blind, ignorant. *a.*

اعمال *i'māl*, applying. *a'māl*, (pl. of عمل) action, conduct. *a.*

اعمي *a'mā*, blind, ignorant; a desert. *a.*

اعيان *a'yān* (pl. of عين), eyes; grandees, nobles. *a'yāni ḥaẓrat*, courtiers. *a.*

آغا *āghā*, a master, lord; an *āgā*. *t.*

اغاريقون *aghārīḳūn* (ἀγαρικὸν) common agaric. *g.*

آغاز *āghāz*, m. beginning, commencement. *āghāz-k.*, to begin. *p.*

اغراق *ighrāḳ*, submersion: in rhetoric it signifies excessive praise or censure. *a.*

آغشته *āghishta*, mixed, macerated, polluted. *p.*

آغل *āghil* (also *aghil*) a sheep-cote in a mountain, an enclosure for sheep &c. in a plain. *aghal*, a bar or bolt. *p.*

اغلاق *ighlāḳ*, m. difficult to be understood, abstruse; an obstacle. *a.*

اغلال *aghlāl* (pl. of غل), yokes or chains for the neck. *a.*

اغلام *ighlām*, m. inflaming with desire, provoking to venery; sodomy. *a.*

اغلب *aghlab*, superior, stronger; adv. most likely, for the most part. *aghlab hai*, it is most likely, it generally happens. *a.*

اغلمش *ughalmish*, a king of Turkestan, descended of the great Jingis Khān. *t.*

اغلي *aghlī*, f. the bolt of a door; same as *ardandā*. *d.*

اغماض *ighmāẓ*, m. dissimulation, superciliousness; ogling, coquetry. *a.*

اغماضي *ighmāẓī*, one who is supercilious, proud. &c. *a.*

اغنيا *aghniyā* (pl. of غني), the rich. *a.*

اغوا *ighwā*, m. seduction, temptation. *ighwā-k.*, a. to seduce, to lead astray. *a.*

آغوش *āghosh*, f. an embrace; the bosom. *p.*

اغيار *aghyār*, (pl. of غير), strangers, foreigners, unknown persons, rivals. *a.*

اغياري *aghyārī*, f. strangeness, rivalry. *a.*

اف *uf*, fye! pooh! for shame! alas! *uf-h.*, to disapprove of, to lament. *uf ho-jānā*, to become ruined. *a.*

آف *āf*, the sun; the musk-deer. *p.*

آفات *āfat*, (pl. of آفت) calamities, evils, misfortunes dangers. *a.*

افاغنه *afāghina* (pl. of افغان), the people of *Afghānistān*, the Afghān race. *a.*

آفاق *āfāḳ* (pl. of افق), horizons, quarters of the heaven, the world or universe, regions. *a.*

افاقت *ifāḳat*, f. } convalescence, recovery
افاقه *ifāḳa*, m. } from a swoon, &c. *a.*

افانين *afānīn* (pl. of افنون), branches. *a.*

آفت *āfat*, f. misfortune, wretchedness, calamity. *āfat-rasīda* or *āfat-zada*, involved in misfortune. *a.*

آفتاب *āftāb*, m. the sun, sunshine. *āftāb-parast*, a worshipper of the sun. *āftāb-parastī*, f. the worship of the sun. *āftāb-gīr*, a parasol. *p.*

افتابه *āftāba*, m. an ewer, a water-pot. *p.*

آفتابي *āftābī*, f. a parasol of a particular form; a target studded with gold. *p.*

افتادگي *uftādagī*, f. a fall, the act of falling. *p.*

افتادن *uftādan*, to fall, to happen.

افتاده *uftāda*, fallen, prostrated. pl. *uftāda-gān*, the fallen, the unfortunate. *p.*

افتان *uftān*, falling. *uftān o khezān*, falling and getting up, met., with great difficulty. *p.*

افتاوا *aftāwā*, m. an ewer (v. *āftāba*). *p.*

افتخار *iftikhār*, m. glory, honour, elegance, gracefulness. *a.*

افترا *iftirā*, f. calumny, slander, false imputation. *a.*

افراختن *afrākhtan* (r. *afrāz*), to raise aloft, to extol. *a.*

افراد *afrād* (pl. of فرد), individuals, singular numbers, single ones. *a.*

افراد *ifrād*, m. withdrawing from society. *a.*

افراز *afrāz*, exalting (used in composition). *p.*

افراسياب *afrāsiyāb*, name of an ancient prince of Tūrān, one of the heroes of the *Shāhnāma*, ultimately slain by Rustam. *p.*

افراط *ifrāṭ*, m. excess, superfluity. *ifrāṭi-akhlāṭ* and *ifrāṭi khūn*, plethora. *a.*

افرنجي *afranjī*, a Frank, or native of Europe, a crusader. *a.*

افروخته *afrokhta*, set on fire, kindled, illumined. *p.*

افروختن *afrokhtan* (r. *afroz*), to set on fire, to burn, to kindle. *p.*

افروز *afroz*, inflaming, enlightening (used in composition.) *p.*

آفريدگار *āfrīda-gār*, m. the Creator. *p.*

آفريدن *āfrīdan* (r. *āfrīn*), to create. *p.*

آفريده *āfrīda*, created, a created being. *p.*

آفرين *āfrīn*, bravo! well done! (in comp.) creating, as *jahān-āfrīn*, creator of the world; m. the Creator. *āfrīn-k.*, a. to praise, to applaud. *p.*

آفرينش *āfrīnish*, f. the creation. *p.*

آفريننده *āfrīnanda*, creating; the Creator. *p.*

افزا *afzā* or *afzā,e*, (r. of *afzūdan*), increasing (used in comp.) *p.*

افزايش *afzāyish*, f. act of increasing or adding. *p.*

افزاينده *afzāyanda*, that which increases. *p.*

افزود *afzūd*, m. increase, addition, abundance; adj. more. *p.*

افزودگي *afzūdagī*, f. increase, addition. *p.*

افزودن *afzūdan* (r. *afzā*), to increase. *p.*

افزون *afzūn*, more, manifold, greater, much, increasing. *p.*

افزوني *afzūnī*, f. increase, enlargement. *p.*

افسانه *afsāna*, m. a tale, fiction, story, romance. *afsāna-go*, m. a romance-teller. *afsāna-go,ī*, f. the profession of a story-teller. *p.*

افسر *afsar*, m. f. a crown, diadem. *p.*

افسردن *afsurdan*, to wither, to flag. *p.*

افسردگي *afsurdagī*, f. dejection, melancholy, lowness or depression of spirits. *p.*

افسرده *afsurda*, dejected, dispirited, melancholy, low-spirited. *afsurda-khāṭir*, depressed, dispirited, afflicted *afsurda-dil*, faint-hearted, low-spirited, dejected. *p.*

افسنتين *afsantīn* (αψινθιον), wormwood. *g.*

افسوس *afsos*, m. vexation, sorrow, concern; interj. ah! alas! *afsos-k.* or *afsos-khānā*, to express sorrow or regret. *p.*

افسون *afsūn*, m. incantation, verses used in spells or enchantments, fascination, sorcery. *afsūn-k.*, a. to enchant, to use spells and incantations. *p.*

افسون‌ساز *afsūn-sāz*, } m. an enchanter, one who
افسون‌گر *afsūn-gar*, } uses spells, a sorcerer. *afsūn-sāzī* or *afsūn-garī*, f. enchantment, witchcraft. *p.*

افشا *ifshā*, m. divulging, publishing. *a.*

افشان *afshān*, dispersing, scattering, (used chiefly in composition; as, *gul-afshān*, strewing roses; *zar-afshān kāghaz*, paper sprinkled with gold). *p.*

افشاندن *afshāndan*, to scatter, disperse. *p.*

افشاني *afshānī*, f. dispersion, sprinkling; scattered over; as, *afshānī kāghaz*, paper sprinkled over with gold dust. *p.*

افشرده *afshurda*, squeezed, filtered. *p.*

افشره *afshura* (for *āb-shora*, q. v.), lemonade, sherbet. *d.*

افصح *afṣaḥ*, very eloquent, speaking very correctly. *a.*

افضال *afẓāl*, (pl. of فضل), graces, favours, virtues. *ifẓāl*, benefiting, making to excel. *a.*

افضل *afẓal*, } more or most excellent. *a*
افضلتر *afẓaltar*, }

افضليت *afẓalīyat*, excellence, pre-eminence. *a.*

افطار *ifṭār*, m. breaking a fast. *ifṭār-k.*, a. to break one's fast in the evening after fasting all day as the Musalmāns do in the month of *Ramaẓān*. *a.*

افطاري *ifṭārī*, that which is proper for fast-breaking. *a.*

افعال *af'āl*, (pl. of فعل), actions, conduct. *a.*

افعي *af'ī* (properly افعى *af'ā*), m. a serpent. *a.*

افغان *afghān*, lamentation: interj. alas! *p.*

افغان *afghān*, the name of a race of people who inhabit the country to the N. W. of Lahore, called also *Paṭhāns*: they are supposed or rather they themselves pretend, to be of Jewish extraction. *a.*

افغاني *afghānī*, of or relating to the *Afghāns*; the *Afghān* language. *a.*

افق *ufk*, m. the horizon; a tract or region of the earth; (poet.) the world. *a.*

افكار *afkār* (pl. of فكر), thoughts, meditations, opinions, counsels. *a.*

افگار *afgār*, wounded; m. a sore (on the back of a horse, &c.) *p.* [position. *p.*

افگن *afgan*, overthrowing, (used in com-

افگندن *afgandan*, to throw down, to cast. *p.*

افگنده *afganda*, overthrown, cast forth. *afgandagī*, f. act of overthrowing. *p.*

افلاس *iflās*, m. bankruptcy, penury, poverty, want; sometimes written *iflāsī*. *a.* [Arabs). *a.*

افلاطون *aflāṭūn*, Plato, (so called by the

افلاك *aflāk* (pl. of فلك), the heavens, heavenly spheres. *a.* [or heavenly spheres. *a.*

افلاكي *aflākī*, celestial, relating to the heavens

افواج *afwāj* (pl. of فوج), armies, crowds. *afwāji-ḳāhira*, a victorious army. *afwāji-shaiyāṭīn*, a host of devils. met. a multitude of children. *a.*

افواه *afwāh* (pl. of فوه), m. mouths; f. doubtful news; fame, report. *a.*

افواهي *afwāhī*, famed, reported, noised about. *a.*

افيم *afīm*, f. opium. *h.*

افيمچي *afīmchī*, m.
افيمن *afīman*, f.
افيمي *afīmī*, m.
} an eater of opium; (fig.) a sot. *h.*

افيون *afyūn*, f. opium. The inspissated juice of the *Papaver somniferum*. *a.*

افيوني *afyūnī*, an opium-eater. *a.*

آقا *āḳā*, m. master; owner. *p.* [dred. *a.*

اقارب *aḳārib* (pl. of قريب), relatives, kin-

اقاقيا *aḳāḳiyā*, the acacia; also the expressed juice of its fruit. *g.*

اقاله *iḳāla*, the cancelling of a sale, on condition of furnishing an equivalent for the original price of the article; breaking a contract. *a.*

اقاليم *aḳālīm*, (pl. of اقليم), climes, regions. *a.*

اقامت *iḳāmat*, f. resting, staying, abode, residence, dwelling. *a.*

اقبال *iḳbāl*, m. prosperity, good fortune, felicity; acceptance of a bond or bill. *iḳbāl-da'wā*, confession of judgment. *a.*

اقبالمند *iḳbāl-mand*, prosperous, of good fortune. *iḳbāl-mandī*, f. prosperity, good fortune. *a. p.*

اقتباس *iḳtibās*, m. borrowing (fire from another); acquiring, procuring, gaining; asking, begging; quotation. *a.* [to imitate. *a.*

اقتدا *iḳtidā*, imitating, following. *iḳtidā-k.*,

اقتدار *iḳtidār*, m. power, authority; excellence, dignity. *a.*

اقتسام *iḳtisām*, m. division, partition. *a.*

اقتصار *iḳtiṣār*, m. abbreviation, abridgment, restriction; determining or fixing the bounds of any thing; failing, wasting. *a.*

اقتضا *iḳtiẓā*, claim, requisition, demand. *a.*

اقدام *iḳdām*, m. intrepidity, resolution, firmness, spirit; endeavour, effort, diligence, attention, care. *iḳdām-namūdan*, to approach. *a.*

اقدس *aḳdas*, very holy, or most sacred. *a.*

اقرار *iḳrār*, m. promise, agreement, assurance, attestation; confession, confirmation; in the language of the law it means the notification or avowal of the right of another upon one's self. *iḳrār-k.*, a. to promise. *iḳrār-nāma*, m. written agreement, indenture, bond, contract, a deed of assent or acknowledgment in general. *iḳrāri 'āmm*, a public acknowledgment, declaration, or confession; a will or testament. *iḳrār-dānapatra*, a conditional deed of gift. *a.*

اقراري *iḳrārī*, one who assents, acknowledges or confesses. *a.*

اقراري اثامي *iḳrārī-asāmī*, m. a prisoner who pleads guilty. *a.*

اقران *aḳrān* (pl. of قرين), equals (in age, rank, &c.). *a.*

اقرب *aḳrab*, most near, more near. *a.*

اقربا *aḳribā* (pl. of قريب), kindred, friends, allies. *a.* [ments. *a.*

اقساط *aḳsāṭ* (pl. of قسط), portions, instal-

اقسام *aḳsām* (pl. of قسم), various kinds, of every sort. *a.*

اقصا *aḳṣā*,
اقصى *aḳṣā*,
} extreme, very or most distant, extremely. *a.* [of land. *a.*

اقطاع *iḳṭā'*, cutting, dividing, an assignment

اقل *aḳall*, less or least, very little. *a.*

اقّل بار *aḳḳal-bār*, the Indian shot-plant (*Canna Indica*), a beautiful flower. The word seems to be a corruption of some Arabic term. (Binning) *d.*

اقلف *aḳlaf*, m. a Muhammadan who for some adequate cause has omitted circumcision, but is not thereby disqualified from giving evidence in court. *a.*

اقليم *iḳlīm*, m. climate, country; according to Moslem geographers, there are seven *aḳālīm* "climates or countries" which occupy a fourth part of the world, called the *rub'i maskūn* "inhabited fourth part." The other three quarters of the globe are supposed to be utterly uninhabitable. (Binning). *g.*

اقوال *aḳwal*, (pl. of قول), words, sayings, agreements, promises. *a.*

اقوام *aḳwām* (pl. of قوم), tribes, nations. *a.*

آک आक *āk* (Dakhanī, *āg*), m. curled flowered gigantic swallowort (*Asclepias gigantea*), celebrated among native practitioners for its many medicinal qualities; a sprout of sugar-cane. *s.*

اک *ik* (for ایک) one (chiefly used in compound expressions as) *ik lautā*, single. *s.*

اکا *ikkā*, single, incomparable, superexcellent; m. an earring of a single pearl; an ornament worn on the wrist, often hollow, containing perfume; a champion, who serves alone, without being attached to any corps. *s.*

اکا *akkā*, m. a father; a dear or intimate friend; f. an elder sister. *d.*

اکابر *akābir* (pl. of اکبر or کبیر) the great or grandees; people of rank. *akābir o aṣāghir*, high and low, rich and poor. *a.*

اکاج अकाज *a-kāj*, m. loss, detriment; hurt, injury, prejudice; uselessness. *s.*

اکاجي अकाजी *a-kājī*, useless (animal, thing, or person); a retarder. *s.*

آکا आकार *ākār* (corruptly *akār*), m. appearance, aspect, shape, statue, likeness; hint, sign, token; the letter आ. *s.*

اکا *a-kār*, اکارت *a-kārat*, } useless, of no avail (properly *a-kārath*). *d.*

اکارته अकारथ *a-kārath*, unprofitable, fruitless, yielding no return, vain. *h.*

اکارن अकारण *a-kāran*, m. absence of cause; adv. causelessly, groundlessly. *s.*

آکاس आकाश *ākās* or *akās*, m. the sky, the firmament, the heavens; space; air; the fifth element of the Hindūs, more subtle than air, æther. *ākās-bānī*, f. revelation, a voice from heaven. *s.*

آکاس برت आकाशवृत्ति *ākās-britti*, f. subsistence not derived from any certain funds, or depending on any particular person; living from hand to mouth. *s.*

آکاس برتي आकाशवृत्ती *ākās-brittī*, one whose subsistence is fortuitous. *s.*

آکاس بیل आकाशबेल *ākās-bel*, f. the air-creeper *Cuscuta reflexa?*): it has no root or leaves, but grows on the tops of trees. *s.*

آکاس پون आकाशपवन *ākās-pawan*, m. a vegetable growing on other trees: air-plant or dodder. (*Cuscuta reflexa*). *s.*

آکاس دیا आकाशदीया *ākās-diyā*, m. a lamp which the Hindūs hang aloft on a bamboo in the month of Kārtik, a beacon (in Dakh., *Akās-diwā*). *s.*

آکاس مکهي आकाशमुखी *ākās-mukhī*, m. a devotee of the Saiva sect: his devotion consists in holding his face up to the sun, so that, after some time, it is difficult for him to hold it in the natural position. *s.*

آکاس منڈل आकाशमण्डल *ākās-manḍal*, m the atmosphere, the celestial sphere. *s.*

آکاس نیم आकाशनीम *ākās-nīm*, m. a plant growing on the *nīm* trees (a kind of *Epidendron*) *s.*

آکاس واني आकाशवाणी *ākās-wānī*, f. a voice from heaven, revelation. *s.*

اکاسي इकासी *ikāsī*, eighty-one. *h.*

آکاسي आकाशी *ākāsī*, aerial, celestial, atmospheric. *ākāsī-barna*, cerulean, azure. *s.* [*ākās*).

آکاش आकाश *ākāsh*, m. the sky (same as

اکال अकाल or आकाल *a-kāl* (or *ākāl*), m. a famine, a general scarcity; unseasonableness, extremity, pinch; adj. unseasonable, untimely, premature. *a-kāl-brishṭi*, untimely rain. *akāl-phal*, a fruit produced out of season. *s.*

اکال *akkāl*, a glutton, an enormous eater. *a.*

اکالنا उकालना *ukālnā*, a. to boil water. *h.*

اکام अकाम *a-kām*, unprofitable, fruitless. *s.*

آکانکشا आकांक्षा *ākānkshā*, f. wish desire, expectation; purpose, intention. *s.*

آکانکشت आकांक्षित *ākānkshit*, desirous; desired, expected. *s.*

آکانکشي आकांक्षी *ākānkshī*, desirous, full of hope, expecting; asking, inquiring. *s.* [one. *h.*

اکانوي इकानव्वे *ikānawwe* or *ikānwe*, ninety-

اکاون इकावन *ikāwan*, fifty-one. *h.*

اکبار *ik-bār* (for *ek bār*), one time. *h. p.*

اکبر *akbar*, very great; a man's name. *a.*

اکبرالراي *akbar-al-rā,ī*, اکبري راي *akbarī-rā,ī*, } presumptive evidence sufficiently strong to convict. *a.*

اکبري *akbarī*, of or relating to the Emperor Akbar; name of a sweetmeat; also of a gold coin worth a guinea and a half of our money. *a.*

اکپیچا *ikpechā*, head-ornament. *h. p.*

اکت उकत or उक्ति *ukat* or *ukti*, f. speech, what is spoken, language; contrivance, invention. *ukat banānā*, to make up a story, to invent, contrive. *ukat l.* to discover, to find out. *s.*

اکت उक्त *ukta*, spoken, used in law documents for "aforesaid, above named." *s.*

اکتارنا उकतानी *uktārnā*, a. to promote, to forward. *h.*

اکتارو उकताऊ *uktārū*, an instigator, promoter. *h.*

اکتالیس इकतालीस *iktālīs*, forty-one. *h.*

اکتانا उकताना *uktānā*, n. to fret, to be melancholy or dejected; to be out of humour with, to be tired of, to tire. *h.*

اکتساب *iktisāb*, m. gain, acquisition. *a.*

اکتفا *iktifā*, f. sufficiency, contentment. *iktifā-k.*, to content one's self; to stop short. *a.*

اکتک इकतक *ik-tak*, staring with a fixed look. *s.*

اکته अकथ *a-kath*, اکتهیه अकथ्य *a-kathya*, } not to be spoken, unfit to be mentioned; unutterable, obscene *s.*

[*grandiflora*).

اکتي *aktī*, f. the agati tree (*Æschynomene*

اکتیس इकतीस *iktīs*, thirty-one. *h.*

اکت उकट *ukaṭ*, contrivance, invention. *h.*

اکٹانا उकटाना *ukṭānā*, a. to dig up slowly a thing which is buried in the ground; to extract a secret gradually and artfully; to pump. *h.*

اکٹنا उकटना *ukaṭnā*, to be dug up, &c. (neut. form of *ukṭānā*; a. to dig up). *h.*

اکٹھا इकठा *ikaṭhā*, اکٹھان इकठान *ikṭhān*, اکٹھورا इकठौरा *ikṭhaurā*, } together, in one and the same place, united. *s.*

اکثر *akṣar*, most, many, much; adv. often, usually, for the most part, generally. *akṣar-auḳāt*, often, frequently, generally. *a.*

اکثریہ *akṣarīya*, for the most part, chiefly. *a.*

اکچت इकचित *ik-chit*, of one mind, unanimous, without wavering. *s.*

اکچھت راج کرنا इकछतराज॰क *ik-chhat rāj-k.*, to rule everywhere. *s.*

اکر अकर *a-kar*, duty-free, exempt from duty. *s.*

آکر आकर *ākar*, f. aborigines; mine, quarry, source; multitude. *s.*

آکر आकर *ākar*, f. the den of a lion or tiger; (conjunct. part. from *ānā*), having come. *h.*

اکرا अकरा *akrā*, dear, costly; f. a kind of grass so called, a kind of vetch. *h.*

اکرام *akrām*, (pl. of کرم), favours, kindnesses, obligations; honour, respect. *a.*

اکرام *ikrām*, m. honouring, complimenting, treating with attention and ceremony. *a.*

اکراہ *ikrāh*, f. horror, aversion, abhorrence, detestation. *a.*

اکرایہ अकराया *akarāyā*, f. ground not properly cleaned for receiving the seed. *s.*

آکرت आकृति *ākṛiti*, f. shape, figure; likeness, image; the body; species. *s.*

اکرترم अकृत्रिम *a-kṛitrim*, inartificial, not made. *s.*

آکرش आकर्ष *ākarsh*, m. attraction, fascination; a magnet, a loadstone; spasm. *s.*

آکرشت आकर्षित *ākarshit*, آکرشٹ आकृष्ट *ākṛishṭa*, } attracted, drawn. *s.*

آکرشک आकर्षक *ākarshak*, m. a magnet, a loadstone, any thing which attracts; adj. attractive, magnetic (also *ākarshik*).

آکرشن आकर्षण *ākarshaṇ*, m. drawing, attraction. *s.*

آکرشی आकर्षी *ākarshī*, attractive. *s.*

اکرکس अकर्कस *a-karkas*, soft, not hard. *s.*

اکرم *akram*, very kind, merciful. *a.*

اکرم अकर्म *a-karm* or *a-karma*, m. bad action, sin, vice, wickedness. *s.*

آکرم आक्रम *ākram*, m. ascending, superiority; surpassing, surmounting; invasion, a seizing. *s.*

اکرما अकर्मा *a-karmā*, idle, unoccupied. *s.*

اکرمک अकर्मक *a-karmak*, intransitive (in gram.). *s.*

اکرمنیہ अकर्मण्य *a-karmanya*, useless, unprofitable, good for nothing. *s.*

اکرمی अकर्मी *a-karmī*, a wretch, sinner. *s.*

اکرنی अकरणी *a-karnī*, inconsistent, indecent, unsuitable, not proper to be done. *s.*

اکروٹ *akroṭ*, m. (for أخروٹ), a walnut. *s.*

اکرور अक्रूर *akrūr*, not cruel, mild, humane, gentle. *s.*

اکڑ अकड़ *akaṛ*, f. crookedness, strut, pride, conceit, airs. *h.*

اکڑا अकड़ा *akṛā*, stiff, affected. *h.*

اکڑانا अकड़ाना *akṛānā*, a. to distress, to impede. *h.*

اکڑباز अकड़बाज़ *akaṛ-bāz*, an affected person, a fop, a swaggerer. *akaṛ-bāzī*, swaggering, foppishness. *h. p.*

اکڑبائی अकड़बाई *akaṛ-bā,ī*, f. the cramp. *h.*

اکڑپکڑ *akaṛ-pakaṛ*, اکڑتکڑ *akaṛ-takaṛ*, اکڑم تکڑم *akṛam-takṛam*, } m. stateliness, affected airs, pride, haughtiness. *h.*

اکڑنا अकड़ना *akaṛnā*, n. to writhe, to ache, to cramp, to be cramped, to become stiff or distorted, as one's limbs; to strut affectedly. *h.*

اکڑو उकड़ू *ukṛū*, m. the posture of sitting on the hams with the soles of the feet on the ground. *ukṛū baiṭhnā*, to sit on the heels with the knees upwards. *h.*

اکڑو अकड़ू *akṛū*, affected, proud, conceited. *h.*

اکڑیت अकड़ैत *akṛait*, an affected person, a swaggerer, a fop. *h.*

اکسار *iksār*, (v. *yak-sār*), similar; of the same sort. *h.*

اکسانا उकसाना *uksānā*, a. to excite, to rouse, to trim (a lamp). *h.*

اکسٹھ इकसठ *iksaṭh*, sixty-one. *h.*

اکسر *iksar* (for *yaksar*), single, in a body, all at once. *p.*

اکسمات अकस्मात *a-kasmāt* (lit. without a wherefore), immediately, accidentally, extempore, unexpectedly, unawares, abruptly. *s.*

اکسنا उकसना *ukasnā*, n. to be excited, moved, to try to move. *h.*

اکسی *aksī*, f. a tree, the leaves and pods of which are eaten as vegetables; probably the same as *akṭī*, *q. v.*

اکسیر *iksīr*, alchemy, chemistry; the philosopher's stone (or rather a calx of quicksilver used in transmuting metals to gold), an elixir, dust, filings. *a.*

اکش अक्ष *aksha*, m. a die, cubic or oblong; the spots on dice. *aksha-bhāg*, m. a degree of latitude. *s.*

اکش अक्षि *akshi*, m. the eye. *akshi-tārā*, f. the pupil of the eye. *s.*

اکش इक्षु *ikshu*, f. sugar-cane. *ikshu-ras*, m. the juice of the sugar-cane. *ikshu-sār*, m. molasses, raw sugar. *ikshu-kānḍ*, m. a species of sugar-cane (*saccharum munja*). *ikshu-mehī*, diabetic. *s.*

اکشانش अक्षांश *akshānsh*, m. a degree of latitude or longitude. *s.*

اکشت अक्षत *a-kshat*, infallible, indelible; remaining, continuing. m. whole grains of rice used in religious ceremonies, fried grain. *akshat-tilak*, f. the ceremony of putting a few grains of rice on the forehead of an idol when addressed, or of a Brāhman when invited to an entertainment. *s.*

اکشر अक्षर *akshar*, m. a letter of the alphabet. *aksharī*, lettered, writing a good hand. *s*

اکشل अकुशल *a-kushal*, unlucky, inauspicious. *s.*

اکشمتي ईक्षुमती *ikshumatī*, f. name of a river in Bengal, the Issamutty. *s.*

اکشوهني अक्षौहिणी *akshauhinī*, f. an army (see *achchhauhinī*). *s.*

اکشي अक्षय *a-kshay*, imperishable, undecayable. *akshayatā*, f. imperishableness. *akshay-briksh*, m. an undecayable tree. *akshay-lok*, m. the imperishable world. *s.*

آکشيپ आक्षेप *ākshep*, m. reproof, sarcasm, abuse. *s.*

اکل *akl*, m. food; eating. *akl-o-shurb*, meat and drink, eating and drinking. *a.*

آکل आकुल *ākul*, confounded, perplexed, confused, distressed, chiefly used in compound words. *s.*

آکلا आकला *āklā*, fleet, swift; peevish. *h.*

اکلا इकला *iklā*, alone, single. (v. *iklautā*). *h.*

اکلاي इकलाई *iklā,ī*, f. loneliness; name of an article of dress. *h.*

اکلانا अकुलाना *akulānā*, n. to be agitated, to be distracted, to be confused, to be out of order, to tire, to weary, to be astonished. *h.*

اکلپت अकल्पित *a kalpit*, not artificial, not made. *s.*

آکلت आकुलित *ākulit*, agitated, distracted. *s.*

آکلتا आकुलता *ākulatā*, f. agitation, distress. *s.*

اکلنا उकलना *ukalnā*, n. the intransitive of *ukālna*, to boil, be boiling. *h.*

اکلني अकुलिनी *a-kulinī*, f. a woman of a low caste or family; adj. bad, base (woman). *h.*

اکلوتا इकलौता *iklautā*, } single, solitary,
اکلونتا इकलौंता *iklauṅtā*, } alone. *s.*

آکلي आकली *āklī*, f. motion, agitation (particularly of a carriage). *h.*

اکليان अकल्याण *a-kalyān*, ominous, unpropitious; disconsolate, uncomfortable. *s.*

اکليسري उकलेसरी *uklesarī*, of or relating to the town of Uklesar, famed for its paper manufacture. *h.*

اکليل الجبل *iklīlu-l-jabal*, m. (the crown of the mountain), an herb smelling like frankincense, rosemary. *a.*

اکليل الملك *iklīlu-l-malik*, m. (the king's crown), melilot. *a.*

اکلينا अकुलीना *a-kulīnā*, of no family, plebeian, of low extraction; ignoble. f. *akulīnī*. *s.*

اکمال *ikmāl*, m. perfection, accomplishing. *a.*

اکمل *akmal*, perfect, very complete, entire, full. *a.*

اکمپت अकम्पित *a-kampit*, firm, unshaken. *s.*

آکمپت आकम्पित *ā-kampit*, shaken, trembling. *s.*

آکمپن आकम्पन *ākampan*, m. shaking, trembling. *s.*

اکمه *akmah*, born blind. *a.*

آکن आकन *ākan*, grass and weeds collected from a ploughed field. *h.*

اکناف *aknāf* (pl. of کنف), environs, borders, confines, sides. *a.*

اکنٹك अकण्टक *a-kanṭak*, free from thorns. *s.*

اکنچن अकिञ्चन *a-kinchan*, poor, needy, destitute. *ākinchan*, m. poverty. *s.*

اکنون *aknūn*, now, at present. *p.*

اکور अकोर *akor*, f. a bribe; coaxing (a cow that has lost her calf, that she may be tractable). *h.*

اکوري अकोरी *akorī*, one who receives a bribe. *h.*

اکول *akūl* (same as اکال), a glutton, &c. *a.*

اکول अकोल *akol*, m. a plant, the oil of which is used in enchantments (*Alangium hexapetalum*). *s.*

اکوند अकन्द *akwand*, m. swallowwort (*Asclepias gigantea*). *h.*

آکها आखा *ākhā*, m. a riddle, a sieve; a bag filled with grain, of which two are carried by a bullock; a pair of grain-bags used as a pannier. *h.*

اکھاڑ उखाड़ *ukhāṛ*, f. rooting up, extirpation. *h.*

اکھاڑا अखाड़ा *akhāṛā*, m. a palæstra, or place for wrestling, a scene; any place of assembly; court, circus. *Indr kā akhāṛā*, Indra's court. *h.*

اکھاڑنا उखाड़ना *ukhāṛnā*, a. to root up, to eradicate, dislocate. *h.*

اکھاڑو उखाड़ू *ukhāṛū*, m. one who digs up or eradicates. *h.*

اکھال उखाल *ukhāl*, m. act of vomiting; an emetic. *ukhāl-pukhāl* (also *ukhāl wakhāl*), m. cholera-morbus, vomiting violently. *h.*

اکھالنا उखालना *ukhālnā*, a. to vomit. *h.*

اکهپاشان आखुपाषाण *ākhu-pāshān*, m. a kind of mineral, a loadstone. *s.*

آکهت आखत or अखत *ākhat*, *akhat*, m. (same as *akshat*), whole or unbroken rice, employed in oblations. *s.*

اکهتر इखत्तर *ikhattar*, seventy-one. *h.*

اکهتيج अखतीज *akhtīj*, the 18th day of *Baisākh*, a Hindū festival. *h.*

اکھٹا इकट्ठा *ikhaṭṭā*, together, in one place. *h.*

اکھٹنا उखटना *ukhaṭnā*, n. to trip, to stumble. *h.*

آکهر आखर *ākhar* (v. آکر), m. the den of a wild beast. *h.*

اکھر अखर *akhar*, plenty, abundance. *d.*

اکھرب अखर्ब *a-kharb*, tall, long, large. *s.*

اکھروٹ अखरोट *akhroṭ*, m. a walnut; the fruit of the *aleurites triloba*. *h.*

اکھڑ अखड़ *akhaṛ*, undisciplined (soldier), barbarous, uncouth, ugly. *h.*

اکھڑا अखड़ा *akhṛā*, rude, ill-shaped. *akhṛā khaṭṭ*, an ill-formed piece of writing. *h.*

اکھڑانا उखड़ाना *ukhṛānā*, a. (same as *ukhāṛnā*), pluck up, eradicate. *h.*

اکھڑنا उखड़ना *ukhaṛnā*, n. (intr. of *ukhāṛnā*), to be rooted up, plucked up, raised up; to slip out (as a bone, &c.). *ukhaṛnā pukhaṛnā*, to be plucked or rooted up. *h.*

اکھل अखल or अखिल *a-khal* or *a-khil*, the whole, all, every. *s.*

اکھل उखल *ukhal*, } m. & f. a wooden mortar for pounding rice or other grain. *s.*
اکھلي उखली *ukhlī*, }

اکھمج उखमज *ukhmaj* (for उष्मज *ushmaj*), gnats, flies, musquitoes, &c., insects produced by heat. *s.*

اکھنڈ अखण्ड *a-khanḍ*, unbroken, entire, the whole. *s.*

اکھنڈت अखण्डित *a-khanḍit*, unbroken, continuous; unrefuted. *s.*

آکھوٹ आखोट *ākhoṭ*, m. the walnut tree. *h.*

اکھي अखय *akhai*, everlasting, not liable to decay. *akhai-bar* or *akhai-bṛikh*, the undecayable tree. *s.*

آکھیا आख्या *ākhyā*, f. name, appellation. *s.*

آکھیات आख्यात *ākhyāt*, said, spoken; denominated, named. *s.*

اکھیات अख्यात *a-khyāt*, unknown, obscure. *s.*

آکھیٹ आखेट *ākheṭ*, m. (v. *āher*), the chase, hunting, pursuing; terror, fright. *s.*

آکھیٹک आखेटिक *ākheṭik*, m. a hound. *s.*

اکھیڑنا उखेड़ना *ukheṛnā*, a. to eradicate, to pluck up, root up. *h.*

اکھیڑوانا उखेड़वाना *ukheṛwānā*, a. to cause to pluck up. *h.*

اکیا अकैया *ahaiyā*, m. one of the sacks or baskets of a pannier. *h.*

اکیرت अकीर्त्ति *a-kīrti*, f. infamy, disgrace. *s.*

اکیس इक्कीस *ikkīs*, twenty-one. *h.*

اکیلا अकेला *akelā*, alone, single, solitary. *h.*

اکیلنا उकेलना *ukelnā*, a. to turn up. *h.*

آگ आग *āg*, f. fire; *āg uṭhānā*, a. to raise disturbance, to enrage, to provoke. *āg bāg-h*, to be hotly enraged. *āg bujhānā*, a. to extinguish; to appease a tumult, to pacify a quarrel, to still resentment. *āg barasnā*, n. to rain fire (applied to the extreme heat of the sun, or to a hot fire of cannon or musketry in battle). *āg barnā*, n. to be enraged; to be very angry. *āg bhaṛkānā*, a. to inflame. *āg bhaknā* and *āg phānknā*, a. to speak idle words, to boast. *āg paṛnā*, n. to be enraged; as *merī bāton se us-par āg paṛtī hai*, he is enraged at my words. *āg denā*, a. to apply the fire, to burn a Hindū corpse. *āg sulgānā*, a. to inflame, to excite sedition, to foment a quarrel clandestinely. *āg-karnā*, a. to make any thing exceedingly warm; to excite envy or anger (used among women). *āg lagānā*, to set fire to, to inflame; to enrage, to raise disturbance. *āg lagāke pānī le dauṛnā*, a. to play tricks, to deceive; to pretend to appease a quarrel which one has purposely excited. *āg lagnā*, n. to take fire, to be enraged, to be very hungry. *āg lage par billī kā mūt ḍhūnḍhnā* or *māngnā*, a. to put off, to delay, or excuse one's self on vain pretences (the literal translation, though highly expressive, would sound somewhat musty). *āg lene ko ānā*, n. to come to get fire, is spoken of a friend who goes to visit another, and leaves him quickly. *āg men pānī ḍālnā*, a. see *āg bujhānā*. *āg men kisī kī jalnā*, or *loṭnā*, or *ghair kī āg men jalnā*, a. to bring reproach upon, to accuse, to suffer for another. *āg men loṭnā*, n. to be afflicted with grief or melancholy. *āg honā*, n. to be enraged; or, as the vulgate hath it, "to flare up." *s.*

آگ *āg*, m. Dakhanī, for *āk*, q.v.

آگا आगा *āgā*, m. the front, the space in front of a house; the fore part of a turban. *āgā lenā*, to take the lead, or precede. *s.*

آگا پیچھا کرنا आगा पीछा करना *āgā-pīchhā-k.* n. to hesitate, to waver, boggle, demur, to prevaricate. *h.*

اگادھ अगाध or आगाध *a-gādh* or *āgādh*, bottomless, unfathomable. *agādhatā*, f. extreme depth, unfathomability. *s.*

آگار आगार *āgār*, m. a house. *s.*

اگار अगार *agār*, avarice, covetousness. *d.*

اگارہ इगारह *igārah*, eleven. *igārahwān*, the eleventh. *s.*

آگاري आगारी *āgārī*, f. money, &c., paid in advance. *s.*

اگاڑا अगाड़ा *agāṛā*, m. the name of a plant said to cure the bite of venomous reptiles (*Achyranthes aspera*). Same as *chirchirā*. *h.*

اگاڑي अगाड़ी *agāṛī*, before, forward, further on; f. the ropes with which a horse's feet are tied; the front, the fore-part. *agāṛī mārnā*, to attack in front, to defeat a hostile army in pitched battle. *agāṛī pichhāṛī lagānā*, to confine (particularly a horse). *h.*

اگاس *agās* (v. *ākās*), the sky, &c. *d.*

اگاسي अगासी *agāsī*, m. f. a turban; a terrace in front of an upper room; the cry of a kite. *h.*

اگال उगाल *ugāl*, m. that which is spit out after chewing any thing (particularly betel leaf). *āp kā ugāl merā adhār*, your worship's leavings are my nourishment, *i.e.* you are my support and benefactor. *h.*

اگالدان उगालदान *ugāl-dān*, m. a spit-box. *h.*

آگامي आगामी *āgāmī*, coming, about to come; future. *s.*

اگانا उगाना *ugānā*, a. to raise, cause to grow. *s.*

اگاؤ आगाऊ *agā,ū*, adv. before, in front. *āgā,ū-jānā*, to advance in order to meet a person coming on a visit; m. an advance of money. *s.*

آگاہ *āgāh*, informed of, acquainted with, intelligent. *p.*

اگاہنا उगाहना *ugāhnā*, a. to collect, to gather, to accumulate. *s.*

آگاهي *āgāhī*, f. intelligence, wariness. *p.*

اگاهي उगाही *ugāhī*, f. usury; the trade of lending money on interest of one fourth, the payment of which is received by instalments. *h.*

آگبوٹ *āg-boṭ*, a steamboat. The latter part of this term is English, the former signifies "fire." *h.* (A word like this can hardly with propriety be inserted in a Dictionary; but it is now so commonly used, that it may be considered a naturalized Hindūstānī term.) Binning.

اگپت अगुप्त *a-gupta*, unhidden, unconcealed. *s.*

اگت उगत *ugat*, growing, springing up; production. *h.*

اگت अगति *a-gati*, dishonoured, disgraced, without character; one whose funeral ceremonies are not performed; f. distress, disgrace, inconvenience, damnation, condemnation. *s.*

آگت आगत *āgat*, come, arrived. *s.*

اگتر अगत्तर *agattar*, coming, arriving. *s.*

اگتي अगती *agtī* (for اَکتي), the agati tree. *s.*

اگٹ अगट *agaṭ*, m. a butcher's stall. *h.*

اگٹنا अगटना *agaṭnā*, a. to collect or assemble. *ugaṭnā*, a. to revile, to give abusive language. *h.*

اگر *agar*, if, though, although, when. *p.*

اگر अगर *agar*,
اگر अगुरु *aguru*, } m. wood of aloes, a kind of fragrant wood, agallochum (*Aquillaria agallocha*): another tree which produces bdellium (*Amyris agallocha*); the *sisu* tree (*Dalbergia sisoo*); light, not heavy. *s.*

اگر उग्र *ugra*, m. wrath, anger; adj. wrathful, cruel, savage. *s.*

اگر अग्र *agra*, m. the forepart of a thing; adj. prior, first. *agra-gāmī*, preceding; m. forerunner. *agra-grās*, m. the first morsel. *agra-sar*, m. a guide; adj. preceding. *s.*

آگر आगर *āgar*, m. a salt-pit. *h.*

اگرا उग्रा *ugrā*, angry, cruel, wrathful. *s.*

اگرار *agrār*, m. a village inhabited entirely by Brāhmans; the quarter of a town or village occupied by Brāhmans. *d.*

اگراس *aggrās* (for *agra-grās*), m. the first morsel. *s.*

اگراس अग्रास *agrās*,
اگراسن अग्रासन *agrāsan*, } m. victuals offered in oblations, sacrifices, &c. to the gods. *s.*

اگرچه *agarchi*, although, though. *p.*

اگرسر अग्रसर *agra-sar*, m. he who goes first, a leader, a chief. *s.*

اگرسوچ अग्रसोच *agra-soch*, m. providence, foresight, precaution, forethought. *s.*

اگرسوچي अग्रसोची *agra-sochī*, provident, endued with foresight. *s.*

اگرو *agrū*, a species of bird, the thrush. *d.*

اگروالا अगरवाला *agar-wālā*, a race of merchants, of the Vais tribe (from Agrohā, a place to the west of Dihlī). *h.*

اگروي *āg-rū,ī*, f. fire-cotton, *i.e.* tinder. *d.*

اگره *agra*, m. the city of Agra; also called Akbar-ābād. *h.*

آگره आग्रह *āgrah*, m. favour; seizing, surpassing, surmounting; power, ability. *s.*

آگرهاين आग्रहायण *āgrahāyan*, m. the first month of the Hindū year (November—December). *s.*

آگرهايني आग्रहायणी *āgrahāyanī*, f. the day of full moon in the month Āgrahāyan; a constellation of three stars, the first of which is Orionis, figured by an antelope's head; hence also *mṛig-shiras*. *s.*

اگري अगरी *agarī*,
اگريا अगरिया *agariyā*, } f. the colour of the wood of aloes. *s.*

آگري आगरी *āgarī*, m. a manufacturer of salt. *h.*

اگڑ *agaṛ* (for *akaṛ*, q.v.), strut, pride. *d.*

آگڑا आगड़ा *āgṛā*, m. an ear of corn or rice which has been blighted. *h.*

اگڑبگڑ अगड़बगड़ *agaṛ-bagaṛ*, m. trifling employment, or talk; trifles, trash; adj. promiscuous, composed of odds and ends. *h.*

اگسانا *ugsānā*, to snuff a candle, to trim a lamp. *d.*

اگست अगस्ति *agasti* (for *agastya*), m. a sage celebrated in Hindū mythology: he is represented of short stature, and to have been born in a water-jar; he is famed for having swallowed the ocean when it had given him offence. At his command the Vindhya mountain prostrated itself, and so remains. Name of a tree (*Æschynomene grandiflora*); name of a star (*Canopus*). *s.*

اگستوار अगस्तवार *agastwār*, name of a small tribe of *rāj-pūts*. *h.*

آگل *āgal*, before, in front. *agal*, m. a bar or bolt. *d.*

اگلا अगला *aglā*, prior, preceding, former, the foremost, the first, the chief, the best; ancestor, ancient; other, second, next. *h.*

آگلانت आगलान्त *āgalānt*, up to the neck. *s.*

اگلنا उगलना *ugalnā*, a. to spit out, to vomit; met. to refund property surreptitiously obtained. *s.*

آگم आगम *āgam*, m. futurity; a Hindū scripture dictated by Mahādeva; a shāstra containing spells and incantations; a shāstra or work on sacred science; (in law) a voucher or document. *āgam-bāndhnā*, to determine the future, to foretell. *āgam-jānī* or *āgam-gyānī*, having the skill of foreknowing, prognosticator. *āgam-bidyā*, f. the art or science of foretelling. *āgam-baktā*, foreteller, predictor; Shiva, one who tells the doctrines of *āgam*. *s.*

اگم अगम *a-gam*, for अगम्य *a-gamya*, impassable, impervious, bottomless, deep, unfordable, unaccomplishable, incomprehensible, unattainable. *s.*

اگم उगुम *ugum*, m. growing, becoming. *d.*

آگمن आगमन *āgaman*, m. coming, arriving, proceeding. *s.*

آگمنا आगमना *āgmanā*, m. the advanced guard; adj. adventurous, venturesome; forward, early (as fruit). *s.*

آگمي आगमी *āgamī*, m one who foretells the future. *s.*

اگميه अगम्य *a-gamya*, deep; impassable, inaccessible, impenetrable, impervious. *s.*

اگن अग्नि *agni* (vulg. *agin*), m. fire; the south-east; (in Hindū mythology) god of fire, and regent of the south-east quarter; also the name of one of the Purānas; the fire of the stomach, the digestive faculty, appetite. *agni-bān*, m. arrow of fire, a rocket. *agni-prastar*, m. fire-stone, flint. *agni-parīkshā*, f. the fiery ordeal, by a heated iron or boiling oil, or passing through fire. *agni-sanskār*, m. funeral ceremonies, as burning a dead body, or any ceremony performed with consecrated fire. *agni-garbha* or *agni-mani*, m. the sun-stone, a fabulous gem, supposed to contain solar heat. *s.*

اگن अगिन *agin*, m. the name of a bird; sort of lark. *h.*

اگن अगुण *a-gun*, unskilful, ineffectual, void of good qualities; m. a defect, a fault. *s.*

اگنا उगना *ugnā*, n. to grow, to spring (as plants); to rise (as the moon). *ugte hī jal jānā*, to be withered as soon as it springs up, is applied to a hope or expectation which is blasted in the bud. *h.*

اگنبان अग्निबाण *agni-bān*, m. a kind of fiery missile, a rocket. *s.*

اگن باو अगिनबाव *agin-bā,o* (or *agni-bā,o*), f. the farcy, in horses; an eruptive disease in men; erysipelas. *s.* [counted. *s.*

اگنت अगणित *a-ganit*, innumerable, not

آگندن *āgandan*, to fill, to cram. *p.*

اگنك अग्निक *agnik*, m. an insect of a scarlet colour, the lady-bird. *s.*

اگنهوتري अग्निहोतृ *agni-hotrī*, m. a Brāhman who maintains a perpetual fire in his house. *s.*

اگني *agnī*, f. (see अग्नि *agni*), fire, &c. *s.*

آگو आगू *āgū*, forward, before; heretofore. *h.*

اگوا अगवा *agwā*, foremost; m., also *agu,ā*, a guide, a forerunner, harbinger; one who adjusts a marriage. *h.*

آگوا आगवा *āgwā*, also *āgū,ā*, m. a pommel. *h.*

اگوار अगवार *agwār*, a portion of corn set apart for village servants, like the customary "sharping corn" in England. *h.*

اگواڑا अगवाड़ा *agwāṛā*, m. the front, the fore-part; the space in front of a house. *h.*

اگواسي अगवासी *agwāsī*, the body of the ploughshare. *h.* [binger (see *agwā*). *h.*

اگواني अगवानी *agwānī*, m. a guide, har-

اگواهي अगवाही *agwāhī*, } f. burning, conflagration (of a city,
اگوائي अगवाई *agwā,ī*, } forest, &c.). *h.* [ship. *s.*

اگوائي अगवाई *agwā,ī*, f. guidance, leader-

اگوچر अगोचर *a-gochar*, imperceptible, unseen, invisible; m. the Invisible, Supreme. *s.*

اگور अगौर *agaur*, m. an advance of rent. *h.*

اگور अगोर *agor*, } m. one who watches
اگوريا अगोरिया *agoriyā*, } over the crops, &c. *agor-batā,ī*, a division of the crop after reaping. *h.*

اگورنا अगोरना *agornā*, a. to watch, to guard. *h.*

اگوريا अगोरिया *agoriyā*, m. watchman, or guard. (v. *agor*). *h.*

اگوڑھ अगूढ़ *a-gūṛh*, easy, manifest, evident. *agūṛh-bhā,o*, open, honest, candid. *s.*

اگوڑي अगोड़ी *agoṛī* or अगोरी *agorī*, in advance, beforehand. *h.* [*nā*. *h.*

اگولنا अगोलना *agolnā*, a. to watch (v. *agor-*

اگوند अगौंद *agaund*, the top of the sugar-cane cut up for seed. *s.*

اگوني अगौनी *agaunī*, f. the going or sending forward to meet and receive a visitant with honour. *agaunī-k.*, to advance to meet the bridegroom at a wedding, or a visitant on the road. *h.*

اگھ अघ *agh*, m. sin, guilt, wickedness. *s.*

آگه *āgah* (for *āgāh*), informed, wary. *p.*

اگھاٹ अघाट *a-ghāṭ*, m. land held in perpetuity and not alienable. *s.*

اگھار आघार *aghār* (v. *agār*), avarice. *d.*

آگھار आघार *āghār*, m. sacred food, which Hindūs place before an idol; ghī, or clarified butter. *h.*

اگھاري अघारी *aghārī*, affected with avarice. *h.*

اگھاڑا अघाड़ा *aghāṛā*, m. name of a plant said to cure the bite of venomous reptiles. *h.*

اگھاڑنا उघाड़ना *ughāṛnā*, a. to discover, to unveil, to pull off. *h.* [or unveils. *h.*

اگھاڑو उघाड़ू *ughāṛū*, m. one who discovers,

اگھانا अघाना *aghānā*, a. to surfeit, to satiate; n. to surfeit, to be satiated; adj. satiated; rich, affluent. *h.*

اگھائي अघाई *aghā,ī*, f. satiety, surfeit. *h.*

اگھڑنا उघड़ना *ugharnā*, n. to be uncovered, opened, pulled off. *h.*

اگھمي अघमय *aghmay*, sinful. *s.*

اگھن अगहन *aghan*, m. the name of the eighth Hindū month (during which the sun is in Scorpio, and the moon is full near Orion's head (November—December). *s.* [grass. *h.*

اگھن گھاس अघिन घास *aghin-ghās*, m. lemon

اگھناشك अघनाशक *agh-nāshak*, adj. purifying, freeing from sin. *s.*

اگھني अगहनी *aghanī*, relating to *aghan*; the produce of that month. *aghanī fasl*, the cold harvest weather. *s.* [terrible. *s.*

اگھور अघोर *aghor*, m. a name of Shiva; adj.

اگھورپنتھ अघोरपंथ *aghor-panth*, m. a particular religious order among Hindūs. *s*

اکھورپنتھي अघोरपंथी *aghorpanthī*, اکھوري अघोरी *aghorī*, } used substantively, professing *aghorpanth*, an order of religious mendicants, who eat every thing, however filthy, even human carcasses; hence, a gross or filthy feeder. *s.*

اکھوري अघोरी *aghorī*, covetous, greedy. *d.*

آگهي *āgahī*, f. (v. *āgāhī*), information, &c. *p.*

آگي आगे *āge*, before, beyond, more, ago, already, in future, formerly, forwards, onwards; hence, or henceforth, rather, sooner. *āge dhar-lenā*, to get before, to outstrip, to surpass, to pass (as a horse in a race). *āge-ānā*, to come forward; to return, to revert; a. to hasten, to accelerate. *āge-lānā*, to bring forward, to advance. *s.*

اگي *age* ! O thou ! (applied to a female). *d.*

آگيا आज्ञा or अज्ञा *āgyā*, *agyā* (or *āgṅyā*), f. command, order. *āgyā-patr*, m. an edict, a written order. *āgyā-bhang*, m. disobedience, insubordination. *āgyā-kār*, or *āgyā-kārī*, obedient, executing orders. *s.*

اگيا अगैया *agaiyā*, a disease which affects the rice plant, which thereby is parched up. *h.*

اگيا अगिया *agiyā*, m. the name of a bird (*Alauda Aggia, Buch.*). *s.*

اگيابيتال अग्याबैताल *agyā-baitāl*, m. a demon who rules over fire. *h.*

اگيات अज्ञात *a-gyāt* or *a-gnyāta*, unknown, inexperienced, ignorant, simple. *agṅyāta-jaubanā* or *-yauwanā*, f. a full-grown girl, arrived at maturity, and surprised at the symptoms which then appear, not knowing to what to attribute her sensations. *s.*

اگياري अगयारी *agyārī*, f. kindling the fire at the time of devotion (by Hindūs). *h.*

اگياگهاس *agyā-ghās*, m. lemon grass. *d.*

اگيان अज्ञान *a-gyān* or *a-gṅyān*, witless, ignorant; m. ignorance. *s.*

اگيانا अगयाना *agyānā*, a. to burn vessels of metal for the purpose of cleaning them. *h.*

اگيان‌پن अज्ञानपन *a-gyān-pan*, state of ignorance. *s.*

اگيانتا अज्ञानता *a-gyānatā*, f. ignorance, stupidity. *s.*

اگياني अज्ञानी *a-gyānī*, ignorant, unwise. *s.*

اگيٹي *ageṭī*, f. a chafing-dish, or brazier; also a flower-pot. *d.*

آگيره आगेरः *āgaira*, m. the first sheaf of the crop, presented to the zamīndār. *h.*

آگين *āgīn*, full (used in comp.). *p.*

اگيه अज्ञ *a-gya*, idiot, stupid, ignorant. *s.*

ال *al*, the, the Arabic definite article (vide Hind. Gram. page 18). *a.*

ال अलि *ali*, m. a large black bee, a scorpion, an Indian cuckoo (*cuculus indicus*), a crow, spirituous liquor. *s.*

آل आल *āl*, f. the name of a tree, from the root of which a red colour is extracted for staining leather, dyeing silk, &c. (*Morinda citrifolia*); m. yellow orpiment. *h.*

آل *āl*, f. children, progeny, descendants, offspring, race, dynasty. N.B. *āl* is commonly used to express a race or family by the mother's side; in contradistinction to *aulād*, a race &c. by the father's side. (Binning). *a.*

آل आलि *āli*, f. a female friend, a damsel. *s.*

آلا आला *ālā*, m. a small recess in a pillar or wall, for holding a lamp, &c.; adj. wet; running (as a sore); land saturated with (rain) water; a basin or hole dug at the root of a tree. *h.*

الا इल्ला *illā*, m. a wart. *h.*

الا *illā*, besides, except, otherwise, unless, if not; sometimes a superfluous negative *na* is added to this particle. *a.*

آلاپ आलाप or अलाप *ālāp*, (corruptly *alāp*), f. prelude to singing; m. intercourse, conversation, association; enumeration of the questions in an arithmetical or algebraic sum. *s.*

آلاپالا *ālā-pālā*, m. the leaves of trees. *d.*

آلاپ‌چاري आलापचारी *ālāp-chārī*, f. the act of tuning the voice previous to singing. *s.*

الاپنا अलापना *alāpnā* or आलापना *ālāpnā*, to tune the voice, to run over the different notes previous to singing, to catch the proper key, to sing, to tune. *s.*

آلات *ālāt*, n. (pl. of آلت), tools, instruments, utensils, apparatus. *a.*

الاتوني *alātūnī*, vague, undetermined. *d.*

الاچا *ilāchā*, m. a kind of silk and thread cloth. *d.*

الاچي इलाची *ilāchī*, f. large cardamums. *ilāchī-bāṅṭnā*, to distribute cardamums, a kind of marriage or wedding ceremony. *ilāchī-panḍā*, a kind of wild fruit. *ilāchī-bonḍā* or *-ḍora*, capsule of cardamums. *ilāchī-dāne*, a kind of sweetmeat. *h.*

الارنا उलारना *ulārnā*, a. to cause to sleep. *h.*

الاغ *ulāgh*, m. an owl. *t.*

الاق *ulāḳ*, f. a kind of small boat. *p.*

الاقي *alāḳī* f. (pl. of القا), questions, problems; misfortunes. *a.*

الالنا उलालना *ulālnā*, a. to overset, to lay over to one side. *s.*

آلام *ālām* (pl. of الم), cares, griefs, misfortunes. *a.*

الامان *al-amān*, m. mercy, quarter; calling for quarter in battle. *a.*

الامان *alāmān*, a German (Lat. *Alemanni*, [*Claudian*). *l.*

آلان आलान *ālān*, m. the post to which an elephant is tied, or the rope that ties him. *s.*

الآن *al-ān*, now, the present time. *al-ān kamā kāna*, now as formerly; just as heretofore, as usual, as formerly. *a.*

الانا अल्लाना *allānā*, n. to bawl, to scream, to squeak. *h.*

الانا *ilānā*, m. race, family, kindred. *ulānā*, act of what is vulgarly called "throwing up in one's teeth," or "reminding one of former services."

الأو अलाव *alā,o*, } m. a bonfire, flame, a
الاوا अल्लावा *allāwā*, } blaze: it also denotes a
الاوۂ अलवः *alāwa*, } fireplace, especially applied to a hole in the front of the shade where the paraphernalia of the Muharram show are deposited, and in which a fire is lighted every evening during the festival. *h.*

الاهنا उलाहना *ulāhnā*, m. reproach, chiding, complaint. *h.*

الايچا इलायचा *ilāyachā*, m. (v. *ilāchā*), a kind of cloth woven of silk and thread. *s.*

الائچي इलायची *ilā,echī* or *ilāyachīn*, f. large cardamums. *s.*

آلايش *ālāyish*, f. filth, pollution. *p.*

آلبال आलबाल *ālbāl*, m. a circular basin round the root of a tree for the purpose of watering it. *s.*

البتہ *al-batta*, certainly, indeed, verily. *a.*

البرز *alburz*, a celebrated mountain in Hamadān, in Persia, famous among the fire-worshippers. *p.*

البهيلا अलभेला *albhelā*, } artless, simple, inno-
البيلا अलबेला *albelā*, } cent; m. a fop, a beau. *albelī*, a belle, a coquette. *albel-pan*, or *albelpanā*, foppishness, frivolity, airs and blandishments. *h.*

الپ अल्प *alp*, little, small, few, short. *alpatā*, f. smallness, minuteness, insignificance. *alpāhār*, moderate, abstemious; m. moderation. *alpāhārī*, moderate. *alpāyu*, short-lived; young. *alp-buddhi*, ignorant, silly. *alp-bal*, feeble, of little strength. *alp-prabhāo*, insignificant, of little weight. *alp-pramān*, of little authority. *alp-pramānak*, credulous, resting on little evidence; of little weight. *alp-shakti*, weak, feeble. *alp-mātr*, a little only; a short time, a few moments. *s.*

الپٹ *ulpaṭ*, m. name of a stroke in sword-play; a reflex or inverted blow. *d.*

الپين *alpīn*, m. (vide *alfīn*, &c.), a pin. *d.*

آلت *ālat*, f. a tool, an instrument, apparatus; the running rigging of a ship; a rope (in the lingo of Indian seamen). *membrum virile; veretrum animalium.* *a.*

التا अलता or आलता *altā* or *āltā*, m. cotton strongly impregnated with the dye of lac, ready to be used for dyeing, &c., principally used by the Hindū women to stain their feet red. *s.*

التباس *iltibās*, being obscure, ambiguity, perplexity, "double entendre." *a.*

التجا *iltijā*, f. a request; flying to in cases of necessity; a petition, refuge, protection. *iltijā-burdan*, to seek refuge. *a.*

التزام *iltizām*, m. being necessary, expedient, being assiduous, taking on one's self. *a.*

التفات *iltifāt*, f. friendship, kindness, obligation, courtesy, respect; (in rhetoric) an apostrophe. *a.*

التماس *iltimās*, m. f. beseeching, petitioning, supplicating, prayer, request. *a.*

التمغا *altamghā* or *āltamghā*, m. a Turkish word, signifying the *red* patent, the impression of the imperial seal affixed to grants &c. being in red ink. It is a grant of land under the royal seal, conveying the property to the first proprietor and his heirs, in perpetuity, and escheating to government only in default of issue, or forfeited by delinquency. It also denotes a kind of tax levied on travellers. Among the Turks it signifies a stamp on gold or silver plate, to certify its being of standard purity. See further, Wilson's Glossary. *t.*

التني अलतनी *altanī*, f. the rope round the neck of an elephant, in which the driver puts his feet, as in stirrups. *h.*

التوا *iltiwā*, hanging back, procrastinating, deferring. *a.*

التها उलथा *ulthā*, m. translation (of a document, &c. *h.*

التهاب *iltihāb*, m. burning, heat. *a.*

التهنا उलथना *ulathnā*, n. to undulate, to be agitated (as the ocean by storms). *h.*

التيام *iltiyam*, allaying, soothing, curing. *a.*

الٹ उलट *ulaṭ*, m. act of upsetting or overturning. *h.*

الٹا उलटा *ulṭā*, reversed, turned back; reverse, contrary, opposite; m. pease-pudding, a kind of pudding made of the meal of any pulse. *ulṭā-pulṭā*, topsy-turvy, higgledy-piggledy, all in confusion. *h.*

الٹانا उलटाना *ulṭānā*, a. to turn upside down, pervert, overset, overturn, thwart. *h.*

الٹانا پلٹانا उलटाना पुलटाना *ulṭānā pulṭānā*, a. to reverse, modify; to interchange. *h.*

الٹ پلٹ उलटपुलट *ulaṭ pulaṭ*, higgledy-piggledy, topsy-turvy; f. confusion; interchange; deception, imposition. *h.*

الٹكنول उलटकँवल *ulaṭ-hanwal*, m. name of a flower. *h.*

الٹنا उलटना *ulaṭnā*, a. to pervert, to subvert, to thwart, to overturn, to reply; n. to be reversed. *ulaṭ-jānā*, (Dakh.), to be proud. *h.*

الٹهانا *ulṭhānā*, a. (same as *ulṭānā*), to pervert, upset, &c. *h.*

الٹهہ پلٹ *ulāṭh-palaṭ* (v. *ulaṭ-palaṭ*). *h.*

الٹهنا *ulaṭhnā* (v. *ulaṭnā*), to turn, &c. *ulthepā,oṅ*, on returning. *ulṭhā mār*, a reverse blow or back stroke. *ulṭhī taḳrīr*, a perverted speech or declaration. *ulṭhī samajh*, a perverse or absurd idea. *h.*

الجوع *al-jū'!* interj. used in complaining of hunger; lit. the hunger! *a.*

الجهانا उलझाना *uljhānā*, a. to entangle; to ravel or entwist (as thread), to involve, to embroil. *h.*

الجهاو उलझाव *uljhā,o*, m. entanglement, perplexity. *h.*

الجهہ پلجهہ جانا उलझपुलझजाना *ulajh-pulajh-j.*, n. (see *ulajhnā*, to be entangled, &c.). *h.*

الجهن उलझन *uljhan*, f. involution, the state of being entangled, complication. *a.*

الجهنا उलझना *ulajhnā* or *ilajhnā*, n. to be entangled, to be involved in a quarrel or difficulties; to quarrel, to debate. *h.*

الجهيڑا उलझेड़ा *uljherā* or *iljherā*, m. the state of being entangled (see *uljhan*). *h.*

الچنا उलचना *ulachnā*, a. to throw out the water from any thing; to drain. *h.*

الحاح *ilḥāḥ*, importunity, urgent solicitation. *a.*

الحاد *ilḥād*, impiety, heresy, idolatry; atheism, unbelief, (as to the Musalmān faith). *a.*

الحاصل *al-ḥāṣil*, in short, in fine. *a.*

الحاق *ilḥāḳ*, m. addition, junction, coupling. *a.*

الحال *al-ḥāl*, now, at present; just now. *a.*

الحان *ilḥān*, m. note, sound, modulation, tune, an air in music. *alḥān* (pl. of *laḥn*), musical notes, melodies. *a.*

الحذر *al-ḥazar*, (used as an interjection) beware! have a care! *a.*

الحفيظ *al-ḥafiẓ*, (lit. the Protector), interj. God preserve us! *a.*

الحق *al-ḥaḳ* or *al-ḥaḳḳ*, true, right; in truth, verily, the truth is. *a.*

الحمد لله *al-ḥamdu-lillāhi*, God be praised! *a.*

الخ *alikh*, (a contraction of الى آخره) used in the sense of "et cætera, and so on." *a.*

الخالق *alkhālaḳ*, f. a coat, vest, garment. *a.*

الڈانا *alḍānā*, to scream out, to shriek. *d.*

الرنا उलरना *ularnā*, n. to lie down, to rest. *h.*

الڑ *alaṛ*, imperfect, not grown up. *d.*

الڑبلڑ अलड़बलड़ *alaṛ-balaṛ*, f. trifling talk or employment. *h.*

الزام *ilzām*, m. blame, reproach; conviction. *a.*

السں अलस or आलस *alas*, *ālas* m. laziness, drowsiness, sloth; adj. lazy, slothful, drowsy. *s.*

السانا अलसाना *alsānā*, n. to be drowsy, to dose, to slacken. *s.*

الستْ अलसट *alasaṭ* or *alasṭā*, or *alasṭā-gī* or *alsaṭī*, f. apathy, sloth, indolence. *s.*

السلام *al-salām*, farewell, peace or safety be upon thee! *a.*

السنه *alsina* (pl. of لسان), tongues, languages. *a.*

آلسيه आलस्य *ālasya*, m. laziness, adj. lazy. (see *alas*). *s.* [slothful. *s.*

آلسي आलस्यी or आलसी *ālasyī*, *ālasī*, drowsy,

السي अलसी *alsī*, f. linseed. (*Linum usitatissimum*. *h.*

الش *ulash* or *ulush*, m. the leavings of a superior. *t.*

الطاف *altāf* m. (pl. of لطف), kindnesses, favours. *a.*

العبد *al-'abd*, a form of counter-signature by a subordinate clerk or officer; lit. the slave or servant. *a*

العظمة لله *al-'aẓamatu-lillāhi*, great is God, an ejaculation expressive of surprise, fear, denial, &c. *a*

الغار *ilghār* or *alghār*, m. rapine, devastation, as during the inroad of a hostile army; the forced march of an army through a district. *p.*

الغرض *al-gharaẓ*, in short, upon the whole, in a word, finally. *a.*

الغوزه *alghūza*, m. a whistle, pipe; or small flageolet. *p.*

الغياث *al-ghiyāṣ*, m. complaint, complaining, demanding justice. interj. alas! help! *a.*

الغيب *al-ghaib*, that which is hidden, secret, or mysterious. *al-ghaib 'ind allāhi*, God knows what is hidden. *a.*

الف *alf*, a thousand. *alif*, the first letter of the Arabic or Persian alphabet. *a.*

الفا *alfā*, m. a kind of dress worn by *faḳīrs*, like a shirt without sleeves, and open at the sides. *a.*

الفاظ *alfāẓ* m. (pl. of لفظ), words, articulate sounds, terms. *a.*

الف بي *alif-be* or *alif-bā-tā*, f. the alphabet. *p.*

الفت *ulfat*, f. friendship, affection, attachment, kindness, familiarity, intimacy. *a.*

آلفته *ālufta*, astonished, frantic, insane. *p.*

الفتي بنده *ulfatī-banda*, attached from friendship (a slave or servant). *a. p.*

الفي *alfī*, f. see الفا *alfā* (cloth, &c.) covered with marks like the letter *alif*. *a.*

الفي *alfī*, الفنات *alfināt*, الفي *alfinnī*, — f. a pin, (so called in Dakhanī): the word is apparently Portuguese.

القا *ilḳā*, m. throwing down, flinging. *ilḳā*, e *ḥajar*, throwing a stone, an offence prohibited by the Muḥammadan law, whereby the person throwing a stone at any article was compelled to purchase it. *a.*

القاب *alḳāb* (pl. of لقب), m. titles, honorary names; forms of address, &c., in letters. *a.*

القصه *al-ḳiṣṣa*, in short, in one word. *a.*

الك अलक *alak*, f. a lock of hair. *s.*

الك *alak*, aside, apart. *d.*

الكا उल्का *ulkā*, f. a firebrand; a meteor, flame, fire. *s.* [curls.

الكاول अलकावलि *alakāvali*, f. a row of side

الكش अलक्ष *alaksh*, الكهه अलख *alakh*, — invisible, unseen: a form of salutation among a class of mendicants. *s.*

الكشن अलक्षण *a-lakshan*, m. a bad sign or ill omen. *s.* [fated. *s*

الكشني अलक्षणी *a-lakshanī*, unfortunate, ill-

الكن *alkan*, stuttering, pronouncing badly. *a.*

الكنندا अलकनन्दा *alak-nandā*, f. a stream that runs from the Himālaya mountains, and falls into the Ganges near Srīnagar. *s.*

الكه **अलख** *a-lakh* (same as *a-laksh*), unseen, unlooked at. *s.*

الكهنامي *alakh-nāmī*, m. a mendicant of the [Saiva sect. *s.*

الگ **अलग** *a-lag*, separate, distinct. *a-lag a-lag*, or *alag-talag*, separately. *s.*

الگا **अलगा** *algā*, separate, apart, distinct, free, loose, unconfined; m. a sandal. *s.*

الگانا **अलगाना** *algānā*, a. to separate, to put one side. *ulgānā*, to cause to leap over. *s.*

الگائي **अलगाई** *algā'ī*, f. separation. *s.*

الگٹ *ulgaṭ*, act of leaping over. *s.*

الگنا *alagnā*, n. to be separated or disjoined. *ulagnā*, n. to spring or bound over. *s.*

الگني **अलगनी** *alagnī*, f. a line for hanging clothes on. *h.*

الگوجا *algojā*, m. (see *alghūza*) a pipe, &c. *p.*

اللنا **उललना** *ulalnā*, n. to be overset, or laid over to one side. *h.*

الله *allāh*, m. God; the Supreme Being. *allāhu akbar*, God is great! an exclamation of surprise, resignation, &c. *allāh, allāh!* Oh wonderful! excellent! *allāh-billah-tallāh*, I swear most solemnly, &c. *a.*

الم **अलम** *alam*, sticks set up for the support of creeping plants (like our vines, &c.). *h.*

الم *alam*, m. pain, grief, affliction. *a.*

الم **अलम** *alam*, enough, abundance; able, adequate, or equal to. *s.*

الماري *almārī*, f. a chest of drawers, a bookcase; (the word is of European origin: for example, the old English term is "almarie;" and the Scotch word "awmrie," or "aumrie," is in common use to this day). *h.*

الماس *almās*, m. a diamond. *almās-tarāsh*, m. diamond-dust; adj. cut into angles (as glass). *p.*

الماسي *almāsī*, cut into facets (like a diamond). *almāsī-rang*, of a diamond colour; m. a bright clear white colour. *p.*

آلمبن **आलम्बन** *ālamban*, m. dependence; a support, protector. *s.*

الم‌غلم *allam-ghallam*, m. trifling talk or business; toying; vanity, idle excuse. *p.*

الملک **उल्मुक** *ulmuk*, m. a firebrand, burning wood, charcoal. *s.*

المناك *alam-nāk*, full of pain or sorrrow. *a. p.*

المنةلله *al-minnatu lillāhi* (God be praised!), an ejaculation expressive of surprise, fear, denial, &c. *a.*

الميره *almaira*, m. (v. *almārī*), a press, &c.

آلنج *ālunj*, a sort of wild plum, a sloe. *p.*

النڈنا *ulanḍnā*, a. (v. *ulenḍnā*), to pour out a liquid. *h.*

النکار **अलंकार** *alankār*, m. ornament or jewel; rhetoric, ornate composition in prose. *s.*

النکرت **अलंकृत** *alankṛita*, adorned, decorated. *s.*

النکهار *alankhār*, the treble notes in music. *d.*

النگ **अलंग** *alang*, f. side, way, corner, intrenchments; *is alang*, this side. *h.*

النگ **उलंग** or **अलङ्ग** *ulang* or *alang*, naked. *s.*

آلنگ *ālang*, intrenchment, trenches. *p.*

آلنگن **आलिङ्गन** *ālingan*, m. the act of embracing. *s.*

النگنا **उलंगना** *ulangā*, n. to bound over, to [overleap. *h.*

النگني **उलंगनी** *alangnī*, f. (v. *alagnī*), a line, &c. *h.*

النگهن **उल्लङ्घन** *ullanghan*, m. the transgressing of a rule or custom; transgression. *s.*

آلنگي **आलिङ्गी** *ālingī*, adj. embracing. *s.*

آلو **आलु** or **आलू** *ālū*, m. an esculent root (*Arum campanulatum*), a potato; *Rat-ālu*, a yam. *ālū,e Shakar-kand*, a sweet potato, &c. *ālū*, in Persian, signifies a plum, but in India the word is taken to signify a potato. It is singular that this vegetable is named by the Persians and Arabs, as by the French, "ground apple," viz. Persian, *sībi zaminī*, Arab. *tuffāḥ-ul-ardh*. *ālū,i bukhārā*, dried plums, prunes. (Binning). *p.*

آلو *ālo*, a portion of unripe corn. *h.*

الو **उल्लू** *ullū*, m. an owl; met. a stupid fellow, a fool. *s.*

الو **उलू** *ulū*, } f. a kind of grass (*Saccharum*
الوا **उलवा** *ulwā*, } *cylindricum, Willden*). *h.*

الواح *alwāḥ* (pl. of لوح), tablets, planks, &c. *a.*

آلوال **आलवाल** *ālwal*, m. a basin for water round the root of a tree. *s.*

الوالامر *ulu-l-amr*, men possessed of command or authority (vide *ūlū*). *a.*

الوان *alwān* (pl. of لون), colours, sorts, kinds; adj. of various sorts and colours. *a.*

الوپ **अलोप** *alop*, concealed, defaced, retired, run out, destroyed; apparent. *alop-ho-j.*, n. to vanish. *s.*

الوپن **उल्लूपन** *ullū-pan*, m. folly, stupidity. *s.*

الوپنا **अलोपना** *alopnā*, a. to conceal, to hide one's self; m. to lie hid, to be concealed. *s.*

الوچه *alūcha*, a kind of small plum. *p.*

آلود *ālūd* (v. *ālūda*), soiled, &c. *p.*

الوداس *ullū-dās*, } stupid as an owl, a fool
الوداسري *ullū-dāsrī*, } or simpleton. *s.*

الوداع *al-widā'*, adieu! fare thee well! *a.*

آلودگي *ālūdagī*, f. contamination, stain, foulness, defilement. *p.*

آلودن *ālūdan*, to stain, defile, pollute. *p.*

آلوده *ālūda*, soiled, stained, smeared or defiled; overwhelmed, immerged, loaded with. *p.*

الوش *ulūsh*, m. (see *ulash*), leavings. *t.*

الوف *ulūf*, thousands (pl. of الف). *a.*

الوك **उलूक** *ulūk*, m. an owl (same as *ullū*). *s*

آلوك आलोक *āloh*, m. sight, looking; light; flattery, panegyric. *s.*

الوكك अलौकिक *a-lauhik*, unpopular, not current, supernatural. *s.* [visibility. *s.*

الوكن अलोकन *a-lokan*, m. disappearance, in-

آلوكن आलोकन *ālokan*, m. sight, seeing, looking. *s.*

الوكهل उलूखल *ulūkhal*, m. bdellium, a gummy substance; a wooden mortar for cleaning rice. *s.*

آلوگاچھ आलूगाछ *ālū-gāchh*, m. the potato tree; the tapioca shrub. *h.*

الول अलोल *alol*, f. gambol (generally applied to a horse); adj. steady. *s.*

الول كلول अलोलकलोल *alol-halol*, f. gambols, wantonness, playsomeness (of young animals). *h.*

الونا अलोणा or अलोना *a-lonā*, fresh, not salt, insipid. *s.* [madan. *p.*

الوند *alvand* or *ālvand*, a mountain in Ha-

الوهيت *ulūhīyat*, } deity, divinity, the divine
الوهيه *ulūhīya*, } essence. *a.*

آله *āla*, m. (see *ālat*), tool, &c. *a.*

اله *ilāh* (v. الله), God, the Supreme Being. *a.*

آلها आल्हा *ālhā*, the name of a Hindū soldier and poet, from whom a species of poetry takes its name. *h.*

الهام *ilhām*, inspiration, revelation. *a.*

الهانا अल्हाना *alhānā*, n. to rejoice, to be cheerful. *h.* [unskilful. *h.*

الهڑ अल्हड़ *alhaṛ*, young, untaught (animal),

الهنا उलहना *ulahnā*, m. complaint, accusation; reproof, chiding. *ulahnā denā*, to reproach, complain, abuse; n. to grow, to vegetate. *h.*

الهى *ilāhī*, divine, the Divine Being; used as an interj., O God! Name of an æra instituted by Akbar. *ilāhī gaz*, the standard yard measure of forty-one fingers, instituted by Akbar. *a.* [musical mode. *h.*

الهيا अल्हैया *alhaiyā*, f. name of a rāgnī or

الهيات *ilāhīyāt*, divine things or studies; metaphysics, theology. *a.*

الهيت *ilāhīyat*, f. divinity, the godhead. *a.*

آلي आली *ālī*, a land measure, equivalent to four *bisīs*; adj. of or belonging to the *āl* tree. *h.*

آلي आली *ālī*, f. damsel, female friend; m. a scorpion. *s.* [of the lotus. *s.*

الي अली *alī*, m. a large black bee, enamoured

الى *ila*, up to, until. *ila-al-ān*, up to the present time. *a.*

آلي आलय *ālai*, m. a house, an abode. *s.*

آليا आलिया *āliyā*, name of a tribe of *banjāras*. *h.*

اليابليا अलैयाबलैया *alaiyā-balaiyā*, f. sacrifice, victim; lighted wisps, with which the Hindūs divert themselves at the season of the Dewālī. *h.*

آليپ आलेप *ālep*, m. liniment, plaster. *s.*

اليچنا उलीचना *ulīchnā*, a. to throw up water, to bale. *h.*

آلي رنگ अलीरंग *ālī-rang*, m. a colour extracted from the *āl* tree (*Morinda citrifolia*). *h. p.*

اليش इलीश *ilīsh*, m. a fish, the hilsa or sable (*Clupea alosa*). *s.*

اليك अलीक *alīk*, m. falsehood, untruth, any thing displeasing or disagreeable; adj. false, unpleasing. *s.* [ciating torment. *a.*

اليم *alīm*, painful. *'azābi alīm*, an excru-

اليڈنا उलेड़ना *ulenḍnā*, a. to pour water. *h.*

آم आम *ām*, m. a mango (fruit of the *Mangifera Indica*), provisions, victuals (undressed); sickness, disease; adj. raw, undressed, unripe. *s.*

ام *umm*, f. a mother. *a.* [ever. *a.*

اما *ammā*, but, moreover, nevertheless, how-

اما अम्मा *ammā*, f. a mother. *s.*

آماتسار आमातिसार *āmātisār*, m. dysentery. *s.*

اماتيه अमात्य *amātya*, m. a minister, counsellor. *s.* [arrows at. *p.*

آماج *āmāj*, m. a mark or butt to shoot

آمادگي *āmādagī*, f. readiness, alertness. *p.*

آماده *āmāda*, prepared, ready, alert. *p.*

آمار *āmār*, calculation, investigation; an account-book or register. *p.*

امارت *imārat*, f. dominion, authority; a district under the government of an *amīr*. *a.*

امارد *amārid*, (pl. of أمرد) beardless youths. *a.*

اماره *ammāra*, domineering, imperious. *a.*

آماس *āmās*, m. swelling. *āmās-h*, to swell, to effect a swelling. *p.*

اماس *ammās*, the conjunction of the sun and moon, the days about new moon. *d.*

اماكن *amākin* (pl. of مكان), mansions, habitations, places. *a.*

امال *imāla*, m. (lit. inclining) a change of vowels in pronunciation as *kitīb* for *kitāb* (a book). *a.*

امام *imām*, m. a priest, a leader in religious matters, patriarch, prelate, chief; a large bead in a rosary, which remains fixed in the hand, and is not turned over in counting (called by the Hindūs *Sumeru*). *a.*

امامباڑا *imāmbāṛā*, m. (also *imāmbaṛī*, f.) a kind of temple in which the festival of the Muharram is celebrated: it is generally a square building with a cupola on the top *h.*

امامت *imāmat*, f. the office of an *imām*. *a.*

امام ضامن *imām-ẓāmin* (or-*ẓāminī*), m. the protecting Imām, or one's guardian saint. *imām-ẓāmin kā rupiya*, a piece of coin dedicated to Imām Ẓāmin: it is fastened on the arm of a person about to leave home as a charm for averting evil: if in want he may spend it, not otherwise. *a.*

امامي *imāmī*, } of or relating to an *imām*,
امامية *imāmīya* } an epithet assumed by the followers of 'Ali. *a.*

امان *amān*, f. grace, mercy, security, safety, protection; as an interj. it denotes, "quarter! spare me!" and is generally sounded *āmān*. *a.*

آمان आमान्न *āmānna*, m. raw rice or grain; provisions undressed. *s.*

امّان अम्मां *ammāṅ* (same as *ammā*), a mother. *s.*

امانا अमाना *amānā*, n. to be contained, to go into. *s.*

امانت *amānat*, f. deposit, charge, any thing given in trust; faith, religion. *amānat-dār*, a trustee, or depositary; adj. faithful, honest. *amānat-dārī*, f. guardianship, agency, trust, charge; faithfulness. *amānat-rakhnā*, a. to consign or deposit. *amānat-daftar*, a registry-office. *amānat-jārī*, assignments of revenue. *amānat-maḥāl*, an estate. *amānat-nāma*, a deed of trust or deposit. *a.*

امانتي *amānatī*, f. goods &c. given in charge. *a.*

امانيه अमाननीय *a-mānanīya*, incredible, not fit to be believed. *s.* [without pride, humble. *s.*

اماني अमानी *a-mānī*, incredulous, inattentive;

اماني *amānī*, f. security; trust, charge, deposit; adj. (applied to land) that which is in charge of a collector on the part of government (in opposition to *ijāra*, that which is farmed). *a.*

امانيه अमान्य *a-mānya* (see *amānanīya*), incredible, not worthy of being believed. *s.*

اماوٹ अमावट *amāwaṭ*, m. the inspissated juice of the mango (v. *amoṭ*). *h.*

اماوس अमावस *amāvas*, } f. the conjunc-
اماوسيه अमावस्य *amāvasya*, } tion of sun and
اماوسي अमावसी *amāvasī*, } moon, the day of new moon. *s.*

امب अम्ब *amb*, m. a mango, a mango tree. *ambu*, m. water. *s.*

امبا अम्बा *ambā*, f. a mother, (same as *ammā*). *s.*

آمبات आम्बात *ām-bāt*, m. a swelling, which comes without pain and goes off as easily, even without medicine, a windy tumour. *s.*

امباري अम्बारी *ambārī*, f. a canopy, a litter used on an elephant or camel. *p.*

امبت अम्बत *ambat*, sour, acid or acrid. *s.*

امبتانا अम्बताना *ambatānā*, n. to grow sour, to be acidulated. *s.* [*nelumbo*). *s.*

امبج अम्बुज *ambuj*, m. the lotus (*Nymphæa*

امبر अम्बर *ambar*, m. clothes, apparel; the sky or atmosphere; a perfume (*ambergris*). *s.*

آمبر आम्बर *āmbar*, f. ambergris (v. *'anbar*). *a.*

امبرائي अम्बराई *ambarā,ī*, f. a mango grove. *s.*

امبرچا अंबर्चा *ambarchā*, m. an ornamental drawing.

امبشٹهه अम्बष्ठ *ambashṭh*, m. a man the offspring of a Brāhman and a Vaisya woman, by occupation a physician. *s.*

امبكا अम्बिका *ambikā*, f. a name of the goddess Pārvatī. *s.*

امبوتي *ambotī*, f. a species of sorrel (*Oxalis corniculata*). *d.* [less. *h.*

امبول अम्बोल *ambol* (for *an-bol*), silent, speech-

امبهوج अम्भोज *ambhoj*, m. the lotus. *s.*

امبيا अम्बिया *ambiyā*, f. a small unripe mango. *s.*

امت *ummat*, f. people, a religious sect, people of the same belief. *a.*

امت अमित *a-mit*, unmeasured, undefined. *s.*

آمّة *āmmat*, one of the ten kinds of wounds compensated by a fine. *a.*

امتحان *imtiḥān*, m. examination, proof, trial, experiment; temptation. *a.*

امتداد *imtidād*, m. protraction, prolongation, prorogation, extension; adj. protracted. *a.*

امتلا *imtilā*, m. repletion, indigestion. *a.*

امتناع *imtinā'*, m. restraint, prohibition. *a.*

امتي *ummatī*, m. a believer in, or follower of, any particular sect. *a.*

امتياز *imtiyāz*, m. discrimination, separation, distinction; pre-eminence; good breeding. *imtiyāz-k.*, a. to discriminate; to treat with distinction. *a.*

امتيازي *imtiyāzī*, having the quality of discriminating, worthy of distinction. *a.*

امٹ अमिट *a-miṭ*, indelible, undefaced. *s.*

امثال *amṣāl* (pl. of مثل), examples, similes, equals, fables, parables. *a.*

امجد *amjad*, very or most glorious. *a.*

امجي *amjī*, f. compulsory service. *d.*

امچور अमचूर *amchūr*, m. parings of the mango, dried in the sun. *s.*

آمد *āmad*, f. arrival, income. *āmad-āmad* or *āmad o raft*, f. access and egress. *āmad-shud* or *āmad o shud*, intercourse, thoroughfare. *p.*

امداد *imdād*, f. act of assisting, aiding, or abetting; succour, help; extending. *a.*

آمدن *āmadan*, (r. *ā* or *āy*) to come. *h.*

آمدني *āmdanī*, f. the season in which any merchandise generally arrives; perquisites; any thing gained over and above; ways and means; income, revenue; import. *p.*

امڈانا उमडाना *umḍānā*, also *umḍā-ḍ.*, a. to cause to overflow, to flood. *h.*

امڈنا उमडना *umaḍnā*, n. to overflow; to let fall (as tears), to shed, to swell and increase or prevail (like a river, clouds, an army, the heart, &c.). *h.*

امر *amr*, m. an order, command; an affair, transaction; (in gram.) the imperative mood. *amr-ba-yad*, lit. "your business is in your own hands," which uttered by a husband and agreed to by a wife, constitutes an irreversible divorce. *a.*

آمر *āmir*, one who orders, a commander, ruler. *a.*

امر آمر आम्र *āmra*, m. the mango tree (*Mangifera indica*). *s.*

امر अमर *a-mar*, undying, immortal, long-lived, perennial, everlasting; a god. *Amara Siṅha*, the name of a Sanskrit lexicographer. . *s.*

امرا आम्रा or अमरा *amrā*, m. name of a fruit; hog-plum (*Spondias mangifera*). *s.*

امرا *umarā* (pl. of امير), nobles, grandees; a noble (generally), but more especially applied to those of a Muḥammadan court. *a.*

امراض *amrāẓ* (pl. of مرض), sicknesses, diseases. *a.*

امراوتي अमरावती *a-marāwatī*, f. the celestial city of Indra. *s.*

امرائي अमराई *amrā,ī*, f. a tope or grove of mangoes. *s.*

امربيل अमरबेल *amar-bel*, m. an epidendron, or parasitical plant similar to the misletoe. *s.*

امرپد अमरपद *amar-pad*, m. the state of an immortal; immortality. *s.*

امرت अमृत *a-mṛit*, m. the water of life, nectar; an antidote; any thing sweet; water; wine; a guava; immortality, final emancipation. *s.*

امرتا { अमरता *amartā* / अमृतता *amṛittā* } f. immortality. *s.*

امرتبان अमृतबान *amrit-bān*, m. a variety of the *kelā*, or plantain. *s.*

امرتي अमृती or इमृती *amṛiti* or *imṛiti*, f. a small vessel for drinking out of; a kind of sweetmeat; a kind of cloth; adj. nectarious. *h.*

امرجاد अमर्याद *a-marjād*, / امرجادا अमर्यादा *a-marjādā*, } f. indignity, dishonour. *s.*

امرد *amrad*, beardless, handsome (a youth). *a.*

آمرز *āmurz*, act of pardoning or forgiving; *āmurz-gār*, he who pardons; an epithet of God. *p.*

آمرزش *āmurzish*, f. pardon, grace, forgiveness of sins (by the Deity). *p.*

آمرس *ām-ras*, inspissated juice of the mango (see *amoṭ*). *s.*

آمرش आमर्ष *āmarsh*, m. anger; wrath; envy, impatience of another's success; peevishness. *s.*

امرلوك अमरलोक *amar-lok*, m. heaven, the region of the immortals. *s.*

امروت अमरूत *amrūt*, m. a guava. (*Psydium pyriferum*). *s.*

امرود *amrūd*, m. a pear; also a guava. *p.*

امروز *imroz* (for *īn-raz*), to-day. *imroz-fardā*, to-day or to-morrow, *i. e.* soon. *imroz fardā-k.*, a. to put off, to procrastinate. *p.*

امر و نهي *amr o nahī*, m. commands and prohibitions, orders and counter-orders, commanding and countermanding; hence, sovereignty, authority. *a.*

امريادا अमर्यादा *a-maryādā*, f. disrespect, indignity. (Same as *a-marjādā*.) *s.*

امريادك अमर्यादिक *a-maryādik*, disrespected. *s.*

امس *ummas*, resolution, firmness, strength. *d.*

امساك *imsāk*, m. parsimony; abstinence; a medicine taken to prolong pleasure; scarcity, want. *a.*

امسال *imsāl* (for *īn-sāl*), this year. *p.*

امسنا उमसना *umasnā*, n. to rot, to putrefy. *h.*

آمش आमिष *āmish*, m. flesh, food, enjoyment; object of enjoyment, a pleasing object. *s.*

امشب *imshab* (for *īn-shab*), to-night. *p.*

آمشول आमशूल *ām-shūl*, m. the cholic, pain arising from indigestion. *s.*

امصار *amsār* (pl. of مصر), cities, large cities. *a.*

امضاي *imẓā,ī*, despatching, transmitting. *a.*

امعان نظر *im'āni naẓr*, looking attentively, contemplating. *a.*

امك अमुक *amuk*, such a one, a certain person. *s.*

امكادهمك अमकाधमका *amkā-dhamkā*, / امكاڈهمكا अमकाढमका *amkā-ḍhamkā*, } m. trifles, trifling; a person of little estimation. *h.*

امكان *imkān*, m. possibility; contingent existence (in opposition to *wujūb*, necessity, or necessary existence). *a.*

امكاني *imkānī*, potential, possible. *a.*

امكهيه अमुख्य *a-mukhya*, inferior, ordinary. *s.*

امل *amal*, m. hope, expectation. *a.*

امل अमल *amal*, m. intoxication. *amalī jins*, intoxicating liquors or drugs. *h.*

امل अम्ल *aml* or *amla*, acid; sour. *s.*

امل अमल *a-mal*, bright, pure, clean, clear. *s.*

املا *imlā*, m. orthography; writing correctly; completing, filling up. *imlā-dān*, one who writes correctly. *imlā-nawīs*, the same. *a.*

آملا आमला *āmla*, m. the emblic myrobalan (*Phyllanthus emblica*). *s.*

املاك *amlāk* (pl. of ملك), possessions, properties (generally applied to land). *a.*

املان अम्लान *amlān*, m. globe amaranth (*Gomphrena globosa*); adj. clean, clear. *s.*

املاك *imlāk*, m. possession, property; land held rent free. *a.*

امل پٿي अमलपट्टी *amal-paṭṭī*, f. the hem of cloth, a kind of stitching. *h.*

املتا अम्लता *amlatā*, f. sourness, acidity. *s.*

املتاس अमलतास *amaltās*, m. *Cassia fistula*. *h.*

آملكا आम्लिका *āmlikā*, f. the tamarind tree. *s.*

املن अमलिन *a-malin*, clean, pure. *s.*

املي इम्ली or इम्लि *imlī* or *imli*, m. the tamarind-tree (*Tamarindus Indica*) and its fruit. *s.*

امم *umam* (pl. of امّت), nations, sects, tribes, herds. *a.*
[difference, stoicism. *s.*

اممتا अममता *a-mamtā*, f. disinterestedness, in-

آمن आमन *āman*, m. winter rice-crop. *h.*

امن *amn*, m. security, safety. *amn-āmān*, m. quarter, crying out for quarter. *amn o āmān*, in safety and security. *a.*

آمنّا *āmannā*, yea, verily; lit. we believe. *a.*

آمناسامنا आम्नासाम्ना *āmnā-sāmnā*, m. opposition, confronting. *h.*

امنڈنا उमंडना *umaṅḍnā*, n. (see *umaḍnā*), to overflow, abound, to swell, to increase, to be poured out. *umaṅḍ umaṅḍ kar ronā*, to weep violently. *h.*

امنڈنا उमंडना *umaṅḍnā*, n. to be proud, conceited. *d.*

امنشیه / امنکهیه } अमनुष्य { *a-manushya*, / *a-manukhya*, } unmanly. *amanushyatā*, unmanliness, inhumanity. *s.*

امنگ उमंग *umang*, f. transport, excessive joy, exultation, ambition. *h.*

امنگل अमङ्गल *a-mangal*, m. a disaster, a calamity; an evil omen, ill luck; adj. inauspicious, unlucky. *s.*
[joy. *h.*

امنگنا उमंगना *umangnā*, n. to advance with

امنگي उमंगी *umangī*, sanguine, desirous, ambitious. *h.*

امنوجوگ अमनोजोग *a-manojog*, m. inattention. *a-manojogī*, inattentive. *s.*

امنونیت अमनोनीत *a-manonīt*, disapproved; reprobate. *s.*
[pleasing. *s.*

امنوهر अमनोहर *a-manohar*, disagreeable, dis-

امنیت *amnīyat*, security, repose, a place of safety. *a.*
[to face. *h.*

آمني سامني आम्नेसाम्ने *āmne-sāmne*, opposite, face

آمنیا आमनिया *āmaniyā*, f. land on which the winter crop of rice is sown. *h.*

اموات *amwāt* (pl. of میت), the dead. *a.*

آموات आमवात *āmvāt*, m. constipation or torpor of the bowels with flatulence and intumescence, the wind being supposed to be chiefly affected. *s.*

امواج *amwāj* (pl. of موج), billows, &c. *a.*

امواس अमवास *amavās*, the new moon. *s.*

اموال *amwāl* (pl. of مال), riches, wealth, goods and chattels, personal property. *a.*
[learn. *p.*

آموختن *āmokhtan*, (r. *āmoz*) to teach; to

آموخته *āmokhta*, learnt, taught, trained. *p.*

آمود आमोद *āmod*, m. fragrance; pleasure. *s.*

امور *umūr* (pl. of امر), business, things, affairs, actions; commanding, ordering. *a.*

امورت अमूर्त्ति *a-mūrti*, formless, unembodied. *s.*

آموز *āmoz*, taught; used in comp., as *dast-āmoz*, taught by the hand, tamed (bird). *p.*

اموگھ अमोघ *a-mogh*, productive, fruitful, effectual, infallible. *s.*

امول अमोल *a-mol*, invaluable, above price. *s.*

امول अमूल *a-mūl*, destitute of root or origin. *s.*

امومت *umūmat*, f. the condition of being a mother, maternity. *a.*

امي अमी *amī*, f. the water of life; nectar. *s.*

آمي आमय *āmaya*, m. sickness, disease. *s.*

امي *ummī*, uneducated, unable to read or write; unknown, unacquainted. *a.*
[rāj-pūts. *h.*

امیتھیا अमेठिया *ameṭhiyā*, name of a tribe of

آمیخته *āmekhta*, mixed, mingled. *p.*

آمیختن *āmekhtan*, (r. *āmez*), to mix, to mingle. *p.*

امید *ummaid* or *ummed*, f. hope, expectation, dependence, trust; (in Hind.) pregnancy. *ummaid-se honā*, to be pregnant. *ummaid-wār*, hopeful, expecting; an expectant, a dependant, a candidate. *ummaid-wārī*, f. expectation, expectancy, dependence. *p.*

امیدهیه अमेध्य *a-medhya*, m. fæces, excrement; adj. impure. *s.*

امیدي *ummedī*, an expectant; adj. hopeful, sanguine. *p.*

امیر *amīr*, m. a nobleman, a grandee; an eastern title nearly answering to Lord. *amīr ul umarā* or *amīri kabīr*, Lord of lords, a title given by eastern princes to their ministers, &c. *amīr-wār* or *amīrānā*, like a noble. *amīr-zāda* or *amīr-zādī*, nobly born; *amīru-l-baḥr*, a commander by sea (hence admiral). *amīrul-mūminīn*, commander of the (true) believers, a title assumed by the Calipha. *a.*

امیري *amīrī*, f. a principality, an earldom, the dignity or office of an *amīr*. *a.*

آمیز *āmez*, mixture; (in compos.) mixed, mixing, fraught with, as *mihr-āmez*, fraught with friendship. *p.*

آمیزش *āmezish*, mingling, mixing; f. mirthfulness, sociability, *bonhomie*. *p.*

امین *amīn*, a commissioner, a trustee, an umpire, an investigator, an arbitrator; a supervisor or officer employed by government to examine and regulate the state of the revenues of a district. *amīn-daftar*, an office for auditing the *amīns*. *a.*

آمین *āmīn*, amen, so be it. *a.*

اميني *amīnī*, f. the office of *amīn*; trust, guardianship; security, secure. *a.*

ان अन *an*, a negative prefix of the same effect as our *un* or *in*, as *an-dekhā*, unseen. In words purely Sanskrit it is prefixed only to those beginning with a vowel, as *an-anta*, endless; but in Hindi it is used indiscriminately before words beginning with vowels or consonants, as *an-ādar*, disrespect, *an-paṛhā*, unread, &c. *s.*
[weapon. *s.*

ان अणि *ani*, m. the edge or point of a sharp

ان अनु *anu*, after (in time, place, and rank), according to, in imitation of. *s.*

آن *ān*, that; he, she, or it. *p.*

آن *ān*, f. time, hour, minute. *a.*

آن आन *ān* (for अन्य), other (for आज्ञा), order, command. *s.*

آن आन *ān*, f. a graceful attitude, an affected gait; affectation, pride. *p.*

آن आन *ān*, f. dignity, honour; modesty, bashfulness; adv. on oath. *ān-mān se*, respectfully, honourably. *h.* [applied to boiled rice). *s*

ان अन्न *ann*, m. food, victuals, (particularly

ان इन *in* and उन *un* (pronouns in the oblique case), these, those, them. *h.*

انا अन्ना *annā*, m. the husband of a nurse. *h.*

آنا आना *ānā*, n. to come, to be, to become. *h.*

آنا आना *ānā*, m. the sixteenth part of a rupī; a measure of land equal to sixteen rūsīs. In most Indian dialects the term *ānā* is conventionally used to denote the fraction $\frac{1}{16}$; thus a man is said to have a four ānā share in a mercantile house, which means that he is entitled to one-fourth of the profits. *ānā-kara*, m. a fee of one *ānā* in the rupī. *h.*

انا *anā*, delay, opportunity; a seasonable hour. *innā*, as to us, verily we (used only in Arabic phrases). *a.*

انابت *inābat*, f. penitence, repentance, conversion, return to the true faith. *a.*

اناتر अनातुर *an-ātur*, healthy, vigorous. *s.*

اناتھ अनाथ *a-nāth*, without a husband, without a protector, without chief or sovereign; helpless, an orphan. *anāthi-banjar*, m. unclaimed land, lands without an owner. *s.* [pronounced *nāj*). *s.*

اناج अनाज *anāj*, m. corn, grain (incorrectly

اناچار अनाचार *an-āchār*, m. improper conduct, neglect of religious observance; adj. immoral, ill-behaved. *an-āchārī*, immoral, indecorous. *s.*

اناچت अनाचित *anāchit*, suddenly, unexpectedly. *anāchitī* or *anāchitī*, f. ignorance, thoughtlessness. *d.*

اناد *an-ād* for अनादि *an-ādi*, without beginning, eternal. *anād-banjar*, land that has been waste from time immemorial. *ānad-bhūmī*, land transferred by mortgage. *unādi-twa*, m. eternity. *s.*

انادر अनादर *an-ādar*, m. affront, disrespect. *s.*

انار *anār*, m. a pomegranate; it also denotes a kind of firework. *p.*

انارپن अनारपन *anārpan*, m. silliness, clumsiness, inexpertness, ignorance. *h.*

انارداند *anār-dāna*, m. a species of millet, so called from its resemblance to the seed of the pomegranate. *p.* [nate. *p.*

اناري *anārī*, of or resembling the pomegra-

اناري अनारी *anārī*, } unskilful, clumsy, inex-
اناڑي अनाड़ी *anāṛī*, } pert; s. a novice, a bungler. *h.*

اناسي उनासी *unāsī*, seventy-nine. *s.*

اناشیہ अनाश्य *an-āshya*, indestructible. *s.*

آنا فآنا *ānan fa-ānan*, constantly, every minute, incessantly. *a.*

اناکار अनाकार *an-ākār*, shapeless. *s.*

آناکاني आनाकाणी *ānā-kānī*, f. turning a deaf ear, overlooking, winking at, purposely neglecting. *ānā-kānā-d.*, to pretend ignorance, to ignore. *h.*

اناکرانتا अनाक्रान्ता *anākrāntā*, f. a sort of prickly nightshade (*Solanum jacquini*). *s.*

اناگمیہ अनागम्य *an-āgamya*, unapproachable, inaccessible. *s.*

انام *anām*, mortals, the world, demons, genii. *a.*

انامت *anāmat* (per metathesin for *amānat*), deposit, trust, &c. *a.* [fingers. *a.*

انامل *anāmil* (pl. of انملہ), fingers, tips of the

آنان *ānān*, those. *ānān-ki*, those who. *p.*

اناناس *anānās*, m. (v. *anannās*), the pine-apple. *Port.*

انانیت *anāniyat*, f. egotism, boasting, arrogance. *a.*

اناهار अनाहार *an-āhār*, m. abstinence, starvation. *an-āhārī*, adj. fasting. *s.* [easy. *s.*

انایاس अनायास *an-āyās*, m. ease, facility; adj.

انب *anab* or *inab*, a kind of grape, the egg-plant. *a.*

آنب आंब *ānb* or *āmb*, m. a mango (v. *ām*). *s.*

انب अम्बु *ambu*, m. water. *s.*

انبا अम्बा *ambā*, f. a mother (same as *ammā*). *s.*

انبار *ambār*, m. magazines, heaps, a stock. *p.*

انباري *ambārī*, f. a canopy; a litter or howdah used on an elephant or camel. *p.*

انباڑا अंबाड़ा *ambāṛā*, m. } the esculent plant
انباڑي अंबाड़ी *ambāṛī*, f. } hibiscus, commonly called the Rozelle (*Hibiscus cannabinus*). *h.*

انباز *ambāz*, m. a partner, an associate. *p.*

انبازي *ambāzī*, partnership, association. *p.*

انبان *ambān*, a kind of soft goat-skin leather; a purse, a clothes-bag, wallet. *p.*

آن‌بان आनबान *ān-bān*, f. spirit, proper pride. *h*

انبت अम्बत *ambat*, sour, acid. *h.*

انبتانا अम्बताना *ambatānā*, n. to be acidulated. *h.*

انبج अम्बुज *ambuj*, m. the lotus (*Nymphæa nelumbo*). *s.*

انبر अंबर *ambar* (v. امبر), sky; clothes. *h.*

انبر *ambar*, m. (corruption of عنبر), amber, &c. *a.*

انبراي अम्बराई *ambarā,ī*, f. a mango grove. *s.*

انبساط *imbisāt*, f. gladness, joy, delight, cheerfulness, recreation, mirth. *a.*

انبکا अम्बिका (see امبکا), the goddess Pārvatī. *s.*

انبل *ambil*, a kind of pottage. *d.*

انبناو अनबनाव *an-banā,o*, m. discord, dissension, misunderstanding. *h.*

انبندهي अनुबन्धी *anubandhī*, connected with, attached. *s.*

انبول अनबोल or अबोल *an-bol* or *am-bol*, speechless. *h.* [course. *p.*

انبوه *amboh*, a crowd, multitude, mob, con-

انبه *amba*, m. a mango (see *ām*). *p.*

انبهاو *anbhā,o*, } m. cultivating or taking possession of land, enjoying
انبهو *anbhau*, } property. *d.*

انبهلاش अनभिलाष *an-abhilāsh*, m. indifference, absence of desire. *an-abhilāshī*, indifferent. *s.*

انبهو अनुभव *anubhav* or *anubhau*, m. comprehension in the mind, judgment, conjecture, experience, result, consequence. *s.* [guessed. *s.*

انبهوت अनुभूत *anubhūt*, experienced, felt,

انبهوج अम्भोज *ambhoj*, m. the lotus (*Nymphæa nelumbo*). *s.*

انبهوگ *anbhog* (v. *anbhā,o*), possession &c. *s.*

آنبي *āmbī*, that which grows spontaneously. *d*

انبيا *ambiyā* (pl. of نبي), prophets. *a.*

انبيا अंबिया *ambiyā*, f. a small unripe mango. *h.*

ان بياها अनबियाहा *an-biyāhā*, unmarried. *s.*

ان بيدها अनबेधा *an-bedhā*, unbored, unperforated. *s.*

انبيق *ambīḳ*, m. a still, an alembic. *a.*

انبيكار *ambīkār*, a sailor, pilot. *d.*

انپاتك अनुपातक *anupātak*, m. a heinous offence short of a capital crime. *s.*

ان پان अनुपान *anu-pān*, m. a vehicle; (in medicine) any thing in which a medicine is mixed, to facilitate the taking of it; or which is swallowed after the medicine. *s.* [drink. *s.*

ان پاني अन्नपानी *ann-pānī*, m. victuals and

انپتيه अनपत्य *an-apatya*, childless, without progeny. *s.*

انپرادھ अनपराध *an-aparādh*, m. innocence; adj. innocent, sinless. *anaparādhī*, innocent. *s.*

ان پراسن अन्नप्राशन *anna-prāsan*, m. a kind of ceremony, the first feeding of children with food made of grain. *s.*

انپڑنا *amparnā*, n. to come to hand. *d.*

انپڑها अनपढ़ा *an-parhā*, illiterate, uninformed. *s.*

انپستهت अनुपस्थित *an-upasthit*, not ready, not present. *s.*

انپل अनुपल *anupal*, m. a second (of time). *s.*

انپن अनिपुण *a-nipun*, unskilled. *s.*

ان پورنا अन्नपूर्णा, f. satiety; name of a goddess, the Ceres of the Hindus. *s.*

آن پورنا आनपूर्णा, n. to happen. *h.*

آنپورو आनुपूर्व *ānupūrv*, f. order, method, a rank, a row. *s.*

انپيكشا अनपेक्ष *an-apekshā*, f. disregard, carelessness, indifference. *s.* [ing. *s.*

انپيكھ अनपेख *an-apekh*, disregarding, unheed-

آنت आन्त *ānt*, f. entrails, gut, tripe. *ānt ā,onā*, n. to be afflicted with the coming down of the rectum. *ānt girnā*, n. to void white glutinous stools. *s.*

انت अंत *ant*, m. end, completion; perdition, destruction; mind, heart, boundary, limit; adj. final, ultimate; adv. after all, at last; (for *antar*) in, within. *ant-ko*, in the end, at the last. *s.*

انت अंत *ant*, m. intelligence, news, account. *h.*

انت अनत *anat*, elsewhere, somewhere else. *s.*

انت उन्नत *unnat*, high, tall. *unnati*, f. increase, prosperity, rising. *s.*

انتاپ अनुताप *anutāp*, m. repentance, regret, remorse. *anutāpī*, penitent. *s.*

انتارا अनुतारा *anutārā*, m. a satellite. *s.*

انتاليس उनतालीस *untālīs*, thirty-nine. *h.*

انتج अन्तज *antaj*, m. a Shūdra, or man of low caste. *s.*

انتخاب *intikhāb*, m. selection, picking; making extracts from books; election, choice. *a.*

انتر अंतर *antar*, within, between, amongst; without, except; on one side, out of the way; m. interval, intermission; period, term; hole, rent; a corner, side, quarter of the heavens; distance, space; heart; a pause, a stop; difference; opportune time; the midst; the heart, the supreme soul; adj. other, similar. *antar-bhāo*, internal or inherent nature. *antar-bhūt*, in the midst. *antar-jāmī*, pervading the inward parts, acquainted with the heart (the Deity). *antar-jāt*, inborn, innate. *antar-dusht*, internally bad, wicked. *antar-dwār*, a private door within a house. *antar-gati*, f. emotions of the heart, inward sensations; adj. forgotten. *antar-manas*, sad, perplexed. *antar-vatnī*, a pregnant woman. *s.*

انتر अन्त्र *antar*, f. the entrails, bowels, viscera. *s.*

انتر अनुत्तर *anuttar*, unable to answer, without reply. *s.* [out. *s.*

انترا अन्तरा *antarā*, central; near; adv. with-

انترا अन्तरा *antarā*, m. a verse, any verse of a song, except the first. *h.*

انتراپت अन्तरापत्य *antarāpatt* (for *antarāpatya*), pregnant, with child, with young (any animal). *s.*

انتراتپ अन्तरातप *antarā-tap*, f. an intermittent fever, a tertian ague. *s.* [space. *s.*

انترال अन्तराल *antarāl*, central; m. included

انتربيد अन्तर्वेद *antarbed*, } f. the region of Kanauj be-
انتربيدي अंतर्वेदी *antarbedī*, } tween the rivers Ganga and Jamunā, commonly called the Du,āb. *s.* [screen. *s.*

انترپٹ अंतरपट *antar-paṭ*, m. a curtain, a

انترت अन्तरित *antarit*, inward, internal. *s.*

انترجال *antarjāl*, m. a stick used in wrestling. *d.*

انترجامي अन्तर्जामी *antarjāmī*, acquainted with the heart, an epithet of Krishna. *s.*

انترچهہ अन्तरिच्छ *antarichh*, } m. the sky, the
انترکش अन्तरिक्ष *antarikṣh*, } air, the firmament. *s.*

انتردهان अन्तर्धान *antardhān*, } m. disap-
انتردهيان अंतर्ध्यान *antardhyān*, } pearance, concealment. *antardhyān-honā*, to disappear. *s.*

آنترک आन्त्रिक *āntrik*, visceral, relating to the bowels. *s.*

انترگنگا अन्तर्गङ्गा *antarganga*, m. a kind of water-plant bearing a white flower. *s.*

انترنگ अन्तरङ्ग *antarang*, m. a relative, a near friend. *s.*

انتري अंत्री *antrī*, f. entrail (v. *antrī*). *s.*

انتريا अंतरिया *antriyā*, m. intermittent, an intermitting fever. *s.*

انتريپ अन्तरीप *antarīp*, m. a promontory. *kumārī antarīp*, Cape Comorin. *s.*

انتريچهہ अन्तरीछ *antarīchh*, } m. the sky;
انتريکش अंतरीक्ष *antarīkṣh*, } adv. in the air; out of sight. *āntarīksh*, heavenly, celestial; m. the firmament. *s.*

انتڙي अन्तड़ी, अन्तरी, or अंत्री *antṛī* or *antrī*, f. entrail, intestine, bowel, gut. *antṛiyān jalnā*, to be very hungry. *antṛī kā bal kholnā*, a. to eat a bellyful after starving. *antṛiyān ḳul huwa-llāh paṛhnā*, n. to be very hungry (the belly saying there is but one God). *antṛiyon men āg lagnā*, to be very hungry. *s.*

انتشار *intishār*, m. confusion, want of regularity; dispersion, explanation. *a.*

انتظار *intiẓār*, m. } looking out (for any
انتظاري *intiẓārī*, f. } person), expectation. *intiẓārī-k.*, a. to expect, to look out for. *a.*

انتظام *intiẓām*, m. disposition, regularity, order, arrangement; the dispensation of Providence or fate. *a.*

انتعاش *inti'āsh*, recovering one's self after stumbling. *a.*

انتفاع *intifā'*, m. profit, advantage. *a.*

انتقال *intiḳāl*, m. transporting, travelling; transferring, circulation (of currency); departure, decease, dying. *a.*

انتقام *intiḳām*, m. revenge, retaliation. *intiḳām-l.*, to retaliate. *a.*

انت کال अन्तकाल *ant-kāl*, m. dying moments, hour of death. *s.*

انتکرن अन्तःकरण *antahkaraṇ*, or *antah-karan*, or *antaskaran*, m. heart, mind, understanding. *s.*

انتم अन्तिम *antim*, final, ultimate. *s.*

انته अन्तः (in comp. same as *antar*). *antah-pātī*, included. *antah-sharīr*, m. the internal and spiritual part of man, conscience, soul. *antah-karan*, m. the understanding, heart, will, conscience, soul. *s.*

انتها *intihā*, f. end, termination, summit; adj. finished, completed, prohibited. *a.*

انته‌پر अन्तःपुर *antaḥ-pur*, m. the inner apartments. *s.*

انتج अन्त्यज *antyaj*, } m. a Shudra,
انتجنم अन्त्यजन्म *antya-janma*, } a man of the lowest cast. *antya-janmanī*, f. a woman of the same cast. *s.*

انتيس उनतीस *untīs*, twenty-nine. *s.*

انتيواسي अन्तेवासी *antevāsī*, m. a disciple, a pupil residing with his teacher. *s*

انتيورن अन्त्यवर्ण *antya-varna*, m. f. a man or woman of the Shudra cast. *s.*

انتيه अनित्य *a-nitya*, not permanent, fleeting, perishable. *anityatā*, f. frailness, transient existence. *a-nitya-datta* or *a-nitya-dattaka*, that which is temporarily granted; a son adopted for a certain term. *s.*

آنٹ आंट *ānṭ*, f. a knot; envy. *h.*

انٹا अंटा *anṭā*, m. a ball, marble. *anṭā-ghar*, m. a billiard-room. *h.*

انٹاچت अंटाचित *anṭā-chit*, unlucky, whose fortune is exhausted (a term of abuse). *h.*

انٹاکوڑي अंटाकोड़ी *anṭākoṛī*, f. a cord with which cattle are tied neck and heels. *h.*

انٹ‌سانٹ आंटसांट *ānṭ-sānṭ*, f. partnership; intrigue. *h.*

انٹنا अंटना *anṭnā*, n. to be contained, to be filled up (a well or tank, &c.). *h.*

آنٹنا आंटना *ānṭnā*, a. to fill (a well or tank), to come or go into, to reach. *h.*

انٹوانا अंटवाना *anṭwānā*, a. to make contain, to cram into, to cause to be filled. *h.*

انٹهلانا अंठलाना *anṭhlānā*, a. to twist, to writhe; n. to swagger, to strut, to give one's self airs, to walk affectedly. *h.*

آنٹهي आंठी *āṇṭhī*, f. stone of fruit; coagulation. *h*

انٹهئي अंठई *anṭha,ī*, f. a tick (the louse that attacks dogs, &c.). *s.*

آنٹي आंटी *ānṭī*, f. a handful; a bundle of grass, &c., a small faggot; a skein of thread, a hank. *h*

انثيان *unṡayānī*, } the two testicles, ears, &c. *a*
انثيين *unṡayain*, }

انج अनुज *anuj*, younger, junior. *s.*

آنجا *ān-jā*, there. *az ān-jā*, thence. *p.*

انجام *anjām*, m. end, termination; accident, vexation; in comp. ending, &c. *p.*

انجاما अनजामा *anjāmā*, barren (land) in which nothing will grow. *h.*

انجاميدن *anjāmīdan*, to terminate, to finish, conclude. *p.*

انجان अनजान *an-jān*, unwitting, unintentional, unknowing, ignorant; m. a stranger. *anjān-h.*, to assume the stranger, to pretend ignorance of a person or thing. *s.*

انجانا अनजाना *an-jānā*, unknown, a stranger ignorant. *an-jāne*, ignorantly, unwittingly. *h.*

انجاني *an-jānī*, f. ignorance, negligence. *h.*

انجائي anjā,ī, a mongrel or hybrid animal. *d.*

انجبار anjabār or injibār, name of a plant from which a drink is prepared for obstinate colds, spitting of blood, &c. *p.* [honey. *s.*

انجبين anjabīn (Arabic form of angabīn),

انجرا anjarā or injarā, m. a nettle. *p.*

انجس अनयश or अनजस an-jas, m. infamy. *s.*

انجل anjal, m. (v. انجلا), two handfuls, &c.

انجل अनजल or अन्नजल ann-jal, m. victuals and drink; Pers. āb o dāna or āb-dāna. *s.*

انجلا अञ्जला anjlā, m. two handfuls, as much as can be held in both hands open; the junction of the two hands to form the shape of a boat; Scottice, a goupen. *s.*

انجلا अनजला an-jalā, unburnt, unscorched. *s.*

انجلي अञ्जलि anjli f. (same as anjlā), it also denotes a mode of salutation by carrying the two hands joined (as above) to the forehead. *s.*

انجم anjum (pl. of نجم), stars, constellations. *a.*

انجماد injimād, m. state of congealing or congelation. *a.*

انجمن anjuman, f. an assembly, meeting, company, banquet. *p.*

آنجن आञ्जन ānjan, } m. a collyrium, an ointment applied to the eye-lashes with a view to blacken and improve them. *s.*
انجن अञ्जन anjan, }

انجن अंजन anjan, m. a kind of grass, much used (in the upper provinces) as food for cattle. *h.*

انجنا अनजना an-janā, unborn; m. an inferior kind of rice. *h.*

آنجنا आञ्जना ānjnā, a. to tinge the eyes with anjan. *s.*

انجنا अञ्जना anjnā, n. to be tinged with anjan; f. the mother of Hanumān; a lizard. *s.*

انجن‌سار अञ्जनसार anjan-sār, m. collyrium. *s.*

انجنكا अञ्जनिका anjanikā, f. a kind of newt or lizard. *s.*

انجنهاري अञ्जनहारी anjanhārī, f. a stye (or stithe) on the eyelids. *h.*

انجني अञ्जनी anjanī, f. a woman perfumed with sandal, &c. a medicinal plant used as a sedative and laxative.

آنجو आंजू ānjū } m. a tear; (see آنسو ānsū). *h.*
آنجهو आंझू ānjhū, }

انجير अञ्जीर anjīr, m. a fig. *p.*

انجيل injīl, m. the New Testament, Gospel. *g.*

آنچ आंच ānch, f. heat, flame of a fire (not of a candle), glare, blaze; (in Dakh.) ashes of cow-dung. *h.*

انچا ऊंचा unchā, high, lofty (for ūnchā). *h.*

انچا anchā, m. the post for letters, a stage or station on the road. *d.*

انچاس उनचास unchās, forty-nine. *s.*

انچاس ऊंचास unchās, f. height, elevation. *h.*

انچان unchān, height, elevation. *d.*

انچانا ऊंचाना unchānā, a. to raise, to take up. *s.*

انچاؤ ऊंचाउ unchā,ū, m. }
انچاهٹ ऊंचाहट unchāhaṭ, f. } elevation, height. *s.*
انچائي ऊंचाई unchā,ī, f. }

انچاهت अनचाहत an-chāhat, not desired. *s.*

انچيت अनचित an-chit, unaware, sudden; adv. suddenly. *h.* [ing *s*

انچيت अनुचित an-uchit, improper, unbecom-

انچر अनुचर anuchar, m. a companion, a follower, an attendant. anucharī, f. a female companion. *s.*

آنچر आंचर ānchar, } m. the hem of a cloak or veil; a border at the end of a veil, shawl, &c. *s.*
انچرا अंचरा anchrā, }

انچل अञ्चल anchal, } m. breast (of a woman or lactescent animal); the hem of a cloak or veil; a border of a veil or shawl. *s.*
آنچل आञ्चल ānchal, }

انچلا अञ्चला anchlā, m. the hem of a cloak, &c., a sheet, used among Jogīs *s.*

آنچنان ān-chun-ān, even as, just as. *p.*

انچ نيچ ऊंचनीच unch-nīch, ups and downs of life, vicissitude, high and low, particulars. *s.*

انچو आंचू ānchū, m. the raspberry. kālā ānchū, the hill bramble. *h.*

آنچه ān-chi, that which, whatsoever. *p.*

انچها अनिच्छा an-ichchhā, f. indifference, absense of desire. *s.*

انچهيلا अनछीला an-chhīlā, unlicked, rude; unpared (as fruit, &c.). *h.*

انچي سڑهي چڑهنا unchī siṛhī chaṛhnā, to to mount a high ladder, *i.e.* to obtain a high rank. *d.*

انچينا anchenā, m. valuation or estimate of growing crops: it is also called kan-kūt, q. v. *d.*

انحراف inhirāf (in Dakh. also inhirāfī), deflection, inversion, change; met. to prove a turncoat; recantation, deviation from the meridian, chiefly applied to the bearing of the temple of Mecca; declination of a heavenly body; a disease, defect, distemper. *a.*

انحصار inhiṣār, m. surrounding, encircling. *a.*

انخفاف inkhifāf, m. levity, lightness. *a.*

انداختن andākhtan (r. andāz), to cast, to throw down. *p.*

انداختا andākhta, cast away, thrown. *p.*

اندار andār, a narrative, story, tale, fiction. *p.*

اندارا इन्दारा indārā, m. a large well built of solid masonry. *h.*

انداز *andāz*, } m. valuation, guess; weighing, measurement; time
اندازه *andāza,* in music; mode, manner; (in comp.) throwing, as *bark-andāz,* a thrower of lightning, a matchlockman. *andāz-paṭṭī,* f. an estimate of the value of a growing crop. *p.*

اندام *andām*, m. body, stature, figure. *andāmi-nihānī, pudendum mulieris. p.*

اندر *andar*, within, inside, inwardly. *p.*

اندر इन्द्र *indra*, m. the king of the Devatās, the regent of the visible heaven; the thunderer. *indra-dwādashī,* the 12th day of the month Bhadra, a festival in honour of Indra. *s.*

اندر अनिद्र *a-nidr*, awake, sleepless. *s.*

اندرا *indirā*, f. the goddess of wealth. *s.*

اندراج *indirāj*, m. becoming extinct (a family); being folded together, insertion. *a.*

اندراسن इंद्रासन *indrāsan*, m. the throne of Indra. *s.*

اندراني इन्द्राणी or इंद्रानी *indrānī*, f. the wife of Indra; the name of a medicine or plant (*Vitex negundo*). *s.*

اندراون *indrāwan* (v. *indrāyan*). *d.*

اندراين इंद्रायण *indrāyan*, f. colocynth, wild gourd; a fruit of beautiful appearance, but bitter taste (*Cucumis colocynthis*); hence a beautiful but worthless person is called *indrāyan kā phal,* the fruit of *indrāyan. s.*

اندربدهو इन्द्रवधू *indra-badhū*, f. name of an insect (a species of acarus, of a scarlet colour like velvet); the wife of Indra. *s.*

اندرپرستهه इंद्रप्रस्थ *indra-prastha*, one of the names of ancient Dihlī. *s.*

اندرپروهتا इन्द्रप्रोहिता *indra-prohitā*, f. the asterism Pushyā. *s.*

اندرپري इन्द्रपुरी *indra-purī*, f. the city of Indra. *s.*

اندرجال इन्द्रजाल *indra-jāl*, m. deception, cheating, juggling; trick or stratagem in war. *indrajālī,* m. a conjuror, juggler; adj. deceptive, unreal. *s.*

اندرجو इन्द्रयव or इन्द्रजौ *indra-jau*, m. name of a medicinal seed that grows on the plant *karā,ījā.* q. v.; (*Sparrow's tongue, Nerium antidysentericum*). *s.*

اندرز *andaraz*, m. last will; last advice, precepts, or admonitions. *p.*

اندرسا अनदर्सा *an-darsā*, m. a kind of fried sweetmeats, a kind of cloth (see *adarsā*). *h.*

اندرنيل इन्द्रनील *indra-nīl*, m. a sapphire. *s.*

اندرنيلك इन्द्रनीलक *indra-nīlak*, m. an emerald. *s.*

اندروار *andarwār* (for *andarūn*) within. *d.*

اندرون *andarūn*, within, inner apartments, interior. *p.*

اندرونه *andarūna*, internal, relating to the inside. *p.*

اندروني *andarūnī*, internal, intrinsic. *p.*

اندري इंद्री *indrī*, } f. the senses (internal
اندري इन्द्रिय *indriya*, and external), organs of action and perception (those of action are the hand, the foot, the voice, the organ of generation and the organ of excretion; those of perception, the mind, the eye, the ear, the nose, the tongue, and the skin); the privities, *membrum virile, veretrum animalium. indrī jullāb,* a diuretic medicine. *indriya-gyān,* m. the faculty of perception, sense, consciousness. *s.*

اندريكها इन्दुरेखा *indu-rekhā*, f. a digit of the moon. *s.*

اندفاع *indifā'*, m. warding off, repelling. *a.*

اندك *andak*, little, small, few. *andakī*, f. a small portion or number. *p.*

اندكار *andakār*, m. } darkness, obscurity;
اندكاري *andakārī*, f. } adj. dark. *d.*

اندلا *andlā* (for *andhlā* q. v.), blind, dark. *d.*

اندمال *indimāl*, m. recovering, getting well of a wound. *a.*

اندن अनुदिन *anudin*, every day, daily. *s.*

آندو आन्दू *āndū*, m. the chain or rope with which the feet of elephants are tied up. *s.*

اندوار इन्दुवार *induwār*, m. the day of the moon, Monday. *s.*

اندوخته *andokhta*, acquired, gained; m. gain, acquisition. *p.*

اندود *andūd* (in comp.), besmeared, encrusted. *p.*

اندور इन्दूर *indūr*, m. a rat, mouse. *s.*

اندوز *andoz*, in comp. gaining, acquiring. *p.*

اندولنا अनदोलना *andolnā*, n. to swing. *s.*

اندوه *andoh*, m. grief, anxiety, trouble; *andoh-gīn,* full of grief, sad, afflicted. *p.*

اندهـ अन्ध *andh*, m. darkness; adj. blind. *andh-tamas,* m. great darkness. *s.*

اندها अंधा *andhā*, adj. blind, dark. *andhā dhūnd,* blind, blindly. *andhā dhūnd ronā,* to weep excessively. *andhā dhūnd luṭānā,* to squander, spend extravagantly. *andhā kū,ā* or *andhā-kūp,* m. a well filled up with rubbish. *andhā-kharch* (Dakh.), prodigality, extravagance. *s.*

اندهارا *andhārā*, dark, obscure. *d.*

اندهاري *andhārī*, f. darkness, obscurity, cloudiness; a blind over a horse's eyes. *d.*

اندهتا अन्धता *andhatā*, f. blindness. *s.*

اندهك अन्धक *andhak*, m. a blind man; a man's name; adj. blind. *s.*

اندهكار अंधकार *andhakār*, m. darkness. *s.*

اندهكارا *andhakārā*, m. } darkness, obscurity,
اندهكاري *andhakārī*, f. } cloudiness. *s.*

اندهلا अन्धला *andhlā* (see اندها *andhā*), blind. *s.*

اندهلاپن अन्धलापन *andhlāpan*, m. blindness; intellectual blindness; acting as if one were blind. *h.*

اندهن इंधन *indhan*, m. fire-wood. *s.*

اندهن अन्नधन *an-dhan*, m. wealth, both in grain and coin, properly *anna-dhan*. *s.*

اندهويا अन्धोया *an-dhoyā*, unwashed, unclean. *s.*

آندهي आंधी *āndhī*, f. storm, hurricane, tempest; a darkening or louring of the sky. *āndhī-h.*, to engage keenly in a bad action. *h.* [darkness. *s.*

اندهيارا अन्धियारा *andhiyārā*, blind, dark; m.

اندهير अंधेर *andher*, m. darkness, misfortune, calamity, injustice, tumult. *andher-k.*, to tyrannize, oppress. *h.*

اندهيرا अंधेरा *andherā*, dark; m. darkness. (See *andhiyārā*). *andherī-koṭhrī*, f. dark room; the belly; the womb. *h.*

اندهيري अन्धेरी *andherī*, f. darkness, a blind for a horse. *s.*

اندهين अनधीन *an-adhīn*, independent. *s.*

انديش *andesh*, thinking, contriving; used in comp. as *bad-andesh* q. v. *p.*

انديشناك *andesh-nāk* or *andesh-mand*, thoughtful, anxious. *p.* [anxiety. *p.*

انديشناكي *andeshnākī* or *andesh-mandī*, f.

انديشه *andesha*, m. thought, meditation, suspicion, care, concern. *andesha-k.*, to reflect, to hesitate, to fear. *p.*

انديشه‌مند *andesha-mand*, full of anxiety. *p.*

ابديشه‌مندي *andesha-mandī*, anxiousness, concern. *p.*

انديشيدن *andeshīdan*, to consider to reflect. *p.*

انديكها अनदेखा *an-dekhā*, not yet seen, undiscovered, invisible. *h.*

انڈ अण्ड *and* (vulgarly آنڈ *ānḍ* or *ānṛ*), m. Palma Christi (*Ricinus vulgaris*). *h.*

انڈ अण्ड *anḍ*, m. an egg; a testicle. *anḍ-kos* or *anḍ-kosh*, a hernia or rupture. *s.*

آنڈ आण्ड or आंड़ *ānḍ* or *ānṛ*, m. a testicle, the scrotum; semen genitale. *s.*

انڈا अण्डा *anḍā* (also *ānḍā*), m. an egg. *s.*

انڈج अण्डज *anḍaj* (lit. egg-born), oviparous, a bird. *s.*

انڈرا *anḍrā* or *ānḍra*, m. an egg. *d.*

انڈكا अण्डका *anḍkā*, m. an egg; also used for *ākhā*, a pannier, or rather one of the bags forming a pannier. *h.*

انڈكوش अण्डकोष *anḍ-kosh*, m. the scrotum, the testicles; rupture, hernia. *s.*

انڈلنا *unḍalnā*, a. to pour out water, &c. *d.*

انڈلنا *anḍalnā*, to consider, to determine or settle. *d.*

انڈو आण्डू *ānḍū*, having large testicles. *ānḍū bail*, a bull. In *Dakhanī* it is said to mean a bull with one testicle. *s.*

انڈوا इण्डूआ *inḍū,ā*, m. a head cushion for carrying a burden on. *h.*

انڈواي *anḍwā,ī*, f. a swelled testicle. *d.*

انڈوي इण्डुई *inḍū,ī*, f. a head or crown ornament; also a cushion, v. *inḍū,ā*. *h.*

انڈي‌سيكنا *anḍe-sehnā*, to bring forth young; to keep one's own house. *anḍe meṅ kī zardī*, applied to one who is raw and inexperienced. *d.*

انڈيل अण्डेल *anḍel*, oviparous; pregnant (bird). *h.*

انڈيلنا उण्डेलना *unḍelnā*, a. to pour water. *h.*

انرادها अनुराधा *anurādhā*, f. the 17th lunar mansion, designated by a row of oblations; stars in Libra. *s.*

انراگ अनुराग *anurāg*, m. affection, love. *s.*

انراگنا अनुरागना *anurāgnā*, n. to be in love with. *s.* [loving, caressing. *s.*

انراگي अनुरागी *anurāgī*, making friendship,

انرته अनर्थ *an-arth*, unmeaning, fruitless, absurd, improper. *s.* [restrained *s.*

انرده अनिरुद्ध *a-niruddha*, unobstructed, un-

انرس अनरस *an-ras*, m. want of flavour or enjoyment; disgust, nauseousness; coolness, distaste, misunderstanding between friends. *s.*

انرس अन्नरस *ann-ras*, m. chyle. *s.*

انرمل अनिर्मल *a-nirmal*, dirty, foul. *s.*

انرني अनिर्णय *a-nirnay*, m. uncertainty. *s.*

انرني अनृणी *an-ṛinī*, unindebted. *s.*

انروپ अनुरूप *anurūp*, like, conformable; m. conformity. *s.*

انروچنيه अनिर्वचनीय *a-nirvachanīya*, } not fit
انروچيه अनिर्वच्य *a-nirvachya*, } to be spoken, indefinable. *s.* [ness. *s.*

انروده अनुरोध *anurodh*, m. service, obliging-

انريت अनरीत *an-rīt*, f. unmannerliness, ill-behaviour. *s.*

آنڑ आंड़ *ānṛ*, m. a testicle (v. *ānḍ*).

انزال *inzāl*, m. emission, sending down; *emissio seminis*. *a.*

انزروت *anzarūt*, m. sarcocolla; (gum-resin, said to be from *Penæa mucronata*). *a. p.*

انزوا *inziwā*, retiring into a corner or cell (a recluse). *a.* [thing. *h.*

آنس आंस *āṅs*, f. the fibrous part of any

انس *ins*, men, mankind, the human race. *a.*

انس *uns*, m. friendship, love, affection, society, companionship. *a.*

انس अंस *aṅs* or अंश *aṅsh*, m. a part, division, share, right, possession; a degree of a circle; a fraction, the numerator of a fraction; essence. *aṅsa-patra*, a deed setting forth the shares of a property between the members of a Hindū family. *aṅsa-hārā*, m. one who takes a share of an estate; a co-heir or joint sharer, &c. *s.*

انساب *ansāb* (pl. of نسب), generations, families. *a.*

انسار अनुसार *anusār*, alike, according to; m. conformity to usage. *anusārī*, adj. following, according with or to. *s.*

انسان *insān*, m. man, mankind. *a.*

انسانس संशांश *ansāns* or *anshānsha*, m. a subdivision, a share of a share. *s.*

انساني *insānī*, of or belonging to humanity, peculiar to man, human. *a.*

انسانيت *insānīyat*, f. humanity, human kindness; affability. *a.*

انسب *ansab*, advisable, most proper. *a.*

انست *anasat*, f. intimacy, use, cheerfulness. *a.*

انسٹھ उनसठ *unsaṭh*, fifty-nine. *s.*

انس دهاري संशधारी *ansdhārī*, successful; (in theology) incarnating. *s.*

انسرنا अनुसरना *anusarnā*, n. to follow a person, to follow on some previous circumstance. *s.*

انسك संसिक *ansik*, a partner; a proprietor. *s.*

انسکھ अनसिख *an-sikh*, unlearned, untaught. *s.*

انسجها अनसमझा *an-samjhā*, not understood. *h.*

انسنا अनसुना *an-sunā*, unheard, disregarded. *h.*

انسندهان अनुसन्धान *anusandhān*, m. inquiry, investigation. *s.*

انسني کرنا अनसुनी करना *ansunī-k.*, a. to pretend not to hear what is spoken; to disregard. *h.*

آنسو आंसू *ānsū*, m. a tear. *ānsū bhar-lanā*, to have the eyes filled with tears. *s.*

انسوار अनुस्वार *anuswāra*, m. the nasal dot or character in Devanagari. *s.*

انسوانسه संसवांस: *answānsa*, m. a measure of land, twenty of which make a *pilwānsa*. *h.*

انس و جن *ins o jinn*, m. men and spirits. *a.*

انسي संसी or संशी *ansī* or *anshī*, a partner, sharer, co-heir. *s.*

انسیکها अनसीखा *an-sīkhā*, uninstructed, untaught. *s.*

انسيين *unsiyain* (for *unsiyaini*), the two testicles. *a.*

انشا *inshā*, writing, composition, elegance of style, the belles lettres. *inshā-pardāzī*, f. writing, letter-writing. *a.*

انشا الله تعالي *in-shā allāhu ta'ālā*, if God the most High willeth; *Deo volente*. *a.*

انشٹ अनिष्ट *an-ishṭ*, undesired, evil, ominous. *s.*

انشٹها अनिष्ठा *an-ishṭhā*, f. unstedfastness, unsteadiness. *s.*

انشدھ अनिषिद्ध *an-ishiddha*, unprohibited, unforbidden. *s.*

انصار *anṣār* (pl. of ناصر), assistants, friends (of Muhammad), applied to the inhabitants of Medina who first embraced the Islām religion. *a.*

انصاري *anṣārī*, a tribe of *Muḥammadan Shaikhs*, supposed to have come originally from Medina. *a.*

انصاف *inṣāf*, m. decision (of a cause); equity, justice. *inṣāf-ṭalab*, one who seeks for justice. *a.*

انصرام *inṣirām*, m. completion, end. *a.*

انضباط *inẓibāṭ*, f. being bound or determined, restraint; self-control. *a.*

انطباع *inṭibā'*, being impressed or stamped, printed. *a.*

انظار *anẓār* (pl. of نظر), looks, eyes. *a.*

انعام *in'ām*, m. a present, a gift. *in'ām-i-ikrām*, an honourable gift. *in'ām-kā-paisā*, prize money. *in'āmi altamghā*, a grant under the royal seal. *in'āmi ḳānūngo*, an assignment of rent-free land to a village accountant. *an'ām*, gifts. *a.*

انعامت *in'āmat*, f. a gift, a benefaction; an assignment of rent-free land. *a.*

انعكاس *in'ikās*, m. being turned upside down; reflexion (from a mirror), repercussion, reverberation. *a.*

انفار *anfār* (pl. of نفر), individuals, persons, soldiers, servants. *a.*

انفاس *anfās* (pl. of نفس), breathings, spirits. *a.*

انفخه *anfikha*, m. rennet, leaven; a substance tending to produce fermentation; a term in medicine. (The word is apparently a corruption of the Arabic *infaḥat*). *d.*

انفصال *infiṣāl*, m. decision, termination (of a cause); division, separation, settling. *infiṣāl-k.*, to settle, to decide (corruptly *infiṣālī*). *a.*

انفعال *infi'āl*, m. shame, confusion, modesty. *a.*

انقباض *inḳibāẓ*, m. detention, constipation. *a.*

انقسام *inḳisām*, m. division, dividing. *a.*

انقضا *inḳiẓā*, m. the expiration of any term; adj. elapsed, ended, fulfilled, accomplished, finished, completed. *a.*

انقطاع *inḳiṭā'*, m. being broken, cut off, cessation, failure, separation, adjustment. *a.*

انقلاب *inḳilāb*, m. revolution, vicissitude, alteration, change, inversion, transposition. *a.*

انقياد *inḳiyād*, m. fidelity, submission, obedience, compliance. *a.*

آنك आंक *ānk*, } m. a letter of the alphabet;
انك अङ्क or संक *ank*, } a figure, a number (in contradistinction to *sūn* or *sunnā*, a dot or cypher); the stamp on coins, plate, &c. *ank-kār*, m. an assayer; a mark (on cloth, pointing out the price); the flank or part above the hip; embrace, the bosom; (for *ang*) a share, portion. *ānk-dār*, a sharer. *s.*

آنك *ānuk*, m. a kettle-drum, a kind of large drum beaten only at one end. *s.*

انكار *inkār*, denial, refusal, disavowal. *a.*

انكانا संकाना *ankānā*, a. to cause to value, to prize, to examine (as cloth), to approve of. *s.*

انكاو संकाव *ankā,o*, m. valuation, appraisement. *h.*

آنكبندي आंकबंदी *ānk-bandī*, f. an adjustment of rents. *h.*

انكت संकित *ankit*, marked, spotted, paged, counted. *s.*

انکت अनुक्त *an-ukt*, not told; m. a trope. *s.*

انکٹا *ankaṭṭā*, } m. a bank, a prop or support,
انکٹہ *ankaṭa*, } a dam or embankment in a river; a lock. *d.*

انکر *ankar*, more or most wicked, very offensive, displeasing or detestable. *a.*

آنکر आंकर *āṅkar* (for *ākar*), having come. *s.*

انکر अंकुर *aṅkur*, } m. the first sprout from
انکر अंकुरा *aṅkurā*, } a seed (after planting), a shoot, a plantlet, a germ. *s.*

انکرم अनुक्रम *anukram*, m. order, method, succession, series. *s.*

انکري अंक्री *aṅkrī*, f. a kind of vetch (*Vicia sativa*); wet grain; a young sprout. *s.*

آنکري आंकरी *āṅkrī*, } f. (also *ankṛī*), the
آنکڑي आंकड़ी *āṅkṛī*, } barb. of an arrow; a circle, a hook, tenter, catch; a tendril, a cirrhus; a fishing-hook. *h.*

آنکس *ān-kas*, that person, whosoever, &c. *p.*

آنکس आंकस, अंकस, अंकुस *āṅkas*, *aṅkas*, or *aṅkus*, m. the iron with which elephants are driven, a goad. *āṅkus mārnā*, to bring to obedience, to reduce to submission. Some European writers (probably the King of Oude's cockney barber) have corrupted the word into "hawkuss" or "horkuss," vid. Lib. of Entertaining Knowledge, vol. The Elephant. p. 15. *s*

انکسار *inkisār* (corruptly *inkisārī*), m. being routed, humility, want of courage, despondency. *a.*

انکساف *inkisāf*, m. being eclipsed (the sun). *a.*

انکشاف *inkishāf*, detection, disclosure. *a.*

انکسي अङ्कुसी or आंकुसी *ankusī* or *aṅkusī*, f. a hook, a tenter. *s.*

انکش अङ्कुश or आंकुश *ankush* or *āṅkush*, same as *āṅkas*, an elephant's goad. *s.*

انکك अंकक *aṅkak*, m. an accountant, arithmetician. *s.*

انکمپا अनुकम्पा *anukampā*, f. tenderness, pity. *s.*

انکنا अंकना *aṅknā*, n. to be valued, prized, examined, approved of; a. to mark, page a book, distinguish a thing by some mark. *s.*

آنکنا आंकना *āṅknā*, a. to mark, to page, to write numbers; to value, to examine, to approve of. *s.*

انکوار अंकवार *aṅkwār*, f. an embrace, the bosom. *aṅkwār bharnā*, to embrace. *s.*

ان کوٹ अन्नकूट *anna-kūṭ*, m. a festival celebrated by Hindūs on the day following the Dewālī, by offering a large quantity of meats to the god. *s.*

انك وديا अङ्कविद्या *anka-vidyā*, f. arithmetic. *s.*

انکور अङ्कूर *ankūr*, } m. a sprout. *s.*
انکور अङ्कूरा *ankūrā*, }

انکوڑا *anhoṛā*, m. a large hook, a kind of grapnel. *d.*

انکول अनुकूल *anukūl*, coinciding, favourable, conformable, acting in concert with. *anukūlatā*, f. coincidence, concert, concord. *ānukūlya*, m. assistance, patronage. *s.*

آن کہ *ān-ki*, he or she who, that which. *p.*

آنکھ आंख *āṅkh*, f. the eye. – *āṅkh-anjanī*, f. a stye on the eyelids. *āṅkh ānī*, to have an inflammation of the eyes, to be blear-eyed. *āṅkh bachānā*, to steal away privately and unseen. *āṅkh badalnā*, to withdraw one's favour or affection from any one. *āṅkh barābar na kar saknā*, (not to be able to look stedfastly in another's face), to be ashamed. *āṅkh band kar lenī*, to turn from another, to treat one with neglect; to die. *āṅkh bharke dekhnā*, to look till one's curiosity is fully satisfied. *āṅkh bhar lānā*, to have eyes full of tears, to be ready to cry. *āṅkh pasārnā*, (obsolete) to open one's eyes, to stare, to be wise and prudent, to discriminate, to discern, to be judicious. *āṅkh pathrānī*. (from *patthar*, a stone), to become dim (the eyes) from long expectation. *āṅkh pharaknī*, to feel a pulsation in the eye, considered as an omen of some desirable event, as the meeting of friends. *is men dāhnī āṅkh jon pharkī, dil men shād hū,ā ki yih shugūn achchhā hai*, On this, feeling a pulsation in the right eye, he (Rājā Dushmanta) rejoiced in his heart, conceiving it to be a favourable omen. *Sakuntalā Nātak*: (a pulsation in the right eye of a man, or the left of a woman, is a favourable omen, the reverse disastrous). *āṅkh phūṭnī*, to be blind. *āṅkh phūṭī, pīṛ ga,ī*, the eye is lost, and the pain is gone (spoken of a contention, which has ceased by the object of it being lost to both parties). *āṅkh-phoṛā*, m. a midge, that flies into the eyes at night. *āṅkh phoṛnī*, to make blind; to expect or watch in vain. *āṅkh phernī*, to shew aversion after friendship (see *āṅkh moṛnī*). *āṅkh pher lenā*, to turn away the eyes (as from grief, displeasure, &c.). *āṅkh phailānā* (see *āṅkh pasārnā*). *āṅkh ṭhanḍī karnī*, to have consolation by meeting friends, to be glad. *āṅkh joṛnī*, to look stedfastly (inelegant). *āṅkh jhapaknā*, (to have eyelids joined, to move them quickly), to fear. *āṅkh churānī*, (to steal eyes), not to attend to, to avert eyes through shame, dislike, &c., to avoid the sight of any one. *āṅkh chaṛhānī*, to be angry; to be intoxicated. *āṅkh chaṛhnā*, to have eyes marked by debauch. *āṅkh chamkānī*, to make the eyes dance (to roll one's eyes) in anger, or as a blandishment. *āṅkh chhipānī* (to hide one's eyes) to be ashamed of an improper act. *āṅkh chīr chīr dekhnā*, and *āṅkh chīrke dekhnā*, to look with great attention and deep meditation; with anger. *āṅkh dābnī*, (to shut one's eyes), to forbid by signs. *āṅkh dikhānī* or *dikhlānī*, (to shew one's eyes), to frighten, to restrain, to brow-beat. *āṅkh dekhke kuchh karnā*, to do any thing after consulting the inclination of another. *āṅkh ḍabḍabānī*, to fill the eyes with tears. *āṅkh ḍhaknī*, (obsolete, to have eyes shut); to die; to be ashamed. *āṅkh rakhnī*, to love, to entertain friendship; to have hope; to discern. *āṅkh surkh karnī*, to be angry. *āṅkh se dekhke kuchh-k.*, to do any thing knowingly and with reflection. *āṅkh se girnā* (to fall from eyes), to become contemptible. *āṅkh senknī*, to contemplate the beauty of any one. *āṅkh kisī se roshan-k.*, (to obtain a look from any one), to meet (visit) a friend or person of rank. *āṅkh kisī kī dekhnī* (to look at one's eyes), to receive education in any one's company. *āṅkh khaṭaknī*, to have pain in the eyes. *āṅkh kholnā* (see *āṅkh pasārnā*). *āṅkh garm karnī* (see *āṅkh senknī*). *āṅkh ghuraknā*, to look at with anger. *āṅkh laṛānī*, to wink as a hint, to communicate a secret by signs. *āṅkh laṛnī*, to encounter the eyes of another; to meet with one's lover unexpectedly. *āṅkh lagānī*, to contract friendship or affection for any one, to fall in love. *āṅkh mārnī*, to wink; to stop any one by a sign; to make amorous signs with the eyes. *āṅkh michawwal*, m. *āṅkh michaulī*, f. blindman's buff (Pers. *sarmāmak*). *āṅkh milānī* (to exchange looks), to contract friendship. *āṅkh milnī*, to look stedfastly. *ānkh minch jānā*, to die, to perish. *ānkh morṇī* (see *ānkh pherni*). *ānkh mūndke ek chīz kā ikhtiyār-k.*, to choose or accept precipitately or inconsistently. *ānkh mūndnī* (see *ānkh band kar lenī*). *ānkh mūndaurā*, m. blindman s buff. *ānkh na rakhnī* (not to have eyes, not to look) to have no hope or expectation; to be mentally blind. *ānkh nam karnā* (see *ānkh bhar lānā*), to have the eyes full of tears. *ānkhoṅ par baiṭhnā* (to sit on eyes), to be beloved, to sit or cause to sit on a very elevated place; to become dignified. *ānkhoṅ kā gulābī karnā* (to have the redness of the eyes), is applied to a look of intoxication or wantonness. *ānkhoṅ meṅ ānā*, to intoxicate (applied especially to wine). *ānkhoṅ meṅ phirnā*, to be always present in one's eyes, to be ever in one's mind. *ānkhoṅ meṅ pen lenā*, to be at ease, secure, &c. *ānkhoṅ meṅ charbī chhānā*, to be wilfully blind, to pretend from pride not to know one's old acquaintance. *ānkhoṅ meṅ khāk ḍālnā* (lit. to throw dust in one's eyes); to commend or puff wares of an inferior quality; to pilfer or snatch away any thing quickly and privately. *ānkhoṅ meṅ khuṭaknā*, to be seen with envy and dislike. *ānkhoṅ meṅ ghar karnā*, to be beloved or esteemed; to persist in one's own erroneous opinions. *ānkhoṅ meṅ rāt kāṭnā* or *lejānā*, to pass the night awake. *ānkheṅ-wālā*, m. (lit. "a man with eyes"), a spy, an inspector, one of the secret police. *ānkheṅ dekhnā*, to study one's temper or inclination; to behave respectfully towards another. *ānkheṅ nīlī pīlī karnī*, to change the colour of the face from excess of anger. *s.*

انکهات *an-hhāt*, m. dislike, aversion. *d.*

انکهال अनुखाल *anukhāl*, m. a creek. *s.*

انکهانا अनखाना or अंखाना *aṅkhānā*, n. to be angry or displeased, to be peevish or fretful. *h.*

آنکهاؤ आंखाऊ *ānkhā,ū*, m. valuation (by the eye without measurement) of a growing crop. *s.*

انکهري अंखरी *aṅkhrī*, } f. the eye, a glance
انکهڑي अंखड़ी *aṅkhṛī*, } of the eye. *s*
انکهيا अंखिया *aṅkhiyā*, }

انکهن *ankhan*, m. the space between two pillars or beams. *d.*

انکهيان अंखियां *aṅkhiyāṅ*, f. the eyes, amorous glances. *s.*

آنگ आंग *āṅg*, a demand on each head of cattle for pasture, an agistment. *h.*

آنگ आङ्ग *āng*, } m. the body, a limb. *āng*
انگ अङ्ग *anga*, } *ho lagnā*, to be firm or confirmed; to have effect; a member, portion. *anganyāsa*, act of touching different parts of the body as a religious exercise. *s.*

انگ अनुग *anug* or *anuga*, m. a follower, a servant; adj. following, succeeding. *s.*

انگا अङ्गा *angā*, m. a coat or upper-garment, a long tunic worn alike by the Hindūs and Musalmans: the former tie it on the left, the latter on the right breast. *s.*

انگا अङ्गा *angā*, f. a nurse, a maid whose business it is to hold, watch, and amuse a child. *h.*

انگار अङ्गार *angār*, } m. embers, sparks;
انگارا अङ्गारा *angārā*, } wrath, rage; a firebrand, fire, a spark, a bit of fire. *angār* or *angāroṅ par loṭnā*, to be highly enraged, particularly from jealousy. *angār kā kīṛā*, m. a salamander. *h.*

انگار अङ्गारि *angāri*, f. a small fire-pan. *s.*

انگاريدن *angārīdan*, } to reckon, compute
انگاشتن *angāshtan*, } suppose, imagine. *p*

انگامي अनुगामी *anugāmī*, following, consequent upon, devoted to, imitating. *s.*

انگبين *angabīn*, m. honey (Arab. *anjabīn*). *p.*

انگت अनुगत *anugat*, m. a follower. adj. gone after, dependent on, attached to. *s.*

انگت इङ्गित *ingit*, m. hint, sign, gesture; motion; inquiry, research. *s.*

انگڈيه *angaḍḍiya*, m. a man who carries money or jewels concealed in his quilted clothes. *h.*

انگراي अङ्गराई *angrā,ī*, f. yawning (v. *angrā,ī*). *h.*

انگرکها अंगरखा *angarkhā*, m. a coat, gown, jacket, doublet, an upper garment. *s.*

انگره अनुग्रह *anugrah*, m. favour, kindness, indulgence. *s.*

انگري अंगुरी *angurī* (same as *angulī*), f. a finger, a finger's breadth. *s.*

انگريز *angrez* or *ingrez* (vulg. *angrej*, &c.), [England.

انگريزي *angrezī*, English, the English language (the term is of Portuguese origin).

انگريکها अंग्रीखा *angrīkhā*, m. a vest, coat, &c. (v. *angarkhā*. *s.*

انگڑانا अङ्गड़ाना *angṛānā*, n. to yawn, to stretch the limbs), to oscitate. *h.*

انگڑاي अङ्गड़ाई or अङ्गराई *angṛā,ī* or *angrā,ī*, f. stretching the limbs, yawning, &c. *h.*

انگڑه अनगढ़ *an-gaṛh*, } unwrought, un-
انگڑها अनगढ़ा *an-gaṛhā*, } formed; uneducated, unlicked, unfinished, unset (as a ring or jewel). *angaṛhī bāt*, inconsistent or ill-arranged speech. *h.*

انگشت *angusht*, f. a finger. *angushti-ḥairat dānton meṅ rakhnā*, to bite the finger, or place it between the teeth to express surprise. *p.*

انگشتان *angushtān*, } m. a ring (particu-
انگشتانه *angushtāna*, } larly the one worn on the thumb); a thimble. *p.*

انگشتري *angushtarī*, f. a ring, particularly one worn on the finger, not applied to that on the thumb. *p.*

انگشت نما *angusht-numā*, one who is pointed at, famous (in a good or bad sense, but in India most frequently in a bad one), notorious. *angusht-numā,ī*, act of pointing out with the finger. *p.*

انگشتهه अङ्गुष्ठ *angushṭha*, m. the thumb. *s.*

انگل उङ्गल or अङ्गुल *ungal* or *angul*, m. the thumb, a finger. *s.*

انگلستان *inglistān* or *anglistān*, England. *p.*

انگلي उंगली, अङ्गली, अङ्गुली *unglī*, *anglī*, or *angulī*, f. a finger, a finger's breadth. *pair kī unglī*, a toe. *kalām kī unglī*, fore-finger. *bīch kī unglī*, middle-finger. *kan unglī*, little finger. *unglī kā nok*, tip of the finger. *unglī kāṭnā*, to be astonished. *s.*

انگليٹ अंगलेट *aṅgleṭ*, f. appearance, person. *h.*

انگلیس *anglīs* or *inglīs*, English, the term is generally applied to an invalided soldier.

آنگ‌مڑی आङ्गमड़ी *āng-maṛī*, f. yawning, stretching the body (a dog, &c.). *h.*

انگمن अनुगमन *anugaman*, m. (the going after) applied to the ceremony of burning a Hindū widow who has heard of her husband's death when from home. *s.*

انگن उङ्गन *ungan*, m. dozing, drowsiness (from opium &c.); greasing a wheel to set it asleep, *i.e.* to prevent creaking. *h.*

آنگن आङ्गन *āngan*, } m. (also *āngnā*) a yard,
انگنا अङ्गना *angnā*, } area, court, inclosed space adjoining to a house. *s.*

انگنا अनगिणा *an-ginā*, uncounted, numberless. *anginā mahīna*, the eighth month of a woman's pregnancy. *h.* [(same as *angan*). *s.*

انگنائی अङ्गनाई *angnā,ī*, f. a yard, area, &c.

انگنت अनगिणत or अनगणित *an-ginat* or *an-ganit*, uncounted, beyond calculation. *s.*

انگنتی अनगिणती *an-gintī*, uncounted, countless, numberless. *s.*

انگنی उङ्गनी *ungnī*, f. drowsiness, &c. (v. *ungan*). *h.*

انگو *angū*, in front, before, preceding. *d.*

انگوارا अङ्गवारा *angwārā*, the proprietor of a small portion of a village; mutual aid in tillage. *h.*

انگوٹ अङ्गोट *angoṭ*, f. appearance, person (same as *angeṭ*). *h.*

انگوٹھا अंगूठा *angūṭhā*, m. thumb. *angūṭhā dikhānā*, an attitude used by women in blandishment, as a token of prohibition, to brave, defy, &c. *angūṭhā chūmnā*, to flatter. *s.* [the finger. *s.*

انگوٹھی अंगूठी *angūṭhī*, f. a ring worn on

انگوچھا अंगोछा *angochhā*, m. a cloth which Hindūs fasten round their waists when bathing, and afterwards wipe themselves with; a towel, a handkerchief. *h.*

انگور *angūr*, m. a grape; granulations in a healing sore. *angūr bannā* or *honā*, to become sound and healthy (applied to a wound). *p.*

آنگورا अङ्गोरा *āngorā*, m. a midge, a gnat. *h.*

انگوری *angūrī*, of or belonging to the grape. *p.*

انگوریہ अंगौरिया *angauriya*, m. a ploughman; also, allowing the use of a plough instead of paying wages in money or kind. *h.*

انگوزہ *angūza*, m. assafœtida. *p.*

انگونگا अंगौंगा *angaungā*, perquisites from the threshing-floor to the Brāhman, Gurū, &c. *h.*

آنگہ *āṅ-gah* (for *āṅ-gāh*) then, at that time. *p.*

انگھ अनघ *an-agh*, blameless, free from guilt. *s.*

انگھڑ *anghaṛ*, stupid, ignorant. *anghaṛ-pan*, m. stupidity. *d.*

انگی अङ्गी *angī*, corporeal, bodily. *s.*

انگیا अङ्गिया *angiyā*, f. m. bodice, stays. *h.*

انگیا अनुज्ञा *anugyā*, f. order, command. *s.*

انگیٹ अङ्गेट *angeṭ*, f. appearance, person. *h.*

انگیٹی *angeṭī*, f. (v. *ageṭī*) a flower-pot. *d.*

انگیٹھی अङ्गेठी or अंगीठी *angeṭhī* or *angīṭhī*, f. a chafing-dish. *h.*

انگیختن *angekhtan* (r. *āngez*,) to excite, stir up. *p.*

انگیز *angez*, exciting; (used in comp.) as *fitna-angez*, strife-exciting. *p.*

انگیزنا *angeznā*, a. to suffer, to experience, to bear, to excite. *p. h.*

انگیکار अंगीकार *angīkār*, m. agreement, promise, acquiescence, avowal, reception, accepting, agreeing to. *angīkār-k.*, to accept, agree to. *s.*

انگیکرت अंगीकृत *angīkṛit*, agreed, promised. *s.*

انل अनिल *anil*, f. wind, breath, air. *s.*

انل अनल *anal*, f. fire, a flame, a plant (*Plumbago zeylanica* and *rosea*). *s.*

انما *inna-mā*, for, surely not, only. *a.*

انما अणिमा *animā*, m. a superhuman faculty; the subtle and invisible state, assumable by austere devotion. *s.*

انماد उन्माद *unmād*, m. madness, extravagance. *s.*

انمادا उन्मादा *unmādā*, mad, insane. *s.*

انمان अनुमान *anumān*, m. inference, logical conclusion, reasoning. *s.*

انمان उन्मान *unmān*, m. a measure of size or quantity. *s.*

آنمانک आनुमानिक *ānumānik*, inferable, subject to inference, probable, specious. *s.*

انمت अनुमति *anumati*, f. order or command, consent, permission. *s.*

انمت उन्मत्त *unmatt* } mad, insane, crazy;
انمد उन्मद *unmad*, } drunk, lustful, furious; salacious. *unmattatā*, f. insanity, intoxication. *s.*

انمرن अनुमरण *anumaran*, m. dying with (a husband), or following in death, applied to a Hindū widow. *s.*

انمکھ उन्मुख *unmukh*, looking upwards. *s.*

انمل अनमिल *anmil*, discordant, heterogeneous. *s.*

انمن अणिमन *animan*, m. the same as *animā*.

انمنا अनमना *anmanā*, thoughtful, agitated, regretting, sad, troubled in mind, sickly, dissatisfied. *s.*

انمنات *anmanāt*, doubt, perplexity. *d.*

انمنانا *anmanānā*, a. to perplex. *d.*

انمول अनमोल *an-mol*, invaluable, beyond price. *s.*

انمیش उन्मेष *unmesh* m. winking, twinkling of the eyelids. *s.*

انميل अन्मेल *an-mel*, heterogeneous; discordant. *s.*

آنن आनन *ānan*, m. face, visage, mouth. f. order. *s.*

آننا आंना *ānnā* (for *ānā*), n. to come. *s.*

آننا आन्ना *ānnā*, a. to bring. *s.*

اننا अन्ना *annā*, a kind of male nurse, the nurse's husband. *h.*

اناناس अनन्नास *anannās*, m. a pine-apple. *h.*

اناناسي *anannāsī*, made like a pine-apple. *h.*

اننت अनन्त *an-ant*, adj. boundless, endless, eternal, infinite; m. a name of the serpent that supports the earth; a name of the god Vishnu; name of several plants; a cord with fourteen knots, which the Hindūs tie on their arm on the fourteenth day of *Bhādoṅ*, Shuklpaksh, which is sacred to Vishnu, and called Anant Chaudas or Chaturdashī. *anantatā*, f. eternity. *anant-rāshi*, f. infinite quantity. *anant-rūp*, multiform. *anant-vāt*, m. rigidity or paralysis of the muscles of the face and neck. *s.*

اننتيه अनन्त्य *an-antya*, infinite, endless; m. infinity, eternity. *s.*

آنند आनन्द *ānand* (or *anand*), m. pleasure, delight; ease, tranquillity, content; God, Supreme Spirit. *ānand-may*, blissful. *s.*

آنندت आनन्दित *ānandit*, overjoyed, delighted. *s.*

انندت अनिन्दित *a-nindit*, unreproachable. *s.*

آنندتا आनन्दता *ānandatā*, f. joy, delight. *s.*

آنندکند आनन्दकन्द *ānand-kand*, source of joy; an epithet of Krishna. *s.*

آنندي आनन्दी *ānandī*, delighted, rejoiced. *s.*

اننس अनंश *an-aṅsa*, m. one who has no share; excluded from a share (of an inheritance) on account of some legal flaw. *s.*

اننگ अनंग *an-aṅg*, m. (literally, bodiless), the god Kāma, the Hindū Cupid. *s.*

انني अन्नी *annī*, a female nurse. *h.*

آنو आंव *āṅw*, m. the glutinous whitish matter or mucus voided by people afflicted with a tenesmus. *s.*

انو अणु *aṇū* or *aṇu*, m. an atom; adj. atomic, minute. *s.*

انوا अनुवा *anuwā*, m. the place where men stand when throwing the *bokā*, or water-bucket. *h.*

ان واد अनुवाद *anuvād*, m. repetition; answer. *s.*

انوادي अनुवादी *anuvādī*, a defendant, opponent. *s.*

انوار *anwār* (pl. of نور), lights, rays of light, splendour. *a.*

انوارت अनिवारित *a-nivārit*, unchecked, unopposed. *s.*

انواسا संवासा *aṅwāsā*, old, stale, seasoned; m. a handful of corn or grass cut in reaping. *h.*

انواسنا संवासना *aṅwāsnā*, a. to season (a new earthen vessel, by letting water remain in it some time), to rinse. *h.*

انواع *anwā'* (pl. of نوع), sorts, kinds, varieties; adj. various, diverse. *anwā' o aḳsām*, all sorts and kinds. *a.*

انوپ अनूप *anūp*, incomparable, best, rare; m. a watery or moist soil. *s.*

انوپان अनूपान *anūpān*, m. a fluid vehicle wherewith to swallow medicine. *s.*

انوت अन्वित *anvit*, connected with, possessed of, fraught with. *s.*

انوٹ अनवट *anwaṭ*, m. a ring furnished with little balls, worn on the great toe. *h.*

انوٹھا अनूठा *anūṭhā*, rare, wonderful, uncommon. *h.*

انودهان अनवधान *an-avadhān*, careless, inattentive; also *an-avadhānatā*, f. carelessness, inadvertence, indifference. *s.*

انور *anwar*, splendid, shining, resplendent. *a.*

انوري *anwarī*, name of a Persian poet. *p.*

انوستها अनवस्था *an-avasthā*, unstable, unsteady; incontinent; f. instability, absence of fixed state; uncertainty; incontinence. *s.*

انوسر अनवसर *a-navasar*, busy, having no leisure; inopportune; m. want of leisure, unseasonableness. *s.*

انوکها अनोखा, अनौखा *anokhā* or *anaukhā*, rare, wonderful, uncommon (generally applied to man). *h.*

انول आंवल *aṅwal*, m. the after-birth, secundines. *aṅwal-nāl*, the navel-string of a new-born infant. *h.*

آنولا आंवला *āṅwalā*, m. a fruit so called, a kind of myrobalans (*Phyllanthus emblica*). *h.*

انولاسار *aṅolāsār*, m. a sort of brimstone so called. *s.*

آنول نال *āṅwal-nāl*, m. the navel-string of a new-born infant. *s.*

انومان *anūmān* (v. *anumān*), inference, logical conclusion. *s.*

انونا अनोना *a-nonā*, without salt. *s.*

آنه *āna* (v. *ānā*), the 16th part of a rupee. *h.*

انه उन्ह *unh* and इन्ह *inh*, oblique plural forms of the pronouns *wuh* and *yih*. (Vide Gram.) *h.*

انوي अन्वय *anvai*, or *anvaya*, m. race, lineage; interpretation; making out the natural order or connexion of poetical style. *s.*

انويشن अन्वेषण *anveshan*, m. inquiry, research, investigation. *s.*

انويشي अन्वेषी *anveshī*, searching, inquisitive. *s.*

انهار *anhār* (pl. of نهر), rivers, streamlets. *a.*

انهار उन्हार *unhār*, f. mode, appearance; adj. like, similar. *s.*

انهان अन्हान *anhān*, m. bathing, washing. *h.*

انهانا अन्हाना *anhānā*, a. to bathe, to wash. *h.*

انهت अनहित *an hit*, unfriendly, hostile; hostility. *s.*

انهتر उनहत्तर *unhattar*, sixty-nine. *h.*

انهدام *inhidām*, m. perdition, act of abolishing, extermination, demolition. *a.*

انهنكار अनहङ्कार *an-ahankār*, m. absence of pride, humility. *an-ahankārī*, humble. *s.*

انهوانا अन्हवाना *anhwānā*, a. to wash, to bathe, to cause to be bathed or washed. *s.*

آنهون आनिहौं *ānihaun*, aor. first pers. sing. of *ānnā*, to bring (obsolete form). *h.*

انهونهار अन्होन्हार *an-honhār*, hopeless, unpromising, improbable. *h.*

انهونا अन्होना *an-honā*, impossible, not to be. *h.*

اني अणि, आणि *ani*, *āni*, m. f., or अणी *anī*, f. the point of a spear, or of an arrow, the stem or prow of a boat, &c. *s.*

اني अन्नी *annī*, f. a nurse or female attendant on a child. *h.*

انيايي अन्याय *a-nyā,e* or *a-nyāya*, m. injustice, outrage; a complaint of injustice. *s.* [lawless. *s.*

انيائي अन्यायी *a-nyāyī*, unjust, unequitable,

انيپروا अन्यपूर्वा *anya-pūrvā*, f. a woman who has been previously married. *s.*

انيت अनीति *a-nīti*, f. injustice, impropriety, rudeness, impolicy, unmannerliness. *s.*

انيتر अन्यत्र *anyatra*, elsewhere. *s.*

انيتها अन्यथा *anyathā*, otherwise, in a different manner; inaccurately; adj. contrary. *s.*

انيدا उनीदा *unīdā*, unshut (eye), sleepless; expanded (as a flower). *s.*

انير *anyar*, very bright, most luminous. *a.*

انيس उनीस *unīs*, nineteen. *h.*

انيس *anīs* or *anīs-jalīs*, m. a companion. *a.*

انيسون *anīsūn*, m. aniseed. *g.*

انيك अनेक *an-ek*, much, many, abundant. *anek-ākār*, multiform. *anek-rūp*, multiform, of various kinds, of variable mind. *anek-kāl*, adv. a long time. *anek gotrā*, one who is a member of more than one *gotrā*, or family. *anek-vidh*, various, of many kinds, in different ways. *s.*

انيكني अनीकिनी *anīkinī*, f. an army; a certain force, one tenth of an *akshauhinī*. *s.*

انيگوتر अन्यगोत्र *anya-gotra*, of another race or lineage. *s.*

انيه अन्य *anya*, other, different. *anya-janam*, m. another birth, regeneration. *anya-manas*, fickle, versatile. *s.*

انيونيه अन्योन्य *anyonya*, reciprocal, mutual. *s.*

آنييار आनेयार *āneyār*, m. the time allotted for agricultural labour in the hot season, from sunrise till noon. *s.*

او *au*, conj. and (more com. *aur*). *h.*

او *o* (in Pers. and Dakh.) third pron. he, she, it; the vocative interj. O!

او अव *ava*, a Sanskrit prefix denoting negation, disrespect, or dispersion; from, down from, off. *s.*

آوا आवा *āwā*, m. a potter's kiln; a furnace. *h.*

آواتي आवाती *āwātī*, f. the coming of an army, the approach of a friend; the season in which merchandize is expected to arrive; advance; rumour, tidings. *h.*

آواجائي आवाजाई *āwā-jā,ī*, f. coming and going, intercourse, dancing attendance upon one. *h.*

اواچيه अवाच्य *a-vāchya*, dumb, speechless. *s.*

اواخر *awākhir* (pl. of آخر), extremes, ends; the last ten days of a lunar month. *a.*

اوادان *awādān* (see *ābādān*), dwelling, &c. *d.*

اواداني *awādānī* (v. اباداني) *d.* [crop. *h.*

اوار उवार *uwār*, ploughing up a standing

اوار अवार *awār*, f. delay; injustice, tyranny. *s.p.*

اوارجه *awārija*, آوارجه *āwārija*, آوارچه *āwārcha*, } m. a diary, a rough note-book or account-book. *p.*

آوارگي *āwāragī*, f. vagrancy, profligacy. *p.*

آواره *āwāra*, vagabond, wanderer. *āwāra-h.*, n. to wander, to be distressed, to be oppressed, to be miserable. *āwāra-k.*, a. to harass, to expel. *p.*

آواز *āwāz*, f. sound, voice, report, fame, echo, a whisper, sentence. *āwāz-uṭhānā*, to raise the voice, to spread a report. *āwāz par kān rakhnā*, to hear, to listen. *āwāz parnā*, to be reported. *āwāz baiṭhnā*, to be suppressed (the voice) from hoarseness or otherwise. *āwāz-baiṭhā*, hoarse. *p.*

آوازا *āwāzā*, آوازه *āwāza*, } m. report, fame, rumour; conversation, loud talking. *p.*

آواس आवास *āwās*, m. a house, a habitation. *s.*

اواسط *awāsiṭ* (pl. of اوسط), middles, the period of a lunar month between the tenth and twentieth days. *a.* [ley (v. supl. Gloss). *h.*

اواسي आवासी *awāsī*, unripe corn, chiefly bar-

آواگمن आवागमन *āwāgaman*, آواگون आवागवन *āwāgavan*, } m. coming and going, transmigration. *s.*

اوال अवाल *awāl*, m. an inclosed space formed by a cluster of peasants' houses. *h.*

آوام *āwām*, m. loan, debt; colour. *p.*

آوان *āwān* (pl. of آن), times, seasons. *a.*

آواهن आवाहन *āwāhan*, m. calling, summons, a respectful invitation. *s.*

اوائي अवाई *awā,ī*, f. approach, advance; a saddle cloth adorned with fringes, &c.; a kind of pickaxe. *h.*

آوائي आवाई *āwā,ī*, آواتي आवाती *āwātī*, } f. rumour, mention, tidings, report. *h.*

اوائل *awā,il* (pl. of اول), m. commencements, &c.; the first ten days of a lunar month, which, consisting of thirty days nearly, is divided into three decades, 1st. *awā,il*, 2nd. *awāsiṭ*, and 3rd. *awākhir*. *a.*

اوباش *aubāsh*, m. a rake, a dissolute fellow; a mixed crowd of all nations and all sorts of people, but especially of the meanest; the mob, the canaille. *aubāsh-h.*, to become depraved or dissolute. *aubāshāna*, like a rake, dissolute. *p.*

اوباشي *aubāshī*, m. rakishness, dissoluteness, attending at games and spectacles. *p.*

اوبالنا *ūbālnā*, a. same as ابالنا *ubālnā*. *d.*

اوبٹ ऊबट or औबट *ūbaṭ, aubaṭ*, impassable, steep, inaccessible. *s.*

اوبلنا *ūbalnā*, same as ابلنا *ubalnā*. *d.*

اوبھ ऊभ *ūbh*, m. oppressive heat, languor brought on by the effect of heat. *h.*

اوبھاجيه अविभाज्य *a-vibhājya* (in law language), indivisible (as property, etc.). *s.*

اوبھٹ औभट *aubhaṭ*, steep, impassable. *s.*

آوبھکت आवभक्ति *āwbhakt*, or *āwbhakti*, آوبھگت आवभगत or आवभगति *āwbhagat* or *āwbhagati*, } f. a civil reception or salutation, welcome, courteousness. *h.*

اوبھنا ऊभना *ūbhnā*, n. to be agitated or oppressed with heat; to be angry or dissatisfied. *h.*

اوپ ओप *op*, f. ornament, beauty, elegance, grace, brightness, polish. *h.*

اوپٹنا *ūpaṭnā*, n. to exceed, &c. (same as اپٹنا *upaṭna*). *d.*

اوپجنا *ūpajnā*, n. to grow, &c. (v. اپجنا *upajnā*). *d.*

اوپچي ओपची *opchī*, m. an armed man, armed with weapons; a man armed in mail. *opchī-khāna*, a guardhouse or post of armed men. *h.*

اوپر ऊपर *ūpar*, above, on, up, upon, upwards, over, outside, past, top. *ūpar-se*, from above. *ṭūfān ūpar se chalā gayā*, the storm has passed over. *s.*

اوپرلا *uparlā*, upper, superficial; m. the surface or outside. *s.*

اوپري ऊपरी *ūparī*, upper or external; foreign, strange. *s.*

اؤُت अऊत *a,ūt* or ऊत *ūt*, m. one who dies without leaving issue; an unmarried man; (in Hindū phraseology) a stupid person, a blockhead. *h.*

اوت ओत *ot*, overplus, surplus; abatement; convalescence, recovering from sickness. *h.*

اوتا ऊता or ओता *ūtā* or *otā*, so much, that much. *h.*

اوتاد *awtād* (pl. of وتد), pegs, props; met. chiefs, nobles (being the props of the state). *a.*

اوتار *ūtār*, m. (for *utār*) descent, reduction in price; ebb tide, or low water.

اوتار अवतार or औतार *avatār* or *autār*, m. birth, descent; incarnation of the deity (the Hindūs reckon the following ten of the god Vishnu:—1st. *matsya*, a fish; 2nd. *kachchhapa*, a tortoise; 3rd. *varāha*, a boar; 4th. *nri-singha*, a man-lion; 5th. *vāmana*, a dwarf; 6th. *parashurāma*; 7th. *rāma*; 8th. *balarāma*; 9th. *buddha*; 10th. *kalki*); a pious or distinguished person in the language of flattery is also called an *avatār*, or incarnation of the deity; a *tīrth*, or sacred place; translation; crossing. *s.*

اوتارن *ūtāran*, m. stripping off, act of dismounting. *d.*

اوتارنا *ūtārnā*, a. same as اتارنا *utārnā*. *d.*

اوتاول *ūtāwal*, m. same as اتاول q. v. *d.*

اوتاولپنا *ūtāwal-panā*, m. haste, urgency. *d.*

اوتر *ūtar*, m. an answer (v. *uttar*). *d.*

اوترنا अवतरना or औतरन *avatarnā* or *autarnā*, n. to descend, especially as an incarnation of the deity. *s.*

اوترنا *ūtarnā*, n. same as اترنا *utarnā*. *d.*

آوتي आवती *āwatī*, f. approach, advance, the season in which merchandise is expected. *h.*

اوتسك औत्सुक *otsuk*, اوتسكيه औत्सुक्य *autsukya*, } m. anxiety, perturbation, regret; eagerness, impatience. *s.*

اوتك ओतिक or ऊतिक *otik* or *ūtik*, that much, or many. *h.*

اوتكرش औत्कर्ष *autkarsh*, m. excellence. *s.*

اوتنا ऊतना or ओतना *ūtnā* or *otnā*, that much or many. *h.*

اوٹ ओट *oṭ*, f. protection, shade, shelter, partition, screen. *oṭ-k.*, to conceal, to screen. *oṭ-h.*, to be concealed. *s.*

اوٹا ओटा *oṭā*, m. a partition-wall, or screen. *h.*

اوٹانا *auṭānā*, a. to make hot, cause to boil. *d.*

اوٹ پٹانگ ऊटपटाङ्ग *ūṭ-paṭāng*, poor, helpless, destitute. *h.*

اوٹ پٹانگي ऊटपटाङ्गी *ūṭ-paṭāngī*, one who speaks inconsiderately, without preparation. *h.*

اوٹ پٹنگ ऊटपटङ्ग *ūṭ-paṭang*, m. absurdity, nonsense, what is without meaning or foundation; adj. poor, helpless, destitute, in disorder. *ūṭ-paṭangī*, the same as *ūṭ-paṭāngī*. *h.*

اوٹن औटन *auṭan*, boiling, evaporation by boiling; m. a knife used for cutting tobacco. *h.*

اوٹنا ओटना *oṭnā*, a. to defend, screen, shelter; to thrumb, to separate the seed from cotton; to catch as a ball. *h.*

اوٹنا औटना *auṭnā*, n. to boil (as milk), to evaporate over fire; to consume with rage or vexation; a. to burn, to parch, or dry. *h.*

اوٹھ ओठ *oṭh*, m. the lip. *s.*

اوٹھانا *ūṭhānā*, a. same as اٹھانا *uṭhānā*. *d.*

اوٹھا بٹھانا ऊठाबिठाना *ūṭhā-biṭhanā*, a. to excite, to stir up, to urge. *h.*

اوٹھائي گيرا ऊठाईगीरा *ūṭhā,ī-gīrā*, m. a kind of robber, who plunders by day; they are commonly followers of an army (same as *uṭhā,ī-gīrā*, q. v.). *h.*

اوٹھنا ūṭhnā, m. same as اٹھنا uṭhnā. d.

اوج auj, m. height, summit, the top; dignity, preferment, promotion. auj i falak, the zenith of the sky. a. p.

اوجاڑنا ūjāṛnā, same as اجاڑنا ujāṛnā. d.

اوجال ūjāl, } (for اجال ujal, &c.) bright,
اوجالا ūjālā, } luminous. d.

اوجڑنا ūjaṛna, n. (v. اجڑنا ujaṛnā), to be desolated. d.

اوجس ओजस ojas, m. light, splendour; manifestation; strength, vitality (especially in the fœtus). s.

اوجل ojal (v. ojhal), privacy, shelter, &c. h.

اوجل ūjal, } (for ujjal and ujlā), clear, bright,
اوجلا ūjlā, } pure, &c. d.

اوجلنا ūjalna (for ujalnā), to shine, &c. d.

اوجھ ओझ ojh, m. entrails, stomach, guts. h.

اوجھا ओझा ojhā, m. a diviner, a wizard, a magician (probably from examining the entrails of a victim like the Roman "aruspex"). h.

اوجھڑ ओझड़ or औझड़ ojhaṛ or aujhaṛ, f. thrust, push; in Dakh. ūjhaṛ denotes awkward, clumsy. h.

اوجھل ओझल ojhal, f. privacy, retirement; adj. private, hid. ojhal-k., to conceal, screen. ojhal-h., to be concealed. h.

اوچار अविचार a-vichār, m. want of judgment or consideration, injustice. s.

اوچارت अविचारित a-vichārit, ill-judged, not investigated, unconsidered. s.

اوچاري अविचारी a-vichārī, m. } destitute of
اوچارني अविचारिणी a-vichāriṇī, f. } consideration, unjust. s.

اوچٹ औचट auchaṭ, } suddenly, unexpect-
اوچك औचक auchak, } edly. h.

اوچل अविचल a-vichal, motionless, unmoved, firm. s.

اوچھ औछ auchh, m. name of a root from which an orange colour is extracted (*Morinda citrifolia*). h.

اوچھا ओछा ochhā, adj. light, of little consequence; mean, base or low-born; absurd, trifling; fruitless. ochhā honā, n. to want. h.

اوچھالنا ūchhālnā, a. same as اچھالنا uchhālnā, q. v. d.

اوچھٹ uchhaṭ, retirement, retreat. d.

اوچھلنا ūchhalnā, n. (for اچھلنا uchhālnā, q. v.). d.

اوچھالني ऊछालनी ūchhālnī, f. the multiplication table. h.

اود ऊद ūd, m. an otter. s.

اودا ओदा odā, wet, moist, damp. h.

اودا ऊदा ūdā, m. brown, of a brown colour. h.

اودات औदात audāt, white, white colour. s.

اوداريہ औदार्य audārya, m. munificence, liberality. s.

اوداسيہ औदास्य audāsya, m. solitude, loneliness. s.

اودان औदान audān, m. gratis, what is given over and above, or without purchase; to boot. s.

اوداهٹ ऊदाहट ūdāhaṭ, } f. brownness of co-
اوداي ऊदाई ūdā,ī, } lour. h.

اودبلاو ऊदबिलाव ūd-bilā,o, m. an otter. s.

اودن ओदन odan, m. boiled rice. s.

اودني ओदनी odanī, f. a plant (*Sida cordifolia*). s.

اودھ अवध avadh, f. the name of ayodhyā, vulg. Oude. avadh or avadhi, agreement, promise, time, boundary. s.

اودھ अवधि avadhi, m. limit, term, period; (used adverbially in comp.), as far as, as long as. s.

اودھ अवधि avdhi (for abdhi), m. the ocean. s.

اودھار ūdhār, m. (same as udhār) debt &c. d.

اودھان अवधान avadhān, cautious, attentive; m. caution, attention. s.

اودھر ऊधर ūdhar, thither, thitherwards, on the other side. h.

اودھم ऊधम ūdhām, m. noise; impudence; rebellion, disturbance, uproar. h.

اودھمي ऊधमी ūdhamī, making noise; impudent; rebellious. h.

اودھو ऊधो ūdho, the name of a friend and companion of Krishna. s.

اودھوت अवधूत avadhūt, m. a kind of religious mendicant. s.

اودھوت अवधूत avadhūt or audhūt, large, gigantic; frightful as to form. s.

اودھي ओधे odhe, adj. possessing a right or title to; m. a proprietor, supreme ruler. s.

اودھيڑنا ūdheṛnā (same as udheṛna q. v.). d.

اودھيہ अवध्य a-vadhya, not fit to be slaughtered. s.

آودي आवदी ā,odī, name of a tribe of jāts. h.

اوديا अविद्य a-vidyā, f. ignorance. s.

اوديچ अवदीच avadīch, the name of a tribe of Gujerātī Brāhmans. s.

اوديس audes, } m. a strange or foreign
اوديسا audesā, } country. audesī, a stranger,
اوديسہ audesa, } a foreigner. s.

اوڈھنگا audhangā, improper, out of place. d.

اور ओर or, f. origin, boundary, limit; way, side (ward). us or, that way. or nibāhnā, to be constant to, to protect (for ever). h.

اور और *aur*, conj. and, also, but; adj. more, other; *aur ek*, another, separate, distinct, else. *aur nahīṅ to*, and (if) not then, and in that case then. *aur hī*, quite different, extraordinary. *h.*

آور *āwar*, in compos. bearing, having; as, *zor-āwar*, powerful, having force. *p.*

اوراد *aurād* (pl. of ورد), daily lessons (of the Kur,ān), commemorations, devotional exercises. *a.*

اوراق *aurāq* (pl. of ورق), leaves of a tree or book. *a.*

آوربهاو आविर्भाव *āvirbhā,o*, m. a developing, manifestation, becoming visible. *s.*

آوربهوت आविर्भूत *āvirbhūt*, unfolded, manifested, appeared. *s.*

آورت आवृत *āvṛit*, enclosed, surrounded. *s.*

آورت आवृत्ति *āvṛitti*, f. order, method; a repetition of the same thing, a resolution. *s.*

آورجه *āwarja*, v. آوارجه a day-book, &c. *p.*

آوردا आवर्दा *āwardā*, f. the allotted period of one's life-time. *s.*

آوردن *āwardun* (r. *ār* or *āwar*), to bring, to relate or record. *p.*

آورده *āwarda*, that which is brought or carried. *āwarda-nawīs*, m. a writer or registrar of accounts as delivered. *p.*

اورده ऊर्द्ध *ūrdh* or *ūrddh*, superior, above. *ūrdh-bāhu*, with arms aloft (*a posture of Jogīs*). *s.*

اوردهپنڈ ऊर्द्धपुण्ड *ūrddh-puṇḍ*, a perpendicular line delineated on the forehead by the *vaishnavas* or worshippers of Vishnu. *s.*

اوردهديهك और्द्धदेहिक *aurdh-dehik*, obsequies; whatever is given or performed in remembrance of the dead. *s.*

اوردهريتا ऊर्द्धरेता *ūrddh-retā*, a kind of ascetic or *rishī*, one who lives in perpetual chastity. *s.*

اوردهسانس ऊर्द्धसांस *ūrdh-sāṅs*, m. a gasp, deep inspiration. *s.*

اورس औरस *auras*, a legitimate child, *i.e.* by a wife of the same tribe. *s.*

اورس چورس *auras chauras*, all around; breadth and length; m. neighbourhood. *d.*

اورما ओरमा *ormā*, m. the name of a particular kind of sewing, stitching together two breadths. *h.*

آورن आवरण *āvaran*, m. a shield, a covering. *s.*

اورنگ *aurang*, m. a throne; places where goods are manufactured for sale. *p.*

اورنگ زيب *Aurang-zeb*, name of one of the Mogul emperors, who died A.D. 1707. *p.*

اورنگ‌زيبي *aurang-zebī*, m. a kind of cloth so called. *p.*

اورنگ‌شاهي *aurang-shāhī*, m. a kind of silk so called. *p.*

اوروانل और्वानल *aurvānal*, m. submarine fire. *s.*

اورودهه अवरोध *avarodh*, m. the seraglio of a palace, the queen's apartment; a place, a covering; hindrance, obstruction. *s.*

اورودهه अविरोध *a-virodh*, absence of contention, quietness. *avirodhī*, m. *avirodhinī*, f. quiet, tranquil. *s.*

اوري ओरी *orī*, a protector, partial; f. the eaves of a house; bank of a pond or rivulet to the water's edge. *h.*

اوڑا ओड़ा *oṛā*, m. a basket, pannier. *h.*

اوڑن ओड़न *oṛan*, m. a shield, target. *h.*

اوڑنا *oṛnā*, a to ward off a blow: it is also used for *oṛhnā*, to put on dress, &c. *d.*

اوڑنا *ūṛnā*, n. (same as اڑنا *uṛnā*) to fly, &c. *d.*

اوڑني *oṛnī* f. (v. *oṛhnī*), a veil, &c. *d.*

اوڑهنا ओढ़ना *oṛhnā*, a. to put on (dress); m. sheet, cloak, or mantle. *h.*

اوڑهني ओढ़नी *oṛhnī*, f. a smaller sheet; a veil or woman's cloak. *h.*

أوڑي अवड़ी *a,oṛī*, f. a kind of basket (used in a sugar-mill. *h.*

اوڑي‌مارنا *ūṛī-mārnā*, to dive, to plunge. *d.*

اوزار *auzār* (pl. of وزر), m. the rigging and implements of a ship or boat; asylums; loads; weapons, tools, apparatus. *a.*

اوزان *auzān* (pl. of وزن), weights, measures. *a.*

اوس ओस *os*, f. dew. *os paṛ jānī*, to fall in value, to be less in demand than formerly. *ūs*, old form of the oblique pron. *us*, him, her, &c. *h.*

اوساره *ūsāra*, m. gamboge. The name seems to be a corruption of the Arabic or Persian name *'uṣāra,e rāwand* (Extract of rhubarb), which this gum, from its yellow colour, was supposed to be.—(Binning.) *h.*

اوسان औसान *ausān*, m. sensation, sense; courage; presence of mind. *h.*

اوسان अवसान *avasān*, m. the end; conclusion; completion; death; boundary, limit. *s.*

اوس‌برگ ओसबर्ग *os-barg*, m. the name of a medicine. *h.*

اوستاد *ūstād*, preceptor, master (v. *ustād*). *p.*

اوستتا अवस्तुता *a-vastutā*, f. insubstantiality, unreality. *s.*

اوستها अवस्था *ava-sthā*, f. state, condition (frequently used in an unfavourable sense); any particular state varying with the progress of time, as youth, age, &c. *s.*

اوستهي अवस्थी *awasthī*, one of the subdivision of Kanaujiya Brāhmans. *s.*

اوسچ औसुच *ausuch*, without consideration, heedless. *h.*

اوسر अवसर or औसर *avasar* or *ausar*, m. time, leisure, occasion, vacation, opportunity. *s.*

اوسر ओसर *osar*, f. a heifer. *h.*

اوسر *ūsar* (same as *ūshar*, q. v.), barren (land). *s.*

اوسرا ओसरा *osrā*, m. turn, vicissitude. *osrā-osrī*, by turns, alternately. *h.*

اوسرلي *ūsarallī*, f. a chameleon. *d.*

اوسط *ausaṭ*, middle, intervening; m. the middle, medium, interval; mediocrity, moderation. *a.*

اوسطي *ausaṭī*, midmost, middling, moderate. *a.*

اوسنا औसना *ausnā*, n. to become musty, to rot, to putrify. *h.*

اوسي *ūse* (old form of the acc. pron. *use*), him, her, &c. *d.*

اوسير औसेर *āuser*, m. anxiety, solicitude. *h.*

اوسيسا ओसीसा *osīsā*, m. the head of a bed; a pillow, a cushion. *h.*

اوش ओष *osh*, f. dew (same as *os*). *h.*

اوش अवश *a-vash*, subject to another, helpless. *s.*

اوش अविष *a-vish*, anti-venomous, not poisonous. *s.*

اوشا उषा *ushā*, name of the wife of Aniruddha, the son of Kāma-deva. *s.*

آوشٹ आविष्ट *āvishṭ*, possessed (by a demon &c.), engrossed (by a feeling). *s.*

اوشٹھ ओष्ठ *oshṭh*, m. the lip, especially the upper. *oshṭh-rog*, m. a morbid affection of the lips. *s.*

اوشٹھي ओष्ठी *oshṭhī*, f. a creeper bearing a red flower, to which the lip is compared (*bryonia grandis*, or *momordica monodelpha*). *s.*

اوشدھ औषध *aushadh* (also *aukhadh*), f. medicine, drug, herb, mineral, cure, remedy, physic, antidote. *s.*

اوشدھي ओषधि, औषधि, or ओषधी *oshadhi*, *aushadhi*, or *aushadhī* (also *aukhadhī*), f. an annual plant or deciduous herb. *aushadhīya*, medicinal, an ingredient of a medicine; *materia medica*. *s.*

اوشر ऊषर *ūshar*, barren (land), a spot with saline soil.

اوششٹ अवशिष्ट *avashishṭ*, left, remaining. *s.*

اوشن ऊषण *ūshan*, m. black pepper. *s.*

اوشواس अविश्वास *a-vishwās*, m. distrust, unbelief suspicion. *a-vishwāsī*, m. *a-vishwāsin*, *a-vishwāsinī*, f. distrustful, unbelieving. *s.*

اوشيش अवशेष *avashesh*, m. residne, remnant, surplus. *a-vishesh*, m. a want of distinction; adj. indiscriminate. *s.*

آوشيك आवश्यक *āvashyak*,
اوشيه अवश्य *a-vashya*,
اوشيك अवश्यक *a-vashyak*, } necessary, indispensable, inevitable, actual; certainly, necessarily, absolutely, positively, really. *avashyakiā* or *āvashyaktā*, necessity. *s.*

اوصاف *auṣāf* (pl. of وصف), praises, commendations, endowments. *auṣāf-i ḥamīda*, noble properties, praiseworthy qualifications. *a.*

اوصيا *auṣiyā* (pl. of وصي), preceptors, guardians, executors, administrators. *a.*

اوضاع *auẓāʻ* (pl. of وضع), breeding, behaviour, politeness, address, manners, &c. *a.*

اوغرا *oghrā*, m. a kind of dish, flummery, a kind of sick-man's gruel, vulgarly called "conji". *p.*

اوقات *auḳāt* (pl. of وقت), times, circumstances. *auḳāt-ba-sarī*, f. pastime, amusement, employment. *auḳāt-ba-sar* or *-ba-sarī k.*, to spend one's time. *a.*

اوقيت *ūḳiyat*, f. an ounce of silver, or a silver coin of that weight, value between six and seven shillings. *a.*

آوك आवक *āvak*, m. insurance or assurance. *h.*

اوك ओक *ok*, m. a house, a dwelling; an asylum, a refuge; sickness at the stomach, inclination to vomit; a draught of water from the hollow of the hand. *h.*

اوك ऊक *ūk*, f. error, slip, mistake. *h.*

اوكاش अवकाश *ava-kāsh*, m. leisure, opportunity, interval, space. *s.*

اوكال औकाल *aukāl*,
اوكالي औकाली *aukālī*, } untimely, out of season; a child born before its time (properly *ava-kāl*, &c.). *s.*

آوكان आवकान *ā,okān* or *āvakān*, straw and grain heaped up. *h.*

اوكت *ūkat* (same as *ukt* or *ukta*), speech, &c. *d.*

اوكل *aukal*, restless, uneasy. *aukal-bekal*, very restless. *d.*

اوكنا ओकना *oknā*, or ऊकना *ūknā*, n. to vomit. *h.*

اوكنا ऊकना *ūknā*, n. to miss, to err, to trip, to mistake. *h.*

اوكھ ऊख *ūkh*, f. sugar-cane (*Saccharum officinarum*). *s.*

اوكھارنا *ūkhārnā*, a. (for اكھارنا *ukhārnā*), to root up, &c. *d.*

اوكھاڑي ऊखाड़ी *ūkhāṛī*, f. a field of sugar-canes. *s.*

اوكھال *ūkhāl*, m. an emetic. *ūkhāl-jullāb*, cholera morbus. *d.*

اوكھالنا *ūkhālnā*, a. (for *ukhālnā*), to vomit. *d.*

اوكھدھ *aukhadh*, f. (for *aushadh*), medicine. *s.*

اوكھراج ऊखराज *ūkh-rāj*, the day on which the planting of the sugar-cane commences, generally attended with some festive ceremonies. *h.*

آوكھل आवखल *ā,okhal* or *āvakhal*, land reclaimed from waste. *h.*

اوكھلي ओखली *okhlī*, f. a wooden mortar. *s.*

اوكيشي अवकेशी *avakeshī*, barren. *s.*

اوگاه औगाह *augāh*, deep, unfathomable. *s.*

اوگاه अवगाह *avagāh*,
اوگاهن अवगाहन *avagāhan*, } m. bathing, ablution. *s.*

اوگت अवगत *avagat*, known, understood. *avagati*, f. knowledge. *s.*

اوگر *ogar*,
اوگرا *ogrā*, } m. a kind of pottage or gruel (corruption of *oghrā*, q. v.). *d.*

اوگن अवगुण *avagun* or औगुण *augun*, m. blemish, vice, defect, demerit, worthlessness. *s.*

اوگنا *ūgnā*, n. (for *ugnā*), to grow, sprout up, &c. *d.*

اوگني अवगुणी *auguni*, vicious, of a bad dis- [position. *s.*

اوگھ ओघ *ogh*, m. multitude, aggregate, collection. *s.*

اوگھٹ औघट *aughaṭ*, steep, inaccessible. *h.*

اوگھڑ *aughaṛ*, awkward, unpleasant, indiscreet. *d.*

اوگي औगी *augī*, f. a whip like a waggoner's, in length about seven cubits, used in training horses; an ornamental edging of superior country shoes (peculiar to Delhi). *h.*

اوگيا अवज्ञा *avagyā*, f. contempt, despite, dis- [regard. *s.*

اوگيت अवगीत *avagīt*, detested, reproached, wicked, vile; m. reproach, blame. *s.*

اول *awwal*, first, best, principal; (for *aulā*) proper, fit; m. beginning; adv. at first. *a.*

اول ओल *ol*, m. name of a vegetable, of which the root is eaten (*Arum campanulatum, Roxb.*); a hostage or personal security for a debt. *h.*

اولا ओला *olā*, m. hail; the name of a sweetmeat. *olā hojānā*, to become cold. *jon sir mundāyā ton ole parc*, I had no sooner got my head shaved, than a shower of hail came on (spoken of one who has just engaged in an enterprise which turns out unfortunate). *h.*

اولا *aulā* (for *aulā*) better, preferable. *awwalan*, in the first place, firstly. *a.*

اولاد *aulād*, f. (pl. of ولد), children, descendants, progeny, offspring. *a.*

اولانيا *a,olāniyā*, a tribe of *jāṭs* so called. *h.*

اولتي ओलती *oltī*, f. (v. *orī*), the eaves of a house. *h.*

اولٹنا *ūlaṭnā* } for *ulaṭnā*, } q. v. *d.*
اولٹھنا *ūlaṭhnā* } and *ulaṭhnā*, }

اولچھن औलछण *aulachhan*, of evil omen, unfortunate; m. a bad omen. *s.*

اولچھنا *ūlachhnā* (for *ulachhnā*). *d.*

اولکشن अवलक्षण *avalakshan*, } of inauspi-
اولکھن औलखन *aulakhan*, } cious or evil omen; m. a bad omen. *s.*

اول‌کوبي ओलकोबी *ol-kobī*, f. the vegetable commonly called knolcole. *h.*

اولنب अवलम्ब *avalamb*, m. asylum, protection; adj. depending, hanging down. *s.*

اولنب अविलम्ब *a-vilamb*, m. quickness, dili- [gence. *s.*

اولنبت अविलम्बित *a-vilambit*, quick, expeditious. *ava-lambit*, alighting, descending; protected, cherished. *s.*

اولندنا *ūlindnā*, n. (for *ulindnā*), to be poured out, &c. *d.*

اولو ऊलू *ūlū*, } f. a kind of grass used in
اولوا ऊलुआ *ūlu,ā*, } thatching (*Saccharum cylindricum*). *h.*

اولو *ūlū*, prefixed to an Arabic noun denotes possessed of, endowed with. *a.*

اولوکت अवलोकित *avalokit*, a *Jain* saint; adj. [seen. *s.*

اولوکن अवलोकन *avalokan*, m. view, sight, inspection. *s.*

اولوکنا अवलोकना *avaloknā*, a. to see, to look. *s.*

اولي अवली *avalī*, or आवलि *āvalī* (vulg. *aulī*), f. a row; a line; a series, a lineage. *ā,olī*, f. mode of estimating the produce of land. *s.*

اولي *aulā*, better, best, most proper. *ūlā*, the first, &c. (fem. of *awwal*). *a.*

اولي *ūlī*, possessed of, endowed with. *ūlī-l-ajniḥa*, winged animals. *ūlī-l'ilm*, possessed of science. *ūlī-l-abṣār*, wise, prudent. *ūlī-l'azm*, resolute. *a.*

اولي *ūllī*, f. a chisel, a carpenter's tool. *d.*

اولي *olī*, m. (same as *ol*), personal security, hostage. *h.*

آولي *ā,ole*, m. twins, (also *ā,ole-jā,ole*). *d.*

آولي आवली *ā,olī*, f. a mode of estimating crops, the produce of one *biswā* is measured, thence the rest inferred. *h.*

اوليا *auliyā* (pl. of ولی), friends, companions (particularly of the prophets); the apostles, the saints, the holy. *auliyā-i-allāh*, friends of God; in law it signifies the next of kin, or other person entitled to exact retaliation (v. *walī*). *a.*

اوليت *awwalīyat*, f. priority, pre-eminence, excellence, superiority. *a.*

اوليتر *aulā-tar*, better, best. *a. p.*

اولي چاولي *aule chā,ole*, a twin, twins. *d.*

اولين *awwalīn* (pl.), the first, former, ancient. *awwalīn o ākhirīn*, the ancients and the moderns. *a.*

اوم ओम् *om*, the mystic name of the Deity prefacing all the prayers and most of the writings of the Hindūs: it is said to imply the Indian Triad or Trinity, Brahma, Vishnu, Shiva. *s.*

اوم अवम *avam*, low, vile, inferior. *s.*

اومس *ūmas*, m. (for *umas*), resolution, &c. *d.*

اومندنا *ūmandnā*, m. (for *umanḍnā*), to be proud, &c. *d.*

اومي ऊमी *ūmī*, f. an ear of corn (half ripe). *h.*

اون ऊण or ऊन *ūn*, f. wool. *gāḍar ānī ūn kon baiṭhī chare kapās*, "I bought the sheep for (furnishing) wool, and she is eating up the cotton" (spoken of any thing done by way of economy which turns out in the end very expensive). *s.*

اون *ūn* (for اُن *un*), oblique pl. of *wuh*, he, &c. *d.*

اون ऊन *ūna*, less, defective, minus; prefixed to a Sanskrit numeral it denotes "one less;" thus *ūna-trinshat*, one less thirty, twenty-nine. So *ūna-trinshatam*, the twenty-ninth; hence the modern forms in Hindūstānī, *untīs*, twenty-nine; *unchālis*, thirty-nine, &c. *s.*

آون *ā,on*, m. fæculent matter, mucus. *d.*

آون आवन *āwan*, m. coming, approach, arrival. *s.*

آون آون आवन आवन *āwan-āwan*, f. tidings of arrival. *s.* [come. *s.*

آونا आवना *āwanā* (old form of *ānā*), n. to

اونا ऊना *ūnā*, m. a kind of sword, a scimitar, a knife, &c., worn down by grinding. *h.*

اوناش अविनाश *a-vināsh*, exception from loss, safety. *a-vināshī*, safe, entire, free from loss, everlasting. *s.*

اونتکا अवंतिका *avantikā*, } f. the name of a city,
اونتي अवंती *avantī*, } Ujjain, anciently Ujjayini. *s.*

اونتيس *ūntīs*, Dakhanī for *untīs*, twenty-nine.

اونٹ ऊंट *ūnṭ*, m. a camel; Dakh. *onṭ* (for *honṭh*), the lip. *h.*

اونٹ کٹار ऊंट कटारा *ūnṭ-kaṭārā*, m. name of a thistle of which camels are fond (*Eschinops echinatus, Roxb.*). *h.*

اونٹنا *aunṭnā*, n. (same as *auṭnā*), to boil. *h.*

اونٹني ऊंटनी *ūnṭnī*, f. a female camel. *h.*

اونٹھ ओंठ *onṭh*, m. the lip (com. *honṭh*). *s.*

اونجري ऊंजरी *ūnjarī* or *unjarī*, f. a small heap of corn set apart (by Musalmāns) in harvest-time in the name of some saint. *h.*

اونچ ऊंच *ūnch*, } high, tall, lofty, steep,
اونچا ऊंचा *ūnchā*, } loud. *ūnch-nīch*, ups and downs, inequality; vicissitudes in fortune, &c. *ūnchā bol bolnā*, to speak with pride. *ūnchā sunnā*, to be hard of hearing. *ūnchā-hānī*, f. deafness. *ūnche bol kā munh nīchā*, the proud ones are degraded. *s.*

اونچاس *ūnchās* (for *unchās*), forty-nine. *d.*

اونچاس ऊंचास *ūnchās*, f. }
اونچان ऊंचान *ūnchān*, m. } elevation, height,
اونچاؤ ऊंचाव *ūnchā,o*, m. } eminence, exaltation, tallness,
اونچاهٹ ऊंचाहट *ūnchāhaṭ*, f. } steepness. *s.*
اونچائي ऊंचाई *ūnchā,ī*, f. }

اونچاليس *ūnchālīs* (for *unchālīs*), thirty-nine. *d.*

اونچانا ऊंचाना *ūnchānā*, a. to raise, elevate. *s.*

اوند *avind* or *āwand*, m. a pan, a vessel. *p.*

اوند अविन्दु *a-vindu*, without point or dot. *s.*

اوندھ ओंध *ondh*, m. the cord with which rafters or frames for thatching on are pulled into their place, and fastened till the roof is finished. *h.*

اوندھا औंधा *aundhā* or ओंधा *ondhā*, upside down, overturned. *aundhā-bakht*, m. misfortune, adverse fortune. *aundhī-peshānī*, short-sighted, unfortunate. *aundhā leṭnā*, n. to lie on one's face. *h.*

اوندھانا औंधाना *aundhānā*, a. to turn upside down, to reverse, to overturn, to spill. *h.*

اوندھنا औंधना *aundhnā*, n. to lower (as the sky. *h.*

اونڈا औंडा *aunḍā*, or ओंडा *onḍā*, deep. *h.*

اونڈيلنا *ūnḍelnā*, a. (for *unḍelnā*), to pour out. *d.*

اونساٹھ *ūnsāṭh*, } (for *unsaṭh*), fifty-nine. *d.*
اونسٹھ *ūnsaṭh*, }

اونسو *ūnsau*, one less a hundred, ninety-nine. *d.*

اونکار ओंकार *onkār*, m. the mysterious syllable *om*. *s.* [son.)

اونگلي *awingillī*, a mode of torture. (v. Wil-

اونگنا *ūngnā*, n. (for *ūnghnā*), to doze. *d.*

اونگھ ऊंघ *ūngh*, f. nodding, sleepiness. *h.*

اونگھاس ऊंघास *ūnghās*, } f. drowsiness, nod-
اونگھائي ऊंघाई *ūnghā,ī*, } ding, sleepiness, drooping (especially from opium). *h.*

اونگھنا ऊंघना *ūnghnā*, n. to nod from sleepiness, to doze, to droop. *h.*

اونگي औंगी *aungī*, f. silence, dumbness. *h.*

اونلا औंला *aunlā*, *ā,onlā*, or *ā,onla*, m. (same as *āmla*), the emblic myrobalan (*phyllanthus emblica*). *aunlā-sār*, m. a sort of brimstone.

اونلاجونلا *aunlā-jaunlā*, a twin, twins. *a.*

اونن *ūnan* (same as انهون *unhon*), those, them (also *ūnū* and *ūnon*). *d.*

آونون आवनौं *āwanaun*, n. (Braj.) to come. *h.*

اونهتر *ūnhattar* (for *unhattar*), sixty-nine. *d.*

اونهون *ūnhūn*, an interjection, denoting refusal or negation. *d.*

اونهين ऊंहीं *ūnhīn* (for *wonhīn*), exactly in that manner, even so. *h.*

اوني ऊणी or ऊनी *ūnī*, woollen, made of wool. *s.*

اوني *ū-ne* (same as اسي *us-ne*), he, by him, &c. *d.* [want of submission. *s.*

اوني अविनय *a-vinay*, m. pertness, wantonness,

اوني پوني औनेपौने *aune-paune*, partially, more or less; on occasion. *h.*

آونيهار आवनेहार *āwanehār*, } the future,
آوني هارا आवनेहारा *āwane-hārā*, } that which is about to come. *s.*

اونيت अविनीत *a-vinīt*, misbehaving, acting improperly. *a-vinītā*, f. an unchaste woman. *s.*

اووادي अविवादी *a-vivādī*, not disputatious. *s.*

اوويك अविवेक *a-vivek*, m. want of discrimination, indiscretion. *avivekatā*, f. indiscreetness, inconsiderateness. *aviveki*, indiscreet, inconsiderate. *s.*

اوهـ अह *ūh*, m. reasoning, logic. *s.*

آوه *āwa*, m. a brick-kiln; a forge. *p.*

اوهو ओहो *oho*, interj. heigho! alas! *h.*

اوئي अई *ū,ī*, interj. Oh! oh fye! *h.*

اوياپت अव्याप्ति *a-vyāpti*, f. the not diffusing itself; not pervading. *s.*

اوياكل अव्याकुल *a-vyākul*, calm, firm, composed. *s.*

آويختن *āwekhtan* (r. *āwez*), to hang by, to cling to, to be suspended. *p.*

آويخته *āwekhta*, suspended, pendulous. *p.*

اوير अवेर *awer* or *aver* (for *a-ber*), delay, lateness, &c. *s.*

اويرا अवीरा *a-vīrā*, f. a childless widow. *s.*

آويز *āwez* or *āwezān* (in comp.) suspending, adhering. *āwez-k.*, a. to hang, to suspend. *p.*

آويزه *āweza*, m. an ear-ring, drops or pendants worn in the ears as ornaments. *p.*

آويزه‌بند *āweza-band*, an ear-ring. *p.*

اويكت अव्यक्त *a-vyakta*, adj. indistinct, unapparent, invisible; m. the Supreme Being, or Universal Spirit; the soul, nature, temperament. *s.*

اويوستها अव्यवस्था *a-vyavasthā*, irregular. *s.*

اويوستهت अव्यवस्थित *a-vyavasthit*, not regulated, undisciplined, not put in order. *s.*

اويي अव्यय *a-vyaya*, m. an indeclinable word, a particle; a name of Vishnu; adj. economical, parsimonious. *s.*

آه *āh*, f. sigh; interj. alas! *āh bharnā*, a. to sigh. *āhi jān-kāh*, a heartrending sigh. *āhi jigar-soz*, a heartburning sigh. *āhi-sard*, a cold or sorrowful sigh. *āh-khainchnī*, f. heaving a sigh. *p.*

اه *uh*, interj. Oh! ah! hah! *p.*

اهي अहि *ahi*, m. a serpent, a snake. *s.*

اه इह *ih* (for *yih*), this. *ih-kāl*, m. this life. *ih-lok*, the present world. *ihī*, this very. *ihī-thān*, here, in this very place. *h.*

آهي आहि *āhi* (Braj.), is, exists. *h.*

اها आहा *ahā*, alas! woe's me! bravo! well done! *d.*

اهار उहार *uhār*, m. a covering, a cover of a litter or palkī for women. *h*

اهار अहार *ahār*, m. starch, glue, paste. *h.*

آهار आहार *āhār* (vulg. *ahār*), m. aliment, food, victuals. *s.*

اهارنا अहारना *ahārnā*, a. to paste, to starch. *h.*

اهالي *ahālī* (pl. of اهل), inhabitants, common people. *ahālī-mawālī*, the people at large, rich and poor. *a.*

اهان अहां *ahāṅ*, interj. do not, no, nay. *h.*

اهانت *ihānat*, f. contempt, disdain, enmity, affront, insult. *a.*

اهاهاها अहाहाहा *ahāhāhā*, interj. used in praise; also expressive of surprise, pain, or pleasure. *s.*

آهبان आह्वान *āhbān*, m. a call, imitation, summons. *s.*

اهيپهين अहिफेन *ahi-phen*, m. the saliva or venom of a snake. *s.*

اهت अहित *a-hit*, an un-friend, enemy; enmity, want of affection; adj. hostile, prejudicial. *ahit-kārī*, inimical, acting unkindly. *ahit-manā*, inimical, hating. *s.*

آهت आहुत *āhut* and आहुति *āhuti*, m. offering, oblations with fire to the deities; a burnt-offering. *s.*

اهتدا *ihtidā*, being directed in the right way (spiritually). *a.*

اهتمام *ihtimām*, f. diligence, solicitude, anxiety, care; inspection, superintendence; a subdivision of a province. *a.*

اهتمام‌دار *ihtimām-dār*, m. a superintendant of the revenues, &c. of an *ihtimām* or district. *a. p.*

اهتمامي *ihtimāmī*, m. a curator or manager. *a.*

آهٹ आहट *āhaṭ*, f. sound, noise, clack. *h.*

اهر अहर *ahar*, name of a tribe of *rāj-pūts*. *h.*

آهر आहर *āhar*, } a small pond, a salt-pit,
آهري आहरी *āharī*, } a drain, a trough for watering cattle. *s.*

آهرجاهر आहरजाहर *āhar-jāhar*, f. coming and going. *h.*

اهرشت अहर्षित *a-harshit*, unhappy, sorrowful. *s.*

اهرمان *ahrimān*, m. the spirit or principle of evil (among the fire worshippers). *p.*

اهرنا उहरना *uharnā*, n. to subside (a swelling or inundation. *h.*

اهرنش अहर्निशि *ahar-nishi*, day and night. *s.*

اهره अहरः *ahra*, m. a reservoir for collecting rain-water to water the fields; fuel made of cowdung. *s.*

اهري अहरी *ahrī*, f. a small pond (v. *āhar*). *h.*

آهستگي *āhistagī* (or *āhastagī*), f. slowness, delay; gentleness, softness. *p.*

آهسته *āhista* (or *āhasta*), gently, slowly; softly, tenderly. *āhista-raw*, slow paced. *p.*

آهستے *āhiste* (vulg. *āste*), gently, slowly, easily. *p.*

آهك *āhak*, m. quicklime, cement, plaster: it also denotes an *abwāb*, or cess upon lime. *āhak-tafta*, quicklime. *p.*

اهل *ahl*, m. people, master; (in comp.) attached to, possessed of, &c., as *ahl ullāh*, people of God, dervises, *faḳīrs*. *ahli ijtihād*, qualified jurists. *ahli khirad*, people of wisdom. *ahli bait*, family (*i.e.* wife and children), but generally means the family of the Prophet. *ahli ḥuḳūḳ*, possessed of rights, or of just claims. *ahli-dil*, dervises, liberal, brave, generous. *ahli-ẕauḳ*, addicted to pleasure, a voluptuary. *ahli rozgār*, skilful, knowing the world. *ahli zamān*, time-servers. *ahli zamīn*, an inhabitant of the earth. *ahli zuhd*, pious, devout. *ahli sunnat*, the followers of the traditional as well as the written law: the Sunnī sect in opposition to that of the Shī'as. *ahli shar'*, a legislator, a lawyer, one who obeys and observes the law of the Prophet. *ahli ṣafā*, possessor of purity; a *ṣūfī*; a voluptuary. *ahli shinākht*, men of intelligence. *ahli ṭā'at*, faithful, obedient to God. *ahli ṭabḳa*, one who does not observe the precepts of *Muḥammad*. *ahli ṭarīḳ*, an observer of the laws of *Muḥammad*. *ahli ẓarf*, noble. *ahli 'irfān*, learned. *ahli 'aḳl*, wise. *ahli 'ilm*, scientific. *ahli faẓl*, virtuous. *ahli kār*, a workman, a clerk. *ahli kitāb*, a learned man; a person of any religion revealed and contained in books (the Musulmāns allow that the Jews and Christians are *ahli kitāb*, whereas the Hindūs are considered as idolaters). *ahli karam*, liberal, generous. *ahli majlis*, an assistant, a member of (genteel) society, a courtier. *ahli-maṣārif*, a proprietor. *ahli-ma'āsh*, the holder of a rent-free tenure. *ahli ma'rifat*, possessed of the knowledge of God. *ahli manṣab*, a minister, a person in office. *ahli naṣrat*, colleagues, coadjutors. *ahli nifāḳ*, infidels, enemies. There is no limit to compounds of this sort: two more I may here add—*ahli saif*, a military man; *ahli ḳalam*, a civilian. *a.*

آهل आहल *āhal*, m. freshness of soil. *h.*

آهلا आहला *āhlā* or *ihlā*, m. inundation, deluge, flood, overflow. *h.*

آهلاد आह्लाद *āhlād*, m. joy, gladness, mirth, festivity. *s.*

آهلادت आह्लदित *āhlādit*, joyful, glad, merry.

اهلاك *ihlāk*, m. destroying, ruining. *a.*

آهلو आहलो *āhlo*, inundation, flood, &c. *h.*

اهلوك इहलोक *ihaloh*, m. this present world. *s.*

اهليا *ahliyā*, f. a wife. *sarā,e ahliyā*, the women's apartments, hence "seraglio."

اهليا अहल्या *ahalyā*, wife of Gotam, and daughter of Brahmā; one of the Apsarās. *h.*

اهليت *ahlīyat*, f. worth, worthiness, excellence; possession. *a.*

اهم *ahamm*, important. *ahammi kār*, important business. *a.*

اهم अहं *aham*, pron. I. *aham-mati*, spiritual ignorance; conceit, self-love. *s.*

اهمال *ihmāl*, m. } negligence, indolence, in-
اهمالي *ihmālī*, f. } attention, delay, carelessness. *a.*

اهن अहं *ahaṅ*, don't, not, no, nay. *h.*

آهن *āhan*, m. iron. *āhan-rubā*, m. a loadstone. *āhan-gar*, an ironsmith or blacksmith. *āhangarī*, the trade of an ironsmith. *p.*

اهنسا अहिंसा *a-hinsā*, f. harmlessness. *s.*

اهنسك अहिंसक *a-hinsah*, harmless, innocuous. *s.*

آهنك आह्निक *āhnik*, m. the constant or daily ceremonies of religion, daily work; adj. daily, diurnal. *āhnikī*, adj. of or belonging to a day. *s.*

اهنكار अहङ्कार *ahankār*, m. egotism, arrogance, haughtiness, pride. *s.*

اهنكاري अहङ्कारी *ahankārī*, } haughty, arro-
اهنكرت अहङ्कृत *ahankṛit*, } gant, proud, an egotist. *s.*

آهنگ *āhang*, m. design, purpose; sound, melody; one of the Persian tunes or modulations in music. *p.*

آهني *āhanī*, } made of iron. *āhanīn-panja*,
آهنين *āhanīn*, } iron-handed or iron-fisted, strong, powerful. *p.*

آهو *āhū*, m. a deer; a vice, defect, fault. *āhū-bara*, m. a fawn. *āhū-chashm*, having eyes like those of a deer. *āhū-gīr*, a deer catcher. *āhū-girī*, the act of catching deer. *p.*

اهو अहो *aho*, interj. O! holla! sign of the vocative, wonderful! *h.*

اهوراتر अहोरात्र *aho-rātra*, adv. day and night. *s.*

آهوان आह्वान *āhvān*, m. summons, respectful invitation. *s.*

اهي अहे *ahe*, interj. O! sign of the vocative. *s.*

اهي इही *ihī* (for *yihī*), this very. *uhī* (for *wuhī*), that very. *h.*

اهيتك अहेतुक *a-hetuk*, careless, without motive. *s*

اهيٹا अहीटा *ahīṭā* or *ahīṭa*, a person appointed to watch the grain when ripe, and see that the dues are paid ere it be removed. *h.*

اهير अहीर *ahīr*, m. a particular caste in India, whose business is to attend on cows; a cowherd. For a full account of this tribe v. Wilson's Glossary. *s.*

اهير अहेर *aher*, f. prey, game, hunting. *aheru*, f. a plant (*Asparagus racemosus*). *h.*

اهيرن अहीरन *ahīran*, } f. a woman of the
اهيرني अहीरणी *ahīrnī*, } caste of *ahīrs*; a
اهيري अहीरी *ahīrī*, } cowherd's wife. *h.*

اهيري अहेरी *aherī*, } m. a sportsman, a
اهيريا अहेरिया *aheriyā*, } hunter, a fowler. *h.*

اي *ai*, interj. O! the vocative particle. *p.*

اي ए *e*, interj. O! a respectful particle of address. *s.*

آئي आई *ā,ī*, f. coming, arrival. *s.*

آئي आयु *āyu*, f. age. *bin-ā,e marnā* is a phrase apparently connected with *āyu*: it signifies, "to die before one's allotted time," or "in spite of fate." *s.*

آيا *āyā*, an interrogative particle, whether or not? interj. ho! hark you! *p.*

آيا आया *āyā*, f. female attendant on children. *h.*

آيات *āyāt* (pl. of آيت), signs, marks; sentences of the *ḳur,ān*. *a.*

اياز *aiyāz*, name of a favourite slave in the household of *Maḥmūd* of *Ghaznī*. *t.*

آياس आयास *āyās*, m. fatigue, weariness. *s.*

اياغ *ayāgh*, m. a cup, a drinking vessel. *p.*

ايال *ayāl* (for *yāl*), f. a horse's mane, the lock between a horse's ears. *p. h*

ايالت *iyālat*, f. dominion, government. *a.*

ايام *aiyām* (pl. of يوم), days, times; season, weather. *a.*

ايامي *aiyāmī*, durable, for a length of time. *a.*

ايانا अयाना *a-yānā*, ignorant; m. a fool. *a.*

ايبا *ibā*, making a sign with the finger for any one to approach (*īmā* denotes a similar sign to signify departure.) *a.*

ايباغيب *ībāghaib*, ايباغيبي *aibā-ghaibī*, ايبوغيبو *aibū-ghaibū*, } suddenly, unexpectedly, all at once. *d.*

ايت अयुत *ayut*, ten thousand, a myriad. *s.*

آيت आयत *āyat*, long, large, wide; m. the sunshine, sunbeam. *s.*

آيت आयत्त *āyaitta*, docile, tractable. *āyattatā*, f. docility, tractableness. *s.*

آيت *āyat*, f. a sign, mark; a sentence of the *ḳur,ān*, contained between (signs) semicolons, or stops nearly equivalent thereto. *āyat-i muṭlaḳ*, a stop (in gram.), only used in the *ḳur,ān*, nearly equal to a comma. *a.*

ايتا एता *etā* or ईता *ītā*, so much, this much (Dakh. now, at present). *a.*

ايتال *ītāl* (for *itāl*), now, at present. *d.*

ايتاوتا एतावता *etā,otā*, on this account, for this reason. *s.*

ايتاونماتر एतावन्मात्र *etāwan-mātra*, thus much, only this. *s.*

ايتدرته एतदर्थ *etad-arth*, therefore, on that account. *s.*

ايتر ईतर *ītar* (v. *itrānā*), affectation; adj. acting affectedly. *h.*

ايتك एतिक *etik*, this much or many. *h.*

ايتلاف *ītilāf*, m. familiarity, friendship, society, connection, company, correspondence. *a.*

ايتم *etam*, m. a large lever for raising water, commonly called a *pacotta*. *d.*

ايتنا एतना *etnā* or *ītnā*, so much. *h.*

ايتوار एतवार *etwār* (v. *itwār*), m. Sunday. *s.*

ايتواري *etwārī*, m. a man confined for debt, who avails himself of the Christian sabbath for appearing abroad. *s.*

آيتي پا,يتي *ā,etī-pā,etī*, low down. *d.*

ايٹ *īṭ*, f. (same as *īṅṭ*), a brick. *s.*

ايٹنا *aiṭnā*, n. to be pulled, dragged. *d.*

ايٹهه ईठ *īṭh*, reverenced, desired, &c. (v. *ishṭa*). *s.*

ايٹي *īṭī*, f. a spear or lance; the cat in boy's play. *īṭī-ḍānḍā*, the ball and crooked stick in the game of chaugān. *d.*

ايثار *īṡār*, presenting, offering. *a.*

ايجاب *ījāb*, m. rendering necessary; (in logic) affirmation (opposite to privation); (in Musalmān law) the first proposal made by one of the parties in negotiating or concluding a bargain. *a.*

ايجاد *ījād*, m. invention; invented. *ījād-h.*, a. to invent. *a.*

ايجاز *ījāz*, abridging, curtailing, epitomizing (a book, &c.). *a.*

آيده आयुध *āyudh*, m. a weapon in general. *s.*

ايدرش ईदृश *īdrish*, thus, such, like this. *s.*

ايدهر ईधर *īdhar* (v. *idhar*), here, hither. *s.*

ايذا *īẕā*, f. pain, trouble, vexation, distress, affliction. *īẕā-dih* or *īẕā-rasān*, one who gives annoyance, &c.; a regular bore. *a.*

ايراب *erāb*, m. the keel of a ship or boat. *d.*

ايراپهير एराफेर *erāpher*, m. } exchange, interchange; dancing attendance. *h.*
ايراپهيري एराफेरी *erāpherī*, f. }

ايراد *īrād*, f. citing, adducing, bringing (a charge). *īrād-k.* to impute blame. *a.*

ايران *īrān*, Persia. *īrān wa turān*, Persia and Tartary, or Persia and Transoxiana. *a.*

ايراني *īrānī*, of or relating to Persia; a Persian; a man of the Shī'a sect. *p.*

ايراوت ऐरावत *airāvat*, the name of Indra's chief elephant. *s.*

ايراوتي ऐरावती *airāvatī*, f. the *Ravī* river in the Panjāb. *s.*

آيربل आयुर्बल *āyurbal*, } f. age, lifetime. *s.*
آيردا आयुर्दा *āyurdā*, }

ايرکها ईर्खा *īrkhā*, } f. emulation, envy, spite. *īrshālu*, envious. *s.*
ايرشا ईर्षा *īrshā*, }

ايرنڈ एरण्ड *erand*, m. or *erandī*, f. the castor-oil plant (*Palma Christi* or *Ricinus communis*). *s.*

ايري एरी *erī*, interj. O! a vocative particle for females. *h.*

ايري پهيري *erī-pherī*, f. exchange, barter, &c. *h.*

ايڑ एड़ *eṛ* or *eḍ*, f. striking with the heel, spurring, a sort of spur, &c. for urging on a horse. *eṛ mārnā*, to spur. *h.*

ايڑکا एड़का *eṛkā*, a large he-goat trained for fighting; a kind of fireworks. *h.*

ايڑگج एड़गज *ergaj*, m. a medicinal plant used for the cure of ring-worms. *s.*

ايڑي एड़ी *eṛī*, f. the heel. *eṛī dekho* (look at your heel) look at home, a phrase used to obviate the effect of an evil eye. *h.*

ايزد *īzid*, God. *īzidī*, divine, any thing bestowed for the love of God. *p.*

ايس ईस *īs*, ⎫ God, a lord, master, su-
ايش ईश *īsh*, ⎭ preme ; a name of *Shiva*. *s.*

آيس आयसु *āyasu*, m. command, order. *h.*

آيس आयुस *āyus*, f. age, lifetime. *s.*

ايسا ऐसा *aisā*, like this, after this manner, sometimes joined to other words, as *mard-aisā*, like a man; *aisā taisā* or *aisā waisā*, so so, indifferent, indifferently. *h.*

ايسان ईशान *īsān* or *īshān*, a name of *Shiva*. *īsān-koṅ*, the north-east. *h.*

ايستا ईशिता *īsitā*, f. lordship, supremacy. *s.*

ايستادگي *īstādagī*, f. erection, stability. *p.*

ايستادن *īstādan* (r. *īst*), to stand, to be erect; to stay. *p.*

ايستاده *īstāda*, erected, set up. *īstāda-k.*, to raise up. *p.*

ايسل *īsal*, m. a winged white ant. *d.*

آيسو आयसू *āyasū*, m. order, command. *h.*

ايسون ऐसों *aisoṅ*, this year. *h.*

ايسي ऐसे *aise*, ⎫ adv. thus; m. this man-
ايسين ऐसें *aisen*, ⎭ ner. *h.*

ايشا ईशा *īshā*, f. the beam or pole of a plough. *s.*

ايشان *eshān* (pl. of *o*), they, those. *p.*

ايشان ईशान *īshān*, m. a name of *Shiva*; light, splendour. *īshān kon*, m. north-east. *s.*

ايشت ईषत *īshat*, adv. a little, somewhat. *s.*

ايشتا ईशिता *īshitā*, f. ⎫ supremacy, one
ايشتوه ईशित्व *īshitwa*, m. ⎭ of the eight attributes of God. *s.*

ايشور ईश्वर *īshwar*, m. ruler, lord; God; a name of *Shiva*, of *Kām-dev*, of *Durgā*, *Lakshmī*, *Saraswatī*, or any other of the *Saktis* or female energies of the deities. *īshwar-ādhīn*, subject to God. *īshwarādhīnatā*, subjection to God. *īshwar-ārādhnā*, f. worship of God. *īshwar-bhāo*, m. the divine nature. *s.*

ايشورتا ईश्वरता *īshwaratā*, f. divine nature; divinity, the godhead. *s.*

ايشوريه ऐश्वर्य्य *aishwarya*, m. grandeur, pomp, state, supremacy, sway; the divine faculties of omnipresence, omnipotence, invisibility, &c. *s.*

ايضاً *aiẓan*, even, also; again; the same; likewise, moreover. *a.*

ايفا *īfā*, m. performing a promise, paying, satisfying. *īfā-k.*, to make good. *a.*

ايك *ek*, one; frequently used like the article *a* or *an*, with us, as *ek mard*, a man, &c.; it is also used in forming compound adjectives in imitation of the Persian, as *ek-dil* or *ek-chit*, of one mind, determined, resolute. *ek-zabān*, of one speech, or of the same mind or sentiments. *ek-se din na rahne*, is applied to a change of condition, most commonly from good to evil, but sometimes the reverse. *ek kī das sunānī*, to reply ten (words) for one (spoken of one who replies in many words, especially in giving abuse). *ek muth*, (Dakh.) agreeing, unanimous. *ek* is frequently united with the following word in writing, as *ekdin* or *ekroz*, one day. *ekdam*, in one instant. *ek ād*, or *ek-ādh*, one half, some few. *ek bār*, once upon a time. *ek-bārgī*, *ekā ek*, or *ekā ekī*, all at once, suddenly. *ek dast* or *ek ḳalam* or *ek-laḳht*, altogether, entirely, utterly. *ek na ek*, either, one or other. *ek dīgar*, one another. *s.*

ايكادش एकादश *ekādash*, eleven. *s.*

ايكادشي एकादशी *ekādashī*, f. the eleventh day of the lunar fortnight. *s.*

ايكادهپتي एकाधिपति *ekādhipati*, m. sole and absolute monarch. *aikādhipatya*, m. absolute sovereignty. *s.*

ايكاكار एकाकार *ekākār*, alike, uniform. *s.*

ايكاكش एकाक्ष *ekāksh*, one-eyed, blind of one eye; m. a crow. *s.*

ايكاكي एकाकी *ekākī*, solitary, alone. *s.*

ايكاگر एकाग्र *ekāgra*, intent, fixed on one object, undisturbed. *ekāgratā*, f. close attention. *s.*

ايكانت एकान्त *ekānt*, aside, apart, alone, solitary, uninhabited. *s.*

ايكانو *ekānaw* or *ekānauwe* (for *ikānawe*), ninety-one. *d.*

ايكاون *ekāwan* (for *ikāwan*), fifty-one. *d.*

ايكاهك ऐकाहिक *aikāhik*, quotidian. *s.*

ايكائي एकाई *ekā,ī*, f. unanimity, unity; solitude, loneliness. *s.*

ايكاء يكي एकाएकी *ekā-ekī*, all at once. *s.*

ايكباچهي एकबाछी *ek-bāchhī*, distribution of any tax or cess levied upon all lands at an equal rate. *h.*

ايكبهكت एकभक्त *ek-bhakt*, worshipping one deity. *ek-bhakti*, of one faith, believing in one deity. *s.*

ايكپتني एकपत्नी *ek-patnī*, f. a faithful wife, one devoted to her husband. *s.*

ايكپكش एकपक्ष *ek-paksha*, m. an associate, a firm ally. *s.*

ايكت अयुक्त *a-yukt* or *a-yukta*, unfit, improper; m. violence, oppression. *s.*

ايكتا एकता *ektā*, f. unity, union, equality. *s.*

ايكتال एकताल *ek-tāl*, m. harmony, unison, adjustment of song, dance and music. *s.*

ايكتاليس *ektālīs* (for *iktālīs*), forty-one. *d.*

ايكتان एकतान *ek-tān*, closely attentive, intent on one object; m. musical unison. *s.*

ايكتر एकत्र *ekatr* or *ekatra*, together, in one place. *s.*

ايكترا एकत्रा *ekatrā*, ⎫ m. a sum total; in-
ايكتره एकत्र *ekatra*, ⎭ terest of one per cent per mouth; adv. together, in one place. *s.*

ايكتراجور एकत्राज्वर *ekatrā-jwār*, m. a tertian ague or fever. *s.*

ايكتها एकथा *ekathā* or *ekthā*, ايكٹها एकठा, एकट्ठा *ekṭhā* or *ekaṭṭhā*, } together, collected; m. a small boat, rowed by one oar. *ekṭhā-k.*, a. to gather, to collect. *s.*

ايکٹک एकटक *ek-ṭak*, m. a fixed look, stare. *s.*

ايکچت एकचित्त *ek-chitt*, intent on, absorbed in one thing; of one mind, agreeing. *s.*

ايكدا एकदा *ekadā*, once, once upon a time. *s.*

ايكدرش एकदृश *ek-drish*, one-eyed. *s.*

ايك دكه سكه एकदुखसुख *ek-dukh-sukh*, sympathizing, sharing joy and sorrow. *s.*

ايكراشي एकराशि *ek-rāshi*, f. a heap, a crowd. *s.*

ايكروپ एकरूप *ek-rūp*, like, similar. *s.*

ايكسا एकसा *eksā*, ايكسار एकसार *eksār*, ايكسان एकसान *eksān*, } similar, identical. *h.*

ايكشرن एकशरण *ek-sharan*, one only refuge, applied to a deity. *s.*

ايكشرير एकशरीर *ek-sharīr*, of one body or blood. *s.*

ايكشن ईक्षण *īkshan*, m. sight, seeing; the eye.

ايكفردي *ek-fardī*, ايكفصلي *ek-faṣlī*, } land producing only one crop annually. *p.*

ايكك एकक *ekak*, ايكل एकल *ekal* } alone, solitary. *s.*

ايككال एककाल *ek-kāl*, m. one or the same time. *ek-kālīn*, coeval, simultaneous, contemporary. *s.*

ايك گاچهي एकगाछी *ek-gāchhī*, f. a canoe hollowed out of one single trunk of a tree. *s.*

ايك گرامين एकग्रामीण *ek-grāmīn*, of the same town or village. *s.*

ايك گرو एकगुरु *ek-guru*, a pupil of the same preceptor. *s.*

ايكلوتا एकलौता *ek-lautā*, only-begotten (son). *s.*

ايكوترا एकोत्रा *ekotrā*, a sum total. *h.*

ايكورن एकवर्ण *ek-varna*, of one caste, of one colour; m. an unknown quantity (in algebra). *s.*

ايكورني एकवर्णी f. *ek-varnī*, beating time by clapping the hands, an instrument which beats time, a castanet. *s.*

ايكونش एकविंश *ekaviṅsha*, the twenty-first. *s.*

ايكونشت एकविंशति *ekaviṅshati*, twenty-one. *s.*

ايكه ईख *īkh*, f. sugar cane (same as *ūkh*). According to the author of the *Arāishi Mahfil*, the word is pronounced *īkh* in the province of Dihlī, and *ūkh* in that of Oude, Lakhnau, &c. *s.*

ايكه *ai-ki*, alas that, pity that. *p.*

ايكهراج ईखराज *īkh-rāj*, the day on which the planting of the sugar-cane commences, generally attended with festive ceremonies. *h.*

ايكهتر *ekhattar* (for *ikhattar*), seventy-one. *d.*

ايكهٹا *ekhaṭṭā* (for *ekaṭhā*), collected, in one place, &c. *d.*

ايكهرا एकहरा *ekahrā*, single, solitary, alone. *s.*

ايكياسي *ekeāsī* (for *ikāsī*), eighty-one. *d.*

ايكيانوي *ekeānawe* (for *ikānawe*), ninety-one. *d.*

ايكيس *ekīs* (for *ikīs*), twenty-one. *d.*

ايكيك एकैक *ekaik*, singly, one by one. *s.*

ايكيلا *ekelā* (for *akelā* or *ikelā*), alone, solitary. *d.*

ايكيه ऐक्य *aikya*, m. oneness, sameness; an aggregate, a total. *s.*

ايگن ऐगुण *aigun*, m. unskilfulness, stupidity. *s.*

ايل *iyyal*, *uyyal* and *ayyul*, a deer, hart, wild goat of the mountains. *a.*

ايل *el*, f. a gold or silver bracelet worn by males only. *d.*

ايلا एला *elā*, f. small cardamums, the seeds of *Electaria cardamomum* or *Alpinia cardamomum*. *s.*

ايلا *īlā* (lit.) swearing; in law, a vow to abstain from having carnal knowledge of a wife for four months, the fulfilment of which is equivalent to a divorce. *a.*

ايلار *ailār* or ايلاڙ *ailāṛ*, on this side. *d.*

ايلچي *elchī*, m. an ambassador, agent, attorney, envoy. *elchī-panā*, m. or *elchī-garī*, f. office or dignity of ambassador, ambassadorship, agency. *elchī-garī-k.*, a. to act the ambassador, &c.; to act for another. *t.*

ايلغار *īlghār* or *elghār* (for *ilghār* q.v.), the forced march of an army through a country. *t.*

ايلفيل *ailfail*, m. abusive language, obscenity. *d.*

ايلم *elam* or *īlam*, m. an auction or public sale. *elam-ḍālnā*, to sell by auction. *d.*

ايلوا एलवा *elwā*, m. aloes. *h.*

ايليا *īlyā*, Elias or Eli; Jerusalem. *a.*

ايلي ايلاله *elī-elāllāh* (for *lā ilāha illā-allāh*), there is but one God. *d.*

ايليوار *ailewār* or *ailewar*, on this side. *d.*

ايما *īmā*, m. sign, nod, wink (indicating departure); emblem, symptom. *a.*

ايمان *īmān*, m. faith, belief, conscience, religion. *īmān-dār*, faithful, true. *īmān-dārī*, f. fidelity, truth. *īmān-lānā*, to believe. *īmān-h.*, to be on oath. *a.*

ايماني *īmānī*, faithful, of the (Musalmān) faith. *a.*

ايملي ऐमली *aimlī*, name of a tribe or caste. *h.*

ايمن एमन *eman*, m. a musical mode. *s.*

ايمن *aiman*, more or most happy, fortunate. *a.*

ايمن *emin* (for *āmin*), secure, safe, void of care. *p.*

ايمني *aimanī* or *eminī*, f. security, protection. *a.*

ایمه **aima** (for *a,imma*, pl. of امام, Imāms, Saints), m. land given as a reward or favour by the king, at a very low rent, a fief (when no rent is paid, it is called *lā-kharāj*); a grant of land, &c., to the people who attend at the tomb of a saint. *aima-dār*, one who holds *aima* land, a feoffee. *aima mauẓa'*, a village given as a charitable endowment to learned or religious persons. *a.*

این **īn** (Pers.), this, these. *ain* (Arab.), where? *īn* (Dakh.), shewing, or exhibiting the teeth.

اینٹ ईंट **īnṭ**, f. a brick. *īnṭ-garī*, brickwork. *īnṭ-wālā*, a brickmaker. *s.*

اینٹا ऐंटा **ainṭā**, m. a snail. *h.*

اینٹایا ईंटाया **īnṭāyā**, m. a kind of dove. *h.*

اینٹکاری ईंटकारी **īnṭ-kārī**, f. brickwork. *h.*

اینٹن **ainṭan**, m. the strings or bands of a spinning wheel. *d.*

اینٹنا ऐंटना **ainṭnā**, n. to twist, to writhe, to be racked with spasms; to walk or move stiffly. *h.*

اینٹنی **ainṭnī**, f. pride, peevishness. *d.*

اینٹو **ainṭū**, proud, peevish; stately. *ainṭū-pana*, stateliness. *d.*

اینٹھ ऐंठ **ainṭh**, f. a coil, twist, convolution, tightening; strut. *īnṭh* (Dakh.) for *īnṭ*, q. v.

اینٹھانا **ainṭhānā**, a. to twist, &c. (in a transitive sense). *h.*

اینٹھنا ऐंठना **ainṭhnā**, a. to tighten; n. to writhe, to cramp, to twist; to strut, to stalk, to walk affectedly. *h.*

اینچ ऐंच **ainch** (also *īnch* and *ainchū*), m. reserve, security, attraction. *ainch-khainch*, quarrelling. *h.*

اینچنا ऐंचना **ainchnā** (or *īnchnā*), a. to draw, to attract, to pull. *h.*

ایندرجالک ऐन्द्रजालिक **aindra-jālik**, m. a juggler, a magician; adj. of or relating to magic, illusory. *h.*

ایندور ईंदूर **īndūr**, m. (also *īndur*), a rat; a mouse. *h.*

آینده **āyanda**, in future, futurity. *p.*

آینده رونده **āyanda-ravanda** (pl. *āyanda-rawandagān*), one who is passing to and fro. *p.*

ایندهن ईंधन **īndhan**, m. firewood. *s.*

ایندنا ऐंडना **aindnā**, n. to strut, to stalk about. *h.*

ایندهوا ईंडुआ **īndhū,ā**, m. a roll or round fold on which a burden is carried on the head; a pad on the top of the head for supporting a water-jar. *h.*

اینک **īnak**, lo! behold! there for you. *p.*

اینگر ईंगुर **īngur**, m. red lead, minium. *p.*

اینو **īnū** or **īno**, this, these. *d.*

ایو एव **eva**, even so, verily, indeed. *s.*

آیو आयु **āyū**, also *āyu*, f. age, lifetime. *s.*

ایواره ऐवारः **aiwāra**, m. a cow-shed (in a jungle). *h.*

ایوان **aiwān**, m. a hall, a gallery, a portico, applied generally to a royal palace. *p.*

ایودهیا अयोध्या **ayodhyā**, f. the name of the country and city of which Rāma was sovereign; the present kingdom of Oude. *s*

ای واي **ai-wā,ī**, } interj. alas! alas! woe is
ای واه **ai-wāh**, } me! *p.*

ایوب **aiyūb**, m. the patriarch Job. *a.*

آیوربل आयुर्बल **āyūrbal**, } f. age, lifetime, du-
آیورداد आयुर्दा **āyūrdā**, } ration of life. *s.*

ایوڑ एवड़ **evar**, m. a flock of goats. *h.*

ایوگیه अयोग्य **a-yogya**, unfit, improper. *s.*

ایوگیتا अयोग्यता **a-yogyatā**, f. want of fitness. *s.*

ایوم एवम **evam**, thus, so, even so. *s.*

آیه आय **āya**, m. receipt, gain, profit. *h.*

آیه **āya** (v. *āyat*), a verse of the *ḳur,ān*. *a.*

ایه ईह **īh** (for *yih*), this, he, she, it. *h.*

ایهان ईहां **īhāṅ** (for *yahāṅ*), here, in this place. *h.*

ایهک ऐहिक **aihik**, of this place; of this present world; worldly, mundane. *s.*

آییتا आयीता **āyītā**, prepared, ready. *s.*

آئین **ā,īn**, m. regulation, law, rules (common law; the laws delivered by *Muḥammad* are called *shar'*, those established by princes *ā,īn*); institute, custom, manner. *p.*

آئینتی پائینتی **ā,īntī-pā,īntī**, low, under, inferior. *d.*

آئین دان **ā,īn-dān**, m. one skilled in the law; but it generally signifies a man who practises on the simplicity of people by his knowledge of law, hence, a pettifogger, a rogue. *p.*

آئینه **ā,īna**, m. a mirror, looking-glass; the kneepan. *ā,īna,e iskandarī*, a celebrated mirror said to have been made by Aristotle, and placed on the summit of a tower built by Alexander the Great at his newly-built city of Alexandria. *p.*

آئینه دار **ā,īna-dār**, m. the mirror-holder, an officer at eastern courts; met. a mendicant. *ā,īna-dārī*, f. the office of holding the mirror. *p.*

آئینه دان **ā,īna-dān**, m. the case of a mirror. *p.*

آئینه ساز **ā,īna-sāz**, m. a mirror-maker. *ā,īna-sāzī*, the trade of mirror-making. *p.*

آئینه فروز **ā,īna-faroz**, or *ā,īna-afroz*, or *ā,īna-zidā,e*, m. an instrument for polishing mirrors. *p.*

آئینه محل **ā,īna-mahall**, m. an apartment of which the walls are covered with mirrors (in eastern palaces). *p. a.*

ب

ب **be**, the second letter of the Arabic alphabet. It is sounded like our *b*, and in numeration by *abjad* it counts two. It is often prefixed to Persian and Arabic words with the sense of by, to, for, &c. In Arabic phrases it is always united to the noun it governs, and sounded *bi*. In Persian it is sounded *ba*, and may be united to its noun, or it may be written separately with the weak or imperceptible *h*. *a. p.*

ب ब **ba**, is the corresponding Devanāgarī letter, and in words from the Sanskrit it is frequently substituted for *v*, as *barāha* for *varāha*. It stands for *baruna*, the god of water: it may also denote the sun, the ocean, or water in general. *h. s.*

بَ बा *bā* (for वा *vā*), conj. or, either. *s.*

بَ *bā*, with, by, possessed of (in opposition to *be*, without, deprived of); frequently used as first member in composition, as in *bā-ābrū*, honourably, respectably. *bā-ittifāḳ*, with unity, harmoniously. *bā-asar*, effectively. *bā-ikhlāṣ*, sincere. *bā-adab*, in accordance with good manners. *bā-ān-ki*, notwithstanding that. *bā-īmān*, faithful, religious. *bā-tadbīr*, prudent, with deliberation. *bā-tamīz*, discreet, judicious. *bā-khabar*, intelligent. *bā-ḥayā*, modest. *bā-shu'ūr*, wise, intelligent. *bā-ḳā'ida*, according to rule. *bā murūwat*, humane. *bā maza*, tasteful, delicious. *bā waṣf* or *bā wujūd*, notwithstanding. *bā waz'*, respectfully. *bā wafā*, sincere, faithful. *p.*

باب *bāb*, m. a chapter, section, or any division of a book; a door; subject, head, affair, business, point, matter, reason, manner, mode, species, method, sort; *bābu-t-taubat*, the door of repentance. In revenue language a head of accounts, a tax, a cess (vide the pl. *abwāb*). *bāb-wār* and *bāb-yāft*, classified, items entered (as fields, &c.) under their proper heads. *bāb-wārī*, f. classification. *a.*

بابا बाबा *bābā*, m. father, sir; in Bengal it is a very common term for boy, girl, child, or any young person. *bābā-jān*, dear father, or dear child. *h.*

بابت *bābat*, f. account, head, article, item; business, affair, matter; on account of. This term, with its compounds, is much employed in revenue accounts; as, *bābat-wār*, according to entry. *bābat-wārī*, f. any thing which is registered or entered in a general statement of accounts. *bābat-yāft*, the particular items of any charge. *bābatī*, any cess or item of revenue: the Persian pl. *bābatān* is also used in the sense of "sundries," miscellaneous items. *a.*

بابر बाबर *bābar*, m. a kind of sweetmeat; a species of grass (v. *beb*). *h.*

بابرچي बाबर्ची *babarchī* (for *bāwarchī*), m. a cook. *bābarchī-khāna*, a cook's shop or kitchen, vulgarly called *bobberchy-conner* by the non-reading Europeans, male and female. *p.*

بابريان बाबरियां *bābariyāṅ*, a head of hair, long and uncut. *d.*

بابل *bābul*, Babel or the city of Babylon. *a.*

بابني बाबनी *bābnī*, f. a snake's hole. *h.*

بابو बाबू *bābū*, m. a child; a prince; master, a title among Hindūs equivalent to our Mr. or Squire, and it is now as common as the latter terms are among us. *h.*

بابول *bābūl* (same as *bābul*), the city of Babylon, Babel. *a.*

بابون बाबों *bāboṅ*, for the sake of. *d.*

بابونه *bābūna*, m. camomile; wild ivy (*Richards*). *p.*

باپ बाप *bāp*, m. father. *bāp-k.*, a. to consider as a father. *bāp-re* or *bāp-merā* (my father!), interj. an exclamation expressive of surprise, grief, &c. *h.*

باپتسما बापतिस्मा *bāptismā*, m. baptism (this word has been recently introduced into the Indian dialects by the Christian Missionaries. *g.*

باپرو बाप्रौ *bāprau*, } helpless, poor, destitute. *h.*
باپڑا बापड़ा *bāpṛā*, }

باپھ बाफ *bāph*, f. steam, vapour. *s.*

باپي बापी *bāpī*, f. a large oblong pond or pool, commonly called a tank. *s.*

بات बात *bāt*, f. speech, language, word; account, subject, question, cause. *bāt bāndhnā*, a. to sophisticate, to prevaricate. *bāt baṛhānā*, a. to prolong a contest. *bāt bigāṛnā*, a. to mar a plot, to spoil. *bāt banānā*, a. to make up a story, to make excuses. *bāt pānā*, a. to accomplish one's wishes, to effect one's purpose. *bāt pherna*, a. to equivocate. *bāt phenknā*, a. to jeer, to mock, to speak at (but not to). *bāt ṭālnā*, a. to put off, to excuse one's self. *bāt chalānā*, a. to converse, to start a subject. *bāt chīt*, f. conversation, chit-chat. *bāt-dharānā*, a. to persist in making excuses, to put off, to evade. *bāt ḍālnā*, a. to throw away one's words, to ask in vain. *bāt rakhnā*, a. to assist, to agree, to comply. *bāt rahnā*, n. to make good one's words, to be fulfilled or accomplished (declarations), to succeed, to overcome, to get the better in arguments, to be accepted, to preserve perfect. *bāt kā batakkaṛ-k.*, to multiply words, talk much on little. *bāt kāṭnā*, a. to interrupt. *bāt kā jān*, in short. *bāt kān ko lenā*, a. to accept, agree to. *bāt kursī-nishīn-h.*, to be approved of (an affair or proposal). *bāt ko pīna*, a. to have patience. *bāt-k.*, a. to converse, to talk, to speak. *bāt kī bāt*, unmeaning orders, commands not expected to be obeyed. *bāt kī bāt meṅ*, in an instant. *bāt gaṛhnā*, n. to speak to the purpose, to (speak so that one's words) have effect or make impression. *bāt ghaṭ-k.*, to determine, settle. *bāt lagānā*, to calumniate. *bāt mārnā*, to turn off, to evade, to divert (a discourse, &c.). *bāt man meṅ basnā*, n. to recollect, remember. *bāt meṅ kuchh-k.*, to perform a business in a word, *i. e.* in a short time, to lose no time in doing any thing. *bāt meṅ girānā*, a. to floor (the opponent) in argument. *bāteṅ sunānā*, a. to abuse, to speak harshly. *bāteṅ sunnā*, a. to receive abuse or harsh reproof. *s.*

بات बात *bāt*, m. pain in the joints, rheumatism. *s*

باتان خاني *bātān khānī*, talkative. *d.*

باتفاق *ba-ittifāḳ* or *bi-ittifāḳ*, with one consent, harmoniously. *a.*

باتن बातिन *bātin*, name of a tract of land in Etawah. *h.*

باتوني बातूनी *bātūnī*, } conversable, entertaining, talkative,
باتونيا बातूनिया *bātūniyā*, }
chatty; a talkative, entertaining, conversable person. *h.*

باتي बाती *bātī*, f. a candle, a wick; a tent or bougie put into a wound to keep it open. *s.*

باٹ बाट *bāṭ*, f. a road, highway. *bāṭ sārū*, a traveller, a wayfarer; m. a weight, or measure of weight, whether of stone or metal. *bāṭ-chhāp*, the stamp on weights and measures to guarantee their being genuine. *bāṭ-chhāpī*, fee for stamping weights, &c. *s.*

باٹا बाटा *bāṭā*, m. a share, portion. *d.*

باٹكا बाटिका *bāṭikā*, m. a villa. *s.*

باٹنا बाटना *bāṭnā* (also *bāṭhnā*), a. to share, to portion out or divide; to spin, to twist. *d.*

باٹي बाटी *bāṭī*, f. a habitation, dwelling-house, home; a garden-house. *s.*

باٹي گھاٹي बाटेघाटे *bāṭe-ghāṭe*, somewhere or other. *h.*

بااثر *bā-asar*, with effect, effective. *p. a.*

باج बाज *bāj*, without, in the absence of. *d.*

باج *bāj*, m. a tax, duty, toll, import, &c.; tribute, originally, that taken by one king from another. *bāj-dār* or *bāj-gīr*, a tax-gatherer, or collector of tribute or revenue. *bāj-guzār*, one who pays taxes, duties, &c. *p.*

باجا बाजा *bājā*, m. a musical instrument; music. *bājā-bajantar*, or *-bajattar*, a band of music. *s.*

باجاگاجا बाजागाजा *bājā-gājā*, m. the sound or clangor of various musical instruments. *s.*

باجرا बाजरा *bājrā*, m. a kind of grain so called; Indian corn (*Holcus spicatus*). *h.*

باجري बाजरी *bājrī*, f. same as *bājra* only of a smaller kind. *h.*

باج‌گاج बाजगाज *bāj-gāj*, m. sound of musical [instruments. *s.*

باجگير *bāj-gīr*, one who receives or collects taxes, &c. *p.*

باجن बाजन *bājan*, m. pl. musical instruments. *h.*

باجنا बाजना *bājnā*, n. to sound (as a musical instrument); to be published; a. to play, strike up or perform on an instrument. *h.*

باجن‌باجا बाजनबाजा *bājan-bājā*, m. pl. musical instruments. *h.*

باجنتري बाजन्तरी *bājantarī*, f. a tax formerly exacted from musicians and dancing-girls. *h.*

باجو बाजू *bājū*, m. a kind of ornament for the arm. *h.*

باجه *bāja*, m. (v. *bājā*), a musical instrument. *s.*

باجي बाजी *bājī*, m. a horse. *s.*

باچا बाचा *bāchā* or *vāchā*, f. speech, affirmation, agreement, promise or pledge. *s.*

باچك बाचक *bāchak* or *vāchak*, speaker; (in grammar) an explanatory particle. *s.*

باچه बाछ *bāchh*, f. selection; the corner of the lip; adj. useless; in revenue language, it denotes the proportionate rate or division either of lands or liabilities attached to them. *bāchh-barār*, an adjustment of liabilities, &c. *s.*

باچها बाछा *bāchhā*, a calf (or young of any [animal). *s.*

باچهل बाछल *bāchhal*, a tribe of *rāj-pūts* about *'Aligarh*, &c. *h*

باچهنا बाछना *bachhnā*, a. to choose, to se- [lect. *h.*

باچيه बाच्य *bāchya* or *vāchya*, m. a sentence (in grammar); adj. speakable, fit to speak. *s.*

باخ *bākhā*, m. (for باخه q. v.) a tortoise. *p.*

باخبر *bā-khabar*, careful, intelligent. *p.*

باختن *bākhtan* (r. *bāz*) to play, to sport with; to endanger. *p.*

باخته *bākhta*, played, lost (by play). *p.*

باخه *bākha*, m. a tortoise or turtle. *p.*

باد *bād*, f. wind. *bād-se bāt-k.*, to go very quickly, to be very swift. *bādi tund*, f. a stormy wind. *bād-paimā* or *bād-raftār*, swift as the wind (generally applied to a horse). *bādi samūm*, f. a hot pestilential wind. *bād-sanj*, idly speculative, vain; one who builds castles in the air. *bādi shurṭa*, f. a fair wind, a favourable wind. *bādi farang*, St. Anthony's fire (the pox?). *bād-farosh*, a musician or minstrel, literally a seller of wind. *bādi mukhālif*, f. a contrary wind. *bādi ṣabā*, f. the morning breeze, a zephyr. *bādi murād*, f. a fair wind; in revenue language it denotes a remission on account of deficient produce. *p.*

باد *bād* (for *bunvād*, precative form of *būdan*, to be;) may it be, or may it continue or be perpetual. (also *bādā*). *p.*

باد बाद *bād* or *vād*, m. accusation; assertion, asseveration, affirmation; a claim or plea; rheumatism. *bād-k.*, a. to argue. *s.*

بادار बादार *bādār*, a large house, granary raised on piles. *h.*

بادام *bādām*, m. an almond, also an Indian fruit resembling the almond, the catapāng of the Malays. *p.*

بادامه *bādāma*, the aurelia or silkworm in its nymphean state; a kind of silk; a dress made of rags sewn together, worn by *faķīrs*. *p.*

بادامي *bādāmī*, almond-coloured; almond-shaped; a kind of eunuch; a kind of dish of which almonds form a main ingredient. *p.*

بادانباد बादानुबाद *bādānubād*, m. altercation, dispute, &c. *s.*

بادباقي *bād-bāķī*, f. subtraction (in arithme- [tic). *p. a.*

بادبان *bād-bān*, m. a sail; a vessel in which a lamp is placed for protection from the wind. *p.*

بادپا *bād-pā*, having feet like the wind, fleet, swift (horse). *p.*

بادخايه *bād-khāya*, m. the rupture. *p.*

بادخور *bād-khor*, m. a disease in horses, from which the hair falls off. *p.*

بادخورا *bād-khorā*, a scald head (*Tinea ca-* [*pitis*). *p.*

بادر बादर *bādar*, a cloud, (v. *bādal*). *h.*

بادر बादुर *bādur*, m. a flying fox; a bat. *s.*

بادرنج *bādranj*, | بادرنگ *bādrang*, | بادرنگين *bādrangīn*, } an orange, a kind of citron, a species of large cucumber. *bādranj būya* or *bādrang boya*, Arabian balm, mountain balm. *p.*

بادريشه *bād-resha*, m. a whirl, a circular piece of wood at the end of a spindle; the round piece of wood at the upper end of a tent-pole. *p.*

بادريه *bādriya*, m. a ventilator suspended to the roof of a house, to increase the circulation of air, and drive away flies. *p.*

بادشاه *bādshāh*, m. a king, a sovereign: this is an Arab corruption of the Persian word *pādishāh*, q. v. *p.*

بادشاهانه *bādshāhāna*, kingly, in the manner [of a king. *p.*

بادشاهت *bādshāhat*, f. a kingdom, government. *p.*

بادشاه‌زاده *bādshāh-zāda*, a king's son, a prince. *bādshāh-zādī*, a princess. *p.*

بادشاهي *bādshāhī*, f. royalty, sovereignty; adj. royal, belonging to a king. *bādshāhī sanad*, a royal tenure, or grant of land rent-free. *p.*

بادشه *bādshah* (same as *bādshāh*), a king, &c. *p.*

بادكش *bād-kash*, m. a fan, a ventilator; a punkah; bellows. *p.*

بادگرد *bād-gird*, a whirlwind. *p.*

بادل बादल *bādal*, m. a cloud. *h.*

بادلا बादला *bādlā*, } m. gold or silver thread,
بادله बादलः *bādla*, } brocade, &c. *h.*

بادلي बादली *bādalī*, silver cloth; cloudiness. *h.*

بادم *bādam* (for *bādām*), an almond; spiceries. *p.*

بادمهره *bād-muhra*, m. an antidote for a [snake's bite. *p.*

بادنجان *bādinjān*, the egg plant. *p.*

بادنما *bād-numā*, m. a weathercock. *p.*

باده *bāda*, m. wine, spirits. *bāda-parast*, addicted to wine. *bāda-kash*, wine-drawer. *bāda-nosh*, or *bāda-gusār*, a wine-bibber. *p.*

بادھ बाध *bādh*, a lesser division of an estate; a plain, a desert. *h.*

بادھ बाध *bādh*, m. prohibition, hindrance; a chord, a string. *s.*

بادھا बाधा *bādhā*, f. pain, anguish. *s.*

بادھت बाधित *bādhit*, obstructed, impeded, pained, tormented. *s.*

بادھك बाधक *bādhak*, one who interrupts, &c. *s.*

بادھن बाधन *bādhan*, m. pain, act of obstructing or opposing. *s.*

بادهوائي *bād-hawā,ī*, f. fruitlessness, uselessness; waste. *p.*

بادھيه बाध्य *bādhya*, what ought to be stopped. *s.*

بادي *bādī*, flatulent, troubled with wind. *p.*

بادي बादी *bādī* (for *vādī*), an accuser, a plaintiff, an enemy. *bādī chor*, an inveterate thief. *s.*

بادي *bādī*, beginner, an author. *a.*

باديان *bādiyān* (also *bādiyāna*), sweet fennel; anise seed. *s.*

باديه *bādiya*, m. a bowl, cup, glass (but generally made of brass or bell-metal). *p.*

باديه *bādiya*, m. a desert, a wilderness. *a.*

باڈه बाढ *bāḍh*, f. stubble. *h.*

باڈهنا बाढना *bāḍhnā*, a. to cut, to shear. *h.*

باذق *bāẕik*, the juice of grapes, slightly boiled. *a.*

بار *bār*, m. load; time, once; a court, a tribunal, sitting of a sovereign to give audience; repetition; fruit; leave, permission, admission; pregnancy. *bār-dār*, loaded, full of fruit; pregnant. *bār-denā*, to load; to give charge; to impose, to give trouble, to encumber; to give admission, to give leave. *ka,ī bār karke*, after several times or turns. *p.*

بار बार *bār*, f. time, occasion, delay; verge, edge; a girl not exceeding sixteen; m. day of the week; door; water; child; hair; prohibition, obstacle. *bār lagānā*, to delay, to hesitate. *s.*

بار बार *bār*, } m. perquisite of the *ahīr* or
بارا बारा *bārā*, } cow-herd in milk, generally the milk of every eighth day. *h.*

بارا *bārā*, m. wind, air, atmosphere. *d.*

بارادري बारादरी *bārādarī* (v. *bārah*), f. a summer-house. *h.*

باراسنگا बारासिंगा *bārāsingā*, m. a stag (*Cervus elaphus*). *h.*

باراكهري बाराखरी *bārākharī*, f. the combination of the consonants (in the Devanāgarī) with the vowel symbols. *h.*

باران *bārān*, m. rain, the rainy season. *p.*

باراني *bārānī*, f. a great coat, or cloak for keeping off the rain; unirrigated land, *i.e.* land depending on the natural rains of the season. *p.*

باراه बाराह *bārāh*, m. a boar, a hog; the third incarnation of Vishnu. *s.*

باراهي बाराही *bārāhī*, f. land; adj. relating to *bārāh*, the third incarnation. *h. s.*

باربار *bār-bār*, repeatedly, often (also *bārambār*). *bār-bārī-k.*, to procrastinate, delay. *p.*

باربٹائي बारबटाई *bār-baṭā,ī*, f. division of the crops by sheaves or shocks, before the corn is trodden out. *h.*

باربر *bārbar*, burden-bearing (ox or ass). *p.*

باربردار *bār-bardār*, m. a porter, a burden-bearer. *p.*

باربرداري *bār-bardārī*, f. expenses of travelling, coolie-hire, carriage-hire, means of conveyance. *p.*

بارج बारिज *bārij* (for *vārija*), m. the lotus. *bārija nayan*, having eyes like the flower of the lotus. *s.*

بارجات *bārjāt*, an oppressive custom, forcing the natives to buy goods above the market price. *p.*

بارجائي *bārjā,e*, a custom of forcing people to buy goods at an exorbitant price; likewise, a free grant of a spot of ground made by the zamindārs and landholders to any of their relatives, the rents of which, to prevent a loss to the donor, are assessed upon the rest of his possessions. *p.*

بارچاپ *bār-chāp*, a kind of cloth. *d.*

بارخاص *bāri-khāṣṣ*, m. private hall of audience. *p.*

بارخاطر *bāri-khāṭir*, load or distress of [mind. *p. a.*

بارخانه *bār-khāna*, m. a warehouse. *p.*

بارخدا *bāri-khudā*, Great God. *p.*

بارد बारिद *bārid* m. (for *vārid*), a cloud. *s.*

بارد *bārid*, cold, frigid; established. *a.*

بارز *bāriz*, a term in arithmetic, the sum total or gross amount. *p.*

بارش *bārish*, f. rain; a shower of rain. *p.*

بارعام *bār-i-'ām*, m. public hall of audience. *p. a*

بارك वारिक *bārik*, m. rain (for *vārik* or *vārid*). *h.*

بارك الله *bārak-allāh* (God prosper you), a phrase expressive of admiration. *a.*

باركش *bār-kash*, lit. "burden-bearing," applied to elephants, carts, porters, &c. *p.*

بارگاه *bārgāh* or بارگه *bārgah*, f. a court, palace, place of audience. *bār-gāh-i-khāṣ*, private court, privy-council chamber. *bārgāh-i-'ām*, public court, where every body is admitted. *p.*

بارگي *bāragī* or *bārgī* (used in comp.), time, or turn. *p.*

بارگير *bārgīr*, m. a horseman (soldier) who does not find his own horse; a beast of burthen. *p.*

بارن वारण *bāran* (for *vāraṇ*), m. forbidding, prohibiting, preventing; an elephant. *s.*

بارنا वारना *bārnā*, n. to leave off, to separate, to quit; a. to forbid, to prohibit. *s.*

بارنا बारना *bārnā*, a. to light, to kindle. *h.*

بارنبار बारंबार *bārambār* (for *bār-bār*), often, repeatedly. *h.*

بارنبه बारंबः *bārumba*, m. fruit of mangoes, revenue derived from mango groves. *h.*

بارندگي *bārandagī*, f. rain, raining. *p.*

بارنده *bāranda*, that which rains or showers. *p.*

بارني वारुणी *bārunī*, f. spirituous liquors. *s.*

بارو बारू *bārū*, f. sand (vide *bālū*); m. a child. *s.*

بارو *bārū* (for *bārūt*), f. gunpowder, saltpetre. *p.*

باروان *bārwān* (for *bārahwān*), the twelfth. *h.*

باروت *bārūt*, } f. saltpetre; gunpowder. *p.*
بارود *bārud*, }

باره वारह *bārah*, land next to or surrounding a village. *h.*

باره बारह *bārah*, twelve. *bārah-darī*, f. a summerhouse (q.d. with twelve doors). *bārah bāṭ honā*, n. to become a vagabond, to be ruined or harassed. *h.*

باره *bāra*, for the sake of, in behalf of, as in the phrase *dar bāra,e man*, in my behalf; (in comp.) turn, time; as, *dū-bāra*, twice, over again. *p.*

بارها *bār-hā*, often, repeatedly. *p.*

بارهسنگا बारहसिंगा *bārah-singā*, m. lit. "a twelve-tiner;" a stag with horns of twelve branches (*Cervus elaphus*). *h.*

باري *bāre*, once, one time; it is used by some authors in the sense of at last, at length, lastly. *p.*

باري *bārī*, m. a name of the Deity, the Creator. *bārī ta'ālā*, the most high God. *a.*

باري बारी *bārī*, f. a garden, an orchard, a house; a window; an ornament worn in the ear and nose; a young girl not exceeding sixteen. *a.*

باري बारी *bārī*, m. the name of a caste of Hindūs whose business it is to sell torches and leaves which are used as platters: the same caste occasionally act as barbers. *h.*

باري *bārī*, tour, turn. *bārī-dār*, an attendant who waits in turn with others. *bārī kī tap*, an intermittent fever. *p.*

بارياب *bār-yāb*, admitted at court or into company; one who has the entrée. *p.*

باريابي *bāryābī*, f. admittance at court or into company; having the entrée. *p.*

باريدن *bārīdan*, to rain, to shower. *p.*

باريك *bārīk*, fine, slender, minute, subtile. *bārīk-bīn*, intelligent, penetrating, quick of apprehension. *bārīk-miyān*, slender-waisted. *p.*

باريكي *bārīkī*, f. subtilty; minuteness. *p.*

باڑ बाड़ *bāṛ*, f. edge; name of a place near Mungīr; a fence, a hedge; a line (of soldiers); a margin. *bāṛ-pakṛānā*, to urge on, to instruct. *bāṛ jhāṛnā* and *bāṛ uṛānā*, a. to fire a volley. *bāṛ-bāndhnā*, a. to inclose a field with thorns. *bāṛ-rakhnā*, *-chirnā*, or *-chirwānā*, a. to sharpen *bāṛ-denā*, or *-dilwānā*, a. to sharpen, to grind, excite, to instigate. *h.*

باڑا बाड़ा *bāṛā*, m. an inclosure; alms, charity. *h.*

باڑو बाड़व *bāṛav*, } m. submarine
باڑوانل बाड़वानल *bāṛavānal*, } fire. *s.*

باڑھ बाढ़ *bāṛh*, f. a flood; promotion, increase. *h.*

باڑھنا बाढ़ना *bāṛhnā*, } n. to increase, go on,
باڑھنو बाढ़नौ *bāṛhnau*, } advance, rise, swell; to be promoted, to amount, lengthen. *h.*

باڑهي बाढ़ही *bāṛhī*, f. usurious profit or interest taken on grain; interest in kind paid upon seed grain. *h.*

باڑي बाड़ी *bāṛī*, a kitchen-garden; a house with the garden, orchard, &c., attached to it; also cotton (see *bārī*). *s.*

باڑيا बाड़िया *bāṛiyā*, m. a whetter (of swords, [knives, &c.). *h.*

باز *bāz*, m. a female falcon, a hawk. *bāz-dār*, m. a falconer. *bāz-dārī*, f. the charge of hawks, keeping falcons. *a.*

باز *bāz*, adv. again, once more. *bāz-ānā*, n. to decline, to leave off; to refuse, to reject, to desist. *bāz rakhnā*, a. to hold back, to prevent, to forbid. *bāz-rahnā*, n. to decline, to reject, to leave off; to refuse; (in comp.) it denotes a player; as, *shaṭranj-bāz*, a chess-player; *ḥuḳḳa-bāz*, a juggler. *p.*

بازار *bāzār*, m. a market: according to Gladwin it denotes a constant and established market, in contradistinction to *hāṭ*, an occasional one. *p.*

بازاري *bāzārī*, belonging to a market; market people, common people. *bāzārī bāt*, low or vulgar language; patois; Billingsgate. *p.*

بازپرس *bāz-purs*, } m. reiterated inquiry;
بازخواست *bāz-khwāst*, } minute investigation. *p.*

بازپسين *bāz-pasīn*, last, hindmost. *p.*

بازرگان *bāzargān* (for *bāzārgān*), m. a merchant, a dealer in the market. *p.*

بازرگاني *bāzargānī*, f. merchandise, traffic, trade commerce. *p.*

بازکردن *bāz-kardan*, to throw open (a door). *p.*

بازگشت *bāz-gasht* or *bāz-gashta*, returned, retreated. *p.*

بازگون *bāz-gūn*, preposterous, upside down. *p.*

بازگير *bāz-gīr*, a falconer; a chronologist, or historian; (for *bāj-gīr*), a collector of revenue. *p.*

بازنده *bāzanda*, playing, a player; a kind of pigeon (vide *khirad-afroz*). *p.*

بازو *bāzū*, m. the arm (plur. *bāzū,ān*); the fold of a door; the side of a bedstead; a friend, a companion; one who repeats the chorus of the *marsiya*; an accompanier in a song. *bāzū denā*, a. to assist, to help, to support. *p.*

بازوبند *bāzū-band*, m. an ornament worn on the arm, a bracelet or an armlet. *p.*

بازي *bāzī*, f. play, sport; a game, a stake at play. *bāzī khānā*, to lose, to be cast; to be cheated. *bāzī pānā*, to be victorious, prosperous. *bāzī-lagānā*, to wager. *bāzī lejānā*, to win, to excel. *p.*

بازيافت *bāz-yāft*, resumption of any thing, the act of resuming alienated lands or property of any kind. *p.*

بازيچه *bāzīcha*, f. fun, play, sport; wagering; [a toy, plaything. *p.*

بازيدن *bāzīdan*, to sport, to play; to gamble. *p.*

بازي‌گاه *bāzī-gāh*, f. a place for exhibiting feats of activity; a theatre. *p.*

بازيگر *bāzīgar*, m. a tumbler, one who exhibits feats of activity. *p.*

بازيگرن *bāzīgaran*, } f. a tumbling-woman,
بازيگرني *bāzīgarnī*, } an actress. *p.*

بازيگري *bāzīgarī*, f. the art of juggling, tumbling, &c. *p.*

باس बास *bās*, f. smell, scent, odour. *bās-* [*banyā*, a perfumer. *s.*

باس बास *bās*, } m. abode, residence, lodg-
باسا बासा *bāsā*, } ing, temporary residence. *s.*

بآساني *ba-āsānī*, with facility, easily. *p.*

باستان *bāstān* (in Persian), ancient, past: in the south of India it is used corruptly for *ba'd az ān*, after, afterwards. *p. d.*

باستو बास्तु *bāstū*, site or foundation of a house. *s.*

باسٹھ बासठ *bāsaṭh*, sixty-two. *h.*

باسديو बासुदेव *bāsudev* (properly *vāsudeva*), name of Krishna, the son of Vasudeva. *s.*

باسر बासर *bāsar* (for *vāsar*), m. a day. *s.*

باسري *bāsrī* or *bāsurī*, f. (v. *bāṅsrī*), a flute, pipe, &c. *s.*

باسق *bāsiḳ*, tall, lofty (palm-tree). *a.*

باسك बासुक *bāsuk*, } m. the name of the
باسكي बासुकी *bāsukī*, } serpent which supports the universe, and which was used as a string to whirl the mountain Mandar in churning the ocean for the *amṛit*, &c. *s.*

باسليق *bāsalīḳ*, f. the great vein in the arm [(*Vena basilica*). *g.*

باسمتي बासमती *bāsmatī*, f. a fragrant kind of rice, also of millet. *h.*

باسن बासन *bāsan*, m. a basin, goblet, pot, [plate, dish, &c. *h.*

باسنا बासना *bāsnā* or *vāsanā*, f. desire, inclination. *s.*

باسنا बासना *bāsnā* or बासना *vāsanā*, a. to scent, to perfume. *s.*

باسي बासी *bāsī*, stale, fusty, perfumed. *bāsī-k.*, to make stale; to vomit. *h.*

باسي बासी *bāsī* or *vāsī*, an inhabitant; (used in comp.), as *ban-bāsī*, or *vana-vāsī*, inhabitant of the woods. *s.*

باسيان बासियान *bāsiyān*, name of a tribe of [*ahīrs*. *h.*

باش *bāsh*, stay, stop, be patient; (in comp.) it denotes being, staying, as *shab-bāsh*, staying for a night. *p.*

باشا *bāshā*, m. a kind of falcon, a hawk. *p.*

باشد *bāshad*, it may be, perhaps. *p.*

باشگيا बासगिया *bāshgiyā*, crops being choked and destroyed by weeds. *h.*

باشنده *bāshanda*, an inhabitant, a dweller. *p.*

باشه *bāsha*, m. a hawk (same as *bāshā*). *p.*

باشين *bāshīn*, a female falcon. *p.*

باصره *bāṣira*, sight, the sense of seeing. *a.*

باطل *bāṭil*, false, vain; absurd, futile, ignorant; abolished. *a.*

باطلي *bāṭilī*, f. vanity, folly, absurdity. *a.*

باطن *bāṭin*, m. the inward part, the heart; adj. internal, hidden, concealed. *a.*

باطني *bāṭinī*, intrinsic, internal. *a.*

باعث *bā'is*, cause, account, occasion, inducement; author, producer; prep. by means or by reason of. *a.*

باغ *bāgh*, m. a garden, orchard, grove. *bāghī sabz dikhānā* or *-dikhlānā*, to excite desire and expectation by deceitful promises. *bāgh-bāgh-honā*, or *hojānā*, n. to be delighted, to rejoice greatly. *p.*

باغات *bāghāt*, pl. gardens, groves, orchards. *p.*

باغايتي *bāghāyatī*, fit for garden cultivation; f. fruit raised in a garden; tax levied on gardens. *h.*

باغبان *bāgh-bān*, m. a gardener. *p.*

باغباني *bagh-bānī*, f. gardening. *p.*

باغچه *bāghcha*, m. a small garden, orchard, &c. *p.* [tumour, a wen. *p.*

باغره *bāghira*, m. an indolent swelling or

باغشاي *bāghshāī*, f. a walk in a garden. *d.*

باغكاري *bāgh-kārī*, f. garden cultivation, business of a gardener. *p.*

باغوالا *bāgh-wālā*, } m. a gardener, the owner
باغوان *bāghwān*, } of a garden. *p. h.*

باغها *bāghhā*, pl. gardens, orchards. *p.*

باغي *bāghī*, a mutineer, traitor, rebel. *a.*

باغيچه *bāghīcha*, a little garden (v. *bāghcha*). *p.*

باف *bāf*, (in comp.) weaving or woven. *kināri-bāf*, a weaver of lace. *zarī-bāf*, a gold-lace weaver; a kind of cloth interwoven with gold. *p.*

بافت *bāft*, web, weaving, tissue, texture. *p.*

بافته *bāfta*, woven; m. a kind of cloth; a colour in pigeons; buttons woven like mohair; (in comp.) it denotes woven, wrought, as *zar-bāfta*, wrought in gold, embroidered. *p.*

بافراط *ba-ifrāt*, in abundance, copiously. *p. a.*

بافنده *bāfanda* or *bāfinda*, a weaver. *p.*

باقر *bāḳir*, abounding in wealth and knowledge, one who is deeply learned. *a.*

باقرخاني *bāḳir-khānī*, f. a kind of bread or cake mixed with butter and milk. Dr. Gilchrist suggests, in his Vocabulary, that this kind of cake took its name from some nobleman called *Bāḳir-khān*, as our word *sandwich* is said to be so named after Lord Sandwich. *a.*

باقلا *bāḳilā*, } m. a bean, a pea, a potherb. *a.*
باقله *bāḳila*, }

باقي *bāḳī*, remnant, remainder, balance, arrears; adj. permanent, durable, eternal. *bāḳī-dār*, owing a balance; a revenue defaulter. *bāḳī-rahnā*, n. to remain, to be left, to be saved. *a.*

باقيات *bāḳiyāt*, remainders, balances, arrears. *a.*

باك *bāk*, m. fear, apprehension. *p.*

باك बाक *bāk* or *vāk*, m. language, dialect, speech; in the language of revenue officers it is used to denote a verbal estimate of the produce without measuring the field. *s.*

باكره *bākira*, an unblemished virgin. *a.*

باكري बाकरी *bākrī*, f. a cow advanced about five months in pregnancy (also a small buffalo). *h.*

باكس बाकस *bākas*, m. a bush of which charcoal is made for the manufacture of gunpowder (*Justicia adhatoda*). *s.*

باكلا बाकला *bāklā*, m. a bean, a potherb (v. *bāḳilā*). *h.*

باكند बाकन्द *bākand*, a portion of the crop, about two-fifths, paid as rent by the cultivators to the zamīndārs. *h.*

باكهر बाखर *bākhar*, } m. name of a drug
باكهل बाखल *bākhal*, } used as a ferment; a house, an inclosure; several houses contained within one inclosure; an area or court-yard. *h.*

باكيه बाक्य *bākya* (for *vākya*), m. (in gram.) a sentence; speech, a word. *s.*

باگ बाग *bāg*, f. a rein, a bridle. *bāg-moṛnā*, to turn the reins: it is applied to the drying up of the small-pox: when the pustules begin to blacken and dry up, they say *sītlā* or *mātā ne bāg moṛī*. *bāg hāth se chhūṭnā*, the power of choice to be lost to any one. *h.*

باگ *bāg* (Dakh. for باگهه), a tiger. *bāg ka paṭṭha*, a tiger's cub.

باگا बागा *bāgā*, m. a vestment; honorary dress. *h.*

باگڈور बागडोर *bāgḍor*, f. a long rein with which horses are led. *h.*

باگر बागर *bāgar*, m. a hedge of thorns or twigs; name of a tract of country belonging to the *rāj-pūts*. *h.*

باگري बागरी *bāgrī*, a native of Bāgar. *h.*

باگم बागम *bāgam*, m. any cultivated spot. *h.*

باگنهك *bāgnakh*, the claws of a tiger set in silver and worn round the neck by a string as a charm against sundry evils. A kind of weapon made of steel, resembling huge claws, and fitting upon the hands. With this instrument the celebrated Sevājee, the Mahratta chief, is said to have murdered the Muḥammadan governor of Bijapūr, while embracing him under pretence of friendship. (Binning). *d.*

باگهه बाघ *bāgh*, } m. a tiger. *bāgh-bakrī*, f.
باگها बाघा *bāghā*, } tiger and goat, a kind of children's play, akin to our "fox and geese". *s.*

باگهنبر बाघंबर *bāghambar*, m. a tiger's skin. *s.*

باگهن बाघन *bāghan*, } f. a tigress. *s.*
باگهني बाघनी *bāghnī*, }

باگهي बाघी *bāghī*, f. a bubo. *h.*

باگي बागी *bāgī*, a horseman, a rider. *s.*

بال बाल *bāl*, f. a girl not arrived at the age of maturity; m. a child under five years old; adj. infantine, childish; ignorant, uninstructed. *s.*

بال बाल *bāl*, m. hair; a child. *bāl bikā na ho,e* (let not the hair be bent or disordered), a mode of inculcating extraordinary care. *bāl-bāl*, hair by hair, every hair. *bāl bāndhī kauṛī mārnā*, to shoot at, not to miss; to act with great care, not to mistake. *s.*

بال *bāl*, m. a wing. *bāl-dār*, winged. *p.*

بال बाल *bāl*, f. an ear of corn; a crack in a cup or glass; m. the thread on which sugar is crystallized. *bāl-dār*, a cracked vessel (of china, glass, &c.). *h.*

بال बालु *bālu*, m. a drug commonly called *elā-bāluk* *s.*

بال *bāl*, m. heart; power. *a.*

بالا *bālā*, above, up; m. top. *bālā-batānā*, or *-denā*, a. to baulk, to circumvent, to dupe; to put off, to disappoint, to prevaricate. *bālā-bālā*, deceitfully, fraudulently; secretly. *bālā-dast*, superior. *p.*

بالا बाला *bālā*, m. a kind of grub which eats the young plants of wheat or barley when about six inches high. *h.*

بالا बाला *bālā*, f. a girl not arrived at the age of maturity; a medicinal and fragrant plant, of the roots of which *ṭaṭṭīs* are made (*Andropagon muricatum*), commonly called by Europeans "cus-cuss"; m. an earring; a male child, a boy. *bālā chānd*, the new moon. *s.*

بالابر *bālābar*, m. part of the *angarkhā* (q.v.) that laps over the thigh. *p.*

بلابند *bālā-band*, m. part of the native dress, a kind of turban; a coat of a particular kind. *p.*

بالابهولا बालाभोला *bālā-bholā*, adj. innocent, artless, as a child; m. an artless child. *s. h.*

بالاپن बालापन *bālā-pan*, m. childhood, infancy; also boyhood. *s.*

بالاپوش *bālā-posh*, m. a coverlet, quilt. *p.*

بالاتپ बालातप *bālātap*, m. the rays of the rising sun. *s.*

بالاتفاق *bi-l-ittifāḳ*, lit. by agreement, by chance. *a.* [(an estate, &c.). *h.*

بالاجمال *bi-l-ijmāl*, in the whole, in the lump

بالاچاند बालाचांद *bālā-chānd*, the new moon. *s.*

بالاخانه *bālā-khāna*, m. an upper room, an upper story, a balcony. *p.*

بالادست *bālā-dast*, superior, high-handed. *p.*

بالاگشتي *bālā-gashtī*, an inspector of police. *p.*

بالان *bālaṅ*, hairs of the head, the hair collectively. *bālaṅ bharā*, full of hair, bristly. *d.*

بالانشين *bālā-nishīn*, seated aloft, superior. *p.*

بالاوپست *bālā o past*, above and below, *i.e.* the heavens above and the earth beneath. *p.*

بالائي *bālā,ī*, s. a horse led for show; any extra tax; adj. external, superficial. *p.*

بالائي مزي *bālā,ī maze* (pl.), m. superficial or hollow pleasures. *p.*

بالائي يافت *bālā,ī-yāft*, f. perquisites. *p.*

بال بچي *bāl-bachche*, pl. children. *s. p.*

بالبنان *bi-l-banān*, with the tips of the fingers; "*monstrari digitis.*" *a.*

بال بهوگ बालभोग *bāl-bhog*, m. an offering to Krishna, presented early in the morning. *s.*

بال پر *bāl-par*, m. adoption of better habits; *bāl par nikālnā*, to turn over a new leaf; to flourish or prosper; to betray one's evil disposition, to begin wicked pranks, to show the cloven hoof. *p.*

بالپن *bāl-pan*, m. (v. *bālāpan*), childhood, &c. *s.*

بالتصريح *bi-t-taṣrīḥ*, distinctly, explicitly. *a.*

بال توڑ बालतोड़ *bāl-toṛ*, m. a pimple, a sore. *h.*

بالجمله *bi-l-jumla*, in short, to conclude. *a.*

بال چهڑ बालछड़ *bāl-chhaṛ*, f. the name of a medicine or perfume. *h.* [happily. *a.*

بالخير *bi-l-khair*, in a good manner, well,

بالذات *bi-ẕ-ẕāt* or *bi-ẕ-ẕāti*, naturally, originally. *bi-ẕātihi*, in its nature or essence. *a.*

بالراج बालराज *bālrāj*,
بالسوريه बालसूर्य *bālsūrya*, } m. lapis lazuli. *s.*

بال رانڈ बालरांड *bāl-rānḍ*, f. a very young widow, or one who lost her husband when she was very young. *s.*

بالش *bālish*, m. a pillow, a cushion. *p.*

بالشت *bālisht*, f. a span; a pillow. *p.*

بالضرورت *bi-ẓ-ẓarūrat* (also *bi-ẓ-ẓarūra*), necessarily, perforce. *a.*

بالعکس *bi-l'aks*, the reverse. *us ke bi-l'aks*, the contrary to that. *a.*

بالغ *bāligh*, m. a youth just arrived at the age of maturity; adj. of age; fem. *bāligha*, marriageable. *a.*

بالفرض *bi-l-farẓ*, granted that, on the supposition or condition that. *a.*

بالفعل *bi-l-fi'l*, in fact, actually; now, for the present moment; in short; in the mean time. *a.*

بالقصد *bi-l-ḳaṣd*, on purpose. *a.*

بالقوت *bi-l-ḳūwat*, by the strength, or power of. *a.* [name of a drug (v. *bālu*). *s.*

بالك बालक *bālak*, m. a young child. *bāluk*,

بالكا बालका *bālkā* or *bālakā*, m. a young follower or disciple of a *jogī* or *sanyāsī*. *s.*

بالكا बालुका *bālukā*, f. sand, gravel. *s.*

بالكاگڑ बालुकागड़ *bālukāgaṛ*, m. a sort of fish. *s.*

بالكامي बालुकामय *bālukāmay*, sandy, gravelly. *s.*

بالكپن बालकपन *bālakpan*,
بالكپنا बालकपना *bālakpanā*,
بالكتوه बालकत्व *bālakatwa*, } m. childhood, boyhood; infancy, childishness. *s.* [together. *a.*

بالكل *bi-l-kull* (or *bi-l-kullīya*), totally, al-

بالكيه बालकीय *bālakīya*, childish, infantine. *s.*

بال گوپال बालगोपाल *bāl-gopāl*, offspring. *s.*

بالله *bi-llāh* (or *bi-llāhi*), by God. *bi-llāhi-l'aẓīm*, by the High God! *a.*

بالم बालम *bālam*, m. a lover, or beloved person; a husband; a kind of cloth. *bālam khīrā*, m. a sort of cucumber, in season in the rains (a variety of *Cucumis sativus*). *h.* [son). *a.*

بالمقطعه *bi-l-muḳṭa'a*, a kind of tenure. (v. Wil-

بالنا बालना *bālnā*, a. to light, to kindle (v. *bārnā*). *h.*

بالند बालन्द *bāland*, name of a tribe inhabiting the southern parts of *Mirzapūr*. *h.*

بالنگو *bālangū*, a species of citron. *p.*

بالني बालिनी *bālinī*, f. the constellation *aswinī*. *s.*

بالو बालू *bālū*, f. sand, gravel. *s.*

بالوبرد *bālū-burd*, land covered with a deposit of sand after an inundation; also, a remission of revenue on that account. *s. p.*

بالوپويت बालोपवीत *bālopavīt*, m. a child's sacrificial thread; a cloth covering the privities (of children). *s.*

بالوچري बालूचरी *bālūcharī*, a kind of silk cloth manufactured in Bālūchar, near Murshidābād. *h.*

بالوفا *bi-l-wafā*, in truth, in reality. *a.*

بالوك बालूक *bālūk*, m. a sort of poison. *s.*

بالي बाली *bālī*, f. a female-child; ear-ring worn in the ear, passing through the centre of it: it also signifies an ear of corn. *s.*

بالي बाली *bālī*, m. name of a monkey, the son of Indra, killed by Rāma. *s.*

باليدگي *bālīdagī*, f. vegetation. *p.*

باليده هونا *bālīda honā*, n. to vegetate. *p. h.*

باليش बालीश *bālīsh*, m. pain in making water, from gravel, &c. *s.*

باليقين *bi-l-yaķīn*, assuredly, certainly. *a.*

بالين *bālīn*, f. a pillow, a cushion. *p.*

باليه बाल्य *bālya*, m. childhood, infancy. *s.*

باليېه बालेय *bāleya*, باليېه‌شاك बालेयशाक *bāleyashāk*, } m. name of a plant *Siphomanthus Indica*). *s.*

بام बाम *bām*, f. an eel (*Ophidium simack, Buch.*); m. the left (side); an enemy. *s.*

بام *bām*, m. an upper story, a terrace; the morning dawn. *p.*

بام *bām*, m. a fathom, a measure of six feet, or three and a half cubits. *d.*

بام‌انگ बामअंग *bām-ang*, m. the left side. *s.*

بامبهي बाम्भी *bāmbhī*, بامبهني बाम्भनी *bāmbhnī*, } f. a snake's hole. *s.*

بامداد *bāmdād* or *bāmdādān*, f. morning, dawn, Aurora; adv. in the morning. *p.*

بامن बामन *bāman* (for *vāmana*), a dwarf, one of the incarnations of Vishnu. *s.*

بامن *bāman*, بامنه *bāmanh*, } m. a Brāhman. *d.*

بامن‌هٿي बामनहट्टी *bāman-haṭṭī*, f. name of a plant (*Ovieda verticellata, Roxb.*). *h.*

بامهن बाम्हन *bāmhan*, m. a Brāhman. *s.*

بامهني बाम्हनी *bāmhnī*, f. a stye on the eyelids; a species of lizard. *h.*

بامهني बाम्हनी *bāmhnī* f. (for *bāhmanī*), the wife of a Brāhman; name of a medicinal herb. *s.*

بان बान *bān*, f. temper, quality, manners; m. a rocket used in battle; the boar or swell of the tide; a kind of rope made of mūnj. *h.*

بان बान *bān* or *vān*, m. an arrow; the name of an asur, son of Rājā Bali. *s.*

بان *bān*, m. name of a tree (*Guilandina moringa*), whose seeds are called *ḥabb-ul-bān*, bennut, or according to some, *Bakain* (*Melia sempervirens*); that which yields benjamin or benzoin (*Styrax benzoe*); a tree the leaves and flowers of which are sweet-scented, called by the Persians *bed-mashk*. *p.*

بان *bān*, keeper or guardian; (used in comp.) as *dar-bān*, a door-keeper, *bāgh-bān*, a gardener. *p.*

بانا बाना *bānā*, m. habit, profession; a kind of weapon; fashion in dress, peculiar to individuals, or bodies taken individually (so regimentals may be called *bānā*); uniformity; the woof (in weaving); a veil. *banā bāndhnā*, to be ready, to be determined. In the Dakhanī dialect it denotes the basin or metal bucket of a *pacotta*, or lever for raising water. *h.*

بانا बाना *bānā*, a. to open or spread out. *h.*

بانات बानात *bānāt*, f. broad-cloth. *h.*

باناتي बानाती *bānātī*, woollen, made of broad-cloth. *h.*

بانان *bāṅān* (v. *bāyān*), the left hand or side. *s.*

بانب बांब *bāmb*, m. (also *bāmb-andhū,ā*), an eel, snake (see *bām*). *h.*

بان بان كرنا बां बांक *bāṅ bāṅ-k.*, to prate idly, to tattle foolishly. *h.*

بانبهني बांभनी *bāmbhnī*, بانبهئي बांभई *bāmbha,ī*, بانبهي बांभी *bāmbhī*, } f. a snake's hole. *h.*

بان‌پرستهه बानप्रस्थ *bāna-prasth*, m. the state of an anchorite or hermit (see *āsram*). *s.*

بانٹ बांट *bānṭ*, m. share, distribution; a weight (*i. e.* the standard by which things are weighed); food given to a cow while milking her. *s.*

بانٹا बांटा *bānṭā*, m. portion, share. *s.*

بانٹ‌چونٹ बांटचोंट *bānṭ-chonṭ*, share, distribution. *s.*

بانٹنا बांटना *bānṭnā*, بانٹهنا बांठना *bānṭhnā*, } a. to share, to distribute, to divide, participate, dispose of. Also *bānṭ-lenā*, the same. *s.*

بانجر बांजर *bāṅjar*, (land) lying waste or fallow. *h.*

بانجه बांझ *bānjh* (Dakh. *bāṅj*), barren (applicable to females, also to land or soil. *s.*

بانجيه वाणिज्य *bāṇijya*, m. trade, commerce, merchandise. *s.*

بانچنا बांचना *bāṅchnā*, a. to read; m. Dakh. *bāṅchnā* (for *bachnā*); n. to escape, to be saved. *s.*

بانچها बांछा *bānchhā*, f. wish, desire. *s.*

بانچهت बांछित *bānchhit*, desired, longed for. *s.*

باندا बान्दा *bāndā*, the name of a place in Bandel-khand. *h.*

باندا बान्दा *bāndā* (for *bandā*), m. kind of plant which grows on trees (*epidendrum*, particularly *tessellatum, Roxb.*). *s.*

بان‌دار बानदार *bān-dār*, a rocket-thrower. *h.p.*

باندر बान्दर *bāndar*, باندرا बान्दरा *bāndrā*, } m. (for *bandar*), an ape, a monkey. *s.*

باندرني बान्दरनी *bāndarnī*, باندري बान्दरी *bāndrī*, } f. a female ape or monkey. *s.*

باندنا *bāndnā* (for *bāndhnā*), a. to tie, to stop, &c. *s.* [finement, imprisonment. *s.*

باندھ बांध *bāṅdh*, m. an embankment; con-

باندھلگوتی बांधलगोती *bāṅdhalgotī*, name of a tribe inhabiting part of Bandel-khand. *h.*

باندھنا बांधना *bāṅdhnā*, a. to tie; to shut; to stop water, to embank; to bind, to fasten; to invent, to contrive, to stop, to pack, to aim, to build, to put, to settle *s.*

باندھنو बांधनू *bāṅdhnū*, m. a mode of dyeing, in which the cloth is tied in different places to prevent the parts tied from receiving the dye; slander, plot, plan; a kind of silk cloth; a kind of parrot. *h.*

باندھو बांधव *bāṅdhav*, m. a relative, a kinsman, a friend. *s.*

باندی बांदी *bāndī*, f. a female slave. *bāndī kā beṭā*, obedient, submissive. In the Dakhanī dialect, *bāndī-bartun*, "slave girls and utensils," the impediments, appropriately so called, of an army on march; the families, baggage, &c. of the Sipāhīs. *h.*

بانڈا बांडा *bāṅḍā*, m. a bird without tail; a serpent which has lost its tail; adj. tail-less, docked. *s.*

بانڈی बांडी *bāṅḍī*, f. a cudgel; a kind of dress; misfortune, calamity. *h.*

بانر बानर *bānar* (for *vānar*), m. a monkey. *s.*

بانس बांस *bāṅs*, m. a bamboo; a measure of about ten feet, used to measure tanks, ditches, or excavations in general (a cube of one *bāṅs* is called a *chaukā*). *bāṅs par charhnā*, n. to be branded with infamy. *s.*

بانسا बांसा *bāṅsā*, m. the bridge of the nose; the channel through which the seeds descend in a drilling-machine. *h.*

بانس پھوڑ बांसफोर *bāṅs-phor*, m. the name of a caste who work or deal in bamboos. *s.*

بانسری बांसरी *bāṅsrī*, بانسری बांसुरी *bāṅsurī*, بانسلی बांसली *bāṅslī*, بانسی बांसी *bāṅsī*, } f. a flute, fife, pipe; a kind of noxious weed in arable land; a purse; adj. made of bamboo. *s.*

بانک बांक *bāṅk*, f. an ornament (half-circle) worn on the arms; a kind of dagger having a curved blade; an exercise with the dagger; a settee. *h.*

بانک बांक *bāṅk*, m. a crook, curvature, bending; a reach or turning of a river; fault, offence, wickedness. *s.*

بانکا बांका *bāṅkā*, m. a fop, a beau, a coxcomb; a buck, a bravo, a bully; a bent trumpet or bugle; f. name of a river; adj. crooked, foppish. *h.*

بانکاچور बांकाचूर *bāṅkā-chūr*, m. a fop, coxcomb, &c. *h.*

بانک پٹا बांकपट्टा *bāṅk-paṭṭā*, m. a kind of fencing with (wooden) dagger and cutlass. *h.*

بانک پن बांकपन *bāṅk-pan*, m. foppishness; debauchery; disorderly conduct. *h.*

بانگ *bāng*, f. sound, voice, cry; the voice of the *mu,azzin* calling *Muhammadans* to prayer; the crowing of a cock. *bāng-mārnā*, a. to cry out, to call. *bāng-denā* (or in Pers. *-bardāshtan*, or *-dādan*), a. to call *Muhammadans* to prayer. *bāngi ṣubḥ*, the call to morning prayer. *bāngi namāz*, the call to prayers in general. *p.*

بانگا बांगा *bāngā*, m. raw cotton (v. *bānga*). *h.*

بانگر बांगर *bāngar*, m. high ground or uplands. *h.*

بانگہ *bānga*, m. a species of cotton produced exclusively in the Dacca district, and indispensably necessary, though not otherwise of superior quality, to form the stripes of some of the finest kinds of muslin. *p.*

بانگی बानगी *bāngī*, f. a pattern, muster. *h.*

بانو *bānū*, f. a lady, a woman of rank. *p.*

بانوا बानूआ *bānū,ā*, m. the name of a water-bird. *h.*

بانواں बांवां *bāṅwāṅ*, the left hand or side. *s.*

بانوسا बानूसा *bānūsā*, m. بانوسی बानूसी *bānūsī*, f. } a kind of cloth. *h.*

بانوی बानवे *bānawwe* or *bānawe*, ninety-two. *h.*

بانہہ बांह *bāṅh*, f. the arm from the shoulder to the elbow; guarantee, protector, or security (as when a person trusts himself in the power of an enemy, a third person being his *bāṅh*, who engages to return him to his house or fort in security). *bāṅh-balī*, strong in the arm. *bāṅh pakaṛnā* or *gahnā*, a. to protect. *bāṅh denā*, a. to assist (see *bāzū denā*). *bāṅh ṭūṭnā*, to be destitute of friends or protectors. *s.*

بانہ *bāna* (for *bānā*), m. dress, uniform, &c. *s.*

بانہیاں बांहियां *bāṅhiyāṅ*, m. a patron. *s.*

بانی *bānī*, a builder, an architect, a composer, author, founder. *a.*

بانی बानी *bānī*, f. the price paid for a work; a fabric or manufacture; ashes; the name of a yellow earth with which potters sometimes ornament their vessels; the thread with which cloth is woven; a weight equal to 80 rupees. *h.*

بانی बानी *bānī*, f. speech, language; name of the goddess of eloquence, *Saraswatī*. *s.*

بانی بونی बानीबोनी *bānībonī*, f. the price of weaving. *h.*

بانی کار *bānī-kār*, an architect; a composer, an author, beginner; an instigator. *p.*

بانی کاری *bānī-kārī*, f. architecture; composition; commencing a business; instigation. *p.*

باو बाओ *bā,o*, f. wind. *bā,o sarnā*, n. to be discharged backwards (wind). *bā,o bāndhnā*, to prevail over an adversary by flattery or invective without argument. *bā,o-khānī*, to live in pleasure and enjoyment; to court one's inspirations; to protract a miserable existence. *s.*

باو बाओ *bā,o* or बाव *bāv*, f. the pox, a bubo. *h.*

باوا बावा *bāwā* (v. *bābā*), father. *bāwā-jān*, dear father. *d.*

باوان बावाँ *bāwān*, the left hand or side. *s.*

باوبتاس बाओबतास *bā,o-batās*, f. calamity, misfortune, particularly such as is believed to result from the evil influence of a demon (see *āsīb*). *h.*

باوبهري كهال *bā,o bharī-khāl*, of no intrinsic value; lit. a skin full of wind. *d.*

باوبهك बाओभक *bā,o-bhak*, } a prattler, tri-
باوجهك बाओझक *bā,o-jhak*, } fling talker. *h.*

باوتا बावता *bā,otā*, } m. a flag or banner; a
باوٹا बावटा *bā,oṭā*, } sail; a sort of armlet worn by women. *s.*

باوجود *bā-wujūd*, notwithstanding. *bā-wujūdi-ānki*, notwithstanding that. *p.*

باور *bāwar*, m. belief, faith, confidence, truth, credit; adj. true, credible. *bāwar-k.*, to credit. *bāwar-h.*, to be credible. *p.*

باور बावर *bāwar*, m. a kind of sweetmeats. *h.*

باورا बावरा *bā,orā* or *bāwarā*, mad, crazy. *s.*

باورچن *bāwarchin*, } f. a cookmaid or female
باورچني *bāwarchinī*, } cook. *t. h.*

باورچي *bāwarchī*, m. a cook. *bāwarchī-khāna*, m. a kitchen, cook-house. "This word seems to be one of those old Persian or Turkish terms, of which several are now preserved in the Hindustanī, which are no longer used by or known to the Turks and Persians. The term implies "confidential person," as a cook unquestionably should be, particularly in the East, where life is so frequently attempted by poison." (Binning). *t.* [art. *t. p.*

باورچيگري *bāwarchīgarī*, f. the culinary

باوري बाओरी *bā,orī*, name of a tribe of vagrants to the west of Delhi. *h.*

باوري बावरी *bā,orī*, } f. a well, pit. *d.*
باوڑي बाओड़ी *bā,oṛī*, }

باوسول बावसूल *bā,o-sūl*, m. the cholic. *s.*

باوصف *bā-waṣf*, yet, notwithstanding. *p. a.*

باوفا *bā-wafā*, faithful, trusty. *p. a.*

باوگ बावग *bāwag*, m. seed-time (same as *bā,onī*). *h.* [tulency. *s.*

باوگولا बावगोला *bā,o-golā*, m. the cholic; fla-

باولا बावला *bā,olā* or *bāwalā*, mad, crazy. *s.*

باولي बाओली *bā,olī*, f. a large well into which people descend to get water; the drag (thing or animal) with which hawks, dogs, &c., are taught to hunt; a trick. *bā,olī denā*, a. to initiate. *h.*

باولينا बावलेना *bā,olenā*, m. the name of a defect in horses. *h.*

باون बावन *bāwan* (for *vāmana*), dwarfish, diminutive; m. the fifth incarnation of Vishnu. *s.*

باون बावन *bāwan*, fifty-two. *h.* [*bāwan*). *s.*

باونا बावना *bā,onā* or *bāwanā*, dwarfish (see

باوني बाओनी *bā,onī*, f. seed-time, sowing. *h.*

باه बाहु *bāhu* or बाह *bāh*, f. an arm. *s.*

باه *bāh*, f. virility, manhood; coitus. *p.*

باها बाहा *bāhā*, a water-course, channel. *h.*

باهبهوشا बाहुभूषा *bāhu-bhūshā*, f. an armlet, an ornament worn round the upper arm. *s.*

باهج बाहुज *bāhuj*, m. sesamum growing wild or spontaneously. *s.*

باهدا बाहुदा *bāhudā*, f. the name of a river said to rise in the Himalaya mountains: probably the modern Behut, the classical Hydaspes. *s.*

باهر बाहर *bāhar* or बाहिर *bāhir*, without, foreign. *s.*

باهر *bāhir*, superior, excellent; open, public. *a.*

باهرا बाहरा *bāharā* or *bāhara*, the man who stands at the well to upset the water from the leathern bucket or *charas*, q. v. *h.*

باهركا *bāhir-kā*, from without, strange. *bāhir-kā ṣāḥib āyā, khabar dījo*; "a strange gentleman is arrived, give notice;" an exclamation used by the darwāns or gatekeepers in Calcutta on the arrival of a stranger, to give notice to the family within. In my time the above sentence was pronounced (by the non-reading gentry), "Barker sawb āyā, cover the Jew!" *s.*

باهره बाहिरह *bāhirah*, m. the left side (in sword exercise, &c.). *s.*

باهري बाहरी *bāharī*, a foreigner, a stranger; outward. *s.*

باهليا बाहुल्य *bāhulyā*, m. } plenty, abun-
باهليتا बाहुल्यता *bahulyatā*, f. } dance, quantity. *s.*

[one with another. *p.*

باهم *bāham*, together, mutually. *bā-ham-digar*,

باهمن बाह्मन *bāhman*, a Brāhman. *s.*

باهمنهٹي बाह्मनहट्टी *bāhman-haṭṭī*, f. name of a plant (*Ovieda verticellata*). *s.*

باهمني बाह्मनी *bāhmanī*, wife of a Brāhman; a Brāhmaness; adj. of or relating to a Brāhman. *bāhmanī badakh*, the *chakwā* or Brāhmany duck. *bāhmanī chīl*, the Brāhmany kite, v. *garuṛ*. *s.*

باهمنيٹا बाह्मनेटा *bāhmaneṭā*, son of a Brāhman; a young Brāhman. *s.*

باهمول बाहुमूल *bāhu-mūl*, m. the armpit. *s.*

باهن बाहन *bāhan*, m. a carriage. *s.*

باهن बाहन *bāhan*, m. fallow land (root of *bāhnā*). *h.*

باهنا बाहना *bāhnā*, a. to plough, to till; to shoot or discharge a weapon; to comb the hair. *h.*

باهيده बाहुयुद्ध *bāhu-yuddh*, m. close fight, personal struggle; boxing, wrestling. *s.*

بائي बाई *bā,ī*, f. mistress, lady (among Mahrattas); a dancing-girl. *bā,ī-jī*, the mother bawd; the old abbess; "la bonne." *h.*

باي बाए *bā,e* or बाई *bā,ī*, f. flatulency; rheumatism. *bā,ī pachnī*, to be mortified, to be depressed, to die away. *bā,ī men bharaknā*, to prate foolishly. *bā,ī sarnā* (see *bā,o sarnā*). *s.*

بايان बायाँ **bāyāṅ**, left (not right); m. the bass part in music, the bass sound (particularly of the *ṭabla, dholak*, and *pakhāwaj*, which are played upon by the left hand). *bāyāṅ pāṅw pūjnā*, to acknowledge the cunning of an artful person. *s.*

بايب बायब **bāyab**, apart, separate, strange, distinct. *yih bāt bāyab hai*, this is another thing; this is a horse of another colour. *h.* [quarter. *h.*

بايب बायब **bāyab** or **bā,ib**, m. the north-west

باي برنگ बाएबिरंग **bā,e-birang**, m. name of a medicinal seed. *s.*

بايد **bāyad**, it is fit, or necessary. *bāyad-shāyad*, as it should be. *p.*

بائيس बाईस **bā,īs**, twenty-two. *h.*

بايسته **bāyista**, that which is becoming or requisite, necessary. *p.*

بائيسي बाईसी **bā,īsī**, f. the royal army, because composed of the troops of the twenty-two *ṣūbas* or provinces then constituting the Mogul empire; a command of 22,000 men. *bā,īsī ṭūṭnā*, to attack with one's whole force. *h.*

بايع **bā,i'** or **bāyi'**, a seller, a merchant. *a.*

بائكا **bā,īkā**, }
بائكو **bā-īkū**, } f. a woman, a wife. *d.*

بائي گولا बाएगोला **bā,e-golā**, m. (see *bā,o-golā*). *h*

باين बायन **bāyan**, m. sweetmeat, &c., which is distributed to friends in marriage feasts, or in commemoration of a success. *s.*

بائين **bā,īn** (v. *bā,olī*), a large well. *d.*

بائين **bā-īn**, along with this, although. *p.*

بائني बाईनी **bā,īnī**, f. a basket in which snakes are carried about for show. *h.*

بائيها बाईहा **bā,īhā**, m. rheumatism. *h.*

بباد बिबाद **bibād** (for *vivād*), m. quarrel, contest. *h.*

بباد **ba-bād**, lit. to the wind, cast away. *p.*

ببادي बिबादी **bibādī** (for *vivādī*), a disputant, plaintiff. *s.* [marriage. *s.*

بباه बिबाह **bibāh** (for *vivāh*), m. matrimony,

ببر बबर **babar**, m. one who crops the manes of horses. *h.*

ببر **babar**, m. a lion, a tiger. *bi-bar* (imper. of *burdan*), bear or carry thou. *p.*

ببرجي **babarjī**, }
ببرچي **babarchī**, } m. (for *bāwarchī*), a cook; so *babarjī-khāna*, a cook-house or kitchen. *p.* [dissension. *h.*

ببراكهيري बबराखेरी **babrā-kherī**, f. quarrelling,

ببرن बिबरण **bibaran** (for *vivaran*), m. interpretation, explanation. *s.* [colour. *s.*

ببرن बिबर्ण **bibarn** (for *vivarna*), faded in

ببروتا बबरूता **babrūtā**, m. a clown, lout, bumpkin, a clumsy young man. *h.*

ببري बबरी **babrī**, f. cropped hair, tresses; the act of cropping (particularly the manes of horses). *h.*

ببري **babarī**, leonine or tigerish; canine, savage. *p.*

ببري बबुरी **baburī**, }
ببور बबूर **babūr**, }
ببول बबूल **babūl**, } f. the name of a tree of the mimosa kind. (There are several species: the commonest is the Arabica, *Rox.*); the acacia tree. The *babūl* produces also a valuable gum, and its bark, being a powerful astringent, is used in tanning by *chamārs*, q. v. *s.* [of fondness. *h.*

ببوا बबुवा **babuwā**, m. a child, a boy (a term

ببهر बभ्रु **babhru**, large, great, tawny, &c.; bald-headed through disease; m. a large ichneumon: the name of a sage; a tawny or brown colour. *s.*

ببهكشا बुभुक्षा **bubhukshā**, f. hunger. *s.*

ببهكشت बुभुक्षित **bubhukshit**, hungry. *s.*

ببهني बभनी **babhnī**, f. (see *bāmhnī*), a stye on the eyelids, a lizard. *h.*

ببهو बिभव **bibhaw** (for *vibhav*), m. substance, wealth; power, grandeur. *s.*

ببي बबै **babai**, m. the seed of a sweet-scented herb (*Ocymum pilosum, Roxb.*); name of a bird. *s.*

ببي बब्बी **babbī**, f. a kiss. *h.*

ببيسي बबेसी **babesī**, f. the piles. *h.*

ببيسيا बबेसिया **babesiyā** or **bawesiyā**, talking nonsense; m. a catamite. *h.*

ببيك बिबेक **bibek**, m. }
ببيكتا बिबेकता **bibekatā**, f. } discrimination, discretion, sense. *s.*

ببيكي बिबेकी **bibekī**, discreet, prudent. *s.*

بپاهونا बपाहोना **bapā honā**, to be raised, established, pitched. *h.*

بپت **bapt** or **bapat**, hidden, secret. *d.*

بپت बिपत **bipat**, }
بپت बिपत्ति **bipatti**, }
بپتا बिपता **biptā**, } f. calamity, misfortune, danger, mischief. *s.*

بپر बिप्र **bipr** (for *vipra*), a man of the sacerdotal caste, a Brāhman. *s.*

بپرا बपुरा **bapurā**, helpless, distressed. *h.*

بپرنا बिपरना **biparnā**, a. to attack, to assault. *h.*

بپريت बिपरीत **bi-parīt**, contrary, opposite; f. mischief, ruin. *s.*

بپل बिपल **bipal**, m. a measure of time, a second, or (as some say) one-sixth of a second. *s.*

بپنس बपंश **bapaṅs**, m. patrimony, a father's share. *s.*

بپوتي बपौती **bapautī** or **bapotī**, f. paternal estate, patrimony, heritage. *h.* [bath. *s.*

بپهارا बफारा **baphārā**, m. vapour, vapour-

بپهرنا बिफरना **bipharnā**, n. to be perverse, refractory, cross, irritated, obstinate, pert. *s.*

بپھي बिफै *biphai* (for *vrihaspati*), m. Thursday. *h.*

بپيتي बपैती *bapaitī*, f. paternal estate. *s.*

بت वित *bit* or वित्त *bitt* (for *vitt*), m. wealth, substance, ability, power, means. *s.*

بت बुत *but*, m. a hazard table; a blow with the fist. *h.*

بت *but*, m. an idol (hence, figuratively, a beloved woman; a darling). *but-parast*, an idolater *but-parastī*, idolatry. *but-tarāsh*, a maker of idols. *p.*

بت *bat*, m. a line drawn to distinguish separate names in a catalogue, or articles in an account. *p.*

بت बत *bat*, m. the worm which is so destructive to shipping (*Teredo*); contraction of *bāt*, a word (used in composition), as *bat-bāharī*, external, foreign. *bat-baṛhā,o*, m. prolixity, talkativeness, chicanery, wrangle. *bat-banā*, an orator, a sophist. *bat-kahāo*, m. talk, conversation. Contraction of *bāt*, wind, used in composition, as *bat-soṅhā-k.*, a. to ventilate. *h.*

بتا वित्ता *bittā*, m. a span, a hand's breadth. *h.*

بتا बुत्ता *buttā*, m. overreaching, fraud, trick, take in. *buttā-denā*, to overreach. *h.*

بتا बता *batā*, m. a bamboo lath; a thin slip of bamboo; an oblong stone on which powders are levigated. *h.*

بتارد बुतारद *butārad*, a name given to an extra cess upon the cultivator. *h.*

بتاس बतास *batās*, f. wind, air. *batās-phenī*, f. a kind of sweetmeats, sugarcakes. *s.*

بتاسا बतासा or बताशा *batāsā*, m. a kind of sweetmeats, sugarcakes (of a spongy texture, q. d. filled with air); a bubble filled with water. *h.*

بتاشا *batāshā*, m. (see *batāsā*), a bubble, &c. *h.*

بتان बतान *batān*, place of assemblage of cattle at night in an open field. *h.*

بتانا बताना *batānā*, a. to point, to shew, to explain, to teach; to appear; m. an upper turban; a small bracelet of metal. *h.*

بتانا बिताना *bitānā*, a. to pass (time), to spend. *s.*

بتانا बुताना *butānā*, } a. to extinguish. *h.*
بتاونا बुतावना *butā,onā*, }

بتاري نيمبو बतारी निंबू *batārī nimbū*, m. the shaddock. *h.*

بتخانه *but-khāna*, an idol temple. *p.*

بتر बतर *batar*, land in a state fit for the plough. *h.*

بتر *batar* or *battar*, worse, very bad (contracted from *bad-tar*). *p*

بتر *batar*, curtailed (animal); destitute of good qualities (see *abtar*). *a.*

بترابندي बित्राबन्दी *bitrā-bandī* (v. *bila-bandī*), a kind of settlement. *h.*

بتراش *but-tarāsh*, an idol-maker, a statuary. *p.*

بترانا बतराना *batrānā*, a. to converse, talk. *s.*

بترن वितरण *bitaran* (for *vitaran*), m. giving charity, alms, a donation. *s.*

بترنا वितरना *bitarnā*, a. to bestow, to grant. *s.*

بتسا बत्सा *batsā*, m. a kind of rice. *h.*

بتسل वात्सल *batsal* (for *vatsal*), kind, loving. *s.*

بتك बतक *batak*, f. (v. بطك), a duck. *p.*

بتكده *but-kada*, an idol temple, a pagoda. *p.*

بتكڑ बतक्कड़ *batakkhaṛ*, loquacious, talkative. *h.*

بتكها बतकहा *bat-kahā*, loquacious, conversible. *h.*

بتكهاو बतकहाव *bat-kahā,o*, m. } loquacity,
بتكهي बतकही *bat-kahī*, f. } conversibleness, discourse, dialogues. *h.*

بتلانا बतलाना *batlānā*, a. to shew, to explain, to point out, to teach, to inform. *h*

بتم بتم *bittam-bittam*, bit by bit, gradually. *d.*

بتنا वितना *bitnā* (see *bītnā*), n. to pass, elapse. *s.*

بتنگ *ba-tang*, lit. in straitness. *ba-tang ānā* or *honā*, to be in great distress. *p.*

بتورا बितौरा *bitaurā*, m. a heap of dried cow-[dung. *h.*

بتوري बतौरी *batauri*, f. a flatulent or œdematous swelling. *h.*

بتوري बतूरी *batūrī*, f. a species of *chanā* (q. v.); a small kind of grain. *h.*

بتورن बतोरन *batoran*, } gathering or collect-
بتولن बतोलन *batolan*, } ing the grain in the time of harvest. *h.*

بتول *batūl*, f. a virgin averse to matrimony, [a nun. *a.*

بتولي बतोली *batolī*, f. buffoonery. *h.*

بتوني बतूनी *batūnī*, a tattler, an idle talker. *h.*

بتوون बतवोन *batwon*, the preparation of land for the reception of the seed. *h.*

بتها विथा *bithā*, f. pain; affliction. *s.*

بتهارنا बिथारना *bithārnā*, a. to cause to scatter, to cause to sprinkle. *h.*

بتهاري बिथारी *bithārī*, f. cleansing the warp. *h.*

بتهرانا बिथराना *bithrānā*, a. to scatter, to sprinkle. *h.*

بتهرنا बिथरना *bitharnā*, or बिथुरना *bithurnā*, n. to be scattered, to be sprinkled. *h.*

بتهوا बथूआ *bathū,ā*, m. name of a kind of greens (*Chenopodium album*); also a kind of weed which grows with the spring crops in the vicinity of water. *h.*

بتهيا बथिया *bathiyā*, a heap of dried cowdung. *h.*

بتي बाती *batī*, f. a word, speech. *s.*

بتي बत्ती *battī*, f. a candle; a wick; a match; a tent or bougie; a stick (of sealing-wax). *s.*

بتي *buttī*, f. provision for a journey. *buttī lekar chaudhīr dhūndnā*, to go in earnest search (of any thing). *d.* [high. *h.*

بتيا बित्तिया *bittiyā*, m. a dwarf, *i.e.* a span

بتيانا बतियाना *batiyānā*, a. to speak, to talk, to say, to converse. *h.*

بتيت बितीत *bitīt*, passed, gone, elapsed. *s.*

بتيس बत्तीस *battīs*, thirty-two. *h.*

بتيسا बत्तीसा *battīsā*, m. a medicine composed of thirty-two ingredients, usually given to mares after foaling. *h.*

بتيسي बत्तीसी *battīsī*, f. any aggregate, consisting of thirty-two parts, hence, a set of teeth. *battīsī dikhānā*, a. to shew the teeth, to laugh; to scoff or make faces at any one. *h.*

بٹ बट *baṭ*, m. name of a tree (*Ficus Indica*); a single *cauṛī*. *s.*

بٹ बट *baṭ*, m. tripe; twist; a wrinkle or fold of the abdomen; (in comp.) contracted for *bāṭ*, a road, as *baṭ-pār*, a highwayman. In Dakh. a weight made of metal or hard stone to weigh with (v. *baṭkharā*). *h.*

بٹ बट *baṭ*, m. }
بٹائي बटाई *baṭā,ī*, f. } a partition, division: in revenue language, division of the crop between the cultivator and zamīndār. *baṭā,ī-dār*, a cultivator who shares his crop with the zamīndār. *h.*

بٹّا बट्टा *baṭṭā*, m. deficiency; exchange or discount; defect, blemish, injury, offence; a ball (of wood or stone); a box in which gems are kept. *baṭṭe-bāz*, a juggler, a trickster. *baṭṭe-bāzī*, f. juggling, trickery, subterfuge. *baṭṭā ḍhār* and *baṭṭā ḍhāl*, level, even. *h.*

بٹار बटार *baṭār*, name of a tribe of *Gūjars*, q. v. *h.* [lusion, &c. (v. *saṭṭā-baṭṭā*). *h.*

بٹاسٹا *baṭṭā-saṭṭā*, m. a kind of armour, col-

بٹان बिटाना *biṭānā*, a. to scatter, to sprinkle. *h.*

بٹانا *baṭānā*, }
بٹانه *baṭāna*, } m. a pea, called in Urdū, *maṭar* (q. v.). *d.*

بٹاؤ बटाऊ *baṭā,ū*, m. a traveller; (in Dakh.) a highwayman. *s.* [ropes, &c. (v. *baṭ*). *h.*

بٹائي बटाई *baṭā,ī*, f. hire paid for twisting

بٹپ बिटप *biṭap*, a tree, a twig. *s.*

بٹ پار बटपार *baṭpār*, }
بٹ پاڑ बटपाड़ *baṭpāṛ*, } m. highwayman, villain, footpad. *h.*

بٹ پاري बटपारी *baṭpārī*, }
بٹ پاڑي बटपाड़ी *baṭ-pāṛī*, } f. highway robbing. *h.*

بٹخ *baṭṭakh*, m. a duck (v. بطك). *h.*

بٹرنا बटुरना *baṭurnā*, to be collected together. *h.*

بٹري बटरी *baṭrī*, f. a small cup. *h.*

بٹکهرا बटखरा *baṭkharā*, m. a weight to weigh with (also written *baṭkara* or *baṭkhara*). *h.*

بٹلون बिटलवण *biṭ-lavan*, m. a kind of medicinal salt. *s.*

بٹلوهي बटलोही *baṭlohī*, or *baṭlo,ī*, f. a brass vessel in which Hindūs dress their food. *h.*

بٹمار बटमार *baṭ-mār*, a highwayman. *baṭ-mārī*, highway robbery. *h.* [pulse. *s.*

بٹماس बिटमास *biṭmās*, m. a coarse species of

بٹموگرا बटमोगरा *baṭ-mogrā*, m. the double jasmine (*Jasminum zambac*). *h.*

بٹنا बटना *baṭnā*, a. to twist, to form by convolution (as ropes); to divide, share; to gain, make profit; n. to be divided, to be twisted; m. an instrument with which ropes are twisted. *h.*

بٹنيا बटनिया *baṭaniyā*, m. proprietor of a *baṭ*, a shareholder. *h.*

بٹوا बटुआ *baṭū,ā* or *baṭwā*, m. a purse, a small bag, generally used for holding betel-nut, &c.; a brass vessel in wich Hindūs dress their food. *h.*

بٹوا बिटवा *biṭwā*, m. a son. *h.*

بٹوار बटवार *baṭwār* (also *baṭwāl*), a tax gatherer who collects a tax levied in kind; a customs or police officer stationed on the road for collecting transit duties. *h.*

بٹوارا बटवारा *baṭwārā*, m. a share, the partition or division of lands, division of a crop in shares. *h.*

بٹوانا बटवाना *baṭwānā*, a. to cause to twist, &c. *h.* [resort. *h.*

بٹور बटोर *baṭor*, m. a gathering, a crowd, a

بٹورا बिटौरा *biṭaurā*, m. a heap of the cakes of dried cow-dung. *h.*

بٹورن बटोरन *baṭoran*, gathering or heaping grain in one place at the time of harvest. *h.*

بٹورنا बटोरना *baṭornā*, a. to gather up, to collect, to purse, to accumulate (in Dakh. *baṭolnā*). *h.*

بٹوري बिटौरी *biṭaurī*, f. a tax on shopkeepers &c. in a village. *h.* [&c. *d.*

بٹولن *baṭolan* (v. *baṭoran*), gathering grain,

بٹونا बिटोना *biṭonā*, a. to scatter, to sprinkle; m. a son (see *biṭwā*). *h.*

بٹوهي बटोही *baṭohī*, m. a traveller, wayfarer. *s.*

بٹه बट्ट *baṭṭa*, an extraordinary allowance paid the military when on field duty. Also, the agio allowance, or rate of expenditure, between rupees of different species. *h.*

بٹهان बठान *baṭhān*, pasture grounds. *h.*

بٹهانا बिठाना *biṭhānā*, a. to cause to sit down, to set, settle. *h.*

بٹهك बिठक *biṭhak*, m. an ant hill. *h.*

بٹهلانا बिठलाना *biṭhlānā*, to cause to be seated, to make one sit down. *h.*

بٹهنا बठिना *biṭhnā*, n. (for *baiṭhnā*), to sit. *h.*

بٹھنا बठना *baṭhnā*, n. to enter: (in Dakh.) to be twisted, plaited, or woven together, as ropes. *h.*

بٹھوا बठुआ *baṭhū,ā* or *baṭhuwā*, a kind of herb. *h*

بٹھئی बटई *batha,ī*, f. the art of making gold thread, also *baṭa,ī*. *h.*

بٹی बट्टी *baṭṭī*, f. a candle; a still for distilling [spirits. *h.*

بٹیا बिटिया *biṭiyā*, f. a daughter. *s.*

بٹیا बटया *baṭyā*, f. a silken cord adorned with three fringes, which women use to tie their hair behind. *h.*

بٹیا बटिया *baṭiyā*, f. a narrow passage, an [alley; a small measure of weight. *h.*

بٹی باز बट्टेबाज *baṭṭe-bāz*, m. a juggler. *baṭṭe-bāzī*, f. performance of a juggler, slight of hand. *h. p.*

بٹیر बटेर *baṭer*, m. f. a kind of quail (*Perdix olivacea, Buch*). *s.*

بٹیس बटेस *bāṭes*, m. a passage, pathway. *h.*

بٹینتھ बटेन्थ *baṭenth*, m. the proprietor or holder of a share (same as *baṭaniyā*). *h.*

بجا *ba-jā*, in place, all right, proper, true, accurate, becoming, fit. *p.*

بجار बिजार *bijār*, m. a bull, a stallion. *h.*

بجاک बजाक *bajāk*, m. a kind of serpent. *h.*

بجالا बिजाला *bijālā*, seedy, turned to seed, abounding in seed. *s.*

بجالانا बजालाना *ba-jā-lānā* (in Pers. *ba-jā āwardan*,), a. to perform, to obey, to execute, to accomplish. *p. h.*

بجان *ba-jān*, to the heart, soul, or life. *ba-jān āmadan*, to be in imminent danger or distress. *ba-jān ranjīdan*, to be vexed to the soul. *p.*

بجانا बजाना *bajānā*, a. to sound, to play upon an instrument of music; to perform, to execute. *h.*

بجانا *bujānā* (for *bujhānā* q. v.), to extinguish, &c. *h.*

بجای *ba-jā,e*, in place of, by way of. *p.*

بجائی बिजाई *bijā,ī*, f. a portion of seed corn which the poorer classes are allowed to take from the field. *h.*

بجایتھ बिजायठ *bijāyath*, m. a kind of ornament for the arm; a bracelet. *h.*

بجبجانا बजबजाना *baj-bajānā*, n. to effervesce with noise in putrefying. *h.*

بجتر *bujattar*, } m. (for *bajantrī*, &c. q. v.)
بجتری *bajattarī*, } a musician, &c. *s.*

بجدھونا *ba-jidd-honā*, n. to be importunate, to insist upon any thing; to tempt, to urge (a person). *a. h.*

بجر बज्र *bajr* (for *vajr*), m. a thunder-bolt; a diamond; adj. hard. *bajr pare us par*, &c., may lightning fall on him, &c.; this is used in cursing any body. *s.*

بجرا बजरा *bajrā*, m. a boat for travelling in, a pleasure boat (of a larger kind, q. d. heavy or hard), commonly called "budge-row". *h.*

بجراگھات बज्राघात *bajr-āghāt*, (lightning-struck), any sudden calamity, especially if viewed as a judgment from heaven. *s.*

بجربٹو बजरबट्टू *bajar-baṭṭū*, m. name of a fruit; a large kind of seed, of which necklaces are made. *h.*

بجربھانگ बज्रभांग *bajar-bhāng*, m. tobacco. *h.* "This appears to have been the first name given to the weed, which was introduced into India, as is supposed, in the time of Jehanghire. It has now been superseded by the European name—see *tambākū*." (Binning.)

بجرکیٹ बज्रकीट *bajr kīṭ*, m. (lit. "lightning-insect"), a species of the armadillo, called by naturalists Pangolin or Manis; and sometimes "the scaly ant-eater".—It is termed in the Dakhnī dialect *khaulā-mānjā*. (Binning). *s.*

بجرنگ बज्रङ्ग *bajrang*, m. a title of Hanumān. *s.*

بجرنگی बज्रङ्गी *bajrangī*, f. a kind of *tilak*, or mark, made on a Hindū's forehead with red lead. *h.*

بجرہ *bajra*, m. a pleasure-boat (v. *bajrā*). *h.*

بجری बिज्री *bijrī*, f. (v. *bijlī*), lightning. *s.*

بجز *ba-juz*, besides, except. *p.*

بجلی बिजली *bijlī*, f. lightning; a thunder-bolt. *h.*

بجنا बजना *bajnā*, n. to be sounded (a bell or gong &c.); *das baje*, ten have sounded, *i.e.* it is ten o'clock; to be famous; m. a rupee (used among brokers). *h.*

بجنا बुजना *bujnā*, m. a cloth used by menstruous women, a pessary. *h.*

بجنا बिजना *bijnā*, m. a fan, a punkah. *s.*

بجنتر *bajantar*, m. (v. *bajantrī*), *d.*

بجنتری बजन्त्री *bajantrī*, m. one who plays upon musical instruments; f. a tax on musicians and female dancers. *bajantrī-mahall*, m. the quarter inhabited by musicians; a brothel. *h.*

بجنس *ba-jins*, in kind, in some sort. *p. a.*

بجنی बजनी *bajanī* or *bajnī*, f. quarrel, fight; uproar, a row. *h.*

بجو *bijū* (also *bijū bā,orā*), m. (v. *bejū*), an animal that feeds on dead carcases, the Indian badger; (some say the ichneumon), *Ursus Indicus*. *h.*

بجوانا बजवाना *bajwānā*, a. to cause to sound, to cause to play on an instrument. *h.*

بجوڑنا बजोड़ना *bajoṛnā*, a. to strike, smite. *a.*

بجوگ बिजोग *bijog* (for *vijog*), m. separation, absence (especially of lovers); adj. parted, separate. *s.*

بجوگی बिजोगी *bijogī*, wretched, one who is separated (from his beloved, &c.). *s.*

بجھا बझा *bajhā*, m. marshy soil. *h.*

بجھارت बुझारत *bujhārat*, adjustment of accounts. *h.*

بجھانا बुझाना *bujhānā*, a. to extinguish, to put out; to damp or depress one's courage, to quench one's thirst, as *piyās bujhānā*. *h.*

بجهانا बुझाना *bujhānā* a. (caus. of *būjhnā*), to explain, to infuse into the mind, to demonstrate, to push as with argument, to persuade, to cause to believe, to take to. *h.*

بجهانا बझाना *bajhānā*, a. (also *bajhāwanā* or *bajhā,onā*), to entangle, to ensnare (as game), to entrap. *h.* [again. *h.*

بجهبجهول *bujhbujhawal*, m. a riddle, guess

بجهرا बुजहरा *bujahrā*, m. a vessel for warm water. *h.*

بجهکانا बिझकाना *bijhkānā*, a. to frighten, to scare, to alarm. *h.*

بجهکنا बिझकना *bijhaknā*, n. to be alarmed, to be startled. *h.*

بجهگاه बिझगाह *bijhgāh*, a scarecrow. *h.*

بجهنا बुझना *bujhnā*, n. to be extinguished, to be put out (as fire, a lamp), to be quenched (thirst), to be dejected (the spirits). *h.*

بجهنا बझना *bajhnā*, to be ensnared, to be caught (as game); to stick. *h.*

بجهوٹ बझवट *bajhwaṭ*, a stalk with ear. *h.*

بجهونتا बुझोंता *bujhontā*, an abstract account of a village proprietary. *h.*

بجهونیا बिझोनिया *bijhoniyā*, name of a tribe of *rāj-pūts* in Jaunpūr. *h.* [burthen. *h.*

بجهیل बुझैल *bujhail*, laden; beast, &c., of

بجي बिजै *bijai* (for *vijaya*), m. triumph. *bijai-dasamī*, the victorious tenth; the tenth of *āsin Shukl Paksh*; the anniversary of Rāma's victory over Rāvana. *s.*

بجیا बिजिया *bijiyā* or *bijayā*, m. hemp, bhang (*Cannabis sativa*). *s.*

بجیدار बजीदार *bajī-dār*, an agricultural servant who takes corn as a recompense for his labour. *h.*

بجيي बिजयी *bijayī* (for *vijayī*), vanquisher, conqueror. *s.*

بچ बिच *bich* (for *bīch*), in the midst, among. *s.*

بچ बच *bach* or *vach*, f. orris root. *s.*

بچ बच *bach*, an inferior tribe of *rāj-pūts* in the district of Jaunpūr. *h.*

بچا बचा *bachā* or बच्चा *bachchā*, m. a child; a young animal. *bachche wālī mūrghī*, the hen with her chickens; the constellation of the Pleiades. *p.*

بچاپا बचापा *bachāpā*, m. safety, escape, deliverance. *h.*

بچار बिचार *bichār* (for *vichār*), m. contrivance, consideration, reflection, judgment, opinion, thought, will. *s.*

بچارا *bichārā* (for *be-chāra*), helpless. *p.*

بچارت बिचारत *bichārat* (for *vichārat*), part. reflecting, thinking. *s.*

بچارت बिचारित *bichārit* (for *vichārit*), judged, considered, matured. *s.*

بچارك बिचारक *bichārak*, an inspector, investigator, judge. *s.*

بچارنا बिचारना *bichārnā*, a. to consider, to reflect, to investigate, to comprehend, to think, to apprehend, to conceive. *s.* [helpless. *p*

بچاره *bichāra* (for *be-chāra*), without resource,

بچاریه बिचार्य *bichārya*, fit for consideration. *s*

بچالي बिचाली *bichālī*, f. straw. *h.*

بچانا बचाना *bachānā*, a. to save, to preserve, to reserve, to protect; to save, to spare; to defend, to guard, to conceal, to leave. (for *bajānā*), to sound a musical instrument. *h.*

بچاو बचाव *bachā,o* or *bachāv*, m. safety, protection; escape, deliverance. *h.*

بچپن बचपन *bach-pan*, m. childhood, infancy. *h.*

بچتر बिचित्र *bichitr* (for *vichitra*), various; wonderful. *s.*

بچتي बचती *bachtī*, f. remainder; surplus, residue; end, conclusion. *h.*

بچرنا बिचरना *bicharnā*, to detail. *bichar bichar kar bolnā*, to speak in full detail. *h.*

بچك बिचक *bichak*, disappointment; fright, alarm. *h.*

بچکانا बिचकाना *bichkānā*, a. to baulk, to disappoint, to break one's promise. (in Dakh.) to frighten, to terrify or threaten. *h.*

بچکانا बचकाना *bachkānā*, small (generally applied to shoes and clothes); m. a dancing boy. *h.*

بچکاني बचकानी *bachkānī*, f. a girl adopted by an old prostitute. *p.* [children, &c. *h.*

بچ کچ बचकच *bach-kach* (generally *kach-bach*).

بچکنا बिचकना *bichaknā*, n. to be disappointed, baulked; to sprain; to run away, to retreat; to withdraw a consent which has been given. (in Dakh.) to start, to be afraid. *h.*

بچکنا बिचकन्ना *bichkannā*, m. an ornament worn in the anterior lobe of the ears. *h.*

بچگان *bachagān* or *bachchagān*, children, young one's (Pers. pl. of *bachcha*). *p.*

بچگانه *bachchagāna*, fit for children; in a childish manner. *bachchagānī*, f. a child's toy or plaything. *p.* [tribe. *h.*

بچ گوتي बचगूती *bach-gūtī*, name of a *rāj-pūt*

بچگي *bachchagī* f. infancy, childhood. *p.*

بچلنا बिचलना *bichalnā*, n. to break one's promise, to slip, to infringe, to turn, to bend. *s.*

بچمنا बिचमना *bichamnā*, a. to tease or torment one with questions. *h.*

بچن बचन *bachan*, m. speech, talk, discourse, word; promise, agreement. *bachan band kar lenā* or *bandh k.*, to bind by promise. *bachan band*, or *bandh, honā*, to promise, to be agreed upon. *bachan pālnā*, to abide by a promise. *bachan tornā*, a. to break one's word. *bachan chhornā*, to break one's promise. *bachan denā*, a. to promise, to agree. *bachan ḍālnā*, a. to question, to ask, to inquire. *bachan lenā*, to receive a promise. *bachan mārnā*, to conclude an agreement. *bachan mānnā*, to obey. *bachan nibhānā*, to abide by a promise. *bachan hārnā*, to promise, to agree, to give one's word. *s.*

بچنا बचना *bachnā*, n. to be saved or spared, to escape, to remain unexpended. *bach-rahnā*, to avoid, to take care against. *h.*

بچناگ बचनाग *bachnāg*, name of a vegetable poison. *s.*

بچن دت बचनदत्त *bachan-datta*, betrothed, [espoused. *s.*

بچوا *bichū,ā*, m. name of a plant. *d.*

بچواني बिचवानी *bichwānī*, بچوليا बिचौलिया *bichauliyā*, بچوئي बिचवई *bichwa,ī*, m. one who interposes, a mediator, an umpire, an arbitrator; an agent or ambassador. *s.*

بچه *bachcha*, m. the young of any animal, an infant, a child. *bachcha-dān*, m. the womb. *bachche-wālī murghī*, f. the hen and chickens; a name given to the Pleiades. *p.*

بچه बछ *bachh*, or بچها बछा *bachhā*, m. a calf. *s.*

بچهاتا बिछाता *bichchātā*, m. a stinging-nettle (*Urtica interrupta*). *h.*

بچها دينا बिछा देना *bichhā-denā*, a. to spread; met. to knock down, to drub, to floor. *h.*

بچهانا बिछाना *bichhānā*, a. to spread; m. a bed, bedding, carpet. (Dakh. *bichhānān*). *h.*

بچه‌دان *bachcha-dān*, m. the womb. *p.*

بچهرا बछरा *bachhrā*, m. a calf. *h.* *bichhrā* (Dakh.) separation.

بچهرانا बिछुराना *bichhurānā*, a. to cause to be separated, to separate or sunder (actively). *s.*

بچهراهٹ *bichhurāhaṭ*, f. separation, act of separating. Also *bichharāhaṭ*. *s.*

بچهرنا बिछुरना *bichhurnā* or बिछरना *bichharnā*, n. to be separated, or set apart, to slide, to slip, to turn away the face. *s.*

بچهرو बछरू *bachhrū*, m. a calf or colt. *s.*

بچهڑا बिछड़ा *bichhaṛā*, m. بچهڑاٹ बिछड़ाट *bichhaṛāṭ*, f. separating, separation, parting asunder. *s.*

بچهڑانا बिछड़ाना *bichhaṛānā*, a. to cause to be separated; to part or divide (actively). *s.*

بچهڑاو बिछुड़ाओ *bichhuṛā,o*, m. act of parting or separating, separation. *s.*

بچهڑاهٹ *bichhṛāhaṭ*, fem. separation, turning [away. *s.*

بچهڑنا बिछुड़ना *bichhuṛnā* or बिछड़ना *bichhaṛnā*, n. to be separated, to turn away. *s.*

بچهڑو बछड़ू *bachhṛū*, m. a colt, a calf. *s.*

بچهلنا बिछलना *bichhalnā*, n. to be separated; to slip, to slide; to slip out of place, to sprain; to turn away the face. *h.*

بچهنا बिछना *bichhnā*, n. to be spread. *h.*

بچهناگ बच्छनाग *bachchh-nāg*, m. name of a vegetable poison. *s.*

بچهو बिच्छू *bichchhū*, بچهوا बिछूआ *bichhū,ā*, m. a scorpion. the sign Scorpio. *s.*

بچهوا बिछूआ *bichhū,ā*, m. a sort of dagger; a small stiletto with a curved or serpentine blade; an ornament worn on the toes. *h.*

بچهوانا बिछवाना *bichhwānā*, a. to cause to spread. *h.*

بچهوڑنا बिछोड़ना *bichhoṛnā*, a. to separate. *h.*

بچهونا बिछौना *bichhaunā* or बिछोना *bichhonā*, m. bedding, carpeting. *h.*

بچهونٹا बछोंटा *bachhonṭā*, m. distribution of an aggregate sum on several individuals. *h.*

بچهوه बिछोह *bichhoh*, بچهوها बिछोहा *bichhohā*, m. separation, absence. *h.*

بچهوي *bichhū,ī*, f. a ring or ornament worn on women's toes. *d.*

بچهي बछी *bachhī*, a female young animal. *p.*

بچهيا बछिया *bachhiyā* (diminutive of *bachhī*), f. a female calf. *h.*

بچهيرا बछेरा *bachherā*, بچهيڑا बछेड़ा *bachheṛā*, m. a colt. *h.*

بچهيري बछेरी *bachherī*, بچهيڑي बछेड़ी *bachheṛī*, f. a foal, filly. *h.*

بحاث *baḥḥās*, a great disputer, controvertist, arguer. *a.*

بحار *biḥār* (pl. of بحر), seas, gulfs, &c. *a.*

بحال *ba-ḥāl*, happy, flourishing, prosperous; reinstated (as in service); restoration to a former condition, or continuing in the present state. *p. a.*

بحالي *ba-ḥālī* adj. of or relating to a former state; f. restoration to a former state or condition. *ba-ḥālī sanad*, a grant restoring a person to the possession of something that he has been deprived of, or confirming to him what he at present enjoys. *p.*

بحث *baḥs*, f. argument, discussion, altercation, controversy, discussion. *baḥs-k.*, to dispute. *a.*

بحثابحثي *baḥsā-baḥsī*, f. controversy, discussion, argumentation. *a.*

بحثنا *bahasnā*, a. to argue, to dispute; to talk. *a.*

بحد *ba-ḥadd*, or بحدي كه *ba-ḥadde ki*, to such a degree that; so that. *p.*

بحر *baḥr*, m. a sea, a gulf, a bay; f. metre in prosody; a fleet. *a.*

بحران *buḥrān*, m. the crisis of any disease (as fever, &c.). *a.*

بحري *baḥrī*, maritime, naval; (for *bahrī*), a kind of falcon. *a.*

بحرين *baḥrain*, lit. the two seas, generally applied to the Mediterranean and the Euxine: it also applies to the two waters, viz. the fresh and the salt. *a.*

بحسب *ba-ḥasb* or *ba-ḥasbe ki*, according to, in accordance, in such a way that. *p. a.*

بحق *ba-ḥaḳḳ* or *ba-ḥaḳḳi*, on account of; in the case of. *p. a.*

بحكم *ba-ḥukm* or *ba-ḥukmi*, under the command of; by dint of. *p. a.*

بحل *biḥil*, (for *bi-hil*, "let alone,") pardon, absolution. *p.*

بحمدالله *ba-ḥamd Illāhī*, by the grace of God, God be praised that. *a.*

بحيرة *buḥaira*, a small sea or inland lake. *a.*

بخار *bukhār*, m. steam, mist, fog; glowing heat from the ground, or such as is felt in a fever; vapour, exhalation. *bukhār-nikalnā*, n. to break out (as an eruption on the skin). *bukhār dil meṅ rakhnā*, a. to entertain enmity or malice in the heart. *a.*

بخارا *bukhārā*, name of a town and country; the ancient Bactria. *p.*

بخاري *bukhārī*, of or relating to Bukhārā, a native of Bukhārā. *p.*

بخت *bakht*, m. fortune, prosperity, luck, felicity. *bakht-āwar*, fortunate. *bakht-balī*, lucky, fortunate. *bakht-bāzī*, f. trying one's fortune. *bakht jalnā*, to lose one's luck, to become unfortunate. *bakht-bīdār*, one whose fortune is wide awake, a prosperous person. *bakht-bargashta*, unfortunate. *bakht-khufta*, one whose fortune is asleep, unlucky. *p.*

بخت *bukht*, m. } a quick-paced camel (gene-
بختي *bukhtī*, f. } rally used to ride on, and not for burthens). *a.*

بختيار *bakhtiyār*, fortunate, prosperous. *bakhtiyārī*, f. prosperity, good fortune. *p.*

بخرا *bakhrā*, } m. share, portion, lot, allow-
بخرة *bakhra*, } ance. *p.*

بخري *bakhrī*, }
بخريت *bakhrait*, } partner, sharer. *p.*

بخش *bakhsh*, m. gift, donation; pay; pardon or forgiveness; share, portion, lot. *bakhsh denā*, to give, to bestow; in comp. it denotes giving, bestowing, forgiving, as *ṡamar-bakhsh*, productive of fruit, *tāj-bakhsh*, bestowing a diadem. *p.*

بخشانا *bakhshānā*, a. to cause to give; to procure pardon for another. *p.*

بخشائش *bakhshā,ish*, f. a favour, forgiveness. *p.*

بخشش *bakhshish*, f. a gift, gratuity. *bakhshish-nāma*, a deed of gift. *p.*

بخشنا *bakhshnā*, a. to give, to bestow, to grant, to spare, to pardon or forgive. *p.*

بخش نامه *bakhsh-nāma*, m. a deed of gift. *p.*

بخشندگي *bakhshandagī*, f. liberality, generosity; forgiveness. *p.*

بخشنده *bakhshanda*, he who bestows; God, the forgiver. *p.* [forgiver. *p. h.*

بخشن هارا *bakhshan-hārā*, m. the bestower, the

بخشي *bakhshī*, m. (lit. the giver), a paymaster; a general, commander-in-chief. *bakhshī-ul-mamālik*, a title or rank, equivalent to commander-in-chief. *bakhshi-khāna*, m. the pay-office; the general's office. *bakhshiyāni a'ẓam*, the supreme commanders. *p.*

بخشيات *bakhshiyāt*, name of a division of the Jaunpūr district. *p.*

بخشيدن *bakhshīdan*, to bestow; to forgive. *p.*

بخشي گري *bakhshī-garī*, f. office of general. *p.*

بخل *bukhl*, m. parsimony, stinginess, avarice, sparingness. *a.* [sition. *p. a.*

بخلاف *ba-khilāf*, on the contrary, in oppo-

بخوبي *ba-khūbī*, in perfection, thoroughly. *p.*

بخود *ba-khud*, lit. to or into self. *ba-khud ānā*, to come to one's self or one's senses. *p.*

بخور *bakhūr*, m. perfume, odour, frankincense. *a.*

بخوشي *ba-khushī*, with pleasure; joyfully. *p.*

بخير *ba-khair*, in welfare, well, good. *p. a.*

بخير *bakhīr*, m. report, news, intelligence. *d.*

بخيل *bakhīl*, a miser, a niggard. *a.*

بخيلي *bakhīlī*, f. stinginess, niggardliness. *a.*

بخيه *bakhiya*, m. a kind of stitching; quilting, sewing very thick and strong. *p.*

بد *bad*, evil, bad; much used in the formation of compounds; as, *bad-akhtar*, of an unlucky star, unfortunate. *bad-akhlāḳ*, of bad habits. *bad-uslūb*, ill-shaped, ill-made; of evil conduct. *bad-aṣl* or *bad-uṣūl*, low-born. *bad-aṭwār*, ill-mannered. *bad-af,āl*, of evil deeds. *bad-i'tiḳād*, mistrustful. *bad-andesh*, inimical, evil-minded. *bad-ā,īn*, of ill manners, observing no religious precepts. *bad-bāṭin*, internally evil. *bad-bakht*, unlucky, unfortunate. *bad-bar*, evil-minded or disposed. *bad-bū*, fœtid; f. stink. *bad-parhez* not controlling one's inclinations and passions; in temperate. *bad-chālī*, of bad conduct. *bad-chashm*, malignant, envious, coveting other men's goods, particularly wives. *bad-ḥāl*, in bad circumstances, ill-conditioned. *bad-ḥawāss*, senseless, stupified. *bad-khiṣāl* or *bad-khaṣlat*, of a bad disposition. *bad-khaṭṭ*, writing ill. *bad-khulk*, of evil nature, ill-disposed. *bad-kho*, of bad habits. *bad-khwāh*, wishing evil. *bad-du'ā*, f. curse. *bad-dil*, suspicious. *bad-dimāgh*, dissatisfied, displeased with every thing. *bad-ḍaul*, ill-shaped, ungraceful. *bad-ẓāt*, low-born, of bad breed, wicked, vicious. *bad-ẓihn*, stupid, slow of apprehension. *bad-rāh*, wicked, sinful. *bad-rikāb*, ill-paced (a horse), also difficult to mount. *bad-rag*, of a bad vein, ill-natured, malevolent. *bad-rang*, bad colour, bad kind. *bad-rau*, ill-paced (a horse). *bad-zabān*, indecent speaker, abuser; f. indecent language, abuse. *bād-zabānī*, f. abuse. *bad-zeb*, ungraceful. *bad-sā'at*, f. an unlucky moment. *bad-saj*, ungraceful, ill-looking. *bad-sirisht*, of a bad composition, ill-natured. *bad-saranjām*, of a bad end. *bad-sigāl*, malevolent. *bad-sulūk*, unfavourably inclined, maltreating. *bad-sīrat*, ill-tempered, of bad disposition. *bad-shakl*, ill-shaped, ill-looking. *bad-shugun*, of evil omen, inauspicious. *bad-ṣūrat*, ugly, ill-conditioned. *bad-ṭarīḳ*, m. bad habit (in a religious sense). *bad-ṭīnat*, malevolent, iniquitous. *bad-ṭīnatī*, f. malevolence, iniquity. *bad-ẓann*, suspicious. *bad-'ahd*, faithless, treacherous. *bad-fi'l*, m. evil deeds; of bad habits (particularly in a religious sense). *bad-farjām*, of evil end or issue, malignant. *bad-kār* or *bad-kirdār*, sinful; a malefactor. *bad-gumān*, suspicious. *bad-go*, slanderous. *bad-guhar*, of bad origin. *bad-lagām*, hard-mouthed (a horse), not obedient to the reins. *bad-mast*, dead drunk. *bad-maza*, of bad taste, unsavory. *bad-mazagī*, unsavoriness, tastelessness; coolness between friends. *bad-mizāj*, of evil temper. *bad-muẓanna*, suspicious. *bad-ma'āsh*, of a bad profession, of an infamous trade. *bad-mu'āmala*, of unfair dealing, roguish. *bad-mihrī*, f. disobligingness, unkindness. *bad-nām*, infamous, calumnious. *bad-nāmī*, f. infamy. *bad-nasal*, of a bad race or breed; a bastard. *bad-naṣīb*, unfortunate. *bad-naẓar*, ill-looking. *bad-na'l*, tripping (a horse). *bad-numā* or *bad-namūd*, ungraceful, inelegant. *bad-nihād*, ill-disposed, of bad intention. *bad-waẓ'*, ill-disposed or ill-behaved. *bad-hazm*, of bad digestion. *bad-hai,at*, ill-formed, misshapen. *bad-yumn*, evil-omened, unpropitious. N.B.—All the preceding adjectives may form abstract substantives by the addition of *ī*, as *bad-akhlāḳī*, depravity of morals. *bad-uslūbī*, malformation, &c. *p.*

بد बद *bad*, f. a bubo, or swelling of the gland. *h.*

بد बिद *bid*, f. a little pit into which children in play endeavour to throw balls or marbles. *h.*

بد बदि *badi*, f. the wane of the moon; the dark half of the lunar mouth, from full moon to new moon. *s.*

بدا बिदा *bidā*, f. dismission; taking leave, farewell, adieu. *bidā-k.*, to bid farewell, to dismiss. *s.*

بدا *bidā*, f. beginning, commencement. *a.*

بدا बदा *badā*, predestined, fated. *h.*

بدابدي बदाबदी *badā-badī*, with emulation or rivalship, contentiously. *h.*

بدارن बिदारन *bidāran* (for *vidāran*), m. act of tearing, breaking, severing, rending, or dividing. *s.*

بدارنا बिदारना *bidārnā*, a. to tear, to rend. *s.*

بدامي बदामी *badāmī*, f. a species of rice. *h.*

بدان *bad-ān* (for *ba-ān*), lit. by that; thereby, thence. *p.* [congratulation, &c.

بداها *badāhā*, m. (v. *badhāwā*), a song of

بداهت *badāhat*, f. an unexpected accident. *a.*

بداهنا बिदाहना *bidāhnā*, a. to turn the plough over a field, after the seed is come up, and also to plough immediately after sowing, for the purpose of covering the seed; to harrow. *h.*

بدايت or بداية *badāyat*, commencement. *a.*

بدايع *badā,i'* (pl. of بديعة), wonders, rarities. *a.*

بدباچا बदबाचा *bad-bāchā*, m. a false or fraudulent *bāch* or division. *h.*

بدبد बुद्बुद *budbud*, m. a bubble. *h.*

بدبدانا बुद्बुदाना *budbudānā*, a. to mutter, to grumble. *h.*

بدت बिदित *bidit*, known, famed, renowned. *s.*

بدتر *badtar*, worse, inferior, very bad. *p.*

بدخ *badakh*, m. a duck (for *baṭakh*). *d.*

بدخشان *badakhshān*, name of a region near the source of the Oxus, famous for its rubies, &c. *p.*

بدر *badr*, m. the full moon. *a.*

بدر *ba-dar* (to the door, or at the door), without, out. *ba-dar-nawīsī*, writing off objectional items of an account; auditing or taxing an overcharged bill. *p.*

بدرا बदरा *badrā*, m. a cloud, cloudiness. *s.*

بدرج *ba-darj*, by insertion, per invoice. *p. a.*

بدرجه *ba-daraja*, in, or to a degree. *p. a.*

بدررو *badar-rau*, f. a drain, a sewer. *p.*

بدرقه *badarḳa* or *badraḳa*, m. a fellow-traveller; a convoy, or guard on the road; any thing ordered to be taken with a certain medicine (as water gruel with salts); a vehicle (in medicine—see *anupān*); also a charge (of one per cent.) formerly levied as the expense for keeping the highways and rivers free from robbers. *badraḳa ḥisāb*, an invoice of goods sent; also transit duty. *p.* [ten thousand dirhams. *p.*

بدره *badra*, m. a bag of money; a weight of

بدري बद्री *badrī*, a place of pilgrimage in the north of India. *s.*

بدري बिदरी *bidrī*, f. a mixture of metals so called; a kind of tutenag inlaid with silver, (so called from Bidar, the name of a city and province), used for *ḥuḳḳas*, &c. *h.*

بدري پترك बदरीपत्रक *badrī-patrak*, m. a sort of perfume, a leaf. *s.*

بدري پهلا बदरीफला *badrī-phalā*, f. a plant, the blue sephalica or nyctanthes. *s.*

بدري چهدا बदरीछदा *badrī-chhadā*, f. a kind of perfume, apparently a dried shell-fish; a tree, a species of the Zizyphus. *s.*

بدري شيل बदरीशैल *badrī-shail*, m. a part of the Himālaya range, and a celebrated place of pilgrimage, the Badrināth of modern travellers; or a town and temple on the west bank of the Alaknanda river in the province of Shrīnagar. *s.*

بدست *ba-dast*, in hand, or into hand. *p.*

بدستور *ba-dastūr*, according to custom; as usual, in the usual manner. *p.*

بدسلا बदसला *badsalā*, m. a hog-sty. *h.*

بدعت *bid'at*, f. violence, oppression, wrong; schism, heresy, blasphemy. *a.*

بدعتي *bid'atī*, a tyrant, oppressor. *a.*

بدق *badaḳ* (same as *baṭ*), a duck. *d.*

بدقت *ba-diḳḳat*, with toil or difficulty. *p. a.*

بدكنا बहकना *badaknā*, n. to move, be moved. *h.*

بدل *badal*, m. exchange, substitution; retaliation; prep. for, on account of. *badal lenā*, a. to exchange, to take in exchange. *badali māl*, m. price, barter. *badal-mushāhara*, m. stipend given in money or kind to public or private servants. *a.*

بدل बद्दल *baddal*, or बदल *badal*, m. cloud. *h.*

بدل *ba-dil*, with the heart, heartily, sincerely. *ba dil o jān*, with heart and soul. *p.*

بدلا बदला *badlā*, m. exchange, lieu, stead, a substitute, recompense, revenge, requital. *badlā lenā*, a. to alter, to revenge. *badle*, in exchange, in return for. *a.* [of the English word. *d.*

بدلا *budlā*, m. a bottle, probably a corruption

بدلام *bad-lām* (for *bad-nām*), infamous, of bad repute. *d.*

بدلانا बदलाना *badlānā*, a. to cause to alter; to change, to put one thing for another. *a.*

بدلائي बदलाई *badlā,ī*, f. price of exchange. *a.*

بدلنا बदलना *badalnā*, a. to change, to alter. *a.*

بدلي बदली *badlī*, f. cloudiness; a small bit of cloud. *a.*

بدلي बदली *badlī*, f. exchange; relief (of watches, &c.); a substitute; a person or thing taken; representation or exchange of some other person or thing. *a.*

بدلي *budlī*, f. a small bottle (v. *budlā*). *d.*

بدن बदन *badan* (for *vadan*), m. the mouth, the countenance. *s.*

بدن *badan*, m. the body. *badan phal-jānā*, n. to be covered with an eruption of pustules. *a.*

بدنا बदना *badnā*, a. to wager, to stake at play, to settle, to predestinate, to take (as witness), to obey, to acknowledge, to agree, not to refuse. *h.*

بدنا *badnā*, m. (for *badhnā*), a kind of pot. *h.*

بدني *badnī*, f. a pipkin of a small size. *d.*

بدني बदनी *badnī*, a contract by which the borrower gives a bond at high interest, and as a further security to the lender, he assigns his crops valued far below the market price. *h.*

بدني *badanī*, of or relating to the body. *a.*

بدو *badū*, infamous. *bado* (for *ba-o*), in or to him, &c. *p.*

بدو *badū*, a tribe of Arabs so called. *a.*

بدوان बिद्वान *bidwān* (for *vidwān*), learned. *s.*

بُدُوح *budūḥ*, an invocation, supposed to possess great power over the invisible world. It has no meaning that I ever heard, but some suppose it to be the name of a certain deceased saint. The word is often written as a charm, and inlaid in letters of gold on sword-blades, &c., to ensure their efficiency. *a.* (Binning). [to laugh at, to ridicule. *h.*

بدورنا बिदोरना *bidornā*, a. to screw; to mock,

بدوڙنا बिदोड़ना *bidoṛnā*, a. to laugh at. *h.*

بدولت *ba-daulat*, by means of, through. *p.a.*

بدون *bidūn*, without, deprived of. *a.*

بده बध *badh*, m. killing, slaying. *badh-daṇḍ*, m. capital punishment. *badh-kāmyā*, f. desire to kill. *badh-kānkshī*, wishing death. *badh-sthān*, m. or *badh-sthalī*, f. a place of slaughter or execution. *s.*

بده बद्ध *baddha*, bound, tied; checked, suppressed; fixed, withheld. *baddha-shikh*, young, a pupil whose hair has not been shaved. *baddha-shikhā*, f. a pungent root, a kind of garlic. *baddha-kop*, one who governs or suppresses wrath. *baddha-mūl*, fast or firmly rooted. *s.*

بده बिध *bidh* (for *vidhi*), f. a sacred precept, rule, common practice, precept, direction; name of Brahmā; manner. *bidhi-bat*, (for *vidhi-vat*), according to rule, law, or precept. *s.*

بده बुध *budh*, m. name of a Hindū deity corresponding to the Odin or Woden of the Saxons, and regent of the planet Mercury; the planet Mercury; Wednesday; a wise man, a sage. *s.*

بده बुद्ध *buddha*, m. a wise or learned man, a sage; a deified teacher, especially of the *Bauddha* sect; the ninth avatār or incarnation of Vishnu, and the apparent founder of Buddhism. *s.*

بده बुद्धि *buddhi*, f. sense, knowledge, understanding. *buddhi-hīn*, senseless. *s.*

بده बिधु *bidhu* (for *vidhu*), m. the moon. *s.*

بدهاتا बिधाता *bidhātā* (for *vidhātā*), m. he who has predestined, *i. e.* the deity Brahmā, providence. *s.* [precept, direction. *s.*

بدهان बिधान *bidhān*, m. common practice,

بدهانجل बद्धाञ्जलि *baddhānjuli*; putting the hands joined to the forehead, saluting respectfully. *s.*

بدهاوا बधावा *badhāwā*, m. a song in congratulation; presents, &c., carried to the house of a woman on the sixth or fortieth day after childbirth. *h.*

بدهاوٹ बिधावट *bidhāwat*, f. perforation. *h.*

بدهاي बधाई *badhā,ī*, f. (same as *badhāwā*), a song, presents, &c. *h.* [gent. *s.*

بدهبهرت बुद्धिभृत *buddhi-bhṛit*, wise, intelli-

بدهبار *budh-bār*, m. the day of Budh, Wednesday. *s.*

بدهت बुधित *budhit*, known, understood. *s.*

بدهجن बुधजन *budh-jan*, m. a wise man. *s.*

بدهر बधिर *badhir*, deaf. *badhirtā*, f. deafness. *s.* [execution, place of slaughter. *s.*

بدهستهان बधस्थान *badha-sthān*, m. place of

بدهك बधक *badhak*, m. a slaughterer, a killer. *s.*

بدهك बधिक *badhik*, a huntsman, sportsman, fowler, killer, slayer. *s.*

بدهمان बुद्धिमान *buddhimān*, m. }
بدهمت बुद्धिमत *buddhimat*, m. } wise, sensible, learned, famed,
بدهمتي बुद्धिमती *buddhimatī*, f. }
known. *s.*

بدهنا बधना *badhnā* (also *bidhnā*), a. to smite, to kill; n. to be wounded. *s.*

بدهنا बधना *badhnā*, m. a kind of pot, with a spout to it, a vessel for drinking water from. *s.*

بدهنا बिधना *bidhnā*, n. to be pierced; m. a name of Brahmā (see *bidhātā*). *s.*

بدهند *bi-dihand* ("let them grant"), a superscription of assent by the emperor on a petition for an assignment of revenue. *p.*

بدهو बधू *badhū*, f. a daughter-in-law, son's wife; a woman, wife, lady (same as *bahū*). *s.*

بدهوا बिधवा *bidhavā* or *bidhwā* (for *vidhavā*), f. widow. *bidhawā*, m. the Deity. *s.*

بدهوار बुधवार *budh-wār*, m. Wednesday. *s.*

بدهوان बुद्धिवान *buddhiwān*, }
بدهوتي बुद्धिवती *buddhiwatī*, } wise, knowing, intelligent. *s.*
بدهونتا बुद्धवन्ता *buddhiwantā*, }

بدهوپاي बधोपाय *badhopāya*, m. instrument or means of putting to death. *s.*

بدهونس बिध्वंस *bidhwaṅs* (for *vidhwaṅs*), m. death, annihilation, demolition. *s.*

بدهونش बधवंश *badha-vansh*, m. the slaughter of a whole race. *s.*

بدهِهين बुद्धिहीन *buddhi-hīn*, ignorant, silly, a fool. *buddhi-hinatā*, f. ignorance, folly. *s.*

بدهي बद्धी *baddhī*, f. an ornament worn round the neck, hanging down to the waist, and crossing behind and before; a belt, a sash, a pair of braces. *h.*

بدهيا बधिया *badhiyā*, f. a bullock, or any castrated animal. *h.*

بدهيندري बुद्धीन्द्रिय *buddhīndriya*, m. an organ of intellect or perception, as the mind, eye, ear, nose, tongue and skin. *s.*

بدهيه बध्य *badhya*, deserving death, condemned to death. *badhyatā*, f. fitness to be killed. *badhya-bhūmi*, f. or *badhya-sthān*, m. a place of public execution. *s.*

بدي *badī*, f. badness, wickedness. *p.*

بدي बदी *badī*, f. the dark half of the lunar month, from full moon to new moon. *s.*

بديا बिद्या *bidyā* (for *vidyā*), f. science, knowledge, intellect. *s.*

بديادهر बिद्याधर *bidyādhar*, m. a Vidyādhara, a species of dancers that perform before the assembled deities in Indra's paradise. *s*

بديارتهي बिद्यार्थी *bidyārthī* (for *vidyārthī*), m. a seeker after knowledge, a student. *s.*

بدياوان बिद्यावान *bidyāwān* (for *vidyāwān*), scientific, learned. *s.*

بديس बिदेश *bides* (for *videsh*), abroad, a [foreign country. *s.*

بديسي बिदेशी *bidesī*, of another country, a traveller, a foreigner. *s.*

بديع *badī'*, rare, strange, wonderful, curious. *a.*

بدين *badīn* (for *ba-īn*), to, for, or in this. *p.*

بديهه *badīha*, m. an extempore, an impromptu, impetuosity, any thing done inconsiderately, an unexpected event; an axiom. *a.*

بديهي *badīhī*, unpremeditated; apparent. *a.*

بڈّا बड़ा *baḍā* (see *baṛā*), great, large. *s.*

بڈّا *buḍḍā*, old, aged; an old man. *d.*

بڈّاپا *buḍḍāpā*, }
بڈّاپن *buḍḍāpan*, } m. old age, senility. *d.*

بڈّارنا बिडारना *bidārnā*, a. to drive away, to turn away; to efface. *s.*

بڈّپن *buḍpan*, also *buḍpanā*, m. old age. *d.*

بڈّها बुड्ढा *buḍḍhā*, aged, old; an old man. *buḍḍhā khabīṣa*, an old sinner (a term of ridicule or reproach). *buḍḍhā-khank*, an old fellow. *s.*

بڈّهاپا *buḍḍhāpā*, }
بڈّهاپن *buḍḍhāpan*, } m. old age, senility. *s.*

بڈّهگنگا बुढगङ्गा *buḍh-gangā*, the old bed of the Ganges, where it has shifted its stream. *h.*

بڈّهيا बढ़िया *baḍhiyā*, m. a disease affecting sugar-cane, Indian corn, &c., which prevents the head from shooting. *h.*

بڈّهيا बुढ़िया *buḍhiyā*, }
بڈّي बुडी *buḍī*, } f. an old woman. *s.*

بذاته *bi-ẕāti-hi*, of itself, independently, by its own essence, personally. *a.*

بذر *baẕr*, m. seed. *baẕr-gar*, a sower. *a. p.*

بذل *baẕl*, m. expense, gift, a portion. *a.*

بذله *biẕla*, m. a garment for daily use of which no care is taken. *a.*

بذله *baẕla*, m. a jest, raillery, pleasantry. *a.*

بر बुर *bur*, f. *Pudenda fœminæ, vulva.* *h.*

بر बर *bar* or *var*, excellent; m. bridegroom, a son in law; a boon, a blessing, a choice, a good; the Indian fig-tree; f. *Asparagus racemosus*; conj. but, moreover, even. *bar-dāī*, giver of a choice or blessing. *s.*

بر बर *bar*, m. breadth (of cloth). *h.*

بر *bar*, f. bosom. *bar-mārnā* and *bar-hānknā*, to boast; fruit, produce, result; prep. on or upon. *bar-ānā*, Pers. *bar-āmadan*, to succeed. *bar-lānā*, Pers. *bar-āwardan*, to accomplish, to bring to a successful issue. *bar-andākhtan*, to overthrow, to vanquish. *p.*

بر बर्रै *barr*, f. a wasp. *h.*

بر *barr*, m. land. *barran wa bahran*, by land and sea. *birr*, a fox-cub. *a.*

برا बरा *barā*, m. cakes made of pulse-meal, and fried in butter or ghī; adj. large, great (for *baṛā*). *s.*

برا बुरा *burā*, bad, worse. *burā mānnā*, a. to take amiss or ill, as an affront, to be affronted or displeased. *burā lagnā*, n. to be unpleasant. *h.*

برا बर्रा *barrā*, m. a kind of rope used in a village game on the 14th of the light half of Kū,ār. v. Wilson. *h.*

برا बिर्रा *birrā*, m. gram and barley sown in the same field. *h.*

برا बुर्रा *burrā*, m. the interior cavity of any thing, the belly of a drum. *d.*

برابر *barābar*, abreast, even, level, like, plain, uniform, smooth, up to, opposite, equal, exact, accurate, alike, straight. *barābar ānā*, to overtake. *barābar-k.*, to smooth, to compose. *barābar-honā*, to terminate, to allow, to suit. *p.*

برابرار बिर्राबरार *birrā barār*, m. collection in [kind. *h.*

برابري *barābarī*, equality; competition, rivalry. *barābarī-k.*, to vie with, to compete with. *p.*

برات बरात *barāt*, f. the company and attendants at a marriage-feast; the marriage procession. *s.*

برات *barāt*, f. a commission, a warrant, assignment, a letter, a draught. *a.*

برات *barāt*, f. the 14th day of the month *Sha'bān*, which is appropriated to the commemoration of ancestors; this is generally called *shabi-barāt*, q.v. *p.a.*

براتي बराती *barātī*, m. an attendant at a marriage procession. *s.*

براٹ विराट *birāṭ*, m. the embodied spirit, name of a king. *s.*

براٹھا बराठा *barāṭhā*, m. a washerman. *s.*

براجنا विराजना *birājnā*, n. to be conspicuous or splendid, to enjoy one's self, to live in health, ease, content, and independence. *s.*

برادر *barādar* or *birādar*, m. brother. *birādar-parwar*, kind to friends and relations. *barādar-khwāndagī*, profession of fraternal affection. *p.*

برادرانه *barādarāna*, like a brother, becoming a brother. *p.*

برادرزاده *barādar-zāda*, a nephew. *p.*

برادرزادي *barādar-zādī*, a niece. *p.*

برادري *barādarī*, f. relationship, brotherhood; adj. brotherly, fraternal. *p.*

براده *burāda*, m. filings, saw-dust. *p.*

برار *barār*, lit. that which brings up, or to pass. *barār-i-kār*, successful accomplishment of an affair; taxation in general. *p.*

برارا बरारा *barārā*, f. a thong, a rope (particularly of a swing). *h.*

براري बरारी *barārī*, m. a shareholder paying his proportion of the *barār* taxation. *p.*

براز *barāz*, m. stool, motion, excrement; fighting (especially in single combat). *a.*

براس बुरास *burās*, anger, rage; adj. angry, vexed, displeased. *d.*

براسي विरासी *birāsī*, eighty-two. *s.*

برآشفته *bar-āshufta*, excited, distracted. *p.*

برافتاد *bar-uftād*, fallen off, dwindled away. *p.*

برافروخته *bar-afrokhta*, set on fire, inflamed. *p.*

براق *burāḳ*, the horse or Pegasus on which Muhammad went one night from Jerusalem to heaven, and thence returned to Mecca. N.B. Our lexicographers, Richardson, and after him Hunter and sundry others, will have it that this spirited quadruped was an *ass*; on what authority I know not. *a.*

براق *barrāḳ*, flashing, shining, brilliant. *a.*

براقي *barrāḳī*, f. brilliancy, splendour. *a.*

برام विराम *birām*, uneasy, unquiet, agitated. *s.*

برآمد *bar-āmad*, f. lit. up coming: issue, expenditure; informing (more particularly of bribery). accusation. *bar-āmad honā*, to ascend, appear, come forth. *p.*

برآمده *bar-āmada*, m. a verandah, balcony; issue, expenditure, disbursement. *p.*

برآمدي *bar-āmadī*, an accuser. *p.*

بران *barān*, time, turn, vicissitude. *d.*

بران *burrān*, sharp, cutting, cleaving. *p.*

برانا बरराना *barrānā*, a. to talk in one's sleep, or in a delirium. *h.*

برانا विराना *birānā*, strange, foreign; belonging to another, of or relating to another. *h.*

برانا विराना *birānā*, a. to mock, to jeer or jibe, to taunt. *h.*

برآنا बरआना *bar-ānā*, n. to succeed, to remain at a distance, to keep aloof, to abstain. *p. h.*

برانداز *bar-andāz*, destroying, upsetting. *p.*

برانوے विरानवे *birānawe*, ninety-two. *s.*

برانس बुरांस *buraṅs*, m. the Rhododendron. *h.*

براؤ बरआव or बराव *bar-ā,o*, abstinence. *p. h.*

براورد *barāward*, f. } calculating, estimating, considering be-

براورده *barāwarda*, m. } fore hand what may be necessary for a feast, &c. *barāward-k.*, a. to strike out (of a muster-roll); to calculate, to estimate, to carry to account. *p.*

براونا विरावना *birā,onā*, a. to vex, to mock. *h.*

براه बराह *barāh* (for *varāh*), m. a boar; the third avatār or incarnation of the deity (among the Hindūs). *s.*

براهٹ बर्राहट *barrāhaṭ*, f. chattering, prating, ranting, talking incoherently in one's sleep. *h.*

براهمن ब्राह्मण *brāhman*, a Brāhman, a man of the priest caste among the Hindūs. *s.*

برهمني ब्राह्मणी *brāhmanī*, f. wife of a Brāhman, a female of the Brāhman caste. *s.*

براهمنيٹا ब्राह्मणेटा *brāhmaneṭā*, m. a young Brāhman. *s.*

براهمنيه ब्राह्मण्य *brāhmanya*, m. the Brāhman sect, Brāhmanism; the state or quality of a Brāhman. *s.*

براهميه ब्राह्म्य *brāhmya*, m. the worship or veneration of Brāhmans; astonishment. *brāhmya-muhūrt*, the dawn of day, from two to four *gharīs* before sun rise. *s.*

براهي बराही *barāhī*, a small species of sugar-cane. *h.*

برائي बुराई *burā,ī*, f. mischief, badness, evil. *burā,ī par uṭhnā*, or *kamar bāndhnā*, to resolve on mischief. *h.*

براي *barā,e*, for the sake of, on account of. *barā,e khur o posh*, "for the purpose of food and clothing"—a kind of settlement of property on a person for life, not transferable. *p.*

برائي *barā,ī*, f. name of a species of grain. *d.*

برايا *barāyā* (pl. of برية), creatures, people, nobles. *a.*

برباد *bar-bād*, thrown away, given to the wind, destroyed, laid waste, ruined. *bar-bād-k.*, or *bar-bād-d.*, to cast away, to misapply, to lavish or squander. *bar-bād-h.*, to be squandered. *p.*

بربٹ *barbaṭ*, m. a sort of bean. *d.*

بربرا *burburā* m. (for *bulbulā*), a bubble. *h.*

بربري बरबरी *barbarī*, f. a large kind of goat (from Barbary). *h.*

بربس बरबस *barbas* m. strength, vigour, prowess, bravery. *s.*

بربط *barbaṭ*, a species of lute or harp. *g.*

بربن बरबन *barban*, a north wind. *h.*

بربولا बुर्बोला *bur-bolā*, scurrilous, abusive. *h.*

بربهسيد बरभसिया *barbhasiyā*, or बुरभसिया *bur-bhasiyā*, affected, an old person who affects the manners of youth. *h.*

برپا *bar-pā*, on foot, erected, established; *bar-pā-k.*, Pers. *bar-pā-dāshtan*, a. to pitch, to raise, to set on foot, excite; *bar-pā honā* or *rahnā*, to be or remain established. *h.*

برت व्रत *brat*, बरत *barat*, or बर्त *bart*, m. a fast, a vow, a meritorious act, rite, or penance; use; part. flaming, blazing. *s.*

برت बिर्त *birt*, a right, custom, privilege. *h.*

برت बरत *barat*, a disease which affects rice crops; a leathern girth or large cable; the rope attached to the bucket of a well. *h.*

برت वृति *briti*, m. a proxy in the performance of religious duty. *s.*

برت वृत्ति *britti* (corruptly *bart*), f. a stipend, a pension, income, estate, means of livelihood. *s.*

برتا बरता *bartā*, that which has been used. *h.*

برتا बिरता *birtā*, m. purpose, substance, power. *s.*

برتا व्रिता *britā*, m. a grant generally of land to a religious person, or to a tenant on certain stipulations. *h.*

برتانا बरताना *bartānā*, a. to distribute, to cause to be used; m. old clothes. *h.*

برتانت वृत्तान्त *brittānt* or *britānt*, m. account, narration, story; intelligence or news; circumstance, mode. *s.*

برتانت پتر वृत्तान्तपत्तर *britānt-pattar*, the record of a decision given by a *panchāyet*. *s.*

برتر *bartar*, higher; exellent, superior. *p.*

برتري *bartarī*, f. eminence, superiority. *p.*

برتش बरतुश *bartush*, land sown with sugar-cane after a rice crop. *h.*

برتمان वर्त्तमान *bartamān*, the present tense in grammar; existent, present; commenced or set in. *s.*

برتن बर्तन or बरतन *bartan*, m. a dish, plate, &c., utensils, vessel, bason. *h.*

برتنا बरतना *baratnā*, a. to consider, to re- [flect. *h.*

برتنا बर्तना *bartnā*, a. to use. *h.*

برتني बरतनी *baratnī* or *bartanī*, f. orthography. *h.*

برتهه बरथ *barath*, land situated in the midst [of jungles. *h.*

برته *brita*, m. (v. *britā*), a grant of land, &c. *h.*

برتها वृथा *brithā*, or व्रथा *brathā* (for *vṛithā*), abortive, vain, in vain. *s.*

برتي व्रती *bratī*, m. one who fasts; adj. engaged in the performance of a vow or penance. *s.*

برتي बिरती *birtī*, m. name of a plant (a species of Panicum). *h.*

برتيا बिरतिया *birtiyā*, a tenant who holds his lands on a fixed unalterable annual assessment. *h.*

برّ تيتر *barr-tītar*, m. the Indian grouse, commonly called rock partridge. *h.*

برج ब्रुज *bruj* (or *burj*), m. a cable, a large track rope, (a small one being called *gun*). *h.*

برج *burj*, m. a bastion, a tower; a sign of the zodiac, a constellation. *a.*

برج ब्रज *braj*, m. a name of a district, containing the several villages of Mathura, Gokul, Brindāvan, &c., about 168 miles in circumference, celebrated as the land where *Krishna* passed his youthful days. *braj-bāsī*, an inhabitant of *Braj*, an armed attendant. *braj-bhāshā* or *bhākhā*, the dialect of Hindī spoken in the district of *Braj*. *s.*

برجا *bar-jā*, in place, true, accurate, right. *p.*

برجتيا बरजतिया *barjatiyā*, m. an innocent kind of snake. *h.*

برجري बुर्जरी *burjarī*, f. a term of abuse applied to a woman, such as brimstone, strumpet, &c. *h.*

برجسته *barjasta*, right, proper, opportune, exact, *à propos*, prompt. *p.*

برجنا बरजना *barajnā*, a. to forbid, to pro- [hibit. *h.*

برجوگ बरयोग *bar-jog*, marriageable (a girl). *s.*

برجي *burjī*, f. a small tower or turret (the cutwater to the pier of a bridge). *a.*

برجيا बिरजिया *birjiyā*, one of the subdivisions of *ahīrs*, q. v. *h.*

برجيس *birjīs*, the planet Jupiter. *p.*

برچخ *barchakh*, m. (v. *barchhā*, &c.), a spear. *p.*

برچن बिरचन *birchan*, m. a kind of flour made from the fruit of the *ber* tree (*Rhamnus jujuba*). *h.*

برچهه वृच्छ *brichchh* (for वृक्ष *vṛiksha*), m. a tree in general, a plant. *s.*

برچها बर्छा *barchhā*, m. } a (long, slender)
برچهي बर्छी *barchhī*, f. } spear, a javelin.
barchhā, *barchhe*, or *barchhī-bardār*, a spearman. *h.*

برچهك बिरछिक *birchhik*, m. (for *vṛischik*), a scorpion; the sign of the zodiac so called. *s.*

برچهيت बर्छैत *barchait*, m. a spearman. *h.*

برچي *barchī*, f. a spear. (v. *barchhī*). *h.*

برحق *bar-ḥakk*, for a certainty, rightful. *p. a.*

برخ *barkh* or *birkh*, little, few, some. *p.*

برخاست *barkhāst*, f. recalling or removing from office, going away; a breaking up of a court of justice. *p.*

برخاستن *bar-khāstan*, lit. to rise up; met. to go away, to cease. *p.*

برخلاف *bar-khilāf*, on the contrary. *p. a.*

برخورد *bar-khurd*, success, enjoyment. *p.*

برخوردار *barkhurdār*, happy, enjoying long life, prosperity (male children are so called, q. d. enjoying the fruits of life). *p.*

برخي *barkhe*, a little, few, somewhat. *p.*

برخيا *barkhiyā*, the father of Āsaf, q. v. *a.*

برد बरद *barad*, m. a bullock, a bull. *s.*

برد बुर्द *burd*, m. lit. carrying off, a term used at chess when only the king (on one side) remains on the board: it is a species of victory, but not so creditable as checkmate. *p.*

برد बिरद *birad*, m. fame, reputation, panegyric. *h.*

برد *bard*, m. cold, frigidity, frosty weather. *burd*, a kind of striped cloth. *burd i yamanī*, striped cloth of Yaman, or Arabia Felix. *a.*

بردار बरदार *bardār*, wide broadcloth. *h. p.*

بردار *bardār*, bearer (in comp.); as *sonṭe-bardār*, stick bearer, &c. *ḥukḳe-bardār* (or more commonly *ḥukḳa-bardār*), the servant who takes care of the *hookah*, or the luxurious *qui hy* pipe. *p.*

برداري *bar-dārī*, act of bearing, means of carriage or conveyance. *p.*

برداشت *bar-dāsht*, f. endurance, patience; stores, supplies. *bardāsht khāna*, a temporary storehouse. *p.*

برداشته *bar-dāshta*, raised up, elevated. *p.*

بردان बरदान *bar-dān* (for *vara-dān*), m. a wedding-gift to a bride from her betrothed; the answer to a prayer addressed to God, or to a saint. *s.*

بردبار *burdbār*, forbearing, mild, patient. *p.*

بردباري *burdbārī*, patience, forbearance. *p.*

بردمند *burdmand*, productive, fruitful. *p.*

بردن *burdan* (r. *bar*), to bear, to carry. *p.*

بردنگ *birdang*, } f. a missile weapon shaped
بردنگي *birdangī*, } like a sword-blade, and made of ivory, horn, or other hard substance. It is thrown with the hand, and much resembles the "boomerang" of New South Wales. (Binning.) *d.*

بردوخته *bar-dokhta*, sewed; fixed or nailed upon. *p.*

برده *barda*, m. and f. a slave. *barda-farosh*, a slave-merchant. *burda* (in comp.) denotes bearing or possessing, as *nām-burda*, named or having a name, the gentleman aforesaid. *h.*

بردھ बरध *baradh*, m. a bullock. *s.*

بردھ वृद्ध *briddha*, old, aged. *s.*

بردھ वृद्धि *briddhi*, f. vegetation, increase. *s.*

بردھ विरुद्ध *biruddha*, opposite, opposed to; against, contrary. *s.*

بردھانا बरधाना *bardhānā*, a. to cause the cow to be bulled. *h.*

بردھنا बरधना *baradhnā*, a. to cover or bull a cow. *h.*

بردي बरदी *bardī*, f. a drove of cattle loaded. *s.*

بردي *bardī* (for *bardiy*), the papyrus. *a.*

برديت बरदैत *bardait*, a panegyrist, a bard. *h.*

برديھي बरदैही *bardaihī*, f. compensation for pasture-ground. *h.*

برڈا बरडा *barḍā*, m. } any kind of sandy, light,
برڈي बरडी *barḍī*, f. } or stony soil. *h.*

بررا बर्रा *barrā*, m. a rope, a cable. *h.*

برز *barz*, m. a sown field, agriculture. *p.*

برزخ *barzakh*, m. interval, bar, partition; interval between death and resurrection, purgatory. *a.*

برزن *barzan*, m. a mansion; a street, especially a large and spacious one, a quarter of a town. *p.*

برس वृष *bris* (for *vṛisha*), m. a bull; the sign or constellation Taurus. *s.*

برس बरस *baras*, m. a year; rain, raining. *s.*

برس बरस *baras*, m. an intoxicating drug made of opium. *h.*

برسا बरसा *barsā*, m. the rainy season (see [barshā]. *s.*

برسات बरसात or बर्षात *barsāt*, rain in general; f. the rainy season, the rains. *s.*

برساتي बरसाती or बर्षाती *barsātī*, f. the name of a disorder in horses; the farcy; adj. relating to rain. *barsātī faṣl*, the rain crop, or what is sown during the rains. *h.*

برساليا बरसालिया *barsāliyā*, a servant engaged in cultivation who contracts for one year's service. *h.*

برسام *barsām*, m. the pleurisy; an inflammation of the diaphragm. *p.*

برسانا बरसाना *barsānā*, a. to shower down; to cause to rain; to winnow grain. *s.*

برساؤ बरसाऊ *barsā,ū*, raining, rainy season. *h.*

برسپتي *brispatī* (for *brihaspatī*), m. Jupiter; Thursday. *s.*

برسچك वृश्चिक *brischik* (or *vṛishchik*), m. a scorpion; the sign Scorpio. *s.*

برسگانٹھ बरसगांठ *baras-gāṅṭh*, f. literally, "the year-knot;" the ceremony of tying a knot on the anniversary birthday of a child: hence it comes to denote a birthday, anniversary. *s.*

برسن बरसन *barsan*, m. rain, or raining. *s.*

برسنا बरसना *barasnā*, n. to rain, to be wet. *s.*

برسنا बिरसना *birasnā*, n. to stay, to remain. *h.*

برسوان बरसवान *baraswān*, anniversary, annual. *s.*

برسوديا बरसोदिया *barsodiyā*, a servant engaged by the year. The word is also written *barsoliyā* and *barsāliyā*. *h.*

برسوڑي बरसौड़ी *barsauṛī*, f. an annual tax or rent. *s.*

برسي बर्सी *barsī*, m. annual ceremony in commemoration of deceased relations. *s.*

برش **बर्ष** ***barsh*** (v. *baras*), m. rain; a year. *s.*

برش **बृष** ***brish*** (for *vṛisha*), m. a bull; the sign or constellation Taurus. *s.* [ness. *p.*

برش ***burrish***, f. cutting, cleaving; sharp-

برشا **बर्षा** ***barshā***, or **बर्खा** ***barkhā*** (for *varshā*), f. the rains, the third season (of the six), from the 15th of *Ashārh* to the 15th of Bhādū, rain. *s.*

برشارت **बर्षाऋतु** ***barshā-***, ***barkhā-***, or ***varshā-ṛitu***, f. the rainy season. *s.*

برشاشن **बर्षाशन** ***barshāshan***, m. yearly pay or subsistence. *s.*

برشاکال **बर्षाकाल** ***barshā-***, ***barkhā-***, or ***varshā-kāl***, m. the rainy season. *s.*

برشانا **बर्षाना** ***barshānā***, a. to cause to rain, to shower down; to rain. *s.*

برشاؤ **बर्षाऊ** ***barshā,ū***, برکھاؤ **बर्खाऊ** ***barkhā,ū***, } part. raining. *s.*

برشبھ **बृषभ** ***brishabh*** (for *vṛishabha*), a bull. *s.*

برشته ***birishta***, fried, broiled. *p.*

برشکال **बर्षकाल** ***barsh-kāl*** or ***varsh-kāl***, m. the rainy season, the rains. *s.* [sary. *s.*

برشوان **बर्षवान** ***barshwān***, annual, anniver-

برشوڑي **बर्षौड़ी** ***barshaurī***, f. an annual tax or rent. *h.*

برص ***baraṣ***, m. the leprosy, more especially the white-spotted or scaly leprosy. *a.*

برطرف ***bar-ṭaraf***, aside, apart; dismissed (as a plaint); also as a subst., discharge; dismissal from office. *bar-ṭaraf-k.*, a. to dismiss, to discharge, to turn off. *bar-ṭaraf-honā*, n. to be dismissed, discharged, or turned off. *p. a.*

برطرفي ***bar-ṭarfī***, f. dismission, discharge. *p. a.*

برعکس ***bar-'aks***, on the contrary, in spite of. *p. a.*

برغبت ***ba-raghbat***, with avidity, eagerly. *p. a.*

برغلانا ***barghalānnā*** (for *warghalānnā*), a. to deceive, to wheedle, &c. *h.*

برف ***barf***, m. f. ice, snow. *barf-parward*, sherbet, &c. cooled in ice. *p.*

برفي ***barfī***, f. a kind of sweetmeat; adj. iced, or cooled by means of ice. *p.*

برق ***barḳ***, f. lightning. *barḳ-andāz* (lit. throwing lightning), a matchlockman; also a watchman, guard, or escort. *a. p.*

برقرار ***bar-ḳarār***, firm, fixed, established. *p. a.*

برقع ***burḳa'***, m. a dress, or kind of veil covering the whole body from head to foot, with eye-holes to it. *burḳa'-posh*, one who wears a *burḳa'*. *a.*

برك **बृक** ***brik***, m. a wolf (properly *vṛika*). *s.*

برکات ***barakāt*** (pl. of برکت), f. blessings, auspiciousness. *bā-barakāt*, fortunate, prosperous; fortunate in every undertaking, and communicating good fortune to every thing one is concerned in; productive of advantage and success. *a.*

برکت ***barakat***, f. a blessing, abundance, prosperity, auspiciousness; an inherent prosperity which produces success or abundance. *a.*

برکت **बिरकत** ***birkat***, m. a kind of ascetics who have relinquished the world; adj. wearied, disgusted with the world, ascetic. *s.*

برکش **बृक्ष** ***briksh*** or ***vṛiksha***, m. a tree. *s.*

برکشيدن ***bar-kashīdan***, to pull up, extract. *p.*

برکلا **बरकला** ***barkalā***, an inferior clan of *rāj-pūts*. *h.*

برکندن ***bar-kandan***, to root up, to eradicate. *p.*

برکه ***birka***, m. a pond, a small well, the basin of a fountain. *a.*

برکھ **बृख** ***brikh***, m. a tree (same as *briksh*). *s.*

برکھ **बर्ष** ***barkh*** (for *varsha*), m. rain. *s.*

برکھا **बर्षा बर्खा** ***barkhā***, f. (see *barshā*), rainy season, &c. *s.*

برکھاسن **बर्षासन** ***barkhāsan***, m. yearly pay. *s.*

برکھبھ **बृषभ** ***brikhabh*** (for *brishabh*), a bull. *s.*

برکھنا **बरखना** ***barakhnā*** (v. *barasnā*), to rain. *s.*

برگ **बर्ग** ***barg***, m. an assembly of people of one class, a multitude of similar things; a class of letters of the same organ, as the dentals, palatines, &c.; the square of a number. *s.*

برگ ***barg***, m. a leaf; knapsack containing provisions or necessaries for a journey; a kind of musical instrument, melody; a kind of warlike apparatus. *p.*

برگا **बरगा** ***bargā***, m. a rafter. *h.*

برگت **बरगत** ***bargat***, m. the Indian fig-tree (*Ficus Indica*). *h.*

برگزيده ***bar-guzīda***, chosen, selected. *p.*

برگشتگي ***bar-gashtagī***, retrocession, apostacy. *p.* [apostatized, rebelled. *p.*

برگشته ***bar-gashta***, changed, turned away,

برگن **बरगन** ***bargan***, partition, a share. *h.*

برگي **बर्गी** ***bargī***, the *Marhaṭās* are so called. *s.*

برگيل **बरगेल** ***bargel***, m. an ortolan (*Alauda*). *h.*

برلا **बुरला** ***burlā***, m. a wasp. *h.*

برلا **बिरला** ***birlā***, scarce, uncommon, rare, wonderful; delicate, fine, thin. *s.*

برما ***birmā***, m. name of a plant (*Trichosanthes incisa*). *d.* [worked with a string. *h*

برما **बर्मा** ***barmā***, m. a kind of gimlet or borer,

برمانا **बर्माना** ***barmānā***, a. to bore. *h.*

برمانا **बिरमाना** ***birmānā***, a. to stop; to tame, to reduce to obedience; to allure. *s.*

برماؤ **बिरमाऊ** ***birmā,ū***, taming, tamed, allured. *s.*

برم بهاٹ **बिर्मभाट** ***birm-bhāṭ***, a subdivision of the *bhāṭ* (or bard) tribe. *h.*

برمحل ***bar-maḥal***, one who is appointed to the charge of a district. *p. a.*

برملا **बरमला** ***barmalā***, public, conspicuous. *h.*

برمنا **बिरमना** ***biramnā***, n. to stop, to remain. *s.*

برمه *birma*, m. (v. *birmā*) name of a plant. *d.*

برمهه बम्हा *barmhā*, the people of Ava are so called, vulgarly the Burmese. *h.*

برمهوتر ब्रम्होतर *barmhotar* (for ब्रह्मोत्र *brahmahotra*), a free grant given to Brāhmans for religious purposes. *s.*

برن बरुण *barun* (for *varuṇa*), m. the god of water; name of a tree (*Cratæva tapia*, or *Capparis trifoliata*). *s.* [even, but even, rather. *s.*

برن बरं or बरन *baran*, conj. moreover, and

برن बर्ण *barna*, or बरन *baran*, m. colour; a class or caste; one of the four tribes among Hindūs, viz. 1. *brāhmana*, 2. *chhatriya*, or *kshatriya*, 3. *vaishya*, 4. *shūdra*; a letter of an alphabet; praise, description; fresh earth carried into hollows by means of water. *baran-k.*, to hire a priest for the performance of a sacrifice or of any religious ceremony. *s.*

برنا बरना *baranā*, a small river near Benares. *s.* [(*Cratæva tapia*). *s.*

برنا बरना *barnā*, m. name of a fruit-tree

برنا बरना *barnā*, n. to burn, to be burnt. *h.*

برنا बरना *barnā*, a. to marry. *s.*

برنا *barnā*, m. a youth; adj. young. *barnā wa pīr*, the young and the aged. *p.*

برنارمتي बर्णारमट्टी *barnār-maṭṭī*, f. coloured soil of two kinds, one tinged with yellow, the other with yellow and white. *h.*

برنج *biranj* (or *birinj*), m. rice; brass. *p.*

برنجاري *birinjārī*, a grain-merchant, a camp-follower (with grain, &c.), a suttler. *p.*

برنجپهل *birinj-phal*, } m. name of a species
برنجپهول *birinj-phūl*, } of rice. *h.*

برنجي *birinjī*, made of brass, brazen. *p.*

برنچ बिरिंचि *birinchi*, or बिरंचि *biranchi* (for *virinchi* or *virancha*—see *bidhātā*), *Brahmā*, the Deity. *s.*

برند बृंद *bṛind* (for *vṛinda*), m. a heap, a multitude, a quantity, an aggregation. *s.*

برندا बृंदा *bṛindā*, f. a sacred plant, commonly called *tulsī* (*Ocymum sanctum*, or sacred basil: this shrub is said to be a female metamorphosed). *s.*

برندابن बृंदाबन *bṛindā-ban*, the forest of *Bṛindā* in the vicinity of *Mathurā*, celebrated as the scene of young *Krishna's* sports with the *Gopīs*; a forest of *tulsī* trees. *s.*

برنده *baranda*, bearing, a bearer. *p.*

برن سنكر बर्णसंकर *barn-sankar*, m. a person of a tribe originating in the intercourse of a man of one tribe with a woman of another. *s.*

برنك *ba-rang*, in kind, in the mode or manner. *p.*

برن مالا बर्णमाला *barn-mālā*, f. an alphabet. *s.*

برنن बर्णन or बरनन *barnan* (for *varnan*), m. description, recital, explanation; praise. *barnan-k.*, to extol, to praise; to describe, to explain. *s.*

برننا बर्णना *barnanā* or *barannā*, a. to describe, praise. *s.*

برني बरणी or बरनी *baranī*, f. an eye-lash. *barnī*, an advance made for cultivation or manufacture. *s.*

برني बिरनी *birnī*, f. a wasp; a small grain. *h.*

برو बरो *baro*, name of a high jungle-grass. *barū*, the kalam or reed used in writing; a tube, conduit, or canal. *h.*

بروا बिरवा *birwā*, m. a plant, a tree; the labourer employed at the basket used in raising water for the purpose of irrigation. *h.*

بروا बरवा *barwā*, f. name of a rāginī in music, by which deer and serpents are said to be tamed. *barū,ā*, a soil consisting of sand and clay. *h.*

بروار बरवार *barwār*, name of a class of people engaged in cleansing and selling rice. *h.*

برواهي बिरवाही *birwāhī*, f. an orchard. *birwāhī-k.*, a. to make an orchard; to inclose with a hedge. *h.*

بروائيك बरवायक *barwā,eh*, name of a class of hereditary *chaukī-dārs*, or watchmen, near the Sewalik hills. *h.* [*barābar.*) *p*

بروبر *barobar*, even, breast to breast. (See

بروپ बिरूप *bi-rūp*, disfigured, ugly. *birūp-h.* to be disgraced. *s.*

بروت *barūt*, f. whiskers, moustaches. *p.*

بروت बरवत *barwat*, f. a kind of snake. *h.*

بروتهي बरोथी *barothī*, name of a tribe of *ahīrs*, in the Mynpūr districts. (v. *ahīr*). *h.*

بروٹ बरवट *barwaṭ*, m. a tumour in the belly. *h.* [washerman; a vestibule. *h.*

بروٹها बरोठा *baroṭhā* or बरौठा *barauṭhā*, m. a

بروج *burūj* (pl. of برج), bastions, towers, celestial signs, more particularly those of the zodiac. *a.*

برودت *burūdat*, f. coldness, chilliness. *a.*

برودھ बिरोध *birodh* (for *virodh*), m. quarrel, enmity, contrariety, opposition. *s.*

برودھي बिरोधी *birodhī*, quarrelsome. *s.*

بروقت *bar-wakt*, in time, *à la bonne heure*, seasonably, opportunely. *p. a.* [absence. *s.*

بروگ बिरोग *birog* (for *virog*), m. separation,

بروگن बिरोगन *birogan*, m. sickness from the absence of a beloved object; adj. f. separated, distressed from separation. *s.*

بروگي बिरोगी *birogī*, a separated or distressed lover; adj. separated. *s.* [(soil). *p.*

برومند *barūmand*, fortunate, happy; fertile

برون *birūn* (for *berūn*), also *burūn*, without, outside, external. *p.*

برونڈها बरौन्धा *baraundhā*, m. cotton-land. *h.*

برونكها बरोङ्खा *baronkhā*, m. a species of sugar-cane with long thin joints. *h.*

بروه बरोंह *barroh*, a name given to the uplands on the right banks of the Jumna. *barwa*, m. the name of a bird that feeds on fish. *h.*

بروے बरवे *barwe*, a kind of measure or cadence in language. *h.*

برہ बिरह *birah*, m. separation, absence (especially that of lovers). *s.*

برہ बिरः *birra*, m. grain and barley sown together in the same field. *h.*

برہ *bara*, also *barra*, a lamb, a kid or fawn; the sign Aries. *ba-rah*, on the road; provisions for a journey. *p.*

برها बरहा *barhā*, m. a channel for the passage of water from a well to a field, or from one field to another; a field where cows feed; a rope or string. *s. h.*

برها बुरहा *burhā*, wicked, bad. *h.*

برها बिरहा *birhā*, m. separation, parting, absence (especially of lovers), a kind of song peculiar to washermen. *s. h.*

برهان *burhān*, m. demonstration, proof. *a.*

برهانا बिरहाना *birhānā*, m. land in which culinary herbs are produced. *h.*

برهائي *barhā,ī* (v. *baṛha,ī*), m. a carpenter. *h.*

برهسپت बृहस्पति *brihaspati* (for *vṛihaspati*), a name of the spiritual preceptor of the Devatās, corresponding to the Thor of the Northmen, and the Jupiter of the ancient Greeks and Romans; the planet Jupiter; Thursday. *s.*

برهسپتبار बृहस्पतिबार *brihaspati-bār*, m. Thursday; *Dies Jovis*. *s.*

برهم ब्रह्म *brahm* or *Brahma*, m. God; the all-pervading, the divine cause and essence of the world, from which all things are supposed to proceed, and to which they return; spirit, the very soul. *brahm-astra*, a fabled weapon which deals infallible destruction to those against whom it is discharged. *brahma-bhoj*, feeding of Brāhmans. *brahma-putra*, m. a kind of poison; the Burampooter river; a place of pilgrimage, probably the source of the stream. *brahma-putrī*, f. the *Saraswatī* river. *brahma-tatwa*, m. the true knowledge of the Supreme Spirit. *brahma-twa*, m. Godhead. *brahma-janma*, m. second or spiritual birth, investiture. *brahma-dāru*, m. the mulberry (*Morus Indica*) *brahma-darbhā*, f. a plant (*Ligusticum ajwaen*). *brahma-daṇḍ*, m. a curse, an anathema. *brahma-daitya*, an apparition, Satan, ghost. *brahma-rākshas*, a kind of ghost or demon. *brahma-rātri*, a night of Brahma, comprehending 1000 *yugas* or ages of the gods, said to be equal to 216,000,000 ages of mortals. *brahma-swarūp*, of the nature or essence of the Godhead. *brahma-sesh*, the leavings of Brāhmans. *brahma-shāsan*, m. an edict or grant, &c. addressed to Brāhmans. *brahma-gya*, m. one who has spiritual wisdom. *brahma-gyān*, m. spiritual wisdom, divine knowledge. *brahma-lok*, m. a division of the universe, the eternal residence of the spirits of the pious. *brahma-nirwān*, m. absorption into the Supreme Being. *brahma-vādī*, m. a follower of the Vedants system of philosophy, one who maintains all things are spirit; an expounder of the Vedas. *brahma-hatyā*, the murder of a Brāhman; sacrilege. *brahma-hatyārā*, (fem. *ī*), one who is guilty of the murder of a Brāhman. *s.*

برهم *bar-ham*, confused, entangled, spoiled; angry, vexed, sullen. *bar-ham darham*, entangled, confused, topsy-turvy. *barham-zan*, an exciter of quarrels, an embroiler. *bar-ham-zanī*, embroiling, putting a stop to, interfering, preventing. *bar-ham-zadan*, to embroil; lit. to strike together. *p.*

برهما ब्रह्मा *brahmā*, m. (see *vidhātā*), the Deity in the character of Creator, or matter personified. *s.*

برهمادي ब्रह्मादय *brahmādaya*, m. any grant or perquisite bestowed on a Brāhman. *s.*

برهمانڈ ब्रह्माण्ड *brahmānḍ*, m. the top of the head; the mundane egg (of the Hindūs); the globe, the world. *s.*

برهماستر ब्रह्मास्त्र *brahmāstra*, m. a fabulous weapon, said to be the gift of Brahmā. *s.*

برهماسن ब्रह्मासन *brahmāsan*, m. a posture suited to devout meditation. *s.*

برهماورت ब्रह्मावर्त्त *brahmāvartta*, m. the country to the north-west of Delhi, lying between the rivers Saraswatī and Drishadwatī. *s.*

برهمبان ब्रह्मबान *brahma-bān* (same as *brahmāstra*). *s.*

برهمچارني ब्रह्मचारिणी *brahma-chārinī*, f. a woman leading a life of continence. *s.*

برهمچاري ब्रह्मचारी *brahma-chārī*, a religious student, a Brāhman, from the time of his investiture by the sacerdotal thread till he becomes a householder; a person who continues with his spiritual teacher studying the Veda, a *pandit*, an ascetic. By the *tantras*, this name is assigned to persons whose chief virtue is the observance of continence, and it is assumed by many religious vagabonds; the life led by a young Brāhman before he becomes a householder. *s.*

برهمچریه ब्रह्मचर्य *brahma-charya* or *brahma-charj*, the profession or way of life of a *Brahma-chārī*. *s.*

برهمرندهر ब्रह्मरन्ध्र *brahma-randhra*, m. the aperture at the crown of the head. *s.*

برهملوك ब्रह्मलोक *brahma-lok*, m. the world of Brahma, the regions above. *s.*

برهمن ब्रह्मन *brahman*, m. a Hindū priest, a Brāhman, or one of the sacerdotal caste. *s.*

برهمنبهوجنا ब्रह्मणभोजना *brahmana-bhojanā*, f. distribution of food to Brāhmans. *s.*

برهمني ब्रह्मणी *brahmanī*, wife of a Brāhman; adj. of or relating to a Brāhman. *s.*

برهمنيٹا ब्रह्मनेटा *brahmaneṭā*, son of a Brāhman. *s.*

برهمهتيه ब्रह्महत्य *brahma-hatya*, m. the murder of a Brāhman. *s.*

برهمي *barhamī*, confusion, sullenness. *p.*

برهن बिरहन *birhan* or *birahan*, (a woman) suffering the pangs of love from the absence of her lover, a female lover whose beloved one is absent. *s.*

برهنگي *barahnagī*, f. nakedness. *p.*

برهنه *barhana* or *barahna*, naked. *barahna-pā*, barefooted. *p.*

برهني *birahnī*, f. (v. *birhan*), sickness from separation, &c. *s.*

برهي बिरही *birhī* (for *virahī*), m. suffering the pangs of love, separate from one's love. *s.*

برهي बर्ही *barhī*, m. a peacock. *s.*

برهيا बिरहिया *birhiyā*, amorous, sensual; suffering the pangs of love. *s.*

برهيلا बरहेला *barhelā*, } m. a wild hog. *s.*
بڑهيلا बड़हेला *baṛhelā*, }

بري बरी *barī*, f. quicklime; a dish made of pulse; a wedding garment, or wedding gifts in general, carried in procession; it also denotes the marriage ceremony and wedding day; adj. strong, powerful. *s.*

بري *barī*, acquitted, free, clear. *barī-dāshtan*, to exempt; (in law) a defendant released by the plaintiff from the demand against him. *barrī*, connected with land in opposition to water. *a.*

بري *bare* (for *bāre*), at last; however. *p.*

بري बुर्री *burrī*, f. sowing by dropping seed from the hand into the furrow, instead of sowing broadcast or with the drill. *h.*

برئي बरई *bara,ī*, or बरै *barai*, m. a seller of betel leaf, a cultivator of betel. *h.*

بريار बरयार *baryār* or बरियार *bariyār*, strong, violent; hence, rich or fertile (soil). *s.*

بريارا बरयारा *baryārā* or बरियारा *bariyārā*, strong, violent; m. a medicinal herb so called. *s.*

بريان *biryān*, fried, roasted, broiled, parched, grilled. *biryān sākhtan*, to fry. *p.*

بريان बिरियाँ *biriyāṅ*, f. time, space of time. *h.*

برياني *biryānī*, f. name of a dish made of flesh and rice. *p.*

بريائي बरियाई *bariyā,ī*, f. boast, exultation. *s.*

بريٹها बरेठा *barethā*, m. a washerman. *h.*

بريٹهن बरेठन *baret̤han*, f. a washerwoman. *h.*

بريج बरेज *barej*, } m. garden for the cul-
بريجا बरेजा *barejā*, } tivation of the be-
بريجه बरेजः *bareja*, } tel. *h.*

بريجا बिरीजा *birījā*, m. *Galbanum*. *s.*

بري‌چڑي बुरीचुड़ी *burī-chuṛī*, f. the screech owl. *h.*

بريدن *burīdan*, to cut, clip, cleave. *p.*

بريده *burīda*, cut, clipped; a field cut by stealth by a cultivator. *p.*

بريرا बरेरा *barerā*, m. a wasp. *h.*

بريز بريز *birez-birez*, overcome by, and yielding to misfortune, or to an enemy. *p.*

بريس बरीस *barīs*, m. a year (v. *baras*). *s.*

بريسري बरेसिरी *baresirī*, a tribe of inferior *rāj-pūts*. *h.*

بريشم *bareshim* (for ابريشم), silk. *p.*

برين बरैन *barain*, f. a (female) seller of betel leaf, or rather cultivator of betel. *h.*

برين *barīn*, on high, higher, sublime. *p.*

بريهٹا बरेहटा *barehṭā*, land of the third quality; also a plot of land on which sugar-cane has been lately grown. *h.*

بڑ बड़ *baṛ*, m. the large Bengal fig-tree (*Ficus Bengalensis*), also called the baniyān tree. *s.*

بڑ बड़ *baṛ* (contraction of *baṛā*), great, large, (used in comp.) as *baṛ-bolā*, a noisy talkative person. *baṛ-bhakū,ā*, a blockhead. *baṛ-peṭā*, big-bellied; a great eater; greedy, avaricious. *h.*

بڑ बुड़ *buṛ*, f. *Vulva fœminea*. *h.*

بڑا बड़ा *baṛā*, large, great, old, senior, principal; it is often used adverbially in the sense of "very, exceedingly." *baṛā bhā,o*, money borrowed at a very high interest. *baṛā miyāṅ*, a form of address to an elderly person—venerable or honoured Sir. *baṛā-k.*, a. to enlarge, to exalt or promote; to extinguish, to put out (a lamp, &c.—to use the direct phrase is esteemed unlucky). *baṛā rasta pakaṛnā*, to enter on the long journey, to die. *baṛe peṭ wālā honā*, to be patient. *s.*

بڑا بهاو बड़ाभाव *baṛā-bhā,o*, a kind of appraisement. *h.*

بڑاپا बड़ापा *baṛāpā*, } m. grandeur, dignity,
بڑاپن बड़ापन *baṛāpan*, } elevation, greatness. *h.*

بڑاڑ बिड़ाड़ *biṛāṛ*, f. a drove of bullocks laden with grain or merchandise. *h.*

بڑانا बुड़ाना *buṛānā*, a. to cause to sink. *h.*

بڑانا बड़ाना *baṛānā*, a. to speak in a dream or in delirium, to talk incoherently in one's sleep. *h.*

بڑاو *baṛāo* (for *baṛhā,o*), m. increase, &c. *h.*

بڑاهي *baṛāhī*, } m. a carpenter: this is a Dak-
بڑائي *baṛā,ī*, } hanī corruption of *baṛha,ī*. *h.*

بڑاي बड़ाई *baṛā,ī*, f. greatness; boasting. *baṛā,ī k.*, to extol; to boast, to vaunt; to magnify. *baṛā,ī-denā*, to honour. *s.*

بڑبڑ बड़बड़ *baṛbaṛ*, f. muttering; the light-headed talk of a person in a delirium. *s*

بڑبڑا बुड़बुड़ा *buṛbuṛā* (v. *bulbulā*), m. a bubble. *d.*

بڑبڑانا बड़बड़ाना *baṛbaṛānā*, a. to mutter, to chatter nonsense, to talk light-headedly. *h.*

بڑبڑاٹ *baṛbaṛāṭ*, } f. muttering in one's
بڑبڑاهٹ *baṛbaṛāhaṭ*, } sleep, as in a fit of
بڑبڑاي *baṛbaṛā,ī*, } delirium. *s.*

بڑبڑيا बड़बड़िया *baṛbaṛiyā*, m. a chatterer, a mutterer. *h.*

بڑپن बड़पन *baṛpan*, } m. greatness, gran-
بڑپنا बड़पना *baṛpanā*, } deur, superiority, adult state. *h.*

بڑت बिड़ता *birtā*, m. } purpose or object;
بڑتي बिड़ती *birtī*, f. } power, ability. *kis birte par tattā pānī?* for what purpose do you call for hot water? a proverbial expression applied to a man who has not done his matrimonial duty over night. *h.*

بڑتي *bartī*, f. (for *barhtī*), increase, advancement, success, promotion. *s.* [cal. *h.*

بڑچود बुड़चोद *burchod*, m. a scoundrel, ras-

بڑڑ *burur*, m. a basket-maker or a mat-maker *d.* [thing falling. *d.*

بڑك बुड़क *burak* (also *buruh*), noise of any

بڑكا बड़का *barkā* (same as *barā*), large; elder (brother or son). *h.* [cylinder of masonry. *h.*

بڑكويان बड़कूयान *barkūyān*, a well without a

بڑكي बिड़की *birkī*, f. (v. *birār*), a drove of bullocks, &c. *h.*

بڑگٹ बड़गट *bar-gat*, the Bengal fig-tree. *s.*

بڑگوجر बड़गूजर *bar-gūjar*, one of the thirty-six royal races of *rāj-pūts*. *h.*

بڑم बुड़म *buram*, the noise of water. *d.*

بڑنا बड़ना *barnā* (for *barhnā*), n. to enter. *h.*

بڑوا बड़वा *barwā*, f. a mare; the nymph Aswinī or the asterism designated by a horse's head. *s.*

بڑواگن बड़वाग्नि *barwāgni*, m. submarine fire. *s.*

بڑوامكه बड़वामुख *barwāmukh*, m. submarine fire; the infernal regions. *s.*

بڑوانل बड़वानल *barwānal*, m. submarine fire; in mythology, a being consisting of flame, but with the head of a mare who sprang from the thighs of Urwā, and was received by the Ocean. *s.*

بڑوتي बड़ोती *barotī*, f. progression, advancing. *d.*

بڑونكها बड़ूंखा *barūnkhā*, m. a kind of sugar-cane with long joints. *h.*

بڑهاپا बुढ़ापा *burhāpā*, m. old age. *h.*

بڑهالانا बढ़ालाना *barhā-lānā*, a. to bring forward, to lead on (an army). *h.*

بڑهانا बढ़ाना *barhānā*, a. to increase; to lengthen; to make advance; to raise, to promote; to extinguish; to shut up (a shop); to remove the table-cloth and eatables, &c. *s.*

بڑهاو बढ़ाव *barhā,o*, m. advancement, prolongation, increase, promotion. *s.*

بڑهاوا बढ़ावा *barhāwā*, m. population; excitement, flattery. *s.*

بڑهاون *barhāwan*, a round cake of cow-dung used as a charm against the effect of the evil eye. *h.*

بڑهائي *barhā,ī*, f. advancement, increase, &c. (v. *barhā,o*). *s.*

بڑهبهس बुढ़भस *burh-bhas*, one who affects in old age the manners of youth. *h.*

بڑهتا बढ़ता *barhtā*, m. } increase, overplus,
بڑهتي बढ़ती *barhtī*, f. } promotion, advancement. *s.*

بڑهل बढ़ल or बड़हल *barhal*, m. a sweet and acid fruit of yellowish red, and nearly round. *h.*

بڑهن बढ़न *barhan*, f. a carpenter's wife (see *barha,ī*). *s.*

بڑهنا बढ़ना *barhnā*, n. to increase, to go on, to proceed, to exaggerate, to grow, to rise, to swell, to be promoted. *s.* [*barhtā*).

بڑهنت बढ़न्त *barhant*, f. increase, &c. (v.

بڑهني बढ़नी *barhnī*, f. a broom; advance made for cultivation, or manufacture, or contract. *h.*

بڑهوا बुढ़वा *burhwā*, old, advanced in years. *s.*

بڑهوتر बढ़ोतर *barhotar*, m. } interest; pro-
بڑهوتري बढ़ोतरी *barhotarī*, f. } fit, advantage, increase. *h.* [*pūts* near Benares. *h.*

بڑهوليا बढ़ोलिया *barholiyā*, a branch of *rāj-*

بڑهي बढ़ी *barhī*, profits (same as *barhotarī*). *h.*

بڑهي बढ़ई *barha,ī*, m. a carpenter. *s.*

بڑهي बुढ़ी *burhī*, } f. an old woman. *h.*
بڑهيا बुढ़िया *burhiyā*, }

بڑهيا बढ़िया *barhiyā*, name of a kind of sugar-millstone extracted from the Chunar quarries; a species of pulse; a grain measure of one *sīr*. *h.*

بڑهيا बढ़िया *barhiyā*, high-priced, costly; name of a small clan of *rāj-pūts*. *h.*

بڑهيا बढ़ैया *barhaiyā*, name of a species of pulse; also a grain measure of about one *sīr*. *barhed*, a species of sugar-millstone from the quarries of Chunar. *h.*

بڑهيريا बढ़ेरिया *barheriyā*, one of the subdivisions of the *chamār* caste. *h.* [swine. *h.*

بڑهيلا बढ़ेला or बड़हेला *barhelā*, m. a wild

بڑي *burrī*, sowing seed by dropping it by the hand into the furrow. *d.* [*barī*). *s.*

بڑي बड़ी *barī*, f. a dish made of pulse (see

بڑي *barī*, f. a fireball made of charcoal for the *hukka* (also called the *gul*). *d.*

بڑيا بهوم बड़ियाभूम *bariyā bhūm*, a rich and fertile soil. *h.*

بڑي مياں बड़ेमीयां *bare miyān*, m. an old man; great sir, addressed to an old man. *h.*

بڑيون مين ملنا बड़यों में मिलना *baryaun men milnā*, to associate with elders, to be grown up. *d.*

بز *buz*, m. a he-goat. *buz-dil*, a coward. *p.*

بز *bazz*, m. fine linen. *a.*

بزا *bazā*, name of a species of bird. *h.*

بزار *bazār*, m. (for *bāzār*, q. v.) a market. *p.*

بزاز *bazzāz*, a cloth-merchant, mercer. *a.*

بزازا *bazzāzā* (also *bazzāza* and *bazzāzistān*), the cloth market. *a. p.*

بزازي *bazzāzī*, f. trade of mercer, haberdashery, the business of a draper. *a. p.*

بزان *bazān* (for *ba'd az-ān*), afterwards, after. *d.*

بزباز *bazbāz*, a kind of spice, mace, nutmeg. *p.*

بزرجمهر *buzurjmihr*, the famous minister of Naushīrwān, king of Persia, who lived in the sixth century of our æra. *p.*

بزرگ *buzurg*, a grandee, a great man; a saint; an elder, an ancestor; adj. great, venerable. *p.*

بزرگان *buzurgān* (pl.), grandees; doctors, saints, sages. *p.*

بزرگانه *buzurgāna*, like a grandee, &c., nobly. *p.*

بزرگزاده *buzurg-zāda*, of a noble race. *p.*

بزرگ‌سال *buzurg-sāl*, aged, stricken in years. *p.*

بزرگ منش *buzurg-manish*, noble-minded. *p.*

بزرگوار *buzurgwār*, ancestor, saint, sage. *p.*

بزرگواري *buzurgwārī*, f. grandeur, reverence, highness, nobility. *p.*

بزرگي *buzurgī*, f. grandeur, exaltation, greatness; reverence, respectability. *p.*

بزغاله *buzghāla*, m. a kid, a young goat. *p.*

بزله *bazla*, m. a jest, a bon mot. *a.*

بزم *bazm*, f. assembly, company, especially at a feast or entertainment. *p.*

بزور *ba-zor*, by main force, on compulsion. *p.*

بزه *baza*, m. a sin, a crime. *baza-kār*, a criminal, a sinner. *p.*

بس बस *bas*, m. opportunity, advantage, power, authority, *bas-ānā*, to be obtained, to come into one's power. *bas-k.*, a. to overpower, to bring to submission. *s.*

بس बिष *bis* (for *vish*), m. venom, poison of reptiles (*aconitum ferox*), &c.; met. it is sometimes applied to bitter things. *bis-dhar*, a snake. *s.*

بس *bas*, enough; plenty; very, a great many. *bas-k.*, a. to stop, to seize, to put an end to. *az bas ki*, inasmuch as, whereas. *p.*

بسا *basā*, much, very. *basā-buzurg*, very great, very noble. *basā auḳāt*, generally, mostly, frequently. *p.*

بسات *bisāt* (for *bisāṭ*), f. means, capital stock, estate. *a.*

بساتي *bisātī* (for *bisāṭī*), one who sells every kind of thing, a pedlar, a haberdasher. *a.*

بسار बिसार *bisār*, loan of seed upon the stipulation of ample repayment after harvest. *h.*

بسارنا बिसारना *bisārnā*, a. to forget. *s.*

بساط *bisāṭ*, f. bedding, carpeting, *bisāṭi shatranj*, a chess-board. *bisāṭi bāzī*, a play-board in general; means, capital, stock, &c. *a.*

بساطي *bisāṭī*, a dealer, pedlar, a haberdasher. *a.*

بساكها बिसाखा *bisākhā*, f. the name of the 16th mansion of the moon. *s.*

بسال बिसाल *bisāl*, great, lofty, extensive. *s.*

بسان बिसान *bisān*, f. an offensive smell (as of fish, onions, &c.). *h.*

بسان *ba-sān*, like, resembling. *p.*

بسانا बसाना *basānā*, a. to people, to colonise, to bring into cultivation, to settle (a country), to build (a city, &c.). *s.*

بسانا बिसाना *bisānā* (for *bisāhnā*), a. to purchase; (for *bisrānā*) to cause to forget, to mislead. *h.*

بساندھ बिसांध *bisāndh*, f. evil odour, a stink. *h.*

بساوري बसावरी *basāwarī*, f. ground-rent, rent paid by villagers who do not occupy any of the village lands. *h.*

بساه बिसाह *bisāh*, f. purchase, buying. *h.*

بساهنا बिसाहना *bisāhnā*, a. to buy, to purchase. *h.*

بساهن बिसाहन *bisāhan*,
بساهند बिसाहिन्द *bisāhind*, } f. stink, fetidness. *h.*

بساهندا बिसाहिन्दा *bisāhindā*, fetid, stinking. *h.*

بسائندھ बिसायंध *bisāyandh* or *bisā,endh*, f. a stink. *h.*

بس‌باس बसबास *bas-bās*, m. a house, a dwelling. *h.*

بسباسه *basbāsa*, m. mace, the envelope of the nutmeg. *a.*

بسبب *ba-sabab*, by reason of, on account of. *p. a.*

بس بس *bis-bis*, the call made to a cat, like our "Puss, Puss." *h.*

بسبسانا बिसबिसाना *bisbisānā*, n. to yield a sound as in the fermentation of putrefying vegetable or of vinous liquors. *h.*

بست *bast* (in comp.—for *basta*), bound, shut, frozen. *bist* (for *bīst*), twenty. *p.*

بست बस्त *bast* or *bastu* (for *vasta*), f. thing, matter, substance; chattels, things, baggage. *basat*, inhabited, cultivated (land). *s.*

بستا *bastā*, m. the cloth in which a bundle is tied up; a bundle, a parcel. *p.*

بستاخ *bustākh*, impudent, rash, audacious. *p.*

بستار बिस्तार *bistār*, m. abundance, prolixity, diffusion. *s.*

بستارنا बिस्तारना *bistārnā*, a. to spread out, to extend, to diffuse. *s.*

بستاري बिस्तारी *bistārī*, ample, diffuse. *s.*

بستان *bustān* (for *būstān*), m. a flower-garden. *p.*

بستاني *bustānī*, relating to a flower-garden. *p.*

بستر *bistar*, m. bedding, carpeting; a bed, &c. *p.*

بستر बस्तर *bastar* (for *vastra*), cloth, garments. *s.*

بسترا बस्त्रा *bastrā*, m. the name of a plant (*Callicarpa Americana*). *h.*

بسترا *bistarā*, a bed, &c., peculiar to *faḳīrs*; the abode of a *faḳīr*. *p.*

بستگي *bustagī*, f. binding, contraction, constipation. *p.*

بستن *bastan* (r. *band*), to bind, shut. *p.*

بستني *bastanī*, f. a cloth for binding together bundles of paper, books, ink-stands, &c. *p.*

بست و بند *bast-o-band*, an agreement, settlement. *p.*

بستوئي बिसतुई *bistū,ī*,
بستوئيا बिसतुइया *bistu,iyā*, } f. a lizard. *h.*

بسته *basta*, m. cloth in which any thing is folded up, a parcel, a bundle (see *bastā*). *p.*

بستي बस्ती *bastī*, f. an abode, a village, a peopled place, population. *s.*

بسد *bussad* or *busadd*, coral and its root. *p.*

بسد बिसद *bisad*, white, pure, clean. *s.*

بسدها बसुधा *basudhā*, f. the world, the earth. *s.*

بسر *ba-sar*, at, or to, an end. *ba-sar ānā*, to come to an end; to succeed, to get away from. *ba-sar jānā*, to be finished, to pass away. *ba-sar-k.*, to bring to an end, to execute; to pass (one's days). *ba-sar le-jānā*, to finish, to execute, to acquit one's self of; to outstrip. *basar-honā*, to be finished, to vie with or rival. *ba-sar āmadan*, to excel, to be pre-eminent. *ba-sar burdan*, to finish. *ba-sar-shudan*, to be finished. *p.*

بسر बिसर *bisar*, m.
بسرات बिसरात *bisrāt*, f. } forgetfulness, oblivion. *s.*

بسرام बिश्राम *bisrām* (for *vishrām*), m. pause, a stop, a point in writing; rest. *bisrām lenā*, to rest, to pass the night (particularly used by wandering *fakīrs*). *s.*

بسرانا बिसराना *bisrānā*, a. to forget, to cause to forget, to mislead. *s.*

بسرانت विश्रान्त *bisrānt* (for *vishrānt*), rested, reposed. *bisrānti*, f. rest, repose, cessation from toil or occupation. *s.*

بسرليجانا *ba-sar-lejānā*, a. to outstrip; to finish, to pass. *p.h.*

بسرنا बिसरना *bisarnā*, n. to forget, to be forgotten. *s.*

بسرنا बिसुरना *bisurnā*, n. to sob. *h.*

بسروچشم *ba-sar-o-chashm*, with head and eye, *i. e.* most carefully, heartily. *p.*

بسط *bast*, diffusiveness, distension. *a.*

بسفاتج *bisfātaj*,
بسفائج *bisfā,ij*, } m. a medicinal root, polypody. *a.*

بس کهپرا बिसखपरा *bis-khaprā*, m. the name of a medicinal plant (*Trianthema pentandra*): it spreads over the ground, and forms a circle of nearly a yard in diameter. *h.*

بس کهوپرا बिसखोपरा *bis-khoprā*, m. the name of an animal of the lizard kind, about a yard long, and said to be venomous (*Lacerta iguana*). *h.*

بسگت बसगित *basgit* or *basgat*, f. residence, homestead, site of a village residence. *h.*

بسما *basmā*, m. staining (particularly men's beards); staining the legs (by the women) so as to have the appearance of having light drawers on, whereas they are in fact naked. *p.*

بسمار बिसमार *bismār*, m. the name of a bush. *h.*

بسمل *bismil*, sacrificed (any animal). *bismil-k.*, to sacrifice an animal. *a.*

بسم الله *bismillāh*, in the name of God: this phrase is generally used by good Musalmāns in the beginning of all actions, written works, &c.; hence *bismillāh-k.*, to begin, to commence. *a.*

بسم الله هوا *bismillāh-hū,ā*, said of a child who has just commenced learning to read. *a.h.*

بسمه *basma*, m. a collyrium, or tincture for dyeing. *p.*

بسمي बिसमय *bismai* (for *vismaya*), m. amazement, astonishment, surprise. *s.*

بسن बसन *basan*, m. a dress, a habit, a suit of clothes, apparel. *s.*

بسن बिसन *bisan*, m. evil, fault; desire, lust. *s.*

بسنا बसना *basnā*, n. to dwell, to abide, to be peopled, to be built (a city, town, &c.). *s.*

بسنا बस्ना *basnā*, m. cloth, a wrapper, pack-cloth. *s.*

بسن پٹ बिसनपट *bisan-pat*,
بسن پن बिसनपन *bisan-pan*, } m. a habit of indulging desire. *h.*

بسن پد बिसनपद *bisan-pad*, a hymn to Vishnu. *s.*

بسنت बसन्त *basant*, f. the spring; one of the *rāgs* or musical modes of the Hindūs; the name of the first of the six seasons, including from the 15th Phāgun to the 15th Baisākh; the small-pox (phrase peculiar to the Bengalīs). *basant-phūlnā*, n. to put forth the blossoms of mustard plants. *āṅkhoṅ meṅ-basant-phūlnī*, to dazzle. *basant kī khabar*, knowledge of or care about futurity. *basant panchamī*, a Hindū festival on the 5th of Māgh, formerly observed as the beginning of spring. *s.*

بسنتي बसन्ती *basantī*, of yellow colour (this was Krishna's favourite colour). *h.*

بسني बिसनी *bisnī*, m. a rake, a debauchee, a lecher; adj. delicate, nice, showy in dress. *h.*

بسني बसनी *basnī*, f. a purse. *h.*

بسو बिश्व *bisva* (for *vishva*), m. the universe, the world. *s.*

بسوا बिस्वा *biswā*, m. the twentieth part (particularly of a *bīghā* of ground). *s.*

بسوار *biswār*, a mixture of spices, &c., for making curry. *d.*

بسواري बसवारी *baswārī*, f. a bamboo-garden. *h.*

بسواس बिश्वास *biswās* (for *vishwās*), m. confidence, faith, sincerity, dependence. *s.*

بسوانسه बिसवांसः *biswāṅsa*, m.
بسوانسي बिसवांसी *biswāṅsī*, f. } a fraction of a *biswā*. *a.*

بس وباس बसोबास *bas o bās*, m. home, country, dwelling-place, residence. *s.*

بسوابرار बिस्वाबरार *biswā-barār*, collecting by the *bīswā*, or twentieth of a *bīghā*, q. v. *h.*

بسور बसौर *basaur*, a bamboo-garden. *h.*

بسورنا बिसूरना *bisūrnā*, a. to cry slowly, to sob. *h.*

بسوکرما विश्वकर्मा *biswa-harmā*, the artificer of the gods; the Indian Vulcan. *s.*

بسولا बसूला *basūlā*, m. a kind of axe used by carpenters, an adze. *h.*

بسولي बसूली *basūlī*, f. an instrument for cutting bricks. *p.*

بسوہ बिस्वा *biswa*, m. the twentieth part, particularly of a *bighā* of ground. *biswa barār*, assessment by the *biswa*. *biswa-dār*, the holder of a share or shares in a coparcenary village. *h.*

بسوہداري बिस्वदारी *biswa-dārī*, a tenure of independent villages. *h.*

بسوي विश्वी *biswī* (for *vishwī*), worldly, belonging to the universe. *s.*

بسوي बिस्वी *biswī*, f. alienation of land, on the payment of fines in advance. *h.*

بسہا विषहा *bis,hā*, venomous (as reptiles). *s.*

بسہرو बिसहरू *bisahrū*, } a buyer; a pur-

بسہروا बिसहरूआ *bisahrū,ā*, } chaser. *h.*

بسہري बिसहरी f. a phlegmon or boil on the hand; a purchaser. *h.*

بسي *base*, abundantly, much, many. *p.*

بسيار *bisyār*, many, much, very, abundant; *bisyārī*, abundance, superfluity. *p.*

بسيت बसीत *basīt*, the head man of a village, also called *mukaddam*, or *pātīl*. *h.*

بسير विषियर *bisiyar*, venomous, poisonous. *s.*

بسيرا बसेरा *baserā*, m. a time before evening when birds return to their nest; a night's lodging; a bird's roost, a bird remaining on its roost. *baserā-k.*, to roost. *h.*

بسيستا विशेषता *bisestā* (for *visheshatā*), f. abundance. *s.*

بسيط *basīt*, simple, uncompounded, elementary. *a.*

بسيکت बसीकत *basīkat*, inhabited, peopled. *h.*

بسيکھ विशेष *bisekh* (for *vishesh*), m. a particular circumstance; adj. peculiar, special, particular; abundant; adv. particularly, specially. *s.*

بسيلا विसेला *biselā*, venomous, poisonous. *s.*

بسيم *basīm*, affable, courteous. *a.*

بسين बिसेन *bisen*, a powerful tribe of *rājpūts*. *h.*

بسيندھا बसेंधा *basendhā*, fetid, stinking. *h.*

بسينڈ बसेंड *basend*, an edible root found in ponds, &c. *h.*

بش विष *bish* (for *visha*), m. venom, poison. *s.*

بشارت *bashārat*, f. glad tidings. *a.*

بشارہ *bashāra*, m. a dream, a vision. *a.*

بشاش *bashshāsh*, in good spirits, pleased, delighted, cheerful. *a.*

بشاشت *bashāshat*, f. cheerfulness, alacrity. *a.*

بشت विशत *bisht*, } m. a kind of *ta'alluk-dār*

بشت विष्ट *bisht*, } or landholder whose office is in the gift of government. *h.*

بشٹھا विष्ठा *bishṭhā*, f. ordure. *s.*

بشٹي विष्टी *bishṭī*, f. rain. *s.*

بشدت *ba-shiddat*, violently, forcibly. *p. a.*

بشر *bashar*, m. man, mankind, mortals. *a.*

بشرام विश्राम *bishrām*, m. rest, ease, pause. *bishrām l.*, to rest, to pass the night (particularly used by wandering fakirs). *s.*

بشرانت विश्रान्त *bishrānt*, rested, reposed. *bishrānti*, f. rest, repose. *s.*

بشرطيکہ *ba-sharṭe-ki*, on the agreement that, so that, on condition that. *p. a.*

بشرہ *bashara* (also *bushara*), m. countenance, the outer skin or cuticle. *a.*

بشري *basharī*, human, relating to man. *a.*

بشريت *bashriyat*, f. humanity, human nature. *a.*

بشکپرہ विषकप्र: *bish-kapra*, m. a species of grass used in medicine (*Trianthema pentandra*). *s.*

بشکنيا विषकन्या *bishkanyā*, f. literally, "Poison-damsel." A female who has been fed on poisons from her infancy. Such damsels, it is said, were sent by former Indian princes as presents to those whom they wished to destroy, as the poisonous constitution of the young lady could immediately infect and kill an unwary lover. Ladies of this description are said to have existed before the days of Columbus, and the importation of a new disease from the new world; otherwise the nature of their poisonous quality might be guessed at. (Binning). *s.*

بشم विषम *bisham*, unequalled (in a bad sense), difficult, bad, excessive, difficult of cure. *s.*

بشم جور विषमज्वर *bisham-jwar*, m. a violent inflammatory fever. *s.*

بشن विष्णु *bishan* (for *Vishnu*), m. (in Hindū mythology) the Deity in the character of preserver. *s.*

بشن پد विष्णुपद *bishan-pad*, m. a particular song in the name of *Vishnu*. *h.*

بشن پريت विष्णुप्रीत *bishn-prīt*, land held rent-free by religious persons, especially followers of *Vishnu*; the term *Bishnottar* has the same signification. *s.*

بشن پريتدار विष्णुप्रीतदार *bishn-prīt-dār*, a class of Brāhmans to whom has been assigned grants of land in the name of *Vishnu*. *h.*

بشنوي विष्णवी *bishno,ī* or *bishnawī*, a worshipper of Vishnu, name of a Hindū sect. *s.*

بشني विज्ञानी *bishnī*, m. a rake, a lecher; adj. delicate, nice, showy in dress. *s.*

بشہا विषहा *bishhā*, venomous (as reptiles). *s.*

بشئي विषयी *bisha'ī* or *bishayī*, sensual, worldly. *s.*

بشي बिषय *bishaya*, m. any object of sense; any thing perceptible by the senses, as colour, smell, flavour, and contrast; an affair, matter. *s.*

بشير *bashīr*, a messenger of glad tidings. *a.*

بشير बिषियर *bishiyar*, venomous. *s.*

بشيش बिशेष *bishesh*, | بشيكه बिशेख *bishekh*, } a particular circumstance, &c. (v. *bisekh*). *s.*

بشيلا बिषेला *bishelā*, venomous. *s.*

بشيشتا बिशेषता *bisheshatā*, f. abundance. *s.*

بصارت *baṣārat*, f. sight, seeing, perceiving. *a.*

بصد *ba-ṣad*, by a hundred, used only in Persian phrases, as *ba-ṣad miḥnat*, with a hundred toils or exertions. *p.*

بصر *baṣar*, m. seeing, discerning, vision, sight, understanding, knowledge. *a.*

بصره *baṣra*, the city commonly called Bassorah, on the Persian Gulf. *a.*

بصل *baṣal*, f. an onion. *a.*

بصورت *ba-ṣūrat*, in the way or manner. *p.a.*

بصير *baṣīr*, seeing (met. blind). *a.*

بصيرت *baṣīrat*, f. sight, perception, circumspection, prudence. *a.*

بصيغه *ba-ṣigha*, in the degree or mode. *p.a.*

بضاعت *biẓā'at*, f. stock (in trade), capital; agency, commission. *a.*

بط *baṭ*, m. a goose, a duck. *a.*

بطال *baṭṭāl*, very foolish or vain; false. *a.*

بطالت *baṭālat*, folly, vanity, falsehood. *a.*

بطخ *baṭakh*, | بطك *baṭak*, } m. or f. (dimin. of *baṭ*), a duck or duckling; a vessel formed in imitation of a duck. *a.*

بطرز *ba-ṭarz*, in the mode or manner. *p. a.*

بطرف *ba-ṭaraf*, aside, apart. *p. a.*

بطريق *ba-ṭarīḳ*, by way of. *p. a.*

بطش *baṭsh*, power, severity, sternness. *a.*

بطل *baṭl*, m. rendering vain, abortive, of no effect. *a.*

بطلان *buṭlān*, abortive; m. falseness, vanity. *a.*

بطن *baṭn*, m. the belly, womb, inside. *baṭnan ba'd baṭnin*, generation after generation. *a.*

بطور *ba-ṭaur*, by way of, in manner of. *p.a.*

بطون *baṭūn*, m. interior part; heart, mind; adj. concealed. *a.*

بطي *baṭī*, slow, dilatory; tedious. *a.*

بطيخ *biṭṭīkh*, a melon, a musk melon. *a.*

بظاهر *ba-ẓāhir*, | بظهور *ba-ẓuhūr*, } in appearance, externally, ostensibly. *p. a.*

بعث *ba'ṡ*, m. exciting motive, cause. *a*

بعد *ba'd*, after, afterwards, subsequent. *a.*

بعد *bu'd*, f. distance, remoteness. *a.*

بعده *ba'dahu*, after which, then, however. *a.*

بعض *ba'ẓ*, | بعضا *ba'ẓā*, | بعضي *ba'ẓe*, } some, certain ones. *a.*

بعضي *ba'ẓī*, some, certain, sundry. *ba'ẓī bāb*, various or miscellaneous items, sundries. *ba'ẓī kharch*, miscellaneous expenses. *ba'ẓī jam'*, aggregate of revenue derived from other sources than the Customs and Excise. *ba'ẓī zamīn*, in official language, denotes land exempted from the payment of revenue under various denominations, as *altamghā*, *aima*, &c. *a.*

بعلبك *ba'lbak*, the city Balbeck in Syria, formerly Heliopolis. *a.*

بعلت *ba-'illat*, by reason, or on account [of. *p. a.*

بعلزبوب *ba'alzabūb*, m. Beelzebub. *a.*

بعوض *ba-'iwaẓ*, in lieu, or instead of. *p. a.*

بعون *ba-'aun*, through the aid of. *p.*

بعيد *ba'īd*, far, distant, absent, remote. *ba'īd 'aḳl se*, foolish, absurd, far from wisdom. *a.*

بعينه *bi-'ainihi*, himself or itself, in person, exactly, clearly. *a.*

بغار *bughār*, | بغاره *bughāra*, } m. a breach in a wall; a gash, a deep wound. *p.*

بغاوت *baghāwat*, f. rebellion, opposition to, and defection from, the rightful Imām; violence, plunder, breach of law. *a.*

بغبغانا *baghbaghānā*, a. to boast; to bill or coo as doves; to low as a camel. *d.*

بغچه *baghcha*, m. a little garden. *p.*

بغدا *bughdā*, m. a cleaver used by cooks or butchers, a knife. *p.*

بغداد *baghdād*, the city of Bagdad. *a.*

بغدي *bughdī*, m. a kind of camel (of high cost). *p.* [*sewa,īā*). *p.*

بغرا *bughrā*, m. macaroni (also called

بغض *bughẓ*, m. malice, spite, revenge, hatred. *h.*

بغل *baghal*, f. the armpit; embrace. *baghal jānā* or *ho-jānā*, to go out of the way. *baghal-meṅ lenā*, to take in one's arms, to embrace. *baghal bajānā*, to be highly pleased, to be in triumph; to jeer, to jest. *baghal sūṅgnā*, to be penitent, to regret. *baghal garm-k.*, a. to embrace a woman. *baghal meṅ dabānā*, a. to get possession of another's goods by fraud. *baghal gandh*, stinking armpits. *baghal-gīr*, an embracer in the Hindustānī mode. *baghal-gīrī*, f. embracing. *baghal-meṅ-mārnā*, to conceal (under one's arms) *baghal meṅ muṇḍī ḍālnā*, to be ashamed. *p.*

بغلانا *baghlānā*, to make way, to get out of the way. *p.* under the armpits. *p.*

بغل بند *baghal-band*, m. a kind of robe tie

بغلي *baghlī*, f. a disorder in camels, rubbing the thigh against the belly; a purse; a kind of dumb-bell used in exercise. *p*.

بغوڑدا *baghordā*, m. a slap with the fists; a kind of short dagger. *d*. [ron. d.

بغولا *baghola* (same as *baglā*), a crane, a heron. d.

بغي *baghī*, tyranny, oppression; rebellion, insurrection; infraction of the laws. adj. rebellious, refractory. *a*.

بغيا *baghiyā*, }
بغيچه *baghīcha*, } m. a small garden, an orchard, a flower-garden. *p*.

بغير *ba-ghair*, without, except, besides, independent of. *p. a*.

بفا *bafa*, f. a kind of scales or dandruff formed on the head. *p*.

بفلير *bafler*, fat, gross, bloated. *d*.

بقا *baḳā*, f. eternity, duration, remaining. *a*.

بقال *baḳḳāl*, a grain-merchant, a shop-keeper. *baḳḳālnī*, a shopkeeper's wife. *a*.

بقايا *baḳāyā* (pl. of بقيه), remains, old balances of revenue, arrears, dues. *baḳāyā,e bāḳī*, arrears on arrears. *a*.

بق بق *baḳ-baḳ*, foolish prattle, talkative. *a*.

بقچه *buḳcha*, m. a small bundle of cloth. *t*

بقدر *ba-ḳadri*, to the extent of. *p. a*.

بقر *baḳar*, m. a bull. *baḳar-'īd*, a festival held in commemoration of Abraham's offering to sacrifice his son. According to the *Muḥammadans* of the Sunnī sect, it was *Isma'īl* that Abraham was about to sacrifice; those of Shī'a persuasion hold that it was Isaac. It may be stated, however, that the name of this son is not mentioned in the Ḳur,ān. *a*.

بقسميه *ba-ḳasamīya*, being on oath. *p. a*.

بقعه *buḳ'a*, m. a house, a place. *a*.

بقلة *baḳlat* or *baḳla*, a potherb. *baḳlat-ul-ḥumaḳā*, m. (the fool's herb) purslain. *a*.

بقم *baḳam*, f. sappan wood (*Cæsalpinia sappan*). *a*.

بقول *buḳūl* (pl. of بقل), plants, potherbs. *a*.

بقول *ba-ḳaul*, according to the word of. *p. a*.

بقية *baḳīyat*, remainder, balance, residue. *baḳīyatu-s saif*, the remnant left by the sword. *a*.

بك बिक *bik* (for *vṛika*), m. a wolf. *s*.

بك बक *bak*, m. name of a bird that feeds on fish (*Ardea torra* and *putea*, *Buch.*). *bak-chāl*, a slow walk or strut like that of the bird called *bak*. *bak-dhyān-lagānā*, to act with dissimulation. *s*.

بك बक *bak*, f. prattle, foolish talk. *bak-jhak* the same. *bak-jhak k.*, to prattle, to chatter, to gabble *bak-lagnī*, talkativeness, garrulity. *s*.

بكا बुक्का *bukkā*, m handful. *h*.

بكا *bakā* or *bukā*, f. crying, a complaint, lamentation. *a*.

بكات *bukāt*, a kind of sweetmeat. *d*.

بكار बिकार *bikār*, m. the change of any thing from its original state; disease. *s*.

بكار बकार *bakār*, amount or value of a crop fixed by an appraiser by word of mouth. *h*.

بكار *ba-kār*, of use, serviceable. *ba-kār-āmadan* or *-ānā*, to be of use. *p*.

بكارا बकारा *bakārā*, m. a forerunner, a harbinger; traveller; intelligence forwarded by word of mouth. *h*.

بكارت *bakārat*, f. virginity, maidenhood. *a*.

بكاس बिकास *bikās*, shining, blooming; expansion, display; pleased, happy, delighted. *s*.

بكال बिकाल *bikāl*, m. the afternoon. *s*.

بكام *ba-kām*, agreeable to one's wish. *p*.

بكانا बिकाना *bikānā* (same as *bikwānā*), to sell, or to cause to be sold. *h*.

بكاو बिकाव *bikā,o*, m. sale. बिकाऊ *bikā,ū*, saleable, for sale. *h*.

بكاول *bakāwal*, m. a cupbearer, a steward; a head cook; superintendant of the kitchen. *p*.

بكاولي *bakāwalī*, relating to a *bakāwal*, q. v. f. cooking materials. *p*.

بكاين बकायन *bakāyan*, f. the name of a tree (*Melia sempervirens*). *h*.

بك بك बकबक *bak-bak*, f. prattle, foolish talk. *bak-bak-k.*, to prattle, to chatter, to gabble. *s*.

بكبكانا बकबकाना *bakbakānā*, n. to prattle, to chatter. *h*.

بكتا बक्ता *baktā*, m. a speaker in general; adj. eloquent, loquacious. *s*.

بكتاش *baktāsh*, name of a famous athlete. *p*.

بكتر *baktar*, m. iron armour, a coat of mail a cuirass. *baktar-posh*, a man clad in armour. *p*.

بكتري *baktarī*, m. an armourer, one who makes coats of mail. *p*.

بكٹ बिकट *bikaṭ*, difficult, terrible. *s*.

بكٹ बुकट *bukaṭ*, }
بكٹا बुकटा *bukṭā*, } m. a claw. *h*.

بكثرت *ba-kaṣrat*, plentifully, in abundance. *p. a*.

بكچا *bukchā*, }
بكچه *bukcha*, } m. a bundle, a wrapper. (v. *buḳcha*). *t*.

بك جهك बकझक *bak-jhak*, f. prattle, foolish talk. *h*.

بكچي बकची *bakchī*, f. the name of a plant, the seed of which is used to cure itch (*Conyza* or *Serratula anthelmintica*). *s*.

بكر *bikr*, f. virginity. *bikr-tornā*, or *bikr-phornā*, a. to deflower. *a*.

بكرا बकरा *bakrā*, a he-goat. (in Dakh. the word is often, but erroneously, applied to a ram). *s.*

بكرار बिकरार *bikrār*, बकराल بكرال बिकराल *bikrāl*, terrific, ugly, hideous. *s.*

بكرم बिक्रम *bikram*, m. great power or strength, prowess, heroism; act of overpowering. *s.*

بكرماجيت बिक्रमाजीत *bikramājīt*, the name of a celebrated sovereign of Ujjain (for *vikramāditya*). *s.*

بكري बकरी *bakrī*, f. a she-goat; m. or f. a goat (generally); (in Dakh. improperly applied to a sheep). *s.*

بكري बिक्री *bikrī*, f. a sale, a demand. *s.*

بكسا बकसा *baksā*, astringent. *baksākat*, astringency. *h.*

بكست बिकसित *bikasit*, expanded, blown (as a flower), delighted. *s.*

بكسنا बिकसना *bikasnā*, n. to blow or expand as a flower, to be delighted, to smile. *s.*

بكسوٗا बकसुआ *baksū,ā*, m. the tongue of a buckle. *h.*

بكسيلا बकसैला *baksailā*, astringent. *h.*

بكل बकुल *bakul*, m. name of a tree (*Mimusops elengi*). *s.*

بكل बिकल *bikal*, restless, uneasy, troubled. *s.*

بكل बक्कल *bakkal*, بكلا बकला *bahlā*, m. skin, rind, shell (of a fruit). *s.*

بكلانا बुकलाना *buhlānā*, n. to talk incoherently to one's self, to act or talk foolishly. *s.*

بكم *bukm* (pl. of ابكم), dumb, mute. *a.*

بكم बक्कम *bakkam* m. (v. بقم), sappan or red wood (*Caesalpinia sappan*). *p.*

بكنا बकना *baknā*, n. to prate, jabber. *s.*

بكنا बिकना *bikn ā*, n. to be sold, to sell (in an intransitive sense, like the French "se vendre"). *bik-jānā*. met. to be dependent on, to be obliged. *s.*

بكني बुकनी *buknī*, f. a kind of digestive powder. *h.*

بكواد बकवाद *bakwād*, f. foolish talk. *s.*

بكوادي बकवादी *bakwādī*, m. one who talks foolishly, an idle talker. *s.*

بكواس बकवास *bakwās*, f. talkativeness; m. an incessant prattler. *s.*

بكوان बिकवान *bikwān*, a subdivision of the *Gaurtagās* (v. Wilson's Gloss.). *h.*

بكوانا बिकवाना *bikwānā*, to cause to be sold. *s.*

بكواها बकवाहा *bakwāhā*, m. بكواهي बकवाही *bakwāhī*, f. chatterer, an idle talker. *h.*

بكوٹنا बुकोटना *bukoṭnā*, n. to lacerate with nails, to scratch, to claw. *h.*

بكولا बकोला *bakolā*, m. a covering for the head, as a piece of blanket &c. used by *faḳīrs*. *h.*

بكولي बकोली *bakolī*, name of a green caterpillar destructive of rice crops. *h.*

بكه बिख *bikh* (for *vish*), m. poison, venom. *bikh-dhar*, a snake (lit. poison-holder). *s.*

بكه बख *bakh*, the world, the universe. *h.*

بكها बखा *bakhā*, m. grass for pasturage. *h.*

بكهار बखार *bakhār*, m. بكهاري बखारी *bakhārī*, f. a storehouse, a granary. *h.*

بكهان बखान *bakhān*, m. explanation, praise, description, account. *s.*

بكهاننا बखानना *bakhānnā* or *bakhān-k.*, a. to praise, to commend; to explain, to define, relate. *s.*

بكهر बखर *bakhar* (v. *bākhar*), a kind of plough; also, a house; an inclosure; a cattle shed. *h*

بكهرنا बिखरना *bikharnā*, n. to be scattered, dispersed, or dishevelled; to become angry, to be amazed or confounded. *h.*

بكهري बखरी *bakhrī*, f. a cottage, a house, a round granary of grass, reeds, and mud, raised on piles. *h.*

بكهريا बखरिया *bakhriyā*, m. a householder. *h.*

بكه كهپرا बिखखपरा *bikh-khaprā*, m. a medicinal plant (*Trianthema petandra*). *s.*

بكه كهوپرا बिखखोपरा *bikh-khoprā*, m. a kind of lizard about a yard long, and said to be venomous (*Lacerta iguana*). *s.*

بكهم बिखम *bikham*, odd (number); difficult. *s.*

بكهمان बिखमान *bikhmān*, m. the name of a medicine or poison. *s.*

بكهها बिखहा *bikhhā*, venomous (as reptiles). *s.*

بكهي बखी *bakhī*, f. the side under the armpit. *h.*

بكهي बिखय *bikhai*, m. any thing perceivable by the five senses; affair, matter, &c. (v. *bishaya*). *s.*

بكهيا बखिया *bakhiyā*, m. a kind of stitch, strong quilting. *h.* [quilt. *h.*

بكهيانا बखियाना *bakhiyānā*, a. to stitch, to

بكهيرنا बखेरना *bakhernā*, a. to scatter. *h.*

بكهيڑا बखेड़ा *bakheṛā*, m. wrangling, a tumult, contention, dispute, uproar. *h.*

بكهيڑيا बखेड़िया *bakheṛiyā*, quarrelsome, a wrangler. *h.*

بكهيي बिखयी *bikhayī*, sensual, worldly. *s.*

بكي बुक्की *bukkī*, f. a cloth brought over the shoulders under the armpits and tied behind; a handful. *bukkī mārnā*, to pass a cloth under the armpits and tie it behind. *h.*

بكي बक्की *bakkī*, talkative, a prater. *s.*

بكي बिक्की *bikkī*, m. a partner (at play, &c.). *h.*

بكيا बिकया *bakiyā*, f. a clasp-knife, a penknife. *h.*

بكيل बकेल *bakel*, twine made from the root of the *dhāk* tree. *h.*

بكيلو बकेलू *bahelū*, m. the root of a grass of which rope is made. *h.*

بگ बग *bag*, m. name of a bird, a crane (same as *bak*). *bag-chāl*, f. walking slowly (like a crane); (contracted for *bāgh*) a tiger, hence *bag chhandā lagnā*, n. to be stupified or petrified with fear, as one feels at the sight of a tiger. *s.*

بگا *buggā*, a fountain, jet d'eau. *d.*

بگار बगार *bagār*, m. pasture-ground: it also denotes forced labour for which no reward is given. *h.*

بگارا *bugārā*, m. a large hole or breach. *p.*

بگارنا बगारना *bagārnā*, a. to throw away; to spread over. *h.*

بگاڑ बिगाड़ *bigāṛ*, m. injury, violation, difference. *bigāṛ-k.*, a. to quarrel, to forfeit friendship. *bigāṛ par ānā*, n. to be ready to quarrel. *h.*

بگاڑنا बिगाड़ना *bigāṛnā*, a. to spoil, to mar, to damage; to cause misunderstanding between friends. *h.*

بگاڑو बिगाड़ू *bigāṛū*, m. a spoiler, violator. *h.*

بگانا *bi-gānā* or *bi-gāna*, strange, foreign, unknown (for *be-gāna*, q. v.). *p.*

بگانگي *bi-gānagī*, strangeness, &c. *p.*

بگپاتي बगपाती *bag-pātī*, f. the side under the armpit. *h.*

بگپانتي बगपान्ती *bag-pāntī*, f. a row or line of [cranes. *h.*

بگت बिगति *bigati*, f. badness, misdemeanor. *s.*

بگچھوٹ बगछूट *bag-chhūṭ*, f. galloping. *bag-chūṭ-dauṛnā*, to set off at full gallop. *h.*

بگدانا बगदाना *bagdānā*, a. to cause to return, to put to the rout. *h.*

بگدنا बगदना *bagadnā*, n. to return, to be [spoiled. *h.*

بگره बिग्रह *bigrah* (for *vigraha*), m. quarrel, strife. *s.*

بگري बगरी *bagarī*, a species of rice, cultivated chiefly in the province of Benares. *h.*

بگرينڈي बगरेण्डी *bagrenḍī*, f. the name of a plant (*Jatropha curcas, Lin.*). *h.*

بگڑ बगड़ *bagaṛ*, m. a kind of rice. *h.*

بگڑا बगड़ा *bagṛā*, m. trouble; cheat, deceit. *bagṛā-k.*, to evade the payment of one's debts, or the performance of a promise. *h.*

بگڑنا बिगड़ना *bigaṛnā*, n. to be spoiled, damaged, or marred, to fail, to miscarry; to quarrel, to disagree, to be enraged. *h.*

بگڑي बिगड़ी *bigṛī*, f. spoil, damage, war, battle, misunderstanding. *h.*

بگڑيا बगड़िया *bagṛiyā*, m. a deceitful person. *h.*

بگسريا बगसरिया *bagsariyā*, a small clan of *rāj-pūts* in the Murādābād districts; also of a branch of Kanauj Brāhmans. *h.*

بگسنا बिगसना *bigasnā*, n. to blow, to expand (a flower). &c. (v. *bikasnā*). *s.*

بگلا बगला *baglā*, बगुला *bagulā*, m. the name of a bird, a white crane or heron, commonly called by Europeans "the paddy bird" (*Ardea torra* and *putea, Buch.*). *baglā-bhagat*, a hypocrite. *h.*

بگمار बुगमार *bugmār*, m. a musketoon or blunderbuss. *h.*

بگندھ बिगन्ध *bigandh*, f. stink, fœtor. *s*

بگولا बगूला *bagūlā*, m. a whirlwind. *h.*

بگھا बिगहा *bighā*, m. a quantity of land containing twenty *kaṭṭhas*, or 120 feet square. *h.*

بگھار बघार *baghār*, m. the spices which are mixed with food to give it relish; seasoning, condiment. *h.*

بگھارنا बघारना *baghārnā*, a. to season. *h.*

بگہٹي बिगहटी *bigahṭī*, rent per *bīghā*, fixed on lands. *h.* [vention, interruption. *s.*

بگھن बिघन *bighan*, m. hindrance, stop, pre-

بگھنا बघना *baghnā*, m. the teeth and nails of a tiger which are hung round the neck of a child to serve as a charm. *s.*

بگہنس बगहंस *bag-hans*, m. the name of a bird, a grey goose. *s.*

بگھنہا बघनहा *baghnahā*, m. name of a medicinal herb with a fragrant root. *s.*

بگھي बघी *baghī*, f. a horse-fly. *h.*

بگھيل बघेल *baghel*, m. the name of a tribe of *rāj-pūts* (lit. tiger's whelps). *h.*

بگھيلا बघेला *baghelā*, m. a *rāj-pūt* of the *baghel* tribe; also a tiger's whelp. *s.*

بگيا बगिया *bagiyā*, }
بگيچا बगीचा *bagīchā*, } f. a little garden. *p. h.*

بگيري बगेरी *bagerī*, f. an ortolan. *h.*

بل बल *bal*, m. a coil, twist, convolution; side, direction. *bal-dār*, crooked, twisted, coiled, convoluted. *bal-denā*, a. to twist. *bal-khānā*, to be twisted. *h.*

بل बल *bal*, m. power, strength; semen virile; the elder brother of Krishna, *Bala-Rāma*; (for *bali*) the king of *Pātāl*, or the infernal regions; a sacrifice, an offering. *bal-be*, interj. bravo! *bal-jānā* or *bal-bal-jānā*, to be sacrificed. *bal-dena* or *bal-karnā*, to sacrifice. *s.*

بل बलि *bali*, an oblation, a religious offering; presentation of food to all created beings; one of the five great sacraments of Hindū religion: it consists in throwing a small parcel of the offering, ghī, rice, or the like, into the open air at the back of the house; an animal fit for an oblation; a king and *Daitya*; also *Mahā-bali*, the virtuous sovereign of *Mahābalipur*, tricked out of the dominions he had obtained over earth and heaven by Vishnu, in the *Vāman* or dwarf *Avatār*, and lost, in consideration of his merits, the sovereignty of Pātāla, or the infernal regions. *s.*

بل बुल *bul*, f. *vulva fœminea*. *h.*

بل बिल *bil*, }
بلا बिला *bilā*, } m. a hole or burrow. *s.*

بلا बला *balā*, m. an aquatic and medicinal plant (*Sida rhombifolia, rhomboidea,* and *cordifolia*). *s.*

بلا *balā*, f. misfortune, calamity, accident, vengeance, evil, or mischief. *balā-zada*, one who is struck with misfortune. *balā-kash*, one who suffers under affliction, &c. *balā-gardān*, that which averts evil. *balā-naṣīb*, one of evil destiny. *a.*

بلا *bilā*, without; *bilā taraddud*, without hesitation. *bilā tawaḳḳuf*, hastily, speedily. *bilā-nāgha*, unhesitatingly, without delay. *a.*

بلا बल्ला *ballā*, m. a pole or boat-hook. *h.*

بلا बिल्ला *billā*, m. a male cat. *s.*

بلا *billā*, m. a breast-plate or badge as worn by peons, policemen, &c.: a tablet or flat piece of metal; also a string confining the hilt of a sword or dagger to the sheath. *d.*

بلا बुल्ला *bullā*, m. a bubble. *h.*

بلابر *balābar*, a kind of jacket. *p.*

بلابل बलाबल *balābal*, strong and weak. *s.*

بلابهيجنا बुलाभेजना *bulā-bhejnā*, a. to send for, to invite. *h.*

بلاپ बिलाप *bilāp*, m. lamentation, complaint. *s.*

بلاپنا बिलापना *bilāpnā*, n. to lament, to bewail. *s.*

بلاتکار बलात्कार *balātkār*, m. violence, oppression, exaction; (in law) the detention of a debtor and violence exercised upon him to recover a debt. *s.*

بلاتمکا बलात्मिका *balātmikā*, f. a sort of sunflower (*Heliotropium Indicum*). *s.*

بلاٹ बलाट *balāṭ*, m. a sort of bean. *h.*

بلاد *bilād* (pl. of بلد), cities, towns, countries, provinces, territories. *a.*

بلادر *balādur*, m. a nut used for marking clothes. *p.*

بلادور *balā-dūr*, averting an evil omen (lit. "far be the evil"). *a. p.*

بلار बिलार *bilār* or बिल्लार *billār*, m. a male cat. *s.*

بلاس बिलास *bilās*, m. pleasure, satisfaction, delight. *s.*

بلاسي बिलासी *bilāsī*, voluptuous, addicted to pleasure. *s.*

بلاش बलाश *balāsh*, m. the phlegmatic humour. *s.*

بلاع *ballāʻ*, an enormous eater, a glutton. *a.*

بلاغت *balāghat*, f. eloquence; maturity. *a.*

بلاق बुलाक *bulāḳ*, m. an ornament worn in the nose. *h.*

بلاکا बलाका *balākā*, f. a sort of crane. *h.*

بلال *bilāl*, the name of the crier who announced to the people when Muhammad said prayers. *a.*

بلالا बिलाला *bilālā* (v. *bilallā*), foolish, simple. *h.*

بلالانا बुलालाना *bulā-lānā*, a. to summon. *h.*

بلالك बलालक *balālak*, m. the Caronda (*Carissa carandas*). *s.*

بلانا बुलाना *bulānā*, a. to call, invite, bid. *h.*

بلانا बिलाना *bilānā*, a. to cause to vanish, to dissipate; to dispose of; to distribute; n. to retire, to vanish, to be lost. *h.*

بلانا बिल्लाना *billānā*, to weep, whine. *h.*

بلاند बिलान्द *bilānd*, f. a span. *h.*

بلانچتا बलाञ्चिता *balānchitā*, f. a sort of *vīnā* or lute, called also *Rāma's* lute. *s.*

بلانوت बलान्वित *balānwit*, strong, powerful. *s.*

بلاو बिलाव *bilā,o*, m. a tom-cat. *s.*

بلاؤ बलाव *balā,o*, any thing very cheaply purchased; adj. dog cheap. *h.*

بلاوا बुलावा *bulāwā*, m. act of calling. *h.*

بلاوڑ बिलावड़ *bilāwaṛ* (v. *bilā,o*), a he-cat. *s.*

بلاول बिलावल *bilāwal*, f. the name of a rāgini in music. *h.*

بلاهٹ बुलाहट *bulāhaṭ*, f. calling, call, summons. *h.*

بلاهر बलाहर *balāhar*, a low-caste servant, a village guide or messenger. *h.*

بلاهي बलाही *balāhī*, m. a worker in hides and leather (v. *chamār*). *h.*

بلائي बिलाई *bilā,ī*, f. a she-cat; a grater for scraping pompions, &c. *bilā,ī-kand*, m. name of a medicine. *s.*

بلاي *balā,e* (same as *balā*), f. accident, misfortune. *balā,e baghma*, trash, stuff, filth, matter. *a.*

بلائي बल्लाई *ballā,ī*, m. a kind of village servant, for cutting wood and preserving the village boundaries. *h.*

بلائي کند बिलाईकन्द *bilā,ī kand*, m. the name of a medicine. *h.*

بلايه बलाय *balāya*, m. a plant (*Capparis trifoliata*). *s.*

بلائين لينا बलाएंलेना *balā,eṅ lenā*, or बलाईलेना *balā,ī lenā*, to draw the hands over the head of another in token of taking all their misfortunes upon one's self, a practice peculiar to females. *h.*

بلب बिल्व *bilb* (for *vilva*), m. the *bel* tree or its fruit. *s.*

بلب *ba-lab*, at the lip, or to the lip, applied to one in great distress, when the soul is "come to the lip;" *balab-ānā*, *i.e.* when he is on the point of death. *p.*

بل بکرا बलबक्रा *bal-bakrā*, m. a person who dies in a battle, &c., without doing any thing. *s.*

بلبل *bulbul*, f. a nightingale: in India, a shrike. The *ḥusainī bulbul* and *sulṭānī bulbul* are two very beautiful species of this little bird, which bear no resemblance whatever to a nightingale; neither is the Persian *bulbul* at all like the English nightingale, but a rather smaller bird of the same genus. The *ḥusainī bulbul* has a white body, wings, and tail, with a black-crested head. The *sulṭānī bulbul* has a reddish or chesnut body and wings, with black crest. Both species have very long tails like the bird of paradise.—Binning. *p.*

بلبلا बुलबुला *bulbulā*, m. a bubble. *s.*

بلبلانا बलबलाना *balbalānā*, n. to ferment (as sour milk, curds, &c.); to be inflamed with lust; to make a noise (a camel) from lust. *h.*

بلبلانا बिलबिलाना *bilbilānā*, n. to be restless, to be tormented with pain, to complain from pain; to weep, to whine, whimper. *h.*

بلبهه बल्लभ *ballabh*, dear, beloved; m. a master, superintendant; a favourite; a friend. *s.*

بلبهانا बलभाना *balbhānā*, a. to allure. *s.*

بلبهدر बलभद्र *bal-bhadra*, m. a strong robust man; the name of Balarāma, Krishna's elder brother. *s.*

بلبهوگ बलभोग *bal-bhog*, taking possession by force of another's right. *h.*

بلبي बलबे *bal-be*, bravo! well done! *h.*

بلبير बलबीर *bal-bīr*, the brave, the heroic; an epithet applied to the brothers *Krishṇa* and *Balarāma* (in the *Prem-sāgar*). *s.*

بل تاڑ बलताड़ *bal-tāṛ*, m. the male palm or toddy tree (*Borassus flabelliformis*). *h.*

بلتكار बलत्कार *balat-kār*, any act of violence, as robbery, rape, &c. *s.*

بلتور बलतोर *bal-tor*, } m. a pimple, a sore, a
بلتوڑ बलतोड़ *bal-toṛ*, } small boil (supposed to be caused by the breaking or pulling out of a hair). *s.*

بلٹنا बिलटना *bilaṭnā*, n. to become bad. *h.*

بلچنا बिलचना *bilachnā*, to extract, to select, as passages from books; to pick, to cull. *h.*

بلحاظ *ba-lihāz*, with regard to. *p. a.*

بلخ *balkh*, a famous city in Bactriana. *balkhī*, belonging to, or made in *Balkh*. *p.*

بلد *balad*, a city, town; a country. *a.*

بلد बलद *balad*, a bullock that carries a burden; a drove of cattle, bullocks, horned beasts. *h.*

بلدار *bal-dār*, crooked, twisted, coiled; m. a species of wheaten cake. *h.* [tries. *a.*

بلدان *buldān* (pl. of بلد), cities, towns, coun-

بلدان बलिदान *bali-dān*, m. act of sacrificing or offering a sacrifice to a deity. *s.*

بلدانه *baladāna*, m. a tax on laden oxen. *h.*

بلداؤ बलदाऊ *baldā,ū*, m. a bullock-driver; a name of Balarāma. *s.* [exaction. *p.*

بلدستي *bal-dastī*, f. unauthorised or oppressive

بلده *balda*, m. a city, a town. *a.*

بلدهائي *baldihā,ī*, compensation for pasture-ground. *h.*

بلدي बलदी *baldī*, } a bullock-driver, or
بلديا बलदिया *baldiyā*, } one who loads bullocks. *s.* [*Balarāma*, Krishna's elder brother. *s.*

بلديو बलदेव *baldev*, a cow-herd; the name of

بلديوا बलदेवा *bal-devā*, f. a medicinal plant commonly called *Trāyumān*. *s.*

بلرا बिलरा *bilrā*, m. a he-cat; a kind of cloth. *s.*

بلرام बलराम *bala-rāma*, the elder brother of Krishna. *s.*

بل رانڈ बलराँड़ *bal-rāṇḍ*, f. a widow who lost her husband while very young. *s.*

بلركهه बलरख *bal-rakh*, m. a person put in charge of property under distraint for arrears of revenue. *s.* [of Gilead. *a.*

بلسان *balasān*, the balsam-tree, balsam, balm

بلست बिलस्त *bilast*, f. a span (v. *bilisht*). *p.*

بلسنا बिलसना *bilasnā*, n. to be pleased, to be satisfied, to be delighted. *s.*

بلسندر बलसुन्दर *balsundar*, name of a kind of (sandy) soil in *'Azim-gaṛh*; clay much mixed with sand. *h.*

بلش *bilish*, } f. a span, the extent from the
بلشت *bilisht*, } tip of the thumb to that of the little finger when stretched. *p.*

بلغار *bulghār*, Bulgaria; Russia-leather. *p.*

بلغم *balgham*, m. phlegm; a running at the nose from cold. *a.*

بلغمي *balghamī*, phlegmatic. *a.*

بلفم *balfam* m. or *balfam kī takhtī*, a school-boy's slate for writing or cyphering. *d.*

بلقيس *balkīs*, the name of the queen of Sheba, according to the Musalmāns. *a.*

بلكانا *balkānā*, n. to bring under one's own possession or charge. *d.*

بلك *bilk*, a spark. *balki*, but, moreover. *bilak*, a gift. *bilik*, adhesiveness. *buluk*, a large prominent eye. *p.*

بلكٹ बलकट *balkaṭ*, rent taken in advance. *h.*

بلكٹي बलकटी *balkaṭī*, f. name of a tax formerly exacted at the commencement of reaping. *h.*

بلكنا बलकना *balaknā*, a. to open; to speak indistinctly from excessive joy or intoxication. *s.*

بلكنا बिलकना *bilaknā*, n. to sob, to cry violently, as a child; to long for, to desire eagerly. *h.*

بلكه *balki*, moreover, on the other hand; but, nay. *p.*

بلكهريا बिल्खरिया *bilkhariyā*, name of a tribe of Rājpūts, so called from Bilkhar in Oude. *h.*

بلكهنا बिलखना *bilakhnā*, a. to see, to look at, perceive, behold; n. to be displeased. *s.*

بلگ बिलग *bilag*, separate; m. separation, difference. *bilag mānnā*, n. to be displeased, angry, offended. *s.*

بلگانا बिलगाना *bilgānā*, a. to separate, to part. *s.*

بلگاو बिलगाव *bilgā,o*, m. separation, parting. *s.*

بلگنا बिलगना *bilagnā*, n. to separate, to be separated, to curdle, to turn (as milk). *h.*

بلگنا बलगना *balganā*, m. a sob; sobbing. *s.*

بللا बिलल्ला *bilallā*, foolish, simple, silly. *h.*

بللانا बिललाना *bilalānā*, n. to lament. *h.*

بلم बिलम *bilam*, m. delay, long stay. *s.*

بلم बल्लम *ballam*, m. a spear. *ballam-bardār*, a spearman; adj. having a very large and broad head. *h.*

بلم बलम *balam*, }
بلما बलमा *balmā*, } m. a lover, a husband. *s.*

بلمانا बिलमाना *bilmānā*, a. to allure, to tantalise. *h.*

بلمب बिलम्ब *bilamb*, m. delay, long stay. *s.*

بلمبنا बिलम्बना *bilambnā*, n. to stay, to tarry, to delay. *s.* [long stay. *s.*

بلمبھ बिलम्भ *bilambh* (for *vilambh*), m. delay,

بلمبھنا बिलम्भना *bilambhnā*, n. to stay, to tarry, delay. *s.*

بلمنا बिलमना *bilamnā*, to delay, tarry; to stop, remain. *s.* [flaccid. *s.*

بلن बलिन *balin*, shrivelled, wrinkled, flabby,

بلنا बलना *balnā*, n. to burn, to be burnt. *h.*

بلند *buland*, high, elevated, exalted, sublime, tall. *buland-pāya*, of high rank. *buland-ḥauṣila*, ambitious, aspiring. *buland-nagar*, of exalted views, aspiring. *buland-himmat*, ambitious, of lofty intention. *p.*

بلندي *bulandī*, f. height, elevation, exaltation. *p.*

بلنگره बलनिग्रह *bal-nigrah*, m. weakening, reducing strength. *s.* [ascend. *h.*

بلنگنا बिलङ्गना *bilangnā*, a. to climb, to

بلني बिलनी *bilnī*, f. a stye or stithe, the disorder in the eyelids. *h.*

بلوا बलवा *balwā*, m. a tumult, riot, sedition, mutiny, alarm. *h.*

بلوا बलुआ *balū,ā* or *baluwā*, sandy. *s.*

بلوالا बलवाला *balwālā*, }
بلوان बलवान *balwān*, } powerful, strong. *s.*

بلوانا बुलवाना *bulwānā*, a. to cause to be called or sent for. *h.*

بلوتا बलवत्ता *balwattā*, f. strength, power. *s.*

بلور *billaur*, m. a kind of stone, crystal; cut glass. *a.* [ing, ennobling. *s.*

بلوردھن बलवर्द्धन *bal-varddhan*, adj. strengthen-

بلورنا बलूरना *balūrnā*, a. to scratch, to tear (with nails). *h.*

بلوري *billaurī*, made of crystal or glass: the forms *bilorī*, *billaurīn*, and *bilorīn* are also in use. *a.*

بلوط *ballūṭ*, m. an acorn, an oak, a chesnut-tree. *a.*

بلوغ *bulūgh*, m. }
بلوغت *bulūghat*, f. } puberty, adolescence, the attaining of a marriageable age. *a.*
بلوغيت *bulūghīyat*, f. }

بلوكنا बिलोकना *bilohnā*, a. to see, to look at. *s.*

بلولا बलूला *balūlā*, m. a bubble (of water). *a.*

بلونا बिलोना *bilonā*, }
بلوونا बिलोवना *bilowanā*, } a. to churn (also *bilaunā*). *s.*

بلونت बलवन्त *balwant*, powerful, strong. *s.*

بلوند *balwand*, powerful, strong. *d.*

بلونگي बिलौङ्गी *bilaungī*, f. a species of grass. *h.*

بله *balah*, weak, silly, simple, ignorant, unskilful. *a.*

بله *billa* m. (v. *billā*), a badge, &c. *d.*

بلهار बलिहार *bali-hār*, m. }
بلهاري बलिहारी *bali-hārī*, f. } sacrifice. *bali-hārī-jāna*, same as *bal-jānā*, to be sacrificed. *s.*

بلهبند बिलहबंद *bilah-band*, m. settlement, regulation. *h.*

بلهبندي बिलहबन्दी *bilah-bandī*, an account of the settlement of a district, specifying the name of each *maḥall*, the farmer of it, and the amount at which it is let. *h.*

بلهرا बिलहरा *bilharā*, m. a kind of basket (long and narrow) generally used for holding *pāns* or betel leaf. *h.*

بلهري बिलहरी *bilahrī*, f. a ladle for taking out oil; a small basket for holding betel leaf. *h.*

بلهن बलहन *bal-han*, m. phlegm. *s.*

بلهي बलही *balhī*, f. a fagot. *h.*

بلهين बलहीन *bal-hīn*, weak, infirm. *bal-hīnatā*, f. weakness, prostration. *s*

بلي बली *balī*, strong, powerful; f. a wrinkle, skin shrivelled by age; the fold of the skin in stout persons upon the upper part of the belly, between the ensiform cartilage and the navel. *s.*

بلي बली *balī*, any thing offered or sacrificed to an idol, such as flowers, rice, goats, &c. *s.*

بلي बल्ली *ballī*, a climber, a vine. *s.*

بلي बल्ली *ballī*, f. a prop, a pole, a long wooden stick to move or steer boats. *ballī-mārnā*, to steer, to push (a boat). *h.*

بلي बिल्ली *billī*, f. a she-cat. *billī-loṭan*, m. valerian. *s.*

بلي *bale*, yes, true, so, well, right. *p.*

بليا لينا बलैयालेना *balaiyā lenā*, to take or invoke another's misfortunes on one's self (v. *balā,eṅ lenā*). *h.*

بليت *balīyat*, misfortune, calamity. *a.*

بليد *balīd*, stupid; a dunce, a simpleton. *a.*

بليسر बलेसर *balesar*, a subdivision of the Gūjar tribe, q.v. *h.*

بليغ *balīgh*, eloquent, mature; copious. *a.*

بليلوٹن बिल्लीलोटन *billī-loṭan*, m. valerian; so named from its effect on cats, which are said to be so delighted with its fragrance, as to roll about in their ecstasies. *h.*

بليله *balela*, m. the belleric myrobalan. *p.*

بليندّا बलेंडा *balenḍā*, m. a whirlwind; a ridge-pole (of a cottage). *h.*

بليندّي बलेंडी *balenḍī*, f. a ridge-pole (of a cottage). *h.*

بليه बल्य *balya*, strong, vigorous; m. semen virile. *s.*

بم बम *bam*, f. a spring (of water); a fathom; a measuring-rod of 3½ cubits. *h.*

بم बम *bam*, an interjection addressed to Shiva; much used by pilgrims to the temple of Baijnāth or Vaidyanāth. *s.*

بم *bam*, f. a bass part in music; a bass or lowest string or drum; having the deepest tone; deep sound (as that of the large pipes of an organ, a drum). *a. p.*

بمان विमान *bimān*, m. the chariot or vehicle of the gods (sometimes serving as a throne, and at others carrying them through the skies self-moving and self-directed). *s.*

بمب बिम्ब *bimb*, m. the name of a tree bearing a red fruit (*Momordica monadelpha* or *Byronia grandis*). *s.*

بمب बम्ब *bamb*, m. a revenue defaulter, one who owes a balance to the state. *h.*

بمبا *bumbā*, m. a pump (from the English). *d.*

بمبو *bambū*, m. a bamboo, the species of cane so called. (This has not been borrowed from the English, as some have supposed, but the English word itself has been derived from the Hindū dialects of Southern India). *d.*

بمبوڈ *bambūḍ*, a disease in elephants, a kind of ulceration of their lower extremities. *d.*

بمبي *bumbī*, f. the navel. *d.*

بمتيلي बमतेले *bamtele*, name of a *rāj-pūt* tribe in the *Du,āb*: they are of low repute. *h.*

بمثل *ba-misl*, like, resembling. *p. a.*

بمجرد *ba-mujarrad*, instantly, immediately. *p. a.*

بمدد *ba-madad*, by aid of, by means of. *p. a.*

بمرتبه *ba-martaba*, in a degree, to some extent. *p. a.*

بمڑي *bamṛī*, interj. alas! *bamṛī mārnā*, to bewail the dead, in the Hindū fashion, namely, by uttering loud cries and slapping the mouth with the hand at the same time. *d.*

بمعه *ba-ma'a* or *ba-ma'ī*, along with. *p. a.*

بمقتضاي *ba-muḳtaẓā,e*, by the exaction of. *ba-muḳtaẓā,e lā-chārī*, through sheer helplessness. *p. a.*

بمكنا बमकना *bamaknā*, n. to swell. *h.*

بمكهه विमुख *bimukh* (for *vimukh*), having the face averted, turned from, averse. *s.*

بمل विमल *bimal* (for *vimal*), free of filth, clean. *s.*

بملا बमला *bamlā*, a hole from which water springs up. *h.*

بمن बमन *baman* (for *vaman*), m. vomit; an emetic. *baman-k.* to vomit, to spew. *s.*

بمن *baman*, a Brahman. *d.*

بمني *bamanī*, a female of the Brāhman caste; of or belonging to the Brāhmanical sect. *d.*

بموجب *ba-mūjib*, on account of, by reason of, in conformity with. *p. a.*

بمهن बम्हन *bamhan*, m. (for *bāhman* or *brāhman*), a Brāhman. *s.*

بمهنگور बम्हनगौर *bamhangaur*, a class of the Gaur Rājpūts. *h.*

بمهني बमहनी *bamhanī*, light red soil. *h.*

بمهنيا बमहनिया *bamhaniyā*, a subdivision of the *Kāchhī* tribe, q. v. *h.*

بمهنيٹا *bamhaneṭā*, m. a young Brāhman. *d.*

بميٹها बमीठा *bamīṭhā*, m. a term applied to anthills (also to a snake's hole) in Upper India. *h.*

بميل बमील *bamīl*, m. the name of a grass. *h.*

بن बन *ban*, m. cotton; a crop of cotton. *h.*

بن बन *ban*, f. a forest, a wood. *ban-jhāṛnā*, *-mārnā*. or *majhāṛnā*, a. to beat the forests. *ban-kanḍā* and *ban-gonṭhā*, cow-dung found in the forests. *ban-jātrā*, f. the pilgrimage through the 84 forests of *Braja*. *s.*

بن *bin*, m. (contract. of ابن), a son. *a.*

بن *bun*, m. coffee before it is ground (for then it takes a new name, *ḳahwa*). *a.* an allowance of grain given to a day labourer. *h.*

بن *bun*, f. basis, root, stem. *p.*

بن बिन *bin*, بنا बिना *binā*, } without, unless. *bin jāne*, without knowing, unwittingly. *bin māre* or *bin tegh shahīd honā*, to be slain without a wound (applied to lovers). *bin māre tauba-k.*, to fear without cause. *s.*

بنا बना *banā*, m. bridegroom; (part. of *bannā*), made, prepared, &c.; land dressed and ready for the seed. *h.*

بنا *binā*, f. foundation, basis. *a.*

بنا बना *bannā*, n. to be made, to be prepared, to be mended or adjusted; to chime, to agree, to fall in with, to do, to answer, to serve, to be, to become, to avail, to counterfeit, to succeed; m. a bridegroom. *banā-banāyā*, ready, finished, complete, entire, perfect. *banā-ṭhannā*, to be fully adorned, decked out. *banā-chunā*, dressed, decked out. *banā-rahnā*, to remain waiting. *h.*

بنا *bannā*, m. a mason, a builder. *a.*

بنا बुन्ना *bunnā*, a. to weave, intertwine. *h.*

بنا बिन्ना *binnā*, a. to knit; to weave; n. to be picked. *h.*

بنابر *binā-bar*, on account of, owing to. *p.*

بنابرين *binā-bar-īn*, therefore, with this view or intent. *p.*

بناپهر बनाफिर *binnāphir*, m. the name of a tribe of *rāj-pūts*. *h.*

بنات बनात *banāt*, f. woollen cloth, broad-cloth. *h.*

بنات *banāt* (pl. of بنت), daughters. *banāti nabāt*, the tender herbage. *a.*

بنات النعش *banātu-n-na'sh*, m. the constellation of the Great Bear. *a.*

بناتي बनाती *banātī*, woollen. *h.*

بنادر *banādir* (pl. of بندر), ports, harbours. *a.*

بناس बिनास *binās*, m. death, annihilation. *s.*

بناسپتي बनासपत्ती *banāspattī* or *banās-patthī*, f. forest leaves. *s.*

بنافر *banāfar*, name of a tribe of *Yadu-bansī rāj-pūts* in Oude. *h.*

بناگوش *binā-goch*, the cavity at the lower part of the ear. *p.* [bring. *h.*

بنالانا बनालाना *banā-lānā*, n. to make and

بنام *ba-nāmi*, in the name of. *p.*

بنانا बनाना *banānā*, a. to do, to make, to fabricate, to prepare, to build, to compose, to perform, to adjust, to adorn, to pluck (a fowl), to mend, to invent, to rectify, to dress (victuals), to mock, to feign. *h.*

بن آنا बनआना *ban-ānā*, n. to succeed (in life), to be fortunate, to prosper. *h.*

بناؤ बनाव *banā,o*, m. dressing, preparing, decking one's self; concord, understanding, reconciliation; making up. *banā,o-k.*, to adorn, bedeck: in the Indian English the word is pronounced and written *bunnow*, and means a "cram," or "tough yarn," a purely made-up story. *h.*

بناوت बिनावत *bināwat*, act of weaving. *h.*

بناوٹ बनावट *banāwaṭ*, f. make, invention, affectation, contrivance, fabrication, fiction, sham. *h.*

بناوٹ बिनावट *bināwaṭ*, f. weaving. *h.*

بناوري बनावरी *banāwarī* or *banā,orī*, f. the act of getting ready, preparation. *h.* [pare. *h.*

بناؤنا बनावना *banā,onā*, a. to make, to pre-

بنائي बिनाई *binā,ī*, f. weaving. *h.*

بناياجانا बनायाजाना *banāyā-jānā*, n. to be making, to be in hand. *h.*

بنايك बिनायक *bināyak* (for *vināyaka*), a name of *Ganesha*. *s.*

بنب बिंब *bimb* or *vimba*, m. the name of a tree bearing a red fruit (*Bryonia grandis, Lin., Momordica monadelpha, Roxb.*). *s.*

بنبا बंबा *bambā*, m. a well; a jet d'eau, the spout of a fountain. *h.*

بنباس बनवास *ban-bās*, m. one who dwells in the forest, a hermit. *s.*

بنباسي बनवासी *ban-bāsī*, adj. dwelling in the forest; f. life of a hermit. *s.*

بنبك बिंबक *bimbuk*, red, fiery, flame-coloured. *s.*

بنبلاو बनबिलाव *ban-bilā,o*, m. a wild cat. *s.*

بنبو *bambū*, the cane called bamboo. *d.*

بن بهانٹا बनभांटा *ban-bhānṭā*, m. wild baingan or egg-plant (*Solanum melongena*). *s.*

بنبي *bumbī*, f. the navel. *d.*

بنبي *bambī*, f. harvest crop; a stack or heap of grain; (same as *khirman*, q. v.). *d.*

بنپرستھ बनप्रस्थ *ban-prasth*, m. a Hindū who has reached the hermit stage of his existence. (v. *āsram*). *s.*

بن پڑنا बनपड़ना *ban-parnā*, n. to succeed, to answer, to suit, to come to a conclusion. *s.*

بنت बनत *banat*, m. lace; a riband studded with spangles. *h.*

بنت *bint* or *binat*, a daughter. *bintu-l-'inab*, wine, daughter of the grape. *a.*

بنتا बनिता *banitā* (for *vanitā*), f. a wife, a woman. *s.*

بن ترائي बनतराई *ban-tarā,ī*, f. wild *tarā,ī*, a kind of plant (*Luffa*). *h.*

بنتريا बनतरिया *bantariyā*, m. a class of people who formerly acted as wood-rangers in Gorakpūr. *h.* [solicitation. *s.*

بنتي बिन्ती *bintī*, f. an apology, submission,

بنٹانا बंटाना *banṭānā*, a. to share, distribute, to participate. *h.* [shared, to distribute. *h.*

بنٹوانا बंटवाना *banṭwānā*, a. to cause to be

بنٹويا बंटवैया *banṭwaiyā*, } one who shares or

بنٹيت बंटैत *banṭait*, } distributes; a divider, distributer. *h.*

بنتھنا *banthnā*, n. to be braided or plaited. *d.*

بنج *banj*, henbane (Arab. form of بنگ). *a.*

بنج बणिज *banij*, m. a merchant, trader; the sixth of the astronomical periods called Karan, corresponding to the half of a lunar day. *s.*

بنج बणिज *banij* or बनज *banaj* (for बणिज्य *banijya*), m. trade, traffic, merchandise. *s.*

بنجارا बनजारा *banjārā*, m. a grain-merchant; also a carrier of grain. The term *banjārā* or *birinjārā* is also applied to a distinct class of vagrants. They are Hindūs, but do not belong to any particular caste or part of the country. They live in tents, and travel about like gipsies. *s.*

بنجاري बनजारी *banjārī*, f. a kind of tent used by banjārās; adj. half-boiled (grain). *h.*

بنجر बनजर *banjar*, f. waste land; land which has not been cultivated for five years and upwards. *banjar-jadid*, land brought into cultivation after lying some time fallow. *banjar kadim*, land left fallow for some years. *banjar-kami*, abatement of rent for fallow land. *banjar khāriji jam'*, waste land excluded from the rental. *h.*

بنجن बनजिन *banjin*, lands close by a village; name of a weed about three feet high, which springs up among harvest crops. *h.*

بنجن बिञ्जन *binjan*, m. sauce, condiments; particularly vegetables dressed with butter, &c. and added to flesh or fish; (in grammar) a consonant. *s.*

بنجھوٹي बंझोटी *banjhoṭī*, f. a medicine taken to produce barrenness. *h.*

بنجيه बणिज्य *banijya*, m. trade, traffic. *s.*

بنچانا बंचाना *bañchānā*, a. to make or hear one read. *s.*

بنچانا *bañchānā* (for *bachānā*), a. to save or protect. *d.*

بنچاو *bañchā,o* (for *bachā,o*), m. safety, protection. *d.*

بنچر बनचर *ban-char*, m. literally, "wood-goer"; any wild animal, such as a monkey, &c.: it also denotes a forester or woodman. *s.*

بنچري बनचरी *bancharī*, a kind of high jungle-grass, of which wild elephants are very fond. *s.*

بنچنا बंचना *banchnā*, n. to be read or perused. *h.*

بند *band*, m. a fastening, a knot, a bandage; binding, literally or figuratively, as a tie, a cord; fetters, imprisonment; an agreement, pledge, or promise; a contract; a regulation; a dyke, mound, dam, or embankment; a verse of a song consisting of two or three couplets; belt, roll, string, joint, knuckle. *band-khāna*, m. a prison. *band-bāndhnā*, to restrain an inundation with dykes. *band-meñ-ānā*, to become a captive. *band-rahnā*, to be engaged in a business. *band-baiṭhnā*, to succeed in an affair. *band pakaṛnā*, to object to the arguments of an opponent. *band-meñ paṛnā*, to become a captive. *band-band-pakaṛnā*, to seize (as rheumatism, &c.) all one's joints. *band-k.* or *band-kar denā*, a. to make fast, to shut or bar (a door). In composition it denotes fastening, enchaining, or fixing, as *na'l-band*, a blacksmith, one who fastens on horses' shoes. *dev-band* (epithet of an ancient hero), the enchainer of demons. In Persian, *band* denotes hope or wish; also "a trick of fence," a stratagem. *band-farmūdan*, to imprison. *p.*

بند *bañd*, the limbs, members. *d.*

بند बिन्द *bind*, f. a spot, dot, mark; the nasal dot *anuswāra*. *s.*

بندا बन्दा *bandā* or बंडा *banḍā*, m. mistletoe, a kind of epidendron (*Epidendron tesselloides*, *Roxb.*). *s.*

بندا बुन्दा *bundā*, m. a drop, point, a dot. *s.*

بندا *bindā*, m. a bundle, a sheaf, a faggot. *d.*

بندا बन्दा *bandā*, a grain-magazine above ground. *h.*

بندارا *bandārā*, m. a shore, or coast. *d.*

بندال बिन्दाल *bindāl*, f. a medicinal herb. *h.*

بندانا *bandānā* (for *bandhānā*), a. to cause to be fastened, &c. *d.*

بندبٹائي बन्दबटाई *band-baṭā,ī*, f. account of each share of assessment in grain. *h.*

بند برداشت *band-bardāsht*, an account of the share of an instalment to be paid by each villager. *p.*

بند بيهري बन्दबेहरी *band-behrī*, f. statement of the amount of each money instalment of a village. *p. h.*

بندپهانته *band-phānta*, an account of the shares of the liabilities of a village. *p. h.*

بندتال बन्दताल *band-tāl* or *-ṭāl*, damming up a water-course for the purpose of irrigation. *h.*

بند حساب *band-ḥisāb*, an abstract account. *p. a.*

بندجمع *bandi jam'*, the act of allotting to each cultivator an equal portion of good and bad lands. *p. a.*

بندر बन्दर *bandar*, m. a monkey, an ape. *s.*

بندر *bandar*, m. a city, an emporium; a port, harbour, a trading town to which numbers of foreign merchants resort, a mart or market. *p.*

بندرا बन्दरा *bandrā*, m. mistletoe (v. *bandā*). *s.*

بندرکهت बन्दरखत *bandar-khat*, m. a sore that does not heal; a running sore, an issue. *s.*

بندري बन्दरी *bandarī*, f. a sort of chintz from Machhlī-bandar; a sword from Rājbandarī; name of a grass used as fodder for cattle. *h.*

بندري बन्दरी *bandrī*, } f. a female mon-
بندريا बन्दरिया *bandariyā*, } key. *s.*

بندسيل *bandi sel*, a contract of sale. *p. e.*

بندش *bandish*, f. lit. tying, binding, or making up; preparing a false story, making up a false account of a transaction, invention, contrivance; elegancy (of style). *bandish-bāndhnā*, a. to contrive; to form a plot. *p.*

بندکشاد *bind-kushād*, m. *semen cito emittens, morbo affectus*. *h. p.*

بندگان *bandagān* (pl. of *banda*), servants, slaves. *p.*

بندگي *bandagī*, f. slavery; devotion; service, compliment. *bandagī meñ khudā,ī-k.*, to affect authority while in servitude. *p.*

بندلي बन्दली *bandlī*, a species of Rohilcund rice. *h.*

بند مدت *bandi muddat*, a stated period for the settlement of an account. *p. a.*

بندنا *bandnā* (for *bandhnā*, q. v.), a. to bind, &c. *d.*

بندنوار बन्दनवार *bandanwār*, f. a wreath or garland of leaves and flowers suspended across gateways on marriages or public festivals. *s.*

بندنويس *band-nawīs*, a clerk, an accountant. *p.*

بندوا *bandū,ā*, m. a prisoner, a captive. *p.*

بندوبست *band-o-bast*, m. literally, "binding and fastening"; settlement, regulation, disposition, arrangement; economy, management, government. *band-o-bastī dawāmī*, permanent settlement. *band-o-bastī mī'ād* or *-sar-sarī*, temporary or summary settlement. *band-o-bastī mulk*, the sum total of the revenue of a kingdom or province. *p.*

بندوبستي *band-o-bastī*, f. arranging, economy; adj. of or relating to settlement, &c. *band-o-bastī parwāna* or *sanad*, patent, warrant, or deed of settlement. *band-o-bastī sar-rishta-dār*, a revenue-officer attached to some courts in Bengal. *p.*

بندوڑ बन्दोड़ *bandoṛ*, f. a female slave. *h.*

بندوق *bandūḳ*, f. a musket. (Whence comes the word *bandūḳ*? It is not known either to the Turks or Persians. The nearest approach to it I have ever heard is the African-Arabic term *bunduḳiyya*, literally signifying "Venetian," and formerly applied to a cross-bow, but in recent times to a gun, as the descendants of the Arabs in Egypt, Morocco, and Barbary obtained these weapons chiefly from Venice.—Binning.) *a.*

بندوقچي *bandūḳchī*, m. a musketeer. *a. t.*

بندول बन्दोल *bandol*, m. the child of a slave. *h.*

بندوها बन्दूहा *bandūhā*, m. a whirlwind. *h.*

بندھ बन्ध *bandh*, m. a pledge, a deposit; m. f. binding, tying, bandage, a tie, or fetter; a bank, a dyke, a mound for confining water; a village boundary; bondage, imprisonment. *bandh men paṛnā* or *ānā*, to become a captive. *s.*

بندھ बन्धु *bandhu*, m. a kinsman, a friend. (v. *bandhū*). *bandhutā*, f. a multitude of relations and friends; relationship, friendship. *bandhutwa*, m. relationship, friendship. *bandhu-jan*, a relation, a friend. *bandhu-datta*, given by a kinsman; m. the property given to a bride by her relatives. *bandhu-hīn*, friendless, relationless. *s.*

بندہ *banda*, a slave, servant. *banda-parwar*, cherisher of servants (a respectful expression used in addressing a superior, *i.e.* your honour). *banda,e-dargāh*, the slave of (your) threshold. *banda-zāda*, son of (your) slave, *i.e.* thine humble servant. *banda-nawāz*, cherisher of servants or dependants. *p.*

بندها *bandahā* (pl.), servants, slaves. *p.*

بندھان बन्धान *bandhān*, m. pension, a fixed allowance to any one; raised earthen embankments for flooding lands; purchase of grain in advance of harvest. *s.*

بندھانا बन्धाना *bandhānā*, a. to bind, fasten, [shut, &c. *s.*

بندھاني बन्धानी *bandhānī*, m. one whose business is to carry stone or timber, &c., over his shoulder; a pensioner; a gunner, an artilleryman. *h.*

بندھائي बन्धाई *bandhā,ī*, f. bond, binding, fastening. *s.*

بندھ تنتر बन्धतन्त्र *bandha-tantra*, m. a complete army, or one with its four divisions of elephants, chariots, horse, and foot, v. *chaturanga*. *s.*

بندھ جيو बन्धुजीव *bandhu-jīv*, m. a flower (*Pentapetes phœnicea*). *s.*

بندھر बन्धुर *bandhur*, m. a flower (*Pentapetes phœnicea*); a drug, commonly called *birang*; a drug called *rishabh*; a crane. *s.*

بندھرا बन्धुरा *bandhurā*, f. a whore, a prostitute. *s.*

بندھك बन्धक *bandhak*, m. a pledge, a pawn; binding, confinement. *s.*

بندھكي बन्धाकी *bandhakī*, f. an unchaste woman, a harlot; a barren woman. *s.*

بندھن बन्धन *bandhan*, m. fastening, bandage; obstacle, hinderance. *bandhan-rajju*, f. any rope used for tying. *bandhan-granthi*, m. the knot of a ligature. *s.*

بندھنا बन्धना *bandhnā*, n. to be tied, to be fastened; to be continuous, to be kept, enclosed, formed, or composed. *bandhī mūṭhī*, an undisclosed intention. *s.*

بندھنا बिन्धना *bindhnā*, a. to sting, to bite; n. to be bored or pierced. *s.*

بندھنالي बन्धनालय *bandhanālay*, m. a prison.

بندھو बन्धू *bandhū*, बन्धु *bandhu*, or बान्धव *bandhava*, a friend, kinsman, but especially a distant cognate, subsequent in right of inheritance to the gentile *Sugotra*: the *bandhu* is of three kinds, the kinsman of the person himself, of his father, and of his mother; a flower (*Pentapetes phœnicea*). *s.*

بندھوا बन्धूआ *bandhū,ā*, m. friend. बन्धुवा *bandhuwā*, a prisoner. *s.*

بندھوانا बन्धवाना *bandhwānā*, to cause to be bound; to accuse. *s.*

بندھواس बन्धवास *bandhwās*, land embanked all around so as to retain the water. *h.*

بندھور *bandhūr*, m. purchase of grain in advance of harvest. *h.*

بندھوك बन्धूक *bandhūk*, m. a shrub bearing a red flower (*Pentapetes phœnicea*); also applied to the *Ixora bandhu*; a tree (*Pentaptera tomentosa*). *bandhūk-pushp*, m. the blossom of the same tree. *s.*

بندھيا बन्धिया *bandhiyā*, an embankment (v. *bandhān*). *s.*

بندھتا बन्ध्या *bandhyā*, f. a childless woman; a barren cow; a perfume called *bālā*. *s.*

بندھيج बन्धेज *bandhej*, m. parsimony; stability, steadiness, persistence. *h.*

بندھي موٹھي बन्धीमूठी *bandhī mūṭhī*, f. an undisclosed intention. *h.*

بندھيه बन्ध्य *bandhya*, barren, unfruitful; detained, confined. *s.*

بندي *bandī*, f. a female slave or servant; m. a prisoner, captive. *bandī-khāna* or *bandī-griha*, a prison-house. In law and revenue language *bandī* denotes agreement, arrangement; distribution, allowance; deduction or charge: it is also the name of a certain dry measure. *p. s.*

بندي बन्दी *bandī*, f. the name of an ornament worn on the forehead; a dress shorter than the Jāma; m. name of a tribe called *Bhāṭ*, a bard. *s.*

بندي बिन्दी *bindī*, f. a spot, dot, mark; the nasal dot *anuswāra*. *s.*

بنديا बुन्दिया *bundiyā*, f. a kind of sweetmeats (like drops). *s.*

بنديجن बन्दीजन *bandī-jan*, m. a kind of ornament; a bard. *h.*

بنديگرھ बन्दीगृह *bandī-griha*, m. a house for [captives. *s.*

بنديلا बुन्देला *bundelā*, a spurious tribe of *rāj-pūts*, who give name to the province of Bundle cund (*Bundel-khand*). *h.*

بنديوان बन्दीवान *bandīwān*, a captive, a pri-[soner. *s*

بنڈا बंडा *banḍā*, m. mistletoe, a kind of epidendron. *h.* [sticks, or straw, &c. *s.*

بنڈا *binḍā*, m. a faggot, a bundle of firewood,

بنڈا बुण्डा *bunḍā*, m. a kind of ornament worn on the ears. *h.* [devil. *h.*

بنڈوها बंडोहा *banḍohā*, m. a whirlwind; a

بنڈي बंडी *banḍī*, f. short robe, a short full *jāma*. *h.*

بنڈي *banḍi*, f. a cart or carriage of any kind, called by Europeans in the Carnatic "a bandy." *d.*

بنڈيري बंडेरी *banḍerī*, f. a ridge-pole, the ridge of a house. *h.*

بنرا बनरा *banrā*, m. a bridegroom. *h.*

بنري बनरी *banrī*, f. a bride. *h.*

بنس बंश *bans* (for *vansha*), m. a descendant, offspring; race, lineage, family; a bamboo. *s.*

بنسا बंसा *bansā*, a species of grass which grows in rice-fields: it is used as fodder for cattle. *h.*

بنساولي बंशावली *bansāwalī*, f. a genealogy. *s.*

بنسبت *ba-nisbat*, with regard to, concerning. *p. a.*

بنسلامي *ban-salāmī*, f. a fee exacted by the *zamīndār* from the cultivator for permission to collect the juice of the forest date-trees. *s. a.*

بنس لوچن बंशलोचन *bans-lochan*, m. the manna or sugar of the bamboo (it has been found by analysis to contain much siliceous earth). *s.*

بنسن विनसना *binasnā*, n. to perish, to become spoiled. *s.*

بنسي बंशी or बनसी *bansī*, f. (for *vanshī*) a flute; a fishing-hook; a kind of wheat with blackish ears; in comp. of the race or lineage. *bansī-baṭ*, m. the fig-tree under which Krishṇa was accustomed to play the lute. *s.*

بنفشه *banafsha*, f. a violet. *p.*

بنك बंक *bank*, m. a bending, a curvature; reach of a river. *s.*

بنكائي बङ्काई *bankā,ī*, f. a bending, a curvature, the reach or bend of a river. *s.*

بنك پتر वणिक्पुत्र *banik-putra*, m. the son of a merchant, a young merchant. *banik-putrī*, a young woman of the Baniyā tribe. *s.* [merce. *s.*

بنك پته वणिक्पथ *banik-path*, m. traffic, com-

بنكٹا बंकटा *bankṭā*, the crop on the field irrecoverably spoiled. *h.*

بنكٹي बनकटी *ban-kaṭī* or *ban-kaṭṭī*, f. a fee paid for cutting timber; the right obtained by clearing a jungle and bringing it under cultivation. *h.*

بنكٹيا बंकटैया *ban-kaṭaiyā*, m. name of a prickly plant (v. *bang-kaṭiyā*). *h.*

بنكر बनकर *bankar*, spontaneous produce of jungle or forest land, such as gums, honey, &c.; also revenue from woods and forests. *h.* [ropes. *h.*

بنكس बनकस *bankas*, grass used in making

بنكنڈا बनकंडा *ban-kanḍā*, cow-dung found in a jungle or forest, and used for fuel. *h.*

بنكهرا बनखरा *bankharā*, lands on which cotton has grown during the past season. *h.*

بن كهنڈ बनखंड *ban-khanḍ*, m. a forest. *s.*

بن كهنڈي बनखण्डी *ban-khanḍī*, m. the name of a celebrated forest in India. *h.*

بنگ *bang*, f. hemp (*Canabis sativa*); an intoxicating potion made from the leaves of hemp. *p.*

بنگ बङ्ग *bang*, f. calx of tin, given internally as an aphrodisiac; name of Bangālā (Bengal). *s.*

بنگا *bingā*, crooked, awry, distorted. *d.*

بنگا बङ्गा *bangā*, m. a joint of bamboo root; a kind of soil; well-water slightly brackish. *h.*

بنگالا बङ्गाला *bangālā*, the province of Bengāl. *bangālī*, m. *bangālin*, f. an inhabitant of Bengal. *s.*

بنگاه *bungāh*, f. baggage, luggage; the tents, stores, furniture, &c., of an army. *p.*

بنگ بهاو वणिग्भाव *banig-bhāo*, m. traffic, trade. *s*

بنگڑي बङ्गड़ी *bangṛī*, f. an ornament worn on the wrist (properly of glass), a bangle or bracelet made of glass or lac. *h.*

بنگكا बङ्गका *bangkā*, an aquatic beetle that eats rice-plants. *h.*

بنگ كٹيا बंगकटिया *bang-kaṭiyā*, a species of solanum resembling a thistle (not of any use). *h.*

بنگكي बङ्गकी *bangkī*, a species of rice cultivated in Benares. *h.*

بنگلا बङ्गला *banglā*, m. kind of thatched house, commonly called by Europeans a "bungalow"; a sort of betel-leaf so called. *h.*

بنگليا बङ्गलिया *bangliyā*, name of a species of rice. *h.* [in forests. *h.*

بنگونٹها बनगौंठा *ban-gaunṭhā*, cow-dung found

بنگي बङ्गी *bangī*, f. a humming-top. *h.*

بنگي *bangī*, m. one who intoxicates himself with bang. *p.*

بنمال बनमाल *ban-māl*, f. a garland of various flowers (usually those of the *tulsī*) reaching to the feet. *s.*

بنمالي बनमाली *ban-mālī*, one who wears a *ban-māl*; an epithet of *Krishṇa*. *s.*

بنمانس बनमानुस *ban-mānus*, m. a man of the woods, a wild man; an oran-ūtang. *s.*

بننا *bannā, binnā, bunnā.* v. بنا.

بنواري बनवारी *banwārī*, m. one of the names of *Krishṇa*. *s.*

بنواس बनवास *ban-vās*, m. separated from one's family, living in a wood; met. disinherited (a son). *s.* [made or formed. *h.*

بنوانا बनवाना *banwānā*, a. to cause to be

بنوائي बनवाई *banwā,ī*, f. price paid for making any thing. *h.* [weaving. *h.*

بنوائي बिनवाई *binwā,ī*, f. price paid for

بنوتسرگ बनोत्सर्ग *banotsarg*, m. a ceremony performed in honour of a newly-planted orchard: it somewhat resembles a marriage ceremony. (v. Wilson's Glossary). *s.*

بنور बंवर *banwar*, m. f. a creeper, vine. *s.*

بنوريا बिनौरिया *binauriyā*, m. name of an herb used as fodder for cattle. *h.*

بنولا बिनौला *binaulā*, m. the seed of the cotton-tree (it is said to be very fattening food for cattle). *binaulā chābnā*, a. to say unpleasant things. *h.*

بنولي बिनौली *binaulī*, f. hail (of a smaller kind). *h.*

بنونا बिनौना *binaunā*, a. to adore, to venerate, to revere, to laud. *s.*

بنونڈ बंवंड *banwanḍ*, m. a creeper, a vine. *h.*

بنويا बनवैया *banwaiyā*, m. maker, manufacturer. *h.* [household furniture. *p.*

بنه *buna* or *bunna*, m. basis, root, domestics,

بنہا बन्हा *banhā*, m. a conjurer. *h.*

بنہار बनिहार *banihār*, a labourer whose services are paid in *bannī*, or in kind. *h.*

بنہیان बन्हियान *banhiyān*, m. a bridegroom. *h.*

بنہائي बन्हाई *banhā,ī*, f. a female conjuror, an enchantress. *h.*

بنہر बिनहर *binahar*, m. a gatherer of cotton. *h.*

بني बनी *banī*, f. a bride. *h.*

بني बनी *banī*, f. a small forest; a wood. *s.*

بني बिनय *binay* (for *vinaya*), m. humility, humble entreaty, courtesy, good-nature. *s.*

بني *banī* (pl. of ابن), sons. *banī-ādam*, sons of Adam; men. *banī isrā,īl*, children of Israel, Israelites. *a*

بني बन्नी *bannī*, a portion of grain given to a labourer as a remuneration for his services. *h.*

بنيا बणिया or बनिया *baniyā* (also *banyā*), m. a shopkeeper, a merchant (usually a corn-chandler), a Hindū money-changer: in Calcutta this term is applied to the Hindū partner or cash-keeper of a European firm. *s.*

بنياد *bunyād*, f. foundation, base, origin. *bunyād ḍālnā*, to lay the foundation, to found (a city, &c.). *p.*

بنياكنڈا बनैयाकण्डा *banaiyā-kanḍā*, m. cow-dung dried for fuel (not made up). *h.*

بنيان बनियां *baniyāṅ* or *banyāṅ*, m. a trader, a merchant (v. *baniyā*). *p.*

بنيان *bunyān*, f. foundation, basis. *a.*

بنياين बनियायन *baniyāyan* or *baniyā,in*, f. wife of a *baniyā* (a trader). *h.*

بنيٹي बनेटी *baneṭī* or बनैटी *banaiṭī*, f. a torch lighted at both ends and whirled round so as to form a double circle of fire. *h.*

بنيج बनीज *banīj*, m. trade, traffic. *s.*

بنيك बनीक *banīk*, m. a merchant, a trader. *s.*

بنيلا बनेला *banelā* or बनैला *banailā*, wild, of the forest. *s.*

بنيني बनैनी *banainī*, f. wife of a *baniyā*. *h.*

بنيوال बनीवाल *banīwāl*, a subdivision of the *Bhangī* caste. *h.*

بو *bū* (for ابو), father; possessed of; generally used in composition with another word, as *bū-l-'ajab*, father of wonder, or possessed of wonder, marvellous. *a.*

بو *bo* or *bū*, f. smell, odour. *bū-kash*, one who inhales the scent or odour of any substance. *p.*

بو बो *bo* (root of *bonā*), sowing, cultivation. *h.*

بو बौ *bau*, the fee or perquisite of the zamīndār whenever a daughter of any cultivator in his village is married. *h.*

بوٗا बूआ *bū,ā*, f. sister; also an aunt by the father's side. *h.*

بوّاب *bawwāb*, a janitor or porter. *a.*

بوادا बवादा *bawādā*, m. a kind of herb, somewhat like turmeric. *h.*

بوآرا बोआरा *bo,ārā*, m. seedtime, sowing. *h.*

بواسطه *ba-wāsiṭa*, by reason, because of. *p.a.*

بواسير *bawāsīr* (pl. of باسور), the piles or hemorrhoids. *a.*

بو الهوس *bu-l-hawas*, desirous; m. a blockhead, a wavering, fickle person. *bu-l-hawasī*, f. whim, caprice. *a.*

بوآنا बोआना *bo,ānā*, a. to cause to sow; n. (from *bū*, smell), to stink, to emit a smell. *h.*

بواه बिवाह *biwāh*, m. marriage. *s.*

بواها बवाहा *bawāhā*, pocky, affected with *lues venerea*. *h.*

بوائي बवाई *bawā,ī*, f. a kibe, or chap on the foot, a chilblain. *s.* [seedtime. *h.*

بوائي बोआई *boā,ī*, f. sowing, the act of sowing;

بوب बोब *bob*, the sowing of grain by the drill. *h.*

بوبا बोबा *bobā*, m. goods and chattels, property; a bundle. *h.*

بوبك *būbak*, m. an old simpleton. *d.*

بوبو बूबू *būbū*, a sister; (in the west of India) a lady (for *bībī*); a favourite concubine, or one of superior rank. *h.*

بوتا बूता *būtā*, m. strength, power, ability. *h.*

بوتا *botā*, m. a young camel. *p.*

بوتات *būtāt* (for *buyūtāt*), m. account of household expense. *a.*

بوتاتي *būtātī*, relating to household expense. *a.*

بوتو बोतू *botū*, m. a he-goat. *h.*

بوته *būta*, m. a crucible, melting-pot; a bush, a shrub. *p.*

بوتي زمين *bautī-zamīn* (corruptly *-jamīn*), land held by the owner of a village in his own possession to give out to the peasants for cultivation. *h. p.*

بوتيمار *būtīmār*, a heron. *p.*

بوٹ बूट *būṭ*, m. a kind of pulse, *chich-pea* (*Cicer arietinum*). *h.*

بوٹ बोट *boṭ*, the finger, finger's breadth. *h.*

بوٹا बूटा *būṭā*, m. a flower, particularly worked on cloth, or painted on paper, &c.; a bush, a shrub. *būṭe-dār*, a flowered (cloth). *būṭā-ḳadd*, applied to describe the small stature and exquisite proportion of a beloved person. *h.*

بوٹي बूटी *būṭī*, f. drugs; flowers or sprigs (on muslin), sprigs of a plant. *h.*

بوٹي बोटी *boṭī*, f. a morsel (or lump) of meat. *h.*

بوجه *ba-wajh* or *ba-wajhe-ki*, in a way; in such a way that. *p. a.*

بوجھ बूझ *būjh*, f. understanding, comprehension. *būjh-ke*, wittingly. *s.*

بوجھ बोझ *bojh*, بوجھا बोझा *bojhā*, } m. a load, weight, ballast of a boat or ship. *bojh pakaṛnā*, to affect a new delicacy or consequence, to give one's self airs (it is generally spoken in raillery). *bojh sir par honā*, applied to a task, the performance of which is become indispensable: in agricultural language the *bojh* or load comprises about five *dhokās* of corn (v. *dhokā*). *h.*

بوجھا بوجھي *būjhā-būjhī*, f. a game among children: one of them is blindfolded, and must guess which of the others touches him. *s.*

بوجھائي बूझाई *būjhā,ī*, f. teaching, instruction. *s.*

بوجھائي बोझाई *bojhā,ī*, f. lading (a cargo). *h.*

بوجھ‌بٹائي बोझबटाई *bojh-baṭā,ī*, f. a mode of division by stacks or bundles of mowed corn. *h.*

بوجھل बोझल *bojhal*, loaded, laden, heavy. *h.*

بوجهل *bū-jahl* (v. *abū-jahl*), adj. foolish. *a.*

بوجھنا बूझना *būjhnā*, a. to understand, to make out or comprehend; to think. *būjh-lenā* (at cards), to settle the account of gain and loss. *s.*

بوجھنا बोझना *bojhnā*, a. to load; to scald or parch rice. *h.*

بوجھيل बोझेल *bojhel*, loaded, burdened. *h.*

بوچ बोच *boch*, m. an alligator. *h.*

بوچا बोचा *bochā*, m. a kind of sedan, a chair-pālkī. *h.*

بوچا बूचा *būchā*, m. *būchī*, f. ear-cropt, without ears. *h.*

بوچڑا *bochṛā*, chipped or notched on the edge. *h.*

بوچنا बूचना *būchnā*, n. to sit in a confined posture, to crouch. *h.*

بوچھار बौछार *bauchhār*, بوچھاڑ बौछाड़ *bauchhāṛ*, } f. driving rain, wind and rain. *h*

بود *būd*, f. existence, being; a dwelling. *būd o bāsh*, residence, dwelling. *p.*

بودا बोदा *bodā*, weak, faint-hearted, low-spirited; m. a buffalo; (in Dakh.) *bodā-kāghaz*, blotting paper. *h.*

بودا *bodā*, m. the nave of a wheel. *d.*

بودار *bo-dār* or *bū-dār*, fragrant, scented; m. a kind of leather so called. *p.*

بودباش *būd-bāsh*, f. existence, subsistence; residence, abode. *p.*

بودر बोदर *bodar*, a place to stand on for those who raise water from a well. *h.*

بودلي बोदली *bodlī*, f. a simple woman, trollop; a woman who lives with a *be-nawā faḳīr*, and dresses like a man. *h.*

بودن *būdan* (root *buw* or *bāsh*), to be. *p.*

بودھ बोध *bodh*, m. understanding, knowledge. *s.*

بودھ बोध *bodh*, m. a security. *h.*

بودھ बौद्ध *bauddha*, m. a Buddhist. *s.*

بودھا बोद्धा *boddhā*, ingenious, intelligent, sensible. *s.*

بودھك बोधक *bodhak*, m. a teacher. *s.*

بودھن बोधन *bodhan*, m. بودھني बोधनी *bodhanī*, f. } knowledge, teaching; awakening, arousing. *s.*

بودھنا बोधना *bodhnā*, a. to wheedle. *s.*

بوڈا *būḍā*, old, aged; m. an old man. *būḍī*, f. an old woman. *d.*

بوڈپن *būḍ-pan* (also *būḍ-panā*), m. old age. *d.*

بوڈھا *būḍhā*, m. an old man; adj. aged. *h.*

بوڈھگنگا बूढगंगा *būḍh-gangā*, the old bed of the Ganges below Hastināpūr, &c. *h.*

بور बोर *bor*, deep; m. studs of gold or silver. *h.*

بور बूर *būr*, barren (land); f. chaff, husk. *būr-kā-laḍḍū*, a sort of sweetmeat made with the husk of grain. The confectioners avow the imposition, and cry out to passengers, "You'll repent if you eat it, or regret your tasting it." Hence great men are sometimes called *būr-kā-laḍḍū*, when they make a practice of encouraging their dependants to hope, but do nothing for them at last. The term also means any person or thing which is fair without and foul within, or that promises well but turns out bad; a well-looking but stupid fellow. *h.*

بورا बूरा *būrā*, m. a coarse kind of sugar; sawdust; powder; redeemable mortgage. *h.*

بورا बोरा *borā*, m. a canvass bag (particularly for holding about two maunds of rice), a sack; a kind of bean like French beans (*Dolichos catsang*). *h.*

بورا बौरा *baurā*, m. mad, insane. *h.*

بوراپا बौरापा *baurā-pā*, بوراپن बौरापन *baurā-pan*, } m. madness, state of insanity. *h.*

بورانا बौराना *baurānā*, n. to be mad, to madden. *h.*

بوراني *būrānī*, f. a kind of food, consisting of the fruit of the egg-plant (*Baingan*) fried in sour milk. *p.*

بوراها बौराहा *baurāhā*, mad, insane. *h.*

بوربچه *bor-bachcha*, m. a leopard. *d.*

بورق *būraķ* or *bauraķ*, m. borax. *a.*

بورنا *būrnā*, a. to shew, to scatter about. *d.*

بورو बोरो *boro*, m. rainbow; marsh rice (Elliot Gloss.); the name of a kind of rice which is cut in March (Hunter). *boro faṣl*, the season of cutting this rice. *h.*

بورو *būrū* or *borū*, a tube, pipe; a reed or [*ķalam* for writing. *p.*

بوره *būra*, borax; nitre for soldering. *p.*

بوره *bora*, m. redeemable mortgage; a sack for holding rice. *h.*

بورها बौरहा *baurhā*, mad, insane. *h.*

بوري बौरी *baurī*, f. mad, an insane woman. *h.*

بوريا *boriyā* or *būriyā*, m. a kind of mat. *būriyā-bāf*, a mat maker. *p.*

بوڙا बोड़ा *boṛā*, m. a kind of bean (*Dolichos* [*catsang*). *h.*

بوڙا *boṛā*, deaf, dull of hearing. *d.*

بوڙمرنا बूड़मरना *būṛ-marnā*, n. to be drowned, to die by drowning. *h.*

بوڙنا बोड़ना *borṇā*, a. to cause to dive. *h.*

بوڙنا बूड़ना *būṛnā*, n. to dive; to drown, to be immerged, to dip. *h*

بوڙها बूढ़ा *būṛhā*, m. an old man; adj. old, aged. *būṛhā-āṛhā*, aged, of mature years. *h.*

بوڙهاپا बूढ़ापा *būṛhāpā*, also *būṛhā-pan*, m. old age. *h.*

بوڙي बूड़ी *būṛī*, f. a point of a spear; a spike in the end of a staff. *h.*

بوڙيا बूड़िया *būṛiyā*, m. a diver. *h.*

بوز *boz*, m. cream-coloured (a horse). *p.*

بوزا *būzā* (vulgarly *bozā*), m. beer. *būze-ḵẖāna*, a beer-shop. a "boozing-ken;" the latter term is probably a corruption of *būze-ḵẖāna*, introduced into Europe by the gypsies. *p.*

بوزاگر *būzāgar*, m. a brewer, a maker of or dealer in the stuff called *būzā*. *p.*

بوزاگري *būzāgarī*, f. brewing (of *būzā*) *p.*

بوزنه *būzna*, also *bozna* and *boznīna*, m. a monkey, an ape. *p.*

بوزه *boza*, m. the name of a bird (*Ibis denudata? Buch.*); a kind of beer (v. *būzā*). *p.*

بوزينه *būzīna*, an ape, monkey. *p.*

بوس *bos* (in compos.) kissing, saluting. *p.*

بوساطت *ba-wasāṭat*, by means of. *p. a.*

بوستان *bostān* or *būstān*, m. a pleasure-garden; name of a celebrated work by the Persian poet and moralist *Sa'dī*. *p.*

بوس وكنار *bos o kinār*, m. kissing and toying; dalliance. *p.*

بوسه *bosa*, m. a kiss. *bosa-bāzī*, f. kissing and toying. *bosa-denā* or *lenā*, to kiss. *p.*

بوسي *bosī*, kissing, used in comp. as *ķadam-bosī*, kissing the feet, *i.e.* obeisance. *p.*

بوسيدن *bosīdan*, to kiss, embrace. *p.*

بوسيده *bosīda*, stale, rotten. *bosīdagī*, f. rottenness; also part. having kissed. *p.*

بوغ *bogh*, a wrapper, a pouch. *bogh-band*, m. the cloth in which any thing (particularly a saddle) is wrapped up. *p.*

بوغرا *boghrā*, m. a dish made of boiled meat, flour, &c. *boghrā nikālnā*, to be well beaten; somewhat akin to our phrase "having his gruel." *p.*

بوغما *boghmā*, m. trumpery, trifles, scraps, rags, &c., the stores of a wallet; ugly and fat (woman). *p.*

بوق *būķ*, m. a trumpet, clarion. *a.*

بوقت *ba-waķt*, at the time, in the time. *p.a.*

بوقلمون *bū-ķalamūn*, m. a chameleon, (hence) any thing of various hues; adj. various, wonderful. *a*

بوقله *boķla* or *būķla*, m. potherb. *a.*

بوك बूक *būk*, land recovered by the recession of a river. *h.*

بوك बोक *bok*, m. a he-goat, a ram, a tup. *s.*

بوكا बूका *būkā*, m. powder; small pearls. *h.*

بوكا बोका *bokā*, m. a basket, pail, or leather bag for throwing water to a higher elevation. *h.*

بوكارا बूकारा *būkārā*, land (previously recovered as *būk*, q. v.), but rendered useless by a deposit of sand. *h.*

بوكرا बोकरा *bokrā*, m. a he-goat. *s.*

بوكري बोकरी *bokrī*, f. a she-goat. *s.*

بوكڑ *bokaṛ*, m. a he-goat (big-bearded). *d.*

بوكنا बूकना *būknā*, a. to powder, to grind, to reduce to powder. *h.*

بوكه *boka*, m. a basket or leather bag used for raising water. *h.*

بول बोल *bol*, m. myrrh. *s.*

بول बोल *bol*, m. speech, talk, conversation; words of a song. *h.*

بول *baul*, m. urine. *baul-dān*, a chamber-pot. *baul-gāh*, the urethra. *a.*

بولا बौला *baulā*, toothless. *h.*

بولا बोला *bolā*, m. a verbal agreement between two parties. *h.*

بولاچالي बोलाचाली *bolā-chālī*, f. conversation. *h.*

بولانا *baulānā* (v. *baurānā*), n. to be mad. *bolāna* (Dakh. for *bulānā*, q. v.). *h.*

بول بالا बोलबाला *bol-bālā*, m. a kind of benediction. *bol-bālā honā*, to prosper. *h.*

بول بهيجنا *bol-bhejnā*, a. to send for, to summon. *d.*

بولتا बोलता *boltā*, m. the faculty of speech; soul, life. *h.*

بول چال बोलचाल *bol-chāl*, f. conversation. *h.*

بولنا बोलना *bolnā*, n. to speak; to sound, to emit sound; to tell, to say. *bol uṭhnā*, to speak out, to exclaim. *bol chālnā*, to converse, speak together. *bole so bolnā*, to speak repeatedly. *h.*

بولنس बोलंस *bolans*, making over one's own share to another. *h.*

بولنسي बोलंसी *bolansī*, the holder of another's share or inheritance; an adopted heir. *h.*

بولي बौली *baulī*, f. settlement direct with the peasant; also a kind of assessment. *h.*

بولي बोली *bolī*, f. speech, dialect, language; conversation, talk. *bolī-k.*, to jeer, to jest. *h.*

بولي ٹهولي बोलीठोली *bolī-ṭholī*, f. jeering, speaking *at* but not *to* a person. *bolī ṭholī sunānā* or *mārnā*, to reproach, to blame. *h.*

بوم *būm*, m. an owl; land, ground, soil. *p.*

بوم *bom*, m. } weeping, wailing, lamentation; interj. alas! *d.*
بومڑي *bomṛī*, f. }

بونا बोना *bonā*, a. to sow, to plant. *s.*

بونا बौना *baunā*, m. a dwarf; the fifth *avatār*, or incarnation of Vishnu. *s.*

بونٹ बोंट *bonṭ*, m. a stalk. *h.*

بونٹ बूंट *būnṭ*, m. a kind of pulse when green (*Cicer arietinum*); the plant of *būnṭ*; adj. little compact and firm (epithet applied to a pony: sometimes used substantively). *h.* [*būnṭ*, q. v. *h.*

بونٹ پلاو *būnṭ pulāw*, m. a *pulāw* made of

بونٹ बोंट *bonṭ*, a finger (same as *angul*). *d.*

بونج *būnj*, mould, mustiness. *būnj-bharā*, very musty. *d.*

بوند बूंद *būnd*, f. drop. *būnd kī būnd* (*sharāb*, understood), very strong wine; doubly-distilled spirits, &c. *s.*

بوند बून्द *būnd*, good, well, excellent; high soaring (generally applied to kites). *h.*

بوندكي *būndakī*, f. a spot. *būndakī-dār*, spotted. *d.*

بوندا बून्दा *būndā*, m. a large drop. *būndā-bāndī*, small and interrupted dropping of rain.

بوندي बून्दी *būndī*, f. drops of rain; name of a place; a kind of sweetmeat in the form of drops. *s.*

بونديلا बुन्देला *būndelā*, name of a tribe of *rāj-pūts*, who give name to the province of Bundlecund (i. e. *Būndel-khand*). *h.*

بونڈ बौंड *baunḍ*, m. a creeper, a vine. *h.*

بونڈا *bonḍā*, m. a capsule, or pod of cotton, &c. *d.*

بونڈر बवंडर *bawanḍar*, m. a whirlwind, a devil. *h.*

بونڈنا बौंडना *baunḍnā*, n. to entwine (creepers or vines). *h.*

بونڈي बोंड़ी *bonḍī*, f. the germ of a plant after the flower is shed. *h.*

بونڈيانا बौंडियाना *baunḍiyānā*, n. to twine; to run irregularly or in a crooked direction, with turnings and windings. *h.*

بونگا बूंगा *būngā* or *bongā*, a stack of straw, a heap of chaff. *h.*

بوني बौनी *baunī*, f. female dwarf. *s.*

بوني बोनी *bonī*, f. the season of sowing. *s.*

بوها बौहा *bauhā*, pocky (v. *bawāhā*). *h.*

بوهائي बौहाई *bauhā,ī*, f. afflicted with venereal disease (a woman). *h.*

بوهرا बोहरा *bohrā*, m. a class of bankers or money-lenders so called. *h.*

بوهني बोहनी *bohnī*, f. the money received for the first sale in the morning by shopkeepers and hucksters: no credit is allowed, nothing but ready money being received on such occasions. *h.*

بوهوديا बोहोदिया *bohodiyā*, m. a man who works with a borrowed plough, or with a spade, &c. (having no plough of his own). *h.*

بوئي बूई *bū,ī*, a word used to frighten children, a goblin, or still more nearly, "bogie." *h.*

بوئي باچه बोईबाछ *bo,ī-bāchh*, assessment to be realized on cultivation. *h.*

بوير बोयर *boyar*, land that is never allowed to lie fallow. *h.*

بويرا बवेरा *bawerā*, sowing, seedtime. *h.*

بويسيا बवेसिया *bavesiyā*, a catamite, sodomite; one who talks nonsense, a babbler. *h.*

بوئيا बोइया *bo,iyā*, m. a small basket. *h.*

بوئيدن *bū,īdan*, to diffuse fragrance. *p.*

به भ *bha*, the aspirate form of the letter ب ब. *s. h.*

به *ba*, prep. by, with, in; generally joined to the word it governs, and then the imperceptible *h* is dropped, as *ba-wajh* or *ba-wajhe*, in such a manner *p.*

بهه बहु *bahu*, much, many, large, great. *s.*

بہ *bih*, good, better. *bih* or *bihi*, a quince. *p.*

بہا *bahā*, m. price, value. *bahā,e khūn*, blood-money (paid to the relations of a person slain). *bahā,e khil'at*, a tax raised in order to defray the expense of honorary dresses. *bahā,e kāghaz*, an allowance for office paper, red tape, &c. *h.*

بهابر भाबर *bhābar*, name of a large forest at the foot of the Sevalic hills. *h.*

بهابهي भाभी *bhābhī*, f. a brother's wife. *h.*

بهابي भावी *bhābī*, future, about to be, predestined. *s.*

بهاپه भाफ *bhāph*, f. steam, vapour. *s.*

بہاپهرنا बहाफिरना *bahā-phirnā* or *bahā-bahā phirnā*, n. to wander; to be in a distressed condition; to be intoxicated. *s.*

بهاپهنا भाफना *bhāphnā*, a. to conceive, to guess, to comprehend. *h.*

بهات भात *bhāt*, advances to ploughmen without any interest. *h.*

بهات भात *bhāt*, m. boiled rice, food. *s.*

بهاتا भाता *bhātā*, m. an extra allowance to troops on service, commonly called batta. *h.*

بهاٹ भाट *bhāṭ*, m. a bard, a minstrel; a genealogist or family bard; name of a tribe. *h.*

بهاٹن भाटन *bhāṭan*, the wife of a bard, a female minstrel. *h.*

بهاٹها भाठा *bhāṭhā*, m. a current or stream, the ebb tide. *h.*

بهاٹهی भाठी *bhāṭhī*, f. bellows. *s.*

بهاٹهي भाठी *bhāṭhī*, f. down the river, with the current. *h.*

بهاٹهيال भाठियाल *bhāṭhiyāl*, m. down, below, down the river, with the stream. *h.*

بهاجر भाजर *bhājar*,
بهاجڑ भाजड़ *bhājaṛ*, } f. flight, running off. *h.*

بهاجن भाजन *bhājan*, m. a plate, a dish, &c.; (in arithmetic) division. *s.*

بهاجنا भाजना *bhājnā*, n. to flee, run away. *h.*

بهاجنا भाजना *bhājnā*, a. to fry. *s.*

بهاجي भाजी *bhājī*, f. greens. *s.*

بهاجي भाजी *bhājī*, f. portion or share of food. *h.*

بهاجيه भाज्य *bhājya*, divisible, to be portioned; m. a portion, a share, an inheritance; (in arithmetic) the dividend. *s.*

بهاچر *bhāchar*, a large earthen pot or jar. *d.*

بہادر *bahādur*, brave, bold, valiant, courageous, invincible; m. a hero, a champion, knight; a title bestowed on military officers. "It is often accompanied with the word *jang*, war; thus, *bahādur jang*, invincible in war. The English (that is to say, Indian-English) language has adopted this word: a "bahauder" indicates a martinet, or proud and haughty mortal dressed in a little brief authority" (Binning.) *p.*

بهادر भाद्र *bhādra*,
بهادرپد भाद्रपद *bhādra-pad*, } m. the fifth solar month (see *bhādoṅ*). *s*

بهادرپدا भाद्रपदा *bhādra-padā*, f. a name common to the 26th and 27th lunar asterisms, distinguished by the epithets prior and subsequent, or *pūrva* and *uttar*. *s.*

بہادري *bahādurī*, f. bravery, gallantry. *p.*

بهادون भादों *bhādoṅ*, m. name of the fifth solar month, August—September (in which the full moon is near *Pūrvabhādrapada*). *s.*

بهادونوي भादोंवी *bhādoṅwī*, of or relating to the month *bhādoṅ*; the autumnal crop. *s.*

بہادينا बहादेना *bahā-denā*, a. (lit. to set afloat), to demolish, to destroy, to ruin, to impoverish, to deprive of felicity or fortune. *s.*

بہار बिहार *bihār*, m. diversion, sport, amusement; name of a province. *bihāra-sthal*, place of amusement. *s.*

بہار *bahār*, f. spring; beauty, elegance, delight. *bahāristān*, m. a place adorned with the blossoms of spring; name of a Persian book by Jāmī. *p.*

بهار भार *bhār*, m. a load, weight, fagot, gravity, a weight of gold equal to 2000 *palas*. *s.*

بهار भार *bhār*, out, without (v. *bāhar*); adj. external, outside. *d.*

بهارا भारा *bhārā*, m. a load, burthen. *s.*

بہاران *bahārān*, the spring season. *p.*

بهاربركش भारबृक्ष *bhār-briksh*, m. a fragrant substance, commonly called *kākshī* considered variously as a vegetable or mineral product. *s.*

بهارت भारत *bhārat* or *bhārata*, m. the heroic poem which contains the account of *Yudhishṭhir's* war; m. name of one of the nine divisions of the world: India proper, so called from Bharata, the son of Dushyanta, whose patrimony it was. *s.*

بهارجا भार्या *bhārjā*, f. a wife; wives of the Rāgs, or deities presiding over the Hindū musical modes. *bhārjātwa*, the condition of a wife. *bhārjāṭik*, m. a henpecked husband. *s.*

بهاردواج भारद्वाज *bhāradwāj*, m. a skylark. *s.*

بہارستان *bahāristān*, abode of spring, or of beauty; name of a Persian work by the poet Jāmī. *p.*

بہارن बुहारन *buhāran*, f. sweepings. *h.*

بہارنا बुहारना *buhārnā*, a. to sweep, to gather. *h.*

بہارني बुहारनी *buhārnī*, f. a broom, a besom. *h.*

بہارو बुहारू *buhārū*, m. a sweeper. *h.*

بهارواه भारवाह *bhār-wāh* (also *bhāra-vāhik*), m. a porter, a bearer of burthens. *s.*

بہاري बुहारी *buhārī*, f. a broom, a besom. *h.*

بهاري भारी *bhārī*, heavy; of importance (met.); big, weighty, fat, large; valuable; patient, steady, grave; strong, thick, troublesome; m. a porter, carrier of burthens. *bhārī-bharkam*, grave, sedate. *bhārī patthar chūmkar chhoṛnā*, to withdraw from a difficult or impracticable undertaking. *s.*

بہاري *bahārī*, vernal, relating to spring. *p.*

بہاري बिहारी *bihārī*, sportive; a name of Krishna; name of a Hindī poet. *s*

بهاريا भार्या **bhāryā**, f. lit. a wife or married woman; a musical mode; the wife of a Rāg or deity presiding over a musical mode. *s.*

بهاڑ भाड़ **bhāṛ**, m. a furnace, kiln (particularly for frying grain). *s.*

بهاڑ भाड़ **bhāṛ**, m. the price of fornication. *bhāṛ-khānā*, a. to live on the wages of prostitution (applied not to the woman but to her dependants). *h.*

بهاڑا भाड़ा **bhāṛā**, m. hire, settled fare, rent; recompense. *h.*

بهاسر भासुर **bhāsur**, m. a husband's elder brother; a species of costus (*Costus speciosus*). *s.*

بهاسکر भास्कर **bhāskar**, resplendent, shining; m. the sun; name of a Hindū astronomer, author of the *Siddhānta Shiromani* and other works. *s.*

بهاسنا भासना **bhāsnā**, n. to be known, to appear. *s.*

بهاسور भास्वर **bhāswar**, shining, radiant; m. the sun, a day; *Costus speciosus*. *s.*

بهاشا भाषा **bhāshā**, f. a dialect, &c. (same as [bhākhā]). *s.*

بهاشت भाषित **bhāshit**, spoken, said. *s.*

بهاکت भाक्त **bhākta**, } m. a follower, a dependant, a retainer. *s.*
بهاکتك भाक्तिक **bhāktik**, }

بهاکسي भाकसी **bhāksī**, f. a kiln. *s.*

بهاکهه भाखा **bhākhā**, f. speech, dialect, language. *s.*

بهاکهنا भाखना **bhākhnā**, a. to speak, to call. *s.*

بهاگ बिहाग **bihāg**, m. name of a rāg in music. *h.*

بهاگ भाग **bhāg**, m. fortune, destiny; share, lot; tax, duty; share in kind; a degree, the 360th part of a circle; a fraction. *bhāg jāgnā*, to be fortunate. *bhāg-baṭā,ī*, apportionment of the shares of a crop. *bhāg-dār*, a sharer. *s.*

بهاگابهاگ भागाभाग **bhāgā-bhāg**, m. running away, flight. *h.*

بهاگ‌بهروسا भागभरोसा **bhāg-bharosā**, comfort, consolation. *d.*

بهاگ‌جانا भागजाना **bhāg-jānā**, n. to run away. *h.*

بهاگڑ भागड़ **bhāgaṛ**, f. flight, a general emigration, escape from immediate danger. *h.*

بهاگڑا बिहागड़ा **bihāgaṛā**, m. (v. *bihāg*). *h.*

بهاگل भागल **bhāgal**, trick, affectation. *h.*

بهاگلپوري भागलपूरी **bhāgalpūrī**, m. a kind of cloth from Bhāgalpūr made of silk and cotton. *h.*

بهاگلي भागली **bhāgalī**, false, mock, imitation. *h.*

بهاگليا भागलिया **bhāgaliyā**, f. imposture, hypocrisy. *h.*

بهاگ‌مان भागमान **bhāgmān**, fortunate. *s.*

بهاگماني भागमानी **bhāgmānī**, f. good fortune. *s.*

بهاگنا भागना **bhāgnā**, n. to flee, to run away. *h.*

بهاگنر भागनर **bhāgnar**, name of a rich alluvial soil on the banks of the Jumna. *h.*

بهاگني भागिनी **bhāginī**, fem. of *bhāgī*, partner, co-heiress, a sister. *s.*

بهاگنيه भागिनेय **bhāgineya**, m. a sister's son. *s.*

بهاگو भागू **bhāgū**, a deserter, a runaway. *h.*

بهاگوار भागवार **bhāgwār**, held upon a joint tenure or share (land). *h.*

بهاگوان भागवान **bhāgawān**, fortunate, prosperous. *s.*

بهاگوت भागवत **bhāgavat**, m. name of one of the *purānas*. *s.*

بهاگوڑا भागोड़ा **bhāgoṛā**, a runaway, a coward. *h.*

بهاگي भागी **bhāgī**, m. a partner, sharer, participator, a co-heir; also a share or portion. *bhāgī-dār*, a sharer, a partner. adj. prosperous. *s.*

بهاگيرته भागीरथ **bhāgīrath**, m. name of a pious king whose austerities brought the river Ganges from heaven. *s.*

بهاگيرتهي भागीरथी **bhāgīrathī**, f. the river Ganges (so called from the pious monarch aforesaid). *s.*

بهاگيل भागेल **bhāgel**, a deserter, a runaway; desertion, flight. *h.*

بهاگيوان भाग्यवान **bhāgyawān**, } fortunate, rich. *s.*
بهاگيونت भाग्यवन्त **bhāgyawant**, }

بهاگيه भाग्य **bhāgya**, m. fortune, destiny. *s.*

بهاگيهين भाग्यहीन **bhāgya-hīn**, poor, wretched, unfortunate. *s.*

بهال भाल **bhāl**, f. the point of an arrow. *h.*

بهال भाल **bhāl**, m. a tribe of *rāj-pūts*. *h.*

بهال भाल **bhāl**, f. the forehead; fortune. *s.*

بهال भाल **bhāl**, m. a bear. *s.*

بهالا भाला **bhālā**, m. a spear (about seven cubits long). *s.*

بهالانك भालाङ्क **bhālānk**, m. a sort of fish, commonly called the *rohi* (*Cyprinus rohita*); a sort of potherb. *s.*

بهالك भालुक **bhāluk**, } m. a bear. *s.*
بهالو भालू **bhālū**, }

بهالنا भालना **bhālnā**, a. to see, to perceive, to look, to contemplate. *h.*

بهالوکولا **bhālū-kolā**, m. a hyena, or, as some say, a hybrid animal between a wolf and a jackal. *d.*

بهاليت भालैत **bhālait**, m. a pikeman, a spearman. *s.*

بهامن भामिन **bhāmin**, angry, passionate. *s.*

بهامني भामिनी **bhāminī**, f. a passionate woman. *s.*

بهان भानु **bhānu**, m. the sun. *s.*

بهان *bhān*, f. (for *bahin*, q.v.), a sister. *d.*

بهان बिहान *bihān*, m. morrow, morning. *h.*

بهانا भाना *bhānā*, a. to please, to suit, to fit, to be approved of. *h.*

بهانا बहाना *bahānā*, a. to make flow, to set afloat, to launch. *s.*

بهانا बिहाना *bihānā*, n. to spend or pass (the time). *h.*

بهانا *bahānā* (for *bahāna*), m. pretence, &c. *p.*

بهانت भांत *bhānt* or भांति *bhānti*, f. manner, mode, method, kind, sort. *h.*

بهانت بهانت *bhānt-bhānt*, various, of many sorts. *h.*

بهانٹ भांट *bhānṭ*, m. a medicinal plant (*Clerodendron infortunatum, Lin.; Volkameria infortunata, Roxb.*). *s.*

بهانٹا भांटा *bhānṭā*, m. the egg-plant (*Solanum melongena*. *s.*

بهانج भांज *bhānj*, f. twist. *s.*

بهانجا भांजा *bhānjā*, m. a nephew, a sister's son. *s.*

بهانجنا भांजना *bhānjnā*, a. to put into circular motion, to twist, to turn on a lathe, to wave, to brandish. *s.*

بهانجي भांजी *bhānjī*, f. a niece, a sister's daughter. *s.*

بهانجي भांजी *bhānjī*, f. interruption, hinderance; tale-bearing. *bhānjī-khor*, m. an interrupter, a tale-bearer. *bhānjī khānā*, a. to give a malicious piece of intelligence. *bhānjī-denā* or *-mārnā*, a. to interrupt, to put a stop to, to break in upon. *h,*

بهان چارا भानचारा *bhān-chārā*, sisterhood, state or relationship of sister. *d.*

بهانڈ भाण्ड *bhānḍ*, m. a mimic, an actor; a small earthen pot: stock, capital. *s.*

بهانڈا भाण्डा *bhānḍā*, m. a large earthen pot; estate, equipage. *bhānḍā-phūṭnā*, n. to lose one's character. *s.*

بهانڈار भाण्डार *bhānḍār*, بهانڈارا भाण्डारा *bhānḍārā*, } m. also *bhānḍār-khāna*, a store, a place where household goods are kept, a storehouse. *s.*

بهانڈاري भाण्डारी *bhānḍārī*, m. a house-steward, a treasurer, purveyor. *s.*

بهانڈن भाण्डिन *bhānḍin*, f. an actress, or female mimic. *s.*

بهانڈنا भाण्डना or भांडना *bhānḍnā*, a. to abuse, to calumniate. *s.*

بهانڈيتي भांडैती *bhānḍaitī*, f. mimickry, buffoonery; a female mimic, an actress. *s.*

بهانڈير भांडीर *bhānḍīr*, m. the Indian fig-tree. *s.*

بهانس *bhāns* (for *bāns* q. v.), m. a bamboo. *d.*

بهانسي *bhānsī* (for *bānsī* q. v.), f. a flute, &c. *d.*

بهانكري भांनकरी *bhānkarī*, f. name of a shrub. *h.*

بهانكڑا भांकड़ा *bhānkṛā*, m. a fop, a parasite. *h.*

بهانگ भांग *bhāng*, f. hemp (*Cannabis sativus*), of which an intoxicating potion is made. *s.*

بهانگرا *bhāngrā*, بهانگي *bhāngī*, } m. one who is addicted to the use of *bhāng*. *s.*

بهانگيرا भांगेरा *bhāngerā*, m. a seller of *bhāng*. *s.*

بهان متي भानमती *bhān-matī*, m. a female juggler, an actress. *s.*

بهان متي भानुमती *bhānumatī*, adj. f. beautiful, handsome. *s.*

بهاننا भानना *bhānnā*, a. to turn (on a lathe), to put into circular motion, to twist, wave, brandish; to break, destroy. *h.*

بهانو भानु *bhānū*, m. the sun. *s.*

بهانوار भानुवार *bhānuwār*, m. Sunday. *s.*

بهانور भांवर *bhānwar*, بهانوري भांवरी *bhānwrī*, } f. revolution, circulation. *bhānwrī phirnā*, to circle; to be sacrificed. *s.*

بهانولي *bhānolī*, f. a sort of bread. *d.*

بهانه *bahāna*, m. pretence, evasion, contrivance, excuse, pretext. *p.*

بهاني बिहाने *bihāne*, early, soon. *h.*

بهاؤ भाव *bhā,o*, m. price, value, rate, friendship. *h.*

بهاو भाव *bhāw*, m. state or condition of being; natural state, disposition, nature; meaning, purpose; sentiment, passion; will, notion, idea; living, being, existence, thing; choice, liking; blandishment; gesticulaation, acting, pantomime, expressing a meaning by signs; a sudden idea or emotion of mind. *bhāw-batānā*, to gesticulate. *s.*

بهاؤ बहाव *bahā,o*, m. flowing, a flood. *s.*

بهاوت भावित *bhāvit*, animated, inspired; thoughtful, anxious, apprehensive, alarmed. *s.*

بهاؤتا भावता *bhā,otā*, amiable, dear, beloved. *h.*

بهاوج भावज *bhāwaj*, f. a brother's wife, also the wife of a wife's brother. *s.*

بهاوك भावक *bhāwak*, m. the external expression of amatory sentiments; a friend, a lover. *s.*

بهاوك भाविक *bhāwik*, natural, innate, sentimental, relating to feeling. *s.*

بهاولي भावली *bhā,olī* or *bhāwalī*, f. rent paid in kind to a *zamīndār*, distribution of crop between the *zamīndār* and cultivator. *bhā,olī-khil*, land recently brought into cultivation. *bhā,olī-pā*, land long cultivated. *h.*

بهاون भावन *bhāwn* or *bhā,on*, regarding, concerning, in respect to. *h.*

بهاونا भावना *bhāvanā* or *bhā,onā*, f. mental perception, recollection, the present consciousness of past ideas or perceptions; imagination; religious and abstract meditation; looking about, observing, investigating; consideration; apprehension, contemplation, thought, doubt, fear, concern. *s.*

بهاونا भावना *bhā,onā* or *bhāwnā*, n. to please. *h.*

بهاوه भावह *bhāwah*, f. a younger brother's wife. *s.*

بهاوي भावी *bhāwī*, بهاوئي भावई *bhāwa,ī*, } future, what is about to be, predestined. *s*

بهاوين भावें *bhāwen*, postpos. masc. in the sentiment, perception, mind, notion; in one's eyes, in sight, near, before, &c. *h.*

بهاويه भाव्य *bhāvya*, what must, will, or ought [to be. *s.*

بهائم *bahā,im* (pl. of بهيمه), beasts, animals, wild beasts. *bahā,imī*, beastly, brutal. *a.*

بهائي बिहाई *bihā,ī*, f. a spirit supposed to tease infants, whispering alternately sad and pleasing things in their ears, which is the cause of their laughing and crying in their sleep or waking. *h.*

بهائي भाई *bhā,ī*, m. brother, also a friend or comrade. *bhā,ī-ans*, also *bhā,ī-pahsī* and *bhā,ī-hissa*, the share or portion of a brother. *s.*

بهائي بانٹ भाईबांट *bhā,ī-bānṭ*, m. fraternal community; a term applied to a village owned by brothers, or descendants from one common stock. *h.*

بهائي بت भाईवत *bhā,ī-bat* (or *bhā,ī-vat*), like a brother, fraternal *s.*

بهائي بند भाईबन्द *bhā,ī-band*, m. brotherhood, brothers, friends, relations; also *bhā,ī-bandī*. *s.*

بهائي چارا भाईचारा *bhā,ī-chārā*, m. } brotherhood,
بهائي چاري भाईचारी *bhā,ī-chārī*, f. } fraternity. *s.*

بهائين भाईन *bhā,īn*, terrible, awful. *h.*

بهبچن बहुबचन *bahu-bachan*, plural (in grammar). *s.*

بهبروت भब्रूत *bhabrūt*, ashes of cow-dung. *s.*

بهبها भबका *bhabhā*, m. an alembic; a kind of drinking-vessel with a large mouth. *s.*

بهبكانا भबकाना *bhabhānā*, a. to kindle, to light; to provoke, to exasperate, to enrage; to spur a horse. *h.*

بهبكنا भबकना *bhabaknā*, n. to be enraged, to rush on with rage; to catch fire; to run with great rapidity (a horse), to bubble (as boiling water), to roar, to grumble. *h.*

بهبكي भबकी *bhabhī*, f. threat. *h.*

بهبل बिहबल *bihbal*, agitated, alarmed, overcome with fear or agitation, unable to restrain one's self. *s.*

بهبوت *bhabūt*, } f. ashes of cow dung (vide
بهبوتي *bhabūtī*, } *bhabhūt*. *s.*

بهبود *bih-būd*, m. } health, vigour, goodness,
بهبودي *bih-būdī*, f. } welfare. *p.*

بهبها बहबहा *bahbahā*, flowing, gliding along; brave, bold; public, notorious. *h.* [fortunate. *s.*

بهبهاگيه बहुभाग्य *bahu-bhāgya*, f. *bahu-bhāgyā*,

بهبهر भभर or भबभर *bhabbhar*, m. solicitude, alarm. *bhabhar bhabhar parnā*, n. to be alarmed, to be frightened. *s.*

بهبهرانا भभराना *bhabhrānā*, a. to swell (particularly the face). to entertain doubts. *h.*

بهبهرنا भभरना *bhabharnā*, n. to be solicitous, to be alarmed, to be frightened. *h.*

بهبهك भभक *bhabhak*, f. sudden bursting forth of flame; forcible expulsion of water from a fountain or pipe; smell arising suddenly. *h.*

بهبهكنا भभकना *bhabhaknā*, n. to simmer, to bubble; to emit steam, to boil. *h.*

بهبهل भबभल *bhabbhal*, fat, corpulent. *h.*

بهبهوت भभूत *bhabhūt*, f. ashes of cow-dung, which ascetics or *jogīs* rub over their bodies. *s.*

بهبهوكا भभूका *bhabhūkā*, m. blaze, flame, explosion; adj. red (as a coal): this is sometimes applied to the splendour of a beloved person's countenance; adj. splendid, beautiful. *h.*

بهپارا भपारा *bhapārā*, } m. steam, vapour,
بهپكارا भपकारा *bhapkārā*, } exhalation. *s.*

بهپتر बहुपुत्र *bahu-putra*, having many children; m. a tree (*Echites scholaris*). *s.*

بهپتري बहुपुत्री *bahu-putrī*, f. a plant (*Asparagus racemosus*). *s.*

بهپتر बहुपत्र *bahu-patra*, m. talc. *s.*

بهپتري बहुपत्री *bahu-patrī*, f. a drug (*Trigonella fœnum græcum*). *s.*

بهپٹ बहुपटु *bahu-paṭu*, very clever. *s.*

بهپرني बहुपर्णी *bahu-parnī*, f. a medicinal plant (*Trigonella fœnum græcum*). *s.*

بهپرواه बहुप्रवाह *bahu-pravāh*, flowing in many streams. *s.*

بهپكنا भपकना *bhapaknā* (same as *bhabhaknā*), to simmer, boil, &c. *d.*

بهپولا भपोला *bhapolā*, m. a blister. *d.*

بهپهارا भफारा *bhaphārā*, m. steam, vapour. *s.*

بهپهل बहुफल *bahu-phal*, fertile, fruitful; m. the Kadamb-tree (*Nauclea cadamba*). *bahu-phalī*, adj. f. fertile; f. the opposite-leaved fig-tree. *s.*

بهپهي बिहफै *bihphai*, m. Thursday. *s.*

بهت बहुत *bahut*, much, many, more, most; *bahut yār honā*, to become more intimate than formerly. *s.* [sonry. *s.*

بهت भित्ति *bhitti*, f. a wall of earth or ma-

بهتا बहता *bahtā*, running (water). *bahte pānī men hāth dhonā*, to pay attention to one's friends, or attend to one's own duty or affairs while the opportunity is favourable; to make hay while the sun shines. *h.*

بهتا भुट्टा *bhuttā*, m. Indian corn or maize, see *bhuṭṭā*. *h.*

بهتا *bhattā*, m. a pair of bellows. *d.*

بهتات बहुतात *bahutāt*, f. excess, abundance. *s.*

بهتار भतार *bhatār*, m. a husband. *s.*

بهتان *buhtān*, m. calumny, aspersion, false accusation. *buhtān bāndhnā*, to calumniate. *a.*

بهتاها भुताहा *bhutāhā*, devilish, peevish, fierce. *s.*

بهتايت बहुतायत *bahutāyat* f. abundance, plenty, multitude. *s.*

بهتر *bihtar*, good, excellent, well, better. *p.*

بهتر बहत्तर *bahattar*, seventy-two. *h.*

بهتر बहुत्र *bahutra*, in many ways or places. *s.*

بهتري *bihtarī*, f. superior excellence, welfare. *p.*

بهترين *bihtarīn*, best, superior. *p.*

بهت‌سا बहुतसा *bahut-sā*, a great deal, very much. *h.*

بهتنا भुतना *bhutnā*, m. a small devil, an imp, [a demon. *s.*

بهتني भुतनी *bhutnī*, f. wife of an imp; a female demon. *s.*

بهتوك बहुत्वक्क *bahu-twakk*, m. the Bhoj or birch-tree. *s.*

بهتوه बहुत्व *bahutwa*, m. plurality, multitude, abundance. *s.*

بهته भत्तः *bhatta*, m. an extra allowance for troops when marching; batta. *h.*

بهتها भुतहा *bhutahā*, devilish, peevish, fierce. *s.*

بهتيانا भुतियाना *bhutiyānā*, n. to be like a devil. *s.*

بهتيجا भतीजा *bhatījā*, m. nephew, brother's son. *s.*

بهتيجي भतीजी *bhatījī*, f. niece, brother's daughter. *s.*

بهتيرا बहुतेरा *bahuterā*, very much. *s.*

بهٹ भट *bhaṭ*, f. misfortune, curse; an oven, a furnace, a kiln. *bhaṭ parnā*, n. to be cursed, to be unfortunate, to be lost (lit. to fall into the kiln). *h.*

بهٹ भट *bhaṭ*, m. a warrior, hero, soldier; a barbarian or outcast of a particular tribe. *s.*

بهٹ भट्ट *bhaṭṭ*, m. a learned man, a philosopher; a title of Mahāratthā Brāhmans. *s.*

بهٹا भट्टा *bhaṭṭā*, a ploughman's wages in kind. *h.*

بهٹا भुट्टा *bhuṭṭā*, m. Indian corn (*Zea mays*); any large bunch, the head or ear of corn ripened. *h.*

بهٹا *bhaṭṭā*, m. a pair of bellows. *d.*

بهٹاچارج भट्टाचार्य *bhaṭṭāchārj* m. (for *bhaṭṭāchārya*), the most learned of the learned; a title given to the Kanaujiya Brāhmans: it is also applied to one who teaches any branch of Sanskrit literature. *s.*

بهٹکا भटका *bhaṭkā*, astray, wandering. *h.*

بهٹکانا भटकाना *bhaṭkānā*, a. to baulk, to mislead, to deceive, to scare, to cause to wander, to lead astray. *h.*

بهٹ‌کٹائي भटकटाई *bhaṭ-kaṭā,ī*, } f. the name
بهٹ‌کٹیا भटकटैया *bhaṭ-kaṭaiyā*, } of a prickly plant (*Solanum Jacquini, Willd.*). *h.*

بهٹکریا भटकरिया *bhaṭ-kariyā*, a class of inferior *rājpūts*. *h.*

بهٹکنا भटकना *bhaṭaknā*, n. to wander about; to go astray, to miss the right path. *h.*

بهٹگور भटगौर *bhaṭ-gāur*, a subdivision of the Gaur *rāj-pūts*, q.v. *h.*

بهٹلا भटुला *bhaṭulā*, m. a kind of bread made from the flour of the *arhar* and other sorts of pulse. *h.*

بهٹناگر भटनागर *bhaṭnāgar*, a tribe of *Kāyaths*. *h.*

بهٹني भिटनी *bhiṭnī*, f. a nipple. *h.*

بهٹو भटू *bhaṭū*, interj. O sister! *h.*

بهٹولر भटोलर *bhaṭolar*, lands allotted to *bhāṭs* or bards; also lands given to Brāhmans. *h.*

بهٹه *bhuṭṭa*, m. Indian corn, any large bunch. *h.*

بهٹها भट्ठा *bhaṭṭhā*, m. a furnace, kiln, oven. *h.*

بهٹهي भट्ठी *bhaṭṭhī*, or भठी *bhaṭhī*, f. a small fire-place, a kind of furnace; a liquor-shop, distillery. *bhaṭṭhī-dār*, one who keeps a spirit-shop. *h.*

بهٹهي‌دار भट्ठीदार *bhaṭṭhī-dār*, a person who manufactures and sells spirituous liquors. *h.*

بهٹهيارا भठियारा *bhaṭhiyārā*, m. (or *bhaṭhiyārī*, f.) a sutler, an innkeeper; one who prepares victuals for travellers in a *sarā*. *h.*

بهٹهيارپن भठियारपन *bhaṭhiyārpan*, m. the business of a *bhaṭhiyārā*. *h.*

بهٹهيارخانه भठियारखान *bhaṭhiyār-khāna*, an inn, a caravanserai. *p.*

بهٹهيارن भठियारिन *bhaṭhiyārin*, } f. a female
بهٹهياري भठियारी *bhaṭhiyārī*, } sutler. *h.*

بهٹهيال भठियाल *bhaṭhiyāl*, with the current, i.e. down the river, and not with the flood tide; m. a kind of *marṣiya*, or elegiac verses sung in praise of *Ḥasan* and *Ḥusain*. *h.*

بهٹهيانا भठियाना *bhaṭhiyānā*, n. to go down the river; to ebb (the tide). *h.*

بهٹي भट्टी *bhaṭṭī*, f. a furnace, a kiln, an oven, a still; name of a *rāj-pūt* tribe. *h.*

بهٹئي भटई *bhaṭa,ī*, f. praise from a poet (*bhāṭ*). *h.*

بهٹيا भटिया *bhaṭiyā*, the poorest kind of land [(in Bundlecund. *h.*

بهٹيارا भटियारा *bhaṭiyārā*, m. (same as *bhaṭhiyārā*), a sutler, an innkeeper. *h.*

بهٹيارپن भटियारपन *bhaṭiyārpan* (see *bhaṭhiyārpan*). *h.*

بهٹيارن भटियारिन *bhaṭiyārin*, } f. a female
بهٹياري भटियारी *bhaṭiyārī*, } sutler. *h.*

بهٹيانا भट्टियाना *bhaṭṭiyānā*, the country of the *bhaṭṭī rājpūts*. *h.*

بهج भुज *bhuj*, m. the arm above the elbow; one of the shorter sides of a right-angled triangle (i.e. the perpendicular or the base.) *s.*

بهجا भुजा *bhujā*, f. the arm above the elbow. *s.*

بهجانا बहजाना *bah-jānā* or बहिजाना *bahijānā*, n. to flow, to go or swim with the stream; to be ruined, to be destroyed. *h.*

بهجانا भजाना *bhajānā*, a. to cause to flee. *h.*

بهجانا भिजाना *bhijānā*, a. to cause to be wet, to wet, to moisten; to cause to send. *h.*

بهجت bahjat, f. joy, pleasure, gladness, cheerfulness, alacrity, beauty, grace, excellence. a.

بهجت भजत bhajat, serving, waiting upon; enjoying carnally. s. [away. s.

بهج جانا भजिजाना bhaji-jānā, n. to flee, to run

بهجن भजन bhajan, m. adoration, worshipping, a hymn; enjoying carnally. bhajan-k., a. to sing; to say prayers, to worship. s.

بهجنا भजना bhajnā, a. to worship, to count one's beads, to adore. s.

بهجنا भजना bhajnā, n. to flee, to run away. h.

بهجنا भुजना bhujnā, m. parched or scorched grain. s.

بهجنگ भुजङ्ग bhujang, } m. a serpent. s.
بهجنگم भुजङ्गम bhujangam, }

بهجنگا भुजङ्गा bhujangā, m. a kind of shrike, commonly called "the king crow" (Lanius cærulescens). bhujange urānā, to be in great distress and poverty; to spread false reports. h.

بهجنيك भजनीक bhajnīk, m. a singer; an adorer. s. [sent. h.

بهجوانا भिजवाना bhijwānā, a. to cause to be

بهجيا भुजिया bhujiyā (same as bhājī), f. greens. h.

بهچ भुच bhuch, barbarous, ignorant. h.

بهچك भचक bhachak, alarmed, aghast, starting. bhachak rahnā, to be amazed or astonished at a sudden and unexpected event. s.

بهچكانا भचकाना bhachkānā, a. to amaze, to strike with astonishment. h.

بهچكنا भचकना bhachaknā, n. to be astonished or amazed. h. [eating. s.

بهچن भचन bhachan (for bhakshan), m. food,

بهچنپا भुचंपा bhuchampā, m. a kind of tree (Kæmpferia rotunda); also a species of fireworks resembling the flower of that tree. s.

بهچنگ भुचङ्ग bhuchang, m. name of a bird (Lanius cærulescens). h.

بهچه भक्ष bhachh (for bhakshh), eatable. s.

بهچهك भक्षक bhachchhak (for bhakshak), a gormandizer, a devourer. s.

بهچهك भिक्षुक bhichchhuk, m. a beggar. s.

بهچهنا भक्षना bhachhnā, a. to eat, to take food. s.

بهچهي भक्षी bhachchhī or bhakshī, m. an eater. s.

بهد भद bhad, f. a slap; a crash. h.

بهدا भद्दा bhaddā, stupid, senseless, dull. h.

بهداك भदाक bhadāk, m. a crash, the noise made by any thing falling; as, bhad or bhadāk se gir parā, it fell with a crash. h.

بهداكا भदाका bhadākā, m. a sound or noise. h.

بهدانه bih-dāna, m. quince seeds, used as a demulcent in certain complaints. p.

بهداهر भदाहर bhadāhar, grain cut when only half ripe. h.

بهدبهد भदभद bhad-bhad, m. sound made by the fall of a fruit, or walking of a person, &c. h.

بهدبهدانا भदभदाना bhad-bhadānā, m. cutting grain when only half ripe; shaking fruit from a tree. h.

بهدبهدانا भदभदाना bhad-bhadānā, a. to make a sound by striking two bodies together; to strike repeatedly; to shake fruit from a tree. h.

بهدبهداهٹ भदभदाहट bhad-bhadāhaṭ, f. sound made by the fall of fruits. h.

بهدر भद्र bhadra, happy, prosperous, lucky; m. prosperity, happiness; a fragrant grass (Cyperus); a wagtail. s.

بهدرا भद्रा bhadrā, m. name of a bird, a lark. s.

بهدرا भद्रा bhadrā, f. an unlucky moment; the 2nd, 7th, and 12th days of the lunar month. s.

بهدرارك भद्रारक bhadrārak, m. one of the 18 minor dwīpas, or divisions of the world. s.

بهدراسن भद्रासन bhadrāsan, m. a throne, a peculiar posture of meditation used by devotees; the legs bent and crossed underneath, and turned so as to bring the ancles in contact with the perineum, whilst the soles of the feet are held close to the sides. s.

بهدراشو भद्राश्व bhadrāshva, m. one of the four mahā-dwīpas into which the known world is divided, or one of the nine khandas or smaller divisions of the continent: in either case it is the east division. s.

بهدراكرن भद्राकरण bhadrā-karan, m. shaving. s.

بهدرپدا भद्रपदा bhadra-padā, f. name of the 26th and 27th lunar asterisms. s.

بهدرپرنا भद्रपर्णा bhadra-parnā, f. a shrub (Pœderia fœtida). s.

بهدرپرني भद्रपर्णी bhadra-parnī, f. a tree (Gmelina arborea); a shrub (Pœderia fœtida). s.

بهدرجو भद्रजौ bhadra-jau, m. the seed of the Echites or Wrightea antidysenterica. s.

بهدرچوڑ भद्रचूड़ bhadra-chūṛ, m. a sort of euphorbia (Euphorbia tirucalli). s.

بهدردار भद्रदारु bhadra-dāru, m. a sort of pine (Pinus devadaru). s.

بهدرشٹ बहुदृष्ट bahu-drishṭa, } experienced. s.
بهدرشي बहुदर्शी bahu-darshī, }

بهدرك भद्रक bhadrak, beautiful, pleasing; respectable, worthy; lucky, fortunate; m. or f. advantage, produce; nature, genius, reason; beauty, goodness, pleasantness; m. a sort of grass (Cyperus pertenuis); a sort of pine (Pinus devadāru). s.

بهدركالي भद्रकाली bhadr-kālī, f. one of the names of a Hindū goddess; a fragrant grass (Cyperus pertenuis or rotundus). s.

بهدرگندهكا भद्रगन्धिका bhadra-gandhikā, f. a creeping plant (Asclepias pseudosarsa, the narrow leaved variety). s.

بهدرمستك भद्रमुस्तक *bhadra-mustak*, m. a fragrant grass (*Cyperus pertenuis*). *s.* [*cordifolia. s.*

بهدرودني भद्रोदनी *bhadrodnī*, f. a plant (*Sida*

بهدرولي भद्रवल्ली *bhadra-wallī*, f. Arabian jasmine (*Jasminum zambac*); the large Bengal creeper (*Gaertnera racemosa*). *s.*

بهدرهونا भद्रहोना *bhadr-honā*, n. to be clean or purified by shaving one's head and beard after mourning, or in a holy place. *s.*

بهدري भद्री *bhadrī*, m. an astrologer; a palmister. *s.*

بهدريو भद्रयव *bhadra-yav*, m. the seed of the *Echites* or *Wrightea antidysenterica*. *s.*

بهدگدهكا बहुदुग्धिका *bahu-dugdhikā*, f. a plant yielding a caustic, milky juice (euphorbia of various sorts). *s.* [sugar-cane. *h.*

بهدوار भदवार *bhadwār*, land prepared for

بهدوريا भदवरिया *bhadawriyā*, name of a tribe of *rāj-pūts*. *h.* [bad. *s.*

بهدوش बहुदोष *bahu-dosh*, full of faults, very

بهدها बहुधा *bahudhā*, in many ways, sorts, &c.; usually, often. *s.*

بهدها बहधा *bahdhā*, f. pain, distress, obstruction, hindrance, prevention. *s.*

بهدهاگت बहुधागत *bahudhāgat*, dispersed, scattered. *s.*

بهدهن बहुधन *bahu-dhan*, wealthy, rich. *s.*

بهدئي भदई *bhada,ī*, the produce of the month *Bhādoṅ*. *s.*

بهديسل भदेसल *bhadesal*, } ill-shaped, ugly,
بهديسلا भदेसला *bhadesalā*, } awkward. *h.*

بهڐا भडा *bhaḍā* or भड़ा *bhaṛā*, a kind of grass used for fodder. *h.* [(v. *ḍakaut*). *h.*

بهڐريا भडरिया *bhaḍariyā*, m. name of a tribe

بهر *bahar*, f. a fleet. *bahrī*, on account of *ba-har*, in every (this is used only in phrases from the Persian). *a. p.*

بهر भर *bhar*, full; as much as, as far as; all, every, size, bulk, whole, up to. *bhar maḳdūr* or *maḳdūr-bhar*, to the best of one's power. *'umr-bhar*, all lifetime. It is sometimes used in composition, without expressing any meaning, unless it is "a," as *ser-bhar*, a ser; *bāṅs bhar*, (the height or length of) a bamboo; *kos bhar*, a kos, whereas *bhar kos* would mean a full kos, &c. *s.*

بهر *bhir* (also *bhiṛ*), m. a species of insect, a wasp, a bee, (perhaps from the Sanskrit *bhring*, q. v.) (?) N.B.—This word occurs repeatedly in the *Ikhwānu-ṣ-ṣafā*, pages 113 to 116. *h.*

بهر बहुर *bahur* or बहुरि *bahuri*, again. *h.*

بهر भर *bhar*, name of one of the aboriginal races of India. *h.*

بهر बहिर *bahir*, out, without. *bahir ānā*, n. to issue, to come out. *bahir-desh*, remote or foreign country. *bahir-mukh*, the neglect of any moral or religious duty; adj. impious. *s.*

بهرا भर्रा *bharrā*, m. a panic. *fauj meṅ bharrā paṛā*, the army was seized with a panic. *h.*

بهرا भरा *bharā*, full, overflowing. *s.*

بهرا बहरा *bahrā*, or बहिरा *bahirā*, deaf. *h.*

بهراتا भ्राता *bhrātā*, } m. brother.
بهراتر भ्रातृ *bhrātṛi*, }

بهراترك भ्रातृक *bhrātrik*, } fraternal, bro-
بهراتريه भ्रात्रीय *bhrātrīya*, } therly. *s.*

بهرارو बहरारू *bahrārū*, m. an upstart, a stranger. *h.*

بهرام *bahrām*, the planet Mars; name of several kings of Persia; Varanes. *p.*

بهرامر भ्रामर *bhrāmar*, m. epilepsy. *s.*

بهرامري भ्रामरी *bhrāmarī*, epileptic. *s.*

بهرامك भ्रामक *bhrāmak*, m. a cheat, a rogue. *s.*

بهرانا भुराना *bhurānā*, a. to wheedle. *h.*

بهرانا बहुराना *bahurānā*, a. to bring back, to cause to return. *h.*

بهرانا बहिराना *bahirānā*, a. to divert, to amuse. *h.*

بهرانا भराना *bharānā*, a. to fill, to cause to fill; to cover (a mare). *s.* [blundering, erring. *s.*

بهرانت भ्रान्त *bhrānta*, whirled, revolved;

بهرانت भ्रान्ति *bhrānti*, f. error, ignorance; revolving, wandering. *s.* [a wanderer. *s.*

بهرانتا भ्रान्ता *bhrāntā*, one who is gone astray,

بهرانتمان भ्रान्तिमान *bhrāntimān*, adj. erring, wandering. *s.*

بهرانتي भ्रान्ती *bhrāntī*, f. erring, wandering. *s.*

بهراوٹ भरावट *bharāvaṭ*, f. act of filling; any thing in which they fill any substance. *s.*

بهربهانڈ भरभांड *bharbhānḍ*, m. name of a prickly poppy (*Argemone Mexicana*). *h.*

بهربهرا भुरभुरा *bhurbhurā*, dry and in a state of powder. *h.*

بهربهرانا भुरभुराना *bhurbhurānā*, a. to throw or sprinkle sugar or salt upon meat. *h.*

بهربهرانا भरभराना *bharbharānā*, a. to swell and be glossy (particularly the face, as in fever). *s.*

بهربهري भरभरी *bharbharī*, f. a swelling, a sore. *bhurbhurī*, a light sandy soil. *h.*

بهرپانا भरपाना *bhar-pānā*, a. to be paid, to receive the full amount; met. is expressed when a person is disappointed; as, *main ne bhar pāyā*, I am paid; or still more idiomatic, "I am paid with a witness." *h.*

بهرپائي भरपाई *bhar-pā,ī*, f. a receipt in full. *h.*

بهرپتوا भरपतवा *bharpatwā*, a subdivision of the *bhar* tribe. *h.*

بهرپور भरपूर *bhar-pūr*, بهرپورن भरपूरन *bhar-pūran*, } overflowing, chokeful, brimful.

بهرپيتي भरपेटी *bhar-peṭī*, pot-bellied. *h.*

بهرت भरत *bharat*, name of Rāma's brother; the son of Dushyanta, and first monarch of all India. *bharat khanḍ*, m. one of the nine divisions of the world, between Lankā and Sumeru, *i.e.* India from Ceylon to Tartary; also the amount of revenue paid by an individual or party. *s.*

بهرت भर्त *bhart*, or भरत *bharat*, m. a mixed metal composed of copper and lead; the name of a bird (a species of lark); the full amount of rent paid by a person. *h.* [bourer. *s.*

بهرت भृत *bhṛit*, m. a servant, a hired la-

بهرت भृति *bhṛiti*, f. wages, hire, maintenance. *s.*

بهرتا भर्ता *bhartā*, m. a cherisher, supporter, a husband. *s.*

بهرتا भर्ता *bhartā*, or भुर्ता *bhurtā*, m. vegetables boiled or fried and broken or pressed in the hand. *s.* [f. reproach, abuse. *s.*

بهرتسنا भर्त्सना *bhartsnā*, m. threat, menace;

بهرت كول *bharat-kūl*, a tribe of Brāhmans so called. *h.*

بهرت ورش भरतवर्ष *bharat-varsh*, m. India (so called from Bharata, son of Dushyanta, its first monarch). *s.* [a slave. *s.*

بهرتي भृत्य *bhṛitya*, m. an attendant, servant,

بهرتي भर्ती *bhartī*, f. completion; filling; loading, cargo; vulgarly used for promotion. *bhartī-k.*, to recruit. *s.* [in the metal called *bhart*. *h.*

بهرتيا भर्तिया *bhartiyā*, m. a brazier, a worker

بهرتيا भृत्या *bhṛityā*, f. hire, wages. *s.*

بهرتيه भृत्य *bhṛitya*, m. a dependant, a servant. *s.*

بهرجانا भरजाना *bhar-jānā*, n. to be filled; to be lined (a bitch); to be broken-winded (a horse from severe exercise). *h.*

بهرجن भर्जन *bharjan*, m. frying, boiling. *s.*

بهرداند *bhar-dānd*, بهرڈانڈ *bhar-ḍānḍ*, } galloping at full speed. *bhar-ḍānḍ phenknā*, to go at full speed. *d.*

بهردواج भरद्वाज *bharadvāj*, m. a skylark. *s.*

بهرحال *ba-har-ḥāl*, by every means, somehow or other. *a. p.*

بهردينا भरदेना *bhar-denā*, a. to pay; to darn; to fill; to reimburse. *h.*

بهرشت भ्रष्ट *bhrasht*, fallen, lost, depraved, debased, polluted, abominable, vicious, dissolute. *bhrasht-k.*, a. to pollute, to seduce. *bhrasht-honā*, n. to be polluted; to calcine. *bhrashta-rājya*, deposed, deprived of a kingdom.

بهرشت भृष्ट *bhrishṭa*, fried. *s.* [case. *p. a.*

بهرصورت *ba-har ṣūrat*, in every aspect, or

بهرطور *ba-har ṭaur*, by every means, by any means, somehow or other. *p. a.*

بهرکا भरका *bharkā*, m. slaked lime. *h.*

بهرکانا भरकाना *bharkānā*, a. to slake (lime). *bhirkānā*, a. to cast, throw, dart. *p.*

بهرکتي भृकुटी *bhṛikuṭi*, f. the eyebrow, a frown, a contraction of the brows. *s.*

بهرکيف *ba-har kaif*, by any means, anyhow. *p. a.*

بهرگ भृगु *bhṛigu*, the name of a celebrated Muni. *s.* [Bhrigu, a tribe of *rāj-pūts*. *h.*

بهرگبنسي भृगुबंसी *bhrigu-bansī*, descended of

بهرم भ्रम *bhram*, or भरम *bharam*, m. error, mistake, doubt, suspicion, apprehension, perplexity; blunder, slip. *s.*

بهرم भ्रमि *bhrami*, f. error, blunder, mistake. *s.*

بهرم भरम *bharam*, m. credit, character. *bharam gańwānā*, n. to lose character. *s.*

بهرمانا भरमाना *bharmānā*, a. to excite by throwing out temptation; to deceive; to perplex, to alarm. *h.* [round, roving, erring.

بهرمت भ्रमत *bhramat*, adj. whirling, going

بهرمر भ्रमर *bhramar*, m. a large black bee; vertigo, epilepsy. *s.*

بهرمکه बहरमुख *bahar-mukh*, m. the neglect or violation of any moral or religious duty; impious. *s.*

بهرمن भ्रमण *bhraman*, m. whirling, going round; walking, roaming. *s.*

بهرمي भ्रमी *bhramī* or भरमी *bharmī*, apprehensive, doubtful, scrupulous, whirling, going round. *s.*

بهرميلا भरमीला *bharmīlā*, ambiguous, doubtful, confounded, scrupulous. *h.*

بهرن भरण or भरन *bharan*, to, up to (same as *tak*). *bharan*, m. cherishing, maintaining, rearing, the act of filling, paying in full. *h.* [door. *h.*

بهرنا भिरना *bhirnā*, to be open or ajar (a

بهرنا बिहरना *biharnā*, n. to rejoice, to take pleasure; a. to enjoy, to delight. *s.*

بهرنا भरना *bharnā*, a. to fill, load, satisfy, perform, discharge (a debt); to undergo, to suffer, to daub; n. to abound, to be filled, to heal (a wound). *h.*

بهرنا भरना *bharnā*, act of filling or completing; to give property in repayment of a debt: it also denotes the vessel that receives the expressed juice of the sugar cane. *h.* [back. *h.*

بهرنا बहुरना *bahurnā*, n. to return, to come

بهرنش भ्रंश *bhransh*, m. falling, declining. *s.*

بهرنگ भृङ्ग *bhṛing*, m. a large bee, enamoured of the lotus, the humble bee. *s.*

بهرنگ راج भृङ्गराज *bhṛing-rāj*, m. name of a kind of shrike (*Lanius Malabaricus*); name of a medicinal herb or spreading shrub (*Eclipta prostrata, Lin. Verbesina prostrata*, or *Verbesina scandens, Roxb.*). *s.*

بهرنگک भृङ्गक *bhringak*, m. a bird, a sort of shrike (*Lanius Malabaricus*). *s.*

بهرنگي भृङ्गी *bhṛingī*, f. a kind of wasp (*Vespa solitaria*), a large black bee, a humble bee. *bhṛingī-phal*, m. the hog plum. *s.*

بهرنگي बहुरङ्गी *bahu-rangī*, of many colours, met. fickle, unsteady. *s.*

بهرني भरनी *bharnī*, f. weft, woof. *s.*

بهرني भरणी *bharaṇī*, f. the name of the second lunar mansion (three stars in *Musca*), figured by the *pudendum muliebre*. *s.* [or load. *s.*

بهروانا भरवाना *bharwānā*, a. to cause to fill

بهروبهنگ भ्रूभङ्ग *bhrū-bhang*, m. a frown. *s.*

بهروپ बहुरूप *bahu-rūp*, adj. multiform; m. mimicry. *s.*

بهروپا बहुरूपा *bahu-rūpā*, m. a chamelion. *s.*

بهروپي बहुरूपी *bahu-rūpī*, } m. an actor, a
بهروپيا बहुरूपिया *bahu-rūpiyā*, } mimic, a person assuming various characters and disguises. *s.*

بهروپيه बहुरूप्य *bahu-rūpya*, m. mimicry. *s.*

بهروتي भरौती *bharautī*, f. a release in full. *h.*

بهروٹا भरोटा *bharoṭā*, m. a load of grass or hay. *h.*

بهروسا भरोसा *bharosā*, m. hope, dependence, faith, confidence. *bharosā k.*, to hope, to rely. *s.*

بهروسو भरोसौ *bharosau* (Braj. for *bharosā*), hope, trust, &c. *s.*

بهرون बहुरों *bahuroṅ*, again, a second time. *h.*

بهرون भ्रूण *bhrūn*, m. pregnancy; a fœtus, a child. *bhrūn-hatyā*, f. murder of the fœtus, causing abortion. *s.*

بهرونا भरौना *bharaunā*, m. a load of wood. *h.*

بهره *bahra*, m. property, fortune; quota, share, portion; profit, gain, advantage. *bahra-mand* or *bahra-war*, or *bahra-andoz*, fortunate, prosperous, profitable. *bahra-mandī*, f. prosperity. *p.*

بهري भरी *bharī*, f. the weight of one sicca rupī, or one *tola*. *s.*

بهري भरे *bhare*, a grass which grows in the jungles, used for thatching and making tatties. *h.*

بهري बिहरी *bihrī*, f. a subscription to raise a certain sum, an assessment, quota, share. *h.*

بهري बुहरी *buhrī*, f. fried or parched barley. *h.*

بهري बहरी *bahrī*, f. a falcon, female hawk (*Falco calidus, Lath.*). *bahrī-bachā*, the male of the same species. *h.*

بهرئي भरई *bhara,ī*, f. a kind of cess or tax. *h.*

بهريا बहरिया *bahriyā*, a stranger. *s.*

بهريا बहुरिया *bahuriyā*, f. a daughter-in-law. *s.*

بهريا भरिया *bhariyā*, land watered by irrigation. *h.*

بهريا *bharyā* (for *bharā*), full, filled. *d.*

بهڑ *bhiṛ*, m. a species of insect, a wasp. *h.*

بهريت भरैत *bharait*, } m. a tenant, a lessee. *h.*
بهريتي भरैती *bharaitī*, }

بهريكها बहुरेखा *bahu-rekhā*, m. pl. wrinkles, furrows. *s.*

بهڑ भड़ *bhaṛ*, m. a large boat, a lighter. *h.*

بهڑ भुड़ *bhuṛ*, f. a hole through which water runs out. *h.*

بهڑا भड़ा *bhaṛā*, a kind of grass, v. *bhaḍā*. *h.*

بهڑانا भिड़ाना *bhiṛānā*, a. to join, to place close to, to close in battle (armies); to cause to fight. *h.*

بهڑائي भिड़ाई *bhiṛā,ī*, f. the closing of two armies in battle. *h.*

بهڑبهڑانا भड़भड़ाना *bhaṛ-bhaṛānā*, to flutter. *h.*

بهڑبهڑيا भड़भड़िया *bhaṛbhaṛiyā*, simple, candid, without guile. *h.*

بهڑبهونجا भड़भूँजा *bhaṛbhūnjā*, m. a man who parches grain; name of a caste of Hindūs whose occupation is to parch grain. *s.*

بهڑبهونجن भड़भूँजन *bhaṛbhūnjan*, f. a woman who parches grain. *s.*

بهڑريا भड़रिया *bhaṛariyā*, m. a conjuror. *h.*

بهڑڑا *bharaṛā*, m. the beleric myrobalan. *d.*

بهڑسائن भड़साईं *bhaṛasā,īṅ*, m. v. *bhāṛ*. *h.*

بهڑک भड़क *bhaṛak*, f. splendour, blaze, flash, show; perturbation, agitation, alarm, starting (in animals). *h.*

بهڑکانا भड़काना *bhaṛkānā*, a. to frighten, to scare; to blow up into flame. *h.*

بهڑکل *bhaṛkal*, a large door or gate. *d.*

بهڑکنا भड़कना *bhaṛaknā*, a. to start, to shrink, to be scared, to be alarmed, to be blown up into a flame. *h.* [coy. *h.*

بهڑکيل भड़केल *bhaṛkel*, wild, untamed, shy,

بهڑکيلا भड़कीला *bhaṛkīlā*, splendid, glittering. *h.*

بهڑنا भिड़ना *bhiṛnā*, n. to close (as two armies), to come together, to be joined, to shoulder, to join, to be placed together, touching each other; to be continuous. *h.*

بهڑنگ भड़ङ्ग *bhaṛang*, simple, undesigning, silly, artless, having the quality of telling secrets without reserve. *h.*

بهڑوا भड़ूआ *bhaṛū,ā*, m. a pimp, one who lives on what a prostitute earns. *h.*

بهڑوائي भड़ूआई *bhaṛū,ā,ī* or *bhaṛwā,ī*, f. panderism, pimping; the wages of prostitution. *h.*

بھڑھا भिड़ा *bhiṛhā*, m. a wolf. *s.*

بھڑیت भड़ैत *bharait*, }
بھڑیتی भड़ैती *bharaitī*, } m. a tenant, lessee. *h.*

بھس भुस *bhus*, m. bran, husk, chaff. *bhus par barāt* (lit. an assignment on chaff), *i. e.* an assignment from whence nothing can be obtained. *s.*

بھس भस *bhas*, m. ashes, cinders. *s.*

بھس भिस *bhis*, the edible root of the lotus. *h.*

بھسانا भसाना *bhasānā*, a. to launch, to set afloat. *s.*

بھساون भसावन *bhasāwan*, a tax on boats carrying grain. *h.*

بھس بھسا भसभसा *bhas-bhasā*, weak, soft, flabby (as meat). *h.*

بھستا बहुसुता *bahu-sutā*, f. a plant (asparagus). *s.*

بھستکا भसतिक्का *bhas-tihhā*, m. a steak, chop, or collop. *h.*

بھسد भसद *bhasad*, f. *pudendum muliebre; mons veneris. s.*

بھسرا भुसरा *bhusrā*, m. a kind of inferior wheat. *h.*

بھسکارنا भुसकारना *bhuskārnā*, n. to hiss (as a snake). *d.*

بھسکارہ भुसकार *bhushāra*, m. the breathing or hissing of a snake. *d.*

بھسکنا भसकना *bhasaknā*, n. to fall, to drop down. *h*

بھسل भुसुल *bhusul* (same as *bhuserā*). *s.*

بھسلنا भिसलना *bhisalnā*, m. to be dazzled (the sight). *h.*

بھسم भस्म *bhasma* or भसम *bhasam*, f. ashes. *bhasma-snān*, art of smearing the body with the ashes of cow-dung. *s.*

بھسمک भस्मक *bhasmak*, m. a disease of the eyes, thickening of the membranes and indistinctness of vision; morbid appetite. *s.*

بھسمگربھا भस्मगर्भा *bhasma-garbhā*, f. the *sisu* tree, or a variety of it (*Dalbergia sisu*). *s.*

بھسمنت भस्मन्त *bhasmant*, m. ashes. *s.*

بھسمی کرت भस्मीकृत *bhasmī-kṛit*, reduced to ashes calcined. *s.*

بھسمی کرن भस्मीकरण *bhasmī-karan*, m. calcining. *s.*

بھسنا भसना *bhasnā*, n. to float. *s.*

بہسنا बहसना *bahasnā*, for بحثنا, q. v. *a.*

بہسو बहुसू *bahu-sū*, f. the mother of many children. *s.*

بھسوری भुसौरी *bhusaurī*, f. }
بھسولا भुसौला *bhusaulā*, m. } the place in a dwelling-house for keeping straw, &c. *s.*

بھسونڈا भुसौंड़ा *bhusaundā*, m. a hole, a cavity, a place to put chaff in. *s*

بھسیرا भुसेरा *bhuserā*, }
بھسیلا भुसेला *bhuselā*, }
بھسیہرا भुसेहरा *bhusehrā*, } m. a place where corn or chaff is kept. *s.*

بہشاکھ बहुशाख *bahu-shākh*, having many branches. *s.*

بہشت *bihisht*, f. Paradise. *bihishtī*, of or belonging to Paradise; m. a water-carrier. *p.*

بہشتر बहुशत्रु *bahu-shatru*, having many enemies. *s.*

بھشٹل भिश्टल *bhishṭal*, f. a foolish or stupid woman. *h.*

بھشرا भशिरा *bhashirā*, f. a sort of beet (*Beta Bengalensis*). *s.*

بہک बहुक *bahuk*, m. a plant (*Asclepias gigantea*). *s.*

بھکاری *bhikārī*, m. a beggar, a mendicant. *d.*

بہکال बहुकाल *bahu-hāl*, m. a long time. *s.*

بہکانا भहकाना *bahkānā*, a. to baulk, to disappoint, to mislead, to deceive. *h.*

بھکت भक्त *bhakt*, m. an adorer, one who has devoted himself to a religious life, a votary, zealot; a Hindū performer, a dancer, a player. adj. attached, devoted, pious; desirous. *bhakta-rāj*, lord of the devout, God. *bhakta-tā*, devotedness, attachment to. *s.*

بھکت भक्ति *bhakti*, f. persuasion, religion, faith, attachment, desire. *s.*

بھکت भुक्त *bhuhta*, eaten, eating. *s.*

بھکتائی भक्ताई *bhaktā,ī*, f. faith, devotedness. *s.*

بھکتمان भक्तिमान *bhaktimān*, m. }
بھکتمت भक्तिमत *bhaktimat*, m. }
بھکتمتی भक्तिमती *bhaktimatī*, f. }
بھکتونت भक्तिवन्त *bhaktiwant*, m. } faithful, devoted, pious.

بھکسا भुकसा *bhuhsā*, name of a forest tribe of *rāj-pūts*. *h.*

بھکسی भकसी *bhahsī*, f. a dungeon, a dark room in which revenue defaulters (in native states) are confined. *h.*

بھکشا भिक्षा *bhikshā*, f. begging; alms. *s.*

بھکشاپاتر भिक्षापात्र *bhikshā-pātra*, m a beggar's bowl, a wallet for collecting alms. *s.*

بھکشت भक्षित *bhakshit*, eaten. *s.*

بھکشک भक्षक *bhahshak*, gluttonous, voracious; a feeder, an eater. *s.*

بھکشک भिक्षुक *bihshuk*, m. a beggar. *s.*

بھکشن भक्षण *bhakshan*, m. eating. *s.*

بھکشنیہ भक्षणीय *bhakshanīya*, eatable, to be eaten. *s.*

بهكشي भक्षी *bhakshī*, m. an eater. *s.*

بهكشيه भक्ष्य *bhakshya*, eatable. *s.*

بهكنا बहकना *bahaknā*, n. to be baulked, to be disappointed, to be deceived, to stray, to be intoxicated. *h.*

بهكنٹك बहुकण्टक *bahu-kanṭak*, m. a prickly plant (*Hedysarum alhagi*); the marshy date tree. *s.*

بهكوءا भकूआ *bhakū,ā*, foolish, stupid. *h.*

بهكوءانا भकूआना *bhakū,ānā*, n. to be stupified. *h.*

بهكوسنا भकोसना *bhakosnā*, a. to devour, to stuff, to eat. *h.*

بهكهاري भिखारी *bhikhārī*, m. a beggar. *s.*

بهكهري भिखरी *bhikhrī*, f. an unfilled grain; a shrivelled grain. *h.*

بهكهنا भखना *bhakhnā*, a. to eat, to devour. *s.*

بهگ भग *bhag*, f. *vulva*; prosperity, supreme power. *s.*

بهگا भुग्गा *bhuggā*, simple, foolish. *h.*

بهگانا भगाना *bhagānā*, a. to drive off, to put to flight. *h.*

بهگانا भिगाना *bhigānā*, a. to wet, moisten. *h.*

بهگت भगत *bhagat*, m. (for *bhakt*, q. v.), a religious mendicant. *bhagat-k.*, to disguise. *bhagat-khelnā*, n. to be disguised, to act (a play), to mimic. *bhagat-honā*, n. to be initiated as a devotee; to be affiliated to a religious order. This is peculiar to the low tribes. The initiation consists in putting a necklace of beads round the neck and marking a circle on the forehead; after which the initiated person is bound to refrain from the use of spirituous liquors and flesh, &c. *s.*

بهگتا भगता *bhagtā*, name of a tribe of *ahīrs*, q. v. *h.*

بهگتانا भुगताना *bhugtānā*, a. to distribute, to requite, to cause to enjoy. *s.*

بهگتاي भगताई *bhagatā,ī*, f. sanctity, life of a devotee. *s.*

بهگتمان भुगतमान *bhugatmān*, fit to enjoy, deserving punishment. *s.*

بهگتن भगतन *bhagtan*, f. wife of a Bhagat; (ironically) a lewd woman, a prostitute, a whore. *h.*

بهگتنا भुगतना *bhugatnā*, a. to enjoy, to suffer, to receive the reward of virtue or punishment of a crime. *s.*

بهگتيا भगतिया *bhagtiyā*, m. a dancing boy. *h.*

بهگل भगल *bhagal*, m. affectation, hypocrisy, trick, deception. *bhagal-nikālnā*, a. to play a trick, to pretend poverty. *h.*

بهگلي گهنا भगलीगहना *bhaglī-gahnā*, m. false jewels, trinkets. *h.*

بهگليا भगलिया *bhagliyā*, m. trick, cheat, imposture; impostor. *h.*

بهگن बहुगुण *bahu-gun*, m. } many times; hav-
بهگنا बहुगुणा *bahu-gunā*, f. } ing many good qualities. *s.*

بهگن भग्न *bhagna*, torn, broken; defeated. *s.*

بهگنا भग्ना *bhagnā* (also *bhaginā*), m. a brother. *s.*

بهگناس भग्नाश *bhagnās*, disappointed. *s.*

بهگندر भगन्दर *bhagandar* or *bhugandar*, m. a fistula (*in ano*). *s.*

بهگندهه बहुगन्ध *bahu-gandh*, m. olibanum. *s.*

بهگندها बहुगन्धा *bahu-gandhā*, f. Arabian jasmine. *s.*

بهگني भगिनी *bhaginī*, or भग्नी *bhagnī*, f. a sister. *s.*

بهگو भग्गू *bhaggū*, m. a deserter, a runaway. *h.*

بهگوان भगवान *bhagwān*, adorable, divine; m. the Deity, the Supreme Being. *s.*

بهگوان भगवाँ *bhagwāṅ*, m. cloth dyed with *geru*, a kind of red colour or ochre. *h.*

بهگوانا भगवाना *bhagwānā*, a. to cause to flee or run away. *h.*

بهگوت भगवत *bhagawat*, divine, glorious; the Deity, the Most High. *h.*

بهگوڑا भगोड़ा *bhagoṛā*, m, a runaway, a deserter. *h.*

بهگونا भिगोना *bhigonā*, a. to wet, to steep. *h.*

بهگونت भगवन्त *bhagawant*, divine, glorious, illustrious; the Deity, the Most High. *s.*

بهگونها भगोंहा *bhagoṅhā*, m. the reddish colour extracted from *gerū*; a kind of ochre. *h.*

بهگيرتهه भगीरथ *bhagīrath*, m. a king whose austerities brought the river Gangā from heaven. *s.*

بهگيل भगेल *bhagel*, f. overthrow, defeat; m. a runaway, a deserter. *h.*

بهل बहल *bahal*, f. a two-wheeled car (for riding in, not for baggage), coach, carriage. *h.*

بهل भल *bhal*, good, well. *bhal-ghoṛiyā*, well-mounted; m. a cavalier. *s.*

بهل भल *bhal*, m. side, direction. *sir ke bhal*, head-foremost. *h.*

بهل बहुल *bahul*, much, many. *s.*

بهلا भला *bhalā*, good, excellent, benevolent, kind, healthy, virtuous, righteous, sound; strange, wonderful, admirable, comical, droll. *bhalā ādmī*, m. a person of respectability, a gentleman; (iron.) a silly fellow. *bhalā changā*, in good order, perfect, in health. *bhalā mānnā*, to take well. *s.*

بهلا बहिला *bahilā*, f. barren (generally applied to cattle). *bahulā* (in S. India), the dark fortnight of the lunar month. *h.*

بهلاٹ भुलाट *bhulāṭ*, f. forgetfulness. *d.*

بهلانا भुलाना *bhulānā*, a. to cause to forget; to inveigle, to mislead, to deceive, to fascinate, to coax. *h.*

بهلانا बहलाना *bahlānā*, a. to divert, to amuse. *h.*

بهلاوا भुलावा *bhulāwā*, m. deception, fraud, a cheat, deceit. *bhulāwā denā*, a. to deceive, to play a trick. *h.*

بهلاوان भिलावाँ *bhilāwāṅ*, } m. a nut used for
بهلاون भिलावन *bhilāwan*, } marking clothes, &c., commonly called Malacca bean (*Semicarpus anacardium*). *s.*

بهلائی भलाई *bhalā,ī*, f. goodness, welfare. *h.*

بهلپن भलपन *bhal-pan*, m. goodness, excellence. *h.*

بهل بهل اجالا भलभलउजाला *bhal-bhal ujālā*, broad day-light. *d.*

بهل پچهی भलपुच्छी *bhal-puchchhī*, f. a plant (*Hedysarum lagopodioides*). *s.*

بهلتوه बहुलत्व *bahulatwa*, m. abundance. *s.*

بهلسنا भुलसना *bhulasnā*, n. to be singed, scorched. *h.*

بهلك भल्लक *bhallak* or भल्लुक *bhalluk*, m. a bear. *s.*

بهلکا भलका *bhalkā*, m. a gold patch fixed on the nose-ring; a kind of bamboo; dawn of day. *h.*

بهلکا भल्लिका *bhallikā*, f. marking nut. *s.*

بهل مانس भलमानुस *bhal-mānus* courteous, polite, humane. *s.*

بهل منسات भलमनसात *bhal-mansāt*, f. humanity. *s.* [ture, benevolence. *s.*

بهل منسي भलमनसी *bhal-mansī*, f. good-na-

بهلنا बहलना *bahalnā*, n. to be diverted, to be amused. *h.*

بهلوك भल्लूक *bhallūk*, m. a bear. *s.*

بهلول *bahlūl* or *bahlol*, a virtuous prince; a joker, one who smiles; a man's name famed in Oriental anecdotes, like our Joe Miller. *a.*

بهلونجي भिलौंजी *bhilaunjī*, f. the seed of the *bhilāwāṅ*. *s.* [glove. *p.*

بهله *bahla*, m. a privy purse, a falconer's

بهلي बहली *bahlī*, f. a two-wheeled car (for riding in, not for baggage), a coach, a carriage. *h.*

بهليا बहलिया *bahaliyā*, m. a huntsman, a kind of retainer armed with bow and arrows. *h.*

بهليم बहलीम *bahlīm*, name of a small tribe of Muhammadans near *Mīrat* and *Dasna*. *h.*

بهم *baham*, together, one with another, one against another. *baham ānā*, to be procured, acquired. *baham pahunchānā*, a. to get, to acquire, to procure. *baham pahunchnā*, to be procured. *p.* [rence. *s.*

بهمان बहुमान *bahu-mān*, m. respect, reve-

بهمبهيري भमभेरी *bhambherī*, f. a butterfly. *h.*

بهمنا भमना *bhamnā*, a. to revolve. *s.*

بهمنيٹا बह्मनेटा *bahmaneṭā*, a young Brāhman. *h.*

بهمورت बहुमूर्त्ति *bahu-mūrti*, multiform. *s.*

بهمول बहुमूल *bahu-mūl*, many-rooted. *s.*

بهمولیه बहुमूल्य *bahu-mūlya*, costly, precious. *s.*

بهمي भमी *bhamī*, f. revolution, whirling; wandering. *s.*

بهمیاں भुमयाँ *bhumyāṅ*, m. landholder. *s.*

بهن बहिन *bahin*, बहन or *bahan* f. a sister. *s.*

بهن भिन्न *bhinn* or *bhinna*, separate, different, other, apart, (in arithm.) a fraction. *bhinn bhinn*, various, severally. *s.*

بهن बिहन *bihan* or *bihin*, m. a seed. *h.*

بهنا बहना *bahnā*, n. to flow, to glide; to float; to blow. *s.* [broiled. *h.*

بهنا भुना *bhunnā*, n. to be fried, dried, parched;

بهنانا भिन्नाना *bhinnānā*, n. to have a singing in the ears, to be giddy; to sound (as shot, and brass pots, &c.). *h.*

بهنانا भुन्नाना *bhunnānā*, a. to fry, parch, &c. *h.*

بهنبهاگهر भिन्नभागहर *bhinn-bhāg-har*, m. division of fractions. *s.*

بهنبهنانا भिनभिनाना *bhinbhinānā* or *bhambhanānā*, n. to buzz (as a fly), to hum (as a bee). *h.*

بهنبهناهٹ भिनभिनाहट *bhinbhināhaṭ*, f. buzz, hum (of bees). *h.*

بهنبهوا भम्भूआ *bhambhū,ā*, an ascetic or *faḳīr* who is pressed by hunger to rob. *h.*

بهنبهورنا भंभोरना *bhambornā*, } a. to bite (and
بهنبهوڑنا भंभोड़ना *bhambhoṛnā*, } mumble as a dog), to worry. *h.*

بهنبهيري भंभेरा *bhambherā*, } f. a butterfly. *h.*
بهنبيري भंबेरी *bhamberī*, }

بهنت भणित *bhanit*, sounded, uttered. *s.*

بهنٹا भण्टा *bhanṭā*, a ploughman's wages in kind; the egg-plant (*Solanum melongena*). *h.*

بهنٹواس भिण्टवास *bhinṭwās*, m. a sort of pulse. *h.*

بهنٹواس भंटवास *bhanṭwās*, m. the name of a grain, the fruit of the *ko,ī*, or water-lily. *h.*

بهنجا भुंजा *bhunjā*, m. parched grain. *h.*

بهنجانا भञ्जाना *bhanjānā*, a. to change (money). *s.* [ing. *s.*

بهنجت भञ्जत *bhanjat*, adj. breaking, destroy-

بهنجك भञ्जक *bhanjak*, adj. who or what breaks, severs. *s.*

بهنجن भञ्जन *bhanjan*, destroying, breaking, demolishing, separating, afflicting; m. breaking, &c. *s.*

بهنڈ भंड *bhanḍ*, m. a mimic, jester, buffoon, actor; confusion, spoiling. *bhanḍ-honā*, n. to be destroyed, spoiled. *h.*

بهنڈ बिहण्ड *bihanḍ*, land cut up by a torrent. *h.*

بهنڈا भण्डा *bhanḍā*, m. a large earthen pot. *bhanḍā phūṭnā*, n. to be disclosed (a secret). *s.*

بهنڈار भण्डार *bhanḍār*, m. a place where household goods are kept, a storehouse. *s.*

بهنڈارا भण्डारा *bhanḍārā*, m. a feast of *jogīs*, *sanyāsīs*, &c. *h.*

بهنڈاري भण्डारी *bhanḍārī*, m. a house-steward, one who has charge of the storehouse, a treasurer. *s.*

بهنڈسار भण्डसार *bhanḍsār*, } f. the provision
بهنڈسال भण्डसाल *bhanḍ-sāl*, } which is previously reserved for years. *s.*

بهنڈسالي भण्डसाली *bhanḍsālī*, m. one who reserves provision for years. *s.*

بهنڈك भण्डक *bhanḍak*, m. a wagtail. *s.*

بهنڈلي भुण्डली *bhunḍlī*, f. a kind of worm covered with hair, the palmer-worm. *h.*

بهنڈوا भण्डौवा *bhanḍauwā*, m. satire, ribaldry. *s.*

بهنڈولي भण्डोली *bhanḍolī*, f. two or more jars borne one over the other. *d.*

بهنڈي भिण्डी *bhinḍī*, f. the name of a vegetable (*Hibiscus esculentus*). *h.*

بهنڈي خانه भिण्डेखानः *bhinḍe-khāna*, m. the room appropriated to the apparatus of the *ḥuḳḳa*. *h.*

بهنڈيريه भण्डेरिया *bhanḍeriyā*, } m. an actor. *s.*
بهنڈيلا भण्डेला *bhanḍelā*, }

بهنڈيلن भण्डेलन *bhanḍelan*, f. an actress. *s.*

بهنسار भिन्सार *bhinsār*, m. dawn of day. *h.*

بهنسرا भंसरा *bhansarā*, a subdivision of the *ahīr* tribe. *h.*

بهنسنا भंसना *bhansnā*, n. to float. *h.*

بهن سنكلت भिन्नसंकलित *bhinna-sankalit*, m. addition of fractions. *s.*

بهنك भणक *bhanak* or भिनक *bhinak*, f. a low sound; a rumour, report; hum of insects. *s.*

بهنك भिन्नक *bhinnak*, m. a heterodox sectary, a seceder, a Bauddha or Buddhist. *s.*

بهنكنا भिनकना *bhinaknā*, n. to buzz as a fly; to be covered with flies, to swarm. *h.*

بهنگ भङ्ग *bhang*, f. hemp (v. *bhāng*). *s.*

بهنگ भङ्ग *bhang*, m. breaking, destruction, defeat, sporting; adj. broken, torn, defeated. *s.*

بهنگا भङ्गा *bhangā*, f. hemp, name of a species of bird; also name of a species of insect. *h.*

بهنگان भङ्गान *bhangān*, m. a sort of fish (*Cyprinus banggana*). *h.*

بهنگ راج भङ्गराज *bhang-rāj*, m. name of a bird. *s.*

بهنگڑا भङ्गड़ा *bhangṛa*, m. the name of an herb (*Eclipta* or *Verbesina prostrata*). *s*

بهنگن भङ्गन *bhangan*, f. the wife of a *ḥalāl-khor*, q.v. *h.*

بهنگن भङ्गन *bhangan*, f. a female drinker of bhang. *s.*

بهنگنا भङ्गना *bhangnā*, f. a kind of fish. *h.*

بهنگنن भिन्नगुणन *bhinna-gunan*, m. multiplication of fractions. *s.*

بهنگوتر भिन्नगोत्र *bhinna-gotra*, m. one not belonging to the same family. *s.*

بهنگوريا भङ्गोरिया *bhangoriyā*, name of a tribe of *tagās*, q.v. *h.*

بهنگهن भिन्नघन *bhinna-ghan*, m. cube of a fraction. *s.*

بهنگي भङ्गी *bhangī*, m. a caste of sweepers, or *ḥalāl-khors*. *h.*

بهنگي भङ्गी *bhangī*, m. a drinker of bhang; f. fraction, division; fraud, trick. *s.*

بهنگي बहङ्गी *bahangī*, f. a bamboo stick with ropes hanging from each end, for slinging baggage to, which is carried on the shoulder. *bahangī-bardār* or *bahangī-wālā*, m. the man who carries the bahangī. *s.*

بهنگيرا भङ्गेरा *bhangerā*, m. one who sells bhang. *s.*

بهنگيرن भङ्गेरन *bhangeran*, f. a woman who sells bhang. *s.*

بهنگيلا भङ्गेला *bhangelā*, m. coarse hempen cloth; also a sack or pannier made from the fibres of the bhang-plant. *s.*

بهنوت भिन्नवत *bhinna-vat*, divided, scattered. *s.*

بهنودر भिन्नोदर *bhinnodar*, m. a half-brother, a brother not by the same mother. *s.*

بهنور बिहनौर *bihnaur*, f. a seed-plot, nursery (for plants). *h.*

بهنور भंवर *bhanwar*, m. a whirlpool, eddy; a large black bee, a creeper. *s.*

بهنورا भंवरा *bhanwrā*, m. a large bee; a climbing plant, creeper. *s.*

بهنوركلي भंवरकली *bhanwar-kalī*, f. a kind of halter (for horses or dogs, &c.). *h.* "In South India this word denotes a swivel." (Binning.)

بهنورگ भिन्नवर्ग *bhinna-varg*, m. square of a fraction. *s.*

بهنوگ भंवग *bhanwag*, a small class of *rāj-pūts*. *h.*

بهن ويوكلت भिन्नव्यवकलित *binna-vyavakalit*, m. substraction of fractions. *s.*

بهنوي बहनोई *bahno,ī*, m. a brother-in-law a sister's husband. *s.*

بهنيؤ बहनेऊ *bahne,ū* (same as *bahno,ī*), a sister's husband. *s.*

بهني बुहनी *buhnī*, f. handsel, first sale, earnest-money. *h.*

بهنيلي बहनेली *bahanelī*, f. an adopted sister. *s*

بهو बहू *bahū*, f. daughter-in-law, son's wife; a wife. *s.*

بهو भौ *bhau*, m. fear, dread, terror. *s.*

بهو भू *bhū*, f. the earth, the world; place, site, land or soil. *s.*

بهو भव *bhav*, m. being, existence; the world; name of Mahādeva. *bhava-sāgar*, the ocean or world of existence. *s.*

بهو भुव *bhuva*, m. heaven, ether, sky, atmosphere. *s.*

بهوٗا भूआ *bhū,ā*, f. father's sister; a worm, caterpillar. *h.*

بهوار बहूआर *bahū,ār*, } m. name of a fruit
بهوار बहुवार *bahuvār*, } (*Cordia myxa*). *s.*

بهواني भवानी *bhawānī*, f. *Parvatī* or *Durgā*, Mahādeva's wife, name of a Hindū goddess, the patroness of those miscreants called *thags*. *s.*

بهوبهل भूभल *bhūbhal*, m. hot ashes. *h.*

بهوپ भूप *bhūp*, m. a king, a sovereign. *s.*

بهوپا भोपा *bhopā*, m. a kind of *fakīr*, a magician. *s.*

بهوپال भूपाल *bhū-pāl*, m. a landlord, a king, rājā. *s.*

بهوپالي भूपाली *bhū-pālī*, f. name of a *rāginī*. *s.*

بهوپت भूपति *bhū-pati*, m. a king, sovereign. *s.*

بهوت भूत *bhūt*, been, become; existing; past; m. a demon, a goblin; a malignant spirit haunting cemeteries, lurking in trees, animating carcases, and deluding or devouring human beings; the preterite tense in grammar; one of the elements, which among the Hindūs are five in number; viz. 1st, the earth; 2nd, the water; 3rd, the fire; 4th, the air; 5th, space or ether. *bhūt honā*, to be distracted with rage. In law it denotes the real fact or state of the case. *s.*

بهوت बहूत *bahūt*, much, many (same as *bahut*). *d.*

بهوتا भोता *bhotā*, blunt, obtuse. *h.*

بهوتاتما भूतात्मा *bhūtātmā*, m. body, vital principle, cause of life. *s.*

بهوتاد *bhūtād*, much, many; excess, abundance. *d.*

بهوتار भूतारि *bhūtāri*, m. assafœtida. *s.*

بهوتاوشٹ भूताविष्ट *bhūtāvishṭa*, possessed by a devil. *s.*

بهوتاویش भूतावेश *bhūtāvesh*, m. possession by a devil. *s.*

بهوت جٹا भूतजटा *bhūt-jaṭā*, f. Indian spikenard (*Valeriana jatamansi*). *s.*

بهوت سنچار भूतसंचार *bhūt-sanchār*, m. possession by evil spirits. *s.*

بهوتك भौतिक *bhautik*, relating to evil spirits. *s.*

بهوت گن भूतगण *bhūt-gan*, m. a class of sprites or goblins. *s.*

بهوت گندها भूतगन्धा *bhūt-gandhā*, f. *Mūra*, a sort of perfume. *s.*

بهوتل भूतल *bhū-tal*, m. the earth, the terrestrial globe. *s.*

بهوت ناشن भूतनाशन *bhūt-nāshan*, m. marking-nut plant (*Semicarpus anacardium*); the Eleocarpus seed. *s.*

بهوتني भूतनी *bhūtnī*, f. a she-demon, an ogress. *s.*

بهوت واس भूतवास *bhūt-vās*, m. beleric myrobalan (*Terminalia belerica*). *s.*

بهوت ورکش भूतवृक्ष *bhūt-vriksha*, m. a tree (*Trophis aspera*); Bignonia Indica. *s.*

بهوت وکريا भूतविक्रिया *bhūt-vikriyā*, f. epilepsy, possession by evil spirits. *s.*

بهوتويتا भवितव्यता *bhavitavyatā*, f. futurity, destiny. *s.*

بهوت ويشي भूतवेषी *būt-veshī*, f. a species of Nebari (*Nyctanthes tristis*). *s.*

بهوتويه भवितव्य *bhavitavya*, what is to be, or become. *s.*

بهوتي भोती *bhotī*, f. labour, work. *h.*

بهوتيهار भोतीहार *bhotīhār*, a labourer. *h.*

بهوٹ भूट *bhūṭ*, land irretentive of water. *h.*

بهوٹ भोट *bhoṭ*, } m. a country, pro-
بهوٹانگ भोटाङ्ग *bhoṭāng*, } bably Bootan. *s.*

بهوٹیا भोटिया *bhoṭiyā*, m. an inhabitant of Bootan. *s.*

بهوج भोज *bhoj*, m. eating, feast; name of a rājā celebrated in the *Singhāsan batīsī*, a sovereign of Ujjain, who is supposed to have flourished about the end of the tenth century: he was a celebrated patron of learned men, and the nine gems or poets are often ascribed to his era; a country, Patna and Bhagalpore. *s.*

بهوجائي भौजाई *bhau-jā,ī*, f. a brother's wife. *s*

بهوجپور भोजपूर *bhoj-pūr*, name of a country near Chhaprā. *s.*

بهوجپتر भोजपत्र *bhoj-patra* or *bhojpattar*, m. the bark of a tree, said to be a kind of birch, used in making long tubes or pipes for the *ḥukka*. *s.*

بهوجکٹ भोजकट *bhoj-kaṭ*, m. the country of Bhoj, the present Bhojpore, or the vicinity of Patna and Bhagalpore. *s.*

بهوجن भोजन *bhojan*, m. eating, food, victuals. *bhojan-k.*, to eat. *bhojan-kharch*, table expenses. *s.*

بهوجنبو भूजम्बू *bhū-jambū*, f. wheat; the fruit of the Vaikunta (*Flacourtia sapida*). *s.*

بهوجنت भूजन्तु *bhū-jantu*, m. an earth-worm. *s.*

بهوجنيه भोजनीय *bhojanīya*, } to be eaten, edi-
بهوجيه भोज्य *bhojya*, } ble; m. food. *s.*

بهوجي भौजी *bhaujī*, f. a brother's wife. *s.*

بهوجيل भूजेल *bhūjel*, m. a species of bird. *s.*

بهوچك भौचक *bhauchak* (inelegant), aghast. *s.*

بهودار भूदार *bhūdār*, m. a hog. *s.*

بهودان भूदान *bhū-dān*, m. a grant of land or of the revenue thereof. *bhū-dāna-patra*, a deed of grant of land, &c. *s.*

بھودھر भूधर **bhū-dhar**, m. a mountain. *s.*

بھوديو भूदेव **bhū-dev**, m. a Brāhman. *s.*

بھوچکر भूचक्र **bhū-chakra**, m. the equinoctial line. *s.*

بہوچن बहुवचन **bahu-vachan**, m. the plural number (in grammar). *s.*

بہودھ बहुविध **bahu-vidh**, various, multiform, of many kinds. *s.*

بھودہ भूदा **bhūda**, a light or sandy soil. *h.*

بھور भोर **bhor**, f. dawn of day. *bhor-honā*, n. to be finished, to be terminated. *h.*

بھور भूर **bhūr**, f. charity given to poor people, alms. *bhūr-bāṅṭnā*, a. to give alms to a numerous assembly of the poor; a spring, fountain. *h.*

بھور भूरि **bhūri** or **bhūr**, much, many. *s.*

بھورا भूरा **bhūrā**, fair, auburn, or brownish (as hair). *h.*

بھورا भोरा **bhorā**, simple, artless, undesigning. *h.*

بھورا भूरा **bhūrā**, land belonging to a village furthest from the inhabitants. *h.*

بہورا बहोरा **bahorā**, m. a shopkeeper or monied man in a village, who makes advances to or on account of the cultivators. *h.*

بھورج پتر भूर्जपत्र **bhūrj-patra**, m. the *Bhoj-patr*, a tree growing in the snowy mountains, a kind of birch; the bark is used for writing on, and for making *hukka* snakes. *s.*

بھوردھامن भूरिधामन **bhūri-dhāman**, splendid, illustrious. *s.*

بھورلابھ भूरिलाभ **bhūri-lābh**, very profitable, m. great gain. *s.*

بھورلوك भूर्लोक **bhūr-lok**, m. the earth. *s.*

بھورنڈي भूरुण्डी **bhū-ruṇḍī**, f. a sort of sunflower (*Heliotropium Indicum*). *s.*

بہورو बहोरो **bahoro**, a kind of sloping pathway for bullocks drawing water from a well. *h.*

بہورنگي बहूरङ्गी **bahū-rangī**, many-coloured, changeable (v. *bahurangī*). *s.*

بھوري भूरी **bhūrī**, light sandy soil. *h.*

بہوريہ बहुव्रीहि **bahu-vrīhi**, m. name of a class of compound words used as attributive; as, *bahu-māl*, having many necklaces. *s.*

بھوڑ भूड़ **bhūṛ**, f. sandy ground, soil in which much sand is mixed. *h.*

بھوڑري भूड़री **bhūṛarī**, corn still remaining in the ear after the process of treading. *h.*

بھوڑل भूड़ल **bhūṛal** or भोड़ल **bhoṛal**, m. talc, mica. *h.*

بھوس भूस **bhūs**, }
بھوسا भूसा **bhūsā**, } m. husk of corn, chaff, straw. *s.*

بھوسا भोसा **bhosā**, m. (also *bhosṛī* f.), *Vulva valde magna*. *s.*

بھوساون भूसावन **bhūsāwan**, a tax on boats carrying grain. *h.*

بھوسرا भूसरा **bhūsrā**, an inferior kind of wheat. *h.*

بھوسوامي भूस्वामी **bhū-swāmī**, m. a landlord, a landholder. *s.*

بھوسورگ भूस्वर्ग **bhū-swarg**, m. the mountain Sumeru. *s.*

بھوسوري **bhūsaurī**, }
بھوسولہ **bhūsaula**, }
بھوسيہرا **bhūsehrā**, } an apartment in a house where straw, &c., is kept. *h.*

بھوسي भूसी **bhūsī**, f. chaff, bran. *s.*

بھوشت भूषित **bhūshit**, adorned, arrayed. *s.*

بھوشن भूषण **bhūshan**, m. ornament, embellishment, jewel. *s.*

بھوشيہ भविष्य **bhavishya**, }
بھوشيت भविष्यत **bhavishyat**, } future, about to be. *s.*

بھوشيت وكتا भविष्यतवक्ता **bhavishyat-vaktā**, m. one who foretells the future, a prophet. *s.*

بھوك भूक **bhūk**, hunger, desire. *d.*

بھوكا भूका **bhūkā**, }
بھوكڑ भूकड़ **bhūkaṛ**, } hungry, destitute, desirous of. *d.*

بھوكدنب भूकदम्ब **bhū-kadamb**, m. a plant (*Ligusticum ajwaen*). *s.*

بھوكس भोकस **bhokas**, m. a wizard, a sorcerer, a magician *h.*

بھوكمپ भूकम्प **bhū-kamp**, m. an earthquake. *s.*

بھوكھ भूख **bhūkh**, f. hunger, appetite. *bhūkhoṅ marnā*, to starve. *s.*

بھوكھا भूखा **bhūkhā**, hungry, starving. *s.*

بھوكھن भूखन **bhūkhan**, m. ornaments, jewels. *s.*

بھوكھنا भोखना **bhokhnā**, a. to bark (see *bhauṅknā*). *s.*

بھوگ भोग **bhog**. m. enjoyment; the food offered to an idol; pleasure, satisfaction; possession; eating, victuals; (in arithm.) the numerator of a fraction. *bhog-bandhak*, a bond granting the use of a pledged article. *bhog-dār*, one in the possession or enjoyment of any property. *bhog-lābh*, usufruct in lieu of interest. *bhog-k.*, to enjoy, to suffer. *s.*

بھوگ भोग **bhog**, m. abuse, rudeness. *h.*

بھوگا भोगा **bhogā**, m. fraud, trick, deceit, illusion, deception, imposition, treachery, roguery, cheat. *h.*

بھوگادھكار भोगाधिकार **bhogādhikār**, m. the possessor of the usufruct of mortgaged or pledged property. *s.*

بھوگبندھك भोगबन्धक **bhog-bandhak**, a mortgage. v. *bhog*. *h.*

بھوگل भूगल **bhūgal**, m. ashes, embers of a fire. *h.*

بھوگنا भोगना **bhognā**, n. to enjoy, to suffer, to live stoically, to take pain and pleasure as they come. *s.*

بھوگول भूगोल **bhū-gol**, m. the terrestrial globe, the earth. *s.*

بهوگوتر भोगोत्र ***bhogotra***, a grant of revenue for the use or enjoyment of an individual, especially a Brāhman or religious person. *s.*

بهوگي भोगी ***bhogī***, jovial, jolly; the person who enjoys or possesses any thing; one who pursues pleasure. *man bhogī karm daridri*, by nature fond of pleasure, but condemned by fate to poverty. *s.*

بهوگهيا भोघिया ***bhoghiyā***, a small basket in which the sower carries his seed. *h.*

بهوگيه भोग्य ***bhogya***, that which may be enjoyed or possessed. *s.*

بهول भूल ***bhūl***, f forgetfulness, an error, mistake, blunder. *h.*

بهولا भोला ***bholā***, simple, artless, undesigning. *h.*

بهولابسرا भूलाबिसरा ***bhūlā-bisrā***, } missing
بهولابهٹکا भूलाभटका ***bhūlā-bhaṭkā***, } the road, generally a person who calls on another in consequence of some accident, &c., not intentionally, to pay a visit. *h.*

بهولانا ***bhūlānā*** (for *bhulānā*), to mislead, &c. *h.*

بهولاناته भोलानाथ ***bholā-nāth***, m. a name of *Mahādeva.* *h.*

بهولنا भूलना ***bhūlnā***, n. to forget, to err, to mistake, to blunder; to miss, to omit, to stray, to be forgotten. *h.*

بهولوک भूलोक ***bhū-lok***, m. the earth, region of mankind. *s.*

بهولي भोली ***bholī***, f. innocent, artless. *bholī-bāteṅ*, innocent prattle. *h.*

بهوم भूमि ***bhūmi*** or ***bhūm***, f. land, soil: the earth, place, scite; the base of any figure in geometry. *s.*

بهوم भौम ***bhaum***, m. the planet Mars. *bhaum-bār*, m. Tuesday. *s.*

بهومپ भोम्प ***bhomp***, m. a horn, &c. (v. *bhoṅp*). *h.*

بهومج भूमिज ***bhūmij***, (lit. earth-born) a caste of low Hindūs. *s.*

بهوم جنب भूमिजम्बु ***bhūmi-jambu***, f. a tree (*Premna herbacea*). *s.*

بهوم چنپک भूमिचम्पक ***bhūmi-champak***, m. a plant (*Kæmpferia rotunda*) *s.*

بهومک भूमिक ***bhūmik***, m. a landholder; a chief. *s.*

بهوم کنپ भूमिकम्प ***bhūmi-kamp***, m. an earthquake. *s.*

بهومي भूमी ***bhūmī***, f. the earth; ground, land, soil. *bhūmī-dār*, a landholder, a headman or chief. *bhūmī-dāhā*, being burnt or reduced to earth (a corpse). *s.*

بهومي भौमी ***bhaumī***, adj. f. earthly, terrestrial. *s.*

بهوميا भूमिया ***bhūmiyā***, a landlord, proprietor of the soil. *h.*

بهوميال भूमयाल ***bhūmyāl***, a resident, native of a place, also one's native country. *d.*

بهوميال भूमियाल ***bhūmiyāl***, proficient, accomplished. *d.*

بهومياوت भूमियावत ***bhūmiyāwat***, f. a general plundering. *h.*

بهومياوتي भूमियावती ***bhūmiyāwatī***, an insurgent chief. *s.*

بهوميرا भोमीरा ***bhomīrā***, f. coral. *h.*

بهون भौं ***bhauṅ***, or भों ***bhoṅ***, f. the eyebrow. *bhauṅ-ṭeṛhī-karnī*, a. to browbeat, to look angrily, raising the eyebrows, to frown, to scowl. *bhau,eṅ tannī*, to knit the eyebrows. *s.*

بهون भवन ***bhawan***, m. a house, a habitation, scite, spot, a temple. *s.*

بهون भुवन ***bhuwan***, m. a world; water; heaven; man, mankind. *s.*

بهونا भौना ***bhaunā***, n. to revolve. *s.*

بهونا भूना ***bhūnnā***, to parch, &c., see بهوننا.

بهوناس भौनास ***bhaunās***, m. a large and strong post to which they fasten elephants. *h.*

بهوناشني भवनाशिनी ***bhavanāshinī***, f. the Sarju river, which flows from the Himālaya into the Gogra. *s.*

بهوناگ भूनाग ***bhū-nāg***, m. an earth-worm. *s.*

بهونائي ***bhaunā,ī***, m. brother-in-law, sister's husband. *d.*

بهون بهاي भूंभाई ***bhūṅ-bhā,ī***, a man invested by a proprietor with a portion of land, which he must not dispose of to others. *h.*

بهونپ भोंप ***bhomp***, } m. a horn, a wind instru-
بهونپو भोंपू ***bhompū***, } ment. *h.*

بهونتها भोंथा ***bhonthā***, } blunt, obtuse. *h.*
بهونتهرا भोंथरा ***bhonthrā***, }

بهونتي भवन्ती ***bhavantī***, a house surrounded by a dead wall. *h.*

بهونچال भौंचाल ***bhauṅ-chāl*** also ***bhūṅ-chāl***, m. an earthquake. *s.*

بهون چنپا भूंचम्पा ***bhūṅ-champā***, m. the name of a plant (*Kæmpferia rotunda*). *s.*

بهوندري भूंदरी ***bhūndarī***, land given rent-free to village servants. *h.*

بهوندنا भोन्दना ***bhondnā***, a. to deceive, to impose upon. *d.*

بهوندو भोंदू ***bhondū***, silly, quiet, mild, artless, simple. *h.* (In Dakh.) deceitful, artful. *h.*

بهونڈا भोंडा ***bhonḍā***, ill-shaped, useless, bad, ugly. *h.*

بهونڈا बहोंडा ***bahonḍā*** or ***bahaunḍā***, land given rent-free to the village chaukīdār or watchman. *h.*

بهونڈپيرا भूंडपैरा ***bhūnḍ-pairā***, unlucky, ill-omened. *h.*

بهونڈري भूंडरी ***bhūnḍarī***, f. a small patch of cultivation alloted rent-free to village servants. *h.*

بهونڈيا भूंडिया ***bhūndiyā***, m. one who cultivates with a borrowed plough or hand instrument. *h.*

بهونر भौंर ***bhaunr*** (v. ***bhanwar***), m. a whirlpool. *s.*

بهونرا भौंरा *bhaunrā*, m. a large bee, or rather beetle, enamoured of the lotus. In Dakh. a whirlpool, an abyss. *s.* [lar. *s.*

بهونرا भौंरा *bhaunrā*, m. a cavern, vault, cel-

بهونركلي भौंरकली *bhaunr-kalī*, f. a kind of halter (for horses or dogs). In Dakh. a swivel. *h.*

بهونري भौंरी *bhaunrī*, f. feathered hair; name of a defect in horses. *s.* [*bhaunrā*). *s.*

بهونري भौंरी *bhaunrī*, f. a female bee (vide

بهونريانا भौंरियाना *bhaunriyānā*, a. to whirl, to turn. *s.*

بهونسا भूंसा *bhūnsā*, m. chaff, bran. *bhūnsā-jins*, all kinds of grain in husk. *h.* [n. to bark. *h.*

بهونسنا भौंसना *bhaunsnā*, or भूंसना *bhūnsnā*,

بهونسي *bhūnsī*, f. damp, mouldiness. *d.*

بهونك भोंक *bhonk*, m. a stab, a thrust. *h.*

بهونكا بهونكي भोंकाभोंकी *bhonkā-bhonkī*, f. stabbing and thrusting. *h.*

بهونكڑا भोंकड़ा *bhonkṛā*, very fat. *h.*

بهونكس भोंकस *bhonkas*, m. a wizard who preys upon children (or men or women), till he brings them to the grave. *h.* [to talk foolishly. *h.*

بهونكنا भौंकना *bhaunknā*, n. to bark; (met.)

بهونكنا भोंकना *bhonknā*, a. to thrust, to drive (as a nail). *h.* [pent. *s.*

بهونگ भुवङ्ग *bhuwang*, m. a snake, a ser-

بهونگائي भूंगाई *bhūnga,ī*, } f. a kind of tax on
بهونگئي भूंगई *bhūngā,ī*, } forest produce: (in Bijpūr, &c.). *h.* [vern, a cellar. *s.*

بهونگهرا भोंघरा *bhon-gharā*, m. a vault, a ca-

بهوننا भूनना *bhūnnā*, a. to parch, to grill, to broil, to toast, to roast, to inflame, to fry. *h.*

بهوننب भूनिम्ब *bhū-nimb*, m. a species of gentian, commonly called *cheraitā* (*Gentiana cherayta*). *s.*

بهونوركلي भौंवरकली *bhaunwar-kalī*, f. a kind of halter (for horses or dogs). *h.*

بهونه भोंह *bhonh*, f. the eyebrow. *s.*

بهونهار भूंहार *bhūnhār*, name of a tribe of Hindūs. *h.* [raneous dwelling. *h.*

بهونهرا भूंहारा *bhūnhārā*, m. a kind of subter-

بهونيا भूनिया *bhūniyā*, m. the headman of a village. *h.*

بهونيارا भूंयारा *bhūnyārā*, m. a cellar, cavern. *d.*

بهونئين भूंईं *bhūn,īn*, f. the earth, a kind of caterpillar (see *bhū,īn*). *h.*

بهوئي भोई *bho,ī* or भूई *bhū,ī*, m. a chair-porter, a pālkī bearer (generally pronounced "boy" by European ladies); a white cat. *h.* [teller. *s.*

بهويا भवैया *bhawaiyā*, m. a dancer, a story-

بهوبيج बहुबीज *bahu-bīj*, having many or much seed; m. the custard-apple (*Annona squamosa*). *s.*

بهويرجيه बहुवीर्य्य *bahu-vīrjya*, m. belleric myrobalan (*Terminalia bellerica*). *s.*

بهوين भूयन *bhūyan*, } m. a chief, holding by
بهويي भूयी *bhūyī* } military service; headman of a village. *h.*

بهوئين भूईं *bhū,īn*, f. the earth, ground; a kind of caterpillar covered with hair and destructive to plants, flowers and trees. *s.*

بهوءين چنپا भूईंचम्पा *bhū,īn-champā*, m. a kind of fireworks, like a flower-pot (resembling that commonly called *anār*). *s.*

بهوءين دگدها भूईंदग्धा *bhū,īn-dagdhā*, gifts at marriages and funerals. *s.* [quake. *s.*

بهوءين ڈول भूईंडोल *bhū,īn-ḍol*, m. an earth-

بهوءينمالي भूईंमाली *bhū,īn-mālī*, a low caste of Hindūs engaged in the vilest offices. *h.*

بهوءينهار भूईंहार *bhū,īn-hār*, a tribe of Hindūs settled in Gorackpūr, &c. *h.*

بهوءينهاري *bhū,īn-hārī*, land let at a low rent to military retainers. *h.* [again, repeatedly. *s.*

بهويوبهويه भूयोभूयः *bhūyobhūya*, again and

بهويه भव्य *bhavya*, prosperous, fit, happy. *bhūya*, again, afterwards. *s.*

بهرانا भहराना *bhahrānā*, n. to shiver, to tremble, to totter, to stagger. *h.*

بهي *bihī*, a quince. *bihī-dāna*, m. quince-seed; (from the adj. *bih*, good), goodness, welfare. *p.*

بهي भय *bhai*, m. fear, terror. *s.*

بهي भी *bhī*, conj. also, too, even, and. *h.*

بهئ भई, fem. of *bhayā*, was, became. *s.*

بهي बही *bahī*, f. a book, not stitched at the sides, but at the ends; a register, book of accounts, a ledger. *bahī-khātā* or *bahī-khasrā*, a day-book. *bahī-paṭwārī*, the village accountant's register. *bahī-mahājan*, a merchant's or banker's book. *h.*

بهيا भैया *bhaiyā*, m. brother, comrade. *s.*

بهيا भया *bhayā*, was, became; past tense of an obsolete verb "to be, to become." *s.*

بهيابانٹ भैयाबाण्ट *bhaiyā-bānṭ*, brotherhood, fraternity. *h.*

بهياپا भैयापा *bhaiyāpā*, } m. brotherhood,
بهياپت भैयापत *bhaiyāpat*, } friendship (also *bhayāpā*, *bhayāpat*). *s.*

بهياتر भयातुर *bhayātur*, terrified, astounded, distracted with fear. *s.*

بهياچارا भैयाचारा *bhaiyā-chārā*, also *bhaiyā-chārī*, a community of brethren, or of people from one stock. *h.*

بهيار बहियार *bahiyār*, lands at a distance from the village. *h.*

بهيارت भयार्त *bhayārta*, frightened, afraid. *s.*

بهي انس भैयंश *bhai-aṅs*, division of property or interests among brothers. *s.*

بهيانك भयानक *bhayānak*, } terrific, fright-
بهياونا भयावना *bhayāwanā*, } ful. *s.*

بهياو *bhiyā,o*, m. marriage, espousals. *d.*

بهيبت भैबट *bhaibat*, } paying and receiving
بهيواد भैवाद *bhaiwād*, } on the footing of one of a fraternity. *h.*

بهيبهيت भयभीत *bhay-bhīta*, frightened, terrified. *s.*

بهيپنسي भैपंसी *bhaipansī*, } the shares of a bro-
بهيحصي भैहिस्सी *bhaiḥiṣṣī*, } therhood, especially in the lands of a village or township. *h.*

بهيت भीत *bhīt*, f. a wall (or breadth of a wall), mound, embankment, the vestige of an old house. *ochhe kī prīt, jon bālū kī bhīt*, the friendship of the mean is like a wall of sand (*i.e.* unstable). *s.*

بهيت भीत *bhīt* or *bhīta*, terrified, afraid, alarmed. *bhīti*, f. fear, alarm. *s.*

بهيت भीति *bhīti*, f. fear, apprehension. *s.*

بهيتا भैता *bhaitā*, m. a stunted crop. *h.*

بهيتر भीतर *bhītar*, within, inside. *s.*

بهيتري भीतरी *bhītarī*, inward, inside, internal. *s.*

بهيتريا भीतरिया *bhītariyā*, m. an inmate, the people who live in a house, not strangers, domestic; men who preside at a temple; those among the guests at a wedding-feast who eat in company with the relatives of the bride: those who partake of the feast without are called *bāhariyā*. *s.*

بهيتو बहेतू *bahetū*, m. a vagabond, vagrant, a wanderer. *s.*

بهيتوري भीतौरी *bhītaurī*, ground-rent paid for the site of a house by a stranger. *s.*

بهيٹ भेट *bheṭ*, f. meeting, interview; a present (to a superior). *bheṭ-bakrā*, a present made to a newly-appointed governor by the villagers. *bheṭ-patra*, a deed of gift on the above occasion. *bhīṭ*, the mound of a tank or artificial pond; the vestige of an old house. *h.*

بهيٹا भीटा *bhīṭā*, m. an old house, a former residence (provided some vestige remain). *h.*

بهيٹن भेटन *bheṭan*, to meet, act of meeting. *h.*

بهيٹنا भेटना *bheṭnā*, n. to meet, to join; to arrive; to make a present (to a superior). *h.*

بهيٹو भेटू *bheṭū*, m. } a stalk, stem. *bhīṭī*, same
بهيٹي भेटी *bheṭī*, f. } as *bhīṭ*, q. v. *h.*

بهيج भेज *bhej*, rent, an instalment. *bhej-barār*, name of a kind of complex tenure (v. Wilson's Gloss.). *h.*

بهيجا भेजा *bhejā*, m. the brain. *h.*

بهيجا भीजा *bhījā*, wet, moist. *h.*

بهيجنا भेजना *bhejnā*, a. to send, to transmit, to utter, ejaculate. *h.*

بهيجنا भीजना *bhījnā*, n. to be wet. *h.*

بهيچك भैचक or भयचक *bhaichak*, alarmed, aghast, starting. *s.*

بهيچنا भीचना *bhīchnā*, a. to squeeze, to compress, to crush. *h.*

بهيد भेद *bhed*, m. secrecy, mystery; difference, kind, sort; disunion, disagreement. *bhed-lenā*, a. to spy, to pry into, to work one's self into confidence, to sound. *s.*

بهي درشي भयदर्शी *bhai-darshī*, fearful, frightful. *s.*

بهيدك भेदक *bhedak*, a breaker, one who breaks or divides, a mischief-maker. *s.*

بهيدكر भेदकर *bhed-kar*, separating, causing disunion. *s.*

بهيدكيا भेदकिया *bhedakiyā*, m. a scout, a spy. *s.*

بهيدو भेदू *bhedū*, m. one who possesses another's secret, a confidant. *s.*

بهيدي भेदी *bhedī*, } intelligent; m. a
بهيديا भेदिया *bhediyā*, } scout, a confidant. *s.*

بهيدي भेदी *bhedī*, m. the ratan. *h.*

بهيديه भेद्य *bhedya*, whatever ought to be kept secret, worthy of secrecy. *s.*

بهير भेर *bher*, f. a kind of pipe, a musical instrument, a kettle-drum. *s.*

بهير भीरु *bhīru*, f. a timid woman; a plant (*Asparagus racemosus*); a sort of prickly nightshade. *s.*

بهير बहीर *bahīr*, } f. the baggage accompany-
بهيڑ बहीड़ *bahīṛ*, } ing an army; also the lines near a camp where the wives and families of the soldiers live. *h.*

بهيرا बहेरा *baherā*, the *beleric myrobalan*. *h.*

بهيراري भैरारी *bhairārī*, f. the name of a Rāginī. *s.*

بهيرو भैरव *bhairav* or *bhairava*, formidable horrible; m. hatred, abhorrence, a name of *Shiva*, but more especially an inferior manifestation of the deity eight of which are reckoned, and severally termed Asitanga, Ruru, Chanda, Krodh, Unmatta, Kupati Bīshan, and Sanghār, all alluding to terrific properties of mind or body; the name of a river; a kind of *rāg* in music. *s.*

بهيروبنا बहीरोबुना *bahīro-bunā*, the baggage accompanying an army. *h*

بهيرون भैरों *bhairoṅ*, m. the name of a *rāg*, or musical mode, sung at dawn in autumn, represented by *Mahādeva* with the Ganges flowing from the hair of his head, and this *rāg* or musical deity issues from *Mahādeva's* mouth (vide Gilchrist's Gram. 4to. p. 276); a name of *Mahādeva*. *s.*

بهيروي भैरवी *bhairavī*, f. the name of a *rāginī*, the wife of *Bhairoṅ rāg*. *s.*

بهيري भेरी *bherī*, m. a piper. *bhairī*, a species of falcon. *s.*

بهيريا बहेरया *baheryā*, name of a clan of *rāj-pūts* in Jaunpūr and Chunār. *h.*

بهيڙ भीड़ *bhīṛ*, f. multitude, crowd, mob; a press of work, trouble, difficulty. *h.*

بهيڙ भेड़ *bheṛ*, m. a ram; f. a sheep, ewe. *s.*

بهيڙ बहीड़ *bahīṛ*, m. baggage, &c. of an army, a camp-follower of any kind. *h.*

بهيڙا बहेड़ा *baheṛā*, m. the name of a fruit (the *beleric myrobalan; Terminalia belerica, Roxb.*). *s.*

بهيڙا भेड़ा m. a ram, Dakh. a wolf. *bhīṛā*, crowded, throng. *h.*

بهيڙبنگه *bhīṛ-banga*, m. the rabble of camp followers, the "*impedimenta*" of an army on march. *d.*

بهيڙبهاڙ भीड़भाड़ *bhīṛ-bhāṛ*, f. a crowd, multitude. *h.*

بهيڙنا भेड़ना *bheṛnā*, a. to shut, to close. *h.*

بهيڙي भेड़ीया *bheṛī*, f. a sheep, an ewe. *s.*

بهيڙيا भेड़िया *bheṛiyā*, m. a wolf. *bheṛiyā-dhasān*, m. a multitude crowded together like sheep in a pen, the act of following the example of another. *s.*

بهيس भेष *bhes* m. (for *bhesh*), appearance, assumed likeness, counterfeit dress, semblance. *bhīs* (for *bhīsha*), the edible root of the lotus plant. *s.*

بهيستهان भयस्थान *bhaya-sthān*, m. seat or part exposed to peril or hurt. *s.*

بهيش भेष *bheṣh*, m. (same as *bhes*), appearance, &c. *s.* [kind of fennel (*Nigella Indica*). *s.*

بهيشج भेषज *bheshaj*, m. a remedy, drug; a

بهيشم भीष्म *bhīshma*, horrible, fearful; m. horror. *s.*

بهيشن भीषण *bhīshan*, horrible, formidable; m. horror; the olibanum tree (*Boswellia thurifera*). *s.*

بهيك भेक *bhek*, m. a toad, a frog. *s.*

بهيك *bhīk*, m. (for *bhīkh*), begging, &c. *d.*

بهيكارك भयकारक *bhaya-kārak*, terrifying, frightening. *s.*

بهيكاري *bhīkārī*, m. a mendicant. *d.*

بهيكه भेख *bhekh*, m. (for *bhesh*) disguise, assumed appearance, dress, &c., semblance. *bhekh-dhārī*, adj. putting on a disguise, assuming an appearance. *s.*

بهيكه भीख *bhīkh*, f. begging, charity, alms. *s.*

بهيكي भेकी *bhekī*, f. the female of the frog, or a small frog; a kind of creeper (*Hydrocotyle Asiatica*). *s.*

بهيگنا भीगना *bhīgnā*, or भींगना *bhīṅgnā*, n. to be wet. *rāt-bhīgnā*, applied to the night passing in mirth and musical entertainment. *h.*

بهيل भील *bhīl*, m. the name of a wild race of mountaineers dwelling especially along the course of the Narmada or Nerbudda, and subsisting chiefly by plunder. *s.*

بهيلا भेला *bhelā*, m. a kind of nut, used for marking clothes (*Semicarpus anacardium*). *s.*

بهيل‌سيل भेलसेल *bhel-sel*, m. alloy of metal (in coinage, &c.). *h.*

بهيلي भेली *bhelī*, f. a lump of coarse sugar (or *gur*), generally consisting of five or six *sīrs*. *h.*

بهيليا बहेलिया *baheliyā*, m. a fowler; the name of a tribe of Hindūs. *h.* [terror. *s.*

بهيم भीम *bhīm*, fearful, terrible; m. horror,

بهيم भीम *bhīm*, or *bhīma*, } the name of one of
بهيم‌سين भीमसेन *bhīm-sen*, } the five Pandu princes, the second brother of *Judhishṭhir* or *Yudhishṭhira*. *s.* [ed. *s.*

بهيمان भयमान *bhayamān*, frightened, alarm-

بهيم‌سيني भीमसेनी *bhīm-senī*, f. a kind of camphire. *h.*

بهيمي भैमी *bhaimī*, f. the eleventh day of the bright half of the month of Māgh. *s.*

بهين *bihīn*, best, most excellent. *s.*

بهين भैं *bheṅ*, the earth, the ground; the bleating of sheep. *bheṅ-bheṅ-k.*, to bleat as sheep *h.*

بهينا भेना *bhenā*, f. a sister. *h.*

بهينا भीना *bhīnā*, wet; m. sister's husband, brother-in law. *h*

بهينت भींत *bhīṅt*, f. a wall (v. *bhīt*). *s.*

بهينٹ भेंट *bheṅṭ*, f. interview; visit; present. *bheṅṭ-mulāḳāt*, f. a meeting. *h.* [sit. *h.*

بهينٹنا भेंटना *bheṅṭnā*, n. to meet with; to vi-

بهينڈ *bheṅḍ*, m. a kind of reed or aquatic plant (*Æschynomene paludosa*), from the stem of which, resembling pith, being exceedingly light, are made a variety of articles. Being a non-conductor of heat, this substance is admirably adapted for making hats, covers for wine-bottles which have been cooled with ice or saltpetre, &c. The article commonly called "rice paper" is nothing more than this substance cut in very thin plates. The plant is also named *sholā* q. v. (Binning). *d.* [in Urdū, *rāmturā,ī*, q. v.). *d.*

بهينڈي *bheṅḍī*, f. name of a vegetable (called

بهينس भैंस *bhaiṅs*, f. a female buffalo. *s.*

بهينسا भैंसा *bhaiṅsā*, m. a male buffalo. *s.*

بهينساداد भैंसादाद *bhaiṅsā-dād*, } m. a
بهينسياداد भैंसियादाद *bhaiṅsiyā-dād*, } kind of ringworm. *s.*

بهينسوندا *bhaiṅsondā*, a tax or cess for the privilege of grazing buffaloes. *h.*

بهينكر भयङ्कर *bhayaṅkar*, terrible, terrific. *s.*

بهينگا भेंगा *bheṅgā*, squint-eyed. *h.*

بهينگنا *bhīṅgnā*, n. (v. *bhīgnā*), to be wet. *h.*

بهيو भेव *bhev*, m. a state, condition; innate property, nature. *s.* [was or became. *h*

بهيو भयो *bhayau* or *bhayo* (Braj. for *bhayā*),

بهيواد *bhaiwād* (v. *bhaibaṭ*), paying, &c. *h.*

بهيهر भीहर *bhīhar*, name of a tribe, supposed to be the aborigines of Rohilcund, Upper Du,āb. *h.*

بهيهو भैहू or भयहू *bhaihū*, f. sister-in-law, younger brother's wife. *s.*

بهئي भई *bha,ī*, fem. of *bhayā*, was, became. *h.*

بي बी *bī*, a vocative particle used in speaking to women; contraction of *bī-bī*, a lady, mistress; conj. (for *bhī*) also, even. *h.*

بي बे *be*, a vocative particle, used contemptuously, as "you rascal," "you sirrah." *h.*

بي *be*, a privative particle or preposition, denoting in the Persian Language "without," "void of." When prefixed to nouns, it forms compound adjectives, corresponding with our words of the same kind beginning with *in*, *un*, *im*, *ir*, &c., or such as end with *less*. All these compound adjectives may again become abstract nouns by the addition of *ī*, as *be-adab*, unmannerly, rude, *be-adab-ī*, unmannerliness, rudeness. It is impossible to give a complete list of these, as the employing of them has no limit but the taste or caprice of the writer. The following list will be found useful in the meantime;—*be-āb*, without water (lustre, temper, dignity, &c.). *be-ābrū*, dishonourable. *be-ittifāḳ*, discordant, without union. *be-aṣar*, without effect. *be-ajal*, lit. without or in spite of fate, untimely (death). *be-iḥtiyāṭ*, incautious, improvident, imprudent. *be-ikhtiyār*, without choice, in spite of one's self. *be-adab*, rude, presumptuous, impudent. *be-adabī*, rudeness, presumptuousness. *be-ārām* (vulg. *bīrām*), restless, sick. *be-asbāb*, having no effects. *be-i'tibār*, not trustworthy. *be-i'tidāl*, uneven. *be-i'tiḳād*, incredulous. *be-iltifāt*, regardless. *be-ulfat*, unsocial, averse to attachment or friendship. *be-imtiyāz*, undistinguishing, ill-bred, rude, unmannerly. *be-intihā*, endless, boundless, infinite. *be-andāza*, immoderate. *be-inṣāf*, unjust. *be-aulād*, childless. *be-īmān*, without conscience, without religion. *be-bā'iṣ*, without reason. *be-bāḳ*, complete, without arrears, paid up in full. *be-bāḳī*, f. completion. *be-bāk*, fearless. *be-bāl o par*, without power. *be-bad*, without blemish. *be-badal*, incomparable, inestimable. *be-bar*, fruitless, barren. *be-barg o bar*, fruitless, barren, poor. *be-bas*, without power, without authority or command; helpless. *be-baṣar*, without sight (generally applied to the mind,) senseless, undiscerning. *be-baḳā*, frail, perishable, not eternal. *be-bal*, without power, weak; wretched, poor. *be-band o bast*, unarranged, without order, unsettled (as a country). *be-bunyād*, groundless, unfounded. *be-bahā*, beyond price, invaluable. *be-bahār*, out of season. *be-bahra*, portionless, unfortunate. *be-pāyān*, boundless. *be-parda*, unveiled, immodest. *be-parwā*, fearless, without reflection, careless. *be-parwā,ī*, f. thoughtlessness, carelessness, independence, tranquillity, indifference. *be-par o bāl*, weak, utterly helpless. *be-parhez*, incontinent. *be-parhezī*, f. incontinence. *be-phāb*, shapeless. *be-pīr*, having no spiritual guide, vicious. *be-pīr*, cruel, pitiless, unfeeling. *be-tāb*, faint, restless. *be-tāṣīr*, of no effect. *be-ta,ammul*, rash. *be-tāl*, out of time (in music); ill-timed. *be-tān*, out of tune. *be-taḥāshā*, inconsiderate. *be-ta'alluḳ*, without connections, independent. *be-taḳṣīr*, innocent, blameless, not guilty, acquitted. *be-takallaf*, without ceremony. *be-tamannā*, content. *be-tamīz*, silly, indiscreet. *be-tawajjuh*, inattentive, unkind. *be-tosha*, unprovided, destitute (a traveller). *be-tawaḳḳu'*, hopeless, without expectation. *be-tah*, bottomless. *be-ṭhaur-ṭhikāne*, groundless. *be-ṣabāt*, unstable, *be-ṣamar*, fruitless, of no result. *be-tadbīr*, incautious, unwitting, inconsiderate. *be-jā*, ill-placed, ill-timed, inaccurate. *be-jāda*, variegated coral. *be-jān*, lifeless, faint; valiant, brave. *be-jān k.*, to deprive of life, to slay. *be-jur,at*, cowardly. *be-jurm*, innocent, faultless. *be-jirm*, without blemish, spotless (a jewel). *be-jigar*, cowardly. *be-jamālī*, f. ugliness, imperfection. *be-jawāb*, unable to answer. *be-chāragī*, f. necessity, helplessness. *be-chāra*, without choice, without remedy, helpless, poor. *be-chāl* and *be-chālī*, unprincipled; f. misdemeanour, ill-behaviour. *be-chirāgh*, lampless, desolated, childless. *be-chashm*, eyeless. *be-chūn*, unparalleled, incomparable. *be-chain*, restless, uneasy. *be-ḥāṣil*, fruitless, without result. *be-ḥāl*, ill-circumstanced. *be-ḥijāb* or *be-ḥijābāna*, unveiled, openly, immodest. *be-ḥadd*, boundless. *be-ḥurmat*, disgraced. *be-ḥurmatī*, f. disgrace. *be-ḥiss*, insensible, senseless. *be-ḥisāb*, countless, immoderate, inconsistent. *be-ḥikmat*, unskilful. *be-ḥawāss*, beside one's self, out of one's senses. *be-ḥayā*, shameless, immodest, impudent. *be-khār*, without thorns; without anxiety, without fear or solicitude. *be-khān o mān*, without house or hall, destitute. *be-khāya*, m. (lit. without a testicle) a eunuch. *be-khabar*, incautious, imprudent; unwitting, unintentional. *be-khabrī*, f. imprudence, heedlessness. *be-kharch*, without (money for) expenditure. *be-khirad*, without understanding, stupid. *be-khar o khāwind*, without a master, without an owner. *be-khaṭar* and *be-khaṭra*, free from danger, safe. *be-khwāb*, sleepless. *be-khwābī*, f. sleeplessness. *be-khwāhish*, without inclination or spirit; without pursuit, object, or hobby-horse. *be-khud*, beside one's self, enraptured. *be-khudī* f. ecstasy, rapture. *be-khur o khwāb*, without inclination to eat or sleep, restless. *be-khwesh*, friendless. *be dākhil*, dismissed, set aside, not admitted (a claim). *be-dād*, unjust, not doing justice, lawless. *be-dād-gar*, m. an oppressor. *be-dādī*, f. injustice, lawlessness. *be-dāsht*, careless, inattentive, negligent. *be-dāshtī*, f. carelessness, inattention (particularly not taking care of cattle). *be-dāgh*, spotless. *be-dāna*, seedless (fruit). *be-dakhl*, ejected. *be-dakhl-karnā*, a. to exclude. *be-dard*, pitiless, unfeeling. *be-dirang*, without delay. *be-daregh*, undeniable, incontestable, readily acknowledged; unsparing, ungrudging, liberal, not refusing. *be-dast o pā*, (having neither hands nor feet) helpless, without power or authority. *be-dastūr*, ill-bred, unusual. *be-da'wā*, free from claims; (in law) one who relinquishes his claim or suit. *be-da'wā patra*, a deed acknowledging the abandonment of a claim or suit. *be-dil*, heartless, dispirited, melancholy, dejected, sad. *be-dilī*, f. dejection, heartlessness. *be-dam*, breathless. *be-damāgh*, ill-tempered, impatient, irritable, easily provoked. *be-damāghī*, f. bad temper, irritability. *be-dawā*, incurable. *be-daulat*, destitute, unfortunate. *be-dhaṛak* or *be-dhaṛkā*, without fear or hesitation. *be-dos*, innocent, faultless (little used). *be-dahshat*, fearless. *be-dayā*, unfeeling. *be-diyānat*, irreligious, unjust. *be-dīn*, without religion. *be-ḍaul*, shapeless; uneducated, ill-bred. *be-ḍhab*, ill-shaped. *be-ḍhang*, uneducated, ill-mannered, ill-bred. *be-ẕauḳ*, having no relish or desire for. *be-rāh*, unprincipled, dissolute. *be-rabṭ*, contrary to rule. *be-raḥm*, merciless. *be-raẓā*, without leave. *be-rū*, shameless, inhuman. *be-roz*, unfortunate. *be-rozī*, destitute of daily bread, unfortunate. *be-rok-ṭok*, without let or hindrance. *be-riyā*, without guile. *be-raib o riyā*, without guile or deceit. *be-rīsh*, beardless (a youth). *be-resha*, without fibre. *be-zabān*, dumb, speechless (applied to the brute creation). *be-zar*, without money or the means of getting it, helpless. *be-zar kharīd*, (taking or getting) without purchase. *be-zan o farzand*, without wife or children. *be-zawāl*, unchangeable, imperishable. *be-zor*, weak, impotent. *be-zahra*, without bile, patient, forbearing; indefatigable; shameless. *be-zeb o zīnat*, ugly and awkward, inelegant in dress and person. *be-zīn*, unsaddled. *be-sākhta*, plain, undisguised, artless. *be-sākhtagī*, artlessness. *be-sāz*, unaccoutred, without apparatus, tools, &c. *be-sāz o sāmān*, without apparatus. *be-sabab*, without reason. *be-satrī*, impudence, barefacedness. *be-saj*, shapeless, ill-made. *be-sukhan*, taciturn. *be-sudh*, senseless, beside one's self; enraptured; entranced; in a faint. *be-sar*, unequalled, peerless. *be-surt*, stupid. *be-sar o pā*, without head or foot, utterly helpless. *be-sar o sāmān*, without apparatus, helpless. *be-salīḳa*, inexpert, without method. *be-sīl*, shameless. *be-shāhid*, without evidence. *be-sharaf*, without honour or dignity. *be-sharm*, shameless, impudent, immodest. *be-shu'ūr*, ignorant, a blockhead. *be-shafḳat*, harsh, unkind, unmerciful. *be-shakk o shubh* or *be-shakk o raib*, certain, doubtless, indubitable. *be-shumār*, countless, numberless, much. *be-ṣabr*, impatient, restless. *be-ṣalāḥ*, ill-advised, headstrong. *be-ẓabṭ*, wanton, irregular, unrestrained. *be-ẓabṭ-rabṭ*, without order or connection. *be-ṭāḳat*, beyond the power of endurance. *be-ṭāḳatī*, non-endurance, weakness. *be-ṭāli'*, destitute of good fortune, unlucky. *be-ṭaraḥ*, ill-mannered, uncivil. *be-ṭalab*, uncalled for, unsought. *be-ṭam'*, free from greediness, disinterested. *be-ṭaur*, ill-mannered. *be-'ibrat*, unwarned by example, unawed. *be-'izzat*, without honour or dignity, disgraced. *be-'aḳl*, stupid, senseless. *be-'adl*, unjust, lawless. *be-'aib*, faultless, without blemish. *be-ghāyat*, boundless. *be-ghil o ghash*, without trouble or anxiety. *be gharaẓ*, independent, disinterested, indifferent. *be-gham*, without anxiety. *be-ghaur*, without consideration. *be-ghairat*, wanton, impudent, infamous, rude. *be-ghairatī*, f. disgrace, &c. *be-fā,ida*, profitless, useless, vain. *be-fikr*, contented, thoughtless, tranquil. *be-fahmīd*, stupid, slow in comprehending. *be-faiẓ*, unprofitable, possessing but not bestowing (as a learned man who does not communicate his knowledge, or a rich man from whose wealth no person receives advantage). *be-ḳābū*, without restraint, out of one's power, secure against surprise or attack. *be-ḳā'ida*, unarranged, irregular, without order or rule. *be-ḳadr*, of no importance, worthless. *be-ḳarār*, restless, unsettled, variable, inconstant. *be-ḳarārī*, f. restlessness, fluctuation, variableness, instability. *be-ḳuṣūr*, faultless, innocent, without fail, completely, entirely. *be-ḳala'ī*, untinned (a pot, &c). *be-ḳaul*, faithless, perfidious. *be-ḳiyās*, inconceivable, contrary to the common order of things, incomprehensible, immense. *be-ḳaid*, unrestrained; irregular. *be-kāj*, or *be-kār*, useless, unemployed. *be-kām*, frustrated, disappointed. *be-karān*, immense, infinite, boundless. *be-kas*, friendless. *be-kasī*, destitution. *be-kafan*, unshrouded. *be-kal*, restless, out of order. *be-kalī*, uneasiness. *be-kam o kāst*, without decrease or diminution, all right, accurate. *be-gāh*, untimely, unseasonable. *be-gumān*, without suspicion, doubtless. *be-gunāh*, innocent, faultless. *be-ghāṭ*, inaccessible, (a river) without steps or a quay to it. *be-lāj*, impudent, shameless. *be-liḥāẓ*, inattentive, undistinguishing, ill-bred, unmannerly. *be-luṭf*, unkind, ungracious. *be-lagām*, unbridled, licentious. *be-lagā,o*, unconnected, inaccessible, candid, categorical, without reserve. *be-mān*, disgraced, dishonourable, dishonoured. *be-mānand*, incomparable, unparalleled. *be-māya*, without means of subsistence, poor, indigent. *be-miṣāl*, incomparable, unequalled. *be-muḥāsaba*, without calculation, at a venture. *be-muhābā*, without respect, unceremonious. *be-maḥall*, out of place, improper. *be-muruwwat*, unkind, cruel. *be-maza*, tasteless, insipid. *be-ma'nī*, foolish, idle, vain, unmeaning, absurd. *be-maḳdūr*, without authority; without resource, miserable, poor. *be-man*, spiritless. *be-minnat*, independent, unwilling to incur obligation. *be-mūjib*, without cause, without reason. *be-mauḳi'* out of place, unapt, unseasonable, inopportune, inconvenient. *be-mihr*, unfriendly, unkind. *be-nām*, without character or reputation. *be-nām o nishān*, without name or character. *be-naṣīb*, unfortunate. *be-naẓīr*, incomparable. *be-namak*, insipid; saltless; ugly, ordinary. *be-nang o nāmūs*, without name or character. *be-nawā*, indigent; m. a kind of *darwesh* who shaves his eyebrows and beard. *be-nawā,ī* begging, mendicancy. *be-nihāyat*, endless, without bound or limit. *be-niyāz*, without want, an epithet of God, the Almighty. *be-wāriṣ*, without heirs. *be-wāriṣ-māl*, property that escheats to the government in default of heirs. *be-wālī*, without protector. *be-wajh*, without cause or reason. *be-waṭan*, without home or native country, an exile. *be-wafā*, faithless, ungrateful. *be-wafā,ī*, f. infidelity, faithlessness. *be-waḳt*, out of season, untimely, ill-timed. *be-waḳr*, or *be-waḳār*, without fame or character, dishonourable. *be-wuḳūf*, ignorant, inexpert, stupid. *be-hamāl*, without compeer, unequalled, unrivalled. *be-himmat*, unambitious, humble, miserly, vile, slothful, lazy, indolent. *be-hunar*, unskilled. *be-hangām*, untimely. *be-hosh*, stupified, senseless. *be-hech*, without reason, purpose, or motive. *p.*

بيا बया *baya*, a person appointed in bazars to measure grain. *h.*

بيا बया *bayā*, or **बैया** *baiyā*, m. the name of the little bird that learns to fetch and carry, &c., and that the Hindūs teach to snatch the ornamental patch or wafer from the foreheads of their mistresses (*Lexia Indica*); an assiser. *biyā*, m. seed.

بيابان *bayābān*, or *biyābān*, m. a desert, a wilderness. *bayabān-gard* or *-naward*, one who traverses the desert, a wanderer. *bayābāni ḳuds*, the wilderness of Jerusalem. *p.*

بياباني *bayābāni*, of or belonging to the wilderness or desert. *p.*

بيابيا *biyā biyā*, come, come; a mode of calling pigeons, falcons, &c. *p.*

بياپار ब्यापार *byāpār*, business, affair. *s.*

بياپاري ब्यापारी *byāpārī*, a man of business in general, a dealer, a trader. *s.*

بياپنا ब्यापना *byāpnā*, n. to provide, occupy, to effect, to operate, to work, to act, to affect or influence. *s.*

بياتها *byāthā* (v. *byāhā*), married. *d.*

بياج ब्याज *byāj*, m. interest; delay. *byāj-khor*, one who takes interest, a usurer. *h.*

بياج ब्याज *byāj*, m. pretence, pretext. *s.*

بياجو ब्याजू *byājū*, m. the principal, or capital sum put out to interest. *h.*

بيادھ ब्याध *byādh*, m. a hunter, fowler. *s.*

بيادھ ब्याधि *byādhi*, m. sickness, ailment, pain, anguish, disease. *s.*

بيادھا ब्याधा *byādhā*, m. a fowler, hunter. *s.*

بيادھت ब्याधित *byādhit*, sick, grieved, pained. *s.*

بيادھي ब्याधी *byādhī*, ill, sick; m. a fowler, hunter. *s.*

بيار बयार *bayār*, f. wind, air. *h.*

بيار *biyār* (imper. of *āwardan*), bring thou. *p.*

بيار बीअर *bī,ar*, m. a hole (of a snake, rat, &c.). *s.*

بيارتھ ब्यार्थ *byārth*, vain, of no effect. *s.*

بياري बियारी *biyārī*, **बिआरी** *bi,ārī*, f. supper. *h.*

بياڙ बीअड़ *bī,aṛ*, seed-bed; evening. *h.*

بياز *byāz* m. (for *byāj*, q.v.) interest, &c. *d.*

بياس ब्यास *byās*, the name of a *muni* or sage, who is said to have compiled the *Vedas*, the *Bhāgavat Purāna* and the *Mahābhārata* (properly *vyāsa*), also the founder of the Vedanta philosophy. *s.*

بياس बियास *biyās*, land cultivated and prepared for being sown in the following year. *h.*

بياسي बयासी *bayāsī*, *byāsī* or *be,āsī*, eighty-two. *s.*

بياض *bayāẓ*, f. whiteness; a common-place book, a blank book. *a.*

بیاکرن व्याकरण *byākaran*, or वैयाकरण *baiyākaran*, m. gammar. *s.*

بیاکرن वैयाकरण *baiyākaran*,
بیاکرنی व्याकरणी *byākaranī*, or
वैयाकरणी *baiyākaranī*,
} m. grammarian. *s.*

بیاکل व्याकुल *byākul*, restless, agitated (in mind), perplexed. *s.*

بیاکھیان व्याख्यान *byākhyān*, m. explanation. *s.*

بیالا बयाला *bayālā*, or बैयाला *baiyālā*, flatulent; also heavy or indigestible (esculents). *s.*

بیالو ब्यालू *byālū* or बियालू *biyālū*, m. supper. *h.*

بیالیس बेआलीस *be,ālīs*, or बयालीस *bayālīs*, forty-two. *h.*

بیان *bayān*, m. explanation, relation. *bayān-k.*, a to explain, to unfold, to relate. *bayān-wār*, explicitly; adj. clear, evident. *a.*

بیان ब्यान *byān*, or बैयान, *baiyān*, m. birth, act of parturition. *char-byān-gā,e*, a cow that has calved four times. *ek-byān jāmak*, having produced two calves at a birth. *s.*

بیانا ब्याना *byānā*, or बैयाना *baiyānā*, to be delivered of young (applied only to brute animals). *s.*

بیانت ब्यान्त *byānt* (see *byān*), birth, &c. *s.*

بیاہ ब्याह, *byāh* or बियाह *biyāh*, m. marriage. *byāh-rachānā*, to celebrate a marriage. *byāh k.*, to marry. *byāh-lānā*, a. to take in marriage, to bring home a wife, to marry. *s.*

بیاہا ब्याहा *byāhā*, बियाहा *biyāhā*, m.
بیاہتا ब्याहता *byāhtā*, बियाहता *biyāhtā*, f.
} married.
byāhā jānā, n. to be married (a man). *byāhī-jānā*, to be married (a woman). *s.*

بیاہ جوگ ब्याहयोग *byāh-jog*, marriageable. *s.*

بیاہنا ब्याहना, *byāhnā* बियाहना, *biyāhnā*, n. to be delivered of young (animal); a. to marry (*i. e.* to give or take in marriage). *s.*

بیاہن ब्याहन *byāhan*, बियाहन *biyāhan*, m. marrying, marriage. *s.*

بیاہن جوگ ब्याहनयोग *byāhan-jog*, fit for marriage, marriageable. *s.*

بیائی बैयाई *baiyā,ī*, f. a weighman's perquisite. *h.*

بیایام ब्यायाम *byāyām*, m. labour, exertion, exercising, practising. *s.*

بیب बेब *beb*, f. name of a grass from which a twine is made; it is also used in thatching. *s.*

بیب बैब *baib*, afar off, at a distance. *h.*

بی بی बीबी *bībī*, f. a lady (vulgarly a wife). *h.*

بیپار बैपार *baipār*, m. traffic, merchandise. *s.*

بیپاری बैपारी *baipārī*, m. a merchant, a trader. *s.*

بیت *bait*, f. a couplet (in poetry); an edifice, house, temple. *bait-bandī*, f. poetry, verse-making. *a.*

بیت बेत *bet*, f. a cane, ratan (*Calamus rotang*). *s.*

بیتال बेताल *betāl* or बैताल *baitāl*, name of a demon supposed to occupy dead bodies. *s.*

بیت الحرام *bait-ul-ḥarām*, m. (sacred house), the temple of Mecca. *a.*

بیت الخلا *bait-ul-khalā*, m. a necessary office, a privy. *a.*

بیت السقر *bait-us-sakar*, m. hell. *a.*

بیت الشرف *bait-ush-sharaf*, the mansion of eminence, the highest mansion of a heavenly body (in astrology). *a.*

بیت الصنم *baitu-ṣ-ṣanam*, an idol temple. *a.*

بیت الله *bait-ullāh*, m. (the house of God), the temple of Mecca. *a.*

بیت المال *bait-ul-māl*, m. lit. the treasure-house; the public treasury or exchequer, into which payments on various accounts are made, and according to the sources from which they are derived, applicable to the support of different classes of persons; an escheat, property that falls to the crown in failure of heirs; met. an unfortunate fellow. (v. Wilson's Glossary.) *a.*

بیت المقدس *bait-ul-muḳaddas*, the temple or city of Jerusalem. *a.*

بیتر बेतर *betra* or *betar*, a cane or willow. *betra-bandī*, an allowance for mats or wicker works for packing goods. *s. p.*

بیترا बैतरा *baitarā*, f. dry ginger. *s.*

بیترنی बैतरणी *baitarnī*, f. a river, according to the Hindūs, which is to be crossed by the dead on their way into the world of spirits, like the Styx of the ancients; a river in Orissa. *s.*

بیتکھیت बीतखेत *bīt-khet*, land cultivated by forced labour. *h.*

بیتل *baitul*, unlucky; vicious (an abbreviation of *bait-ul-māl*). *a.*

بیتن *be-tan*, impersonal. *be-tan māl*, an escheat; property devolving on the state from want of legal claimants. *p.*

بیتنا बीतना *bītnā*, n. to pass, elapse (as time); to occur, come to pass. *s.*

بیتیت व्यतीत *byatīt* (for *vyatīt*), passed elapsed. *s.*

بیٹ बीट *bīṭ*, f. dung of any animal; a factitious salt containing sulphur. *s.*

بیٹ बीट *bīṭ*, a kind of agistment, an allowance per head of cattle, paid to the cowherd. *h.*

بیٹا बेटा *beṭā*, m. a son, a child, a boy. *beṭā kar-lenā*, to adopt a son. *h.*

بیٹنا बीटना *bīṭnā*, a. to spill, to scatter. *h.*

بیٹھ बेठ *beṭh*, sandy unproductive soil. *bīṭh*, f. the dung of birds. *baiṭh*, value of the government share of produce, the amount settled on land. *h.*

بیٹھا बीठा *bīṭhā*, m. an annular cushion put on the head for carrying a pot of water. *h.*

بیٹھا बैठा *baiṭhā*, m. a paddle. *h.*

بیٹھانا बैठाना *baiṭhānā*,
بیٹھارنا बैठारना *baiṭhārnā*,
بیٹھالنا बैठालना *baiṭhālnā*,
} a. to cause to sit down. *h.*

بیٹھاو बैठाव *baiṭhā,o*, m. position, allocation, situation. *h.*

بیٹھائي बैठाई *baiṭhā,ī*, f. seating, allaying. *d.*

بیٹھك बैठक *baiṭhak*, f. } a seat, a place where
بیٹھکا बैठका *baiṭhkā*, m. } people meet to sit and converse, a bench; also, the act or state of sitting, sitting; a kind of exercise. *h.*

بیٹھلانا बैठलाना *baiṭhlānā*, a. to cause to sit. *h.*

بیٹھن बेठन *beṭhan*, m. the envelope in which cloth purchased is folded up, to which the purchaser is entitled; pack-cloth. *s.*

بیٹھنا बैठना *baiṭhnā*, to sit, to be idle; to ride (on a horse); to visit a person in grief for the purpose of condolence; to sit in *dharnā*, q. v.; to subside or abate; to perch (as a bird). *h.*

بیٹھوان बैठवान *baiṭhwān*, flat. *h.*

بیٹي बेटी *beṭī*, f. a daughter, a damsel. *h.*

بیج बीज *bīj*, m. seed; *Sperma genitale* (*viri aut mulieris*). *s.* [rest. *s.*

بیجابرکھنڈ बीजाबरखण्ड *bījābarkhand*, m. a fo-

بیجار बीजार *bījār*, seedy, abounding in seed. *s.*

بیجائي बीजाई *bījā,ī*, f. a perquisite of a certain allowance of seed-grain. *h.*

بیجر बीजर *bījar*, soil in which the cerealia are generally grown. *h.*

بیجك बीजक *bījak*, m. a ticket tied to goods, or on bags (of grain, &c.), to mark their contents, price, &c.; a list, an invoice. *s.*

بیجکھاد बीजखाद *bīj-khād*, advance of seed and food to agriculturists. *h.*

بیجگنت बीजगणित *bīja-ganit*, name of an ancient Hindū work on algebra. *s.*

بیجلا बैजिला *baijilā*, a species of black pulse. *h.*

بیجمار बीजमार *bīj-mār*, failure of germination. *h.*

بیجنا बीजना *bījnā*, m. a kind of fan. *bejnā* (Dakh. for *bhejnā*), to send. *s.*

بیجنتي बैजन्ती *baijantī*, f. a flag or standard; the standard of *Vishṇu*. *s.*

بیجنتي مالا बैजन्तीमाला *baijantī-mālā*, f. a necklace worn by *Vishṇu* in his several forms. It was believed to be composed of the following jewels produced from the five elements: viz. the sapphire from earth, the pearl from water, the ruby from fire, the topaz from air, and the diamond from space or ether. *s.*

بیجو बेजू *bejū*, m. the name of an animal that feeds on carcasses (*Ursus Indicus*, Shaw; Indian badger. Pennant). *h.*

بیجوار बीजवार *bījwār*, perquisites of the lower classes, consisting of a portion of seed-corn from the field. *h.*

بیجوت *be-jot*, untilled (as land) a farm that is given up by the cultivators. *p. h.*

بیجھا बेझा *bejhā*, m. a butt, or mark for archers. *s.*

بیجھڑا बेझड़ा *bejharā*, m. a mixed crop, generally grain and barley. *h.*

بیجھنا बीझना *bījhnā*, a. to tear up the earth with the hoofs (a bull); to push, to shove, to shoulder. *h.*

بیجھونیا बीझोनिया *bījhoniyā*, a tribe of *rājpūts* in Jaunpūr. *h.*

بیجھیریا बीझेरया *bījheryā*, name of a clan of *rājpūts* in the district of Gorackpur. *h.*

بیجي बीजी *bījī*, f. a weasel, a mongoose (*Viverra ichneumon*). *h.* [*Urdū*, *shāl*. q. v. *d.*

بیجیسر *bījīsar*, m. a species of tree called, in

بیچ बीच *bīch*, in, into, among, in the midst, between, during; m. middle, centre; difference; quarrel, hostility. *bīch-parnā*. n. to differ, to raise a quarrel between. *bīch kī unglī*, f. the middle finger. *bīchoñ bīch*, the very middle. *h.* [traffic. *d.*

بیچاباچي *bechā-bāchī*, f buying and selling,

بیچابیچ बीचाबीच *bīch-ā-bīch*, the middle, in the middle. *d.*

بیچاره *be-chāra*, helpless, wretched; pl. *be-chāragān*. *bechāragī*, helplessness. *s.*

بیچ بچاو बीचबिचाव *bīch-bichā,o*, m. mediation, interposition, arbitration. *bīch-bichā,o-k.*, to mediate, to interpose. *h.*

بیچرا बीचड़ा *bīchrā*, m. a bed for growing plants to be transplanted. *h.*

بیچنا बेचना *bechnā*, a. to sell, to dispose of. *h.*

بیچواني बीचवानी *bīchwānī*, } m. an umpire, an
بیچوائي बीचवाई *bīchwā,ī* } arbitrator, a middle-man. *h.* [tent pitched without a pole. *p.*

بیچوبه *be-choba* m. (lit. poleless), a kind of

بیچھا बीछा *bīchhā*, } m. a scorpion; the sign
بیچھو बीछू *bīchhū*, } Scorpio. *s.*

بیخ *bekh*, f. root; origin, foundation. *bekh-kan*, an extirpator, a judge (as extirpating thieves); also, a thief (as destroying the subjects). *p.*

بید बैद *baid*, m. a physician, a man of the medical caste. *s.*

بید बेद *bed* (for *veda*), m. the name of the Hindū scriptures (namely, 1st, *ṛig*, 2nd, *sāma*, 3rd, *yajush*, 4th, *atharva*), which are believed to have been revealed by Brahma, and arranged in the present order by a sage called *Vyāsa* or *Veda-vyāsa*; met. certainty, faith. *s.*

بید *bed*, a willow; ratan. *bed-bāf*, one who works on ratans, a basket-maker. *bed-bāfī*, weaving with ratans (as the bottoms of chairs and the panels of doors or windows). *bed-mushk*, musk-willow, celebrated for its fragrance. *p.*

بید *bīd*, a street or lane. *d.*

بیدار *bedār*, awake, *bedār-bakht*, fortunate. *bedār-dil*, alert, watchful, quick of apprehension. *bedār-dilī*, f. alertness, quickness of apprehension. *p.*

بیداري *bedārī*, f. wakefulness, state of being awake. *p.*

بیدانت बेदान्त *bedānt* (for *vedānta*), m. the name of a particular Hindū philosophical system. *s.*

بيداني बेदान्ती *bedāntī*, m. one who is conversant in the *bedānt* school of philosophy. *s.*

بيدانگ बेदाङ्ग *bedāng*, a class of studies or sciences, subservient to the *Vedas*. *s.*

بيدائي बैदाई *baidā,ī*, f. practice of physic. *s.*

بيدر बीदर *bīdar*, a sort of rake or harrow worked by oxen. *h.*

بيدستر *bedastar*, the castor beaver. *p.*

بيدق *baidaḳ*, the pawn at chess. *a.*

بيدك बैदिक *baidik*, m. a reader of the *Veda*, a Brāhman well versed in the *Vedas*. *s.*

بيدك बैदक *baidak*, m. the practice or science of physic. *s.*

بيدكا बेदिका *bedikā*, f. an altar, platform. *s.*

بيدلت *be-dalat* (for *be-daulat*), unlucky. *d.*

بيدن बेदन *bedan*, } f. pain, sickness, ache. *s.*
بيدنا बेदना *bednā*, }

بيدوا बेदवा *bedwā*, m. a reader of the Vedas. *s.*

بيده बेध *bedh*, m. bore, crack, hole. *s.*

بيدها बीधा *bīdhā*, settlement, arrangement. *h.*

بيدهڑك बेधड़क *be-dhaṛak*, } fearless, without
بيدهڑكا बेधड़का *be-dhaṛkā*, } doubt. *p. h.*

بيدهنا बेधना *bedhnā*, a.. to pierce, to perforate. *s.*

بيدهي बेधी *bedhī*, } m. a borer, one who
بيدهيا बेधिया *bedhiyā*, } perforates pearls gems, &c. *s.*

بيدي बेदी *bedī*, f. an altar, a platform. *s.*

بيڈا बीडा *bīḍā*, m. a mound, a cluster of mounds. *h.*

بير बीर *bīr*, m. a hero; a brother; adj. brave. *s.*

بير बीर *bīr*, f. a sister; a tusk; pasturage, grass land. *h.*

بير बीर *bīr*, m. a jewel worn in the ear; in the Delhi and Sāgar territory it denotes pasturage. *h.*

بير बैर *bair*, m. enmity, revenge. *bair-l.*, a. to revenge. *s.*

بير बेर *ber*, m. the name of a fruit (*Zizyphus jujuba*), also the name of the tree; jujubes; time, vicissitude; delay, while; the lotus of the ancients. *s.*

بيرا बीरा *bīrā*, m. a betel-leaf made up, &c. (see *bīṛā*), a quid of tobacco, a cheroot or cigar. *s.*

بيرا बीरा *bīrā*, m. (same as *bīran*) a brother. *h.*

بيرار *berār*, a village registrar or accountant. *d.*

بيراق *bairāḳ* (for *bairaḳ*), a banner, a standard. *p.*

بيراكهيري बैराखेरी *bairākherī*, f. quarrelling. *h.*

بيراگ बैराग *bairāg* or *bairāgya*, m. penance, devotion, the act of leaving the pleasures of the world. *s.*

بيراگا बैरागा *bairāgā*, m. a small crooked stick, which a *Bairāgī* places under his armpit to lean upon as he sits. *s.* [also the same as *bairāgā*. *s.*

بيراگن बैरागन *bairāgan*, f. a female *bairāgī*;

بيراگي बैरागी *bairāgī*, austere, recluse; m. the religious ascetic who abandons terrestrial objects, thoughts, passions; a kind of wandering *faḳir*, who practises certain austerities. *s.* [*rāg*). *s.*

بيرگيه बैराग्य *bairāgya*, m. penance (v. *bai-*

بيرانا बेराना *berānā*, m. a grove of *ber* trees. *h.*

بيرباني *bīr-bānī*, f. a man's own wife. *h.*

بيربهٹي बीरबहुट्टी *bīr-bahuṭṭī*, } f. a small in-
بيربهوٹي बीरबहूटी *bīr-bahūṭī*, } sect with a back of a bright red colour; the scarlet or lady-fly, commonly called the "Rain insect," as it makes its appearance when the first rains have fallen. It is covered with a downy exterior resembling velvet, and of a scarlet colour. *h.* [peatedly. *s.*

بيربير बेरबेर *ber-ber*, often, frequently, re-

بيرتا बीरता *bīrtā*, f. heroism, valour, prowess. *s.*

بيرج बीर्य *bīrj*, m. power, strength; seed; *sperma genitale*. *s.*

بيرق *bairaḳ*, m. a banner, ensign, colours. *p.*

بيركه बैरख *bairakh*, m. a banner, ensign, colour (corrupted from *bairaḳ*). *h.*

بيرن बैरण *bairan*, f. a female enemy. *s.*

بيرن बीरन *bīran*, m. a brother. *h.*

بيرن बीरण *bīran* (also *bīranākhar*), a kind of tough grass spreading over uncultivated lands. *h.*

بيرون *berūn*, out, outside. *berūn-jāt*, country, in opposition to town. *berūn-jātī*, rustic, country-bred. *p.*

بيري बेरी *berī*, f. the tree of *Zizyphus jujuba*. *s.*

بيري बेरी *berī*, f. a betel leaf made up with spices, &c.; the colour which adheres to the lips from chewing betel. *s.*

بيري बीरी *bīrī*, f. a betel-leaf made up with spices, &c.; the colour which adheres to the lips from chewing betel; a composition, which being rubbed on the teeth, stains their interstices of a reddish colour. *h.*

بيري बैरी *bairī*, m. an enemy, an adversary. *s.*

بيريه बीर्य *bīrya* (for *vīrya*), m. valour, &c. *s.*

بيريز *beriz*, m. sum total, the entire revenue of a farm; also a government tax. *h.*

بيڙ बेड़ *beṛ*, m. an inclosure. *beṛ bandī-h.*, to inclose a field. *h.*

بيڙا बेड़ा *beṛā*, m. a raft, a float; the raft which is floated by the Muhammadans in honour of *khwāja-khiẓr*. Besides the anniversary *beṛā* offered to propitiate him, hundreds of smaller ones with lamps may be seen on Thursdays of the month *Bhādoṅ* particularly, which are offered by the Muhammadans to this saint. *beṛā bāndhnā*, a. to collect a crowd. *beṛā pār-k.* or *lagānā*, to relieve from distress, to remove difficulties, to help one through a business (lit. to ferry over a raft). *beṛā kisī kā pār honā*, to be propitious, to succeed; in Dakh. it denotes a fence or inclosure. *s.*

بيڑا बीड़ा *bīṛā*, m. a betel-leaf made up with a preparation of the areca nut, spices, and chanām. *bīṛā uṭhānā*, a. to undertake a business. *bīṛā ḍālnā*, a. to propose a premium for the performance of a task (the expressions originate in a custom that prevailed of throwing a *bīṛā* of betel into the midst of an assembly, in token of proposal to any person to undertake some difficult affair then requisite to be performed, and the person who took up the betel bound himself to perform the business in question). *h.*

بيڑا बीड़ा *bīṛā*, m. a thong tied to the hilt of a sword by which it is retained in the scabbard, a sword-knot. *h.*

بيڑها बेढ़ा *beṛhā*, m. paling, railing, inclosure; adj. bent, crooked. *h.*

بيڑهنا बेढ़ना *beṛhnā*, a. to inclose with a fence, to pound (cattle, &c.); to drive away cattle (as in a foray). *h.*

بيڑي बेड़ी *beṛī*, f. iron fastenings to the legs of criminals or of quadrupeds; the baskets used to irrigate fields with. *bīṛī*, a small parcel of betel nut (v. *bīṛā*). *h.* [Hindūs, dimin. of *beṛā*. *h.*

بيڑيا बेड़िया *beṛiyā*, m. the name of a caste of

بيز *bez*, in comp. diffusing, dispersing. *p.*

بيزار *bezār*, displeased, angry, out of humour; (vul.) sick. *p.* [pleasure. *p.*

بيزاري *bezārī*, f. anger, bad humour, dis-

بيس बैस *bais*, m. the third of the four Hindū castes, whose especial duties are agriculture and trade; a name of a tribe of *rāj-pūts*, giving its name to the province of *Baiswāṛā*, in Oude; a prince of that tribe formerly reigned at *Dunḍla-kherā*. His dominions, which extended over a great part of the province of Oude, on the north bank of the Ganges, are still called *Baiswāṛā*. *s.*

بيس बीस *bīs*, twenty. *bais* (for *vayas*), age. *s.*

بيسا बीसा *bīsā*, m. a score; a dog which has twenty nails. *s.*

بيساكه बैसाख *baisākh*, m. the first solar month of the Hindūs, the full moon of which is near *Vishākha* (four stars in Libra and Scorpio); April—May. *s.*

بيساكها बैसाखा *baisākhā* or बैशाखा *baishākhā*, m. a crutch; a club armed with iron; a club consecrated in the month of *Baisākh*. *s.*

بيساكهي बैसाखी *baisākhī*, growing in the month of *Baisākh*; f. a large kind of myrobalan or citron fruit; the day of full moon in the month *Baisākh*. *s.*

بيسانڈو बैसांडू *baisānḍū*, sedentary, idle. *h.*

بيست *bīst*, twenty, a score. *p.*

بيستون *be-sutūn*, of no foundation, insignificant. *besitūn* or *bīstūn*, name of a celebrated mountain in Persia. *p.*

بيسر बीसर *bīsar*, gleanings left in the field for the lower orders to gather. *h.* [nose. *h.*

بيسر बेसर *besar*, f. the small ring worn in the

بيسرا बेसरा *besarā*, f. a kind of falcon, the female or hen bird of the species called *dhotī*, q. v. (*Falco nisus*). *h.*

بيسرا बेसुरा *be-surā*, out of tune. *h.*

بيسك बैसक *baisak*, a spot in a jungle to which cattle are sent out to graze: the term is also applied to an old and worn-out animal. *h.*

بيسك *baisak* (for *baiṭhak*), a seat, sitting. *d.*

بيسلانا *baislānā*, a. to cause to sit, to set. *d.*

بيسن बेसन *besan*, m. the flour or meal of pulse, particularly of chuna (*Cicer arietinum*): the same is used as a substitute for soap. *h.*

بيسنا *baisnā*, n. (for *baiṭhnā*) to sit, to remain. *d.*

بيسندر बैसंदर *baisandar*, m. fire, or its deity. *s.*

بيسنوٹي बेसनौटी *besnauṭī*, f. a cake made of peameal. *h.* [caste. *s.*

بيسني बैसनी *baisnī*, f. a female of the Bais

بيسني बेसनी *besanī*, made or mixed with besan. *h.*

بيسوا बेस्वा *beswā*, f. a courtesan, a prostitute. *s.*

بيسواڑا बैसवाड़ा *baiswāṛā*, m. the residence of *Bais*, the nativity of *Bais*, q. v. *h.*

بيسي बीसी *bīsī*, f. twenty; a score, a measure of grain; also a land measure equal to 20 nails. *s.*

بيسا बेस्या *besyā*, f. a prostitute, a harlot, a courtesan. *s.*

بيش *besh*, more; good, proper, well, excellent, elegant, delightful. *besh-ḳarār*, trustworthy. *besh-bahā* or *besh-ḳīmat*, of great value, costly, precious. *p.*

بيشا *beshā*, m. a forest, jungle (v. *besha*). *p.*

بيش ازبيش *besh-az-besh*, a great deal. *p.*

بيشتر *beshtar*, better, more, exceeding, generally, for the most part. *s*

بيشنو बैष्णव, बैष्णौ *baishnau*, relating to Vishnu. m. a kind of mendicant, a follower of Vishnu. *s.*

بيشنوي बैष्णवी *baishnavī* or *bīshnavī*, a follower of Vishnu. *baishnavottar*, lands granted rent free to the worshippers of Vishnu, especially those of the mendicant order. *s.*

بيش وكم *besh o kam*, more or less; not much, a moderate quantity. *p.*

بيشه *besha*, m. a forest, a jungle; a desert. *p.*

بيشي *beshī*, f. excess, surplus, increase, increased assessment. *beshī jam'*, increase of revenue on that of last year. *beshī zamīn*, increase in the lands under cultivation. *p.*

بيض *baiẓ*, m. a mark fixed to public writings by the magistrate or any principal officer. *a.*

بيضا *baiẓā*, m. the sun; whiteness. *yadi baiẓā dikhānā*, a. to distinguish one's self in any work (an allusion taken from the luminous hand of Moses). *a.*

بيضانه *baiẓāna*, m. the perquisite of the magistrate, &c. for marking public papers. *a.*

بيضاوي *baiẓāwī*, f. the author of a book, containing a commentary on the *ḳur,ān*. *a.*

بيضوي *baiẓawī*, fashioned in the shape of an egg. *khaṭṭ-i-baiẓawī*, m. a form of the Persian *Nasta'līḳ* character, in which the curved tails of the letters are segments of an oval; opposed to *khaṭṭ i āftābī*, in which they are portions of a circle. *a.*

بيضه *baiza*, m. an egg, a testicle. *a.*

بيطار *baiṭār*, a horse-doctor. *a.*

بيع *bai'* or *bī'*, f. buying and selling; commerce, selling. *bai'-k.*, to sell. *bai' bi-l-wafā*, a conditional sale, depending on the final decision of the seller; also a pawn or pledge. *bai' bi-l wafā-dār*, a person having the use of an article conditionally sold to him in acquittance of a debt. *bai'-nāma*, a deed of sale *bai' paṭṭā*, a lease or sub-lease obtained by purchase. *bai' sulṭānī*, a sale by order of government. *bai' taljīh*, a temporary sale. *bai'-dār*, a purchaser, a possessor by purchase. *a.*

بيعانه *bai'āna*, m. earnest-money. *a.*

بيع بالوفادار *bai'bil-wafā-dār*, a person having the possession and usufruct of a property on its conditional sale to him. *p.*

بيعت كرنا *bai'at-k.*, a. to become a disciple of some saint. *a. h.*

بيعدار *bai'dār*, a proprietor by purchase. *a.p.*

بيك बीक *bīk*, m. (same as *bih*), a wolf. *s.*

بيكا बीका *bīkā*, crooked, awry; injured, damaged. (v. *bāl.*) *h.*

بيكال बैकाल *baikāl*, m. afternoon. *s.*

بيكٹر *behaṭṭar*, ruffianly, brutal, cruel. *d.*

بيكس *behas*, a kind of grass used for fodder; adj. helpless, destitute. *h. p.*

بيكسي *be-hasī*, f. destitution, forlornness. *p.*

بيكنٹھ बैकुण्ठ *baikunṭh*, m. a name of *Vishṇu*; the heaven or paradise of *Vishṇu*. This name was also applied in the time of Ja'fir Khān to a kind of pit, in which revenue defaulters were confined until they paid the demands against them: in this sense it was evidently used ironically on the part of the Musalmāns in ridicule of the Hindūs. *s.*

بيكھ बेष *bekh*, m. a habit, dress, garb. *s.*

بيكھٹ बैखट *baikhaṭ*, a sale, selling. *h.*

بيگ बेग *beg*, m. celerity, haste, rapidity; adv. quickly, soon; dung. *s.*

بيگ *beg*, a *Mughal* title corresponding with lord, master, &c. *t.*

بيگا *bīgā* (v. *bīkā*), awry, crooked. *d.*

بيگار बैगार *baigār*, a name of the *Kharwār* tribe. *h.*

بيگار बेगार *begār*, m. a person forced to work with or without pay. *begār pakaṛnā*, to press one into service. *p.*

بيگاري बेगारी *begārī*, f. the act of pressing or forcing to work. *begārī lenā*, a. to take forcibly or press, with or without paying for. *begārī-pakṛelā*, m. a pressed man; one compelled to work. *p.*

بيگانگي *begānagī*, f. strangeness, shyness. *p.*

بيگانه *begāna*, strange, not domestic, foreign, unknown; m. a stranger, a foreigner. *p.*

بيگڑ *begaṛ*, m. gold-tinsel; tinfoil; varnish. *d.*

بيگم *begam*, f. a lady, a queen: women of rank are called begams (pl. *begamāt*). *t.*

بيگما *begmā*, f. (dimin. of *begam*) a young lady of rank. *t.*

بيگن बैगन *baigan*, m. the egg-plant (*Solanum melongena*). *h.*

بيگنتي बैगन्ती *baigantī*, f. a sort of wood. *s.*

بيگني *begnī*, f. the wife of a *beg*. *t.*

بيگها बीघा *bīghā*, m. a measure of land consisting in Bengal of 20 *kaṭṭhās* or 120 feet square, or 1600 square yards, which is nearly ⅓ of an English acre; in the Upper Provinces it is nearly ⅝ of an acre. *bīghā dām*, settlement of revenue at so much per *bīghā*. *bīghā-dām*, rate levied per *bīghā*. *bīghā-daftarī*, a record of the measurement of lands in a district. *s.*

بيگي बेगी *begī*, quick, swift, speedily. *s.*

بيل बैल *bail*, m. a bull, an ox; met. a blockhead (in which last sense the Scotch say, "a stot"). *s.*

بيل बेल *bel*, m. the name of a fruit (*Cratæva* or *Ægle marmelos*). *bel* or *beli*, f. a creeper, climber, tendril (of a vine); descendants, offspring. *s.*

بيل बेल *bel*, m. the name of a flower (*Jasminum zambac*). *bel-phalne*, to attain one's precise or utmost wish. *h*

بيل *bel*, a spade, hoe, mattock; a spot in which the receiving-pans are placed, where sugar is manufactured; a creeper, a tendril, a pole for directing a boat; a well. *p.*

بيلا बेला *belā*, f. a while, a time. *s.*

بيلا बेला *belā*, f. name of a shrub (*Jasminum zambac*); a cup; an instrument of music resembling a fiddle. *h.*

بيلا *belā*, m. a bag of money carried in the hand of a person of rank for distribution among the poor. *belā-bardār*, one of the retinue of a great man, who scatters money among the populace. *belā-kharch*, expenditure in alms-giving. *p.*

بيلا बैला *bailā*, m. a species of bird. *h.*

بيل بوٹا बेलबूटा *bel-būṭā*, m. a shrub, bush, or creeper; flowers (on cloth). *h.*

بيلچا *belchā*, بيلچك *belchak*, بيلچه *belcha*, } m. a small spade, a hoe, a small mattock. *p.*

بيلدار *beldār*, m. a pioneer; a class of Hindūs employed in digging. *p.*

بيلقان *bailkān*, name of a city in Armenia near the Caspian. *p.*

بيلك *belak*, f. a small mattock; the iron point of an arrow. *p.*

بيلكي बेलकी *belkī*, m. a cattle-breeder, a grazier. *h.*

بيلن बेलन *belan*, m. a rolling-pin. *s.*

بيلنا बेलना *belnā*, m. a rolling-pin; a. to spread out, to laminate. *s.*

بيلني बेलनी *belanī*, m. a branch; a small rolling-pin. *h.*

بيلو बेलू *belū*, m. act of rolling. *h.*

بيلو बेलौ *be-lau*, dispirited, heartless. *p. h.*

بيلي बेली *belī*, f. a creeper, climber; tendril (of a vine). *s.*

بيم *bīm*, m. fear, terror, dread, danger. *p.*

بيما बीमा *bīmā*, m. insurance; also the rate of insurance, or the per-centage paid for that purpose. *h.*

بيمات बेमात *bemāt*, f. a stepmother. *bemātbhā,ī*, a brother born of a different mother by the same father (a half-brother by the father's side). *s.*

بيماتر वैमात्र *baimātra*, m. a brother born of a different mother by the same father. *s.*

بيمار *bīmār*, sick, indisposed. *bīmār-khāna*, m. an hospital. *p.*

بيماردار *bīmār-dār*, an attendant on a sick person, a nurse. *p.*

بيمارداري *bīmār-dārī*, attendance on the [sick. *p.*

بيماري *bīmārī*, f. sickness, illness. *p.*

بيمان बीमां *bīmāṅ* (v. *bīmā*), m. insurance. *h.*

بين बीन *bīn*, f. a kind of stringed musical instrument, having a long narrow body, and a large dried calabash at either end to concentrate the sound. It is strung with steel wires. *s.*

بين बेण *ben*, बेणु *benu*, or बैन *bain*, f. a flute, pipe, fife. *s.*

بين बैन *bain*, m. f. a word, speech. *s.*

بين *baiyan*, m. explanation, interpretation. *baiyin*, clear, evident, manifest. *a.*

بين *bīn*, see thou (r. of *dīdan*); in comp. seeing, as *'ālam-bīn*, world-seeing, an epithet applied to the sun. *p.*

بين *bain*, among, between, interval. *a.*

بينا बैना *bainā*, m. sweetmeats, cakes, &c. distributed at marriages. *s.*

بينا बैना *bainā*, m. an ornament worn on the [forehead. *h.*

بينا *bīnā*, clear-sighted, discerning. *p.*

بينا बेना *benā*, m. a fan; the name of a grass, *khas-khas* (*Andropogon muricatum*). *s.*

بيناپ *be-nāp*, unmeasured, unsurveyed. *be-nāp kā paṭṭā*, a lease guaranteeing that the average rates of land remain as before. *p. h.*

بينائي *bīnā,ī*, f. sight, vision. *p.*

بين بين *bain-bain*, betwixt and between, so so, passable, tolerable, middling. *a.*

بينتنا *bīṅtnā*, a. to cut (clothes). *d.*

بينت बेंट *beṅt*, } m. a handle of an axe, hoe,
بينٹا बैंटा *baiṅṭā*, } &c. *h.*

بينج *bīṅj* (for *bīj*), m. seed, grain. *d.*

بينجني बैंजनी *bainjnī*, purple (the colour of the *Solanum melongena*). *h.*

بينچ *bīṅch* (for *bīch*), in the midst. *d.*

بينچنا बेंचना *beṅchnā*, a. to sell. *beṅch-ḍālnā*, to sell off. *h.*

بيند बीन्द *bīnd*, m. a reed, a rush. *h.*

بيندا बैन्दा *baindā*, m. a mark on the forehead, as a preparative of devotion among the Hindūs. *bīndā*, a kind of rope made of grass or fibres of the *arhar* plant. *h.*

بيندهنا बीन्धना *bīndhnā*, a. to bore. *s.*

بيندهنا बेन्धना *bendhnā*, a. to plait, to braid. *h*

بيندي बैन्दी *baindī*, f. an ornamental circlet made with a coloured earth or unguent on the forehead and between the eyebrows; an ornament worn by women on the forehead. *h.*

بينڈا बींड़ा *bīnḍā*, m. a roll of paper; a kind of rope made of grass, or the fibres of the *arhar* plant. *h.*

بينڈا बेंड़ा *benḍā*, crooked; met. absurd. *h.*

بينڈهنا बेंढ़ना *benḍhnā*, a. to plait, to braid. *s.*

بينڈي बैंडी *bainḍī*, act of throwing up water from a pond or reservoir with a basket, for the purpose of irrigation. *h.*

بينڈي बींडी *bīnḍī*, f. the hair twisted (or [plaited) behind, (a tail). *s.*

بينسي बैंसी *baiṅsī*, a subdivision of the *Gūjar* tribe. *h.*

بينش *bīnish*, f. seeing, discernment. *p.*

بينگ बेङ्ग or बेंग *beng*, m. (for *vyanga*), a frog, puddock, toad. *s.*

بينگ ब्यंग *byang*, m. (for *vyangya*), sar-[casm. *s.*

بينگت बेङ्गत *bengat*, seed given to an indigent peasant at the time of sowing, to be repaid with interest in harvest. *h.*

بينگن बैंगन *baingan*, m. the egg-plant (*Solanum melongena*). *h.*

بينگني बैंगनी *baingani*, purple (the colour of the *Solanum melongena*). *h.*

بينودها बेनौधा *benaudhā*, the country between Allahabad and Sarwar. *h.*

بيني बेनी *benī*, f. the hair twisted behind. *s.*

بيني *bīnī*, f. the nose. *bīnī-burīda*, one whose nose is cut off (a common mode of punishment in the East). *p.*

بيوا *bewā*, f. a widow. *p.*

بيواپا *bewā-pā*, } state or situation of widow-
بيواپن *bewā-pan*, } hood. *p. h.*
بيوائي *bewā,ī*, }

بيوار *bewār*, account, explanation. *d.*

بیوان बेवान *bewān*, m. the vehicle or self-moving car of a Hindū deity; a (Hindū) bier. *s.*

بیوپار ब्योपार *byopār*, m. trade, traffic, business. *s.*

بیوپاري ब्योपारी *byopārī*, or बेपारी *be,opārī* (same as *baipārī*), a merchant. *s.*

بیوت *buyūt* (pl. of بیت), houses. *a.*

بیوت *bīwat*, fit (of a suit of clothes, &c.). *d.*

بیوتات *buyūtāt* (additional plural of *buyūt*, pl. of *bait*, a house): the term is used in several senses as outhouse, house-expense, house-tax, &c. *a.*

بیورا ब्योरा *byorā*, or बेवरा *beorā* also *by,aurā*, m. difference, distinction; account, explanation, history, detail of circumstances, an account of particulars, or detailed account (in book-keeping). *h.*

بیوریوار बेवरेवार *beore-wār*, explicitly, distinctly. *h.*

بیوگ बियोग *biyog*, m. separation (generally of lovers. *s.*

بیوگي बियोगी *biyogī*, m. a lover suffering the pain of absence. *s.*

بیونت ब्योंत *byont*, m. shape, the act of cutting out clothes. *h.*

بیونتنا ब्योंतना *byontnā*, a. to cut or shape clothes. *h.*

بیونگا ब्योंगा *byongā*, m. the instrument with which leather is scraped and cleaned. *byongā phirā nahīn*, his hide has not been curried yet (said of a spoilt child, &c.). *n.*

بیونگي ब्योंगी *byongī*, f. (see *byongā*). *h.*

بیوه *bewa*, f. a widow. *p.*

بیوهار ब्योहार *byohār*, or बेवहार *be,ohār*, m. profession, calling, negociation, transaction, money-lending, custom. *s.*

بیوهر ब्योहर *byohar*, or बेवहर *be,ohar*, m. a loan. *s.*

بیوهرا ब्योहरा *byoharā*, or बेवहरा *be,oharā*, بیوهریا ब्योहरिया *byohariyā*, or बेवहरिया *be,ohariyā*, } a trader, a money-lender. *s.*

بیوي *bewī* or *bewī-zan*, a widow. *p.*

بیه बेह *beh*, m. a hole, a perforation. *s.*

بیهده *behuda* (for *be-hūda*), foolish, stupid, silly. *p.*

بیهرا बेहरा *behrā*, بیهره बेहरः *behra*, } m. grass kept for pasturage. *h.*

بیهري बेहरी *behrī*, f. a subscription, instalment. *behrī-barār*, collection on shares of the revenue in kind. *behrī-bandī*, an allowance for repairing roads, &c. *behrī-dār*, the holder of a *behrī*. *h.*

بیهڑ बेहड़ *behaṛ* or *bīhaṛ*, uneven, abrupt, rugged, waste land, land full of ravines. *h.*

بیهش *behush* (for *be-hosh*), senseless. *p.*

بیهلا *behlā*, m. a bag of money carried by great men to be distributed in charity when travelling, &c. *behlā-bardār*, the carrier of the *behlā* (v. *belā*). *h.*

بیهن बेहन *behan*, a nursery for rice plants; *bīhan* seed. *h.*

بیهنا बेहिन्ना *behinnā*, m. a comber, a carder (of cotton). *h.*

بیهنور बेहनौर *behnaur*, m. a nursery for rice plants. *h.*

بیهودگي *be-hūdagī*, f. absurdity, frivolity *p.*

بیهوده *be-hūda*, absurd, idle, vain, fruitless, unprofitable. *be-hūda-go*, a babbler. *p.*

بیهوش *be-hosh*, senseless, insane. *p.*

بیهوشي *be-hoshī*, f. senselessness, insanity. *p.*

بیهین *bīhīn*, better, best, swift-paced. *p.*

بیي व्यय *byai*, m. expense, expenditure. *s.*

بییا बैया *baiyā* (v. بیا *bayā*), the name of a little bird. *s.*

بییهار व्ययहार *byayhār*, m. expense, expenditure. *s.*

پ

پ *pe*, the third letter of the Persian and Hindūstānī alphabets. It does not occur in the language or alphabet of the Arabs, and the letter *f* or *b* is substituted for it in such Persian words as are adopted into the Arabic language: thus, *fārsī* for *pārsī*, and *bādshāh* for *pādshāh*. In reckoning by *abjad*, *pe* is the same as *be*, viz. two.

پ प *pa*, m. the corresponding Sanskrit letter in that language denotes the wind; Æolus, the god of the wind; a nourisher or protector; act of drinking: as a termination (in Sanskrit words) it denotes supporting, cherishing, holding, also drinking; as from *bhū*, the earth, *bhūpa*, a king; lit. the earth-protector. *s.*

پا पा *pā*, a masculine termination added to Hindūstānī substantives or adjectives to denote abstract quality; as, *buṛhāpā*, old age, from *buṛhā*, old. *h.*

پا *pā*, m. the leg, the feet; *pā ba-zanjīr*, having the foot in chains, fettered. *pā dar rikāb*, foot in stirrup, ready, alert. *pā-shikasta*, broken-footed, infirm, reduced; in comp. (as the root of *pā,īdan*) it denotes permanency, continuation; as, *kam-pā*, of short duration, transitory; *der-pā*, permanent. *p.*

پانداز *pā-andāz*, m. a carpet spread at the entrance of a room, on which the feet are cleansed. *p.*

پابند *pā-band*, m. a rope with which the fore-feet of a horse are tied. *pā-band honā*, n. met. to be married. *p.*

پابوس *pā-bos*, kissing the feet, *i.e.* adoring, worshipping, revering. *pā-bos honā*, n. to worship, to reverence, to adore, to pay respect. *p.*

پابوسي *pā-bosī*, f. worship, reverence, adoration. *pā-bosī-k.*, a. to worship, to reverence. *p.*

پاپ पाप *pāp*, m. a crime, a sin, a fault. *s.*

پاپا पापा *pāpā*, m. a weevil, an insect bred in rice; also a father (v. *bābā*). *h.*

پاپاتما पापात्मा *pāpātmā*, m. a sinner, a reprobate. *h.*

پاپ‌بدھ पापबुद्धि *pāp-buddhi*, evil-minded, wicked. *s.*

پاپ‌پت पापपति *pāp-pati*, m. a paramour, a gallant. *s.*

پاپ‌پرش पापपुरुष *pāp-purush*, m. a personification of all sin. *s.*

پاپ‌چیلي पापचेली *pāp-chelī*, f. a plant commonly called *Aknidhi* (*Cissampelos hexandra*). *s.*

پاپ‌درشي पापदर्शी *pāp-darshī*, malevolent, looking at faults. *s.*

پاپ درشون पापदृश्वन *pāp-dṛishwan*, conscious of guilt, knowing an act to be wicked. *s.*

پاپر पापर *pāpar*, a fertile soil. *h.*

پاپ‌روگ पापरोग *pāp-rog*, m. a disease considered as the punishment of sin in a former life; small-pox, leprosy. *s.*

پاپڑ पापड़ *pāpaṛ* or *pāpar*, m. a thin crisp cake made of any grain. *pāpaṛ belnā*, to undergo great labour or pain. *s.*

پاپڑا पापड़ा *pāpṛā*, m. a kind of plant (*Gardenia latifolia Roxb.*). *s.*

پاپڑاکھار पापड़ाखार *pāpṛākhār* (in Dakh. *pāpaṛkhār*), m. ashes of the plantain tree (*Musa paradisiaca*), used instead of salt for seasoning the cakes called *pāpaṛ*. *s.*

پاپ‌سنمت पापसंमित *pāp-sammit*, equal in sin. *s.*

پاپشٹھ पापिष्ठ *pāpishṭha*, very wicked. *s.*

پاپ‌کر पापकर *pāp-kar*, wicked, abandoned. *s.*

پاپ‌کرت पापकृत *pāp-kṛit*, } sinful, wicked; a sinner. *s.*
پاپ‌کرتا पापकर्ता *pāp-kartā*, }

پاپ‌گره पापग्रह *pāp-grah*, m. any ill-omened aspect of the stars, as the conjunction of the sun or Budh with the moon in its last quarter. *Rahu*; Saturn; Mars. *s.*

پاپ‌گھن पापघ्न *pāp-ghna*, removing sin. *s.*

پاپ‌مت पापमति *pāp-mati*, of a corrupt mind, depraved. *s.*

پاپ‌مکت पापमुक्त *pāp-mukta*, freed from sin. *s.*

پاپن पापिन *pāpin*, } a female delinquent, sinner, criminal, &c. *s.*
پاپني पापनी *pāpnī*, }
or पापिनी *papinī*, }

پاپ‌ناشي पापनाशी *pāp-nāshī*, purifying, sin-destroying. *s.*

پاپوش *pā-posh*, f. a slipper. *p.*

پاپي पापी *pāpī*, m. a sinner, criminal. *s.*

پاپیا पापिया *pāpiyā*, the castor-oil tree. *h.*

پاپیاده *pā-piyāda*, on foot, walking. *p.*

پات पात *pāt*, m. falling; sin, wickedness; a leaf; an ornament worn in the upper part of the ear; a draft or cheque on a banker. *pāton ā-lagnā*, applied to trees, indicates the fall of their leaves in autumn; met. it signifies that one's power or ability is exhausted: it is often applied to patience exhausted by the scorn of a beloved person, or to a destitute condition from adverse fortune. *s.*

پات पाति *pāti*, m. a master, lord, husband. *s.*

پاتا पाता *pātā*, m. a leaf; adj. preserved, protected. *s.*

پاتابه *pā-tāba*, m. a sock; the straps of sandals, &c. *p.*

پاتال पाताल *pātāl*, m. regions (according to the Hindūs) under the earth, or towards the south pole, inhabited by a serpentine race; infernal regions, hell; a sort of apparatus for calcining and subliming metals, formed of two earthen pots, the upper one inverted over the lower, and the two joined together by their necks with cement, and placed in a hole containing fire. *s.*

پاتبندي *pāt-bandī*, a statement of the assets and debts of an estate. *h.p.*

پاتت पातित *pātit*, lowered, depressed, humbled. *s.*

پاتر पात्र *pātr* or *pātra*, m. a vessel in general, a plate, a cup, a jar, &c.; a leaf; a receptacle of any kind; what holds or supports; adj. worthy, able, eligible, fit, capable. *s.*

پاتر पातृ *pātṛi*, who or what protects or nourishes. *s.*

پاتر पात्त्र *pāttra*, m. a preservative from sin, a preserver, a saviour. *s.*

پاتر पातर *pātar* or पातुर *pātur*, f. a prostitute, a dancing-girl; adj. weak, lean. *pātur-bāz*, a whoremonger. *h.*

پاتر *pātar*, m. a moth, a butterfly. *d.*

پاترتا पात्रता *pātratā*, f. capacity, fitness. पातृता *pātṛitā*, m. a plant (*Ocymum pilosum*). *s.*

پاترتا पात्त्रता *pāttratā*, f. the quality of a preservative from sin. *s.*

پاترني *pātarnī*, f. (of *pātar*), a butterfly. *d.*

پاتریا पातुरिया *pāturiyā*, a whoremonger. *h.*

پاتک पातक *pātak*, m. sin, crime, vice. *s.*

پاتک पातुक *pātuk*, m. an aquatic animal of a large size; figuratively the water-elephant. *h.*

پاتک पातिक *pātik*, m. the Gangetic porpoise. *s.*

پاتکوا पातकवा *pātakwā*, m. a messenger. *s.*

پاتکي पातकी *pātakī*, criminal, wicked. *s.*

پاتلي पातिली *pātilī*, f. a small earthen pot used by religious mendicants. *s.*

پاتنجل पातञ्जल *pātanjal*, m. the Yog system of philosophy. *s.*

پاتھر पाथर *pāthar*, m. a stone (same as *patthar*). *s.*

پاتھنا पाथना *pāthnā*, a. to make up cow-dung into cakes for fuel. *h.*

پاتھیه पाथेय *pātheya*, m. provender, provisions for a journey. *s.*

پاتي पाती *pātī*, f. a letter, note, epistle; a leaf. *s*

پاتیله *pātīla* (also *pātila*), a kind of wide-mouthed saucepan used by confectioners. *p.*

پات पाट *pāṭ*, m. breadth (of cloth or of a river); tow; it also signifies a note or obligation to pay a sum of money for one's own account on an appointed day. It is often usual to accept these *pāṭs* from creditable persons, in payment of the arrears of the *zamīndārs* or renters. *h.*

پات पाट *pāṭ*, m. silk; a millstone; a throne, a seat; a board, shutter, plank, flap; a plank on which washermen beat clothes, the leaf of a door. *s.*

پات *pāṭ*, m. a bed or plot in a garden or field. *s.*

پاٹا पाटा *pāṭā*, m. a plank on which washermen beat clothes. *s.*

پاٹ رانی पाटरानी *pāṭ-rānī*, f. the queen, the principal wife of a rāja. *s.*

پاٹ کرم पाटकृम *pāṭ-kṛim* or *pāṭ-kiram*, m. a silkworm. *s.*

پاٹل पाटल *pāṭal*, m. rose-colour or pink. *s.*

پاٹلا पाटला *pāṭalā*, f. the trumpet flower (*Bignonia suaveolens*). *s.*

پاٹل پتر पाटलिपुत्र *pāṭali-putra*, m. the name of a city, supposed to be the ancient Palibothra and the modern Patna. *s.*

پاٹلوپل पाटलोपल *pāṭalopal*, m. a ruby. *s.*

پاٹمبر पाटम्बर *pāṭambar*, m. silk cloth, silk garment. *s.*

پاٹن पाटन *pāṭan*, f. a roof; m. name of a city, commonly called Patna; old inflect. plur. of *pāṭ*, a millstone (for *pāṭoṅ*). *h.*

پاٹن पाटिन *pāṭin*, m. a sort of fish described as having many teeth. *s.*

پاٹنا पाटना *pāṭnā*, a. to roof, to cover, to shut; to fill, to irrigate, to water, to pay; to overstock; to accumulate, to pile, to fill up. *h.*

پاٹو पाटव *pāṭav*, clever, sharp, dexterous; m. cleverness, talent, eloquence. *s.*

پاٹوک पाटविक *pāṭavik*, cunning, crafty, fraudulent; clever, dexterous. *s.*

پاٹونی पाटूनी *pāṭūnī* or पाटौनी *pāṭaunī*, m. a ferryman. *h.*

پاٹھ पाठ *pāṭh*, m. a lesson, reading; studying the Vedas or sacred writings. *s.*

پاٹھا पाठा *pāṭhā*, m. a young animal full grown (generally expressive of a goat or elephant); a youth or young wrestler. *h.*

پاٹھان पाठान *pāṭhān*, m. bdellium. *s.*

پاٹھ بھو पाठभू *pāṭh-bhū*, f. a place where the Vedas are read or studied. *s.*

پاٹھت पाठित *pāṭhit*, instructed, taught. *s.*

پاٹھ سالا पाठशाला *pāṭh-sālā* or *pāṭh-shālā*, f. a school, a college. *s.*

پاٹھ شالنی पाठशालिनी *pāṭh-shālinī*, f. a small bird (*Gracula religiosa*). *s.*

پاٹھک पाठक *pāṭhak*, m. he that gives lessons, a teacher, a professor; a lecturer, a public reader of the sacred writings, or a Pandit who declares what is the law; a spiritual preceptor; a title of Brāhmans. *s.*

پاٹھکا पाठहिका *pāṭhikā*, f. a small shrub (*Abrus precatorius*). *s.*

پاٹھ مار पाठमार *pāṭh-mār*, a courier or messenger, sent from place to place. *h.*

پاٹھ منچری पाठमञ्चरी *pāṭh-mancharī*, f. a small bird (*Gracula religiosa*). *s.*

پاٹھن पाठन *pāṭhan*, m. lecturing, teaching. *s.*

پاٹھی पाठी *pāṭhī*, m. a teacher (the same as *pāṭhak*); a plant (*Plumbago zelanica*); f. a young goat; a kind of fish. *s.*

پاٹھین पाठीन *pāṭhīn*, m. a sort of fish (*Silurus boalis*); a public reader or lecturer on the Purānas. *s.*

پاٹھیہ पाठ्य *pāṭhya*, adj. to be read or studied. *s.*

پاٹی पाटी *pāṭī*, f. the side pieces of a bedstead; a kind of mat; a board on which children learn to write; divisions of the hair which is combed towards the two sides and parted by a line in the middle; a kind of sweetmeat; m. a sort of fish, described as having many teeth. *s.*

پاٹیر पाटीर *pāṭīr*, m. a pungent root, a sort of radish; sandal. *h.*

پاجامہ *pā-jāma*, m. trousers, long drawers. *p.*

پاجی *pājī*, mean, base. *pājī-parast*, a patroniser of mean upstarts. *pājī-mizāj*, of a mean disposition. *p.*

پاجیانہ *pājiyanā*, meanly, in the manner of the base. *p.*

پاجی پنا *pājī-panā*, m. meanness, baseness. *p.*

پاجی مزاج *pājī-mizāj*, mean-spirited, base-souled. *p. a.*

پاچ पाच *pāch*, a sort of gem, emerald. *h.*

پاچک पाचक *pāchak*, digestive, tonic; m. a cook; the bile which assists in digestion; a digestive, a stomachic, a solvent. *s.*

پاچک *pāchak*, m. cow-dung dried for fuel. *p.*

پاچل पाचल *pāchal*, whatever promotes digestion. *s.*

پاچن पाचन *pāchan*, digestive, suppurative; m. a medicinal preparation an infusion of various drugs, chiefly carminatives or gentle stimuli, given to bring the vitiated humours to maturity, a diet-drink, a digestive (v. *pāchak*). *s.*

پاچنک पाचनक *pāchanak*, m. borax. *s.*

پاچنی पाचनी *pāchanī*, f. a sort of myrobalan (*Terminalia chebula*). *s.*

پاچہ *pācha*, m. (sheep's foot), foot. *p.*

پاچھ पाछ *pāchh*, m. the act of inoculating, inoculation. *h.*

پاچھنا पाछना *pāchhnā*, a. to inoculate. *h.*

پاچھے पाछे *pāchhe*, پاچھین पाछें *pāchhen*, } after, afterwards, behind, in the absence of (v. *pīchhe*). *s.*

پاد पाद *pād*, m. the foot; a foot, a quarter; the foot or line of a stanza; emission of wind downwards. *pād-mārnā*, to emit wind backwards. *s.*

پادارده पादार्द्ध *pādārddha*, m. half a line of a stanza. *s.*

پاداسن पादासन *pādāsan*, m. a foot-stool. *s.*

پاداش *pādāsh*, } m. revenge, retaliation;
پاداشت *pādāsht*, } recompense, retribution, reward. *p.*

پادانگشٹھ पादाङ्गुष्ठ *pādāngushṭh*, m. the great toe. *s.*

پادانگشٹکا पादाङ्गुष्ठिका *pādāngushṭhikā*, f. an ornament or ring worn on the great toe. *s.*

پادانون पादानोन *pādā-non*, m. black salt, prepared by melting common salt with a small proportion of *myrobalans*: it contains sulphur. *h.*

پاداهت पादाहत *pādāhat*, kicked, trodden, touched by the foot. *s.*

پادپ पादप *pādap*, m. a footstool, a cushion for the feet. *s.*

پادپا पादपा *pād-pā*, f. a shoe, a slipper. *s.*

پادپرکشالن पादप्रक्षालन *pād-prakshālan*, m. washing the feet. *s.*

پادپرنام पादप्रणाम *pād-pranām*, m. bowing to the feet, prostration. *s.*

پادپ رها पादपरुहा *pādap-ruhā*, f. a creeping or parasite plant. *s.*

پادپرهار पादप्रहार *pād-prahār*, m. a kick. *s.*

پادتل पादतल *pād-tal*, m. the sole of the foot; adv. under the feet. *s.*

پادج पादज *pādaj*, m. a *sūdra*, a man of the fourth caste. *s.*

پادچاپلیه पादचापल्य *pād-chāpalya*, m. beating or shuffling with the feet. *s.*

پادچار पादचार *pād-chār*, on foot. *s.*

پادچاري पादचारी *pād-chārī*, m. a footman, a foot soldier. *s.*

پادچتور पादचत्वर *pād-chatwar*, m. the religious fig-tree (*Ficus religiosa*). *s.*

پادداري पाददारी *pād-dārī*, f. a chap in the feet, a chilblain. *s.*

پادراز *pā-durāz*, contented, tranquil, at ease. *p.*

پادراکیڑا पाद्राकीड़ा *pādrā-kīrā*. the ant lion, an insect which constructs a hole in the ground as a trap for ants, on which it feeds. *h.*

پادروهن पादरोहण *pād-rohan*, m. the Indian fig-tree. *s.*

پادري *pādrī*, m. a Christian priest of any denomination (the word was introduced into India by the Portuguese).

پادزهر *pādzahr*, m. the name of a medicine, expeller of poison (*Bezoar stone*). *p.*

پادسپهوٹ पादस्फोट *pād-sphoṭ*, m. kibe, chilblain, an ulcer in the foot. *s.*

پادشاکها पादशाखा *pād-shākhā*, f. a toe. *s.*

پادشاه *pādshāh*, a king, a sovereign (same as *bādshāh*). *pādshāh-zāda*, a prince. *pādshāh-zādī*, a princess. *p.*

پادشاهانا *pādshāhānā*, fit for, or worthy of a king; kingly. *p.*

پادشاهت *pādshāhat*, f. sovereign power, royalty. *p.*

پادشاهي *pādshāhī*, f. royalty; adj. of or belonging to a king, royal. *p.*

پادشبد पादशब्द *pād-shabd*, m. the sound of feet. *s.*

پادشوتھ पादशोथ *pād-shoth*, m. swelling of the feet, gout. *s.*

پادك पादुक *pāduk*, who or what goes on foot, or with feet. *s.*

پادکا पादुका *pādukā*, f. a shoe, a slipper. *s.*

پادکٹك पादकटक *pād-kaṭak*, m. an ornament for the feet or toes. *s.*

پادگرهن पादग्रहण *pād-grahan*, m. respectful obeisance, touching the feet of a superior. *s.*

پادگنڈر पादगण्डिर *pād-ganḍir*, m. morbid enlargement of the legs and feet. *s.*

پادگهابرا पादघाबरा *pād-ghābrā*, frightened out of one's wits. *h.*

پادمول पादमूल *pād-mūl*, m. the heel. *s.*

پادنا पादना *pādnā*, to emit wind (backwards). *s.*

پادو पादू *pādū*, f. a shoe. *s.*

پادودك पादोदक *pādodak*, m. water for the feet, especially that in which the feet of a Brāhman have been washed. *s.*

پادوك पादविक *pādvik*, m. a traveller, a wayfarer. *s.*

پادولميك पादवल्मीक *pād-valmīk*, m. morbid enlargement of the legs and feet. *s.*

پادها पाधा *pādhā*, m. a schoolmaster. *s.*

پادهارك पादहारक *pād-hārak*, m. one who takes or steals with his feet. *s.*

پادهت पादहत *pād-hat*, trodden on, kicked, struck with the feet. *h.*

پادهرش पादहर्ष *pād-harsh*, m. tingling of the feet, caused by pressure upon the crural nerves. *s.*

پادي पादी *pādī*, footed, having feet; m. a footed aquatic animal, an amphibious animal. *s.*

پادي पादी *pādī*, rice in the husks. *h.*

پادیه पाद्य *pādya*, m. water for washing the feet. *s.*

پادیه پاتر पाद्यपात्र *pādya-pātra*, m. a metal vessel for washing the feet. *s.*

پاڈها पाढा *pāḍhā*, m. a hog-deer (v. *pāṛhā*). *s.*

پاڈهي पाढी *pāḍhī*, f. the act of crossing a river. *h.*

پار पार *pār*, m. the opposite bank or shore; adv. over, across, on the other side, through. *pār-k.*, to ferry over, to cross; to finish; to perforate; to relieve; to carry off. *pār-ho-janā*, to escape; to attain refuge. *s.*

پارا *pārā*, m. a sentinel or sentry; a watchman. *d.*

پارا पारा *pārā*, m. quicksilver, mercury; f. a river, said to flow from the Pāriyātr mountains, a portion of the Vindhya chain. *pāre-kā kāfūr*, calomel. *s.*

پاراپار पारापार *pārāpār*, m. the two banks of a river. *s.*

پاراشر पाराशर *pārāshar*, m. a name of the poet Vyāsa; the rules of Vyāsa for the conduct of the mendicant orders. *s.*

پاراشري पाराशरी *pārāsharī*, m. the religious mendicant, who, having passed through the three stages of student, householder, and ascetic, leads a vagrant life, and subsists upon alms. *s.*

پاراوار पारावार *pārāwār*, on both sides (of a river); m. limit (of sea); sea, ocean. *s.*

پاراوت पारावत *pārāwat*, m. a sort of ebony (*Diospyros glutinosa*). *s.*

پاراوتي पारावती *pārāwatī*, f. a river in the peninsula; the fruit of the *Annona reticulata*; a form of song peculiar to the cowherds. *s.*

پارايں पारायण *pārāyan*, m. totality, completeness; the act of reading a *Purān* continually, without expressing its meaning. *s.*

پاراينك पारायणिक *pārāyanik*, m. a lecturer, a reader of the Purānas. *s.*

پاربهاويه पारिभाव्य *pāribhāvya*, m. a drug, a sort of costus (*Costus speciosus*). *s.*

پاربهدر पारिभद्र *pāri-bhadra*, m. the coral tree (*Erythrina fulgens*); the nimb tree; a sort of pine (*Pinus devadaru*); the *surul*; also a sort of pine (*Pinus longifolia*). *s.*

پارپاتر पारिपात्र *pāripātra*, m. name of a mountain, apparently the central or western portion of the Vindhya chain, which skirts the province of Mālwa. *s.*

پارپنتهك पारिपन्थिक *pāripanthik*, m. a robber, a thief, a highwayman. *s.*

پارتتهيا पारितथ्या *pāritathyā*, f. a trinket worn on the forehead where the hair is parted. *s.*

پارتوشك पारितोषिक *pāritoshik*, gratifying, giving satisfaction; m. a reward, gratuity. *s.*

پارتهكيه पार्थक्य *pārthakya*, m. severalty, individuality, difference. *s.*

پارتهو पार्थिव *pārthiv*, earthen, terrestrial; ruling the earth; m. a king; an earthen vessel. *s.*

پارجات पारिजात *pārijāt*, m. a tree that grows in paradise: the coral tree (*Erythrina fulgens*). *s.*

پارجايك पारजायिक *pār-jāyik*, m. an adulterer. *s.*

پارچه *pārcha*, m. fragment, piece, scrap; cloth, web, a piece of cloth. *p.*

پارد पारद *pārad*, m. quicksilver. *s.*

پاردارجيه पारदार्य *pār-dārjya*, m. adultery. *s.*

پاردارك पारदारिक *pār-dārik*, m. an adulterer. *s.*

پاردرشون पारदृश्वन *pār-drishwan*, long-sighted, far-seeing, wise. *s.*

پاردنڈك पारदण्डक *pār-dandak*, m. name of a country, part of Orissa. *s.*

پاردیشك पारदेशिक *pār-deshik*, foreign, abroad; m. a traveller, a foreigner. *s.*

پارديشي पारदेशी *pār-deshī*, f. } belonging
پارديشيه पारदेश्य *pār-deshya*, m. } to another
country; m. a traveller, one gone to another country; a foreigner. *s.*

پارس पारस *pāras*, m. the philosopher's stone; a touchstone for gems; adj. Persian. *s.*

پارس *pāris* or *pārs*, m. Persia. *p.*

پارسا *pārsā*, abstemious, chaste, watchful; a holy man, a devotee. *p.*

پارسال *pār-sāl*, the year before; last year. *p.*

پارسائي *pārsā,ī*, f. chastity, purity, abstinence, holiness. *p.*

پارس‌پتهر पारसपत्थर *pāras-patthar*, } m. the
پارس‌پتهل पारसपत्थल *pāras-patthal*, } philo-
sopher's stone. The *pāras patthar*, according to Hindū legends, was a stone which, on touching any metal, immediately converted it into gold. It was found in ancient times by a grasscutter, who, accidentally touching it with his scythe, was astonished to find that implement turned into gold. It then found its way into the hands of the rājā of that part of the country, who one day, in a fit of generosity, presented this invaluable stone to a Brāhman. The Brāhman, not knowing the virtue of the gift, and being displeased at receiving a present apparently so worthless, threw the stone into the Nerbudda. When he was informed of what he had done, struck with shame and remorse, he plunged into the river in order to recover it if possible, but the water was so deep, that he could not reach the bottom. That part of the Nerbudda is said to be unfathomable, hence, unfortunately, no man has, ever since, found the stone aforesaid (Binning). *s.*

پارس‌پيپل पारसपीपल *pāras-pīpal*, m. the name of a tree (*Hibiscus populneoides, Roxb.*); also the tulip tree. *s.*

پارسك पारसिक *pārsik*, m. Persian. *s.*

پارسي *pārsī*, m. a Persian, the Persian language; a follower of Zoroaster; a fire-worshipper. *p.*

پارسيك पारसीक *pārsīk*, m. (same as *pārsī*), Persian, the kingdom of Persia; a Persian horse, &c. *s.*

پارشد पारिषद *pārishad*, m. a spectator, a person present at an assembly. *s.*

پارشو पारशव *pārshav*, m. the son of a Sūdra woman by a Brāhman; a son by another's wife, an adulterine; an iron weapon. *s.*

پارشو पार्श्व *pārshwa*, near, proximate, by the side of; m. a side, flank. *s.*

پارشوبهاگ पार्श्वभाग *pārshwa-bhāg*, m. the side, flank. *s.*

پارشوشول पार्श्वशूल *parshwa-shūl*, m. spasm of the chest, stitch. *s.*

پارشوك पार्श्विक *pārshwik*, lateral; m. a partisan, a sidesman, a companion. *s.*

پارشوگت पार्श्वगत *pārshwa-gat*, close to, beside. *h.*

پارشيك पारशीक *pārshīk*, same as *pārsīk*, Persian, &c. *s.*

پارشيه पारुष्य *pārushya*, m. aloe wood or *agallochum*: in law, this term denotes harshness or violence. *danda-pārushya*, assault and battery. *vāk-pārushya*, slander, calumny, libel. *s.*

پارك पारक *pārak*, what purifies, protects, cherishes; what enables one to cross (a river) or go through the world. *s.*

پارکانکشي पारिकाङ्क्षी *pārikānkshī*, m. an ascetic, one who lives in devout contemplation. *s.*

پارکهي पारखी *pārkhī*, m. an examiner. *s.*

پارگ पारग *pārag*, crossing, going over or beyond the world. *s.*

پارگت पारगत *pār-gat*, crossed, gone over; pure, holy; a Jin, or Jain, deified teacher. *s.*

پارل पारल *pāral*, m. name of a plant (*Bignonia chelonoides* or *Bignonia suaveolens, Roxb.*). *s.*

پارلوکك पारिलौकिक *pārilaukik*, belonging to the next world. *s.*

پارمارتهك पारमार्थिक *pārmārthik*, preferable, best, most desirable. *s.*

پارمپرج पारम्पर्य *pāramparj*, m. traditional instruction, tradition, continuous order or succession. *s.*

پارمپرجوپديش पारम्पर्योपदेश *pāramparjopadesh*, m. traditional instruction. *s.*

پارن पारण *pāran*, m. a cloud; eating or drinking after a fast. *s.*

پارنايه पारिणाय *pārināya*, m. property received at the time of marriage by a woman. *s.*

پارنا पारना *pārnā*, a. to finish, to perform. *s.*

پارنا पारना *pārnā*, m. breaking a fast. *s.*

پاروار पारवार *pārwār*, on both sides (of a river); quite through, through and through. *s.*

پاروت पार्वत *pārvat*, m. a tree called the large nimb (*Melia sempervirens*). *s.*

پاروتي पार्वती *pārwatī*, f. daughter of *parwat*, a mountain, q.d. mountain-born; the goddess *Durgā*, the wife of *Shiva*; the olibanum tree (*Boswellia thurifera*); another tree (*Celtis orientalis*). *s.*

پاروتيه पार्वतीय *pārvatīya*, adj. mountainous. *s.*

پارون पार्वण *pārvan*, m. the general funeral ceremony to be offered to all the manes at the *Parva* or junction of the sun and moon, at which double oblations to the ancestors are offered. *s.*

پاره *pāra*, m. a strap, a slip, a piece, a bit; *pāra-doz*, m. a patcher; a tent-maker, or one who applies the leather parts in tents, screens, &c. *p.*

پاري पारी *pārī*, f. time, tour, turn. *s.*

پارياتر पारियात्र *pāriyātra*, m. name of a mountain (same as *pāripātra*). *s.*

پاريندر पारीन्द्र *pārīndra*, m. a lion; a large snake (*boa*). *s.*

پارينه *pārīna*, ancient, past, elapsed. *pārīna daftar*, an ancient record. *p.*

پاڙ पाड़ *pāṛ*, f. a scaffold. *s.*

پاڙا पाड़ा *pāṛā*, m. a quarter of a town, ward; (in Dakh.) a calf. *h.*

پاڙپڙنا *pāṛ-paṛnā*, to sustain an injury, to receive a blow. *d.*

پاڙنا पाड़ना *pāṛnā*, a. to let fall; to collect lamp-black; (Dakh.) to finish, to accomplish. *h.*

پاڙوا पाड़वा *pāṛwā* (same as *salkh*, q. v.). *d.*

پاڙها पाढ़ा *pāṛha*, m. a hog-deer (*Cervus porcinus*). *h.*

پاڙهي पाढ़ी *pāṛhī*, f. crossing a river (when travelling on it); a young buffalo, a calf. *h.*

پازهر *pāzahr*, f. bezoar stone. *p.*

پاس पास *pās*, m. a rope, a noose (v. *pāsh*). *s.*

پاس पास *pās*, near, about, at, in the possession of. *s.*

پاس *pās*, m. watch, guard, defence; a space of about three hours (the same as *pahr*, q. v.), observance, preservation. *pās i khāṭir*, attention to (one's) wishes. *p.*

پاسا पासा *pāsā*, m. a die (pl. *pāse*, dice), the long dice with which *chaupar* is played); a throw of dice. *s.*

پاسبان *pās-bān*, m. a watchman, guard, sentinel; a shepherd, protector. *p.*

پاسباني *pāsbānī*, f. watch, guard, protection, keeping. *p.*

پاستان *pāstān*, former, of yore. *p.*

پاسداري *pās-dārī*, f. watching, guardianship. *p.*

پاسنگ *pā-sang*, m. a weight or make-weight, an equipoise, a balance. *p.*

پاسي पासी *pāsī*, f. a net; a rope with which the legs of a horse are bound. *s.*

پاسي पासी *pāsī*, m. a fowler; one whose business is to make *tāṛī* or *tāṛī* (so named from the rope round his leg when he climbs the *tāṛ* tree). *s.*

پاسي *pāsī* (from *pās*), a watchman; (ours were called "watchy," from "watch," in my young days). *p.*

پاش *pāsh*, (in comp.) scattering, sprinkling. *p.*

پاش पाश *pāsh*, m. a fetter, chain, tie; the string for fastening tame animals, the net or noose for catching birds, deer, &c.; a noose, a weapon of combat. *s.*

پاشا पाशा *pāshā*, m. a die, a throw of dice. *s.*

پاشان पाषाण *pāshān*, m. a stone. *s.*

پاشان‌بهيدي पाषाणभेदी *pāshān-bhedī*, m. a plant (*Plectanthus scutellaroides*). *s.*

پاش‌بدهه पाशबद्ध *pāsh-baddha*, noosed, snared, caught, bound. *s.*

پاش‌پاش *pāsh-pāsh*, broken to pieces, shivered. *d.*

پاش‌بندهه पाशबन्ध *pāsh-bandh*, m. a noose, a snare, a halter, a net. *s.*

پاشت पाशित *pāshit*, tied, fettered, bound. *s.*

پاش‌چاتيه पाश्चात्य *pāsh-chātya*, adj. behind, being behind, subsequent; western. *s.*

پاشك पाशक *pāshak*, m. a die, particularly the oblong die used to play *chaupar*. *s.*

پاشك पाषक *pāshak*, m. an ornament for the feet. *h.*

پاشنڈ पाषण्ड *pāshanḍ*, } m. a heretic, an impostor, a sectarian, a Jaina, a Bauddha or Būddhist. *s.*
پاشنڈي पाषण्डी *pāshanḍī*, }

پاشنه *pāshna* or *pāshina*, m. the heel. *p.*

پاشويه *pā-shoya*, m. feet-washing. *p.*

پاشي *pāshī*, f. diffusion, scattering. *p.*

پاشي पाशी *pāshī*, m. one armed with a net or noose. *s.*

پاشيدن *pāshīdan*, to sprinkle, to scatter. *p.*

پاك *pāk*, pure, clean, upright. *pāk-burdan*, to carry clean off. *pāk-sokhtan*, to burn or be burnt utterly. *p.*

پاك पाक *pāk*, m. an electuary medicine, a confection. *s.*

پاكباز *pāk-bāz*, undefiled (generally applied to the mind). *p.*

پاكبازي *pāk-bāzī*, f. purity (generally of mind. *h.*

پاك پهل पाकफल *pāk-phal*, m. the Caronda (*Carissa carondus*). *s.*

پاك دامن *pāk-dāman*, chaste, pure. *p.*

پاكدامني *pāk-dāmanī*, f. chastity, purity. *p.*

پاك رنجن पाकरञ्जन *pāk-ranjan*, m. the leaf of the *Laurus cassia*. *s.*

پاك رو *pāk-rau*, upright in conduct. *p.*

پاكڑ पाकड़ *pākaṛ*, } the citron-leaved
پاكڑيا पाकड़िया *pākaṛiyā*, } Indian fig-tree (*Ficus venosa*). *h.*

پاك زاده *pāk-zāda*, a washerman. *d.*

پاك ستهان पाकस्थान *pāk-sthān*, m. a kitchen. *s.*

پاك سنڑسي पाकसंड़सी *pāk-sanṛsī*, f. a table-vice, a bench-vice (this is a modern name for the instrument which was introduced by Europeans). *h.*

پاك شالا पाकशाला *pāk-shālā*, m. a kitchen. *s.*

پاكشيه पाक्ष्य *pākshya*, belonging to a side or party. *s.*

پاك صاف *pāk-ṣāf*, pure, clean, undefiled, unpolluted. *a. p.*

پاك صافي *pāk-ṣāfī*, f. purity, sanctity. *p.*

پاكل पाकल *pākal*, producing maturity, suppurative; m. *Costus speciosus*. *s.*

پاكل पाकलि *pākali*, m. a plant (*Bauhinia candida*). *s.*

پاكلي पाकली *pākalī*, f. a sort of cucumber (*Cucumis usitatissimus*). *s.*

پاكنا पाकना *pāknā*, n. to boil in syrup. *s.*

پاكها पाखा *pākhā*, m. a shed, any small building leaning against the wall of a yard or area. *h.*

پاكهان पाषाण *pākhān* or *pāshān*, m. a stone. *s.*

پاكهر पाखर *pākhar*, f. an iron armour for the defence of a horse or elephant. *h.*

پاكهنڈ पाखण्ड *pākhanḍ* or पाषण्ड *pāshanḍ*, m. wickedness, deceit, hypocrisy, heresy, a heretic, a heterodox Hindū, adopting the exterior marks of the classes, but not respecting the ordinances of the Vedas. *s.*

پاكهنڈي पाखण्डी *pākhanḍī* or पाषण्डी *pāshanḍī*, deceitful, hypocritical, heretical, wicked. *s.*

پاكي *pākī*, f. purity, cleansing. *pākī-lenā*, a. to shave or pluck hair from parts concealed. *p.*

پاكيزگي *pākīzagī*, f. cleanliness, purity, neatness. *p.*

پاكيزه *pākīza*, clean, pure, neat. *pākīza-rau*, innocent, of pure conduct. *p.*

پاكيه पाक्य *pākya*, m. *Bitlaban*, a medicinal salt, impregnated with iron; nitre, saltpetre. *s.*

پاگ पाग *pāg*, f. a turban; syrup; a poll-tax formerly levied on all males over twelve years of age. *s.*

پاگا पागा *pāgā*, m. a troop of horse; (among *Marhattās*) a stud. *h.*

پاگر पागुर *pāgur*, m. act of chewing the cud; rumination. *h.*

پاگرانا पागुराना *pāgurānā*, a. to chew the cud, to ruminate. *h.*

پاگل पागल *pāgal*, m. a fool, idiot, madman (a word peculiar to Bengal, and vulgarly sounded *pogle*). *h.*

پال पाल *pāl*, m.f. shelter; a sail; a small tent; layers of straw, leaves, &c., between which unripe mangoes are ripened; a dyke or dam; crown lands kept in the hands of government. *h.*

پالا पाला *pālā*, m. frost, hoar frost, snow; trust, charge; cherishing, protecting, fostering; a heap of earth made by children to separate the two parties in a game called *kabaḍḍī*; leaves of a tree named *jhaṛberī* (a species of *Zizyphus*) *pālā-paṛna*, n. to snow. *pāle-paṛnā*, to fall within the power of another. *s.*

پالاش पालाश *pālāsh*, green; belonging to the palās tree, made of its wood; m. green colour. *s.*

پالاش كهنڈ पालाशखण्ड *pālāsh-khanḍ*, m. a country in India, the western part of Behar. *s.*

پالاگن पालागन *pā-lāgan*, m. obeisance performed by embracing the feet; reverence, respect, veneration. *s.*

پالان *pālān*, m. pack-saddles, dorsers. *p.*

پالت पालित *pālit*, cherished, nourished. *s.*

پالايش *pālāyish*, f. filtration, percolation. *p.*

پالغز *pā-laghz*, a slip of the foot, a stumble; met. error, ruin. *p.*

پالك पालक *pālak*, one who protects, nourishes, &c. m. a kind of green (a species of spinach); a bedstead. *s.*

پالك पालिक *pālik* or *pālak*, m. a cherisher, a protector, a guardian, a watchman, a preserver. *pālak-putr*, adopted son. *pālak-beṭa*, a boy who has been bought of his parents, hence a slave. *s.*

پالك جوهي पालकजूही *pālak-jūhī*, f. name of a medicinal tree (*Justicia nasuta*, also *Ixora undulata Roxb.*) *h.*

پالكري पालकरी *pā-lakrī*, f. blocks of wood placed under the feet of a bed to raise it (it is the custom to have two such blocks ready to raise the head of a bed, to give it a sloping position). *h.*

پالكڑا पालकड़ा *pālakṛā*, m. a child adopted as a son. *palakṛī*, an adopted daughter. *h.*

پالكي पालकी *pālkī*, f. a litter, a sedan, commonly called by Europeans *palankeen*. *pālkī-sawār*, one who rides in a *pālkī*. *pālkī-nishīn*, entitled to be carried in a *pālkī* (formerly this privilege was granted to individuals by a king or viceroy). *h.*

پالن पालन *pālan*, m. bringing up, rearing, breeding. *s.*

پالنا पालना *pālnā*, a. to bring up, to breed, to educate; to guard, to protect; m. a cradle. *s.*

پالند पालिन्द *pālind*, m. a sort of jasmine (*Jasminum pubescens*). *s.*

پالندهي पालिन्धी *pālindhī*, f. a plant commonly called *teorī* (*Convolvulus turpethum*) the black sort. *s.*

پالنك पालङ्क *pālank*, m. olibanum tree (*Boswellia thurifera*); a sort of beet-root (*Beta Bengalensis*); a hawk. *s.*

پالنكي पालङ्की *pālankī*, } f. incense, the gum
پالنكيا पालङ्क्या *pālankyā*, } or resin of the olibanum. *s.*

پالهنگ *pā-lahang*, m. a tether, a halter. *p.*

پالي पाली *pālī*, who or what nourishes or protects; m. a cowherd; f. a battle between birds; a place where birds fight; a covering of a pot. *h.*

پاليز *pālez*, f. a melon-field. *p.*

پاما पामा *pāmā*, f. cutaneous eruption, herpes, scab. *s.*

پامار पामारि *pāmāri*, m. sulphur. *s.*

پامال *pā-māl*, } trodden under foot, ruined,
پايمال *pā,e-māl*, } devastated. *p.*

پامالي *pā-mālī*, } f. ruin, devastation. *p.*
پايمالي *pā,e-mālī*, }

پامر पामर *pāmar*, adj. wicked, vile, base; stupid, idiot, fool. *s.* [lour. *p.*

پامردي *pā-mardī*, f. strength; resolution, valour. *p.*

پامري पामरी *pāmarī*, f. silken clothes, silk dress; the wife of a man of inferior caste. *h.*

پامن पामन *pāman*, diseased with herpes. *s.*

پان पान *pān*, m. act of drinking; drink in general; betel leaf (leaves of *Piper betel*); (in Dakh.) a leaf (of any plant in general). *pān uṭhānā* or *pān lenā* (to accept or take the betel leaf), to consent, to agree. *s.*

پان पाणि *pāni*, m. the hand. *s.*

پانا पाना *pānā*, a. to get, to acquire, to find, to enjoy, to suffer, to overtake, to reach, to accept, to obtain; m. a plant growing in stagnant water. *s.*

پان بهج पाणिभुज *pāni-bhuj*, m. the glomerous fig-tree. (*Ficus glomerata*). *s.*

پانپ पांप *pāmp*, sin, crime (v. *pāp*); also agony, anguish, torture. *h.*

پان پاتر पानपात्र *pān-pātra*, m. a glass, a drinking vessel. *s.*

پانپي पांपी *pāmpī*, wicked, criminal, sinful. *h*

پانت पांत *pānt*, f. a line (of writing); a rank of soldiers, a row. *s.*

پانتر पांतर *pāntar*, m. a desert field. *s.*

پانتهہ पान्थ *pānth*, m. a traveller. *s.*

پانتي पांती *pāntī*, f. a row. *s.*

پانجر पाञ्जर *pānjar*, m. the ribs, the side; a side or quarter (synon. with *ṭaraf*). *s.*

پانچ पांच *pānch*, five; (in Dakh.) an emerald. *s.*

پانچال पाञ्चाल *pānchāl*, belonging to the country of Panchāl; m. the sovereign of Panchāl; the company or association of five trades, viz. carpenter, weaver, barber, washerman, and shoemaker. *s.*

پانچ جهٹانك पांचछटांक *pānch chhaṭānk*, a toll of five *chhaṭānks* (q. v.) in a *rūpī's* worth of rice or paddy, established in large cities to defray the expense of inspectors of weighmen, stationed in the bāzārs, &c. to prevent fraud in the weight and measure of commodities sold therein. *h.*

پانچوان पांचवां *pānchwān*, the fifth. *s.*

پانچي *pānchī*, f. a kind of weed growing in tanks and pools. *d.*

پاندان पानदान *pān-dān*, m. a box for holding betel and its apparatus. *s. p.*

پانڈ पाण्डु *pānḍu*, pale or yellowish white; m pale or yellowish white colour; name of an ancient king of India, and nominal father of the five Pānḍava princes; f. a plant commonly called Mashani (*Glycine debilis*). *s.*

پانڈبهوم पाण्डुभूम *pānḍu-bhūm*, m. a country with a light-coloured soil. *s.*

پانڈپتر पाण्डुपुत्र *pānḍu-putra*, m. son of Pānḍu, either of the Pānḍava princes. *s.*

پانڈتي पाण्डिती *pānḍitī*, f. scholarship, learning. *s.*

پانڈر पाण्डर *pānḍar* or पाण्डुर *pānḍur*, pale or yellowish white; m. pale or yellowish white colour. *pānḍar*, the many flowered jasmine. *pānḍur*, the white leprosy; vitiligo. *s.*

پانڈرا पांडरा *pānḍrā*, m. a species of sugar-cane. *s.*

پانڈرپشپكا पाण्डरपुष्पिका *pānḍar-pushpikā*, f. a plant commonly called *sitalā* (perhaps *Phrynium dichotomum*). *s.*

پانڈردرم पाण्डुरद्रुम *pānḍur-drum*, m. a plant (*Echites antidysenterica*). *s.*

پانڈشركرا पाण्डुशर्करा *pānḍu-sharkarā*, f. light-coloured gravel (*disease*). *s.*

پانڈكمبل पाण्डुकम्बल *pānḍu-kambal*, m. a kind of stone, limestone or marble. *s.*

پانڈلوما पाण्डुलोमा *pānḍu-lomā*, f. a plant (*Glycine debilis*). *s.*

پانڈمرتكا पाण्डुमृत्तिका *pānḍu-mrittikā*, f. the opal, a pale soil. *s.*

پانڈناگ पाण्डुनाग *pānḍu-nāg*, m. a plant (*Rotleria tinctoria*). *s.*

پانڈو पाण्डव *pānḍav* or *pānḍava*, a descendant of king *Pānḍu*, but more especially his five sons distinguished in the great wars detailed in the *Mahābhārata*. *s.*

پانڈُورن पाण्डुवर्ण *pāṇḍu-varna*, adj. white; m. whiteness. *s.*

پانڈُوا पांडुवा *pāṅḍuwā*, m. a light-coloured soil; a mixed soil of clay and sand. *s.*

پانڈي पाण्डे *pāṅḍe*, } m. a title of Brāhmans,
پانڑي पाण्ड़े *pāṅṛe*, } a priest, a teacher. *s.*

پانزده *pānzdah*, fifteen. *panzdahum*, fifteenth. *p.*

پانس पांस *pāṅs*, m. manure, a dunghill. *pāṅs ho jānā*, n. to rot, to become mellow (land). *s.*

پانسُ पांसु *pāṅsu*, f. a rib, the rib bones. *s.*

پانسا पांसा *pāṅsā*, m. (lit. a throw), a die (v. *pāsā*) *h.*

پانسنا पांसना *pāṅsnā*, a. to manure. *h.*

پانسو पांसौ *pāṅsau*, } five hundred. *pāṅsū*, a
پانسي पांसै *pāṅsai*, } rib bone. *s.*

پانسي पांसी *pāṅsī*, a net for carrying grass or straw. *h.*

پانش पांशु *pāṅshu*, m. manure. *s.*

پانش پتر पांशुपुत्र *pāṅshu-putra*, m. a pot-herb (*Chenopodium album*). *s.*

پانشج पांशुज *pāṅshuj*, m. salt extracted from soil, rock or fossil salt. *s.*

پانشکا पांशुका *pāṅshukā*, f. a fragrant plant (*Pandanus odoratissimus*). *s.*

پانشکاسیس पांशुकासीस *pāṅshukāsīs*, m. sulphuret of iron. *s.*

پانشل पांशुल *pāṅshul*, m. a kind of tree (*Cisalpinia bonducella*). *s.*

پانك पांक *pāṅk*, m. a bog, mire, mud, slough, quagmire. *s.*

پانكت पंक्त *pāṅkta*, linear, in line or row. *s.*

پانگ पांग *pāṅg*, mud left by inundations; alluvial soil. *h.*

پانگا पांगा *pāṅgā*, m. culinary salt, obtained from the sea-sand, as by the process in use on the sea-coast of Bengal. *h.*

پان گرهن पाणिग्रहण *pāṇi-grahan*, m. marriage, the junction of the hands of the bride and bridegroom. *pāṇi-grahanik*, matrimonial. *s.*

پان گرهيتا पाणिगृहीता *pāṇi-gṛihītā*, f. a bride, one wedded according to the ritual. *s.*

پانن पाणिनि *pāṇini*, m. a *muni* and inspired grammarian. *s.*

پانِنيه पाणिनीय *pāṇinīya*, belonging to Pāṇini the grammarian. *s.*

پانو पांव *pāṅw*, m. leg, foot. *pāṅw utarnā*, to be dislocated (the foot). *pāṅw uṭhānā* or *chalānā*, to go quickly. *pāṅw uṛānā*, to interfere unprofitably in any one's affairs. *pāṅw baṛhānā*, to take the lead among one's equals; to desist from one's former courses. *pāṅw bhar-jānā*, numbness of the feet, sleeping of the feet. *pāṅw-pāṅw* or *pāṅoṅ-pāṅoṅ*, on foot. *pāṅw par pāṅw rakhnā*, to imitate or adopt the conduct of another; to walk in the steps of another; to sit at ease, to sit cross-legged. *pāṅw-paṛnā*, to entreat submissively. *pāṅw pakaṛnā*, to beseech submissively; to prevent one from going. *pāṅw pūjnā*, to honour another; to avoid another. *pāṅw phailākar sonā*, (lit. to sleep with legs extended) is applied to signify that a person is in perfect content and security. *pāṅw phallānā*, to insist, be obstinate. *pāṅw phūk phūk rakhnā*, to do any thing carefully. *pāṅw pīṭnā*, to stamp with impatience. *pāṅw tale malnā*, to give one pain, to annoy. *pāṅw-toṛnā*, to desist from visiting any person; also to visit one very often; to be tired. *pāṅw ṡābit rakhnā*, to persevere firmly in a resolution. *pāṅw jamānā*, to stand firmly. *pāṅw chal-jānā*, to totter, to become unstable. *pāṅw dho dho pīnā* (lit. to drink the water with which one's feet are washed) expresses perfect confidence. *pāṅw ḍālnā*, to prepare for and commence an undertaking. *pāṅw ḍignā*, to slip. *pāṅw ragaṛnā*, to go about foolishly and unprofitably; to be in the agonies of death. *pāṅw zamīn par na ṭhaharnā* is used to indicate excessive joy. *pāṅw-sonā*, to be numbed, to sleep (the foot). *pāṅw se pāṅw bāndhnā* to watch one close. *pāṅw se pāṅw bhiṛānā*, to be near. *pāṅw ḳā,im-k.*, to occupy a fixed habitation; to adopt a new resolution. *pāṅw kā anguṭhā*, m. the great toe. *pāṅw kāmpnā* or *thartharānā*, to fear to attempt any thing. *pāṅw kisī kā ukhāṛnā*, to move any person from his place, from his intention or resolution. *pāṅw kisī kā gale meṅ ḍālnā*, to convict one by his own arguments. *pāṅw kī unglī*, f. or *pāṅw kā anguṭhā*, m. a toe. *pāṅw gāṛnā*, to plant one's feet, to stand immoveable. *pāṅw lagnā*, to make obeisance. *pāṅw nikālnā*, to exceed one's proper limits; to withdraw from an undertaking; to be a ringleader in a criminal action. *dabe pāṅw ānā*, to come gently and unperceived as a spy. *s.*

پانوروٹي पांवरोटी *pāṅw-roṭī*, f. a kind of loaf. *h.*

پانوڑا पांवड़ा *pāṅwṛā*, m. a cloth or carpet spread for great personages to walk on. *h.*

پانون पांवों *pāṅoṅ* (for *pāṅwoṅ*, pl. of *pāṅw*), the feet; the first *nūn*, being nasal, is generally omitted in writing, and a *hamza* substituted, as *pā,oṅ*. *h.*

پانهر पान्हर *pānhar*, m. a kind of reed. *h.*

پاني पानी *pānī*, m. water; lustre, &c.; sperm; *pānī bharnā*, to confess inferiority. *pānī paṛnā*, n. to rain. *pānī pī pī kosnā*, to curse excessively (i.e. till the throat being dry must be moistened by drinking). *pānī jānā*, n. to be afflicted with the *fluor albus*; to be disgraced; to shed tears. *pānī chalnā*, n. to be afflicted with the *fluor albus*. *pānī d.*, to offer a libation of water to satisfy the manes of a deceased person after the corpse has been burnt. *pānī se patlā-k.*, to abash, put to shame. *pānī kā bulbulā* (a bubble of water) indicates instability; *pānī-k.*, a. to abash; to facilitate. *pānī-marnā*, n. to dry up, to be evaporated; to exhibit signs confirming a suspicion. *pānī mārnā*, or *pānī toṛnā*, to draw, in nautical phrase; as, *yih jahāz kitnā pānī mārtā* (or *toṛtā*) *hai*? "What is the draught of this ship? How much does she draw?" *pānī meṅ āg lagānā*, to revive a contention which had subsided; *pānī na-māṅgnā*, to be slain with a single stroke (of the sword &c.), and die instantly. *s.*

پانياملك पानीयामलक *pānīyāmalak*, m. a fruit (*Flacourtia cataphracta*). *s.*

پانيتي पायती *pānyatī*, f. the foot of a bed. *s.*

پانيه पानीय *pānīya*, drinkable, to be drunk. *s.*

پانيه پرشٹھج पानीयपृष्ठज *pānīya-prishṭhaj*, m. an aquatic plant (*Pistia stratioites*). *s.*

پانيه مولك पानीयमूलक *pānīya-mūlak*, m. a plant (*Serratula anthelmintica*). *s.*

پانيه نکل पानीयनकुल *pānīya-nakula*, m. an otter. *s.*

پاو पाव *pā,o*, m. a quarter, fourth part. *s.*

پاوت पावित *pāvit*, purified. *s.*

پاوتكي पावतकी *pā,o-takī* or पावटकी *pā,o-ṭakī*, f. the present fee of a *ḳānūn-go* (q.v.), allowed by government, at the rate of four ānās per hundred rupees, on the net revenue of each district, to defray the expenses of the establishment. *h.*

پاوتي पावती *pā,otī*, f. what one gets, gain, income; *pā,ūtī*, a kind of lamp. *h.*

پاوزهر *pā,o-zahr*, the bezoar stone. *d.*

پاوس पावस *pāwas*, m. the rainy season. *s.*

پاوك पावक *pāwak*, purifier, purificatory; m. fire; a saint, a person purified by religious abstraction; a tree the wood of which is used to procure fire by attrition (*Premna spinosa*); lead wort (*Plumbago zeylanica*); marking-nut plant (*Semicarpus anacardium*. *s.*

پاولا पावला *pā,olā*, m. a quarter of any coin, as of a rupee, &c. *s.*

پاومان पावमान *pāwamān*, purificatory. *s.*

پاون पावन *pāwan*, sacred, holy, purifying; m. water; penance, purification by acts of austerity: the eleocarpus seed; a kind of grass (*Costus*). *s.*

پاءون पाओं *pā,oṅ* (pl. of *pā*), feet. *pā,oṅ par tesha mār-lenā*, to hit one's own feet with the adze, i.e. to occasion one's own failure. *pā,oṅ dhūl*, calamity, misfortune. *h.*

پاون دهون पावनध्वनि *pāwan-dhwani*, a conch shell. *s.*

پاونا पावना *pāwnā*, a. to get, to obtain, &c. (see *pānā*); m. a plant growing in stagnant water. *s.*

پاوي पावी *pāwī*, who or what purifies. *s.*

پاهات पाहात *pāhāt*, m. the mulberry tree (*Morus Indica*). *h.*

پاهان पाहाण *pāhān*, } m. a stone; the head-
پاهن पाहण *pāhan*, } man of a village. *s.*

پاهل पाहल *pāhal*, the ceremony of initiation into the Sikh religion and community. *h.*

پاهن पाहुन *pāhun*, m. a guest. *s.*

پاهنا पाहुना *pāhunā*, m. a guest; son-in-law. *s.*

پاهني पाहुनी *pāhunī*, f. a female guest. *s.*

پاهو पाहू *pāhū*, m. a person, individual. *h.*

پاهي पाही *pāhī* (also *pāhī-asāmī*), m. a non-resident cultivator. *pāhī-kāsht*, cultivation by non-residents. *h. p.*

پاءي पाए *pā,e*, m. a peasant residing in one village, and cultivating land belonging to another village. *h.*

پاءي पाइ *pā,ī*, } f. a coin, the fourth part
پاءين पाईं *pā,īn*, } of an āna. *s.*

پاءي पाइ *pā,ī*, } f. pins used by weavers to
پاءين पाईं *pā,īn*, } wind off the warp from; the word *pā,ī* is frequently used for *pāhī*, q. v. a non-resident, &c. *h.*

پاءي *pā,e*, m. foot, leg, the foot or stand of a table, chair, &c. *pā,e-band* (tied by the leg), met. encumbered with a family. *pa,e bāḳī*, remainder, balance in hand. *pa,e-takht*, m. the royal residence, or place of general residence of the royal family. *pā,e-turāb*, m. the first stage of a journey (it is usual to make one short stage at the commencement of a journey, and there to wait a few days to collect every thing necessary). *pā,e-jāma*, drawers, trousers. *pā,e ḥisāb lānā*, to settle accounts. *pā,e-dām*, m. a gin, a springe, a snare, a noose. *pā,e-zanjīr*, (chained by the leg) met. encumbered with a family. *pā,e-zih*, m. a loop or slip-knot tied to the legs of falcons, &c.; a staple. *pā,e zeb*, a female ornament, worn round the ankles. *pā,e lagnā*, n. to make obeisance by embracing the feet (a token of respect paid by the Hindūs to Brāhmans). *pā,e-māl*, trampled on, ruined, utterly subdued. *pā,e-māl-k.*, to trample on, to destroy, to lay waste, to ravage. *pā,e-mālī*, f. destruction, ravage, ruin, occasioned by an army or cattle overrunning and trampling fields, &c.; *pā,e-mardī*, f. courage, resolution. *p.*

پايا *pāyā*, m. the foot of a bedstead, &c. *p.*

پاياب *pāyāb*, fordable, within man's depth; m. a ford. *p.*

پايابي *pāyābī*, f. quality of being fordable. *p.*

پايان *pāyān*, m. } end, extremity; comple-
پاياني *pāyānī*, f. } tion. *p.*

پاي‌پوش *pā,e-posh*, a shoe, a slipper. *p.*

پاءي‌تابه *pā,e-tāba*, m. a sock, a sandal. *p.*

پايٿه पायठ *pāyaṭh*, m. a scaffold. *h.*

پائجامه *pā,e jāma*, m. drawers, trousers. *p.*

پائخانه *pā,e-ḵẖāna*, m. a necessary, a privy. *p.*

پائيدار *pā,e-dār*, firm, steady, durable, permanent. *p.*

پائيداري *pā,e-dārī*, permanency, stability. *p.*

پائيري *pā,erī*, f. foundation, basis. *d.*

پايس पायस *payas*, made of milk or water; m. an oblation of milk, rice, and sugar. *s.*

پايز *pāyiz*, the autumnal season. *p.*

پائيزهر *pā,e-zahr*, the bezoar stone. *p.*

پايك पायिक *pāyik*, m. a messenger, harbinger; a foot-soldier. *s.*

پائي‌كار *pā,e-kār*, a person who purchases goods from the manufacturer to sell to the merchant; a non-resident labourer hired to cultivate land. *p.*

پائي‌كاشت *pā,e-kāsht*, (land) let out to non-resident tenants; *pā,e-kāsht zamīn*, land cultivated by peasants not residing upon the spot. *p.*

پائيگاه *pā,e-gāh*, m. rank, dignity; a stable. *p.*

پايل पायल *pāyal* or पायिल *pāyil*, firm of foot, steady, easy paced (elephant); f. an ornament for the feet; a bamboo ladder. *p.*

پائي‌مال *pā,e-māl*, subdued, trampled under foot. *p.*

پائي مالي *pā,e-mālī*, devastation, destruction. *p.*

پائي‌موز *pā,e-moz*, m. a kind of pigeons. *p.*

پائين *pā,īn*, low, lower, under, the lower part. *p.*

پائين पाईं *pā,īn*, f. pins used by weavers to wind off the warp from. *h.*

پاینت पायिंत *pāyint*, پاینتي पायंती *pāyantī*, پائینتي पाइंती *pā,intī*, } f. the foot of a bed, the side towards the feet. *s.*

پائیني *pā,īnī*, f. inferiority, lowness. *p.*

پاینده *pāyanda*, firm, permanent. *p.*

پایه *pāya*, m. a step, degree; rank, dignity; the foot of a table, chair, &c.; the foundations of a building. *p.*

پاییز *pāyīz*, autumn; met. old age. *p.*

پبتر पवित्र *pabitr*, undefiled, nice, clean; m. the Brāhmanical cord. *pabitra-tā*, f. purity, holiness. *s.*

پبترا पवित्रा *pabitrā*, m. a Brāhmanical thread; a string of silken beads; a knotted piece of *Kūsha* grass used in religious ceremonies of the Hindūs. f. holy basil (*Ocymum sanctum*); a river a little to the north-west of Hardwar, the *Pabar*; the 12th of the light fortnight of Shrāwan, a festival in honour of Vishnu. *p.*

پبتري पवित्री *pabitrī*, f. a ring of *Kūsha* grass (*Poa cynosuroides*), or of gold, silver, or copper, worn on the ring-finger and fore-finger by Hindūs during religious worship. *s.*

پپاسا पिपासा *pipāsā*, f. thirst. *pipāsit*, *pipāsan*, or *pipāsu*, thirsty. *s.*

پپٹا पिप्पटा *pippaṭā*, f. a kind of sweetmeat. *s.*

پپرماس *paparmās*, the shaddock or pampelmase (*Citrus decumanus*). *d.*

پپڑا पपड़ा *papṛā*, m. a crust, a scale. *s.*

پپڑي पपड़ी *papṛī*, f. a scab, a scale, scurf; thin cakes of bread; scales formed by the drying up of moist earth. *s.*

پپڑیاکت पपड़ियाकत *papṛiyā-hat*, پپڑیاکتھ पपड़ियाकथ *papṛiyā-kath*, } f. a kind of white-coloured *kath* (ex. of *Mimosa catechu*). *h.*

پپڑیلا पपड़ीला *papṛīlā*, scurfy, scabby. *s.*

پپل पिप्पल *pippal*, m. the holy fig-tree (*Ficus religiosa*). *s.*

پپلك पिप्पलक *pippalah*, m. a nipple. *s.*

پپلي पिप्पली *pippalī*, f. long pepper (in Dakh. *piplī*). *pippalī-mūl*, m. the root of long pepper. *s.*

پپني पपनी *papnī*, f. the eyelash. *h.*

پپوٹا पपोटा *papoṭā*, f. the eyelid. *s.*

پپہا पपिहा *papihā*, پپیہا पपीहा *papīhā*, } m. a sparrow-hawk (*Falco nisus*). *h.*

پپي *pīppī*, the dregs or lees of any thing when poured out or drained. *d.*

پپیا पपैया *papaiyā*, m. a kind of child's whistle; name of a tree and of its fruit (the *Papaw* tree; *Carica papaya*). *h.*

پپیتکي पिपीतकी *pipītakī*, f. the 12th of the month Vaisakh, when giving away water is an act of merit. *s.*

پپیلك पिपीलक *pipīlak*, m. a large black ant. *s.*

پپیلکا पिपीलिका *pipīlikā*, f. the common small red ant. *s.*

پت पत *pat*, f. good name, honour, character. *s.*

پت पत *pat* or पति *pati*, m. a lord, master, husband. *pati*, m. a leaf. *s.*

پت पत्ति *patti*, m. a company, a platoon, consisting of one chariot, one elephant, three horse, and five foot. *s.*

پت पित *pit* or पित्त *pitt*, m. bile, gall. *s.*

پت पुत *put*, m. a hell to which the childless are said to be condemned. *s.*

پتا पिता *pitā*, m. a father. *s.*

پتا पित्ता *pittā*, m. bile, the gall-bladder; met. anger, emotion of mind. *pittā marnā*, to subside (anger). *pittā nikālnā*, to chastise. *s.*

پتا पता *patā*, m. a sign, mark, symptom, hint, direction, address (or place where one is directed), a label; a book of instructions and regulations for rent collectors. *patā-rakhnā* or *-lagānā*, to seek for, to endeavour to find out. *h.*

پتا पत्ता *pattā*, m. a leaf; a trinket. *pattā honā*, to run away, to flee. *s.*

پتاکا पताका *patākā*, f. a standard, flag, banner. *s.*

پتاکي पताकी *patākī*, m. an ensign, a standard-bearer. *s.*

پتال पताल *patāl* or पत्ताल *pattāl*, m. (in Hindū mythology) the infernal regions, or a place under the earth (v. *pātāl*). *s.*

پتامہ पितामह *pitā-maha*, a paternal grandfather; a name of *Brahma*, the great father of all. *s.*

پتامہي पितामही *pitāmahī*, a father's mother. *s.*

پتانبر पितांबर *pitāmbar*, m. a silk cloth of a yellow colour, a dress worn by *Krishna*. *s.*

پتاءي पुताई *putā,ī*, the act of plastering; price paid for plastering. *p.*

پتبرت पतिब्रत *patibrat*, m. chastity, modesty. *s.*

پتبرتا पतिब्रता *patibratā*, f. chaste (woman). *s.*

پت پاپڑا पितपापड़ा *pit-pāpṛā*, m. name of a medicinal plant (*Oldenlandia biflora*). *s.*

پتپتي पतपिती *patpitī*, the grass warbler, a small bird. *h.*

پتپڑ पतपड़ *patpaṛ*, land susceptible of alluvial deposits. *h.*

پتپڑي पतपड़ी *patpaṛī*, surface of soft land caked by sunshine after rain. *h.*

پت پرانا पतिप्राणा *pati-prāṇā*, f. a faithful wife. *s.*

پت پنکت पत्तिपंक्ति *patti-pankti*, f. a line of infantry. *s.*

پتت पतित *patit*, abject, fallen, guilty, abandoned. *s.*

پتت پاون पतितपावन *patit-pāwan*, purifying the guilty (an epithet of the Deity). *s.*

پتتو पतित्व *patitwa*, m. the conjugal state. *s.*

پت جور पित्तज्वर *pitt-jwar*, m. bilious fever. *s.*

پت جهڑ पतझड़ *pat-jhaṛ*, without leaves; f. the fall of the leaf, autumn. *pat-jhaṛ honā*, to lose its leaves in autumn (a tree); met. to decay (a person from age). *h.*

پت جهڑي पतझड़ी *pat-jhaṛī*, f. autumn. *h.*

پت دن पतदिन *pat-din* or *pati-din*, daily, always, constantly. *s.*

پتر पत्र *patra* or पत्तर *pattar*, m. a leaf; the leaf of the *Laurus cassia*; the leaf of a book, gold leaf, &c.; a sheet or plate of metal, a letter, epistle; a deed. *s.*

پتر पुत्र *putr* or *putra*, m. a son, a child. *s.*

پتر पितर *pitar*, m. (pl.) fathers, ancestors. *s.*

پتر पितृ *pitṛi* (same as *pitā*), a father (this form is used in compound words). *s.*

پترا पत्रा *patrā*, m. an almanac; an ephemeris. *s.*

پترانك पत्राङ्क *patrānk*, m. page, paging. *s.*

پترانگ पत्राङ्ग *patrāng*, m. red sanders (*Pterocarpus santalinus*); red or sappan wood (*Cæsalpinia sappan*); the *Bhojpatr*, a tree so called; a kind of birch. *s.*

پترائي पितराई *pitrā,ī*, m. a kinsman, a paternal relation from three generations. *s.*

پترائي पितराई *pitrā,ī*, f. verdigris, sub-acetate of copper. *s.*

پتربندھ पितृबन्धु *pitṛi-bandhu*, m. a remote or cognate kinsman by the father's side. *s.*

پتربهكت पितृभक्ति *pitṛi-bhakti*, f. filial duty to a father. *s.*

پتربهوجن पितृभोजन *pitṛi-bhojan*, m. food offered to the manes. *s.*

پترپتر पितृपितृ *pitṛi-pitṛi*, m. a paternal grandfather. *s.*

پترپراپت पितृप्राप्त *pitṛi-prāpta*, received from a father, patrimonial. *s.*

پترپرسو पितृप्रसू *pitṛi-prasū*, f. a father's mother. *s.*

پترپشپ पत्रपुष्प *patra-pushp*, m. a red sort of basil (*Ocymum pilosum*). *s.*

پترپشپك पत्रपुष्पक *patra-pushpak*, m. a kind of birch from the bark of which ḥukka snakes are made. *s.*

پترپكش पितृपक्ष *pitṛi-paksha*, } m. the first or
پترپكهہ पितरपख *pitar-pakh*, } dark fortnight of the lunar month *Asin*. *s.*

پترپوترين पुत्रपौत्रीण *putra-pautrīn*, descended from son to son. *s.*

پترترپن पितृतर्पण *pitṛi-tarpan*, m. the part of the hand between the middle finger and the thumb, sacred to the manes; gifts in honour of deceased relatives, distributed at the *shrāddhas* or funeral ceremonies; the act of throwing water out of the right hand at seasons of ablution, by way of offering to the manes. *s.*

پترتتهہ पितृतिथि *pitṛi-tithi*, m. day of new moon on which she rises invisible. *s.*

پترتيرتهہ पितृतीर्थ *pitṛi-tīrth*, m. Gāyā, the city so called, where the performance of funeral sacrifices is thought to be peculiarly efficacious; the part between the middle finger and the thumb, sacred to the manes. *s.*

پترجگ पितृयज्ञ *pitṛi-jag*, m. obsequial rites. *s*

پترجيو पुत्रजीव *putra-jīv*, m. a tree, from the fruit of which necklaces are made, of supposed prolific efficacy (*Nigella putrangiva*). *s.*

پتردان पितृदान *pitṛi-dān*, m. gift in honour of deceased ancestors. *s.*

پتررنجن पत्ररञ्जन *patra-ranjan*, m. embellishing a page, illuminating, gilding. *s.*

پترستهان पितृस्थान *pitṛi-sthān*, m. a guardian, a protector; the abode of the manes. *s.*

پترسوسا पितृस्वसा *pitṛi-swasā*, f. an aunt, father's sister. *s.*

پترشرا पत्रशिरा *patra-shirā*, f. the vein or fibre of a leaf. *s.*

پترشرادھ पितृश्राद्ध *pitṛi-shrāddha*, m. the obsequial ceremony of a father. *s.*

پترشريني पुत्रश्रेणी *putra-shrenī*, f. a plant (*Salvinia cucullata*). *s.*

پترك पितृक *pitṛik*, paternal, ancestral, obsequial. *s.*

پتركا पुत्रिका *putrikā*, f. a daughter; a doll. *putrikā-putra*, m. the son of a daughter, appointed to raise issue for the father. *s.*

پتركا पत्रिका *patrikā*, f. a leaf, a page, a writing, a letter. *s.*

پتركارج पितृकार्य *pitṛi-kārj*, m. obsequial rites. *s.*

پتركاميا पुत्रकाम्या *putra-kāmyā*, f. wish, or affection for, progeny. *s.*

پتركرم पितृकर्म *pitṛi-karm*, m. } obsequial
پتركريا पितृक्रिया *pitṛi-kriyā*, f. } rites. *s.*

پتركپت पत्रगुप्त *patra-gupta*, m. a species of euphorbia. *s.*

پترگره पितृगृह *pitṛi-grih*, m. burial-ground. *s.*

پترگن पितृगण *pitṛi-gan*, m. a class of progenitors, the sons of the Rishis or Prajāpatis. *s.*

پترگهاتك पितृघातक *pitṛi-ghātak*, a son who is hostile to his father; a parricide. *s.*

پترلوك पितृलोक *pitṛi-lok*, m. the world or sphere of the manes: it is variously situated, but principally in the *Bhuvar* region, or mid-heaven. *s.*

پترمندر पितृमन्दिर *pitṛi-mandir*, m. the paternal mansion; a cemetery. *s.*

پترناڑكا पत्रनाड़िका *patra-nāṛikā*, f. the fibre or vein of a leaf. *s.*

پترنگ पत्रङ्ग *patrang*, m. red sanders (*Pterocarpus santilanus*). *s.*

پترنگا पतरिङ्गा *patringā*, m. name of a bird, the flycatcher (*Merops viridis*). *h.*

پترو पितरौ *pitarau*, m. (dual), the two parents. *s.*

پتروپسکر पत्रोपस्कर *patropaskar*, m. a tree (*Cassia esculenta*). *s.*

پترورن पत्रोर्ण *patrorna*, m. a plant (*Bignonia indica*). *s.*

پترون पितृवन *pitṛi-van*, m. a cemetery; a place where dead bodies are burnt. *s.*

پترویه पितृव्य *pitṛivya*, m. a paternal uncle. *s.*

پترهن पितृहन *pitṛi-han*, m. a parricide. *s.*

پتري पुत्री *putrī*, f. a daughter. *patrī*, a note, an epistle. *s.*

پتریشٹ पुत्रेष्टि *putreshṭi*, f. a sacrifice performed for obtaining children. *s.*

پتریا पतरिया *patariyā* or पतुरिया *paturiyā*, f. a prostitute. *patariyā-bāz*, a whoremonger. *h.*

پتریگیه पितृयज्ञ *pitṛi-yagya*, m. obsequial rites. *s.*

پتسنگهت पत्रिसंहति *patti-sanghati*, f. a body of troops. *s.*

پتسیوا पतिसेवा *pati-sevā*, f. devotion to a husband. *s.*

پتکا पतका *patkā*, m. a girdle, a sash. *zarī-patkā*, a gold sash granted by the Peshwa as a badge of honour to his officers. *h. p.*

پتکي पतुकी *patukī*, f. a small pot, a pan. *h.*

پتگهن पित्तघ्न *pitta-ghna*, antibilious *s.*

پتگهني पित्तघ्नी *pitta-ghnī*, f. a plant (*Menispermum glabrum*). *s.*

پتگهني पतिघ्नी *pati-ghnī*, f. the murderess of her husband; a line on the hand indicating that a woman will be treacherous to her husband. *s.*

پتل पत्तल *pattal*, f. a plate or trencher formed of leaves. *s.*

پتل पित्तल *pittal*, bilious; m. brass; the *bhojpatr*, or birch tree, of which the bark is used for writing upon. *s.*

پتلا पतला *patlā*, fine, thin (cloth or liquids); lean, meagre, delicate. *h.*

پتلا पुतला *putlā*, m. an image, effigy, idol. *s.*

پتلا पित्तला *pittalā*, f. a plant (*Jussieua repens*). *s.*

پتلان पितलाना *pitlānā* or पित्तलाना *pittlānā*, n. to be contaminated with verdigris (as food, especially of an acid quality, kept in copper vessels). *s.*

پتلاءي पतलाई *patlā,ī*, f. thinness, fineness, meagreness. *h.*

پتلکا पुतलिका *putlikā* or पुत्तलिका *puttalikā*, m. an image, an idol. *s.*

پتلو पतलो *patlo*, m. the dead leaves fallen from a tree; the leaves cut from the culm of a reed (*Saccharum spontaneum*), and used for thatching. *s.*

پتلي पुतली *putlī*, f. the pupil of the eye; an image, puppet, idol, doll; the frog of a horse-hoof. *putlī-kā-tārā-k.*, to honour or esteem as the apple of the eye. *s.*

پتلي पित्तली *pittalī*, brazen, made of brass. *s.*

پتمبرا पतिंबरा *patimbarā*, f. a bride choosing her husband; a pungent seed (*Nigella indica*). *s.*

پتمئي पतमई *patma,ī*, sowing fresh sugar cane after cutting the old. *h.*

پتن पतन *patan*, m. the act of falling. *s.*

پتن पत्तन *pattan*, m. act of ordering goods from a manufacturer. *h.*

پتن पत्तन *pattan*, m. a city, town; chiefly used in comp., as *srīrang-pattan* Seringapatam. *s.*

پتن جمع خرچ *patan jam'i kharch*, a monthly treasury account, specifying the receipts and disbursements arranged under the different heads for each month. *h. p.*

پتنگ पतङ्ग *patang*, m. sappan wood. *h.*

پتنگ पतङ्ग *patang*, } m. a moth; a (child's)
پتنگا पतंगा *patangā*, } paper kite; the sun. *s.*

پتنگا पतङ्गा *patangā*, m. a spark. *patangā honā*, to go rapidly about a business. *h.*

پتني पत्नी *patnī*, f. a wife. *patnī-bhāg*, division of property among a man's widows. *s.*

پتني पत्तनी *pattanī*, commissioned, manufactured by order. *h.*

پتوا पतौवा *patauwā*, m. a leaf. *s.*

پتوار पतवार *patwār*, } f. a rudder or helm. *h.*
پتوال पतवाल *patwāl*, }

پتورت पतिव्रत *pati-vrat*, m. chastity. *s.*

پتورتا पतिव्रता *pativratā*, f. a chaste and faithful wife. *s.*

پتوریا पतूरिया *patūriyā*, f. a prostitute. *h.*

پتونتي पत्वन्ती *patwantī*, f. a wife devoted to her husband. *s.*

پتوه पतोह *patoh*, } f. daughter-in-law, son's
پتوهو पतोहू *patohū*, } wife. *s.*

پته पथ *path*, m. a road, path, highway. *s.*

پتهدرم पथिद्रुम *pathi-drum*, m. a sort of *khyar* (*Mimosa alba*). *s.*

پتهر पत्थर *patthar*, m. a stone; *patthar-bāzī*, f. throwing stones, playing with stones. *patthar pānī ho jānā*, the melting of a stony heart; a difficult task to be facilitated. *patthar pasījnā*, to be softened or melted (a stony heart). *patthar chhātī par rakhnā*, to be patient by compulsion, or from being without remedy. *patthar sā phenk mārnā*, to reply rashly, without understanding the meaning of one's question. *patthar se sir phoṛnā* or *mārnā*, to teach or instruct a fool. *patthar honā*, to be heavy; to be stable, to stand still; to be unmerciful. *s.*

پتهرانا पथराना *pathrānā*, n. to become hard (a boil); to be petrified. *s.*

پتهراو पत्थराओ *pathara,o*, act of stoning. *s.*

پتهرپهوڑ पत्थरफोड़ *patthar-phoṛ*, m. a woodpecker (*Picus*). *h.*

پتھرچٹا पत्थरचटा *patthar-chaṭā*, m. name of a kind of greens; a skin-flint; name of a serpent; name of a fish; adj. one attached to his own house, who remains there even in distress. *h.*

پتھرچور पत्थरचूर *patthar-chūr*, m. name of a plant (*Plectranthus aromaticus, Roxb.*). *s.*

پتھرکلا पथरकला *pathar-kalā*, m. a firelock. *s.*

پتھری पथरी *pathrī*, f. the flint of a musket; a gizzard; grit, gravel; stone in the bladder. *s.*

پتھریلا पथरीला *pathrīlā*, stony (as soil). *s.*

پتھک पथिक *pathik*, m. a passenger, a traveller. *s.*

پتھن पथिन *pathin*, m. a division of hell. *s.*

پتھیا पथ्या *pathyā*, f. yellow myrobalan (*Terminalia chebula*). *s.*

پتھیہ पथ्य *pathya*, proper, fit, suitable, agreeing with (chiefly with respect to diet). *s.*

پتی पत्ती *pattī*, f. a leaf; hemp, of which an intoxicating potion is made; the hem of cloth; (for *pati*, q.v.), a husband, lord, or master. *s.*

پتی पतै *patai*, straw or grass thrown over a field to protect the fresh planted roots from the sun. *s.*

پتیا पतिया *patiyā*, f. a written opinion given by *Pandits* on a point of Hindū law; a letter, a small note. *s.*

پتیا पितिया *pitiyā*, a paternal uncle, father's brother. *s.*

پتیارا पतियारा *patiyārā*, m. belief, confidence, dependence. *s.*

پتیانا पतियाना *patiyānā*, a. to confide in, to trust, to depend on, believe. *s.*

پتیت पतीत *patīt*, m. uncultivated, waste land. *h.*

پتیت‌کمی *patīt-kamī*, f. a decrease, occasioned by lands being left uncultivated. *h.p.*

پتیری पतीरी *patīrī*, f. a kind of mat. *s.*

پتیل पतील *patīl*, thin, fine. *h.*

پتیل *patīl*, m. a match for a lamp, a link-stock, a candle-wick. *patīl soz*, f. the stand or support of a lamp. *p.*

پتیلا पतीला *patīlā*, m. a pan, a pot. *h.*

پتیلہ *patīla* (v. *patīl*), a match, &c. *p.*

پٹ पट *paṭ*, m. a shutter, the valve of a folding-door; a sound; adj. upside down, overturned. *h.*

پٹ पट *paṭ*, m. the sound resulting from the falling or beating of any thing. *s.*

پٹ पट *paṭ*, m. cloth, coarse cloth or canvas, a checkered cloth on which chess &c. may be played. *s.*

پٹ पटु *paṭu*, clever, dexterous, skilful, diligent, sharp. *s.*

پٹ पट्ट *paṭṭ*, m. wove silk; a plant (*Corchorus olitorius*) from the fibres of which, called jute, a coarse sackcloth and cordage are prepared; a royal grant or order written on copper, stone, &c. *s.*

پٹ पुट *puṭ*, m. a menstruum, solvent, flux. *s.*

پٹا पटा *paṭā*, m. a foil, a wooden scimitar for cudgelling with; a board on which Hindūs sit, whilst eating their meals or performing religious ceremonies. *paṭe-bāz*, a fencer, a cudgel-player; met. a coquette, a wanton, a strumpet; *paṭā kāṭnā*, a. to discharge from service. *h.*

پٹا पट्टा *paṭṭā*, m. a lock of hair; a dog-collar; name of harness; f. an ornament for the forehead. *paṭṭā turānā*, to flee, to run away. *h.*

پٹا पट्टा *paṭṭā*, m. a deed, particularly a title-deed to land; a grant or lease, specifying the quantity of land possessed by each tenant, and the amount of rent with which it is charged. *paṭṭā-dār*, one who holds his lands by a written engagement. *paṭṭā dah-sāla*, a lease for ten years. *paṭṭā janājāt*, leases granted to tenants individually. *paṭṭā ta'alluḳ*, a dependent lease. *paṭṭā ṭhīkā*, a deed assigning land for farming on certain conditions. *s.*

پٹا *puṭṭā*, m. an ant-hill, a snake's hole. (Snakes are usually to be found in old ant-hills, where the ground is burrowed in every direction to a considerable extent.—B.) *d.*

پٹاپٹ पटापट *paṭāpaṭ*, m. the sound of beating, or of the falling of drops of rain. *s.*

پٹاپر पटापर *paṭāpar*, m. name of a fruit. *h.*

پٹاتڑانا पट्टा तुड़ाना *paṭṭā turānā*, n. to run away. *h.*

پٹاخا *paṭā<u>kh</u>ā*, m. (properly *paṭākā*) a cracker, a squib. *h.*

پٹارا पिटारा *piṭārā*, m. a large basket, a portmanteau, square boxes much used by persons travelling. A couple of them are slung by ropes to either end of a bamboo, called a bahangī, and thus carried by a man who runs alongside of the palanquin.—(B). *d.*

پٹارو पिटारू *piṭārū*, m. an order of mendicants (v. *aghorī*). *s.*

پٹاری पिटारी *piṭārī*, f. a small basket, a portmanteau, a hamper, a pannier. *s.*

پٹاری पिटारी *piṭārī*, f. a weevil, an insect bred in rice, &c. *s.*

پٹاک पटाक *paṭāk*, m. a crash, explosion, report of artillery; a kind of bird. *h.*

پٹاکا पटाका *pāṭākā*, / پٹاکھا पटाखा *paṭākhā*, } m. a squib, cracker, fireworks; f. a flag, a banner. *h.*

پٹالن *paṭālan*, m. a regiment, a battalion. (The Urdū version of the English word is *palṭan*). *d*

پٹانا पटाना *paṭānā*, a. to irrigate, to water; to place the beams on the roof of a house; to pay money; to prepare a *chaukā* with cow-dung dissolved in water. *h.*

پٹاو पटाव *paṭāw*, irrigating, flooding a field; roofing a house with tiles, &c. *h.*

پٹ‌پٹ पटपट *paṭpaṭ*, f. the sound of beating. *s.*

پٹپٹیا पिटपिटिया *piṭpiṭiyā*, adj. combing or carding (wool, cotton, &c.). *h.*

پٹتا पटुता *paṭutā*, f. / پٹتوہ पटुत्व *paṭutwa*, m. } expertness, adroitness; eloquence. *s.*

پٹ‌دیوی पट्टदेवी *paṭṭ-devī*, f. a principal queen. *s*

پترا **पटरा** *paṭrā*, m. a plank to sit on, a plank on which a washerman beats clothes; unripe grain (*Cicer arietinum*). *paṭrā kar denā*, a. to deprive one of his power or strength, to convict an adversary and leave him without reply. *h.*

پٹ‌رانی **पटरानी** *paṭ-rānī*, f. a queen who is installed or consecrated along with the king. *s.*

پترنگ **पट्टरङ्ग** *paṭṭ-rang*, m. a plant used in dyeing (*Cæsalpinia sappan*). *s.*

پتري **पटरी** *paṭrī*, f. a tile. *s.*

پتري **पटरी** *paṭrī*, } f. a plank to write on; the
پتڑي **पटड़ी** *paṭṛī*, } vanes of a Venetian window; a firm seat on horseback; a narrow slip or plank of wood. *h.*

پتڑا **पटड़ा** *paṭṛā*, m. a plank, &c., see *paṭrā*.

پٹ‌سال **पटसाल** *paṭ-sāl*, m. a college, a reading-room, a school-house. *s.*

پتسن **पटसन** *paṭ-san*, m. a plant. *h.*

پتشاك **पट्टशाक** *paṭṭ-shāk*, m. a sort of pot-herb (*Corchorus capsularis*). *s.* [of the teeth. *s.*

پتك **पिट्टक** *piṭṭak*, m. the tartar or excretion

پتكا **पटका** *paṭkā*, m. a cloth worn round the waist, a girdle. *zarī paṭkā*, the golden girdle, an ensign conferred by the *Peshwā* on generals who are invested with authority immediately by him. *paṭkā bāndhnā*, to determine on, or prepare for any act. *paṭkā-pakaṛnā*, a. to hinder, to obstruct. *s.*

پتكاجانا **पटकाजाना** *paṭkā jānā*, n. to fall from one's rank or estimation. *h.*

پتكارنا **पटकारना** *paṭkārnā*, } a. to dash against
پتكانا **पटकाना** *paṭkānā*, } any thing, to throw on the ground with violence; to knock. *h.*

پتكن **पटकन** *paṭkan*, f. a knock, a fall; *paṭkan khānā*, to fall down. *h.*

پتكنا **पटकना** *paṭaknā*, a. to dash against any thing, to throw on the ground with violence, to knock; n. to crackle (as wood in the fire), to sputter, to fret. *h.*

پتكني‌دينا **पटकनी देना** *paṭkanī-denā*, a. to dash on the ground, to throw against any thing with violence. *h.* [the ground, &c. (same as last). *h.*

پتكي‌دينا **पटकीदेना** *paṭkī-denā*, a. to dash on

پتل **पट्टिल** *paṭṭil*, m. a plant (*Cæsalpinia bonducella*). *s.*

پتلودهر **पट्टिलोध्र** *paṭṭilodhra*, m. a tree, the bark of which is used as an astringent; the red species of the *lodh* (*Symplocos racemosa*). *s.*

پتن **पटन** *paṭan*, m. roofing. *h.*

پتن **पट्टन** *paṭṭan*, m. the name of a city. *h.*

پتن **पट्टन** *paṭṭan*, act of ordering goods from a manufacturer. *h.*

پتنا **पटना** *paṭnā*, n. to be paid, to be procured, to fill, to be watered, to be covered, to be roofed, &c.; m. name of a city in Behar. *h.*

پتنا **पिटना** *piṭnā*, n. to be beaten. *h.*

پتنكاش **पिटङ्काश** *piṭankāsh*, m. a species of pike (*Esox scolopax*). *s.*

پتنكاكي **पिटङ्काकी** *piṭankākī*, f. colocynth. *s.*

پتني **पटनी** *paṭnī*, m. a ferryman. *h.*

پتني **पट्टनी** *paṭṭanī*, commissioned goods, or goods made to order. *h.* [purpet. *s.*

پتو **पट्टू** *paṭṭū*, m. a kind of woollen cloth,

پتوا **पटुआ** *paṭū,ā* or *paṭwā*, m. a man who strings pearls, a braider, a maker of fringe and tape. *s.*

پتوا **पटवा** *paṭwā*, irrigation. *paṭwā-zamīn*, land artificially watered. *h. p.*

پتوا **पटुआ** *paṭū,ā*, m. tow made from the *Hibiscus cannabinus*. *h.*

پتوار **पटवार** *paṭwār*, } m. one who keeps
پتواري **पटवारी** *paṭwārī*, } accounts of lands, a land-steward: he keeps the accounts of the rents realized in his village or department, and accounts for them to his superior. The *paṭwārī* is also employed on the part of the husbandman, to keep an account of his receipts and disbursements, and no village is without one of these. *h.* [to water. *h.*

پتوانا **पटवाना** *paṭwānā*, a. to provide money;

پتوت **पटुत** *paṭut*, m. } vigour, virility, acti-
پتوتا **पटुता** *paṭutā*, f. } vity, skill. *s.*

پتوتن **पटोतन** *paṭotan*, m. roofing with planks or boards, transom. *h.*

پتوكا **पटुका** *paṭūkā*, m. a cloth worn round the waist, a girdle. *paṭūkā bāndhnā*, a. to determine on or prepare for any act. *paṭūkā pakaṛnā*, to hinder, to obstruct. *s.*

پتوني **पटौनी** *paṭaunī*, m. a ferryman. *h.*

پتوهيا **पटोहिया** *paṭohiyā*, m. an owl. *h.*

پتويگر *paṭwīgar*, m. (v. *paṭū,ā*), a braider, &c. *h.*

پته **पठ** *paṭh*, } m. a young full-grown ani-
پتها **पट्ठा** *paṭṭhā*, } mal, a youth, a wrestler; a sinew, a tendon; a plant with long leaves. *a.*

پته **पट्ट** *paṭṭa*, a lease, &c. (*paṭṭā*). *h.*

پتها **पुट्ठा** *puṭṭhā*, m. the buttock, the hip (of an animal). *h.*

پتهان **पठान** *paṭhān*, name of a race or dynasty that reigned in Delhi; also an *Afghān* race settled in Rohilcund. *h.*

پتهانا **पठाना** *paṭhānā* or *piṭhānā*, } a. to send,
پتهونا **पठौना** *paṭhaunā*, } to despatch. *h.*

پتهت **पठित** *paṭhit*, read, studied; recited. *h.*

پته‌دار **पट्टदार** *paṭṭa-dār*, a leaseholder. *h.*

پتهن **पठन** *paṭhan*, m. reading, reciting. *h.*

پتهنگا **पठिङ्गा** *paṭhingā*, shelter, refuge. *d.*

پتهيا **पठिया** *pāṭhiyā*, f. a young full-growu animal, generally applied to kids, fowls, &c. *h.*

پٹھیا पठैया *paṭhaiyā*, part. sent, despatched. *h.*

پٹي पट्टी *paṭṭī*, f. plaster; a bandage, a fillet; a quarter of a place; the side pieces of the frame of a bedstead; a written order, charter, or patent, a list, statement, or invoice; documents of any kind; laths of split bamboo; spokes of a wheel; a row; a kind of sweetmeat; divisions of the hair which is combed towards the two sides, and divided by a line in the middle. *paṭṭī pakaṛke hilte rahnā*, expresses excessive weakness and laziness. *paṭṭī toṛnā*, to be bedrid. *paṭṭī se paṭṭī milānā*, expresses the most intimate proximity. *s.*

پٹي *puṭṭī*, a basket for catching fish. *d.*

پٹیا पटिया *paṭiya*, f. a slate or slab of stone. *s.*

پٹیت पटैत *paṭait*, m. a cudgel-player. *h.*

پٹي دار *paṭṭī-dār*, a patentee; a person who holds a tenure by *paṭṭī*; one who has a share in a coparcenary village or estate. *paṭṭī-dārī*, a coparcenary tenure. *h. p.* [grass eaten by elephants. *h.*

پٹیرا पटेरा *paṭerā*, m. papyrus; a kind of long

پٹیل पटेल *paṭel*, m. cudgelling; sovereignty; a title among the *Kunbī* tribe; a title of Marhattas, the headman of a village. *paṭel ḍālnā*, a. to interrupt, to throw obstacles in the way of a business; to beat. *h.*

پٹیلا पटेला *paṭelā* or पटैला *paṭailā*, m. a kind of large and flat-bottomed boat used for merchandise on the Ganges; a log or beam used to roll or harrow ground. *h.* [to beat. *h.*

پٹیلنا पटीलना *paṭīlnā*, a. to exact, to subdue,

پٹیلي पटेली *paṭelī*, f. a flat-bottomed boat. *h.*

پٹیما पटीमा *paṭīmā*, m. the planks on which cloth is spread for printing. *s.*

پٹینا पटीना *paṭīnā* or *paṭainā*, m. the name of a bird, the green fly-catcher (*Merops viridis*). *h.*

پٹیوار *paṭṭīwār*, according to shares or assessments (v. *paṭṭī*). *h. p.* [shipping. *s.*

پجاپا पुजापा *pujāpā*, m. the apparatus of wor-

پجانا पुजाना *pujānā*, a. to fill, to accomplish; to cause to worship. *h.*

پجاوا *pajāwā* (v. *pajāwa*) a brick-kiln. *p.*

پجاونا पुजावना *pujāwanā*, a. to cause to worship. *s.* [kiln. *p.*

پجاوه *pajāwa*, m. (corrupt. of *pazāwa*), a brick-

پجر *pajar*, distillation, dripping; also a fountain, jet d'eau. *d.*

پجرنا *pajarnā*, to drop, ooze, distil. *d.*

پجوانا पुजवाना *pujwānā*, to cause to worship, to cause to fill or complete. *s.*

پجوڑا पजौड़ा *pajauṛā*, low, mean, shabby. *h.*

پجیب पजेब *pajeb*, f. an ornament for the feet. *p.*

پچ पिचु *pichu*, m. a sort of leprosy. *s.*

پچاڈالنا पचाडालना *pachā ḍālnā*, n. to digest, to rot. *s.*

پچارا पुचारा *puchārā*, m. a thin coat of clay for laying on a wall; the sponge of a gun. *puchārā phernā*, to sponge a gun. *puchārā denā*, to lay a thin coat of clay on the walls of a house; to whitewash a wall. *h.*

پچاس पचास *pachās*, fifty. *pachāswān*, the fiftieth. *s.*

پچاسي पचासी *pachāsī*, eighty-five. *s.*

پچانا पचाना *pachānā*, a. to digest; to cause to rot; to rot, to ferment. *s.* [five. *s.*

پچانوي पचानवे *pachānawwe*, *pachānwe*, ninety-

پچاو पचाव *pachā,o*, m. digestion. *s.*

پچ پچ पचपच *pach-pach*, m. the noise made by walking in damp places; adj. soft or plashy, as soil, or rotten vegetable matter and mud. *h.*

پچپچا पिचपिचा *pichpichā*, soft, flaccid, moist, flabby, watery. *h.* [to be wet; to sweat. *h.*

پچپچانا पचपचाना *pachpachānā*, n. to be damp,

پچپن पचपन *pachpan*, fifty-five. *h.*

پچتانا पचताना *pachtānā*, n. to regret, repent; to grudge, to grieve. *h.*

پچتاو पचताव *pachtā,o*, } m. penitence, re-
پچتاوا पचतावा *pachtāwā*, } pentance, concern, grief. *h.* [cloth. *h.*

پچتولیا पचतोलिया *pachtoliyā*, m. a kind of

پچٹ पिचट *pichchaṭ*, m. inflammation of the eyes, ophthalmia. *s.*

پچر पच्चर *pachchar*, f. a wedge. *pachchar-mārnā*, a. to tease, to harass, to distress. *h.*

پچک पिचुक *pichuk*, m. a plant (*Vangueria spinosa*). *s.* [large nail. *d.*

پچڑا *pachṛā*, m. a kind of wedge, a spike or

پچرس *puchras*, m. a kind of bronze, a composition of iron and other metals. *d.*

پچکا पिचुक्का *pichukkā*, m. a squirt. *h.*

پچکارا पुचकारा *puchkārā*, m. (same as *puchārā*) a thin coat of clay, sponge of a gun. *puchkārā phernā*, to whitewash a wall. *h.* [syringe. *h.*

پچکاري पिचकारी *pichkārī*, f. a squirt, a

پچکانا पिचकाना *pichkānā*, a. to squeeze, to press together. to shrivel, to wrinkle, to burst. *h.*

پچکنا पिचकना *pichaknā*, n. to be squeezed; to be shrivelled. *h.*

پچکھا पचखा *pachkhā*, f. six days from *shrāvaṇa* to *revatī*, on which days several kinds of work are unlawful. *s.* [or divisions (a house). *h.*

پچکھنا पचखना *pachkhanā*, having five parts

پچل पिचुल *pichul*, the tamarisk tree; a plant (*Barringtonia acutangula*); the diver or water-crow. *s.*

پچلڑا पचलड़ा *pachlaṛā*, consisting of five rows or strings, as a necklace, &c. (v. *pāṅch laṛā*). *pachlaṛī*, f. a necklace consisting of five strings. *h.*

پچلونا पचलोना *pachlonā*, m. a medicine composed of five kinds of salt. *s.*

پچمپچا पचम्पचा *pachampachā*, f. a species of curcuma (*Curcuma xanthorhizon*). *h.*

پچمحلا पचमहल्ला *pachmaḥallā*, consisting of five stories, rooms, or apartments (a house). *h.*

پچمرد पिचुमर्द *pichu-mard*, } m. the nimb tree
پچمند पिचुमन्द *pichu-mand*, } (*Melia azad-dirakhta*). *s.*

پچميل पचमेल *pachmel*, mixed, confused. *s.*

پچن पचन *pachan*, what cooks or matures, &c. *s.*

پچنا पचना *pachnā*, n. to be digested; to rot; to take pains, to labour, to be consumed. *s.*

پچنڈ पिचण्ड *pichanḍ* or पिचिण्ड *pichinḍ*, m. the belly. *s.*

پچنڈکا पिचण्डिका *pichanḍikā*, f. the instep. *s.*

پچنڈل पिचण्डिल *pichanḍil* or पिचिण्डिल *pichinḍil*, big bellied, corpulent. *s.*

پچوتره पचोतरा *pachotara*, m. a duty of five per cent. on merchandise (v. *panchatara*). *s.*

پچوکا पचूका *pachūkā*, m. a squirt, a syringe. *h.*

پچواءي पचवाई *pachwā,ī*, } f. an intoxicating
پچوي पचवी *pachwī*, } drink made from rice. *h.*

پچور पिचोर *pichor*, garden-ground &c. in rear of a tank. *h.*

پچوني पचौनी *pachaunī*, f. the stomach. *s.*

پچھ पक्ष *pachh* or पख *pakh*, m. confirmation, protection, defence; partiality; a feather; a fortnight, or division of the month. *s.*

پچھ पिच्छ *pichchh*, m. the tail of a peacock, a tail in general. *h.*

پچھ पुच्छ *puchchh*, f. a tail. *s.*

پچھار पुछार *puchhār*, m. asking, investigation. *h.*

پچھاڑ पछाड़ *pachhāṛ*, f. a fall, throwing down; the act of winnowing. *pachhāṛ khānā*, to fall down; to suffer pain. *s.*

پچھاڑنا पछाड़ना *pachhāṛnā*, a. to throw down, to abase, to conquer, to upset. *h.*

پچھاڑي पिछाड़ी *pichhāṛī*, f. the rear; the hinder part of an animal; the ropes by which a horse's hind legs are tied; adv. in the rear, behind. *pichhāṛī mārnā*, to attack in rear. *h.*

پچھاں पछाँ *pachhāṅ*, m. the west, the setting of the sun. *s.*

پچھاننا पिछानना *pichhānnā*, a. to know, to be acquainted with, to recognise. *h.*

پچھ پاءوں هونا *pichh pā,oṅ honā*, to retreat, fall back, withdraw. *d.*

پچھتانا पछताना *pachhtānā*, n. to regret, to repent of, to feel vexed. *s.*

پچھتاوا पछतावा *pachhtāwā*, m. regret, concern, grief, contrition, repentance. *s.*

پچھتر पचहत्तर *pachhattar*, seventy-five. *h.*

پچھتکا पिच्छितिका *pichchhitikā*, f. the sisu (*Dalbergia sisu*). *s.*

پچھڑجانا पछड़जाना *pachhaṛ-jānā*, n. to be overcome. *h.*

پچھڑنا पछड़ना *pachhaṛnā*, n. to fall, to tumble. *h.*

پچھلا पिछला *pichhlā*, hindermost, last; modern, recent (in opp. to ancient). *pichhle pāṅw haṭnā* to withdraw from one's agreement. *h.*

پچھلا पिच्छिला *pichchhilā*, f. the silk cotton tree (*Bombax heptaphyllum*); a potherb (*Basella rubra* and *lucida*); a timber tree (*Dalbergia sisu*), an esculent root (*Arum Indicum*). *s.*

پچھل پاءي पिछलपाई *pichhal-pā,ī*, f. an ugly or frightful woman, one who is a satire upon the sex, an ogress. *h.*

پچھل دلا पिच्छलदला *pichchhal-dalā*, f. the jujube (*Zizyphus jujuba*). *s.*

پچھلن पिछलन *pichhalan*, m. sliding, slipping. *h.*

پچھلن *pichhalan*, next, second, again. *d.*

پچھلنا पिछलना *pichhalnā*, n. to slip, to slide. *s.*

پچھم पच्छम *pachchham* or पच्छिम *pachchhim*, west, western. *s.*

پچھنا पछना *pachhnā*, m. the act of scarifying (tattooing); inoculating; a scarificator (name of instrument). *h.*

پچھني पछनी *pachhnī*, f. scarifying (tattooing. *h.*

پچھوا पछवा *pachhwā*, f. western wind. *s.*

پچھواڑا पिछवाड़ा *pichhwāṛā*, m. } rear, rear-
پچھواڑي पिछवाड़ी *pichhwāṛi*, f. } wards, hindermost; the back yard of a house. *h.*

پچھوان पिछवान *pichhwān*, tailed, having a tail. *h.*

پچھوت पिछूत *pichhūt*, afterwards, behind; m. back of a house. *s.*

پچھورا पिछौरा *pichhaurā*, } m. a cloth or sheet
پچھوڑا पिछौड़ा *pichhauṛā*, } worn round the waist, or thrown carelessly over the head, a tablecloth. *h.*

پچھوري पिछौरी *pichhaurī*, } f. a small cloth,
پچھوڑي पिछौड़ी *pichhauṛī*, } &c.; a headkerchief. *h.*

پچھوڑنا पछोड़ना *pachhoṛnā*, a. to winnow with a basket used for this purpose. *h.*

پچھوڑي *pachhoṛī*, f. a sheet, cloth, &c. *d.*

پچھويا पुछवैया *puchhwaiyā*, m. an inquirer, interrogator. *s.*

پچھي पच्छी *pachchhī*, m. an ally, an assistant, an advocate, patron; a bird. *s.*

پچھياو पछियाव *pachhiyāw*, f. a westerly wind. *s.*

پچھيت पिछेत *pichhet*, m. the back of a house; a yard or compound behind a house. *s.*

پچي पची *pachchī*, adherent, joined; (met. in music) in unison. *pachchī-kārī*, f. mosaic; patching or darning of damaged cloth. *pachchī honā*, n. to be stuck together as with glue; to be in unison; to be strongly attached by love. *h.*

پچيس पचीस *pachīs*, twenty-five. *s.*

پچیسي पचीसी *pachīsī*, f. a game, so called, played with cowries instead of dice. It is so named from the highest throw, which is twenty-five. *s.*

پخ *pakh*, interj. Oh! bravo! well done! *pikh*, get away! begone! *p.*

پخال *pakhāl* f. (for *pakhāl*), a large leather bag for carrying water, generally on bullocks. *s.*

پختري *pukhtarī*, f. cakes (or bread) which are laid over dishes when bringing to table, and under which the meat is kept warm; cakes embued with clarified butter, from being laid over certain greasy dishes, as *dopiyāza*, &c. These cakes are very soft and savoury, whence *māmā pukhtariyāṅ khānā*, to eat cakes of this description prepared by his mother, is applied to a person accustomed to luxury and incapable of labour or fatigue. *p.* [of the world. *p.*

پختگي *pukhtagī*, dressing, ripeness, experience

پختن *pukhtan* (r. *paz*), to cook, to bake; met. to concoct in the mind, or imagine, to entertain an idea. *p.*

پخته *pukhta*, dressed (as victuals); ripe; sly, knowing, experienced (in the world), wise; built of cut or polished stones (a house). *pukhta karnā*, to make strong. *pukhta-kārī*, sound workmanship. *pukhta-mizāj*, of mature disposition, experienced. *p.*

پخش *pakhsh*, trodden, expanded, withered. *p.*

پد पद *pad*, m. the foot; footstep; rank, character; (in gram.) a word; place, station; a foot or a line in a stanza; (in law) a head, title, or topic of legal or judicial proceedings. *s.*

پدا पिद्दा *piddā*, m. a species of small bird. *h.*

پدابهشکت पदाभिषिक्त *padābhishikta*, anointed or installed in rank or office. *s.*

پدات पदात *padāt* or *padāti*, m. a footman, a foot-soldier, a pedestrian; a pawn (in chess). *s.*

پداتك पदातिक *padātik*, a peon, a footman or foot-soldier; a pawn (in chess). *s.*

پدارته पदार्थ *padārth*, m. a thing, substance, a good, a blessing; a rarity; a delicacy, or exquisite food; the meaning of a word; a category or predicament in logic, of which seven are maintained, viz. substance, quality, action, identity, variety, relation, and nonentity. *s.*

پدارگه पदार्घ *padārgh* (for *padārghya*), an offering of curds, honey, &c. to a guest or Brāhman. *s.*

پداس पदास *padās*, f. inclination to break wind backwards, flatulency. *s.*

پداسا पदासा *padāsā*, m. one who is inclined to break wind; adj. flatulent. *s.*

پداسن पदासन *padāsan*, m. a footstool. *s.*

پدانا पदाना *padānā*, a. to cause to break wind, (met.) to frighten, or to put to flight. *s.*

پدانك पदाङ्क *padānk*, m. footmark, vestige. *s.*

پدبي पदबी *padbī*, f. title, titular name, surname, patronymic; rank, character; a path. *s.*

پدبهنجن पदभञ्जन *pad-bhanjan*, m. explanation

پدچیت पदच्युत *pad-chyut*, fallen from dignity, disgraced. *s.*

پدر *padar* (in Hind. *pidar*), a father. *pidar-mizājī*, a representative father, or one who has adopted a son. *p.* [bottom, beneath. *d.*

پدر *padar* (same as *tah*, q. v.), fold, &c.;

پدرانه *padarāna*, paternally, like a father. *p.*

پدرود *padrūd*, leave, dismissal, farewell; *padrūd-k.*, to bid adieu. *p.*

پدري *padarī*, paternal, fatherly. *p.*

پدڑي पिदड़ी *pidṛī*, f. a tomtit. *h.*

پدك पदक *padak*, m. an ornament of the neck; (in Dakh.) a flat plate of gold or other metal; badge. *s.*

پدکرم पदक्रम *pad-kram*, m. step, pace. *s.*

پدم पदम *padam* or पद्म *padma*, m. the lotus (*Nelumbium speciosum, Willd.* or *Prunus cerasus*): it is often confounded with the water-lily (*Nymphæa*); ten billions, according to the *Shāstr*, or one thousand billions, according to the *Dastūr-ul-'amal* or the royal ordinances of *Akbar*. *s.*

پدما पद्मा *padmā*, f. the goddess of riches, *Lakshmī*; a small tree (*Hibiscus mutabilis*). *s.*

پدمات पद्माट *padmāṭ*, m. a sort of cassia (*Cassia tora*). *s.*

پدماسن पद्मासन *padmāsan*, m. a posture in religious meditation, sitting with the thighs crossed, one hand resting on the left thigh, the other held up with the thumb upon the heart, the eyes directed to the tip of the nose; a seat made in the shape of a lotus. *s.*

پدماکر पद्माकर *padmākar*, m. a large deep pond, in which the lotus does or may grow. *s.*

پدماوت पद्मावत *padmāvat*, name of a celebrated princess, whose adventures are related in a romance entitled *Padwāwatī*. *s.*

پدماوتي पद्मावती *padmāvatī*, f. the wife of the sage *Jaratkāru*; the main stream of the Ganges between the Ķāsimbāzār river and the sea. *s.*

پدم پتر पद्मपत्र *padma-patra*, m. a sort of *costus* (*Costus speciosus*). *s.* [(*Webera corymbosa*). *s.*

پدم پشپ पद्मपुष्प *padma-pushp*, m. a shrub

پدم چارني पद्मचारिणी *padma-chārinī*, f. a small tree (*Hibiscus mutabilis*). *s.*

پدم درشن पद्मदर्शन *padma-darshan*, m. the resin of the *Pinus longifolia*. *s.*

پدم راگ पद्मराग *padma-rāg*, m. a ruby. *s.*

پدمك पद्मक *padmak*, m. a kind of leprosy. *s.*

پدم کاشته पद्मकाष्ठ *padma-kāshṭh*, m. a fragrant wood, used as a cooling and tonic medicine. *s.*

پدمکي पद्मकी *padmakī*, m. the *Bhojpatra* or birch tree. The bark is used for writing upon, wrapping shawls, &c. *s.*

پدم مکهي पद्ममुखी *padma-mukhī*, f. a sort of

پدمني पद्मनी *padmani* or पद्मिनी *padminī*, f. a description of women, the most excellent of the four classes into which womankind is divided by the Hindūs (the names of the other three are *chitrinī, sankhinī,* and *hastinī*). *s.*

پدموتر पद्मोत्तर *padmottar*, m. safflower. *s.*

پدم ورنك पद्मवर्णक *padma-varnah*, m. a species of costus (*Costus speciosus*). *s.*

پدنا पदना *padnā*, پدو पद्दू *paddū*, پدوڑا पदोड़ा *padoṛā*, having a propensity for breaking wind backwards; met. a coward. *s.*

پدودك पदोदक *padodak*, m. water in which the feet of a Brāhman have been washed, and which it is a meritorious deed for inferiors to drink. *s.*

پدوي पदवी *padwī*, f. rank, character, title, road, path (v. *padbī*). *s.*

پدھارنا पधारना *padhārnā*, n. to take leave, to go away, to depart; to arrive. *s.*

پدھان पिधान *pidhān*, m. a covering, a cover or concealment; a lid; a wrapper or cloak. *s.*

پدھت पद्धति *paddhat*, پدھتي पद्धती *paddhatī*, f. a road, line, row; manner, custom; a treatise on a particular science; ritual; a title or titular name. *s.*

پدي पद्दी *paddī*, f. an alley, a way. *h.*

پديد *padīd*, open, public, clear, evident, manifest, conspicuous, visible. *p.*

پديه पद्य *padya*, m. metre, verse.

پڈا पडा *paḍā*, m. the boundary of a field. *h.*

پذير *pazīr* or *pizīr*, (in comp.) denotes taking, receiving, admitting, being possessed of or endowed with; as, *zīnat-pazīr*, adorned, possessed of ornament; *ṣafā-pazīr*, endowed with integrity, pure, sincere. *p.*

پذيرفتن *pazīraftan* (r. *pazīr*), to receive, to accept; to admit, to sustain. *p.*

پذيره *pizīra*, acceptable, agreeable. *p.*

پر पर *par*, other, strange, foreign, distant. *par-des*, abroad: conj. but, over, through, after, at, by, for, of; post-position, on, upon, notwithstanding. *s.*

پر प्र *pra*, prep. (in comp.) forth, for, forward, off, away. *s.*

پر *par*, m. a feather, a quill, wing. *par-jalnā* or *ṭūṭnā*, to be without power or ability. *par-jhāṛnā* or *girānā*, to prepare to fly; to get new feathers after moulting. *par nikālnā*, to display on acquiring power those qualities which remained concealed in poverty or a low station; to shew the cloven foot. *p.*

پر परु *paru*, m. a knot or joint in a reed. *s.*

پر *pur*, full, complete, loaded, charged; used (in comp.) as *pur-nūr*, illustrious, lit. full of light. *p.*

پر पुर *pur*, m. f. a city, town. *pur-bāsī* or *pura-vāsī*, a dweller in a city, a citizen. *s.*

پرا परा *parā*, prep (in comp.) back, backward, reverse, over. *s.*

پرا पुरा *purā*, m. a large village, town; (in comp.) apartment; as, *ran-purā*, the women's apartment. *s.*

پرا परा *parā*, m. a company; a body (of troops); a rank, file, or row. *s.*

پرابليه प्राबल्य *prābalya*, m. power, vigour, predominance. *s.*

پرابھو प्राभव *prābhava*, m. superiority, pre-eminence. *s.*

پرابھو पराभव *parābhav*, m. discomfiting, overcoming. *s.*

پرابھوت पराभूत *parābhūt*, defeated, overcome. *s.*

پراپت प्राप्त *prāpta* or *parāpat*, m. income, produce, gain; advantage, benefit; acquired, attained; proper, right. *s.*

پراپت प्राप्ति *prāpti*, f. gain, income, advantage, acquiring, obtaining, success. *s.*

پراپت प्रापित *prāpit*, procured, obtained. *s.*

پراپتارتھ प्राप्तार्थ *prāptārtha*, successful, having gained an object. *s.*

پراپتاوسر प्राप्तावसर *prāptāvasar*, opportune, seasonable, finding an occasion. *s.*

پراپت بدھ प्राप्तबुद्धि *prāpta-buddhi*, enlightened, instructed; recovering, becoming conscious. *s.*

پراپت كال प्राप्तकाल *prāpta-kāl*, fated, one whose fated time has come; opportune. *s.*

پراپك प्रापक *prāpak*, adj. procuring, obtaining. *s.*

پراپن प्रापण *prāpan*, m. obtaining. *s.*

پراپيه प्राप्य *prāpya*, attainable, obtainable. *s.*

پرات प्रात *prāt* or प्रातः *prātah*, m. morning, dawn of day. *prāta-samai, prāta-kāl*, the same. *s.*

پرات परात *parāt*, پراتي पराती *parātī*, f. a large plate (of brass). *h.*

پراتپدك प्रातिपदिक *prātipadik*, m. the crude form of a noun, without affixes. *s.*

پرات پريه परातप्रिय *parāt-priya*, m. a kind of reed (*Saccharum spontaneum*). *s.*

پراتر प्रातर *prātar*, adv. morning, dawn. *prātar-bhojan*, m. the morning meal. *s.*

پراتم पुरातम *purātam*, پراتن पुरातन *purātan*, old, aged. *s.*

پراتھمك प्राथमिक *prāthamik*, first, initial. *s.*

پراتھميه प्राथम्य *prāthamya*, m. firstness, priority. *s.*

پراتييك प्रात्ययिक *prātyayik*, trusty, confidential; m. a surety. *s.*

پراٹھا पराठा *parāṭhā*, m. bread made with butter (or *ghī*), and of several layers like a pie-crust. *h.*

پراجاپتيا प्राजापत्या *prājāpatyā*, f. giving away the whole of one's property before entering upon the life of an ascetic or mendicant. *s.*

پراجاپتيه प्राजापत्य *prājāpatya*, m. a form of marriage, the gift of a girl respectfully by her father to her lover; a name of Allahabad or Prayāg; a sort of penance, eating once a day for three days in the morning, once in the night for three days, subsisting three days on food given as alms, and fasting three days more; a particular sacrifice performed before appointing a daughter to raise issue in default of male heirs; the asterism *Rohinī*.

پراجت पराजित *parājit*, conquered, defeated. *s.*

پراجي पराजय *parājai* or *parājaya*, m. overthrow, defeat, discomfiture. *s.*

پراجيمان पराजयमाण *parājaimān*, adj. overcoming, conquering, surpassing. *s.*

پراچار प्राचार *prāchār*, contrary to rectitude, deviating from the ordinary institutions and observances. *s.*

پراچارج प्राचार्य *prāchārj*, m. a scholar, a pupil. *s.*

پراچت पराचित *parāchit*, m. a fine or penance imposed on religious occasions as the price of absolution, atonement, expiation. *s.*

پراچي प्राची *prāchī*, east, eastern; f. the east. *s.*

پراچير प्राचीर *prāchīr*, m. a bound hedge, a fence, a wall, a rampart. *s.*

پراچين पराचीन *parāchīn* or प्राचीन *prāchīn*, old, of former times, ancient; f. a broad hedge, a fence, a wall. *s.*

پراچينا प्राचीना *prāchīnā*, f. a plant (*Cissampelos hexandra*). *s.*

پراچيناملك प्राचीनामलक *prāchīnāmalak*, m. a fruit (*Flacourtia cataphracta*). *s.*

پراچين‌پنس प्राचीनपनस *prāchīn-panas*, m. a tree (*Ægle marmelos*). *s.*

پراچينتا प्राचीनता *prāchīnatā*, f. antiquity. *s.*

پراچيه प्राच्य *prāchya*, eastern; m. the eastern country, south and east of the Saraswatī. *s.*

پرادربهاو प्रादुर्भाव *prādur-bhāo*, m. appearance, manifestation. *s.*

پرادكشنيه प्रादक्षिण्य *prādakshinya*, m. circumambulation. *s.*

پرادن परादन *parādan*, m. a horse of the Persian breed. *s.*

پرادهانيه प्राधान्य *prādhānya*, m. supremacy, superiority. *s.*

پرادهكار पराधिकार *parādhikār*, m. another person's office or post. *parādhikār-charchā*, f. officiousness, interference with another's concerns. *s.*

پرادهين पराधीन *parādhīn*, in the power of another, dependent. *s.*

پرادهينتا पराधीनता *parādhīnatā*, f. subjection, dependence. *s.*

پراديش प्रादेश *prādesh*, m. place, country. *s.*

پراڈوواك प्राड्विवाक *prāḍ-vivāk*, m. a judge, a magistrate. *s.*

پرارو परारु *parāru*, m. a kind of gourd (*Momordica charantia*). *s.*

پراربده प्रारब्ध *prārabdh*, f. fortune, lot, fate, predestination, chance; adj. begun. *s.*

پرارته परार्थ *parārth*, having another object or sense; designed by another; m. for the sake of another. *parārth-vādī*, officious, meddling. *s.*

پرارتهت प्रार्थित *prārthit*, asked begged, solicited. *s.*

پرارتهك प्रार्थक *prārthak*, asking, an asker, a soliciter. *s.*

پرارتهنا प्रार्थना *prārthnā*, f. asking, petition, prayer. *s.*

پرارتهنيه प्रार्थनीय *prārthnīya*, to be asked or begged; m. the third or Dwāpar age of the world. *s*

پراردهوه परार्द्ध *parārdhwa*, m. a lack of lacks of crores, or a number equal to half the term of Brāhma's life. *s.*

پرارنبه प्रारम्भ *prārambh*, m. beginning, commencement. *s.*

پراس परास *parās*, m. the name of a tree (*Butea frondosa*); oakum, made of the bark of that tree. *s.*

پراس प्रास *prās*, m. a bearded dart. *s.*

پراس परासु *prāsu*, dead, expired. *s.*

پراساد प्रासाद *prāsād*, m. a temple, a palace. *s.*

پراست परास्त *parāst*, defeated. *s.*

پراستا परासुता *parāsutā*, f. death, extinction; drowsiness. *s.*

پراسچت पराश्चित *prāschit*, m. atonement, expiation. *s.*

پراسك प्रासक *prāsak*, m. a die, dice. *s.*

پراسنگك प्रासङ्गिक *prāsangik*, innate, inherent. *s.*

پراشر पराशर *parāshar*, the father of the poet Vyāsa. *s.*

پراشرت पराश्रित *parāshrit*, subject, dependent. *s.*

پراشري पराशरी *parāsharī*, m. a beggar, a wandering mendicant. *s.*

پراشري पराश्रय *parāshrai*, dependent, relying upon another; m. dependence. *s.*

پراشريا पराश्रया *parāshrayā*, f. a parasite plant. *s.*

پراك पराक *parāk*, m. a religious obligation of an expiatory kind, fasting for twelve days and nights, and keeping the mind attentive and organs subdued; a sacrificial sword. *s.*

پراك प्राक *prāk*, before, prior, preceding; east, eastern; at dawn, early. *s.*

پراكار प्राकार *prākār*, m. an inclosure, a fence, a rampart, particularly a surrounding wall elevated on a mound of earth. *s.*

پراك‌پهلگني प्राकफल्गुणी *prāk-phalgunī*, f. the eleventh lunar asterism. *s.*

پراكتن प्राक्तन *prāktan*, old, prior, former. *prāktan-karma*, m. any act formerly done; fate, destiny. *s.*

پراكرت प्राकृत *prākṛit*, low, common, vulgar; natural; belonging to the *Prakṛiti*, illusory, material m. a dialect derived from the *Sanskṛit*. *s.*

پراکرت بهاشا प्राकृतभाषा *prākṛit bhāshā*, f. a popular dialect formed from the *Sanskṛit* language. In the *Sanskṛit* plays, the illiterate, and generally the females, speak *Prākṛit*. The *Prākṛit* and *Pāli* are very clearly *Sanskṛit* corrupted, smoothed down, and simplified. Some have maintained that, on the contrary, *Sanskṛit* is merely a refinement on the former. This is about as rational as saying that *Latin* was derived from the present *Italian* or *Spanish*. *s.*

پراکرت پرلي प्राकृतप्रलय *prākṛit-pralai*, m. the total dissolution of the world. *s.*

پراکرت جور प्राकृतज्वर *prākṛit-jwar*, m. common or usual fever. *s.*

پراکرت متر प्राकृतमित्र *prākṛit-mitra*, m. a natural friend or ally. *s.*

پراکرم पराक्रम *parākram*, m. ability, power, valour. *s.*

پراکرمي पराक्रमी *parākramī*, bold, powerful, stout. *s.*

پراک کال प्राक्काल *prāk-kāl*, m. former age or time. *s.*

پراگ पराग *parāg*, m. the pollen or farina of a flower; fragrant powder used after bathing; the name of a mountain. *s.*

پراگ प्राग *prāg*, m. the ancient name of *Ilāhābād*, vulg. *Allahabad*. *s.*

پراگ بهاو प्रागभाव *prāg-bhā,o*, m. prior existence; superiority, excellence. *s.*

پراگبهاو प्रागभाव *prāg-abhā,o*, m. antecedent privation, non-existence of a thing which may yet be; the non-possession of property which may yet be possessed. *s.*

پراگ جيوتش प्राग्ज्योतिष *prāg-jyotish*, m. a country, *Kāmrūp*, part of Assam, the scene of Brahma's penance. *s.*

پراگ گامي प्रागगामी *prāg-gāmī*, going before, a precursor. *s.*

پراگلبهيه प्रागल्भ्य *prāgalbhya*, m. confidence, boldness, arrogance. *s.*

پراگندگي *parāgandagī*, f. dispersion, defeat. *p.*

پراگنده *parāganda*, dispersed, scattered. *p.*

پراگيا प्राज्ञा *prāgyā*, f. knowledge, understanding; a clever woman. *s.*

پراگيتوه प्राज्ञत्व *prāgyatwa*, m. learning, wisdom. *s.*

پراگيمان प्राज्ञमान *prāgya-mān*, m. respect for learned men. *prāgya-mānī*, adj. respecting learned men. *s.*

پراگيه प्राग्र्य *prāgya*, chief, principal. *s.*

پراگيه प्राज्ञ *prāgya*, wise, clever; m. a *paṇḍit*; a learned or clever man. *s.*

پراگيي प्राज्ञी *prāgyī*, f. the wife of a Brāhman; a clever woman. *s.*

پرال पराल *parāl*, f. straw, stubble. *s.*

پرالبده प्रालब्ध *parālabdh*, f. fate, predestination, venture, chance. *s.*

پرامادیه प्रामाद्य *prāmādya*, m. a tree (*Justicia adhenatoda*); madness, frenzy, intoxication. *s.*

پرامانك प्रामाणिक *prāmāṇik*, adj. possessing authority; a president, the chief of a trade; a learned man, one able to quote his authorities. *s.*

پرامانيه प्रामाण्य *prāmāṇya*, m. authority, proof. *s.*

پرامرش परामर्श *parāmarsh*, m. counsel, advice, consideration, reflection, discrimination, judgment. *s.*

پرامودهنا परामोधना *parāmodhanā*, m. coaxing, wheedling. *s.*

پران पुराण *purāṇ* or *purāṇa*, m. the Hindū mythological books, generally reckoned eighteen in number (v. preface to Wilson's translation of the *Vishṇu purāṇa*). *s.*

پران प्राण *prāṇ* or *parāṇ*, m. breath; soul, life; sweetheart, mistress; poetical talent or inspiration; a title of Brahma, the supreme spirit; an aspiration in the articulation of letters. *s.*

پران परान्न *parānna*, adj. living at another's expense; m. food supplied by another. *s.*

پرانا पुराण *purāṇā*, old, ancient. *s.*

پرانا पराना *parānā*, n. to run, to flee. *s. p.*

پرانا पुराना *purānā*, a. to fill, to make full; also (in Dakh.) to pierce, to bore, to string pearls. *h.*

پرانا पिराना *pirānā*, n. to have pain, be painful. *s.*

پراناپهاري प्राणापहारी *prāṇāpahārī*, deadly, fatal. *s.*

پراناده‌ناته प्राणाधिनाथ *prāṇādhināth*, m. a husband, as lord over life. *s.*

پرانانت प्राणान्त *prāṇānt*, m. death. *s.*

پرانانتك प्राणान्तिक *prāṇāntik*, fatal, destructive of life; m. murder. *s.*

پرانايام प्राणायाम *prāṇāyām*, m. breathing in a peculiar way through the nostrils during the mental recitation of the names or attributes of some deity: the *Vaidyas* close the right nostril with the thumb, and inhale through the left; then they close both nostrils, and finally open the right for exhalation. *s.*

پران بادہ प्राणबाध *prāṇ-bādh*, m. extreme peril, fear of life. *s.*

پران بهوجي परान्नभोजी *parānna-bhojī*, living at another's cost. *s.*

پران پت प्राणपति *prāṇ-pati*, m. soul's lord, a husband. *s.*

پران پرتشٹها प्राणप्रतिष्ठा *prāṇ-pratishṭhā*, m. the ceremony of imparting life to an idol. *s.*

پران پردا प्राणप्रदा *prāṇ-pradā*, f. a medicinal plant, commonly called *riddhi*. *s.*

پرانت प्रान्त *prānt*, m. edge, margin, border, end. *s.*

پران تياگ प्राणत्याग *prāṇ-tyāg*, m. abandoning life, dying, suicide. *s.*

پرانٹها पराँठा *parāṅṭhā*, m. a kind of cake, paste. *h.*

پرانجل प्राञ्जलि *prānjali*, f. putting the hands together to the forehead, a mark of respect. *s.*

پران دهارن प्राणधारण *prāṇ-dhāran*, m. sustenance, supporting life. *s.*

پرانسا परानसा *parānsā*, f. the practice of medicine, administering remedies. *s.*

پران‌سم प्राणसमा *prān-samā*, f. a wife, considered as equal to life. *s.*

پران‌سنيم प्राणसंयम *prān-sanyam*, m. a peculiar religious exercise, suspending breath. *s.*

پرانك प्राणक *prānak*, m. an animal or sentient being; a plant (*Celtis orientalis*). *s.*

پرانمي प्राणमय *prān-mai*, endowed with breath or life. *prān-mai-kosh*, m. one of the cases or receptacles of the soul, the vital or organic case. *s.*

پران‌ناتهه प्राणनाथ *prān-nāth*, m. a husband. *s.*

پراننت प्राणान्त *prānant*, m. a sort of collyrium. *s.*

پراننتي प्राणान्ती *prānantī*, f. sneezing, hiccup. *s.*

پران‌ويي प्राणव्यय *prān-vyai*, m. loss of life, death. *s.*

پران‌هاري प्राणहारी *prān-hārī*, } deadly, mortal. *s.*
پران‌هر प्राणहर *prān-har*, }

پراني प्राणी *prāṇī*, endowed with life, an animal. *s.*

پران‌ياترا प्राणयात्रा *prān-yātrā*, f. support of life, subsistence. *s.* [animals. *s.*

پراني‌پيڑا प्राणीपीड़ा *prānī-pīṛā*, f. cruelty to

پرانيش प्राणेश *prānesh*, m. a husband, as sovereign of life. *s.*

پرانيشا प्राणेशा *prāneshā*, f. a wife. *s.*

پراني‌ماتا प्राणीमाता *prānī-mātā*, f. a mother. *s.*

پراني‌هت प्राणीहित *prānī-hit*, favourable or good for living beings. *s.*

پراني‌هنسا प्राणीहिंसा *prānī-hinsā*, f. doing harm to a living creature. *s.*

پراوٹ प्रावट *prāvat*, m. barley. *s.*

پراورت परावर्त्त *parāvart*, m. reversal of a sentence. *parāvart-byavahār*, m. appeal (in law). *s.*

پراورت परावृत्त *parāvṛitt*, reversed (as a judgment). [cloak. *s.*

پراورت प्रावृत *prāvṛit*, m. veil, a wrapper, a

پراورت प्रावृत्ति *prāvṛitti*, f. an inclosure, a fence, a hedge. *s.* [about July and August. *s.*

پراورش प्रावृष *prāvṛish*, f. the rainy season,

پراورشايني प्रावृषायणी *prāvṛishāyanī*, f. cowach (*Carpopogon pruriens*). *s.*

پراورشينيه प्रावृषेण्य *prāvṛishenya*, m. the *Kadamb* tree (*Nauclea cadamba*). *s.* [fulness. *s.*

پراوينيه प्रावीण्य *prāvīnya*, m. cleverness, skil-

پراه पराह *parāh*, f. flight, a general emigration; m. the next day. *s.*

پراهن पराह्न *parāhna*, m. the afternoon, the latter part of the day. *s.*

پرايا पराया *parāyā*, strange, foreign, belonging to another. *s.*

پرايت परायत्त *parāyatt*, dependant, subject. *s.*

پرائچه *parā.icha* (pl. of *pārcha*, Gılch.) scraps, bits, &c. *p.*

پرايشچت प्रायश्चित्त *prāyashchitt*, m. expiation, penance. *prāyashchitt-vidhi*, f. rules for penance. *s.*

پراين परायण *parāyan*, m. adherence to a pursuit, attachment to, dependence on; adj. adhering or attached to, depending upon. *s.* [death. *s.*

پراين प्रायण *prāyan*, m. death, voluntary

پرايه प्राय *prāya*, adj. like, resembling; (in comp.) m. fasting to death, as a religious act; quantity, abundance. *s.*

پرب परब *parb*, m. gem, a flat diamond. *h.*

پرب परब *parab*, m. a holiday, anniversary feast, a sacred day. *s.* [travelling, journey. *s.*

پرباس प्रवास *prabās*, m. residing abroad,

پرباسي प्रवासी *prabāsī*, one who resides abroad, a foreigner, stranger, traveller. *s.*

پرباسي पुरबासी *pur-bāsī*, the inhabitants of a city or town. *s.*

پربال प्रवाल *prabāl*, m. coral. *s.*

پرباني *parbānī*, f. a species of tax assessed on the cultivators of the soil. *a.*

پرباه प्रवाह *prabāh*, m. tide, stream. *s.*

پربت पर्वत *parbat*, m. a mountain. *s.*

پربتي पर्वती *parbatī*, m. a mountaineer, a highlander. *s.*

پربتي पर्वती *parbatī*, f. } a production of the hills; a kind of pumpkin. *s.*
پربتيا पर्वतिया *parbatiyā*, m. }

پربدهه प्रबुद्ध *prabuddha*, wise, learned. *s.*

پربرهم परब्रह्म *par-brahm*, m. the supreme being. *s.*

پربس परबस *par-bas*, dependent, precarious, depending on the will of another. *s.*

پربسي परबसी *par-basī*, f. dependence. *s.*

پربل परबल *par-bal* or प्रबल *pra-bal*, predominant, superior, prevalent, violent. *s.*

پربلا परबला *par-balā* or प्रबला *prabalā*, predominant, &c. (v. *par-bal*). *s.* [periority. *s.*

پربلتا प्रबलता *prabalatā*, f. predominance, su-

پربندهه प्रबन्ध *prabandh*, m. a kind of song; style, composition (of a discourse); continuous application, uninterruptedness; a connected discussion or narrative; *prabandh-kalpnā*, f. a fiction, a work of imagination. *s.*

پربوده प्रबोध *prabodh*, m. vigilance, wakefulness; understanding, wisdom; consciousness, awaking; demonstration consolation, persuasion. *s.*

پربودهتا प्रबोधिता *prabodhitā*, f. a species of the *Atiyagatī* metre. *s.*

پربودهن प्रबोधन *prabodhan*, m. awakening, arousing; instructing; persuasion, prejudice. *s.*

پربها प्रभा *prabhā*, f. splendour; light. *s.*

پربهات प्रभात *prabhāt*, m. dawn, morning. *s.*

پربهاتي प्रभाती *prabhātī*, sung in a tune (or *rāginī*), peculiar to morning. *s.*

پربهاس प्रभास *prabhās*, m. a place of pilgrimage in the west of India. *s.*

پربهاشا परिभाषा *paribhāshā*, f. a technical term; the interpretation of a grammatical rule of Pāuini; (in medicine) prognosis; abuse, ridicule. *s.*

پربهاكر प्रभाकर *prabhā-kar*, m. the sun; the moon; lit. the light maker. *s.*

پربهاكيٹ प्रभाकीट *prabhā-kīṭ*, f. the fire-fly. *s.*

پربهاگ परभाग *par-bhāg*, m. excellence, superiority; good fortune; residue, remainder. *s.*

پربهان प्रभान *prabhān*, m. light, radiance. *s.*

پربهانجن प्रभाञ्जन *prabhānjan*, m. a tree (*Hyperanthera morunga*). *s.*

پربهاو प्रभाव *prabhāw*, m. power, strength, influence, prosperity, felicity; majesty, dignity; spirit. *s.*

پربهاو परिभाव *pari-bhā,o*, m. disrespect, contempt, disgrace. *s.*

پربهت प्रभुत *prabhut*, m. } ability, government, liberty,
پربهتا प्रभुता *parbhutā*, f. } option, superiority, influence, legislation. *s.*

پربهرت परभृत *par-bhrit*, cherished or nourished by a stranger, fostered, adopted; m. the Indian cuckoo, which is supposed to leave its eggs in the nest of the crow to be hatched. *s.*

پربهرت प्रभृति *prabhriti*, f. manner, kind; et cetera, others, rest (in comp.). *s.*

پربهرم परिभ्रम *paribhram*, m. wandering, going about, error. *s.*

پربهرشٹ परिभ्रष्ट *paribhrashṭ*, fallen, degraded, deprived of. *s.*

پربهو प्रभव *prabhaw*, born, produced; superior, powerful; the operative cause or immediate origin of being. *s.*

پربهو प्रभु, प्रभू *prabhū*, m. commander, lord, master, principal; adj. strong, able, eternal. *s.*

پربهو परिभव *paribhav*, m. disrespect, disgrace. *s.*

پربهوبهكت प्रभुभक्त *prabhū-bhakt*, faithful, devoted. *s.*

پربهوگ परिभोग *paribhog*, m. possession, enjoyment. *s.*

پربهوم परभूमि *par-bhūmi*, f. a foreign or an enemy's country. *s.*

پربهيد प्रभेद *prabhed*, m. kind, sort, difference. *s.*

پربيس प्रवेश *prabes*, m. admittance, access. *s.*

پربيسي प्रवेशी *prabesī*, penetrating, entering. *s.*

پربين प्रवीण *prabīn*, knowing, intelligent, accomplished, skilful. *s.*

پربينتا प्रवीणता *prabīnatā*, f. knowledge, skill. *s.*

پرپ पर्प *parp*, m. a wheel chair. *s.*

پرپاٹي परिपाटी *paripāṭī*, f. order, method, arrangement, arithmetic. *s.*

پرپاك परिपाक *paripāk*, m. maturity, perfection; cleverness; digestion. *s.*

پرپاكني परिपाकिनी *paripākinī*, f. a drug (*Convolvulus turpethum*). *s.*

پرپالت परिपालित *paripālit*, protected, cherished. *s.*

پرپالن परिपालन *paripālan*, m. protecting, cherishing. *s.*

پرپتامه प्रपितामह *prapitāmaha*, m. a paternal great-grandfather. *s.*

پرپتامهي प्रपितामही *prapitāmahī*, f. a paternal great grand-mother. *s.*

پرپٹ पर्पट *parpaṭ*, m. a medicinal plant with bitter leaves (*Oldenlandia biflora* or *Gardenia latifolia*). *s.*

پرپٹ درم पर्पटद्रुम *parpaṭ-drum*, m. bdellium. *s.*

پرپٹي पर्पटी *parpaṭī*, f. a thin crisp cake made of any pulse. *s.*

پرپد परपद *par-pad*, m. eminence, high station; final felicity. *s.*

پرپرانا परपराना *parparānā*, n. to smart. *h.*

پرپراهٹ परपराहट *parparāhaṭ*, f. acrimony, smarting. *h.*

پرپرگره परपरिग्रह *par-parigrah*, m. the family or dependants of another. *s.*

پرپشٹ परपुष्ट *par-pushṭ*, m. the *Kokila* or Indian cuckoo. *s.*

پرپشٹا परपुष्टा *par-pushṭā*, f. a harlot, a whore; a parasite plant. *s.*

پرپشكرا परिपुष्करा *paripushkarā*, f. a sort of cucumber (*Cucumis madraspatanus*). *s.*

پرپكوه परिपक्व *paripakwa*, cooked, mature; shrewd; digested. *paripakwatā*, f. maturity; perfection; shrewdness; digestion. *s.*

پرپلايت प्रपलायित *prapalāyit*, routed, defeated. *s.*

پرپلاين प्रपलायन *prapalāyan*, m. flight, running away. *s.*

پرپلايي प्रपलायी *prapalāyī*, m. a fugitive, one who deserts his cause. *s.*

پرپلت परिप्लुत *pariplut*, immersed, inundated, bathed. *s.*

پرپلو परिप्लव *pariplav*, m. bathing, immersing, inundation. *s.*

پرپنا प्रपुन्ना *prapunnā*, f. a sort of grass (*Hedysarum alhaji*). *s.*

پرپناڑ प्रपुनाड़ *prapunāṛ*, m. a sort of cassia (*Cassia tora*). *s.*

پرپنتهي परिपन्थी *paripanthī*, m. an enemy, a robber, a bandit. *s.*

پرپنچ प्रपञ्च *prapanch* or परपञ्च *parpanch*, m. fraud, cheat, imposition, deceit, treachery, art, artifice; opposition; prolixity, copiousness in style; error, illusion. *s.*

پرپنچت प्रपञ्चित *prapanchit*, erring, mistaken; deceived, beguiled; declared fully, treated at length. *s.*

پرپنچي प्रपञ्ची *prapanchī* or परपञ्ची *parpanchī*, insidious, fraudulent, artful. *s.*

پرپوتا परपोता *parpotā*, m. a great-grandson. *h.*

پرپوتي परपोती *parpotī*, f. a great-granddaughter. *h.*

پرپوتر प्रपौत्र *prapautra*, m. a great-grandson. *prapautri*, f. a great-granddaughter. *s.*

پرپوجت परिपूजित *paripūjit*, served, worshipped, adored. *s.* [adoring. *s.*

پرپوجن परिपूजन *paripūjan*, m. worshipping,

پرپورکا प्रपूरिका *prapūrikā*, f. a prickly nightshade (*Solanum jacquini*). *s.* [ful. *s.*

پرپورن परपूर्ण *prapūrṇa* or *parpūran*, brim-

پرپورن परिपूर्ण *paripūrna*, full, complete, content. *paripūrnatā*, f. completion, satiety. *s.*

پرپونڈریك प्रपौण्डरीक *prapaunḍarīk*, m. a small herbaceous plant, used in medicine, and as a perfume, commonly called *punderyā*. *s.*

پرپهل प्रफुल्ल *praphull*, blown, as a flower; smiling, glad; shining. *praphull-nayan*, having full or sparkling eyes. *praphull-vadan*, having a cheerful smiling countenance. *s.*

پرپهلت प्रफुल्लित *praphullit*, blossoming, in blossom; gay, lively, cheerful. *s.*

پرپیٹه परपैठ *parpaiṭh*, m. a duplicate (of a bill of exchange). *h.*

پرپیل परिपेल *paripel*, m. a fragrant grass (*Cyperus rotundus*). *s.* [a stratum. *h.*

پرت परत *parat*, m. a fold, ply, layer, crust,

پرت प्रति *prati*, Sansk. prep. (used in comp.) it generally denotes repetition, continuity, retaliation, or retribution. *s.*

پرتا परता *partā*, m. a reel (for winding thread). *h.*

پرتا परता *partā*, agreeable to, conformable with. *purtā*, fully, completely. *s.*

پرتاب *partāb*, m. the range of a musket, arrow, &c. *p.*

پرتاپ प्रताप *pratāp*, m. splendour; courage, glory, potency, prosperity, felicity. *s.*

پرتاپ परिताप *paritāp*, m. pain, anguish; a division of hell. *s.*

پرتاپس प्रतापस *pratāpas*, m. the gigantic asclepias with white flowers. *s.*

پرتاپن प्रतापन *pratāpan*, m. a hell. *s.*

پرتاپ‌وان प्रतापवान *pratāp-wān*, } glorious,
پرتاپي प्रतापी *pratāpī*, } potent. *s.*

پرتارت प्रतारित *pratārit*, cheated, deceived. *s.*

پرتارك प्रतारक *pratārak*, m. a cheat. *s.*

پرتارن प्रतारण *pra-tāran*, m. } fraud, cheating,
پرتارنا प्रतारणा *pra-tārnā*, f. } deceit. *s.*

پرتال परताल *partāl*, also *partāl-jarīb*, remeasurement of a field. *s. p.*

پرتان प्रतान *pratān*, m. a disease, fainting, epilepsy. *s.*

پرتبنب प्रतिबिम्ब *pratibimb*, also *pratibimbh*, m. an image or picture, the reflection of an image or figure from a mirror. *s.* [prohibition, obstacle. *s.*

پرتبندہ प्रतिबन्ध *pratibandh*, m. interruption,

پرتبندهك प्रतिबन्धक *pratibandhak*, one who forbids, impedes, or interrupts; m. an impediment. *s.*

پرتبها प्रतिभा *pratibhā*, f. understanding, intellect; sharpness; light, splendour. *s.*

پرتبهاو प्रतिभाव *pratibhā,o*, m. corresponding character or disposition. *s.* [vided. *s.*

پرتبهن प्रतिभिन्न *pratibhinn*, separated, di-

پرتبهو प्रतिभू *pratibhū*, m. a surety. *s.*

پرتبهي प्रतिभय *pratibhai*, formidable, fearful; m. fear. *s.*

پرتبهیدن प्रतिभेदन *pratibhedan*, m. piercing, penetrating; dividing. *s.*

پرتپادن प्रतिपादन *pratipādan*, m. gift; ascertaining, determining. *s.*

پرتپال प्रतिपाल *pratipāl*, m. patronising, tuition, fostering, rearing, breeding, cherishing. *s.*

پرتپالك प्रतिपालक *pratipālak*, m. cherisher, patron. *s.* [rishing, &c. (v. *pratipāl*). *s.*

پرتپالن प्रतिपालन *pratipālan*, m. act of che-

پرتپالنا प्रतिपालना *pratipālnā*, a. to foster, cherish, rear. *s.*

پرتپت प्रतिपत *pratipat*, f. the first day of a lunar fortnight; rank, consequence. *s.*

پرتپت प्रतिपत्ति *pratipatti*, f. fame, reputation; knowledge, ascertainment. *s.*

پرتپد प्रतिपद *pratipad*, f. the first day of a lunar fortnight; adv. step by step, continually. *s.*

پرتپرسو प्रतिप्रसव *pratiprasav*, m. precept for an act which, under other circumstances, is forbidden. *s.*

پرتپرش प्रतिपुरुष *pratipurush*, adv. every man, man by man. *s.*

پرتپن प्रतिपन्न *pratipann*, known, certain. *s.*

پرتپوجك प्रतिपूजक *pratipūjak*, m. a reverer, one who does homage. *s.*

پرتپوجن प्रतिपूजन *patripūjan*, m. exchange of civilities, mutual reverence; offering homage. *s.*

پرتپهل प्रतिफल *pratiphal*, m. return, requital, retaliation. *s.* [melody. *s.*

پرتتال प्रतिताल *pratitāl*, m. a kind of air or

پرتجهوا प्रतिजिह्वा *pratijihvā*, f. the uvula, or soft palate. *s.*

پرتجیون प्रतिजीवन *pratijīvan*, m. resuscitation. *s.*

پرتچنتن प्रतिचिन्तन *pratichintan*, m. thinking repeatedly, meditating. *s.*

پرتچهہ परतच्छ *partachh*, obvious, present, apparent, public; adv. before, in the presence. *s.*

پرتچهایا प्रतिच्छाया *pratichhāyā*, f. an image, a statue, a picture. *s.*

پرتدان प्रतिदान *pratidān*, m. the return of a deposit; barter; giving back, or in return for. *s.*

پرتدشا प्रतिदिशा *pratidishā*, adv. everywhere, all around. *s.*

پرتدن प्रतिदिन *pratidin*, day after day, daily. *s.*

پرتدهوان प्रतिध्वान *pratidhwān*, m. } echo, resonance. *s.*
پرتدهون प्रतिध्वनि *pratidhwani*, f. }

پرتراتر प्रतिरात्र *pratirātra*, m. every night. *s.*

پرتران परित्राण *paritrān*, m. preserving, protecting. *s.*

پرترکشن प्रतिरक्षण *pratirakshan*, m. preserving. *s.*

پرتروپ प्रतिरूप *pratirūp*, m. a picture, an image. *s.*

پرترودھ प्रतिरोध *pratirodh*, m. opposition, impediment. *s.*

پرترودهك प्रतिरोधक *pratirodhak*, } m. a thief,
پرترودهي प्रतिरोधी *pratirodhī*, } a robber. *s.*

پرتسپردھا प्रतिस्पर्द्धा *pratisparddhā*, f. emulation, rivalry. *s.*

پرتسپردهي प्रतिस्पर्द्धी *pratisparddhī*, envious, emulous; refractory. *s.*

پرتسر प्रतिसर *pratisar*, m. cicatrizing; a form of incantation; a string worn round the hand at nuptials. *s.*

پرتسرگ प्रतिसर्ग *pratisarg*, m. the portion of a Purān, which treats of the destruction and renovation of the world; secondary creation by agents of one Supreme Being. *s.*

پرتسیایه प्रतिश्याय *pratisyāya*, m. catarrh. *s.*

پرتشٹ परितुष्ट *paritushṭ*, pleased, delighted. *s.*

پرتشٹهہ प्रतिष्ठ *pratishṭh*, famous. *s.*

پرتشٹها प्रतिष्ठा *pratishṭhā*, f. consecration of a monument erected in honour of a deity, or of the image of a deity; celebrity, renown; endowment of a temple; portioning a daughter; a form of metre, consisting of a stanza of four lines of four syllables each. *s.*

پرتشٹهان प्रतिष्ठान *pratishṭhān*, m. site, situation; the capital of the early kings of the lunar dynasty, opposite to Allahabad; the capital of Sālivāhan in the Dukhin. *s.*

پرتشٹهت प्रतिष्ठित *pratishṭhit*, famous, celebrated; consecrated; endowed; situated, established. *s.*

پرتشدھ प्रतिषिद्ध *pratishiddha*, forbidden, prohibited. *s.*

پرتشنکا प्रतिशङ्का *pratishankā*, f. constant fear or doubt. *s.*

پرتشیا प्रतिश्या *pratishyā*, f. catarrh. *s.*

پرتشیدھ प्रतिषेध *pratishedh*, prohibition, exception, contradiction. *s.*

پرتکار प्रतिकार *pratikār*, m. revenge, retaliation; remedying, counteracting. *s.*

پرتکرما प्रतिकर्मा *pratikarmā*, m. retaliation, requital; remedy, redress. *s.*

پرتکریا प्रतिक्रिया *pratikriyā*, f. return, requital; remedying, counteracting. *s.*

پرتکشن प्रतिक्षण *pratikshan*, adv. momentarily, every moment. *s.*

پرتکول प्रतिकूल *pratikūl*, contrary, adverse, inverted; contradictory, perverse. *s.*

پرتکولتا प्रतिकूलता *pratikūlatā*, f. opposition, hostility. *s.*

پرتگرجن प्रतिगर्जन *pratigarjan*, echoing, reverberating. *s.*

پرتگره प्रतिग्रह *pratigrah*, m. proper donation to Brāhmans; the acceptance of such a gift. *s.*

پرتگهات प्रतिघात *pratighāt*, m. a return blow, rebound; warding off a blow; preventing. *s.*

پرتگهاتن प्रतिघातन *pratighātan*, m. killing, slaughter. *s.*

پرتگهاتي प्रतिघाती *pratighātī*, repelling, hostile, opposed to. *s.*

پرتگیا प्रतिज्ञा *pratigyā* or *pratignyā*, f. an agreement, compact, stipulation, engagement, promise; (in logic) the proposition, the assertion to be proved. *pratigyā-patrak*, m. a bond, a written contract. *s.*

پرتگیات प्रतिज्ञात *pratigyāt*, promised, agreed, admitted, asserted. *s.*

پرتل परतल *partal*, m. f. the baggage of a horseman, carried all on one bullock or *ṭaṭṭū* (a pony). *partal kā ṭaṭṭū*, a pack-horse, a bat-horse. *h.*

پرتل प्रतल *pratal*, m. one of the seven divisions of the lower regions. *s.*

پرتلا परतला *partalā*, m. a sword-belt. *h.*

پرتلنبهه प्रतिलम्भ *pratilambh*, m. censure, reviling, abuse. *s.*

پرتلوم प्रतिलोम *pratilom*, left, not right; reverse, inverted; low, vile, base. *s.*

پرتم *pirtam*, the earth, the world. *d.*

پرتم परतम *partam*, greatest, supreme. *s.*

پرتما प्रतिमा *pratimā*, f. likeness, image, statue, picture. *p.*

پرتماس प्रतिमास *pratimās*, every month, monthly. *s.*

پرتمان प्रतिमान *pratimān*, m. resemblance, image, picture. *s.*

پرتموشکا प्रतिमूषिका *pratimūshikā*, f. a kind of rat. *s.*

پرتنا पृतना *pṛitnā*, f. an army; a division consisting of 243 elephants, as many chariots, 729 horses, and 1215 foot. *s.*

پرتناد प्रतिनाद *pratinād*, m. echo, resonance. *s.*

پرتندھ प्रतिनिधि *pratinidhi*, m. a resemblance, image; a surety; a substitute. *s.*

پرتنش प्रतिनिश *pratinish*, by night, every night. *s.*

پرتو *partau* or *partav*, m. light, the sunbeams, rays of light, enlightenment. *p.* [ply. *s.*

پرتواچ प्रतिवाच *prativāch*, f. an answer, a re-

پرتوادي प्रतिवादी *prativādī*, m. a defendant, a respondent. *s.* [neighbouring. *s.*

پرتواسي प्रतिवासी *prativāsī*, a neighbour,

پرتواکيه प्रतिवाक्य *prativāhya*, m. a reply, an answer. *s.* [echo. *s*

پرتوچن प्रतिवचन *prativachan*, m. a reply, an

پرتوش परितोष *paritosh*, m. pleasure, delight. *s.* [(*Betula*). *s.*

پرتوشا प्रतिविषा *prativishā*, f. a plant

پرتومب प्रतिविम्ब *prativimb*, m. a resemblance, image, shadow. *s.*

پرتوني प्रतूणी *pratūnī*, f. pain shooting from the rectum along the bowels. *s.*

پرته परितः *parita*, around, all round. *s.*

پرتھ पृथु *prithu*, m. the fifth monarch of the solar dynasty in the second age; the name of an ancient rājā, son of *Vena*, rājā of *Bettūr*. He was married to a form of the goddess *Lakshmī*, taught men to cultivate the earth, &c. &c.; f. a pungent seed (*Nigella Indica*); a medicinal substance commonly called *Hingupatrī*. *s.* [morial custom. *s.*

پرتھا प्रथा *prathā*, f. fame, celebrity; imme-

پرتھاس प्रतिहास *pratihās*, m. a shrub. (*Nerium odorum*). *s.* [declared. *s*

پرتھت प्रथित *prathit*, famous, celebrated;

پرتھت प्रथिति *prathiti*, f. celebrity, notoriety. *s.*

پرتھت प्रतिहत *pratihat*, disappointed, opposed, obstructed; overthrown. *s.*

پرتھت प्रतिहति *pratihati*, f. disappointment. *s.*

پرتھك प्रथुक *prathuk*, m. the young of any animal. *s.*

پرتھك प्रथक *prathak* or पृथक *prithak*, separate, apart. *prithak-parnī*, f. a plant (*Hemionites cordifolia*). *prithak-twa*, m. individuality, separateness. *prithak-twachā*, f. a plant, commonly called *Mūrva* (*Sanseviera zeylanica*). *prithak-krit*, separated, sundered. *prithak-karan*, m. separating, distinguishing. *s.*

پرتھگ آتما पृथगात्मा *prithag-ātmā*, individualised spirit, or that of an individual as detached from the universal spirit. *prithag-gun*, having distinct properties. *prithag-vidh*, various, diversified. *s.*

پرتھم प्रथम *pratham*, first, in the first place. *pratham-sāhas*, the first or lowest degree of punishment. *s.*

پرتھمي प्रथमी, पिरथमी, पृथमी *prathmī*, *pirthamī*, or *prithamī*, f. the world, earth, ground. *s.*

پرتھنسا प्रतिहिंसा *pratihinsā*, f. retaliation, revenge. *s.*

پرتھودر पृथूदर *prithūdar*, large-bellied, corpulent; m. a ram. *s.*

پرتھوي पृथ्वी *prithwī* or पृथिवी *prithivī*, f. the earth. *prithivī-tal*, m. the surface of the ground. *prithwī*, f. a pungent seed (*Nigella Indica*); a medicinal substance and condiment, *Hingupatrī*. *s.*

پرتھوي بھر पृथ्वीभर *prithwī-bhar*, m. a species of the *atyasti* metre. *s.*

پرتھوي پال पृथिवीपाल *prithivī-pāl*,
پرتھوي پت पृथिवीपति *prithivī-pati*,
پرتھوي ناتھ पृथिवीनाथ *prithivī-nāth*, } m. a king, a sovereign; lit. cherisher or lord of the earth. *s.*

پرتھي पृथी *prithī* or *pirthī*, the earth. *s.*

پرتھي پال पृथीपाल *prithī-pāl*,
پرتھي ناتھ पृथीनाथ *prithī-nāth*, } king, sovereign; lit. cherisher or lord of the earth. *s.* [ground. *h.*

پرتي परती *partī*, f. waste or uncultivated

پرتيادشٹ प्रत्यादिष्ट *pratyādisht*, removed, set aside; informed, warned; declared. *s.*

پرتياديش प्रत्यादेश *pratyādesh*, m. information, apprising, warning, declaration. *s.*

پرتياشا प्रत्याशा *pratyāshā*, f. hope, expectation, desire. *pratyāshī*, hoping. *s.*

پرتياگ परित्याग *parityāg*, m. abandonment, quitting. *parityāgī*, adj. abandoning. *s.*

پرتياھار प्रत्याहार *pratyāhār*, m. (in gram.) combination of two or more letters of the alphabet to form a class of letters. *s.*

پرتيپکار प्रत्युपकार *pratyupahār*, m. a return of kindness or assistance. *pratyupakārī*, adj. returning a kindness. *s.*

پرتيت प्रतीत *pratīt* or परतीत *partīt*, famous, renowned; f. faith, confidence. *partīt-k.*, to examine, to believe, to trust. *s.*

پرتيت प्रतीति *pratīti*, f. knowledge, understanding; fame, notoriety. *s.*

پرتيتپن प्रत्युत्पन्न *pratyutpanna*, reproduced, regenerated; multiplied; m. the product of a multiplication. *s.*

پرتيتر प्रत्युत्तर *pratyuttar*, m. a retort, or return of answer for answer. *s.*

پرتيتھان प्रत्युत्थान *pratyutthān*, m. rising from a seat as a mark of respect *s.*

پرتيچي प्रतीची *pratīchī*, f. the west quarter. *pratīchīn* or *pratīchya*, western. *s.*

پرتيدگمن प्रत्युद्गमन *pratyudgaman*, m. rising from a seat, going forth to meet any one. *s.*

پرتير प्रतीर *pratīr*, m. a shore or bank. *s.*

پرتيشمن प्रत्यश्मन् *pratyashman*, m. red chalk. *s.*

پرتيك प्रतीक *pratīk*, contrary, adverse, reversed; m. a limb, a part. *s.*

پرتیک प्रत्यक् *pratyak*, subsequent, uniform. *pratyak-parnī* or *pratyak-pushpī*, f. a plant (*Achyranthes aspera*). *pratyak-shrenī*, f. a plant, commonly called *Dantī*; a plant (*Salvinia cucullata*). *s.*

پرتیکار प्रतीकार *pratīkār*, m. revenge, retaliation; obviating, remedying. *s.*

پرتیکت परित्यक्त *parityakt*, void, deprived of; abandoned. *s.*

پرتیکت प्रत्युक्ति *pratyukti*, f. a rejoinder, a reply. *s.*

پرتیکش प्रत्यक्ष *pratyaksh*, perceptible, evident, apparent. *pratyaksh-darshan*, m. an eye-witness. *pratyaksh-pramān*, ocular or visible proof. *s.*

پرتیکشا प्रतीक्षा *pratīkshā*, f. regard to, consideration, expectation. *pratīkshak*, adj. expecting; looking at. *pratīkshan*, m. looking to, considering; expecting. *pratīkshī*, expecting. *s.*

پرتیکشي प्रत्यक्षी *pratyakshī*, adj. seeing, perceiving. *pratyakshī-krit*, manifested, made visible. *s.*

پرتیہ प्रत्यहः *pratyaha* or प्रत्यहम् *pratyaham*, every day, from day to day. *s.*

پرتینت प्रत्यन्त *pratyant*, bordering, contiguous. m. the country of *Mlechhas* or savages. *s.*

پرتینگ प्रत्यङ्ग *pratyang*, m. an organ of perception; adv. on the body, or the limbs severally. *s.*

پرتیننتر प्रत्यनन्तर *pratyanantar*, adv. next in succession. *s.*

پرتیواپ प्रतीवाप *pratīvāp*, m. calcining or fluxing metals; throwing one substance into another, adding any thing to a medicine during or after decoction; a public calamity, a plague. *s.*

پرتیوایہ प्रत्यवाय *pratyavāya*, m. disappearance, non-production. *s.*

پرتیوش प्रत्यूष *pratyūsh*, m. the morning, dawn. *s.*

پرتیوگ प्रतियोग *pratiyog*, m. opposition, contradiction; co-operation, association. *prati-yogitā*, f. mutual co-operation; opposition. *pratiyogī*, m. an opponent; a partner, an associate. *s.*

پرتییک प्रत्येक *pratyek*, each, every, one by one. *s.*

پرتیي प्रत्यय *pratyay* or *pratyaya*, m. belief, faith, trust, confidence. *pratyayit*, trusted, confidential. *pratyayī*, trusting, believing. *s.*

پرتییمان प्रतीयमान *pratīyamān*, adj. being believed or trusted. *s.*

پرج पर्ज *parj*, f. name of a musical mode or *rāginī*; a handle of a shield. *parj-dār*, basket-hilted (scimitar). *s.*

پرجا पर्जा *parjā* or प्रजा *prajā*, f. a subject, a tenant, a renter; people; progeny. *prajā-dharm*, m. the duty of children or subjects. *prajā-hit*, good for children or subjects; kind to them. *s.*

پرجاپت प्रजापति *prajā-pat* or *prajā-pati*, m. a name of Brahma; the epithet common to ten divine personages, who were first created by Brahma: a prince, lord of subjects; father; son-in-law, daughter's husband; potter. *s.*

پرجاءي *parjā,e*, f. custom, manner; place, room. *s.*

پرجت परजित *parjit*, conquered, subdued. *s.*

پرجتن परजतन *parjatan*, } m. travelling. *s.*
پرجٹن परजटन *parjaṭan*, }

پرجن परिजन *parijan*, m. attendants, followers, suite. *s.*

پرجنک पर्जङ्क *parjank*, m. a bedstead. *s.*

پرجني पर्जनी *parjanī*, f. a sort of *curcuma* (*Curcuma zanthorhizon*). *s.*

پرجوٹ परजवट *parjawaṭ*, m. quit-rent, tax. *s.*

پرجولت प्रज्वलित *prajwalit*, blazing, radiant. *s.*

پرجیایہ पर्याय *parjyāya*, m. order, arrangement, series; manner, kind; opportunity; a series of of synonyms for one term. *s.*

پرجیٹن पर्यटन *parjyaṭan*, m. wandering about, roaming. *s.*

پرجینت पर्यन्त *parjyant*, m. limit, term, boundary. *s.*

پرجینک पर्यङ्क *parjyank*, m. a bedstead. *s.*

پرجیوسان पर्यवसान *parjyavasān*, m. end, conclusion. *s.*

پرجیون प्रजीवन *prajīvan*, m. livelihood, subsistence. *s.*

پرچ पिरिच *pirich*, a saucer. *h.*

پرچا पर्चा *parchā*, f. (v. *parīchhā*) trial, examination; m. demonstration, proof. *s.*

پرچار परचार *parchār* or प्रचार *prachār*, m. publication, disclosure; appearance; custom, usage; conduct; currency. *s.*

پرچارک परिचारक *parichārak*, m. a servant, an attendant. *s.*

پرچانا परचाना *parchānā*, a. to introduce to a person, to engage in conversation. *s.*

پرچت *parchat*, mark, trace, effect. *d.*

پرچت प्रचित *prachit*, m. a species of metre. *s.*

پرچت परिचित *parichit*, known, acquainted with. *s.*

پرچر प्रचुर *prachur*, much, many. *s.*

پرچرت प्रचरित *pracharit*, pursued, practised (as an art). *s.*

پرچرجیا परिचर्य्या *paricharjyā*, f. service, dependence; veneration, worship. *s.*

پرچلک पुर्चेक *purchak*, f. deceit, trick, coaxing. *h.*

پرچلت प्रचलत् *prachalat*, prevailing, circulating, customary. *prachalit*, current, recognised (as a law). *prachalan*, m. being customary or current. *s.*

پرچم *parcham*, a flag, streamer, vane, tassel, pennant, ensign. *p.*

پرچنا परच्ना *parachnā*, n. to be tried, introduced, to be made acquainted, &c. *s.*

پرچنڈ प्रचण्ड *prachanḍ*, excessively hot or burning; intolerable; wrathful, passionate, raging, mighty, predominant. *prachanḍ-mūrti*, m. a tree (*Tapia crataeva*). *s.*

پرچو पर्चौ *parchau*, m. examination, &c. (v. *parchā*). *s.*

پرچودت प्रचोदित *pra-chodit*, prescribed, directed; sent. *pra-chodan*, m. saying, enjoining, prescribing; a rule, a law; sending, directing.

پرچودني प्रचोदिनी *pra-chodinī*, f. a prickly night-shade (*Solanum jacquini*). *s.*

پرچوني पर्चूनी *parchūnī*, f. the act of selling flour, meal, &c. *h.*

پرچونیا पर्चुनिया *parchūniyā*, m. a meal-merchant, a seller of flour. *h.* [cloth, web. *p.*

پرچه *parcha*, m. fragment, scrap, bit, rag,

پرچها पर्छा *parchhā*, m. self-grown paddy; a spindle for winding thread on; adj. cleared up (as the sky after rain). *h.*

پرچها पृच्छा *prichchhā*, f. asking, question. *s.*

پرچها परिच्छा *parichchhā*, f. examination. *s.*

پرچهان पर्छाँ *parchhāṅ*, پرچهانون पर्छाँवाँ *parchhāṅwāṅ*, پرچهاءين पर्छाईं *parchhā,iṅ*, } f. image (*from shade or reflection*), shadow, shade. *parchhā,iṅ apnī se bhāgnā*, to be frightened at one's own shadow. *s.*

پرچهت परिच्छित *parichchhit*, examined; proper name, grandson of *Arjuna*. *s.*

پرچهتي पर्छत्ती *parchhattī* or पर्छती *parchhatī*, f. a small thatch thrown over mud walls. *s.*

پرچهتي *parchhaṭī*, same as the last. *d.*

پرچهد प्रच्छद *parchchhad*, m. a wrapper, a cover. *s.* [defect in another. *s.*

پرچهدر परछिद्र *par-chhidra*, m. a fault or

پرچهك पृच्छक *prichchhak*, m. an inquirer, an investigator. *s.*

پرچهن प्रच्छन्न *prachchhann*, covered, clothed; disguised, private, secret, concealed; partial, not universal; m. a private door, a lattice, a loop-hole. *s.*

پرچهن पृच्छण *prichchhan*, m. asking, inquiring. *s.*

پرچهنا परछना *parachhnā*, a. to move a lamp or candle over the heads of a bride and bridegroom, to drive away evil spirits, propitiate good ones, &c.; to kindle (a fire). *h.* [dressing, inviting. *s.*

پرچهنا प्रच्छणा *prachchhanā*, f. asking, ad-

پرچهيد परिछेद *pari-chhed*, m. segment, division; section, chapter. *s.*

پرچي परिचय *pari-chai*, m. acquaintance, intimacy. *pari-cheya*, adj. to be known as an acquaintance. *s.* [viated from. *s.*

پرچيت प्रच्युत *pra-chyut*, fallen from, de-

پرچيل प्रचेल *prachel*, m. a yellow, fragrant wood. *s.* [ful. *p.a.*

پرحذر *pur-ḥazar*, full of caution, very care-

پرخاش *parkhāsh*, m. war, battle, conflict; commotion, disturbance, tumult; violence, injury, oppression; severe inquisition. *p.*

پردا *pardā* (for *parda*), m. a veil, a screen, &c.; adv. to-morrow, the day after to-morrow. *p.*

پرداخت *pardākht*, f. patronising. *p.*

پرداختن *pardākhtan* (r. *pardāz*), to finish, to accomplish; (hence) to leave off, to have done. *p.*

پردادا पर्दादा *pardādā*, m. a great-grandfather by the father's side. *h.*

پردادي पर्दादी *pardādī*, a great-grandmother by the father's side. *h.*

پردار परदार *par-dār*, f. another's wife. *par-dār-gaman*, m. adultery. *s.*

پرداز *pardāz*, performing, finishing, &c.; (used in comp.) as *kār-pardāz*, effecting the business. *p.*

پردان प्रदान *pradān*, m. gift, donation. *s.*

پردانا *pardānā*, a. to conceal, to keep behind a screen (inelegant). *p.*

پردچهنا *pradachhinā*, پردکشنا *pradakshinā*, } प्रदक्षिणा { f. going round an object to which respect is intended, with the right hand always towards it (a religious or superstitious ceremony); circuit, circumambulation. This is precisely the ceremony called *deasail*, practised formerly among the Highlanders, and alluded to by Scott in the "Chonicles of the Canongate." *s.*

پردر प्रदर *pradar*, m. a disease of women (*menorrhagia*). *s.* [another. *s.*

پردروهي परद्रोही *par-drohī*, tyrannizing over

پردرشن प्रदर्शन *pradarshan*, m. shewing; explaining; prophesying. *pradarshak*, m. a teacher, an expounder, a prophet. *pradarshit*, mentioned; explained, prophesied. *s.* [perty. *s.*

پردرويه परद्रव्य *par-dravya*, m. another's pro-

پردش प्रदिश *pradish*, پردك प्रदिक *pradik*, } f. intermediate point of the compass, or half quarter. *s.*

پردکشنا *pradakshinā* v. *pradachhinā*.

پردکه परदुःख *par-dukh*, m. the pain of another. *s.*

پردگي *pardagī*, f. a modest, chaste woman, one who confines herself to home. *p.*

پردمن *parduman*, (for प्रद्युम्न *pradyumna*) *Kāma* (or Cupid), son of *Kṛishṇa*, was married to *Ratī*. *s.*

پردن पर्दन *parddan*, m. wind downwards, letting wind. *s.*

پردوار पुरद्वार *pur-dwār*, m. a city gate. *s.*

پردوش प्रदोष *pradosh*, m. evening, the first part of the night; fault, offence, defect. *s.*

پردوش परदोष *par-dosh*, m. another's fault. *par-dosh-kīrthan*, m. scandal, slander. *s.*

پردويشي परद्वेषी *par-dweshī*, hostile, inimical. *s.*

پرده *parda*, m. a curtain, a screen; the sail of a ship; a musical tone or melody, a key or mode (in music); modesty. *parda parda dekhnā*, to pry or inquire secretly into any matter. *parda parda-k.*, to do a thing secretly or privately. *parda,e bīnī*, the cartilage that separates the nostrils. *parda-poshī*, the act of

concealing a blemish. *parda chhornā*, to let fall a curtain; to lay aside concealment. *parda-dār*, confidentia.. *parda-dar*, a betrayer of secrets. *parda-darī*, betraying of secrets. *parda-rakhnā*, to give obscure hints, or relate a matter in such terms as only to be understood by part of the hearers. *parda-fāsh*, betraying secrets. *parda-k.*, to conceal. *parda kisī kā phāṛnā* or *kholnā*, to reveal the faults of another. *parda-nishīn*, remaining behind the curtain, modest. *parde meṅ sūrāḵẖ-k.*, spoken of a woman who secretly indulges in licentious practices. *parda,e haft-rang*, lit. the veil of seven colours, the world, worldly vicissitudes and vanities. *p.* [disc of the sun. *s.*

پردهہ परिधि *paridhi*, m. circumference; the

پردهان प्रधान *pardhān*, or *pradhān*, m. nature, the natural state of any thing, or the cause of the material world; the Supreme God; chief, principal; the first companion of a king, his minister, his eunuch, or confidant; a courtier, a minister of state, a president, leader, chief. *pradhān-tā*, f. excellence, supremacy. *pradhān-dhātu*, m. semen virile. *pradhān-mantrī*, m. prime-minister. *pradhānottam*, eminent, illustrious. *s.* [clothes. *s.*

پردهان परिधान *paridhān*, m. a lower garment,

پردهرم परधर्म *par-dharm*, m. another's duty or business. *s.*

پردهن परधन *par-dhan*, m. another's wealth. *par-dhan-āswādan-sukh*, m. feeding luxuriously at another's expense. *s.*

پردهونس प्रध्वंस *pradhwaṅs*, m. destruction, loss. *pradhwaṅsī*, destroying, annihilating. *s.*

پرديپ प्रदीप *pradīp*, m. a lamp. *s.*

پرديپن प्रदीपन *pradīpan*, m. a mineral poison of a red colour and caustic nature. *s.*

پرديس परदेश *pardes*, m. a foreign country; adj. of another country, abroad. *s.*

پرديسي परदेशी *par-desī*, m. foreigner, a stranger. *s.*

پرديش प्रदेश *pradesh*, m. a place in general, a district; a foreign country, abroad. *s.*

پرديوتا पुरदेवता *pur-devtā*, f. the tutelary deity of a town. *s.*

پرديہ प्रदेह *pradeh*, m. unguent, unction. *s.*

پررو परुह *par-ru*, m. a potherb (*Eclipta prostrata*). *s.*

پرزه *purza*, m. a scrap (generally applied to paper), piece, bit, rag, frippery. *purze honā*, to be severely wounded in battle. *p.* [dividual. *s.*

پرس पुरुष *purus* or *purush*, m. a man, an in-

پرس परस *paras*, m. act of touching, a touch. *s.*

پرس *purs*, (in comp.) asking, inquiring. *p.*

پرس परुस् *parus*, m. the knot or joint of a cane or reed. *s.*

پرسا *pursā*, m. condolence, inquiring kindly into one's condition. *p.*

پرسا पुर्सा *pursā*, of a man's height, the extent of a man's reach when extending the arms and fingers (a fathom). *s.*

پرساد प्रसाद *prasād*, m. favour, kindness, blessing, propitiousness; viand, victuals, food that has been offered to the deities; leavings of a great man or spiritual guide. *s.*

پرسادهن प्रसाधन *prasādhan*, m. accomplishing, effecting. *prasādhak*, one who accomplishes. *prasādhit*, accomplished, completed. *s.*

پرسادهن परिसाधन *parisādhan*, m. accomplishing; determining. *s.* [monly called *siddhi*. *s.*

پرسادهي प्रसाधनी *prasādhanī*, f. a drug com-

پرسادي प्रसादी *prasādī*, offered to deities. *s.*

پرسار प्रसार *prasār*,
پرسارن प्रसारण *prasāran*, } m. spreading, expanding. *prasārit*, stretched, expanded. *prasārī*, adj. spreading, expanding *s.*

پرسال *par-sāl*, last year (*pār-sāl*). *p.*

پرساله *pur-sāla*, aged, full of years. *p.*

پرسان *pursān* (v. *purs*), asking, inquiring; (used in comp.) as *aḥwāl-pursān*, inquiring after one's condition. *p.*

پرسپر परस्पर *paraspar*, mutually, reciprocally. *parasparānumati*, f. mutual concurrence or assent. *parasparopakārī*, an ally, an associate. *s.*

پرسپهٹ प्रस्फुट *prasphuṭ*, blown, expanded. *s.*

پرست *parast*, (in comp.) adorer, worshipper; as, *ḵẖudā-parast*, a worshipper of God; *but-parast*, an idolater, worshipper of idols; *ātash-parast*, a worshipper of fire, a *guebre* of the sect of Abraham, Zoroaster, or the Magi; *ḵẖud-parast*, a worshipper or admirer of himself, selfish or self-conceited. *p.*

پرستاب प्रस्ताव *prastāb*, m. mention, occasion, opportunity. *s.*

پرستابک प्रस्ताविक *prastābik*,
پرستاوک प्रस्ताविक *prastāvik*, } suggested by previous mention, well-timed, a-propos, opportune, seasonable. *s.*

پرستار *parastār*, m. an adorer; a slave. *p.*

پرستاو प्रस्ताव *prastā,o*, m. opportunity, season; eulogium. *s.* [ment, introduction. *s.*

پرستاونا प्रस्तावना *prastā,onā*, f. commence-

پرستت प्रस्तुत *prastut*, celebrated, praised; said, declared; accomplished, done. *s.*

پرستر प्रस्तर *prastar*, m. a stone; a jewel. *s.*

پرستش *parastish*, f. devotion, act of worshipping. *p.*

پرستش خانه *parastish-ḵẖāna*, m.
پرستش گاه *parastish-gāh*, f. } a place of worship, church, temple, mosque. *p.*

پرستنده *parastanda*, a worshipper. *p.*

پرستهہ प्रस्थ *prasth*, expanding, spread; m. a measure of quantity, 48 double handfuls; table-land on the top of a mountain. *prasth-pushp*, m. a sort of *tulsī*, or basil, with small leaves. *s.*

پرستهاپن प्रस्थापन *prasthāpan*, m. sending away, mission. *prasthāpit*, sent, despatched. *s*

پرستهان प्रस्थान *prasthān*, m. going forth, setting out, departure. *s.*

پرستیدن *parastīdan*, to worship, to adore. *p.*

پرسدھ प्रसिद्ध *prasiddha*, celebrated, renowned; adorned, ornamented. *prasiddhi*, f. fame, celebrity. *s.*

پرسراو प्रस्राव *prasrāv*, m. urine. *s.*

پرسرم परिश्रम *parisram* or *parishram*, m. fatigue, weariness. *s.*

پرسرمي परिश्रमी *parisramī*, active, laborious. *s.*

پرسش *pursish*, f. inquiry, asking (generally means asking after health, &c.). *p.*

پرسکار पुरस्कार *puraskār*, m. honouring, worshipping. *s.*

پرسکت प्रसक्त *prasakta*, eternal, constant; obtained, attained; attached to, devoted to; adv. continually. *prasakti*, f. adherence, attachment to. *s.*

پرسکندکا प्रस्कन्दिका *praskandikā*, f. } purging, پرسکندن प्रस्कन्दन *praskandan*, m. } diarrhœa. *s.*

پرسماپت परिसमाप्त *parisamāpta*, finished, completed. *parisamāpti* f. & *parisamāpan*, m. entire, completion. *s.*

پرسمرت प्रस्मृति *prasmṛiti*, f. forgetfulness, forgetting. *s.*

پرسميپد परस्मैपद *parasmaipad*, m. the transitive or active form of a verb (in Gram.). *s.*

پرسن प्रसन्न *prasann* or *prasanna* or *parsan*, rejoiced, pleased; gracious, kind. *prasann honā*, n. to acquiesce; to like. *prasann-karnā*, to please. *prasannatā*, f. favour, kindness. *prasann-mukh* or *prasann-mukhī*, smiling, agreeable looking. *s.*

پرسنا *parasnā*, a. to worship, to adore. *p.*

پرسنا परसना *parasnā*, a. to touch. *s.*

پرسنبندھ परसम्बन्ध *par-sambandh*, m. relation or connection with another, *par-sambandhī*, related to another, belonging to another. *s.*

پرسنتا प्रसन्नता *prasannatā*, f. acquiescence; kindness. *s.*

پرسنسا प्रशंसा *prasansā*, f. praise, eulogy. *s.*

پرسنکهيا परिसङ्ख्या *parisankhyā*, f. complete enumeration. *parisankhyāt*, enumerated. *s.*

پرسنگ प्रसङ्ग *prasang*, m. association; mention; insertion. *prasang na lagnā*, not to associate with. *s.*

پرسو प्रसव *prasav*, m. the act of bearing a child. *prasav-bandhan*, m. the foot-stalk of a leaf or flower. *s.*

پرسو प्रसू *prasū*, f. a mother. *s.*

پرسوت प्रसूत *prasūt* or परसूत *parsūt*, m. a flower, fruit; the disease called *fluor albus* or the whites; part. born, produced. *prasavat*, bearing. *prasūti*, f. bringing forth, birth; offspring. *s.*

پرسوتا प्रसूता *prasūtā*, } a woman who پرسوتي प्रसौती *prasautī*, } has borne a پرسونتي प्रसवन्ती *prasavantī*, } child; a puerperal woman. *s.*

پرسورام *parsurām* (for परशुराम *parashurāma*), the first of the three *Rāmas*, and the sixth incarnation or *avatār* of *Vishnu*. He was the son of *Jamadagni*, and was contemporary with *Dāsharatha Rāma*. He is called *Jāmadagni*, and the deity descended in this form to destroy the *Kshatriyas* (or *Chhatrīs*), who were become tyrannical. *Renukā*, wife of *Jamadagni*, was interrupted in bringing water from the river by *Kārtavīrjārjuna*, a prince of the *Kshatriyas*, who was sporting in the water with his thousand wives, for which *Parashurāma's* father (*Jamadagni*) cursed him. The *Kshatriya* prince killed *Jamadagni*, and *Jāmadagni* (the son of the latter) vowed not to leave a *Kshatriya* on the face of the earth. He is said to have extirpated them twenty-one times, the women with child each time producing a new race. They say there has been no *Kshatriya* since that period, those so called being of spurious breed (or *Varnasankars*). *s.*

پرسون परसों *parson*, the day before yesterday; the day after to-morrow. *s.*

پرسون प्रसून *prasūn*, born, produced; m. a flower, a bud; fruit. *s.*

پرسوي प्रसवी *prasavī*, adj. having or bearing young. *s.*

پرسه *pursa*, m. condolence, kind inquiry. *p.*

پرسيا परसिया *parsiyā*, m. a reaping-hook, a sickle. *h.*

پرسياوشان *parsiyāwshān* or *parsiyāwishān*, m. maiden-hair (*Pteris lunulata*). *p.*

پرسيدن *pursīdan*, to ask, to inquire. *p.*

پرسيمن परिसीमन् *parisīman*, m. boundary, extreme limit. *s.*

پرش परश *parash*, m. a kind of gem. *s.*

پرش पुरुष *purush*, m. a man, a male human being; God, the Supreme Being. *purushā*, ancestors. *purushārth*, m. a human object, as the gratification of desire, discharge of duty, &c.; adv. on account of man. *purushādhikār*, m. manly office or duty. *purushādham*, m. an outcast. *purushāshī*, m. a rākshas, a cannibal. *purushāyu*, m. life of man. *purushtā*, f. *purushtwa*, m. manhood, manliness, valour. *purush-dweshī*, m. *purush-dweshinī*, f. misanthropic. *purush-kār*, m. manly act, virility; exertion. *purush-mātr*, of the height of a man. *purushottam*, m. an excellent or superior man. *purush-varjit*, depopulated. *s.*

پرش परुष *parush*, m. harsh and contumelious speech, abuse; yellow Barleria; a sort of tree (*Xylocarpus granatum*). *parush-bachan*, m. *parush-vāch*, f. *parushokti*, f. harsh language, abuse. *parushoktik*, m. an abuser. *s.*

پرش परशु *parashu*, m. an offensive weapon resembling a hatchet. *s.*

پرشا पुरुषाः *purushā*, people of old, predecessors, ancients. *s.*

پرشاپ परिशाप *parishāp*, m. cursing, reviling. *s.*

پرشاد परशाद *parshād* or *prashād*, m. favour, kindness, food, &c. (v. *prasād*). *s.*

پرشارتھ पुरुषार्थ *purushārth*, m. that which is becoming a man, as valour, generosity, &c. *s.*

پرشاسن प्रशासन *prashāsan*, m. governing, ruling. *s.*

پرشانت प्रशान्त *prashānt*, calmed, tranquillised. *prashānti*, f. calm, tranquillity. *prashāntātmā*, peaceful, composed in mind. *s.*

پرشب प्रशाव (for प्रसव) *prashab*, m. the act of bringing forth (young). *prashab-honā*, n. to be delivered (of young). *s.*

پرشدھ परिशुद्ध *parishuddha*, cleaned, purified; discharged, paid. *s.*

پرشرام परशुराम *parashurām*, see پرسورام. *s.*

پرشٹ पृष्ट *pṛisht*, asked, inquired. *s.*

پرشٹا प्रष्टा *prashṭā*, adj. asking, demanding; a questioner. *s.*

پرشٹھ पृष्ठ *pṛishṭh*, m. the back, the rear. *pṛishṭh-dṛishṭi*, m. a bear (from looking behind him). *s.*

پرشٹھ प्रष्ठ *prashṭh*, a leader; prior, preceding; chief, best. *prashṭhī*, the wife of a leader. *s.*

پرشچھد पुरश्छद *purashchhad*, m. a sort of grass (*Saccharum cylindricum*). *s.*

پرشرانت परिश्रान्त *parishrānt*, wearied, exhausted. *parishrānti*, f. fatigue, labour. *s.*

پرشرم परिश्रम *parishram*, m. labour, toil, fatigue. *parishramī*, laborious. *s.*

پرشست प्रशस्त *prashast*, happy, well, right, good, excellent. *prashasti*, f. excellence, eminence, eulogy. *s.*

پرشعور *pur-shu'ūr*, wise; most sagacious. *p. a.*

پرشکار परिष्कार *parishkār*, m. splendour, decoration, initiation, purification. *s.*

پرشکرت परिष्कृत *parishkṛit*, adorned, embellished; purified by initiatory rites. *parishkṛit-bhūmi*, f. a ground prepared for a sacrifice. *s.*

پرشمن प्रशमन *prashaman*, m. killing, slaughter; pacifying. *s.*

پرشن प्रश्न *prashn*, m. a question. *prashn-dūtī*, f. a riddle, an enigma. *s.*

پرشن‌پرني पृश्निपर्णी *pṛishniparnī*, f. a plant (*Hemionites cordifolia; Hedysarum lagopodioides*). *s.*

پرشنسا प्रशंसा *prashansā*, f. praise, applause, flattery. *s.*

پرشنسن प्रशंसन *prashansan*, m. praising, eulogizing. *prashansanīya*, to be praised, praiseworthy. *prashansit*, praised. *s.*

پرشنکا पृश्निका *pṛishnikā*, f. an aquatic plant (*Pistia stratioites*). *s.*

پرشنکنیہ परिशङ्कनीय *parishankanīya*, adj. to be doubted, to be apprehended. *s.*

پرشني प्रश्नी *prashnī*, f. an aquatic plant (*Pistia stratioites*). *s.*

پرشودھ परिशोध *parishodh*, m. cleansing, purifying; discharging (a debt). *s.*

پرشوس परश्वस *par-shwas*, the day after to-morrow. *s.*

پرشوش परिशोष *parishosh*, m. drying, evaporation. *s.*

پرشیش परिशेष *parishesh*, m. remainder, completion. *s.*

پرضرور *pur-ẓarūr*, very necessary, most essential *p. a.*

پرکا पृक्का *pṛikkā*, f. a gramineous plant (*Trigonella corniculata*). *s.*

پرکاج परकाज *par-kāj*, m. the business or affairs of another. *s.*

پرکاجي परकाजी *par-kājī*, attentive to the business or interest of others, serving others, beneficent. *s.*

پرکار *pur-kār*, thick, coarse, fat; efficient, well executed. *p.*

پرکار *parkār*, compasses. *parkārī*, done with compasses (v. *pargār*). *p.*

پرکار प्रकार *prakār*, manner, method, kind, sort. *s.*

پرکاري *purkārī*, f. thickness, coarseness. *p.*

پرکاس प्रकाश *prakās* or *parkās*, m. light, daylight; adj. clear, apparent. *s.*

پرکاسي *prakāsī*, m. a discoverer. *s.*

پرکاش प्रकाश *prakāsh*, m. light, daylight, sunshine; expansion, diffusion, manifestation; adj. open, manifest, blown, expanded; famous, celebrated clear, apparent. *prakāsaktā*, f. manifestation, luminousness. *prakāshit*, evident, manifest, promulgated. *prakāshak*, what irradiates, manifests; an illuminator. *prakāshmān*, splendid, radiant. *prakāshan*, m. illuminating, making manifest. *prakāshī*, m. a discoverer. *s.*

پرکالہ *parkāla*, m. a spark; pane of glass. *p.*

پرکان परकान *parkān*, m. a trunnion. *h.*

پرکانا परकाना *parkānā*, a. to accustom, to habituate. *h.*

پرکانڈ प्रकाण्ड *prakāṇḍ*, m. the stem of a tree, excellence, happiness. *s.*

پرکپت प्रकुपित *prakupit*, enraged, incensed. *s.*

پرکتھا परिकथा *parikathā*, f. a tale, a story. *s.*

پرکٹ प्रकट *prakaṭ*, displayed, manifest. *prakaṭit* or *prakaṭ-kṛit*, manifested, made visible. *s.*

پرکٹ पकेट *parkaṭ*, m. a heron. *s.*

پرکٹي पर्कटी *parkhaṭī*, f. the waved-leaf fig tree (*Ficus infectiosa*). *s.*

پرکر प्रकर *prakar*, m. aloe wood (*agallochum*). *s.*

پرکرت प्रकृति *prakṛit* or *prakṛiti*, f. property, quality, nature; the passive or material cause of the world; a goddess, the personified will of the Supreme Being in the creation, identified with Māyā; a stanza of four lines, each line containing twenty-one syllables; temperament, predominance of one of the humours. *prakṛiti-taral*, volatile, fickle. *prakṛiti-stha*, natural, innate. *s.*

پرکرت प्रकृत *prakṛit*, made, accomplished. *s.*

پرکرش प्रकर्ष *prakarsh*, m. (in gram.) the effect of the prefix *pra* upon roots. *s.*

پرکرشٹ प्रकृष्ट *prakṛisht*, chief, principal. *prakṛishṭatwa*, m. eminence. *s.*

پرکرم प्रक्रम *prakram*, m. proceeding, going, leisure, opportunity. *s.*

پرکرما परिक्रमा *parikramā*, f. act of going round to the right, by way of adoration, circumambulation, a superstitious ceremony (v. *pradakhina*). *s.*

پرکرن प्रकरण *prakaran*, m. topic, subject; paragraph, section; prologue, prelude; a book. *s.*

پرکري परिक्रय *parikray*, m. redeeming, purchasing back. *s.*

پرکريا प्रक्रिया *prakriyā*, f. bearing royal insignia. *s.*

پرکشالن प्रक्षालण *prakshālan*, m. cleaning, washing. *prakshālit*, washed. *s.*

پرکشپت प्रक्षिप्त *prakshipt*, thrown, cast, hurled. *s.*

پرکشت परिक्षित *parikshit*, a king, son of Abhimanyu, and grandson of Arjun. *s.*

پرکشيتر परक्षेत्र *par-kshetr*, m. another's field, another's body, another's wife. *s.*

پرکشين प्रक्षीण *prakshīn*, decayed, wasting. *s.*

پرکلپت परिकल्पित *parikalpit*, made, invented. *s.*

پرکلش परिक्लिश *pariklish*, m. vexation, trouble. *pariklisht*, vexed, annoyed. *s.*

پرکمپ प्रकम्प *prakamp*, m. shaking, trembling. *prakampamān*, adj. shaking, trembling violently. *prakampan*, id.; m. a hell. *s.*

پرکنا परकना *parakhnā*, n. to be habituated, to acquire a habit; to inspect, examine, prove, try. *s.*

پرکوپ प्रकोप *prakop*, m. irritation, provocation. *prakopit*, irritated. *prakopan*, m. irritating, provoking *p.*

پرکھ परख *parakh*, f. examination, trial, proof, inspection. *s.*

پرکھ पुरुष *purukh*, m. a man (*vir*), a male human being. *s.*

پرکھا पुरखा *purukhā* or पुर्खा *purkhā*, m. an old man. *s.*

پرکھا परिखा *parikhā*, f. a moat surrounding a fort, &c. *s.*

پرکھانا परखाना *parkhānā*, a. to cause to examine, try, prove, or inspect. *s.*

پرکھاوني परखावनी *parkhāvanī*, f. examination; assaying of coin, &c. *s.*

پرکھاءي परखाई *parkhā,ī*, f. the price paid for examination, trial, proof, inspection; the act of examining *s.*

پرکھر प्रखर *prakhar*, very hot or acrid. *s.*

پرکھنا परखना *parakhnā*, a. to inspect, to examine, to prove. *s.*

پرکھي पुरखे *purukhe* or पुर्खे *purkhe*, m. (pl. of *purkhā*), ancestry, ancestors. *s.*

پرکھي परखी *parkhī*, m. a banker who examines and proves money. *s.*

پرکھيات प्रख्यात *prakhyāt* or परिख्यात *parikhyāt*, famous, celebrated. *prakhyāti* or *parikhyāti*, fame, notoriety. *s.*

پرکھيا परखैया *parkhaiyā*, } m. an inspector,
پرکھيرا परखेरा *parkherā*, } examiner, prover, especially of coins. *s.*

پرکيرت प्रकीर्ति *prakīrti*, f. fame, celebrity. *prakīrtit*, declared, explained; celebrated. *s.*

پرکيرتن परिकीर्तन *parikīrttan*, m. telling, talking of, boasting. *s.*

پرکيرن प्रकीर्ण *prakīrn*, promulgated, published; expanded; m. a *chauri*, a cow-tail used as a fan; a chapter. *s.*

پرکينه *pur-kīna*, malicious, spiteful. *p.*

پرکيه परकीय *parkīya*, belonging to another. *parkiyā*, f. another's wife or mistress. *s.*

پرگاچھ परगाछ *pargāchh*, m. epidendron. *h.*

پرگار *pargār*, f. a pair of compasses. *p.*

پرگاري *pargārī*, f. work done with compasses. *p.*

پرگاڑھ प्रगाढ़ *pragāṛh*, much, excessive; hard, difficult; hard, firm; m. pain, privation, penance. *s.*

پرگاه *pargāh*, straw, rubbish, any thing worthless. *p.*

پرگٹ प्रगट *pragaṭ* or *pargaṭ*, obvious, notorious, public, manifest. *s.*

پرگٹتا प्रगटता *pragaṭatā*, f. visibility, publicity. *s.*

پرگٹنا प्रगटना *pragaṭnā*, n. to appear, be made public. *s.*

پرگرهن प्रग्रहण *pragrahan*, m. taking, seizing, assuming. *s.*

پرگلبھ प्रगल्भ *pragalbh*, bold, ready, resolute, strong. *pragalbhatā*, f. energy, boldness; power. *s.*

پرگمن प्रगमन *pragaman*, m. progress, advance. *s.*

پرگنات *parganāt*, } pl. of *pargana* (the last
پرگنجات *parganajāt*, } form may be called the pedantic or barbarous plural), used in revenue documents. *p.*

پرگناتي *parganātī*, of or relating to baronies. *parganātī-jam'*, the amount of the revenue received at the head office of the *pargana* from the several subdivisions composing such *pargana*, after deducting the charges of collecting in each. *parganātī-kharch*, charges of a district to be deducted from the gross revenue. *parganātī-nirkh*, rates of valuation, &c. *p.*

پرگنه *pargana*, m. an inferior division of a country (less than a *zil'*), nearly equalling a barony; the largest division of land in a *zamīndārī*. *pargana dār*, m. the superior officer of a *pargana*; lord of the barony. *pargana-wār*, according to district (settlement, &c.).

پرگو *pur-go*, talkative, loquacious. *p.*

پرگوپن प्रगोपन *pragopan*, m. protection, preservation. *s.*

پرگوءي *pur-go,ī*, f. loquacity, volubility of tongue. *s.*

پرگھٹ प्रघट *praghaṭ* or *parghaṭ*, apparent, clear. *s.*

پرگھٹي प्रघटी *praghaṭī* or परघटी *parghaṭī*, f. a mould in which silver or gold is cast, previous to working it; apparency, clearness. *s.*

پرگھن प्रघन *praghan*, m. a sort of bean (*Phaseolus mungo*). *s.*

پرگيا प्रज्ञा *pragyā*, f. a clever woman; understanding, wisdom. *pragyāwān*, wise. *s.*

پرگيات प्रज्ञात *pragyāt*, known, understood, notorious. *s.*

پرگیان प्रज्ञान *pragyān*, m. knowledge, wisdom; adj. wise, learned. *s.*

پرگیری *pargīrī*, f. an ortolan (a species of *Alauda*). *p.*

پرگیه प्रज्ञ *pragya*, wise, learned. *s.*

پرلا परला *parlā*, of the other side. *h.*

پرلاپ प्रलाप *pralāp*, m. unmeaning prattle; discourse. *s.*

پرلوبھ प्रलोभ *pralobh*, m. desire, cupidity. *pralobhan*, m. allurement, attraction. *s.*

پرلوٹھن प्रलोठन *pralothan*, m. rolling on the ground, tossing. *pralothit*, adj. rolling, tossing. *s.*

پرلوک परलोक *par-lok*, heaven, paradise. *par-lok-gam*, m. death. *s.*

پرلی प्रलय *parlai* (for *pralaya*), a general destruction, such as at the flood or resurrection; death, dissolution, fainting, syncope; (met.) vexation, fatigue, oppression, languor, disgust. *s.*

پرلیپک प्रलेपक *pralepak*, who or what anoints, besmears. *s.*

پرم परम *param*, best, first, supreme; used in comp. as, *paramātmā*, m. the Supreme Being, the soul of the universe. *paramādwait*, m. pure unitarianism. *paramārth*, m. superior aim, the best end; virtue; spiritual knowledge; the best sense. *paramārthī*, seeking the best end, religious. *paramāgati*, translation to heaven, beatitude. *paramānu*, m. an atom, the lowest measure of weight, or time. *paramānn*, m. an oblation of rice to progenitors. *param-ānand*, supreme pleasure, chief object of refuge. *param-gati*, f. eternal felicity. *paramāyu*, m. the longest period of life. *param-rāj*, m. a supreme monarch. *param-hans*, an ascetic, a religious man who has subdued all his senses. *s.*

پرم *purum* or *prum*, a lead and sounding-line used on board ship (the word is borrowed from the Portuguese *prumo*, plummet). *prum-ḍālnā*, to heave the lead. *h.*

پرما प्रमा *pramā*, f. true knowledge; consciousness, perception. *s.*

پرماتامهه प्रमातामहः *pramātā-maha*, m. a great-grandfather on the mother's side; f. *pramātāmahī*. *s.*

پرماد प्रमाद *pramād*, m. inadvertence, carelessness, error. *pramādī*, heedless, inconsiderate. *s.*

پرمارتھ परमार्थ *paramārth*, m. the first pursuit, the chief end, virtue, merit. *s.*

پرمارتھی परमार्थी *paramārthī*, religious, virtuous. *s.*

پرمان प्रमाण *pramān* or *parmān*, m. cause, motive; limit; proof, attestation, verification, authority, instance, example; adj. actual, authentic, substantial, real. *parmān-charhnā*, to rise to a high rank (the word is used sometimes as a man's name). *pramānabhāo*, m. absence of proof. *pramān-purush*, m. an umpire, an arbitrator. *pramānī-karan*, establishing or admitting as authority or proof. *s.*

پرمان परिमाण *parimān*, m. dose, quantity; proportion. *s.*

پرمانک प्रमाणिक *pramānik*, proper, creditable; reverend; m. chairman of an assembly; (in Bengal) a chief of a tribe among the inferior castes. *pramānikā*, f. a species of the *anushṭubh* metre. *s.*

پرمپد परम्पद or परमपद *param pad*, m. eminence, high station, heaven, beatitude. *s.*

پرمپر परम्पर *parampar*, traditionary, hereditary; m. a great-great-grandson. *s.*

پرمپرا परम्परा *paramparā*, f. tradition; communication from one to another in succession; series succession; race, lineage. *paramparīn*, hereditary traditional. *s.*

پرمت परमत *par-mat*, m. a different opinion. *s.*

پرمت परिमित *parimit*, measured, regulated. *parimitāhār* or *parimit-bhuj*, eating moderately, temperate. *s.*

پرمت प्रमित *pramit*, known, understood, proved; measured. *pramitāksharā*, f. a species of the *jagati* metre. *s.*

پرمتھا प्रमथा *pramathā*, f. yellow myrobalan (*Terminalia chebula*). *s.*

پرمتھالی प्रमथालय *pramathālay*, m. hell, or abode of pain. *s.*

پرمد प्रमद *pramad*, mad, intoxicated, impassioned; m. joy, delight. *pramadā*, f. a woman, a handsome woman. *s.*

پرمد प्रमुद *pramud* or *pramudit*, pleased, glad. *s.*

پرمدھام परमधाम *param-dhām*, m. paradise. *s.*

پرمکھ प्रमुख *pramukh*, chief, principal, best, first; m. a chief, a sage; a tree used for dyeing (*Rottleria tinctoria*). *pramukh-twa*, m. superiority, predominance. *s.*

پرمگن प्रमग्न *pramagn*, immersed, drowned. *s.*

پرمل परिमल *parimal* or परमल *parmal*, fragrant; m. trituration of perfumes, and the scent arising from it; parched grain of *jo,ār* or *bājrā*, q. v. (*Holcus sorgum* and *spicatus*). *s.*

پرملان परिम्लान *parimlān*, soiled, stained; withered, impaired. *s.*

پرمن *pirman*, the yard of a sail (see پروان). *h.*

پرمند परिमन्द *parimand*, slow, dull. *s.*

پرمنڈل परिमण्डल *parimanḍal*, m. a ball, a globe, a circle. *parimanḍaltā*, f. rotundity. *s.*

پرموچن प्रमोचन *pramochan*, m. liberating, setting free. *pramochanī*, a sort of cucumber. *s.*

پرمود प्रमोद *pramod*, m. pleasure, delight. *pramodit* or *pramodī*, happy, delighted; delighting. *s.*

پرموه प्रमोह *pramoh*, m. fascination; fainting, insensibility. *s.*

پرموهن परिमोहन *parimohan*, m. fascinating, beguiling. *parimohī*, m. *parimohinī*, f. adj. fascinating, bewitching. *s.*

پرمیشور परमेश्वर *param-eshwar*, m. the first and supreme Lord, God, the Almighty. *s.*

پرمیو परमेव *parmew*, } m. a (venereal) clap;
پرمیه प्रमेह *prameh*, } a gleet, any urinary affection. *s.*

پرن परन *paran*, f. a very quick time in music. *h.*

پرن प्रण *pran*, m. promise, resolution, vow. *s.*

پرنانی *parnānī*, great-grandmother. *h.*

پرن पर्ण *parn* or *parna*, m. a leaf, betel leaf; the palās tree (*Butea frondosa*). *parn-wallī*, f. the same tree. *parn-shālā*, f. a hut of leaves, a hermitage. *parn-latā*, f. the betel plant. *parn-nar*, m. a man of leaves, an effigy stuffed with leaves, made to represent a person deceased whose body cannot be found. *s.*

پرناد प्रणाद *pranād*, m. a disease of the ear, a buzzing in the ear. *s.*

پرناس पर्णासि *parnāsi*, m. a sort of basil (*Ocymum sanctum*) with small leaves. *s.*

پرناش प्रणाश *pranāsh*, m. loss, destruction. *pranāshī*, destroying.

پرنال प्रणाल or प्रनाल *pranāl*, m.
پرناله परनाला *parnāla*, m.
پرنالي प्रणाली or प्रनाली *pranālī*, f. } a conduit, a gutter, a drain. *s.*

پرنام परिणाम *parinām*, m. maturity, fulness, end, last stage; sequel, result. *parinām-darshī*, who looks forward or to the end. *s.*

پرنام प्रणाम or प्रनाम *pranām*, aslo *parnām*, m. salutation, bow, adoration. *s.*

پرنانا परनाना *par-nānā*, a great-grandfather (by the mother's side). *s.* [sance. *s.*

پرنپات प्रणिपात *pranipāt*, m. salutation, obei-

پرنپتن प्रणिपतन *pranipatan*, m. saluting, bowing. *s.* [obeisance. *s.*

پرنت प्रणति *pranati*, f. salutation, reverence,

پرنت परन्तु *parantu*, but, however, on the other hand; afterwards, also. *s.*

پرنتر परन्त्र *parantra*, subservient, dependent. *s.*

پرند *parand*, m. a bird. *parand-ho-jānā*, to move with great rapidity. *p.*

پرندر पुरन्दर *purandar*, m. a sort of pepper (*Piper chavya*). *s.*

پرنده *paranda*, flying; a bird. *parande kā par na mārnā kisī jāgah meṅ*, is used to express a place quite inaccessible. *p.*

پرندهان प्रणिधान *pranidhān*, m. great effort, stress; profound meditation; access, entrance. *s.*

پرن‌ماچال पर्णमाचाल *parn-māchāl*, m. the *kamrāngā*, an acid fruit (*Averrhoa carambola*). *s.*

پرنو प्रणव *pranav*
پرنوك प्रणवक *pranavak*, } m. the mystical name of the deity. *s.* [a hermitage. *s.*

پرنوتج पर्णोटज *parnoṭaj*, m. a hut of leaves,

پرنور *pur-nūr*, illustrious, enlightened. *p.*

پرني प्रणय *pranay*, m. affection, regard; asking, solicitation; final emancipation; trust, confidence; reverence, obeisance. *pranayī*, affectionate, kind, intimate; m. a husband or lover. *s.*

پرني प्रणी *pranī*, resolute, bold, determined. *s.*

پرني *purnī*, f. a ferule, a tube, a thimble; the ramrod-pipes of a musket; a bugle or oblong bead. *d.*

پرني पर्णी *parnī*, m. a tree (*Butea frondosa*); f. an aquatic plant (*Pistia stratiotes*); the leaf of the assafœtida(?). *s.* [patron. *s.*

پرنيا पुरनिया *puraniyā*, m. an old man; a

پرنيا पुरणिया, पुरणैया, पुरैनिया *puraniyā*, *puranaiyā*, or *purainiyā*, m. name of a district and town in Bengal (vulg. *Poorneah*). *h.*

پرنيان *parniyān*, m. a kind of fine painted silk (from China); also garments made of the same. *p.*

پرو पर्व *parv*, m. a festival, a holiday; *parv-kārī*, a Brāhman who performs ceremonies for hire out of season. *parv-gāmī*, a man who associates with his wife on festival days. *s.*

پرو पुरु *puru*, m. name of the sixth monarch of the lunar line; the farina of a flower; f. the name of a river to the north-west of the Saraswatī. *s.*

پروا *parwā*, f. care, concern, anxiety, vexation; inclination, affection, concupiscence, desire rest, quiet. *kuchh parwā nahīṅ*, (vulg. *kuch-parwā-nīṅ*), no matter, it is of no consequence. *p.*

پرو. पुर्वा *purwā*, f. an easterly wind. *s.*

پروا परिवा *pariwā*, f. the first day of the moon's increase or wane. *s.*

پرواد परिवाद *parivād*, m. abuse, reproach, accusation. *parivādak* or *parivādī*, an accuser, a plaintiff, a calumniator. *s.*

پروار परिवार *pariwār*, m. family, dependants. *pariwār-tā*, f. subjection, dependence. *s.* [position. *s.*

پروارن प्रवारण *pravāran*, m. prohibition, op-

پرواري *parwārī*, fattened or fatted. *p.*

پرواز *parwāz*, flying, flight. *parwāz-karnā*, n. to fly. *parwāz-kunān*, flying, on the wing. *p.*

پرواس परिवास *parivās*, m. abiding, abode. *s.*

پرواس प्रवास *pravās*, m. a foreign country or residence, dwelling away from home. *pravāsat*, adj. absent, dwelling abroad. *pravāsan*, m. sojourning abroad, exile. *s*

پرواسي *pravāsī*, a foreigner, one from abroad; one living away from home. *s.* [city. *s.*

پرواسي पुरवासी *pur-vāsī*, adj. inhabiting a

پروال पर्वाल *parwāl*, m. a disease of the eyelids, in which the eyelashes fall, a stye or stithe. *h.*

پروان परवान *parwān*, m. the yard (of a sail); *parwān chhaṛhnā*, to grow up (a phrase peculiar to women). *h.*

پروانا पुर्वाना *purwānā* (caus. of *purānā*), to cause to be filled. *h.*

پروانجات *parwānajāt*, m. (pl. of *parwāna*), orders; passes, licenses. *p.* [mission. *p.*

پروانگي *parwānagī*, f. command, order, per-

پروانه *parwāna*, m. a grant, or letter, under a great seal, from any man of power to a dependant; an order, a pass, a licence, leave, command, a precept, warrant; a butterfly, a moth. *parwāna kisī kā honā*, to be desperately in love with any one (an allusion to the moth and the candle). *p.*

پرواه *parwāh*, f. (the same as *parwā*, q. v.), care, concern, &c. *p.* [overflowing. *s.*

پرواه परिवाह *parivāh*, m. an inundation, an

پرواه प्रवाह *pravāh*, m, stream, current of a river. *s.*

پرواهكا प्रवाहिका *pravāhikā*, f. diarrhœa. *s.*

پرواءي *parwā,ī*, one who stands in need of, necessitated, wanting, having occasion for. *p.*

پروبهاگ प्रविभाग *pravibhāg*, m. division, a part. *s.* [titioned, shared. *s.*

پروبهكت प्रविभक्त *pravibhakt*, divided, par-

پروپديش परोपदेश *paropadesh*, m. giving advice, admonishing. *s.* [of others, beneficence. *s.*

پروپكار परोपकार *paropakār*, m. the helping

پروپكاري परोपकारी *paropakārī* aiding others, beneficent, hospitable. *s.*

پروت पर्वत *parvat*, m. a mountain, a hill. *parvat-āshray* or *parvat-vāsī*, living in the mountains. *parvat-kāk*, m. a raven. *parvatīya*, mountainous; m. a mountaineer. *s.* [of fish (*Silurus pabda*). *s.*

پروت पर्वित *parvit* or पर्वत *parvat*, m. a kind

پروتساه प्रोत्साह *protsāh*, m. effort, exertion; stimulus. *protsāhit*, instigated, stimulated. *protsāhak*, m. instigator. *protsāhan*, m. inciting, stimulating. *s.*

پروتي परौती *parautī*, land which is kept out of cultivation for a short time, in order that the soil may recover its strength. *h.*

پروتيا पर्वतिया *parvatiyā*, m. a kind of pumpkin. *s.* [gence. *s.*

پروجن परोजन *parojan*, m. purpose, use, exi-

پرودها पुरोधा *purodhā*, m. the family priest. *s.*

پرور *parwar*, (in comp.) a patron, protector, nourisher, cherisher; educated, cherished, as *gharīb parwar*, cherisher of the poor. *sāya-parwar*, educated in the shade or at home; soft, delicate, knowing little of the world. *p.*

پرور पर्वर *parwar*, m. the name of a kind of gourd (*Trichosanthes dioica, Roxb.*). *s.*

پرور प्रवर *pravar*, m. offspring, race. *s.*

پرور प्रविर *pravir*, m. a yellow fragrant wood. *s.*

پرواجك परिव्राजक *parivrājak*, m. a religious mendicant. *s.*

پرورت प्रवर्त्त *pravartta*, engaged in, undertaking; m. excitement, stimulus. *s.*

پرورت प्रवृत्त *pravritta*, fixed, determined; engaged in, occupied. *pravritti*, f. activity, occupation, active life; perseverance; addiction to; tidings, intelligence; continuous flow, stream; Ujjain, or any holy place; (in arith.) the multiplier. *s.*

پرورت परिवृत्त *parivritta*, gone round, revolved; exchanged. *s.*

پرورت परिवर्त्त *parivartta*, m. going or turning back, revolving; exchange, requital; the end of a period of four ages, destruction of the world. *s.*

پرورتك प्रवर्त्तक *pravarttak*, inciting, stimulating; m. an instigator. *s.*

پرورجيا परिव्रज्या *parivrajyā*, f. the life of a religious mendicant. *s.*

پروردگار *parwardagār*, m. the cherisher; an epithet of the Deity. *p.*

پروردن *parwardan*, to cherish, rear, foster. *p.*

پرورده *parwarda*, bred, reared, brought up (used substantively) a slave, a protegé. *p.*

پرورش *parwarish*, f. breeding, fostering, rearing, patronising, education, protection. *p.*

پروللت प्रवरललित *pravar-lalit*, m. a species of the *ashtī* metre. *s.* [risher. *p.*

پرورنده *parwaranda*, cherishing, the che-

پروروس पुरूरवस् *purūravas*, the son of Buddha, and second king of the lunar dynasty. *s.*

پروري *parwarī*, f. education; m. one who educates; (in comp.) cherishing, rearing. *p.*

پروڑه प्रौढ़ *prauṛh*, able, clever, full grown; confident, bold. *prauṛhi*, f. enterprise, confident exertion; investigation. *prauṛhā*, a woman from 30 years of age to 55. *prauṛhatā*, f. strength, firmness, breadth. *s.* [hood. *s.*

پروس परोस *paros*, m. vicinity, neighbour-

پروسا परोसा *parosā*, m. a dish which is sent to a friend. *s.*

پروستي *parwastī*, f. cherishing, patronising: especially applied to the cherishing of old servants past work; care, protection, favour (probably a corruption of the Persian word *parwarish*). *d.*

پروسن प्रवसन *pravasan*, m. going or dwelling abroad *s.*

پروسنا परोसना *parosnā*, a. to take up dinner, to distribute, serve up, to divide. *s.*

پروسندهه पर्वसन्धि *parv-sandhi*, m. the full and change of the moon. *s.*

پروسي परोसी *parosī*, m. a neighbour. *h.*

پروسيا परोसैया *parosaiyā*, m. a distributor of victuals to the guests, one who serves up dinner, a waiter. *s.* [dent. *s.*

پروش परवश *par-vash*, subservient, depen-

پروشٹ परिविष्ट *parivishṭ*, surrounded, enclosed. *s.*

پروشٹ प्रविष्ट *pravishṭ*, entered, engaged in. *s.*

پروشٹهه प्रोष्ठ *proshṭh*, m. a sort of carp (*Cyprinus prausius*). *proshṭh-padā*, f. the 26th and 27th asterisms, containing the stars in the wing of Pegasus. *praushṭh-pad*, m. the month Bhadr (August—Sept.). *praushṭh-padī*, f. full moon in Bhadr. *s.*

پروشني परोष्णी *paroshnī*, f. a cockroach. *s.*

پروكت प्रोक्त *prokt*, said, declared. *s.*

پروكش परोक्ष *paroksh*, invisible; absent, past; m. an ascetic, a hermit; invisibility, absence; (in gram.) past time or tense. *s.*

پروکشن प्रोक्षण *prokshan*, m. killing animals in sacrifice, immolation, slaughter; sprinkling, with water, &c.; a text to be recited when animals are offered. *prokshit*, sprinkled; killed, offered in sacrifice.

پروکهيات प्रविख्याति *pravikhyāti*, f. celebrity, renown. *s.* [*dioica*). *s.*

پرول परवल *parval*, m. a plant (*Tricosanthes*

پرونا पिरोना *pironā* or *paronā*, a. to thread (as a needle), to string (as pearls), to spit. *h.*

پرونکا पर्वणिका *parvanikā*, f. specks attended with pain on the edge of the cornea of the eye. *s.*

پروه प्रवह *pravah*, m. one of the seven Vāyus or winds. *s.* [of leather. *h.*

پروها परोहा *parohā*, m. a water-bucket made

پروهت पुरोहित *purohit* (also प्रोहित *prohit*), m. a priest who presides at the performance of religious ceremonies; family priest. *s.*

پروهتاني पुरोहितानी *purohitānī*, f. the wife of a *purohit*, or priest, q.v. *s.*

پروهن परोहन *parohan*, m. carriage, vehicle, instruments of transportation. *s.*

پرويا पुर्वैया *purwaiyā*, f. easterly wind. *s.*

پروياده परिव्याध *parivyādh*, m. a tree (*Pterospermum acerifolia*); a sort of reed growing in water (*Calamus fasciculatus*). *s.*

پرويٹ प्रवेट *pravet*, m. barley. *s.*

پرويدن परिवेदन *parivedan*, m. anguish, pain; marriage. *s.* [a chief. *s.*

پروير प्रवीर *pravīr*, best, excellent; m. a hero,

پرويس प्रवेश *praves* or *pravesh*, m. entering, arriving. *s.*

پرويشٹن परिवेष्टन *pariveshtan*, m. surrounding; circumference. *pariveshtit*, enclosed, surrounded, covered. *s.* [serving up food. *s.*

پرويشن परिवेषण *pariveshan*, m. surrounding;

پرويشن प्रवेशन *praveshan*, m. the entrance; entering. *praveshak*, who enters; m. an entry. *s.*

پرويکشن प्रवेक्षण *pravehshan*, m. foreseeing. *pravekshit*, foreseen. *pravekshyat*, adj. foreseeing. *s.*

پرويل प्रवेल *pravel*, m. the yellow variety of the kidney bean. *s.*

پروين *parvīn*, m. the Pleiades. *p.*

پروين प्रवीण *pravīn*, intelligent, skilful, wise. *s.*

پروينتا प्रवीणता *pravīnatā*, f. wisdom, intelligence, skill. *s.*

پرويني प्रवेणी *pravenī* or प्रवेणि *praveni*, f. the hair twisted and undecorated, as worn by women in the absence of their husbands. *s.*

پرهار प्रहार *prahār*, m. the act of beating, a stroke *s.*

پرهار परिहार *parihār*, m. disrespect. *s.*

پرهاري प्रहारी *prahārī*, m. one who beats or strikes. *s.*

پرهاس प्रहास *prahās*, m. loud laughter. *prahāsī*, laughing aloud, causing laughter. *s.*

پرهاس परिहास *parihās*, m. jest, joke, jeer; mirth, pastime. *parihās-vedī*, m. a jester, a wag. *s.*

پرهت परहित *par-hit*, friendly, benevolent, good for another. *s.*

پرهر प्रहर *prahar*, m. a watch of the day or night; a division of time, consisting of 8 *gharīs* or about 3 hours. *s.*

پرهرشت प्रहर्षित *praharshit* or प्रहृष्ट *prahrisht*, delighted, very happy. *s.*

پرهرشني प्रहर्षिणी *praharshinī*, f. a species of the *atijagatī* metre. *s.*

پرهرن परिहरण *pariharan*, m. seizing, taking; leaving, abandoning. *s.*

پرهرن کلکا प्रहरणकलिका *praharan-kalikā*, f. a species of the *sarkarī* metre. *s.*

پرهرنا परिहरना *pariharnā*, a. to leave, to forsake, to abandon, to desert, to take away, clear off. *s.*

پرهري प्रहरी *praharī* or पहरिया *pahriyā*, m. a watchman, a sentinel. *s.*

پرهسر पुरःसर *pura-sar*, one who goes first, a leader, a preceder. *s.*

پرهسن प्रहसन *prahasan*, m. loud laughter, mirth; sarcasm, ridicule, irony. *prahasat*, adj. laughing heartily. *s.* [mine. *s.*

پرهسنتي प्रहसन्ती *prahasantī*, f. Arabian jas-

پرهلاد प्रह्लाद *prahlād*, m. pleasure, joy; the name of Hiranyāksha's pious son, and regent of one division of Pātāl. *prahlādit*, rejoiced, delighted. *s.*

پرهيز *parhez*, m. abstinence, forbearance, continence, control of the passions. *badī-parhez*, abstaining from evil. *parhez-k.*, a. to control one's passions; to abstain from; to observe a regimen. *p.*

پرهيزگار *parhez-gār*, one who controls his passions, abstinent, temperate. *p.*

پرهيزگاري *parhez-gārī*, f. abstinence, control of the passions. *p.*

پرهيزي *parhezī*, fit for a person under a regimen (also the same as *parhez-gār*, q.v.). *p.*

پرهيلکا प्रहेलिका *prahelikā*, f. an enigma, a riddle. *s.* [prived of, deserted by. *s*

پرهين परिहीण *parihīn*, waned, faded; de-

پري परे *pare*, beyond, yonder. *pare rahnā*, to remain at a distance. *s.*

پري *parī*, f. a fairy. *parī-paikar* or *parī-chihra*, angelical, fairy-faced. *p.*

پري *purī*, f. fulness, completion. *p.*

پري पुरी *purī*, f. (same as *pur*, &c.), a city town. *s.*

پري प्रिय *priya*, m. beloved, dear; m. a husband, a lover; a sort of drug commonly called *Riddhi*. *s.*

پريا प्रिया *priyā*, m. beloved, dear, a sweetheart, *he priye*, my dear! *s.*

پرياس प्रयास *prayās*, m. trouble, labour, desire or pursuit of any object. *s.* [tidings. *s.*

پرياکهيه प्रियाख्य *priyākhya*, announcing good

پرياگ प्रयाग *prayāg*, m. the modern Allahabād, a celebrated place of pilgrimage at the confluence of the Ganges and Jamunā, together with the supposed subterraneous addition of the Saraswatī, according to the Hindū creed: in comp. it applies to several places of reputed sanctity, as, *Deva-prayāg*, *Rudra-prayāg*, *Karna-prayāg* &c. *s.*

پريال प्रियाल *priyāl*, m. a tree commonly called *piyāl* (*Buchanania latifolia*). *s.*

پريان प्रयाण *prayān*, m. going forth, departure; death, march, invasion. *prayān-kāl*, time of departure, death. *s.* [ing kindly. *s.*

پريبهاشن प्रियभाषण *priya-bhāshan*, m. speak-

پريت प्रीत *prīt*, kind, affectionate, beloved, dear. m. delight. *s.*

پريت प्रीति *prīt* or *prīti*, f. love, friendship; the second of the 27 astronomical *yogs*. *prīti-pūrvak*, adv. through kindness; *prīti-dān*, m. a friendly present. *prīti-dāya*, m. a gift of affection. *prīti-mān*, kind, affectionate. *s.*

پريت प्रेत *pret* or परेत *paret* adj. dead; m. a spirit of the dead, a ghost. *pret-paksh*, m. the dark half of the month. *pret-karm*, m. funeral rites. *pret-grih*, m. a cemetery. *pret-lok*, m. the region of disembodied spirits, in which they remain one year, or until the obsequies are completed. *pret-nadī*, f. the river of hell. *s.* [yarn). *h.*

پريتا परेता *paretā*, m. a reel (for winding

پريتا प्रियता *priyatā*, f. love, affection. *s.*

پريتر प्रियतर *priyatar*, dearer, more beloved. *s.*

پريتم प्रीतम *prītam* or प्रियतम *priyatam*, dearest, most beloved; m. a lover, a husband. *s.*

پريتن प्रयत्न *prayatna*, m. continued effort, exertion; act, action; caution, care. *prayatna-wān*, active, zealous, persevering. *s.* [yarn). *h.*

پريتنا परेतना *paretnā*, a. to reel (thread or

پريتني प्रेतनी *pretnī*, a female *pret* or ghost, a ghostess. *s.* [testing (gold or silver). *s.*

پريچها (परीछा for परीक्षा) *parīchhā*, f. trying,

پريچهك (परीछक for परीक्षक) *parīchhak*, m. one who tests or examines. *s.*

پري‌خوان *parī-khwān*, m. a magician, one who "calls spirits from the vasty deep." *p.*

پري‌دار *parī-dār*, one who controls fairies; also one who is spell-bound by fairies. *p.*

پريدرشن प्रियदर्शन *priya-darshan*, handsome, good-looking. m. a tree (*Mimusops kauki.*) *s.*

پريدن *parīdan*, to fly, to soar on the wing. *p.*

پريدهاوي परीधावी *parīdhāvī*, m. the forty-first year of the Indian cycle. *s.*

پريرت प्रेरित *prerit*, sent, directed, despatched. *s.*

پري‌رخسار *parī-rukhsār*, angelic, fairy-cheeked. *p.*

پريرن प्रेरण *preran*, } m. the act of sending;
پريرنا प्रेरना *prernā*, } command. *s.*

پري‌رو *parī-rū*, fairy-faced, a beautiful woman, plur. *parī-rūyān*. *p.*

پريزاد *parī-zād*, fairy-born, *i.e.* beautiful. *p.*

پري‌ستان *parī-stān*, m. the region of the fairies. *p.*

پريسکه प्रियसख *priya-sakh*, m. a tree (*Mimosa catechu.*) *s.* [friend, a confidante. *s.*

پريسکهي प्रियसखी *priya-sakhī*, f. a female

پريسنديش प्रियसन्देश *priya-sandesh*, m. a tree bearing a fragrant flower (*Michelia champaca*). *s.*

پريش पुरीष *purīsh*, m. fæces, excrement. *s.*

پريشان *pareshān*, distressed, wretched, dispersed perplexed, dishevelled, ruined. *pareshān-hāl*, distressed in condition. *pareshān-kahnā*, to talk foolishly. *p.* [dispersion, destruction. *p.*

پريشاني *pareshānī*, f. distress; perplexity;

پريشٹه प्रेष्ठ *preshṭh*, most or very dear. *preshṭhā*, f. a wife. *s.*

پريك प्रियक *priyak*, m. a tree (*Nauclea cadamba*); another tree (*Pentaptera tomentosa*). *s.*

پريکار प्रियकार *priya-kār*, or प्रियकृत *priya-krit*, kindly, doing good, a benefactor. *s.*

پريکت प्रयुक्त *prayukta*, endowed with, possessing; connected with; compact. *s.* [proof. *s.*

پريکشا परीक्षा *parīkshā*, f. examination, trial,

پريکشا प्रेक्षा *prekshā*, f. seeing, viewing, observing. *s.*

پريکشت परीक्षित *parīkshit*, the name of the grandson of *Arjuna*; adj. examined, tried, proved. *s.*

پريکشت प्रेक्षित *prekshit*, seen, beheld, looked at. *s.* [mines, &c. *s.*

پريکشك परीक्षक *parīkshak*, one who exa-

پريکشن परीक्षण *parīkshan*, m. trial, experiment, examination. *s.* [spectacle, sight. *s.*

پريکشن प्रेक्षण *prekshan*, m. a public show,

پريکها परेखा *parekhā*, m. repentance, regret, concern. *h.*

پريکها परेखा *parekhā*, f. (corrupted for *parīkshā* or *parīchhā*, &c.), trial, examination, search. *s.*

پريم प्रेम *prem*, m. love, friendship; *prem-sāgar*, name of a well-known Hindī work so called, which details the history of *Krishna*. *s.*

پريمان प्रियमाण *priyamān*, beloved, affectionate. *s.*

پريمبهوك प्रियम्भावुक *priyam-bhāvuh*, become dear to. *priyam-bhāvuktā*, f. amiability, becoming beloved. *s.*

پريمپر प्रेमपर *prem-par*, affectionate, loving. *s.*

پريمرنگ‌راتا प्रेमरङ्गराता *prem-rang-rātā*, coloured with the dye of love; strongly in love, enamoured. *s.* [(*Datura*). *s.*

پري‌موه पुरीमोह *purī-moh*, m. the thorn apple

پريمي प्रेमी *premī*, affectionate; a lover. *s.*

پرين पुरेन *puren*, f. the placenta; the plant of the *lotus*. *h.*

پرينگ प्रियङ्गु *priyangu*, m. a medicinal plant and perfume, or fragrant seed; panick seed (*Panicum italicum*). *s.* [moon. *s.*

پريوا परीवा *parīwā*, f. the first day of the

پريوا परेवा *parewā*, m. a pigeon. *h.*

پريواد परीवाद *parīvād*, m. reproof, censure, abuse. *s.* [flatterer. *s.*

پريوادي प्रियवादी *priya-vādī*, sweet spoken, a

پريوار परीवार *parīwār*, m. dependants, family, retinue. *s.* [flow. *s.*

پريواه परीवाह *parīwāh*, m. inundation, over-

پريوجك प्रयोजक *prayojak*, who or what causes or induces any act; who or what deputes or appoints; m. a founder or instituter of any ceremony; a legislator. *s.*

پريوجن प्रयोजन *prayojan*, m. cause, motive, need, occasion; intention, design; use, exigence. *prayojan-wān*, designing, purposing. *prayojanī*, necessary, requisite. *s.*

پريوجيه प्रयोज्य *prayojya*, m. capital, principal; a servant, a slave. *s.* [barter. *s.*

پريورت परीवर्त्त *parīvartta*, m. exchange,

پريورني प्रियवर्णी *priya-varnī*, f. a creeping plant (*Echites frutescens*). *s.*

پري‌وش *parī-wash*, fairy-like, angelic. *p.*

پريوگ प्रयोग *prayog*, m. occasion, cause, motive, object, result; device, contrivance; example, comparison; act, action. *prayogī*, having some object in view, calculated for a particular purpose. *s.*

پريه परेह *pareh*, m. soup made of rice (v. *palew*). *h.*

پريه परेह *pareh*, } m. land watered after

پريها परेहा *parehā*, } ploughing, or flooded before the final ploughing and levelling of the ground. *h.*

پريه प्रिय *priya*, dear, beloved (see پري).

پريهاس परीहास *parīhās*, m. mirth, sport, amusement. *s.*

پڑا पुड़ा *puṛā*, m. a large parcel (of physic, &c.). *paṛā*, m. the boundary of a field. *h.*

پڑاپانا पड़ापाना *paṛā-pānā*, a. to find, to get easily. *h.*

پڑاپڑ पड़ापड़ *paṛāpaṛ*, with reiterated strokes. *s.*

پڑانا पड़ाना *paṛānā*, a. to put to sleep, to lay down, to cause to repose; to cull, to gather, pluck. *h.*

پڑاو पड़ाव *paṛāw*, m. halting, resting, sleeping; halting-place; camp, encampment; an army; a crowd, assembly. *h.*

پڑپڑانا पड़पड़ाना *paṛpaṛānā*, n. to prattle, to chatter; to throb with pain (as the tongue from an acid substance). *paṛpaṛ-rahnā*, to chat, prattle. *h.*

پڑجانا पड़जाना *paṛ-jānā*, n. to lie down; to cease, as the wind; to repose; to abate. *h.*

پڑچھٹي पड़छटी *paṛchhaṭī*, f. a small thatch thrown over mud walls. *d.*

پڑرهنا पड़रहना *paṛ-rahnā*, n. to be utterly helpless, to be in a regular fix. *d.*

پڑم *paṛam*, m. a coarse kind of cotton cloth used for tents, &c. *d.* [immodesty. *d.*

پڑمرگي पड़मर्गी *paṛ-margī*, f. shamelessness,

پڑنا पड़ना *paṛnā*, n. to repose, to lie down; to fall; to befall, to happen; to encamp; to drop; to be confined to bed by sickness. *h.*

پڑوا *paṛwā*, m. a large boat; a ferry boat. *d.*

پڑوانا पिड़वाना *piṛwānā*, a. to cause to press, squeeze. *h.*

پڑوس पड़ोस *paṛos*, m. neighbourhood. *s.*

پڑوسن पड़ोसिन *paṛosin*, f. a female neighbour. *s.*

پڑوسي पड़ोसी *paṛosī*, m. a male neighbour. *s.*

پڑوي पड़वी *paṛwī*, a sort of sugar-cane sown in autumn. *h.*

پڑها पढ़ा *paṛhā*, read, learned, of much reading. *paṛhā-gunā*, a learned, experienced man. *s.*

پڑهانا पढ़ाना *paṛhānā*, a. to teach to read, to instruct, to teach to speak (or sing) as birds. *s.*

پڑهن पढ़न *paṛhan*, f. reading, the act of reading. *s.*

پڑهن पढ़िन *paṛhin*, f. a mullet. *h.*

پڑهنا पढ़ना *paṛhnā*, a. to read, to repeat, to say, to speak, to quote or recite. *paṛhne-wālā*, m. reader. *s.*

پڑهنت पढ़न्त *paṛhant*, f. study, reading; a spell. *s.*

پڑهوانا पढ़वाना *paṛhwānā*, a. to cause to be taught reading (v. *paṛhānā*). *h.* [made. *h.*

پڑي पुड़ी *puṛī*, f. a skin with which a drum is

پڑي पड़ी *paṛī*, f. a measure (v. *paimāna.*) *d.*

پڑيا पुड़िया *puṛiyā*, f. a parcel (of physic, &c.), a dose of medicine in powder. *s.*

پڑيا पड़िया *paṛiyā*, f. a female buffalo calf. *h.*

پڑي‌رهنا पड़ेरहना *paṛe-rahnā*, n. to be in a hopeless or desperate state. *d.*

پڑيل पढ़यल *paṛyal*, f. sweepings. *h.*

پز *puz* or *paz*, (in comp.) cooking, baking; framing or contriving (in the mind). *p.*

پزاوا *pazāwā*, پزاوه *pazāwo*, } f. a brick-kiln. *p.*

پژمردگي *pazhmurdagī*, f. rottenness, faded state. *p.*

پژمردن *pazhmurdan*, to wither, fade, decay. *p.*

پژمرده *pazhmurda*, withered, faded, drooping. *p.*

پس *pas*, after, behind; at length, then, therefore, finally. *pas-andāz*, savings, something laid up to provide for old age or want of employment; labourers, &c. call it *māya ī tawakkul*. *p.*

پسا पसा *pasā*, m. two handfuls, as much as can be held in both hands open (same as *ānjlā*, q. v.). *s.*

پساب *pisāb* or *pishāb* (for *peshāb*), m. the act of pissing, urine. *p.*

پساچ पिसाच *pisāch* (for पिशाच *pishāch*, q. v.) m. a spectre, apparition, vision, a demon. *s.*

پساچي पिसाची *pisāchī* or पिसाचनी *pisāchnī*, f. a female spectre, an ogress. *s.*

پسارا पसारा *pasārā*, m. expansion, the act of spreading out. *pasārā-k.*, to procrastinate and find obstacles to an easy matter. *s.*

پسارنا पसारना *pasārnā*, a. to spread; to distend; to stretch out, to expand, to open. *s.*

پساري पसारी *pasārī*, m. one who sells spices (v. *pansārī*). *h.*

پسان पिसान *pisān*, m. meal, flour. *s.*

پسانا पिसाना *pisānā*, a. to reduce to meal, flour, or powder; to grind. *s.*

پسانا पसाना *pasānā*, a. to skim; to pour off superfluous water. *s.*

پساءي पसाई *pasā,ī*, f. a kind of rice. *h.*

پساءي पिसाई *pisā,ī*, f. price paid for grinding. *s.*

پس‌پا *pas-pā* or *pas-pā,e*, sitting cross-legged (like the Asiatics). *p.*

پس‌پال पशुपाल *pasu-pāl* or *pashu-pāl*, پس‌پالك पशुपालक *pasu-pālak* or *pashu-pālak*, } m. lit. beast-feeder; a cowherd, a cow-feeder. *s.*

پسپالن पशुपालन *pasu-pālan*, the rearing and tending of cattle, one of the duties of the *Vaisya* caste. *s.*

پس‌پاهونا *pas-pā honā*, n. to decline; to fall in the rear, to slink behind; to retreat, to flee, to desist from an attempt. *p. h.*

پس‌پوت पुसपूत *pus-pūt* (for पुष्यपुत्र *pushya-putra*), adopted son. *pus-pūt k.*, to adopt as a son. *s.*

پست *past*, below, low. *past-fitrat*, of inferior understanding, of a mean disposition. *past-himmat*, unambitious. *past o buland dekhnā*, to consider and take precautions against the vicissitudes of fortune. *pas-at*, behind thee. *p.*

پستان *pistān*, m. the breasts, bubbies. *p.*

پستانا पछताना *pastānā*, n. to regret, repent. *s.*

پستك पुस्तक *pustak*, f. a book, a volume. *s.*

پسته *pista*, m. a pistachio nut. *p.*

پستي *pastī*, f. inferiority, lowness. *p.*

پستئي رنگ *pista,ī rang*, m. pea-green. *p.*

پس‌خورده *pas-khurda*, m. leavings (of food), dregs, offal. *p.*

پسر पसर *pasar*, f, grazing cattle at night. *h.*

پسر *pisar*, m. a boy, a son, a child. *pisar-zāda*, a grandchild. *pisar i khwānda*, an adopted son. *pisri akhyāfī*, a step-son, son of a wife by a former husband. *pisri-mutabannā*, an adopted son. *pisar-khwāndagī*, adoption of a son. *p.*

پسرنا पसरना *pasarnā*, n. to be spread, stretched out, expanded. *s.*

پس‌رو *pas-rau*, or *pas-raw*, m. a follower; dependants; train, equipage. *p.*

پسروي *pas-rawī*, f. following; equipage. *p.*

پسري *pisarī*, f. boyhood, infancy. *p.*

پسطول *pistol* or *pistūl*, a pistol. *e.*

پس‌غيبت *pas ghaibat*, in one's absence. *p.*

پس‌قد *pas-kad* or *-kadd*, a dwarf (properly *past-kadd*). *p. a.*

پس‌كش *pas-kash*, m. recoil, retraction. *p.*

پسلانا पिसलाना *pislānā*, a. to cause to grind. *h.*

پسلي पसली *paslī*, f. a rib, the præcordia. *paslī pharaknī*, a thrilling over the ribs, is applied to a perception of the condition of an absent person. *h.*

پس‌مانده *pas-mānda*, left behind, a survivor. *p.*

پسنا पिसना *pisnā*, n. to be reduced to meal, to be ground; to be ruined, distressed; (met.) to be desperately in love. *h.*

پسند *pasand*, f. choice, approbation; (in comp.) agreeable to, pleasing, as *dil-pasand*, pleasing the heart. *pasand-h*, to please. *p.*

پسنديدن *pasandīdan*, to approve of, to be agreeable. *p.*

پسنديده *pasandīda*, chosen, approved of, agreed to. *p.*

پسنگا *pasangā*, m. (the same as *pāsang*), a [weight, &c. *p.*

پسو पशु *pasū* or *pashū*, (see پش) m. a beast; an animal. *s.*

پسو पिसू *pisū* or *pissū*, m. a flea. *h.*

پس‌وپيش *pas o pesh*, m. lit. behind and before; evasion, prevarication. *pas o pesh-k.*, a. to prevaricate. *p.*

پسوجنا पसूजना *pasūjnā*, a. to stitch. *h.*

پسهي पसही *pas,hī*, f. a kind of wild rice, growing in shallow ponds. *h.*

پسيج *pasīj*, provision for a journey; adj. ready, prepared. *p.*

پسيجنا पसीजना *pasījnā*, n. to perspire, to sweat, to melt; to compassionate. *s.*

پسين *pasīn*, last, posterior, modern. *p.*

پسيني *pasīnī*, modern, recent; *pl. pasīniyān*, the moderns. *p.*

پسينا पसीना *pasīnā*,
پسيو पसेव *pasew*,
پسيوها पसेवहा *pasewhā*, } m. perspiration, sweat. *s.*

پشُ पशु *pashu*, m. an animal, a beast; cattle. *pashu-pāl*, m. a herdsman. *pashu-pālan*, m. tending or rearing cattle. *pashutā*, f. *pashutwa*, m. nature of an animal, bestiality. *pashu-dharm*, m. action or property of animals; promiscuous cohabitation, the marrying of widows. *pashu-rāj*, m. a lion. *pashu-rajju*, m. a string for fastening cattle. *pashu-roman*, m. the hair of an animal. *pashu-kriyā*, f. copulation. *pashu-gāyatrī*, f. a verse whispered into the ear of an animal about to be sacrificed. *s.*

پشاب पिशाब *pishāb* (for *peshāb*), m. urine. *p.*

پشاچ पिशाच *pishāch*, m. a sprite, a fiend, a spectre; an infernal imp or ghost, described as fierce and malignant. *pishāch-dru*, m. a tree supposed to be haunted by goblins (*Trophis aspera*). *pishāch-grasta*, possessed of a demon, a demoniac. *pishāchnī*, f. a female sprite. *s.*

پشان पषान *pashān*, m. a stone, a rock. *s.*

پشپ पुष्प *pushp* or *pushpa*, m. a flower, the menses; the car of Kuvera; specks on the eye, albugo. *pushpānjalī*, f. presenting flowers held in both hands hollowed. *pushpa-path*, m. the vulva. *pushpa-pur*, the city of Pātāliputra or Palibothra. *pushpa-phal*, m. elephant or wood-apple. *pushpa-chāmar*, m. a plant (*Artemisia*); a fragrant plant (*Pandanus odoratissimus*) having a large bushy flower. *pushpa-dant*, m. the elephant of the north-west quarter. *pushpa-ras*, m. the honey of flowers. *pushpa-rakta*, m. a shrub (*Hibiscus phœniceus*). *pushpa-renu*, m. the farina of flowers. *pushpa-rochan*, m. a plant (*Mesua ferrea*). *pushpa-sār*, m. the honey of flowers. *pushpa-samay*, m. spring. *pushpa-shūnya*, flowerless. *pushpa-karaṇḍak*, m. Avantī or Ujjain, or the grove in its vicinity, sacred to Mahādeva. *pushpa-ketu*, m. calx of brass. *pushpa-kīṭ*, m. any insect affecting flowers. *pushpa-mās*, m. spring. *pushpa-vāṭī*, f. a flower-garden. *pushpa-wat*, flowery. *pushpa-hīn*, flowerless. *pushpa-hīnā*, f. the glomerous fig-tree; a woman whose menstruation has ceased. *pushpī*, flowering. *s.*

پشپانجن पुष्पाञ्जन *pushpānjan*, m. the calx of brass. *s.*

پشپت पुष्पित *pushpit*, flowered, in flower. *pushpitā*, f. a woman during menstruation. *pushpitāgrā*, f. a form of metre. *s.*

پشپك पुष्पक *pushpak*, m. calx of brass, the car of Kuvera, god of riches; specks on the eye; a bracelet of jewels; green vitriol. *pushpakāsīsh*, m. the green sulphate of iron. *s.*

پشپكا पुष्पिका *pushpikā*, f. the tartar of the teeth; the mucus of the glans penis or urethra. *s.*

پشپلول पशुपल्वल *pashu-palval*, m. a fragrant grass (*Cyperus rotundus*). *s.*

پشت *pusht*, f. ancestry, a generation of progenitors; the back; a second, an assistant. *pusht ba pusht*, generation by generation. *pusht-pāṅw*, m. an inflammation or phlegmon on the upper surface of the foot. *pusht par kisī ke rahnā*, (lit. to be at the back of one, or to back one) to support steadily. *pusht panāh*, an ally, a support. *pusht-khAm*, hump-backed. *pushti dast kisī par mārnā* or *pushti pā mārnā*, to reject, to abandon. *pusht denā* (in Pers. *pusht-dādan*), to flee, run away (lit. turn one's back, "*terga dare*"). *p.*

پشتا पिशिता *pishitā*, f. spikenard. *s.*

پشتارا *pushtārā*, m. a load, burden for carrying on the back. *p.*

پشتانا *pashtānā*, to regret, repent. *d.*

پشتاوا *pashtāwā*, m. regret, remorse. *d.*

پشتخار *pusht-khār*, m. an artificial hand of ivory, &c., set in a long handle to scratch the back with. *p.*

پشتك *pushtak*, a vice in horses, plunging and kicking up behind. *p.*

پشتو *pushtū*, the *Afghan* language. *p.*

پشته *pushta*, m. a buttress, a prop; a bank, a quay; a hill, an eminence; heap, load, a bundle. *p.*

پشته‌بندي *pushta-bandī*, embankments of a river. *p.*

پشتي *pushtī*, m. backing, alliance, aid; a prop; the cover of a book. *pushtī-bān*, an ally, a supporter; *pushtī-bānī*, f. alliance, aid; support. *pushtī-k.*, to assist, to support, to second, to back. *p.*

پشٹ पुष्ट *pushṭ*, nourished, fat; restorative, provocative. *pushṭānga*, fat. *s.*

پشٹ पुष्टि *pushṭi*, f. nourishing. *pushṭi-du*, adj. nourishing. *pushṭi-dā*, f. a plant (*Physalis flexuosa*). *pushṭi-kar*, m. any nutritive substance, a provocative food.

پشٹپ पिष्टप *pishṭap*, m. a world, a division of the universe. *s.*

پشٹتا पुष्टता *pushṭatā*, f. fatness; invigoration, restorative power. *s.*

پشٹك पिष्टक *pishṭak*, m. a disease of the eyes, opacity of the cornea. *s.*

پشٹي पुष्टई *pushṭa,ī*, f. adj. restorative, provocative. *s.*

پشچات पश्चात् *pashchāt*, after, afterwards, behind; westward. *pashchāt-tāp*, m. repentance. *s.*

پشچم पश्चिम *pashchim*, west, western; behind, after. *s.*

پشكا पशुका *pashukā*, f. any small animal. *s.*

پشكر पुष्कर *pushkar*, m. the sky, heaven; a lotus (*Nelumbium speciosum* or *Nymphæa nelumbo*); a drug (*Costus speciosus*); a place of pilgrimage called Pokar in the province of Ajmīr; one of the seven great *dwīpas* or divisions of the world; a mountain in the same *dwīpa*; a pond or lake. *pushkar-mūlak*, m. the root of the *costus speciosus*. *s.*

پشكرني पुष्करिणी *pushkarinī*, f. a large pond, a lake. *s.*

پشكل पुष्कल *pushkal*, excellent, best; much, many; full, complete; m. the mountain Meru; the holy place, Pushkar. *s.*

پشکش *pish-kash* (for *pesh-kash*), a present, a tribute. *p.*

پشکل *pishkil*, dung of sheep, deer, &c. *p.*

پشم *pashm*, f. wool, hair (*pubes tum maris tum fœminæ*). *pashm par mārnā*, to be perfectly contented and independent, to despise, disregard. *pashm samajhnā*, to despise. *pashm na ukharnā*, to suffer nothing from the enmity of another, not a hair of the head to be touched (spoken in great contempt of an adversary). *p.*

پشمك *pashmak*, a kind of sweetmeat. *p.*

پشمي *pashmī*, پشمين *pashmīn*, پشمينه *pashmīna*, } woollen, made of wool. *p.*

پشن पिशुन *pishun*, wicked, relentless, cruel; vile, low; stupid, a fool; m. a spy, an informer. *pishun-vākya* or *pishun-vachan*, m. evil speech, slander. *s.*

پشنا पिशुना *pishunā*, f. a gramineous plant (*Trigonella corniculata*). *s.*

پشنگ पिशङ्ग *pishang* or *pishangī*, tawny, brown. *pishtangatā*, f. tawniness. *s.*

پشنگ *pashang*, a mattock, spade, hoe; also a man's name, the father of *Afrāsiyāb*. *p.*

پشواز *pishwāz*, f. a gown, a female dress. *p.*

پشه *pasha* or *pashsha*, a gnat, a fly, a mosquito. *p.*

پشهريتکي पशुहरीतकी *pashu-harītakī*, f. the hog-plum. *s.*

پسيز *pashīz*, a small piece of money. *p.*

پشيمان *pashemān*, ashamed, abashed, disgraced, penitent. *p.*

پشيماني *pashemānī*, f. regret, penitence, remorse. *p.*

پشيه पुष्य *pushya*, m. the eighth lunar asterism, comprising three stars, of which one is Cancer; the month *Paus* (Dec.—Jan.). *pushya-putr*, an adopted son. *s.*

پك पिक *pik*, f. name of a bird (*Cuculus Indicus*); the *kokila*. *pik-bayanī*, having a voice like the pik. *s.*

پك पिक्क *pikk*, m. a young elephant. *s.*

پك पक्क *pakk*, پک पका, पक्का *pakā* or *pakkā*, } ripe; boiled, dressed (opposite to raw); baked (as bricks), made of brick; cunning, knowing. *pakkā-k.*, to establish a claim, or an agreement, or a proposition, so that no doubt or subject of dispute can remain; to build with bricks. *pakā-pakāyā*, ready cooked. *pakkā-ghar*, a house built of baked bricks or stone. *pakkā-chiṭṭhā*, an authenticated, revised, or accredited account. *pakkā-ser*, a ser of full and standard weight. *s.*

پکار पुकार *pukār*, f. *pukārā*, m. a cry a shout. *h.*

پکاردينا पुकारदेना *pukār-denā*, a. to proclaim publicly, to call. *h.*

پکارنا पुकारना *pukārnā*, a. to call aloud, to bawl out, to cry; to call or summon. *h.*

پکاکش पिकाक्ष *pikāksha*, m. a vegetable and perfume, commonly called *rochanī*. *s.*

پکانا पकाना *pakānā*, a. to ripen; to dress victuals, to cook, to bake. *s.*

پکانگ पिकाङ्ग *pikāng*, m. a small bird, called also *chātakiya*. *s.*

پکانند पिकानन्द *pikānand*, m. the spring season. [*s.*

پکاو पकाव *pakāw*, m. suppuration. *pakā,ū*, suppurative. *s.*

پکاي पकाई *pakā,ī*, f. dressing, ripeness. *s.*

پکبندھ पिकबन्धु *pik-bandhu*, m. the mango tree. *s.*

پکبيني पिकबयनी *pik-bayanī* or पिकबैनी *pik-bainī*, f. possessing a voice like the *kokila*. *s.*

پکپن पकपन *pakpan*, m. ripeness; cunning, cleverness, expertness. *s.*

پکتشول पक्तिशूल *pakti-shūl*, m. inflammation of the bowels, cholic. *s.*

پکڈنڈي *pakdanḍī*, f. a footpath. *d.*

پکڑ पकड़ *pakaṛ*, f. the act of seizing, seizure, capture; objection, difficulty. *h.*

پکڑانا पकड़ाना *pakṛānā*, a. to cause to be caught, seized, or laid hold of; to deliver over or give in charge. *h.*

پکڑبندي *pakaṛ-bandī*, f. proof, evidence; capture, seizing. *d.*

پکڑنا पकड़ना *pakaṛnā*, a. to catch, to lay hold of, to seize, to apprehend; to object. *h.*

پکش पक्ष *paksh*, m. half a lunation, a fortnight; a partisan, a friend; a side, a flank. *pakshāghāt*, m. palsy, hemipelgia. *paksha-pāt*, m. partisanship, partiality. *paksha-pātī*, m. a partisan, an adherent. *paksha-pātitā*, f. adherence, friendship. *pakshatā*, f. the taking up a side, partiality. *paksha-dhar*, m. a partisan. *s.*

پکشي पक्षी *pakshī*, m. *pakshinī*, f. a bird. *pakshi-rāj*, m. king of the birds, *Garuḍa*. *pakshi-shālā*, f. a nest, an aviary. *s.*

پکلا पकला *paklā*, m. a sore between the toes, produced by moisture. *h.*

پکنا पकना *paknā*, n. to be dressed or cooked; to ripen; to suppurate (as an inflammation, boil, &c.); to turn grey (hairs). *s.*

پکو पक्व *pakwa*, ripe, cooked, mature, perfect; able, shrewd; grey (the hair); digested. *pakwāshay*, m. the abdomen, the stomach. *pakwa-kṛit*, m. the *nimb* tree, the leaves of which are used to induce suppuration. *s.*

پکوان पकवान *pakwān* or पक्वान्न *pakwānna*, m. sweetmeats, victuals fried in melted butter or oil, cookery of any kind. *s.*

پکوانا पकवाना *pakwānā*, a. to cause to be dressed or cooked; to cause to ripen. *s.*

پکواي पकवाई *pakwā,ī*, f. price paid for cooking. *h.*

پکوڑا पकोड़ा *pakoṛā*, m. پکوڑي पकोड़ी *pakoṛī* or पकौड़ी *pakauṛī*, f. } a kind of dish made of peameal *s.*

پکھ पख *pakh* (for **पक्ष** *paksha*, q.v.), m. a period of fifteen days, fortnight, half a lunation; two; assistance, protection. *s.* [of a bow. *d.*

پکھاٹا पखाटा *pakhāṭā*, m. the horn or corner

پکھارنا पखारना *pakhārnā*, a. to wash. *s.*

پکھال पखाल *pakhāl*, f. } a large leather
پکھالا पखाला *pakhālā*, m. } bag for carrying water usually double, and thrown over the back of a bullock; also a leathern bag for raising water from a well. *s.*

پکھالي पखाली *pakhālī*, m. a water-carrier. *s.*

پکھان पखान *pakhān* (for *pākhān*), } m. a
پکھانا पखाना *pakhānā*, } stone. *s.*

پکھاوج पखावज *pakhāwaj*, f. a kind of drum, a timbrel. *h.*

پکھاوجي पखावजी *pakhāwajī*, m. one who beats the *pakhāwaj*; a drummer. *h.*

پکھراج पुखराज *pukhrāj*, m. a topaz; name of a lunar mansion. *h.*

پکھروٹا पखरौटा *pakhrauṭā*, m. a bit of gold or silver leaf covering a *bīṛā* or mouthful of betel. *h.*

پکھڑي पखड़ी *pakhṛī*, f. a petal, or flower-leaf. *h.*

پکھوا *pakhwā* or *pakhū,ā*, m. a side, wing, flank, gable end of a house. *d.*

پکھوٹا पखौटा *pakhoṭā*, m. a wing, fin of a fish; side or flank. *d.* [blade. *s.*

پکھوڑا पखौड़ा *pakhauṛā*, m. the shoulder-

پکھیرو पखेरू *pakherū*, m. a bird. *s.*

پکھیس पखेस *pakhes*, m. mark, stamp. *h.*

پگ पग *pag*, m. the foot. *pag paṭ tār bajnā*, to beat time with the foot. *pag-danḍī*, f. by-path. *pagdanḍī-lenā*, to track, to trace. *s.*

پگا पगा *pagā*, m. a rope fastened round the neck of a bullock, a tether. *h.*

پگار पगार *pagār*, mud kneaded for building or plastering walls; (in Dakh.) pay, salary, wages. *s.*

پگاه *pagāh*, f. dawn of day, morning, twilight. *p.*

پگاهتر *pagāhtar*, f. early dawn of day. *p.*

پگ‌دھارنا पगधारना *pag-dhārnā*, n. to travel, to depart. *s.* [chew the cud. *h.*

پگرانا पगुराना *pagurānā*, n. to ruminate, to

پگڑي पगड़ी *pagṛī*, f. a turban; a species of poll-tax (v. *pāg*). *pagṛī aṭaknā*, to be obstinate, to persist or persevere. *pagṛī chhapaṭnā*, a. to act falsely or treacherously. *h.*

پگلا पगला *paglā*, foolish (phrase peculiar to Bengal and the eastern parts of Hindūstān). *h.*

پگنا पगना *pagnā*, n. to be dipped in or covered with syrup; (met.) to be in love. *s.*

پگها पगहा *paghā*, m. (the same as *pagā*), a rope, tether. *h.* [or steel. *h.*

پگهال पघाल *paghāl*, m. a kind of hard iron

پگهايا पघाया *paghāyā*, m. a dealer in cloth, metals, &c. *h.*

پگهلانا पिघलाना *pighlānā*, a. to melt, to fuse; to soften (an angry or a hard person), to assuage. *s.*

پگهلاو पिघलाव *pighlāw* or *pighlā,o*, m. fusion. *s.*

پگهلنا पिघलना *pighalnā*, n. to melt or be melted, to be in fusion. *s.*

پگهيا पघैया *paghaiyā*, m. a trader in cloth, iron, &c. *h.*

پگيا पगिया *pagiyā*, f. a turban. *h.*

پل पल *pal*, m. a moment; the sixtieth part of a *gharī* or *dand* (2½ *pals* are equal to one minute). *pal mārte*, immediately, instantly, in the twinkling of an eye. *pal mārnā*, to wink, to move the eyelid. *p.*

پل *pul*, m. a bridge, an embankment, a causeway. *pul-guzār*, a bridge toll. *pul bāndhnā*, a. (to make a bridge) to limit; to abound. *p.*

پلا पला *palā*, m. a spoon, ladle for taking out oil, &c. *pulā*, m. a small bundle of plants or sticks. *h.* [*harāmī pillā*, a bastard. *h.*

پلا पिल्ला *pillā*, m. a pup, a whelp, cub;

پلا पल्ला *pallā*, m. space, distance; assistance; a border of cloths; a sheet (generally applied to chintz or shawl); a bag; *labium vulvæ*; one shutter of a door, &c.; border, margin. *h.*

پلا *pallā*, m. one scale (or side of a pair of scales). *pallā-bāndhna*, to enter the lists against an enemy. *pallā-kash*, partial. *pallā-kashī*, partiality. *palle par kisī ke ānā*, to assist, to favour, to side with any one. *palle-dār*, a porter who has bags to carry burdens. *palle-dārī*, f. the business of a porter. *p.*

پلاد पलाद *palād*, m. f. a *Rākshas* or demon, male or female. *s.* [humour. *s.*

پلاگن पलाग्नि *palāgni*, m. the bile, the bilious

پلاس *palās*, m. very coarse cloth. *p.*

پلاس पलाश *palās* or *palāsh*, m. a tree so called, on which the lac insect feeds (*Butea frondosa*). *palās pāpṛā*, m. the seeds of the *Butea frondosa*, used in medicine. *s.*

پلاسي पलाशी *palāsī*, m. name of a village (vulg. *Plassey*), famous for one of our earlier victories in India. *s.*

پلاش पलाश *palāsh*, m. a tree (see *palās*).

پلاشاکھيه पलाशाख्य *palāshākhya*, m. assafœtida. *s.* [clinata; the *palās* tree. *s.*

پلاشك पलाशक *palāshak*, m. curcuma re-

پلاشي पलाशी *palāshī*, f. lac; m. a goblin; a sort of mimusops (*m. kauki*). *s.*

پلاکش प्लाक्ष *plāksha*, m. the fruit of the *hibiscus populneoides*. *s.*

پلان पलान *palān*, a space of ground between two occupied lots, left for future disposal. *h.*

پلان *palān*, } m. (corruption of *pālān*), a
پلانا *palānā*, } packsaddle. *p.*

پلانا पलाना *palānā*, a. to run away, to flee, to escape. *s.*

پلانا पिलाना *pilānā*, a. to cause to drink; to ply with drink. *h.*

پلانا पलान्ना *palānnā*, a. to saddle a horse or bullock. *p.*

پلانڈ पलाण्डु *palāṇḍu*, m. an onion. *s.*

پلانگ पलाङ्ग *palāng*, m. the Gangetic porpoise. *s.*

پلاني पलानी *palānī*, f. } thatching. *h.*
پلاو पलाव *palāw*, m. }

پلاو प्लाव *plāv*. m. submersion. *s.*

پلاو *pulā,o* (properly *pilāv*), m. a kind of dish made up of rice, spices, and flesh or fowl. *hawā kā pulā,o*, a castle built in the air. "Lord Byron has been laughed at by many an 'old Indian' for writing this word 'pilaff,' making it rhyme with 'quaff,' but the fact is, that his lordship's Anglified term comes much nearer to the real word, which is Persian, than our barbarous Indian corruption of it." *p.* (B.)

پلاونا पलावना *palā,onā*, n. to flee, to run away. *s.*

پلايمان पलायमान *palāyamān*, adj. running away. *s.*

پلاين पलायन *palāyan*, m. flight, retreat. *palāyan-parāyan*, fugitive. *s.*

پل بندي *pul-bandī*, f. an embankment, dykes or mounds raised to prevent inundations; keeping a bridge &c. in repair, also a tax levied for that purpose; sodomy. *pul-bandī-k.*, to ravish, to violate. *p.*

پلپل *pilpil*, m. pepper. *p.*

پلپلا पिलपिला *pilpilā* or पुलपुला *pulpulā*, soft, flabby, flaccid. *h.*

پلپلانا पिलपिलाना *pilpilānā*, a. to soften. *h.*

پلپلانا पुलपुलाना *pulpulānā*, n. to fear, to dread; to take a morsel into the mouth, and from the want of teeth being unable to chew, to turn it about. *h.*

پلپلاهٹ पिलपिलाहट *pilpilāhaṭ*, f. softness. *h.*

پلپلاهٹ पुलपुलाहट *pulpulāhaṭ*, f. fear; the act of turning about a morsel in the mouth. *h.*

پلت प्लुत *plut*, m. the protracted utterance of a vowel, being three times the length of a short vowel. *s.*

پلتها مارنا पलथा मारना (also पलठामारना) *palthā* (or *palṭhā*) *mārnā*, n. to sit down on the ground resting on the buttocks. *h.*

پلتهي पलथी *palthī*, f. a mode of sitting on the buttocks. *h.*

پلٹا पलटा *palṭū*, m. turn, stead, exchange, recompense, revenge, retaliation. *h.*

پلٹانا पलटाना *palṭānā*, a. to cause to turn, to convert. *h.*

پلٹاکهانا पलटा खाना *palṭa khānā*, a. to turn over head and heels; to overturn, to be tilted, to rebound. *h.*

پلٹالينا *palṭā-lenā* (v. *palaṭ-l.*), to revenge, &c. *h.*

پلٹاو पलटाव *palṭāw* or *palṭā,o*. m. contradiction, reaction, rebound. *h.*

پلٹ لينا पलटलेना *palaṭ-lenā* or *palṭā-lenā*, a. to take in return, to revenge, to exact retribution. *h*

پلٹن पलटन *palṭan*, f. a battalion, a regiment. *h*

پلٹنا पलटना *palaṭnā*, n. to return, to turn back; to retreat; to overturn, to rebound; to change. *h.*

پلٹها مارنا पलठा मारना *palṭhā-mārnā*, n. to sit down on the ground resting on the buttocks. *h.*

پلج पुलिज *pulij*, that land which is cultivated for every harvest, being never allowed to lie fallow. *h.*

پلچنا पिलचना *pilachnā*, n. to adhere. *h.*

پلڑا पलड़ा *palṛā*, m. a scale, *i.e.* one side of a pair of scales. *h.*

پلڑي पिलड़ी *pilṛī*, f. a kind of forced meat. *h.*

پلسات *pīlsāṭ*, f. yellowness, yellow hue. *d.*

پل سراط *pul sirāṭ* or *puli sirāṭ*, m. the bridge, over which Musalmāns pass into paradise.—N. B. the wicked are sure to fall thence into the bottomless pit. *p. a.*

پلشت *pilisht*, polluted impure, unclean; (met.) f. an adulteress, a strumpet. *p.*

پلك पलक *palak*, f. the eyelid; a moment; *palak daryā*, m. clouds; *palak mārnā* or *-maṭkānā*, a. to wink. *p.*

پلكت पुलकित *pulkit*, joyful, rejoiced. *s.*

پلكش प्लक्ष *plaksha*, m. waved-leaf fig-tree (*Ficus infectoria*); another tree (*Hibiscus populneoides*); the holy fig-tree (*Ficus religiosa*); one of the seven *Dwīpas* or divisions of the world. *s.*

پلكي पुलकी *pulkī*, m. a sort of Kadamb (*Nauclea cadamba*). *s.*

پلن पुलिन *pulin*, m. an island of alluvial formation, a small island or bank left in a river upon the falling of waters. *s.*

پلنا पिलना *pilnā*, a. to attack, to assault; n. to be bruised, thrashed, trodden, pressed, ground. *s.*

پلنا पलना *palnā*, n. to be reared; to be fattened, to thrive. *s.*

پلند पुलिंद *pulind*, m. a barbarian, an outcast, one inhabiting mountains and forests. *s.*

پلندا पुलिन्दा *pulindā*, m. a bundle, a parcel. *h.*

پلنگ पलङ्ग *palang*, m. a bed (without curtains), a bedstead. *palang-posh*, m. a coverlet, a counterpane: this last compound is commonly called a "*palampore*" by Europeans. *palang tīn chor*, "the bed and three thieves," the constellation called "Charles's wain" (B.) *p.*

پلنگ *palang*, m. a tiger, a panther, a leopard. *palang-afgan*, tiger killer, a fierce warrior. *p.*

پلنگ पुलिङ्ग *puling* or पुंल्लिङ्ग *pullinga*, the masculine gender. *s.*

پلنگڑي पलङ्गड़ी *palangṛī*, f. a small bedstead. *h*

پلنگي *palangī*, of or relating to a tiger, tiger-like, fierce, ferocious. *p.*

پلو प्लव *plav*, m. a diver, a bird so called (*Pelicanus fusicollis*); waved-leaf fig-tree (*Ficus infectoria*); a sort of grass (*Cyperus rotundus*); fragrant grass in general. *s.*

پلو पल्लव *pallav*, m. a sprout, a shoot, a branch with the leaves attached. *s.*

پلو पल्लू *pallū*, m. the hem of a garment, the border of a garment. *pallū-dār*, a garment with gold or silver border. *h.*

پلو पिल्लू *pillū*, m. } a worm. *s.*
پلوا پلوآ पिलुआ *pilū,ā*, }

پلوار पलवार *palwār*, m. a kind of boat of 15 to 20 tons burden for carrying goods; applied chiefly to the slow heavy craft in the Sunderbuns: it is considered to have come originally from Dacca. *h.*

پلواري पलवारी *palwārī*, m. a boatman, people belonging to a boat or *palwār*. *h.*

پلوانا पलवाना *palwānā*, a. to cause to be reared or nourished. *s.*

پلوٹها पलौठा *pallauthā* or *palauṭhā*, first-born (q. d. *pahilā uṭhā* or *pahlā uṭhā*). *h.*

پلوك पल्लवक *pallavak*, m. a kind of fish (*Cyprinus denticulatus*). *s.*

پلول पलवल *palwal*, m. the name of a plant (*Trichosanthes dioica, Roxb.*). *palwal-latī*, the plant of *palwal*). *s.*

پلون प्लवन *plavan*, m. a deluge, an inundation. *s.*

پله *palla*, m. a side (as of scales), (v. *pallā*). *p.*

پله *pula*, soft, tender; hollow. *d.*

پلها प्लिहा *plihā*, f. the spleen (v. *plīhā*). *s.*

پلهانا पुलहाना *pulhānā*, a. to persuade. *s.*

پلهن प्लिहन *plihan*, m. the spleen. *s.*

پلهنڈا पल्हिण्डा *palhinḍā* or *palihṅḍā*, m. }
پلهنڈي पल्हिण्डी *palhinḍī* or *palihṅḍī*, f. } a shelf upon which water-pots are placed, a place where water is kept. *h.*

پلي पिलई *pila,ī*, f. the spleen; a disease from enlargement or inflammation of the spleen. *s.*

پلي पली *palī*, f. a ladle used to take out oil with. *h.*

پلي पल्ली *pallī*, f. a small village; a house lizard. *h.*

پلئي पलई *pala,ī*, f. a young branch or spray of a tree. *h.*

پليت *palīt* (for *palīd*), polluted, unclean. *p.*

پليت पलीत *palīt*, m. a ghost, spirit of the dead. *h.*

پليتا पलीता *palītā*, m. a match (of a gun); a candle. *palītā chāṭ-jānā*, to flash in the pan. *p.*

پليتهن पलेथन *palethan*, m. dry flour laid under and over bread when it is rolled. *palethan pakānā*, to contrive the ruin of any one. *palethan nikālnā*, a. to beat severely. *h.*

پليد *pilīd* or *palīd*, unclean, polluted. *p.*

پليدي *palīdī*, f. uncleanness, excrement. *p.*

پليؤ पलेव *pale,o*, m. soup, pounded rice or flour put into soup to thicken it. *palev* or *pale,ā*, land watered after ploughing. *h.*

پليها प्लीहा *plīhā*, f. } the spleen; the organ,
پليهن प्लीहन *plīhan*, m. } or the disease of it; enlargement of the mesenteric glands. *s.*

پليهار प्लीहारि *plīhāri*, m. the holy fig-tree (*Ficus religiosa*), deemed an enemy to spleen. *h.*

پليهشتر प्लीहशत्रु *plīha-shatru*, } m. a medicinal
پليهگهن प्लीहघ्न *plīha-ghna*, } plant, commonly called Rohinī or Roherā (*Andersonia rohitaka*). *s.*

پمپا पम्पा *pampā*, f. a river in the south of India. *s.*

پن पुन *pun*, पुनः *puna*, or पुनि *puni*, again, also, afterwards. *puna-puna* or *puna-punar*, again and again, repeatedly. *s.*

پن पुन *pun* (for पुण्य *punya*), m. virtue, virtuous action, charity; (opposite to fault); merit. *s.*

پن पिन *pin*, m. a sound, noise. *s.*

پن पण *pan*, m. an aggregate number, consisting of twenty *gaṇḍās* (q. v.), that is, eighty *kauṛīs* (and sixteen *paṇs* make a *kāhan*); a vow; promise; a bet, a wager, a stake at play: it is also used to denote money in general; wages, hire, price; business; an agreement, a stipulation or clause in an agreement; (contr. of *pān*), as, *pan-baṭṭa*, m. a betel-box. *s.*

پن पन *pan*, a termination affixed to nouns, answering to the English terminations *ship, hood, ness*, &c., as, *laṛak-pan*, childhood, *bālak-pan*, boyhood. *h.*

پن *pan*, conj. but, yet, for. *d.*

پنا पना *panā*, a termination added to words to denote trade, state, or condition (also the same as *pan*), as *jauharī-panā*, the trade of a jeweller. *h.*

پنا पुन्ना *punnā*, a. to abuse, revile. *h.*

پنا पन्ना *pannā*, m. a beverage; the upper part of a shoe; a termination answering to *pan*, q.v. *h.*

پنا पन्ना *pannā*, m. an emerald; a leaf. *s.*

پنا पिन्ना *pinnā*, m. a cake of mustard-seed remaining after the expression of the oil, which is given to cows, &c., for food. *s.*

پنارا पनारा *panārā*, m. } a drain or pipe by
پناري पनारी *panārī*, f. } which water runs off from the roof of a house, a spout. *s.*

پناك पिनाक *pināk*, m. the bow of *Shiva*, a musical instrument of one string shaped like a bow, the trident of Shiva. *s.*

پناكي पिनाकी *pinākī*, f. a sort of viol. *s.*

پناگ पुन्नाग *punnāg*, m. a tree from the flowers of which a yellowish dye is prepared (*Rotleria tinctoria*). *s.*

پنالا पनाला *panālā*, m. } (see *panārī*); a spout.
پنالي पनाली *panālī*, f. } *panalī parnā*, to be very fat (a horse). *s.*

پناتا पनाना *panānā*, a. to cause the milk to come into the udder of animals. *h.*

پناه *panāh*, f. shade, shelter; protection; asylum, refuge. *panāh-dih*, a protector. *panāh kisī se māngnā*, to seek protection, to avoid; used in comp. as *jahān-panāh*, asylum of the world, your Majesty. *'adālat-panāh*, refuge of justice, your Worship. *p.*

پن بٹا पनबट्टा *pan-baṭṭā*, m. a betel-box. *h.*

پنبه *pumba*, m. cotton. *pumba ba-gosh*, deaf (lit. having cotton in the ear). *pumba-dahan*, silent in company, taciturn; mealy-mouthed. *pumba-doz*, a carder of cotton. *p.*

پنبهتا पनभत्ता *pan-bhattā*, m. a mixture of water and boiled rice (for drinking). *h.*

پنبهٹا पनभट्टा *pan-bhaṭṭā*, m. a betel-box. *h.*

پنبئی *pumba,ī*, made of cotton. *p.*

پنپانا पंपाना *pampānā* or पनपाना *panpānā*, a. to cause to flourish, to promote the prosperity of another; to refresh (little used). *h.*

پنپنا पनपना *panapnā*, a. to commence increasing in bulk (a man, tree, &c.); to prosper, to flourish, to thrive, to shoot, to be refreshed, restored. *h.*

پنپناتا पिनपिनाना *pinpinānā*, n. to twang, to whiz. *h.*

پنپناهت पिनपिनाहट *pipināhaṭ* or पनपनाहट *panpanāhaṭ*, f. the whizzing of an arrow or shot. *h.*

پنتوا पनतवा *pantawā*, m. a kind of sweetmeat. *h.*

پنتھ पन्थ *panth*, } m. a road; a sect, a religious order. *s.*
پنتھا पन्था *panthā*, }

پنتهی पन्थी *panthī*, m. a traveller; a sectary, a follower of any peculiar sect or master; generally used in comp., as *kabīr-panthī*, a follower of *Kabīr*. *s.*

پنج पुञ्ज *punj*, m. an aggregate, the whole, a heap. *s.*

پنج *panj*, five. *naye panj*, of five years old. *male panj*, of ten years old (these applied to horses only). *panj 'aibi shar'ī*, very vicious (possessed of five vices, i.e. robbery, adultery, gaming, drunkenness, falsehood). *panj-āyat*, the five chapters of the *ḳur,ān*, which are read during the mourning of a Musalmān. *panj tani pāk*, the five holy persons, i.e. *Muḥammad*, *Alī*, *Fāṭima*, *Ḥasan*, and *Ḥusain*. *p.*

پنجاب *panjāb*, m. the country inhabited by the Sikhs, so called from its being watered by five rivers. *p.*

پنجابی *panjābī*, of or belonging to the *Panjāb*; the language of the Sikhs. *p.*

پنجارا *panjārā*, m. a cotton-carder. *d.*

پنج انگشت *panj angusht*, m. cinq-foil. *p.*

پنجاه *panjāh*, fifty. *panjāhum*, fiftieth. *p.*

پنجت पिञ्जट *pinjaṭ*, m. the concrete rheum of the eyes. *s.*

پنجر पिञ्जर *pinjar*, yellow, tawny, reddish yellow; m. a bay or chesnut horse; yellow orpiment. *s.*

پنجر पञ्जर *panjar*, m. or *panjrī*, f. a rib. *s.*

پنجر पिञ्जर *pinjar*, } m. a cage; a trap. *pinjrā honā*, n. to be or grow lean. *s.*
پنجرا पिञ्जरा *pinjrā*, }

پنجری पञ्जरी *panjarī*, f. a rib. *s.*

پنج سال *panj sāl*, m. five years; a five-year old (horse). *p.*

پنج ساله *panj-sāla*, of five years, quinquennial. *p.*

پنجشنبه *panj-shamba*, Thursday. *p.*

پنج عیب *panj-'aib*, very vicious (v. *panj*). *p.a.*

پنجکا पञ्जिका *panjikā*, f. the register or journal of Yama, the record of human actions. *s.*

پنجکا पिञ्जिका *pinjikā*, f. a roll of cotton from which the thread is spun. *s.*

پنجگانه *panj-gāna*, fivefold. *p.*

پنجگوشه *panj-gosha*, } five-cornered, pentangular, quintuple, fivefold. *p.*
پنجگنا *panj-gunā*, }

پنجگنج *panj-ganj*, the five senses, the five stated daily prayers enjoined on all good *Musulmāns*; the name of a collection of five treatises on Arabic Grammar. *p.*

پنجلی पिञ्जली *pinjlī*, f. two blades of *kusa* grass, used as a vessel. *s.*

پنجم *panjum*, the fifth. *p.*

پنجن पिञ्जन *pinjan*, m. a bow used for cleaning cotton. *s.*

پنجوش पिञ्जूष *pinjūsh*, m. the wax of the ear. *s.*

پنجول पिञ्जूल *pinjūl*, m. the wick of a lamp. *s.*

پنجه *panja*, m. a claw, the bunch of fives; a sort of link or torch resembling the five fingers, which is also called *panj-shākha*, a hand made of ivory, &c., to scratch the back. *panja-phernā*, to overcome, to overpower. *panja-k.*, a kind of wrestling wherein the antagonists lock their fingers together. *panja-kash*, m. an iron instrument resembling a hand, with which wrestlers exercise themselves by locking their fingers into those of the instrument; a kind of bread bearing the marks of five fingers. *p.*

پنجیارا पिञ्जियारा *pinjiyārā*, m. one whose business is to beat and separate cotton. *h.*

پنجیت पिञ्जेट *pinjeṭ*, m. the concrete rheum of the eyes. *s.*

پنجیری पञ्जीरी *panjīrī*, f. a medicine composed of sugar, ghī, flour, &c., given to puerperal women; caudle. *s.*

پنچ पञ्च *panch*, five; m. a council, an assembly, a meeting, a company; arbitrators. *panchādhyāy*, m. five readings or chapters; f. the aggregate of five chapters of the *Shrī Bhāgavat*, detailing the sports of *Krishna* with the *Gopīs*. *panchāgni*, m. five fires amidst which a devotee performs penance. *panchāmla*, m. the aggregate of five acid plants, viz. the jujube, pomegranate, sorrel, spondias, and citron. *panchāng*, m. five modes of devotion: silent prayer, burnt offering, libation, bathing idols, and feeding Brāhmans; an almanac; reverence by extending the hands, bend ing the knees and head and in speech and look. *panch-bandh*, m. a fine equal to the fifth part of any thing lost or stolen. *panch-bhadra*, m. a horse with five auspicious marks; a sauce of five ingredients. *panch-bhūt*, m. the five elements: earth, air, fire, water, and ether (*ākās*). *panch-bhūtātmā*, m man as formed of the five elements. *panch-pātra*, m. five vessels; an offering made in five vessels. *panch-prān*, m. the five airs supposed to be in the body. *panch-parnī*, f. a small shrub. *panch-piriyā*, any person, Hindū or other, who worships the five pīrs or saints of the *Musalmāns*; a caste of *halālkhors*. *panch-pallav*, m. the aggregate of five sprouts used in religious ceremonies: viz. spondia, rose-apple, *bel* or marmelos, citron, and wood-apple. *panch-panchanakh*, m. five kinds of animals allowed to be killed and eaten: hare, porcupine, alligator, rhinoceros, and tortoise. *pancha-tapā* m. an ascetic making penance between four fires and the sun above. *panch-tīrthī*, f. five places of pilgrimage: Vishrānti, Saukar, Naimish, Prayāg, and Pushkar; bathing on the day of the equinox. *pancha-ratna*, m. five precious objects: as, gold, diamond, pearl, ruby, amethyst. *pancha-sugandhak*, m. five aromatic drugs: cloves, nutmeg, camphor, aloe wood, and *kakkola*. *pancha-sūnā*, m. pl. five things by which animal life may be accidentally destroyed: the fire-place, the slab on which condiments are ground, the broom, the pestle and mortar, and the water-pot. *pancha-shākhā*. m. the hand. *pancha-karma*, m. five actions of the body or modes of evacuation. *pancha-koshā*, m. pl. the five sheathes supposed to invest the soul. *pancha-kol*, five spices: pepper, ginger, &c. *pancha-kon*, m. a pentagon. *panch-khanā*, consisting of five stories. *panch-gun*, five times, five-fold. *pancha-gavya*, five articles derived from the cow: milk, curds, ghī, urine, and dung. *pancha-lakshan*, m. a Purāna, comprehending five topics: the creation of worlds, their destruction, the genealogies of gods and heroes, the reigns of Manus, and the actions of their descendants. *pancha-loh*, m. a compound of five metals: copper, brass, tin, lead, and iron. *pancha-māsya*, m. the koil or Indian cuckoo. *pancha-mūl*, m. the aggregate of five roots: the *bel*, Premna longfolia, cassia, Gilmena arborea, and the trumpet-flower. *pancha-mūlī*, f. the aggregate of five smaller roots; Hedysarum gangeticum, H. lagopodioides, Solanum melongena, S. jacquini, and Tribulas lanuginosus. *pancha-mahā-yagya*, m. the five great sacraments of the Hindūs, or the worship of spirits, progenitors, gods, Vedas, and mankind, by offerings of perfumes and flowers; obsequial rites, oblations with fire, the study of the Vedas, and hospitality. *pancha-nad*, m. the *Panjāb*, or country of five rivers. *pancha-nakh*, m. any animal having five toes, as the elephant, tortoise, tiger, &c. *panchendriya*, m. the five organs of sense, viz. eye, ear, nose, tongue, and skin; or those of action, as hands, feet, windpipe, anus, and parts of generation. *s.*

پنچ पनच् ***panach***, f. a bowstring. *s.*

پنچادھیاءي पञ्चाध्याई ***panchādhyāī***, f. the aggregate of the five chapters of the *Bhāgavat Purāna*, comprising a detail of the sports of *Krishna* with the *Gopis*. *s.*

پنچال पञ्चाल ***panchāl***, deceitful, cunning; m. a country in the north of India. *h.*

پنچامرت पञ्चामृत ***panchāmrit***, m. a kind of sweetmeat made of five ingredients; or the term may be applied to the ingredients separately; and these are said to be curdled milk, cream, ghī, honey, and sugar. *s.* [a lion. *s.*

پنچانن पञ्चानन ***panchānan***, m. a name of *Shiva*;

پنچاون पञ्चावन ***panchāvan***, fifty-five. *h.*

پنچایت पञ्चायत ***panchāyat***, f. a meeting of any particular society, generally as a court of inquiry; a jury, an inquest, originally consisting of five members. *panchāyati-jātī*, an arbitration by persons of the same caste as the litigant parties. *panchāyati-khāngī*, a domestic settlement of family quarrels, &c. *panchāyati-sarkār*, a court held by public authority. *panchāyat-nāma*, the written award of a court of arbitration. *s.*

پنچایتي पञ्चायती ***panchāyatī***, f. (same as *panchāyat*, q. v.); also relationship, affinity: the sentence or award of a *panchāyat* court. *s.*

پنچتا पञ्चता ***panchatā***, f. death, dissolution of the five elements of the body. *s.*

پنچتتو पञ्चतत्व ***pancha-tatwa***, m. the five elements or principles according to the Hindūs, viz. fire, earth, air, water, and ether or space; the five essentials of certain rites. *s.*

پنچتر पञ्चत्र ***panchatra***, a fee or duty of five per cent. levied from a successful litigant. *s.*

پنچتو पञ्चत्व ***panchatwa***, m. death, dissolution. *s.*

پنچدس पञ्चदश ***panchadas*** or ***panchadash***, the fifteenth. *s.* [fold. *s.*

پنچدھا पञ्चधा ***panchadhā***, in five ways, five-

پنچک पञ्चक ***panchak***, f. a bowstring; adj. five, relating to five, made of five, &c.; m. an aggregate of five. *s.*

پنچک पञ्चक ***panchak***, taxes levied by the *zamīndārs*, over and above the fixed revenue. *h.*

پنچکھن पञ्चखन ***panchakhan***, also ***panchakhanā***, consisting of five floors or stories (a house, &c.). *s.*

پنچکي पनचक्की ***pan-chakkī***, f. a water-mill. *s.*

پنچگویہ पञ्चगव्य ***pancha-gavya***, m. five things derived from the cow, as, milk, curds, &c. *s.*

پنچلڑا पञ्चलड़ा ***panch-laṛā***, consisting of five rows or strings (a necklace, &c.). *h.*

پنچلڑي पञ्चलड़ी ***panchlaṛī***, f. a necklace of five rows. *s.*

پنچم पञ्चम ***pancham*** or ***panchama***, the fifth; m. name of a *rāg*; also of a *sur*, or musical note. *s.*

پنچمي पञ्चमी ***panchamī***, also ***panchamīn***, f. the fifth day of the moon. *s.*

پنچوترہ पञ्चोतर ***panchotara***, m. a transit duty of five per cent.; a deduction from rent, &c., of five per cent.; a custom-house, a toll-house. *s.*

پنچورا पञ्चोरा or पनचोरा ***panchorā***, m. an earthen vessel with a narrow neck, and having a hole in the bottom. When filled with water and the mouth stopped, no water flows from the hole below till the hand, or whatever stopped the mouth, be removed (it is used as an experiment to illustrate the doctrine of the *horror vacui* by the followers of Aristotle). *h.*

پنچون पञ्चों ***panchoṅ***, m. associates, friends. *s.*

پنچونشت पञ्चविंशति ***pancha vinshati***, five-and-twenty. *s.* [the twenty-fifth. *s*

پنچونشتتم पञ्चविंशतितम ***panchavinshatitam***,

پنچھالا पञ्छाला ***panchhālā***, m. the tail of a paper kite. *s.*

پنچھي पञ्छी ***panchhī***, m. a bird. *s.*

پند ***pand***, m. advice, admonition, moral maxim. *p.*

پندا *pindā*, young fruit just formed. *d.*

پندار *pindār* (root of *pindāshtan*), m. thought, imagination; pride, self-opinion; (in comp.) imagining, &c. *pand-ār*, one who takes or listens to advice. *p.*

پندرواڑا *pandrawāṛā*, m. a fortnight. *d.*

پندرہ **पन्द्रह** *pandrah*, fifteen. *pandrahwāṅ* and *pandrahwīṅ*, the fifteenth. *s.*

پندهلانا **पंधलाना** *pandhlānā*, a. to coax, to wheedle. *h.*

پنڈ **पण्ड** *panḍ*, m. a catamite, a eunuch. *s.*

پنڈُ **पण्डु** *panḍu*, m. the name of a sovereign of ancient *Delhī*, and nominal father of *Yudhishṭhira* and the other four *Pānḍava* princes. *s.*

پنڈ **पिण्ड** *pinḍ*, m. body, person; balls made of flour or rice, and offered to the manes at a religious ceremony of Hindūs: they are afterwards thrown into the river or given to cows. *pinḍ parnā*, to follow, to pursue, to be intent on. *pinḍ chhuṛānā*, to avoid, to escape. *pinḍ-pushp*, m. the flower of the *asoka* tree (*Jonesia asoca*); the China rose; a lotus; a flower (*Tabernæmontana coronaria*). *pinḍ-pushpak*, m. a pot-herb (*Chenopodium album*). *pinḍ-phalā*, f. a bitter gourd. *pinḍ-tailak*, m. incense, olibanum. *pinḍ-dān*, m. presentation of the obsequial cakes. *pinḍ-gos*, m. gum myrrh. *pinḍ-mustā*, f. a sort of grass (*Cyperus pertenuis*). *pinḍ-mūl*, m. the carrot (*Daucus carota*). *pinḍ-vīj*, m. a flowering shrub (*Oleander odorum*). *s.*

پنڈا *pinḍā*, m. body, person; a lump of clay; a bundle or ball of string; balls of flour or rice (vide *pinḍ*). *s.*

پنڈا **पण्डा** *panḍā*, m. a minister or priest who presides at the temple of an idol; f. wisdom, science. *s.*

پنڈادهکاری **पिण्डाधिकारी** *pinḍādhikārī*, m. the superintendant of a funeral, usually the nearest relation, to whom belongs the right of presenting the funeral cake. *s.*

پنڈار **पिण्डार** *pinḍār*, m. a tree (*Trewia nudiflora*). *s.*

پنڈارا **पिण्डारा** *pinḍārā*, m. a plunderer, pillager (among *Marhaṭṭās*). *h.*

پنڈالو **पिण्डालु** *pinḍālū*, m. name of a fruit (*Trewia nudiflora, Lin.; Rottlera indica, Willd.*); an esculent root, described as sweet, cooling, and diuretic; (in Dakh.) yam. *s.*

پنڈبی **पण्डुबी** *panḍubī*, f. a waterfowl, the coot, the diver. *h.*

پنڈت **पण्डित** *panḍit*, m. a learned Brāhman; adj. learned; an honorary title signifying doctor or philosopher. The *panḍits* are the only men who understand the *Sanskṛit*, the language in which the ancient writings of the Hindūs are composed. *s.*

پنڈتانی **पण्डितानी** *panḍitānī*, f. the wife of a *panḍit*. *s.*

پنڈتائی **पण्डिताई** *panḍitā,ī*, f. learning, scholarship. *s.*

پنڈت‌خانہ *panḍit-khāna*, m. (a corruption of *bandī-khāna*) a prison, lock-up house. *h. p.*

پنڈریک **पुण्डरीक** *punḍarīk*, m. the elephant of the south-east quarter; a sort of snake (*amphisbæna*); a sort of leprosy; a white lotus. *s.*

پنڈریک **पुण्डरीयक** *punḍarīyak*, m. a flower (*Hibiscus mutabilis*); a drug commonly called *punḍeriyā*. *s.*

پنڈک **पण्डुक** *pinḍuk*, m. a turtle-dove. *s.*

پنڈری *pinḍrī* also **پنڑی** *pinṛī*, the leg, shin; calf of the leg. *h. d.*

پنڈلا **पिण्डिला** *pinḍilā*, f. a sort of cucumber (*Cucumis madraspatanus*). *s.*

پنڈلی **पिण्डली** *pinḍlī*, f. the calf of the leg. *h.*

پنڈو *panḍū*, fruit in general. *d.*

پنڈوری **पण्डूरी** *panḍūrī*, f. the name of a bird (*Falco*). *h.*

پنڈول **पिण्डोल** *pinḍol*, f. a kind of white earth (used for whitewashing walls). *pinḍoli*, f. orts, leavings of a meal. *s.*

پنڈی **पिण्डी** *pinḍī*, f. the upper part of a *Shiva-ling*; a lump of any thing that may be contained in the fist; a small clue or ball of string; a small altar of sand a cubit square, on which oblations are offered to the manes of deceased persons; the same as *pinḍ*, balls made of rice, &c., offered to the manes; a long gourd (*Cucurbita lagenaria*); a sort of palm (*Phœnix dactylifera*); a flowering shrub (*Tabernæmontana coronaria, flor. plen.*) *s.*

پنڈیتک **पिण्डीतक** *pinḍītak*, m. a tree (*Vangueria spinosa*); a shrub (*Tabernæmontana coronaria*). *s.*

پنڈیتگر **पिण्डीतगर** *pinḍītagar*, m. a plant, a species of the *Tabernæmontana*. *s.*

پنڈیاین **पण्डियायन** *panḍiyāyan*, f. the wife of a *pānḍe*, or priest, q.v. *s.*

پنر **पुनर्** *punar* or **पुनराय** *punarāya*, again. *punar-bhū*, f. a widow re-married. *punar-utthan*, m. resurection. *punar-janmā*, re-born, born again. *punar-ukta*, repeated; m. tautology. *punar-ukti*, f. repetition. *punar-navā*, f. hog-weed (*Boerhavia diffusa-alata*). *s.*

پنربس **पुनर्बसु** *punarbasu* or *punarvasu*, m. the seventh mansion of the moon; Castor and Pollux. *s.*

پنس **पनस** *panas*, m. the bread-fruit tree (*Artocarpus integrifolia*). *s.*

پنسا **पनसा** *pansā*, insipid; f. a pustule, pustular and phlegmonoid inflammation of the skin. *s.*

پنسارهٹا **पंसारहटा** *pańsārhaṭā*, f. dealing in spices &c. *h.*

پنسارهٹا **पनसारहट्टा** *pansār-haṭṭā*, m. a quarter where there are many druggists' shops. *h.*

پنساری **पनसारी** *pansārī*, m. a druggist, a dealer in groceries, spices, herbs, &c. *h.*

پنسال **पनसाल** *pansāl*,
پنسالا **पनसाला** *pansālā*,
پنسلا **पनसल्ला** *pansallā*,
} m. a stand where water is provided for passengers. *s.*

پنستوہ **पुंस्त्व** *puństwa*, m. semen virile; virility. *s.*

پنسون **पुंसवन** *puńsavan*, m. a festival held on the mother's perceiving the first signs of a conception. *s.*

پنسوئی **पनसोई** *panso,ī*, f. a small boat so called, vulg. *panchway*. *h.*

پنسیری **पंसेरी** *pańserī*, f. a weight or measure of five sers. *h.*

پنشچهن **पुंश्चिह्न** *pańshchihna*, m. the penis. *s.*

پنک पङ्क *pank*, m. mud, mire, clay. *pank-prabhā*, f. the hell of mire. *pank-dhūm*, m. a division of hell. *pank-shukti*, f. a cockle. *pank-kīr*, m. a lapwing. *pank-grāh*, m. the *makar*, a marine monster. *pank-gaṛak*, m. a small fish (*Macrognathus pancalus*). *pank-vās*, m. a crab. *s.*

پنکار पङ्कार *pankār*, m. an aquatic plant (*Vallisneria*, also *Trapa bispinosa*). *s.*

پن کپڑا पनकपड़ा *panhapṛā*, m. soft cloth wetted and applied to a wound or sore. *s. h.*

پنکتي पङ्क्ती *panktī*, f. a line, a row; a stanza of four lines of ten syllables each. *s.*

پنکج पङ्कज *pankaj*, m. a lotus. *s.*

پنکرچر पङ्कृचर *pankṛichar*, m. an osprey. *s.*

پنکشتر पुन्नक्षत्र *punnakshatra*, m. an asterism under which males are procreated. *s.*

پنکوکڑي *pankūkṛī*, f. }
پنکوّا *pankawwā*, m. } a water hen. *d.*

پنکھ पङ्ख *pankh*, m. a feather, wing. *s.*

پنکھا पङ्खा *pankhā*, m. a fan. *s.*

پنکھڑي पङ्खड़ी *pankhṛī*, f. a petal, flower-leaf. *h.*

پنکھي पङ्खी *pankhī*, f. a small fan; a bird. *s.*

پنکھي पङ्खी *pankhī*, f. a kind of woollen cloth, which comes from the hilly countries. *h.*

پنکھيا पङ्खिया *pankhiyā*, f. a small fan; m. a kind of *faḳīr* who fans every body; a wicked man. *s.*

پنکي पिनकी *pinkī* (for *pīnak*), f. intoxication from eating opium; drowsiness, nodding. *h.*

پنکيرہ पङ्केरुह *pankeruh*, m. the Indian crane. *s.*

پنگ पिङ्ग *ping*, tawny. *ping-chakshu*, m. a crab. *ping-kapishā*, f. a cockroach. *s.*

پنگ पङ्गु *pangu*, lame, a cripple. *s.*

پنگ पन्नग *pannag*, m. a serpent. *s.*

پنگا पङ्गा *pangā*, lean, soft, delicate. *s.*

پنگاچا पनगाचा *pangāchā*, m. a field covered and saturated with water. *h.*

پنگاس पङ्गास *pangās* or पिङ्गाश *pingāsh*, m. name of a fish (*Silurus sagittatus Buch* or *Pimelodius pangasius*). *h.*

پنگت पङ्गत *pangat*, f. a row, or line. *s.*

پنگتا पङ्गुता *pangutā*, f. deformity, lameness. *s.*

پنگل पिङ्गल *pingal*, m. art of measuring verses; name of a fabulous being in the form of a serpent, to whom a treatise on prosody is ascribed; adj. tawny, pale; the fifty-first year of the Hindū cycle. *s.*

پنگل पङ्गुल *pangul*, m. a horse of a glossy or silvery white colour. *s.*

پنگلا पङ्गला *panglā*, bandy-legged, lame. *s.*

پنگلکا पिङ्गलिका *pingalikā*, f. a sort of crane. *s.*

پنگو पङ्गू *pangū*, (for *pangu*, q. v.), a cripple, lame, &c. *s.*

پنگوٹي पनगोटी *pan-goṭī*, f. chicken-pox. *h.*

پنگورا पिङ्गूरा *pingūrā*, }
پنگولا पिङ्गूला *pingūlā*, } m. a cradle. *h.*

پنگھٹ पनघट *panghaṭ*, m. a passage to a river, a stair, a quay for drawing water. *s.*

پنگھورا पंघूरा *panghūrā*, }
پنگھولا पंघूला *panghūlā*, } m. a cradle, same as *pingūrā*, &c. *h.*

پنلنگ पुंलिङ्ग *puṅ-ling*, m. the male organ; the masculine gender. *s.*

پنم *punam*, religious merit, the reward of merit in futurity. *d.*

پنم *punim* (v. *badr*), the full moon. *d.*

پنمار पनमार *panmār*, a soil submerged so as to be incapable of cultivation. *s.*

پنملا *panmallā*, m. a betel garden. *d.*

پنوار पंवार *paṅwār* or *puṅwār*, m. the name of a plant (*Cassia obtusifolia*); name of a *rāj-pūt* tribe *s*

پنوارا पंवारा *paṅwārā*, m. a story, tale, fable. *h.*

پنوارا पनवारा *panwārā*, m. a plate or dish made of leaves. *s.*

پنواري पंवारी *paṅwārī* or पनवारी *panwārī* f. a betel-garden. *s.*

پنواريا पंवारिया *paṅwāriyā*, m. a bard, a story-teller. *h.*

پنواڑا पंवाड़ा *paṅwāṛā*, m. a story, fable, tale. *h.*

پنواڑي पंवाड़ी *paṅwāṛī*, f. a betel-garden. *s.*

پنواڑيا पंवाड़िया *paṅwāṛiyā*, m. a bard, a story-teller. *h.*

پنوانا पुनवाना *punwānā*, a. to cause to be abused or reproached by another. *h.*

پنولا पनोला *panolā*, land watered after ploughing. *h.*

پنه पुनः *puna*, again (see *pun*). *puna-puna*, repeatedly. *s.*

پنها *panhā*, wide, broad, spacious. *p.*

پنهارا पनहारा *panhārā*, m. a man who carries water in pots on his head. *s.*

پنهارن पनहारिन *panhārin*, }
پنهاري पनहारी *panhārī*, } f. a woman who carries water on her head; a faithless person, promise-breaker. *s.*

پنهان *pinhān*, secret, hidden, concealed. *p.*

پنهانا पनहाना *panhānā*, a. to cause the milk to come into the udder of animals. *h.*

پنهانا पिनहाना *pinhānā*, a. to dress, to put on (clothes). *h.*

پنهاني *pinhānī*, f. concealment, secrecy. *p.*

پنه پنا पुनः पुना *puna-punā*, f. the *Pumpun* river in Behar. *s.*

پنهرا पनहरा *panharā*, m. }
پنهرن पनहरिन *panharin*, f. } a man or woman carrying water pots on the head. *s.*

پنهي पनही *panhī*, f. a slipper. *s.*

پنهياءي पनहियाई *panhiyā,ī*, afflicted with the *fluor albus*. *s.*

پنهين *panhīn*, f. (the same as *panhī*), a [slipper. *s.*

پني पुण्य *punya*, m. virtue, a good action; fame; adj. pure, holy, righteous. *punya-bhū*, or *punya-bhūmi*, f. the holy land of the Hindūs, bounded on the north by the Himālaya, on the south by the Vindhya, and on the east and west by the sea; the mother of a male child. *punya-phal*, m. the reward of good actions. *punya-tṛin*, m. white, *kusa* grass. *punya-tīrtha*, m. a holy shrine. *punya-darshan*, m. the blue jay. *punya-sthān*, m. a sacred place. *punya-shīl*, virtuous. *punya-karmā*, pious, virtuous. *punya-gandh*, m. the champak flower (*Michelia champaca*). *punya-lok*, m. paradise. *punya-wān*, virtuous, pious. *s.*

پني पन्नी *pannī*, f. tinfoil; m. name of a tribe [of *Paṭhāns*. *h.*

پني पिन्नी *pinnī*, f. a kind of sweetmeat. *h.*

بنيا पनिया *paniyā*, m. water; a water-snake, or any thing living in water. *s.*

پنيا पुण्या *punyā* (v. پنيه), f. the commencement of collection for the new year. *s.*

پنياتما पुण्यात्मा *punyātmā*, charitable, virtuous. *s.*

پنيارا पनियारा *paniyārā*, inundated. *s.*

پنياك पिण्याक *piṇyāk*, m. assafœtida. *s.*

پنيالا पनियाला *paniyālā*, m. the name of a fruit (*Flacourtia catafracta*). *s.*

پنيانا पनियाना *paniyānā*, a. to irrigate, to [water. *s.*

پنياءي पुण्याई *punyā,ī*, f. a virtuous action, performed (according to those who hold the doctrine of metempsychosis) in one state of existence, the reward of which is received in a future transmigration; merit of an ancestor rewarded in the person of his descendants. *s.*

پنيت पुनीत *punīt*, pure, clean. *s.*

پنير *panīr*, m. cheese. *panīr-māya*, rennet. *p.*

پنيري *panīrī*, cheesy, or made of cheese. *p.*

پنيرك पनीरक *panīrak*, } f. a young flower-
پنيري पनीरी *panīrī*, } tree. *h.*

پنيودي पुण्योदय *punyoday*, m. good fortune, as reward of the meritorious acts of a former life. *s.*

پنيه पुण्य *punya*, virtue, &c. (v. پني); the first day of the collections, when the head officer of government in this department sits in state at the *kachahrī* or office, and adjusts the amount of the revenue to be collected in the ensuing year. *s.*

پنيه पण्य *panya*, m. any saleable article; adj. saleable, vendible. *panya-sālā*, a market. *s.*

پنيه पनीहा *panīhā*, m. a water-snake; any thing living in water, an aquatic animal. *s.*

پو *po* (same as *par*), on, upon, at. *d.*

پو पौ *pau*, f. the one or ace on dice; a stand where water is provided for passengers; an overflooding of low lands in the rainy season. *pau phaṭnā*, to dawn (the morning). *h.*

پوا पौवा *pauwā*, m. a quarter; a weight or measure of a quarter of a *ser*. *s.*

پوا पोआ *po,ā*, m. a very young serpent; a nursling of any animal; a plant. *s.*

پوا पूआ *pū,ā*, m. a pancake. *s.*

پواج *pawāj*, mean people (pl. of *pājī*). *p.*

پواڑا *pawāṛā*, m. narration or explanation of a story. *d.*

پوال पुवाल *puwāl*, f. straw (also *po,ār*). *s.*

پوانا पोआना *po,ānā*, a. to warm by the sun or the steam of water, to bask. *s.*

پواءي पवाई *pawā,ī*, f. a chain fastened to horses' legs to prevent their being stolen; chains with which the legs of a criminal are fastened; the leg of a boot or stocking. *s.*

پوپ पूप *pūp*, m. a cake. *s.*

پوپالي पूपाली *pūpālī*, f. a cake made of meal or barley, half-baked or fried. *s.*

پوپلا पूपला *pūplā*, f. a sort of sweet cake, fried. *s.*

پوپلا पोपला *poplā*, one whose teeth are fallen [out, toothless. *h.*

پوپني पोपनी *popnī*, f. a wind instrument (of music) made by children of the seeds of mango and the leaves of the *Borassus*; any wind instrument. *h.*

پوپهٹنا पोफटना *po-phaṭnā*, also *pauphaṭnā*, to break forth as the daylight, to dawn. *po-phaṭī*, f. daybreak. *s.*

پوت पोत *pot*, f. a boat. *s.*

پوت पोत *pot*, m. nature, disposition, quality; glass beads; an assessment on cultivated fields. *h.*

پوت پوت पूत *pūt*, m. a son; the young of any animal. *pūt-zambūrā*, m. a young monkey. *s.*

پوت पूति *pūti*, f. purity, purification. *s.*

پوت पवित *pavit*, purified, cleansed. *s.*

پوت पिवत् *pivat*, adj. drinking. *s.*

پوتا पोता *potā*, m. grandson, son's son. *s.*

پوتا *potā*, m. the scrotum, the testicles. *p.*

پوتاتما पूतात्मा *pūtātmā*, m. a saint, an ascetic; a man of a cleanly person, or purified. *s.*

پوتپهل पूतफल *pūt-phal*, m. the jack-fruit. *s.*

پوتپهلا पूतिफला *puti-phalā*, f. a plant (*Psoralea corilifolia*). *s.*

پوتپهلي पूतिफली *pūti-phalī*, f. a medicinal plant (*Serratula anthelmintica*). *s.*

پوتج पोतज *potaj*, m. an animal that produces young at once without the intervention of any medium; elephants and some other animals being supposed to carry the young without the aid of an ovarium or uterus. *s.*

پوتر पौत्र *pautra*, (v. *potā*), a grandson, son's [son. *s.*

پوتر पवित्र *pavitr* or *pavitra*, pure, clean, free from sin, m. the brahmanical cord. *s.*

پوترا पवित्रा *pavitrā*, m. a knotted piece of *kusha* grass used in purification, the brahmanical thread; a string of silken beads. f. holy Basil (*Ocymum sanctum*); a river north-west of Haridwār, the *Pabar*; the twelfth of the light fortnight of *Shrāwan*, a festival in honour of Vishnu. *s.*

پوترا पोतरा *potrā*, m. baby-cloths, clouts. *h.*

پوترتا पवित्रता *pavitratā*, f. purity, sanctity, *s.*

پوترک पौत्रिक *pautrik*, belonging to a son, or a grandson. *s.*

پوتري पुतरी *pūtrī*, f. a puppet, an image. *s.*

پوتري पवित्री *pavitrī*, f. a ring of *kusha* grass (*Poa cynosuroides*), or of gold, silver, or copper, worn on the ring-finger and fore-finger by Hindūs during religious worship. (v. *pavitrā*). *s.*

پوتري पौत्री *pautrī*, a grand-daughter, son's daughter. *s.*

پوتڑا पोतड़ा *potṛā*, m. baby-cloths, clouts, *h.*

پوتڑي पोतड़ी *potṛī*, f. the after-birth. *h.*

پوتشارجا पूतिशारिजा *pūti-shārijā*, f. the pole or civet cat. *s.*

پوتک पूतिक *pūtik*, m. grey bonduc (*Cæsalpinia bonducella*). *s.*

پوتکاشٹھ पूतिकाष्ठ *pūti-kāshṭh*, m. a sort of pine (*Pinus devadaru*). *s.*

پوتکامکھ पूतिकामुख *pūtikā-mukh*, m. a bivalve [shell. *s.*

پوتکرنک पूतिकर्णक *pūti-karnak*, m. fetid ulceration of the ear. *s.*

پوتلا पुतला *putlā*, m. a puppet, an image. *s.*

پوتلک पौत्तलिक *pauttalik*, m. a worshipper of idols. *s.*

پوتلي पुतली *pūtlī*, f. a small puppet; the apple of the eye. *s.*

پوتنا पोतना *potnā*, a. to plaster, to besmear. *h.*

پوتنا पूतना *pūtnā*, f. name of a giantess, who was killed by *Krishna*; yellow myrobalan (*Terminalia chebula*); atrophy and wasting in a child, ascribed to the influence of the female fiend *Pūtnā*. *s.*

پوته *pota* (v. *poṭā* also *foṭa*), the scrotum. *p.*

پوتھ पोथ *poth*, m. glass beads, nature, &c. (v. *pot*). *h.*

پوتھا पोथा *pothā*, m. a large book especially a manuscript book written on long separate leaves of paper or palmyra connected by a string through the centre. *s.*

پوتھکي पोथकी *pothkī*, f. red pimples on the [eyelids. *s.*

پوتھلا पोथला *pothlā*, m. a porter's load, especially of grain. *h.*

پوتھي पोथी *pothī* (also *pūthī*), f. a book like *pothā*, only of a smaller size. *s.*

پوتھي पोथी *pothī*, f. a clove of garlic. *h.*

پوتي पोती *potī*, f. a grand-daughter, a son's daughter; f. the young (female) of any animal. *s*

پوتيا पोतिया *potiyā*, m. a cloth worn at time of bathing; the name of a plaything. *h.*

پوتينڈ पूत्यंड *pūtyanḍ*, m. the musk-deer; an insect with a fetid smell, the fetid bug. *s.*

پوٹ पोट *poṭ*, f. a bundle, a bale, a package; a spout. *h.*

پوٹ पूट *pūṭ*, m. name of a bone lying over the tail of a cow. *h.*

پوٹا पोटा *poṭā*, m. an unfledged bird; the eyelid, the crop or craw (of birds); stomach; the mucus of the nose, snot; f. a woman having a beard. *h.*

پوٹکي पुट्की *pūṭkī*, f. the anus, a term of abuse. *h.*

پوٹگل पोटगल *poṭ-gal*, m. a reed (*Arundo tibialis*); a sort of grass (*Saccharum spontaneum*). *h.*

پوٹلا पोटला *poṭlā*, m. a large bundle. *h.*

پوٹلي पोटली *poṭlī*, } f. a small bundle, a
پوٹلکا पोटलिका *poṭlikā*, } small packet. *h.*

پوٹھ पूठ *pūṭh*, m. the buttock, the hip. *h.*

پوٹھا पूठा *pūṭhā*, m. the paper or pasteboard cover of a book; (in Dakh.) *poṭhā*, m. the stomach; the crop of a bird. *s.*

پوجا पूजा *pūjā*, f. devotion, worshipping, veneration, homage to superiors; idolatry or idol worshipping (by Hindūs). *s*

پوجاري पुजारी *pūjārī*, } a worshipper, an
پوجک पूजक *pūjak*, } adorer, an idolater, a priest having the charge of an idol temple. *s.*

پوجت पूजित *pūjit*, adored, worshipped. *pūjat*, adj. adoring, worshipping. *s.* [of adoration. *s.*

پوجمان पूजमान *pūjamān*, venerable, worthy

پوجن पूजन *pūjan*, m. act of adoration, &c. *s.*

پوجنا पूजना *pūjnā*, a. to adore, to venerate, (but being a Hindū word it generally means) to idolatrize; to elapse, as time; to be accomplished. *s.*

پوجنيه पूजनीय *pūjanīya*, worthy of adoration; right worshipful. *s.*

پوجيمان पूज्यमान *pūjyamān*, being reverenced or respected. *s.* [father-in-law. *s.*

پوجيه पूज्य *pūjya*, venerable, adorable; m. a

پوچ *pūch*, absurd, obscene, inordinate. *pūch-go* or *pūch-bāf*, an obscene babbler. *pūch pā dar hawā*, nonsensical. *p.*

پوچھ पूछ *pūchh*, f. inquiry, investigation. *s.*

پوچھپچار *pūchh-pichār*, investigation discovery. *d.*

پوچھاپاچھا पूछापाछा *pūchhā-pāchhā*, m. investigation, inquiry. *s* [terrogation. *s.*

پوچھپچھ पूछपछ *pūchh-pachh*, f. inquiry, in

پوچھنا पूछना *pūchhnā*, a. to ask, to inquire; (in Dakh.) *pochhnā*, to wipe, to clean. *s.*

پوچھي पूछी *pūchhī*, f. the tail of a fish. *s.*

پوچي *pūchī*, an insect. *d.*

پوچيات *pūchiyāt*, foolish prattle. *p.*

پود *pūd*, warp, web, cloth in the loom. *p.*

پوددار *pod-dār* (for *foṭa-dār*), m. a person whose business it is to assay coin, or examine whether it is sterling or not; an examiner of coin; also a cash-keeper, a clerk whose business is to reckon and examine money. *p.*

پودنا पोदना *podnā*, m. } the name of a bird
پودني पोदनी *podnī*, f. } (*Sylvia olivacca*). *h.*

پودھ पौध *paudh*, } m. a young tree or plant
پودھا पौधा *paudhā*, } for transplantation. *h.*

پودھيلا पौधेला *paudhelā*, ground on which plants are sown for transplantation. *h.*

پودينه *podīna*, m. mint (*Mentha sativa*). *p.*

پور पोर *por*, f. the space or interval between two joints or articulations (in the body, or of a bamboo, sugar-cane, &c.). *por-por*, every joint. *s.*

پور *pūr* (in Dakh. *por*), m. a son. *p.*

پور पूर *pūr*, a city, town, village; much used in comp., as *Sulṭān-pūr*, Sultan's town, Kingston. *s.*

پور पौर *paur*, f. a gate, door; m. a fragrant grass. *h.*

پورا पूरा *pūrā*, entire, complete, exact, full, perfect, total, ripe. *pūrā-k.*, a. to fill, to reimburse, to fulfil, accomplish; (in Dakh.) *porā*, m. a complete set or assortment of any thing. *s.*

پورانك पौराणिक *paurānik*, belonging to the Purānas; m. a Brāhman well read in the Purānas. *s.*

پوراءي पूराई *pūrā,ī*, f. fulness, satisfaction, welfare. *s.* [adj. eastern; former, ancient. *s.*

پورب पूरब *pūrab* or पूर्ब *pūrba*, m. the east;

پوربارده पूर्बार्द्ध *pūrbārddha*, m. the former or prior half. *s.*

پوربي पूर्बी *pūrbī*, f. the name of a *rāginī*, sung before evening; adj. eastern, from the east; a kind of rice from the east of Bengal. *s.* [tion. *d.*

پورپڑنا *pūr-parnā*, to discharge an obliga-

پورت पूरित *pūrit*, filled complete. *s.*

پورت पूर्त्ति *pūrtt* or *pūrtti*, f. fulness. *s.*

پورتي पूर्त्ती *pūrttī*, adj. filling, completing. *s.*

پورسکھيه पौरसख्य *paurasakhya*, m. fellow-citizenship. *s.*

پورش पूरुष *pūrush*, m. man (see *purush*). *s.*

پورش पौरुष *paurush*, m. the height of a man with both arms elevated; virility; semen virile. *paurushtā*, f. manhood, manliness. *s.*

پورك पूरक *pūrak*, adj. filling, completing. *s*

پورن पूर्ण *pūrṇa* or पूरण *pūran*, complete, perfect. *pūrn-pātr*, m. a full cup or vessel; a vessel filled with clothes or ornaments which are scrambled for by the guests at a festival; a vessel filled with 256 handfuls of rice given to the superintending priest at a religious ceremony. *pūran polī*, f. a kind of bread *pūrna-kām*, satisfied, satiated. *pūrna-kumbh*, m. a vessel filled with holy water, used at the consecration of a king; a full cup or jar. *s.*

پورن पूरण *pūran*, adj. filling, completing; m act of filling, making up; multiplication; a fragrant grass (*Cyperus rotundus*). *s.*

پورنا पूर्णा *pūrnā*, a. to weave (as a spider); n. to be filled. *chauk pūrnā*, to make chequers or squares. *s.*

پورناهت पूर्णाहुति *pūrnāhuti* or *pūrnāhut*, f. the oblation presented at the conclusion of a religious sacrifice; the final oblation, the consummation. *s.*

پورنما पूर्णिमा *pūrnimā*, पौर्णिमा *paurnimā*, or पूर्णमा *pūrnamā*, } f. the day
پورن‌ماسي पूर्णमासी *pūrnamāsī* or पौर्णमासी *paurnamāsī*, } of full
پورنواسي पूर्णवासी *pūrnawāsī*, } moon. *s.*

پورنماس पूर्णमास *pūrnamās*, m. a monthly sacrifice offered on the day of full moon. *s.*

پورني पूरणी *pūrnī*, f. the cross threads in weaving a piece of cloth. *s.*

پورو पूर्व *pūrva*, m. the east; adj. first, prior, former, ancient, of yore; before, in front of. *pūrvābhyās*, m. former practice or experience. *pūrva-parvat*, m. the eastern mountain, from behind which the sun is supposed to rise. *pūrva-paksh*, m. a proposition, the first part of an argument; the first half of a lunar month. *pūrva-dish* or *pūrva-dik*, f. the eastern region. *pūrva-desh*, m. the eastern country. *pūrva-deh*, m. a former body, a prior existence. *pūrva-rātr*, m. the first part of the night. *pūrva-sandhyā*, f. dawn. *pūrva-shail*, m. the eastern mountain. *pūrva-kāl*, m. former time. *pūrva-kālīn*, ancient. *pūrva-krit*, done formerly, in a prior existence. *pūrva-gangā*, f. the Nermada, formerly called the Ganges. *pūrva-lakshan*, m. prognostic. *s.*

پوروا पूर्वा *pūrvā*, m. a small village. *s.*

پوروا पोरुआ *porū,ā*, m. a joint or phalanx of the fingers; a joint of a tamarind. *s.*

پوروابهادرپد पूर्वाभाद्रपद *pūrvā-bhādrapad*, m. the 26th lunar asterism. *s.* [the east. *s.*

پوروابهمکهه पूर्वाभिमुख *pūrvābhimukh*, facing

پوروابهالگني पूर्वाफाल्गुनी *pūrvā-phālgunī*, f. the 11th lunar asterism. *s.*

پورواردھ पूर्वार्द्ध *pūrvārddha*, the first half. *s.*

پورواشاڑھا पूर्वाषाढ़ा *pūrvāshārhā*, f. the first *Āshārhā*, or 20th lunar asterism, containing two stars, one of which is Alpha Sagittarii. *s.*

پوروال पोरवाल *porwāl*, name of a mercantile caste of Hindūs in Malwa. *h.*

پورواهن पूर्वाह्न *pūrvāhna*, m. the first portion of the day. *s.*

پوروبهادرپدا **पूर्वभाद्रपदा** *pūrva bhādrapadā*, f. the first of two lunar asterisms called *bhādrapadā*, the 26th of the whole. *s.*

پوروپهلگني **पूर्वफल्गुनी** *pūrva-phalgunī*, f. the first *phalgunī*, or eleventh lunar asterism, figured by a conch, containing two stars, one of which is Leonis. *s.*

پوروج **पूर्वज** *pūrvaj*, born before, elder, born in the east. *pūrva-jā*, m.pl. ancestors, the deified progenitors of mankind. *s.*

پورودیهك **पौर्वदेहिक** *paurva-dehik*, belonging to a former body or existence. *s.*

پوروك **पूर्वक** *pūrvak*, prior, before, preceding. *s.*

پوروك **पौर्विक** *paurvik*, prior, primary, former. *s.*

پورووتر **पूर्वोत्तर** *pūrvottar*, m. the north-east. *s.*

پوروهتیه **पौरोहित्य** *paurohitya*, m. the office of family priest. *s.*

پوروي **पूर्वी** *pūrvī*, of or belonging to the eastern region, oriental; f. name of a *rāginī* in music; a kind of rice from the east or Bengal. *s.*

پوري **पोरी** *porī*, f. a joint of bamboo, &c.; a stiff strong kind of soil. *s.*

پوري **पूरी** *pūrī*, f. a kind of fresh cake, fried in butter or ghī. *s.*

پوري **पौरी** *paurī*, f. a gate, a door. *s.*

پوریا **पौरिया** *pauriyā*, m. a doorkeeper, a porter. *s.*

پوریا **पूरिया** *pūriyā*, f. the name of a musical mood or *rāginī*. *h.*

پوڑا **पूड़ा** *pūṛā*, m. a kind of cake made of peameal. *h.*

پوڑها **पौढ़ा** *pauṛhā*, wide, broad, extensive. *h.*

پوڑها **पौढ़ा** *pauṛhā* or **पोढ़ा** *poṛhā*, strong, firm. *s.*

پوڑهاءي **पौढ़ाई** *pauṛhā,ī* or **पोढ़ाई** *poṛhā,ī*, f. strength, firmness; breadth. *s.*

پوڑهنا **पौढ़ना** *pauṛhnā*, n. to lie down, to sleep. *h.*

پوڑي **पोड़ी** *poṛī* or **पौड़ी** or *pauṛī*, a stiff strong species of soil. *h.*

پوز *pūz*, m. lip of a horse. *p.*

پوزش *pozish*, f. excuse, palliation, apology, pretence, pretext. *s.*

پوزمال *pūzmāl*, m. a cord twisted tight round a horse's lip or ear to enable the farrier to manage him. *p.*

پوزه *pūza*, m. the lip (of a horse particularly). *p.*

پوزي *pūzī*, f. part of the ornamental accoutrements of a horse. *p.*

پوس **पूस** *pūs*, m. the name of the ninth solar month, the full moon of which is near *pushya*, the eighth lunar asterism. *s.*

پوست *post*, m. crust, skin, rind; poppy plant; an infusion of the poppy formerly much used as a slow poison. *post bar post*, crust upon crust, or skin upon skin. *p.*

پوستي *postī*, m. one who intoxicates himself with infusion of poppy-heads; (met.) a lazy indolent person. *p.*

پوستین *postīn*, leathern (garment); a fault, blemish. *postīn-doz*, a furrier, or maker of leathern garments. *p.*

پوسنا **पोसना** *posnā*, a. to breed, to rear, to educate, to nourish, to tame. *s.*

پوش *posh*, (in comp.) covering, wearing, as *pā-posh*, (covering the feet) shoes, slippers; *sabz-posh*, clothed in green; *kulah-posh*, wearing a hat or cap. *p.*

پوش **पूष** *pūsh*, m. the eighth mansion of the moon, containing three stars in Cancer; the mulberry (*Morus Indica*). *s.*

پوش **पोष** *posh*, m. nourishing, cherishing. *s.*

پوش **पौष** *paush*, m. the ninth Hindū solar month (see *pūs*). *s.*

پوشاك *poshāk*, f. vestments, dress, habit, garments, especially costly ones. *p.*

پوشاكي *poshākī*, fit for making garments (cloth). *p.*

پوشپ **पौष्प** *paushpa*, flowery, floral. *s.*

پوشپك **पौष्पक** *paushpak*, m. the oxide of brass, used as a collyrium. *s.*

پوشپي **पौष्पी** *paushpī*, f. a name of the city of Pataliputra or Palibothra. *s.*

پوشٹك **पौष्टिक** *paushṭik*, preservative, protective; nutritive. *s.*

پوشش *poshish*, f. dress, garments, vestment, concealing, covering. *p.*

پوشك **पोषक** *poshak*, m. a nourisher, cherisher. *s.*

پوشكرني **पौष्करिणी** *paushkarinī*, f. a large pond or reservoir. *s.*

پوشن **पोषण** *poshan*, m. bringing up, rearing, fostering, cherishing. *s.*

پوشنا **पोषणा** *poshnā*, a. to breed, rear, foster, cherish, tame. *s.*

پوشي **पौषी** *paushī*, day of full moon in the month *paush* or *pūs*. *s.*

پوشیدگي *poshīdagī*, f. concealment. *p.*

پوشیدن *poshīdan*, to conceal, to hide, to cover or veil over. *p.*

پوشیده *poshīda*, concealed, covered. *p.*

پوشیه **पोष्य** *poshya*, adj. to be cherished. *poshya-putra*, m. an adopted son. *poshya-varga*, m. a class of persons or objects to be cherished, as parents, children, guests, and the sacred fire. *s.*

پوكري *pokrī*, m. a blackguard, a low fellow. *pokrī-log*, low, vile people (*quere*, Is not this word of French or English origin?). *d.*

پوكه **पूष** *pūkh*, m. the eighth mansion of the moon, comprising three stars in Cancer. *s.*

پوكهر **पोखर** *pokhar*, } m. a pond, a tank,
پوكهرا **पोखरा** *pokharā*, } a lake. *s.*

پوكهنا **पोखणा** *pokhnā* (v. *poshnā*), to breed, &c.

پوگ पूग *pūg*, m. the betel-nut tree (*Areca faufel* or *catechu*); a heap, a quantity; the fruit of the faufel, the betel nut. *pūg-phal*, m. the areca-nut. *s.*

پوگروٹ पूगरोट *pūg-roṭ*, m. the marshy date-tree (*Phœnix* or *elate paludosa*). *s.*

پوگنڈ पोगण्ड *pogaṇḍ*, m. a boy from five to fifteen years old. *s.*

پول *pol*, family, offspring; a litter of cubs or young of beast or bird. *d.*

پول पोल *pōl*, a court-yard; a gate; a ward or quarter of a town, having its own gateway. *h.*

پولا पूला *pūlā*, m. a bundle of grass or straw. *pūle tale guzrān karnā* (lit. to live under a bundle of straw), implies a very destitute condition. *s.*

پولا पोला *polā*, m. soft, hollow. *h.*

پولاد *polād* or *pūlād*, m. steel in general; the finest Damascus steel, which, with that of Ḳum, is esteemed the best in the East. *p.*

پولچ पोलच *polach* (also *polich*), land constantly under cultivation. *h.*

پولک पोलक *polak*, m. strawbands at the end of a staff, used with a charkhī to frighten and restrain a furious elephant. *a.*

پولي पोली *polī*, f. a term of abuse, simpleton. *h.*

پولي *polī*, f. a honeycomb. *d.*

پولي पूली *pūlī*, f. a small bundle of any grass or straw, &c.; a small quantity of corn given at harvest to village officers and servants. *s.*

پولي पौली *paulī*, f. a gate, a door. *h.*

پوليا पोलिया *poliyā* or पौलिया *pauliyā*, a gate-keeper, a janitor. *h.*

پوليا *pūliyā*, the poolias are persons who profess a species of Muḥammadanism, extremely corrupted by the Indian superstitions. The Muḥammadan Arabs in India propagated their religion by buying slaves, to whom, after they had been circumcised, and instructed in their doctrine, they gave their freedom; the latter in time became a distinct people, inhabiting the coast of India from Goa, round the peninsula to Madras: they go by the above name in Malabar, and by that of Coolies on the Coromandel. *d.*

پوليچي *pūlichī*, m. a degraded race of men who inhabit the forests of Malabar, where they are not permitted to build huts, but are obliged to make a kind of nest upon the trees: when they are pressed by hunger they howl, to excite compassion from those passing: the charitable deposit some rice or other food at the foot of a tree, and retire with all possible haste, to give the famished wretch an opportunity of taking it without meeting with his benefactor. *d.*

پومچها पोम्चा *pomchā*, m. a shady kind of cloth, a dress from *Jayanagar*. *h.*

پوں पूँ *pūṅ*, m. a sound of the emission of wind backwards. *h.*

پون पौन *paun* or पवन *pawan*, f. air, wind. *pawan-byādhi*, m. wind, as affected morbidly, or rheumatism, &c. *pawan chakkī*, f. a windmill. *pawan*, m. regent of the winds, and of the north-west quarter. *pawan kā pūt*, m. the son of Pawan, i.e the ape *Hanumān*. *s.*

پون पौन *paun*, one quarter less (than any given number); three quarters. *paun tīn*, two and three-quarters. *s.*

پون पिवन् *pivan*, adj. drinking. *s.*

پون *pūn*, m. a ferule or cap of metal; mounting of a sword-hilt, walking-cane, &c. *d.*

پونا पोना *ponā*, a. to make bread; to string (pearls), to thread (as a needle). *h.*

پونا पौना *paunā* or *ponā*, m. a spoon with holes in it like a colander, for skimming, &c. *h.*

پونال पवनाल *pavanāl*, m. a kind of grain (*Andropodon saccharatus*). *s.*

پونٹا पोंटा *ponṭā*, m. snot, &c. (v. *poṭā*). *h.*

پونٹهي पोंठी *ponṭhī*, f. a kind of small fish (*Cyprinus chyrsopareius, Buch.*). *s.*

پونجي पूंजी *pūnjī*, f. a capital in trade, stock, principal sum. *s.*

پونچ *pauṅch* (for *pahunch*), f. arrival, arriving. *d.*

پونچنا *pauṅchnā*, n. to arrive, to come. *d.*

پونچه पूंछ *pūnchh*, f. a tail. *s.*

پونچهار पूंछार *pūnchhār*, tailed, having a tail. *s.*

پونچهلا पूंछला *pūnchhlā*, a tail. *s.*

پونچهن पोंछन *poṅchhan*, m. any thing thrown away after wiping; a rag, &c. with which any thing is wiped. *h.*

پونچهنا पोंछना *poṅchhnā* or पूंछना *puṅchhnā*, a. to wipe, to clean, to expunge. *h.*

پونڈا पौंडा *paunḍā*, m. a kind of sugar-cane. *s.*

پونڈرک पौण्ड्रक *paunḍrak*, m. the pale straw-coloured species of sugar-cane; a man of a mixed caste, from the Vaisya and female of the distiller caste, whose business it is to boil sugar. *s.*

پونڈروردهن पौण्ड्रवर्द्धन *paunḍra-varddhan*, m. one of the divisions of central India (Behar). *s.*

پونڈهنا पौंढना *paunḍhnā*, a. (v. *pauṛhnā*) to repose, lie down. *h.*

پونربهو पौनर्भव *paunar-bhava*, m. one of the sons or heirs admitted by the old Hindū law, the son of a woman from a second marriage. *s.*

پونرکت पौनरुक्त *paunar-ukta*, m. tautology. *s.*

پونسلاءي पूनसलाई *pūnsalā,ī*, f. a thin roller, on which cotton is prepared for spinning. *h.*

پونسون पौंसवन *pauṅ-savan*, m. a religious ceremony performed when signs of conception appear. *s.*

پونکا पोंका *ponkā*, m. the ship-worm (*Teredo navalis*). *h.*

پونکنا पोंकना *ponknā*, n. to be fluxed. *h.*

پونگا पोंगा *pongā*, m. a blockhead; a sort of drum; a thin joint of bamboo; adj. empty. *h.*

پونگڑا *pūngṛā*, m. a male child, a boy. *d.*

پونگي पूंगी *pūngī* or *paungī*, f. flute, pipe; a kind of pipe played upon by the jugglers. *h*

پونو पूनौ *pūnau*, پونون पूनों *pūnon*, } f. the day of the new moon. *s.*

پوونون पोवनौं *powanaun* (Braj. for *ponā*, q.v.), to thread a needle, to make bread, &c. *h.*

پونه पौनह *paunah*, m. a spoon with holes in it like a colander, for skimming, &c. (see *paunā*). *h.*

پوني पूनी or पूणी *pūnī*, f. rolls of cotton prepared for spinning. *h.*

پونے पौने *paune*, prefixed to a number denotes a quarter less, as *paune tīn*, a quarter less three, or two and three-fourths. *h.*

پوني पौनी *paunī*, a collective name for the lower castes, such as barbers, shoemakers, &c. *h.*

پونيو पून्यो *pūnyo*, f. the day of the new moon. *s.*

پووا पौवा *pauwā*, m. a quarter; a quarter of a ser. *h.*

پوه पोह *poh*, f. dawn of day. *h.*

پوه पौह *pauh*, m. a stand where water is kept ready for travellers. *h.*

پوها पोहा *pohā*, the cattle of a village, permitted to graze on waste land. *h.*

پوهدا पोहदा *pohdā*, m. a young tree &c. *h.*

پوهنا पोहना *pohnā*, a. to make bread. *h.*

پوي पवी *pavī*, a dyke cut either to let water in or out. *h.*

پوءي पोय *po,e*, f. پويا पोया *poyā*, m. } a kind of vegetable (*Basella alba vel rubra*). *h.*

پويالس पूयालस *pūyālas*, m. suppuration at the joints, white swelling. *s.*

پوئيدن *pū,īdan* or *po,īdan*, to run, to wander. *h.*

پويرا पवेरा *paverā*, act of sowing seed by the hand. *h.*

پوين पूयन *pūyan*, پويه पूय *pūya*, } m. pus, matter, discharge, from an ulcer. *s.*

پويه *poya* or *pūya*, m. a canter or hand-gallop. *p.*

پوئيس पोईस *po,īs*, inter. ho! hallo! (calling to people in the road to get out of the way), have a care. *p.*

په फ *pha*, the aspirate of the letter प *pa*.

په पः *pa*, (for *par*), on, in, at; conj. but, yet, used chiefly in verse. *h.*

په पह *pah*, f. dawn; *pah-phaṭnā*, n. to dawn, to grow luminous. *h.*

پهاٹ फाट *phāṭ*, division of revenue, assessment among the sharers in joint tenantry. *h.*

پهاٹك फाटक *phāṭak*, m. a gate; a large shutter; an obstruction, impediment, a check; the bar of a court of justice, where the plaintiff and defendant take their station; a watchman in charge of a gate. *phāṭak-bandī*, imprisonment, safe custody, under lock and key. *h.*

پهاٹنا फाटना *phāṭnā*, n. to be torn; to be broken, split, rent &c. *s.*

پہاڑ पहाड़ *pahāṛ*, m. a mountain. *pahāṛ sī rāten*, long and tedious nights (especially of sorrow) *h.*

پهاڑا फाड़ा *phāṛā*, torn, broken, split, rent. *s.*

پہاڑا पहाड़ा *pahāṛā*, m. (in arithmetic) the multiplication table; a story or fable. *h.*

پهاڑكهانا फाड़खाना *phāṛ khānā*, a. to worry; to bite and gnaw. *s.*

پهاڑكهاؤ फाड़खाऊ *phāṛ khā,ū* or *-khā,o*, m. a ravenous beast. *s.*

پهاڑنا फाड़ना *phāṛnā*, a. to tear, to rend; to split; to break; to cleave (as wood). *s.*

پہاڑي पहाड़ी *pahāṛī*, f. a hill, a small mountain; adj. of or relating to the hills. *pahāṛī bhang*, henbane. *h.*

پہاڑيا पहाड़िया *pahāṛiyā*, m. a mountaineer; adj. belonging to the mountains. *h.*

پهاگ फाग *phāg*, m. red powder thrown over one in the time of the Holī; the act of throwing coloured powders in the Holī, the gambols of the Holī (in Dakh.) the forms *phāk* and *phak-ṛā*, are used. *s.*

پهاگن फागन *phāgan* or फागुन *phāgun*, (also *phālgun*). the name of the eleventh month, the full moon of which is near *pūrvaphālgunī*. (Feb.—March). *s.*

پهال फाल *phāl*, m. a ploughshare. *s.*

پهال फाल *phāl*, f. a lump of betel-nut (*Areca*); a step. *h.*

پهالسا फालसा *phālsā*, m. name of a fruit (*Grewia Asiatica*). (in Dakh.) *phālisa*, a shrike. *h.*

پهالگن फाल्गुन *phālgun*, the eleventh month (v. *phāgun*); a tree (*Pentaptera arjuna*). *s.*

پهالگني फाल्गुनी *phālgunī*, f. day of the full moon in the month Phālgun, on which the Holī festival is celebrated; a name common to the eleventh and twelfth lunar asterisms, distinguished by the epithets *pūrvā* and *uttarā*. *s.*

پهالنا *phālnā*, a. to spring, leap, jump. *d.*

پهالي *phālī*, f. a kind of small pillow, a child's napkin. *d.*

پهانپنا फांपना *phāmpnā*, n. to swell. *h.*

پهانپهڑ फांफड़ *phāmphar*, m. a hole, an orifice. *h.*

پهانت फांत *phānt*, m. a village register. *h.*

پهانٹا *phānṭā*, m. a branch of a tree, a neck of land. *d.*

پهانج *phānj*, a noose, snare, &c. (v. *phāndā*). *d.*

پهانجنا *phānjnā*, a. to chop, to score. *d.*

پهاند फांद *phānd*, پهاندا फांदा *phāndā*, } m. a noose, a net; met. perplexity, difficulty. *h.*

پهاندنا फांदना *phāndnā*, to leap, jump, or spring over; to imprison, to tie, to ensnare or entrap. *s.*

پهاندي फांदी *phāndī*, f. a bundle of 50 or 100 sugar-canes. *s.* [&c.). *h.*

پهانس फांस *phāns*, m. a splinter (of bamboo,

پهانس फांस *phāns*, } m. a noose; an impedi-
پهانسا फांसा *phānsā*, } ment; (in Dakh.) a die for playing. *s.*

پهانسنا फांसना *phānsnā*, n. to noose; to throttle, to choke; to be perplexed; to be impeded; to stick (as in mud). *s.*

پهانسي फांसी *phānsī*, f. a noose, a loop. *phānsī parnā*, n. to be hanged. *phānsī denā*, a. to strangle, to hang. *phānsī lagānā*, a. to kill one's self by strangling. *s.*

پهانسيگار फांसीगार *phānsī-gār*, } a strangler,
پهانسيگر फांसीगर *phānsī-gar*, } a sneaking sort of highwaymen, of recent notoriety under the name of *thags* (vulg. *thugs*), who first strangle the unwary traveller, then take possession of his money, &c. *h.*

پهانك फांक *phānk*, f. a slice, or piece of fruit. *h.*

پهانكڑ फांकड़ *phānkar*, } m. a fop, a vain
پهانكڑا फांकड़ा *phānkrā*, } silly fellow. *h.*

پهانكنا फांकना *phānknā*, a. to chuck into the mouth from the palm of the hand (grain, meal, &c.); to squander; (in Dakh.) to elapse (as time); to vanish (as clouds, &c.). *h.*

پهانكي फांकी *phānkī*, f. a slice, or piece of [fruit. *h.*

پهانكي फांकी *phānkī*, f. (in logic) an objection. *s.*

پها फाव *phāw*, m. a small quantity given above the quantity purchased, to boot. *h.*

پهاوڑا फावड़ा *phāwarā* or *phā,orā*, m. a mattock, a spade, a hoe. *h.*

پهاءوڑي फावड़ी *phā,orī*, f. a crutch on which a *jogī* leans; a piece of wood, or staff, with a support at each end, which is held in both hands and laid horizontally, in performing the exercise of *ḍanḍ*; an instrument like a small rake or hoe for removing a horse's dung. *h.*

پهاها फाहा *phāhā*, m. a flock of cotton, wet with *'atar*, or scented water; a plaster, a pledget. *h.*

پهايا फाया *phāyā*, } m. a plaster, a blister. *h.*
پهايه फायः *phāya*, }

پهب फब *phab*, f. embellishment, ornament, [dress. *h.*

پهبتا फबता *phabtā*, pertinent, fitting. *h.*

پهبتي फबती *phabtī*, f. ornament, conjecturing what a person is by his dress. *phabtī kahnā*, a. to say or conjecture by one's dress what sort of person, or of what caste, he is. *h.*

پهبكنا फबकना *phabaknā*. n. to shoot forth (as branches); to grow, sprout. *h.*

پهبن फबन *phaban*, f. embellishment, orna- [ment. *h.*

پهبنا फबना *phabnā*, n. to become, to fit. *h.*

پهبيلا फबीला *phabīlā*, becoming, fit, proper. *h.*

پهپ फुप *phup*, पहुप *pahup*, or पुहप *puhap*, a flower (v. *pushp*). *s.*

پهپا *phupā*, } m. the husband of a paternal
پهپو *phupū*, } aunt (v. *phupphā*). *h.*

پهپكار फुपकार *phuphār*, f. bubbling, blowing or breathing into any liquid. *h.*

پهپها फुप्फा *phupphā*, m. the husband of a paternal aunt. *h.*

پهپهسا फफसा *phaphsā*, swelled; insipid. *h.*

پهپهكار फुफकार *phuphhār*, f. the hissing of a snake. *h.*

پهپهكارنا फुफकारना *phuphhārnā*, n. to hiss (a [snake). *h.*

پهپهندي फफुन्दी *phaphundī* or फफून्दी *phaphūndī*, f. mould (on fruit, bread, &c., from dampness). *h.*

پهپهو फुफू *phuphū*, m. the husband of a pa- [ternal aunt. *h.*

پهپهولا फफोला *phapholā*, m. a blister. *phaphole phūṭne*, n. to be blistered; (it is figuratively applied to the mind); hence it signifies to be afflicted. *phaphole dilke phorne*, to satisfy a revenge that has long been rankling in one's breast. *s.*

پهپهوندي फफून्दी *phaphūndī*, f. mouldiness. *h.*

پهپهي फुप्फी *phupphī*, f. a paternal aunt; father's sister. *h.*

پهپهياساس फुफियासास *phuphiyā-sās*, f. the sister of a father-in-law. *h.*

پهپهياسسر फुफियासुसुर *phuphiyā-susur* or -ससुर *-sasur*, m. the husband of a father-in-law's sister. *s.*

پهپهيرا फुफेरा *phupherā*, m. } descended from or
پهپهيري फुफेरी *phupherī*, f. } related through a paternal aunt. *phupherā bhā,ī*, the son of a paternal aunt. *phupherī bahin*, daughter of the same. *h.*

پهت फुत *phut*, interj. expressive of contempt. *s.*

پهتر *phattar*, m. a stone. *phattar kā phūl*, lichen, rackmoss. *phattar bandī*, stone work, masonry, paving. *d.*

پهتري *phattarī* or *phattrī*, f. a flint. *d.*

پهتكار फुतकार *phuthār*, arrogant, disdainful. *s.*

پهٹ फिट *phiṭ*, m. curse, malediction; adv. fye! *phiṭ-phiṭ*, curse on it! fye upon it! *h.*

پهٹ फुट *phuṭ*, separated, odd, unpaired. *h.*

پهٹا फटा *phaṭā*, m. a crack. *phaṭe men pā,on denā*, to interfere in any thing. *h.*

پهٹانا फिटाना *phiṭānā*, a. to beat up and mix, to froth. *phuṭānā* (tr. of *phuṭnā*), to increase, &c. *h.*

پهٹ پڑنا फटपड़ना *phaṭ parnā*, n. to be produced plentifully; to become fat suddenly; to be confounded with too much business. *āsmān phaṭ parnā*, n. to rain hard. *h.*

پهٹپهٹانا फटफटाना *phaṭphaṭānā*, a. to shake or flap the wings, as birds just going to fly; to give a sound, as the shoes of a person walking. *h.*

پهٹك फटक *phaṭak* or फटिक *phaṭik*, m. crystal. *h.*

پهٹك फिटिक *phiṭik*, a snare, net, cage. *a.*

پهٹكار फिटकार *phiṭkār*, f. curse, malediction, removing something to a distance. *h.*

پهٹكارنا फिटकारना *phiṭkārnā*, a. to curse. *h.*

پهٹكر फुटकर *phuṭkar*, odd, unpaired; separate, dispersed (as a horseman). *h.*

پهٹكري फिटकिरी, फिटकरी, or फटकरी, *phiṭkirī*, *phiṭkarī*, or *phaṭkarī*, (in Dakh.) *phaṭakrī*, f. alum, saltpetre. *s.*

پهٹكنا फटकना *phaṭaknā*, a. to winnow; to dust, to shake or knock off any light thing which slightly adheres, as crumbs from a table-cloth or dust from a table; n. to be separated; m. the tape in a pellet bow which strikes the ball. *s.*

پهٹكي फटकी *phaṭkī*, f. a fowler's net; a large cage; a rope tied to a tree to frighten birds with its sound; (in Dakh.) saltpetre, alum. *h.*

پهٹكي फुटकी *phuṭkī*, f. a blot, spot, stain; adj. odd, not paired. *h.*

پهٹنا फटना *phaṭnā*, a. to be torn, split, rent; to be broken, burst, cracked; (in Dakh.) to be paid off or liquidated (a debt). *s.*

پهٹنا फुटना *phuṭnā*, n. to increase, to obtain advancement. *d.*

پهٹي آنكهي *phaṭī-ānkhī*, blear eyed. *d.*

پہچان पहचान *pahchān*, f. acquaintance, knowledge. *h.*

پہچاننا पहचानना *pahchānnā*, a. to know, to recognise, to distinguish or discriminate, to understand or percieve. *h.*

پهخ پهخ *phikh phikh*, the imitative sound uttered by birds. *d.*

پهدپهدانا फदफदाना *phadphadānā*, n. to ferment (as sour milk, curds, &c.); to be inflamed with lust (v. *balbalānā*). *h.*

پهدكنا फुदकना *phudaknā*, to jump, to leap, to hop (applied to small birds), to dance about in token of delight. *h.*

پهدكي फुदकी *phudkī*, f. the name of a bird (*Certhia tula*). *h.*

پهڈي *phaḍḍī*, finally, at last; hence. *d.*

پهر फुर *phur*, true, right. *h.*

پهر फुर्र *phurr*, m. the noise of a bird, as a partridge or quail, suddenly taking wing, or of a small quantity of gunpowder exploding. *h.*

پهر फिर *phir*, again, then, afterwards, any more. *h.*

پہر पहर *pahar*, m. a division of time consisting of seven and a half *gharīs*; or, more strictly speaking, the *pahar* is the fourth part of the natural day or night, and consequently it must vary in length from six to nine *gharīs*, according to the season of the year and the latitude of the locality. For example: in the province of *Kashmir*, in the north of India, the *pahar* of the day at midsummer will be nearly nine *gharīs*, and that of the night about six, while at *Cape Comorin*, in the extreme south, there is very little variation during the whole year (v. *gharī*). *s.*

پهر फर *phar*, m. a fruit; a shield. *s*

پہرا पहरा *pahrā*, m. a watch, a sentinel; tour of watch; a corporal and six. *pahre-wālā*, a sentinel, watchman, guard. *pahrā denā*, to watch. *pahre meṅ ḍālnā*, to confine in a guard. *pahre meṅ paṛnā*, to be confined in a guard. *s.*

پهراٹا फर्राटा *pharrāṭā*, m. a piece of bamboo; a sound made by the flying of a flag, or the breathing of a horse. *h.*

پهراس फरास *pharrās* m. the name of a tree (its leaves resemble those of the *Cypress* or of the *Tamarisk*, and make a whistling noise in the wind, whence the name). *h.*

پهرانا फिराना *phirānā*, to cause to turn, to whirl, to return, to change, to roll, to shift, to wander. *h.*

پهرانا फर्राना *pharrānā*, n. to fly (as a flag). *s.*

پہرانا पहराना *pahrānā*, also *pahirānā*, a. to cause to dress, to clothe, to dress. *s.*

پهراو फिराव *phirāv* or *phirā,o*, m. turning, a return, restitution, rotation. *h.*

پہراون पहिरावन *pahirāwan*, m. } vestments
پہراوني पहिरावनी *pahirāwanī*, f. } bestowed
on guests at a wedding, dress, clothing. *s.*

پہراوني पहिरावनी *pahirāwnī* or पहरावनी *pahrā,onī*, f. a woman who dresses the guests at a wedding, a tire-woman. *s.*

پهراءي फिराई *phirā,ī*, f. act of returning. *h.*

پهرپڑنا *phir-paṛnā*, to be dissatisfied. *d.*

پهرپهرانا फुरफुराना *phurphurānā*, n. to tremble; to wave (as hair in the wind). *h.*

پهرپهري फुरफुरी *phurphurī*, f. trembling, quivering, tremor, palpitation. *h.*

پهرپهند फरफन्द *pharphand*, m. deceit, trick, wickedness. *h.*

پهرپهنديا फरफन्दिया *pharphandiyā*, deceitful, treacherous, wicked. *h.*

پهرت फिरत *phirat*, m. rejected things; money paid by a lewd woman to her paramour. *h.*

پهرت फुर्त *phurt*, f. activity, alertness. *s.*

پهرتابارا *phirtā-bārā*, m, a whirlwind. *d.*

پهرتارهنا फिरता रहना *phirtā rahnā*, n. to wander, to perambulate, to walk about. *h.*

پهرتي फिरती *phirtī*, returning, homeward-bound. *phirtī kā bhāṛā*, the hire of a return boat, carriage, &c. *h.*

پهرتي फुर्ती *phurtī*, f. activity, quickness. *s.*

پهرتيلا फुर्तीला *phurtīlā*, quick, nimble, active. *s.*

پهرجانا फिरजाना *phir-jānā*, to return, to revolt; to be distorted; to warp. *h.*

پهرچا फरचा *pharchā*, m. fair weather; dispersion or clearing away (of a crowd of people, or of clouds, &c.); a decision, definitive sentence. *h.*

پهرچانا फरचाना *pharchānā*, a. to decide, to give a final sentence or decree. *h.*

پهرچها फरछा *pharchhā*, m. fair weather (same as *pharchā*), adj. pure, honest; fair (not cloudy). *pharchhā-k.*, a. to clean, to settle, to sweep. *pharchhā-h.*, to clear up, to become fair (the weather). *h.*

پهرچهانا फरछाना *pharchhānā*, a. to clean, to wipe, to settle. *h.*

پهرسا फरसा *pharsā*, m. an axe, a hatchet. *s.*

پهرك फरक *pharak*, f. fluttering, palpitation; m. a shield. *h.* [to flutter. *h.*

پهركانا फरकाना *pharkānā*, a. to agitate, cause

پهركنا फरकना *pharaknā*, n. to flutter, vibrate, to throb, to writhe, &c. (v. *pharaknā*). *h.*

پهركي फिरकी *phirkī*, f. a whirligig; any thing turning as on an axis; a reel for thread. *h.*

پهرنا फिरना *phirnā*, a. to turn, to return, to walk about, to whirl, to wheel, to wander, to change, to revolt. *h.*

پهرنا पहरना *paharnā* or पहिरना *pahirnā*, a. to put on clothes, to dress, to clothe one's self, to wear. *s.*

پهرني फिर्नी *phirnī*, f. a whirligig, any thing turning on an axis; a whirlwind. *h.*

پهرو पहरू *pahrū*, پهروا पहरुआ *pahru,ā*, } m. a watchman, a sentinel (also *pahrū,ā*). *s.*

پهروانا फिरवाना *phirwānā*, to cause to be returned. *h.*

پهروك फरुवक *pharuvak*, m. a betel-box. *s.*

پهروها फरूहा *pharūhā*, m. an instrument for raking together. *h.*

پهره *pahra*, m. a watchman, sentinel. v. *pahrā*. *s.*

پهرهاري फुरहारी *phurhārī*, f. horripilation. *s.*

پهرهرا फरहरा *pharahrā*, پهرهري फरहरी *pharahrī*, } m. a vane, a pendant; adj. half-dried. *s.*

پهري फरी *pharī*, f. a shield, a target. *s.*

پهري फरी *pharī*, f. one of several fishes. *h.*

پهري पहरी *paharī*, پهريا पहरिया *pahriyā*, } m. a watchman, a sentinel; a village servant and messenger, also employed to keep watch. *s.*

پهريا फरिया *phariyā*, f. a kind of bordered vestment, worn by Hindūs; a contractor for reaping. *h.*

پهڙ फड़ *phaṛ*, f. a gaming-house where dice are played; a place where goods are exposed for sale; the shafts or pole of a carriage. *phaṛ-bāz*, m. a player at dice, a gamester; a prater, a talkative fellow. *phaṛbāzī*, f. gambling, playing at dice. *h.*

پهڙاپهڙي *phaṛā-phaṛī*, f. war, battle, fight. *d.*

پهڙانا फड़ाना *phaṛānā*, a. to cause to be torn, split, or cleaved. *h.*

پهڙپهڙات *pharpharāt*, پهڙپهڙاهت *pharpharāhat*, } agitation, flutter, disquietude. *h.*

پهڙپهڙانا फड़फड़ाना *pharpharāṇā*, n. to flutter, to wave, to twinkle, to move with convulsive motion. *h.*

پهڙپهڙيا फड़फड़िया *pharphaṛiyā*, m. flutterer; adj. swift, quick. *h.* [ing, &c. *h.*

پهڙك फड़क *pharak* (v. *pharah*), f. flutter-

پهڙكانا फड़काना *phaṛkānā*, a. to cause to flutter, to cause convulsive motion in the muscles, &c.; (met.) to shew. *h.*

پهڙكنا फड़कना *phaṛaknā*, n. to flutter, to vibrate with convulsive, involuntary motion, as the eyelids and other muscles; to throb, to palpitate, to writhe (the shoulders). *h.*

پهڙكي फड़की *phaṛkī*, f. a coarse screen. *h.*

پهڙنا पहुड़ना *pahuṛnā*, n. to lie down, rest, sleep. *h.*

پهڙنگا फड़िङ्गा *phaṛingā*, f. a cricket. *s.*

پهڙيا फड़िया *phaṛiyā*, m. a pedlar, a retailer; the keeper of a gaming-house or dice table. *h.*

پهڙيا फुड़िया *phuṛiyā*, f. a sore, a pimple, a boil. *h.*

پهس *phus*, a voice, sound, noise. *d.*

پهساكو फसाकू *phasākū*, bad tobacco (inelegant). *h.*

پهسانا फसाना *phasānā*, a. to cause to stick (as in mud, &c.); to catch, to entangle; to cause to be imprisoned, to squash. *h.*

پهسانڈي *phusānḍī*, f. mouldiness; scum. *d.*

پهساو फसाव *phasāv* or *phasā,o*, m. sticking, entanglement. *h.* [ing, stinking. *h.*

پهساهندا फुसाहिन्दा *phusāhindā*, adj. disgust-

پهسپهسا फसफसा *phasphasā*, flabby, loose, not rigid. *h.* [per. *h.*

پهسپهسانا फुसफुसाना *phus-phusānā*, n. to whis-

پهسپهسانا फिसफिसाना *phis-phisānā*, n. to be terrified. *h.*

پهسپهساوٹ फुसफुसावट *phus-phusāwaṭ*, f. پهسرپهسر फुसरफुसर *phusar-phusar*, m. } whispering, buzzing in the ear. *h.*

پهسكا फुस्का *phuskā*, weak, without strength; slack (as a knot). *h.*

پهسكانا फसकाना *phaskānā*, a. to burst, to split, to break; to loosen or slacken. *h.*

پهسكٹ *phaskaṭ*, squatting in the oriental fashion (vide *chār-zānū*). *d.*

پهسكڑ फसकड़ *phaskaṛ*, m. sitting on the ground with legs extended. *h.*

پهسكنا फसकना *phasaknā*, n. to split, to burst, to break. *h.* [slide, err. *s*

پهسلانا फिसलाना *phislānā*, a. to cause to slip,

پھسلانا फुसलाना *phuslānā*, a. to coax, to wheedle, to instigate, to entice. *h.*

پھسلاءو फुसलाऊ *phuslā,ū*, m. a wheedler, instigator. *phuslā,o*, wheedling, coaxing, flattery. *h.*

پھسلاهٹ फिसलाहट *phislāhaṭ*, f. slipperiness; a slip, an error. *phuslāhaṭ*, cajolery, seduction. *s.*

پھسلبنڈا *phisal-baṇḍā*, m. sliding down a smooth bank, a favourite sport with children. *h. d.*

پھسلن फिसलन *phislan*, m. act of slipping or sliding; error. *h.* [to err; adj. slippery. *s.*

پھسلنا फिसलना *phisalnā*, n. to slip, to slide,

پھسلونیا फुसलौनिया *phuslauniyā*, m. a wheedler, a coaxer. *h.* [slippery. *h.*

پھسلها फिसलहा *phisalhā*, m. slipping; adj.

پھسلي *phaslī* (v. *paslī*), f. a rib, &c. *d.*

پھسنا फसना *phasnā*, n. to be stuck (as in mud or in a narrow passage); to be caught, to be imprisoned, ensnared, entangled, involved; to be impeded. *h.*

پھسیارا फसियारा *phasiyārā*, m. a strangler, a *ṭhag* (v. *phānsī-gār*). *h.*

پھش फिश *phish*, interj. pish! pshaw! *h.*

پھق *phak*, a sound, voice, noise. *d.*

پھکا फक्का *phakkā*, m. a small quantity of parched grain to be chucked into the mouth. *h.*

پھکا *phikkā* (v. *phīkā*), vapid, tasteless, &c. *d.*

پھکارنا फिकारना *phikārnā*, a. to uncover the head, to unplait the hair of the head. *h.*

پھکانا फिकाना *phikānā*, a. to cause or teach to throw. *h.*

پھکڑ फक्कड़ *phakkaṛ*, m. wrangling, mutual abuse, raillery. *phakkaṛ-bāz*, an abuser, an indecent chatterer. *h.* [with rudeness. *h.*

پھکڑي फकड़ी *phakṛī*, f. the act of treating

پھککا फक्किका *phakkikā*, f. a sophism; a trick, illusion, fraud. *s.* [blown into a flame. *h.*

پھکنا फुकना *phuknā*, to be inflated, to be

پھکنا फुकना *phuknā*, m. a bladder. *h.*

پھکني फुकनी *phuknī*, f. blow-pipe; a fire-lock or pistol. *h.*

پھکوڑیا फकोड़िया *phakoṛiyā*, m. a fop, an absurd prattler, an indecent talker. *h.* [ity. *h.*

پھکوڑیات फकोड़ियात *phakoṛiyāt*, f. absurd-

پھکیا फकिया *phakiyā*, f. a slice, a piece of fruit. *h.* [&c.). *h.*

پھکیت फिकैत *phikait*, m. a thrower (of a spear,

پھگوءا फगुआ *phagū,ā*, m. the same as *holī*; presents made during the *holī* holidays. *s.*

پھگنا *phugnā*, m. to swell, puff out, enlarge. *d.*

پھل फल *phal*, m. fruit; effect, result, advantage, reward, equivalent; the iron head of a spear or arrow, &c.; children, progeny; a blade (of a sword &c.); a sort of fragrant berry and drug commonly called *kakoli*; a nutmeg; a ploughshare; the quotient of a sum. *phal-āpekshā*, f. regard to, or expectation of, consequences. *phal-āshī*, living on fruits. *phal-ākānkshī*, f. hope or expectation of good consequences. *phal-bhog*, m. enjoyment of reward or consequences; usufruct. *phal-bhogī*, who receives the profits. *phal-pāk*, m. the ripening of fruit; the fulness of consequences; the *Coronda*. *phal-pāk-āntā*, f. an annual plant, dying after bearing fruit. *phal-pānā*, a. to reap the reward of (good or bad actions). *phal-prāpti*, f. obtaining the fruit or desired result. *phal-trik* or *phal-tray*, m. three sorts of fruits collectively; the three myrobalans collectively. *phal-janak*, producing fruit. *phal-chamas*, m. the bark of the Indian fig, ground and eaten with curds by way of penance. *phal-siddhi*, f. attaining an object, reaping the fruit of an act. *phal-sampad*, or *phal-sampat*, f. prosperity, success. *phal-shreshṭha*, m. (best of fruits) the mango. *phal-kāmnā*, f. desire of reward or consequences. *phal-khanḍan*, m. disappointing. *phal-grahi*, adj. bearing fruit. *phal-nirvṛitti*, f. final consequence or result. *phal-nishpatti*, f. producing fruits, or desired results. *phal-nivṛitti*, f. cessation of consequences. *phal-hāni*, f. loss of fruit or profit. *s.*

پھل फल *phal*, form, shape, figure. *d.*

پھل फुल्ल *phulla*, m. blown, opened, expanded (as a flower). *s.*

پہل पहल *pahal*, m. a flock of cotton; beginning, aggression; the side of a rectangular figure. *h.*

پہلا पहला *pahlā* (also पहिला *pahilā*), first, the first; before, rather; soon. *pahle pahal*, at first, in the first instance. *h.* [ract. *d.*

پھلا *phullā*, m. a disease of the eye, a cata-

پھلاس फलास *phalās*, f. a leap, spring, bound; m. a step, a stride. *h.*

پھلاسرا फुलासरा *phulāsarā*, m. flattery. *h.*

پھلانا फलाना *phalānā*, a. to cause to produce. *s.*

پھلانا फुलाना *phulānā*, a. to cause to swell; to fatten; (met.) to make proud by flattery. *s.*

پھلانگ फलाङ्ग *phalāng*, f. a stride, leap, bound. *h.*

پھلبجھول پھل بجھول फलबुझौवल *phal-bujhauwal*, m. the name of a game (also called *mankelā*), "think of a number, double it, add ten to it, take five from it, &c., how much remains?" "twenty-one?" "the number was eight." *h.*

پھلبھوگ फलभोग *phal-bhog*, m. usufruct, receiving the produce or profits of any thing. *s.*

پھلپور फलपूर *phal-pūr*, m. common citron (*Citrus medica*). *s.*

پھلپھلاري फलफलारी *phal-phalārī*, f. variety of fruits or of dishes made of fruit. *s.*

پھلت फलित *phalit*, fruitful, prolific. फलत् *phalat*, yielding fruit, profit, &c. *s.*

پھلتارتھ फलितार्थ *phalitārth*, m. a meaning implied though not expressed. *s.*

پھل تاڑ फलताड़ *phal-tāṛ*, m. the fruit-bearing *tāṛ*, the female palm. *s.*

پهلجهڙي फुलझड़ी *phuljhaṛī*, f. a kind of firework like a fountain. *s.*

پهلد फलद *phalad*, پهلداتا फलदाता *phal-dātā*, } adj. yielding fruit; m. one who rewards a benefactor. *phalad*, m. a tree. *s.*

پهلدار फलदार *phal-dār*, fruitful, bearing fruit. *h. p.*

پهلدامن फुल्लदामन *phulla-dāman*, m. a species of the *Atidhriti* metre. *s.*

پهلڈا *phalḍā*, پهلڑا *phalṛā*, } m. the blade of a sword, knife, &c. *d.*

پهلسنا फिलसना *philasnā*, n. (per *metathesin*, for *phisalnā*), to slip. *h.*

پهلك फलक *phalak*, m. a shield; a bone; the os frontis; a plant (*Mesua ferrea*). *s.*

پهلكا फुलका *phulkā*, inflated, puffed up; light; m. a blister; an area or arena for wrestlers; a kind of cake or small loaf. *s.*

پهلكارنا फुलकारना *phulkārnā*, n. to inflate, to swell out, as a snake does his hood, to expand. *s.*

پهلكاري फुलकारी *phulkārī*, m. flowered cloth. *s.*

پهلكر फलकर *phal-kar*, a branch of revenue arising from the rent of orchards; profits of an estate arising from fruit-trees thereon. *s.*

پهلكرشن फलकृष्ण *phal-krishna*, m. a small fruit of a black colour (*Carissa carandas*). *s.*

پهلكوشك फलकोषक *phal-koshak*, m. the scrotum or testicles. *s.*

پهلكيشر फलकेशर *phal-keshar*, m. the cocoanut tree. *s.*

پهلكي फलकी *phalkī* or پهلكي फल्लकी *phallakī*, armed with a shield; m. a sort of fish caught in ponds, commonly called *Phala,sī* (*Mystus capirat*). *s.*

پهلكي फुलकी *phulkī*, f. a cake or raised bread, fritters. *s.*

پهلگ फल्गु *phalgu*, f. the *Ficus oppositifolia*; a river which is said to run underneath *Gya*; a red powder, usually of the root of wild ginger, coloured with sappan-wood, and thrown over one another by the Hindūs at the *Holī* festival. *s.*

پهلگن फल्गुन *phalgun*, m. the month *Phālgun*. *phalgunī*, same as *phālgunī*. *s.*

پهلن फलन *phalan*, m. fructifying, bearing fruit. *s.*

پهلنا फलना *phalnā*, n. to bear fruit; to produce; to be fortunate. *s.*

پهلنتا फलन्ता *phalantā*, fruitful, bearing fruit. *s.*

پهلنگ *phalang*, f. a stride, leap, bound. *d.*

پهلو *pahlū*, m. the side; the wing of an army. *pahlū tihī-k.*, a. to refuse, to decline, to evade. *p.*

پهلوا फलूआ *phalū,ā*, m. a knotted fringe. *h.*

پهلواري फुलवारी *phulwārī*, پهلواڙي फुलवाड़ी *phulwāṛī*, } f. a flower-garden. *s.*

پهلوان फलवान् *phalwān*, fruitful, fruit-bearing. *s.*

پهلوان फुल्लवान् *phulla-wān*, blossoming, blowing. *s.*

پهلوان *pahalwān* or *pahlawān*, m. a hero, a champion, a stout fellow, a wrestler. *p.*

پهلواني *pahalwānī* or *pahlawānī*, f. heroism. *p.*

پهلوت फलवत् *phal-wat*, adj. fruit-bearing. *s.*

پهلوتما फलोत्तमा *phalottamā*, f. the highest reward, arising from sacred study. *s.*

پهلوٹا पहिलौटा *pahilauṭā*, first-born. *h.*

پهلودي फलोदय *phaloday*, m. profit, result; happiness. *s.* [results. *s.*

پهلوديش फलोद्देश *phaloddesh*, m. regard to results. *s.*

پهلوري फुलौरी *phulaurī*, f. bread or cake made of fruit and pulse, and fried in *ghī* or oil. *s.*

پهلوي *pahlavī*, of or relating to a hero; the language of Persia in its transition from the Zand to that now spoken. *p.* [beating. *h.*

پهلهتها फुलहथा *phul-hatthā*, m. cudgelling, beating. *h.*

پهلي पहले *pahle* or पहिले *pahile*, at first, in the first place, soon, rather *pahle pār*, on the other side. *h.*

پهلي फली *phalī*, m. a sort of fish, commonly called *Phala,ī*. (*Mystus kapirat*); f. a shield; a medicinal plant, commonly called *Priyangu*. *s.*

پهلي फिल्ली *phillī*, f. the leg. *h.*

پهلي फुल्ली *phullī*, f. a disorder in the eye, the *albugo*; (in Dakh.) an ornament worn in the nose; the tumbler nail of the cock of a musket. *phullī hūn*, the star pagoda, a gold coin worth three and a half rupees, or seven shillings sterling.

پهلي फली *phalī*, پهليا फलिया *phaliyā*, } f. a cod, a pod (or the seed) of any leguminous plant, but particularly of peas; a loop. *phalī-kash*, m. a hook for drawing the strings through the holes by which the walls of a tent are laced to the top; adj. fruitful, prolific. *s.*

پهليانا फलियाना *phaliyānā*, n. to bear fruit. *s.*

پهليرها फलेरुहा *phaleruhā*, f. the trumpet-flower, (*Bignonia suaveolens*). *s.*

پهليري *phulerī*, f. romping, playing. *d.*

پهليل फलेल *phulel*, m. oil impregnated with the essence of flowers by steeping them in it. *s.*

پهليه फल्य *phalya*, m. a bud, a flower. *s.*

پهن फण or फन *phan*, m. the hood of a snake; his expanded neck. *phan uṭhānā*, a. to spread the hood, as a snake. *phan-dhar*, *phan-kar*, *phan-wān*, a snake. *phan-manī*, m. a jewel supposed to be in the head of a snake. *s.*

پهن *pahan*, m. width, breadth, ampleness; adj. wide, widely, extensive. *p.*

پهنا फना *phanā*, a snake's hood; the forecastle of a ship. *s.*

پهنّا *phunnā*, m. the silk lash of a whip. *d.*

پهنا *pahnā*, broad, wide, extensive. *p.*

پهنا पहन्ना *pahannā* or पहिन्ना *pahinnā*, a. to wear, to dress, to put on; m. dress, clothing. *s.*

پهنانا पहनाना *pahnānā*, a. to clothe, cause to be dressed. *s.* [raiment. *s.*

پهناوا पहनावा *pahnāwā*, m. dress, clothes,

پهناوار *pahnāwār*, } ample, wide, broad, spa-
پهناور *pahnāwar*, } cious. *p.*

پهنائي *pahnā,ī*, width, spaciousness. *p.*

پهنپهنانا फनफनाना *phanphanānā*, n. to hiss (as a snake); to spring up suddenly (as a fast-growing plant); to move about briskly (as a playful child). *s*

پهنپه फंफ *phamph*, land that requires to be left fallow for some time. *h.*

پهنجپترکا फञ्जिपुत्रिका *phanji-putrikā*, f. a plant (*Salvinia cucullata*). *s.*

پهنجکا फञ्जिका *phanjikā*, f. a plant, (*Siphonanthus indica*); a species of *Hedysarum* (*H. alhāgi*). *s.*

پهنجهك फणिज्झक *phanijjhak*, m. a plant, called also *marua*. *s.*

پهنجهكا फणिज्झका *phanijjhakā*, f. a plant, commonly called *Rām Dūti*, apparently a sort of basil with small leaves. *s.*

پهنچ पहुंच *pahunch*. m. arrival; access, admittance; sagacity, penetration; a receipt. *h.*

پهنچا पहुंचा *pahunchā*, m. the wrist. *h.*

پهنچانا पहुचाना *pahunchānā*, a. to send, to carry, convey; to cause, to occasion, to bring about. *h.*

پهنچنا पहुंचना *pahunchnā*, n. to arrive, to reach, to come, to amount, to befall. *h.*

پهنچوانا पहुंचवाना *pahunchwānā* (caus. of *pahunchānā*), to cause to be carried, conveyed, &c. *h.*

پهنچي पहुंची *pahunchī*, f. an ornament worn on the wrist, a kind of bracelet. *h.*

پهندا फन्दा *phandā*, m. a noose, a net; perplexity, difficulty. *h.* [to leap. *h.*

پهندانا फन्दाना *phandānā*, a. to cause to jump,

پهندلانا फन्दलाना *phandlānā*. a. to catch in a snare, to entrap. *h.*

پهندنا फन्दना *phandnā*, n. to be imprisoned. *h.*

پهندنا फुन्दना *phundnā*, m. a tassel. *h.*

پهنس *phannas*, m. the jack fruit, also the tree bearing the same. *d.*

پهنسانا फंसाना *phańsānā*, a. to ensnare, to involve. *h.*

پهنساو फंसाव *phańsāw* or *phańsā,o*, m. entanglement. *h.* [stick (v. *phasnā*). *h.*

پهنسنا फंसना *phańsnā*, n. to be entangled, to

پهنسوانا फंसवाना *phańswānā* (caus. of *phańsānā*) to cause to be ensnared, strangled &c. *h.*

پهنسي फुनसी *phunsī*, f. a pimple. *h.*

پهنسيارا फंसियारा *phańsiyārā*, } m. a foot-pad
پهنسيگار फंसीगार *phańsī-gār*, } who strangles passengers or travellers: the term is more especially applied to a well-known organized gang, called *ṭhags* (vulg. *thugs*). *s.*

پهنكا फङ्का *phankā*, m. a handful (or rather mouthful) of any thing eaten by being chucked into the mouth. *phankā mārnā*, a. to eat by chucking into the mouth, to chuck food into the mouth. *h.*

پهنكا पह्निका *pahnikā*, f. a plant (*Pistia stratioites*). *s.*

پهنكار फुंकार *phunkār*, f. the hiss of a snake. *s.*

پهنكارنا फुंकारना *phunkārnā*, n. to hiss (as a snake). *s.*

پهنكاري फुंकारी *phunkārī*, f. hissing of a snake. *phunkārī mārnā*, to hiss (a snake). *s.*

پهنكنا फिंकना *phinknā*, n. to be thrown. *s.*

پهنكهيل फणिखेल *phani-khel*, m. a quail *s.*

پهنكي फङ्की *phankī*, f. same as *phankā*, q. v.

پهنكيشر फणिकेशर *phanī-keshar*, m. a plant (*Mesua ferrea*.) *s.*

پهنگا फङ्गा or फनगा *phangā*, m. a grasshopper. *s.*

پهنگك फिङ्गक *phingak*. m. the fork-tailed shrike. *s.*

پهنگني *phungnī*, f. a pimple or pustule. *d.*

پهنگي फुङ्गी *phungī*, f. a sprout, bud, the point of an ear of corn, &c. *h.*

پهننگ फुनङ्ग *phunang*, f. top, summit. *h.*

پهنو फुन्नो *phunno*, f. *penis puerilis*. *h.*

پهنو पह्नव *pahnav*, m. the name of one of the degraded Kshatriya races sentenced by Sagar to wear beards. *s.* [rain. *h.*

پهنهار फुंहार *phuńhār*, f. the small drops of

پهنهارا फुंहारा *phuńhārā*, m. a fountain, a jet d'eau. *h.*

پهنئي पहुनई *pahuna,ī*, f. hospitality. *s.*

پهني फनी *phanī*, m. a serpent; a wedge. *s.*

پهني फुन्नी *phunnī*, } f. a tassel, a knot;
پهنيا फुनिया *phuniyā*, } *penis puerilis*. *h.*

پهنيشور फणीश्वर *phanīshwar*, } m. the great
پهنيندر फणीन्द्र *phanīndra*, } serpent *Ananta*. *s.*

پهوءا फूआ *phū,ā*, m. the husband of a father's sister; a lizard. *h.*

پهوپها फूफा *phūphā*, } m. an uncle, the hus-
پهوپهو फूफू *phūphū*, } band of a father's sister. *h.*

پهوپهو फूफू *phūphū*, } f. an aunt, applied
پهوپهي फूफी *phūphī*, } only to a father's sister. *h.*

پهوپهيرا फूफेरा *phūpherā*, of or relating to a paternal aunt. *phūpherā-bhā,ī*, a cousin, son of a paternal aunt. *h.*

پهوٹ फूट *phūṭ*, f. a kind of melon (*Cucumis momordica, Roxb.*); a ripe cucumber bursting elastically (as the *Cucumis utilatissimus, Roxb.* and *Momordica mixta. Roxb.*); odd, unpaired; difference of opinion; separation; a flaw. *phūṭ parnā*, to have disagreement, to arise (dissension). *phūṭ phūṭ*, or *phūṭ kar ronā*, n. to weep excessively. *phūṭ rahnā*, n. to be broken; to be dispersed; to be unpaired. *phūṭ honā*, n. to be divided in opinion. *s.*

پهوٹا फूटा *phūṭā*, broken, cracked. *phūṭā dūdh*, [m. whey. *s.*

پهوٹ بکهيرا फूटबिखेरा *phūt-bikherā*, confused, dispersed. *s.*

پهوٹلا फूटला *phūṭlā*, bad or false (coin). *s.*

پهوٹن फूटन *phūṭan*, f. wrangling, disagreement, misunderstanding. *s.*

پهوٹنا फूटना *phūṭnā*, n. to be broken; to be dispersed, to be separated; to be unpaired; to burst; to be made public; to arise (as a smell), or to burst forth. *s.*

پهوٹنا *phūṭnā*, to get promotion, advancement. *d.*

پهوٹي फूटी *phūṭi*, f. disagreement, disparity. *s.*

پهوريري *phūrīrī*, f. extravagance, prodigality. *d.*

پهوڑا फोड़ा *phoṛā*, m. a boil, a sore. *h.*

پهوڑا फौड़ा *phauṛā*, m. a mattock, spade, hoe. *h.*

پهوڑنا फोड़ना *phoṛnā*, a. to break, to burst; to disclose, to divulge. *phor-k.*, to be wounded. *s.*

پهوڑني फोड़नी *phoṛnī*, f. explaining, &c. (v. *taujīh*). *h.*

پهوس फूस *phūs*, m. old, dry grass or straw. *phūs men chingārī ḍālnā*, to excite contention or strife. *h.*

پهوسرا फूसरा *phūsrā*, } m. a rag, or bundle of
پهوسڑا फूसड़ा *phūsṛā*, } rags. *s.*

پهوسي फूसी *phūsī*, f. chaff, rubbish. *s.*

پهوك फोक *phok*, m. dregs, sediment; adj. hollow. *h.*

پهوکٹ फोकट *phokaṭ*, m. an indigent person. *h.*

پهوکر फूकर *phūkar*, m. a fine sensible young fellow. *h.*

پهوکڑ फोकड़ *phokaṛ*, m. dross, refuse, trash. *h.*

پهوکل *phokal*, empty, void. *d.*

پهوکنا फूकना *phūknā*, to blow. *s.*

پهول फूल *phūl*, m. a flower, a blossom; boss, stud, bunch of ribands, cockade; a kind of bell metal; an attack or assault; the menses, of which children are the fruit; bones of a dead person, after the fleshy parts are burned; lights or fire (seen at night); a swelling; a ceremony performed among Musalmāns in honour of a deceased person on the third day after his death, on which occasion a portion of the *ḳur,ān* is recited and flowers are placed on trays in the midst of the assembly. *phūl uṭhnā*, to be performed (the funeral ceremony above mentioned), to complete the forty days of mourning. *phūl parnā*, n. to break out (a fire). *phūl baiṭhnā*, n. to be glad. *phūl jānā*, n. to swell, to be delighted; to become fat *phūl-paṭṭī*, a cockade; a knot of ribands. *phūl jharnā*, n. to speak eloquently; to fall from a lamp (drops of burning oil). *s.*

پهولا फोला *pholā*, m. a blister. *h.*

پهولا फूला *phūlā*, swelled, blossomed. *phūlā na samānā*, not to be able to contain one's self from delight, to be overjoyed. *phūlā-phalā*, flourishing. *s.*

پهولاو फूलाव *phūlāv* or *phūlā,o*, m. swelling. *s.*

پهولجهاڑ फूलझाड़ *phūl-jhāṛ*, } (also *phūl-*
پهولجهڑي फूलझड़ी *phūl-jhaṛī*, } *chaṛī*), f. a species of fireworks. *h.*

پهولکوبي फूलकोबी *phūl-kobī*, f. cauliflower. *h.*

پهولنا फूलना *phūlnā*, n. to blossom, to blow; to be pleased, to be in health and spirits, *i. e.* to bloom; to swell, to be inflated. *phūl-jānā*, n. to swell; to be delighted, to be pleased; to become fat. *phūl-uṭhnā*, n. to be performed (a ceremony in honour of the dead). *s.*

پهولي फूली *phūlī*, f. a disorder in the eye, the *albugo*; adj. flowered, having a flower. *s.*

پهون फूं *phūn*, m. a fop, an affected person, a rake, a swaggerer. *d.*

پهونپهي फोंफी *phonphī*, f. a pipe, a tube; any thing perforated or hollow. *h.* [(v. *pāhunchnā*).

پهونچنا *pahūnchnā* or *pahonchnā*, n. to arrive. *h.*

پهوندنا *phūndnā*, m. (for *phundnā*), a tassel. *d.*

پهونك फोंक *phonk*, f. the notch of an arrow; adj. hollow, not solid (particularly jewels). *h.*

پهونك फूंक *phūnk*, f. act of blowing, a puff, a blast. *phūnk-phūnk-ke pāṅw dharnā*, a. to act or walk carefully and cautiously. *phūnk-denā*, to set on fire. *s.*

پهونکار फूंकार *phūnkār*, f. hissing (as a snake), snorting. *s.* [snake), to snort. *s.*

پهونکارنا फूंकारना *phūnkārnā*, n. to hiss (as a

پهونکنا फूंकना *phūnknā*, a. to blow, to inflame, set on fire. *s.*

پهونوار फूंवार *phūnwār*, } f. small drizzling
پهونهار फोंहार *phonhār*, } rain, Scotch
پهونهي फूंही *phūnhī*, } mist. *h.*

پهونيارا *phūniyārā*, m. a jet d'eau. *h.*

پهوها फूहा *phūhā*, m. an artificial pap or nipple made of cotton, &c., by means of which milk is given to an infant when in want of its mother. *h.*

پهوهار फूहार *phūhār* (the same as *phonhār*), mist, &c.

پهوهڑ फूहड़ *phūhaṛ*, undisciplined, uneducated; stupid; obscene, foolish, rude (applied to women); f. a bad housewife, a slut or slattern. *h.*

پهوهڑا फूहड़ा *phūhṛā*, talking obscenely. *h.*

پھوھڑپن फूहड़पन *phūhaṛpan*, } m. stupidity,
پھوھڑپنا फूहड़पना *phūhaṛpanā*, } obscenity,
folly, silliness, affectation. *h.*

پھوھي फूही *phūhī*, f. small rain. *h.*

پھوياں *phūyāṅ* (also *phū,īṅ*), small rain. *d.*

پھہار फुहार *phuhār*, f. drizzling showers. *h.*

پھہرانا फहराना *phahrānā*, a. to make fly (a banner). *h.* [&c.). *h.*

پھہرنا फहरना *phaharnā*, n. to fly (as a banner,

پہيا पहिया *pahiyā*, m. a wheel (of a carriage, &c.). *h.*

پھيپس *phīpas*, flabby, flaccid. *d.*

پھيپسا *phīpsā*, } m. the lights or lungs. *d.*
پھيپھڑا *phephṛā*, }

پھيپھڑي फेफड़ी *phephaṛī*, f. inability to move; adv. again, afterwards. *h.*

پھيٹ फेट *pheṭ*, f. the waist when bound with a belt. *h.* [band without a fringe. *h.*

پھيٹا फेटा *pheṭā*, m. a small turban; a waist-

پھيٹنا फेटना *pheṭnā*, a. to mix by trituration. *h.*

پھير फेर *pher*, m. turning, turn, return, change; meander, maze, curvature, twisting, coil, fold; difficulty, distance; circumference; equivocation, ambiguity; adv. again, back. *pher paṛnā*, n. to differ. *pher-phār*, alternate. *pher phār-k.*, a to alternate. *pher denā*, a. to restore, give back. *pher meṅ ḍālnā*, a. to throw obstacles in the way of another. *pher-khānā*, a. to wind (as a river); to go round about; to meet with perplexities. *h.*

پھيرو फेरु *pheru*, m. a jackal. *h.*

پھيرا फेरा *pherā*, m. turning, circuit; a roll; a wooden frame with which lime, sand, &c. is measured. *h.*

پھيرا *pherā*, m. a set or assortment (as a set of chessmen, a dinner service, &c.). *d.*

پھيراپھيري फेराफेरी *pherā-pherī*, f. walking backwards and forwards, going and coming; returning, alternating. *h.* [men. *d.*

پھيربوٹي *pher-boṭī*, f. the paunch and abdo-

پھيرنا फेरना *phernā*, a. to return, to invert, to revert; to turn away, to make to walk backwards and forwards; to bring or carry back, to shift; to plaster, to stroke. *hāth phernā*, to caress, to fondle. *sir par hāth phernā*, a. to deceive by coaxing. *h.*

پھيرو फेरव *pherav*, fraudulent, crafty; a rogue, a cheat; malicious, injurious. *h.*

پھيري फेरी *pherī*, f. going round to the right by way of adoration; (v. *parikramā*); the knuckles. *h.*

پھيري *pherī*, f. a set or assortment (v. *pherā*). *d.*

پھيريدار फेरीदार *pherī-dār*, m. a vagabond, a vagrant. *h. p.*

پھيري والا फेरीवाला *pherī wālā*, m. a pedlar. *h.*

پھيڑنا *pheṛnā*, a. to accomplish, perform; to pay or liquidate a debt. *d.*

پھيك फीक *phīk*, f. the point of a scourge. *h.*

پھيكا फीका *phīkā*, weak, vapid, tasteless, insipid; pale, sallow, light (in colour). *h.*

پھيلانا फैलाना *phailānā*, a. to spread, to expand, to diffuse, to widen, to publish, to proclaim, to branch out. *pāṅw phailānā*, to insist, to be obstinate. *hāth phailānā*, a. to beg. *h.*

پھيلاو फैलाव *phailāw*, m. spread, expansion, diffusion, extent; plenty, profusion (also *phailā,o*). *h.*

پھيلاوا फैलावा *phailāwā*, m. prolixity. *h.*

پھيلنا फैलना *phailnā*, n. to be spread; to be expanded; to be diffused; to become public, to spread abroad (as news, &c.). *h.*

پہيلي पहेली *pahelī*, f, a riddle, an enigma. *s.*

پھين फेन *phen*, } m. foam, froth. *phen*, cuttle-
پھينا फेना *phenā*, } fish bone, supposed to be the indurated foam of the sea *s.*

پھينانا फैनाना *phainānā* or फेनाना *phenānā*, n. to foam. *s.* [frothing. *s.*

پھينايمان फेनायमान *phenāyamān*, adj. foaming,

پھينٹ फेंट *pheṅṭ* or फैंट *phaiṅṭ*, f. waist-band, belt, fob. *pheṅṭ-bāndhnā*, to get ready, to resolve. *h.*

پھينٹا फेंटा *pheṅṭa* or फैंटा *phaiṅṭā* f. a small turban; a waist-band; a fob. *h.*

پھينٹنا फेंटना *pheṅṭnā*, a to mix, to beat (as eggs, &c.), to triturate. *h.*

پھينٹي फेंटी *pheṅṭī*, f. a skein (of thread, &c.). *h.*

پھينچنا पींचना *phīṅchnā* or *phīṅch-ḍālnā*, a. to wash cloth, to rinse, to squeeze. *h.*

پھينس फेनुस *phenus*, m. beestings; the first milk of a cow, &c. after calving. *s.*

پھينك फेंक *pheṅk*, f. throw, cast. *pheṅk-denā*, a. to throw away, to fly a hawk after game; to rush off on horseback at full speed. *h.*

پھينكا फींका *phīṅkā*, (v. *phīkā*) pale, dim, &c. *h.*

پھينكاو फेंकाव *pheṅkāw*, requiring to be thrown. *h.*

پھينكنا फेंकना *pheṅknā*, a. to throw, to fling, to let fly (a hawk), to set off (a horse) at full speed. *h.*

پھينگڑا *pheṅgṛā*, lame, club-footed. *d.*

پھينل फेनिल *phenil*, frothy, foamy; m. the soap-plant (*Sapindus detergens*); the fruit of the jujube; the fruit of the *vangueria spinosa*. *s.*

پھيني फेनी *phenī*, f. a kind of sweetmeat. *s.*

پي पी *pī* or पिय *piya*, beloved; m. a lover, a sweetheart a husband. *s.*

پي *pī* f. fat, grease, tallow. *p.*

پي *pai*, m. the foot, the heel; a nerve, tendon, sinew. *pai ānā*, n. to have a splint (a horse). *pai-k.*, a. to pursue, to seize, to be importunate. *pai-ā-pai*, step by step, successively. *p.*

پي पै or पय *pai*, m. milk, any thing to drink; (postposition) on, upon, over, nevertheless, yet; but. *s.*

پي पय *pai*, f. a fault, vice, blemish. *h.*

پيا पिया *piyā*, beloved; m. a husband, a lover, sweetheart. *h.*

پياده *piyāda*, m. a footman, a foot soldier; a *pawn* at chess; a species of foot soldiers employed as servants or attendants: they are armed with swords and targets, and sometimes carry matchloks. *piyāda-pā*, on foot. *p.*

پيار प्यार *pyār* or पियार *piyār*, m. f. love, affection; name of a tree and its fruit. *pyār-k.*, a. to fondle. *s.*

پيار पयार *payār*, a species of grass. *h.*

پيارا प्यारा *pyārā* or पियारा *piyārā*, m. beloved; *pyārā jānnā*, a. to esteem. *s.*

پياري प्यारी *pyārī* or पियारी *piyārī*, f. beloved, pleasant, a sweetheart. *h.*

پياز *piyāz*, f. an onion. *piyāzī*, of or resembling an onion. *piyāzī rang*, m. a reddish colour, crimson. *p.*

پياس प्यास *pyās* or पियास *piyās*, f. thirst. *pyās bujhānā*, a. to quench thirst. *pyās lagnā*, n. to be thirsty. *pyās mārnā*, a. to suffer thirst. *pyās marnā*, n. applied to thirst which vanishes without drinking. *s.*

پياسا प्यासा *pyāsā* or पियासा *piyāsā*, m. thirst; adj. thirsty; *pyāse marnā*, n. to be very thirsty. *s.*

پياسي प्यासी or पियासी *pyāsī*, f. a kind of fish. *s.*

پيال पियाल *piyāl* or प्याल *pyāl*, f. name of a fruit (*Chironjia sapida, Roxb., Buchanania latifolia*). *s.*

پيال पयाल *payāl*, पैयाल *paiyāl*, or प्याल *pyāl*, f. straw, dried grass. *s.*

پياله *piyāla* or *pyāla*, m. a glass, a cup; a priming pan (of a musket, &c.). *piyāla niwāla*, food and drink (in the slang of debauchees). *piyāla bharnā*, to be proud, conceited. *piyāla honā* (in the language of *fakīrs*), to die. *p.*

پيالي *piyālī*, f. a small cup or goblet. *p.*

پيام *payām*, m. a message, news, advice, intelligence. *p.*

پيامبر *payāmbar*, a message-bearer, a prophet. *p.*

پيامبري *payāmbarī*, f. office of prophet. *p.*

پيان पयान *payān* or पैयान *paiyān*, m. departure. *s.*

پيانا पियाना *piyānā* or प्याना *pyānā*, a. to give drink, to cause to drink; to water or irrigate. *s.*

پيب पीब *pīb*, f. pus, matter, purulent running. *s.*

پيبيانا पीबियाना *pībiyānā*, n. to suppurate. *s.*

پيبياهٹ पीबियाहट *pībiyāhaṭ*, f. suppuration. *s.*

پيپ *pīp* (same as *pīb*), pus, matter, &c. *d.*

پيپا *pīpā*, m. a pipe, barrel, cask. *e.*

پيپل पीपल *pīpal*, m. a species of fig-tree (*Ficus religiosa*); f. long pepper (*Piper longum*). *s.*

پيپلا पीपला *pīplā*, m. the point of a sword; (in Dakh.) long pepper. *h.*

پيپلامور पीपलामूर *pīplā-mūr*, پيپلامول पीपलामूल *pīplā-mūl*, } m. the root of the long pepper-tree. *s.*

پيت पीत *pīt* or पीति *pīti*, f. love, affection. *pīt kī pīt rahe aur mīt kā mīt hāth lage*, let friendship continue, and the sweets of it will be obtained; as an adjective, *pīt* denotes yellow. *s.*

پيتا पीता *pītā*, m. a father (for *pitā*). *d.*

پيتامبر पीताम्बर *pītāmbar*, m. a silk cloth of a yellow colour, a kind of dress (generally worn by young *Krishṇa*); vulg. a silk cloth. *s.*

پيتپادا पीतपादा *pīt-pādā*, f. a small bird, the *myna* (*Turdus salica*). *s.*

پيتپرني पीतपर्णी *pīt-parnī*, f. a plant called *bichhati*; a kind of nettle (*Tragia involucrata*). *s.*

پيتپشپ पीतपुष्प *pīt-pushp*, m. a species of *karnikārā*; a sort of *Tabernæ montana*. *s.*

پيتپشپي पीतपुष्पी *pīt-pushpī*, f. yellow Barleria. *s.*

پيتپهل पीतफल *pīt-phal*, m. *Trophis aspera*. *s.*

پيتتا पीतता *pītatā*, f. yellowness. *s.*

پيتتند पीततुण्ड *pīt-tuṇḍ*, m. the taylor-bird (*Sylvia sutoria*). *s.*

پيتچندن पीतचन्दन *pīt-chandan*, m. a yellow species of sandal wood. *s.*

پيتدار पीतदारु *pīt-dāru*, m. a sort of pine (*Pinus devadaru*; also *Pinus longifolia*). *s.*

پيترا पैतरा *paitarā*, m. flourishing about before cudgelling, &c. *h.*

پيترس पीतरस *pīt-ras*, m. turmeric. *s.*

پيترکت पीतरक्त *pīt-rakt*, m. a yellow-coloured gem. *s.*

پيترک पैतृक or पैत्रिक *paitrik*, paternal, ancestral, hereditary; inherited from a father. *paitrik-bhūmi*, f. fatherland, a paternal estate. *s.*

پيتسار पीतसार *pīt-sār*, m. sandal; a yellow gem, topaz, a tree (*Alangium hexapetalum*) *s.*

پيتسپهٹك पीतस्फटिक *pīt-sphaṭik*, m. a yellow gem, topaz. *s.*

پيتشال पीतशाल *pīt-shāl*, m. a tree (*Pentaptera*). *s.*

پيتك पैत्तिक *paittik*, bilious. *s.*

پيتكاشٹه पीतकाष्ठ *pīt-kāshṭh*, m. yellow sanders. *s.*

پيتكند पीतकन्द *pīt-kand*, m. the carrot. *s.*

پيتگهوشا पीतघोषा *pīt-ghoshā*, f. a sort of creeper with yellow flowers. *s.*

پيتل पीतल *pītal*, m. brass. *s.*

پيتلا पीतला *pītlā*, brazen, made of brass. *s.*

پيتلا पैतला *paitalā*, shallow. *s.*

پيتلوه पीतलोह *pīt-loh*, m. yellow brass, queen's metal. *s.* [a sweetheart, a husband. *s.*

پيتم पीतम *pītam*, most beloved; m. a lover,

پيتمبر पीतम्बर *pītambar*, m. (v. *pītāmbar*), a silk cloth of a yellow colour; vulg. a silk cloth. *s.*

پيتمستك पीतमस्तक *pīt-mastak*, m. a small bird (*Loxia philippensis*). *s.* [topaz. *s.*

پيتمن पीतमणि *pīt-mani*, m. a yellow gem, a

پيتمنڈ पीतमुण्ड *pīt-muṇḍ*, m. a gallinule. *s.*

پيتن पीतन *pītan*, m. the hog-plum (*Spondias magnifera*); a tree (*Pentaptera tomentosa*); the waved-leaf fig-tree. *s.* [mine. *s.*

پيتيوتهي पीतयूथी *pīt-yūthī*, f. yellow jas-

پيٹ पेट *peṭ*, m. the belly; pregnancy, the womb; the bore (of a gun, &c.); cavity, capacity. *peṭ ānā*, n. to be purged. *peṭ bāndhnā*, a. to eat less than one's appetite demands. *peṭ baṛhānā*, a. to eat voraciously, to encroach on the share or rights of another. *peṭ bhar*, bellyful. *peṭ bharnā*, a. to fill one's belly; to be satisfied. *peṭ pālnā*, a. to be able to live decently; to be selfish. *peṭ pānī honā*, n. to be violently purged, have watery stools. *peṭ paknā*, n. to burst with laughter. *peṭ-posū* or *peṭ-posū,ā*, glutton. *peṭ poṅchan*, the last child of a woman. *peṭ phūlnā*, n. to burst with laughter. *peṭ pīṭh ek honā*, n. to be greatly emaciated. *peṭ pīṭh batānā*, to evince extreme weakness, to act submissively. *peṭ jārī honā*, n. to be fluxed, to be purged. *peṭ jalnā*, n. to be very hungry. *peṭ chalnā* or *chhūṭnā*, n. to be purged, have a diarrhoea. *peṭ dikhānā*, a. to complain of poverty and hunger. *peṭ ḍālnā*, a. to procure abortion. *peṭ rakhānā*, a. to get with child. *peṭ rahnā*, n. to be pregnant. *peṭ se*, pregnant. *peṭ se honā*, n. to be pregnant. *peṭ kā pānī na hilnā*, n. is applied to the steady motion of a horse, &c. which does not agitate the rider. *peṭ ka parda*, m. the omentum. *peṭ kāṭnā*, a. to pinch one's belly, to starve one's self; (in Bengal) to be griped. *peṭ kā dukh denā*, a. to starve. *peṭ ke pāṅw bāhir nikālnā*, to perpetrate villainy; to shew the cloven foot. *peṭ kī āg*, f. maternal affection; hunger. *peṭ kī āg bujhānā*, to eat something. *peṭ kī bāteṅ*, f. bosom secrets. *peṭ girānā*, a. to cause an abortion. *peṭ girnā*, n. to miscarry (a female). *peṭ gaṛgaṛānā*, n. to have *borborygmi*. *peṭ lag jānā*, n. to be starving with hunger. *peṭ lag rahnā*, n. to be very hungry. *peṭ mārnā*, a. to commit suicide, to stab one's self. *peṭ meṅ paiṭhnā*, n. to worm one's self into the secrets of another, to become intimate. *peṭ meṅ lenā*, to bear or put up with, to endure. *peṭ wālī*, f. pregnant. *peṭ kaṛbaṛānā*, n. to have a griping or inclination to stool. *s.*

پيٹا पेटा *peṭā*, f. a large basket. *s.*

پيٹارا पेटारा *peṭārā*, m. a large basket, a portmanteau. *h.*

پيٹارتهو पेटार्थू *peṭārthū*, **پيٹارتهي पेटार्थी** *peṭārthī*, } gluttonous, epicurean. *s.*

پيٹك पेटक *peṭak*, m. a basket for holding clothes, &c. *s.*

پيٹنا पीटना *pīṭnā*, a. to beat, to thrash, to dash, to strike, to knock, comminute. *chhātī pīṭnā*, to lament, repent. *muṅh pīṭnā*, to wrinkle one's mouth in anger. *s.*

پيٹو पेटू *peṭū*, gluttonous, epicurean. *s.*

پيٹوكها पेटौखा *peṭaukhā*, m. a looseness, purging, flux. *h.*

پيٹهه पीठ *pīṭh*, f. the back. *pīṭh kā bāṅs*, the spine. *pīṭh par hāth phernā* a. to encourage, to pat on the back. *pīṭh phernā*, a. to turn one's back, to depart, to flee, to leave, to withdraw. *pīṭh ṭhaknā*, to encourage. *pīṭh denā*, n. (*terga dare*) to run away, to flee; to turn, to shrink from, to veer; to turn away in displeasure. *pīṭh ke pīchhe paṛnā*, to seek shelter of any one. *pīṭh ke pīchhe ḍāl lenā*, to afford an asylum, to protect. *pīṭh lagānā*, a. to throw down in wrestling. *pīṭh lagnā*, n. to have a sore on the back (a horse); to mount a horse. *s.*

پيٹهه पीठ *pīṭh*, m. a stool, a seat, a chair. *s.*

پيٹهه पैठ *paiṭh*, m. a duplicate (of a bill of exchange); entrance, admission, access. *s.*

پيٹهه *peṭh*, a village or small town; used in comp. like the words *pūr*, *paṭṭan*, *ābād*, &c. *d.*

پيٹها पेठा *peṭhā*, m. a kind of gourd. *s.*

پيٹها पीठा *pīṭhā*, m. a kind of food made of rice and flour. *s.*

پيٹهالنا पैठालना *paiṭhālnā*, a. to force in, to make penetrate, to thrust, to push in, to introduce, to insinuate. *s.*

پيٹهنا पैठना *paiṭhnā*, n. to rush in, to penetrate, to enter, to pervade. *h.*

پيٹهوتا पीठौता *pīṭhautā*, m. page of a book. *s.*

پيٹهيا पेठिया *peṭhiyā*, a market, a bazar. *h.*

پيٹهيا ٹهونك पीठियाठोंक *pīṭhiyā ṭhonk*, closely. *s.* or *h.*

پيٹي पेटी *peṭī*, f. a belly-band; a portmanteau; a large basket, a box, a tumbril; the thorax, chest. *peṭī larnā* or *mārnā*, a. to copulate. *peṭī sharīk*, a coparcener in land. *s.*

پيٹيا पेटिया *peṭiyā*, m. a pension, daily food. *s.*

پيج पैज *paij*, f. a vow, a promise. *paij-k.*, a. to make a vow. *h.*

پي جانا पीजाना *pī-jānā*, a. to drink to the point of intoxication, to absorb; to stifle one's passions; to refrain from answering. *h.*

پيچ *pech*, m. twist, revolution, coil; a screw; perplexity, difficulty; deceit; complication. *pech uṭhānā*, a. to suffer loss or distress. *pech ukhaṛnā*, n. to loose (the twist of any thing). *pech bāndhnā*, a. to grapple in wrestling. *pech paṛnā*, n. to become difficult or intricate, to occur as an obstacle, to be entangled. *pech chalnā*, n. to prevail by stratagem. *pech chunnā*, a. to bind the twists of a turban with care. *pech-dār*, twisted, coiled. *pech-dar-pech*, coil within coil, entangled. *pech denā*, a. to circumvent, to deceive, to twist, &c. *pech ḍālnā*, a. to throw obstacles in the way; (in playing with paper kites) to entangle the string of an adversary's kite. *pech-k.*, a. to deceive, to trick, to complicate; to seize in wrestling, to grapple. *pech khānā*, a. to be perplexed, to fall into difficulties, to sustain a loss. *pech khulnā*, n. to be untwisted or unscrewed. *pech kholnā*, a. to untwist, to unscrew. *pech lenā*, a. to fight paper kites (each party endeavours to entangle and cut the string of his adversary's kite); to meet, to embrace. *p.*

پيچ पीच *pīch*, f. rice-water, rice-gruel (see *pīchh*). [*colocasia*. *s.*

پيچو पेचु *pechu*, m. an esculent root (*Arum*

پيچا पेचा *pechā*, m. an owl. *s.*

پيچان *pechān*, twisted, coiled. *p.*

پيچانيدن *pechānīdan*, to cause to be coiled or twisted. *p.*

پيچ تاب *pech-tāb*, or *pech o tāb*, m. restlessness, alarm, suspense, perplexity; folds, twisting, knots. *pech tāb khānā*, a. to suffer distress or anxiety, to be vexed. *p.*

پيچش *pechish*, f. inflection, contortion, writhing; trouble, perplexity; pain in the bowels, *tenesmus*, gripes; circumvention, contention. *p.*

پيچك पेचक *pechak*, m. an owl. *s.*

پيچك *pechak*, f. a ball or clue of thread; the bottom on which thread is wound. *p.*

پيچنا पीचना *pīchnā*, a. to tread under foot. *h.*

پيچو पीचू *pīchū*, m. the fruit of the capparis. *h.*

پيچوان *pechwān*, twisted (generally applied to *ḥuḳḳa* snakes). *p.*

پيچ وتاب *pech-o-tāb*, m. restlessness, alarm, suspense, perplexity (v. *pech-tāb*). *p.*

پيچه पीछ *pīchh*, f. rice-water, or that in which rice has been boiled, rice-gruel, slip-slop. *h.*

پيچها पीछा *pīchhā*, (also *pīchhal* and *pīchhū*), m. the hinder part, the rear; pursuit, persecution, absence. *pichhā-phernā*, a. to leave, withdraw. *pīchhā-k.*, to pursue, to chase; to recoil (a gun, &c.). *pīchhā lenā*, to pursue, to importune. *s.*

پيچهوا पीछवा *pīchhwā*, m. the hinder part (of a saddle particularly). *s.*

پيچهوت पीछूत *pīchhūt*, rearwards, afterwards.

پيچهي पीछे *pīchhe* or *pīchhen*, after, behind. *pīchhe parnā*, n. to dance attendance, to importune, to dun, to persecute; to be outstripped. *pīchhe ḍālnā*, a. to leave behind, to outstrip. *pīchhe lagnā*, to pursue, to set after. *s.*

پيچيدگي *pechīdagī*, being twisted. *p.*

پيچي *pīche* (for *pīchhe*, q. v.) behind, &c. *d.*

پيچيدن *pechīdan*, to twist or coil (as a worm &c.) in a reflective or neuter sense. *p.*

پيچيده *pechīda*, twisted, coiled. *p.*

پيخال *paikhāl*, m. dung of birds. *p.*

پيخنا पेखना *pekhnā*, m. a puppet-show; a plaything; the artifices and pretences of a woman. *h.*

پيخورا *pīkhurā*, m. a drunkard, a sot. *d.*

پيدا *paidā*, born, created, produced, exhibited, discovered, manifest, evident, invented. *paidā-k.*, a. to discover, to produce, to find, to get, to earn, to invent, to procure. *paidā-wār*, m. produce of a field, fruit, profit of trade, &c. *paidā-honā*, to be born, to be created; to be found, to be earned, to be produced. *p.*

پيدايش *paidā,ish*, f. birth, existence; earnings, production, profit. *p.*

پيداوري *paidāwarī*, f. statement of the produce of land. *p.*

پي در پي *pai dar pai*, successively, repeatedly, one after another. *p.*

پيدڑي पीदड़ी *pīdṛī*, f. a tomtit. *h.*

پيدل पैदल *paidal*, on foot; m. infantry. *s.*

پير पीर *pīr*, f. pain, sickness; feeling, pity, compassion. *s.*

پير *pīr*, m. Monday; an old man; a saint, spiritual guide. *pīri ṭarīḳat*, a spiritual leader (among the Sūfīs). *p.*

پير पैर *pair*, m. the foot. *h.*

پيرا पीरा *pīrā*, yellow (v. *pīlā*). *h.*

پيرا *pairā*, (in comp.) adorning, from,

پيراستن *pairāstan*, to adorn, decorate. *p.*

پيراك पैराक *pairāk*, m. a swimmer. *h.*

پيراكي पैराकी *pairākī*, f. swimming, the art of swimming, a female swimmer. *h.*

پيرامن *pīrāman*, پيرامون *pīrāmūn*, } m. a circuit, circumference, environs, adjacent places; the skirt, lappet, or flap of a garment; adv. about, around. *p.*

پيران *pīrān*, m. charity lands (bestowed on the poor in honour of a saint); also land granted for the erection and preservation of a tomb over a *Musalmān* saint or man of piety; Pers. pl. old men, saints, sages. *p.*

پيرانا पैराना *pairānā*, a. to make float or swim. *h.*

پيرانه *pīrāna*, elderly, like an old man; growing old; belonging to, or connected with, or worthy of, a saint. *p.*

پيراو पैराव *pairāw* or *pairā,o*, deep, or beyond man's depth, where it is necessary to swim. *h.*

پيراوا *pairāwā*, tillage, cultivation; a garment, clothing, (a corrupt form of *pairāhan*). *d.*

پيراهن *pairāhan*, m. a long robe, a kind of loose vest; a shirt or shift. *p.*

پيرائي पीराई *pīrā,ī*, m. name of a tribe or caste who beat a kind of drum called *ḍhol*, q. v. *h.*

پيرائي पैराई *pairā,ī*, f. place of swimming, or distance over which it is necessary to swim; art of swimming; wages for teaching to swim. *h.*

پيرايه *pīrāya*, m. an ornament. *p.*

پيرپا *perpā*, m. a large earthen vessel. *d.*

پيرپال *pīr-pāl* (v. *pīrān*), a grant of land to a *pīr*, &c. *p. s.*

پيرپتاري *pīr-pattārī*, f. an agate. *d.*

پيرت *pīrt* (for *prīt*, q.v.), love, friendship. *d.*

پيرزاده *pīr-zāda*, m. the son or disciple of a *pīr*; a mendicant, also a priest attached to a mosque. *p.*

پيرزال *pīr-zāl*, پيرزاله *pīr-zāla*, پيرزن *pīr-zan*, } an aged woman. *p.*

پیرمرد *pīr-mard*, an old man. *p.*

پیرنا पैरना *pairnā*, n. to swim, to float. *h.*

پیرنا *pernā*, a. to sow, to plant. *d.*

پیرو पेरू *perū*, m. a kind of bird, a turkey-fowl. *h.*

پیرو *pai-rau* or *pai-rav*, following, a follower. *p.*

پیروج *peroj*, m. the turquoise (see *fīroza*). *p.*

پیروز *pīroz*, victory; adj. victorious. *p.*

پیروي *pai-ravī*, f. following, pursuit, hunting after. *p.*

پیري *pīrī*, f. old age, decrepitude. *p.*

پیري पैरी *pairī*, f. an ornament worn on the legs. *h.*

پیڑ पेड़ *peṛ*, f. a tree, a plant; trunk or stem of a tree. *peṛ lagānā*, a. to plant trees. *h.*

پیڑ पीड़ *pīṛ*, f. pain, labour (in childbirth). *s.*

پیڑ *pair*, noise of a blow, or knock. *d.*

پیڑا पेड़ा *peṛā*, m. a kind of sweetmeat made with curds; a globular mass of leaven prepared for baking. *s.*

پیڑا पीड़ा *pīṛā*, f. pain, sickness, anguish. *pīṛā-kar*, giving pain, afflicting. *s.*

پیڑت पीड़ित *pīṛit*, sick, afflicted, pained. *s.*

پیڑك पीड़क *pīṛak*, what causes pain. *s.*

پیڑنا पेड़ना *peṛnā*, a. to press (oil by means of a mill), to squeeze, to rack. *s.*

پیڑو पेड़ू *peṛū*, m. the belly, below the navel; the pubes; (for *perū*) a turkey-fowl. *h.*

پیڑھا पीढ़ा *pīṛhā*, m. a stool, a seat. *s.*

پیڑھا بندھ पीढ़ाबन्ध *pīṛhā-bandh*, m. a preface or preliminary discourse to a book. *s.*

پیڑھي पीढ़ी *pīṛhī*, f. a small stool; a race or series of generations, progenitors, or descendants. *pīṛhī ba pīṛhī*, for successive generations. *s.*

پیڑي पेड़ी *peṛī*, f. a kind of sweetmeat made with curds; a kind of betel leaves; the indigo plant after being once cut; the trunk of a tree. *h.*

پیڑي पैड़ी *paiṛī*, f. a ladder, a staircase, a flight of steps; the inclined plane leading to a reservoir of water, on which the oxen travel for the purpose of drinking, or drawing water for irrigation. *h.*

پیزار *paizār*, f. a slipper, a shoe. *paizārā paizārī*, f. fighting, or mutual beating with slippers. *paizār-paṭṭī* or *-kārī*, act of beating with slippers. *paizār-khor*, abject, mean, base (q.d. fit or deserving to be beaten with slippers). *paizār se*, an expression of contempt signifying It concerns not or affects not me, I care not. *paizār khānā*, a. to be beaten with slippers. *h.*

پیزنه *pezna*, m. a sieve; a riddle. *p.*

پیس *pes*, the leprosy *p.*

پیسا पैसा *paisā*, m. the name of a copper coin nearly equal to our halfpenny; the sixty-fourth part of a rupī: in common parlance it is used for money in general (as we say "the dibs" or "the browns"). *paisā uṛānā*, a. to spend extravagantly; to take the money of another by theft or deceit. *paisā pherphār-k.*, a. to turn the penny. *paisā dubonā*, a. to sink money, to lay out money without return. *paisā dubnā*, n. to be sunk (money). *paise son darbār bandnā* (Dakh.), to bribe. *paisā khānā*, a. to spend extravagantly, to waste; to subsist by wages or the produce of labour; to take bribes; to embezzle. *paise lagānā*, a. to lay out or expend money. *paise wālā*, monied; worth one *paisā*. *h.*

پیساچ पीसाच *pīsāch*, m. an evil spirit that haunts the places where dead bodies are burnt or buried. *s.*

پیساچ पैशाच *paisāch*, demoniac, diabolical; applied to a kind of unfair Hindū marriage, such as the violation of a girl when asleep or unconscious. *s.*

پیسار पैसार *paisār*, m. access, ability, admission. *h.*

پیسندازي *paisandāzī*, rich, wealthy. *d.*

پیسنا पीसना *pīsnā*, a. to grind, to triturate, to bruise, to powder; to gnash (the teeth); m. the corn or grain for grinding. *pīs pās-k.*, to grind down, to triturate. *s.*

پیسنا *paisnā*, n. to enter, to plunge in. *d.*

پیسوني पयस्विनी *payasvinī*, f. milch-cow. *s.*

پیسي *pesī*, affected with leprosy. *p.*

پیسیا पयस्या *payasyā*, f. a shrub (*Asclepias rosea*); a medicinal kind of moon-plant. *s.*

پیش *pesh*, promoted, advanced, respected, confided in, possessing influence; m. before, front; the vowel point ُ, called *zamma* by the Arabs, is named *pesh* by the Persians and people of India; (as a prep.) before, in front of. *pesh āmad*, f. access, admittance. *pesh-ānā*, to come to pass, to happen, to await; to treat, to behave, to negotiate. *pesh band*, m. the belt that passes over a horse's breast to prevent the saddle's slipping back. *pesh bandī*, f. foresight, timely preparation. *pesh-bīn*, prudent, wise. *pesh-khima*, m. a tent or other baggage sent on before. *pesh-dast*, surpassing, one who excels. *pesh-dastī*, f. excelling, surpassing, pre-eminence, pre-excellence. *pesh-ras*, early (fruit, grain, &c.). *pesh-raft*, making impression, successful, efficient, effectual (generally applied to words that are attended to). *pesh-rav*, a precursor; the advanced guard. *pesh-ravī*, f. act of preceding. *pesh-ḳabẓ*, m. a kind of dagger. *pesh-ḳadamī*, f. alacrity, alertness, activity. *pesh-namāz*, m. he that precedes in saying prayer. *pesh-nihād*, m. custom, regulation, habit, example, model, profession. *pesh-giriftan*, to adopt, select. *p.*

پیشاب *peshāb*, m. urine. *peshāb-band*, m. [strangury. *p.*

پیشاچ पैशाच *paishāch*, demoniacal, belonging to a pisāch or goblin; m. a mode of marriage, the ravishment of a girl by her lover (v. *paisāch*). *s.*

پیشاني *peshānī*, f. the forehead, the brow. *p.*

پیشتر *pesh-tar*, before, prior, formerly, heretofore. *peshtar az īn*, before now, heretofore, *pesh az ān ki* or *peshtar az ān ki*, before that, "antea quam." *p.*

پیشکار *pesh-kār*, m. a deputy, agent, assistant, a minister, a manager. *p.*

پیشکاری *pesh-kārī*, f. deputyship. *p.*

پیشکش *pesh-kash*, m. a present, a tribute; a fine, tribute, or quit-rent, paid to government as an acknowledgment for any tenure. *pesh-kashī bāzār*, a tax upon stalls in a public market. *peshkashī*, of or relating to land held under a quit-rent. *p.*

پیشگاه *pesh-gāh*, f. a portico. *p.*

پیشگي *peshgī*, f. an advance; earnest-money given on confirming an agreement, &c. Scotticè, "arles penny." *peshgī-dar*, a lender of money to enable a person to pay in advance. *p.*

پیشن पेषण *peshan*, m. reducing to powder; a hand-mill, muller, any apparatus for grinding or pounding; a plant, a sort of *euphorbia* with three lobes, commonly called *tekāntā-sij*. *s.*

پیشني पेषणी *peshanī*, f. a stone slab on which condiments are ground with a muller. *s.*

پیشنیه पैशुन्य *paishunya*, m. depravity, wickedness. *s.*

پیشوا *peshwā*, m. a leader, a guide; a title of the *Marhaṭṭa* minister. *p.*

پیشواز *peshwāz*, f. a gown, a female dress. *p.*

پیشواءي *peshwā,ī*, f. office of *peshwā*, the honourable meeting and reception of a visitor. *p.*

پیشور *peshaur* (properly *peshāwar*), m. name of a country and city between the Indus and Kābul. *h.*

پیشوري *peshaurī*, f. a kind of slipper, made in *Peshaur*; a kind of rice. *p.*

پیشه *pesha*, m. trade, profession; custom, habit, practice; in comp. it denotes an agent or doer, as *jaur-pesha*, an oppressor. *p.*

پیشه‌وار *pesha-wār*, } m. an artisan, craftsman
پیشه‌ور *pesha-war*, } or artificer. *p.*

پیشي *peshī*, f. an advance; precedency, superior rank. *p.*

پیشي पेशी *peshī*, f. spikenard (*Valeriana atamansi*). *s.*

پیشین *peshīn*, anterior, ancient, prior, former; m. the afternoon. *p.*

پیشینیان *peshīniyān*, (pl.) the ancients. *p.*

پیغار *paighār*, m. a ditch, a furrow. *p.*

پیغام *paighām*, m. a message. *p.*

پیغاماپیغامي *paighāmā-paighāmī*, f. mutual messages, mediation, correspondence. *p.*

پیغامبر *paighām-bar*, m. a prophet, a messenger, an apostle. *p.*

پیغامبري *paighām-barī*, f. mission, office of a prophet. *p.*

پیغمبر *paigham-bar*, m. the same as (*paighām-bar*), a prophet, &c. *p.*

پیغمبري *paighambarī*, mission of a prophet. *p.*

پیک पीक *pīk*, f. the juice of the betel-leaf chewed and spit out. *pīk-dān*, m. a vessel for holding betel spittle; (in Dakh.) m. ripened produce of a field; crop, harvest. *p.*

پیک *paik*, m. a messenger, a runner; a watchman employed as a guard at night; likewise a footman or runner employed on the business of the lands. *p.*

پیکار पैकार *paikar*, m. a dealer, agent, or broker; one who goes about with goods for sale, a pedlar or hawker. *h.*

پیکار *paikār*, war, battle, contest. *p.*

پیکان *paikān*, f. the head of an arrow or javeline; also any pointed missile; (plur. of *paik*) armed militia or watchmen; also revenues of lands for their maintenance. *p.*

پیکر *paikar*, m. face, countenance, visage, form, appearance; a portrait, a likeness; used in comp. it denotes similitude, as *koh-paikar*, like a mountain, "instar montis." *p.*

پیکڑا पैकड़ा *paikaṛā*, m. } iron chains on a
پیکڑھا पैकढ़ा *pai-kaṛhā*, m. } culprit's legs; or-
پیکڑي पैकड़ी *paikaṛī*, f. } namental rings
worn on the ankles. *s.*

پیکنا *pīknā*, n. to be produced, to ripen, to grow. *d.*

پیکھنا पेखना *pekhnā*, m. play, farce, sham, comedy. *h.*

پیکھنا पेखना *pekhnā*, a. to see, to behold. *s.*

پیکھنیا पेखनिया *pekhniyā*, m. a player, an actor. *h.*

پیکي पैकी *paikī*, m. one who carries about a *ḥuḳḳa* for hire at a fair or in a camp. *h.*

پیگشتي *paigashtī*, a collector of market dues; a policeman who patrols at night; a guard who goes about from station to station. *d.*

پیگو पैगु *paigū*, m. a sort of green-coloured stone (imported from Pegu). *h.*

پیل *pīl*, m. an elephant; the name of the bishop at chess. *pīl-band*, m. a term used at chess to express that a bishop and two pawns mutually support each other. *h.*

پیل पेल *pel*, a shove, push, thrust. *s.*

پیل पीलु *pīlu*, m. a tree; see *pīlū*. *s.*

پیل पैल *pail*, n. prop. a sage, the promulgator of the Rig-Veda. *s.*

پیل पेल *pel*, } m. a testicle; fault, oppres-
پیلا पेला *pelā*, } sion; a prop, a support. *h.*

پیلا पीला *pīlā*, yellow. *s.*

پیلا पैला *pailā*, m. a vessel for measuring grain. *h.*

پیلار *pailār*, removed in time by a whole unit. *pailār kā baras*, the year before last, or the year after next. *d.*

پیلام पीलाम *pīlām*, m. satin. *Chin.*

پیلاءي पीलाई *pīlā,ī*, f. yellowness. *s.*

پیلبان *pīl-bān*, m. an elephant driver or keeper; one who has charge of elephants. *p.*

پیلبانی *pīl-bānī*, f. the business of taking care of elephants. *p.*

پیلپا *pīlpā*, afflicted with elephantiasis. *p.*

پیل‌پال पेलपाल *pel-pāl*, pushing, shoving. *s.*

پیلپایہ *pīl-pāya*, m. (an elephant's foot, hence) a pillar, a column. *p.*

پیلپاعی *pīl-pāe*, name of a sage; vulg. [Pilpay. *p.*

پیلپرنی पीलुपर्णी *pīlu-parnī*, f. a plant (*Bryonia grandis*). *s.*

پیلتن *pīl-tan*, having a body like that of an elephant, gigantic. *p.*

پیل‌دندان *pīl-dandān*, elephant's tooth [ivory. *p.*

پیلڑ पेलड़ *pelaṛ*, }
پیلڑا पेलड़ा *pelṛā*, } m. a testicle. *h.*

پیلک पीलक *pīlak*, m. the large black ant; it is also the name of a pretty little bird called the oriole or mango-bird. [push. *s.*

پیل‌مارنا पेलमारना *pel mārnā*, a. to shove, to

پیل‌مرغ *pīl-murgh*, a turkey-fowl. *p.*

پیلن *pailan*, m. the first-born (child, &c.); adv. first, foremost, in the first place. *d.*

پیلنا पेलना *pelnā*, to shove, to push; to stuff, to cram (particularly *in coitu*); to express, to squeeze out. *s.*

پیل‌نشین *pīl-nishīn*, an elephant rider. *p.*

پیلو पीलु *pīlū*, m. the name of a tree (*Salvadora persica*; also in the Dakhin, *Careya arborea, Roxb.*), also applied to all exotic trees; the blossom of the *Saccharum sara*; an insect. *s.*

پیلو पेलू *pelū*, a wrestler, an athlete. *s.*

پیلور *pailwar*, yonder, on that side (v. *pare*). *d.*

پیلور *pīlawar*, a pedlar, a druggist. *p.*

پیلہ *pīla*, m. a silkworm, the silkworm's cone or envelope. *p.*

پیلہڑ पेल्हड़ *pelhaṛ*, }
پیلہڑا पेल्हड़ा *pelhṛā*, } m. a testicle. *h.*

پیلی पीली *pīlī*, f. a gold *mohur*. *s.*

پیلے *paile*, (for *pahile*), first, at first. *d.*

پیلی‌بهیت पीलीभीत *pīlī-bhīt*, the name of a town in Rohilkhand. *h.*

پیلیور *pailewar*, yonder, on that side. *d.*

پیم पेम pem, m. love, friendship. *s.*

پیما *paimā*, (in comp.) measuring, traversing. *p.*

پیمان *paimān*, m. a promise, agreement, treaty, confirmation, security, an oath, asseveration, convention, compact. *p.*

پیمانہ *paimāna*, m. a goblet; a certain measure for goods, dry or liquid. *paimāna 'umr kā bharnā*, a. to fill up the measure of one's age, *i.e.* to die or kill. *p.*

پیماعی *paimā,ī*, }
پیمائش *paimā,ish*, } f. measuring; the measure or survey of a country; measurement and allotment of lands. *paimā,ish-dār*, a surveyor. *paima,ishī kampās*, a trigonometrical survey (by theodolite and compass). *p.*

پیمبر *payambar*, m. (the same as *paighāmbar*), a prophet, &c. *p.*

پیمبری *payambarī*, f. the mission or office of a prophet, prophecy. *p.* [lover. *s.*

پیمی पेमी *pemī* (for *premī*), affectionate, a

پین पें *pain*, or پئین पइं *pa,īn*, m. a reservoir of water, a rill. *s.*

پین पीन *pīn*, heavy, fat, corpulent. *s.*

پین पें *pen*, m. an imitative sound. *h.*

پینا पैना *painā*, m. a goad; adj. sharp. *h.*

پینا पीना *pīnā*, a. to drink; to smoke (tobacco); m. act of drinking; the dregs or refuse (of linseed, &c.); the oil-cake. *s.*

پینالا पैनाला *painālā*, m. a gutter, a spout. *s.*

پینام पैनाम *painām*, a division of a province (like the Ridings of Yorkshire). *h.*

پینانا पैनाना *paināna*, a. to sharpen. *h.*

پینتالیس पैंतालीस *paintālis*, forty-five. *h.*

پینتانا पैंताना *pentānā* or पैंताना *paintānā*, m the foot of a bed, the side towards the feet. *s.*

پینتیس पैंतीस *paintīs*, thirty-five. *s.*

پینٹھ पेंठ *penṭh*, f. a market, a mart. *painṭh*, a duplicate bill of exchange (v. *peṭh*). *h.*

پینجنا पींजना *pīnjnā*, a. to clean cotton from the seeds. *h.*

پینجنی पैंजनी *penjnī* or पैंजनी *painjnī*, f. little bells fastened round the feet of pigeons and of children. *s.*

پینچ *pench* (for *pech*), twisting, &c. *d.p.*

پینچا पैंचा *painchā*, m. return, retribution, a loan, repayment of a loan. *h.*

پینچنا पैंचना *painchnā*, a. to winnow. *h.*

پیندا पेंदा *pendā*, m. the bottom (of a vessel, box, pot, &c.), breach of a cannon. *h.*

پینڈ पींड *pīnḍ*, m. a roller. *h.*

پینڈ पेंड *penḍ* or पैंड *painḍ*, f. pace, step; a rising ground, eminence. *h.*

پینڈا पैंडा *painḍā*, m. a road, highway, path. *painḍā mārnā*, a. to stop a road, to rob in the road. *s.*

پینس पीनस *pīnas*, m. a disease in the nose, cold, catarrh. *s.*

پینس पीनस *pīnas*, f. a kind of sedan or *pālkī*, a kind of boat or barge, a pinnace. *h.*

پینسٹھ पैंसठ *painsaṭh*, sixty-five. *s.*

پینسی पीनसी *pīnasī*, adj. having a cold. *s.*

پينك पीनक *pīnak*, f. intoxication and drowsiness from opium; stupefaction. *h.*

پينگ पेंग *peng*, f. the exertion made by people in a swing, when two persons keep the swing in motion without assistance from bystanders; m. the name of a bird (*Gracula chattareah, Buch.*). *h.*

پيننا *pennā*, to clothe, put on (clothes). *d.*

پيني पेनी *penī* or *painī*, f. sharp (v. *painā*). *h.*

پيو पिउ *pi,ū* or *pīw*, adj. dear; m. a sweetheart, a lover. *s.*

پيوا पीवा *pīwā*, f. water, drink. *s.*

پيودهر पयोधर *payodhar*, m. a woman's breast; a sort of rush (*Scirpus kysoor*); a fragrant grass (*Cyperus rotundus*). *s.*

پيودهك पयोधिक *payodhik*, m. a cuttle-fish bone. *s.*

پيور पयोर *payor*, m. the *khayar* (*Mimosa catechu*). *s.*

پيوري पीवरी *pīvrī*, f. a plant (*Asparagus racemosus*). *s.*

پيوڙي पेवड़ी *pewṛī*, f. a kind of yellow colour (said to be obtained from the urine of a cow fed on the flowers of *Butea frondosa*, or, according to others, on the leaves of the mango-tree). *h.*

پيوس पीयूस *pīyūs* or पेयूस *peyūs*, m the milk of a cow for some days after calving, biestings. *s.*

پيوست *paiwast*, f. junction, connection, friendship. *p.*

پيوستگي *paiwastagī*, f. attachment; contiguity. *p.*

پيوستن *paiwastan*, (r. *paiwand*), to join, unite, tie. *p.*

پيوسته *paiwasta*, joined; adv. always, continually; m. the year before last. *paiwasta-abrū*, whose eyebrows join above the nose. *p.*

پيوسي पेवसी *pewsī*, f. the milk of a cow some days after calving. *s.*

پيوشني पयोष्णी *payoshnī*, f. a river that flows from the Vindhya mountains. *s.*

پيوكڙ पीवक्कड़ *pīwakkaṛ* or *pewakkaṛ*, m. a tippler, a toper. *h.*

پيوند *paiwand*, m. junction, conjunction, connection; a relative or kindred; a patch; a graft or bud. *paiwand kārī*, f. patching, cobbling. *p.*

پيوندهه पयोनिधि *payo-nidhi*, m. the ocean. *s.*

پيوندي *paiwandī*, engrafted. *paiwandī ber*, m. an engrafted *ber* (*Zizyphus jujuba*). *paiwandī múchheṅ*, f. the mustachios joining the beard. *paiwandī gudṛī*, patched garments. *p.*

پيوورت पयोव्रत *payo-vrat*, m. living upon milk for a month as an expiation; offering of milk to Vishnu. *s.*

پيه *pīh*, f. grease, tallow. *p.*

پيه पिय *piya*, dear, beloved. See *piyā*.

پيهر पीहर *pīhar*, m. kindred, relationship, mother's family. *h.*

پي هم *pai ham*, thickly, close together. *p.*

پيهو पीहू *pīhū*, m. a flea. *h.*

پيا पैया *paiyā*, m. a wheel; an allowance of half an *ānā* on each *rupī* of revenue set apart for the *paṭwārī*, or village accountant. *h.*

پيهي पैहै *paihai* (Braj), aorist of *pāwanauṅ*, to get, acquire. *h.*

پييو पीयू *pīyū*, beloved, dear, m. husband, lover. *s.*

پييوس पेयूस *peyūs* or *pīyūs*,
پييوش पेयूष *peyūsh* or *pīyūsh*, } m. the food of gods, ambrosia, nectar; the milk of a cow during the first seven days after calving. *s.*

پييه पेय *peya*, m. water, milk, drink. *s.*

پيئي पेई *pe,ī* or पेयी *peyī*, f. a small basket, a portmanteau. *h.*

ت

ت *tā* or *te*, the third letter of the Arabic and the fourth of the Persian alphabet. In numeration by *abjad* it stands for 400.

ت त *ta*, the corresponding letter of the Devanāgarī alphabet: it has various odd significations in Hindī, as, a thief; nectar; an outcast or barbarian; the flank; a tail; crossing; a wicked man; a tree. *s.*

ت ति *ti*,
تا ता *tā*, } in the Braj or old Hindī dialect is the inflect. of the third pers. pron. sing. him, her, it: the syllable *ti* also denotes three in a few compounds, as *ti-bārā*, thrice; a house with three doors. *h.*

تا *tā*, to, until, so far as, even to, in order that, to the end that, in such a manner that. *tā bazīst*, while life remains. *tā bakai*, how many, how much, till what time, when, to what length. *tā chand*, how many, by how much, how long. *tā chand bār*, how often, or many times. *tā chunīn*, hitherto, thus far. *tā ḥāl*, till now, yet, hitherto. *tā zandagī*, during life. *tā dami zīst*, while life remains. *tā kujā*, how far. *tāki*, so that, to the end that, till, until, so long, whither. *tā maḳdūr*, to the best of one's power; as much as possible. *tā-ham*, yet, nevertheless. *tā hanoz*, yet, still, hitherto, till now. *p.*

تاب *tāb*, f. power; heat; endurance, brooking; twisting; rage, fury; light, splendour; contortion. *tāb tillī*, f. an induration of the spleen attended with or preceded by fever; *splenitis*, ague-cake. *tāb-dār*, bright, luminous; twisted. *tāb-denā*, a. to twist. *tāb lānā*, a. to be able to bear. *p.*

تابا *tābā*, m. a frying-pan (v. *tāba*). *p.*

تابان *tābān*, resplendent, splendid, glittering. *p.*

تاباني *tābānī*, f. splendour, light. *p.*

تابدان *tāb-dān*, m. a lattice, a skylight; a window of coloured panes of glass: it is generally of carved wooden work, with small variegated panes inserted in the open interstices. *p.*

تابڑتوڑ ताबड़तोड़ *tābaṛ-toṛ*, successively, repeatedly. *h.*

تابستان *tābistān*, m. the hot weather, summer. *p.*

تابستاني *tābistānī*, resembling or appertaining to summer, pleasant as the summer. *p.*

تابش *tābish*, f. heat; brilliancy, splendour. *p.*

تاب‌طاقت *tāb-ṭāḳat*, f. power, ability. *p. a.*

تابع *tābi'*, dependent, subject. *tābi'-dār* (much used in Hindūstān, though ungrammatical), dependant, follower. *tābi'-dārī*, allegiance, obedience, fidelity. *tābi'-k.*, a. to control, to subject. *a.*

تابعون *tābi'ūn*, } m. (pl. of تابع) followers,
تابعين *tābi'-īn*, } attendants; the term is applied *par excellence* to those Musalmān doctors who followed the immediate *aṣḥāb*, or companions of the prophet *Muḥammad*. *a.*

تابناك *tāb-nāk*, hot, passionate; brilliant. *p.*

تابندگي *tābandagī*, f. brilliancy, light. *p.*

تابنده *tābanda*, shining, luminous. *p.*

تابوت *tābūt*, m. a coffin, a bier; the ark of the covenant, presented by God to Adam, and which (according to the *Musalmāns*) contained the portraits of all the prophets. *tābūt-gar*, a coffin-maker. *a.*

تابه *tāba*, m. a frying-pan, a skillet. *p.*

تاپ ताप *tāp*, m. warmth, heat; fever; met. affliction of mind, distress, passion. *tāp-tillī*, f. (same as *tāb-tillī*) induration of the spleen, &c. (under *tāb*). *tāp-ṭhand*, fever and shivering; ague. *s.*

تاپاك *tāpāk*, m. friendship, the anguish of love, solicitude of friendship, affection. *p.*

تاپت तापित *tāpit*, inflamed; distressed, pained. *s.* [does penance, an ascetic. *s.*

تاپس तापस *tāpas*, m. a devotee, one who

تاپك तापक *tāpak*, m. fever, morbid heat; adj. burning, inflaming. *s.* [flaming. *s.*

تاپن तापन *tāpan*, m. the sun; heating, in-

تاپنا तापना *tāpnā*, n. a. to bask in the sun, or a fire, to warm one's self at (or over) a fire, to warm, to heat. *s.*

تاپي तापी *tāpī*, f. name of the *Tāptī* or *Surāt* river; a name of the Jumna river; adj. oppressed by heat, heated. *s.*

تاپي *tāpī*, f. a bricklayer's trowel. *d.*

تاپيه ताप्य *tāpya*, m. a mineral substance, sulphuret of iron, procured from the Tāpī river. *s.*

تات तात *tāt*, m. father; hot, warm, heated. *tāta*, venerable, respectable. *s.*

تاتا ताता *tātā*, m. hot, heating (food). *s.*

تاتار *tātār*, m. a Tartar, the Tartars. *p.*

تات‌پرج तात्पर्ज *tātparj*, } m. object, purpose;
تاتپريه तात्पर्य *tātparya*, } meaning, purport, explanation; the apprehension of an implied wish or thought; need, occasion. *s.* [time. *s.*

تاتكالك तात्कालिक *tātkālik*, of that very

تاتل तातल *tātal*, }
تاتي ताती *tātī*, } hot, warm *s.*

تاتنو तातनौ *tātnau*, } of this, that, him, her,
تاتني तातनी *tātnī*, } it. *h.*

تاتي ताते *tāte* or *tā-teṅ*, from that, thence, thereby. *h.*

تاٹ *ṭāṭ*, m. hemp; tow or flax; sackcloth; a very coarse kind of cloth made of hemp, commonly called "gunny." *d.* [in the ear. *s.*

تاٹنك ताटंक *tāṭank*, m. an ornament worn

تاءثر *ta,aṣṣur*, m. penetration, passing through, impression. *a.*

تاثير *tāṣīr*, f. penetration, passing through; an effect or impression (pl. *tāṣīrāt*, effects, &c.). *a.*

تاج *tāj*, m. a crown, a diadem; a cap; a crest, the comb of a bird; name of a suit in cards; the pack (*ganjīfa*) consists of eight suits (*rang*), each containing twelve circular cards, viz. a king or *mīr*, a *wazīr*, and spots from one to ten: in every suit the *mīr* is the highest card, and the *wazīr* the second: the suits are divided into two classes, I. *Beshbar*, in which, after the *mīr* and *wazīr*, the highest numbers, from 10 to 1, are most powerful; these are, 1. *tāj* (a cap), 2. *zar-i-sufaid* (a silver coin, or the moon), 3. *shamsher* (a scimitar), 4. *ghulām* (a slave or boy). II. *Kambar*, in which the lowest numbers from 1 to 10 are most powerful: these are, 1. *ḳimāsh* (representing a loaf of bread), 2. *barāt* (an oblong inscribed with characters representing a warrant or assignment), 3. *chang* (a harp), 4. *zar-i-surkh* (gold coin, or the sun); the *mīr* of every suit is seated on a throne under a canopy, and the *wazīr* on horseback; except that, of *zar-i-surkh*, the *mīr* represents the sun, mounted on a tiger, and the *wazīr* also rides a tiger; of *ghulām*, the *mīr* rides on an elephant and the *wazīr* on a bullock; and of *chang*, the *wazīr* is mounted on a camel. *p.*

تاج‌بخش *tāj-bakhsh*, a great king, an emperor, one who gives away crowns. *p.* [crown. *p.*

تاجدار *tāj-dār*, m. a king, one who wears a

تاجداري *tāj-dārī*, f. royalty, sovereignty. *p.*

تاج‌خروس *tāj-i-kharos*, m. the cock's-comb flower (*Amaranthus*, or *Celosia*). *p.*

تاجر *tājir*, a merchant, a trader. *a*

تاجور *tāj-war*, m. a prince, a king. *p.*

تاجوري *tāj-warī*, f. royalty, sovereignty. *p.*

تاخ *tākh*, m. a veil; firewood; darkness. *p.*

تاخت *tākht*, f. assault, attack, incursion, invasion. *tākht-k.*, a. to assault. *p.*

تاخت‌تاراج *tākht-tārāj* or *tākht o tārāj*, m. assault and plunder, depredation, devastation. *tākht o tārāj-k.*, a. to ruin, depopulate. *p.*

تاختن *tākhtan*, to assault, to rush upon; to invade, to plunder; to gallop or run fast. *p.*

تاءخر *ta,akhkhur*, m. delay; retarded, postponed, following. *a.*

تاخير *tākhīr*, f. delay, procrastination, impediment. *tākhīr-k.*, a. to delay, to postpone. *a.*

تاداتميه तादात्म्य *tādātmya*, m. likeness, similarity. *s.* [or it, &c. *s.*

تادرشيه तादृश्य *tādrishya*, such like, like him

تاديب *tādīb*, f. correction, chastisement, amendment, erudition; (in law) a notice or summons. *tādīb-k.*, a. to instruct, to correct. *a.*

تار *tār*, m. a thread; a wire, the string of a musical instrument; a note in music; dark, obscure, also darkness, obscurity. *tār-bāndhnā*, to continue or repeat an action without interruption. *tār ṭuṭnā*, n. to be disjointed, to be separated. *tāri 'ankabūt*, spider's web, cobweb. *tār-kash*, m. a wire-drawer. *tār-kashī-k.*, a. to draw wires. *p.*

تار तारि *tāri*, f. a key, clasping of the hands. *s.*

تارا तारा *tārā*, f. and m. a star; the apple of the eye; n. pr. the name of the wife of *Rājā Bali*. *tārā-path* or *tārā-manḍal*, m. the firmament, the starry sphere. *tāre-ginnā*, a. to count the stars, *i.e.* to get no sleep. *s.*

تاراج *tārāj*, m. plunder, devastation. *tārāj*, *k.*, to devastate, lay waste, spoil. *p.*

تارپتار तारपतार *tār-patār*, dispersed, &c. *h.*

تارتاربولنا *tār-tār bolnā*, to speak in detail, or circumstantially. *d.*

تارتميه तारतम्य *tārtamya*, m. distinction, discrimination. *s.*

تارتوڑ तारतोड़ m. a kind of sewing, or needle-work, open work, pulling out some threads, &c. *h.*

تارخ *tārakh*, the root of the tongue, the palate. *tārakh ko jīb naiṅ lagānā*, to prattle much. *d.*

تارك तारक *tārak*, m. a protector, a preserver. *s.*

تارك *tārik*, a deserter. *tāriku-d-dunyā*, abandoning the world, abstinent, sober, chaste; m. an anchorite, a hermit. *a.*

تارك *tārak*, m. the crown of the head; a hill, heap, head, top, summit. *p.*

تاركا तारिका *tārikā*, f. the apple of the eye, a star. *s.*

تاركك तार्किक *tārkik*, m. a philosopher, a logician, a sophist. *tārkikā*, belonging to the science of reasoning, logical. *s.*

تارن तारण *tāran*, m. a raft, a float; the act of freeing; salvation, deliverance; one that exempts, sets free, or delivers. *tāran-taran*, the saviour and the saved (v. *taran*). *s.*

تارنا तारणा or तारना *tārnā*, a. to free, to rid, to exempt from further transmigration, to absolve, to save. *s.*

تارني तारिणी *tārinī*, f. a goddess peculiar to the Jains; a name of Durgā; m. a deliverer. *s.*

تارو तारू *tārū*, m. the palate. *s.*

تاري *tārī*, f. darkness, obscurity. *p.*

تاري तारी *tārī*, f. the clapping of hands; a key; abstraction, absence of mind, absorption in thought or devotion. *s.*

تاري توڑنا *tāre toṛnā*, to act deceitfully. *d.*

تاريخ *tārīkh*, f. date, era; annals, history. *tārīkh-ul-hijrat*, the era of the *hijra*. *tārīkh-wār*, periodically, according to dates; at stated times or dates. *a.*

تاريك *tārīk*, dark; obscure. *tārīk-chashm*, blind, dim-sighted. *p.*

تاريكي *tārīkī*, f. darkness, obscurity. *p.*

تاڑ ताड़ *tāṛ*, m. the palmyra, or "toddy-tree." *tāṛ ban*, a grove or "tope" of palmyra trees. The Indian-English word "tope" is originally Tamul. Dr. Gilchrist errs in stating that it does not belong to any Indian language.—(Binning). *tāṛ-patra* (also *tāla-patra*), the palm-leaf prepared for writing on; a document so written. (*Borassus flabelliformis*). *tāṛ-phal* the gelatinous pulp of the palmyra. *s.*

تاڑ ताड़ *tāṛ*, f. understanding. *tāṛ-bāz*, intelligent, quick of apprehension. *tāṛ-bāzī*, quickness of apprehension. *h. p.*

تاڑا *tāṛā*, m. a wink, &c. (v. *ghamza*). *d.*

تاڑك ताड़क *tāṛak*, m. a reprover, punisher. *s.*

تاڑن ताड़न *tāṛan*, } m. beating, whipping;
تاڑنا ताड़ना *tāṛanā*, } admonition, reproof, penalty, punishment. *tāṛanā-k.*, a. to reprove, punish, &c. *s.*

تاڑنا ताड़ना *tāṛnā* (or *tāṛ-jānā*), a. to understand, conceive, to comprehend to guess. *h.*

تاڑنك ताड़ङ्क *tāṛank*, m. an ornament worn in the ear. *s.*

تاڑنيه ताड़नीय *tāṛnīya*, reprovable, worthy of punishment. *s.*

تاڑي ताड़ी *tāṛī*, f. the juice of the palmyra-tree, vulg. *toddy*. *tāṛī-wālā*, a man who climbs palmyra-trees, and extracts the juice therefrom. *s.*

تاڑي ताड़ी *tāṛī*, f. hilt of a dagger. *h.*

تاز *tāz* (r. of *tākhtan*), running, race, assault. *tāz o tag*, toil and labour. *p.*

تازگي *tāzagī*, f. freshness, plumpness, fatness, tenderness, greenness; pleasure. *p.*

تازه *tāza*, fresh; fat; young, green, tender, raw; happy, pleased. *tāza-k.*, a. to renew, to refresh, to re-create. *tāza-kār*, one who renews. *tāza-kārī*, act of renewal. *tāza-honā*, n. to be in good case, to increase, to flourish. *tāza-ba-tāza*, fresh and blooming. *tāza-dam*, m. good spirits, hilarity, cheerfulness. *tāza-wārid*, new-comer, or, as nicknamed in India, "a griffin." *p.*

تازي *tāzī*, Arabian; the Arabic language; Arabian (horse). *tāzī kuttā*, a greyhound. *tāzī khāna*, dog-kennel. *p.*

تازيانه *tāziyāna*, m. a whip, a scourge; *tāziyāna-jaṛnā*, *-lagānā*, or *-mārnā*, a. to apply the whip, to scourge. *p.*

تازيدن *tāzīdan*, to run, to rush upon. *p.*

تازيك *tāzīk*, one who is ignorant of Persian, or one who speaks it with an Arabian accent and idiom; a colt of a mixed breed, or an Arabian colt reared in another country. *p.*

تاس तास *tās*, m. the cards, a game at cards; (for *tāsh*, q.v.), brocade, cloth of gold. *h.* "The word *tās* (Persian *tāj*) is applied to the Indian playing-cards, in contradistinction to *ganjifa*, the European pack. The Indian pack contains eight suits, each suit consisting, of a king, a *wazīr* or minister, and ten cards having various figures represented on them, from one to ten in number."—(Binning.) [&c. *h.*

تاسو तासु *tāsu* (Braj.), him, her, it, or of him,

تاسف *ta,assuf*, m. brooding over affliction, pining, lamenting, grief, regret. *a.*

تاسفا *ta,assufan*, with grief, or regret. *a.*

تاسکو तासुकौ *tāsu-kau*, of him, her, it. *h.*

تاس‌ناس *tās-nās*, destruction, (v. *satyānās*). *d.*

تاش ताश़ *tāsh*, m. cloth of gold, brocade, tinsel, gold foil. *h.*

تاغ *tāgh*, m. the poplar; the elm; tamarisk; a pomegranate; an ensign-staff. *h.*

تاغي *tāghī*, (properly طاغي) rebellious. *a.*

تافتن *tāftan*, to shine; to twist or spin; to turn away the face. *p.*

تافته *tāfta*, m. a kind of silk, taffeta; a colour in pigeons and horses, glossy cream-colour. *p.*

تاقي *tāḳī*, defective (horse), having the eyes of two different colours; f. a kind of hat. *t.*

تاک ताक *tāk*, f. a look, a glance; an aim, the act of aiming, point (of a dog). *tāk bāndhnā*, a. to covet, to point as a dog. *tāk-rahnā*, n. to aspire. *s.*

تاک *tāk*, f. a vine, a creeper; grasses. *p.*

تاکاتاکي ताकाताकी *tākā-tākī*, f. mutual staring. *s.*

تاک‌باک ताकबाक *tāk-bāk*, f. nick of time. *h.*

تاکنا ताकना *tāknā*, a. to stare at, to aim, to peep, to see, to spy, to view, to look for. *s.*

تاکيد *tākīd*, f. confirmation; superintendence; ascertaining, injunction. *tākīd-k.*, a. to enjoin strictly, to urge, to press. *s.*

تاکيدي *tākīdī*, emphatic (in grammar). *a.*

تاگ ताग *tāg*, } m. a thread. *tāg-toṛ*, m.
تاگا तागा *tāgā*, } lace. *h.*

تاگنا तागना *tāgnā*, a. to thread. *h.*

تال ताल *tāl*, m. a pond; chime, time in music; slapping the hands together or against the arms previous to fighting; the name of a musical instrument of bell-metal or brass (a kind of cymbal), played with a stick; name of a fruit and tree, the palm-tree (*Borassus flabelliformis*). *tāl-be-tāl*, out of tune. *tāl denā*, to chime, to slap the hands before fighting. *tāl mārnā* or *-ṭhoknā*, a. to strike the hand against the arms preparatory to wrestling. *s.*

تالا ताला *tālā*, m. a lock of a door; a lid of a vessel &c. *s.*

تالاب *tālāb*, } m. an artificial pond, a reservoir
تالاو *tālāw*, } of water, a tank. *p.*

تالاکهيا तालाख्या *tālākhyā*, f. a perfume. *s.*

تالپتر तालपत्र *tāl-patra*, m. a hollow cylinder of gold worn in the ear. *s.*

تالپرني तालपर्णी *tāl-parnī*, f. a sort of anise (*Anethum panmorium*). *s.*

تالپشپک तालपुष्पक *tāl-pushpak*, m. a medicinal application to the eyes. *s.*

تالشپتري *tālish patrī*, f. name of a restringent plant; a fragrant stomachic (*Flacourtia cataphracta*).

تالک तालक *tālak*, m. a bolt, a latch. *s.*

تالم *ta,allum*, m. melancholy, grief, torment. *a.*

تال‌مکهانا तालमखाना *tāl-makhānā*, m. the name of a medicinal herb (*Barleria longifolia*). *h.*

تالمولي तालमूली *tāl-mūlī*, f. a plant (*Curculigo orchioides*). *s.*

تالو तालू *tālū*, m. the palate, the slit in the roof of the mouth; a disorder in horses, the lampreys. *s.*

تالورنت तालवृन्त *tāl-vṛint*, m. a fan. *s.*

تالي ताली *tālī*, f. a key; clapping of the hands; a species of the mountain palm (*Corypha taliera*); a plant (*Flacourtia cataphracta*). *tālī ek hāth se bajnī* is used to express an impossibility. *tālī bajānā*, a. to clap the hands, not in token of approbation, but censure and ridicule, to hoot, to clap the hands in ridicule of any one. *tālī mārnā*, a. to hoot, to damn (in a theatrical sense); also to applaud. *s.*

تاليف *tālīf*, f. composition, compiling; connecting; reconciling or joining in friendship. *a.*

تاليقه *tālīḳa*, m. a list, catalogue, inventory (corrup. of *ta'līḳā*, q.v.). *a.*

تام *tāmm*, perfect, entire, complete, full. *a.*

تاما तामा *tāmā*, } m. copper. *s.*
تامبا ताम्बा *tāmbā*, }

تامبرا ताम्रा *tāmbrā*, m. a copper colour (in pigeons); a false stone resembling a ruby. *s.*

تامبول ताम्बूल *tambūl*, m. betel-leaf, the areca nut. *s.*

تامبول‌راگ ताम्बूलराग *tāmbūl-rāg*, m. a kind of pulse (*Ervum lens*). *s.*

تامبول‌ولي ताम्बूलवल्ली *tāmbūl-wallī*, f. a small plant bearing a pungent leaf (*Piper betel*), which, with the areca nut, caustic lime, or chunām, catechu, &c. form the *pān* or betel of the Asiatics. *s.*

تامبولي ताम्बूली *tāmbūlī*, f. betel (*Piper betel*) or its leaf; m. the *pān* bearer; a servant who prepares and furnishes the *pān*. *s.*

تام‌چيني तामचीनी *tām chīnī*, f. enamelled copper. *s.*

تامر ताम्र *tāmra*, m. copper; a coppery red; a dark red kind of sandal wood. *tāmra-paṭṭ*, m. a copper-plate, such as Hindū grants of land &c. are frequently engraved upon. *tāmra-parnī*, f. a river in Dekhan, and the district in its vicinity. *tāmra-pushp*, m. a kind of ebony (*Bauhinia variegata*); a plant (*Kempferia rotunda*). *tāmra-pushpā*, f. a trumpet flower (*Bignonia suaveolens*). *tāmra-pushpī*, f. *Lythrum fruticosum*. *tāmra-phal*, m. *Alangium hexapetalum*. *tāmra-sār*, m. a red kind of sandal (*Pterospermum santolinum*). *tāmra-kār*, m. a coppersmith. *tāmra-karnī*, f. the female elephant of the western quarter. *tāmra-garbha*, m. blue vitriol, or sulphate of copper. *tāmra-vṛiksha*, m. a sort of sandal wood. *tāmra-varnī*, f. the blossom of sesamum. *tāmra-wallī*, f. Bengal madder (*Rubia manjith*). *tāmra-vīj*, m. a kind of vetch. *s.*

تامراک ताम्राक *tāmrāku*, m. one of the eighteen divisions of the known continent. *s.*

تامرس तामरस *tāmras*, m. a lotus (*Nymphæa nelumbo*); copper; gold. *s.*

تامرك ताम्रिका *tāmrik*, m. a coppersmith, a brazier. *s.*

تامركا ताम्रिका *tāmrikā*, } f. a copper vessel for
تامري ताम्री *tāmrī*, } marking time, a copper cup of prescribed capacity and perforated by a small hole at the bottom, answering the purpose of an hour glass: it is put into a vessel of water, the water gradually filling it, and the sinking of the cup marks the time that has elapsed. *s.*

تامڑا तामड़ा *tāmṛā*, m. a gem of inferior value, of a copper colour. *s.*

تامس तामस *tāmas*, m. darkness, illusion, irascibility; adj. partaking of or influenced by the principle of inertness, ignorance, or mental darkness; inert, stupid, ignorant. *s.* [dark. *s.*

تامسي तामसी *tāmsī*, irascible, vindictive,

تامل *ta,ammul*, meditation, reflection; purpose. *ta,ammul-k.*, a. to collect one's self; to consider, to reflect. *a.*

تامليپت तामलिप्त *tām-lipt*, f. a district in the south of Bengal, Tamluk. *s.*

تاملكي तामलकी *tāmalkī*, f. a plant (*Flacourtia cataphracta*). *s.* [of copper. *s.*

تاميسور तामेश्वर *tāmeswar*, m. calx or scoriæ

تان तान *tān*, *m.* f. a note in music, tone; stretching, tension, knitting (the eye-brows). *tān tornā*, a. to crack a joke; to drop a word which shall excite quarrelling or induce conversation, to animadvert; to strike up a tune. *s.*

تان *tān*, m. a species of vervain. *d.*

تانا ताना *tānā*, m. the warp, the threads that are extended lengthwise upon a loom. *tānā-bānā-k.*, a. to fidget, to dance attendance. *tāne tānnā*, to wander here and there without profit. *s.*

تانا ताना *tānā* (for *tāwnā*), a. to heat, assay, twist. *s.* [nate. *a.*

تاناتريز *tānā tarez* (for طعن‌تعريز), unfortu-

تانبا तांबा *tāmbā* (in Dakh. *tāmbaṭ*) m. copper. *tāmbaṭ-gar*, a worker in copper, brass, &c., a plumber. *s. d.* [the chase. *d.*

تانبا *tāmbā*, food for a falcon or bird of

تانبڑا तांबड़ा *tāmbṛā*, m. a copper-colour (in pigeons); a false stone resembling a ruby. *s.*

تانبيل *tāmbel*, a tortoise, turtle. *d.*

تانت तांत *tānt*, m. f. catgut, sinew, the string of a musical instrument. *tānt bājī aur rāg būjhā*, he understood from the first word. *tānt bāndhnā*, to put to silence an idle talker. *s.*

تانت तांत *tānt*, m. a loom, a weaving apparatus; also thread, fibre, &c. *h.*

تانتا तांता *tāntā*, m. a string (of camels, horses, &c.), a drove; train, series. *s.*

تانترك तान्त्रिक *tāntrik*, m. a scholar; a follower of the doctrine taught by the Tantras. *s.*

تانتي तांती *tāntī*, m. a weaver. *s.*

تانڈا *tānḍā*, m. a caravan of merchandise carried on bullocks, mules, camels, &c.; a large body of travellers or traders travelling together for mutual security. *d.*

تانڈو ताण्डव *tānḍav*, m. dancing, especially with violent gesticulation, and particularly applied to the frantic dancing of the god *Shiva* and his votaries. *s.*

تانس *ta,annus*, m. acquaintance. *a.*

تانگا तांगा *tāngā*, m. a small two-wheeled car (without covering, and on which one person only can sit): (in Dakh.) it means the rostrum or forepart of a Hindū car, to which the bullocks are yoked. *tāngā-sawār*, one who rides on a *tāngā*. *h.*

تانگل *tāngal*, m. a small tank or pond. *d.*

تاننا तानना *tānnā*, a. to extend, to stretch, to expand, to pull; to knit (the eye-brows). *tambū-tānnā*, to pitch tents. *s.* [elder brother. *h.*

تانو تांऊ *tān,ū*, m. a paternal uncle, father's

تاني तानी *tānī*, f. the warp of cloth (v. *tānā*). the price paid for weaving. *s.*

تاني *ta,annī*, f. delay, procrastination. *a.*

تانيث *tānīs*, f. the feminine gender. *a.*

تاو ताव *tāw*, m. heat; passion, rage; strength, power; splendour, dignity; twist, coil, contortion. *tāw denā*, a. to twist; to stroke the whiskers; to beat (as iron). *tāw-khānā* or *tāw pech khānā*, n. to be heated, to be angry. *p.* or *s.* [assay; speed. *h.*

تاو ताव *tāw*, m. a sheet of paper: proof, trial,

تاو ताऊ *tā,ū*, m. a paternal uncle, father's elder brother. *h.*

تاوان *tāwān*, m. retaliation, recompense; debt; fine, mulct; loan. *tāwān* is used in opposition to *ḳiṣāṣ*, and means the price paid for blood. *tāwān bāndhnā* or *lenā*, a. to fine, to mulct. *tāwān lagānā*, a to amerce. *p.* [loan. *p.*

تاواني *tāwānī*, f. compensation; debt; fine;

تاوت तावत् *tāwat*, so much, so far, so many, until, the correlative to *yāwat*. *s.*

تاونا तावना *tāwnā*, a. to heat, to raise heat by blowing with a bellows; to prove, to assay; to twist. *s.*

تاويل *tāwīl*, f. explanation, elucidation, interpretation, paraphrase. *a.* [plexity. *p.*

تاه *tāh*, f. a plait, fold, ply, multiplicity, per-

تاهِ ताहि *tāhi*, pron. to him, her, it, or that. *h.*

تاهري ताहिरी *tāhirī*, f. a kind of dish, viz. rice boiled with *baṛī*, which consists of pulse (*Phaseolus radiatus*) ground in a wet state and mixed with ginger, pepper, &c., and dried in small lumps. *h.*

تاهل *ta,ahhul*, m. marrying, establishing a family. *a.*

تائي ताई *tā,ī*, f. an aunt, paternal uncle's wife, father's elder brother's wife; an earthen frying-pot. *h.*

تايا ताया *tāyā*, m. a father's eldest brother. *h.*

تائب *tā,ib*, repenting, penitent. *a.*

تائت ताइत *tā,it*, m. an amulet, a charm. *h.*

تائيد *tā,īd*, f. aid, assistance; corroboration; a written voucher in corroboration of a claim. *tā,īd-nawīs*, an assistant clerk. *a.*

تائيدات *tā,īdāt* (pl. of تائيد), helps, aids, [&c. *a.*

تائيرا *tā,erā*, born of a father's elder brother. *tā,erā bhā,ī*, m. or *tā,erī bahin*, f. a cousin. *d.*

تب तब *tab*, then, at that time; afterwards. *tab-tak*, *tab-torī*, *tab-ta,īṅ*, or *tab-lag*, till then, up to that time. *s.*

تبار *tabār*, m. people, nation; a tribe, family. *shahriyārī 'ālī tabār*, a monarch of an illustrious house. *p.*

تبارا तिबारा *tibārā*, thrice, or three times; m. a hall or room with three doors. *s.*

تبارك *tabāruk*, blessing, being blessed. *tabāraka*, used in Arabic phrases, as *allāhu tabāraka wa ta'ālā*, God, he is, or may he be, blessed and exalted. *a.*

تباره *tibāra*, thrice, three times (v. *tibārā*). *s.*

تباه *tabāh*, bad, wicked, depraved, abject, spoiled, ruined, wretched. *tabāh-ḥāl*, ruined. *p.*

تباهي *tabāhī*, f. wickedness, depravity, ruin, wreck, perdition. *tabāhī khānī*, a. to be afflicted. *tabāhī-zada*, ruined, afflicted, distressed. *p.*

تباين *tabāyun*, difference, contradiction, inconsistency; (in arithm.) incommensurability. *a.*

تبحر *tabaḥḥur*, m. profound learning. *a.*

تبختر *tabakhtur*, walking very stately. *a.*

تبدل *tabaddul*, m. } change, alteration, substitution; difference,
تبديل *tabdīl*, f. } transposition. *tabdīli makān*, migration. *a.*

تبر *tabar*, m. a hatchet, an axe. *tabar-bardār*, an axe-bearer, a woodcutter. *tabar-zan*, a woodcutter, a hatchet-man. *tabar zīn*, m. a horseman's battle-axe. *p.*

تبرع *tabarru'*, doing any thing voluntarily; giving gratuitously. *a.*

تبرك *tabarruk*, m. benediction, congratulation; a portion of presents (or what is left of food presented to great men, &c.), given to their dependants, sacred relics. *tabarrukan*, by way of blessing. The word is employed idiomatically in the sense of making use of, or tasting any thing (used in a respectful sense); for example: after the arrival of a visitor, the *ḥuḳḳā* is introduced: the host offers it to his guest, who will probably say, *awwal āp tabarruk farmāiye*, "Do you, Sir, first make use of it." (Binning.) *a.*

تبرگون *tabar-gūn*, hollow-backed (a horse). *p.*

تبريد *tabrīd*, f. act of cooling, refreshing. *a.*

تبريز *tabrīz*, the city of Tabrīz or Tauriz, in Persia. *p.*

تبريزي *tabrīzī*, belonging to Tabrīz. *Shams tabrīzī*, name of a distinguished saint or *ṣūfī*. *p.*

تبسم *tabassum*, m. a smile. *a.*

تبصر *tabaṣṣur*, m. sight, distinct perception, attentive consideration. *a.* [subjection. *a.*

تبعيت *tab'iyat*, f. obedience, dependence,

تبلق *tablaḳ*, a bundle or file of papers. *a.*

تبليس *tablīs*, playing the devil. *a.*

تبنچه *tabancha*, m. a pistol. *tabancha mārnā*, a. to shoot with or fire a pistol. *t.*

تبني *tabannī*, f. adoption (of a son, &c.). *a.*

تبه *tabah* (for *tabāh*, q. v.), bad, wicked, &c. *p.*

تبهي तबही *tab-hī*, at that very time. *tabhī-to*, then, indeed. *tab-hī-se*, thence, thenceforth. *s.*

تبي तबै *tabai* (in Dakh. *tabīch*), exactly then. *h.*

تبيعت *tabī'at*, f. following, dependence. *a.*

تپ तप *tap*, f. heat, warmth; m. the hot season, summer; prayer, adoration, devotion, penance. *s.*

تپ *tap*, f. a fever. *tap utarnā*, n. to go off (a fever). *tap chaṛhnā*, n. to come on (a fever). *tapi-diḳḳ*, f. a hectic fever. *tapi ghib*, f. a tertian fever. *tap-kā mūt jānā*, n. the breaking out of an eruption on the lips after a fever. *tapi larza*, m. an ague. *tapi muḥriḳ*, m. an ardent or burning fever. *tapi naubat*, f. intermittent fever. *tap-khāla* or *tap-uchhlī*, f. pimples on the face; cutaneous eruption. *p.* [*jogī*. *s.*

تپا तपा *tapā*, m. a worshipper, an ascetic, a

تپا तप्पा *tappā*, m. division, district, parish. *h.*

تپاري तिपारी *tipārī*, f. a fruit, commonly called Cape gooseberry or Brazil cherry. *h.*

تپاس तपास *tapās*, f. sunshine, the sunbeams; toil, labour. *s.*

تپاك *tapāk*, m. affection, esteem, regard, love, zeal, ardour; consternation, affliction. *p.*

تپان *tapān*, palpitating, growing hot. *p.*

تپانا तपाना *tapānā*, a. to pour a libation. *h.*

تپانا तपाना *tapānā*, a. to heat, to warm, to make another person warm himself at the fire, or in the sun. *s.*

تپانا तुपाना *tupānā* or *topānā*, a. to have buried, to cause to cover. *h.*

تپت तप्त *tapta* or तपत *tapat*, hot, warm, fervent, burning with heat, pain, or sorrow; *tapti* or *tapat*, f. heat. *tapta-krichchhra*, m. a sort of penance, drinking hot water, milk, or ghī, for three days. *s.*

تپخاله *tap-khāla*, m. breaking out on the lips after a fever, the thrush. *p.*

تپرهاءو तपरिहाउ *taparihā,ū*, land cultivated in small patches among the uncultivated portions of an estate. *h.* [an acclivity. *h.*

تپري तपरी *taprī*, f. a mound, a small height,

تپس तपस् *tapas*, m. religious austerity, penance, self-denial; the region inhabited by devotees after death; virtue, duty: thus the *tapas* of a Brāhman is sacred learning, of a *Kshatriya*, the protection of subjects, &c. *s.*

تپسون तपस्विन् *tapaswin*, } m. a devotee, a
تپسوي तपस्वी *tapaswī*, } *jogī*. *s.*

تپسوني *tapaswinī*, f. a female devotee. *s.*

تپسي तपसी *tapasī* or तपस्सी *tapassī*, m. devotee, performer of austere devotion; adj. devout, ascetic. *tapasī machhlī*, f. the mango-fish (*Polynemus paradiseus*). *s.*

تپسيا तपस्या *tapasyā*, f. austere devotion, prayer, penance, mortification of self. *s.*

تپسيه तपस्य *tapasya*, m. the month Phālgun. *s.*

تپش *tapish*, f. affliction; heat, warmth. *p.*

تپشي *tapshī* (v. *tapasī*), devotee, &c. *s.*

تپشيا *tapashyā* (v. *tapasyā*), austerity, &c. *s.*

تپك *tapak*, m. favour, friendship; a sledge-hammer. *p.* [musket. *t.*

تپك तुपक *tupak*, f. (for *topak*, q. v.), a

تپكچي *tapakchī*, m. an officer formerly employed in the management of revenue affairs. The duties of this functionary are fully described in the Ayeen Akbery. The etymology of the word seems to be doubtful.

تپكنا तपकना *tapaknā*, n. to throb, to palpitate. *tapaknā phoṛe kā*, the throbbing of a phlegmon or boil when coming to suppuration. *h.*

تپن तपन *tapan*, f. heat, glow, fervour, warmth; m. the sun; a division of hell; the hot season; mental distress, grief. *s.*

تپنا तपना *tapnā*, n. to be glorified; to glow, to frisk about; to burn with pain or grief. *s.*

تپني तपनी *tapnī*, f. the Godavarī river. *s.*

تپودهن तपोधन *tapodhan*, m. a devotee, an ascetic. *s.* [India, or holy land. *s.*

تپووٹ तपोवट *tapowaṭ*, m. a part of central

تپه तपः *tapa*, m. a division of land smaller than a *pargana*. *h.*

تپي तपी *tapī*, m. a devotee, a worshipper. *s.*

تپيدن *tapīdan*, to palpitate, tremble, &c.; (as a sub.) agitation, &c. *tapīdan-wār*, in a troubled condition. *p.* [at that time. *s.*

تت तत् *tat*, that, used in comp. as *tat-kāl*,

تت तत *tat* or तत्त *tatt*, m. an element, principle (see *tatwa*). *s.*

تت तित *tit*, there, thither, that way. *s.*

تتا तत्ता *tattā*, hot, warm, zealous, wrathful. *s.*

تتار *tatār*, m. (the same as *tātār*) a Tartar. *p.*

تتار ततार *tatār*, f. embrocation, pouring of warm water on a diseased part. *h.*

تتارنا तातारना *tatārnā*, a. to embrocate. *h.*

تتال *tittāl*, artful, deceitful; a knave or cheat. *tittālī*, deceitfulness. *d.*

تتانا तताना *tatānā*, a. to warm, heat. *s.*

تتبع *tatabbu'*, m. imitation; continuation. *tatabbu'-k.*, to search diligently, to explore, to examine; to follow, to imitate. *a.* [gent, adept. *s.*

تتپر तत्पर *tatpar*, engaged, addicted to, dili-

تت چهن तत्क्षण *tat-chhan* (for *tat-kshaṇ*), at that time, then. *s.*

تتر तत्र *tatra*, there, therein, in that case. *s.*

تتر तित्तिरि *tittiri* or *tittir*, m. the francoline partridge; the name of a *Muni*, one of the early teachers of the black Yajur-veda; the Yajur-veda. *s.*

تترانا तुतराना *tutrānā*, n. to lisp, to speak imperfectly as a child. *h.* [*bittar*, dispersed. *h.*

تتربتر तितरबितर *titar-bitar* or तित्तरबित्तर *tittar-*

تتربهوت तत्रभवत *tatra-bhawat*, venerable, reverend. *s.*

تتري ततरी *tatrī*, f. a playful or wanton girl. *h.*

تتري *tatarī* (for *tātārī*), of or relating to Tartary. *p.*

تتك *tutak*, the deck of a ship. *d.*

تتكال तत्काल *tat-kāl*, at that time, then; m. present, time being. *tat-kāla-dhī*, m. a man wise for the time being, having presence of mind. *s.*

تتكش तितिक्षु *titikshu*, } patient, re-
تتكشت तितिक्षित *titikshit*, } signed. *s.*

تتكشا तितिक्षा *titikshā*, f. patience, resignation, endurance. *s.*

تتكشن तत्क्षण *tat-kshan*, at that time, instantly; m. time being. *s.*

تتل तितिल *titil*, m. one of the seven *karans* or astronomical periods; a sweetmeat made of sesamum ground and baked with sugar. *s.*

تتلانا तुतलाना *tutlānā*, n. to lisp, to speak imperfectly as a child. *h.*

تتلي *titlī*, f. (for *tītrī*) a butterfly. *h.*

تتمبا तितिम्बा *titimbā*, m. obstacle, impediment, stratagem. *h.*

تتمه *tatimma*, m. an appendix, supplement, continuation, remainder, balance. *a.*

تتميم *tatmīm*, f. consummation, completion. *a.*

تتنا तितना *titnā*, m. } so many, that much or
تتني तितनी *titnī*, f. } many. *titne meṅ*, in so much time. *s.*

تتو तत्व *tatwa* or तत्त्व *tattwa*, m. truth, reality, primary principle, essence; the real nature of the soul considered as one with the divine spirit; mind, intellect; a first principle, an axiom; slow time in music; a musical instrument. *s.*

تتوگيان तत्वज्ञान *tatwa-gyān*, one who is inspired, divine; m. knowledge of divine truth. *s.*

تته तिथ *tith* or तिथि *tithi*, f. a lunar day. *s.*

تته तथ *tath*, true, right, perfect. *s.*

تته तुत्थ *tutth*, m. a collyrium extracted from the *amomum xanthorhiza*; blue vitriol, sulphate of copper, applied to the eyes. *s.*

تتها तथा *tathā*, f. power, ability, might. *h.*

تتها तथा *tathā*, so, thus, and, thence, in that manner. *s.*

تتهاپ तथापि *tathāpi*, then even, nevertheless. *s.*

تتهاست तथास्तु *tathāstu*, be it so, yes. *s.*

تتهاگت तथागत *tathāgat*, m. a *Jain* or *Buddha*, a divine teacher. *s.*

تتهانجن तुत्थाञ्जन *tutthānjan*, m. blue vitriol [applied to the eyes. *s.*

تتهرا ततहरा *tutahrā*, m. } a vessel for warm-
تتهري ततहरी *tatahrī*, f. } ing water, a kettle. *h.*

تتهکشي तिथिक्षय *tithi-kshay*, m. day of new moon. *s.*

تتئي तुतई *tuta,ī*, f. a vessel with a spout *h.*

تٹ तट *taṭ*, m. bank of a river, shore, a field. *s.*

تٹ *taṭ*, fortifications of a city; also the environs or outskirts of a town. *d.*

تٹا *taṭṭā*, m. a screen; vulg. *tattah*. *d.*

تٹاپا *tuṭāpā*, m. helplessness, inability. *d.*

تٹستهه तटस्थ *taṭastha*, m. an indifferent person, one neither a friend nor a foe. *s.*

تٹتانا *taṭ-taṭānā*, a. to pain or vex greatly. *d.*

تٹکارنا *tiṭkārnā*, a. to urge on a horse by uttering any sound. *d.*

تٹنا *tuṭnā* (for *ṭūṭnā*), to be broken, to burst. *d.*

تٹو *taṭṭū*, } m. a pony, a sorry horse of a
تٹوا *taṭṭū,ā*, } small kind. *d.*

تٹواني *taṭwānī*, f. a female or mare pony. *d.*

تٹولنا *taṭolnā*, m. to feel (with the hand), to grope, touch. *d.*

تٹهه *taṭh* or *tuṭh*, the crash made by the breaking of wood. *d.*

تثليث *taṣlīṣ*, f. trinity; dividing into three parts; trine (the aspect of the planets). *a.*

تثنيه *taṣniya*, m. dual (number). *a.*

تج तज *taj*, f. the bay tree, or its bark (*Laurus cassia*); (as a verbal root), abandoning, forsaking. *s.*

تجار *tujjār*, m. a merchant, (pl. of تاجر properly, "merchants," but generally used as a singular noun in Hindūstānī). *a.*

تجارت *tijārat*, f. trade, commerce. *a.*

تجاري तिजारी *tijārī*, f. a tertain fever or ague. *s.*

تجاسر *tajāsur*, boldness, intrepidity. *a.*

تجاوز *tajāwuz*, m. diversity, departing or deviating, offending. *tajāwuz-k.*, a. to err, to deviate, to stray. *a.*

تجاهل *tajāhul*, m. pretending ignorance, connivance, apathy, indifference. *a.*

تجدد *tajaddud*, m. } renovation, renewal. *a.*
تجديد *tajdīd*, f. }

تجربت *tajribat*, } m. experiment, trial, proof,
تجربه *tajriba*, } experience, assay, probation. *tajriba-kār*, expert, conversant in. *tajriba-kārī*, f. experience. *a.*

تجرد *tajarrud*, m. solitude; celibacy; living in solitude. *a.*

تجري तिजरी *tijarī*, f. a tertian fever or ague. *s.*

تجريد *tajrīd*, f. solitude, celibacy, separation; (properly, rendering solitary). *a.*

تجزي *tajazzī*, f. separating into small pieces, analysis. *a.*

تجسس *tajassus*, m. spying, exploring, search, inquiry, curiosity, inquisitiveness, espionage. *tajassus-k.*, a. to pry into, to search diligently. *a.*

تجلجل *tajaljul*, commotion, sinking into the earth. *a.*

تجلي *tajallī*, f. splendour, brilliancy, lustre, clearness; pl. *tajalliyāt*, lustres, illuminations. *a.*

تجمل *tajammul*, m. dignity, retinue. *a.*

تجنا तजना *tajnā*, a. to abandon, to desert, to quit, to leave. *taj-d.*, to give up. *s.*

تجنب *tajannub*, withdrawing, ceasing. *tajannub-k.*, to refrain, or desist, or withdraw from. *a.*

تجنيس *tajnīs*, f. resemblance, analogy; equivocation; punning to the eye instead of the ear. *tajnīsi khaṭṭī*, writing words alike to the eye which are pronounced differently, according to the short vowel employed; a sort of equivoque in writing, as *pal*, *pil*, and *pul*, in the following line from Saudā, *mauji chashmi 'āshiḳān de tor pal meṅ pil ke pul*, "the waves from the eyes of lovers would instantly demolish a bridge by their shock." In the original manuscript, the three words *pal*, *pil*, and *pul*, present to the eye the same appearance, viz. *pl*, or *pe* and *lām* only. *a.*

تجويز *tajwīz*, f. approbation; inquiring into, examining; considering, contrivance, sentence, judgment, trial, plan, permission. *tajwīz-nāma*, a written decree, judgment, or resolution. *a.*

تجويزي *tajwīzī*, tried, determined. *a.*

تجويف *tajwīf*, f. hollowing, making concave. *a.*

تجهيز *tajhīz*, f. burial; arranging, adorning. *tajhīzi lashkar-k.*, a. to raise an army. *a.*

تچانا तचाना *tachānā*. a. to parch, to scorch. *h.*

تچنا तचना *tachnā*, n. to be heated, to parch. *h.*

تچه तुच्छ *tuchh*, contemptible, despicable worthless, void, empty. *s.*

تچهدر तुच्छद्रु *tuchcha-dru*, m. the castor-oil tree (as having no sap). *s.*

تچهك तक्षक *tachhak* (for *takshak*), m. one of the principal *nāgas* or serpents of Pātāla; a snake of a middle size and of a red colour. *s.*

تچهن तिच्छन *tichchhan*, (for *tīkshna*) sharp, virulent, bitter, severe. *s.*

تحاشي *taḥāshī*, excepting against (any measure), by saying *ḥāshā*, "God forbid," by "no means." *a*

تحالف *taḥāluf*, conspiring, leaguing; (in law) the swearing of both the plaintiff and the defendant. *a.*

تحائف *taḥā,if* (pl. of تحفه), rarities, curiosities; presents, choice articles. *a.*

تحت *taḥt*, m. below, the inferior part; possession. *taḥt-uṣ-ṣarā* or *ṣarā*, m. under the earth. *taḥt-ush-shu,ā'*, m. change of the moon, conjunction with the sun. *taḥti-taṣarruf* or *-farmān* or *-ḥukūmat* subjection, dominion, jurisdiction. *taḥt-lafẓī*, verbally, literal translation, interlinear translation. *taḥt meṅ lānā*, a. to conquer, to subjugate. *a.*

تحتاني *taḥtānī*, (applied to letters or points in dictionaries) small, short, under. *a.*

تحذير *taḥẕīr*, threatening, cautioning. *a.*

تحرك *taḥarruk*, m. motion, movement. *a.*

تحرير *taḥrīr*, f. writing correctly; manumission; adj. written, dated. *taḥrīri uḳlīdas*, Euclid's Elements. *a.*

تحريص *taḥrīṣ*, f. stimulation. *taḥrīṣ karnā*, a. to stimulate, to entice, to allure. *a.*

تحريف *taḥrīf*, f. changing, inverting, transposing letters, forming an anagram, cutting the point of a *ḳalam* obliquely; pl. *taḥrīfāt*, changes, anagrams. *a.*

تحريك *taḥrīk*, f. movement; exciting desire, temptation, commotion, encouragement. *taḥrīk denā*, a. to touch, to move, to affect, to encourage. *taḥrīk-k.*, a. to tempt, to instigate. *a.*

تحريمه *taḥrīma*, m. the commencement of prayer, when all worldly thoughts are forbidden, assumption of a pilgrim's garb. *a.* [dolence. *a.*

تحسر *taḥassur*, m. grieving, regretting; con-

تحس نحس *taḥs-naḥs*, spoilt, broken, dispersed, overthrown, destroyed, unfortunate (the last part is significant, the first redundant). *a.*

تحسين *taḥsīn*, f. approbation, applause, acclamation. *taḥsīn-k.*, to applaud, praise. *a.*

تحصيل *taḥṣīl*, f. collection (particularly revenues), it also denotes the district allotted to a collector; gain, acquisition, profit, attainment; pl. *taḥṣīlāt*, collections, acquisitions; districts. (vide Wilson.) *a.*

تحصيلدار *taḥṣīl-dār*, m. a collector, a tax-gatherer; an officer employed for a fixed salary to collect the revenues of a district. *a.*

تحصيلداري *taḥṣīl-dārī*, f. office or rank of collector; collectorship, tax-gathering. *a.*

تحصيلنا *taḥṣīlnā*, a. to collect, to gather a tax; hence, to oppress, to afflict. *a.*

تحفت *tuḥfat* (v. *tuḥfa*), a rare gift or present. *tuḥfat-ul-mūminīn*, "Rare gift of the orthodox"; a well-known book on medicine, written in Persian, but compiled from a great variety of other works in Sanskrit, Arabic, &c.—(Binning.) *a.*

تحفجات *tuḥfajāt* (barbaric pl. of تحفه), rarities, curiosities, presents. *a.*

تحفگي *tuḥfagī*, f. excellence, rarity, beauty, neatness, elegance. *a.*

تحفه *tuḥfa*, a curiosity; a present; adj. rare, uncommon, excellent, admirable, nice, choice, beautiful, wonderful, odd, singular. *tuḥfa ma'jūn*, a wag. *a.*

تحقق *taḥaḳḳuḳ*, m. ascertainment, certain knowledge, verification. *a.*

تحقير *taḥḳīr*, f. despising, scorn, neglect, disdain. *taḥḳīr-k.*, to despise. *a.*

تحقيق *taḥḳīḳ*, f. ascertaining, investigation, trial, verification, exactness, precision; truth, certainty; adj. authentic, actual, real, indubitable, apparent; indeed; pl. *taḥḳīḳāt*. *a.*

تحقيقانه *taḥḳīḳāna*, according to truth. *a.*

تحقيقي *taḥḳīḳī*, sure, certain, confirmatory. *a.*

تحكم *taḥakkum*, m. commanding, ruling, dominion, power, authority; usurping authority; condemning, passing sentence. *a.*

تحكيم *taḥkīm*, f. arbitration, authority. *a.*

تحليف *taḥlīf*, exacting an oath. *a.*

تحليل *taḥlīl*, m. digestion, concoction, solubility; making lawful. *taḥlīl honā*, n. to waste, to consume. *taḥlīl-karnewālā*, digestive. *a.*

تحمل *taḥammul*, m. patience, endurance, long-suffering, resignation, forbearance, truce, peace, meekness, humility. *taḥammul-k.*, to endure. *a.*

تحميد *taḥmīd*, f. the utterance of the Arabic phrase, "*al ḥamdu lillāhi*," praise be to God. *p.*

تحميل *taḥmīl*, f. burthening, imposing a load on; importuning, asking more than one's right. *a.*

تحور *taḥawwur*, m. haste, celerity; anger. *a.*

تحويل *taḥwīl*, f. trusts, charges, cash; return, renovation; change, transfer; passing of the sun, moon, or a planet from one sign to another; pl. *taḥwīlāt*, revolutions, &c. *taḥwīli taṣarruf*, embezzlement. *a.*

تحويلدار *taḥwīl-dār*, m. a cash-keeper, a treasurer. *a. p.* [of cash-keeper. *a. p.*

تحويلداري *taḥwīl-dārī*, the office or situation

تحيت *taḥiyat*, f. a salutation, congratulation, prayer, benediction. *a.* [nishment. *a.*

تحير *taḥaiyur*, m. amazement, wonder, asto-

تخارج *taḳhāruj*, lit. mutual disbursement; (in the language of the law) a composition entered into by some heirs for their share of the inheritance, in consideration of some specific thing, which for the time being excludes them from such inheritance. *a.*

تخالص *taḳhāluṣ*, liberation, manumission. *a.*

تخالف *taḳhāluf*, m. opposition, enmity. *a.*

تخت *taḳht*, m. a throne. *taḳht baḳht* or *taḳht o baḳht*, throne and fortune; used as a form of benediction, particularly by women, to signify wedlock and wealth. *taḳht par baiṭhālnā*, a. to enthrone. *taḳht par baiṭhnā*, n. to reign. *taḳht chhoṛnā*, a. to abdicate a throne. *taḳht-dār*, m. a king. *taḳht-dārī*, sovereignty. *taḳhti-rawān*, m. a travelling throne, a throne on which the king is carried; also a kind of sedan carried on mules or camels, in which women commonly travel. *taḳht se utarna*, a. to dethrone. *taḳht nishān*, seating on or bestowing thrones. *taḳht nishīn*, m. a king, a prince. *taḳht-nishīnī*, f. accession to the throne, reign. *taḳht yā taḳhta*, either a throne or a bier (spoken on engaging in a desperate enterprise). *p.*

تختپوش **takht-posh**, a covered stage or platform. *p.*

تختگاه **takht-gāh**, f. the royal residence, metropolis, seat of government. *p.*

تختہ **takhta**, m. a plank, a board; a stool; a bier; a sheet of paper. *takhta-bandī*, f. wainscot. *takhta-gardan*, thick, broad, and straight-necked (a horse). *takhta-nard*, m. backgammon. *p.*

تختي **takhtī**, f. a small plank; a little board like a slate which children write on; a signet of stone; the breast; a kind of amulet. *p.*

تخريب **takhrīb**, f. devastation, destruction, razing or laying waste (a country, &c.). *a.*

تخصيص **takhṣīṣ**, f. particularity, peculiarity, appropriating, preserving for one's self. *a.*

تخصيصي **takhṣīṣī**, special cess, not liable to division. *a.*

تخفيف **takhfīf**, making light, lifting up; despising; abbreviating; abatement, relief, remission, abridgment, decrease, diminution, decay, alleviation; softening the pronunciation of letters, or changing one for another *euphoniæ gratia*. *takhfīfi taṣdī*, banishing care; relieving pain or trouble. *a.*

تخلخل **takhalkhul**, putting on or wearing the ornament called *khalkhāl*, q. v. *a.*

تخلص **takhalluṣ**, m. the titular name assumed by poets, as Saudā was the *takhalluṣ* of *Mirzā Muḥammad Rafī*. *a.*

تخلف **takhalluf**, m. retiring, deferring, remaining behind. *a.*

تخلل **takhallul**, m. disturbance, discord, dissension, interruption. *a.*

تخليص **takhlīṣ**, release, freedom. *a.*

تخليہ **takhliya**, m. evacuating; privacy; manumission (of a slave); divorce (of a wife). *a.*

تخم **tukhm**, m. seed; an egg; a testicle; sperm. *tukhmi bālangū*, m. a seed of a cooling quality. *tukhmi bad*, low bred. *tukhmi raiḥān*, m. the seed of *Ocymum pilosum*. *tukhm-rez*, a sower. *tukhm-rezī*, f. scattering seed, sowing. *tukhm-sokht*, land in which seed has not germinated. *tukhmi kāhū*, m. seed of lettuce (*Lactuca sativa*). *tukhmi katān*, m. linseed. *p.*

تخمہ **tukhma**, m. indigestion. *a.*

تخمير **takhmīr**, f. fermentation, leavening. *a.*

تخميناً **takhmīnan**, by guess, hypothetically, by appraisement; adv. nearly, about. *a.*

تخمينہ **takhmīna**, m. guess, appraisement, conjecture, valuation. *a.*

تخنہ **takhna**, m. the ankle or ankle-joint. *h.*

تخويف **takhwīf**, f. terrifying; threatening. *a.*

تخيل **takhaiyul**, m. fancying, imagining, supposing; suspicion; pl. *takhaiyulāt*, suspicions, &c. *a.*

تخيم **takhaiyum**, the pitching of a tent. *a.*

تد तद **tad**, then, at that time, afterwards, in that case, therefore, so soon. *tad-antar*, after that, after which. *tad-bhī*, still, nevertheless, however, notwithstanding. *tad to*, then, in that case. *tad se*, thence, since that time. *tad-hī*, at that very time, in that case only. *s.*

تدا तदा **tadā**, then, at that time. *s.*

تدابير **tadābīr** (pl. of تدبير), deliberations, &c. *a.*

تداخل **tadākhul**, mutual insertion or entrance. *a.*

تدارك **tadāruk**, m. chastisement, retaliation; provision, preparation (particularly to obtain justice); the instruments and means used to procure justice, as writing, lawyers, witnesses, &c.; remedy, precaution, reparation. *tadāruk-k.*, a. to provide against, to prepare, to oppose, to chastise. *a.*

تدافع **tadāfu'**, repelling, resisting. *a.*

تدان **tadān**, then, at that time. *d.*

تداول **tadāwul**, m. tradition. *a.*

تداوي **tadāwī**, f. cure, remedying. *a.*

تدبير **tadbīr**, f. deliberation, counsel, opinion, advice; government, regulation, order; in the language of the law, it means a declaration of freedom made to a slave, to be established after the master's death; pl. *tadbīrāt*, counsels, deliberations; regulations. *tadbīri salṭanat* or *tadbīri mamlukat*, f. politics, administration of government. *tadbīri ghiẓā*, f. regimen. *a.*

تدرو **tadarw**, m. a pheasant (to whose gait that of a mistress is compared). *p.*

تدري तिदरी **ti-darī**, three-doored. *s.*

تدريج **tadrīj**, f. gradation, scale. *a.*

تدريس **tadrīs**, f. giving lectures. *a.*

تدفين **tadfīn**, m. burial, sepulture. *a.*

تدننتر तदनन्तर **tadanantar**, thereafter. *s.*

تدهارا तिधारा **tidhārā**, m. the name of a plant (*Euphorbia antiquorum*); the meeting of three streams (in Dakh. *tidhārī*). *s.*

تدهر तिधर **tidhar**, thither, in that direction. *h.*

تدهن तद्धन **taddhan**, miserly, niggardly. *s.*

تدهي तधी or तदही **tadhī**, at that very time, in that case. *s.*

تدهين **tad,hīn**, f. anointing. *a.*

تدين **tadaiyun**, m. religiousness, sanctity. *a.*

تڈا तडा **taḍā**, m. an island. *h.*

تڈا **tiḍḍā** (for *ṭiḍḍā*), a grasshopper, a locust. *d.*

تڈاك तडाक **taḍāk**, splendid, gaudy. *h.*

تڈاكا तडाका **taḍākā**, m. noise of beating. *h.*

تڈاگ तडाग **taḍāg**, m. a tank, pond. *h.*

تڈاوا तडावा **taḍāwā**, m. a crash, crack. *h.*

تڈايا तडाया **taḍāyā**, m. report, rumour (v. *hāhā*). *h.*

تڈي **tiḍḍi**, a troop of men. *d.*

تذبذب **tazabzub**, agitation, commotion. *a.*

تذرو **tazarw** (v. *tadarw*), a pheasant. *p.*

تذکرت *tazkirat,* } m. memory, remembrance;
تذکره *tazkira,* } a memoir, billet, schedule, obligation, handwriting; biographical memoirs, especially of poets. *tazkiratan*, by way of mention, memoir or memorial. *a.*

تذکير *tazkīr*, f. masculine gender; commemoration, bringing to memory, mentioning, recording, admonishing. *a.*

تذليل *tazlīl*, f. abasement, depression. *a.*

تذهيب *tazhīb*, art of gilding, illumination of manuscripts. *a.*

تر *tar*, moist, wet, fresh, green, young, juicy; a particle, by the adding of which, Persian adjectives form their comparative degree; as *khūb*, good, fair; *khūb-tar*, better, fairer. *p.*

تر तर *tar* (for *tale*), underneath, below. *h.*

تر तरु *taru*, m. a tree in general. *s.*

تر त्रि *tri*, three (used only in composition). *s.*

ترا तिरा *tirā* (for *terā*), they, thine, of thee. *s.*

ترا तरा *tarā*, the bottom of any thing. *h.*

ترا *turā* (for *tūrā*), to thee, or thee. *p.*

تراب *turāb*, m. earth, ground, dust. *a.*

ترابي *turābī*, earthen or earthly. *a.*

ترادف *tarāduf*, m. succession; adj. uninterrupted, carrying double (a horse). *a.*

ترار तरार *tarār*, rapid, quick. *h.*

ترارا तरारा *tarrārā*, m. rapidity. *tarrārā bharnā*, to gallop, to rush on at full speed. *h.*

ترازو *tarāzū*, f. a scale, a balance. *tarāzū ho-jānā*, to hit right through (an arrow). *p. h.*

تراس तिरास *tirās* or त्रास *trās*, f. thirst. *tirās ānā* or *lagnā*, a. to be thirsty. *s.*

تراس त्रास *trās*, m. alarm, fear, dread. *trās-dāyī*, terrifying, occasioning dread or alarm. *s.*

ترسا त्रासा *trāsā*, } afraid, terrified. *s.*
تراست त्रासित *trāsit*, }

تراسي तिरासी *tirāsī*, eighty-three. *s.*

تراش *tarāsh*, f. cutting, paring, shape, form. *tarāsh ḍālnā*, a. to pare off or away; (in comp.) cutting or trimming; as, *ḳalam-tarāsh*, a penknife. *p.*

تراش خراش *tarāsh kharāsh*, f. form, shape, (particularly good); neatness of form. *p.*

تراشنا *tarāshnā* (in Pers. *tarāshīdan*), a. to cut, to chip; to shave; to shape, to cut out. *apne ta,īṅ tarāshnā*, to be vain, to value or esteem one's self above others. *p.*

تراشه *tarāsha*, m. shaving, splinter, clip. *p.*

تراق or تراك *taraḳ* &c., a crack, the noise of any thing splitting or breaking. *p.*

تراكڑي तराकड़ी *tarākṛī*, f. the beam of a balance. *h.*

تراكم *tarākum*, accumulation, heaping up. *a.*

تران तरान *tarān*, m. revenue, income. *h.*

تران त्राण *trān*, m. safety; protection deliverance; a coat of mail. *trān-k.*, a. to free, to protect. *trān-kartā*, a deliverer. *s.*

ترانا तर्राना *tarrānā*, n. to grudge, grumble, murmur. *h.*

ترانا तिराना *tirānā* or तराना *tarānā*, a. to cause to pass over or swim, to save. *s.*

ترانا *turānā*, rice boiled and kept overnight in cold water. *d.*

ترانكرتا त्राणकर्ता *trān-kartā*, m. a protector. *s.*

ترانوي तिरानवे *tirānawwe* or तिरान्वे *tirānwe*, ninety-three. *s.*

ترانه *tarāna*, m. modulation, harmony, voice, song, melody, symphony, trill, shake, quaver; a kind of song. *tarāna-pardāz*, composing songs. *p.*

تراني त्राणी *trānī*, m. a saviour, a protector. *s.*

تراو तिराव *tirāw* or तराव *tarāw*, m. swimming. *s.*

تراوش *tarāwish*, f. distillation, dripping, exudation. *p.*

تراوي *tarāwī*, } certain extra prayers offered
تراويح *tarāwīḥ*, } up by the more devout among the Moslems. These are always performed during the Ramazān fast, but pious persons often repeat them every morning. *a.*

تراه त्राह *trāh* or त्राहि *trāhi*, an exclamation denoting mercy! pardon! *trāhi-trāhi-k.*, a. humbly to ask mercy; to complain, to repent of a sin. *trāhi-kār*, m. cry for mercy. *s.*

تراءي तराई *tarā,ī*, f. a marsh, mead, meadow; low ground flooded with water, upon which rice is generally cultivated. *tarā,ī khewā*, living in or near water (a waterfowl, water spaniel, &c.). *tarā,ī*, a species of cucumber. *h.*

ترايمان त्रायमाण *trāyamān*, adj. preserving, a preserver. *s.*

ترائن तराइन *tarā,in*, m. stars, constellations. *s.*

ترب तर्ब *tarb*, f. a musical tone. *h.*

ترب *turb*, m. a radish (for *turāb*, q. v.) earth, &c. *p.*

ترباچك तिरबाचक *tirbāchak*, m. an agreement confirmed three times. *s.*

تربانتين *tirbāntīn*, turpentine. *g.*

تربت *turbat*, f. a tomb, a sepulchre. *a.*

تربتي *turbatī*, sepulchral. *a.*

تربتر *tar-ba-tar*, completely wet. *tar-ba-tar honā*, n. to drip with wet, (but generally) to be covered with blood. *p.*

تربد *tarbad* or *turbud*, m. a purgative Indian root; turbith (*Convolvulus turpethum*). *p.*

تربج *tarbuj*, } (also *tarbuza*, *tarbūz*, & *tarbūza*),
تربز *tarbuz*, } m. a water-melon (*Curcurbita citrullus*). *p.*

تربهنگا त्रिभङ्गा *tribhangā* or तिरभङ्गा *tirbhangā*, standing awry, or bending (properly with legs, loins, and neck bent). *s.*

تربهنگي त्रिभङ्गी *tribhangī* or तिरभङ्गी *tirbhangī*, an epithet of *Krishṇa*; name of a species of poetical measure. *s.*

تربھون त्रिभुवन *tri-bhuwan*, m. the three worlds, *i.e.* heaven, earth, and hell, the universe. *tri-bhuwan-ujāgar*, splendour of three worlds. *tri-bhuwan-sundarī*, the beauty of the three worlds, a lady's name. *s.*

تربيت *tarbiyat*, f. education, instruction, tuition, breeding, correction. *tarbiyat-pizīr*, docile, tractable. *tarbiyat-k.*, a. to educate, to instruct. *a.*

تربيع *tarbī'*, f. dividing into four, making a quadrangular or square figure; (in astrology) a quadrangular aspect of the stars, quadrature. *a.*

تربيني त्रिबेणी *tri-benī* or तिरबेणी *tir-benī*, f. lit. three braids of hair, applied to the confluence of three rivers (v. *triveni*). *h.*

ترپا त्रपा *trapā*, f. an unchaste woman. *trapā-raṇḍā*, f. a whore. *s.*

ترپاد त्रिपाद *tri-pād*, m. fever, or the demon of fever, described as having three feet and three heads. *s.*

ترپانا तुरपाना *turpānā*, a. to stitch, to darn; to hem. *h.*

ترپت तृप्त *tripta*, pleased, satisfied. *tṛipti*, f. pleasure, satisfaction. *triptātmā*, contented. *s.*

ترپتاك त्रिपताक *tri-patāk*, m. the forehead marked naturally with three horizontal lines. *s.*

ترپتھ त्रिपथ *tri-path*, m. a place where three roads meet. *s.* [pod. *s.*

ترپد तिरपद *tirpad* or त्रिपद *tri-pad*, m. a tri-

ترپدي त्रिपदी *tri-padī*, f. a creeper (*Cissus pedata*); the girth of an elephant. *s.*

ترپر त्रिपुर *tri-pur*, f. a district of Bengal, the modern Tippera. *s.*

ترپن तर्पण *tarpan*, m. a libation of water to the manes of deceased ancestors; satisfaction, gratification, satiety. *s.*

ترپن तिरपन *tirpan*, fifty-three. *s.*

ترپن तुरपन *turpan*, a kind of stitch. *h.*

ترپنا तुरपना *turapnā*, a. to sew (in a particular manner), to stitch. *h.*

ترپنڈ त्रिपुण्ड *tri-puṇḍ*, m. three curved horizontal lines delineated on the forehead by the *Shaivas* and *Shaktas*, or the followers of Shiva and Shakti respectively. *s.*

ترپوليا तिरपौलिया *tirpāuliyā* or त्रिपौलिया *tri-pauliyā*, m. a building with three doors or arches. *s.h.*

ترپھلا तिरफला *tirphalā* or त्रिफला *triphalā*, m. the name of a medicine composed of three kinds of myrobalan (v. *itrī-phal*). *s.*

ترپھنا तरफना *taraphnā*, n. to flutter, to tremble, to palpitate, to writhe, wriggle, toss, jump, spring; to be very desirous. *h.*

ترت तुर्त *turt* or तुरत *turat*, ترتاو तुर्ताव *turtāw*, ترت‌پھرت तुर्तफुर्त *turt phurt*, } instantly, quickly, directly, presently, immediately. *s.*

ترتا तिरता *tirtā*, treble, threefold. *h.*

ترتاليس *tirtālīs* (for *tetālīs*), forty-three. *d.*

ترترا तुर्तुरा *turturā*, nimble, active; flippant. *h.*

ترترا तरतरा *tartarā*, m. a kind of dish. *h.*

ترتراتا ततराता *tartarātā*, very greasy; dropping with moisture. *h.*

ترترانا ततराना *tartarānā*, to bluster, to boast. *h.*

ترترانا तिरतिराना *tirtirānā*, n. to trickle, to drop. *h.*

ترتراهٹ ततराहट *tartarāhaṭ*, f. bluster, boast. *h.*

ترتري *turturī*, f. a kind of horn or trumpet of great length, generally used at funerals, commonly called the Coleroon horn. *d.*

ترتيه तृतीय *tṛitīya* or *tirtīya*, the third. *tṛitīya-prakṛiti*, f. the neuter gender, m. a eunuch. *s.*

ترتيب *tartīb*, f. arrangement, disposition, order, method. *tartīb denā*, a. to put in order, &c. *a.*

ترتيبي *tartībī*, orderly, methodical. *a.*

ترتيل *tartīl*, reciting with a clear voice. *a.* [*s.*

ترتي‌پھرتي तुर्तीफुर्ती *turtī phurtī*, hastily, quickly.

ترٹي त्रुटी *truṭi*, f. loss, destruction. *h.*

ترجگت त्रिजगत *tri-jagat* (also *trijag*) the three worlds (v. *trilok*). *s.*

ترجمان *tarjumān*, m. a translator; (vulg. called in the Levant), dragoman or drogaman. *a.*

ترجماني *tarjumānī*, f. office of interpreter. *a.*

ترجمه *tarjama* or *tarjuma*, m. translation, interpretation. *tarjama-navīs*, m. a translator. *a.*

ترجن तर्जन *turjan*, m. wrath, anger. *s.*

ترجني तर्जनी *tarjanī*, f. the fore-finger. *s.*

ترجيح *tarjīḥ*, f. gaining a superiority, preference, excellence, pre-eminence. *tarjīḥi bilā murajjaḥ*, unreasonable preference. *tarjīḥ rakhnā*, a. to excel, to surpass. *a.*

ترجيع‌بند *tarjī'-band*, a kind of stanza, in which one line recurs at stated intervals. *a. p.*

ترجيون तरुजीवन *taru-jīvan*, m. the root of a tree. *s.*

ترچھا तिरछा *tirchhā*, crooked, across, crosswise, bent, awry; perverse; affected, foolish. *tirchhā dekhnā*, a. to squint. *tirchhā lagnā*, n. to strike obliquely. *tirchhī āṅkh-k.*, a. to look angrily, to cast unkind looks. *tirchhī nazar*, leer, ogle. *s.*

ترچھانا तिरछाना *tirchhānā*, a. to crook, to place in a transverse position; to be perverse; to be affected. *s.*

ترچھٹ तरछट *tarchhaṭ*, f. dregs, sediments. *h.*

ترچھيانا तिरछियाना *tirchhiyānā*, n. to edge, to go obliquely (little used, the proper expression being *katrānā*). *s.* [ness, mercy, lenity. *h.*

ترحم *taraḥḥum*, m. pity, compassion, kind-

ترخنا *tarakhnā*, to warp, crack, split. *d.*

ترخيم *tarḵẖīm*, f. abbreviation, contraction, apocope (in grammar). *a.*

تردد *taraddud*, m. irresolution; contrivance, debating; rejecting, hesitation, fluctuating, suspension of judgment, anxious consideration. pl. *taraddudāt*, as *taraddudāti dunyavī*, attention to, or anxiety about, worldly affairs. *a.*

تردست *tar-dast*, expert, active, adroit. *p.*

تردستي *tardastī*, f. activity, handiness, adroitness, expertness. *p.*

تردش त्रिदश *tridash*, m. a god, a deity. *tridashāhār*, m. god's food, *amṛit*, or *ambrosia*. *s.*

تردلا त्रिदला *tridalā*, f. a creeping plant (*Cissus pedata*). *s.*

تردنڈي त्रिदण्डी *tri-daṇḍī*, a Shiva mendicant, so called from his carrying as his symbol three slender staves, typical of his command over thoughts, words, and actions. *s.*

تردوش त्रिदोष *tri-dosh*, m. effervescence of the three humours, viz. phlegm, bile, and *atrabilis*. *s.*

ترديد *tardīd*, f. opposing. *ḥarfi tardīd*, the disjunctive conjunction *yā*, or. *a.*

ترديف *tardīf*, f. following, subjoining. *a.*

ترراتر त्रिरात्र *tri-rātra*, m. three nights collectively. *s.*

ترس तर्स *tars*, m. compassion, mercy. *tars khānā*, to compassionate, to feel pity. *h.*

ترس तिरस *tiras*, indirectly, covertly; crookedly, awry; a particle of abuse or depreciation. *s.*

ترس *tars*, m. fear, terror. *p.*

ترسا *tarsā*, m. one who is not a Musalmān; a Christian; an infidel, a pagan, a worshipper of fire, a guebre. *p.*

ترسان *tarsān*, fearful, timid, afraid. *p.*

ترسانا तर्साना *tarsānā*, a. to cause to long, to tantalize, teaze. *s.*

ترسپرن त्रिसुपर्ण *tri-suparna*, m. a portion of the Rig and Yajur Vedas. *s.*

ترست त्रस्त *trasta*, timid, fearful. *s.*

ترسٹھ तिरसठ *tirsaṭh*, sixty-three. *s.*

ترسكار तिरस्कार *tiraskār*, m. } disrespect,
ترسكريا तिरस्क्रिया *tiraskriyā*, f. } abuse, reproach. *s.*

ترسكرت तिरस्कृत *tiraskṛit*, reviled, abused. *s.*

ترسل *tarassul*, m. doing (any thing) softly, or easily. *a.*

ترسن तरसना *tarasnā*, n. to long, to desire anxiously; to beg, to entreat, to supplicate, to pity. *s.*

ترسناك *tars-nāk*, timid, cowardly. *p.*

ترسندهيا त्रिसन्ध्या *tri-sandhyā*, the three periods of the day, dawn, noon, and eve. *s.*

ترسول त्रिशूल *trisūl*, m. a trident or three-pronged lance (the weapon borne by Mahādeva). *s.*

ترسوں तर्सों *tarsoṅ*, the third day past or to come (not including the present, *i.e.* two days intervening). *h.*

ترسيدن *tarsīdan*, to fear, to dread. *p.*

ترسيل *tarsīl*, f. sending, transmitting. *a.*

ترش तर्ष *tarsh*, m. thirst, wish, desire. *s.*

ترش *tursh*, sour, harsh; ill-tempered, crabbed. *tursh-rū*, cynical, morose, surly, stern, hard-favoured, ugly. *tursh-ṭab'* or *-mizāj*, sour-tempered, harsh. *p.*

ترشا तृषा *tṛishā*, f. thirst, desire; a plant (*Commelina salicifolia*). *tṛishā-want*, thirsty. *s.*

ترشائي *turshā,ī*, f. sourness, harshness, acidity. *p.* [late. *p.*

ترشانا *turshānā*, to become sour, to acidu-

ترشت तर्षित *tarshit* or तृषित *tṛishit*, thirsty. *s.*

ترشٹبھ त्रिष्टुभ *trishṭubh*, f. a sort of metre or stanza consisting of three lines. *s.*

ترشح *tarashshuḥ*, m. sweating, exuding; dripping, distilling; a small rain. *a.*

ترشرن त्रिशरण *tri-sharan*, m. a sanctified teacher of the Jaina sect, the refuge of the three worlds. *s.*

ترشرنگ त्रिशृङ्ग *tri-shring*, m. a hill with three peaks; a triangle. *s.*

ترشرنگي त्रिशृङ्गी *tri-shringī*, m. a kind of fish (*Cyprinus denticulatus*). *s.*

ترشك तुरुष्क *turushka*, m. incense; name of a country (perhaps Tūrān, now called Turkistān). *turushkā*, m. pl. its inhabitants. *s.*

ترشن तर्षण *tarshan*, m. thirst, thirsting; it is also used metaphorically. *s.*

ترشنا *tarashnā*, n. to be cut or pared. *p.*

ترشنا तृष्णा *tṛishṇā*, f. thirst; ambition, desire, avarice. *trishṇā-kshay*, m. content, resignation, patience. *s.*

ترشنج तृष्णज *trishnaj*, thirsty, longing for. *s.*

ترشوانا *tarashwānā*, to cause to be cut. *p.*

ترشول त्रिशूल *trishūl*, m. a trident (the weapon borne by Mahādeva). *s.*

ترشه *tarsha*, a species of fruit. *tursha*, a kind of sorrel, wild sorrel. *p.*

ترشي *turshī*, f. sourness, acidity, harshness. *turshī-bādī*, acid (or) flatulent (a medical term). *p.*

ترصد *taraṣṣud*, m. expectation, hope. *a.*

ترصيع *tarṣī'*, adorning with jewels or gold; an ornate style in prose or verse. *a.*

ترغيب *targhīb*, f. exciting desire, temptation, stimulation. *targhīb denā*, a. to set a-gog, to tempt, to excite or induce. *a.*

ترقب *taraḳḳub*, m. contemplating, expecting, hoping. *a.*

ترقنا *taraḳnā*(for *taṛaknā*,q.v.),n.to split,&c.*d.*

ترقي *taraḳḳī*, f. promotion, preferment; increase; making progress in learning, proficiency; pl. *taraḳḳiyāt*, preferments, advances. *a.*

ترقيق *tarḳīḳ*, f. softening, thinning, dilution, rarefaction. *a.*

ترقيم *tarḳīm*, f. writing, noting, marking. *a.*

ترك *turk*, m. properly a Turk, which in Persian takes many other meanings; a soldier; a *Musalmān*. *turk-sawār*, m. a horseman, cavalier. *turk-mizāj*, savage or of a *Tartarly* disposition; wicked, sly, depraved. *a. p.*

ترك *tark*, m. abandoning, leaving, deserting. *tark i adab*, disrespect, rudeness; *tark i dunyā*, abandonment of the world and its vanities. *a.*

ترك तरक *tarak*, f. a beam, a rafter. *h.*

ترك तर्क *tark*, m. doubt, discussion; logic; a proposition (in logic). *tarka-vidyā*, f. the science of reasoning, logic. *s.*

ترك तर्कु *tarku*, f. a spindle or distaff, an iron pin upon which the cotton is first drawn out. *s.*

تركا त्रिका *trikā*, f. a triangular frame or bar across the mouth of a well to support the rope of the bucket. *s.*

تركاري तर्कारी *tarkārī*, f. esculent vegetables. *h.*

تركالدرشي त्रिकालदर्शी *trikāl-darshī*, m. one who sees the past, present, and future; a *rishi* or divine sage; a name of Buddha. *s.*

تركالگيه त्रिकालज्ञ *trikāla-gya*, m. one who knows the past, present, and future; a name of Buddha. *s.*

تركپنڈ तर्कुपिण्ड *tarku-pinḍ*, m. }

تركپيٹهي तर्कुपीठी *tarku-pīṭhī*, f. } a ball of clay upon the lower end of the spindle to assist in giving it a rotatory motion. *s.*

تركت तर्कित *tarkit*, doubtful, disputed. *s.*

تركتاز *turk-tāz*, }

تركتازي *turk-tāzī*, } depredation, attack; feigned anger. *p.*

تركٹ तर्कुट *tarkuṭ*, m. drawing out the cotton upon the distaff or upon the wheel. *s.*

تركٹ त्रिकट *trikaṭ*, m. a plant (*Ruellia longifolia*). *s.*

تركٹ त्रिकटु *trikaṭu*, }

تركٹا तिरकुटा *tirkuṭā*, } m. a mixture of dry ginger, long pepper, and black pepper. *s.*

تركٹي तर्कुटी *tarkuṭī*, f. a spindle or a distaff. *s.*

تركس *tirkas*, bent, crooked, cornerwise, diagonally. *d.*

تركستان *turkistān*, the country of the (eastern) Turks, Transoxiana. *p.*

تركش *tarkash*, m. a quiver. *tarkash-band*, wearing a quiver. *p.*

تركشان तर्कुशाण *tarku-shān*, m. a small whet stone for sharpening spindles. *s.*

تركل तर्कुल *tarkul*, m. the fruit of the *tāṛ* tree (*Borassus flabelliformis*). *s.*

تركل तर्किल *tarkil*, m. *Cassia tora*. *s.*

تركلاسك तर्कुलासक *tarkulāsak*, m. a concave shell or saucer in which the lower end of the spindle is placed and whirled round. *s.*

تركن तर्किन *tarkin*, m. a logician, a disputant, a follower of the *Tarka-shāstra*. *s.*

تركنٹك त्रिकण्टक *tri-kanṭak*, m. a sort of fish (*Silurus*), a plant (*Ruella longifolia*). *s.*

تركني *turkanī*, (lit.) a female Turk, a Turcomān woman. In India the term denotes any Musalmān female. *p.*

تركوٹ त्रिकूट *tri-kūṭ*, m. a three-peaked mountain; name of a mountain in the peninsula; sea salt prepared by evaporation. *s.*

تركون त्रिकोण *tri-kon*, m. a triangle; the vulva. *s.*

تركه *tarika* or *tarikat*, m. the estate of a deceased person, a bequest, a legacy. *a.*

تركها तर्खा *tarkhā*, rapid (a stream). *h.*

تركها तिरखा *tirkhā* (for *tṛishā*), f. thirst; desire. *s.*

تركهاونت *tirkhāwant* (for *trishāwant*), thirsty. *s.*

تركهنٹي तिरखुंटी *tir-khunṭi*, }

تركهونٹي तिरखूंटी *tirkhūnṭī*, } f. a trivet. *h.*

تركي तर्की *tarkī*, f. an ornament for the ear made of the leaves of the *tāṛ* tree; m. a logician, a disputant; same as *tarkin*, q.v. *s.*

تركي *turkī*, m. a kind of horse; adj. of or belonging to a Turcomān or Tartar; the language spoken by the Turcomāns. *turkī tamām hū,ī*, spoilt, destroyed. *p.*

تركيب *tarkīb*, f. composition, mixture, cement, make, form, mechanism. *tarkīb-k.*, a. to organize; pl. *tarkībāt*, mixtures, compositions. *a.*

تركيبي *tarkībī*, composed, mixed, artful, artificial. *a.*

ترگ तुरग *turag*, m. a horse. *turag-brahmachāryak*, m. enforced celibacy, continence arising merely from the absence of women. *s.*

ترگرت त्रिगर्त्त *tri-gartta*, m. a country in the north-west division of India, apparently part of Lahore. *s.*

ترگرتا त्रिगर्त्ता *tri-gartta*, f. a lascivious, woman, a wanton. *s.*

ترگن त्रिगुण *tri-gun*, thrice, triple; possessing the three *gunas* or properties of beings; m. the aggregate of those three properties *s.*

ترگي तुरगी *turagī*, f. a plant (*Physalis flexuosa*); m. a horseman. *s.*

ترل तरल *taral*, capricious, changeable, fickle, inconstant, ticklish, volatile, unsteady, libidinous, wanton. *s.*

ترلا तरला *tarlā*, m. a kind of bamboo; lower, nethermost. *h.*

ترلوچن त्रिलोचन *tri-lochan*, a name of *Mahādeva* or *Shiva*. *s.*

ترلوك त्रिलोक *tri-lok*, m. } the universe, the
ترلوكي त्रिलोकी *tri-lokī*, f. } world as consisting of three distinct departments, *i.e.* heaven, earth, and the regions under the earth. *trilokī-nāth*, Lord of the universe. *s.* [three roads. *s.*

ترمارگي त्रिमार्गी *tri-mārgī*, f. the meeting of

ترمتي तुरमती *turmatī*, f. the name of a hawk (*Falco cyanellus, B.*; *fasciatus B.*; *Tinnunculus dubius*). *h.*

ترمدھ त्रिमधु *tri-madhu*, m. a portion of the Rig-Veda; a student of that portion. *s.*

ترمرا तिमिरा *tirmirā*, m. a spot of oil, &c. swimming on water; an ocular spectrum, or spark appearing before the eye, from the internal state of that organ. *h.*

ترمرانا तिमिराना *tirmirānā*, n. to vibrate, to dazzle, to thrill, to shake; to sparkle as grease or oil swimming on water. *h.*

ترمراهٹ तिमिराहट *tirmirāhaṭ*, f. vibration. *h.*

ترمري तिमिरी *tirmirī*, f. darkness; vertigo. *s.*

ترمس *turmis*, a kind of millet, lupine, Turkey corn. *p.* [three peaks. *s.*

ترمکٹ त्रिमुकुट *tri-mukuṭ*, m. a mountain with

ترمني *turamnī*, f. an instrument for rasping cocoa-nuts. *d.*

ترمورت त्रिमूर्ति *tri-mūrti*, f. trinity; the three principal Hindu deities, Brahma, Vishnu, and Shiva; m. a Jaina saint. *s.*

ترن तरण *taran*, m. a raft, a float; Swarga or paradise; crossing over, passing; escape, deliverance; one who is delivered. *s.*

ترن तृण *tṛin* or *tṛina*, m. grass. *tṛinatā*, f. the state or property of grass. *tṛin-jāti*, m. the vegetable kingdom. *tṛin-jambh*, graminivorous. *tṛin-rāj*, m. a palmyra-tree. *tṛin-wat*, like grass; worthless. *s.*

ترن तरुण *tarun*, young, juvenile, adult; m. a young man; a kind of plant (*Achyranthes aspera?*). *s.*

ترن तरणि *tarani*, m. the sun, a ray of light; a float or raft; f. a ship, a boat; the succotrine aloe (*A. perfoliata*); a plant (*Hibiscus mutabilis*). *s.*

ترنا तरना *tarnā*, n. to pass over, to be ferried; to be saved. *s.*

ترنا तिरना *tirnā*, n. to swim, to float. *h.*

ترناپن तरुणापन *tarunā-pan*, m. adolescence, youth, puberty. *s.*

ترناترکیت त्रिणात्रिकेत *trinātriket*, m. a portion of the Yajur Veda; a follower of that branch of the Veda. *s.*

ترناگن तृणाग्नि *triṇāgni*, m. conflagration of chaff; burning of a criminal wrapped up in straw. *s.*

ترناءي तरुणाई *tarunā,ī*, f. adolescence, youth, puberty. *s.* [rectly. *s.*

ترنت तुरन्त *turant*, instantly, quickly, di-

ترنت तरन्त *tarant*, m. a fog; a torrent of rain; the ocean. *s.*

ترنتي तरन्ती *tarantī*, f. a boat. *s.*

ترنج *turunj*, m. a citron, an orange. *a.*

ترنجبين *taranjabīn*, m. manna (produced from the *Hedysarum alhagi*); (by this name some call) honey mixed with lime-juice, &c. *p.*

ترنڈ तरण्ड *taranḍ* or *taranḍī*, f. a raft, a float made of bamboos; the float of a fishing-line. *s.*

ترنس तृणस *tṛinas*, grassy, made with grass. *s.*

ترنش त्रिंश *trinsha*, the thirtieth. *s.*

ترنشت त्रिंशत् *trinshat*, thirty. *s.*

ترنگ तरङ्ग *tarang*, f. wave, emotion; becoming state and dignity; whim, conceit, caprice. *s.*

ترنگ तुरङ्ग *turang*, m. a horse. *s.*

ترنگ त्रङ्ग *trang*, m. f. the city of Harischandra, suspended, it is supposed, in the air. *s.*

ترنگبين *tarangabīn*, m. manna (v. *taranjabīn*). *s.*

ترنگني तुरंगनी *turangnī*, f. a dragon-fly. *h.*

ترنگني तरङ्गिणी *taranginī*, f. a river. *s.*

ترنگي तरङ्गी *tarangī*, braggart, fantastical, whimsical. *s.* [*flexuosa*). *s.*

ترنگي तुरङ्गी *turangī*, f. a plant (*Physalis*

ترنم *tarannum*, m. a song, modulation. *a.*

ترنوت तृणवत *tṛina-vat*, grass-like, good for nothing. *s.* [(see *tarani*). *s.*

ترني तरणी *taranī*, f. a ship, a vessel, a boat

ترني तरुणी *tarunī*, a young female, a young wife. *s.*

ترو तरव *tarav*, m. (v. *taru*) a tree. *s.*

تروار तर्वार *tarwār*, f. a sword, scimitar (com. *talwār*). *s.* [and frisky. *p.*

تروتازه *tar o tāza*, new, fresh; cheerful, fresh

ترور तरवर *tarwar*, m. a large tree; also a shrub, a small species of cassia. *s.*

تروٹکي त्रोटकी *troṭakī*, f. a Rāginī, one of the female personifications of music. *s.*

تروٹي त्रोटी *troṭī*, f. the beak of a bird; a kind of pike (*Esox scolopax*). *s.*

ترورت پرني त्रिवृत्पर्णी *trivṛit-parnī*, f. a pot-herb (*Hilancha repens*). *s.*

ترورگ त्रिवर्ग *tri-varga*, m. three human objects, as, love, duty, and wealth; three conditions of a state, prosperity, evenness, and decay; the three qualities of nature, purity, blindness, and depravity. *s.*

ترورنك त्रिवर्णक *tri-varnak*, m. a plant (*Ruellia longifolia*). *s.* [swordsman, fencer. *s.*

ترورِيا तर्वरिया *tarwariyā*, m. a sword; a

تروندا तिरौंदा *tiraundā*, m. buoy, beacon. *h.*

تروهت तिरोहित *tirohit*, covered, concealed, hidden. *s.*

ترويدي त्रिवेदी *tri-vedī*, a Brāhman who professes to have read three of the Vedas. *s.*

تروینی त्रिवेणी *triveni*, f. the confluence of three rivers, more especially applied to that of the Ganges, the Jamuna, and (as supposed) the Saraswatī (underground) at Ilāhābād, which last city is so called by the Hindūs. *s.*

تره *tara*, m. garden herbs, pottage, greens. *p.*

ترهت तिर्हुत *tirhut*, f. name of a district (vulg. *Tirhoot*). *s.*

ترهتیا तिर्हुतिया *tirhutiyā*, belonging to Tirhut, [grown in Tirhut. *s.*

تره‌تیز *taratez*, ترہ‌تیزک *taratezak*, } m. garden cresses (*Lepidium sativum*). *p.*

ترهي तुरही *turhī*, تري तुरी *turī*, } f. a trumpet, a clarion. *h.*

ترئي तरई *tara,ī*, f. a star. *s.*

تري तरे *tare* (for *tale*), under, beneath. *s.*

تري तिरी *tirī*, also त्रय *tray*, three. *s.*

تري तरी *tarī*, f. a boat. *s.*

تري तुरी *turī*, f. a brush or fibrous stick used by weavers to clean the woof; a painter's brush; a trumpet (see *turhī*). *h.*

ترئي तुरई *tura,ī*, f. the name of a kind of cucumber (*Cucumis acutangulis, Roxb.*). *s.*

تري *tarī*, f. moisture; water, in opposition to *khushkī*, dry land; wet lands applied to the cultivation of rice and other vegetables requiring much moisture; sugar. *tarī se*, by water. *p.*

تریا तिरिया *tiriyā* or त्रिया *triyā*, f. a woman, maid, female wife. *tiriyā bed*, the science of women, knowledge of woman. *tiriyā charitr*, m. female wiles. *tiriyā rāj*, amazon country, petticoat government. *s.*

تریا तरैया *taraiyā*, f. a star. *s.*

تریاق *tiryāḳ*, m. in Persian denotes treacle of *Baghdād*, esteemed an antidote against poison; (but in Hindūstānī always means) opium; an antidote in general. *a.*

تریاق فاروق *tiryāḳ fārūḳ*, m. the name of a medicine, an antidote to poison. *a.*

تریاما त्रियामा *tri-yāmā*, f. the Yamunā or Jumna river. *s.*

تریامك त्रियामक *tri-yāmak*, m. sin, as the impeder of the three objects of life. *s.*

تریاقي *tiriyāḳī* or *tiryāḳī*, m. an opium-eater. *a.*

تري بري तिरीबिरी *tirī birī*, dispersed. *h.*

تريپر त्रैपुर *trai-pur*, m. the city of Tipperah in Bengal. *s.*

تریت तरेत *taret*, m. a buoy. *h.*

تریتا त्रेता *tretā*, f. the name of the second Hindū *yug* or æra, the silver age (v. *yug*). *s.*

تریتاگن त्रेताग्नि *tretāgni*, the three sacred fires of the Hindūs. *s.*

تریڑا तरेड़ा *tareṛā*, m. the falling of water from a spout, or from any height. *h.*

تریز *tarīz*, the pieces in a vestment that are cut transversely or diagonally. *p.*

تریشت त्रियष्टि *tri-yashṭi*, m. a medicinal plant (*Mollugo pentaphylla*). *s.*

تریکه *tarīka* (v. *tarika*), property left by a deceased person. *a.*

ترین *tarīn*, sign of the superlative degree in Persian; as *khūb*, fair. *khūb-tarīn*, fairest, most fair. *p.*

تریند तिरेन्द *tirend*, تریندا तिरेन्दा *tirendā*, } m. the float of a fishing-line, a float or floater (a buoy). *h.*

تریودش त्रयोदश *trayodash*, m. تریودشي त्रयोदशी *trayodashī*, f. } the thirteenth (used only in dates), as the 13th of the half lunation or lunar month. *s.*

تریودیه त्रैविद्य *traividya*, m. a man versed in the three Vedas, or possessing three sciences. *s.*

تریه तुरीय *turīya*, m. the Divine Being, or Universal Spirit. *s.*

تري त्रयी *trayī*, f. the three Vedas; a plant (*Conyza serratula*). *trayī-dharma*, m. duties or rites enjoined by the three Vedas. *s.*

تڙ तड़ *taṛ*, m. party, division, faction; an imitative sound. *h.*

تڙا तड़ा *taṛā*, m. an island. *h.*

تڙاڙا तड़ाड़ा *taṛāṛā*, m. throwing water. *h.*

تڙاڙنا *taṛāṛnā*, a. to rear up (a horse). *d.*

تڙاقا *taṛāḳā*, m. sound of a blow, noise made by striking. *d.*

تڙاکا तड़ाका *taṛākā*, m. the sound of striking; adj. pretty, showy, gaudy. *h.*

تڙاکڙي तड़ाकड़ी *taṛākṛī*, f. the beam of a balance. *h.*

تڙاگ तड़ाग *taṛāg*, m. a pond, a tank deep enough for the growth of the lotus; a trap for catching deer. *h.*

تڙانا तुड़ाना *tuṛānā*, a. to break, to cause to be broken or changed (as money). *h.*

تڙاوا तड़ावा *taṛāvā*, m. show, ostentation, vanity. *h.*

تڙایا तड़ाया *taṛāyā*, m. foppishness, wearing smart clothes. *taṛāyā-dār*, m. one who dresses well, and is particular in having fine and well-made clothes. *h.*

تڙپ तड़प *taṛap*, f. haste, hurry; outrageousness, explosion, fury; leap, jump. *h.*

تڙپانا तड़पाना *taṛpānā*, a. to put in great agitation; to cause to flutter, stumble. *h.*

تڙپڑا तड़पड़ा *taṛpaṛā*, m. the noise of falling water. *h.*

تڙپڙي तड़पड़ी *taṛpaṛī*, f. flutter, agitation. *h.*

تڙپنا तड़पना *taṛapnā*, تڙپهنا तड़फना *taṛaphnā*, } n. to flutter, to palpitate; to be very desirous about any thing, to be agitated, to jump, to spring, to bound, to wriggle, to toss. *h.*

ترپهه तड़फ *taraph*, f. perplexity, timidity, agitation. *h.*

ترپهانا तड़फाना *tarphānā*, a. (same as *tarpānā*), to cause to flutter or agitate. *h.*

ترپهڑانا तड़फड़ाना *tarpharānā*, n. to flutter, to palpitate. *h.*

ترپهڑاهٹ तड़फड़ाहट *tarpharāhaṭ*, f. act of fluttering, palpitation. *h.*

ترپهنا तड़फना *taraphnā*, m. (see *tarapnā*). *h.*

ترپيلا तड़पीला *tarpīlā*, hasty, hurrying. *h.*

ترترانا तड़तड़ाना *tartarānā*, n. to trickle, to drop, to patter, to bluster, to welter; to warp or crack with noise (as a plank exposed to the sun). *h.*

ترتراهٹ तड़तड़ाहट *tartarāhaṭ*, f. the act of dropping. *h*

ترخ *tarakh*, } a cleft, fissure, crevice, split, or
ترق *taraḳ*, } crack. *d.*

ترس *taras*, m. a hyena. *d.*

ترقنا *taraḳnā* (also *tarakhnā*), n. to be cracked, to be split (see *taraknā*). *p.*

ترکا तड़का *tarkā*, m. dawn of day. *tarke*, in the morning, early. *h.*

ترکان तड़काना *tarkānā*, to cause to be cracked. *h.*

ترکنا तड़कना *taraknā*, n. to be cracked, to be split. *h.*

تڑواٹ तुड़वाट *turwāṭ*, breakage, fracture. *h.*

تڑوان तुड़वाना *turwānā*, a. to cause to break, to cause to be devoured. *h.*

ترور *tarwar*, name of a shrub (*Cassia auriculata*), the bark of which is used in tanning. *d.*

تري بري *tirī-birī*, mishmash, medley. *d.*

ترايد *tazāyud*, m. increase, augmentation. *a.*

ترك *tuzuk*, m. retinue, pomp; regulation, ordinance, institutes. *t.*

ترکيه *tazkiya*, m. purifying; in law it signifies a case in which a certain number of special witnesses bear testimony to the competency of other witnesses who are giving evidence in any cause; the former being denominated the *Muzakkīs*, or purgators. *a.*

ترلزل *tazalzul*, m. commotion, agitation, trepidation; an earthquake. *a.*

تزويج *tazwīj*, taking unto one's self a wife. *a.*

تزوير *tazwīr*, f. imposture, fraud, deceit, stratagem; deception, lie. *a.*

تزيلا *tazelā*, m. a *tāzī*, or Arabian colt. *p.*

تزيين *tazyīn*, f. dressing one's self, decoration, ornament, honour, jewel. *a.*

تس तिस *tis*, inflect. pron. that, which, &c. *tis-uparānt*, moreover. *tis-par* or *tis-pe*, besides, over and above, whereupon, moreover, yet, nevertheless, then, after that, thereon, whereat. *tis-par-bhī*, thereon, nevertheless. *h.*

تس तिस *tis* (for *trish*), f. thirst. *s.*

تس तुस *tus*, m. the husk of corn or rice. *s.*

تسار तुसार *tusār*, m. ice, frost, or snow (see *tushar*). *s.*

تسامح *tasāmuḥ*, m. reciprocal indulgence, mutual kindness and forgiveness; double meaning. *a.*

تساوي *tasāwī*, f. similarity, sameness, equality, neutrality. *a.*

تساهل *tasāhul*, m. conniving at, pardoning; carelessness. *a.*

تسبيح *tasbīḥ*, f. the act of praising God by repeating the sentence *subḥān-allāh* "glory be unto the Lord;" a rosary, a chaplet of beads (not applied to a Hindū rosary). *tasbīḥ-khāna*, a chapel. *tasbīḥ-khwān*, saying prayers; a person hired to pray for another, a private chaplain. *tasbīḥ-khwānī*, the office of a chaplain. *a.*

تسخر *tasakhkhur*, m. ridicule; subduing, making tractable. *a.*

تسخير *taskhīr*, f. imprisoning, taking a strong hold, subduing, captivating. *taskhīri-kulūb*, captivating hearts. *a.*

تسديس *tasdīs*, f. divided into six parts; a sextile aspect of the stars. *a.*

تسر तसर *tasar*, m. a shuttle; a kind of coarse silk, the produce of a particular worm (*Bombyx paphia*) that feeds on the asin (*Terminalia alata globra*), &c *s.*

تسرا तिसरा *tisrā*, } m. third person,
تسرايت तिसरायत *tisrāyat*, } an umpire. *h.*

تسطير *tasṭīr*, writing, delineating. *a.*

تسع *tis'*, nine. *tus'*, a ninth part. *a.*

تسع مائة *tis'a mi,at*, nine hundred (used in dates of the *hijra*). *a.*

تسكر तस्कर *taskar*, m. a stealer, a thief, a robber, a kind of potherb (*Medicago esculenta*); a tree (*Vangueria spinosa*). *taskaratā*, f. thievishness, thieving. *s.*

تسكري तस्करी *taskarī*, f. theft, robbery; a passionate woman. *s.*

تسكين *taskīn*, f. consolation, comfort, pacifying. *taskīn denā*, a. to appease, to pacify, to soothe, to calm, to assuage. *taskīn-bakhsh*, assuasive, mitigating, consolatory, an anodyne. *a.*

تسلا तसला *taslā*, m. a vessel used by the Hindūs wherein to dress their victuals. *h.*

تسلسل *tasalsul*, m. connecting like a chain, association of ideas, infinite series, succession; flowing as water. *a.*

تسلط *tasalluṭ*, m. command, sway, absolute rule. *a.*

تسلي *tasallī*, f. consolation, comfort, solace. *tasallī denā*, a. to assure, to secure, to animate, to exhilarate. *a.*

تسليم *taslīm*, f. delivery, consignment; recommending to the care or protection of another; a respectful mode of salutation which consists in lowering the right hand until the knuckles nearly touch the ground, then gradually raising the body and lifting the hand to the crown of the head. This salutation is more respectful than the *kornish*, q.v.; health, security *taslīm-k.*, to give up with resignation; to resign, surrender, cede; to do homage; pl. *taslīmāt*. *taslīmāt-bajā lānā*, to make obeisances. *a.*

تسمه *tasma*, m. a thong, a strap of leather. *tasma khaincknā*, a. to strangle. *tasma-kash*, a strangler, a mute. *tasma-bāzī*, a game played by the lower orders: it consists in coiling up a leather strap and then inserting a pin, &c. This game may be seen in our own country fairs. *p.*

تسميه *tasmiya*, m. nomination, giving a name to, pronouncing the formula "*bism Illāh*." &c. *a.*

تسنن *tasannun*, m. the becoming a *sunnī* (v. *sunnī*). *a.*

تسنيم *tasnīm*, name of a fountain in paradise. *a.*

تسوت तिसूत *tisūt*, m. name of a medicine. *h.*

تسو तस्सू *tassū*, m. a measure of nearly one inch. *h.*

تسوانسي तिस्वांसी *tiswānsī*, the twentieth of a *biswānsī*, q.v. *h.*

تسويد *taswīd*, f. making black; the draft of a letter, &c., a rough copy, sketch, plan, delineation. *a.*

تسهيل *tas,hīl*, rendering easy, facilitating. *a.*

تش तिष *tish*, f. thirst; wish, desire. *s.*

تش तुष *tush*, m. the husk or chaff of rice, &c. (*Beleria myrobalan*). *s.*

تشابه *tashābuh*, m. similitude, resemblance, likeness. *a.*

تشار तुषार *tushār*, m. frost, cold; thin rain, mist; ice or snow. *s.*

تشارا तुषारा *tushārā*, cold, frosty. *s.*

تشاريف *tashārif* (pl. of تشريف), honours, &c. *a.*

تشاكل *tashākul*, m. mutual resemblance. *a.*

تشانل तुषानल *tushānal*, m. a conflagration of chaff; a capital punishment; twisting dry straw round the limbs of a criminal, and setting it on fire. *s.*

تشبه *tashabbuh*, m. resemblance, similitude. *a.*

تشبيه *tashbīh*, f. a simile, comparison, allegory, metaphor. *ḥarf-i tashbīh*, adverbs of similitude. *a.*

تشت *tasht*, m. a platter, a basin, a charger, a salver. *p.*

تشت तुषित *tushit*, m. a subordinate deity, one of a class of thirty-six. *s.*

تشتت *tashattut*, m. dispersion, dissipation. *a.*

تشتري तश्तरी *tashtarī*, } f. a salver, a small
تشتڑي तश्तड़ी *tashtaṛī*, } plate, a saucer. *h.*

تشٹ तुष्ट *tushṭa*, pleased, satisfied. *tushṭi*, f. pleasure, content. *tushṭatā*, f. delight, satisfaction. *s.*

تشخص *tashakhkhus*, m. identifying, particularizing, appropriation. *a.*

تشخيص *tashkhīs*, f. distinguishing perfectly (a word much used by physicians, to denote their having ascertained the disorder of a patient, *diagnosis*); valuation; assessment. *a.*

تشدد *tashaddud*, m. seizing and holding firmly; adj. strong, robust; corroborated, confirmed. *a.*

تشديد *tashdīd*, f. consolidating, corroborating; name of an orthographical mark placed over letters, which denotes that they should be doubled. *a.*

تشرع *tasharru'*, m. the ordinances of a prophet, particularly the laws of *Muḥammad*; acting agreeably to those ordinances. *a.*

تشريح *tashrīḥ*, f. anatomy; a skeleton or anatomical preparation; act of dissecting a body; explanation or declaration. *'ilm-ut-tashrīḥ*, the science of anatomy. *a.*

تشريحي *tashrīḥī*, of or relating to anatomy. *a.*

تشريف *tashrīf*, f. honouring, exalting; investing with a splendid robe.. *tashrīf-i ḳabūlī*, sublime admiration. *tashrīf arzānī farmānā*, and *tashrīf farmānā*, mean only to go, or to come, *tashrīf lejānā*, to go, and *tashrīf lānā*, to come, *i.e.* to honour with one's presence (never said of one's self, except by a king). *a.*

تشريك *tashrīk*, becoming an associate or partner. *a.*

تشفي *tashaffī*, f. consolation; becoming calm (after anger). calmness. *a.*

تشكك *tashakkuk*, m. doubting. *a.*

تشنا तिष्णा *tishnā*, f. thirst; temptation. *s.p.*

تشنج *tashannuj*, m. the cramp, convulsion, spasm. *a.*

تشنك *tashank*, m. an iron instrument for piercing walls. *p.*

تشنگان *tishnagān* (pl. of *tishna*), the thirsty ones. *p.*

تشنگي *tishnagī*, f. thirst; temptation. *p.*

تشنه *tishna*, thirsty. *tishna,e khūn*, blood-thirsty. *tishna-k.*, a. to make thirsty; (met.) to create desire, to tempt. *tishna-lab*, of dry lips, thirsty. *tishna-labī*, thirstiness. *p.*

تشنيع *tashnī'*, f. disparaging, slandering; taunting, reproaching. *a.*

تشوير *tashwīr*, anguish, distress of mind. *a. p.*

تشويش *tashwīsh*, confusion; distraction; anxiety, grief, disquietude, alarm, apprehension. *a.*

تشهد *tashahhud*, m. making a profession of religious sentiments; avowing belief in the unity of the Deity and the mission of *Muḥammad*: this is done by declaring (in Arabic), "I profess that there is no god but God; and I acknowledge that *Muḥammad* is the apostle of God." *a.*

تشهير *tashhīr*, f. proclaiming, publishing; marking a criminal, public exposure such as carrying a criminal through a city mounted on an ass, &c. *a.*

تشيا तिष्या *tishyā*, f. } emblic
تشيپسپ तिष्यपुष्प *tishyapushp*, m. } myrobalan (*Phyllanthus emblica*), or auspicious flower. *s.*

تشيخ *tashaiyukh*, m. ostentatious pretence to, or display of, rank or dignity. *a.*

تشيع *tashaiyu'*, m. professing to be of the Muhammadan sect called *Shī,a*, or a follower of *'Alī*. *tashaiyu'-mazhab*, heresy: the sect of *Shī'a*, followers of *'Alī*. The Turks, Arabs, and Tartars are generally *Sunnis*, and consider themselves orthodox; the Persians again are mostly *Shī'as*, and are viewed by the orthodox as little better than so many of the wicked (v. *Shī'a*). *a.*

تشين *tashaiyun*, m. displaying of state, dignity. *a.*

تشيه तिष्य *tishya*, m. the eighth lunar mansion, figured by an arrow, and containing three stars, of which one is Cancri; adj. auspicious, fortunate. *s.*

تصاعد *taṣā'ud*, m. ascending, becoming difficult. *a.*

تصانيف *taṣānīf* (pl. of تصنيف), compositions, books, literary works. *a.*

تصاوير *taṣāwīr* (pl. of تصوير), pictures. *a.*

تصحيح *taṣ,ḥīḥ*, f. rectification, correction, verifying, illustrating, attestation. *a.*

تصحيحه *taṣ,ḥīḥa*, m. muster (especially of cavalry horses). *dāgh i taṣḥīḥa*, the office in which the horses employed in service are marked. *a.*

تصحيف *taṣ,ḥīf*, f. making an error in writing; changing the diacritical points so as to alter the pronunciation and meaning of a word. *a.*

تصدق *taṣadduḳ*, m. alms; giving alms (particularly with a religious view); sacrificing, devoting. *taṣadduḳ honā*, to become a sacrifice, to become devoted heart and soul to a beloved object. *a.*

تصديع *taṣdī'*, f. the headache; trouble, perplexity; pl. *taṣdī'āt*, troubles. *taṣdī'-dih*, troublesome, giving trouble. *a.*

تصديق *taṣdīḳ*, f. verifying, attesting, acknowledging as true, appeal. *taṣdīḳ-bilā taṣawwur*, presupposition. *a.*

تصرف *taṣarruf*, m. possession, use; expenditure, disposal, embezzlement, extravagance. *taṣarruf-ẓāmin* or *-ẓāminī*, security for possesion (of a property). *taṣarruf-k.* or *-meṅ lānā*, a. to take or get possession of; pl. *taṣarrufāt*, (in general acceptation for) the sum total of expenses, supernatural powers (of holy men). *a.*

تصرفي *taṣarrufī*, f. common provisions given to dependants, &c. (in opposition to *khāṣṣa*, being what the master and his company eat). *a.*

تصريح *taṣrīḥ*, f. evidence, manifestation. *a.*

تصريف *taṣrīf*, f. conjugation, declension, inflection (in gram.); changing, turning, converting. *a.*

تصغير *taṣghīr*, f. diminution, a diminutive noun. *a.*

تصفيه *taṣfiya*, m. purifying, particularly the mind from ill-will; reconciling, reconciliation, purgation. *a.*

تصليب *taṣlīb*, f. crucifixion. *a.*

تصميم *taṣmīm*, f. resolve, determination. *a.*

تصنع *taṣannu'*, artifice, speciousness, display. *a.*

تصنيف *taṣnīf*, f. invention, composition, authorship; pl. *taṣnīfāt*, compositions. *a.*

تصور *taṣawwur*, m. contemplation, meditation, reflection, fancy, conception, preconception, apprehension. *taṣawwur-k.*, to imagine. *a.*

تصوف *taṣawwuf*, m. the theology of the *ṣūfīs* or mystics of the east; mysticism, contemplation. *a.*

تصوير *taṣwīr*, f. a picture, an image. *taṣwīr banānā* or *khainchnā*, a. to draw, &c. to paint. *a.*

تضاد *taẓādd*, m. contradiction, contrariety, absurdity, inconsistency. *a.*

تضحيك *taẓḥīk*, f. mocking, derision, ridicule. *a.*

تضرع *taẓarru'*, m. supplication; lamenting, humbling one's self, submission. *a.*

تضعيف *taẓ'īf*, doubling, duplication. *a.*

تضمين *taẓmīn*, f. giving satisfaction for an injury; comprehending or including one thing in another; inserting the verses of another in one's own poem; giving security; intrusting with another; lending on interest; putting in a purse or strong box. *taẓmīn-k.*, to insert the verses of another in one's own poem, making the one correspond with the other. *a.*

تضييع *taẓyī'*, f. spoiling, wasting, idling (away time). *taẓyī' auḳāt*, idling away time; ennui, weariness. *a.*

تطابق *taṭābuḳ*, m. similarity, congruity, analogy, coherence, cohesion. *a.*

تطاول *taṭāwul*, m. usurpation, oppression, tyranny, conquest, rudeness, insolence. *a.*

تطبيق *taṭbīḳ*, f. comparing, likening; confronting (as two armies). *a.*

تطلع *taṭallu'*, arising. *taṭallu'u-sh -shams*, the rising of the sun. *s.*

تطوع *taṭawwu'*, doing a good action which one is not obliged to do, an act of supererogation. *a.*

تطويل *taṭwīl*, f. extending, lengthening, prolonging, stretching out, prorogation. *a.*

تطهير *taṭhīr*, f. purification, purgation, sanctification. *a.*

تظلم *taẓallum*, m. groaning under oppression, injustice, injury. *a.*

تعارف *ta'āruf*, m. mutual acquaintance; rule, fashion, custom; handing or offering any thing to another person (used in a respectful or polite sense). *a.*

تعاطي *ta'āṭī*, mutual giving or surrender; a silent kind of bargain, when the vendor hands over an article to the buyer, and the latter gives him the price without speaking. *a.*

تعاقب *ta'āḳub*, m. pursuit; persecuting; alternate succession, following. *a.*

تعال *ta'āl* (lit. be exalted), *ta'āl allāhu*, or *ta'āl-ta'āl!* interj. Good God! bravo! well done! *a.*

تعالي *ta'ālā* (used adjectively), the Most High. *a.*

تعاون *ta'āwun*, m. assistance, conspiring. *a*

تعب *ta'b*, m. labour, lassitude, weariness. *a.*

تعبد *ta'abbud*, being pious; devotion. *a.*

تعبير **ta'bīr**, f. explanation, interpretation (particularly of dreams); attribute, quality; pl. *ta'bīrāt*. *ta'bīr-go*, m. an interpreter of dreams. *a.*

تعبئه **ta'bi,a**, } تعبيه **ta'biya**, } m. arranging (household furniture); drawing up (an army), training, exercising. *a.*

تعجب **ta'ajjub**, m. wondering, admiration, astonishment, amaze, surprise. *a.*

تعجيل **ta'jīl**, f. agility, haste, despatch, expedition. *a.*

تعداد **ti'dād** or **ta'dād**, m. number; computation, enumeration, a list or invoice. *a.*

تعدد **ta'addud**, plurality, numbering, multiplying. *a.*

تعدي **ta'addī**, f. extortion, exorbitancy, oppression, wrong, injury, tyranny, violence, cruelty. *a.*

تعذر **ta'azzur**, m. apology (pl. *ta'azzurāt*). *a.*

تعذيب **ta'zīb**, torture, punishment. *a.*

تعذير **ta'zīr**, f. apologizing, subterfuge, excuse (little used). *a.*

تعرض **ta'arruz**, m. resisting, preventing, hindrance, obstacle, opposition, impediment. *a.*

تعريض **ta'rīz**, f. enlarging; making conspicuous; rendering obnoxious; being ambiguous in speech, or hinting at a subject obscurely; rendering intricate; making writing illegible; not dressing meat sufficiently; opposing, objecting; barter, exchange of one commodity for another; statement of particulars of landed property, deposited in a collector's office. *a.*

تعريف **ta'rīf**, f. praising; asserting; explaining, description; a table of rates of export and import duties, hence the European term "tarif." *ta'rīf ul-majhūl bil-majhūl*, explaining in terms as little understood as the thing intended to be explained. *a.*

تعريفي **ta'rīfī**, commendable; notable. *a.*

تعزيت **ta'ziyat**, f. condolence, lamentation; *ta'ziyat-nāma*, m. letter of condolence. *a.*

تعزير **ta'zīr**, f. punishment of a discretionary kind, such as the law does not precisely specify, correction, reproof, censure, reprimand. *a.*

تعزيل **ta'zīl**, f. removing or deposing from office, dismissal. *a.*

تعزيه **ta'ziya**, m. condolence, comforting; a representation or model of the tomb of *Hasan* and *Husain*, which is thrown into the river at the anniversary of the *muharram*. *ta'ziya khāna*, m. the place of the *Ta'ziya*. *ta'ziya-dār* or *-gīr*, m. one who observes the mourning in the *muharram*. *ta'ziya lenā*, a. to observe the mourning during the *muharram*. *a.*

تعشق **ta'ashshuk**, m. falling in love, making love, being in love. *a.*

تعصب **ta'assub**, m. prejudice for or against, i.e. prejudice or partiality, bigotry, superstition. *a.*

تعطل **ta'attul**, m. idleness; having no bracelets or other ornaments. *a.*

تعطيل **ta'tīl**, f. rendering useless; abandoning, neglecting; laying waste; vacation from school or from office. *ta'tīl kā roz*, a holiday, a sabbath (that of the *Muhammadans* is Friday). *a.*

تعظم **ta'azzum**, m. magnificence, grandeur, pride, arrogance. *a.*

تعظيم **ta'zīm**, f. reverence, respect, honour; treating with ceremony and respect, honouring, gentility, politeness. *a.*

تعفن **ta'affun**, m. stink, fœtor. *a.*

تعفيت **ta'fiyat**, effacing; adjusting. *a.*

تعقب **ta'akkub**, m. pursuing, punishing, tracing (intelligence). *a.*

تعقيد **ta'kīd**, causing to unite, joining. *a.*

تعقير **ta'kīr**, f. wounding desperately. *a.*

تعقل **ta'akkul**, m. understanding, perceiving; informing. *a.*

تعلق **ta'alluk**, m. relationship, connection, dependence; consideration, reflection; commerce, correspondence; property, possession, appertaining; a manor, lordship, a lease in perpetuity, a subdivision of a *zila'* or county, the latter consisting of several *ta'alluks*. *a.*

تعلقات **ta'allukāt**, pl. connections, concerns. *ta'allukāti dunyawī*, worldly concerns. *a.* [&c. *a.*

تعلقجات **ta'allukajāt** (pl. of تعلقه), lordships,

تعلقدار **ta'alluk-dār**, m. a landholder, the holder or proprietor of a *ta'alluk*. *ta'alluk-dārī*, the tenure, office, or estate of a *ta'alluk-dār*. *ta'alluk-dārī hakk*, the dues or rights of a *ta'alluk-dār*. *a. p.*

تعلقه **ta'alluka**, m. connection, relationship; lordship, possession of land, fee, manor; possessor of an estate, a lord of a manor, landlord, feoffee. *ta'alluka,e jadīd*, new dependencies. *ta'alluka,e kadīm*, old possessions. *ta'alluka,e zabar-dastī*, an estate seized by main force. *h.*

تعلل **ta'allul**, m. an excuse, pretext, refusal. *ta'alluli 'alīl*, a weak excuse. *a.* [study. *a.*

تعلم **ta'allum**, m. learning, being taught;

تعلي **ta'allī**, f. exalting one's self, appearing conspicuous. *a.*

تعليق **ta'līk**, f. a kind of writing used by the Persians; suspension; delaying. *a.*

تعليقه **ta'līka**, m. an inventory, a list. *a.*

تعليل **ta'līl**, f. causing one to make an excuse occasioning; changing one of the weak letters for another (in Arabic grammar); pl. *ta'līlāt*. *a.*

تعليم **ta'līm**, f. teaching, instruction, tuition; copying fine writing accurately; pl. *ta'līmāt*. *a.*

تعمق **ta'ammuk**, m. deepness; penetrating, going deep into. *a.*

تعميد **ta'mīd**, propping up; baptizing. *a.*

تعمير **ta'mīr**, f. rebuilding, repairing; making a place habitable, productive, and populous; pl. *ta'mīrāt*, repairs, &c. *a.*

تعمين **ta'mīl**, causing to act, putting in force (a decree, &c.). *a.*

تعميه *ta'miya*, m. act of rendering blind; an enigma; concealing the meaning of a sentence or discourse (generally applied to a chronogram after the manner of *abjad*, q.v., when the clause which should give the date fails in accuracy, and the excess or defect is obscurely indicated by another word; ex. gr. *az ḥauẓi laṭīf āb bardār*, draw water from the pellucid cistern. The letters in *ḥauẓi laṭīf* make 943, from which, subtracting those of *āb* (1 + 2 = 3), we have the date required, viz. 940. *a.*

تعويذ *ta'wīẕ*, m. having recourse to the Deity; asking protection; a charm, an amulet; a structure of brick or stone-work over a grave. *a.*

تعويق *ta'wīḳ*, f. suspending, preventing, delaying, averting. *a.*

تعهد *ta'ahhud*, m. agreement, a promise or pledge; rent; a lease, a contract. *ta'ahhud-dār*, the holder of an agreement or lease. *a.*

تعيش *ta'aiyush*, m. rejoicing; procuring a livelihood by labour and industry. *a.*

تعيل *ta'aiyul*, land held by a member of a royal family, more especially applied to the Delhī family, a royal appanage. *ta'aiyul shāhī*, the royal domains (around Delhī). *a.*

تعين *ta'aiyun*, m. manifesting, establishing, appointing, assigning, deputing; *ta'aiyunāt*, appointments. *a.* [tion. *a.*

تعيين *ta'yīn* or *ta'īn*, f. appointing, deputa-

تعينات *ta'yināt*, m. appointments, command, a garrison; business. *a.*

تعيناتي *ta'yinātī*, the object or business of an appointment, &c.; duty, service; a detachment of troops, a guard; any number of individuals nominated for some special duty. *a.* [one another. *a.*

تغابن *taghābun*, mutual deception, cheating

تغار *taghār*, m. a tub, bucket, trough, pail, platter. *p.* [bucket. *p.*

تغاري *taghārī*, f. a small tub, trough, or

تغافل *taghāful*, (sometimes *taghāfulī*), m. negligence, inadvertency, being absorbed, as in sleep, &c. *taghāful-shi'ār*, careless. *a.*

تغاير *taghāyur*, m. differing from each other, discrepancy. *a.*

تغذيه *taghẕiya*, m. food, nourishment. *a.*

تغريب *taghrīb*, banishment, transportation; imprisonment. *a.*

تغلب *taghallub*, m. taking advantage, cheating, imposition, forgery, embezzlement. *a.*

تغلبي *taghallubī*, f. adulteration, forgery. *a.*

تغمه *taghma*, m. a mark which artists put on their productions, device on a shield, a medal. *p.*

تغني *taghannī*, f. singing, cooing, celebrating a mistress in verse, contentment. *a.*

تغير *taghīr*, f. alteration, change; adj. changed, discharged, dismissed. *taghīr-k.*, a. to remove (from an office), to dismiss, to alter. *a.* [moval. *a.*

تغير *taghaiyur*, m. change, alteration, re-

تغيري *taghīrī*, f. the state of alteration or change, revolution, discharge, dismission. *a.*

تغيير *taghyīr* (v. *taghīr*), alteration &c. *a.*

تف *tuf*, m. spittle, saliva, a curse. *p.*

تف *taf*, m. vapour, steam, mist. *p.*

تفاخر *tafākhur*, m. boasting, vaunt. *a.*

تفارق *tafāruḳ*, m. division, separation. *a.*

تفاريق *tafārīḳ* (pl. of تفرقه), intervals, divisions, instalments. *a.*

تفاوت *tafāwut*, m. distance; difference, distinction, disparity; distant, separate, far away, remote, absent. *tafāwut bolnā*, a. to prevaricate. *a.*

تفاوق *tafāwuḳ*, commensurability (in arith.). *a.*

تفاول *tafāwul*, m. (v. *tafawwul*), presage &c. *a.*

تفت *taft*, heat, warmth; adj. hot, warm. *p.*

تفتگي *taftagī*, f. heat, ardour; anxiety. *p*

تفته *tafta*, hot, burning; quick-lime. *p.*

تفته‌دل *tafta-dil*, grieved at heart. *p.*

تفتيش *taftīsh*, f. examination, inquiry, search, investigation, research. *a.*

تفجر *tafajjur*, m. suppuration. *a.*

تفحص *tafaḥḥuṣ*, m. investigation, inquiry, search, disquisition. *a.* [gance. *a.*

تفخر *tafakhkhur*, m. pride, boasting, arro-

تفراخ *tafrākh*, a blow, a slap. *d.*

تفرج *tafarruj*, m. recreation, amusement, relaxation of mind, contemplation of natural scenery. *tafarruj-gāh*, a place of recreation. *a.* [ment. *a.*

تفرح *tafarruḥ*, m. leisure, ease, refresh-

تفرس *tafarrus*, m. intelligence, understanding; judging from physiognomy. *a.*

تفرقه *tafriḳa*, m. division, separation, dispersion; distress, divorce. *tafriḳa-k.*, to separate, to distribute; pl. *tafārīḳ*. *a.*

تفره *tafra*, affected magnificence, pride. *t.*

تفريح *tafrīḥ*, f. rejoicing, exhilarating; amusement. *tafrīḥi ṭab'*, ease of mind, cheerfulness, hilarity. *a.*

تفريد *tafrīd*, f. retiring, leading a solitary life (especially for the purpose of devotion). *a.*

تفريس *tafrīs*, f. breaking, tearing in pieces. *a.*

تفريق *tafrīḳ*, f. separation, division; partition, participation; jealousy, misunderstanding; department. *tafrīḳ-k.*, a. to analyze. *tafrīḳ-nāma*, a deed settling the shares claimed by different parties. *a.*

تفسيده *tafsīda*, burnt, warmed, heated, chapped or cracked through heat. *p.*

تفسير *tafsīr*, f. explanation, commentary, paraphrase, an interpretation of the *ḳur,ān*. *a.*

تفصيل *tafṣīl*, f. explanation, analysis; separation, division; detail or particulars of an account, and the like. *tafṣīl-k.*, to explain at full length. *tafṣīl wār*, in full detail. *a.*

تفضل *tafazzul*, m. excelling; deserving. *a.*

تفضيح *tafzīh*, f. disgrace, disrepute. *a.*

تفضيل *tafzīl*, excellence, pre-eminence. *ismi tafzīl*, the comparative or superlative degree. *a.*

تفقد *tafakkud*, m. kindness; searching for a thing lost, inquiring diligently. *a.*

تفكر *tafakkur*, m. reflecting, meditating; cogitating, considering; anxiety. *a.*

تفكه *tafakkuh*, m. admiring; penitence; enjoyment of any thing. *a.*

تفنگ *tufang*, f. a musket (properly any tube through which any thing is blown). *tufangchī*, a musketeer. *tufangī*, musketry, firing of muskets. *p.*

تفنن *tafannun*, m. amusement, pastime. *a.*

تفوق *tafawwuk*, m. pretending to a superiority over others; doing any thing by degrees. *a.*

تفول *tafawwul*, m. presaging happily, taking a good omen from a name, &c. *a.*

تفويض *tafwīz*, f. resigning, committing to another, recommending, confiding to another; marrying a wife without a fortune. *a.* [ing. *a.*

تفهم *tafahhum*, m. understanding, conceiv-

تفهيم *tafhīm*, f. teaching, instructing. *a.*

تقابل *takābul*, m. encountering, being drawn up in mutual opposition. *a.*

تقادم *takādum*, m. being ancient; in law, it signifies such a distance of time as suffices to prevent punishment. It operates in a way similar to our statutory limitations. *a.*

تقارب *takārub*, m. approaching one another; (in versification) name of a measure. *a.*

تقاضا *takāzā*, m. dunning, exacting, urgency, importunity; exacting by means of a suit at law. *takāzā,e sinn*, the customs or habits of different ages, as of childhood, youth, manhood, &c. *takāzā,e shadīd*, inexorable dunning. *a.*

تقاضاىي *takāzā,ī*, importunate, solicitous. *a.*

تقاطر *takātur*, m. distilling drop by drop; raining. *a.*

تقاعد *takā'ud*, backwardness, dilatoriness. *a.*

تقاوت *takāwat*, f. piety, abstinence, continence. *a.*

تقاوي *takāwī*, f. strengthening, assisting (particularly tenants); vying, contending with; money advanced to cultivators at the time of sowing. *a.*

تقبض *takabbuz*, mutual surrender, or silent exchange of an article and its cost. *a.*

تقدس *takaddasa*, lit. "He is pure, or holy." *takaddasa wa ta'ālā*, an epithet of the Deity, "He is Holy and Most High." *takaddus*, holiness, sanctity. *a.*

تقدم *takaddum*, m. priority, pre-eminence. *a.*

تقدمه *takaddama*, final adjustment or audit of an account. *a.*

تقدير *takdīr*, f. fate, predestination, the Divine decree, the ordination of Providence. *a.*

تقديس *takdīs*, f. sanctity, purity, sanctification, sanctifying; magnifying. *a.*

تقديم *takdīm*, f. giving precedence, priority, precedence, performance. *takdīm-k.*, a. to perform, to put before, to give precedence to. *a.*

تقرب *takarrub*, propinquity, nearness, approximation; access; association. *a.*

تقرر *takarrur*, m. being established; confirmation, ratification, approbation. *a.*

تقريب *takrīb*, m. recommendation, mention, occasion, conjunction, cause, pretence, motive, approaching, proximity, probability. *takrīb-k.*, a. to commend, to prepare a person for the reception of another. *a.*

تقريبًا *takrīban*, near to, about, nearly. *a.*

تقرير *takrīr*, f. confession; relation, oration, recital, detail, narration. *takrīr-k.*, to relate. *a.*

تقريس *takrīs*, f. congealing, cooling. *a.*

تقسيم *taksīm*, f. division (in arithmetic); dividing, distributing. *taksīm-k.*, a. to distribute. *taksīm-dār*, the divisor. *taksīm-hone kī rakm*, the dividend. *taksīmi jam'*, assessment upon the lands of a country. *a.*

تقشف *takashshuf*, m. living poorly, being scantily fed and coarsely clothed. *a.*

تقصير *taksīr*, f. (lit. deficiency) fault, error, crime. *taksīr-mand*, guilty, criminal. *taksīr-wār*, blameable, criminal; pl. *taksīrāt*, crimes. *a.*

تقطير *taktīr*, f. distilling, dropping (particles of urine), strangury. *a.*

تقطيع *taktī'*, f. the cæsura or pause in reading poetry; scanning of verse; dissection. *a.*

تقلب *takallub*, m. conversion, change, transmutation. *a.*

تقليب *taklīb*, m. conversion, change. *a.*

تقليد *taklīd*, f. imitation, counterfeiting, forgery. *taklīd-k.*, to ape, to imitate. *a.*

تقليدي *taklīdī*, imitated, forged, false (as stone, &c.), counterfeit (as a coin). *a.*

تقليل *taklīl*, f. diminishing, causing to look less, reduction, diminution. *a.*

تقوىٰ *takwā*, m. piety, abstinence, the fear of God. *ahli-takwā*, pious people, men of piety. *a.*

تقوي *takawwī*, f. assisting (particularly tenants by advances, remitting rents, &c.). *a.*

تقويت *takwiyat*, f. corroboration, strengthening, establishing, confirming, confidence, strength, assurance, comfort, reliance, trust, aid. *a.*

تقويم *takwīm*, f. making straight, adjusting; an almanack, ephemeris, calendar. *a.*

تقي *takī*, pious, devout; name of a celebrated Hindūstānī poet. *tukā*, piety, fear of God. *a.*

تقيد *taḳaiyud*, m. attention, diligence, industry, application; superintending, overseeing, care, assiduity; pl. *taḳaiyudāt*. *a.*

تقيه *taḳīya*, m. pious fraud or subterfuge, allowable in certain cases; for instance, a Shī'a visiting Mecca as a pilgrim is allowed to practise *taḳīya*, and call himself a Sunnī. *a.*

تك तुक *tuk*, f. one line of a poem; a rhyme; a moment. *tuk-ek*, for one moment. *h.*

تك तक *tak*, (postpos.) till, to, up to, while, toward, near to; f. a scale, balance; aim. *tak-bāndhnā* or *-lagānā*, to gaze, to stare. *h.*

تكا तिक्का *tikkā*, m. a small piece of flesh; a steak, a slice; a chop or collop. *tikkā-boṭī-k.*, to tear to small pieces (a prey). *h.*

تكا *tukkā*, m. a sort of arrow blunt at the end; a small hill or mountain; an eminence. *p.*

تكاپو *takāpū*, also *takāpū,ī*, diligent search; bustling about in all directions. *p.*

تكار तिकार *ti-kār*, three ploughings. *h.*

تكاسل *takāsul*, m. indolence, negligence, carelessness. *a.* [of bamboos. *s.*

تكاكشيري तुकाक्षीरी *tukākshīrī*, f. the manna

تكاليف *takālīf* (pl. of تكليف), difficulties, distresses. *a.* [ture. *p.*

تكان तकान *takān*, m. motion, agitation, ges-

تكانا तकाना *takānā*, a. to take aim. *h.*

تكان دينا (in Persian تكانيدن), to shake, to jolt, to agitate, to brush off. *p*

تكاهل *takāhul*, m. negligence, remissness. *a.*

تكبر *takabbur*, m. arrogance, haughtiness, pride, insolence of office. *a.*

تكبري *takabburī*, f. haughtiness. *a.*

تكبير *takbīr*, f. repeating the (Musulmān) creed, or only saying "*Allāhu akbar*," "God is great," upon particular occasions. *a.*

تكت तिक्त *tikta*, bitter; fragrant; m. bitterness; fragrance. *tikta-bhadrak*, m. a kind of cucumber (*Trichosanthes diœca*). *tikta-patra*, m. a cucurbitaceous plant (*Momordica mixta*). *tikta-parwan*, f. a potherb (*Hilancha repens*), a plant (*Menispermum glabrum*). *tikta-tumbī*, f. a bitter gourd. *tikta-dugdhā*, f. a medicinal kind of moon-plant. *tikta-rohinikā*, f. a medicinal plant. *tikta-sār*, m. *mimosa catechu*. *tikta-sāk*, m. a plant (*Capparis trifoliata*). *tikta-gandhā*, f. a plant (*Lycopodium imbricatum*). *tikta-wallī*, f. a plant (*Aletris hyacinthoides*). *s.*

تكتك तिक्तक *tiktak*, m. a kind of gourd (*Trichosanthes diœca*); a sort of Gentian (*G. cherayta*). *s.*

تك تك तकतक *tak-tak*, m. the sound of feet. *h.*

تك تك तिकतिक *tik-tik*, f. a sound used in driving a cart. *h.*

تكتكا तिक्तिका *tiktikā*, f. a bitter gourd. *h.*

تكثير *taksīr*, f. augmenting, enlarging, increasing, multiplying. *a.*

تكثيف *taksīf*, rendering thick, condensation. *a.*

تكدد *takaddud*, toil, labour; hardship. *a.*

تكدر *takaddur*, m. dregs, dulness, moroseness. *a.*

تكذيب *takzīb*, f. accusing of falsehood, giving the lie. *takzīb-d.*, to give the lie. *a.*

تكر तक्र *takra*, m. buttermilk with a fourth part water. *s.*

تكراٹ तक्राट *takrāṭ*, m. a churning stick. *s.*

تكرار *takrār*, f. repetition, tautology; altercation, contention, dispute; the chorus or burden of a song. *a.* [troublesome, argumentative. *a.*

تكراري *takrārī*, adj. importuning, seizing,

تكرر *takarrur*, m. repeating, reiterating, persevering, repetition. *a.*

تكريم *takrīm*, f. honour, reverence, respect; treating with respect, honouring. *a.*

تكڑي *tukṛī*, f. a flight or swarm (of birds or insects). *d.*

تكسر *takassur*, m. being broken or shattered, spent or debilitated; carrying (figures in arithmetic); folding up the wings, as a bird when about to cease from flight. *a.*

تكسل *takassul*, m. sickness, indolence. *a.*

تكسير *taksīr*, f. breaking to pieces; carrying (figures in arithmetic); dividing so as to produce a fraction. *a.*

تكش *tukkash* (cor. of *tarkash*), m. a quiver. *p.*

تكششلا तक्षशिला *taksha-shilā*, f. the name of a city in Panjāb (the Taxila of Ptolemy). *s.*

تكشك तक्षक *takshak*, m. one of the *Nāgas* or serpents of the lower regions; a snake of a middle size and of a red colour. *s.*

تكشن तिक्ष्ण *tikshan*, pungent, hot; angry, passionate; sharp, acute, ardent, bitter, severe. *s.*

تكشن तक्षन *takshan*, m. a carpenter. *s.*

تكشني तक्षणी *takshanī*, f. a carpenter's adze. *s.*

تكفل *takafful*, m. taking security; becoming security for another; bail. *a.*

تكفير *takfīr*, f. covering, expiating a crime, doing penance or paying a mulct as atonement; guiltiness; humbling one's self before another (putting the hand upon the breast, and inclining the head); shewing distant respect; accusing one of impiety calling him infidel, making one an unbeliever. *a.*

تكفين *takfīn*, f. putting on the winding-sheet, laying in the coffin, &c., shrouding, sepulture. *a.*

تكل तुक्कल *tukkal*, f. } a kind of paper kite. *h.*
تكلا तुकला *tuklā*, m. }

تكلا तकला *taklā*, m. a spindle. *h.*

تكلف *takalluf*, m. inconvenience, ceremony; extravagance, profusion; preparation. *takalluf bar taraf*, waving ceremony. *takalluf-mizāj*, ceremonious; pl. *takallufāt*. *takallufāti darbār*, lit. extravagances of a court, expending much. *takallufāti rasmi*, ceremonious attention, empty compliments. *takallufāti majlis*, the ceremonies of society, etiquette. *a.*

تكلم *takallum*, m. conversation. *a.*

تكلي तुकली *tuklī* f. a paper kite (child's). *h.*

تكلي तकली *taklī*, f. a weaver's reel. *h.*

تكليف *taklīf*, f. ceremony, imposition of a burthen; trouble, difficulty, molestation, distress, inconvenience, ailment, affliction, annoyance. *taklīf denā*, a. to annoy. *taklīf-k.*, to take the trouble; pl. *taklīfāt*, ceremonies, &c. *a.*

تكمله *takmila*, m. perfection, completion. *a.*

تكمه *tukma*, m. a button, a loop, an eye loop. *tukma,e jaib kholnā*, a. to open the purse, to loosen the purse-strings. *p.*

تكميل *takmīl*, f. completing, finishing, perfection, excellence. *a.*

تكنا तकना *taknā*, a. to observe, to aim at, to watch; n. to be looked at, or stared at. *h.*

تكوا तकूआ *takū,ā*, or *takwā*, m. a spindle. *h.*

تكواهي तकवाही *takwāhī*, f. watching, overseeing, superintending, looking sharp after (as after a silversmith). *h.*

تك‌ودو *tak o dau*, fatigue, running about. *p.*

تكوري *takore*, a small kettle-drum. *d.*

تكونيا तिकोनिया *tikoniyā*, three-cornered, triangular. *s.*

تكه *tukha*, m. (see *tukkā*), a blunt arrow. *p.*

تكه *takha*, a goat. *takha-rīsh*, beard on the chin only, like a goat. *tikka*, a slice, a bit. *p.*

تكهار तुखार *tukhār*, m. (see *tusār*) ice, &c. *s.*

تكهارنا तिखारना *tikhārnā*, a. to confirm, to prove, to establish by argument; to trifallow, or plough three times; to inquire earnestly. *h.*

تكهان तखान *takhān*, m. a carpenter. *s.*

تكهراكرنا तिखराकरना *tikhrā-karnā*, a. to trifallow, to plough three times. *h.*

تكهري तखरी *takharī*, f. scales of a balance. *h.*

تكيني तकीनी *takīnī*, f. a small pillow. *h.*

تكيه *takya*, m. a pillow, a *faķīr's* stand; the reserve of an army. *takya-dār*, a *faķīr*, dervise. *takya denā*, a. to receive respectfully. *takya-k.*, v.a. to support, to encourage. *takya kisī par-k.*, a. to depend upon. *takya kalām* or *sukhan-takya*, m. a cant word introduced into one's conversation without any meaning. *takya lagānā*, a. to lean. *takya-nishīn*, a *faķīr*, a dervise. *p.*

تگ *tag*, running, toiling, a gallop. *p.*

تگ तग *tag* (same as *tak*, postpos.) up to, till, &c. *h.*

تگا तग्गा *taggā*, f. a strand or thread of a twist. *h.*

تگا तगा *tugā*, f. the manna of bamboos. *h.*

تگاپو *tagāpū*, f. bustle, toil, labour; also *tag o pū*. *p.*

تگادو *tagādau* (v. *tag-dau*), fatigue, &c. *p.*

تگانا तगाना *tagānā*, a. to cause to be quilted, to get stitched together. *h.*

تگائي तगाई *tagā,ī*, f. the price paid for quilting, &c.; act of quilting. *h.*

تگٹ *tagaṭ*, gold or silver tinsel. *d.*

تگ‌دو *tag-dau* (also *tag o dau*), f. fatigue, running about on business, or in search of employment. *p.*

تگر तगर *tagar*, m. a tree (*Tabernæmontana coronaria*). *s.*

تگرگ *tagarg*, m. hail, a hail storm. *p.*

تگڑ *tagaṛ*, a plate of metal; any thin flat piece of metal. *d.*

تگم तिग्म *tigma*, hot, pungent; sharp; m. heat, pungency. *s.*

تگن तिगुण *tigun*, m. a tone in music; adj. threefold. *s.*

تگنا तगना *tagnā*, a. to quilt, to stitch together. *h.*

تگنا तिगुना *tigunā*, threefold, triple. *s.*

تگوپو *tag-o-pū*, search, inquiry, bustle. *p.*

تگوتاز *tag-o-tāz*, gallop, running. *p.*

تگهڑي तघड़ी *taghṛī*, f. a girdle, a zone. *h.*

تگي तग्गी *taggī*, f. a strand or thread of a twist. *ti-taggī*, a thread of three strands. *chau-taggī*, of four strands; a kind of fishing-line not used with a rod. *h.*

تگيانا *tagyānā*, a. to cause to run or gallop. *p.h.*

تگيڑنا *tageṛnā*, to pursue closely, to chase. *d.*

تل तल *tal*, m. depth, bottom; the place underneath; the sole of the foot. Dakh. (for *tale*), under, beneath. *s.*

تل तुल *tul*, alike, like; m. the breadth of a field. *tul baiṭhnā*, n. to be weighed against valuable things which are to be given in alms; to sit straight and compact (as in a boat, which might be overset by sitting uneven or carelessly). *tul rahnā*, n. to stand front to front, or opposed. *s.*

تل तिल *til*, a plant bearing an oily seed (*Sesamum orientale*); the seed of the sesamum; a mole on the face; a moment, an instant. *tiloṅ meṅ tel nahīṅ kahnā* (lit. to say there is no oil in the seeds of sesamum), to say snow is black, to deny the most evident truth, to swear black is white. *s.*

تل *tall*, a hillock, a hill, a heap. *a.*

تلا तला *talā*, m. the sole of a shoe; the bottom of any thing; protection; a leathern fence worn by archers on the left arm. *s.*

تلا तुला *tulā*, f. a balance, a pair of scales; the seventh sign, Libra; a measure or weight of gold and silver, 100 *palas*, or about 145 ounces troy; the act of being weighed against gold or any kind of valuable substance, which is afterwards given to the priests. *s.*

تلا *tillā*, m. (for طلا) the golden border of a turban. *a.p.*

تلابيج तुलाबीज *tulā-bīj*, m. the berry of the *abrus precatorius*, from which the jeweller's weight is taken. *s.*

تلاپريكشا तुलापरीक्षा *tulā-parīkshā*, an ordeal by balance; the accused is accurately weighed, then removed, and certain prayers, &c. said; then he is weighed again, and if lighter than before it is an infallible sign of his innocence: if equal or heavier, he is deemed guilty. *s.*

تلادان तुलादान *tulā-dān*, n. a gift of gold to Brāhmans equal in weight to the person of the donor. *s.*

تلاداني *tillā-dānī*, f. a housewife or small bag for holding needles, thread, &c. *a. p.*

تلاتل तलातल *talātal*, m. the region under the earth; one of the seven divisions of hell. *s.*

تلاٹا *talāṭā*, m. the east, downwards. *d.*

تلار *talār* (v. *tale*), underneath, below. *d.*

تلاسنا *talāsnā*, } a. to rub the palms of the
تلاشنا *talāshnā*, } hands, or the soles of the feet. *d.*

تلاش *talāsh*, f. search, study, inquiry. *talāshī*, one who searches goods, &c. *p.*

تلاشي *talāshī*, f. annihilation; dispersion. *a.*

تلاطم *talāṭum*, m. buffeting, dashing; (particularly with reference to the waves of the ocean). *a.*

تلافي *talāfī*, f. compensation, recompense. *a.*

تلاقي *talāḳī*, f. meeting, interview, reunion. *a.*

تلاكوٹ तुलाकोटि *tulā-koṭi*, f. an ornament of the feet or toes; a hundred millions. *s.*

تلاكوش तुलाकोश *tulā-kosh*, m. a sort of ordeal by weighing the accused (v. *tulā-parīkshā*). *s.*

تلام *tilām* (pl. of تلم), servants, &c. *a.*

تلامذ *talāmiz*(pl.of تلميذ),students, scholars.*a.*

تلانا *tilānā*, m. a kind of song. *p.*

تلانا तलाना *talānā*, a. to cause to fry. *h.*

تلانا तुलाना *tulānā*, a. to cause to be weighed. *s.*

تلاو तलाव *talāw* (for *tālāb*), m. a tank, a pond, reservoir of water. *p.*

تلاوا *tulāwā*, m. an advanced guard, forlorn hope, a patrol or reconnoitering party. *t.*

تلاوا तुलावा *tulāwā*, m. part of a Hindūstānī carriage, which rests on the axle-tree arm, and supports the body of the carriage. *s.*

تل اوپر तलऊपर *tal-ūpar*, upside down, confused. *s.*

تلاوت *talāwat* or *talāwat*, f. meditation, reading (particularly the *ḳur,ān*,as an act of religion). *a.*

تلاوڑي तिलावड़ी *tilāwṛī* or *tilā,oṛī*, f. the name of a plain in the vicinity of Sirhind, abounding in robbers: hence it is applied to any situation of danger. *h.*

تلاؤں तलाओं *talā,oṅ*, low grounds. *s.*

تلائي तिलाई *tilā,ī*, f. a small frying-pan. *h.*

تلبر तिलबर *tilbar*, m. a species of bird. *h.*

تلبيس *talbīs*, f. cheating, fraud, fallacy, imposture; mixture, confusion; misrepresentation; concealing (the truth, the faults of goods on sale); failing in proving one's allegations; a knave; covering. *a.*

تلپٹ तलपट *talpaṭ*, ruined, destroyed, more especially crops by the trampling of cattle. *h.*

تلپنا तलपना *talapnā*, } a. to flutter to pal-
تلپهنا तलफना *talaphnā*, } pitate, to be restless. *h.*

تلپچٹ तिलपिच्चट *til-picchaṭ*, m. a sweetmeat made of ground sesamum. *s.*

تلپرني तिलपर्णी *til-parnī*, f. red sanders (*Pterocarpus santolinus*). *s.*

تلپنج तिलपिञ्ज *til-pinj*, } m. barren sesamum,
تلپيج तिलपेज *til-pej*, } bearing no blossom, or yielding no oil. *s.*

تليپهلا तुलिफला *tuli-phalā*, f. the *Simul*, or silk-cotton tree. *s.*

تلتلانا तुलतुलाना *tultulānā*, n. to become soft (from moisture), as a mud wall in the rains, as a sore or boil when suppurating, or a fruit getting ripe. *h.*

تلتلانا तलतलाना *taltalānā*, n. to shake. *h.*

تلتيل तिलतैल *til-tail*, m. sesamum oil. *s.*

تلجية *taljiyat*, a forced or wrong interpretation of the words of a contract. *a.*

تل چاولي तिलचावली *til-chāwlī*, f. mixture composed of rice and sesamum seeds; a mixture of black and grey hairs in the head. *s. h.*

تل چٹا तिलचट्टा *til-chaṭṭā*, m. a cockroach, (*Blatta*). *s. h.* [kind of sweetmeat. *s.*

تل چوري तिलचूरी *til-chūrī*, f. the name of a

تلچوه तलचुअ *talchu,a*, a light soil above clay. *h.*

تلچهٹ तलछट *talchhaṭ*, f. dregs, refuse, scum, sediment, offals, leavings. *h.*

تلچهنا तिलछना *tilachhnā*, a. to flutter, palpitate, be restless. *h.*

تلخ *talkh*, bitter, acrimonious, rancid; malicious, sorrowful. *talkh-rū*, morose. *talkh-dāna*, darnel, tares. *talkh-kām*, bitter to the palate. *talkh-k.*, to embitter, to aggravate. *talkh-go*, plain-spoken, harsh. *talkh-mizāj*, ill-tempered. *p.*

تلخا *talkhā*, m. grain parched and pounded, and then mixed up into a paste with water; the gall-bladder. *p.*

تلخي *talkhī*, f. bitterness, malice, rancour. *p.*

تلدهين तिलधेनु *til-dhenu*, f. sesamum made up in the shape of a cow for the purpose of being presented to the Brāhmans. *s.*

تلذذ *talazzuz*, m. delight, pleasure, charms. *a.*

تلڑا तिलड़ा *tilaṛā*, m. } a necklace or any ornament of three strings. *h.*
تلڑي तिलड़ी *tilaṛī*, f. }

تلسي तुलसी *tulsī* or *tulasī*, f. the name of a plant worshipped by the Hindūs, holy basil (*Ocymum sanctum*). *Tulsī* or *Tūlasī*, was a nymph beloved by *Krishṇa*, but by him turned into this plant. *tulsī-dās*, name of a *gosā,īṅ* and a celebrated Hindū poet. *tulsī dāna*, a gold ornament. *tulsī kā hīrā* beads made of the wood of the *tulsī* plant. *s.*

تل‌شکري तिलशकरी *til-shakarī*, f. a kind of sweetmeat made of sesame and sugar. *s.*

تلطف *talaṭṭuf*, m. kindness, obligingness, blandishment, favour. *talaṭṭuf-k.*, to shew kindness. *a.*

تلف *talaf*, m. ruin, destruction, loss; prodigality, consumption, expense. *talafu-l māl khalafu-l'umr*, the loss of riches is the prolongation of life. *talaf-k.*, a. to waste, to consume. *talaf-honā*, n. to be unfortunate, to meet with a loss. *a.*

تلفظ *talaffuẓ*, m. expression, pronunciation, utterance. *a.*

تلفيق *talfīḳ*, collecting; sewing together. *a.*

تلقا *tilḳā*, m. reprehension; arriving at, meeting with, falling upon, encountering in battle. *a.*

تلقين *talḳīn*, f. instructing, informing; the admitting of a person into any order in society, and initiating him in its laws, &c.; religious instruction, funeral service. *talḳīn-k.*, a. to instruct, to inform, to teach. *a.*

تلك तिलक *tilak*, m. the mark which Hindūs make on their forehead with coloured earths or unguents; a freckle, a mole, a natural mark on the body; a title (especially in comp.) implying pre-eminence; a commentary. *a.*

تلك *tilak*, f. a gown, a sleeveless robe. *p.*

تلك तलक *talak* (v. *tak*), (postpos.) up to, as far as, until. *h.*

تلكا तिलका *tilakā*, spotted, freckled; chief, principal; f. a kind of necklace. *s.*

تلكا तुलिका *tulikā*, f. a small bird, said to resemble the wagtail. *s.*

تلكا तल्लिका *tallikā*, f. a key. *s.*

تلكالك तिलकालक *tilkālak*, m. a mole on the body; a man so marked. *s.* [mum. *s.*

تلكٹ तिलकट *tilkaṭ*, m. the farina of sesa-

تل‌كٹ तिलकुट *til-kuṭ*, m. the name of a sweetmeat composed of pounded sesamum and sugar. *s. h.*

تلگ तलग *talag* (v. *talak*), up to, until. *h.*

تلملانا तलमलाना *talmalānā*, n. to be tantalized, to grieve, to be agitated. *h.*

تلمي तिलमय *til-may*, made of sesamum. *s.*

تلميذ *talmīẕ*, m. a student, a scholar, disciple, pupil. *a.*

تلميور तिलमयूर *til-mayūr*, m. a kind of peacock, marked with spots resembling the seed of sesamum. *s.*

تلن तलन *talan*, m. frying, fried meat. *h.*

تلنا तलना *talnā*, a. to fry, or n. to be fried. *h.*

تلنا तुलना *tulnā*, n. to be weighed in a balance; to be drawn up in array (as one army against another). *h.* [*lung jānā*, to amble. *d.*

تلنگ *tulung*, a kind of pace in a horse. *tu-*

تلنگا तिलङ्गा *tilangā* or *tilingā*, m. an inhabitant of Tailang, in which the soldiers were first clothed and disciplined in the European manner; hence, a soldier. *s*

تلنگا तिलङ्गा *tilangā*, m. } a kind of (child's) paper kite; the
تلنگي तिलङ्गी *tilangī*, f. }
Tininga or Telugu language. *h.*

تلوا तिलुवा *tilu,ā* or *tilwā*, m. a kind of sweetmeat (eaten particularly by the Hindūs when the sun enters Capricorn). *s.*

تلوا तलुवा *talū,ā* or तलवा *talwā*, m. the sole of the foot, the heel. *talwā chāṭnā* or *talwe tale hāth dharnā*, a. to flatter. *talwe sahlāne* (lit. to stroke the soles of the feet), signifies excessive flattery, adulation. *talwoṅ se āg lagnī* (lit. burning in the soles of the feet) implies excessive anger. *s.*

تلوار तलवार *talwār*, f. (same as *tarwār*), a sword. *s.*

تلواسنا तलवासना *talwāsnā*, a. to wear out, spoken in reference to the feet of an animal, which are worn by treading on hard rocky ground. *h.*

تلواسه *talwāsa*, m. commotion, astonishment. *p.*

تلوانا *talwānā*, } n. to have blistered feet from the heat of the sun. *d.*
تلواءي جانا *talwā,e-jānā*, }

تلوتما तिलोत्तमा *tilottamā*, f. name of an *apsarā* or dancing-girl in the court of Indra. *s.*

تلوٹ *tilwaṭ*, a kind of sweetmeat. *d.*

تلودن तिलौदन *tilaudan*, m. a dish of milk, rice, and sesamum. *s.*

تلوريا तलवरिया *talwariyā*, f. a scimitar; m. a swordsman; one armed with a scimitar, a sword-player. *s.*

تلون *talawwun*, m. changing colours like a chameleon; fidgeting, restlessness, capriciousness. *talawwun-ṭab'* or *-mizāj*, capricious, whimsical, fretful. *talawwun-mizājī*, f. capriciousness, fickleness of disposition. *a.*

تلونها तिलौंहा *tiloṅhā*, (spoken of a lamp) sloped so that the oil may reach the wick. *s.*

تلها तिलहा *tilhā*, oily. *tilhā,ī*, oiliness. *s.*

تلہڑو तलिहड़ू *talihṛū*, inferior, next, below, one who acts at the command of another. *s.*

تلي तली *talī*, f. the sole of a shoe; the bottom of any thing; beneath, under; impalpable powder. *s.*

تلي तिल्ली *tillī*, f. the spleen or milt. *tap tillī*, f. disorder of the spleen. *s.*

تلي तले *tale*, below, down, underneath. *tale ūpar*, upside down; confused. *tale tale dekhnā*, a. to see clandestinely. *tale kī zamīn ūpar honī*, is used to express great disturbance and confusion. *s.*

تلي तुली *tulī*, f. a steelyard; a fibrous stick or brush used by weavers for cleansing the wool; a painter's brush. *s.*

تليا तलैया *talaiyā*, f. a small pond. *s.*

تليپان तुल्यपान *tulya-pān*, m. drinking together. *s.*

تليني तलीनी *talīnī*, f. a kind of beetle, the wings of which are used for blistering, as a substitute for cantharides. This insect makes its appearance chiefly during the rainy season. *h.*

تليه तुल्य *tulya*, like, equal. *s.*

تليها तलैहा *talaihā* or *tilaihā*, m. a turtle-dove. *h.*

تم तम *tam* or तमः *tama*, m. darkness, gloom; the third of the qualities incident to the state of humanity; the *tama-gun*, or property of darkness, whence proceed folly, ignorance, mental blindness, worldly delusion, passion, anger, &c.; sorrow, grief. *s.*

تم *tamm* (for *tamma*), it is complete. *tammal-kitāb*, the book is finished; finis. *a.*

تم तुम *tum* (2d pers. pron. pl.), you. *tum-āp*, you yourself. *tum-ko*, to you. *tum-tanau*, gen. pl. your, of you. *s.*

تم तिमि *timi*, m. a fabulous fish, said to be [one hundred *Yojans* long. *s.*

تماثل *tamāṡul*, equal division of an estate. *a.*

تماچا *tamāchā*, | تماچه *tamācha*, } m. a slap, a box, a blow, a thump, a cuff. *p.*

تماخرامارنا *tamākhrā mārnā*, a. (inelegant) to reproach in jest; to put on airs of consequence in poverty. *h.*

تماخو *tamākhū* (Dakh. for *tamākū*), tobacco.

تمادي *tamādī*, f. perseverance; a long time; (in law) a limitation as to time which bars a civil prosecution. *a.*

تمارا *tumārā* (for *tumhārā*), your. *d.*

تمارض *tamāruẓ*, m. feigning a disease. *tamāruẓ-k.*, to feign sickness, to "sham Abram." *a.*

تماسخ *tamāsukh*, m. effacing, transforming, metamorphosing, transmigration (of souls). *a.*

تماشا *tamāshā*, m. an entertainment, show, a spectacle; sight. *tamāshā-k.*, a. to see; to take a walk; to jeer, to jest. *tamāshā-bīn*, a sight-seer, rake, epicure. *tamāshā-bīnī*, f. luxury, libertinism; sometimes contracted into *tamāsh*, as *tamāsh-bīn*, a rake, an epicure, a whoremaster. *tamāsh-bīnī*, f. raking, whoring. *a.*

تماشاگاه *tamāshā-gāh*, f. a spectacle, a place [for holding a show. *a. p.*

تماشائي *tamāshā,ī*, m. a spectator, looker on; a rake, an epicure. *a.*

تماكو *tamākū*, | تماكهو *tamākhū*, } tobacco (v. *tambākū*). *h.*

تمال तमाल *tamāl*, m. the name of a tree, noted for the dark hue of its blossoms (*Xanthocymus pictorius*); the sectarial mark made with sandal, &c. *s.*

تمالك तमालक *tamālak*, m. a potherb (*Marsilea dentata*). *s.*

تمالكا तमालिका *tamālikā*, f. a district in Bengal, the modern *Tamluk*. *s.*

تمالي तमाली *tamālī*, f. a plant used as an [emollient *s.*

تمام *tamām*, entire, perfect, complete. *tamām-tar*, wholly, completely. *tamām shud*, it is finished. *tamām-k.*, to perfect, to complete, to finish. *tamām honā*, n. to be finished, to die. *a.*

تمامي *tamāmī*, f. completion, totality, the whole; brocade, cloth of gold, tissue. *a.*

تمانا तुमाना *tumānā*, a. to cause to be carded. *h.*

تمائي तुमाई *tumā,ī*, f. the price of carding. *h.*

تمبا तुम्बा *tumbā*, m. a hollowed gourd; the rind of a gourd in which beggars carry water, &c. *s.*

تمبا *tambā*, | تمبان *tambān*, } m. trousers, drawers. *p.*

تمباكو तम्बाकू *tambākū*, m. tobacco: the word, though of foreign origin, is now quite naturalized in the language. *h.*

تمبالو तम्बालू *tambālū*, a brass vessel in which Hindūs dress their food; a small round brass pot for water. *d.*

تمبو तम्बू *tambū*, m. a tent; (in Dakh.) an eel. *h.*

تمبول तम्बोल *tambol*, m. the betel leaf. *tambol ānā*, to bleed from the bridle (a horse's mouth). *h.*

تمبولن तम्बोलिन *tambolin*, a woman who sells betel leaf; a kind of tree. *h.*

تمبولي तम्बोली *tambolī*, m. a caste whose business is to sell betel leaf. *h.*

تمبومچهي *tambū-machhī*, a species of lam-[prey. *h.*

تمبي तुम्बी *tumbī*, f. a long gourd (*Cucurbita lagenaria*); a small hollow gourd; the rind of a gourd in which beggars carry water, &c.; a kind of pipe. *s.*

تمبيا तम्बिया *tambiyā* or तुम्बिया *tumbiyā*, m. a pot. *h.*

تمت तमत *tamat*, desirous, longing. *s.*

تمت तिमित *timit*, wet, moist; steady, fixed. *s.*

تمتع *tamattu'*, m. enjoyment, delight, pleasure; using, gaining. *a.*

تمتمانا तमतमाना *tamtamānā*, m. to grow red (in the face); to glow, to sparkle, to twinkle, to flash. *s.*

تمتمانا *timtimānā*, to dance in time to music. *d.*

تمتماهت तमतमाहट *tamtamāhaṭ*, f. the state of growing red (in the face). *s.*

تمتنو तुमतनौ *tumtanau* (for *tumhārā*), your [yours. *h.*

تمثال *timṡāl*, resemblance, picture. *a.*

تمثل *tamaṡṡul*, m. imitating, resembling; applying allegories. *s.*

تمثيل *tamṡīl*, f. comparison, similitude; allegory, parable, prologue, an example; pl. *tamṡīlāt*, parables, &c. *tamṡīl lānā*, a. to allegorize, to speak in parables. *tamṡīlan*, allegorically. *a.*

تمجيد *tamjīd*, f. the glorification of God; hence, the hymn or prayer that is pronounced from the minarets an hour and a half before dawn. *a.*

تمر तिमिर *timir*, m. darkness, obscurity. *s.*

تمر *tamar*, m. a date. *tamari-hind* or *tamari-hindī*, f. a tamarind. *a.*

تمرد *tamarrud*, m. refractoriness, stubbornness, disobedience, insolence, rebellion. *a.*

تمردي *tamarrudī*, refractoriness, &c. *d.*

تمس तमस *tamas*, m. (v. *tam*) darkness. *s.*

تمسرا तमिस्रा *tamisrā*, f. a dark night, one during the wane of the moon; m. the dark half of the month from the full to the change. *s.*

تمسخر *tamaskhur*, m. buffoonery. *a.*

تمسك *tamassuk*, m. a note of hand, bond, obligation, receipt; pl. *tamassukāt*. *a.*

تمسوني तमस्विनी *tamaswinī*, f. night. *s.*

تمش तिमिष *timish*, m. a kind of pumpkin gourd, a water melon. *s.*

تمغا *tamghā* (v. *al-tamghā*), stamp, mark, brand; a species of tax; royal charter, seal. *t.*

تمك तमक *tamak*, f. vanity, arrogance, pride; f. growing red in the face. *s.*

تمكا तमका *tamkā*, m. a stroke of the sun. *h.*

تمكن *tamakkun*, possessing authority. *a.*

تمكنا तमकना *tamaknā*, n. to grow red in the face; to be enraged without cause, or to break out into violence at a temperate and reasonable speech. *h.*

تمكنت *tamkanat*, f. dignity, authority. *a.*

تمكين *tamkīn*, f. majesty, dignity, authority, power. *a.* [beleric myrobalan. *s.*

تمل तुमुल *tumul*, m. tumult, combat, uproar;

تملق *tamalluḳ*, m. cajoling, flattery, adulation, ceremony. *a.*

تمليك *tamlīk*, possessorship, property. *tamlīk-nāma*, a deed of transfer. *a.*

تمن *tuman*, m. brotherhood, connection, caste, &c.; bevy, crowd, troop, squadron (properly, ten thousand) (see *tomān*). *tuman bāndhnā*, a. to collect a body of troops. *tuman-dār*, the commander of a *tuman*. *tuman-dārī*, f. the command of a *tuman*. *p.*

تمنا *tamannā*, f. request, wish, prayer, supplication, petition. *a.*

تمنا तुमना *tum-nā* (for *tum-ko*), to you, you. *d.*

تمنچه *tamancha*, m. a pistol. *p.*

تمنگل तिमिङ्गिल *timingil*, m. (v. *timi*) a fabulous colossal fish, the father of the sea serpent. *s.*

تمنگلگل तिमिङ्गिलगिल *timingilgil*, m. a fabulous fish, larger than the preceding. *s.*

تمني *tamannī*, f. request, &c. (see *tamannā*). *a.*

تموز *tamūz*, name of a Syrian month (July). *a.*

تموگن तमोगुण *tamo-gun* (v. *tam*), m. the principle of darkness, delusion, &c. *s.*

تموج *tamauwuj*, agitation (of waves, &c.) *a.*

تموگهن तमोघ्न *tamo-ghna*, m. a name of the legislator Buddha; lit. destroyer of darkness. *s.*

تمول *tammawwul*, f. riches, becoming rich. *a.*

تموليتي तमोलिप्ती *tamo-liptī*, f. the district of Tamluk, in Bengal. *s.* [passion, fear, &c. *s.*

تمورت तमोवृत *tamo-vṛit*, overcome with rage,

تمه तुम्ह *tumh* (for *tum*), you. *h.*

تمهارا तुम्हारा *tumhārā* (2d pers. pron. gen. pl.), your, yours, of you. *h.*

تمهوں तुम्हों *tumhoṅ* (inflect. pl. of *tum*), you. *h.*

تمهيد *tamhīd*, f. disposition, arrangement, settlement, management, confirmation, preliminary, preamble, preface, preparation, introduction. *tamhīd-k.*, a. to dispose, &c. (pl. *tamhīdāt*). *a.*

تمهيں तुम्हें *tumheṅ*, you, or to you. *h.*

تميز *tamīz*, f. judgment, discernment, discretion, sense. *ḥarfi-tamīz*, an adverb. *a.* [guished. *a.*

تميز *tamaiyuz*, m. being discerned, or distin-

تن *tan* (तन for तनु *tanu*) m. f. the body, person. *tan-āsānī*, f. bodily ease. *tan-parwarī*, f. luxury, voluptuousness. *tani-tanhā*, alone, solitary. *tan-durust*, sound in body, healthy, vigorous. *tan-durustī*, f. health, vigour. *tan-dih*, a person of application. *tan-dihī*, f. application, exertion, attention. *tan-denā*, a. to pay attention. *tan o man mārnā*, to restrain one's desires and be silent. *p. s.* [them, these. *h*

تن तिन *tin* (infl. pl. of the correl. pr. *so*), whom,

تن तुन्न *tunn*, m. name of a tree, of which the wood, resembling mahogany, is used for furniture; f. the flower of the tree (used for dyeing a yellow colour) (*Cedrela toona, Roxb.*); adj. tormented, vexed, injured, cut, broken. *s.* [sit upright. *s.*

تنا तना *tannā*, a. to stretch, to pull tight; n. to

تناخوري *tanā-khorī* (for *tanhā-khorī*), solitary living or enjoyment. *d.*

تناد *tanādd*, being dispersed, flight. *a.*

تنازع *tanāzu'*, m. wrangling, strife. *a.*

تنازل *tanāzul*, m. descent, decline (falling of price, losing rank, &c.); leaping from a horse in order to fight. *a.*

تناسب *tanāsub*, m. resembling, relation, proportion. *a.* [psychosis. *s.*

تناسخ *tanāsukh*, m. transmigration, metem-

تناسل *tanāsul*, m. generation; uninterrupted descent through a series of generations. *a.*

تنافر *tanāfur*, flying from each other, retiring, contending for pre-eminence (before a judge.) *a.*

تنافي *tanāfī*, f. expelling, pursuing, persecuting; denial (that another has performed any thing as that he has paid a debt). *a.*

تناقض *tanāḳuẓ*, contradiction; (in law) the advancing of two incompatible claims to the same property. *a.*

تناقل *tanāḳul*, mutual communication. *a.*

تنانا तनाना *tannānā*, n. to twang; to have a sharp pricking pain from inflammation. *h.*

تناور *tan-āwar*, corpulent, stout. *p.*

تناول *tanāwul*, m. eating. *tanāwul-k.*, a. to eat. *a.*

تناهي *tanāhī*, f. finishing, completing, arriving at the end, or place of destination. *a.*

تنبا *tambā*, m. a kind of drawers, very wide, almost like petticoats. *p.*

تنباكو तमाकू *tambākū*, m. tobacco: the word, though of European or American origin, is now naturalized in the Indian tongues. *h.*

تنبالو तमालू *tambālū*, m. an earthen pot (for cooking), a pipkin, a small metal pot (of brass or tinned iron). *h.*

تنبان *tambān*, m. drawers, trousers. *p.*

تنبو तम्बू *tambū*, m. a tent, pavilion. *h.*

تنبور *tambūr*, تنبورا *tambūrā*, } m. a kind of Turkish guitar; also a drum. *a.*

تنبول तम्बोल *tambol*, m. the betel leaf. *tambolānā*, n. to bleed from the bridle (a horse's mouth). *s.*

تنبولن तम्बोलिन *tambolin*, f. a woman whose business is to sell betel leaf; name of a tree. *s.*

تنبولي तम्बोली *tambolī*, m. name of a caste whose business is to sell betel leaf. *s.*

تنبه *tanabbuh*, m. bashfulness, modesty; admonition, advice; animadversion, reproof. *a.*

تنبي *tanabbī*, f. a beam, a rafter. *d.*

تنبيا तम्बिया *tambiyā*, m. a pot. *h.*

تنبيه *tambīh*, f. admonition, correction, beating, punishment. *tambīh-k.* or *-d.*, to chastise. *a.*

تنت तन्तु *tantu*, m. a thread, offspring, race. *s.*

تنت तन्ति *tanti*, m. a weaver. *s.*

تنتر तन्त्र *tantr* or *tantra*, m. name of a Hindū scripture; charm, enchantment; the term *tantra* is also applied to a religious treatise teaching peculiar and mystical formulæ or rites, for the worship of the deities, or for the attainment of superhuman power. It is mostly in the form of a dialogue between Shiva and Durgā, who are the peculiar deities of the *Tāntrikas*; demonstration, clear and right conclusion; raiment, vesture; a medicament, a drug. *s.*

تنتري तन्त्री *tantrī*, m. a musician. *s.*

تنتڙي तिन्तिड़ी *tintiṛī*, m. the tamarind tree. *s.*

تنتكيت तन्तुकीट *tantu-kīṭ*, m. a silk-worm. *s.*

تنتنانا तनतनाना *tantanānā*, n. to twang, to tingle. *h.*

تنتنانا तुनतुनाना *tuntunānā*, n. to sound. *h.*

تنتناهٹ तनतनाहट *tantanāhaṭ*, f. sharp pricking pain, from inflammation. *h.*

تنتو *tantū* (same as تنت), a thread, &c. *s.*

تنٹا *tanṭā*, تنٹل *tanṭal*, } m. wrangling, altercation; adj heinous. *tanṭalmārī*, quarrelsome. *d.* [*teori. s*

تنٹي तिण्टी *tinṭī*, f. a plant commonly called

تنجيم *tanjīm*, f. astrology; act of predicting any thing from the aspect of the stars. *a.*

تنخنخ *tanakhkhnukh*, m. clearing the throat, hemming, hawking. *a.*

تنخواه *tankhwāh*, f. wages, an assignment (on the revenues); an order or draft for money. *tankhwāh-dār*, one who receives salary, a holder of an order for wages. *tankhwāh-dārī*, f. receiving pay, service. *p.*

تند तुन्द *tund*, m. the belly; f. the navel. *tund-parimārj* or *-parimṛij*, m. a lazy man, passing his time in stroking his belly. *s.*

تند तिन्दु *tindu*, m. a species of ebony from the fruit of which a resin is obtained that is used for caulking vessels (*Diospyros glutinosa*). *s.*

تند *tund*, active, hot, spirited, fierce, sharp, severe, acrid. *tund-kho*, warm, passionate, fretful. *tund-raftār*, fast-going. *tund-zabān*, eloquent, talking rapidly. *tund-mizāj*, hot-headed, passionate. *tund honā*, n. to be angry, to be displeased. *p.*

تندر *tandar* or *tundar* (also *tundur*), m. thunder; the nightingale. *p.*

تندرا तन्द्रा *tandrā*, f. lassitude, weariness, syncope. *tandrālu*, slothful, overcome with sleep or fatigue. *s.*

تندرست *tan-durust*, sound in body, healthy. *p.*

تندرستي *tan-durustī*, f. bodily health. *p.*

تندري तन्द्री *tandrī*, f. sleepiness; lassitude, exhaustion. *s.*

تندكوپي तुन्दकूपी *tund-kūpī*, f. the navel. *s.*

تندكي तिन्दुकी *tindukī*, f. the resinous fruit of the ebony called *tindu*. *s.*

تندل तुन्दिल *tundil*, having a prominent navel. *s.*

تندم *tanaddum*, m. penitence, bashfulness, modesty. *a.*

تندور *tandūr*, m. (see *tanūr*) an oven. *a.*

تندي *tundī*, f. fierceness, acrimony, &c. *p.*

تنڈ *tunḍ*, تنڈكا *tunḍkā*, } a large piece of wood. *d.*

تنڈل तण्डुल *tanḍul*, m. rice (cleaned from the husk); any grain after threshing and winnowing; a vermifuge plant. *s.*

تنڈل तण्डुलु *tanḍulu*, f. a plant of which the seeds are used as a vermifuge. *s.*

تنزع *tanazzu'*, m. quarrelling, wrangling. *a.*

تنزل *tanazzul*, m. descent, declining slowly, diminution; condescending. *a.*

تنزه *tanazzuh*, m. being pure, modest, free from vice or stain. *a.*

تنزيل *tanzīl*, f. revelation; the *ḳur,ān*; causing (a traveller) to alight, receiving him hospitably. *a.*

تنزيه *tanzīh*, f. purifying, cleansing, keeping at a distance from every thing unclean. *tanziya*, m. inspiring with desire. *a.*

تنسل *tanassul*, m. pedigree, genealogy. *a.*

تنسيخ *tansīkh*, abrogation, quashing (of a decision). *a.*

تنصر *tanaṣṣur*, mutual help; conversion to [Christianity. *a.*

تنصيف *tanṣīf*, f. dividing in the middle or into two equal parts. *a.*

تنظير *tanẓīr*, f. resembling, beholding. *a.*

تنظيم *tanẓīm*, f. ordering, arranging; composing verses; threading pearls. *a.*

تنعم *tana''um*, happiness, enjoyment. *a.*

تنعيم *tan'īm*, m. bestowing abundance; saying. *na'm*, yes, in confirmation (of a debt, &c.). *a.*

تنفر *tanaffur*, m. aversion, disgust. *a.*

تنفس *tanaffus*, m. respiration, breathing. *a.*

تنقيح *tanḳīḥ*, f. cleaning, polishing; deciding disputes, investigation, search, ascertaining, verification of accounts, &c. *a.*

تنقيه *tanḳiya*, m. cleaning (the bowels), purging; winnowing grain. *a.*

تنك *tunak* or *tunuk*, slight, weak, delicate, effeminate; a thin cake or fritter. *tunak-ḥawāss*, sensible, sensitive. *tunak-ḥawāssī*, f. sense, sensibility. *tunak-ẓarf*, (lit. a weak vessel), talebearer, tatler. *tunak-mizāj*, whimsical, captious, peevish, fretful. *p.*

تنك तनुक *tanuk* or तनक *tanak*, little, small; adv. slightly, in a small degree. *s.*

تنكا तिनका *tinkā*, m. a straw, a bit of the stalk of grass. *tinkā dānton men lenā*, to make submission, confess inferiority or ask for quarter. *tinke chunne*, (lit.) to pick straws, applied to one who is intoxicated. *h.*

تنكار *tinkār*, m. borax (in Dakh. *tankār*). *p.*

تنكنا तिनकना *tinaknā*, n. to flutter, palpitate, to throb. *h.* [skin. *s.*

تنكوپ तनुकूप *tanu-kūp*, m. a pore of the

تنكي तुनकी *tunkī*, f. a fine kind of bread or wafers, thin as muslin. *s.*

تنگ तुङ्ग *tung*, high, elevated; m. a tree (*Rottleria tinctoria*); top, vertex, height. *s.*

تنگ *tung*, m. a vessel with a long and narrow neck; a body of troops. *p.*

تنگ *tang*, strait, tight, narrow; wanting, scarce, barren; m. a horse-belt, girth; a bag, a sack, half a horse's, bullock's, or camel's load, a bell. *tang-ānā*, n. to be distressed, to be exhausted, to be dejected. *tang-chashm*, miserly, niggard. *tang-ḥāl*, poor, distressed, straitened in circumstances. *tang-ḥālī*, f. poverty, distress, narrow circumstances. *tang-dast*, poor, distressed; miserly. *tang-dastī*, f. parsimony, poverty, want. *tang-dil*, miserly, niggard. *tang-dilī*, f. niggardliness, stinginess, parsimony. *tang-dahan*, small-mouthed; an epithet of a sweetheart. *tang-k.*, a. to distress; to contract. *tang-l.*, a. to tighten, to take in (a knot or buckle). *p.*

تنگا तङ्गा *tangā*, m. a denomination of money, equal to two *paisa*. *h.*

تنگ‌بهدر तुङ्गभद्र *tung-bhadra*, m. a restive elephant, or one in rut; f. a river in Mysore, the *Tumbhadr*. *s.*

تنگ‌چاءي *tang-chā,ī*, f. tightness, closeness; scarcity, distress, difficulty; stinginess, parsimony. *p.*

تنگي तुङ्गी *tungī*, f. a kind of basil (*Ocymum gratissimum*). *s.*

تنگي *tangī*, f. want; a bag, a sack. *tangī-k.*, a. to be parsimonious, to act the miser. *p.*

تنگيانا *tangiyānā*, to tighten; to make a horse gallop. *h.*

تنماتر तन्मात्र *tanmātra*, that merely. *s.*

تنو तनू *tanū*, m. (v. *tan*) the body. *s.*

تنوايه तुन्नवाय *tunna-vāya*, m. a tailor. *s.*

تنور *tanūr* or *tannūr*, m. an oven, a stove. *a.*

تنومند *tanū-mand* or *tano-mand*, robust, corpulent. *p.*

تنوير *tanwīr*, f. illumination, enlightening. *a.*

تنوين *tanwīn*, f. nūnation, *i.e.* marking the final letters with double vowel points, which gives them the additional syllable of *an*, *in*, or *un* (vide Hind. Gram. pp. 19, 20). *a.*

تنه *tana*, m. a stalk, stock, trunk, stem. *p.*

تنها *tanhā*, alone, solitary, singular, unique; private, apart; only, single. *p.*

تنهاءي *tanhā,ī*, f. loneliness, solitude. *p.*

تني तनी *tanī*, f. a string with which garments are tied. *h.*

تني तिन्नी *tinnī*, f. a kind of rice. *h.*

تني तनय *tanay*, m. a son; a male descendant. *s.*

تني तनी *tanī*, } f. a daughter or female
تنيا तनया *tanayā*, } descendent. *s.*

تنيا तनिया *taniyā*, m. a kind of covering for the waist. *h.*

تنين *tinnīn*, a large serpent, a dragon; the constellation Draco. *a.*

تو तो *to*, a correlative particle; introducing the second clause of a conditional proposition, as *jo tū āwegā, to pāwegā*, If thou wilt come, *then* shalt thou receive; an expletive, ornamental, or strengthening the expression, as *main to ātā thā, par usne āne na diyā*, I was *in fact* coming, but he prevented me. *s.*

تو तौ *tau*, then, in that case, moroever, that, also, for, yes, well. *tau bhī*, even then, still, nevertheless. *tau-lon* or *tau-lag*, then, in that case, till then. *s*

تو तू *tū*, pron. thou. *tū-tū*, sound of calling a dog. *h.*

توا *tawā*, m. the iron plate on which bread is baked; the part of a *ḥuḳḳa* to which tobacco is fixed, or the tobacco itself; an iron mirror. *p.*

توا *tawwā*, m. (v. *tāba*) a frying-pan. *tawwe po kī khilṭī honā*, to be restless, uneasy. *d.*

توابع *tawābi'* (pl. of تابع), followers, dependants. *a.*

تواتر *tawātur*, m. continuation, succession. *a.*

تواجد *tawājud*, mutual extacies, rapture. *a.*

توار तुअर *tū,ar*, f. a kind of pulse (*Cytisus cajan*). *s.*

توارا तिवारा *ti-wārā*, m. a hall with three doors. *s.*

توارد *tawārud*, m. unintentionally inserting the sense of another in one's own poems; corresponding by letter. *a.* [annals, chronicles. *a.*

تواريخ *tawārīkh* (pl. of تاريخ), dates; histories,

تواسي तिवासी *tivāsī*, stale, three days old. *s.*

تواسي *tivāsī*, a small embroidered carpet. *p.*

تواضع *tawāẓu'*, f. humility, attention, pretended kindness, empty compliments. *tawāẓu'i-samarkandī*, false politeness, pretended kindness, empty compliment, "*Punica fides.*" *tawāẓu'k*, to offer as a present. *a.*

توافق *tawāfuḳ*, m. concord, agreement; (in arithmetic) the relation between two numbers which have a common divisor; as 6 and 8, both divisible by 2. *a.*

توالد *tawālud*, successive generations. *a.*

توالي *tawālī*, f. continuation, succession. *a.*

توام *tau,am* or *taw,am*, m. a twin. *a.*

توامان *tau,amān* or *tawāmān* (dual), twins. *a.*

توان *tawān*, power, strength, ability; strong, able, powerful: (as an impers. verb) it is possible. *p.*

توانا *tawānā*, powerful, able; strong. *p.*

تواناءي *tawānā,ī*, f. power, ability. *p.*

توانستن *tawānistan* (r. *tawān*), to be able, &c. *p.*

توانگر *tawāngar*, rich, powerful. *p.*

توانگري *tawāngarī*, f. opulence, power. *p.*

تواوا तुवावा *tuwāwā*, m. the name of a bird. *h.*

تواءي *tawā,ī*, f. distress, misfortune. *p.*

توباه *taubāh*, f. penitence, &c. (v. *tauba*). *a.*

توبڑا तोबड़ा *tobṛā* (also *tobra* or *tobṛa*), m. the bag out of which horses eat their corn. *h.*

توبند *toband*, a kind of petticoat. *d.*

توبه *tauba*, m. penitence, conversion; promising to sin no more. *tauba-dhāṛ*, f. the sound of punishing, &c. *a.*

توبيخ *taubīkh*, f. reproach, speaking harshly. *a.*

توپ *top*, f. a cannon, a gun. *top-andāz*, a cannonier. *top-chalānā*, *-chornā*, *-dāghna*, *-lagānā*, or *-mārnā*, a. to cannonade. *top-khāna*, m. a park of artillery, the place where cannon and artillery stores are kept, an arsenal (naval or military). *t.*

توپ तोप *top*, a wood, an orchard of palmettoes, or of cocoa-nut trees; a tuft of trees. *h.*

توپانا तोपाना *topānā* or तुपाना *tupānā*, a. to have buried, to cause to cover. *h.*

توپچي *top-chī*, m. a conductor of artillery, a commissary of ordnance, a bombardier. *t.*

توپڑا तोपड़ा *topṛā*, m. a fly, a kind of pigeon. *h.*

توپك *topak* or *tūpak*, f. a musket. *t.*

توپنا तोपना *topnā*, to bury, to cover. *h.*

توپي *topī* (Port. "*topo*"), a hat such as Europeans wear. *topī-wālā*, a "topi-man," an European in general. *port.*

توت *tūt*, m. the mulberry tree. *a.*

توتا तोता *totā*, m. a male parrot; the cock of a matchlock. *h.*

توتا तूता *tūtā*, } m. blue vitriol, tutty, sulphate of copper. *s.*
توتك तूतक *tūtak*, }

توتلا तोतला *totlā*, a stutterer, a stammerer; adj. lisping. *h.* [a child. *h.*

توتلانا तोतलाना *totlānā*, n. to lisp, speak like

توتن तूतन *tūtan*, m. chips, clippings, filings, fragments. *h.*

توتنا तोतनी *totnā*, a. to weave tape or riband. *h.*

توتي तोती *totī*, f. (the female of *totā*), a parrot. *h.*

توتي *totī*, f. a singing bird (*Loxia rosca*). *p.*

توتئي तूतई *tūta,ī* or *tuta,ī*, f. a vessel with a spout. *h.* [phate of copper. *s.*

توتيا तूतिया *tūtiyā*, m. blue vitriol, tutty, sul-

توٹا *toṭā*, m. loss, deficiency (for *tonṭā*), a cartridge. *d.*

توٹاپا *tūṭāpā*, m. helplessness. *d.*

توٹکا तोटका *toṭkā*, m. a charm, amulet, philter. *s.*

توٹنا *tūṭnā*, n. to break, be broken, &c. (v. *ṭuṭnā*). *d.*

توجه *tawajjuh*, f. turning towards, regarding, attending to; kindness, favour, obligingness; pl. *tawajjuhāt*, favours, &c. *a.*

توجيه *taujīh*, f. calling one's attention; explaining, accounting for; adjustment of accounts; assessment; a description-roll. *taujīh-nawīs*, a keeper of description-rolls. *a.* [cassia. *s.*

توچا त्वचा *twachā*, f. skin; bark, rind; woody

توحيد *tauḥīd*, f. unity, believing in the unity of the Deity. *a.*

تودري *todrī*, f. the seed of mallows. *p.*

توده *tūda* or *toda*, m. the butt, or mark, at which arrows are shot; a mound, a heap, a stack; *toda,e ṭūfān*, accusing, charging with crime; a calumniator. *p.*

توديع *taudī'*, bidding adieu; dismissing, &c. *a.*

تور तोर *tor* or तोड़ *toṛ*, f. a kind of pulse; a net thrown over a woman's palkī. *tor* (in the eastern dialect), pron. second p. sing. gen. thy, thine. *h.*

تور तुवर *tuwar*, m. the name of a tribe among *Rājpūts*. *h.*

تورا त्वरा *twarā*, f. haste, speed, hurry. *s.*

تورات *taurāt* (v. توريت), the Pentateuch. *a.*

توران *tūrān*, the name of the country to the north-east of Persia, generally called Tartary, Transoxiana, Turcomania, Turkistān. *p.*

توراني *tūrānī*, a native of Tūrān, a Tartar. *p.*

تورت त्वरित *twarit*, swift, quick; speedily; m. despatch, haste. *s.*

تورگ तवर्ग *ta-varga*, m. the dental class of letters beginning with त. *s.*

تورن तोरण *toran*, m. strings of flowers suspended across gateways on occasions of public festivals; the ornamented arch of a door or gate. *s.*

تورن तूर्ण *tūrna*, quick, swift, expeditious. *s.*

توره तोरह *torah*, m. a dish of various meats presented to others by great men; a nobleman, a minister; pride. *torah-bandī*, f. the sending out of trays of food as presents. *torah-posh*, m. a covering for dishes, &c. *h.* [pet. *h.*

تورهي तोरही *torhī* (prop. *turhī*), m. a trum-

توري तोरी *torī*, f. a kind of cucumber. *h.*

توري तुवरी *tuwarī*, f. a kind of lentil (*Cytisus cajan*). *s.*

توريت *taurīt*, f. the Old Testament, more particularly the Pentateuch. *a.*

توڑ तोड़ *toṛ*, m. the breach made by a gun, &c.; the strength of a current; whey. *toṛ-phoṛ*, m. breaking, plain speaking. *toṛ-tāṛ*, m. breaking and destroying, plain speaking. *toṛ-joṛ*, cutting out (as cloth by a tailor); arranging a speech, &c. *toṛ-denā*, a. to break to pieces, to spoil. *toṛ-ḍālnā*, a. to break and destroy, to pull down. *toṛ-k.*, to make a breach (as a ball). *toṛ-kasr*, fractions (in arithmetic). *toṛ-l.*, a. to gather, to pluck (fruit); (for *tor*, q. v.) a net, &c. *s.*

توڑا तोड़ा *toṛā*, m. scarcity, want; a purse, a bag containing one thousand *rupīs*; the match of a gun; a bank, an island: a bar; a ploughshare; a piece of rope; an ornament like a chain. *toṛe-dār*, a matchlock. *h.* [be broken or changed, as money. *s.*

توڑانا तोड़ाना *toṛānā* or *tuṛānā*, a. to cause to

توڑتا तोड़ता *toṛtā* or *toṛtā*, m. a dried pod of *torī* (q.v.) kept for seed. *h.* [on the wrist. *h.*

توڑل तोड़ल *toṛal*, m. a large thick ring worn

توڑل مل तोड़लमल *toṛal-mal*, a man's name, a statesman who flourished in Akbar's reign. *h.*

توڑنا तोरना *toṛnā*, a. to break, tear, rend, demolish; to grind (as grain); to change (as coin); to pluck or gather (fruit, flowers); to reduce (in arith.). *dam toṛnā*, a. to be at the point of death. *roṭī toṛnā*, a. to eat the bread of idleness. *toṛnā joṛnā* expresses absolute power over any thing. *s.*

توڑني *toṛnī*, f. a claim (for debt, &c.), dunning. *toṛnī denā* or *toṛnī lagānā*, to tighten, to distress. *d.*

توڑوانا तोड़वाना *toṛwanā* or *tuṛwānā*, a. to cause to be broken or changed, as coin. *s.*

توڑواءي तोड़वाई *toṛwā,ī* or *tuṛwā,ī*, f. price paid for breaking or changing coin, discount. *s.*

توڑه *toṛa*, the match of a gun. *toṛa-dār*, a matchlock. *h.* [up to. *s.*

توڑي तोड़ी *toṛī*, f. mustard seed; adv. till,

توز *tūz*, ornaments, trappings of a bow, saddle, &c.; the under bark of a tree used in Cashmīr for writing upon in lieu of paper; name of a town in Khuzistān in Persia. *tos* (Dakh.), powder in medicine; dust. *p.* [at Tūz. *s.*

توزي *tuzī*, a kind of shawl-stuff manufactured

توسدان *tos-dān*, a cartridge-box. *d.*

توسط *tawassuṭ*, m. mediation; introduction; also a mediator or introducer. *a.*

توسل *tawassul*, m. conjunction, copulation; introduction (to another person). *a.*

توسن *tausan*, m. a horse; a young unbroken horse; a high-blooded noble steed, a war-horse; a plump horse; a horse with a hard mouth, or unmanageable. *p.*

توسنا *tūsnā*, n. to fade, wither (a flower). *d.*

توش तोष *tosh*, m. pleasure, joy. *s.*

توشدان *tosh-dān*, m. a pouch, a cartridge-box. *p.*

توشك *toshak*, f. a quilt, a mattress. *toshak-khāna*, (same as *tosha-khāna*), m. a wardrobe, a place where furniture is kept. *p.*

توشه *tosha*, m. provision, particularly of a traveller, or those which are carried with the funeral of a deceased person, to support him during his journey to the other world; viaticum. *tosha-khāna*, m. a wardrobe, a place where furniture is kept, a store-room. *p.*

توشيح *taushīḥ*, f. a kind of acrostic. *a.*

توصيف *tauṣīf*, f. description, commendation. *a.*

توضو *tawaẓẓū*, f. performing the ablution before praying; arriving at the age of puberty, when ablution must be performed. *a.*

توضيح *tauẓīḥ*, f. publishing, illustrating, statement of collections, &c. *a.*

توطن *tawaṭṭun*, m. fixing one's residence in a foreign country; taking up one's abode. *a.*

توغدار *toghdār*, m. the bustard, (*otis*). *d.*

توفير *taufīr*, f. increase; perfecting, augmentation of revenue. *a.*

توفيق *taufīḳ*, f. the completion of one's wishes, the favour, grace, or guidance of God. *a.*

توقر *tawaḳḳur*, m. respect, honour, modesty, mildness. *a.*

توقع *tawaḳḳuʻ*, f. request; hope, desire, expectation; wish, trust, reliance. *a.*

توقف *tawakkuf*, m. patience; delay; procrastination; hesitation, tediousness. *a.*

توقير *taukīr*, f. honouring, respecting, treating with ceremony, reverence. *a.*

توك त्वक *twak*, f. the bark of the bamboo; bark in general, skin. *twak-kshīrā*, f. the manna of the bamboo. *twak-kandūr*, m. a sore or wound. *s.*

توكارنا तूकारना *tūkārnā*, a. to thou (French *tutoyer*, from *tū*). *s.*

توكل *tawakkul*, m. trust in God, reliance on, faith in, or resignation to, the divine will or destiny. *a.*

توكيل *taukīl*, keeping in custody, imprisonment. *a.* [*taul-tāl*, weighing and measuring. *s.*

تول तौल *taul* or तोल *tol*, m. weight, weighing.

تول तूल *tūl*, m. (for *tulya*), resembling. *s.*

تولا तोला *tolā*, m. one rupī weight; a denomination of weight, consisting of a number of *māshas*, which varies in different parts of India. *tolā-dār*, a weighman, one who weighs coins or goods in a market. The standard *tolā*, or sicca weight of Calcutta, is 12¼ *māshas*, agreeably to the following table:—

		Grains troy.
4 *panks*	= 1 *dhān* or grain ..	·44916
4 *dhān*	= 1 *ratti*	1·79666
8 *ratti*	= 1 *māsha*	14·37333
12¼ *māshas*	= 1 *tolā*	179·66666 *s.*

تولا तौला *taulā*, an intoxicating liquor made from the flowers of the Mahwa tree. *h.*

تولا *tawallā*, m. hope; attachment. *a.*

تولانا तौलाना *taulānā*, a. to cause to be weighed. *s.*

تولائي तौलाई *taulā,ī*, f. the price of weighing. *s.*

تولت *tuwalat*, / تولة *tuwala*, } a misfortune; a philter or charm used by a wife to conciliate the affections of her husband. *a.*

تولد *tawallud*, m. birth, nativity; adj. begotten, born, generated. *a.*

تولنا तोलना *tolnā* or तौलना *taulnā*, a. to weigh, to balance; to confront (as two armies). *taulnā nazroṅ men*, to estimate the worth of any one. *s.*

تولنالي तूलनाली *tūl-nālī*, f. a thick roll of cotton, from which it is drawn out in spinning. *s.*

تولوائي तौलवाई *taulwā,ī*, f. the price of weighing. *s.*

تولة तोल *tola*, m. a denomination of weight (v. *tolā*). *s.*

تولة *tuwala*, misfortune, evil. *tiwala*, a charm, amulet, philter. *a.*

تولي तूली *tūlī*, f. a steelyard; a weaver's fibrous stick or brush; a painter's brush, or a fibrous stick used as one; a rod dipped into crucibles to try the contents. *s.*

تولي तौली *taulī*, f. / توليا तौलिया *tauliyā*, m. } a vessel used by Hindūs. *h.*

توليت *tawliyat*, f. appointing one as governor, deputy, or superintendant; trusteeship. *tawliyat nāma*, deed of trusteeship. *a.*

توليد *tawlīd*, f. procreating, generation, birth; assisting at a birth. *a.*

توم *tūm*, a dry measure of twelve Arcot *sers*; a conduit or channel. *d.*

تومان *tomān*, m. a myriad, 10,000; a sum of money equal to 10,000 Arabic silver drachmas (which are about one-third less than those of the Greeks; also, a sum equal to fifteen dollars and a half); districts into which a kingdom is divided, each being supposed to furnish 10,000 fighting men: when, for example, a province is put down for seven *tomāns*, it implies that such province must hold 70,000 men ready for the field on the requisition of the sovereign. It also denotes a Persian gold coin, at present worth about ten shillings. It was formerly worth from twenty to twenty-five shillings. *p.*

تومري तूमरी *tūmrī*, f. the snout of a crocodile, alligator, &c. *h.*

تومڑا तोमड़ा *tomṛā*, m. / تومڑي तोमड़ी *tomṛī*, f. } a hollowed gourd (*Cucurbita lagenaria*). *s.*

تومنا तूमना *tūmnā*, a. to card or arrange (wool or cotton) with the finger, preparatory to combing. *h.*

توميا तूमिया *tūmiyā*, m. thread made of carded cotton, in opposition to that made of that which has only been beaten (called *dhunā rū,ī*). *h.*

تون तून or तुन *tūn*, m. a quiver; name of a tree the wood of which resembles mahogany, and is used for furniture (*Cedrela tuna*). *s.* [manner. *h.*

تون तों *toṅ* (Braj. तौं *tauṅ*), so, in that

تون तौन *taun* (correl. of *jo* or *jaun*), that, that same. *h.*

تونبا तूंबा *tūmbā*, m. a hollowed gourd, the rind of a gourd in which beggars carry their water, &c. *s.*

تونبي तूंबी *tūmbī*, f. a small *tūmbā*, q. v.; the snout of a crocodile, alligator, &c. *s.*

تونبي तूंबी *tūmbī*, f. a kind of pipe (chiefly used by those who exhibit snakes). *s.*

تون تان كرنا तूंतांकरना *tūṅ-tāṅ karnā*, a. to dispute, to wrangle, to abuse. *h.*

توند तोंद *toṅd*, f. a large belly, a pot-belly. *s.*

توندار तोंदार *toṅdār*, / توندالا तोंदाला *toṅdālā*, } pot-bellied. *s.*

توندي तोंदी *toṅdī*, f. the navel. *h.*

تونديل तोंदैल *toṅdail*, / تونديلا तोंदैला *toṅdailā*, } pot-bellied, gor-bellied, corpulent. *s.*

تونسنا तौंसना *tauṅsnā*, n. to be heated in the sunshine, to be overcome with heat. *h.*

تونگا *tūngā*, m. a reed, a flag or rush. *d.*

تونگر *tawangar*, rich, wealthy; powerful. *p.*

تونگري *tawangarī*, f. riches, wealth, opulence; power. *p.* [even. *s.*

تونهين तोंहीं *toṅhīṅ*, at that instant, then

تونير तूणीर *tūnīr*, m. a quiver. *s.*

توور तुवर *tūwar*, m. a tribe of Rājputs; a bull without horns; a beardless man, a eunuch. *h.*

توه तोहि *tohi*, to or for thee, thee. *h.*

توهم *tawahhum*, m. suspicion, imagination. *a.*

توهن तूहिन *tūhin*, m. snow, ice, or frost. *s.*

توهو तौहू *tauhū*, / توهي तौही *tauhī*, } then even, nevertheless, still, in that case only, at that very time. *s.*

توهي तूही *tū-hī*, thou thyself, thou even. *s.*

توهي तोही *tohī*, pron. to or for thee, thee. *h.*

توهين *tauhīn*, f. enervating, relaxing, scoffing. *a.*

تويه तोय *toya*, m. water. *toya-pippalī*, f. a plant (*Jussieua repens*). *toya-prasādan*, m. the clearing nut plant (*Strychnos potatorum*): the nut being rubbed upon the inside of a water-jar occasions the precipitation of the impurities of the water poured into it. *toya-pushpī*, f. trumpet flower. *toya-da*, m. a fragrant grass (*Cyperus rotundus*). *toya-dhar*, m. a pot-herb (*Marsilia dentata*). *toya-kām*, m. a sort of cane (*Calamus fasciculatus*). *toya-krichchha*, m. a sort of penance, drinking nothing but water for a fixed period. *toya-wallī*, f. a kind of gourd (*Momordica charautia*). *s.*

ته थ *tha*, the aspirated form of ت त *ta*. *s. h.*

ته *tah*, f. fold, plait; the bottom, beneath. *tah bāzārī*, ground-rent of a stall in the market. *tah ba-tah*, plait by plait, every fold. *tah ba-tah-k.*, a. to pile one upon another. *tah-band*, m. a cloth worn round the waist, and passing between the legs. *tah-pech*, m. a cap or cloth worn under the turban. *tah-khāna*, m. a cavern, a cellar, a room under ground, a lower story, a vault. *tah darz*, new. *tah-degī*, f. the scrapings of a pot, the burnt part of victuals that sticks to the bottom of a pot. *tah-denā*, a. to tinge slightly. *tah-kar rukho*, (lit. fold and lay it by, *i.e.* keep it to yourself) is used to express the speaker's independence, or not wanting the thing spoken of. *tah mārnā*, a disease of a horse from excessive thirst, affecting the flanks. *tah-nishīn honā*, n. to subside, to settle. *tah o bālā-k.*, a. to subvert, to overthrow. *p.*

ته *tih*, bottom, void, empty. *p.*

تها था *thā* (auxil. v. past t.), was. *h.*

تهاپ थाप *thāp*, f. a tap, a pat, a slap, paw; the sound of a small drum. *h.*

تهاپا थापा *thāpā*, m. a mark of the paw; gleanings of corn, &c. left on the field after harvest. *h.*

تهاپنا थापना *thāpnā*, a. to patch (as a wall with cow-dung); to tap; f. a religious ceremony performed at a certain season at Āgra and in its vicinity. *s.*

تهاپي थापी *thāpī*, f. the noise of tapping; the instrument with which potters beat their earth, or with which terraces are beaten. *h.*

تهاتي थाती *thātī*, / تهاتهي थाथी *thāthī*, } f. a trust, what is given in charge. *s.*

تهاٹ *thāṭ*, state, dignity; abundance. *d.*

تهار थार *thār*, m. a large dish, a tray. *h.*

تهارو तिहारौ *tihārau*, m. / تهارے तिहारे *tihāre*, m. / تهاري तिहारी *tihārī*, f. } your, of you (in the old Braj. dialect). *h.*

تهاكنا थाकना *thāknā*, n. to fatigue, to be tired. *h.*

تهال थाल *thāl*, m. a tray, a large dish. *h.*

تهالا थाला *thālā*, m the place at the root of a tree for holding water; the excavation in which a tree is to be planted; a large flat dish. *s.*

تهالي थाली *thālī*, f. a salver, a platter, a flat dish, a tray, a hole about the root of a tree for holding water. *s.*

تهالي तिहाली *tihālī*, a species of cotton pod. *h.*

تهام थाम *thām*, / تهامبه थाम्भ *thāmbh*, } m. a post, a pillar, support, an obstacle. *s.*

تهامنا थामना *thāmnā*, / تهامبهنا थाम्भना *thāmbhnā*, } a. to support; to shield, to protect, to shelter; to prevent, to withhold; to stop, to pull up (a horse), to bear, to assist, to resist. *s.*

تهامجان *thāmjān*, (probably from *thāmnā*, "to support" and *jāngh*, "the thigh;" m. a kind of sedan-chair commonly called a "Tonjohn". *h.*

تهان थान *thān*, m. a piece of cloth; a stall for cattle, a manger; a piece (of coin), as *ek thān ashrafī*, one gold mohur. *tinoṅ thān*, the private parts of a male (lit. the three bits or parts). *h.*

تهاں तहाँ *tahāṅ*, there, thither. *tahāṅ tahāṅ*, in each place. *h.*

تهانا थाना *thānā*, m. a station, a guard; the inside of the lines of an army *thānā dār* (or *thāne-dār*) the officer in charge of a *thānā*. *s.*

تهانا थाना *thānā*, m. a heap of bamboos. *h.*

تهانا तहाना *tahānā*, a. to fold, to ply, to wrap. *p.*

تهانبهنا थाम्भना *thāmbhnā*, a. (v. *thāmnā*) to support, &c. *s.*

تهاناداري *thānā-dārī*, f. the office of a station-master; adj. of or relating to such office. *thānā-dārī abwāb*, a cess for defraying the expense of station-master. *h. p.*

تهانگ थाङ्ग *thāng*, f. a den of thieves. *h.*

تهانگي थाङ्गी *thāngī* or *thāngī-dār*, m. a receiver of stolen goods. *thāngī-dārī*, the receiving of stolen goods. *h.*

تهانولا थाँवला *thāoṅlā*, m. the mound about the root of a tree for holding water. *h.*

تهانه थान *thāna*, m. (see *thānā*) a station, guard; pl. *thānajāt* or *thānahāt*. *thāna-dār*, a sentinel, guardian. *h.*

تهاني थानी *thānī*, stationary resident; a permanent cultivator; a householder, master of the house; f. a den of thieves. *h.*

تهاون *tahāwun*, negligence, sloth. *a.*

تهاه थाह *thāh*, f. bottom, ford. *s.*

تهاهي थाही *thāhī*, f. fordableness. *s.*

تهاءي तिहाई *tihā,ī*, f. the third part; the third part of a piece of cloth for making trousers. *s.*

تهايت तिहायत *tihāyat* or *tihā,et*, m. a third person; a court of inquiry, three or four persons by whom any cause is arbitrated; an arbitrator. *s.*

تهبازاري *tah-bāzārī*, ground rent for a stall in a market. *p.*

تهپانا थुपाना *thupānā*, a. to cause to be supported, propped, or plastered. *h.*

تهپڑ थप्पड़ *thappaṛ*, } m. a box, a slap, claw,
تهپڑا थपड़ा *thapṛā*, } cuff. *h.*

تهپڑي थपड़ी *thapṛī*, f. the clapping of hands. *thapṛī-bajānā*, a. to clap the hands. *thapṛī mārnā*, a. to damn, (in the theatrical sense); to hoot. *h.*

تهپك थपक *thapak*, m. a pat, a tap. *h.*

تهپيڑا थपेड़ा *thapeṛā*, m. a slap, a box, a clout; the scalp. *h.*

تهتر तिहत्तर *tihattar*, seventy-three. *h.*

تهتك *tahattuk*, m. being torn or worn out (as a veil, &c.); disgrace, dishonour. *a.*

تهتكارنا थुतकारना *thuthārnā*, a. to drive away scornfully. *h.*

تهتهانا थुथाना *thuthānā*, n. to frown, to scowl, or pout. *muṅh thuthānā*, to make a wry face. *h.*

تهتهني थुथनी *thuthnī*, f. the mouth of a horse, camel, &c. *s.*

تهٹا *thaṭā*, (for *ṭhaṭhā*), m. fun, jest, joking. *d.*

تهٹكنا *thaṭaknā*, n. to stop, stagnate. *d.*

تهجانا *thijānā*, a. to astonish, to congeal. *d.*

تهم جانا *thaj-jānā*, n. to be fixed (the eyes). *d.*

تهجد *tahajjud*, m. a form of prayer said during the night; wakefulness; sleeping sound. *a.*

تهجنا *thijnā*, n. to be astonished; to become senseless and motionless, to be congealed. *d.*

تهجي *tahajjī*, f. spelling. *ḥurūfi-tahajjī*, the letters of the alphabet. *a.*

ته خانه *tah-k͟hāna*, m. a cave, grotto, cellar, vault, an apartment under ground. *p.*

تهديد *tahdīd*, f. terrifying, threatening, menace, threat. *a.*

تهڈي *thuḍḍī*, f. the chin; parched grain. *thaḍḍī*, the guard of a sword hilt. *d.*

تهذيب *tahẕīb*, f. purifying, adjusting, adorning, edification. *tahẕībi ak͟hlāq*, civilization, good breeding. *a.*

تهر थर *thar*, m. a lion's or tiger's den. *s.*

تهر थिर *thir*, fixed, stable, settled. *s.*

تهرا तिहरा *tihrā*, triple, threefold. *h.*

تهرانا तिहराना *tihrānā*, a. to tertiate, to do (any thing for) the third time, to triple. *h.*

تهرانا थर्राना *tharrānā*, n. to tremble, to shake. *h.*

تهرانا थिराना *thirānā*, n. to settle (as liquor). *s*

تهراوٹ तिहरावट *tihrāwaṭ*, f. triplication. *h.*

تهرتا थिरता *thiratā*, f. firmness, stability. *s.*

تهرتهر थरथर *tharthar*, adj. trembling. *h.*

تهرتهرانا थरथराना *thartharānā*, n. to tremble, to quiver, to shiver, to shake; a. to make tremble. *h.*

تهرتهراهٹ थरथराहट *thartharāhaṭ*, } f. tremor,
تهرتهري थरथरी *thartharī*, } shaking, trembling, quivering. *h.*

تهرتهرنا थरथरना *thartharnā*, n. to tremble, to shake, to quiver, to shiver. *h.*

تهركنا थिरकना *thirahnā*, n. to set one's feet off well in dancing, to dance with expressive action and gesture; (in Dakh.) to hover (a bird, &c.). *h.*

ته رو *tah-rū*, m. the stuffing of a saddle. *p.*

تهرهرانا थरहराना *tharharānā*, } n. to tremble,
تهرهرنا थरहरना *tharharnā*, } shake. *h.*

تهري तिहरे *tihare*, thy, of thine, your. *h.*

تهڑدلا थुड़दिला *thuṛ-dilā*, adj. miserly, narrowly. *h. p.*

تهس نهس तहसनहस *tahas-nahas*, ruined, destroyed, dispersed. *h.*

تهك थक *thak*, } m. clot, lump (congealed).
تهكا थक्का *thakkā*, } *thakke ke thakke*, congealed, thick, conglomerated. *h.*

تهكا थका *thakā*, tired, weary, over-fatigued. *thakā-bakkā*, or *thakā-pikkā*, or *thakā-phakkā*, distracted, troubled. *s.*

تهكانا थकाना *thakānā*, a. to tire, to harass, to weary. *s.*

تهكانا थुकाना *thukānā*, to cause to spit, to cause to reproach. *h.*

تهكت थकित *thakit*, wearied, stopped, motionless, astonished. *s.*

تهك تهك थकथक *thak thak*, very wet, drenched. *h.*

تهك تهكانا थुकथुकाना *thuk-thukānā*, n. to spit on the mention of any disease, as a preservative against it, or as a caution against the influence of an evil eye. *h.*

تهكنا थकना *thaknā*, n. to be wearied, to tire, to fatigue. *s.*

تهكهاءي थुकहाई *thukhā,ī*, f. base, contemptible (q. d. fit to be spit upon). *h.*

تهگلا *thiglā*, m. a binding; a patch. *d.*

تهل थल *thal*, m. place, firm or dry ground; a lion's or tiger's den. *thal-berā*, m. place of abode and means of attaining one's desires. *thal-char*, moving on land, terrestrial (an animal). *s.*

تهلتهلانا थलथलाना *thal-thalānā*, } n. to undu-
تهل تهل كرنا थलथलकरना *thal-thal-karnā*, } late, fluctuate (as a thick or glutinous fluid), to shake (as the flabby flesh of a fat man). *h.*

تهل تهل थुलथुल *thul-thul*, gently falling, or dropping (as water from a small height) (see *chul-chul*). *h.*

تهلكنا थलकना *thalaknā*, n. to tremble, palpitate. *h.*

تہلکہ *tahluka*, m. ruin, perdition; consternation, alarm; pang, agony. *a.*

تهليا थलिया *thaliyā*, f. a salver, a platter, a flat dish, generally of brass. *s.*

تہليل *tahlīl*, f. acknowledging the true God, by repeating (in Arabic) the sentence, "*Lā ilāha illā-llāhu. wa muhammadun rasūlu-llāhi*," "there is no god but God, and Muhammad is God's apostle." *a.*

تهم थम *tham*, تهمب थम्ब *thamb*, تهمبا थम्बा *thambā*, تهمبه थम्भ *thambh*, } m. a pillar, a post, a prop or support; any thing that restrains. *s.*

تهمانا थमाना *thamānā*, a. to stop, to restrain, to quiet. *s.*

تهمبهنا थम्भना *thambhnā*, n. (see *thamnā*).

تہمت *tuhmat*, f. suspicion of guilt; accusation, charging one with a crime. *tuhmat-lagānā* or *-denā*, or *-karnā*, a. to belie, &c., to accuse one falsely. *a.*

تہمتي *tuhmatī*, suspicious; ignominious (in Dakh.) a calumniator, a slanderer. *a.*

تهمڑا थमड़ा *thamṛā*, thick, corpulent. *h.*

تهمنا थमना *thamnā*, تهمبنا थम्बना *thambnā*, تهمبهنا थम्भना *thambhnā*, } n. to stand still, to stop, to cease, to be restrained, to be supported. *s.*

تهن थन *than*, m. udder. *than-dār*, an animal with a large udder, or having an udder. *s.*

تهن तिहिं *tihin*, pron. plur. those very, them, themselves. *h.*

تہن तुहिन *tuhin*, m. frost, snow; ice. *s.*

تہنال *tah-nāl*, m. the mounting at the upper end of a scabbard. *p.*

تہنامہ *tahnāma*, a treaty of peace; a bill of articles or items agreed upon by two parties. *p.*

تهنبهنا थम्भना *thambhnā*, n. to stop, &c., v. *thamnā*. *s.*

تهنڈ *thanḍ*, تهنڈك *thanḍak*, } coldness, coolness (met.) a refreshing sensation. *thanḍ-kālā* or *thanḍ-kāla*, cold weather, cold season. *d.*

تہنشان *tah-nishān*, inlaid, particularly iron with gold. *p.*

تهني थनी *thanī*, f. the name of a blemish in horses. *thunī* (Dakh.) a column, a pillar. *h.*

تہنيت *tahniyat*, f. congratulation. *a.*

تهنيسري थनेसरी *thanesarī*, تهنيشوري थनेश्वरी *thaneshwarī*, } m. Brāhman of Thaneshwar, a famous shrine in *Kuru-kshetra*, near Karnāl. *s.*

تهنيلا थनेला *thanelā*, m. inflamed breast (of a woman) name of an animal. *s.*

تهوپ थोप *thop*, m. an ornament at the end of the bamboo of a palkī, &c., head, topping. *h.*

تهوپڑا *thopṛā*, m. the jaw (same as *jabhṛā*). *d.*

تهوپنا थोपना *thopnā*, a. to support, to prop; to plaster; to pile, to heap. *h.*

تهوپي थोपी *thopī*, f. box, thump. *h.*

تهوپيانا थोपियाना *thopiyānā*, n. to trickle. *h.*

تهوترا थोतरा *thotrā*, bruised and spoiled, as the head of a mallet; toothless. *h.*

تهوتڑا थूतड़ा *thūtṛā* (for *thūthṛā*), the mouth. *h.*

تهوتلا थोतला *thotlā*, blunt, toothless. *h.*

تهوتهه थोथ *thoth*, m. the mouth. *s.*

تهوتها थोथा *thothā*, m. the name of a medicine; an arrow without a point; adj. hollow, empty; toothless. *thothī bāt*, f. word without meaning. *h.*

تهوتهڑا थूथड़ा *thūthṛā*, m. mouth. *h.*

تهوتهلا थोथला *thothlā*, blunt, not sharp. *h.*

تهوتهنا थूथना *thūthnā*, m. تهوتهني थूथनी *thūthnī*, f. } the mouth of a horse, camel, &c. *s.*

تہور *tahawwur*, m. intrepidity, daring; plunging inconsiderately into any business; fury; oppression. *a.*

تهور थोर *thor*, تهورا थोरा *thorā*, تهوڑا थोड़ा *thoṛā*, } a little, small, scarce, seldom, some, less. *thoṛā bahut*, more or less. *thoṛā*, a little. *thoṛā thoṛā*, a little, by degrees. *thoṛā thoṛā honā*, n. to be ashamed, to shrink with shame. *thoṛe se thoṛā*, very little. *h.*

تهوڑ थोड़ *thoṛ*, m. the spathe of a plantain tree before it shoots from the stem. *s.*

تہوع *tahawwuʻ*, m. sickness at the stomach. *a.*

تهوك थोक *thok*, m. amount, heap, ready money; share, portion. *thok-dār*, m. a wholesale dealer. *h.*

تهوك थूक *thūk*, m. spittle; the gossamer. *thūk chāṭnā*, to break one's promise. *thūk denā*, a. to leave, to give up. *thūk lagākar chhoṛnā*, a. to treat with sovereign contempt. *thūk lagānā*, a. to apply spittle (a term of abuse and of most indecent meaning). *h.*

تهوكنا थूकना *thūknā*, a. to spit. *h.*

تهولي *thūlī*, a kind of sweet dish. *d.*

تهون तिहूँ *tihūn*, three, all three. *h.*

تهونبا थूँबा *thūmbā*, a lump of earth put on the end of a lever as a balance. *h.*

تهوني थूणी or थूनी *thūnī*, f. تهونيه थूण्य *thūnya*, m. } a post, pillar, column. *h.*

تهوهر थोहर *thohar* or थूहर *thūhar*, m. the name of a plant (*Euphorbia neriifolia, Roxb.*). *h.*

تهوئي थवई *thawaī*, m. a mason, a bricklayer, an architect. *s.*

تهئي थई *tha,ī*, f. a heap of clothes, &c. *h.*

تهي *tihī* (in modern Persian *tuhī*), empty, vain. *pahlū tihī-k.*, a. to abstain. *tihī-dast*, empty-handed, poor. *tihī-dastī*, poverty. *tihī-dimāgh*, ignorant, empty-headed. *p.*

تهي तुही *tuhī*, thee, or to thee. *h.*

تهير थीर *thīr*, tranquil, calm, smooth. *s.*

تهيكر थीकर *thīkar*, تهيكرا थीकरा *thīkrā*, m. the duty of keeping the village watch, taken by the villagers in turn. *h.*

تهيگلي थेगली *thoglī*, f. a patch (on a garment). *h.*

تهيلا थैला *thailā*, m. تهيلي थैली *thailī*, f. تهيليا थैलिया *thailiyā*, f. a purse tied round the waist; a bag; the scrotum. *h.*

تهين तहीं *tahīn*, thither, there, in that same place, in that very direction. *h.*

تهينگا थेंगा *thengā*, m. a club, a stick. *h.*

تهيوا थेवा *thewā*, m. a stone set in a ring. *h.*

تهيه *tahīya*, m. preparation, provision, putting in order. *a.*

تهيئي تهيئي थेईथेई *the,ī the,ī* or थेयीथेयी *theyī-theyī*, f. merry-making. *the,ī the,ī k.*, to make merry. *h.*

تي ते pron. they, those; postpos. from, by, with, than. *s.*

تي तै *tai*, so many. *tai-ber*, so often. *h.*

تيا तिया *tiyā*, f. a woman, a wife. *s.*

تياجيه त्याज्य *tyājya*, fit to be forsaken, avoided. *s.*

تيار *taiyār* (for طيّار), ready, prepared, finished, complete; alert. *p.*

تياري *taiyārī*, f. readiness, activity, &c. *p.*

تياگ त्याग *tyāg*, m. abdication, leaving, abandonment, renouncing. *tyāg-d.*, to renounce. *s.*

تياگنا त्यागना *tyāgnā*, a. to leave, to abandon, to desert, to forsake, to quit, to abdicate. *s.*

تياگن त्यागिन *tyāgin*, تياگي त्यागी *tyāgī*, leaving, relinquishing; m. a religious ascetic who renounces worldly objects. *s.*

تياني तियाने *tiyāne* (also *tī,āne*), name of a small charge on revenue; v. *jot-jarībī*. *h.*

تيبير तैबेर *tai-ber*, so many times, so often. *h.*

تيپچي तेपची *tepchī*, f. a kind of stitch. *h.*

تيت तीत *tīt*, تيتا तीता *tītā*, bitter, pungent, hot, acrid. *s.*

تيتا तेता *tetā*, so much, that much. *s.*

تيتاليس तेतालीस *tetālīs*, forty-three. *h.*

تيتر तीतर *tītar*, m. a partridge (*Perdix Francolinus*). *tītar ke munh lachhmī*, (lit. good fortune proceeds from the mouth of the partridge, *which is a small bird of little estimation*), a saying used when a person of mean understanding is chosen to decide in matters of which he is incompetent to judge. *s.*

تيتر तैत्तिर *taittir*, m. a flock of partridges; a francoline partridge. *s.*

تيتري तीतरी *tītrī*, f. a butterfly; the name of a medicine. *h.*

تيتريك तैत्तिरीयक *taittirīyak*, m. a follower of the Tittiri branch of the Yajur-veda. *s.*

تيتريه तैत्तिरीय *taittirīya*, relating to the Tittiri branch of the Yajur-veda. *s.*

تيتل तैतिल *taitil*, m. one of the astronomical periods called *Karans*. *s.*

تيتيس तेतीस *tetīs*, thirty-three. *s.*

تيج तेज *tej*, m. ardour, splendour, glory, strength, energy; sharpness, pungency. *tejmān* or *tejwant*, glorious. *s.*

تيج तीज *tīj*, f. the third day of the lunar fortnight. *s.*

تيجا तीजा *tījā*, m. the third day after the death of a relation, on which oblations are offered (used among Musalmāns), also the offerings so made. *s.*

تيج پات तेजपात *tej-pāt*, m. cassia; the leaf of the laurus cassia. *s.*

تيجس तेजस *tejas*, m. splendour, lustre; dignity, strength, power; semen virile. *tejas-kar*, restorative, invigorating, tonic. *s.*

تيجسوي तेजस्वी *tejaswī*, glorious, splendid. *s.*

تيجمان तेजमान *tejmān*, تيجونت तेजवन्त *tejwant*, glorious, illustrious. *s.*

تيجنا त्यजना *tyajnā*, a. to quit, to abandon, to resign. *s.*

تيجنك तेजनक *tejnak*, m. a kind of reed (*Saccharum sara*). *s.*

تيجني तेजनी *tejnī*, f. a plant (*Alètris hyacinthoides*). *s.*

تيجوتي तेजवती *tejwatī*, f. an aromatic plant (*Pothos officinalis*). *s.*

تيجومنته तेजोमन्थ *tejo-manth*, m. a tree (*Premna spinosa*). *s.*

تيجومي तेजोमय *tejo-may*, luminous, glorious. *s.*

تيجووتي तेजोवती *tejo-watī*, f. a plant bearing a fruit resembling pepper. *s.*

تيچهن तीछन *tīchhan*, ardent, sharp. *s.*

تير तीर *tīr*, m. the bank of a river, the shore of the sea; near, close at hand. *s.*

تير *tīr*, m. an arrow; the planet Mercury; the fourth solar month of the Persian year (corresponding to the Hindū *Shrāvan* or *Sāwan*); a beam. *tīr-andāz*, an archer. *tīr-andāzī*, f. archery. *tīr-bārān*, a punishment, in which the culprit is shot with arrows. *tīr-partāb*, the range of an arrow, bow-shot distance.

tīr chalānā, a. to shoot an arrow. *tīr-<u>kh</u>ākī*, f. a kind of arrow (light and with a small head). *tīr-<u>kh</u>urda*, wounded by an arrow. *tīr-ras*, a bow-shot, the range of an arrow. *tīr-kash*, an aperture, loop-hole. *tīr-gar*, m. a maker of arrows. *tīr-garī*, f. arrow-making. *tīri nāwak*, m. an arrow discharged through a tube. *p.*

تیرا तेरा *terā*, of thee, thy, thine. *h.*

تیرا *tīrā* (Dakh. for *tīr*), an arrow. *p.*

تیربھکت तीरभुक्ति *tīr-bhukti*, m. Tirhut, a province in the east of central Hindustān, on the north of Behar (now famed for its indigo). *s.*

تیرتھ तीर्थ *tīrth* or *tīrath*, m. pilgrimage (a Hindū term), especially holy places along the course of sacred streams. *tīrth-kār*, a holy personage. *s.*

تیرتھ راج तीर्थराज *tīrth-rāj*, the city of Ilāhābād (vulg. Allahabad). *s.*

تیرتھ‌راجي तीर्थराजी *tīrth-rāji*, f. the city of Benares. *s.*

تیرج तीरज *tīraj*, an abstract of a long list of accounts, &c. (v. Wilson). *h.* [moon. *s.*

تیرس तेरस *teras*, f. the thirteenth day of the

تیرس तेरस *terus*, the third year past or to come, year before last, or year after next. *h.*

تیرگي *tīragī*, f. darkness, obscurity. *p.*

تیرمار *tīr-mār*, a viper, a viper's teeth. *p.*

تیرن तीर्ण *tīrna*, crossed, passed over; spread. *tīrna-padī*, f. a plant (*Curculigo orchioides*). *s.*

تیرنا तैरना *tairnā* or *tīrnā*, a. to swim, to cross over. *s.*

تیره तेरह *terah*, thirteen. *terah-tezī*, the first thirteen days of the month *ṣafar*, which are considered to be unlucky. *h.p.*

تیره *tīra*, dark, obscure. *tīra abr*, m. black clouds. *tīra-ba<u>kh</u>t*, or *-rozgār*, unfortunate. *tīra-rozī*, misfortune, adversity. *tīra-dil*, blackhearted, malicious; m. an apostate, an outcast. *tīra-rang*, black. *p.*

تیرهان *terahān*, तेरहां } the thirteenth. *h.*
تیرهوان *terahwān*, तेरहवां }

تیڑها *teṛhā*, crooked, bent, awry, uneven. *d.*

تیز *tez*, sharp, pungent, acute, hot, strong, impetuous, violent, swift. *tez-āb*, m. nitrous acid, aquafortis. *tez-pāt*, m. the name of an aromatic leaf (*Laurus cassia*). *tez-par*, high-flying, swift-flying. *tez-raftār* or *-raw*, fast-going. *tez-ṭab'*, quick of apprehension. *tez-'aḳl*, or *-fahm*, intelligent, quick of apprehension. *tez-ḳadam*, or *-gām*, swift, active, quick, fast-going. *tez-nā<u>kh</u>un*, sharp-nailed. *tez-nigāh*, keen-sighted. *p.* [vum). *p.*

تیزک *tezak*, m. cress, cresses (*Lepidium sati-*

تیزي *tezī*, f. sharpness, pungency, swiftness. *p.*

تیس तीस *tīs* (for *trinshat*), thirty. *s.*

تیس *tais*, a he-goat (especially one that is old and rank); also a stag. *a.*

تیسا तैसा *taisā*, like that, so, in that manner; in like manner; at the same moment. *h.*

تیسرا तीसरा *tīsrā*, the third. *tīsre*, thirdly. *h.*

تیسوان तीसवां *tīswān*, the thirtieth. *h.*

تیسي तीसी *tīsī*, f. flax (*Linum usitatissimum*. *s.*) [ter's, an adze. *p.*

تیشه *tesha*, f. a kind of axe used by carpen-

تیغ *tegh*, m. a scimitar, a sword. *tegh ba dast*, sword in hand. *tegh-zan*, a swordsman. *teghi dallākī*, barber's sword, a cant term (in Persia) for *ustura*, a razor. *p.*

تیغا *teghā*, } m. a short, broad scimitar. *teghā-numā*, a sword like a scimitar.
تیغه *tegha*, }
tegha-bāz, a sword-player, a hero. *p.*

تیقظ *tayaḳḳuẓ*, watchfulness, vigilance. *a.*

تیقن *tayaḳḳun*, knowing for certain, prying into, ascertaining. *a.*

تیکت त्यक्त *tyakta*, left, resigned, abandoned. *s.*

تیکٹھ तीकठ *tīkaṭh*, m. posteriors. *h.*

تیکشن तीक्ष्ण *tīkshna* or *tīkshan*, hot, warm, pungent, ardent; zealous, active; keen, intelligent; angry, passionate; sharp, penetrating. *tīkshna-patra* or *tīkshna-phal*, m. coriander. *tīkshna-pushpa*, m. cloves. *tīkshna-tail*, m. resin; the milky juice of the *euphorbia*; spirituous liquor. *tīkshna-ras*, m. saltpetre. *tīkshna-shūk*, m. barley. *tīkshna-karman*, active, zealous. *tīkshna-kanṭak*, m. thorn-apple (*Datura metel*). *tīkshna-kand*, m. onion. *tīkshna-gandh*, m. *Morunga hyperanthera*; the gum olibanum tree; small cardamons. *tīkshna-gandhā*, f. mustard-seed; orris root; *Pandanus odoratissimus*. *s.*

تیکور तीकुर *tīkūr*, f. a starchy substance obtained from the root of the *curcuma angustifolia*. *h.*

تیکها तीखा *tīkhā*, pungent, hot; angry, passionate; sharp, penetrating. *s.*

تیکهر तीखुर *tīkhur*, f. a starchy substance obtained from the root of the *cucurma angustifolia*, *Roxb.* *h.*

تیکهي तीखी *tīkhī*, f. a sharp tone in music. *s.*

تیل तेल *tel* or तैल *tail*, m. oil. *tail*, storax, gum benzoin, incense. *tel chaṛhānā*, a. to anoint the head, shoulders, hands, and feet of the bride and bridegroom with oil mixed with turmeric. *s.*

تیل तीयल *tiyal*, f. a suit of females' clothes. *h.*

تیل چورکا तैलचौरिका *tail-chaurikā*, f. a cockroach (an oil-stealer). *s.*

تیلسالا तैलिसाला *taili-sālā*, f. an oil-mill. *s.*

تیل سپهٹك तैलस्फटिक *tail-sphaṭik*, m. a sort of gum (amber?). *s.*

تیلکٹ तैलकिट्ट *tail-kiṭṭ*, m. the oil cake, made of the oily seed after expression. *s.*

تیلمالي तैलमाली *tail-mālī*, f. a wick, the cotton of a lamp. *s.*

تیلن तेलिन *telin*, f. wife of an oil-seller. *s.*

تیلنگ तैलङ्ग *tailang*, m. the modern Carnatic. *tailangā*, an inhabitant of Tailang, a sepoy. *s.*

تیلني तैलिनी *tailinī*, f. the wick of a lamp. *s.*

تیلي तेली *telī* or तैली *tailī*, m. name of a caste whose business is to sell oil, an oilman, an oil grinder; adj. oily. *s.*

تيلي तीली *tīlī*, f. a bar; leg, calf of the leg. *h.*

تيليا तेलिया *teliyā*, m. name of a colour, dark bay. *teliyā-surang*, light bay coloured. *h.*

تيم *tem*, freshness, verdure. *d.*

تيمار *tīmār*, m. care, attention, regimen of the sick; infirmity, sickness, indisposition, affliction. *p.*

تيمم *tayammum*, m. purifying before prayer with sand or dust, when water cannot be had. *a.*

تيمن तेमन *teman*, m. wetting; moisture, damp, a sauce or condiment. *s.*

تيمني तेमनी *temnī*, f. a chimney, a fire-place. *s.*

تين तैं *taiṅ*, 2nd pers. pron. thou. *h.*

تين तें *teṅ*, postpos. from, by, with, in, (used chiefly in the Bhākhā dialect).

تين *teṅ*, (Dakh. for *ta,īṅ*), to, up to. *ke teṅ*. is much used in this dialect in place of *ko*, as the sign of the dat. and acc. cases. *d.*

تئيں तईं *ta,īṅ* (postpos.), up to, to; it is generally used with the possessive *apne*, in the sense of "*self*," as *apne ta,īṅ*, own self. *h.*

تين तीन *tīn*, three; *tīn rahmī ķānūn*, the rule of three (in arithmetic). *tīn thān*, m. the private parts; also the penis (only). *tīn terah*, dispersed, scattered. *s.*

تينتاليس तैंतालीस *teṅtālīs*, forty-three. *h.*

تينتيس तैंतीस *taiṅtīs* or तेंतीस *teṅtīs*, thirty-three. *h.*

تيندو तेंदू *tendū*, m. the name of a fruit (*Diospyros ebenum or glutinosa*). *s.*

تيندوا तेंदुआ *teṅdu,ā*, m. a leopard (*Felis leopardus*). *h.*

تيور तीवर *tīwar*, m. a hunter, one who lives by killing and selling game; a fisherman. *s.*

تيور तेवर *tewar*, m. vertigo, giddiness; countenance, physiognomy. *h.*

تيور तीव्र *tīvra*, much, excessive; hot, pungent. *tīvra-vedanā*, f. excessive pain, the torments of damnation. *s.*

تيورا तीव्रा *tīvrā*, f. a river in the east of Bengal. *s.*

تيورانا तेवराना *te,orānā*, n. to have a swimming in the head, to be faint, to stagger, to fall down senseless from a blow. *h.*

تيورس तेवरस *te,oras*, m. the third year past or to come, the year before last, or the year after next. *s.*

تيورهي तेवरही *teorhī*, } f. a frown. *teorī charhānā*, a. to frown. *teorī charhnā*, n. a frown to come on. *h.*
تيوري तेवरी *teorī*,
تيوڙي तेवड़ी *teoṛī*,

تيوري तीवरी *tīwarī*, f. the wife of a hunter. *s.*

تيون त्यूं *tyūṅ*, त्यों *tyoṅ*, or तेवों *teoṅ*, so, in like manner, at the same time. *h.*

تيون तेवन *tewan*, m. a garden, a pleasure-ground; play, sport. *s.*

تيوندها त्योंधा *tyondhā* or तेवोंधा *teoṅdhā*, dim-sighted, purblind. *h.*

تيوهار तेवहार *te,ohār*, m. a holyday, a festival. *h.*

تيه तिय *tiya* or तीय *tīya*, f. a woman, a wife. *s.*

تيه तेह *teh*, m. wrath, rage, vehemence. *h.*

تيها तेहा *tehā*, m. stedfastness, firmness, speaking with warmth, vehemence, peremptoriness, perseverance. *h.*

تيهر तेहर *tehar*, f. a female ornament worn round the ankles. *h.*

تيهو *taihū*, m. a small partridge; adj. empty. *p.*

تيهي तेही *tehī*, exactly then, instantly, immediately. *h.*

تيئيس तेईस *te,īs*, twenty-three. *h*

تييل तीयल *tīyal*, f. a suit of female's clothes. *h.*

تييه तीय *tīya*, f. a woman, wife. *s.*

ٹ

ٹ ट *ṭa*, the fifth letter in the Hindūstānī alphabet: its sound does not occur in the Arabic or Persian alphabets; and it differs from that of *te* in being formed by the forcible application of the tip of the tongue to the roof of the mouth, instead of the roots of the teeth. *h.*

ٹابر टाबर *ṭābar*, f. a small lake. *h.*

ٹابرا *ṭābrā*, m. a water-pot. *d.*

ٹاپ टाप *ṭāp*, f. a stroke with the fore-foot of a horse; the sound of a horse's hoof in travelling; a frame made of bamboo, for catching fish. *h.*

ٹاپا टापा *ṭāpā*, m. a hen-coop. *ṭāpā-ṭo,ī-h.* or *ṭāpā-ṭoiyā-k.*, a. to trifle; to grope, to rummage. *h.*

ٹاپا *ṭāpā*, } m. a sort of boat or raft. *d.*
ٹاپرا *ṭāprā*,

ٹاپر *ṭāpar*, a sheet, a wrapper, &c. *d.*

ٹاپنا टापना *ṭāpnā*, n. to paw with the fore-feet (as a horse expecting his corn); to whore (low phrase). *h.*

ٹاپو टापू *ṭāpū*, m. an island. *h.*

ٹاٹ टाट *ṭāṭ*, m. canvas, sackcloth; hemp or tow. *ṭāṭ-bāf*, m. a weaver of canvas. *ṭāṭ-bāfī*, f. embroidery. *h.*

ٹاٹك टाटक *ṭāṭak*, fresh, new, recent; a charm, juggling. *h.*

ٹاٹي टाटी *ṭāṭī*, f. a screen, a matted shutter. *h.*

ٹار टार *ṭār* (v. *ṭāl*), evasion, &c. *h.*

ٹارنا टारना *ṭārnā*, n. to evade, prevaricate, put off, postpone; a. to drive out of the way, to move, to prevent. *h.*

ٹاري टारी *ṭārī*, f. distance, remoteness. *h.*

ٹاڑي टाड़ी *ṭāṛī*, f. a small axe. *h.*

ٹاكن *ṭākan* (v. *ṭāṅghan*) a kind of horse. *d.*

ٹکي *ṭākī* (v. ٹانکي), f. a venereal chancre; a natura. basin or fountain in a rock. *d.*

ٹال टाल *ṭal*, f. shuffling, evasion, rejecting a request; f. a heap (of grain, &c.), a stack, a rick; baldness from age; a turn or trick in wrestling. *ṭāl-k.*, a. to put off; to heap. *ṭāl mārnā*, a. to heap; to turn the scale fraudulently in weighing. *h.*

ٹالا टाला *ṭālā*, m. evasion, &c.; a rick, heap, stack; a quagmire, decayed vegetable matter; a piece of stagnant water. *ṭālā-bālā batānā*, a. to put off, to drive away, to deceive. *h.*

ٹالاٹولي टालाटोली *ṭālā-ṭolī*, f. }
ٹال‌ٹول टालटोल *ṭāl-ṭol*, m. } evasion, prevarication, putting off, shuffling. *h.*
ٹال‌مٹول टालमटोल *ṭāl-maṭol*, m. }

ٹالنا टालना *ṭālnā*, a. to evade, to prevaricate; to avert or put off; to drive out of the way, to ward off, to remove, to prevent. *h.*

ٹالي टाली *ṭālī*, f. a kind of musical instrument. *h.*

ٹامبرا *ṭāmbrā*, m. a water-pot (v. *ṭābrā*). *d.*

ٹانا टानना *ṭānnā*, a. to stretch, to pull. *h.*

ٹانٹ टांट *ṭānṭ*, f. the crown of the head. *h.*

ٹانٹھا टांठा *ṭānṭhā*, powerful, strong, firm, solid. *h.*

ٹانٹھاءي टांठाई *ṭānṭhā,ī*, f. solidity. *h.*

ٹانچ टांच *ṭānch*, }
ٹانچڑا टांचड़ा *ṭānchṛā*, } perverse, audacious, troublesome. *h.*

ٹانچھامارنا *ṭānchhā-mārnā*, a. to hamstring a horse, cow, &c. *d.*

ٹانڈ टांड *ṭānḍ*, f. a stage, a raised seat, platform. *h.*

ٹانڈا टांडा *ṭānḍā*, m. a venture (of goods); a caravan or a large company of travelling merchants; name of a place in Oude; the goods of a *banjārā*, q.v. *h.*

ٹانک टांक *ṭānk*, m. a weight equal to four *māshas* (see *tolā*). *s.*

ٹانک टांक *ṭānk*, f. an iron pin; a stitch; solder for uniting metals. *h.*

ٹانکا टांका *ṭānkā*, m. a stitch; a tub made of stones; solder. *ṭānke lagānā*, a. to stitch, to solder. *h.*

ٹانکر टांकर *ṭāṅkar*, m. a blackguard, a lecher, a libertine. *s.*

ٹانکنا टांकना *ṭāṅknā*, a. to stitch, to cobble. *h.*

ٹانکھ टांख *ṭāṅkh*, a reservoir for water, a tank. *h.*

ٹانکي टांकी *ṭāṅkī*, f. a venereal chancre; a square piece cut out of a melon to examine its quality. *h.*

ٹانکي टांकी *ṭāṅkī*, f. a chisel. *s.*

ٹانگ टांग *ṭāng*, f. the leg. *ṭāng uṭhānā*, a. to copulate. *ṭāng-denā*, a. to hang up, to hang; (lit. to give the leg) to be a catamite. *h.*

ٹانگڑي *ṭāngṛī*, f. the foot, the leg. *d.*

ٹانگن टांगन *ṭāngan*, m. (see *ṭānghan*). *h.*

ٹانگنا टांगना *ṭāngnā*, a. to hang up, to dangle, to hang by a string, &c., not on a peg. *h.*

ٹانگھن टांघन *ṭānghan*, m. a kind of horse, a pony. *ṭānghan-numā*, like a *ṭānghan*. *h. p.*

ٹانگي टांगी *ṭāngī*, f. a hatchet. *h.*

ٹاننا टानना *ṭānnā*, a. to stretch, to pull. *h.*

ٹبر टब्बर *ṭabbar*, m. family (v. *tabār*). *h.*

ٹبہ *ṭibba*, m. a rising ground, a height; a sand-bank or shoal (in the sea). *d.*

ٹبھانا टिभाना *ṭibhānā*, a. to give a small daily allowance, such as merely to save from starving. *h.*

ٹبھاو टिभाव *ṭibhāw*, m. a small daily allowance. *h.*

ٹبھک टुभक *ṭubhak*, f. the sound of water dropping; sound of gurgling. *h.* [a sound. *h.*

ٹپ टप *ṭap*, m. spring, leap, bound; a drop;

ٹپا टप्पा *ṭappā*, m. the post-office; a raft, a catamaran; a relay of palanquin bearers; the name of a mode in music; the bound of a ball, &c.; a sort of hook; a jump, a bound. *ṭappā mārnā*, a. to sew or stitch with intervals; to read in a desultory manner. *ṭappā khānā*, a. to bound or ricochet (a shot). *h.*

ٹپا टपा *ṭapā*, an island in a river. *h.*

ٹپال *ṭappāl*, m. the post for letters; a mail or packet; relays of runners or carriers, for the conveyance of letters or other things; the post-office. *ṭappālī* or *ṭappālwālā*, the postman, a runner or carrier of letters. *d.*

ٹپانا टपाना *ṭapānā*, a. to cause to jump over, to cause to leap, to make bound. *h.* [to cover. *h.*

ٹپانا टुपाना *ṭupānā*, a. to have buried, to cause

ٹپ‌پڑنا टपपड़ना *ṭap-paṛnā*, a. to thrust one's self into other people's concerns, to intermeddle, to interfere. *h.*

ٹپ‌جانا टपजाना *ṭap-jānā*, n. to jump over. *h.*

ٹپڑي *ṭipṛī*, f. stocks (for the legs); a bookbinder's press (v. *shikanja*). *d.*

ٹپس टिप्पस *ṭippas*, f. pride, arrogance. *h.*

ٹپک टपक *ṭapak*, f. pain, throbbing; sound made by dropping. *ṭapak paṛnā*, a. to drip. *ṭapak-navīs*, m. one who reports erroneously what he pretends to have overheard. *h.*

ٹپکا टपका *ṭapkā*, m. a drop of rain; fruit falling when ripe (particularly mangoes), a windfall. *h.*

ٹپکا टिपका *ṭipkā*, m. a stain of any colour applied by the finger; the focus of a burning lens. *h.*

ٹپکانا टपकाना *ṭapkānā*, a. to cause to drip, to distil. *h.*

ٹپکاو टपकाव *ṭapkā,o*, m. distillation, dripping. *h.*

ٹپکنا टपकना *ṭapaknā*, n. to drop when ripe; to drip, to distil; to throb, to palpitate. *h.*

ٹپکي टपकी *ṭapkī*, f. (diminutive of *ṭapkā*) a small drop, &c. *ṭapkī paṛnī 'aurat kī*, to be wanton (a woman). *h.*

ٹپن टिप्पन *ṭippan*, f. annotation, comment. *s.*

ٹپي टिप्पनी *ṭippanī*, f. gloss, comment. *s.*

ٹپنا टपना *ṭapnā*, a. to jump over. *h.*

ٹٹا टट्टा *ṭaṭṭā*, m. a screen. *h.*

ٹٹانا टटाना *ṭaṭānā*, n. to be dried (vulgar). *h.*

ٹٹبھ टिट्टिभ *ṭiṭṭibh*, m. a bird (*Parra jacana* or *goensis*). *s.*

ٹٹپونجیا टटपूंजिया *ṭaṭpūnjiyā* or *ṭuṭpūnjiyā*, a man of broken fortune, a bankrupt. *h.*

ٹٹر टट्टर *ṭaṭṭar*, m. a matted shutter. *h.*

ٹٹري टट्टरी *ṭaṭṭarī*, f. a lie, a falsehood; a kettle-drum. *s.*

ٹٹري टटिरी *ṭaṭirī*, f. name of a bird, sandpiper (*Tringa goensis*). *h.*

ٹٹڑي टटड़ी *ṭaṭṛī* (also *ṭaṭṭarī*), f. the crown of the head; a fence, a hedge. *h.*

ٹٹکا टटका *ṭaṭkā*, fresh, new, recent. *h.*

ٹٹکا टुटका *ṭuṭkā* (v. *ṭoṭkā*), m. a charm, a superstitious remedy. *h.*

ٹٹکارنا टिटकारना *ṭiṭkārnā*, a. to urge an animal by making the noise *ṭiṭkārī*, q. v. *h.*

ٹٹکاري टिटकारी *ṭiṭkārī*, f. the noise made by drawing the tongue from the roof of the mouth, to make horses, &c. proceed. *h.*

ٹٹو टट्टू *ṭaṭṭū*, m. a pony, a small horse. *h.*

ٹٹواني टटवानी *ṭaṭwānī*, f. a pony mare. *h.*

ٹٹولنا टटोलना *ṭaṭolnā*, a. to feel for, to grope, to search for by feeling with the hand, to touch, to handle. *h.*

ٹٹھیا टठिया *ṭaṭhiyā*, f. a flat dish used by Hindūs. *h.*

ٹٹي टट्टी *ṭaṭ ī*, f. a screen, a matted shutter; a necessary office; a frame for illumination. *ṭaṭṭī bandhnā*, n. to draw up (men in a close rank). *shikār kī ṭaṭṭī kī oṭ baiṭhnā*, a. to do secretly; to form an ambuscade. *h.*

ٹٹیا टटिया *ṭaṭiyā*, f. a screen, a matted shutter. *h.*

ٹٹیہرا टटीहरा *ṭaṭīhrā*, m. } a sandpiper (*Tringa goensis*); a kind of rattle.
ٹٹیہري टटीहरी *ṭaṭīhrī*, f. } *ṭaṭīhrī se āsmān thāmā jā,egā*, will the sky be supported by the sandpiper? applied to a person who undertakes an enterprise far above his strength; (this bird is said to sleep with its legs extended upwards, as if to prop the firmament). *s.*

ٹچا टुच्चा *ṭuchchā*, m. a rake, a blackguard. *h.*

ٹخنا *ṭakhnā*, } m. (prop. *ṭahnā*), the ankle
ٹخنہ *ṭakhna*, } joint. *h.*

ٹڈا टिड्डा *ṭiḍḍā*, m. } a locust; a grasshopper. *h.*
ٹڈي टिड्डी *ṭiḍḍī*, f. }

ٹر टर *ṭar*, intoxicated; inattentive, regardless, like one intoxicated. *h.*

ٹرا टर्रा *ṭarrā*, wicked, vicious (particularly a horse); stout. *h.*

ٹرانا टर्राना *ṭarrānā*, a. to chatter. *s.*

ٹرٹر टरटर *ṭarṭar*, f. chattering. *s.*

ٹرٹرانا टरटराना *ṭarṭarānā*, a. to chatter. *s.*

ٹرٹري टरटरी *ṭarṭarī*, f. chattering. *s.*

ٹرخل *ṭarkhal*, m. a contemptuous epithet for a woman, a low-priced trull. *h.*

ٹرم ٹرم *ṭurm ṭurm*, noise made by frogs. *d.*

ٹرنا टरना *ṭarnā*, n. to flinch, retire (v. *ṭalnā*). *h.*

ٹسر टसर *ṭasar*, m. (v. *tasar*), a kind of silk. *s*

ٹسک टसक *ṭasak*, f. shooting pain, stitch, throb. *h.* (actively); n. to shoot with pain. *h.*

ٹسکانا टसकाना *ṭaskānā*, a. to move or shake

ٹسکنا टसकना *ṭasaknā*, n. to move, to shake; to have pain; to decline in quality. *h.*

ٹسکنا टुसकना *ṭusaknā*, n. to cry, to weep. *h.*

ٹسنا टसना *ṭasnā*, n. to burst (as tight clothes, or a pillow stuffed too full), to split, to crack. *h*

ٹسوي टसवे *ṭaswe*, m. tears. *h.*

ٹک टक *ṭak*, f. temper, nature, disposition, a look, a stare. *ṭak bāndhnā*, a. to stare. *ṭak lagānā*, a to expect, to long for. *h.*

ٹک टुक *ṭuk*, a little. *ṭuk-eh*, a little way. *h.*

ٹکا टका *ṭakā*, m. a copper coin equal (in northern India) to two *paise*; money in general. *h.*

ٹکانا टिकाना *ṭikānā*, a. to retain, to fix in any place, to stop, to billet, to lodge, to station. *h.*

ٹکاءو टिकाऊ *ṭikā,ū*, durable, stationary. *h.*

ٹکاو टिकाव *ṭikāw*, m. stability, residence. *h.*

ٹکاءي टकाई *ṭakā,ī*, f. a tax, duty, collection, imposition; a cheap trull. *h.*

ٹکٹکي टिकटिकी *ṭikṭikī*, f. a lizard. *h.*

ٹکٹکي टकटकी *ṭakṭakī*, f. staring, fixed look. *ṭakṭakī-lagānā* or *-bāndhnā*, a. to fix one's looks on an object. *h.*

ٹکٹھي टिकठी *ṭikṭhī*, f. a teapoy or three-footed stool. *h.*

ٹکدیشي टक्कदेशी *ṭakka-deshī*, m. a potherb (*Chenopodium album*). *s.*

ٹکر टक्कर *ṭakkar*, f. shoving, pushing, shouldering, knocking against, striking a blow, the knocking of head to head, equality. *ṭakkar pahāṛ se lenī*, to enter the lists against an antagonist of greatly superior force. *ṭakkar khānā*, n. to stumble; to be dashed against any thing; to meet with a loss or misfortune. *ṭakkar mārnā*, a. to knock against; met. to pray, from their striking their heads on the ground; to curse. *h.*

ٹکر टुकर *ṭukar*, } m. a piece, a bit. *ṭukrā-*
ٹکرا टुकरा *ṭukrā*, } *purza*, m. scraps, clippings, shavings. *ṭukar-gadā*, one who begs for bits of bread, &c. *h.p.*

ٹکرانا टकराना *ṭakrānā*, a. to knock together the heads of two people; to dash on something; to grope in a dark place or passage. *h.*

ٹکري टिकरी *ṭikarī*, a kind of soil which is irretentive of moisture. *h.*

ٹکڑ टिक्कड़ ṭikkaṛ, f. a thick loaf of bread. ṭakkar, resemblance, comparison. h.

ٹکڑا टुकड़ा ṭukṛā, m. } a bit, a portion, morsel. h.
ٹکڑی टुकड़ी ṭukṛī, f. }

ٹکڑی ṭukṛī, f. a band, company, party. ṭukṛī-dār, a commander of a company. ṭikṛī, the spreading hog-weed (*Boerhavia diffusa*). d.

ٹکڑی टिकड़ी ṭikṛī, f. a wafer, &c. (v. ṭiklī). h.

ٹکسا टुकसा ṭuksā, a little. h.

ٹکسال टकसाल ṭaksāl, f. a mint. ṭaksāl charhnā, n. to be educated. ṭaksāl bāhar, uneducated, unpolished, rude, unclassical. ṭaksāl kā khoṭā, spoilt in education. s.

ٹکسالی टकसाली ṭaksālī, } m. an officer, a master of the mint. h.
ٹکسالیا टकसालिया ṭaksāliyā, }

ٹکلی टिकली ṭiklī (also ṭikkalī), f. a wafer, a small round cake; an ornament worn on the forehead, a spangle. h.

ٹکمک دیکھنا ṭukmuk dekhnā, a. to stare, to fix one's look. d.

ٹکنا टकना ṭaknā, a. to stare at (v. tāknā); n. to be stitched, to be studded with gems or embroidery. h.

ٹکنا टिकना ṭiknā, n. to stop, to remain in any place, to be detained. h.

ٹکوء टकूआ ṭakū,ā, m. a spindle. s.

ٹکور टिकोर ṭikor, m. a cataplasm, poultice. h.

ٹکور टकोर ṭakor, f. a fillet, tap, the sound of a drum (v. ṭakorā). h.

ٹکورا टकोरा ṭakorā, m. a fillip, a tap; a very small unripe mango; the sound of a drum. h.

ٹکورنا टकोरना ṭakornā, a. to foment. h.

ٹکونا टकौना ṭakaunā, m. (see ṭakā) a copper coin. h.

ٹکھنا टखना ṭakhnā, m. the ankle-joint. h.

ٹکی टकी ṭakī, f. staring, fixed look; aim. h.

ٹکی टिक्की ṭikkī or ṭikī, f. a small loaf of bread. ṭikkī lagānā, a. to form a connection, to make interest; to earn a scanty livelihood. h.

ٹکیا टिकिया ṭikiyā, f. a small cake, a little cake of charcoal for the ḥuḳḳa; a wafer, a bolus. h.

ٹکیت टकेत ṭaket or टकैत ṭakait, } rich, possessed of ready money, a monied man. h.
ٹکیٹا टकेटा ṭakeṭā, }

ٹگر टगर ṭagar, m. borax; wanton play or sport; wandering of the mind, confusion, perplexity. h.

ٹگرا टगरा ṭagrā, squint-eyed. h.

ٹگرانا टगराना ṭagrānā, }
ٹگھرانا टघराना ṭaghrānā, } a. to roll or make roll (in a transitive sense). h.
ٹگھلانا टघलाना ṭaghlānā, }

ٹگرنا टगरना ṭagarnā, }
ٹگھرنا टघरना ṭagharnā, } n. to roll or be rolled (intransitively). h.
ٹگھلنا टघलना ṭaghalnā, }

ٹگھلنا टिघलना ṭighalnā or टघलना ṭaghalnā, n. to be melted, to rarefy. h.

ٹلا टल्ला ṭallā, m. *impetus sive succussus in coitu.* ṭalle-navīsī, f. unprofitable employment, wasting of time. h.

ٹلانا टलाना ṭalānā, a. to cause to disappear, to cause to give way. h.

ٹلپ टलप ṭalap, a bit, a piece, morsel. h.

ٹل جانا टलजाना ṭal-jānā, n. to get out of the way; to disappear, to vanish. h.

ٹل ملانا टलमलाना ṭal-malānā, to totter; to tantalize. h.

ٹلنا टलना ṭalnā, n. to give way, to shrink from, to withdraw or retire from; to disappear. h.

ٹلوءا टिलूआ ṭilū,ā, m. a flatterer. h.

ٹلوءا टलूआ ṭalū,ā, m. a man who watches over a ṭāl, q. v. h.

ٹلی टल्ले ṭalle, m. *congressus, sonitus collisionis in coitu.* ṭalle-navīsī, f. unprofitable employment. h.

ٹلیا टिलिया ṭiliyā, f. a young hen. h.

ٹم ٹم टिमटिम ṭimṭim, m. a sound. ṭam-ṭam (vulg. ṭom-ṭom), a small drum, also the sound of such a drum. h.

ٹمٹمانا टिमटिमाना ṭimṭimānā, n. to give a faint light. h.

ٹمکی ṭamkī, f. a small drum, a gong. ṭamkī-pīṭnā, a. to issue a proclamation. d.

ٹمل ṭamil, the language of the Hindūs of a considerable part of Southern India, extending from Madras to Cape Comorin. It has been erroneously called by Europeans "Malabars," although it is not spoken or understood in Malabar. d.—(Binning).

ٹمنا ṭumnā, a. to vex, irritate (v. chhernā). d.

ٹن टन ṭan, m. twang; pride, conceit, vanity. ṭan-ṭan, an imitative sound, like our "ding-dong," &c. h.

ٹنا टना ṭanā, m. *pudendum muliebre, clitoris.* h.

ٹنانا टनाना ṭanānā, a. to extend, stretch. s.

ٹنٹا टण्टा ṭanṭā, m. wrangling, altercation squabble. h.

ٹنٹنانا टुनटुनाना ṭunṭunānā, a. to tune slowly. h.

ٹنچ टञ्च ṭanch, miserly, hard, untractable. h.

ٹنخواہ ṭan-khwāh, (in law) an assignment. p.

ٹنڈ टुण्ड ṭunḍ, m. a hand or branch that has been cut off. h.

ٹنڈا टुण्डा ṭunḍā, handless, whose hands have been cut off, or one born without hands; the knob in the back part of a turban. ṭunḍe-dār, a turban which has a knob in the hinder part. h.

ٹنڈی टुण्डी ṭunḍī, f. the navel; adj. handless. ṭunḍiyāṅ bāndhnā or charhānā, or kasnā, a. to tie the hands behind the back. h.

ٹنڈیرا टण्डेड़ा *ṭanḍera* (see *tirendā*), a float. *h.*

ٹنک टनक *ṭanak*, f. a harsh sound. *h.*

ٹنک टङ्क *ṭank*, m. a weight of four *māshas*; a sword, a sacrificial knife; a hatchet or stone cutter's chisel; a spade, a hoe; borax; a kind of elephant or wood apple. *ṭank-pati*, m. the master of the mint. *ṭank shālā*, f. a mint. *s.*

ٹنکا टङ्का or टनका *ṭankā*, m. the jingle (of plates, dishes, &c. *h.*

ٹنکار टङ्कार *ṭankār*, f. the twang (of a bow-string); surprise, wonder; fame, notoriety. *s.*

ٹنکانک टङ्कानक *ṭankānak*, m. the mulberry (*Morus indica*). *s.*

ٹنکنا टंकना *ṭanknā*, n. to be stitched. *h.*

ٹنکورنا टङ्कोरना *ṭankornā*, n. to twang. *h.*

ٹنگ टङ्ग *ṭang*, m. the leg; borax. *h.*

ٹنگا टुङ्गा *ṭungā*, m. scut, a short tail. *h.*

ٹنگ टंगा *ṭangā*, a large reedy kind of grass growing on high ground (*Saccharum procerum*). *h.*

ٹنگار टुङ्गार *ṭungār*, f. pecking, nibbling fruit, &c., more for amusement than from appetite. *h.*

ٹنگٹنگاذ *ṭingṭingānā*, a. to twang or sound a single string of a musical instrument. *d.*

ٹنگ جانا टङ्गजाना *ṭang-jānā*, n. to hang, to be hung or suspended (also *ṭangnā*). *h.*

ٹنگری टङ्गरी *ṭangrī*, } f. the leg, the thigh. *h.*
ٹنگڑی टङ्गड़ी *ṭangṛī*, }

ٹنگنا टङ्गना *ṭangnā*, n. to hang (v. *tang-jāna*). *h.*

ٹنگنی टङ्गिनी *ṭanginī*, f. a plant (*Cissampelos hexandra*). *s.*

ٹنیا टुंइया *ṭuniyā*, tiny. *ṭuniyā totā*, a kind of parrot. *h.*

ٹوءا टोआ *ṭo,ā*, f. act of feeling or groping. *h.*

ٹوءاٹوءی टोआटोई *ṭo,ā-ṭo,ī*, f. searching, feeling for, feeling (with the hand). *h.*

ٹوبنا *ṭobnā*, a. to hang, suspend. *d.*

ٹوپ टोप *ṭop*, m. a hat, a cap, a head, a cover, a thimble; bait; a stitch. *h.*

ٹوپا टोपा *ṭopā*, m. a covering for the head, a helmet, a cap (v. *ṭop*). *h.*

ٹوپنا *ṭopnā*, a. to hang, suspend. *d.*

ٹوپی टोपी *ṭopī*, f. a hat. *ṭopī-wālā*, one who wears a hat, or an animal with a comb, crest, &c. The term was once used to express the Persian or *Moghul* troops, but it is now generally applied to Europeans. *h.*

ٹوٹ टूट *ṭūṭ*, f. fracture, breaking; misunderstanding or coolness between friends, harm, loss, deficiency; a passage omitted in the writing of a book, which is afterwards written in the margin. *ṭūṭ-parnā*, n. to break in upon, to rush in, to be collected in crowds. *ṭūṭ-jānā*, n. to be broken; to become ill, pine. *ṭūṭ-rahnā*, n. to be distressed, to be weary, to be reduced to poverty, to pine away; to be separated. *s.*

ٹوٹا टूटा *ṭūṭā*, broken; m. want, deficiency, loss, failure. *ṭūṭā-phūṭā*, fragments, broken to pieces. *s.*

ٹوٹا टोटा *ṭoṭā*, m. loss, deficiency; a cartridge; a candle's end. *h.*

ٹوٹرو टोटरू *ṭoṭrū*, m. a kind of turtle-dove. *h.*

ٹوٹکا टोटका *ṭoṭkā*, m. a charm, an amulet, a philter. *h.*

ٹوٹنا टूटना *ṭūṭnā*, n. to break, to be broken; to break forth, to rush upon, to assault. *s.*

ٹورا टोरा *ṭorā*, m. a ledge extending out from a wall, to keep off the weather, without pillars, eaves. *h.*

ٹوڑی टोड़ी *ṭoṛī*, f. the name of a musical mode or *rāginī*. *h.*

ٹوسی टूसी *ṭūsī*, f. a bud, a young flower. *h.*

ٹوک टोक *ṭok*, f. hindrance, prevention; the influence of an evil eye. *h.*

ٹوک टूक *ṭūk*, } m. a piece, a little, a particle,
ٹوکا टूका *ṭūkā*, } an atom, a bit; a single beat of a drum. *h.*

ٹوکاپٹا टोकापट्टा *ṭokā-paṭṭā*, a permanent lease or *paṭṭā*. *h.*

ٹوکاٹوکی टोकाटोकी *ṭokā-ṭokī*, } f. hindrance and
ٹوک ٹاک टोकटाक *ṭok-ṭāk*, } prevention. *h.*

ٹوکرا टोकरा *ṭokrā*, m. a large basket (without a lid); (in Dakh.) a broad shallow basket, a wicker boat covered with leather, for crossing a river, &c. *ṭokrā-denā*, to beat another person at a game. *h.*

ٹوکری टोकरी *ṭokrī*, f. a small basket without a lid. *h.*

ٹوک کر بولنا *ṭok kar bolnā*, a. to speak from experience. *d.*

ٹوکنا टोकना *ṭoknā*, a. to interrogate, to prevent, to challenge, to accost, to envy; to look at with an evil eye. *h.*

ٹول टोल *ṭol*, m. a company, a society; a hamlet. *ṭol mārnā*, a. to dash one top against another while in motion. *h.*

ٹولا टोला *ṭolā*, m. a quarter or particular part of a town. *h.*

ٹولا टोला *ṭolā*, m. } a set of any thing, such as
ٹولی टोली *ṭolī*, f. } of chessmen, &c.; a complete assortment. *h.*

ٹولغی *ṭūlghī*, f. fun, jesting, joking. *d.*

ٹولی टोली *ṭolī*, f. a company, society, crowd. *h.*

ٹوم टूम *ṭūm*, m. trifles; an ornament; a frame for pigeons to perch on. *ṭūm-ṭām*, m. a few trifles; an ornament. *ṭūm-denā*, a. to push gently. *h.*

ٹومنا टूमना *ṭūmnā*, a. to push or jog gently, to strike softly, so as to draw a person's notice. *h.*

ٹون टूं *ṭūn*, m. *ventris crepitus*. *ṭūn-h.*, a. *crepitum ventris edere*. *h.*

ٹونا टोना *ṭonā*, m. enchantment, fascination; a wedding song. *h.*

ٹوناٹامن टोनाटामन *ṭonā-ṭāman*, m. } hocus-
ٹوناٹانی टोनाटानी *ṭonā-ṭanī*, f. } pocus, juggling. *h.*

ٹونٹا टोंटा *ṭonṭā*, m. a cracker, a serpent in fireworks; a joint of bamboo, &c.; a cartridge; handless. *h.*

ٹونٹي टोंटी *ṭonṭī*, f. a spout. *h.*

ٹونڈي टूंडी *ṭūnḍī*, f. the navel; a small branch or stump of a tree, broken at the end and leafless. *h.*

ٹونگ टूंग *ṭūng*, f. (v. *ṭungār*) pecking, &c. *h.*

ٹونگاٹانگي टूंगाटांगी *ṭūngā-ṭāngī*, f. pecking and nibbling. *h.*

ٹونگنا टूंगना *ṭūngnā*, a. to peck, to nibble, to chew straws, &c. for amusement; to pick; to piddle. *h.*

ٹونوا टोनवा *ṭonwā*, m. a kind of hawk (see *ṭonā*). *h.*

ٹونہا टोन्हा *ṭonhā* or टौन्हा *ṭaunhā*, m. a juggling man, a conjuror. *h.*

ٹونہاءي टोन्हाई *ṭonhā,ī*, f. a juggling woman, a female conjuror. *h.*

ٹوه टोह *ṭoh*, watching secretly, espionage. *h.*

ٹھ ठ *ṭha*, the aspirated form of ٹ ट *ṭa*. *s. h.*

ٹھا ठा *ṭhā*, m. a sound made by striking one thing on another. *h.*

ٹھاٹ ठाट *ṭhāṭ*, m. the frame of thatch on which the straw is laid; arrangement, adjustment. *h.*

ٹھاٹھ ठाठ *ṭhāṭh*, m. state, dignity, equipage, pomp; conveniency, plenty. *h.*

ٹھار ठार *ṭhār*, m. determination; snow, frost. *h.*

ٹھاڑا ठाड़ा *ṭhāṛā*, erect, straight. *h.*

ٹھاڑھ ठाढ़ *ṭhāṛh*, steep, lofty. *h.*

ٹھاڑھا ठाढ़ा *ṭhāṛhā*, m. }
ٹھاڑھي ठाढ़ी *ṭhāṛhī*, f. } erect, straight. *h.*

ٹھاڑھنا ठाढ़ना *ṭhāṛhnā*, n. to be erect, to stand. *h.*

ٹھاڑھو ठाढ़ौ *ṭhāṛhau*, erect, standing. *h.*

ٹھاسنا ठासना *ṭhāsnā*, a. to stuff, to cram, to ram down. *h.*

ٹھاکر ठाकुर *ṭhākur*, m. the divinity; an idol; a lord, master, chief (among *rājpūts*); a landholder; a barber. *ṭhākur-bāp*, a grandfather. *ṭhākur-mā*, a grandmother. *ṭhākur-sevā*, lit. the service of an idol, applied to a grant of revenue for the support of an idol temple. *s.*

ٹھاکراني ठाकुरानी *ṭhākurānī*, }
ٹھاکراين ठाकुरायन *ṭhākurāyan*, } f. a goddess, a lady, the wife or daughter of a *ṭhākur*. *h.*

ٹھاکراءي ठाकुराई *ṭhākurā,ī*, rank or office of a *ṭhākur*. *h.*

ٹھاکرباري ठाकुरबारी *ṭhākurbārī*, f. }
ٹھاکردوارا ठाकुरद्वारा *ṭhākur-dwārā*, m. } an idol temple. *s.*

ٹھال ठाल *ṭhāl*, m. }
ٹھالا ठाला *ṭhālā*, m. } a branch of a tree, &c. *h.*
ٹھالي ठाली *ṭhālī*, f. }

ٹھالا ठाला *ṭhālā*, disengaged, at leisure. *h.*

ٹھاں ठां *ṭhāṅ*, m. a place, station, residence. *h.*

ٹھاں *ṭhāṅ*, a place for tying up an animal. *d.*

ٹھانا *ṭhānā*, m. place, station. *ṭhānā-dār*, station-master or keeper. *h.*

ٹھانٹھو ठानठू *ṭhānṭhū*, worthy of belief, trusty (vulgar); m. the report of a musket. *h.*

ٹھانس *ṭhāṅs*, coughing, a cough. *d.*

ٹھانسا ठांसा *ṭhāṅsā*, m. stuffing, wadding of a gun, &c. *h.*

ٹھانسنا ठांसना *ṭhāṅsnā*, a. to stuff, to cram. *h.*

ٹھاننا ठान्ना *ṭhānnā*, a. to resolve, to determine, to be intent on, to set one's heart on; to settle. *h.*

ٹھانو ठांव *ṭhāṅw* (also *ṭhā,oṅ*), f. a residence, place. *s.*

ٹھپا ठप्पा *ṭhappā*, m. an instrument for stamping leather with, a die, a stamp, a printing type; printing. *h.*

ٹھپنا ठपना *ṭhapnā*, a. to strike, to beat. *h.*

ٹھٹ ठट *ṭhaṭ*, m. bank, shore, margin. *s.*

ٹھٹھ ठठ *ṭhaṭh*, m. throng, crowd. *h.*

ٹھٹھا ठट्ठा *ṭhaṭṭhā*, m. fun, sport, joking, jest; name of a place. *ṭhaṭṭhe-bāz* or *ṭhaṭhā-mizāj*, a jester, a humorous person, a funny fellow; adj. jocular. *ṭhaṭṭhe-bāzī*, f. jesting, sporting, joking, fun. *ṭhaṭṭhā-k.* or *-mārnā*, to jest, to deride. *h.*

ٹہٹہ टहटह *ṭahṭah*, }
ٹہٹہا टहटहा *ṭahṭahā*, } m. beauty, freshness, or splendour, conspicuous at a distance. *h.*

ٹھٹھانا ठठाना *ṭhaṭhānā*, a. to strike, to beat; to beat one's own head, &c., in token of vexation; to harass one's self. *h.*

ٹھٹھر ठट्ठर *ṭhaṭṭhar*, m. the frame made of bamboo for thatching, shell of a house. *h.*

ٹھٹھر ठिठुर *ṭhiṭhur* (also *ṭhiṭhir*), f. numbness, torpor. *h.*

ٹھٹھرا ठिठरा *ṭhiṭhrā* or ठिठुरा *ṭhiṭhurā*, numbed, benumbed, torpid. *h.*

ٹھٹھرا ठठरा *ṭhaṭhrā*, m. a fence. *h.*

ٹھٹھرانا ठिठुराना *ṭhiṭhurānā*, a. to benumb, to chill. *h.*

ٹھٹھراہٹ ठिठराहट *ṭhiṭhrāhaṭ*, f. numbness, torpor. *h.*

ٹھٹھرنا ठिठिरना, ठिठरना or ठिठुरना, *ṭhiṭhirnā*, *ṭhiṭharnā* or *ṭhiṭhurnā*, n. to be numbed, benumbed, to be chill. *h.*

ٹھٹھري ठठरी *ṭhaṭhrī*, f. the frame of a matted screen, the frame (bamboo-work) of a thatched roof, shell of a house; a bier; a skeleton, a very thin person. *h.*

ٹھٹھک ठिठक *ṭhiṭhak*, f. the state of standing amazed. *ṭhiṭhak-rahnā* or *-jānā*, n. to stop short. *h.*

ٹھٹھکنا ठठकना *ṭhaṭhaknā* or ठिठकना *ṭhiṭhaknā*, n. to stop, to stagnate, to stand amazed, to draw back in surprise, to shrink. *h.*

ٹهٹهور ठठोर *ṭhaṭhor*, ٹهٹهول ठठोल *ṭhaṭhol*, } a banterer, a wag, a jester; adj. jocose. *h.*

ٹهٹهولي ठठोली *ṭhaṭholī*, f. fun, humour, sport, joking. *h.*

ٹهٹهيرا ठठेरा *ṭhaṭherā*, m. a brazier, a tinker. *ṭhaṭhere ṭhaṭhere kī badla,ī*, a bargain between two people equally acute or knowing; diamond cut diamond; the stalk of the *jo,ār* (*Holcus sorgum*). *h.*

ٹهٹهيري ठठेरी *ṭhaṭherī*, f. a brazier's wife, a female brazier, or tinker. *h.*

ٹهچرا ठचरा *ṭhachrā*, m. wrangling, quarrelling. *h.*

ٹهخ ٹهخ *ṭhakh-ṭhakh* also *ṭhakh-ṭhakhī*, chattering, a chatterer. *d.*

ٹهڈا ठड्डा *ṭhaḍḍā*, m. the beak of a paper kite. *h.*

ٹهڈي ठुड्डी *ṭhuḍḍī*, f. the chin; parched grain; *ṭhuḍḍī pakarnā*, a. to flatter, to curry favour. *h.*

ٹهر ठिर *ṭhir*, f. frost, coldness. *h.*

ٹهرا ठर्रा *ṭharrā* or ठरा *ṭharā*, f. a kind of wine or spirituous liquor; a kind of shoe worn by villagers. *h.*

ٹهرا ठिहरा *ṭihrā*, m. a small village. *h.*

ٹهرانا ठिराना *ṭhirānā*, a. to cause to congeal. *h.*

ٹهراو ठराव *ṭharā,o*, settlement, determination (properly *ṭhahrāo*). *h.*

ٹهرر ठरर *ṭharar*, ٹهرك ठरक *ṭharak*, } m. snoring. *ṭharak pārnā*, n. to snore. *h.*

ٹهرنا ठिरना *ṭhirnā*, n. to freeze, to be chilled. *h.*

ٹهري ठर्री *ṭharrī*, f. (see *ṭharrā*) wine. *h.*

ٹهريا ठरिया *ṭhariyā*, m. a kind of earthen hukka. *h.*

ٹهس ठस *ṭhas*, *ṭhis*, or *ṭhus*, an imitative sound, as of a musket ill charged, or flashing in the pan. *h.*

ٹهسا ठस्सा *ṭhassā*, m. a mould or form into which plates of metal, &c. are beaten to take the form of pastes of ornaments, &c.; a type in printing; a stamp or impression on coins, &c.; pride, vanity. *h.*

ٹهساٹهس ठसाठस *ṭhasā-ṭhas*, filled; crowded. *h.*

ٹهسانا ठुसाना *ṭhusānā*, a. to cause to stuff. *h.*

ٹهسك ठसक *ṭhasak*, f. state, dignity. *h.*

ٹهسكنا ठुसकना *ṭhusaknā*, n. *peditum ciere, suppedere*; to weep (but not aloud). *h.*

ٹهسكنا ठसकना *ṭhasaknā*, a. to break a piece off any vessel of earthenware, by knocking two vessels together, without completely destroying it. *h.*

ٹهسكي ठुसकी *ṭhuskī*, f. *ventris crepitus surdus*. *h.*

ٹهسنا ठुसना *ṭhusnā*, n. to be stuffed, crammed. *h.*

ٹهسني ठसनी *ṭhasnī*, f. a rammer. *h.*

ٹهك ठहक *ṭahak*, f. pain in the joints. *h.*

ٹهكانا ठिकाना *ṭhikānā*, m. residence, place, station, abode, dwelling; boundary, limit; *ṭhikānā ḍhūnḍhnā*, a. to seek a residence, or employment. *ṭhikānā-k.*, a. to account, to search or trace an affair to its commencement. *ṭhikāne lagānā*, a. to put to death, to kill, to waylay, to make away, to assassinate; to establish, to settle, to prove; to find out one's residence. *ṭhikāne lagnā*, n. to be killed, to die, to be put an end to. *ṭhikānā lagānā*, a. to establish, to settle, to prove; to find out one's residence. *h.*

ٹهك ٹهك ठकठक *ṭhak ṭhak*, m. f. hard work, harassing labour, difficulties; a sound. *h.*

ٹهكٹهكانا ठकठकाना *ṭhakṭhakānā*, a. to pat, tap, sound. *h.*

ٹهكٹهوا ठकठौवा *ṭhak-ṭhauwā*, f. a small boat so called, a shallop. *h.*

ٹهك ٹهكيا ठकठकिया *ṭhak-ṭhakiyā*, m. a stickler, a wrangler. *h.*

ٹهكٹهيلا ठकठेला *ṭhakṭhelā*, stuffed together in a crowd, crowded. *h.*

ٹهكرا ठिकरा *ṭhikrā*, m. a fragment of an earthen vessel, a shard; a vessel for carrying fire; such as *fakīrs* use. *h.*

ٹهكرانا ठुकराना *ṭhukrānā*, a. to kick or strike with the toes. *h.*

ٹهكراءي ठकुराई *ṭhakurā,ī*, f. lordliness, nobility; the state or rank of *ṭhākur*. q.v. godship, divinity. *h.*

ٹهكراين ठकुरायन *ṭhakurāyan*, f. the wife or daughter of a *ṭhākur*, a female divinity or idol. *h.*

ٹهكڑا ठुकड़ा *ṭhukṛā*, m. a bit, a piece (of bread). *h.*

ٹهكنا टहकना *ṭahaknā*, n. to pain. *h.*

ٹهكنا टुहुकना *ṭuhuknā*, n. to cry. *h.*

ٹهگ ठग *ṭhag*, m. a robber, a cheat: the term is more especially applied of late to the miscreants called *phansīgars*, or stranglers. q.v. *ṭhag-bidyā* or *-bāzī*, f. cunning, art, fraudulent dexterity. *ṭhag lānā*, a. to rob, to cheat. *ṭhag lenā*, a. to cheat. *h.*

ٹهگانا ठगाना *ṭhagānā*, n. to be cheated; a. to cheat, to deceive. *h.*

ٹهگاءي ठगाई *ṭhagā,ī*, f. robbery, theft, cheating. *h.*

ٹهگن ठगिन *ṭhagin*, f. a female *ṭhag*. *h.*

ٹهگنا ठगना *ṭhagnā*, a. to cheat, to deceive. *h.*

ٹهگني ठगनी *ṭhagnī*, f. a female robber, or cheat. *h.*

ٹهگوري ठगौरी *ṭhagaurī*, f. cheating, robbing. *h.*

ٹهگئي ठगई *ṭhaga,ī* or *ṭhagī*, f. the practice of strangling, &c. (v. *ṭhag*), cheating, robbing. *h.*

ٹهگيا ठगिया *ṭhagiyā*, m. a cheater, a robber. *h*

ٹهل टहल *ṭahal* (also *ṭahal-ṭakor*), f. housewifery, housekeeping, duty, service, task, business, work, job, use, drudgery. *ṭahal-k.*, a. to serve, to drudge. *ṭahal lagānī*, n. to dance attendance. *h.*

ٹهلانا टहलाना *ṭahlānā*, a. to lead about, to cause to walk backwards and forwards (as a horse or child); to make dance attendance. *h.*

ٹهل ٹكور टहलटकोर *ṭahal-ṭakor*, f. housewifery, &c., the same as *ṭhahal*. *h.*

تہلنا टहलना *ṭahalnā*, n. to walk backwards and forwards, to take the air, to rove, to ramble. *h.*

تہلني टहलनी *ṭahalnī*, f. a housewife. *h.*

تہلوا टहलूआ *ṭahlū,ā*, m. a manager of household concerns, a servant. *h.*

تہلوئي टहलूई *ṭahlūī*, f. a housewife. *h.*

تہليا ठिलिया *ṭhiliyā*, f. a waterpot. *h.*

تہمك ठुमक *ṭhumak*, f. the act of waving, or walking with a graceful, easy air. *ṭhumak-chāl*, f. a dignified pace, stately gait, graceful carriage. *h.*

تہمكا ठुमका *ṭhumkā*, short, of low stature. *h.*

تہمكنا ठुमकना *ṭhumakhnā*, n. to walk with grace and stateliness, to strut, to walk with dignity. *h.*

تہمكي ठुमकी *ṭhumkī*, lazy; f. the playing of a paper kite, to keep it up when the wind is light. *h.*

تہنا टहना *ṭahnā*, m. a branch or large bough. *h.*

تہنا ठना *ṭhannā*, n. to be fixed, to be ascertained. *h.*

تہناك ठनाक *ṭhanāk*, m. a clinking noise. *h.*

تہنتہنانا ठनठनाना *ṭhanṭhanānā*, n. to jingle, to rattle. *h.*

تہنڈ ठंड *ṭhanḍ*, f. coldness, a cold *h.*

تہنڈا ठंडा *ṭhanḍā*, cold; free from weeds (a soil). *ṭhanḍā parnā*, n. to abate (anger, virility, or wantonness). *ṭhanḍā-k.*, a. to make cold; to extinguish; to comfort, to assuage. *ṭhanḍā honā*. n. to become cold; to be extinguished; to be comforted, or pacified; to rest; to lose virility. *kalejā ṭhanḍā honā*, n. to be pleased, to be happy (by seeing a friend, son, &c., after a long separation); to have one's revenge gratified. *h.*

تہنڈائي ठंडाई *ṭhanḍā,ī*, f. refrigerant (medicine); the intoxicating drug made of *bhang*. *h.*

تہنڈك ठंडक *ṭhanḍak*, } f. coldness, coolness. *h.*
تہنڈهك ठंढक *ṭhanḍhak*, }

تہنڈها ठंढा *ṭhanḍhā* (v. *ṭhanḍā*), cold. *h.*

تہنڈي ठंडी *ṭhanḍī*, cold. *ṭhanḍī sāṅs bharnī*, a. to sigh, to heave a cold sigh. *h.*

تہنك ठिनक *ṭhinak* or ठुनुक *ṭhunuk*, f. sob. *h.*

تہنكانا ठुनकाना *ṭhunkānā*, a. to cause to knock, hammer. *h.*

تہنكنا ठनकना *ṭhanakhnā*, n. to throb, to shoot (as a pain); to jingle, tinkle. *h.*

تہنكنا ठिनकना *ṭhinakhnā* or ठुनुकना *ṭhunuknā*, n. to sob. *h.*

تہنگنا ठिङ्गना *ṭhingnā*, short, dwarfish. *ṭhingnā,ī*, f. lowness of stature. *h.*

تہني टहनी *ṭahnī*, f. a branch. *h.*

تہور ठौर *ṭhaur*, f. place, residence; adv. upon the spot. *ṭhaur rahnā*, n. to be murdered, to be knocked down lifeless upon the spot. *h.*

تہور ठोर *ṭhor*, f. beak, bill. *h.*

تہوڑي ठोढ़ी *ṭhoṛī*, f. the chin. *h.*

تہوس ठोस *ṭhos*, solid, firm, compact. *h.*

تہوسا ठोसा *ṭhosā*, m. the thumb presented in token of denial (a mode peculiar to women). *h.*

تہوسائي ठोसाई *ṭhosā,ī*, f. solidity, firmness. *h.*

تہوسنا ठोसना *ṭhosnā*, a. to stuff, cram in; to stab. *h.*

تہوكا टहोका *ṭahokā*, m. a blow, a thump. *h.*

تہوكا *ṭhokā*, m. reproof, chiding, scolding. *d.*

تہوكر ठोकर *ṭhokar*, f. a blow, a stroke, a thump; tripping or striking the foot against any thing, a kick, stumble; a stumbling-block. *ṭhokar khānā*, n. to trip, to stumble; to meet with a loss or misfortune; to encounter obstacles or difficulties. *ṭhokar lagnā*, n. to strike the foot against (a stumbling-block or obstacle). *h.*

تہوكرا ठोकरा *ṭhokrā*, m. a fillip; adj. hard [(as bad bread). *h.*

تہوكن ठोकन *ṭhokan*, m. act of beating, &c. *h.*

تہوكنا ठोकना *ṭhoknā*, a. to beat, to strike; to drive (as a stake). *h.*

تہولا ठोला *ṭholā*, m. a cup for the food and drink of a bird in a cage; the knuckles. *ṭholā mārnā* a. to strike with the knuckles. *h.*

تہوں टहों *ṭahoṅ*, m. the voice of a new-born child. *h.*

تہونا ठिवना *ṭhiwnā*, m. the knee (see *ṭhewnā*). *s.*

تہونتہ ठूंठ *ṭhūnṭh*, m. a stump, a branch of a tree broken off at the end and leafless; an amputated hand. *h.* [bird. *h.*

تہونتہ ठोंठ *ṭhonṭh*, f. the beak or bill of a

تہونتہا ठूंठा *ṭhūnṭhā*, having the hand amputated; having its branches lopped and leafless (a tree). *h.*

تہونتہي ठूंठी *ṭhūnṭhī*, f. stubble. *h.*

تہونتيا ठूंटिया *ṭhūnṭiyā*, mutilated, lopped off; m. a eunuch. *h.*

تہونسنا *ṭhoṅsnā*, a. to stuff (see *ṭhosnā*). *d.*

تہونكنا ठोंकना *ṭhoṅknā*, a. to knock, to hammer; to drive (as a stake); to thrust with the finger, to fillip, to drive, to beat. *ṭhoṅk-d.*, to hammer, to knock. *pīṭh-ṭhoṅknā*, to pat on the back. *h.*

تہونگ ठोंग *ṭhong*, f. the act of striking with a finger or beak, pecking. *h.*

تہونگا ठोंगा *ṭhongā*, m. striking with the beak. *h.*

تہونگانا ठोंगाना *ṭhongānā*, } a. to peck, to strike
تہونگنا ठोंगना *ṭhongnā*, } with the beak. *h.*

تہاكا ठहाका *ṭhahākā*, m. a peal, a succession of loud sounds, explosion. *ṭhahāke kī mulāḳāt*, f. meeting with great demonstrations of friendship. *h.*

تہرانا ठहराना *ṭhahrānā*, a. to fix, settle, to come to a decision or determination. *h.*

تہراو ठहराव *ṭhahrā,o*, m. settlement, fixture, permanence; proof. *h.*

تہرنا ठहरना *ṭhaharnā*, n. to stop, rest, remain, stay, be determined. *h.*

ٹھئي ठई ṭha,ī, f. (past tense of ṭhānnā), to resolve, fix, &c. *h.*

ٹھیپ ठीप ṭhīp, f. a kind of lamp. *h.*

ٹھیپي ठेपी ṭhepī, f. a cork, a plug, stopper; *ṭhepī muṅh meṅ denā*, n. to be silent. *h.*

ٹھیٹھ ठेठ ṭheṭh, pure, genuine; contentious. *h.*

ٹھیس ठेस ṭhes, m. f. a knock, a blow, tripping against a stone, &c., a shove, a push, a thrust. *h.*

ٹھیسرا ठेसरा ṭhesrā, m. sneer, oblique reflection or inuendo. *h.*

ٹھیسنا ठेसना ṭhesnā, a. to pierce; to knock against; to stuff, to cram, to ram in; to eat ravenously. *h.*

ٹھیک ठेक ṭhek, f. a support, a prop; a large sack filled with grain; a portable granary. *h.*

ٹھیک ठीक ṭhīk, exact, even, accurate, complete, just, fit, proper, reasonable, true, regular, right; (met.) parsimonious; m. sum, addition. *ṭhīk ānā*, to fit, to suit. *ṭhīk-k.*, a. to put to rights; to correct; to beat; to adjust. *h.*

ٹھیکا ठेका ṭhekā, m. a plug, a stopper. *h.*

ٹھیکا ठीका ṭhīkā, m. hire, fare, fixed price; work done by contract, a task. *h.*

ٹھیک‌ٹھاک ठीकठाक ṭhīk-ṭhāk, quite right, right and tight. *ṭhīk-ṭhāk-k.*, to set to rights, to adjust. *h.*

ٹھیکرا ठीकरा ṭhīkrā, m. a broken piece of earthenware. *h.*

ٹھیکري ठीकरी ṭhīkrī, f. a broken piece of earthenware; *mons veneris*; the upper or moveable jaw of the cock of a musket. *ṭhīkrī-chunnā*, a. to evince madness. *h.*

ٹھیکم‌ٹھیک ठीकमठीक ṭhīkam-ṭhīk, exactly, truly, rightly, quite right. *h.*

ٹھیکم‌ٹھیکا ठीकमठीका ṭhīkam-ṭhīkā, m. abuse. *h.*

ٹھیکي ठेकी ṭhekī, f. act of resting on the way (a porter carrying a load). *ṭhekī lagānā* or *denā*, a. to rest (a porter carrying a load). *h.*

ٹھیلا ठेला ṭhelā, m. a push, a shove. *ṭhelā-ṭhelī*, f. shoving and shouldering. *h.*

ٹھیلنا ठेलना ṭhelnā, a. to shove, to push, to move forward by pushing. *h.*

ٹھیلنا ठेलना ṭhelanā, m. acting the buffoon. *h.*

ٹھینٹھ ठेंठ ṭhenṭh, pure, genuine; contentious. *h.*

ٹھینٹھي ठेंठी ṭhenṭhī, f. a cork, a plug; a ball of ear-wax; a *dhotī* or cloth, reaching no further than the knee. *h.* [a tool (*penis*). *h.*

ٹھینگا ठेंगा ṭhengā, m. a stick, a small club;

ٹھینگاباجنا ठेंगाबाजना ṭhengā-bājnā, a. to spoil, destroy. *h.*

ٹھینگنا ठेंगना ṭhengnā, short, dwarfish. *h.*

ٹھیونا ठेवना ṭhewnā or ठेउना ṭhe,unā, m. the knee, the pastern (of a horse). *s.*

ٹھیي ठये ṭhaye, past tense of ṭhānnā, to fix, resolve, &c. *h.*

ٹیپ टीप ṭīp, f. a note of hand, a cheque; drawing a card; raising the voice in singing, the noting of any thing; f. the act of pressing, compressing. *ṭīp-ṭāp*, f. ornament; the act of pressing or compressing. *ṭīp lenā*, a. to draw a card. *h.*

ٹیپڑي टीपड़ी ṭīpṛī, f. wooden stocks or thumbscrews used for torture; an instrument in which the prepuce of a boy is fixed when undergoing the operation of circumcision. *h.*

ٹیپنا टीपना ṭīpnā, a. to press, to compress, to grope, to feel, to squeeze. *h.*

ٹیٹا टीटा ṭīṭā, f. *lingula vulvæ mulierum*. *h.*

ٹیٹلي टीटली ṭīṭlī, f. the name of a medicine. *h.*

ٹیٹوا टेटवा ṭeṭwā, m. the head of a snake. *h.*

ٹیخنا ṭīkhnā, n. to cry, as a partridge. *d.*

ٹیڈي टीडी ṭīḍī, f. a locust. *h.*

ٹیر टीर ṭīr, f. a transverse piece in cloths, or a breadth cut diagonally. *h.*

ٹیر टेर ṭer, f. tune; voice. *h.*

ٹیرا टेरा ṭerā, m. a curtain; squint-eyed, cock-eyed. *h.*

ٹیرنا टेरना ṭernā, n. to bawl, to roar to, to call loudly, to shout, to halloo; to tune. *h.*

ٹیڑا टेड़ा ṭeṛā, m. the trunk of a tree; an instrument for twisting coarse thread or twine. *ṭeṛā hilānā*, a. to be afflicted with the venereal disease. *a.*

ٹیڑھا टेढ़ा ṭeṛhā, crooked, bent. *ṭeṛhā-beṛā*, crooked. *ṭeṛhā-k.*, a. to bend, to crook. *h.*

ٹیڑھاءي टेढ़ाई ṭeṛhā,ī, f. crookedness. *h.*

ٹیڑھي टेढ़ी ṭeṛhī, f. pride, vanity, haughtiness; perverseness. *h.*

ٹیڑي टीड़ी ṭīṛī, f. a locust (same as ṭīḍī). *h.*

ٹیس टीस ṭīs, f. a throb, throbbing, a shooting pain. *ṭīs mārnā*, n. to throb. *h.*

ٹیسنا टीसना ṭīsnā, n. to palpitate, to throb. *h.*

ٹیسو टेसू ṭesū, m. the blossoms of the palās tree (*Butea frondosa*); a kind of play. *h.*

ٹیسوا ṭeswā, m. a tear (also ṭaswā, q.v.). *h.*

ٹیک टीक ṭīk, f. an ornament for the head and neck. *h.*

ٹیک टेक ṭek, f. a prop, pillar; a promise, vow. *ṭek rahnā*, n. to lean upon. *h.*

ٹیکا टीका ṭīkā, m. inoculation; a mark made on the forehead by Hindūs; a badge of sovereignty; an ornament worn on the forehead; the nuptial gifts. *ṭīkā bhejnā*, a. to send the nuptial gifts, which are presented by the relations of the bride to the bridegroom. *h.*

ٹیکا टीका ṭīkā, f. a commentary or gloss. *h.*

ٹیکا ṭekā, m. trust, reliance, confidence, support. *d.*

ٹیکان ṭekān, m. a height, elevation. *d.*

ٹیکر टेकर *ṭehar*, ٹیکرا टेकरा *ṭekrā*, } m. (also *ṭīkar*, &c.) a height, a rising ground; high lands of indifferent quality. *h.*

ٹیکري टीकरी *ṭīkarī*, a small field of inferior land. *h.*

ٹیکڑا *ṭekṛā*, m. a height, rising ground. *d.*

ٹیکن टेकन *ṭekan*, m. a prop, support. *h.*

ٹیکنا टेकना *ṭeknā*, a. to support, to prop. *h.*

ٹیکیت टीकैत *ṭikait*, invested with the *ṭīkā* or badge of sovereignty. *s.*

ٹیگرا टेगरा *ṭegrā*, m. a rising ground. *h.*

ٹیل टील *ṭīl*, f. a young hen; a woman (name given in contempt). *h.*

ٹیلا टीला *ṭīlā*, ٹیلها टीलहा *ṭīlhā*, } m. a rising ground, a ridge, a low hill. *h.*

ٹیلنا टेलना *ṭelnā*, a. to remove. *h.*

ٹیلوءا टेलूआ *ṭelū,ā*, m. a beam. *h.*

ٹیم टेम *ṭem*, f. snuff of a candle; the flame of a candle or lamp. *h.*

ٹیم ٹام टेमटाम *ṭem-ṭām* or *ṭīm-ṭām*, m. dressing. *h.*

ٹینا टेना *ṭenā* (mas. of *ṭenī*), a particular breed of fowls *h.*

ٹینٹ टेंट *ṭenṭ* or टींट *ṭīnṭ*, m. the ripe fruit of *karīl*; a speck on the eye. *h.*

ٹینٹا टेंटा *ṭenṭā*, m. a large ripe fruit of *karīl*; a fizgig; speaking inconsiderately. *h.*

ٹینٹر टेंटर *ṭenṭar*, m. name of a fruit. *h.*

ٹینٹوءا टेंटूआ *ṭenṭū,ā*, m. the windpipe, the throat. *h.*

ٹینٹي टेंटी *ṭenṭī*, f. name of a fruit; speaking inconsiderately. *h.*

ٹین ٹین टें टें *ṭen-ṭen*, an imitative sound, inarticulate sound. *h.*

ٹینك टेंक *ṭenk*, f. shelter, support; recognising. *h.*

ٹینگرا टेंगरा *ṭengrā*, m. ٹینگري टेंगरी *ṭengrī*, f. } the name of a fish (*Silurus*). *s.*

ٹینگي टेंगी *ṭengī*, f. teazing. *h.*

ٹیني टेनी *ṭenī*, m. a particular breed of fowls; adj. tiny, small. *h.*

ٹیو टेव *ṭew* or *ṭe,o*, f. habit, custom. *h.*

ٹیوا टेवा *ṭewā*, m. calculation of nativity; habit, custom. *h.*

ٹیوري *ṭe,orī* (v. *ṭe,orī*), a frown, &c. *h.*

ٹیوکي टेवकी *ṭewkī*, f. a prop, a pillar. *h.*

ٹیونا टेवना *ṭewnā*, a. to sharpen. *h.*

ٹیہرا टेहरा *ṭehrā*, m. a village. *h.*

ٹیہلا टेहला *ṭehlā*, m. the customs of marriage. *h.*

ث

ث *se* or *sā*, 4th letter of the Arabic alphabet. It does not occur, strictly speaking, in words of Persian or Indian origin. Its sound, among the Arabs, is that of *th* in the English word *thin*, but the Persians and Indians give it the sound of *s*. It is one of the radical letters, never being employed in the formation of derivatives; and in the reckoning by *abjad* it stands for 500. When Persian words are introduced into Arabic writings, this letter is sometimes used instead of *te* or *sīn*, as *Kayūmars* for *Kayūmart*, and *Tahmūras* for *Tahmūras*. *s.*

ثابت *sābit*, firm, constant, durable, stable, proved, confirmed, established, fixed. *sābit rahnā*, n. to adhere to a person. *sābit-ḳadam*, immoveable, stable, resolute, permanent, constant. *sābit-k.*, to confirm, to establish, to render durable, to prove by witness. *a.*

ثابت خاني *sābit-ḳhānī*, an armed retainer or sentinel. *a.*

ثاقب *sāḳib*, shining, splendid; sublime, high. *a.*

ثالث *sālis*, the third; an umpire, arbitrator mediator. *sālis salāsa*, m. trinity. *sālis bil-ḳhair*, an unprejudiced arbitrator. *a.*

ثالث نامه *sālis-nāma*, m. a deed of award. *p.*

ثالثه *sālisa*, f. an arbitress, mediatrix. *a.*

ثالثي *sālisī*, f. arbitration, mediation. *a.*

ثالوث *sālūs*, the Trinity. *sālūsi aḳdas*, the most holy Trinity. *a.*

ثامن *sāmin*, the eighth. *a.*

ثاني *sānī*, m. ثانيه *sāniya*, f. } second; the second. *sānī ul-ḥāl*, another time. *sānī mulāḥaza*, re-inspection, revisal. *sāniyan*, secondly, in the second place. *a.*

ثبات *sabāt*, m. permanency, stability, firmness, resolution, constancy. *a.*

ثبت *sabt*, f. stability, permanency, firmness, *sabt-k.*, a. to inscribe, to subscribe, to write. *a.*

ثبوت *sabūt* or *subūt*, m. firmness, stability, permanency, confirmation by evidence. *a.*

ثرا *sarā*, opulent, rich; m. the earth. *a.*

ثروت *sarwat*, f. wealth, multitude. *a.*

ثريا *suraiyā*, m. the Pleiades. *a.*

ثعلب *sa'lab*, m. a fox (pl. *sa'ālib*). *a.*

ثعلب مصري *sa'labi miṣrī*, m. salep (the root of a species of orchis, considered, particularly in the East, to be a strong restorative and aphrodisiac). *a.*

ثفل *sufl*, dregs, sediment, refuse. *a.*

ثقات *siḳāt* (pl. of ثقه), trusty friends. *a.*

ثقالت *saḳālat*, f. weight, heaviness. *a.*

ثقل *siḳl*, m. gravity, weight; indigestion, heavy load. *a.*

ثقه *siḳa*, m. confidence; a confidant, a trusty friend. *a.*

ثقيل *saḳīl*, heavy; lazy, phlegmatic; indigestible. *a.*

ثلاث *salās*, three. *sulās*, by three. *a.*

ثلاثي *sulāsī*, triangular, any thing made up of three parts, triple; (in gram.) triliteral. *a.*

ثلث *suls*, m. the third part. *a.*

ثمر *samar*, m. fruit; produce, advantage, profit; offspring. *samar-bakhsh*, productive of fruit. *a.*

ثمره *samra* or *samara*, m. fruit; profit, reward, recompense; offspring. *a.*

ثمن *saman*, m. price, value. *a.*

ثمن *sumun* or *sumn*, m. the eighth part. *a.*

ثمين *samīn*, costly, precious. *a.*

ثنا *sanā*, f. praise, applause, eulogy. *sanā-khwān*, one who praises. *sanā-gustar*, one who scatters praises. *a.*

ثواب *sawāb*, m. the future reward of virtue; a virtuous action, reward, premium. *a.* [stars. *a.*

ثوابت *sawābit* (pl. of ثابت), m. the fixed

ثوب *suub*, m. a robe, a vestment. *a.*

ثور *saur*, m. a bull; the sign Taurus; twilight, crepuscule; the name of a mountain near Mecca. *a.*

ثياب *siyāb* (pl. of ثوب), m. clothes, robes. *a.*

ثيبه *saiyiba*, f. a young woman who has consummated her marriage; *femina cujus periit virginitas*. *a.*

ج

ج *jīm* or *jīm-i-tāzī*, the fifth letter of the Arabic alphabet, the sixth in the Persian, and the seventh in the Hindūstānī. It has the sound of *j* in *judge*. In Arabic it is a radical letter. In enumeration by *abjad* it stands for the number three. It is sometimes used: 1st, for *sh*, as *kāj* for *kāsh*, would that! 2nd, for *g* (particularly in conformity to Arabic pronunciation), as *faranj* for *farang*, Europe; 3rd, for the final imperceptible *he*, as *fīrozaj* for *fīroza*, a turquoise. Again, for *j* are used, 1st, *t*, as *tārāt*, for *tārāj*, plunder; 2nd, *zh*, as *kazhdum* for *kajdum*, a scorpion; 3rd, *g*, as *akhshīg* for *akhshīj*, contrary. In some rare instances it is redundant, as *debāj* for *debā*, brocade.

ج ज *ja*, is the corresponding letter in the Devanāgarī alphabet. It is used for *z*, in such Arabic and Persian words as have found their way into the Hindī dialect, thus, *hājirī* for *hāzirī*, breakfast. In many words borrowed from the Sanskrit, *j* is substituted for *y*, particularly in the dialects of Bengal, Tirhoot, &c. When added to a pure Sanskrit substantive it denotes born, sprung, or produced from such substantive, as *anḍaj*, a bird, the egg-born, from *anḍa*; *vārij*, the lotus, lit. sprung from water.

جا *jā*, f. a place. *jā-ba-jā* or *hama-jā*, everywhere. *jā-nishīn*, m. a locum tenens, a deputy, a successor, vicegerent. *p.*

جا जा *jā*, the old inflected form of the rel. pron. *jo* or *jaun*, whom, which. *h.*

جاب जाब *jāb*, m. muzzle for large cattle; net for fruit; a sort of grass. *h.*

جابر *jābir*, a despot, a tyrant. *a.*

جابسال *jāb-sāl* and *jāb-sālī* (for *jawāb-sawāl*, &c.), conversation, reply, rejoinder. *a.*

جابي जाबी *jābī*, f. muzzle for small cattle. *h.*

جاپ जाप *jāp*, m. repeating inaudibly passages from the *Shāstras*, charms, names of a deity; silent meditation; counting one's beads (a Hindū term not applicable to Musalmāns). *s.*

جاپك जापक *jāpak*, } m. one who counts his
جاپي जापी *jāpī*, } beads, or who recites to himself. *s.*

جاپلوسي *jāplūsī*, f. flattery, adulation (more commonly *chāplūsī*). *p.*

جاپن जापन *jāpan*, m. spending or passing away time. *s.*

جاپهل *jāphal* (v. *jā,e-phal*), nutmeg. *d.*

جات जात *jāt*, born, produced; a child, offspring. *jāt* or *jāti*, f. kind, sort, cast, sect, tribe, class, birth, production, lineage, race. *jāt-pānt* or *jāt-pānti*, f. pedigree. *jāt-bhā,ī*, a brother by caste. *jāti-swabhāw*, m. specific or generic character or nature. *jāti-lakshan*, m. generic distinction or characteristic; mark of tribe or caste. *jāti-hīn*, outcaste. *s.*

جاتا رهنا जाता रहना *jātā-rahnā*, to go away entirely, to vanish. *h.*

جاتر यात्रु *jātru*, m. a pilgrim, wayfarer. *s.*

جاترا जात्रा (for यात्रा *jātrā*), f. a moment (generally implies a fortunate moment); pilgrimage; departure, march, journey; a religious festival, especially a procession of idols, a fair. *jātrā-karan*, m. setting forth on a march. *s.*

جاترك यात्रिक *jātrik*, } m. a pilgrim, a travel-
جاترو जात्रू *jātrū*, } ler. *s.*
جاتري जात्री *jātrī*, }

جاتك जातक *jātak*, m. a mendicant; astrological calculation of a nativity. *s.*

جات‌كرم जातकर्म *jāt-karma*, m. a sacrificial ceremony directed to be performed at the birth of a child. *s.*

جاتو जातू *jātū*, a *rājpūt* tribe in Karnal, of whom many have now become Musalmāns. *h.*

جاتي जाती *jātī*, f. kind, tribe (same as *jāti*); the great-flowered jasmine (*Jasminum grandiflorum*); mace, nutmeg. *jāti-patrī*, f. mace. *jāti-phal*, m. nutmeg (same as *jā,e-phal*, q.v.). *jātī-ras*, m. gum myrrh. *s.*

جاتيندهه जात्यन्ध *jātyandh*, born blind. *s.*

جاتيه जात्य *jātya*, well-born, of good family. *s.*

جاٹ जाट *jāṭ*, m. the name of a tribe among the *rājpūts* (for a full account of this celebrated clan, vide Wilson's Glossary). *h.*

جاٹل जाटलि *jāṭli*, m. f. a plant (*Bignonia suaveolens*). *s.* [tribe *h.*

جاٹلي जाटली *jāṭlī*, a subdivision of the *gūjar*

جاتو जातू *jātū*, name of a *rājpūt* tribe. *h.*

جاتوا जातुवा *jātuwā* or जातूआ *jātū,ā*, a branch of the *chamār* tribe, q. v. *h.*

جاٹھ जाठ *jāṭh*, m. the axis of an oil or sugar mill which presses the grain or the canes; a post placed by Hindūs in the centre of a tank to mark that its water has been dedicated to a deity. *s.*

جاثي *jās̤ī*, one who is kneeling. *a.*

جاجت *jā-jat*, f. the series of binary combinations of letters beginning with *jīm*, the first being *jīm alif* or *jā*, the second *jīm te* or *jat*, &c. *a.*

جاجك जाजक (for याजक) *jājak*, m. a Brāhman who presides at the performance of a religious ceremony. *s.* [or on the tabor. *h.*

جاجك जाजक *jājak*, m. a player on cymbals

جاجم जाजम *jājam*, f. a cloth thrown over the carpet to sit on. *h.*

جاجن याजन *jājan*, m. the act of conducting a sacrifice or causing its performance. *s.*

جاجيه याज्य *jājya*, m. property or presents earned by officiating at sacrifices. *s.*

جاچت याचित *jāchit*, asked, begged. *s.*

جاچك जाचक (for याचक) *jāchak*, m. a solicitor; a beggar; a person who goes about singing for charity. *s.*

جاچنا जाचना (for याचना) *jāchnā*, a. to want, to need, to require, to implore, to solicit; f. asking, begging. *s.*

جاداد *jā-dād*, f. a place, station, service, employment, consignment. *p.* [*jāda*, q. v.). *p.*

جادج *jādaj*, m. a pathway, road (same as

جادو जादव *jādaw* (for यादव *yādava*), m. a descendant of Yadu; the lineage of *Krishṇa* as descended from Yadu; a name of *Krishṇa*. *s.*

جادو *jādū*, m. enchantment, conjuring, juggling. *jādū-chalānā*, a. to practise incantations. *jādū-gar*, m. an enchanter, conjuror, juggler, magician. *jādū-garnī*, f. a sorceress. *jādū-garī*, f. magic, necromancy. *p.*

جادو जादो *jādo*, m. one of the low castes in a village, employed in menial offices. *h.*

جادون जादों *jādoṅ*, name of a tribe of *rājpūts*. *h.*

جاده *jāda*, m. a pathway, a road, manner, practice, the right road. *a.* [stupidity. *s.*

جاڈيه जाड्य *jāḍya*, m. coldness, apathy; folly,

جاذب *jāẕib*, alluring, attractive; drawing (as a plaster). *jāẕib kāg͟haẕ*, blotting-paper. *a.*

جاذبت *jāẕibat*, } attracting; charm, grace,
جاذبه *jāẕiba*, } loveliness. *a.*

جار *jār*, m. neighbour. *jāri mulāsiḳ*, a near neighbour. *jārr*, giving *kasra* to the last letter of a word. *ḥarfi-jārr*, a particle which gives to the noun a termination in *kasra*, or the short *i*. *a.*

جار जार *jār*, m. a gallant, a paramour. *s.*

جار जार *jār*, m. virulence, violence. *h.*

جارج जारज *jāraj*, m. f. an adulterine, the child of a woman by her paramour. *s.*

جارل जारल *jāral*, m. a kind of wood (*Lagerstrœmia flos reginæ*). *h.*

جارن जारन *jāran*, m. fire-wood, fuel. *s.*

جارنا जारना *jārnā*, } a. to burn, to kindle,
جارنون जारनौं *jārnauṅ*, } to inflame, to light. *s.*

جارو जारू *jārū*, burning, inflaming. *s.*

جاروب *jārūb*, m. a broom, or the sweeper who uses it. *jārūb-kash*, m. sweeper. *jārūb-kashī*, f. the act or office of sweeping. *p.*

جاري *jārī*, running, flowing, proceeding, current, customary, in force (a law). *jārī-k.*, a. to begin, to set on foot. *jārī honā*, n. to pass current, to be in force, to proceed; (as business) to flow. *jārī rupaiya*, a current rupī, current coin in general. *a.*

جاري *jārī*, Indian millet (v. *jo,ār*). *d.*

جاريه *jāriya*, f. a maid-servant. *a.*

جاڑ जाड़ *jāṛ*, m. the gums (of the teeth). *h.*

جاڑا जाड़ा *jāṛā*, m. cold, coldness; the winter. *s.*

جاڑي जाड़ी *jāṛī*, f. a row of teeth. *h.*

جاڑيه जाड्य *jāṛya*, coldness, apathy, indifference. *s.*

جازم *jāzam*, f. a cloth thrown over a carpet to sit on (same as *jājam*). *h.*

جازم *jāzim*, having the property of rendering the last letter of a word inert or not followed by a short vowel. *a.*

جاس जासु *jā-su*, } (old form of pron.) from
جاسو जासू *jā-sū*, } whom or from which, whereby. *h.*

جاسندي *jāsundī* (v. *jāsūn*) the shoe-flower. *d.*

جاسوس *jāsūs*, m. a spy, emissary. *a.*

جاسوسي *jāsūsī*, f. spying, espionage. *jāsūsī-k.*, a. to play the spy. *a.*

جاسون *jāsūn*, } a species of China rose;
جايسون *jā,esūn*, } the shoe-flower (*Hibiscus Syricus*, or *Hibiscus sinensis*). In Urdū it is called *gaṛhal*, and in Hindī *jawā* or *japā*, q. v. (Binning.) *d.*

جاکڑ जाकड़ *jākaṛ*, a pledge, &c. (v. *jāṅkaṛ*). *h.*

جاکھر जाखर *jākhar*, a subdivision of the *jāṭ* tribe. *h.*

جاکھن जाखन *jākhan*, the wooden foundation of the brickwork of a well. *h.*

جاگ जाग *jāg*, m. a religious sacrifice, vigils. *s.*

جاگ जागु *jāgu*, m. one who watches. *s.*

جاگا जागा *jāgā*, m. the name of a caste of Hindūs (same as *bhāṭ*, q. v.). *h.*

جاگا *jāgā* (for *jagah*), a place, situation. *d.*

جاگابندي जागाबन्दी *jāgā-bandī*, f. drowsiness, sleepiness. *s.*

جاگت जागत *jāgat*, f. waking, vigilance. *s.*

جاگتي جوت *jāgtī-jot* (for जागतीज्योति *jāgtī-jyoti*), possessed of or exerting miraculous power. *s.*

جاگرت जागर्ति *jāgarti*, f. waking, vigilance. *s.*

جاگرن जागरण *jāgaran*, m. vigil, wakefulness, sitting up at night (in a religious ceremony or prayer); vespers. *s.*

جاگري जागरी *jāgrī*, f. coarse sugar, molasses, refuse of sugar; sugar of the palmyra tree. *h.*

جاگنا जागना *jāgnā*, n. to be awake, to awake. *s.*

جاگو जागू *jāgū*, wakeful, watchful. *s.*

جاگو जागू *jāgū*, } f. place, situation (v. *jagah*). *h.*
جاگه जागह *jāgah*, }

جاگير *jāgīr*, f. land given by government as a reward for services, or as a fee; a pension (in land). *jāgīr-dār*, m. the holder of a fee or *jāgīr* (v. Wilson). *p.*

جاگيك याज्ञिक *jāgyik*, m. a sacrificer, the institutor of a sacrifice. *s.*

جاگيه याज्ञिय *jagiyā*, fit for sacrifice. *h.*

جال *jāl*, forged, counterfeited (cor. for *ja'l*, q. v.). *a.*

جال जाल *jāl*, m. a net, a sash; a window, a lattice, an eyelet or loophole; magic, conjuring, supernatural deception. *jāl-dār*, reticulated. *jāl-silāhī*, f. a coat of mail. *jāl-lakṛī*, f. valerian. *s.*

جالا जाला *jālā*, m. cobweb; a net, a pellicle; a jar; a speck on the eye, a cataract. *s.*

جالس *jālis*, one who sits; one of a company. *a.*

جالك जालिक *jālik*, m. a spider; a fisherman; a hunter using nets. *s.*

جالكي जालिकी *jālikī*, m. a cheat, a rogue, a conjuror or juggler; one who employs nets for a livelihood. *s.*

جالم जाल्म *jālm*, m. a low man, one of a degraded tribe; adj. cruel, harsh; rash, inconsiderate. *s.*

جالنا *jālnā*, a. to burn, set on fire. *d.*

جالندهر जालन्धर *jālandhar*, m. a country in the north-west of India, perhaps the modern *Jallindhar*. *jālandharā*, an inhabitant of Jālandhar. *s.*

جالني जालिनी *jālinī*, f. a painting-room. *s.*

جالي जाली *jālī*, illusory, deceptive; f. network; the integument in which a fœtus is enveloped; a coil, caul; lattice, grate; an ox-muzzle. *jālī parnā* expresses the hardening of the stone of a mango. *s.*

جاليا जालिया *jāliyā*, m. a cheat, a rogue, a conjuror. *s.*

جالينوس *jālīnūs*, Galen, the celebrated Greek physician. *s.*

جام *jām*, m. a goblet, cup, glass, any vessel for drinking out of, a bowl; a mirror. *jām-i-jam* or *jām-i-jamshīd*, the mirror of *Jamshīd*, in which he saw whatever he wished. *jām-i jahān-numā*, a pharos. *jām-i lab-rez*, a bumper. *p.*

جام जाम *jām*, m. the rose-apple (*Eugenia jambos, &c.*); a watch of the day or night (v. *pahr āṭh-jām*, ever, perpetually. *s.*

جام *jām*, m. the guava (*Psidium pyriferum*). *d*

جاما *jāmā*, m. garments, clothes. *p.*

جاماتا जामाता *jāmātā*, m. son-in-law, daughter's husband. *s.*

جاماتر जामातृ *jāmātṛi*, m. a daughter's husband, a son-in-law; a husband, a lord or master; the sunflower (*Helianthus annuus*). *s.*

جامبب जाम्बव *jāmbab*, m. the rose-apple, the fruit. *s.*

جامبوت जाम्बुवत *jāmbu-wat*, m. a fabulous bear, father-in-law to *Krishṇa*. *s.*

جامد *jāmid*, styptic. *ismi jāmid*, concrete, a noun not derived from any root, and from which no word is derived. *a.*

جامدار *jāma-dār* (v. *jāma*), the keeper of a wardrobe. *jāmadār-khāna*, the house where wardrobes are kept. *p.*

جامداري *jāma-dārī*, f. office of keeping the wardrobes; the guards or keepers (collectively). *p.*

جامداني *jāmdānī*, f. a kind of cloth in which the flowers are wove in, and not worked (generally muslin); a kind of leather basket; (applied to utensils of metal, &c.) flowered, sculptured, or embossed. *p.*

جامرول जामरूल *jāmrūl*, m. the Malay or star-apple (*Eugenia malaccensis*). *h.*

جامع *jāmi'*, completing, comprehending, collecting. *jāmi' ul kamālāt*, most learned, skilled in all sciences, containing the essence of all perfection; all, whole, universal, collective; f. a great mosque, temple, or cathedral, where the prayer called *khutba* is repeated on Fridays. "The mosque, and all its attached buildings, generally comprising a caravansary, an almshouse, a school, &c., is termed the *jāmi'*, while the sanctuary or place of worship is called the *masjid*."—(Binning.) *a.*

جامگي *jāmgī*, f. a salary; a match of a gun. *p.*

جامن जामन *jāman*, f. m. a fruit and tree so called (*Calyptranthes caryophyllifolia*; also *Eugenia jambolana*). *s.*

جامن जामन *jāman*, m. sour milk used to coagulate fresh milk, rennet. *h.*

جامني जामिनी *jāminī*, f. (for *yāminī*), night. *s.*

جامني जामनी *jāmnī*, Grecian, Mahometan, or their language. *s.*

جاموس *jāmūs*, m. a buffalo (Arab. form of the Persian *gāwmesh* or *gāmesh*, q. v.). *a.*

جامونت जामवन्त *jāmawant*, m. a fabulous bear; father-in-law to *Krishṇa*. *s.*

جامه *jāma*, m. a garment, robe, vest, a flowered sheet or shawl, a kind of chintz. *jāma-khāna*, a wardrobe. *jāma-dānī*, f. portmanteau. *jāma-zeb*, becoming one's clothes. *jāma-wār*, fit to make clothes of, sufficient for a *jāma*. *p.*

جامي जामी *jāmī*, f. a virtuous and respectable woman; a sister. *s.*

جامي *jāmī*, name of a celebrated Persian poet; adj. of or relating to a cup. *p.*

جان *jān*, f. m. life, soul spirit, mind; a sweetheart. *jān-āfarīn*, animator, creator of life (an epithet of God). *jān-bāz*, risking life, venturesome, daring. *jān bāzī*, f. the risking of life in battle, or working at any thing as if life depended on success. *jān-bāzī-k.*, a. to risk life in a business *jān-ba<u>kh</u>sh*, f. animator, bestower of life, forgiver of a capital crime. *jān-ba<u>kh</u>shī*, f. animation, vivification, pardon of a capital crime. *jān bar ḥaḳḳ* (or *ba-ḥaḳḳ*) *taslīm-k.*, to expire, to give up the ghost. *jān-bar honā*, n. to survive, to outlive *jān ba lub honā*, n. to be at the point of death. *jān par ānā* or *parnā*, n. to be exposed to imminent danger. *jān par khelnā*, a. to run the hazard. *jān par naubat ānī*, n. to be in imminent danger of life. *jān parnā*, n. to be refreshed. *jān-tarāsh*, weakening. *jān taslīm-k.*, a. to resign one's life. *jān chhuṛānā*, n. to escape, to get rid of. *jān-dār*, life-posessing; an animal (generally implies strength), powerful, active. *jān-supār*, resigning one's life into the hands of another (an epithet of a lover). *jān-sitān*, life-destroying (as poison or a snake, &c.). *jān-soz*, heart-inflaming beloved. *jān se mārnā*, a. to kill. *jān-fishān*, ready to sacrifice one's life for another, zealous, fervent. *jān-fishānī*, f. zeal, devotedness, extreme diligence. *jān-fishānī-k.*, a. to strain every nerve. *jān-kāh*, life-reducing, pathetic, affecting. *jān kisī par denā*, a. to love excessively; to die, to fall a sacrifice. *jān-kandan*, gasping in the agonies of death. *jān-kandanī*, anguish of soul. *jān-gudāz*, life-consuming, debilitating. *jān-mārnā* or *khānā*, to overcome, to exhaust, to deject, to oppress, to vex, to perplex, to plague. *jān meṅ jān ānā*, n. to be satisfied, to be comforted. *jān-nisār*, devoted, sacrificing one's life. *p.*

جان जान *jān*, m. a conjuror, an astrologer; adj. knowing, wise. *jān būjhke*, knowingly. purposely. *s.*

جان जानु *jānu*, m. the knee. *jānu-phalak*, m. the knee-pan or patella. *jānu-sandhi*, f. the knee-joint. *s.* [the genii. *a.*

جان *jānn*, m. a demon or devil, the race of

جان *jāṅ* (for *jahāṅ*), where, whither. *d.*

جانا जाना *jānā*, n. to go, to be, to pass, to reach. *jātā rahnā*, n. to be lost, to be missing, to disappear, to go away, to pass away entirely. *s.*

جانان *jānān*, } handsome, lovely; a sweet-
جانانه *jānāna*, } heart, mistress. *p.*

جانب *jānib*, f. part, side. *jānib-dār*, a supporter, a second. *jānib-dārī*, supporting, seconding. *a.*

جان بوجهكي *jān-būjh-ke*, knowingly, purposely. *s.*

جانبين *jānibain*, (du. of جانب), mutual, on both sides. *jānibain se*, reciprocally, alternately. *a.*

جان پہچان जानपहचान *jān-pahchān*, m. an acquaintance, an intimate friend. *s.*

جانت जांत *jānt*, f. a wooden trough for raising water. *s.* [standing. *h.*

جانت जानत *jānat*, adj. knowing, under-

جانتا जांता *jāntā*, m. f. a stone mill for grinding corn, a handmill of two stones one over the other; a bellows. *jāntā-kal*, f. (same as *jānt*) a wooden trough. *s.* [assay, proof. *h.*

جانچ जांच *jānch*, m. trial, examination, test,

جانچنا जांचना *jānchnā*, a. to examine, to inquire into, to ascertain, to try, to prove, to assay. *h.*

جانكڑ जांकड़ *jānkaṛ*, m. money (or other pledge) left for a thing purchased, while it is carried away to be finally approved. *h.*

جانگر जांगर *jāngar*, m. the thigh and leg. *s.*

جانگل जाङ्गल *jāngal*, m. the francoline partridge. *s.*

جانگل जाङ्गुल *jāngul*, m. poison, venom. *s.*

جانگل जाङ्गुलि *jānguli*, } m. a snake-
جانگلك जाङ्गुलिक *jāngulik*, } catcher, a dealer in antidotes, a man who pretends chiefly by charms to cure the bite of snakes, &c. *s.*

جانگلي जाङ्गुली *jāngulī*, f. knowledge of poisons, of charms and antidotes; a potherb (*Luffa acutangula*). *s.*

جانگھ जांघ *jāngh*, f. the thigh. *s.*

جانگھل जांघल *jānghal*, m. a kind of heron (*Ardea Indica*). *s.*

جانگھیا जांघिया *jānghiyā*, m. a kind of breeches that do not cover the thigh. *s.*

جاننا जानना *jānnā*, a. to know; to understand, to comprehend; to suppose, to trust, to believe. *h.*

جاننون जाननौं *jānnauṅ* (old form), (v. *jānnā*); to know, understand, &c. *h.*

جانو जानो *jāno*, that is to say; *videlicet*, understand, suppose; to wit, namely. *h.*

جانوا *jānwā*, a belt, brāhminical thread, a Hindū rosary. *d.* [ture. *p.*

جانور *jānwar*, m. an animal, any living crea-

جانون जानौं *jānauṅ* (old form of *jānā*), to go, move, &c.; it is also used in the sense of *jāno*, q.v., that is, suppose, &c. *h.* [away. *h.*

جانہار जानहार *jānhār*, adj. going, passing

جاني जानी (for ज्ञानी) *jānī*, m. an astrologer, a fortune-teller. *s.*

جاني *jānī*, m. a lover, a friend; adj. of or relating to the life or soul. *jānī dushman*, an enemy desirous of one's life. *p.*

جاني انجاني जाने अनजाने *jāne anjāne*, wittingly or unwittingly. *h.*

جاني دينا जाने देना *jāne denā*, a. to liberate, to let go; to excuse, to pass over (as a fault). *jāne do*, never mind, let alone, don't. *h.*

جاوا *jāwā*, a kind of gruel or potage. *d.*

جاوان जावां *jāwāṅ*, a twin, twins. *s.*

جاوت यावत *jāvat*, as much as, as many as, as long as, until. *s.*

جاوتري जावत्री *jāwatrī* or जावित्री *jāwitrī*, f. mace, a kind of spice. *s.* [long as life. *s.*

جاوجيون यावज्जीवन *jāvajjīvan*, for life, as

جاود *jāwid*,
جاودان *jāwidān*,
جاودانه *jāwidāna*, } eternal, perpetual, everlasting. *p.*

جاوداني *jāwidānī*, eternity, the next world. *p.*

جاوك जावक or यावक *jāwak*, m. the red colour procured from the lac insect (v. *altā*). *s.*

جاوني بهاشا जावनीभाषा *jāvanī bhāshā*, the language of the *Javans* (i. e. Greeks or Muhammadans), q. v. *s.*

جاويد *jāwīd*,
جاويدان *jāwīdān*, } always, eternal, everlasting. *p.*

جاويداني *jāwīdānī*, f. eternity. *p.*

جاه *jāh*, f. dignity, rank, grandeur. *jāh o jalāl*, dignity, grandeur, splendour, magnificence. *p.*

جاه जाहि *jāhi* (pron. in the dative case), to whom, to whomsoever (*Bhāshā*). *h.*

جاهل *jāhil* ignorant, barbarous, brutal. *a.*

جاهلي *jāhilī*, ignorance; paganism (vide next word). *a.*

جاهليّت *jāhiliyyat*, f. ignorance, folly, "Muhammadans use the term *ayyāmi jāhiliyyat* (days of ignorance) to denote the times previous to the manifestation of *Islām*, or what they consider the true faith. St. Paul uses a similar phrase with reference to the days before the diffusion of Christianity (Acts xvii. 30). —(Binning). *a.*

جاهي जाही *jāhī*, f. the name of a flower *Jasminum grandiflorum*); a fire-work resembling that flower. *s.*

جاءي *jā,e*, f. a place (see *jā*). *jā,e bāsh* place of residence. *jā,e i'tirāz*, the time or place of opposition. *jā,e zarūr*, f. the necessary. *jā,e-gham*, the place or time of grief. *jā,e nishīn*, a successor, "locum tenens." *jā,e namāz*, a carpet for praying on. *p.*

جاءي जाई *jā,ī*, f. a daughter; particip. f. born. *s.*

جايا जाया *jāyā*, particip. m. born; m. a son; f. a wife, one wedded according to the perfect ritual. *s.*

جاياپتي जायापती *jāyā-patī*, m. du. husband and wife. *s.*

جايپتري जायपत्री *jāyapatrī*, f. mace, a kind of spice. *s.*

جاءي پهل जायफल *jā,e phal* or *jāya-phal*, m. nutmeg (*Myristica moschata*). *s.*

جاءيداد *jā,e-dād*, f. an assignment on land for the maintenance of any establishment, such as troops, &c.; assets, funds; employment. *p.*

جائز *jā,iz*, lawful, permitted, right, proper, warrantable, authorized; m. a joist, a beam. *jā,iz ki*, possibly, it may be that. *a.*

جايزه *jā,iza*, m. examination, reviewing, confronting; benignity. *a.*

جاءيس जाएस *jā,es*, a tribe of *sūraj-bansī rājpūts*. *h.*

جايسون *jā,esūn*, the shoe-flower. v. *jasūn*. *d.*

جائفه *jā,ifa*, a wound or stab, such as is punishable by a fine. *a.*

جاءيگاه *jā,e gāh*, place, situation. *p.*

جاءيگير *jā,e-gīr*, lit. holding a place, permanent; pension. *jā,e-gīr-dār*, a possessor of *jāgīr* land. *jā,e-gīrī*, employed by holding a pension or consignment. *p.*

جاءيل जाइल *jā,īl*, land twice ploughed. *h.*

جب जब *jab*, when, at the time when. *jab-tab*, now and then. *jab-tak*, or *-talak*, or *-torī*, till when, as long as. *jab-jab*, whenever. *jab se*, since. *jab-ki*, at the time when, when. *jab-kā tab*, at the time when, at the proper moment. *jab-kabhī*, or *jab-kabhū*, whenever. *jab-lag*, till, when. *jab-na-tab*, now and then, perpetually. *jab-hī*, at the very time when. *s.*

جبا जुबा *jubā* (for *yuvā*), young. *s.*

جبا *jibā*, tribute, revenue. *jubā*, Saturday. *p.*

جبار *jabbār*, omnipotent; m. a conqueror; a revenger; a tall palm-tree; the constellation Orion. *a.*

جبال *jibāl* (pl. of جبل), mountains. *a.*

جبان *jabān*, timid, abject; m. a coward. *a.*

جباه *jibāh* (pl. of جَبهه), foreheads. *a.*

جبتي जुबती *jubatī* (for *yuvatī*), f. a young woman, a damsel. *s.*

جبدا जबद्दा *jabaddā*, rigid, stiff, awkward. *h.*

جبدنا जबदना *jabadnā*, n. to be filled, to be folded. *h.*

جبدي जबदी *jabdī*, f. a species of rice cultivated in Rohilkhand. *h.*

جبديا जबद्दिया *jabaddiyā*, ill-shaped. *h.*

جبر *jabr*, m. oppression, violence, strength, force, power; the reduction of fractions to integrals. *jabr se*, by violence, violently. *jabr nuksān*, making good a deficiency (as if two horses are to be given to two persons, one to each; if they are not equally good, saddle and bridle are given with the worst). *al-jabr wa-l-mukābala*, algebra. *a.*

جبرًا *jabran*, oppressively, by violence. *a.*

جبراعيل *jabrā'īl*,
جبراءيل *jabrā,īl*,
جبريل *jabrīl*,
جبرين *jabrīn*, } m. the archangel Gabriel. *a.*

جبروت *jabrūt*, omnipotence, dominion, heaven, the unity of God. *'ālami jabrūt*, the highest or empyreal heaven. *a.*

جبري *jabarī*, f. oppression, injury. *a.*

جبڑا जबड़ा *jabṛā*, m. (v. *jabhā*) the jaw. *h.*

جبڑيبند *jabṛī-band*, the lock-jaw. *d.*

جبل *jabal*, m. a mountain, a hill. *a.*

جبلت *jibillat*, f. essence, quality, disposition, temperament, constitution, creation, form. *a.*

جبلقوم *jabalkūm*, m. an amethyst. *a.*

جبلي *jibillī*, natural, innate, essential, in general. *a.*

جبن *jubun*, m. pusillanimity, cowardice. *a.*

جبه *jubba*, m. a kind of long vest, resembling a shirt; a coat of mail. *a.*

جبها जभा *jabhā*, m. the jaw. *h.*

جبهارا जिभारा *jibhārā*, abusive, talkative. *h.*

جبهڑا जभड़ा *jabhṛā*, m. the jaw. *h.*

جبهه *jabha*, m. the forehead. *a.*

جبهه‌سائي *jabha-sā,ī*, beseeching, begging earnestly (lit. rubbing one's forehead on the ground). *a.p.*

جبهيا जभिया *jabhiyā*, ugly, uncouth. *h.*

جبين *jabīn*, f. the forehead. *jabīn-sā,e* or *farsā,e*, rubbing the forehead on the ground (in prayer or supplication). *p.*

جپ जप *jap*, m. silent repetition of the name of God, muttering prayers, charms, &c., adoration, repeating the bead-roll (to speak in the mind). *jap-parāyan*, m. a man devoted to religious meditation. *jap-tap*, m. devotion, adoration. *jap-māl* or *-mālā*, f. a rosary. *s.*

جپا जपा *japā*, f. the flower of the plant *hur* (*Cleome viscosa*). *s.*

جپت जपत *japat* (old form of pres. part. from *japnā*), repeating internally or mentally the name of God. *s.*

جپنا जपना *japnā*, a. to count one's beads, to repeat the name of God internally, to recite the bead roll; (in Dakh.) to wait for, to expect. *s.*

جپنون जपनौं *japnauṅ* (Braj for *japnā*, q.v.). *s.*

جپي تپي जपीतपी *japī-tapī*, m. an adorer. *s.*

جت जुत or युत *jut*, joined; (in comp.) with, possessed of; as *dharm-jut*, virtuous. *s.*

جت जित *jit*, where, wheresoever (Braj). *s.*

جت जत *jat*, f. manner, fashion, kind. *s.*

جت जति *jati* or *jat*, f. a kind of musical rhythm (generally sung at the *holī*). *s.*

جت यति *jati* (for *yati*), m. a sage whose passions are under subjection; a religious mendicant, especially one of the Jaina sect. *s.*

جت जतु *jatu*, m. lac, a red dye analogous to cochineal. *s.*

جتا जुता *jutā*, m. the rope connecting the irrigating basket with its handle. *h.*

جتا जिता *jitā* or जित्ता *jittā*, whatever much, as much as, or (in the pl.) as many as. *jittā-kī*, for all that, notwithstanding. *h.*

جتاتما जितात्मा *jitātmā*, self-subdued, void of passion. *s.*

جتارا जतारा *jatārā*, } m. lineage, family, ge-
جتاڑا जताड़ा *jatāṛā*, } nealogy, a dynasty. *h.*

جتانا जताना *jatānā*, a. to caution, to remind, to warn, to admonish, to inform of, to proclaim. *s.*

جتانا जिताना *jitānā*, a. to cause to win or conquer. *h.*

جتانا जुताना *jutānā*, to conglutinate; n. to be joined, to yoke; to be tilled. *s.*

جتائي जुताई *jutā,ī*, arable; f. tillage. *s.*

جتبر *jitbar*, means of living; housewifery. *d.*

جتپترك जतुपुत्रक *jatu-putrak*, m. a man of piece, at chess or backgammon. *s.*

جتر जतर *jatar*, cultivated land. *h.*

جتر जत्रु *jatru*, m. the collar-bone, the clavicle. *s.*

جتراني जत्रानी *jatrānī*, a tribe of *jāts* in Rohilkund. *h.*

جتك जतुक *jatuk*, m. lac, assafœtida. *s.*

جتكا जतुका *jatukā*, f. a plant commonly called *chakwat*; a bat. *s.*

جتكرودھ जितक्रोध *jit-krodh*, one who has subdued anger. *s.*

جتن जतन, यतन *jatan* or यत्न *jatna*, m. striving, exertion, perseverance, energy, carefulness, remedy, care. *s.*

جتنا जितना *jitnā*, m. } how much soever, so
جتني जितनी *jitnī*, f. } much, as much as, as many. *jitne meṅ*, in as much (time) as. *h.*

جتناءيگي *jatnā,egī*, also *jatnāgī* and *jatnā,-engī*, f. care, caution. *d.*

جتنوان यत्नवान *jatnawān*, } persevering, dili-
جتنوت यत्नवत *jatnawat*, } gent, making an exertion. *s.*

جتني जतनी, यत्नी *jatnī*, careful, persevering, energetic. *s.*

جتنيه यतनीय *jatanīya*, to be exerted or persevered, to be made as an effort. *s.*

جتوانا जुत्वाना *jutwāna*, a. to cause to be joined or yoked. *s.*

جتوري जित्वरी *jitwarī*, victorious, triumphant; f. the city of Benares. *s.*

جتها जथा *jathā*, m. a company, band, party, class. *jathā-bāndhnā*, a. to form a party. *s.*

جتها जथा *jathā* (for *yathā*), as, so, like, according to. *jathā-jog*, or *jathā-jogya*, in a proper manner. *s.*

جتهارتھ जथार्थ *jathārth*, in fact, exactly, truly. *s.*

جتي जती or यती *jatī*, faithful to the marriage bed (a man); a sage with subdued passions; religious person, devotee; a particular order of devotees. *s.*

جتيا जित्या *jityā*, conquerable, vincible. *s.*

جتيانا जुतियाना *jutiyānā*, a. to beat one with a shoe or slipper (deemed an act of great degradation). *h.*

جتيك जितेक *jitek*, as much as, as many as. *h.*

جتيندري जितेन्द्री, जितेन्द्रिय or यतेन्द्रिय *jitendrī*, *jitendriya*, or *jatendriya*, m. one who has completely subdued his passions, a sage, an ascetic. *jitendriyā*, adj. having subdued the senses. *jitendriyatā*, f. continence, subjugation of the senses. *s.*

جٹ जटि *jaṭi*, f. waved-leaf fig-tree (*Ficus venosa*). *s.*

جٹ जट *jaṭ*, m. (the same as *jāṭ*), a class of *rājpūts*. *h.*

جٹ जट *jaṭ,* }
جٹا जटा *jaṭā,* } f. matted hair, as worn by *Shiva* and by ascetics; the long hairs occasionally clotted together and brought over the head so as to project like a horn from the forehead, at other times allowed to fall carelessly over the shoulders; the root of a tree, a fibrous root; spikenard. *jaṭā dhārī,* one whose hair is matted; f. the cock's-comb flower (*Celosia cristata*). *s.*

جٹا जटा *jaṭā,* m. (v. *jaṭ* or *jāṭ*) a tribe of *rājpūts. h.*

جٹّا *juṭṭā,* m. a span; the space from the tip of the thumb to the tip of the forefinger when stretched. *d.*

جٹّاجوٹ जटाजूट *jaṭā-jūṭ,* f. the matted hair of *Shiva,* rolled on his head. *s.*

جٹال जटाल *jaṭāl,* adj. wearing clotted hair. *s.*

جٹالا जटाला *jaṭālā,* f. spikenard. *s.*

جٹاماسي जटामासी *jaṭā-māsī,* }
جٹامانسي जटामांसी *jaṭā-mānsī,* } f. Indian spikenard (*Valeriana jatamansi*). *s.*

جٹانا जुटाना *juṭānā,* a. to conglutinate. *s.*

جٹايو जटायू *jaṭāyū,* the name of a fabulous bird mentioned in the story of *Rāmachandra* and *Rāvana*; bdellium. *s.*

جٹت जटित *jaṭit,* clotted, matted; set or studded with jewels; f. set work of jewels. *s.*

جٹك जुटक *juṭak,* m. f. the matted hair of *Shiva* or of ascetics; any knot or fillet of hair. *s.*

جٹل जटिल *jaṭil,* having matted or entangled hair; m. a lion; f. Indian spikenard; long pepper; orris-root. *s.*

جٹل जटुल *jaṭul,* m. a freckle, a mark. *s.*

جٹن जटिन *jaṭin,* m. waved-leaf fig-tree. *s.*

جٹنا जटना *jaṭnā,* a. to pilfer, steal, snatch. *s.*

جٹنا जुटना *juṭnā,* n. to close with, to engage in close fight, to unite, to close, to join (as the edges of a wound), to stay, to wait. *s.*

جٹني जटिनी *jaṭinī,* adj. having clotted hair. *s.*

جٹھاني जिठानी *jiṭhānī,* f. the wife of a *jeṭh,* q. v., *i. e.* the wife of a husband's elder brother. *s.*

جٹھر जठर *jaṭhar,* m. the belly. *jaṭhar-nud,* m. *Cassia fistula. s.*

جٹھرا जठरा *jaṭharā,* hard, firm; bound, tied. *s.*

جٹھرام जठराम *jaṭharām,* m. dropsy. *s*

جٹھرانل जठरानल *jaṭharānal* m. the pangs of hunger. *s.*

جٹھي *jaṭhī,* }
جيٹھي *jeṭhī,* } m. a wrestler, a servant who shampoos or kneads the limbs after bathing. *d.*

جثّه *jussa* m. the body, the figure of the human body. *a.*

ججمان जजमान (for यजमान) *jajmān,* m. an employer of priests at a sacrifice; the person who institutes its performance and pays the expenses of it; a customer, a person to whose custom Brāhmans, barbers, and some others, have a legal claim (the hereditary Brāhman or barber, &c., of a village must be paid his fees, whether you choose to employ him or another person). *s.*

ججماني जजमानी *jajmānī,* f. the stipend paid by a *jajmān,* q.v.; the wife of a *jajmān. s.*

ججھ जुझ *jujh,* m. an engagement, a battle. *s.*

ججھاؤ باجنا जुझाउ बाजना *jujhā,u bājnā,* n. to sound or strike up (as warlike instruments in battle.) *s.*

ججھوٹيا जिझोटिया *jijhoṭiyā,* a low caste of Kanaujiyā Brāhmans. *h.*

ججي जिजी *jijī* or *jijjī,* a foster-mother; a wet-nurse; also a maid that takes care of children. *h.*

ججيا जिजिया *jijiyā,* f. a sister; a dug, breast. *h.*

جچا *jachā* or *jachchā,* f. a woman in child-birth and for forty days after; a lying-in woman. *p.*

جچاوٹ जचावत *jachāwaṭ,* f. test, trial, examination, proof. *h.*

جچنا जचना *jachnā,* n. to be examined, tried, proved. *h.*

جحيم *jaḥīm,* a large hot fire, hell; the damned. *a.*

جد जद *jad,* as, while, whilst, when, so soon, at the time when. *jad-tak, -talak,* or *-lag,* till, until, yet, whilst, as long as, while. *jad na tad,* constantly. *s.*

جدّ *jadd,* m. a grandfather; an ancestor; dignity, glory (of God), happiness, prosperity; pl. *ajdād. a.*

جدّ *jidd,* m. trial, endeavour, effort, study. *jidd o jahd-k.,* a. to endeavour, to strive. *jidd o kudd,* m. expostulation, endeavour, exertion. *a.*

جدو यदु *jadu,* m. (v. *yadu*) name of a celebrated family of which sprung *Krishna. jadu-nāth,* chief of the Yadus, an epithet of *Krishna. s.*

جدا *judā* (in Pers. *jidā*), separate, away, absent, different. *judā judā,* various, one by one, severally. *judā judā kahnā,* a. to particularize. *p.*

جدال *jidāl,* m. altercation, contest. *jang o jidāl,* m. fighting and quarrelling. *a.*

جداول *jadāwil* (pl. of جدول), lines, rivulets; columns in a book, &c. *a.*

جدائي *judā,ī,* f. separation, absence.

جدباتدبا जदबातदबा *jadbā-tadbā,* m. unmeaning expression; so so. *s.*

جدبر *jidbar,* means of subsistence; furnishing, &c., of a house; stock in trade, and plenishing or fixings. *d.*

جدبنسي जदुबंशी *jadu-bansī,* of or belonging to the family of *Jadu* or *Yadu. s.*

جدپ *jadapi* (for यद्यपि *jadyapi* or *yadyapi*), though, although, notwithstanding. *s.*

جدري *judrī,* f. the small-pox. *a.*

جدل *jadal*, m. fighting, battle, encounter, altercation. *a.*

جدوار *jadwār*, m. zedoary (*Kœmpferia zedoar*). *a.*

جدول *jadwal*, f. lines drawn in a book, as ruling, or to separate the margin; a rivulet; a table, an astronomical table. *jadwal paṭṭī* or *jadwal-kash*, a rule, consisting of a card of pasteboard and threads on which the paper is pressed, and thus becomes ruled. *a.*

جدولي *jadwalī*, lined, ruled. *a.*

جده जुद्ध, युद्ध *juddh*, m. battle, war, contest. *s.*

جدهر जिधर *jidhar*, where, wherever, whither, there. *jidhar tidhar*, whither, thither, whithersoever, everywhere. *jidhar niwān udhar pānī ḍhaltā hai*, where is a declivity, thither flows the water, applied in the sense of "evil unites with evil." or "misfortunes never come single." *s.*

جدهشٹهر युधिष्ठिर *judhishṭhir* (prop. *yudhishṭhira*), m. the elder of the five Pāṇḍava princes. *s.*

جدهمان युधमान *judhmān*, adj. fighting, warring. *s.*

جدي *jadī*, m. a kid, a he-goat; the sign or constellation Capricorn. *a.*

جدي *judai*, m. the polar star. *a.*

جدي *jaddī*, ancestral, belonging to ancestors, paternal (estate, &c.). *a.*

جديپ यद्यपि *jadyapi* (for *yadyapi*), though, although. *s.*

جديد *jadīd*, new, modern, fresh. *a.*

جڈهن *jaḍhan* (v. *jaṛhan*), a species of rice. *h.*

جذام *juẕām*, m. leprosy, more especially the black or eating leprosy, the worst form of the disease (v. *koṛh*). *juẕām-k͟hāna*, m. a lazaretto. *a.*

جذب *jaẕb*, m. allurement, attraction, absorption, drawing (as a plaster). *jaẕb honā*, n. to be absorbed. *jaẕb-k.*, to attract or absorb. *a.*

جذبه *jaẕba*, m. passion, rage, fury; violent desire. *a.*

جذر *jaẕr*, m. origin, root; the square root (in arithmetic); (for *jazr*) the ebb-tide *a.*

جر जर *jar*, f. a root; m. a fever. *s.*

جر *jarr*, m. drawing, dragging; the base, foundation, foot of a mountain; the vowel *kasra* at the end of words; (in law) dragging forth an offender for public punishment. *a.*

جرا जरा *jarā*, f. decrepitude, old age; a tree (*Mimusops kauki*); a female demon. *s.*

جرا *jurrā*, m. a kind of hawk. *a.*

جراب *jurrāb*, m. a sock, stocking. *a.*

جرات *jur,at*, f. courage, audacity, boldness, bravery, temerity, valour. *a.*

جراتر जरातुर *jarātur*, infirm from old age. *s.*

جراح *jarrāḥ*, m. a surgeon, an anatomist. *a.*

جراحت *jarāḥat*, f. a wound, a sore. *a.*

جراحي *jarrāḥī*, f. surgery; adj. of or relating to surgery, chirurgical. *a*

جراد *jarād*, m. a locust. *a.*

جرادينا जुरा देना *jurā denā*, a. to procure. *h.*

جرار *jarrār*, warlike, valiant; numerous. *a.*

جراسنده जरासन्ध *jarāsandh*, name of a *kshatriya rājā*, sovereign of Magadha, father-in-law to Kansa, and foe to *Krishṇa*, who was slain in single combat by Bhīma. *Jarāsandha-jit*, Bhīma, the third of the Pāṇḍu princes. *s.*

جرانا जुराना *jurānā*, n. to be comforted, pacified; a. to procure. *h.*

جرانا जराना *jarānā*, a. to burn; to kindle; to make jealous. *s.*

جرانس जरांश *jarāns*, m. paroxysm of a fever. *s.*

جراو जुराव *jurā,o*, m. procurement. *h.*

جراون जुरावन *jurāwan*, procurable. *h.*

جراي जरायु *jarāyu*, m. the womb, the uterus. *s.*

جرايج जरायुज *jarāyuj*, viviparous, born from the womb. *s.*

جرائم *jarā,im* (pl. of جريمه), sins, crimes, offences. *jarā,im k͟hafīfa*, light or petty offences. *jarā,imi sangīn*, heinous offences. *a.*

جرت जरत *jarat*, old, ancient; infirm, decayed. *s.*

جرتي जरती *jaratī*, f. an old woman. *s.*

جرتل जर्तिल *jartil*, m. sesamum growing wild. *s.*

جرته जरुथ *jaruth*, m. skinniness, flesh flaccid with old age. *s.*

جرٹها जरठा *jarṭhā*, hard, solid; cruel, harsh; old, decayed; m. decrepitude. *s.*

جرجر जर्जर *jarjar*, m. Indra's banner or emblem; an aquatic plant (*Vallisneria*); adj. old, infirm. *s.*

جرجريكا जर्जरीका *jarjarīkā*, rugged, full of holes, old, decayed. *s.*

جرح *jarḥ*, a wound; (in law) an offence against the person. *a.*

جرس *jaras*, m. a bell (on a horse's neck). *a.*

جرسام *jirsām*, m. the pleurisy. *a.*

جرعه *jur'a*, m. a drop, one draught. *a.*

جركل *jarkul*, the whole extent, &c. *h.*

جرگا जरगा *jargā*, the name of a grass given as fodder to horses, &c. *h.*

جرم *jirm*, m. the body of any thing inanimate; a globe; a flaw or crack. *jirmi ḳamar*, the body of the moon; pl. *ajrām*. *a.*

جرم *jurm*, m. a crime, fault, sin. *a.*

جرمانه *jurmāna* or *jaramāna*, (properly *jarīmāna*), m. a fine, a penalty. *a.*

جرمبها जृम्भा *jṛimbhā*, f. gaping, yawning. *s.*

جرمبهني जृम्भिनी *jṛimbhinī*, f. a kind of mimosa (*Mimosa octandra*). *s.*

جرن जरण or जरन *jaran*, f. the act of burning; m. cumin-seed; a plant yielding a pungent seed (*Nigella Indica*); old age, becoming old and infirm. *s.*

جرن जर्ण *jarna*, old, decayed. *s.*

جرنا जरना *jarnā*, n. to burn, to be on fire. *s.*

جرنا *jirnā*, to dry up, to wither. *d.*

جرنا जुरना *jurnā*, n. to be procured, or obtained, to come to hand; to be joined. *s.*

جرنون जुरनौं *jurnaun̈* (old form), n. to unite, to be joined. *h.* [female. *h.*

جروءا जुरुवा *jurū,ā* or *juruwā*, f. a woman, a

جره *jurra*, m. a hawk, a falcon (also applied to any male bird). *p.* [ewer. *p.*

جره *jarra*, m. a jar, an earthen vessel, an

جري *jarī*, valiant, intrepid. *a.*

جريا जिरिया *jiriyā*, name of a species of rice cultivated in Benares. *h.*

جريان *jiryān*, m. flowing, running; flux (of blood, urine, &c.). *jiryāni āb* or *jiryāni mazī*, *fluor albus*. *jiryāni shikm*, dysentery. *jiryāni manī*, *gonorrhea simplex*, gleet. *a.*

جريب जरीब *jarīb*, f. a sort of wooden dart with an iron point. *jarīb chalānā*, to throw the *jarīb*. *h.*

جريب *jarīb*, f. a measuring-chain or rope; a land measure of 60 *gaz* square, or 3600 square *gaz*; a corn measure (of 384 *madds*, or about 768 lb.). *jarīb-amīn* or *jarīb-kash*, m. a land-surveyor. *jarīb-kashī*, f. mensuration (of land), the office of a land-surveyor. *a.*

جريته *jarīṭa*, m. brushwood, brambles. *h.*

جريده *jarīda*, a register, an account-book; adj. alone, separate, solitary, unattended (when travelling), unencumbered. *a.*

جريلا जुरेला *jurelā* (also *jarelā*), m. a species of rice grown in Rohilkhund. *h.*

جريمانه *jarīmāna*, m. penalty, forfeit, fine. *a.*

جريمه *jarīma*, m. a crime, a fault; also a fine, mulct, or pecuniary punishment. *a.*

جڑ जड़ *jaṛ*, f. a root, origin, foundation; m. an inanimate body, a blockhead. *jaṛ kā bhed*, the nature, quality, or essence (of a thing); adj. cold, chilly, stolid. *s.*

جڑا जड़ा *jaṛā*, m. cold, frost, winter; stupidity, dulness, sluggishness; f. cowach. *s.*

جڑات जुड़ाट *juṛāt*, annexation, joining. *h.*

جڑانا जुड़ाना *juṛānā*, a. to cause to join, to get mended; to tear the hair in token of grief or vexation; to cause to couple. *h.*

جڑانا जड़ाना *jaṛānā*, n. to be or feel cold. *s.*

جڑانا जड़ाना *jaṛānā*, a. to cause to stud, to cause to set jewels. *s.*

جڑاو जड़ाव *jaṛāw*, m. }
جڑاوت जड़ावत *jaṛāwat*, f. } the act of setting jewels. *s.*

جڑاءو जड़ाऊ *jaṛā,ū*, set or studded with jewels. *s.*

جڑاور जड़ावर *jaṛāwar*, }
جڑاول जड़ावल *jaṛāwal*, } f. warm clothes, winter dress. *s.*

جڑاءي जड़ाई *jaṛā,ī*, f. price of setting jewels; the act of setting jewels. *s.*

جڑاءي जुड़ाई *juṛā,ī*, f. the price of joining, mending, &c. *h.*

جڑپ *juṛap* (for *jhuṛap*), a thicket, a brake. *d.*

جڑپيڑ जड़पेड़ *jaṛ-peṛ*, f. root and branch. *jaṛ-peṛ se-ukhāṛnā*, a. to extirpate. *h.*

جڑت जड़ित *jaṛit*, set or studded with jewels. *s.*

جڑتا जड़ता *jaṛatā*, f. coldness, chilliness; apathy, stolidity; immoveableness, stiffness, rigidity, torpor. *s.*

جڑكريه जड़क्रिय *jaṛ-kriya*, dilatory, working slowly. *s.*

جڑل जड़ल *jaṛul*, m. a freckle, a mark. *s.*

جڑن जड़न *jaṛan*, f. the act of setting jewels. *s.*

جڑنا जड़ना *jaṛnā*. a. to strike, to shake off; to join, to make adhere; to stud, to set jewels, to fix. *h.*

جڑنا जुड़ना *juṛnā*, n. to unite, to be joined. *s.*

جڑوات *juṛwāt*, }
جڑواءي *juṛwā,ī*, } f. the state of being joined, adhesion. *d.*

جڑوانا जड़वाना *jaṛwānā*, a. to cause to be set or studded with jewels. *s.*

جڑوٹ जड़वट *jaṛwaṭ*, f. the trunk of a tree. *h.*

جڑوي जड़वी *jaṛwī*, f. the name given to the small shoots of the rice plant when it first springs from the ground. *h.*

جڑها जुढ़ा *juṛhā*, m. twins, a pair. *h.*

جڑهن जड़हन *jaṛhan*, m. a large species of rice cropped at the end of the rainy season. *h.*

جڑي जड़ी *jaṛī*, f. the root of a medicinal herb. *jaṛī būṭī*, f. medicinal herbs, drugs. *s.*

جڑيا जड़िया *jaṛiyā*, m. a jeweller, one who sets jewels; a striker. *s.* [bles. *h.*

جڑيٹا जड़ीटा *jaṛīṭā*, m. brushwood, bram-

جز *juz*, besides, except. *p.*

جز *juz*, m. a part, portion; foot of a verse; "a section of the *ḳur,ān*; (pl. *ajzā*). The holy book of the Moslems consists of 114 chapters called *sūra*, (pl. *suwar*), the aggregate of which is divided into 30 sections, as above mentioned. Each of these sections is also subdivided into two portions, called *ḥizb* (pl. *aḥzāb*)."—Binning. A division of a book consisting of eight leaves; ingredient. *juz-bandī*, f. binding of a book. *juz-ras*, penitent, sagacious; frugal, economical. *juz-rasī*, f. frugality, economy, &c. *juz o kull*, totally, entirely, great and small. *juz-dān*, m. a cloth in which books are wrapped up, a portfolio. *juz-gīr*, m. an instrument used for keeping a book open when reading or writing; a portfolio. *juzi lā-yatajazzā*, an indivisible atom, any thing too small to be divided. *a.*

جزا *jazā*, f. retaliation, requital, return, retribution; compensation, reward. *a.*

جزاك الله *jazāk-allāh*, may God reward thee! *a.*

جزائر *jazā,ir*, m. (pl. of جزيره), islands. *a.*

جزائل *jazā,il*, m. a large musket, a wall-piece, swivel. *jazā,il-andāz* or *jazā,ilchī* (vulg. *jazailchī*), one who fires a wall-piece. *a.*

جزبز *jizbiz*, offended, displeased. *p.*

جزر *jazr*, m. the ebb-tide, the reflux of the sea; a term in arithmetic signifying duplification. *jazr o madd*, the ebb and flow of the sea. *a.*

جزم *jazm*, m. deciding, determining, resolving; amputation; the orthographical character *jazm*, which is placed over a letter to shew that it is inert or has no vowel following it. *a.*

جزو *jazw*, subduing. *juzw*, a particle. *jazu,a*, a part or portion. *a.*

جزوي *juzwī*, a little, in part, a few; pl. *juzwiyāt*, parts, portions, particulars. *a.*

جزئات *juz,iyāt* or *juziyāt* (pl. of جزئة), trifles, minutiæ. *a.*

جزيره *jazīra*, m. an island, a peninsula. *a.*

جزيه *jizya* or *jazya*, m. a tribute, capitation tax levied by the *Musalmāns* on their subjects of another faith; a poll-tax. *a.*

جس जस *jas* (for यश), m. name, character, celebrity, reputation, fame, splendour, praise, luck. *jas-apajas*, m. good or bad, fame or infamy. *s.*

جس जिस *jis*, infl. pron. (of *jo*), that, what, who, whom. *jis jis*, that which, whatever, some or other. *jis-jis*, whichever, each of which. *jis jagah*, where, wherever. *jis-ṭaraḥ*, in what manner, according to, as. *jis-ṭaraf*, wherever. *jis-dam*, when, while, whilst. *jis-ḳadr*, to what degree, as, as much as, whatever, whatsoever. *jis-kā*, whose, of whom. *jis-kā khā,e uske dayān meṅ denā*, (Dakh.) explained by *namak-ḥarāmī-k.*, to evince ingratitude. *jis-kisī-kā*, of whomever. *jis-kisī-ko* or *jis-ko*, whom, to whom. *s.*

جس *jas* (Dakh. for *jast*), pewter. *d.*

جسارت *jasārat*, f. boldness, presumption, temerity, daring, intrepidity. *a.*

جسام *jisām* or *jusām*, large-bodied. *a.*

جسامت *jasāmat*,
جسامي *jusāmī*, } f. corpulency, bulkiness. *a.*

جساور जसावर *jasāwar*, a small tribe of *rājpūts* in Mathura. *h.*

جسپت जसपत *jaspat*,
جسپتي जसपति *jaspatī*, } reputable, renowned. *s.*

جست *jast*, m. a leap, jump; leaping, spring. *jast-k.* or *mārnā*, a. to jump, &c. *just*, seeking, searching. *p.*

جست जस्त *jast*,
جستا जस्ता *jastā*, } m. pewter, prince's metal. *h.*

جستا *justā*, m. power, strength (from *jussa*). *a.*

جستن *jastan* (r. *jah*), to spring, to leap. *p.*

جستن *justan* (r. *jū* or *jū,e*), to seek or search. *p.*

جست جو *just jū*,
جست وجو *just o jū*, } f. searching, seeking. *p.*

جسته *justa*, sought for, searched. *p*

جسته *jasta*, m. tin, pewter; (part. of *jastan*), having sprang or leaped. *p. h.*

جستي जस्ती *jastī*, made of tin or pewter. *h.*

جسد *jasad*, the body; pl. *ajsād*. *a.*

جسدا जसुदा *jasudā*, f. (v. *jasodā*). *s.*

جسدهات *jis-dhāt*, as, in the manner in which. *d.*

جسر *jisr*, a bridge. *jasr*, a large strong (camel). *a.*

جسسكام यशस्काम *jasas-kām*, desirous of glory, ambitious. *s.*

جسسكر यशस्कर *jasas-kar*, conferring glory. *s.*

جسسوان यशस्वान *jasas-wān*,
جسسوي यशस्वी *jasasnī*, } famed, renowned. *s.*

جسطرح *jis-ṭaraḥ*, in which way, in whatever manner. *h. a.*

جسطرف *jis-ṭaraf*, in which direction, whithersoever. *h. a.*

جسم *jism*, m. body of any animated being. *jismi jamādī*, mineral body. *jismi jauharī*, constitutional parts. *jismi ḥaiwānī*, animal body. *jismi nabātī*, vegetable body. *a.*

جسماني *jismānī*, belonging to a body, corporeal, material, carnal. *a.*

جسمانيت *jismāniyat*,
جسميت *jismiyat*, } f. materiality, corporeality. *a.*

جسمتي जसुमती *jasumatī*,
جسومتي जसोमती *jasomatī*,
جسودا जसोदा *jasodā*, } f. the foster-mother of *Krishṇa*, and the wife of *Nanda*. *s.*

جسوقت *jis-waḳt*, at the time when. *h.*

جسونت जसवन्त *jaswant*,
جسوي जसवी *jaswī*,
جسي जसी *jasī*, } famous, illustrious, renowned. *s.*

جسيم *jasīm*, corpulent, large-bodied. *a.*

جشٹ जुष्ट *jushṭa*, m. the crumbs or remnants of a meal. *s.*

جشٹا जुष्टा *jushṭā*, served, obliged, worshipped. *s.*

جشٹمدھ यष्टिमधु *jashti-madhu*, m. liquorice, or the root of the *abrus precatorius*, which is used for it. *s.*

جشكك जुष्कक *jushkah*, m. the water of boiled pulse, pease soup. ..

جشن *jashn*, m. a feast, a festival (chiefly applied to royalty). *jashni wazn*, the ceremony of weighing the royal personage. *p.*

جشني *jashnī*, voluptuous, luxurious. *p.*

جعبه *ja'ba* (also *ja'bat*), m. a quiver. *a.*

جعد *ja'd*, f. a ringlet, a lock of hair. *a.*

جعفر *ja'far*, a man's name; a river (large or small). *a.*

جعفري *ja'farī*, f. a kind of cupola; a sort of screen (the interstices of the frame being lozenged); lattice-work; the purest kind of gold; the name of a yellow flower (called also *gul i ashrafī*, *Linum trigynum*). *a.*

جعل *ja'l*, } base, forged or counterfeit (a
جعلي *ja'lī*, } coin, &c.). *ja'l-sāz*, a forger, a cheat. *ja'l-sāzī*, forgery. *ja'l-kāghaz*, a forged document. *a.*

جعليت *ja'līyat*, forging, counterfeiting. *a.*

جغرافيه *jughrāfiya*, m. geography (γεωγραφια). *g.*

جف *jaff* or *juff*, a troop or body of men; an old man; any thing hollow. *a.*

جفا *jafā*, f. oppression, violence, injury, injustice. *jafā-kār*, or *-pesha*, or *-jū*, or *-shi'ār*, an oppressor. *jafā-kārī*, *&c.*, the act or habit of oppressing. *p.*

جفت *juft*, m. evenness, parity, a pair, a couple, a match. *juft giriftan*, to marry. *p.*

جفته *jufta*, bent, wrinkled; running together (the threads in cloth). *p.*

جفتي کهانا *juftī khānā*, a. to copulate, to pair (as birds). *p. h.*

جفر *jafar*, m. the art of making amulets or charms. *h.*

جفه *jaffa* or *juffa*, a hoop; a crowd. *a.*

جقجق *jakjak*, nonsensical talk, twaddle. *p.*

جك जक *jak*, m. when treasure, &c. is buried, an animal (sometimes a man) is killed and buried with it as a guard. This animal is called *jak*, and receives orders to allow no one else to take up the treasure, &c.; (met.) a miser, called also *jak kā gumashta*. *s.*

جکڑبند जकड़बंद *jakar-band*, tight. *h.*

جکڑنا जकड़ना *jakarnā*, a. to tighten, to draw tight, as a knot; to bind, to fasten, to tie, to pinion. *h.*

جکه जख *jakh* (for *yaksha*), m. a fairy, an attendant of Kuvera, the Indian Plutus (see *jak*). *s.*

جکهني जखनी *jakhnī* (for *yakshanī*), f. a fairy, the fem. of *jakh*. *s.*

جگ जुग *jug* (for युग *yuga*), m. a period, one of the four great Hindū periods or ages, the Sat or Krit, Tretā, Dwāpar, and Kali; a term used in the game of chausar (the opposite of a blot, two or more men standing on the same square); a pair. *jug phornā* or *phutnā*, a. to cause a difference between two friends, to fall out. *jug-jug*, constantly, eternally. *s.*

جگ जग *jag*, m. the world, the universe. *jag-bandhu*, m. friend of the world. *jag-jagat*, m. the universe; a feast, entertainment; sacrifice, a religious ceremony; *jag-ādhār*, support of the universe, God. *s.*

جگا *jagā* (v. *jagah*), a place; name of a division of the *bhāt* tribe. *h.*

جگاجوت *jagājot* (for जगाज्योति *jagājyoti*), f. splendour, much light. *s.*

جگاکرنا *jagā-karnā*, to stand, to settle. *d.*

جگال जुगाल *jugāl*, two, a pair. *s.*

جگالنا जुगालना *jugālnā*, a. to chew the cud. *h.*

جگالي जुगाली *jugālī*, f. the cud. *h.*

جگانا जुगाना *jugānā*, a. to be careful of, to keep with care; to lend labour, *i. e.* to assist another in his work, in expectation of similar assistance hereafter. *h.*

جگانا जगाना *jagānā*, a. to awaken, to arouse [from sleep. *s.*

جگانت युगान्त *jugānt*, m. the end of an age, destruction of the world. *jugānt-bandhu*, m. a real friend. *s.*

جگانجگ जुगानुजुग or युगानुयुग *jugānujug*, ages of ages, from age to age; during successive ages. *s.*

جگپت युगपत *jug-pat*, at one time, at once; together, conjointly. *s.*

جگ پتي जगपती *jag-patī*, m. a king; q. d. lord of the universe. *d.*

جگپسا जुगुप्सा *jugupsā*, f. } censure, abuse,
جگپسن जुगुप्सन *jugupsan*, m. } reviling. *s.*

جگپست जुगुप्सित *jugupsit*, censured, abused. *s.*

جگت जगत *jagat*, m. the world; a buttress. *jagat-prān*, m. air, wind. *jagat-dukhī*, a tyrant. *jagat-kartā*, m. the creator of the world, Brahma. *jagat-kshay*, m. destruction of the world. *s.*

جگت जुगत *jugat*, f. address, dexterity, contrivance, wit, a pun, art. *jugat bolnā*, a. to pun. *jugat-bāz*, a punster. *jugat-bāzī*, f. quibble, pun, witticism, economy. *s. p.*

جگتا जगता *jagtā*, not sleeping, awake. *s.*

جگتجاگر जगत उजागर *jagat-ujāgar*, enlightening the world. *s.*

جگتر *jaggatar* (v. *jag*), the world, universe. *d.*

جگتي जुगती *jugatī*, artful, clever, cunning; economical, facetious, punning. *s.*

جگتي जगती *jagatī*, f. the earth, the world; mankind; a sort of metre; adj. moveable, transitory. *s.*

جگتيتل जगतीतल *jagatī-tal*, m. the world, the earth, sublunary things. *s.*

جگٹا *jigaṭā*, clammy. *jigaṭā,ī*, clamminess. *d.*

جگجگا जगजगा *jagjagā*, m. brass tinsel, very thin plates of brass used in decoration. *h.*

جگجگانا *jigjigānā*, n. to shine, to glitter. *d.*

جگجگاهٹ जगजगाहट *jagjagāhaṭ*, f. splendour, much light, glitter. *h.*

جگجگي जिगजिगी *jigjigī*, f. an exclamation expressive of surprise and pleasure. *jigjigī-k.*, a. to fawn or wheedle. *h.*

جگجگيا जिगजिगिया *jigjigiyā*, fawning, wheedling *h.*

جگدادھار जगदाधार *jagad-ādhār*, m. air, wind; support of the universe. *s.*

جگدنبا जगदम्बा *jagadambā*, f. mother of the world; an epithet of a Hindū goddess, wife of Mahādeva. *s.*

جگدوناش जगद्विनाश *jagad-vināsh*, m. destruction of the world, the expiration of a Kalpa. *s.*

جگدیش जगदीश *jagad-īsh*, m. lord of the universe, Vishnu or Shiva. *s.*

جگر जगर *jagar*, m. armour, coat of mail. *s.*

جگر *jigar*, m. the life, vitals, heart, mind. *jigar-band*, the bowels or entrails; met. a son. *jigar-soz*, tormenting. *jigar-jigar digar-digar*, mine is mine, and yours is yours, or every one knows where his own shoe pinches. *jigar-afgār* or *-chāk* or *-figār*, heart-broken. *jigar-tafta*, heart-burnt (as in love or fever). *jigar-kharāsh*, heart-rending. *jigar khur* or *jigar khwār*, a mischievous enchanter, supposed to be able to steal the liver of any person by incantations. *jigar-doz*, heart-piercing. *jigar-sokhta*, burnt in the heart (from love or sorrow). *jigar kādī*, anxiety or uneasiness and trouble of mind. *jigar-gosha*, (lit.) lobe of the liver; met. a child or beloved object. *p.*

جگري *jigarī*, belonging to the liver or heart; liver-coloured. *'akīk i jigarī*, carnelion. *jigarī dāgh*, m. indelible stain or mark; natural spot; inconsolable grief. *p.*

جگل जुगल or युगल *jugal*, } two, a pair,
جگم जुगम or युग्म *jugam*, } brace. *s.*

جگمگا जगमगा *jagmagā*, glittering, brilliant. *h.*

جگمگانا जगमगाना *jagmagānā*, n. to glitter. *h.*

جگمگاهٹ जगमगाहट *jagmagāhaṭ*, f. glitter splendour, much light, great brilliancy. *h.*

جگنا जगना *jagnā*, n. to be awake, to awake. *s.*

جگناتھ जगन्नाथ *jagan-nāth*, m. lord of the universe; a form of *Vishṇu*, known to Europeans as Juggernaut: "the great temple of this deity is situated on the coast of Orissa, and the great annual feast, called *rath jātrā*, is there held in the month of July, when the huge car of the idol is brought forth from the temple. Formerly pilgrims were wont to cast themselves under the wheels of the car in order to be crushed to death as a meritorious exit from this world, ensuring happiness in the next, but this horrible practice has been prohibited by the British Government."—Binning. *s.*

جگناسا जिज्ञासा *jignāsā*, f. a wish to be informed, an inquiry, investigation. *s.*

جگناسیه जिज्ञास्य *jignāsya*, fit to be known or inquired into. *s.*

جگنبنسي जगनबंसी *jagan-bansī*, a tribe of Brāhman zamīndārs in *Fatihpūr*. *h.*

جگنسوتر यज्ञसूत्र *jagna-sūtra*, } m. (v. *upa-*
جگنوپویت यज्ञोपवीत *jagnopavīt*, } *nayan*)
the sacrificial cord or thread worn by the three first classes of Hindūs. *s.*

جگنو जुगनू *jugnū*, m. the fire-fly (*Lampyris*).

جگنون जगनूं *jugnūn*, a jewel worn about the neck. *h.*

جگني जुगनी *jugnī*, f. glow-worm, an ornament worn round the neck; also a small grain from which oil is extracted. *h.*

جگنیشور जगनेश्वर *jagneshwar* (v. *jageshwar*). *s.*

جگنیه यज्ञ *jagnya*, m. a sacrifice or religious ceremony in which oblations are presented. *s.*

جگوپبیت जगोपवीत *jagopabīt*, m. see *jagyopavīt*.

جگه जगह *jagah*, f. place, station, quarter, room, vacancy, stead. *jagah chhoṛnā*, a to leave a blank. *h.*

جگهر जगहर *jaghar*, m. wakefulness (occasioned by apprehension of disease); coughing at night, vigils, vespers. *s.*

جگهن जघन *jaghan*, m. *mons veneris*; the hips and loins. *s.*

جگهنیا जघन्या *jaghanyā*, m. a sūdra or man of the fourth caste. *s.* vile, base. *s.*

جگهنیه जघन्य *jaghanya*, last; hindmost, low;

جگیشور जगेश्वर *jageshwar* (also *jagneshwar* or *jaggīsar*), m. god of the universe, a name of *Vishṇu* and *Shiva*. *s.*

جگیاسا जिज्ञासा *jigyāsā*, f. asking, inquiring. *s.*

جگي جگي जिगीजिगी *jigī-jigī*, f. an exclamation expressive of surprise and pleasure. *h.*

جگیشا जिगीषा *jigīshā*, f. emulation, wish to overcome. *s.*

جگیوپویت यज्ञोपवीत *jagyopavīt*, m. the sacrificial cord worn by the first castes of Hindūs. *jagyopavītī*, m. a man invested with the sacred cord. *s.*

جگیه यज्ञ *jagya*, m. a sacrifice. *jagya-bhūmi*, f. place prepared for sacrifice. *jagya-pātra*, m. a sacrificial vessel. *jagya-purush*, m. a name of *Vishṇu*. *jagya-pasu*, m. a horse; any animal offered in sacrifice. *jagya-sthān*, m. a place of sacrifice. *jagya siddhi*, f. performance of a sacrifice; obtaining the objects of a sacrifice. *jagya-sūtra*, m. the sacrificial cord worn by the three first classes of Hindūs. *jagya-shālā*, f. a place of sacrifice. *jagya-karma*, m. a sacrificial act or ceremony. *s.*

جگیه यज्ञिय *jagiya*, proper for or suitable to a sacrifice. *jagiya-des*, f. the country of the Hindūs that in which their rites are in force; properly, the country in which the black deer or antelope is native. *s.*

جل *jull*, f. a housing or covering for an elephant, bullock, &c. *a.*

جل जुल *jul*, m. deceit, cheating, a trick. *jul-bāz*, a knave, a cheat. *jul-bāzī*, f. knavery. *h. p.*

جل जल *jal*, m. water; frigidity (physical or moral); also name of a jungle shrub; adj. cold, stupid, apathetic. *jal-pachchhī*, f. water-fowl. *jal-jal*, full of water, wet. *jal-thal*, ground half covered with water, marshy ground. *jal-krīṛā*, sporting or playing in the water. *jal-char*, any creature that moves in water, an aquatic animal. *s.*

جل *jall*, great, glorious, eminent. *jalla* (3rd pers. sing.), is eminent. *jalla jalālu-hu*, eminent is His glory; *jalla shānu-hu*, eminent is His majesty —phrases applied only to God. *a.*

جلا *jilā*, f. splendour, lustre, brightness; enamel; scouring, polishing; emigration. *jilā-kār*, a polisher, scourer. *jilā waṭan-k.*, a. to abandon one's country, to exile one's self. *jilā waṭanī*, banishment, expulsion. *jilā waṭan honā*, to become an exile. *a.*

جلا जला *jalā* or *jallā*, m. a lake, a mass of water, tank or reservoir. *s.*

جلاب *jullāb*, m. a purge; q. d. drawing (from *jalaba*, he drew), and in this sense it is generally used in India. Freytag, on the authority of Golius, gives it, in his Arabic Lexicon, as unconnected with *jalaba*, and describes it as a mixture of water and syrup (perfumed with rose-water), as if derived from the Pers. *gul*, a rose, and *āb*, water. *jullāb-kā tel*, castor-oil. *a.*

جلا بلا जलाबला *jalā-balā*, جلابھنا जलाभुना *jalā-bhunā*, heated, scorched, burnt up; fretful, passionate, hot-tempered. *h.*

جلاپا *jalāpā*, envy, anger, rage, spite. *jalāpā-khur*, an envious person. *d.*

جلاد *jallād*, m. an executioner; (and hence, as an adj.) cruel, hard-hearted (q. d. one who excoriates; from *jild*, the skin). *jallādi falak*, the planet Mars. *a.*

جلادت *jalādat*, f. activity, agility, strength. *jalādat-āsār*, or *-shi,ār*, brave, valorous. *a.*

جلادھار जलाधार *jalādhār*, m. a pond, a lake, a reservoir. *s.*

جلادي *jallādī*, f. the office of an executioner; cruelty, villainy. *a.*

جلاردرا जलार्द्रा *jalārdrā*, wet, charged with moisture. *s.*

جلارنو जलार्णव *jalārnav*, m. a deluge, a great flood; the rainy season; the sea of fresh water. *s.*

جلاسا जलासा *jalāsā*, a pool of water, a tank. *s.*

جلاشي जलाशय *jalāshay*, m. a pond, a lake, a reservoir; the ocean; a fragrant grass (*Andropogon muricatum*); adj. stupid, dull, cold. *s.*

جلاکار जलाकार *jalākār*, m. appearance of water. *s.*

جلاکھ जलाखु *jalākhu*, m. an otter or water-cat. *s.*

جلال *jalāl*, m. dignity, state, majesty, grandeur, splendour, power. *a.*

جلالت *jalālat*, f. dignity, &c. (same as *jalāl*). *a.*

جلالکا जलालुका *jalālukā*, جلالوکا जलालोका *jalālokā*, f. a leech. *s.*

جلالي *jalālī*, glorious, illustrious; it also denotes an æra reckoned from the time of *Jalāl-ud-dīn*, Malik Shāh, son of Alp Arslān, of the Saljūk dynasty of Persia, commencing at the vernal equinox A. D. 1079. *a.*

جلاليا *jalāliyā*, a fine species of wheat with reddish ears. *a.*

جلاليه *jalāliya*, m. a person who worships the more terrible attributes of the Deity; the followers of *Saiyid Jalāl Bukhārī*; a kind of pigeon. *a.*

جلامبکا जलाम्बिका *jalāmbikā*, f. a well. *s.*

جلامي जलामय *jalāmay*, full of water, wet. *s.*

جلانا जलाना *jalānā*, a. to burn, to kindle, to inflame, to light; to make one jealous. *s.*

جلانا जिलाना *jilānā*, a. to give life to, to recover any thing almost dead; to foster, to patronise. *jilā-denā*, to revive or bring to life (the dead). *s.*

جلانچل जलाञ्चल *jalānchal*, m. a natural water-course or channel; a plant (*Vallisneria*). *s.*

جلاءو जलाऊ *jalā,ū*, act of burning, a burner. *s.*

جلاوتي *jalāwatī* (a corruption of *jilā-waṭan*, q. v.), emigration. *h.*

جلاون जलावन *jalāwan*, f. firewood. *s.*

جلاه *julāh*, جلاها *julāhā*, جله *julah*, m. a weaver, of the Muḥammadan religion; met. a fool, a blockhead. *julāh-ḍāṛhī*, f. a short round beard, such as *julāhs* usually wear. *h.*

جلاءي *julā,ī* (Dakh. for *julāh*, q. v.). *julā,ī-wāṛī*, the ward inhabited by weavers. *d.*

جلائني *julā,inī*, a weavers's wife, or a female weaver. *d.*

جلبدبد जलबुदबुद *jal-budbud*, m. a bubble of water. *s.*

جلبرهمي जलब्रह्मी *jal-brahmī*, f. a potherb (*Hilancha repens*). *s.*

جلبل जलबल *jal-bal*, burnt up, consumed with fire. *s.*

جلبندھ जलबन्धु *jal-bandhu*, m. a fish. *s.*

جلبندهك जलबन्धक *jal-bandhak*, m. a dam, a dike, rocks and stones impeding a current. *s.*

جلبھو जलभू *jal-bhū*, m. a cloud; an aquatic plant (*Commelina salicifolia* or *bengalensis*). *s.*

جلبهي जलवही *jal-bahī*, f. swimming, striking with the arms and legs in the water. *s.*

جلپ जल्प *jalp*, m. dissension, wrangling; prate, babble. *s.*

جلپاك जल्पाक *jalpāk*, m. a chatterer, talking much and foolishly. *s.*

جلپان जलपान *jalpān*, m. drinking (of water), eating, taking light food between meals a luncheon. *s.*

جلپاءي जलपाई *jalpā,ī*, f. the *Eleocarpus serratus*; an olive. *h.*

جلپپلي जलपिप्पली *jal-pippalī*, f. an aquatic plant (*Commelina salicifolia*, &c.). *s.*

جلپت जलपति *jal-pati*, m. *Varuna*, the lord of waters. *s.*

جلپرشٿجا जलपृष्ठजा *jal-prishṭhajā*, f. an aquatic plant (*Pistia stratiotes*). *s.*

جلپريه जलप्रिय *jal-priya*, m. the chātak (*Cuculus melanoleucos*); a fish. *s.*

جلپيپل जलपीपल *jal-pīpal*, a herb somewhat resembling the pepper plant. *s.*

جلتاپك जलतापिक *jal-tāpik*, جلتال जलताल *jal-tāl*, m. the *hilsa* or sable fish (*Clupea alosa*). *s.*

جل‌ترنجي जलतरञ्जी *jal-taranjī*, f. name of a musical instrument (v. next word). *s.*

جل‌ترنگ जलतरङ्ग *jal-tarang*, m. the musical glasses or harmonicon; playing on glasses or china bowls by rubbing the edges; a brass vessel in which water is put, and the edges are beaten with two sticks. *s.*

جل‌ترنگي जलतरङ्गी *jal-tarangī* (v. *jal-tarang*). *s.*

جلتهل जलथल *jal-thal*, m. ground half covered with water, marshy ground. *s.*

جلج जलज *jalaj*, m. a fish; a lotus; a shell. *s.*

جلجا जलजा *jaljā*, f. a plant, a sort of *Bassia* growing in or near the water; adj. water-born, aquatic. *s.*

جلجلا जलजला *jaljalā*, indignant, outrageous. *h.*

جلجلانا जलजलाना *jaljalānā*, n. to be indignant. *h.*

جلجلاهت जलजलाहट *jal-jalāhaṭ*, f. indignation, rage, passion, anger. *h.*

جل‌جنت जलजन्तु *jal-jantu*, m. an aquatic animal (a porpoise, shark, &c.). *s.*

جلجنتکا जलजन्तुका *jal-jantukā*, f. a leech. *s.*

جل‌چر जलचर *jal-char*, m. aquatic, moving in water (as birds, but not fish). *h.*

جلد *jald*, expeditious, quick, brisk, fast, hasty, fierce. *jald-bāz*, expeditious, fleet, hasty. *jald-bāzī*, f. haste. *jald-raw*, swift of motion. *jald-ḳadam*, fleet. *jald-mizāj*, passionate. *p.*

جلد *jild*, f. the skin, leather; the binding of a book; a volume, book. *jild-k.*, to bind a book. *jild-gar*, m. a bookbinder. *a.*

جلد जलद *jalad*, m. a cloud; a fragrant grass (*Cyperus rotundus*). *s.*

جلداشن जलदाशन *jal-dāshan*, m. the sāl tree (*Shorea robusta*). *s.*

جلدهِ जलधि *jala-dhi*, m. the ocean. *s.*

جلدهارا जलधारा *jal-dhārā*, m. a stream or current of water. *s.*

جلدهر जलधर *jal-dhar*, m. a cloud; the ocean; a grass (*Cyperus rotundus*). *s.*

جلدي *jaldī*, f. quickness, rashness; (in Dakh.) *jalde*, quickly, speedily. *p.*

جلڈمب जलडिम्ब *jal-ḍimb*, m. a bivalve shell. *s.*

جلرنج जलरञ्ज *jal-ranj*, m. the *vak*, a kind of crane. *s.*

جلرنک जलरङ्क *jal-rank*, m. a kind of crane, feeding on small fish and haunting swamps. *s.*

جلرنک जलरङ्कु *jal-ranku*, m. a gallinule. *s.*

جلس *jils*, m. a companion. *a.*

جلسا *julasā* (pl. of جليس), companions. *a.*

جلسا‌خطيبي *jalsā khaṭībī*, f. the sitting down of the *khaṭīb* or reader of the *ḳur,ān*, between the reading of the first and second *khuṭba*, q. v. *a.*

جلساعي जलशाई *jalsā,ī* (lit. sleeping on the water), an epithet of *Vishṇu*, when, after the destruction of the universe, he alone of all beings remains floating on the water, on a leaf of the *bar*, or *Ficus Indica*, or on the great snake. *s.*

جلسوت जलसूत *julsūt*, f. a guinea-worm (*Filaria medinensis*). *s.*

جلسوچ जलसूचि *jal-sūchi*, m. a fish, a sort of pike (*Esox scolopax*); the Gangetic porpoise; an aquatic plant (*Trapa bispinosa*); f. a leech. *s.*

جلسيني जलसेनी *jal-senī*, f. sleeping in water by way of mortification; a fish. *s.*

جلسه *jalsa*, m. posture, situation, seat, post, state. *a.*

جلشي जलशय *jal-shay*, m. *Vishṇu* sleeping on the water (see *jalsā,ī*). *s.*

جلف *jalaf*, m. a miser; mean, base, despicable; pl. *ajlāf*, mean wretches. *a.*

جلکا जलिका *jalikā* or जलुका *jalukā*, f. a leech. *s.*

جلکاک जलकाक *jal-kāk*, m. the diver or water-crow. *s.*

جلکانکش जलकाङ्क्ष *jal-kānksha*, m. an elephant. *s.*

جلکپ जलकपि *jal-kapi*, m. the water-ape or Gangetic porpoise. *s.*

جلکر जलकर *jalkar*, the produce of the fisheries, or the revenue thereon assessed. *s.*

جلکرات जलकिराट *jal-kirāṭ*, m. a shark; a large alligator. *s.*

جلکريڙا जलक्रीड़ा *jal-krīṛā*, f. sporting or gamboling in the water, bathing. *s.*

جلککٹي जलकुक्कुटी *jal-kukkuṭī*, f. the black-headed gull. *s.*

جل‌ککڑ जलकुक्कड़ *jal kukkaṛ*, m. a waterfowl; a diver. *s.*

جلکنتل जलकुन्तल *jal-kuntal*, m. an aquatic plant (*Vallisneria*). *s.*

جلکنٹک जलकण्टक *jal-kanṭak*, m. an aquatic plant (*Trapa bispinosa*), a crocodile. *s.*

جلکوپي जलकूपी *jal-kūpī*, f. a whirlpool; a pond, a spring, a well. *s.*

جلکورم जलकूर्म *jal-kūrma*, m. the Gangetic porpoise. *s.*

جلکيش जलकेश *jal-kesh*, m. an aquatic plant (*Vallisneria*). *s.*

جلگ *jalag* (for *jab-lag* or *jab-talak*), until. *d.*

جلگلم जलगुल्म *jal-gulm*, m. a whirlpool; a turtle, a tortoise; a pond, a lake. *s.*

جل‌لتا जललता *jal-latā*, f. a wave, a billow. *s.*

جلم *jalam* (for *janam*), birth, birthright. *s.*

جل‌مارجار जलमार्जार *jal-mārjār*, m. an otter. *s.*

جلمارگ जलमार्ग *jal-mārg*, m. a drain or issue from a pond. *s.*

جلمانس जलमानुष *jal-mānus*, m. a waterman, a mermaid, the water-kelpie, a small species of monkey. *s.*

جلمکشکا जलमक्षिका *jal-makshikā*, f. a water insect. *s.*

جلمنڈل **जलमंडल** ***jalmandal,*** m. a kind of tarantula or large spider, the bite of which is said to be fatal. *s.*

جلمورت **जलमूर्त्ति** ***jal-mūrti,*** m. Shiva, of whom one form is water, implying his omnipresence. *s.*

جلمي **जलमय** ***jalmai,*** watery ; m. flood, inundation. *s.*

جلن **जलन** ***jalan,*** m. burning, heat ; passion, [vexation. *s.*

جلنا **जलना** ***jalnā,*** n. to burn, to be kindled ; met. to be enraged. *jal-uṭhnā*, n. to break out (as fire). *jal-bujhnā*, n. to brand, to burn to ashes. *jal-paknā*, n. to be in a passion, to rage. *jale par non lagānā* (to throw salt on a burn), to triumph over, to insult. *s.*

جلنا **जुलना** ***julnā,*** to meet, to be united. *h.*

جلنار ***julnār*** (Arab. form of *gulnār*), the pomegranate flower. *a. p.*

جلندر **जलन्दर** ***jalandar,***
جلندهر **जलन्धर** ***jalandhar,*** } m. the dropsy, ascites ; lit. that which has water ; hence it is applied to flat alluvial land, as the *Jalandar du,āb.* *s.*

جلندهه **जलनिधि** ***jal-nidhi,*** m. the ocean. *s.*

جلنرگم **जलनिर्गम** ***jal-nirgam,*** m. a drain, a watercourse ; a pipe along a wall for carrying off water ; a waterfall. *s.*

جلنكل **जलनकुल** ***jal-nakul,*** m. an otter. *s.*

جلنيلي **जलनीली** ***jal-nīlī,*** f. *vallisneria.* *s.*

جلنيم **जलनीम** ***jalnīm,*** m. the name of a drug ; lit. the *water-nīm* (*Herpestes monniera*), a bitter herb which grows on the banks of tanks, &c. *s.*

جلو ***jilau,*** f. a rein (of a horse's bridle) ; retinue, court, equipage. *jilau-dār*, attendant. *jilau-khāna*, an area, vestibule, porch, antechamber. *a.*

جلوا ***jilwā,*** m. the meeting of the bride and bridegroom (in presence of the relations). *jilwe kā gīt*, m. epithalamium. *a.*

جلوانا **जलवाना** ***jalwānā,*** a. (causal of *jalānā*) to cause to be burnt or set on fire. *s.*

جلوت ***jalwat*** or ***jilwat,*** f. splendour, lustre. *a.*

جلوتسرگ **जलोत्सर्ग** ***jalotsarg,*** a kind of ceremony (v. *banotsarg*). *s.*

جلوچهواس **जलोच्छ्वास** ***jalochchhwās,*** m. a drain or channel carrying off an excess of water. *s.*

جلودر **जलोदर** ***jalodar,*** m. dropsy. *s.*

جل ورشچك **जलवृश्चिक** ***jal-vrishchik,*** m. a prawn or shrimp (water-scorpion). *s.*

جلورگي **जलोर्गी** ***jalorgī,*** f. a leech. *s.*

جل وڙال **जलविड़ाल** ***jal-viṛāl,*** m. an otter. *s.*

جلوس ***julūs,*** m. accession (to a throne) ; the reign or æra of a monarch. *a.*

جلوسي ***julūsī,*** of or during the reign (of a king, &c.). *julūsī ṭonṭā*, m. a light cartridge. *a.*

جل وشو **जलविषुव** ***jal-vishuv,*** m. the autumnal equinox, close of the annual rains. *s.*

جلوكا **जलोका** ***jalokā*** or ***jalaukā,***
جلوكس **जलौकस** ***jalaukas,*** } f. a leech. *s*

جلوه ***jalwa*** or ***jilwa,*** m. splendour, lustre ; the bridal bed or ornaments. *jalwa-gar*, splendid, conspicuous. *jalwa-garī*, f. conspicuity, splendour ; blandishments, affectation. *a.*

جلويا **जलवैया** ***jalwaiyā,*** m. a burner. *s.*

جل ويده **जलव्यध** ***jal-vyadh,*** m. a kind of fish, a sort of pike. *s.*

جلهه **जलह** ***jalah,*** m. a small piece of water, a lake or pond ; a summer-house. *s.*

جله ***julah,*** m. (v. *julāh*) a weaver, &c. *p.*

جلهاس **जलहास** ***jal-hās,*** m. cuttle-fish bone, considered as the indurated foam of the sea. *s.*

جلي ***jalī,*** plain, apparent ; large, plain (handwriting). *faṣli jalī*, a season before the commencement of the rains, in which a crop of rice is cut. *a.*

جليا **जलिया** ***jaliyā,*** m. a fisherman. *s.*

جليب ***jaleb,*** m. attendants, equipage, suit (cor. from *jilau*). *a.*

جليب طاس ***jaleb-ṭās,*** m. the goglet in which water is cooled with nitre. *a.*

جليبي ***jalebī,*** f. belonging to the retinue. *a.*

جليبي **जलेबी** ***jalebī,*** f. a kind of sweetmeats. *h.*

جلي پرنون لگانا **जलेपर नोन लगाना** ***jale par non lagānā,*** to triumph over, to insult (lit. to throw salt on one who is burned). *h.*

جليچهيا **जलेच्छया** ***jalechchhayā,*** f. a plant (*Heliotropum indicum*) *s.*

جليس ***jalīs,*** m. a companion. *a.*

جليشور **जलेश्वर** ***jaleshwar,*** m. Varuna, the god of water ; the ocean. *s.*

جليل ***jalīl,*** great, glorious, illustrious. *jalīlu-l-ḳadr*, august, illustrious. *a.*

جلينتر **जलयन्त्र** ***jal-yantra,*** m. a water-work, a machine for raising water. *jal-yantra-grih*, m. a house erected in the midst of water, or subterraneous apartments constructed on the bank of a river, for retiring to in the hot season ; a summer-house. *a.*

جليندهن **जलेन्धन** ***jalendhan,*** m. submarine fire. *s.*

جليو ***jalew,*** m. attendants, equipage, suit. *a.*

جم ***jam,*** name of an ancient king of Persia, famed for his pomp and magnificence. *p.*

جم **जम** ***jam*** (for **यम** *yama*), adj. twin, fellow, one of a pair ; m. the Pluto of the Hindūs ; he is regent of the world below, or of the realms of death, and judge of departed souls. *jam-dūt*, the messenger of death, of the same import as the Arabic term *malaku-l-maut.* *jam diyā*, m. a candle or illumination sacred to Pluto, lighted on the 13th of *Kārtik*, *krishn paksh*, *i.e.* three days before the *Dewālī*. *s.*

جم **जिम** ***jim,*** like, as, in such manner as. *h.*

جم *jamm*, a multitude. *jammi ghafīr*, a vast multitude, including the high and the low. *a.*

جماد *jamād*, m. a stone or fossil. *jamādāt*, minerals, fossils. *a.*

جمادي *jamādā* or *jumādā*, name of the fifth and sixth Muhammadan lunar months. *a.*

جمادي الاول *jamādā-l-awwal*, جمادي الاولى *jamādā-l-ūlā*, } the first *jamādā*, the fifth month of the lunar year of the Musalmāns: it contains thirty days. *s.*

جمادي الثاني *jamādā-s-sānī*, جمادي الآخر *jamādā-l-ākhir*, } the second or latter *jamādā*, the sixth lunar month of the Musalmāns, consisting of twenty-nine days. *a.*

جماع *jimā'*, f. *coitus, concubitus. a.*

جماعت *jamā'at*, f. a crowd, a party, an assembly, a troop, meeting, society, senate, congregation. *a.*

جمال *jamāl*, m. beauty, elegance. *a.*

جمال گوٹا जमालगोटा *jamāl-goṭā*, m. the name of a purgative nut (*Jatropha curcas: croton triglium*). *h.*

جمالي *jamālī*, m. a kind of musk melon (red-fleshed); adj. amiable (the Deity). *s.*

جمانا जिमाना *jimānā*, a. to feed, to entertain. *s.*

جمانا जमाना *jamānā*, a. to collect; to sum up; to coagulate, to freeze or make ice; to congeal; to pace in the manege. *h.*

جماو जमाव *jamā,o*, m. a crowd or multitude, collection, accumulation; coagulation. *h.*

جماوٹ जमावट *jamāwaṭ*, f. coagulation, agglutination, congelation. *a.*

جماوڑا *jamā,oṛā*, m. an assembly, a crowd, a collection; place of assembling. *d.*

جماهنا जमाहना *jamāhnā*, to gape, to yawn. *s.*

جماهي जमाही *jamāhī*, gaping or yawning. *s.*

جماهير *jamāhīr* (pl. of جمهور), nations, kingdoms; states, republics. *a.*

جماءي जमाई *jamā,ī*, m. a son-in-law. *s.*

جمب जम्बु *jambu*, f. a fruit-tree, the rose-apple (*Eugenia jambu*). *s.*

جمبال जम्बाल *jambāl*, m. an aquatic plant (*Vallisneria*). *s.* [(*Pandanus odoratissimus*). *s.*

جمبالا जम्बाला *jambālā*, m. a fragrant plant

جمب دويپ जम्बुद्वीप *jambu-dwīp*, m. one of the purānic divisions of the earth, the central one, including Hindūstān, or the known world. *s.*

جمبک जम्बुक *jambuk*, m. a jackal; a low man; the rose-apple. *s.*

جمبو *jambū* (v. *jambu*). *d.*

جمبول जम्बूल *jambūl*, m. a fragrant plant (*Pandanus odoratissimus*); the rose-apple. *s.*

جمبهيري जम्भीरी *jambhīrī*, جمبير जम्बीर *jambīr*, } m. the lime or citron; a kind of basil with small leaves. *s.* [a dagger. *p.*

جمبيا *jambiyā* (for *janbiya*), a kind of weapon,

جمپتي जम्पती *jampatī*, (m. dual) husband and wife. *s.* [perpetually. *h.*

جم جم जमजम *jam-jam*, always, constantly,

جمد *jamd*, m. congelation, connection. *a.*

جمدگني जमदग्नी *jamadagnī*, name of *Parasurāma's* father. *s.* [senger. *s.*

جمدوت जमदूत *jam-dūt*, m. death's mes-

جمدهر जमधर *jamdhar*, جمدهڑ जमधड़ *jamdhaṛ*, } m. a dagger (lit. death-bearer); "a large dagger resembling a *kaṭār*, but having a kind of basket hilt protecting the hand."—(Binning.) *s.*

جمراج जमराज *jamarāj*, the king of death, the Hin‧ū Pluto (v. *jam*). *s.*

جمست *jamast*, f. a kind of blue stone or mineral substance, supposed to be a specific against fainting and palpitation of the heart. *d.*

جمش *jammash*, a species of bird of chase. *d.*

جمشيد *jamshīd* (v. *jam*), name of a celebrated Persian king, the founder of Persepolis. *a.*

جمع *jam'*, f. a congregation, conjunction, collection, accumulation, assembly, amount, sum total, whole revenue generally, amount assessed, plural number. *jam'-ānā*, or *-āmadan*, to assemble. *jam'-bandī*, f. accounts of the revenues, settlement of the revenues. *jam'-jhartī*, a periodical account. *jam'-kharch*, debit and credit, cash account. *jam'-dār*, m. a native officer of the army so called; the head of any body, as guides, *harkāras*, &c. *jam'-k.*, to collect. *jam'-honā* or *-shudan*, to be collected or assembled. *jam'-dārī*, the business or rank of a *jam'dār*. *jam' o-kharch*, m. account of receipt and disbursement, account current. *jam' o kharch-k.*, a. to make up or balance an account. *jam' wāṣil-bākī*, an account stating payments periodically due, with the amount received and the arrears. *a.*

جمعات *jam'āt* (pl. of جمع), additions, collections. *a.* [Thursday. *a. h.*

جمعرات *jum'a-rāt* (v. *jum'a*), Friday eve, *i.e.*

جمعگي *jum'gī*, f. the weekly allowance to schoolboys, paid on a Friday; also presents given on a Friday by schoolboys to their preceptor. *a.*

جمعه *jum'a*, m. Friday (on which day Musalmāns assemble to pray at the great mosque). *a.*

جمعرات *jum'a-rāt*, f. Thursday (q. d. eve of Friday). *a. h.*

جمعيت *jam'aiyat* or *jam'īyat*, f. collection; wealth; recollection, reflection. *jam'aiyat-i-khāṭir*, peace of mind. *a.*

جم غفير *jammi ghafīr*, m. a great multitude. *a.*

جمک जमक *jamak*, f. the state of succeeding or going on well. *h.*

جمک जमक or यमक *jamak*, twin, fellow, one

of a pair; m. repeating of a word in different significations (in rhetoric). *s.*

جمكانا जमकाना *jamkānā*, a. to adjust, to go on well, to settle; to assemble, to crowd together. *h.*

جمكنا जमकना *jamaknā*, n. to succeed, to go on well, to fit. *dūkān jamkī*, buyers and sellers are collected in the shop. *laṛā,ī jamkī*, the fight was joined. *majlis jamkī*, the assembly is full. *muḳaddama jamkā*, the cause is begun to be debated. *h.*

جمكوڙا *jamkūṛā*, m. a kind of covering for the head and shoulders, worn during rainy weather: it is made of reeds or palm leaves plaited. *d.*

جمگهٹ जमघट *jamghaṭ*, m. crowd, multitude. *s.*

جمل यमल *jamal*, m. a pair, a brace. *s.*

جمل *jamal*, a camel; a kind of fish. *a.*

جمل *jumal*, (pl. of جملة, q. v.) the whole sum; *ḥisābi jumal*, the reckoning by *abjad*. *a.*

جملگي *jumlagī*, f. the totality, the whole. *p.*

جملة *jumla*, m. the whole sum, aggregate, total; a sentence. *fi-l-jumla*, upon the whole. *min jumla* or *az ān jumla*, from or out of the whole. *a.*

جمن *jamun*, coagulation, congelation; curds, jelly; rennet or acid employed for curdling milk. *d.*

جمنة जमुना *jamunā*, f. (for *yamunā*) name of a well-known river, the Jumna; (in mythology) twin sister of *Yama*. *s.*

جمنا जमना *jamnā*, n. to germinate, to grow. *s.*

جمنا जमना *jamnā*, n. to be coagulated or frozen; to be collected, to adhere, to stick; to pace in the manège. *h.*

جمنوٹا जमनौटा *jamnauṭā*, } m. a certain
جمنوٹيا जमनौटिया *jamnauṭiyā*, } consideration given to one who becomes security for another, generally five per cent. on the amount. *h.*

جموءا जमोआ *jamo,ā*, indigo planted before the rains, and irrigated by artificial means. *h.*

جموٹ जमूवट *jamūwaṭ* or *jamū,aṭ*, the foundation of a well, or the festive ceremony held on the occasion of laying the foundation of a well. *h.*

جموگ जमोग *jamog*, transfer of liabilities by mutual consent, a conditional mortgage. *h.*

جموگدار जमोगदार *jamog-dār*, a person who lends a landed proprietor a sum of money, and recovers that money from the cultivators. *h.*

جموگنا जमोगना *jamognā*, a. to ascertain. *h.*

جمهانا जमहाना *jamhānā*, n. to gape, to yawn. *s.*

جمهاءي जमहाई *jamhā,ī*, f. gaping, yawning. *jamhā,ī lenā*, a. to gape, to yawn. *s.*

جمهور *jumhūr*, universal, all; m. high heaps of sand; a republic, populace, community. *a.*

جمي जम्मी *jammī*, a species of tree or plant so called. *h.*

جميا जमैया *jamaiyā*, a kind of grass (in the province of Delhi); Thursday. *h.*

جميرات जुमेरात *jume-rāt*, f. (for *jum'e-rāt* or *jum'a-rāt*), Thursday. *a. h.*

جميع *jamī'*, the whole, all; universal. *jamī'an*, altogether; universally. *a.*

جميعت *jamī'at*, f. a concourse, an assembly, a multitude. *a.*

جميل *jamīl*, beautiful, elegant (fem. *jamīla*). *a.*

جن जन *jan*, m. a person, individual, mankind: in comp. it denotes plurality, as *strī-jan*, women. *s.*

جن जनु *janu*, m. birth, engenderment. *s.*

جن जुन *jun*, m. time. *h.*

جن जिन *jin*, (infl. pl. of rel. pron.) whom, what; (a negative particle) no, not; (a prohibitive particle) don't. *h.*

جن जिन *jin*, m. a deified saint, according to the heretical sect of *Jin* and *Budh*. *s.*

جن *jinn*, m. a genius, spirit, demon. *a.*

جنا जना *janā*, a person, individual; (part. pass. of *jannā*) born, a son. *s.*

جنا जना *jannā*, n. to produce young, to be delivered of a child; to be born. *s.*

جناب *janāb*, f. side, brink, margin; majesty, highness, excellency; vestibule, threshold. *janābi'ālī*, your majesty, your or his excellency. *a.*

جنابت *janābat*, f. pollution, loss of sperma. *a.*

جناپك ज्ञापक *jnāpak* (or *gyāpak*), m. an instructor. *s.*

جناپن ज्ञापन *jnāpan* (or *gyāpan*), m. act of causing to know, instruction. *s.*

جنات ज्ञात *jnāta* (or *gyāta*), known, understood. *jnāti*, a father, a kinsman. *s.*

جنات *jannāt*, (pl. of جنّة), gardens. *jinnāt* (pl. of *jinn*), genii, demons. *a.*

جناجات जनाजात *janā-jāt*, man by man, one by one (person). *h.*

جناح *jināḥ* or *janāḥ*, f. a pinion, wing. *a.*

جنازة *janāza*, m. a bier, a hearse, a funeral. *janāza rawān*, (met) a horse. *a.* [hall. *s.*

جناشري जनाश्रय *janāshray*, m. a temporary

جناغ *janāgh*, a contract, a bargain. *junāgh*, a stirrup-leather, saddle-cloth, surcingle. *p.*

جنان *jinān*, (pl. of جنّة) gardens (planted with trees), the regions of paradise. *a.*

جنان ज्ञान *jnān* (v. *gyān*), m. knowledge. *s.*

جنانا जनाना *janānā*, a. to deliver, to bring to bed; to inform, to remind, to tell, to warn (little used. *jatānā* being substituted for it); m. midwifery. *s.*

جنانتك जनान्तिक *janāntik*, m. secret communication, whispering, speaking aside. *s.*

جناو जनाव *janāw* or *janā,o*, m. a signal. *h.*

جناور *janāwar*, m. an animal. *d.*

جناءي जनाई *janā,ī*, f. a midwife. *janā,ī ṣadḳa*, alms given at the birth of a child. *s.*

جناية or جنايت *jināyat*, f. any prohibited act committed upon the person or property, such as murder, maiming, &c. *a.*

جنب *jamb*, a side, a part, a tract of country. *a.*

جنب *junub*, defiled, polluted. *a.*

جنبا *janibā*, m. support, seconding; countenancing, assistance, partiality. *a.*

جنبان *jumbān*, trembling, stirring, moving, (root of *jumbānīdan*) in comp. causing to move or stir, shaking (actively.) *p.*

جن‌بچي *jan-bachche* (*āl-aulād*), family, offspring. *d.*

جنبش *jumbish*, f. agitation, motion, gesture. *p.*

جنبك जम्बुक *jambuk*, } m. a jackal. *s.*
جنبو जम्बू *jambū*,

جنبوديپ जम्बूदीप *jambūdīp* for जम्बुद्वीप *jambu-dwīp*, m. one of the seven parts of the world. *s.*

جنبهيري जम्भीरी *jambhīrī*, f. a fruit of the lime kind. *s.*

جنبي *jambī* (properly *jambīy*), lateral. *a.*

جنبيدن *jumbīdan*, to be moved or agitated. *p.*

جنبير *jambīr*, the lime tree and fruit (*Citrus medica*). *s.*

جنبيه *jambiya*, a kind of side weapon, a large dagger worn at the side. *a.*

جنت जन्तु *jantu*, m. an animal, a beast. *s.*

جنت जनित *janit*, produced, born. *s.*

جنت *jannat*, f. paradise, heaven. *jannatu-l-bilād*, the paradise of regions, an epithet applied (very questionably) to Bengal. *jannat i'adan*, f. the garden of Eden. *jannati māwā*, the paradise of rest. *jannati ni'm* or *na'īm*, the garden of pleasure. *jannat-makān* or *-naṣīb* or *-ārāmgāh*, one whose abode or portion is paradise. *a.*

جنت *janat*, birth, being born. *d.*

جنتا जन्ता *jantā*, m. an instrument for drawing wire. *s.*

جنتا जनिता *janitā*, m. a father, a parent. *s.*

جنتا जनता *janatā*, f. mankind a number of men. *s.*

جنتار जन्तार *jantār*, m. an amulet, a charm. *s.*

جنتانا जन्ताना *jantānā*, n. to be squeezed, pressed. *h*

جنتپهل जन्तुफल *jantu-phal*, m. glomerous fig-tree (*Ficus glomerata*). *s.*

جنتر मन्त्र or यन्त्र *jantr*, m. an instrument, an engine; a musical instrument; an amulet; juggling; an observatory; a dial; an astrological or magic diagram. *jantr-mantr*, m. juggling, conjuring, enchanting by figures and incantations. *s.*

جنترنا यन्त्रणा *jantranā*, m. pain, anguish, affliction. *s.*

جنتري जन्त्री or यन्त्री *jantrī*, m. an instrument for drawing wire; a conjuror, a juggler, a wizard; f. an almanack, a register, more especially the Indian Army and Civil List, commonly called "the Gentry-book." *s.*

جنتري जनित्री *janitrī*, f. a mother. *s.*

جنتگهن जन्तुघ्न *jantu-ghna*, m. a vermifuge. *s.*

جنتلا जन्तुला *jantulā*, f. a grass (*Saccharum spontaneum*). *s.*

جنتي *jannatī*, relating to paradise, heavenly. *a.*

جنجال जञ्जाल *janjāl*, m. trouble, difficulty, plague, embarrassment, misfortune. *s.*

جنجال जञ्जाल *janjāl*, m. a swivel, a large musket. *h.*

جنجالي जञ्जाली *janjālī*, m. one who molests; a gun mounted on a camel or elephant. *s.*

جنجانور जनजानवर *jan-janwār*, m. man and beast. *s. p.*

جند *jund*, a medicinal substance found in the castor beaver. *d.*

جندرا जन्द्रा *jandrā*, m. a pitchfork, a kind of rake used in the north-west provinces. *h.*

جندوليا जन्दौलिया *jandauliyā*, name of a small clan of *rājpūts* in Banda. *h.*

جنرو जनरव *jan-rav*, m. noise, clamour, sound of human voices. *s.*

جنس *jins*, f. genus, kind, species, sort, family, race; goods, merchandise, moveables, grain, commodities, produce. *jinsi bashar*, mankind, *genus humanum*. *jinsi kāmil*, first-rate crops. *jinsi-adnā*, an inferior article. *jinsi a'lā* or *'ālī*, any article of the best quality. *a.*

جنسرت *jansruti* (v. *jan-shruti*), news, &c. *s.*

جنسوار *jinswār*, a distinct statement relative to crops. *jinswār jam'bandī*, a detailed statement of the rents levied upon each kind of crop. *p.*

جنسواري *jinswārī*, separately, distinctly. *p.*

جنسي *jinsī*, in kind, in goods (paid, &c.). *a.*

جنسيت *jinsiyat*, homogeneousness, sameness, or similarity of kind. *a.*

جنشرت जनश्रुति *jan-shruti*, f. news, tidings, report. *s.*

جنطيانا *janṭiyānā*, m. the herb gentian. *a.*

جنك जनुक *januk*, to wit, though, although. *h.*

جنك जनक *janak*, m. a father; name of a king, sovereign of Mithilā, and father of *Sītā*. *s.*

جنكا जनिका *janikā*, m. a pun, "double entendre." *h.*

جنك‌پر जनकपुर *janak-pur*, m. the metropolis of *rājā Janak*, *Sītā's* father, in the district of Tirhut. *s.*

جنگ जुङ्ग *jung*, f. emotion, impulse; a volume containing several books; m. f. a pother's (*Convolvulus argenteus*). *h.*

جنگ *jang*, m. battle, war, combat, fight. *jang-āzmūda*, a veteran; warlike, brave. *jang-āwar*, a champion, a hero. *jang-āwardan*, to fight, to stand the brunt of battle. *jang-jo*, contentious, litigious. *jang o jadal*, m. battle, conflict, brawl, squabble, altercation. *jangi zargarī*, a goldsmith's quarrel: the term is applied to a collusive dispute between two parties in order to defraud a third. *p.*

جنگال *jangāl*, m. verdigris (v. *zangār*). *p.*

جنگامشتي *jangā-mushṭī*, f. boxing. *p. h.*

جنگاہ *jangāh*, f. the field of battle (q. d. *jang gāh*). *p.*

جنگت जुङ्गित *jungit*, outcast, deserted, injured. *s.*

جنگرا जंगरा *jangrā*, m. the haulm or stalk of autumnal crops. *h.*

جنگل जङ्गल *jangal*, adj. desert, waste; m. a forest, a wood, a jungle. *jangal-burī*, f. act of clearing woodlands. *jangal phirnā* or *-jānā*, n. (lit. to walk in, or go to, the wood); to ease one's self. *s.*

جنگلا जङ्गला *janglā*, wild, untamed; m. name of a *rāginī*, or musical mode; woody country, forest. *s.*

جنگله *jangla*, a coppice or thicket; a kind of flowered cloth; a medley of tunes. *s.*

جنگلي जङ्गली *janglī*, wild, savage; a barbarian, boor, clown. *janglī-ām*, wild mango. *janglī-bādām*, wild almond. *janglī billī*, f. a wild cat. *janglī piyāz*, squills (*Erythronium Indicum*). *janglī-champā*, the red jasmine. *janglī singhārā*, m. hermodactyl. *janglī-sarv*, wild cypress. *janglī-kabūd*, the bustard. *janglī-kaṅwār*, hill aloe. *janglī-kawwā*, m. a raven. *s.*

جنگم जङ्गम *jangam*, m. a kind of *faḳīr*, who has matted hair, and rings a bell. *h.*

جنگم जङ्गम *jangam*, removeable, moveable, in motion; a mendicant. *s.*

جنگھ जिङ्घि *jinghi*, Bengal madder (*Rubia manjith*). *s.*

جنگھا जङ्घा *janghā*, f. the thigh, the leg. *s.*

جنگھارا जङ्घारा *janghārā*, the name of a large and turbulent tribe of *rājpūts*. *h.*

جنگھلا जंघला *jaṅghalā*, name of a rate or clause in a lease. *h.*

جنگي *jangī*, m. a combatant, a warrior; adj. of or relating to war, warlike, martial, military, quarrelsome. *p.*

جنگيزخان *jangīz khān*, n. the name of one of those atrocious scourges of the human race, vulgarly called "renowned conquerors." He was of Tartar or Moghul origin, and born in A.D. 1154. *p.*

جنلوك जनलोक *janlok*, m. one of the seven *lokas* or divisions of the world: the region inhabited by pious men after their decease. *s.*

جنم जन्म *janam* or *janma*, m. birth; metempsychosis of the Hindūs; life, existence. *janmāshṭamī*, the eighth day of the dark half of Bhādra, being the anniversary of the birthday of *Krishṇa*. *janam-bhūm* or *janma-bhūmi*, also *janam bhum*, f. birthplace. *janma-* or *janam-patrī*, f. horoscope, nativity. *janma-patrī kī bidhi milnā*, to meet one's fate, to receive one's destined award. *janam-jalā*, burned or spoiled from its birth, originally bad. *janmad* or *janma-dātā*, a father. *janam-din*, m. birthday. *janam-rogī*, valetudinarian. *janma-sthān*, birthplace, native land. *janma-kīl*, m. *Vishṇu*, the bolt or stay of life. *janam-lagan*, f. the moment of birth, horoscope. *s.*

جنمانا जन्माना *janmānā*, a. to beget; to make vegetate. *s.*

جنمانتر जन्मान्तर *janmāntar*, m. regeneration, another birth, another state of existence. *janmāntarīya*, acquired in a former birth. *s.*

جنماندھ जन्मान्ध *janmāndha*, born blind. *s.*

جنمن जन्मन *janman*, m. birth. *janmin*, an animal, a living being. *s.*

جنمنا जनमना *janamnā*, n. to be born. *s.*

جنموتسو जन्मोत्सव *janmotsav*, m. a festival held on the anniversary of *Krishṇa's* birthday. *s.*

جنمي جي जन्मेजय *janmejai*, the son of *rājā Parīkshit*. *s.*

جنن जनन *janan*, m. birth, production; family, race. *s.*

جننا जनना *jannā*, n. to produce young, to be delivered. *s.*

جننگم जनङ्गम *janangam*, m. a *Chanḍāl*, a man of a degraded tribe. *s.*

جنني जननी *jananī*, f. a mother, the actual mother of a child, in contradistinction to a stepmother; tenderness, compassion. *s.*

جنو जनो *jano*, m. the brāhmanical thread (v. *janew*); adv. like as, as. *s.*

جنواد जनवाद *jan-vād*, m. news, rumour, report. *s.*

جنواسا जनवासा *janwāsā*, m. the place at the bride's house where the bridegroom and his train are received. *s.*

جنواءي *janwā,ī*, a son-in-law. *d.*

جنوب *janūb*, m. the south. *a.*

جنوبي *janūbī* (f. *janūbiya*), southern. *a.*

جنوداهرن जनोदाहरण *janodāharan*, m. fame, glory. *s.*

جنون *janūn*, m. madness, insanity, phrensy; a demoniac. *a.*

جنوں *janoṅ*, probably, perhaps. *d.*

جنوني *janūnī*, mad, insane; passionate. *a.*

جنهار जुन्हार *junhār*, m. a kind of grain (comprising many species, of which Indian corn is one). *h.*

جنهار जन्हार *janhār*, } man by man, every
جنهاءي जन्हाई *jan-hā,ī*, } one. *s.*

جنهاءي जुन्हाई *jun-hā,ī*, } f. the moonlight. *h.*
جنهيا जुन्हैया *junhaiyā*, }

جنهر *janhar*, a branch of the Gujar tribe. *h.*

جنهري जुन्हरी *junhrī*, f. a kind of grain. *s.*

جني *jinnī* or *jinniy*, a jinn, a demon or spirit. *a.*

جني जनी *janī*, f. a maid-servant; daughter-in-law; a woman in general; a mother; birth, production; (in Dakh.) a fainting fit to which lying-in women are subject.

جنيا जन्या *janyā*, f. the friend of a mother; the relation or companion of a bride, a bridesmaid. *s.*

جنيبت *janībat*, a she camel entrusted to a person to bring provisions on. *a.*

جنيت जनेत *janet*, f. the company and attendants at a wedding. *s.*

جنيرا जनेरा *janerā*, a tall species of millet. *h.*

جنيلا *janelā*, a window. *d.*

جنين *janīn*, fœtus, embryo. *a.*

جنيو जनेव *jane,o*, *janew* or जनेऊ *jane,ū*, m. the brāhmanical thread; a flaw in a jewel. *h.*

جنيوا जनेवा *janewā*, f. the name of a fragrant grass (*dūb*-grass, *Agrostis linearis*). *h.*

جنيه जन्य *janya*, m. a father; the friend or companion of a bridegroom. *s.*

جنيه *jinnīya*, a female *jinnī*, q.v. *a.*

جو जो *jo*, if, that, as, when; rel. pron. who, which, what. *jo-jo*, whoever. *jo-chīz*, what, whatever, or -soever. *jo kuchh*, whatever or whatsoever. *jo ko,ī*, whoever. *jo ki*, though, although, whichever. *h.*

جو जौ *jau*, if, that, when. *jau-loṅ*, as long as. *h.*

جو *jo* or *jū*, a river, a brook, a rivulet; in comp. seeking, as *jang-jo*, one who seeks battle or strife. *p.*

جو जौ, जव or यव *jau*, m. barley (*Hordeum hexastichon*); the measure of a barley-corn, equal to six mustard-seeds; the mark between the joints of the fingers. *jau-jau ḥisāb lenā*, a. to take a strict account. *jau-farosh i gandum-numā*, one who sells only barley, while he exhibits wheat; a cheat, a hypocrite. *s. p.*

جو जू *jū* (v. *jī*), lord! master! sir! *h.*

جوا जवा *jawā*, m. a clove of garlic; a kind of stitch in needlework. *jawe-dār*, sewed in a particular manner; (in Dakh.) a kind of grub or worm. *h.*

جوا जवा *jawā*, m. mark in the joints of the fingers; name of a flower (*Hibiscus rosa sinensis*). *s.*

جوءا जूआ *jū,ā* or जुवा *juwā*, m. a yoke of a carriage or plough; a die, dice; a game, gambling. *jū,ā khelnā*, a. to play dice, to gamble. *jū,e khāna*, a gambling house. *jū,e-bāz*, a gambler. *s.*

جوا जुवा *juvā* (for युवा *yuva*), young, a young man, or one of the virile age. *s.*

جواب *jawāb*, m. an answer, any thing answering to another. *jawābi bā ṣawāb*, m. a proper answer; an answer full of sound sense. *jawāb bālā*, a kind of benediction (*i. e.* may your advice prevail). *jawāb-dār* or *jawāb-dih*, a respondent or surety; adj. responsible, accountable, amenable. *jawāb denā*, a. to be accountable for, to be amenable or responsible, to reply; to discharge, to dismiss one from his office (in Bengal the English language has been enriched with an additional verb from this source; hence, when a lady rejects a gentleman's matrimonial overtures, the inconsolable swain is said to have been *jawābed*). *jawāb sawāl*, (corruptedly *jāb-sāl*), m. altercation, conversation. *jawāb sawālī*, m. reply, rejoinder. *jawābi ḳāfī*, m. a definitive answer. *jawāb nāma*, m. a writing fixed to the winding-sheet, on the breast of a good Musalmān deceased, which it is intended that Munkir and Nakīr (q. v.) should read, in case the poor soul should be too much flurried to answer their questions. *raddi jawāb* or *jawābu-l-jawāb*, m. reply, rejoinder. *a.*

جوابي *jawābī*, m. a respondent; a kind of bill of exchange the price of which is not paid till notice is received of the bills having been paid; the chorus, especially in repeating a *marsiya* or elegy. *jawābī sawālī*, m. a mediator, an ambassador, an agent, an attorney. *a.*

جواپشپ *jawā-pushp*, m. the China-rose. *s.*

جوات जूआट *jū,āṭ*, } m. a yoke. *s.*
جوءاٹهه जुआठ *jū,āṭh*, }

جواد *jawwād*, liberal, beneficent. *a.*

جواد *jawād*, m. civet; probably a corruption of the Arabic *zubād*. *d.*

جوار *jawār*, m. neighbourhood, propinquity. *a.*

جوءار जोआर *jo,ār* or ज्वार *jwār*, f. the name of a grain, Indian corn (*Holcus sorgum, sorgum vulgaris*); flood-tide; also *jawār*. *jo,ār-bhāṭā*, the flood-tide and ebb-tide. *juwār* or *jawār*, a species of millet. *juwār*, m. large maize. *h.*

جوارا जुवारा *juwārā*, m. large maize. *jawārā*, m. Indian corn; as much land as can be ploughed by a pair of bullocks. *h.*

جوارس *jawāras*, m. } a stomachic medicine,
جوارش *jawārish*, f. } the Arabic form of *gawārish* (q. v.) *a. p.*

جواري जुआरी *ju,ārī*, जूआरी *jū,ārī* or जुवारी *juwārī*, m. a gambler; a thread stretched over the bridge of a musical instrument, beneath the cords, whereby the sound is said to be improved. *h.*

جواري जवारी *jawārī*, f. great millet (v. *jawār* and *jārī*). *h.*

جواز *jawāz*, a wooden mortar; a sugar-mill; an oil-mill. *p.*

جواز *jawāz*, m. permission, lawfulness, propriety. *a.*

جوازيت *jawāzīyat*, legality, allowability. *a.*

جواس यवास *jawās*, } m. a prickly bush on
جواسا जवासा *jawāsā*, } which cattle and camels browse, and of which *ṭaṭṭīs* are made (*Hedysarum alhagi*). *s.*

جواكهار जवाखार *jawākhār*, name of a medicine; an impure species of saltpetre. *s.*

جوال *jawwāl*, one who travels about much. *jiwāl* (pl. of *jūl*), walls or parapets (of wells). *a.*

جوال *juwāl*, a bag, sack; the half of a (horse) load; the human body; deceit, fraud. *p.*

جوالا ज्वाला *jwālā*, f. flame, fire. *jwālā-jihvā*, flame-tongued, a name of Agni, or fire. *s.*

جوالا जवाला *jawālā*, m. grain mixed with barley, as food for cattle. *s.*

جوالامكهه ज्वालामुख *jwālā-mukh*, } f. a vol-
جوالامكهي ज्वालामुखी *jwālā-mukhī*, } cano, a place where inflammable gases break forth from the soil; especially one near Balkh, to which pilgrimages are made from Hindūstān. *s.*

جوالي जवाली *jawālī*, f. mixed wheat; gram mixed with barley as food for cattle. *h.*

جوان *jawān*, young, youthful; m. a youth, lad, man, adult. *jawān-bakht*, of blooming prospects. *jawān-pan* or *-panā*, m. youth. *jawānī ṣāliḥ*, m. a fine youth.—N. B. The term *jawān* agrees more nearly with the Latin "juvenis" than with our word "youth." *p.*

جوانا जिवाना *jiwānā*, a. (v. *jimānā*) to cause to live, to vivify, to feed, to foster. *s.*

جوانامرگ *jawānā-marg*, f. death in the bloom of youth. *jawānā-marg marnā*, n. to die prematurely. *p.*

جوانان *jawānān*, (Pers. pl.) youths, young men, heroes. *p.*

جوانانه *jawānāna*, bravely, gallantly, heroically. *p.*

جوانسا *jawānsā*, m. (v. *jawāsā*). *s.*

جوانكر जवाङ्कुर *jawānkur*, m. the young shoots of barley presented by Brāhmans to their disciples at the feast of Naurātr. *s.*

جوانمرد *jawān-mard*, brave, generous, manly; m. a fine young fellow, a brave fellow, a hero. *p.*

جوانمردي *jawān-mardī*, f. generosity, manliness, heroism. *p.*

جواني *jawānī*, f. youth, adolescence; season of youth: the term is nearly equivalent to what we call, "coming of age". *p.*

جواني यवानी *jawānī*, f. a plant (*Ligusticum ajwaen*). *s.*

جواني *jawānī*, f. a daughter's husband. *d.*

جواهر *jawāhir*, m. a jewel, essence, gem: it is, strictly speaking, the plural of *jauhar*, but in the Hindūstānī it is used singularly; hence the extra pl. form *jawāhirāt*, jewels, gems, &c. *a.*

جواهرخانه *jawāhir-khāna*, the jewel office, a storehouse for jewels. *a.p.*

جواهرنگار *jawāhir-nigār*, ornamented with jewels. *a.p.*

جواهري *jawāhirī*, a jeweller, dealer in jewels. *a.*

جواءي जवाई *jawā,ī*, m. a son-in-law. *s.*

جوبن जोबन *joban* or जौबन *jauban*, m. youth, puberty; (met.) breast, bubby. *joban-watī* or *-matī*, adj. f. at the age of puberty, fit to be married. *s.*

جوپ यूप *jūp*, m. a sacrificial post to which the victim is bound; a trophy; a column erected in honour of a victory. *s.*

جوپهل यवफल *jau-phal*, m. a medicinal plant (*Wrightea antidysenterica*). *s.*

جوت जोत *jot*, f. cultivation, cultivated land; tenure of a cultivator, also rent paid by the cultivator. *jot-dār*, a husbandman, one who has a tenure. *h.*

جوت जोत *jot* or जोति *joti* (for *jyoti*), f. brilliancy, lustre; the sunbeams; the flame of a candle or lamp; vision. *jot-mān*, luminous, bright. *joti-sarūp*, luminous (an epithet of God). *s.*

جوتا जोता *jotā*, the point of the beam of the plough on which the drag rests. *h.*

جوتا जूता *jūtā*, m. a shoe, a slipper: collectively, it means the "pair of shoes" or slippers: it also denotes the rope connecting the irrigating basket with the handle. *h.*

جوتا जोता *jotā*, جوتار जोतार *jotār*, جوتيا जोतिया *jotiyā*, m. a ploughman, a husbandman, a cultivator of land, tilling his own ground. *s.*

جوتخوره जूतखोरः *jūt-khora*, جوتن‌خوره जूतनखोरः *jūtan-khora*, one who has been beaten with slippers; adj. infamous, degraded. *h.*

جوتري जवत्री *jawatrī*, f. mace; the nutmeg. *s*

جوتش जोतिष *jotish*, m. astrology, astronomy. *s.*

جوتشي जोतिषी *jotishī*, relating to astrology; an astrologer, an astronomer. *s.*

جوتك जौतुक *jautuk* (v. *yautuk*), a nuptial present, dower. *s.*

جوتك जोतिक *jotik*, جوتكه जोतिष *jotikh*, m. astrology, astronomy. *jotik-bidyā*, the astronomical (or rather astrological) science. *s.*

جوتكهورا जूतखोरा *jūt-khorā*, beaten with slippers; infamous (v. *jūt-khora*). *s.*

جوتكهي जोतिषी *jotikhī*, جوتكي जोतिकी *jotikī*, m. an astrologer, an astronomer. *s.*

جوتمان जोतमान *jotmān*, splendid, bright. *s.*

جوتن जोतन *jotan*, m. ploughing; a ploughman. *s.*

جوتنا जोतना *jotnā*, a. to yoke; to plough, till. *s.*

جوته जूथ or यूथ *jūth*, m. a flock, herd; a multitude of birds; a company (v. *jathā*). *s.*

جوتهالي जूथाली *jūthālī*, also *jūthelī*, land bearing two harvests annually. *h.*

جوتهوار जूथवार *jūthwār*, corporate, joint, possessed in common. *h.*

جوتهي जूथी *jūthī*, f. a sort of jasmine (*Jasminum auriculatum*). *s.*

جوتي जूती *jūtī*, f. a shoe, a slipper. *jūtī-khor*, beaten with slippers; mean, abject. *jūtī-paizār*, f. a scuffle. *jūtī-kārī* or *jūtī-mār*, act of beating with slippers. *h.*

جوتي जोती *jotī*, f. the string which suspends the scale of a balance; the string which goes round the neck of a bullock to fasten the yoke. *h.*

جوتي जुवती or युवती *juvatī*, f. a young woman, one from sixteen to thirty; a damsel. *s.*

جوتيا जोतिया *jotiyā*, a ploughman (see *jotā*). *h.*

جوتيال जूतियाल *jūtiyāl*, a class of hereditary watchmen located in the tract under the Siwalik hills. *h.*

جوتيان जूतियां *jūtiyāṅ*, land bearing two crops in the course of one year. *h.*

جوتي‌سوروپ जोतिस्वरूप *joti-swarūp*, luminous, self-resplendent, an epithet of the Deity. *s.*

جوٹ जोट *joṭ*, m. a fellow, peer, one of a pair, a match; equal, even, not odd. *joṭ bāndhnā*, v. to pair. *h.*

جوٹ जूट *jūṭ*, m. the matted hair of Shiva; the clotted hair of an ascetic. *s.*

جوٹيال जूटियाल *jūṭiyāl* (v. *barwā,ek*), a kind of watchman. *h.*

جوجن जोजन or योजन *jojan* (for *yojan*), m. a measure of four *kos*; joining, union; the Supreme Being, the soul of the world. *s.*

جوجهنا जूझना *jūjhnā*, n. to fight; to be killed in battle. *jūjh-marnā*, to die fighting. *s.*

جوچني जौचनी *jau-chanī*, f. a mixed crop of barley and *chanā*. *h.*

جود *jūd*, m. a present, liberality, munificence, beneficence. *a.*

جودت *jaudat*, f. ingenuity, intelligence, quickness of apprehension, benignity. *a.*

جودها जोधा or योद्धा *joddhā*, m. a warrior, a hero, a brave fellow. *s.*

جودهاپن योधापन *jodhāpan*, m. heroism, bravery. *s.*

جودهن जोधन or योधन *jodhan*, m. fighting, battle. *s.*

جودهي योधी *jodhī*, m. a warrior. *s.*

جور *jaur*, m. violence, oppression. *jaur-pesha*, an oppressor, a tyrant. *a.*

جور ज्वर *jwar*, m. a fever. *jwar-nāshak*, antifebrile, febrifuge. *s.*

جوراپها ज्वरापहा *jwarāpahā*, f. a plant (*Medicago esculenta*). *s.*

جوراج जुवराज or युवराज *juva-rāj*, m. a king's son, the heir apparent, appointed to the empire. *s.*

جوراجيه युवराज्य *juva-rājya*, m. the dignity of heir apparent and associate in the throne. *s.*

جوراگن ज्वराग्नि *jwarāgni*, m. feverish heat, the hot paroxysm of fever. *s.*

جورو जोरू *jorū*, f. a wife, a woman. *h.*

جوري ज्वरी *jwarī*, febrile, feverish. *s.*

جوڑ जोड़ *jor*, m. junction, connexion; joints, joining, a patch, a seam, society. *jor-denā*, a. to cast up, to add the sum. *jor-tor*, m. contrivance, mechanism, joining. *jor-jār*, m. savings, collecting by small quantities, scraping together. *h.*

جوڑ जूड़ *jūr*, cold; m. coldness, the cold. *h.*

جوڑا जूड़ा *jūrā*, m. cold; the hair done up in a knot behind; the hinder part of a turban; a rope of grass (v. *jūna*). *h.*

جوڑا जोड़ा *jorā*, m. joining, connexion; a pair, a couple; a pair of shoes; a suit (of clothes); alchymy; a rope of twisted grass made to support a round-bottomed jar. *h.*

جوڑا जिवड़ा *jivrā*, m. life, soul; sweetheart, beloved; annual wages to washermen, &c. *h.*

جوڑائي जोड़ाई *jorā,ī*, f. the act or profession of joining, &c.; price of joining. *h.*

جوڑتي जोड़ती *jortī*, f. calculation, reckoning. *h.*

جوڑگڑتي *jor-gartī*, f. a companion, consort; wife. *d.*

جوڑن जोड़न *joran*, m. solder; rennet. *joran-hārā*, a joiner. *h.*

جوڑنا जोड़ना *jornā*, a. to join, to mend, to patch; to add together; to reckon, to add up; to get or rather to save and scrape a fortune, &c., to fabricate, to cement, to solder, to unite, to tie, to invent, to contrive. *h.*

جوڑوان *jorwān*, f. a companion, helpmate, consort, wife. *d.*

جوڑي जोड़ी *jorī*, f. a pair, a couple; a small pond. *s.*

جوڑي जूड़ी *jūrī*, f. an ague; a small bundle of sugar-cane (v. Wilson's Glossary). *h.*

جوڑيماري जूड़ीमारी *jūrīmārī*, f. land in actual possession. *h.*

جوز *jauz*, m. a nut; nutmeg. *jauzu-l-māsal*, the thorn-apple. *a.*

جوزا *jauzā*, m. the sign Gemini; also Orion. *a.*

جوس जूस or यूष *jūs*, m. broth (Lat. *jus*), pease-soup, pease-porridge; the water in which pulse has been boiled.

جوسق *jausak*, a palace; a lofty edifice. *a.*

جوسي जोसी *josī* or जोषी *joshī*, m. an astrologer, an astronomer. *s.*

جوسي जोसी *josī*, m. the name of a tribe of Hindūs. *h.*

جوش *josh*, m. heat; ebullition; passion; lust. *josh-kharosh*, m. anger, passion, rage. *joshi khūn*, m. ebullition of the blood (the name of a disease). *p.*

جوش जूष *jūsh*, broth (see *jūs*). *s.*

جوشان *joshān*, boiling, foaming (as waves). *p.*

جوشانده *joshānda*, m. a decoction. *p.*

جوشت योषित *joshit*, f. a woman. *s.*

جوشش *joshish*, f. heat, ebullition; violent desire, fervour, emotion. *p.*

جوشن *jaushan*, m. a cuirass, armour, coat of mail. *p.*

جوشي जोषी *joshī*, m. an astrologer, a low caste of Brāhmans employed in casting nativities. *s.*

جوشيدن *joshīdan*, to boil, to foam; met. to be enraged. *p.*

جوع *jū'*, f. hunger, appetite. *jū'u-l-bakar* or *jū'u-l-kalb*, voracious, gluttonous. *a.*

جوف *jauf*. m. the interior cavity (of any thing; hence a drum called *mujawwaf*). *a.*

جوق *jauk*, m. a troop or body of men. *jauk jauk*, in troops. *a.*

جوك जोंक *jok*, f. a leech, v. *jonh*. *s.*

جوكا यूका *jūkā*, f. a louse. *s.*

جوكنا *johnā* (for *jokhnā*), to weigh. *d.*

جوكوب *jau-kob*, half-pounded, coarsely ground (q. d. reduced to particles like barleycorns). *p.*

جوكه जोख *jokh*, f. weight, weighing. *h.*

جوكهار यवक्षार *javakhār*, m. saltpetre, nitre, nitrate of potash. *s.*

جوکهاءي जोखाई *johkhā,ī*, f. a weighman's perquisite. *h.*

جوکهم जोखिम *johkim*, f. a risk, venture, peril, achievement, enterprise. *jokhim uṭhānā*, n. to run the hazard, to venture. *h.*

جوکهمي जोखिमी *johhimī*, m. one who risks. *h.*

جوکهنا जोखना *johhnā*, a. to weigh. *h.*

جوکهون जोखों *johhoṅ*, f. a risk, venture; danger, harm, damage. *h.*

جوگ जोग or योग *jog*, m. junction, union, meeting; fitting; a fortunate moment, opportunity; penance, devotion; spiritual worship, or union with the Supreme Being by means of abstract contemplation; certain divisions of a great circle, measured upon the ecliptic (see Asiat. Res. vol. ix. p. 365); propriety, fitness; adj. possible, capable, fit. In comp. it answers to our termination *able*, in the sense of fitness, as *bar-jog*, marriageable (lit. fit for a husband). *s.*

جوگ जोग *jog*, the name of the person upon whom a draft or bill of exchange is drawn. *h.*

جوگا जोगा *jogā* (for *yogya*), fit, proper, able, capable, adequate, advisable, apposite. *s.*

جوگابهياس जोगाभ्यास *jogābhyās*, m. life and practice of a devotee, penance, austerity. *s.*

جوگاسن योगासन *jogāsan*, m. the position in which the devotee sits to perform the *jog* or religious meditation. *s.*

جوگپٿ योगपट्ट *jog-paṭṭ*, m. a cloth drawn round the lower extremities of a squatting ascetic. *s.*

جوگت जुगत *jūgat*, f. manner, mode; skill, cleverness; a pun, or double meaning. *jūgat-bāz*, a punster, or rather one who is fond of uttering double meanings. *jūgat-bāzī*, punning. *s. p.*

جوگتا जोगता *jogtā* (for *yogyatā*), f. suitableness, capability, ability, fitness. *s.* [&c. *h.*

جوگتي जुगती *jūgatī* (v. *jugatī*), artful, clever,

جوگسيوا योगसेवा *jog-sevā*, f. practising religious abstraction. *s.*

جوگمايا जोगमाया or योगमाया *jog-māyā*, f. a deceptive power which *jogīs* are supposed to possess, a power of assuming various forms. *s.*

جوگن जोगिन *jogin*, f. a female (of *jogī*, q.v.) devotee. *s.* [*rus ascita*). *s.*

جوگناوك योगनाविक *jognāvik*, m. a fish (*Silu-*

جوگ‌ندرا योगनिद्रा *jog-nidrā*, f. light sleep, wakefulness. *s.*

جوگني जोगनी *jognī* or जोगिनी, योगिनी *joginī*, f. a class of female deities attendant on the goddess *Debī*, a female fiend or sprite; in astrology, spirits governing periods of good and ill luck. *s.*

جوگواهي योगवाही *jog-vāhī*, m. a menstruum or medium for mixing medicines; f. alkali; quicksilver. *s.*

جوگي जोगी or योगी *jogī*, m. a Hindū ascetic; a magician, a conjuror; a caste of Hindūs who are commonly weavers. (The people of this caste do not burn, but bury their dead, and the women are sometimes buried alive with their husband's corpse). *s.*

جوگيا जोगिया *jogiyā*, m. name of a colour; f. the name of a *rāginī* or musical mode; a kind of pigeon. *h.*

جوگيتا योग्यता *jogyatā*, f. fitness, ability. *s.*

جوگيسر जोगेसर *jogesar*, } m. a devotee, an
جوگيش जोगेश *jogesh*, } adorer. *s.*

جوگيشور योगेश्वर *jogeshwar*, m. a name of *Shiva*; a devotee, an adorer; a magician. *s.*

جوگيه जोग्य or योग्य *jogya*, accomplished, fit, capable. *s.*

جول ज्वल *jwal*, m. flame, blaze, light. *s.*

جول झूल *jūl*, } m. guile, fraud, deceit. *jolā*
جولا जोला *jolā*, } *denā*, a. to deceive. *iolā* or *jūlā*, a land measure of sixteen *bisīs*. *h.*

جولان *jaulān*, moving, springing, wandering. *jaulān-gāh*, f. a place for (military) exercise, a playground. *jaulān-garī*, f. galloping fast, fleetness. *p.*

جولان *jawalān*, walking round; motion, agitation. *a.*

جولاني *jolānī*, f. strength of mind (or body), quickness of apprehension; fleetness. *p.*

جولاه *jolāh*, also *jūlāha*, *jūlāhī*, and *jūlā,ī*, a weaver (v. *julāh*). [fire. *s.*

جولت ज्वलित *jwalit*, burnt, consumed by

جولکا ज्वलका *jwalkā*, f. flame. *s.*

جولگ जौलग *jau-lag* (for *jab-lag*), until, as long as. *h.* [or fire. *s.*

جولن ज्वलन *jwalan*, burning, blazing; Agni

جوله जोला *jola* or *jūla*, a tract of land containing sixteen *bisīs*. *h.*

جولي जोली *jolī*, m. a companion, a playfellow. *h.*

جوليده *jolīda*, scattered, confused. *p.*

جومدهيه यवमध्य *jau-madhya*, m. a form of penance, diminishing the food daily during the dark fortnight, fasting on the new moon, and gradually augmenting the food till the full moon. *s.*

جون जों *joṅ*, as, when. *joṅ-toṅ*, as before, "in statu quo;" in some way. *joṅ toṅ karke*, in any way, by any means, as it could be done. *joṅ kā toṅ*, unaltered, "in statu quo." *h.*

جون जूं *jūṅ*, f. a louse. *jūṅ-munhā*, smooth-faced, hypocritical (lit. with a small mouth). *h.*

جون जौन *jaun*, (rel. pro.) he who, that which. *h.*

جون जून *jūn* or जौन *jaun*, m. time. *h.*

جون जवन or यवन *javan* (for *yavana*), m. a Greek, or a Musalmān; the country Ionia or Greece; a courser, a fleet horse. *s.*

جون जोन *jon* or जोनि, योनि *joni*, m. f. *pudendum mulieris*. *jaun*, m. *jaunī*, f. belonging to the womb or place of origin, uterine; connected by female alliance. *s.*

جونا जूना *jūnā*, m. a rope of grass; a ring of twisted grass laid under a round-bottomed jar to prevent it from oversetting. *h.*

جونار जौनार *jaunār*, f. a feast, entertainment; land ready for the seed. *s.*

جونال जौनाल *jaunāl*, land in constant cultivation, or cultivated alternately for spring and autumn crops. *h.*

جونتري *jauṅtarī*, mace (spice so called). *d.*

جونچي जौंची *jauṅchī*, a kind of disease in barley or wheat, the ears producing no grain. *h.*

جونڈري जौंडरी *jaunḍrī*, } f. the name of a grain (*jū,ar* or *jo,ar*, *Holcus sorgum*). *h.*
جونڈي जौंडी *jaunḍī*,
جونري जूनरी *jūnrī*,

جونڑا जौंड़ा *jauṅṛā*, payment of village servants in kind. *h.*

جونرا بهونرا जौंरा भौंरा *jauṅrā-bhauṅrā*, m. retirement, privacy. *h.*

جونك जोंक *jonk*, f. a leech: *jonk lagānā*, a. to apply leeches. *s.*

جونكر जोंकर *joṅkar*, in any way, by any means. *h.*

جونكنا जौंकना *jauṅknā*, a. to rail, to scold. *h.*

جونگك जोङ्गक *jongak*, m. aloe wood or agallochum. *h.*

جون لنگ योनिलिङ्ग *joni-ling*, m. the clitoris. *s.*

جون ناسا योनिनासा *joni-nāsā*, f. the upper part of the vulva, or the union of the labia. *s.*

جونهين जोंहीं *joṅhīṅ*, as soon as, the moment when. *h.*

جونيرسا योन्यर्शा *jonyarsā*, m. an affection of the vulva, menorrhagia or prolapsus uteri. *s.*

جووا जुवा *jūwā*, m. a yoke. *s.*

جووت जोवत *jowat*, looking, seeing (pres. part. of *jowanauṅ*). *h.*

جوون यौवन *jauvan*, m. youth, manhood. *jauvan-darp*, m. pride of youth, rashness, conceit. *jauvan-dasā*, f. the period of youth. *jauvan-wān*, m., *jauvan-vatī*, f. youthful. *s.*

جوونون जोवनौं *jowanauṅ* (Braj.), to look, to see. *h.*

جوه जूह *jūh*, m. a yoke. *s.*

جوها जिह्वा *jivhā*, f. tongue (see *jihvā*). *s.*

جوهر *jauhar*, m. a gem, jewel, pearl; bright, glittering; skill, knowledge; matter, substance, essence (distinguished from accident); virtue, worth, merit; blackish marks in the steel of well-tempered scimitars. *jauhar-dār*, a scimitar marked with *jauhar*. *a.*

جوهر *johar* or *jūhar*, name given to an act of desperation peculiar to the Hindūs. When in a siege the men find themselves unable to resist their assailants, as a last resource they destroy all their wives and children within the place; then, sword in hand, they desperately meet the foe, and fight to the last. *johar-k.*, a. to kill one's self, to commit suicide. *p.*

جوهر जोहर *johar*, a large pond or lake; inundated land. *h.*

جوهرات *jauharāt* (pl. of *jauhar*), gems, jewels, &c. *a.*

جوهرفرد *jauhari fard*, m. an indivisible atom; (met.) a person unrivalled or unequalled. *a.*

جوهري *jauharī*, m. a jeweller, a lapidary; adj. essential. *a.*

جوهڑ जूहड़ *jūhaṛ* or जोहड़ *johaṛ*, m. pits filled with water at the bottom of mountains; a large pond or lake. *h.*

جوهنا जोहना *johnā*, a. to expect, to look out for. *h.*

جوهي जूही *jūhī*, f. jasmine (*Jasminum auriculatum*); a kind of fireworks. *s.*

جوهيا जोहिया *johiyā*, name of a tribe of *rājpūts*. *h.*

جوئي जोय *jo,e* or *joya*, f. a wife. *s.*

جوئي *jo,e* or *jū,e*, f. a rivulet, a brook. *p.*

جوئي जूई *jū,ī*, an insect destructive to certain crops. *h.*

جويا *joyā*, } one who searches for; an inquirer; a seeker. *joyanda yābanda*, lit. the seeker (is a) finder, *i.e.* search and you shall find. *p.* [*jū,ā*). *s.p.*
جويان *joyān*,
جوينده *joyanda*,

جوئباز *jū,e-bāz*, a dice player, a gambler (v.

جوئيدن *jo,īdan*, to seek, to search. *p.*

جوين *jauwīn*, made of barley (bread). *p.*

جه झ *jha*, the aspirate form of ج ज *ja*. *s.h.*

جها झहा *jahā*, f. a plant, the flowers of which resemble those of the *kadamb*. *s.*

جهابا झाबा *jhābā*, m. a leathern pot for measuring oil, *ghī*, &c. *h.*

جهابر झाबर *jhābar*, f. marshy land on which water lies, and which produces rice. *h.*

جهاپ *jhāp* (for *jhāṅp*), a matted shutter. *h.*

جهاپا झापा *jhāpā*, m. a narrow-mouthed basket. *h.*

جهاپنا *jhāpnā* (for *jhāṅpnā*), to cover, &c. *h.*

جهات *jihāt*, duties on manufactures. *a.*

جهاٹ झाट *jhāṭ*, m. an arbour, a bower, a place overgrown with creepers, a thicket. *s.*

جهاٹا झाटा *jhāṭā*, f. jasmine. *s.*

جهاٹيكا झाटीका *jhāṭīkā*, f. a plant (*Flacourtia catafracta*). *s.*

جهاج *jahāj* (for *jahāz*), a ship. *a.*

جهاجها झाझा *jhājhā*, m. an intoxicating mixture, made with *bhang* or hemp. *h.*

جهاجهر झाझर *jhājhar*, m. cymbals or bells for the ankles. *s.*

جهاد झाद *jhād*, land on which jungly bushes grow. *h.*

جهاد *jihād*, m. war (especially that which is waged by Musalmāns against infidels or idolaters). *a.*

جهاڈ *jhāḍ*, (in Dakh.) a tree in general. *d.*

جهاڈا झाडा *jhāḍā*, land which remains under water during the rains; a swamp. *h.*

جهار जुहार *juhār*, f. Hindū salutation, obeisance. *h.*

جهاري झारी *jhārī*, m. a pitcher with a long neck and a spout to it, an ewer; (for *jhāṛī*) forest, wood, underwood. *h.*

جهاڑ झाड़ *jhāṛ*, m. bushes, brambles, bush, shrub, underwood; a kind of fireworks; a lustre or chandelier, the same as *pan-shākha*, q. v.; a purge; continued rain. *jhāṛ bāndhnā*, to rain without ceasing. *jhāṛ-pahāṛ*, digression. *jhāṛ-phūnk*, f. juggling, conjuring, hocus-pocus (particularly to cure the bite of a snake or a disease). *jhāṛ-jhaṭak*, f. sweeping. *jhāṛ-jhankhār*, m. brambles a purge. *jhāṛ-jhūṛ*, f. sweepings; perquisites; a thicket. *jhāṛ-kā-namak*, potass, impure carbonate of potass. *jhāṛ-khanḍ*, full of brambles, &c. bushy; the forest of *Baijnāth*. "In southern India *jhāṛ* denotes a tree in general; as the words *darakht*, *per*, *gāchh*, &c. do in the north"—(Binning). *h.*

جهاڑا झाड़ा *jhāṛā*, m. a stool, purge. *jhāṛā-jhapṭe-jānā*, n. to go to the necessary. *jhāṛā-jhapṭā lenā*, a. to search. *dūkān-jhāṛā*, m. sweeping of a (druggist's) shop, compound medicine. *jhāṛā phirnā* or *jhāṛā jhuṭkā phirnā*, a. to walk among the bushes, which means to go to the necessary. *jhāṛā denā*, n. to submit to search. *h.*

جهاڑدينا झाड़देना *jhāṛ-denā*, } a. to sweep
جهاڑڈالنا झाड़डालना *jhāṛ-ḍālnā*, } out or away,
to brush, to clear away. *h.*

جهاڑکهنڈ झाड़खड *jhāṛ-khanḍ*, adj. bushy; m. a forest, the forest of *Baijnāth*. *s.*

جهاڑن झाड़न *jhāṛan*, f. sweepings; a coarse cloth for wiping furniture, a dishclout. *h.*

جهاڑنا झाड़ना *jhāṛnā*, a. to sweep, to brush, to shift, to clean; to strain, knock off, dash, flap; to strike fire (as with a flint), to beat (bushes &c.). *jhāṛ-pachhoṛ-kar dekhnā*, to test, try, examine. *jhāṛnā phūnknā*, to exorcise, to repeat spells. *jhāṛ denā*, a. to brush, to clear away. *jhāṛ ḍālnā*, to sweep out or away. *h.*

جهاڑنت झाड़न्त *jhāṛant*, entirely. *h.*

جهاڑو झाड़ू *jhāṛū*, m. f. a broom, a sweeper by caste and occupation; a comet. *jhāṛū-kash* or *-bardār*, m. a sweeper; the caste of *ḥalāl khor*, q. v. *h.*

جهاڑي झाड़ी *jhāṛī*, f. forest, wood, underwood, brushwood, bush, brake, shrub. *h.*

جهاز *jahāz*, m. a ship, the tree of a camel's saddle; a portion in the disposal of the wife; funeral apparatus; *vulva, pudenda mulieris*. *jahāz par*, aboard. *jahāz-shikanī*, f. shipwreck. *a.*

جهازي *jahāzī*, m. a sailor; f. a kind of scimitar; adj. naval, nautical. *a.*

جهاكري झाकरी *jhākarī*, } f. a kind of milk-
جهاكڑي झाकड़ी *jhākaṛī*, } pail. *h.*

جهاگ झाग *jhāg*, m. foam, froth (of the ocean), scum. *h.*

جهال झाल *jhāl*, m. sharpness, heat, fieryness (as of pepper); acrimony; a large basket; joining or soldering of metals. *h.*

جهال *juhhāl* (pl. of جاهل), ignorant (people), fools, simpletons. *a.*

جهالت *jahālat*, f. brutality, barbarism, ignorance. *a.*

جهالر झालर *jhālar*, f. a fringe. *jhālar-dār*, having a fringe, mounted with a fringe *h.*

جهالرا झालरा *jhālrā*, m. a spring (of water). *h.*

جهالري झालरी *jhālrī*, f. cymbals. *h.*

جهالنا झालना *jhālnā*, a. to season (pickles); to polish, to clean (plate); to solder. *h.*

جهام झाम *jhām*, a large instrument in the shape of a hoe used for excavating earth in well-sinking. *h.*

جهاما झामा *jhāmā*, m. pumice-stone, bricks burnt to cinder. *h.*

جهامر झामर *jhāmar*, m. a small whetstone, used chiefly by housewifes for sharpening their spindles, needles, &c. *s.*

جهامك झामक *jhāmak*, m. a burnt or vitrified brick. *s.*

جهان *jahān*, m. the world. *jahān jahān*, much, many. *jahān-āfirīn*, the creator of the world. *jahān-bān*, a sovereign. *jahān-bīn*, world-seeing, the Almighty; a traveller. *jahān-panāh*, asylum of the world, (addressed to kings) your majesty, sire. *jahān-tāb*, warming the world (the sun). *jahān-soz*, world-inflaming. *jahān-gīr*, world-grasping; name of a Great Mogul, the contemporary of James the First. *jahān-dār*, ruler of the world, world-possessor, a king. *jahān-dārī*, f. sovereign power. *jahān-dīda*, one who has seen the world, experienced. *jahān-gard*, m. a traveller. *jahān-numā*, world-exhibiting (a lofty tower, &c.). *p.*

جهان जहाँ *jahān*, where, wheresoever, in the place which. *jahāṅ tahāṅ*, wherever, where, there, here and there. *jahāṅ tahāṅ phirnā*, n. to straggle, to wander. *jahāṅ-jahāṅ*, wherever. *jahāṅ kā tahāṅ*, everywhere, in the same place as before. *jahāṅ kahīṅ*, wherever. *jahāṅ tak*, as far as. *jahāṅ se*, whence. *h.*

جهانپ झाँप *jhāmp*, m. a matted shutter; (in Dakh.) a large cage or inclosure of wicker-work for keeping fowls, &c. *s.*

جهانپنا झाँपना *jhāmpnā*, a. to cover, to shut. *h.*

جهانٹ झाँट *jhānṭ*, f. the hair of the private parts; *pubes*. *h.*

جهانجه झाँझ *jhānjh*, f. anger, passion, pet, rage; stillness, dreariness; impatience (in a horse expecting his corn). *h.*

جهانجه झाँझ *jhānjh*, f. cymbals. *s.*

جهانجها झाँझा *jhānjhā*, m. the name of an insect, caterpillar, cabbage-worm. *h.*

جهانجهٹ झाँझट *jhānjhaṭ*, m. wrangling, squabbling, quarrelling. *s.*

جهانجهي झाँझी *jhānjhī*, f. a kind of play (children in the month of *āsin* go about at night, dancing, begging, and carrying on their heads earthen pots perforated on all sides, within which lamps are kept burning). *h.*

جهانجهيا झाँझिया *jhānjhiyā*, passionate, furious. *h.*

جهاندن *jahāndan*, to cause to leap; to urge on (a horse). *p.*

جهانسا झाँसा *jhānsā*, m. love, lust, desire; eagerness. *h.*

جهانسنا झांसना *jhānsna*, a. to debauch, to seduce, to wheedle, to coax; to be inclined, to be agog, to be intent or set on, to covet. *s.*

جهانسو झांसू *jhānsū*, m. a flatterer, a seducer. *h.*

جهانسه झांसा *jhānsa* or *jhānsā*, m. an assessment formed by general estimate without regular data. *h.* [deer, flock of birds, &c. *h.*

جهانك झांक *jhānk*, f. a peep; m. a herd of

جهانك जहानक *jahānak*, m. the period of the total destruction of the world. *s.*

جهانكا جهونكي झांकाझोंकी *jhānka-jhonkī*, f. peeping. *h.* [underwood. *h.*

جهانكڑ झांकड़ *jhānkaṛ*, m. bushes, brambles,

جهانكنا झांकना *jhānknā*, a. to peep, to spy. *h.*

جهانكه झांख *jhānkh*, m. a kind of deer. *h.*

جهانگي झांगी *jhāngī*, a kind of bramble and brushwood. *h.*

جهانگير *jahān-gīr*, (lit.) the seizer of the world; (met.) a sovereign; also the name of one of the Great Moguls, the son and successor of Akbar. *p.*

جهانگيري *jahān-gīrī*, f. the name of a sort of bracelet; adj. of or relating to Jahāngīr; royal, princely. *p.*

جهانوا झांवा *jhānwā*, } m. pumice-stone;
جهانوان झांवां *jhānwān*, } bricks burnt to cinders. *s.*

جهانورا झांवरा *jhānwrā*, black, dusky. *h.*

جهانولي झांवली *jhānwlī*, f. a wink, coquetry; hot wind. *jhānwlī-bāz*, a coquette. *jhānwlī lenā*, a. to ogle. *h.*

جهاني *jahānī*, worldly, a human being. *p.*

جهانيان *jahāniyān*, pl. mortals, creatures, worldly people. *p.*

جهانيدن *jahānīdan*, to impel, to cause to leap, to put to the gallop (a horse). *p.*

جهاءو झाउ *jhā,ū* or झावु *jhāwu*, m. name of the tamarisk-tree, called also in Persian *shora-gaz*, from its growing in marshy ground (*Tamarix Indica* or *Divica*), (in Arabic) *aṡl*. *s.*

جهاور झावर *jhāwar*, flat or low land flooded by the rains, same as *jhābar*. *h.*

جهاءين झाईं *jhā,īn*, f. shadow; a freckle or black mark on the face (not a mole). *h.*

جهبا झब्बा *jhabbā*, m. a tassel. *h.*

جهبرا झबरा *jhabrā*, covered with long hair (the ears of animals). *h.*

جهبكانا झबकाना *jhabkānā*, a. to astonish. *h.*

جهبوءا झबूआ *jhabū,ā* or *jhabbū,ā*, long-haired (cattle or dogs); bent, curved, bending as the bough of a tree. *h.*

جهبي झब्बी *jhabbī*, f. trappings. *h.*

جهبيا झबिया *jhabiyā*, m. the name of an ornament. *h.*

جهپ झप *jhap*, a trice, quick; quickly. *jhap-se*, quickly. *jhap-khānā*, n. to be overset (a paper kite in flying). *h.*

جهپاٹ झपाट *jhapāṭ*, f. quickness. *h.*

جهپا جهپي झपाझपी *jhapā-jhapī*, f. haste, hurry. *h.*

جهپاس झपास *jhapās*, f. a shower. *h.*

جهپاسيا झपासिया *jhapāsiyā*, deceitful, fraudulent. *h.*

جهپانا झपाना *jhapānā*, n. to take a nap. *h.*

جهپٹ झपट *jhapaṭ*, f. a snatch, a spring (as of a tiger). *jhapaṭ-lenā*, a. to snatch, to seize. *h.*

جهپٹا झपट्टा *jhapaṭṭā*, m. assault, sudden attack; the spring of a tiger; a snatch. *jhapaṭṭā mārnā*, a. to snatch. *h.*

جهپٹنا झपटना *jhapaṭnā*, n. to snatch, to spring, to attack suddenly, to pounce upon, to fly at. *h.*

جهپك झपक *jhapak*, f. act of fanning, winking, &c. *h.*

جهپكا झपका *jhapkā*, m. a snatch, spring (v. *jhapkī*), a puff or gust of wind. *a.*

جهپكانا झपकाना *jhapkānā*, a. to wink, to twinkle. *h.*

جهپكنا झपकना *jhapaknā*, n. to fan, to move to and fro (a fan); to spring (as a tiger); to snatch; to wink. *h.*

جهپكي झपकी *jhapkī*, f. a snatch, a spring (as of a tiger), drowsiness, wink, twinkle. *h.*

جهپلانا झपलाना *jhaplānā*, a. to wash, to rinse. *h.*

جهپيٹ *jhapeṭ*, } Dakhanī forms of *jhapaṭ*,
جهپيٹنا *jhapeṭnā*, } &c. q. v. *d.*

جهت *jihat*, f. account, cause, reason; side, surface, form, manner, mode. *a.*

جهٹ झट *jhaṭ*, quick, quickness. *jhaṭ-se* or *jhaṭ-paṭ*, quickly, hastily. *s.* [bush. *s.*

جهٹ झटि *jhaṭi*, m. a small tree, a shrub, a

جهٹاس झटास *jhaṭās*, m. flap, clap, a shower of rain blown with a strong wind. *h.*

جهٹالنا झुटालना *jhuṭālnā*, a. to assert falsely, to pretend; to prove to be false, to prove one in the wrong; to pollute victuals by touching them, &c. *muṅh jhuṭālnā*, a. to eat something. *muṅhā-muṅh jhuṭālnā*, a. to give a man the lie before his face. *h.*

جهٹ پٹ झटपट *jhaṭ-paṭ*, quickly, hastily. *s.*

جهٹتي झटिति *jhaṭiti*, quickly, instantly. *s.*

جهٹك झटक *jhaṭak*, f. twitch, stitch, toss, throw, jerk, shake. *h.*

جهٹكا झटका *jhaṭkā*, that which is beheaded or torn to pieces; torn by a sudden jerk; (in Dakh.) a shake, a sudden jerk or knock. *jhaṭkā karnā*, a. to steal, to pilfer; to make haste. *h.*

جهٹكانا झटकाना *jhaṭkānā*, a. to shake. *h.*

جهٹکنا झटकना *jhaṭaknā*, a. to touse, to shake, pull, jerk; n. to shake, to become lean. *jhaṭak lenā*, a. to snatch. *h.* [to belie, to falsify. *h.*

جهٹلانا झुटलाना *jhuṭlānā*, also *jhuṭhlānā*, a.

جهٹنا *jhaṭnā*, n. to become thin, to diminish; to argue, to dispute. *s.*

جهٹهالنا झुठालना *jhuṭhālnā*, } to falsify, &c.
جهٹهلانا झुठलाना *jhuṭhlānā*, } (same as *jhuṭālnā*, q. v.)

[*rājpūts* in the upper Duāb. *h.*

جهٹیانا झटियाना *jhaṭiyānā*, a small clan of

جهجنا *jhijnā*, n. to become lean, to pine. *d.*

جهجه झझ *jhajh*, m. a long beard. *h.*

جهجها झझा *jhajhā*, a violent wind with rain. *h.*

جهجهر झज्झर *jhajjhar*, m. a goglet. *h.*

جهجهرکا झझरका *jhajharkā*, } m. early dawn
جهجهلکا झझलका *jhajhalkā*, } before it is easy to distinguish objects. *s.*

جهجهری झझरी *jhajhrī*, a window, a lattice. *h.*

جهجهک झिझक *jhijhak*, f. start. *h.*

جهجهکانا झिझकाना *jhijhkānā*, n. to start. *h.*

جهجهکارنا झझकारना *jhajhkārnā*, a. to browbeat, to speak snappishly. *h.*

جهجهکنا झिझकना *jhijhaknā*, also *jhujhaknā*, n. to start, to feel the sensation of the limbs being asleep, or as if pins and needles were striking into them. *h.* [meat. *h.*

جهجهلا झझला *jhajhlā*, m. a kind of sweet-

جهجهلکا झझलका *jhajhalkā* (v. *jhajharkā*). *h.*

جهد *jihd* or *jahd*, m. struggle, endeavour, exertion, effort, diligence, care, application, assiduity. *a.*

جهر *jihar*, m. a female oblation. *jhar*, speaking loud enough to be heard by the company. *a.*

جهر झर *jhar*, f. heavy rain, the heat from a fire. *jhar-barnā*, to burn furiously, to be all in flames. *h.*

جهربیری *jharberī* (v. *jharber*), the jujube. *h.*

جهرا *jharrā*, m. a spring, a fountain, a jet d'eau. *d.*

جهرپهنا झरफना *jharaphnā*, n. to spar, to fight (as cocks, &c.), to contend. *h.*

جهرجهر झरझर *jharjhar*, m. a goglet. *h.*

جهرجهر झिरझिर *jhir-jhir*, running in a slender stream (water, &c.). *h.*

جهرجهرا झिरझिरा *jhir-jhirā*, very thin. *s.*

جهرجهرانا झिरझिराना *jhirjhirānā*, n. to trickle, to rill, to flow in a small stream. *s.*

جهرمٹ झुरमट *jhurmaṭ*, m. a multitude, crowd, assembly, ball; a battle, conflict; a shawl twisted round the head. *h.*

جهرمٹانا *jhurmuṭānā*, n. to fade, decay. *d.*

جهرنا झरना *jharnā*, m. a skimmer; a spring, a cascade; n. to spring, to flow; to fall off (as fruit leaves, &c., from the tree). *h.*

جهرنا झुरना *jhurnā* n. to wither, to fade (from grief), to pine. *h.*

جهروا झरुवा *jharuwā* or झरुआ *jharū,ā*, m. a nutritious kind of grass resembling *panik*. *h.*

جهروکها झरोखा *jharokhā*, m. a lattice, a window. (in Dakh.) *jharūkā*, the same. *h.*

جهری झुरी *jhurī*, f. a wrinkle (of the body). *h.*

جهری झिरी *jhirī*, f. a cricket; withered wheat, blight. *h.*

جهریانا झुरियाना *jhuriyānā*, a. to weed; to wipe clean, and plaster a house, &c. *h.*

جهڑ झड़ *jhaṛ*, f. heavy rain; the heat from a fire; m. a kind of lock. *h.*

جهڑ झुड़ *jhuṛ*, m. a bush, a bramble. *h.*

جهڑاتا झड़ाता *jhaṛātā*, m. the close of the fruit season. *h.* [hurry. *s.*

جهڑاجهڑ झड़ाझड़ *jhaṛā-jhaṛ*, hastily, in a

جهڑاك झड़ाक *jhaṛāk*, } m. speed, haste,
جهڑاکا झड़ाका *jhaṛākā*, } hurry. *jhaṛāk-jhaṛāk*, in great haste. *h.*

جهڑاکها झड़ाखा *jhaṛākhā*, m. a skylight. *h.*

جهڑانا झड़ाना *jhaṛānā*, a. to get swept; to cause to be exorcised. *h.*

جهڑبرانا झड़बराना *jhaṛbarānā*, n. to burn, to be all in flames. *h.*

جهڑبیر झड़बेर *jhaṛ-ber*, m, } a wild ber-tree,
جهڑبیری झड़बेरी *jhaṛ-berī*, f. } jujubes (*Zizyphus jujuba*). *h.*
جهڑبیل झड़बेल *jhaṛ-bel*, f. }

جهڑپ झड़प *jhaṛap*, f. heat, fieryness (as of pepper), acrimony, contention. *h.*

جهڑپ *jhuṛup*, brushwood, bushes, underwood. *d.*

جهڑپاجهڑپی झड़पाझड़पी *jhaṛpā-jhaṛpī*, f. fighting (particularly birds), sparring. *h.*

جهڑپانا झड़पाना *jhaṛpānā*, a. to fight (cocks or other birds); to make to spar or contend. *h.*

جهڑپنا झड़पना *jhaṛapnā*, a. to spar, fight, contend. *h.*

جهڑت *jhaṛat*, falling off, &c. (v. *jhaṛan*). *d.*

جهڑتی لینا *jhaṛtī-lenā*, to take an account, to search, to rummage; to examine. *d.*

جهڑجهڑات *jhiṛjhiṛāṭ*, chiding, scolding. *jhaṛjhaṛāṭ*, flapping, shaking. *h.*

جهڑجهڑانا झिड़झिड़ाना *jhiṛjhiṛānā*, n. to be enraged, to rail, to storm. *h.*

جهڑجهڑانا झड़झड़ाना *jhaṛjhaṛānā*, a. to flap, to shake, to jerk. *h.*

جهڑك झिड़क *jhiṛak*, threat, augury, jerk. *h.*

جهڑکا جهڑکی झड़काझड़की *jhaṛkā-jhaṛkī* also *jhiṛkā-jhiṛkī*, f. mutual wrangling. *h.*

جهڑکنا झड़कना *jhaṛaknā* or झिड़कना *jhiṛakna* also *jhiṛkānā*, a. to browbeat, to speak snappishly, to threaten, to jerk. *h.*

جهڑکي झड़की *jhaṛkī* or झिड़की *jhiṛkī*, f. rebuff, snappishness, frowning, jerk, repercussion. *h.*

جهڑمتانا *jhuṛmutānā*, n. to wither, to fade. *d.*

جهڑن झड़न *jhaṛan*, f. the act of falling off (as fruit from the tree); snuff. *h.*

جهڑنا झड़ना *jhaṛnā*, n. to fall off (as fruit from the tree); to emit, to drop, to fall, to pour, to shake, to strain, to be sounded (the *naubat*), to be discharged (a volley). *h.*

جهڑوانا झड़वाना *jhaṛwānā*, to cause to be swept. *h.*

جهڑوتا झड़ोता *jhaṛotā*, m. the end of the season (of fruit, &c.); adj. going out of season. *h.*

جهڑي झड़ी *jhaṛī*, f. continued rain, showers, wet weather; perquisites; procession in honour of a saint, &c. *h.*

جهك झक *jhak*, f. passion, emotion. *jhak-mārnā*, a. to act fruitlessly, or absurdly, to talk nonsense. *jhak margī*, f. the acting fruitlessly or absurdly, talking nonsense, prattling. *h.*

جهكا جهك झकाझक *jhakā-jhak*, shining, glittering with gold and silver, &c., brocade. *h.*

جهكانا झुकाना *jhukānā*, a. to cause to stoop, to tilt, to bend downwards; to nod, or make nod. *h.*

جهكاو झुकाव *jhukāw* or *jhukā,o*, m. the state of being bent downwards. *h.*

جهكاوٹ झुकावट *jhukāwaṭ*, f. stooping, nodding. *h.*

جهك جهوري झकझोरी *jhak-jhorī*, f. scrambling and wrangling, snatching. *h.*

جهكري झकरी *jhakrī*, f. a milkpail (or vessel). *h.*

جهكڑ झक्कड़ *jhakkar*, m. a squall, a storm, a tempest, a "Nor-wester." *s.*

جهكنا झकना *jhaknā*, a. to rave, to chatter, to reflect, to lament. *h.*

جهكنا झुकना *jhuknā*, n. to nod, to bow, to stoop, to be bent downwards as the bough of a tree, to be tilted; to be angry, to be perplexed. *h.*

جهكني झुकनी *jhuknī*, f. affliction, suffering. *h.*

جهكور झकोर *jhakor*, f. loss, misfortune. *is be-ārāmī se bahut jhakor pā,ī*, this illness has reduced him much. *h.*

جهكورا झकोरा *jhakorā*, m. raining, a shower, a squall, a gust. *h.*

جهكورنا झकोरना *jhakornā*, a. to drive, as wind and rain in a squall, to shake. *h.*

جهكورنون झकोरनौं *jhakornaun* (Braj), v. *jhakornā*. *h.*

جهكول झकोल *jhakol*, f. the act of shaking in the water. *h.*

جهكولنا झकोलना *jhakolnā*, a. to shake. *h.*

جهكهنا झखना *jhakhnā*, n. to rave, to chatter, to weep. *h.*

جهكي झकी *jhakī*, passionate, wrathful. *h.*

جهكي झक्की *jhakkī*, m. one who talks to himself; a prater, an idle talker. *h.*

جهگا झगा *jhagā*, m. cloth; an upper garment or vest, a coat, a gown. *h.*

جهگڑ झगड़ *jhagaṛ*, m. a kind of hawk. *h.*

جهگڑا झगड़ा *jhagṛā*, m. wrangling, quarrelling, squabble, strife. *jhagṛā pakaṛnā*, a. to engage in another's quarrel. *jhagṛā-ragṛā*, m. squabbling and wrangling. *h.*

جهگڑانا झगड़ाना *jhagṛānā*, a. to set a-wrangling. *h.*

جهگڑالن झगड़ालिन *jhagṛālin*, f. } quarrelsome, contentious. *h.*
جهگڑالو झगड़ालू *jhagṛālū*, m. }

جهگڑنا झगड़ना *jhagaṛnā*, a. to wrangle, to quarrel, to cavil, to squabble. *h.*

جهگلا झगुला *jhagulā*, m. a child's frock or shirt. *h.*

جهل झल *jhal*, f. passion, anger, jealousy; the heat from a fire. *jhil* (v. *jhīl*), a morass, &c. *h.*

جهل *jahl*, m. ignorance, irreligion, stupidity. *a.*

جهلا झुल्ला *jhullā*, m. a shirt, or vest that covers the body from the shoulder downwards. *h.*

جهلا *juhalā*, (pl. of جاهل) ignorant people. *a.*

جهلابور झलाबोर *jhalābor*, splendid, shining, glittering with jewels; f. splendour. *s.*

جهلاجهل झलाझल *jhalājhal*, luminous, resplendent; f. splendour, glitter. *s.*

جهلار झलार *jhalār*, m. a thicket, a copse, underwood. *h.*

جهلانا झुलाना *jhulānā*, a. to swing, to shove a swing in which others are, to rock (a cradle); to dangle, to hang; to make another (as a dun) dance after one. *h.*

جهلانا झलाना *jhalānā*, a. to repair, to solder. *h.*

جهلجهل झलझल *jhaljhal*, m. glare, glitter. *h.*

جهلجهلانا झलझलाना *jhaljhalānā*, n. to glitter; to be in a passion; to throb, to ache, to smart. *h.*

جهلجهلاهٹ झलझलाहट *jhaljhalāhaṭ* (contr. *jhaljhalāṭ*), f. glitter, splendour; smarting. *h.*

جهلخانه *jhil-khāna*, jail-house. *d.*

جهلڈي *jhulḍī*, } f. a fold, wrinkle. *d.*
جهلڑي *jhulṛī*, }

جهلسانا झुलसाना *jhulsānā*, a. to cause to singe. *h.*

جهلس دينا झुलसदेना *jhulas-denā*, a. to sear, to singe. *h.*

جهلسنا झुलसना *jhulasnā* or झुलसजाना *jhulas jānā*, n. to be singed, scorched. *h.*

جهلك झलक *jhalak*, f. brightness, glitter, glare, refulgence; reflection of light. *jhuluk*, drowsiness, slumber. *h.*

جهلكا झलका *jhalkā*, }
جهلكاٹ झल्काट *jhalkāṭ*, } m. a blister. *h.*

جهلكار झलकार *jhalkār*, m. brightness, light, splendour. *h.* [to make bright, to burnish. *h.*

جهلكانا झलकाना *jhalkānā*, a. to cause to shine,

جهلكانا झुलकाना *jhulkānā*, a. to scorch, to singe (as the small feathers of a plucked fowl). *h.*

جهلكنا झलकना *jhalaknā*, n. to shine, to glare. *h.*

جهلكي झलकी *jhalkī*, f. a glance. *h.*

جهلگا झिलगा *jhilgā*, m. the netted bottom of a bed or couch when worn out and separated; adj. a couch or bed is said to be *jhilgā* when the bottom is worn out or broken. *h.*

جهلم झिलम *jhilam*, f. armour, a coat of mail; the vizor of a helmet. *jhilām kā ṭop*, an iron helmet. *h.* [crowd, &c. (v. *jhurmaṭ*). *h.*

جهلمٹ झुलमट *jhulmaṭ*, m. a multitude,

جهلمل झिलमिल *jhilmil*, m. a kind of gauze; a shutter, a Venetian blind *h.*

جهلملا झिलमिला *jhilmilā*, thin, sparkling. *h.*

جهلملانا झिलमिलाना *jhilmilānā*, n. to undulate, as the flame of a candle or as water, to twinkle, to scintillate. *h.*

جهلملي *jhilmilī*, a kind of cloth so called. *d.*

جهلنا झलना *jhalnā*, a. to fan, to move to and fro (as a fan); n. to be soldered or repaired. *h.*

جهلنا झुलना *jhulnā*, n. to swing, to dangle. *h.*

جهلنگ *jhilang*, of first rate quality, applied to cloth, &c. *d.*

جهلنگا झिलङ्गा *jhilangā*, m. a kind of soldier, also same as *jhilgā*, q. v. *h.*

جهلني *jhalnī*, f. a sieve (*ghirbāl*). *d.*

جهلوان झुल्वाँ *jhulwāṅ*, m. a wreath or garland of flowers. *h.* [*nā*, q.v.

جهلوانا झलवाना *jhalwānā*, a. causal of *jhal-*

جهلهايا झलहाया *jhalhāyā*, suspicious, jealous. *h.*

جهلي झिल्ली *jhillī*, f. a cricket. *s.*

جهلي झिल्ली *jhillī*, f. a thin skin, a pellicle; the membrane in which the fœtus is enveloped (*secundines*); the caul (*omentum*). *h.*

جهلي *jhullī*, a fold or wrinkle, plaits in cloth. *d.*

جهلي *jahlī*, lazy; passionate. *a.*

جهما جهم झमाझम *jhamā-jham*, raining heavily, and during the whole day. *h.*

جهماكا झमाका *jhamākā*, m. a heavy shower; quickness, haste. *h.*

جهم جهم झमझम *jham-jham*, heavy continued rain (v. *jhamā-jham*). *h.*

جهمجهمانا झमझमाना *jhamjhamānā*, n. to shine, to glitter, to sparkle; (in Dakh.) *jhumjhumānā*, to smart or feel (pain as after a blow), &c. *h.*

جهمر *jhammar*, a flight of birds, a swarm of flies, &c. *d.*

جهمر جهمر झमरझमर *jhamar-jhamar*, drop by drop (a kind of small rain). *h.*

جهمك झमक *jhamak*, f. glitter, splendour. *h.*

جهمكا झमका *jhamkā*, m. splendour, refulgence; the clash or clatter of metallic substances. *h.*

جهمكا झुमका *jhumkā*, m. the bell-shaped pendant of an ear-ring; the wain, *Ursa Major*; a bunch of flowers or fruit; name of a flower (*Gloriosa superba*). *h.*

جهمكانا झमकाना *jhamkānā*, a. to cause to shine, to make glitter, to cause to dance. *h.*

جهمكڑا झमकड़ा *jhamakṛā*, m. splendour, beauty. *h.* [dance. *h.*

جهمكنا झमकना *jhamaknā*, n. to glitter; to

جهمكي झमकी *jhamkī*, f. glare, lustre, brilliancy. *h.* [madan sect so called. *a.*

جهمي *jahmī* (properly *jahmīyat*) a Muham-

جهن झुन *jhun*, f. a slight resemblance. *h.*

جهن झन *jhan*, m. the sound of platters, or any vessel of metal, striking against one another, clash of arms, as swords, &c. *h.* [whom. *h.*

جهن जिहिं *jihiṅ*, inflect. pron. what, who,

جهن जह्नु *jahnu*, m. the name of a king or saint. *jahnu-tanyā*, f. (Jahnu's daughter) a name of the Ganges; Jahnu having drunk up its waters, and then released them at the intercession of the god, is considered the parent of the stream. *s.*

جهنٹ झुण्ट *jhunṭ*, m. a shrub, a bush. *s.*

جهنٹي झिण्टी *jhinṭī*, f. a shrub (*Barleria cristata*). *s.* [tribe, q. v. *h.*

جهنجر *jhinjar*, a subdivision of the *gūjar*

جهنجوتي *jhinjotī*, name of a musical mode. *d.*

جهنجور *jhinjūr* (also *jhinjur*), the morning twilight, or dawn of day. *d.*

جهنجوڑنا *jhinjoṛnā*, to gnaw, to pull asunder with the teeth, as a dog &c. does flesh. *d.*

جهنجها झञ्झा *jhanjhā*, f. wind, wind and rain, a gale; raining in large drops; a sharp clanging sound, jangling. *s.*

جهنجهانل झञ्झानिल *jhanjhānil* also *jhanjhāwāt*, m. wind with rain, a high wind in the rainy season, a typhoon or tempest frequent in the south-west monsoon. *s.* [perplexity, incumbrance, *h.*

جهنجهٹ झंझट *jhanjhaṭ*, m. wrangling;

جهنجهٹي झंझटी *jhanjhaṭī*, perplexing. *h.*

جهنجهري झञ्झरी *jhanjhrī*, f. a lattice. *h.*

جهنجهكار झंझकार *jhanjhkār*, f. clinking, tinkling, ringing. *s.*

جهنجهلانا झुञ्झलाना *jhunjhlānā*, n. to be peevish or fretful, to be petulant or irritable, to rage, to storm. *h.* [ness, rage, fury. *h.*

جهنجهلاهٹ झुञ्झलाहट *jhunjhlāhaṭ*, f. peevish

جهنجهن झनझन *jhan-jhan*, m. an indistinct noise like the jangling of metal ornaments, a ringing, a rattling. *s.*

جهنجهنا झुनझुना *jhunjhunā*, m. a child's rattle. *h.*

جهنجهنا झनझना *jhanjhanā*, peevish, fretful. *h.*

جهنجهنانا झनझनाना *jhanjhanānā* (also *jhunjhunānā*), n. to tinkle, to clink, to tingle, to ring, to rattle. *s.*

جهنجهناهٹ झनझनाहट *jhanjhanāhaṭ*, f. peevishness; clinking, tinkling. *h.*

جهنجهني झुनझुनी *jhunjhunī*, f. little bells worn on the feet. *h.*

جهنجهني झिनझिनी *jhinjhinī*, f. the tingling sensation felt when a limb is asleep. *h.*

جهنجهوڑنا *jhinjhoṛnā*, a. to break with the teeth, as a dog does a bone, &c. (v. *jhinjoṛnā*). *d.*

جهنجيا झंजिया *jhañjiyā*, a species of *ser* in the lower Duāb. *h.*

جهنڈ झुण्ड *jhunḍ*, m. crowd, swarm, flock; the buzzing noise of a crowd; a clump of trees. *jhunḍ ke jhunḍ*, dense crowds. *h.*

جهنڈا झण्डा *jhanḍā* or झुण्डा *jhunḍā*, m. a banner, a flag, an ensign, a streamer. *h.*

جهنڈو झण्डू *jhanḍū*, petals or foliage of a tree, &c.; a lock of hair. *h.*

جهنڈولا झण्डूला *jhanḍūlā*, with thick, handsome foliage (a tree); with a fine head of hair (a child). *h.*

جهنڈي झुण्डी *jhunḍī*, f. a bush, thicket, jungle, a tuft of grass. *jhanḍī*, a banner, a flag-staff. *h.*

جهنك झणक or झनक *jhanak*, } f. ringing,
جهنكار झनकार *jhankār*, } tinkling,
clinking; clank, tingle, rattle. *s.*

جهنكارنا झनकारना *jhankārnā*, a. to ring, to make sound. *h.*

جهنكاڑ झंकाड़ *jhankāṛ*, a tree without leaves. *h.*

جهنكنا झणकना or झनकना *jhanaknā*, a. to tinkle, to clink, to tingle, to ring. *s.*

جهنكواءي *jhanakwā,ī*, acute rheumatism. *d.*

جهنكهاڑا झंखाड़ा *jhankhāṛā*, } m. an elk; also
جهنكهڑا झंखड़ा *jhankhaṛā*, } a tree without
leaves. *h.*

جهنكهنا झंखना *jhankhnā*, } n. to be hor-
جهنكهنون झंखनौं *jhankhnaun*, } ror-struck,
to have the hair stand on end, to shudder, to rave, to chatter, to lament. *h.*

جهنگا झंगा *jhangā*, m. an upper garment or vest; a coat, a gown. *h.*

جهنگور *jhingūr*, m. a cockroach. *d.*

جهنم *jahannam*, m. hell; *gehenna*, according to the Musalmāns *Jahannam*, is divided into seven portions, appropriated severally to wicked Moslems, Christians, Jews, Sabæans, Gebrs, idolaters, and hypocrites. *a.* [infernal. *a.*

جهنمي *jahannamī*, hellish, belonging to hell;

جهنوان झनवाँ *jhanwāñ*, m. a kind of rice. *h.*

جهنوانا झँवाना *jhañwānā*, n. to tan (in the sun); a. to wash the feet by rubbing *jhañwāñ*, q.v. *h.*

جهنهڈا झिनहड्डा *jhin-haḍḍā*, raw-boned. *s.*

جهوا जिह्वा *jihvā*, f. the tongue. *jihvā-swād*, m. licking, lapping. *jihvā-mal*, m. the fur of the tongue. *s.*

جهوا झौवा *jhawwā*, m. a tree (*Tamarix Indica*) with the tender branches of which baskets are made (same as *jhā,ū*); a large basket (without a cover), made from the twigs of the tree so called. *s.*

جهوپا झूपा *jhūpā*, m. a pile of mangoes or other fruit. *h.*

جهوٹ झूठ *jhūṭ*, } false, untrue; m. a lie, a
جهوٹه झूठ *jhūṭh*, } falsehood. *jhūṭ-sach*, mis-
representation. *jhūṭ-sach lagānā*, to misrepresent, to calumniate. *jhūṭh-mūṭh*, false, untrue, falsely. *s.*

جهوٹا झूटा *jhūṭā*, } m. liar, false; leavings
جهوٹها झूठा *jhūṭhā*, } of food, offal, refuse;
(among Hindūs) that which has touched food and is thereby defiled. *jhūṭhā chāṭnā*, a. to eat leavings, to be very wretched. *jhūṭhī na pūchhnā*, a. to refuse even common civility. *s.*

جهوٹالنا *jhūṭālnā*, to prove false. *d.*

جهوٹهن *jhūṭhan*, } land yielding a
جهوٹهيايل *jhūṭhiyā,il*, } double crop. *h.*

جهوجه झोझ *jhojh*, m. a nest; the stomach; a pendulous belly. *h.*

جهوجها झोझा *jhojhā*, m. the stomach; name of an inferior class of Musalmāns in the Du,āb, &c., chiefly converts from Hinduism. *h.*

جهوجهرو झोझरू *jhojhurū*, a kind of grass on which camels and horned beasts feed. *h.*

جهود *juhūd* or *jahūd* (for *yahūd*), a jew. *a.p*

جهورا झूरा *jhūrā*, withered. *h.*

جهورا झोरा *jhorā*, the stalk of a leguminous plant (such as *moṭh*, q. v.), used as fodder. *h.*

جهورنا झूरना *jhūrnā*, a. to pound, to grind; to shake fruit from the tree; n. to pine. *h.*

جهوڑ झौड़ *jhauṛ*, f. squabbling; sounding all the strings of a musical instrument at once. *h.*

جهوڑ झूड़ *jhūṛ*, m. a bush, a bramble. *jhūṛ-jhāṛ*, a thicket. *h.*

جهوسا झूसा *jhūsā*, m. mizzling rain.

جهوسي झूसी *jhūsī*, f. name of a town near Ilāhābād. *h.*

جهوك झोक *jhok*, f. a jolt, push, shove, a puff, a gust of wind; a bunch, a cluster of grapes, &c. *h.*

جهوكا झोका *jhokā*, m. a blow, a contact, collision; a gust, a blast, a breeze. *jhokā bā,okā*, a current of wind. *h.*

جهوكنا झोकना *jhoknā*, a. to cast, to throw. *d.*

جهوكند झोकन्द *jhokand*, the spot on which the *jhokkiyā* (q. v.) stands. *h.*

جهول झोल *jhol*, m. puckering or wrinkling (as ill-made clothes); a litter, brood, farrow, hatch, a birth. *h.*

جهول झूल *jhūl*, f. body-clothes of cattle, housings; a bag, a wallet, a knapsack; a swing. *h.*

جهول *jahūl*, extremely ignorant. *a.*

جهولا झोला *jholā*, m. a stroke of the sun; the palsy; a knapsack, a wallet; a bleak cold wind which affects the wheat crop. *h.*

جهولا झूला *jhūlā*, m. a swing, the rope on which people swing; (in Dakh.) a cradle. *h.*

جهولنا झूलना *jhūlnā*, n. to swing (for exercise); to swing, to dangle, to hang, to oscillate; m. a kind of poem *h.*

جهولن جاترا झूलनजात्रा *jhūlan-jātrā*, a Hindū festival kept about new moon in August, in honour of *Krishna* and his mistress Rādhā. Idols representing these personages are placed in a chair suspended from the roof of the temple or house, and swung to and fro, while offerings of fruits, &c., are presented. The brāhmins are feasted, and love songs of the most indelicate description chanted all night. This festival is usually celebrated for five days and nights.—(Binning.) *s.*

جهوله झोलः *jhola*, a cold wind which affects wheat by drying up the ears. *h.*

جهولي झूली *jhūlī*, f. a cloth or sheet made into a fan for winnowing grain when there is no wind; a hammock or swinging cot. *h.*

جهولي झोली *jholī*, f. a wallet, a sack. *h.*

جهوم झूम *jhūm*, m. abundance of foliage; waving, undulating. *jhūm-jhūm*, m. gathering of the clouds. *jhūmā-jhūm*, repeated attack. *h.*

جهومجهل झूमझल *jhūmjhal*, anger, fury, storming. *h.* [(met.) a battle, an engagement. *h.*

جهومك झूमक *jhūmak*, f. an assembly, a ball;

جهومكا झूमका *jhūmkā*, m. the bell-shaped pendant of an ear-ring; the constellation of the Bear, also (like *jhumkā*, q. v.), the *Gloriosa superba*, a beautiful flower growing wild in India. *h.*

جهومكي झूमकी *jhūmkī*, f. a kind of ear-ring (see *jhumkā*). *h.*

جهومنا झूमना *jhūmnā*, n. to wave, to move the head up and down, to slumber, to move loose, to gather (the clouds). *h.* [of muslin. *h.*

جهونا झूना *jhūnā*, m. a ripe cocoa-nut, a kind

جهونپا झोंपा *jhompā*, m. a bunch of fruit; a cloth with eyelets which covers the whole body; a spike. *h.*

جهونپڑا झोंपड़ा *jhomprā*, m. } a small hovel,
جهونپڑي झोंपड़ी *jhomprī*, f. } a cottage, a hut, chiefly made up of bamboo; a thatched roof or shed. *s.*

جهونٹا झोंटा *jhonṭā*, m. also *jhonṭī*, f. the hair on the back part of the head; the motion of a swing. *jhonṭā denā*, a. to shake one's head with violence. *h.*

جهونٹر झूंटर *jhūnṭar*, } f. ground that pro-
جهونٹهر झूंठर *jhūnṭhar*, } duces two crops yearly. *h.* [*ṭhan*, f. leavings. *h*

جهونٹهن جهانٹهن झूंठनझांठन *jhūnṭhan jhān-*

جهونٹي झोंटी *jhonṭī*, f. (v. *jhonṭā*) the hair, &c.

جهونجه झूंझ *jhūnjh*, m. a bird's nest. *h.*

جهونجهل झूंझल *jhūnjhal*, f. petulance, peevishness, rage. *h.*

جهوند झूंद *jhūnd*, a heap, crowd; an association. *h.* [in a coparcenary village. *h.*

جهوندي झूंदी *jhūndī*, a lot or parcel of land

جهونڈي झूंडी *jhūndī*, f. a bush, a clump of grass, the amount due from each sharer in a *bhaiyā chārā* estate. *h.* [fruit. *h.*

جهونرا झोंरा *jhonrā*, m. a bunch, a cluster (of

جهونرا झौंरा *jhaunrā*, tawny. *h.*

جهونسا झौंसा *jhaunsā*, greatly burnt or scorched. *h.*

جهونك झोंक *jhonk*, f. a shove or push in swinging; the impulse of a squall or sudden blast of wind. *jhonk denā*, a. to set fire to (particularly straw, &c.); to throw dust, &c.; to throw away (the lives of men uselessly). *jhonk khānā*, n. to roll. *h.*

جهونك *jhonk* (for *jonk*), a leech. *d.*

جهونكنا झोंकना *jhonknā*, a. to cast, to push, to throw, to toss, to cast fuel (into an oven). *h.*

جهونكيا झोंकिया *jhonkiyā*, the man who keeps up the fire when sugar is boiling. *h.*

جهونگا झूंगा *jhūngā*, m. bramble, brushwood. *h.*

جهونمنا *jhūnmnā* (v. *jhūmnā*), to wave, &c. *h.*

جهونيا *jhonaiyā*, a division of the Kurmī tribe. *h.*

جهوها झूहा *jhūhā*, a large stack of *bājra* or *Holcus sorghum*, amounting to from ten to twenty *bojh* or loads. *h.*

جهيز *jahez*, m. a portion, whatever a wife carries with her to her husband's house, paraphernalia. *a.*

جهيسي झीसी *jhīsī*, m. a shower. *h.*

جهيكنا झीकना *jhīknā*, } n. to grieve, to
جهيكهنا झीखना *jhīkhnā*, } be vexed, to la-
جهينكنا झींकना *jhīnknā*, } ment, to think of any thing with sorrow, to recommend any thing seriously. *s.*

جهيل झील *jhīl*, f. a shallow lake or morass. *h.*

جهيلنا *jhelnā*, to brush off; to waft away; to fan; to swing gently. *jhel-lenā*, to grasp; to hold in the arms. *d.*

جہیم *jahīm* (also *jaḥīm*), hell, or rather that subdivision of it which is allotted to idolators. *a.*

جہیں जहीं *jahīṅ*, in whatever place, wherever. *h.*

جهين झीन *jhīn*,
جهينا झीना *jhīnā*, } fine, subtile, thin. *h.*

جهينكنا झींकना *jhīṅknā*, same as *jhīknā*, q. v.

جهينگا झींगा *jhīngā*, f. shrimp, a prawn; m. (*Cucumis acutangulus, Lin.; Luffa acutangula, Roxb.*). *h.*

جهينگٹ झींगट *jhīngaṭ*, m. a steersman. *h.*

جهينگر झींगुर *jhīngur*, m. the name of an insect, a cricket. *h.*

جي जी *jī*, m. life, soul, spirit. *jī uṭhānā*, a. to withdraw one's friendship or desire. *jī ā-jānā*, to have the mind suddenly fixed (on any thing). *jī burā-k.*, a. to vomit, to have a nausea; to be displeased. *jī baṛhānā*, n. to be moderately desirous. *jī bikharnā*, n. to faint. *jī bhar-jānā*, n. to be at ease and contented. *jī bhar-ānā*, n. to be touched with compassion or seized with grief. *jī bahlānā*, a. to amuse one's self; to dissipate reflection. *jī pānā*, a. to understand one's temper; n. to be highly pleased, to escape from misfortune. *jī pānī-k.*, a. to harass, to tease, to plague, to perplex. *jī par kisī ke chalnā*, a. to obey one. *jī par khelnā*, to run the hazard (see *jān par khelnā*). *jī pasījnā*, *-pighalnā*, or *-pighal-jānā*, n. to be compassionate, to feel affection. *jī pakṛā jānā*, n. to be sorry. *jī phaṭ-jānā*, n. to be broken-hearted. *jī phir-jānā*, n. to be contented; to be satiated or disgusted. *jī jalānā*, a. to befriend; to plague, to perplex. *jī jalnā*, to be vexed or troubled in mind. *jī chāhnā*, a. to desire. *jī chhipānā* or *-churānā*, a. to do a work carelessly or lazily, to neglect. *jī chalānā*, a. to act bravely. *jī chalnā*. to desire. *jī dān-k.*, a. to grant life, to pardon a capital crime. *jī dhaṛaknā*, n. to have a palpitation of the heart. *jī ḍūb jānā*, n. to faint. *jī rakhnā*, n. to be easily pleased; to please. *jī se utar-jānā*, n. to sink in the opinion of another; to be broken-hearted. *jī se mārnā*, to kill. *jī karnā* and *honā*, a. to desire, to wish for. *jī kholke kuchh-k.*, a. to do with pleasure, cheerfully. *jī kī amān māngnī*, a. to preface a discourse with excuses. *jī ke badal jī denā*, a. to take up the cause of another. *jī ghaṭ-jānā*, n. to detest. *jī lagānā*, a. to excite desire or love; to fix or apply the mind. *jī lagnā*, a. to contract affection for any person or thing, to hanker after. *jī lenā*, a. to penetrate one's thoughts; to excite one's desire; to kill. *jī mārnā*, a. to mortify one's desire, to displease. *jī matlānā*, to be sick at the stomach, to feel nausea. *jī milānā*, a. to contract friendship. *jī meṅ ānā*, n. to come into the mind, to occur to the recollection. *jī meṅ jal-jānā*, n. to be tormented with envy or jealousy. *jī meṅ jī ānā*, n. to be comforted. *jī meṅ ghar-k.*, n. to be pleasant, agreeable, or acceptable. *jī nikalnā*, n. to die; to desire or love excessively; to fear exceedingly. *jī hārnā*, n. to be discouraged, depressed; to be deterred by cowardice, to lose heart. *jī haṭ-jānā*, n. to detest. *s.*

جي जी *jī*, yes; sir, master, you sir. *h.*

جي जे *je*, pron. who, which, what. *h.*

جي जै *jai*, as much as, as many as. *h.*

جي जै *jai* or जय *jaya*, m. f. triumph, promotion, advancement, preferment, victory, bravo! huzza! all hail. *jai-jai-kār*, m. rejoicings, cheers, triumph, exultation. *jai-jai-kār k.*, to huzza, to shout. *jai-māl*, f. garland of victory. *s.*

جئي जई *ja,ī*, oats; the grain was introduced into India by the British. *h.*

جيا ज्या *jyā*, f. a mother; the earth; a bow-string. *s.*

جيانا जियाना *jiyānā*,
جيانون ज्यानौं *jyānauṅ*, } a. to vivify, to restore to life, to foster. *s.*

جيب *jaib*, f. the breast, the heart; the breast or collar of a garment. *a.*

جيب जेब *jeb* (also *jaib*), f. a pocket. *jeb-katra*, m. a pickpocket. *jaibī ḵẖāṣṣ*, a privy purse. *p.*

جيب *jīb* (v. *jībh*), the tongue. *jīb-ulaṭnā*, to express clearly. *jīl-chhilnī*, a tongue-scraper. *d.*

جيبكا जीविका *jībikā*, f. pension, livelihood. *s.*

جيبه जीभ *jībh*, f. the tongue. *jībh baṛhānā*, n. to be loquacious and abusive; to pursue pleasures beyond one's reach. *jībh pakaṛnā*, a. to silence, to interrupt one's discourse; to criticise minutely. *jībh-jhukānā*, to pretend to wealth falsely. *jībh chāṭnā*, a. to long after or covet unattainable enjoyment. *jībh chalānā*, n. to boast beyond one's ability. *jībh dābke bāt kahnā*, a. to speak with reserve. *jībh kāṭnā*, a. to forbid by signs; (from the Persian) to grant the request of a petitioner; to be struck with terror or astonishment. *jībh nikālnā*, to put out the tongue (met.) to be extremely fatigued, thirsty. *s.*

جيبهارا जीभारा *jībhārā*, plain-spoken, loquacious. *s.*

جيبهي जीभी *jībhī*, f. an instrument for cleaning the tongue; a bit of a bridle. *jībhī-machhlī*, a sole fish. *s.* [*jebī*, of the pocket. *h. p.*

جيبي *jībī*, of or relating to the tongue, lingual.

جيبير जैबेर *jai-ber*, as many times, as often as. *s.*

جيپال जयपाल or जैपाल *jaipāl*, m. a king, a sovereign (name of several celebrated Hindū princes), a plant or tree (*Croton triglium*). *s.*

جيپتر जयपत्र *jai-patra*, m. record of victory; in law, the written and sealed award of the judge in favour of either party. *s.*

جيت जीत *jīt*, f. winning, victory, success. *jīt-patra*, a favourable decree. *s.*

جيت जयत, जैत *jait* or जेत *jet*, m. name of a plant (*Æschynomene sesban*); name of a musical mode. *s.*

جيتا जीता *jītā*, alive. *jīte jī*, when alive, in one's lifetime; (for *jetā*), over, more, above. *jītā honā*, n. to be over. *s.*

جيتا जीता *jītā*, m. mutual assistance in tillage, also allowing the use of a plough and bullocks instead of paying wages in money or kind. *h.*

جيتا जेता *jetā*, as much as, so much. *jetā ki*, though, although. *s.* [decision. *h.*

جيتاپتر जीतापत्र *jītā-patr*, m. a favourable

جيت آلو जीतालू *jīt-ālū*, arrowroot. *h.*

جيتب जीतब *jītab*, m. life, existence. *s.*

جيترا जैत्रा *jaitrā*, m. a conqueror, a victor. *s.*

جيترته जैत्ररथ *jaitra-rath*, m. a hero, a victor. *s.*

جيتري जैत्री *jaitrī*, victorious, triumphant. *s.*

جيتك जेतिक *jetik*, as many, as much. *s.*

جيتنا जीतना *jītnā*, a. to win, to conquer, to overcome. for *jitnā*, as much as, or, as many as. *s.*

جيتو जीतू *jītū*,
جيتونت जीतवन्त *jītwant*,
جيتويا जीतवैया *jītwaiyā*, } m. a conqueror, a winner at play. *s.*

جيتي जैती *jaitī*, a kind of weed (v. *jaichī*).

جيتيا जीतिया *jītiyā*, f. name of a Hindū fast, with sacrifice to and worship of *Devī* (*jītiyā bart*), observed by women who have lost several children, to preserve the remainder. *s.*

جيتيرا *jīterā*,
جيتيره *jītera*, } m. mutual assistance in tillage (v. *jītā*). *h.*

جيٹ जेट *jeṭ*, f. heap, accumulation. *h.*

جيٹھ जेठ *jeṭh*, adj. best, eldest (brother where there are several); m. husband's elder brother; name of the second Hindū month (the full moon of which is near *jyeshṭhā*) (May—June). *jeṭh-ra'iyat*, the head of the "ryots" or cultivators in a village (v. *jeshṭhā*). *s.*

جيٹھا जेठा *jeṭhā*, m. elder, first-born; the first and strongest tint obtained from *kusum* (*Carthamus tinctorius*). *s.*

جيٹھاني जेठानी *jeṭhānī*, f. the wife of a husband's elder brother. *s.*

جيٹھرا जेठरा *jeṭhrā*, elder, first-born; husband's elder brother. *s.*

جيٹھ رعيت *jeṭh-ra'iyat*, m. the head villager who conducts the ordinary business thereof. *h. a.*

جيٹھنڈا जेठुंडा *jeṭhuṇḍā*, the share or right of the eldest son. *h.*

جيٹھوت जेठौत *jeṭhaut*, m. the son of a husband's elder brother. *s.*

جيٹھي مدھ जेठीमधु *jeṭhī-madhu*, m. liquorice (*Glycirrhiza glabra*). *s.*

جيجيونتي जयजयवन्ती or जैजैवन्ती *jaijaiwantī*, f. name of a *rāginī*, or musical mode. *h.*

جيچي जैची *jaichī*, a kind of weed which grows up with the spring crops, and yields a kind of oil. *h.*

جيد *jaiyid*, excellent, elegant, arable; pure money of standard weight. *jīd*, a slender and beautiful neck. *jayad*, slenderness of the neck. *a.*

جيدھر जीधर *jīdhar*, whithersoever (v. *jidhar*). *h.*

جيڈھك जयढक or जैढक *jaiḍhak* (also *jaiḍhāk*), m. a kind of drum. *s.*

جيدھون जयधुनि *jai-dhwani*, m. shout of victory. *s.*

جير जेर *jer*, m. the membrane in which the fœtus is enveloped, the after-birth, *secundines*. *h.*

جيرا जियरा *jiyarā*, m. life, soul; (met.) beloved. *s.*

جيرا जीरा *jīrā*,
جيرك जीरक *jīrak*, } m. cummin-seed. *s.*

جيران *jīrān* (pl. of جار), neighbours. *a.*

جيرن जीरन *jīran* or जीर्ण *jīrna*, old; digested; withered, decayed; m. an old man. *jīrni*, f. old age, decay; digestion. *jīrnatā*, f. old age, infirmity, decay. *jīrna-vastra*, m. old, worn or tattered raiment. *s.*

جيرن وردھنك जीर्णवृद्धक *jīrna-vradhnak*, m. a fragrant grass (*Cyperus rotundus*). *s.*

جيسا जैसा *jaisā*, as, such as, like; *jaisā chāhiye*, as occasion may require, as it ought, sufficiently. *jaisā-taisā*, as well as. *jaisā kā taisā*, precisely the same. *jaisā ki*, as though, as when. *s.*

جيسوار *jaiswār*,
جيسوارا *jaiswārā*, } name of certain low-caste tribes. *h.*

جيش *jaish*, an army, troops; enjoyment, pleasure. *a.*

جيشبد जयशब्द *jai-shabda*, m. a shout or song of victory, the exclamation *jai jai*. *s.*

جيشٹ जेष्ट *jeshṭ*,
جيشٹھ जेष्ठ *jeshṭh*, } eldest, chief, &c. (same as *jeṭh*, q. v.). *s.*

جيشٹھا जेष्ठा *jeshṭhā*, f. one of the mansions of the moon (the eighteenth, Antares and two other stars in Scorpio). *s.*

جيغه *jīgha* or *jegha*, an ornament of gold and jewels worn in the turban. p.

جيف *jaif* or *jiyaf*, (pl. of جيفه), carcases, dead bodies. *a.*

جيفه *jīfa*, m. a dead and putrefying carcase; [a corpse; adj. unclean. *a.*

جيكا जीका *jīkā* (for *jīvikā* or *jībikā*), f. pension, livelihood, means of living. *s.*

جيل जेल *jel*, m. a string or line of captives chained together; a string of buckets passed over the Persian wheel; a jail or prison; also *jel-khāna*, the same. *h.*

جيل जील *jīl*, f. a high note or tone in music, [the treble. *p.*

جيلي जेली *jelī*, a kind of pitchfork or rake for collecting and adjusting the ears of corn on a threshing-ground. *h.*

جيمار जीमार *jī-mār*, capital, deserving death (as a crime); mortifying one's desires. *s.*

جيمال जयमाल *jai-māl* or *jaya-māl*, f. necklace or garland of victory. *s.*

جيمان जयमान or जैमान *jaimān*, victorious. *s.*

جيمن जैमिनि *jaimini*, m. a celebrated saint and philosopher, founder of the *Uttara-Mīmānsā* school. *s.*

جيمنا जीमना *jīmnā*, a. to eat, to feed one's [self. *s.*

جيمنگل जयमङ्गल *jai-mangal*, m. the royal elephant. *s.*

جين जीन *jīn*, m. an old man (v. *jīrna*). *s.*

جين जैन *jain*, m. a Jaina, a follower of the heterodox sect so called from worshipping a number of *Jins*, or divine teachers, as incarnations of the Deity; they deny the authority of the Vedas, and disregard the distinction of castes. *s.*

جينا जीना *jīnā*, n. to live; m. living, life. *s.*

جينتي जयन्ती *jayantī*, f. a tree (*Æschynomene sesban*); a flag, a banner. *s.* [to wrinkle. *h.*

جينگترانا जीङ्गुराना *jingurānā*, a to corrugate,

جيني जयिनी *jayinī*, victorious. *jainī*, of or relating to the sect of Jains, q. v. *s.*

جيو जीव *jīw*, m. life, soul. जीउ *jīu*, a sweetheart, a lover; interj. bravo! *s.*

جيو ज्यो *jyo*, life, soul, (same as *jīw*). *jyo par dnā*, to come into extreme difficulty. *jyo chhī kahnā*, to shew aversion, to abhor. *jyo señ uṭhnā*, to pass away from life. *d.*

جيوات जीवातु *jīvātu*, m. a drug for re-animating the dead; life, existence. *s.*

جيواتما जीवात्मा *jīvātmā*, m. the vital principle or spirit. *s.*

جيوادهار जीवाधार *jīvādhār*, m. (the receptacle of life) the earth. *s.* [a village. *h.*

جيوار जैवार *jaiwār*, the head inhabitants of

جيوار जेवार *jewār*, a clan of *rājpūts*. *h.*

جيوان जयवान *jai-wān*, victorious. *s.*

جيوانتك जीवान्तक *jīvāntak*, m. a fowler, a bird-catcher, *s.*

جيوپترك जीवपुत्रक *jīv-putrak*, m. a plant bearing seeds which are used in rosaries. *s.*

جيوت जीवित *jīwit*, m. life existence. *jīwit, kāl*, m. duration of life. *s.*

جيوت जीवत *jīwat*, living, alive; spirited, bold; victorious. *jīwat-pati*, f. a wife whose husband is alive. *jiwat-tokā*, f. a woman whose children are living. *s.*

جيوت ज्योति *jyoti*, f. light, splendour. *s.*

جيوتا जीविता *jīwitā*, living, alive. *s.*

جيوتسنا ज्योत्स्ना *jyotsnā*, f. moonlight. *jyotsnā-priya*, m. the *chakor* or Greek partridge. *jyotsnā-vriksha*, m. the tripod or tree of a lampstand, a candlestick. *s.* [a night of full moon. *s.*

جيوتسي ज्योत्स्नी *jyotsnī*, f. a moonlight night,

جيوتش ज्योतिष *jyotish*, m. astronomy, astrology. *jyotish-mān*, luminous, radiant. *s.*

جيوتشك ज्योतिष्क *jyotishk*, m. a heavenly body, a planet, a star. *s.* [ger. *s.*

جيوتشك ज्योतिषिक *jyotishik*, m. an astrolo-

جيوتشي ज्योतिषी *jyotishī*, f. a star, a planet; m. an astronomer an astrologer. *s.*

جيوتيا जीवतिया *jīvtiyā*, f. (same as *jītiyā*, q.v.)

جيوتيرته ज्योतीरथ *jyotī-rath*, m. the pole-star. *s.*

جيوتيش जीवितेश *jīwitesh*, m. (lord of life) a name of Yama; a husband, a lord; a drug to revive the dead. *s.*

جيوتيش जीवितेशा *jīwiteshā*, adj. ruling life (applicable to objects of reverence or affection). *s.*

جيوٹ जीवट *jīwaṭ*, lively, spirited, bold. *s.*

جيوتهـ जियौठ *jiyauṭh*, brave, courageous. *s.*

جيوجيو जीवजीव *jīv-jīv*, m. a kind of bird, supposed to be a pheasant (v. *jīvanjīv*). *s.*

جيودهن जीवधन *jīv-dhan*, m. live stock; wealth in flocks and herds. *s.* [sure of land. *h.*

جيوري जेवरी *jewrī*, f. a cord, a string, a mea-

جيوڙا जीवड़ा *jīwṛā* or जियूड़ा *jiyūṛā*, m. life, soul; sweetheart, beloved; annual wages to washermen and others. *s.*

جيوڙا जेवड़ा *jewṛā* or *je,oṛā*, m. cord, string; perquisites of village servants. *h.*

جيوڙي जेवड़ी *jewṛī* or *je,oṛī*, f. a cord, string; a worm. *h.* [articulation. *s.*

جيوستهان जीवस्थान *jīvasthān*, m. a joint, an

جيوسو जीवसू *jīv-sū*, f. the mother of living children. *s.*

جيوك जीवक *jīvak*, m. a tree (*Pentaptera tomentosa*); a medicinal plant; an animal, a living being. *s.*

جيوكا जीविका *jīvikā*, f. pension, livelihood. *s.*

جيوكوٿهي *jīva-koṭhī*, a house or hospital for vermin, &c., such as may be seen at Surat. *s.*

جيوگر जीवगर *jīw-gar*, resolute, bold. *s.*

جيومار जीवमार *jīv-mār*, capital (same as *jī-mār*, q. v.) [the body. *s.*

جيومندر जीवमन्दिर *jīv-mandir*, (temple of life)

جيون जीवन *jīwan*, m. life, existence, livelihood; water; a son. *jīwan-birt*, a stipend allowed to the family of an old deceased servant. *s.*

جيون ज्यूं *jyūñ* or ज्यों *jyoñ*, how much, the more so, when, as, as if. *jyūñ kā tyūñ*, precisely the same. *h.*

جيونا जीवना *jīwnā*, n. to live, be alive. *s.*

جيونا जेवना *jewnā*, a. to eat. *s.*

جيونار जेवनार *jewnār* or *je,onār*, f. a treat, feast, entertainment; (for *jaunāl*, q. v.) land in constant cultivation. *s.*

جيونت जयवन्त *jai-want*, victorious. *s.*

جيونت जीवन्त *jīwant*, living, alive. *s.*

جيونتك जीवन्तिक *jīwantik*, m. a fowler, a bird-catcher. *s.*

جيونتكا जीवन्तिका *jīwantikā*, f. a parasite plant (*Epidendron tesseloides*, &c.); a plant (*Menispermum glabrum*). *s.*

جيونتي जीवन्ती *jīwantī*, f. a tree (*Celtis orientalis*); a plant (*Menispermum glabrum*); the Sam or Sāen tree (*Mimosa albida*); yellow myrobalan (*Terminalia chebula*). *s.*

جيونجيو जीवञ्जीव *jīvanjīv*, m. a kind of bird, supposed to be a pheasant; the *chakor* or Greek partridge. *s.* [subsistence. *s.*

جيونوپايه जीवनोपाय *jīvanopāya*, m. means of

جيونوشدهه जीवनौषध *jīvanaushadh*, m. a drug to revive the dead. *s.*

جيونی जीवनी *jīvanī*, f. jasmin. *s.*

جيوي जीवी *jīvī*, living, alive; a living being. *s.*

جي هارنا जीहारना *jī-hārnā*, to be discouraged, depressed from fear. *s.*

جيہر जेहर *jehar*, f. m. the name of an ornament. *h.*

جيہڑ जेहड़ *jehaṛ*, f. a pile of pots filled with water and placed one over the other, in order to be carried on the head; a ceremony preparative to marriage, in which pots filled with water are piled over one another, the whole crowned with a bowl of *sharbat*, and the friends watch by it during the night. *h.*

جي هو जैहौ *jai-hau* (Braj), you may or will go. *h.* [will go, will be. *h.*

جي هي जैहै *jai-hai* (Braj), he, &c. may or

جيي जयी *jayī*, victorious, triumphant. *s.*

جييا जेया *jeyā*, conquerable, fit to be conquered. *s.*

جييشٹھ ज्येष्ठ *jyeshṭha*, best, pre-eminent; oldest, older. *jyeshṭhāṅsa*, the eldest son's share, the right of primogeniture; m. the second Hindū month (May—June). *jyeshṭhatā*, f. seniority, pre-eminence. *jyeshṭha-tāt*, m. a father's elder brother. *jyeshṭha-varna*, m. a Brāhman. *s.*

جييشٹھا ज्येष्ठा *jyesṭhā*, f. the eighteenth lunar mansion comprising three stars, of which one is Scorpionis; the middle finger. *s.*

چ

چ *che* or *chīm*; called also *jīm-i fārsī* or *jīm-i 'ajamī* (*i.e.* the Persian *jīm*, the Arabs not having it in their language), the seventh letter of the Persian alphabet and the eighth of the Hindūstānī. It sounds like *ch* in the English words "cherry, cheek". It is sometimes permuted, 1st, into *zh*, as *kāzh* for *kāch*, glass; a pine-tree: 2nd, into *z*, as *pizishk* for *pichishk*, a physician or apothecary. 3rd, into *sh*, as *kāshī* for *kāchī*, made of glass: lastly, by the Arabs it is changed into *j*, and sometimes into *ṣ* or *sh*, as *kāj* for *kāch*, and *ṣīn*, China, for *chīn*, *shatranj* for *chaturang*, chess. In reckoning by the *abjad* it represents three, the same as *jīm*. *h. p.*

چ च *cha*, is the corresponding letter in the Devanagarī alphabet. In Sanskrit it is a symbol for the God Shiva, a thief, a tortoise, &c. *s.*

چا *chā*, f. tea. *chā-dān*, m. a teapot. *p.*

چابک *chābuk*, m. active, alert; a horsewhip (in this sense it is only found in the works of *Khusrū*, and it is probably Hindī). *chābuk-bāzī*, f. whipping, lash. *chābuk-dast*, nimble, active, alert, quick, beautiful. *chābuk phaṭkārnā*, a. to crack a whip. *chābuk-sawār*, m. a horse-breaker, a jockey; a good rider; a horse-broker. *chābuk-sawārī*, f. jockeyship, &c. *chābuk mārnā*, a. to whip, to lash. *p.*

چابکی *chābukī*, f. activity, alertness, despatch, patch, celerity. *p.*

چابنا चाबना *chābnā*, a. to chew, to masticate. *chāb chāb bāteṅ karnī*, a. to mince one's words, to speak little and haughtily. *s.*

چابڼ *chābnā*, a. to thrust in (a pin, nail, &c.), to prick. *d.*

چابا *chābū*, (in comp.), chewing, a chewer. *h.*

چابهٹ پاڑنا चाभटपाड़ना *chābhaṭ pāṛnā*, a. to craunch, to crush. *h.*

چابي चाबी *chābī*, f. a key. The word is inelegant, and chiefly used in Bengal: it is apparently of Portuguese origin. *h.*

چاپ चाप *chāp*, m. a bow; also the refuse of the *jhar berī*, after the leaves are beaten from it. *chāp-jarīb*, gross measurement of the lands on an estate. *h.*

چاپاتي *chāpātī*, f. a thin cake of fine bread. *d.*

چاپ پٹ चापपट *chāp-paṭ*, m. a tree (*Buchanania latifolia*). *s.*

چاپڑے चापड़े *chāpṛe*, cakes of cow-dung, which, when dry, are used as fuel. *h.*

چاپل चापल *chāpal*, m. unsteadiness. *s.*

چاپلوس *chāplūs*, m. a flatterer, a wheedler. *p.*

چاپلوسي *chāplūsī*, m. flattery, wheedling. *p.*

چاپنا *chāpnā* (v. *chāṅpnā*), to join; to cram, &c. *h.* [ing-net. *h.*

چاپهند चाफन्द *chāphand*, m. a kind of fish-

چاتر चातुर *chātur*, clever, able, cunning, wise; in comp. (from *chatur*) four. *chātur-varnya*, m. the aggregate of the four castes. *chātur-vaidya*, m. a priest versed in the four Vedas. *s.*

چاتر चातर *chātar*, m. a large net, a seine. *h.*

چاتري चातुरी *chāturī*, f. } cleverness, dex-
چاتريہ चातुर्य *chāturya*, m. } terity, cunning. *s.*

چاتک चातक *chātak*, m. name of a bird (*Cuculus melanoleucos*). *s.*

چاتوال चात्वाल *chātwāl*, m. a hollow made in the ground to receive a burnt-offering; any hole in the ground. *s.*

چاٹ चाट *chāṭ*, f. longing, wish, relish, taste; habit, custom, "bonne bouche". *chāṭ lenā*, a. to lick up. *h.*

چاٹا चाटा *chāṭā*, the vessel that receives the juice of the sugar cane as it drops from the mill. *h.*

چاٹنا चाटना *chāṭnā*, to lick, to lap. *h.*

چاٹي चाटी *chāṭī*, f. a churn. *h.*

چاچا चाचा *chāchā*, m. a father's brother, paternal uncle (Lat. patruus). *h.*

چاچر चाचर *chāchar*, m. the pole round which they play at the festival of the *holī*; a fair or assemblage of people collected after the *holī*. *h.*

چاچي चाची *chāchī*, f. father's sister, or father's brother's wife, aunt. *h.*

چادر *chādar*, f. a sheet, tablecloth, mantle, veil; a cascade. *chādar bichhānā*, a. to lay the cloth. *h.*

چار चारु *chāru*, beautiful, pleasing, elegant. *s.*

چار चार *chār*, four. *chār abrū*, m. a kind of dervise who shaves his eyebrows and whiskers. *chār-ānkh* or *chār-ānkheṅ* (v. *chār-chashm*). *chār-ungal*, m. palm (four inches). *chār-unglī*, f. hand's breadth. *chār-āīna*, m. iron armour. *chār-bālish*, m. a throne, couch, or sofa. *chār-bāng*, sensible, quick, intelligent, alert. *chār-bīsī*, m. fourscore. *chār-pāra*, divided into four, four-pieced. *chār-ṭūk*, broken (into four pieces). *chār-tak*, ambling, pace of a horse. *chār-tak chalnā*, to amble. *chār-jāma*, m. a kind of saddle (without a tree). *chār-chashm*, f. meeting, interview, the eyes of two people meeting. *chār-khāna*, chequered; m. a kind of cloth. *chār-dīwārī* or *-dīwālī*, f. a court-yard, inclosure, area. *chār zānū*, a mode of sitting, as tailors sit at work. *chār-zānū baiṭhnā*, n. to squat, to sit oriental fashion, with the legs crossed in front. *chār-sāl*, a horse of four years old. *chār-sū*, a cross-road, two roads crossing each other. *chār-shāna*, tough, hardy. *chār-ẓarb*, sensible, intelligent, generally applied to slaves. *chār-khūnṭā*, quadrangular. *chār-maghz*, m. a walnut; an earthen ball with which children play. *chār-nazaren-k.*, an interview to take place (v. *chār-chashm*). *chāron ṭaraf* and *chāron or*, the four sides or quarters, *i. e.* all around, on all sides. *p.*

چار *chār* (v. *chāra*), remedy, help, &c. *chār-nā-chār*, nolens volens. *p.*

چار *chār*, pepper soup, commonly called by Europeans "*mulligatawny*" which is a corruption of its name in the Tamul language. *d.*

چارا *chārā* (for چاره q.v.), remedy, aid, &c. *p.*

چارا चारा *chārā*, m. forage, fodder; bait for fish; a young plant. *chāra ḍālnā*, to bait. *h.*

چارپایه *chār-pāya*, m. a quadruped. *p.*

چارپائي *chār-pā,ī*, f. a bedstead, a bed. *chār-pā,ī par parnā*, n. to get sick; a litter for carrying the sick. *p.*

چارپتھ चारपथ *chār-path*, m. a meeting of roads, quadrivium. *s.*

چارتا *chār-tā* (for *chār-tār*), a lute with four strings. *p.*

چارچند *chār-chand*, fourfold, quadruple. *p.*

چارده *chār-dah*, fourteen, the full moon. *p.*

چاردهم *chār-dahum*, the fourteenth, the full moon. *p.*

چاردیهات *chār-dīhāt*, an estate formed of the land belonging to four villages. *p.*

چارشنبه *chār-shamba*, Wednesday. *p.*

چارقب *chār-ḳab*, an article of dress so called; a kind of vest; also a kind of mirror. *p.*

چارگنا चारगुणा *chār-gunā*, fourfold, quadruple. *p. s.*

چارم *chārum*, *chārumī* or *chārumīn*, the fourth. *p.*

چارن चारण *chāran*, m. a dancer or mimic, a kind of bard, a panegyrist. *s.*

چارناچار *chār-nā-chār*, certainly, inevitably, by force, right or wrong, nolens volens. *p.*

چاروا *chārwā*, m. a pony, quadruped. *chārwā-dār*, m. a groom, one who lets horses. *p.*

چارواك चारवाक *chārvāk*, the head of a tribe of atheists; a sophist, a sceptic, an atheist. *s.*

چاروان *chārwān*, m. } the fourth; more usually
چاروين *chārwīn*, f. } *chauthā*, &c. *h.*

چارولي *charolī*, f. kernel of a nut. *d.*

چاروناچار *chār-o-nā chār*, nolens volens, &c. *p.*

چاروي चार्वी *chārvī*, f. a beautiful woman, understanding, intellect; moonlight; light, splendour. *s.*

چاره *chāra*, m. remedy, cure, help, aid; expedient. *chāra-sāz* or *-gar*, one who remedies. *chāra-sāzī* or *-garī*, remedying, curing, &c. *p.*

چاره चार: *chāra*, m. forage, fodder, food for cattle; truss, sheaf, grass; a young plant; a bait for fish. *chāra ḍālnā*, a. to bait. *h.*

چارياري *chāryārī*, m. a sect of Musalmāns who venerate equally the four successors of *Muhammad*. The Shi'as apply this term to the Sunnīs. *p.*

چاريك *chār-yak*, one of four, a fourth. *p.*

چاڑ चाड़ *chāṛ*, f. turf; a hurt, a wound, a knock; a lever. *chāṛ-paṛnā*, to be necessary. *h.*

چاڑي *chāṛī*, slander, calumny, backbiting. *chāṛī khānā*, to delight in calumny, &c. *d.*

چاس चास *chās*, f. ploughing, cultivation. *chās-k.*, a. to plough. *h.*

چاسا चासा *chāsā*, m. a cultivator, a ploughman, a husbandman. *h.*

چاسکو *chāshū* (for *chāksū*, q. v.), a kind of medicine. *d.*

چاسنا चासना *chāsnā*, a. to plough, to till. *h.*

چاسني चासनी *chāsnī*, a pan in which the juice of the sugar-cane is boiled. *h.*

چاسي चासी *chāsī*, m. (v. *chāsā*) a ploughman; f. cultivation, tillage. *h.*

چاشت *chāsht* or *chāsht-gāh*, f. the middle hour between sunrise and the meridian; also what is eaten at that time, breakfast, a collation. *chāsht-namāz*, morning prayer. *p.*

چاشني *chāshnī*, f. flavour, relish, a mixture of sweet and sour; a specimen; syrup. *p.*

چاشنيگير *chāshnīgīr*, a taster, a servant whose duty it is to watch over the kitchen of princes, and to taste every dish brought to table as a security against poison—(Binning). *p.*

چاق *chāḳ*, active, alert; well, in good health; erect, a horse ready to cover; in spirits. *chāḳ chau-band*, healthy and vigorous. *t.*

چاقو *chāḳū*, m. a clasp-knife, a penknife. *p.*

چاك *chāk*, m. a narrow opening intentionally left in clothes; a rent, a slit, a fissure. *chāk-k.*, a. to rend, to slit, to tear, to split. *chāk-girebān*, with collar torn, afflicted. *s.*

چاك चाक *chāk*, m. a potter's wheel; a wheel of any kind; rings of earth for forming a well; a millstone, mill. *s.*

چاکٹ *chākaṭ*, a kind of bracelet. *d.*

چاکر *chākar*, m. a servant, attendant. *p.*

چاکران *chākarān* (pl.), servants. *chākarān-zamīn*, lands exempted from revenue dues, and appropriated to the maintenance of public officers and servants. *p.*

چاکري *chākarī*, f. service, attendance; a grant in a village for personal services, service land. *p.*

چاكسو chāksū, m. the name of a medicine (a small black seed) for diseases of the eyes. *p.*

چاكو chākū, m. a claspknife, a penknife. *p.*

چاكهنا चाखना chākhnā, a. to enjoy, to relish, to taste. *s.*

چاكي चाकी chākī, f. (v. chakkī), a mill-stone. *h.*

چال चाल chāl, f. habit, custom; gait, pace. *chāl pakaṛnā*, n. to prevail. *chāl-chalnā*, n. to behave. *chāl-ḍhāl*, f. manners, behaviour, breeding, politeness. *chāl-milnā*, n. to smell a rat. *s.*

چال चाल chāl, f. a colour in horses, roan; m. the thatch or roof of a house. *h.*

چالا चाला chālā, m. motion, departure; (met.) a lucky moment. *s.*

چالا chālā, } laborious, active, hard-
چالاك chālāk, } working, alert, fleet, nimble, ingenious, clever. *chālāk-dast*, expert of hand. *chālāk-dastī*, expertness. *p.*

چالاكي chālākī, f. activity, alertness, nimbleness, celerity; boldness. *p.*

چالان chālān, invoice, bill of lading; transportation. *p.*

چالش chālish, f. exertion in battle; manner, conduct; a graceful gait. *p.*

چالك चालक chālak, laxative. *s.*

چالن चालन chālan, m. a sieve, a strainer. *s.*

چالنا चालना chālnā, a. to sift; n. to be mischievous. *s.*

چالنهار चालनहार chālan-hār, a sifter. *s.*

چالني चालनी chālnī, f. a sieve, a strainer. *s.*

چاله चालह chālah, f. the name of a fish (sort of sprat. (*Clupea cultrata, Buch*). *s.*

چالي चाली chālī, roguish, wicked, mischievous. *h.*

چاليس चालीस chālīs, forty. *chālīs-sutūn*, a pavilion, palace, &c., having forty (*i. e.* a great many) pillars. *s.*

چاليسا चालीसा chālīsā, m. a dimness of sight which is supposed to come on at forty years of age, and often to be removed on approaching the forty-eighth or fiftieth year; the fortieth year of any era, or of the century; an aggregate of forty, a period of forty days; a quarantine. *s.*

چاليسوان चालीसवां chālīswāṅ, the fortieth; hence a festival or ceremony held on the fortieth day after child-birth, death of a relation, &c. *s.*

چاليسي चालीसी chālīsī, f. quarantine; a period of forty days' abstinence kept after the death of a relation, child-birth, &c. *s.*

چام चाम chām, m. hide, skin, leather. *chām ke dām chalāne*, a. to stretch to the utmost a temporary authority (lit. to give currency to coins of leather). *chām-chorī*, adulterous connection with another man's wife. *s.*

چامر चामर chāmar, m. the tail of the Bos grunniens, used to whisk off flies, &c. *chāmar-pushpa*, m. the betel-nut tree (*Areca faufel* or *catechu*). *s.*

چاميكر चामीकर chāmīkar, m. gold. *s.*

چانپ चांप chāmp, f. the lock of a gun; the stocks, the rack. *chāmp chaṛhānā*, a. to cock a gun; to punish or torment by squeezing the ear with the lock of a gun. *h.*

چانپنا चांपना chāmpnā, a. to join; to stuff, to cram, to thrust in, to press. *h.*

چانٹنا चांटना chānṭnā, a. to press, to squeeze. *h.*

چانٹي चांटी chānṭī, cesses levied or "squeezed" from artisans and others. *h.*

چانچري चांचरी chāncharī, a kind of inferior grain, as *mung* or *jawār*. *h.*

چانچليه चाञ्चल्य chānchalya, m. unsteadiness. *s.*

چاند चांद chānd, m. the moon; the crown of the head; a white spot in the forehead of cattle and many other things which are moon-like; name of an ornament; a month; a target (to shoot at). *chānd chhipānā*, a. to change as the moon. *chānd-rāt*, night of the new moon; end of the month. *chānd-tārā*, a robe made of flowering muslin, &c. *chānd-mārnā*, a. to fire at a mark. *chānd ne khet kiyā*, the moon has risen. *s.*

چاندا चांदा chāndā, m. a common station of the revenue survey; a subscription to raise a certain sum; an assessment, quota, share. *h.*

چاندر चान्द्र chāndra, lunar; m. the moon-gem; a lunar month; the light fortnight. *s.*

چاندراين चान्द्रायण chāndrāyan, m. an expiatory fast; diminishing one's food by a mouthful every day during the dark half of the month, and increasing it in like manner during the light half. *s.*

چاندربهاگا चान्द्रभागा chāndra-bhāgā, f. a river in the Panjāb, the Chināb. *s.*

چاندرمس चान्द्रमस chāndramas, m. the constellation *Mriga shira*; stars in Orion. *s.*

چاندم चांदम chāndam, name of a clan of *rājpūts*. *h.*

چاندنا चांदना chāndnā, m. light. *chāndnā pakh*, m. the light fortnight of the moon. *s.*

چاندني चांदनी chāndnī, f. the moonbeams; name of a flower; a white cloth spread over a carpet; any thing white and shining. *chāndnī chauk*, m. a wide and public street or market, that of Delhi being celebrated in its way. *chāndnī-rāt*, f. a moonlight night. *chāndnī-karan*, the practice of Brāhmans, &c. of wounding themselves in order to extort alms or payment of a debt. *chāndnī kā mārā-jānā*, n. to be affected with a disease, supposed to proceed from a stroke of the moon (a horse). *s.*

چانده chānda (v. chāndā), a revenue station. *h.*

چاندي चांदी chāndī, f. silver (pure), plate; the crown of the head. *s.*

چانڈ चांड chānḍ or चाड़ chāṅṛ, f. a prop, support. *h.*

چانڈال चाण्डाल chānḍāl, m. an impure or degraded caste, a Pariah, an outcaste. *chānḍālī*, f. a woman of the same tribe. *s.*

چانك चांक chāṅk, } m. a stamp fixed on a
چانكا चांका chāṅkū, } stack or heap of grain, or a piece of cow-dung placed on the same to protect it from the evil eye. *h.*

چانگلا चाङ्गला *chānglā*, m. a colour in horses. *h.*

چاننا *channā* (v. *chāndnā*), light. *d.*

چانول चांवल *chāṅwal*, m. rice (v. *chāwal*). *h.*

چاو चाव *chāw* or *chā,o*, m. eagerness, pleasure, taste; a measure equal to four fingers; a kind of bamboo. *chā,o-chochlā* or *chā,o-choz*, fondness, endearment, fondling, tenderness, love. *h.*

چاوڑي चावड़ी *chāwṛī*, f. name of a place in Dehlī; a caravansary, a building for the accommodation of wayfarers, commonly called a "choultry." *h.*

چاول चावल *chāwal*, m. rice (cleared of the husk, and not dressed). *h.*

چاه चाह *chāh*, f. desire, wish, love, liking, affection, choice, want, appetite. *chāh-chit* or *chāh o choz*, love, affection, dalliance. *h.*

چاه *chāh*, m. a pit, a well. *chāhi zanakh*, f. the dimple of the chin. *chāh-kan*, m. a well-digger. *p.*

چاها चाहा *chāhā*, m. love, affection, will. *h.*

چاهاچهي चाहाचही *chāhā-chahī*, f. the love of one's country. *h.*

چاهت चाहत *chāhat*, f. desire, will, love. *h.*

چاهرا *chāhirā*, } a tribe of *rājpūts*, in Hi-
چاهل *chāhil*, } sar. *h.*

چاهك चाहक *chāhak*, affectionate, friendly. *h.*

چاهنا चाहना *chāhnā*, a. to love, to like, to desire, to wish for, to demand, to choose, to need, to require, to pray, to approve, to ask, to attempt, to try, to look, see, watch, observe. *chāh-rahnauā*, to keep on the alert, to continue watching. *h.*

چاهو चाहो *chāho*, either, choose, or, whether. *h.*

چاهي *chāhī*, of or relating to a well. *chāhī*, f. or *chāhī-zamīn*, land irrigated from wells. *p.*

چاهي चाही *chāhī* or چهي चही *chahī*, f. a snipe (*Scolopax gallinago*). *h.*

چاهيتا चाहीता *chāhītā*, agreeable, desirable; m. a sweetheart, a beloved one. *h.*

چاهيتي चाहीती *chāhītī*, f. a mistress, a sweetheart. *h.* [it behoves, it is necessary. *h.*

چاهيے चाहिये *chāhiye* (impers. v.), it is proper,

چاي चाय *chāya* or चाए *chā,e*, m. eagerness, pleasure, taste. *chā,e choz*, affection. *h.*

چاءين चाईं *chā,in*, } f. scald
چاءين جوءين चाईंजूईं *chā,in jū,in*, } head. *h.*

چاءين चाईं *chā,in*, m. name of a low class of Hindūs; the seed of tamarind; scald head. *h.*

چبانا चबाना *chabānā*, a. to chew, to gnaw, to masticate. *chabā-chabā-ke bāt karnī*, a. to speak with study or preparation; also without reserve; or haughtily and scornfully. *s.*

چباولا चिबावला *chibā,olā* or चबावला *chabā-olā*, also *chibāwalā*, childish, puerile. *h.*

چباءي चबाई *chabā,ī*, f. mastication, chewing. *s.*

چبك चिबुक *chibuk*, f. the chin. *h.*

چبكني *chubuknī*, f. a puncture or wound with any sharp-pointed instrument. *d.*

چبل चिबिल *chibil*, } unpolite, boyish. *chi-*
چبلا चिबिल्ला *chibillā*, } *billā-pan*, boyishness. *h.*

چبلانا चबलाना *chablānā*, a. to chew slowly. *s.*

چبني هڏي चबनीहड्डी *chabnī-haḍḍī*, f. cartilage, grissel. *h.* [chew, &c. *s.*

چبوانا चबवाना *chabwānā*, a. to cause to

چبوترا चबूतरा *chabūtrā*, } m. a terrace or
چبوتره चबूतरः *chabūtara*, } mound to sit and converse on; a custom-house, a tribunal or court of justice, a police-station, a guard-house; a market-place; a boundary-mark. *h.*

چبهانا चुभाना *chubhānā*, a. to stick into, to thrust into, to pierce, to goad, to stab, to prick. *h.*

چبهك चभक *chabhak*, f. sting. *h.*

چبهكي चुभकी *chubhkī*, a dip, a dive, a plunge in water. *h.*

چبهنا चुभना *chubhnā*, n. to prick, to be stuck or thrust into, to pierce, to penetrate; to be pierced, pricked, stabbed. *s.*

چبهونا चुभोना *chubhonā*, a. (v. *chubhānā*) to stick into, to stab, sting, &c. *h.*

چبينا चबेना *chabenā*, m. } parched grain, to
چبيني चबेनी *chabenī*, f. } exercise the teeth with when more substantial food is not at hand. *s.*

چپ *chap*, left, the left hand. *chap o rāst*, to the left and to the right. *p.*

چپ चुप *chup*, silent; gratis, for nothing; interj. silence! (the word *rah* or *raho* being understood). *chup-chāp*, quite still; silently, stealthily. *chup-lagnī* or *chupkī lagnī*, n. to be struck dumb. *h.*

چپا चप्पा *chappā*, m. a hand-breadth, a span. *h.*

چپات *chapāt*, a slipper having a heel piece; an English shoe or slipper, in contradistinction to the Oriental shoe, &c., which wants the heel piece. *d.*

چپاتا चपाता *chapātā*, m. } a thin cake of un-
چپاتي चपाती *chapātī*, f. } leavened bread. *h.*

چپاچپ चुपाचुप *chupā-chup*, silent; furtively. *h.*

چپانا चपाना *chapānā*, a. to abash, to place one thing on another, to pile. *h.* [nous. *h.*

چپٹا चिपटा *chipṭā*, clammy, viscous, gluti-

چپٹا चपटा *chapṭā*, flattened, compressed, shallow; level or even (as ground, &c.). *s.*

چپٹانا चिपटाना *chipṭānā*, a. to sod, to turf, to apply patches, to stick. *h.*

چپٹانا चपटाना *chapṭānā* or *chipṭāna*, to flatten; to glue, to fasten, to cause to adhere. *h.*

چپٹ باز चपटबाज़ *chapaṭ-bāz*, *femina libidini sapphicæ indulgens.* *chapaṭ-bāzī*, *congressus libidinosus duarum mulierum.* *h. p.*

چپٹنا चपटना *chapaṭnā*, n. to be flattened, also to stick, &c. *h.*

چپٹنا चिपटना *chipaṭnā*, n. to stick, to adhere. *h.*

چپٹهي चपटिही *chapṭihī*, f. the name of an insect. *h.*

چپٹي चपटी *chapṭī*, f. *congressus mulierum. chapṭī laṛnā* or *khelnā*, n. *libidini sapphicæ indulgere. h.*

چپ چاپ चुपचाप *chup-chāp*, silent, perfectly still, furtively, by stealth. *h.*

چپچپا चिपचिपा *chip-chipā*, clammy, viscid, glutinous. *s.*

چپ چپاتي चुपचुपाते *chup-chupāte*, silently, secretly. *h.*

چپ چپانا चुपचुपाना *chup-chupānā*, n. to keep silence, to move quietly and secretly. *h.*

چپچپانا चिपचिपाना *chipchipānā*, n. to adhere, to cohere. *h.*

چپچپاهٹ चिपचिपाहट *chipchipāhaṭ*, f. viscosity, glutinousness, stickiness. *h.*

چپخ *chippakh*, m. a sparrowhawk. *p.*

چپرا चिपरा *chiprā*, m. gum (of the eyes). *h.*

چپراس चपरास *chaprās*, f. a buckle, a breastplate, clasp, badge. *h.*

چپراسي चपरासी *chaprāsī*, m. a messenger, or other servant, so called from his wearing a *chaprās. h.*

چپرنون चुपरनौं *chuparnauṅ*, a. (Braj) to varnish, cover, smooth, anoint. *h.*

چپري चपरी *chaprī*, a puddle, also a kind of small pulse. *h.*

چپڑا चुपड़ा *chupṛā*, plausible though false. *h.*

چپڑا चपड़ा *chapṛā*, m. a kind of lac; clear land. *h.*

چپڑانا चपड़ाना *chapṛānā*, a. to falsify, to

چپڑاو चपड़ाऊ *chapṛā,ū*, brazenfaced; m. brazen. *h.* slippers. *h.*

چپڑاها चिपड़ाहा *chipṛāhā*, bleared (as the eyes). *h.*

چپڑ چپڑ चपड़चपड़ *chapaṛ-chapaṛ*, f. the noise that a person's mouth makes when eating. *h.*

چپڑنا चपड़ना *chapaṛnā*, n. to flee, to run away; to desist, to deny. *h.*

چپڑنا चुपड़ना *chupaṛnā*, a. to varnish, to anoint, to cover, to smooth, to palliate. *h.*

چپڑي चपड़ी *chapṛī* or चिपड़ी *chipṛī*, f. cakes of cow-dung. *h.*

چپڑي चुपड़ी *chupṛī*, f. oiled, greasy; smooth, plausible. *chupṛī-bāt*, flattery, soft words. *chupṛī roṭī*, cakes rich with clarified butter. *chupṛī ālū*, the yam. *h.*

چپقلش *chapḳalish*, f. crowding, want of room. *t.*

چپك चिप्पक *chippak*, shallow; m. f. name of a bird, the goat-sucker. *h.*

چپكا चपका *chavkā* m. the goat-sucker; (*Caprimulgus*). *h.*

چپكا चुपका *chupkā*, quiet, silent, mute. *chupke*, quietly, silently, with little noise. *chupke-kahnā*, so speak in a whisper, or in a very low voice. *h.*

چپكانا चपकाना *chapkānā*, a. to make adhere, to stick on; to compress; to threaten. *h.*

چپكن चपकन *chapkan*, f. a kind of vest, a sort of coat. *chapkan-dār*, m. a vest like a *chapkan. h.*

چپكنا चिपकना *chipaknā*, n. to stick, to adhere; to spread or sink (as ink on damp paper); to be compressed. *chipak jānā*, n. to be sold on account of its sweetness; to fall in love at first sight. *h.*

چپكنا चपकना *chapaknā* (also *chipaknā*), n. to collapse. *h.*

چپكو *chupko*, gratis, for nothing. *d.*

چپكه चिप्पख *chippakh*, m. a sparrowhawk. *p.*

چپكي चुपकी *chupkī* (fem. of *chupkā*), silent, also silence; (in Dakh.) *chupke*, gratis. *h.*

چپل *chapal*, filthy, brutal, beastly. *p.*

چپل चप्पल *chappal*, f. a slipper. *chappal mārnā*, to beat with a slipper. *h.*

چپل चपल *chapal*, trembling, tremulous, wavering, unsteady; swift, expeditious; wanton, restless, volatile; adv. swiftly. *s.*

چپلا चपला *chapalā*, f. the goddess Lakshmī or fortune; lightning; a whore. *s.*

چپلاتمك चपलात्मक *chapalātmak*, of a fickle or inconstant nature. *s.*

چپلپن *chapal-pan*, volatileness, agility. *d.*

چپلتا चपलता *chapalatā*, f. fickleness, inconstancy. *s.*

چپلسيند *chappal-senḍ*, the prickly pear (called in the north *nāg-phanī*). *d.*

چپلگڑي *chapalgiṛī*, a kind of lizard. *d.*

چپن चप्पन *chappan*, m. a lid or cover of a pot (large). *h.*

چپنا चपना *chapnā*, n. to be abashed, to be bashful in company, to blush, to submit, to stoop, to be crushed or squeezed. *h.*

چپنا चिपना *chipnā*, n. to be concealed. *h.*

چپني चपनी *chapnī*, f. a lid, a cover, top (small) the knee-pan. *chapnī bhar pānī meṅ* (or *leke*) *ḍūb marnā*, (lit. to drown one's self in a saucerful of water) to be greatly abashed. *chapnī chāṭnī*, (to lick the pot-lid) to be contented with a little. *h.*

چپو चप्पू *chappū*, m. a paddle, an oar. *chappū mārnā*, a. to row. *h.*

چپوٹي चपोटी *chapoṭī*, f. an old worn-out turban. *h.*

چپ وراست *chap o rāst*, m. (lit. left and right) unsteadiness, want of principle, carelessness. *p.*

چپهال चफाल *chaphāl*, f. a place surrounded with marshes and mire. *h.*

چپي चिप्पी *chippī*, f. a patch on paper. *h.*

چپي चप्पी *chappī*, f. kneading the limbs. *h.*

چپي चुप्पी *chuppī*, f. silence. *h.*

چپيٹ चपेट *chapeṭ*, m. the palm of the hand with the fingers extended; f. a sudden misfortune, risk; a slap, a blow. *s.*

چپيٹا चपेटा *chapeṭā*, m. a slap, a blow. *s.*

چپيٹا चपेटा *chapeṭā*, illegitimate; m. a bastard, or as we say in the vernacular "a bye blow". *h.*

چت चित *chit*, f. look, glance, sense; adj. supine, lying flat on the back. *chit-k.*, to throw (one's adversary) on his back (a term in wrestling), to discomfit, overcome in battle. *h.*

چت चित *chit* or चित्त *chitt*, m. f. intellect, mind, life, soul, heart, memory. *chit-chā,e*, pleasing to the mind, what the heart desires. *chit-chor*, heart-stealing or -alluring. *chit denā*, to pay attention. *chit-karnā*, to make up one's mind. *chit-lānā*, to be attentive, to apply to. *chit-lagan*, amusing, pleasant. *s.*

چت *chit*, (in Dakh.) blotted, foul, stained. *chit-k.* or *chit-pit-k.*, to blot paper when writing; to spoil a copy. *d.*

چتا चिता *chitā*, a funeral pile, a heap of dried wood on which dead bodies are burned. *s.*

چتا चित्ता *chittā*, m. name of a medicinal plant (*Plumbago zeylanica*). *s.*

چتا चित्ता *chittā*, m. application of a blister; white; adj. lying down, reclining. *h.*

چتابھوگ चित्ताभोग *chittā-bhog*, m. consciousness of pain or pleasure, attention of the mind to its own sensations. *s.*

چتاپنڈ चितापिण्ड *chitā-pinḍ*, offerings of cakes to the manes at the time of burning the corpse. *s.*

چتاچوڑک चिताचूड़क *chitā-chūṛak*, m. a mark where a funeral pile has been, a mausoleum, a monument. *s.*

چتارنا चितारना *chitārnā*, m. to paint. *s.*

چتاروهن चितारोहण *chitārohan*, ascending the funeral pile (a widow); burning with the dead body of a husband. *s.*

چتاري चितारी *chitārī*, m. a painter. *d.*

چتاکھا चिताखा *chitākhā*, f. a funeral pile. *s.*

چتانا चिताना *chitānā*, a. to caution, to warn, to apprise, to advise, to remind. *s.*

چتانگ चिताङ्ग *chitāng*, supine (applied to animated beings). *h.* [*chitānā*), to caution, &c. *s.*

چتاونا चितावना *chitā,onā* or *chitāwnā*, a. (see

چتاوني चितावनी *chitā,onī* or *chitāwnī*, f. a token; admonition, warning. *s.*

چت پت *chit-pit*, stained, defiled. *d.*

چت پٹ *chit-paṭ*, a game at wrestling. *d.*

چتپرسنتا चित्तप्रसन्नता *chitta-prasannatā*, f. happiness, gaiety. *s.*

چتر चित्र *chitra*, m. a picture; painting, delineation; writing, &c.; a circular ornament, a sectarial mark on the forehead; the mirage, or fallacious appearance of water on a sandy plain when heated by the sun. *chitr-sālā* or *-sārī*, a gallery of pictures. *s.*

چتر चतुर *chatur*, cunning, sly, shrewd, wise, knowing, expert; four. *s.*

چتر *chatr* or *chatra*, m. an umbrella. *p.*

چترا चतरा *chatrā* or चतुरा *chaturā*, wise, intelligent, cunning. *s.*

چترا चित्रा *chitrā*, f. name of the fourteenth mansion of the moon (*Spica virginis*); adj. variegated, speckled. *s.*

چترانگ *chitrāng*, m. a kind of snake; a plant (*Plumbago zeylanica*); yellow orpiment; vermilion. *s.* [(v. *chaturtā*). *s.*

چترائي चतुराई *chaturā,ī*, f. cunningness, &c.

چتربچتر चित्रविचित्र *chitr-bichitr*, of various colours. *s.* [an epithet of *Vishṇu*. *s.*

چتربهج चतुर्भुज *chatur-bhuj*, having four arms;

چتربهجي चतुर्भुजी *chatur-bhujī*, having four arms; an epithet of *Devī*. *s.*

چتربهدر चतुर्भद्र *chatur-bhadra*, m. the four objects of human pursuit (v. *chatur-varga*). *s.*

چتربهوجن चित्रभोजन *chitr-bhojan*, m. change of diet, eating of unusual food. *s.*

چترپادا चित्रपादा *chitra-pādā*, f. the *mainā*, a small bird so called. *s.*

چترپدا चित्रपदा *chitra-padā*, f. a creeper (*Cissus pedata*); a kind of metre. *s.*

چترپرنکا चित्रपर्णिका *chitra-parnikā*, } f. a plant
چترپرني चित्रपर्णी *chitra-parnī*, } (*Hemionitis cordifolia*); Bengal bladder (*Rubia manjeth*) *s.*

چترتا चतुरता *chaturtā*, f. cunning, slyness wisdom, knowledge, dexterity. *s.*

چترته चतुर्थ *chaturth*, the fourth. *s.* [day. *s.*

چترتهي चतुर्थी *chaturthī*, f. the fourth lunar

چتردش चतुर्दश *chaturdash*, fourteen. *s.*

چتردشي चतुर्दशी *chaturdashī*, the fourteenth day of the moon's age. *s.*

چتردك चतुर्दिक *chaturdik*, the four sides, all around (v. *chāron ṭaraf* and *chāroṅ or*, under *chār*). *s.*

چترسر चतुरस्र *chatur-asra*, four-cornered, quadrangular. *s.*

چترشالا चित्रशाला *chitra-shālā*, f. a gallery of pictures, a picture-room. *s.* [painter. *s.*

چترکار चित्रकार *chitra-kār*, m. a portrait-

چترکاري चित्रकारी *chitra-kārī*, f. portrait-painting. *s.*

چترکوٹ चित्रकूट *chitra-kūṭ*, m. a mountain in Bandelkhand, the modern Compteh, and first habitation of Rāma in his exile. *s.*

چترگپت चित्रगुप्त *chitra-gupta*, m. a name of Yama; Yama's registrar, said to record the good and evil deeds of men: the recording angel. *s*

چترگر चित्रगर *chitra-gar*, m. a portrait-painter. *s.*

چترگريو चित्रग्रीव *chitr-grīv* or *chitra-grīva*, spotted neck; the name of the king of the pigeons in the *Akhlāqi Hindī*. *s.*

چترل चित्रल *chitral*, m. variegated or spotted (the colour). *s.*

چترمار *chatar-mār*, m. toadstool, mushroom. *p.*

چترمکھ चतुर्मुख *chatur-mukh*, having four faces; an epithet of Brāhma. *s.*

چترمول *chittar-mūl*, m. name of a plant (*Plumbago zeylanica*), called in Urdu *chittā*, q. v. *d.*

چترنا चितरना *chitarnā*, a. to paint. *s.*

چترنگي *chitrangī* (explained by *haft-rangī*), versatile, unsteady, deceitful. *d.*

چترني चित्रिणी *chitrinī*, f. the second division of women (the first being called *padminī*, q. v.). *s.*

چترنيترا चित्रनेत्रा *chita-netrā*, f. a small bird, the *mainā*. *s.*

چتروچتر चित्रविचित्र *chitra-vichitra*, of various colours. *s.*

چتروَرگ चतुर्वर्ग *chatur-varga*, m. the four objects of human pursuit, viz. *dharma*, *artha*, *kāma*, and *moksha* (virtue, wealth, lust, and final beatitude), q. v. *s.*

چتروَرن चतुर्वर्ण *chaturvarṇa*, m. the four classes or castes of Hindūs. *s.*

چترونش चतुर्विंश *chaturvinsha*, the twenty-fourth. *s.*

چترونشت चतुर्विंशति *chaturvinshati*, twenty-four. *s.*

چترويدي चतुर्वेदी *chatur-vedī*, a Brāhman who has read (or professes to have read) the four Vedas. *s.*

چتري चतरी *chatrī*, f. a canopy, veil, a parasol; a tent, pavilion. *p.*

چتريگ चतुर्युग *chatur-yug*, m. the aggregate of the four *yugs* or ages of the world. *s.*

چتڑ *chittar*, the buttocks, hips, thighs. *d.*

چتڑان بجانا *chitaṛān bajānā*, to rejoice, to evince pleasure. *d.*

چتشپتھ चतुष्पथ *chatush-path*, m. a place where four roads meet. *s.*

چتشپد चतुष्पद *chatush-pad*, m. or *chatush-padī*, f. a metre or stanza consisting of four *pads* or lines. *s.*

چتشپدا चतुष्पदा *chatush-padā*, m. a quadruped. *s.*

چتکار चित्कार *chit-kār*, m. a cry, a scream. *s.*

چت کبرا चितकबरा *chit-kabrā*, } piebald, speckled, spotted. *s.*
چتلا चितला *chitlā*,

چتل चित्तल *chittal* or چيتل चीतल *chītal*, m. the spotted deer (*Cervus axis*). *h.*

چتنا चितना *chitnā*, n. to look, appear, seem. *h.*

چتنا चितना *chitnā*, n. to be painted. *s.*

چتوان चित्तवान *chittawān*, kind-hearted, amiable. *s.*

چتوبھرم चित्तविभ्रम *chitta-vibhram*, m. madness, derangement. *s.*

چتون चितवन *chitwan*, f. a sight, a look. *h.*

چتونا चितौना *chitaunā*, } a. to see, to look at, to behold. *h.*
چتونوں चितौनौं *chitaunauṅ*,

چتھاڑنا चिथाड़ना *chithāṛnā*, a. to tear to pieces; to fill a paper with writing; to abuse, revile, treat with indignity. *h.*

چتھٹ चितहट *chithaṭ*, f. reluctance, repugnance. *h.*

چتھڑا चिथड़ा *chithṛā*, m. a rag, tatter. *h.*

چتھڑيا चिथड़िया *chithaṛiyā*, tattered, ragged, clothed in rags. *h.*

چٹي चिट्टी *chiṭṭī*, f. a scar, a spot, freckle, &c.; a kind of serpent; a *kauṛī* worn smooth with rubbing. *chiṭṭī-dār*, speckled. *chiṭṭī lānā*, a. to scar. *h.*

چٹي *chiṭṭī*, f. mildew or rot in cloth. *chiṭṭī khānā*, to become mildewed or rotten, as damp cloth. *d.*

چتيا चित्या *chityā*, f. a funeral pile. *s.*

چتيرا चितेरा *chiterā*, m. a person who paints flowers, &c. on wood, a painter. *s.*

چتينوں चितैनौं *chitainauṅ*, a. to see, to look at, to behold. *h.*

چتيه चित्य *chitya*, m. a monument, or any mark of the site of a funeral pile. *s.*

چٹ चिट *chiṭ*, f. rag, scrap.. *chiṭ ukhaṛnā*, n. to splinter, or have small pieces knocked off (furniture). *chiṭṭ* (corruptly for *chit*, q.v.), mind, &c. *h.*

چٹ चट *chaṭ*, quickly, instantly; f. an excoriation, a sore, scab, chancre; the noise of breaking, snap. *chaṭ bhasam*, eating up the whole, licking the platter clean. *chaṭ de ṭūṭnā*, n. to snap short, to break. *chaṭ-k.*, a. to eat, to dissipate, to devour. *chaṭ-h.*, to be dissipated or consumed. *h.*

چٹا चुट्टा *chuṭṭā*, m. (see *choṭī*) a lock of hair left on the top of the head, &c.

چٹا चिट्टा *chiṭṭā*, white, fair; m. a silver coin. *chiṭṭā ukhāṛnā*, n. to splinter, or knock small pieces off furniture. *h.*

چٹا चट्टा *chaṭṭā*, m. a schoolboy. *s.*

چٹا *chaṭṭā*, m. a frock-coat, a jacket. *d.*

چٹابٹا चट्टाबट्टा *chaṭṭā-baṭṭā*, m. the name of a plaything, a kind of rattle or clapper. *h.*

چٹاچٹ चटाचट *chaṭāchaṭ*, m. reiterated sound. *s.*

چٹاخا *chaṭākhā*, m. (properly *chaṭākā*) a crash, an explosion, a smack (as in kissing). *h.*

چٹاک चटाक *chaṭāk*, f. a crash, an explosion; adj. intelligent. *h.*

چٹاکا चटाका *chaṭākā*, } m. a crash, &c. (v. *chaṭākhā*). *h.*
چٹاکھا चटाखा *chaṭākhā*,

چھٹالنا चुटालना *chuṭālnā*, a. to wound. *h.*

چٹان चटान *chaṭān* or *chaṭṭān*, f. rocky ground, a block of stone. *h.*

چٹانا चटाना *chaṭānā*, a. to make lick, or lap up; m. the ceremony of feeding a child for the first time. *h.*

چٹانا चुटाना *chuṭānā*, a. to wound. *h.*

چٹائي चटाई *chaṭā,ī*, f. a mat. *chaṭā,ī bichhānā*, a. to mat, to spread a mat. *h.*

چٹ پٹ चटपट *chaṭ-paṭ*, hastily, in a hurry, instantly. *h.*

چٹ پٹا चटपटा *chaṭ-paṭā*, active, hasty; stout; meat dressed with little sauce or gravy. *h.*

چٹ پٹانا चटपटाना *chaṭ-paṭānā*, n. to be agitated, to flutter, to palpitate, to wince. *h.*

چٹ پٹاهٹ चटपटाहट *chaṭ-paṭāhaṭ*, f. agitation, flurry, flutter, palpitation. *h.*

چٹ پٹي चटपटी *chaṭ-paṭī*, f. haste, hurry, quickness, agility, restlessness. *h.*

چٹ پٹیا चटपटिया *chaṭ-paṭiyā*, active, quick, alert; hot with spice; restless, fidgety. *h.*

چٹجیرا चटजीरा *chaṭ-jīrā*, m. name of a tree. *h.*

چٹخنا *chaṭakhnā*, n. (v. *chaṭaknā*) to crack, split, &c. *h.*

چٹري चटरी *chaṭrī*, name of an herb used as fodder for cattle. *h.* [tree (v. *chaṭ-jīrā*). *h.*

چٹ زيره चटजीरः *chaṭ-zīra*, m. the name of a

چٹ ساري चटशारी *chaṭ-sārī*, } f. a school,
چٹ سال चटशाल *chaṭ-sāl*, } academy. *s.*

چٹک चटक *chaṭak*, m. a sparrow; f. a hen-sparrow; a crash, a crack, a smack; intelligence, gaudiness; glitter, splendour, prime of life; adj. intelligent, quick. *chaṭak se*, deceiving. *chaṭak se jānā*, to pay with the fore top-sail. *chaṭak-wā,ī*, f. quickness. *h.*

چٹکا चिटका *chiṭhā*, m. a kind of grass or grain; mucus, slime, a place where dead bodies are burnt. *h.*

چٹکا चटका *chaṭkā*, m. scarcity. *chaṭkā lagānā*, a. to thirst, to wish. *h.*

چٹکارا चिटकारा *chiṭkārā*, m. a speck, a scar. *chiṭkārā lagānā*, a. to brand; a clack with the tongue, occasioned by an acrid taste. *h.*

چٹکارنا चटकारना *chaṭkārnā*, a. to urge cattle by the clacking noise made by drawing the tongue from the palate. *h.* [from last). *h.*

چٹکاري चटकारी *chaṭkārī*, f. (verbal noun

چٹکانا चटकाना *chaṭkānā*, a. to crack (as a whip); to snap the fingers (in rejoicing), to split; to fire off a musket; to irritate. *h.*

چٹکلا चुटकुला *chuṭkulā*, m. pleasantry, facetiousness, wit, humour; (see *ṭoṭkā*) conundrum. *h.*

چٹکلاسا चुटकुलासा *chuṭkulāsā*, amusing. *h.*

چٹکنا चटकना *chaṭaknā*, } n. to crackle (as
چٹکهنا चटखना *chaṭakhnā*, } charcoal or wood on fire); to crack, as a whip; to split. *h.*

چٹکنا चटकना *chuṭkanā*, m. a slap, a box, a blow. *h.*

چٹکي चुटकी *chuṭkī*, f. a pinch, snapping of the fingers; the hammer of a gun; a mode of printing cloth, or *gulbadan*; name of an ornament worn on the toes. *chuṭkī bharnā*, or *lenā*, a. to nip, to pinch; to throw out provoking insinuations. *chuṭkiyoṅ meṅ uṛānā*, to put one off with a joke. *h.*

چٹکي चिटकी *chiṭhī*, f. sunshine. *h.*

چٹکیلا चटकीला *chaṭkīlā*, splendid, glittering. *h.*

چٹلا चुटला *chuṭlā*, f. a lock of hair, a queue, &c. (v. *chaṭī*). *s.*

چٹنا चटना *chaṭnā*, m. voracious (man). *h.*

چٹني चटनी *chaṭnī*, f. a kind of acid sauce (or marmalade); a voracious woman. *h.*

چٹوا चटुआ *chaṭū,ā*, m. a kind of plaything; a sort of hawk. *h.* [up. *h.*

چٹوانا चटवाना *chaṭwānā*, a. to cause to lick

چٹوخا चटोखा *chaṭokhā*, m. a kind of dove. *h.*

چٹور चटोर *chaṭor*, } m. an epicure. *h.*
چٹورا चटोरा *chaṭorā*, }

چٹوکها चटोखा *chatokhā*, m. (v. *chatokhā*).

چٹه चिट्ठः *chiṭṭa*, an account of all the lands of a village. *h.*

چٹه *chuṭṭa*, m. a cheroot or cigar. *d.*

چٹها चट्ठा *chaṭṭhā*, m. a tit-bit, dainties. *h.*

چٹها चिट्ठा *chiṭṭhā*, m. a memorandum of money paid, or the pay of servants of the state; a rough note or account, journal or day book. *chiṭhā-'amaldārī*, a deed conveying a proprietary right. *h.*

چٹهي चिट्ठी *chiṭṭhī*, f. a note, a letter; an order or demand. *chiṭhī-ṭalab* or *ṭalab-chiṭṭhī*, f. a summons. *chiṭṭhī-pātī* or *-pattar*, f. epistolary correspondence. *h.*

چٹي चिट्टी *chiṭṭī*, f. the hen of the little birds called amaduvades (*Fringilla amandava*). *h.*

چٹي चट्टी *chaṭṭī*, f. scarcity, want. *h.*

چٹیا चुटिया *chuṭiyā*, m. a spy to thieves, the head of a gang of thieves; f. a lock of hair left on the head when the rest is shaved. *h.*

چٹیا चटिया *chaṭiyā*, m. a pupil, a scholar. *s.*

چٹیانا चुटियाना *chuṭiyānā*, a. to wound. *h.*

چٹیکار *chaṭṭekār*, m. a Portuguese or half-caste; an Anglo-Indian or Eurasian. *d.*

چٹیلا चुटीला *chuṭīlā*, wounded, bruised. *h.*

چچ चुचि *chuchi*, f. the female breast or bosom. *s.*

چچا चचा *chachā* or *chachchā*, m. paternal uncle, father's brother. *h.*

چچانا चुचाना *chuchānā*, n. to drop, to be drenched with water, to be dripping wet with sweat, water, &c. *h.* [wife. *d.*

چچاني *chichānī*, f. aunt, father's brother's

چچر चचर *chachar*, (land) that after having lain fallow has been cultivated (or ploughed) for one year. *h.*

چچرا चचरा *chachrā*, m. the name of a tree. *h.*

چچڑ चुचड़ *chuchchaṛ*, m. large breasts. *s.*

چچڑهي کهينچنا चिचढ़ी खेंचना *chichṛhī khainchnā*, n. to scrawl, to score. *h.*

چچڑي चिचड़ी *chichṛī*, f. a tick or louse (of dogs and sheep). *h.*

چچکارنا चुचकारना *chuchkhārnā*, a. to fondle, to chirp to, to cheer by making the noise occasioned by drawing in the breath with lips protruded. *h.*

چچکاري चुचकारी *chuchkhārī*, f. blandishment. *h.*

چچل चचल *chachchal*, m. large breasts. *h.*

چچندر चिचुन्दर *chichundar*, m. a musk-rat. *h.*

چچنڈا चिचिंडा *chichindā*, m. the name of a vegetable (*Beta vulgaris*). *h.* [*nā*). *h.*

چچوانا चुचवाना *chuchwānā*, n. (v. *chuchā-*

چچورنا चचोरना *chachornā*, } a. to suck (a

چچوڑنا चचोड़ना *chachoṛnā*, } dry substance from which nothing can be obtained). *h.*

چچونڈا चिचोंडा *chichonḍā* (same as *chichinḍā*). *chichonḍā honā*, to be still, motionless. *d.*

چچهانا *chuchuhānā*, to sing, to whistle, to warble as birds. *p.*

چچهيا चचहिया *chachahiyā*, m. a whistler. *h.*

چچي *chichī*, f. a woman's bosom, nipple, or teat. *d.* [brother's wife, aunt. *h.*

چچي चच्ची *chachchī* or चची *chachī*, f. father's

چچيانا चिचियाना *chichiyānā*, n. to squeak, to shriek, to bleat. *h.*

چچير चचीर *chachīr*, m. a line, stripe, score. *h.*

چچيرا चचेरा *chacherā*, descended from or related through a paternal uncle, as *chacherā bhā,ī*, m. a cousin, son of paternal uncle; *chacherī bahin*, daughter of paternal uncle. *h.*

چخ *chakh*, f. (scattering, dispersing) in Hind. variance, rupture, quarrel. *p.*

چخا چخي *chakhā-chakhī*, f. wrangling. *p.*

چخماخ *chakhmākh* (v. *chaḳmāḳ*), f. a flint. *p.*

چخي *chakhe*, begone, away, avaunt. *p.*

چداس चुदास *chudās*, f. lust, lasciviousness. *h.*

چداسا चुदासा *chudāsā*, m. } desirous of copu-

چداسي चुदासी *chudāsī*, f. } lating. *h.*

چدانا चुदाना *chudānā*, a. *viri amplexibus se submittere (mulier)*. *h.*

چداءي चुदाई *chudā,ī*, f. copulation. *h.*

چدر *chaddar*, f. a sheet, a table-cloth, a cloth of more than one breadth. *chaddar-andāzī*, a marriage ceremony among the Sikhs; when a man marries a widow a sheet is thrown over the parties. *chaddar bichhānā*, a. to lay the cloth. *p.*

چدکڑ चुदक्कड़ *chudakkaṛ*, m. a salacious person *qui coitu frequenti fruitur*. *h.*

چدنا चुदना *chudnā* n. *feminam subigere*. *h.*

چدوانا चुदवाना *chudwānā* (v. *chudānā*). *h.*

چدواءي चुदवाई *chudwā,ī*, f. the hire of prostitution. *h.*

چدويا चुदवैया *chudwaiyā*, m. (v. *chudakkaṛ*) *h.*

چڈها चड्ढा *chaḍḍhā*, m. the groin, a bubo; (in Dakh.) *chaḍḍā*, the same. *h.*

چر चर *char*, m. a ford, shoal; an island in the current of a river, a sand-bank; sound made by tearing cloth, &c.; a wag-tail. *h.*

چر चुर *chur*, an imitative sound. *h.*

چر चर *char*, m. forage, pasture; food; adj. going, removable; used in comp. as *jal-char*, that which moves in the water, aquatic. *s.*

چر चिर *chir*, adj. long (time), a long time. *s.*

چرا *chirā*, why? how? *chirā-ki*, because that. *charā*, pasturing, grazing. *p.*

چرا चर्रा *charrā*, m. thunder. *h.*

چراچر चराचर *charāchar*, moveable, locomotive; shaking, unsteady; sky, atmosphere, heaven. *s.*

چراغ *chirāgh*, m. a lamp, light. *chirāgh-baṛhānā* or *-ṭhanḍā-k.*, a. to put out, to extinguish (a lamp). *chirāgh-dān*, m. a stand for a lamp. *chirāgh meṅ battī paṛnā*, an expression to denote that evening sets in, that it grows dark, and that it is time to light the lamp. *p.*

چراغان *chirāghān*, pl. lamps, a display of lamps, a general illumination. *p.*

چراغپا *chirāgh-pā*, rearing (a horse). *p.*

چراغي *chirāghī*, f. a present made to the *mullā* for offering up oblations at the tomb of a saint; a grant of land bestowed for the same purpose; alms given to beggars who walk the streets at night, as the class called *naḳsh-bandī*; a present to soothsayers. *p.*

چراك चराक *charāk*, m. an animal that grazes. *s.*

چراگاه *charā-gāh*, f. a pasture, a meadow. *p.*

چران *charān*, चरान m. lea fallow, a meadow, a salt marsh or meadow by the sea-shore. *s.*

چران *charān* (v. *charand*), grazing, &c. *p.*

چرانا चराना *charānā*, a. to graze, to pasture. *s.*

چرانا चुराना *churānā*, a. to steal, to filch. *s.*

چرانا चिराना *chirānā*, a. to cause to tear, to split. *h.* [to smart. *h.*

چرانا चर्राना *charrānā*, n. to burst; to ache,

چراند चिरांद *chirānd*, f. the smell of burning leather, hair, &c. *h.*

چرانڈي *chirānḍī*, f. an alley, a bye-lane. *d.*

چراو *chirā,o*, m. a rent, a fissure. *d.*

چراو चराव *charāw* or *charā,o*, m. pasture-ground. *s.*

چراي चिरायु *chirāyu*, long-lived; m. a deity, [a divinity. *s.*

چرايندہ *charā,inda* or *charāyanda*, grazing; m. a grazier. *p.*

چرائي चराई *charā,ī*, f. the price paid for pasturage, or rent thereof. *p. h.*

چرائتا चिराइता *chirā,eta*, m. a species of gentian so called (*Gentiana chirayita*). *s.*

چرايہ चिरायुः *chirāyu*, of long existence. *s.*

چرب *charb*, fat, thick, gross, viscous, oily; also *charab*, an overmatch. *charb-dast*, active, ingenious; (met.) a thief. *charb-zabān*, agreeable, conversable, entertaining. *charb-ghizā*, dainties, viands. *p.*

چربانا चरबाना *charbānā*, a. to brace a drum. *h.*

چربرا *charbarā*, active, alert, expert. *d.*

چربرانا *charbarānā*, to practise plausibility, to speak smoothly. *d.*

چربرائيگي चरबराइगी *charbarā,egī*, f. expertness, dexterity, activity. *h.*

چربنا *charabnā*, to overcome, prevail. *d.*

چربي *charbī*, f. fat, suet, grease. *charbī-dār*, fat, not lean. *charbī-kī jhillī*, f. caul of fat covering the bowels. *p.*

چرپٹا *charapṭā*, a small or slight wound. *d.*

چرپر चरपर *charpar*, m. (see *charphar*). *h.*

چرپرا चरपरा *charparā*, acrid, hot (as pepper); smart (in conversation). *h.*

چرپرانا चरपराना *charparānā*, n. to smart. *h.*

چرپراہٹ चरपराहट *charparāhaṭ*, f. smarting, pungency. *h.* [nious. *h.*

چرپريا चरपरिया *charpariyā*, active, inge-

چرپوز *charpūz* (in Hindī *char-pūj*), useless, stupid, miserly, wicked, mean. *p.*

چرپھر चरफर *charphar*, m. activity, cleverness, quickness. *h.* [quick. *h.*

چرپھرا चरफरा *charpharā*, active, clever,

چرت चुर्त *churt* or चर्त *chart*, f. nap, drowsiness, nodding. *h.*

چرت चरित *charit*, } m. instituted or peculiar
چرتر चरित्र *charitr*, } observance or conduct; story, adventures; nature, temper, behaviour, disposition, conduct, carriage, quality, humour, use, custom, talent. *s*

چرتکت चिरतिक्त *chir-tikta*, m. a kind of gentian (*Gentiana cherayta*). *s.*

چرتن चिरत्न *chiratna*, old, ancient, antiquated, long-lasting. *s.*

چرتي चरती *chartī*, m. one who does not fast. *s.*

چرٹ चरट *charaṭ*, m. a wagtail. *s.*

چرجيونا चिरजीवना *chir-jīwnā*, n. to live long, to be of a great age. *s.*

چرجيوي चिरजीवी *chir-jīvī*, long-lived. *s.*

چرچا चर्चा *charchā*, m. f. talking over past events, recapitulating former occurrences; inquiry, investigation; argument, report, discourse, consideration, careful perusal, attention to business, discussing, mentioning, prevalence; practising or cultivating (science, &c.); adoration; performing by smearing the body with sandal-wood, &c. *s.*

چرچٹا चिरचिट्टा *chirchiṭṭā* or *chirchiṭṭa*, m. name of a species of grass. *h.*

چرچر चरचर *charchar*, m. prating, chattering; an imitative sound. *h.* [ing. *h*

چرچرا चरचरा *charcharā*, talkative, chatter-

چرچرا चिरचिरा *chirchirā*, m. name of a medicinal plant, said to be of sovereign virtue to one bitten by a venomous reptile, or stung by a scorpion, &c. (*Achyranthes aspera*); a child. *h.*

چرچرا चुरचुरा *churchurā*, crisp, acrid. *h.*

چرچرانا चरचराना *charcharānā* or, चिरचिराना *chirchirānā*, n. to crackle (as wood in the fire), to sputter, to chew with a crackling noise, to chide. *h.*

چرچراہٹ चिरचिराहट *chirchirāhaṭ*, f. peevishness. *h.*

چرچري चुरचुरी *churchurī*, f. dregs, sediment. *h.*

چرچک चर्चक *charchak*, m. an arguer. *s.*

چرچنا चर्चना *charchnā*, a. to consider, to reflect, to apprehend, to conceive. *s.*

چرچنا चरचना *charachnā*, to smear or plaster the body with sandal-wood. *s.*

چرچون चरचूं *char-chūn*, m. an imitative sound, as of a carriage-wheel, &c.; idle prattle. *h.*

چرچيت चर्चैत *charchait*, m. a reasoner, a mentioner. *s.* [prater. *s.*

چرچيلا चरचेला *charchelā*, m. a chatterer, a

چرخ *charkh*, m. a wheel (particularly a potter's); the sky, the heavens; the celestial globe, the sphere; fortune, chance, circular motion; a cross-bow, a bow in a very tense state; a hyena. *charkh chaṛhnā*, n. to dress or adorn one's self; to turn, as in a lathe. *charkh-pūjā*, a penitential ceremony observed by the lower orders of Hindūs on the day when the sun enters Aries, for the expiation of their own sins, or of those of other people who can afford to pay well for it. They are suspended, by an iron hook passed through the skin of the back, to one end of a lever, which is raised on the top of a high pole, and whirled round by means of a rope fixed to the other end. This penance is, of course, of great virtue, but rather disagreeable to the flesh; hence rich people prefer having it done by deputy. *charkh-andāz*, an expert archer. *charkhi dawwār*, m. the sky, the heavens, the firmament. *charkh-zan*, m. spinner. *charkh-zanī*, f. a spinning-wheel, spinning. *charkh mārnā*. n. to circulate (as the blood). *p.*

چرخا *charkhā*, } m. a spinning-wheel, a reel;
چرخہ *charkha*, } adj. thin, weak, nag, jade, garran. *p.*

چرخل *charkhal*, aged and decrepit. *d.*

چرخي *charkhī*, f. a spinning-wheel; a pulley; the instrument with which the seed is separated from cotton; a globe; a kind of fireworks, catherine-wheels; a dumb waiter; the pulley by which water is raised from a well; a round piece of wood fixed over the top of a tent pole upon which the fly of the tent rests. *charkhī fānūs*, a kind of magic lantern, a revolving lantern made of some transparent substance with pictures all round. *p.*

چرز *charz*, m. a small species of bustard (*Otis Bengalensis*). *p.*

چرس चरस *charas* or चर्स *chars*, m. the exudation of the flowers of hemp collected with the dew and prepared for use as an intoxicating drug; a leathern bucket, an urn. *h.*

چرس *churs* or *churus*, spite, envy, jealousy. *d.*

چرسا चरसा *charsā*, m. a hide, a skin. *h.*

چرستهايي चिरस्थायी *chira-sthāyī*, long-enduring, long-lasting. *s.*

چرسي *chursī*, spiteful, envious. *d.*

چرغ *chargh*, m. a kind of hawk. *p.*

چرغد *charghad*, m. a cricket. *p.*

چرغنا *churaghnā*, n. (properly *churugnā*) to prate, to prattle. *h.*

چرغينه *charghīna*, wicked, villainous. *p.*

چرك *chirk*, m. dirt, filth, ordure; matter. *chirk-ālūd*, filthy, &c. *p.*

چرك चरक *charak*, m. leprosy; name of a treatise on medicine; applied also to the author. *s.*

چرك *churuk*, the chirping of little birds. *d.*

چركا चरका *charkā*, m. white-spotted (as from a leprosy); a small wound, a scratch. *p.*

چركاري चिरकारी *chir-kārī*, dilatory, tedious, slow. *s.*

چركال चिरकाल *chir-kāl*, m. a long period; always, eternally. *chir-kāl-se*, long ago. *s.*

چركت *chirkat*, dirt, filth, ordure. *p.*

چركٹ चिरकुट *chirkuṭ*, m. a bit, piece, a rag. *s.*

چركٹ चुरकुट *churkuṭ*, m. powder. *h.*

چركٹا चरकटा *charkaṭā*, m. the person who cuts forage for cattle, elephant-keeper's mate. *s.*

چركٹيا चिरकुटिया *chirkuṭiyā*, a tatterdemalion, ragged. *s.*

چركريا चिरक्रिया *chir-kriyā*, dilatory, tedious, slow. *s.*

چركن *chirkan* (v. *chirk*), filth, &c. *p.*

چركنا चिरकना *chiraknā*, n. to have a scanty stool. *h.*

چركها चरखा *charkhā*, m. (v. *charkhā*) a wheel, &c. *p.*

چركهاو *charkhā,ū*, a beast, quadruped. *d.*

چركهي चरखी *charkhī*, f. (v. *charkhī*). *p.*

چركي चरकी *charkī*, m. a leper. *s.*

چركي चुरकी *churkī*, f. lock of hair. *h.*

چركين *chirkīn*, filthy, dirty, slovenly; m. dung. *p.*

چرگنا चुरुगना *churugnā* or चुरगना *churagnā*, n. to gabble, to prattle, to chirp. *h.*

چرم चर्म *charm*, m. leather, a skin, a hide; a shield. *charm-tarang*, m. a wrinkle, a fold of the skin. *charm-kār* or *charmār*, m. a shoemaker, a currier, or worker in leather. *charm-may*, made of leather. *s.p.*

چرم चरम *charam*, last, ultimate; west, western. *charamāchal* or *charama-kshmābhrit*, m. the western mountain behind which the sun is supposed to set. *s.*

چرمار चर्मार *charmār* (same as *charm-kār*), m. a worker in leather. *s.*

چرم چٹکا चर्मचटका *charm-chaṭkā*,
چرم چٹي चर्मचटी *charm-chaṭī*, } f. a bat. *s.*

چرمرا चुर्मुरा *churmurā*, an imitative sound. *h.*

چرمن चर्मन *charman*, m. skin, hide, bark, &c.; a shield; the hide upon which a student sits, usually that of an antelope. *s.*

چرمنوتي चर्मण्वती *charmanwatī* (also *charmavatī*), f. a river that runs across Bandelkhand into the Ganges, the modern Chambal. *s.*

چرمي चर्मी *charmī*, made of leather. *s.*

چرمينه *charmīna*, made of leather. *charmīna-doz*, m. a shoemaker. *charmīna-farosh*, m. one who sells shoes. *p.*

چرن चरण or चरन *charan*, m. the foot; the feet of a verse; shoes; feeding, grazing. *charanābharan*, m. an ornament on the feet. *charan-patit*, prostrate, fallen at the feet. *charan-patan*, m. prostration. *charan-sevā*, f. service, devotion. *charanodak* (v. *charaṇāmṛita*). *s.*

چرنا चरना *charnā*, n. to graze, to feed (as ewes, &c.). *s.*

چرنا चरना *charnā*, m. half-trousers. *charnā charhānā*, a. to put on half-trousers. *h.*

چرنا चिरना *chirnā*, n. to be torn, to split. *h.*

چرنامرت चरणामृत *charanāmṛita*, m. the water with which an idol's or Brāhman's feet have been washed. *charanāmṛita lenā*, to wash the feet of a guest and sip the water.

چرنتن चिरन्तन *chirantan*, old, ancient, long-lasting *s.*

چرنٹي चिरण्टी *chiranṭī* or *chirinṭī*, f. a woman, married or single, who continues to reside after maturity in her father's house, a young woman. *s.*

چرنجي चिरंजी *chiranjī*,
چرنجيو चिरंजीव *chiranjīv*, } long-lived, a kind of benediction, "May you live a long time!" *s.*

چرنجيون चिरञ्जीविन *chiran-jīvin*, m. a crow; Vishnu; adj. long-lived. *s.*

چرند *charand*,
چرنده *charanda*, } m. a beast, quadruped. *charand o parand*, m. beasts and birds. *p.*

چرنڈول *chirandūl*, a species of lark. *d.*

چرنودك चरणोदक *charanodak*, m. (same as *charanāmrit*, q. v.) *s.*

چرنی चरनी *charnī*, f. a feeding-trough. *h.*

چرنی चरन्नी *charannī*, f. a quarter of a rupī (*chār āne*). *h.*

چروا चरुआ *charū,ā*, m. a large pot. *h.*

چروانا चरवाना *charwānā*, a. (see *charānā*). *s.*

چروانا चिरवाना *chirwānā*, a. to cause to tear or to be torn. *h.*

چرواها चरवाहा *charwāhā*, m. a grazier, a shepherd. *s.*

چرواهی चरवाही *charwāhī*, f. wages of a shepherd paid in grain. *s.*

چروائی चरवाई *charwā,ī*, f. price paid for pasturage. *s.*

چروتر चरोतर *charotar*, a life-rent grant. *h.*

چروری चिरौरी *chraurī*, f. beseeching, begging, requesting. *h.*

چرون चर्वण *charvan*, m. chewing, masticating. *s.*

چرونجی चिरौंजी *chironjī*, f. nut of the *Chironjia sapida* (v. *piyāl*), and the tree. *h.*

چرویا *chawaiyā*, } m. a grazier, a shepherd,
چرویه *charwaiya*, } a herdsman in general. *d.*

چرویل *chirwel*, m. the chay-root or Indian madder. *d.*

چری चरी *charī*, f. unripe corn cut for the food of cattle; adj. moveable, locomotive; trembling, unsteady. *s.*

چری चुरी *churī*, f. bangles or rings made of glass, &c., and worn on the wrist; a kind of bracelet; a small well. *s.*

چری चुर्री *churrī*, f. dregs, refuse. *h.*

چریا चर्या *charyā*, f. perseverance in religious austerities, due observance of all rites. *s.*

چڑ चड़ *chaṛ*, m. sound made by breaking a branch. *h.*

چڑ चुड़ *chuṛ*, f. *vulva*; an imitative sound. *h.*

چڑ चिढ़ *chiṛ*, f. vexation, irritation; aversion, antipathy. *chiṛ nikālnā*, a. to banter. *h.*

چڑا चिड़ा *chiṛā*, m. a sparrow. *s.*

چڑالو *chiṛālū*, peevish, fretful. *d.*

چڑانا चिढ़ाना *chiṛānā*, a. to vex, irritate, mock, provoke, offend, jeer. *h.*

چڑانا *charānā* (Dakh. for چڑهانا), to raise, &c.

چڑاو *charā,o*, m. ascent, flood-tide. *d.*

چڑاوا *charāwā*, m. an offering (to an idol); jewels, &c. presented by a betrothed damsel to her intended. *d.*

چڑبڑ بولنا یا کرنا चड़बड़ बोलना or -करना *charbar-bolnā* or *-karnā*, a. to chatter, to prattle. *h.*

چڑبڑیا चड़बड़िया *charbaṛiyā*, m. chatterer. *h.*

چڑپڑا चिड़पिड़ा *chirpirā*, fiery, hot (as pepper), acrid. *h.*

چڑپڑانا चड़पड़ाना *charparānā*, to smart, to palpitate, to flutter, to throb. *h.*

چڑپڑاهٹ चिपिड़ाहट *chirpirāhaṭ*, f. acrimony. *h.*

چڑچڑ चड़चड़ *charchar*, m. an imitative sound. *h.*

چڑچڑا चिड़चिड़ा *chiṛchiṛā*, m. the name of a plant (*Achyranthes aspera*); cross, peevish, crabbed, fretful. *h.*

چڑچڑانا चड़चड़ाना *charcharānā*, n. to crack. *h.*

چڑچڑاهٹ चिड़चिड़ाहट *chiṛchiṛāhaṭ*, f. peevishness, fretfulness. *h.*

چڑر चड़र *charar*, } m. an imitative sound. *h.*
چڑڑ चड़ड़ *charar*, }

چڑنا चिड़ना *chiṛnā*, n. to be vexed irritated, provoked, to fret. *h.*

چڑندول *chiṛandol*, m. a species of lark. *d.*

چڑوا चुड़आ *churu,ā* or *churwā*, m. a dish prepared from parched rice. *s.*

چڑھ चढ़ *chaṛh*, lit. rise; increase or augmentation of rent. *h.*

چڑھ चिढ़ *chiṛh*, f. abhorrence, abomination, dislike, vexation, provocation (v. *chiṛ*). *h.*

چڑهانا चढ़ाना *chaṛhānā*, a. to make ascend. &c.; to offer up (oblations); to string a bow, or to brace a drum; to raise, lift, advance, apply, put, spread, bend, dye (with colour), pull, to draw on, cock, fix (a bayonet), run. *h.*

چڑهانا चिढ़ाना *chiṛhānā*, a. (v. *chiṛānā*). *h.*

چڑهاو चढ़ाव *chaṛhāw* or *chaṛhā,o*, m. ascent, rise, acclivity, attack, rank, dignity; flood-tide; offerings made to idols; raising in price or rent. *h.*

چڑهائی चढ़ाई *chaṛhā,ī*, f. (from *chaṛhānā*) ascent, acclivity, attack, assault, rank, dignity, price paid for ascending, riding, embarking, &c. *h.*

چڑهبنا चढ़बना *chaṛhbannā*, a. to find an opportunity. *h.*

چڑهتا चढ़ता *chaṛhtā*, increase of price, making of additional profit, settlement of revenue at a progressively increasing price. *chaṛhtā paṭṭā*, a lease for a term of years the rent progressively increasing. *chaṛhtā honā*, to be excelling, rising, &c. *h.*

چڑهتی चढ़ती *chaṛhtī*, f. advantage, gain, rise. *h.*

چڑهکے चढ़के *chaṛhke*, avowedly, designedly, excellently. *h.*

چڑهنا चढ़ना *chaṛhnā*, n. to ascend, to mount, to advance, to attack, to embark, to board, to rise, to climb, soar, spread, swell, ride; to elapse, or pass over (as time); to be strung (a bow); to be braced (a drum); to be offered up (a sacrifice). *chaṛhnā utarnā*, n. to hire, and dismiss; *congressus*. *h.*

چڑهنا चिढ़ना *chiṛhnā*, n. to be vexed, fret, take offence. *h.*

چڑهندار चढ़न्दार *chaṛhan-dār*, m. a passenger, supercargo. *h.*

چڑهنی चढ़नी *chaṛhnī*, f. preparations for battle. *h.*

چڑهوا चढ़ौवा *chuṛhauwā*, m. a shoe rising up over the heel of the wearer. *h.*

چڑھوان चढ़वां *chaṛhwāṅ*, rising high. *h.*

چڑھوانا चढ़वाना *chaṛhwānā*, to cause to be raised. *h.*

چڑھوي चढ़वी *chaṛwī*, f. raising (rent, &c.). *h.*

چڑھویا चढ़वैया *chaṛwaiyā*, m. one who ascends, mounts, &c., a rider. *h.*

چڑھي चढ़ी *chaṛhī*, f. preparations for battle. *h.*

چڑھیت चढ़ैत *chaṛhait*, m. (v. *chaṛhaiyā*) one who ascends, &c., also the same as *chaṛhaitā*. *h.*

چڑھیتا चढ़ैता *chaṛhaitā*, m. a trooper who does not ride his own horse, a rider. *h.*

چڑي चिड़ी *chiṛī* or *chuṛī*, a bird, a hen-sparrow. *s.*

چڑیا चिड़िया *chiṛiyā*, f. a bird; a kind of sewing. *chiriyā-khāna*, m. aviary. *h.*

چڑیا चिड़िया *chiṛiyā*, f. a hen-sparrow. *s.*

چڑیل चुड़ैल *churail*, f. the ghost of a woman who died while pregnant; a hag, fury; a dirty woman, slut, slattern. *h.*

چڑیمار चिड़ीमार *chiṛī-mār*, m. a birdcatcher, a fowler. *h.*

چسانا चुसाना *chusānā*, a. to give or cause to suck. *h.*

چسپان *chaspān*, viscous, slimy, coherent. *p.*

چسپیدگي *chaspīdagī*, f. love, affection, attachment, coherence. *p.*

چسپیده *chaspīda*, joined to, stuck, adhered; addicted to, liking, fond of, attached. *p.*

چست *chust*, active, fleet, ingenious; narrow, straight, tight. *chust chālāk*, active, alert, fleet. *p.*

چستا *chastā*, m. tripe, the straight gut, the rectum. *p.*

چستا *chustā*, tight, fitting well (as clothes). *p.*

چستان *chistān*, m. an enigma; lit. *chīst ān*, "what is that?" *p.*

چسته *chusta*, m. runnet. *p.*

چستي *chustī*, f. activity, alertness, fleetness. *p.*

چسك चसक *chasak*, f. pain, aching, throbbing pain, a stitch (sharp lancinating pain). *h.*

چسکا चसका *chaskā*, m. love, ardent desire, a relish, habit, custom. *h.*

چسکر चुसक्कर *chusakkar*, m. one in the habit of sucking, (met.) a tippler. *s.*

چسکنا चसकना *chasaknā* or चुसकना *chusaknā*, n. to throb, to ache. *h.*

چسکي चुसकी *chuskī*, f. a mouthful of drink. *s.*

چسنا चसना *chasnā*, n. to burst or split (as tight clothes). *h.*

چسني चुसनी *chusnī*, f. a child's coral, a stick for a child to suck. *s.*

چسي चस्सी *chassī*, f. a species of itch peculiar to the palms of the hand and soles of the feet, said to be occasioned by insects. *h.*

چسي चुस्सी *chussī*, f. the juice of fruits. *h.*

چش *chash*, (in comp.) tasting, having the flavour of, as *namak-chash*, having the flavour of salt. *p.*

چشت चषति *chashati*, m. decay, infirmity. *s.*

چشك *chashak*, f. a tasting. *p.*

چشك चषक *chashak*, m. a vessel for drinking spirits, a wine-glass, &c., any drinking vessel; spirituous liquour. *s.*

چشم *chashm*, m. f. the eye; hope, expectation. *āhū-chashm*, fawn-eyed, soft-eyed (an epithet expressive of beauty). *chashmi bad dūr*, avaunt malicious glances. *chashm ba rāh hona*, n. to wait for, to expect. *chashmi-bīmār*, m. an eye that looks half-closed (from modesty, an epithet applied to beauty). *chashm poshī*, f. turning away the eyes, affecting not to see or hear a petitioner, &c., connivance. *chashmi tar*, m. a moist eye, *i.e.* a weeper. *chashm-tarī*, f. moist eyes, full eyes, weeping. *chashm-khāna*, the socket of the eye. *chashmi khūn-ālūd*, fiery eyes, eyes filled with blood, murderous looks. *chashm-dāsht*, f. hope, confidence. *chashm-zakhm*, m. viewing with an evil eye; a misfortune. *chashm-numā,ī*, f. reproof. *chashm o chirāgh*, dearly beloved. *p.*

چشمك *chashmak*, f. winking. *chashmak* (called also *chāksū* and *kishmizaj*), the seed of *Cassia absus*, used as a remedy in diseases of the eyes. *p.*

چشمه *chashma*, m. spectacles; a fountain. *chashma,e ḥaiwān*, the fountain of life or immortality. *chashma,e nūr*, the fountain of light, the sun. *p.*

چشیدن *chashīdan*, to taste, to experience. *p.*

چشیده *chashīda* (in comp.), having tasted, encountered, or experienced. *p.*

چغتا *chaghattā*, m. the name of a *Mughal* tribe, of which is descended the house of *Tīmūr*. *t.*

چغد *chughd*, m. the small screech-owl. *p.*

چغر *chaghar*, m. a wall-eyed horse. *p.*

چغربا *chagharbā*, m. revelry. *p.*

چغل *chughhal* or *chughal-khor*, m. a tell-tale, a talebearer, backbiter, informer. *chughal-khorī*, f. the act of backbiting. *p.*

چغلي *chughlī*, f. talebearing. *chughlī-khānā*, a. to backbite, to tell tales, to inform. *p.*

چفت *chaft*,
چفته *chafta*, } m. a prop, an arbour. *p.*

چق *chiḳ*, f. a kind of screen used to keep out the glare; large blinds in front of a house. *t.*

چقاچاق *chuḳāchāḳ*, f. (v. *chaḳāchaḳ*). *t.*

چقچقي *chaḳchaḳī*, f. a kind of musical instrument made of wood, used by the *Mughals*. *t.*

چقر *chuḳḳar*, m. outlet of a fountain. *t.*

چقماق *chaḳmāḳ*,
چقمق *chaḳmaḳ*, } f. the steel for striking fire from a flint; the lock of a gun. *t.*

چقماقي *chaḳmāḳī*, f. a firelock. *t.*

چقندر *chuḳandar*, m. beet-root (*Beta vulgaris*). *p.*

چك चक *chak*, m. landed property, an estate, a farm; also a portion of land divided off. *chak-bandī*, f. defining or marking the boundaries of an estate. *chak-barār*, collecting the rent of a *chak*. *chak-nāma*, a register of a *chak*, also a grant for holding the same. *chak-ṭukṛā*, a plot or parcel of a landed estate. *s.*

چك चक *chak*, m. a shepherd, a goatherd. *h.*

چك चिक *chik*, f. a pain in the loins; a screen made of split bamboos. *h.*

چك चिक्क *chikk*, m. a musk-rat. *h.*

چكا चिक्का *chikkā*, f. a mouse. *h.*

چكا चक्का *chakkā*, m. coagulated milk; a carriage-wheel, a circle, a circular lump of earth, a round sod of turf; adj. thick (as *dahī*, &c.). *s.*

چكاٹی جانا चकाठेजाना *chakāṭe jānā*, n. to be in astonishment or perplexity. *d.*

چكاچاك चकाचाक *chakāchāk*, f. the sound of the stroke of a dagger, clashing of swords. *p.*

چكاچوندھ चकाचौंध *chakāchaundh*, f. the state of being dazzled; radiance. *h.*

چكار चुक्कार *chukkār*, m. the roaring of a lion.

چكارا चिकारा *chikārā* or *chikāra*, m. a kind of antelope found on the banks of the Jumna; a kind of fiddle. *chukārā*, customs duty. *h.*

چكارنا चिकारना *chikārnā*, n. to squeak. *s.*

چكاره *chikāra*, m. a kind of antelope, the four-horned antelope (v. *chikārā*). *h.*

چكاره *chikāra*, useless, worthless; lit. of what use? "cui bono?" *p.*

چكاری चिकारी *chikārī*, f. an insect like a musquito; smut (obscenity). *h.*

چكاری *chikārī*, useless, worthless, contemptible. *p.*

چكان *chakān*, dropping, distilling. *p.*

چكان चक्कान *chakkān*, thick (*bhang*, &c.); blot, blotted, smeared. *h.*

چكانا चुकाना *chukānā*, a. to finish, complete, to settle; to fix the price of. *h.*

چكاوٹ चिकावट *chikāwaṭ*, black clayey soil. *h.*

چكاور चकावर *chakāwar*, m. the name of a disease in horses. *h.*

چكاوك *chakāwak*, m. a lark. *p.*

چكاوی चकावी *chakāwī*, f. a ring-worm. *s.*

چكائی चुकाई *chukā,ī*, f. (v. *chukautā*), a task, agreement, adjustment, decision. *chukā,ī denā*, to escape one's notice, to give one the slip. *h.*

چكت चकित *chakit*, timid, fearful, astonished. *s.*

چكت चक्कात *chakkat*, the loss of a *chak*, or whole plot of ground, by diluvion or inundation. *h.*

چكت चुकत *chukat*, a settlement, a contract. *h.*

چكتا *chakattā*, m. (v. *chaghattā*) name of a *Mughal* family. *t.*

چكتا चकता *chaktā*, m. a scraping of the skin, a scrape, a scar; a slice, &c. *chaktā denā* or *lenā*, to scar. *h.*

چكتانا चकताना *chaktānā*, a. to sod, to turf. *h.*

چكتسا चिकित्सा *chikitsa*, f. attendance of a physician on a patient; application of remedies, healing, curing. *s.*

چكتسك चिकित्सक *chikitsak*, m. a physician. *s.*

چكتی चकती *chaktī*, f. the hide of a rhinoceros (of which shields are made); a patch of leather, a slice, compressed, flattened, a patch; the round of a cheese; a round plate of metal, &c. *h.*

چكتی चुकती *chuktī*, f. settlement, decree or sentence (of a court, &c.). *h.*

چكٹ *chihaṭ*, sticky, adhesive, gummy. *d.*

چكٹ चिक्कट *chikkaṭ*, filthy, covered with grease and dirt. *h.*

چكٹا चिकटा *chikṭā*, m. a kind of *tasar* cloth. *h.*

چكٹھا चिकठा *chikṭhā*, filthy, greasy; m. an oil-merchant. *h.*

چكٹی चिकटी *chikṭī*, a sticky or clayey soil. *h.*

چكچكا चकचका *chakchakā*, shining, resplendent. *h.*

چكچكی चकचकी *chakchakī*, f. a kind of dagger worn on the waist: "it also denotes a small knife, one or two of which are often worn in the same sheath with a dagger, similar to the appendages to a Highlandman's dirk."—(Binning.) adj. resplendent. *h.*

چكچھوندی चकछूंदी *chakchhūndī*, f. a musk-rat (*Sorex cærulescens, Shaw; S. cæruleus, Turton*). *h.*

چكر चक्कर *chakkar* or चक्र *chakra*, m. a wheel; a circle, or any thing revolving in a circle; a whirlwind or whirlpool; a weapon used principally by the Sikhs, an iron ring which they throw with great dexterity. It was with this instrument (called *sudarshana chakra*) that *Nārāyana* cut off the head of the *Asur Rāhu*, when, after churning the ocean, the *Surs* (or gods) and *Asūrs* fought for the *amṛita* or nectar; a circular course, the lounge (in manège); (met.) a misfortune, scrape, perplexity. *chakkar bardeshī*, compound interest. *ghoṛe ko chakkar denā*, to lounge a horse. *chahoṅ chakkar meṅ*, on the four sides, on all sides. *chakkar mārnā*, to wheel or whirl round. *chakra dārī*, m. a peacock; *Vishṇu*. *chakra-vān*, circular, ring-shaped. *chakra-vat*, in rotation, revolving like a wheel. *chakra-vartī*, m. an emperor, a sovereign of the world; twelve princes beginning with Bharat are especially considered *Chakra-vartīs*; a title of Brāhmans in Bengal. *s.*

چكر चिकुर *chikur*, m. hair; lock of hair. *s.*

چكر चुक्र *chukr*, m. sorrel; sourness; acid seasoning. *s.*

چكرا चकरा *chakrā*, m. a kind of dish made of pulse. *h.*

چكرا चिकुरा *chikurā*, rashly criminal, inconsiderately guilty, punishing or injuring others without consideration. *s.*

چكراكار चक्राकार *chakrākār*, circular. *s.*

چكرانی चकरानी *chakrānī*, f. woman servant. *p.*

چكربا चकरबा *chakarbā*, m. revelry. *chakarbā machānā*, a. to revel. *h.*

چکربردیشي चकरबरदेशी *chakar-bardeshī*, compound interest (Gladwin). *h.*

چکرت चक्रित *chakrit*, astonished, amazed, timid, fearful. *s.*

چکرکا चुक्रिका *chukrikā*, f. wood sorrel (*Oxalis monodelpha*) or (*Rumex vesicarius*). *s.*

چکرمکر *chakar-makar*, m. evasion, trick, subterfuge. *p.*

چکرواك चक्रवाक *chakrvāk*, m. name of a bird, the ruddy goose (*Anas casarca*). *s.*

چکرورتي चक्रवर्ती *chakravartī*, a prince, a ruler: in Bengal the word is corrupted into "*chuckerbutty*," or, still worse, "*chokerbotty*." *s.*

چکرورده‌ي चक्रवृद्धि *chakra-vriddhī*, compound interest. *s.*

چکرها *chaharihā*, m. a good servant, a person fit for (in want of) service; one habituated to service. *p.*

چکري चुक्री *chukrī*, a fractional division of land. *h.*

چکري चक्री *chakrī*, f. a round plate on which bread is rolled; a whirligig or plaything; (v. *chaklā*) an assembly of singers. *s.*

چکریٹها चक्रेठा *chakreṭhā*, having large eyes. *h.*

چکریلا चक्रेला *chakrelā*, round, circular. *s.*

چکڑ *chikhaṛ*, m. mud, mire, a swamp, clay, compost. *d.*

چکڑ चुक्कड़ *chukkaṛ*, m. a small tank or pit. *h.*

چکس चक्कस *chakkas*, m. a perch for birds (particularly falcons), roost. *h.*

چکس चिक्कस *chikkas*, m. barley meal. *s.*

چکسوني चकसूनी *chaksūnī*, f. the name of a grass. *h.*

چکسا *chiksā*, } m. a kind of pulville or perfumed powder of many ingredients. *d.*
چکسه *chiksa*, }

[m. ophthalmia. *s.*

چکش चक्षु *chakshu*, m. the eye. *chakshu-rog*,

چکل चिकिल *chikil*, m. mud, mire. *s.*

چکلا चकला *chaklā*, m. a brothel; a kind of cloth made of silk and cotton. *h.*

چکلا चकला *chaklā*, adj. wide, broad, round; m. a division of a country, containing several parganas; a round plate on which bread is rolled. *chakle-dār*, m. the governor of a province or county. *chakle-dārī*, f. the government of a province or county. *chaklā-kharch*, expenses of a *chaklā*. *chaklā-nawīs*, the accountant of the revenues and charges of a *chaklā*. *s.*

چکلا *chaklā*, m. a log of wood; trunk of a tree; a block or mass. *d.*

چکلان चकलाना *chaklānā*, a. to extend in breadth, to widen. *h.*

چکلاءي चकलाई *chaklā,ī*, f. breadth, width. *h.*

چکلنا चिकलना *chikalnā*, a. to masticate, to chew (slowly). *h.*

چکلنا *chakalnā*, to squeeze, to press upon. *d.*

چکما चकमा *chakmā*, m. a game at cards; a boot, a stocking. *h.*

چکماك *chakmāk*, } the steel for striking fire with. *chakmāk kā patthar*, a flint. *t.*
چك‌مك *chakmak*, }

چکمه *chakma*, m. a boot, a stocking (v. *chakmā*). *h.*

چکن *chikan*, m. a particular mode of working flowers on muslin or other cloth. *chikan-doz* or *-gar*, m. one who performs *chikan* work. *chikan-kārī*, the making of *chikan*. *p.*

چکن चिकिन *chikin*, flat-nosed. *s.*

چکن चिक्कण *chikkan*, } clean, polished; beautiful (persons); bland, soft, mild; unctuous,
چکنا चिकणा *chiknā*, }
چکنا चिक्किणा *chikkinā*, }

greasy; incontinent, lewd, wanton. *chikhnā-bāsan* or *-gharā banna*, n. to be incontinent, incorrigible, deaf to admonition. *chiknā chāndā*, beautiful. *chiknī jorū*, f. a slippery wife. *chiknī supārī*, f. a kind of betel-nut, prepared by boiling. *chiknī ṣūrat*, prosperous, affluent, flourishing. *chiknī miṭṭī*, f. clay, potters' earth. *s.*

چکنا चिकना *chiknā*, m. oil, grease. *s.*

چکنا चुकना *chuknā*, n. to have finished or completed, to be fixed; to be agreed upon, adjusted. *h.*

چکناٹ चिकनाट *chiknāṭ*, oiliness, fatness. *h.*

چکناچور चकनाचूर *chaknā-chūr*, m. scraps, small pieces, atoms, filings. *chaknā-chūr-h.*, to be dashed to pieces. *chaknā-chūr-k.*, to shatter to pieces. *h.*

چکنامه *chaknāma*, m. a statement shewing the boundaries of a *chak*, q. v. *h. p.*

چکنانا चिकनाना *chiknānā*, a. to clean, to polish, to smooth. *s.*

چکناوت चिकनावत *chiknāwat*, } f. a clayey, fat, or loamy soil. *h.*
چکناوٹ चिकनावट *chiknāwaṭ*, }

چکناهٹ चिकनाहट *chiknāhaṭ*, f. cleanness, smoothness, polish; greasiness; beauty. *s.*

چکناءي चिकनाई *chiknā,ī*, f. fat of meat; wantonness; gloss, smoothness, polish. *s.*

چکنیا चिकनिया *chikniyā*, m. a beau, a spark. *h.*

چکو चक्कू *chakkū*, m. a claspknife, a penknife. *p.*

چکوا चकवा *chakwā*, m. name of a bird, the ruddy goose or Brāhmanī duck (*Anas casarca*); whirlpool. *s.*

چکوائین चकवाईं *chakwā,īn*, a small class of *rājpūts* in the district of Ghāzīpūr. *s.*

چکوتا चुकौता *chukautā*, m. a task, an agreement, an adjustment, a settlement in full. *h.*

چکوترا चकोत्रा *chakotrā* or *chakoturā*, m. a fruit of the lime kind, a citron; pompelmoose, shaddock (*Citrus decumanus*). *h.*

چکوٹ *chakoṭ*, delicious, savoury. *d.*

چکوٹا चकौटा *chakauṭā* or *chakauṭa*, m. fixed rates of rent, money-rate, settlement. *h.*

چکور चकोर *chakor*, m. the *Bartavelle* or Greek partridge (*Tetrao rufus, Lin.; Perdix rufa, Lath.*), said to be enamoured of the moon, and to eat fire at the full moon. *s.*

چکورا चिकोरा *chikorā*, restless, inconstant. *h.*

چکورنا चिकोरना *chikornā*. a. to peck. *h.*

چکوري चकोरी *chakorī*, f. (v. *chakor*). *h.*

چکونڈ चकवण्ड *chakwānd*, name of a common weed bearing a long legume, and used as a pot-herb. *h.*

چکوندا चकौंदा *chakaundā*, } m. a
چکونڑ चकौंड़ *chakaunṛ* or *chakwaṅr*, } species of cassia (*Cassia obtusifolia*), esteemed a remedy for ringworms. *s.*

چکوي चकवी *chakwī* (f. of *chakwā*, q. v.), a species of duck. *s.*

چکھ चख *chakh* (for *chakshu*), m. the eye. *s.*

چکھانا चखाना *chakhānā*, a. to cause to taste, to give a specimen of. *s.*

چکھرن चिखुरन *chikhuran*, m. a weed. *h.*

چکھرنا चिखुरना *chikhurnā*, a. to weed. *h.*

چکھاچکھي चखाचखी *chakhāchakhī*, f. discord. *h.*

چکھ चिखर *chikhar*, the husk of the *chanā*, [q. v. *h.*

چکھنا चखना *chakhnā*, a. to relish, taste. *s.*

چکھواءي चिखुरवाई *chikhurwā,ī*, f. wages for weeding. *h.*

چکھوري चिखूरी *chikhūrī*, f. a squirrel. *h.*

چکئي चकई *chaka,ī*, f. the name of a plaything, a whirligig; a duck, the female of *chakwā*, q.v. *s.*

چکي चक्की *chakkī*, f. a millstone, grinder; a handmill; the timber of a gunlock; the kneepan; a thunderbolt. *chakkī-nāma*, a kind of song sung by women at weddings while grinding a perfumed powder. *chakkī-nāwarī*, presentation of said powder to the bride and bridegroom. *s.*

چکي चुक्की *chukkī*, f. deceit, fraud. *chukkī denā*, a. to deceive, to play tricks. *h.*

چکي चिक्की *chikkī*, f. a rotten betel nut; adj. flat-nosed. *s.* [gle-eyed. *s.*

چکیٹھا चकेठा *chakeṭhā*, with large eyes, gog-

چکیدگي *chakīdagī*, f. a drop, distillation. *p.*

چکیدن *chakīdan*, to drop, to trickle. *p.*

چکیده *chakīda*, dropped, distilled. *p.*

چگانا चगाना *chugānā*, a. to cause to peck. *h.*

چگاءي *chugā,ī*, f. pasturage. *h.*

چگلنا चगलना *chagalnā*, a. to eat without appetite. *h.* [ment. *h.*

چگن चुगन *chugan*, f. a plait or fold in a gar-

چگنا चुगना *chugnā*, n. to peck, to pick up food with the beak. *chug lenā*, a. to select, to choose. *h.*

چگونگي *chigūnagī*, f. circumstance, manner. *p.*

چگونه *chigūna*, how? of what kind? *p.*

چگیر चगेर *chager*, f. a flower-pot (also *chaṅger*, q. v.) *h.*

چل चल *chal*, f. going, dispersion; variation, departure from truth, failure in the performance of a promise, or accomplishment of a prediction. *chal-denā*, a. to march as an army; to beguile. *s.*

چل चुल *chul*, f. itch, scratching. *h.*

چل *chil* (contraction of چهل), forty. *p.*

چل चुल्ल *chull*, m. a blear eye.

چل चिल्ल *chill*, m. the Bengal kite (*Falco cheela*). *s.*

چل चलु *chalu*, m. water taken up in the palm of the hand for rinsing the mouth. *s.*

چلا *chillā*, m. the forty days of Lent, during which the religious fraternities in the east shut themselves up in their cells, or remain at home; also the holy place where *faḳīrs* abide; quarantine; the period of forty days after child-bed, during which a woman remains unclean. *chillā khainchnā*, to keep quarantine. *p.*

چلا चिल्ला *chillā*, m. the string of a bow; gold threads put in the border of a turban. *chillā khainchnā*, to bend a bow; to prepare for battle. *chillā chaṛhānā*, a. to bend a bow. *h.*

چلا चुल्ला *chullā*, blear-eyed. *s.*

چلاچل चलाचल *chalāchal*, } f. the bustle of
چلاچلي चलाचली *chalāchalī*, } setting out on a journey, &c., setting about any thing; adj. tremulous, unsteady; moveable and stationary. *s.*

چلان चलान *chalān*, f. clearance; remittance; an invoice, an announcement of despatch a pass or passport. *chalān-dār*, one who has charge of an invoice or despatch. *s.*

چلانا चुलाना *chulānā*, a. (v. *chūlanā*) to distil, to cause to drip. *h.*

چلانا चिल्लाना *chillānā*, n. to scream, to shriek. *h.*

چلانا चलाना *chalānā*, a. to impel, to set a-going, to drive; to fire a musket, to shoot at, to do, to hasten, to forward, to send, to accustom, to act, to advance, to throw, to thrust, to use, to walk. *s.*

چلاءو चलाउ *chalā,ū*, going; frail, inconstant, fickle; on the point of death. *s.*

چلاو चलाव *chalāw* or *chalā,o*, m. habit, custom. *s.*

چلاو चुलाव *chulāw*, m. a kind of dish consisting of plain boiled rice. *p.*

چلاوا चलावा *chalāwā*, m. motion, custom; going. *s.*

چلاون آمدني *chalāwan-āmdanī*, invoice or statement of revenue sent. *h.p.*

چلاء وني *chalā,onī*, passing, current (a coin). *d.*

چلاهٹ चिल्लाहट *chillāhaṭ*, f. cry, outcry. *h.*

چل بچل चलबिचल *chal-bichal*, m. error, mistake. *s.*

چلبدھرا चलबिधरा *chalbidhrā*, restive. *h.*

چلبدھراهٹ चलबिधराहट *chalbidhrāhaṭ*, f. restiveness. *a.*

چلبلا चुलबुला *chulbulā*, restless, fidgetting; airy, gay. *chulbulā-pan*, m. gaiety. *h.*

چلبلاگي *chulbulāgī*, f. liveliness, airiness. *d.*

چلبلانا चुलबुलाना *chulbulānā*, n. to be restless, to fidget (little used). *h.*

چلبلاهٹ चुलबुलाहट *chulbulāhaṭ*, gaiety, airiness. *h.*

چلبليا चुलबुलिया *chulbuliyā*, restless, fidgetting; airy, gay. *h.*

چلپاسہ चलपासः *chalpāsa* or चिलपासः *chilpāsa*, m. a lizard. *h.*

چلپھير चलफेर *chal-pher*, m. motion. *h.*

چلت चलत *chalat*, current, saleable, vendible. *s.*

چلت चलित *chalit*, current, usual; shaking, trembling, gone, departed; m. moveable or personal property. *s.*

چلتا चलता *chaltā*, m. the name of a tree (*Dillenia Indica*), producing an acid fruit; going, moving, passable. *chaltī chīz*, f. a saleable commodity, passable coin, &c. *h.*

چلتر चलित्र *chalitr*, m. (v. *charitr*), conduct, nature, &c. *s.*

چلتري *chalitrī*, gay, sportive, changeable, inconstant, affected. *s.*

چلتو चल्तू *chaltū*, land in cultivation. *h.*

چلتہ *chilta*, m. the lining of iron armour. *p.*

چلتي चलती *chaltī*, cultivated lands; adj. moving, passing. *h.*

چلچت चलचित्त *chal-chitt*, fickle, inconstant; m. fickleness. *chal-chittatā*, f. fickleness, inconstancy. *s.*

چلچل चुलचुल *chulchul*, m. wantonness, inconstancy. *s.*

چلچلانا चुलचुलाना *chulchulānā*, n. to itch, to titillate. *s.*

چلچلانا चिलचिलाना *chilchilānā*, n. to shriek, to scream, to screech. *h.*

چلچلاو चलचलाव *chalchalāw*, m. preparation for journey or departure. *s.*

چلچلي चुलचुली *chulchulī*, f. (v. *chulchul*). *s.*

چلدل चलदल *chal-dal*, m. the holy fig-tree. *s.*

چلرا *chilrā*, m. Sunday; adj. a few, some. *d.*

چلڑ चिल्लड़ *chillaṛ*, f. (v. *chilhāṛ*) a louse. *chillaṛ mārnā*, a. to louse. *h.*

چلڑاہ चिलड़ाहा *chilṛāhā*, lousy. *h.*

چلغوزہ *chalghoza*, m. a kind of nut, like the pistachio. *p.*

چلك चिलक *chilak*, f. refulgence, glitter. *h.*

چلك चिलिक *chilik*, f. twitch, stitch. *h.*

چلك चलुक *chaluk*, m. the hand hollowed, as for holding a little water; a small pot, a gallipot; a handful of water. *s.*

چلكنا चिलकना *chilaknā*, n. to glitter, to shine. *h.*

چلم चिलम *chilam*, m. f. the part of a *ḥukka* which contains the tobacco and the charcoal ball. *h.*

چلمچي चिलमची *chilamchī*, f. a wash-hand basin of metal, with a cover to it; part of a *ḥukka* fixed under the *chilam*. *h.*

چلمردان *chil-mardān*, m. the leather fixed to the vacant part of the tree of a saddle. *p.*

چلمن चिलमन *chilman*, f. (v. *chilwan*) a screen, &c. *h.*

چلن चलन *chalan*, m. habit, custom, process, course, conduct, behaviour; ceremony; currency; adj. current *chalan chalnā*, n. to behave. *s.*

چلنا चलना *chalnā*, n. to go, to proceed, to walk; to go off, to pass (as coin), to blow, to flow, to behave, to sail, to work, to answer, to succeed, to last, to serve, to stand. *chal nikalnā*, n. to turn out vicious, to exceed bounds. *chale-jānā* or *chale-chalnā*, n. to go along. *s.*

چلنتا चलनता *chalantā*, passing, moveable; vendible, saleable. *s.*

چلندري *chalandarī*, f. a place where water is supplied gratis to travellers as an act of charity or religious merit (called in Urdu *pansālā*, q. v.). *d.*

چلني चलनी *chalnī*, f. a sieve; adj. current, circulating (as coin); usual. *s.*

چلو चुल्लू *chullū*, m. a handful, the palm of the hand contracted so as to hold water. *chullū bhar pānī meṅ ḍūb marnā*, to perish from drowning in a handful of water, to be greatly abashed (v. *chapnī bhar pānī meṅ ḍūb marnā*). *chullū chullū sādhnā*, a. to get a habit of drinking by gradual increase. *chullū meṅ ullū honā*, to be intoxicated with a mouthful. *s.*

چلو चलो *chalo*, interj. away, begone; come away. *chalū*, m. the ceremony described under *ācha-man*. *s.*

چلوا चलवा *chalwā*, f. a kind of fish; the anchovy (*Clupea cultrata*). *s.*

چلوان चिलवान *chilwān*, m. a shutter. *h.*

چلواءي चिलवाई *chilwā,ī*, f. (v. *chīh*) mud, &c. *h.*

چلون चिलवन *chilwan*, f. a screen for keeping out the glare, a Venetian blind, lattice. *h.*

چلونا चलौना *chalaunā*, m. a small stick with which the spinning-wheel is turned. *s.*

چلويا *chalwaiyā*, m. one who moves about a great deal. *d.*

چلہ *chilla*, m. (v. *chillā*) a bow-string; a period of forty days, &c. *p. h.*

چلہارا चुल्हारा *chulhārā*, lascivious, lewd. *h.*

چلہاي चुल्हाई *chulhā,ī*, f. lewd, libidinous (woman). *h.*

چلہلا चिलहला *chilahlā*, splashy, muddy, slimy.

چلہوانس चिल्हवांस *chilhwāṅs*, m. the flesh of a kite (the eating of which is said to produce madness); screaming like a kite. *s.*

چلہورنا चिलोरना *chilhornā*, a. to peck. *h.*

چلي चिल्ली *chillī*, f. a kind of dish made of eggs; m. a blockhead, one who plays mischievous pranks. *h.*

چلي चुल्ली *chullī*, f. the support placed below a stack of straw, &c.; a fire-place, a chimney; staddles. *h.*

چليپا *chalīpā*, m. a cross. *p.*

چليندريہ चलेन्द्रिय *chalendriya*, sensitive, sensual, not having subdued the senses or passions. *s.*

چم *cham*, an easy air (in walking); prepared, arranged. *p.*

چم चिमि *chimi*, m. a parrot; a plant from the fibres of which coarse cloth and rope are made. *s.*

چما चुमा *chumā*, m. (v. *chūmā*) a kiss; also *chummā*. *chumā-chāṭī*, f. dalliance. *h.*

چمار चमार *chamār*, m. a worker in leather, a shoe-maker, a tanner, a currier. *chamār-kār*, a man of low caste who works in hides and leather. *s.*

چمارني चमरनी *chamārnī* } f. the wife of a
چماري चमारी *chamarī*, } *chamār*, q. v. *s.*

چماغ *chumāgh* } a mace, a club; a baton
چماق *chumāḳ*, } with an iron knob at the end. *p.*

چمان *chamān*, walking haughtily or gracefully; giving one's self airs. *p.*

چمانا चुमाना *chumānā*, a. to cause to kiss. *s.*

چماؤن चमाऊं *chamā,ūṅ* or *chamā,ū*, f. slippers or shoes fixed to pattens. *h.*

چماءي चमाई *chamā,ī*, copper-coloured. *h.*

چماين चमायन *chamāyan*, a small clan of the *gūjar* tribe in Panipat Bargar. *h.*

چمبا चम्बा *chambā*, m. a tribe of beggars who cut or scarify their skin. *s.*

چمبر *chambar*, sphere, an orb, a wheel, globe, circle, disk. *p.*

چمبر चिम्बूर *chimbur*, a kind of grass. *h.*

چمبك चुम्बक *chumbak*, m. a kisser, a lecher; a rogue, a cheat; a loadstone; an extract (from a book, &c.); a general scholar, one who knows parts in a variety of books; the upper part or middle of a balance. *s*

چمبل चम्बल *chambal*, f. the name of a river in Bandelkhand; a log of wood with grooves, fixed on the banks of canals, and used in drawing water for irrigation. *h.*

چمبن चुम्बन *chumban*, m. kissing, embracing. *s.*

چمبو चम्बू *chambū*, m. a narrow-necked vessel for holding water. *s.*

چمبيلي चमेली *chambelī*, f. a flower (*Jasminum grandiflorum*). *s.*

چمپ चम्प *champ*, mountain ebony (*Bauhinia variegata*). *s.*

چمپا चम्पा *champā*, m. the name of a tree bearing a fragrant yellow flower (*Michelia champaca*). *champā kālī*, f. a necklace each piece of which resembles the unblown flowers of the *champā*. *champā-kelā*, m. a small kind of plantain or banana. *champā-watī* f. the district of Champā or Bhagalpore (abounding in ebony trees). *s.*

چمپٹ هونا चम्पट होना *champaṭ-honā* or *hojānā*, n. to vanish, to disappear, to scamper off, to run away. *h.*

چمپك चम्पक *champak*, m. a kind of tree bearing a yellow fragrant flower (*Michelia champaca*) a division of the jack-fruit. *s.*

چمپك برني चम्पकबर्णी *champak-barṇī*, } of the
چمپئي चम्पई *champa,ī*, } colour of the *champā* flower, *i. e.* gold-coloured. *s.*

چمپو चम्पू *champū*, f. a work in which the same subject is continued through alternations of prose and verse. *s.*

چمپي चम्पी *champī*, orange-coloured. *s.*

چمتكار चमत्कार *chamatkār*, m. amazement, splendour, astonishment, surprise. *s.*

چمتكار चमत्कार *chamatkār*, f. name of a grass; haste. *h.*

چمتكاري चमत्कारी *chamatkārī*, astonishing, surprising; sagacious, acute. *s.*

چمتكرت चमत्कृत *chamatkṛit*, surprised, astonished. *s.*

چمٹا चिमटा *chimṭā* or *chumṭā*, m. tongs. *h.*

چمٹانا चिमटाना *chimṭānā*, a. to make adhere or cling to. *h.* [cleave to. *h*

چمٹ رهنا चिमट रहना *chimaṭ-rahnā*, n. to

چمٹنا चिमटना *chimaṭnā*, n. to adhere, to cling to. *h.*

چمٹها चिमठा *chimṭhā*, elastic, tough. *h.*

چمٹي *chumṭī*, f. an ant; a nip or pinch. *d.*

چمٹي كاٹنا चिमटी काटना *chimṭī-kāṭnā*, a. to pinch. *h.*

چمچ *chamach*, } m. (properly چمچہ) a spoon,
چمچا *chamchā*, } a ladle. *chamach-boza*, name of a bird, the spoonbill. *p.* [m. a bat. *h.*

چمچڑخ चमचड़ख *chamchaṛakh*, lean, meagre;

چمچما चिमचिमा *chimchimā*, m. oil become viscous by age. *h.*

چمچمانا चमचमाना *chamchamānā*, n. to tingle, to sleep, to sparkle, to shine, to glitter. *h.*

چمچماهٹ चमचमाहट *chamchamāhaṭ*, f. brightness. *h.*

چمچمہ *chimchima*, m. (v. *chimchimā*) oil, &c. *h*

چمچه *chamcha*, m. a spoon. *chamcha-bhar*, a spoonful. *chamcha-har-degī*, one who intermeddles in every one's affairs: Scottice, "one who puts his spoon in everybody's kail." *p. h.*

چمر चमर *chamar*, m. a flapper made of a cow's tail to drive away flies; the tail of the *bos grunniens*. *s.*

چمراوت चमरावत *chamrāwat* (also *chamrāwaṭ*,) the perquisites of a *chamār*, q.v. *h.*

چمربگلي चमरबगली *chamar-baglī*, f. a bittern. *h.*

چمرکهه चमरख *chamrakh*, f. the apparatus of a spinning-wheel; (met.) a lean woman. *s.*

چمري चमरी *chamrī*, f. the yak or *bos grunniens*, of whose tail-hairs the *chaurī* is usually made. *s.*

چمڑا चमड़ा *chamṛā*, m. leather, a hide, a skin. *chamṛā-udheṛnā, -chhuṛānā, -khainchnā*, or *nikālnā*, a. to flay. *s.*

چمڑا चिमड़ा *chimṛā*, tough, ductile, flexible, hardy. *h.*

چمڑانا चिमड़ाना *chimṛānā*, n. to toughen, to grow tough. *h.*

چمڑاهٹ चिमड़ाहट *chimṛāhaṭ*, f. toughness, flexibility. *h.*

چمڑاءي चिमड़ाई *chimṛā,ī*, f. power, rigour, flexibility. *h.*

چمڑنا चिमड़ना *chimaṛnā*, n. to adhere (same as *chimaṭnā*). *h.*

چمڑي चिमड़ी *chimṛī*, infrangible (a quill for instance), hard. *h.*

چمس चमस *chamas*, m. a vessel used at sacrifices for drinking the juice of the acid asclepias, a kind of ladle or spoon; a plant commonly called *khetvaprā* (*Mollugo pentaphylla*). *s.*

چمسا चिमसा *chimsā*, glutinous (as oil by long keeping). *h.*

چمك चमक *chamak*, f. glitter, splendour, glare. *chamak-ṭamak*, f. splendour, refulgence. *h.*

چمك चुम्मक *chummak* (also *chammak*), m. a loadstone. *s.*

چمکار चुमकार *chumkār*, m. (also *chumkārī*), f. a sound with the lips by which dogs and horses are called. *h.*

چمکارنا चुमकारना *chumkārnā*, a. to coax, to speak kindly to, to sooth (by drawing in the breath with protruded lips). *h.*

چمکانا चमकाना *chamkānā*, a. to cause to glitter; to provoke, make to start; to wave, to brandish, to brighten; to display. *h.*

چمکاو चमकाव *chamkāw*, m.
چمکاهٹ चमकाहट *chamkāhaṭ*, f. } glitter, splendour, much light; flourish. *h.*

چمکتا चमकता *chamaktā*, bright, brilliant. *h.*

چمکنا चमकना *chamaknā*, n. to glitter, to shine, to flash, to glare, to startle; to prosper; to be angry. *h.*

چمکي चमकी *chamkī*, f. glitter; a spangle. *d.*

چمگادڑ चमगादड़ *chamgādaṛ*, m.
چمگدڑي चमगुदड़ी *chamgudṛī*, f.
چمگيدڑ चमगीदड़ *chamgīdaṛ*, m. } a large bat, the flying fox; in Dakhanī the form used is *chamgadal*. *h.*

چمل चम्मल *chammal*, m.
چملا चमला *chamlā*, m.
چملي चमली *chamlī*, f. } a mendicant's cup, a begging-dish. *h.*

چمل *chummal*, m.
چملي *chumlī*, f. } a ring made of grass or twigs, placed under water-pots to keep them in an upright position (called in Urdu *biṭhā* and *jūnā*, q. v.). *d.*

چمن *chaman*, m. a bed in a garden, a parterre. *chaman-band*, m. a gardener. *chaman-bandī*, art of gardening. *chaman-bandī-k.*, a. to lay out a garden. *chamanī-dahr*, terrestrial abode. *chaman-zār*, a meadow. *p.*

چمنستان *chamanistān*, m. a flower-bed. *p.*

چمني *chamanī*, of or belonging to a flower-bed. *p.*

چمو चमू *chamū*, f. an army; a squadron, a division of an army. *h.*

چموٹا चमोटा *chamoṭā*, m.
چموٹي चमोटी *chamoṭī*, f. } a razor-strap. *s.*

چموکن चमूकन *chamūkan*, m. a tick or louse infesting cattle. *h.*

چميٹا चमेटा *chameṭā*, m. box, thump, blow. *s.*

چن चन *chan* or *chin*, m. a kind of sugar-cane. *h.*

چن चिन्न *chinn*, m. a kind of grain (*Panicum miliaceum*. *h.*

چنا चणा or चना *chanā*, m. gram, a kind of pulse, chick pea (*Cicer arietinum*), fitches, vetches: on this pulse horses are chiefly fed in India. It is also much used by people, and is grown in all parts of the East. Its Persian name is *nukhūd*. *s.*

چنا *channā*, m. (v. *chāndnā*) light. *d.*

چنا चुन्ना *chunnā*, a. to gather, to pick, to choose; to pick up food (as birds); to place in order, to arrange; to plait; m. *ascarides*. *darwāza chunnā*, a. to close a door with bricks. *h.*

چنار *chinār* or *chanār*, m. a poplar-tree, a plane-tree. *p.*

چناکا चनाका *chanākā*, m. (v. *chanak*). *h.*

چنال *chināl*, m. a kind of high-heeled slipper. *d.*

چنان *chunān*, like that, such as that. *p.*

چنانا चुनाना *chunānā*, a. to cause to pick, to choose; to array or dress one's self, &c. *chunā lenā*, a. to plait (cloth); to kill by building a person into a wall. *h.*

چنانا *chanānā*, a. to reflect or cast back (a shadow). *d.*

چنان‌چنين *chunān-chunīn*, in this and that manner; (met.) evasion, subterfuge. *p.*

چنانچه *chunānchi* or *chunān-ki*, so that, in such manner that, accordingly. *p.*

چناوٹ चुनावट *chunāwaṭ*, f. a plait, act of plaiting. *h.*

چنبا चंबा *chambā*, m. a tribe of beggars who cut or scarify their skin. *h.*

چنبار *chambār*, m. (v. *chamār*) a tanner, &c.; also an executioner. *d.*

چنبر *chambar*, a cover (*sarposh*) for the *chilam* of a *ḥuḳḳa*. *chambarī-gardan*, stocks, pillory, necklace, handkerchief, dog's collar. *p.*

چنبري *chambarī*, round, circular. *p.*

چنبك चुंबक *chumbak*, m. a magnet; a quotation, an extract. *s.*

چنبك चिंबुक *chimbuk*, m. the chin. *h.*

چنبل चंबल *chambal*, چنبلا चंबला *chamblā*, (v. *chammal*), a beggar's cup. *h.*

چنبو चंबू *chambū*, m. a narrow-necked vessel for holding water, commonly called a goglet. *h.*

چنبیلی चंबेली *chambelī*, f. the name of a flower (*Jasminum grandiflorum*). *h.*

چنپا चंपा *champā*, چنپك चंपक *champak*, (same as *champā*) name of a tree and its blossom (*Michelia champaca*). *champā-kalī*, f. a necklace resembling the buds of the *champā* flower. *champā-kelī*, f. a species of plantain. *champak-barnī*, of the colour of the *champā* flower, which is of a beautiful yellow. *h.*

چنپت *champat* (v. چمپت هونا), to run off, &c. *h.*

چنپو चंपू *champū*, m. (v. *chappū*) a paddle, an oar. *h.*

چنت चुनत *chunat*, f. plaiting (cloths), plaits. *h.*

چنت चिन्त *chint*, چنتا चिन्ता *chintā*, f. reflection, consideration, thought, care, doubt, anxiety, danger, peril, risk. *chintā-par*, thoughtful, anxious. *chintā-mani*, f. m. a fabulous gem, supposed to yield to its possessor whatever he may think of. *chintā-wat*, thinking, thoughtful. *chintā-veshman*, m. council-house or room. *s.*

چنتاكل चिन्ताकुल *chintākul*, adj. disturbed in thought, distracted by an idea. *s.*

چنتانا चिन्ताना *chintānā*, a. to cause to study. *s.*

چنتت चिन्तित *chintit*, thoughtful, anxious, reflective. *s.*

چنتن चिन्तन *chintan*, m. study, reflection. *s.*

چنتنا चिन्तना *chintanā*, a. to study, to think. *s.*

چنتیا चिन्तिया *chintiyā*, f. reflection, consideration, thinking. *s.*

چنٹ चण्ट *chant*, m. a miser. *h.*

چنچ चञ्चु *chanchu*, f. the beak of a bird. *s.*

چنچا *chinchā*, m. tamarind stones, used by children for playing with. *d.*

چنچر चंचर *chanchar*, land left untilled for one, two, or three years. *h.*

چنچل चञ्चल *chanchal*, unsteady, shaking, playful; fickle, inconstant; restless, wanton; perishable; m. a lecher, a libertine. *chanchal-hṛiday*, capricious, fickle, false-hearted. *s.*

چنچلا चञ्चला *chanchalā*, f. lightning. *s.*

چنچلانا चञ्चलाना *chanchalānā*, n. to be playful, wanton, or restless. *s.*

چنچلاهٹ चञ्चलाहट *chanchalāhaṭ*, f. restlessness, unsteadiness, wantonness. *s.*

چنچلاءي चञ्चलाई *chanchalā,ī*, f. چنچل پنا चञ्चलपना *chanchal-panā*, m. gaiety, wantonness. *s.*

چنچلتا चञ्चलता *chanchalatā*, f. perishableness; restlessness, fickleness. *s.*

چنچنا चुनचुना *chunchunā*, m. *Ascarides*. *h.*

چنچنانا चञ्चनाना *chanchanānā*, n. to throb or shoot (as a boil, &c.); to make the noise that butter does in a frying-pan. *h.*

چنچنانا चिनचिनाना *chinchinānā*, n. to scream, to squeak, to squall. *h.*

چنچي *chanchī*, a cloth wrapper or cover for a book. *d.*

چنچناهٹ चञ्चनाहट *chanchanāhaṭ*, f. a throb, throbbing, a shooting pain. *h.*

چنچني चुनचुनी *chunchunī*, f. *Ascarides*. *h.*

چند *chand*, some, few (interrogatively), how much? how often? when? *chand dar chand*, several, various. *chand roza*, of few days, transitory. *har-chand*, or *har-chand-ki*, although, nevertheless, notwithstanding, however, with all that, so much the more. *p.*

چند चन्द *chand* (also *chandā*, m. the moon. *chand-mukh*, *-mukhī* or *-badanī*, moon-faced, *i.e.* beautiful as the moon. *s.*

چندا चन्दा *chandā*, m. assessment, contribution, subscription. *chandā uṭhānā*, to subscribe or contribute, to get up a subscription. *p.*

چنداليا चन्दालिया *chandāliyā*, a caste of sweepers. *s.*

چندان *chandāṅ*, many, numbers, more, as many as, how many soever, so much, so greatly. *p.*

چندانكه *chandāṅki*, as many, as much, whatever, so greatly; how much soever. *p.*

چندانه *chandāna*, sundry, or miscellaneous; a variety of petty taxes formerly levied by the Mogul Government, such as those on musicians, showmen, &c. *p.*

چندر चन्द्र *chandar* or *chandra*, m. the moon. *chandra-rekhā* or *chandra-lekhā*, f. a digit of the moon. *chandra-gol* or *chandra-mandal*, m. the orb or sphere of the moon. *chandra-mani*, m. the moon gem. *chandra-vaṅshī*, m. a descendant of the moon (v. *chandra-baṅsī*). *s.*

چندرا चन्द्रा *chandrā*, bald; wise, intelligent. *h.*

چندراتپ चन्द्रातप *chandrātap*, m. moonlight. *s.*

چندرانا चन्द्राना *chandrānā*, n. to be withered or dried up (a tree); to cease to grow. *h.*

چندربنسي चन्द्रबंशी *chandra-bansī* (for *chandra vanshī*), lit. descendants of the moon, name of a race or dynasty of the *Kshatriyas*. *s.*

چندربهاگا चन्द्रभागा *chandra-bhāgā*, f. the name of a river, the Chenab, one of the five streams of the Panjāb. *chandra-bhāg*, a mountain, part of the Himālaya range, from which the river above mentioned is said to flow. *s.*

چندررين चन्द्ररेणु *chandra-renu*, m. a plagiarist, a poetical thief. *s.*

چندرجوت चन्द्रजोत *chandra-jot*, f. moonshine; a blue light. *s.* [small cardamums. *s.*

چندرسنبهو चन्द्रसंभव *chandra-sambhava*, f.

چندرك चन्द्रक *chandrak*, m. the eye in a peacock's tail; a finger-nail. *s.*

چندركا चन्द्रिका *chandrikā*, f. moonlight, moonbeams; a small fish (*Zeus oblongus*). *s.*

چندركانت चन्द्रकान्त *chandra-kānta* or *chandra-kāntā*, m. a species of gem, supposed to be formed of the congelation of the rays of the moon. *s.*

چندركلا चन्द्रकला *chandra-kalā*, f. a digit or one-sixteenth part of the moon's orb or diameter; a lunar crescent. *s.*

چندرگپت चन्द्रगुप्त *chandra-gupta*, m. the registrar of Yama's court. *s.*

چندرگرهن चन्द्रग्रहण *chandra-grahaṇ*, m. a lunar eclipse. *s.* [*podium album*).

چندرل चन्द्रिल *chandril*, m. a potherb (*Cheno-*

چندرليكها चन्द्रलेखा *chandra-lekhā*, f. a digit of the moon; a plant (*Serratula anthelmintica*). *s.*

چندرما चन्द्रमा *chandramā*, m. the moon. *s.*

چندرمكهي चन्द्रमुखी *chandra-mukhī*, moon-faced, *i.e.* having a face beautiful as the moon. *s.*

چندرنا चन्दरना *chandarnā*, n. (v. *chandrānā*). *h.*

چندروالا चन्द्रवाला *chandra-wālā*, f. large cardamums. *s.*

چندروپل चन्द्रोपल *chandropal*, m. moon-gem. *s.*

چندرودي चन्द्रोदय *chandroday*, m. an awning, a cloth or sheet spread over the open courts of Hindū houses, &c. upon festival occasions; moon-rise; a kind of collyrium. *s.*

چندرولري चन्द्रवल्लरी *chandra-vallarī*, f. a kind of asclepias (*a. acida*); rue. *s.*

چندرهار चन्द्रहार *chandra-hār*, m. a sort of necklace composed of circular pieces of gold, silver, &c. *s.*

چندلا चन्दला *chandlā*, bald (v. *chandrā*), m. baldness. *h.*

چندن चन्दन *chandan*, m. sandal wood or tree (*Syrium myrtifolium* or *Santalum album*). *s.*

چندنا *chandnā*, m. (v. *chāndnā*) light, &c. *d.*

چندنهار *chandan-hār*, an ornament worn on the head by women: it is shaped like a half-moon. *d.*

چندوا चन्दवा *chandwā*, m. a small canopy, an awning; (in Dakh.) *chandwā machhī*, the pomflet fish. *h.*

چندها चुन्धा *chundhā*, dim-sighted, blinkard; bad and crabbed (as a handwriting). *h.*

چندهلا चुन्धला *chundhlā*, m. a blinkard. *h.*

چندهلانا चुन्धलाना *chundhlānā*, n. to be purblind, to see dimly. *h.*

چندي *chande*, a few, some; sometime. *p.*

چندي चुन्दी *chundī*, f. a procuress, a bawd.

چندي *chindī*, f. a small piece, a fragment; rags, a scrap of cloth, a tatter. *chindī-chindī-k.*, to break or reduce into small pieces. *d.*

چنديا चन्दिया *chandiyā*, f. the crown of the head. *s.*

چنديا चन्दैया *chandaiyā*, deep places. *h.*

چنديري चन्देरी *chanderī*,
چنديل चन्देल *chandel*, } f. name of a place. *h.*

چنديل चन्देल *chandel*,
چنديل चन्दील *chandīl*,
چنديلا चन्देला *chandelā*, } m. the name of a tribe of *rājpūts* who claim descent from the moon (v. Elliott). *s.*

چنديلي चन्देली *chandelī*, f. a fine species of cotton fabric (made at Chandel). *h.*

چندين *chandīn*, so much, so many. *p.*

چنديه *chandīna*, a variety of petty taxes (v. *chandāna*). *p.*

چنديها चन्दीहा *chandīhā*, silvery, white. *h.*

چنڈ चण्ड *chanḍ*, fierce, violent, passionate, hot, warm; pungent, acrid. *s.*

چنڈا चण्डा *chanḍā*, f. a name of the goddess Durgā, applied especially to her incarnation for the purpose of destroying the demon Mahes Asur; a passionate or furious woman. *s.*

چنڈل चण्डल *chanḍal*,
چنڈال चण्डाल *chanḍāl*, } m. an inferior caste of Hindūs; a man of the lowest of the mixed tribes, born from a Sudra father and Brāhmanī mother; (met.) a miser, a merciless wretch, an outcast. *s.*

چنڈالن चण्डालिन *chanḍālin*, f. the female of *chanḍāl*. *s.* [Bhangīs. *h.*

چنڈاليا चण्डालिया *chanḍāliyā*, a tribe of the

چنڈاول चण्डावल *chanḍāwal*, m. the rear guard. *h.* [fierceness. *s.*

چنڈتا चण्डता *chanḍatā*, f. warmth, pungency,

چنڈكا चण्डिका *chanḍikā*, f. a name of Durgā (v. *chanḍā*). *s.* [warm. *s.*

چنڈوت चण्डवत *chanḍwat*, passionate, violent,

چنڈوا चंडवा *chanḍavā*, the shaft of a plough share. *h.*

چنڈول चण्डोल *chanḍol*, m. (for *chanḍāwal*) the rear-guard; a sort of sedan; the name of a bird, a species of the lark; a plaything consisting of four little earthen pots joined together. *h.*

چنڈي चण्डी *chanḍī*, f. a name of Durgā (v. *chanḍā*). *chanḍī-kusum*, m. red oleander. *s.*

چنري चुनरी *chunrī*, f. a mode of dyeing cloths, in which they are tied in different places previous to dipping them in the dye, so as to prevent the parts tied from receiving the colour; also the cloths dyed in this manner. *h.*

چنسر चन्सुर *chansur*, m. cress, cresses (*Lepidium sativum*). *h.*

چنك चनक *chanak*, f. the bursting of the husk of a seed by exposure to the sun. *h.*

چنك चणक *chanak*, m. a kind of pulse (v. *chanā*). *chank* (v. *shank*), a conch shell. *s.*

چنكنا चनकना *chanaknā*, n. to burst and fall out (as a seed from the husk). *h.*

چن كهاءو *chun-khā,ū*, m. a bird; a beggar. *d.*

چنگ चिनग *chinag*, f. *ardor urinæ*. *h.*

چنگ *chang*, f. a claw; the hand expanded; a kind of guitar, a harp; fame, report; a paper-kite which they fly at night; the name of a suit at cards (v. *tāj*). *p.*

چنگا चङ्गा *changā*, healthy, cured, sound. *changā banānā*, a. to correct, to punish, to put to right, to chastise. *bhalā changā*, in health and vigour; perfect, good. *h.*

چنگا चिङ्गा *chingā*, m. a chicken. *h.*

چنگاري चिनगारी *chingārī*, f. a spark (of fire). *h.*

چنگال *changāl*, m. (v. *changal*). *p.*

چنگ باو चङ्गबाव *chang-bā,o*, m. the name of a disorder. *h.*

چنگٹ चिङ्गट *chingaṭ*, m. a shrimp or prawn. *s.*

چنگر चङ्गर *changar*, m. a tray, a trough. *h.*

چنگڑا चिङ्गड़ा *chingṛā*, m. } a prawn, shrimp. *s.*
چنگڑي चिङ्गड़ी *chingṛī*, f. }

چنگل *changul*, m. a claw, a talon. *p.*

چنگل चुङ्गल *chungal*, a handful of any thing dry, as *chullū* denotes a handful of liquid. *h.*

چنگنا चिनगना *chinagnā*, n. to throb, to shoot (as a boil, &c.); to cry, to screech. *h.*

چنگني चिङ्गनी *chingnī*, f. a chicken. *h.*

چنگور चङ्गूर *changūr*, excellent. *h.*

چنگهاڑ चिङ्घाड़ *chinghāṛ*, } f. scream, clamour.
چنگهاڑا चिङ्घाड़ा *chinghāṛā*, }
chinghār-marnā or *chinghāṛen mārnā*, n. to scream. *h.*

چنگهاڑنا चिङ्घाड़ना *chinghāṛnā*, n. to scream, to screech (applied properly to the elephant). *h.*

چنگي चुङ्गी *chungī*, f. a tax gathered daily from grain merchants, being as much grain as can be taken up in a man's fist; illegal abstraction of handfuls of market produce. *chūngī-penth*, a market held on condition of giving a small portion of each saleable article to the zamīndār. *h.*

چنگي चिङ्गी or चिनगी *chingī*, f. a spark of fire (v. *changārī*); a wicked dwarf. *chingī-jharnā*, *-chhūṭnā*, or *-nikalnā*, n. to sparkle. *h.*

چنگي *changī*, m. one who plays on the *chang* or harp, a harper. *p.*

چنگير चङ्गेर *changer*, f. a flower-pot, a tray. *h.*

چنگيرا चङ्गेरा *changerā*, m. a large basket; a trough or tray. *h.*

چنگيري चङ्गेरी *changerī*, f. a small basket. *h.*

چنگيل चङ्गेल *changel*, name of an herb which grows amidst old buildings, the seed of which is used in medicine, and termed *khabājī*. *h.*

چنلي متي *chunlī-miṭṭī* or *-maṭī*, potters' earth. *h.*

چنميا चनमिया *chanamiyā*, a tribe of *rājpūts*. *h.*

چنن चुनन *chunan*, m. rumple, crease. *h.*

چننا चुन्ना *chunnā*, a. to gather (v. چنا).

چنوان चनवान *chanwān*, a small species of millet. *h.*

چنوانا चुनवाना *chunwānā*, a. to cause to pick, choose, arrange, &c. (v. *chunānā*). *h.*

چنوٹا चुनौडा *chanauṭā*, m. (the same as *chunauṭī*, q. v.) the folding of the cloth called *sārī* worn by the women. *h.*

چنوٹي चुनौटी *chunauṭī*, f. a box for holding the lime used to chew along with betel; a small spoon used to take out the lime. *s.*

چنوٹي चुनौटी *chunauṭī*, f. encouraging troops in the time of battle, for which purpose there is an officer in Indian armies; selecting from an army the fittest men for a desperate enterprise. A practice which formerly prevailed at Benares: on the 11th of *Jaiṭh Shuklpaksh* the inhabitants were wont to swim across the river, and, forming themselves into two parties, to fight with swords, clubs, &c. *h.*

چنور चंवर *chanwar*, m. a kind of flapper to drive away flies. *s.*

چنه चिन्ह *chinh*, m. (for चिह्न *chinha*) a scar, a mark, spot, stain; symbol, token, feature; signature. *chinh chaṛhānā*, to stigmatize. *s.*

چنهار चिन्हार *chinhār*, m. } an acquaintance; ac-
چنهاري चिन्हारी *chinhārī*, f. }
quaintanceship. *s.*

چنهت चिन्हित *chinhit*, marked, known. *s.*

چنهوانا *chinhwānā*, to cause to be recognised. *h.*

چني चनी *chanī*, a small species of *chanā* or gram. *h.*

چني चुन्नी *chunnī*, f. a small ruby; *ascarides*. *h.*

چنيادا चनियादा *chaniyādā*, also *chane,ādā*, land under a crop of *chanā* or gram. *h.*

چنيٹه चनेठ *chaneṭh*, f. spices given to cattle, drugs for oxen. *h.*

چنيده *chinīda*, selected, chosen. *p.*

چنين *chunīn*, like this, such as this. *p.*

جو चौ *chau*, m. a back tooth; ploughshare. *h.*

چو चौ *chau*, same as *chār*, four, but used only in comp. as *chau-bag͟hlā*, m. a kind of jacket, not open under the arms. *chau-bandī*, f. giving a horse new shoes (v. *khol-bandī*); the fastenings of baggage. *chau-bhīr*, on all sides, all round. *chau-pāra*, made of four pieces. *chau-pas*, all around, on all sides. *chau-pās*, all round, around. *chau-pahal*, four sides or four-sided, a square bottle. *chau-pahlū* or *chau-pahra*, during four pahars, *i.e.* half the natural day, or twelve hours. *chau-pahra-denā*, to break in a horse, by giving a twelve hours' spell of it. *chau-tah* or *chau-tahā*, of four folds. *chau-dhīr*, *-dhir*, *-ras*, *-kudhan*, *-kudan*, or *-khūt*, on all four sides, all around. *chau-jugī*, belonging to the four *jugs* or ages of the world: the term is used to denote "of vast antiquity." *chau-goshī*, f. an animal whose ears are slit (particularly a horse: these are generally taught to amble). *chau-maḥalla*, of four stories (a house). *chau-mukhī*, four-faced. *chau-mek͟hā*, tying the elbows behind. *h.*

چو *chū*, such as, like, when; how? *p.*

چو चवि *chavi*, f. the pepper plant which yields long pepper. *s.*

چوا चौवा *chauwā*, m. quadruped (particularly oxen), a handbreadth. *h.*

چوءا चोआ *cho,ā* or चूआ *chū,ā*, m. the name of a perfume; the pod, or skin of any kind of pulse; a windfall (fruit); name of a plant used as a potherb (*Amaranthus oleaceus*). *h.*

چوءا *chū,ā* (for *chūhā*), a rat, a mouse. *chū,e-dān*, a mouse-trap. *d.*

چوءار चोआर *cho,ār*,
چوءاڑ चोआड़ *cho,āṛ*, } m. a mountain robber, an outlaw mountaineer, a brigand. *h.*

چوالا चवाला *chawālā*, m. a chair, sedan (cor. of *chaupālā*). *h.*

چواليس चौआलीस *chau,ālīs* or *chawālīs*, forty-four. *s.*

چوءان चूआन *chū,ān* or चुआन *chu,ān*, f. a reservoir, a cistern. *chū,ān khā,ī*, f. a deep ditch with water springing at the bottom. *s.*

چوءان चोआन *cho,ān*, f. dropping, dripping. *h.*

چوانا चिवाना *chiwānā*, m. a place for the cremation of the dead. *h.*

چوءانا चोआना *cho,ānā* or *chuwānā*, a. to cause to drip, to distil, to filter, to draw off. *h.*

چوءاني चौअन्नी *chau,annī*, f. a (silver) four ānā piece, a quarter rupī. *h.*

چواو चवाव *chawāw*, m. a report, slander. *s.*

چواءي चौवाई *chauwā,ī*, f. a tempest, hurricane, commotion (q. d. wind blowing from four quarters). *s.*

چواءي चवाई *chawā,ī*, m. reporter, backbiter. *s.*

چوب *chob*, f. wood; a post; a drumstick, a stick, a club. *chob-kārī* or *kār-chobī*, f. beating with a stick; a kind of embroidery. *p.*

چوبا *chobā*, m. a stake, post. *p.*

چوباچهه चौबाछः *chau-bāchha*, a kind of tax or levy of revenue on four specified things (v. Wilson). *h.*

چوبار चौबार *chau-bār*,
چوبارا चौबारा *chau-bārā*, } m. a summer-house; an assembly, court; town-hall; a shed, a police-station. *h.*

چوبان *chūbān* (v. *chūpān*), a shepherd. *p.*

چوبچه *chaubachcha*, m. (cor. of *chah-bachcha*, q. v.) a vat, a cistern, a reservoir attached to a tank or well. *p.*

چوبچيني *chob-chīnī*, f. the name of a medicine, China root (*Chinā smilax*). *p.*

چوب‌دستي *chob-dastī*, f. a staff, stick. *p.*

چوب‌دار *chob-dār*, m. a servant whose business is to announce the arrival of company, a mace-bearer. *p.*

چوبر चौबर *chaubar*, stout, robust, bold. *h.*

چوبك *chobak*, f. a drumstick. *p.*

چوبه चूभ *chūbh*, m. pricking, puncture. *h.*

چوبها चोभा *chobhā*, m. a nail; a kind of victuals given upon great occasions, marriages, &c.; prey; puncture. *h.*

چوبهنا चूभना *chūbhnā*, n. to be stuck, or thrust into; to pierce, to be goaded or stabbed, to penetrate. *h.*

چوبي चौबे *chaube* (corrup. of *chatur-vedī*, q. v.), m. a Brāhman acquainted with the four *Vedas* (now applied to the descendants of such, though not learned). *s.*

چوبي *chobī*, wooden; made of wood. *p.*

چوبيس चौबीस *chaubīs*, twenty-four. *s.*

چوبيسا चौबीसा *chaubīsā*,
چوبيسه चौबीसः *chaubīsa*, } a track of land containing twenty-four villages, occupied by one tribe. *s.*

چوبين *chobīn*, wooden, made of wood. *p.*

چوپ चोप *chop*, f. desire, wish, hope. *h.*

چوپا चौपा *chaupā*,
چوپار चौपार *chaupār*,
چوپال चौपाल *chaupāl*, } m. four-footed, a quadruped. *s.*

چوپاڑ चौपाड़ *chaupāṛ* (also *chaupār* & *chaupāl*), m. a kind of summer-house or pavilion (generally built jointly by several people, as a resting-place common to them all); a quadruped, an animal a beast. *s.*

چوپالا चौपाला *chaupālā*, m. a litter, sedan. *s.*

چوپان *chaupān* or *chūpān*, m. a cowherd, or shepherd. *chūpānī*, the office of shepherd. *p.*

چوپاءي चौपाई *chaupā,ī*, f. a sort of metre, a verse consisting of four long feet or short lines, chiefly used in Braj compositions. *s.*

چوپايه चौपाय *chaupāya*, m. an animal, a beast, quadruped. *p.*

چوپتري चौपत्री *chaupatrī*,
چوپتي चौपत्ती *chaupattī*, } f. a small tract, an essay, a pamphlet, a pocket-book. *s.*

چوپٹ चौपट *chaupaṭ*, ruined, destroyed, levelled, plain. *chaupaṭ-k.*, to level, to destroy. *h.*

چوپڑ चौपड़ *chaupaṛ*, f. the name of a game played with long dice, also the cloth on which it is played; also a summer-house (v. *chaupār*). *s.*

چوپڑ चूपड़ *chūpaṛ*, m. grease. *h.*

چوپڑي चूपड़ी *chūpṛī*, adj. f. oiled, greasy, unctuous. *chūpṛī bāt*, f. flattery, soft words. *chūpṛī roṭī*, f. cakes rich with clarified butter. *h.*

چوپنا चोपना *chopnā*, a. to throw water from a *dauri*, q. v. *h.*

چوپہلا चौपहला *chau-pahlā*, m. a kind of sedan (v. *chau-pālā*). *h.*

چوت चूत *chūt*, f. *vulva*. *chūt-salāmī*, fees paid by a bridegroom to the *ḍūṛī* on the morning after his nuptials. *chūt-marānī*, a strumpet, a harlot. *s.*

چوتارا चौतारा *chautārā*, m. a four-stringed musical instrument, a guitar. *h.*

چوتال चौताल *chautāl* or *chautāla*, m. a mode in music. *s.*

چوترا चौतरा *chautarā* (v. *chautara*). *h.*

چوترکا चौतरका *chautarkā*, m. a mitre; a kind of tent. *h.*

چوترہ चौतरः *chautara*, m. (v. *chabūtara*) a terrace or mound to sit and converse on, a tribunal. *h.*

چوتڑ चूतड़ *chūtaṛ*, m. the backside, buttock, hip. *chūtaṛ bajānā*, n. to be overjoyed. *chūtaṛ sakoṛnā*, a. to loiter, to hang back. *chūtaṛ se kān gāṅṭhnā*, to speak in parables, to use far-fetched expressions. *h.*

چونکي کھئالي चौत्कीखैआली *chautkī-khai,ālī*, a sum paid to the *zamīndār* for the privilege of weighing the grain of the cultivators. *h.*

چوتھ चौथ *chauth*, f. the fourth lunar day; the fourth part; a species of tribute, consisting of one fourth the regular government assessment, demanded by the *Marhaṭṭās* from the neighbouring princes, Hindū and Musalmān alike, as the price of forbearing to ravage their countries. This is the same as the "blackmail" formerly levied by the Highland Scottish chiefs on their more wealthy and less warlike neighbours of the lowlands. *s.*

چوتھ चोथ *choth*, m. cow-dung. *h.*

چوتھا चौथा *chauthā*, the fourth. *chauthe*, in the fourth place, fourth: (in Dakh.) *shauthā*, denotes a kind of palanquin, sometimes called a "dooly." *s.*

چوتھاءي चौथाई *chauthā,ī*, f. the fourth part, a quarter; a fine equal to one-fourth of the revenue. *s.*

چوتھي चौथी *chauthī*, f. the fourth day; a ceremony performed on the fourth day after marriage. *s.*

چوتھيا चौथिया *chauthiyā*, m. one who receives the *chauth*; a quartan ague; name of a measure for grain nearly equal to a *ser* (q. v.). *s.*

چوتيا चूतिया *chūtiyā*, m. a blockhead. *chūtiyā shahīd*, m. a cully, a dupe. *s.*

چوتيا चौतीया *chautīyā*, f. a quartan (ague) *s.*

چوتيس चौतीस *chautīs*, thirty-four. *s.*

چوٹ चोट *choṭ*, f. a hurt, a blow, damage; fall; spite, effort, attempt, assiduity, desire, wish, aim tip of the toe, folding a blanket, &c., as a covering for the head and shoulders. *choṭ par choṭ*, one misfortune follows another, misfortunes come not single. *choṭ bāndhnā*, a. to defend; to bind up the edge of a sword &c.; to restrain by magic. *choṭ khānā*, to receive a blow, to be hurt; to suffer loss. *h.*

چوٹ चूट *chūṭ*, m. a crack, a noise, a peculiar mode of folding a blanket or sheet. *h.*

چوٹا चोटा *choṭā*, m. discount or premium independent of interest; treacle. *h.*

چوٹا चोट्टा *choṭṭā*, m. a thief. *h.*

چوٹي चोटी *choṭī*, f. a lock of hair left on the top of the head, the plait or tie of hair behind, a queue; top, summit; a petticoat. *choṭī kā honā*, to excel, be pre-eminent, or unrivalled. *h.*

چوٹيانا चोटियाना *choṭiyānā*, a. to seize by the hair, also to wound, to hurt. *h.*

چوج चोज *choj*, m. subtleness, beauty. *h.*

چوج *chūj*, *chūjā*, and *chūja* (v. *chūz*, &c.). *p.*

چوجي चोजी *chojī*, subtle, fine. *h.*

چوچلا चोचला *chochlā*, m. playfulness, blandishments, endearing arts and expressions, coquetry. *h.*

چوچي चूची *chūchī*, f. (v. *chūṅchī*) the breast, pap, &c. *h.*

چوحدا *chau-ḥaddā*, چوحدي *chau-ḥaddī*, } the neighbourhood, environs; surrounding country. *d.*

چودا *chaudā* (for *chaudah*), fourteen. *p.*

چوداني चौदानी *chaudānī*, f. چودانيا चौदानिया *chaudāniyā*, m. } an ornament (formed of four pearls) worn in the ears. *h.*

چودري *chaudrī* (for *chaudharī* q. v.), head man, &c. *d.*

چودس चौदस *chaudas*, f. the fourteenth day [of the moon. *s.*

چودنا चोदना *chodnā*, a. to copulate. *h.*

چودنت चौदन्त *chau-dant*, crossing their teeth in fight (elephants); sturdy, robust, stout. *s.*

چودنتي चौदन्ती *chaudantī*, f. boldness. *s.*

چودوان चौदवाँ *chaudwāṅ*, the fourteenth. *s.*

چودوانسا चोदवाँसा *chodwāṅsā*, whorish, libidinous, addicted to fornication. *h.*

چودهان चौदहाँ *chaudahāṅ*, the fourteenth. *s.*

چودہ चौदह *chaudah*, fourteen. *s.*

چودھر चौधर *chaudhar*, robust, active, vigorous, corpulent. *h.*

چودھراءي चौधराई *chaudharā,ī*, f. the business, office, or dignity of a *chaudharī*, q.v. *h.*

چودھرايت चौधरायत *chaudharāyat*, a *chaudharī's* fees of office. *h.*

چودھري चौधरी *chaudharī*, m. the head man of a trade; a village chief or headman; in Bengal, a title of landholders superior to a *ta'alluḳ-dār*, q. v. *h*

چودهوان चौदहवां *chaudahwān*, the fourteenth. *s.*

چودهير *chaudher*, all around. *d.*

چوڈول चौडोल *chauḍol*, m. a kind of sedan with two poles. *h.*

چور चोर *chor*, m. a thief, robber; adj. sly, hidden, false, treacherous. *chor-bālū*, f. a quicksand. *chor-pahrā* or *-pahra*, the scouts of an army. *chor-jahāz*, a pirate ship, a privateer. *chor-chakār*, m. a thief. *chor-khāna*, m. bye-room, concealed drawer. *chor-darwāza*, m. trapdoor. *chor-dhor*, m. plaintiff and defendant; all the parties of a law suit; a thief and what he has stolen. *chor-rāh* or *-rasta*, a secret path. *chor-zamīn*, a quagmire, bog. *chor-siṛhī*, f. back-stairs. *chor-khiṛkī*, f. a back-door, a bye-door. *chor-galī*, f. a bye-road, back-lane. *chor lagnā*, n. to be injured, to damage. *chor lagnā sham' ko*, n. to waste a candle by a thief being attached to it. *chor-maḥal*, m. the apartments of the concubines of great men. *chor-mandūrā*, m. a game played by children. *chor-mahīchnī*, f. hide and seek. *chor-nimak*, contraband salt (chiefly used in Cuttack).

چور चूर *chūr*, m. powder, filings, atoms; bruised. *chūr-chūr*, broken to atoms. *chūr rahnā*, n. to sot. *chūr-k.*, a. to break into small pieces. *chūr honā*, n. to be broken into small pieces; to be enamoured of, to be in love; to be tired. *nashe meṅ chūr honā*, n. to be helplessly intoxicated. *s.*

چور चौर *chaur*, a large open space in a forest; an extensive tract of low land. *h.*

چورا चौरा *chaurā*, m. a terrace or mound to sit and converse on; the place where Hindū widows are burnt; also a kind of bean (v. *chaulā*). *h.*

چورا चूरा *chūrā*, m. filings; saw-dust; grain reduced to coarse particles to be chucked into the mouth. *s.*

چوراسته *chau-rāsta* (v. *chau-rāhā*), a cross-road. *h. p.*

چوراسي चौरासी *chaurāsī*, eighty-four; a subdivision of a *pargana*, amounting to eighty-four villages. *s.*

چوراسي चौरासी *chaurāsī*, f. morris bells worn on the ankles by dancing girls. *h.*

چورانا चोराना *chorānā*, a. to steal. *s.*

چورانوي चौरानवे *chaurānawwe* or चौरान्वे *chaurānwe*, ninety-four. *s.*

چوراها *chau-rāhā*, چوراهه *chaurāha*, चौराहा m. a cross-road; the junction of four roads; the meeting of the boundaries of four villages. *h. p.*

چورپشپي चोरपुष्पी *chor-pushpī*, f. a kind of grass (*Andropogon aciculatum*). *s.*

چورپهره *chor-phara* or *-pahra*, the vanguard of an army; (lit.) "the sly sentry." *d.*

چورس चौरस *chauras*, level, even. *h.*

چورس *chauras*, all around, on the four sides. *d.*

چورساءي चौरसाई *chaurasā,ī*, f. equality of surface, evenness. *h.*

چورسانا चौरसाना *chaurasānā*, a. to level. *h.*

چورسي चौरसी *chaurasī*, a granary above ground. *h*

چورما चूर्मा *chūrmā*, m. a kind of sweetmeat made of sugar and crumbled bread. *h.*

چورن चूरन *chūran* or चूर्ण *chūrṇa*, m. powder, dust; a powder composed of medicines for promoting digestion, aromatic powder, pounded sandal, &c.; fossil alkali, efflorescent salt. *chūrna-kuntal*, m. a lock of hair, a curl. *chūrna-khanḍ*, m. pebble, gravel, hardened fragments of earth or brick; limestone nodule, commonly called *kankar*. *s.*

چورنا चूर्णा *chūrnā*, a. to reduce to very small peices, or to atoms. *s.*

چورنگ चौरङ्ग *chaurang*, m. a practice of the sword exercise; cutting the four legs of an animal off at one blow. *chaurang kāṭnā*, a. to cut off the four legs of an animal at one blow. *chaurang-mārnā*, a. to lose the use of the limbs by illness; to hamstring a quadruped. *s.*

چوره *chūra*, a small bit, a fragment. *d.*

چوري चोरी *chorī*, f. a theft, robbery, stealth. *chorī-chorī*, by stealth, clandestinely. *s.*

چوري चूरी *chūrī*, f. a species of bread rich with *ghī*; a kind of bracelet. *h.*

چوري चौरी *chaurī*, f. a summer-house. *h.*

چوڑ चूड़ *chūṛ*, m. a silver or gold ornament worn by the Hindū widows; the ring fastened to elephant's teeth. *h.*

چوڑ चोड़ *choṛ*, m. a boddice, a jacket.

چوڑ चूड़ *chūṛ* (also *chūṛā* and *chūṛī*), a crest, a top-knot, a ring, an amulet, the bracelet put on a bride at the time of marriage. *chūṛā-bhandāra*, an allowance for the maintenance of the junior members of a zamīndār's family. *s.*

چوڑ चौड़ *chauṛ*, spoiled, destroyed. *h.*

چوڑا चौड़ा *chauṛā*, wide, broad. *chauṛā chaklā*, extensive, spacious. *h.*

چوڑا चूड़ा *chūṛā*, f. a single lock of hair left on the crown of the head at the ceremony of tonsure; a peacock's crest; any crest, plume, diadem; head, top, summit; a kind of bracelet; m. the rings fastened to elephants' teeth; a kind of ornament; a kind of food made of parched rice. *chūṛā-mani*, m. a jewel worn in a crest, or a diadem; the Gunjā (*Abrus precatorius*). *chūṛā-wat*, crested, having a lock of hair on the top of the head. *s.*

چوڑالا चूड़ाला *chūṛālā*, f. a kind of grass (*Kyllinga monocephala*); adj. crested, having a lock of hair on the crown of the head. *s.*

چوڑان चौड़ान *chauṛān*, m. f. breadth, width, extension. *h.*

چوڑانا चौड़ाना *chauṛānā*, a. to increase in breadth, to expand, to widen. *h.*

چوڑاءي चौड़ाई *chauṛā,ī*, f. breadth, width, extension; boasting. *chauṛā,ī-mārnā* or *-karnā*, a. to boast, to give one's self airs. *h.*

چوڑچوپٹ चोड़चौपट *chauṛ-chaupaṭ*, abandoned, vicious, damaged. *h.*

چوڑي चूड़ी *chūṛī*, f. bangles or rings made of glass, &c., and worn on the wrist (v. *chūrī*). *chūṛī dār*, drawers, or sleeves, made too long, so as to be crumpled into plaits. *h.*

چوز chūz, m. a young hawk, a hawk that has not hunted. p.

چوزا chūzā, a kite, (also v. chūza). p.

چوزه chūza, m. a chicken, a young bird. chūza-bāz, an old woman who keeps a young gallant, an old woman fond of striplings. p.

چوس चौस chaus, m. flour, powder; land four times tilled. h.

چوسٹھ चौसठ chausaṭh, sixty-four. s.

چوسر चौसर chausar, m. (v. chaupar) a kind of game played with oblong dice; also the cloth, &c. on which it is played. s.

چوسري chausarī, a female ornament worn round the neck. d.

چوسنا चूसना chūsnā, a. to suck. s.

چوسنگھا चौसिंघा chausinghā, a. raised mound indicating where the boundaries of four villages meet. h.

چوسني चूसनी chūsnī, f. a child's coral, a sucking-stick for children. s.

چوشيه चोष्य choshya, suckable, any thing (especially fruit) capable of being sucked, as a mango, &c. s.

چوغه chogha (v. قبا), a kind of garment. d.

چوک चूक chūk, f. an error, inadvertency, blunder, mistake. h.

چوک चूक chūk, adj. sour, acid; m. a medicine made of boiled lemon-juice and pomegranates. s.

چوک चौक chauk, m. a square, an open place in a city where the market is held, and where also the chief of the police-office is stationed; a market; (according to Gladwin it denotes) "a constant daily market, or place of sale in towns, for all articles of wearing apparel and other second-hand goods, the commodities here sold being, for the most part, not new; or if new, coarse of their kind;" a court-yard; a custom at the marriage of Hindūs and Musalmāns of making a square space of coloured meal, in which the bride and bridegroom are seated on chairs, &c. chauk-bharnā or -pūrnā, a. to form a square space of coloured meal, in which at marriages the bride and bridegroom are seated on chairs, &c. chauk-paṭṭā, a seat on which the people sit and eat in the ceremony above mentioned. chauk-nikās, a tax on all goods sold in the chauk. chauk-mārā, smuggling; evading the market tax. h.

چوکا चूका chūkā or chakā, m. a kind of sorrel (Rumex vesicarius); also rice. s.

چوکا चूका chūkā, m. a kind of earthen pot. h.

چوکا चौका chaukā, m. the space in which Hindūs dress their victuals; a square slate of marble, &c.; the four front teeth; the cube of a measure called bans. h.

چوکاباگ चोकाबाग chokābāg, seeds sown immediately after a fall of rain. h.

چوکٹ चौकट chaukaṭ, f. (v. chaukhaṭ) frame of a door, &c. s.

چوکدهن chau-hudhan, on all four sides. d.

چوکري चौकरी chaukarī, a measure of grain, a quarter of a chautiyā, q. v. h.

چوکر चोकर chokar, } m. husk of wheat,
چوکڑ चोकड़ chokaṛ, } bran. h.

چوکڑ चौकड़ chaukaṛ, good, well, fine, excellent. h.

چوکڑا चौकड़ा chaukaṛā, m. a ring of two pearls worn in each ear; also a division of crop, the cultivator giving a fourth part to the zamīndār. s.

چوکڑي चौकड़ी chaukaṛī, f. a bound, a spring; a ring of pearls worn by men in the ears. chaukaṛī bharnā, a. to leap, to bound. chaukaṛī bhūlnā, n. to forget one's bound, i. e. to be fascinated, to have one's senses benumbed. chaukaṛī mār baiṭhnā, n. to squat. h.

چوکس चौकस chaukas, cautious, watchful, alert, diligent, active, clever, intelligent; full weight. h.

چوکسي चौकसी chaukasī, f. diligence; four people employed together, or eating out of the same dish or plate; m. an assayer, an examiner. h.

چوکساٸي चौकसाई chaukasā,ī, f. attention, circumspection, watchfulness, caution. h.

چوکله चौकलः chaukla, an assemblage of the smaller divisions of a province, the jurisdiction of a faujdār, q. v. h.

چوکنا चूकना chūknā, n. to blunder, to mistake, depart from, err, miss, fail. h.

چوکنا चौकन्ना chaukannā, cautious, alert, circumspect, sly, wary. h.

چوکور चौकोर chaukor, } four-cornered,
چوکونا चौकोना chau-konā, } square, or quadrangular. s.

چوکھ चोख chokh, adj. sharp, pungent; also chūkh, m. the name of a medicine, orris-root, orrice or iris root. h.

چوکھا चोखा chokhā, pure, unadulterated, genuine, good, fine, sharp, pungent, keen; clever, dextrous; pleasing, delightful, beautiful; m. a station where four boundaries meet. h.

چوکھا चौखा chaukhā, a station where four boundaries meet. h.

چوکھاٸي चोखाई chokhā,ī, f. purity, sharpness. h.

چوکھٹ चौखट chaukhaṭ, m. f. frame of a door; the upper and lower piece of the frame of a door. s.

چوکھونٹا चौखूंटा chaukhūnṭā, square. h.

چوکھي चौखी chaukhī or चोखी chokhī, adj. f. sharp (tone in music). h.

چوکي चौकी chaukī, f. a chair, a stool; guard, or watch; the post where a guard is stationed; a custom-house; a police-station; an ornament worn on the breast. chaukī-dār, m. a watchman. chaukī-dārī, the business of a watchman; the pay or hire of a watchman. chaukī-d., to watch, to mount guard. chaukī mārnā, a. to smuggle. h.

چوکي चविकी chavikī, f. Piper chavya. s.

چوگا चोगा chogā, m. food of birds brought up from the crop; food of birds in general. chogā-badalnā, a. to bill, to caress as doves by joining bills. h

چوگان चौगान *chaugān*, m. a plain, a desert. *h.*

چوگان *chaugān*, m. a game resembling what in Scotland they call "shinty," and in some parts of England, "shinney," or "hockey," or "bandy," but played on horseback; also the crooked stick or club used in playing the game. *chaugān-gāh*, shinty-ground. *chaugān-bāz*, a shinty player. *chaugān-bāzī*, the playing of shinty. This game has been improperly described as "cricket," "golf," &c., to which it bears no resemblance whatever. It is simply the good old game of "shinty," played by mounted horsemen, each armed with a long stick like a shepherd's crook. The players are divided into two parties, the object of each being either to carry off the ball from the adverse party, or to force it over a certain boundary-line. *p.*

چوگانه चौगाणः *chaugāna*, fourfold, quadruple. *s.*

چوگاني चौगानी *chaugānī*, f. a straight (*ḥuḳḳa* pipe or) tube for smoking through. *h.*

چوگڈّا चौगड्डा *chaugaḍḍā*, a place where the boundaries of four villages meet. *h.*

چوگرد *chaugird*, on all four sides, all around; m. environs, vicinity. *p.*

چوگڑا चौगड़ा *chaugaṛā*, m. a rabbit, a hare. *h.*

چوگنا चौगुणा *chaugunā*, fourfold, four times. *s.*

چوگوشه *chau-gosha*, a kind of oblong tray. *p.*

چوگوشیا चौगोषिया *chau-goshiyā*, m. a *turki* horse; a horse with slit ears. *h.*

چوگهرا चौघरा *chau-gharā*, m. a small box with four partitions for holding betel leaf, nut, chunam, and spices, which are chewed together, or for perfumes, &c.; also a wooden frame for holding four chatties or pots. *s.*

چول चूल *chūl*, f. a tenon, the part of joiners' work which fits into another (as a dove-tail); a pivot upon which a door turns as on a hinge; an axle-tree arm. *chūleṅ-ukhaṛnā* or *-dhīlī honā*, n. to be tired, worn out with labour. *h.*

چول चौल *chaul*, the ceremony of tonsure. *s.*

چولا चूला *chūlā* f. a crest (also *chūlat*), name of a tribe of *Tagās*. *h.*

چولا चोला *cholā*, m. (v. *cholī*); a bodice, a waistcoat, a jacket; a garment worn by a bride at her marriage; a small betel-basket; a country, the modern Tanjore: the name is supposed to apply to a part of Bīrbhūm in Bengal. *s.*

چولا चौला *chaulā* (also *chaurā*), name of a kind of bean much cultivated in India (*Dolichos sinensis*). *h.*

چولا *chūlā*, also *chūla* & *chūlyā* (for *chūlhā*), m. a fireplace. *d.*

چولاءي चौलाई *chaulā,ī*, f. a kind of vegetable (*Amaranthus polygamus*). *h.*

چولڑا चौलड़ा *chaulaṛā*, m. } a necklace of four
چولڑي चौलड़ी *chaulaṛī*, f. } strings. *h.*

چول کرم चौलकर्म *chaul-karma*, m. the ceremony of tonsure, cutting off all the hair from the head of a child three years old, except one lock on the crown. *s.*

چولها चूल्हा *chūlhā*, m. } a fire-place. *s.*
چولهي चूल्ही *chūlhī*, f. }

چولي चोली *cholī*, f. a bodice, a waistcoat, the body of a gown, a jacket; a small betel basket. *s.*

چوما चूमा *chūmā*, m. a kiss; *chūmā-chāṭī*, f. dalliance, kissing and toying. *s.*

چوماس चौमास *chau-mās*, lands tilled during the *chau-māsā*, q. v. *s.*

چوماسا चौमासा *chau-māsā*, } m. the space of
چوماسه चौमासः *chau-māsa*, } four months,
applied particularly to the rainy season (from June to September). *s.*

چومسیا चौमस्या *chau-masyā*, } a ploughman
چومسیه चौमस्यः *chau-masya*, } hired for a
term or season of four months. *s.*

چومکپتهر चूमकपत्थर *chūmak patthar*, m. a magnet (v. *chumbak*). *s.*

چومکه चौमुख *chau-mukh*, m. a lamp-stand with four partitions; a name of Brāhma. *s.*

چومکها चौमुखा *chau-mukhā*, adj. having four burners (a lamp); m. a lamp-stand with four partitions; a kind of *paṭā*, q. v. *s.*

چومکهي चौमुखी *chau-mukhī*, f. a name of a Hindū goddess; the seed of a tree called in Sanskrit *rudrāksha* (*Scævola lobella* or *Eleocarpus ganitrus*). *s.*

چومن चूमन *chūman*, m. act of kissing. *s.*

چومنا चूमना *chūmnā*, a. to kiss. *s.*

چون *chūṅ*, such as, like; interrog. how when? conj. because, inasmuch as. *chūṅ-ki*, whereas, since. *p.*

چون चून or चूण *chūn*, m. flour, pulse coarsely ground; lime. *s.*

چون चौवन *chauwan*, fifty-four. *h.*

چونا चूना *chūnā*, n. to leak, to drop, to ooze, to be distilled, to be filtered; to drop from the tree when ripe (fruit). *s.*

چونا चूना *chūnā*, m. lime; *chunam*. *chūnā-pazni*, f. a dancing girl. *chūnā lagānā*, a to defame. *s.*

چونارو चूनारू *chūnārū*, } m. a lime-burner or
چوناري चूनारी *chūnārī*, } worker in lime. *s.*

چونان *chūnān*, like that, just as if, such as. *p.*

چون بي چگون *chūni be chigūn*, without likeness, incomparable, an epithet of the Deity. *p.*

چونپ चोंप *chomp* or चौंप *chaump*, f. wish, desire, fondness, alacrity, avidity; a gold ornament worn on the front teeth. *h.*

چونتالي चौंताली *chauntālī*, cotton pods in which the fibre is equal to one-fourth of the whole produce. *h.*

چونترا चौंतरा *chauntarā* (v. *chabūtara*), a terrace or mound to sit and converse on; a custom-house; a police-office. *h.*

چونترو चूंत्रू *chūntrū*, the head man of a district. *h.*

چونتھنا चोंथना chonthnā, a. to scratch, to claw. h.

چونتیس चौंतीस chauṅtīs, thirty-four. h.

چونٹا चूंटा chūṅṭā, m. a large ant. h.

چونٹلا चोंटला chonṭlā, m. the ribbon with which hair is tied or braided at the end; false hair mixed with the real. h.

چونٹنا चूंटना chūṅṭnā, / چونٹھنا चूंठना chūṅṭhnā, a. to gather (a flower); to claw, to pinch. h.

چونٹي चोंटी choṅṭī, f. the hair braided behind; a tuft of hair left at the top of the head when all the rest is shaved off; queue, top, apex, summit, pinnacle; an ornament worn on the head by women. *choṅṭī āsmān par ghisnā*, n. to be very vain or aspiring. *choṅṭī-kaṭ*, a slave. *choṅṭī kaṭwānā*, to be a slave, to be obedient. *choṅṭī kisī kī hāth meṅ ānā*, a. to have a power over one, to subdue. h.

چونٹي चूंटी chūṅṭī, f. a small ant. h.

چونچ चोंच chonch, f. beak, bill; a point. s.

چونچرا chūṅ chirā, wrangling, altercation (lit. when or how, and wherefore). p.

چونچلا चोंचला choṅchlā, m. playfulness (v. chochlā). h.

چون چون chūṅ-chūṅ, the noise of birds. d.

چونچه chauṅcha, the fourth reservoir to which water by the *daurī* (q. v.), for irrigation is raised. h.

چونچهاٹ चूंचहाट chūṅchahāṭ, f. singing of birds. h.

چونچي चूंची chūṅchī, f. breast, bubby, dug, nipple. s.

چوندھا चूंधा chūndhā, / چوندھلا चोंधला chondhlā, (also chūndhlā), dim, purblind, dim-sighted. h.

چوندھلانا चोन्धलाना chonhhālnā, n. to be purblind, to see dimly. h.

چوندھي चोन्धी chondhī, f. dimness, dulness of sight. h.

چوندھیانا चौंधियाना chaundhiyānā, n. to be confused, to be frightened out of one's senses, to be amazed, to be dazzled. h.

چوندي choṅdi, f. fraud, deceit, trick. d.

چونڈا चोंडा choṅḍā, m. the head; hair braided on the of top the head; a kind of well where the water is near the surface of the ground. h.

چونڈو चौंडू chauṅḍū, m. a blockhead. h.

چونڈول chauṅḍol (v. chauḍol), a sedan. s.

چونر चवंर chawaṅr or chauṅr, a flapper. s.

چونرا चौंरा chauṅrā, m. an apartment under ground for grain. h.

چونري चौंरी chauṅrī, f. an instrument for driving away flies, a fly-flapper; a police-station, where the kotwāl or petty magistrate resides. s.

چونسر चौंसर chauṅsar, m. the name of a game, the same as *chausar*; a garland of flowers. s.

چونك चौंक chaunk, f. the act of starting. h

چونکانا चौंकाना chaunkānā, a. to waken, to rouse up. h.

چونکنا चौंकना chaunknā, n. to start, to boggle, to start up from sleep. *chaunk-uṭhnā*, n. to start up, to wince. *chaunk-paṛnā* or *-ānā*, n. to bounce up. h.

چونکنا चोंकना chonknā, a. to prick, to goad. h.

چونکه chūṅki, when that, whereas, since. p.

چونکیل चौंकेल chaunkel, an untamed animal, a boggler, a horse that starts. h.

چونگا चौंगा chaungā, m wheedling. *changā-k.*, a. to wheedle one out of money. h.

چونگا चोंगा chongā, m. a funnel; (in Dakh.) a sort of bread. h.

چونگلا चोंगला chonglā, m. a joint of bamboos, used to send letters in. h.

چونگي चूंगी chūngī, f. toll, tax, duty, a small pipe or tube. h.

چونگي चौंगी chaungī, f. wheedling. *chaungī-bāz*, m. a wheedler. *chaungī-bāzī*, f. sharping, &c. h.

چونلائي chauṅlā,ī, a species of plant (*Pertulaca quadrifica*). d.

چونه chūna (for chūnā), lime, chunam. h.

چونما चूंमा chūṅmā (for chūmā), kissed. h.

چوني चूनी chūnī, f. pulse split or ground very coarsely; a spark, or small ruby, or other gem. h.

چووا चोवा chowā, m. a perfume; the pod or skin of any kind of pulse; a wind-fall (fruit). h.

چووا चौवा chauwā, m. a quadruped (particularly oxen); a handbreath. h.

چووائي चौवाई chau-wā,ī, f. a tempest, a hurricane (wind blowing from the four quarters). s.

چوون चौवन chauwan, fifty-four. h.

چوونا चूवना chūvnā, / چوونون chūwanauṅ, n. to drop, to leak, to ooze, to exude. s.

چوها चूहा chūhā, m. a rat, a mouse. *chohā*, a small well. *chūhe-dān*, m. a mouse-trap. *chūhe-mār* or *chūh-mār*, m. a sparrow-hawk, cormorant, a mouser. h.

چوهان चौहान chauhān, m. a caste of *rāj-pūts*.

چوهتر चौहत्तर chauhattar, seventy-four. h.

چوهٹا चौहट्टा chauhaṭṭā, m. a market where four roads meet. s.

چوهڑ चूहड़ chūhaṛ, m. the act of hunting by deceiving game with a stalking horse. h.

چوهڑا चूहड़ा chūhṛā, m. a Hindū sweeper (v. *ḥalāl-khor*), the lowest caste of village servants. h.

چوهڑنچلا चोहड़नीचला chohaṛ-nichlā, m. the lower jaw. h.

چوهڑي चूहड़ी chūhṛī, f. wife of a *ḥalāl-khor* or sweeper. h.

چوهلا चोहला *chohlā*, m. a large peg or pin. *h.*

چوهنا चूहना *chūhnā*, a. to suck. *s.*

چوئي *cho,ī*, the pip of an orange. *d.*

چوهي चूही *chūhī*, f. a mouse, a she mouse or rat; (in Dakh.) *chūwī*, the same. *h.*

چويا चोया *choyā*, m. husk of grain, the scale of a fish; a hole dug in the sandy bed of a river which has dried up, in which water is found, a rivulet. *h.*

چوئل चोईल *cho,īl*, land lying low and always moist

چويه चव्य *chavya*, pepper (*Piper chavya*). *s.*

چه छ *chha*, the aspirate form of چ च. *s.h.*

چه *chah*, m. (for *chāh*) a well, a pit. *p.*

چه *chi*, pron. inter. what? when joined to another word the mute *h* is dropped, as *chi-gūna*, in wnat manner, how? *p.*

چه *cha*, a termination annexed to Persian nouns (chiefly names of lifeless things) to form diminutives, as *kū-cha*, a small street, form *kū*. *p.*

چه छः *chha*, six. *chha-dām*, a very small denomination of money, hence any thing of little value. *chha-sāt*, trick, cheat, juggle. *chha-kur*, a division of crops in which the zamīndār gets only a sixth part. *s.*

چه चह *chah*, a platform, a pier head. *h.*

چهاپ छाप *chhāp*, f. stamp, print, copy, a seal; impression of a stamp or seal; the government stamp on coins, papers, &c.; an official stamp in general. *h.*

چهاپا छापा *chhāpā*, sectarial marks representing a lotus, trident, &c., delineated on the body by the *Vaishnavas* or worshippers of *Vishṇu*; m. edition, print, seal, &c. *chhāpā-vidyā*, f. the art of printing. *chhāpe-wālā*, a printer. *chhāpe-khāna*, a printing-office. *h.*

چهاپتي छापती *chhaptī*, a coarse seal of cow-dung and mud affixed to a pile of grain on the threshing-floor to prevent its removal. *h.*

چهاپنا छापना *chhāpnā*, a. to print, to stamp. *h.*

چهاپه *chhāpa* (v. *chhāpā*), a mark, stamp, &c. *h.*

چهات छात *chhāt*, f. roof; adj. thin, feeble, emaciated. *s.*

چهاتا छाता *chhātā*, m. a large umbrella. *s.*

چهاتر छात्र *chhātra*, a scholar, disciple, a pupil. *s.*

چهاتي छाती *chhātī*, m. f. a small umbrella, a parasol. *s.*

چهاتي छाती *chhātī*, f. breast; dug. *chhātī-bhar*, breast high. *chhātī bhar-ānā*, n. to weep. *chhātī bhar-jānā*, n. to be chest-foundered. *chhātī par patthar rakhnā*, a. to have patience. *chhātī par mūng dalnā* (lit. to grind pulse on the breast), to do any thing in presence of another person by which he is vexed. *chhātī phaṭnī*, one's heart to be broken with grief or sorrow; to sympathise. *chhātī pīṭnā*, a. to regret, to repent, to lament. *chhātī ṭhoknā*, a. to encourage; to assure. *chhātī ṭhanḍī honā*, to be pleased, overjoyed. *chhātī jalnā*, to have the heartburn; to lament. *chhātī kā patthar*, nuisance, pest. *chhātī kā jam* (lit. the destroyer of the heart), applied to a person or thing the presence of which is unpleasant, a pest, a nuisance. *chhātī kholke milnā*, to meet frankly. *chhātī gadrānī*, the swelling of the breast in young women. *chhātī lagānā*, a. to lament, to grieve. *chhātī (se) lagānā*, a. to fondle. *chhātī nikālke chalnā*, n. to stalk, to strut. *h.*

چهاج छाज *chhāj*, m. a basket or fan (for winnowing corn). *h.*

چهاجنا छाजना *chhājnā*, n. to thatch; to befit, to become. *s.*

چهاچه छाछ *chhāchh* (in Dakh. *chhāch*), butter-milk, also (same as *chhāj*) a winnowing basket. *h*

چهادان छादान *chhādān*, m. a water-bag.

چهادت छादित *chhādit*, covered, concealed. *s.*

چهادن छादन *chhādan*, m. the act of covering; a covering, a screen, &c. *s.*

چهار छार *chhār*, f. ashes; a large clod of earth; (for *chhāṛ*, q. v.) the bank of a river, hence *chhār-chiṭṭhī*, a permit or pass over a river. *h.*

چهار *chihār* or *chahār*, four. *chahār-pāya*, a quadruped. *chahār-chand*, fourfold. *chahār-bālish*, m. throne (Indian) with four cushions. *chahār-sū*, square, market-place. *chahār shamba*, Wednesday. The contracted form *chār*, q. v., is more usual in compound words. *p.*

چهارتك *chahār-tak* or *-tag*, m. a gallop. *p.*

چهارچهبيلا छारछबीला *chhār-chhabīlā*, m. a fragrant moss.

چهارده *chahār-dah*, fourteen. *p.*

چهاردهم *chahār-dahum*, the fourteenth. *p.*

چهارم *chahārum*, the fourth. *p.*

چهارو छारू *chhārū*, m. the thrush (disease so called), a blister. *h.*

چهاڑ छाड़ *chhāṛ*, f. a bank of a river; alluvium, land gained from a river. *chhāṛ chiṭṭhī*, f. permit, pass; (in Dakh.) for *jhāṛ*, a tree. *h.*

چهاڑچهڑيلا छाड़छड़ेला *chhāṛ chhaṛelā*, m. name of a medicinal herb. *h.*

چهاك छाक *chhāk*, m. ready prepared food carried out by labourers and husbandmen when they proceed to their daily work, a luncheon; (in Dakh.) a cup, an ewer. *h.*

چهاكنا छाकना *chhāknā*, a. to clear the water of a well, &c. *s.*

چهاگ छाग *chhāg*, m. a he-goat. *s.*

چهاگكا छागिका *chhāgikā*, f. a she-goat. *s.*

چهاگل छागल *chhāgal*, f. a leathern bottle with a spout to it, a goat-skin; m. a goat. *s.*

چهاگي छागी *chhāgī*, f. a she-goat. *s.*

چهال छाल *chhāl*, f. peel, skin, rind, bark. *chhāl-utārnā*, to peel, to decorticate. *h.*

چهالا छाला *chhālā*, m. a blister, a pustule, pimple. *h.*

چهاليا छालिया *chhāliyā*, f. a kind of betel nut. *s.*

چهان छान *chhān*, f. a roof, a frame of bamboo for thatching. *h.*

چهان छां *chhāṅ*, f. shade, shadow; reflection, image. *chhāṅ bāṅh*, f. auspices. *s.*

چهانا छाना *chhānā*, a. to thatch, to shade, to roof, to spread. *chhā-jānā*, n. to spread, to lie, to overshadow. *chhā-lenā*, a. to cloud, to overspread, to darken. *s.* [decorate. *h.*

چهانا चिहाना *chihānā*, a. to embellish, to

چهان بچهان छानबिछान *chhān-bichhān*, / چهان بنان छानबिनान *chhān-binān*, } m. search, investigation. *h.*

چهانتا छान्ता *chhāntā*, additional sowing of seed among a growing crop of rice. *h.*

چهانٹ छांट *chhāṅṭ*, f. refuse, parings, &c.; selection, fashion of clothes. *chhāṅṭ-k.*, a. to vomit, to disgorge. *chhāṅṭ lenā*, a. to select, to choose. *chhāṅṭ-chhaṭāw*, m. retrenchment. *h.*

چهانٹن छांटन *chhāṅṭan*, f. cutting, slip, chip. *h.*

چهانٹنا छांटना *chhāṅṭnā*, a. to separate the husk from grain by pounding it in a mortar; to pare, to clip, to prune, to lop, to trim, to dress, to select; to vomit. *h.* [net. *h.*

چهاند छांद *chhāṅd*, f. a tether, a trammel, a

چهاندا छांदा *chhāṅdā*, m. share, part (among *fakīrs*). *h.* [fasten, to tie. *h.*

چهاندنا छांदना *chhāṅdnā*, a. to tether, to

چهانڈنا छांडना *chhāṅḍnā*, a. to vomit; to emit; to leave, to let go, to release, to abandon, to lose. *h.*

چهانس छानस *chhānas*, m. chaff. *h.*

چهاننا छान्ना *chhānnā*, a. to strain, to sift; to search, to investigate. *chhān-lenā*, a. to cull, to select *chhān-mārnā*, a. to search, to rummage, to explore. *h.*

چهانو छांव *chhāṅw*, / چهانوا छांवा *chhāṅwā*, / چهانه छांह *chhāṅh*, / چهاءون छाओं *chhā,oṅ*, } f. shadow; the reflection of any object in a mirror, &c. *chhāṅh-bāṅh*, f. auspices. *s.* [six. *s.*

چهانوی छानवे *chhānwe* or *chhānawe*, ninety-

چهان هارا छांहारा *chhāṅ-hārā*, umbrageous. *h.*

چهانی चिहानी *chihānī*, / چهاءی चिहाई *chihā,ī*, } f. a place for the burning of the dead. *h.*

چهاوا *chhāwā*, m. an elephant aged from ten to twenty years. *d.*

چهاونا छावना *chhāwnā*, a. (v. *chhānā*), to thatch, &c. *h.*

چهاونی छावनी *chhāwnī* also *chhā,onī*, f. cantonments, barracks or huts for soldiers; thatching, the act of thatching. *s.*

چهاهین छाहीं *chhāhīṅ* f. discoloration. *h.*

چهاءی छाई *chhā,ī*, f. ashes. *s*

چهاءی छिहाई *chhihā,ī*, f. a crematory. *h.*

چهایا छाया *chhāyā*, f. shade, reflected image darkness, obscurity; m. apparition, spectre, shade (met.) somewhat resembling; a mode in music. *chhāyā-path*, m. æther, the firmament. *chhāyā-pād*, fixing the time by observing the shadow of an object. *chhāyā-taru*, m. a large tree that gives shadow and shelter. *chhāyā-mitra*, m. a parasol. *s.*

چهایانٹ छायानट *chhāyānaṭ*, m. name of a *rāg* or musical mode. *s.*

چهاءین छाईं *chhā,īṅ*, f. discoloration. *s.*

چهب छब *chhab*, f. beauty, splendour, brilliancy; shape, form, figure. *chhab-takhtī*, f. handsomeness. *chhabi-chhīn*, small in shape, deficient in splendour, small, slender. *s.*

چه‌بچه *chah-bacha*, m. a vat, a cistern. *p.*

چهبڑا छबड़ा *chhabṛā*, m. a kind of basket. *h.*

چهبیس छब्बीस *chhabbīs*, twenty-six. *s.*

چهبیلا छबीला *chhabīlā*, handsome, comely, m. a fop. *s.*

چهپ छप *chhap*, m. squash, plash, the sound of an object falling in water. *chhap-chhap*, the sound occasioned by water when struck with the hand. *h.*

چهپا छिपा *chhipā*, close, bidden, concealed. *chhipā-rahnā*, n. to abscond. *chhipā-chhipī*, underhand, secretly. *h.*

چهپاکا छपाका *chhapākā*, m. a splash, a squash; the sound produced by striking water. *h.*

چهپانا छिपाना, छुपाना or छपाना, *chhipānā*, *chhupānā* or *chhapānā*, a. to conceal, to hide. *h.*

چهپانا छपाना *chhapānā*, a to cause to print. *h.*

چهپاو छिपाव *chhipāw* or *chhipā,o*, m. concealment. *h.*

چهپاونی छिपावनी *chhipāwanī*, f. clandestine cultivation of land. *h.*

چهپاءی छपाई *chhapā,ī*, f. edition; the price of printing, the act of printing. *h.*

چهپر छप्पर *chhappar*, m. thatched roof. *chhappar-band*, m. a thatcher. *chhappar-bandī*, f. thatching or the price of thatching. *h.*

چهپرکهاٹ छप्परखाट *chhapar-khāṭ*, / چهپرکهٹ छप्परखट *chhapar-khaṭ*, } m. a bedstead with a tester and curtains. *h. s.*

چهپری छपरी *chhaprī*, f. a puddle. *h.*

چهپک *chhapak*, a shock, dashing against an object, collision; a bruise or dent. *d.*

چهپکا छिपका *chhipkā*, m. sprinkling. *h.*

چهپکانا छपकाना *chhapkānā*, a. to dash or throw water. *h.*

چهپکلی छिपकली *chhipkalī*, / چهپکی छिपकी *chhipkī*, } f. a lizard. *h.*

چهپن छप्पन *chhappan*, fifty-six. *h.*

چهپنا छपना *chhapnā*, छिपना *chhipnā* or छुपना *chhupnā*, n. to be concealed, to be hidden, to be absent, to disappear, to lurk. *chhip-jānā*, n. to retire, to withdraw. *h.* [stamped. *h.*

چهپنا छपना *chhapnā*, n. to be printed or

چهپوانا छपवाना *chhapwānā*, a. to have printed, to cause to be printed. *h.*

چهپئي छपय *chhapai* or छपई *chhapa,ī*, m. (*i. e.* consisting of six feet) a kind of measure in Hindī verse. *h.*

چهت छत *chhat*, f. a roof, a cloth stretched across the roof of a room; a platform. *chhat-banānā*, *-pāṭnā*, or *-lagānā*, a. to ceil, to cover the inner roof of a building. *s.*

چهت छिति *chhiti*, f. (for *kshiti*), the earth. *s.*

چهتا छत्ता *chhattā*, m. a honeycomb. *h.*

چهتر छत्तर *chhattur*, a covering placed on a heap of winnowed corn. *h.*

چهتر छत्तर *chhattar* or छत्र *chhatr*, m. an umbrella. *chhatr-bhang*, m. widowhood; subversion of dominion, loss of empire, deposition, &c. *chhatr-pati* or *-dhārī*, one entitled to carry an umbrella, *i. e.* a rājā, prince, &c.; a house set apart for the charitable entertainment of strangers or guests; a shed, an open building; a choultry or resting-place for travellers, &c. *h.*

چهتر छत्रा *chhatrā*, f. a kind of fennel (*Anethum sowa*), a pungent seed, coriander; a mushroom; anise. *s.* [spread. *h.*

چهترانا छितराना *chhitrānā*, a. to scatter, to

چهترنا छितरना *chhitarnā*, n. to be scattered, to be spread about. *h.*

چهترني छत्रिणी *chhatrinī*, a female of the *chhatrī* or military caste; adj. bearing a parasol. *s.*

چهتري छत्री *chhatrī*, f. a tester, or covering of a bed, a small umbrella; a small ornamented pavilion generally built over a place of interment; a frame made of bamboos for pigeons to settle upon; the poop of a ship; (for *kshatriya*) the second of the four Hindū castes. *s.*

چهتري छितरी *chhitrī*, f. a kind of small basket without lid or handle (generally applied to an old worn-out basket). *h.*

چهتنار छतनार *chhatnār*, bunchy, flat. *h.*

چهتني छितनी *chhitnī*, f. a basket (without a cover, like a tray).

چهتور छत्वर *chhatwar*, m. a house, a dwelling; a bower, an arbour. *s.*

چهتور छत्तूर *chhattūr*, an article placed upon a heap of grain, such as a cake of cow-dung, &c., to protect it from the evil eye. *h.*

چهتوڑنا *chhitoṛnā*, a. to asperse, to sprinkle. *d.*

چهتهرا छुतहरा *chhutahrā*, defiled by touching, foul, corrupt, polluted (applied to vessels, dishes, &c.). *h.*

چهتي क्षिती *chhiti*, f. the earth. *chhiti-chhān*, covering the earth, prostrate on the ground. *chhiti-chhān-honā*, to be dispersed or scattered. *s.*

چهتيس छत्तीस *chhattīs*, thirty-six. *s.*

چهتيسي छत्तीसी *chhattīsī*, f. an excessively lewd woman (q. d. one who knows thirty-six postures in the way of copulation, and who pretends modesty), a prude; adj. prudish. *h.*

چهٹ छुट *chhuṭ*, but, except, save; (cont. of *choṭā*, little, small: used in comp. as) *chhuṭ-bhaiyā*, m. middling class of people. *chhuṭ-panā*, m. childhood. *h.*

چهٹا छटा *chhaṭā*, f. splendour, brilliancy, lustre, refulgence. a glory; assemblage, number; a straight or continuous mark or line. *chhaṭṭā*, the sixth. *chhiṭṭā*, the rind or husk of a hard seed or of fruit stones. *s.*

چهٹابها छटाभा *chhaṭābhā*, f. lightning. *s.*

چهٹاپا छुटापा *chhuṭāpā*, m. littleness, small ness. *h.*

چهٹان छुटान *chhuṭān*, } f. leisure, time. *h.*
چهٹاني छुटानी *chhuṭānī*, }

چهٹانك छटांक *chhaṭānk*, f. the sixteenth part of a *ser*, about two ounces avoirdupois. *s.*

چهٹاو छटाव *chhaṭāw* or *chhaṭā,o*, act of clearing rice from the husk. *h.*

چهٹائي छुटाई *chhuṭā,ī*, f. rescue, escape. *h.*

چهٹپٹانا छटपटाना *chhaṭpaṭānā*, n. to toss, to tumble about, to flounder. *h.*

چهٹپن छुटपन *chhuṭ-pan*, } m. childhood, infancy. *s.*
چهٹپنا छुटपना *chhuṭ-panā*, }

چهٹك *chhaṭak* (same as *chhaṭānk*, q. v.)

چهٹكا छुटका *chhuṭkā*, diminutive, little, small, less, younger, junior, least. *s.*

چهٹكار छुटकार *chhuṭkār*, } m. exemption, liberty, liberation, disengagement; (in Dakh.) *chhuṭkārī*, f. the same. *h.*
چهٹكارا छुटकारा *chhuṭkārā*, }

چهٹكانا छिटकाना *chhiṭkānā*, a. to dissipate, to disperse, to squirt, to scatter, to desert. *h.*

چهٹكانا छुटकाना *chhuṭkānā*, a. to release, to set at liberty. *h.*

چهٹكرا छुटकरा *chhuṭharā*, m. deliverance. *h.*

چهٹكنا छिटकना *chhiṭaknā*, n. to be scattered, dissipated, to spread. *chhiṭaknā chāndnī kā*, the diffusion of moonlight. *h.*

چهٹكني छिटकनी *chhiṭkanī*, f. a bolt. *h.*

چهٹكهيلا छुटखेला *chhuṭkhelā*, dissolute. *s.*

چٹكهيلي छुटखेली *chhuṭkhelī*, f. dissoluteness. *h.*

چٹكي छिटकी *chhiṭkī*, f. small spot, speck. *chhiṭkī-ḍālnā*, a. to splash. *chhiṭkī-denā*, a. to flecker, to spot, to mark with strokes or touches. *chhiṭkī-k.* or *-lagānā*, a. to spot, to speck, &c. *h.*

چهٹنا छटना *chhaṭnā*, m. a kind of sieve; n. to decay, to separate, to be pruned, to be picked out. *h.*

چهٹنا *chhaṭnā*, n. to be cut to a point and obliquely (a *ḳalam*); to be cut aslant; to be reduced. *d.*

چھٹنا छुटना *chhuṭnā*, n. to be adrift, discharged, got rid of, to be let go; to be let off or go off (a gun, &c.); to be left or abandoned; to slip (from), to escape, to be liberated, to be loose, dishevelled (the hair); to cease, to get loose, to leave, to remain, to slip away, to be dismissed. *h.* [cast. *h.*

چھٹوا छिटुवा *chhiṭuwā*, m. sowing broad-

چھٹواں छटवां *chaṭwāṅ*, the sixth. *h.*

چھٹوتي छुटौती *chhuṭautī*, f. a remission of revenue on the part of government. *h.*

چھٹھ छठ *chhaṭh* or छट्ठ *chhāṭṭh*, f. the sixth lunar day. *s.*

چھٹھا छटहा *chhaṭhā*, waspish, peevish. *h.*

چھٹھا छठा *chhaṭhā*, the sixth. *s.*

چھٹھي छठी *chhaṭhī* or छट्ठी *chhaṭṭhī*, the sixth; f. a religious ceremony performed on the sixth day after child-birth. *chhaṭhī kā dūdh yād dilānā*, a. to correct. *s.*

چھٹي छुट्टी *chhuṭṭī*, f. discharge, leave of absence, time, leisure, cessation, disengagement, intermission, dismission, permission, freedom. *h.*

چھج छज *chhaj*, bushy, a thicket. *h.*

چھجا छज्जा *chhajjā*, m. gallery; the expanded branches of a tree. *h.*

چھچھا *chhichchā* (v. *chhūchhā*), empty, &c. *d.*

چھچھڑا छिचड़ा *chhichṛā*, m. sink, slough (of a wound), skin, thin skin or pellicle. *h.*

چھچھڑيل छिचड़ैल *chhichṛail*, lean, skinny. *h.*

چھچھکارنا *chhachhkārnā*, to reprove, chide. *d.*

چھچھکارنا छुचकारना *chhuchkārnā*, a. to drive away contemptuously; to set on or encourage a dog. *h.*

چھچھکارنا *chhuchhkārnā*, to whistle. *d.*

چہچہا चहचहा *chahchahā* or चुहचुहा *chuhchuhā*, deeply coloured. *h.*

چہچہا *chahchahā*, m. the song of a bird, especially the melody of the nightingale. *chahchahe mārnā*, a. to sing (birds). *p.*

چہچہات चहचहाट *chahchahāt*, } f. the
چہچہاہٹ चहचहाहट *chahchahāhaṭ*, } singing or talking (of birds). *p. h.*

چہچہانا चुहचुहाना *chuhchuhānā*, n. to glow as a colour, to dye a deep colour. *h.*

چہچہانا चहचहाना *chahchahānā*, a. to sing (as a nightingale), to whistle, to warble (as birds). *p.h.*

چھچھڑا छिछड़ा *chhichhṛā*, m. the prepuce. *h.*

چھچھڑي छछड़ी *chhachhaṛī*, f. the root of a certain tree (of the *phapond*). *h.*

چھچھکارنا छुछकारना *chhuchhkārnā*, a. to drive away contemptuously; to set on or encourage a dog. *h.*

چھچھلا छिछला *chhichhlā*, shallow. *h.*

چھچھلائي छिछलाई *chhichhla,ī*, f. shallowness. *h.*

چھچھلي छिछली *chhichhlī*, f. the play of ducks and drakes. *chhichhlī khelnā*, a. to play at ducks and drakes. *h.*

چھچھلي छुछली *chhuchhlī*, f. the play of a dog or cat with game, &c. *h.*

چھچھوندر छुछुंदर *chhuchhundar*, m. } the
چھچھوندري छुछुंदरी *chhuchhundarī*, f. } musk-rat or shrew; a mole; a sort of squib let off from the hand. *chhuchhundarī chhoṛnā*, to calumniate, to excite wrath. *s.* [jure, to exorcise. *h.*

چھچھوانا छुछवाना *chhuchhwānā*, a. to con-

چھچھورا छिछोरा *chhichhorā*, } trifling, pue-
چھچھوڑا छिछोड़ा *chhichhoṛā*, } rile, airy. *h.*

چھچھوندر छुछूंदर *chhuchhūndar*, f. mole, musk-rat (*Sorex cærulescens, Shaw*); squib. *chhuchhūndar chhoṛnā*, a. to backbite, to calumniate, to excite resentment. *s.*

چہچہيا चहचहिया *chahchahiyā*, m. a whistler. *h.*

چھدام छदाम *chha-dām*, m. a denomination of money equal to six *dāms* or two *damṛīs*, being the fourth part of a *paisā*. *h.*

چھدانا छिदाना *chhidānā*, a. to cause to pierce, to perforate. *s.*

چھدر क्षुद्र *chhudra*, mean, low, little, trifling. *s.*

چھدر छिद्र *chhidra*, m. a hole, a vacuity, a perforation; fault, defect, flaw. *s.*

چھدرت छिद्रित *chhidrit*, perforated, pierced, having holes or openings. *s.*

چھدم छद्म *chhadma*, } m. disguise, mas-
چھدمن छद्मन *chhadman*, } querade; trick, deceit, fraud. *chhadma-tāpas*, m. a religious hypocrite, a false brother. *s.*

چھدنا छिदना *chhidnā*, n. to be pierced, bored. *s.*

چھدھا क्षुधा *chhudhā*, f. hunger. *s.*

چھر छर *chhar*, f. spikenard; shaft, pole, pike, staff, flagstaff, flag. *h.*

چھرا छर्रा *chharrā*, m. a small shot. *h.*

چھرا छुरा *chhurā*, m. a large knife, an amputating knife; a razor. *chhurā-chhurī*, f. snickasnee, fighting with knives; at daggers drawn. *s.*

چھرچھوبي छरछोबी *chhar-chhobī*, f. jakes, a privy. *h.*

چھرد छर्द *chhard* or छर्दि *chhardi*, f. vomiting, sickness, retching. *s.*

چھردکارپ छर्दिकारिपु *chhardikā-ripu*, m. small cardamums (an anti-emetic). *s.*

چھرندا छरिन्दा *chharindā*, alone, single, free, not burdened (as a traveller).

چہرہ *chihra*, m. face, visage, countenance, air, description-roll. *chihra likhnā*, a. to write a description-roll (soldier's). *chihra-likhānā*, a. to enlist; to take service and horses. *chihra-paṭṭī*, a descriptive roll. *p.*

چہرہ جنا *chahra-junnā*, to calumniate. *d.*

چھري छुरी *chhurī*, f. a knife, a scalpel. *chhurī tale dam lenā*, a. to be patient in difficulties. *chhurī kaṭārī*, f. snickasnee, a fight with knives; quarrel. *s.*

چھڑ छड़ *chhaṛ*, f. the pole of a spear; spikenard; straw, stubble, pedule, stalk. *h.*

چھڑا छड़ा *chhaṛā*, m. an ornament made of pearls worn in the ears. *h.*

چھڑا छड़ा *chhaṛā*, apart, alone, solitary. *s.*

چھڑانا छुड़ाना *chhuṛānā*, a. to set free, to free, to liberate, to extricate, to get rid of, to discharge, to remove, to dismiss, to cause to be freed; to separate, to except. *h.*

چھڑاوا छुड़ावा *chhuṛāwā*, m. a liberator, deliverer. *h.* [charge. *h.*

چھڑائي छुड़ाई *chhuṛā,ī*, f. dismissal, dis-

چھڑکانا छिड़काना *chhiṛkānā*, a. to cause to sprinkle. *h.* [sprinkling. *h.*

چھڑکاو छिड़काव *chhiṛkāw* or *chhiṛkā,o*, m.

چھڑکنا छिड़कना *chhiṛaknā*, a. to sprinkle. *chhiṛak-kar-bechnā*, to sprinkle water on stale or faded vegetables or fruits to make them appear fresh; to puff off goods. *h.*

چھڑکوانا छिड़कवाना *chhiṛakwānā*, a. to cause another to sprinkle. *h.*

چھڑنا छड़ना *chhaṛnā*, a. to beat rice to separate the husk from it. *h.*

چھڑنا छिड़ना *chhiṛnā*, n. to be vexed, touched, excited, plagued, to fret, to take offence. *h.*

چھڑوانا छुड़वाना *chhuṛwānā*, a. to cause to be set free, let off, or released. *h.*

چھڑوتي छुड़ौती *chhuṛautī*, f. ransom. *h.*

چھڑي छड़ी *chhaṛī*, f. a switch, wand, cane, rod; a procession of the followers of Shāh Madār. *chhaṛī-dār*, a mace-bearer, usher of the rod. *h. p.*

چھڑیاچھات *chhaṛyā-chhāṭ*, solitary, alone. *d.*

چھڑیلا छड़ीला *chhaṛīlā*, f. a kind of fragrant moss, potters' earth. *h.*

چہکا चहका *chahkā*, m. a kind of fire-works; the smarting of a wound by the application of medicine. *chahkā lagānā*, a. to burn the skin slightly by fomenting. *h.*

چھکا छक्का *chhakkā*, m. the sixth (at cards, &c.); a cage with a net attached to it. *chhakkā-pakkā ronā*, to weep very violently. *chhakkā-panjā-k.*, a. to deceive, to play tricks. *s.*

چھکاچک کرنا *chhakā-chak-k.*, to satiate, to gratify, to satisfy. *d.*

چہکار चहकार *chahkār*, f. singing or chirping of birds. *h.*

چہکارنا चहकारना *chahkārnā* (v. *chahaknā*), to whistle or sing as birds. *h.*

چھکانا छकाना *chhakānā* or *chhikānā*, a. to pamper, to cloy, to satiate; to chastise. *h.*

چھکائي छिकाई *chhikā,ī*, f. (v. *fārigh-khaṭṭāna*) a deed of release. *h.*

چھکائي छकाई *chhakā,ī*, f. satiety, satisfaction. *h.*

چھکر छकुर *chhakur*, a division of crops, when the *zamīn-dār* gets one-sixth. *h.*

چھکڑ छक्कड़ *chhakkaṛ*, f. a slap, blow, cuff. *h.*

چھکڑا छकड़ा *chhakṛā*, m. a cart or car. *h.*

چھکڑانا छकड़ाना *chhakṛānā*, a. to slap, cuff. *h.*

چھکن छिक्कन *chhikkan*, m. sneezing. *h.*

چہکنا चिहिकना *chihiknā*, a. warbling of the nightingale, &c.; the sound of fire-works. *h.*

چہکنا चहकना *chahaknā*, n. to whistle (birds). *h.*

چھکنا छकना *chhaknā*, n. to be content, satiated; to be afflicted, harassed; to be astonished. *chhak-j.*, to be satisfied or satiated. *h.*

چھکني छिकुनी *chhikunī*, f. a wand, a stick. *h.*

چہکیٹ चहकैट *chahkaiṭ* or *chahkaiṭh*, brawny, stout. *h.*

چھگ छग *chhag*, m. a he-goat. *s.*

چھگري छगरी *chhagrī*, f. a small she-goat. *s.*

چھگل *chhagal* (v. *chhāgal*), a leathern bottle. *d.*

چھگلي छगली *chhaglī*, f. a she-goat; a kind of convolvulus (*C. argenteus*, or, more probably, *C. pes-capræ*). *s.*

چھگني छगुनी *chhagunī*, f. a child's coral. *h.*

چھل छल *chhal*, m. fraud, trick, deception, knavery, artifice, evasion, excuse, subterfuge, pretence; (in law) a misdemeanor; a legal quibble or deceit. *chhal-bal*, *chhal-chhidr*, or *chhal-chhidram*, m. plot, stratagem. *chhal chhidrī*, deceitful, fraudulent. *s.*

چہل चुहल *chuhal* or *chahal*, f. mention; cheer, jollity, mirth, festivity. *chuhal-puhal* or *chahal-pahal*, merriment, festivity, good cheer. *chuhal-k.*, a. to carol, &c. *h.*

چہل *chihal* or *chihil*, forty. *chihal-tah*, f. coat of mail. *chihal-manār* or *-sutūn* (the forty towers or pillars), a name given to the ruined city of Persepolis: the term *chihal sutūn* is now applied to any pavilion or palace supported by *forty*, *i. e.* a great number of pillars. *chihal ḳadamī*, f. walk, ramble; a custom at the funerals of Musalmāns of stepping back forty paces from the grave, and again advancing to it before reading the service over. *p.*

چہل चहल *chahal*, name of a strong kind of soil ranking between *rauslī* and *dānkar*, q. v. *h.*

چہلا चहला *chahlā* or चिहला *chihlā*, m. mud, ooze, slime; a splinter of wood. *chihlā nikalnā*, n. to fatigue, to be tired. *chihlā-k.*, a. to split to pieces. *h.*

چہلا चुहला *chuhlā*, m. a large wooden peg, a tent-pin. *h.*

چھلا छल्ला *chhallā*, m. a ring of gold or silver worn for ornament on the finger and toes: in Dakh. it means a blister; a pock or pustule. *chhalle-dār*, annular. *h.*

چھلانا छुलाना *chhulānā*, a. to cause to touch. *h.*

چھلانگ छलांग *chhalāng*, f. skipping, jumping; a spring, skip, leap. *chhalāngeṇ mārnā*, a. to spring, to jump. *h.*

چهلاوا छलावा *chhalāwā*, m. *ignis fatuus*. *chhalāwā-d.*, to mislead, to lead one a wild-goose chase. *chhalāwā-ho-jānā*, to elude one's search or pursuit. *h.*

چهل پهل चहलपहल *chahal-pahal*, also *chuhal-puhal*, f. jollity, merriment, cheer. *h.*

چهل چهدر छलछिद्र *chhal-chhidra*, m. plot, stratagem. *chhal-chhidrī*, deceitful, fraudulent. *s.*

چهلچهلانا छलछलाना *chhalchhalānā*, a. to murmur. *h.*

چهلچهلانا छुलछुलाना *chhulchhulānā*, a. to make water slowly (as mares, &c. in heat). *h.*

چهلچهلاهٹ छलछलाहट *chhalchhalāhat*, f. murmur. *h.*

چهلڑ छिल्लड़ *chhillar*, m. the husk of *chanā*, [q. v. *h.*

چهلك छलक *chhalak*, f. running over, overflow. *s.*

چهلکا छिलका *chhilkā*, m. crust, husk, peel, scale, rind, bark, skin. *chhilkā utārnā*, a. to blanch, to peel. *h.*

چهلکانا छलकाना *chhalkānā*, a. to spill. *s.*

چهلکنا छलकना *chhalaknā*, n. to be spilt, to overflow. *s*

چهلکنا *chhilaknā*, n. to glitter to shine. *d.*

چهلکنا छुलकना *chhulaknā*, a. to make water slowly (as mares, &c. in heat). *h.*

چهلکه *chhilka*, m. (v. *chhilkā*), crust, &c. *h.*

چهلم *chihlum*, the fortieth, generally applied to the fortieth day after the decease of a parent, &c., which concludes the period of mourning among Musalmāns. *p.*

چهلنا छलना *chhalnā*, a. to deceive, to cheat, to evade, to make excuses; m. tricking, deceiving. *h.*

چهلنا छिलना *chhilnā*, n. to be excoriated, to be worn or rubbed away. *h.*

چهلنا चहलना *chahalnā*, n. to be fatigued, to grow tired. *h.*

چهلنگ छलंग *chhalang*, f. skip, bound, &c. *h.*

چهلنگنا छलङ्गना *chhalangnā*, n. to skip, to bound. *h.*

چهلني छलनी *chhalnī*, battered; f. a sieve. *chhalnī-k.*, a. to batter. *h.*

چهلو छुल्लू *chhullū*, boyish, silly. *h.*

چهلوانا छिलवाना *chhilwānā*, a. to cause to be skinned or excoriated. *h.*

چهلوري छलोरी *chhalorī* or छिलौरी *chhilorī* or *chhilaurī*, f. a whitlow, blister, felon. *h.*

چهلوهلا छुलोहला *chhulohlā*, } boyish, puerile,
چهلهلا छुलुहला *chhuluhlā*, } finical. *h.*

چهلها चिहलहा *chihlahā*, splashy, muddy, slimy. *h.*

چهلي चहली *chahlī*, the wheel on which the rope revolves at the top of a well. *h.*

چهلي चुहली *chuhlī*, comic, mirthful. *h.*

چهلي छल्ली *chhallī*, f. skin, bark, rind, &c. *s.*

چهلي छली *chhalī*, } deceitful, fraudulent,
چهليا छलिया *chhaliyā*, } betrayer, artful, treacherous, false, perfidious; m. a cheat, a deceiver. *s.*

چهما छिमा *chhimā* or छमा *chhamā*, f. pardon, quarter, forgiveness, absolution. *chhimā-k.*, to pardon, to excuse. *s.*

چهماجوگ छिमाजोग *chhimā-jog*, venial, pardonable. *s.*

چهمچهمانا छमछमाना *chhamchhamānā*, n. to shine, to glitter; to sound. *h.*

چهمنا छमना *chhamnā*, a. to pardon, to forgive. *s.*

چهمنڈ छमण्ड *chhamand*, m. an orphan, a fatherless son. *s.*

چهن छिण, छिन *chhin* or छण, छन *chhan*, m, a moment or instant. *chhin bhar meṅ*, in a moment. *chhin-bidhaṅs*, m. fading, frail, passing away quickly. *s.*

چهن छन *chhan*, m. a sound made by the falling of a drop of water upon a warm plate. *h.*

چهن छिन्न *chhinna*, cut, divided. *chhinna-saṅshaya*, free from doubt, confident. *s.*

چهن चहुं *chahuṅ*, four. *chahuṅ-or*, on all sides. *s.*

چهن चिह्न *chihna*, m. mark, spot, sign (v. *chinh*). *s.*

چهنا छन्ना *chhannā*, n. to be strained; m. a sieve, a cloth through which any thing is sifted; the cells formed by bees in their hives. *h.*

چهنا छिन्ना *chhinnā*, f. a whore, a harlot, a tree (*Menispermum glabrum*). *s.*

چهناك छनाक *chhanāk*, m. the sound of a drop of water falling on a hot plate, hissing; the sound of the breaking of earthenware. *h.*

چهنال छिनाल *chhināl*, f. a harlot, prostitute. *chhināl-pan* or *-panā*, m. harlotry, prostitution. *h.*

چهنالا छिनाला *chhinālā*, m. fornication. *chhinālā-k.*, a. to whore. *h.*

چهنانا छिनाना *chinānā*, a. to seize, snatch, pluck. *h.*

چهناو छिनाव *chhināw* or *chhinā,o*, m. seizure. *h.*

چهن بدهنس छिनबिधंस *chhin-bidhaṅs*, fading, frail, passing away quickly. *s.*

چهن بهن छिन्नभिन्न *chhinna-bhinna*, cut up, destroyed, scattered. *s.*

چهنت चिह्नित *chihnit*, marked, known or distinguished; measured, identified. *chihnit-nāma*, a specification of land with its boundaries. *s. p.*

چهنٹاو छण्टाव *chhanṭāw*, m. detachment on forage; beating rice to clear it from the husk. *h.*

چهنٹائي छण्टाई *chhanṭā,ī*, f. cleaning or separating (grain, &c.); the price paid for cleaning. *h.*

چهنٹنا छण्टना *chhanṭnā*, n. to grow thin; to diminish; to be extracted or separated *h.*

چهنٹوانا छनटवाना **chhanṭwānā**, a. to cause to clean rice; to cause to select, prune, lop, clip. *h.*

چهن چك चहुँचक **chahuṅ-chak**, circumjacent, all around. *s.*

چهنچهنانا छनछनाना or छनछनाना **chhanchhanānā**, m. to simmer; to sound; to smart, to pain. *h.*

چهند छन्द **chhand**, m. measure of verses (particularly applied to the metre of the Vedas); a measure (in music); meaning, intention, purport, opinion; wish, desire; adj. solitary, secret, private. *s.*

چهندا छन्दा **chhandā**, m. (v. *chhāndā*) a share. *h.*

چهندبند छन्दबन्द **chhand-band**, m. trick, cheating, deceiving. *s.*

چهندپاتن छन्दपातन **chhand-pātan**, m. a hypocrite, a false ascetic. *s.*

چهن دش चहुँदिश **chahuṅ-dish**, circumjacent, all around. *s.*

چهندنا छन्दना **chhandnā**, n. to be tied. *h.*

چهندوگ छन्दोग **chhandog**, m. a reciter or chanter of the Sāma Veda. *s.*

چهندي छन्दी **chhandī**, deceitful. *s.*

چهن روها छिन्नरुहा **chhinna-rūhā**, f. name of a tree (*Menispermum glabrum*). *s.*

چهنك छणिक or छनिक **chhanik**, perishable, temporary, momentary, inconstant, uncertain. *s.*

چهنكانا छंकाना or छनकाना **chhankānā**, a. to concentrate, to cause to strain. *h.*

چهنكانا छिंकाना or छिनकाना **chhinkānā**, a. to cause to stop, to cause to seize, to cancel, to strike out. *h.*

چهنكاهٹ छंकाहट or छनकाहट **chhankāhaṭ**, f. concentration, causing to strain. *h.*

چهنكنا छिनकना **chhinaknā**, a. to winnow, to sift; n. to go away offended; to blow the nose. *h.*

چهنكوانا छिंकवाना **chhinkwānā** (v. *chhinkānā*), to cause to be stopped, &c. *h.*

چهنگلي छिंगुली **chhingulī**, } f. the little
چهنگليا छुंगलिया **chhungliyā**, } finger. *h.*

چهنلا छिनला **chhinalā**, m. a fornicator, a whoremonger. *h.*

چهنوانا छिनवाना **chhinwānā**, a. to cause to snatch. *h.*

چهنوانا छनवाना **chhanwānā**, a. to cause to sift or strain. *h.*

چهن ويشكا छिन्नवेशिका **chhinna-veshikā**, f. a plant, also called *Uknidhi* (*Cissampelos hexandra*). *s.*

چهنهاءي छंहाई **chhanhā,ī**, f. shadiness. *s.*

چهنيك छिणेक or छिनेक **chhinek**, a little while. *s.*

چهو छवि **chhavi**, f. beauty, splendour. *h.*

چهو **chhū**, the act of blowing or exorcising on uttering a prayer or incantation. *d.*

چهوءا छोआ **chho,ā**, m. treacle. *h.*

چهوءانا छुआना **chhū,ānā** (v. *chhulānā*), to cause to touch. *h.*

چهوءاني छुआनी **chhū,ānī**, f. caudle given to a lying-in woman. *h.*

چهواو छुवाव **chhuwāw**, m. resemblance, likeness. *h.*

چهوپ छोप **chhop**, m. a coat of paint, &c. *chhop-chhāp-k.*, a. to shuffle up; to plaister or repair a wall, &c. *h.*

چهوپنا छोपना **chhopnā**, a. to fill up, to shut, paint, dye. *h.*

چهوت छूत **chhūt** or छोत **chhot**, f. defilement; contamination, touch. *chhūt-lagnā* or *paṛnā*, to be infectious (a disease); to infect a person by touch. *h.*

چهوٹ छूट **chhūṭ**, f. remission, leaving; remission of revenue; striking off hand or playing loose in fencing; radiance or splendour of jewels; reflection of a mirror, &c.; giving money off hand or at will to jugglers, &c. at entertainments. *h.*

چهوٹا छोटा **chhoṭā**, little, small, less, younger, &c. *chhoṭā-baṛā*, varied, variegated, various, great and small, high and low. *h.*

چهوٹا چاند **chhoṭā chānd**, m. name of a climbing plant (*Ophioxylon serpentinum*) the root of which is said to be an excellent remedy for snake bites. This root, dried and powdered, is applied externally to the bitten part, and a decoction of it is given to the wounded person to drink, to the extent of a pint in twenty-four hours—(Binning). *d.*

چهوٹاءي छोटाई **chhoṭā,ī**, f. smallness, littleness. *h.*

چهوٹنا छूटना **chhūṭnā**, n. to escape, cease, get loose, leave, remain, slip away, to be discharged, dismissed. *h.*

چهوٹوتي छूटौती **chhūṭautī**, f. (v. *chhūṭ*) remission of rent or revenue. *h.*

چهوچها छूछा **chhūchhā**, empty, hollow; m. conjuration. *h.*

چهوچهلا छूछला **chhuchhlā**, m. foolish, silly, empty. *h.*

چهوچهو छोछो **chhochho**, f. a nurse; bosom. *chhochho-k.*, a. to fondle. *h.*

چهوچهي छूछी **chhūchhī**, contemptible, despicable, mean; f. a pipe, tube. *h.*

چهور छौर **chhaur**, m. shaving of the head or beard, the office of barber. *s.*

چهور छोर **chhor**, m. border; edge; end; a towboat. *chhaur*, a large stack of *juwār* or *bajrā*, q.v., collected for fodder; walking a boundary. *h.*

چهورا चहोरा **chahorā**, a fine sort of rice. *h.*

چهورا छोरा **chhorā** (for *chhokrā*), a boy. *chhorā-chhorī*, boy and girl, children. *h.*

چهورن छोरण **chhoran**, m. abandoning, leaving. *h.*

چهورنا चहोरना **chahornā**, a. to transplant. *h.*

چهوري छोरी **chhorī**, f. a girl. *h.*

چهوڑ छोड़ *chhor*, چهوڑا छोड़ा *chhoṛā*, چهوڑاو छोड़ाव *chhoṛāw*, چهوڑاوا छोड़ावा *chhoṛāwā*, m. release, deliverance, setting free, omission, leaving, sparing. *s.*

چهوڑاونا छोड़ावना *chhoṛāonā*, a. to set free, deliver, dismiss, separate, except. *h.*

چهوڑچٹهي छोड़चिट्ठी *chhoṛ-chiṭṭhī*, f. a deed of release, a pass, a permit; a deed of divorce or abandonment of a betrothed girl. *h.*

چهوڑنا छोड़ना *chhoṛnā*, a. to let go, to emit fire, forgive, forsake, desert, loose, omit, pardon, release, shoot, fire (a gun), spare, abandon, abstain, breathe; resign, discharge, lay aside. *h.*

چهوڑوتي छोड़ौती *chhoṛautī*, f. ransom. *h.*

چهوکرا छोकरा *chhokrā*, m. a boy. *h.*

چهوکري छोकरी *chhokrī*, f. a girl. *h.*

چهوکن छौकन *chhaukan*, m. a scrambler. *h.*

چهوکنا छौकना *chhauknā*, a. to scramble. *h.*

چهوکي छूकी *chhūkī*, f. a gnat. *h.*

چهول *chhaul*, joy, merriment. *d.*

چهولا छोला *chholā*, m. gram; also one who cuts the standing sugar-cane. *h.*

چهولنا छोलना *chholnā*, a. to peel, skin, excoriate; to pare, to scrape. *h.*

چهولني छोलनी *chholnī*, f. a scraper. *h.*

چهوله *chhola* (v. *chholā*), gram, &c. *h.*

چهوليا छौलिया *chhauliyā*, cheerful, happy. *d.*

چهون छहूँ *chahūṅ*, four. *chahūṅ-or*, on all sides. *chahūṅ-chakr* or *-dis*, circumjacent, all around. *s.*

چهونا छूना *chhūnā*, a. to touch, to meddle with, to feel. *h.*

چهونا छौना *chhaunā*, m. young of any animal. *h.*

چهونچلاکرنا छोंचला करना *chhonchlā-k.*, a. to fondle. *h.*

چهونچهي छोंछी *chhonchhī*, f. bodkin, case for needles; a small cup for children. *h.*

چهونك छोंक *chhoṅk* or छौंक *chhauṅk*, f. seasoning, relish. *h.*

چهونکن छोंकन *chhoṅkan* or छौंकन *chhauṅkan*, m. spices with which food is seasoned. *h.*

چهونکنا छौंकना *chhauṅknā*, a. to season. *h.*

چهوني छौनी *chhaunī*, f. barracks, cantonment. *h.*

چهوني छोनी *chhonī*, f. the earth. *s.*

چهوه छोह *chhoh*, m. affection; anger. *s.*

چهوهرا छोहरा *chhohrā*, m. a boy; child. *h.*

چهوهي छोही *chhohī*, affectionate; angry. *s.*

چهوئي छूई *chhū,ī*, f. chalk. *h.*

چهويا छवैया *chhawaiyā*, m. a thatcher. *h.*

چهہارا छुहारा *chhuhārā*, m. date, date fruit (*Phœnix dactylifera*). *h.*

چهہانا छुहाना *chhuhānā*, a. to whitewash. *h.*

چهہاوٹ छुहावट *chhuhāwaṭ*, f. touch. *h.*

چهہتر छिहत्तर *chhihattar*, seventy-six. *h.*

چهي चही *chahī*, f. warbling; a snipe. *h.*

چهئي छई *chha,ī*, pulmonary consumption. *s.*

چهئي छई *chha,ī*, abolished; f. a thatched roof on a boat; a stuffed pad to prevent bullocks being hurt when loaded. *s.*

چهي छय *chhai*, f. mortality, frailty, destruction. *chhai-rog* (vul.) *chha,ī rog*, consumption. *s.*

چهي छे *chhe* (for *chha*), six. *h.*

چهي छी *chhī*, interj. tush! tut! fye! *h.*

چهيا छया *chhayā*, چهيا छैया *chhaiyā*, m. victim; shade, shadow; a boy. *s.*

چهيا चुहिया *chuhiyā*, m. a little mouse. *h.*

چهياسٹه छियासठ *chhiyāsaṭh* or छयासठ *chayāsaṭh*, sixty-six. *s.*

چهياسي छियासी *chhiyāsī*, eighty-six. *s.*

چهياليس छियालीस *chhiyālīs*, forty-six. *h.*

چهيانوي छियानवे *chhiyānawwe*, ninety-six (in Dakh. *chhiyānaw*). *s.*

چهيپ छीप *chhīp*, f. discoloration or spot on the skin; fishing rod; the act of a buffalo's pushing with his horn. *h.*

چهيپنا छीपना *chhīpnā*, a. to print cloths; to push with the horn as a buffalo; to draw up the rod in fishing. *h.*

چهيپي छीपी *chīpī*, m. cotton printer or stamper; a flapper or whisk to drive away flies. *h.*

چهيتر छेत्र *chhetr*, m. a geometrical figure; field, land, plantation; a sacred or holy place, as Banāras, &c. *chhetr-phal*, m. the measurement (or superficial contents) of a field, or of a triangle, or other geometrical figure. *s.*

چهيتر छीतर *chhītar*, m. brogue, shoe. *h.*

چهيتري छेत्री *chhetrī* (v. *chhatrī*), a man of the military caste. *h.*

چهيٹ छीट *chhīṭ*, f. spot, chintz (v. *chhīṅṭ*). *h.*

چهيٹنا छीटना *chhīṭnā*, a. to scatter, to sprinkle. *h.*

چهيجنا छीजना *chhījnā*, n. to decrease, to pine away. *dekhā-dekhī kīje jog, chhīje kāyā bāṛhe rog*, they who merely imitate others in austerity, waste away, and their diseases increase. *h.*

چهيچهڑا छीछड़ा *chhīchhaṛā*, m. flesh tough as leather, and uneatable, the skinny part of meat. *chhīchhaṛā-k.*, to tear to pieces, to flay. *h.*

چهيد छेद *chhed*, m. a hole, a mouth, an opening; the denominator of a fraction, the divisor. *s.*

چهيدا छेदा *chhedā*, m. a little insect destructive to corn: the disease occasioned by it. *s.*

چهيدا छीदा *chhīdā*, thin, not close (said of a person or animal whose legs are much separated), also applied to trees, crops of corn, &c., which are scattered or straggling. *h.*

چهيدک छेदक *chhedak*, m. that which penetrates, any thing to bore a hole with. *s.*

چهيدن छेदन *chhedan*, m. act of piercing, boring, a hole, an orifice; (in criminal law) mutilation, the cutting off of a limb, &c. *s.*

چهيدنا छेदना *chhednā*, a. to pierce, to bore. *s.*

چهير क्षीर *chhīr*, m. milk; (for *sīr*) the lessee's own cultivation of a farm, &c. *s.*

چهيرنا छेरना *chhernā*, a. to have a bad digestion. *h.*

چهيروگ छैरोग *chhai-rog*, m. pulmonary consumption. *s*

چهيري छेरी *chherī*, f. a she-goat. *h.*

چهيڙ छेड़ *chheṛ*, f. the act of irritating, vexing, &c. (v. *chheṛnā*). *chheṛ-chhāṛ* or *chheṛ-khānī*, f. stricture, animadversion; the act of vexing, &c. *h.*

چهيڙا छेड़ा *chheṛā*, m. touch, provocation, excitement. *h.*

چهيڙنا छेड़ना *chheṛnā*, a. to irritate, to vex, to fret, to trouble, to abuse, to aggress, to stir up, to interrupt; to play on a musical instrument. *h.*

چهيک छेक *chhek*, domesticated, tame (as a bird or beast). *h.*

چهيکا छीका *chhīkā*, m. a sling for carrying baskets, &c. (v. *chhīṅkā*). *s.*

چهيکتوٹ *chhīktūṭ*, m. a wanderer, a vagabond. *d.*

چهيکنا छेकना *chheknā*, a. to stop, detain, prevent, restrain. *h.*

چهيکوکت छेकोक्ति *chhekokti*, f. indirect speech, insinuation, double-entente, hint. *s.*

چهيل चहेल *chahel* or चिहेल *chihel*, wet oozy land. *h.*

چهيل छैल *chhail*, چهيلا छैला *chhailā*, m. fop, beau. *chhail-pan* or *chhailā-pan*, m. spruceness, foppishness. *h.*

چهيلو छेलु *chhelu*, m. a medicinal plant (*Conyza anthelmintica*). *s.*

چهيلا *chhelā*, m. a he-goat. *d.*

چهيل‌چکنيا छैलचिकनिया *chhail-chikniyā*, m. a coxcomb, fop, an exquisite. *h.*

چهيل‌چهبيلا *chhelchhabelā*, free, unrestrained. *d.*

چهيلن छीलन *chhīlan*, f. parings, scrapings. *h.*

چهيلنا छीलना *chhīlnā*, a. to peel, to skin, to excoriate, to pare, to erase, to scrape. *chhīlnā chhālnā* or *chhīl-chhāl-k.*, a. to pare, to peel, &c. *h.*

چهيلي *chhelī*, f. a she-goat. *d.*

چهيم क्षेम *chhem*, f. welfare. *chhem-kushal*, f. welfare, happiness. *s.*

چهيمنڈ छेमण्ड *chhemanḍ*, m. a fatherless son. *s.*

چهيمنکري क्षेमङ्करी *chhemankarī*, f. a sort of kite (*Falco ponticerianus*). *s.*

چهيمي छीमी *chhīmī*, f. a pod, legume, husk. *h.*

چهين छीन or क्षीण *chhīn*, wasted, emaciated, decayed; slight, slender. *s.*

چهينا छेना *chhenā*, m. curd; a small kind of cymbal. *h.*

چهينا *chhīnā*, to bite, sting; also same as *chhūnā*, to touch, q. v. *d.*

چهينا छीना *chhīnnā*, a. to pull, to tear, to pluck, to rob, to snatch. *chhīnā chhānī-k.*, a. to scramble; *chhīn-lenā*, a. to snatch up, to seize, to take possession of, to bereave. *h.*

چهينٹ छींट *chhīṅṭ*, f. chintz, spotted cotton cloth. *h.*

چهينٹا छींटा *chhīṅṭā*, m. shot, spot, splash; a field in which peas and linseed have been sown broad cast. *chhīṅṭā mārnā*, a. to sprinkle. *h.*

چهينٹنا छींटना *chhīṅṭnā*, a. to sprinkle, irrigate. *h.*

چهينٹب छींटब *chhīṅṭab*, sowing broad cast. *h.*

چهينچنا छींचना *chhīnchnā*, a. to throw out water. *s.*

چهينچنا छेंचना *chhenchnā*, a. to mince, to hack, to pound. *h.*

چهينک छींक *chhīṅk*, f. sneezing, sneeze. *chhīṅk-lānewālā*, a sternutatory (medicine). *h.*

چهينک छेंक *chheṅk*, f. sequestration of goods. *chheṅk-lenā*, a. to confiscate. *h.*

چهينکا छींका *chīṅkā*, m. a network of strings to hang any thing in (as a burthen at either end of a pole), the cords of a *bahangī*, an ox muzzle. *s.*

چهينکاو छेंकाव *chheṅkāw*, m. sequestration of goods. *h.*

چهينکنا छेंकना *chheṅknā*, a. to detain, to prevent, to stop, to retain, to bar, to restrain, arrest. *h.*

چهينکنا छींकना *chhīṅknā*, n. to sneeze. *s.*

چهينکويا छेंकवैया *chheṅkwaiyā*, m. a confiscator. *h.*

چهينو *chhīnū*, (in comp.) snatching. *d.*

چهيني छेनी *chhenī*, f. (v. *chhewnī*) a chisel, punch, piercer. *h*

چهيو छेव *chhew*, m. a mark, a piece of wood cut off. *chhew mārnā*, a. to line out, to mark. *h.*

چهيوا छेवा *chhewā*, m. spaces, comma, &c. *h.*

چهيور छेवुर *chhewur*, m. cuticle, skin. *h.*

چهيول छियूल *chhiyūl* or *chhī,ūl*, a kind of jungle tree (called also *dhāk*, q. v.). *h.*

چهيونا छेवना *chhewnā*, a. to pierce, or to bleed a *tār* tree, to extract *tāṛī*; to mark. *s.*

چهيوني छेवनी *chhewnī*, f. a chisel, punch, piercer. *h.*

چاهيے चाहिये *chahiye*, becoming, necessary, [expedient. *h.*

چي चय *chay*, m. an assemblage, a multitude; a heap, a mound of earth. *s.*

چيبهر चीभर *chībhar*, land which remains long moist. *h.*

چيپڑ चीपड़ *chīpaṛ*, f. rheum of the eyes. *h.*

چيپنا चेपना *chepnā*, a. to stick together. *h.*

چيت चैत *chait*, m. the Hindū name of the twelfth month, the full moon of which is near *chitrā* (March—April). *s.*

چيت चेत *chet*, m. memory, remembrance, thought, perception, consciousness, circumspection. *s.*

چيت च्युत *chyut*, fallen, dropped; fallen off, deviated strayed. *s.*

چيتا चीता *chītā*, m. a leopard or panther (*Felis jubata*, *Schreb.*; hunting-leopard, *Pennant*); name of a medicinal plant (*Plumbago zeylanica*). *s.*

چيتا चीता *chītā*, m. wish, desire, thought; understanding, wisdom; painting. *s.*

چيتا चेता *chetā*, m. an adviser, a monitor. *s.*

چيتر चैत्र *chaitra*, the twelfth Hindū month (v. *chait*). *s.*

چيتڑ चीतड़ *chītaṛ*, m. hips, buttocks. *chītaṛ teknā*, to sit down, to get rest. *h.*

چيتل चीतल *chītal*, m. a certain animal of the forest, some think the spotted deer (perhaps a leopard or panther, or some other spotted animal); adj. spotted, speckled. *s.*

چيتن चेतन *chetan*, m. reason, rationality, caution; soul, self; intelligence, wisdom; adj. alive, living, feeling. *s.*

چيتنا चेतना *chetnā*, a. to remember, to think of, to advise, to reflect, to be aware, to recover the senses, to be roused. *chetanā*, f. action. *s.*

چيتنا चीतना *chītnā*, a. to draw; to paint; to wish, think, or imagine. *h.*

چيتنيه चैतन्य *chaitanya*, m. soul, spirit, the Deity considered as the essence of all being; reason, understanding, perception, the possession of the proper use of the faculties; adj. in possession of the senses, awake, sensitive, cautious, attentive, aware, perceiving; an animal or sentient being. *s.*

چيته *chīta* (v. *chītā*), a medicinal plant. *s.*

چيتهنا चीथना *chīthnā*, to rend, to tear. *h.*

چيتي चैती *chaitī*, the harvest of the month *chait*, q. v. *s.*

چيٹ चेट *cheṭ*, m. a servant, a slave. *s.*

چيٹك चेटक *cheṭak*, f. a miracle; a deception. *h.*

چيٹهي चीठी *chīṭhī*, f. a note, letter, billet. *h.*

چيٹي चेटी *cheṭī*, f. a female servant. *s.*

چيچك *chechak*, f. the small-pox. *p.*

چيخ *chīkh*, f. a scream, screech, &c. *chīkh mārnā*, a. to scream, to screech, to cry. *s.*

چيخنا *chīkhnā*, a. to roar, to scream. *s.*

چيدن *chīdan* (r. *chīn*), to gather, to glean. *p.*

چيده *chīda*, selected, culled, gathered. *p.*

چير चीर *chīr*, m. rent, slit, strip; attire; the act of tearing, rending, &c. *chīr nikalnā*, n. to break through troops. *s.*

چير चीर *chīr*, f. cloth; a sort of cloth for women; the pine tree (*Pinus longifolia*). *s.*

چيرا चेरा *cherā*, m. (v. *chelā*) a slave, &c. *s.*

چيرا चीरा *chīrā*, m. incision, cut, wound, slit; maidenhead; turban. *chīrā utārnā*, to deflower. *chīrā-band* or *chīrā-wālī*, a virgin. *s.*

چيراي चेराई *cherā,ī*, f. slavery, servitude. *s.*

چيرايتا चेरायता *cherāyatā*, f. *Gentiana cherayta*. *s.*

چيرنا चीरना *chīrnā*, a. to rend, to tear, to split, to cleave, to harrow. *h.*

چيرو चेरू *cherū*, name of a wild tribe in Mīrzāpur, &c. *h.*

چيره *chīra*, powerful; rude, uncivil. *p.*

چيره *chīra*, m. a turban; maidenhead (v. *chīrā*). *s.*

چيري चीरी *chīrī*, f. the ends or hem of a gar- [ment.

چيري चेरी *cherī*, } f. a slave-girl, a girl servant. *s.*
چيڑي चेड़ी *cheṛī*, }

چيريتا चीरैता *chīraitā*, m. the gentian plant (*Gentiana cherayta*). *h.*

چيڑا चेड़ा *cheṛā*, m. a servant, a slave. *s.*

چيڑي चेड़ी *cheṛī*, f. a female servant (v. *cherī*).

چيز *chīz*, f. thing, commodity. *p.*

چيزبست *chīz-bast*, f. chattels, baggage. *p. s.*

چيزي *chīze*, something, a little. *p.*

چيست *chīst* (for *chi-ast*), what is it? *p.*

چيستان *chīst-ān*, (lit. "what is that?") m. an enigma, a riddle. *p.*

چيشٹا चेष्टा *cheshṭā*, f. application, endeavour, motion, exercise, search, appearance; bodily act or function. *s.*

چيك चीक *chīk*, f. mud, slime (v. *chīkar*). *h.*

چيكٹ चीकट *chīkaṭ*, f. a mixture of oil and dust; adj. greasy or dusty (as cloth); a sort of clayey soil. *h.*

چيكٹي चीकटी *chīkṭī*, f. a clayey soil. *h.*

چيكر चीकर *chīkar*, } f. mud, slime, land that has been recently irrigated. *h.*
چيكڑ चीकड़ *chīkaṛ*, }

چيكھ चीख़ *chīkh*, f. (v. *chīkh*) a scream, &c. *s.*

چيكھر चीखुर *chīkhur*, m. a squirrel. *h.*

چيكھنا चीखना *chīkhnā*, a. to taste; (v. *chīkh-nā*). *s.*

چيل चील *chīl*, f. a kite (*Falco cheela, Lath.*). *chīl-jhapaṭṭā mārnā*, to snatch. *s.*

چيل चैल *chail*, land twice tilled. *h.*

چيلا चैला *chailā*, m. a billet of wood cut for burning, &c. *h.*

چيلا चेला *chelā*, m. a slave brought up in the house, a pupil, a disciple, a servant. *s.*

چيلر चीलर *chīlar*, f. a large louse. *h.*

چيلكا *chelkā*, m. a slave disciple. *h.*

چيله *chīla*, m. a thin cake made of rice-flour and cocoa-nut milk. *d.*

چيلھ चील्ह *chīlh*, f. (v. *chīl*) a kite. *s.*

چيلهار चील्हार *chīlhār*, } f. a large louse. *h.*
چيلهڑ चील्हड़ *chīlhaṛ*, }

چيلي चेली *chelī* (f. of *chelā*), a female slave. *s.*

چين चैन *chain*, m. ease, relief, repose, tranquillity; a calm at sea; denying a bet in gaming, imposture; cultivated land; a low caste of Hindūs. *h.*

چين *chīn*, f. fold, plait, wrinkle. *chīn-abrū-h.* or *chīn ba jabīn-honā*, n. to frown. *chīn par chīn honā*, n. to become wrinkled from fat. *chīn ḍālnā*, a. to crease. *chīn lenā*, n. to crumple. *chīn mānnā*, a. to acquiesce or submit to blame or loss; root of *chīdan*, used in comp. denoting to collect, gather; as *gul-chīn*, one who culls flowers. *sukhan-chīn*, one who gathers tales, an eaves-dropper. *p.*

چين *chīn*, m. China. *p.*

چين चीन *chīn*, m. a sort of grass (*Panicum miliaceum*); a sort of cloth. *s.*

چينا *chīnā*, n. to ooze, to leak. *d.*

چينا चेना *chenā*, *chīnā*, or *chainā*, m. millet (*Panicum Italicum*). *h.*

چينپ चेंप *cheṅp*, m. the acrid resin of fruits and trees. *h.*

چين پشٹھ चीनपिष्ट *chīn-pishṭha*, m. minium or red-lead (brought in cakes or lumps from the hills on the north-west of Bengal). *s.*

چينٹھنا चींथना *chīṅthnā*, n. to be bruised by being trod upon. *h.*

چينٹا चैंटा *chaiṅṭā*, m. a black ant. *h.*

چينٹي चींटी *chīṅṭī*, f. small ant. *h.*

چينچ चेंच *chench*, a kind of herb which springs up in uncultivated places during the rains. *s*

چينچ پينچ चेंच पेंच *cheṅch-peṅch*, m. brats, young ones. *h.*

چين چين كرنا चेंचेंकरना *cheṅ-cheṅ karnā*, n. to chatter, to chirp, to murmur, to grumble, to squeak. *h.*

چينچي चेंची *cheṅchī*, f. a needle-case. *h.*

چيند *chend*, m. a lock of hair left on the top of the head. *d.*

چيندول *chendūl*, m. a ball to play with. *d.*

چينڑا चेंड़ा *cheṅṛā*, young, little. *h.*

چين كپور चीनकपूर *chīn-kapūr*, m. camphor. *s.*

چينه *chaina*, an inferior kind of millet. *h.*

چينھ चीन्ह *chīnh*, m. a mark, a token by which any thing is known. *s.*

چينها चीन्हा *chīnhā*, m. an acquaintance. *s.*

چينهنا चीन्हना *chīnhnā*, a. to know, to recognise. *s.*

چينهوں चीन्हौं *chīnnhauṅ* (v. *chīnhnā*). *s.*

چيني चीनी *chīnī*, f. sugar of a coarse kind (perhaps from *chīn*, China), in opposition to *miṣrī*, sugar-candy, from *miṣr*, Egypt). *h.*

چيني *chīnī*, belonging to or produced in China, Chinese; f. the face of a watch. *p.*

چيور चीवर *chīvar*, m. the tattered dress of a mendicant, especially that of a Bauddha. *s.*

چيورن चीवरिन *chīvarin*, m. a Bauddha or Jaina mendicant. *s.*

چيوڑا चीउड़ा *chī,ūṛā* or *chyūṛā*, m. rice parched in a certain mode and eaten dry. *s.*

چيولي चेवली *chevalī* or *che,olī*, f. a kind of silk (cloth). *h.*

چيونٹا चीऊंटा *chī,ūṅṭā* or *chyūṅṭā*, m. large black ant. *h.*

چيونٹي चीऊंटी *chī,ūṅṭī* or *chyūṅṭī*, f. a small ant. *chī,oṅṭī* (Dakh.) a nip or pinch with the nails of a thumb and finger. *h.*

چيهرا *chehrā*, a descriptive roll of a servant. *p.*

چيهي चीही *chīhī* or *chīhe*, a subdivision of the *gūjar* tribe. *h.*

ح

ح *ḥe*, commonly called *ḥā,i muhmala* and *ḥā,i ḥuṭṭī*, the sixth letter of the Arabic alphabet, the eighth in Persian, and the ninth in Hindūstānī. It does not occur in words purely Persian, nor is there in Sanskrit any letter corresponding to it. Its sound is much akin to our *h* in *haul*, only the aspiration is stronger, and formed deep in the throat. In reckoning by *abjad* it stands for eight. Being the initial letter of *ḥuẓūr-navīs*, or Secretary of State, it is affixed to royal grants as a mark of attestation by that officer. *a.*

حاتم *ḥātim*, a judge; a black crow (probably from decisions being formed by augury from that bird); the name of an Arab chief of the tribe of *Ṭā,ī*, famed for his boundless liberality, whence (met.) liberal, generous, bountiful; for example, a man of great liberality is styled "the *ḥātim* of the age." *a.*

حاج *ḥājj*, a pilgrim to Mecca. *a.*

حاجات *ḥājāt* (pl. of حاجت), wants, necessities. *a.*

حاجب **ḥājib**, m. a porter, a door-keeper; a chamberlain, a privy-counsellor; a curtain, a screen; the eyebrow. *a.*

حاجت **ḥājat**, f. necessity; poverty; hope, wish, need, want. *ḥājat-barār* or *-rawā*, producing or supplying what is needed. *ḥājat raf' karnā*, a. to relieve one's necessities; to go to the necessary. *ḥājat-mand*, necessitous, indigent; hoping, depending. *ḥājat-mandī*, f. indigence, destitution. *a.*

حاجز **ḥājiz**, that which hinders or intervenes. *a.*

حاجي **ḥājī**, m. a Musalmān who has made the pilgrimage to Mecca. *ḥājī ul ḥaramain*, a pilgrim to both the sacred places, *i. e.* Mecca and Medina. *a.*

حاجي احمق **ḥājī-aḥmaḳ**, } two mock pil-
حاجي بيوقوف **ḥājī bewuḳūf**, } grims who perform a conspicuous part in the Muḥarram festival. Their tricks, antics, and conversation are very similar to those of "Symmie and his brither," the two mock friars who generally appeared in the burlesque pageants, ridiculing the Pope and priesthood of Rome, performed in Scotland about the time of the Reformation—(Binning). N.B. The church of Rome herself had for ages countenanced and encouraged these saturnalia before the Reformation was thought of. In the palmy days of Popery such mummeries were regarded as utterly harmless; but in the hands of the reformers they of course became highly offensive. *a.*

حاد **ḥādd**, acrid, sharp, bitter, sour, ardent, fiery, poignant, caustic. *a.*

حادث **ḥādis**, new, just appearing. *ḥādis honā*, n. to appear, to emerge, to happen. *a.*

حادثه **ḥādisa**, m. a novelty, an event, an occurrence; a misfortune, calamity. *a.*

حادق **ḥādiḳ**, } ingenious, industrious, skilful,
حاذق **ḥāẕiḳ**, } penetrating, intelligent, excelling. *a.*

حار **ḥārr**, hot, ardent; difficult, laborious. *a.*

حارصه **ḥāriṣa**, a slight wound or scratch. *a.*

حاسد **ḥāsid**, envious; m. an enemy. *a.*

حاشا **ḥāshā**, besides. *ḥāshā-lillāh*, interj. God forbid, by no means. *ḥāshā-ka* and *ḥāshā-la-ka*, far be it from thee. *ḥāshā-ka-llāh*, God preserve thee from it. *a.*

حاشيه **ḥāshiya**, m. a margin, hem, border; a marginal note; people of inferior rank, attendants, retinue, troops; facings of a military uniform. *ḥāshiya-gawāh*, a witness to the execution of a deed (he writing his name on the *ḥāshiya* or margin). *a.*

حاصل **ḥāṣil**, m. produce; acquiring; profit; corn; a tax, duty, custom, revenue; *ḥāṣili bāzār*, m. collections or duties of a market. *ḥāṣil zamīn*, land under cultivation and paying revenue. *ḥāṣilī-ẓarb*, the product of multiplication. *ḥāṣil-k.*, a. to acquire, to get; to gain; to produce; to collect; to learn. *ḥāṣili-kalām*, in short, briefly. *ḥāṣil honā*, to be got or attained. *a.*

حاصله **ḥāṣila**, cultivated or cropped land. *a.*

حاضر **ḥāẓir**, present, ready, willing, content. *ḥāẓir-bāsh*, (be ready) a constant attendant. *ḥāẓir-bāshī*, f. constant attendance. *ḥāẓir-jawāb*, pert, answering wittily. *ḥāẓir-jawābī*, f. repartee; readiness of reply. *ḥāẓir-rahnā*, n. to attend, to wait on. *ḥāẓir-ẓāmin*, m. bail, security for the appearance of another, a bondsman. *ḥāẓir-ẓāminī*, f. the act of giving bail for another; a bail-bond. *ḥāẓir o nāẓir*, present and seeing (an epithet of God). *ḥāẓir-honā*, n. to be at hand, to be ready, to consent. *h.*

حاضرات **ḥāẓirāt**, f. commanding or imprisoning demons, &c.; raising the devil. *a.*

حاضراتي **ḥāẓirāṭī**, f. the commanding of evil spirits, &c.; m. a conjuror, a necromancer. *a.*

حاضران **ḥāẓirān**, } (pl. of حاضر) people pre-
حاضرين **ḥāẓirīn**, } sent, or those who are or were present. *a.*

حاضري **ḥāẓirī**, f. breakfast, desert; levee, presence, audience, muster-roll; an offering made to a saint. *ḥāẓirī khānā*, a. to breakfast. *a.*

حاطه **ḥāṭa**, premises, an inclosure; a courtyard (in Anglo-Indian phraseology) a compound. *a.*

حافظ **ḥāfiẓ**, m. a guardian, governor, preserver; having a good memory; one who has the whole *ḳur,ān*, by heart; the poetical name of a celebrated poet of Persia (*Muḥammad Shamsu-d-dīn* of *Shīrāz*). *ḥāfiẓi-daftar*, keeper of the records in an office. *a.*

حافظه **ḥāfiẓa**, m. a retentive memory. *a.*

حاكم **ḥākim**, m. a ruler, a governor, a commander, a master; pl. *ḥākimān*. *a.*

حاكمانه **ḥākimāna**, judicially, magisterially, with authority. *a.*

حاكمي **ḥākimī**, of or belonging to a ruler; f. office of ruler, a magistracy. *a.*

حال **ḥāl**, m. state, condition; business, affair; present time, present tense (in gram.); in revenue language, the actual state of the collections; extasy; (pl. *aḥwāl*). *ḥāl-ābādī*, land under present cultivation (having formerly been waste). *ḥāl-ākār*, present revenue. *ḥāl-bāḳī*, current balance. *ḥāl-chalanī*, present currency. *ḥāl-ānā*, n. to be inspired, to be thrown into extasies. *ḥāl-ān-ki*, whereas, though, yet, however, even, although, notwithstanding. *ḥāl ḥāl chalnā*, n. to go, or walk quickly. *ḥāl-sāl*, this present year. *a.*

حالا **ḥālā**, an instalment of revenue. *ḥālā* or *ḥālaṇ*, now, at present. *a.*

حالات **ḥālāt**, f. (pl. حالت) present states or conditions; circumstances, cases. *a.*

حالت **ḥālat**, f. condition, circumstance, posture of one's affairs; case. *a.*

حالحاصل **ḥāl-ḥāṣil**, the actual produce or revenue of a tract of land. *ḥāl-ḥāṣili*, actually producing. *a.*

حالدار **ḥāl-dār**, a village officer next to the *paṭwārī*, q. v. *ḥāl-dārī*, a tax formerly levied (in Bengal) on marriages. *a. p.*

حالف **ḥālif**, one who makes oath or affidavit. *a.*

حالم **ḥālim**, m. cress, cresses (*Lepidium sativum*). *a.*

حالي **ḥālī**, modern, new; present, now, soon; current (coin); government assessment. *a.*

حام **ḥām**, the second son of Noah, from whom (according to the Musalmāns) the Indians are descended. *a.*

حامد *ḥāmid*, m. one who praises (God). *a.*

حامض *ḥāmiẓ*, sour, bitter, salt. *a.*

حامل *ḥāmil*, m. a carrier, porter, bearer; f. pregnant (a woman). *ḥāmili matan*, a commentary rehearsing, or annexed to the text. *ḥāmili zamīn*, the bearer of the earth; the personage among the Greeks and Romans who held a similiar office was Atlas; among the Hindūs it is *Sheshnāg*, a great serpent. *a.*

حامله *ḥāmila*, f. pregnant, fruitful (a tree). *a.*

حامي *ḥāmī*, m. a protector, a defender, a guardian. *ḥāmī bharnā*, a. to consent, to confirm. *a.*

حاميه *ḥāmiya*, a protectress; a protective body. *a.*

حانث *ḥānis*, m. a perjurer. *a.*

حاوي *ḥāwī*, containing, collecting, comprehending; a collector. *a.*

حائط *ḥā,iṭ*, a wall, an inclosure. *a.*

حائك *ḥā,ik*, m. a weaver. *a.*

حائل *ḥā,il*, restraining, intervening; m. (used substantively) a shelter, defence, protection. *a.*

حب *ḥubb*, f. love, affection; friendship. *ḥubbu-l-waṭan*, love of one's country. *a.*

حب *ḥabb*, f. a pill; a grain; a berry. *a.*

حباب *ḥubāb*, m. a bubble. *ḥubāb uṭhnā*, n. to bubble. *ḥubābī*, of or resembling a bubble; full of bubbles. *a.*

حباري *ḥubārā*, a species of bustard. *a.*

حبذا! *ḥabbazā*, excellent! bravo! *a.*

حبس *ḥabs*, m. retention, imprisonment; prison; a prisoner; a bank, mound, dam; a tank, pond, reservoir. *ḥabsu-l-baul*, m. a retention of urine; a strangury. *ḥabsu-n-nafas*, suffocation. *ḥabsi dam*, m. retaining the breath, which some *faḳīrs* do as a religious act for a very long time (this is esteemed a means of prolonging life, on the very philosophic principle, that every man has a predestined number of inspirations to make, and the more slowly these are performed, the longer will be the period of his existence); an asthma. *a.*

حبش *ḥabash* (pl. *ḥubshān*), an Abyssinian or Ethiopian. *a.*

حبشن *ḥabshin*, } an Abyssinian woman, a
حبشني *ḥabshinī*, } negress, a slave. *a.*

حبشه *ḥabasha* or *ḥabashat*, Ethiopia, people of Ethiopia; also people of Southern Arabia. *a.*

حبشي *ḥabshī*, Abyssinian or Ethiopian, a Caffre, a negro, a slave. *a.*

حبل *ḥabl*, m. rope, cord, tendon; a league, alliance, compact. *ḥablu-l-warīd*, the jugular vein. *a.*

حبوب *ḥubūb* (pl. of حب), pills, grains. *a.*

حبوبات *ḥubūbāt*, vegetables, potherbs; articles formerly furnished gratis to men in authority, consisting of sheep, milk, eggs, blankets, hides, &c. *a.*

حبه *ḥabba*, m. one berry, one grain, one seed; a particle, part; a measure equal to two barleycorns; a pill. *a.*

حبيب *ḥabīb*, a lover, sweetheart, a friend, a mistress. *a.*

حتي *ḥattā*, until, so that, in such a manner, and thus. *ḥattā-l-maḳdūr*, or *-imkān*, or *-wus'*, to the best of one's ability. *a.*

حج *ḥajj*, m. act of moving round, or going to a place; pilgrimage to Mecca. *ḥajju-l-farz*, the enjoined pilgrimage to Mecca, which should be performed once in his lifetime by every good Musalmān. *amīru-l-ḥajj*, the officer in charge of a caravan of pilgrims, generally a man of high rank and dignity. *a.*

حجاب *ḥijāb*, m. modesty, bashfulness, shame; a veil, curtain; night. *ḥijāb uṭhnā*, n. to be lost (the sense of shame); to be removed (a screen). *ḥijāb-chashmī*, sheep's-eyed. *ḥijāb-k.*, a. to cover, hide, conceal; to shame. *ḥijāb khānā*, n. to blush. *a.*

حجاب *ḥujjāb* (pl. of حاجب), porters, doorkeepers, chamberlains. *a.*

حجابي *ḥijābī*, modest, veiled; f. secrecy. *a.*

حجاج *ḥujjāj* (pl. of حاج), pilgrims to Mecca. *a.*

حجاج *ḥajjāj*, a tyrant, oppressor. *ḥajjāj bin yūsuf*, name of a notorious petty tyrant who was governor of *'Irāḳ 'Arab*, under 'Abdu-l-Malik, about the year of our æra 685. *a.*

حجاز *ḥijāz*, m. lit. prohibiting or separating; Mecca, and the adjacent country, Arabia Petræa. According to some authorities Arabia is divided into five parts, *Tihāma, Najd, Hijāz, 'Urūz*, and *Yaman*: *Hijāz* is the chain of mountains extending from *Yaman* to *Syria*, and has this name as separating the territories of *Najd* and *Tihāma*. *a.*

حجام *ḥajjām*, m. a cupper, phlebotomist, scarifier; a barber, a shaver. *a.*

حجامت *ḥajāmat*, f. cupping, scarifying, shaving. *ḥajāmat-k.*, to shave, "faire la barbe." *a.*

حجامني *ḥajjāminī*, a barber's wife. *a.*

حجامي *ḥajjāmī*, f. the profession of a cupper or barber, shaving. *a.*

حجب *ḥajab*, m. interposing, secluding, excluding, fencing round. *a.*

حجت *ḥujjat*, an argument, proof, reason; altercation, disputation, controversy. *a.*

حجتي *ḥujjatī*, a sound reasoner; a disputatious person, a sophist; a wrangler, a caviller. *a.*

حجر *ḥajar*, m. a stone; hindrance, prohibition: in law, annulment. *ḥajaru-l-aswad*, m. the black stone in the temple of Mecca. *ḥajaru-t-tīs*, the bezoar-stone. *ḥajaru-d-dam*, the blood-stone. *ḥajaru-l-ḳamar*, the moonstone (*Selenites*). *ḥajaru-l-yahūd*, m. a calcareous stone used in medicine; jew's-stone, resembling an olive or acorn, found in Palestine (*Helmintholithus Judaicus*). *a.*

حجرتان *ḥajratān*, du. gold and silver. *a.*

حجره *ḥujra*, m. a cell, closet, chamber. *ḥujra,e khāṣṣ*, a private closet. *a.*

حجله *ḥajla*, m. (vulg. *ḥujla*) the female partridge; the ornamented chamber where the bride sits, the curtain which hangs before her, the marriage bed. *a.*

حجم ḥajm, thickness, bigness; cupping, scarifying. *a.*

حد ḥadd, f. a boundary, limit; an impediment; a definition; a starting-post; punishment agreeable to the laws of *Muḥammad*, which fix the exact number of lashes, &c., to be inflicted for certain crimes. *ḥadd bāndhnā*, a. to bound, to terminate. *ḥadd-bast* or *hadd-bandī*, the settlement and demarcation of boundaries. *ḥadd-bhar-k.*, a. to do one's best. *ḥaddi shar'*, the extremity of the law, legal punishment. *ḥadd-se-afzūn*, or *-ziyād*, or *-ziyāda*, beyond bounds, excessively. *ḥadd-k.*, a. to push any thing to extremity; to go beyond bounds. *ḥadd mārnā*, a. to punish. *a.*

حداد ḥaddād, m. a blacksmith; a jailer. *a.*

حدت ḥiddat, f. the edge of a sword; passion, vehemence, impetuosity, poignancy, virulence. *a.*

حدث ḥadaṡ or **ḥadṡ**, m. any thing existing for the first time, recently happening, novelty, contingency, event, accident; an accidental cause of impurity, according to Musalmān traditions, whereby it becomes unlawful to commence or finish a prayer without previously undergoing ablution. *a.*

حدوث ḥudūṡ, m. novelty, invention. *a.*

حدود ḥudūd (pl. of حد), limits, confines, boundaries. *ḥudūdi shar'iya*, penal laws. *ḥudūdi arba'*, boundaries of the four sides of an estate. *a.*

حديث ḥadīṡ, m. a history, a tradition; the traditional sayings of *Muḥammad*, which now bear the force of laws. *ḥadīṡ-k.*, a. to forswear, to abjure, to renounce. *a.*

حديد ḥadīd, m. iron; a helmet. *a.*

حديقه ḥadīḳa, an inclosed garden, a palm plantation; name of a Persian poetical and mystical work by *Ḥakīm Sanāyī*. *a.*

حذر ḥażar, m. caution, prudence; fear. *a.*

حذف ḥażf, m. taking away, ejecting, cutting off a letter or syllable of a word, apocope. *ḥażf-k.*, a. to omit, contract, reject. *a.*

حر ḥurr, free, well-born, genteelly born. *ḥarr*, being hot, warmth, boiling. *a.*

حراث ḥurrāṡ (pl. of حارث), husbandmen. *a.*

حراج ḥirāj (pl. of حرجه), troops of camels; thickets, brakes. *a.*

حراج ḥarrāj (for هراج), an auction, a sale. *a.*

حرارت ḥarārat, f. heat; a burning fever; warmth, zeal. *ḥarārati dīnī*, f. religious fervour, fanaticism. *ḥarārati gharīzī*, f. natural heat. *a.*

حراست ḥirāsat, f. care, watching, guarding. *ḥirāsat-k.*, a. to take care of, to govern. *a.*

حراض ḥarrāẓ, one who prepares ashes of alkali; a lime-burner, a maker of plaster or cement. *a.*

حراف ḥarrāf, ingenious, clever; pleasant, facetious, talkative, chatty. *a.*

حرام ḥarām, unlawful, forbidden, sacred, wrong. *ḥarām rakhnā*, a. to prohibit, to deem a thing sacred or forbidden. *ḥarām-khor*, m. one who lives on the wages of iniquity. *ḥarām-zāda*, unlawfully begotten, a bastard; generally used as a term of abuse, such as rogue, scoundrel, &c. *ḥarām-zādī*, f. a wicked woman, a strumpet. *ḥarām zādagī*, f. rascality, roguery. *ḥarām-zādagī-k.*, a. to abuse, to ill treat. *ḥarām-maghz*, spinal marrow. *ḥarām-kār*, m. a fornicator. *ḥarām-kārī*, f. forbidden acts (but particularly adultery and fornication). *ḥarām kā māl*, good for nothing. *ḥarām khānā*, a. to receive the wages of iniquity. *a.*

حرامي ḥarāmī, m. a robber, an assassin, a rogue. *ḥarāmī pillā*, a bastard. *a.* [na. *a.*

حرامين ḥarāmain, (dual) Mecca and Medi-

حرب ḥarb, f. war, battle. *ḥarb-gāh*, f. field of battle. *a.*

حربا ḥirbā, m. a chameleon. *a.*

حربه ḥarba, m. arms, warlike apparatus. *a.*

حربي ḥarbī, relating to war, bellicose; (in law) an infidel, as being considered by the "true believers" a fair subject of hostility. *a.*

حرث ḥarṡ, m. ploughing, sowing, cultivating; a ploughshare. *a.*

حرجه ḥaraja or **ḥarajat**, a troop of camels; a thicket, shrubbery. *a.*

حرز ḥirz, m. an amulet, a charm; a fortification, an asylum, a place of refuge, custody, safe keeping of goods or valuables. *a.*

حرس ḥirs, m. (v. *ḥarāsat*) care, &c. *a.*

حرص ḥirṣ, f. desiring eagerly; greediness, avidity; ambition, avarice. *a.*

حرصاها ḥirṣāhā, } **حرصي ḥirṣī**, } greedy, avaricious, covetous; ambitious. *a.*

حرف ḥarf, m. a letter of the alphabet; a particle (in grammar); inverting, changing, turning (as a coat); a crooked pen; writing diagonally; a margin, side; a word; the summit of a mountain. *ḥarf-āshnā*, being just able to read, knowing the letters. *ḥarf-ānā*, n. the approach of infamy, to be incurred (infamy). *ḥarf-andāz*, cunning, artful. *ḥarf-andāzī*, f. cunning, artifice, art. *ḥarf-baiṭhālnā* or *-jamānā*, a. to compose for printing. *ḥarf par ungli rakhnā*, a. to criticise. *ḥarf pakaṛnā*, a. to censure, to criticise. *ḥarfi tardīd*, disjunctive conjunction. *ḥarfi tashbīh*, the adverb of similitude. *ḥarfi ta'rīf*, the definite article. *ḥarfi tankīr*, the indefinite article. *ḥarfi sharṭ*, conditional conjunction. *ḥarfi ṣaḥīḥ*, a consonant. *ḥarfi 'illat*, a long vowel (*i. e. alif, wāo*, or *ye*). *ḥarf-gīr*, m. a critic: it rather denotes the contemptible little vermin of criticism whose abilities extend no further than to detect an error of the press or so, hence, adj. captious. *ḥarf-gīrī*, f. criticism, captiousness. *ḥarf-lānā*, a. to asperse, to defame, to blot, to brand, to blemish. *ḥarf o ḥikāyat*, f. disputing, doubting. *a.*

حرفاحرفا ḥarfan ḥarfan, letter by letter, syllable by syllable, literal or literally. *a.*

حرفات ḥarfāt, (pl. of حرف), letters, &c. *a.*

حرفت ḥirfat, f. } **حرفه ḥirfa**, m. } trade, art, profession; skill, ingenuity, cleverness, cunning. *ahli ḥirfa*, men of skill, artists. *a.*

حركات ḥarakāt, (pl. of حركت), movements, proceedings; the vowel-points. *a.*

حرکت *ḥarakat*, motion, action, conduct, procedure; prevention, hindrance; a short vowel. *ḥarakat-k.*, a. lit. to move; generally it means to commit an improper action. *a.*

حرکتي *ḥarakatī*, m. an interrupter. *a.*

حرم *ḥaram*, sacred, forbidden; m. the sacred inclosure of the temple of Mecca; f. a concubine, a wife, a daughter, the women's apartments, a seraglio (vulg. *ḥarem*). *a.*

حرمان *ḥirmān*, m. repulse, disappointment. *a.*

حرمت *ḥurmat*, f. dignity, character; chastity, honour; reverence. *ḥurmat toṛnā*, a. to disgrace. *ḥurmat denā*, a. to bestow honour, to exalt; to lose one's character, to incur disgrace. *ḥurmat-k.*, a. to treat honourably and respectfully. *ḥurmat lenā*, a. to violate, to ravish; to disgrace. *a.*

حرور *ḥurūr*, heat, warmth. *a.*

حروف *ḥurūf*, (pl. of حرف) letters, &c. *ḥurūfi hijā* or *ḥurūfi tahajjī*, the letters of the alphabet, an alphabet. *a.*

حریر *ḥarīr*, m. silk, silken cloth. *a.*

حریره *ḥarīra*, m. a kind of pap of milk and flour, caudle. *a.*

حریري *ḥarīrī*, f. a very thin kind of paper. *a.*

حریص *ḥarīṣ*, covetous, greedy, gluttonous. *a.*

حریف *ḥarīf*, clever, cunning; pleasant, facetious; m. a rival, an enemy; an associate, a partner or opponent at play, a friend. *a.*

حریفي *ḥarīfī*, cleverness; rivalry, enmity. *a.*

حریم *ḥarīm*, m. a sacred place, a sanctuary; the enclosure of the temple of Mecca; a house or dwelling. *a.*

حزب *ḥizb*, a portion of the *ḳur,ān*, being a sixtieth part of the whole volume. *a.*

حزم *ḥazm* or *ḥazam*, vigilance, industry, steadiness, caution, resolution. *a.*

حزن *ḥuzn*, m. grief, sadness, affliction. *a.*

حزین *ḥazīn*, sad, afflicted, melancholy, grieved, doleful. *a.*

حزیني *ḥazīnī*, f. grief, sadness, affliction. *a.*

حس *ḥiss*, m. sense, sentiment, feeling, imagination; sympathy. *ḥissi bāṭinī*, internal sense. *ḥissi ẓāhirī*, external sense. *ḥissi mushtarik*, common sense. *a.*

حساب *ḥisāb*, m. computation, calculation, arithmetic, accounts. *ḥisāb pāk-k.*, to clear accounts. *ḥisāb-dān*, m. an arithmetician. *ḥisāb rakhnā*, a. to keep accounts of, to register. *ḥisāb ṣaf-k.*, a. to settle accounts. *ḥisāb kitāb*, m. accounts. *ḥisāb-k.*, a. to calculate. *ḥisāb lenā*, a. to take accounts. *ḥisāb-nawīs*, m. an accountant. *a.*

حسابي *ḥisābī*, proper, accountable, accurate, just; f. calculation; m. an accountant. *a.*

حساس *ḥassās*, possessed of the five senses; m. (used substantively) an animal. *a.*

حسام *ḥusām*, f. a sharp sword. *a.*

حسان *ḥussān* or *ḥassān*, very good or very beautiful. *a.*

حسب *ḥasab*, m. pedigree, nobility; computation; measure, proportion; value; way, mode or manner; religion. *ḥasab-nasab*, m. pedigree. *a.*

حسب *ḥasb*, agreeably, conformably, according to, in conformity with; m. computing, reflecting upon, considering; quantity, measure, proportion, value; sufficiency; number. *ḥasbu-l-imkān*, as far as possible. *ḥasbu-l-ḥukm*, agreeably to orders. *ḥasbu-l-ma'mūl*, agreeably to custom. *ḥasbi ḥāl* or *ḥasbi wāḳi'a*, agreeably to circumstances, as exigency may require. *ḥasbi dil-khwāh*, agreeably to one's desire. *a.*

حسد *ḥasad*, f. envy, malice, emulation, ambition. *ḥasad-pesha*, envious, ambitious. *a.*

حسرت *ḥasrat*, f. regret, grief, desire. *ḥasrat-zada*, struck with regret, woe-begone, afflicted. *a.*

حسن *ḥasan*, good, beautiful, elegant; (often used as a man's name) the eldest of 'Alī's two sons. *Ḥasan Maimandī*, name of the vizir of Sultān Maḥmūd of Ghaznī. *a.*

حسن *ḥusn*, m. beauty, elegance, goodness. *ḥusni ikhtiyār*, free-will. *ḥusni tadbīr*, excellent management, sound policy. *ḥusni khiṭāb*, elegance of address. *ḥusni khulḳ*, a good disposition. *ḥusni rā,e*, prudent counsel, sound judgment. *ḥusni 'ahd*, good faith, trustworthiness. *ḥusni ẓann*, m. a good opinion, a favourable judgment. *a.*

حسود *ḥasūd*, envious, spiteful, malignant. *ḥusūd*, envy, malice, spite. *a.*

حسین *ḥasīn*, beautiful, elegant. *a.*

حسین *ḥusain*, good, beautiful; a man's name, the second of the two sons of 'Alī, who both suffered martyrdom. *a.*

حسیني *ḥusainī*, of or relating to *ḥusain*; a species of grape. *ḥusainī-bulbul* (v. *bulbul*), a species of bird of melody. *ḥusainī kabāb*, a kind of stew. *a. p.*

حشاش *ḥushāsh*, } m. the remains of life,
حشاشه *ḥushāsha*, } last breathings of a dying man. *a.*

حشاش *ḥashshāsh*, a forager, a grasscutter. *ḥashshāsh-bashshāsh* (for *hashshāsh*), merry, hilarous. *a.*

حشر *ḥashar* or *ḥashr*, m. a meeting, congregation, concourse; the general resurrection of the dead. *yaumu-l-ḥashar*, day of resurrection. *a.*

حشرات *ḥasharāt* (pl. of حشره), the buzzing noise of a crowd; reptiles, insects, animalcules. *ḥasharātu-l-arẓ*, reptiles. *a.*

حشره *ḥashara* or *ḥasharat*, a reptile, an insect. *a.*

حشري *ḥashrī*, violent and impetuous (a stallion). *a.*

حشفه *ḥashfa*, m. *glans penis*. *a.*

حشم *ḥasham*, m. pomp, equipage, suite. *a.*

حشمت *ḥashmat*, f. state, dignity; equipage, retinue, train, parade. *a.*

حشو *ḥashū* or *ḥasho*, m. stuffing a pillow, cushion, bed, &c.; also whatever they are stuffed with; people of the meanest condition; small camels. *ḥashw minhā* or *ḥasho minhā,ī*, subtraction, deduction; the quantity deducted; (in revenue language) rent-free. *a.*

حصار *ḥiṣār*, m. an enclosure, a fence; a fortified place, a castle; besieging. *a.*

حصاري *ḥiṣārī*, those who are besieged. *a.*

حصانت *ḥaṣānat*, f. firmness, stability, durability, steadiness; chastity, continence. *a.*

حصبا *ḥaṣbā*, gravel, pebbles. *a.*

حصر *ḥaṣr*, m. a siege, blockade; reckoning, counting, number. *a.*

حصص *ḥiṣaṣ* (pl. of حصه), shares, lots, portions. *a.*

حصن *ḥiṣn*, m. a castle, fortification. *ḥiṣni ḥaṣīn*, an impregnable fortress; the title of a book of Musalmān traditions. *a.*

حصول *ḥuṣūl*, m. acquisition; profit, advantage, produce, getting or attaining. *a.*

حصه *ḥiṣṣa*, m. share, lot, portion, division. *ḥiṣṣa i ḥākimī*, the share of produce to which the king or ruler is entitled. *ḥiṣṣa-dār*, a sharer. *ḥiṣṣa-dārī*, f. sharing, being entitled to a share; copartnership. *ḥiṣṣa-rasad*, an equal share, a proportional part. *ḥiṣṣa-kashī*, distribution of shares. *ḥiṣṣa i hālī*, a ploughman's share or wages in kind. *a.*

حصيت *ḥiṣṣait*, a shareholder. *a.*

حصير *ḥaṣīr*, m. a mat for sitting on. *a.*

حصين *ḥaṣīn*, strong; fortified. *a.*

حضار *ḥuẓẓār* (pl. of حاضر), those present, spectators, auditors, assistants. *a.*

حضانت *ḥaẓānat* or *ḥiẓānat*, the bringing up of children in the Musalmān faith. *a.*

حضر *ḥaẓar*, m. residence, resting, remaining in a place, presence; rest or repose (in opposition to *safar*, journeying, moving about). *a.*

حضرت *ḥaẓrat*, f. presence; dignity; majesty, highness, &c. (a title addressed to the great, such as our words Excellency, Eminence, Holiness, &c.). *ḥaẓrat ẓilli subḥānī*, m. his majesty, the shadow of God, the king. *ḥaẓrat 'īsā*, Jesus Christ. *a.*

حضور *ḥuẓūr*, m. presence, appearance, attendance: court, government; the town or station at which the chief authority is resident (the other towns and places subject to the same authority are termed *ghaibat*); used also in the sense of "your honour," "your highness." *ḥuẓūri pur-nūr*, his illustrious majesty. *ḥuẓūr-ṭalab*, being called to the presence, summoning attendance. *ḥuẓūr-navīs*, a private secretary. *a.*

حضوري *ḥuẓūrī*, m. an attendant; f. presence; adj. of or belonging to the court, royal. *a.*

حضيض *ḥaẓīẓ*, low; (substantively) the lower extremity or surface of any thing; the foot of a mountain; (in astronomy) the lower apsis in an eccentric orbit (opposed to *auj*, the zenith). *a.*

حطام *ḥuṭām*, any thing brittle or dry, minute or paltry; worldly goods. *a.*

حطب *ḥaṭab*, firewood. *ḥaṭib*, very lean, thin, lank (like a stick). *a.*

حظ *ḥaẓẓ*, m. pleasure, delight; flavour, taste; good fortune, felicity. *ḥaẓẓi nafsānī*, sensual pleasures. *a.*

حظر *ḥaẓr*, m. prohibition, seclusion, forbidding; harshness, rudeness. *a.*

حظوظ *ḥuẓūẓ* (pl. of حظ), pleasures, &c. *a*

حفاظت *ḥifāẓat*, f. memory; custody, guardianship, protection. *ḥifāẓat-k.*, a. to preserve, to defend; to repeat from memory; to keep in memory. *a.*

حفصه *ḥafṣa*, one of the wives of Muḥammad. *a.*

حفظ *ḥifẓ*, m. memory; custody, guardianship, protection. *ḥifẓi marātib*, observing etiquette, attention to the rank, &c., of persons addressed. *a.*

حفل *ḥafl*, m. an assembly, council, congregation. *a.*

حق *ḥaḳḳ*, just, right, true; m. the Deity; justice, rectitude; lot, portion; equity. *ḥaḳḳ adā-k.*, a. to render every one his due. *ḥaḳḳu-s-sa'ī*, m. the wages of labour, recompense for trouble. *ḥaḳḳu-llāh*, the rights of God, punishment inflicted for religious offences. *ḥaḳḳu-n-nās*, the rights of man, punishment of crimes against society. *ḥaḳḳu-n-nāẓirīn*, something left after a banquet for the servants or spectators. *ḥaḳḳ ta'ālā*, God is great, the Almighty. *ḥaḳḳ jall o jalāl*, the Deity in all his splendour. *ḥaḳḳi ḥawāla-dār*, the allowance of grain given to *shaḥnas* (q. v.), generally at the rate of a seer (*ser*) and a-half to every maund (*man*). *ḥaḳḳ-dār*, proprietor. *ḥaḳḳ ḥaḳḳ-k.*, n. to be very hungry. *ḥaḳḳi-zamīndārī*, a zamīndār's proprietary right. *ḥaḳḳ-shinās*, knowing and performing one's duty; rendering to every one his due; grateful. *ḥaḳḳ-shināsī*, gratitude. *ḥaḳḳi-kamīnchārī*, *-sayānchārī* or *-thokdārī*, dues and fees to *kamīns* or village servants, generally amounting to 3 per cent. *ḥaḳḳ men*, with respect to. *ḥaḳḳ-nā-ḥaḳḳ*, right or wrong. *ḥaḳḳ-nā-shinās*, ungrateful, undutiful. *ḥaḳḳ honā*, n. to die. *a.*

حقًا *ḥaḳḳan̲*, really, truly. *ḥaḳḳā*, by God. *a.*

حقارت *ḥiḳārat*, f. contempt, scorn, affront, disgrace, vileness, baseness. *a.*

حقاني *ḥaḳḳānī*, true, perfect, divine. *a.*

حقائق *ḥaḳā,iḳ* (pl. of حقيقت), truths. *a.*

حق بهينٹ *ḥaḳḳ-bheṇṭ*, presents made to native officers in authority. *a. h.*

حقنه *ḥuḳna*, m. a syringe, a squirt, a clyster-pipe, a clyster, a glister. *a.*

حقوق *ḥuḳūḳ* (pl. of حق), rights, duties. *a.*

حقه *ḥuḳḳa*, m. the pipe, &c., in which tobacco is smoked; a grenade or bomb; a box for holding jewels or drugs. *ḥuḳḳa-bardār*, the servant who prepares the *ḥuḳḳa*. *ḥuḳḳe bāz*, a juggler; a grenadier. "*ḥuḳḳa*, although an Arabic word, signifies a pipe only in India: no Arab would use it in this sense. The word signifies, in Arabia, Egypt, and Syria, a small round box or casket."—Binning. *a.*

حقيت *ḥaḳḳiyat*, f. right, share, proprietorship, claim, property. *a.*

حقير *ḥaḳīr*, contemptible; thin, lean; vile. *ḥaḳīr-jānnā*, a. to contemn, to despise. *a.*

حقيري *ḥaḳīrī*, contemptibleness; leanness. *a.*

حقيقت *ḥaḳīḳat*, f. account, narration, relation, explanation; truth, sincerity. *ḥaḳīḳat-nāma*, a written statement of particulars. *a.*

حقيقتًا *ḥaḳīḳatan̲*, really, truly. *a.*

حقيقي *ḥaḳīḳī*, real, true, certain, accurate, just, own. *ḥaḳīḳī bhā,ī*, a full brother. *a.*

حك *ḥakk*, m. erasure, scratching out. *ḥakk-k.*, a. to erase. *ḥakk-h.*, to be erased. *a.*

حكاك *ḥakkāk*, m. a cutter and polisher of precious stones; a lapidary. *a.*

حكام *ḥukkām* (pl. of حاكم), governors, rulers, commanders, magistrates. *a.*

حكامي *ḥukkāmī*, a term applied to grants of land made by the officers of government. *a.*

حكايات *ḥikāyāt* (pl. of حكايت), tales, &c. *a.*

حكايت *ḥikāyat*, f. a history, romance, story, tale, narration. *ḥikāyat-k.*, to relate. *a.*

حكم *ḥukm*, m. order, command, decree, permission. *ḥukm-uṭhānā* or *-nikālnā*, a. to draw at cards. *ḥukm-andāz*, obedient to directions; an archer, one who hits the mark (with an arrow, bullet, &c.). *ḥukm-nāma*, m. a written order. *a.*

حكم *ḥakam*, m. an umpire, a mediator, an arbitrator. *ḥikam*, knowledge, science, wisdom, &c. *a.*

حكما *ḥukamā* (pl. of حكيم), philosophers, sages; physicians; wise men in general. *a.*

حكمت *ḥikmat*, f. wisdom, knowledge; skill, cleverness; philosophy, mystery; principle. *a.*

حكمتي *ḥikmatī*, clever, philosophic. *a.*

حكمي *ḥukmī*, obedient to directions (generally applied to medicine). *a.*

حكومات *ḥukūmāt* (pl. irreg.), orders, rules. *a.*

حكومت *ḥukūmat*, f. dominion, sovereignty, government, jurisdiction, authority. *ḥukūmati 'adl*, a just award, a decision by just arbitrament. *a.*

حكي *ḥakkī*, m. an erasing-knife. *a.*

حكيم *ḥakīm*, a sage, philosopher; a physician, a doctor, in the general sense of the term. *a.*

حكيمانه *ḥakīmāna*, like a sage, wisely. *a.*

حكيمي *ḥakīmī*, f. the practice of medicine; adj. of or relating to men of wisdom. *a.*

حل *ḥall*, m. solution, loosening, untying. *ḥall-kārī*, f. gilding. *ḥall-k.*, a. to loosen, to solve, to dissolve, discuss, to dilute. *ḥall-honā*, to be solved, overcome (as difficulties). *a.*

حلاج *ḥallāj*, m. a comber, a carder of cotton. *a.*

حلال *ḥalāl*, legal, legitimate, lawful, right; (a woman) laying aside mourning for the death of her husband at the expiration of a hundred days (during which time she is not by law allowed to marry). *ḥalāl-khor*, m. a person of the lowest caste, generally a sweeper, or employed in the meanest and dirtiest occupations, so called because every thing is lawful food to him. *ḥalāl-khorī*, f. the business or state of a sweeper, &c.; a female sweeper, &c. *ḥalāl-k.*, a. to slay according to the forms prescribed by the *Muḥammadan* religion; to murder; to marry. *a.*

حلاله *ḥalāla*, f. a woman married again with her first divorcer, after she had been divorced by her second husband. *a.*

حلاوت *ḥalāwat*, f. sweetness; deliciousness. *a.*

حلب *ḥalab*, the city of Aleppo in Syria. *a.*

حلبه *ḥulba*, fenugreek, tragacanth. *a.*

حلبي *ḥalabī*, of or belonging to Aleppo, made in Aleppo (a mirror). *a.*

حلتيت *ḥiltīt* (also *ḥiltīṡ*), assafœtida. *a.*

حلف *ḥalf*, an oath, a vow. *ḥalf-nāma*, an affidavit, a declaration upon oath. *ḥalf durogh*, perjury, false-swearing. *a.*

حلق *ḥalq*, } m. the wind-pipe, the throat.
حلقوم *ḥulqūm*, } *ḥalq par chhurī achhnā* (explained by *kāwish honā*), to be menaced. *a.*

حلقه *ḥalqa*, m. a ring, a circle; a loop, a button-hole; a kind of fireworks; a knocker (of a door); a village circuit or boundary-line. *ḥalqa-ba-gosh*, a slave, a servant, *i.e.* one who wears a ring in his ear as a badge of servitude. *ḥalqa-ba-goshī*, f. servitude, slavery. *ḥalqa-zan*, one who knocks. *a.*

حلقي *ḥalqī*, guttural letters, (ح خ ه ع غ). *a.*

حلم *ḥilm*, m. coolness, temperateness; mildness, affability, gravity. *be-ḥilm*, merciless, severe. *a.*

حلوا *ḥalwā*, m. a kind of sweetmeat made of flour, ghī, and sugar. *ḥalwā-sohan*, m. name of a sweetmeat. *ḥalwā-machhī*, the pomflet fish. *ḥalwā nikālnā*, a. to beat severely. *a.*

حلوان *ḥalwān*, m. a kid, a lamb. *a.*

حلوائي *ḥalwā,ī*, m. a confectioner; a maker or vendor of *ḥalwā*, q. v.; name of a caste or tribe in the lower Du,āb. *a.*

حلواين *ḥalwāyan*, f. a confectioner's wife; the appellation of a caste or tribe in the lower Du,āb. *a.*

حلول *ḥulūl*, m. descent; stopping or sojourning; entering or penetrating; transmigration. *a.*

حلوه *ḥalwa* (v. *ḥalwā*), sweetmeat. *a.*

حلويات *ḥalwiyāt* (pl.), sweetmeats. *a.*

حله *ḥulla*, m. a robe, a garment. *a.*

حله *ḥalla* (for *ḥamla*), assault, attack. *h.*

حلي *ḥulī*, f. jewels, ornaments. *a.*

حليم *ḥalīm*, mild, affable, unassuming, tractable; a kind of food dressed in the *Muḥarram*. *a.*

حمار *ḥimār*, m. a male ass; the wild ass. *ḥammār*, an ass-driver. *a.*

حماري *ḥimārī*, asinine, stupid; f. stupidity. *a.*

حماقت *ḥimāqat*, f. folly, stupidity. *a.*

حمال *ḥammāl*, a porter, a carrier of burthens, a pālkī-bearer. *a.*

حماله *ḥamāla* or *ḥamālat*, bearing, becoming pregnant. *ḥammāla*, fem. (of *ḥammāl*), a woman who bears burdens, &c. *a.*

حمام *ḥammām*, m. a warm-bath, a bagnio. *a.*

حماما *ḥamāmā*, stone parsley, Jamaica pepper. *a.*

حمامي *ḥammāmī*, a bath or bagnio-keeper. *a.*

حمايت *ḥimāyat*, f. protection, defence, guardianship, patronage, countenance. *ḥimāyat-k.*, a. to defend, to patronise. *a.*

حمايتي *ḥimāyatī*, deliverer, protector. *a.*

حمائد *ḥamā,id* (pl. of حميده), praiseworthy qualities; laudable deeds or conduct. *a.*

حمائل *ḥamā,il*, f. a sword-belt hung from the shoulders; a necklace of flowers; a small *ḳur,ān* suspended to the neck as an amulet. *ḥamā,il-k.*, to sling across the shoulders (a gun or sword). *a.*

حمد *ḥamd*, f. praise (of God). *a.*

حمر *ḥamr*, حمرا *ḥamrā*, red, of a red colour; m. bitumen, naphtha. *a.*

حمق *ḥumḳ* or *ḥumuk*, m. foolishness, stupidity, inadvertency. *a.*

حمقا *ḥumaḳā* (pl.), fools, stupid fellows. *a.*

حمل *ḥaml*, m. a burden, a load. *ḥaml-k.*, a. to load, to impute, to accuse, to ascribe; the fruit (of the womb), pregnancy; fruit (of any kind). *ḥamal*, the first sign of the zodiac, called Aries or the ram. *a.*

حمله *ḥamla*, m. an attack, onset, storming, an assault; (fig.) *concubitus*. *a.*

حمي *ḥummā*, a fever (pl. *ḥummayāt*). *a.*

حميت *ḥamīyat*, f. ardour, impetuosity, zeal; a nice sense of honour. *a.*

حميد *ḥamīd*, حميده *ḥamīda*, praised; laudable, glorious. *akhlāḳi ḥamīda*, praiseworthy disposition. *auṣāfi-ḥamīda*, laudable qualifications. *a.*

حميل *ḥamīl*, m. a son of a whore, a bastard; a surety; herbs, sticks, &c., carried down by the stream. *a.*

حنا *ḥinnā*, f. the tree with which the Indians stain their hands and feet (*Lawsonia inermis*). *a.*

حنائي *ḥinnā,ī*, of the colour of *ḥinnā*. *a.*

حنجر *ḥanjar*, حنجرا *ḥanjarā*, حنجره *ḥanjara*, m. the throat, the gullet, the windpipe. *a.*

حنظل *ḥanẓal*, wild gourd, colocynth. *a.*

حوا *ḥawwā*, Eve, the mother of mankind. *a.*

حوادث *ḥawādis̤* (pl. of حادثه), accidents, occurrences; misfortunes, calamities. *a.*

حوادثات *ḥawādis̤āt*, occurrences, misfortunes. *a.*

حواري *ḥawārī*, m. having a white skin; a washerman, fuller; a friend, a companion; an apostle, a disciple or apostle (of Jesus Christ); a friend, associate, companion (of *Muḥammad*). *a.*

حواس *ḥawāss* (pl. of حاسّه), the senses. *ḥawāss-bākhta*, out of one's senses. *ḥawāssi khamsa*, the five senses. *a.*

حواشي *ḥawāshī* (pl. of حاشيه), followers, attendants; margins, borders. *a.*

حواصل *ḥawāṣil*, m. (pl. of حوصله q. v.), stomachs, &c.; an animal of whose skin they make garments; a pelican. *a.*

حوالات *ḥawālāt*, حوالجات *ḥawālajāt*, f. (pl. of حواله) things given in charge, trusts, deposits. *a.*

حوالدار *ḥawāl-dār* (for *ḥawāla-dār*), m. a military officer of inferior rank, vulg. havildar. *a. p*

حواله *ḥawāla*, m. charge, custody, care. *ḥawāle*, in the charge or care of any one, &c. *a.*

حوالدار *ḥawāla-dār*, one employed to protect the grain before it is stored; a steward or agent employed for the management of a village. *a.*

حوالي *ḥawālī*, f. environs, outskirts, suburbs. *ḥawālī,e shahr*, environs of a city. *a.*

حوت *ḥūt*, f. fish; the sign Pisces. *a.*

حور *ḥūr*, حوري *ḥūrī*, f. a virgin of paradise; a celestial bride promised by Muhammad to all good Musalmāns in the next world; a black-eyed nymph. *a.*

حوزه *ḥauza*, m. a track, side, part, middle. *a.*

حوصله *ḥauṣila* or *ḥauṣala*, m. the stomach, maw, crop; (met.) resolution, desire, ambition, capacity, spirit. *ḥauṣila-mand*, ambitious, aspiring. *a.*

حوض *ḥauẓ*, m. a reservoir, a pond, the basin of a fountain, a tank, vat. *a.*

حول *ḥaul*, changing, returning; passing by or over; detaining; power, strength; deceit; a year. *ḥawal*, squinting, blind of an eye. *a.*

حولدار *ḥawaldār* (for *ḥawāl-dār*, q. v.). *a. p.*

حويلي *ḥawelī*, house, dwelling, habitation; lands in the vicinity of towns, the revenues of which were devoted to the support of the military garrison. *a.*

حي *ḥaiy*, alive; a family, a tribe. *ḥaiy kaiyūm*, eternal, immortal. *ḥaiy lā-yamūt*, eternal imperishable. *a.*

حيا *ḥayā*, f. modesty, shame. *ḥayā-dār*, modest, possessed of modesty. *a.*

حيات *ḥayāt*, f. life. *ḥayāti tāza*, new life, regeneration (used to express recovery from severe illness), the pleasure derived from meeting with a friend. *a.*

حياتي *ḥayātī*, existence, life. *a.*

حيازت *ḥiyāzat*, lit. accumulation; (in law) joint acquisition of an article (having no owner) by two or more persons. *a.*

حيثيت *ḥais̤iyat*, f. ubiquity, universality; capacity, ability, merit; conditional proposition. *a.*

حيدر *ḥaidar*, a lion, a man's name. *ḥaidar-ābād*, Hyderabad, name of a city in the Deccan, and of another in Guzerat. *ḥaidarī*, of or belonging to Haidar. *a.*

حيران *ḥairān*, perplexed, astonished, confounded, disturbed, fatigued. *a.*

حيراني *ḥairānī*, f. astonishment, perturbation, confusion or distraction of mind. *a.*

حيرت *ḥairat*, f. stupor, perturbation, astonishment. *ḥairat-afzā*, increasing one's amazement; astonishing. *ḥairat-zada*, struck with astonishment. *a.*

حيرتي *ḥairatī*, astonished, bewildered. *a.*

حيز *haiyiz*, m. a place, part, a tract of ground; a court-yard, an area. *a.*

حيص بيص *haiṣbaiṣ*, f. perplexity, hesitation, suspense, a perplexed business, a dilemma. *a.*

حيض *ḥaiẓ*, f. the menses. *waladu-l-ḥaiẓ*, a term of reproach. *a.*

حيضي *ḥaiẓī*, a wicked brat. *a.* [sure. *a.*

حيطه *ḥīṭa*, m. a court, a place, an enclo-

حيف *ḥaif*, m. iniquity, violence, oppression; interj. ah! alas! *ḥaif bāshad ki*, 'twere a pity that. *a.*

حيفي *ḥaifī*, grief, sorrow, regret. *a.*

حيل *ḥiyal* (pl. of حيله), tricks, stratagems. *a.*

حيله *ḥīla*, m. stratagem, deceit, pretence, trick. *ḥīla-bāz*, artful, a cheat. *ḥīla-bāzī*, knavery, artfulness. *ḥīla-sāz* or *ḥīla-gar*, a knave, "an artful dodger;" *ḥīla-sāzī*, *ḥīla-garī*, knavery. *a.*

حين *ḥīn*, m. time, interval or period of time. *ḥīnī ḥayāt*, life-time. *a.*

حيوان *ḥaiwān*, m. a brute or irrational animal, in contradistinction to *insān*, a human being. *a.*

حيوانات *ḥaiwānāt*, animals, living creatures. *a.*

حيواني *ḥaiwānī*, brutal, beastly. *a.*

حيوانيت *ḥaiwānīyat*, brutality; in contradistinction to *insānīyat*, humanity. *a.*

حيوت *ḥayāt* or *ḥai,at*, life, existence. *a.*

خ

خ *khe*, called *khā,e manḳūṭa* or *khā,e mu'jama*, the seventh letter of the Arabic, the ninth of the Persian, and tenth of the Hindūstānī alphabets, has the sound of the Greek χ: it is a guttural letter, formed by compression of the top of the throat near the mouth, and contains a mixture of the sounds of *k* and *h*: it has no corresponding sound in the English language, but is expressed by the Scottish pronunciation of *ch* in the word Auchtermuchty. In *abjad* it stands for 600. *a. p.*

خا *khā* (v. *khā,īdan*), in comp. chewing or gnawing; as, *ṭūṭī,e shakar-khā*, the sugar-chewing parrot. *p.*

خاتم *khātim*, a ring worn on the fingers; a seal. *khātimu-l-ambiyā*, the seal of prophets, i.e. *Muḥammad*. *a.*

خاتمه *khātima*, m. conclusion, epilogue, finis, end. *khātima bandī*, f. a kind of workmanship, of which they make bows; the ceiling of a roof. *a.*

خاتون *khātūn*, f. a lady, a matron. *khātūn-i jannat*, the queen of heaven (the title given to Fātima the daughter of *Muḥammad*). *p.*

خاد *khād*, a kite; a falcon; an eagle. *p.*

خادم *khādim*, m. a servant. *khādimu-ṭ-ṭulabā*, a public teacher, a professor (of a college). *khādim-i dargāh*, a servant who takes care of a tomb (mosque, &c.). *a.* [tombs, mosques, &c. *d.*

خادمان *khādimān*, pl. servants in charge of

خادمه *khādima*, a female servant. *a.*

خادمي *khādimī*, f. service, serving. *a.*

خار *khār*, m. a thorn, spine, thistle, bramble; a spur, a cock's spur. *khār ānkhon kā*, an eye-sore, disagreeable. *khār-bunān*, roots of thorns or brambles. *khār-bast* or *khār-bandī*, a fence or hedge; a stockade. *khār-pusht*, m. a porcupine (*Hystrix*). *khār-khār*, disquietude. *khār-dār*, troublesome, arduous, barbed, thorny. *khār-kash*, a woodcutter. *khār-kan*, one who digs or plucks up thorns. *khār o khas*, m. sweepings, any thing vile. *p.*

خارا *khārā*, a stone of extreme hardness; a species of waved silk; adj. flinty or hard, as a stone. *khārā-sang*, a kind of marble. *p.*

خارج *khārij*, external, without, beyond, outcast. *khārij-k.*, a. to exclude. *khārij-honā*, to be excluded, exempted. *khārij jam'*, land separated from the revenue, and sold by the zamindārs; it is hereditary, and consequently alienable by the holder of it, whether by deed, gift, or otherwise. *a.*

خارجه *khārija*, m. the word at the bottom of a page, which is repeated at the beginning of the next, an asterisk, a catch word. *a.*

خارجي *khārijī*, m. a seceder, a schismatic, a rebel; a sect of *Muḥammadans* who do not reckon 'Alī among the legal successors of the prophet: they are the mortal enemies of the *Rāfiẓīs* or *Shī'as*, who reject *Abū-bakr*, *'Umar*, and *'Uṣmān*, while *Sunnīs* consider the four as legal successors. Yet the *Shī'as* apply the term *khārijī* to the *Sunnīs*. *a.*

خارز *khāraz*, a dish prepared of eggs. *d.*

خارش *khārish*, } f. the itch, the scab, the
خارشت *khārisht*, } mange. *p.*

خارشتي *khārishtī*, mangy, itchy, scabby. *p.*

خاري *khārī*, f. (for *khwārī*) meanness, ignominy. *p.*

خازن *khāzin*, a treasurer, custodier. *a.*

خاستن *khāstan* (r. *khez*), to rise up, to go away. *p.*

خاسته *khāsta*, (in comp.) risen, sprung up. *p.*

خاشاك *khāshāk*, m. sweepings, chips, leaves, shavings, rubbish. *p.*

خاص *khāṣṣ*, excellent, noble, pure, unmixed; particular, private, what is kept for the king's (or master's) private use, own, proper, peculiar, single, gentle: in revenue language the term is applied to lands the rents of which are not leased out, but collected immediately by the officers of government, appointed for that sole purpose. *khāṣṣ-ajīr*, private or domestic servants or slaves. *khāṣṣ-le,o*, land under the management of the sovereign. *khāṣṣ-chela*, the head disciple in a monastery. *khāṣṣ-ḥāl*, a rent-free tenure. *khāṣṣ-maḥāl*, districts under the management of government. *khāṣṣ-navīs*, a private secretary; a government clerk or accountant. *khāṣṣ-navīsī*. of or relating to government clerks or accountants. *khāṣṣ-zamīn*, land of which the revenue is collected directly by government. *khāṣṣ-bardār*, m. a servant who in a great man's retinue carries a firelock. *khāṣṣ-ta'alluḳ*, lands exclusively belonging to government, from the original proprietors having died without heirs. *khāṣṣ khawāṣṣ*, attendants, domestics, ministers, properties, qualities. *khāṣṣ-maḥal*, m. private apartment, the apartments of married women (in opposition to *khurd maḥal*, or apartments of the concubines); (met.) first-married wife. *khāṣṣ o 'ām*, noble and plebeian. *a.*

خاصان ***khāṣṣān***, pl. the noble; persons of high rank. *a.*

خاصة ***khāṣṣat***, special, private. *khāṣṣatan*, especially, in particular. *a.*

خاصدان ***khāṣṣ-dān***, m. a wallet, a portmanteau. *p.*

خاصگي ***khāṣṣagī***, f. excellence, nobility; peculiarity. *p.*

خاصه ***khāṣṣa***, excellent, pure, noble, elegant, good, charming, delightful, pretty, fine, virtuous; m. dinner, more particularly a king's meal; a kind of fine cotton cloth. *a.*

خاصي ***khāṣṣī***, excellent, noble. *a.*

خاصيت ***khāṣṣiyat***, f. quality, peculiarity, innate property, natural disposition. *a.*

خاطب ***khāṭib***, a preacher, a public speaker. *a.*

خاطر ***khāṭir***, f. the heart, soul, inclination, memory, propensity, account, sake, will, choice. *khāṭir-āzurda*, melancholy, dejected, sad. *khāṭir-āshufta*, distressed, dispirited, agitated. *khāṭir-jam'*, collected, comforted, contented, tranquil, at ease; f. satisfaction, assurance, encouragement. *khāṭir-jam'ī*, f. comfort, confidence. *khāṭir-khwāh*, agreeable to one's wishes. *khāṭir-dārī*, encouragement, comfort, gratification, satisfaction. *khāṭir-dāsht*, f. complaisance, regard. *khāṭir rakhnā*, a. to conciliate, to encourage, to comfort, to quiet. *khāṭir-k.*, a. to fondle; to be desirous of pleasing; to encourage, to comfort. *khāṭir men rakhnā*, a. to remember. *khāṭir men lānā*, a. to regard, to attend to. *khāṭir-nishān*, imprinted on the memory, by heart. *khāṭir-nishīn*, fixed in the memory, by heart; chosen, beloved. *a.*

خاطرًا ***khāṭiran***, willingly; by heart or memory. *a.*

خاطف ***khāṭif***, seizing, snatching, removing. *a.*

خافي ***khāfī***, occult, concealed. *a.*

خاقان ***khāḳān***, m. a king, emperor (the term is generally applied to the sovereign of China and Chinese Tartary). *a.*

خاقاني ***khāḳānī***, royal, imperial; name of a most celebrated poet of Persia. *a.*

خاك ***khāk***, f. dust, earth. *khāk-bāzī*, f. playing with dust. *khāk-phānknā*, a. to wander, to stray. *khāk-toda*, m. a butt or mark of earth, for shooting arrows at. *khāk chhānnā*, (lit. to sift the dust) expresses excessive labour and exertion in fruitless search. *khāk ḍālnī*, is used to express the concealing of those things from the disclosure of which disgrace may be expected. *khāk-rob*, m. a sweeper, a menial servant of the lowest caste. *khāk-roba*, m. sweepings. *khāk-zād*, earth-born, made of dust. *khāk-sār*, base, mean, lowborn, a humble suppliant. *khāk-sārī*, f. meanness, humility. *khāk sir par uṛānā*, a. to lament. *khāk siyāh-k.*, a. to plunder and lay waste a country, to depredate. *khāk-sho*, m. a person in the mint who washes the ashes to recover any particles of bullion which may have fallen; the man who prepares earth for brick-making or pottery. *khāk-k.*, a. to waste, to ruin, to demolish. *khāk men milānā*, a. to destroy, to spoil, to demolish. *khāk men milnā*, n. to die, to perish; to be ruined, demolished. *khāk ho jānā*, n. to moulder or pine away. *a.*

خاكا ***khākā***, m. a plan, sketch, draft, outline, delineation. *p.*

خاكتوده ***khāk-tūda***, a mark or butt of earth for shooting at. *p.*

خاكدان ***khāk-dān***, m. a place where rubbish is placed; also a sack, &c. in which it is carried; (met.) the world. *p.*

خاكستر ***khākistar***, f. ashes; calx of metals. *khākistar-honā*, n. to be calcined or reduced to ashes. *p.*

خاكستري ***khākistarī***, ash-coloured. *p.*

خاكشي ***khākshī***, f. a small weight used by goldsmiths; a kind of red bramble; a small red seed used in medicine, chiefly as an eye-salve. *p.*

خاكي ***khākī***, dusty, terrestrial, earthen; a Hindū mendicant who smears his body with the ashes of cow-dung; the name of a kind of arrow. *khākī anḍā*, m. an addled egg, wind egg; a term of reproach. *p.*

خاكيان ***khākiyān***, pl. a denomination of *Muhammadan faḳīrs*. *p.*

خاگ ***khāg***, an egg. *khāgīna*, m. fried eggs, a kind of dish made of eggs, an omelet, pancake, &c. *p.*

خال ***khāl***, m. a mole on the face (black and ornamental); an artificial spot made for ornament; a maternal uncle, mother's brother. *khāl-khāl*, thick, close, thickly spread; little, scarce; adv. occasionally, now and then. *a*

خالا ***khālā***, f. maternal aunt, mother's sister. *khālā kā ghar* or *khālā māmā kā ghar*, (lit. the house of one's aunt) signifies a place of rest and security. *a.*

خالاتي ***khālātī***, descended from or related to the maternal aunt. *khālātī bhā,ī*, a cousin, son of maternal aunt. *a.*

خالاوي ***khālā,ī***, m. the husband of a mother's sister, (same as *khālū*). *a.*

خالص ***khāliṣ***, pure, sincere; m. a friend. *a.*

خالصه ***khāliṣa***, pure, sincere; m. the exchequer, or royal office for the collection and receipt of the revenues, and for the determination of causes relating thereto; land held immediately from government. *khāliṣa kachahrī*, the exchequer office. *khāliṣa sharīfa*, the royal exchequer. *a.*

خالق ***khāliḳ***, the Creator, the Deity. *a.*

خالو ***khālū***, maternal uncle, husband of a mother's sister. *a.*

خاله ***khāla***, (v. *khālā*), f. a mother's sister. *a.*

خالي ***khālī***, empty, vacant; pure, mere, only, unmixed; unoccupied, unemployed. *khālī-hāth*, empty-handed, pennyless, unarmed. *khālī-mahīna*, the month Shawāl; lit. the vacant month, so called from being the only month in which no festival takes place. *p.*

خام ***kh**ām*, raw, unripe, immature. *khām-āmdanī*, gross receipts of revenue in rupees of sort. *khām-pāra*, a term of abuse, applied to a woman who has been cohabited with before the age of maturity. *khām-shurwā*, m. half boiled soup. *khām-shob*, half-washed, rinsed *khām-ṭab'*, foolish, dull. *khām-ṭab'ī*, stupidity, perversity. *khām-ṭama'*, entertaining vain desires. *khām-ṭama'ī*, a depraved or vain desire. *khām-'aḳlī*, m. folly, weak understanding. *khām-kārī*, awkwardness, unskilfulness. *p.*

خامش ***khāmush***, silent, } same as *khāmosh*, *khāmoshī*. *p.*
خامشي ***khāmushī***, f. silence, }

خاموش ***khāmosh***, silent; m. a disease in [horses. *p.*

خاموشي ***khāmoshī***, f. silence, taciturnity. *p.*

خامه ***khāma***, m. a pen, a writing-reed. *khāma-dān*, m. a pen-case. *p.*

خامي ***khāmī***, f. rawness, unripeness; loss. *p.*

خان ***khān***, m. lord, prince, a title principally used by *paṭhāns*: in Persia this title is applied to a prince or governor of a province, but in Hindūstān it signifies the lowest order of *Mughal* nobility. *p.*

خانجات ***khānajāt*** (pl. of خانه), houses, dwellings, mansions, &c. *p.*

خان‌خانان ***khān-khānān***, lord of lords, a [prime-minister. *s.*

خاندار ***khān-dār***, } properly *khāna-dār*, q. v. under *khāna*. *p.*
خانداري ***khān-dārī***, }

خاندان ***khāndān***, m. family, household. *khāndān kī 'alāmat*, f. armorial bearings. *p.*

خانسامان ***khānsāmān***, m. a house-steward. *p.*

خانساماني ***khānsāmānī***, f. the household department, including all expenditures on that score. *p.*

خانقاه ***khānḳāh***, }
خانقه ***khānaḳah***, } f. a monastery, a religious establishment for holy men. *p.*
خانگاه ***khānagāh***, }

خانگي ***khāngī***, domestic; f. a prostitute. *p.*

خانم ***khānam***, a lady, a woman of rank, a princess. *p.*

خانمان ***khānmān***, also *khān-o-mān*, m. household furniture, domestic, every thing belonging to the house. *khānmān-kharāb*, ruined, desolated. *p.*

خانواده ***khānawāda***, a family household; the mistress of a family; adj. noble, of an ancient family. *p.*

خانه ***khāna***, m. house, place, dwelling; a drawer, a partition, compartment; department. *khāna-ābād*, a benediction, meaning, may your house flourish. *khāna-ba-dosh*, (used substantively) a traveller, a pilgrim, a gypsey, rover, sojourner. *khāna-bar-andāz*, a prodigal, a spendthrift. *khāna-pardāzī*, domestic management, economy. *khāna-jang*, quarrelsome, a brawler. *khāna-jangī*, f. domestic strife, civil war, skirmish, duel, bickering. *khāna-khāna*, cellular. *khāna-kharāb*, ruined. *khāna-kharābī*, f. ruination. *khāna-khudā*, master of a house. *khāna-dār*, m. family man. *khāna dārī*, f. the state of the master of a family. *khāna-dāmād*, a son-in-law, who lives in the house of his father-in-law. *khāna-dost*, fond of staying at home (a term of abuse). *khāna-zād*, the child of a slave. As the last member of a compound *khāna* denotes place or residence, as *kutub-khāna*, a book-house, library. *p.*

خانه‌باري ***khāna-bārī***, a family house. *p.*

خاور ***khāwar***, m. the west, but often used by poets for the east, also for the sun. *p.*

خاوران ***khāwarān***, the east and west; the name of a district in *khurāsān*, the birthplace of the poet Anwarī. *p.*

خاوري ***khāwarī***, solar, western; also eastern. *p.*

خاوند ***khāwind*** or ***khāwand***, m. lord, master, husband. *khāwind-k.*, to marry (a woman). *p.*

خاوندانه ***khāwindāna***, in the manner of a lord or master. *p.*

خاوندي ***khāwindī***, f. dominion, mastership. *p.*

خائف ***khā,if***, timid, pusillanimous, afraid. *a.*

خائن ***khā,in***, a deceiver, a traitor. *a.*

خايه ***khāya***, m. a testicle; an egg. *khāya-bardār*, a cringing fellow. *khāya-bardārī-k.*, a. to cringe. *khāya chumānā*, a. to disregard, to be disobedient, to be stubborn, not to submit to obedience. *khāya sahlānā*, a. to curry favour. *khāya-kashīda*, m. an eunuch. *p.*

خائيدن ***khā,īdan***, to gnaw, to chew. *p.*

خباثت ***khabāsat***, f. wickedness, depravity. *khabāsati jibillī*, innate depravity. *a.*

خباز ***khabbāz***, m. a baker. *khabbāzī*, f. baking, the business of a baker. *a.*

خبث ***khubs***, m. malice, malignity, spitefulness, perfidy, impurity. *a.*

خبر ***khabar***, f. news, advices, rumours, report, fame, account. *khabar basant kī pūchhnī*, to ask after the *basant*, q.v., expresses extreme ignorance or negligence. *khabari khiẓarī*, report, sudden news, guessing what is to happen [*khiẓar* (v. *khwāja khiẓar*), was a prophet, skilled in divination, and hence, when from certain symptoms the public guess at the intentions of government, &c., intelligence of such intentions, &c., is called *khabari khiẓarī*]. *khabar-dār*, careful, cautious; informed; m. an informer, a spy, a scout; interj. have a care! *khabar-dārī*, f. caution, care; informing. *khabar rakhnā*, n. to be informed, acquainted. *khabar-'aṭar*, intelligence, news. *khabar-k.* or *denā*, a. to apprise, to inform. *khabar-gīr*, a spy, an informer; a protector, a patron. *khabar-gīrī*, f. spying, informing; aiding, protecting. *khabar lenā*, a. to accommodate, to allow, to give, to take care of, to look after, to inquire into. *khabar honā*, n. to be informed. *a.*

خبرت ***khibrat***, f. wisdom, learning; experience, experiment, trial, proof. *a.*

خبط ***khabṭ***, m. making a mistake; madness, insanity. *a.*

خبطي ***khabṭī***, erring; mad, insane. *a.*

خبيث ***khabīs***, wicked, malignant, impure; m. an evil spirit. *a.*

خبيثات ***khabīsāt***, (pl.) things impure. *a.*

خبيثي ***khabīsī***, f. a malignant woman. *a.*

خبير ***khabīr***, knowing, wise, skilful, learned. *a.*

ختك ***khutak*** or ***khuttak***, m. a club, a stick. *p.*

ختكا ***khutkā***, m. a club; the penis. *p.*

ختم ***kh*atm**, m. conclusion, seal, end; (used adjectively) done, finished. *khatmu-'l-ambiyā* or *-mursalīn*, the last of the prophets or apostles, Muhammad. *khatm-k.*, to conclude. *khatm-h.*, to be finished. *a.*

ختمي ***kh*atamī**, a complete perusal of the kur,ān, from beginning to end. *a.*

ختن ***kh*atan**, m. circumcision; feast; the nearest relations to a woman; a son-in-law. *a.*

ختن ***kh*utan**, a district of Tartary famed for musk; also Tartary. *p.*

ختنه ***kh*atna**, m. circumcision. *a.*

ختیاں ***kh*atiyāṅ**, flax, lint, linen stuff. *d.*

خجالت ***kh*ijālat**, f. bashfulness, shame. *a.*

خجسته ***kh*ujista**, happy, fortunate, auspicious, blest. *p.*

خجل ***kh*ajal**, modest, bashful, ashamed. *a.*

خجلت ***kh*ijlat**, f. shame (v. *khijālat*). *khijlat uṭhānī*, or *-khānī*, n. to blush. *khijlat-zada*, struck with shame, utterly abashed. *a.*

خچاخچ ***kh*achā*kh*ach**, the sound of a spear or battle-axe, or of treading in clay or mire. *h.*

خچر ***kh*achchar**, m. a mule. *khachchar-bān*, a mule driver, a muleteer. *h.*

خچرخچر ***kh*achar-*kh*achar**, } m. an imitative
خچڑخچڑ ***kh*achaṛ-*kh*achaṛ**, } sound. *h.*

خد ***kh*add**, the cheek, the face. *a.*

خدا ***kh*udā**, m. God. *khudā-parast*, worshipping God. *khudā-tars*, fearing God, virtuous. *khudā-dād*, (*Deodatus*) given or bestowed by God; an epithet applied to part of the Mysore territory under Tippū Sultān. *khudā-khudā karke*, with difficulty, by hook or by crook. *khudā ḥāfiz*, adieu, farewell. *khudā-kare*, would to God. *khudā kyā kare*, what will fate produce? or what is the will of God? (an expression used in doubtful circumstances). *khudā ke māre honā*, to be unfortunate, to suffer by the decrees of fate. *khudā na karda* or *-na khwāsta*, God forbid. *p.*

خدام ***kh*uddām** (pl. of خادم), domestics, servants, ministers. *a.*

خداوند ***kh*udā-wand**, m. possessor, master, husband. *khudāwandi ni'mat*, (lit. beneficent master) a form of address to superiors, a patron; rich, opulent. *p.*

خداوندگار ***kh*udāwandigār**, God, the creator of the universe. *p.*

خداوندي ***kh*udāwandī**, f. lordship, sovereignty, divinity, providence. *p.*

خداءي ***kh*udā,ī**, f. the Godhead, divinity; the world. *khudā,ī rāt*, singing hymns and watching all night, a religious feast kept by women. *khudā,ī raḥm*, a kind of food given to the poor in completion of a vow. *khudā,ī ghar men ānā*, used to express pride from the accession of fortune. *p.*

خدايا ***kh*udāyā**, O God! O Lord! *p.*

خداءي تعالی ***kh*udā,e-ta'ālā**, God the supreme, the Almighty. *p. a.*

خدايگان ***kh*udāyagān**, a great king; a lord paramount. *p.*

خدشه ***kh*adsha**, m. fear, alarm, danger, doubt, question, apprehension, solicitude. *a.*

خدم ***kh*adam** (pl. of خادم), servants, domestics, retinue, attendants. *p.*

خدمات ***kh*idmāt** (pl. of خدمت), services, situations, appointments. *p.*

خدمت ***kh*idmat**, f. service, employment, office, appointment, duty, use; the royal presence. *khidmat-k.*, a. to serve, to attend, to wait on; (met.) to satirize, to beat. *khidmat-gār*, m. a male domestic who waits at table, a servant. *khidmat-gārnī*, a female domestic. *khidmat-gārī*, f. attendance, ministry. *a.*

خدمتگذار ***kh*idmat-guzār**, an attendant; adj. forward, obliging, ready to serve. *p.*

خدمتگذاري ***kh*idmat-guzārī**, f. service, devotedness, readiness to oblige or serve. *p.*

خدمتي ***kh*idmatī**, of or belonging to service, one who is employed; an official. *p.*

خدنگ ***kh*idang**, m. an arrow, the white poplar tree; a wood of which arrows are made. *p.*

خديو ***kh*adīv** or ***kh*adev**, a king, a mighty monarch or ruler, a great prince, a sovereign. *khadīv i Hind*, the sovereign of India. *p.*

خر ***kh*ar**, m. an ass. *khar bā tashdīd*, very stupid. *khari dashtī*, m. a wild ass, onager. *khari dajjāl*, the ass of Dajjāl (the latter was a notorious liar). *p.*

خراب ***kh*arāb**, bad, depraved; ruined, depopulated, deserted, lost, miserable; spoiled, waste, worthless (as land unfit for cultivation). *kharāb-ḥāl* or *kharāb-aḥwāl*, ruined as to circumstances. *kharāb-khasta*, ruined, desolated. *kharāb-karke kahnā*, a. to miscall. *a.*

خرابات ***kh*arābāt**, f. a tavern, a brothel. *a.*

خراباتي ***kh*arābātī**, m. a haunter of taverns and brothels; a rake, a debauchee. *a.*

خرابه ***kh*arāba**, m. devastation, ruin; adj. depraved, bad, ruined, desolated. *a.*

خرابي ***kh*arābī**, f. badness, depravity; ruin, desolation, mischief; misery, affliction. *a.*

خراٹا ***kh*arrāṭā**, m. snoring. *kharrāṭā mārnā*, to snore, to snort. *h.*

خراج ***kh*irāj** or ***kh*arāj**, m. tax, duty, rent, revenue, tribute. *khirāj-guzār*, a tributary. *khirāj lagānā*, a. to impose a tax, to assess. *a.*

خراجي ***kh*arājī** or ***kh*irājī**, (lands) paying rent, taxable, subject to taxation. *a.*

خراد ***kh*arād**, f. a lathe. *kharād chaṛhnā*, n. to be polished (as a clown by intercourse with the society of a city). *a.*

خرادنا ***kh*arādnā**, a. to turn in a lathe; (met.) to worry, to torment. *a.*

خرادي ***kh*arādī**, m. a turner, a carpenter. *a.*

خراسان ***kh*urāsān**, name of an extensive and rich country to the north-east of Persia. *p.*

خراساني ***kh**urāsānī*, of or relating to Khurāsān. ***kh**urāsānī ajwān*, black henbane. *p.*

خراش ***kh**arāsh*, m. excoriation, scraping, scratching; (used in comp. as) *dil-**kh**arāsh*, wounding or irritating the heart. *p.*

خراشنا ***kh**arāshnā*, to scratch, excoriate. *d.*

خراشه ***kh**arāsha*, m. scales or filings of iron, small debt. *p.*

خراشيدن ***kh**arāshīdan*, to scratch, excoriate. *p.*

خراط ***kh**arāṭ*, f. a turner's lathe. ***kh**arrāṭ*, a turner. *a.*

خراطي ***kh**arāṭī*, m. a turner; adj. turned. *a.*

خراطين ***kh**arāṭīn*, m. an earth-worm. *a.*

خرافات ***kh**urāfāt* (pl. of خرافت), fables, tales, romances, ludicrous sayings, smut. *a.*

خرافت ***kh**urāfat*, a fable, tale, romance. *a.*

خرام ***kh**irām*, f. pace, gait, stately gait. ***kh**irām-k.*, n. to march, to pace. ***kh**ush-**kh**irām*, walking elegantly. *p.*

خرامان ***kh**irāmān*, walking in a stately manner, moving gracefully. *p.*

خراميدن ***kh**irāmīdan*, to walk proudly or [gracefully. *p.*

خربزه ***kh**arbuza*, خربوزه ***kh**arbūza*, خرپوزه ***kh**arpūza*, m. a musk-melon, a cucumber. *p.*

خرج ***kh**arj* (v. ***kh**arch*), expenditure, &c. *a.*

خرجنا ***kh**arajnā*, to expend; to sell. *a. h.*

خرجي ***kh**urjī*, خرجين ***kh**urjīn*, a wallet, saddle-bag. *p.*

خرچ ***kh**arch*, m. expenditure, expense, price. ***kh**arch-i**kh**rājāt*, expenditure. ***kh**arch-ḥisāb*, a village account. ***kh**archi **kh**airāt*, a charge for charitable endowments. ***kh**archi mufaṣṣil*, provincial charges. ***kh**archi nānkār*, subsistence money for the zamīndār of a village, &c. ***kh**arch honā*, a. to be expended. *p.*

خرچنا ***kh**arachnā*, a. to expend; to sell. *p. h.*

خرچنگ ***kh**archang*, m. a crab (fish so called); a kind of herb. *p.*

خرچو ***kh**archū*, prodigal, expensive. *a.*

خرچه ***kh**archa*, m. costs of law-suits. *a.*

خرچي ***kh**archī*, f. price of stupration; prodigal; provision for a journey. *a.*

خرچين ***kh**urchīn*, a wallet, bag. *p.*

خرخاوند ***kh**ar-**kh**āwind*, m. master, owner, possessor (spoken contemptuously, like our vulgate, "a man as keeps a donkey of his own") *p.*

خرخر ***kh**ur-**kh**ur* or ***kh**ar-**kh**ar*, purring (of a cat). ***kh**ar-**kh**ar-k.*, a. to purr (like poor puss). *p.*

خرخرا ***kh**ar**kh**arā*, m. snoring. *a.*

خرخرانا ***kh**ar**kh**arānā*, to snore loudly. *h.*

خرخشه ***kh**ar**kh**asha*, m. a tumult, crowd; quarrelling; plea, litigation. *p.*

خرد ***kh**irad*, f. intellect, sense, wisdom. ***kh**irad-afroz*, illumining the intellect, name of a Hindūstanī book. ***kh**irad-mand* or *-war*, wise, sagacious. ***kh**irad-mandī*, or *-warī*, wisdom, sagacity. *p.*

خرد ***kh**urd*, minute, small, little. ***kh**urd-sāl*, of tender age. *p.*

خردخام ***kh**urd-**kh**ām*, bruised, broken, ground [small. *p.*

خردل ***kh**ardal*, mustard; mustard-seed. *a.*

خردمند ***kh**iradmand*, wise, intelligent. *p.*

خرده ***kh**urda*, a fragment, scrap, particle; small coins, small change (of money); pedlars small or trifling wares. *p.*

خردي ***kh**urdī*, f. childhood, infancy. *p.*

خرزهره ***kh**ar-zahra*, m. rhododaphne or rose bay (*Nerium oleander*). *p.*

خرس ***kh**irs*, m. a bear. ***kh**irs-bāzī*, f. rudeness, romping, bear's play. ***kh**irs-bachcha*, a young bear. *a.*

خرسك ***kh**irsak*, a kind of child's game, leap-frog, blindman's buff. *p.*

خرسند ***kh**ursand*, contented, satisfied, pleased. *p.*

خرسندي ***kh**ursandī*, f. content, pleasure, mirth. *p.*

خرسنگ ***kh**arsang*, m. a rival; a large stone. *a.*

خرشيد ***kh**urshīd* or ***kh**urshaid*, the sun. *p.*

خرطوم ***kh**arṭūm*, m. the proboscis of an elephant. *a.*

خرف ***kh**arif*, an old dotard. *a.*

خرفه ***kh**urfa*, m. that which is plucked from a tree; autumnal fruit. *a.*

خرفه ***kh**urfa*, m. purslain (*Portulaca oleraces*). *p.*

خرق عادت ***kh**arḳi'ādat*, f. contrary to nature; of unusual occurrence, a miracle; pl. ***kh**arḳi 'ādāt*, miracles, marvels. *a.*

خرقه ***kh**irḳa*, m. a religious mendicant's habit, made up of patches. ***kh**irḳa-posh*, a mendicant, a darwesh. *a.*

خرگاه ***kh**argāh*, f. a tent, pavilion, tabernacle; the royal tent, court, or palace. *p.*

خرگوش ***kh**argosh*, m. a hare, a rabbit. *p.*

خرم ***kh**urram*, pleasant, delightful; cheerful, pleased. ***kh**urram-dil*, of a cheerful disposition. *p.*

خرما ***kh**urmā*, m. a date (the fruit of the *Phœnix dactylifera*). *p.*

خرمست ***kh**ar-mast*, athletic; stupid. *p.*

خرمن ***kh**irman*, m. harvest; a barn. *p.*

خرموش ***kh**ar-mūsh*, a large species of rat. *p.*

خرمهره ***kh**ar-muhra*, m. the small shells called *kauṛī* (*Cypræa moneta*). *p.*

خرمي ***kh**urramī*, f. cheerfulness. *p.*

خرنفس ***kh**ar-nafs*, *magnum penem habens*. *a.*

خروار ***kh**ar-wār*, an ass-load, a measure varying from 700 to 850 lb weight. *p.*

خروج ***kh**urūj*, m. sally, egress; exodus. *a.*

خروس ***kh**urūs*, m. a dunghill cock. *p.*

خروش ***kh**arosh*, m. a crash, a loud noise, a tumult, a shout, clamour. *p.*

خروشان ***kh**aroshān*, making a loud noise. *p.*

خروشيدن ***kh**aroshīdan*, to shout, make a noise. *p.*

خريت ***kh**arīyat*, asininity, stupidity. *p.*

خريد ***kh**arīd*, f. purchase. ***kh**arīd-faro**kh**t* or ***kh**arīd o fаro**kh**t*, buying and selling. ***kh**arīd kā mol*, m. prime cost. *p.*

خريدار ***kh**arīdār*, m. a purchaser, buyer. *p.*

خريداري ***kh**arīdārī*, f. buying, purchasing, traffic, commerce; demand. *p.*

خريدن ***kh**arīdan*, to buy, purchase. *p.*

خريدنا ***kh**arīdnā*, a. to purchase, to buy. *p. h.*

خريده ***kh**arīda*, purchased, bought. *p.*

خريدي ***kh**arīdī*, purchasing; of or relating to buying. *p.*

خريطه ***kh**arīṭa*, m. a purse, packet, bag, mail; (letters are sent in India enclosed in small oblong bags, diversified according to the quality of the person to whom sent, being more or less rich or embroidered agreeably to their rank); (met.) a letter. *a.*

خريف ***kh**arīf*, f. autumn, the autumnal harvest; the first crop in the year, consisting chiefly of rice, which is sown in *baisākh* and gathered in *bhādon*. *a.*

خريفي ***kh**arīfī*, f. grown in harvest, autumnal. *a.*

خز ***kh**azz*, f. a coarse kind of silk cloth. *a.*

خزان ***kh**izān* or ***kh**azān*, f. autumn, the falling of the leaves. *p.*

خزانچي ***kh**azānchī*, m. a treasurer, a cash-keeper. *a.*

خزانه ***kh**azāna*, m. a treasury, magazine, granary, repository; treasure; the chamber of a gun. ***kh**azāna-dār*, a musket with a chamber. ***kh**azāna,e 'āmira*, m. the royal treasury. *a.*

خزاني ***kh**izānī*, autumnal; fading. *p.*

خزائن ***kh**azā,in* (pl. of خزانه), treasuries. *a.*

خزف ***kh**azaf*, earthenware, crockery. *a.*

خزينه ***kh**azīna*, m. (v. ***kh**azāna*) a treasury. *a.*

خس ***kh**as*, f. the name of a grass, of the roots of which *ṭattis* are made (*Andropogon muricatum*); a thistle, a weed in general; a lettuce. ***kh**as-posh*, covered with thorns. ***kh**as o **kh**ār* or ***kh**as o **kh**āshāk*, m. litter of things, rubbish, stuffs. *p.*

خس ***kh**ass*, lettuce. ***kh**assu-l-ḥimār*, wild lettuce. *a.*

خسارت ***kh**isārat*, f. loss, damage; perfidy, fraud; plunder, devastation. *a.*

خساست ***kh**asāsat* (v. ***kh**issat*), stinginess, &c. *a.*

خسانده ***kh**isānda*, m. an infusion (in medicine). *p.*

خسپيدن ***kh**uspīdan*, to sleep, slumber. *p.*

خست ***kh**issat*, f. stinginess, parsimony; vileness, baseness, meanness. *a.*

خست ***kh**ast*, wounded, sick (v. ***kh**asta*). *p.*

خستك ***kh**istak* (for ***kh**ishtak*), f. codpiece. *p.*

خستگي ***kh**astagī*, f. a wound, a sore; sickness; fatigue, exhaustion. *p.*

خسته ***kh**asta*, wounded; sick, infirm. ***kh**asta-ḥāl*, or *-jān*, or *-jigar*, or *-dil*, grieved, afflicted. ***kh**asta-ḥālī*, &c., grief, affliction. *p.*

خسخس ***kh**as-**kh**as* (v. ***kh**as*), grass, &c. *p.*

خسر ***kh**usar*, m. a fathe -in-law. *p.*

خسر ***kh**asar* or ***kh**asr*, m. damages, loss, injury, fraud; depreciation in value. *a.*

خسرو ***kh**usrau* or ***kh**usrū*, m. name of a celebrated king, Cyrus or Chosroes; a king in general; name of a celebrated poet of Dihlī. *p.*

خسروانه ***kh**usrawāna*, kingly, princely. *p.*

خسروي ***kh**usrawī*, belonging to a king, royal, imperial. *p.*

خسك ***kh**asak*, rubbish, a species of triangular thorns, caltrops. *p.*

خسوف ***kh**usūf*, m. an eclipse of the moon. *a.*

خسيس ***kh**asīs*, penurious, sordid; ignoble. *a.*

خشت ***kh**isht*, f. a brick or tile. ***kh**isht-paz* or *-zan*, a brickmaker. ***kh**ishti-pīrūza* or *-fīrūza*, turquoise-coloured bricks. *p.*

خشتك ***kh**ishtak*, a small brick, an arm-hole piece. *p.*

خشتي ***kh**ishtī*, made of brick. *p.*

خشخاش ***kh**ash**kh**āsh*, / خشخش ***kh**ash**kh**ash*, m. the poppy-seed or plant. *p.*

خشك ***kh**ushk*, dry, withered. ***kh**ushk-damāgh*, grieved. ***kh**ushk-damāghī*, f. grief. ***kh**ushk-sāl*, a general dearth, a dry year, a drought. ***kh**ushk-sālī*, f. drought, sterility. ***kh**ushk-maghz*, dry-brained, a fool or simpleton. *p.*

خشكه ***kh**ushka*, m. boiled rice. *p.*

خشكي ***kh**ushkī*, f. dryness, dearth occasioned by drought; dry land; high lands not flooded with water, and upon which millet and other grains not requiring much moisture are cultivated; adv. by land (in opposition to *tarī*, by water). *p.*

خشم ***kh**ashm*, m. anger, passion, rage, fury. ***kh**ashm-ālūd*, deformed with rage. ***kh**ashm-nāk* or ***kh**ashm-gīn*, passionate, angry. *p.*

خشن ***kh**ashin*, rough, severe, rude. *a.*

خشنود ***kh**ushnūd*, contented, satisfied. *p.*

خشنودي ***kh**ushnūdī*, f. satisfaction, pleasure, content. *p.*

خشوع *khushū'*, humiliation, humility. *a.*

خشونت *khushūnat*, f. asperity, rigidness, disdain, fierceness, indignation. *a.*

خصال *khiṣāl*, خصائل *khaṣā,il*, (pl. of خصلت) habits, good qualities, talents, virtues. *a.*

خصلت *khaṣlat*, f. habit, custom; quality, property, mode, talent, virtue, disposition, nature. *a.*

خصم *khaṣm*, m. an enemy, antagonist. *khaṣmi jānī*, a mortal foe. *khaṣam*, a husband. *khaṣam-mū,ī*, a widow, a woman whose husband is dead. *khaṣam-wālī*, f. a woman whose husband is alive, or as the law hath it, a woman under coverture. *a.*

خصمانه *khaṣamāna*, like a husband; taking care of, husbanding, housewifery. *a.*

خصمي *khaṣmī*, f. enmity, hatred. *khaṣmī,e jānī*, enmity unto death, mortal enmity. *a.*

خصوص *khuṣūṣ*, m. an affair, business, thing, particular; doing any thing particular; adv. particularly. *a.*

خصوصاً *khuṣūṣan*, particularly, especially. *a.*

خصوصيت *khuṣūṣiyat*, m. peculiarity, singularity, attachment, friendship. *a.*

خصومت *khuṣūmat*, f. enmity, strife, litigation, contention, quarrelling. *a.*

خصي *khaṣī*, m. a castrated animal (particularly a goat); an eunuch. *a.*

خصيب *khaṣīb*, the palm-tree. *a.*

خصيه *khuṣiya*, m. a testicle. *a.*

خضاب *khiẓāb*, m. tincture; tinging the nails and hair, but particularly the beard. *khiẓābi āhinī-k.*, a. to shave the beard. *a.*

خضر *khiẓar* or *khiẓr*, name of a prophet, commonly called *khwāja khiẓr*, see the word *khwāja*. *a.*

خضوع *khuẓū'*, humility, humiliation. *a.*

خط *khaṭṭ*, m. a letter, epistle; a line, stripe, lineament; writing, handwriting, chirography; moustaches, beard; name of a place in Arabia where spears are manufactured. *khaṭṭi istiwā*, the equator. *khaṭṭ ānā* or *nikalnā*, n. to appear (the beard). *khaṭṭ banānā* or *banwānā*, a. to shave the beard. *khaṭṭi jadī*, the tropic of Capricorn. *khaṭṭ-khuṭūṭ*, correspondence by letter. *khaṭṭi sabz*, the first appearance of a beard. *khaṭṭi-sharīf*, a royal order or firman, vulgarly called the "Haty sherif." *khaṭṭi sarṭān*, the tropic of Cancer. *khaṭṭi 'amūd*, a perpendicular line. *khaṭṭ kitābat*, correspondence. *khaṭṭi mutawāzī*, a parallel line. *khaṭṭi mustadīr*, a circular line. *khaṭṭi mustaķīm*, a right line. *khaṭṭi munḥanī*, a curved line. *a.*

خطا *khaṭā*, f. a mistake, error, fault, crime. *khaṭā-bakhsh*, m. a forgiver of errors, &c. *khaṭā-k.*, a. to err, to miss. *khaṭā-h.*, to fail, to be deficient. *a.*

خطا *khaṭā*, the country of Scythia beyond the Imaus, Northern China, thence called Cathay by Marco Polo and other early travellers. *p.*

خطاب *khiṭāb*, m. a title; conversation, speech, address. *khiṭāb-k.*, to address, accost. *a.*

خطابت *khiṭābat*, f. preaching, eloquence, rhetoric. *a.*

خطاط *khaṭṭāṭ*, a good writer or penman. *a.*

خطاءي *khaṭā,e* (v. *khaṭā*), Cathay. *khaṭā,ī*, of or belonging to Cathay or China. *a.*

خطب *khaṭb* or *khaṭab*, m. marrying, betrothing, contracting a marriage; a thing, cause, work. *a.*

خطبا *khuṭabā* (pl. of خطيب), preachers. *a.*

خطبه *khuṭba*, m. a sermon or oration delivered after Divine service every Friday, in which the preacher blesses *Muḥammad*, his successors, and the reigning sovereign. *a.*

خطر *khaṭar*, m. recollection, coming into the mind, thought, remembrance; danger, risk, fortune. *khaṭar-nāk*, frightful, dangerous. *a.*

خطرا *khaṭrā*, خطره *khaṭra*, m. danger, fear, risk, venture. *khaṭra-raf'-k.*, a. to ease nature. *khaṭra na-k.*, a. to make no bones of. *khaṭre men ḍālnā*, a. to endanger, to risk, to venture. *a.*

خطمي *khaṭmī* or *khiṭmī*, marshmallows. *a.*

خطور *khuṭūr*, m. coming, passing, entering; occurring, recollection, remembrance, dignity. *a.*

خطوط *khuṭūṭ* (pl. of *khaṭṭ*), epistles, letters. *khaṭṭ-khuṭūṭ*, letters, epistolary correspondence. *a.*

خطوطي *khuṭūṭī*, linear (demonstration, or measurement). *a.*

خطه *khiṭṭa*, m. a boundary line; a region, country, territory. *a.*

خطي *khaṭṭī*, lineal, literal; a spear made at the place called *khaṭṭ* in Arabia. *a.*

خطيب *khaṭīb*, m. a preacher. *a.*

خطيبي *khaṭībī*, f. the office of preacher. *a.*

خطير *khaṭīr*, great, honourable, dignified. *a.*

خف *khiff*, light (of weight or morals), undignified. *khuff*, m. a boot. *a.*

خفا *khafā*, f. a secret, a concealment. *a.*

خفا *khafā*, angry, vexed, enraged. *p.*

خفاچه *khaffācha*, a band of plundering Arabs. *p*

خفت *khuft*, sleep, the act of sleeping. *p.*

خفت *khiffat*, f. lightness of weight, levity of conduct, want of dignity, affront, disgrace. *khiffat i rā,ī*, weakness of intellect. *a.*

خفتا *khaftā* or *khafta*, mad, lunatic. *d.*

خفتان *khaftān*, a vest worn under a coat of mail. *p.*

خفتن *khuftan* (r. *khusp*) to sleep. *p.*

خفته *khufta*, asleep, sleeping; pl. *khuftagān*, those asleep; met. the dead. *p.*

خفقان **khafakān**, m. palpitation, hysterics: "it is described by native physicians as convulsions attended with fainting fits, weeping, deafness, palpitation of the heart, and slight delirium."—Binning. *a.*

خفقاني **khafakānī**, subject to palpitation. *a.*

خفگي **khafagī**, f. displeasure, anger. *p.*

خفه **khafa**, angry, enraged, vexed. *p.*

خفي **khafī**, a fine hand-writing (opposed to *jalī*); adj. secret, concealed. *a.*

خفيف **khafīf**, light, of no weight or consequence, of light character, immoral, undignified. *khafīfi dā,ira*, the centre of a circle. *khafīf-h.* to feel affronted. *h.*

خفيفه **khafīfa**, trivial, petty. *khafīfajarā,im*, petty offences. *khafīfa duzdī*, petty larceny or theft. *khafīfa mukaddama*, a trivial suit or case. *a.*

خفيه **khufya** or **khufyat**, disguised, concealed. *khufyatan*, secretly. *khufya-navis*, m. one whose business is to write intelligence secretly. *khufya-navisī*, the office of secret intelligencer. *a.*

خل **khall**, m. vinegar. **khill**, a friend. *a.*

خلا **khalā**, m. vacancy, vacuity. *khalā-malā*, unfeigned friendship. *a.*

خلاب **khilāb**, m. mire, clay, filth. *p.*

خلاتي **khalātī** (v. *khalerā*), descended from a maternal aunt, &c. *a.*

خلاص **khalāṣ**, m. freedom, release; adj. free, liberated, redeemed, done, out. *khalāṣ-patra*, a deed of release. *khalāṣ-k.*, a. to release. *khalāṣ honā*, n. to be freed, to emit; to calve, to be brought to bed; *emissio seminis, semen emittere*. *a.*

خلاصه **khulāṣa**, also **khulāṣat**, m. essence, the best part of any thing; abstract, abridgment, conclusion, inference, moral; spacious, roomy: in Dakh. it is vulgarly used for *khalāṣ*, freedom, free, &c. *a.*

خلاصي **khalāṣī**, f. freedom, liberation, discharge; m. a native sailor or artilleryman, a tent-pitcher; vulgarly called by Europeans *Clashee*. *a.*

خلاف **khilāf**, m. opposition, contradiction; falsehood. *khilāfi rā,e*, against one's opinion or will. *khilāfi shar'* against law and justice. *khilāfi 'akl*, contrary to reason. *a.*

خلافت **khilāfat**, f. the office of caliph, deputyship, lieutenancy, &c.; imperial dignity, monarchy; more especially the succession of princes who ruled at Damascus and Bagdad from the time of Muḥammad to that of Hūlagū Khān. *a.*

خلاق **khallāk**, (super. of *khalk*, used substantively) the Creator, the Almighty. *a.*

خلال **khilāl**, m. a toothpick; middle; ruin, damage, defect. *a.*

خلالت **khalālat**, f. sincere friendship; bits of meat sticking between the teeth. *a.*

خلان **khullān** (pl. of خليل), intimate friends. *a.*

خلائق **khalā,ik** (pl. of خلق), men, people, the creation, created beings. *a.*

خلت **khullat**, f. friendship. *a.*

خلخال **khalkhāl**, m. a ring of gold or silver worn round the ankle with bells attached to it. *a.*

خلد **khuld**, m. eternity, paradise. *khallad* (used benedictively) may (God) extend or prolong. *a.*

خلش **khalish**, m. and f. putting a stop to, interruption, solicitude, suspicion. *khalish uṭhānā*, a. to reconcile; to excite enmity. *p.*

خلص **khalaṣ**, m. a sincere friend. *a.*

خلط **khilṭ**, m. one of the four humours of the human body. *khalṭ*, confusion, mixture. *khilṭi fāsid*, canker of a sore; *cacochymia*. *a.*

خلطه **khilṭa**, m. conversation, company. *khulṭa*, partnership, association. *a.*

خلطين **khalṭīn** or **khulṭīn**, water in which dates have been steeped, mixed with that of raisins, and boiled together until they ferment and become spirituous: it is not a prohibited liquor. *a.*

خلع **khal'**, stripping, removing (from office). *khul'*, in its primitive sense, means to draw off or dig up. In law it signifies agreement entered into for the purpose of dissolving connubial connection, in lieu of a compensation paid by the wife to her husband out of her property. *a.*

خلعت **khil'at**, m. and f. dress; a robe of honour, with which princes confer dignity on subjects. It is given to a person invested with a new office, or as a token of confirmation in that he holds. This dress of honour is likewise presented by men of rank to visitors of distinction, but it is generally in pieces, and not made up: the number of pieces and their quality are in proportion to the rank of the persons to whom they are presented: sometimes it is sent as a present. "The *khil'at* is not necessarily a dress. Sometimes arms, jewels, or other valuables are presented, without any articles of attire, although in most cases a turban and shawl form part of the gift."—Binning. *khil'at pahrānā* or *-denā*, a. to invest with a robe of honour. *a.*

خلف **khalaf**, m. a successor, an heir, a favourite son, posterity, descendants; (adjectively) depraved, corrupted. *khulf*, breach of promise. *a.*

خلفا **khulafa** (pl. of خليفه), successors, princes, caliphs. *khalafan*, successively, uninterruptedly. *a.*

خلق **khulk**, m. nature, quality, good disposition; custom, manner. *a.*

خلق **khalk**, f. creation, people, mankind. *khalku'llāh*, God's creatures. *a.*

خلقان **khulkān**, worn-out garments. *a.*

خلقت **khilkat**, f. the creation, people, populace, the world. *a.*

خلقي **khalkī**, natural, innate; relating to the world or to mankind. *a.*

خلقيت **khalkīyat**, f. the creation, the universe, the human race. *a.*

خلگا **khalgā** (for *kalgā*, q. v.), name of a flower, cockscomb. *h.*

خلگي **khalgī** (for *kalghī*, q. v.), an aigrette, &c. *p.*

خلل **khalal**, m. interruption, disturbance, confusion, prejudice, damage, injury, ruin. *khalali damāgh*, m. (lit. injury of the brain) madness, melancholy. *khalal-damāgh*, mad, hare-brained, hot-headed, confused. *a.*

خللي ***kh**alalī*, a disturber, mischief-maker. *a.*

خلنجان ***kh**ulanjān*, the root galangale. *a.*

خلنگ ***kh**ulang* (for *kulang*, q. v.), a crane or heron. *p.*

خلو ***kh**ulū*, m. vacuity, empty space. *a.*

خلوت ***kh**alwat*, also ***kh**ilwat*, f. retirement, solitude, privacy; a closet, private apartment, private conference. ***kh**alwat-**kh**āna*, m. a retirement, private apartment. ***kh**ilwat i saḥīḥ*, complete and lawful retirement, as that of married folks, where there is no legal or natural impediment to the carnal act in marriage. ***kh**alwat-gāh*, f. a retirement. ***kh**alwat-guzīn* or ***kh**alwat-nishīn*, retired; (met.) a hermit. ***kh**alwat o jalwat meṅ*, in private and in public. *a.*

خلوتي ***kh**alwatī*, a hermit; a familiar friend, intimate. ***kh**alwatī rāg*, m. soft plaintive music. *a.*

خلوص ***kh**ulūṣ*, m. purity, sincerity, candour, integrity, friendship, affection. *a.*

خله ***kh**ala*, a rudder, helm; trifles, idle talk; pricker, goad; a decree or written document signed by a judge. *p.*

خليده ***kh**alīda*, punctured, pricked, stung. *p.*

خليرا ***kh**alerā*, descended from or related to a maternal aunt; as, ***kh**alerā bhā,ī*, m. the son of a maternal aunt; ***kh**alerī bahin*, f. the daughter of the same. *a.*

خليطه ***kh**alīṭa*, m. (cor. of ***kh**arīṭa*, q. v.) ***kh**alīṭa,e ṭūfān*, an exciter of disturbance, calumniator, a mischief-making wicked person. *a.*

خليفه ***kh**alīfa*, m. a sovereign, (vulg.) the caliph; a successor, particularly applied to the successors of *Muhammad*; (in Hind.) cooks, tailors, &c. are called ***kh**alīfa*; a fencing-master; a monitor (as the elder boys at school become). *a.*

خليق ***kh**alīḳ*, kind, of good disposition. *a.*

خليل ***kh**alīl*, a sincere and intimate friend. ***kh**alīlu-l-lāh*, the friend of God, the patriarch Abraham, also styled *al-**kh**alīl*, the friend. *a.*

خم ***kh**am*, twisted, crooked, coiled; m. a coil, fold, ply, curl, ringlet; that part of a noose which encircles the neck. ***kh**am andar **kh**am*, twist within twist, curling locks. ***kh**am ṭhoknā, bajānā*, or *-mārnā*, a. to strike the arms previous to wrestling, &c. ***kh**am-dār*, twisted, curled, bent, crooked. *p.*

خم ***kh**um*, m. a jar, an alembic, a still. ***kh**um charhānā*, a. to boil cloths preparatory to washing. *p.*

خمار ***kh**umār*, m. sickness, headache, &c., the effects of drink; intoxicating; languishing appearance of the eyes, the effect of love, or of drowsiness, or drinking, &c. ***kh**umār-ālūd* or *-ālūda*, intoxicating (eyes). ***kh**umār-**kh**āna*, m. a tavern. ***kh**umār-shikanī* f. any thing to alleviate sickness arising from intoxication, such as tea, soda-water, &c. ***kh**ammār*, m. a great drunkard. *a.*

خماري ***kh**umārī*, one who is drunk. *a.*

خماسي ***kh**umāsī*, consisting of or relating to the number five; a word of five letters; a sort of magic pentagon. *a.*

خمانا ***kh**amānā*, a. to twist, to curl, to coil. *p.*

خمچي ***kh**amchī*, a kind of lash or whip. *d.*

خمخانه ***kh**um-**kh**āna*, a wine-vault, a tavern. *p.*

خمر ***kh**amr*, m. wine in particular, and all strong liquors in general; covering, hiding; fermenting, leavening. *a.*

خمرك ***kh**amrak* (for *kamrakh*), name of a fruit (*Averrhoa carambola*). *h.*

خمرمحال ***kh**amr-maḥāll*, a branch of revenue arising from the sale of arrack and other spirituous liquors. *p.*

خمره ***kh**umra*, m. a small mat of palm leaves for kneeling on at prayers; a small drum carried by beggars; a small earthen pot in which leaven is prepared and kept. *a.*

خمس ***kh**ams*, five (used only in Arabic phrases). ***kh**ums*, the one-fifth; (in law) a double tithe, or 20 per cent. levied on the owners of land in which there are valuable mines of metals, &c. *a.*

خمسه ***kh**amsa*, five; an aggregate of five poetical pieces. *a.*

خمكده ***kh**um-kada*, a tavern. *p.*

خمنا ***kh**amnā*, a. (from ***kh**am*) to bend, to bow. *d.*

خم وچم ***kh**am o cham*, m. coquetry, the blandishments of a mistress; elegant, graceful. *p.*

خموش ***kh**amosh*, silent, dumb; pl. ***kh**amoshān*, the mute ones, the dead. *p.*

خموشي ***kh**amoshī*, f. silence, muteness. *p.*

خميازه ***kh**amiyāza*, m. gaping, yawning, stretching. ***kh**amiyāza-kash*, one who yawns. ***kh**amiyāza **kh**aiṅchnā*, a. to receive the punishment of one's faults or crimes. *p.*

خميدگي ***kh**amīdagī*, f. crookedness. *p.*

خميدني ***kh**amīdanī*, fit to be bent. *p.*

خميده ***kh**amīda*, awry, crooked, bent. ***kh**amīda-ḳadd*, bent in form or stature. *p.*

خمير ***kh**amīr*, } m. leaven, whatever is used
خميره ***kh**amīra*, } to ferment. *a.*

خميري ***kh**amīrī*, plain steel, *i.e.* steel devoid of *jauhar* or "water," which the Orientals consider an indispensible qualification to good steel; adj. leavened. *d.*

خن ***kh**inn*, m. the hold of a ship. *a.*

خناس ***kh**annās*, m. the devil; (met.) a wicked person. *a.*

خناسي ***kh**annāsī*, devilish, satanic; f. devilishness. *a*

خناق ***kh**unāḳ*, m. the quinsy, suffocation; strangulation. *a.*

خنبي كرنا ***kh**umbī karnā*, to bleach clothes. *d.*

خنث ***kh**unṡ*, } m. a hermaphrodite; as-
خنثي ***kh**unṡā*, } phodel. *a.*

خنجر ***kh**anjar*, m. a dagger, a poniard, (Scotticè "whinger"). *a.*

خنجري ***khanjarī***, f. a mode of printing or staining silk (*gulbadan*, q. v.); a small tambourine. *a.*

خندان ***khandān***, smiling, laughing. *p.*

خندق ***khandaḳ***, m. a ditch, fosse, moat. *a.*

خنده ***khanda***, m. laughter; a laughing-stock. *khanda-rū*, of a smiling countenance. *khanda rū,ī*, mirth, cheerfulness. *khanda-zan* or *-zanān*, one who sets up a laugh. *p.*

خنديدن ***khandīdan***, to smile, to laugh. *p.*

خلزير ***khinzīr***, a wild boar, a hog, a swine. *a.*

خنزيري ***khinzīrī***, hoggish; f. a hog-sty. *a.*

خنك ***khunuk***, cold, temperate, cool; fortunate. *p.*

خنكي ***khunukī***, f. coldness, temperateness; prosperity. *p.*

خنگ ***khing***, m. cream-coloured horse, a steed. *p.*

خنگا ***khingā***, m. an athletic clown; able-bodied. *p.*

خنيا ***khunyā***, m. melody, singing. *khunyā-gar*, m. musician, minstrel, singer. *khunyā-garī*, f. minstrelsy. *p.*

خو ***kho***, f. habit, custom, disposition, nature. *kho-bo*, f. habits, manners. *kho-gar*, *-pizīr* or *-girifta*, accustomed. *kho ḍālnā*, a. to habituate, to adopt a habit, to introduce a custom. *p.*

خواب ***khwāb***, m. sleep; a dream. *khwāb-ālūda* or *khwāb-nāk*, sleepy. *khwāb-āwar*, sleep-producing, soporific (in medicine). *khwāb-khiyāl*, m. spectre, phantom, delusion. *khwāb-dekhnā*, a. to dream. *khwāb-gāh*, sleeping-apartments, bed-room. *p.*

خوابيده ***khwābida***, sleeping, asleep, drowsy. *p.*

خواتين ***khawātīn*** (Arab. pl. of خاتون) ladies. *p.*

خواجه ***khwāja***, m. master; a man of distinction, a rich merchant, a gentleman, a governor. *khwāja-tāsh*, a fellow-servant, companion. *khwāja khizar*, the name of a prophet skilled in divination, and who is said to have discovered the water of life; hence he is considered as the saint of waters: the *Muḥammadans* offer oblations to him of lamps, flowers, &c., placed on little rafts, and launched on the river, particularly on Thursday evening in the month of *bhādoṅ*; and it is in his honour that the feast of *Berā*, q.v. is held. *khwāja-zāda*, m. young master. *khwāja-sarā*, m. an eunuch. *p.*

خوار ***khwār***, poor, distressed; deserted, abandoned, friendless; wretched, contemptible, ruined. *khwār dāshtan*, to hold in contempt; (in comp.) devouring, &c., as *khūn-khwār*, bloodthirsty, a tyrant. *p.*

خوارج ***khawārij*** (pl. of خارجي), heretics, schismatics. *a.*

خوارزم ***khwārazm***, a country to the east of the Caspian Sea, near the mouth of the Oxus, Chorasmia. *p.*

خوارق ***khawāriḳ*** (pl. of خارق), contrary to nature, unusual things, miracles. *a.*

خواري ***khwārī***, f. baseness, distress. *p.*

خواست ***khwāst***, f. desire, wish, request. *khwāst-gār*, m. candidate, competitor, bidder. *khwāst-gārī*, request, petition. *p.*

خواستار ***khwāstār***, a petitioner, a wisher. *p.*

خواستن ***khwāstan*** (r. *khwāh*), to wish, desire. *p.*

خواسته ***khwāsta***, desired, wished. *khudā na khwāsta*, God forbid. *p.*

خواص ***khawāṣṣ*** (pl. of خاص), domestics; grandees, ministers of state; properties, qualities; a page; a favourite. *khawāṣṣ o 'awāmm*, m. nobles and plebeians. *khawāṣṣ-purā*, the apartments allotted to domestics, &c. *a.*

خواصي ***khawāṣī***, m. the place where one sits behind a great man upon an elephant. *a.*

خوان ***khwān***, m. a tray. *khwān-posh*, m. a cloth for covering a tray, a tray lid; (root of *khwāndan* in comp.) reading, reciting. *p.*

خوانچه ***khwāncha***, m. a small tray. *p.*

خواند ***khwānd***, (in comp.) reading, reciting. *khwānd-kār*, a schoolmaster, one who teaches reading. *p.*

خواندن ***khwāndan***, to read, to recite, to declare. *p.*

خوانده ***khwānda***, read; (adjectively) having the knowledge of reading and writing. *nā-khwānda*, ignoramus, one who cannot read. *p.*

خوانسالار ***khwān-sālār***, } m. a house-steward
خوانسامان ***khwān-sāmān***, } (v. *khān-sāmān*). *p.*

خواننده ***khwānanda***, a reader, repeater. *p.*

خواني ***khwānī***, f. (in comp.) reading, recitation. *p.*

خوانين ***khawānīn*** (pl. of خان), lords, nobles. *p.*

خواه ***khwāh***, conj. either, or, whether; (in comp.) wishing, desiring, as *taraḳḳī-khwāh*, wishing increase. *daulat-khwāh*, wishing prosperity. *khāṭir-khwāh*, the desire of one's heart. *khwāh ma khwāh* or *khwāh na khwāh*, willing or not, *nolens volens*; certainly, positively, at all events. *p.*

خواهان ***khwāhān***, wishing, desirous. *p.*

خواهر ***khwāhir*** or ***khwāhar***, f. a sister. *p.*

خواهرانه ***khwāharāna***, sisterly, like a sister. *p.*

خواهش ***khwāhish***, desire, wish, inclination; request. *khwāhish-rakhnā*, or *-karnā*, a. to wish, to desire. *khwāhish-mand*, desirous, solicitous. *p.*

خواهنده ***khwāhanda***, he who asks or wishes; a petitioner, asker. *p.*

خوب ***khūb***, good, excellent, well, beautiful, pleasing, amiable. *khūb-rū*, or *-ṣūrat*, beautiful, well-favoured; pl. *khūbān*, the fair ones, the fair sex. *p.*

خوباني ***khūbānī***, f. the name of a fruit, species of the apricot; an apricot with the kernel of an almond inserted. *p.*

خوبتر ***khūbtar***, more beautiful. *khūbtarīn*, most excellent or most beautiful. *p.*

خوبروئي ***khūb-rū,ī***, } f. beauty, comeliness
خوبصورتي ***khūb-ṣūratī***, } of face or form. *p.*

خوبکلان *khūbkalān*, m. name of a seed of a cooling quality. *p.*

خوبي *khūbī*, beauty, goodness, excellence, [virtue. *p.*

خوجه *khoja*, m. an eunuch. *p.*

خود *khod*, m. a helmet, a steel headpiece. *p.*

خود *khud*, pron. self, own. *khud-ārā*, adorning one's self, proud. *khud ba-khud*, of one's own accord. *khud badaulat*, you, your worship, sir. *khud-bīn*, self-conceited, proud, arrogant, presumptuous. *khud-bīnī*, f. pride. *khud-parast*, self-conceited, *-parastī*, self-conceit. *khud-pasand*, self-complacent, self-conceited. *khud-ṣanā*, an egotist. *khud-dār*, self-restraining, content. *khud-rā,ī*, headstrong, opinionative. *khud rukhṣatī*, leaving a service of one's own accord, in which case it is customary to deduct something from wages. *khud-ro*, or *-rusta*, wild, any thing growing of itself without being sown. *khud-ziyān-kār*, injuring one's self. *khud-sita,ī*, laudation of one's self. *khud-sar*, headstrong, obstinate. *khud-gharaẓ*, selfish. *khud-farosh*, an egotist, a braggart. *khud-kāsht*, cultivating one's own field. *khud-kām*, one who follows his own pleasure, a libertine. *khud-karda*, made by one's self. *khud-kushī*, suicide. *khud-munḍā*, a dervise, the disciple of no saint or *pīr*. *khud-numā*, self-displaying; proud, vain. *p.*

خودکاشت *khud-kāsht*, cultivating one's own field. *khudkāsht zamīn*, land cultivated by ryots residing on the spot. *p.*

خودها *khudhā*, selves, themselves. *p.*

خودي *khudī*, f. selfishness, pride, vanity. *p.*

خور *khur*, adj. worthy, fit, proper; m. food; the sun; (in comp.) devouring, as, *mardum-khur*, man-devouring, *i.e.* a fierce warrior. *khur o posh*, food and raiment. *p.*

خورا *khurā*, worthy, suitable; eating voraciously. *p.*

خوراب *khurāb*, dirty water, a floodgate. *p.*

خوراك *khurāk*, f. food, victuals, provisions, daily food, eatables; one meal, one dose (of medicine). *khurāki afyāl*, food of elephants; a tax formerly levied by the Mogul princes for that purpose. *p.*

خوراكي *khurākī*, f. daily allowance of food, or money to purchase it, subsistence money. *p.*

خورجين *khurjīn*, } m. a wallet, a portmanteau. *p.*
خورچين *khurchīn*, }

خورد *khurd*, small. *khurd-sāl*, young. *khurd-maḥall*, m. the apartments of the concubines of great men. *p.*

خوردگي *khurdagī*, f. small change of money. *p.*

خوردن *khurdan*, to eat; to drink; (met.) to suffer; act of eating or drinking. *p.*

خوردني *khurdanī*, f. provisions, eatables. *p.*

خورده *khurda* (from *khurdan*, q. v.), eaten; afflicted; having experienced. *p.*

خورده *khurda* (from *khurd*), small, minute; m. crumb, scrap; a blemish; small change of money, small coins or wares. *khurda bechnā*, to sell by retail, or in small quantities. *khurda,e ambān*, crumbs in a wallet. *khurda bīn*, m. a caviller, a criticiser. *khurda pakaṛnā*, a. to criticise; to buzz and cavil at minute errors. *khurda farosh*, m. a retailer, a huckster. *khurda-k.*, a. to change coin. *khurda-gīr* a criticiser. *p.*

خوردگتا *khurda-gaṭā*, m. } changing of money,
خوردگي *khurdagī*, f. } giving pieces of smaller value for one of a larger value. *p. h.*

خوردي *khurdī*, f. childhood, infancy. *p.*

خورديا *khurdiyā*, m. a money-changer. *p.*

خورسند *khursand*, happy, contented; adv. with alacrity, swiftly, quickly. *khursandī*, contentment, &c. *p.*

خورش *khurish*, f. eating and drinking. *p.*

خورشيد *khurshaid* or *khurshīd*, m. the sun. *p.*

خورم *khurram*, pleasant, joyful. *p.*

خورمي *khurramī*, joy, mirth, pleasure. *p.*

خورنده *khuranda*, an eater; a gormandizer; (met.) children. *khuranda,e bisyār* a numerous family. *p.*

خورنق *khawarnak*, } the palace of king Bah-
خورنه *khawarna*, } rām Gor in Babylonia, celebrated for its magnificence. *p.*

خوره *khura*, m. the leprosy; that which eats or devours; that which suffers or endures. *p.*

خوري *khurī* (in comp.), eating, devouring, &c. *p.*

خوزاده *khuzāda* or *khūzāda*, m. } naturally
خوزادي *khuzādī* or *khūzādī*, f. } beautiful, unadorned; or, as the poet hath it, "when unadorned adorned the most." *p.*

خوش *khush*, pleased, delighted, excellent, delicious, cheerful, amiable, healthy, elegant, good, willing, glad, happy, content, merry, pleasant, sweet. *khush-āb*, abounding in good water, moist, fresh. *khush-akhtar*, of lucky stars, fortunate. *khush-uslūb*, well-proportioned, neat, elegant in form. *khush-aṭwār*, well-bred. *khush-iḳrār*, abounding in promises. *khush-ilḥān* or *khush-āwāz*, tuneful, melodious. *khush-ilhānī* or *khush-āwāzī*, tunefulness, melody. *khush-āmad*, f. flattery. *khush-āmadī*, a flatterer. *khush-āhang*, with a sweet voice. *khush-āyand* or *-āyanda*, flattering (caresses); grateful, wholesome, amiable, agreeable, pleasing, charming. *khush-bāsh*, free to stay or depart. *khush-bo* or *khush-bo-dār*, fragrant, odoriferous. *khush-bayān*, eloquent. *khush-prakār*, well-proportioned, well-shaped. *khush-poshāk*, well-dressed. *khush-tarāsh*, well-made. *khush-tarkīb*, elegant in form. *khush-taḳrīr*, eloquent. *khush-jauhar*, of fine water (steel, jewels). *khush-chashm*, sweet-eyed. *khush-chhab*, graceful, well-shaped or proportioned. *khush-ḥāl*, happy, fortunate, in pleasant circumstances. *khush-khāl* (lit. having a good mole), a mistress, a sweetheart. *khush-khāna*, m. an aviary. *khush-khabarī*, f. glad tidings. *khush-khirām*, of a graceful gait. *khush-kharīd*, f. paying ready money, purchasing in private sale. *khush-khaṭṭ*, elegant writing. *khush-khiṣāl*, *-khaṣlat*, *-khulk*, or *-khū*, affable, of good disposition, well-bred. *khush-khwār*, a good liver, one who lives well. *khush-khwān*, one who reads or sings sweetly. *khush-khurāk*, one who lives well. *khush-dāman*, f. mother-in-law, wife's or husband's mother. *khush-dil*, happy, pleased. *khush-dimāgh*, cheerful, gay. *khush-dahān* or *-dahan*, having a beautiful or pleasing mouth. *khush-ẓāyiḳa*, high-flavoured, grateful to the taste. *khush-rang*, pleasant in colour. *khush-raftār*, graceful (in walking). *khush-rau* or *-rav* pleasant-paced. *khush-rū*, beautiful. *khush-zabān*, eloquent, plausible. *khush-zamzama*, sweet or melodīvas in singing. *khush-sakhra*, a pleasant, humorous fellow. *khush-salīka*, of a pleasant manner or method. *khush-salīkagi*, pleasantness of method. *khush-sawād*, of pleasant environs (a city). *khush-tāli'*, of good destiny, fortunate. *khush-tab'*, jocular, merry. *khush-tab'ī*, jocularity, pleasantness. *khush-zāhir*, handsome. *khush-'inān*, tractable (a horse). *khush-fi'l*, of proper conduct. *khush-kadd*, well-shaped, of elegant stature (a mistress). *khush-kat*, well-shaped, nicely cut out. *khush-kumāsh*, of good texture or quality. *khush-k.*, to make glad, to please, to gratify. *khush-gap*, conversable, pleasant, chatty. *khush-giristan*, to weep copiously. *khush-go*, eloquent. *khush-guzrān*, one who enjoys life. *khush-gawār*, sweet to the taste, easy of digestion. *khush-maza*, delicious. *khush-ma'āsh*, well-fed. *khush-nishīn*, pleasantly seated. *khush-nasīb*, fortunate. *khush-naghma*, of sweet melody. *khush-nigāh*, of pleasant aspect. *khush-nawā*, having a sweet voice. *khush-numā*, beautiful, neat, pretty. *khush-navīs*, writing an elegant hand. *khush-niyat*, well-disposed, amiable. *khush-wakt*, happy, pleased, delighted. *khush o-khurram*, cheerful, gay. *khush-hazm*, of easy digestion. *khush-honā*, to be pleased, to be satisfied, to rejoice. *p.*

خوشا *khushā*, interj. hail! joy! happy! how fortunate! *p.*

خوش‌الحاني *khush-ilhānī*, f. melody, sweetness of voice. *p.*

خوشباش *khush-bāsh*, persons who enjoy lands rent-free, upon condition of serving the government in a military capacity when called upon: the term is also extended to people of middling circumstances, who do not cultivate their lands themselves, but hire servants to do it, while they hold other employments. *p.*

خوشبو *khush-bo*, f. perfume, odour; adj. odoriferous. *khush-bo-dār*, aromatic. *p.*

خوشبوئي *khush-bo,ī*, f. sweet fragrance. *p.*

خوشتر *khushtar*, more pleasant, &c. *p.*

خوشترين *khushtrarīn*, most pleasant, &c. *p.*

خوشخريد *khush-kharīd*, an off-hand purchase, without advance or dispute, a very rare thing in India. *p.*

خوشروز *khush-roz*, a day of festivity or diversion; a festival. *p.*

خوش‌گذران *khush-guzrān*, happy, merry. *p.*

خوشگوار *khush-gawār*, pleasant, delicious. *p.*

خوشنود *khushnūd*, pleased, contented, delighted. *p.*

خوشنودي *khushnūdī*, f. pleasure, delight. *p.*

خوشه *khosha*, m. an ear of corn; a bunch (of grapes, &c.); an ear-ring, a spike. *khosha-chīn*, a gleaner. *p.*

خوشي *khushī*, f. delight, pleasure, cheerfulness, gaiety. *khushī khushī* or *khushī se*, happily, with pleasure, cheerfully. *p.*

خوشيدن *khoshīdan*, to grow dry, to fade, wither. *p.*

خوض *khauz*, confederating; purposing, resolving, intending, considering, consulting. *a.*

خوف *khauf*, m. fear. *khauf-rajā*, m. (fear and hope) suspense. *khauf-nāk*, frightful, terrifying. *a.*

خوك *khūk* (also خوگ *khūg*), m. a hog, a wild boar. *p.*

خوكرده *khū-karda*, habitual or habituated. *p.*

خوگير *khogīr*, m. the stuffing of a saddle, a pad, a packsaddle. *khogīr-doz*, m. a saddle-maker. *p.*

خول *khol*, m. a case, sheath, hollow (Hind. *khol*). *h.*

خولنجان *kholanjān*, m. the herb galangal. *p.*

خون *khūn*, m. blood; murder. *khūn-āb* or *-āba*, tears of blood. *khūn-āshām*, ferocious, cruel. *khūn-afshānī*, bloodshed, murder. *khūn-ālūda*, stained with blood. *khūn-bār* (raining blood), weeping blood (generally spoken of the eyes of a lover). *khūn-bahā*, m. the price of blood, fine or mulct of retaliation for murder. *khūni jigar-pīnā* or *khānā*, a. to work one's self to death. *khūn chāṭnā*, to be stained with blood (a weapon). *khūn-chakan*, dropping blood. *khūn-kharāba*, m. bloody work, deeds of death, murder on either side. *khūn-khwār*, an animal that feeds on blood, a murderer. *khūn-khwāragi* or *khūn-khwārī*, ferocity, bloodshed, cruelty. *khūn-khwāh*, thirsting or wishing for blood. *khūn-dār*, bloody, sanguine. *khūn-rez*, a murderer (lit. shedding blood). *khūn sir charnā*, n. to be distracted by assassinating a person. *khūn sufaid-k.*, to be unkind, to be displeased. *khūni siyāvashān*, dragons' blood, a kind of gum extracted from the Calamus draco. *khūn-fishān*, one who sheds blood, a murderer. *khūn-k.*, a. to assassinate, to kill. *khūn-girifta*, doomed to be slain. *khūn-nāb* or *-nāba*, (same as *khūn-āb*) tears of blood. *p.*

خوناب *khūnāb*, } blood, bloody water, tears
خونابه *khūnāba*, } mixed with blood. *p.*

خونچه *khuncha*, m. a small tray. *p.*

خوني *khūnī*, m. a murderer. *p.*

خونين *khūnīn*, bloody, blood-coloured. *p.*

خويد *khaved* (also *khavīd* and *khavaid*), m. a green field, a sown field; green grass cut for cattle. *p.*

خويش *khwesh*, pron. own; self; m. a kinsman, a son in-law, a family. *khwesh-karābat*, kinsmen, relations. *p.*

خويشاوند *khweshāwand*, a kinsman, a relative. *p.*

خويشاوندي *khweshāwandī*, f. consanguinity, relationship. *p.*

خويشتن *khweshtan*, self, own; a relation. *p.*

خويشي *khweshī*, f. relationship, affinity. *p.*

خهي *khahe*, interj. bravo, well done. *p.*

خيابان *khayābān*, m. a flower-bed. *p.*

خيار *khiyār*, m. choice, election; a cucumber; a second rate land of two species. *a.*

خيارچنبر *khiyār-chambar* (v. *amaltās*), the cassia fistula. *p.*

خياري *khayārī*, f. a kind of violet. *a.*

خيارين *khiyārain*, m. du. cucumbers (of two kinds), the cucumber and musk melon. *a.*

خياط *khaiyāt*, m. a tailor. *khiyāt*, f. a needle. *a.*

خيال ***kh*iyāl**, m. imagination, fancy, thought, consideration; phantom, delusion, vision; a kind of song. *khiyālī bāṭil*, foolish imagination. *khiyāl-bāndhnā*, to rear a structure in the imagination; castle-building in the air. *khiyāl-bandī*, castle-building. *khiyāl-parast*, a visionary, a castle-builder. *khiyāl-paṛnā*, to pursue an object. *khiyāl pulāw pakānā*, a. to indulge in vain speculations or absurd fancies, to build castles in the air. *khiyāl-chhoṛnā*, a. to be out of conceit with. *khiyālī khilāfat*, ambition. *khiyālī khām*, a vain, ridiculous idea. *khiyāl-k.*, to imagine, to fancy, to look forward. *a.*

خيالات ***kh*iyālāt**, (pl. of حيال) imaginations. *khiyālāti lā-ṭā,il*, ill-grounded expectation. *a.*

خياله ***kh*iyāla**, a phantom, an illusion. *a.*

خيالي ***kh*iyālī**, fanciful, capricious, fantastical. *a.*

خيبر ***kh*aibar**, m. name of town of Hijāz in Arabia Petræa, near which there is a pass between two ranges of mountains, and hence the name of several similar places in various parts of the East, the famous Khyber pass at Peshawur among others.—(Binning.) *a.*

خيچه ***kh*īcha**, poor land, and which produces only *callāi*, and of this but one crop per annum. *a.*

خيانت ***kh*iyānat**, f. perfidy, treachery, embezzlement. *a.*

خير ***kh*air**, good, best, well; f. goodness, health, happiness. *khairu-l-bashar*, the best of men, the prophet *Muḥammad*. *khairu-n-nisā*, the best of women, *Fāṭima*. *khair-andesh*, a well-wisher, a friend. *khair-bād*, may he prosper. *khair-khabar*, news, intelligence. *khair-khwāh*, a friend, a well-wisher. *khair-khwāhī*, goodwill, friendship. *khair o'āfiyat*, f. health, welfare. *a.*

خيرات ***kh*airāt**, alms, deeds of charity; land given in charity, principally to Musalmāns: it is by custom hereditary and alienable. *khairāt-zamīn*, land given for charitable endowments (to Musalmān *faqīrs*). *a. p.*

خيراتي ***kh*airātī**, intended for charitable purposes, given (or to be given) or received in charity. *a.*

خيرگي ***kh*īragī**, f. darkness, wickedness, malignity. *p.*

خيره ***kh*īra**, dark; wicked, malignant, vain. *khīra-rā,ī*, of dark or wicked intentions. *p.*

خيريت ***kh*airiyat**, f. welfare, happiness. *s.*

خيز ***kh*ez**, (in comp.) rising, leaping, bounding, galloping, capering; springing up (vegetation). *p.*

خيزان ***kh*ezān**, } rising, springing up (as
خيزي ***kh*ezī**, } flowers, &c.). *p.*

خيزيدن ***kh*ezīdan**, to rise, spring up. *p.*

خيشوم ***kh*aishūm**, m. the nose, the cartilaginous part of it; nasal letters; the ridge or summit of a mountain. *a.*

خيل ***kh*ail**, m. horsemen, cavalry; a body of men, a troop of horse, an army. *a.*

خيلا ***kh*ailā**, a woman having many moles (a great beauty among the Arabs). *a.*

خيلا ***kh*elā**, a playful, foolish (girl). *khelā pā,enchā*, unsteady, foolish, inconsistent, unchaste (woman). *h.*

خيلتاش ***kh*ail-tāsh**, a fellow-soldier, a comrade; name of a famous athlete. *p.*

خيلي ***kh*aile**, many, much, very. *p.*

خيمه ***kh*īma** or ***kh*aima**, m. a tent, pavilion. *khīma-doz*, a tent-maker. *khaima-zadan*, to pitch a tent. *khaima-zan*, a pitcher of tents. *a.*

خيمه گاه ***kh*īma-gāh**, f. a camp, an encampment. *a. p.*

د

د **dāl**, called *dāl i muhmala*, is the eighth letter in the Arabic, the tenth in the Persian, and the eleventh in the Hindūstānī alphabets: its sound is much softer and more dental than that of our *d*: in reckoning by *abjad* it stands for four: in Persian it is sometimes permuted into *t*, as *bat-tar* for *bad-tar*, worse; in the classic period of the Persian language *dāl* seems to have been pronounced *ẕāl*, whenever a vowel preceded, as *gumbaẕ*, a dome, for *gumbad*; *ustāẕ*, a preceptor, for *ustād*; and in good Persian MSS. written four hundred years ago or upwards the *dāl*, thus permuted, is generally marked with a dot, *ẕāl*. The letter *dāl* (denoting *dāda*, "granted") used formerly to be affixed to *zamīndārī* and other grants by the head native revenue officer under the British government in Bengal. *a. p.*

د द **da**, in Sanskrit added as a termination to a substantive, denotes giving, bestowing; as, from *sukh* or *sukha*, pleasure, comes *sukh-da* or *sukha da*, giving or bestowing pleasure (similar to the Persian *dih* or *bakhsh*, q.v. as *ārām-dih* from *ārām*). *s.*

داب **dāb**, m. custom, manner, institution; situation, condition; vehement, or forcible propulsion. *dābi ṣuḥbat*, m. good manners, civilization. *a.*

داب **dāb**, magnificence, pomp, ostentation. *p.*

داب **dāb**, fear, dread; awe reverence. *d.*

داباگن दावाग्नि **dābāgni**, } m. conflagration of
دابانل दावानल **dābānal**, } a forest (v. *dāvāgni*). *s.*

دابه **dābbat**, a reptile, a beast of burden. *dābbatu-l-arẓ*, the second beast mentioned in the Apocalypse. *a.*

دابت **dābat**, an imprecation, a curse. *d.*

دابنا दाबना **dābnā**, a. to press down, to suppress, to snub, to squeeze. *dāb-rakhnā*, a. to conceal, to steal and conceal; to press, particularly with the thighs, to retain by pressure, to grip (as money). *dāb-lenā*, a. to outgrow. *h.*

دابي दाबी **dābī**, f. a measure of about ten handfuls (of autumn crop, &c.). *h.*

دات दात **dāt**, m. liberality, bountifulness (for *dānt*) the tooth. *s.*

داتا दाता **dātā**, } liberal, generous, a
داتار दातार **dātār**, } giver. *s.*

داتر दात्र **dātr** or **dātra**, m. a kind of sickle, a large knife. *h.*

داتر दातृ *dātṛi*, m. a donor, a giver, giving. *s.*

داتن दातन *dātan*, f. a toothbrush, or rather a piece of wood for cleansing the teeth (Dakh. *dātūn*). *s.*

داتويه दातव्य *dātavya*, to be given, what may or ought to be given. *s.*

داج *dāj*, m. darkness, a dark night. *a.*

داخل *dā<u>kh</u>il*, entering, penetrating, arriving; taking possession; entry in a book; (adjectively) entered, produced. *dā<u>kh</u>il <u>kh</u>ārij-k.*, a. to transfer property (by taking out the name of the former proprietor from the deed or register, and inserting that of the new). *dā<u>kh</u>il-k.*, a. to cause to enter or arrive, to place or fix in; to produce, to include, to insert. *dā<u>kh</u>il hṇā*, n. to enter, to arrive, to penetrate, to belong, to appertain, to be inserted. *dā<u>kh</u>il-daftar*, entered upon the record. *dā<u>kh</u>il-dār*, an occupant. *dā<u>kh</u>il-nāma*, a warrant or deed of possession; a conveyance. *dā<u>kh</u>il <u>kh</u>ārij*, erasure of an entry. *a.*

داخلا *dā<u>kh</u>ilā*, داخله *dā<u>kh</u>ila*, m. a receipt for money; a list, or entry; a muster-roll; a concern or business; a connexion. *a.*

داخلنامه *dā<u>kh</u>il-nāma*, m. a warrant of possession. *a.*

داخلي *dā<u>kh</u>ilī*, contained, belonging to, inherent, included in. *a.*

داد दाद *dād*, m. a ringworm, herpes. *dād-mardan*, m. a plant used to cure the ringworm (*Cassia alata*). *s.*

داد *dād*, f. a gift, giving; law, equity, justice; revenge; (in comp.) it denotes given, bestowed, as *<u>kh</u>udā-dād*, given by God. *dād bedād-k.*, a. to demand justice. *dād-<u>kh</u>wāh*, m. a plaintiff, a petitioner of justice. *dād-<u>kh</u>wāhī*, f. demanding justice, instituting a suit. *dād-dihish*, f. liberality; a present. *dād denī*, a. to praise one's actions properly. *dād-ras*, a redresser of grievances. *dād-rasī*, redress of grievances, justice. *dād ko pahunchnā*, n. to arrive at justice; to obtain justice. *dād-gar*, m. administrator of justice. *dād-gustarī*, diffusion or administration of justice. *dād lenī*, a. to take vengeance. *dād milnī*, n. to obtain redress. *dād o bedād*, crying out for justice. *dād o sitad*, lit. giving and taking, traffic. *p.*

دادا दादा *dādā*, m. a paternal grandfather; elder brother. *h.*

دادار *dād-ār* or *dād-āwar*, m. the distributor of justice, an epithet of the Deity. *p.*

دادر दादुर *dadur*, m. a frog. *s.*

دادرا दादरा *dādrā*, m. a kind of song. *h.*

دادروا दादुरवा *dādurwā*, m. a frog (same as *dādur*). *s.*

دادمردن दादमर्दन *dād-mardan*, m. the name of a plant applied to cure the ringworm (*Cassia alata*). *s.*

دادن *dādan* (r. *dih*), to give, to bestow. *p.*

دادني *dādnī*, f. advances; money advanced for the provision of goods or merchandise of any kind. *p.*

دادو दादू *dādū*, name of a famous *fakīr*, born in the state of Jaipur, and founder of a sect. *dādū-panthī*, followers of *dādū*. *h.*

داده *dāda*, given, or having given; (used in comp.) as *tāb-dāda*, inflamed. *p.*

داذهنا दाधना *dādhnā*, n. to burn. *s.*

دادي दादी *dādī*, f. paternal grandmother. *h.*

دادي *dādī*, a plaintiff, a complainant. *dādī-faryādī*, a complainant, one suing for justice. *p.*

دار *dār*, m. a dwelling, a mansion, seat, country habitation; according to Gladwin, a single-roofed house, surrounded with walls, with a door or entry, is termed a *bait* or room; a *manzil* or tenement, on the contrary, is a place composed of different rooms, such as a man may reside in with his family: a *dār*, or mansion, on the other hand, is a place consisting of various rooms or tenements, with an open court. *dāru-l-amān*, m. the house of safety, a country with which there is peace. *dāru-l-bakā*, the house of eternity, i.e. the next world. *dāru-l-bawār*, m. the dwelling of perdition, hell. *dāru-l-<u>kh</u>ilāfat* or *dāru-s-saltanat*, *dāru-l-imārat* or *dāru-l-ḥukūmat*, f. the royal residence, the seat of empire; (met.) capital, metropolis. *dāru-l-ḥarb* (lit. the mansion of war), a country where the Musalmān religion does not prevail. *dāru-s-salām*, house of salvation, heaven. *dāru-sh-shar'*, a court of law or religion. *dāru-sh-shafā* or *dāru-l-maraẓ*, m. an hospital. *dāru ẓ-ẓarb*, f. the mint. *dāru-l-'adālat*, a court of justice. *dāru-l-'ilm*, a school or college. *dāru-l-'iwaẓ*, house of retribution. *dāru-l-fanā*, the frail house, (met.) the world. *dāru-l-ḳarār*, house of rest, the grave. *dāru-l-mukāfāt*, house of retaliation. *dār o dasta*, house and family. *a.*

دار *dār*, m. a gallows, a gibbet, an impaling stake. *dār par khainchnā*, a. to impale. *dār-kash*, the hangman; (in comp.) it means possessing, a possessor, a lord, a master; as, *ḥiṣṣa-dār*, a partaker. *āb-dār*, adj. watery, resplendent; m. a person intrusted with the charge of water for drinking. *'amal-dār*, a tax gatherer. *dār-gīr*, m. seizing (particularly thief-taking); tumult, conflict. *dār madār*, m. agreement, stipulation, adjustment of a dispute. *p.*

دار दार *dār*, f. (v. *dāl*), pulse, vetches. *s.*

دار दारु *dāru*, m. wood, timber; a sort of pine (*Pinus devadaru*). *s.*

دار दार *dār*, دارا दारा *dārā*, f. a wife; (in Dakh.) for *ḍāṛh*, jaw tooth, grinder. *s.*

دارا *dārā*, possessor, sovereign; Darius. *p.*

دارادهين दाराधीन *dārādhīn*, dependent on a wife, subject to her. *p.*

داراب *dārāb*, name of a Persian king, the father of Darius. *p.*

دارائي *dārā,ī*, f. (vulg. *daryā,ī*) red silk cloth; sovereignty; adj. of or belonging to Darius. *p.*

دارج दारुज *dāruj*, made of wood, wooden. *s.*

دارچيني *dār-chīnī*, f. cinnamon. *s. p.*

دارد दारद *dārad*, m. a sort of poison brought from the country called *Darad*. *s.*

داردر दारिद्र *dāridr* or दारिद्र्य *dāridrya*, m. wretchedness, poverty, indigency. *dāridr-khednā* (lit. to drive out poverty), a superstitious or religious ceremony. They take a sieve or winnowing-basket, and beating it in every corner of the house, exclaim, *ishwar paitho, dāridr niklo!* "Enter, O God! depart, O Poverty!" *s.*

داردري दारिद्री *dāridrī*, wretched, poor, unfortunate, indigent. *s.*

داڑھيه दार्ढ्य *dārḍhya*, m. hardness, firmness, stability. *s.*

داراستري दारुस्त्री *dāru-strī*, f. a doll. *s.*

دارمدار *dār-madār*, settlement of a quarrel. *p.*

دارمي दारुमय *dārumay*, made of wood, wooden. *s.*

دارکا दारिका *dārikā*, f. a daughter. *dārikā-dān*, m. giving a daughter in marriage. *s.*

دارن दारण *dāran*, m. the clearing nut plant (*Strychnos potatorum*). *s.*

دارن दारुण *dāruṇ*, austere, unfeeling, horrible, fearful, shocking; m. horror, horribleness; lead wort (*Plumbago zeylanica*). *s.*

دارنشا दारुनिशा *dāru-nishā*, f. a plant (*Curcuma xanthorrhizon*). *s.*

دارو दारू *dārū*, f. spirituous liquors; gunpowder. *dārū-sīsā*, (lit.) powder and lead, ammunition, military stores. *h.*

دارو *dārū*, f. medicine. *dārū darman*, application of medicine. *dārū lagnī*, to take effect (medicine). *p.*

داروڑا दारूड़ा *dārūṛā*, m. } wine, spirituous li-
داروڑي दारूड़ी *dārūṛī*, f. } quor. *h.*

داروغانه *dāroghāna*, pay of a *dārogha*. *p.*

داروغگي *dāroghagī*, f. superintendence; the station of *dārogha*, q. v. *p.*

داروغه *dārogha*, m. the head man of an office, the prefect of a town or village; a superintendant of the police, &c.; an overseer. *p.*

داروکا दार्विका *dārvikā*, } f. a sort of collyrium
داروي दार्वी *dārvī*, } from an infusion of the *Curcuma xanthorrhizon*; a sort of potherb. *s.*

دارومدار *dār o madār*, reconciliation, settlement of a dispute or quarrel. *p.*

دارهردرا दारुहरिद्रा *dāru-haridrā*, f. a kind of curcuma (*C. xanthorrhizon*). *s.* [war. *s.*

داري दारी *dārī*, f. a female slave taken in

دارين *dārain*, (dual.) the two worlds, *i. e.* the present and future life. *a.*

داڑك दाड़क *dāṛak*, m. a tooth, a tusk. *s.*

داڑم दाड़िम *dāṛim*, } m. a pomegranate,
داڑمب दाड़िम्ब *dāṛimb*, } the tree or its fruit. (*Punica granatum*). *dāṛim-priya*, m. the parrot, as being fond of the pomegranate. *dāṛim-pushpak*, m. a medicinal plant (*Andersonia rohitaka*). *s.*

داڑه दाढ़ *dāṛh*, f. a jaw-tooth, a grinder. *dāṛh mārnā*, to gnash or grind the teeth in wrath, anguish, &c. *h.*

داڑها दाढ़ा *dāṛhā*, m. a large tooth, a tusk. *h.*

داڑهکا दाढ़िका *dāṛhikā*, } f. beard; tendril.
داڑهي दाढ़ी *dāṛhī*, } *dāṛhī banānā* or *mūṇḍnā*, a. to shave (in Dakh. *dāṛī*). *s.*

داس दास or दाश *dās*, m. a male slave, a servant; a Sūdra, or man of the fourth caste. *dāsatā*, f. or *dāsatwa*, m. slavery. *dās-dāsī*, the female slave of a slave; male and female slaves. *s.*

داس *dās*, m. a sickle, a scythe. *p.*

داسا दासा *dāsā*, m. a piece of wood sticking out from a wall to support the thatch (or *chhappar*, q.v.); a reaping-hook. *h.*

داسپور दासपूर *dās-pūr* or दाशपुर *dāsh-pur*, m a fragrant grass (*Cyperus rotundus*). *s*

داستان *dāstān*, f. a story, fable, tale. *p.*

داسه *dāsa*, m. a reaping-hook (v. *dāsā*). *h.*

داسي दासी *dāsī*, f. a maid-servant. *dāsī-putra*, m. the son of a slave-girl. *h.*

داسيه दास्य *dāsya*, m. slavery, servitude. *s.*

داش दाश *dāsh*, m. a servant (v. *dās*). *s.*

داشت *dāsht*, f. bringing up, breeding, taking care of, patronage; service. *p.*

داشتن *dāshtan* (r. *dār*), to keep, to possess, to have, to place, to deposit. *p.* [province. *s.*

داشيرك दाशेरक *dāsherak*, m. Mālwā, the

داعي *dā'ī*, m. a well-wisher, one who prays for the welfare of another; a plaintiff; one who instigates another to any thing, instigator, author, cause. *a.*

داعيه *dā'iya*, m. petition, plaint, desire, wish; cause, source. *a.*

داغ *dāgh*, m. spot, stain, mark, scar, a freckle, a mark made by burning with a hot iron brand, stigma, cautery; (adjectively) wounded, cauterized, having many scars. *dāgh bar bālā,e dāgh*, one misfortune following another. *dāgh chaṛhānā* or *lagānā*, a. to vilify, to defame. *dāgh-dār*, spotted, marked. *dāgh denā*, a. to mark by burning with a hot iron, cauterize; to blemish. *dāgh lānā*, a. to vilify. *dāgh lagnā*, n. to be damaged. *dāgh honā*, to be cauterized or scarred. *p.*

داغنا *dāghnā*, a. to cauterize, to mark by burning with a hot iron; to fire (a gun, &c.). *p. h.*

داغي *dāghī*, spotted, stained. *dāghī-k.*, a. to stain, to blemish. *p.*

داك दाक *dāk*, m. a donor, one who makes presents, especially to Brāhmans; a sacrificer, one who pays the expenses of the ceremony and employs the officiating priests. *s.*

داكشايني दाक्षायिणी *dākshāyinī*, f. pl. the twenty-seven lunar mansions, considered as the daughters of Daksha and wives of the moon; f. the nymph and asterism *Rohinī*; a plant (*Croton polyandrum*). *a.*

داكش كنتها दाक्षिकन्था *dākshi-hanthā*, f. a place to the north of India, in the country of Vahlīk or Balkh. *dākshi-kanthīya*, produced or born in *Dākshi-kanthā*. *s.*

داكشيه दाक्ष्य *dākshya*, m. cleverness, dexterity, ability. *s.*

داكه दाख *dākh*, f. a raisin. *s.*

داگ दाग *dāg*, m. spot, scar, &c. (v. *dāgh*). *h.*

داگنا दागना *dāgnā*, a. to cauterize, &c. (v. *dāghnā*). *h.*

دال दाल *dāl*, f. pulse, vetches, a kind of split pea, much used for food, as a soup used along with boiled rice, what we call curry or mulligatawny; a sort of grain (*Paspalum frumentaceum*). *dāl galnī kisī kī*, n. to have an advantage, to avail. *kuchh dāl meṅ kālā hai*, "there is something wrong;" "there is a flaw in the indenture;" lit. there is something black in the *dāl*, or pea soup. *s.*

دال *dāll*, significant, expressive, typical. *a.*

دالا दाला *dālā*, f. colocynth. *s.*

دالان *dālān*, m. a hall. *dar-dālān*, m. an outer hall. *p.* [mon. *h.*

دالچيني *dāl-chīnī* (for *dār-chīnī*), f. cinna-

دالدر दालिद्र *dālidr*, m. (v. *dāridr*) poverty. *s.*

دالدري दालिद्री *dālidrī*, m. (v. *dāridrī*) poor. *s.*

دالم दालिम *dālim*, m. pomegranate (v. *dāṛim*). *s.*

داله *dāla*, a peculiar kind of tenure (in the Du,āb). *h.*

دام *dām*, m. a net, a snare; a quadruped. *p.*

دام दाम *dām*, f. m. a rope, any kind of string. *s.*

دام दाम *dām*, m. price; the name of a copper coin; in the *āyīni akbarī*, and consequently in most revenue accounts, the *dām* is considered to be the fortieth part of a rūpī. The dām, or one-fortieth of a rūpī, was divided into eight parts, called *damṛī*. Two damṛis make one *pā,olā*, and two pā,olās one *adhelā*, or half a dām. Since the time of Akbar, however, the dām has greatly fallen off in value, so that at present, in Upper India, it is only one-twenty-fifth of a paisa, or one-sixteen-hundredth of a rūpī. *h.*

دام *dāma*, may (it) be perpetual. *dāma mulku-hu*, may his kingdom be everlasting. *a.*

داما दामा *dāmā*, m. a rope, a string, a cord. *s.*

داماد *dāmād*, m. a son-in-law. *p.*

دامادي *dāmādī*, f. relationship of son-in-law. *p.*

داماساه दामासाह *dāmāsāh*, name of a merchant, who, dying insolvent, his effects were divided among his creditors in proportion to their claims. *h.*

داماساهي दामासाही *dāmāsāhī*, f. proportioning, equal assessment, dividend (of a bankrupt's property); composition of a debt. *h.*

دامان *dāmān* (v. *dāman*), a skirt, &c. *p.*

دامبهك दाम्भिक *dāmbhik*, hypocritical; m. a hypocrite; a kind of crane (*Ardea nivea*). *s.*

دامچه दामचः *dāmcha*, m. the platform on which a person is posted to protect crops. *h.*

دامداري *dāmdārī*, a branch of revenue arising from birdcatchers, players, and musicians. *p.*

دامعة *dāmi'at*, a wound causing the blood to flow. *a.*

داملپت दामलिप्त *dām-lipta*, m. a country, the modern district of Tamluk. *s.*

دامن *dāman*, m. a skirt of a garment; sheet (of a sail on ship-board); the foot or declivity of a mountain. *dāman pakaṛnā*, a. to prevent, to oppose; to take protection, to take refuge. *dāman phailānā*, a. to beg, to petition, to desire. *dāman tale chhipānā*, to protect; to commit crimes secretly. *dāman jhāṛkur uṭhnā*, to rise quickly in displeasure. *dāman jhaṭak lenā*, a. to refuse, to decline clownishly. *dāman chhuṛānā*, a. to escape, to get rid of, to come off. *dāman-dār*, wide (as cloth). *dāman dabā baiṭhnā*, to intrude upon. *dāman se lagnā*, to depend upon, to claim protection. *dāman-gīr*, attached to, depending on; demanding justice, an accuser. *dāman-gīrī*, f. attachment, friendship, applying for justice, arraignment. *p.*

دامن दामिनि *dāmini*, } f. lightning. *s.*
دامني दामिनी *dāminī*, }

دامني दामनी *dāmnī*, relating to the artemisia flower; f. a string, a rope, especially for tying cattle. *s.*

دامنه *dāmana*, m. a skirt, &c. (v. *dāman*). *p.*

دامني *dāmanī*, f. scrap of the shroud kept by relations of the deceased; a saddle-cloth, furniture, housings; an ornament worn on the forehead. *p.*

دامودد *dām-o-dad* (v. *dad-o-dām*), wild beasts, quadrupeds in general. *p.*

دامودر दामोदर *dāmodar*, m. a name of *Krishṇa*; Yasodā, his foster-mother, having in vain passed the folds of a rope round his body, whilst a child, to keep him in confinement. *s.*

دامي दामी *dāmī*, f. an assessment. *dāmī lagānā*, a. to assess. *dāmī wāṣilāt*, gross assets of a village. *h.*

دامي *dāmī*, m. a sportsman, a fowler. *p.*

دامية *dāmiyat*, a contusion or wound sufficient to make the blood appear but not to flow. *a.*

دان दान *dān*, m. charity, alms, act of giving or bestowing, gift; any thing demanded by law or custom, as toll, &c.; a religious rite, in which the Brāhmans pronounce a certain charm or incantation over any thing, in the wish of a happy futurity, and give it as a present to another person; the fluid that flows from the temples of an elephant in rut. *dān-pati*, m. a liberal or munificent man. *dān-pattar* or *dān-patra*, m. a deed of conveyance, a deed of gift by which land is conveyed to Brāhmans. *dān-pattar-dār* a Brāhman to whom lands have been assigned. *dān-pun*, m. charity, alms. *dān-dharma*, m. almsgiving, charity; the rules for making donations. *dān-shīl*, liberal, munificent. *dān-yogya*, fit for, or meriting a donation. *s.*

دان *dān*, in comp. denotes knowing, understanding, as *ḳadar-dān*, knowing the value or quality (of persons). *nukta-dān*, subtle, penetrating. *p.*

دان *dān*, m. an affixment; a place, a stand; generally used in comp. as *ḳalam-dān*, a pen-case. *sham'-dān*, a candle-stick. *chā-dān*, a tea-pot. *p.*

دانا *dānā*, wise, learned. *dānā,e dahr*, wise, the learned of the age. *p.*

دانا दाना *dānā*, m. grain, corn, berry (for *dāna*. *p.*). *h.*

داناءي *dānā,ī*, f. wisdom, knowledge. *p.*

دانت दांत *dānt*, m. a tooth. *dānt unglī kāṭnā*, a. to bite the finger, is a term expressive of being surprised, amazed, or perplexed. *dānt bājnā*, chattering of the teeth, squabbling, sparring, wrangling. *dānt patthar po ghasnā* (Dakh., explained by *hawas-k.*), to aim at, to desire. *dānt par chaṛhānā*, to detract from the virtues or praise of another. *dānt pīsnā*, a. to gnash the teeth, to grin. *dānt tale unglī dabānā* or *-kāṭnā*, to stand in amaze, to be amazed, to wonder. *dānt-rakhnā* or *-honā kisī par*, to desire any thing exceedingly; to hate. *dānt-salsulānā* (Dakh.)

to ache (the teeth). *dānt kā dard*, tooth-ache. *dānt kaṭī roṭī khānā*, to be united in intimate friendship. *dānt kaṭkaṭānā*, a. to gnash the teeth *dānt kachkachānā*, to grin, to shew the teeth. *dānt khaṭṭe-k.*, to dishearten, to displease. *dānt kholne*, to disclose the teeth, to grin. *dānt-lānā* or *-nikālnā*, to teeth, to grow (as teeth). *dānt lagnā*, m. trismus or locked-jaw. *dānt-nikālnā*, to laugh, to grin; to express or confess inability and helplessness. *dānton zamīn pakaṛnī* (lit. to bite the ground), to be reduced to extremities, to suffer great pain. *dānton mārnā*, a. to gnash the teeth (with anger). *s.*

دانتاکلکل दाँताकिलकिल *dāntākilkil*, f. quarrel. *s.*

دانت تنکا दाँततिंका *dānt-tinkā*, the act of taking a straw or a piece of grass in the teeth to deprecate wrath, or as a token of complete submission. *h.*

دانتن दाँतन *dāntan*, m. a tooth-brush (v *dātan*). *s.*

دانتي दाँती *dāntī*, f. the tooth of a saw or other instrument, cog of a wheel; a rake; a harrow; a kind of sickle. *dāntī-paṛnā*, n. to be notched or indented (as the edge of a sword). *dāntī denā*, a. to insist upon. *dāntī lagnā*, to have a locked jaw. *s.*

دانڈ दाँड *dānḍ*, m. oppression, injustice, injury; fine, punishment. *s.*

دانڈامینڈا दाँडामेंडा *dānḍā menḍā*, m. the frontier, or boundary between the lands of two proprietors. *h.*

دانڈو *dānḍū*, a ball for playing with; also a bat for striking the same. *d.*

دانڈورگي *dānḍorgī*, f. mischief, wickedness. *d.*

دانڈي दाँडी *dānḍī*, f. a balance; m. a rower, a waterman. *s.*

دانست *dānist*, f. knowledge, opinion. *p.*

دانستن *dānistan* (r. *dān*), to know, to consider. *p.*

دانسته *dānista*, having known, knowingly. *p.*

دانستگي *dānistagī*, } f. knowledge, science,
دانش *dānish*, } learning. *p.*

دانشمند *dānish-mand*, } wise, learned; *dānish-*
دانشور *dānish-war* } *mandī* or *-warī*, learning, wisdom, science. *p.*

دانق *dānaḳ*, } f. a small denomination of mo-
دانك *dānk*, } ney, the sixth part of a *dīnār*; a
دانگ *dāng*, } weight, the fourth part of a drachm; the sixth part of a city; it is used conventionally as a sixth part in general. *a. p.*

دانگ दाँग *dāng*, a hill or precipice; the summit of a mountain. *h.*

دانگر *dāngar*, a superannuated horned beast, (met.) a fool, idiot. *h.*

دانگي दाँगी *dāngī*, a name given to the *bīn* [*dela rājpūts*. *h.*

دانندہ *dānanda*, he that knows; skilled. *p.*

دانو दाँव *dānw*, m. ambuscade, ambush, snare; power, opportunity; time, turn, vicissitude; twisting of one another in wrestling. *dānw-baiṭhnā*, n. to lie in ambush. *dānw pakaṛnā*, a. to wrestle. *dānw chalānā*, a. to take advantage of. *dānw chalnā*, n. to have the advantage. *h.*

دانو *dānw*, m. a stake, a wager; a throw, or cast of the dice (properly, *dā,o* or *dāw*). *p.*

دانو दानव *dānaw* of *dānava*, m. (see [illegible]) demon, a giant, a Titan. *s.*

دانوان दाँवान *dānwān*, m. burning stubble, &c.; a conflagration in a forest. *s.*

دانوري दाँवरी *dānwarī*, f. a rope which fastens bullocks together when threshing (v. *daurī*). *h.*

دانه *dāna*, m. a grain, seed, speck, pimple, corn. *dāna-badalnā*, a. to caress as birds do by joining bills. *dāna badlawwal*, billing, caressing as birds do by joining bills. *dāna-bandī*, a cursory survey or partial measurement or weighment to ascertain the produce of each field. *dāna pānī*, m. food, victuals. *dāna-dār*, granulated; having the appearance of being granulated; containing grain. *dāna dān-k.*, to mingle, confound, or destroy. *dāna-kesh*, m. a kind of embroidered neckcloth, worn in cold weather over the cloak. *p.*

داني दानी *dānī*, charitable, liberal, bountiful. *s.*

داني *dānī*, f. place, pot; used in comp. as *tel-dānī*, f. an oil-pot (abstract form from *dān*, knowing) in comp., as, *ghaib-dānī*, knowledge of the mysterious. *p.*

داني‌زاد *dāne-zād*, m. a miser, avaricious. *d.*

دانيزه *dānīza* (also *dānīzha*), a lentil. *p.*

دانيه दानीय *dānīya*, worthy of having any thing given, worthy or fit to be given. *s.*

داو दाव *dāw*, m. a bill, or kind of hatchet with a hooked point; vicissitude, turn, opportunity; stake, wager, a stroke at a game; a throw of the dice, &c. *dāw-bāndhnā* or *-badnā*, a. to bet, wager. *p. h.*

داو दाव *dāv* or *dāva*, m. a forest, a forest on fire (Pers. *dāw*, v. *dānw*, a wager, &c.). *s.*

داءو दाऊ *dā,ū*, m. an appellation of a father or of an elder brother; used by contraction for *Baladeva*, the foster brother of *Krishṇa*. *h.*

داءو *dā,ū*, fraud, deceit, cheating. *dā,o-ghā,o*, feint or stratagem in war, &c. *d.*

داوا दावा *dāwā*, m. a male nurse; the husband of a *dā,ī*, q. v. *h.*

داواگن दावाग्नि *dāvāgni*, } m. the conflagra-
داوانل दावानल *dāvānal*, } tion of a forest kindled by a tempest or some other cause. *s.*

داءود *dā,ūd*, the name of the prophet David. *a.*

داودي *dā,ūdī*, f. a shrub that bears a flower like camomile (*Chrysanthemum Indicum*); a kind of armour; coat of mail, so named from its being supposed to have been originally made by Dā,ūd, just as we employ the terms Ferrara and Joe Manton. *a.*

داور *dāwar*, m. a sovereign, a judge, God. *p.*

داوري *dāwarī*, f. sovereignty, royalty. *p.*

داون *dāwan* (v. *dāman*), m. a skirt, &c. *d.*

داون दावन *dāwan*, m. the process of threshing by means of bullocks, &c. (v. *dāwnā*). *h.*

داونا दावना *dāwnā*, a. to thresh, to tread; m. the act of treading out the grain (v. *dā,en*). *h.*

داه दाह *dāh*, m. f. burning, ardour; combustion, conflagration; morbid heat; cautery. *dāh-jwar*, m. inflammatory fever. *dāh denā*, to light the funeral pile. *dāh rakhnā*, to grudge. *dāh-sar*, m. a place where dead bodies are burnt. *dāh-haran*, m. the root of a fragrant grass (*Andropogon muricatum*), woven into screens and kept wet for excluding the heat. *dāh-karma*, or *-karana*, or *-kriyā*, the act or ceremony of burning a dead body. *s.*

داها *dāhā*, m. the ten days of the *muharram*, in which the tombs of *hasan* and *husain* are carried about and thrown into the river, or other water (v. *dahā*). *p.*

داهك दाहक *dāhak*, burning, inflammatory; cauterizing, caustic; m. a plant (*Plumbago zeylanica*). *s.*

داهن दाहन *dāhan*, m. burning, cauterizing. *s.*

داهنا दाहना *dāhnā*, a. to burn, to scorch. *s.*

داهنا दाहिना *dāhinā* or **दाहना** *dāhnā*, right (not left). In Sanskrit *dakshina* signifies south or right, because, according to the Hindūs, the earth, the navel of which corresponds to Hindūstān, has its head to the west, its feet to the east, the right side to the south, and the left to the north; or perhaps the term has arisen from the position of eastern people in adoration of the rising sun. In Arabic, the word *shamal* denotes north, or left, and this agrees with the manner in which the Roman augurs determined the regions of the heavens, according to Livy. It may be further stated, that in the Gaelic dialects south and north are synonymous terms with right and left respectively. *s.*

داهي *dāhī*, shrewd, ingenious, penetrating. *a.*

داي दाय *dāy* or *dāya*, m. paternal property, inheritance. *dāya-bhāg* or *dāya-vibhāg*, m. division of property amongst different heirs. *s.*

داءي दाई *dā,ī*, f. a milk-nurse; a midwife. *dā,ī pilā,ī*, f. a wet-nurse. *dā,ī janā,ī*, f. a midwife. *dā,ī ko sompnā*, a. to put out to nurse. *dā,ī khilā,ī*, a dry nurse. *dā,ī-garī*, f. midwifery. *p. h.*

داءي दाई *dā,ī*, m. a giver, generally used in composition, as, *dukh-dā,ī*, giving or occasioning pain. *s.*

دايا दाया *dāyā*, m. demand, claim, plaint. *h.*

دايا *dāyā*, m. a male nurse, the husband of a *dā,ī*, q. v. *p. h.*

داياپورتن दायापवर्तन *dāyāpavartan*, m. privation, forfeiture of property. *s.*

داياد दायाद *dāyād*, m. son; kinsman, near or remote; an heir. *s.*

دايادو दायादव *dāyādav*, m. heir, kinsman. *s.*

دايادي दायादी *dāyādī*, f. a daughter, an heiress. *s.*

دايت दायित *dāyit*, condemned, sentenced; awarded, adjudged. *s.*

دايجا दायजा *dāyajā* or **दाइजा** *dā,ejā*, m. a dowry, portion, nuptial present. *s.*

دائر *dā,ir*, encircling. *dā,ir o sā,ir*, going the circuit (judges, &c.); absolute, invested with authority. *a.*

دائره *dā,ira*, m. a circle, a ring, circumference, orbit; a tambourine; a monastery. *dā,ira-dār*, the head of a monastery, the lord abbot, prior, &c. *a.*

دايك दायक *dāyak* or **दाइक** *dā,ik*, m. a giver (v. *dā,ī*). *s.*

دائم *dā,im*, always, perpetual, permanent. *dā,imu-l-habs*, perpetually imprisoned. *dā,imu-l-khamr*, a sot, drunkard. *dā,imu-l-maraz*, always sick. *a.*

دائماً *dā,iman*, perpetually, everlastingly. *a.*

دائمي *dā,imī*, } f. perpetuity, eternity. *dā,imī*, adj. perpetual, everlasting. *a.*
دائمية *dā,imīyat*, }

داءين दाएँ *dā,en*, the tying of a number of bullocks together for the purpose of treading out the grain from the ear. *h.*

داءين باءين दाएँ बाएँ *dā,en-bā,en*, on the right and left. *h.*

داءين *dā,in*, hill estates (v. *dūn*). *a.*

دايه *dāya*, a female attendant, a nurse. *p.*

دب *dubb*, m. state, constitution, condition, custom, manner, property, quality; a bear. *dubbi asghar*, the lesser bear. *dubbi akbar*, the greater bear; (met.) a fool. *a.*

دبا दबा *dabā*, m. ambush. *dabā mārnā*, to lie in wait. *h.*

دبا दिबा *dibā*, m. (for *divā*) day, daylight. *s.*

دبارا *dubārā* (for *do-bārā*), } a second time, over again. *p.*
دباره *dubāra* (for *do-bāra*), }

دباسي *dubāsī* (same as *dobhāshiyā*, q. v.), an interpreter, a manager or factotum. *d.*

دباغ *dabbāgh*, m. a currier, a tanner. *a.*

دباكر दिबाकर *dibākar* (for *divākar*), m. (lit. the day-maker) the sun. *s.*

دبانا दबाना *dabānā*, a. to press down; to snub, to chide, to keep under, to check, curb, restrain, awe, depress, suppress. *dabā-lenā*, a. to encroach upon. *dabā-mārnā*, a. to overcome, to get the better of; to crush to death. *h.*

دب آنا दबआना *dab-ānā*, n. to advance. *h.*

دباو दबाव *dabāw*, m. strength, power, authority; pressure, crush, resignation, submissiveness. *dabāw mānnā*, a. to stand in awe. *h.*

دباي ڈالنا दबाए डालना *dabā,e ḍālnā*, a to keep concealed, to hide (generally furtively). *h.*

دبدبه *dabdaba*, m. dignity, state, pomp. *a.*

دبدها दुबधा *dubdhā*, f. doubt, suspense, uncertainty, a dilemma. *s.*

دبر *dubur*, f. the backside, posteriors; podex; end, conclusion. *a.*

دبرا दबरा *dabrā*, a marsh, a puddle; a small field. *h.*

دبز *dabz*, thick, coarse (as cloth). *p.*

دبستان *dabistān*, m. a school. *dabistāni mazāhib*, "School of religious sects;" the title of a celebrated work in the Persian language: the author of this singular and very interesting work is unknown, but it has generally been attributed to Muhsin Fānī, a native of Kāshmīr, who lived in the 17th century. From its Indianized style and idiom it is evidently not the production of a Persian.—Binning. *a.*

دبستاني *dabistānī*, m. a student or scholar; adj. of or belonging to a school. *p.*

دبسي दुबसी *dubsī*, the per-centage allowed to government farmers on the revenue paid to government, being two in twenty, or ten per cent. *h.*

دبكانا दबकाना *dabkānā*, a. to snub, to check, to chide, to threaten, to awe, to daunt; to conceal, to hide. *h.*

دبكر दबकर *dabkar*, f. a trap, a snare. *h.*

دبكنا दबकना *dabaknā*, n. to crouch, to be awed, to lie in ambush, to sculk, to lurk, to set (a dog), to twinkle. *dabak-ānā, -jānā* or *-rahnā*, n. to sneak, to skulk. *dabak baiṭhnā*, n. to crouch. *h.*

دبكني दबकनी *dabaknī* (v. *dabkī*), ambush, &c. *d.*

دبكي दबकी *dabkī*, f. ambush, crouching. *dabkī mārnā*, to lie in ambush (a tiger, &c.). *h.*

دبكيل दबकेल *dabkel*, } m. skulking, a
دبكيلا दबकीला *dabkīlā*, } skulker. *h.*

دبلا दुबला *dublā*, thin, lean, poor, barren, weak. *dublā-pā*, m. leanness, emaciation. *s.*

دبلاپا दुबलापा *dublāpā*, m. } thinness,
دبلاپنا दुबलापना *dublāpanā*, m. } leanness. *s.*
دبلاءي दुबलाई *dublā,ī*, f. }

دبنا दबना *dabnā*, n. to be snubbed, to crouch, to shrink, to be pressed down, mowed down, to give way, to be awed; to be concealed. *dab-jānā*, n. to retire, to withdraw, to be mortified. *dab-chalnā* or *-nikalnā*, n. to be awed, to be overpowered. *dab-marnā*, n. to be crushed to death. *dabe pā,oṅ*, with silent steps, softly, gently. *h.*

دبنگ दबङ्ग *dabang* or *dabing*, } ill-bred,
دبنگا दबङ्गा *dabangā* or *dabingā*, } brutish, foolish, barbarous; m. a dolt, lout, clown. *h.*

دبوچنا दबोचना *dabochnā*, a. to conceal, to hide (generally furtively), to strangle. *h.*

دبور *dabūr*, f. zephyr, the west wind. *a.*

دبوس *dabūs*, m. a club, a mace. *a. p.*

دبوس दबोस *dabos*, m. a flint. *h.*

دبوسا *dabūsā*, m. the cabin of a ship, stern. *a.*

دبوسنا दबोसना *dabosnā*, to tope, to tipple. *h.*

دبه *dabba*, m. a leathern vessel for holding oil. *h.*

دبهاشيا दुभाषिया *dubāshiyā*, m. (lit. the "*bilingual*") an interpreter; also an agent in general, like the continental "commissaire." *s.*

دبهك दुभुक्ष *dubhuk*, m. a famine, a scarcity. *s.*

دبي दुबे *du-be* (for *dwi-veda*), a Brāhman learned in two of the four Vedas. *s.*

دبيا दबिया *dabiyā*, m. a measure of about ten handfuls (of corn, &c.). *h.*

دبير *dabīr*, m. a writer, a secretary, a notary. *p.*

دبيل दबेल *dabel*, m. subject, person under dominion. *h.*

دبيلا दबीला *dābīlā*, m. the name of a medicine; a paddle. *h.*

دبيه दिव्य m. (for *divya*) an oath; adj. pure, unpolluted, divine. *s.*

دبيهرا दबेहरा *dabehrā*, a large ploughshare. *h.*

دبيهري दबेहरी *dabehrī*, a kind of light plough. *h.*

دپٹ दपट *dapaṭ*, f. a course, a gallop. *h.*

دپٹا दुपट्टा *du-paṭṭā*, } m. a kind of veil or a
دپٹه दुपट्टः *du-paṭṭa*, } piece of linen in which there are two breadths. *dupaṭṭa tānke sonā*, "to draw the sheet (over one's head) and sleep," is used to express a state of security, and also to denote resigning one's self to die. *dupaṭṭā hilānā* or *phirānā*, to hold out a flag of truce, to offer to surrender (a fort). *h.*

دپٹانا दपटाना *dapṭānā*, a. to put to the gallop. *h.*

دپٹنا दपटना *dapaṭnā*, n. to gallop, to rush; a. to rebuke, to reprimand. *h.*

دپدپانا दपदपाना *dapdapānā*, } a. or
دپدپ كرنا दपदपकरना *dap-dap-karnā*, } n. to shine. *h.* splendour. *h.*

دپدپاهٹ दपदपाहट *dapdapāhaṭ*, f. shining,

دپستا दुपसता *dupastā*, pregnant. *h.*

دپو दपू *dapū*, f. the anus (vulgar term). *h.*

دپهريا दुपहरिया *du-pahriyā*, m. a kind of flower (*Pentapeles Phœnicea*); adj. meridian. *h.*

دت दुत *dut*, interj. away, begone, avaunt. *dut-dabak*, reproof, reprimand. *s.*

دت दुत *dut* or दुति *duti*, f. light, splendour, beauty; spite, malice. *s.*

دت दिति *diti*, f. one of the wives of Kasyapa, and mother of the *Daityas*, or infernal race, opposed to the gods. *s.*

دت दत्त *datta*, given, presented; m. the name of a king; a title or surname of a man of the Vais or third caste. *s.*

دت दत्ति *datti*, f. gift, donation. *s.*

دتاتمن दत्तात्मन् *dattātman*, m. a youth or orphan who gives himself to adoptive parents. *s.*

دتادينا दुत्तादेना *duttā denā*, a. to drive away scornfully; to deceive, to baulk, to cheat. *h.*

دتاره दुतारः *du-tāra*, m. a kind of shawl (v. *dotārā*). *s.*

دتانا दुताना *dutānā*, a. to press down; to snub, to chide, to keep under. *h.*

دتانپكرمن दत्तानपकर्मन् *dattānapakarman*, m. non-resumption of gifts. *s.*

دت پردانك दत्तप्रदानिक *datta-pradānik*, m. resumption of a gift. *s.*

دترا दतरा *datarā*, } m. a large rake used for
دتره दतरः *datara*, } gathering high grass together into a cocklet: *kilwā,ī*, q. v. is a small implement of the same kind. *h.*

دتكار दुतकार *dutkār*, m. reproof. *s.*

دتكارنا दुतकारना *dutkārnā*, a. to reprove. *s.*

دتكاري दुतकारी *duthārī*, f. a reproof, reprimand. *s.*

دتك پتر दत्तकपुत्र *dattak-putra*, m. a son given away by his natural to adoptive parents; one of the twelve heirs acknowledged by the old Hindū law. *s.*

دتنا दतना *datnā*, n. to oppose, to confute, to fight. *h.*

دتون दतवन *datwan* or दतौन *dataun*, m. a tooth-brush (made of a twig). *s.*

دتوئي दतोई *dato,ī*, f. land which has been lately cropped with the grain called *bājrā* or *jwār*, q. v. *h.*

دتيا दितिया *ditiyā*, f. the second lunar day (v. *dūj*). *s.*

دتيه दित्य *ditya*, m. a Titan, a demon (v. *ditī*). *s.*

دٹا *daṭṭā*, m. a cork, a stopper, a plug. *d.*

دٹانا *daṭānā*, a. (v. *dabkānā*) to snub, &c. *d.*

دٹنا दटना *daṭna*, a. to oppose, &c. (same as *datnā*, q. v.). *h.*

دٹهون दिठवन *diṭhwan*, the *ekādashī* or eleventh day of the bright half of the month *kārtik*, on which there is a festival dedicated to *Vishṇu*. *h.*

دٹهونا दिठौना *dithaunā*, m. a patch, an artificial mole on the face. *h.*

دثار *disār*, a mantle, an upper garment. *a.*

دجا दुजा *dujā* (for *dūjā*), second, other. *s.*

دجّال *dajjāl*, m. a liar, an impostor; antichrist. *a.* [the river Tigris. *a.*

دجله *dijla* or *dajla*, also *dajlat*, m. a lake;

دچ दच *dach*, a homestead (East Oude). *h.*

دچار *du-chār*, a meeting, an interview. *p.*

دچت दुचित *duchit*, } of two minds, wavering, doubtful, one whose mind is bent on two different courses, absent in mind. *s.*
دچتا दुचित्ता *duchittā*, }

دچتائي दुचिताई *duchittā,ī*, f. suspense, absence of mind, unsteadiness. *s.* [ways. *h.*

دچله दुचल्लः *du-challa*, m. a roof sloping two

دچند *du-chand*, twice, double. *p.*

دچوبه *du-choba*, two poled (tent). *p.*

دچھ दच्छ *dachh*, learned, scientific, able; proper name of a most ancient sage, father-in-law of Mahādeva (v. *daksha*). *s.* [south. *s.*

دچھن दच्छिन *dachchhin* (for *dakshiṇa*), m. the

دچھنا दच्छिना *dachchhinā*, f. (for *dakshinā*) reward to a Brāhman for performing religious ceremonies; fee. *s.*

دچھناين दच्छिनायन *dachchhināyan*, m. the sun's progress from north to south, winter solstice. *s.*

دچھي दच्छी *dachchhī*, dexterous, capable, able, well qualified. *s.*

دخ *dakh*, a throng or company; good for adapted to. *dukh*, a daughter. *p.*

دخ *dakhkh* or *dukhkh*, smoke. *a.*

دخان *dukhān*, smoke; fumes of tobacco. *a.*

دخاني *dukhānī*, abounding in smoke. *a.*

دخت *dukht*, } f. a daughter, a girl, a virgin. *dukhtar-ah*, a little girl or daughter. *p.*
دختر *dukhtar*, }

دخل *dakhl*, m. entrance; access; possibility or practicability; produce, income, receipt; intrusion, interference, disturbance, molestation. *dakhl pānā*, a. to have access. *dakhl-k.*, a. to meddle, to interrupt, to take possession. *a.*

دخلدار *dakhl-dār*, a partner, an accomplice. *a. p.*

دخمه *dakhma*, a coffin, a tomb, a receptacle for the dead. *p.* [nue. *a.*

دخول *dukhūl*, entrance, access; income, reve-

دخيل *dakhīl*, intimate, familiar; admitted, allowed entrance; m. a friend, a confidant a protegé, one who claims protection or mercy; (in law) an occupant, or the party in possession. *a.*

دد *dad*, a rapacious animal, beast of prey, forest full of game. *p.*

ددا *dadā*, f. a maid-servant, a nurse. *p. t.*

ددچھر *dadachhar*, evil omen, misfortune. *d.*

ددر दद्रु *dadru* or दद्रू *dadrū*, m. cutaneous and herpetic eruption. *dadru-rogin*, diseased by herpes. *s.*

ددري *dadrī*, unripe corn, chiefly barley. *h.*

ددله *du-dila*, wavering, doubtful. *p.*

ددلانا ददलाना *dadlānā*, a. to chide, to snub. *h.*

ددودام *dad o dām*, a fierce rapacious animal (as a lion, tiger, &c.); a wild beast in general; also a harmless animal, as a goat, sheep, &c. *p.*

ددوڑا ददोड़ा *dadoṛā*, m. a bump (occasioned by the bite of an insect). *h.*

ددھ दधि *dadhi*, m. sour, thick milk, coagulated milk. *dadhi kādo*, coagulated milk and clay thrown by people at each other in sport on a holiday held in honour of *Krishṇa* on his birth-day. *s.*

ددھ दिधि *didhi*, f. firmness, stability. *s.*

ددھ दुद्धि *duddhi*, f. a kind of medicinal root (v. *duddhī*). *s.*

ددھار दुधार *dudhār*, giving milk, a milch cow. *s.*

ددھارا *du-dhārā*, two edged (sword). *h.*

ددھ پشپكا दधिपुष्पिका *dadhi-pushpikā*, f. a flower (*Clitorea ternata*). *s.*

ددھ پھل दधिफल *dadhi-phal*, m. the elephant or wood-apple. *s.*

ددھي दुद्धी *duddhī*, f. name of a medicinal herb (*Euphorbia hirta* and *thymifolia*). *s.*

ددھياني दध्यानी *dadhyānī*, f. a medicinal plant. *s.*

ددهيچ दधीच *dadhīch*, the name of a Muni or saint, who devoted himself to death, that the gods might be armed with his bones in lieu of thunderbolts, to destroy the demon *Tārak*. *s.*

ددهيل दुधैल *dudhail*, f. milch, giving milk. *s.*

دديال ददियाल *dadiyāl*, m. descent, pedigree, ancestors, paternal grandfather's family. *h.*

دڈي *diḍḍī*, f. a wicket, a small door. *d.*

در *dar*, m. a door, a gate. *dar-ba-dar*, from door to door. *dar o dīwār dekhnī*, expresses solitude and anxious expectation; prep. in, at, on, into. *dar ānā*, n. to come in, to arrive, to penetrate. *dar pai e jān honā*, n. to be desirous of the death of another, to persecute to the uttermost. *dar pai honā*, n. to follow, to prosecute, to persecute. *dar ṣūrat*, in case, provided, should, suppose that. *p.*

در *dar* from *darīdan*, (in comp.) tearing, rending, as *mardum-dar*, man-destroying. *p.*

در दर *dar*, m. price, rate, a number or quantity fixed as a standard. *h.*

در दुर *dur*, as the first member of a compound (like the Greek δυς) denotes bad, evil, ill, unfortunate, difficult; as *dur-bāchya* or *dur-bachan*, m. scurrility, abuse. *dur-bal*, weak, nerveless, faint. *dur-balatā*, f. faintness, weakness. *dur-jan*, m. a bad man, an enemy. *dur-din*, day of adversity. *dur-nām*, m. infamy. *dur*, (in Dakh.) an ornament worn in the ear. *s.*

در *durr*, m. a pearl. *durr-afshān* (scattering pearls), eloquent. *durr-rez*, eloquent. *durri yatīm*, a priceless pearl. *a.* [gone. *p. a.*

در *dur* (contr. of *dūr*), avaunt! away! be-

درا दरा *darā*, m. (cor. from *dara*) the highway; f. a cave, a grotto; a valley. *p.*

درا *darā* or *dirā*, a bell. *p.*

دراتما दुरात्मा *dur-ātmā*, vile, wicked, bad; m. a rascal, a villain. *s.*

دراج *durrāj*, m. the black partridge. *a.*

دراج *darrāj*, a hedgehog; a malignant whisperer. *a.*

دراجارة *dar-ijāra*, a sublease of a farm. *p. a.*

دراچار दुराचार *dur-āchār*, } wicked, immo-
دراچاري दुराचारी *dur-āchārī*, } ral, irreligious, profligate, one of infamous conduct. *s.*

دراد هرش दुराधर्ष *dur-ādharsh*, m. white mustard. *s.* [rent. *h.*

درار दरार *darār*, m. a crack, a fissure, rift,

دراروه दुरारोह *dur-āroh*, of difficult ascent; m. the palm-tree, the date-tree. *s.* [tree. *s.*

دراروها दुरारोहा *dur-ārohā*, f. the silk cotton-

دراز *darāz*, long, tall, extended. *darāz-dast*, long-handed (*longi-manus*), (met.) oppressive. *darāz-gosh*, long-eared, an ass or a hare. *darāz-dastī*, f. oppression, tyranny. *p.*

درازي *darāzī*, f. extension, length. *darāzī,e, 'umr*, length of life. *p.*

دراكشا द्राक्षा *drākshā*, f. a grape. *s.*

دراگهما द्राघिमा *drāghimā*, m. length. *s.*

درالاپ दुरालाप *dur-ālāp*, m. abusive or scurrilous language, abuse. *s.* [ment. *s.*

درالبه दुरालभ *dur-ālabh*, difficult of attain-

درالبها दुरालभा *dur-ālabhā*, f. a prickly plant, the Jawāsā (*Hedysarum alhagi*). *s.*

درامد *dar-āmad*, entrance; (in law) the return of a process. *dār-āmad bār-amad*, entrance and egress, receipt and disbursement. *p.*

دران *darān*, (in comp.) tearing, rending. *p.*

درانا दर्राना *darrānā*, n. to go straight and quickly, to go on fearlessly and boldly; adj. straight forward. *h.*

درانا दुराना *durānā*, a. to conceal, to hide. *h.*

درانتي दरांती *darāntī*, f. a sickle. *h.*

دراني *durrānī*, m. the name of a tribe of *Paṭhāns* or *Afghāns*, inhabiting the country about *Ḳandhār*. They are said to have got this name from wearing pearls in the ear; they are also called *Abdālīs*. *p.*

دراوك द्रावक *drāvak*, diuretic; solvent, discutient. *s.*

دراوكا द्राविका *drāvikā*, f. saliva. *s.*

دراوكر द्रावकर *drāv-kar*, m. a kind of borax. *s.*

دراوڑ द्राविड़ *drāviṛ*, m. the name of the country which terminates the peninsula of India; the coast of Coromandel, or the country in which Tamul is spoken its northern limits appear to be between the twelfth and thirteenth degrees of north latitude; in a more general sense it applies to four other countries, *Karnāṭ*, *Gujjarāt*, *Mahārāshṭr*, and *Tilinga*; a native of *Drāviṛ*; a Brāhman of *Drāviṛ*. *s.*

دراوڑك द्राविड़क *drāviṛak*, m. zedoary (*Curcuma zerumbet*); black salt. *s.* [fusing. *s.*

دراون द्रावन *drāvan*, m. the clearing nut;

دراها *du-rāhā*, a road branching into two different directions. *p.*

دراهم *darāhim* also *darāhīm* (pl. of درهم). *a.*

دراءي *darā,ī*, f. contradiction. *harza darā,ī*, f. chattering, idle talk. *darā,e* (v. *darā*), a bell. *p.*

درايت *dirāyat*, knowledge, sense, science; manner, mode; quality. *a.*

دراين ولا *dar īn wilā*, at this time; in this case; by these presents. *p. a.*

درب दर्ब *darb* (cor. of *dravya*), m. prosperity, wealth; metal, substance, matter. *s.*

دربار *darbār*, m. house, dwelling, court, hall of audience. *darbār bāndnā*, (Dakh.) to fix or secure the court; to give a bribe. *p.*

درباري *darbārī*, of or belonging to the court; a courtier; the elegant and polished language of the court, in contradistinction to *bāzārī*, q. v. *p.*

دربان *dar-bān*, m. a doorkeeper, porter. *p.*

درباني *darbānī*, f. the office of doorkeeper. *p.*

دربدر *dar-ba-dar*, from door to door, a wandering mendicant, a vagrant. *p.*

دربدھ दुर्बुद्धि *dur-buddhi*, silly, ignorant. *s.*

دربڑ *darbaṛ*, war, battle, contest. *d.*

دربست *dar-bast* (for *dar o bast*, q. v.), all, entire. *p.*

دربستہ *dar-basta*, bound, tied, fastened. *p.*

دربل दुर्बल *dur-bal*, infirm, powerless, weak; thin, emaciated; poor. *s.*

دربلتا दुर्बलता *dur-balatā*, f. infirmity, poverty. *s.*

دربند *dar-band*, a bar, bolt (of a door). *p.*

دربندي *dar-bandī*, f. a statement of the different rates of a village; also assessing the prices of produce. *p.*

دربھ दर्भ *darbh*, m. *kusa*, or sacrificial grass (*Poa cynosuroides*); a kind of reed (*Saccharum spontaneum* or *cylindricum*). *s.*

دربھاگیہ दुर्भाग्य *dur-bhāgya*, unfortunate, unlucky. *s.*

دربھاو दुर्भाव *dur-bhāo*, m. bad disposition, ill-temper; bad behaviour, ill manners. *s.*

دربھچھ *durbhichh* for *dur-bhiksha*, m. a scarcity, a famine. *s.*

دربہرا दरबहरा *darbahrā* or *durbahrā*, an intoxicating spirit drawn from rice. *h.*

دربھکش दुर्भक्ष *dur-bhaksha*, hard to eat. *s.*

دربھکش दुर्भिक्ष *dur-bhiksha*, m. scarcity, famine. *s.*

دربھگا दुर्भगा *dur-bhagā*, f. a wife disliked by her husband; an ill-tempered woman. *s.*

دربھگرہ दुरभिग्रह *dur-abhigrah*, m. a tree (*Achyranthes aspera*). *s.*

دربھگرھا दुरभिग्रहा *dur-abhigrahā*, f. cowach. *s.*

درپ दर्प *darp*, m. pride, arrogance, boasting. *s.*

درپن दर्पण *darpan*, m. a mirror, a looking-glass. *s.*

درپي *dar-pai*, following, in pursuit of, intent upon. *p.*

درپيش *dar-pesh*, lit. in front. *dar-pesh-honā*, to await (one), to come to pass. *p.*

درت द्रुत *drut*, quick, swift; flown, escaped, run away. *drut-pad*, m. a quick pace; adv. quickly. *s.*

درت दुरित *dur-it*, sinful, wicked; m. sin. *s.*

درتر दुरुत्तर *dur-uttar*, unanswerable. *s.*

درج *durj*, m. a little casket in which they deposit gems. *a.*

درج *darj*, m. comprising, holding; a closet, a place for writing, or any thing written on, a volume. *darj-k.*, a. to write, to copy, to enter, to fold. *a.*

درجات *darjāt* (pl. of درجہ), steps, degrees, &c. *a.*

درجات दुर्जात *dur-jāt*, inauspiciously born; improper; m. misfortune, calamity; disparity, impropriety. *s.*

درجات दुर्जाति *dur-jāti*, vile, wicked, low, outcast. *s.*

درجر दुर्जर *dur-jar*, indigestible. *s.*

درجن दुर्जन *dur-jan*, bad, wicked, malicious; m. a bad man, an enemy. *s.*

درجنتاي दुर्जनताई *dur-janatā,ī*, f. or *dur-janatwa*, m. enmity, malignity, wickedness, villainy. *s.*

درجہ *darja* (properly *daraja*). m. step, stair, gradation, degree, rank, station; act (of a play); a degree of a circle. *darja ba darja*, step by step, gradually. *a.*

درجي दुर्जय *dur-jay*, difficult to be overcome, invincible. *s.*

درجي *darjī* (for *darzī*), a tailor. *p. h.*

درحالتيکہ *dar-ḥālate-ki*, } in case that; on the
درحاليکہ *dar-ḥāle-ki*, } supposition that. *p. a.*

درحوالہ *dar-ḥawāla*, a sublease or tenure. *p. a.*

درحوت *darḥot*, advance (Wilson's Gl.).

درخا *du-rukhā*, that which is the same on both sides, not having a wrong side. *p.*

درخت *darakht* or *dirakht*, m. a tree. *p.*

درخشان *darakhshān*, shining, brilliant. *p.*

درخشاني *darakhshānī*, } f. brilliancy,
درخشندگي *darakhshandagī*, } splendour. *p.*

درخشندہ *darakhshanda*, bright, shining; a shiner. *p.*

درخواست *dar-khwāst*, f. application, request, entreaty, proposal, desire, wish, demand, petition, appeal, or petition of appeal. *p.*

درد *dard*, m. pain, affliction; pity, sympathy. *dard-ālūd*, overwhelmed in grief. *dard-āmez*, piteous, feelingly. *dard-ānā*, to be affected with pity, &c. *dard-angez*, pitiable, exciting compassion. *dard-ras*, grieved, afflicted. *dardi zih*, m. the pangs of labour, throe. *dardi-sar*, m. or *dard-sarī*, f. the head-ache; trouble, vexation. *dard-sharik*, sympathetical. *dardi shikam*, m. colic. *dardi farzandī*, m. paternal affection. *dard-khānā*, to feel pity; to suffer the pangs of childbirth. *dard-mand* or *dard-nāk*, afflicted; compassionate, sympathizing. *dard-mandī*, f. affliction. *p.*

درد *durd*, f. sediment, dregs, lees. *p.*

دردا *dardā*, interj. alas! woe's me! *p.*

دردا दरदा *dardā*, f. a country bordering on Kashmir; m. name of a tribe of barbarians. *s.*

دردامن *dar-dāman*, a skirt, ornament of a gown or robe. *p.*

دردر दरदर *dardar*, m. cinnabar. *h.*

دردر दरिद्र *daridr*, poor, needy, wretched; m. poverty, indigence. *s.*

دردرا दरदरा *dardarā*, half pounded, coarsely ground. *h.*

دردرتا दरिद्रता *daridratā*, f. poverty, indigence, want, wretchedness. *s.*

دردرش दुर्दर्श *dur-darsh*, difficult to be seen or met with. *s.*

دردرشٹ दुर्दृष्ट *dur-dṛishṭa*, ill-seen, ill-examined; looked at with an evil eye; m. bad luck, misfortune. *s.*

دردرو दद्रु *dardrū*, m. cutaneous eruption, herpes. *dardrū-rogī*, afflicted with herpes. *s.*

دردري दरिद्री *daridrī*, poor, destitute, needy. *s.*

دردشا दुर्दशा *dur-dashā*, f. calamity, misfortune. *s.* [unconquerable. *s.*

دردم दुर्दम *dur-dam*, difficult to be subdued,

دردن दुर्दिन *dur-din*, m. a dark or cloudy day, rainy weather. *s.*

درديو दुर्दैव *dur-daiv*, m. bad luck, misfortune. *s.*

درڑھ दृढ *driṛh*, firm, strong, immoveable; bulky, massive. *driṛh-bhakti*, faithful, devoted. *driṛh-sauhṛid*, firm in friendship, constant. *driṛh-kārī*, persevering, determined. *driṛh-mushti*, close-fisted, miserly. *driṛh-nis,chay*, certain, confirmed, undoubted. *s.*

درڑھابھکت दृढाभक्ति *driṛhā-bhakti*, f. a faithful mistress or wife. *s* [prove. *s.*

درڑھانا दृढाना *driṛhānā*, a. to strengthen, to

درڑھانگ दृढाङ्ग *driṛhāng*, firm-bodied, hard; m. a diamond. *s.* [firm in battle. *s.*

درڑھايدھ दृढायुध *driṛhāyudh*, m. a hero, one

درڑھبندھني दृढबन्धिनी *driṛh-bandhinī*, f. a creeper (*Echites frutescens*). *s.* [nut. *s.*

درڑھپھل दृढफल *driṛh-phal*, m. the cocoa-

درڑھتا दृढता *driṛhatā*, f. strength, firmness. *s.*

درڑھسکندھ दृढस्कन्ध *driṛha-shandh*, m. a sort of Mimusops. *s.*

درڑھسوترکا दृढसूत्रिका *driṛh-sūtrikā*, f. a plant from the fibres of which bowstrings are made. *s.*

درڑھلوما दृढलोमा *driṛh-lomā*, having coarse or stiff hair; m. a wild hog; bristles. *s.*

درز *darz*, m. sewing; a rag, a slip of cloth, a long strip of cloth, a narrow shred; a rent, split, or fissure in a garment, &c. *p. a.* [knocker. *p.*

درزن *darzan*, f. a needle. *dar-zan*, a door-

درزي *darzī*, m. a tailor. *darzin* or *darzinī*, a tailor's wife. *p.*

درس *dars*, m. reading, learning to read; a lecture, lesson. *dars denā*, a. to teach to read. *dars lenā*, a. to read a lesson. *a.*

درس दर्श *dars* or दरस *daras*, m. seeing, sight; the conjunction of the sun and moon, or the day of new moon. *s.*

درست *durust*, right, fit; proper, just, true, well, safe, sound, entire, straight, accurate. *durust rakhnā*, a. to admit, to allow. *durust-k.*, a. to arrange, to adjust, to rectify. *p.*

درست दर्शित *darsit*, visible, apparent, shewn, displayed, seen. *s.*

درستگو *durust-go*, one who speaks the truth. *p.*

درسته *du-rasta*, a double row or avenue (of trees, &c.), one on each side of the way. *p.*

درستي *durustī*, f. reformation, amendment; truth, rectitude, soundness. *p.*

درسک दर्शक *darsak*, who or what shews, displays, explains; an exhibitor. *s.*

درسلک द्रुसल्लक *dru-sallah*, m. a tree (*Chironjia sapida*). *s.*

درسن दर्शन *darsan*, m. sight, seeing, looking; aspect, interview, appearance; a shāstra, one of the six philosophical systems; visiting a sacred shrine. *darsan-pratibhū*, m. a surety for appearance. *darsan dhārī*, beautiful. *s.*

درسني दर्शनी *darsanī*, f. a bill of exchange payable at sight; offering, present; adj. handsome, sightly. *darsanī jawān*, a beautiful youth. *s.*

درسني هنڈي *darsanī-hunḍī*, f. a bill of exchange, or money order, payable at sight. *h.*

درسنيه दर्शनीय *darsanīya*, beautiful, handsome; visible, to be seen. *darsanīya-mānī*, vain, conceited, thinking one's self handsome. *s.*

درشا दृशा *drishā*, f. the eye (also *drishī*). *s*

درشت *durusht*, rough, hard, stiff, rigid; stern, morose, oppressive, fierce. *p.*

درشتي *durushtī*, f. severity, fierceness. *p.*

درشٹ दृष्ट *drishṭa*, seen, visible. *drishṭa-wān* or *drishṭa-wat*, seeing, having seen. *s.*

درشٹ दृष्टि *drishṭi* or *drishṭ*, f. sight, vision; eye. *drishṭi-pāt* or *drishṭi-nipāt*, m. a look, a glance. *drisht kūṭ*, m. an enigma, a riddle. *s.*

درشٹانت दृष्टान्त *drishṭānt*, m. an example, illustration; a parable, a simile. *s.*

درشٹ کرت दृष्टिकृत *drishṭi-hrit*, m. a flower (*Hibiscus mutabilis*). *s.*

درشٹھ दुरिष्ठ *durishṭha*, very bad, most wicked; m. great crime, extreme wickedness. *s.*

درشن दर्शन *darshan*, m. sight, interview. *s.*

درشني दर्शनी *darshanī*, at sight (v. *darsanī*). *s.*

درشوپم दृशोपम *drishopam*, m. the white lotus (*Nelumbium speciosum*). *s.*

درشي दृशी *drishī*, f. the eye (also *drishā*). *s.*

درشيه दृश्य *drishya*, visible, to be seen, beautiful; m. (in arithm.) a given quantity or number. *drishya-twa*, m. vision, sight. *s.*

درصورت *dar-ṣūrat*, in case that; suppose that. *p.*

درفشان *darafshān*, shining, splendid. *p.*

درفشه *durufsha*, a sword. *p.*

درک *dark*, m. understanding, knowledge, comprehending, (in law) a contingency, a possible event. *a.*

درک दृक *drik* or *drig*, m. the eye. *drik-karn*, m. a snake (lit. whose eyes are his ears; the snake having no external ear). *s.*

درکا दरका *darkā*, m. crack, crevice, cranny. *h.*

درکات *darakāt* (pl. of درکت), steps for descending, descents. *a.*

درکار *dar-kār*, necessary, wanting. *p.*

درکانا दरकाना *darkānā*, a. to cause to crack, split. *h.*

درکت *darakat*, descent, bottom. *a.*

درکلم द्रुकिलिम *dru-kilim*, m. a tree, a sort of pine (*Pinus devadāru*). *s.*

درکنا दरकना *daraknā*, n. to split, to rend, to be torn, to crack. *h.*

درکنار *dar-kinār*, on one side, apart, out of the way, out of the question. *p.*

درکها दुरुखा *du-rukhā* (from the Pers. *du-rukhā*, q. v.). *h.*

درکهال दरखाल *darkhāl*, a cattle enclosure. *h.*

درکهي *durkhī*, an insect whose ravages are very destructive to indigo, when the plant is young. *h.*

درگ दृग *drig*, m. the eye, the vision. *drig-gol* or *drig-mandal*, m. a small circle within the great circles of the armillary sphere, accompanying each planetary orbit. *s.*

درگ दुर्ग *durga*, impenetrable, impassable, inaccessible, unattainable; m. a strong fort, a difficult pass or defile. *durga-karma*, m. difficult enterprise. *s.*

درگا दुर्गा *durgā*, f. the goddess Durgā, the wife of Shiva, and mother of Kārtikeya and Ganesha; also called Umā, Bhavānī, and Pārvatī, a goddess of terrific and irascible temper, particularly worshipped at the Durgā-pūjā held in Bengal in the month of Aswin; (met.) a word; name of a Hindū book containing the narration of the goddess Durgā. *s.*

درگا *du-raggā*, capricious, whimsical (v. *do*). *p.*

درگادهکاري दुर्गाधिकारी *durgādhikārī*, } m. the governor of a fort. *s.*
درگادهيکش दुर्गाध्यक्ष *durgādhyaksha*, }

درگاشرين दुर्गाश्रयण *durgāshrayan*, m. taking refuge in a fortress. *s.*

درگانومي दुर्गानवमी *durgā-navamī*, f. the ninth of the light half of Kārtik, sacred to Durgā as Jagaddhātrī. *s.*

درگاه *dargāh*, f. a place, court; threshold, door; a mosque. *p.*

درگت दुर्गत *dur-gat*, poor, indigent, afflicted. *s.*

درگت दुर्गति *dur-gati*, f. hell; poverty, meanness, abjectness. *s.*

درگبنسي *durag-bansī*, a tribe of *rājpūts*. *h.*

درگذر *dar-guzar*, passing over, excusing. *dar-guzar-k.*, to excuse, overlook, to pass by. *p.*

درگذرنا *dar-guzarnā*, n. to decline, to leave off, to refrain from, to pass by, to excuse. *p.*

درگرفت کرنا *dar-girift karnā*, a. to catch, seize, to captivate. *p.*

درگم दुर्गम *durgam*, difficult of access, unattainable; deep, profound (v. *durga*). *s.*

درگمتا दुर्गमता *durgamatā*, f. depth, profundity *s.*

درگنده दुर्गन्ध *dur-gandh*, fœtid; f. stink, stench. *dur-gandh ānā*, to stink. *dur-gandhī*, ill-smelling. *s.*

درگه *dar-gah* (same as *dar-gāh*), a court. *p.*

درگهٹ दुर्घट *durghaṭ*, difficult of accomplishment, arduous. *s.*

درگير *dar-gīr*, effective; inflaming. *p.*

درلبه दुर्लभ *dur-labh*, difficult to be procured, scarce, rare; excellent, eminent; dear, beloved; m. a plant, a sort of hedysarum. *s.*

درلبها दुर्लभा *dur-labhā*, f. a sort of prickly nightshade. *s.*

درلکشن दुर्लक्षण *dur-lakshaṇ*, m. an unlucky mark, a mark or sign of evil omen. *s.*

درلانا *dar-lānā*, a. to comprise. *p. h.*

درم द्रुम *drum* or *druma*, m. a tree; a tree of Swarga or paradise. *drum-nakh*, m. a thorn or claw of trees. *s.*

درم *diram*, money, specie; a small coin so named (v. *dirham*). *p.*

درما दरमा *darmā*, m. a kind of mat. *h.*

درمامي द्रुमामय *drum-āmay*, m. lac, the animal dye, or disease of trees. *s.*

درمان *darmān*, m. medicine, cure. *p.*

درماندگي *dar-māndagī*, f. misery, distress, penury, misfortune. *p.*

درماندن *dar-māndan*, to be in distress. *p.*

درمانده *dar-mānda*, helpless, destitute, without remedy. *p.*

درماها *dar-māhā*, m. } monthly wages, salary.
درماهي *dar-māhī*, f. } *dar-māhā-dār*, one who receives monthly wages. *p.*

درمت दुर्मति *dur-mati*, silly, ignorant, simple, a blockhead; also *dur-matī*, f. folly, foolishness. *s.*

درمس दुरमुस *durmus*, m. a pounder, an instrument for pounding pavements with, a rammer. *h.*

درمکه दुर्मुख *dur-mukh*, foul-mouthed, scurrilous; ugly, hideous. *s.*

درمن *darman*, m. drug, remedy. *p.*

درمنا दुर्मना *dur-manā*, sad, distressed, sorrowful. *s.*

درموليه दुर्मूल्य *dur-mūlya*, dear, of an exorbitant price; m. dearness, any thing of high price. *s.*

درم وياده द्रुमव्याधि *drum-vyādhi*, m. lac (v. *drumāmay*). *s.*

درمه *darmah* (for *dār-māhā*), pay, wages. *d.*

درميان *darmiyān*, m. interval, middle; postpos. during, in the course of, before, in view. *darmiyān denā*, a. to employ as a mediator. *p.*

درمياني *darmiyānī*, midmost; m. a mediator. *p.*

درميدها दुर्मेधा *dur-medhā*, dull, stupid, ignorant. *s.*

درميشور द्रुमेश्वर *drumeshwar*, m. (the lord of trees) the palm tree. *s.*

درنا दुरना *durnā*, n. to be hidden, concealed or absent; to lurk, disappear. *h.*

درنام दुर्नाम *dur-nām*, m. infamy, bad name, obloquy, slander. *dur-nāmī*, infamous. *s.*

درناما दुर्नामा *dur-nāmā*, m. piles or hæmorrhoides. *s.*

درنت दुरन्त *dur-ant*, ending ill, having a bad end. *s.*

درند *darind* or *darand*, درنده *darinda* or *daranda*, } tearing; rapacious, fierce, ravenous (animal). *p.*

درنگ *dirang*, m. delay, hesitation; late. *p.*

درنگا *du-rangā*, of two colours, capricious, fickle. *p.*

درنگي *dirangī*, f. lateness, tardiness. *p.*

درنوار दुर्निवार *dur-niwār*, difficult to be stopped, irresistible. *s.*

درنيت दुर्नीत *dur-nīt*, ill-behaved, ill-governed, impolitic, m. (or *dur-nīti*, f.) misconduct, impolicy. *s.*

درو *dirau*, m. reaping, cutting corn at harvest. *dirau-k.*, a. to reap. *p.*

درو दर्व *darv* or *darw*, m. prosperity, wealth, substance, metal, matter. *s.*

درواچيه दुर्वाच्य *dur-vāchya*, m. abuse, ill-omened speech. *s.*

دروازه *darwāza*, m. door. *darwāza ṭhoknā*, a. to knock at a door. *darwāza ma'mūr-k.*, a. to close a door. *p.*

دروازي *darwāzī*, m. a warden, a keeper of the city. *p.*

دروان *darwān*, m. a doorkeeper. *p.*

دروبست *darobast*, all, entire; the whole of an estate, as opposed to a *ḳismat*, or share of it. *p.*

دروچن दुर्वचन *dur-vachan*, m. abuse; ill-omened speech. *s.*

درود *darūd*, f. congratulation, benediction, salutation, blessing. *p.*

درودكار *darūd-kār*, درودگر *darūd-gar*, } m. a carpenter. *p.*

درودكاري *darūd-kārī*, درودگري *darūd-garī*, } f. carpentry, the trade or art of a carpenter. *p.*

درودن *dirūdan* (r. *dirū* or *dirau*), to reap, to mow. *p.*

درورت दुर्वृत्त *dur-vṛitt*, vile, wicked, leading a low or infamous life; a cheat, rogue, juggler, a blackguard. *dur-vṛitti*, f. disreputable life, degrading business, juggling. *s.*

دروڑ द्रविड़ *draviṛ*, m. a man of an out-cast tribe, descended from a degraded *Kshatrī*. *s.*

دروڑي द्रविड़ी *draviṛī*, f. one of the rāginīs or female personifications of music. *s.*

دروش दरोश *darosh*, m. an awl; a lancet. *s.*

دروغ *darogh*, m. a lie, falsehood; false. *darogh-ḥalfī*, perjury, false-swearing. *darogh-go*, m. a liar. *darogh-go,ī*, f. the telling of lies. *p.*

دروغي *daroghī*, false, lying; a liar. *p.*

درون *darūn*, in, within; m. interior; the heart, bowels. *p.*

درون द्रोण *dron*, m. a measure of capacity, the same as an *ādhak*; a measure of four *ādhaks*; the sixteenth part of a *kharī*, or forty-eight gallons; a weight of thirty-six *sers*, or about sixty-four pounds avoirdupois; name of the military preceptor of the Pandu princes; a raven, the carrion crow. *s.*

درون كاك द्रोणकाक *dron-kāk*, m. a raven. *s.*

درونكي द्रौणिकी *draunikī*, f. a vessel holding a *dron* by measure. *s.*

درون مكهه द्रोणमुख *dron-mukh*, m. (also *dronī-mukh*) the capital of a district; the principal of four hundred villages. *s.*

درون ناشن द्रविणनाशन *dravin-nāshan*, m. a plant. (*Hyperanthera morunda*). *s.*

درونه *darūna*, m. the heart. *p.*

دروني *darūnī*, internal; intrinsic. *p.*

دروني مكهه द्रोणीमुख *dronī-mukh*, v. *dron-mukh*.

دروه द्रोह *droh*, m. spite, malice, hatred; injury, wrong, mischief; rebellion. *droh-chintan*, m. injurious design, malice prepense. *s.*

دروهاٹ द्रोहाट *drohāṭ*, m. a sort of metre, the *dohā*, or stanza of Hindī poetry. *s.*

دروهي द्रोही *drohī*, دروهيا द्रोहिया *drohiyā*, } spiteful, malicious, inimical, mischievous, rebellious. *s.*

دروي दर्वी *darvī*, f. a ladle or spoon. *s.*

درويارجن द्रव्यार्जन *dravyārjan*, m. gain, acquisition of wealth. *s.*

دريوزه *darweza*, m. beggary, mendicancy. *p.*

درويش *darwesh*, m. a dervise, beggar, a religious mendicant. *p*

درويشانه *darweshāna*, like a *darwesh*, q. v. *p.*

درويشي *darweshī*, f. life or state of a *darwesh*. *p.*

درويه द्रव्य *dravya*, m. wealth, substance; an object in general; elementary things, as earth, water, fire, air, æther, time, space, soul and intellect; a drug, a medicament. *dravya-sanchaya*, m. accumulation of wealth. *dravya-wat* or *dravya-wān*, rich, wealthy *s.*

درويه *du-rūya*, double, two-faced. *p.*

دره *dara*, also *darra*, m. a valley or glen between hills, with a stream flowing or winding through it; a depth, a pass. *p.*

دره *dira* (properly *durra*), m. a scourge. *a.*

درهردي दुर्हृदय *dur-hṛiday*, bad-hearted, evil-minded. *s.*

درهم ***dar-ham***, angry, higgledy-piggledy, confounded. *dar-ham bar-ham*, confused. *p.*

درهم ***darham*** or ***dirham***, m. money; a silver coin, of which from twenty to twenty-five have at different times passed current for a *dīnār*, and the latter being nearly equal to a ducat or sequin, about nine shillings of our money, it follows that the *darham* is about five pence sterling. "The *dirham* is said to have originally been an unstamped piece of silver, shaped like a date stone. About fifty years after the death of the prophet Muhammad it was altered into a round form and stamped. Its value in these days is uncertain."—(Binning.) *a.*

درهمي ***dar-hamī***, f. confusion, disorder. *p.*

درهي दरही ***darhī***, f. the name of a fish, sort of carp (*Cyprinus*). *h.*

دري दरी ***darī***, f. a cave, a grotto; a valley [(v. *darā*). *h.*

دري दुरी ***durī***, f. the two on dice, the deuce. *p.*

دري ***darī***, f. a small carpet; a dialect of the Persian language, the origin and peculiarities of which are variously defined by Persian lexicographers. Some allege its distinctive mark to be when the form of the word is complete, without contraction, as in the words *bago ishkam*, said to be *Darī*, whereas the forms *go* and *shikam* are *Pārsī*. Others make it the dialect of a certain district, comprehending *Balkh*, *Bukhārā*, *Badakhshān*, *Marw-Shāh-Jahān*, and *Bāmiān*. The name is by some said to be derived from *dara*, a valley among hills, which corresponds with its origin in *Badakhshān* and the mountainous parts of *Kandhār*. Others assert that it was spoken at the court of the monarchs of the *Kaianian* dynasty, and derive the name from *dar*, a gate, or *dargāh*, a court. *p.*

دريا ***daryā***, m. the sea; any large river; the waters. *daryā-barār* and *daryā-barāmad*, lands reclaimed from a river. *daryā-burd* and *daryā-shikast*, lands cut away by the encroachments of a river. *daryā-kā kaf*, foam of the sea; "meer-schaum." *daryā,e maghrib*, the western ocean. *p.*

درياچه ***daryācha***, m. a lake, a ditch, a pool. *p.*

دريافت ***daryāft***, f. conceiving, understanding. *daryaft-k.*, to understand, to perceive. *p.*

درياءي ***daryā,ī***, of or belonging to the sea or river, marine. *daryā,ī ādmī*, a mer-man. *daryā,ī totā* (lit. the sea parrot), the flamingo, also called *rāj-hańs*. *p.*

دريبا दरीबा ***darībā*** or ***darebā***, m. a stall (in a market) where betel is sold. *h.*

دريچه ***darīcha***, m. a window. *p.*

دريدن ***darīdan***, to tear, to rend. *p.*

دريده ***darīda***, torn. *darīda-dahan*, plain-spoken, saying whatever comes uppermost. *p.*

دريس दरेस ***dares***, a road, margin, any line very straight. *h.*

دريغ ***daregh*** or ***diregh***, m. a sigh, sorrow, repugnance, disinclination; interj. alas! *daregh-k.*, a. to withhold. *daregh khurdan*, to grieve, to be afflicted. *p.*

دريغا ***dareghā*** or ***direghā***, interj. alas! *p.*

دريكان द्रेक्काण ***drekkān***, m. the regent of one-third of a planetary sign, the Decanus of European astrology. *s.*

دريودهن दुर्योधन ***duryodhan***, the elder of the Kuru princes, one of the heroes of the *Mahābhārata*. *s.*

دريوزه ***daryūza***, beggary, begging. *p.*

دڙچنا ***daṛachnā***, n. to fit tight. *d.*

دڙكنا दड़कना ***daṛaknā***, n. to split, to be rent or torn, to crack. *h.*

دڙكي ***duṛkī***, f. (v. *dulkī*) a trot. *d.*

دڙه दिढ़ ***diṛh*** (for *dṛiṛh*, q. v.), firm, immoveable. *s.*

دڙهتا दिढ़ता ***diṛhatā***, f. firmness, strength. *s.*

دڙهانا दिढ़ाना ***diṛhānā***, a. to prove (the strength of a thing), to strengthen. *s.*

دڙهمنڈا दढ़मुंडा ***daṛh-munḍā***, shaven, beardless. *h.*

دڙهيل दढ़ियल ***daṛhiyal***, having a long beard. *h.*

دڙيڙا दड़ेड़ा ***daṛeṛā***, m. hard, impetuous rain. *h.*

دڙيلا ***daṛelā***, m. a rush of water, a water-fall. *d.*

دزد ***duzd***, m. a thief, robber. *p.*

دزدي ***duzdī***, f. the act of stealing, theft, robbery; stealth. *p.*

دزديده ***duzdīda***, stolen, pilfered. *p.*

دژم ***dizham***, melancholy, grieved; black, dark. *p.*

دس दस or दश ***das***, ten. *dasoń-disā*, the ten regions or quarters. *dasoń-dwār*, the ten passages for the actions of the faculties, viz. the ears, eyes, nostrils, mouth, penis, anus, and the crown of the head. *s.*

دس दिस ***dis*** (for *dish*), } f. side, quarter,
دسا दिसा ***disā*** (for *dishā*), } point (of the compass). *disā-k.*, a. to travel. *disā-jānā* or *-phirnā*, to go into the fields (for a privy). *s.*

دسا दशा ***dasā*** (for *dashā*), f. condition, state, circumstances. *s.*

دساد दुसाद ***dusād***, m. name of a low caste (v. *dosād*). *h.*

دسادهيه दुःसाध्य ***du-sādhya***, difficult, arduous. *s.*

دساسول दिशाशूल ***disā-sūl***, m. (v. *dishā-shūl*), an unlucky day. *s.*

دساله ***das-sāla***, decennial; a decennial settlement. *h.*

دسانس दशांश ***dasāńs***, m. the tenth part. *s.*

دساور दिसावर ***disāwar***, m. (v. *desāwar*) a foreign country, a climate. *s.*

دساوري दिसावरी ***disāwarī***, f. a kind of betel leaf; a kind of dove, foreign (goods). *s.*

دسپرش दुःस्पर्श ***du-sparsh***, difficult or unpleasant to be touched; m. a plant (*Hedysarum alhagi*). *du-sparshā*, f. a prickly sort of nightshade. *s.*

دست ***dast***, m. hand, cubit; stool, purge, evacuation; (in Dakh.) a shoulder of mutton, the forequarter of an animal. *dast-afshān*, one who dances, or moves the hands in dancing, &c. *dast-āmoz*, tame, familiarized, tractable; skilful, dexterous. *dast-andāz*, he who commences a business; an oppressor. *dast-āwar*, purgative, effective (as medicine). *dast-āwez*, f. signature, a note of hand, bond, title-deed, &c. *dast ba dast*, from hand to hand, quick, expeditious; ready-money purchase. *dast-burd*, m. superiority, advantage, victory. *dast bardār honā*, n. to leave business, to desert, to decline. *dast-bardārī*, f. cessation, relinquishment. *dast bar sar honā*, n. to be unable to execute one's intention, to be distressed, weak, poor, or wretched. *dast basta*, with close hands (a token of respect). *dast ba sar honā*, a. to salute in the eastern manner by putting the hand to the head. *dast ba ḳabẓa*, sword in hand, ready for battle. *dast-buḳcha*, m. cloth in which a small bundle is wrapped up. *dast-band*, a string of pearls or precious stones used as ornaments by women. *dast-bos honā*, *dast-bosī-k.*, to kiss hands, to salute. *dast baiʻ honā*, n. to become a disciple. *dast panāh*, m. tongs. *dast-chālāk*, nimble-fingered, a thief. *dast-chālākī*, f. a civil war, duel; stealth. *dast-ḵhatt*, m. signature; a manuscript, chirography. *dast-darāz*, m. an oppressor. *dast-darāzī*, f. oppression. *dast-ras*, able, affording protection or aid. *dast-ras honā*, n. to be able, to afford. *dast-rasī*, f. ability, assistance. *dast-shifā*, successful in curing diseases (a physician). *dast-ṭalab*, a beggar. *dast-farosh*, m. a pedlar. *dast-faroshī*, f. peddling. *dast-ḳudrat*, power, ability, strength. *dast-kār*, m. a handicraftsman; dexterous. *dast-kārī*, f. handicraft; dexterity. *dast-kash*, a led horse; a guide (of the blind); a captive, a beggar. *dast-girifta*, one who is taken by the hand; a protégé. *dast-gīr*, a patron, protector, a saint. *dast-girī*, f. aid, help, assistance, support, protection. *dast-lāf*, the first money received in the morning by dealers. *dast-māl*, m. a handkerchief. *dast-nigar* or *-nigarān*, needy, one in want. *dast-o baghal*, caressing, embracing. *dast o girebān honā*, to be engaged in combat; "to be at it tooth and nail." *dast-yāb*, attainable, procurable. *p.*

دستا दस्ता *dastā*, m. zinc, tutanag; *lapis calaminaris*. *h.*

دستار *dastār*, m. a turban. *dastār-band*, m. a servant whose business it is to make up the turban. *dastār ḵhwān*, a tablecloth. *p.*

دستان *dastān* (for *dāstān*), a tale or romance; (pl. of *dast*) the hands. *p.*

دستانه *dastāna*, m. a glove, a gauntlet. *p.*

دسترخوان *dastar-ḵhwān*, m. (properly *dastār-ḵhwān*) a tablecloth; strictly speaking, it is a round piece of cloth or leather, &c., spread on the ground, on which the food is laid out, and around which the guests squat and fall to. There is no *table* in the case. *p.*

دستك *dastak*, f. clapping of the hands, rapping at a door; a pass, passport, summons; commission. *p.* [ture. *p.*

دست‌كاري *dast-kārī*, f. handiwork, manufacture.

دستكانه *dastakāna*, a fee for serving a writ or summons, or for a passport, &c. *p.*

دستكي *dastakī*, f. a pocket-book, a tweezer-case; a falconer's glove. *p.*

دستگاه *dastgāh*, } f. power, ability,
دستگه *dast-gah*, } strength. *p.*

دستور *dastūr*, m. custom, fashion, mode, manner; a minister, senator; model, regulation. *a.p.*

دستورالعمل *dastūru-l-ʻamal*, m. a rule, regulation, model; a body of instructions and tables for the use of revenue officers under the native governments. *a. p.*

دستوري *dastūrī*, f. perquisites paid to servants by one who sells to their master, a gratuity varying in amount in different places from one to three per cent.; leave, licence, congé. *p.*

دسته *dasta*, m. a handle; a pestle; a quire of paper; a bundle consisting of twenty-four arrows; a handful; a skein of thread; a division of an army, a brigade. *dasta-dār*, m. commander of a *dasta*. *p.*

دستي *dastī*, f. a torch or link that is carried in the hands; a kind of present or handsel given to native officials; adj. of or relating to the hand. *dastī muhar*, the sign manual. *p.*

دستيار *dastyār*, an assistant, coadjutor, minister. *p*

دستج दुस्त्यज *dus-tyaj*, difficult to be relinquished or parted with. *s.*

دسخط *daskhatt*, m. (for *dast-ḵhatt*) a signature. *daskhatti khāṣṣ*, the royal signature. *p. a.*

دسخطي *daskhattī*, of or relating to a signature. *p. a.*

دسر दुस्सर *dussar*, m. double stakes at dice, &c., playing double or quits. *h.*

دسرا *dusrā* (for *dūsrā*), the second. *h.*

دسران *dasrān*, a kind of trick in wrestling. *d.*

دسرتھ दशरथ *dasarath* (for *dasharath*), name of an ancient *rājā* of Ayodhyā or Oude, father of *Rāma*, the latter being called *dāsharath*. *s.*

دسم दसम *dasam* or दशम *dasham*, m. the tenth. *s.*

دسم दुःसम *du-sam*, improper, unseasonable. *s.*

دسمي दसमी *dasamī* or दशमी *dashamī*, f. the tenth day of a lunar month. *s.*

دسمي दुःसमय *du-samay*, m. time of affliction, distress. *s.*

دسن दसन *dasan* or दशन *dashan*, m. a tooth. *s.*

دسنا दिसना *disnā*, n. to be seen, to appear; a. to see. *s.*

دسوان दसवाँ *daswāṅ*, the tenth. *daswāna*, a tenth part (added to the revenue, &c.). *s.*

دسوترا दसोतरा *dasotarā*, } ten per cent.; a
دسوتره दसोतरः *dasotara*, } tenth part. *h.*

دسوكھا दसोखा *dasokhā*, m. moulting (of birds). *dasokhā jhārnā*, to moult. *h.*

دسوں‌دسا दसोंदिसा *dasoṅ-disā*, the ten regions or quarters of the world. *s.*

دسوں‌دوار दसोंदुआर *dasoṅ-dwār* (see *das*). *s.*

دسوندھا दसौंधा *dasauṅdhā*, } m. a panegy-
دسوندھي दसौंधी *dasauṅdhī*, } rist, a bard. *h.*

دسه दुःसह *du-sah*, intolerable, difficult to be borne. *s.*

دسهرا दसहरा *dasahrā* or *das,harā*, the tenth of *Jaith shukl paksh*, which is the birthday of *Gangā*. Whoever bathes in the *Gangā* on that day is purified from ten sorts of sins; the tenth of *āsin shukl paksh*, on which, after the worship and religious ceremonies performed during nine nights (*navarātri*) they throw the images of *Devī* into the river. On this day *Rāma* marched against *Rāvana*, on which account it is called *Vijai Dasamī*. The day is celebrated with great pomp by Hindū princes, the weapons and instruments of war are hallowed, and, if war be intended, the campaign is then opened. *s.*

دسي दसी *dasī*, f. thread; the unwoven threads at the end of a piece of cloth. *s.*

دسي दस्यु *dasyu*, m. an enemy, a thief, an oppressor, a violator, &c. *dasyu-vṛitti*, f. theft, dishonest mode of subsistence. *s.*

دسيرہ *du-sera*, a weight of two *sers*. *p.*

دسيلا दसीला *dasīlā*, in good circumstances. *s.*

دش दश *dash*, ten (v. *das*). *s.*

دش दिश *dish*, } f. region, quarter, point (of
دشا दिशा *dishā*, } the compass). *s.*

دشا दशा *dashā*, f. state, condition, circumstance; period or time of life, age. *dashā-phal*, m. result of circumstances or of condition of life. *dashā-vishesh*, m. peculiar circumstances or condition. *s.*

دشارن दशार्ण *dashārn*, m. a country in central Hindūstān, south-east of the Vindhya mountain. *s.*

دشارنا दशार्णा *dashārnā*, f. a river rising in the Vindhya mountain, the Dosarene of the ancients. *s.*

دشارہ दशार्ह *dashārh*, m. a country in the south of India, the kingdom of Yadu, or its people. *s.*

دشاسن दुःशासन *du-shāsan*, ungovernable, intractable. *s.*

دشاشول दिशाशूल *dishā-shūl*, m. a sign in the heavens, consulted on commencing a journey; the quarters towards which it is considered unlucky to travel on particular days. *s.*

دشالا दुशाला *du-shālā*, m. a pair of shawls. *h.*

دشانش दशांश *dashānsh*, m. the tenth part. *s.*

دشانك दशानिक *dashānik*, m. a plant (*Croton polyandrum*). *s.*

دشاوتار दशावतार *dashāvatār*, (he of the ten incarnations) a name of *Vishnu*. *s.*

دشپر दशपुर *dash-pur*, m. a fragrant grass (*Cyperus rotundus*); a district, part of Malwa in Bandelkhand. *s.*

دشپراپ दुष्प्राप *dush-prāp* (also *dush-prāpya*), difficult of attainment, remote, unattainable. *s.*

دشپرش दुष्पर्श *dushparsh* (f. *dushparshā*), not to be touched, unpleasant to the touch; m. a plant (*Hedysarum alhagi*). *s.*

دشپرکرت दुष्प्रकृति *dush-prakṛiti*, of a bad nature or disposition. *s.*

دشت *dasht*, m. a desert, forest; a plain. *p.*

دشترا दशत्रा *dashatrā*, ten per cent.; a tenth. *s.*

دشتي *dashtī*, wild, savage; uncouth. *p.*

دشٹ दुष्ट *dushṭ*, bad, wicked, depraved, low, vile; enemy. *dushṭ-bhā,o*, innately bad. *dushṭ-bhā,otā*, f. innate depravity. *dushṭa-tā*, f. wickedness, badness. *dushṭ-chārī* (f. *dushṭ-chārinī*), wicked. *dushṭ-chetā*, malevolent; stupid. *dushṭ-mati*, wicked, depraved. *s.*

دشٹ दिष्ट *dishṭ*, f. (for *dṛishṭ*, q. v.) sight, view. *s.*

دشٹبندهك दिष्टबन्धक *dishṭbandhak*, the pledge of real property, such as land, houses, &c. *s.*

دشٹا दुष्टा *dushṭā*, f. a depraved woman, a harlot. *s.*

دشٹتا दुष्टता *dushṭatā*, f. wickedness, depravity. *s.*

دشچرا दुश्चरा *dush-charā*, acting ill, behaving wickedly. *s.*

دشچرت दुश्चरित *dush-charit*, misbehaving, doing or designing ill; m. evil purpose or action, misconduct. *s.*

دشرتھ दशरथ *dasharath* (see *dasarath*). *s.*

دشست दशसत *dash-sat*, a thousand. *s.*

دشرسہسر दशसहस्र *dash-sahasra*, a myriad. *s.*

دشکامج ويسن दशकामजव्यसन *dash-kāmaja-vyasan*, ten vices proceeding from *kāma* or desire: viz. hunting, gambling, sleeping during the day, abusiveness, lechery, drunkenness, dancing, singing, playing, and hypocrisy. *s.*

دشکر दुष्कर *dush-kar*, difficult to be done. *s.*

دشکرت दुष्कृत *dushkrit*, } m. sin, crime, wicked-
دشکرم दुष्कर्म *dushkarm*, } ness, evil-doing. *s.*

دشکرتي दुष्कृती *dush-kṛitī*, } m. a criminal, an
دشکرمي दुष्कर्मी *dushkarmī*, } evil-doer; adj. wicked. *s.*

دشکل दुष्कुल *dush-kul*, m. a low family or race. *dush-kulīn*, of a low family. *s.*

دشکھ दुष्ख *dushkh*, m. pain in general. *s.*

دشگرام दशग्राम *dash-grām*, m. a district of ten villages. *s.*

دشگن दशगुण *dash-gun*, ten times, tenfold. *s.*

دشلکشن दशलक्षण *dash-lakshan*, m. an aggregate of ten marks or attributes. *s.*

دشم दशम *dasham*, tenth (v. *dasam*), *s.*

دشمال दशमाल *dash-māl*, m. a collection of ten garlands. *s.*

دشمن *dushman*, m. an enemy. *dushmanī jānī*, a deadly foe. *dushman-kām*, a calamity (q. d. the wish of an enemy); adj. wretched, ruined. *p.*

دشمني *dushmanī*, f. hatred, detestation, enmity. *p.*

دشمول दशमूल *dash-mūl*, m. a tonic prepared from the roots of ten plants. *s.*

دشمي दशमी *dashamī*, f. the tenth day of a lunar fortnight; the tenth and last stage of human life; the last ten years of a century; adj. very old. *s.*

دشن दशन *dashan*, m. a tooth. *s.*

دشنام *dushnām*, m. abuse, scurrility. *p.*

دشنہ *dashna*, m. a poignard. *p.*

دشوار *dushwār*, difficult, arduous. *p.*

دشواري *dushwārī*, f. difficulty. *p.*

دشہرا दशहरा *dashahrā*, m. (see *dasahrā*). *s.*

دشي दशी *dashī*, f. thread (v. *dasī*). *s.*

دشيل दुःशील *du-shīl*, ill-behaved, reprobate. *s.*

دشيلا दशीला *dashīlā*, same as *dasīlā*, q.v. *s.*

دشيندريه दशेन्द्रिय *dashendriya*, the ten organs of sense and action, viz. skin, eye, tongue, nose, ear, organ of speech, hand, foot, anus, and pudendum. *s.*

دعا *du'ā*, f. benediction, salutation, congratulation, prayer, wish, imprecation. *du'ā,e khair*, a prayer for one's welfare. *du'ā,e daulat*, praying for one's prosperity, benediction. *du'ā-k.*, or *-māngnī*, a. to wish for, to pray for. *du'ā-go*, one who is uttering a benediction, a well-wisher. *du'ā-go,ī*, f. the act of blessing. *a.*

دعائيه *dū'ā,iya*, benediction, prayer, &c. *a.*

دعوا *da'wā*, m. (v. دعوي) claim, &c. *a.*

دعوات *da'wāt* (pl. of دعوت), prayers, convocations, invitations. *a.*

دعوت *da'wat*, f. invitation, convocation; a feast, an entertainment; pressing people to become Musalmāns; pretension, exorcism, invocation of the powers of darkness. *a.*

دعوتي *da'watī*, one who is invited, a guest. *a.*

دعوا *da'wā*, } f. a law-suit; claim, pretension, دعوي *da'wī*, } plaint. *da'wī-dar*, or *da'wā-dār*, a plaintiff, a claimant. *da'wedārī*, a selfish motive, prejudice. *da'wī ghalat*, a plea of error. *a.*

دغا *daghā*, f. deceit, imposture, treachery. *daghā-bāz*, a cheat, impostor, traitor. *daghā-bāzī*, imposition. *p.*

دغانا *daghānā*, a. to cause to fire a gun; to cause any thing to be marked. *p.*

دغاءي *daghā,ī*, f. price paid for marking. *p.*

دغدغا *daghdaghā*, } m. alarm, disturbance, دغدغه *daghdagha*, } tumult. *a.*

دغل *daghal*, m. vice, corruption, treachery, depravity; luxuriant and entangled herbage; a villain, a pickpocket; adj. false, deceitful; base (as coin). *daghal-faṣal*, treachery, deceit, depravity. *a.*

دغلا *daghlā* (for *daglā*), a kind of quilted under-garment. *h.*

دغلي *daghlī*, treacherous, deceitful. *a.*

دغلي *daghlī*, f. treachery, villainy, fraud. *p.*

دغنا *daghnā*, n. to be fired off (as a gun); to be marked, to be branded. *p.*

دغوليا *dagholiyā*, m. an impostor. *a.*

دغيلا *daghīlā*, stained, spotted; deceitful. *p.*

دف *daf* (or *daff*), m. a small tambourine. *p.*

دفاتر *dafātir* (pl. of دفتر), books. *a.*

دفالي *dafālī*, m. he whose business is to play on the tambourine. *p.*

دفائن *dafā,in*, (pl. of دفينه q.v.) things buried or hidden, more particularly hidden or buried treasures. *a.*

دفتر *daftar*, m. a book, journal, record. *daftar-khāna*, m. an office, a counting-house. *daftar kharch*, office charges. *daftar-dār* or *daftar-nawīs*, a registrar, a recorder. *daftar-dārī*, &c., office of registrar. *p.*

دفتربند *daftar-band*, } m. a man employed in دفتري *daftarī*, } preparing articles of stationery, and in ruling and binding office books. *p.*

دفتي *daftī*, } f. the boards of the binding of دفتين *daftīn*, } a book, pasteboard. *p.*

دفرقليا *dafar ḳaliyā*, tasteless victuals, a dish in which much broth, vegetables, &c. are mixed, to make it go the further; slops, wishwash. *a.*

دفع *daf'*, m. repulsion, averting, preventing. *daf'-dār*, m. an officer so called, whose rank corresponds with that of our serjeant. *a.*

دفعات *dafa'āt* (pl. of دفعه), times, &c. *a.*

دفعتًا *daf'atan*, often, all at once. *a.*

دفعه *daf'a*, time, a moment, one time. *daf'a ba daf'a*, from time to time, repeatedly. *a.*

دفعيه *daf'īya*, a preventive means of averting evil, &c. *a.*

دفله *dafla*, m. a smaller tambourine. *p.*

دفن *dafn*, m. burial, hiding, concealing. *dafn-k.*, a. to bury, to hide, to conceal. *a.*

دفنانا *dafnānā*, a. to bury, to inter. *a. h.*

دفينه *dafīna*, m. buried, or hidden treasure, hoard. *a.*

دق *diḳḳ*, m. teazing, trouble, &c.; adj. vexed, angry, fretful, peevish (v. *diḳḳat*). *diḳḳ-k.*, a. to perplex, to plague. *diḳḳ-dār*, troublesome, teazing. *diḳḳ-dārī*, f. trouble, vexation. *a.*

دق *daḳ*, a kind of cloth; a darwesh's dress. *p.*

دق *daḳḳ*, subtile, minute, thin. *tapi-daḳḳ*, f. a hectic fever. *a.*

دقاق *diḳāḳ*, minute, intelligent; m. a shred; a chip. *daḳḳāḳ*, a corn grinder. *a.*

دقايق *daḳā,iḳ* (pl. of دقيقه), subtleties; difficulties; flour meal; minutes, moments; minutiæ. *a.*

دقت *diḳḳat*, f. abstrusity, difficulty, trouble, uneasiness, diligence, close application; industry, accuracy; a subtile or minute thing. *a.*

دق ولق *daḳḳ o laḳḳ*, m. an extensive and uncultivated plain. *a.*

دقيق *daḳīḳ*, difficult, abstruse; fine, minute; m. flour, meal. *a.*

دقيقه *daḳīḳa*, m. a minute, a moment of time; any thing small, a subtle question, a trifling business. *a.*

دك दिक *dik*, m. quarter, region, point (of the compass). *s.*

دكاكين *dakākīn* (pl. of دكان), shops. *a. p.*

دكال *du-kāl*, m. famine, scarcity. *d.*

دكان *dukān* or *dukkān*, f. a shop. *p.*

دكپال दिक्पाल *dik-pāl*, } m. the ten supporters or masters of ten sides; *i.e. Brāhma*, for upwards; *Ananta*, for downward; *Indra*, for east; *Agni*, for south-east; *Yama*, for south; *Nairṛita*, for south-west; *Varuna*, for west; *Vāyu*, for north-west; *Kuvera*, for north; *īshāna*, for north-east. *s.*
دك‌پت दिक्पति *dik-pati*, }

دكڑا दुकड़ा *dukṛā*, m. the fourth part of a [paisā. *h.*

دكڑي दुकड़ी *dukṛī*, f. a snaffle. *h.*

دكش दक्ष *daksha*, a son of *Brāhma*, said to have been born from the thumb of his right hand, for the purpose of peopling the world. *Daksha* is said to have had sixty daughters, of whom twenty-seven are represented as wives of the moon and lunar asterisms; a scholar, a pandit, a clever man; adj. clever, able, dexterous. *s.*

دكشادهور دهونسكرت दक्षाध्वर ध्वंसकृत *dakshādhwar-dhwańs-kṛit*, m. a name of Shiva, from his having disturbed on some occasion a sacrifice prepared by Daksha, to which he had not been invited. *s.*

دكشن दक्षिण *dakshin*, right (not left); south, southern. *dakshin-pūrvā*, f. the south-east quarter. *s.*

دكشنا दक्षिणा *dakshinā*, f. a present to Brāhmans at a sacrifice, a fee; donation to Brāhmans; personified as a goddess, and said to be born from *Krishṇa's* right side; a figure of Durgā, in which the right side is said to be advanced. *s.*

دكشناچل दक्षिणाचल *dakshināchal*, m. the Malay mountain. *s.*

دكشناگن दक्षिणाग्नि *dakshināgni*, m. one kind of sacred fire, placed in the south. *s.*

دكشنامكهه दक्षिणामुख *dakshinā-mukh*, adj. turning the face southwards. *s.*

دكشناين दक्षिणायन *dakshināyan*, southing, &c. (v. *dakhināyan*). *s.* [erly. *s.*

دكشنين दक्षिणेन *dakshinen*, southward, southerly. *s.*

دكشنيه दक्षिण्य *dakshinya* or दक्षिणीय *dakshinīya*, deserving a reward. *s.*

دك‌شول दिक्शूल *dik-shūl*, m. an inauspicious planetary conjunction. *s.* [fied. *s.*

دكشي दक्षी *dakshī*, capable, able, well-qualified. *s.*

دكوڑي *dikoṛī*, f. a wasp, a hornet. *d.*

دكهه दुःख *dukh*, m. ache, pain; labour, fatigue; annoyance, distress. *dukh-bhāgin* or *dukh-bhāgī*, suffering, having pain as his portion. *dukh-bharnā*, a. to labour, to toil. *dukh-bahul*, distressful, abounding with pain. *dukh pānā*, n. to be afflicted. *dukhh-jīvī*, living in pain. *dukh-chinna*, afflicted, distressed. *dukh-dā,ī*, *dukh-dānī*, or *dukh-dāyak*, troublesome, vexatious. *dukh-dagdha*, consumed with pain, distressed. *dukh-sāgar*, m. ocean of troubles, the world; deep distress. *dukh-kar*, causing pain. *dukh-labhya*, to be obtained with trouble. *dukh kā mārā* afflicted. *dukh kā hartā* or *dukh-hartā*, dispeller of grief. *dukh-haraṇ*, anodyne. *dukh-han*, removing pain. *s.*

دكهاري दुखारी *dukhārī*, afflicted, pained, sick. *s.*

دكهانا दिखाना *dikhānā*, a. to shew, to display. *h.*

دكهانا दुःखाना *dukhānā* a. to inflict pain. *s.*

دكهاو दिखाव *dikhāw* or *dikhā,o*, m. exhibition, shew. *h*

دكهاءو दिखाऊ *dikhā,ū*, comely, fit to be shewn. *h.*

دكهاءي दिखाई *dikhā,ī*, f. exhibition, shewing. *dikhā,ī denā*, to appear, to present itself. *h.*

دكهت दुःखित *dukhit*, afflicted, grieved, pained. *s.* [pāts (Elliot). *h*

دكهت दिखित *dikhit*, name of a tribe of *rāj*-

دكهڑا दुःखड़ा *dukhṛā*, m. misfortunes, calamities. *s.*

دكهلانا दिखलाना *dikhlānā*, a. to shew, to exhibit, to denote, to direct. *h.*

دكهلاءي दिखलाई *dikhlā,ī*, f. shew, appearance. *dikhlā,ī denā*, to appear, to be apparent. *h.*

دكهلاوا दिखलावा *dikhlāwā*, m. show, pageantry. *h.*

دكهن दखन *dakhun* or दखिन *dakkhin* (for *dakshina*), m. the south, hence the Deccan. *s.*

دكهن दुःखिन *dukhin*, suffering pain, afflicted, sick. *s.* [f. southerly wind. *s.*

دكهنا दखिना *dakkhinā* or *dakhnā*, southern;

دكهنا दुखना *dukhnā*, n. to ache, to pain, to smart. *dikhnā*, n. to appear, to be seen. *s.*

دكهناين दखिनायन *dakkhināyan* (for *dakshināyan*), m. southing. *dakkhināyan sūraj*, the winter solstice, sun's southing, the period of the sun's being in the southern hemisphere, southern declination. *s.*

دكهني दखनी *dakhnī*, *dakhanī* or दखिनी *dakhinī*, southern; of or belonging to the Deccan or southern India; (generally things or persons from the south). *dakhnī pūdīna*, horse mint. *s.*

دكهويا दिखवैया *dikhwaiyā*, m. a spectator. *h.*

دكهي दुःखी *dukhī*, afflicted, in distress or pain, sick, suffering (bodily or mentally). *s.*

دكهيا दुःखिया *dukhiyā*, in distress or pain, unfortunate, poor, indigent. *s.*

دكهيارا दुःखियारा *dukhiyārā*, afflicted, in pain, grieved, sick. *s.*

دگ दिग *dig*, m. quarter, side, way, wards (as *uttar dig*, northwards); the natives reckon ten *digs* or *diks* (v. *dik-pāl*); point (of the compass). *s.*

دگانه *du-gāna*, m. (for *do-gāna*) two prostrations at prayer; (in the dialect of women) two intimate female friends, sworn sisters. *p.*

دگپال *dig-pāl*, m. (v. *dik-pāl*) the ten guardian deities of the quarters and points. *s.*

دگج दिग्गज *dig-gaj*, lit. elephants that support the four quarters of the earth; (met.) great. *s.*

دگدگا दगदगा *dagdagā*, shining, bright. *h.*

دگدگانا दगदगाना *dagdagānā*, n. to glow, to gleam, to twinkle. *h.*

دگدگانا दिगदिगाना *digdigānā*, n. to chatter (as teeth). *s.*

دگدگاهٹ दगदगाहट *dagdugāhaṭ* (contr. *dagdagāṭ*), f. splendour, sparkling, twinkling (as of a star). *h.*

دگدگي *dugdugī*, f. the cavity at the bottom of the throat. *d.*

دگدھ दग्ध *dagdha*, burnt, scorched, consumed. *dagdha-kāk*, m. a raven, or perhaps the carrion crow. *s.*

دگدھ दुग्ध *dugdha*, m. milk. *dugdha-phen*, m. the froth or skim of milk, syllabub, cream. *dugdha-phenī*, f. a small medicinal shrub. *dugdha-tā*, f. milkiness, the nature of milk. *dugdha-tāliya*, m. milk and mangoes, mango fool. *s.*

دگدھا दग्धा *dugdhā*, name of a tribe of inferior Brāhmans on the borders of Allahabad. *h.*

دگدھکا दुग्धिका *dugdhikā*, f. a sort of asclepias (*A. rosea*); the Hindī derivative *Dudhī* is also applied to *Euphorbia hirta* and *thymifolia*. *s.*

دگدھن दुग्धिन *dugdhin*, } milky, having milk. *s.*
دگدھي दुग्धी *dugdhī*, }

دگدھنا दगधना *dagadhnā*, a. to burn; to tease, to vex; to chide, to threaten, to upbraid, to revile, to pester. *s.*

دگدھنکا दुग्धिनिका *dugdhinikā*, f. a red sort of *Apang* (*Achyranthes aspera*). *s.*

دگر *digar* (for *dīgar*), again, once more; another; pl. *digarān*, others. *p.*

دگڑ दगड़ *dagaṛ*, a kettle-drum. *h.*

دگڑا दगड़ा *dagṛā*, m. the highway. *h.*

دگڑانا दगड़ाना *dagṛānā*, a. to propel, to roll. *h.*

دگڑنا दगड़ना *dagaṛnā*, n. to disbelieve a true testimony. *h.*

دگسول दिगशूल *dig-sūl*, m. an unlucky day for travelling in a particular direction. *s.*

دگلا दगला *daglā*, m. a kind of quilted vest worn as armour or under armour. *h.*

دگمبر दिगम्बर *digambar*, naked; m. an order of Hindū ascetics who go naked: they are worshippers of *Shiva*; an order of ascetics of the sect of *jains*; they either go naked or are clad in cloth dyed with red chalk. *s.*

دگمگانا दगमगाना *dagmagānā*, m. to tremble. *h.*

دگن दुगण *dugan*, } (also *dugunā*), twofold,
دگنا दुगणा *duganā*, } double. *dugan*, m. the second tone in music. *s.*

دگنت दिगन्त *dig-ant*, m. the horizon. *s.*

دگنتر दिगन्तर *dig-antar*, m. the aerial space, the atmosphere. *s.*

دگوان दिगवान *digwān*, } m. a watchman,
دگوار दिगवार *digwār*, } guard. *s.*

دگ ويبهاگ दिग्विभाग *dig-vibhāg*, m. a quarter or point of the compass. *s.*

دگ وجي दिग्विजय *dig-vijay*, m. subjugation of an extensive country, either in arms or controversy. *dig-vijay-kram*, m. invasion, going forth to conquer the world. *dig-vijayī*, a conqueror of the world, a subjugator of vast territories. *s.*

دگ وياپي दिगव्यापी *dig-vyāpī*, spreading through space. *s.*

دگهي दिघी *dighī*, } f. a large tank or reser-
دگي दिग्गी *diggī*, } voir, in form of an oblong quadrangle: corrupted by Europeans into *diggy*. *s.*

دل *dil*, m. heart, mind, soul. *dilā*, O heart! *dil-ārā*, beloved; an epithet of a sweetheart. *dil-ārām*, m. (lit. heart-easing) a sweetheart. *dil-āzār*, m. (lit. heart-tormenting) a sweetheart. *dil-āzurda*, afflicted in heart or mind. *dil-āsā*, m. comfort, soothing, encouragement, consolation. *dil-afgār*, broken-hearted. *dil-āgāh*, wise, wary, wide-awake. *dil-āwar* or *dil-āwarān*, bold, resolute, valiant. *dil-āwez*, transporting. *dil-bākhta*, deluded in heart or mind. *dil baṭornā*, to dishearten, to deject. *dil ba dil*, mutual love, interchange of hearts. *dil bar*, m. a sweetheart. *dil-barī*, f. comfort, pacification. *dil baṛhānā*, a. to hearten, to encourage. *dil-bastagī*, f. friendship, love, anguish, attachment. *dil-basta*, afflicted; attached, enamoured. *dil-band*, attractive, heart-stealing; (met.) a son. *dil bahlānā*, a. to amuse, to divert. *dil bahalnā*, n. to be amused, diverted. *dil pānā*, to find out what is pleasing to any one. *dil pizīr*, grateful to the soul, amiable. *dil par kisī ke chalnā*, n. to be obedient. *dil-pasand*, agreeable to the heart, desirable. *dil phernā*, to disincline. *dil pīchhe paṛnā*, to forget one's sorrow. *dil-taftagī*, burning of the heart, love, or any strong emotion of the mind. *dil-tafta*, heart-burnt, distracted by love, &c. *dil-tang*, distressed, mournful, sad. *dil-tangī*, distress, grief, sadness. *dil toṛnā*, to disappoint, to mortify. *dil-jalnā*, to be moved or affected. *dil-jam'*, collected in mind, at ease. *dil-jo* or *-jū*, one who is desirous to please. *dil-jū,ī*, a desire of pleasing. *dil churānā*, a. to steal the heart of any one; to abstain from any thing, to be deterred and desist from an enterprise. *dil-chasp*, beloved, pleasant. *dil-chal* or *-chalā*, brave, resolute, generous; persevering. *dil chalnā*, to desire. *dil-chalī*, f. bravery, resolution. *dil-chor*, inattentive; timid. *dil-kharāsh*, (lit. heart-scratching) vexatious. *dil-khasta*, broken-hearted, sorely grieved. *dil-khwāh*, m. desire, affection; beloved. *dil-khush*, glad, contented. *dil-dāda*, one who has given away his heart. *dil-dār*, m. a lover, a mistress, a sweetheart. *dil-doz*, heart-piercing. *dil-dihī*, cheerfulness, alacrity. *dil dekhnā*, to study one's temper. *dil denā*, n. to lose one's heart, to be in love. *dil-rubā*, m. (lit. heart-ravishing), a sweetheart. *dil rakhnā*, to possess one's heart, to gratify. *dil-resh*, afflicted; m. a sweetheart. *dil-zada*, struck in the heart. *dil-sāz*, heart-pleasing, delightful. *dil-sard*, cold-hearted, indifferent, averse. *dil-sitān*, heart-alluring, beautiful. *dil-sokhta*, afflicted. *dil-soz*, affecting, moving. *dil-soz i khāna-tarāsh*, an enemy under the semblance of a friend. *dil-shād*, rejoiced at heart, cheerful, gay. *dil-shuda*, one whose heart is gone, enamoured. *dil-shikasta*, broken-hearted, sorely afflicted. *dil-faroz*, (heart-enlightening) delightful, recreating, pleasant, refreshing. *dil-fareb*, heart-alluring, beautiful, enchanting, lovely. *dil-figār*, melancholy, mournful, pensive; an epithet of a sweetheart. *dil kā phapholā phoṛnā*, a. to rip up old sores, to renew a half-forgotten grief. *dil-kash*, (lit. heart-attracting) chosen, approved of, beloved; pleasant. *dil-kushā*, heart-expanding, exhilirating. *dil-gudāz*, heart-melting. *dil-gurda*, courage. *dil-garmī*, f. friendship, warm-heartedness. *dil-lagānā*, to apply the mind, to act with earnestness. *dil-gīr*, melancholy, sad, low-spirited, afflicted, grieved. *dil-lagnā*, n. to apply to, to be attentive. *dil-mānnā* to follow the inclination of the heart (v. *man-māntā*). *dil-murgh*, m. a kind of arrow. *dil meṅ ḍālnā*, a. to put in one's mind (spoken of God), to inspire. *dil* *men khub jānā*, n. to obtain a place in one's heart; to possess one's heart. *dil men ghar-k.*, to contract intimate friendship. *dil-nishīn*, impressed on the heart or mind. *dil-nawāz*, soothing the mind, conciliating; beloved; an epithet of a sweetheart. *dil-nawāzī*, f. blandishment. *dil-nihād*, any object on which the heart is fixed, a beloved one. *dil o jān*, heart and soul; tooth and nail. *dil o jān se*, heartily, with heart and soul. *dil o damāgh*, m. ambition, pride, stateliness. *dil haṭ-jānā*, n. to be averse. *dilī dil*, a secret, kept secret. *p.*

دل दिल *dil*, a small eminence; the site of an old village. *h.*

دل दल *dal*, m. a large army; the leaf of a tree; a heap, a quantity. *dal-wāl*, commander of an army; thickness. *dal-dār*, fleshy, thick. *s*

دل दल *dal*, m. wild rice. *h.*

دلا *dallā*, m. a lump, a piece. *d.*

دلاڈھک दलाढक *dalāḍhak*, m. sesamum growing wild; an aquatic plant (*Pistia stratioites*); a plant commonly called Nagesar (*Mesua ferrea*); a tree (*Mimosa sirisha*); a sort of jasmine (*Jasminum pubescens*). *s.*

دلار दुलार *dulār*, m. love, affection. *h.*

دلاك *dallāk*, a barber, a shampooer, a waiter at a bath. *a.*

دلاكي *dallākī*, of or relating to a barber, &c. *teghi dallākī*, a razor, lit. the barber's sword. *a. p.*

دلاسا *dilāsā*, m. comfort, consolation. *p.*

دلال दलाल *dalāl*, name of a tribe of *jāṭs*. *h.*

دلال *dallāl*, m. a broker, a salesman. *a.*

دلال *dalāl*, m. looking (haughtily or amorously) through half-shut eyes; looking with affected anger (as lovers); *cinædus libidine infamis*. *a.*

دلالت *dalālat* or *dilālat*, f. direction, indication, sign, token, argument, demonstration; brokerage. *a.*

دلاله *dallāla*, f. a procuress; an old go-between. *a.*

دلالي *dallālī*, f. brokerage; the business of a broker. *a.*

دلامل दलामल *dalāmal*, m. a tree (*Vangueria spinosa*). *s.*

دلانا दिलाना *dilānā*, a. to cause to give, to occasion, to administer, to consign, to assign, to cause to yield, to cause to give up. *h.*

دلانا दुलाना *dulānā*, a. to agitate, to toss, to shake. *s.*

دلانا दलाना *dalānā*, a. to grind coarsely, to cause to be ground. *s.*

دلاو दुलाव *dulāw*, m. agitation. *s.*

دلاور *dilāwar*, brave, intrepid. *p.*

دلاوري *dilāwarī*, f. intrepidity, bravery. *p.*

دلائي दुलाई *dulā,ī*, f. a kind of veil or covering, made of two breadths and used by females. *h.*

دلائل *dalā,il* (pl. of دليل), proofs, arguments. *a.*

دل بادل दलबादल *dal-bādal*, m. a mass of clouds; a large army; a large tent. *s.*

دلبازي *dil-bāzī*, f. palpitation of the heart. *p.*

دلبند *dul-band*, turban, or the fine cloth of which a turban is made up. *p.*

دلپشپي दलपुष्पी *dal-pushpī*, f. a fragrant plant (*Pandanus odoratissimus*). *s.*

دلتي दुलत्ती *du-lattī*, f. a kick or fling with the two hind legs of a quadruped. *du-lattī mārnā*, to wince, to kick with the two hind legs. *h.*

دلداپيشگير *daldā-peshgīr*, a bed-screen. *p.*

دلدر दलिद्र *dalidr*, m. } poverty, want,
دلدرتا दलिद्रता *dalidratā*, f. } destitution. *s.*

دلدري दलिद्री *dalidrī*, poor, indigent, wretched. *s.*

دلدل *duldul*, m. a hedgehog; the name of the horse of *'Alī*, the prophet's son-in-law; (met.) fat. *a.*

دلدل दलदल *daldal*, f. a quagmire, a slough, a bog. *h.*

دلدلا दलदला *daldalā*, quaggy, boggy. *h.*

دلدلانا दलदलाना *daldalānā*, n. to shake, to undulate. *h.*

دلدلاهٹ दलदलाहट *daldalāhaṭ*, f. tremor. *h.*

دلدهردي दलदहृदय *dalad-hṛiday*, broken-hearted, cut to the heart. *s.*

دلدلي दलदली *daldalī*, swampy, quaggy. *h.*

دلڑا दुलड़ा *dulaṛā*, double-stringed, twofold, of two rows; m. a double-stringed necklace (also *dulṛī*, f.). *h.*

دلسوسا दलसूसा *dal-sūsā*, f. the fibre or vein of a leaf. *s.*

دلفن *dulfin* or *dilfin*, } a dolphin. *g.*
دلفين *dulfīn* or *dilfīn*, }

دلق *dalk* (properly *dilk*), m. a mendicant's habit, made of patches and shreds. *dalk-posh*, a mendicant or one who wears the *dalk*; ragged, clothed in rags. *a.*

دلك दलक *dalak*, f. glitter, splendour. *h.*

دلك پاٹ दलकपाट *dalak-pāṭ*, m. a folded petal or leaf. *s.*

دلكنا दलकना *dalaknā*, n. to glitter, to shine. *h.*

دلكوش दलकोष *dal-kosh*, m. a sort of jasmine (*Jasminum pubescens*). *s.*

دلكي दुलकी *dulkī*, f. a trot; the movement of a dog. *dulkī jānā* or *-chalnā*, n. to trot (particularly as a dog). *h.*

دلگنجنا दलगंजना *dalganjanā*, a kind of rice (v. *dhān*). *h.*

دل مسل كرنا दलमसल करना *dal masal karnā*, a. to thrash, to crumple. *h.*

دلمه *dulma*, a tarantula. *dalama*, new cheese. *p.*

دلميان दुलमियान *dulmiyān*, a small purse. *h.*

دلن दलन *dalan*, m. the act of dividing into two parts; breaking, cleaving. *s.*

دلنا दलना *dalnā*, a. to grind coarsely, to split pulse. *s.*

دل‌نرموك दलनिर्मोक *dal-nirmok*, m. the *Bhojpatr* tree, the bark of which is used for wrapping woollens in and for *hukka* snakes. *s.*

دلو *dalv*, m. a bucket, an urn; the sign Aquarius; the hopper of a mill. *a.*

دلوالي दिलवाली *dilwālī*, m. an inhabitant of *Dillī* or *Dihlī*. *dillī ke dilwālī munh chiknā peṭ khālī*, the inhabitants of *Dihlī* appear to be opulent, when in fact they are starving (a proverb used to express the vanity and indigence prevalent in that city). *h.*

دلوانا दलवाना *dalwānā*, a. to cause to be coarsely ground. *s.*

دلوانا दिलवाना *dilwānā*, a. to cause to pay or give. *h.*

دلوه दुलोह *du-loh*, } a scimitar made of two
دلوهي दुलोही *du-lohī*, } plates of steel joined together. *h.*

دلويا दिलवैया *dilwaiyā*, m. one who causes to give or to pay. *h.*

دلويا दलवैया *dalwaiyā*, m. one who grinds. *s.*

دلها दुल्हा *dulhā*, m. a bridegroom. *h.*

دلهارا दलहारा *dal-hārā*, m. one whose business is to sell grain. *s.*

دلهارن दलहारन *dal-hāran*, } f. a woman whose
دلهاري दलहारी *dal-hārī*, } business is to deal in grain. *s.*

دلهن दलिहन *dalihan*, f. any sort of pulse which may be split, as *dāl*. *s.*

دلهن दुल्हन *dulhan*, }
دلهن दुल्हिन *dulhin*, } f. a bride. *h.*
دلهيا दुल्हैया *dulhaiyā*, }

دلي दली *dalī*, f. a clod of clay or mould. *s.*

دلي दिल्ली *dillī*, f. the city of Delhī, the metropolis of Hindūstān, called also *Shāhjahān-ābād*. *h.*

دلي *dilī*, appertaining or belonging to the heart; hearty, sincere. *p.*

دليا दलिया *daliyā*, half-ground or coarsely-pounded grain; split pulse, ground more finely than *dāl*, q. v. *s.*

دليپ दिलीप *dilīp*, the name of a king, whose seat was Hastināpur or Delhi, one of Rāma's ancestors. *s.*

دلير *diler*, intrepid, bold, brave; insolent, impudent, presumptuous. *p.*

دليرانه *dilerāna*, bravely, heroically. *p.*

دليري *dilerī*, f. bravery, boldness, impudence, daring. *p.*

دلي گندهه दलेगन्धि *dale-gandhi*, m. a plant (*Echites scholaris*). *s.*

دليل *dalīl*, f. argument, proof, demonstration; a guide, director. *a.*

دليلي *dalīlī*, argumentative; a good arguer. *a.*

دليمه दलीमः *dalīma*, name of a clan of *tagās* in Murādābād (v. *gaur tagā*). *h.*

دلينتي दलेंती *dalentī*, f. a hand-mill. *s.*

دم *dam*, m. blood. *damu-l-akhwain*, dragon's blood (*Sanguis draconis*). *a.*

دم *dam*, m. breath, life; boasting; spring; ambition; cheerfulness; a moment; the stewing over a slow fire. *dam ulaṭnā*, n. to breathe one's last; to relinquish one's usual habits. *dam-ā-dam*, incessantly, continually. *dam-bāz*, m. a wheedler, deceiver. *dam-bāzī*, f. wheedling, deceiving. *dam i bāz-pasīn*, the last breath, the last moment. *dam bāndhnā*, n. to be attentive. *dam-ba-khud*, silent, keeping one's breath within himself. *dam ba dam*, perpetually. *dam-band*, an alembic. *dam bharnā*, n. to boast. *dam-pukht*, m. a stew, a kind of *pulāw*. *dam phūlnā*, to breathe short. *dam phūṅknā*, to breathe, inspire. *dum ṭūṭnā*, n. to die. *dam jagnā*, n. to speak, to talk. *dam churānā*, a. to feign death. *dam chaṛhnā*, n. to pant, to respire. *dam-chūṛā*, m. the name of a kind of firework which burns at intervals. *dam chhoṛnā*, a. to breathe, to expire. *dam-kham*, edge or temper of a scimitar, &c. *dam-dār*, elastic. *dam-dilāsā* or *dam o dilāsā*, m. encouragement, comfort, soothing, coaxing. *dam denā*, a. to wheedle, to coax, to inveigle, to deceive; to leave to simmer (a stew, &c.). *dam-raftan*, to expire. *dam roknā*, a. to suffocate, breathe short. *dam rakhnā*, n. to be content with a little. *dam-zadan*, to breathe, to live or exist; to keep silence; to hesitate. *dam-zanī*, hesitation; maintaining silence. *dam sādhnā*, a. to stop one's breath, when feigning death, or as some ascetics do, as religious exercise, for hours together (v. *ḥabs i dam*). *dam-sāz*, concordant, harmonious. *dam se ṭālnā*, a. to turn off with a joke. *dami shamsher*, m. the edge of a sword. *dam-k.*, a. to blow (as a fire); to blow, as a conjuror when juggling or exorcising. *dam-kash*, silent. *dam-kashī*, silence. *dam khā-jānā* or *-rahnā*, n. to be crestfallen. *dam khānā*, n. to be deceived; to be silent; to be dressed over a slow fire (a stew, &c.). *dam khainchnā*, n. to be silent. *dam lagnā*, n. to be desirous. *dam lenā*, a. to take breath, to rest. *dam mārnā*, a. to speak; to boast. *dam nāk meṅ ānā*, to be fatigued to death; to gasp for life; to be much distressed. *dami naḳd*, ready (as dinner, &c.). *dam-nikalnā*, n. to die. *dam honā*, n. to be stewed, to be left on the fire after cooling, as a *pulāw*, &c. *p.*

دم *dum*, f. tail, end, extremity. *dum-dār*, tailed, having a tail. *dum dabānā*, a. to run away, to put the tail between the legs. *dum dabā-jānā* or *dum 'alam-k.*, n. to run away. *dum-kā-tārā*, a comet. *dum lāba-k.*, to wag the tail (as a dog or cat when pleased). *dum men ghusnā*, to take protection. *p.*

دم दम *dam*, m. taming, subduing; self-command, endurance of austerities; subduing the senses or passions. *s.*

دمار *damār*, ruin, destruction. *a.*

دماغ *dimāgh* or *damāgh*, m. the brain; pride, haughtiness; the organ of smell. *dimāgh tāza-k.*, a. to be pleased. *damāgh chaṛhnā*, to be proud with excess of wealth. *damāgh-k*, a. to be vain, proud, haughty, or rather to act proudly, &c. *damāgh honā*, n. to be vain, haughty, proud. *a.*

دماع *dummā'*, tears, from old age or sickness, sap dripping from the vine in spring. *a.*

دماغي *damāghī*, vain, frivolous, proud. *p.*

دماما *damāmā*, }
دمامه *damāma*, } m. a kettledrum. *p.*

دمان *damān*, powerful, terrible, fierce. *p.*

دمانا दमाना *damānā*, n. to bend (with elasticity). *h.*

دمانك *damānak*, m. a blunderbuss, a carcane. *p.*

دمبھ दम्भ *dambh*, m. arrogance, pride, boast, ostentation, hypocrisy. *s.*

دمبھي दम्भी *dumbhī*, proud, ostentatious; m. a hypocrite, an impostor. *s.*

دمپتي दम्पती *dampatī*, husband and wife. *s.*

دمچي *dumchī*, f. a crupper. *p.*

دمدمانا दमदमाना *damdamānā*, a. to shake (as the branch of a tree). *h.*

دمدمه *damdama*, m. a cavalier, (in fortification) a mound, a raised battery. *h.*

دمڑا दमड़ा *damṛā*, m. gold, silver, riches. *s.*

دمڑي दमड़ी *damṛī*, f. the eighth part of a *paisā*, or very nearly three *dāms*; in the emperor Akbar's time the *damṛī* was rated one-eighth of a *dām*, or one-three-hundred-and-twentieth of a *rūpī*. *damṛī ke tīn tīn honā*, n. to be ruined, demolished. *h.*

دمس كرنا *dimmas-karnā*, to lay down turf, to place the sods and pound them with a rammer. *d.*

دمشق *dimashḳ* or *damishḳ*, Damascus in Syria. *a.*

دمك दमक *damak*, f. ardour, glitter; m. a tamer, a subduer (of passions). *s.*

دمكا दमका *damkā*, a hillock, an eminence. *h.*

دمكنا दमकना *damaknā*, n. to shine. *h.*

دمكلا दमकला *damkalā*, m. a squirt, a fire-engine; a jack or crane (for raising weights). *h.*

دمل *dummal*, m. a boil, a swelling, a felon, an imposthume, an abscess. *a.*

دملي *dummalī*, f. a small boil or swelling. *a.*

دم مدار *dam-madār*, a kind of superstitious ceremony (v. Wilson's Glossary). *h. p.*

دمن *dimn*, the orbicular dung of cattle, &c. *a.*

دمن दमन *daman*, taming, subduing; m. a hero; a kind of flower (*Artemisia*). *s.*

دمن *daman* (Pers. cor. of *damayantī*), the heroine of a tale in the Mahābhārata. *s. p.*

دمنا दमना *damnā*, n. to glitter, to flash; to bend with elasticity, to spring. *h.*

دمنها दुमुंहा *dumunhā*, having two mouths; m. name of a serpent, which has two mouths (*Amphisbæna*). *s.*

دموست दमवस्त *damwast*, name of a low tribe of *rāj-pūts* in the Benares district. *h.*

دموي *damwī*, plethoric, bloody. *a.*

دمه *dama*, m. pair of bellows; an asthma. *p.*

دمي *damī*, f. a kind of *ḥuḳḳa*, or instrument for smoking; adj. inflated. *p.*

دمئي दमई *dama,ī*, f. amount of assessment. *h.*

دمياط *dimyāṭ*, Damietta (in Egypt). *a.*

دمياطي *dimyāṭī*, f. a kind of fine cloth made at Damietta, dimity. *a.*

دميتا *damītā*, rich, prosperous, wealthy. *d.*

دميدگي *damīdagī*, f. blowing (as wind); blowing as a flower, sprouting. *p.*

دميدن *damīdan*, to blow, to expand; to break forth (as the dawn of day). *p.*

دميده *damīda*, blown, expanded, vegetated; broke forth (as the dawn of day). *p.*

دميه दम्य *damya*, subjected, tamed; m. a steer, a young bullock. *s.*

دن दिन *din*, m. day. *din ba-din*, day by day. *din bharne* expresses time spent in pain and trouble. *din paṛnā*, n. to be unfortunate. *din phirnā*, n. to begin to prosper (after adversity). *din-jyotis*, m. sunshine, daylight. *din chaṛhānā*, a. to commence any business late in the day; to eat the bread of idleness, or earn one's wages without labour. *din chaṛhnā*, the day being far advanced; the period of a woman's menstruation being protracted. *din-dhaule* or *din diwāle*, in daylight. *din-diyā*, daylight. *din ḍhalnā*, n. to grow late, to decline (the sun). *din kāṭnā*, to pass time with difficulty. *din ko din, rāt ko rāt, na jānnā*, n. (lit. not to perceive that day is day, and that night is night) to be totally absorbed in thought or business. *din khulnā*, n. to begin to prosper after adversity. *din gaṅwānā*, a. to spend time carelessly. *din mundnā*, n. to grow late, to close the day. *s.*

دنا दन्ना *dannā*, m. *membrum virile*. *h.*

دنا *dannā*, large, great, ample. *d.*

دناءت *danā,at*, f. meanness, baseness. *a.*

دناتي दिनाती *dinātī*, time of a plough's working in the course of a single day; daily work of labourers. *s.*

دنارمبھ दिनारंभ *dinārambh*, m. morning. *s.*

دنانت दिनान्त *dinānt*, m. evening, close of day. *s.*

دنائي दिनाई *dinā,ī*, f. a tetter, ringworm. *h.*

دنبال *dumbāl*, } m. a tail; the stern of a vessel; the rudder; after, behind. *dumbāla-dār*, tailed. *sitāra,e dumbāla-dār*, a comet. *p.*

دنباله *dumbāla*, }

دنبل *dumbal*, m. a boil, an imposthume, a bubo (v. *dummal*). *p.*

دنبه *dumba*, m. a kind of sheep with a thick tail. *p.*

دنپا *dampā*, fat, thick, corpulent. *d.*

دنت दन्त *dant*, m. a tooth; an elephant's tusk. *dant-pīr* or *dant-shūl*, the toothache. *dant-shān*, m. a dentifrice composed chiefly of the powdered fruit of the Chebulic myrobalan and green sulphate of iron. *dant-māṅs*, m. the gums. *dant-mal*, m. the tartar of the teeth. *s.*

دنتاولي दंतावली *dantāwalī*, a harrow or rake. *h.*

دنتارود दन्तार्वुद *dantārvud*, m. a disease of the teeth, ulceration of the gums. *s.*

دنت پترك दन्तपत्रक *dant-patrak*, m. a kind of jasmine (*Jasminum pubescens*), the petals resembling teeth in colour and shape. *s.*

دنت پشپ दन्तपुष्प *dant-pushp*, m. a plant, the flower of which is compared to a tooth (*Strychnos potatorum*). *s.*

دنتر दन्तुर *dantur*, having large tusks, tusked [(an elephant). *s.*

دنت دهاون दन्तधावन *dant-dhāvan*, m. a tree yielding an astringent resin (*Mimosa catechu*); a plant (*Mimusops elengi*); a tooth-brush, or fibrous stick used for cleaning the teeth. *s.*

دنت شٹھ दन्तशठ *dant-shaṭh*, m. elephant or wood-apple; common lime (*Citrus acida*); a plant bearing an acid fruit (*Averrhoa carambola*). *dant-shaṭhā*, f. wood sorrel (*Oxalis monodelpha*). *s.*

دنتهل दंथल *danthal*, } the bare stalks of *bājrā*,
دنتهلا दंथला *danthlā*, } *jwār*, &c.; the roots of *chanā* left in the ground after the crop is cut. *h.*

دنتي दन्ती *dantī*, toothed, tusked; m. an elephant. *dantī-vīj*, m. a strong purgative nut, the fruit of the croton. *s.*

دنتيل दन्तेल *dantel* or दन्तैल *dantail*, tusked. *s.*

دنتيلا दन्तेला *dantelā*, m. an elephant with large tusks, or a boar or any animal with prominent tusks. *s.*

دنتيه दन्त्य *dantya*, dental (a class of letters). *s.*

دند *dand*, enmity, hatred. *d.*

دند दुन्द *dund* or *dundu*, a kind of kettle-drum (same as *dundubhī*). *s.*

دند *dand*, m. a rib, a tooth; a weaver's toothed instrument; adj. poor, destitute, stupid. *p.*

دندارو दन्दारू *dandārū*, m. a blister, a pimple. *h.*

دندان *dandān*, m. a tooth. *dandān-gīr*, biting (horse). *dandān-misrī*, f. a kind of sweetmeat. *p.*

دندانه *dandāna*, m. the tooth of a saw, &c. *p.*

دندبهي दुन्दुभी *dundubhī* or *dundubhi*, m. a kettle-drum. *s.*

دندکا दुन्दका *dundkā*, m. a sugar-mill. *h.*

دندم दुन्दम *dundam*, m. a kettle-drum. *s.*

دندمار दुन्दुमार *dundumār*, m. a sort of red worm. *s.*

دندنانا दन्दनाना *dandanānā*, n. to enjoy one's self, to be contented and independent, to live at one's ease. *h.* [light. *d.*

دندوالي दिनदिवाले *din-divāle*, m. broad day-

دندي *dandī*, m. an enemy, an adversary. *d.*

دنڈ दण्ड *dand*, m. a stick, a staff; punishment, castigation by amercement, or putting to death; fine, penalty; a measure of time, or twenty-four minutes. *dandā-dandī*, f. single-stick, cudgelling. *dand-tāmrī*, f. a perforated copper vessel of given capacity placed in a vessel full of water: after filling by degrees it sinks, marking a certain portion of time. *dand-dhakkā*, f. a sort of drum. *dand-nīti*, f. the system of ethics taught by Chāṇakya. *s.*

دنڈا *dandā*, m. a post or stake; the pole of a carriage. *d.* [erect. *s.*

دنڈايمان दण्डायमान *dandāyamān*, standing

دنڈپال दण्डपाल *dand-pāl*, m. a small kind of fish (*Cyprinus barbiger*)?

دنڈت दण्डित *dandit*, punished, fined. *s.*

دنڈك दण्डक *dandak*, m. a sort of metre, a stanza of which exceeds twenty-seven syllables. *s.*

دنڈکا दण्डका *dandakā*, f. a country on the north-east coast of the peninsula containing the forest *dandak-āranya*, in which Rāma dwelt. *s.* [bearer. *s.*

دنڈن दण्डिन *dandin*, m. a staff or mace-

دنڈنا दण्डना *dandnā*, } a. to inflict a
دنڈيچنا दण्डीचना *dandīchnā*, } penalty; to investigate. *s.*

دنڈنيه दण्डनीय *dandnīya*, } punishable, de-
دنڈيه दण्ड्य *dandya*, } serving punishment. *s.*

دنڈوت दण्डवत *dandwat*, f. a Hindū mode of salutation, something like our military salute. *s.*

دنڈي दण्डी *dandī*, m. (v. *ḍandī*) a mendicant (who carries a staff); also same as *dasta*, a handle; the penis. *h.*

دنڈي *dandī*, f. a pole, staff, or post; the yard of a sail; the beam of a pair of scales. *d.*

دنڈيا *dandiyā* (v. *ḍandiyā*), a kind of garment. *d.*

دنڈيچنا *dandīchnā*, same as *dandnā*, q. v.

دنش दंश *dansh*, m. a gad fly; a tooth; the sting of a snake. *s.*

دنشت दंशित *danshit*, bitten, stung. *s.*

دنش مول दंशमूल *dansh-mūl*, m. a plant (*Hyperanthera morunga*). *s.* [stinging. *s.*

دنشن दंशन *danshan*, m. the act of biting or

دنشي दंशी *danshī*, f. a small gadfly. *s.*

دنشير दंशेर *dansher*, noxious, mischievous. *s.*

دنکا दुंका *dunkā*, m. a crumb, a scrap. *h.*

دنکر दिनकर *dinkar*, m. (lit. the day-maker) the sun. *s.*

دنگ *dang*, astonished; careless, foolish. *p.*

دنگا दङ्गा *dangā*, m. wrangling, confusion, mutiny, sedition, rebellion. *dangā-bāz*, mutinous, turbulent. *h.* [division of an estate. *h.*

دنگاني दुंगानी *dungānī*, f. a small fractional

دنگري दुंग्री *dungrī*, f. a coarse kind of cloth. *h.*

دنگست दंगस्त *dangast*, name of a clan of *rājpūts* in Ghāzipūr. *h.*

دنگل दङ्गल *dangal*, m. a kind of chair. *h.*

دنگل *dangal*, m. a crowd, an assembly. *p. t.*

دنگيا दङ्गया *dangayā*, } turbulent, mutinous,
دنگيت दङ्गैत *dangait*, } quarrelsome. *h.*

دنمان दिनमान *din-mān*, m. the length of day. *s.*

دنوندها दिनौंधा *dinaundhā*, m. dysopia, or day-blindness. *s.* [animals). *s.*

دني दिनी *dinī*, aged (generally applied to

دني *danī*, mean, paltry, base. *a.*

دنيا *dunyā*, f. the world (either as being near and present, or as worthless); (met.) people. *dunyā po uṭhāne paṛnā*, to be proud or haughty (Dakh.). *dunyā-dār*, worldly, worldly-minded. *dunyā-dārī*, f. economy. *dunyā-ṭalab*, one who is eager in seeking the good things of this world. *dunyā wa mā fī-hā*, the world and whatever therein is. *a.*

دنياوي *dunyāwī*, دنيوي *dunyawī*, } worldly, of the world. *a.*

دنية *danīyat*, f. vice, meanness, defect. *a.*

دو *do*, two. *do-ātasha*, double-distilled. *sharābi do-ātasha*, double-distilled liquor, *i.e.* very strong. *do-* or *du-bāra*, twice. *do-barābar*, double, equal to two. *do-bhāshiyā*, m. an interpreter. *do-pāra*, halved. *do-pāya*, two-legged, a biped, *i.e.* a man. *do-* or *du-paṭṭā*, m. (two-breadthed) a kind of veil in which there are two breadths. *do-paṭṭā tānke sonā*, to draw the sheet over one's head (either from security and carelesness, or after death). *do-paṭṭā hilānā* or *phirānā*, n. to hold out a flag of truce, to offer to surrender (a fort). *do-partā*, double, of two folds. *do-palkā*, (m. having two eyelids) a kind of pigeon; a kind of stone for a ring. *do-pahar*, f. mid-day, noon. *do-pahrī*, of noon, meridian. *do-pahriyā* or *du-pahriyā*, of noon, meridian; m. a kind of flower (*Pentapetes phœnicea*). (*do-piyāza*, m. a kind of stew (v. p 392). *do-paikar*, the sign Gemini.) *do-tārā* or *du-tārā*, m. (double-threaded); a kind of shawl; a guitar with two strings. *do-tahī*, f. (two-plied, double); cloths that are lined. *do-ṭūk*, two-pieced; clear, plain, clean. *do-ṭūk honā*, n. to be adjusted, to be completed. *do-jiyā*, pregnant. *do-jī se honā*, n. to be pregnant. *do-jīwā* (v. *do-jiyā*). *do-chār*, f. interview. *do-* or *du-chittā*, wavering, doubtful, in suspense, absent (in mind). *do-* or *du-chitā,ī*, f. suspense, absence of mind. *do-* or *du-challā*, m. a roof sloping two ways. *do-* or *du-chand*, twice, double. *do-* or *du-choba*, two-poled (tent). *do-khammā*, m. a kind of *ḥukka*-snake with two bends, such as that of the *gurguṛī*, or hubble-bubble. *do-dāmī*, f. flowered muslin, the flowers worked with a needle. *do-* or *du-dila*, wavering, doubtful, in suspense, absent in mind. *do-* or *du-dhārā*, adj. two-edged (sword). *do-* or *du-rāhā*, m. a road dividing into two, leading different ways. *do-* or *du-rukhā*, that which is the same on both sides, not having a wrong side. *do-* or *du-raggā*, capricious, whimsical; m. a mongrel, a person of double breed, having good qualities on one side, and bad on the other, so as not to be depended on. *do-rung*, piebald, of two colours; hypocrite. *do-* or *du-rungā*, capricious; double-dealer. *do-rangī*, f. the property of having two colours, capriciousness, duplicity, hypocrisy, double-dealing, deceit; of two colours, capricious, double-faced. *do-* or *du-roya*, double, two faced. *do-zānū baiṭhnā*, to sit in the Persian fashion, namely, kneeling down and sitting back on the heels (v. *chār-zānū baiṭhnā* and *sari pā baiṭhnā*). *do-sirhā*, tête-à-tête. *do-sūtā*, m. a kind of cloth, the threads of which are double. *do-* or *du-serā*, a weight of two *sīrs*. *do-ẓarbī* or *do-nalī*, double barrelled (a gun). *do-ṭarfī*, mutual, on both sides. *do-kāl*, m. both worlds. *do-kasī*, two-personed, fit for two persons. *do-kalā*, m. irons on the feet of criminals; a double padlock. *do-kohā*, m. a camel, not the dromedary of this country, but the two-bunched animal (*Camelus Bactrianus*). *do-gaṇḍī chittī*, a fomenter of quarrels; a go-between, one who flatters both parties in a dispute (allusion to a game among children, who rub a tamarind seed on one side till a mark is made, then throw it like a die: the caster wins if the mark turn up: the seed thus prepared is called *chittī*, and if it be fraudulently marked on both sides, so as always to win, it is called *do-gaṇḍī*). *do-ghariyā*, m. the space of two-hours. *do-laṛā*, m. a double-stringed necklace. *do-* or *du-loh* and *do-* or *du-lohī*, f. a scimitar made of two plates of steel joined together. *p. s.*

دو द्वि *dwi* (prefixed in comp.), two. *s.*

دو *dau* (in comp.), running, as *nek-dau*, running well. *p.*

دوءا दूआ *dū,ā*, m. the two or deuce at cards, [dice, &c. *p. s.*

دوا *dawā*, f. medicine, a remedy. *dawā-pizīr*, susceptible of cure. *a.*

دوا *diwā*, a lamp (v. *diyā*). *d.*

دوا दिवा *divā*, m. (v. *dibā*), a day. *s.*

دواب *dawābb*, m. (pl. of دابّة), animals, quadrupeds, cattle, beasts. *a.*

دواب *duwāb*, دوابه *duwāba*, } m. the country (we call the Du,āb) between the Ganges and Jamunā: the term may be applied to any flat region lying between two rivers. *p.*

دواپر द्वापर *dwāpar*, m. the third *yuga* or age of the Hindūs, corresponding to the brazen age of the Romans, and comprising 864,000 years (v. *yuga*); doubt, uncertainty. *s.*

دوات *dawāt*, f. an inkstand, ink. *a.*

دواتن दिवातन *divatan*, daily, diurnal. *s.*

دوادس द्वादश *dwādas*, twelve. *s.*

دوادسي द्वादशी *dwādasī*, f. the twelfth lunar day, reckoned from new or full moon. *s.*

دوادش द्वादश *dwādash* (v. *dwādas*), twelve. *s.*

دوادشي द्वादशी *dwādashī*, the twelfth day of the lunar fortnight. *s.*

دوادو *daw-ā-dau*, دوادوي *daw-ā-dau,ī*, } f. labour and fatigue, toil, trouble. *p.*

دوءار *do,ār*, m. (properly *dawwār*) vertigo, giddiness. *a.*

دوار *dawwār*, round. *charkhi dawwār*, the revolving heavens. *a.*

دوار द्वार *dwār*, m. or f. a door, a gate, gateway, passage; a means, an expedient, the medium or way by which a thing is effected. *dwār-pāl*, m. a doorkeeper. *dwār-pālī*, f. the office of a doorkeeper. *s.*

دوار दवार *dawār*, f. fire that breaks out in woods. *s.*

دوارا द्वारा *dwārā*, m. a door; (prep.) by means [of. *s.*

دوارابتي द्वाराबती *dwārābatī*, دواراوتي द्वारावती *dwārāvatī*, دواركا द्वारिका *dwārikā* or *dwārkā*, } f. name of a Hindū holy place on the bank of the Western sea, near the mouth of the gulf of Katch, once the capital of *Krishṇa*, and supposed to have been submerged by the sea. *dwārikā-nāth*, master of *dwārikā*, an epithet of *Krishṇa*. *s.*

دواراتر दिवारात्र *divā-rātra* m. or *divā-rātri*, f. a day and night (Pers. *shabāna-roz*, q. v.). *s.*

دواروليبهج द्वारबलिभुज *dwār-wali-bhuj*, m. the Vak, a sort of crane (*Ardea nivea*). *s.*

دوارن द्वारिन *dwārin*, دواري द्वारी *dwārī*, } m. a porter, a warder, a doorkeeper. *s.*

دوازده *duwāzdah*, twelve. *duwāzdah-jausaḳ*, or *-mil*, the twelve signs of the zodiac. *p.*

دوازدهم *duwāzdahum*, the twelfth. *p.*

دوازدهي *duwāzdahī*, a dozen. *p.*

دواسپه *do-aspa*, quick, expeditious; lit. having two horses, *i.e.* having one horse to relieve another, or having a relay of horses. *p.*

دوآشيانا *do-āshiyānā*, m. (with two rooms) a kind of tent. *p.*

دواكر दिवाकर *divā-kar*, m. the sun. *s.*

دواگن दवाग्नि *davāgni*, m. a wood on fire, conflagration of a forest. *s.*

دوءال *do,āl*, f. a leather strap, a belt. *do,āl-pā*, web-footed; a fabulous race with legs like thongs, who are said to deceive and devour unwary travellers. *p.*

دوال *diwāl* (v. *dīwār*), a wall. *d.*

دوالا दिवाला *diwālā*, m. bankruptcy, insolvency. *h.*

دوالي दिवाली *divālī*, f. (v. *dewālī*) name of a [Hindū festival. *s.*

دوءالي *dū,ālī*, f. (properly *do,āl*) a leather strap, a belt. *dū,ālī band*, a *sipāhī* (having a leather belt). *p.*

دواليب *dawālīb* (Ar. pl. of دولاب), wheels. *p.*

دوام *dawām*, m. perpetuity, persevering; always, eternally. *'alq-d-dawām*, continually, assiduously, incessantly. *dawām band o bast*, perpetual settlement. *a.*

دوامدهيه दिवामध्य *divā-madhya*, m. mid-day, [noon. *s.*

دوان *dawān*, running, walking fast. *p.*

دوانده दिवान्ध *divāndh*, blind by day; m. an owl. *s.*

دوانش दिवानिश *divā-nish*, m. day and night. *s.*

دوانيدن *dawānīdan*, to cause to run, to drive about. *p.*

دوب दूब *dūb*, f. name of a grass (*Agrostis linearis*). *s.*

دوباز *dobāz*, m. a kind of pigeon; a sort of [child's kite. *p.*

دوباسي *do-bāsī* (for *du-bhāshiyā*), an interpreter. *h.*

دوبر दोबर *dobar*, double, twofold. *s.*

دوبر दूबर *dūbar*, weak, lean, difficult. *s.*

دوبڑوگهسڑو दूबड़ूघसड़ू *dūbṛū-ghasṛū*, unknown, insignificant, helpless, hiding through weakness. *h.*

دوبسوي दोबिसवी *do-biswī*, an allowance of two *biswas* out of twenty, or ten per cent. *h.*

دوبهك दूभक *dūbhak*, f. a scarcity, a famine. *s.*

دوبهاشيا दोभाषिया *do-bhāshiyā* (vulg. *dobash*), a man skilled in two tongues, an interpreter. *s.*

دوبهيان दोभयान *dobhayān*, (with two hands) two-fisted, ambi-dextrous; strong. *s.*

دوبي दोबे *dobe*, m. the knowing two Vedās; a title of Brāhmans. *s.*

دوبيا दूबिया *dubiyā*, f. a kind of green, grass green. *s.*

دوپستا दोपस्ता *dopastā* or *dūpastā*, pregnant. *h.*

دوپ द्विप *dwip*, m. a plant (*Mesua ferrea*). *s.*

دوپته द्विपथ *dwi-path*, m. a place where two roads meet. *s.*

دوپد द्विपद *dwi-pad*, two-footed; m. a biped, including gods, demons, men, and birds. *s.*

دوپيازه *do-piyāza*, a kind of rich stew made with butter, onions, and sundry other good things. *p.*

دوت दूत *dūt*, m. an ambassador, messenger, a go-between, an angel who passes between God and mortals. *s.*

دوتا *dotā*, }
دوتاو *dotāw*, } double, doubled, bent, bending the body; a kind of cloth. *p.*
دوتاه *dotāh*, }

دوتكا दूतिका *dūtikā*, f. a female messenger, a confidant. *s.*

دوتي दूती *dūtī*, f. a female messenger, a confidant, a procuress, a go-between, a bawd; (for *dyuti*) refulgence. *s.*

دوتيا दूतिया *dūtiyā*, }
دوتيه द्वितीय *dwitīya*, } second, the second. *dwitīyā*, f. (a second self) a wife legally wedded according to the Vedic rites; the second day of a lunar fortnight. *s.*

دوتيابها द्वितीयाभा *dwitīyābhā*, f. a scitamineous plant (*Curcuma zanthorrhiza*). *s.*

دوج दूज *dūj*, f. the second lunar day. *s.*

دوج द्विज *dwi-ja*, (lit. twice-born) a man of any of the three first classes of Hindūs, but particularly a Brāhman, whose investiture with the sacrificial string is considered as a second birth. *dwija-dās* or *dwija-sevak*, a man of the fourth or servile caste, a Sūdra, as being the servant of the *dwija* classes. *s.*

دوجا दूजा *dūjā*, second, another. *s.*

دوجا द्विजा *dwi-jā*, f. a plant (*Siphonanthus Indicus*); gum olibanum. *s.*

دوجاتي द्विजाती *dwijātī* (v. *dwija*), twice-born. *s.*

دوجايني द्विजायनी *dwi-jāyanī*, f. the sacrificial string worn by the first three castes. *s.*

دوجبر दूजबर *dūj-bar*, m. a man who marries a second wife, a bigamist. *s.*

دوجپتني द्विजपत्नी *dwija-patnī*, f. the wife of a *dwija*, a Brāhmanī woman. *s.*

دوجپريا द्विजप्रिया *dwija-priyā*, f. the moon-plant (*Asclepias acida*). *s.*

دوج كتست द्विजकुत्सित *dwija-kutsit*, m. a tree (*Cordia myxa*). *s.*

دوجنما द्विजन्मा *dwi-janmā*, twice-born, a [Brāhman. *s.*

دوجها दोझा *dojhā*, married to a second wife. *s.*

دوجيرا दोजीरा *dojīrā*, }
دوجيره दोजीरः *dojīra*, } a kind of rice (v. *dhān*). *h.*

دوجيو दोजीवा *do-jīwā*, pregnant. *s.*

دوچه दोच: *docha*, the second reservoir to which water is raised for the purpose of irrigation. *h.*

دوحة *dauḥat*, a grove, orchard, nursery. *a.*

دوخت *dokht*, f. sewing, a stitch. *p.*

دوختن *dokhtan* (r. *doz*), to stitch, to sew; to pin, as with an arrow. *p.*

دوخته *dokhta*, stitched, fixed (the eye or sight). *p.*

دود *dūd*, m. smoke, vapour. *dūdi dil* or *dūdi dam*, a sigh. *dūd-ālūda*, smoky. *p.*

دودآلود *dūd-ālūd*, smoked, perfumed; name of a town and river in India. *p.*

دودمان *dūdmān*, m. generation, race. *p.*

دودنا दोदना *dodnā*, a. to deny. *h.*

دودھ दूध *dūdh*, m. milk; the juice (or milk) of certain bushes. *dūdh-adhārī*, living on milk. *dūdh baṛhnā*, n. to be weaned. *dūdh-bhātī*, f. same as *dūdhā-bhātī*, q. v. *dūdh-bhā,ī*, m. foster-brother. *dūdh pilānā*, to suckle. *dūdh-pilā,ī*, f. a wet-nurse. *dūdh-haṇḍī*, f. a vessel for holding milk. *s.*

دودھا दूधा *dūdhā*, a kind of rice (v. *dhān*). *h.*

دودھا द्विधा *dwidhā*, of two kinds, in two ways. *s.*

دودھا *dūdhā*, m. lamp-black. *p.*

دودھابھاتي दूधाभाती *dūdhā-bhātī*, f. a ceremony performed the fourth day after marriage, wherein the bride and bridegroom eat milk, boiled rice, and sugar, together. *s.*

دودھاتُ द्विधातु *dwi-dhātu*, having two natures. *s.*

دودھار दूधार *dūdhār*, } giving much milk,
دودھل दूधल *dūdhal*, } milch. *s.*

دودھي दूधी *dūdhī*, milky, containing milky juice; f. starch; name of several plants with milky juice, as various species of *Asclepias*, *Echites*, *Euphorbia*, &c., *Asclepias rosea*, &c. *s.*

دودھيا दूधिया *dūdhiyā*, milky; m. name of several plants with milky juice (v. *dūdhī*). *dūdhiyā-patthar*, a white stone of which plaster is made and utensils are formed; the opal. *h.*

دور दूर *dūr*, f. distance; adj. far, distant, remote. *dūr-andesh*, provident, foreseeing, penetrating, sagacious, wise, prudent. *dūr-bād*, God forbid. *dūr bhāgnā*, n. to abstain from, to abominate, to shun. *dūr-bīn*, m. a spy-glass, a telescope; having the quality of shewing a distant object; far-seeing; (met.) prudent, provident, ingenious. *'aḳli dūr-bīn*, far-seeing reason, solid judgment. *dūr-pār*, God forbid (a female phrase). *dūr-darāz*, f. far-distant. *dūr-drish* or *dūr-darshī*, long-sighted, far-seeing; m. a learned man, a teacher; a vulture. *dūr-drishṭi* or *dūr-darshan*, long-sightedness, foresight. *dūra-stha*, remote, far off. *dūr-k.*, to remove, to reject. *dūr-gāmī*, going far. *dūr-vāsī* (f. *dūr-vāsinī*), residing in a distant country; outlandish. *dūr-h.*, to be removed or dispelled. *dūr ho*, be gone, avaunt, be off. *s. p.*

دور *daur*, m. revolution (of time or of any body), circular motion; the windlass or capstan of a ship; a species of argument, reasoning in a circle; age, vicissitude, circuit. *daur daur*, m. prosperity. *a.*

دور दौर *daur*, the slings attached to a basket for irrigation. *h.*

دور दोर *dor*, land ploughed twice; when ploughed thrice it is called *te,ār*; when four times, *chawar* (Ell.). *h.*

دورا दौरा *daurā*, m. a large basket (without cover). *h.*

دوراتميه दौरात्म्य *daurātmya*, m. wickedness, depravity. *s.*

دورادور *dūr-ā-dūr*, very far, to a great distance. *p.*

دوران *daurān*, m. time, age; fortune, vicissitude; a revolution, period, a circle, cycle. *daurāni sar*, m. a swimming in the head. *a.*

دورانديش *dūr-andesh*, far-seeing, of deep reflection. *p.*

دورانديشي *dūr-andeshī*, f. prudence, forethought. *p.*

دوربھاگيه दौर्भाग्य *daurbhāgya*, m. ill luck, misfortune. *s.*

دورجنيه दौर्जन्य *daurjanya*, m. wickedness, depravity. *s.*

دورتا दूरता *dūratā*, f. remoteness, distance. *s.*

دورخي *do-rukhī*, f. a kind of bow. *p.*

دورس दोरस *do-ras*, a mixture of two soils. *h.*

دورکت द्विरुक्त *dwir-ukt*, said twice, repeated. *dwir-ukti*, f. repetition. *s.*

دورگندھ दौर्गन्धि *daurgandhi*, f. fœtor, bad smell. *s.*

دورولیه दौर्बल्य *daurvalya*, m. weakness, debility. *s.*

دوروا दूर्वा *dūrvā*, f. bent grass, the *Dūb* (*Panicum dactylon*). *s.*

دوروپ द्विरूप *dwi-rūp*, of two forms. *s.*

دوره *daura*, m. going round, circulation (particularly of the wine-cup). *a.*

دورو *do-rū*, m. two-faced, a kind of small drum played on both ends. *p.*

دوري *dūrī*, f. distance, separation. *p.*

دوري दोरी *dorī*, f. a chain or line with which lands are measured. *h.*

دوري दौरी *daurī*, f. a basket (without lid); a rope wherewith a string of cattle are bound together, as in the case of a number of bullocks when threshing, or rather treading out the corn: it also denotes a kind of sling-basket used in irrigation. *h.*

دوري‌بھوت दूरीभूत *dūrī-bhūt*, remote, far off. *s.*

دوري‌کرت दूरीकृत *dūrī-kṛit*, removed, dispelled. *s.*

دوڑ दौड़ *dauṛ*, f. run, incursion, attack, assault, endeavour, race, struggle, effort, career, military expedition. *dauṛ-dhūp*, labour and fatigue. *dauṛ-dhūp-k.*, to use great labour and exertion for the accomplishment of any object; to bustle, to toil. *h.*

دوڑا दौड़ा *dauṛā*, m. a large basket (without lid); a highwayman (who robs on horseback). *s.*

دوڑاپا *dauṛāpā*, a village runner or messenger. *h.*

دوڑادوڑي दौड़ादौड़ी *dauṛā-dauṛī*, f. running, race, hurry. *h.*

دوڑاك दौड़ाक *dauṛāh*, m. a racer, a runner. *h.*

دوڑانا दौड़ाना *dauṛānā*, a. to cause to run, to drive, to impel, to actuate, to expedite. *h.*

دوڑاها दौड़ाहा *dauṛāhā*, m. a messenger, a courier, a guide. *h.*

دوڑنا दौड़ना *dauṛnā*, n. to run, to gallop, course, drive; to assault, rush, invade; to toil. *dauṛnā dhāpnā*, to run violently; to use great exertion, to toil. *h.* [a messenger. *h.*

دوڑها दौड़हा *dauṛahā*, m. a harbinger, a guide,

دوڑي दौड़ी *dauṛī*, f. a drawn game at *chaupaṛ*. *h.*

دوز *doz*, (in comp.) sewing, piercing; as *zar doz*, an embroiderer; *dil-doz*, heart-piercing. *p.*

دوزخ *dozakh*, m. hell; (met.) the belly. *p.*

دوزخي *dozakhī*, m. hellish; the people of hell, *i.e.* the damned; (met.) a glutton. *p.*

دوزه *doza*, a kind of prickly plant; gum lac, a kind of wax for fixing handles on knives, &c. *p.*

دوزيره *dozīra*, m. a kind of rice. *p.*

دوس दिवस *divas*, m. a day. *s.*

دوس दोष *dos*, m. crime, fault, blame. *dos honā*, n. to be sick after childbirth, from neglect of regimen. *s.*

دوساد दोसाद *dosād* or *dusād*, m. a low caste residing in and about Patna, whose business it is to remove carcases, and to be executioners; hog-keepers. *h.* [crops a year. *h.*

دوساهي दोसाही *do-sāhī*, lands yielding two

دوسپتاه द्विसप्ताह *dwi-saptāh*, m. a fortnight. *s.*

دوست *dost*, m. a friend, a sweetheart. *dost-dār*, m. (vulg. *dosdār*) a friend, a sweetheart. *dost-dārī*, f. (vulg. *dosdārī*) friendship, love. *p.*

دوستانه *dostāna*, friendly, like a friend. *p.*

دوستي *dostī*, f. friendship, love, affection. *p.*

دوسر दूसर *dūsar*, m. the second. *s.*

دوسرا दूसरा *dūsrā*, the second, other; an equal, a match. *dusre*, secondly. *s.*

دوسري दोसरी *do-sarī*, the ploughing of land twice; also land twice ploughed; when ploughed three times it is called *te-sarī*; when four times, *chau-sarī*. *h.*

دوسنا दोषना *dosnā*, a. to accuse, to blame. *s.*

دوسي दोषी *dosī*, faulty, criminal. *s.*

دوسي दोसी *dosī*, m. thick, sour milk; a Musalmān milkman. *h.*

دوش *dosh*, the shoulder; a kind of lac (v. *doya*); adv. last night. *p.*

دوش दोष *doṣh*, m. (v. *dos*) crime, fault, blame, blemish, defect, sin, offence; disorder of the humours or functions of the body. *dosh-kalpan*, m. reprehending, condemning. *dosh-grāhī*, censorious, malicious. *dosh-honā*, to be sick after childbirth from neglect of regimen. *s.*

دوشاله *do-shāla*, a kind of plaid made of two shawls sewn together; a single breadth of a shawl is never worn by Indians. *h.* [animal. *s.*

دوشپه द्विशफ *dwi-shaph*, m. a cloven-footed

دوشت दूषित *dūshit*, calumniated, falsely accused (especially of adultery); contaminated, corrupted, violated; blamed, censured. *s.*

دوشتا दूषिता *dūshitā*, f. a girl who has been violated. *s.*

دوشك दूषक *dūshak*, ill, low, contemptible. *s.*

دوشك दोषिक *doshik*, } faulty, defective; bad,
دوشن दोषिन *doshin*, } wicked, criminal. *s.*

دوشمال *doshmāl*, m. a towel used by butchers, &c. *p.*

دوشن दोषण *doshan*, m. objection, blame. *dūshan*, blame, fault, defect, offence. *doshin*, faulty. *s.*

دوشنا दोषना *doshnā*, a. to accuse, to blame. *s.*

دوشوان दोषवान *dosh-wān*, }
دوشوت दोषवत *dosh-wat*, } faulty, defective, wicked, bad. *s.*
دوشي दोषी *doshī*, }

دوشي दूषी *dūshī*, } f. the secretion or
دوشيكا दूषीका *dūshīkā*, } rheum of the eye. *s.*

دوشيزگي *doshīzagī*, f. virginity. *p.*

دوشيزه *doshīza*, f. a virgin. *p.*

دوشينه *doshīna*, m. a shoulder-load; adj. of, or relating to last night. *p.*

دوشيه दूष्य *dūshya*, reprehensible, vile, bad. *s.*

دوغ *dogh*, m. butter-milk. *p.*

دوغله *doghla* (properly *dāghūl*), a mongrel. *p.*

دوغله بازي *dūghla-bāzī*, f. horse exercise with throwing the javelin, and which the Arabs call "*la'bu-l-jarīd*." *p.*

دوفصلي *do-faṣlī*, land that produces two crops in a year. *p.*

دوك दोक *dok*, m. a two-year-old foal. *h.*

دوك *dūk*, m. a spindle. *p.*

دوكان *dūkān*, f. a shop, a workshop. *dūkān-dār*, a shopkeeper. *dūkān-dārī*, f. the keeping of a shop. *p.* [keeper. *p.*

دوكاني *dūkānī*, f. shopkeeping; m. a shop-

دوكه दोष *dokh*, m. a crime, a fault, blame, vice (see *dosh*). *s.*

دوكهك दोषक *dokhak*, m. an objector. *s.*

دوكهنا दोषना *dokhnā*, a. to accuse, to calumniate, to blame. *s.*

دوكهي दोखी *dokhī*, a raised mound indicating the junction of two boundaries. *h.*

دوكهي दोषी *dokhī*, an offender, a criminal. *s.*

دوگانا *dogānā*, دوگانه *dogāna*, double, twofold; m. two genuflexions in prayer. *h. p.*

دوگاڑا दोगाड़ा *dogāṛā* or *dugāṛā*, twice, double; a musket carrying two balls. *h.*

دوگر दोगर *dogar*, name of a marauding tribe in the north-west of India. *h.*

دوگلا दूगला *dūglā*, دوگله दूगलः *dūgla*, a sling-basket of large size, round and deep, used for the purposes of irrigation. *h.*

دوگن द्विगुण *dwi-gun*, twice, twofold, doubled. *dwi-gunī-bhūt* or *dwi-gunī-krit*, doubled, increased. *s.*

دوگنا दूगुणा *dū-gunā*, double, two-fold. *s.*

دول दोल *dol*, m. the mast of a ship. *h.*

دول *daul*, state, condition; statement of revenue items. *a.*

دول दोल *dol*, m. swinging; a festival on the fourteenth of Phālgun, the swinging of the juvenile *Krishna*; a litter, a swinging cot, a *dūlī*, a swing. *dol-māl*, *k.*, to wave, swing, undulate; to hesitate. *s.*

دولاب *dūlāb*, m. a wheel for drawing water with. *p.*

دولاوه दोलावः *do-lāwa*, a well having two well-buckets and ropes. *h.*

دولايمان दोलायमान *dolāyamān*, swinging, being swung; perplexed, vacillating. *s.*

دولت *daulat*, f. happiness, felicity, riches, wealth; fortune, prosperity, state, empire or kingdom; cause, occasion, effect, means. *daulat-khāna*, m. (house of fortune) a palace, a house (your house). *daulat-khāna,e khāṣṣ*, a royal residence, the king's palace. *daulat-sarā*, f. house, palace (your house, being a respectful mode of address). *daulat-mand*, wealthy, rich, fortunate. *a.*

دولڑ दोलड़ *dolaṛ*, دولڑا दोलड़ा *dolaṛā*, double, of two rows, &c. *h.*

دولکا दोलिका *dolikā*, f. a swing. *s.*

دولم *dūlam* (v. *nāṭh*), nonentity, nonexistence. *d.*

دولمال کرنا दोलमालकरना *dolmāl-karnā*, a. to wave, to swing, to undulate, to hesitate. *s.*

دولها दूल्हा *dūlhā*, m. a bridegroom. *h.*

دوءم *dū,am*, second; inferior, second sort. *p.*

دوما दूमा *dūmā*, دومه दूमः *dūma*, the name of a leathern case in which they import tea from Thibet into Garhwāl, and Kamā,on: it contains about six pounds. *h.*

دومٹ दोमट *do-maṭ*, m. a mixture of two soils, clay and sand. *h.*

دومٹکار दोमटिकार *domṭihār*, name of a subdivision of the Brāhman tribe. *h.*

دومکه द्विमुख *dwi-mukh*, دومنها दोमुँहा *do-muṅhā*, having two mouths; m. a kind of serpent (*Amphisbana*) (also *dwimukh-āhī*). *dwi-mukh*, f. a leech. *s.*

دومين *dū,amīn* (same as *dū,am*), the second. *p.*

دون *dūn*, base, mean, ignoble, poor, vile. *dūn-himmat*, mean-spirited, of a base disposition. *a.p.*

دون दौँ *dauṅ*, f. fire, a flame. *s.*

دون दोँ *doṅ*, a fractional division of an estate. *h.*

دون दून *dūn*, a valley (the etymology of the word is learnedly discussed in Elliot's Glossary). *h.*

دونا दोना *donā* or दौना *daunā*, m. the name of a flower (a species of *Artemisia*); southernwood. *s.*

دونا दौना *daunā* or दोना *donā*, m. a leaf folded up in the shape of a cup for holding betel, flowers, or boiled rice, &c.; a basket or bucket made of large leaves. *h.*

دونا दूना *dūnā*, double, twofold. *h.*

دونالي दोनाली *do-nālī*, two-barrelled (a gun). *s.*

دونجا दौँजा *daunjā*, m a scaffold. *h.*

دوند द्वन्द *dwand*, دوندوه द्वन्द्व *dwandwa*, m. a pair, a couple (especially male and female); union of the sexes, or coupling. *dwandwa-chārī*, the ruddy goose, flying in couples. *s.*

دوند *davind*, a runner, a racer. *p.*

دونر दोँर *doṅr*, m. name of a species of snake. *h.*

دونکنا दोँकना *donknā*, n. to growl. *h.*

دونکي दोँकी *doṅkī*, f. bellows. *h.*

دونگڑا दूँगड़ा *dūngṛā* or दौँगड़ा *daungṛā*, دونگڑه *dūngṛa* or *daungṛa*, a heavy shower. *h.*

[(v. *do-nālī*). *s.*

دونلي दोनली *do-nalī*, two-barrelled (a gun)

دونون दोनोँ *donoṅ*, the two, both. *donoṅ waḳt milne*, expresses the evening twilight. *h.*

دوءو दोउ *do,ū* (v. *donoṅ*), both, the two. *h.*

دووداس दिवोदास *divodās*, a king of Benares, and founder of the Indian school of medicine. *s.*

دوودھ द्विविध *dwi-vidh*, of two kinds, in two ways. *s.*

دوها दोहा *dohā*, m. a couplet (*bhākhā*). *s.*

دوهان दोहान *dohān*, m. a young bullock, a steer. *s.*

دوهاءو दोहाव *dohā,o*, the zamīndār's perquisite of milk from the cultivator's cows. *h.*

دوهاءي दोहाई *dohā,ī* or दुहाई *duhā,ī*, f. crying out for justice, exclamation; an oath, plaint (q.d. twice alas). *duhā,ī tihā,ī-k.*, to make reiterated com plaints. *h.*

دوهتا दोहता *dohtā*, m. a grandson (daughter's son), son-in-law. *s.*

دوهتر दौहित्र *dauhitr*, m. daughter's son. *s.*

دوهتري दौहित्री *dauhitrī*, f. daughter's daughter. *s.*

[with both hands. *h.*

دوهتڑ दोहत्तड़ *do-hattaṛ*, m. a blow or slap

دوهتي दोहती *dohtī*, f. a grand-daughter (daughter's daughter). *s.*

دوهد दोहद *dohad*, m. wish, desire, the longing of a pregnant woman. *dohad-lakshan*, fœtus, embryo. *dohadānvitā* or *dohad-watī*, a pregnant woman longing for any thing. *s.*

دوهر दोहर *dohar*, m. a double sheet; a sheath; the old bed of a river; land yielding two crops in a year. *dohur*, a sandy sub-soil. *h.*

دوهرا दोहरा *dohrā*, double, twofold (v. *dolaṛ*); m. a distich. *h.* [peat. *h.*

دوهرانا दोहराना *dohrānā*, a. to double, to re-

دوهراو दोहराव *dohrāw*, m. act of doubling, repetition. *h.* [woman. *s.*

دوهرديا द्विहृदया *dwi-hṛidayā*, f. a pregnant

دوهڑكا दोहड़िका *dohaṛikā*, f. the Prākrit metre called *Dohā*, a stanza of four lines, containing thirteen and eleven syllabic instants alternately. *s.*

دوهلوتي दोहलवती *dohal-watī*, for *dohad-watī*, v. *dohad.* [to Brāhmans. *h.*

دوهلي दोहली *dohlī*, service lands; lands given

دوهن दोहन *dohan*, m. milking; a milk-pail. *dohin* (f. *dohinī*), a milker. *s.*

دوهنا दोहना *dohnā*, a. to milk. *s.*

دوهني दोहनी *dohnī*, f. a vessel for holding milk; a milking-pail. *s.*

دوهيا दूहिया *dūhiyā*, m. a kind of fireplace. *h.*

دوئي दूई *dū,ī*, f. duality, separation or dispersion, in opposition to unity. *s.*

دوي द्वै *dwai*, two (same as *do*). *s.*

دوياگن द्वयाग्नि *dwayāgni*, m. a plant (*Plumbago zeylanica*). *s.*

دويپ द्वीप *dwīp*, m. an island, a large portion of the earth, a clime, a region. This word is applied by the Hindūs to seven imaginary divisions of the world, represented as seven concentric continents, separated from each other by circumambient oceans. Reckoning from the central one, they are called *Jambu, Kas, Plaksh, Sālmalī, Kraunch, Sāk*, and *Pushkar*. The central Dwip, *Jambu*, or the known continent, is again portioned into ten divisions, likewise termed *Dwīps*; viz. *Kuru, Chandra, Varun, Saumya, Nāg, Kumārikā, Gabhastimān, Tāmrapūrn, Kaseru*, and *Indra*. *s.*

دويپي द्वीपी *dwīpī*, m. an islander; a tiger. *s.*

دويت द्वैत *dwait*, m. doubt, separation; duplication, duality, or assertion of two principles, as spirit and matter (in philosophy). *dwait-vādī*, m. a philosopher who asserts two principles. *s.*

دويدن *dawīdan*, to run, flow; to make haste. *p.*

دويدھ द्वैध *dwaidh*, m. doubt, division into two parts; adj. twofold, of two sorts. *s.*

دويدهيكرن द्वैधीकरण *dwaidhīkaraṇ*, m. separating. *s.* [a double entendre. *s.*

دويرتھ द्वयर्थ *dwyarth*, of two meanings or senses,

دوي سلاءي दिवेसलाई *dive-salā,ī*, f. (v. *diyā-salā,ī*) a match for kindling a lamp. *d.*

دويش द्वेष *dwesh*, m. enmity, aversion. *s.*

دويشي द्वेषी *dweshī*, hostile, adverse; m. an enemy. *s.*

دويشيه द्वेष्य *dweshya*, hateful, detestable. *dweshyatā*, f. aversion, detestableness. *s.*

دويم *dūyam* or *doyum*, } the second. *p.*
دويمين *dūyamīn*, }

دويوپپادك दिव्योपपादुक *divyopapāduk*, of heavenly birth, divine. *s.*

دويه दिव्य *divya*, divine, celestial; beautiful, charming; an ordeal; an oath. *divya-panchāmṛit*, m. a mixture of five ingredients, ghī, curds, milk, butter, and sugar. *divya-dharmī*, virtuous, agreeable. *divya-ratna*, m. the famous gem *chintāmaṇi*. *divya-ras*, m. quicksilver. *divya-vastra*, clothed in celestial raiment. *s.*

ده *dih*, m. a village. *dih-khudā*, the headman in a village; (in comp.) it signifies giving, occasioning; as *ārām-dih*, giving ease or comfort. *taṣdī'-dih*, troublesome. *p.*

ده *dah*, ten. *dah-chand*, tenfold, ten times. *dah-chandagī*, f. tenfold (it is a word with which they return a salutation). *dah dar dunyā, sattar dar ākhirat*, a benediction of *faḳīrs*, meaning, charity will be returned sevenfold in the next world (it is probably a corrupt Persian phrase, *dah dar dunyā sitān dar ākhirat*, "give in this world and receive in the next") —so says Hunter, and so copy his copyists; but in the latter case it must be written *dih*, not *dah*. It is much more likely that the proverbial expression in question is from the Persian "*dah dar dunyā, ṣad dar ākhirat*," "ten in this world (is, or yields) a hundred in the next." *dah yak*, tenth part. *p.*

دهه दह *dah*, m. very deep water; whirlpool, a pool or eddy in a river; abyss. *kaṅwal-dah*, a place abounding with the lotus or water-lily. *s.*

دها *dahā*, m. the ten days of the *Muḥarram*; the models of the tombs of *ḥasan* and *ḥusain*, or the model of a building containing the tombs, which are carried about in procession during those ten days. On the tenth day, the tombs are buried, or in some places thrown into water; the building, if made of cheap materials, shares the same fate; if costly, it is carried back and deposited in the *dargāh* or *karbalā*. *p.*

دهابا धाबा *dhābā*, an upper story of a house; a terraced roof. *h.*

دهابري *dhābrī*, f. a pigeon-house, a dovecot. *d.*

دهابهائي धाभाई *dhā-bhā,ī*, m. foster-brother. *s.*

دهاپ धाप *dhāp*, f. a measure of length; as far as a man can run without taking breath; according to Elliot it signifies one quarter of a *kos*, or nearly half a mile: it is also applied to a *ghāṭ* or passage; also, a large expanse of low ground. *s.*

دهات धात *dhāt* or धातु *dhātu*, m. metal; the Sanskrit root or crude form of a word; a mineral; a principle or humour of the body; an organ of sense; an elementary substance or property; f. *semen virile*. *dhātu-bhṛit*, promoting the animal secretions. *dhātu-vādī*, m. an assayer, a mineralogist. *s.*

دهات *dihāt*, m. (Arab. pl. of *dih*) villages; the country, as opposed to towns. *p.*

دهاتپ धातुप *dhātup*, m. the alimentary juice or chyle. *s.*

دهاتراجك धातुराजक *dhātu-rājah*, m. *semen virile*. *s.*

دهاترپشپكا धातृपुष्पिका *dhātṛi-pushpikā*, f. a tree (*Grislea tomentosa*). *s.*

دهاتركا धात्रिका *dhātrikā*, f. emblick myrobalan. *s.*

دهاتري धात्री *dhātrī*, f. a nurse (v. *dhā,e*); a mother; the earth; emblick myrobalan. *s.*

دهاتشيكهر धातुशेखर *dhātu-shekhar*, m. green vitriol. *s.*

دهاتكاشيش धातुकाशीश *dhātu-kāshīsh*, m. red sulphate of iron. *s.*

دهاتكي धातकी *dhātkī*, f. a tree (*Grislea tomentosa*). *s*

دهاتمارني धातुमारिणी *dhātu-mārinī*, f. borax. *s.*

دهاتماكشك धातुमाक्षिक *dhātu-mākshik*, m. a sulphuret of iron. *s.*

دهاتوپل धातूपल *dhātūpal*, m. chalk. *s.*

دهاتولبه धातुवल्लभ *dhātu-vallabh*, m. borax. *s.*

دهاتويري धातुवैरी *dhātu-vairī*, m. sulphur. *s.*

دهاٹي धाटी *dhāṭī*, f. advancing towards, or confronting an enemy. *s.*

دهاچك *dhāchak*, dread, aversion. *d.*

دهاڈا धाडा *dhāḍā*, water falling from above, a waterfall. *s.*

دهار धार *dhār*, f. a line, lineament; stream, current; edge of a sword, &c.; sharpness. *dhār par mārnā* or *dhār mārnā*, to contemn, to despise. *s.*

دهار धार *dhār*, m. debt; slight sprinkling of rain; end, bound, limit. *s.*

دهار धार *dhār*, a hollow tree inserted in the mouth of wells to prevent their falling in. *h.*

دهار दुहार *duhār*, m. a milker. *s.*

دهارت धारित *dhārit*, upheld, sustained. *s.*

دهارا धारा *dhārā*, f. stream, a current. *dhārā-sār*, m. a heavy shower, a large drop of rain. *s.*

دهارباچه धारबाछ *dhār-bāchh*, an even or general distribution of charges, rates, &c. *s.*

دهاردهرنا धारधरना *dhārdharnā*, to winnow. *h.*

دهاردهورا धारधूरा *dhār-dhūrā*, the boundary formed by a stream. *h.*

دهارك धारक *dhārak*, m. a debtor. *s.*

دهارمك धार्मिक *dhārmik*, virtuous, pious, just. *s.*

دهارن धारण *dhāran*, m. act of upholding, bearing, having, keeping, &c. *s.*

دهارنا धारणा or धारना *dhārnā*, a. to uphold, to bear, support, keep, place, sustain; to pour (water); to owe; f. continuance in rectitude, keeping in the right way; fortitude, firmness; memory. *s.*

دهارني धारणी *dhārnī*, f. any tubular vessel of the body. *s.*

دهاري धारी *dhārī*, f. a line, lineament; a small buttress. *dhārī-dār*, lined, striped; name of a plant used in dyeing (*Lythrum fruticosum, Lin.*; *Grislea tomentosa, Roxb., pl. cor.*); (in comp.) bearing, holding. *s.*

دهاڑ धाड़ *dhāṛ*, f. } a crowd, a multitude;
دهاڑا धाड़ा *dhāṛā*, } falling of water from above; a robbery. *h.*

دهاڑس *dhāṛas*, courage, confidence (v. *ḍhāras*). *d.*

دهاڑنا दहाड़ना *dahāṛnā*, n. to roar (as a tiger). *h.*

دهاك धाक *dhāk*, f. pomp, glory; renown, fame; fear, terror; name of a tree (*Butea frondosa*); a poet. *h.*

دهاك *dahāk*, m. the place of tens in arithmetic. *p.*

دهاكر धाकर *dhākar*, m. a mongrel. *h.*

دهاكرا धाकरा *dhākarā*, } name of a small tribe
دهاكره धाकरः *dhākara*, } of *rājpūts*, in the districts of Agra. *h.*

دهاكها धाखा *dhākhā*, m. a swing; name of a tree (*Butea frondosa*). *h.*

دهاگا धागा *dhāgā*, m. a thread. *dhāgā ḍālnā*, a. to quilt. *h.*

دهالا धाला *dhālā*, } a stream, a current; a
دهاله धालः *dhāla*, } kind of cess, about one ānā in the *rupī*, levied on villagers. *h.*

دهام धाम *dhām*, m. a dwelling, a place, a house. *s.*

دهاما धामा *dhāmā*, m. a large cane basket. *h.*

دهامن धामन *dhāman*, a species of grass of a good quality, found in the Bhattī territory. *h.*

دهامن धामिन *dhāmin*, m. a kind of serpent (which is said to suck cows, and to be otherwise harmless); a kind of wood; a kind of bamboo. *h.*

دهامني धामनी *dhāmnī*, f. vein, any tubular vessel of the body. *s.*

دهاموت धामवत *dhām-wat*, splendid, luminous, illustrious. *s.*

دهاميان धामियान *dhāmiyān* (pl. of *dhāmī*), name of a sect, followers of Prānāth, a Hindū reformer who flourished in the 17th century in *Bundelkhand*. *h.*

دهان धान *dhān*, m. rice before it is separated from the husk. Of the *dhān* there are many species, for an account of which v. Ell. Gloss. *dhān-kāṭī*, the season for cutting rice. *s.*

دهان *dahān* or *dihān*, the mouth, an orifice. *p.*

دهانا धाना *dhānā*, n. to run, to make haste, to toil and labour, to drudge; to worship. *s.*

دهانا दुहाना *duhānā*, a. to cause to milk. *s.*

دهانا दहाना *dahānā*, a. to burn, to set on fire. *s.*

دهانا धाना *dhānā*, } the *gond* portion of a vil-
دهانه धानः *dhāna*, } lage, which is always separated from the rest (v. *gond*). *h.*

دهاندهل धांधल *dhāndhal*, f. wrangling, subterfuge, trick, juggle, chicanery. *s.*

دهاندهلپنا धांधलपना *dhāndhal-panā*, m. trickery, roguery, chicanery, subterfuge. *h.*

دهاندهلي धांधली *dhāndhlī*, m. a wrangler; adj. quarrelsome. *h.*

دهاندهنا धांधना *dhāndhnā*, a. to gormandize. *h.*

دهانسنا धांसना *dhāṅsnā*, a. to cough (a horse). *h.*

دهانسي धांसी *dhāṅsī*, f. a cough (of a horse). *h.*

دهانشك धानुष्क *dhānushk*, m. an archer, a bowman. *s.*

دهانشكا धानुष्का *dhānushkā*, f. a tree (*Achyranthes aspera*). *s.*

دهانك धानुक *dhānuk*, m. a bowman; a watchman armed with a bow; name of a caste of hill people using bows and arrows, employed as archers, fowlers, house guards, and several menial occupations, both of the house and field, wherever they reside: the females are especially in request as midwives. *s.*

دهانگر धांगर *dhāngar*, m. a caste whose business is to dig the earth. *h.*

دهانويا धांवैया *dhāṅwaiyā*, m. a thresher or seller of rice. *h.*

دهانه *dahāna*, m. the bit of a bridle; the mouth of a water-bag; any thing which covers the mouth. *p.*

دهاني धानी *dhānī*, f. a kind of rice in the husk; a light green colour; a good soil, fit for grain. *s.*

دهانيه धान्य *dhānya*, m. corn, especially rice; coriander; a measure equal to four sesamum seeds. *dhānya-rāj*, m. barley. *dhānya-wat*, abounding in corn. *s.*

دهاو धाव *dhāw*, m. a plant used in dyeing; *Grislea tomentosa* (v. *dhārī*). *s.*

دهاوا धावा *dhāwā*, m. running; over-running an enemy's country, attack, assaulting; a stock, a store; crowding together; name of a tree. *dhāwā-mārnā*, n. to go expeditiously from a distant place, to run on or about. *s.*

دهاوت धावत *dhāwat*, running, going fast. *dhāwit*, gone, run away; run to, advanced; purified, cleansed. *s.*

دهاوك धावक *dhāwak*, running, swift; cleaning, what cleanses. *s.*

دهاومان धावमान *dhāwamān*, running, going fast. *s.*

دهاون धावन *dhāwan*, m. act of running, motion; cleansing, purifying. *s.*

دهاونا धावना *dhāwnā*, n. to rang., to roam, to rove; to run, to run at, to attack; to trudge; to worship. *s.*

دهاونكا धावनिका *dhā,onikā*, f. a prickly nightshade. *s.*

دهاوني धावनी *dhā,onī*, f. a creeping plant (*Hedysarum lagopodioides*). *s.*

دهاه धाह *dhāh*, f. cry, noise. *dhāh mārnā*, n. to cry, to groan. *h.*

دهاءي दहाई *dahā,ī*, f. the figure ten; the tenth part; the decimal place of figures in arithmetic. *p.*

دهاءي दुहाई *duhā,ī*, f. (v. *dohā,ī*) crying out for justice; exclamation, oath, plaint. *duhā,ī tihā,ī-k.*, to make reiterated complaints. *h.*

دهاءي धाए *dhā,e* or *dhā,ī*, f. a nurse that gives milk, a wet-nurse. *s.*

دهاءي مارنا धाइमारना *dhā,e mārnā*, n. to cry, to groan. *dhā,e mār ronā*, n. to cry, to groan, to weep bitterly. *h.*

دهاين دهاين धांयधांय *dhā,eṅ dhā,eṅ*, f. the report of a cannon heard at a distance; a sound made by burning any thing. *h.*

دهبا धब्बा *dhabbā*, m. a stain on cloth. *h.*

دهباشي *dah-bāshī*, m. a commander of ten men; a person having a place of trust; a valet. *p. t.*

دهبلا धुबला *dhublā*, m. a petticoat or any loose garment for covering the legs. *h.*

دهپ धप *dhap*, m. noise, voice, sound, crack (also same as *dhappā*). *d.*

دهپا धप्पा *dhappā*, m. a stain on cloth; a slap, box, thump, blow; deception. *h.*

دهپاڑ धपाड़ *dhapāṛ*, m. running, a race. *h.*

دهپيا धपिया *dhapiyā*, a fourth part of a *kos*; supposed to be so named from *dhāv*, running, being such a distance as a man may run in a single race without stopping to take breath. *h.*

دهت धत *dhat*, f. a word used to encourage elephants. *h.*

دهت दहित *dahit*, burnt, scorched. *dahat*, burning, scorching. *s.*

دهتا धुत्ता *dhuttā*, m. trick, deception. *dhuttā denā*, a. to deceive. *s.*

دهتا दुहिता *duhitā*, } f. a daughter. *duhitā-pati*, m. a son-in-law, a daughter's husband. *s.*
دهتر दुहितृ *duhitṛi*, }

دهتكارنا धतकारना *dhatkārnā*, a. to reprove. *h.*

دهتورا धतूरा *dhatūrā*, m. the name of a plant (*Datura*, or thorn-apple). *s.*

دهتوريا धतूरिया *dhatūriyā*, a cheat, an impostor. *s.*

دهتينگر धतीनगर *dhatīngar*, } ignoble, spurious. *h.*
دهٹينگر धटीनगर *dhaṭīngar*, }

دهج धज *dhaj*, f. shape, form; attitude, posture, figure, appearance, person. *dhaj palaṭnā*, to change one's attitude in fencing. *s.*

دهجا धजा *dhajā*, f. a slip of cloth, a standard, a flag; a ship's pendant; also the pole to which the strip of cloth is attached; m. attitude, posture. *s.*

دهج بهنگ धजभंग *dhaj-bhang*, m. impotency. *s.*

دهجي धज्जी *dhajjī*, f. a slip of cloth or paper, a shred. *dhajjiyāṅ uṛānā*, a. to disgrace, to expose one to infamy. *dhajjiyāṅ-k.*, a. to tear to pieces. *h.*

دهجير धजीर *dhajīr*, f. (v. *dhajjī*). *h.*

دهجيلا धजीला *dhajīlā*, well-looking, personable. *s.* [to frighten. *d.*

دهچکچانا धचकचाना *dhachhachānā*, a. to terrify,

دهچکنا धचकना *dhachahnā*, n. to give way, to sink (as a bog, slough, &c.). *h.*

دهدهچهر धधच्छर *dhadhachchhar* (also *dadhachchhar*), m. (lit. burnt letters). In Hindī versification, certain words or letters, which are reckoned by poets to be unlucky. Thus the Devanāgarī letters *ha, ga, na*, in the beginning of a verse, *ra, sa, ja*, in the middle, and *ka, ṭa, jha*, in the end of a sentence are of this description. *s.*

دهدهکنا धधकना *dhadhaknā*, n. to blaze. *h.*

دهر *dahr*, m. time, an age, custom, habit, mode, manner, solicitude; the world; atheism; fortune, chance, adversity, danger. *a.*

دهر धुर *dhur*, m. beginning; limit, end; extremity. *dhur se dhur tak*, from beginning to end. *dhar*, side, direction; a rope or line. *h.*

دهرا धरा *dharā*, f. (lit. holding or containing) the earth. *s.*

دهرا दुहरा *duhrā*, double, two-fold. *h.*

دهرا दिहरा *dihrā* or *dihurā*, m. an idol-temple. *s.*

دهراج धिराज *dhirāj*, m. a potentate, a monarch. *s.*

دهران दुहराना *duhrānā*, a. to fold, to double, to repeat. *h.*

دهرانا धिराना *dhirānā*, a. to threaten. *h.*

دهرانا धराना *dharānā*, a. to owe. *s.*

دهراوٹ धरावट *dharāwaṭ*, land ascertained and apportioned by estimate, not measured. *h.*

دهراونا धरावना *dharāwanā*, f. a woman married a second time. *h.*

دهرب ध्रुब *dhrub*, m. the pole; adj. true, right. *s.*

دهرپد धुरपद *dhur-pad*, m. burden of a song; a kind of song in the Hindī or Braj *bhākhā* dialects. *s.*

دهرت धृत *dhṛit*, possessed, held. *dhṛiti*, f. steadiness, firmness; a stanza of four lines, of eighteen syllables each. *dhṛiti-mān* or *dhṛiti-mat*, firm, steady. *dhṛitātmā*, calm, collected. *s.*

دهرتا धरता *dhartā*, } discount and commission. *h.*
دهرته धरतः *dharta*, }

دهرتا धर्ता *dhartā*, m. a debtor. *s.*

دهرت‌راشٹر धृतराष्ट्र *dhṛita-rāshṭra*, m. the name of a king, the father of Duryodhana and uncle to the Panḍu princes. *s.*

دهرتري धरित्री *dharitrī*, } f. the land, the earth; *dhartī kā phūl*, m, a mushroom, a fungus or toadstool. *s.*
دهرتي धर्ती *dhartī*, }

دهردهمکنا धरधमकना *dhar-dhamaknā*, n. to proceed with tumultuous rapidity; to move with violence: to rush. *h.* [light. *h.*

دهرسانجه धुरसांझ *dhur-sānjh*, f. dusk, twi-

دهرکار धिरकार *dhirkār*, m. (v. *dhikkār*). *s.*

دهرکال धिरकाल *dhirkāl*, m. the name of a caste of people who work on bamboos. *h.*

دهرم धर्म *dharm*, *dharma*, or *dharam*, m. justice, virtue, righteousness, or those attributes personified; business, profession; usage, practice, manner, mode, observance of sects, castes, &c.; duty, especially that enjoined by the *Vedas*. *dharma-bhāginī*, f. a virtuous and amiable wife. *dharma-patra*, m. glomerous fig-tree (*Ficus glomerata*). *dharma-putra*, a name of *Yudhishṭhira*. *dharma-patnī*, f. a man's first wife and of the same caste. *dharma-pradhān*, eminent in piety. *dharma-twa*, m. morality, piety; inherent nature or property. *dharma-chārī*, virtuous, moral. *dharma-chārinī*, f. a virtuous wife. *dharma-chintā*, f. or *dharma-chintan*, m. virtuous reflection. *dharma-drohī*, wicked, immoral. *dharma-dhwajī*, m. a hypocrite, a religious impostor, one who makes a livelihood by assumed devotion. *dharma-rāj*, m. a name of *Yama* or Pluto, of *Yudhishthira*, also of *Arjuna*; a king in general; a kingdom where justice is administered. *dharma-rāj-k.*, to govern justly. *dharam* or *dharm-sālā*, or *dharma-shālā*, a place where alms are distributed. *dharma-rodhī*, illegal, immoral. *dharma-sabhā*, f. a tribunal, a court of justice. *dharma-sanhitā*, f. a code of laws, as that of *Manu*, &c. *dharma-shāstra*, a code of laws, any work on the subject. *dharma-shīl*, devout, virtuous. *dharma-karya*, m. an indispensable act of religion. *dharma-kriyā*, f. righteous and legal conduct, religious act. *dharma kshetra*, m. a plain near Dehli, the scene of the great battle between the Kurus and Pandus. *dharma-grahan*, m. observance of the law or religious institutes. *dharma-gya*, knowing one's duty, conversant with virtue. *dharma-gyān*, knowledge of duty or virtue. *dharma-mūl*, m. the foundation of law (the Vedas). *dharma-may*, moral, righteous. *dharma-nibandh*, m. piety, practice of virtue. *dharma-nibandhī*, pious, holy, practising virtue. *dharma-nishpatti*, f. duty, religious observance, discharge of duty. *dharma-wān* or *dharma-wat* (fem. *dharma-watī*). virtuous, pious, just. *dharma-vivāh*, m. legal marriage of five sorts, viz. *Brāhma*, *Daiva*, *ārsha*, *gāndharba*, *prājāpatya*. *dharma-vivechan*, m. judicial investigation. *s.*

دهرمات धर्मात *dharmāt*, } virtuous, just, holy, pious. *s.*
دهرماتما धर्मात्मा *dharmātmā*, }

دهرماتر धर्मातर *dharmātar*, a charitable grant. *s.*

دهرمادهرم‌پريکشا धर्माधर्मपरीक्षा *dharmā-dharma-parīkshā*, f. ordeal by drawing lots or slips of white and black paper. *s.*

دهرمادهکاري धर्माधिकारी *dharmādhikārī*, } m. a judge, a magistrate. *s.*
دهرمادهيکش धर्माध्यक्ष *dharmādhyaksh*, }

دهرماسن धर्मासन *dharmāsan*, m. the seat of justice, the bench. *s.*

دهرمانسار धर्मानुसार *dharmānusār*, m. conformity to law or virtue, practice of duty. *s.*

دهرماوتار धर्मावतार *dharmāvatār*, m. an incarnation of *Dharma*, the god of justice, used as a term of respect to high personages. *s.*

دهرمشٹه धर्मिष्ठ *dharmishṭha*, very virtuous, inclined to the performance of duty. *s.*

دهرم‌گور धर्मगौर *dharm-gaur* (v. *gaur Brāhman*). *h.*

دهرمن धर्मन *dharman*, m. a sort of tree; a kind of large snake (not poisonous). *s.*

دهرموپديش धर्मोपदेश *dharmopadesh*, m. moral or religious instruction. *dharmopadeshak*, m. a guru, or spirituous preceptor. *s.*

دهرمي धर्मी *dharmī*, virtuous, religious. *s.*

دهرن धरण *dharan*, f. a beam; accent, tone; the navel (or rather the umbilical vein, perhaps the aorta or cœliac artery, as it is said to pulsate), which is supposed by the Hindū physicians to be occasionally removed from its place, and thus to occasion various morbid symptoms. This is called *dharan ḍignī* or *nāf ṭalnā* or *-ukharnā*, and the cure is attempted by friction of the belly; m. holding, possessing; a female breast. *s.*

دهرنا धरना *dharnā*, a. to place, to put down; to give in charge; to hold, to seize, to catch, to lay hold of. *dharnā-denā* or *-baiṭhnā*, a mode of extorting payment of a debt or compliance with any demand. See Asiat. Res. vol. iv. art. 22; also Wilson's Glossary. *s.*

دهرنا दुहरना *duharnā*, m. to be folded or doubled up. *h.*

دهرنگا धरिंगा *dharingā*, a kind of rice. *h.*

دهرني धरणी *dharnī*, f. the earth; pressing into service, compelling to work. *dharnī-dhar*, m. a mountain; name of *Sheshnāg*, a serpent who upholds the earth; and of *Vishnu* in the form of a tortoise and of a boar. *dharnī-sūtā*, f. (earth-born) a name of *Sītā*, the wife of *Rāma*, having been turned up from the soil by a plough. *dharnī-kand*, m. an esculent root or bulb. *s.*

دهرني धरनी *dharnī*, } m. a dun (v. *dharnā*). *h.*
دهرنيت धरनेत *dharnet*, }

دهرو ध्रू *dhrū*, m. (for *dhruva*) the pole (of the earth) the polar star. *s.*

دهرو ध्रुव *dhruv*, fixed, stable; true, right; m. the polar star, the north pole. *dhruv-tārā*, m. the polar star. *s.*

دهروا ध्रुवा *dhruvā*, f. a plant (*Hedysarum gangeticum*); a small tree, from the fibres of which bow-strings are made; the first stanza of a song, repeated as a burden; a virtuous woman. *s.*

دهرواना धरवाना *dharwānā*, a. to cause to be placed. *s.*

دهروپد ध्रुवपद *dhruv-pad*, m. a kind of song. *s.*

دهروت *dharūt*, a trust, deposit, substitute; a pawn or pledge. *d.* [guess. *h.*

دهروكي धरौकी *dharaukī*, ascertainment by

دهروهر धरोहर *dharohar*, f. a trust, a charge, any thing given in charge, a deposit. *h.*

دهري *dahrī*, temporal, relating to time or fortune (v. *dahr*). *a.*

دهري धुरी *dhurī*, f. an axle, a pole. *h.*

دهري दहरी *dahrī*, stiff clay soil in low grounds. *h.*

دهريا *dahriyā*, m. an atheist. *a.*

دهريانا धुरियाना *dhuriyānā* or *dhariyānā*, n. to throw dust; to winnow, sift, to separate the good from the bad grain. *s.*

دهريچا धरीचा *dharīchā*, m. the second husband of a Hindū widow among the lower classes. This connection being contrary to the spirit of the Hindū institution, is formed without any particular ceremony, except marking the bride's head with minium. *h.*

دهڙ धड़ *dhaṛ*, m. the body, carcase, trunk; adj. (Dakh.) firm, strong. *dhaṛ jīv ko taṛānā*, to consider, reflect. *h.*

دهڙا धड़ा *dhaṛā*, m. a party; a weight. *dhaṛā bāndhnā*, a. to make up a standard to weigh by, with bricks, or any thing else, as by having one weight (of a pound suppose), it is doubled, quadrupled, and so on, till the weight requisite is obtained. *h.*

دهڙاکا धड़ाका *dhaṛākā*, m. a crash, report of a gun, explosion. *h.* [to palpitate. *h.*

دهڙدهڙانا धड़धड़ाना *dhaṛ-dhaṛānā*, n. to flutter,

دهڙدهڙجلنا दहड़दहड़जलना or धड़धड़जलना, *dahaṛ-dahaṛ-jalnā* or *dhaṛ-dhaṛ-jalnā*, n. to burn furiously. *dhaṛ-dhaṛ rahnā*, n. to flutter, to palpitate. *h.*

دهڙك धड़क *dhaṛak*, f. palpitation; fear. *h.*

دهڙکا धड़का *dhaṛkā*, m. fear, doubt, suspense; palpitation; thunder. *h.* [alarm. *h.*

دهڙکانا धड़काना *dhaṛkānā*, a. to frighten, to

دهڙکنا धड़कना *dhaṛaknā*, n. to palpitate; to blaze. *h.*

دهڙکها धड़खा *dhaṛakhā*, m. the sound of hammering, &c.; frightening, alarming; a scarecrow; a crowd (also *dhaṛakkā*). *h.*

دهڙگتي *dhargutti*, peace of mind, comfort. *d.*

دهڙلا धड़ल्ला *dhaṛallā*, m. the sound of hammering, &c.; frightening, alarming; bullying, bravado; a scarecrow; a crowd. *h.*

دهڙنگ धड़ंग *dhaṛang*, naked, bare. *h.*

دهڙوا धड़ुआ *dhaṛū,ā* or धड़वा *dhaṛwā*, m. the name of a bird, a kind of maina or jay. *h.*

دهڙواءي धड़वाई *dhaṛwā,ī*, the *paṭwārī* who weighs grain, so named from *dhaṛī*, a measure of five *sers*, which is generally considered his perquisite at the harvest. *h.*

دهڙي धड़ी *dhaṛī*, f. a line, particularly the black lines made on the lips with *missī*; a weight of five *sers*, the quantity weighed at once. *h.*

دهڙي दिहुड़ी *dihuṛī*, f. threshold, door. *dihuṛī-dār*, doorkeeper. *h.*

دهس धस *dhas*, a kind of soil, sloping ground, sterile sandy eminences. *h.*

دهسا धुस्सा *dhussā*, m. flannel, a kind of coarse stuff made of shawl wool. *h.*

دهسان धसान *dhasān*, } m. a slough, bog, quagmire, a swamp. *h.*
دهساو धसाव *dhasāw*, }

دهسانا धसाना *dhasānā*, a. to cause to be thrust into. *h.* [*tura fastuosa*). *s.*

دهستور धुस्तूर *dhustūr*, f. the thorn-apple (*Da-*

دهسکنا धसकना *dhasaknā*, n. to give way, to sink (as a quagmire or slough). *h.*

دهسم धसम *dhasam*, m. a swamp, a quagmire. *h.*

دهسن धसन *dhasan*, f. a quagmire; the state of being thrust into. *h.*

دهسنا धसना *dhasnā*, n. to be pierced, stuck into, to be penetrated, to be thrust into, to sink, to enter. *h.*

دهسني *dah-sanī*, belonging to ten years; a book of accounts, registers, &c., for the space of ten years. *p. a.* [sers. *s.*

دهسيرا दहसेरा *dahserā*, m. a weight of ten

دهش *dahash*, stupified with amazement, striking with astonishment or consternation. *a.*

دهش *dihish*, charity, bounty, liberality. *p.*

دهشت *dahshat*, f. fear, dread. *dahshat-angez*, horrible, hideous. *dahshat-zada*, panic-struck. *dahshat-nāk*, alarming, dreadful. *a.*

دهقان *dihḳān*, m. a villager, headman of a village. *p. a.*

دهقاني *dihḳānī*, m. a villager, a husbandman; f. agriculture, the profession of a husbandman. *a. p.*

دهقانيت *dihḳānīyat*, } rusticity, boorishness;
دهقانيه *dihḳānīya*, } husbandry, agriculture. *a.*

دهك दहक *dahak*, f. ardour, conflagration. *h.*

دهك धिक *dhik*, interj. expressing contempt and aversion, reproach or menace; fie! shame! *s.*

دهكا धक्का *dhakkā*, m. a shove, jolt, push. *dhakkā denā*, a. to shove, to push. *h.*

دهكار धिक्कार *dhikkār*, m. curse, anathema, reproach; disrespect. *s.* [to curse. *s.*

دهكارنا धिक्कारना *dhikkārnā*, a. to reproach,

دهكاري धिक्कारी *dhikkārī*, f. damnation, a curse; adj. damned, cursed. *s.*

دهكانا दहकाना *dahkānā*, a. to burn, to kindle; to ruin, destroy, lose; to cause to regret; to heat (iron, &c.). *h.*

دهكدهك धकधक *dhakdhak*, m. palpitation, perturbation, apprehension. *h.* [tate. *h.*

دهكدهكانا धकधकाना *dhakdhakānā*, n. to palpi-

دهكدهكي धुकधुकी *dhukdhukī* or धकधकी *dhakdhakī*, f. consideration, reflection; perturbation, anxiety, apprehension; an ornament worn on the breast. *h.*

دهك‌ره‌جانا धकरहजाना *dhak-rah-jānā* or *dhak-hojānā*, to be confounded at a sudden disaster. *h.*

دهكڑپكڑ धुकड़पुकड़ *dhukaṛ-pukaṛ*, f. palpitation, agitation. *h.*

دهكڑي धुकड़ी *dhukaṛī*, f. a purse. *h.*

دهكم‌دهكا धक्कमधक्का *dhakkam-dhakkā*, m. shoving and jostling. *h.*

دهكنا दहकना *dahaknā*, n. to burn, to be burnt, to be ruined, lost, destroyed; to regret. *h.*

دهكيل धकेल *dhakel*, m. shove, push, thrust. *h*

دهكيلنا धकेलना *dhakelnā*, a. to shove, to push, to jostle. *dhakel-denā*, a. to push, to precipitate. *h.*

دهكيلو धकेलू *dhakelū*, m. one who pushes. *h.*

دهگدهگانا *dhagdhagānā*, n. to shine, to glitter. *d.*

دهگڑ धगाड़ *dhaggaṛ*, } m. a paramour. *dhag-*
دهگڑا धगड़ा *dhagṛā*, } *gaṛ-bāz*, f. an adultress. *ḳāẓī-* or *bakhshī-kā dhaggaṛ*, independent of judge or general, a fig for the parson and squire (an expression of pride and independence). *h.*

دهگولنا धगोलना *dhagolnā*, n. to roll, to wallow. *h.*

دهگي *dahaggī*, heat, warmth. *d.*

دهل दहल *dahal*, a quicksand, a quagmire. *h.*

دهل *duhal*, m. a kind of drum. *p.*

دهلا *dahlā*, m. the ten (at cards). *p.*

دهلان दहलान *dahlān*, name of a tribe of *Jagas* in the upper Du,āb. *h.*

دهلانا दहलाना *dahlānā*, a. to agitate. *h.*

دهلانا धुलाना *dhulānā*, a. to cause to wash. *h.*

دهلاءي धुलाई *dhulā,ī*, f. washing; price of washing. *h.* [or peon. *h.*

دهلائت धलाइत *dhalā,it*, an armed attendant

دهلنا दहलना *dahalnā*, n. to shake, tremble to fear. *h.*

دهلوانا धुलवाना *dhulwānā*, a. (v. *dhulānā*) to get washed; to cause to be washed. *h.*

دهلي दिहली *dihlī*, f. a threshold. *s.*

دهلي *dihlī*, m. name of a city, the metropolis of Hindūstān (v. *dillī*), generally called by Musalmāns *shāh-jahān-ābād*, and by Europeans Delhi. *p.*

دهليانا धुलियाना *dhuliyānā*, a. (v. *dharyānā*). *s.*

دهليز *dahlīz*, f. a portico, a threshold. *dahlīz khundlānā*, "treading the threshold"; a ceremonial visit paid by a young man about to be married, to the parents of his intended bride. *p.*

دهلينڈي धुलेंडी *dhulenḍī* or *dhulainḍī*, f. the second day of the *holī*, on which it is the practice to scatter a kind of fine red powder; the first day of the month of Chait, in which they scatter ashes. *s.*

دهم *dahum*, tenth, the tenth (day). *p.*

دهماچوكڑي धमाचौकड़ी *dhamā chaukṛī*, f. noise, tumult, bustle. *h.*

دهمادهم धमाधम *dhamādham*, the sound of stamping, thumping. *h.*

دهمار धमार *dhamār*, m. name of a chime, or time in music; the same as *dhamāl*, q. v.; running through fire on religious occasions (among Muhammadan *faḳīrs*). *h.*

دهماكا धमाका *dhamākā*, m. a kind of cannon carried on an elephant. *h.*

دهمال धमाल *dhamāl*, m. a species of music; a kind of song which they sing during the saturnalia of the *holī*; (also *dhammāl*), running through fire on religious occasions (among Musalmān *faḳīrs*). *h*

دهمچا धिमचा *dhimchā*, m. a kind of tamarind. *h.*

دهمدهمانا धमधमाना *dhamdhamānā*, a. to make a noise (with the feet, by running about over-head). *h.*

دهمدهوسر धमधूसर *dhamdhūsar*, corpulent. *h.*

دهمردا *dah-mardā*, a kind of cart capable of carrying ten men. *p.*

دهمس *dhamas* or *dhammas*, a kind of mallet. *dhammas-k.*, to lay down turf, and pound the same with a mallet. *h.*

دهمك धमक *dhamak*, f. noise of footsteps overhead, thumping; an echo; threat, threatening, awe; m. a blacksmith. *h.*

دهمكا धमका *dhamkā*, m. great heat; threatening, chiding, thump, noise produced by the fall of a heavy body. *h.*

دهمكانا धमकाना *dhamkānā*, a. to threaten, to chide, to snub, to cow, to daunt. *h.*

دهمكاهٹ धमकाहट *dhamkāhaṭ*, f. threatening, chiding. *h.*

دهمكنا धमकना *dhamaknā*, n. to throb, to shoot (as the pain of a headache); to palpitate; to thump; to flash, to glimmer. *h.*

دهمكي धमकी *dhamkī*, f. threatening, snubbing. *h.*

دهمكيلا धमकीला *dhamkīlā*, m. a bright colour. *h.*

دهملا धुमला *dhumlā*, blind, dim-sighted. *s.*

دهملاءي धुमलाई *dhumlā,ī*, f. gloominess. *h.*

دهمنا धमना *dhamnā*, n. to be grieved, to be amazed. *h.*

دهمني धमनी *dhamnī*, f. a vein, an artery. *s.*

دهموكا धमोका *dhamokā*, m. a kind of tambourine. *h.*

دهن धुन *dhun*, f. inclination, propensity, application, diligence, perseverance, ardour, ambition, assiduity; pains in the bones. *s.*

دهن धुन *dhun* or धुनि *dhuni*, f. musical sound.

دهن धन *dhan*, m. fortune, prosperity, an expression of praise, thanks, riches, wealth, opulence; adj. fortunate; interj. well-done! how fortunate! *dhan-pati*, m. the god of riches, Kuvera. *dhan-patr*, m. an inventory of property. *dhan-priya*, fond of wealth. *dhan-tṛishnā*, f. covetousness. *dhan-dāyī*, liberal, munificent; m. a benefactor. *dhan-darp*, m. pride of wealth. *dhan-daṇḍ*, m. fine, amercement. *dhan-sampatti*, f. accumulation of wealth. *dhan-garbit*, purse proud. *dhan-lobh*, m. desire of wealth, greediness. *dhan-mānnā*, to thank. *dhan-mad*, proud of wealth, inflated. *dhan-vyay*, m. expenditure, extravagance. *dhan-hīn*, poor. *dhan-vān*, affluent, wealthy. *s.*

دهن धनु *dhanu*, m. a bow, the sign Sagittarius. *s.*

دهن *dahan*, m. mouth (v. *dahān*). *p.*

دهن *duhn*, m. oil, ointment. *a.*

دهن दहन *dahan*, f. sultriness, conflagration; m. burning, combustion; fire, Agni; the marking-nut plant; lead-wort (*Plumbago zeylanica, &c.*); a gold coin, in value six rupis. *s.*

دهن दुहन *duhan*, m. milking. *s.*

دهنا दहना *dahnā* or दहिना *dahinā*, right, the opposite of left. *s.*

دهنا दहना *dahnā*, n. to burn, to be burnt. *s.*

دهنا दुहना *duhnā*, n. to be milked; to milk (Gilc.). *s.*

دهنا धुन्ना *dhunnā*, a. to comb, to card; to beat. *sir dhunnā*, to beat one's head with vexation, &c. *s.*

دهنادهكاري धनाधिकारी *dhanādhikārī*, m. an heir. *dhanādhikārinī*, an heiress. *s.*

دهنادهيكش धनाध्यक्ष *dhanādhyaksh*, m. a man of wealth. *s.*

دهناڈهيه धनाढ्य *dhanāḍhya*, wealthy, affluent. *s.*

دهنارتهي धनार्थी *dhanārthī*, seeking for wealth, covetous. *s.*

دهنارجن धनार्जन *dhanārjan*, m. acquisition of wealth. *s.*

دهناسري धनाश्री *dhanāsrī*, f. name of a *rāginī* or musical mode. *s.*

دهناسيٹهه धन्नासेठ *dhannā-seṭh*, successful; true-speaking. *h.*

دهناشا धनाशा *dhanāshā*, f. the desire of wealth. *s.*

دهناندهه धनान्ध *dhanāndh*, blinded by wealth or riches, purse-proud. *s.*

دهن پٹ धनुःपट *dhanu-paṭ*, m. a tree (*Buchanania latifolia*). *s.*

دهن پريا धनप्रिया *dhan-priyā*, f. a vegetable (*Ardisia solanacea*). *s.*

دهنتر धनत्तर *dhanattar*, opulent, powerful; name of a physician in the court of *Indra*. *s.*

دهنتهيا धनथिया *danthiyā*, a field on which rice has been cut. *h.*

دهن چڑي *dhanchiṛī*, f. the hornbill (*Buceros*); also called *dhanes, ghanes*, or *ghan chiṛī*. *d.*

دهند *dhund*, an attempt, design; a thought, an idea. *h.*

دهند धनद *dhanad*, liberal, munificent. *s.*

دهندا *dhandā* (v. *dhandhā*), business, &c. *d.*

دهند *dahand* or *dihand*, one who is able and willing to give or pay; "a good man on change." *p.*

دهندهه धुंध *dhundh*, m. dim-sightedness; haziness. *h.*

دهنده *dihanda*, a giver; adj. generous, liberal. *p.*

دهندها धंधा *dhandhā*, m. business, employment, work, avocation, occupation. *h.*

دهندهار धंधार *dhandhār*, m. solitary, lonely. *h.*

دهندهاري धंधारी *dhandhārī*, f. solitude, loneliness. *h.*

دهندهالا धंधाला *dhandhālā*, f. a procuress, a bawd. *h.*

دهندهرانا धुंधराना *dhundhrānā*, n. to be dull, misty. *s.*

دهندهکا धंधका *dhandhkā*, m. a kind of drum. *h.*

دهندهکار धुंधकार *dhundh-kār*, m. darkness, mistiness. *h.*

دهندهكي धंधकी *dhandhkī*, m. a small drum. *h.*

دهندهلا धंधला *dhandhlā*, m. deception, trick. *h.*

دهندهلا धुंधला *dhundhlā*, foggy, misty, dull. *h.*

دهندهلانا धंधलाना *dhandhlānā*, a. to trick. *h.*

دهندهلاءي धुंधलाई *dhundhlā,ī*, f. dimness, cloudiness. *h.*

دهندهمار धुंधमार *dhundhumār*, m. an insect [(*Coccinella*). *s.*

دهندهيلا धुंधेला *dhundhelā*, knavish. *h.*

دهنڈلات *dhanḍlāt*, coming and returning without effecting one's purpose; wandering about uselessly. *d.* [clamation. *d.*

دهنڈورا *dhanḍorā*, m. (v. *ḍhanḍhorā*) a pro-

دهنڈهولنا *dhanḍholnā*, a. (v. *ṭaṭolnā*) to feel or grope (for an object). *d.*

دهنردهاري धनुर्धारी *dhanur-dhārī*, } m. an ar-
دهنردهر धनुर्धर *dhanur-dhar*, } cher, one armed with a bow; a name of *Arjuna*. *s.*

دهنرلتا धनुर्लता *dhanur-latā*, f. the moon-plant. *s.*

دهنرمالا धनुर्माला *dhanur-mālā*, f. a plant, from the fibres of which bowstrings are made. *s.*

دهنسنا धंसना *dhansnā*, n. (v. *dhasnā*) to be pierced or penetrated, to be stuck into, thrust into; to sink, to enter. *s.*

دهنسو धनसू *dhan-sū*, m. the fork-tailed shrike. *s.*

دهنش धनुष *dhanush*, m. a bow. *dhanush-dharā*, a ceremony in honour of *Shiva*. *s.*

دهن‌شاكها धनुःशाखा *dhanu-shākhā*, f. a plant, of the fibres of which bowstrings were formerly made (*Sanseviera zeylanica*). *s.*

دهنشٹها धनिष्ठा *dhanishṭhā*, f. the twenty-fourth mansion of the moon, the dolphin: it is figured by a drum. *s.*

دهنك धनुक *dhanuk*, f. a bow. *dhanuk-dhārī*, m. an archer. *dhanuk-bā,e*, f. tetanus. *dhanuk-dhar*, m. armed with a bow, an epithet of *Krishṇa*. *dhanuk-dharā*, m. a ceremony in honour of *Shiva*. *s.*

دهنك धनिक *dhanik*, pious; m. a creditor. *s.*

دهنك धनक *dhanak*, f. embroidery, lace. *h.*

دهن‌كٹي धनकटी *dhan-kaṭī*, f. the season for cutting rice. *s. h.*

دهن‌كٹي धनकटी *dhan-kaṭī*, f. a kind of cloth. *h.*

دهنكر धनकर *dhankar*, a kind of stiff soil producing rice (*dhān*), which can be ploughed and sown only in the event of sufficient rain falling. it also denotes a field which has been cropped with rice during the previous season. *h.* [(cotton). *s.*

دهنكنا धुनकना *dhunaknā*, a. to card or comb

دهنكه धनुष *dhanukh*, m. a bow (v. *dhanuk*). *s.*

دهنكي धनुकी *dhanukī*, f. the bow with which cotton is cleaned; adj. arched. *s.*

دهنگار धुंगार *dhungār*, m. seasoning with which any thing is fried. *h.*

دهنگارنا धुंगारना *dhungārnā*, a. to season with spices. *h.* [pression. *h.*

دهنگانا धिंगाना *dhingānā*, m. clamour, op-

دهنگر *dhangar*, m. a cowherd, shepherd. *d.*

دهنماني धनमानी *dhanmānī*, thankful; interj. well-done! bravo! *s.*

دهنمد धनमद *dhan-mad*, intoxicated with wealth, purse-proud. *s.*

دهننا धुन्ना *dhunnā*, a. to card or comb (cotton); to beat one's head with vexation. *s.*

دهننتر धनन्तर *dhanantar*, } the name of a
دهننتري धनन्तरी *dhanantarī*, } physician in the court of Indra; adj. wealthy, rich; powerful, strong. *s.*

دهننجيا धनंजया *dhananjayā* or *dhanan-jaya*, m. conqueror of wealth; a name of *Arjuna*; fire, or its deity; a tree (*Pentaptera arjuna*). *s.*

دهن‌نوٹا धनोटा *dhan-noṭā*, m. cross-beams that sustain the supports of thatch. *h.*

دهنوا धन्वा *dhanwā*, m. an arid country, a desert; a firm spot, land. *s.*

دهنوا धुंवा *dhunwā*, m. smoke, vapour. *s.*

دهنوان धनवान *dhanwān*, } wealthy, possessed
دهنونت धनवन्त *dhanwant*, } of substance. *s.*

دهنوپل दहनोपल *dahnopal*, m. the sun gem, a crystal lens. *s.*

دهنون दहनौं *dahnaun*, n. to burn, to be burnt. *s.*

دهنونتر धन्वन्ततरि *dhanwantari*, v. *dhanantar*.

دهنوي धुन्वी *dhunwī*, f. the bow with which cotton is carded. *s.*

دهنوي धन्वी *dhanwī*, m. an archer; a name of *Arjuna*; a tree (*Pentaptera arjuna*); a wag, a wit, a sharp or shrewd man. *s.*

دهنويواس धन्वयवास *dhanwayvās*, m. a plant (*Hedysarum alhagi*). *s.*

دهنها धनहा *dhanhā*, m. a cultivator of rice; adj. (of a country) in which rice is cultivated. *s.*

دهنهاو धुनिहाव *dhunihā,o*, m. pains in the bones. *h.*

دهنهري धनहरी *dhan-harī*, m. a thief, a pilferer; f. a sort of perfume, commonly called *chor*. *s.*

دهني धनी *dhanī* or धन्य *dhanya*, rich, wealthy, fortunate; an epithet of the Deity; m. owner, proprietor. *dhanya-bhāg*, happy destinies. *s.*

دهني धुनी *dhunī*, f. (v. *dhūnī*) persevering, &c. *s.*

دهني धनी *dhanī*, f. a beam. *h.*

دهنيا धनिया *dhaniyā*, m. coriander seed (*Coriandrum sativum*). *dhaniye kī khoprī meṅ pānī pilānā* a. to harass, to disturb, to tantalize. *s. h.*

دهنيا धुनिया *dhuniyā*, a carder or comber (of cotton). *s.*

دهنياك धन्याक *dhanyāk*, m. a plant bearing a small pungent seed used as a condiment (*Coriandrum sativum*). *s.*

دهنياني *dhanyānī*, a lady, mistress; also one who has control; same as *mukhtār*. *d.*

دهنيت *duhniyat*, f. oil, ointment, fatness. *a.*

دهنيس धनेश *dhanes*, m. the name of a bird with a very large bill (*Buceros*). *s.*

دهنيشور धनेश्वर *dhaneshwar*, m. the god of riches, Kuvera. *s.*

دهنيمي *dah-nīmī*, five per cent. (lit. half of ten, or ten halves). *p.*

دهنيه दहनीय *dahnīya*, fit to be burnt, combustible. *s.*

دهنيه धन्य *dhanya*, fortunate; interj. well done! (v. *dhan*). *s.*

دهنيها धुनेहा *dhunehā*, m. a carder of cotton, a comber. *s.*

دهنيهاو धुनीहाव *dhunīhāw*, m. pains in the bones (v. *dhun*). *h.*

دهو धौ *dhau*, f. a kind of wood (*Lythrum fruticosum, Lin.; Grislea tomentosa, Rox. Pl. Cor.*). *s.*

دهو धव *dhava*, m. a husband; a tree (*Grislea tomentosa*). *s.*

دهوا धवा *dhawā*, m. a caste of pālkī-bearers who are Musalmāns. *h.*

دهوءا धोआ *dho,ā*, m. a present of fruit. *h.*

دهوان धूआँ *dhū,āṅ* or *dhuwāṅ*, m. smoke (v. *dhūṅwā*). *s.*

دهواندهار धूआँधार *dhuwāṅdhār*, a mass of smoke; adj. smoky. *s.*

دهوانكش ध्वांक्ष *dhwānksh*, m. any aquatic bird feeding on fish, as a crane, a gull, &c. *s.*

دهوب धोब *dhob*, m. washing. *h.*

دهوبن धोबिन *dhobin*, f. a washerwoman. *h.*

دهوبي धोबी *dhobī*, m. a washerman. *h.*

دهوپ धूप *dhūp*, f. sunshine, sunlight. *h.*

دهوپ धूप *dhūp*, f. a perfume burnt by Hindūs at the time of worshipping, the aromatic vapour which arises from the combustion of any fragrant gum or resin. *dhūp-dānī*, f. a pot for keeping *dhūp*. *s.*

دهوپ धोप *dhop*, f. a kind of sword; race, running; exertion. *h.*

دهوپانگ धूपाङ्ग *dhūpāng*, m. turpentine. *s.*

دهوپ بركش धूपवृक्ष *dhūp-brikh*, m. a species of pine (*Pinus longifolia*). *s.*

دهوپكالا धूपकाला *dhūp-kālā*, m. the hot weather. *s.*

دهوپنا धूपना *dhūpnā*, a. to smear with pitch, to perfume. *s.*

دهوپيليان धूपेलियाँ *dhūpeliyāṅ*, f. the prickly heat. *h.*

دهوت धौत *dhaut*, washed, cleaned, purified. *s.*

دهوتا धोता *dhotā*, false, treacherous, perfidious. *s.*

دهوترا *dahotrā*, m. tithe, tenth part. *p.s.*

دهوت‌شل धौतशिल *dhaut-shil*, m. chrystal. *s.*

دهوتي धोती *dhotī*, f. a cloth worn round the waist, passing between the legs and fastened behind; m. a kind of falcon, the female of which is called *besarā*, q. v. *s.*

دهوجا ध्वजा *dhwajā*, f. (v. *patākā*) a flag, banner, &c. *dhwajī*, a standard-bearer. *s.*

دهور धूर *dhūr*, f. dust. *s.*

دهور धूर *dhūr*, the twentieth part of a *biswā*; also a kind of coarse grass. *h.*

دهور धौर *dhaur*, m. a large kind of dove. *h.*

دهورا धौरा *dhaurā* (v. *dhaulā*), white. *s.*

دهورا धोरा *dhorā*, m. the name of a medicine; adj. white. *h.*

دهورادينا धूरादेना *dhūrā denā*, a. to deceive, to wheedle, to take in. *h.*

دهورت धूर्त *dhūrt*, cunning, artful, crafty, knavish, mischievous; a knave, a cheat, a gamester. *s.*

دهورتتا धूर्तता *dhūrtatā*, f. knavery, trickery. *s.*

دهورتك धौर्तिक *dhaurtik*, knavish, dishonest. *s.*

دهوردهاني धूरधानी *dhūrdhānī*, m. a tall stout fellow; f. a firelock (without a chamber). *h.*

دهورسنجها धूरसंझा *dhūr-sanjhā*, m. evening. *s.*

دهوركٹ धूरकट *dhūrkaṭ*, an advance of rent paid by villagers to the zamīndār. *h.*

دهوركي धूरकी *dhūrkī*, the twentieth part of a *dhūr*. *h.*

دهورن धोरणि *dhorani*, f. tradition. *s.*

دهوري धूरी *dhūrī*, f. an axletree, a strand of a rope. *s.*

دهوري धौरी *dhaurī*, a bull's hide cut into two pieces (said to be a corruption of *adhaurī*, q.v.). *h.*

دهوريابيلا धूरियाबेला *dhūriyā-belā*, m. a species of jessamine. *h.*

دهورياملار धूरियामल्लार *dhūriyā-mallār*, m. name of a musical mode (particularly sung in the beginning of the rains). *h.*

دهوڑ धोड़ *dhoṛ*, m. a sort of water-snake. *s.*

دهوسا धोसा *dhosā*, m. a coarse kind of shawl. *h.*

دهوسادهاسي धूसाधासी *dhūsā-dhāsī*, f. cramming and stuffing. *h.*

دهوسر धूसर *dhūsar*, grey; m. grey (the colour). *s.*

دهوسنا धूसना *dhūsnā*, a. to ram, to stuff; to butt (as horned cattle). *h.*

دهوك धोक *dhok*, f. salutation, bowing down to idols. *h.*

دهوكا धुवका *dhuvkā*, f. the first stanza of a song, repeated as a burden. *s.*

دهوكا धोका *dhokā*, / دهوكه धोकः *dhoka*, } name of a measure (v. *dabiyā*). *h.*

دهوكڑ धोकड़ *dhokar*, robust, athletic. *h.*

دهوكها धोखा *dhokhā*, m. deceit, deception; disappointment; doubt, hesitation; a scarecrow; any thing imaginary, not real, a vapour resembling water at a distance (Fr. *mirage*). *dhokhā denā*, a. to deceive. *dhokhā-khānā*, to be deceived. *h.*

دهول धूल *dhūl* or धूलि *dhūli*, f. dust. *s.*

دهول धौल *dhaul*, f. a thump, a rap, a slap; a kind of sugar-cane. *dhaul-jaṛnā*, or *-lagānā*, or *-mārnā*, a. to thump. *dhaul-lagnā*, n. to suffer loss. *h.*

دهول धवल *dhaval*, white; handsome, beautiful; a tree (*Grislea tomentosa*); an inferior mode of music. *dhaval-paksh*, the fortnight of the moon's increase. *dhaval-mṛittikā*, f. chalk. *dhavalī-kṛit*, *dhavalī-bhūt*, or *dhavalit* made white. *s.*

دهولا दिहूला *dihūlā*, / دهوله दिहूलः *dihūla*, } a species of rice grown in the Benares district. *h.*

دهولا धौला *dhaulā*, white. *dhaulāgir* (for *dhavalagiri*), m. name of a mountain. *s.*

دهولانا धौलाना *dhaulānā*, a. to thump, to box, to slap. *h.*

دهولاءي धौलाई *dhaulā,ī*, f. whiteness. *s.*

دهول دهاني धूलधानी *dhūl-dhānī*, dispersed, perplexed. *d.*

دهول دهپا धौलधप्पा *dhaul-dhappā*, m. thumping and slapping. *h.*

دهولك धूलक *dhūlak*, m. poison. *s.*

دهول گچهك धूलिगुच्छक *dhūli-guchchhak*, m. the red vegetable powder thrown about at the *Holi* festival. *s.*

دهوليانا धौलियाना *dhauliyānā*, a. to thump, to box, to slap. *h.*

دهوليدهويا धूलीधोया *dhūlī-dhoyā*, a washer of refuse or dust. *s.*

دهوم धूम *dhūm*, f. tumult, bustle; fame, report, pomp. *dhūm-dhām*, pomp and noise, &c. *h.*

دهوم धूम *dhūm*, m. smoke, vapour. *dhūm-prabhā*, f. a division of hell, the hell of smoke. *dhūm-ketu*, m. a comet, a falling star. *s.*

دهوما धूमा *dhūmā*, m. the name of a colour (like that of smoke) compounded of black and red. *s.*

دهوم دهام धूमधाम *dhūm-dhām*, f. pomp, parade; tumult, bustle, noise. *h.*

دهومرا धूमरा *dhūmrā*, / دهوملا धूमला *dhūmlā*, } m. tumult, bustle, uproar, confusion; adj. smoke-coloured, purple-coloured. *s.*

دهون धौं *dhauṅ*, m. a weight of twenty *sīrs*; conj. whether. *h.*

دهون ध्वन *dhwan* or ध्वनि *dhwani*, m. sound, the sound of a drum. *dhwan-modī*, m. the humble bee. *dhwani-wālā*, f. the *vīnā* or lute; a pipe, a fife, a trumpet. *s.*

دهون *dhūn*, m. a loud report, an explosion. *d.*

دهونا धूना *dhūnā*, m. resin. *s.*

دهونا धोना *dhonā*, a. to wash, to cleanse. *dhō-dhā-kar*, having thoroughly washed and cleansed. *s.*

دهونان धूँआँ *dhūṅāṅ*, m. smoke, vapour. *s.*

دهونت ध्वनित *dhwanit*, sounded, making noise. *s.*

دهونتال धौंताल *dhauntāl*, rich, wealthy; strong, stout; bold; vicious, mischievous. *s.*

دهونتالي धौंताली *dhauntālī*, f. riches; strength, courage; viciousness, mischievousness. *s.*

دهونج धौंज *dhaunj*, f. contemplation, thought, consideration, reflection. *s.*

دهونچا धोंचा *dhonchā*, four and a half; a term in use among surveyors, so *ponchā* denotes five and a half. *h.*

دهوندها धोंधा *dhondhā*, m. a small mound of earth; (met). a potbelly, a large belly. *h.*

دهوندهر धूँधर *dhūndhar*, f. fogginess, dulness. *s.*

دهوندهرا धूँधरा *dhūndharā*, foggy, dull, gloomy. *h.*

دهونددهون كار धूँधूँकार *dhūṅ-dhūṅ-kār*, / دهونددهون كال धूँधूँकाल *dhūṅ-dhūṅ-hāl*, } m. heavy rain, obscuring the whole heaven; gloomy weather, gloominess; desolateness; name of a game. *s.*

دهونڈا धोंडा *dhonḍā*, m. (same as *dhonḍī*, q.v.) *h.*

دهونڈنا *dhūnḍnā*, a. (v. *ḍhūnḍhnā*) to seek for. *d.*

دهونڈي धोंडी *dhonḍī*, f. a kind of grass which grows in rice-fields, and sometimes chokes the plant. *h.*

دهونرا धूँरा *dhūṅrā*, the chimney of a sugar-cane mill. *h.*

دهونس धौंस *dhauṅs*, m. assault, attack, threatening. *h.*

دهونس ध्वंस *dhwaṅs*, m. loss, destruction. *s.*

دهونسا धौंसा *dhauṅsā*, m. a large kettledrum. *h.*

دهونست ध्वंसित *dhwaṅsit*, lost, destroyed. *s.*

دهونس دهڑلا धौंसधड़ल्ला *dhauṅs dhaṛallā*, m. blustering, bullying, tumult, the impetuous assault of a crowd or body of men. *h.*

دهونسن ध्वंसन *dhwaṅsan*, m. loss, destruction. *s.*

دهونسي ध्वंसी *dhwaṅsī*, f. a mote in a sunbeam; adj. destructive. *s.*

دهونسيا धौंसिया *dhauṅsiyā*, the leader of a hue and cry, or *posse comitatus*. *h.*

دهونك धौंक *dhauṅk*, f. breathing, panting; the asthma. *h.*

دهونك धूनक *dhūnak*, m. resin. *s.*

دهونكا धूँका *dhūṅkā* (v. *dhūṅrā*), chimney, &c. *h.*

دهونكنا धौंकना *dhauṅknā*, a. to blow with a bellows. *h.*

دهونكني धौंकनी *dhauṅknī*, f. bellows. *h.*

دهونوا धूंवा *dhūṅwā* or *dhuwāṅ*, m. smoke. *dhūṅwādhār*, much smoke; smoky; beautiful, adorned. *s.*

دهونوارا धूंवारा *dhūṅwārā*, m. a chimney; a hole to let out smoke. *s.*

دهونوارانا धूंवाराना *dhūṅwārānā*, a. to smoke. *s.*

دهونوالا धोंवाला *dhoṅwālā*, a passage for smoke, a chimney. *s.*

دهونور धूंवर *dhūṅwar*, of a blue or dark grey [colour. *h.*

دهوني धूनी *dhūnī*, f. persevering; smoke; fumigation by way of exorcising one possessed, or as a medical application; a fire lighted by a Hindū ascetic, over which he sits, imbibing the smoke, by way of penance. It is often practised by them, in the manner of *dharnā*, to extort compliance with their demands; hence *dhūnī denā*, a. to dun, to importune: to smoke. *dhūnī-lagānī*, *dhūnī lenā*, a. to insist obstinately or persevere in a demand; to inhale smoke or undergo fumigation as a penance. *s.*

دهووا धोवा *dhowā*, washed, cleansed. *s.*

دهوها धूहा *dhūhā* (also *dhū,ā*), m. a scarecrow. *h.*

دهوئي धोई *dho,ī* or *dhū,ī*, f. pulse which has been soaked previous to boiling; a mash. *h.*

دهوئينڈيڈكار धोयेंडीडकार *dho,eṅḍī-* or *dho,-eṅdhī-ḍakār*, f. a sour belch. *h.*

دهي दही *dahī* (vulgarly *dhai*), m. thick sour milk, coagulated milk. *dahī-wālā*, m. a seller of sour milk. *s.*

دهي धी *dhī*, f. a daughter; sense, intelligence; adj. (Beng.) famed, renowned. *s.*

دهيا धिया *dhiyā*, f. a daughter. *s.*

دهيان ध्यान *dhyān*, m. consideration, reflection, thought, advertency, meditation, especially mental contemplation of the divinity. *dhyān-yog*, the practice of religious abstraction. *s.*

دهيانا ध्याना *dhyānā* or *dhyānnā*, to think on, adore, know. *s.*

دهيانون ध्यानौं *dhyānauṅ*, } (Braj) (v.
دهياونون ध्यावनौं *dhyāwanauṅ*, } *dhyānā*). *s.*

دهياني ध्यानी *dhyānī*, considerate, contemplative, religious. *s.* [on. *s.*

دهيانيه ध्यानीय *dhyānīya*, adj. to be meditated

دهياونا ध्यावना *dhyāwanā*, to meditate, &c. *s.*

دهيٹ *dhīṭ* (v. *dhīṭh*), bold, impudent, &c. *d.*

دهيدا धीदा *dhīdā*, f. a virgin, a maid. *s.*

دهير धीर *dhīr*, gentle, patient, firm, resolute; m. patience, slowness, deliberateness, forbearance; resolution, firmness. *s.* [sedate. *s.*

دهيرا धीरा *dhīrā*, gentle, patient, deliberate,

دهيرا धेरा *dherā*, squint-eyed. *h.*

دهيرتا धीरता *dhīratā*, f. patience, firmness, fortitude (also *dhīratwa*). *s.*

دهيرج धीरज *dhīraj* or धैर्य *dhairj*, m. steadiness, firmness, patience. *dhīrjawān*, patient. *dhairj-kalit*, steady, calm, assuming composure. *s.*

دهيري धीरी *dhīrī*, f. the pupil of the eye. *s.*

دهيريا धीरिया *dhīriyā*, f. a daughter. *h.*

دهيڑ दहेड़ *daheṛ*, m. a species of bird (*Coracias*). *h.*

دهيڑ धीड़ *dhīṛ* (v. *ḍhīṛh*), pregnancy, &c. *h.*

دهيري كوا *dherī kauwā*, a large black crow. *d.*

دهيز *dihez*, m. a dowry, a portion, every thing a wife carries with her to her husband. *p.*

دهيشكت धीशक्ति *dhī-shakti*, f. an intellectual faculty or power of the understanding. *s.*

دهيك *dah-yak*, an allowance of ten per cent. of revenue (for the farmer). *p.* [*racias*). *h.*

دهيل दहेल *dahel*, m. the name of a bird (*Co-*

دهيلا धेला *dhelā*, m. half a *paisā*. *h.*

دهيلا दुहेला *duhelā*, difficult, arduous. *h.*

دهيم धीम *dhīm*, m. slowness, gentleness. *h.*

دهيما धीमा *dhīmā*, slow, lazy; gentle, mild, temperate; abated, allayed. *dhīme-dhīme*, gently, softly. *h.*

دهيمان धीमान *dhīmān*, wise, intelligent. *s.*

دهيماءي धीमाई *dhīmā,ī*, f. slowness, gentleness. *h.* [sible, wise. *s.*

دهيمت धीमत *dhīmat* (fem. *dhīmatī*), sen-

دهيمر धीमर *dhīmar*, m. a fisherman; name of a caste of fishermen. *s.*

دهين धीन *dhīn*, m. slowness, gentleness. *h.*

دهين धेनु *dhenu*, f. a cow, a milch cow, one which calved not long since. *s.*

دهيندريه धीन्द्रिय *dhīndriya*, m. an intellectual organ, organ of perception, as the mind, the eye, ear, &c. *s.*

دهينڈي दहेंडी *daheṅḍī* or *dahaiṅḍī*, f. a vessel in which sour milk is kept. *s.*

دهينگ धींग *dhīṅg*, m. a paramour. *h.*

دهينگادهانگي धींगाधांगी *dhīṅgā-dhāṅgī*, f. teasing. *h.* [cuffs. *h. s.*

دهينگامشٹي धेंगामुष्टी *dheṅgā-mushṭī*, f. fisti-

دهينگر दहेंगर *daheṅgar*, m. a vessel for carrying sour milk in (particularly at festivals). *s. h.*

دهينگڑا धींगड़ा *dhīṅgṛā*, m. a paramour. *h.*

دهينو धेनू *dhenū*, f. a milch cow. *s.*

دهنون दहनौं *dahnauṅ*, n. to burn. *s.*

دهيو दहयौ *dahyau* (past part.), burnt. *s.*

دهيوان धीवान *dhīwān*, intelligent, wise. *s.*

دهيوت धैवत *dhaiwat*, m. the sixth note of the gamut. *s.*

دهينور धींवर *dhīṅwar*, } a fisherman. *dhīwarī*,
دهيور धीवर *dhīwar*, } f. a fisherman's wife; a harpoon for catching fish. *s.*

دهيه दुह्य *duhya*, to be milked, milkable. *s.*

دئي दई *da,ī*, part. fem. given; gift; m.f. the Deity, destiny. *da,ī lagnā*, to be unfortunate. *da,ī-mārā*, struck by the Deity, accursed. *s.*

دي *dī*, yester; as *dī-roz*, yesterday; *dī-shab*, yesternight. *p.*

ديا दया *dayā*, f. a gift; affection, tenderness, sympathy, kindness, favour. *dayā-sīl* or *dayā-shīl*, affectionate. *dayā-kār*, *dayā-krit*, *dayā-yukt*, *dayā-yut*, kind, compassionate, benevolent. *dayā-mān*, charitable. *s.*

ديا दिया *diyā*, given (past part. of *denā*); m. a gift. *h.*

ديا दिया *diyā*, m. lamp. *diyā-salā,ī*, f. a match for kindling a lamp. *s.*

ديا दैया *daiyā*, f. a mother; the stand that children run to in playing hide and seek. *h.*

ديار *diyār*, m. (pl. of دار) a country, region. *diyār-bakr*, Mesopotomia. *a.*

ديّاڑا देआड़ा *de,āṛā*, m. a white ant-hill. *h.*

دياڑا दियाड़ा *diyāṛā*, alluvion, an island formed in the bed of a river. *h.*

ديال दयाल *dayāl* or दयालु *dayālu*, generous, liberal, gracious, kind, tender, compassionate. *dayālu-twa*, m. tenderness. *s.*

ديانت *diyānat*, f. conscience, honesty, justice, piety, virtue. *diyānat-dār*, honest, just, conscientious. *diyānat-dārī*, honesty. *a.*

دياوان दयावान *dayā-wān*, } (also *dayā-wat*,
ديايت दयायुत *dayā-yut*, } *dayā-want*), kind, generous, humane, tender. *s.*

ديبا *debā*, m. brocade, cloth of gold. *p.*

ديباجه *debāja*, } m. preface, exordium, in-
ديباچه *dībācha*, } troduction, preamble of a manuscript volume, which portion is generally illumined. *p.*

ديبدار देबदार *debdār*, m. the mast tree (*Uvaria longifolia*). *s.*

ديبرا देबरा *debrā*, left, opposite of right. *h.*

ديبق *debaḳ* (v. *debā*), brocade, &c. *p.*

ديبي देबी *debī*, f. a Hindū goddess, especially Durgā; a queen. *s.*

ديبي दैबी *daibī*, by chance, accidentally. *s.*

ديپ दीप *dīp*, m. a lamp; an island; the world, as supposed to consist of several islands. The Hindū philosophers say that the terrestrial globe contains seven *dīps* or islands, encompassed by seven seas, the whole land and water measuring 7,957,752 *yojanas*. *s.*

ديپالي दीपाली *dīpālī*, f. a row of lamps; the day of new moon in the month Aswin or Kārtik, a festival with nocturnal illuminations in honour of Kārtikeya (commonly called *dewālī* or *dīwālī*). *s.*

ديپبرکش दीपवृक्ष *dīp-briksha*, m. the stand or stem of a lamp; candlestick. *s.*

ديپپشپ दीपपुष्प *dīp-pushp*, m. the champac (*Michelia champaca*). *s.*

ديپت दीप्त *dīpta*, luminous, radiant. *dīpti*, f. light, lustre. *s.*

ديپدان दीपदान *dīp-dān*, land assigned to Brāhmans on the banks of rivers, to deprecate river encroachments; offering of a lamp to an idol. *s.*

ديپدهوج दीपध्वज *dīp-dhwaj*, m. lamp-black. *s.*

ديپشکها दीपशिखा *dīp-shikhā*, f. the flame of a lamp. *s.*

ديپك दीपक *dīpak*, m. a light, a candle, a lamp; an aromatic seed (*Ligusticum ajwaen*); a kind of fireworks; name of a *rāg*, or musical mode, sung at noon in the hot weather; adj. making luminous, kindling, inflaming. *s.*

ديپکٹ दीपकिट्ट *dīp-kiṭṭ*, m. lamp-black, soot. *s.*

ديپکوپي दीपकूपी *dīp-kūpī*, } f. the wick of
ديپکهوري दीपखोरी *dīp-khorī*, } a lamp. *s.*

ديپن दीपन *dīpan*, adj. inflaming, light or heat-exciting, tonic, stimulant. *s.*

ديپمالا दीपमाला *dīp-mālā*, } f. a row
ديپمالکا दपिमालिका *dīp-mālikā*, } of lamps, an illumination. *s.*

ديت *diyat*, f. the law of retaliation, when a fine is paid for murder, wounding, or maiming (in cases of murder it is exacted when the homicide is committed any other way than with sword, dagger, &c.). *a.*

ديت दयित *dayit*, beloved, dear, desired. *s.*

ديت दैयत *daiyat*, } m. a demon, an evil spirit,
ديتيه दैत्य *daitya*, } a Titan, or giant, in Hindū mythology. *daitya-yug*, m. an age of the demons, consisting of 12,000 divine years, or the sum of the four yugs or ages of men. *s.*

ديتا दयिता *dayitā*, f. the beloved one, a wife. *dayitā dhīn*, subject to a wife, hen-pecked. *s.*

ديتلا द्युतिला *dyutilā*, f. a plant (*Hemionites cordifolia*). *s.*

ديتيه दैत्य *daitya*, m. a demon (v. *daiyat*). *s.*

ديٹه दीठ *dīṭh*, *dīṭhi*, } f. sight, view, looking,
ديٹهي दीठी *dīṭhī*, } glance. *s.*

ديجا देजा *dejā* or दैजा *daijā*, m. a dowry, a portion which the wife brings to the husband in marriage; presents made by the bride's family to the bridegroom, chiefly with a view to secure a husband of higher rank. *h.*

ديجو देजू *dejū*, m. part of a portion or dowry. *h.*

ديجور *daijūr*, m. the night of conjunction of sun and moon; a dark night, without moonlight; every thing black. *p.*

ديچهت दीछित *dīchhit*, a tribe of Kanaujiyā Brāhmans; also for *dīkshit*, q. v. *h.*

ديد *dīd*, m. and f. sight, seeing, show, spectacle. *dīd-bāzī*, f. looking about one, taking air reconnoitering. *dīd wā dīd*, m. interview. *p*

ديدار *dīdār*, m. sight, look; interview, seeing (a person); an overseer or inspector. *dīdār-kharch*, charges for the support of an overseer. *p.*

ديدارو *dīdārū*, well-looking (fellow), personable, presentable. *p.*

ديدبازي *dīdbāzī*, f. looking about, recreation; amorous ogling. *p.*

ديدبان *dīd-bān*, a guard, vidette. *p.*

ديدباني *dīd-bānī*, f. watching, guarding. *p.*

ديدن *dīdan* (r. *bīn*), to see; (met.) to encounter, to experience, to perceive in general. *p.*

ديدني *dīdanī*, fit to be looked at. *p.*

ديده *dīda*, m. the eye; a sight, a thing seen; a wanton or impudent eye; (met.) impudence; *dhoyā dīda*, an eye void of shame, wanton, impudent. *dīda rezī*, f. fatiguing to the eyes (as minute objects, &c.). *dīda kholnā*, a. to consider maturely. *dīda-wān* or *-bān*, the sight (of a gun, &c.). *dīda o dānista*, knowingly, wittingly, purposely. *dīda o dil se*, with heart and soul. *dīde nile pile-k.*, (Dakh.) to be enraged: it is sometimes used in comp., denoting seen or experienced, as *jahān-dīda*, one who has seen the world. *p.*

ديدهت दीधित *dīdhit*, f. a sunbeam, a ray of light; light in general. *s.*

دير *dair*, m. a temple where idols are worshipped (in Arab. a convent, a monastery). *p.*

دير *der*, f. delay, tardiness, slowness. *der-pā*, durable. *der-pā,ī*, f. durability. *der-gāh*, always. *p.*

ديرا डेरा *derā*, m. a dwelling, a tent. *h.*

ديرگه दीर्घ *dīrgh* or *dīrgha*, long. *dīrghāyu*, m. long life. *dīrghāyus*, long-lived; m. the silk-cotton tree (*Bombax heptaphyllum*). *dīrgha-bans*, of ancient family. *dīrgha-pād*, long-footed, a heron. *dīrgha-patra*, long-leaved; m. garlic. *dīrgha-patrā*, f. a sort of Eugenia. *dīrgha-patrak*, m. garlic; a thorny plant, a kind of Bassia, growing in marshy places. *dīrgha-parna*, long-leaved, Longifolium. *dīrgha-paksha*, m. the fork-tailed shrike. *dīrgha-pallav*, having long shoots; m. the sun-plant (*Crotolaria junica*). *dīrgha-phal*, m. a plant (*Cassia fistula*). *dīrgha-tanu*, long-bodied, tall. *dīrgha-jangal*, m. a kind of fish. *dīrgha-janghā*, long-thighed; m. a crane; a camel. *dīrgha-jihwā* or *dīrgha-jibhā*, long-tongued; m. a snake. *dīrgha-jīv*, m. long life. *dīrgha-jīvī*, long-lived. *dīrgha-drishṭi* or *dīrgha-darshī*, far-seeing, provident; a wise man, a prophet. *dīrgha-rātra*, m. a long night, a long period. *dīrgha-rogī*, being long ill. *dīrgha-sūtra*, or *dīrgha-sūtrī*, dilatory, slow, tedious. *dīrgha-sūtratā*, f. dilatoriness, tediousness. *dīrgha-swar*, m. a long vowel, a long-note. *dīrgha-shākh*, m. the Sāl tree (*Shorea robusta*). *dīrgha-kāl*, m. a long time. *dīrgha-kanṭak* or *dīrgha-kandhar*, m. a sort of crane (*Ardea nivea*). *dīrgha-kesh*, long-haired. *dīrgha-kīl*, m. a tree (*Alangium hexapetalum*). *dīrgha-mūl*, having a long root; m. a kind of Bilwā tree; a sort of sensitive plant. *dīrgha-mūlā*, f. a creeper (*Echites frutescens*); also *dīrgha-mūlī*, a plant (*Hedysarum alhagi* or *Gangeticum*). *dīrgha-nidrā*, f. (long sleep) death. *dīrgha-nishwās*, m. a long or deep sigh. *dīrgha-varna*, m. a long vowel. *dīrgha-vrint*, m. a plant (*Bignonia Indica*). *dīrgha-vrintikā*, f. a plant (*Mimosa hectandra*). *s.*

ديروز *dī-roz*, yesterday. *p.*

ديري *derī*, f. lateness, delay, slowness. *derī-lagnā*, to be late, slow, &c. *p.*

ديرين *derīn*, / ديرينه *derīna*, } old, ancient; wise, cunning. *p.*

ديڑپيلا *deṛ-pelā*, m. a swelled testicle. *d.*

ديڑه *deṛh* (for ڈيڑه), one and a half. *d.*

ديس देश *des*, m. country, territory, region. *des-tyāg*, abandoning one's country (v. *desh*). *s.*

ديس देस *des*, a day (cor. of *divas*). *d.*

ديساكه देसाख *desāhh*, m. name of a *rāginī* or musical mode sung at noon in the spring. *h.*

ديساور देशावर *desāvar* or *disāvar*, m. a foreign country. *s.*

ديساوري देशावरी *desāvarī* or *disāvarī*, m. a kind of betel leaf; a kind of dove. *s.*

ديس بهاءي देशभाई *des-bhā,ī*, m. a fellow-countrymen. *h.*

ديسكار देशकार *deskār*, m. or *deskārī*, f. name of a *rāginī* or musical mode sung in the morning. *h.*

ديسنا दीसना *dīsnā*, n. to look, to appear. *s.*

ديسوال देसवाल *deswāl*, name of a tribe of *gaur tagās*. *h.*

ديسي देशी *desī*, of the same country, belonging to a country, indigenous, local; f. appearance. *s.*

ديسي दीसे *dīse*, adj. like; adv. likely. *s.*

ديش देश *desh*, m. country, region, territory. *desh-āchār*, m. the custom of the country. *desh-bhāshā*, f. the language of the country, the vernacular dialect. *desh-tyāg*, m. abandoning one's country, emigration. *desh-dharm*, m. the law or usage of the country. *desh-nikālā*, m. banishment, exile. *desh-vyavahār* or *desh-beohār*, m. local usage

ديشاٹن देशाटन *deshāṭan*, m. wandering through the country. *s.*

ديشادهپت देशाधिपति *deshādhipati*, m. the ruler of a country, governor, king. *s.*

ديشاكه देशाख *deshāhh*, m. a *rāginī* v. *desākh*.

ديشانتر देशान्तर *deshāntar*, / ديشاور देशावर *deshāvar*, } m. a foreign country. *s.*

ديشاوري देशावरी *deshāvarī*, m. v. *desāvarī*.

ديشب *dī-shab*, last night. *p.*

ديشكار देशकार *desh-kār*, m. or *desh-kārī*, f. name of a *rāginī* v. *deskār*.

ديشي देशी *deshī*, / ديشيه देश्य *deshya*, } belonging to a country, local, v. *desī*. *s.*

ديغ *degh*, f. a pot, a caldron, generally written *deg*. *p.* [&c. *p.*

ديغچه *deghcha* (dimin. of *degh*), a small kettle,

ديكشا दीक्षा *dīkshā*, f. sacrificing, offering oblations; receiving the initiatory *mantra* or incantation. *s.*

ديكشت दीक्षित *dīkshit*, initiated; performed (as the Dīkshā ceremony). *s.* [initiator. *s.*

ديكشتر दीक्षितृ *dīkshitṛi*, m. spiritual father,

ديكها देखा *dekhā*, seen; m. a sight. *dekhā-dekhī*, f. emulation, competition, the looking at each other, or being within sight (of objects). *s.*

ديكهانا देखाना *dekhānā*, a. to shew, exhibit. *s.*

ديكهاى देखाई *dekhā,ī*, f. appearance, shewing. *s.*

ديكهت दीखित *dīkhit* (v. *dikhit*). *h.*

ديكهلانا देखलाना *dekhlānā*, a. to shew, to exhibit. *s.*

ديكهنا देखना *dekhnā*, a. to see, to look, behold, to observe, to inspect, to experience. *dekhnā-bhālnā*, to see, to look at. *s.*

ديكهنا दीखना *dīkhnā*, n. to look, to appear, seem. *s.*

ديكهويا देखवैया *dekhwaiyā*, m. a spectator, [looker-on. *s.*

ديگ *deg*, f. a caldron, a pot. *p.*

ديگدان *deg-dān*, m. a fireplace, a trivet. *p.*

ديگچه *degcha*, m. } a pot, a small caldron. *p.*
ديگچي *degchī*, f. }

ديگر *dīgar*, other, another; again. *p.*

ديگشو *deg-sho*, m. a scullion. *p.*

ديگمبر *dīgambar* or देगम्बर *degambar* (v. *digambar*), naked, &c. *s.*

ديمارنا देमारना *de-mārnā*, a. to dash on the ground, to throw, to stamp. *h.*

ديمك दीमक *dīmak*, f. the white ant. *h.*

دين दीन *dīn*, poor, needy, distressed; humble. *dīn-dayāl*, merciful to the poor. *dīn-bandhū*, the friend of the poor, and *dīna-nāth*, master of the poor, are epithets of the Deity. *dīn-chetan*, distressed, dejected. *dīn-mukh*, downcast, of melancholy aspect. *s.*

دين *dīn*, m. faith, religion. *dīn-dār*, virtuous, religious. *a.*

دين *dain*, m. debt. *dain-dār*, m. a debtor. *daini mu'ajjal*, a debt payable on demand. *daini muwajjal*, a debt of which payment is deferred. *a.*

دين दैन *dain*, diurnal, daily; m. poverty, wretchedness. *s.*

دين देन *den*, m. (verb. noun) to give, giving. *den-len*, m. (giving and taking) traffic, pecuniary transactions, debts and credit. *s.*

دينا देना *denā* (also दीना *dīnā*), a. to give, to grant, to yield; to allow, to permit; to emit, let, resign; to cause, to produce, to lay (eggs); m. giving. *denā pānā*, profit and loss; settling of one's affairs. *denā-lenā* (v. *den-len*), traffic, &c. *s.*

دينار *dīnār*, m. the name of a coin, a ducat. *dīnār i surkh*, gold coin; according to Gladwin, the *dīnār* is a silver coin, estimated at ten *dāms*, or sixpence sterling of our money, reckoning the *dām* at one-fortieth of a rūpī. "The actual value of the dīnār is not known. It is at present merely a nominal or imaginary coin. The Persian *tūmān*, a gold coin worth about ten shillings, is said to contain 10,000 dīnārs, which would make the dīnār somewhat less than one-twentieth of a farthing."—(Binning.) *p.*

دينتا दीनता *dīnatā*, } f. poverty, indigence; humility. *s.*
دينتاى दीनताई *dīnatā,ī*, }

دينك दैनिक *dainik*, diurnal, daily. *s.*

دينكي दैनिकी *dainikī*, f. a day's hire or wages. *s.*

دينگي *dongī*, f. bounty, liberality. *d.*

دين لين देंलें *den-len*, m. pecuniary transactions upon interest, debts and credits, gambling. *s.*

دينو दीनौ *dīnau* (Braj), third pers. sing. past tense of *denau*, to give. *s.*

دينيه दैन्य *dainya*, m. poverty, humbleness, meanness, covetousness. *s.*

ديو *dew*, m. a demon, a sprite, a devil. *p.*

ديو देव *dew*, m. a god; a husband's brother; a term applicable to a Brāhman, also to a man of the Kāyath class. *dew-thān*, f. a temple, place of idols; (met.) the rain. *s.*

ديو दैव *daiv*, divine, celestial; m. destiny, fate. *daiv-chintā*, f. fatalism, reliance on fate. *daiv-chintak*, m. a fatalist. *daiva-gya*, prophetic, acquainted with fate; m. an astrologer. *daiva-gyā*, a female fortune-teller. *daiv-lekhak*, an astrologer. *daiv-vānī*, f. a voice from heaven. *daiv-yug*, m. an age of the gods. *s.*

ديو दयौ *dayau* or दैयौ *daiyau* (Braj), gave, given, past of *denaun*. *s.*

ديو दीवि *dīvi*, m. the blue jay. *s.*

ديوا देवा *dewā*, m. a god, a deity; a giver, a liberal man; f. a flower (*Hibiscus mutabilis*); a plant (*Marsilea quadrifolia*). *s.*

ديوا दीवा *dīwā*, m. (v. *diyā*) a lamp. *s.*

ديوات दैवात *daivāt*, by chance, fatally, unavoidably; at length. *s.*

ديوار *dīwār*, f. a wall; the bridge of the nose. *p.*

ديوار *dīwār*, the "genius loci," or god under whose special care a village is placed (supposed to be a corruption of *dih-wār*). *p.*

ديوارگيري *dīwār-gīrī*, f. tapestry or hangings [on a wall. *p.*

ديواگت देवागत *dewāgat* or *daivāgat*, f. sudden misfortune, accident. *s.*

ديوال देवाल *dewāl*, m. a giver. *s.*

ديوال *dīwāl*, f. a wall (same as *dīwār*). *p.*

ديوالا देवाला *dewālā*, m. bankruptcy. *h.*

ديوالبند *dewāl-band*, a soldier. *p.*

ديوالى देवालई *dewā-la,ī* or देवालेई *dewā-le,ī*, f. barter, traffic. *s.*

ديوالي देवाली *dewālī* (also *dīwālī*), f. a Hindū festival celebrated on the day of the new moon of *Kārtik*, when the Hindūs, after bathing in the Ganges, perform a *shrāddha*, and at night worship *Lakshmī*: the houses and streets are illuminated all night, and in Hindūstān the night is universally spent in gaming. *s.*

ديوالي *dīwālī*, f. a leather strap, a belt. *h.*

ديوالي देवालय *dewālai* or *dewālaya*, m. a temple of idols; the residence of the gods, heaven. *s.*

دیوالیا देवालिया *dewāliyā*, a bankrupt, q. d.; one who has been fleeced or cleaned out at *dewālī*, q. v. *s.* [*den*). *s.*

دیوالیٔی देवालेई *dewāle,ī*, f. traffic (v. *len-*

دیوان *dīwān*, m. a tribunal; a steward; the collector-general of a province on the part of his majesty (next in rank to the *nāzim*), whose business it is to superintend the lands and collections, and the remittances of them to court, to grant *sanads* under his seal (with the approbation of the *nāzim*), to *zamīndārs*, *jāgīrdārs*, &c. The steward of any man of rank, as the title is now adopted by the principal servants of the *zamīndār*, and those of English gentlemen, are also called *dīwān*. The term is sometimes used to express the bags in which the records and other papers are kept: it is also applied to a book or collection of poetical pieces of the species called *ghazal* and *ḳaṣīda*, q. v., the rhymes of the different poems ending successively with every letter in the alphabet. *dīwāni a'lā*, m. a prime minister, *wazīr*. *dīwāni khāṣṣ*, m. privy-council chamber. *dīwān-khāna*, a tribunal, an office; a court, hall, hall of audience. *dīwāni 'ām*, public hall of audience. *p.*

دیوانپن *dīwāna-pan*, madness, insanity. *p. h.*

دیوانگی *dīwānagī*, f. insanity, madness. *p.*

دیوانه *dīwāna*, mad, insane, inspired. *p.*

دیوانی *dīwānī*, the office of the king's *dīwān*, and superintendence of the administration of civil justice. *p.* [heaven, firmament. *s.*

دیوپتھ देवपथ *dev-path*, m. the celestial path,

دیوپوجا देवपूजा *dev-pūjā*, f. the worship of the gods, idolatry. *s.*

دیوبلبھ देवबल्लभ *dev-ballabh*, m. a tree used in dyeing (*Rottleria tinctoria*). *s.*

دیوبھون देवभवन *dev-bhavan*, m. the holy fig-tree; paradise; a temple. *s.*

دیوپوجك देवपूजक *dev-pūjak*, a worshipper of the Deity. *s.*

دیوت द्यूत *dyūt*, m. gaming, playing with dice, &c. *dyūtādhikārī*, the keeper of a gaming-house. *dyūt-pūrnimā*, f. the day of full moon in *Kārtik*, the night of which is spent in games of chance, in honour of *Lakshmī*. *dyūt-sabhā*, f. a gaming-house or assembly. *dyūt-kār*, m. a gaming-house keeper, a gambler. *s.*

دیوتا देवता *dewtā*, f. a Hindū god, a deity, divinity; a respectful address used towards Brāhmans, such as "your holiness," "your godship." *s.*

دیوتاڑ देवताड़ *dev-tāṛ*, m. a kind of grass (*Andropogon serratus*). *s.*

دیوتر देवतरु *dev-taru*, m. the holy fig-tree; a tree of paradise, the tree of plenty; any venerable and ancient tree, generally the place of assembling in a village. *s.* [nature. *s.*

دیوتوه देवत्व *devatwa*, m. divinity, divine

دیوتیرتھ देवतीर्थ *dev-tīrth*, m. the tips of the fingers, sacred to the gods. *s.*

دیوٹ दीवट *dīwaṭ*, f. a lamp-stand. *s.*

دیوٹھان देवठान *dew-ṭhān*, f. the second day of the moon of *Kārtik shukl paksh*, on which *Vishṇu* awakes from his sleep of four months.

دیوٹی देवट्टी *devaṭṭī*, f. a sort of gull (*Larus ridibundus*). *s.*

دیوٹی *de,oṭī*, a torch, a lamp. *d.*

دیودارو देवदारु *dev-dāru*, m. a species of pine (*Pinus devadaru*): in Bengal it is usually applied to a medicinal tree (*Uvaria longifolia*); and in the peninsula to another tree (*Erythroxylon sideroxyloides*). *s.*

دیودانی देवदानी *dev-dānī*, f. a creeper, commonly called *Hātīghosh*. *s.*

دیودت देवदत्त *deva-datta*, given by a deity: this is frequently a man's name among Hindūs, and it is curious to observe how names of the same or similar import are found in various languages, such as *Allāh-bakhsh*, *Khudā-dād*, Theodore, Diodati, Gottsched, &c. *s.*

دیودھانیه देवधान्य *dev-dhānya*, m. a sort of grain (*Andropogon saccharatus*). *s.*

دیودھوپ देवधूप *dev-dhūp*, m. a fragrant resin (bdellium) used in incense. *s.* [ther. *s.*

دیور देवर *dewar*, m. husband's younger bro-

دیورانی देवराणी *dewrānī*, *diwrānī*, or द्योरानी *dyorānī*, f. husband's younger brother's wife. *s.*

دیوروپی देवरूपी *dev-rūpī*, godlike, of divine form. *s.*

دیوڑی *de,oṛī* (for *ḍe,oṛhī*), a gate, &c. *d.*

دیوس *daiyūs*, m. a contented cuckold, or one who winks at the fornication of his female relatives from interested motives (also *daiyūṣ*). *a.*

دیوسبھا देवसभा *dev-sabhā*, f. an assembly of the gods. *s.* [mons. *p.*

دیوستان *dew-stān*, f. the habitation of de-

دیوستھان देवस्थान *deva-sthān*, f. temple, place of idols. *s.*

دیوسوه देवस्व *deva-swa*, m. the property applicable to religious purposes, endowments. *s.*

دیوك देवक *devak*, divine, godlike. *daivak*, an astrologer, an almanac maker. *s.*

دیوك *dīwak*, a weevil, a moth, the white ant. *p.*

دیوکاشٹھ देवकाष्ठ *dev-kāshṭha*, m. a kind of pine (*Pinus devadāru*). *s.* [cresses. *h.*

دیوکانڈر देवकांडर *dev-kānḍar*, m. water-

دیوکردم देवकर्दम *dev-kardam*, m. a fragrant paste of sandal, agallochum, camphor, and saffron-flower. *s.*

دیوکری देवकिरी *dev-kirī*, f. one of the female personifications of the modes of music. *s.*

دیوکسم देवकुसुम *dev-kusum*, m. cloves. *s.*

دیوکنڈ देवकुण्ड *dev-kunḍ*, m. a natural spring. *s.*

دیوکی देवकी *devakī*, the daughter of Devaka, wife of Vasudeva, and mother of *Krishṇa*. *s.*

دیوکیه देवकीय *devakīya*, divine, belonging to a divinity. *s.*

دیوگاندھاری देवगान्धारी *dev-gāndhārī*, f. one of the *rāginīs*, or female personifications of music. *s.*

ديوگاين देवगायन ***dev-gāyan***, m. a celestial quirister. *s.*

ديوگرهه दिवगृह ***deva-griha***, a house or temple dedicated to a deity; a celestial or planetary sphere. *s.*

ديوگري देवगिरी ***dev-girī*** (also *dev-gīrī*), f. name of a musical note or *rāginī*. *s.*

ديوگندم ***dev-gandum*** (lit. devil's wheat), rye. *p.*

ديوگيه दैवज्ञ ***daivagya***, an astrologer, an almanac maker. *s.*

ديول देवल ***dewal***, m. a temple where idols are worshipped, a temple, a pagoda. *s.*

ديولتا देवलता ***dev-latā***, f. double jasmine. *s.*

ديولوک देवलोक ***dev-lok***, m. heaven, paradise, any of the celestial worlds. *s.*

ديولي दीवला ***dīvlī***, f. a small lamp. *s.*

ديولي देवली ***dewlī***, f. a fish scale; the scale or scab of small pox; a small lamp. *h.*

ديوماس देवमास ***dev-mās***, m. the eighth month of pregnancy. *s.*

ديوناگري देवनागरी ***deva-nāgarī***, f. the character used by the Hindūs in their sacred writings. *s.*

ديونامروا देवनामरवा ***dewnā-marwā***, m. the name of a shrub (*Ocymum*). *s.*

ديونرمت देवनिर्मित ***dev-nirmit***, created (by God), natural. *s.*

ديونل देवनल ***dev-nal, dī,ūnal***, or ***de,onal***, a kind of reed (*Arundo Bengalensis*), the stem of which is used for writing. *s.*

ديوننذا देवनिन्दा ***dev-nindā***, f. contempt of the gods, atheism. *s.*

ديوننذک देवनिन्दक ***dev-nindak***, a reviler of the gods, an unbeliever. *s.*

ديوواني देववाणी ***dev-vānī***, f. the language of the gods, Sanskrit. *s.*

ديووتر ***devotar***, land held rent-free in the name of Hindū deities, ostensibly for the provision of all the necessaries of divine worship.—Gladwin. *h.*

ديووتهان देवोत्थान ***devotthān***, f. a place of idols, a temple. *s.*

ديووديان देवोद्यान ***devodyān***, m. a sacred grove. *s.*

ديوور देववर ***dev-var***, m. a divine boon or blessing. *s.*

ديوورت देवव्रत ***dev-vrat***, m. vow to a deity. *s.*

ديوورکش देववृक्ष ***dev-vrihsh***, m. a tree (*Echites scholaris*); a tree of heaven or paradise; a plant yielding a fragrant resin (*Bdellium*). *s.*

ديوه दैव: ***daiva***, divine, relating to a divinity. *s.*

ديوهرا देवहरा ***dewhrā***, m. a temple where idols are worshipped. *s.*

ديوي दैवी ***daivī*** (v. *daibī*), fate, destiny; adv. accidentally, fatally. *s.*

ديوي देवी ***devī***, f. (v. *debī*) a goddess; the goddess Durgā; a queen; a plant (*Trigonella corniculata*). *s.*

ديويکوٹ देवीकोट्ट ***devī-koṭṭ***, m. a town, the city of Vān, probably Davicotta on the Coromandel coast. *s.*

ديويه दैव्य ***daivya***, m. fate, fortune. *s.*

ديه देह ***deh***, f. the body. *deh durānā*, to conceal or cover one's nakedness. *deh sambhālnā*, to keep one's spirits, to be firm, to recover one's self. *deh-tyāg*, m. voluntary death, death in general. *deh-chyut*, detached from the body (as excrements or the spirit). *deh-kshay*, m. disease, sickness. *deh-wat* or *deh-wān*, corporeal, embodied. *deh-yātrā*, f. death. *s.*

ديه देहु ***dehu***, (Braj) 2d pers. sing. imper. of *denaun*, to give. *s.*

ديه ***dīh***, / **ديهه** ***dīha***, } a town or village. *p.*

ديهات ***dīhāt*** (pl. Arab.), villages; the country, as opposed to cities. *p.*

ديهاتم وادي देहात्मवादी ***dehātma-vādī***, m. a *chārvāk*, a materialist. *s.*

ديهاتي ***dīhātī***, of or relating to a village or villages. *dīhātī-jam'*, the amount of revenue receivable at the *dīh*, from the several villages composing such division, after deducting the charges of collection in each. *p.*

ديهدار ***dīh-dār***, a person appointed to attach the harvest of villagers, that the revenue may be secured. *dīh-dār <u>kh</u>arch*, expenses of a *dīh-dār*. *p.*

ديهداري ***dīh-dārī***, office of a village keeper; adj. of or relating to a village keeper. *dīhdārī-salāmī*, a tax of one *rūpī* annually, collected from every *dīh* or village of a district, to defray the expenses of a *dīh-dār* or person deputed on the part of him who has the charge of the collection, to hinder the cultivators from carrying off their crops till they have paid up their revenues. *p.*

ديهرا देहरा ***dehrā***, m. a temple where idols are worshipped by *jains*; a Hindū temple. *s.*

ديهلي देहली ***dehlī***, f. the threshold of a door, the lower part of the wooden frame of a door, or a raised terrace in front of it. *h.*

ديهن देहिन ***dehin***, / **ديهي देही** ***dehī***, } corporeal, embodied, living. *s.*

ديهو दैहौ ***daihau***, (Braj) second plur. aor. of *denaun*. *s.*

ديهي ***dīhī***, of or belonging to the village, a peasant. *p.*

ديية देय ***deya***, fit or proper to be given. *s.*

ڈ

ڈ ड ***ḍa***, is the twelfth letter in the Hindūstānī alphabet. Its sound is very nearly that of our own *d* in *did, done*; and it differs from that of *dāl* from its being uttered by applying the tip of the tongue to the roof of the mouth or palate. It is sometimes used instead of *dāl*, *ḍanḍ* for *danḍ*, a staff, and when not at the beginning of a word, it is frequently converted into *ṛ*, as *taḍā* or *taṛā*, an island. *h.*

ڈاب डाब *ḍāb*, f. the name of a grass (*Poa cynosuroides*). *s.*

ڈاب डाब *ḍāb*, m. a sword-belt; an unripe cocoa-nut. *h.*

ڈابر डाबर *ḍābar*, m. a vessel for washing hands in; a small round tank; low ground where water settles. *ḍābar-nainī*, having large eyes (epithet applied to women; *ḍābar* in Panjābī signifies great). *h.*

ڈابك डाबक *ḍābak*, m. fresh water drawn from a well. *h.*

ڈابھ डाभ *ḍābh*, m. name of a sacrificial grass (v. *kusha*); a forest. *h.*

ڈاٹ डाट *ḍāṭ*, f. threatening, snubbing, browbeating, checking. *h.*

ڈاٹنا डाटना *ḍāṭnā*, a. to snub, to check, to threaten, to browbeat (also *ḍāṅṭnā*, q. v.) *h.*

ڈار डार *ḍār*, f. a branch, a bough; a rank, row. *ḍār kī ḍār*, a succesion of ranks; a band, troop. *h.*

ڈارم डारिम *ḍārim*, m. (v. *dāṛim*) a pomegranate. *h.*

ڈارنا डारना *ḍārnā*, a. (v. *ḍālnā*) to throw, &c. *h.*

ڈاڑھ डाढ़ *ḍāṛh*, f. a jaw-tooth or grinder. *ḍāṛh*- (or *ḍāṛheṅ*) *-mārnā*, to grind or gnash the teeth from rage, despair, &c. *s.*

ڈاڑھي डाढ़ी *ḍāṛhī*, f. the beard. *s.*

ڈاك डाक *ḍāk*, f. a post (for the conveyance of letters, also relay of horses or of pālkī-bearers). *ḍāk-chaukī*, a stage where a relay of horses is posted. *ḍāk-ghar*, a post-office. *h.*

ڈاك डाक *ḍāk*, perpetual vomiting. *ḍāk-lagnī*, to be seized with constant vomiting. *h.*

ڈاك डाक *ḍāk*, m. husband of a *ḍākinī*, q.v. *s.*

ڈاکا डाका *ḍākā*, m. an attack by a gang of armed robbers. *ḍākā-paṛnā*, *-denā*, or *ḍālnā*, a. to rob. *h.*

ڈاکرا डाकरा *ḍākarā*, m. name of a good kind of soil. *h.*

ڈاکن डाकिन *ḍākin*, f. same as *ḍākinī*, q. v.

ڈاکنا डाकना *ḍāknā*, a. to vomit. *h.*

ڈاکني डाकिनी *ḍākinī*, f. a female imp, a witch, whose evil eye causes children to pine and die: she is said to consume their liver; (met.) a termagant. *s.*

ڈاکو डाकू *ḍākū*, m. a robber, pirate. *h.*

ڈاکي डाकी *ḍākī*, gluttonous, voracious. *h.*

ڈاکيا डाकिया *ḍākiyā*, m. a robber; a postman. *h.*

ڈاکيت डाकैत *ḍākait*, m. one of a gang of robbers, commonly called a "*dacoit*." *h.*

ڈاکيتي डाकैती *ḍākaitī*, f. robbery by gangs. *h.*

ڈال डाल *ḍāl*, f. a branch, a bough; a basket for raising water. *ek ḍāl*, of one piece, without joining. *h.*

ڈالا डाला *ḍālā*, m. a litter, a large branch. *h.*

ڈالم डालिम *ḍālim*, m. a pomegranate (v. *dāṛim*).

ڈالنا डालना *ḍālnā*, a. to throw down, to fling, to cast, to pour, to lay, to push, to set, to shake, to submit, to throw, to thrust, to destroy, to throw away, to cause, to occasion, to produce, to excite. *ḍāl-denā*, a. to throw away, to cast, to occasion. *h.*

ڈالي डाली *ḍālī*, f. a tray, or rather a couple of trays fastened by slings for carrying presents; hence a present of fruit, &c.; a basket of fruit, &c.; a branch a bough. *h.*

ڈامر डामर *ḍāmar*, m. pitch, resin; a torch. *h.*

ڈانٹ ڈپٹ डांटडपट *ḍāṅṭ-ḍapaṭ*, f. gallop, swiftness. *h.*

ڈانٹنا डांटना *ḍāṅṭnā*, a. to snub, to threaten (also *ḍāṭnā*). *h.*

ڈانٹھ डांठ *ḍāṅṭh*, the refuse of harvest floors. *h.*

ڈانٹھل डांठल *ḍāṅṭhal*, m. pedicle, petiole, footstalk. *h.*

ڈانٹھي डांठी *ḍāṅṭhī*. f. a straw, stubble, pedicle, stalk. *h.*

ڈانڈ डांड *ḍāṅḍ*, high ground (opposed to *ḍābar*, low ground). *h.*

ڈانڈ डांड *ḍāṅḍ*, m. retaliation, penalty, revenge, fine, forfeit; an oar; the back-bone; a stick; a line. *ḍāṅḍ bharnā*, a. to pay a fine, or undergo a penalty. *ḍāṅḍ lenā*, to fine, to amerce. *s.*

ڈانڈا डांडा *ḍāṅḍā*, m. landmarks; road. *ḍāṅḍā-meṅḍā*, m. the frontier boundary between the lands of two proprietors. *s.*

ڈانڈنا डांडना *ḍāṅḍnā*, a. to retaliate, to take revenge, to fine, to punish. *s.*

ڈانڈي डांडी *ḍāṅḍī*, m. a rower, a waterman. *s.*

ڈانس डांस *ḍāṅs*, m. the sting of a reptile; a large mosquito. *s.*

ڈانك डांक *ḍāṅk*, m. foil (under precious stones); the sting of a scorpion. *s.*

ڈانکي *ḍāṅkī*, voracious, gluttonous; m. a glutton. *d.*

ڈانگ डांग *ḍāṅg*, f. a stick, a club; the greatest height or summit of a mountain. *h.*

ڈانگر डांगर *ḍāṅgar*, ڈانگرا डांगरा *ḍāṅgrā*, } thin, lean; m. a lean beast, a starveling, superannuated horned cattle; the flowering stem of radishes or mustard. *h.*

ڈانواڈول डांवाडोल *ḍāṅwāḍol*, or *ḍāṅwāṅḍol*, m. wandering without house or home, ruined, destitute. *ḍāṅwāḍolī*, f. state of destitution, wandering without a home. *h.*

ڈانورو डांवरू *ḍāṅwrū*, m. a tiger's cub or whelp. *h.*

ڈاوان *ḍāwāṅ*, left, left hand. *d.*

ڈاوانڈول *ḍāwāṅḍol* (v. *ḍāṅwāḍol*). *d.*

ڈاہ डाह *ḍāh*, f. malice, spite, rancour, envy, jealousy. *s.*

ڈاہك डाहुक *ḍāhuk*, m. a gallinule. *s.*

ڈاہل डाहल *ḍāhal*, m. the name of a country, also *Tripura*. *s.*

ڈاهنا डाहना **ḍāhnā**, n. to be malicious, to burn with spite; to be fuzed (as metal); to heat metal. *s.*

ڈاهي डाही **ḍāhī**, malicious, spiteful, envious. *s.*

ڈاین डायन **ḍāyan** (also **ḍā,en** or **ḍāyin**), f. a witch. *s.*

ڈب डब **ḍab**, m. strength, power, authority; a kind of pocket; the leather with which oil-pots are made. *ḍab-gar*, m. a currier. *h.*

ڈبا डब्बा **ḍabbā**, m. a leathern vessel for holding oil. *h.*

ڈبا डिब्बा **ḍibbā**, m. a small box. *h.*

ڈبانا डुबाना **ḍubānā**, a. to cause to sink, to immerse, to dip; to demolish, ruin, destroy. *h.*

ڈباو डुबाव **ḍubāw**, out of man's depth, deep (enough to drown in); m. drowning. *h.*

ڈبڈبانا डबडबाना **ḍabḍabānā**, m. to be filled with water or tears (an eye). *ānsū ḍabḍabānā*, to be on the point of shedding tears. *h.*

ڈبرا डबरा **ḍabrā**, } m. marshy land, a puddle,
ڈبره डबरः **ḍabra**, } a small pond (Scottice, "a dub"). *ḍabrā-ḍahrā*, m. a puddle. *h.*

ڈبري डबरी **ḍabrī**, division of profits among the village community according to their respective shares. *h.*

ڈبريا डिबरिया **ḍibriyā** or डबरिया **ḍabriyā**, left-handed. *h.*

ڈبس डबस **ḍabas**, m. provisions, sea-stock, stores. *h.*

ڈبسي डुबसी **ḍubsī**, inundated land, or land liable to be flooded. *h.*

ڈبكا डबका **ḍabkā**, m. fresh water drawn from a well; adj. fat, corpulent. *h.*

ڈبكنا डबकना **ḍabahnā**, n. to glitter. *h.*

ڈبكي डुबकी **ḍubkī**, f. a dip, a dive. *h.*

ڈبنا डुबना **ḍubnā**, n. to sink, be immersed. *h.*

ڈبو डब्बू **ḍabbū**, m. an iron spoon. *h.*

ڈبوانا डुबवाना **ḍubwānā**, a. (v. *ḍubānā*) to cause to be sunk, drowned, or destroyed. *h.*

ڈبونا डबोना **ḍabonā** or डुबोना **ḍubonā**, a. (same as *ḍubānā*). *nām ḍubonā*, to vilify, to disgrace. *h.*

ڈبودينا डुबोदेना **ḍubo-aenā**, a. to exhaust, to ruin, to demolish; to drown, to immerse. *h.*

ڈبه **ḍibba**, m. a soldier's cartridge-box. *d.*

ڈبي डिब्बी **ḍibbī**, f. a cartouche-box, a small box of any kind. *h.*

ڈبيا डिबिया **ḍibiyā**, f. a small box (for medicines, &c.). *h.*

ڈپٹنا डपटना **ḍapaṭnā**, n. to call out, to shout; to gallop; to rebuke. *h.*

ڈپرا **ḍaprā**, a sort of musical instrument. *d.*

ڈپھ डफ **ḍaph**, m. (for *daf*) a kind of musical instrument, a small drum. *h.*

ڈپھارنا डफारना **ḍaphārnā**, n. to cry bitterly, to blubber, to roar. *h.*

ڈپھالي डफाली **ḍaphālī** (for *dafālī*), m. a kind of *fakīr*, who plays upon a musical instrument called *daf*; (met.) a chatterer. *p.*

ڈٹا डट्टा **ḍaṭṭā**, m. a plug, spigot, a cork. *h.*

ڈٹنا डिटना **ḍiṭnā**, a. to see; to take aim, to look at. *s.*

ڈٹنا डटना **ḍaṭnā**, n. to stop, to stand still. *h.*

ڈٹھا डठा **ḍaṭhā**, m. a stalk. *h.*

ڈٹھنا डिठना **ḍiṭhnā**, a. to see, &c. (v. *ḍiṭnā*). *s.*

ڈٹھيارا डिठियारा **ḍiṭhiyārā**, seeing, possessed of vision, the opposite of blind. *s.*

ڈڈكا डुडका **ḍuḍkā**, a kind of disease in the rice plant. *h.*

ڈر डर **ḍar**, m. f. fear, dread. *ḍar-poknā*, a coward. *h.*

ڈراك डराक **ḍarāk**, fearful, frightened. *h.*

ڈرابو **ḍarābū**, m. a coward; adj. timid. *d.*

ڈرالو डरालू **ḍarālū**, timid, fearing. *s.*

ڈرانا डराना **ḍarānā**, a. to frighten, to terrify; adj. frightful, terrible. *s.*

ڈراءو डराउ **ḍarā,ū**, terrible, terrific. *h.*

ڈراونا डरावना **ḍarāwnā**, a. to frighten, to terrify. *ḍarāwanā*, frightful, terrifying, tremendous. *h.*

ڈرپ डरप **ḍarap**, adj. afraid. *h.*

ڈرپنا डरपना **ḍarapnā**, n. to be afraid. *h.*

ڈرپوكنا डरपोकना **ḍarpoknā**, a coward. *h.*

ڈركا डरक्का **ḍarakkā**, m. terror, fright. *h.*

ڈرنا डरना **ḍarnā**, to fear, to be frightened. *h.*

ڈرويا डरवैया **ḍarwaiyā**, fearful; (met.) a coward. *h.*

ڈريانا डुरियाना **ḍuriyānā**, } a. to lead
ڈرياليـنا डुरियालेना **ḍuriyā lenā**, } about (as a horse), to lead in hand. *h.*

ڈڑهمنڈا डढ़मुण्डा **ḍaṛhmunḍā**, having the beard cropped, shaved, deprived of beard. *s.*

ڈڑهيل डढ़ियल **ḍaṛhiyal**, having a long beard. *s.*

ڈس डस **das**, m. the string by which scales are suspended (or held in the hand); the threads of the warp at the end of a piece of cloth which are left unwoven; the end of a piece of cloth. *s.*

ڈسنا डसना **ḍasnā**, a. to bite or sting (as a venomous animal). *s.*

ڈسونا डसौना **ḍasaunā**, m. bedding. *h.*

ڈف **ḍaf**, a kind of tambourine (v. *daf*). *d.*

ڈفالي **ḍafālī** (for *dafālī*), one who plays on the *ḍaf*. *d.*

ڈفر **ḍafar**, sail of a ship. *d.*

ڈك डुक **ḍuk**, m. a blow with the fist. *h.*

ڈکار डकार *ḍakār*, f. a belch, eructation. *ḍakār lenā*, to belch. *h.*

ڈکارنا डकारना *ḍakārnā*, n. to belch; to bellow, to low. *ḍakār-baiṭhnā* or *-jānā*, n. to embezzle. *h.*

ڈکڈکانا डकडकाना *ḍakḍakānā*, m. (v. *ḍagḍagānā*), to shake, burn, &c. *h.*

ڈکرانا डकराना *ḍakrānā*, n. to cry bitterly. *h.*

ڈکریا डुकरिया *ḍukariyā*, f. old (woman). *h.*

ڈکوت डकौत *ḍakaut*, ڈکوتیا डकौतिया *ḍakautiyā*, m. a caste of Hindūs descended from a Brāhman on the father's, and a Gwālin on the mother's side. They subsist on alms, and are skilled in astrology. They are considered by all decent people as troublesome vagabonds. *h.*

ڈکوري *ḍakorī*, f. a wasp, a hornet. *d.*

ڈکي *ḍikkī*, an attack, an onslaught, butting with the horns (an animal). *d.*

ڈکیت डकैत *ḍakait*, m. a robber, a pirate (vulg. *dacoit*). *h.* [coity). *h.*

ڈکیتي डकैती *ḍakaitī*, f. robbery (vulg. *da-*

ڈگ डग *ḍag*, f. a pace, one step (measure). *h.*

ڈگا डग्गा *ḍaggā*, m. a lean long-legged horse, a rosinante, a garran. *h.*

ڈگانا डिगाना *ḍigānā*, a. to cause to shake, move. *h.*

ڈگڈگانا डुगडुगाना *ḍugḍugānā*, n. to sound a kettle drum, to twinkle. *h.*

ڈگڈگانا डगडगाना *ḍagḍagānā*, n. to shake; to burn brightly, to burn clear (charcoal). *ḍagḍagākar pānī pīnā*, to drink greedily, or a large quantity at a draught. *h.*

ڈگر डगर *ḍagar*, f. a road, a path, a highway. *h.*

ڈگرا डग्रा *ḍagrā*, a kind of vessel. *h.*

ڈگرانا डगराना *ḍagrānā*, a. to propel, to roll. *h.*

ڈگرجانا डिगरजाना *ḍigar-jānā*, n. to go away. *h.*

ڈگرنا डगरना *ḍagarnā*, n. to travel, to walk on the road, to roll. *h.*

ڈگمگ डगमग *ḍagmag*, adj. unsteady, tottering; f. the act of shivering, tottering. *h.*

ڈگمگانا डगमगाना *ḍagmagānā*, n. to shiver, to totter, to stagger. *h.*

ڈگنا डिगना *ḍignā*, n. to shrink, to go back, to relapse, to slide from the right path; to shake, to vibrate, to tremble, to quaver, to move, to slip to stumble. *h.* [tle. *s.*

ڈلي डुलि *ḍuli*, f. a small turtle; a female tur-

ڈلا डला *ḍalā*, m. a large lump, a clod, a large basket. *h.* [swing. *h.*

ڈلانا डुलाना *ḍulānā*, a. to move, to shake, to

ڈلک डलक *ḍalak*, m. a sling, a basket, a *ḍālī*, carried on men's shoulders by means of a stick and ropes, like the beam and strings of a balance; presents of fruit, sweetmeats, &c., are generally sent in this manner; glitter. *h.*

ڈلکا डुलिका *ḍulikā*, f. a small bird resembling a wagtail. *s.* [*gānā*). *d.*

ڈلملانا डलमलाना *ḍalmalānā*, n. (v. *ḍagma-*

ڈلنا डुलना *ḍulnā*, n. to walk with a peculiar twisting of the body; (a gait much affected by women). *h.* [a lid). *h.*

ڈلوا डलवा *ḍalwā*, m. a large basket (without

ڈلوانا डलवाना *ḍalwānā*, a. (from *ḍālnā*) to cause to throw, &c. *h.*

ڈلي डली *ḍalī*, f. a lump (of sugar, meat, &c.). *h.*

ڈلیا डलिया *ḍaliyā*, m. a basket (without cover, like a tray); a lump of meat, &c. *h.*

ڈلیاجھاڑ डलियाझाड़ *ḍaliyā-jhāṛ*, (lit. the brushing out of the basket) the conclusion of the sowing season. *h.*

ڈم डिम *ḍim*, m. a dramatic entertainment dramatic exhibition of battle or tumult. *s.*

ڈمب डिम्ब *ḍimb*, m. an egg; a chrysalis; the bladder; the spleen; the uterus; any young animal. *s.*

ڈمبکا डिम्बिका *ḍimbikā*, f. a libidinous woman. *s.*

ڈمبھ डिम्भ *ḍimbh*, m. pride, vanity; any young animal; a fool, an idiot, a blockhead. *s.*

ڈمبھا डिम्भा *ḍimbhā*, f. an infant. *s.*

ڈمرو डमरू *ḍamrū*, m. a small drum shaped like an hour-glass, held in one hand and beaten with the fingers. *s.*

ڈنڈ डण्ड *ḍanḍ*, m. the arm above the elbow, a kind of exercise, placing the hands on the ground, and then bending down so as almost to touch the earth with the breast. *ḍanḍ-pel*, one who exercises himself at the *ḍanḍ*. *s.* [*sbœna*). *s.*

ڈنڈ डुण्डु *ḍunḍu*, m. a kind of snake (*Amphi-*

ڈنڈا डण्डा *ḍanḍā*, m. a staff, an ensign-staff; the beam of a pair of scales. *s.*

ڈنڈا डण्डा *ḍanḍā*, a collector of market dues. *h.*

ڈنڈازني *ḍanḍā-zanī*, name of a mode of torture (v. Ell. Gl.). *h. p.* [(*Amphisbœna*). *s.*

ڈنڈبھ डुण्डुभ *ḍunḍubh*, m. a kind of snake

ڈنڈر डिण्डिर *ḍinḍir*, m. cuttle-fish bone, considered to be congealed foam of the sea. *s.*

ڈنڈم डिण्डिम *ḍinḍim*, m. a musical instrument; a kind of small drum or tabor; a plant bearing a small fruit (*Carissa carandas*). *s.*

ڈنڈوارا डण्डवारा *ḍanḍwārā*, a south wind. *h.*

ڈنڈوت डण्डवत *ḍanḍwat* or डण्डौत *ḍanḍaut*, also *ḍanḍāwat*, a Hindū salutation, obeisance. *h.*

ڈنڈي डण्डी *ḍanḍī*, f. a handle; the beam of a pair of scales; m. any one who bears a staff, a weighman; a mendicant who carries a staff in his hand. *pagḍanḍī*, f. a footpath. *s.*

ڈنڈي डण्डी *ḍanḍī*, f. the tube of the corolla of the *Nyctanthes arbortristis*, which is used for dye ing. *h.*

ڈنڈیا डण्डिया *ḍanḍiyā*, m. a kind of garment for women; a collector of market duties. *h.*

ڈنڈیر डण्डीर *ḍanḍīr*, f. a line, stripe, score, lineament. *h.*

ڈنک डङ्क *ḍank*, m. the sting of a reptile or insect, particularly a scorpion. *ḍank mārnā*, to sting. *h.*

ڈنکا डङ्का *ḍankā*, m. a double drum, a kettle-drum; the sound of the kettle-drum. *h.*

ڈنکارنا *ḍankārnā*, n. (v. *ḍakārnā*) to bellow, &c. *d.*

ڈنکاءي डङ्काई *ḍankā,ī*, f. wages of a beater of [the kettle-drum. *s.*

ڈنکني डङ्किनी *ḍankinī*, f. a witch (v. *ḍākinī*). *s.*

ڈنکیانا डङ्कियाना *ḍankiyānā*, a. to sting (as a reptile). *h.*

ڈنکیلا डङ्कीला *ḍankīlā*, armed with a sting. *h.*

ڈنگر डिङ्गर *ḍingar*, m. a fat man; a servant, a slave, a rogue, a cheat, a low or depraved man. *s.*

ڈنگوارا टङ्गवारा *ḍangwārā*, ڈنگوارہ डङ्गवारः *ḍangwāra*, } reciprocal assistance in tillage. *h.*

ڈوا डवा *ḍawā*, m. a large wooden spoon. *h.*

ڈوب डोब *ḍob*, m. a dip, a dive, a plunge; a dip (in dye or colouring). *ḍob-denā*, a. to dip in dye. *h.*

ڈوب डूब *ḍūb*, m. a dip, a dive, immersion. *h.*

ڈوبا डोबा *ḍobā*, m. a reservoir; fainting. *h.*

ڈوباچر डूबाचर *ḍūbāchar*, ڈوبارا डूबारा *ḍūbārā*, } m. an island or bank left in the channel of a river; any low ground liable to be flooded. *h.*

ڈوبانا डूबाना *ḍūbānā*, ڈوبونا डूबोना *ḍūbonā*, } a. to sink or cause to sink, to immerse. *h.*

ڈوباءي डूबाई *ḍūbā,ī*, an unconditional bribe. *h.*

ڈوبنا डूबना *ḍūbnā*, n. to dive; to be drowned; to be immersed; to set, to sink; to be absorbed in business or study; to be destroyed, ruined. *dil-ḍūbnā*, a. to faint. *h.*

ڈوبونا डूबोना *ḍūbonā*, a. to sink (v. *ḍūbānā*).

ڈور डोर *ḍor*, f. string, cord, thread, rope; m. a fillet of thread or cord tied round the arm or wrist. *h.*

ڈورا डोरा *ḍorā*, m. thread, line; edge of a sword, &c.; a ladle; a capsule (of poppy, &c.). *ānkh kā ḍorā*, a blood-shot eye, vessels distended with blood on the tunica conjunctiva of the eye (from intoxication or other cause). *ḍore ḍālnā*, a. to stitch a quilt; to utter a long-continued sound like the amaduvade (*Fringilla Amandava*). *kis chiṭṭī ne ḍore ḍāle? ṭukṛe ho ho lāl laṛā hai*, What female amaduvade uttered this prolonged strain? (at hearing which) the male has fought so desperately. *gardan kā ḍorā*, a graceful motion of the neck in dancing. *h.*

ڈورک डोरक *ḍorak*, m. a string, a fillet of thread, &c. (v. *ḍor*).

ڈوري डोरी *ḍorī*, f. a string, cord, thread. *h.*

ڈوریا डोरिया *ḍoriyā*, m. striped muslin; lace; a dog-keeper. *h.*

ڈوریوالا डोरीवाला *ḍorī-wālā*, m. a ropemaker. *h.*

ڈوریهار डोरीहार *ḍorīhār*, m. a pedlar who goes about selling laces, thread, &c. *h.*

ڈوریہ डोरिय *ḍoriya*, m. a kind of lace. *h.*

ڈوڑ डोड़ *ḍoṛ*, name of a race of *rājpūts*, said to be now extinct. *h.*

ڈوڑهي डौढ़ी *ḍauṛhī*, f. a threshold, &c. (v. *ḍewṛhī*); adj. one and a half, or half as much as (any quantity); raised one half higher (a tone in music). *h.*

ڈوک डोक *ḍok*, f. vomiting. *h.*

ڈوکرا डोकरा *ḍokrā*, old, ancient, an old man. *h.*

ڈوکري डोकरी *ḍokrī*, f. old (woman). *h.*

ڈوکنا डोकना *ḍoknā*, n. to vomit. *h.*

ڈوکي डोकी *ḍokī*, f. vomiting. *h.*

ڈوگر *ḍogar* (for *ḍongar*), a mountain. *d.*

ڈول डोल *ḍol*, m. a leathern bucket for drawing water; a rich black soil. *h.*

ڈول डौल *ḍaul*, m. manner, method, mode; shape, fashion, form; estimate of assets for the purpose of assessments. *ḍaul-paṭṭa*, the rent-roll of a farm. *h.*

ڈولا डोला *ḍolā*, m. a swing; a kind of sedan a bier on which a corpse is carried f. a wife from an inferior family, married by a person of rank who gives a present to her parents, she ranks below wives of equal family, but above concubines. *ḍolā denā*, a. to give a daughter to a superior by way of tribute, manner, coition. *s.*

ڈولا डौला *ḍaulā*, a limit, boundary. *h.*

ڈولچہ डोलचः *ḍolcha*, m. ڈولچي डोलची *ḍolchī*, f. } a small bucket for drawing water. *h.*

ڈولڈول डोलडोल *ḍol ḍol*, m. roving, perambulating. *h.*

ڈولنا डोलना *ḍolnā*, to move, to shake, or be shaken; to roam, ramble, rove; to swing. *s.*

ڈولہ डोलः *ḍola*, m. manner; coition (a phrase). *h.*

ڈولي डोली *ḍolī*, f. a kind of sedan, an inferior sort of palanquin commonly called "a dooly." *s.*

ڈوم डोम *ḍom*, ڈومڑا डोमड़ा *ḍomṛā*, } m. a low caste of Hindūs; a caste of Musalmāns, the men of which are musicians, and the females sing and dance in the company of females only (v. *domnī*). *h.*

ڈومن پنا डोमनपना *ḍoman-panā*, m. the art practised by the *Ḍom* caste. *h.*

ڈومني डोमनी *ḍomnī*, f. a female of the caste [called *Ḍom*. *h.*

ڈونجا डौंजा *ḍaunjā*, m. a scaffold. *h.*

ڈونڈا डूंडा *ḍūnḍā*, m. a bullock with only one horn. *h.*

ڈونڈي डोंडी *ḍonḍī* or डौंडी *ḍaunḍī*, f. publication by beat of drum. *h.*

ڈونر डोंर *ḍonr*, ڈونرا डोंरा *ḍonrā*, } f. a kind of snake. *h.*

ڈونگا डोंगा *ḍongā*, m. a spoon; a canoe; a trough. *ḍūngā*, deep. *h.*

ڈونگر डोंगर *ḍongar*, a mountain, a hill. *h.*

ڈونگري *ḍongrī*, a hill, a mountain. *d.*

ڈونگي डोंगी *ḍongī*, f. (v. *ḍongā*) a spoon, &c., a small boat. *h.*

ڈوني *ḍonī*, f. a boat or ship, a canoe, a coasting vessel. "The word is commonly applied to all vessels manned and commanded by natives, as *jahāz* is to all commanded by Europeans."—(Binning). *d.*

ڈوهي डूही *ḍūhī*, alluvial formations, a mark of village boundaries. *h.*

ڈوئي डोई *ḍo,ī*, f. a wooden spoon, ladle; an oar, a paddle. *h.*

ڈھابا ढाबा *ḍhābā*, m. a net; the eaves of a house, extending three or four cubits beyond the wall, so that people may sit under them. *h.*

ڈھاٹا ढाटा *ḍhāṭā*, m. a handkerchief tied over the head and over the ears. *h.*

ڈھاٹھي ढाठी *ḍhāṭhī*, f. rack, torment, torture; a noose or gin fastened on a horse's nose. *h.*

ڈھار ढार *ḍhār*, m. a declivity, shield, target; a heap of corn. *h.*

ڈھاڑس ढाड़स *ḍhāṛas*, f. and m. firmness of mind, confidence, animation, encouragement, comfort. *ḍhāras bandhānā*, a. to encourage, to comfort, to keep in spirits. *ḍhāṛas denā*, a. to animate. *h.*

ڈھاڑن ढाड़िन *ḍhāṛin*, f. a female musician. *h.*

ڈھاڑهس ढाढ़स *ḍhāṛhas*, m. (v. *ḍhāṛas.*) *h.*

ڈھاڑهن ढाढ़िन *ḍhāṛhin*, f. }
ڈھاڑهي ढाढ़ी *ḍhāṛhī*, m. } a kind of musician, a singer. *h.*
ڈھاڑي ढाड़ी *ḍhāṛī*, m. }

ڈھاک ढाक *ḍhāk*, m. name of a tree (*Butea frondosa*). *h.*

ڈھاکا ढाका *ḍhākā*, m. a thick wood of *ḍhāk* trees; a city or district, *Ḍhacca* or *Ḍacca*. *h.*

ڈھال ढाल *ḍhāl*, m. declivity, slope; f. shield, target. *h.*

ڈھالا *ḍhālā*, m. a bough or branch of a tree. *d.*

ڈھال‌بھول ढालभोल *ḍhāl-bhol*, complete transfer by sale. *h.*

ڈھالنا ढालना *ḍhālnā*, a. to cast (metal in fusion); to pour out, to tilt, to spill; (met.) to do mischief, to mar. *h.*

ڈھالو ढालू *ḍhālū*, slant, sloping; spoiling, doing mischief, casting, &c. *ḍhālū bhar-k.*, a. to shift goods, &c. occasionally over shallows, &c. *h.*

ڈھالوان ढालवां *ḍhālwāṅ*, sloping, declivitous; cast (metal). *h.*

ڈھالي ढाली *ḍhālī*, m. a warrior armed with a shield, a shield-bearer; f. a bough or branch. *h. d.*

ڈھان ढान *ḍhān*, m. hedge, inclosure. *h.*

ڈھانا ढाना *ḍhānā*, a. to break, to knock down or raze a building, &c. *h.*

ڈھانپنا ढांपना *ḍhāṅpnā*, a. to cover, to conceal. *h.*

ڈھانچا ढांचा *ḍhāṅchā*, m. a frame, a plan. *h.*

ڈھانس *ḍhāṅs*, a cough, a cold. *d.*

ڈھانسا ढांसा *ḍhāṅsa*, m. calumny, undeserved abuse, defamation. *h.*

ڈھانسنا ढांसना *ḍhāṅsnā*, a. to blame, to accuse. *h.*

ڈھانکنا ढांकना *ḍhāṅknā*, a. to cover, to shut. *h.*

ڈھانگ ढांग *ḍhāng*, f. a precipice, cliff. *h.*

ڈھاها ढाहा *ḍhāhā*, m. the precipitous or high bank of a river. *h.*

ڈھائي ढाई *ḍhā,ī*, two and a-half. *h.*

ڈھب ढब *ḍhab*, m. shape, form, manners, breeding, behaviour, mode, method, knack, knowledge fashion, style, way, address, dexterity, art, position. *h.*

ڈھبرا ढबरा *ḍhabrā*, turbid. *h.*

ڈھبکا ढिबका *ḍhibkā*, m. protuberance. *h.*

ڈھبوا ढबूआ *ḍhabū,ā*, m. a copper coin equal to a *paisā*. *h.*

ڈھبوس *ḍhabūs*, fat, corpulent. *d.*

ڈھبيلا ढबीला *ḍhabīlā*, well-made, graceful. *h.*

ڈھپ‌ڈھپانا ढपढपाना *ḍhap-ḍhapānā*, a. to thump a drum (as children do). *a.*

ڈھپنا ढपना *ḍhapnā*, n. to be covered, concealed, hidden; m. a cover, covering. *h.*

ڈھٹھا ढट्ठा *ḍhaṭṭhā*, m. a plug, a cork. *h.*

ڈھٹھائي ढिठाई *ḍhiṭhā,ī*, f. forwardness, impudence, audacity, presumption, pertness. *s.*

ڈھٹھيا ढठिया *ḍhaṭhiyā*, }
ڈھٹيا ढटिया *ḍhaṭiyā*, } f. a cord used instead of a bridle. *h.*
ڈھٹي ढट्टी *ḍhaṭṭī*, }

ڈھچا *ḍhichchā*, m. a blow of the head (from a fighting ram, &c.). *d.*

ڈھڈا ढड्डा *ḍhaḍḍā* (v. *ḍhaḍḍī*). *h.*

ڈهڈها डहडहा *ḍahḍahā*, flourishing, blossoming, green, fresh, pleasing. *h.*

ڈهڈهانا डहडहाना *ḍahḍahānā*, n. to flourish, to blossom. *h.*

ڈھڈي ढड्डी *ḍhaḍḍī*, a term applied to low ground. *h.*

ڈهر डहर *ḍahar*, a road, path, low lands flooded with water. *h.*

ڈهرا डहरा *ḍahrā*, m. a pond, a pool. *h.*

ڈھڑکوا ढड़कौआ *ḍhar-kauwā*, m. a raven. *s.*

ڈھرکھا ढरखा *ḍharkhā*, }
ڈھرلا ढरला *ḍharlā*, } m. a scarecrow. *h.*

ڈھڑوا ढड़वा *ḍhaṛwā*, m. the name of a bird, a kind of *mainā*, q.v. *h.*

ڈهڑهور डिढ़ोर *ḍhiṛhor*, name of an inferior tribe of *ahīrs* in Benares. *h.*

ڈهك डहक *ḍahak*, m. f. a cavern, abyss, a pitfall. *h.*

ڈهك ढक *ḍhak*, m. a weight. *h.*

ڈهك ढक्क *ḍhakk*, m. the city or district of *Ḍhacca* or *Dacca*: covering or disappearance. *h.*

ڈهكا ढक्का *ḍhakkā*, m. f. a large or a double drum. *s.*

ڈهكار ढकार *ḍhakār*, f. (cor. for *ḍakār*, q. v.). *ḍhakār lenā*, n. to belch. *h.*

ڈهكانا डहकाना *ḍahkānā*, a. to deceive, to disappoint, to baulk, to tantalize; to spoil, to throw away uselessly. *h.*

ڈهكل دينا *ḍhakal-denā*, a. to dismiss a complaint; to reject a suit or claim, to quash. *d.*

ڈهكلي ढुकली *ḍhuklī*, f. a machine for raising water. *h.*

ڈهكنا ढकना *ḍhaknā*, m. a lid, a cover. *h.*

ڈهكنا ढकना *ḍhaknā*, a. to cover, to conceal; *h.*

ڈهكنا ढुकना *ḍhuknā*, n. to enter, to penetrate; to take aim; to have regard for, inclination to, to sympathize. *h.*

ڈهكني ढकनी *ḍhaknī*, f. a lid, cover (of a pot). *h.*

ڈهكيل ढकेल *ḍhakel*, m. a push, shove. *ḍhakel denā*, to push, to precipitate. *h.*

ڈهكي لگانا ढुक्कीलगाना *ḍhukkī lagānā*, a. to take aim. *h.*

ڈهكيلنا ढकेलना *ḍhakelnā*, to push, thrust, shove. *h.*

ڈهكيلو ढकेलू *ḍhakelū*, m. one who pushes, &c. *h.*

ڈهگ ढिग *ḍhig*, m. (v. *dig*) side, quarter, near. *s.*

ڈهگار *ḍhigār*, a store, a heap. *d.*

ڈهلانا ढलाना *ḍhalānā*, a. to cause to cast (metal), to cause to pour. *h.*

ڈهلانا ढुलाना *ḍhulānā*, a. to cause to be carried; to spill (water, &c.). *h.*

ڈهلاءي ढुलाई *ḍhulā,ī*, f. act of carrying; price paid for carrying, or for transporting. *h.*

ڈهلڑ ढिल्लड़ *ḍhillaṛ*, lazy, indolent. *h.*

ڈهلك ढलक *ḍhalak*, f. rolling, tilting. *h.*

ڈهلكا ढलका *ḍhalkā*, m. blear-eyed; spilling. *h.*

ڈهلكانا ढलकाना *ḍhalkānā*, a. to tilt, to overturn, to spill, to pour, to roll. *h.*

ڈهلكنا ढलकना *ḍhalaknā*, n. to roll, to be tilted, to be spilt; to become loose (a girdle). *h.*

ڈهلملانا ढलमलाना *ḍhalmalānā*, n. to move from side to side, to totter. *h.*

ڈهلنا ढलना *ḍhalnā*, n. to be cast (a metal); to be poured out, to spill; to roll; to be inclined. *din ḍhalnā*, to decline (the day towards evening). *ḍhalti phirti chhāṅw*, (lit. rolling and turning shade) is applied to the changeable state of worldly concerns; (met.) to a person of a capricious or unsteady temper. *h.*

ڈهلنا ढुलना *ḍhulnā*, n. to be poured out, to be spilt, to roll. *h.*

ڈهلوانا ढुलवाना *ḍhulwānā*, a. (v. *ḍhulānā*). *h.*

ڈهليت ढलैत *ḍhalait*, m. a person in the equipage of great men armed with sword and buckler; a constable, a targeteer; "a peon who waits on the person of a European in authority: he wears a silver badge, but his target has been laid aside."—(Binning.) *h.*

ڈهليتي ढलैती *ḍhalaitī*, of or relating to a *ḍhalait*; f. situation of *ḍhalait*. *h.*

ڈهمڈهمي ढिमढिमी *ḍhimḍhimī*, f. a tambourine. *h.*

ڈهملانا ढमलाना *ḍhamlānā*, n. to roll. *h.*

ڈهنا ढना *ḍhanā*, n. to be demolished, razed, destroyed (v. *ḍhahnā*). *h.*

ڈهنڈهنا ढुंढना *ḍhunḍhnā*, a. to seek, search for. *ḍhunḍhnā ḍhanḍhnā*, to search for. *h.*

ڈهنڈهوانا ढुंढवाना *ḍhunḍhwānā*, a. to cause to seek. *h.*

ڈهنڈهورا ढंढोरा *ḍhanḍhorā*, m. publication by beat of drum; (in Dakh.) *ḍhanḍorā* (for *ḍhanḍhorā*) *piṭāna*, to proclaim by beat of drum. *h.*

ڈهنڈهوريا ढंढोरिया *ḍhanḍhoriyā*, m. a proclaimer, a public crier. *h.*

ڈهنڈهوءي ढंढोई *ḍhanḍho,ī*, the scum of the sugar-cane juice when boiling. *h.*

ڈهنگ ढंग *ḍhang*, m. behaviour, manners, breeding, gracefulness, mode, method. *h.*

ڈهنيك ढनेक *ḍhanek*, m. the name of a bird with a very large bill (*Buceros*). (v. *dhanes*). *h.*

ڈهو *ḍhau*, deep water, an eddy; a deep pool in a river. *d.*

ڈهوا ढूआ *ḍhū,ā*, m. a bank, a mound raised as a boundary. *h.*

ڈهوا ढोआ *ḍho,ā*, m. fruit and flowers presented by inferiors on festival days. *h.*

ڈهوانا ढवाना *ḍhawānā*, a. to cause to be cast down, razed, or demolished. *h.*

ڈهوٹا ढोटा *ḍhoṭā*, m. a child. *h.*

ڈهور ढोर *ḍhor*, m. cattle. *h.*

ڈهورا ढोरा *ḍhorā*, m. the tomb, carried about in *muḥarram*; name of an insect very destructive to *chanā*, &c. *h.*

ڈهوروا ढूरवा *ḍhūrwā*, m. a pea. *h.*

ڈهوري ढोरी *ḍhorī*, f. eagerness, ardour. *h.*

ڈهوڑها ढोढ़ा *ḍhoṛhā*, m. (v. *ḍhorā*). *h.*

ڈهوڑي डिहोड़ी *ḍihoṛī* (for *de,oṛhī*), a threshold. *h.*

ڈهوسر ढूसर *ḍhūsar*, m. a caste of Hindūs. *h.*

ڈهوك ढोक *ḍhok*, f. salutation, obeisance. *h.*

ڈهوكا ढोका *ḍhokā*, small stones of an inferior quality extracted from the Chanār quarries. *h.*

ڈھوکا **ढूका** *ḍhūkā*, m. tapping or shoving, by way of calling the attention of one spoken to. *ḍhūkā denā*, a. to peep; to tap. *h.*

ڈھوکنا **ढोकना** *ḍhoknā*, a. to drink, to tope. *h.*

ڈھوکنا **ढूकना** *ḍhūknā*, n. to shut, to close; to steal on, to draw nigh, to approach; to go into, to enter. *h.*

ڈھول **ढोल** *ḍhol*, m. a kettle-drum. *h.*

ڈھولا **ढोला** *ḍholā*, name of a famous lover in Hindūstān; a boy. *h.*

ڈھولک **ढोलक** *ḍholak*,
ڈھولکی **ढोलकी** *ḍholkī*, } f. a small drum. *h.*

ڈھولکیا **ढोलकिया** *ḍholkiyā*, m. a person that plays on the *ḍholak*. *h.*

ڈھولن **ढोलन** *ḍholan*, m. a friend, a sweetheart. *h.*

ڈھولنا **ढोलना** *ḍholnā*, m. a little amulet in the shape of a drum. *h.*

ڈھولی **ढूली** *ḍhūlī* or **ढोली** *ḍholī*, f. a bundle of one hundred betel leaves; m. a drummer. *h.*

ڈھولیا **ढोलिया** *ḍholiyā*, m. a drummer. *h.*

ڈھونا **ढोना** *ḍhonā*, a. to take up, take away, to carry. *h.*

ڈھونچا **ढोंचा** *ḍhoṅchā* or **ढौंचा** *ḍhauṅchā*, four and a half. *h.*

ڈھونڈ **ढोंड** *ḍhoṅḍ* (also *ḍhoṅḍh*), m. a capsule or seed-vessel, especially of the poppy. *h.*

ڈھونڈھ **ढूंढ** *ḍhūṅḍh*, m. f.
ڈھونڈھن **ढूंढन** *ḍhūṅḍhan*, m. } seeking, a search. *s.*

ڈھونڈھاڑ **ढूंढर** *ḍhūṅḍhaṛ*,
ڈھونڈھ ڈھانڈھ **ढूंढढांढ** *ḍhūṅḍh-ḍhāṅḍh*, } m. strict search, inquiry, quest, investigation. *s.*

ڈھونڈھنا **ढूंढना** *ḍhūṅḍhnā* or *ḍhūṅḍhnā ḍhāṅḍhnā*, a. to seek, to search for. *s.*

ڈھونڈھیا **ढूंढया** *ḍhūṅḍhiyā*, m. name of a kind of *faḳīr*, of the sect of *Jains*. *h.*

ڈھونڈی **ढूंडी** *ḍhūṅḍī*, the pod of gram. *h.*

ڈھونڑڈھانڑ **ढूंड़दांड़** *ḍhūṅṛ-ḍhāṅṛ*, m. search. *s.*

ڈھونڑھنا **ढूढ़ना** *ḍhūṅṛhnā*, a. (v. *ḍhūṅḍhnā*), to search. *s.*

ڈھونگ *ḍhong*, fraud, trickery, deceit. *d.*

ڈھونگیا *ḍhonyiuā*, fraudulent, deceitful. *d.*

ڈھوہ **ढोह** *ḍhoh* (also *ḍhūh*), elevated grounds in the midst of ravines. *h.*

ڈھوہا **ढूहा** *ḍhūhā*, a scarecrow, a mound of earth (v. *ḍhū,ā*). *h.*

ڈھہ پڑنا **ढहपड़ना** *ḍhah-parnā*,
ڈھہنا **ढहना** *ḍhahnā*,
ڈھہے پڑنا **ढहे पड़ना** *ḍhahe-paṛnā*, } n. to fall, to be demolished, to tumble down (a house), to be razed, destroyed. *h.*

ڈھی **ढी** *ḍhī*, a high bank of a river. *ḍhe*, a subdivision of the *Jāṭ* tribe. *h.*

ڈھیا **ढैया** *ḍhaiyā*, m. a measure of two and a half *sers*. *ḍhaiyā ṭekār*, desolated. *h.*

ڈھیپا *ḍhepā*, a large lump or clod of earth; arable land; adj. bulky, corpulent. *d.*

ڈھیٹھ **ढीठ** *ḍhīṭh*,
ڈھیٹھا **ढीठा** *ḍhīṭhā*, } forward, impudent, familiar, presumptuous, confident, tame, pert; seen. *s.*

ڈھئی دینا **ढई देना** *ḍhā,ī denā*, a. to force an invitation, by fixing one's self in a house till dinner comes on table. *h.*

ڈھیر **ढेर** *ḍher*, m. a heap; a parcel; adj. much, abundant, enough. *h.*

ڈھیرا **ढेरा** *ḍherā*, adj. squinting, squint-eyed. *h.*

ڈھیری **ढेरी** *ḍherī*, f. a heap, also a sharer in landed property. *h.*

ڈھیڑ *ḍheṛ* (for *ḍheṛh*, q. v.), a pariah, an outcast. *d.*

ڈھیڑھ **ढेढ़** *ḍheṛh*, m. name of a tribe of workers in leather; a low caste of Hindūs so called; a crow. *h.*

ڈھیڑھ **ढीढ़** *ḍhīṛh*, m. pregnancy; a large belly. *h.*

ڈھیڑھی **ढेढ़ी** *ḍheṛhī*, f. an ornament worn in the ear. *h.*

ڈھیڑی **ढेड़ी** *ḍheṛī*, f. (v. *ḍher*), a heap, &c. *h.*

ڈھیگ *ḍhīg*, a heap, a store. *d.*

ڈھیل **ढील** *ḍhīl*, f. looseness, remissness; laziness, inattention, delay, caution, foresight. *ḍhīl lenā*, to give way, to yield. *h.*

ڈھیلا **ढीला** *ḍhīlā*, loose, not tight; remiss; lazy, inattentive, dilatory. *h.*

ڈھیلا **ढेला** *ḍhelā*, m. a lump of earth, a clod; a pellet made of clay for shooting at birds. *ḍhelā-chauth*, f. the fourth day of the bright fortnight in *Bhādoṅ*, a festival on which the Hindūs pelt each other with clods. *h.*

ڈھیلائی **ढीलाई** *ḍhīlā,ī*, f. remissness, looseness. *h.*

ڈھیلی ڈوری دینا *ḍhelī ḍorī denā*, to act remissly. *d.*

ڈھین **ढेन** *ḍhen*, f. a milch cow (for *dhenu*). *h.*

ڈھینڈس **ढेंडस** *ḍheṅḍas*, m. a kind of gourd. *h.*

ڈھینڈھا **ढेंढा** *ḍheṅḍhā*, m. pregnancy, a large belly. *h.*

ڈھینڑس **ढेंड़स** *ḍheṅṛas*, m. a kind of gourd. *h.*

ڈھینڑی **ढेंड़ी** *ḍheṅṛī*, f. the capsule of the poppy (or of the cotton tree), a poppy head; an ornament worn in the ear. *h.*

ڈھینکا **ढेंका** *ḍheṅkā*, m. a machine for pounding with. *h.*

ڈھینکھر **ढींखर** *ḍhīṅkhar*, a kind of harrow, consisting of a bundle of thorns tied together, and drawn by bullocks. *h.*

ڈھینکلی **ढेंकली** *ḍheṅklī*, f. a mode of joining breadths of cloth or of cutting out cloth; a machine for drawing water, being a lever supported on a long post, having a bucket suspended to one end and a weight of earth or stone to the other. *h.*

ڈھینکي **ढेंकी** ***ḍhenkī***, f. (same as *ḍhenkā*). *h.*

ڈھیئو **ढेअ** ***ḍhe,ū***, m. a wave. *h.*

ڈھیہا **ढेहा** ***ḍhehā***, m. a kind of *faḳīr*; a tribe of *jāṭs*. *h.*

ڈھیہا **ढीहा** ***ḍhīhā*** or **ढेहा** ***ḍhehā***, m. a rising ground; mounds. *h*

ڈیٹھ **डीठ** ***ḍīṭh***, f. sight, a look, a glance, vision. *ḍīṭh-band*, enchanting the sight, preventing one's seeing by conjuration; a juggler. *ḍīṭh-bandī*, f. the act of enchanting the sight, &c. *h.*

ڈیرا **डेरा** ***ḍerā***, ڈیرہ **डेरः** ***ḍera***, m. a dwelling, a tent; adj. squint-eyed. *h.*

ڈیڑ **डेड़** ***ḍeṛ***, f. (v. *ḍāṛh*), a tooth. *ḍeṛeṅ mārnā*, to gnash or grind the teeth from grief, rage, &c. *h.*

ڈیڑھ **डेढ़** ***ḍeṛh***, one and a half. *ḍeṛh-pāw*, three-eighths. *ḍeṛh-pauwā*, a weight, three-eighths of a *ser*. *ḍeṛh īnṭ kī masjid judī banānī*, (lit. to make a separate temple of a brick and a half) to withdraw, from pride, from the society of others. *ḍeṛh bakāyan miyāṅ bāgh meṅ* (lit. the gentleman is in his garden consisting of a tree and a half); (the bakāyan, *Melia sempervirens*, is a tree of no use or estimation); applied to a person who assumes consequence without cause. *h.*

ڈیڑھ گت **डेढ़गत** ***ḍeṛh-gat***, f. a kind of dance. *h.*

ڈیگ **डेग** ***ḍeg***, m. step, pace. *h.*

ڈیل **डील** ***ḍīl***, m. f. stature, body, size, bulk; ploughed land. *h.*

ڈیل **डेल** ***ḍel***, ڈیلا **डेला** ***ḍelā***, m. a lump of earth. *h.*

ڈین **डैन** ***ḍaiṅ***, m. wings of birds. *s.*

ڈین **डयन** ***ḍayan***, m. a car or litter carried on men's shoulders; a pālkī, a dooly; flying, flight. *s.*

ڈینا **डेना** ***ḍenā***, m. a log tied to the neck of a vicious ox. *h.*

ڈینا **डैना** ***ḍainā***, m. a branch, a bough. *h.*

ڈینگ **डींग** ***ḍīng***, m. boasting, gasconading, *ḍīng-mārnā*, a. to make a boast. *h.*

ڈینگي **डींगी** ***ḍīngī***, f. a boat, a ferry-boat. *ḍīngī-wālā*, a boatman, a ferryman. *h.*

ڈیوڑھا **डेवढ़ा** ***ḍeoṛhā***, half as much again; a mode of reckoning used to denote interest in kind or grain at the rate of fifty per cent. *h.*

ڈیوڑھانا **डेवढ़ाना** ***ḍeoṛhānā***, a. to take once and a half more; to receive back the sum lent with fifty per cent. interest. *h.*

ڈیوڑھي **डेवढ़ी** ***ḍe,oṛhī***, f. a threshold, a door, antechamber. *ḍeoṛhī-dār*, a doorkeeper. *h.*

ڈیولا **डेवला** ***ḍewalā***, ڈیولہ **डेवलः** ***ḍewala***, also *ḍe,olā*, &c., mounds, high ground. *h.*

ڈیہ **डीह** ***ḍīh***, m. a haunt, a place, a dwelling, village; also the site of a deserted village. *p.*

ڈیہا **डीहा** ***ḍīhā***, m. a small bank or mound. *h.*

ڈیہڑ **डेहड़** ***ḍehuṛ***, f. a volley, several muskets discharged at once. *h.*

ڈیہڑي **डेहड़ी** ***ḍehuṛī***, f. threshold, &c. (v. *ḍeoṛhī*). *h.*

ذ

ذ ***ẕāl***, called *dāli mu'jama*, is the ninth letter of the Arabic alphabet, the eleventh Pers., and thirteenth Hind. Its existence in Persian, except as a substitute for *dāl*, q. v., appears very doubtful, nor does it exist in the Sanskrit and Indian dialects thence derived: it is pronounced by the Arabs like *th* in the English word *thou*; but in Hindūstānī its sound is not to be distinguished from that of *ze*, which is exactly our own letter *z*. In reckoning by *abjad* it stands for 700. *h.*

ذابح ***ẕābiḥ***, a sacrificer, a butcher. *sa'du-ẕ-ẕābiḥ*, two bright stars in the left horn of Capricorn. *a.*

ذات ***ẕāt***, f. a mistress, possessor; the soul, essence, substance, nature; the person viewed as the body and soul, in opposition to *badan*, the material body; caste. *ẕāt-jānā*, n to be outcast. *ẕāt-dena*, a. to give up one's caste or relinquish the benefits of one's religion by eating, &c. with a person of another sect; also to give caste, or receive into any sect as a member. *ẕat ke gun nikālnā*, to act wickedly, to shew the nature of the beast, to exhibit the cloven foot. *ẕāt-lenā* or *-mārnā*, a. to deprive another of caste, by touching his food, &c. *h.*

ذاتي ***ẕātī***, ذاتیلا ***ẕātīlā***, essential, natural, innate (opposed to *ṣifātī*, acquired or artificial). *a.*

ذاف ***ẕāf***, m. sudden death. *a.*

ذاکر ***ẕākir***, remembering, grateful, one who remembers or praises God. *a.*

ذاهل ***ẕāhil***, careless, forgetful. *a.*

ذائق ***ẕā,iḳ***, tasting, one who tastes. *a.*

ذائقه ***ẕā,iḳa***, m. the sense of tasting, the palate, relish, taste. *a.*

ذبح ***ẕabḥ***, f. a sacrifice, slaughter. *ẕabḥ-k.*, n. to sacrifice; to kill (animals for food agreeably to the *Muḥammadan* law), to slaughter. *a.*

ذبیح ***ẕabīḥ***, sacrificed; m. a sacrifice. *ẕabīḥu-l-lāh*, the sacrifice of God; a name of Isma'īl (not of Isaac), the son of Ibrāhīm (Abraham). *a.*

ذخائر ***ẕakhā,ir*** (pl. of ذخیره), victuals, provision, treasures, stores. *a.*

ذخر ***ẕukhr***, ذخیره ***ẕakhīra***, m. treasure, provisions, victuals, stores. *a.*

ذر ***ẕarr***, ذرا ***ẕarrā***, m. an atom, a little (v. *ẕarra*). *a.*

ذرات ***ẕarrāt*** (pl. of ذره), atoms, particles. *a.*

ذراره ***ẕarāra***, m. particles scattered from any thing pounding. *a.*

ذراع *zirā'*, m. a yard; a cubit; two bright stars in the head of Gemini. *a.*

ذروت *zirwat* and *zurwat*, f. the summit, pinnacle; majesty, pomp. *a.*

ذره *zarra*, m. an atom, a particle, a little. *zarra-wār*, humble, lowly, a mere atom. *a.*

ذري *zarrī*, an atom, a small particle. *a.*

ذريعه *zarī'a*, m. medium, means. *zarī'e (se)*, by means of, &c. *a.*

ذريت *zurrīyat*, f. race, lineage, offspring. *a.*

ذعاف *zu'āf*, m. deadly venom. *a.*

ذعف *zu'uf* (pl. of ذعاف), poisons. *a.*

ذقن *zaḳan*, m. the chin, the beard. *chāhi zaḳan*, m. a dimple in the chin. *a.*

ذكا *zakā*, m. vivacity, acuteness of genius, penetration. *zukā*, m. the sun. *a.*

ذكاوت *zakāwat*, f. brightness of genius, acuteness. *a.*

ذكر *zikr*, m. remembrance, memory, commemoration, mention; praise, fame, recital, relation; reciting the *Kur,ān*, repeating the names, attributes, and praises of God. *zikr-k.*, to mention.

ذكر *zakar*, m. *membrum virile*, male; the masculine gender. *a.*

ذكوره *zakūra*, m. the male sex. *a.*

ذكي *zakī*, acute, ingenious; fiery, flaming. *zakīyu-l-ma'ī*, of a splendid genius. *a.*

ذل *zull*, m. baseness, meanness. *zill*, m. gentleness, ease. *a.* [sequiousness. *a.*

ذلالت *zalālat*, f. abjectness, baseness; ob-

ذلام *zulām*, m. the cholic. *a.*

ذلت *zullat* or *zillat*, f. baseness, meanness, (for *zallat*) error, blunder. *a.*

ذلق *zalḳ*, m. a prompt and ready or eloquent tongue. *ḥarfu-z-zalḳ*, lingual letter, as *re*, *lām*, *nūn*. *a.*

ذلك *zālik* or *zālika*, dem. pron. that. *a.*

ذلل *zalal*, baseness, meanness. *a.*

ذليل *zalīl*, abject, submissive, mean, contemptible, wretched, base. *a.*

ذم *zamm*, m. blame, reproach, accusation, detraction. *a.*

ذمائم *zamā,im* (pl. of ذميمت), crimes, misdeeds; base qualities. *a.*

ذمه *zimma*, m. trust, charge, obligation, subjection, duty, service, fidelity, lineage. *zimma lenā*, a. to take charge, to take care of, to take upon one's self. *a.*

ذمي *zimmī*, an infidel (*i.e.* a person who is not a *Musalmān*) subject to a *Muḥammadan* government. *a.*

ذميم *zamīm*, blameable, culpable. *a.*

ذنب *zanab*, a tail; (in astronomy) the tail of the dragon, the descending node. *a.*

ذنب *zamb*, m. a crime, sin, fault. *a.*

ذنوب *zunūb* (pl. of ذنب), crimes. *a.*

ذو *zū*, a lord, a master; (in comp.) implies possessed of or endowed with, as *zū-l-jalāl*, glorious, splendid. *zū-l-janāḥ*, "the winged one," name of the horse of *Ḥusain*, the son of *'Alī*. *zū-l-ḳa'da*, and *zū l-ḥijja* (see *zī-ḳa'da* and *zī-ḥijja*). *zū-ma'nī* (probably intended for *zu-l-ma'nain*), a pun, a joke, a double entendre. *zu-l-faḳār*, name of *'Alī's* sword. *zū-l-ḳurbā*, a kinsman. *zū-l-nūn*, name of a celebrated saint and sūfy. *zū-l-ḳarnain*, lord of the two horns (*i. e.* of the East and West), an epithet of Alexander the Great. *zū-zanab*, tailed (a comet). *a.*

ذواق *zawwāḳ*, m. a taster. *a.*

ذوانب *zawānib* (pl. of ذنب), tails. *a.*

ذوق *zauḳ*, m. taste, delight, joy, pleasure, voluptuousness. *zauḳ se*, with pleasure, willingly, with all my heart. *a.*

ذوي *zawī* (ob. pl. of ذو), lords, masters, possessors. *zawī-l-ikrām*, held in veneration. *a.*

ذهاب *zahāb*, departure, failure (of one's senses, &c.). *a.*

ذهب *zahab*, gold, the yolk of an egg. *a.*

ذهل *zahl*, m. forgetting, leaving, carelessly abandoning. *a.*

ذهن *zihn*, m. understanding, memory, genius, ability. *zihni daḳīḳ*, a subtle genius. *a.*

ذهول *zahūl*, m. oblivion, forgetting. *a.*

ذهين *zahīn*, sagacious, ingenious. *a.*

ذي *zī* (obl. case of *zū*), a lord, a master; (in comp.) possessed of, endowed with, as *zī-hosh*, sensible, *zī-rūḥ*, rational, spiritual. *a.*

ذي حجه *zī-ḥijja*, m. the name of the last month of the *Muḥammadan* year, on the 10th day of which month is the festival of *baḳar'īd*. *a.*

ذي قعده *zī-ḳa'da*, the eleventh month of the *Muḥammadan* lunar year, consisting of thirty days. *a.*

ذيل *zail*, m. the skirt of a garment, the train of a robe, the last, hinder, or supplementary part of any thing, the sequel, that which follows or is annexed, as a list of particulars mentioned in a letter. *a.*

ر

ر र *re* or *rā*, called *rāe muhmala*, and *rāe ghair manḳūṭa*, is the tenth letter in the Arabic, twelfth in the Persian, and fourteenth in the Hindustānī alphabets. In reckoning by *abjad* it stands for 200. Its sound is that of *r* as pronounced by the Scotch and Irish; that is, it is much more marked than the English *r*. It is interchangeable with *lām*; as *dajra* for *dajla*, the river Tigris; *tarwār* for *talwār*, a sword. In Hindī, besides *lām* it is also interchanged with *ṛa*: as *daṛaknā* for *daraknā*, to split. In almanacks it is the astronomical character for the moon, and in dates it denotes the month *rabī'u-l-awwal*. *a. h. p.*

راب राब *rāb*, f. syrup. *h.*

رابڑي राबड़ी *rābṛī*, f. a kind of food like pap. *h.*

رابطا, *rābiṭa*, conjunction, bond, connection. *a.*

راين, रावण *rāban* or *rāvan* (for *rāvaṇa*): it is said that *Vishṇū* having an inclination for war, occasioned a Brāhman to curse his two doorkeepers, *Jaya* and *Vijaya*, wishing that they might be born on earth three times, after each time returning to their original forms of porters to the deity. By this means *Vishṇū* contrived to be nearly matched on earth, so as to have a good battle. They first appeared as *Hiraṇyākshha* and *Hiraṇyakashipu*, then as *Rāvaṇa* and *Kumbhakarṇa*, and lastly as *Shishupāl* and *Dantavaktra*, in each of which characters they opposed the deity in different *avatārs*. *s.*

رابنا, *rābnā*, n. to toil, to labour. *d.*

راپي, *rāpi*, a currier's knife. *d.*

رات, रात *rāt*, f. night. *rāt thoṛī aur sāng bahut* is applied to express a hurry of business with little time to perform it in, or as our vernacular hath it, "the devil to pay and no pitch hot;" also great expense with a small income. *ban jo kuchh ban sake jawānī meṅ*; *rāt thoṛī hai aur bahut hai sāng*, acquire whatever you can in the season of youth, the task is arduous and the time short (*ars longa, vita brevis*: *Hippoc.*). *rāton-rāt*, in the middle of the night. *ādhī-rāt*, midnight. *s.*

راتا, राता *rāta*, red; dyed; coloured. *s.*

راتب, *rātib*, m. daily allowance of food (to animals, particularly dogs and elephants); allowance, portion, provision. *a.*

راتبه, *rātiba*, m. salary, stipend, pay. *rātiba khur*, a stipendiary, a pensionary. *a.*

راتر, रात्रि *rātri*,
راتري, रात्री *rātrī*, } f. the night (v. *rāt*). *rātri-char*, moving at night; m. a goblin, a fiend; a thief, a robber; a guard, a patrol. *s.*

راتنا, रातना *rātnā*, a. to dye (with colour), to stain; to be strongly attached or in love (lit. stained with the dye of love). *s.*

راتوندها, रातौंधा *rātaundhā*, m. night blindness, nyctalopia. *s.*

راتهوڑ, *rāthoṛ*, strong, firm. *d.*

راج, राज *rāj*, m. government, sovereignty, kingdom, reign, sway; (in comp.) king, prince. *rāj-bansī*, descendant of a king; a *rājpūt* tribe. *rāj-bhūban* or *rāj-bhavan*, m. a royal residence, a palace. *rāj-bhog*, m. victuals placed before idols at noon. *rāj-pat* or *-pati*, m. a Hindū title, prince. *rāj-patnī*, f. a queen. *rāj-pāṭṭ*, a king's cushion, throne. *rāj-tilak*, the royal mark on the forehead, the ceremony of coronation. *rāj-tejas*, m. majesty, kingly dignity. *rāj-judhwā*, m. a rebel, one making war against a king. *rāj-jogya*, suitable for a king, princely. *rāj-darshan*, m. a levee, an audience. *rāj-droh*, m. oppression; rebellion. *rāj-drohī*, a rebel, a traitor. *rāj-daṇḍ*, m. punishment ordered by the king; sceptre. *rāj-dwār*, the gate of a palace or royal residence. *rāj-dhurā*, f. royal state or function, government. *rāj-dharm*, m. royal duty; the duties of the military caste. *rāj-dhan*, m. royal revenue or right to property. *rāj-rāj*, m. kings of kings, an emperor. *rāj-rog*, a mortal disease; consumption. *rāj-sabhā*, f. a royal assembly, the royal court. *rāj-sattā*, f. majesty, royal dignity. *rāj-sarp*, m. the king-serpent, a boa. *rāja-swa*, m. royal revenue or tax. *rāj-sevak*, a courtier, a royal attendant. *rāj-shāsan*, m. a royal edict. *rāj-kārj*, m. royal duties, state affairs. *rāj-kul*, m. a royal race; a prince. *rāj-kumār* or *rāj-kuṅwar*, m. a king's son, a prince. *rāj-kanyā*, f. a princess. *rāj-gādī*, f. a king's cushion a throne. *rāj-guru*, m. the king's spiritual preceptor. *rāj-lakshan*, m. royal insignia, any natural mark indicating royalty. *rāj-lekh*, m. a royal letter or order. *rāj-mārg*, m. a royal road, one passable for horses and elephants, and 40 cubits broad. *rāj-mandir*, a palace, a royal residence. *rāj-nīti*, f. the art of government, the duties of a prince, both in peace and war; name of a work on the art of government. *rāj-wat*, royal, kingly. *rāj-wansī* or *rāj-vaṅsya*, of royal descent, a *rājpūt*. *rāj-vījī*, springing from a royal race. *s.*

راج, राज *rāj*, m. a mason, bricklayer. *p.*

راجا, राजा *rājā*, m. a king, a prince. *s.*

راجادهراج, राजाधिराज *rājādhirāj*, m. supreme ruler of princes, king of kings. *s.*

راجاگيا, राजाज्ञा *rājāgyā* or *rājāgnyā*, f. a command from the sovereign, a royal *farmān*. *s.*

راجاو, राजाऊ *rājā,ū*, kingly, royal. *s.*

راجاورت, राजावर्त *rājāvart*, m. a kind of diamond, v. *rāj-paṭṭ*. *s.*

راجاولي, राजावली *rājāvalī*, f. a line of kings, a dynasty or royal genealogy. *s.*

راجبنسي, राजवंशी *rāj-baṅsī*, m. descendant of a *rājā*; the name of a *rāj-pūt* tribe. *s.*

راجبها, राजबहा *rāj-bahā*, the main channel, the principal or common branch of a canal. *s.*

راجپتر, राजपुत्र *rāj-putr*, a prince; a *kshatrī* or man of the military caste. *s.*

راجپتري, राजपुत्री *rāj-putrī*, a princess. *s.*

راجپٹ, राजपट्ट *rāj-paṭṭ*, m. a gem, said to be an inferior kind of diamond brought from *Virāṭ Des*, a country in the north-west of India; a tiara or royal fillet; f. a king's cushion, a throne. *s.*

راجپوت, राजपूत *rāj-pūt*, m. a descendant of a *rājā*; the name of a celebrated military caste. *s.*

راجپوتانا, राजपूताना *rāj-pūtānā*, the country of the *rāj-pūts*. *s.*

راجپوتي, राजपूती *rāj-pūtī*, f. courage, prowess [in war. *s.*

راجپهوڑا, राजफोड़ा *rāj-phoṛā*, m. a carbuncle or large boil, generally rising on the back of the neck, and which commonly proves fatal. The famous Hyder Ali died of this carbuncle; and in 1713 Dr. Hamilton obtained for the East-India Company a considerable grant from the Emperor Furrokhseir as a reward for having cured that prince of this dangerous malady."—(Binning.) *h.*

راجتوه, राजत्व *rājatwa*, m. sovereignty, kingcraft. *s.*

راجدهر, राजधर *rāj-dhar*, m. the prime minister [of a *rājā*. *s.*

راجدهاني, राजधानी *rāj-dhānī*, f. the metropolis, seat of empire or of government. *s.*

راجراني, राजरानी *rāj-rānī*, a queen, royal consort. *s.*

راجس, राजस *rājas*, m. lust, sensuality; adj. relating to the quality of passion. *s.*

راجستهان, राजस्थान *rājasthān*, the country of the *rāj-pūts*, also called *rāj-pūtānā*. *h.*

راجسويه, राजसूय *rāj-sūya* or राजसू *rajsū*, m. a sacrifice performed only by an universal monarch, attended by his tributary princes, as in the case of *Yudhishṭhira* and others. *s.*

راجكر राजकर *rāj-kar*, m. the royal tribute, king's taxes. *s.*

راج کشیر राजकशेरु *rāj-kasheru*, m. a fragrant grass (*Cyperus*). *s.*

راجکیه राजकीय *rājakīya*, royal, kingly. *s.*

راج گریو राजग्रीव *rāj-grīv*, m. a flat fresh-water fish. *s.*

راجنا राजना *rājnā*, n. to shine, to be adorned. *s.*

راج نیل राजनील *rāj-nīl*, m. the emerald. *s.*

راجواڑا राजवाड़ा *rāj-wāṛā*, m. the country of *rājās*; the royal domains. *s.*

راجه राजः *rāja*, m. (v. *rājā*) a king. *s.*

راج هاسك राजहासक *rāj-hāsak*, m. a large fish (*Cyprinus niloticus*). *s.*

راج هنس राजहंस *rāj-hańs*, m. a white goose with red legs and bill; the flamingo. *s.*

راجي *rājī*, hoping, asking, interceding; a client. *a.*

راجي राजी *rājī*, f. a row, a line. *s.*

راجيادهكار राज्याधिकार *rājyādhikār*, m. government of a kingdom; right or title to a sovereignty. *s.*

راجيسور *rājeswar*, راجيشور *rājeshwar*, राजेश्वर m. a sovereign prince, a lord, a governor. *s.*

راجيندر राजेन्द्र *rājendra*, m. an emperor. *s.*

راجيو राजीव *rājīv*, m. a large fish (*Cyprinus niloticus*). *s.*

راجيوگيه राजयोग्य *rāj-yogya*, befitting a prince. *s.*

راجيه राज्य *rājya*, m. government, kingdom, sovereignty. *rājya-bhrashṭa* or *rājya-chyut*, deposed, fallen from royalty. *rājya-bhrans*, m. or *rājya-chyuti*, f. deposal or loss of a kingdom. *rājya-bhang*, m. subversion of sovereignty. *rājya-rakshā*, f. protection or defence of a kingdom. *s.*

راچنا राचना *rāchnā*, n. to be affected or imbued with love, to be strongly attached. *s.*

راچه राछ *rāchh*, m. apparatus. *s.*

راچهس राछस *rāchhas*, m. (for *rākshas*) a demon, the name of the evil spirits of the Hindūs. *s.*

راچهس بياه राछसब्याह *rāchhas-byāh*, a sort of devil's marriage, which consists in the violent seizure and rape of a girl after the destruction of all her relatives. *s.*

راچهسني राछसनी *rāchhasnī*, f. a female demon. *s.*

راچهسي राछसी *rāchhasī*, (fem. of *rāchhas*) a she-devil; adj. devilish, demoniacal. *s.*

راح *rāḥ*, wine; enjoying satisfaction. *a.*

راحت *rāḥat*, f. quiet, repose, ease, tranquillity. *a.*

راحله *rāḥila*, a company travelling together for mutual security, a caravan. *a.*

راحم *rāḥim*, compassionate, merciful. *a.*

راخ *rākh*, ashes (same as *rākh*, q. v.). *d.*

راد राद *rād* (also *rādh*), f. pus, matter. *h.*

رادها राधा *rādhā*, the name of *Krishṇa*'s mistress, who is also called *rādhikā*. *s.*

رادهانگري राधानगरी *rādhānagarī*, m. a kind of silk cloth made at Rādhānagar. *s.*

رار रार *rār*, راڙ राड़ *rāṛ*, f. wrangling, quarrel, fray, contention. *h.*

راري रारी *rārī*, راڙي राड़ी *rāṛī*, f. a coarse kind of grass; adj. quarrelsome, contentious. *h.*

راڑه राढ़ *rāṛh*, m. name of that portion of Bengal which lies west of the Ganges. *h.*

راڑهي राढ़ी *rāṛhī*, a native of *Rāṛh*, a Brāhman from that place. *h.*

راڙي *rāṛī*, the sharp point of an arrow, or pen. *d.*

راز *rāz*, m. a secret, a mystery. *rāz-posh*, one who conceals a secret. *rāz-poshī*, the concealing of a secret. *rāz-dār*, trusty, faithful, confident; a mason, a bricklayer. *rāzi nihufta*, a hidden secret. *rāz-niyāz*, secrets of lovers, loving prattle. *p.*

رازق *rāziḳ*, m. sustainer, cherisher, affording sustenance, a title of the Deity. *a.*

رازي *rāzī*, of or relating to a secret. *p.*

راس रास *rās*, m. the name of a Hindū festival including songs and dances, celebrated in the month of *Kārtik*, in commemoration of the dances performed by *Krishṇa* and the *Gopīs*. *rās-dhārī*, a dancing-boy who imitates the *rās* of *Krishṇa*. *rās-yātrā*, f. the *rās* festival. *rās*, f. heap; a sign of the zodiac. *rās-chakr*, or *rāsa-chakra*, m. the zodiac (v. *rāshi*). *s.*

راس रास *rās*, f. reins of a bridle; usury; corn separated from the chaff; adoption. *rās-ānā*, to be agreeable. *rās-biṭhānā* or *-lenā*, a. to adopt a son. *rās-nishīn*, an adopted son. *h.*

راس *rās*, m. the head; a head of cattle (*i. e.* one ox or one horse). *rāsu-s-saraṭān*, the summer solstice. *rāsu-l-jadī*, the winter solstice. *rās fakaṭ*, a horse of middling breed. *rās kalān*, a horse of high caste. *rāsu-l-māl*, the principal or capital stock. *a.*

راست *rāst*, right, true, good, just, sincere; right (opposite of left); straight, even, level; actually, certainly. *rāst ānā*, n. to regain one's temper, to be set to rights. *rāst-bāz*, faithful, to be depended on (lit. one who plays or acts fair). *rāst-bāzī*, f. fidelity. *rāst-mu'āmala*, proper, just, of good actions, of upright conduct. *p.*

راستا *rāstā*, راسته *rāsta*, m. a road, a street. *p.*

راستي *rāstī*, f. truth, sincerity, fidelity, justice, loyalty, rectitude. *p.*

راسخ *rāsikh*, firm, durable, constant, rooted; sincere, learned. *a.*

راسنا रास्ना *rāsnā*, f. a plant (*Mimosa octandra*); another plant (the serpent *Ophioxylon?*); a sort of perfume. *s.*

راسو *rāsū*, m. a mongoose (*Viverra mungo*). *p.*

راسي, रासी *rāsī*, of middling breed (a horse); indifferent, so so. *h.*

راش, राशि *rāshi*, m. a heap, a quantity; a sign of the zodiac; a part and its divisor, or numerator and denominator. *rāshi-bhāg*, m. a fraction. *rāshi-bhog*, m. passage of a planet through a sign of the zodiac. *rāshi-chakra*, m. the zodiac. *rāshi-kṛit*, heaped, piled. *rāshi-karan*, m. heaping, piling. *s.*

راشٹر, राष्ट्र *rāshṭra*, m. a realm, a country. *s.*

راشٹرکا, राष्ट्रिका *rāshṭrikā*, f. a prickly night-shade (*Solanum jacquini*). *s.*

راشد, *rāshid*, pious, faithful, orthodox, following the right path. *a.*

راشي, *rāshī*, m. one who bribes. *a.*

راضي, *rāẓī*, satisfied, contented, agreed, pleased, willing. *rāẓī ba riẓā*, God willing. *a.*

راضي نامه, *rāẓī-nāma*, m. an acknowledgment of a cause being finally settled, given by the plaintiff: the defendant gives a *ṣāfī-nāma*, a general release. *a.*

راعي, *rā'ī*, a shepherd, a manager. *a.*

راغ, *rāgh*, m. a declivity, the lower part of a mountain; the top of a hill; a pleasant verdant meadow; a villa, a summer-house. *p.*

راغب, *rāghib*, willing, wishing; adj. desirous, curious. *a.* [*Shī'a*, q. v. *a.*

رافضي, *rāfiẓī*, m. a heretic, particularly a

رافع, *rāfi'*, elevating, exalting; repelling; carrying off. *a.*

راقب, *rāḳib*, m. a rival, an observer. *a.*

راقم, *rāḳim*, m. one who writes, a writer. *rāḳimu-l-ḥurūf*, the writer of these letters, *i. e.* of this epistle, of this book, &c. *a.*

راکا, राका *rākā*, f. full moon, the day of full moon; (in Dakh.) a cup made of the palmyra. *s.*

راکب, *rākib*, m. a rider; adj. mounted (on a horse, ship, &c). *a.*

راکتي, *rākṭī*, an ornament worn by women, also called *sis-phūl* and *sūraj*: its Arabic name is *ḳurṣ*, and this ornament, under that name, has been fully described by Mr. Lane in his well-known work on the Modern Egyptians. *d.*

راکس, राकस *rākas*, } m. demon, an evil spirit; adj. demo-

راکشس, राक्षस *rākshas*, } niacal. *rākshas-byāh*, m. a form of marriage, the violent seizure and rape of a girl after the repulse or destruction of her relatives. *s.*

راکشسي, राक्षसी *rākshasī*, f. a female fiend, the female of *rākshas*: adj. demoniacal. *rākshasī belā*, the period between sunset and dark. *s.*

راکهه, राख *rākh*, f. ashes (of cow-dung). *s.*

راکهات, राखात *rākhāt*, lands set apart for grazing. *h.*

راکهس, *rākhas*, same as راچهس, q. v. *s.*

راکهس پتا, *rākhas pattā*, the aloe plant. *d.*

راکهس گڈہ, *rākhas-gaḍḍa*, devil's root, a species of air-plant (*Bryonia epigæa*). *d.*

راکهسي بيلا, राखसी बेला *rākhasī-belā*, twilight, time when evil spirits are abroad. *h.*

راکهنا, राखना *rākhnā*, a. to keep, put. *s.*

راکهي, राखी *rākhī*, f. an amulet, or string which Hindūs tie round their arms on a certain festival, held in the full moon of *Srāvana* or *Sāwan*, in honour of *Krishṇa*. *s.*

راگ, राग *rāg*, m. a mode in music (six in number, viz. *Bhairav*, *Mālav*, *Sārang*, *Hinḍol*, *Vasant*, *Dīpak*, and *Megh*), music, song, tune; anger, passion; love. *rāg chhānā*, n. to be in concert. *rāg-rang*, m. music. *rāg-sāgar*, m. a song composed of many *rāgs* or musical modes. *rāg-mālā*, f. the name of a treatise on music (nothing more than a collection of pictures, exhibiting the traditional history of the primary and subordinate modes and the subjects appropriated to each). *s.*

راگ چون, रागचून *rāg-chūn*, m. a tree yielding an astringent resin, the wood of which is used in dyeing (*Mimosa catechu*). *s.*

راگنا, रागना *rāgnā*, a. to begin to sing. *s.*

راگني, रागिणी *rāginī*, f. a mode in music (wives of *rāgs*, thirty in number). *s.*

راگهو, राघव *rāghav*, m. a sort of fish. *s.*

راگي, रागी *rāgī*, f. a singer; a libertine; a lover; adj. passionate. *s.*

راگي, *rāgī*, f. name of a grain commonly called by Europeans Natchenny (*Cynosurus coracanus*); also called *lachhnā* and *manṛūā*. *d.*

رال, राल *rāl*, f. resin; the fragrant exudation of the *Shorea robusta*; pitch; saliva. *s.*

رالا, *rālā*, m. a kind of millet. *d.*

رام, *rām*, obedient; m. a domestic, one who receives orders. *p.*

رام, राम *rām* or *rāma*, m. a name common to three incarnations of *Vishṇu*, viz. 1. *Parashu-rāma*, the son of the Muni *Jamadagni*, born at the commencement of the second or Treta jug, for the purpose of punishing the tyrannical kings of the *Kshatrī* race; 2. *Rāma-chandra*, the son of *Dasaratha*, king of Oude, born at the close of the second age to destroy the demons who infested the earth, and especially *Rāvana*, the king of Ceylon; 3. *Bala-rāma*, the elder brother of *Krishṇa*, born at the end of the third age. *rām-bhati*, f. calling out for redress, complaint. *rām-kahānī*, the *rāmāyana*; a long story. *rām-duhā,ī*, f. an asseveration of *Rāma*, or the Deity. *rām-dhanush*, the rainbow. *rām-rām*, a Hindū form of salutation. *s.*

رامانندي, रामानन्दी *rāmānandī*, m. a kind of Hindū ascetic, followers of *Rāmānand*; believers in *Rāma*. *s.*

راماوت, रामा :त *rāmāvat*, m. the system or tenets of a sect of Hindū ascetics. *s.*

راماوتار, रामावतार *rāmāvatār*, m. the seventh incarnation of *Vishṇu*, in the form of *Rāmachandra* q.v. for the purpose of destroying the tyrant *Rāvana*. *s*

رامائن, रामायण *rāmāyaṇ* or *rāmāyaṇa*, f. an epic poem by *Vālmīki*, containing the history of *Rāma*. Poems on the same subject and under the same title have been composed by other authors. *s.*

رامبهت, रामभति *rāmbhati*, f. calling out for redress, complaint. *s.*

رامبهنا, रामभना *rāmbhnā*, n. to low, to bellow, cry out. *s.*

رامپي, राम्पी *rāmpī* (v. *rāṅpī*), f. a shoemaker's knife. *h.*

رامتري, रामतुरई *rāmtura,ī*, f. the name of a vegetable, ochra (*Hibiscus esculentus*). *h.*

رام تلسي, रामतुलसी *rām-tulasī*, f. a plant (*Ocymum gratissimum*). *s.*

رامجني, रामजनी *rāmjanī*, f. a Hindū dancing-girl, a prostitute (vulg. Rum Johney). *s.*

رامچندر, रामचन्द्र *rāmachandra*, was son of *Dasharatha*, and conqueror of *Lankā* or Ceylon. He was the seventh *avatār*, when the deity descended for the purpose of destroying *Rāvana*, who having (for his devotion) a promise from *Brahmā* that he should not suffer death by any of the usual means, was become the tyrant and pest of mankind. The *Devatās* came in the shape of monkeys, as *Rāvana* had gained no promise of safety from them; hence *Hanumān* was *Rāma's* general. *Rāmachandra's* mother's name was *Kaushalyā*, his younger brother *Bharata* was son of *Kaikeyī*, who was the cause of *Rāma's* going to the desert to perform devotions, on the banks of the *Pampā-nadī*, insisting that her son should reign the fourteen years that *Rāma* employed in the devotion. It was while performing his devotion (or during his stay in the forests) in company with *Lakshmana* (his brother by *Sumitrā*) that *Rāvana* appeared as a beggar, while he was absent hunting, and enticed away *Shītā*, which gave rise to the war detailed in the *Rāmāyaṇa*. *Shītā* was daughter of *Janaka Rājā*, who had promised to give her to any person who could break a certain bow, which was done by *Rāmachandra*. When in the forest, he drew a circle round *Shītā*, and forbade her to go beyond it, and left *Lakshmana* to take care of her; but *Lakshmaṇa* hearing some noise which alarmed him for his brother, left her to seek him: then it was that *Rāvana* appeared and enticed her out of the circle (*gaṇḍī*), and carried her off in his flying chariot: in the air he was opposed by the bird *Jaṭāyu*, whose wings he cut and escaped. *Rāmachandra* reigned in Oudh (*Ayodhya*) before Christ 1600. *s.*

رامبٹاءي, रामबटाई *rāmbaṭā,ī*, f. division of the crop between the landlord and tenant. *h.*

رامدهاءي, रामधाई *rām-dhā,ī*, an asseveration on oath by *Rāma* (also *rām-duhā,ī*). *h.*

رامچيرا, रामचेरा *rāmcherā*, m. (lit. slave of *Rāma*) a man's name, particularly that of a slave. *s.*

رامسر, रामसर *rāmsar*, m. the name of a wood; the name of a kind of reed. *s.*

رامش, *rāmish*, harmony, modulation; hilarity, mirth; rest, ease. *rāmish-gar*, a musician. *p.*

رامكري, रामकरी *rāmkarī*, | **رامكلي, रामकली** *rāmkalī*, | **رامكيلي, रामकेली** *rāmkelī*, } f. name of a *rāginī* or musical mode. *s.*

رام گر, रामगिरि *rām-giri*, m. Rāma's mountain, a name especially applied to a mountain called *Kompts* or *Chitr-kūṭ*, in Bundelkhand, and also to another near Nagpore, called now *Rām-ṭek*. *s.*

رامون, राममून *rāmmūn*, m. a kind of goat. *h.*

ران, *rān*, f. the thigh. *rān tale dabānā*, to press one under one's thigh; to subdue; to have completely in one's power. *rān se rān bāndhnā*, a. to guard or watch diligently; used in comp. in the sense of driving, managing, as *kām-rān*, prosperous (lit. driving one's business, or desire). *p.*

رانا, राणा or **राना** *rānā*, m. a Hindū prince or *rājā*, in central India; a tribe of *rāj-pūts*. *h.*

رانبهنا, रांभना *rāmbhnā*, n. to low, to bellow, cry out. *s.*

رانپي, रांपी *rāmpī*, f. an iron instrument for scraping leather. *s.*

رانجها, रांझा *rānjhā*, | **رانجهن, रांझन** *rānjhan*, | **رانجهنا, रांझना** *rānjhnā*, } m. an estimable person, a sweetheart. *s.*

راندا, *rāndā*, a carpenter's plane. *d.*

راندپڑوس, रांदपड़ोस *rāndpaṛos*, m. neighbourhood. *h.*

راندن, *rāndan*, to expel, to drive out, to drive off or away. *p.*

راندنا, *rāndnā*, a. (Hind. form of *rāndan*) to expel, &c. *p.*

راندني, रांदनी *rāndnī*, f. parsley. *h.*

رانده, *rānda*, rejected, abandoned. *p.*

راندهنا, रांधना *rāndhnā*, a. to cook, to dress food. *s.*

راندهنيا, रांधनैया *rāndhanaiyā*, a cook, a baker. *s.*

رانڈ, रांड *rānḍ*, f. a widow; a woman. *rānḍ kā sānḍ*, lit. "a widow's stallion," *i. e.* a gallant, or "cavaliere serviente," hence, a base, contemptible fellow. *s.*

رانڈا, रांडा *rānḍā*, barren; the mango-fish without roes are so called. It is particularly applied to unproductive trees, such as the male palm, &c. *s*

رانڈاپا, रांडापा *rānḍāpā*, m. widowhood. *s.*

رانگ, रांग *rāng*, f. | **رانگا, रांगा** *rāngā*, m. } pewter, tin. *s.*

رانگبهرا, रांगभरा *rāngbharā*, m. a toyman. *h.*

راني, राणी or **रानी** *rānī*, f. a (Hindū) queen or princess. *s.*

راو, राव *rāw* or *rā,o*, a prince, a Hindū title. *ra,o krishak*, the headman of a village.

راوت, रावत *rāwat*, m. a hero; a sweeper (of a particular caste). *h.*

راوٹي, रावटी *rāwṭī*, f. a kind of tent. *h.*

راوچاو, रावचाव *rāwchāw*, f. gaiety, amusement, merriment, mirth; affection, endearment. *h.*

راورا, रावरा *rāwarā* or *rā,orā*, | **راورو, रावरौ** *rāwarau* or *rā,orāu*, } (pron. in Braj-Bhākhā) yours, of you. *h.*

راول, *rāwal*, a soldier, military. *d.*

راون रावण *rāwan*, son of *Vishravā* and *Kaikasī*, was king of *Lankā*; he carried away *Shītā*, and lost his kingdom to her husband *Rāmachandra*, q. v. *s.*

راوند *rāwand*, rhubarb. *p.*

راوي *rāwī*, m. an historian, the author of a fable, romance, fiction, &c., a narrator. *a.*

راويان *rāwiyān*, راويين *rāwiyīn*, } pl. historians, narrators. *p.a.*

راهُ राहु *rāhu*, m. Typhon, or the dragon that is supposed to devour the sun or moon during an eclipse; the ascending node. *rāhu-grās* or *rāhu-grāh*, m. an eclipse. *s.*

راه *rāh*, f. road; manner. *rāh-āward*, a present brought by one who has been on a journey. *rāh bāndhnā*, to refuse admittance, to stop one's progress. *rāh batānā*, to discharge, dismiss; to guide. *rāh-bar*, m. a guide, conductor. *rāh-barī*, f. guidance. *rāh par ānā*, to find the road which had been lost; to mend one's manners. *rāh-paṛnā*, to establish mutual confidence. *rāh chhoṛnā*, to give way. *rāh-kharch*, charges of the road, travelling expenses. *rāh-dār*, m. a collector of duties (on the road). *rāh-dārī*, f. collection of duties (on roads). *rāh dikhānā*, a. to make one wait for. *rāh dekhnā* or *taknā*, to expect, to wait for. *rāh denā*, to give one access. *rāh ḍālnā*, to establish a custom. *rāh rāh chalnā*, to continue in one's usual practice or mode of conduct. *rāh rakhnā*, to keep up an intercourse. *rāh-rav* or *-rau*, a traveller, a wayfarer. *rāh rawish*, f. manners, habits, customs. *rāh-zan*, m. a highwayman. *rāh-zanī*, f. highway robbery. *rāh-sir*, just, right. *rāh kāṭnā*, to travel a road; to quit a path or take a short cut. *rāh karnā*, to contract friendship. *rāh khoṭī karnī*, to linger on the road. *rāh guzar*, m. road, way; a traveller. *rāh-gīr*, m. a traveller, wayfarer. *rāh lagnā*, to follow one's own devices. *rāh lenā*, n. to go, to depart. *rāh-mār*, a highway robber. *rāh-mārnā*, a. to waylay, to rob; to lay one under restraint, to ruin one's prospects in life. *rāh marnā*, the trace of a path being effaced. *rāh nāpnā*, to walk about idly, to employ one's self unprofitably. *rāh-nāma*, a road-book. *rāh nikālnā*, to devise a new mode of conduct. *rāh-numā*, m. a conductor, guide, leader. *rāh-numā,ī*, f. leading. *rāh-wār*, ambling, a pace (in horsemanship), a gait generally taught to *ṭāngans*. *rāhwārī*, f. ambling (a horse). *p.*

راهب *rāhib*, a monk, a Christian priest. *p.*

راهدار *rāh-dār*, an officer employed in collecting land duties, also a road patrol. *p.*

راهداري *rāh-dārī*, an authorized branch of revenue, arising from duties collected from travellers by the officers of government stationed on the high roads for the protection of passengers. It was formerly levied on goods passing and repassing the public roads. In Bahar there were, in many districts, *chaukīs* or stationary guards, for the protection of the roads, known by the name of *chaukī rāhdārī*, on account of which revenue was collected and paid into the *nizāmat*; in Dakhanī, the term *rāh-dārī* denotes a guide; a passport, a warrant, a permit. *rāh-dārī kī chiṭṭhī*, a passport, a permit. *p.*

راهو राहू *rāhū*, m. (v. *rāhu*) name of a [demon. *s.*

راهن *rāhin*, m. a mortgager, one who borrows on a pledge or pawn. *a.*

راهنا राहना *rāhnā*, a. to roughen a millstone (by digging little pits in its surface with a small pickaxe). *h.*

راهي *rāhī*, m. a traveller, wayfarer. *p.*

راي राए or राय *rā,e*, m. a (Hindū) prince, a chief. *rā,e rāyān*, m. a Hindū title (lit. the chief of princes); the *dīwān* of the *khāliṣa* or chief treasurer: according to Gladwin the *rā,e rāyān* is the principal officer under the *dīwān* of the provinces, who has the immediate charge of the crown lands, and is the superintendant of the *khāliṣa*. *s.*

راءي राई *rā,ī*, f. a species of (*sarson*) mustard; a kind of mustard-seed with very small grains (*Sinapis ramosa*). *raī-kā,ī*, broken to atoms. *h.*

راي *rā,e* or *rā,ī*, f. wisdom, opinion, thought, counsel. *rā,ī buland*, exalted understanding. *rā,ī zadan*, to broach or express an opinion. *a. p.*

راءيا राइया *rā,iyā*, m. chaff of wheat, bran. *h.*

راءيا राइया *rā,iyā*, m. species of mustard with large seeds. *s.*

رايات *rāyāt* (pl. of رايت), standards, banners, especially of an army in motion; (met.) a camp. *a.*

راي بانس राएबांस *rā,e-bāns*, m. a kind of spear. *h.*

راي بيل राएबेल *rā,e-bel*, f. a kind of flower. *h.*

رايت *rāyat*, f. a standard, a banner. *a.*

راءيتا रायता *rā,etā*, m. pumpkins, &c., pickled in sour milk. *h.*

رائج *rā,ij*, customary, current, usual, common. *rā,iju-l-waqt*, the fashion or custom of the time. *a.*

رائحه *rā,iḥa*, m. fragrance, perfume; an odour. *a.*

راءيگان *rā,egān*, gratis, gratuitous; in vain. *p.*

راءيمني रायमनी *rā,e-manī*, راي منيا रायमनिया *rā,e-maniyā*, } m. a kind of rice (in the husk). *h.*

رائيا राईया *rā,iyā*, m. chaff; mustard (v. راءيا).

رب *rabb*, m. a lord, protector, preserver; a name of God. *rabbu-l-'ālamīn*, God, preserver of the world. *rabbu-l-'ibād*, God, the protector of his servants. *a.*

رب रबि *rabi*, m. (for *ravi*) the sun. *s.*

رب *rubb* or *rub*, m. juice, rob, syrup. *rubbu-s-sūs*, extract of liquorice. *p. a.*

ربا *rubā*, (in comp.) ravishing, stealing; as *dil-rubā*, heart-ravishing. *p.*

رباب *rabāb*, a kind of violin, a rebeck. *ribāb*, (Ar. pl. of *rubb*) inspissated juices. *p.*

رباني *rabābī*, ربابيا *rabābiyā*, } m. a player on the *rabāb*. *p.*

رباط *ribāṭ*, an hotel, an inn, a caravanserai; a rope, a ligament (pl. *ribāṭāt*). *a.*

رباطي *ribāṭī*, an innkeeper. *a.*

رباعي *rubā'ī*, f. a quatrain, a stanza of four lines. *a.*

رباعيات *rubā'iyāt*, quatrains (pl. of *rubā'ī*). *a.*

ربانا *rabānā*, to cause to toil or labour. *d.*

رباني *rabbānī*, divine, godly. *a.*

رباءيدن, *rubā,idan*, to seize, to carry off. *p.*

ربٻار, रबिबार *rabi-bār* (for *ravi-bār*), m. Sunday. *h.*

ربڈا, रबड़ा *rabḍā*, fatigued, wearied. *h.*

ربڑ, रबड़ *rabaṛ*, f. fatigue, fruitless labour, trudging. *h.*

ربڑا, रबड़ा *rabṛā*, fatigued, worn down. *h.*

ربڑانا, रबड़ाना *rabṛānā*, a. to fatigue, to cause to run about uselessly. *h.*

ربڑنا, रबड़ना *rabaṛnā*, n. to fatigue one's self, to run about fruitlessly. *h.*

ربڑي, रबड़ी *rabṛī*, f. thick milk; a kind of porridge made of Indian corn. *h.*

ربط, *rabṭ*, m. connection, friendship, practice, habit, use, binding. *a.*

ربع, *rub'*, m. fourth part, a quarter. "*rub' maskūn*, the fourth part of the world, which is believed to be peopled, while the remaining three quarters are supposed to be uuinhabitable."—(Binning.) *a.*

ربنا, *rabba-nā*, interj. Oh! Our Lord! *a.*

ربوب, *rubūb* (pl. of *rubb*), syrups. *a.*

ربودن, *rubūdan* (r. *rubā*), to rob, to carry off. *p.*

ربي, *rabī*, m. (v. *rabi* or *ravi*) the sun. *s.*

ربيب, *rabīb*, m. a step-son, son by a former husband. *a.*

ربيبار, रबीबार *rabī-bār*, m. Sunday. *s.*

ربيبه, *rabība*, f. step-daughter, daughter by a former husband. *a.*

ربيع, *rabī'*, f. the spring; the spring harvest, or grain sown in October and November and cut in the spring months (March-April), as peas, wheat, &c. *rabī'u-l-awwal*, the third month, and *rabī'u-l-ākhir* or *rabī'u-s-sānī*, the fourth month of the *Muhammadan* year. The ninth and twelfth days of the former are festivals. *a.* [ing to the spring, vernal. *a.*

ربيعي, *rabī'ī*, produced in the spring, belong-

رپ, रिपु *ripu*, m. an enemy. *ripu-tā*, f. enmity. *s.* [slipperiness; chase. *h.*

رپٹ, रपट *rapaṭ*, f. fatigue, hard labour;

رپٹنا, रपटना *rapaṭnā*, n. to slip, to slide. *h.*

رپرپانا, रपरपाना *raprapānā*, n. to gallop hard. *h.*

رپنا, रुपना *rupnā*, n. to be at bay, to stop. *h.*

رپهرا, रुपहरा *rupahrā*, made of silver. *s.*

رپئي, रुपए *rupa,e* (pl. for *rupaye*, &c.), rupees. *s.*

رپيه, रुपया *rupayā* or रुपैया *rupaiyā*, } m. a rupee, a

رپيه, रुपिया *rupiyā* or रुपीया *rupīyā*, } well-known coin, nearly equal to two shillings. *h.*

رت, रत *rat*, f. (contr. of *rāt*, q. v.). *rat-jagā*, watching all night on religious occasions (a female ceremony), vigil. *rat-aundhā*, blindness at night, *Nyctalopia*. *rat-aundhiyā* or *-andhlā*, blind at night. *rat meṅ honā*, n. to be in fault. *s.*

رت, ऋतु or रितु *ṛitu* (vulg. *rut*), f. season, weather: the Hindūs divide the year into six seasons, viz. *basant*, *grishma*, *varshā*, *sharad*, *hima*, and *shishira*. the menstrual evacuation. *ṛitu-prāpta*, fruitful, productive in due season. *ṛitu-snān*, m. bathing after menstruation. *ṛitu-matī*, f. a woman during the menstruation. *s.*

رت, रत *rat*, occupied or engaged in, intent on; m. coition, copulation. *s.*

رت, रति *rati*, f. love; venery, coition; Venus (wife of Cupid, v. *ratī*). *rati-kriyā*, f. copulation. *s.*

رتارتهني, रतार्थिनी *ratārthinī*, f. a libidinous woman, a harlot. *s.*

رتارتهي, रतार्थी *ratārthī*, libidinous, lewd. *a.*

رتالو, रतालू *ratālū*, m. a yam (*Dioscorea*). *s.*

رتانا, रताना *ratānā*, n. to rut, to be lewd. *s.*

رتانا, रिताना *ritānā*, a. to cause to empty. *s.*

رتاوا, *ratāwā*, an attack, assault, more particularly a sudden inroad into an enemy's territory. *d.*

رتايني, रतायनी *ratāyanī*, f. a whore, a harlot. *s.*

رتبه, *rutba*, m. rank, dignity, degree, stair, step. *a.* [rejoicings at night. *h.*

رتجگا, रतजगा *rat-jagā*, m. vigils, night-watchings,

رت ستورا, रतिसत्वरा *rati-satwarā*, f. a plant (*Trigonella corniculata*), perhaps considered as an aphrodisiac. *s.*

رتكيل, रतकेल *rat-kel*, m. venery, coition. *s.*

رتگهٹ, *rat-ghaṭ*, toil and trouble. *d.*

رتن, रतन *ratan* or रत्न *ratna*, m. a jewel, gem, a precious stone; the pupil of the eye. *ratna-jaṛit* or *-jaṭit*. set with jewels. *ratna-may*, gemmed, made of gems. *ratna-wat*, having gems. *s.*

رتنار, रतनार *ratnār*, m. red colour. *h.*

رتناكر, रत्नाकर *ratnākar*, m. the ocean; a jewel mine. *s.* [gems. *s.*

رتناولي, रत्नावली *ratnāwalī*, f. a necklace of

رتن جوت, रतनजोत *ratan-jot*, name of a plant; name of a medicine, said to be good for the eyes. *s.*

رت ندهي, रतनिधि *rat-nidhi*, m. a wagtail. *s.*

رتن سنگهاسن, रत्नसिंहासन *ratna-singhāsan*, m. a throne studded with jewels. *s.*

رتن كندل, रत्नकन्दल *ratna-kandal*, m. coral. *s.*

رتن مالا, रत्नमाला *ratan-mālā*, f. a necklace of precious stones; name of a book in astronomy; a flower. *s.*

رتن منجري, रत्नमंजरी *ratna-manjarī*, f. name of a flower, also the name of one of the thirty-two images supporting the throne of king Bikram. *s.*

رتن ورکش, रत्नवृक्ष *ratna-vṛiksh*, m. coral. *s.*

رتنيان, रतनियाँ *ratniyāṅ*, m. a kind of rice. *h.*

رتواهي, रतवाही *ratwāhī*, f. an attack in the night; a concubine who comes at night. *s.*

رتوندھ रतौंधा *rataundhā*, m. blindness at night, *nyctalopia*. *s.*

رتوندھیا रतौंधिया *rataundhiyā*, blind at night. *s.*

رتھ रथ *rath*, m. a car, a war-chariot, a four-wheeled carriage (not used for baggage), a coach. *rath-bān* or *rath-wān*, m. a coachman. *rath-bānī* or *rath-wānī*, f. coachmanship. *rath-kār*, m. a coachmaker. *rath-yātrā*, f. a procession of chariots, applied to the procession of the car of *Krishṇa* as *Jagannāth* on the second of the light fortnight of *Ashāṛh*. *s.*

رتھانگ रथाङ्ग *rathāng*, m. a wheel; the ruddy goose (*Anas casarca*). *s.*

رتھوان रथवान *rathwān*, m. a carriage-driver. *s.*

رتھوانی रथवानी *rathwānī*, f. the office of carriage-driving. *s.*

رتھی रथी *rathī*, m. the owner of a chariot, a man riding in a carriage, a charioteer. *s.*

رتی रती *ratī*, the Venus of the Hindūs, wife of *Kāmadeva* (or Cupid), who was son of *Vishṇu* and *Rukminī*: he was consumed by the fiery rage of *Mahādeva*, for interrupting him in his devotions, and *Ratī*, disconsolate for the loss of her husband, implored *Mahādeva's* mercy, who promised that she should meet him again in the house of *Shambara rājā*, whither she repaired and took service under the name of *Māyāvatī*: here, as she was one day cleaning a large fish, she discovered a child in its belly, which she immediately knew to be her husband Cupid, or *Kāmadeva*, whom (under the name of *Pradyumna*) the tyrant had thrown into the ocean: he at first took *Ratī* for his mother, but remembering the promise of *Mahādeva*, he knew his wife, and the god of love was again united to the goddess of pleasure: hence, however, *Ratī* is considered as both mother and wife of *Kāmadeva*. *s.*

رتی रती *ratī* or रत्ती *rattī*, f. a weight equal to eight barleycorns; fortune. *ratī chamaknī*, to begin to prosper, to flourish. *s.*

رتیوت रतीवत *ratīwat*, } fortunate, prosperous. *s.*
رتیونت रतीवन्त *ratīwant*, }

رٹ रट *raṭ*, f. repetition, iteration. *s.*

رٹ گھٹ *raṭghaṭ*, f. labour and toil. *d.*

رٹنا रटना *raṭnā*, a. to repeat, to iterate, to order or demand repeatedly. *s.*

رج रज *raj*, f. dust; menses; farina of flowers, (in Dakh.) a bellyful. *s.*

رج रज *raj* (for *rajas*), m. the second of the qualities incident to the state of humanity, the quality of passion or sensuality (v. *rajo-guṇ*). *s.*

رج ऋजु *ṛiju*, straight; also applied to moral rectitude. *s.*

رج रज्जु *rajju*, m. a rope, a cord, a tie, a string. *s.*

رجا *rajā*, f. hope, prayer, supplication, intercession. *a.*

رجال *rijāl*, m. (pl. of رجل) men. *rijālu-l-ghaib*, m. (by the Hindūs called *yoginī*) an invisible being which moves in a circular orbit round the world: on the 1st, 9th, 16th, and 24th days of a lunar month his station is in the east; on the 3rd, 11th, 18th, and 25th, in the south-east; on the 5th, 13th, 20th, and 28th, in the south-east; on the 4th, 12th, 19th, and 27th, in the south-west; on the 6th, 14th, 21st, and 29th, in the west; on the 7th, 15th, and 22nd, in the north-west; on the 2nd, 10th, 17th, and 25th, in the north; and on the 8th, 23rd, and 30th, in the north-east: his influence on each day is especially exerted during nine *gharis*, or three hours thirty-six minutes, at the close of that *tith* or lunar day; and in that interval it is unfortunate to begin a journey towards the station of this being, or in such a direction as to place him on the right hand. *a.*

رجالا *rijālā* (for *ruẕālā*), mean, vile, base. *a.*

رجائی *rajā,ī* (for *raẓā,ī*, q. v.), a quilt. *h.*

رجب *rajab*, m. the seventh month of the Muhammadan year: it is also called *rajabu-l-murajjab*, or the sacred *rajab* (from *rajaba*, to fear, to reverence), because in the time of paganism it was unlawful to go to war in that month. *s.*

رجت रजत *rajat*, m. silver. *s.*

رجت रजित *rajit*, affected, moved, attracted, excited. *s.*

رج جانا रजजाना *raj-jānā*, n. to be satisfied. *h.*

رجز *rajaz*, a species of metre or verse. *a.*

رجس रजस *rajas*, m. the second condition of humanity (v. *rajo-guṇ*); dust, pollen; menstruation. *rajas-walā*, f. a woman during menstruation. *s.*

رجعت *raj'at* or *rij'at*, f. a return; returning to earth after death: the word in its primitive sense means restitution; in law, it signifies a husband returning to or receiving back his wife after divorce, and restoring her to her former situation. *a.*

رجك रजक *rajak*, m. a washerman. *s.*

رجکی रजकी *rajakī*, f. a washerman's wife, or a washerwoman. *s.*

رجل *rajul*, m. a man (pl. *rijāl*). *a.*

رجم *rajm*, m. detestation, repulse, dejection; stoning to death; the punishment for adultery, according to the Muhammadan law (founded on the Jewish law). *a.*

رجنی रजनी *rajnī*, f. night. *rajnī-char*, a *rākshas* or goblin; a thief; a watchman. *rajnī-kar*, m. the moon. *rajnī-gandh*, m. the tuberose (*Polianthes tuberosa*). *rajnī-mukh*, m. beginning of night, evening. *rajnī-hāsā*, f. a flower (*Nyctanthes arbor tristis*) which blossoms at night and diffuses a powerful scent after sunset. *s.*

رجو रज्जू *rajjū*, m. f. rope, cord, thread, string. *s.*

رجواڑا रजवाड़ा *rajwāṛā*, m. a kingdom, a country under the control of a *rājā*. *s.*

رجوبندھ रजोबन्ध *rajo-bandh*, m. suppression of menstruation. *s.*

رجوع *rujū'*, m. return, turning towards, appearing; reference. *rujū'-k.*, to appeal or have recourse to a higher authority. *rujū' lānā*, a. to turn towards, to side with, to submit, to yield. *a.*

رجوگن रजोगुण *rajo-guṇ*, m. one of the three characters or dispositions assigned by the Hindūs to the human mind: they are, 1. *satwa*, benevolence; 2. *raja* love of sensual enjoyment, or of pleasure; 3. *tama* irascibility, or promptitude to the vindictive passions these are all exhibited in the Hindū Trinity: in *Brahma*, *raja* prevails; in *Vishṇu*, *satwa*; and in *Shiva* *tama*. *s.*

رجوليت *rajūliyat*, f. virility. *a.*

رجهانا रिझाना *rijhānā*, a. to please; (met.) to plague, to tease, to perplex. *s.*

رجهوار रिझवार *rijhwār*, } having the quality of being pleased, easily gratified. *s.*
رجهواڑ रिझवाड़ *rijhwāṛ*,
رجهويا रिझवैया *rijhwaiyā*,

رچ रुच *ruch* or रुचि *ruchi*, f. desire, wish, avidity, desire of, or pleasure from, eating; light, lustre. *s.*

رچا ऋचा or रिचा *richā*, f. a peculiar sort of prayer from the *Veda*, a magical invocation. *s.*

رچانا रचाना *rachānā*, a. to set to work, to set a-going; to make, to do; to make merry; to stain the hands, feet, &c. with *ḥinnā* or *mendhī*; to celebrate. *s.* [*ḥinnā*, q. v. *s.*

رچاوٹ रचावट *rachāwaṭ*, staining with

رچت रचित *rachit* or *rachita*, done, made, or written by, generally used in comp., as *Vyāsa-rachita*, composed by *Vyāsa*. *s.*

رچك रचक *rachak*, m. a maker, a composer. *a.*

رچنا रचना *rachnā*, n. to be made, to be prepared, to be set to work; to be employed, to be about (a business); to stain, to colour; to love, to like; to keep time in music; to penetrate; to predestinate; a. to make, to form, to compose; f. creation, invention; created thing, work, workmanship. *s.*

رچنا रुचना *ruchnā*, a. to excite desire; n. to be agreeable, to gratify. *s.* [ing. *s.*

رچوا रचवा *rachwā*, m. act of making or form-

رچها रच्छा *rachchhā*, f. protection, assistance, patronage; shadowing, safety. *s.*

رچهك रच्छक *rachchhak*, m. a protector, a keeper, a guard, a watchman, a redeemer. *s.*

رچهن रच्छन *rachchhan*, m. (v. *rachchhā*) act of protecting, &c. *s.*

رحل *raḥl*, m. departing, travelling; a mansion, a resting-place. *riḥl*, f. a support for a book. *a.*

رحال *riḥāl*, a kind of desk or stool on which the *ḳur,ān* is placed. *a.*

رحلت *riḥlat*, f. marching (particularly to the other world); death. *riḥlat-k.*, n. to die. *a.*

رحم *raḥm*, m. mercy, kindness, pity. *raḥm-āshnā*, a friend to mercy. *raḥm-ā.*, pity or mercy (to affect one). *raḥm khānā*, to feel pity. *raḥm-dil*, tender-hearted, merciful, kind. *a.*

رحم *riḥm* or *riḥam*, the womb. *a.*

رحمان *raḥmān*, merciful, forgiving (an epithet of God). *a.*

رحماني *raḥmānī*, divine. *a.*

رحمت *raḥmat*, f. pity, mercy, kindness. *raḥmatu-l-lāh 'alai-hi*, the mercy of God be upon him! *a.*

رحمن *raḥman* (for *raḥmān*), merciful, gracious. *a.*

رحيق *raḥīḳ*, the best wine, pure wine; the real stuff. *a.*

رحيل *raḥīl*, a journey, departure. *a.*

رحيم *raḥīm*, merciful (an epithet of God, also applied to the prophet *Muḥammad*). *a.*

رخ *rukh*, m. the cheek; the castle at chess; face, point, side, quarter. *rukh pheruā* or *badalnā*, a. to be inattentive; to reject; to turn away from; to be angry, to be displeased. *rukh denā*, a. to familiarize. *rukh rakhnā*, a. to continue friendship, to maintain friendly intercourse. *rukh-k.*, n. to attend to; to pursue (a prey); to make for (a place). *p.*

رخام *rukhām*, m. alabaster, marble. *sang i rukhām*, alabaster stone. *a.*

رخت *rakht*, m. goods and chattels, property, apparatus, furniture, apparel. *rakht o matā'*, personal property, exclusive of cash or bullion. *p.*

رخسار *rukhsār*, } m. the cheek, the air, mien, complexion. *p.*
رخساره *rukhsāra*,

رخش *rakhsh*, lightning, splendour, effulgence; the name of Rustam's famous horse, q. v. *p.*

رخشان *rakhshān*, shining, resplendent. *p.*

رخشندگي *rakhshandagī*, f. refulgence, brightness. *p.*

رخشنده *rakhshanda*, flashing, shining. *p.*

رخشيدن *rakhshīdan*, to flash, to shine, to glitter. *p.*

رخصت *rukhṣat*, f. leave, license, congé, dismission, discharge, permission, indulgence. *rukhṣat lenā*, to take one's leave, to depart. *rukhṣat-d.* or *k.*, to dismiss. *rukhṣat-h.*, to be dismissed, to depart. *a.*

رخصتانه *rakhṣatāna*, m. a parting present. *a.p.*

رخصتي *rukhṣatī*, f. any thing given at parting. *a.*

رخم *rakham*, name of a species of eagle, shaped like a vulture, and of the size of a raven. *a.*

رخن *rukhan* (v. *rukh*), the cheek, &c. *d.*

رخنه *rakhna*, m. a fracture, a hole, a notch, a cleft, perforation, flaw. *p.* [the lips. *s.*

رد रद *rad*, m. a tooth. रदछद *rad-chhad*, m.

رد *radd*, m. rejection, repulsion, resistance, refutation; (met.) vomiting. *raddu-l-'ajz 'alą-ṣ-ṣadr*, the antistrophe, repeating at the end of a verse the same word with which it begins, or beginning another with the word which terminated the preceding; a kind of rondeau. *radd-badal*, f. argument, discussion, altercation. *raddi jawāb*, a replication or rejoinder. *raddi salām*, returning compliments. *radd-nāma*, a deed of abrogation. *radd-k.*, to reject, repel; to refute, to oppose (in arguing); to vomit. *radd-h.*, to be rejected or refuted; to be abrogated (a law). *a.*

ردا *ridā*, f. a cloak or mantle (worn by dervises); an upper garment of fine linen unsewed (or sewed, if made of other cloth), reaching to the middle of the leg; any kind of cloak put on when going out. *a.*

ردا रद्दा *raddā*, m. a layer of a wall, the work of a day. *h.* [or *Shiva*. *s.*

ردر रुद्र *rudr*, m. name or form of *Mahādeva*

ردراکش रुद्राक्ष *rudrāksha*, m. a tree (*Eleocarpus ganitrus*). *s.* [(v. *durgā*). *s.*

ردراني रुद्राणी *rudrānī*, the wife of *Mahādeva*

ردن रदन *radan*, m. a tooth. *s.*

ردن रुदन *rudan*, m. (v. *rodan*) weeping, crying; a tear, tears. *s.*

رده *rada*, m. a row, a layer or line. *d.*

ردهه ऋद्ध *riddha*, prosperous, thriving. *s.*

ردهه ऋद्धि or रिद्धि *riddhi*, f. name of a medicinal plant; increase, growth, prosperity; a name of Pārvatī. *s.*

ردهه रुद्ध *ruddha*, obstructed, stopped, impeded.

ردهر रुधिर *rudhir*, m. the blood. *s.*

ردي *raddī*, rejected; m. rejected things. *a.*

رديف *radīf*, f. a man riding behind another on the same horse; the rhyming word of a *ghazal* or *kasīda*. *a.*

رديه *radīya*, m. rejection, refutation; a doctrine directly opposing another. *raddīya,i dīni musalmānī*, "Refutation of Mahomedanism." *a.*

رز *raz*, f. a vineyard; a battle; a castle. *p.*

رزاق *razzāk*, an epithet of the Deity, the great provider of daily bread. *a.*

رزاقي *razzākī*, f. an attribute of the Deity, providing daily bread. *a.*

رزال *rizāl* (properly *ruzāl*), mean, worthless. *a.*

رزالپن *rizāl-pan*, } m. meanness, baseness,
رزالپنا *rizāl-panā*, } worthlessness. *a. h.*

رزاله *rizāla* (properly *ruzāla*), worst, after the best has been picked out, mean, vile. *a.*

رزق *rizk*, m. food, wealth, a pension, allowance, support, subsistence, daily bread. *a.*

رزم *razm*, m. war, battle, combat. *razm-gāh*, f. the field of battle. *p.*

رس रस *ras*, m. juice, humour, essence; flavour, taste; mercury or quicksilver; a kind of grass that overspreads fallow fields; (in rhetoric) expresses the passions which a composition describes or is calculated to excite. These are stated to be nine, viz. 1. *Sringār-ras*, expressing love, or the intercourse between and mutual feeling of lovers; 2. *Hāsya-ras*, the ludicrous style; 3. *Karunā-ras*, the pathetic; 4. *Bīr-ras*, the heroic or epic, describing deeds of courage and martial prowess; 5. *Raudr-ras*, describing or exciting rage or indignation; 6. *Bhayānak-ras*, the terrible, describing the fear and terrible apprehension of the writer; 7. *Vibhatsa-ras*, expressing aversion; 8. *Shānt-ras*, expressing confidence and security; 9. *Adbhut-ras*, the marvellous, expressing astonishment; taste, of which are reckoned six, viz. sweet, sour, salt, bitter, acrid, astringent. *ras-gholnā*, to become friendly (Dakh.); perhaps it should be *ris-gholnā*, which would signify to dissolve one's wrath. *ras-nivritti*, f. loss of taste, flavour, &c. *s.*

رس *ras*, (in comp.) arriving, happening, touching at. *faryād-ras*, one whom lamentation reaches, *i.e.* a protector, a preserver. *p.*

رس रिस *ris*, f. anger, passion, vexation. *s.*

رسا *rasā*, arriving; quick of apprehension, skilful, capable, clever. *p.*

رسا रस्सा *rassā*, m. rope, cable. *h.*

رساتل रसातल *rasātal*, m. the regions below, *pātāla*. *s.*

رسال रसाल *rasāl*, m. the sugar-cane, the mango tree (*Mangifera Indica*). *s.*

رسالت *risālat*, f. mission, apostleship. *a.*

رسالسا रसालसा *rasālsā*, f. a tubular vessel of the body, a nerve, a tendon, &c. *s.*

رساله *risāla*, m. mission, sending a letter, &c.; a book, an essay, a small tract; a troop of horse. *risāla-dār*, the commander of a troop of horse. *risāla-dārī*, f. the command of a troop of horse, the rank or office of a *risāla-dār*. *a.*

رسام *rassām*, m. a delineator. *a.*

رسان *rasān*, (in comp.) conveying, bearing; as *muzhda-rasān*, conveying glad tidings. *p.*

رسانا रसाना *rasānā*, a. to solder. *h.*

رسانا रिसाना *risānā* or *rusānā*, n. to be displeased, to be angry, to be vexed. *s.*

رسانجن रसाञ्जन *rasānjan*, m. a collyrium prepared with the calx of brass or with the *Ammonium anthorrhiza*. *s.*

رسانيدن *rasānīdan*, to send, to forward. *p.*

رساول रसावल *rasāval*, m. a kind of dish (rice and the juice of sugar-cane boiled together). *s.*

رسائي *rasā,ī*, f. access, entrance; wisdom, quickness, apprehension, cleverness, skill. *p.*

رساين रसायन *rasāyan*, m. chemistry; a medicine composed of mercury, or other metals. *s.*

رساين रसायन *rasāyan*, m. slowness, mildness *h.*

رسايني रसायनी *rasāyanī*, m. a chemist. *s.*

رسبتي *ras-batī*, a port-fire (v. *rasaut*). *s.*

رسبهسمن रसभस्मन *ras-bhasman*, m. calx or oxide of mercury. *s.*

رسپشپ रसपुष्प *ras-pushp*, m. a muriate of mercury formed by subliming in close vessels a mixture of sulphur, mercury, and common salt. *s.*

رست *rast*, free, secure, firm, steady. *p.*

رست *rust*, growth, increase; adj. courageous, hearty, bold. *p.*

رستا *rastā*, m. road, a path (v. *rasta*). *p.*

رستخيز *rastakhīz*, m. the last day, the day of judgment or resurrection. *rustakhez*, newly sprung up. *p.*

رستگار *rasta-gār*, free, safe, liberated; virtuous, generous. *p.*

رستگاري *rastagārī*, f. salvation, liberation. *s.*

رستم *rustam*, name of a celebrated warrior; hence this term is applied to a hero in general: he was one of the twelve champions of Persia. His combat with *Asfandiyār* is famous in the East: it lasted two days, and as the brazen body of his enemy was proof against his arrows, he at last killed him with his mace. He was son of *Zāl*, who was son of *Sām*, son of *Narimān*. He was general of *Kaikā,ūs*, and considered by the Persians descended from *Māmūn*, son of Benjamin, son of Jacob. He overcame *Afrāsiyāb*, king of *Turkistān*, who was joined by the Indians and Tartars; nevertheless he fell into disgrace with his master, principally on account of his rejecting the religion of *Zoroaster*, and it was upon this occasion he killed *Kaikā,ūs's* son *Asfandiyār*, above mentioned. *Rustam* himself is said to have been killed by the wound of an arrow in an engagement with *Bahman* (or *Artaxerxes Longimanus*), son of *Asfandiyār*; but according to the *Shāhnāma*, he was treacherously murdered by his own bastard brother. *p.*

رستمي *rustamī*, f. valour, heroism; adj. of or resembling *Rustam*. *p.*

رستني *rustanī*, f. a vegetable. *p.*

رستن *rastan* (r. *rah*), to escape, to be saved. *p.*

رستن *rustan* (r. *rū*), to grow, to flourish. *p.*

رسته *rusta*, m. a road, path, street, a row or line of warehouses; partic. saved, escaped. *p.*

رسته *rasta*, m. a market-town; partic. grown, sprung up (vegetation). *p.*

رسد *rasad*, f. store of grain laid in for an army, &c., grain, provision. *rasad-beshī*, an increase of revenue. *p.* [creasing. *p.*

رسدي *rasadī*, progressively increasing or de-

رسدهات रसधातु *ras-dhātu*, m. quicksilver. *s.*

رسرا रसरा *rasrā*, m. rope, a cable. *h.*

رس راج रसराज *ras-rāj*, m. quicksilver. *s.*

رسري रसरी *rasrī*, f. string, cord. *h.*

رس سندور रससिन्दूर *ras-sindūr*, m. a sort of artificial cinnabar, made with zinc, mercury, blue vitriol, and nitre, fused together, and used as an escharotic. *s.*

رسك रसिक *rasik*, flavoured, tasteful; witty, facetious; m. a libertine. *s.*

رسكاءي रसिकाई *rasikā,ī*, f. cunningness, shrewdness, amourousness. *s.*

رسكرپور रसकपूर *ras-karpūr* or *-kapūr*, m. corrosive white sublimate, or a muriate of mercury similar to it, but perhaps milder; at least if we may trust to the dose assigned by eastern physicians, as stated in the *Makhzanu-l-Adwiya*, *i. e.* from one and three-quarters to three and a-half grains. To prepare it, quicksilver is triturated with red bole (*v. gerū*), marine salt, and a substance containing vitriolic acid. The *Bhāva Prakāsha* orders alum; the *Makhzanu-l-Adwiya* vitriol of zinc or copper; but the *Sukhabodha* directs sulphur; and in the last case the mass is to be moistened with the juice of the bark of the *Amrā* tree (*Spondias mangifera*). It is then sublimed in close earthen vessels. *s.*

رسگيا रसज्ञा *rasa-gyā*, f. the tongue, the palate. *s.*

رسگيه रसज्ञ *rasa-gya*, acquainted with tastes, or with the sentiments expressed in poetry; a poet, an alchymist, a physician. *rasa-gya-tā*, f. poetical skill; knowledge of flavours, alchymy. *s.*

رسل *rasal*, m. sending news. *rusul*, (pl. of *rasūl*) prophets, messengers, angels. *rasal rasā,it* epistolary correspondence. *a.*

رسلي *rusulī*, a wen, an excrescence. *d.*

رسم *rasm*, f. custom; law; model, plan; a game among children, the laws of which are, that one puts a question to another, who is obliged to reply in words which do not contain either of the three letters *re*, *sin*, or *mīm*, which compose the word *rasm*. If one of these should be found in his answer, he is condemned, as a penalty, to imitate the voice of any animal which may be directed by the questioner. *a.*

رسمسا रसमसा *ras-masā*, wet with perfumed essences or perspiration. *s.*

رسمسانا रसमसाना *rasmasānā*, n. to be wet with perfumed essences or perspiration. *s.*

رسمسيلا रसमसीला *rasmasīlā*, wet (little used) (v. *rasmasānā*). *s.*

رسمي *rasmī*, customary; middling, second sort; usage, custom. *a.*

رسميات *rasmiyāt* (pl. of رسمي), usages, customs, &c. *a.* [a ropedancer. *a.*

رسن *rasan*, m. string, cord, rope. *rasan-bāz*,

رسن रसुन *rasun*, m. garlick. *s.*

رسنا रसना or रशना *rasanā*, f. the tongue, a woman's girdle. *s.*

رسنا रिसना *risnā*, n. to drop slowly, to be angry, to be vexed. *h.*

رسنا रुसना *rusnā*, n. to be angry, displeased, to have a misunderstanding with a friend. *h.*

رسوا *ruswā*, disgrace, infamy; adj. infamous, ignominious, dishonoured. *p.*

رسواد रसवाद *raswād*, exciting quarrels. *s.*

رسوان रसवान *ras-wān*, well-flavoured, tasteful, applied to a composition, &c. *s.*

رسواءي *ruswā,ī*, f. ignominy, infamy. *p.*

رسوت रसौत *rasaut*, } f. (also *ras-wat*), a kind
رسوته रसूथ *rasūth*, } of collyrium, extracted from the root of the *Amonium anthorrhizum*, *Roxb.* *h.*

رسوتي रसवती *ras-watī*, tasteful, luscious. *s.*

رسوخ *rusūkh*, m. } firmness, constancy,
رسوخيت *rusūkhiyat*, f. } steadiness, steady friendship. *a.*

رسول *rasūl*, m. a messenger, an apostle; the prophet *Muhammad* (pl. *rasūlān*). *a.*

رسولي *rasūlī*, f. mission, apostleship; (in Dakh. same as *rusulī*). *a. d.*

رسوم *rusūm* (pl. of رسم), a fee, duties, taxes, postage of letters, customs. *rusūm-dār*, one who holds particular perquisites. *rusūmi chaudharī*, fees and perquisites of the headman of a village or of a trade. *rusūmi khazāna*, fees charged at the public treasury on all receipts and payments. *rusūmi khazānchī*, fees paid to the treasurer. *rusūmi kānūngo*, a small fee to the *kānūngo* levied on the revenue collections. *a.*

رسومات, *rusūmāt* (barbarous pl. of *rusūm*), customs, &c. *a.* [&c. *h.*

رسونت, रसौंत *rasoṅt* (v. *rasaut*), collyrium,

رسوئي, रसोई *raso,ī*, f. victuals; cook-room, kitchen. *s.* [of food. *s.*

رسوئيا, रसोइया *raso,iyā*, m. a cook, a dresser

رسها, रिसहा *ris,hā*, passionate, wrathful. *s.*

رسي, रसी *rasī*, humorous; impassioned. *s.*

رسي, रसे *rase*, softly, gently. *h.*

رسي, रस्सी *rassī*, f. a string, a cord, a rope. *s.*

رسيا, रसिया *rasiyā*, m. an epicure, one who enjoys life, a voluptuary. *s.*

رسيانا, रसियाना *rasiyānā*, n. to be moist, to be juicy; to commence ripening, to ooze. *s.*

رسيانا, रिसियाना *risiyānā*, n. to be vexed, to be angry, to be provoked. *s.*

رسيد, *rasīd*, f. acknowledgment of arrival, or receiving; a receipt. *p.*

رسيدن, *rasīdan*, to arrive, to reach. *p.*

رسيده, *rasīda*, arrived, at hand; used in comp. as *miḥnat-rasīda*, one to whom misfortune has arrived. *p.*

رسيلا, रसीला *rasīlā*, juicy, luscious; voluptuous, rakish. *s.*

رسيندر, रसेन्द्र *rasendra*, m. quicksilver; the philosopher's stone. *s.*

رسيه, रस्य *rasya*, juicy; m. blood. *s.*

رش, ऋषि or रिषि *ṛishi*, m. (also *ṛikhi*) a sage, saint. There are several orders of *ṛishis*, as the *Maharshi*, *Devarshi*, *Rājarshi*: the uncompounded name is especially applied to seven ancient sages, beginning with *Vashishṭha*, and in astronomy to the seventh asterism of the Greater Bear. The *ṛishi* of a *mantra* or prayer in the Vedas is the sage by whom it was composed or recited. *s.*

رشته, *rishta*, m. a string, line; series; relationship, connection, kin. *rishta-dār*, m. a relation, a kinsman. *rishta-dārī*, f. relationship, affinity. *p.*

رشتي, रश्ती *rashtī*, a bonus paid by the cultivator in consideration of being allowed to reclaim waste lands. *h.*

رشٹ, रुष्ट *rushṭ*, angry, displeased. *s.*

رشٹ پشٹ, रिष्टपुष्ट *rishṭ-pushṭ* (for *hṛishṭa-pushṭ*), fat, corpulent, stout. *s.*

رشٹك, रिष्टक *rishṭak*, m. the soap-berry plant (*Sapindus*). *s.*

رشحه, *rash,ḥa*, dripping, drop, sweat, juice. *a.*

رشد, *rashad* or *rushd*, m. rectitude, being in the right way (spiritually). *a.*

رشف, *rashf*, a drop; sipping. *a.*

رشك, *rashk*, m. malice, spite, envy, emulation, jealousy. *p.*

رشكي, *rashki*, envious, spiteful. *p.*

رشم, रश्मि *rashmi*, m. a ray of light. *s.*

رشنا, रशना *rashnā*, f. the tongue, a woman's girdle. *s.*

رشوت, *rishwat*, f. a bribe. *rishwat khur-dan*, to take a bribe. *rishwat khur*, one who takes bribes. *rishwat khurī*, f. the taking of a bribe. *rishwat-denā*, to bribe. *rishwat-khānā*, to be bribed, lit. to swallow the bribe. *a.*

رشوتي, *rishwatī*, one who takes bribes. *a.*

رشي, ऋषी *ṛishī*, f. the wife of a *ṛishi*. *s.*

رشيش, ऋषीश *ṛishīsh*, m. chief of the *ṛishis*. *s.*

رشيد, *rashīd*, sagacious, intelligent, wise; m. a guide, a conductor. *hārūna-r-rashīd*, the name of a celebrated Caliph of *Bāghdād*, known to readers of the Arabian Nights as *Haroun al raschid*. *a.*

رصاص, *raṣāṣ*, m. tin, lead. *raṣṣāṣ*, a tinman, a worker in tin or lead. *a.*

رضا, *razā* or *rizā*, f. consent, acquiescence; permission, leave. *razā-paṭṭī*, list of holydays, feasts, &c., in the course of the year, on which days public offices are closed. *razā-jo*, one who seeks the gratification of another. *razā-jo,ī*, the gratifying of another. *razā-mand*, acquiescing, consenting, permitting, willing. *raza-mandī*, f. consent, acquiescence; permission. *a.*

رضاعت, *razā,at*, f. act of sucking. *a.*

رضاعي بهاءي, *razā'ī bhā,ī*, a foster-brother. *a.h.*

رضاءي, *razā,ī*, f. a quilt, a headgear, a comforter. *a. p.*

رضوان, *rizwān*, m. good pleasure; paradise, also the name of the porter of paradise. *a.*

رضواني, *rizwānī*, of or belonging to paradise. *a.*

رطب, *raṭb*, moist, green, fresh, tender. *raṭbu-l-lisān*, fresh on people's tongues, *i. e.* frequently spoken of with praise. *a.*

رطب, *ruṭab*, m. (pl. *arṭab*) ripe dates. *a.*

رطل, *raṭal*, m. a pound weight, consisting of twelve ounces; a cup of wine. *a.*

رطوبت, *raṭūbat* or *ruṭūbat*, f. humidity, moisture; freshness (pl. *ruṭubāt*). *a.*

رعايا, *ri'āyā* (pl. of رعيت), subjects, tenants: it should properly be *ra'āyā*, hence the term *Raya* applied to the Christian subjects of the Porte. *a.*

رعايت, *ri'āyat*, f. observation, respect, honour; kindness, favour; guarding, protecting, paying attention; remission, indulgence. *ri'āyati khāṭir-k.*, to pay regard to another's feelings, to gratify. *ri'āyat-k.*, to observe, to take care of. *a.*

رعايتي, *ri'āyatī*, m. a favoured person, a protégé, a tenant to whom abatement of rent is made. *a.*

رعب, *ra'b* or *ru'b*, m. fear, terrifying, trembling with fear. *a.*

رعد, *ra'd*, m. thunder, fulmination. *a.*

رعشه, *ra'sha*, m. the shaking palsy. *a.*

رعنا, *ra'nā*, moving gracefully; beautiful, lovely graceful, delicate. *a.*

رعناءي, *ra'nā,ī*, f graceful gait; beauty, loveliness, grace. *a.*

رعونت, *ru'ūnat*, f. pride, haughtiness. *a.*

رعيت, *ra'īyat* or *ra'aiyat*, f. a subject, tenant; (vulg. *ryot.*) *ra'īyat-āzār*, an oppressor. *ra'īyat-parwar* or *ra'īyat-nawāz*, a cherisher of subjects, a protector. *ra'īyat-parwarī*, or *-nawāzī*, protection, cherishing of subjects. "*ra'īyatwārī faiṣala*, settlement of land rents made with the cultivators themselves, without the intervention of any zemindar or landlord, commonly known as the *ryotwary* system."—Binning. *s.*

رعيتي, *ra'aiyatī*, f. subjection, tenancy; adj. of or relating to a *ra'īyat* or tenant. *a.*

رغب, *raghb*, m. } strong desire, avidity;
رغبت, *raghbat*, f. } wish, curiosity; esteem, affection, pleasure. *a.*

رغم, *raghm*, m. looking down, shame, reproach; repugnance, abhorrence; contempt. *a.*

رف, *raff*, m. shining, glittering; eating much; kissing (a woman) with the tips of the lips; sucking (the lips) when kissing; sucking milk (a colt); defending, preserving; favouring, serving; honouring; swelling with moisture (herbage; winking or twinkling with the eye; moving tremulously; sewing any garment in order to lengthen it. *a.*

رفا, *rafā*, m. mending (a garment), cementing broken friendship, quieting, pacifying, peace, tranquillity. *a.*

رفاقت, *rafākat* (vulg. *rifākat*), f. society, companionship, friendship. *a.*

رفاه, *rafāh*, } f. content, affluence, en-
رفاهيت, *rafāhiyat*, } joyment of life, repose, quiet, tranquillity. *a.*

رفت, *raft*, (in comp.) going, motion, as *āmad-raft*, coming and going. *ruft*, sweeping. *ruft-rūb*, a clean sweep; a broom. *p.*

رفتار, *raftār*, f. gait, pace, walk. *p.*

رفت گذشت, *raft-guzasht* or *raft o guzasht*, past and gone. *p.*

رفتگي, *raftagī*, f. departure. *p.*

رفتن, *raftan* (r. *rav*), to depart, to go away, to depart this life. *p.*

رفتن, *ruftan* (r. *rūb*), to sweep, to brush. *p.*

رفتني, *raftanī*, fit to go, transient. *p.*

رفت وروب, *ruft o rūb*, clean sweeping; a broom. *p.*

رفته, *rafta*, gone, past, defunct. *p.*

رفته رفته, *rafta-rafta*, going, in the act of going, by degrees, gradually, in process of time. *p.*

رفض, *rifẓ* or *rafẓ*, m. schism, heresy; abandoning (particularly one's religion). *a.*

رفضي, *rafẓī*, m. a heretic (v. *rāfiẓī*). *a.*

رفع, *raf'*, m. elevation, promotion, ascending; finishing, completing, settling, deciding; repelling. *raf' daf'*, deciding, settling, finishing. *raf' i sharr*, settling a dispute, deciding a difference; getting rid of a dispute. *raf'-nāma*, a deed of compromise. *raf'-k.* to remove, to decide a lawsuit. *raf'-h.*, to be removed, to be decided (a suit). *a.*

رفعت, *raf'at*, f. elevation, promotion, dignity, eminence, nobility. *a.*

رفق, *rifk*, benevolence, kindness, courtesy. *a.*

رفقا, *rufakā* (pl. of رفيق), companions (more especially in travelling). *a.*

رفو, *rafū*, m. darning, a darn. *rafū-chakkar*, making one's escape, stealing off. *rafū chakkar meṅ ā-jānā*, to be lost in astonishment. *rafū-gar*, m. a darner. *rafū-garī*, f. the employment of darning. *rafū-honā*, to run away, to retire. *a.*

رفيع, *rafī'*, high, sublime, elevated, exalted. *rafī'u-sh-shān*, a person of dignity, a nobleman of high rank. *rafī'u-l-kadar*, of high estimation. *a.*

رفيف, *rafīf*, the Daurian lily (*Lilium dauricum*). *a.*

رفيق, *rafīk*, m. a friend, ally, associate, companion (especially in a journey). *a.*

رق, *rakk*, m. parchment, vellum. *a.*

رقاب, *rikāb* (pl. of رقبه), necks; slaves. *a.*

رقاص, *rakkāṣ*, a dancer, a jumper; the balance-wheel of a watch. *a.*

رقاع, *rikā'* (pl. of رقعه), notes, &c.; also a species of handwriting. *a.*

رقبه, *rakba*, m. inclosure; esplanade; environs. *rakba-bandī*, an account of all the lands, cultivated and otherwise, pertaining to a village. *rakaba*, the neck; a slave purchased with money. *a.*

رقت, *rikkat*, f. thinness, minuteness, subtileness; affection; pity, sympathy, tenderness; weeping. *a.*

رقص, *rakṣ*, m. a dance, a ball; dancing. *a.*

رقص, *rakaṣ*, } ambling, capering, skipping
رقصان, *rakaṣān*, } about, dancing. *a.*

رقعات, *ruk'āt* (pl. of رقعه), notes; a collection of epistles. *a.*

رقعه, *ruk'a*, m. a bit, a piece; a note, epistle, card. *ruk'a-wār*, paper fit for writing letters on. *s.*

رقم, *rakam*, f. writing; handwriting, character; a mode of arithmetical notation, chiefly taken from the initials of the Arabic words denoting the numbers; one character in the notation above described; arithmetic; manner, kind, method, sort; a royal edict. *rakam-siwā,e*, that which is in excess of a stipulated sum. *rakam-k.*, to write. *rakam-h.*, to be written. *a.*

رقمي, *rakamī*, written, committed or reduced to writing, marked. *a.*

رقو, *rakū*, a styptic, any thing applied to stanch a bleeding. *a.*

رقوب, *rukūb*, m. expecting, watching, contemplating the stars, waiting. *a.*

رقيب, *rakīb*, m. a rival, an enemy; one who watches, a guardian. *a.*

رقيق, *rakīk*, subtile, minute, thin, fine. *a.*

رقيمه, *rakīma*, m. an epistle, note, letter. *a.*

رك *rak*, rage, indignation; a row, a line; (for *rag*.) a vein, a nerve. *p.*

رك रुक *ruk*, m. stoppage, hindrance. *rik* (v. *rig*), one of the four Vedas. *s.*

رکاب *rikāb*, f. a stirrup. *rikāb-dār*, an attendant when riding, a companion. *rikāb-dawāl*, a stirrup leather. *a. p.*

رکاب *rikāb*, f. a dish, a plate. *rikāb-dār*, keeper of the dishes. *p.*

رکابي *rikābī*, f. a dish, a plate; a kind of *rupī* current in Lakhnau. *rikābī mazhab*, parasitical. *p.*

رکاز *rikāz*, valuable fossils or mines, treasures buried in the earth. According to Gladwin, there are three legal terms which particularly belong to mines and buried treasures, and which are employed for the use of distinction: *ma'dan*, the place in which the ore or metal is naturally produced; *kanz*, treasure, or the property buried in the ground; and *rikāz*, applied equally to either—to *ma'dan* literally, and to *kanz* metaphorically. In all parts of Asia it is a common practice to bury treasure: treasures are hidden in the ground on the commencement of a war or other troubles, and it frequently happens that, the depositors perishing, the treasure remains concealed, perhaps for many years, till it be discovered by accident, and at a time when no legal claimants are to be found. *a.*

رکانا रुकाना *rukānā*, a. to cause to inclose, to surround, to stop, to hinder. *s.*

رکاو रुकाव *rukāw*, m. hindrance, prevention. *s.*

رکاوٹ रुकावट *rukāwaṭ*, f. prevention, stoppage, hindrance, delay. *s.*

رکائز *rakā,iz* (pl. of رکاز, q.v.), treasures, &c. *a.*

رکت रिक्त *rikta*, empty, void, deprived of; m. (also *riktatā*, f.) vanity. *rikta-hasta*, empty-handed. *s.*

رکت रकत *rakat* or रक्त *rakt* or *rakta*, m. the blood; adj. red. *rakta-pā*, f. a leech. *rakta-pāt*, m. spilling of blood. *rakta-chandan*, m. red sandal-wood. *rakta-chūrn*, m. red lead. *rakta-dhātu*, m. red chalk or red orpiment; copper. *rakta-lochan*, red-eyed. *rakta-may*, bloody, consisting of blood. *rakta-varn*, of red colour. *rakta-hīn*, bloodless. *s.*

رکتال रक्तालु *raktālu*, m. a sort of yam (*Dioscorea purpurea*). *s.*

رکتامبر रक्ताम्बर *raktāmbar*, dressed in red. *raktāmbarā*, m. any vagrant devotee wearing red garments. *s.*

رکت پت रक्तपित्त *rakta-pitt*, m. } a painful
رکت پتي रक्तपित्ती *rakt-pittī*, f. } and itchy
eruption supposed to arise from excess of blood and bile; hæmorrhages from the mouth, nose, rectum, and cuticle; a plant used for the cure of this disease: in Dakh. it denotes the black or eating leprosy. *s.*

رکت کوڑھ रक्तकोढ़ *rakt-koṛh*, m. a kind of leprosy in which the part affected is red. *s.*

رکتگلم रक्तगुल्म *rakta-gulm*, m. a disease, a hard lump in the abdomen of the female after conception; a clot of blood. *s.*

رکس *rakkas*, an answer; the north. *d.*

رکش रूक्ष *ruksh*, harsh, unkind; rough, hard, rugged, uneven. *s*

رکش ऋक्ष *ṛiksh*, m. a bear; a constellation. *s.*

رکشا रक्षा *rakshā*, f. } preservation, pro-
رکشن रक्षण *rakshan*, m. } tection. *rakshan*, adj. protecting, guarding. *s.*

رکشت रक्षित *rakshit*, preserved protected, [kept. *s.*

رکشس रक्षस *rakshas*, m. an evil spirit. *s.*

رکشك रक्षक *rakshak*, m. a preserver, protector. *s.*

رکشیمان रक्ष्यमाण *rakshyamān*, preserved, pro- [tected. *s.*

رکعت *rak'at*, a genuflexion; gesticulations, &c., performed when reading the *kur,ān*. *a.*

رکم रुक्म *rukma*, m. the name of the brother-in-law of *Krishṇa*, and the son of *Bhīshmaka*. *s.*

رکمي रुक्मिणी *rukminī*, f. the name of one of *Krishṇa's* wives, and sister of *Rukma*. *s.*

رکن *ruhn*, m. a pillar, a prop, aid, support; a grandee; the feet of a verse (pl. *arkān*). *a.*

رکن रुकन *rukan*, f. stopping. *s.*

رکنا रुकना *ruknā*, n. to stop, rest, be inclosed; hindered, prohibited. *s.*

رکوب *rukūb*, riding, mounted on; perpetration (of a crime). *rakūb*, any one mounted; any beast, &c. on which people ride. *a.*

رکوع *rukū'*, bowing the head in humility and reverence, as in prayer, or towards one of old age. *a.*

رکویا रुकवैया *rukwaiyā*, m. a preventer. *s.*

رکھ रिखि *ṛikhi* or *ṛikh*, m. a sage, a saint. *s.*

رکھا रुखा *rukhā* (for *rūkhā*), plain, dry, stale (bread). *s.*

رکھانا रखाना *rakhānā*, a. to give in charge, to cause to keep, put, place. *rakhā-lenā*, a. to take in charge. *s.*

رکھاءي रुखाई *rukhā,ī*, f. plainness, dryness (of bread, &c.); unkind looks, indifference. *s.*

رکھك रखक *rakhak* (for *rakshak*), a keeper, protector, &c. *s.*

رکھن रखन *rakhan* (for *rakshan*), m. keeping, charge, protection, preservation. *s.*

رکھنا रखना *rakhnā*, a. to keep, to put, to place, to have, to hold, to possess to lay, to set, to station, to leave, to own, to stop, to save, to reserve. *rakh-chhoṛnā*, a. to place; to keep; to have; to give in charge. *rakh-denā*, a. to put down, to place; to keep, to put by. *rakh-lenā*, a. to take in charge, to take into keeping or service. *s.*

رکھنہار रखनहार *rakhan-hār*, m. a watchman, a guard. *h.*

رکھوارا रखवारा *rakhwārā*, } m. a keeper, a
رکھوال रखवाल *rakhwāl*, } guard; a shep-
رکھوالا रखवाला *rakhwālā*, } herd, cowherd,
or goatherd. *s*

رکهولي रखवाली *rakhwālī*, f. keeping, guarding, grazing cattle, tribute or fees paid to a chief for protection of one's property; "black mail." *s.*

رکهوان रखवाना *rakhwānā*, a. to cause to keep. *rakhwā-lenā*, a. to take in charge. *s.*

رکهواءي रखवाई *rakhwā,ī*, f. the price paid for keeping, &c *s.*

رکهي रिखी *rikhī*,m. (for *rishi*),a sage,a saint.*s.*

رکهي रखी *rakhī*, f. a tribute, or rather "black mail," paid to a Sikh chief for protection; m. a protector, guardian; grass which has been preserved for cattle, cut down and dried, hay. *s.*

رکهيا रखिया *rakhiyā*, f. protection, keeping. *s.*

رکهيا रखैया *rakhaiyā*, m. a guardian, keeper. *s.*

رکيب *rakīb*, a stirrup; a beast for riding upon, a companion in riding. *p.*

رکيبي *rikebī*, f. a dish, a plate. *p.*

رکهيس *rikhīs*, رکهيش *rikhīsh*, } ऋषीश { m. the chief of the *rikhis* or saints, an arch-saint. *s.*

رکهيل *rahhel*, رکهيلا *rakhelā*, } an assault, attack. *d.*

رکهيلنا *rukhelnā*, a. to assault, attack. *d.*

رکيك *rakīk*, fine, minute, subtile, thin. *a.*

رگ *rag*, f. a vein, a fibre. *rag utarnā*, n. to be appeased; to have a rupture. *rag-dār*, veined; m. cloth in which the threads are uneven, so that some appear like veins; a wicked brat. *rag-resha*, m. every vein, veins and fibres; every thing, all. *rag-zan*, m. a surgeon, a bleeder, a phlebotomist. *rag-zanī*, f. venisecton, phlebotomy. *rag chaṛhnā*, to be obstinate, pettish, or proud. *rag marnā*, n. to lose virility, become impotent. *ragi gardan*, pride. *p.*

رگ بيد ऋगवेद *rig-bed* (v. *rig-ved*). *s.*

رگت *ragat* (for *rakat*), the blood. *d.*

رگڑ रगड़ *ragaṛ*, f. rubbing, attrition. *h.*

رگڑا रगड़ा *ragarā* or *ragṛā*, m. quarrelling; rubbing, poishing; name of a collyrium. *ragṛā-jhagṛā*, m. quarrel, debate, discussion. *h.*

رگڑنا रगड़ना *ragaṛnā*, n. to rub, to scour, to fret, to excoriate, to grind. *h.*

رگستان *rigistān* (for *registān*), a sandy region. *p.*

رگن रुग्न *rugna*, bent, crooked, curbed; diseased, sick. *s.*

رگنا रगना *ragnā*, to be attached to, to be in [love with. *s.*

رگ وبد ऋग्वेद *rig-ved*, m. the first of the four Vedas (v. *ved* or *veda*). *s.*

رگهو रघु *raghu*, a sovereign of Oude, the great-grandfather of *Rāmā-chandra*. *raghu-bans* (for *raghu-vansa*, m. the race of Raghu; a poem by Kālidās. *s.*

رگيد रगेद *raged*, f. pursuit, chase. *h.*

رگيدنا रगेदना *ragednā*, a. to pursue, to chase. *h.*

رل रुल्ल *rull*, land that requires to be left fallow for a year or two in order to recover its vigour. *h.*

رلانا रलाना *ralānā*, a. to mix, to pound together. *h.*

رلانا रुलाना *rulānā*, a. to make one cry or weep; to vex, to displease, to afflict. *s.*

رلنا रलना *ralnā*, n. to be mixed, ground down. *rulnā*, to be rolled or planed, to be smoothened. *h.*

رم *ram*, m. flight, elopement. *ram-khur*, one who takes to flight. *ram-khurda*, taken to flight. *ram rahnā*, to elope, to remain concealed. *ram-k.*, n. to flee, to fly, to run away. *p.*

رما रमा *ramā*, f. a name of *Lakshmī*, the wife of *Vishṇu*, and goddess of prosperity. *s.*

رماء *ramā*, usury, increase, excess. *a.*

رماز *rammāz*, m. a proposer of riddles, enigmas, &c.; one who speaks mysteriously. *a.*

رمال *rammāl*, m. a soothsayer, a fortune-teller, prophet, conjuror. *a.*

رمال *rumāl* (for *rū-māl*), a pocket-handkerchief, a towel. *p.*

رمان *rummān*, the pomegranate. *a.*

رمانا रमाना *ramānā*, a. to entice, to beguile, to take possession of. *s.*

رماني *rummānī*, resembling a pomegranate. *a.*

رمت रमत *ramat*, adj. pleasing, sporting. *s.*

رمچيرا रमचेरा *ramcherā*, m. a slave; a name frequently given to slaves. *s.*

رمجهول रमझोल *ramjhol*, a kind of ornament for the foot. *h.*

رمدو پهتو रमदूफट्टू *ramdū phaṭṭū*, m. pl. the populace, the vulgar (comp. of two names peculiar to the lowest ranks, as in English, Tom, Dick, and Harry, or tag, rag, and bobtail). *h.*

رمز *ramz*, m. a wink, nod, sign; a riddle, enigma, mysterious talking, ambiguous expression. *a.*

رمضان *ramazān*, m. the name of the ninth *Muhammadan* month, during which those who profess that religion are interdicted from eating, drinking, and conjugal duty between the morning dawn and appearance of the stars at night: in short, this is their Lent. On the 27th of this month the *ḳur,ān* began to descend from heaven, and every prayer offered up on that night (called *lailatu-l-ḳadr*, q.v.) will be complied with. Also prayers offered up on the 19th, 21st, and 23rd days of this month are supposed to be peculiarly efficacious. *a.*

رمضاني *ramazānī*, of or relating to the fast of *ramazān*; a name given to one born in that month, called in Anglo-Indian, "Rum Johney." *a.*

رمق *ramaḳ*, m. the last breath, the departing soul or spirit. *a.*

رمل *raml*, m. sand. *ramal*, geomancy, foretelling by figures. *a.*

رمن रमण *ramaṇ*, m. playing, sporting, dalliance, amorous sport, act of copulation. *s.*

رمن, रमना *ramnā*, a. to reap enjoyment, to copulate. *s.*

رمنا, रमना *ramnā*, n. to turn; to roam, to go, to range, to wander. *h.*

رمنا, रमना *ramnā*, } m. a park, a chase (for game),
رمنه, रमनः *ramna*, } a place to roam in. *s. p.*

رمني, रमणी *ramnī*, also रमणीय *ramanīya*, pleasant, agreeable; a beautiful or excellent woman. *ramanīyatā*, f. pleasantness. *s.*

رمنيك, रमणीक *ramnīk*, pleasant, agreeable. *s.*

رمنيه, रमण्य *ramanya*, m. sport, pleasure, dalliance. *s.*

رموز *rumūz* (pl. of رمز, q.v.), winks; enigmas. *a.*

رمه, *rama*, a flock, a herd; a multitude, an army. *p.*

رميدن, *ramīdan*, to fly in terror. *p.*

رميده, *ramīda*, terrified, afflicted, alarmed. *p.*

رميك, रम्यक *ramyak*, m. one of the minor Dwīpas, or divisions of the world, lying to the north of Ilāvrit. *s.*

رميم, *ramīm*, carious, putrified, decayed. *a.*

رن ऋण *ṛiṇ*, m. borrowing, debt; negative quantity in algebra. *ṛin-shodhan*, m. discharge of a debt. *ṛin-grast*, involved in debt. *ṛin-mār*, m. one who does not pay his debts. *ṛin-mukti*, f. or *ṛin moksh*, m. discharge of a debt. *s.*

رن रण *raṇ*, m. battle, war. *raṇ-bhūmi*, f. a battle-field. *raṇ-stambh*, m. a trophy, a pillar. *raṇ-kāmī*, desirous of battle, warlike. *s.*

رنانگن, रणाङ्गन *ranāngan*, m. a field of battle. *s.*

رن‌باس रनबास *ran-bās*, m. the seraglio of a rājā, the female apartments. *s.*

رن‌بن रनबन *ran-ban*, m. a wilderness. *s.*

رنبها, रम्भा *rambhā*, f. a courtesan, a harlot; a plantain or banana. *s.*

رنج *ranj*, m. grief, affliction, anguish of mind, offence, disgust. *p.*

رنجت, रञ्जित *ranjit*, moved, affected. *s.*

رنجش, *ranjish*, f. grief, affliction. *p.*

رنجك, रञ्जक *ranjak*, what excites or affects; what colours, &c.; m. a colourist, a painter, a dyer; a stimulus, an inciter of affection, &c.; biliary humour on which vision depends; f. priming-powder; the touch-hole of a gun. *ranjak uṛānā*, a. to burn priming, to flash in the pan. *ranjak pilānā*, a. to prime. *ranjak-dān*, m. priming-pan. *s.*

رنجن رञ्जन *ranjan*, m. colouring, dyeing; affecting, exciting passion; red sandal or sapan wood; (in Dakh.) a large jar. *s.* [firm. *p.*

رنجور *ranjūr* or *ranjwar*, sick, afflicted, in-

رنجوري, *ranjūrī*, f. sickness, grief. *p.*

رنجه, *ranja*, sorrow, trouble, pain. *p.*

رنجيدگي, *ranjīdagī*, f. affliction. *p.*

رنجيدن, *ranjīdan*, to be grieved or vexed. *p.*

رنجيده, *ranjīda*, afflicted, vexed. *ranjīda-khāṭir*, afflicted in mind. *p.*

رند, *rind*, m. a reprobate, a drunkard, a debauchee, a vagabond *p.* [brasure. *s.*

رندا, रन्द्रा *randā*, m. a hole, a loophole, an em-

رندا, *randā*, } m. a plane (for smoothing
رنده, *randa*, } wood). *p.*

رندانه, *rindāna*, licentious, disorderly. *p.*

رلدنا, रुँदना *rundnā*, n. to be trod or trampled on. *h.*

رنده, *randa*, m. a hole, &c. (v. *randā*.) *s.*

رندهر, रन्ध्र *randhra*, m. a hole, a fissure, a chasm; a fault, a defect. *s.*

رندهنا, रूँधना *rundhnā* or *rundh-jānā*, n. to be constrained, afflicted, surrounded. *h.* [tuals). *s.*

رندهنا, रन्धना *randhnā*, n. to be boiled (vic-

رندي, *rindī*, f. trick, fraud, debauchery. *p.*

رنڈ, रुण्ड *ruṇḍ*, m. the trunk, the headless body. *s.*

رنڈ, रण्ड *ranḍ*, m. the name of a tree, the castor-oil plant, *Palma Christi* (*Ricinus vulgaris*). *s.*

رنڈا, रण्डा *ranḍā*, f. a plant (*Salvinia cucullata*); a widow. *s.*

رنڈاپا, रण्डापा *ranḍāpā*, }
رنڈاپرو, रण्डापरो *ranḍāparo*, } m. widow-
رنڈاپن, रण्डापन *ranḍāpan*, } hood. *p.*
رنڈاپنا, रण्डापना *ranḍāpanā*, } [or dress. *s.*

رنڈسالا, रण्डसाला *ranḍsālā*, m. widows' weeds

رنڈك, रण्डक *ranḍak*, m. a barren tree. *s.*

رنڈوا, रण्डूआ *ranḍū,ā*, m. a widower. *s.*

رنڈي, रण्डी *ranḍī*, f. a woman, a wench; (in Dakh.) a prostitute. *ranḍī-bāz*, a wencher, a whoremonger. *ranḍī-bāzī*, f. whoredom, fornication. *s.*

رنڈيا, रण्डिया *ranḍiyā*, f. a widow, a woman. *s.*

رنز, *ranz* or *runz*, m. rice. *a.*

رنس, रंस *rans*, f. a ray, a sunbeam. *s.*

رنك, रंक *rank*, m. a poor man, a miser; adj. niggardly, avaricious. *h.*

رنگ, *rang*, m. colour; manner, method, hue, paint. *rang utarnā*, to become pale; to be grieved. *rang uṛ-jānā*, to change colour, to be afraid. *rang-āmez*, painted, gaudy; variable. *rang-āmezī*, f. being variegated. *rang-ba-rang*, of various hues or sorts. *rang bigaṛnā*, changing the state or condition of any thing. *rang-bhang*, spoiling of sport. *rang-bhūm*, a place of amusement, theatre, palæstra. *rang-chaṛhnā*, to be elated with liquor. *rang dekhnā*, to look at or examine the state, condition, result, conclusion, or consequence of any thing. *rang-ḍhang*, a brilliant or pleasing sight. *rang rātnā*, to become attached to any one. *rang-raliyāṅ*, merriment, pleasure, mirth, pleasant society of a lover. *rang-rūp*, m. colour, form, appearance. *rang-rez*, m. a dyer, one whose business is to dye. *rang-*

-ezī, f. dyeing. *rang fak hojānā*, to grow pale (from fear, astonishment). *rang karnā*, to enjoy, to lead a life of pleasure. *rang lagānā*, to colour; to excite a quarrel. *rang mārnā*, to win (in gaming, an expression taken from the game of *chaupar*). *rang-mahal* or *-mahall*, an apartment dedicated to voluptuous enjoyment. *p.*

رنگ रङ्ग *rang*, m. dancing, acting, singing, amusement, merriment, pleasure; suit (at cards). *rang-bhūti*, f. the day of full moon in the month Aswin, the night of which is devoted to *Lakshmī*, and spent in playing ancient chess, dancing, &c. *rang-bhūmi*, f. a field of battle; a stage, a theatre, a place where dancing is exhibited (also *rang-shālā*, f.). *s.*

رنگارا *rangārā*, a colourer, a dyer. *d.*

رنگارنگ *rangārang*, various, many-coloured, of various kinds. *p.*

رنگانا रङ्गाना *rangānā*, a. to colour, to tinge. *p.*

رنگاوٹ रङ्गावट *rangāwaṭ*, f. colour, colouring. *p. h.*

رنگائي रङ्गाई *rangā,ī*, f. the price paid for dyeing; a certain space of time, during which a cloth is dyed. *p. h.*

رنگت *rangat*, f. colour, dye, tint. *p.*

رنگترا *rangtarā*, m. a kind of orange (this name was given by *Muhammad Shāh* instead of *sangtarā*, q. v.). *p.*

رنگرس रङ्गरस *rangras*, m. delight, melody, pleasure. *s.*

رنگڑھا रणगढ़ा *ran-garhā*, m. lines of intrenchment. *s.*

رنگنا रङ्गना *rangnā*, a. to colour, to dye. *p.*

رنگوائي रङ्गवाई *rangwā,ī*, f. the price paid for colouring (particularly for dyeing). *p.*

رنگویا रङ्गवैया *rangwaiyā*, m. a dyer. *p.*

رنگي *rangī*, m. a dyer; f. chintz, the colour of which will not stand washing; a kind of cloth peculiar to the city of *Khairābād*. *p.*

رنگي रङ्गी *rangī*, impassioned, having propensity or passion. *s.*

رنگیت *rangīt*, a vulture having a white body and yellow neck, commonly called "Pharaoh's chicken." *d.*

رنگیلا रङ्गीला *rangīlā*, gaudy, fine, showy, airy, buxom; m. a rake, a man of pleasure. *p. h.*

رنگین *rangīn*, coloured, gaudy. *p.*

رنگیني *rangīnī*, f. the state of being coloured. *p.*

رن‌مار ऋणमार *riṇ-mār*, m. one who does not pay his debts. *s.*

رنواس रनवास *ranwās*, m. the seraglio of a rājā. *s.*

رنوتساه रणोत्साह *ranotsāh*, m. prowess, valour. *s.*

رن‌ون रणवन *ran-van*, m. a wilderness. *s.*

رنہٹ रहट *ranhaṭ*, m. a wheel for raising water (same as *rahaṭ*). *h.*

رني ऋणी *riṇī*, } indebted; m. a debtor. *s.*
رنیا ऋणिया *riṇiyā*, }

رو *rū*, m. face, surface; sake; cause, reason. *rū-posh*, hiding one's face, concealed. *rū-dār*, m. a man of rank and dignity. *rū-dārī*, f. rank, dignity; flattery, complaisance. *rū-denā* (Pers. *rū-dādan*), to occur, to appear or present itself, to happen. *rū-se*, according to, by way of. *rū-shināś*, an acquaintance, one whose face is known, a cap acquaintance. *rū-shināsī*, f. intimacy, acquaintance. *rū-gardān*, turning away the face, deserting, abandoning. *rū-gardān-k.*, a. to turn away the face, to abandon; to beat. *p.*

رو *raw*, (in comp.) going; as *pesh-raw*, preceding, going, or singing before another. *raw-denā*, to copulate (used among women). *p.*

رو *ro*, (in comp.) growing, as *khud-ro*, growing of itself. *p.*

رو रव *raw* or *rava*, m. a voice, sound. *s.*

رو रवि *ravi*, m. the sun. *ravi-kānt*, m. the sun-stone, a sort of crystal. *ravi-mārg*, m. the sun's path. *rāvi-mandal*, m. the disc of the sun. *s.*

روا *rawā*, right, proper, accurate. *rawā-dār*, an approver, chooser, consenter, one who judges or deems (a thing) right. *rawā-dāshtan*, to deem proper, to allow or countenance. *p.*

روا रवा *rawā*, m. gold or silver filings; a grain or particle of sand, dust, gunpowder, &c. *h.*

رواتب *rawātib* (pl. of راتب, q. v.), necessaries of life, &c. *h.*

رواج *riwāj*, f. usage, custom, fashion; adj. customary, current, vendible. *riwāju-l-mulk*, custom of the country. *a.*

روارو *rawārau*, } f. going, travelling. *p.*
رواروي *rawāravī*, }

روءاس रोआस *ro,ās*, f. inclination to weep. *s.*

روءاسا रोआसा *ro,āsā*, inclined to cry, vexed, displeased, afflicted. *s.*

روافض *rawāfiz* (pl. of رافض), heretics, particularly *Shī,as*. *a.*

رواق *ruwāk*, a portico, a gallery, a balcony. *a.*

روان *rawān*, life, soul; running, flowing; text; reading. *rawān-āsā*, soul-refreshing. *rawān-k.*, a. to set a-going; to despatch, to forward, to send; to make current. *rawān-h.* (Pers. *rawān shudan*) to depart, to set forth. *p.*

روءان रोआँ *ro,āṅ*, m. hair of the body, wool, down. *s.*

روءانا रोआना *ro,ānā*, a. to make cry, to vex, to displease. *s.*

روانس रवाँस *rawāṅs*, m. a kind of bean (*Dolichos sinensis*). *h.*

روانگي *rawānagī*, f. running, flowing; passing, travelling, going. *p.*

روانه *rawāna*, m. a pass, passport; adj. despatched, departed. *rawāna honā*, n. to flow; to be despatched, to be in motion, to go, to pass. *p.*

رواني *rawānī*, f. a course, proceeding. *p.*

روءائي रोआई *ro,ā,ī*, f. lamentation. *s.*

روایات *riwāyāt* (pl. of روایت), histories, narrations. *a.*

روايت *riwāyat*, f. a history, narrative, tale, fiction, fable. *riwāyati ṣaḥīḥ*, indubitable report; a title bestowed upon two different treatises on the *sunnat* or traditions of *Muḥammad*. *riwāyati mash,hūr*, celebrated reports; a work of considerable authority. *a.*

روب *rob* or *rūb*, (in comp.) sweeping. *p.*

روباه *robāh*, f. a fox. *robāh-bāz* or *robāh-wash*, one who acts slily or deceitfully. *robāh-bāzī*, f. stratagem, wile, trick, deceit, evasion, subterfuge; spying; endeavouring to find out a secret; pumping a person for that same purpose. *p.*

روبراه *rū-ba-rāh*, fit for business, adjusted, prepared; reformed, returned from an erroneous course. *p.*

روبرو *rū-ba-rū*, m. presence; face to face, before. *p.*

روبكار *rū-ba-kār*, ready for business, intent on; pl. *rū-ba-kārāt*, causes, &c. brought to court. *p.*

روبكاري *rū-ba-kārī*, f. proceeding (of a cause). *p.*

روبه *robah* (for *robāh*), a fox, q. v. *p.*

روپ रूप *rūp*, m. beauty; shape, appearance, face, picture, manner, mode, method; silver. *rūp-rat*, killed or calcined silver. *rūp-sāgar*, ocean of beauty. *rūp-nidhān*, receptacle or abode of beauty. *s.*

روپ *rop*, m. the stalk of grass or corn when growing. *d.*

روپا रूपा *rūpā*, m. silver. *s.*

روپت रोपित *ropit*, planted, raised. *s.*

روپجست रूपजस्त *rūp-jast*, m. pewter. *h.*

روپر रोपर *ropar*, transplanted rice; a rate in a lease for crops of rice raised by transplanting. *h.*

روپك रोपक *ropak*, who or what plants, raises, &c. *s.*

روپن रोपण *ropan*, m. the act of planting or [raising. *s.*

روپنا रोपना *ropnā*, a. to transplant. *s.*

روپنا रोकना *ropnā*, a. to defend, to obstruct. *h.*

روپوان रूपवान *rūpwān*, beautiful, handsome. *s.*

روپوتي रूपवती *rūpwatī*, a beautiful woman. *s.*

روپوش هونا *rū-posh honā*, n. to be concealed, to hide one's face, to abscond. *p. h.*

روپوشي *rū-poshī*, f. hiding, absconding. *p.*

روپونت रूपवन्त *rūpawant*, well-shaped, elegant, beautiful. *s.*

روپهلا रूपहला *rūpahlā*, } silvered, made of
روپهنا रूपहना *rūpahnā*, } silver. *s.*

روپي रूपी *rūpī*, beautiful, shapely; (in comp.) in form of, having the shape of. *s.*

روپيه रूपयः, रूपियः, रूपीयः, or रूपैयः, *rūpaya*, *rūpiya*, *rūpīya*, and *rūpaiya*, a rūpī; a well-known coin so called. The Calcutta sicca rūpī is worth about two shillings, and the silver of it better than English standard silver by 2¾*d*. the ounce. By the regulations of Government passed in May 1793, it should weigh 179⅝ grains (troy weight). *s.*

روت *rūwat*, friendly attention, kindliness; also gracefulness, beauty, splendour. *d.*

روتا रौता *rautā* (v. *rā,etā*), pumpkins, &c. *h.*

روٹ रोट *roṭ*, } m. thick bread; (met.) sweet-
روٹا रोटा *roṭā*, } meats offered to *Hanūmān*. *s.*

روٹھا روٹھي रूठारूठी *rūṭhā-rūṭhī*, f. mutual coolness, misunderstanding. *s.*

روٹھنا रूठना *rūṭhnā*, n. to have a misunderstanding with a friend, to be cool, to quarrel. *s.*

روٹھني रूठनी *rūṭhnī*, quarrelsome; f. the name of a species of sensitive plant (*Mimosa natans*). *s.*

روٹي रोटी *roṭī*, f. bread (in the general sense), any cake toasted on a gridiron, &c. without yeast: our European loaf made with yeast is properly called *k͟hamīrī roṭī*. *s.*

روج रूज *rūj*, m. the name of an insect very troublesome to birds. *h.*

روج *roj*, (in Bengal) corrup. of *roz*, a day. *p.*

روج रोज *roj*, } m. lamentation. *h.*
روجڑا रोजड़ा *rojṛā*, }

روجھ रोझ *rojh*, m. the *nīl gā,o*, or white-footed antelope (*Antilope picta*). *s.*

روجھا रूझा *rūjhā*, (an animal or bird more particularly) much teased by the insect *rūj*, q. v. *h.*

روچك रोचक *rochak*, a stomachic, something taken to excite appetite. *s.*

روچنا रोचना *rochanā*, m. a yellow pigment, supposed to be the concrete bile of the cow, used as a medicine, a dye, and perfume. *s.*

روچھ रूछ *rūchh*, stern; m. a violator. *s.*

روح *rūḥ*, f. soul, spirit. *rūḥu-l-ḳuds*, the holy spirit, the angel Gabriel. *rūḥu-l-lāh*, the Spirit of God. Jesus Christ. *rūḥ aʻẓam*, sulphuric acid (pl. *arwāḥ*). *a*

روحاني *rūḥānī*, spiritual. *a.*

رود *rod* or *rūd*, m. a river; the string of a musical instrument. *p.*

رودا *rodā*, m. a gut or sinew used as a bow-string; the branch of a creeper. *p.*

روداد *rūdād*, m. account of circumstances, narrative. *rūdādi tajwīz* or *rū,edādi tajwīz*, statement of the investigation of a complaint or suit at law. *p.*

رودخانه *rūd-k͟hāna*, m. the bed or channel of a river. *p.*

رودر रौद्र *raudra*, fearful, terrific, wrathful, m. wrath, rage, heat. *raudratā*, f. fierceness. *s.*

رودن रोदन *rodān*, m. weeping, crying, tears. *s.*

روده *rūda*, a gut, an intestine, string of a bow or of a musical instrument. *p.*

رودھ रोध *rodh*, m. a bank, a shore. *s.*

رودھن रोधन *rodhan*, adj. impeding, obstructing; m. an obstacle, the act of impeding. *s.*

رور रोर *ror* or रौर *raur*, f. noise, clamour. *s.*

رورا *rorā*, m. a blackguard, a profligate. *d.*

رورو रौरव *raurav*, formidable, terrific; m. one of the divisions of hell. *s.*

روروكر रोरोकर *rorokār* (lit. with repeated weeping), with difficulty, with labour and pain. *s.*

روڑا रोड़ा *roṛā*, m. name of a caste of the *kshatrī* or military class. *h.*

روڑا रोड़ा *rorā* (or *roṛā*), m. a stone, a fragment of stone or brick. *bāṭ-kā roṛā*, a stumbling-block (in one's path). *s.*

روڑھ रूढ़ *rūṛh*, hard, stiff, rough, grim, cross. *s.*

روز *roz*, m. a day. *roz bā'-aish*, a good day (to you). *roz-ba-roz*, daily, constantly. *roz-bih*, fortunate days, happy times, prosperity. *roz o shab*, day and night, always, constantly. *rozi dād*, day of retribution, the last day. *rozi shumār*, day of reckoning. *rozi maidān*, day of battle; (lit.) of the field. *p.*

روزانه *rozāna*, daily, daily pay, a pension. *p.*

روزگار *roz-gār*, m. service; earning; the world, time, age. *rozgār-k.*, a. to serve; to earn. *p.*

روزگاري *roz-gārī*, one who earns his daily bread. *roz-gāre*, for or during some time. *p.*

روزمره *roz-marra*, m. daily conversation, common discourse; always, daily. *p.*

روزن *rauzan*, m. a hole, a window. *p.*

روزنامچه *roz-nāmcha*, } m. a daily account-
روزنامه *roz-nāma*, } book. *p.*

روزه *roza*, m. fast, Lent. *roza-dār*, m. one who fasts or keeps Lent. *p.*

روزي *rozī*, f. daily food or portion. *rozī-dih*, one who bestows daily food. *p.*

روزينه *rozīna*, m. daily pay. *rozīna-dār*, m. one who receives daily wages. *p.*

روس रोष *ros*, m. anger, rage. *ros-k.*, to be angry, to be displeased. *s.*

روس *raus*, f. (for *ravish*, q.v.) an avenue, &c. *p.*

روسپي *rūspī*, a courtesan, a harlot. *p.*

روستا *rostā* or *rūstā*, } m. a village; a peasant,
روستاءي *rostā,ī*, } a villager. *p.*

روسل रोसल *rosal*, } light soil of a good
روسلي रोसली *rosalī*, } quality. *h.*

روسنا रोसना *rosnā* or रूसना *rūsnā*, n. to be angry, to be displeased, to have a misunderstanding with a friend, to quarrel. *s.*

روس واهن रोषवाहन *ros-vāhan*, angry, displaying wrath. *s.*

روسي रूसी *rūsī*, f. scurf. *s.*

روسياه *rū-siyāh*, black in the face; (met.) disgraced, unfortunate, criminal. *p.*

روسياهي *rū-siyāhī*, f. disgrace, criminality. *p.*

روش *ravish*, f. custom, fashion, institution, law, rule; an avenue, walk, passage, way. *p.*

روشن *roshan*, bright, splendid, manifest, conspicuous. *roshan-chaukī*, f. a kind of serenade, with pipes and small tabors, round the apartment of a great man when he retires to rest: the same kind of music used on other occasions. *roshan-dān*, m. a small hole for admitting light. *roshan-dil*, of an enlightened mind. *roshan-damāgh*, snuff. *roshan-rā,e*, of enlightened understanding. *roshan-zamīr*, enlightened (in mind). *roshan-ṭab'*, of a bright genius. *roshan 'akl*, of enlightened mind. *roshan-k.*, to illumine. *roshan-gar*, an illuminator. *p.*

روشن रोषण *roshan*, m. } angry, passionate. *s.*
روشنا रोषणा *roshanā*, f. }

روشنا *roshanā*, light, splendour; the name of one of Alexander's queens, called by the Greeks Roxana. *p.*

روشناءي *roshnā,ī*, f. light, splendour; ink. *p.*

روشني *roshnī*, f. light, splendour. *p.*

روضت *rauẓat* or روضه *rauẓa*, m. a garden, a mausoleum, a shrine or tomb of a reputed saint. *a.*

روغن *raughan*, m. grease, oil, boiled butter, varnish. *raughani-balsān*, balsam. *raughani-talkh*, m. oil of mustard. *raughan-josh*, a kind of dish. *raughan-dāgh*, m. a vessel for boiling butter in. *raughani-zard*, m. boiled butter. *raughan-farosh*, m. an oil-merchant. *raughan-kā-tel*, varnish, oil. *p.*

روغني *raughanī*, greasy, oily; buttery. *p.*

روف *ra,ūf*, forgiving, merciful. *a.*

روك रोक *rok*, m. ready money, cash. *s.*

روك रोक *rok*, f. prevention, prohibition, hindrance. *s.*

روك रूह *rūh*, f. to boot, over and above. *h.*

روك ٹوك रोकटोक *roh-ṭok*, challenge, obstruction. *be-rok-ṭok*, without let or hindrance. *s.*

روكڑ रोकड़ *rokaṛ*, f. } ready money, cash;
روكڑي रोकड़े *rokṛe*, m. } prompt payment in cash. *rokaṛ-bahī*, a cash-book. *s.*

روكڑيا रोकड़िया *rokaṛiyā*, m. a cash-keeper, a treasurer. *s.*

روكن रूहन *rūhan*, f. to boot (v. *rūh*). *h.*

روكن रोकन *rokan*, f. an obstacle. *s.*

روكنا रोकना *roknā*, a. to inclose, to surround, to stop, to prevent, to detain, to interrupt, to prohibit. *s.*

روكو रोकू *rokū*, m. a preventer. *s.*

روكھ रूख *rūkh*, m. a tree. *rūkh chaṛhā*, m. a monkey (q. d. a climber of trees); adj. plain, unseasoned (bread or food). *s.*

روكھا रूखा *rūkhā*, dry, plain; rough, harsh, unkind; simple, unseasoned. *rūkhā sūkhā*, plain, blunt, harsh (words). *s.*

روكھاني रूखानी *rūkhānī*, f. a carpenter's chisel. *h.*

روكھاءي रूखाई *rūkhā,ī*, f. plainness, staleness, roughness, dryness, unfriendliness. *s.*

روكھڑ रूखड़ *rūkhar*, m. a kind of small tree; name of a class of *jogīs* or ascetics. *h.*

روکهڙا रूखड़ा *rūkhṛā*, m. a small tree. *h.*

روکهن रूखन *rūkhan*, to boot, over and above. *h.*

روکهي रूखी *rūkhī*, f. a squirrel. *s.*

روگ रोग *rog*, m. sickness, disease. *rog-bhū*, f. (the seat of disease) the body. *rog-rāj*, m. (the king of diseases) consumption. *rog-shānti*, f. cure or alleviation of disease. *rog-shāntak*, m. an alleviator of sickness, a physician. *rog-grasta*, sick, diseased. *rog-lakshan*, m. symptom of disease. *rog-har* or *rog-hārī*, curative; m. a physician. *s.*

روگي रोगी *rogī*, روگیا रोगिया *rogiyā*, روگیل रोगील *rogīl*, روگیلا रोगीला *rogīlā*, sick, ailing; lazy; an invalid (fem. *roginī* and *rogīlī*). *s.*

رولا रौला *raulā*, m. noise, tumult, sedition, alarm. *h.*

رولانا रोलाना *rolānā*, a. to cause to cry. *s.*

رولنا रोलना *rolnā*, a. to plane, to polish, to smooth. *rol-lenā*, to select, to pick: *Saudā* says, *Ki jiskī khāk se letī thī khalk, motī rol*, From the earth of which people picked out pearls. *h.*

رولي रोली *rolī*, f. a mixture of rice, turmeric, and alum, of which they form the *tilak* (q. v.) marked on the forehead of a Hindū. *h.*

روم *rūm*, the Eastern Roman empire; the present Turkish empire, Greece, Romelia, Asia Minor. *a.*

روم रोम *rom*, m. down, small hair of the body. *rom-kūp*, m. a pore of the skin. *rom-bikār*, m. horripilation (v. *romānch*). *s.*

رومال *rūmāl*, m. a handkerchief, a towel. *p.*

رومالي *rūmālī*, m. a kind of pigeon; a mode of exercising the arms by turning the *mugdars* over the head; a sodomite; a handkerchief worn about the head. *p.*

رومانچ रोमाञ्च *romānch*, m. horripilation, erection of the hair of the body, occasioned by extreme delight. *romānchit*, having the hair of the body erect; delighted, enraptured. *s.*

روماولي रोमावली *romāvalī*, f. a line of hair on the belly. *s.*

رومٹي रूमटी *rūmṭī*, f. subterfuge, trick, wrangling. *h.*

رومس रोमश *romas*, روم‌وت रोमवत *rom-wat*, hairy, woolly. *s.*

رومك रौमक *raumak*, روم‌لون रौमलवण *raum-lavan*, m. a kind of salt procured from a salt lake near the town of Sāmbhar in the district of Jainagar. *s.*

رومي *rūmī*, of or belonging to *rūm* (q. v.), a native of *Rūm* or Turkey; f. gum mastic. *s.*

روون रवन *ravan*, m. a lord, husband, lover. *s.*

روين *rūin*, down, fine wool. *d.*

رونا रोना *ronā*, n. to cry, to weep; to be displeased, to be melancholy; adj. addicted to crying; m. lamentation, grief. *ro-denā*, n. to cry, to weep; to be displeased, to be filled with indignation. *ronī ṣūrat*, adj. a sad countenance; f. a melancholy countenance. *s.*

رونا रोना *ronā*, m. (v. *rawā*) gold-filings, &c. *h.*

روانا रवन्ना *rawannā*, m. a servant who attends at the gate of the women's apartments to purchase articles that are required. *h.*

رونا रौना *raunā*, m. bringing home a wife to consummate a marriage. *h.*

روںپنا रोंपना *rompnā*, a. to plant, to transplant. *s.*

رونٹ रोंट *ronṭ*, f. trick, subterfuge. *h.*

رونٹگي रोंटगी *ronṭgī*, f. quarrelling, trickery. *h.*

رونٹنا रोंटना *ronṭnā*, a. to deny. *h.*

رونٹي रोंटी *ronṭī*, f. trick, subterfuge. *h.*

رونٹیا रोंटिया *ronṭiyā*, treacherous. *h.*

روندن रौंदन *raundan*, m. trampling, treading under foot. *s.*

روندنا रौंदना *raundnā*, روندھنا रौंधना *raundhnā*, a. (also *rondhnā*) to trample, to tread down, to ride over. *h.*

رونده *ravanda*, a goer, a traveller. *p.*

روندھنا रूंधना *rūndhnā*, a. to surround, to inclose (as with a hedge); to watch; n. to be restrained; to be confounded, astonished. *s.*

رونڈي *rondī*, fraud, deceit; villainy. *d.*

رونق *raunaḳ*, f. beauty, elegance, splendour, ornament, gaiety; (met.) order, symmetry. *raunaḳ afzā honā*, n. to be graced by the presence of any high personage, as a king, &c.: it may also denote to grace a place or person with a visit (as when a person of consequence honours a place with his presence). *raunaḳ-dār*, possessed of splendour, beautiful. *a.*

رونگٹا रूंगटा *rūngṭā*, m. the short hairs of the body. *rūngṭe khaṛe honā*, n. the standing of the hairs on end (from cold, fear, &c.). *s.*

رونگٹي रोंगटी *rongṭī*, f. wrangling, trickery, deception. *h.*

رونگهٹ रूंघट *rūnghaṭ*, f. dirt, filth. *h.*

روانه *rawanna*, m. a pass, a permit. *p.*

روهت रोहित *rohit*, m. a species of fish (*Cyprinus rohita*). *s.*

روهٹ रोहट *rohaṭ*, f. weeping, crying, tears. *h.*

روهس रोहिष *rohis*, روهش रौहिष *rauhish*, m. a sort of grass; the *rohi*, a kind of fish; a deer said to resemble an ass. *s.*

روهگ रोहग *rohag*, m. the name of a mountain, Adam's peak in Ceylon. *s.*

روهن रोहण *rohaṇ*, m. name of an ancient *rājā*. *s.*

روهن रौहिण *rauhiṇ*, m. sandal wood. *s.*

روهني रोहिणी *rohiṇī*, f. the name of the fourth mansion of the moon, figured by a wheeled carriage, comprising *Aldebaran* and four other stars in *Taurus*. *s.*

روهنییه रौहिणेय *rauhineya*, m. an emerald. *s.*

روهو रोहू *rohū*, m. f. the name of a fish (*Cyprinus denticulatus*, Buch.). *s.*

روئي रुई *rū,ī*, f. cotton. *rū,ī-dār*, quilted with cotton, stuffed with cotton. *h.*

روئي *rū,e* (v. *rū*), face, surface. *p.*

روئي *ro,ī*, (in comp.) growing (v. *ro*). *p.*

رويا *raviyā*, m. (for *raviya*, q.v.), custom, &c. *p.*

رويت *royat*, f. shape, appearance; seeing; aspect of the planets. *a.* [plant. *p.*

روئيدگي *rū,īdagī*, f. vegetation, growth of a

روئيدن *rū,īdan* or *rō,īdan*, to grow, to vegetate (a plant). *p.*

روئين *ro,īn*, m. brass, bell-metal. *ro,īn-tan*, a hero, an epithet of *Isfandiyār*, whose body was impenetrable to weapons. *p.*

روئين रोएं *ro,eṅ*, f. the hair on the arms, &c., bristle, pile, nap, down. *ro,eṅ badalnā*, n. to become sleek and fat (a horse), to change his coat. *s.*

رويه *raviya*, m. custom, fashion, institution, law, rule, mode of procedure. *p.*

روئيها रुईहा *rū,īhā*, m. a seller of cotton. *h.*

ره *rah*, f. a road, path; time or turn (*i. e.* twice, three times, &c.). *p.*

رها *rahā*, release, escape. *rahā-h.*, to release. *p.*

رهان *rihān* (pl. of رهن), pawns, pledges. *a.*

رهاو रहाव *rahāw*, m. stay, halt, delay, abode, residence, continuance. *h.*

رهائي *rahā,ī*, f. liberation, escape, relief, acquittal, discharge, freedom, release. *p.*

رهائس रहाइस *rahā,is*, } f. stay, delay, halt,
رهائش रहाइश *rahā,ish*, } abode, residence. *h.*

رهبان *rah-bān*, one who guards the way. *p.*

رهبان *ruhbān* (pl. of راهب), monks, &c. *a.*

رهباني *rah-bānī*, f. guardianship of the way. *p.*

رهبر *rah-bar*, m. a guide, a conductor. *p.*

رهبري *rah-barī*, f. guidance, direction, shewing the road. *p.*

رهت रहित *rahit*, destitute, deprived of, void of. *rahat*, staying, remaining. *s.*

رهتي रहते *rahte*, in the presence of, during the existence of, notwithstanding. *h.*

رهتي جاتي रहतेजाते *rahte-jāte*, before and behind, in the presence or absence of. *d.*

رهٿ रहट *rahaṭ*, f. a wheel for drawing water with. "This wheel has a long string of pots, fastened together, laid over it, which pots continually descend empty into the well or river and come up full. The wheel itself is acted upon by another horizontal wheel, which is turned by a bullock."—(Binning). *h.*

رهٿا रहटा *rahṭā*, m. a spinning-wheel. *h.*

ره جانا रहजाना *rah-jānā*, n. to wait, to stay, to delay, to desist, to give up. *h.*

رهچولا रहचोला *rahcholā*, m. flattery, agreeable conversation. *h.*

رهرو *rah-raw*, m. a traveller, a wayfarer; follower or sectary. *p.*

رهروان *rahrawān*, pl. followers, wanderers. *p*

رهروي *rahrawī*, f. traversing the road. *p.*

رهڙو रहड़ू *rahṛū*, m. a cart, a waggon. *h.*

رهزن *rah-zan*, f. a highwayman, a robber. *p*

رهزني *rahzanī*, f. act of plundering, highway robbery. *p.* [under foot. *h.*

رهس रहस *rahas*, m. trampling, treading

رهس रहस *rahas*, m. waggery, merriment; solitude, privacy; copulation; adj. secret, private, solitary (little used). *s.* [rejoice. *s.*

رهسنا रहसना *rahasnā*, n. to be pleased, to

رهسيه रहस्य *rahasya*, private, secret; m. a secret, a mystery. *s.*

رهکل रहकल *rahkal*, } m. a small cannon, a
رهکلا रहकला *rahkalā*, } swivel; a cart. *h.*

رهگذار *rah-guzār*, m. a pass, a road; a wayfarer, a traveller. *p.*

رهگذر *rah-guzar*, an event, occurrence; a wayfarer, a traveller. *p.*

رهگذري *rahguzarī*, f. a passage, the highway; m. a wayfarer, a traveller. *p.*

رهگرا *rahgirā*, m. a traveller. *rahgirā,ī*, f. travelling, journeying. *p.*

رهگير *rah-gīr*, m. a traveller, wayfarer. *p.*

رهلا रहला *rahlā*, m. a kind of pulse (*chanā*, *Cicer arietinum*). *h.* [wayman. *p. h.*

رهمار रहमार *rah-mār*, m. a robber, a high-

رهن *rihn* or *rahn*, m. a pledge, a pawn, any thing given in security for a loan; in the language of the law, it means the detention of a thing, on account of a claim, which may be answered by means of that thing, as in the case of debt. *a.*

رهن रहन *rahan*, f. manner, method. *s.*

رهنا रहना *rahnā*, n. to stay, to stop, to remain, to be, to exist, to last, to stand, to continue to live, to inhabit, to dwell, to escape. *rahne-wālā*, an inhabitant. *s.*

رهنامه *rah-nāma*, m. a map or book of roads. *p.*

رهنٿ रहंट *rahanṭ* (v. *rahaṭ*), a wheel, &c. *h.*

رهنما *rah-numā*, } one who shews the road,
رهنماي *rah-numā,e*, } a guide, a conductor, a pilot. *p.*

رهنمائي *rah-numā,ī*, f. guidance, pilotage. *p.*

رهنمون *rah-namūn*, m. a guide, escort, pilot, a conductor. *p.*

رهنموني *rahnamūnī*, f. guidance, pilotage. *p.*

رهنهار रहनहार *rahanhār*, remaining, abiding; a dweller. *h.* [chased. *h.*

رهوا रहवा *rahwā*, m. a slave. one not pur-

رهوار *rahwār*, m. ambling, smooth-going horse, a sound roadster. *p.*

رهواس *rahwās*, a residence, also a resident. *d.*

رهوائي रहवाई *rahwā,ī*, f. house-rent. *h.*

رهون *rahūn*, any thing pawned, property mortgaged. *a.*

رهويا रहवैया *rahwaiyā*, m. an inhabitant, a dweller or occupant. *h.*

رهيدن *rahīdan*, to escape, to be liberated. *p.*

رئي रई *ra,ī*, f. a churning-staff; bran. *h.*

ري रे *re*, m. } a vocative particle used by way
ري री *rī*, f. } of disrespect or admiration, such as holla! sirrah! bravo! O! *s.*

ري *rai*, name of the capital of Persian *'Irāḳ* (Parthia): there is another city of the name in *Khurāsān* (Bactriana). *p.*

ري *raiy*, giving water to drink. *a.*

ريا *riyā*, m. hypocrisy, dissimulation, subterfuge, evasion, affectation. *a.*

رئات *ri,āt* (pl. of رئة), f. the lungs. *a.*

رياحين *riyāḥīn* (pl. of ريحان), odoriferous herbs. *a.*

رياست *riyāsat*, f. government, command, dominion. *a.*

رياض *riyāẓ* (pl. of روضة), gardens. This word (both in the pl. and sing.) is a favourite title of numerous books on various subjects; such as *rauẓatu-s-ṣafā*, the garden of "purity," name of a universal history. *a.*

رياضت *riyāẓat*, f. abstinence, austerity. *a.*

رياضتي *riyāẓatī*, m. a devotee, an ascetic. *a.*

رياضي *riyāẓī*, m. mathematics, the abstract sciences. *a.*

ريان *raiyān*, juicy, sappy, flourishing. *a.*

ريائي *riyā,ī*, m. a hypocrite, sophist. *a.*

ريب *raib*, m. doubt, suspicion, scandal; necessity; bad fortune. *be raib o riyā*, without dissimulation, guileless, undisguised. *a.*

ريباس *rebās*, name of a sour plant, sorrel. *p.*

ريپه रेफ *reph*, m. the letter *r* with the inherent short vowel. *s.*

ريت रेत *ret*, f. sand; filings. *s.*

ريت रीत *rīt* or रीति *rīti*, f. custom, usage, rite, habit, regulation, rule, observance. *s.*

ريت रेत *ret* or रेतः *reta*, m. *sperma genitale* (*viri aut mulieris*), seed in general. *s.*

ريت *ret* (v. *renṭ*), snivel, snot. *d.*

ريتا रेता *retā*, m. sand; filings. *s.*

ريتا रीता *rītā*, empty, void, deprived of. *s.*

ريتائي रेताई *retā,ī*, f. price paid for filing or polishing. *h.*

ريتل रेतल *retal*, } sandy, abounding in sand.
ريتلا रेतला *retalā*, } *retal*, f. sand, sandy ground. *s.*

ريتن रेतन *retan*, m. *semen virile*. *s.*

ريتنا रेतना *retnā*, a. to file, to polish, to thrumb. *h.*

ريتوا रेतुआ *retū,ā*, m. a file-man, a filer, a polisher. *h*

ريتة रेतः *reta*, m. *semen virile*. *s.*

ريتي रेती *retī*, f. sandy ground on the shore of a river; a file. *s.*

ريتيانا रेतियाना *retiyānā*, a. to file, to polish. *h.*

ريتيلا रेतीला *retīlā*, sandy, gritty. *s.*

ريٹها रीठा *rīṭhā*, m. the name of a fruit, soapwort, soap-nut (*Sapindus saponaria*). *s.*

ريٹهيا रीठिया *rīṭhiyā*, f. a small *rīṭhā*, q. v. *s.*

ريجه रीझ *rījh*, f. choice, approbation, love, desire, wish; pleasing, satisfying. *rījh pachānā*, a. to conceal one's gratification. *rījh pachā,ū*, m. a person who conceals his inclination. *s.*

ريجهنا रीझना *rījhnā*, n. to be pleased, to be gratified, to be delighted. *s.*

ريجهوار *rejhwār*, m. (v. *rījhwār*) pleased. *s.*

ريچه रीछ *rīchh*, m. a bear (f. *rīchhnī*). *s.*

ريح *rīḥ*, f. wind, odour, exhalation. *a.*

ريحان *rīḥān*, m. an odoriferous plant, sweet basil. *tukhmi rīḥān*, m. the seed of *Ocymum pilosum*. *raiḥān*, favour, support; a blade of corn. *a.*

ريحاني *rīḥānī*, of or relating to, or smelling of *rīḥān*; m. a species of Arabic handwriting so called. *a.*

ريحي *rīḥī*, windy, flatulent. *a.*

ريخ *raikh*, loose, relaxed; straddling wide with the thighs; having a prolapsus ani; m. a prolapsus ani. *a.*

ريخ *rīkh*, m. thin excrement in diarrhœa. *rīkh nikalnā*, a term of abuse. *p.*

ريختن *rekhtan* (r. *rez*), to pour out, to scatter. *p.*

ريختة *rekhta*, scattered; m. the Hindūstānī language is called *rekhta*, being a mixed dialect; a Hindūstānī ode; mortar, plaster. *p.*

ريداس रैदास *raidās*, m. name of a *faḳīr*, the leader of a Hindū sect. *s.*

رير रीर *rīr*, m. noise, clamour, outcry. *s.*

ريريانا रीरियाना *rīriyānā*, n. to cry (as a child); to murmur; a. to importune, to beg earnestly. *s.*

ريڑه रीढ़ *rīṛh*, f. the backbone. *h.*

ريڑهي रीढ़ी *rīṛhī*, f. a young mango. *h.*

ريز *rez*, (in comp.) pouring, scattering, dropping, shedding, &c.; as *ashk-rez*, shedding tears; *khūn-rez*, shedding blood, a murderer; *durr-rez*, scattering pearls. *rez-k.*, a. to begin to speak or talk (as young birds). *p.*

ريزان *rezān*, scattering, pouring, used in comp. *p.*

ريزش *rezish*, f. a running at the nose; a running, flowing in small quantities, pouring, scattering. *s.*

ريزگي *rezgī*, a scrap, a bit, piece; small coin (as quarter-rupī pieces, &c.). N.B. I have ventured to make an alteration here, for which I have to apologize if wrong. In Hunter, *reza* and *rezgī* are said to denote "four-rupī pieces," which most assuredly would be no *small coin*. I believe the author meant "a fourth, or quarter-rupī piece," or, which is the same thing, a four-*ānā* piece: finally, I never heard of a *four-rupī* piece in my life.—(D. F.) *p.*

ريزه *reza*, m. a scrap, piece, bit; small coin (as quarter-rupī pieces, &c.); a kind of cock; children employed in mason-work, &c., who receive half, one-third, &c., of a man's pay. *reza khaṭṭ*, fine-striped, thin-lined. *reza-reza*, m. scraps, pieces; adj. in pieces, broken. "*reza* and *rezgī* are, as far as I can learn, used to signify small coin of any description, equivalent to our word 'change.'"—(Binning.) *p.*

ريزي *rezī*, f. mercy, clemency; (in comp.) scattering, shedding. *p.*

ريس *rīs*, f. equality. *h.*

ريس रीस *rīs*, f. anger, wrath, vexation. *s.*

ريسمان *resmān*, f. string, cord, thread, rope. *p.*

ريش *resh*, m. a wound, a sore, pus, matter; (in comp.) wounding, &c., as *dil-resh*, wounding the heart. *p.*

ريش *rīsh*, f. beard. *rīsh banānā*, to shave. *rīsh-khand*, laughing, risible, ridiculous. *rīsh-khandī*, f. risibility; a laughing-stock, a proverbial saying when a man does any thing unworthy of his beard. *p.*

ريشاءيل *rīshā,īl*, having a long beard. *p.*

ريشم *resham*, m. silk (v. *abresham*). *p.*

ريشمي *reshmī*, } ريشمينه *reshmīna*, } silken, woven or made of silk. *p.*

ريشه *resha*, m. fibre, stringiness of a mango. *resha-dār*, fibrous. *p.*

ريعان *ra'ān*, the prime or best part of any thing. *a.*

ريغل *rīghal*, dry, thin, lean. *p.*

ريكه रेख *rekh*, } ريكها रेखा *rekhā*, } f. a line, mark, streak; writing; fate, destiny. *s.*

ريكهان रेखान *rekhān*, land beyond the reach of river water. *h.*

ريگ *reg*, f. sand. *regi-rawān*, movable sand, quicksand. *reg-māhī*, f. a scink (*Lacerta scincus*). *p.*

ريگاري *regārī*, a furrow (properly *reghārī*). *s.*

ريگر रेगर *regar*, m. (v. *legar*) black soil, &c. *h.*

ريگروان *regi-rawān* or *reg-rawān*, moving sand; name of a famous sandhill to the north of *Kābul* (v. Sir Alex. Burnes's Cabool, p. 157). *p.*

ريگزار *reg-zār*, a sandy region. *p.*

ريگستان *registān*, m. the region of sand, a sandy place, a strand. *p.*

ريگهاري रेघारी *reghārī*, f. a furrow. *s.*

ريلا रेला *relā*, m. a flood; a line or string of animals; rushing, rush, push, shove, assault. *h.*

ريل پيل रेलपेल *rel-pel*, } ريل چهيل रेलचेल *rel-chhel*, } f. abundance, plenty; crowd, bustle. *h.*

ريلنا रेलना *relnā*, a. to shove, to push, to rush. *h.*

ريم *rīm*, f. pus, matter, humour, dregs, dross, lees, rheum. *p.*

ريمي *rīmī*, purulent, full of pus or matter. *p.*

رين रैन *rain*, f. night, from the end of twilight till daybreak. *s.*

رين रेण *ren* or रेणु *renu*, f. sand, powder, dust. *s.*

رينٹ रेंट *renṭ*, m. (v. *rahaṭ*) snivel, snot; a wheel for drawing water with. *h.*

رينٹا रेंटा *renṭā*, m. snot, snivel. *h.*

رينچه रींछ *rīnchh*, m. a bear (same as *rīch*). *s.*

رينڌهنا रींधना *rīndhnā*, a. to dress (victuals), to cook. *s.*

رينڌي रेंदी *rendī*, f. a small melon. *h.*

رينڈ रेंडु *rendu*, f. dust (same as *renu*). *s.*

رينڈ रेंड *renḍ*, f. } رينڈي रेंडी *renḍī*, m. } رينڑ रेंड़ *renṛ*, m. } *Palma Christi* (*Ricinus vulgaris*). *renḍī kā tel*, m. castor-oil. *s.*

رينك रेंक *renk*, f. braying (as an ass). *h.*

رينكنا रेंकना *renknā* or रैंकना *rainknā*, n. to bray (as an ass). *h.*

رينگنا रींगना *rīngnā* or रेंगना *rengnā*, n. to creep, to plod. *s.*

رينگني रेंगनी *rengnī*, f. name of a medicinal herb (v. *bhaṭ-kaṭaiyā*). *h.*

ريو *rev*, fraud, deceit, stratagem; (in Dakh.) a ford. *p.*

ريوا रेवा *rewā*, f. the Nerbudda or Narmadā river, which rises in the mountain Amrkūṭ in the province of Gondwana, and falls into the sea below Baroach. *s.*

ريوت रेवत *rewat*, name of an ancient *rājā*, who was the father-in-law of *Balarāma*. *s.*

ريوتي रेवती *rewatī*, f. the twenty-seventh mansion of the moon, consisting of ζ *Piscium* and thirty-one other stars, and figured by a tabor; the name of *Balarāma's* wife, daughter of *Rewat*. *s.*

ريوڙي रेवड़ी *rewṛī*, f. a kind of sweetmeat. *rewṛī ke pher men parnā*, n. to be involved in difficulties (this alludes to a game on the principle of geometrical progression, wherein one party bets that he will eat one of these sweet cakes so many times doubled, and is confounded at finding the same amount to a quantity far beyond his expectation): the same term also applies to a similar game founded on arithmetical progression, such as the well-known feat of gathering up a hundred stones, &c. (placed at the distance of one yard asunder) in the space of an hour. *h.*

ريوند *rewand* or *rewandi chīnī*, f. rhubarb. *p.*

رئہ *ri,a*, m. the lungs. *gātu-r-ri,a*, m. an inflammation in the lungs, the peripneumony. *a.*

ریہ, रेह *reh*, f. (*miṭṭī*) fossil alkali, used for washing and making soap. *h.*

ریہر, रेहर *rehar*, barren (soil or land). *h.*

ریہڑو, रेहड़ू *rehṛū*, m. a sled, a sledge. *h.*

ریہلا, रेहला *rehlā*, m. a vetch. *h.*

ریہوپیہو, रेहूपेहू *rehū-pehū*, f. abundance. *h.*

ریہی, रेही *rehī*, f. fossil alkali. *s.*

رئیس *ra,īs*, m. a prince, a chief, head, principal, president, commander, captain, pilot; citizen. *a.*

ڑ

ڑ ड़ *ṛa*, the fifteenth letter of the Hindūstānī alphabet. Its sound differs from that of *re* by being uttered with the tip of the tongue turned up towards the roof of the mouth. It differs very little in sound from the letter *ḍa*, with which it is often interchanged, and in the Devanāgarī alphabet the same character represents both. In reckoning by *abjad* it counts to 200, the same as *re*. It is very rarely used as the first letter of a word, there being, so far as we have been able to discover, only one solitary vocable under this class, viz.:

ڑوڑا *ṛoṛā*, m. a stone, a fragment of stone or brink (v. *roṛā*). *s.*

ز

ز *ze*, called *zā,e mu'jama* or *zā,e manḳūṭa*, the eleventh letter of the Arabic, the thirteenth Persian, and sixteenth in the Hindūstānī alphabets: its sound is that of the English *z*. In reckoning by *abjad* it stands for seven. In almanacks it stands for Saturday, and for the sign Scorpion. In Persian poetry it is used with the vowel *i* for *az*, *zi baski* for *az baski*, inasmuch as. This letter does not occur in the Sanskrit alphabet: hence, in Indian dialects of Sanskrit origin, such as the Hindī and Bengalī, it is generally changed into *j*, as *roj* for *roz*, a day. *jīn* for *zīn*, a saddle. *a. p. h.*

زا *zā*, (in comp.) born, descended, as *mīr-zā*, born of a noble, a mirza. *p.*

زاج *zāj*, m. copperas, vitriol. *zāji sufaid*, m. alum. *a.*

زاد *zād*, m. increase; food, provisions. *zādi rāh* or *zādi rāḥila*, m. way charges, provisions. *a.*

زاد *zād*, m. } born (a son, a child); used in
زاده *zāda*, m. } comp. as *ādmī-zād*, a man,
زادی *zādī*, f. } one born of the human race.
parī-zād, born of a *parī* or fairy, a beautiful woman. *shah-zāda*, a prince. *shah-zādī*, a princess. *p.*

زادن *zādan* (for *zā,īdan*), to bring forth young. *p.*

زار *zār*, m. desire, wish; a groan, lamentation; afflicted. *zār-zār* or *zār-nālī*, great grief or lamentation. *zār-o nizār*, emaciated (through grief). *p.*

زار *zār*, (in comp.) implies place, multitude, as *gul-zār*, m. a garden of roses. *p.*

زاری *zārī*, f. crying, sighing, groaning, lamentation, weeping. *p.*

زاغ *zāgh*, m. a crow. *zāghi-ābī*, a coot. *p.*

زاگ *zāg*, m. (v. *zāj*) copperas, vitriol. *p.*

زال *zāl*, old, decrepit, grey-haired (man or woman); the name of the father of *Rustam*, and son of *Sām*, son of *Narīmān*. He was so called because he came into the world with white hair, and a red countenance; the former like that of an old man, the latter of golden hue. *p.*

زان *zān* (for *az-ān*), from that, therefore. *p.*

زانکہ *zān-ki* (for *az-ān-ki*), because that, inasmuch as. *p.*

زانگاه *zān-gāh* (or *-gah*), from that time. *p.*

زانو *zānū*, m. the knee, the lap. *p.*

زانی *zānī*, m. an adulterer, a whoremonger, a fornicator. *a.*

زانیہ *zāniya*, f. a whore, a strumpet, an adulteress. *a.*

زاویہ *zāwiya*, m. an angle (in geometry); a corner, a retired place, &c. *a.*

زاہد *zāhid*, m. a monk, a hermit, a recluse; adj. religious, devout. *a.*

زاہدانہ *zāhidāna*, devoutly, like a *zāhid*. *p.*

زاہدی *zāhidī*, f. continence, devotion, leading the life of a *zāhid* or recluse. *p.*

زائچہ *zā,icha*, m. horoscope, astronomical table. *a.*

زائد *zā,id*, redundant, superfluous. *zā,idu-l-waṣf*, beyond description. *a.*

زائدن *zā,īdan*, to bring forth young. *p.*

زائر *zā,ir*, visiting, a visitor, one who visits holy places. *a.*

زائل *zā,il*, deficient, failing, perishing, vanishing. *a.*

زاینده *zāyanda*, one who brings forth. *p.*

زباد *zabād* or *zubād*, civet (perfume so called). *p. a.*

زبان *zabān* or *zubān*, f. the tongue; language dialect, speech. *zabān-āwar*, eloquent, voluble. *zabān-āwarī*, eloquence. *zabān-baṛhānā*, n. to chatter, to prattle. *zabān-bandī*, a written deposition. *zabān par chaṛhnā*, n. to be public; a. to learn by heart. *zabān par lānā*, a. to speak, to say. *zabān pakaṛnā*, a. to prevent one from speaking, to criticize. *zabān palaṭnā*, a. to equivocate, to retract, to eat one's words. *zabān chalānī*, to give abuse. *zabān dābnā*, a. to hold one's tongue. *zabān dābke kahnā*, to detract in whispers. *zabān-dān*, a poet. *zabān darāz*, abuse. *zabān-darāzī-k.*, a. to give abuse. *zabān-denā*, a. to promise. *zabān ḍālnā*, a. to ask, to put a question. *zabān-zad honā*, n. to be public. *zabān kāṭnā*, to grieve, to lament; to interrupt one's speech. *zabān karnī*, to speak foolishly, or inconsiderately. *zabān kholnā*, to let the tongue loose, to speak out. *zabān men paṛnā*, n. to be blamed. *zabān hārnā*, a. to promise. *zabān hilānā*, a. to speak. *p.*

زبانہ *zabāna*, m. flame (particularly of a candle). *p.*

زبانی *zabānī*, traditional, verbal; by word; from the tongue or statement of (any one). *p.*

زبد *zubd*, زبده *zubda*, زبدة *zubdat*, m. (from *zabad*, to churn) the best of any thing; cream, butter. *zubdatu-n-no,īnān*, the cream or essence of princes. *a*

زبر *zabar*, above, superior; the vowel-point *fatḥa* or short *a*. *zabar-dast*, vigorous, violent, oppressive. *zabar-dastī*, f. violence, oppression; violently, forcibly. *zabar-dastī-k.*, a. to oppress, to force. *zabar-k.*, a. to oppress. *zabar honā*, n. to have the upper hand. *p.*

زبرجد *zabarjad*, m. a kind of emerald, a chrysolite, a topaz, a beryl, jasper. *p. a.*

زبري *zabarī*, violence, oppression. *p.*

زبرين *zabarīn*, upper, superior. *p.*

زبس *zi-bas* (for *az-bas*), in abundance, plentifully. *zi-baski*, inasmuch as. *p.*

زبور *zabūr*, f. the psalms of David. *a.*

زبون *zabūn*, bad, ill, unlucky, wicked; a dupe, a capture. *p.*

زبوني *zabūnī*, f. vileness, infirmity, &c. *p.*

زبيب *zabīb*, currants; adj. sweet. *a.*

زپاٹا *zapāṭā*, noise of a bird's wing. *d.*

زٹل *zaṭal* (for *jaṭāl*), f. chattering, talking much and foolishly, quibbling, tattle. *zaṭal hānknā*, to quibble. *h.*

زجاج *zujāj*, m. a glass, a cup. *a.*

زجر *zijr*, m. threatening; an impediment; opposition, violence. *a.*

زچ *zich* (for *jich*), m. teazing. *h.*

زچا *zachā* (for *jachā*), a lying-in woman. *d.*

زحل *zuḥal*, the planet Saturn. *a.*

زحمت *zaḥmat*, f. disquietude, pain, trouble, injury, sickness, affliction. *a.*

زحمتي *zaḥmatī*, one who is afflicted or troubled. *a.*

زخ *zakh* (for *zakhm*), a sore, an ulcer. *p.*

زخار *zakhkhār*, raging, overflowing, full and swelling (the ocean). *a.*

زخام *zakhām* (for *zukām*), a cold, a catarrh. *d.*

زخم *zakhm*, m. a wound, sore, scar, cut. *zakhm-rasā*, a deep wound. *zakhm khānā*, n. to be wounded. *zakhmi kārī*, a mortal wound. *p.*

زخمه *zakhma*, the bow or plectrum of a musical instrument. *p.*

زخمي *zakhmī*, wounded; killed by a wound. *p.*

زد *zad*, beating, striking, smiting. *p.*

زدگي *zadagī*, percussion, a blow; used in comp., as *dahshat-zadagī*, being panic-struck. *p.*

زدن *zadan* (r. *zan*), to strike, to beat; to raise a noise. *p.*

زدني *zadanī*, worthy of being beaten. *p.*

زدوكوب *zad o kob*, m. beating, assault and battery. *p.*

زده *zada*, struck, affected by; arrayed, drawn up; used in comp., as *dahshat-zada*, panic-struck. *ṣaff-zada*, drawn up in a row. *p.*

زر *zar*, m. gold, riches, wealth, money. *zar-parast*, venal, selfish. *zari ja'farī*, gold of the purest kind. *zar-kharīd*, purchased (as a slave). *zar-khez*, rich (a country), producing gold and silver. *zar-dār*, wealthy. *zar-doz*, embroidered. *zar-dozī*, f. embroidery. *zari surkh*, m. gold; pure gold of a red colour, gold coin; name of a suit in cards (v. *tāj*). *zari sufaid*, m. silver; a suit in cards. *zar-gar*, m. a goldsmith. *zar-garī*, f. the business of a goldsmith; a kind of dialect. *zari-gul*, the yellow stamina of a rose. *zari naḳd*, ready money, cash. *zar-nigār*, gilt. *p.*

زراتشت *zarātusht*, زرادشت *zarādusht*, Zoroaster, the founder of the sect of Magi or fire-worshippers. *p.*

زراعت *zirā'at*, f. agriculture, husbandry, sown field, tillage, cultivation. *a.*

زرافه *zarāfa* or *zurāfa*, the giraffe. *a.*

زرباف *zar-bāf*, brocade, cloth of gold. *p.*

زربافي *zarbāfī*, brocaded, embroidered. *p.*

زربفت *zarbaft*, m. brocade, cloth of gold. *p.*

زربفتي *zar-baftī*, made of cloth of gold. *p.*

زرد *zard*, yellow, pale, livid. *zard pīlak*, m. the name of a bird (v. *pīlak*). *zard-rang*, yellow; (met.) bashful. *zard-rū,ī*, f. bashfulness. *zard-gosh*, hypocritical, malignant. *p.*

زردآلو *zard-ālū*, m. an apricot. *p.*

زردچوب *zard-chob*, f. yellow wood, turmeric (*Curcuma longa*). *p.*

زردشت *zardusht* (v. *zarātusht*), Zoroaster. *p.*

زردك *zardak*, f. a carrot; adj. yellowish. *p.*

زردوست *zar-dost*, fond of gold, venal. *p.*

زرده *zarda*, m. a kind of *pulāw*, dressed with saffron. *p.*

زردي *zardī*, f. yellowness, paleness (from fear or sorrow); the yolk of an egg; the jaundice. *p.*

زرضامني *zar-ẓāminī*, security for money payment. *p. a.*

زرع *zar'*, sowing, a sown field, seedtime. *a.*

زرق *zarḳ*, m. turning the eyes; (in Pers.) hypocrisy, fraud; detraction. *ẓarḳ-barḳ*, shining, glittering, splendid clothes, gaudy apparel. *a.*

زرگر *zar-gar*, a goldsmith, jeweller. *p.*

زرگري *zar-garī*, business of a goldsmith. *p.*

زرنباد *zurumbād*, zedoary, a Chinese root. *p.*

زرنه *zarna*, زرني *zarnī*, زرنيخ *zarnīkh*, m. arsenic, orpiment (perhaps corrupted from *αρσενικον*). *p.*

زره *zirah* or *zirih*, f. iron armour made with rings. *zirah-posh*, a man clad in iron armour. *p.*

زري *zarī*, f. any thing woven with gold thread. *zarī-bāf*, a manufacturer in gold threads. *zarī-bāfī*, the trade of gold-lace working. *p.*

زريح *zarīḥ*, f. a railing or lattice-work surrounding a temple or tomb. *a.*

زرين *zarrīn*, golden. *zarrīn-murgh*, m. the name of a bird; (met.) the sun. *p.*

زرينه *zarīna*, golden, made of gold. *p.*

زشت *zisht*, deformed, ugly, inhuman, hideous. *zisht-kho*, of unseemly habits, of a wicked disposition. *zisht-rū*, ugly, ill-favoured. *zisht-go*, an obscene speaker. *p.*

زشتي *zishtī*, f. ugliness, deformity; (met.) evil, wickedness. *p.*

زعاف *zu'āf*, m. sudden death (by poison). *a.*

زعفران *za'farān*, f. saffron (hence Ital. *zafferano*). *a.*

زعفراني *za'farānī*, f. a yellow colour. *a.*

زعم *za'm* or *zu'm*, f. thinking, presuming, speaking from belief; vanity, arrogance. *a.*

زغال *zughāl*, charcoal, live coal. *p.*

زغن *zaghan*, f. a kite; a black sparrow. *p.*

زغند *zaghand*, f. sally, flight, levity. *p.*

زفاف *zifāf*, m. leading the bride home to her husband's house. *a.*

زقوم *zakkūm*, a kind of thorny tree; an infernal tree (mentioned in the *Kur,ān*), the fruit of which is said to be the heads of devils whereof the damned shall eat. *a.*

زك *zak* or *zik*, f. injuring, deceiving, disappointing. *zak uṭhānā*, n. to be ashamed. *zak denā*, a. to put to shame. *a.*

زكاة *zakāt*, f. alms, a portion of a Musalmān's property given in charity agreeably to the rules laid down in the *Kur,ān*. *a.*

زكام *zukām*, m. rheum, defluxion, a cold. *a.*

زكاوت *zakāwat*, f. probity, purity, ingenuity. *a.*

زكوات *zakwāt* or *zakawāt*, pl. alms. *a.*

زكوة (pronounced) *zakāt*, alms (v. *zakāt*). *a.*

زكي *zakī*, pure, pious; continent; m. one who regularly pays the *zakāt*, q. v. *a.*

زلازل *zalāzil* (pl. of زلزله), earthquakes, commotions; (met.) misfortunes, afflictions. *a.*

زلال *zulāl*, adj. pure, limpid, wholesome; m. water which is pure, &c. *a.*

زلزله *zalzala*, m. an earthquake. *a.*

زلف *zulf*, f. a curling lock, a ringlet, whisker. *zulfi pareshān*, dishevelled locks. *zulfi tābdār*, curling locks. *zulfi darāz*, long locks. *zulfi 'ambarīn*, perfumed (with ambergris) locks. *p.*

زلفي *zulfī*, f. a sword-knot; the chain by which a door is fastened. *p.*

زلل *zalal*, m. erring, blundering; stumbling, falling; deficiency, loss. *a.*

زلو *zalū*, f. a leech. *p.*

زله *zalla*, m. victuals carried home by the guests from an entertainment. *p. a.*

زليخا *zalīkhā* (generally pronounced *zulaikhā*), the name of Potiphar's wife: the loves of *Yūsuf* (Joseph) and *Zulaikhā* form the subject of several Persian poems. *p.*

زمام *zamām*, f. a rein, a bridle. *a.*

زمان *zamān*, } m. time, an age; the world;
زمانه *zamāna*, } fortune; the heavens; tense.
zamāna-sāz, a turncoat. *zamāna-sāzī-k.*, to practise flattery or obsequiousness, to turn with the tide. *zamāna muwāfik*, fortunate. *h.*

زمبور *zambūr*, m. a vice, nippers, forceps. *h.*

زمرد *zumurrud*, m. an emerald. *p.*

زمردين *zumurrudīn*, of the colour of an emerald. *p.*

زمره *zumra*, m. a troop, a group, crowd, multitude. *a.*

زمزم *zamzam*, m. the name of a well at Mecca, called also Hagar's well. *a.*

زمزمه *zamzama*, m. singing; a concert. *a.*

زمستان *zamistān*, m. winter; wisdom. *p.*

زمستاني *zamistānī*, wintry, winterly. *p.*

زمن *zaman*, m. (v. *zamān*) time, fortune, &c. *p.*

زمهرير *zamharīr*, m. cold, intense cold. *zamharīrī*, intensely cold. *a.*

زميدار *zamī-dār* (for *zamīn-dār*, q.v.). *p.*

زمين *zamīn*, f. the earth, ground, soil; a region, country; the ground of a picture. *zamīn-bos honā*, n. to make a profound bow. *zamīn par se kuchh parā pānā*, to be overjoyed at finding unexpectedly the object of one's wishes. *zamīn pakaṛnī*, to persevere obstinately in any design, to insist. *zamīn meṅ gar-jānā*, to be greatly ashamed. *p.*

زميندار *zamīn-dār*, a landlord, a landholder (in reality a revenue farmer, or what, in Ireland, is called a middleman). As the term *zamīn-dār* differs widely in its signification from our ideas of a landlord, it may be proper to add, on the authority of Gladwin, that under the *Moghal* government the term was applied to a person who held a tract of land immediately of government, on condition of paying the rent of it. He was first in rank among the landholders. If a *zamīndār* was unable to pay up the amount of his engagements with government at the end of the year, such a part of his *zamīndārī* was sold as would discharge the balance. If he was dispossessed of the management of his *zamīndārī*, he was nevertheless exclusively responsible for all debts incurred by him during his possession, unless a mortgage was given on the *zamīndārī*, or the money borrowed applied to the payment of the revenue. *Zamīndārs*, by the nature of their tenures, had no longer a right to their lands than whilst they paid their revenues; and in case of failure, the sale of their land was a more just and useful recompense to government than subjecting them to corporeal punishment. Should they, however, at any time have been prevented fulfilling their engagements by unavoidable accidents rather than by their own mismanagement, equity would point out what indulgence they might be entitled to on that account. *p.*

زميندارانه *zamīn-dārāna*, the allowance to a *zamīndār* when set aside. *p.*

زميندارني *zamīn-dārnī*, the wife of a *zamīndār*.

زميداري *zamīn-dārī*, f. the office of a *zamīndār*; the land or estates held by him as above described. *p.*

زميني *zamīnī*, of or relating to the earth. *p.*

زن *zan*, f. a woman, a wife. *zan-h.* or *-lenā*, to marry. *zan-murīd*, hen-pecked. *zan*, from *zadan*, in comp. denotes smiting, striking; as *rah-zan*, a high wayman. *p.*

زنا *zinā*, f. adultery, fornication. *zinā-zāda*, a bastard. *zinā-kār*, m. an adulterer, a fornicator. *zinākārī*, f. adultery, fornication, harlotry. *a.*

زنابير *zanābīr* (pl. of زنبور), hornets, bees. *a.*

زنابيل *zanābīl* (pl. of زنبيل), baskets, wallets. *a.*

زناخا *zanākhā*, a serpent; also explained as *band i kafan*, the fastening of a winding-sheet. *d.*

زنار *zunnār* or *zanār*, f. a belt, the Brāhmanical thread, a Hindū rosary (from Gr. ζωναριον). *g.a.*

زناردار *zanār-dār*, a Brāhman, one who wears the thread. *p.*

زنان *zanān* (pl. of *zan*), wives, women; part. (of *zadan*, in comp.) striking. *p.*

زنانه *zanāna*, female, feminine, effeminate, womanly; m. female apartments, a seraglio. *h.*

زناني *zanānī*, of or relating to women, female, effeminate. *p.*

زنبق *zambak*, a flower, the jasmine, lily, iris. *a.*

زنبور *zambūr*, m. a hornet, a bee. *a.*

زنبورك *zambūrak*, f. a small gun. *p.*

زنبوره *zambūra*, m. a hornet, large bee; the point of a musical stringed instrument called in Hindī *kengrī*; a small gun. *zambūr-chī*, a fusileer. *a.*

زنبيل *zambīl*, f. a basket; a purse, a wallet. *p.*

زنجبيل *zanjabīl*, f. dry ginger. *a.*

زنجف *zinjif*, f. fringe, border, edging, &c. *p.*

زنجلب *zan-jalab*, a cuckold; also a man who is a pimp or pander to his own wife. *p.*

زنجلبي *zan-jalabī*, cuckoldom, &c. *p.*

زنجي *zanjī*, of or relating to *Zanj* or *Zanguebar*, a country in Africa from which they import slaves into Arabia and Persia. *a.*

زنجير *zanjīr*, f. a chain, fetters. *zanjīr-zāminī*, chain security, a number of persons binding themselves severally and jointly as security. *p.*

زنجيري *zanjīrī*, one bound in chains; (especially) one who is mad or insane. *p.*

زنجيريان *zanjīriyān*, pl. mad people, maniacs, those in chains. *p.*

زنخ *zanakh*, زنخدان *zanakhdān*, } m. the chin, the pit in the chin. *p.*

زندان *zindān*, m. a prison, a jail or gaol. *p.*

زنداني *zindānī*, a prisoner, captive. *p.*

زندقه *zandaka*, impiety, heresy, atheism. *a.*

زندگاني *zindagānī*, f. life, living, existence. *p.*

زندگي *zindagī*, f. life, living. *p.*

زنده *zinda*, alive, living. *zinda-dil*, alive at heart, cheerful. *zinda-k.*, to bring to life. *p.*

زنديق *zandīk* or *zindīk*, an infidel, a fire-worshipper, an atheist, one of a bad religion. *a.*

زنك *zanak*, زنكه *zanka*, } f. a little woman. *p.*

زنگ *zang*, m. rust; the country of Zanguebar, in Africa. *zang lagnā*, n. to become rusty. *p.*

زنگار *zangār*, m. verdigris, rust. *p.*

زنگازوري *zangā-zorī*, f. strife, quarrelling. *d.*

زنگالود *zang-ālūd*, rusty, covered with rust. *p.*

زنگاري *zangārī*, rusty, covered with verdigris. *p.*

زنگوله *zangūla*, m. a bell, cymbal. *p.*

زنگي *zangī*, m. an Ethiop, negro. *p.*

زنهار *zinhār* (v. *zīnhār*), care, caution, &c. *p.*

زنيه *zanya* or *zanyat*, fornication. *ibnu-z-zanyati*, a bastard. *a.*

زواجر *zawājir* (pl. of زاجرة), prohibition, forbidden things. *zawājiri shar'ī*, things prohibited by the divine law. *p.*

زوار *zawwār*, a visitor, a pilgrim. *a.*

زوال *zawāl*, m. decline, misery, wretchedness. *zawāl-pizīr*, transitory, fading. *a.*

زواوي *zawāwī* (pl. of زاويه), corners, angles. *a.*

زواهر *zawāhir* (pl. of زاهره), flowers, ornaments. *a.*

زوايا *zawāyā* (pl. of زاويه), angles, corners. *a.*

زوائد *zawā,id* (pl. of زائده), additions, augmentations. *a.*

زوج *zauj*, m. couple, a pair, alike, a spouse, [a husband. *a.*

زوجه *zauja* or زوجة *zaujat*, f. a wife. *a.*

زود *zūd*, quick, swift, soon, suddenly. *zūd-tar*, more speedily, very soon. *zūd-tarīn*, with all speed. *p.*

زور *zor*, m. force, strength, power, vigour; violence, effort, weight. *zor-āzmā*, a tried athlete. *zor-āwar*, powerful, strong. *zor-denā*, a. to aid, to support, to assist. *zor-k.*, a. to compel; to exercise. *zor-mārnā*, a. to endeavour. *p.*

زور *zūr*, m. a lie, a falsehood, adulteration; a false deity, an idol. *zaur*, m. going on a pilgrimage. *a.*

زوري *zūrī*, f. a lie; m. a liar. *a.*

زورق *zaurak*, a small ship, a skiff. *a.*

زورمند *zor-mand*, robust, powerful. *zor-mandī*, strength. *p.*

زوري *zorī*, f. force, strength (in comp.). *p.*

زوزن *zauzan* or *zūzan*, name of an ancient city in *Khuzistan*. *p.*

زوفه *zūfa* (from ὑσσωπος), hyssop. *a. g.*

زون *zūn*, a fop, a beau; adj. base. *d.*

زه *zih*, f. a bowstring; offspring, childbirth. *dardi zih*, the pangs of childbirth; interj. good! excellent! *p.*

زهاد *zuhhād* (pl. of زاهد), religious men. *a.*

زهار *zihār*, m. a bladder; the lower part of the belly; *mons veneris*. *mū,e zihār*, m. *pubes, pecten*. *p.*

زهد *zuhd*, m. continence, devotion, abstinence. *zuhd-kesh*, devout. *a. p.*

زهدان *zih-dān*, m. the womb, matrix. *p.*

زهر *zahr* or *zahar*, m. poison. *zahr-ālūd*, poisoned. *zahr-dār*, poisonous. *zahri ḳātil* or *zahri halāhal*, m. deadly poison. *zahar khānā kisī par*, to imitate an act unsuitable to one's state or condition, to ape the condition of one's superiors. *p.*

زهره *zahra*, m. bile, gall-bladder; spirit, boldness, pluck. *zahra āb honā*, n. to be much distressed, to be terrified. *p.*

زهره *zuhra*, f. the planet Venus. *a.*

زهري *zahrī*, venomous, poisonous. *p.*

زهي *zihī*, *zahe*, or *zahī*, bravo! well done! admirable! there! lo! behold! *p.*

زهير *zahīr*, reduced (by sickness), thin; sad, melancholy, low-spirited. *a.*

زياد *ziyād*, زيادت *ziyādat*, زيادتي *ziyādatī*, زياده *zīyāda*, } augmentation, surplus, addition; adj. great, excessive; more, too much. *ziyāda-k.*, a. to augment, to increase; (met.) to take away whatever is on the dinner-table. *ziyāda-go*, an intolerable babbler. *a.*

زيارت *ziyārat*, f. pilgrimage, visiting. *ziyārat-gāh*, a place to which pilgrimage is made. *a.*

زيان *ziyān*, m. loss, damage, deficiency. *p.*

زيب *zeb*, ornament, elegance, beauty. *zeb denā*, to suit, to become; (in comp.) adorning, as *aurang-zeb*, throne-adorning, the name of a celebrated Great Mogul. *p.*

زيبا *zebā*, adorned, beautiful. *p.*

زيباءي *zebā,ī*, f. beauty, gracefulness. *p.*

زيبائش *zebā,ish*, f. ornament, elegance. *p.*

زيبق *zībaḳ*, m. quicksilver. *a.*

زيبنده *zebanda*, adorning, decorating. *p.*

زيبيدن *zebīdan*, to adorn, to decorate. *p.*

زيتون *zaitūn*, m. an olive-tree. *a.*

زيج *zīj*, m. astronomical tables, of which there are several in the Persian language; a mason's rule. *a.*

زيد *zaid*, m. increasing, adding, augmentation; a fictitious name employed in exemplifying the rules of Arabic grammar, or cases in law, like our once well-known personages, John Nokes and Thomas Stiles, recently defunct. *a.*

زير *zer*, under, below; the vowel-point called by the Arabians *kasra*, corresponding to *i*, in *fit*. *zer-andāz*, m. the cloth, or carpet, which is spread under a *ḥuḳḳa*. *zer-bār honā*, to be indebted, to undergo a great expense. *zer band*, a martingal. *zer-dast*, m. a subject, a vassal; adj. powerless, under command. *zer-k.*, a. to overpower, to subdue. *p.*

زير *zīr*, f. a fine soft sound, the smallest string of a lute, &c., the treble. *p.*

زيرا *zīrā*, m. cummin-seed (*Cuminum cyminum*). *s.*

زيرا *zīrā*, زيراكه *zīrāki*, } because, because that, since, on account of. *p.*

زيربريان *zer biryān*, m. name of a kind of dish. *p.*

زيربم *zer-bam*, a pair of small kettle-drums. *d.*

زيرزميني *zer-zamīnī*, a chamber under ground. *p.*

زيرك *zīrak*, ingenious, intelligent, sagacious, penetrating, acute. *p.*

زيركي *zīrakī*, f. acuteness, intelligence. *p.*

زيرمشق *zer mashḳ*, m. one or two pieces of leather or pasteboard joined together, and commonly painted or ornamented, placed on the knee when writing, the paper being laid upon this support. *p. a.*

زيرنگي *zīrangī*, f. the cantharides beetle, or Spanish fly. *d.*

زيره *zīra*, m. (v. *zīrā*) cummin. *s.*

زيرين *zerīn*, inferior, lower, lowermost. *p.*

زيست *zīst*, f. life, living, existence. *p.*

زيف *zaif*, light or clipt money, current, but not receivable at the public treasuries. *a.*

زيستن *zīstan* (r. *zī*), to live, to exist. *p.*

زيل *zīl* (v. *zīr*), the treble in music. *p.*

زيل *zail*, removing, leaving off. *a.*

زين *zīn*, m. a saddle. *zīn bāndhnā*, a. to saddle. *zīn-posh*, m. a cloth fastened over the saddle, housing. *zīn-gar*, m. a saddler. *p.*

زين *zain*, ornament, honour. *a.*

زينب *zainab*, name of one of *Muḥammad's* wives. *a.*

زينت *zīnat*, f. ornament, beauty, elegance, dress, decoration. *a.*

زينه *zīna*, m. a ladder, stairs, steps. *p.*

زينهار *zīnhār*, m. care, caution, protection, defence, patronage; interj. take care! beware! on no account! *p.*

زيور *zewar*, m. jewels, ornaments (of gold, silver, &c.); (pl. *zewarāt*). *p.*

ژ

ژ *zhe*, called *zāe fārsī* or *'ajamī*, the fourteenth letter of the Persian alphabet, and seventeenth Hindūstānī, has no corresponding character in the Arabic or Sanskrit alphabets: its sound is that of *s* in the English word *pleasure*, or of *z* in *azure*, or of the French *j* in *jour*; it is sometimes changed into *j*, as *pajmurda* for *pazhmurda*. *p.*

ژاژ *zhāzh*, m. idle, trifling or indecent speech; a kind of thistle. *zhāzh-khā,s*, a trifler, one who speaks obscenely. *p.*

ژاله *zhāla*, m. dew, hoar-frost, hail. *p.*

ژنده *zhinda*, m. a patched garment. *p.*

ژولیده *zholīda*, intricate, entangled. *zholīda-mū*, entangled hair. *p.*

ژیان *zhiyān*, formidable, rapacious, terrible. *sheri zhiyān*, a fierce lion, a ferocious tiger. *p.*

س

س *sīn*, usually named *sīni muhmala* or *sīni ghair manḳūṭa*, the twelfth letter in the Arabic, the fifteenth in the Persian, and eighteenth in the Hindūstānī alphabets: its sound is that of the English *s*, or of the Sanskrit *sa*: in reckoning by *abjad* its value is sixty: in almanacks it represents the sun, and a sextile aspect of the planets. It is also used as an abbreviation for the word *salām*, salutation. *a. p. h.*

س स *sa*, prefixed to Sanskrit substantives, denotes "with," "possessed of," or "related to," as *sa-jīva*, alive. *sa-bal*, powerful. *sa-gotra*, related to one family. *su*, as a prefix, corresponds to the εὖ of the Greek (in opposition to *dur*, δυς, bad), and denotes "goodness, facility, excellency, or excess;" as *su-panth*, the good or right way. *su-labh*, easy of attainment, in opposition to *dur-labh*, difficult in the attainment: again, *su-dur-labh* denotes excessively difficult to attain. *s.*

س सु *su*, in the Braj dialect, is used as a postposition, denoting from, by, with, of, &c., as *jā-su*, from or of whom; it is also used sometimes for the correl. *so*, he, she, it, they, &c. *h.*

سا सा *sā*, added to a substantive denotes similitude, as *kuttā*, a dog. *kuttā-sā*, dog-like: as an adjective adjunct it appears sometimes superfluous, but generally intensive, as *baṛā*, large. *baṛā-sā*, largish, or very large (v. Hind. Gram. p. 108, c.). *kālā-sā*, blackish. *p. h.*

سابدهان सावधान *sābadhān* (v. *sāvadhān*), attentive, cautious. *s.*

سابر साबर *sābar*, m. an elk, or, more properly speaking, a large species of stag; a leather of elks' or any kind of deers' hide for bedding. *sābar mantr*, m. a spell composed in colloquial language. *s.*

سابر साबर *sābar*, m. a small anvil. *h.*

سابع *sābi'*, the seventh. *sābi'an*, seventhly, in the seventh place. *a.*

سابق *sābiḳ*, former, preceding, formerly, of yore, time past. *sābiḳu-l-an'ām*, former bounties. *sābiḳan*, as formerly, agreeably to former practices. *a.*

سابقه *sābiḳa*, preceding, past, ancient; m former friendship, previous intimacy. *a.*

سابل साबल *sābal*, m. an iron crow or lever. *h.*

سابن *sābun*, سابون *sābūn*, } m. (v. *ṣābūn*) soap. *a.*

سابوت साबूत *sābūt*, whole, entire. *s.*

سابونگر *sābūn-gar*, m. a soap-boiler or soap-manufacturer. *p.*

ساپ साप *sāp*, m. imprecation, curse. *s.*

ساپرادھ सापराध *sāparādh*, faulty, offending. *a.*

ساپن सापन *sāpan*, m. the name of a disorder in which the hair gradually falls off. *h.*

ساپن सापिन *sāpin*, f. a female snake. *s.*

ساپنا सापना *sāpnā*, a. to curse. *s.*

ساپھلیه साफल्य *sāphalya*, m. productiveness, fruitfulness. *s.*

سات सात *sāt*, seven. *sāth pānch-h.*, to be in doubt, to be unable to decide what to do. *sāt samundar*, the name of a game. *s.*

ساتاروهن सातारोहण *sātārohan*, m. a dog who associates with (six) wolves. *s.*

ساتبهاءي *sāt-bhā,ī*, (lit. the seven brothers) a species of thrush so called from the birds being gregarious, and frequently seven of them are found together.—(Binning). *d.*

ساتسار सातिसार *sātisār*, dysenteric, afflicted with dysentery. *s.*

ساتو *sāto* (for *sātoṅ*), the seven. *sāto mūṅ sarāhnā*, to praise or extol very much. *d.*

ساتوان सातवाँ *sātwāṅ*, m. the seventh. *s.*

ساتور सातूर *sātūr*, a knife, a butchers' chopping knife. *p.*

ساتوك सात्विक *sātwik*, spontaneous, sincere, relating to or proceeding from the *satwa* quality; sincere, good, true, gentle, amiable, &c. *s.*

ساتوین सातवीं *sātwīṅ*, f. the seventh. *s.*

ساتھ साथ *sāth*, with, together, along with, m. a troop, company, society. *sāth is-ke*, along with this, besides, moreover. *sāth us-ke*, along with that, although, notwithstanding. *sāth denā*, to join, to associate with. *sāth-wālā*, a comrade, a companion. *sāthoṅ sāth*, together with, along with. *s.*

ساتھن साथिन *sāthin*, f. a female companion. *s.*

ساتھي साथी *sāthī*, m. a companion, comrade, ally, associate. *sāthī sāth*, together, in one company. *s.*

ساتي *sātī*, the sixth (in Dukh.), for *sāthī*. *a.d*

سات‌بات साटबाट *sāṭ-bāṭ*, f. combining, leaguing, confederating. *h.*

ساٹھ साठ *sāṭh*, sixty (in Dakh. *sāṭ*). *s.*

ساٹهي साठी *sāṭhī*, m. a kind of rice produced in the rains (so called because it ripens in sixty days from the time of sowing). *s.*

ساٹهيه साठ्य *sāṭhya*, m. vice, villainy. *s.*

ساج साज *sāj*, m. preparation, harness, accoutrements. *s.*

ساج *sāj*, m. the teak-tree (*Tectona grandis*). *p.*

ساجد *sājid*, m. one who is prostrate in adoration; an adorer, a worshipper. *a.*

ساجن साजन *sājan*, m. a sweetheart, a lover. *s.*

ساجنا साजना *sājnā*, a. to prepare, to dress, to decorate, to regulate; n. to become, to fit, to suit. *s.*

ساجها साझा *sājhā*, m. partnership, association. *h.*

ساجهي साझी *sājhī*, m. a partner, an associate. *h.*

ساچ साच *sāch*, true, real, correct. *s.*

ساچق *sāchaḳ*, m. hinna presented to the bride the day of marriage; wedding gifts of various kinds. *t.*

ساحت *sāḥat*, an area or inclosed space, court, quadrangle; shore or coast; tract of country. *a.*

ساحر *sāḥir*, m. an enchanter, a magician, a necromancer (fem. *sāḥira*). *a.*

ساحري *sāḥirī*, f. enchantment, magic, necromancy. *a.*

ساحل *sāḥil*, m. the sea-shore. *a.*

ساخت *sāḵẖt*, f. make, construction, manufacture; pretence. *p.*

ساختگي *sāḵẖtagī*, f. make, effort; art. *p.*

ساختن *sāḵẖtan* (r. *sāz*), to make or form; to counterfeit. *p.*

ساخته *sāḵẖta*, made, formed; counterfeited, false, surreptitious. *p.*

ساد *sād*, f. desire, wish; adj. (v. *sādh*). *s.*

سادات *sādāt*, lords (pl. of سيد, q. v.). *a.*

سادج *sādaj*, Indian spikenard. *p.*

سادر सादर *sādar*, with respect, respectfully. *s.*

سادرا सादरा *sādrā*, m. a kind of song. *h.*

سادرشيه सादृश्य *sādṛishya*, m. likeness, resemblance. *s.*

سادس *sādis*, the sixth (f. *sādisa*). *a.*

سادسا *sādisā* or *sādisan*, sixthly, in the sixth place. *a.*

سادگي *sādagī*, f. plainness, want of ornament, artlessness, simplicity, openness. *p.*

ساده *sāda*, plain, white, unadorned, simple; artless, open, sincere. *sāda-dil*, artless, simple, stupid. *sāda-ṭaurī*, f. gentleness, affability; simplicity, stupidity. *sāda-kār*, m. a (kind of) goldsmith, a plain worker in gold or silver, who makes articles which are after ornamented by other hands. *sāda-lauḥ*, artless, simple, stupid (q.d. *tabula rasa*). *sāda-waẓ'ī*, f. artlessness, simplicity, stupidity. *p.*

سادھ साध *sādh* or साधु *sādhu*, adj. virtuous, good, holy; m. a religious person, a saint, a mendicant. *sādhu*, a merchant; f. desire, wish, inclination. *sādhu-sīl*, virtuous, righteous. *s.*

سادھارن साधारण *sādhāraṇ*, in common, common. *sādhāran-dharm*, m. universal duty, law common to all castes. *s.*

سادھپشپ साधुपुष्प *sādhu-pushp*, m. a flower (*Hibiscus mutabilis*). *s.*

سادھتا साधुता *sādhutā*, f. goodness, honesty, piety. *s.*

سادھك साधक *sādhak*, completing, perfecting, finishing; who or what effects; holy; m. a devotee; a practiser. *s.*

سادھن साधन *sādhan*, m. the act or means of accomplishing, effecting; practice. *s.*

سادھنا साधना *sādhnā*, a. to familiarize gradually to any habit; to teach, to learn, to rectify, to use, to practise, to regulate, to pacify; to settle, to determine, to accomplish. *s.*

سادھنا साधना *sādhanā*, f. the act of familiarizing by habitude; solicitation, contrivance, devotion; practice, accomplishment. *s.*

سادھو साधू *sādhū*, pious, honest; m. a merchant; a kind of mendicant. *s.*

سادھورکش साधुवृक्ष *sādhu-vṛiksh*, m. the Kadamb tree (*Nauclea Cadamba*). *s.*

سادھيه साध्य *sādhya*, practicable, easy; m. the twenty-second astronomical *yug*. *s.*

سار सार *sār*, best, excellent; m. the pith or sap of trees, &c.; strength, vigour; the essence or vital part of any thing, quintessence; value, worth; manure; iron; the piece used in playing at *chaupar*. *sār-varjit*, pithless, sapless. *s.*

سار *sār*, a particle denoting plenty, magnitude, or similitude; as *koh-sār*, a mountainous country; *'ambar-sār*, full of ambergris; *shāh-sār*, like a king; sometimes used for *sar*, the head, as *sigūn-sār*, inverted, with the head undermost; a camel; the name of a black bird of a musical note. *p.*

سار सार *sār*, m. a cowhouse. *s.*

سار *sār* (v. *sā*), like, resembling. *d.*

سارا सारा *sārā*, all, the whole; m. wife's brother, brother-in-law (v. *sālā*). *s.*

سارا *sārā*, pure, excellent, sweet-smelling, undefiled; as *'ambari sārā*, the most odoriferous ambergris. *p.*

سارارتھ सारार्थ *sārārth*, m. abridgment. *s.*

ساربان *sār-bān*, m. a camel-driver. *p.*

سارپي सार्पी *sārpī*, f. the ninth lunar asterism. *s.*

سارتا सारता *sārtā*, f. strength, substance, essence. *s.*

سارتھك सार्थक *sārthak*, profitable, substantial. *s.*

سارتھي सारथी *sārathī*, m. a charioteer. *s.*

ساردا सारदा *sāradā*, f. a name of the goddess *Saraswatī*; also a name of *Durgā*. *s.*

سارس सारस *sāras*, m. } a species of heron,
سارسي सारसी *sārasī*, f. } the Indian crane, male and female (*Ardea antigone*). *s.*

سارسوت सारस्वत *sāraswat*, the people of the *Saraswat* country, or the north-west part of the province of Delhi. *s.*

سارق *sāriḳ*, a thief, a plunderer (pl. *sāriḳīn*), from which, perhaps, the word "Saracen;" as "Cossack," from *ḳazzāḳ*. *a.*

ساركا सारिका *sārikā*, f. a kind of bird (*Turdus salica*), but the name is applied also to the *mainā* (*Gracula religiosa*). *s.*

سارلوه सारलोह *sār-loh*, m. steel. *s.*

سارنا सारना *sārnā*, a. to mend, to perform, to complete, to make, to manure. *s.*

سارنده *sārinda* (v. *sārangī*), a fiddle. *d.*

سارنگ सारङ्ग *sārang*, m. name of a musical mode or *rāg*; a peacock; a snake, a serpent; a cloud; the voice of a peacock; a deer; a woman; water; the name of a country; a lamp; the *nymphæa lotus*. *sārang ne sārang gahyo, sārang bolyo ā,e; jau sārang sārang kahe, sārang muṅh taiṅ jā,e*, a peacock seized a snake; a cloud thundered; if the peacock utter his cry, the snake will escape from his mouth (it is said to be a peculiarity of the peacock, that on hearing thunder he utters a cry of pleasure, and dances for joy). *s.*

سارنگي सारङ्गी *sārangī*, f. a musical instrument like a fiddle. *h.*

سارنگيا सारङ्गिया *sārangiyā*, m. a fiddler. *h.*

سارو सारू *sārū*, f. a kind of bird, a species of blackbird or starling. *h.*

ساروت सारवत *sār-vat*, substantial, having pith, substance, &c. *s.*

ساروان *sār-wān*, a camel-driver; name of a mountain south of *Samarḳand*. *p.*

ساروبهوم सार्वभौम *sārva-bhaum*, m. a universal monarch. *s.*

سارولوكك सार्वलौकिक *sārva-laukik*, prevailing throughout the universe, universally known. *s.*

سارووركك सार्ववर्णिक *sārv-varnik*, of every kind, belonging to every tribe. *s.*

ساري सारी *sārī*, f. cream; a dress consisting of one piece of cloth worn by Hindū women round the body and passing over the head. *s.*

ساري *sārī*, passing, penetrating, pervading, flowing; infecting, contagious. *a*

ساڑهو साढ़ू *sāṛhū*, m. a wife's sister's husband. *s.*

ساڑهي साढ़ी *sāṛhī*, m. the spring harvest, or grain cut in the spring. *h.*

ساڑهي साढ़े *sāṛhe*, } one half more; this word
ساڑي साड़े *sāṛe*, } prefixed to any common numeral denotes that the half of a unity is to be added to such numeral, as *sāṛhe chār*, four and a half; when added to an aggregate number, it signifies that half the aggregate is to be added, as *sāṛhe sau*, 150, *i. e.* a hundred with half a hundred added. *s.*

ساڑي साड़ी *sāṛī*, f. (the same as *sarī*) cream, &c.; it also denotes the single garment worn by females in Bengal. *s.*

ساز *sāz*, m. arms, apparatus, accoutrements, harness, furniture; a musical instrument; concord. *sāz-bāz*, trim, dressy; m. ornament, apparatus. *sāzkār* proper, consonant, concordant. *sāz-yarāḳ*, m. warlike instruments, furniture, baggage. *sāz*, in comp. denotes making, effecting, as *zinda-sāz*, making alive, resuscitating. *p.*

سازا *sāzā*, partnership, companionship. *d.*

سازش *sāzish*, combination, collusion, confederacy. *p.*

سازشي *sāzishī*, collusive, fraudulent. *p.*

سازنده *sāzinda* or *sāzanda*, m. a maker, a musical performer. *p.*

سازوار *sāzwār*, agreeing, well-arranged. *p.*

سازور *sāzwar*, accoutred, armed. *p.*

سازي *sāzī*, f. abstract form of *sāz*, in composition, as *zinda-sāzī*, resuscitation. *p.*

ساس सास *sās* or *sāsu*, a mother-in-law. *s.*

ساس *sās*, m. a bug, a flea, a louse. *p.*

ساست शास्ति *sāsti*, f. (for *shāsti*) command, correction. *s.*

ساسن शासन *sāsan*, m. (for *shāsan*) order, command; a patent, a grant; act of punishing. *s.*

ساسنا सासना *sāsnā*, a. to chastise, to admonish (v. *sāāsnā*). *s.*

ساعت *sā'at*, f. a moment, minute, hour; a watch or clock. *sā'at-sāz*, a watchmaker. *a.*

ساعد *sā'id*, f. the arm from the wrist to the elbow, the fore-arm. *a.*

ساعي *sā'ī*, m. one who attempts or endeavours; a recommender; adj. earnest, eager. *a.*

ساغر *sāghar*, m. a bowl, cup, goblet. *sāghar-kash*, one who drains his cup; a regular toper. *p.*

ساغري *sāgharī*, f. the space between the tail and anus of a horse. *p.*

ساق *sāḳ*, f. the leg, the trunk of a tree, the stalk of an herb. *a.*

ساقط *sāḳiṭ*, falling. *sāḳiṭ honā*, n. to be degraded. *a.*

ساقي *sāḳī*, m. a cupbearer, a page. *sāḳiyā* (poetic vocative), O cupbearer! *a.*

ساقيان *sāḳiyān*, (pl. of *sāḳī*), cupbearers. *p.*

ساكا साका *sākā*, m. an era. *sākā-k.*, a. to establish an era; (met.) to distinguish one's self by heroic actions. *sāke-bandh*, m. a king who has established an era in consequence of his fame and worth. *s.*

ساكار साकार *sākār*, having form or shape. *s*

ساكت *sākit*, silent, quiet, at rest. *a.*

ساكشات साक्षात *sākshāt*, before, in presence, in sight; as, like; evidently, manifestly. *s.*

ساكشي साक्षी *sākshī*, witnessing, seeing, attesting; an eyewitness, an evidence. *s.*

ساكشيه साक्ष्य *sākshya*, m. testimony, evidence. *s*

ساكن *sākin*, m. an inhabitant; adj. quiet, peaceable; a quiescent letter, *i.e.* a consonant not followed by a vowel. *a.*

ساكوت *sākūt*, silent, quiescent. *a.*

ساكهه साख *sākh*, f. trust, credit, reputation. *s.*

ساكهه साख *sākh*, f. season, time. *h.*

ساكها साखा *sākhā* (for *shākhā*), f. a branch of a tree. *s.*

ساكهي साखी *sākhī*, m. an evidence, a witness. *s.*

ساكهيات साख्यात *sākhyāt*, (for *sākshāt*) evident, conspicuous; adv. before, in the presence of. *s.*

ساگ साग *sāg*, m. greens, edible vegetables, culinary herbs. *sāg-pāt*, m. greens; petty dues paid in kind to village officials. *sāg-pāt honā*, n. to become soft. *s.*

ساگر सागर *sāgar*, m. the sea, the ocean. *s.*

ساگمڑي *sāgmaṛī*, rice fields, cultivated ground, lands in full crop. *d.*

ساگو. सागू *sāgū*, sago, a tree of the palm species: a flour is made from this tree, which, formed into bread, when fresh from the oven, eats like hot rolls: when hard, it requires being soaked in water before it is used. Three of these trees are sufficient to maintain a man a year, and an acre properly planted will afford subsistence for one hundred for that time. *h.*

ساگوان *sāgwān* (v. *sāgūn*), teak. *h.*

ساگوتي सागौती *sāgautī*, f. meat, flesh. *h.*

ساگون सागून *sāgūn* or *sāgaun*, f. teak wood, or tree (*Tectona grandis*). *h.*

سال साल *sāl*, m. name of a common timber tree (*Shorea robusta, Rox. Pl. Cor.*), a thorn, spine; perforation, bore, mortice, a hole made by driving a pin into the ground, &c.; a jackal; f. a house, place; a school. *s.*

سال *sal*, m. a year. *sāli āyanda*, next year. *sāli ḥāl*, the present year. *sāl-ḥāṣil*, yearly produce. *sāl-khurda*, old. *sāl-girah*, f. birthday, on every anniversary of which an additional knot is tied on a string kept for this purpose; *sāl gasht*, old, in years. *sāli guzashta*, last year. *sāl-hā-sāl*, annually. *p.*

سالا साला *sālā*, m. a wife's brother, brother-in-law (the term is used also in a grossly abusive sense); (in comp. for *shālā*) it denotes house, place, as *pāṭh-sālā*, a place for reading, a school. *s.*

سالار *sālār*, m. a chief, head, leader, prince, captain. *sālāri ḳāfila*, the chief of a caravan, leader of a troop. *p.*

سالانه *sālāna*, yearly, annual; annually. *p.*

سالبه *sāliba*, (in logic) a negative sentence. *a.*

سالبيه *sālbiya*, sage (*Salvia*). *p.*

سالپرني सालपर्णी *sāl-parnī*, f. a shrub (*Hedysarum gangeticum*). *s.*

سالپشپ सालपुष्प *sāl-pushp*, m. a shrub (*Hibiscus mutabilis*). *s.*

سالرس सालरस *sāl-ras*, m. the resinous juice of the Sāl tree. *s.*

سالسا सालसा *sālsā*, m. sarsaparilla. *h.*

سالستري *sālistrī*, m. a farrier. *d.*

سالك *sālik*, going; m. a traveller; (met.) a devotee; a class of *Muḥammadans* who observe the law and lead a domestic life; (pl. *sālikān*). *a.*

سالگرام सालग्राम *sālagrām*, m. a schistous stone, containing the impression of one or more ammonites, conceived by the Hindūs to represent *Vishṇu*. *s.*

سالم सालम *sālam*, good fertile land. *h.*

سالم *sālim*, safe, free, perfect. *a.*

سالن सालन *sālan*, } m. meat, fowl, or fish,
سالنا सालना *sālnā*, } dressed with spices and eaten with rice: the dish called (by Europeans) curry: the curry used by the Hindūs consist of vegetable only. *h.*

سالنا सालना *sālnā*, a. to perforate, to bore, to prick; n. to ache, to be in pain, to smart. *s.*

سالو सालू *sālū*, m. a kind of red cloth (dyed with *morinda*). *s.*

سالوار *sālwār*, by or according to the year. *p.*

سالواهن सालिवाहन *sālivāhan*, m. name of a celebrated sovereign.

سالوتر सालोतर *sālotar*, } m. a farrier, a
سالوتري सालोतरी *sālotarī*, } horse-doctor.
sālotarī, f. farriery, veterinary practice. *s.*

سالوس *sālūs*, m. } hypocrisy, trick, subter-
سالوسي *sālūsī*, f. } fuge, fraud. *p.*

ساله *sāla*, in comp. with any numeral denotes so many years old; as *si-sāla*, three years old. *p.*

سالها *sālhā*, (Pers. pl. of *sāl*) years. *p.*

سالهاي سال *sālhā,e sāl*, a course or series of years, several years. *p.*

سالي साली *sālī*, f. sister-in-law, wife's sister, especially younger sister. *s.*

سالي *sālī*, annual, relating to the year; f. land taken by the year. *p.*

ساليان *sāliyān* (irreg. pl.), years. *p.*

ساليانه *sāliyāna*, annual; m. a yearly salary, an annuity. *sāliyāna-dār*, an annuitant. *s.*

سالينه *sālīna*, annually, year by year. *p.*

سام साम *sām*, f. a ferule (same as *sāmī*). *s.*

سام साम *sām* or *sāma-veda*, m. the third Veda, the text of which is sung. *s.*

سام *sām*, a celebrated hero in old Persian romance, father to *Zāl*, and grandfather to *Rustam*. *p.*

سام ابرص *sāmm-abraṣ*, a large and venomous kind of lizard. *a.*

ساماما सामा *sāmā*, f. provisions, eatables of various sorts (also same as *sāmagrī*, q. v.). *s.*

ساماجك सामाजिक *sāmājik*, m. an assistant or spectator at an assembly. *s.*

سامان *sāmān*, m. furniture, apparatus, instruments, tools; measure, quantity; understanding, reason, intellect; custom, habit, mode, order, proportion; opulence, power; probity; a laudmark. *sāmāni-jangī*, m. warlike apparatus. *be sar o sāmān*, destitute, indigent, helpless; stupified, brainless; immense, boundless, endless (applied to affairs). *p.*

سامانيا सामान्या *sāmānyā*, f. a prostitute, a girl common to all. *s.*

سامانيه सामान्य *sāmānya*, common, general, universal. *sāmānya-lakshan*, m. a generic character. *s.*

سامبر साम्बर *sāmbar*, m. an elk (v. *sābar*). *s.*

سامبهر साम्भर *sāmbhar*, m. the name of a town near Ajmīr, in the vicinity of which is a lake from which salt is extracted; the salt itself. *s.*

سامدرك सामुद्रिक *sāmudrik*, f. palmistry, chiromancy, fortune-telling, the art of physiognomy. *s.*

سامر सामर *sāmar*, m. a kind of salt (v. *sāmbhar*). *s.*

سامرتهه सामर्थ *sāmarth*, f. } ability,
سامرتهيه सामर्थ्य *sāmarthya*, m. } power. *s.*

سامرتهي सामर्थी *sāmarthī*, powerful, mighty, able, capable. *s.*

سامري *sāmirī*, name of a magician, said to have been contemporary with Moses; adj. Samaritan. *a.*

سامع *sāmi'*, m. a hearer, a listener. *a.*

سامعه *sāmi'a*, hearing, the ear. *a.*

سامگري सामग्री *sāmagrī*, f. furniture, tools, apparatus, articles, materials; scenery. *s.*

سامنا सामना *sāmnā*, m. front, facing, confronting. *sāmnā-k.*, to confront, to encounter. *s.*

سامني सामने *sāmne*, opposite,. before, confronting. *s.*

سامهنا साम्हना *sāmhnā*, m. the front, facing, confronting. *sāmhnā-k.*, to confront, to encounter. *s.*

سامهني साम्हने *sāmhne*, } before, in front, op-
سامهي साम्ही *sāmhī*, } posite, confront-
سامي सामी *sāmī*, } ing. *s.*

سامي *sāmī*, sublime, exalted. *a.*

سامي सामी *sāmī*, f. a ferule; arable land. *s.*

سامييه सामीप्य *sāmīpya*, m. proximity. *s.*

سان *sān*, like; m. likeness; sign; similitude. *sān gumān*, m. understanding and imagination. *p.*

سان सान *sān*, f. a whetstone, a grindstone. *p. s.*

سان सानु *sānu*, m. table-land, level ground on the top of a mountain. *s.*

سان بجهانا सानबुझाना *sān bujhānā*, a. to make one understand by hints. *h.*

سانبهر सांभर *sāmbhar*, m. name of a town near Ajmere; also a kind of salt extracted from a lake in the vicinity. *s.*

سانپ सांप *sāmp*, m. a snake, serpent. *s.*

سانپن सांपन *sāmpan*, f. a female snake. *s.*

سانت सांत *sānt* (v. *shānt*), calm, tranquil. *s.*

سانتا सांता *sāntā*, m. the sugar-cane. *h.*

سانتون सान्त्वन *sāntwan*, m. conciliation, reconcilement. *s.*

سانتي सांती *sāntī*, f. instead, stead. *h.*

سانٹ सांट *sānṭ*, f. joining, sticking; confederacy, collusion; a stick for threshing corn with, a flail. *h.*

سانٹا सांटा *sānṭā*, m. a stick or whip with which elephants are beaten at the time of fight; a spur. *h.*

سانٹھ सांठ *sānṭh*, f. (v. *sānṭ*) joining, &c. *h.*

سانٹھنا सांठना *sānṭhnā*, a. (v. *saṭūnā*) to apply; to join (thread), to splice, to stick together &c. *h.*

سانجھ सांझ *sānjh*, f. evening (Dakh. *sānj*). *s.*

سانجھا सांझा *sānjhā*, m. } images of cow-dung
سانجھي सांझी *sānjhī*, f. } made by children
in the month *āsin, krishṇa paksh*, to represent idols. *s.*

سانچ सांच *sānch*, } true, proper, real. *sānch*
سانچا सांचा *sānchā*, } *ko ānch kyā*(?), pure gold fears not the flame. *s.*

سانچا सांचा *sānchā*, m. a mould, a matrice. *h.*

سانحات *sāniḥāt* (pl. of سانحه), events, occurrences. *a.*

سانحه *sāniḥa*, an event, occurrence. *a.*

ساندا *sāndā*, a limb, members of the body. *d.*

ساندهيه सान्निध्य *sānnidhya*, m. proximity, vicinity. *s.*

سانڈ सांड *sānḍ* or *sānṛ*, m. a bull; a stallion; (met.) an impudent extravagant fellow. *rānḍ-kā-sānḍ*, (lit.) "a widow's bull," that most contemptible of male bipeds, commonly called "a kept man." *s.*

سانڈا सांडा *sānḍā*, m. name of an animal resembling the lizard (the oil of which is said to have restorative powers). *h.*

سانڈني सांडनी *sānḍnī* or *sānṛnī*, f. a female camel, a dromedary. *sānḍnī-sawār*, one who rides on a camel. *h.*

سانڑ सांड़ *sānṛ* (v. *sānḍ*), a bull, &c. *s.*

سانڑني सांड़नी *sānṛnī* (v. *sānḍnī*). *h.*

سانس सांस *sāns*, f. breath, sigh. *sāns ulṭī lenī*, to gasp in agony. *sāns bharnā*, to sigh, to regret. *sāns ruknā*, to be smothered or throttled. *sāns roknā* or *sāns rūknā*, a. to smother, to throttle. *s.*

سانسا सांसा *sānsā*, m. imagination, reflection, fancy, fear, apprehension. *s.*

سانسارك सांसारिक *sānsārik*, worldly, of this world. *s.*

سانسنا सांसना *sāṅsnā*, a. to snub, to distress, to threaten. *s.*

سانك सांक *sāṅk*, f. fear; the asthma. *s.*

سانك सांक *sāṅk*, f. a lump of sweetmeat, particularly of *jalebī*. *h.*

سانكر सांकर *sāṅkar*, سانكري सांकरी *sāṅkrī*, سانكل सांकल *sāṅkal*, f. a chain; a kind of female ornament; a strait, a narrow lane; (met.) difficulty; adj. tight, narrow, close, straight, strict. *s.*

سانكهو सांखू *sāṅkhū* or *sāṅkho*, m. a bridge; a kind of wood (*Shorea robusta*). "*sāṅkho*, 'a bridge' is denoted as Bengālī by Shakspear; but this word is commonly used in the Carnatic."—(Binning.) *h.*

سانكهيه सांख्य *sāṅkhya*, m. a system of philosophy so called, ascribed to Muni Kapila. *s.*

سانگ सांग *sāṅg*, f. a spear or javelin all of iron; adj. having all the members. *s.*

سانگ सांग *sāṅg*, m. disguise, mimickry, acting; a scene. *sāṅg-k.*, a. to act foolishly. *sāṅg lānā*, to imitate, to mimic. *h.*

سانگس सांगुस *sāṅgus*, سانگوس सांगूस *sāṅgūs*, f. a kind of fish, skate. *s.*

سانگهر सांघर *sāṅghar*, m. a wife's son by a former husband. *h.*

سانگي सांगी *sāṅgī*, f. a support on which the pole of a cart is propped. *h.*

سانگيت सांगीत *sāṅgīt*, m. song, &c. (v. *san-gīt*). *s.*

ساننا सानना *sānnā*, a. to knead, to mix up flour, dough, earth, &c. *h.*

ساننا सानना *sānnā*, a. to whet, to impregnate, to stain, to soil. *s.*

سانوا सांवा *sāṅwā*, m. the name of a very small grain (*Panicum frumentaceum, Roxb.*). *s.*

سانوان सांवां *sāṅwāṅ*, m. (v. *sāṅwā*). *s.*

سانوچيت *sāṅw-chīt*, tranquil, without care or anxiety. *d.*

سانولا सांवला *sāṅwlā* or *sā,oṅlā*, of a dark or sallow (complexion). *s.*

ساني सानी *sānī*, f. chaff or straw mixed with grain (particularly that from which oil has been expressed), as food for cattle. *h.*

ساءو साऊ *sā,ū*, tractable; m. a relative. *s.*

ساوج सावज *sāwaj*, savage, wild; m. sport, game (*i. e.* wild animals for the chase). *s.*

ساودهان सावधान *sāvadhān*, careful, attentive, cautious. *s.*

ساودهاني सावधानी *sāvadhānī*, f. care, caution. *s.*

ساوك सावक *sāwak*, m. a child, the young of animals. *s.*

ساوكاس सावकाश *sāvakās* or *sāvakāsh*, m. leisure, opportunity. *s.*

ساون सावन *sāwan*, m. the name of the fourth Hindū month, the full moon of which is near *Sravanā* or *a Aquilæ*. *sāwan hare na bhādoṅ sūkhe* (flourishing in summer and not fading in autumn) is applied to express continuance in the same state or situation. *s.*

ساونت सावन्त *sāwant*, brave, valiant; a hero, a warrior. *s.*

ساونتي सावन्ती *sāwantī*, f. bravery, heroism. *s.*

ساءونگي साऊंगी *sā,ūngī* (v. *sāngī*). *h.*

ساؤنلا सांवला *sā,oṅlā*, dark, sallow (v. *sāṅwlā*). an innocent person. *s.*

ساه साह *sāh*, m. a merchant, a shopkeeper;

ساهايه साहाय *sāhāya*, m. friendship, fellowship, alliance, succour. *s.*

ساهتيه साहित्य *sāhitya*, m. society, association, connexion. *s.*

ساهس साहस *sāhas*, m. violence; courage, spirit, valour, resolution. *s.*

ساهسي साहसी *sāhasī*, violent; resolute, undaunted, determined. *s.*

ساهل साहिल *sāhil*, m. a plumb-line; a porcupine. *h.*

ساهن साहन *sāhan*, fem. of *sāh*, q. v. *s.*

ساهوكار साहूकार *sāhūkār*, m. a great merchant; a banker. *s.*

ساهوكاري साहूकारी *sāhūkārī*, f. traffic, trade, commerce, exchange of money. *s.*

ساهول साहूल *sāhūl*, m. a plummet. *h.*

ساهي साही *sāhī*, f. a porcupine. *s.*

ساءي *sā,e* or *sā,ī*, (in comp.) rubbing, polishing; diffusing; resembling. *p.*

سايا *sāyā*, m. shade (v. *sāya*). *p.*

سايبان *sāyabān*, a canopy, the roof or fly of a tent; a parasol, an umbrella. *p.*

سائبة *sā,ibat*, f. a female slave manumitted; also a she-camel set at liberty under a vow. *a.*

سائيدن *sā,īdan*, to rub, grind, polish. *p.*

سائر *sā,ir*, m. the whole; the remainder; going, walking, wandering; tax, duty levied on personal property, in opposition to that levied on land, which is denominated *māl*; "land customs: duty levied on transit of goods: this tax has lately been abolished."—(B.) *a.*

سائرجات *sā,irjāt* (barbarous pl. of سائر), taxes on personal property, transit duties. *s.*

سأيس *sā,īs*, m. a groom, a horsekeeper. *a.*

سأيسي *sā,īsī*, f. the business of a groom. *a.*

سائل *sā,il*, m. one who asks, an interrogator, questioner; a beggar, a mendicant. *a.*

سائمه *sā,ima*, a term applied to camels, goats, &c. (v. pl. *sawā,im*). *a.*

ساءين साईं *sā,īn*, m. lord, master, your worship; (met.) a *faḳīr*; the Deity; an imitative sound (as of wind). *s.*

سايڼكال सायंकाल *sāyankāl*, m. eveutide, evening. *s.*

سايه *sāya*, m. shadow, shade, protection; an apparition; a petticoat. *sāya-parwarda*, brought up in the shade, delicately reared. *sāya tale ānā*, a. to take protection. *sāya kisī kā parnā*, to imitate the manner of another. *sāya-dār*, shady; a protector. *sāya honā kisī ko*, a demon appearing to or possessing any one. *p. s.*

سب सब *sab*, all, every, the whole, total (inflected plural *sabhoṅ*). *sab miṣrī kī haiṅ ḍaliyāṅ* (all are pieces of sugar), is applied to the equality of state, form, &c. *sab kuchh*, every thing, all. *sab ko,ī*, everybody, every one, all. *sab-khawwā*, omnivorous, one who eats all kind of food without exception. *s.*

سبا *sabā*, a country in Arabia Felix, where they suppose *Balḳis*, the queen who visited Solomon, to have reigned. *a.*

سبابه *sabbāba*, the forefinger. *a.*

سباس सुबास *subās*, f. perfume, fragrance, odour. *s.*

سباع *sibā'* (pl. of سبع), lions, wild beasts. *a.*

سباقت *sabāḳat*, excelling, &c. (v. *sabḳat*). *a.*

سبان *sabāṅ* (v. *ṣabāṅ*), to morrow. *d.*

سبب *sabab*, m. cause, reason, motive; relationship, affinity, instrument; on account of, by reason of. *a.*

سببيت *sababīyat*, f. cause, motive. *a.*

سبت *subbat*, f. reproach, slander, disgrace, injury, villainy; the podex. *a.*

سبحان *subḥān*, m. praising, glorifying (God); a title of the Deity. *subḥāna-llāh*, interj. O God! O holy God! *ḥaḳḳ subḥāna-hu*, God the most holy! *a.*

سبحاني *subḥānī*, divine, relating to God. *a.*

سبحه *subḥa* or *sabḥa*, m. a rosary; a chaplet for repeating prayers. *subḥa-gardān*, one who is counting the beads. *subḥa-gardānī*, the act of counting the beads. *a.*

سبد सब्द *sabd* or *shabd*, m. sound, voice; a song (among *Nānak-panthīs*, q.v.); a word, a noun. *s.*

سبد *sabud*, m. a basket. *p.*

سبدرا सबदरा *sabdarā*, m. the bowsprit of a vessel. *h.* [gent. *s.*

سبدھ सुबुद्धि *subuddhi*, wise, clever, intelli-

سبرت *sabart*, m. a hare, a rabbit. *h.*

سبرن सुबर्ण *subarn*, m. (v. *suvarṇa*) gold. *s.*

سبز *sabz*, green, fresh; grey-coloured (a horse). *sabz bāgh dikhānā*, a. to deceive. *sabz dhūmā*, m. a kind of pigeon. *sabz-rang*, of black complexion. *sabz-roshan*, m. a kind of pigeon. *sabz-ḳadam*, unfortunate, unlucky, ill-omened. *sabz honā*, n. to flourish. *p.*

سبزك *sabzak*, m. the jay bird (*Coracias*). *p.*

سبزوار *sabzawār*, namo of several districts and towns in Persia. *p.*

سبزه *sabza*, m. verdure; incipient beard, bloom; a green stone worn in the ear as an ornament; the jay bird; the sweet basil (*Ocymum basilicum*). *p.*

سبزي *sabzī*, f. greenness; greens, culinary vegetables; an intoxicating potion made of *bhang*. *sabzī manḍī*, f. a place where vegetables are sold. *p.*

سبسبانا सबसबाना *sabsabānā*, n. (v. *sursurānā*) to creep as a snake, &c. *h.* [family. *a.*

سبط *sibṭ*, m. a grandchild; progeny; a tribe,

سبع *sab'*, seven; *sab' saiyāra*, the seven planets. *sub'*, the seventh part, a seventh. *a.*

سبق *sabaḳ*, m. a lesson, lecture, reading. *a.*

سبقت *sabḳat*, f. excelling, surpassing, preceding, aggression. *a.*

سبك *subuk*, light (either in weight or character), debased, unsteady. *subuk-bār*, lightly burdened, *expeditus*. *subuk-pāe*, light of foot, a courier. *subuk-khez*, vigilant, alert. *subuk-dastī*, expedition. *subuk-dosh*, light-hearted. *subuk-raw*, light of step, travelling quickly. *subuk-rūḥ*, of a cheerful spirit, jovial. *subuk-sār*, light-headed, contemptible. *subuk-ser*, soon satisfied. *subuk-mizāj*, of a fickle temper, irresolute. *p.*

سبكاءي *subkā,ī*, سبكي *subkī*, سبكئي *subka,ī*, } f. lightness, levity, frivolousness; rashness, folly; affront, indignity, dishonour. *p.*

سبل सबल *sabal*, powerful, forcible. *sabbal*, a crow, an iron lever. *s.* [stitutions. *a.*

سبل *subul* (pl. of سبيل), ways, means, in-

سبلاءي सबलाई *sabalā,ī*, f. power, force, strength. *s.* [ened. *s.*

سبندھ सुबन्ध *su-bandh*, well secured or fast-

سبو *sabū*, m. a cup, a glass, an ewer, a jar, a pitcher. *p.*

سبوتر सबोतर *sabotar*, everywhere. *s.*

سبوچه *sabūcha*, m. a pitcher, jar, ewer. *p.*

سبورا सबूरा *sabūrā*, m. *instrumentum in membri virilis forma, e corio concinnatum, quo mulieres libidinosæ utuntur.* *h.*

سبوس *sabūs*, m. bran, chaff, sawdust. *p.*

سبھ सुभ *subh*, good, pleasant, agreeable, happy, auspicious. *s.*

سبھا सभा *sabhā*, f. an assembly, meeting, company. *sabhā-pati* or *sabhā-nāyak*, m. the president of an assembly. *sabhā-sad*, m. one of a company, an assistant, an assessor. *s.*

سبھاسبھ सुभासुभ *subhāsubh*, m. good and evil, lucky and unlucky. *s.*

سبھاسد सभासद *sabhā-sad*, one who sits or deliberates in an assembly. *s.*

سبھاو सुभाव *subhāv* or *subhā,o*, m. nature, natural state, property, disposition; good disposition; adj. well-disposed, of good disposition. *s.*

سبھتا सुभिता *subhitā*, f. welfare, security. *s.*

سبھٹ सुभट *subhaṭ*, m. a champion, a hero. *s.*

سبھدر सुभद्र *subhadra*, auspicious, fortunate. *s.*

سبھکا सभिक *sabhik*, one who presides at an assembly or feast. *s.*

سبھگا सुभगा *subhagā*, f. well-favoured; a woman who is loved by her husband, and is the mother of a thriving family. *s.* [the whole. *s.*

سبھوں सभों *sabhoṅ* (inflect. pl. of *sab*), 'all,

سبھي सभय *sabhay*, fearful; timidly. *s.*

سبھيتا सुभीता *subhītā*, m. time, leisure, opportunity, convenience. *s.*

سبھيت सभ्यता *sabhyatā*, f. politeness, refinement in manners. *s.*

سبھيه सभ्य *sabhya*, trusted, confidential, faithful; m. an assistant at an assembly, an assessor. *s.*

سبير सबेर *saber*, early, soon, in good time. *s.*

سبيرا सबेरा *saberā*, m. morning, the dawn of day. *s.*

سبيري सबेरे *sabere*, in the morning, early, soon (more commonly *sawere*, q. v.). *s.*

سبيل *sabīl*, f. a road, way, path; mode, manner; water distributed to thirsty travellers during the first ten days of the *muḥarram*. *sabīl-k.*, to obtain money by borrowing or begging. *a.*

سپات *sapāt*, pure, clean. *d.*

سپاتر सुपात्र *supātr*, good, worthy; a good or able man; a vessel of earthenware, &c. *s.*

سپاٹا *sapāṭā*, a leap, bound, spring. *d.*

سپارا सुपारा *supārā*, m. *glans penis*. *h.*

سپارش *sipārish* or *supārish*, f. a recommendation, intercession, introduction. *p.*

سپاره *sipāra* (for *sī-pāra*), lit. thirty sections, a portion of the *ḳur,ān*. *p.*

سپاري सुपारी *supārī*, f. betel-nut (*Areca catechu*); *glans penis*. *h.*

سپاس *sipās*, f. praise, thanksgiving. *p.*

سپاه *sipāh*, f. (used in the pl.) soldiers, an army. *sipāh phir jānī*, implies a revolt or treachery in an army. *sipāh-garī*, f. the military profession. *p.*

سپاهي *sipāhī*, m. a soldier, military. *p.*

سپاءي *sipā,ī*, f. a tripod, trivet, a three-legged stool or table, a trench. *p.*

سپت सप्त *sapt* or *sapta*, seven. *sapt-ṛikh* (for *saptarshī*), m. the seven principal stars in the constellation of the Bear, Charles's Wain. *s.*

سپت सुप्त *supt*, m. sleeping, asleep, numbed; m. sleep. *s.*

سپت सपुत *saput*, a good son (v. *saputra*).

سپتاه सप्ताह *saptāh*, } m. a week, the
سپتاها सप्ताहा *saptāhā*, } eighth day after any other day. *s.*

سپتت सप्तति *saptati*, seventy. *s.*

سپتدس सप्तदश *saptadas* or *saptadash*, seventeen. *s.*

سپتر सुपुत्र *suputra* and सपुत्र *saputra*, m. a good and dutiful son. *s.* [*cassia*. *s.*

سپتر सुपत्र *supatra*, m. the leaf of the *Laurus*

سپتما सप्तमा *saptamā*, the seventh. *s.*

سپتمي सप्तमी *saptamī*, f. the seventh *tithi* or lunar day. *s.* [sleep. *s.*

سپتوتھت सुप्तोत्थित *suptotthit*, risen from

سپتونشت सप्तविंशति *saptaviṅshati*, twenty-seven. *s.* [the twenty-seventh. *s.*

سپتونشتتم सप्तविंशतितम *saptaviṅshatitam*,

سپتھ सपथ *sapath*, f. an oath, an asseveration. *supath*, m. a good road; good conduct. *s.*

سپچھ सुपच्छ *supachchh* (for *supaksh*), m. the party which has justice on its side; the fortunate half of the month, *i. e.* from the new to the full moon. *s.*

سپچھي सुपच्छी *supachchhī* (for *supakshī*), m. an advocate of the just cause. *s.*

سپد सपदि *sapadi*, this instant, immediately. *s.*

سپر *sipar*, f. a shield, target. *sipar-dārī* f. protecting, shielding. *p.*

سپرا सिप्रा *siprā*, f. a river near Ujjain. *s.*

سپرتشٹھا सुप्रतिष्ठा *supratishṭhā*, f. consecration, erection of a temple, &c. *s.*

سپرد *supurd* or *sipurd*, f. charge, keeping, care, trust; delivering or giving over (property). *supurd-nāma*, a deed of delivery. *supurd-k.*, a. to give in charge, to recommend to one's care, to consign. *p.*

سپردا सपर्दा *sapardā*, m. a musician attending on singing-women. *s.*

سپرداءي सपर्दाई *sapardā,ī*, f. the corps of musicians attending a dancing-girl. *s.*

سپردگي *sipurdagī*, charging, consigning. *p.*

سپردن *sipurdan* (r. *sipār*), to give in charge, to consign, to hand over. *p.*

سپردي *supurdī*, f. the article, &c., given up. *p.*

سپردھا स्पर्द्धा *spardhā*, f. envy, emulation, rivalry. *s.*

سپردھي स्पर्द्धी *spardhī*, envious, emulous. *s.*

سپرز *supurz*, m. the spleen, the milt. *p.*

سپرسن सुप्रसन्न *suprasanna*, well-pleased, favourable. *s.*

سپرش स्पर्श *sparsh*, m. touch, contact. *s.*

سپرکاش सुप्रकाश *suprakāsh*, manifest, public. *s.*

سپرها स्पृहा *spṛihā*, f. desire, wish. *spṛihī*, desirous. *s.*

سپري *siparī*, completed, concluded. *p.*

سپڑانا *sapṛānā*, a. to catch, to arrest. *d.*

سپڑنا *saparnā*, n. to be caught, to be involved. *d.*

سپشٹ स्पष्ट *spashṭ*, evident, manifest, clear. *s.*

سپكش सपक्ष *sapaksh*, m. a partisan, one of the same party. *supaksh*, m. the party which has justice on its side; the fortunate half of the month, i. e. from the new to the full moon. *supakshi*, an advocate of the just cause. *s.*

سپلك *siplak*, m. a small lizard, commonly to be found in houses, and which lives by catching flies and insects. *d.*

سپلو सपल्लव *sapallav*, possessed of sprouts, shoots, twigs (v. *pallav*). *s.*

سپن सप्न *sapn*, سپنا सपना *sapnā*, } m. a dream. *sapn-dosh*, m. *pollutio nocturna*. *sapnā-bichārī*, m. an interpreter of dreams. *s.*

سپند *sipand*, m. a kind of seed (v. *ispand*); wild rue. *p.*

سپندي *sipandī*, f. fumigation by wild rue. *p.*

سپوت सुपूत *supūt* or सपूत *sapūt*, m. a tractable or dutiful son. *s.* [(a son). *s.*

سپوتاءي सपूताई *sapūtā,ī*, f. being good, &c.

سپورن *sapūran*, full, the full moon. *d.*

سپولا सपोला *sapolā*, سپوليا सपोलिया *sapoliyā*, } m. a young snake, just hatched. *s.*

سپه *sipah* (contr. of *sipāh*). *sipah-sālār*, m. a general, commander in-chief. *p.*

سپهاٹك स्फाटिक *sphāṭik*, crystalline; m. crystal. *s.*

سپهٹ स्फुट *sphuṭ*, blown, opened, expanded (as a flower); apparent, manifest, known. *s.*

سپهٹك स्फटिक *sphaṭik* or *sphaṭak*, m. crystal. *sphaṭik-may*, made of crystal. *s.*

سپهٹي स्फटी *sphaṭī*, f. alum. *s.*

سپهر *sipahr*, m. the sphere, the celestial globe, fortune, time, the world. *p.*

سپهر *si-pahar*, m. سپهري *si-pahrī*, f. } (comp. of *si*, three, and *pahar*, a watch), afternoon. *p.*

سپهري सफरी *saphrī*, f. a small glistening fish, commonly called *punthi*; a sort of carp (*Cyprinus sephore*). *s.* [or art. *p.*

سپه‌گري *sipah-garī*, f. the military profession

سپهل सफल *saphal*, bearing fruit, productive; (literally or figuratively) profitable. useful. *suphal*, bearing good fruit, fruitful. *s.*

سپهوٹك स्फोटक *sphoṭak*, m. a boil, a tumor. *s.*

سپهورت स्फूर्ति *sphūrti*, f. throbbing, palpitating. *s.*

سپهين सुफेन *suphen*, m. cuttle-fish bone. *s.*

سپياري सुपियारी *supiyārī*, f. the areca or betel-nut. *h.*

سپيد *saped* (v. *safed*), white. *p.*

سپيده *supaida* (for *sufaida*), dawn of day. *p.*

سپيدي *supaidī*, f. whiteness, light (of the advancing dawn). *p.*

ست सत *sat*, m. power, strength, essence; soul; the principle of goodness, the true God, the all-pervading Spirit; touch; juice, sap; virtue, truth, sense; adj. true, right, actual, good, virtuous; adv. actually. *s.*

ست सित *sit*, white; the planet Venus. *s.*

ست सुत *sut*, m. a son, a male child; used in comp. as *swātī-sut*, a pearl (q. d., the issue of Arcturus; from a popular belief that in October, when the sun's longitude corresponds to that of Arcturus, drops of rain falling into shells are converted into pearls). *s.*

ستا सत्ता *sattā*, m. power, strength; seven (in cards); f. being, existence; goodness, excellence. *s.*

ستا सुता *sutā*, f. a daughter, a female child. *s.*

ستا *sitā*, ستاد *sitād*, } taking, receiving. *satād*, many, numerous. *p.*

ستاده *sitāda*, taken, carried away; (for *istāda*, q. v.) set up, erected, placed, deposited. *p.*

ستار *sitār*, m. a kind of guitar with three strings. *sitār-bāz*, m. one who plays on the guitar. *p.*

ستار *sattār*, m. one who covers. *sattāru-l-'uyūb*, He who hideth sins (with the veil of forgiveness and mercy); God. *a.*

ستار सुतार *sutār*, m. a carpenter, a wheelwright; time, opportunity. *s.* [a son. *s.*

ستارتهي सुतार्थी *sutārthī*, desirous of having

ستارگان *sitāragān* (pl. of *sitāra*), stars. *p.*

ستاره *sitāra*, m. a star; a kind of firework; name of a musical instrument with three strings, a guitar. *sitāra-peshānī*, having a star in the forehead (reckoned a fault in a horse). *sitāra-shinās*, *sitāra-dān*, or *sitāra-shumur*, m. an astrologer or astronomer. *sitara-shināsī*, the astrological art. *p.*

ستاري सुतारी *sutārī*, f. an awl, a bodkin. *s.*

ستاري *sitārī*, f. a rope, twisted with three strings. *p.* [guitar. *p.*

ستاريا *sitāriyā*, f. m. one who plays on the

ستاسي सत्तासी *sattāsī*, eighty-seven. *s.*

ستان *sitān*, in comp. seizing, taking, as *kishwar-sitān*, one who seizes a country. *p.*

ستان *stān*, a termination denoting place, situation; added to words ending in a vowel, as *hindūstān*, the place or country of the Hindūs; if the word end with a consonant, *istān* is employed, as *gul-istān*, a rose-garden. *p.*

ستانا सताना *satānā*, a. to tease, to vex, to fret, to trouble, to afflict, to interrupt. *s.*

ستاندن *sitāndan*, to seize, to take away. *p.*

ستانك सिताङ्क *sitānk*, m. a kind of fish (*Lacerta scincus*). *s.* [seven. *s.*

ستانوي सत्तान्वे *sattānwe* or *sattānawe*, ninety-

ستاني *sitānī*, f. (abstract form of *sitan*) seizing. *p.*

ستاو सताऊ *satā.ū*, m. f. teaser, tormentor. *s.*

ستاوک स्तावक *stāvak*, m. a praiser, a panegyrist. *s.*

ستاون सत्तावन *sattāwan*, fifty-seven. *s.*

ستائیس सत्ताईस *sattā,īs*, twenty-seven. *s.*

ستائش *sitā,ish*, f. praise, returning thanks. *p.*

ستبدھ स्तब्ध *stabdha*, stopped, blocked, shut up. *s.*

ست بھکھا सतभिषा *satbhikhā*, the twenty-fifth mansion of the moon, containing 100 stars, the chief of which is λ *Aquarii*. *s.*

ستپاتر सत्पात्र *sat-pātra*, m. a virtuous person. *s.*

ستپتر सत्पुत्र *sat-putra*, m. a virtuous son. *s.*

ستپتھ सत्पथ *sat-path*, m. a good road; correct conduct or doctrine. *s.*

ستپرش सत्पुरुष *sat-purush*, m. a worthy or spirited man. *s.*

ستپھل सत्फल *sat-phal*, m. the pomegranate. *s.*

ستت स्तुति *stuti*, f. m. praise, eulogy. *s.*

ستچنہ सितचिन्ह *sit-chinh*, m. a sort of fish (*Lacerta scincus*). *s.*

ستدن *sitadan* (for *sitāndan*), to seize, &c. *p.*

ستر सत्तुर *sattur*, m. an enemy (for *shatru*). *s.*

ستر सत्तर *sattar*, seventy. *s.*

ستر *satr*, m. concealing, covering, veiling, suppressing; privities. *a.*

سترا *sutrā*, adorned, ornamented, neat, beautiful. *d.*

سترابہترا सत्तराबहत्तरा *sattarā-bahattarā*, old, decrepit, doting; lit. seventy to seventy-two, which in India is reckoned a very advanced age. *s. h.*

سترانا सतराना *satrānā*, n. to be angry, vexed. *h.*

ستردن *siturdan*, to shave, scrape, to pull out the hair. *p.*

سترگ *siturg*, *saturg*, or *suturg*, big, bulky, corpulent; quarrelsome, passionate. *p.*

سترہ सतरह *satrah*, seventeen. *s.*

سترھواں सतरहवाँ *satrahwān*, the seventeenth. *s.*

ستري स्त्री *strī*, f. a woman, a wife. *strī-jit*, m. a henpecked husband. *strī-dharm*, m. duty of women; the menstrual excretion. *strī-rājya*, m. the kingdom of women, a country placed by some in the direction of Bhot. *strī-ling*, m. the feminine gender. *strī-vas*, m. subjection to women. *s.*

ستري सितरी *sitrī* or *sittarī*, f. sweat, perspiration. *s.*

سترين स्त्रैण *strain*, female, feminine; m. the nature of woman. *s.*

ستساٹھ सतसठ *sat-saṭh*, sixty-seven. *s.*

ستسنگ सत्सङ्ग *sat-sang*, m. association with the good. *s.*

ستسئی सतसई *satsa,ī*, } f. the name of a
ستسیا सतसैया *satsaiyā*, } book written by
Bihārī-lāl (an inhabitant of Go,āliyār), containing 700 distichs or *dohās*, in *braj-bhākhā* or *-bhāshā*. *Braj-bhākhā barnī kabin bahu bidh buddhi bilās, sab kaa bhūkhan Satsaiyā karī Bihārī Dās*, the poets, each according to his capacity, have displayed the beauties of the *Braj-bhāshā*, but *Bihārī Dās* composed the *Satsaiyā*, which is the jewel of the whole. *s.*

ستکار सत्कार *satkār*, m. reverence, respect; hospitable treatment; doing good, a pious action; act of regarding, rewarding, distinguishing; (Beng.) burning the dead. *s.*

ستکاري सत्कारी *satkārī*, m. one who burns the dead. *s.*

ستکرم सत्कर्म *sat-karma*, m. a good act, piety, virtue; hospitality; funeral obsequies. *s.*

ستکریا सत्क्रिया *satkriyā*, f. funeral obsequies, virtue, charity; salutation, welcome, courtesy; hospitality. *s.*

ستکھن सतखन *satkhan*, of seven divisions or stories (a house, &c.). *s. p.*

ستلڑا सतलड़ा *satlaṛā*, sevenfold, of seven strings or rows (a necklace, &c.). *h.*

ستلڑي सतलड़ी *satlaṛī*, f. a necklace of seven strings. *h.*

ستلوک सतलोक *satlok* (for *satyaloka*), the abode of Brahmā. called also *brahmā-loka*, to which living beings once translated are exempted from further birth. *s.*

ستم *sitam*, m. tyranny, oppression, injury, violence. *sitam-dīda*, or *-rasīda*, or *-zada*, or *-kash*, oppressed, injured, subjected to tyranny. *sitam-kushta*, a martyr to tyranny. *p.*

ستم सत्तम *sattam*, best, excellent; most venerable, most virtuous. *s.*

ستماسا सतमासा *satmāsā*, m. a feast given in the seventh month of pregnancy. *s.*

ستمگار *sitam-gār*, } m. a tyrant, an oppressor;
ستمگر *sitam-gar*, } adj. tyrannical, oppres-
ستمور *sitam-war*, } sive. *p.*

ستمگاري *sitam-gārī*, } f. tyranny, oppression,
ستمگري *sitam-garī*, } injury, violence. *p.*
ستموري *sitam-warī*, }

ستمي सतमी *satmī*, f. the seventh lunar day. *s.*

ستن सुतन *sutan* (pl. of *sut*), sons. *h.*

ستن स्तन *stan*, m. the female bosom, breast. *stan-mukh*, m. a nipple. *s.*

ستنبھ स्तम्भ *stambh*, m. a post, a pillar; hindrance, obstruction. *s.*

ستنبھن स्तम्भन *stambhan*, m. stopping, obstruction; a styptic. *s.*

ستنگ सितङ्ग *sitang*, m. palsy, numbness, being chilled with cold. *s.*

ستنگي सितङ्गी *sitangī*, palsied, numbed. *s.*

ستو सत्त्व *sattwa* or *satwa*, m. the principle of goodness or truth; one of the three *gunas* or properties of beings; substance, thing; vigour, power, essence; a substantive noun. *s.*

ستو स्तव *stav*, m. praise, panegyric. *s.*

ستو सत्तू *sattū*, m. parched grain, reduced to meal and made into a paste. *sattū-khora, pæderastes, pædicator, præposteræ veneri addictus.* *s.*

ستوا सतूआ *satū,ā* or *satuwā*, m. same as *sattū*; adj. (applied to a kind of ginger), pulverable, free from threads or fibres. *satū,ā sankrānt*, the entering of the sun into *Aries*, on which day the meal of parched grain is distributed to the Brāhmaṇs. *h.*

ستوانسا सत्वांसा *satwāṇsā*, m. a child born in the seventh month; also an entertainment given to a woman by her parents in the seventh month of her pregnancy. *s.*

ستوپل सितोपल *sitopal*, m. chalk or a similar mineral; crystal. *s.*

ستوتا सत्त्वता *sattwatā*, f. purity, goodness. *s.*

ستوتر स्तोत्र *stotra*, m. praise, eulogium. *s.*

ستودن *sitūdan* (r. *sitā,e*), to praise. *p.*

ستوده *sitūda*, praised, laudable. *sitūda-ṣifat*, possessed of laudable qualities. *p.*

ستور *sator* or *sutūr*, m. an animal, quadruped, beast of burden, cattle. *p.*

ستور सत्वर *satwar*, quick, expeditious; quickly. *satwartā*, f. quickness, speed. *s.*

ستوڑا *satoṛā*, annihilated. *d.*

ستوكه सतूक *satūka*, base coin (Gladw.). *h.*

ستوگن सत्त्वगुण *sattwagun*, m. the quality of truth. *s.*

ستون *satūn* or *sutūn*, also *situn*, m. a pillar, a column, a prop. *chihal-sitūn*, of forty pillars (a palace, &c.). *p.*

ستونتا सतवन्ता *satwantā*, good, virtuous, chaste, honest, truthful; renowned. *s.*

ستونچا सतौंचा *satoṅchā*, seven and a half. *h.*

ستوه *satoh* or *sutūh*, f. distress, affliction, uneasiness, indigence; adj. melancholy, helpless. *p.*

ستوه सत्त्व *satwa*, m. goodness, &c. (v. ستو).

ستهاپت स्थापित *sthāpit*, set up, established, firm, erected. *s.*

ستهاپن स्थापन *sthāpan*, m. setting up, establishing, fixing, erecting. *s.*

ستهاپنا स्थापना *sthāpanā*, f. ordering, arranging. *s.*

ستهالي स्थाली *sthālī*, f. (v. *thālī*) a tray, &c. *s.*

ستهان स्थान *sthān*, m. place, situation, abode; a section, a chapter; office, station. *s.*

ستهاني स्थानी *sthānī*, having place, abiding, permanent. *s.*

ستهاور स्थावर *sthāwar*, firm, stationary, immoveable. *s.*

ستهايك स्थायुक *sthāyuk*, stationary, firm, steady. *s.*

ستهايي स्थायी *sthāyī*, steady, firm, unchangeable. *sthāyī-bhā,o*, m. permanent condition. *s.*

ستهت स्थित *sthit*, steady, firm; resolved, decreed, established. *sthiti*, f. stay, being fixed or stationary. *s.*

ستهتر सतहत्तर *sathattar*, seventy-seven. *s.*

ستهر स्थिर *sthir*, firm, fixed, permanent; hard, solid; cool, collected, constant, calm, tranquil, mild, settled; peace. *sthir-chetā*, firm, resolute, constant. *sthir-mati*, steady, deliberate. *s.*

ستهرا सुथरा *suthrā*, good, well, excellent, beautiful, elegant, neat, adorned. *h.*

ستهراتما स्थिरात्मा *sthirātmā*, firm, resolute, steady. *s.*

ستهراساهي सुथरासाही *suthrāsāhī*, m. a follower of *Suthrāsāh*, a religious mendicant. *h.*

ستهراو सथराव *sathrāw*, m. a heap of slain (in battle). *h.*

ستهراءي सुथराई *suthrā,ī*, f. goodness, beauty; neatness, elegance. *h.*

ستهرتا स्थिरता *sthirtā*, f. stability, firmness; fortitude. *s.*

ستهل सिथल *sithal* (v. *shītal*), cooled, cold, benumbed with fear. *s.*

ستهل स्थल *sthal*, m. place, region, dry land; part (of a book). *sthal-sīmā*, m. a boundary, a landmark. *s.*

ستهلج स्थलज *sthalaj*, terrene, produced on land. *s.*

ستهن सुथन *suthan*, m. trousers. *h.*

ستهوارا सथवारा *sathwārā*, a kind of sweetmeat given to a child-bed woman. *h.*

ستهول स्थूल *sthūl*, fat, corpulent, large, coarse. *sthūl-buddhi*, stupid, dull. *sthūltā*, f. bulkiness, coarseness. *s.*

ستهوليه स्थौल्य *sthaulya*, m. bulk, size. *s.*

ستهونا स्थूणा *sthūnā*, f. the post or pillar of a house. *s.*

ستهيا सथिया *sathiyā*, m. a surgeon; a mark in form of a cross, the four arms of which are bent at right angles, prefixed in vermilion by Hindūs to their account-books at the commencement of a new year: the same figure is formed on the ground with flour at marriages and other ceremonies. *h.*

ستهيرج स्थैर्य *sthairj*, m. firmness, stability, fortitude. *s.*

ستي सत्य *satya*, true, perfect, accurate. *s.*

ستي सती *satī*, f. a woman who burns herself on her husband's funeral pile; adj. chaste, virtuous, constant. *satī-twa*, m. virtue, chastity in a wife. *s.*

ستي *satī* (also *sitī*), postp. from, with (the same as *se*, q. v.). *d.*

ستيا *sattiyā*, power, strength. *d.*

ستياتما सत्यात्मा *satyātmā*, m. a virtuous and upright man. *s.*

ستياناس सत्यानाश *satyānās*, m. (a term of imprecation, signifying) depravation, destruction. *satyānās-jānā* or *-honā, kisī kā*, n. to be depraved, destroyed, ruined, &c. *satyānās karnā kisī kā*, a. to do mischief to another, to make ruin, to be destroyed or ruined. *s.*

ستياناسي सत्यानाशी *satyānāsī*, depraved, bad, destroyed, damaged; name of a thorny plant, a kind of thistle, the juice of which is of a yellow colour and very acrid. It is used as a caustic. *s.*

ستيانرت सत्यानृत *satyānṛit*, m. commerce, trade, traffic (being a mixed practice of truth and lies). *s.*

ستيتا सत्यता *satyatā*, f. truth, integrity, virtue. *s.*

ستيرتھ सतीर्थ *satīrth*, m. a fellow student, the pupil of the same spiritual preceptor. *s.*

ستيز *sitez*, contention, battle, combat. *p.*

ستيزه *siteza*, m. controversy, altercation, quarrelling, contention, battle. *siteza-kho*, quarrelsome. *p.*

ستيساكشي सत्यसाक्षी *satya-sākshī*, m. a veracious witness. *s.*

ستيلا सतीला *satīlā*, powerful, strong. *s.*

ستيم सत्यम *satyam*, indeed, verily, a particle of interrogation and asseveration. *s.*

ستيلوك सत्यलोक *satyalok*, m. (v. *satlok*). *s.*

ستيواد सत्यवाद *satya-vād*, m. truth, speaking truly. *s.*

ستيوادي सत्यवादी *satya-vadī*, one who speaks the truth. *s.*

ستيوار सतीवार *satīwār*, } f. a tomb, grave,
ستيواڑ सतीवाड़ *satīwāṛ*, } burning-ground; the place where a widow has been burned. *s.*

ستيوچن सत्यवचन *satya-vachan*, m. a true statement. *s.*

ستيه सत्य *satya*, true, sincere, honest; m. truth; an oath. *satya* or *satya-yug*, the first Yug or golden age, comprising 1,728,000 years; the uppermost of the seven worlds, the abode of Brahmā, or world of truth. *s.*

ستيها सतेहा *satehā*, m. (v. *sathiyā*). *h.*

ستييگ सत्ययुग *satya-yug*, m. the first of the four *yugas* or ages (v. *yug* or *yuga*) *s.*

سٹا सिट्टा *siṭṭā*, f. (v. *bhuṭṭā*) Indian corn. *h.*

سٹابٹا सट्टाबट्टा *saṭṭā-baṭṭā*, m. an amour, combination; collusion, plot, cabal, intrigue. *s.*

سٹاسٹ सटासट *saṭāsaṭ*, f. adhering together. *h.*

سٹانا सटाना *saṭānā*, a. to unite, to stick, to make to adhere. *h.*

سٹپٹانا सटपटाना *saṭpaṭānā*, n. to be confounded, to be surprised. *s.*

سٹ‌دينا *saṭ-denā*, to throw away, to deem a thing of no value. *d.*

سٹك सटक *saṭak*, f. an elastic rod, thick at one end and thin at the other. *h.*

سٹكاري सिटकारी *sitkārī*, fusiform, tapering. *h.*

سٹكانا सटकाना *saṭhānā*, a. to baulk, to disappoint, to cause to disappear. *h.*

سٹكاءي सटकाई *saṭkā,ī*, f. (explained *utār-chaṛhāo*) lowering and raising; vanishing at the point as a tapering body, disappearance. *h.*

سٹكن सुटकुन *suṭkun*, f. a rod. *h.*

سٹكنا सटकना *saṭaknā*, n. to run away, to disappear, to flee. *h.*

سٹكنا सुटुकना *suṭuknā*, a. to swallow by gulps and with a noise. *h.*

سٹل सतल *saṭal*, f. foolish prattle, falsehood. *h.*

سٹلي सतली *saṭalī*, f. chattering nonsense, falsehood. *h.*

سٹنا सटना *saṭnā*, n. to join, to adhere, to stick, to unite; (in Dakh.) to cast away. *h.*

سٹھ सठ *saṭh*, cunning; ignorant. *s.*

سٹھائي सिठाई *siṭhā,ī*, f. insipidity, tastelessness. *s.*

سٹھوڑا सठोड़ा *saṭhoṛā*, m. a sweetmeat, consisting of meal, sugar, ginger, spices, &c. (particularly given medicinally to childbed women, and distributed, as caudle is to gossips). *h.*

سٹھي सिट्ठी *siṭṭhī*, f. dross, lees. *h.*

سٹھيانا सठियाना *saṭhiyānā*, n. to be turned of sixty years, to be decrepit, or in one's dotage. *s.*

سٹي सटी *saṭī*, f. zedoary (*Curcuma zerumbet* or *Curcuma amada*). *s.*

سٹي सिट्टी *siṭṭī*, f. whistling. *h.*

سٹيا सटिया *saṭiyā*, f. a stick. *s.*

سٹيا सटिया *saṭiyā*, f. a daughter. *h.*

سٹي‌سٹي सटीसटी *saṭī saṭī*, joined, glued, stuck together, crowded. *h.*

سٹيك सटीक *saṭīk*, having a commentary annexed. *s.*

سج सज *saj*, m. f. shape, ornament, appearance, preparation. *saj-dār*, well-shaped, handsome. *saj-dhaj*, f. preparation and appearance. *s.*

سجا सज्जा *sajjā*, armed, accoutred, decorated; f. dress, decoration, armour. *s.*

سجات सजाति *sajāti*, of or belonging to the same caste or kind. *sujāti*, of a good tribe or species. *s.*

سجاد *sajjād*, adoring, bowing the head and body in adoration. *a.*

سجاده *sajjāda*, m. a carpet or mat on which *Muḥammadans* kneel at prayers; an altar; a mosque. *a.*

سجان सुजान *sujān*, well-informed, wise, intelligent. *s.*

سجانا सुजाना *sujānā*, a. to cause to swell. *s.*

سجانا सजाना *sajānā*, a. to cause to prepare. *s.*

سجاو सजाव *sajāw*, m. preparation, ornament. *s.*

سجاوٹ सजावट *sajāwaṭ*, f. preparation; contrivance. *s.*

سجايا *sajāyā* (pl. of سجية), dispositions, qualities, nature. *a.*

سجاءي सजाई *sajā,ī*, f. the price paid for making belts or scabbards; preparation. *s.*

سجدار सजदार *saj-dār*, well-shaped, handsome. *s. p.*

سجده *sijda*, m. touching the ground with the forehead as an act of adoration or worship to God. *sijda-gāh*, f. the place of performing the *sijda*. *a.*

سج دهج सजधज *saj-dhaj*, f. preparation and appearance. *s.*

سجسي सुजसी *su-jasī*, renowned, illustrious. *s.*

سجع *saj'*, m. rhyme, metre, cadence, poesy. *saj'-go*, an eloquent speaker. *a.*

سجل *sijill*, m. a register, the decree of a judge, written attestation of a notary, seal of a judge (*sigillum*). *sijil*, the recording angel; adj. right, proper, good, well-arranged. *a.*

سجل सजल *sajal*, watery, filled with or containing water. *s.* [more. *h.*

سجلا सजला *sajlā*, m. third brother of four or

سجن सजन *sajan* or सज्जन *sajjan*, well-born, respectable, good, virtuous; m. f. a sweetheart, a mistress, a respectable person. *s.* [kind. *s.*

سجن सुजन *sujan*, virtuous, good, respectable,

سجنا सजना *sajnā*, n. to be prepared; to fit, to become, to beseem; a. to dress, to ornament, to adjust, to rectify. *sajanā*, m. f. (same as *sajan*) a sweetheart, &c. *s.*

سجنا *sujnā*, n. to appear, to be manifest. *d.*

سجنتا सुजनता *sujantā*, f. goodness, kindness. *s.*

سجنجل *sajanjal*, spectacles, a mirror; adj. pure, clear. *a.*

سجوانا सजवाना *sajwānā*, a. (caus. of *sajānā*) to get prepared, to have rectified. *s.*

سجود *sujūd*, an act of prostration with the forehead touching the ground; adoration. *a.*

سجهانا सिझाना *sijhānā*, a. to tan, to boil, to melt. *s.* [understand. *h.*

سجهانا सुझाना *sujhānā*, a. to shew, to make

سجهنا *sujhnā*, n. to appear (v. *sujnā*). *d.*

سجي सज्जी *sajjī*,
سجيمتي सज्जीमती *sajjīmatī*,
سجينون सज्जीनून *sajjīnūn*, } f. a kind of mineral alkali, *natrum*; impure carbonate of soda. *s.*

سجيل *sajjīl* or *sijjīl*, m. hard stones, or bricks made from them, and hardened in hellfire, on which are inscribed the names of men, with a catalogue of their sins. *a.*

سجيلا सजीला *sajīlā*, well-shaped, beautiful, handsome. *s.*

سجيو सजीव *sajīv*, alive, endowed with life. *s.*

سجيه *sajīya*, disposition, temper, nature. *a.*

سچ सच *sach*, true; m. truth; adv. indeed; in earnest, actually. *sach-much*, true, truly. *s.*

سچ सचि *sachi*, m. friendship, intimacy, connexion. *s.*

سچ सुच *such*, pure, undefiled, clear. *s.*

سچا सच्चा *sachchā*, true, genuine, real, honest, sincere; m. a truth-teller. *s.*

سچانا सिचाना *sichānā*, a. to irrigate. *h*

سچاهٹ सचाहट *sachāhaṭ*,
سچاي सचाई *sachā,ī*, } f. also *sachchā,ī*, truth, veracity, probity, authenticity. *s.*

سچت सुचित *suchit*, attentive, cautious; easy in mind; free from anxiety, at leisure. *s.*

سچچ *sachich*, really, verily, in fact. *d.*

سچدانند सच्चिदानन्द *sachidānand*,
سچدانند सच्चिदानन्द *sachchidānand*, } m. Brahmā, or the supreme Spirit. *s.*

سچراچر सचराचर *sacharāchar*, all, whether animate or inanimate. *s.*

سچك सुचक *suchak*, cautious, reflective. *s.*

سچکنا सुचकना *suchaknā*, n. to be astonished or startled. *s.* [lity to move. *s.*

سچل सचल *sachal*, moveable, having the abi-

سچنتا सुचिन्ता *suchintā*, f. due reflection. *s.*

سچوتي सचौटी *sachauṭī*, f. veracity, sincerity; the habit of speaking the truth. *s.*

سچها सिच्छा *sichchhā* (for *sikshā*), f. a sermon, tuition; learning. *s.* [teacher. *s.*

سچهك सिच्छक *sichchhak*, m. a preacher, a

سچيت सुचेत *suchet*, attentive, cautious, contented, happy. *s.*

سچيت सचेत *sachet*,
سچيتن सचेतन *sachetan*, } on one's guard, with caution or consideration, attentive, alert, aware, cautious, sensible, rational. *s.*

سچيچ *sachīch*, true, veracious. *d.*

سچيشٹ सचेष्ट *sacheshṭ*, active, making an effort. *s.*

سحاب *saḥāb*, a cloud; quicksilver. *a.*

سحاف *saḥāf* or *suḥāf*, m. consumption. *a.*

سحبان *saḥbān*, name of an Arabian orator whose eloquence is said to have been unrivalled. *a.*

سحر *siḥr*, m. enchantment, magic. *siḥr-bāz*, a magician. *siḥr-bāzī*, enchantment. *saḥar*, m. dawn of day. *a.*

سحرگاه *saḥār-gāh*, the morning, the dawn. *p.*

سحرگاهي *saḥar-gāhī*,
سحري *saḥarī*, } early, relating to the dawn. *p.*

سحور *saḥūr*, the meal which Musalmāns make a little before dawn, during the month of *Ramaẓān*, to enable them to fast till night. *a.*

سخا *saḵẖā*,
سخاوت *saḵẖāwat*, } f. liberality, generosity. *a.*

سخت *saḵẖt*, hard, strong; difficult; obdurate; stingy; wretched, troublesome, violent, very cruel, painful, austere, rigid, severe; adv. very, exceedingly, violently. *saḵẖt-andāz*, an archer. *saḵẖt sust kahnā*, to speak sharply or severely, to rebuke. *saḵẖt-gīr*, holding fast (an animal of chase). *a.p.*

سختي **sakhtī**, f. hardness; obduracy; stinginess, indigence; distress. *sakhtī ko pīnā* (Dakh.), to endure, to bear with patience. *p.*

سخره **sukhra**, } derision, ridicule, a ridi-
سخريه **sukhriya**, } culous person; a drudge, or one who is pressed to labour without any remuneration. *a.*

سخن **sukhan**, **sakhun**, or **sukhun**, m. speech, language; thing, business, affair. *sukhan-pardāz*, eloquent. *sukhan-takya*, m. a prop word, an expletive (as the wise men call it). *sukhan-jān*, eloquent. *sukhan-chīn*, an eavesdropper, a spy, an informer. *sukhan-dān*, intelligent, eloquent; m. a poet. *sukhan-ḍālnā*, a. to ask, to question, to interrogate. *sukhan-sāz*, an orator, a speechifier. *sukhan-sanj*, a weigher of words; a poet, a wise man; adj. prudent. *sukhan i ghaibī*, f. second sight, inspiration. *sukhan-fahm*, intelligent, quick of apprehension. *sukhan-fahmī*, f. intelligence, understanding, apprehension. *sukhan-go*, an orator. *sukhan-war*, eloquent. *sukhan-warī*, eloquence. *p.*

سخي **sakhī**, liberal, munificent. *a.*

سد **sadd**, f. a wall, barrier, impediment, ditch, rampart, an obstruction of any kind, an obstacle. *saddi jawāb*, a rejoinder. *saddi da'wī*, a bar to a claim. *saddi ramaḳ*, m. the last remains of life, the agonies of death. *saddi Sikandar*, Alexander's wall. *saddi rāh*, a bulwark, a barrier. *a.*

سد सद **sad**, fresh, flourishing. *s.*

سد सद **sad**, an ode or poem. *h.*

سدا सदा **sadā**, always, perpetually. *sadā-phal*, m. a fabled fruit, eating of which confers long life, &c.; a kind of lemon; adj. constantly bearing fruit (epithet of a tree), the cocoa-nut tree; the glomerous fig-tree; the jack (*Artocarpus integrifolia*); the Bel (*Ægle marmelos*). *sadā suhāgan*, f. the name of a bird (*Trogon dilectus*, *Buch. MSS.*); name of a flower (*Hibiscus Phœniceus*, the white variety); a kind of *faḳīr* dressed like a woman. *s.*

سداب **sudāb**, m. the herb rue. *a. p.*

سدابرت सदाब्रत **sadā-brat** or **sadā-bart** (for *sadāvrat*), m. alms, or food distributed daily to the poor, to travellers, &c. *s.*

سداتما सदात्मा **sadātmā**, good, virtuous. *s.*

سداچار सदाचार **sadāchār**, m. virtuous conduct. *s.*

سداشو सदाशिव **sadā-shiv**, m. a name of [Shiva. *s.*

سداگت सदागति **sadāgati**, m. final happiness or emancipation; the Supreme Spirit. *s.*

سدان **suddān**, with, along with. *d.*

سدانرت सदानर्त **sadānart**, m. a wagtail. *s.*

سدانند सदानन्द **sadānand**, always happy. *s.*

سداورت सदाव्रत **sadāvrat**, m. alms (v. *sadābrat*).

سدبهاو सद्भाव **sad-bhā,o**, m. a pure or holy nature; good temper, amiability, goodness. *s.*

سدتر सदुत्तर **sad-uttar**, m. proper or good reply. *s.* [profligate. *s.*

سدراچار सुदुराचार **su-dur-āchār**, very wicked,

سدرة **sidrat**, a species of the lote tree. *sidra-tu-l-muntaha*, a tree in Paradise, the mansion of the angel Gabriel. *a.*

سدرڑه सुदृढ़ **su-dṛiṛh**, solid, firm, very hard. *s.*

سدرسن सुदर्शन **su-darsan** or **su-darshan**, handsome, good-looking; m. the discus or missile weapon of *Krishṇa* or *Vishṇu*. *s.*

سدرش सदृश **sadṛish**, alike, resembling. *sadṛishatā*, f. likeness. *s.* [attained. *s.*

سدرلبه सुदुर्लभ **su-dur-labh**, very difficult to be

سدره **sidra** (v. *sidrat*), a tree in Paradise. *sidra-nishīnān*, the angels. *a.*

سدسيه सदस्य **sadasya**, any person present at an assembly, spectator, &c. *s.*

سدشکر सुदुष्कर **su-dush-kar**, very difficult. *s.*

سدگت सद्गति **sad-gati**, f. felicity or fortune; good conduct; salvation. *s.*

سدگن सद्गुण **sad-gun**, good, virtuous, eminent. *s.*

سدمد **sud-mud** (explained *hū-ba-hū*, q. v.), quite, perfectly, exactly. *d.*

سدن सदन **sadan**, m. a place, house, mansion. *s.*

سدنتي सुदन्ती **su-dantī**, f. the female elephant of the south-west quarter. *s.*

سده **sudda**, m. (in medicine) an obstruction; scybala; stoppage of the nose, coryza; a threshhold. *a.*

سدھ सिद्ध **sidh** or **siddha**, accomplished, effected; celebrated, famous; valid (in law); demonstrated, proved (in logic); finished; m. a class of demigods inhabiting Indra's heaven; a saint, a holy man, he who has subjected to his will the eight *siddhis* (v. *ashṭa-siddhi*), an adept, a magician; the 21st of the astronomical *yogs*; adj. successful; ready; completed, accomplished. *siddha-dhātu* or *siddha-ras*, m. quick-silver. *siddha-ras*, adj. mineral, metallic. *siddha-sādhan*, the performance of magical rites, the materials employed in alchymical processes. *s.*

سدھ सिद्धि **sidh** or **siddhi**, f. success, accomplishment of an object; the entire completion of any undertaking, or attainment of any object; prosperity, success; the result or fruit of the adoration of the gods, or of ascetic severities; the supposed acquirements of supernatural powers by the completion of magical, mystical, or alchymical rites and processes; accuracy, correctness, indisputable conclusion or position; validity (in law); one of the astronomical *yogs*. *s.*

سدھ सुध **sudh** or **sudhi**, f. memory, remembrance, sensation, consciousness; notice, care, intelligence; adj. accurate, correct; pure, unpolluted. *be sudh*, beside one's self. *sudh-budh*, f. sense, sensation, perception, care. *sudh-lenā*, to take care of, to accommodate, to look after, to inquire into. *s.*

سدھا सुधा **sudhā**, m. nectar, ambrosia, the honey of flowers. *s.*

سدھارنا सुधारना **sudhārnā**, a. to adorn, to adjust, to arrange, to mend. *s.*

سدھارنا सिधारना **sidhārnā**, n. to go, to depart, to set off. *s.*

سدھاکر सुधाकर *sudhākar*, } m. moonlight, the
سدھانس सुधांसु *sudhānsu*, } moon, being the supposed repository of *Sudhā*, the beverage of the Gods. *s.*

سدھان सुधां *sudhāṅ* or *suddhāṅ*, together, [with. *s.*

سدھانا सधाना *sadhānā*, a. to train animals; to perform. *s.*

سدھانا सुधाना *sudhānā*, a. to put in mind, to [cause to remember. *s.*

سدھانت सिद्धान्त *siddhānt* or *siddhānta*, m. result, consequence, truth established by demonstration; a system of science, particularly of geometry, astronomy, &c., of which there are several in Sanskrit of great antiquity, as the *Sūrya-siddhānta*, the *Brahma-siddhānta*, &c. *s.*

سدھانتی सिद्धान्ती *siddhāntī*, m. one acquainted with the truths which are founded on demonstration, a follower of the Mīmānsā philosophy. *s.*

سدھاوٹ सिधावट *sidhāwaṭ*, f. candour, simplicity. *s.*

سدھرمی सधर्मी *sadharmī*, observing the same customs or laws. *s.*

سدھرنا सुधरना *sudharnā*, n. to be correct, to be mended, to be or seem right or good, to avail, to succeed. *s.*

سدھمنا *sudh-munnā*, well-shaped, handsome. *d.*

سدھنا सधना *sadhnā*, n. to be fully instructed [or disciplined. *s.*

سدھوا सधवा *sadhwā*, f. a wife whose husband is living. *s.*

سدھی सुधी *sudhī*, m. a pandit, a learned or [wise man. *s.*

سدھی *siddhī*, f. a species of hemp, the leaves of which cause intoxication. *d.*

سدی सदय *saday*, benevolent, compassionate. *s.*

سدی सुदी *sudī*, f. the light half of the lunar month, *i. e.* from new to full moon. *s.*

سدیا सद्या *sadyā* or सदिया *sadiyā*, f. the female of the little bird called *Amadavat*; m. a kind of *faḳīr*. *h.*

سدیش सदेश *sadesh*, in front, before, near, proximate; of the same country or place. *s.*

سدیہ सद्य *sadya*, that instant, then. *s.*

سدیھ सदेह *sadeh*, bodily, in the body. *s.*

سڈا सड़ा *saḍā* (v. *saṛā*), rotten &c. *h.*

سڈول सुडौल *su-ḍaul*, } well-shaped, pretty,
سڈھال सुढाल *su-ḍhāl*, } handsome, elegant,
سڈھب सुढब *su-ḍhab*, } graceful. *suḍauldehī*, f. gracefulness of shape, handsomeness. *s.*

سر सिर *sir*, m. the head, top. *sir uṭhāte hī pāmāl hojānā*, to be crushed in the commencement of one's undertaking. *sir uṭhānā*, a. to rebel, to rise up against one. *sir papolnā bhejā khānā*, a. to shew kindness externally and harbour enmity in one's breast. *sir par chaṛhānā*, a. to spoil (a child, &c.); to raise an inferior above one's self; to shew respect *sir par khāk ḍālnā*, to throw ashes on the head; n. to lament. *sir parastī-k.*, a. to protect, to aid. *sir phirānā*, a. to labour in vain. *sir phernā*, n. to revolt from obedience. *sir pīṭnā*, n. to lament. *sir toṛnā*, a. to subdue. *sir-chaṛhā* proud, haughty. *sir chaṛhānā*, to exalt, to assume, to be arrogant; to shew respect. *sir chaṛhke marnā*, to lay the guilt of one's blood at the door of another. *sir dharnā*, to be obedient. *sir dulānā* or *sir dhunnā*, to shake the head from affliction. *sir-de-de-mārnā*, to be desperate. *sir-ḍūb*, perfectly wet. *sir se sirwāhe* or *sir se sirwāh*, the turban is for the head, or turbans are like the head; to express that without a chief the people fall into ruin and confusion. *sir se kafan bāndhnā*, to engage in a desperate undertaking, giving up all regard to one's own safety. *sir kāṛhnā*, n. to become conspicuous. *sir-kaṭā*, beheaded. *sir karnā*, to begin. *sir ko ḳadam-k.*, to go quickly but with respect. *sir khujānā*, to court punishment. *sir ke bhal*, headlong. *sir ke zor*, with all one's might. *sir-girī*, the comb of a cock, crest of a bird. *sir lagnā*, to endure hardship. *sir mārnā*, to be at great pains, to search diligently. *sir munḍānā*, to quit one's connexions and adopt a life of mendicity. *sir-mailā honā*, to have the menses. *sir niwānā*, n. to be humble, to be obedient. *s.*

سر सुर *sur*, m. an angel, one of the gods or inhabitants of the celestial world; tone, melody, accent, song, note; a vowel. *sur milānā*, a. to sing in tune. *s.*

سر सर *sar*, m. an arrow; a reed of which arrows are made (*Saccharum sara, Roxb.*); (for *saras*) a pond, a tank, a lake. *s*

سر *sar*, m. the head, top, pinnacle, origin, point, beginning, chief, principle; intention, end, aim, will, love, desire. *sar-afrāz*, exalted. *sar-afganda*, cast down, abashed. *sar-andāz*, warlike, intrepid; a kind of veil worn by women when they go abroad. *sar-bāz*, intrepid, risking one's life or head. *sar-bāzī*, intrepidity, recklessness of life. *sar-basta*, closed, shut, hidden; inextricable; wearing a turban. *sar-ba-sar*, all, the whole, entirely. *sar-buland*, eminent, glorious, exalted. *sar-bulandī*, f. exaltation. *sar-ba-muhr*, sealed. *sari-pā baiṭhnā*, to sit backwards on the heels with the knees upwards, to squat. *sar-pech* or *sar-pesh*, m. an ornament of gold, silver, or jewels, worn in front of the turban. *sar-tāj*, a chief. *sar-tez*, sharp pointed. *sar-ḵhud*, independent, being one's own master. *sar-ḵhush*, cheerful, gay, merry; tipsy. *sar-ḵhushī*, gaiety, &c. *sar-daraḵhtī*, a tax on trees, orchards, &c. *sar-dard*, m. headache, trouble, perplexity. *sar-dardī*, vexation. *sari-rāh*, m. the high road, the higher part of the road. *sar-zada*, depraved, ill-bred. *sar-zamīn*, f. the earth; country, region; limits, confines. *sar-zor*, mutinous, rebellious, disobedient. *sar-zorī*, f. mutiny, rebellion, disobedience. *sar-zer*, humbled. *sari-sāl*, the commencement of the year. *sari shām*, evening, early in the evening. *sar-kob*, m. superintending, looking after; beating the head; overlooking, overtopping. *sar-guzār*, desperate. *sar-guzasht*, f. an event, accident, transaction, account of circumstances. *sar-garān*, tipsy, drunk; proud. *sar-gardān*, distressed, humbled; confounded, stupefied; wandering, straying. *sar-gardānī*, f. distress, confusion, amazement, stupefaction. *sar-garm*, intent on; attentive; inflamed with love. *sar-garmī*, f. application, attention; love, or being in love. *sar-garoh* or *-guroh*, m. the chief of the troops, &c., leader, commander; a chief of *faḳīrs*, a provincial. *sar-mast*, intoxicated (with wine, lust, power, &c.). *sar-mastī*, f. intoxication. *sar-mashḳ*, a copy (for writing). *sar-nigūn*, hanging the head, abashed; vile; backward, topsy-turvy, upside down. *sari nau*, anew, afresh, over again; commencement. *sar-navisht*, f. destiny, fortune, fate. *sar o pā*, all, the whole; m. a vest with which princes honour their subjects (v. *khil'at*). *sar-k.*, a. to make head, to accomplish, to perform, to execute; to obtain victory. *p.*

سر *sirr*, m. a secret, a mystery. *a.*

سرا *sarā*, f. a caravanserai; a house, a mansion. *sirā* or *sarā*, (in comp.) singing, warbling, as *bulbuli dāstān-sirā*, the warbling nightingale. *p.*

سرا सरा *sarā*, m. an earthen cover of a pot. *s.*

سرا *sarā*, m. a tree from which bows are made. *a.*

سرا सिरा *sirā*, m. head, end, extremity. *s.*

سرا सुरा *surā*, f. spirituous liquor. *s.*

سرا *surrā*, m. the sword-fish. *d.*

سراب *sarāb* or *surāb*, m. a vapour resembling the sea at a distance, formed by the rays of the sun or moon on a sandy plain, glare (Fr. *mirage*). *a.*

سراپ सराप *sarāp* or *srāp*, m. cursing, an imprecation. *sarāp denā*, to curse. *s.*

سراپا *sarāpā*, m. the whole body, figure; adv. totally, from end to end. *sarāpā tak*, from head to foot. *p.*

سراپردہ *sarāparda*, m. a royal tent, pavilion (vide also *sar-parda*). *p.*

سراپنا सरापना *sarāpnā*, a. to curse. *sarāp-denā*, to imprecate or invoke curses. *s.*

سرات सिरात *sirāt*, cold, becoming cold. *s.*

سراج *sirāj*, m. a candle, a lamp; the sun. *sirāju-d-daula*, the lamp or sun of the state; a man's name; the *nawwāb* or viceroy of Bengal, who in 1756 took Calcutta, and caused the death of 131 Englishmen, by confining them in a close dungeon, bore this high-sounding title. In some of the newspapers and chronicles of the day, at home, he figures under the more Christian appellation of Sir Roger Dowler. *a.*

سراج *sarrāj*, m. a saddler; a groom. *a.*

سراجال सिराजाल *sirājāl*, m. enlargement of the vessels of the eye. *s.*

سراجنا सिराजना *sirājnā*, a. to create, produce, form (Gilc.). *s.*

سراچہ *sarācha*, m. a tent, surrounded with an inclosure; an inner apartment. *p.*

سرادار *sarā-dār*, one who has charge of a caravanserai. *p.*

سرادکي सादकी *srādkī*, m. the name of a tribe [of Hindūs. *h.*

سرادھ श्राद्ध *srādh*, m. funeral obsequies, consisting in offering rice and fruits, &c. to the manes of ancestors. *s.*

سرازیر *sarāzīr*, sloping (little used). *p.*

سراسر *sarāsar*, all, the whole, entirely. *p.*

سراسري *sarāsarī*, f. the name of an ornament worn on the head, going all round the head; summary. *p.*

سراسیمگي *sarāsīmagī*, f. amazement, perturbation, perplexity. *p.*

سراسیمہ *sarāsīma*, amazed, confounded, disturbed; distressed. *p.*

سراغ *surāgh*, m. search, inquiry; sign, mark, trace; spying. *surāgh lenā*, a. to search, to seek, to inquire for, to spy. *p.*

سرامد *sarāmad*, perfect, complete, accomplished; master of any art, &c.; chief (q. d. arrived at the summit). *p.*

سرانا सिराना *sirānā*, n. to cool; a. to make cold; to set afloat, to set off, to despatch. *s.*

سرانجام *sar-anjām*, m. apparatus, utensils, furniture, goods and chattels, materials, ingredients; conclusion, end, accomplishment. *saranjām-k.*, to conclude, finish, prepare. *saranjām-h.*, to be concluded. *p.*

سرانديپ *sarāndīp*, the island of Ceylon. *a. s.*

سرانگشت *sar-angusht*, the tip of the finger. *p.*

سراو सराव *sarā,o*, m. a lid, or a shallow cup used as such. *s.*

سراوك सरावक *sarāwak* (for *shrāwak*), m. name of a Hindū tribe; the believers of the Jain religion; the laity. *s.*

سراون सरावन *sarāwan*, m. a harrow. *h.*

سراون श्रावण *srāvaṇ* (for *shrāvaṇ*), the month *sāvan*, q. v. *s*

سراه *sarāh* (v. *sarā*), a kind of tree. *a.*

سراه सराह *sarāh*, f. praise, commendation. *h.*

سراهن सराहन *sarāhan*, m. the act of praising. *h.*

سراهنا सराहना *sarāhnā*, a. to praise, to commend, to approve, to applaud. *h.*

سراي *sarā,e*, f. (v. *sarā*) a mansion, an inn. *sarā,e dīgar*, the next inn, *i. e.* the world to come. *p.*

سراي सराई *sarā,ī*, f. a small cover. *s.*

سرايت *sirāyat*, f. contagion, pestilence. *a.*

سرايچہ *sarā,e-cha*, m. (v. *sarācha*) a tent, &c. *p.*

سرائيدن *sarā,īdan*, to sing, to play on an instrument. *p.*

سرايندہ *sarā,inda* or *sarāyanda*, singing, a [singer. *p.*

سرب *surb* or *surub*, m. lead. *p.*

سرب सर्ब *sarb* (for *sarva*), all, the whole. *s.*

سربدا सर्बदा *sarbadā* (for *sarvadā*), always, perpetually, at all times. *s.*

سربر सरबर *sarbar*, m. (v. *sarobar* or *sarovar*) a pond, an artificial tank. *s.*

سربراہ *sar-ba-rāh*, f. supply; travelling expenses, or cash to pay them. *sarbarāh-kār*, a commissary of supplies. *p.*

سربراهي *sar-ba-rāhī*, f. the act of providing supplies for a journey, &c.; direction, arrangement. *p*

سربس सरबस *sarbas* or *sarbasu* (for *sarvasva*), m. every thing, the whole property. *s.*

سرب گهن सर्बगहन *sarb-gahan*, m. a total eclipse. *s.* [m. nutmeg. *s.*

سربهہ सुरभि *surabhi*, fragrant, sweet-smelling;

سرپ सर्प **sarp, sarpa,** or सरप **sarap,** m. a serpent. *sarpa-phanaj* or *sarpa-mani,* m. the snake-stone, a gem said to be found in the head of a snake. *sarpa-chhatra,* m. a mushroom. *sarpa-gandhā,* f. a plant, perhaps the same as Ophioxylon. *sarpa-han,* m. (the snake-killer) an ichneumon, a mungoose. *s.*

سرپت सुरपति **sur-pati,** m. a name of Indra, ruler of the gods. *s.*

سرپت सरपत **sarpat,** } m. a kind of reed, or
سرپتا सरपता **sarpatā,** } reed grass (*Saccharum procerum, Rox.*). *s.*

سرپٹ सरपट **sarpaṭ,** f. galloping. *sarpaṭ-dauṛnā* or *-phenknā,* to gallop off. *sarpaṭ-dauṛānā,* to put one's horse to a gallop. *h.*

سرپر सुरपुर **sur-pur,** m. the city of the immortals, Indra's capital. *s.*

سرپرده **sarparda,** m. name of a Persian musical mode, supposed to have been published by *Amīr Khusraw,* of *Dihlī.* *p.*

سرپنجگي **sar-panjagī,** strength of fist. *p.*

سرپوش **sarposh,** m. a cover, a lid. *p.*

سرپھٹور सिरफटौवर **sir-phaṭauwar,** wrangling; affectation of civility with internal hatred. *s.*

سرپھوڑي **sir-phoṛī,** f. a headache. *sar-phoṛī,* labour in vain. *d.*

سرپيچ **sar-pech,** a diadem; a turban, an ornament in front of a turban *p.*

سرت सुरत **surat** or **surt,** f. consideration, reflection, memory, attention, caution, accuracy; copulation, coition. *s.*

سرت शरत **sarat,** the name of one of the six seasons; comprising *āsin* and *kārtik.* *s.*

سرت सरित **sarit,** } f. a river in general, a
سرتا सरिता **saritā,** } stream. *s.*

سرتا सुरता **surtā,** considerate, mindful, prudent, intelligent; accurate. *s.*

سرتابي **sar-tābī,** f. disobedience. *p.*

سرتول **sartol,** equal, a compeer, consort. *d.*

سرتيز **sar-tez,** headstrong, obstinate. *p.*

سرتيلا सुरतीला **surtīlā,** considerate, prudent. *s.*

سرٹ सरट **saraṭ,** m. a kind of lizard, a chamelion. *h.*

سرٹھٹھور सिरठठौवर **sir-ṭhaṭhauwar,** } m. sa-
سرٹھٹھول सिरठठौवल **sir-ṭhaṭhauwal,** } lutation (with displeasure). *s. h.*

سرج सर्जी **sarjji,** f. natron, alkali. *s.*

سرج **sarj,** m. a saddle. *a.*

سرجن सुरजन **surjan,** m. (v. *sajan*), a respectable person. *s.*

سرجنا सिरजना **sirajnā** or सृजना **srijnā,** a. to create, to produce, to form. *s.*

سرجنهار सृजनहार **srijan-hār,** m. the Creator. *s.*

سرجو सरजू **sarjū,** f. name of a river. *s.*

سرچشمه **sar-chashma,** m. a spring, a fountain, a source or fountain-head. *p.*

سرچنگ **sar-chang,** repulse, rout; labour, fatigue; a kick. *p.*

سرچوٹ **sir-choṭ,** disgust, aversion. *d.*

سرحد **sar-hadd,** f. boundary, extremity, frontier, limit, confines. *p.*

سرخ **surkh,** red. *surkh-bādā,* m. the name of a disorder, St. Anthony's fire. *surkh-bed,* f. a kind of cane; name of a medicinal plant. *surkh-posh,* dressed in red. *surkh-rū,* honourable, "*nulla culpa pallescens.*" *surkh-rū,ī,* f. honour, character, fame. *surkh sufaid,* (red and white) fair. *p.*

سرخا **surkhā,** m. grey colour in horses. *p.*

سرخاب **surkhāb,** m. name of a bird (*Anas casarca*); also a species of lark. *surkhāb kā par lagnā,* to do any thing expeditiously. *sir par surkhāb kā par honā* n. to be proud. *p.*

سرخط **sarkhaṭṭ,** m. an agreement to hire service; bill of sale, certificate of service performed. *p.a.*

سرخه **surkha,** red tincture; a kind of pigeon; name of the son of *Afrāsiyāb.* *p.*

سرخي **surkhī,** f. redness; blood; brick-dust. *p.*

سرخيل **sar-khail,** a general or commander of an army or division. *p. a.*

سرخيلي **sar-khailī,** office of general. *p.*

سرد **sard,** cold, damp. *sard-k.,* a. to cool, to pacify. *sard-ser,* cool (place). *sard-mihr,* a cool or lukewarm friend. *sard-mihrī,* coolness in friendship. *p.*

سرد शरद **sarad,** f. name of one of the six seasons (v. *sarat*). *s.*

سردا सरदा **sardā,** m. a kind of musk or water melon. *h.*

سردابه **sardāba,** m. the cold-bath. *p.*

سردار **sar-dār,** m. a chief, a head man. *p.*

سرداري **sar-dārī,** f. chiefship. *p.*

سردست **sar-dast,** the hand from the wrist to the finger ends. *p.*

سردوال **sar-dawāl** or **sir-dawāl,** f. reins of a bridle, headstall. *p.*

سردهوپ सुरधूप **sur-dhūp,** m. resin, turpentine. *s.*

سردي **sardī,** f. a cold, coldness, dampness; the cold weather. *p.*

سرراس **sarirās,** alike, the same. *d.*

سررشته **sar-rishta,** m. an office, employment; connexion, affinity; a rope, thread, cord; desire. *p.*

سررشته‌دار **sar-rishta-dār,** } chief native reve-
سرشتدار **sarishtadār,** } nue officer in a district; supervisor of revenue matters. *p.*

سررو **sari rū,** f. the cephalic vein in the arm. *p.*

سرزد **sar-zad,** happening. *sar-zad honā,* to occur, to take place; to be perpetrated. *p.*

سرزن *sar-zan*, (lit.) striking the head, rebellious, disobedient. *p.*

سرزنش *sar-zanish*, f. reproof, rebuke. *p.*

سرزني *sar-zanī*, act of striking the head, disobedience. *p.*

سرس सिरिस *siris*, m. the name of a species of acacia (*Mimosa seris*). *s.*

سرس सुरस *suras*, sweet, well-flavoured, [juicy. *s.*

سرس सरस *saras*, } best, excellent, prime;
سرسا सरसा *sarsū*, } more, abundant, plenty. *s.*

سرسام *sarsām*, m. delirium, frenzy, a tumor, or inflammation of the brain; adj. stupefied. *p.*

سرساعي सरसाई *sarsā,ī*, f. increase, abundance, excellence. *s.*

سرسبز *sar-sabz*, fresh, verdant; prosperous, [fortunate, happy. *p.*

سرسبزي *sar-sabzī*, f. verdure, greenness; prosperity, happiness. *p.*

سرسر सरसर *sar-sar*, } noise of a snake
سرسرات सरसराट *sarsarāṭ*, } when creeping. *h.*

سرسرانا सरसराना *sarsarānā*, } n. to creep along,
سرسرانا सुरसुराना *sursurānā*, } to make the noise a snake does when creeping. *h.*

سرسراهٹ सुरसुराहट *sursurahāṭ* or *sarsarāhaṭ*, f. creeping (sensation), titillation; the noise of a snake in creeping. *h.*

سرسري *sarsarī*, easy, facile, careless. *p.*

سرسري सुरसुरी *sursurī*, f. titillation; an insect bred in grain. *h.*

سرسوت सरस्वत *saraswat*, elegant. *s.*

سرسوتي सरस्वती *saraswatī*, f. the wife of Brahmā, the goddess of speech and eloquence, the patroness of music and the arts, and the inventress of the Sanskrit language, and of the Devanāgarī characters; the river commonly called Sarsūti. *s.*

سرسون सरसों *sarson*, f. a kind of mustard seed or plant (*Sinapis dichotoma, Roxb.*). *s.*

سرسينگ सिरसींग *sirsīng*, rebellious, mutinous. *s.*

سرش *sirish* (v. *siris*), the acacia. *s.*

سرشار *sarshār*, full, brimful, redundant, glutted; intoxicated. *p.*

سرشاري *sarshārī*, f. fulness, intoxication. *p.*

سرشپ सर्षप *sarshap*, m. a sort of mustard (*Sinapis dichotoma*); a kind of poison. *s.*

سرشت *sarisht*, f. nature, temperament, constitution, disposition, complexion; intellect. *p.*

سرشته *sirishta*, mixed, created. *p.*

سرشٹ सृष्ट *srishṭ*, created, made; f. also सृष्टि *srishṭi*, the creation, the world, the universe, nature, natural property. *srishṭi-kartā*, the creator of the universe. *s.*

سرشف *sarshaf*, m. mustard seed. *p.*

سرشك *sarashk* or *sirishk*, m. a tear. *p.*

سرطان *saraṭān*, m. a crab; the sign Cancer; a cancer; a disease incident to the feet of cattle. *a.*

سرعت *sur'at*, haste. *sur'atan*, quickly. *a.*

سرغنه *sarghana*, m. a chief; a great personage; adj. abovementioned, aforesaid. *p.*

سرف *sarf* or *saraf*, m. extravagance. *a.*

سرفراز *sar-farāz*, exalted, eminent, distinguished (same as *sar-afrāz*). *p.*

سرفرازي *sar-farāzī*, f. exaltation, distinction, promotion (also *sar-afrāzī*). *p.*

سرفه *surfa*, a moth, caterpillar; a cough. *p.*

سرقه *sariḳa*, m. plagiarism, theft. *a.*

سرك *sarak*, a noose, a snare. *d.*

سركا *sirkā* (for *sirka*), vinegar. *p.*

سركار *sar-kār*, f. the king's court; government; estate, property; a district comprehending several *parganas*; m. a superintendant; a title by way of respect given to a person present or absent, such as your highness, your honour. *p.*

سركاري *sar-kārī*, f. superintendence; adj. belonging to the state, or to the government. *p.*

سركانا सरकाना *sarkānā*, a. to remove, to put on one side, to remove out of the way. *h.*

سرکڑا सरकड़ा *sarkaṛā*, m. a reed (*Saccharum procerum, Roxb.*). *s.*

سركش *sar-kash*, disobedient, rebellious, mutinous. *p.*

سركشي *sar-kashī*, f. disobedience, mutiny, rebellion, revolt. *p.*

سركنا सरकना *saraknā*, n. to be moved, to move, to stir, to be set aside, to get out of the way. *h.*

سركنا सुरुकना *suruknā*, a. (v. *suṛuknā*) to swallow by gulps, to sip. *h.*

سرکنڈا सरकण्डा *sarkanḍā*, m. (v. *sarkaṛā*) a kind of reed, of which mats are made. *s.*

سركه *sirka*, m. vinegar. *sirka-fishānī*, (lit. scattering vinegar) reproach, sarcasm. *p.*

سرکھا सुरखा *surkhā*, a tall plant running up without a due proportion of leaves. *h.*

سرکھپ सिरखप *sir-khap*, resolute (soldier), adventurous. *s. h.*

سرکھپي सिरखपी *sir-khapī*, f. resolution, perseverance, enterprise. *s. h.*

سركي सिरकी *sirkī*, f. a kind of reed of which mats are made, reed-grass (the upper joint of *Saccharum procerum, Roxb.*); a sort of mat to keep off rain. *h.*

سرگ सर्ग *sarg* or *sarga*, } m. the heaven;
سرگ‌لوك सर्गलोक *sarg-lok*, } the firmament; the sky (properly *swarga*, q. v.). *s.*

سرگپتالي सर्गपताली *sarg-patālī*, squint-eyed; (an ox or cow) having one horn pointing upwards, and the other downwards. *s.*

سرگشتگي *sar-gashtagī*, f. astonishment, affliction. *p.*

سرگشته *sar-gashta*, afflicted, astonished, at a loss, wandering, perplexed. *p.*

سرگم सरिगम *sari-gam*, the gamut; sol-fa-ing, sol-mization. *s.*

سرگن सरगुण *sargun*, filled with or possessed of all good qualities, an epithet of the Deity. *s.*

سرگوش *sari-gosh*, m. the ear. *p.*

سرگوشي *sargoshī*, f. whispering, deliberation. *p.*

سرگين *sargīn*, m. dung, especially cow-dung. *p.*

سرل सरल *saral*, m. name of a fragrant wood (*Pinus longifolia, Roxb.*); a bird (*Pavo bicalcarata*); adj perpendicular, straight; plain, artless, honest, simple, upright. *s.*

سرلا सरला *saralā*, upright, tall, straight; f. a variety of the plant called Teorī. *s.*

سرم श्रम *sram*, m. f. fatigue, toil, pains. *s.*

سرم *saram*, the ridge-pole of a house. *d.*

سرما *sarmā*, m. winter; the cold season. *p.*

سرماءي *sarmā,ī*, m. winter clothing; adj. wintry, of or relating to the cold season. *p.*

سرمايه *sarmāya*, m. stock in trade, capital. *p.*

سرمد *sarmad*, eternal everlasting. *sarmadan*, eternally, for ever. *a.*

سرمدي *sarmadī*, eternal, perpetual, divine. *a.*

سرمست *sar-mast*, dead drunk. *p.*

سرمغزن *sarmaghzan*, m. trouble, vexation, labour, perplexity, fatigue. *p.* [*plex*). *a.*

سرمق *sarmaḳ*, m. (v. *surma*) orach (*Atri-*

سرمکه सरमुख *sarmukh*, (cor. of *sammukh* or *sanmukh*, q. v.) before, in front. *s.*

سرمنڈل *sarmandal*, name of a musical instrument. *d.*

سرمه *surma*, m. a collyrium (generally considered to be antimony, but what is used in India is an ore of lead). *surma-ālūda*, whose eyes are stained with *surma*. *surma-dān* or *surma-dānī*, a box, &c., for holding *surma*. *surma honā*, n. to be reduced to an impalpable powder. *p.* [ish. *p.*

سرمئي *surma,ī*, of the colour of *surma*, grey-

سرن सरन *saran*,
سرنا सरना *sarnā*, } f. an asylum, shelter, protection. *s.*

سرنا सरना *sarnā*, n. to be performed, to be carried on, to issue, to be ended. *h.*

سرنا *surnā*, m. a kind of pipe, a clarion. *p.*

سرناچي *surnā-chī*, m. a clarion (or a hautboy) player. *p.*

سرناگت सरनागत *saranāgat*, one who comes for shelter, a refugee. *saranāgata-vatsal*, merciful to those who come for sanctuary, an epithet of the Deity. *s.*

سرنامه *sarnāma*, m. title, address, superscription of a letter. *p.*

سرناءي *surnā,ī*, m. (v. *surnā-chī*) a piper, &c. *p.*

سرناي *surnā,e*, m. (v. *surnā*). *p.*

سرنجام *sar-anjām* (v. سرانجام), apparatus, &c. *p.*

سرنجامي *saranjāmī*, means of support. *p.*

سرنگ सुरङ्ग *surang*, f. a mine, a hole cut in a wall to break into a house, a gallery, subterraneous passage; m. red colour; adj. red coloured, bay or chesnut (horse). *surang-dhātu*, m. red chalk. *s.*

سرنگ शृङ्ग *sṛing*, m. a precipice; a horn. *s.*

سرنگي शृङ्गी *sṛingī*, horned, crested; name of a saint. *s.*

سرو सर्व *sarv* or *sarva*, all, the whole. *sarva-bhā,o*, m. whole disposition, all one's thoughts and purposes. *sarva-bhaksha*, omnivorous, all-devouring. *sarva-bhūt*, m. all the elements, all created things. *sarva-priya*, universally beloved; loving all. *sarva-pūrnatā*, f. entire completion, complete preparation. *sarva-tejas*, m. all-splendour, omnipotence. *sarva-tejomay*, comprising or consisting of all splendour or power. *sarva-jit*, all-subduing, incomparable; m. the twenty-first year of the cycle. *sarva-jagat*, f. the universe. *sarva-darshi*, all-seeing. *sarva-dukh-kshay*, m. end of all pain, final emancipation. *sarva-daman*, all-subduing. *sarva-dhārī*, f. the 22nd year of the cycle. *sarva-dhan*, m. whole property; (in arith.) total of a sum in progression. *sarva-rātra*, m. the whole night. *sarva-samtā*, f. sameness or identity with all things; equanimity, equal regard for all. *sarva-swāmī*, m. master of all, universal monarch. *sarva-sah*, al.-enduring; m. bdellium. *sarva-kārī*, m. the maker of all things. *sarva-kāl*, m. all seasons or times. *sarva-kālīn*, of all times or seasons. *sarva-ga* or *sarva-gat*, all-pervading, omnipresent. *sarva-gandh*, m. a class of four aromatics, or *kakkol*, cloves, agallochum, and gum benjamin. *sarva-gya*, omniscient. *sarva-gyatā*, f. omniscience. *sarva-lok*, m. the universe. *sarva-may*, universal, comprehensive. *sarva-nāsh*, m. universal destruction. *sarva-nām*, m. a pronoun. *sarva-vid* or *sarva-vedī*, omniscient, all-wise. *sarva-hār*, m. total confiscation. *s.*

سرو *sarv*, m. the cypress tree. *sarv-ḳadd*, or *sarv-andām*, or *sarv-ḳāmat*, of cypress stature; graceful and majestic. *sarvi rawān*, moving majestically. *p.*

سروا सरवा *sarwā*, m. a cup; wife's brother; brother-in-law; adj. excelling. *s.*

سروا सुरवा *surwā*, m. a ladle in form of a hand with which clarified butter is thrown into the fire for a burnt offering. *s.*

سرواتما सर्वात्मा *sarvātmā*, m. the universal spirit, all beings collectively. *s.*

سرواڌهکار सर्वाधिकार *sarvādhikār*, m. general control or superintendence. *sarvādhikārī*, m. a general superintendant. *s.*

سروارتهم सर्वार्थम *sarvārtham*, for all; on account of all. *s.* [to all. *s.*

سرواسري सर्वाश्रय *sarvāsray*, giving shelter

سروال *sarwāl*, m. trousers, breeches. *a.*

سروانگ सर्वाङ्ग *sarvāng*, m. the whole body. *s.*

سروپ सरूप *sarūp*, like, resembling; with form, with appearance; m. (for *swarūp*) appearance, a spectacle; own or natural shape or form; appearance, identity. *surūp*, beautiful, handsome. *sarūpatā*, f. likeness, resemblance. *s.*

سروپي सरूपी *sarūpī*, in its own shape, as it really appears. *s.*

سروتا सरोता *sarotā*, }
سروترا सरोत्रा *sarotrā*, } m. a kind of scissors for cutting betel-nut. *h.*

سروتپات सिरोत्पात *sirotpāt*, m. redness and inflammation of the eyes. *s.*

سروتر सर्वत्र *sarvatra*, everywhere, in all places, at all times. *s.*

سروتوبهدر सर्वतोभद्र *sarvato-bhadra*, everywhere auspicious; m. a temple or palace of a square form, with an entrance opposed to each point of the compass. *s.*

سروتها सर्वथा *sarvathā*, in all ways, by all means, assuredly. *s.*

سروج सरोज *saroj*, m. the lotus; lit. "the lake-born." *s.*

سرود *sarod*, m. a song, modulation, melody. *p.*

سرودا सर्वदा *sarvadā*, always, at all times. *s.*

سرودي *sarodī*, m. a singer. *p.*

سرور *surūr*, m. pleasure, joy, cheerfulness. *a.*

سرور *sarwar*, m. a chief, principal, leader; name of a *Muhammadan* saint. *sarwari kā,ināt* (chief of the world or of creatures) *Muhammad*. *p.*

سرور सरवर *sarvar*, m. a pond, a tank, a lake. *sarwar*, adj. equal. *s.*

سروري *sarwarī*, f. chiefship, leadership. *p.*

سروس सर्वस *sarvas, sarvasu*, }
سروسو सर्वस्व *sarvaswa*, } m. the whole, every thing, all substance or property. *sarvaswa-dand*, fined in all one's property; m. (also *sarvaswa-haran*) confiscation of a whole property. *s.*

سروش *sarosh*, m. an angel; a voice from heaven; the seventeenth day of the solar month. *p.*

سروكار *sarokār*, m. business. *p.*

سروگ सरोग *sarog*, sick, diseased. *sarvag*, all-pervading. *s.*

سرولا सरोला *sarolā*, m. a kind of sweetmeat. *h.*

سرون श्रवण *sravan*, m. the ear; the act of hearing; the twenty-third mansion of the moon, composed of the three principal stars in *Aquila*. *s.*

سرونج सरौंज *saraunj*, f. a kind of seed. *s.*

سروور सरोवर *sarovar*, m. a lake or large pond. *s.*

سرووشدهرس सर्वौषधिरस *sarvaushadi-ras*, m. the juice or infusion of a number of plants as used at a royal inauguration. *s.*

سرووشدهگن सर्वौषधिगण *sarvaushadhi-gan*, m. a class of certain principal drugs, consisting of Mūra, Valeriana, Jatamansi, Orris root, &c. *s.*

سره *sara*, current (as coin); good, worthy. *p.*

سروهي सरोही *sarohī*, f. a kind of scimitar. *h.*

سرهانا सिरहाना *sirhānā*, m. a pillow; the place where the head rests, when a person is asleep or dead; the head of a bed or tomb. *s.*

سرهنا सहेना *sarhnā*, m. the scale of a fish. *h.*

سرهنگ *sarhang*, m. a general, commander, captain, chief, overseer, a foot-soldier; adj. disobedient, violent, rebellious, strong. *p.*

سرهي सुरही *surhī*, a kind of grass growing on neglected or uncultivated lands. *h.*

سري सरी *sarī*, f. the shaft of an arrow; a reed of which arrows are made. *s.*

سري सिरी *sirī* (v. *sir*), the head. *s.*

سري श्री *srī* or *shrī*, a name of *Lakshmī* the wife of *Vishṇu* and goddess of prosperity; beauty; it is written as a mark of respect, something like our Master or Sir at the beginning of Hindū proper names of persons, as *Srī Lallū Lāl*, the author of the *Prem Sāgar*. *s.*

سري *sarī*, f. chiefship; adj. good. *p.*

سري *sare*, a term equivalent to our *a* or *per*, in such phrases as "how many rupees a yard," or "per yard?" *sare gaz kai rupae?* *h.*

سري सिर्री *sirrī*, mad, insane. *h.*

سرياني *suryānī*, Syriac (tongue), a Syrian. *a.*

سرپا *sare-pā*, }
سرپاءو *sare-pā,o*, } all, the whole; from top to toe. *p.*

سريپت श्रीपति *srī-pati*, *Vishṇu*, the husband of *Lakshmī*. *s.*

سريپهل *srīphal* (for *shrī-phal*), a cocoa-nut. *s.*

سريت सुरैत *surait* or *sarait*, }
سريتن सुरैतिन *suraitin* or *saraitin*, } f. a paramour, a mistress, a concubine. *s.*

سريجو सरेजो *sarejo* or *sarejav*, m. shelter, protection, patronage. *s.*

سرير *sarīr*, m. a throne; a cot or bedstead. *a.*

سرير शरीर *sarīr*, m. (for *sharīr*) body, constitution. *sarīrī*, corporeal. *s.*

سريراگ श्रीराग *srī-rāg*, m. name of a musical mode or *rāg*, appropriated to the afternoon in winter. It proceeds from the womb of the earth. *s.*

سريش *saresh*, m. glue, starch. *p.*

سريشٿه श्रेष्ठ *sreshṭh* (for *sreshṭha*), best, most excellent, pre-eminent. *s.*

سريع *sarī'*, quick, nimble, ready. *sarī'u-t-tāsīr*, ready, penetrating. *sarī'u-z-zawāl*, soon passing away; fading, frail. *a.*

سريكا *sarekā*, like, as, that, so (also much used as an expletive without any meaning, but conveying some slight emphasis). *d.*

سريكها सरेखा *sarekhā*, f. the ninth mansion of the moon, consisting of five stars, probably in *Cancer*; cunning, sly. *s.*

سريكها सरीखा *sarīkhā*, like, resembling, so. *h.*

سري‌مت श्रीमत *srī-mat*, prosperous, fortunate, wealthy, opulent. *s.* [sperity. *s.*

سري‌مد श्रीमद *srī-mad*, intoxication of pro-

سرين *surīn*, f. the buttocks, the hips, the thighs. *p.* [hum. *s.*

سريو सरेव *sarew*, m. patronage, shelter, asy-

سڙ सिड़ *siṛ*, f. madness, insanity. *h.*

سڙا सिड़ा *siṛā*, mad, insane. *h.*

سڙا सड़ा *saṛā*, rotten, musty, stinking. *h.*

سڙانا सड़ाना *saṛānā*, a. to cause to rot; to make ferment, to steep. *h.*

سڙاند सड़ांद *saṛānd*, f. a disagreeable smell. *h.*

سڙاهٹ सड़ाहट *saṛāhaṭ*, f. rottenness. *h.*

سڙاهند सड़ाहिन्द *saṛāhind*, f. a disagreeable smell, smell of putrid meat. *h.*

سڙبللا सिड़बिलिल्ला *siṛ-bilillā*, mad, insane. *h.*

سڙپ सुड़प *suṛap*, f. sipping or sucking up (as broth), or the noise made thereby. *h.*

سڙپن सिड़पन *siṛ-pan*, m. madness, insanity. *h.*

سڙپنا सुड़पना *suṛapnā*, n. to sip. *h.*

سڙك सड़क *saṛak*, f. the high road, a path. *saṛak-phāṅsī*, f. a noose. *h.*

سڙك *saṛak*, a game bag (v. *shikār band*); adj. drunk, intoxicated. *d.*

سڙكنا सुड़कना *suṛuknā*, n. to gulp at, to swallow. *h.*

سڙكي सुड़क्की *suṛakkī* or सुड़की *suṛkī*, f. act of suddenly slackening the string of a paper kite. *h.*

سڙن सड़न *saṛan*, f. rottenness, putrefaction. *s.*

سڙن सिड़न *siṛan*, f. mad or insane (women). *h.*

سڙنا सड़ना *saṛnā*, n. to rot; to ferment. *h.*

سڙي सिड़ी *siṛī*, mad, insane (v. *sirrī*). *h.*

سڙي *siṛī*, f. stairs, steps, a ladder. *d.*

سڙيل सड़ियल *saṛiyal*, rotten, stinking. *h.*

سزا *sazā*, f. (literally) one's desert; (generally means) correction, punishment, retribution. *sazā-denā* or *-karnā*, lit. to give one his desert, generally used in the sense of "to punish, to castigate." *p.*

سزاوار *sazā-wār*, worthy, excellent, able, applicable, meritorious. *p.*

سزاواري *sazā-wārī*, f. worthiness, excellence. *p.*

سزاور *sazā-war* (v. *sazā-wār*), worthy, &c. *p.*

سزاول *sazāwal*, m. a tax-gatherer, a land steward, an officer employed at a monthly salary, to collect the revenues of a district, the zamindār of which has fallen in arrear. *t.*

سزاولي *sazāwalī*, f. the business of a *sazāwal*; adj. relating to a *sazāwal*. *t.*

سس सस *sas* (for *shashi*), m. the moon; the sky, the heavens. *s.*

سسا ससा *sasā*, m. a hare (Dakh. *sassa*). *s.*

سسار सुसार *susār*, m. a cook, a dresser and seller of provisions. *h.*

سست *sust*, relaxed, lazy, negligent, slow, dilatory, languid, feeble, indolent. *sust-i'tiḳād*, incredulous, fickle. *sust-paimān*, unsteady to one's engagement. *p.*

سستا सस्ता *sastā*, cheap, easy to procure. *h.*

سستاگي *sastāgī*, f. cheapness. *d.* [to rest. *s.*

سستانا सस्ताना *sastānā* or सुस्ताना *sustānā*, n.

سستاءي सस्ताई *sastā,ī*, f. cheapness. *h.*

سستر *sustar*, a string for making images move or dance. *d.*

سستھ सुस्थ *susth*, well, healthy. *susthatā*, f. health. *s.* [resolute. *s.*

سستھر सुस्थिर *susthir*, firm, steady, stable;

سستي *sustī*, f. relaxation, laziness, negligence, dilatoriness; cheapness, lowness of price. *sustī tornā*, to break one's laziness, to become active. *sustī bechnā*, to sell cheap. *p.*

سسر शिशिर *sisir*, f. one of the six seasons, including from the 11th of Paus to the 11th of Phāgun; dew. *s.*

سسر सुसर *susar* or *sasur*, } m. a father-in-law,
سسرا सुसरा *susrā*, } the father of either husband or wife. *s.*

سسرار सुसरार *susrār*, } f. father-in-law's house
سسرال सुसराल *susrāl*, } or family. In Calcutta, &c., the term is jocosely applied to a jail or prison, just as we call the pawnbroker's shop "the mansion of mine uncle." *s.*

سسكارنا सुसकारना *suskārnā*, n. to sibilate, to hiss (as a snake). *h.*

سسكنا सिसकना *sisaknā*, n. to sob. *h.*

سسكي सिसकी *siskī*, f. sobbing. *siskiyāṉ bharnā*, to sob. *h.* [plenty. *s.*

سسمي सुसमय *susamay*, m. a good season,

سسنشي ससंशय *sasanshay*, doubtful, uncertain. *s.* [able smell. *h.*

سسياءيند सिसियाईंद *sisiyā,īnd*, a disagree-

سسير ससियर *sasiyar*, m. the moon (v. *sasī*). *s.*

سسيه सस्य *sasya*, m. fruit; corn, grass. *s.*

سشپت सुषुप्त *sushupt*, fast asleep. *sushupti*, f. deep sleep. *s.*

سشٹاچار शिष्टाचार *sishṭāchār*, m. humility, complaisance, obligingness. *s.*

سشٹاچاري शिष्टाचारी *sishṭāchārī*, obliging, humble; f. a treat, a feast. *s.*

سشنك सशङ्क *sashank*, fearful, doubtful. *s.*

سشوك सशोक *sashok*, sorrowful, sad, sadly. *s.*

سشيه शिष्य *sishya* or *shishya*, m. a disciple, a scholar, a pupil. *s.*

سشيل सुशील *su-shīl*, well-disposed, good-natured, of good manners, polite. *s.*

سشيلت सुशीलता *su-shīlatā*, f. goodness of disposition, good nature, affability. *s.*

سطح *saṭh*, f. a platform, a terrace, a flat roof; surface, superficies, area. *a.*

سطحي *saṭḥī*, superficial, flat. *a.*

سطر *saṭar*, f. a line, row, rank, series, lineament; delineating, describing. *saṭar-bandī*, f. ruling, lines for writing on. *a.*

سطوت *saṭwat*, dominion, majesty, power, authority, awfulness; force, violence. *a.*

سعادت *sa'ādat*, f. felicity, happiness, good fortune. *sa'ādat-mand*, fortunate, prosperous, happy. *sa'ādat-mandī*, f. prosperity. *a.*

سعاية *si'āyat*, labour expected from a half-free servant; calumny, accusation: according to Gladwin, by *si'āyat* is meant work or labour of any kind. It is a principle of the *Muḥammadan* law that no person can remain partially a slave, but that any circumstance, which in its nature establishes the emancipation of a part, provides for, and necessarily induces, the eventful emancipation of the whole; and hence the rule, that a slave, partially emancipated, works out the remainder of his value at an ascertained rate. *a.*

سعتر *sa'tar*, f. *origanum*; a woman that loves a woman; *instrumentum in modum virgæ virilis, confectum ex serico vel simili materia, quo, ad medium corporis sibi alligato meretrices utuntur*. *a.*

سعد *sa'd*, m. felicity, prosperity, propitiousness. *a.*

سعدي *sa'dī*, the celebrated poet and moralist of Shirāz, author of the Gulistan, &c. *a.*

سعديت *sa'dīyat*, state of felicity. *a.*

سعدين *sa'dain* (du.), two fortunate planets, such as Jupiter and Venus. *a.*

سعي *sa'i*, f. endeavour, attempt, effort, enterprise, purpose. *a.*

سعيد *sa'īd*, fortunate, happy, august. *a.*

سعير *sa'īr*, that portion of hell which is destined for idolaters. *a.*

سفارت *sifārat*, f. making peace (between others); writing, collecting, or binding a book. *a.*

سفارش *sifārish*, f. recommendation, introduction. *p.* [troduction. *s.*

سفارش‌نامه *sifārish-nāma*, m. a letter of in-

سفاك *saffāk*, m. a shedder of blood. *a.*

سفاكي *saffākī*, the act of bloodshed. *a.*

سفال *safāl*, m. meanness of rank, depression; descent, fall. *a.*

سفال *sifāl*, m. earthenware; (in Hindī) glazed earthenware. *p.*

سفالي *sifālī*, earthen, made of earthenware. *p.*

سفانت *sifānat*, f. the art of ship-building. *a.*

سفاهت *safāhat*, f. stupidity, folly, buffoonery; insolence. *a.*

سفت *saft*, firm; thick, close (a cloth). *p.*

سفت *saft*, f. drinking a great deal without quenching thirst. *sift*, soft pitch. *a.*

سفتجة *siftajat* or *siftaja*, the act of giving a bill of exchange or letter of credit, the amount to be payable, with interest, at a distant time and place: it also denotes the delivery of property to another by way of loan, and not by way of trust, in order that the other may deliver it to some friend of his, and the object of it is to avoid the dangers of the road. *a.*

سفتن *suftan* (r. *sumb*), to bore (a pearl, &c.). *p.*

سفته *sufta*, bored, pierced (a pearl). *p.*

سفر *safar*, m. journey, voyage, travel. *safar-k.*, a. to travel; (met.) to go, to depart, to retire, to die. *as-safar wasīlatu-ẓ-ẓafar*, travel produces advantage. *a.*

سفرجل *safarjal* or *safarjil*, a quince. *a.*

سفره *sufra*, m. a tablecloth, napkin; a large leathern bag for holding food, so formed as to serve also for a table when spread out on the ground; the anus. *p.*

سفري *safarī*, f. travelling provisions. *safarī ām*, m. a guava (*Psidium pyriferum*). *p.*

سفك *safk*, shedding, effusion (of blood). *a.*

سفل *sufl* or *sifl*, m. meanness (of origin), ignoble, inferior. *a.*

سفلگي *siflagī*, meanness, stinginess. *p.*

سفله *safla* (vulg. *sifla*), ignoble, mean, contemptible; stingy, miserly; envious. *safla-dān*, m. a cup or plate to throw scraps, bones, &c. on. *a.*

سفلي *suflī*, infernal, lower, inferior. *a.*

سفوف *sufūf*, m. a medicine taken dry and unmixed, a powder (in opposition to an electuary). *a.*

سفيد *sufaid*, *safed*, or *sufīd*, white. *safed-tulsī*, the white basil. *safed muḥammad*, a kind of esculent root (*Fluggea leucopyrus*). *p.*

سفيدا *safedā*, m. white lead. *p.*

سفيدار *safedār*, m. the name of a wood, the white poplar. *p.*

سفيده *sufaida*, the dawn of day; whiteness; white lead; hair powder. *p.*

سفيدي *sufaidī*, f. whiteness; leprosy. *p.*

سفير *safīr*, m. an envoy, ambassador. *a.*

سفينه *safīna*, m. a ship, a vessel, boat; a blank book, common-place book. *a.*

سفيه *safīh*, foolish, stupid, ignorant. *a.*

سقا *sakkā*, m. a water-carrier; a cup-bearer; the pelican, "so called from a tradition, which deposes that when on one occasion there befel a severe drought at Mecca, a number of these sagacious birds brought water in their large beaks for the relief of the inhabitants of that sacred city."—(Binning). *a.*

سقاوا *sakāwā*, a cold bath; a washing room. *a.*

سقايه *sakāya*, m. a bath; a drinking vessel. *a.*

سقر *sakar*, m. hell, or rather that portion of it which is allotted to the Magi or fire-worshippers v. *jahannam*). *a.*

سقط *sakat*, m. abuse, abusive language; an error, blunder, mistake, defect; any thing of a base or useless nature, merchandise of a perishable quality, either spoiled or spoiling. *sakt*, fire; sparks struck from a steel. *sakat honā*, n. to die (applied to brute animals); to miscarry. *a.*

سقطي نامه *sakti-nāma*, m. a casualty list of horses which have died in the cavalry. *a. p.*

سقف *sakf*, f. roof, ceiling, canopy; the sky; a platform. *a.*

سقفي *sakfī*, f. a beam, a rafter. *a.*

سقلات *sakalāt*, *sikalāt*, سقلاط *suklāt*, } scarlet cloth. *p.*

سقمونيا *sakmūniyā*, m. scammony (Hippoc. and Diosc. σκαμμωνια, dried juice exuding from the root of *Convolvulus scammonea*). *g.*

سقنقور *sakankūr*, m. a skink (*Lacerta scincus*). *a.*

سقيم *sakīm*, sick, infirm, weak. *a.*

سك शुक *suk* (for *shuk*), m. a parrot. *s.*

سك *suk* (for *sukh*), m. repose, comfort. *sakh* (for *sankh*), m. a kind of conch, a shell. *d.*

سكها *sukhā* (for *sūkā*), dry (v. *sūkhā*). *d.*

سكات *sakāt*, f. silence; adj. silent. *a.*

سكار सकार *sakār*, m. dawn of day, morning. *s.*

سكارن सकारण *sakāran*, having a cause, originating from a cause. *s.*

سكارنا सकारना *sakārnā*, a. to accept (a bill of exchange, &c.). *s.*

سكاري सकारी *sakārī*, f. dawn of day, morning. *s.*

سكاك *sakkāk*, m. a cutler, one who makes knives. *a.*

سكاكي *sakkākī*, f. the business of a cutler. *a.*

سكال सकाल *sakāl* or *sukāl*, adv. betimes, early in the morning; dawn of day, morning. *sukāl*, m. goodness of seasons, plenty, cheapness, abundance. *s.*

سكان *sukkān*, m. a rudder, helm; (pl. of *sakīn*) inhabitants. *a.*

سكانا सकाना *sakānā*, n. to be grieved, to feel tired. *h.*

سكاني *sukkānī*, m. a steersman (in Indian-English orthography, "sea conny"). *a.*

سكبينج *sikbīnaj*, m. sagapenum, a kind of gum-resin (Gr. σαγαπηνον, Hippoc. and Dioscor.). *g.*

سكت सकत *sakat* or *sakti*, f. ability, strength, power; the energy of a deity; the female organ as the counterpart of the phallic personification of *Shiva*, and worshipped by a sect of Hindūs, hence called Sāktas. *s.*

سكتا सिकता *siktā*, f. gravel or stone (the disease). *s.*

سكتپهلا सक्तुफला *saktu-phalā*, f. a tree (*Mimosa suma*). *s.*

سكتك सक्तुक *saktuk*, m. a species of poison. *s.*

سكته *sakta*, m. a trance, an apoplexy, a pause, vacancy. *a.*

سكٿ सकट *sakaṭ*, bad, vile; m. a small tree (*Trophis aspera*); a cart; the name of a Hindū holiday. *s.*

سكٿا सुकटा *sukṭā*, lean, thin, dry, emaciated. *siktā*, m. a fragment of an earthen vessel, a shard. *s.*

سكٿي सुकटी *sukṭī*, lean, thin, emaciated, dry; f. dried fish. *s.*

سكچ सकुच *sakuch*, f. shrinking, awe, fear, shame. *s.*

سكچانا सुकचाना *sukchānā* or सकुचाना *sakuchānā*, a. to abash; also n. to be abashed, to be afraid. *s.*

سكچنا सुकुचना *sukuchnā* or सकुचना *sakuchnā*, n. to fear, to be afraid of, to be in awe of, to be abashed, to apprehend, to be apprehensive. *s.*

سكديو शुकदेव *sukdev*, m. the name of the son of *Vyāsadeva*: he was famed for his sanctity, and he is the narrator of the *Bhāgavat purāna*, composed by his father *Vyāsa*. *s.*

سكر शुक्र *sukr* or *sukra*, m. the planet Venus (the Freya of the Saxons: hence *sukr-bār*, Friday, *i.e.* Freya's day); (*Sperma genitale*). *sukar*, easy, practicable. *s.*

سكر *sukr*, m. any intoxicating drink, wine; intoxication. *sukkar*, m. sugar. *a.*

سكرا सकरा *sakrā*, small (not having room enough), narrow, straight. *s.*

سكرات *sakarāt*, f. agony, fainting. *sakarāti maut*, senselessness, the point of death. *a.*

سكرانا सकराना *sakrānā*, a. to straiten, to deprive of necessary room; to cause to accept (a bill, &c.). *s.*

سكرانت सक्रान्त *sakrānt*, f. entering of the sun into a new sign. *s.*

سكرانتي *sakrāntī* (v. *sakrānt* or *sanhrāntī*). *s.*

سكراءي सकराई *sakrā,ī*, f. smallness, want of room. *s.*

سكرت सुकृत *su-kṛit*, well done, well performed; virtuous, pious; properly, ably; f. virtue, a good action; moral merit, kindness, bounty. *sukṛitī*, virtuous, good, benevolent. *s.*

سكرمك सकर्मक *sakarmak*, transitive (verb, in grammar). *s.*

سكري सिकरी *sikrī*, f. a staple (of a lock). *h.*

سكريا सुक्रिया *sukriyā*, f. a good action, moral merit. *s.*

سكڑنا सुकड़ना *sukaṛnā* or *sikuṛnā*, n. to be shrunk, to shrink; to draw in, to collect, to gather up, to constrain, to shrivel, to dwindle. *s.*

سكل सकल *sakal*, all, the whole, every. *s*

سکل शुक्ल *sukla* or *sukal*, white. *sukal pachchh* (for *shukla paksha*), moonlight, the light half of the month; a title of Brāhmans. *s.*

سکلیکرم शुक्लीकर्म *sukli-karm*, m. soap (q. d. whitening, making white). *s.*

سکلیه सकुल्य *sakulya*, m. a kinsman, one of the same family. *s.*

سکمار सुकुमार *sukumār* (v. *sukwār*), youthful, tender, soft, delicate, feeble. *s.*

سکن शकुन *sakun*, m. (v. *sagun*) an omen. *s.*

سکن *sakin*, m. a dwelling. *sakn*, the inmates or inhabitants of a house. *a.*

سکنا सकना *saknā*, n. to be able. *s.*

سکنا सिकना *siknā*, n. to be toasted or parched. *h.*

سکنا *suknā*, n. (v. *sūknā*) to become dry. *d.*

سکنٹك सकण्टक *sakanṭak*, thorny, prickly, troublesome, perilous; m. an aquatic plant (*Vallisneria*). *s.*

سکنج *sukunj*, an ulcer on the lip, a fetid breath. *a.*

سکنجبین *sakanjabīn*, f. oxymel; lime-juice or other acid mixed with honey or sugar. *p.*

سکندر *sikandar* (v. *Iskandar*), Alexander the Great. *p.*

سکندري *sikandarī*, of or relating to Alexander. *p.*

سکندریه *sikandarīya*, the city of Alexandria. *p.*

سکندھ स्कन्ध *skandh*, m. the shoulder; a section, portion, division; a canto of a poem, as of the *Bhāgavat* or *Mahābhārat*, the trunk of a tree. *s.*

سکنه *sakana* (pl. of (ساکن), inhabitants. *a.*

سکني शकुनी *sakunī*, m. one who understands omens; a bird (from which an omen is inferred). *s.*

سکوار सुकवार *sukwār*, delicate, feeble. *s.*

سکوپ सकोप *sakop*, angry, displeased. *s.*

سکوت *sukūt*, f. silence, quietness, peace. *sakūt*, adj. silent, quiet. *a.*

سکوچ सकोच *sakoch*, m. regard, respect, esteem. *s.*

سکورا सकोरा *sakorā*, m. a small earthen vessel. *h.*

سکوري सकोरी *sakorī*, f. a saucer. *h.*

سکوڑنا सकोड़ना *sakoṛnā*, n. to shrink, to draw up (the limbs), to gather up, to shrivel, to tighten; a. to contract, to draw up. *s.*

سکون *sukūn*, being quiet; having no vowel (a consonant); tranquillity, ease, dwelling. *a.*

سکونت *sakūnat*, f. dwelling, habitation, residence, tranquillity. *a.*

سکه *sikka*, m. a coining die; an impression on money; sterling, current; stamped coin; name of a weight equal (in Bengal) to 7 dwt. and 11·5511 grains. *p.a.*

سکھ सुख *sukh*, m. ease, tranquillity, easy circumstances, content, happiness, pleasure, delight. *sukh pānā*, a. to get ease, leisure, rest, &c. *sukh-pūrvak*, easily, without difficulty. *sukh-bhāg*, m. happiness, good fortune. *sukh-bhāgī*, happy, delighted. *sukh chain*, m. ease, rest, leisure, tranquillity. *sukh-dān*, m. the act of giving ease or comfort. *sukh-dā,ī* or *sukh-dāyak*, a giver of ease, a comforter. *sukh-dhām* or *sukh-bās*, abode of happiness. *sukh-sādhya*, easy of accomplishment. *sukhi-swabhā,o*, m. a happy or contented disposition. *sukh-may*, full of happiness, delightful. *s.*

سکھ सिख *sikh*, m. a disciple, scholar, pupil; a follower of *Nānak*; the people of the *Panjāb*. *s.*

سکھا सखा *sakhā*, m. a friend, a companion. *s.*

سکھا शिखा *sikhā*, f. a lock of hair on the crown of the head: a queue (v. *choṭī*); flame of a lamp. *s.*

سکھارتھ सुखार्थ *sukhārth*, for the sake of ease, happiness, &c. *sukhārthī*, seeking happiness. *s.*

سکھاسواد सुखास्वाद *sukhāswād*, m. well-flavoured, delightful; m. enjoyment, flavour. *s.*

سکھالا सुखाला *sukhālā*, easy, facile. *s.*

سکھانا सुखाना *sukhānā*, a. to dry; to cause to evaporate, to emaciate, to cause to pine away. *s.*

سکھانا सिखाना *sikhānā*, } a. to teach; (met.) to admonish, to chastise. *s.*
سکھاونا सिखावना *sikhāwanā*, }

سکھاءي सिखाई *sikhā,ī*, f. teaching, instruction. *s.*

سکھپال सुखपाल *sukhpāl*, m. a kind of *pālkī*. *s.*

سکھت सुखित *sukhit*, tranquil, happy. *s.*

سکھ‌تلا सुखतला *sukh-talā*, m. a piece of leather placed on the sole within a shoe. *s.*

سکھتوه सखित्व *sakhitwa*, m. friendship. *s.*

سکھد सुखद *sukhad*, salubrious, pleasant, conferring pleasure. *s.*

سکھداس सुखदास *sukh-dās*, m. a very superior and delicious kind of rice. *s.*

سکھدرسن सुखदर्शन *sukh-darsan*, m. a shrub, the juice of which is given for the ear-ache (*Crinum Asiaticum* and *Zeylanicum*). *s.*

سکھر शिखर *sikhar*, m. three or more strings tied together forming a support to hang any thing on; the cords of a *bahangī*, in which the baskets rest; top, summit, peak, pinnacle. *s.*

سکھرن सिखरन *sikharan*, m. a kind of dish made of coagulated milk and sugar. *s.*

سکھ‌ساون *sukh-sāwan*, } a palanquin. *d.*
سکھ‌سوان *sukh-sawān*, }

سکھلانا सुखलाना *sukhlānā*, a. (v. *sukhānā* to dry, &c. *s.*

سکھلانا सिखलाना *sikhlānā*, a. (v. *sikhānā*) to instruct. *s.*

سکھناود सिखनावद *sikhnāwad*, m. tuition, instruction. *s.*

سکھلن स्खलन *skhalan*, m. stumbling, slipping, tripping. *s.*

سکھودي सुखोदय *sukhoday*, m. realization or ocurrence of pleasure. *s.*

سکھي सखी *sakhī*, f. a friend, companion (female confidant, &c., to a woman); a kind of *faḳīr* who dresses like a woman. *s.*

سکھي सुखी *sukhī*, } at ease, happy, tranquil, contented, comfortable, pleasant. *s.*
سکھيا सुखिया *sukhiyā*, }

سکھيات सुख्यात *sukhyāt*, celebrated, famous. *sukhyāti*, f. fame, celebrity. *s.*

سکھي جن सखीजन *sakhī-jan*, f. a female friend or confidante. *s.*

سکھيچها सुखेच्छा *sukhechchhā*, f. hope or desire of happiness. *s.*

سکھيه सख्य *sakhya*, m. friendship. *s.*

سکي اڑانا *sukke uṛānā*, a. to render hopeless, to reduce to despair. *d.* [distress. *s.*

سکيت सकेत *saket*, narrow, strait; f. want,

سکيتنا सकेतना *saketnā*, a. to tighten, to straiten. *s.*

سکيلا सकेला *sakelā*, m. a kind of iron. *h.*

سکيلنا सकेलना *sakelnā*, n. to shrink, to shrivel, to gather up (the limbs, as a tortoise). *h.*

سگ *sag*, m. a dog. *sagi-bāzārī*, a common cur. *sag-bacha*, m. a pup, a whelp. *sag-davī*, f. running about fruitlessly. *sag-zāda*, son of a bitch. *sagi-shikārī* or *-tāzī*, a hunting dog. *sag-lagī*, f. flattery, servitude. *p.*

سگا सगा *sagā*, m. kin, relative, related (of the same parents), full, own, as *sagā bhā,ī*, own brother. *s.*

سگال *sigāl*, thought, suspicion, word; enmity, calumny. *bad-sigāl*, of evil thoughts, malevolent. *p.*

سگاوت सगावत *sagāvat*, } f. relationship, by the same parents,
سگاءي सगाई *sagā,ī*, }
consanguinity; betrothing for marriage; second marriage of a woman of low tribe. *sagā,ī-k.*, a. to contract a marriage, to affiance, to betroth. *s.*

سگپت सुगुप्त *sugupt*, secret, well hidden; adv. secretly, privily. *sugupti*, f. closeness, secrecy. *s.*

سگ پہتا सगपहता *sag-pahtā*, m. greens dressed with pulse. *s.*

سگٹ *sagaṭ*, the same, alike; similar. *d.*

سگرا सगरा *sagrā* or *sigrā*, every, the whole. *s.*

سگرو सिगरौ *sigrau* (Braj.) for *sigrā*, all, every. *h.*

سگرءي सुगराई *sugra,ī*, f. name of a musical mode or *rāginī*, sung in the afternoon. *h.*

سگڑ सगड़ *sagaṛ* or *saggaṛ*, m. a cart. *s.*

سگسار *sag-sār*, name of an imaginary monster, with the head of a dog, the yellow face of a dragon, the hair of a goat, the ears of an elephant, and blue eyes; (met.) an avaricious man. *p.*

سگل *sagal*, all, every, the whole. *d.*

سگم सुगम *sugam*, that which goes well, good, easy, easily accomplished, practicable, accessible; plain, intelligible. *s.* [omen. *s.*

سگن सगुन *sagun*, *sugun*, or *sugan*, augury, an

سگن सगुण *sagun*, endowed with properties, qualities, &c. *s.*

سگند सुगन्द *sugand*, } f. odour, fragrance; adj. fragrant,
سگندھ सुगन्धि *sugandhi*, }
odoriferous. *sugand-rāe*, name of a flower. *sugandsānā*, perfumed. *sugandhitā*, f. fragrance, such as produced by the trituration of perfumes. *s.*

سگوتر सगोत्र *sagotra*, being of one family, related; m. a distant kinsman. *s.* [flesh. *h.*

سگوتي सगोती *sagotī*, f. animal food, meat,

سگھڑ सुघड़ *sughaṛ*, elegant, accomplished, beautiful, virtuous. *s.* [plishment. *h.*

سگھڑاءي सुघड़ाई *sughṛā,ī*, f. elegancy, accom-

سگھن सघन *saghan*, thick (as a head of hair). *s.*

سگيان सुज्ञान *sugyān*, m. sound knowledge, wisdom, sagacity. *s.*

سگيان सज्ञान *sagyān*, } possessed of knowledge, sagacious, wise, intelligent. *s.*
سگيانا सज्ञाना *sagyānā*, }
سگياني सज्ञानी *sagyānī*, }

سل *sill*, m. a consumption, a hectic fever. *a.*

سل *sal*, m. a kind of grasshopper; the mantis or leaf insect. *d.*

سل सिल *sil*, } f. a stone on which spices, &c. are ground, or knives
سلا सिला *silā*, }
sharpened; a stone (in general), a rock. *s.*

سلا सिला *silā* (for *shilā*), gleanings of a cornfield. *silā-hār*, m. a gleaner. *h.*

سلاجت सिलाजित *silājit*, m. storax. *s.*

سلاح *silāḥ*, f. arms, weapons, implements of war, armour. *silāḥ-posh*, one who is armed. *silāḥ khāna*, an armoury or arsenal. *silāḥ-dār*, a sword- or armour-bearer, an esquire. *silāḥ-shor*, a fencing-master, a champion, a gladiator; a breaker or trainer of horses. *a.*

سلاخ *sallākh*, m. a skinner (in Dakh.) *salākh*, an iron chisel used for breaking through walls, &c. *a.*

سلارس सिलारस *silāras*, m. (v. *silājit*) storax. *s.*

سلاست *salāsat*, f. facility, ductility, easiness, gentleness; perspicuity, clearness. *a.*

سلاسل *salāsil*, lightning darting to a great distance; (pl. of *silsila*) chains. *a.*

سلاطين *salāṭīn* (pl. of سلطان), kings, rulers. *a.*

سلاکا सलाका *salākā*, f. a rule, a ruler; a probe. *s.*

سلام *salām*, m. salutation; peace, safety. *salām-k.*, to salute; to give up, to desist, to refrain, bid adieu. *salām-'alek* (for *salāmun 'alaika*), peace be upon thee. *salām-'alaikum* (for *salāmun 'alaikum*), peace be upon you: these are forms of salutation used by one Musalmān towards another. *salām-lenā*, a. to return the salutation. *a.*

سلامت *salāmat*, f. safety, salvation, recovery, tranquillity, health. *salāmat-raw*, an economist. *salāmat-rawī*, f. economy, good management; the word is often used adverbially, as "*wuh Hindūstān men salāmat pahunchā*," he arrived safe or safely (*i.e.* in safety) in India. *a.*

سلامتي *salāmatī*, f. a kind of coarse cloth. *h.*

سلامي *salāmī*, f. salute; a present given to a landlord for granting a lease, or a present given on receiving an office; a pavement of stones across the bed of a watercourse; an Irish bridge. *a.*

سلانا सिलाना *silānā*, a. to cause to sew, to stitch. *s.*

سلانا सुलाना *sulānā*, a. to cause to sleep; to kill, to murder. *sulā-denā*, a. to kill, to murder. *s.*

سلاءي सिलाई *silā,ī*, f. the price of sewing; seam, sewing. *s.*

سلاءي सलाई *salā,ī*, f. a needle, or piece of wire for tingeing the eyelids with a collyrium; also used for depriving people of sight, which is effected by drawing it while hot close over the eyes of the sufferer; a lead pencil. (in Dakh.) *salā,ī-dār*, striped (as cloth) with narrow stripes. *s.*

سلب *salb*, m. a negative argument in logic; plunder. *salbi kullī*, general negation. *salbi juz,ī*, special negation. *a.*

سل بٹا सिलबट्टा *sil-baṭṭā*, m. two stones with which spices, paint, &c. are ground. *s.*

سلبھ सुलभ *sulabh*, easy, easily attained; *salabh* (for *shalabh*, q.v.) a locust, a grasshopper. *s.*

سلپ शिल्प *silpa* (for *shilpa*, q.v.), art, &c. *s.*

سل پٹ सिलपट *sil-paṭ*, smooth, even, level. *s.*

سلپچي सिलपची *silapchī*, f. a wash-hand basin, ewer (v. *chilamchī*). *h.*

سلتا सलिता *salitā*, f. a river, a stream. *s.*

سلج सलज्ज *sa-lajj*, affected with shame, bashful. *s.*

سلجھانا सुलझाना *suljhānā*, a. to unravel, to disentangle. *h.*

سلجھنا सुलझना *sulajhnā*, n. to be unravelled or disentangled. *h.*

سلچھن सुलच्छन *su-lachhan*, m. (for *su-lakshana*) an auspicious mark; beauty, excellence; adj. auspicious. *s.*

سلح *silah* (v. *silāh*), arms, weapons (as sword, club, and bow). *a.*

سلح پوش *silah-posh*, one who is armed. *a. p.*

سلح خانہ *silah-khāna*, an armoury, an arsenal. *a. p.*

سلح دار *silah-dār*, m. an armour-bearer, an esquire, an armed attendant. *a.*

سلحشور *silah-shor*, a champion, gladiator; horse-breaker. *a.*

سلخ *salakh*, f. the end of the month, or the day of the new moon. *a.*

سلس *sals* (properly *salis*), easy, docile, gentle, mild, ductile. *a.*

سلسال *salsāl*, limpid water; waving like a chain. *a.*

سلسبيل *salsabīl*, s. pure running water; name of a fountain in Paradise; adj. flowing, limpid. *a.*

سلسلاٹ *sulsulāṭ*, piercing, rankling. *d.*

سلسلانا सलसलाना *salsalānā*, n. (v. *sarsarānā*) to creep as a snake. *h.*

سلسلانا *salsalānā*, n. (v. *khaṭaknā*) to pierce (a thorn); to rankle; to offend; to doubt. *d.*

سلسلاهٹ *silsilāhaṭ*, f. concatenation. *salsalāhaṭ*, crawling, tickling. *a. h.*

سلسل بول *silsili baul*, m. a diabetes, a morbid copiousness of urine. *a.*

سلسلہ *silsila*, m. a chain, series, concatenation, succession. *a.*

سلسلي *sulsalī* (v. *jhaṛī*), continued rains. *d.*

سلطان *sulṭān*, m. a prince, a sovereign, a king, an absolute monarch, an emperor. *a.*

سلطاني *sulṭānī*, belonging to a prince, sovereign, princely. *sulṭānī bulbul*, the royal bulbul, a species of that bird (v. *bulbul*); f. dignity or office of *sulṭān*; a kind of broad cloth. *a.*

سلطنت *salṭanat*, power, dominion, sovereignty. *a.*

سلف *salaf*, past, preceding, former (times); m. ancestors; money advanced for merchandize, &c.; a purse, a bag; the past, former times. *silf*, brother-in-law, husband of a wife's sister. *a.*

سلف *suluf* or *sulf*, a small ship, a bark, (evidently a corruption of "sloop"). *d.*

سلفا *sulfā*, m. little balls of tobacco smoked in a *hukka*, without the intervention of a tile. *h.*

سلفچي *silafchī* (v. *silapchī*), an ewer. *h.*

سلك *silk*, m. a thread, string; order, series, train; a road, a path. *a.*

سلك بندي *silk-bandī*, an account of the daily receipts of revenue made out at the end of the month, when the whole is added together, and formed into one total. *a. p.*

سلکشن सुलक्षण *sulakshan*, } (v. *su-lachhan*),
سلکهن सुलक्खण *su-lakhkhan*, } an auspicious mark; adj. of good omen, auspicious, clearly distinguished by marks, &c. *s.*

سلکهن *sulakhhan*, clever, expert. *d.*

سلكي सलकी *salkī*, f. the root of the *Nymphæa lotus*. *s.*

سلكي सल्लकी *sallakī*, f. the gum olibanum tree (*Boswellia thurifera*). *s.*

سلگ *salag*, intimacy, friendship. *a.*

سلگات *sulgāt*, the place where the Hindūs burn their dead. *d.* [to kindle. *s.*

سلگانا सुलगाना *sulgānā*, a. to light, to inflame,

سلگنا सुलगना *sulagnā*, n. to light, to be kindled; to burn without smoke or flame. *s.*

سلگي *salgī*, sociable, attached, tame, domesticated (as an animal). *d.*

سلل सलिल *salil*, m. water; liquid in general. *s.*

سلم *salam*, m. peace, safety; saluting, submitting, cultivating, peace, friendship; adj. free from fault or flaw. *sallama*, may he protect or preserve; as, *sallama hu Allāh ta'ālā*, may God the Most High preserve him (used in Arabic forms of prayer). *sullam*, m. a staircase, a ladder. *a.*

سلم सल्लम *sallam*, m. a kind of coarse cloth. *h.*

سلم *silim*, (in the language of the law) a contract of sale, causing an immediate payment of the price, and admitting a delay in the delivery of the wares. *a.*

سلمي *salmā*, name of a woman; also the name of a tribe and mountain in Arabia. *a.*

سلنا सलना *salnā*, n. to pierce, prick, perforate; m. a rivulet. *h.*

سلو सल्लू *sallū*, m. a thong, narrow slips of leather with which shoes are stitched. *h.*

سلو सल्लो *sallo*, foolish (a woman). *h.*

سلوانا सिलवाना *silwānā*, a. (caus. of *silānā*) to cause to be sewn. *s.*

سلوانا सुलवाना *sulwānā*, a. (caus. form of *sulānā*) to cause to be put to sleep. *s.*

سلوپ सलूप *salūp*, m. a little, very little. *s.*

سلوت *salwat*, f. contentment, cheerfulness, felicity. *a.*

سلوك *sulūk*, m. road, way; manner, mode; intercourse; usage, treatment. *sulūk-k.*, a. to treat, to proceed with. *a.*

سلوك श्लोक *sloh* (for *shloka*, q. v.), a couplet, or stanza of two lines. *s.*

سلول सलोल *salol*, playful, wanton. *s.*

سلون सलोन *salon*, salted food; name of a district. *s.*

سلونا सलोना *salonā*, salted, salt, seasoned, tasteful, beautiful, interesting; dark-complexioned; nutbrown; (met.) intelligent, piquant (in opposition to insipid or dull). *s.*

سلونو सलूनो *salūno*, f. the full moon in *Sāwan*, at which time the ornament called *Rākhī*, q. v., is tied round the wrist. *s.*

سلوني सलोनी *salonī*, seasoned, tasteful; beautiful (when applied to a mistress). *s.*

سلي सिली *silī*, f. a whetstone, a hone; a small kiln; the grain and chaff on the threshing-floor before winnowing. *s.*

سلي सिली *silī*, f. the trunk of a tree; plank; a large species of teal, commonly called the "whistling teal," from the sharp cry of this bird. *h.*

سليس *salīs*, easy, not abstruse, simple. *salīs-navīs*, writing a plain or easy hand. "Pray whence comes this word *salīs?* It is used in Hindī and also in the corrupt Persian of India, but I do not think it is to be found in any real Persian composition, and I never yet met with any native of Persia who understood it or had ever heard of it. I do not think it a legitimate Arabic or Persian word: perhaps it is a corruption of *sahl*."—(Binning). The forms *salīs* and *salīsī*, though not used in the Arabic language, are undoubtedly from the root *salisa*, one of whose meanings is, "he was easy to manage," or "obedient." Moreover, the forms *salis* and *salāsat* are given by Golius as genuine Arabic words, in the sense of "easy, &c.," "facility, &c." Finally, the Indians and Persians have coined many *Arabic* words unknown to the Arabs themselves.—(D. F.) *a.*

سليسي *salīsī*, f. facility, clearness. *a.*

سليش श्लेष *slesh*, m. a pun, a double meaning, an equivoque in writing or speaking, as in the following lines, *kīkar pākar tār, jāman phalsā āmilā; sew kadam kachnār, pīpal rattī tāna taj*, (this seems to be a catalogue of trees; it also means) God has been kind to you; that which you desired is obtained; adore his footsteps; silly woman! leave not your lover for a moment. *s.*

سليقه *salīka*, m. nature, genius, good disposition, knack, knowledge, dexterity, address. *salīka shi'ār*, of good disposition. *salīka,e guft o gū*, m. polite conversation. *salīka,e majlis*, m. good breeding. *ṣāḥib-salīka*, a man of taste and discernment, a well-informed person. *a.*

سليم *salīm*, pacific, mild, affable; perfect, healthy. *salīmu-ṭ-ṭab'*, affable, mild, pacific. *a.*

سليمان *sulaimān*, Solomon, the son of David. *a.*

سليماني *sulaimānī*, of or belonging to Solomon; m. an onyx; f. the state or dignity of Solomon. *a.*

سليمي *salīmī*, name of a species of cloth. *a.*

سم *samm*, m. poison, venom. *a.*

سم *sum*, m. a hoof, foot (of a horse, &c.). *p.*

سم सम *sam*, all, whole, entire; similar, alike; used as a prefix (in comp.) like the Latin *con* and the Greek συμ or συν, as *sam-bandh*, *con*-nection, συμ-πλοκη or συν-δεσις. *s.*

سم सम *sam*, a tone, note (in music). *h.*

سما समा *samā*, m. time, season; plenty, abundance; state, condition; concord, harmony, union. *samā-bandhnā*, to be in concert. *s.*

سما *samā*, m. the heavens, the sky, the firmament; a canopy; altitude. *a.*

سماپت समाप्त *samāpt* or *samāpta*, also *samapit*, accomplished; finished, perfected. *samāpti*, f. accomplishment, the whole, conclusion, end, finis. *s.*

سماپن समापन *samāpan*, m. conclusion, completion. *samāpanna*, finished, completed. *s.*

سمات *samāt* or *simāt*, f. a sign, mark. *simāt*, (pl. of *simat*) signs, marks (made by burning). *a.*

سماج समाज *samāj*, m. multitude, number, assembly; apparatus; society. *s.*

سماجت *samājat*, f. deformity, shamefulness, turpitude; adulteration; entreaty, humiliation (used adjectively) deformed, filthy, base. *a.*

سماجي समाजी *samājī*, f. musicians that attend to dancers. *s.*

سماچار समाचार *samāchār*, m. information, tradition, news, account of circumstances or health, &c.; adj. equal in virtuous conduct. *s.*

سماحت *samāhat*, f. beneficence, liberality. *a.*

سمادر समादर *samādar*, m. respect, reverence. *s.*

سمادھ समाधि *samādhi* or *samādh*, f. the tomb of a *jogī*, particularly where Hindūs, from religious motives, submit to be buried alive; an exercise of austerity among *jogis*, whereby they are supposed to acquire the power of suspending during their pleasure the connection between their soul and body. *s.*

سمادھان समाधान *samādhān*, m. religious meditation; promising, declaring; ease, comfort, consolation, reconciliation, adjustment, pacification, settlement, the act of satisfying. *s.*

سمار समार *samār*, crop-ploughing. *h.*

سمارت स्मार्त *smārt*, a follower of the law-books. *s.*

سمارك स्मारक *smārak*, what causes to remember or call to mind. *s.*

سماروغ *samārūgh*, m. a white mushroom resembling an egg. *p.*

سماس समास *samās*, m. contraction, abridgment; composition of words. *s.*

سماط *simāṭ*, an order, a series. *sumāṭ*, a table covered with victuals. *a.*

سماع *samā'*, m. hearing, listening; singing, a song; extasy occasioned by hearing singing, particularly among darweshes when hearing hymns; the sense of hearing. *a.*

سماعت *samā'at*, f. hearing. *a.*

سماعي *samā'ī*, what has been heard, traditional; (in gram.) irregular. *h.*

سماق *sumāḳ*, m. sumach (*Rhus coriaria*); porphyry, the hardest species of marble. *a.*

سماق پالان *sumāḳ-pālān*, a vessel for boiling rice: it consists of two pots, one fitting into the other, the inner pot being perforated full of small holes: when the rice is boiled, this inner vessel is lifted out, leaving the water strained off in the exterior pot. *p.*

سماکھيہ समाख्या *samākhyā*, f. fame, reputation. *s.*

سماکھيات समाख्यात *samākhyāt*, famed, celebrated, notorious. *s.*

سماگت समागत *samāgat*, arrived; met, encountered, united. *samāgati*, f. arrival; meeting, union; similar condition or progress. *s.*

سماگم समागम *samāgam*, m. union, association, intercourse, meeting. *s.*

سم الفار *sammu-l-fār*, } m. arsenic; (lit.)
سم الکھار *sammu-l-khār*, } poison for mice or rats, ratsbane. *a.*

سمالو समालु *samālū*, m. the name of a plant (also called *meṇrī*; *Vitex trifolia* and *negundo*). *h.*

سمالي समाली *samālī*, f. a collection of flowers, a nosegay. *s.*

سمان समान *samān*, equal, adequate, similar, alike, akin, one, uniform, same; f. equality, level. *samān-janmā*, of equal age. *samān-kālīn*, of the same period. *s.*

سمان समां *samāṅ*, m. (v. *samā*) time, season, state. *s.*

سمان सम्मान *sammān*, m. respect, homage. *s.*

سمانا समाना *samānā*, n. to be contained in (v. *amānā*). *s.*

سمانتا समानता *samāntā* or *samānatā*, f. likeness, resemblance, equality. *s.*

سمانيہ सम्मान्य *sammānya*, respectable, honourable. *s.*

سماو समाव *samāv*, m. room, space. *s.*

سماوي *samāwī*, heavenly, celestial. *a.*

سماويش समावेश *samāvesh*, m. entrance. *s.*

سماعي समाई *samā,ī*, f. endurance, patience, firmness; power, capability. *s.*

سمبا सुम्बा *sumbā*, m. a sponge staff, a ramrod. *h.*

سمباد संवाद *sambād*, m. conversation, intelligence, news of the day. *s.*

سمبت संवत *sambat*, m. a year, an era. *sambat bāndhnā*, to establish an era, to distinguish one's self by illustrious actions. *s.*

سمبدھ संबुद्धि *sambuddhi*, f. the vocative case. *s.*

سمبندھ संबंध *sambandh*, m. affinity, relation, relationship; rhyme, metre; the genitive or possessive case in grammar. *s.*

سمبندھي संबंधी *sambandhī*, m. relation; son or daughter's father-in-law; adj. related to, connected with, belonging. *s.*

سمبودھن संबोधन *sambodhan*, comfort, soothing, encouragement; calling, addressing; vocative. *s.*

سمبھ संभु *sambhu*, m. a parent, a progenitor. *s.*

سمبھارنا संभारना *sambhārnā*, } a. to support,
سمبھالنا संभालना *sambhālnā*, } to prop, to sustain, to assist, to help; to shield, to protect, to stop, to retain, to check. *s.*

سمبھاشن संभाषण *sambhāshan*, m. conversation, discourse. *s.*

سمبھاو समभाव *sam-bhā,o*, of like nature or property; equability, sameness. *s.*

سمبھاوت संभावित *sambhāvit*, possible. *s.*

سمبھاونا संभावना *sambhāwnā*, f. probability; fitness, competency; considering, reflecting; the sense of the potential mood. *s.*

سمبھرم संभ्रम *sambhram*, m. esteem, respect, awe, value. *s.*

سمبھلنا संभलना *sambhalnā*, m. to be supported, to be propped or erected; to stand, to stop, to be firm, to recover one's self from a fall, &c. *s.*

سمبھو संभव *sambhav*, possible; fit, right, proper; m. capacity, appropriateness; possibility, compatibility. *s.*

سمبهوجن संभोजन *sambhojan*, m. a meal taken together, a convivial party. *s.*

سمبهوگ संभोग *sambhog*, m. enjoyment, coition. *s.* [ist. *s.*

سمبهوگي संभोगी *sambhogī*, sensual; a sensual-

سمبهوم समभूमि *sam-bhūmi*, f. even ground. *s.*

سمپادت संपादित *sampādit*, attained, accomplished, gotten. *s.*

سمپادك संपादक *sampādak*, m. one who attains or accomplishes. *s.*

سمپادن संपादन *sampādan*, m. gaining, attaining, accomplishing. *s.*

سمپت संपत *sampat* or संपत्ति *sampatti*, f. affluence, wealth, prosperity, success; a sort of medicinal root. *s.*

سمپٹ संपुट *samput*, m. the closely shutting of any cavity; a box with its lid shut; a casket. *s.*

سمپد सम्पद *sampad*, } f. wealth, pro-
سمپدا सम्पदा *sampadā*, } sperity; advancement, excellence; a necklace of pearls. *s.*

سمپراپت संप्राप्त *samprāpta*, attained, obtained. *samprāpti* f. obtaining, acquisition. *s.*

سمپرت संप्रति *samprati*, now, at this present time. *s.*

سمپردان संप्रदान *sampradān*, m. gift, donation; the dative case in grammar. *s.*

سمپرداي संप्रदाय *sampradāy* or *sampradāya*, m. traditional doctrine banded down from one teacher to another. *s.* [ing, accomplishing. *s.*

سمپرسادهن संप्रसाधन *samprasādhan*, m. effect-

سمپرستهان संप्रस्थान *samprasthān*, m. setting out on a journey. *s.*

سمپرك सम्पर्क *sampark*, m. mixture, contact, union, copulation. *s.*

سمپريت संप्रीत *samprīt*, well pleased, delighted. *samprīti*, f. affection, delight. *s.*

سمپن संपन्न *sampann* or *sampanna*, perfect, complete, endowed with; accomplished, obtained; prosperous, thriving. *s.*

سمپورن संपूर्ण *sampūrn* or *sampūrna*, perfect, full, finished, all, the whole. *sampūrnatā*, f. fulness, completion. *s.*

سمت सुमत *sumat*, friendly, well or kindly disposed. *sumati*, f. friendship, benevolence; good conscience. *s.*

سمت समिति *samiti*, f. sameness, likeness. *s.*

سمت *samt*, f. a way, path, a part, side, quarter, towards. *samtu-r-rās*, the point of the heavens directly over head, called in astronomy the *zenith*. *simat*, a mark (made especially by burning). *a.*

سمت सम्मत *sammat*, assented or agreed to, concurred in; conformable to; m. opinion, sentiment. *sammati*, f. wish, desire; agreement, assent, approbation; opinion, sentiment. *s.*

سمت सम्मित *sammit*, like, similar; of equal measure; measured. *s.*

سمتا समता *samtā* or *samatā*, f. equality, similarity, similitude, parallelism, resemblance, comparison, parity. *s.* [duction, birth. *s.*

سمتپت समुत्पत्ति *samutpatti*, f. origin, pro-

سمتپن समुत्पन्न *samutpanna*, born, produced. *s.*

سمتسو समुत्सव *samutsav*, m. festivity. *s.*

سمٹ सिमट *simaṭ*, f. act of collecting, condensing or constringing; tone, elasticity. *h.*

سمٹنا सिमटना *simaṭnā*, n. to be concentrated, to shrink. *simaṭ-jānā*, n. to shrivel, to shrink. *h.*

سمجه समझ *samajh*, f. comprehension, understanding, knowledge, opinion, thought. *s.*

سمجهانا समझाना *samjhānā*, a. to make comprehend, to explain, to convince, to describe, to inform, to satisfy, to undeceive, to warn, to admonish, to instruct, to apologise. *s.*

سمجهاوا समझावा *samjhāwā* (v. *samjhautī*), explaining, &c. *s.*

سمجهائش समझाइश *samjhā,ish*, f. tampering with, subornation, instructing in false evidence. *h.*

سمجهنا समझना *samajhnā*, a. to comprehend, to understand; to suppose, think, conceive, deem, fancy, perceive; to come to an understanding with. *s.*

سمجهوار समझवार *samajhwār*, prudent, wise, considerate. *s.*

سمجهوتي समझौती *samjhautī*, f. act of explaining, convincing or giving confidence. *s.*

سمچا समचा *samuchā*, full, complete. *s.*

سمچت समुचित *samuchit*, quite right, fit, in a proper manner. *s.*

سمچي समुच्चय *samuchchay*, m. assemblage, collection; conjunction of words or sentences. *s.*

سمداي समुदाय *samudā,e* or *samudāya*, aggregate, quantity, number; adj. together, collected. *s.*

سمدر समुद्र *samudr* or *samudra*, m. the sea, ocean. *samudra-phen* or *samudra-kaph*, m. (lit. the froth of the ocean) the dorsal scale or bone of the cuttle-fish (*Sepia officinalis*). *samudra-taṭ* or *samudra-tīr*, m. the sea-coast. *samudra-lavan*, m. sea-salt. *samudra-vahni*, m. submarine fire. *s.*

سمدرار समुद्रारु *samudrāru*, m. a shark; a fabulous large fish, perhaps intended for the whale. *s.*

سمدرانت समुद्रान्त *samudrānt*, m. the sea-shore; adv. as far as the sea. *s.*

سمدرانتا समुद्रान्ता *samudrāntā*, f. a shrub (*Hedysarum alhagi*); the cotton plant; a gramineous plant (*Trigonella corniculata*). *s.*

سمدرسوكه समुद्रसोख *samudr-sokh*, m. name of a medicine (*Convolvus argenteus*). *s.*

سمدرشي समदर्शी *sam-darshī*, impartial, equally viewing both sides. *s.*

سمدرك समुद्रिक *samudrik*, f. palmistry, fortune-telling; the art of physiognomy. *samudrik-bidyā*, f. the art of palmistry. *s.*

سمدركي समुद्रिकी *samudrikī*, m. a fortune-teller (by means of palmistry); a physiognomist. *s.*

سمدريه समुद्रिय *samudriya*, marine, oceanic. *s.*

سمدكهه समदुःख *sam-dukh*, sympathizing, sharing another's pain (Pers. *ham-dard*). *s.*

سمدم *sum-dum*, very corpulent. *p.*

سمدور *sam-dūr*, the sea, a large river. *d.*

سمده समिध *samidh*, f. fuel; especially pieces of wood prepared for burning in the ceremony of the *homa*, q. v. *s.*

سمدهملاوا समधमिलावा *samadh-milāwā*, m. the mutual embracing of two *samdhīs*, q. v. *s.*

سمدهن समधन *samdhan* or *samdhin*, f. child's mother-in-law. *s.*

سمدهي समधी *samdhī*, m. child's father-in-law; (in Dakh.) the relationship between two persons whose children are married to each other; relationship such as held between the parents of a husband and wife. *s.* [of a child's father-in-law. *s.*

سمدهيانا समधियाना *samdhiyānā*, m. the family

سمدي समुदय *samuday*, m. ascent, rise (as of the sun, &c.). *s.* [m. remembrance. *s.*

سمر समर *samar*, m. war, battle, conflict. *sumir*,

سمر *samar*, m. evening conversations; night, darkness; time; a vestibule; an adventure befalling any one. *sumur*, narration; a small lake. *a.*

سمرپت समर्पित *samarpit*, made over, consigned. *s.*

سمرپن समर्पण *samarpan*, m. act of entrusting or giving (a thing) in charge to another. *s.*

سمرت *smṛiti*, f. recollection, memory; a body of laws, such as those compiled by Manu. *s.*

سمرته समर्थ *samarth*, m. strength, power; adj. strong, capable. *samarthatā*, f. power, ability. *s.*

سمرتهك समर्थक *samarthak*, m. aloe wood (*Amyris agallocha*). *s.*

سمرتهي समर्थी *samarthī*, strong, powerful. *s.*

سمرجاد समर्याद *samarjād*, correct in conduct. *s.*

سمرن स्मरण *smaran* or सुमरन *sumran*, m. remembrance (continual theme), mentioning; f. a small rosary. *s.*

سمرنا सुमरना *sumarnā* or *sumirnā*, a. to remember, to keep in memory; to mention. *s.*

سمرنيه स्मरणीय *smaranīya*, fit to be remembered. *s.*

سمروت *samrūt* (v. *samarth*), strength, &c. *d.*

سمسار *samsār*, a family; household; tribe. *samsār karnā*, to live, to domesticate one's self; to provide for self and family. *d.* [whole. *s.*

سمست समस्त *samast* or *samasta*, all, the

سمسرگ संसर्ग *samsarg*, m. association, relation. *s.*

سمسم सुमसुम *sumsum*, f. the noise of moist wood when burning, simmering. *h.*

سمسم *samsam*, m. a fox. *simsim*, the grain sesame. *a.*

سمسيا *samsiyā*, m. an exercise among Asiatic poets, wherein one writes or speaks an imperfect verse or stanza, which is to be filled up by another. *s.*

سمشان श्मशान *smashān*, or *samshān* m. a cemetery, a place where dead bodies are burned, a burning ground. *samshān-bāsī*, (living in the *samshān*) an epithet of *Mahādeva*. *s.*

سمع *sam'*, m. hearing; the ear. *a.*

سمك *samk*, m. height, depth, profundity. *samak*, a fish on which the earth is supposed to rest; a fish in general; the sign *Pisces*. *az samak tā samāk*, from the bottom of the abyss to the pinnacle of heaven. *a.*

سمكهه सम्मुख *sammukh*, facing, in front. *sammukhīn*, before, in front of. *s.*

سمگده सम्मुग्ध *sammugdha*, fascinated, bewildered, stupified. *s.*

سمل समल *samal*, dirty, muddy, filthy. *s.*

سملا समला *samlā*, a crop that, after having been checked, has recovered. *h.*

سمن *saman*, m. jasmine, lily of the valley. *p.*

سمن सुमन *suman*, m. wheat; the plant *dhatūrā* (q. v.); a flower in general; adj. of good disposition, fair, handsome. *s.*

سمن *samn*, butter, grease, tallow. *a.*

سمنجس समञ्जस *samanjas*, proper, right, fit; m. propriety, fitness. *s.*

سمند *samand*, m. a horse of noble breed, a steed; bay (colour of a horse). *p.*

سمندر समुन्दर *samundar*, m. (also *samandar*) (v. *samudra*) the ocean. *s.*

سمندر *samandar*, m. a salamander. *a. p.*

سمندرپهل समुन्दरफल *samundar-phal*, m. name of a medicine. *s.* [foam of the sea. *s.*

سمندرپهين समुन्दरफेन *samundar-phen*, m.

سمندرسوك *samundar-soh* (v. *samudr-sokh*) *s.*

سمندركهار *samundar-khār* (corrup. of *samm-l-fār*), arsenic; ratsbane. *a.*

سمنده *sammandh*, m. (v. *sambandh*) connection. *s.* [auspicious. *s.*

سمنگل सुमङ्गल *sumangal*, very fortunate or

سمنوهر सुमनोहर *sumanohar*, very agreeable, pleasing, charming. *s.*

سمو समो *samo*, m. season, time. *s.*

سموات *samwāt* (pl. of سما), the heavens, skies (properly *samāwāt*). *s.*

سمواد संवाद *samvād*, m. communication of intelligence, information, news. *s.*

سموت संवत *samvat*, } m. a year, gene-
سموتسر संवत्सर *samvatsar*, } nerally used in Hindū chronological dates. *s.*

سموتسري संवत्सरी *samvatsarī*, f. annual ceremony. *s.* [plete. *s.*

سموچا समूचा *samūchā*, entire, whole, com-

سمود सम्मोद *sammod*, m. pleasure, delight. *s.*

سمور *samūr*, m. a weasel, a marten, a sable; fur, sable skin. *a.*

سموسه *samosa*, m. a kind of small pastry of minced meat of a triangular form; a shawl or handkerchief, &c., doubled diagonally to throw over the shoulders. *samosa-waraḳī*, a species of tart. *p.*

سموم *samūm*, f. a hot pestilential wind (commonly called the *simoom*). *a.*

سمون *samūn*, fat; (pl. of سمن) butter. *a.*

سمونا समोना *samonā*, a. to cool warm water by mixing cold water with it. *s.* [ber. *s.*

سموه समूह *samūh*, m. assemblage, heap, num-

سموه सम्मोह *sammoh*, m. ignorance, folly, beguilement, stupefaction. *s.* [tured. *s.*

سموهت सम्मोहित *sammohit*, beguiled, enrap-

سمهالنا *samhālnā*, a. (v. *sambhālnā*) to support, &c. *s.*

سمي *samī*, m. a namesake. *a.*

سمئي सम्मई *samma,ī*, the pipe of a drill plough, generally made of a hollow bamboo. *h.*

سمي समय *same* or समै *samai*, سميا समैया *samaiyā*, } m. time, season, fit or proper time, leisure, opportunity. *s.*

سميپ समीप *samīp*, proximate, near, at hand. *s.*

سميپتا समीपता *samīpatā*, f. proximity, contiguity. *s.*

سميپي समीपी *samīpī*, f. proximity, nearness. *s.*

سميت समेत *samet*, with, along with, together with. *s.*

سميٹ समेट *sameṭ*, f. an astringent, a medicine used by women *ad constringendam vulvam*. *s.*

سميٹنا समेटना *sameṭnā*, a. to constringe, to compress, to cause to shrivel or shrink; to collect together, to amass; to fold up (a carpet). *h.*

سمير समीर *samīr*, m. wind, air. *s.*

سميرو सुमेरु *sumeru*, m. the sacred mountain Sumeru, allegorically represented as composed of gold and gems. It is supposed by the Hindūs to be the residence of the gods, as Olympus was with the Greeks. In astronomical works it denotes the north pole. *s.*

سميك सम्यक *samyak*, all, wholly; properly, fitly. *s.* [an equation. *s.*

سميكرن समीकरण *samīkaran*, m. (in algebra)

سميل सुमेल *sumel*, suitable, affable, of pleasing manners. *s.* [leisure, opportunity. *s.*

سمين समें *sameṅ* or *samaiṅ*, m. time, season,

سمين *samīn*, fat, plump, well-fed. *a.*

سن सुन *sun*, insensible, without sensation, palsied. *sun-karne-wala*, a narcotic medicine. *s.*

سن सन *san*, m. name of a plant. (*Crotolaria juncea*); a kind of flax or hemp; a tree (*Pentaptera tomentosa*). *s.*

سن सं *saṅ* (v. *sam*), a prefix like the Latin *con*, or the Greek συν.

سن *sinn*, m. an age, period of life; a tooth; the nib of a pen. *san*, a year. *sinn e sāl*, age, period of life. *a.*

سنا *sanā*, m. the plant senna. *a.*

سنا *sunā* (for *sonā*), gold. *d.*

سنا सुन्ना *sunnā*, a. to hear, to listen; m. a cypher. *s.*

سنا सन्ना *sannā*, n. to be impregnated, stained, soiled, to be kneaded, mixed up (as dough, earth, &c.). *h.*

سنابه सुनाभ *sunābh*, m. a mountain, part of the ranges of Southern India. *s.*

سناپٹ सुनापट *sunāpaṭ*, f. stillness, dreariness. *s.* [ning or end. *s.*

سناتن सनातन *sanātan*, eternal, without begin-

سناته सनाथ *sanāth*, having a master or husband; accompanied by a master or husband. *sanāthā*, f. a woman whose husband is living. *s.*

سناٹا सन्नाटा *sannāṭā* or *sunnāṭā*, m. the roaring of the waves; rumbling noise made by wind and rain at a distance. *h.*

سنار सुनार *sunār*, m. a goldsmith. *s.*

سنارن सुनारिन *sunārin*, سنارني सुनारनी *sunārnī*, } f. a goldsmith's wife. *s.*

سناري सुनारी *sunārī* (or *sunāṛī*), clever, skilful. *h.* [goldsmith. *s.*

سناري सुनारी *sunārī*, f. the business of a

سناري सुनारी *su-nārī*, a good, handsome woman; adj. clever. *s.*

سناڑي सुनाड़ी *sunāṛī*, clever, alert, skilful. *h.*

سناسي सन्नासी *sannāsī*, m. (v. *sanyāsī*) name of a class of devotees. *s.*

سنامكي *sanā-makkī*, m. senna of Mecca. *a.*

سنان *sinān*, f. the sharp point (of a spear, arrow, needle, &c.). *a.*

سنان स्नान *snān*, m. bathing, ablution. *s.*

سنانا सुनाना *sunānā*, a. to cause to hear, to inform, to advise, to tell, to bid, to warn. *s.*

سنانيه स्नानीय *snānīya*, ablutionary. *s.*

سناوني सुनावनी *sunā,onī*, f. tidings of any one having died abroad. *s.*

سناي *sanāy*, f. the senna plant. *h.*

سنبل *sumbul*, m. spikenard (to which the locks of a mistress are compared). *sumbul i hindī*, m. the spikenard (*Valeriana jatamansi, Roxb.*). *sumbul i khaṭā,ī*, *Angelica*. *p.*

سنبل *sumbul*, m. a flower (especially of an odoriferous plant). *a.*

سنبل کهار *sumbul-khār*, m. arsenic, orpiment. *d.*

سنبله *sumbula*, m. the sign *Virgo*. *a.*

سنبوسه *sambosa*, m. (v. *samosa*). *p.*

سنبهالنا संभालना *sambhālnā*, a. to support, to uphold, to stop, to restrain. *s.*

سنبهري सुनबहरी *sunbahrī*, f. name of a disease (*elephantiasis*). *s.*

سنپات सनपात *sanpāt* or सन्निपात *sannipāt*, m. the name of a disease in which the body is seized with universal chilliness, deliquium (it is explained by the Hindū physicians to be that in which the three humours, bile, phlegm, and atrabilis, are corrupted). *s.*

سنپارا *sampārā*, m. one who charms and catches snakes. *d.*

سنپت संपत *sampat*, f. (v. سمپت) prosperity. *s.*

سنپڑنا *samparnā*, n. to become captive. *d.*

سنپولا संपोला *sampolā*, } m. a young snake. *s.*
سنپولیا संपोलिया *sampoliyā*, }

سنپیرا संपेरा *samperā*, m. a snake-keeper, one who charms and catches snakes. *s.*

سنت *sunnat*, f. (lit. a religious ceremony necessary to be performed; q. d. that which is constantly repeated or performed): it denotes, first, circumcision, hence *sunnat-k.*, a. to circumcise: it is also applied to denote the traditions of *Muhammad*, ordinance. *sunnati mu'akkad*, a rule or command which must be obeyed literally and immediately. *sanat*, f. the repetition of the same course of the sun, with its concomitant changes; a year. *a.*

سنت सन्नति *sannati*, f. reverence, obeisance. *s.*

سنت सन्त *sant*, m. a kind of ascetic, a saint; adj. pious, virtuous, devout. *s.*

ستنا सन्ता *santā*, depraved; miserly. *h.*

سنتاپ सन्ताप *santāp*, m. heat, burning heat; sorrow, pain, affliction, misery, repentance. *s.*

سنتاپي सन्तापी *santāpī*, sad, sorrowful, afflicted. *s.*

سنتان सन्तान *santān*, m. race, lineage; progeny, offspring, children. *s.*

سنتپت सन्तप्त *santapta*, distressed, afflicted. *s.*

سنتت सन्तति *santati* or *santat*, f. race, &c. (v. *santān*). *s.*

سنتشٹ सन्तुष्ट *santusht*, satisfied, gratified, content, delighted. *s.*

سنتنا संतना *santanā*, f. palliation, consolation, act of appeasing. *santanā-k.*, a. to appease, to still, to quiet, to lull, to comfort. *s.*

سنتوش *santosh*, } सन्तोष { m. continence, content, joy, delight,
ستنوکه *santokh*, } patience, satiety, satisfaction. *santokh-k.*, to be content, to be patient. *s.*

سنتوکهي सन्तोषी *santokhī* (for *santoshī*), patient, contented, consoled, gratified. *s.*

سنتي सन्ते *sante*, adv. instead, stead. *h.*

سنتي सन्ती *santī*, m. a succedaneum. *h.*

سنٹه संठ *santh*, depraved; miserly. *s.*

سنج *sanj*, in comp. denotes one who weighs or examines; as, *naghma-sanj* or *tarāna-sanj*, a measurer of sounds, *i. e.* a musician; *sukhan-sanj*, a weigher of words, *i. e.* an orator. *sinj*, adj. elected, chosen; m. a choice. *sunj*, m. the red (*ber*) jujube tree. *p.*

سنجاب *sanjāb*, m. ermine, the grey squirrel (v. next word). *p.*

سنجاف *sanjāf*, f. border (tacked to the outer part of a garment), flouncing. *p.*

سنجافي *sanjāfī*, adorned with a border (cloths). *p.*

سنجکت संयुक्त *sanjukt*, joined, compounded, connected; endowed with, possessed of. *s.*

سنجم संयम *sanjam*, m. restraint, forbearance; soberness, abstinence from particular food on certain days. *s.*

سنجمي संयमी *sanjamī*, sober, temperate, abstemious; a saint, a sage, one who subdues his passions. *s.*

سنجنا संजना *sanjanā*, m. (v. *sahajnā*) a species of tree. *s.*

سنجوگ संयोग *sanjog*, m. junction, adherence, association; accident, event, chance. *s.*

سنجوگن संयोगन *sanjogan*, f. wife of a *sanjogī*, q. v. *s.*

سنجوگي संयोगी *sanjogī*, m. an ascetic who does not observe a vow of continence, but has a family. *s.*

سنجوونا संजोवना *sanjowanā*, a. to prepare. *s.*

سنجها संझा *sanjhā*, f. evening; a particular prayer said in the forenoon, at noon, and in the evening. *s.*

سنجهنا संझना *sanjhnā*, m. (v. *sahajnā*) a species of tree. *s.*

سنجیدگي *sanjīdagī*, f. gravity, considerateness. *p.*

سنجیدن *sanjīdan*, to weigh (lit. or fig.). *p.*

سنجیده *sanjīda*, weighty, grave, considerate, weighed. *p.*

سنجیون संजीवन *sanjīvan*, m. animating, bringing to life. *s.*

سنجیوني संजीवनी *sanjīvanī*, that which vivifies. *sanjīvanī bidyā*, art of vivifying. *s.*

سنچار सचार *sanchār*, m. entrance, penetration; beginning, commencement; the entering of the planets into a new sign; difficult progress; a gem supposed to be in the head of a serpent. *s.*

سنچارکا संचारिका *sanchārikā*, f. a female messenger, a bawd, a go-between. *s.*

سنچت संचित *sanchit*, collected, hoarded up. *s.*

سنچتا संचिता *sanchitā*, f. a plant (*Salvinia cucullata*). *s.*

سنچکار *sanchkār*, } sound, noise. *d.*
سنچل *sanchal*, }

سنچهیپ संक्षेप *sanchhep*, abridged, short. *s.*

سنچهيپن संक्षेपन *sanchhepan*, m. an abridgment, conciseness, brevity. *s.*

سنچي संचय *sanchai*, m. heap, quantity, number; purse, capital, stock, store, saving, heaping up, hoard. *sanchayī*, who collects, gathers, hoards up. *s.*

سند *sanad*, f. signature, a deed, the seal of a magistrate; a patent grant or charter, from a man in authority; a prop, any thing on which one leans or is supported; relation, connexion. *sanad-wār*, in conformity with the charter (v. Wilson). *a.*

سند *sund*, insensibility; stupidity; a swoon; adj. insensible, stupid; lifeless. *d.*

سندان *sindān*, f. an anvil; the iron on which the knocker of a door strikes. *p.*

سندديواني *sanad-dīwānī*, a grant, or writing for holding land, being that by which all *zamīndārīs* are held. *p.*

سندر सिन्दुर *sindur*, m. (also *sindūr*) red lead. *s.*

سندر सुन्दर *sundar*, beautiful, fair, handsome, good, virtuous. *s.*

سندرا सुनिद्रा *sunidrā*, f. sound sleep. *s.*

سندرتا सुन्दरता *sundaratā*, } f. beauty,
سندرتاءي सुन्दरताई *sundartā,ī*, } goodness. *s.*

سندرشن संदर्शन *sandarshan*, m. looking, presenting. *s.*

سندروس *sundaros*, m. sandarak or sanda racha; a resin supposed to be produced by the *Juniperus communis*, but now proved to exude from a species of thuia (*Thuia articulata, Vahl.*). *a. p.*

سندري सुन्दरी *sundarī*, f. a fair or handsome woman, beauty, goodness, virtue, a small timber tree (*Heritiera minor*). *s.*

سندس *sundus*, brocade, silk wrought with gold or silver. *a.*

سندسي *sundusī*, made of brocade, brocaded. *a.*

سندگدھ संदिग्ध *sandigdh*, doubted, questioned, doubtful. *s.*

سندور सिन्दूर *sindūr*, m. red-lead, minium. *s.*

سندورا सिन्दूरा *sindūrā*, m. a box for rouge or paint. *h.*

سندوري *sandorī*, f. a narrow passage; an alley, a lane. *d.*

سندھ सिन्धु *sindhu* or *sindh*, m. sea, ocean; the Indus; the name of a district, the country along the Indus or *Sindh*; name of a musical mode or *rāginī*. *sindhu-pushp*, m. a conch. *sindhu-lavan*, m. rock-salt. *s.*

سندھ सन्धि *sandhi*, m. union, junction; peace, pacification; a crack; a hole. *s.*

سندھ सन्निधि *sannidhi*, f. proximity. *s.*

سندھان सन्धान *sandhān*, m. spying, prying into secrets. *sandhān pānā*, a. to trace, to discover. *s.*

سندھان सन्निधान *sannidhān*, m. proximity. *s.*

سندھانا सन्धाना *sandhānā*, m. } pickle, acid
سندھاني सन्धानी *sandhānī*, f. } preparation of the *bel* and other fruits. *h.*

سندھاوٹ सुन्धावट *sundhāwaṭ*, m. smell, perfume, odour, scent, an earthy smell. *s.*

سندھب सन्धब *sandhab* (for *saindhav*), m. the name of a kind of salt, rock salt. *s.* [*sindh*). *s.*

سندھو सिन्धू *sindhū*, m. the ocean, &c. (v.

سندھيا सन्ध्या *sandhyā*, f. twilight, either morning or evening, a period of time, forenoon, afternoon, or mid-day; religious abstraction; meditation, repetition of *mantras* (q. v.), sipping water, &c., to be performed by the three first classes of Hindūs, at particular and stated periods in the course of every day, especially at sunrise, sunset, and also, though less essentially, at noon. *sandhyā-samay*, m. evening twilight. *sandhyā-kāl*, m. twilight. *s.*

سندي *sanadī*, held by written deeds or charters. *a.*

سنديس सन्देश *sandes*, } m. a message, news,
سنديسا सन्देसा *sandesā*, } tidings, informa-
سنديسو सन्देसू *sandesū*, } tion (properly *sandesh*, &c.). *s.*

سنديسي सन्देशी *sandesī* or *sandeshī*, m. a messenger. *s.*

سنديہ सन्देह *sandeh*, m. suspicion, doubt, apprehension, hesitation, anxiety. *s.*

سنديہي सन्देही *sandehī*, doubtful, scrupulous, suspicious. *s.*

سنڈ सण्ड *sanḍ*, m. a eunuch. *sunḍ*, the trunk or proboscis of an elephant. *s.*

سنڈا सण्डा *sanḍā*, strong, fat, stout; hardened excrement, *scybala*. *h.*

سنڈاس सण्डास *sanḍās*, m. a necessary, a water-closet (opening into the streets), a sink. *h.*

سنڈاسا सण्डासा *sanḍāsā*, m. large pincers. *s.*

سنڈاسي सण्डासी *sanḍāsī*, m. (cor. of *sanyāsī*); a caste of Hindū ascetics. *s.*

سنڈاسي सण्डासी *sanḍāsī*, } f. tongs, small
سنڈسي सण्डसी *sanḍsī*, } pincers. *s.*
سنڑسي संड़सी *sanṛsī*, }

سنڈھا *sunḍhā*, m. the hump on the back of a camel, bullock, &c. *d.*

سنسا संसा *sanśā*, m. dread, doubt, apprehension. *s.*

سنسار संसार *sanśār*, m. the world, the universe. *s.*

سنسار सुनसार *sunsār*, m. a kind of ornament. *h.*

سنسارك संसारिक *sanśārik*, } worldly, of this
سنساري संसारी *sanśārī*, } world. *s.*

سنسان सुनसान *sunsān*, void, still, silent, dreary, lonely, desolate. *s.*

سنسپرش संस्पर्श *sanśparsh*, m. touching, contact, laying hold of, perception. *s.*

سنستھان संस्थान *sanśthān*, m. shape, form, make, fabrication; a place where four roads meet; a vicinity, a neighbourhood. *s.*

سنسر सुनसर *sunsar*, m. the name of an ornament. *h.*

سنسرگ संसर्ग *sansarg*, m. union, proximity, contact, familiarity, meeting, interview; sexual attachment. *s.*

سنسرگي संसर्गी *sansargī*, familiar, acquainted, friendly, sociable, an acquaintance. *s.*

سنسكار संस्कार *sanskār*, m. completing, accomplishing, perfecting; an essential and purificatory rite among the Hindūs; purification, consecration. *s.*

سنسكرت संस्कृत *sanskrit*, wrought, made, artificially produced; excellent, best; decorated, ornamented; the *Sanskrit* language, the language of the gods, being supposed a perfect tongue, formed by infallible rules. *s.*

سنسكرتانياي संस्कृतानुयायी *sanskritānuyāyī*, following or imitating the *Sanskrit*, or language of the gods. *s.*

سنسگر संसगर *sansgar*, productive, fertile. *s.*

سنسنانا सनसनाना or संसनाना *sansanānā*, n. to jingle, to ring; to faint; to simmer. *h.*

سنسناهٹ संसनाहट *sansanāhat*, f. an imitative sound; ringing, jingling; simmering; fainting. *s.*

سنسو *sansau*, m. apprehension (v. *sansai*). *s.*

سنسوتر सयासूत्र or सनसूत्र *san-sūtr*, m. packthread. *s.*

سنسي संसय *sansai*, } m. apprehension, fear,
سنشي संशय *sanshai*, } doubt, uncertainty.
sanshayāpanna, affected with doubt, hesitating; doubtful, uncertain. *sanshayātmā*, m. a sceptic. *sanshayālu*, doubting, sceptical. *sanshayān*, dubious, uncertain. *s.*

سنك सिनक *sinak*, m. blowing the nose, snot. *h.*

سنك संक *sank*, } fear, terror, doubt, sus-
سنكا संका *sankā*, f. } picion. *s.*

سنكاتر सुनकातर *sunkātar*, m. a kind of snake. *h.*

سنكار संकार *sankār*, f. a sign, nod, wink, beckoning. *s.*

سنكارنا संकारना *sankārnā*, a. to beckon, to nod, to wink, or make a signal. *s.*

سنكٹ संकट *sankat*, narrow, contracted; m. vexation, misfortune, pang, agony, pain, anguish. *sankat chauth*, name of a Hindū holyday in the month of *Māgh*, sacred to *Ganesha*. *s.*

سنكچت संकुचित *sankuchit*, unblown, unopened; abashed. *s.*

سنكچي संकची *sankchī*, f. a skate. *s.*

سنكر सङ्कर *sankar*, m. mixing, blending; a mixed or degraded caste proceeding from the promiscuous intercourse of the four castes. *s.*

سنكرات संक्रात *sankrāt*, } f. the sun's en-
سنكرانت संक्रान्ति *sankrānti*, } tering into a new sign. *s.*

سنكرانت संक्रान्त *sankrānt*, past, gone, transferred from one to another; entered (into a new sign of the zodiac). *s.*

سنكرانتي *sankrantī*, f. (v. *sankrāt*.) *s.*

سنكرش सन्निकर्ष *sannikarsh*, m. proximity. *s.*

سنكرشن संकर्षण *sankarshan*, m. attracting, drawing; a name of *Balarāma*, the elder brother of *Krishna*. *s.*

سنكرم संक्रम *sankram*, m. going, moving, travelling; the passage of a planet through the zodiac. *s.*

سنكشيپ संक्षेप *sankshep*, m. abridgement, abbreviation, conciseness, compression. *s.*

سنكل *sankal*, m. a chain. *d.*

سنكل संकल *sankal*, m. collection, quantity; addition (in arithm.). *s.*

سنكل संकुल *sankul*, crowded, confused, filled so as to be impervious. *s.*

سنكلپ संकल्प *sankalp*, m. volition, resolve; the act of promising, or vowing religiously. *sankalp-k.* (v. *sankalpnā*.) *s.*

سنكلپنا संकल्पना *sankalpnā*, a. to give alms (by making a religious vow), to vow. *s.*

سنكلت संकलित *sankalit*, heaped, piled; added; m. addition. *s.*

سنكلن संकलन *sankalan*, m. contact, junction; [addition. *s*

سنكنا सिनकना *sinaknā*, a. to blow the nose. *h.*

سنكوچ संकोच *sankoch*, m. shame, bashfulness, reserve, diffidence; shutting, closing, contraction; a skate (*Raia sancura*). *s.*

سنكوچن संकोचन *sankochan*, m. the act of shrinking, astringing, causing to shrink. *s.*

سنكوچي संकोची *sankochī*, bashful, reserved, diffident. *s.*

سنكه संख *sankh*, m. a conch which the Hindūs blow; a kind of ornament, a shell. *s.*

سنكه संख *sankh*, simple, artless. *dapol sankh*, promising much and performing nothing. *h.*

سنكهاهلي संखाहुली *sankhāhulī*, name of a medicinal plant (*Andropogon aciculatum?*). *s.*

سنكهني संखिनी *sankhinī*, f. a description of woman (the worst of all, very devils in look and nature). *s.*

سنكهيا संख्या *sankhyā*, f. a number, a numeral; counting the numbers, one, two, three, &c. *sankhiyā*, m. a kind of poison, arsenic. *s.*

سنكهيتا संख्यता *sankhyatā*, f. number, numeration, counting. *s.*

سنكيت संकेत *sanket*, m. engagement, agreement; sign, gesture. *sanket-sthān*, m. a place of assignation. *s.*

سنكيرتن संकीर्तन *sankīrttan*, m. celebrating, praising, honour, glorification. *s.*

سنكيرن संकीर्ण *sankīrna*, crowded, confused. *s.*

سنگ संग *sang*, m. a stone; weight. *sangi āsiyā*, a millstone. *sangi-baṣrī*, zinc. *sang-tarāsh*, m. a stonecutter. *sang-tara*, m. a kind of orange. *sang-taul*, equal in weight. *sangi-jirāḥat*, a species of steatites. *sangi khārā*, flint. *sang-dāna*, m. the gizzard. *sang-dil*, hard-hearted. *sang-reza* and *sang-rezī*, m. gravel. *sangi-sulaimānī*, m. agate, onyx. *sangi-sumāḳ*, porphyry. *sang-lākh*, stony, rocky. *sangi maṣāna*, m. the gravel, the stone. *sangi marmar*, m. marble. *sangi miḳnāṭīs*, the loadstone. *sangi-mūsā*, a black stone so called. *sangi-yasham*, m. a kind of jasper or agate. *s.*

سنگ संग *sang*, in the company of, along with; m. association, company, union, meeting, joining. *s.*

سنگ *sing* (for *sīng*), a horn. *d.*

سنگا सिङ्गा *singā*, m. trumpet (of horn). *s.*

سنگار सिङ्गार *singār*, ornament, dress, embellishment, decoration. *singār-ras*, m. one of the nine *rasas* (v. *ras*). *s.*

سنگارنا सिङ्गारना *singārnā*, a. to dress, to decorate, to embellish. *s.*

سنگارهار सिङ्गारहार *singār-hār*, m. the weeping nyctanthes (*Nyctanthes arbor tristis*). *s.*

سنگاريا सिङ्गारिया *singāriyā*, m. one whose business is to dress an idol. *s.*

سنگپش *sang-push*, سنگ‌پشت *sang-pusht*, سنگپوست *sang-post*, } m. a tortoise, a turtle. *p.*

سنگت संगत *sangat* or संगति *sangati*, f. meeting, union, association, intercourse, coition; collection, congregation, company, society; a place where the *Sikhs* celebrate their religious ceremonies. *sangat*, m. friendship, acquaintance; union, meeting; adj. right, proper, well. *s.*

سنگترا *sangtarā*, سنگتره *sangtara*, } m. a kind of orange, the name of which was changed by *Muḥammad Shāh* into *rangtarā*, on account of its beautiful colour. *h.*

سنگتي संगती *sangatī*, m. f. companion, comrade. *s.*

سنگخوارك *sang-khwārak*, سنگخواره *sang-khwāra*, } a species of bird, called by the Arabs *ḳaṭā*. *p.*

سنگر संगर *sangar*, m. lines, entrenchment; war, battle; misfortune, calamity; promise, agreement. *s.*

سنگرام संग्राम *sangrām*, m. battle, war. *s.*

سنگره संग्रह *sangrah* or *sangraha*, m. a compilation, an abridgment; quantity, collection. *s.*

سنگرهن संग्रहण *sangrahan*, m. collecting, compiling. *s.*

سنگرهني संग्रहणी *sangrahanī*, m. name of a disorder, an irregular state of the bowels, costiveness alternately with a diarrhœa. *s.*

سنگڑا सिंगड़ा *singṛā*, m. a powder-horn. *s.*

سنگڑي सिंगड़ी *singṛī*, f. a small powder-horn for priming. *s.*

سنگسار *sangsār*, m. one who stones (to death), a slinger. *p.*

سنگساري *sangsārī*, f. the act of stoning to death. *p.*

سنگستان *sangistān*, m. a stony country. *p.*

سنسکار सस्कार *sanskār*, m. idea, notion, impression. *s.*

سنگسنگوٹي *sing-singoṭī*, a general term for horned beasts. *d.*

سنگسي संगसी *sangsī*, f. pincers, forceps. *s.*

سنگشوئي *sangsho,ī*, f. washing rice, &c. before dressing. *p.*

سنگ‌کوپي *sang-kūpī*, f. name of a plant used in medicine (*Volkemeria inermis*). *d.*

سنگم संगम *sangam*, m. coition; meeting, conflux, union; planetary conjunction. *s.*

سنگن‌لينا *sungun lenā*, a. to act the spy. *h.*

سنگوپن संगोपन *sangopan*, m. hiding, concealment. *s.*

سنگوٹي सिंगौटी *singauṭī*, f. a polishing-tool made of horn; an ornament of metal on the horns of a bullock. *s.*

سنگهه सङ्घ *sangh*, m. flock, number; a heap, a quantity. *s.*

سنگهه सिंह *singh*, m. a lion; the sign Leo; a name or title common among the Hindūs and Sikhs. *singh-parnī*, f. a plant (*Justicia adhenatoda*). *singh-puchhī*, f. a plant (*Hedysarum lagopodioides*). *singh-keshar*, m. a lion's mane; a plant (*Mimusops elengi*). *singh-nād*, m. war-cry, war-whoop. *singh-nādak*, m. the roar or yelp of a lion; war-cry. *singh-nādakā*, f. *Hedysarum alhagi*. *s.*

سنگهات संघात *sanghāt*, m. companionship, society, assemblage. *s.*

سنگهاتي संघाती *sanghātī*, m. a companion, a friend. *s.*

سنگهار संहार *sanghār*, m. destruction, loss; the destruction of the world; making away, killing, murdering; adj. killed. *s.*

سنگهارنا संहारना *sanghārnā*, a. to kill, to make away with. *s.*

سنگهاڑا सिंघाड़ा *singhāṛā*, m. *trapa natans*; water chestnut or water caltrops; a handkerchief folded diagonally. *s.*

سنگهاسن सिंहासन *singhāsan*, m. a throne. *singhāsan battīsī*, name of a Hindī work of fiction. *s.*

سنگهانا सुंघाना *sunghānā*, a. to cause to smell, to inhale. *s.*

سنگهاوٹ सुंघावट *sunghāwaṭ*, f. odour, perfume. *s.*

سنگهپور सिंहपौर *singh-paur*, سنگهپول सिंहपौल *singh-paul*, سنگهدوار सिंहद्वार *singh-dwār*, } m. the royal gate or entrance to a palace; that on which is placed the effigy of the lion. *s.*

سنگهت संहत *sanghat*, compact, close, collected. *sanghati*, f. assemblage, heap, union; compactness. *sanghattā*, f. compactness, approximation. *s.*

سنگهتا संहिता *sanghitā*, f. an arrangement of the text of the Vedas; a compendium, a collection of laws, &c. *s.*

سنگهل सिंहल *singhal*, m. tin, brass; cassia [bark; Ceylon. *s.*

سنگهني सिंहनी *singhanī*, f. a lioness. *s.*

سنگهيا संघिया *sanghiyā*, m. a companion. *s.*

سنگي *sangī* (v. *sangīn*), stony, heavy. *p.*

سنگي सङ्गी *sangī*, uniting with, attached, lustful; m. a companion, an accomplice. *s.*

سنگيا सिंगिया *singiyā*, m. a kind of poison. *s.*

سنگيا संज्ञा *sangyā*, f. a noun; a metaphor, an idiomatical phrase. *s.*

سنگيت संगीत *sangīt*, m. music, singing, a concert; the exhibition of song, dancing, and music, as a public entertainment; the art of dancing and music. *sangīt-darpan*, name of a book on music. *sangīt-nāch*, a kind of dance. *s.*

سنگين *sangīn*, stony, heavy, weighty; solid, thick; f. a bayonet; "from the Turkish *süngü*, a spear, bayonet. The Persians call this weapon *sarnaiza*, but never *sangīn*."—(D.) *p.*

سنگيني *sangīnī*, f. a load; solidity. *p.*

سنلگن संलग्न *sanlagna*, joined, adherent. *s.*

سنمان सम्मान *sanmān*, m. respect, esteem, reverence. *s.*

سنماني सम्मानी *sanmānī*, adj. polite, civil; respectful. *s.*

سنمكه सम्मुख *sanmukh*, opposite, confronting. *s.*

سنّنا सना *sannā*, n. to be impregnated; be stained, soiled, smeared, or defiled; to be kneaded, mixed up (as flour, dough, earth, &c.). *h.*

سننا सुनना *sunnā*, a. to hear, to listen; m. a dot, cipher. *s.*

سنوات *sanwāt*, n. (pl. of سنة) years; old coin current at a depreciated rate after a certain number of years; *rupīs*, of old date which still pass at a discount, commonly called *sunaut* rupees, in opposition to *sicca* rupees. *a.*

سنوارنا सँवारना *sanwārnā*, a. to prepare, to dress, to decorate, to adjust, to adorn, to arrange, to accomplish. *h.*

سنوح *sunūḥ*, happening, an occurrence. *a.*

سنورنا सँवरना *sanwarnā*, n. to be dressed, to be decorated, to be prepared, to suit, to prosper, &c. *h.*

سنون *sanūn* or *sunūn*, m. (pl. of سنة) years. *sanūn*, tooth-powder, dentrifice. *a.*

سنهت सन्निहित *sannihit*, near, at hand. *s.*

سنهرا सुनहरा *sunahrā*, golden, made of gold. *s.*

سنّي *sunnī*, lawful; m. an orthodox *Muhammadan*, who reveres equally the four successors of *Muḥammad*, and hence called also *chār-yārī* (the Turks are *sunnīs*, the Persians are *shī'as*, q. v.). *a.*

سنيا सनिया *saniyā*, m. a kind of *tasar* cloth. *h.*

سنياس सन्यास *sannyās*, m. abandonment of all worldly things. *s.*

سنياسي संन्यासी *sannyāsī*, m. a Brāhman of the fourth order, a religious mendicant. *s.*

سنيت सुनीत *sunīt*, well-behaved, politic; m. (also *sunīti*, f.) propriety of behaviour, good conduct, policy. *s.*

سنيچر सनीचर *sanīchar*, m. Saturn; Saturday. *s.*

سنيچرا सनीचरा *sanīcharā*, unlucky (fellow); m. name of a mountain near to Go,āliyār. *s.*

سنيکت संयुक्त *sanyukt*, joined, united with. *s.*

سنيم संयम *sanyam*, m. piety, abstinence, forbearance. *s.*

سنيمي संयमी *sanyamī*, abstinent, temperate. *s.*

سنين *sanīn* (for *sangīn*) a bayonet. *d.*

سنيلك सुनीलक *sunīlak*, m. the blue shrike, the emerald or sapphire. *s.*

سنيوگ संयोग *sanyog*, m. accident, chance event; union, association. *s.*

سنيه स्नेह *sneh* or *saneh*, m. friendship, love, affection; oil. *sneh-wān*, affectionate. *s.*

سنيهي स्नेही *snehī* or *sanehī*, kind, affectionate, friend, lover, mistress. *s.*

سو सौ *sau*, a hundred. *sau sir kā honā*, implies excessive perseverance or obstinacy (lit. possessing one hundred heads, of which if one be cut off, the others still remain). *s.*

سو *sū* (for *su*), (in comp.) good, as *sū-ḍhāl*, neat, elegant. *sū-ḍaul*, beautiful or well-shaped. *s.*

سو सिव *siva*, m. Shiva, the Deity in the character of the destroyer. *s.*

سو *sū*, f. a side, direction, part; towards, in the direction of. *p.*

سو सो *so*, correl. pron. that same. *so,ī* or *sohī*, that very. *h.*

سو शव *sav*, m. a dead body. *h.*

سو *so* (v. *son*), with, from. *d.*

سوا सवा *savā*, with a quarter, a quarter more, as *sawā tīn*, three and a quarter. *h.*

سوا सोआ *so,ā*, m. fennel (*Anethum sowa*, *Roxb.*). *s.*

سوا सूआ *sū,ā* or सूवा *sūvā*, m. a parrot, a parroquet; a needle with which gunny-bags are sewed, a packing-needle; an awn of corn. *s.*

سوا शिवा *sivā*, f. a name of the goddess *Pārvatī* (q. v.). *s.*

سوا *siwā*, more, better; besides, except, without; beyond or past (an object); over and above. *a.*

سوابق *sawābiḳ* (pl. of سابقة) past events. *a.*

سوابهاوك स्वाभाविक *swābhāvik*, natural, peculiar, inherent. *s.*

سوات स्वाति *swāti*, f. the star Arcturus, the fifteenth mansion of the moon. *s.*

سواتست स्वातिसुत *swāti-sut*, the issue of Arcturus; a pearl (v. *sut*). *s.*

سواچنا सवाचना *sawāchnā*, a. to test, to try, to prove. *h.*

سواد स्वाद *swād* or सवाद *sawād*, m. relish, flavour, taste, sweetness, pleasure. *s.*

سواد स्वादु *swādu*, sweet, savoury, dainty, agreeable, desired. *s.*

سواد *sawād*, m. blackening, soot, smoke; environs; reading; ability. *a.*

سوادك स्वादक *swādak*, سوادل स्वादल *swādal*, } delicious, relishing, of high flavour. *s.*

سوادهپتيه स्वाधिपत्य *swādhipatya*, m. supreme sway, sovereignty. *s.*

سوادهكار स्वाधिकार *swādhikār*, m. own or peculiar office or station. *s.*

سوادهين स्वाधीन *swādhīn*, independent, being one's own master; absolute, despotic; a neuter verb. *s.*

سوادهينتا स्वाधीनता *swādhīnatā*, سوادهيني स्वाधीनी *swādhīnī*, } f. independence, liberty. *s.*

سوادي स्वादी *swādī*, m. a taster. *s.*

سوار *sawār*, m. a rider; mounted (on a horse, carriage, ship, or any thing else); cavalry, a trooper; (met.) drunk, tipsy. *sawār-kār*, a good rider, a jockey. *sawār-kārī*, f. good riding, jockeyship. *p.*

سوار सोअर *so,ar*, m. the chamber of a puerperal woman. *s.*

سوار सिवार *siwār*, m. green vegetation, at the bottom of pools or other water (*Vallisneria spiralis* or *octandra*). *s.*

سوار सूअर *sū,ar*, m. a hog, a wild boar. *s.*

سواراجيه स्वाराज्य *swārājya*, m. final felicity. *s.*

سوارتهه स्वार्थ *swārth*, having one's own object; m. mundane affairs, desire, &c.; selfishness. *s.*

سوارتهك स्वार्थिक *swārthik*, answering its object, expressing its own or literal meaning; succeeding in one's purpose; effective, successful, useful. *s.*

سوارتهي स्वार्थी *swārthī*, selfish, self-gratifying. *s.*

سواري सूअरी *sū,arī*, f. a sow (v. *sū,ar*). *s.*

سواري *sawārī*, f. riding; equipage, suite. *p.*

سوءاس सूआस *sū,ās*, m. a kind of rice. *h.*

سواس सुवास *suvās*, m. a pleasant or respectable dwelling, an agreeable smell. *s.*

سواس स्वास *swās*, سواسا स्वासा *swāsā*, } m. respiration, breath, life. *s.*

سواف *suwāf*, m. death, a mortal disease (especially among cattle). *a.*

سواك *siwāk*, m. rubbing the teeth; a dentrifice. *a.*

سواگت स्वागत *swāgat*, m. welcome, salutation. *s.*

سوال *suwāl*, m. interrogatory, question, proposition, request. *suwāl-k.*, to ask, to question, to beg or solicit alms: pl. *suwālāt*. *a.*

سوالا सिवाला *siwālā*, m. a temple of Mahādeva. *s.*

سوالي *suwālī*, m. a questioner; the person who sings the *marsiya* (q. v.). *a.*

سوامتوه स्वामित्व *swāmitwa*, m. mastery, superiority, sovereignty. *s.*

سوامي स्वामी *swāmī*, m. master, owner, lord, proprietor; a husband, a lover; a prince, a monarch; the Divine Being; a spiritual preceptor; the *Dandī fakīrs* are so called. *swāmī-droh*, m. injuring one's master, treachery. *s.*

سوان स्वान *swān*, m. a dog, a hound. *s.*

سوانا सुवाना *suwānā*, a. to cause to sleep. *s.*

سوانا सिवाना *siwānā* or *siwāna*, m. verge, limit, boundary. *s.*

سوانح *sawāniḥ* (pl. of سانحه), accidents, occurrences, incidents, events. *sawāniḥ-nigār* or *sawāniḥa-nigār*, a news-writer, intelligencer; an officer stationed by the Mogul government in distant provinces, to transmit weekly to court an account of all public transactions, such as the collections of revenues, the management of lands, and the state of the country (barbarous plur. *sawāniḥāt*). *a.*

سوانگ सवांग *sawāng* or स्वांग *swāng*, m. mimicry, acting, imitation, disguise, sham. *swāng-lānā*, to imitate. *s.*

سوانگي सवांगी *sawāngī* or स्वांगी *swāngī*, m. an actor, a mimic. *s.*

سوانه *siwāna*, m. verge, limit (v. *siwānā*). *s.*

سواءي सवाई *sawā,ī*, m. a title of the rājā of Jaipūr; a quarter more; as *sawā,ī-tīn*, three and a quarter. *s.*

سواءي *sawā,ī*, f. the venereal disease, syphilis. *d.*

سواءي *siwā,e*, except, besides, beyond, over and above (v. *siwā*). *a.*

سوايا सवाया *sawāyā*, a quarter added. *s.*

سوائم *sawā,im* (pl. of سائمه), flocks, herds: according to Gladwin the term is understood to imply camels, oxen, goats, and other animals which subsist for the greater part of the year on pasture; wherefore, if they live but half the year in pasture, and are fed for the other half upon forage, they do not fall under the description of *sawā,im*. *a.*

سوباس सूबास *sū-bās*, m. a pleasant dwelling; f. fragrance, perfume. *s.*

سوبر सूबर *sūbar*, impure, alloyed (silver). *h.*

سوبرن सूबरन *sūbaran*, m. good and pure gold; adj. golden, made of gold. *s.*

سوبس सूबस *sū-bas*, m. a pleasant dwelling. *s.*

سوبها सोभा *sobhā*, f. beauty, splendour; ornament, dress, decoration, embellishment. *s.*

سوبهاگيه सौभाग्य *saubhāgya*, m. auspiciousness, good fortune; the fourth astronomical *yog*. *saubhāgya-wān*, fortunate. *s.*

سوبهاو सोभाव *sobhāw* or **स्वभाव** *swabhāw*, m. nature, natural property or disposition; custom, practice, fashion, habit, temper, disposition. *sūbhāw*, m. good disposition, good nature; adj. well-disposed. *s.*

سوبهايمان सोभायमान *sobhāyamān*, beautiful, splendid, conspicuous, adorning. *s.*

سوبهنا सोभना *sobhnā*, n. to become, to befit. *s.*

سوبهوم स्वभूमि *swabhūmi*, f. own land, native country. *s.* [nowing corn with. *s.*

سوپ सूप *sūp*, m. a kind of basket for win-

سوپابينا सूपाबेना *sūpābenā*, m. name of a bird, a swallow (*Hirundo apus batassia, Buch.*). *s.*

سوپارا सूपारा *sūpārā*, m. *glans penis*. *h.*

سوپاري सूपारी *sūpārī*, f. betel-nut. *s.*

سوپان सोपान *sopān*, f. a ladder, a scale. *s.*

سوپن स्वप्न *swapna*, m. sleeping, dreaming. *swapna-bichār*, m. interpretation of dreams. *swapna-bichārī*, m. an interpreter of dreams. *swapna-dosh*, m. nocturnal pollution. *s.*

سوپهل सुफल *sū-phal*, of good fruit, useful. *s.*

سوپياري सुपियारी *sūpiyārī*, f. betel-nut for chewing. *s.*

سوت सूत *sūt*, m. thread, yarn; a silver thread; a stamen (in botany), a tendril; a bard; a charioteer; a carpenter. *sūt-bunti*, needle work. *s.*

سوت सौत *saut*, f. rival (wife), contemporary wife (one wife is *saut* to another). *s.*

سوت सोत *sot*, m. f. }
سوتا सोता *sotā*, m. } a spring, a fountain, a jet d'eau, a rivulet, an arm (of the sea). *sotā*, m. sleeping; sleep. *s*

سوتر सूत्र *sūtra*, m. a thread; a rule, a precept. *s.*

سوتك सूतक *sūtak*, m. uncleanness produced by the birth of a child or a miscarriage. *s.*

سوتكا सूतिका *sūtikā*, f. a woman recently delivered. *s.*

سوتل सुतल *sutal*, m. hell, or a place three stages under the surface of the earth. *s.*

سوتلا सूतला *sūtlā*, m. reins of a carriage; the little skin that rises backwards near the nails, at the end of the fingers. *h.*

سوتلي सूतली *sūtlī*, f. string, twine. *s.*

سوتن सौतन f. (v. *saut*) a rival wife. *s.*

سوتنا सूतना *sūtnā*, n. to sleep. *s.*

سوتنتر स्वतन्त्र *swa-tantr*, independent, absolute. *s.* [absoluteness. *s.*

سوتنترتا स्वतन्त्रता *swatantratā*, f. independence,

سوته सोथ *soth*, f. swelling, rising. *s.*

سوتهن सूथन *sūthan*, f. drawers. *h.*

سوتهني सूथनी *sūthnī*, f. drawers; an edible root (*Dioscorea fasciculata, Roxb.*). *h.*

سوتي सूती *sūtī*, made of cotton thread. *s.*

سوتياداه सौतियादाह *sautiyā-dāh*, }
سوتياڈاه सौतियाडाह *sautiyā-ḍāh*, } f. malice of a rival wife, *i.e.* "malice of the most virulent quality." The following verse contains undeniable truth. *kahe hain is 'ālam men bihtar hai maut, walekin na ho sāmhne uske saut*, "they have said that in this world it is better to die at once than to endure the presence of a rival wife."—Binning. *s.*

سوتيلا सौतेला *sautelā*, belonging or related to *saut*, of one father by different mothers, as *sautelā-bhāī*, step-brother. *sautelā-bahin*, step-sister. *s.*

سوتيماس सूतीमास *sūtīmās*, m. the last month of pregnancy. *s.*

سوج सूज *sūj* or **सोज** *soj*, f. swelling, rising. *s.*

سوجا सूजा *sūjā*, m. a borer, a gimlet, an auger, an awl. *s.*

سوجن सूजन *sūjan*, f. swelling. *swajan*, m. a distant kinsman. *s.*

سوجنا सूजना *sūjnā*, n. to swell, to rise. *s.*

سوجنا *sūjnā*, n. to be known or perceived. *d.*

سوجنيه सौजन्य *saujanya*, m. kindness, goodness. *s.*

سوجه सूझ *sūjh*, f. sight, perception. *s.*

سوجه सोझ *sojh*, f. straightness, directness. *h.*

سوجها सोझा *sojhā*, straight, direct. *h.*

سوجهنا सूझना *sūjhnā*, a. to be visible, to be seen, to appear, to seem, to be able to see. *h.*

سوجي सूजी *sūjī*, m. a tailor; f. a needle. *s.*

سوجي सूजी *sūjī*, f. meal, flour (ground coarse); the "simola" of the Italians. *h.*

سوچ सोच *soch*, m. consideration, reflection, thought, meditation. *s.*

سوچ सौच *sauch*, m. washing, ablution (particularly the private parts) on going to the necessary. *s.*

سوچار सुविचार *suvichār*, m. deliberate or due consideration. *s.*

سوچت सुचित *sū-chit*, thoughtless, easy, at leisure; careful, attentive, occupied. *s.*

سوچك सूचक *sūchak*, m. a teacher, an instructor; a needle (for *shūchak*), a spy, an informer. *s.*

سوچن सुवचन *suvachan*, m. eloquence, elegant diction. *s.*

سوچنا सोचना *sochnā*, a. to consider, to meditate, to advert. *s.*

سوچه स्वच्छ *swachchh* or *sawachchh*, pure, clean, clear, transparent. *swachchhatā*, f. purity, transparency. *s.* [fine, slender; shrill. *s.*

سوچهم सूक्ष्म *sūchham* or *sūchhma*, subtile,

سوچهمتا सूक्ष्मता *sūchhamtā* or *sūchhmatā*, f. subtileness, minuteness; shrillness. *s.*

سوچهند स्वच्छन्द *swachhand*, according to one's own opinion or inclination, unrestrained, uncontrolled; self-willed. *s.*

سوچي सूची *sūchī*, f. a needle. *s.*

سوچي پتر सूचीपत्र *sūchī-patr*, m. an index (to a work). *s.*

سوخت *so**kh**t*, burnt; a revoke at cards. *p.*

سوختگي *so**kh**tagī*, f. burning; vexation, heart-burning. *p.*

سوختن *so**kh**tan*, (r. *soz*) to burn. *so**kh**tanī*, fit to be burnt. *p.* [m. a slow-match, tinder. *p.*

سوخته *so**kh**ta*, burnt. *so**kh**ta-dil*, heart-burnt;

سود *sūd*, m. profit, interest, gain, usury. *sūd-battā*, profit and loss. *sūd-khor*, an usurer. *p.*

سودا *saudā*, m. melancholy; love; ambition; desire, concupiscence; madness; atrabilis. *a.*

سودا *saudā*, m. trade, traffic; marketing. *saudā sulaf*, m. traffic, barter. *p.*

سوداگر *saudāgar*, m. a merchant. *saudā-garī*, f. merchandise. *p.*

سوداي *saudā,ī*, mad, insane, melancholy. *a.*

سودخور *sūd-**kh**or*, m. a usurer, a publican. *p.*

سودخوري *sūd-**kh**orī*, f. borrowed money. *p.*

سودر सूद्र *sūdr*, m. (for *shūdra*) the fourth or lowest caste of the Hindūs. *s.*

سودر सोदर *sodar*, } m. (for *sahodar*, q. v.)
سودرا सोदरा *sodarā*, } born of the same mother, uterine; m. an own brother. *s.*

سودراني सूद्रानी *sūdrānī*, } f. a female of the
سودرني सूद्रनी *sūdranī*. } *sūdr* caste. *s.*

سودمند *sūd-mand*, profitable, advantageous, beneficial. *p.* [ableness. *p.*

سودمندي *sūdmandī*, f. advantage, profit-

سودن *sūdan* (r. *sā,e*) to wear, to rub. *p.*

سوده *sūda*, rubbed, dissolved; m. a powder. *p.*

سودھ सोध *sodh*, f. discharge (of debt); correction, search, inquiry, collation. *s.*

سودھ सुविध *suvidh*, of a good kind, in a good or easy way, easily. *s.*

سودھا सूधा *sūdhā*, proper, true; straight; simple, artless. *s.* [ness. *s.*

سودھاي सूधाई *sūdhā,ī*, f. simplicity, artless-

سودھرم स्वधर्म *swadharma*, m. the peculiar duty appropriate to each of the four classes of Hindūs; such as praying of a Brāhman, fighting of a soldier, &c. *s.*

سودھنا सोधना *sodhnā*, a. to pay, to discharge (a debt), to liquidate; to collate; to refine metals. *s.*

سودي *sūdī*, (money) borrowed at interest. *p.*

سوديش स्वदेश *swadesh*, m. native country, home. *s.*

سوڈول सुडौल *sū-ḍaul*, } well-shaped, ele-
سوڈھال सुढाल *sū-ḍhāl*, } gant. *s. h.*

سور *suwar* (pl. of سوره), chapters of the *ḳur,ān*. *a.*

سور स्वर *swar*, m. tone, voice; a vowel. *s.*

سور सूर *sūr*, m. a hero; the sun; (contr. of *sūrdās*, q. v.); (cor. of *shūla*) tenesmus. *s.*

سور सौर *saur*, solar; name of a fish. *s.*

سورا सूरा *sūrā*, m. (same as *sūr*) a hero, &c. *s.*

سورات *saurāt*, avarice, greediness. *d.*

سوراتر सिवरात्रि *sivarātri*, m. a festival held on the fourteenth of the dark fortnight in the month of *Phālguna* (February-March), in honour of the anniversary of the birth of *linga* or *phallus*. *s.*

سوراخ *sūrā**kh***, m. a hole, orifice, passage. *p.*

سورانا *saurānā*, } to be helpless, to
سوراي جانا *saurāe-jānā*, } be beyond patience or endurance. *d.*

سوربھ सौरभ *saurabh*, m. fragrance, saffron. *s.*

سوربير सूरबीर *sūr-bīr*, m. a champion, a hero. *s.*

سورت *sūrat*, a chapter of the *ḳur,ān*, of which there are 114. *saurat*, sovereign power, despotism. *a.* [*dhārī*, heroic. *s.*

سورتا सूरता *sūrtā*, f. valour, heroism. *sūrtā-*

سورٹھ सोरठ *soraṭh*, f. name of a musical mode or *rāgnī*. *s.* [*bhākhā*). *s*

سورٹھا सोरठा *sorṭhā*, m. name of a metre (in

سورج सूरज *sūraj* or सूर्य *sūrj* (for *sūrya*), m. the sun. *sūrj-sankrānti*, f. the sun's entrance into a new sign. *sūraj-gahan* or *sūrya-grahan*, m. eclipse of the sun. *sūrj-manḍal*, m. the orb or disc of the sun. *s.*

سورجاست सूर्यास्त *sūrjāst*, m. sunset. *s.*

سورج مکھي सूरजमुखी *sūraj-mukhī* or *sūraj-mukhī*, sunflower (*Helianthus annuus*); a kind of fan. *s.*

سورجودي सूर्योदय *sūrjoday*, m. sunrise. *s.*

سورداس सूरदास *sūrdās*, name of a Hindī poet and singer who was blind; hence a blind man is called *sūrdās*. *s.*

سورگ स्वर्ग *swarg*, m. the sky, the first heaven (of the Hindūs). *swarg-ārohan*, ascending to heaven. *swarga-gaman*, m. going to heaven. *swarga-lok*, m. paradise. *s.*

سورگت स्वर्गति *swar-gati*, f. going to heaven, future felicity, death. *s.*

سورگي स्वर्गीय *swargīya*, स्वर्ग्य *swargya*, or *swargī*, celestial. *s.* [dise. *s.*

سورلوك स्वर्लोक *swar-lok*, m. heaven, para-

سورما सूरमा *sūrmā*, } bold, brave. *sūrmā-*
سورمان सूरमाँ *sūrmāṅ*, } *pan*, m. bravery. *s.*

سورمار *sūr-mār*, brave, valiant. *d.*

سورماس सौरमास *saur-mās*, m. a solar month. *s.*

سورملار सूरमलार *sūr-malār* or *sūr-mallār*, m. name of a musical mode or *rāginī*. *h.*

سورن स्वर्ण *swarna*, m. gold. *swarna-pushpī*, f. the *Cassia fistula*; a medicinal sort of moon-plant. *swarna-chūṛā*, m. the blue jay. *swarna-gairik*, m. a kind of ochre, golden ochre. *swarna-kshīrī*, f. a medicinal kind of moon-plant, said to be brought from the Himālaya mountain. *s.*

سورن सुवर्ण *suvarn*, of good tribe, of good colour, bright; m. gold; a sort of sandal-wood; a red chalk or ochre. *suvarna-ganit*, m. (in arith.) allegation medial. *s.*

سورن सवर्ण *savarn*, like, resembling; of the same class or kind. *s.*

سورن सूरन *suran*, m. an edible tuberous root (*Arum campanulatum, Roxb.*). *s.*

سورنجان *sūranjān*, f. name of a medicine (*Hermadactylus, Gol.*). *a.*

سورنك स्वर्णक *swarnak*, golden, of gold. *s.*

سوروپ स्वरूप *swa-rūp*, m. own or natural shape, form, appearance, or identity; similar, like. *s.*

سوره *sūra*, m. a tale, story, fable, a chapter of the ḳur,ān (of which there are 114). *a.*

سوريار सौरियार *sauriyār*, sizeable. *h.*

سوريوديه सूर्योदय *sūryodaya*, m. the rising of the sun. *s.*

سوريه सूर्य *sūrya*, m. the sun. *sūrya-grahaṇ*, an eclipse of the sun. *sūrya-bansī*, of the solar race; the name of a tribe of *Kshatriyas*, who claim their descent from the sun (v. *sūraj*). *s.*

سوز *soz*, m. burning; vexation, heart-burning; ardour; a stanza of a *marsiya* or elegiac poem. *soz-gudāz*, m. burning and melting; an impassioned style in poetry. *soz-nāk*, burning, ardent. *p.*

سوزاك *sozāk*, m. a gonorrhœa, clap. *p.*

سوزان *sozān* (v. *soz*), burning, &c. *p.*

سوزش *sozish*, f. burning, solicitude, pain, vexation. *p.*

سوزن *sūzan*, f. a needle; pricker (of a gun). *p.*

سوزندگي *sozandagī*, f. a conflagration. *p.*

سوزنده *sozanda*, m. burning, kindling, a burner. *p.*

سوزني *soznī*, f. a kind of coverlet. *p.*

سوزيدن *sozīdan*, to burn (in a transitive or intransitive sense). *p.*

سوس *sūs*, m. liquorice (*Glycyrrhiza*). *a.*

سوس सूस *sūs*, m. a porpoise (*Delphinus*). *s.*

سوست स्वस्ति *swasti*, a formula of benediction or approbation, so be it, it is well, amen, &c. *swasti vāchan*, m. a religious rite preparatory to any important observance, in which the Brāhmans strew boiled rice on the ground, and invoke the blessings of the gods on the ceremonies about to commence. *swasti-mān*, happy, auspicious. *s.*

سوسمار सूसमार *sūsmār*, m. a porpoise (*Delphinus*). *s.p.*

سوسن *sosan*, f. a lily. *a.*

سوسنا *sosnā*, to bear, to endure. *d.*

سوسنديس सूसंदेस *sūsandes*, m. good tidings. *s.*

سوسني *sosnī*, f. a bluish colour. *p.*

سوسه सूसः *sūsa*, m. gasping, panting. *s.*

سوسي सूसी *sūsī*, f. a kind of cloth. *h.*

سوغات *saughāt*, f. a rarity, present, curiosity. *p.*

سوغاتي *saughātī*, given as a present or memorial, fit for a present, (hence) rare. *p.*

سوفار *sūfār*, m. and f. the notch of an arrow or needle. *p.*

سوك सूक *sūk*, m. (for *shukra*) the planet Venus; Friday. *s.*

سوك सोक *sok*, m. the holes in a bedstead through which the strings for bracing it pass. *h.*

سوك सोक *sok*, m. affliction, grief, lamentation. *s.*

سوكا सूका *sūkā*, dry, withered (v. *sūkhā*). *s.*

سوكا सूका *sūkā*, m. a quarter of a rupī piece. *h.*

سوكارج स्वकार्य *swakārj*, m. own business or duty. *s.*

سوكاس सूकास *sūkās*, m. leisure, opportunity. *s.*

سوكتا सुवक्ता *suvaktā*, eloquent. *s.*

سوكٹا सूकटा *sūkṭā*, lean, weak. *s.*

سوكٹمب स्वकुटुम्ब *swakuṭumb*, m. own family. *s.*

سوكر सूकर *sūkar*, m. a hog, a wild boar; the hog-deer. *saukar*, m. *saukarī*, f. hoggish, swinish. *s.*

سوكرت स्वकृत *swakrit*, done or made by one's self, self-performed. *s.*

سوكرم सुविक्रम *suvikram*, m. prowess, valour. *s.*

سوكشم सूक्ष्म *sūkshma*, little, small, minute, fine, subtle. *sūkshmatā*, f. fineness, subtlety. *sūkshma-buddhi*, shrewd, acute; f. mental acumen. *sūkshma darshī*, sharp-sighted, acute. *s.*

سوكل स्वकुल *swakul*, m. own family or race. *s.*

سوكن सौकन *saukan*, f. a rival wife. *h.*

سوكنا सूकना *sūknā*, n. to dry, to become dry. *s.*

سوكناپا सौकनापा *saukanāpā*, m. rivalry between wives of the same husband. *h.*

سوكوا सूकवा *sūkwā*, m. a kind of vetch. *h.*

سوكها सूखा *sūkhā*, dry; m. dry tobacco eaten with betel-leaf; a consumption, atrophy; the croup in children. *sūkhā-dhān*, rice burnt up by the sun's rays. *sūkhā-lagnā* (Dakh.), to be hungry, to be lean or emaciated. *s.*

سوكهـ چهڑي सूखछड़ी *sūkh-chhaṛī*, f. a consumption, atrophy. *s.*

سوكهم *sūkham*, abstracted &c. (v. *sūchham*). *s.*

سوكهنا सूखना *sūkhnā*, n. to dry, to evaporate, to fall away, to pine away, to shrivel, to wither. *s.*

سوكهنا सोखना *sokhnā*, a. to soak up, to absorb. *s.*

سوكي सूकी *sūkī*, f. a quarter of a rupī piece. *s.*

سوکیه स्वकीय *swahīya*, m. } own, belonging
سوکیا स्वकीया *swahīyā*, f. } or relating to one's self. *s.*

سوگ सोग *sog*, m. affliction, grief, lamentation. *p. s.*

سوگا सूगा *sūgā*, m. a parroquet. *s.*

سوگند *saugand*, f. an oath, an asseveration. *saugand-khānā* or *-khurdan*, to make oath, to swear. *s.*

سوگنداسوگندي *saugandā-saugandī*, f. mutual asseveration upon oath. *p.*

سوگندھ सुगंध *sū-gandh* or सौगन्ध *saugandh*, f. perfume, fragrance (also *saugandhya*); adj. fragrant. *sūgandh-sanā*, impregnated with perfume. *s.*

سوگني सौगुणी *sauguṇī*, a hundred-fold. *s.*

سوگوار *sogwār*, grievous, afflicting. *p.*

سوگواري *sogwārī*, f. affliction, grief, sorrow. *p.*

سوگي सोगी *sogī*, afflicted, grieved, sorrowful. *p. s.*

سوگيات स्वज्ञाति *swagyāti*, f. kindred, kin; m. a kinsman. *s.*

سوگيانه *sogyāna*, m. mourning clothes. *p.*

سول सूल *sūl*, m. f. cholic; a trident, pike, dart, the point of a spear; a thorn; compassion, tenderness.

سول सूल *sūl*, m. situation, condition. *h.*

سولاس सविलास *savilās*, wanton, sportive. *s.*

سولپ स्वल्प *swalp*, very small, very few. *s.*

سوله सोलह *solah*, sixteen. *s.*

سولهوان सोलहवाँ *solahwāṅ*, the sixteenth. *s.*

سولي सूली *sūlī*, f. an impaling stake; a name of Mahādeva. *sūlī-denā* or *-chaṛhānā*, to impale. *s.*

سوم सूम *sūm*, m. a miser (Ar. *shūm*, q. v.). *h.*

سوم सोम *som* or *soma*, m. the moon; the moon-plant (*Asclepias acida*); Monday; a mountain or mountainous range so called. *somwār*, m. Monday. *s.*

سوم‌پتر सोमपत्र *som-patra*, m. a sort of grass (*Saccharum cylindricum*). *s.*

سوم‌تيرتھ सोमतीर्थ *som-tīrth*, m. a place of pilgrimage in the west of India. *s.*

سومراج सोमराज *som-rāj* or *som-rājī*, m. black cumin-seed (*Serratula anthelmintica, Roxb.*). *s.*

سومك सौमिक *saumik*, lunar. *s.*

سومنات *somanāt*, m. an idol; name of a celebrated idol temple in Guzerat. *s. p.*

سومناتھ सोमनाथ *soma-nāth*, m. the god Mahādeva. *s.*

سوم‌وار सोमवार *som-wār*, m. Monday. *s.*

سوم‌وت सोमवत *som-wat*, lunar, like the moon. *s.*

سون सून *sūn*, empty, vacant; silent, dreary; (in arith.) a cypher, or what in school phraseology is called "an ought." *s.*

سون सोन *son*, m. name of a river; name of a flower, a kind of jasmine (*Bignonia indica*). *s.*

سون सूनु *sūnu*, m. a son. *s.*

سون सौं *soṅ*, f. an oath, an asseveration. *khudā kī soṅ*, a phrase equivalent to "I swear by God." *h.*

سون सों *soṅ*, postp. from, with (v. *se*). *h.*

سونا सोना *sonā*, n. to sleep; (met.) to die; m. gold. *sone kā nawālā*, an expensive banquet, a delicious morsel. *s.*

سونا सूना *sūnā*, empty, deserted; the following lines contain a "jeu de mots" on the various meanings of *sonā* and *sūnā*:—*Sonā lene pī gaye, sūnā kargaye des; sonā milā, na pī phire, rūpā hogaye kes*, my love went to earn *gold*, and left the country *desolate*: I could not *sleep* (or he found *gold*), my love returned not, my hair became silver. *s.*

سوناش स्वनाश *swanāsh*, m. self-destruction. *s.*

سونپنا सौंपना *sompnā* or सौंपना *saumpnā*, a. to deliver over, to commit any thing to the care or charge of another. *s.*

سونپھ सौंफ *suṅph*, f. anise seed (*Pimpinella anisum*). *h.*

سونتنا सूंतना *sūṅtnā*, } a. to strip leaves of
سونتھنا सूंथना *sūṅthnā*, } vegetables; to draw a sword. *h.*

سونٹ सूंट *sūṅṭ*, f. silence. *sūṅṭ bharnā*, to depart in silence. *sūṅṭ-mārnā*, to maintain silence, to be silent. *h.*

سونٹا सोंटा *sonṭā*, m. a club, mace, pestle. *sonṭe-bardār*, a mace-bearer; a person in the retinue of the great, armed with a short curved club. generally covered with silver. *h.*

سونٹانا *sonṭānā*, a kind of sweetmeat. *d.*

سونٹھ सोंठ *sonṭh*, f. dry ginger; (met.) a miser. *sonṭh kī sī nās le rahnā*, n. to endure, to wait patiently, to suffer. *sonṭh kī nās na lenā*, to be very covetous. *s.*

سونٹھوراءي सोंठूराय *sonṭhūrā,e*, hard, miserly, a ludicrous expression, q. d. chief of misers). *h.*

سوندرج सौन्दर्य *saundarj*, m. beauty, comeliness. *s.*

سوندھا सोंधा *soṅdhā*, m. a composition of fragrant substances used for washing the hair; smelling like that of a new earthen vessel when wetted, or from parching of pulse. *s.*

سوندھاهٹ सोंधाहट *soṅdhāhaṭ*, f. fragrance: a smell like that of new earth. *s.*

سوندھنا सोंधना *soṅdhnā*, a. to rub cloth in mud, preparatory to washing; to mix, to smear. *h.*

سوندھي सोंधे *soṅdhe*, fragrant, smelling like new earth. *s.*

سوندي सोंदी *soṅdī*, f. the wash in which washermen steep their cloth. *h.*

سونڈ सूंड *sūṅḍ*, f. proboscis of an elephant. *s.*

سونڈا सूंडा *sūṅḍā*, m. a weevil, or small insect in corn. *h.*

سونڈکا सूंडका *sūṅḍkā*, m. saddle-cloth, or pillow under a saddle; the hump on the back of a camel, bullock, &c. *h.*

سونڈھ सूंढ *sūṅḍh* (v. *sūṅḍ*). *s.*

سونرا सौंरा *sauṅrā*, m. soot, or any thing of a black colour. *s.*

سونڑی सूंड़ी *sūṅṛī*, m. a distiller and vender of spirituous liquors. *s.*

سونڑی مشخصی *sūṅṛī-mushakhkhaṣī*, a tax on the vendors of spirituous liquors. *s.a.*

سونس सूंस *sūṅs* (*sūs*), a porpoise. *s.*

سونسار *sauṅsār*, family (wife and children); tribes. *sauṅsārī*, a housewife. *d.* [*sum*). *h.*

سونف *sauṅf*, f. aniseed (*Pimpinella ani-*

سونگ *saung*, m. (v. *sawāng*), mimicry, &c. *d.*

سونگا सूंगा *sūṅgā*, m. the clitoris. *h.*

سونگر स्वनगर *swanagar*, m. one's own or native town, city, or country. *s.*

سونگرا सूंगरा *sūṅgrā*, m. a buffalo calf. *h.*

سونگھ सूंघ *sūṅgh*, f. smell, inhaling. *s.*

سونگھا सूंघा *sūṅghā*, staunch (as a dog); (used substantively) a person employed in Mahratta armies, who is said to be able to detect hidden treasure or grain by the smell of the earth. *s.*

سونگھن सूंघन *sūṅghan*, f. any thing to smell or to snuff; the act of smelling. *s.*

سونگھنا सूंघना *sūṅghnā*, a. to smell, to inhale. *s.*

سونگھنی सूंघनी *sūṅghnī*, f. snuff. *s.*

سونوگھن सोनोघन *sonoghan*, m. sign, signal, hint, symbol. *h.*

سونہہ सोंह *soṅh*, f. an oath. *soṅh denā*, a. to adjure. *soṅh ḍālnā*, a. to conjure. *soṅh khilānā*, a. to adjure, to swear, to administer an oath. *h.*

سونہرا सोनहरा *sonahrā*, } golden. *sonahlā pā-*
سونہلا सोनहला *sonahlā*, } *nī*, m. gilding. *s.*

سونہیں सोंहीं *soṅhīṅ*, before, in front of. *s.*

سونیا सोनिया *soniyā*, m. one who separates gold from ashes, &c. in the mint. *s.*

سونیہ शून्य *sūnya*, m. a dot, a cipher. *s.*

سوورت स्ववृत्ति *swavṛitti*, f. own or peculiar duty or occupation. *s.*

سوہ सोह *soh*, f. ornament, dress, decoration. *s.*

سوہا सूहा *sūhā*, red, crimson; m. name of a musical mode, or *rāg*. *sūhā-kusumbhā*, red as the dye of safflower. *h.*

سوہاگا सोहागा *sohāgā*, m. borax. *s.*

سوہان *sohān*, m. a file. *p.*

سوہن सोहन *sohan*, pleasing; m. a lover, a friend. *s.*

سوہن सोहन *sohan*, m. f. a kind of sweetmeat. *h.*

سوہن सोहन *sohan*, f. a file; a whetstone. *p*

سوہنا सोहना *sohnā*. n. to become, to beseem a. to weed. *s.*

سوہی सोही *sohī*, before, in front. *h.*

سوئی सूई *sū,ī*, f. a needle. *sū,ī kā seṅbal*, a bubble. *sū,ī ke nāke se khudā,ī ko nikālnā*, applied to express the performance of things apparently impossible. *sū,ī-gal*, (lit. needle-melter) a very acid kind of lemon so called, as it is said that if a needle be thrust into it, it will melt away. *s.*

سوئی सोई *so,ī*, that very, he himself, &c. *h.*

سوئی *sū,e*, f. (or *sū*) side, path, quarter, towards. *p.*

سوئیا सुइया *sū,iyā*, pointed (as a needle). *s.*

سویا सवैया *sawaiyā*, a quarter more. *h.*

سویا सुवैया *suwaiyā*, m. a sleeper. *s.*

سویت स्वेत *swet* (for *shwet*), white. *s.*

سویچھا स्वेच्छा *swechchhā*, f. wilfulness, following one's own inclination. *s.*

سوید स्वेद *swed*, m. heat, sweat, perspiration. *s.*

سویدا *suwaidā*, black, blackish. *a.*

سویدج स्वेदज *swedaj* or *swaidaj*, engendered by heat (as insects). *s.*

سویر सवेर *sawer*, early, in good time. *s.*

سویرا सवेरा *sawerā*, m. morning, the dawn of day. *s.*

سویرن स्वैरण *swairan*, m. an adulterer. *s.*

سویرنی स्वैरिणी *swairinī*, f. an adulteress, a wanton woman. *s.*

سویرے सवेरे *sawere*, early in the morning. *s.*

سویری स्वैरी *swairī*, uncontrolled, self-willed. *s.*

سویشی सुवेषी *suveshī*, well-dressed, decorated. *s.* [agreeing, promise. *s.*

سویکار स्वीकार *swīkār*, m. avowal, consent,

سویمبر स्वयंवर *swayambar* or *swayamvar*, m. a girl's selecting a husband for herself. *s.*

سویمبرا स्वयंवरा *swayambarā* or *swayamvarā*, f. a girl choosing her husband. *s.*

سویمبھو स्वयम्भू *swayambhū*, m. Brahmā, the self-existent. *s.*

سوین सेवैं *sawaiṅ*, vermicelli. *s.*

سویہ सव्य *savya*, left, left hand; south, southern; reverse, contrary, backward. *s.*

سہ *si*, three. *si-bandī*, m. a militia soldier employed in collecting revenues. *si-pāya*, m. a tripod, trivet. *si-pahar*, afternoon. *si-pahal*, trilateral. *si-chand*, thrice. *si-dara*, three-doored (room, &c.) *si-sāla*, triennial. *si-shash*, three sixes (at dice). *si-karrar*, three times as much. *si-gosha*, a triangle. *si-yak*, three aces (at dice). *p.*

سہا *suhā*, m. an obscure star in the constellation of the Greater Bear. *a.* [charming. *s.*

سہاتا सुहाता *suhātā*, agreeable, pleasant,

سهارا सहारा *sahārā*, m. hope, dependence, assistance, aid, association, concord, gentleness. *sahārā-k.*, a. to abet. *s.*

سهارته सहार्थ *sahārth*, synonymous, having the same meaning. *s.*

سهارنا सुहारना *suhārnā*, a. to trail, to drag. *h.*

سهاگ सुहाग *suhāg*, m. auspiciousness, good fortune; such ornaments as are worn by married women while their husbands are alive; (met.) affections of a husband, caress, act of endearment. *suhāg-piṭārā* or *-purā*, m. a casket of jewels presented by the bridegroom to his bride. *suhāg-lahar*, f. a cool refreshing breeze. *s.*

سهاگا सुहागा *suhāgā*, m. borax. *s.*

سهاگن सुहागन *suhāgan*, f. a woman beloved by her husband; a favourite wife; a married woman whose husband is alive. *s.*

سهال सुहाल *suhāl*, m. } bread (or cakes)
سهالي सुहाली *suhālī*, f. } fried in butter. *h.*

سهانا सुहाना *suhānā*, agreeable, pleasant; n. to be agreeable, to please, to be liked or approved of. *h.*

سهانا सहाना *sahānā*, m. name of a musical mode. *h.*

سهاءو सहाऊ *sahā,ū*, tolerable, endurable. *sahā,o*, bearing, endurance. *s.*

سهاون सुहावन *suhāwan*, agreeable, charming, [refreshing. *s.*

سهاونا सुहावना *suhāwanā*, n. to be agreeable, to please, to be liked or approved of; adj. agreeable, pleasant, charming. *s.*

سهاءي सहाई *sahā,i*, } m. an aider, a helper,
سهاءي सहाय *sahā,e*, } an assistant. *s.*

سهاي सहाय *sahāy* or *sahāya*, } f. aid, help,
سهاءي सहाई *sahā,ī* or *saha,e*, } assistance,
سهايتا सहायता *sahāyatā*, } friendship. *s.*

سهايك सहायक *sahāyak*, m. a succourer, an aider, an assistant, an ally. *s.*

سهاءوان सहायवान *sahā,e-wān*, befriended, assisted, accompanied. *s.*

سهت सहित *sahit*, accompanied by, in company with, together with, along with. *s.*

سهتو सहत्व *sahatwa*, m. sufferance, endurance; association, union. *s.*

سهج सहज *sahaj*, easy, not difficult; adv. easily. *sahaj-subhāva-ki*, with natural ease. *s.*

سهجنا सहजना *sahajnā*, m. a tree which supplies the place of horse-radish (*Guilandina morunga, Lin., Hyperanthera morunga, Roxb.*). *s.*

سهچاري सहचारी *sahachārī*, } m. a companion,
سهچر सहचर *sahachar*, } an attendant. *s.*

سهچري सहचरी *sahacharī*, f. a wife; a confidante. *s.*

سهرا सिहरा *sihrā*, m. a chaplet, a garland, wreath (worn on the head by a bridegroom and bride at the marriage ceremony). *h.*

سهرانا सहराना *sahrānā*, सहिराना *sahirānā*, o *sihrānā*, n. to thrill, to have the hairs stand on end; a. to tire, to harass, to tease, to titillate, to stroke, to rub gently. *h.*

سهراءو सिहराऊ *sihrā,ū*, tiresome, tedious. *h.*

سهراون सहरावन *sahrāwan*, f. titillation. *h.*

سهردي सुहृदय *suhṛiday*, good-hearted. *s.*

سهرنا सिहरना *siharnā*, n. to shiver, to shake with cold; to scrape. *h.*

سهرنا सुहरना *suharnā*, n. to trail, to be dragged. *h.*

سهري सहरी *sahrī*, f. the name of a fish, the small carp (*Cyprinus chrysopareius, Buch.*). *s.*

سهس सहस *sahas*, m. the month Agrahāyan (Nov.-Dec.); the winter season; strength, power. *s.*

سهسا सहसा *sahasā*, quickly, rashly. *s.*

سهسان सहसान *sahsān*, patient, enduring. *s.*

سهسر सहस्र *sahasr* or *sahasra*, a thousand. *sahasrāksh*, thousand-eyed, Argus-eyed, all-perceiving. *sahasra-jug*, m. a period of a thousand ages. *sahasra dant*, m. a sort of sheat fish (*Silurus pelorius*). *s.*

سهسري सहस्री *sahasrī*, m. commander of a thousand. *s.*

سهسيه सहस्य *sahasya*, m. the month Paush (Dec.-Jan.). *s.*

سهشن सहिष्णु *sahishnu*, patient, enduring. *sahishnutā*, f. patience, resignation. *s.*

سهكار सहकार *sahakār*, m. a fragrant sort of mango; assistance. *s.*

سهكارتا सहकारिता *sahakāritā*, f. co-operation, assistance. *s.* [associate, helper. *s*

سهكاري सहकारी *sahakārī*, m. an assistant,

سهگمن सहगमन *sahagaman*, m. going with, accompanying; a woman's burning herself on the funeral pile with her deceased husband. *s.*

سهل *sahl*, easy, not difficult, simple, soft. *a.*

سهلا सुहला *suhlā*, m. a kind of song. *h.*

سهلانا सहलाना *sahlānā*, a. to stroke, to rub gently, to tickle. *khāya sahlānā*, to flatter. *h.*

سهلاهٹ सहलाहट *sahlāhaṭ*, f. gentle rubbing, stroking, titillation. *h.*

سهم *sahm*, m. an arrow; the transverse beam of a house; a lot, a portion, share; the segment of a circle, segment; a versed sine. *a.*

سهم *sahm*, *saham* or *sahim*, m. terror, fear, dread; gravity, venerableness. *sahm-nāk* or *sahmgīn*, frightful; horrible, terrific. *p.*

سهمان *sahmāṅ*, frightened. *p.*

سهمانا *sahmānā*, a. to frighten, to terrify. *p. h.*

سهمرن सहमरण *sahamaran*, m. concremation, a widow's burning herself with the corpse of her husband. *s.*

سهمنا *sahamnā*, n. to fear, to be alarmed. *p.h.*

سہن सहन *sahan*, patient, enduring, suffering, bearing; m. endurance. *s.* [support. *s.*

سہنا सहना *sahnā*, n. to bear, to endure, to

سہنک *sahnak*, f. (properly *ṣaḥnak*) a plate, dish, &c. *a.*

سہنکار सहनकार *sahan-kār*, سہنہار सहन्हार *sahan-hār*, } sufferable, bearable, tolerable. *s.*

سہو *sahū* or *sahw*, f. an error, mistake, fault, inadvertency. *sahwi ḳalam*, a slip of the pen. *sahwi kātib*, an error of the copyist. *sahwu-l-insān min al-lisān*, a man's fall is from the tongue. *a.*

سہواً *sahwan*, erroneously, inadvertently. *a.*

سہواس सहवास *sah-vāsa*, dwelling with (another). *sah-vāsī*, fellow resident. *s.*

سہوٹی सहौटी *sahauṭī*, f. a kind of door-frame. *h.*

سہودر सहोदर *sahodar*, descended from one mother, as *sahodar-bhā,ī*, full brother. *s.*

سہول सहोल *sahol*, m. a plummet. *h.*

سہولت *sahūlat* (also *sahūliyat*), f. facility, ease, smoothness, plainness. *a.*

سہولی *suhūlī*, slow, lazy. *a.*

سہویا सहवैया *sahwaiyā*, m. a sufferer. *s.*

سہی सही *sahī*, an emphatic particle; certainly, undoubtedly, it is true, very well! *h.*

سہی *sahī*, straight; f. a cypress-tree. *sahī salāmat*, safe and sound. *sahī-ḳadd*, tall and graceful as the cypress-tree. *p.*

سہیارنا सहियारना *sahiyārnā*, a. to arrange. *h.*

سہیجنا सहेजना *sahejnā*, a. to try; to adjust; to provide. *h.*

سہیل *suhail*, m. the star Canopus. *a. p.*

سہیلا *suhailā*, a kind of descriptive or eulogistic song. *d.*

سہیلی *suhailī*, of or relating to Canopus; a man's name. *anwārī suhailī*, (lit. rays of Canopus) name of a celebrated version of Pilpay's fables, written in Persian by *Ḥusain Vā'iz*. *p.*

سہیلی सहेली *sahelī*, f. female companions in a seraglio, handmaids, concubines. *s.*

سہیہ सह्य *sahya*, adj. to be borne or suffered. *s.*

سئی सई *sa,ī*, f. a wire-chain. *h.*

سی *sī*, thirty. *sī,um*, thirtieth. *p.*

سی से *se*, postpos. from, with, out of, since, to, through, than. *h.*

سی से *se* and सी *sī*, inflected forms of *sā*, q.v. *h.*

سی सै *sai*, one hundred; f. success. *s.*

سیاح *saiyāh*, m. a traveller, a pilgrim. *a.*

سیاحت *siyāḥat*, سیاحی *saiyāḥī*, } f. travelling, a journey, voyage, pilgrimage. *a.*

سیادت *siyādat*, f. dominion, rule, sovereignty, reigning, governing. *a.*

سیار *saiyār*, m. a wanderer, a person taking the air, or travelling for amusement; wandering, moving. *a.*

سیار सियार *siyār* or स्यार *syār*, m. a jackal. *s.*

سیارہ *saiyāra*, m. a planet (pl. *saiyāragān*). *a.*

سیاست *siyāsat*, f. government, administration of justice; punishment, pain, chastisement, pang, agony. *siyāsat men honā*, n. to be in pain. *a.*

سیاق *siyāḳ*, m. arithmetic or enumeration by the Arabic alphabet, accounts. *a.*

سیاقت *siyāḳat*, f. conflict, contest; driving, stimulating, urging onward, counting. *a.*

سیال *saiyyāl*, flowing rapidly like a torrent. *a.*

سیال सियाल *siyāl*, m. a jackal. *s.*

سیالاپوکا स्यालायोका *syālā pokā*, m. a barnacle (Bang.). *h.*

سیال کانٹا सियालकांटा *siyāl kānṭā*, m. "jackal's thorn," the prickly poppy (*Argemone Mexicana*). *h.*

سیالہ *saiyāla*, m. a torrent. *a.*

سیام श्याम *syām*, m. a name of a bird; an epithet of *Krishna*; name of a musical mode or *rāginī*; adj. dark, or dark blue. *syām chiṛī*, name of a bird. *s.*

سیاما श्यामा *syāmā*, m. name of a bird; f. (black) an epithet of the goddess Kālī. *s.*

سیامتا श्यामता *syāmatā*, f. blackness. *s.*

سیان सयान *sayān* or सियान *siyān*, m. cunning, shrewdness. *syānpan* or *siyānpan*, m. cunning, art. *p.*

سیان स्यान *syān*, f. name of a bird. *h.*

سیانا स्याना *syānā*, सियाना *siyānā*, or सयाना *sayānā*, cunning, artful, clever; prudent; grown up, mature. *h.*

سیانپ स्यानप *syānap*, سیان پن स्यानपन *syān-pan*, سیان پنا स्यानपना *syān-panā*, } m. cunning, art, artfulness. *h.*

سیاوڑہ स्यावढ़ *syāwaṛh*, small heaps of grain set apart for the poor. *h.* [*ris lunulata*). *p.*

سیاوشان *siyāwashān*, m. maiden-hair (*Pte-*

سیاہ *siyāh*, black. *siyāh-bakht*, unfortunate. *siyāh-posh*, clad in black. *siyāh-tālū*, black-mouthed (a horse); abusive, one whose curses prevail. *siyāh-chashm*, black-eyed, unkind. *siyāh-dil*, black hearted, malevolent. *siyāh-rū*, black-faced, unlucky, disgraced. *syāh-roz*, of a dark day, unfortunate. *siyāh-rozī*, *siyāh-ṭāli'*, of unlucky destiny. *siyāh-ṭāli'ī*, bad luck, adverse fortune. *siyāh-fām*, black. *siyāh-ḳalam-k.*, a. to delineate. *siyāh-kār*, wicked, tyrannical. *siyāh-kāsa*, a sordid wretch. *siyāh-k.*, to take an account of. *siyāh-mast*, dead drunk. *p.*

سیاہا *siyāhā*, m. an account-book or written account, a list, inventory. *p.*

سیاہ آمدنی *siyāh-āmdanī*, a running treasury account of the collections, as received day by day from the respective renters. *p.*

سياه‌گوش *siyāh-gosh*, m. name of an animal (*Felis caracal, Gmel.; Persian lynx, Penn.*). *p.*

سياه‌موجودات *siyāh maujūdāt*, an account of the daily receipts, remittances, and disbursements. *a. p.*

سياهي *siyāhī*, f. blackness, ink, blacking. *p.*

سيب *seb*, m. an apple. *sebi samarkand*, the apple of Samarkand, famed for its excellency. *sebi ghab-ghab*, the chin. *p.*

سيپ सीप *sīp*, f. a shell; a kind of mango. *h.*

سيپاره *sī-pāra*, m. a section of the *kur,ān* (Arab. *juz*), one out of the 30 sections into which the whole book is divided. This is a division quite independent of the *sūras* or chapters of the work, of which there are in all 114, of great inequality in length. *p.*

سيپل सीपल *sīpal*, s. a fragment of earthenware. *h.*

سيپهل सीफल *sīphal*, m. the name of a fruit (*Cratæva* or *Ægle marmelos*). *s.*

سيپي सीपी *sīpī*, f. a shell. *h.*

سيت सीत *sīt*, f. cold, chilness; dew, wetness, moistness. *sīt-jwar*, m. ague. *sīt-kāl*, winter, the dewy season. *s.*

سيت सेत *set*, white. *set-dīp*, the white island, or a minor division of the world so called, and supposed by Wilford to be Britain. *s.*

سيت सेतु *setu* or *set*, m. a bridge. *setu-bandh* (v. *set-bandh*). *s.*

سيتا सीता *sītā*, name of the wife of Rāma and daughter of Janaka Rājā (v. *rāmachandra*). *sītā-phal*, m. the custard-apple (*Annona squamosa*). *s.*

سيتارت सीतार्त *sītārt*, affected with cold, being numbed with cold. *s.*

سيتانگ सीताङ्ग *sītāng*, m. palsy, chilness. *s.*

سيتباءي *sīt-bā,ī*, f. the palsy. *d.*

سيت‌بندھ सेतुबन्ध *setu-bandh* or *set-bandh*, the ridge of rocks extending from the south extremity of the Coromandel coast towards the island of Ceylon, supposed to have been formed by Hanuman at the command of Rāma as a bridge for the passage of his forces. Our seamen call it Adam's bridge. *s.*

سيترس सीतरस *sīt-ras*, m. the flux, dysentery. *s.*

سيتل सीतल *sītal*, cool, cold; stupefied, benumbed (with fear, &c.). *sītal-pāṭī*, f. a kind of fine cool mat. *sītal-chīnī*, f. allspice (*Myrtus pimenta*). *s.*

سيتلا सितला *sitlā*, f. small-pox. *s.*

سيتلتا सीतलता *sītalatā*, f. coolness. *s.*

سيتنا सैतना *saitnā* or *setnā*, to take care of, to keep carefully, to husband. *h.*

سيتھ सीथ *sīth*, m. boiled rice, or rice sowins, or gruel. *s.*

سيتھاوار सैथावार *saithāwār*, name of an agricultural tribe located near Benares. *h.*

سيتي सीती *sītī*, f. the plant magnolia. *h.*

سيتي *setī*, postp. (v. *se*) from, &c. *d.*

سيٹھ सेठ *seṭh*, m. a wholesale merchant, a banker. *s.*

سيٹھ सीठ *sīṭh*, f. dregs of betel, or any thing that has been chewed. *s.*

سيٹھا सीठा *sīṭhā*, insipid, tasteless, weak, pale, pithless, sickly. *s.*

سيٹھن सेठन *seṭhan*, a whisk, a kind of brush; female of a *seṭh*, q. v. *h.*

سيٹھنا सीठना *sīṭhnā*, m. } lascivious songs
سيٹھني सीठनी *sīṭhnī*, f. } sung by women at weddings. *h.*

سيٹھي सीठी *sīṭhī*, f. (v. *sīṭh*). *s.*

سيٹي सीटी f. whistling. *sīṭī-bāz*, a whistler. *sīṭī-bajānā*, a. to whistle. *sīṭī-bandhnā*, or *-gum honā*, or *-bhūlnā*, n. to be distracted, confounded, to become senseless. *h.*

سيج सेज *sej*, f. a bed, bedding; a layer of straw for a horse. *sej-band*, m. a cord for fastening bedding to the bedstead. *s.*

سيج सीज *sīj*, m. a species of euphorbia, the milky hedge-plant (*Euphorbia neriifolia, Roxb.* or *antiquorum*). *s.*

سيجنا सीजना *sījnā*, n. to exude, to filtrate, to sweat; to seethe, to boil, to dissolve or become soft by boiling; to be received (as money), liquidated (as a debt). *h.*

سيچن सेचन *sechan*, m. sprinkling, aspersion. *s.*

سيچنا सींचना *sīchnā*, a. to water, to irrigate. *s.*

سيخ *sīkh*, f. a spit, a skewer. *p.*

سيخ‌پا *sīkh-pā*, rearing (a horse); a rearer. *p.*

سيخچه *sīkhcha*, m. a skewer, a small spit. *p.*

سيخياكباب *sīkhiyā kabāb*, m. meat roasted on a spit. *p.*

سيد *saiyid*, m. a lord, a prince: the title is assumed by all those Musalmāns who are or pretend to be descendants of the prophet *Muḥammad* through his son-in-law and successor *'Alī*, and his daughter *Fāṭima*. *saiyidu-l-anām* (the prince of men and of all living creatures); *saiyidu-l-bashar* (the prince of mortals); *saiyidu-l-mursalīn* or *-ambiyā* (the head of the apostles, or prophets), are epithets of *Muḥammad*. *a.*

سيدخانه *sed-khāna*, m. a necessary, a privy (for *ṣiḥḥat-khāna*, q. v.). *a. p.*

سيدزاده *saiyid-zāda*, the son or descendant of a *saiyid*. *a. p.*

سيدنا सेदना *sednā*, a. to stupe, to foment. *h.*

سيدھ सीध *sīdh*, straight; opposite; accurate. *s.*

سيدھا सीधा *sīdhā*, straight, right direct; opposite; simple; fair, candid; m. provisions, victuals (undressed), forage. *sīdhā karnā*, to straighten; in Dakh. the word means right, in opposition to left, as *sīdhī ṭaraf*, to the right side or hand. *s.*

سيدھاءي सीधाई *sīdhā,ī*, } f. straightness; sim-
سيدھي सीधाई *sīdhī*, } plicity; candour *s.*

سير *ser*, full, satiated, tired. *ser-ānā* or *-honā*, n. to be distressed, tired of life. *ser-chashm*, contented. *p.*

سير सेर *ser*, m. name of a weight of nearly two pounds avoirdupois: the Calcutta factory *ser* weighs 1 lb. 13 oz. 13·86 drs. avoirdupois, and the bazaar *ser* 2 lb. 0 oz. 13·853 drs. *s.*

سير सीर *sīr*, damp, raw, cool. *h.*

سير सीर *sīr*, m. husbandry, agriculture; lands in a village cultivated by the hereditary proprietors: hence first-rate land. *s.*

سير *sīr*, m. garlic, water-mint. *p.*

سير *sair*, f. perambulation, taking the air; perusal (of a book); amusement, moving about. *sair-k.*, a. to take the air, to travel; to read, to peruse, to view or contemplate a beautiful landscape scene from an eminence. *sair-gāh*, f. passage, pass, thoroughfare. *a.*

سير *siyar* (pl. of سيرت), virtues, morals, qualities, dispositions. *a.*

سيرا सीरा *sīrā*, cool; m. a kind of sweetmeat made of meal and sugar. *h.*

سيراب *serāb*, moist, succulent; fresh, blooming. *p.*

سيرابه *serāba*, a kind of food composed of curds and garlic. *p.*

سيرابي *serābī*, freshness, humidity, succulence. *p.*

سيرانا सेराना *serānā*, a. to set afloat; to despatch; to cool (v. *sirānā*). *h.*

سيرت *sīrat*, f. disposition, temperament, nature, qualities, conduct, manners. *a.*

سيرك सीरक *sīrak*, f. cool, coolness. *h.*

سيروا सेरुवा *serū,ā*, m. the head and foot parts of a bed frame. *s.*

سيره *ser,h*, m. a sail (evidently a corruption of the English word, but universally used by lascars or Indian seamen.—B.)

سيري *serī*, f. satiety, repleteness. *p.*

سيڙا सीड़ा *sīṛā*, m. a channel through which fields are watered; overflowing field. *s.*

سيڙهي सीढ़ी *sīṛhī*, f. a ladder, stair, step. *h*

سيزده *sīzdah*, thirteen. *sīzdahum*, thirteenth. *p.*

سئيس *sa,īs*, m. a groom, a horsekeeper. *p.*

سيس सेस *ses*, m. (for *sheṣha*) name of a serpent who supports the earth; end. *s.*

سيس सीस *sīs*, m. the head; a freckle, flame, spike (Beng.). *sīs-chaṛhānā*, to exalt, to amuse, to be arrogant. *sīs-phūl*, m. an ornament for the head worn by females. *s.*

سيسا सीसा *sīsā* (also *sīsak*), m. lead. *s.*

سيسر सेसर *sesar*, m. the gripe of a bow; name of a play at cards. *h.*

سيسناگ *sesnāg* (v. *seshnāg*). *s.*

سيسون सीसों *sīsoṅ* or *sīso*, m. a kind of wood, or name of a tree (*Dalbergia sissū, Roxb.*). *s.*

سئيسي *sa,īsī*, f. the office of a groom or horsekeeper (v. *sa,īs*). *p.*

سيش सेष *sesh* (for *sheṣha*), remainder, end; the king of the serpent race: a large thousand-headed snake, at once the couch and canopy of *Viṣhṇu*, and the upholder of the world, which rests on one of his heads. *s.*

سيش‌ساي सेषसाई *seṣh-sā,ī* (for *sheṣha-shā,ī*), the sleeper on the serpent *seṣha* or *ananta*, an epithet of *Viṣhṇu*. *s.*

سيشناگ सेषनाग *seṣh-nāg*, the serpent *seṣha*, and the king of *Pātāl*, q. v. *s.*

سيف *saif*, m. a sword. *saif-bān*, m. a rocket which has a sword attached to its tail. *saif-zabān*, one whose curses prevail. *sīf*, bank, margin, shore. *a.*

سيفي *saifī*, f. cursing, imprecation. *a.*

سيكر सीकर *sīkar* (for *shīkar*), small rain. *s.*

سيكري सीकरी *sīkrī*, f. a wire chain. *s.*

سيكڙا सैकड़ा *saikaṛā* or *saikṛā*, m. a hundred; a hundred per cent. *s.*

سيكه सीख *sīkh*, f. admonition, instruction, lesson, learning, study. *s.*

سيكه शेष *sekh*, f. (for *sesh*) the end; an appendix. *s.*

سيكهرن सेखरन *sekhran*, m. a kind of food. *s.*

سيكهنا सीखना *sīkhnā*, a. to learn, to acquire. *s.*

سيگاره सीगारः *sīgāra*, thick cloth. *h.*

سيل सेल *sel*, m. a spear; (in Dakh.) name of a fish, a species of carp. *s.*

سيل सील *sīl*, m. (for *shīla*) nature, quality, disposition; good conduct or disposition, steady observance of law and morals; complaisance, civility, benevolence, humanity, politeness, generosity. *āṅkhoṅ meṅ sīl honā*, n. to be polite, generous, &c. *s.*

سيل सील *sīl*, f. cold, dampness. *s.*

سيل *sail*, f. flowing; a current, a torrent, flood; walking or going about for amusement. *a.*

سيل सैल *sail* (for *shail*), m. a mountain. *s.*

سيلا सीला *sīlā*, damp, cool, moist. *s.*

سيلا सेला *selā*, m. a kind of sheet constituting a part of dress, especially worn, and given in presents in the Dakhin; a royal tiger. *h.*

سيلاب *sailāb*, abounding with water, a flood, torrent, or inundation. *a. p.*

سيلابي *sailābī*, f. a flood, a torrent, deluge; land watered by inundations. *a. p.*

سيلاني *sailānī*, fond of walking, or going about for amusement, fond of perambulation, &c. *a. h.*

سيلوان सीलवान *sīlwān*, of a good disposition, amiable, virtuous, benevolent. *s.*

سيلي सेली *selī*, f. a necklace (of threads) worn by *fakīrs*, a sash, a belt; (Beng.) a tetter, a mole, a discoloration in the face, &c. *h.*

سيلي *selī*, f. a blow with the edge of the open hand, a slap, a cuff. *p.*

سيليا सेलिया *seliyā*, m. tabby, puss. *h.*

سيم *siyum*, the third: this word is apt to be confounded with *si-um*, the thirtieth. *p.*

سيم *sīm*, m. silver. *sīm-andūd*, covered over with silver. *sīm-parast*, venal, selfish. *sīm-bar*, with a bosom like silver. *sīm-tan*, with a body fair as silver. *sīm-gūn*, silver-coloured. *p.*

سيم सेम *sem*, m. f. the flat bean; leprosy producing discoloration of the skin. *s.*

سيما *sīmā*, m. the forehead, face, countenance, aspect, similitude. *p.*

سيما सीमा *sīmā*, f. limit, restriction, boundary. *sīmā-sandhi*, m. the meeting of two boundaries. *sīmā-vṛiksha*, m. a tree serving as boundary mark. *s.*

سيماب *sīmāb*, m. quicksilver, q.d. silver-water. *p.*

سيمابي *sīmābī*, of the colour of quicksilver. *p.*

سيمبا *sīmbā*, the glanders (disease in horses). *d.*

سيمانه *sīmāna*, bordering, relating to boundaries. *s.*

سيمرغ *sīmurgh*, m. (lit. of the size of thirty birds) a fabulous bird that haunts the mountain *ḳāf*, q. v.; a griffin (v. *'anḳā*). *p.*

سيمل सेमल *semal*, m. a coarse kind of cotton, or the tree producing it (*Bombax heptaphyllum*). *s.*

سيمي *sīmī*, } made of silver. *p.*
سيمين *sīmīn*, }

سيميا *sīmiyā*, m. alchymy, magic, enchantment, necromancy; poetry, rhetoric. *p.*

سين सेन *sen*, m. a hawk, a falcon. *s.*

سين सीन *sīn*, a large metal tray or salver. The word is probably a corruption of the Arabic name of the same utensil, namely *ṣiniyya*. The Persians call it *majmū'a*.

سين सें *seṅ* (for *se*), from, with, by. *h.*

سين सैन *sain*, f. a wink, sign, token, hint, a signal. *sain-k.*, a. to beckon. *s.*

سين सयन *sayan* or सैन *sain*, m. sleep, repose. *s.*

سين सैन *sain* or *sen*, } f. an army. *s.*
سينا सेना *senā* also *sainyā*, }

سينا सेना *senā*, m. an officer who collects the revenue in a village; a commander of an army. *h.*

سينا सेना *senā* (v. *sewnā*), to hatch eggs, to bring forth chickens, &c. *s.*

سينا सीना *sīnā*, a. to sew, to stitch: in the conj. part. we meet with the form *sī-sā-kar*, "having sewn up." It is doubtful whether *sānā* be in use in the sense of sewing. *s.*

سيناپت सेनापति *senā-pati*, a general, the commander of an army; m. a title given to prime ministers, particularly a title of the *rājā* of Berar. *s.*

سيناسيني सैनासैनी *sainā-sainī*, f. mutual tokens, signs, hints, or signals. *s.*

سيناني सेनानी *senānī*, m. the commander of an army. *s.*

سينبل सेंबल *sembal*, } the silk cotton tree. *s.*
سينبهل सेंभल *sembhal*, }

سينت सेंत *seṅt*, gratis, of no expense. *h.*

سينتاليس सैंतालीस *saiṅtālīs*, forty-seven. *s.*

سينتاو सैंताव *saiṅtā,o*, m. arrangement. *h.*

سينت‌ميت सेंतमेंत *seṅt-meṅt*, gratis, free of cost. *h.*

سينتنا सेंतना *seṅtnā* or सैंतना *saiṅtnā*, a. to adjust, to put to rights. *h.*

سينتي *saiṅtī*, f. a dart, a javelin. *d*

سينتيس सैंतीस *saiṅtīs*, thirty-seven. *s.*

سينٹها सेंठा *seṅṭhā*, m. } a kind of reed (of which *moṛhās* or stools are made), reed grass (*Saccharum sara, Roxb.*). *h.*
سينٹهي सेंठी *seṅṭhī*, f. }

سينچ सींच *sīṅch*, watering fields, irrigation. *h.*

سينچاسيچاي *sīṅchā-sīchā,ī*, artificial irrigation of land. *s.*

سينچاي सींचाई *sīṅchā,ī*, f. the price paid for irrigation. *s.*

سينچنا सींचना *sīṅchnā*, a. to irrigate, to water. *s.*

سينچي सींची *sīṅchī*, f. the season of watering fields, &c. *s.*

سيند सेंद *seṅd*, f. name of a vegetable (*Cucumis madraspatanus*). *h.*

سيندور सेंदूर *sendūr*, m. red lead, minium. *s.*

سيندکچريا *send-kachriyā*, m. (v. *send*). *h.*

سيندنا *sendnā*, to water, to irrigate, to draw water. *d.*

سيندهه सेंध *sendh*, m. a hole made in a wall by thieves. *s.*

سيندها सेंधा *sendhā*, m. rock salt. *s.*

سيندهنا सेंधना *sendhnā*, a. to mine, to dig. *s.*

سيندهو सैन्धव *saindhav* or *sendhav*, produced or born in Sindh; m. a horse; rock-salt; (v. *sendhā*). *s.*

سيندهي सेंधी *sendhī*, f. the juice of the wild date-tree (*Phœnix sylvestris, Roxb.*). *h.*

سيندهيا सेंधिया *sendhiyā*, m. poison; a thief making a *sendh*, q. v., a housebreaker; name of a Mahratta tribe (probably so named as originating on the banks of the river *Sindh*). *h.*

سينڈ *seṅḍ*, m. the milk-plant or spurge (*Euphorbia*), of which there are many species. *d.*

سينك सेंक *seṅk*, m. toasting, fomentation. *seṅk sāṅk k.*, to toast or warm. *h.*

سينك सींक *sīṅk*, f. the culm of the grass (*Andropogon muricatum*) of which brooms are made. *h.*

سينکا सींका *sīṅkā*, m. a groove. *h.*

سينکر सींकर *sīṅkar*, m. the flower of the *sīṅk*, q. v. *sīnkur*, m. beard. *h.*

سينکڑا सैंकड़ा *seṅkṛā* or सैंकड़ा *saiṅkṛā*, hundred. *h.*

سينكنا सेंकना *señknā*, a. to toast, to warm before, or with, any thing hot; to foment, to incubate (eggs). *h.*

سينكيا सींकिया *sīñkiya*, striped. *h.*

سينگ सींग *sīng*, m. a horn. *s.*

سينگا सींगा *sīngā*, m. a horn (musical). *s.*

سينگر सैंगर *saiñgar*, m. the bean of *samī*, q.v. *h.*

سينگري सेंगरी *sengrī*, f. a pod, siliqua (particularly the siliqua of the radish). *h.*

سينگڑا सींगड़ा *sīngṛā*, m. a powder-horn. *s.*

سينگهاتي محال *sīnghāṭī-maḥāll*, a tax or toll raised on horned cattle. *h.*

سينگي सींगी *sīngī*, f. name of a kind of fish (*Silurus pungentissimus, Buch.*); a small horn (musical); a cup for cupping. *singī lagānā*, a. to cup. *s.*

سينگيا सींगिया *sīngiyā*, m. a kind of poison. *s.*

سينوياں *señwiyāñ*, m. macaroni, vermicelli. *d.*

سينه सींह *sīñh*, m. a hedgehog. *s.*

سينه *sīna*, m. the breast. *sīna-afgār* or *figār*, wounded in the bosom, afflicted, grieved in heart. *sīna-bāz*, the name of a bird. *sīna-basta*, locked up in the heart, a secret. *sīna-band*, m. stays, bodice. *sīna-chāk* or *-resh*, torn or wounded in heart. *sīna-zan* or *-kob*, one who beats his breast at the festival of the *Muḥarram*. *sīna-zanī*, f. beating the breast. *sīna-zor*, robust, proud of strength. *sīna-zorī*, f. strength, robustness, force; pride of power. *sīna-sokhta* or *-soz*, tormented or distressed in mind. *sīna-ṣāf*, one whose bosom is pure, disinterested. *sīna-koṇḍī*, the nightmare. *p.*

سينهوءا सेंहुआ *señhū,ā*, m. a tetter. *s.*

سيني *sīnī*, f. a salver, tray, trough. *p.*

سينيه सैन्य *sainya*, f. an army. *s.*

سيو सेव *sew*, m. a kind of sweetmeat. *h.*

سيو *sew*, m. an apple (v. *seb*). *p.*

سيو सेव *sev*, } f. service, worship, attend-
سيوا सेवा *sewā*, } ance on a superior. *s.*

سيوار सेवार *sewār*, m. (v. *sivār*) vegetation, &c. *s.*

سيواري सेवारी *sewārī*, f. sugar that has been [purified with *siwār*, q. v. *s.*

سيوتي सेवती *sewtī*, f. a white rose (*Rosa glandulifera, Roxb.*). *s.*

سيوٹ *sewaṭ*, extremity, summit. *d.*

سيورا सेवरा *sewrā*, m. half-baked earthenware; also used for *sevṛā*. *h.*

سيورغال *suyūrghāl*, an assignment of land for charitable purposes; a grant of land revenue without any stipulation of military service or other conditions. *p.*

سيوڑا सेवड़ा *sewṛā*, m. *trophis aspera*. *s.*

سيوڑا सेवड़ा *sevṛā*, a mendicant of the Jain sect. *h.*

سيوك सेवक *sewak*, m. a servant, a worshipper. *s.*

سيوكاءي सेवकाई *sewakā,ī*, f. service. *s.*

سيولي सीवली *sīvlī*, m. name of a caste whose business is to draw juice from the date or *tāṛ* trees, &c. *a.*

سيوم *siwum*, the third, thirdly. *p.*

سيون सीवन *sīwan*, m. sewing, a seam. *sevan*, m. act of serving. *s.*

سيونا सेवना *sewnā*, a. to brood, to rear, to sit, to incubate, to hatch; to attend on, to serve. *s.*

سيونٹها स्यूंठा *syūnṭhā*, m. tongs. *h.*

سيوني सीवनी *sīwanī*, f. the frenum of the prepuce. *s.*

سيوءين सेवईं *sewa,īñ*, f. vermicelli, maca-[roni. *s.*

سيه *siyah* (for *siyāh*), black. *N.B.* For its various compounds look under *siyāh*. *p.*

سيه सीह *sīh* or *seh*, m. a hedgehog. *h.*

سيهتهنا सेहथना *sehathnā*, a. to whisk. *h.*

سيهرن सैहरन *saiharan*, f. sufferance. *s.*

سيهرني सैहरनी *saiharnī*, m. sufferer. *s.*

سيهنڈ सेहुण्ड *sehunḍ*, m. a species of *Euphorbia*, or, indeed, a general name for plants of that kind. *s.*

سيهي सेही *sehī*, a porcupine, hedgehog. *h.*

سيئم *si,um* (properly سي‌أم *sī-um*), the thirtieth (from *sī*, thirty). I have frequently observed that the ordinal of *sī* is formed by the more explicit mode of employing *bīst o dahum*, probably to avoid its being mistaken for *siyum* or *siwum*, the third. *s.*

ش

ش *shīn*, called *shīni mu'jama* or *shīni manḳūṭa*, is the thirteenth letter of the Arabic, the sixteenth of the Persian, and the nineteenth of the Hindūstānī alphabets. Its sound is that of *sh* in English, or *ch* (as *cheval*) in French, and of *sc* (as *scimia*) in Italian: in reckoning by *abjad* its value is 300; it is used as an abbreviation for the word *shamāl*, the North.

श *sha* (or first sibilant) of the Sanskrit generally represents the Persian and Arabic *shīn*; but the Sanskrit letter *sha* is very frequently changed into *sīn* in Hindūstānī; as *sarīr*, the body (for *sharīr*). Again, the Sanskrit *sha* (or second sibilant) is generally changed into *kh*, as *khaṭ* (for *shaṭ*), six.

شا *shā* (for *shād*), joyful, glad. *p.*

شاب *shābb*, m. a young man under thirty-four years of age. *a.*

شاباش *shābāsh*, interj. (for شادباش) bravo! excellent! rest you merry. *p.*

شاباشي *shābāshī*, f. praise, applause. *p.*

شابش *shābash*, cont. from شاباش, q. v. *p.*

شابي *shābī*, likeness, resemblance (for *shabīh*). *d.*

شاپ शाप *shāp*, m. oath, affirmation by oath or ordeal; curse, imprecation. *shāp-grasta*, suffering under a curse. *s.*

شاپت शापित *shāpit*, sworn, cursed. *s.*

شاپودھار, शापोद्धार *shāpoddhār*, m. deliverance from a curse. *s.*

شاٹك शाटक *shāṭak*, m. } a petticoat. *s.*
شاٹي शाटी *shāṭī*, f. } [lainy. *s.*

شاٹھیہ शाठ्य *shāṭhya*, m. wickedness, vil-

شاخ *shā<u>kh</u>*, f. a bough, branch (of a tree); stalk of corn or a flower, &c.; a horn. *shā<u>kh</u>-dār*, branchy, horned. *shā<u>kh</u> dar shā<u>kh</u>*, branched out, or diffused. *shā<u>kh</u>i za'farān* (lit. a twig of saffron) is applied to a proud person, who estimates too highly his own worth. *shā<u>kh</u> shāne* is applied to various reports, calumnies, or complaints. *p.*

شاخچہ *shā<u>kh</u><u>ch</u>a*, m. a small branch, a twig. *p.*

شاخدهنه *shā<u>kh</u>-dahana*, m. a small powder-flask for priming. *p.* [den. *p.*

شاخسار *shā<u>kh</u>-sār*, f. (full of branches), a gar-

شاخول *shā<u>kh</u>ūl*, m. name of a grain (*Cytisus cajan*). *p.*

شاخه *shā<u>kh</u>a*, m. the pillory, a yoke. *p.*

شاد *shād*, pleased, delighted, cheerful, exulting. *shād-<u>kh</u>wār*, voluptuous; f. an adulteress, a strumpet. *shād-dil*, cheerful, delighted, happy. *shād-kām*, joyous, happy, contented. *shād-kāmī*, f. gladness, happiness; delight, content. *p.*

شاداب *shādāb*, fresh, verdant, moist, pleasant, agreeable, succulent. *p.*

شادابي *shādābī*, freshness, moisture, &c. *p.*

شادان *shādān* (v. *shād*), pleased, &c. *p.*

شادمان *shād-mān*, pleased, delighted, joyful. *p.*

شادماني *shād-mānī*, f. pleasure, delight, joy. *p.*

شاده *shāda*, glad, cheerful; m. wine. *p.*

شادي *shādī*, f. pleasure, delight; marriage, festivity, rejoicing. *shādī-marg*, f. an easy death, death from joy; dying easily, or from joy. *p.*

شاديات *shādiyāt*, fees paid at marriages. *p.*

شاديانه *shādiyāna*, relating to marriage or rejoicings. *shādiyāna bajānā*, a. to triumph. *p.*

شاذ *shāẕẕ*, uncommon, miraculous, wonderful; irregular adv. seldom. *a.*

شار *shār* (v. *shārah*), a starling. *p.*

شارح *shāriḥ*, m. a commentator; a guard placed over fields, against birds, &c. *a.*

شارع *shāri'*, f. a high road. *shāri''i'ām*, m. a public road, a highway. *a.*

شارق *shāriḳ*, m. the sun. *a.*

شارك *shārak*, } m. a species of starling famed
شارو *sharo*, } for its talkativeness. *p.*

شاريرك शारीरिक *shārīrik*, bodily, corporeal. *s.*

شاست शास्ति *shāsti*, f. a command, an order; governing, ruling; punishment. *s.*

شاستر शास्त्र *shāstr* or *shāstra*, an order or command; Hindū religious books, Hindū law, scripture: Hindū sciences, or scientific works, especially such as are considered to be of divine origin or authority. *shāstrag* or *shāstra-gya*, versed in the Shāstras, skilled in law and religion. *shāstra-viruddh*, contrary to law. *s.*

شاستارتھ शास्त्रार्थ *shāstrārth*, m. argument, debate, dispute, discussion, discourse. *s.*

شاسترانسار शास्त्रानुसार *shāstrānusār*, m. conformity to sacred ordinances. *s.*

شاستروكت शास्त्रोक्त *shāstrokta*, said or declared in a sacred work. *s.*

شاستري शास्त्री *shāstrī*, skilled in Hindū law or religious books. *shāstrī achchhar*, the Devanāgarī character; lit. the character of the *shāstr*. *shāstriya*, scriptural, authorized by the sacred institutes. *s.*

شاسن शासन *shāsan*, m. an order, an edict; a deed, a written contract; governing, ruling. *shāsan-patra*, m. a plate of copper, a stone or sheet of paper, &c. on which an edict or grant is inscribed. *s.*

شاسنيه शासनीय *shāsanīya*, to be governed or directed. *s.* [punishment. *s.*

شاسيه शास्य *shāsya*, punishable, deserving

شاش *shāsh*, urine. *shāsh-dān*, bladder, urinal. *p.*

شاشيدن *shāshīdan*, to make water. *p.*

شاطر *shāṭir*, wanton; clever, sly: (substantively) a chess-player; an expert player in general; a messenger. *a.*

شاعر *shā'ir*, m. a poet. *a.*

شاعري *shā'irī*, f. poesy, poetry, poetic compositions. *a.* [diligent, busy. *a.*

شاغل *shāghil*, attentive, occupied, employed,

شافع *shāfi'*, deprecating, interceding; (sub.) a patron, an advocate. *a.*

شافعي *shāfi'ī*, n. prop.; one of the chiefs of the four principal sects of the *Muḥammadan* religion; adj. following the sect of *Shāfi'ī*. *a.*

شافه *shāffa*, m. a bougie, a pessary, a suppository. *a.*

شافي *shāfī*, healing, salutary, one who healeth. *shāfī,i ḥaḳīḳī*, an epithet of the Deity. *a.*

شاق *shāḳḳ*, } difficult, perplexing, trouble-
شاقه *shāḳḳa*, } some. *a.*

شاك शाक *shāk*, m. a potherb or vegetable; one of the seven Dwīpas or divisions of the world; an era, especially that of Sālivāhana, commencing 76 or 78 years after the Christian era. *s.*

شاكت शाक्त *shākta*, m. a worshipper of the female principle. *s.*

شاكر *shākir*, grateful, praising, thanking. *a.*

شاكل शाकल *shākal*, f. a mixture of sesamum seed, fruits, *ghī*, barley, coarse sugar &c., used in oblations to the gods. *s.*

شاكمبهري शाकम्भरी *shākambharī*, f. a city supposed to be the modern Sāmbhar in Ajmere. *shākambhariya*, m. a salt brought from a lake in the vicinity of Sāmbhar. *s.*

شاكني शाकनी *shākni*, f. a female divinity of an inferior character, attendant especially on *Shiva* and *Durgā*. *s.* [a tree. *s.*

شاكها शाखा *shākhā*, f. a branch, the branch of

شاكهي शाखी *shākhī*, m. a tree. *s.*

شاكي *shākī*, m. a complainer, a backbiter; adj. lamenting, querulous. *a.*

شاگرد *shāgird*, m. a scholar, disciple, apprentice; a servant. *shāgird-pesha*, m. a servant. *shāgirdi rashīd*, m. a complete scholar, an apt scholar. *p.*

شاگردي *shāgirdī*, f. learning, studying, apprenticeship. *p.*

شال शाल *shāl*, f. a shawl; m. name of a common timber-tree (*Shorea robusta, Roxb.*), a thorn; a jackal; a kind of fish (*Ophiocephalus urahl*). *shāl-bāb*, m. shawl cloths. *shāl-bāf*, m. a shawl-weaver. *s.*

شال शालि *shāli*, m. rice; especially applied to a white rice growing in deep water, and a red sort requiring only a moist soil. *s.*

شالا शाला *shālā* (more commonly *sālā*), in comp. a house, a hall, place, &c., as *pāṭh-shālā*, a reading-room; *shastra-shālā*, a storehouse for arms or weapons. *s.* [*sarum gangeticum*). *s.*

شالپرني शालपर्णी *shālparnī*, f. a shrub (*Hedy-*

شالملي शाल्मली *shālmalī*, the silk-cotton tree (*Bombax heptaphyllum*). *s.*

شالواهن शालिवाहन *shālivāhan* or *sālivāhan*, a sovereign whose capital was Pratisthān in the Dekhan, and who founded the Saka era. *s.*

شالي शाली *shālī*, m. a weaver of shawls and similar articles; rice, paddy; adj. made of shawl. *s. p*

شام *shām*, f. evening; m. Syria, also the city of Damascus. *shām ke murde ko kab tak ro,iye* is applied to express a circumstance which is likely to be a subject of regret for life. The expression is taken from the custom among the relatives of a person who dies, of venting loud lamentations while the corpse remains in the house; if he die in the morning it is soon removed, but if towards evening, it remains till next morning, in which case the mourners are apt to be overtaken by sleep. *p.*

شام श्याम *shām*, a name of *Krishna*. *s.*

شاما श्यामा *shāmā*, m. the little bird generally called *sāma*; name of a grain (*Panicum colonum* or *frumentaceum*). *s.* [*cum colonum*). *p.*

شاماخ *shāmākh*, m. name of a grain (*Pani-*

شامبك शाम्बुक *shāmbuh*, m. a bivalve shell. *s.*

شامت *shāmat*, f. bad fortune; adversity. *shāmit*, rejoicing or laughing at another's misfortune. *a.*

شامتي *shāmatī*, adj. unfortunate. *a.*

شامخ *shāmikh*, high, elevated; proud. *a.*

شامك शामुक *shāmuk*, m. a kind of *helix*, of the shell of which lime is made (Beng.). *s.*

شامگاه *shām-gāh*, f. evening, eventide. *p.*

شامل *shāmil*, together; with, along with; adj. united, confederated; communicating, comprehending. *shāmili ḥāl*, connected from circumstances, of similar circumstances. *shāmil-k.*, a. to blend. *a.*

شاملات *shāmilāt* (pl. of شامله), partnership, affairs in common. *a.*

شامه *shāmma*, m. the sense of smelling. *a.*

شامي *shāmī*, f. supper, the evening meal; adj. Syrian, relating to Syria or Damascus. *a. p.*

شاميانه *shāmiyāna*, m. a canopy, awning. *p*

شامي لگانا शामी लगाना *shāmī lagānā*, a. to shoe with iron. *h.* [grindstone. *s.*

شان शाण *shān*, m. a touchstone; a whet or

شان *shān*, f. business, affair; dignity, state, condition, degree; constitution, nature, disposition. *shān-dār*, a person of state and dignity, or man of rank. *a.* [these, those *p.*

شان *shān*, m. a honeycomb; (for *eshān*) they,

شانت शान्त *shānt*, calm, tranquil, pacified, appeased, hushed, allayed; meek, humble. *shānti*, f. quiet, stoicism; rest, repose, remission, alleviation. *s.*

شانزده *shānzdah*, sixteen. *p.*

شانزدهم *shānzdahum*, the sixteenth. *p.*

شانه *shāna*, m. a comb, a crest; the shoulder. *shāna-dān*, a comb-case. *shāna-sar*, the bird called *hudhud* or hoopoe. *p.* [berty. *d.*

شاني *shānī*, of age, arrived at the age of pu-

شاه *shāh*, m. a king; a title assumed by *faḳīrs*; the king (in chess); (in comp.) royal, noble; excellent, first-rate. *shāh-bāz*, m. a royal falcon. *shāh-balūṭ* m. chesnut. *shāh-khurdi*, f. a kind of sweetmeats used on great occasions. *shāh-tīr*, m. a beam. *shāhi-khāwar*, m. the sun. *shāh-rāh*, f. the highway. *shāh zādagī*, f. the period of the minority of a prince; youthful folly, foolish pride. *shāh-zāda*, m. a prince (generally means the prince royal). *shāh-zādī*, a princess. *shāh-gām*, adj. pleasant-paced (a horse); name of a particular pace of a horse. *shāhi-gardūn*, m. the sun. *shāh-nāma*, f. a celebrated epic poem, containing a history of the kings of Persia, written by Firdausī about the year of Christ 1000. *shāhi mashriḳ* or *shāhi nīmroz*, m. the sun. *shāh-wār*, princely, fit for a king. *p.*

شاه آلو *shāh-ālū*, m. a cherry. *p.*

شاهانه *shāh-āna*, royal, princely; a kind of dress worn by a bridegroom. *p.*

شاهپر *shāh-par*, the largest feather in a wing. *p.*

شاه تره *shāh-tara*, m. *Oldenlandia biflora*. *p.*

شاهد *shāhid*, m. a witness; (in Pers.) a sweetheart; a female friend, a beloved object. *shāhidi ḥāl*, a witness of facts. *shāhidi-roz*, m. the sun. *a.*

شاهدي *shāhidī*, f. evidence, testimony, attestation. *a.* [good rider. *p.*

شاه سوار *shāh-sawār*, an expert horseman, a

شاهنشاه *shāhanshāh*, m. king of kings, an emperor, a title adopted by the old kings of Persia *shāhanshāhi falak*, m. the sun. *p*

شاهنشاهي *shāhanshāhī*, f. empire; adj. imperial. *p.*

شاهوا *shāhwā*, } royal, noble, worthy of a
شاهوار *shāhwār*, } king; a fine pearl. *p.*

شاهي *shāhī*, f. royalty, reign, sovereignty; a follower of the sect of *'Alī*: adj. royal. *p.*

شاهين *shāhīn*, m. a royal white falcon. *p.*

شايان *shāyān*, legal, worthy, suitable, agreeable. *p.*

شائبه *shā,iba*, doubt, suspicion. *a.*

شايد *shāyad*, possibly, probably, may be so, perchance, perhaps. *p.*

شايستگي *shāyastagī*, f. affability, fitness, aptitude, convincing. *p.*

شايستن *shāyastan* (r. *shāy*), to be fit or becoming, to suit. *p.*

شايسته *shāyasta*, worthy, honourable, suitable, proper, well-bred, polite. *shāyasta-mizāj*, affable, mild, good-tempered. *p.* [distressed. *a.*

شائع *shā,i'*, divulged, published, diffused;

شائق *shā,iḳ*, full of desire, lascivious. *a.*

شب *shab*, f. night. *shab-bāsh*, one who stays all night, a lodger. *shab-bāshī*, f. staying all night, nightly lodging. *shab ba-khair*, good night, salutation at night. *shabi barāt*, f. the fourteenth day of the month Sha'bān, on which the Musalmāns make offerings and oblations in the names (if not to the manes) of deceased relations (v. *barāt*). *shab-bedār*, waking, or watching all night, sleepless. *shab-bedārī*, f. nocturnal vigil. *shab-para*, m. a bird of night (as a bat, owl, &c.). *shabi tār* or *shabi tārīk*, a dark night. *shab-khwābī*, f. night-clothes. *shab-khūn*, m. a night attack. *shab-khūnī*, f. robbery at night. *shab-khezī*, rising at night (to pray). *shab-gard*, a watchman. *shab-gardī*, f. watching at night. *shabi māh*, f. light night, moonlight. *shab o roz*, night and day. *p.*

شب *shabb*, m. alum. *a.*

شبا *shabā*, a nocturnal attack. *d.*

شباب *shabāb*, m. youth, prime of life. *a.*

شباروز *shabā-roz*, night and day, *i.e.* always. *p.*

شباشب *shabā-shab*, in the night-time, during the night. *p.*

شبان *shubān*, m. a shepherd, pastor. *p.*

شبانروز *shabān-roz*, night and day, the civil day of twenty-four hours (νυχθήμερον). *p.*

شبانگاه *shabān-gāh*, } f. the evening; a lodg-
شبانگه *shabān-gah*, } ing-place for the night, a fold for cattle. *p.*

شبانه *shabāna*, nocturnal, by night. *shabāna-roz*, the civil day of twenty-four hours. *p.*

شباهت *shabāhat*, f. similarity, resemblance. *a.*

شب بو *shab-bo*, m. (or *guli shab-bo*) the *Polianthes tuberosa*. *p.*

شب چراغ *shab-chirāgh*, lit. the night-lamp, a carbuncle, a brilliant gem; a glow-worm, a fire fly. *p.*

شبچراغك *shab-chirāghak*, a glow-worm, a fire-fly (lit. the little night-lamp). *p.*

شبخيز *shab-khez*, one who rises at night for the purpose of praying; adj. pious, devout. *p.*

शब्द شبد *shabd*, m. a sound in general, a word, a declinable word, as a noun or pronoun (v. *sabd*). *shabd-chor*, m. a plagiary. *shabd-shāstr*, etymology, the science of grammatical inflection. *shabd-bedhī*, m. one who has the skill of shooting an arrow, &c. upon an unseen person on hearing a sound made by him. *shabd-kār*, sounding, sonorous. *shabd-yoni*, f. a radical word. *s.*

شبديز *shabdez*, a horse of a dark rusty colour, a horse of noble breed, name of a famous horse belonging to *Kai Khusrū*, an ancient Persian king. *p.*

شبديگ *shab-deg*, f. a dish composed of meat and turnips left to boil gently all night on the fire. *p.*

شبر *shibr*, a span, a palm. *a.*

شبرنگ *shab-rang*, black, dusky, obscure. *p.*

شبستان *shabistān*, } a bed, a bedchamber, a
شبستاني *shabistānī*, } king's bedchamber. *p.*

شبع *shab'*, fulness, satiety. *a.*

شب قدر *shabi ḳadr*, the night of power, the 27th of *Ramaẓān*, on which the *ḳur,ān* is said to have descended from heaven. *p. a.*

شبك *shabak* (pl. of شبكه), nets, &c. *a.*

شبكارنا *shibkārnā*, to make a whizzing noise like that of a switch. *d.*

شبكور *shab-kor*, night-blind. *p.*

شبكوري *shab-korī*, f. the night-blindness. *p.*

شبكه *shabaka*, m. a net, a lattice, a reticulated veil. *a.*

شبكيان *shabkiyāṅ*, f. (pl.) venetian blinds. *d.*

شبگاه *shab-gāh*, f. night-place to keep any thing in; night-time. *p.*

شبگز *shab-gaz*, (lit. night-stinger) a flea. *p.*

شبگشت *shabgasht*, f. a bridal procession, headed by the bridegroom, perambulating the town with lights, music, &c. on the night previous to the performance of the marriage ceremony.—(Binning.) *p.*

شبگون *shab-gūn*, dark as night, black. *p.*

شبگير *shab-gīr*, m. a cricket; a nightingale, or any animal that sings at night; a servant that works or travels in the night-time; early dawn. *p.*

شبنم *shab-nam*, f. night moisture, dew; m. a kind of cloth; very fine muslin or gauze. *p.*

شبو *shabū*, an agate, a jar, a [illegible]-cloth. *p.*

شبه *shibh* or *shabah*, an image, resemblance, similitude. *a.*

شبه *shiba* or *shaba*, an agate, a bead, a coral. *p.*

شبه शुभ *shubh*, happy, well, fortunate, auspicious, beautiful; m. good, happiness; one of the astrological *yogs*. *shubh-phal*, m. happy result. *shubh-shīl*, of a good disposition. *shubh-kar*, propitious, producing good. *shubh-karma*, m. virtuous act, reputable occupation. *shubh-lagna*, an auspicious moment. *s.*

شبهاچار शुभाचार *shubhāchār*, virtuous. *s.*

شبهاشبه शुभाशुभ *shubhāshubh*, happy and unfortunate, good and evil. *s.*

شبهانگ शुभाङ्ग *shubhāng*, handsome, elegant; f. a handsome woman. *s.*

شبهدنتي शुभदन्ती *shubh-dantī*, f. the female elephant of the north-west quarter. *s.*

شبهر शुभ्र *shubhra*, white, shining; m. white (the colour). *shubhra-kṛit*, the 36th year of the Indian cycle. *s.*

شبهگ शुभग *shubhag*, fortunate, propitious. *s.*

شبهنکر शुभङ्कर *shubhankar*, auspicious, conferring happiness. *s.*

شبهه *shubha*, m. doubt, suspicion, uncertainty. *a.*

شبینه *shabīna*, stale, last night's. *p.*

شبیه *shabīh*, alike, resembling; f. a picture, likeness, resemblance. *a.*

شپا शप्पा *shappā*, m. a butt or mark for archers. *h.*

شپت शप्त *shapta*, cursed, anathematized; m. a sort of grass (*Saccharum cylindricum*). *s.*

شپته शपथ *shapath*, m. an oath, confirmation of the truth by oath or ordeal; an imprecation, a curse. *s.*

شپر *shappar* | شپرك *shapparah* | شپره *shappara* } (for *shab-para*), a night-flyer, a bat. *p.*

شپن शपन *shapan*, m. an oath, &c. (same as *shapath*, q.v.). *s.*

شپهري शफरी f. a small fish (*Cyprinus sophore*). *s.*

شت शत *shat*, m. a hundred. *shat-sahasra*, m. a hundred thousand. *shat-varsh*, m. a century. *s.*

شتا *shitā*, m. winter, the cold season. *a.*

شتا *shattā*, distinct, different, various. *a.*

شتا *shattā*, ingenious, clever, cunning. *d.*

شتاب *shitāb*, m. haste, quickness; adj. quick, speedy; quickly, expeditiously, soon. *shitāb-bāz*, hasty, expeditious. *p.*

شتابان *shitābān*, hastening, hurrying. *p.*

شتابي *shitābī*, quick, hastily; f. speed. *p.*

شتالنا *shitālnā*, a. to actuate, to urge on, incite. *d.*

شتالنگ *shitālang*, m. the ankle. *p.*

شتاه *shattah* (for شطاح *shaṭṭāḥ* ?) meretricious, lewd, obscene. This word occurs in the Guli Bakāwali, p. 157, l. 4. *a. h.*

شتبهشا शतभिषा *shat-bhishā*, f. the twenty-fifth lunar mansion, containing 100 stars. *s.*

شتپاد शतपाद *shat-pād*, | شتپدي शतपदी *shat-padī*, } f. a centipede, jaulus. *s.*

شتدر शतद्रु *shatadru* or शितद्रु *shitadru*, the Sutlej river in the Panjāb. *s*

شتلکش शतलक्ष *shat-laksh*, m. a hundred lakhs, ten millions. *s.*

شتمولي शतमूली *shat-mūlī*, f. a plant (*Asparagus racemosus*). *s.*

شتر *shutur*, m. a camel. *shutur-bān*, a camel-driver (or keeper). *shuturī be mahār*, incorrigible, wild, refractory. *shutur-sawār*, mounted on a camel. *shuturi ṣāliḥ*, the camel of the prophet Ṣāliḥ (v. *ḳur,ān*, sūrat 7). *shutur-ghamza*, wickedness, deceit. *shutur-ḳaṭār*, a string of camels; a series, line, row, &c. *shutur-kīna*, bearing malice (for which the camel is remarkable). *shutur-gām*, a camel-step. *shutur-gāw*, the cameleopard. *shutur-murgh*, m. an ostrich. *shutur-nāl*, f. a small gun carried on a camel. *p.*

شتر शत्रु *shatru*, m. an enemy. *shatru-bhāv*, like an enemy, as bad as an enemy. *s.*

شترتا शत्रुता *shatrutā*, f. enmity, malignity. *s.*

شترتن शितिरत्न *shiti-ratna*, m. a sapphire. *s.*

شتسارك शितिसारक *shiti-sārak*, m. a sort of ebony (*Diospyros glutinosa*). *s.*

شتري *shuturī*, f. a kind of kettledrum; a colour so called. *p.*

شتگن शतगुन *shat-gun*, a hundredfold. *s.*

شتم *shatm*, m. contempt, contumely, reproach, outrage, injury, villainy, abuse not amounting to slander (pl. *shutūm*). *a.*

شتویدهي शतवेधी *shat-vedhī*, m. a sort of dock or sorrel (*Oxalis monadelpha* or *Rumex vesicarius*). *s.*

شتهل शिथिल *shithil*, loose, lax, flaccid, flabby, languid, inert. *shithil-bal*, weakened, relaxed. *shithilā*, f. looseness, relaxation. *s.*

شتي *shattā*, distinct, divided, various. *a.*

شٹ षट *shaṭ*, six (used in compound words from the Sanskrit) (v. *khaṭ*). *s.*

شٹپد षटपद *shaṭ-pad*, | شٹچرن षटचरण *shaṭ-charan*, } m. a bee (lit. six-footed). *s.*

شٹرس षटरस *shaṭ-ras*, six tastes (v. *khaṭ-ras*). *s.*

شٹشاستر षटशास्त्र *shaṭ-shāstr* (v. *khaṭ-shāstr*). *s.*

شٹکون षटकोन *shaṭ-kon*, m. a hexagon; Indra's thunderbolt. *s.*

شٹه शठ *shaṭh*, wicked, depraved, perverse. *shaṭhatā*, f. wickedness, depravity. *s.*

شج *shajj*, a wound or personal injury short of destroying life. *a.*

شجاج *shijāj* (pl. of شج or شجه), (v. Wilson). *a.*

شجاع *shujā'*, brave, intrepid, bold. *a.*

شجاعت *shujā'at* (also *shujā'atī*), f. bravery, valour. *a.*

شجر *shajar*, } m. a tree, a plant. *shajratu-*
شجرة *shajrat*, } *l-ḥukm*, the tree of judgment, a fabulous tree which is said to have given unerring decisions on knotty points of dispute. *a.*

شجرنامه *shajar-nāma*, } m. a list of saints or
شجره *shajara*, } holy predecessors, given to disciples (in the manner of a genealogical table). *a.*

شجع *shaja'*, bravery, intrepidity. *a.*

شجعا *shuja'ā*, } (pl. of شجيع) the brave, the
شجعان *shuj'ān*, } warlike. *a.*

شجيا शय्या *shajyā*, f. a bed, a couch, a sofa. *s.*

شجيع *shajī'*, brave, intrepid. *a.*

شچ शुचि *shuchi*, white, clean, pure. *shuchitā*, f. purity. *shuchi-mani*, m. crystal. *s.*

شحناءي *shaḥnā,ī*, } f. superintendence, po-
شحنگي *shaḥnagī*, } lice. *a. p.*

شحنه *shaḥna*, m. a viceroy, lieutenant, representative; a *peon* or servant of a tax-gatherer. *a.*

شخ *shakh*, hard ground, top of a hill, peak of a mountain. *p.*

شخص *shakhs*, m. a person, body, individual. *a.*

شخصيت *shakhṣiyat*, f. nobility, rank, humanity. *a.*

شد *shud*, was, became, went. *p.*

شد *shadd*, force, running to battle; the mark *tashdīd*, reduplication of a letter. *a.*

شدا *shaddā*, m. the banners which are carried with the *ta'ziya*, in the *Muḥarram*. *a.*

شداد *shidād*, strong, violent, vehement. *a.*

شدآمد *shud-āmad*, custom, usage. *p.*

شدائد *shadā,id* (pl. of شديدة), adversities, troubles, tribulations, disagreeable events. *a.*

شدبود *shud-būd*, so so, indifferently. *p.*

شدت *shiddat*, f. violence, force, vehemence; adversity, affliction, difficulty. *a.*

شدكار *shudkār*, m. ground tilled and sown; a person whose business it is to examine the state of the harvest; survey, valuation. *p.*

شدن *shudan* (r. *shav*), to be, to become. *p.*

شدني *shudanī*, probable; f. a possible event or occurrence. *p.*

شدومد *shadd o madd*, emphasis, energy; reading emphatically with due stress on the proper syllable. *a.*

شده *shuda*, become, past, gone. *p.*

شدھ शुद्ध *shuddha*, accurate, correct; pure, clean, unpolluted; alone, singular, unique. *shuddhamati*, of pure and sincere purpose, guileless; intelligent. *s.*

شدھ शुद्धि *shuddhi*, f. purity, purification; innocence established by ordeal or trial; acquittal. *s.*

شدھتا शुद्धता *shuddhatā*, purity, cleanness, correctness. *s.*

شديد *shadīd*, difficult; afflicting; violent, strong, intrepid. *a.*

شڈ षड *shaḍ* (for *shaṭ*), in comp. six. *s.*

شڈنگ षडङ्ग *shaḍ-anga*, the six principal parts of the body, viz. two hands, two feet, the head, and the waist: it also denotes the six supplementary parts of the Vedas; adj. having six parts or members. *s.*

شڈودھ षड्विध *shaḍ-vidh*, in six ways, of six kinds. *s.*

شڈونشت षड्विंशति *shaḍ-vinshati*, twenty-six. *s.*

شڈونشتتم षड्विंशतितम *shaḍ-vinshatitam*, the twenty-sixth. *s.*

شر शर *shar*, m. a sort of reed or grass (*Saccharum sara*); an arrow. *s.*

شر *sharr*, f. wickedness, depravity, malignancy. *a.*

شر शिर *shir* or *shira*, m. the head. *s.*

شرا *shirā* or *shirạ*, m. purchase, sale, traffic. *sharā*, an eruption of pimples on the skin. *a.*

شرا शिरा *shirā*, any vessel of a tubular form, as a vein, a nerve, a gut. *s.*

شراب *sharāb*, f. wine, spirituous liquor. *sharābi partukālī* or *-partugālī*, port wine. *sharābaṉ ṭahūrā*, nectar. *sharāb-khāna*, m. a tavern. *sharāb-zada*, overcome with wine. *sharāb-khur*, a winebibber. *a.*

شرابور शराबोर *sharā-bor*, soused, dripping wet. *h.*

شرابي *sharābī*, m. a drunkard, a winebibber; adj. intoxicated. *a.*

شراٹ शराटि *sharāṭi*, f. a sort of bird (*Turdus ginginianus*). *s.*

شراٹا शराटा *sharāṭā*, m. sound, noise, voice. *h.*

شرادھ श्राद्ध *shrāddha*, faithful, believing; m. (v. *srāddha*) funeral obsequies, &c. *s.*

شرار *sharār*, m. a spark of fire. *a.*

شرارت *sharārat*, f. vice, wickedness, depravity, villainy. *a.*

شرارة *sharāra*, a spark of fire, flash, gleam. *a.*

شراسن शरासन *sharāsan*, m. a bow. *s.*

شرافت *sharāfat*, f. nobility. *a.*

شراكت *sharākat*, f. partnership. *a.*

شرال शिराल *shirāl*, veiny, tendinous. *s.*

شرالي शराली *sharālī*, f. a bird (the same as *sharāṭi*, q. v.). *s.*

شرانت श्रान्त *shrānt*, wearied, fatigued; calmed, tranquil. *shrānti*, f. weariness. *s.*

شراو शराव *sharāo*, m. a lid or cover; a shallow cup or dish, a platter. *s.*

شراوك श्रावक *shrāvak*, m. the lay votary of a Buddha or Jina. *s.*

شراون श्रावण *shrāvan*, m. the month Sāvan (July-August). *s.* [in Sāvan. *s.*

شراوني श्रावणी *shrāvanī*, f. the day of full moon

شرائط *sharā,it* (pl. of شريطه), agreements, stipulations; signs, marks. *a.*

شرائين *sharā,īn* (pl. of شريان), arteries. *a.*

شرب *shurb*, drink, drinking. *akl o shurb*, food and drink. *a.*

شربت *sharbat*, m. sherbet, beverage, drink; the dose of a medicine. *sharbat-dār*, m. a servant who has charge of the water, wine, &c., a butler. *a.*

شربتي *sharbatī*, f. a kind of lime or lemon; name of a colour. *a.*

شربهہ शरभ *sharabh*, m. a fabulous animal, supposed to have eight legs and to inhabit the snowy mountains. *s.*

شرت श्रुत *shrut*, heard, understood; m. sacred science, holy writ. *shruti*, f. the Vedas. *s.*

شرت‌کال शरत्काल *sharat-kāl*, m. the autumnal season. *sharat-kālīn*, autumnal. *s.*

شرٹ शरट *sharaṭ*, m. a lizard, a chameleon; safflower, the plant. *s.*

شرجو शरयु *sharju*, f. the Serju river. *s.*

شرجا *shirjā* (also شرزه *shirza*), the erysipelas. *s.* [allowance, pay, rate. *s.*

شرح *sharḥ*, f. explanation, commentary;

شرد शरद *sharad*, f. the season of autumn, or the sultry season; the two months succeeding the rains, fluctuating from August to November. *s.*

شرددهان श्रद्धधान *shraddadhān*, adj. trusting, believing, venerating. *s.*

شردها श्रद्धा *shraddhā*, f. respect, reverence; faith, belief; wish, desire; purity. *shraddhā-jukta* or *shraddhānwit*, believing, faithful. *shraddhā-rahit*, unbelieving. *shraddhā-kṛit*, done with faith. *shraddhā-may* or *shraddhā-wān*, full of faith, believing, trusting. *s.*

شردهال श्रद्धालु *shraddhālu*, believing, faithful; desirous; f. a pregnant woman longing for any thing. *s.*

شرر *sharar*, sparks of fire; malice. *a.*

شرزه *sharza*, raging, fierce, roaring. *p.*

شرط *sharṭ*, f. condition, agreement, stipulation; wager; sign, mark, signal. *sharṭ-bart*, f. advantage, success, profit, succeeding in one's undertaking. *us kām se kuchh sharṭ-bart hū,ī*, did you get any thing by that transaction? *a.*

شرطه *shurṭa*, favourable, agreeable (wind). *p.*

شرطي *sharṭī*, conditional; f. a lottery. *a.*

شرع *shar'*, m. the precepts of *Muḥammad*, law, equity; a high road. *a.*

شرعي *shar'ī*, conformable to the *shar'*, lawful, religious; f. trousers. *a.*

شرعيت *shar'iyat*, law, justice; the laws of the *ḳur,ān*. *a.*

شرف *sharaf*, m. nobility, eminence, rank, excellency. *a.* [dees. *a.*

شرفا *shurafā* (pl. of شريف) nobles, gran-

شرف‌بخش *sharaf-bakhsh*, conferring honour. *a. p.*

شرفياب *sharaf-yāb*, honoured, exalted. *a. p.*

شرق *sharḳ*, m. the east; rising. *a.*

شرقي *sharḳī*, eastern, oriental. *a.*

شرك *shirk*, m. company, society, partnership; paganism, infidelity (*i.e.* ascribing plurality to the Deity). *a.* [sociates. *a.*

شركا *shurakā* (pl. of شريك), partners, asso-

شركت *shirkat*, f. going partners; partnership society. *a.*

شركرا शर्करा *sharkarā*, m. clayed or candied sugar; gravel (the disease). *s.*

شرگال शृगाल *shṛigāl*, m. a jackal. *s.*

شرل शरल *sharal*, upright, honest. *sharaltā*, f. honesty. *s.*

شرم श्रम *shram*, m. fatigue, toil, pain. *s.*

شرم *sharm*, f. bashfulness, modesty, shame. *sharm-nāk*, bashful, modest. *p.*

شرما शर्म्मा *sharmmā*, happy, glad; m. a name common to Brāhmans. *s.* [fatigue. *s.*

شرمارت श्रमार्त्त *shramārtta*, overcome with

شرماشرمي *sharmā-sharmī*, modestly. *p.*

شرمانا *sharmānā*, n. to be abashed, to feel shame, to be ashamed. *p. h.*

شرماؤ *sharm-ā,ū*, شرمزده *sharm-zada*, شرمسار *sharm-sār*, شرمگين *sharm-gīn*, } bashful, ashamed, modest, abashed. *p.*

شرمساري *sharmsārī*, شرمگيني *sharmgīnī*, } f. bashfulness, modesty; shame, disgrace. *p.*

شرمل शरमल्ल *shar-mall*, m. a small bird, considered as a variety of the Salic or Maina (*Turdus gosalica*). *s.*

شرمن श्रमण *shraman*, m. an ascetic, one devoted to religious meditation for the purpose of obtaining final emancipation. *s.*

شرمندگي *sharmandagī*, f. bashfulness, shame. *p.*

شرمنده *sharmanda*, bashful, modest, ashamed. *p.*

شرمندي *sharmindī*, f. the bashful tree, a species of acacia (*Mimosa pudica*). *d.*

شرمي श्रमी *shramī*, wearying, tiring; undergoing fatigue; laborious. *s.*

شرميلا *sharmīlā*, bashful, modest. *p.*

شرن शरण *sharaṇ* (v. *saraṇ*), m. a house, shelter, asylum; a protector. *sharan-ārthī*, unfortunate, suing for protection. *sharan-āgat*, one who comes for protection or refuge. *s.*

شرنکھل शृङ्खल *shṛinkhal*, m. a belt or chain worn round a man's body; a chain or fetter in general. *s.*

شرنگ शृङ्ग *shṛing*, m. a horn, a peak. *shṛingi*, f. a sort of sheat fish (*Silurus singio*). *s.*

شرنگار शृङ्गार *shṛingār*, m. love; copulation; red lead. *s.*

شرنگاري शृङ्गारी *shringārī*, feeling or relating to the passion of love; stained with red lead; m. dress, decoration. *s.*

شرنگي शृङ्गी *shṛingī*, horned, crested, peaked. *s.*

شرنية शरण्य *sharanya*, to be protected, miserable, helpless; m. a protection; a protector; a shelter, a house. *s.*

شرو शिरो *shiro*, in comp. for शिरः *shira*, head. *shiro-ratna*, m. or *shiro-manī*, f. a gem worn in a crest or on the top of the head. *shiro-rog*, m. disease of the head. *s.*

شروال *sharwāl* (for *shalwār*), trousers, [breeches. *p.*

شروت श्रोत *shrot*, m. the ear; the current of a stream. *s.*

شروتا श्रोता *shrotā*, m. a hearer.

شروتوية श्रोतव्य *shrotavya*, adj. to be heard, to be listened to. *s.*

شروري शर्वरी *sharvarī*, f. night; a woman. *s.*

شروشٹھا श्रविष्ठा *shravishṭhā*, f. the twenty-fourth lunar asterism. *s.*

شروع *shurū'*, m. begining, commencement. *shurū'āt*, pl. commencements. *a.*

شرون श्रवण *shrawaṇ* (v. *sravaṇ*), the ear, &c. *shravanendriya*, the organ of hearing, the ear. *s.*

شرونا श्रवणा *shravanā*, f. the twenty-third lunar asterism, represented by three footsteps. *s.*

شره *sharah*, m. desire, appetite, avidity, gluttony. *a.*

شره शिरः *shira*, m. the head. *shira-pīṛā*, f. head-ache. *shira-kapālī*, m. a devotee carrying a human skull as his emblem. *s.*

شري श्री *shrī* (v. *srī*), a name of *Lakshmī*; fortune, prosperity; beauty, lustre; the three objects of life; love, duty, and wealth. *s.*

شريان *shiryān* or *sharyān*, f. an artery. *a.*

شريپھل श्रीफल *shrī-phal*, m. a fruit-tree (*Ægle marmelos*). *s.*

شري جت श्रीयुत *shrī-jut*, } illustrious, fortunate. *s.*
شري جكت श्रीयुक्त *shrī-jukta*, }

شري چكر श्रीचक्र *shrī-chakra*, m. a magical diagram; the circle of the globe or earth. *s.*

شرير शरीर *sharīr*, m. the body of any animated being. *sharīr-bandhak*, m. a hostage. *sharīr-sanskār*, purification of the body by various ceremonies at conception, birth, initiation, death, &c. *s.*

شرير *sharīr*, vicious, wicked. *a.*

شري راگ श्रीराग *shrī-rāg*, m. the third of the musical modes. *s*

شري رس श्रीरस *shrī-ras*, m. turpentine. *s.*

شريري शरीरी *sharīrī*, corporeal, relating to the body. *s.*

شريش शिरीष *shirīsh*, a kind of tree (*Acacia* [*sirisa*). *p.*

شريشٹھ श्रेष्ठ *shreshṭh*, best, most excellent, pre-eminent, oldest, senior. *shreshṭhatā*, f. superiority, excellence. *s.*

شريعت *sharī'at*, f. the laws of *Muḥammad*; law, justice, equity. *a.*

شريف *sharīf*, noble, eminent, excellent, illustrious; a title given to the rulers of Mecca. *a.*

شريفة *sharīfa*, m. a custard-apple (*Annona squamosa*). *a.*

شريك *sharīk*, m. a partner, a friend. *a.*

شريمت श्रीमत *shrīmat* (fem. *shrīmatī*), wealthy, prosperous, illustrious, beautiful. *s.*

شريمكھ श्रीमुख *shrī-mukh*, m. the seventh year of the Indian cycle. *s.*

شريني श्रेणी *shrenī*, f. a line, row, range. *s.*

شري هستني श्रीहस्तिनी *shrī-hastinī*, f. the sunflower (*Heliotropium indicum*). *s.*

شريية श्रेयः *shreya*, m. good fortune, final happiness. *s.*

شست *shast*, f. aim; a large fishing-hook (not used in angling with the hand, but left attached to a strong line which is fastened to the shore); the handle of a bow; a thumb-stall (used to defend the thumb in pulling the string of a bow). *p.*

شست *shist*, f. assessment on land, the balance of dues uncollected. *h.*

شستر शस्त्र *shastr* or *shastra*, m. a weapon in general, a sword, a scimitar. *shastra-dhārī*, possessed of weapons. *shastra-kār*, m. an armourer. *s.*

شسترابهياس शस्त्राभ्यास *shastrābhyās*, m. military exercise. *s.*

شستن *shustan* (r. *shū*) to wash. *p.*

شستني *shustanī*, fit or ready for being washed. *p.*

شست و شو *shust o shū*, m. washing or cleansing. *p.* [*shusta guft-gū*, pure language. *p.*

شستة *shusta*, washed; dressed, prepared.

شسية शस्य *shasya*, m. corn, grain in general. *shasya-bhakshak*, graminivorous. *s.*

شش शुश *shush*, m. the lungs; the noise made by a person setting on a dog (Gil.). *dardi shush*, the peripneumony. *shush-k.*, to set dogs on by calling *shush*. *p. h.*

شش *shash* or *shish*, six. *shash o panj* (sixes and fives), confusion, perplexity. *p.*

شش शिशु *shishu*, m. the young of man or animal; a pupil. *s.*

ششپال शिशुपाल *shishupāl*, m. the sovereign of a country in the central part of India or Chhedi, slain by *Krishṇa*. *s.*

ششتا शिशुता *shishutā*, f. childhood, pupilage. *s.*

ششٹ षष्टि *shashṭi*, sixty. *s.*

ششٹ शिष्ट *shishṭa*, obedient, docile, ordered, disciplined. *shishṭa-sabhā*, f. a council of state, an assembly of chief officers. *shishṭa-samāchār*, m. history of eminent persons. *s.*

ششٹاچار शिष्टाचार *shishṭāchār*, well-behaved, m. (v. *sishṭāchār*) humility, complaisance, good manners, &c. *s.*

ششٹتا शिष्टता *shishṭatā*, f. good behaviour, urbanity, civility, docility. *s.*

ششر शिशिर *shishir*, cold, chilly. *shishir-kāl*, m. the cold season, from Jan. to March. *s.*

ششستهلي शशस्थली *shashasthalī*, f. the Doab, the country between the Ganges and Jumna rivers. *s.*

ششٹھ षष्ठ *shashṭha*, the sixth. *s.*

ششخانه بندوق *shish-khāna bandūk*, } a rifle-gun
ششخانه تفنگ *shish-khāna tufang*, }
(so called from its commonly having six grooves in the barrel. *p.*

ششدر *shash-dar*, m. a cube, a die; adj. wonderful; confounded, perplexed. *p.*

ششك शशक *shashak*, m. a hare or rabbit. *s.*

ششك शिशुक *shishuk*, m. a porpoise, a fish resembling a porpoise. *s.*

ششك शुष्क *shushk*, dry, dried. *shushkatā*, f. dryness. *s*

ششكارنا शुशकारना *shushkārnā*, n. to encourage or stimulate a dog to the chase by the sound *shush*. *h.* [to the chase. *h.*

ششكاري शुशकारी *shushkārī*, f. impelling a dog

ششليكها शशिलेखा *shashi-lekhā*, f. a digit of the moon. *s.*

ششم *shashum*, the sixth. *p.*

ششماهي *shash-māhī*, half-yearly; the half-yearly accounts of a village. *p.*

ششي शशी *shashī*, m. the moon. *s.*

ششيه शिष्य *shishya*, m. a disciple, scholar, pupil. *s.*

شصت *shaṣt*, sixty (properly *shast*). *p.*

شطاح *shaṭṭāḥ*, meretricious, lascivious, obscene *a.*

شطرنج *shaṭranj*, f. chess. *shaṭranj-bāz*, a chess-player. *shaṭranj-bāzī*, f. chess-play. *a.*

شطرنجي *shaṭranjī*, m. a man who excels in chess; f. a kind of spotted carpet. *shaṭranjī-bāf*, m. a carpet-weaver. *a.*

شعار *shi'ār*, m. an under garment; mark, signal, sign; habit, custom; in comp. it denotes distinction, habit, &c., as *karam-shi'ār*, distinguished for generosity. *a.*

شعاري *shi'ārī*, customary, habitual. *a.*

شعاع *shu'ā'*, f. light, splendour, lustre, the rays of the sun, sunshine. *a.*

شعاعي *shu'ā'ī*, radiant, full of rays. *a.*

شعب *shi'b*, a pass through mountains. *a.*

شعبان *sha'bān*, m. the eighth Arabian month: the fourteenth day is a festival (called *barāt*, q. v.): on this day an angel is supposed to examine a record, on which is written the names of the living. *a.*

شعبد *shu'bad*, } sleight of hand, juggling,
شعبده *shu'bada*, } conjuration. *shu'bada-bāz*, a juggler, conjuror. *a.*

شعبه *shu'ba*, a small water-channel, a cleft on a mountain, especially where water stands. *shi'ba*, a path through mountains. *a.*

شعر *shi'r*, m. poetry. *shi'r-khwānī*, f. reading or studying poetry. *a.*

شعرا *shu'arā* (pl. of شاعر), poets. *a.*

شعري *shi'rā*, excelling in poetry; the day-star. *a.*

شعري *shi'rī*, poetic, relating to poetry. *a.*

شعله *shu'la*, m. fame, blaze, light, flash. *shu'la-afshān* or *shu'la-fishān*, dispersing or scattering flames. *shu'la-bār*, raining fire or flames. *shu'la-dār*, *shu'la-zan*, or *shu'la-war*, flaming, resplendent, brilliant. *shu'la-rukh*, having resplendent cheeks. *a.*

شعور *shu'ūr*, m. wisdom, intelligence, knowledge, good management. *a.*

شغال *shaghāl* or *shighāl*, m. a jackal. *shaghāl-khor*, (lit. a jackal eater) a term applied to a gang of freebooters on the Oude frontier. *p.*

شغب *shaghab*, noise, tumult. *p.*

شغل *shughl*, m. occupation, employment. *a.*

شفا *shifā* (for *shifā,a*), f. recovery from sickness, convalescence; medicine, remedy, cure. *shifā khāna* or *dāru-sh-shifā*, a hospital, a lazaretto. *a.*

شفاعت *shafā'at*, f. deprecation, intercession, recommendation, entreaty. *a.*

شفاف *shaffāf*, transparent, clear, very thin. *a.*

شفافي *shaffāfī*, f. transparency, clearness. *a.*

شفت *shafat*, m. the mouth, the lip. *a.*

شفتالو *shaftālū*, m. a peach; the colour of the flower of the peach-tree. *p.*

شفعه *shuf'a*, m. any possession coveted. *ḥakki shuf'a*, right of pre-emption in favour of a person whose possessions adjoin to a land offered for sale. *a.*

شفق *shafaḳ*, f. evening, twilight; the horizon; condolence, sympathy, kindness; fear. *a.*

شفقت *shafḳat* or *shafaḳat*, f. condolence, clemency, compassion, mercy; kindness, affection, commiseration, sympathy. *shafaḳat-nāma*, a letter of condolence. *a.*

شفقي *shafaḳī*, of or resembling the evening, twilight. *a.*

شفيع *shafī'*, advocate, patron; possessing a right of pre-emption founded on contiguity. *shafī'i jār*, the occupant of ground which is simply in the neighbourhood of another estate. *shafī'i khalīṭ*, the occupant of ground in actual contact, or intermixed with another estate (the right of pre-emption is stronger in the latter than in the former case). *a.*

شفيعا *shafī'ā*, m. a kind of Persian character or handwriting. *a.*

شفيق *shafīḳ*, merciful, compassionate; affectionate. *a.*

شق *shaḳḳ* or *shiḳḳ*, m. trouble, labour, suspense; dawn of day; a fissure, crack, rent; a large division of a country. *shaḳḳ honā*, n. to be torn, to be split, rent, &c. *shiḳḳ*, the half, one side; trouble, difficulty; (met.) a brother, a friend. *a.*

شقاقل *shaḳāḳul*, a wild carrot. *p.*

شقاوت *shaḳāvat*, f. misery, disgrace, poverty, villany. *a.*

شقائق *shaḳā,iḳ*, m. a tulip. *shaḳā,iḳu-n-nu'man* or *shaḳā,iḳi nu'māni*, the anemone; (pl. of *shaḳīḳa*, q. v.) cracks, &c. *a.*

شقدار *shiḳḳ-dār*, m. an officer appointed to collect the revenue from a certain division of land; adj. perplexing, uncertain. *a. p.*

شقداري *shiḳḳ-dārī*, f. the business of a *shiḳḳ-dār*, perplexity, uncertainty. *a. p.*

شقوق *shuḳūḳ* (pl. of شق), fissures, crevices, &c. *a.*

شقه *shuḳḳa*, m. a royal order, a letter (especially from a superior). *a.*

شقي *shaḳī*, wretched, miserable; villanous, vicious. *a.*

شقيقه *shaḳīḳa*, m. a crack or fissure; the temples of the head. *a.*

شك *shakk*, m. doubt, suspense, uncertainty. *shikk*, an upper garment. *shukk*, division, schism, difficulty, trouble. *a.*

شك शक *shaka*, m. a sovereign who gives his name to an era, especially applied to Sālivāhana; a particular caste, the followers or descendants of Sālivāhana. *s.*

شك शुक *shuk*, m. a parrot. *s.*

شكار *shikār*, m. hunting, chase; prey, game; plunder; perquisites. *shikār-bāz*, m. a sportsman. *shikār-band*, m. cords, &c. for tying game in, or to be tied to a horse's saddle. *shikār-gāh*, f. place for hunting in. *p.*

شكارچي *shikārchī*, m. a sportsman. *p.*

شكاري *shikārī*, relating to hunting, &c.; m. a fowler, a sportsman. *p.*

شكاف *shikāf*, a fissure, crack, crevice. *p.*

شكافتن *shikāftan* (r. *shikāf*), to split, to break, to rend. *p.*

شكايت *shikāyat*, f. lamentation, complaint, accusation. *a.*

شكت शक्त *shakta*, able, capable, strong. *shaktatā*, f. ability. *shakti*, f. ability, power, strength; the energy or active power of a deity, personified as his wife, such as *Gaurī*, the wife of *Shiva*; *Lakshmi*, the wife of *Vishṇu*. *shakti-mān*, powerful. *shakti-hīn*, powerless. *s.*

شكت शुक्ति *shukti*, f. a pearl oyster; a small shell, a cockle. *s.*

شكتمان शुक्तिमान *shuktimān*, m. one of the seven principal mountains of India. *s.*

شكٹ शकट *shakaṭ*, m. a cart. *s.*

شكٹكا शकटिका *shakaṭikā*, f. a small cart, a toy-cart. *s.*

شكر *shukr*, m. thanks, gratitude. *shukr-guzār*, grateful. *shukr-guzārī*, f. gratitude. *shukri ni'mat*, an acknowledgment of favour. *shakr*, f. *vulva, coitus*. *a.*

شكر *shakar* or *shakkar*, f. sugar. *shakar bhatā* or *shakar-pāra*, m. a kind of sweetmeat made of rice, butter, and sugar. *shakar-khand*, smiling sweetly, speaking gently with a smile of love; charming, gracious, amiable. *shakar-rez*, scattering sugar, mellifluous. *shakar-farosh*, a seller of sugar; (met.) a mistress. *shakar-guftār*, speaking agreeably, eloquent. *shakar-lab*, sugar-lipped. *p.*

شكر शक्र *shakra*, a name of Indra. *shakra-dhanus*, m. Indra's bow, the rainbow. *shakra-bhūbhavā*, f. colocynth (*Cucumis coloquintida*). *shakra-gop*, m. a red insect (*Coccinella*, or lady-bird). *s.*

شكر शुक्र *shukra* or *shukr*, m. the planet Venus; *semen virile*. *shukr-wār*, m. Friday. *s.*

شكرًا *shukran*, thankfully, gratefully. *a.*

شكراشن शक्राशन *shakrāshan*, m. a medicinal plant (*Wrightea antidysenterica*). *s.*

شكران *shukrān*, m. gratitude, thanksgiving. *a.*

شكرانه *shukrāna*, m. a fee paid by plaintiff or defendant on the cause being decided in his favour. *a.*

شكرپاره *shakar-pāra*, m. a kind of sweetmeat (v. under *shakar*). *p.*

شكرستان *shakaristān*, a plantation of sugar, a sugar-chest, sugar-refinery. *p.*

شكرقند *shakar-ḳand*, m. sweet potatoes (*Convolvulus batatas*). *p.*

شكروار शुक्रवार *shukr-wār*, m. Friday. *s.*

شكره *shikra*, m. a hawk, falcon (*Falco*). *p.*

شكري *shakarī*, f. a kind of *phālsā* so called (*Grewia Asiatica*). *p.*

شكرينه *shakarīna*, a kind of confection. *p.*

شكست *shikast*, f. deficiency, loss, defeat; adj. broken, odd, uneven, unpaired. *shikast-khurda*, broken off, interrupted, defeated. *p.*

شكستگي *shikastagī*, f. defeat, &c. *p.*

شكستن *shikastan* (r. *shikan*), to break. *p.*

شكسته *shikasta*, m. broken, dispersed; a kind of writing. *shikasta-bāl*, broken-winged, distressed, wretched. *shikasta-bālī*, f. distress, wretchedness, affliction. *shikasta-pā*, infirm, reduced. *shikasta-ḥāl*, distressed. *shikasta-ḥālī*, f. state of indigence or distress. *shikasta-khāṭir*, distressed in mind, afflicted, offended. *shikasta-dil*, distressed, afflicted. *shikasta-dilī*, f. distress, affliction. *shikasta-wa'da*, (broken engagements) faithless. *p.*

شكشا शिक्षा *shikshā*, f. learning, study. *shikshā-shakti*, f. dexterity, skill. *s.*

شکشت शिक्षित *shikshit*, skilful, clever; disciplined, docile, studied. *s.*

شکشک शिक्षक *shikshak*, a learner, a teacher. *s.*

شکفت *shikift*, m. wonder, astonishment. *p.*

شکفته *shukufta*, flourishing, expanded. *p.*

شك كيت शुककीट *shuk-kīt*, m. a caterpillar. *s.*

شکل *shakl*, f. shape, form, effigy, appearance, semblance, mode. *shakl-navīs*, m. a portrait-painter. *a.*

شکل शुक्ल *shukl* or *shukla*, white. *shuklatā*, f. whiteness. *shukla-paksha*, the light fortnight of the lunar month, from new to full moon. *shukla-kanthak*, m. a kind of gallinule or water-hen. *s.*

شکل शकुल *shakul*, m. a fish. *shakul-gand*, m. a kind of fish, the gilt-head. *shakul-ārbhak*, m. a sort of gilt-head (*Sparus emarginatus*). *s.*

شکم *shikam* or *shikm*, m. the belly; a clause or paragraph in a composition. *shikam-banda* or *shikam-parwar*, an epicure, glutton. *p.*

شکمي *shikamī*, subordinate, dependent, included. *p.*

شکن शकुन *shakun*, m. any lucky or auspicious mark or omen. *shakuni*, m. a bird; one of the astronomical periods called *karans*. *s.*

شکن *shikan*, f. shrinking, shrivelling, constringing; a curl, ply, fold, furrow; (in comp.) it denotes breaking, overthrowing, &c.; as *dushman-shikan*, foe-breaking, overthrowing the enemy. *p.*

شکنا *shaknā*, n. to doubt, to fear, to be perturbed. *d.*

شکنجه *shikanja*, m. the rack or torture; stocks (for the legs); boards in which binders press books; a press; rack, torment, torture. *p.*

شکني *shikanī*, f. (abstract of *shikan*), breaking, &c. *p.*

شکو *shakau*, }
شکوا *shakwā*, } m. complaining, upbraiding. *shakwā-nāma*, a letter of complaint. *a.*

شکوفه *shikūfa* or *shukūfa*, a flower. *p.*

شکوه *shakoh*, *shikoh*, or *shukūh*, f. dignity, state, pomp, grandeur, magnificence. *dārā-shikoh*, in pomp like Darius. *p.*

شکوه *shakwa*, }
شکوي *shakwā*, } complaint, upbraiding. *a.*

شکها शिखा *shikhā*, f. point, top, crest; a lock of hair on the crown of the head; flame. *shikhāwal*, crested, pointed. *s.*

شکهر शिखर *shikhar*, m. the top of a mountain or hill, peak, point, end. *s.*

شکهري शिखरी *shikhrī*, crested, pointed. *s.*

شکهي शिखी *shikhī*, crested, having a lock of hair on the top of the head; m. a peacock. *s.*

شکي *shakkī*, doubtful, perplexing. *shakkī-mizāj*, undetermined, wavering, hesitating. *a.*

شکيب *shakeb* or *shikeb*, patience, endurance. *p.*

شکيبا *shakebā*, patient, long-suffering. *p.*

شکيبائي *shakebā,ī*, f. patience, exerting patience, toleration, long endurance. *p.*

شکيبيدن *shikebīdan*, to be patient. *p.*

شکيتا शक्यता *shakyatā*, f. possibility. *s.*

شکيل *shakīl*, }
شکيلا *shakīlā*, } well-shaped, handsome. *a.*

شکيه शक्य *shakya*, possible, practicable. *s.*

شگار *shagār*, a jackal. *shigār*, any thing eatable. *p.*

شگاف *shigāf*, m. split, rent, fissure, crack, crevice; (in comp.) splitting, rending. *p.*

شگال *shagāl* or *shigāl*, a jackal. *p.*

شگرف *shigarf* or *shigraf*, rare, fine, good, beautiful, excellent, glorious, great. *p.*

شگفت *shigift* or *shikift*, m. wonder, astonishment. *p.*

شگفتگي *shiguftagī*, f. expansion, delight, astonishment. *p.*

شگفتن *shiguftan*, to blossom, expand (a flower). *shigiftan*, to be amazed; also to have patience. *p.*

شگفته *shigufta*, expanded, blown (as a flower). *shigufta honā*, n. to be blown (a flower); to be delighted. *p.*

شگن *shugun*, m. an auspicious omen. *p.*

شگني *shugunī*, }
شگنيا *shuguniyā*, } m. a diviner, a soothsayer, an augur. *p.*

شگوفه *shagūfa*, m. a flower, a bud. *shagūfa lānā*, to bud, to put forth young shoots; to produce something new and wonderful. *p.*

شگون *shugūn*, m. augury, omen. *p.*

شگونيا *shugūniyā*, m. a diviner, an augur. *p.*

شل *shal*, a species of stained leather; one who can take nothing in his hands (from sickness). paralytic, having the hand luxated. *p. a.*

شلا शिला *shilā*, f. a stone, a rock; a flat stone on which condiments are ground with a muller. *s.*

شلاپشپ शिलापुष्प *shilā-pushp*, m. storax or benzoin. *s.*

شلاجت शिलाजतु *shilā-jatu* or शिलाजित *shilā-jit*, m. bitumen, red chalk. *s.*

شلادهات शिलाधातु *shilā-dhātu*, m. chalk, red chalk; an aluminous earth of a white colour. *s.*

شلارس शिलारस *shilā-ras*, m. incense, benjamin or olibanum. *s.*

شلاق *shalāk*, flagellation; *coitus*. *a.*

شلاکا शलाका *shalākā*, f. a thin slip of bamboo, serving, when tipped with sulphur, for a match; a ruler; a fibrous stick used as a brush or pencil. *s.*

شلاگها श्लाघा *shlāghā*, f. praise, flattery. *s.*

شلاگهيه श्लाघ्य *shlāghya*, praiseworthy, venerable. *s.*

شلامي शिलामय *shilā-may*, made of stone. *s.*

شلاولكا शिलावल्का *shilā-valkā*, f. a medicinal substance said to be of cooling and lithonthriptic properties, commonly called Silābāk; a sort of lichen or moss. *s.*

شلايين *shalāyīn*, disgustingly importunate. *p.*

شلبه शलभ *shalabh*, m. a grasshopper, a locust. *s.*

شلبين शलबीन *shalbīn*, vice in a horse. *h.*

شلپ शिल्प *shilp*, m. any manual or mechanical art. *shilp-kār* or *shilpī*, an artisan. *shilp-karm*, m. handicraft. *shilp-vidyā*, f. art, manual skill. *shilpi-shāstra*, m. a treatise on works of art. *shilpi-shālā*, f. a workshop. *s*

شلپني शिल्पिनी *shilpinī*, f. a drug commonly called *Lahānasipi*, described as sweet and cooling, and bearing seeds of tonic and restorative properties. *s.*

شلپي शिल्पी *shilpī*, an artist or artisan; belonging to a mechanical profession. *s.*

شلتاق *shiltāḳ*, a dispute with one upon false grounds; litigation, tumult. *p.*

شلتاقي *shiltāḳī*, quarrelsome, litigious. *p.*

شلخ *shalkh*, a round (of musketry, &c.), a discharge: *sperma viri*; *vulva*. *a.*

شلڈي *shilḍī* (v. *siṛī*). mad, insane. *d.*

شلغم *shalgham*, m. a turnip. *p.*

شلق *shalaḳ*, } f. a round, a discharge (of
شلك *shalak*, } fire-arms); a blow; *coitus*. *a.*

شلك शल्लक *shallak*, m. a plant (*Bignonia indica*). *s.*

شلكي शल्लकी *shallakī*, f. the gum olibanum tree (*Boswellia thurifera*). *shallakī-drav*, m. incense, olibanum. *s.*

شلوار *shilwār* or *shalwār*, m. trousers. *p.*

شلوك श्लोक *shlok*, m. a verse, a stanza. *s.*

شلوكا शलूका *shalūkā*, m. a child's bib. *h.*

شليتا शलीता *shalītā*, } m. a canvas sack, &c.
شليته शलीतः *shalīta*, } in which baggage is fastened previously to being loaded on cattle. *h.*

شليشما श्लेष्मा *shleshmā*, m. the phlegmatic humour in the body. *s.*

شليودهار शल्योद्धार *shalyoddhār*, m. extraction of foreign substances from the body. *s.*

شليهشاستر शल्यशास्त्र *shalya-shāstra*, m. that part of surgery which treats of the extraction of extraneous substances lodged in the body. *s.*

شم शम *sham*, m. quiet of mind, stoicism, indifference; abstract meditation on God; final happiness. *s.*

شما *shumā* (pl. of *tū*, sec. pers. pron.), you. *p.*

شماتت *shamātat*, f. rejoicing at the calamity or misfortunes of another. *a.*

شمار *shumār*, m. counting, computing, numbering, reckoning; used (in comp.) as *sitāra-shumār* star-counting, watchful. *p.*

شماري *shumārī*, f. counting, &c.; a rosary. *p.*

شمال *shamāl* or *shimāl*, m. the north; the north wind; the left hand. *shimāl-rū*, facing the north. *shimāl-numā*, the mariner's compass. *a.*

شمالي *shimālī*, northern. *a.*

شمامه *shamāma*, a perfumed pastile. *a.*

شمائل *shamā,il* (pl. of شمال), excellences, virtues, talents, abilities; northerly winds, or regions of the north. *a.*

شمبالي शम्बाली *shambālī*, f. the chaste tree (*Vitex negundo*). *h.*

شمبوك शम्बूक *shambūk*, m. a bivalve shell; a conch shell; a snail. *s.*

شمبه *shamba*, a day of the week; Saturday. *p.*

شمبهپر शुम्भपुर *shumbha-pur*, m. a city and district, perhaps the modern Sambhalpūr in the district of Gondwānā. *s.*

شمت शमित *shamit*, pacified, quiet, calm. *s.*

شمر *shimar*, the name of one of *Yazīd's* generals, who slew *Husain* in the plains of *Karbalā*, and hence the word now signifies vile, infamous, &c. *a.*

شمردگي *shumurdagī*, counting, enumeration. *p.*

شمردن *shumurdan* (r. *shumār*), to count, reckon. *p.*

شمرده *shumurda*, counted, numbered. *p.*

شمس *shams*, m. the sun. *shamsu-d-dīn*, the sun of the true faith. *shamsu-d-daula*, the sun of the state (men's names). *a.* [rosary. *s.*

شمسه *shamsa*, m. little tassels affixed to a

شمسي *shamsī*, solar. *shamsī ḳamarī*, (solar and lunar); a perquisite taken by the officers of government, being the difference between the pay for a lunar and solar month; a monthly period of three or four days, during which the female attendants in the women's apartments have leave of absence. *a.*

شمشاد *shamshād*, m. the box-tree (*Meninsk*); (met.) applied to the form of a mistress. *p.*

شمشان श्मशान *shmashān*, m. a cemetery. *shmashān-wāsī*, a goblin, a sprite abiding in cemeteries. *s.*

شمشير *shamsher* or *shimshīr*, f. a scimitar, sword. *shamsher-bāz*, a sword-player, a gladiator. *shamsher-bāzī*, f. the use of the sword. *shamsher-bahādur* (ironically), a useless, worthless fellow. *shamsher-zan*, a swordsman. *p.*

شمع *sham'*, f. a lamp, a candle; wax. *sham'-dān*, m. a candlestick. *sham'-sāz*, a chandler, a candle-maker. *sham'-rukh* or *sham'-rū*, ruddy, radiant, resplendent. *a.*

شمعي *sham'ī*, of or relating to a candle, waxen. *sham'ī-rang*, flame-colour. *a.*

شمله *shamla*, m. the end of a turban or *kamar-band*, sometimes tucked into the folds and sometimes left flying loose; a kind of shawl for tying round the waist. *a.*

شمن शमन *shaman*, m. killing animals for sacrifice, immolation; mental tranquillity, calmness. *s.*

شمن *shaman*, an idol or image; idolatry; an idol-temple; an idolater. *p.*

شمه *shamma*, m. an atom, a particle, a little; perfume, odour; habit, custom. *a.*

شمي शमी *shamī*, tranquil, pacific; f. a legume or pod; a tree (*Acacia suma*); a shrub (*Serratula anthelmintica*). *s.*

شميانه *shamiyāna*, a kind of canopy. *p.*

شمي پتري शमीपत्री *shamī-patrī*, f. a sort of sensitive plant (*Mimosa pudica*). *s.*

شمير शमीर *shamīr*, m. a small variety of the *Mimosa suma*. *s.*

شميم *shamīm*, } odour, perfume. *a.*
شميمه *shamīma*, }

شن शण *shan*, m. hemp (*Cannabis sativa*); Bengal *San*, a plant from which a kind of hemp is prepared (*Crotolaria juncea, &c.*). *s.*

شن शनि *shani*, m. the planet Saturn. *shani-wār*, m. Saturday. *s.*

شنا *shinā* or *shanā*, swimming. *p.*

شناخت *shinākht*, f. knowledge, understanding. *p.*

شناختن *shinākhtan* (r. *shinās*), to know, to recognise. *p.*

شناس *shinās*, (in comp.) knowing, intelligent, intimate with; as *ḥaḳḳ-shinās*, knowing what is right; upright, conscientious. *p.*

شناسا *shināsā*, one who knows. *p.*

شناسائي *shināsā,ī*, f. acquaintance, knowledge. *p.*

شناسي *shināsī*, f. (in comp.) knowing. *p.*

شناور *shināwar*, a swimmer. *p.*

شناوري *shināwarī*, f. act of swimming. *p.*

شناه *shināh* (v. *shinā*), swimming. *p.*

شنبالي *shambālī*, f. the chaste tree (*Vitex negundo*). *d.*

شنبه *shamba*, m. Saturday. *p.*

شنپريه शनिप्रिय *shani-priya*, m. the emerald or sapphire. *s.*

شنٹهي शुण्ठी *shunṭhī*, f. dry ginger. *s.*

شنڈ शुण्ड *shunḍ*, m. an elephant's trunk. *s.*

شنڈ शण्ड *shanḍ*, m. a bull at liberty. *s.*

شنسپا शिंशपा *shinspā*, a tree (*Dalbergia sisu*). *s.*

شن سوتر शणसूत्र *shan-sūtra*, m. the fibre or flax of the sun-plant, or string made from it; cordage, twine. *s.*

شنعت *shun'at*, baseness, brutality, turpitude, crime. *a.*

شنقار *shunḳār*, m. a falcon. *p.*

شنك शङ्कु *shanku*, m. the trunk of a lopped tree; a javelin, a pin, a stake; the gnomon of a dial; the scate fish (*Raia sankur*). *s.*

شنكا शङ्का *shankā*, f. fear, apprehension doubt. *shankā-may*, fearful. *shankā-hīn*, free from doubt or fear. *s.*

شنكت शङ्कित *shankit*, alarmed; doubtful. *s.*

شنكر शङ्कर *shankar*, a name of *Mahādeva*; a celebrated teacher of the Vedanta philosophy. *s.*

شنكرا शङ्करा *shankarā*, m. name of a musical mode or *rāginī*. *s.*

شنكرابهرن शङ्कराभरण *shankarābharan*, m. name of a musical mode. *s.*

شنكراچارج *shankarāchārj* (for *shankarāchārya*), name of a Hindū ascetic, celebrated for having eradicated the sect of *Jains*. *s.*

شنكراچاري *shankarāchārī*, the followers of *Shankarāchārj*, q. v. *s.*

شنكري *shankarī*, a name of *Pārvatī*. *s.*

شنكوچ शङ्कोच *shankoch*, m. a scate fish. *s.*

شنكه शङ्ख *shankh*, m. a conch, a shell; a large number, ten or a hundred billions. *s.*

شنكهني शङ्खिनी *shankhinī*, f. a description of woman, described as tall with long hair, neither thin nor stout, of irascible disposition and strong passions. *s.*

شنگ *shang*, amorously playful, beautiful, elegant, handsome; a thief, a robber. *p.*

شنگرف *shangarf*, m. cinnabar, vermilion. *p.*

شنو *shinau*, } hearing, a hearer. *shanū*, the
شنوا *shinawā*, } cypress, wild plum-tree. *p.*

شنوار शनिवार *shani-wār*, m. Saturday. *s.*

شنيد *shinīd*, hearing, listening. *p.*

شنيدن *shinīdan* (r. *shinau*), to hear, listen. *p.*

شنيده *shinīda*, heard, perceived. *p.*

شنير शनीर *shanīr*, m. a rock or small island in the midst of the river Sone; an island enclosed by the branches of the Sarju where it falls into the Ganges. *s.*

شنيشچر शनैश्चर *shanaishchar*, m. the planet Saturn. *s.*

شني شني शनैःशनै *shanai-shanai*, slowly, tardily. *s.*

شنيع *shanī'*, base, abominable, shocking, adulterous. *a.*

شنيعه *shanī'a*, turpitude, abomination. *a.*

شنيه शून्य *shunya*, m. empty, void; m. a cypher. *s.*

شو *sho* or *shū*, (in comp.) washing. *shau*, a husband. *p.*

شو शव *shav*, m. a dead body, a corpse. *s.*

شو शिव *shiv* or *shiva*, m. the Deity in the character of the destroyer. *s.*

شوا शिवा *shivā*, f. the goddess *Durgā*, the consort of *Shiva*. *s.*

شوارع *shawārī* (pl. of شارع), high roads. *a.*

شواس श्वास *shwās*, m. breath, breathing. *s.*

شوال *shawwāl*, m. the tenth month of the *Muhammadan* year, on the first day of which the festival of *Bairām* or *'id* is celebrated, being the first day after the *Musalmān* Lent, and on this day it is customary to make presents, &c. *a.*

شوالا शिवाला *shivālā*, } m. a temple of
شوالي शिवालय *shivālay*, } *Shiva.* *s.*

شوان श्वान *shwān*, m. a dog. *shwānā*, f. a bitch. *s.*

شوب *shob*, m. washing. *p.*

شوبها शोभा *shobhā*, f. light, lustre, splendour, beauty. *s.*

شوبهانجن शोभाञ्जन *shobhānjan*, m. a tree, the *Sajinā* or *Sahajnā* (*Hyperanthera morunga*) of which the blossoms and leaves are esculent and the root used as horse-radish, besides various medicinal uses. *s.*

شوبهت शोभित *shobhit*, beautified, decorated. *s.*

شوبهمان शोभमान *shobhamān*, fair, splendid, radiant. *s.*

شوبهن शोभन *shobhan*, beautiful, handsome, auspicious; m. the fifth Yog. *s.*

شوپري शिवपुरी *shiv-purī*, f. the city of Benares. *s.*

شوتر श्वित्र *shwitra*, m. whiteness of the skin, vitiligo. *shwitrī*, affected with vitiligo. *s.*

شوتهه शोथ *shoth*, m. swelling. *shotha-ghna*, removing swellings. *shotha-ghnī*, f. hog-weed (*Boerhavia diffusa*). *s.*

شوچ शौच *shauch*, m. purification, ablution; purity, cleanness. *s.*

شوچت शोचित *shochit*, sorrowful, afflicted. *s.*

شوخ *shokh*, mischievous, playful, saucy, brisk, cheerful, sly, humorous, wanton; strong, insolent, presumptuous. *shokh-chashm* or *dīda*, of a wanton look, lewd, impudent. *p.*

شوخي *shokhi*, f. mischief, humour, sauciness, &c., coquetry. *p.*

شودر शूद्र *shūdra*, m. a man of the fourth or servile caste. *s.*

شودري शूद्री *shūdrī*, f. the wife of a *Shūdra*. *s.*

شودهات शिवधातु *shiv-dhātu*, m. the milk stone, opal or chalcedony. *s.*

شودهك शोधक *shodhak*, what cleanses, purifies; (in arith.) the subtrahend. *s.*

شودهن शोधन *shodhan*, m. cleaning, purifying, correcting; (in arith.) subtraction; payment, acquittance; green vitriol. *s.*

شور शूर *shūr*, m. a hero; a boar. *s.*

شور *shor*, m. cry, noise, outcry; adj salt, very bitter. *shor-angez*, exciting tumults. *shor-bakht*, unfortunate, wretched, infamous. *shor-bor*, very wet. *shor-zamīn*, f. salsuginous ground, barren land. *shor-pusht*, quarrelsome, noisy. *shor-shār*, *shor-shūrr*, *shor-sharāba* or *shor-shaghab*, m. noise, tumult, disturbance, bustle, clamour. *p.*

شور शवर *shavar*, m. a barbarian inhabiting the mountainous districts of India, and wearing the feathers of the peacock, &c., as decorations. *s.*

شورا *shūrā*, agreement, convention, mixture. *a.*

شوراتر शिवरात्रि *shiva-rātri*, m. a festival held on the fourteenth of the dark fortnight in the month of Phalguna (Feb.-March) (v. *siva-rātri*). *s.*

شوربا *shorbā*, m. broth, soup. *p.*

شورپ शूर्प *shūrp*, m. a winnowing basket. *s.*

شورتا शूरता *shūratā*, f. heroism, prowess. *s.*

شورش *shorish*, f. tumult, insurrection, confusion. *p.*

شورن शूरण *shūran*, m. an esculent root (*Arum campanulatum*); a plant (*Bignonia indica*). *s.*

شوره *shora*, marshy, barren ground; m. nitre, saltpetre. *shora-gar*, m. a manufacturer of saltpetre. *shore kā tezāb* or *'araḳi shora*, nitric acid. *p.*

شوريت *shoriyat*, saline quality. *p.*

شوريدن *shorīdan*, to be distracted, &c. *p.*

شوريده *shorīda*, disturbed, mad, desperately in love; faint, dejected. *shorīda-ḥāl*, mad, &c. *shorīda-khāṭir*, dejected, melancholy. *p.*

شوريه शौर्य *shaurya*, m. valour, heroism. *s.*

شوسادهن शवसाधन *shav-sādhan*, m. a mystical ceremony performed with a dead body. *s.*

شوسر श्वशुर *shwasur*, m. a father-in-law, a wife's or husband's father. *s.*

شوشرو श्वश्रू *shwashrū*, f. a mother-in-law. *s.*

شوشه *shosha*, m. an ingot; chips, rubbish, filth; a particle, a part; a lock of hair left on the top of the head. *p.*

شوق *shauḳ*, m. desire, inclination, love; gaiety, cheerfulness; curiosity. *shauḳ-zauḳ*, m. pleasure, delight, gratification. *a.*

شوقي *shauḳī*, loving, cheerful, desirous. *a.*

شوقين *shauḳīn*, intent upon, desirous; lascivious; m. a fancier, amateur. *a.*

شوقيه *shauḳiya*, m. the part of an epistle which follows the complimental address. *a.*

شوك शोक *shok*, m. sorrow, grief. *shok-bhang*, m. dissipating sorrow. *s.*

شوكت *shaukat* f. state, dignity, magnificence, majesty. *shaukatu-l-ba'īr*, a thistle. *a.*

شوكاپٹ शूकापुट्ट *shūkā-puṭṭ*, m. a gem, perhaps amber. *s.*

شوكارت शोकार्त्त *shokārtta*, pained, affected by sorrow. *s.*

شوكر शूकर *shūkar*, m. a hog. *s.*

شوكشم शूक्ष्म *shūkshma*, minute, small, subtile. *s.*

شوك كيٹ शूककीट *shūk-kīṭ*, m. a caterpillar. *s.*

شوكه शोष *shokh*, m. drying; intumescence pulmonary consumption. *s.*

شوكهن शोषण *shokhan*, m. suction, sucking, drying up. *s.*

شول शूल *shūl*, m. a pike, a dart; a sharp pain, cholic, gout, &c.; an astrological *Yog*. *shūl-shatru*, m. the castor-oil plant (*Ricinus communis*). *shūl-hat*, m. assafœtida. *s.*

شولا शोला *sholā*, m. *Æschynomene paludosa* (*Roxb.*), the wood of which, being very light and spongy, is used by fishermen for floating their nets: a variety of toys, such as artificial birds and flowers, are made of it: garlands of these flowers are used in marriage ceremonies: when charred it answers the purpose of tinder. *h.*

شولا *shūlā*, m. a brick-kiln. *d.*

شوله *shola*, m. a dish consisting of rice and pulse boiled together, and given to sick persons. *p.*

شولي शूली *shūlī*, suffering sharp pain, having the cholic, &c. *s.*

شوم *shūm*, black; unfortunate, unhappy, disgraceful, vile; miser, niggard *shūm-ṭab'*, ill-tempered. *shūm-ḳadam*, unlucky, bad (omen). *shūm-mizāj*, stingy. *a.*

شوماري *shomārī*, lazy, indolent; also laziness, indolence. *d.*

شومڑا *shūmṛā*, m. } ugly, miserly, avaricious. *a.*
شومڑي *shūmṛī*, f. }

شومڑي *shūmṛī*, f. a kind of fried food. *h.*

شومي *shūmī*, } f. stinginess, niggardliness. *a.*
شوميت *shūmiyat*, }

شون शोण *shon*, m. the Sone river, which falls into the Ganges above Patna; a flower (*Bignonia indica*); a red sort of sugar-cane. *s.*

شونت शोणित *shonit*, red, crimson, purple; m. blood, saffron. *s.*

شونتوپل शोणितोपल *shonitopal*, m. a ruby. *s.*

شونڈك शौण्डिक *shaunḍik*, m. a distiller and vender of spirituous liquors. *s.*

شونڈكي शौण्डिकी *shaunḍikī*, f. a female keeper of a tavern or dram-shop. *s.*

شون رتن शोणरत्न *shon-ratna*, m. a ruby. *s.*

شونيه शून्य *shūnya*, empty, void; m. the air, sky, ether; a vacuum; a cypher. *shūnyatā*, f. vacuity, vanity, unreality. *shūnya-vādī*, m. an atheist, a Bauddha. *s.*

شوهر *shauhar*, m. a husband. *p.*

شوي *shoī*, (in comp.) washing. *p.*

شويت श्वेत *shwet*, white; m. white (the colour); the planet Venus; the sixth of the fabulous mountains encircling the globe; one of the minor *dwīpas*, or divisions of the world, *shwet-dwīp*, called also *chandra-dwīp*. *shwet-dhātu*, m. chalk; the milk-stone, opal or chalcedony. *shwet-sarp*, m. a tree (*Tapia cratæva*); a white snake. *shwet-hastī*, m. a white elephant. *s.*

شويتارك श्वेतार्क *shwetārk*, m. gigantic swallow-wort (*Asclepias gigantea*) with white flowers. *s.*

شه *shah*, m. a king; check (at chess); in comp means great, large, excelling, &c. *shah-zor*, stout, gallant, strong, brave, heroic. *shah-zorī*, f. valour, heroism. *shah-sawār*, a good rider, a jockey, a horse-breaker. *shah-māt*, check-mate. *p.*

شهاب *shihāb* or *shahāb*, m. bright stars, falling stars; twinkling, shining; red; flame. *a.*

شهاد *shahād*, m. evidences, witnesses. *a.*

شهادت *shahādat*, f. evidence, testimony; martyrdom. *a.*

شهامت *shahāmat*, f. generosity, bravery. *a.*

شهانه *shahāna*, royal, princely (clothes, &c.). *p.*

شهبالا *shah-bālā*, m. the companion of a bridegroom. *p. h.*

شهبندر *shah-bandar*, m. a royal or free port; the principal officer at a sea-port. *p.*

سهبندري *shah-bandarī*, f. the office or situation of *shah-bandar*. *p.*

شهپر *shah-par*, m. strongest feather in a bird's wing. *p.*

شهتره *shahtara*, m. *Oldenlandia biflora*. *p.*

شهتوت *shahtūt*, a mulberry. *p.*

شهتير *shahtīr*, m. a beam. *p.*

شهچال *shah-chāl*, f. a term used at chess when the king only can move. *p. h.*

شهد *shahd*, m. honey (cor. *shahat*, *sahat*, or *shat*). *shahad-makkhī*, f. a bee. *p.*

شهدا *shuhadā* (pl. of شهيد), martyrs. *a.*

شهدا शुहदा *shuhdā*, m. a rake, prodigal, debauchee, blackguard, scoundrel, vagabond. *shuhdā-shikasta*, ruined and wretched. *h.*

شهداپن शुहदापन *shuhdā-pan*, raking, rakishness, debauchery, dissoluteness. *h.*

شهر *shahr*, m. a lunar month. *a.*

شهر *shahr*, m. a city. *shahr-āshob*, a disturber of the peace of a city, a mistress; a kind of verses; *shahr-panāh*, f. wall or entrenchments round a town. *shahr-pūrā*, m. suburbs. *shahr-khabrā*, m. a quidnunc, an intelligencer. *shahr-dār*, m. a birdcatcher, a huntsman. *shahr-gharīb*, m. a stranger, a traveller. *p.*

شهرت *shuhrat*, f. renown, fame; divulging, celebrating. *a.*

شهرخ *shah-rukh*, } m. a term used at chess.
شهرخا *shah-rukhā*, } According to Hyde it simply denotes a check to the king with a castle or rook (as we call it). I have recently examined this subject, however, and I find that it means a divergent check on the part of the knight, or any inferior piece, at once attacking the king and the castle (which latter is the best piece on the Oriental board); such a *coup* generally leads to victory. *p.*

شهرگ *shahrag*, f. the great vein in the arm. *p.*

شهرگشت *shahr-gasht*, a marriage procession; a patrol. *p.*

شهروا *shah-rawā*, (lit.) "king's currency," depreciated money, made of leather. *p.*

شهرة *shuhra*, m. fame, rumour, report, reputation. *shuhra,e āfāq*, renowned. *a.*

شهري *shahrī*, m. a citizen; adj. of or belonging to the city. *p.*

شهريار *shahryār*, m. a prince, a king. *p.*

شهرياري *shahryārī*, f. royalty, sovereignty. *p.*

شهريت *shahriyat*, f. peopling, cultivating. *p.*

شهزاده *shahzāda*, a prince. *p.*

شهزادي *shahzādī*, a princess. *p.*

شهلا *shahlā*, having dark grey eyes, with a shade of red. *a.*

شهناءي *shahnā,ī*, a clarion, a hautboy. *p.*

شهنشاه *shahanshāh*, } a great king, an emperor. *p.*
شهنشه *shahanshah*, }

شهنشاهي *shahanshāhī*, f. sovereignty, empire. *p.*

شهوار *shah-wār*, worthy of a king, regal; the most precious kind of pearl. *p.*

شهوت *shahwat*, f. concupiscence, lust, desire, appetite. *shahwat-angez*, lust-exciting, lascivious. *shahwat-parast*, addicted to lasciviousness. *a.*

شهوتي *shahwatī*, lascivious, lustful. *a.*

شهود *shuhūd* (pl. of شاهد), evidences, testimonies; adj. manifested. *a.*

شهور *shuhūr* (pl. of شهر), months. *a.*

شهي *shahī*, f. royalty; adj. royal, kingly. *p.*

شهيد *shahīd*, killed; (sub.) a martyr (any *Muḥammadan* killed in battle is so called). *shahīd honā*, n. to be killed; (met.) to fall desperately in love. *a.*

شي *shai*, f. a thing, an object. *a.*

شياد *shaiyād*, an impostor, a cheat. *a.*

شياطين *shayāṭīn* (pl. of شيطان), devils, demons. *a.*

شيالو शयालु *shayālu*, sleepy, slothful, sluggish. *s.*

شيالك श्यालक *shyālah*, m. a wife's brother. *s.*

شيالكي श्यालकी *shyālkī*, f. a wife's sister. *s.*

شيام श्याम *shyām* or *shyāma*, black or dark blue; m. a sacred fig-tree at Prayāg or Allahabad. *shyāmatā*, f. blackness. *shyām-bhās*, black as jet. *s.*

شياما श्यामा *shyāmā*, f. a small singing bird with black plumage, commonly called *shāmā*. *s.*

شياماك श्यामाक *shyāmāk*, m. a kind of grain, called also *sāṅwāṅ* (*Panicum frumentaceum* or *colonum*). *s.*

شيامل श्यामल *shyāmal*, black or dark blue. *s.*

سيب *sheb*, m. a descent, declivity; adv. under, below. *p.*

شيپهالكا शीफालिका *shīphālikā*, f. a flower (*Nyctanthes arbor-tristis*). *s.*

شيت शीत *shīt*, cold, chilly; m. cold, numbness, frigidity; cold weather, or the rainy, dewy, and cold season. *shītatā*, f. coldness. *shīt-kāl*, m. cold season. *shīt-har*, removing cold. *s.*

شيتارت शीतार्त्त *shītārtta*, chilled, suffering from cold. *s.*

شيتاشمن शीताश्मन *shītāshman*, m. the moon-gem, crystal. *s.*

شيتانس शीतांशु *shītānsu*, m. camphor. *s.*

شيتل शीतल *shītal*, cool, cold, benumbed; m. or *shītaltā*, f. cold, coldness. *s.*

شيتهليه शैथिल्य *shaithilya*, m looseness, laxity, flaccidity. *s.*

شيتيه शैत्य *shaitya*, m. cold, coldness. *s.*

شيخ *shaikh* (vulg. *shekh*), m. a venerable old man; a chief, a prelate; a title taken by the descendants of the prophet, and given to those who become proselytes to *Muḥammadanism*. *a.*

شيخن پور *shekhan-pūr*, m. a town inhabited by descendants of the prophet. *a. h.*

شيخوخت *shaikhūkhat*, } f. old age. *a.*
شيخوخيت *shaikhūkhiyat*, }

شيخي *shekhī* or *shaikhī*, f. boasting, bragging, domineering. *a.*

شيد *shaid*, deceit, hypocrisy. *shed* or *shīd*, the sun; clear, shining. *p.*

شيدا *shaidā*, mad; deeply in love. *p.*

شير *sher*, m. a tiger, a lion. *sheri ābī*, m. an alligator. *sheri ḳālī*, (the effigy of a tiger) a person only fit to be looked at, a braggart. *sheri gardūn*, m. the sun; the sign Leo. *h.*

شير *shīr*, m. milk. *shīr-khurda*, a suckling. *shīr-dār*, milk, giving much milk. *shīr-shakar*, a kind of silk cloth; affection. *shīr-garm*, milk-warm, lukewarm. *shīr-māl*, f. bread made with milk. *shīr-mast*, a fine plump suckling. *p.*

شيراز *shīrāz*, a city in the south of Persia, celebrated as the birthplace of the poets *Sa'dī* and *Ḥāfiẓ*. *p*

شيرازه *shīrāza*, m. the stitching of the back of a book; sewing buttonholes. *shīrāza-bandī*, f. the binding of a book. *p.*

شيرازي *shīrāzī*, of or relating to Shīrāz, a native of that place. *p.*

شيرانه *sherāna*, fierce as a tiger or lion. *p.*

شيرخشت *shīr-khisht*, a species of manna. *p.*

شيرش शीर्ष *shīrsha*, m. the head. *shīrsha-chhed*, m. decapitating. *s.*

شيرن शीर्ण *shīrnā*, thin, small; wasted, decayed. *s.*

شيرنتا शीर्णता *shīrnatā*, f. emaciation, withering. *s.*

شيرني *shernī*, f. a lioness, a tigress. *p. h.*

شيرني *shīrnī*, f. (cor. of *shīrīnī*) sweetmeats, [illegible] memory of saints, &c. *p.*

شيروا *shīrwā*, m. broth, soup. *d.*

شيره *shīra*, m. syrup, juice of fruit, new wine, must. *shīra,e rewand*, gamboge. *shīra,e* the sap of existence essence of life. *p.*

شيري *shīrī*, f. part of a ship; adj. milky. *p.*

شيري *sherī*, f. boldness, fierceness; adj. of or relating to a tiger or lion. *p.*

شيرين *shīrīn*, sweet; pleasant, gentle, affable; f. beauty, splendour. *shīrīn-zabān*, eloquent, sweet-spoken, affable. *shīrīn-zabānī*, f. eloquence, affability. *shīrīn-lab'*, of gentle manners or mild disposition. *p.*

شيريني *shīrīnī*, f. sweetness; eloquence. *p.*

شيش शेष *shesh*, m. remainder, leavings, rest, balance; end; the serpent *Shesh-nāg*. *shesh-rātri*, f. the last watch of the night. *shesh-kāl*, the last term, time of death. *s.*

شيش *shīsh*, m. lead (in Urdū *sīsā*). *d.*

شيشاوستها शेषावस्था *sheshāvasthā*, f. the last state or condition of life. *s.*

شيش‌شاعي शेषशाई *sheṣha-shā,ī* (*seṣh-sā,ī*), he who sleeps on the serpent *Sheṣha*, *Vishṇu*. *s.*

شيشم शीशम *shīsham*, f. a kind of wood (*Dalbergia sissoo*, *Roxb.*), the Indian rosewood. *s.*

شيش‌ناگ शेषनाग *sheṣh-nāg*, m. the serpent *Sheṣha*, king of the lower regions (v. *seṣh-nāg*). *s.*

شيشه *shīsha*, m. glass, a bottle, a glass. *shīsha-bāshā*, very delicate, tender. *shīsha-gar*, a glass-maker. *shīsha-garī*, f. glass-making. *shīsha-maḥall*, a glazed palace or house, an apartment fitted up with mirrors. *p.*

شيشي *shīshī*, f. a small glass, a phial. *p.*

شيطان *shaiṭān*, m. the devil, Satan. *shaiṭān kī ānt*, the devil's guts, or any thing long and winding (as a lane). *h.*

شيطاني *shaiṭānī*, devilish, diabolical. *a.*

شيطنت *shaiṭanat* f. devil's tricks, wickedness. *a.*

شيعه *shī'a*, m. a follower of the sect of *'Alī*, a sectary (see Sale's Koran, Prelim. Disc. sect. 8). *a.*

شيعي *shiya'ī*, of or belonging to the sect of *'Alī*, a Shiyaite. *a.*

شيفته *shefta*, distracted, mad, enamoured. *p.*

شيكر शीकर *shīkar*, m. thin rain or rain driven by wind. *s.*

شيكهر शेखर *shekhar*, m. a garland of flowers worn on the crown of the head; a crest. *s.*

شيگهر शीघ्र *shīghra* or *shīghar*, expeditious, quick, hasty, fast; adv. soon, quick, speedily; m. parallax. *shīghratā*, f. quickness. *shīghra-gāmī*, swift-going. *s.*

شيل शील *shīl*, m. nature, quality, disposition, good conduct or disposition, observance of the laws and morals; adj. well-disposed, well-behaved. *s.*

شيل शैल [illegible], [illegible]ous, rocky, mountaineer; m. a mountain; bitumen, storax; a sort of collyrium. *s.*

شيلان *shīlān*, a tablecloth. *p.*

شيلم *shīlam*, birdlime, cement. *d.*

شيلوان शीलवान *shīl wān*, of good or amiable disposition, well-conducted. *s.*

شين शयन *shayan*, m. sleep; a bed, a couch; copulation. *s.*

شين *shīn*, a kind of large tray. *d.*

شين *shain*, disgrace, shame. *shīn*, a miser. *shaiyin*, shameful. *a.*

شيو शैव *shaiv*, m. a worshipper of *Shiva*. *s.*

شيوال शैवाल *shaivāl*, m. an aquatic plant (*Vallisneria octandra*). *s.*

شيون शेवन *shewan* or *shīwan*, grief lamentation. *s.*

شيوه *shewa*, m. business, trade, profession; manner, habit, custom; amorous looks. *shewa-dār*, an artist, a tradesman; expert, skilful, clever. *p.*

شيه *shiya*, } the neighing of a horse. *p.*
شيهه *shīha*, }

شيين श्येन *shyen*, m. a hawk. *shyenī*, f. the female hawk. *s.*

ص

ص called *ṣād i muhmala* or *ṣādi ghair mankūṭa*, the fourteenth letter of the Arabic alphabet, the seventeenth Persian, and the twentieth Hindūstānī. Strictly speaking, this letter is purely Arabian or Semitic, but in a few Persian words it has, in modern times, been substituted for the original *sīn*, to distinguish such words from others of a different signification, as *ṣad* originally *sad*, one hundred, and *shaṣt* originally *shast*, sixty (to prevent their being confounded with *sad*, a wall, and *shast*, an aim): it has no corresponding letter in the Sanskrit alphabet, and in Persia and India its pronunciation is hardly distinguishable from that of *sīn*; but among the Arabs its sound is stronger than that of the latter, and with a mixture of *w*. In reckoning by *abjad* its value is ninety. It is used as an abbreviation for *ṣafar*, the name of the second month in the Arabian kalendar. Also, being the initial of the title *ṣuba-dār*, q. v., it is usually affixed by him as a cypher to zamīndārī grants, as a mark of authentication. *a.*

صابر *ṣābir*, patient, enduring. *a.*

صابري *ṣābirī*, f. patience, endurance. *a.*

صابن *ṣābun*, } m. soap; hence Gr. Σάπων. *a.*
صابون *ṣābūn*, }

صابوني *ṣābūnī*, m. a soapmaker; f. a mixture of almonds, honey, and oil of sesame, a species of sweetmeat. *a. p.*

صاحب *ṣāḥib*, m. a lord, master, companion; adj. possessed of, endowed with, &c. *ṣāḥibi ikhtiyār*, possessed of free election, or option. *ṣāḥibi akhlāk*, possessed of good morals or of good manners. *ṣāḥibi tāj*, possessed of the crown, a king. *ṣāḥibi takht*, possessor of the throne, a king. *ṣāḥibi tamkanat*, possessed of dignity: it is also used in composition without the ṣafat, as ṣāḥib-jamāl, beautiful. ṣāḥib-khāna, master of the house. ṣāḥib-dil or ṣāḥib-naẓar, intelligent, a man of worth and sanctity. ṣāḥib-kamāl, perfect, excellent. ṣāḥibi murauwat, (in law) a gentlemen (lit. man of politeness). a.

صاحبان ṣāḥibān (Pers. pl. of صاحب), masters, gentlemen, &c. ṣāḥibān i 'ālī shān, the gentlemen of high dignity, generally applied to the Honourable E. I. Company, or their European servants in India. a.

صاحب‌قران ṣāḥib-ḳirān, m. an invincible hero, a great emperor; lit. lord of the auspicious conjunction, i.e. one who was born under a peculiarly favourable aspect of the planets, as was the case with Tīmūr or Taimūr (vulgarly called Tamerlane), who is accordingly called ṣāḥib-ḳirān by his biographers. One of the emperors of Delhī, Shāh-jahān had also the title of ṣāḥib-ḳirānī ṣānī, the second lord of the conjunction. a.

صاحب‌قراني ṣāḥib-ḳirānī, the state or dignity [of a ṣāḥib-ḳirān. a.

صاحبه ṣāḥiba, f. a lady, mistress. a.

صاحبي ṣāḥibī, f. rule, command, lordship; a kind of grape so called. ṣāḥibī-k., a. to lord, to rule, to govern. a.

صادر ṣādir, produced, derived, happened, arrived, passed, issued. ṣādir-honā or -shudan, n. to be produced, derived, emerged, issued, &c. a.

صادق ṣādiḳ, true, just, sincere. ṣādiḳu-l-ḳaul, speaking truth, sincere of speech. a.

صادقي ṣādiḳī, f. sincerity, truthfulness. a.

صاع ṣā', the bat for playing at chaugān, or horse shinty; a dry measure of four mudds, each mudd being equal to one and one-third raṭl: according to Wilson it is a grain measure of about seven to eight pounds. a.

صاعقه ṣā'iḳa, lightning, a thunderbolt. a.

صاف ṣāf, clean, clear, pure, candid, innocent. ṣāf-dil, of a pure heart. ṣāf-dilī, f. purity of heart or mind. a.

صافي ṣāfī, f. clearness, purity; sincerity, candour; a filter, or cloth through which drinks, medicines, &c. are strained; a dishclout or cloth for wiping with; adj. pure, clean, &c. (v. ṣāf). ṣāfī-nāma or ṣāfī-khaṭṭ, m. a general release, discharge from an obligation (v. rāẓī-nāma under rāẓī). a.

صالح ṣāliḥ, good, apt, fit, proper; m. a man of probity and honour; a sedate steady person (opposite to enthusiast); name of a patriarch. a.

صالحاً ṣāliḥan, justly, uprightly. a.

صالحه ṣāliḥa, f. (of صالح), virtuous, chaste. a.

صامت ṣāmit, silent, inanimate, irrational. a.

صانع ṣāni', m. creator, framer, artificer. a.

صائب ṣā,ib, right, straight; hitting the mark. a.

صائم ṣā,im, one who fasts; (adjectively) thirsty. ṣā,imu-d-dahr, one who fasts always. a.

صبا ṣabā, f. a gentle breeze; an easterly breeze, a morning breeze. a.

صباح ṣabāḥ, f. the morning, dawn of day; name of a bird. ṣabāḥu-l-khair or ṣabāḥ-kum bi-l-khair (morning salutation), good day, good morning to you. 'alā-ṣ-ṣabāḥ, on or in the morning. a.

صباحت ṣabāḥat, f. beauty, gracefulness. a.

صباغ ṣabbāgh, m a dyer, one whose business is to dye. a.

صبان ṣabān or ṣubān, to-morrow. d.

صبائي ṣabā,ī, of or relating to a gentle breeze. a.

صبح ṣubḥ, f. morning, dawn. ṣubḥ-khezā or -kheziyā, a set of thieves who rise early in the morning and steal before people are awake. ṣubḥ-dam, dawn of day. ṣubḥi ṣādiḳ, dawn of day. ṣubḥi kāẓib, the false dawn, just before daybreak. ṣubḥ-gāh or -gahān, the early dawn. ṣubḥ-gāhī, of or relating to the early dawn. a.

صبحاً ṣubḥan, in the morning, at dawn. a.

صبر ṣabr, f. patience, endurance. ṣabr-k., a. to wait. ṣabir, a species of aloes. a.

صبوح ṣabūḥ, the dawn of day; a morning draught; wine which is drunk in the morning. a.

صبوحي ṣabūḥī, a wine-bottle, a morning draught. ṣabūḥī-kash, one who takes his morning draught, or as the Scotch have it still more literally "his morn." a.

صبور ṣabūr, patient, mild, enduring. a.

صبوره ṣabūra, m. (v. سبورا sabūrā). a.

صبوري ṣabūrī, f. patience, forbearance. a.

صبي ṣabī, m. a boy, a youth, a minor. a.

صبيان ṣubyān or ṣibyān, pl. boys, youths. a.

صبيح ṣabīḥ, beautiful; of a fine complexion. a.

صبيه ṣabiya, f. a damsel, a girl, child; a daughter. a.

صحاب ṣiḥāb (pl. of صاحب), companions. a.

صحابت ṣaḥābat, f. society, companionship; the companions of Muḥammad. a.

صحاري ṣaḥārā or ṣaḥārī (pl. of صحرا), deserts. a.

صحاف ṣaḥḥāf, m. a bookbinder, a bookseller, a librarian. a.

صحائف ṣaḥā,if (pl. of صحيفه ṣaḥīfa), pages, leaves, books. a.

صحب ṣaḥb, } (pl. of صاحب), companions,
صحبان ṣuḥbān, } friends, associates. a.

صحبت ṣuḥbat, f. companionship, society; an assembly, a fair; coition; discourse. ṣuḥbat-barār, an acquaintance. ṣuḥbat-barārī, being acquainted, acquaintance. ṣuḥbat-dārī, f. keeping company with associating, acquaintance. a.

صحبتي ṣuḥbatī, a companion, a comrade. a.

صحت ṣiḥḥat, f. health, entireness, perfection, integrity, accuracy. ṣiḥḥat-khāna, m. a necessary. a.

صحرا ṣaḥrā, m. a desert, a plain. ṣaḥrā-nishīn, m. a hermit living in the desert. ṣaḥrā-naward or ṣaḥrā-gard, wandering in the desert. a.

صحرائي ṣaḥrā,ī, } wild, desert; relating to
صحرائيا ṣaḥrā,iyā, } the desert. a.

صحره ṣaḥra (for صحرا), a desert, &c. a.

صحن *ṣaḥn*, m. a court-yard, an area; a large cup or goblet; a small dish or plate, a kind of cloth. *a.*

صحنك *ṣaḥnak*, f. (v. *sahnak*) a plate, dish. *a.*

صحيح *ṣaḥīḥ*, accurate, just, pure, perfect, entire, sound, certain. *ṣaḥīḥ-k.*, a. to sign, to correct, to rectify. *a.* [letter. *a.*

صحيفه *ṣaḥīfa*, m. a book, a leaf, a page, a

صخره *ṣakhra*, name of a jinn or demon; a rock. *a.*

صد *ṣad*, hundred. *ṣad-pā* or *ṣad-pāya*, a centipede. *ṣad-manī*, being a hundred *mans* (vulgarly "maunds") in weight. *p.*

صدا *ṣadā*, f. sound, tone, echo, voice, noise. *a.*

صدارت *ṣadārat*, f. the office of prime minister or of chief justice, *a*

صداع *ṣudā'* m. vertigo, megrim, headache. *a.*

صداق *ṣadāḳ*, a marriage settlement made by the husband on the wife. *a.*

صداقت *ṣadāḳat*, f. sincerity, friendship. *a.*

صدبرگ *ṣad-barg*, m. (lit. a hundred leaves), a kind of flower (*Rosa glandulifera, Roxb.*). *p.*

صددر *ṣad-dar*, the hundred gates, the title of one of the books of the Pārsīs. *p.*

صدر *ṣadr*, f. the breast; exaltation, pre-eminence; chief, supreme; government. *ṣadri a'ẓam*, the prime minister. *ṣadri ṣudūr*, the chief judge, the lord chancellor. *ṣadr dīwānī 'adālat*, the supreme court of justice, the Company's chief civil court in India. *ṣadr fauj-dārī 'adālat*, the chief criminal court (v. Wilson's Glossary). *a.*

صدرنج *ṣad-ranj*, (lit. the hundred vexations) the game of chess (so called). *p.*

صدرنشين *sadr-nishīn*, one who holds the first dignity, or sits in the highest place; a prime minister, president of an assembly. *a.p.* [pearl. *a.*

صدف *ṣadaf*, f. a shell, a pearl, mother of

صدق *ṣidḳ*, m. truth, veracity, sincerity. *a.*

صدقه *sadḳa*, m. alms; propitiatory offerings; voluntary alms in contradistinction to those enjoined by law. *ṣadḳe-jānā* or *-honā*, n. to become a sacrifice for the welfare, &c. of another; to become entirely devoted to another. *ṣadḳe-k.* to sacrifice one's self for the salvation of another. *a.*

صدمه *ṣadma*, m. a blow, a stroke of fortune, adversity, collision, an adventure. *a.*

صدوار *ṣad-wār*, an aggregate or company of a hundred. *p.* [&c. *a.*

صدور *ṣudūr*, (pl of صدر) breasts; ministers,

صدوق *ṣadūḳ*, } true, faithful, a sincere friend.
صديق *ṣadīḳ*, } *ṣiddīḳ*, a faithful witness of the truth, an epithet applied to Joseph, &c. *a.*

صدي *ṣadī*, a century, a centenary. *p.*

صراحت *ṣarāḥat*, f. being pure or genuine; palpableness; pureness; adj, pure, unadulterated. *a.*

صراحتًا *ṣarāḥatan*, publicly, evidently clearly. *a.*

صراحي *ṣurāḥī*, a goblet, a jug, a long-necked flask. *ṣurāḥī-bardār*, the carrier of the flask or goblet. *ṣurāḥī-dār*, shaped in the form of a *ṣurāḥī* (a pearl). *a.*

صراط *ṣirāṭ*, f. a road; the bridge over the bottomless pit, across which good Moslems expect to pass into Paradise. *ṣirāṭu-l-mustaḳīm*, the right way, i. e. the *Muḥammadan* religion. *ṣurāṭ*, a long sword. *a.*

صراف *ṣarrāf*, m. a banker, a money-changer, an officer employed to ascertain the value of different currencies, vulgarly called a *shroff*; hence, according to Gladwin, the Anglo-Indian term *shroffing*, which signifies "the examining, sorting, and weighing the various kinds of rupīs, to fix each to its distinct species, discard the refuse, and settle the *bāṭṭa* upon all, according to the price of the day, in order to establish the value in standard or sicca rupīs." *a.*

صرافه *ṣarrāfa*, m. the place where bankers transact their business, a bank, an exchange. *a.*

صرافي *ṣarrāfī*, f. banking, money-changing. *a.*

صرصر *ṣarṣar*, f. a cold boisterous wind. *a.*

صرع *ṣar'*, f. the epilepsy, the falling sickness; a mode, a species. *a.* [mixed. *a.*

صرف *ṣirf*, merely, only, alone, pure, un-

صرف *ṣarf*, changed or expended; m. expenditure; the orthographical and etymological parts of grammar; dexterity; increase, gain; changing, turning, converting; vicissitudes of fortune. *ṣarf o naḥw*, f. etymology and syntax, grammar in general. *ṣarf-honā* or *-shudan*, to be squandered or expended. *a.*

صرفه *ṣarfa* or *ṣurfa*, f. expense; profusion, profit, surplus, redundancy, addition; the twelfth mansion of the moon, a star in the tail of Leo. *a.*

صرفي *ṣarfī*, m. an etymologist, a grammarian; adj. grammatical. *a.* [silver). *a.*

صره *ṣurra*, m. a purse (filled with gold or

صريح *ṣarīḥ*, apparent, palpable, evident. *a.*

صريحًا *ṣarīḥan*, clearly, openly, plainly. *a.*

صرير *ṣarīr*, grating, scratching sound of a pen, or of a door on rusty hinges. *a.*

صعب *ṣa'b*, hard, difficult, arduous, rough, troublesome, disagreeable, disobedient, stubborn, perverse. *a.*

صعوبت *ṣu'ūbat*, f. difficulty, trouble. *a.*

صعود *ṣu'ūd*, m. ascent, surmounting. *a.*

صعوه *ṣa'wa*, a kind of sparrow with a red head, a sort of waterfowl. *a.*

صغار *ṣighār* (pl. of صغير), small. *ṣighār o kibār*, the small and great, the populace at large. *a*

صغر *ṣighar*, smallness, minuteness. *a.*

صغرا *ṣugharā* (pl. of صغير), the small, the inferiors. *a.* [of a syllogism. *a.*

صغرىٰ *ṣughrā*, less, least; m. the minor term

صغير *ṣaghīr*, slender, inferior, junior. *ṣaghīr-sinn*, of tender age. *a.*

صغيري *ṣaghīrī*, f. infancy, childhood. *a.*

صف *ṣaff*, f. series, order, line, rank, file, row, a mat. *ṣaff-ārā*, a marshaller of troops. *ṣaff-ārā,ī*, the act of marshalling troops. *ṣaff-bāndhnā*, to draw up in ranks. *ṣaffi-jang*, f. the ranks of war, the field of battle. *ṣaff-ṣaff*, in military order, in battle-array. *ṣaff-dar*, a rank-breaker, a valiant warrior. *ṣaff-dari jang*, the disperser of the ranks of war, a title frequently given to a successful commander. *a.*

صفا *ṣafā*, f. purity, cleanness; pleasure, content. *ṣafāan ṣāf* (smack smooth), without a trace or vestige. *a.*

صفات *ṣifāt* (pl. of صفت), good qualities. *a.*

صفاتي *ṣifātī*, artificial, acquired (applied to qualities not innate). *a.*

صفاك *ṣaffāk* (for سفاك *saffāk*, q. v.). *a.*

صفاهان *ṣifāhān*, Ispahan in Persia. *p.*

صفاهاني *ṣifāhānī*, a native of, or relating to Ispahan. *parda,e ṣifāhānī*, a species of melody peculiar to Ispahan, said to resemble the Scottish melodies. *p.*

صفاءي *ṣafā,ī*, f. purity, cleanness. *ṣafā,ī batānī*, to reject a petition without ceremony, to refuse flatly. *a.*

صفت *ṣifat*, f. praise; quality, attribute; manner, description; a noun adjective; like, resembling. *a.*

صفحه *ṣafḥa*, m. a page, surface, face. *a.*

صفر *ṣafar* or *ṣafaru-l-muẓaffar*, m. the second month of the *Muḥammadan* year. On the 20th day of this month is held the festival of *Sar-o-tan*, in commemoration of the junction of the head and body of *Ḥusain*. The 28th and the last days of this month are reckoned unfortunate; the former on account of *Ḥasan's* being poisoned by his wife; the latter, because destructive vegetables are supposed to be produced on that day. *ṣifr*, m. a cipher. *a.*

صفرا *ṣafrā*, m. bile, yellow. *a.*

صفراوي *ṣafrāwī*, } bilious. *ṣafrā,ī-mizāj*, of
صفراي *ṣafrā,ī*, } a bilious constitution. *a.*

صفوت *ṣafwat*, purity, cleanness. *a.*

صفوف *ṣufūf* (pl. of صف), ranks, lines. *a.*

صفهان *ṣifahān* (for *Ispahān* or *Isfahān*, q. v.), a city of Persia, formerly the capital of that empire. *p.*

صفهاني *ṣifahānī*, a native of *Sifahān* or *Ispahān*. *p.*

صفي *ṣafī*, pure, just, righteous; the name of a Persian dynasty that reigned from 1503 to 1736, founded by *Shāh Ismā'īl ṣafī*, and overturned by *Nādir Shāh*. *a.*

صفير *ṣafīr*, f. sound, whistling, a hissing noise, blowing, singing (as a bird); a sapphire. *a.*

صفيل *ṣafīl* (for *faṣīl*), an entrenchment, fortification. *d.*

صلا *ṣalā*, voice, invitation, information, annunciation. *ṣilā* (for *ṣila*, q. v.), conjunction, &c. *a.*

صلابت *ṣalābat*, f. firmness, hardness, severity; majesty, awe, dignity. *a.*

صلات *ṣalāt*, prayer, especially one of the five stated prayers enjoined on good Musalmāns in the course of the twenty-four hours; the first chapter of the *ḳur,ān*. *a.*

صلاح *ṣalāḥ*, f. peace, concord, treaty; rectitude, integrity; advice, counsel; adj. advisable. *a.*

صلاحيت *ṣalāḥiyat*, f. virtue, chastity, integrity. *a.*

صلب *ṣalb*, f. crucifixion; burning; teasing, fretting, vexing. *ṣulb*, the loins, offspring. *a.*

صلبي *ṣulbī*, descended from, begotten by. *a.*

صلح *ṣulḥ*, f. peace, reconciliation, treaty, truce, concord. *ṣulḥi ikhtiyārī*, a voluntary reconciliation. *ṣulḥi ḳahrī*, compulsory composition. *ṣulḥi kull*, f. perfect reconciliation, definitive treaty. *ṣulḥ-nāma*, a treaty of peace. *a.*

صلحا *ṣulaḥā* (pl. of صالح), the pious, the just; men of wisdom or counsel. *a.*

صلحه *ṣulḥa* (also *ṣulḥat*), m. friendship. *a.*

صلعم *ṣal'am*, a contraction (added often to the name of *Muḥammad*), formed from the abbreviation of the words *ṣallą-l-lāh 'alaihi wa sallam*, the blessing and peace of God be with him. *a.*

صلوات *ṣalwāt* (pl. of صلوة), prayers, benedictions. *a.*

صلوة *ṣalāt*, f. prayer, benediction; compassion, or mercy of God. *a.*

صله *ṣila*, m. conjunction, connection; a present. *ṣila,e riḥm*, intercourse with relatives within the forbidden degree. *ḥarfi ṣila*, a conjunctive particle. *a.*

صلي *ṣallą* (3rd pers. pret. used precatively), may he bless, or may he be gracious; as, *ṣallą-l-lāh 'alaihi* or *'alaihim*, may God be gracious unto him or them. *a.*

صليب *ṣalīb*, hard, three-cornered; m. a crucifix, a cross. *a.*

صم *ṣumm* (pl. of اصم), deaf. *ṣummun bukm*, deaf and dumb. *a.*

صمت *ṣamt*, f. silence. *ṣimmat*, adverse fortune. *ṣamut*, silent. *a.*

صمد *ṣamad*, a lord, a master of a family; the Most High; perpetual, eternal. *a.*

صمدان *ṣamadān*, }
صمداني *ṣamadānī*, } everlasting, eternal, divine. *a.*
صمدي *ṣamadī*, }

صمصام *ṣamṣām*, f. a sharp sword. *a.*

صمغ *ṣamagh*, gum. *ṣamaghi ḥamāmā*, gum ammoniac. *ṣamaghi 'arabī*, gum arabic. *a.*

صموت *ṣamūt*, silent. *a.*

صميم *ṣamīm*, } pure, unmixed, sincere. *a.*
صميمي *ṣamīmī*, }

صناديد *ṣanādīd* (pl. of صنديد), kings, princes, chiefs, &c. *a.*

صناديق *ṣanādīḳ* (pl. of صندوق), boxes, trunks. *a.*

صناع *ṣanā'* or *ṣannā'*, industrious, dexterous, very skilful. *ṣunnā'* (pl. of *ṣāni'*), artificers, workmen. *a.*

صناعت *ṣinā'at*, f. art, trade, profession. *a.*

صنائع *ṣanā,i'*, arts, contrivances; miracles. *a.*

صندل *ṣandal*, m. sandal-wood. *a.*

صندلاسا *ṣandalāsā*, صندلوتا *ṣandalauṭā*, } m. a flat stone on which sandal-wood is ground. *h. a.*

صندلاني *ṣandalānī*, a dealer in sandal-wood. *a.*

صندلي *ṣandalī*, of the colour of sandal-wood; made of sandal-wood; f. a kind of chair; name of a city of Kashmīr; m. a sort of eunuch; one whose parts of generation have been entirely extracted. *a.*

صندوق *ṣandūḳ*, f. and m. a box, a trunk, a chest. *ṣandūḳi turbat*, a sarcophagus. *a.*

صندوقچه *ṣandūḳ-cha*, m. صندوقچي *ṣandūḳchī*, f. } a small box, a casket. *a.*

صندوقه *ṣandūḳa*, a coffer, a casket, a bier. *a.*

صندوقي *ṣandūḳī*, like a box (applied to a tomb, or to the scabbard of a sword made in that form). *a.*

صنع *ṣan'* or *ṣun'*, creation, work, action, preparation. *ṣin'*, clever-handed. *a.*

صنعت *ṣan'at*, f. profession, trade, art; mystery, miracle. *san'at-gar*, an artist. *a.*

صنف *ṣinf*, species, kind, sort. *a.*

صنم *ṣanam*, m. an idol; a mistress, lover, sweetheart; the name of a game among children: one says *ṣanam ā,ī*, the idol or sweetheart is come; and asks whence? in which dress is she clothed? what does she eat? &c.; with whatever letter the answer to the first question begins, those to the others must begin with the same, otherwise the person failing is condemned, by way of penalty, to imitate the voice of some animal, as a cock or ass, &c. *a.*

صنم خانه *ṣanam-ḵẖāna*, صنم كده *ṣanam-kada*, } m. an idol temple. *a. p.*

صنوبر *ṣanaubar*, m. fir, pine, any cone-bearing tree. *a.*

صواب *ṣawāb*, m. (hitting the mark) rectitude; a virtuous action, a happy issue, success. *a.*

صوب *ṣaub*, m. side, tract, way. *a.*

صوبجات *ṣūbajāt* (pl. of صوبه), provinces. *a.*

صوبه *ṣūba*, m. a province, one of the large divisions of the Mogul empire, such as Bengal, Bahar, &c.; a governor (term peculiar to Hindūstān). *a.*

صوبه‌دار *ṣūba-dār*, m. the chief (or lieutenant) of a province; a military officer among Indian troops, whose rank corresponds to that of captain. *a. p.*

صوبه‌داري *ṣūba-dārī*, the office of lieutenant of a province; viceroyalty. *ṣūba-dārī abwāb*, taxes imposed by the *ṣūba-dār* in addition to the fixed rates. *ṣūba-dārī parwāna*, an order issued by a *ṣūba-dārī*. *a. p.*

صوت *ṣaut*, f. sound, voice, clamour, noise, calling for help, shout, shriek of distress. *a.*

صور *ṣūr*, a trumpet, a clarion. *ṣiwar* or *ṣuwar* (pl. of *ṣurāt*), figures, forms. *a.*

صورت *ṣūrat*, f. form, face, countenance, appearance, portrait; manner; condition, state. *dar ṣūrat* or *dar ṣūrate-ki*, in case, provided that. *ṣūrat-āshnā*, an acquaintance. *ṣūrati ḥāl*, f. a written statement of facts. *ṣūrat-ḥarām*, plausible, whose appearance promises much more than events will justify specious, superficial, fair without and foul within. *ṣūrat nāma*, a written account of an estate or transaction. *a.*

صورتاً *ṣūratan*, apparently, extrinsically. *a.*

صورتبند *ṣūrat-band*, صورتگر *ṣūrat-gar* } m. a painter or statuary, a maker of effigies. *ṣūrat-bandī* or *ṣūrat-garī*, f. the art or profession of painting or statuary. *a. p.*

صوري *ṣūrī*, exterior, apparent. *a.*

صوف *ṣūf*, m. wool, and applied to silk, thread, and cotton. *a.*

صوفي *ṣūfī*, wise, pious, intelligent; m. a *ṣūfī*, or one of a peculiar sect of Musalmān devotees (so called), who are said to be freethinkers or pantheists on matters of religion: outwardly they conform to the vulgar creed, but are looked upon with great suspicion by the more orthodox. *a.*

صوفيان *ṣūfiyān*, pl. religious brethren of the sect of *ṣūfīs*. *a.*

صولت *ṣaulat*, f. violence, fury, impetuosity. *a.*

صوم *ṣaum*, m. fasting, a fast; one who fasts; a Christian church; silent. *ṣaum ṣalāt*, f. fasting and prayer. *a.*

صومع *ṣauma'*, صومعه *ṣauma'a*, } m. a monastery, a cloister, a cell, a hermitage. *a.*

صهبا *ṣahbā*, a kind of red wine. *a.*

صهيل *ṣahīl*, the neigh (of a horse). *a.*

صياد *ṣaiyād*, m. a hunter, a fowler. *a.*

صيادي *ṣaiyādī*, f. hunting, fowling, shooting, &c. *a.*

صيام *ṣiyām*, fasting. *shahri ṣiyām*, the month of fasting, *i.e.* *ramaẓān*. *a.*

صيان *ṣiyān*, m. keeping, preserving, laying [up. *a.*

صيانت *ṣiyānat*, f. defence, guarding, keeping, preserving, support. *a.*

صيت *ṣīt*, fame, renown, celebrity. *a.*

صيد *ṣaid*, f. game, prey, animal pursued, fished for, &c. *ṣaid-andāz*, or *-bāz*, or *-gar*, a sportsman. *ṣaid-andāzī*, the pursuit of game, the chase, &c. *a.*

صيرف *ṣairaf*, صيرفي *ṣairafī*, } m. a banker or money-changer; an examiner of coins, jewels, and precious stones; a deceiver, a cheat (v. *ṣarrāf*). *a.*

صيغ *ṣayyigh*, m. a liar, an inventor of fictions. *a.*

صيغه *ṣīgha*, m. a mould (for casting metal); a word declinable and derivative; the mood of a verb, conjugation, derivation; trade, profession; a form of words used in marriage ceremonies and other occasions, such as the adoption of children, &c. *a.*

صيف *ṣaif*, summer, especially May and June. *ṣaiyif*, the summer rains. *a.*

صيقل *ṣaiḳal*, m. scouring, polishing, clearing, furbishing; the polishing instrument. *ṣaiḳal-gar*, a polisher, an armourer. *a.*

صيقلي *ṣaiḳalī*, scoured, polished. *a.*

صين *ṣīn* (for *chīn*), the empire of China. *a.*

صيني *ṣīnī*, relating to China, Chinese; a fine kind of porcelain. *a.*

صيهون *ṣaihūn*, Mount Sion. *a.*

ض

ض *ẓād*, called *ẓādi mu'jama* or *ẓādi manḳūṭa*, the fifteenth letter of the Arabic alphabet, the eighteenth Persian, and the twenty-first in Hindūstānī: this letter is purely Arabic, and is said to have a mixed sound of *d*, *th*, and *w*, only to be acquired from natives of Arabia Proper; but in Persia and India its sound is the same as that of *ze*: in reckoning by *abjad* it stands for 800.

ضابط *ẓābiṭ*, m. a governor, ruler, master, possessor. *ẓābiṭu-l-kull*, omnipotent (God), ruler of all. *a.*

ضابطگي *ẓābiṭagī*, being according to law or rule. *a. p.*

ضابطه *ẓābiṭa*, m. canon, ordinance, law, rule, regulation; a list, a catalogue. *a.*

ضاحك *ẓāḥik*, satirist, mocker; name of a poet. *a.*

ضارب *ẓārib*, beating, bruising, striking, stamping, coining. *a.*

ضال *ẓāll*, straying; m. a prevaricator. *a.*

ضامن *ẓāmin*, m. a surety, a sponsor, security, bail. *ḥāẓir-ẓāmin*, security for personal appearance. *māl-ẓāmin*, security for the discharge of a debt. *a.*

ضامن‌دار *ẓāmin-dār*, one who has bail or security, a person bailed. *a. p.*

ضامني *ẓāminī*, f. surety, bail. *ẓāminī ḳabūl karnā*, to admit as bail. *a.*

ضائع *ẓā,i'*, lost, destroyed, perished, fruitless, abortive. *ẓā,i' karnā*, to lose, to destroy, to apply, (labour, &c.) to no purpose. *a.*

ضبط *ẓabṭ*, m. government, direction, discipline; confiscation of property; regulation, check, control. *ẓabṭ karnā*, to confiscate, sequestrate, to take possession, to rule over, to watch, to preserve, to restrain, to control. *ẓabṭ o rabṭ*, rules and regulations. *a.*

ضبطي *ẓabṭī*, m. a confiscator; f. confiscation, sequestration; adj. seized, confiscated. *a.*

ضجور *ẓajūr*, melancholy, peevish, fretful. *a.*

ضحا *ẓuḥā*, ضحي *ẓuḥā*, } m. breakfast-time, that part of the day, about half-way between sunrise and meridian (*i. e.* the brightest part of the day). *'īdu-ẓ-ẓuḥā*, f. name of a festival celebrated on the 10th of *ẕi-ḥijj*, when an animal is sacrificed in commemoration of Abraham's sacrifice of his son *Ismā'īl*. According to the *Sunnī* sect it was *Ismā'īl* and not *Isaac* that Abraham was about to sacrifice. Some *Shī'as* maintain, like us, that it was *Isaac*. *a*

ضحاك *ẓaḥḥāk*, name of a Persian king famed for his cruelty and oppression.

ضخامت *ẓaḵhāmat*, f. being great, thick, and bulky. *h.*

ضد *ẓidd*, f. contrary, opposite. *ẓidd-k.*, to oppose, to spite, to contradict. *a.*

ضدي *ẓiddī*, perverse, contradictory, naughty and unmanageable (as a child). *a.*

ضدين *ẓiddain* (dual of ضدّ), opposites, any two things that are totally opposed to each other, as east and west, &c. *a.*

ضر *ẓarr*, m. loss, damage, injury, distress. *a.*

ضراب *ẓirāb*, m. fighting, fencing, conquering; *coiens*. *ẓarrāb*, a coiner, mint-master. *a.*

ضرب *ẓarb*, f. a blow; violence; multiplication in arithmetic; mode (of speech), form, species; striking; stamping, coining money, struck. *ẓarbu-l-maṡal*, f. a proverb. *dāru-ẓ-ẓarb*, f. the mint office. *ẓarb-zabānī*, the multiplication table. *a.*

ضربات *ẓarbāt* (pl. of ضربه), blows. *a.*

ضربه *ẓarba* or *ẓarbat*, a blow, one single blow. *a.*

ضرر *ẓarar*, m. injury, damage, detriment, loss, ruin; affliction, anguish. *a.*

ضروب *ẓurūb* (pl. of ضرب, q. v.), modes of speech, &c. *a.*

ضرور *ẓarūr*, necessary, expedient, unavoidable. *pur-ẓarūr*, highly necessary. *jā,e ẓarūr* or *jā-ẓarūr*, a place of necessity, a privy. *jā-ẓarūr phirnā*, to pay a visit to the necessary. *a.*

ضرورت *ẓarūrat*, f. force, violence, compulsion, constraint; want, indigence, necessity. *bi-ẓ-ẓarūrat*, necessarily, by compulsion. *a.*

ضرورتاً *ẓarūratan*, necessarily, per force. *a.*

ضروري *ẓarūrī*, necessary, a thing needful. *a.*

ضروريات *ẓarūriyāt* (pl. of *ẓarūrī*), things needful, necessaries, requisites. *a.*

ضرير *ẓarīr*, blind (made so, not born so). *a.*

ضعف *ẓa'f* or *ẓu'f*, m. infirmity, weakness, imbecility of mind or body. *a.*

ضعفا *ẓu'afā* (pl. of ضعيف), weak persons. *a.*

ضعيف *ẓa'īf*, weak, infirm, impotent, emaciated, feeble, frail, old. *ẓa'īf-ḥāl*, distressed in circumstances. *a.*

ضعيفي *ẓa'īfī*, weakness, exhaustion. *a.*

ضل *ẓall*, ضلال *ẓalāl*, ضلالت *ẓalālat*, } m. an error, fault, vice, ruin, perdition. *a.*

ضلع *ẓil'* or *ẓila'*, f. a side, part; a district, a division (in newspaper phraseology called a zillah); a column (in the page of a book); (in Hindūstān) the art of speaking with double meaning, so that the chain of both senses be uninterrupted through the discourse. *a.*

ضلعدار *ẓila'-dār*, m. an officer who has the charge of the revenues of a *ẓila'*. *ẓila'-dārī*, f. the office or situation of *ẓila'-dār*. *a. p.*

ضلل *ẓalal*, m. an error, crime. *a.*

ضم *ẓamm*, m. contraction, conjunction, incorporation; the mark or primitive vowel *pesh*, or short *u*, like our *u* in *push*. *a.*

ضماد *ẓamād*, f. a bandage or fillet for binding the head or a wound; a plaster, or embrocation. *a.*

ضمار *ẓimār*, (in law) any thing disputed or uncertain, as debts, &c. *a.*

ضمان *ẓamān*, ضمانت *ẓamānat*, } m. the being security or surety for another. *ẓamānat-nāma*, a deed of suretiship. *a.*

ضماناً *ẓamānan*, by way of security. *a.*

ضمانت *ẓamānat*, m. ضمانه *ẓamāna*, f. } suretiship, a bail-bond. *a.*

ضمائر *ẓamā,ir* (pl. of ضمير), personal pronouns, &c. *a.*

ضمن *ẓimn*, m. the cover of a letter; the contents, any thing comprehended, contained, or inserted, subject, an idea, conception; suretiship, an obligation; aid, favour. *a.*

ضمناً *ẓimnan*, comprehensively, by the bye. *a.*

ضمه *ẓamma*, the short vowel *u*; the whiskers. *a.*

ضمير *ẓamīr*, f. the mind, heart, thought, reflection, sense, conscience, conception, idea, comprehension; the personal pronoun. *a.*

ضميران *ẓamīrān*, sweet basil. *p.*

ضميري *ẓamīrī*, pronominal; of or relating to the mind. *a.*

ضميمه *ẓamīma*, an addition, augmentation. *a.*

ضمين *ẓamīn*, m. a sponsor a surety. *a.*

ضوا *ẓiwā*, ضيا *ẓiyā*, } f. light, splendour, brilliancy, resplendence. *a.*

ضوابط *ẓawābiṭ* (pl. of ضابطه), laws, rules, &c. *a.*

ضيافت *ẓiyāfat*, f. a feast, a banquet, convivial entertainment; hospitality; invitation. *a.*

ضيغم *ẓaigham*, ضيغمي *ẓaighamī*, } m. a lion; adj. biting, tearing, devouring. *a.*

ضيف *ẓaif*, hospitable, convivial; m. a stranger, a guest. *a.*

ضيفان *ẓīfān* or *ẓaifān*, pl. guests, strangers. *a. p.*

ضيق *ẓīḳ*, m. anguish, vexation, melancholy, affliction, anxiety, doubt, oppression of spirit, or any thing that tortures the mind, hippishness. *ẓīḳu-n-nafas*, m. the asthma. *ẓaiḳ* or *ẓaiyiḳ*, contracted, narrow; (met.) a narrow-hearted miser. *a.*

ط

ط *ṭo,e* or *ṭā*, called *ṭā,e muhmala* or *ṭa,e ghair manḳūṭa*, the sixteenth letter of the Arabic alphabet, the nineteenth Persian, and twenty-second Hindūstānī. This letter is purely Arabic or Semitic, but it is sometimes introduced in certain Persian words which were originally written with *te*, as *ṭabarzad* for *tabarzad*, sugar-candy. It has no corresponding character in Sanskrit, and in Arabic its genuine sound is stronger and harsher than that of the *te*. In reckoning by *abjad*, it stands for 9, and in almanacks for the sign Capricorn.

طاب *ṭāb*, sweet, agreeable, good, pure, excellent. *a.*

طابق *ṭābiḳ*, corresponding, agreeing with. *a.*

طارم *ṭārim*, m. any building of a circular form with an arched or cupola roof; the vault of heaven. *p.*

طاري *ṭārī*, happening, intervening, evident. *a.*

طاس *ṭās*, m. brocade; a cup, goblet, bowl, the vessel in which water is cooled. *a.*

طاسه *ṭāsa*, m. a kind of drum. *ṭāsa-nawāz*, one who plays on the *ṭāsa*. *ṭāsa-nawāzī*, f. beating the *ṭāsa*, q. v. *a.*

طاعات *ṭā'āt* (pl. of طاعت), acts of devotion. *a.*

طاعت *ṭā'at*, f. devotion, obedience, obsequiousness. *a.*

طاعن *ṭā'in*, m. an asperser, a slanderer, a calumniator. *a.*

طاعون *ṭā'ūn*, plague, pestilence. *a.*

طاغي *ṭāghī*, violent, refractory; m. an insurgent, a leader of rebels. *a.*

طافح *ṭāfiḥ*, overflowing (pond or cistern); (met.) dead drunk, full of liquor. *a.*

طاق *ṭāḳ*, m. an arched building, cupola; a recess in a wall, a window; unique, singular; odd (not even); fold, ply. *ṭāḳi azraḳ*, the azure vault of heaven. *ṭāḳ par rakhnā*, a. to refuse, to disobey; neglect, to abandon (to lay on the shelf). *ṭāḳ-juft*, m. the game of odd or even. *do-ṭāḳ*, two-fold. *si-ṭāḳ* three-fold. *ṭāḳ honā*, to be accomplished, to be superior. *a. p.*

طاقت *ṭāḳat*, f. strength, power, force, patience, ability. *ṭāḳat se ṭāḳ honā*, to be weak, feeble, powerless. *a.*

طاقچه *ṭāḳcha*, m. (dim. of *ṭāḳ*) a little recess, a niche; a small window. *a.*

طاقه *ṭāḳa*, a single garment or piece of cloth. *p.*

طاقي *ṭāḳī*, wall-eyed (a horse); f. froth of urine. *a.*

طاقيه *ṭāḳiya*, a fillet, especially one worn under the head-dress; a balcony, a cornice, a pent-house. *a. p.*

طالب *ṭālib*, asking, demanding, interrogating, m. an inquirer. *ṭālibi dunyā*, worldly-minded. *ṭālibi'ilm* or *ṭālibu-l-'ilm*, searching after knowledge, a student. *a*

طالح *ṭāliḥ*, wicked, villanous. *a.*

طالع *ṭāli'*, rising (as the sun), arising, appearing; m. fortune, prosperity; destiny (good or bad); the dawn. *ṭāli'-āzmā,ī*, m. trying one's fortune. *ṭāli'-shinās*, an astrologer, a fortune-teller. *ṭāli'-mand*, fortunate; wealthy. *ṭāli'-mandī*, f. fortune, prosperity; wealth. *ṭāli'-war*, fortunate; wealthy. *a.*

طالوط *ṭālūṭ*, king Saul, so called by the *Muḥammadans*. *a.*

طامات *ṭāmāt*, } statutes, laws; doubtful words,
طامان *ṭāmān*, } without certainty. *a.*

طامع *ṭāmi'*, covetous, greedy, desirous. *a.*

طامعه *ṭāmi'a*, avarice, greediness. *a.*

طاءوس *ṭā,ūs*, m. a peacock (ταως). *a.*

طاءوسي *ṭā,ūsī*, f. a kind of ornamental handwriting; adj. of or relating to the peacock. *ṭakht i ṭā,ūsī*, the peacock throne, *i.e.* the throne of the emperors of Delhi, which was adorned with jewels, so as to resemble a peacock's tail. *a.*

طاهر *ṭāhir*, pure, unsullied, chaste. *a.*

طائر *ṭā,ir*, flying; m. a bird. *ṭā,ir-khāna*, an aviary. *a.*

طائف *ṭā,if*, circumambulating, night patrole; a vision in a dream; vile thoughts or suggestions of Satan; a city in *Hijāz*. *a.*

طائفه *ṭā,ifa*, m. people, nation, tribe, a troop, a band (particularly of musicians and dancing women), suit, equipage. *a.* [the science of physic. *a.*

طب *ṭibb*, f. medicine, magic. *'ilmu-ṭ-ṭibb*,

طبابت *ṭabābat*, f. the practice of physic. *a.*

طباخ *ṭabbākh*, m. a cook. *a.*

طباشير *ṭabāshīr*, f. the sugar of the bamboo. *a.*

طباق *ṭabāḳ*, m. a vessel for kneading dough in. *a.*

طباقي كتا *ṭabāḳī kuttā*, a sponger. *a. h.*

طبانجه *ṭabānja*, } m. a slap, box, or blow. *p.*
طبانچه *ṭabāncha*, }

طبائع *ṭabā,i'* (pl. of طبيعت), natures, &c. *a.*

طبرزد *ṭabarzad*, sugar-candy, conserve of roses; fine hard white sugar. *p.*

طبع *ṭab'*, f. nature, genius, temperament, quality, disposition. *ṭab'-zād*, original invention. *a.*

طبعي *ṭab'ī*, natural, constitutional. *a.*

طبعيت *ṭab'īyat*, f. nature, temperature, constitution, health, property, essence. *a.*

طبق *ṭabaḳ*, m. a cover; a plate, a tray, a dish; a leaf, a disk; gold leaf, tinfoil, &c.; story of a house, a platform; consecutive, one thing following another. *a.*

طبقچه *ṭabaḳcha*, a small plate or tray. *a. p.*

طبقڑي *ṭabaḳṛī*, a small box. *d.*

طبقه *ṭabḳa*, m. a story, floor, stage, degree, class order, rank, shelf. *a.*

طبل *ṭabal*, m. a drum, a tambourine. *ṭabl-bāz* or *-zan*, a drummer *a.*

طبلق *ṭablaḳ*, m. a bundle of papers. *a.*

طبلك *ṭablak*, f. a little drum. *a.*

طبله *ṭabla*, m. a small tambourine; a large wooden dish in which fruits are exposed for sale. *a.*

طبنچه *ṭabancha*, a slap, blow, cuff. *p.*

طبيب *ṭabīb*, m. a physician. *a.*

طبيبي *ṭabībī*, f. the business of a physician, adj. of or relating to the healing art. *a.*

طبيخ *ṭabīkh*, cooked, dressed. *a.*

طبيعت *ṭabī'at*, f. disposition, temperament, constitution, essence, property. *ṭabī'at-shinās*, m. a physician. *a.*

طبيعي *ṭabī,ī*, natural, innate, intrinsic. *'ilmi ṭabī'ī*, natural science, in opposition to *'ilmi ilāhī*, divinity or metaphysics. *a.*

طبيلا *ṭabīlā* (for *ṭawīla*), a stable. *d.*

طپان *ṭapān* (for *tapān*), palpitating. *p.*

طپش *ṭapish* (for *tapish*), heat, agitation. *p.*

طپيده *ṭapīda* (for *tapīda*), agitated, heated. *p.*

طحال *ṭiḥāl*, spleen, the milt. *ṭuḥāl*, a disease in the spleen. *a.* [of Tripoli. *a.*

طرابلس *ṭarābalus* (also *ṭarābalūs*), the city

طراح *ṭarrāḥ*, m. an architect. *ṭarrāḥī*, f. architecture. *a.*

طرار *ṭarrār*, m. a pickpocket, a cutpurse. *a.*

طراره *ṭarrāra*, m. quickness, expedition. *ṭarrāra bharnā*, a. to stretch out or bound (as a horse at full speed). *ṭarrāra-zabān*, chattering, eternal clack. *a.*

طراري *ṭarrārī*, f. quickness, fluency. *a.*

طراز *ṭirāz* or *ṭarāz*, m. lace, fringe, embroidery, &c., any ornament on the border of a garment; (in comp.) adorning, as *debāja-ṭirāz*, a composer of prefaces or exordiums (which are generally written in the most highly ornamented style). *a.*

طرازو *ṭirāzū*, a balance, a pair of scales. *p.*

طرازي *ṭirāzī*, f. abstr. (of *ṭirāz*) adorning. *a.p.*

طراوت *ṭarāwat*, f. freshness, verdure. *a.*

طرب *ṭarab*, f. cheerfulness, mirth, hilarity, joy. *ṭarab-angez*, exciting mirth or joy. *bazmi ṭarab*, a festive assembly. *a.*

طرح *ṭarḥ* or *ṭaraḥ*, f. manner, mode; position, establishment; ejection, throwing. *ṭaraḥ-dār*, beautiful, well-shaped. *ṭaraḥ-dārī*, beauty, elegance. *a.*

طرز *ṭarz*, f. form, manner, fashion. *a.*

طرف *ṭarf* or *ṭaraf*, f. direction; side, margin, corner, quarter, extremity; towards. *ṭarfi ṣānī*, the other side, "pars altera;" a defendant; an enemy; (met.) a wife. *ṭaraf-dār*, m. a partisan, a follower, a sectary, an assistant, a subordinate officer of revenue and police; adj. partial, prejudiced. *ṭaraf-dārī*, f. following, partiality, &c. *a.* [eye. *a.*

طرفةالعين *ṭurfatu-l-'ain*, the twinkling of an

طرفگي *ṯurfagī*, rareness, wonderfulness. *a. p.*

طرفه *ṯurfa*, wonderful, strange, any thing new, rare, or agreeable. *a.*

طرفيل *ṯarfīl*, m. trefoil, clover. *a.*

طرفين *ṯarfain* (du. of *ṯaraf*), both sides, both parties. *a.*

طرق *ṯuruḳ* (pl. of طريق), ways, modes, &c. *a.*

طره *ṯurra*, m. an ornament worn in the turban; a ringlet, a curl; a nosegay; a plume of feathers. *a.*

طريق *ṯarīḳ*, f. way, road; manner, custom, fashion; rite, religion, profession. *a.*

طريقت *ṯarīḳat*, f. } way, path; manner,
طريقه *ṯarīḳa*, m. } mode; religion, sect; the better sort of people. *ahli ṯarīḳa*, people devoted to religion, generally means the sect of *ṣūfīs*. *a.*

طست *ṯasat*, *ṯassat*, or *ṯissat*, a small cup, a bowl. *a.*

طشت *ṯasht*, m. (Pers. تشت) a large basin, ewer, or cup. *ṯasht az bām honā* or *paṛnā*, the secret to be divulged. *a.*

طعام *ṯa'ām*, m. victuals; eating. *ṯa'ām-bakhsh*, a ladle, a tureen-spoon for serving out broth, &c. *a.*

طعم *ṯu'm*, } m. food, bait, dinner, provi-
طعمه *ṯu'ma*, } sions. *a.*

طعن *ṯa'n*, m. blame, disapprobation, reviling; chiding; striking with a spear. *a.*

طعنه *ṯa'na*, m. taunting, reproach, ignominy, disgrace, aspersion. *ṯa'na-zan*, a reproacher, taunter, asperser. *ṯa'na-zanī*, f. taunting, reproaching. *a.*

طغرا *ṯughrā*, m. the royal titles prefixed to public papers; a sort of writing. *t.*

طغيان *ṯughyān*, m. rebellion, sedition, perverseness, insolence. *a.*

طغياني *ṯughyānī*, f. excess, a flood, overflowing. *a.*

طفل *ṯifl*, m. an infant, a young animal. *a.*

طفلانه *ṯiflāna*, infantine, childish. *a. p.*

طفلي *ṯiflī*, } f. infancy, childhood. *a.*
طفوليت *ṯufūliyat*, }

طفيل *ṯufail*, f. a parasite, a glutton; one who uninvited accompanies one of the guests to a feast; (used as a preposition) by means of, through the merits or agency of. *a.*

طفيلي *ṯufailī*, parasitical. *a.*

طل *ṯall*, dew; being bedewed (the earth). *a.*

طلا *ṯilā*, m. gold; gold fringe; an ointment, liniment, embrocation. *ṯilā-bāfī*, f. gold tissue. *ṯilā-sāz* or *ṯilā-kār*, m. a gilder. *ṯilā-kārī*, gilding, the trade of a gilder. *p.*

طلاق *ṯalāḳ*, f. divorce, repudiation (for further explanation, v. Wilson's Glossary). *a.*

طلاقت *ṯalāḳat*, eloquence, glibness of tongue. *a.*

طلاوا *ṯilāwā*, m. (v. *ṯilāwa*). *a.*

طلاوت *ṯalāwat*, f. grace, beauty, elegance. *a.*

طلاوه *ṯilāwa*, m. night watch, rounds, picket. *a.*

طلائي *ṯilā,ī*, } golden, made of gold, or
طلايانه *ṯilāyāna*, } covered with gold. *p.*

طلايه *ṯilāya*, m. night watch, rounds, picket. *a*

طلب *ṯalab*, f. pay, wages, salary; desire, wish, inquiry, demand, request; application, sending for; (in comp.) seeking, searching; as *ārām-ṯalab*, ease-seeking, an epicure. *ṯalab-k.*, to seek for, to demand, to require, to summon. *a.*

طلبا *ṯulabā* (pl. of طالب), lit. seekers; students. *a.*

طلبانه *ṯalbāna*, m. daily pay to constables, &c., paid by those they guard, &c. *a. p.*

طلبچٹھي *ṯalab-chiṭhī*, f. a summons, citation. *a. h.*

طلبدار *ṯalab-dār*, desirous; asking, inquiring; m. one who receives pay; one who searches for any thing. *ṯalab-dārī*, f. search, inquiry. *a. p.*

طلبگار *ṯalab-gār*, desirous; a searcher. *a. p.*

طلبگاري *ṯalab-gārī*, f. desiring, wishing, inquiring. *a. p.*

طلبنامه *ṯalab-nāma*, a summons, citation. *a.*

طلسم *ṯilsam*, or *ṯilasm*, or *ṯalism*, m. a talisman; any thing to cause astonishment, wonder, marvel. *a.*

طلسمات *ṯilasmāt*, talismans, spells. *a.*

طلسماتي *ṯilasmātī*, } magical, talismanic. *a.*
طلسمي *ṯilismī*, }

طلعت *ṯal'at*, } aspect, countenance, appear-
طلعه *ṯal'a*, } ance. *khush-ṯal'a*, of auspicious aspect, of pleasant countenance. *a.*

طلف *ṯalf*, m. a gift, a present. *a.*

طلفا *ṯalfā* or *ṯalfan*, gratis. *a.*

طلق *ṯalḳ* (for تلك), m. talc, mica. *p.*

طلق *ṯalḳ*, m. divorce, repudiation. *a.*

طلوع *ṯulū'*, m. rising (as the sun, &c.). *a.*

طليعه *ṯalī'a* (also *ṯalī'at*), the vanguard or picket, an advanced post, the forlorn hope; a spy, a sentinel. *a.*

طماچه *ṯamācha* (for *ṯamāṅcha*), a slap, &c. *p.*

طماع *ṯammā'*, covetous, wishful, extremely greedy. *a.*

طمانچه *ṯamāṅcha*, m. a pistol; a slap, blow, box, thump, &c. *ṯamāṅcha-jaṛnā*, or *-lagānā*, or *-mārnā*, *a.* to give a slap. *ṯamāṅche se muṅh lāl rakhnā*, to conceal one's poverty from pride or high spirit. *a.*

طمانيت *ṯamāniyat*, f. rest, repose, tranquillity. *a.*

طمطراق *ṯumṯurāḳ* (vul. *ṯumṯaṛāḳ*), m. magnificence, grandeur. *p.*

طمع *ṯam'* or *ṯama'*, f. avarice, desire, covetousness, greediness, avidity. *a.*

طمنچه *ṯamancha*, a pistol. *p. t.*

طناب *ṭanāb*, f. a tent rope; a measure for measuring land, formerly made of rope. *a.*

طناز *ṭannāz*, facetious, jocose, jocund, ludicrous, playful, mirthful. *a.*

طنب *ṭunub*, a tent rope. *a.*

طنبور *ṭambūr*, m. a Turkish guitar with six wires or strings (Menin.); a drum (in Hindūstān). *a.*

طنبوراني *ṭambūrānī*, a player on the *ṭambūr*. *a.*

طنبورہ *ṭambūra*, m. a small kind of guitar (v. *ṭambūr*). *a.*

طنز *ṭanz*, f. mirth, joking, pleasantry; ridiculing, sneering, taunting. *a.*

طنزاً *ṭanzan*, tauntingly, sneeringly. *a.*

طنس *ṭanas*, great darkness. *a.*

طنطنہ *ṭanṭana*, m. sound, fame; rumour; pomp, dignity, state. *a.*

طنين *ṭanīn*, humming, buzzing. *a.*

طواسي *ṭiwāsī* (for *tiwāsī*) a kind of carpet. *p.*

طواف *ṭawāf*, f. turning, encompassing, pilgrimage. *a.*

طوالت *ṭawālat*, prolonging, prolixity. *a.*

طوائف *ṭawā,if*, f. (pl. of طائفہ) troops, bands (particularly of dancing girls); tribes, nations. *mulūku-ṭ-ṭawā,if*, the kings of the Gentiles; generally applied to the princes who succeeded Alexander the Great in Persia, also applied to the petty sovereigns who succeeded the Arabs in Spain, &c. *a.*

طوبىٰ *ṭūbā*, m. the name of a tree in Paradise, whose fruit is said to be most delicious; adj. excellent, sweet. *a.*

طور *ṭaur*, m. mode, manner; condition, state. *ṭūr*, m. a mountain, particularly Mount Sinai. *a.*

طوس *ṭūs*, name of a city in Persia, the birthplace of the poet Firdausī. *p.*

طوسي *ṭūsī*, f. a colour so called; a kind of purple; adj. of or belonging to the city of *ṭūs* in Persia. *a.*

طوطا *ṭoṭā*, m. (for توتا) a parrot. *h.*

طوطي *ṭūṭī*, f. a parrot, a parroquet. *ṭūṭī ke se honṭh mal ḍālnā*, lit. to rub or twist one's parrot-like lips, is used by way of an affectionate or friendly admonition. *p.*

طوطيا *ṭuṭiyā*, report, tale, slander. *p. h.*

طوع *ṭau'* obeying, obedience. *a.*

طوعاً *ṭau'an*, willingly; *ṭau'an wa karhan*, willingly or unwillingly, nolens volens. *a.*

طوف *ṭauf*, m. surrounding, perambulating; pilgrimage, the procession round the temple of Mecca. *a.*

طوفان *ṭūfān*, m. an inundation or deluge; the universal deluge; a hurricane, a storm of wind and rain (anal. to Gr. τυφων); (met.) a quarrelsome person. *ṭūfān lenā*, (Dakh.) to defame, to calumniate. *a.*

طوفاني *ṭūfānī*, stormy; (met.) quarrelsome, boisterous. *a.*

طوق *ṭauḳ*, m. a collar; a necklace, chain, a ring. *ṭauḳi zanjīr*, irons, manacles. *ṭauḳi-zanjīr k.*, to imprison, to manacle. *a.*

طول *ṭūl*, m. length; adj. long, tall, extensive, lasting long. *a.*

طولاً *ṭūlan*, lengthwise, by length. *a.*

طولاني *ṭūlānī*, lengthy, long, prolix; f. prolixity. *a.*

طوليدون *ṭūlīdūn*, m. fox's grapes, nightshade [(*Solanum nigrum*). *a.*

طومار *ṭūmār*, m. a book, a volume, a roll, an account-book, a story. *jam'i ṭūmār*, the produce, or collection of a land recorded in Government books. *ṭūmār-navīs*, an accountant. *a.*

طوي *ṭū,ī* or *ṭo,ī*, a feast, an entertainment. *a.p.*

طويل *ṭawīl*, long, tall, prolix. *a.*

طويلہ *ṭawīla*, m. a long rope with which cattle are tied, a tether, foot-band, fetter; hence, a stable, a stall. *a.*

طهارت *ṭahārat*, f. purity, cleanliness, sanctity; ablution, ceremonial purification. *a.*

طهر *ṭuhr*, m. purification, cleanliness, purity. *a.*

طهور *ṭahūr*, purifying, cleansing. *sharābi ṭahūr* a purifying draught (from the fountain of Paradise). *a.*

طي *ṭai*, m. rolling up, folding. *ṭai-k.*, a. to fold, to roll up; to constrain; to abridge; to travel, to pass over, to traverse. *a.*

طيار *ṭaiyār*, flying, fleet (horse or arrow); a winged animal in general; quicksilver. *a.*

طياري *ṭaiyārī*, readiness, promptness. *a. p.*

طيب *ṭaiyib*, good, sweet, agreeable. *ṭīb*, m. perfume, odour; essence. *a.*

طيبات *ṭaiyibāt* (pl. of طيّبة), good works, &c.; pleasures. *a.*

طير *ṭair*, m. flying; a bird (v. *ṭā,ir*). *a.*

طيران *ṭairān* or *ṭaiyarān*, flight; (pl. of طير) birds. *a.*

طيراني *ṭairānī*, belonging to birds, volatile. *a.*

طيش *ṭaish*, m. levity, folly, anger, passion. *a.*

طيطو *ṭīṭū*, also *ṭīṭuwā* or *ṭīṭuwī*, a kind of water-fowl, a species of the bird called *ḳaṭā*. *p. a.*

طيف *ṭaif*, a phantom, spectre, apparition, a ghost. *a.*

طين *ṭīn*, earth, clay, mud, loam. *a.*

طينت *ṭīnat*, f. a piece of clay; nature, temperament, disposition, genius. *bad-ṭīnat*, of a wicked disposition. *a.*

طيني *ṭīnī*, earthy, made of clay. *a.*

طيور *ṭuyūr* (pl. of طير), birds. *a.*

طيوري *ṭuyūrī*, m. a dealer in birds. *a.*

ظ

ظ **ẓo,e** or **ẓā**, called *ẓā,e mu'jama* or *ẓā,e manḳūṭa*, the seventeenth letter of the Arabic alphabet, the twentieth Persian, and twenty-third Hindūstānī. This letter is purely Arabic, and has not any corresponding character in the Sanskrit: in reckoning by *abjad* it stands for 900.

ظالم **ẓālim**, m. a tyrant; adj. tyrannical, barbarous, cruel, oppressive; (met.) applied by the poets to a beloved person or mistress. *ẓālim-gudāz*, a destroyer of oppressors, an epithet applied to a king who maintains justice and good order. *a.*

ظالمي **ẓālimī**, f. tyranny, oppression. *a. p.*

ظاهر **ẓāhir**, apparent, manifest; m. the outward or external appearance, in opposition to *bāṭin* (the intrinsic). *ẓāhir-bīn*, one who looks only to the exterior. *ẓāhir o bāṭin*, outwardly and inwardly, appearance, and inward qualities. *a.*

ظاهرًا **ẓāhirā** or **ẓāhiran**, evidently, apparent, to all appearance, ostensibly. *a.*

ظاهري **ẓāhirī**, external, apparent. *a.*

ظبي **ẓabī**, m. a deer, a chevril, a gazelle. *a.*

ظرافت **ẓarāfat**, f. beauty; politeness, elegance, gallantry; wit, humour, jocularity. *a.*

ظرف **ẓarf**, m. a vase, vessel; adj. ingenious; in gram. an adverb. *ẓarfi zamān*, adverb of time. *ẓarfi makān*, adverb of place. *a.*

ظرفي **ẓarfī**, f. a kind of sweetmeat. *a. d.*

ظروف **ẓurūf**, (pl. of ظرف) vessels; adverbs, &c. *a.*

ظريف **ẓarīf**, ingenious, polite, gallant; witty, jocose, elegant in conversation. *a.*

ظريفانه **ẓarīfāna**, ingeniously; jocosely. *a.p.*

ظفر **ẓafar**, m. victory. *ẓafar-nāma*, m. a congratulatory letter on the occasion of a victory: it is also the title of several works; one on morality, attributed to Buzurjmihr, the vizier of Naushīrwān; another is a complete history of the life and conquests of Tīmūr (Tamerlane), by 'Alī, of Yazd. The latter work was translated into French, and thence done into English. *a.*

ظفرتكيه **ẓafar-takya**, m. a kind of stiletto or dirk; a long sharp iron prong. *a.p.*

ظل **ẓill**, m. shadow. *ẓillu-l-lāh*, the shadow of God. *ẓillu-l-lāh fi-l arẓi*, the shadow of God upon earth (epithets applied to a king, emperor, &c.). *ẓillu-hu*, his shadow *ẓillu-humā* (du.), the shadow of them both. *ẓillu-hum*, their shadow; employed in Arabic phrases of benediction, as *dāma-ẓillu-hu*, *-ẓillu-humā* or *-ẓillu-hum*, may his or their shadow be prolonged; meaning, in plain English, may he or they long prosper. *a.*

ظلام **ẓalām**, m. darkness. *ẓallām*, a great oppressor, an atrocious tyrant. *a.*

ظلم **ẓulm**, m. oppression, injustice, extortion; a heavier assessment than people can bear. *a.*

ظلمات **ẓulmāt**, f. darkness, regions of darkness; a dark place where the water of immortality is said to be. *a.*

ظلمت **ẓulmat**, f. darkness, obscurity. *a.*

ظلمي **ẓulmī**, unjust, addicted to tyranny. *a*

ظلميت **ẓulmīyat**, f. oppression, tyranny. *a.*

ظلوم **ẓalūm**, cruel, most oppressive, tyrannical. *a.*

ظله **ẓulla**, m. a covering, any thing shady, a cloud. *a.*

ظليل **ẓalīl**, shady, affording shelter. *a.*

ظما **ẓamā**, being very thirsty. *a.*

ظن **ẓann**, m. suspicion, jealousy, opinion, thought, idea. *a.*

ظنون **ẓunūn**, m. suspecting, thinking, supposing: (pl of *ẓann*) suspicions, thoughts, opinions. *a.*

ظني **ẓannī**, supposed, suspected. *a.*

ظهار **ẓihār**, m. a formula of repudiation, or saying what is tantamount to and has the effect of regular divorce, as "You are my mother," or "I sucked the same breast as you;" a penance is requisite to do away the effect of such a speech. *a.*

ظهر **ẓuhr**, m. mid-day, or a little time after the sun has passed the meridian, when it is most sultry. *a.*

ظهر **ẓahr**, f. the back; the external part. *a.*

ظهور **ẓuhūr**, m. appearing, arising, apparency. *ẓuhūr men ānā*, to come to pass, to present itself. *a.*

ظهير **ẓahīr**, m. an assistant, associate, ally; a poetical name of a Persian poet of Faryāb, hence called *ẓahīr Faryābī*. *a.*

ع

ع **'ain**, called *'aini muhmala* or *'aini ghair manḳūṭa*, the eighteenth letter of the Arabic alphabet, the twenty-first Persian, and twenty-fourth Hindūstānī. This letter is peculiarly Arabic or Semitic, and has no analogous sound in Sanskrit. It is of the class of guttural letters, being formed in the lower part of the throat, by a compression of the fauces stronger and deeper than that used in the formation of the *hamza*, or initial *alif*. Its sound has been compared by Meninski to the voice of a calf calling its mother, which is a pure absurdity. In reckoning by *abjad* it stands for 70. In Persian words introduced into Arabic it is sometimes substituted for *alif*, as *la'l* for *lāl*. On the other hand the *'ain* of Arabic words introduced into Hindūstānī is, by the common people, sounded like *alif*.

عابد **'ābid**, m. an adorer, a votary; a worshipper of God; a recluse. *a.*

عابر **'ābir**, passing over, a passenger. *a.*

عاج **'āj**, ivory. *takhti 'āj*, an ivory throne. *a.*

عاجز **'ājiz**, impotent, weak, exhausted, dejected, hopeless. *a.*

عاجزانه **'ājizāna**, weakly, hopelessly. *a. p.*

عاجزي **'ājizī**, f. submissiveness, humility, supplication. *'ājizī-k.*, to implore humbly. *a.*

عاجل *'ājil*, one who is hastening, fleeting; adj. transitory, agile. *a.*

عاد *'ād* (pl. of عادت), customs, &c.; name of an ancient and sinful Arab tribe, to whom the prophet Hūd was sent. *a.*

عادت *'ādat*, f. habit, custom, usage. *'ādat karnā*, a. to adopt a habit, to introduce a custom, to accustom. *a.*

عادتي *'ādatī*, customary, habitual; m. (met.) [a catamite. *a.*

عادل *'ādil*, just, upright, sincere. *a.*

عادي *'ādī*, passing; superseding; transgressing; unjust, wicked; accustomed, addicted; m. an enemy. *'ādī-k.*, to addict. *a.*

عاذر *'āẕir*, making excuses; m. an apologist; the scar of a wound. *a.*

عار *'ār*, f. bashfulness, modesty; reproach, disgrace, ignominy, shame. *a.*

عارس *'āras*, f. a bride (v. *'arūs*). *a. d.*

عارض *'āriẓ*, m. the cheek; an accident; a muster-master, also the general of an army. *a.*

عارضنامه *'āriẓ-nāma*, particulars of receipts or revenues. *a. p.*

عارضه *'āriẓa*, m. any thing necessary to be done, an accident, an event; an obstacle, impediment; sickness. *a.*

عارضي *'āriẓī*, accidental, not inherent; adventitious, casual. *a.*

عارف *'ārif*, wise, sagacious, ingenious; m. a holy man. *a.*

عارفانه *'ārifāna*, wisely, acutely, piously. *p. a.*

عاري *'ārī*, naked, free from, void of. *a.*

عاريت *'āriyat*, f. borrowing any thing which is itself to be returned: it differs from *ḳarẓ*, inasmuch as in the latter term it is not understood that the identical articles are returned, but simply their equivalent; when a man borrows an umbrella it is *'āriyat* (provided always the said man return the said article), when he borrows a shilling it is *ḳarẓ* (v. *udhār*). *a.*

عاريتي *'āriyatī*, that which is borrowed, not intrinsic. *'āriyatī mū,e*, false hair, borrowed locks. *a.*

عازم *'āzim*, applying the mind to an undertaking, intending, determining. *a.*

عاس *'āss*, a patrol, a night-watch. *a.*

عاشر *'āshir*, m. } the tenth. *a.*
عاشرت *'āshirat*, f. }

عاشق *'āshiḳ*, a lover, an inamorato. *a.*

عاشقان *'āshiḳān*, pl. the lovers. *a.*

عاشقانه *'āshiḳāna*, in the manner of a lover. *a.*

عاشقه *'āshiḳa*, f. an inamorato. *a.*

عاشقي *'āshiḳī*, f. being in love; love-making, amorousness. *a.*

عاشورا *'āshūrā*, m. the first ten days of the *Muḥarram*. *a.*

عاشورخانه *'āshūr-ḳhāna*, a temporary kind of house for the celebration of the *Muḥarram* festival; a house for the reception of the banners, &c., used in the *Muḥarram* procession. *a. p.*

عاصم *'āṣim*, virtuous, chaste, protected, safe. *abū 'āṣim* (father of safety), *i.e.* barley broth. *a.*

عاصي *'āṣī*, disobedient, criminal, rebellious; m. and f. a rebel, a sinner. *a.*

عاطر *'āṭir*, odoriferous, benevolent, generous, [noble. *a.*

عاطفت *'āṭifat*, kindness, benevolence, affection. *a.*

عاطله *'āṭila*, vain, useless; void or destitute [of. *a.*

عافيت *'āfiyat*, f. health, safety. *ḳhair o 'āfiyat*, safe and sound. *a.*

عاق *'āḳḳ*, disobedient, rebellious. *a.*

عاقبت *'āḳibat*, f. the end, conclusion; successive adv. finally, at last. *'āḳibat-andesh*, reflecting on the end, prudent, prescient, looking into futurity. *'āḳibatu-l-amr*, in fine, finally. *a.*

عاقرقرحا *'āḳarḳarḥā*, m. the herb pellitory. *a.*

عاقل *'āḳil*, wise, sensible; m. a sage. *a.*

عاقلان *'āḳilān*, pl. the wise, the sages. *a. p.*

عاقلي *'āḳilī*, wisdom, intelligence. *a.*

عاقلانه *'āḳilāna*, prudently, wisely. *a. p.*

عاكف *'āḳif*, assiduous, diligent. *'āḳifāni ka'ba*, those who are assiduous in their attendance at the temple of Mecca. *a.*

عالم *'ālam*, m. the world, the universe, time, state, condition; people, mankind in general. *'ālamibālā*, or *'ulwī*, or *-'alwī*, the heavens, the people of the heavens. *'ālami siflī*, the earth. *'ālami ghaib*, the world of absence, a future state; the world of spirits. *'ālamgīr*, conquering the universe; the name or title of Aurang-zeb. *'ālami ṣūrat*, the visible or external world. *'ālami ma'nī*, the spiritual or invisible world. *a.*

عالم *'ālim*, sage, intelligent, learned. *'ālimi ghaib*, prescient, conversant with what is hidden. *a.*

عالم آرا *'ālam-ārā*, world-adorning. *a. p.*

عالم افروز *'ālam-afroz*, world-illumining; the sun. *a. p.*

عالمانه *'ālimāna*, wisely, like a sage. *a. p.*

عالمپناه *'ālam-panāh*, the asylum of the world, a king, &c. *a. p.*

عالمتاب *'ālam-tāb*, that which warms or illumines the world; the sun. *a. p.*

عالمگرد *'ālam-gard*, } world traversing, a great traveller. *a. p.*
عالمنورد *'ālam-naward*, }

عالمي *'ālamī*, worldly, mundane, existing in this world. *a.*

عالميان *'ālamiyān*, m. people of this world, men, mankind in general. *a.*

عالي *'ālī*, high, sublime, eminent, grand. *'ālī-tabār*, of high or noble lineage. *'ālī-jāh* or *'ālī shān*, of high rank or dignity (although these two terms are nearly synonymous, yet, according to Morier, the former is by far the higher title). *'ālī maḳām*, of high station, of illustrious rank; the word is much used in composition, particularly in letters from inferiors. *'ālī-ḥaẓrat*, *'ālī-jāh*, *'ālī-janāb* or *'ālī-ḳadr*, &c. all denote high in rank, station, &c. *'ālī-khāndān*, of a high family. *'ālī-fiṭrat*, or *-manish*, or *-himmat*, high-minded, magnanimous. *a.*

عام *'āmm*, common, public, plebeian; the vulgar, the common people. *khāṣṣ o 'āmm*, high and low, peculiar and popular. *a.*

عامرة *'āmira*, royal, imperial; abundant, rich, inhabited. *a.*

عامل *'āmil*, m. an agent, a superintendant of the finances, collector of the revenues; a ruler, governor. *a.*

عاملنامه *'āmil-nāma*, a warrant or power from Government, authorizing a person to take possession of any thing; a power of attorney. *a. p.*

عامله *'āmila*, one word that governs another (in gram.). *a.*

عاملي *'āmilī*, the harvest year. *a.*

عامي *'āmī*, blind, ignorant. *a.*

عامي *'āmmī*, general, common; relating to the common people, ignorant, vulgar. *a.*

عائد *'ā,id*, turning towards, happening, referring to, coming back, being restored (as money lent, &c.), returning. *a.*

عبا *'abā*, a kind of cloak or habit worn by darweshes. *a.*

عباد *'ibād* (pl. of عبد) servants, slaves. *'ibādu-l-lāh*, servants of God. *'ubbād* (pl. of *'ābid*), holy men.

عبادت *'ibādat*, f. divine worship, adoration. *'ibādat-gāh*, a place of worship. *a.*

عبادتي *'ibādatī*, a worshipper, an adorer. *a.*

عبارت *'ibārat*, f. style (in writing), speech, a word, dialect, idiom; a trope, or figure; a phrase. *'ibārati rangīn*, the flowery or metaphorical style of writing peculiar to the later Persian and Indian chroniclers. *a.*

عباس *'abbās*, m. a man's name; name of a plant, marvel of Peru (*Mirabilis jalapa*). *a.*

عباسي *'abbāsī*, name of a flower; adj. red. *a.*

عبث *'abaṡ*, vain, idle, absurd, trifling, profitless; adv. in vain, uselessly. *a.*

عبد *'abd*, m. a servant (of God), a devotee; a slave. *a.*

عبديت *'abdīyat*, servitude, slavery. *a.*

عبراني *'ibrānī*, } Hebraic, the Hebrew
عبرانيه *'ibrāniya*, } language. *a.*

عبرت *'ibrat*, f. an example, warning; (met.) fear. *'abirat*, f. weeping; grief. *a.*

عبرت بخش *'ibrat-bakhsh*, } exemplary. *a. p.*
عبرت نما *'ibrat-numā*, }

عبري *'ibrī*, Hebrew, Hebraic. *a.*

عبوديت *'ubūdiyat*, f. servitude, devotion, subjection, reverence *a.*

عبور *'ubūr*, m. passing, crossing (a river); a ford or pass. *a.*

عبهر *'abhar*, the narcissus, jasmine. *a.*

عبهري *'abharī*, of or relating to the narcissus. *a.*

عبيد *'ubaid*, a slave, servant; devotee. *a.*

عبير *'abīr*, ambergris, saffron, or any other grateful perfume; a kind of powder used at the saturnalia of the *holī*. *a.*

عبيري *'abīrī*, of or resembling saffron. *a.*

عتاب *'itāb*, m. reproach, rebuke, anger, displeasure. *a.*

عتاق *'itāḳ*, the manumission of a slave. *a.*

عجالت *'ijālat*, haste, speed; anticipation. *a.*

عجائب *'ajā,ib*, wonders, curiosities. *'ajā,ib o gharā,ib*, wonders, curiosities, strange things. *'ajā,ibu-l-makhlūḳāt*, the wonders of the creation. *a.*

عجائبات *'ajā,ibāt* (additional pl. of the preceding), wonders, &c. *a. p.*

عجب *'ajab*, wonderful, rare, &c. *'ujb*, m. pride, haughtiness. *a.*

عجز *'ajz*, m. weakness, impotence, submission, wretchedness. *a.*

عجلت *'ajlat*, f. haste, speed, velocity. *a.*

عجم *'ajam*, m. barbarians, all people not Arabian; Persians; countries not Arabian; Persia. *a.*

عجمي *'ajamī*, Persian, barbarian. *a.*

عجوبة *'ujūba* (vulg. *'ajūba*), wonderful, m. a wonder. *a.*

عجوز *'ajūz*, the winter solstice. *a.*

عجول *'ajūl*, hasty, quick, expeditious. *a.*

عجيب *'ajīb*, wonderful, surprising, rare, astonishing. *a.*

عجين *'ajīn*, plaster, paste. *a.*

عدالت *'adālat*, f. a court of justice; justice, law, equity. *'adālat-panāh*, asylum of justice. *a.*

عدالتين *'adālatain*, (dual) the two courts of justice, *i.e.* the civil and the criminal. *a.*

عداوت *'adāwat*, f. enmity, hatred, strife. *a.*

عدت *'iddat*, the time of probation which a divorced woman must wait before she can be re-married. *a.*

عدد *'adad*, m. number. *'adadi auwal*, a prime number *'adadi ṣaḥīḥ*, a whole number, a unit. *'adadi ẕātī* or *adadi muṭlaḳ*, a cardinal number. *a.*

عددي *'adadī*, numeral, numerical. *a.*

عدل *'adl*, m. justice, equity. *'adl-k.*, a. to administer justice. *a.*

عدم *'adam*, m. non-existence, non-entity, nothing, privation; cessation, discontinuance. *'adami ṡabūt*, the want of proof or confirmation. *a.*

عدن *'adan*, f. Eden, Paradise; name of a town in the south of Arabia, Aden. *a.*

عدو *'adū*, m. an enemy, a foe. *a.*

عدول *'udūl*, m. declining, refusing, disobeying. *'udūli-ḥukmī*, disobedience to a positive order, receding, deserting, returning; (pl. of *'ādil*) just men. *a.*

عديل *'adīl*, alike, equal; just, equitable; m. a distributor of justice. *a.*

عديم *'adīm*, destitute, deprived, not to be found. *'adīmu-l-miṣāl*, incomparable. *a.*

عذاب *'aẕāb*, m. pain, misfortune, torment, martyrdom, punishment. *a.*

عذار *'iẕār*, also *'uẕār*, the face, the cheeks. *a.*

عذر *'uẕr*, m. excuse, apology. *'uẕr-khwāh*, one who begs pardon of another. *'uẕr-khwāhī*, f. an apology, an excuse. *a.*

عرابه *'arāba*, a kind of cart (v. *arāba*); (in Dakh.) a magazine for military stones. *t.*

عرابچي *'arābchī*, the driver of an *'arāba*. *t.*

عراق *'irāḳ*, name of a territory between Persia and Arabia, which is divided into two portions, viz. *'irāḳi 'arab*, the ancient Babylonia or Chaldea, and *'irāḳi 'ajam*, comprehending Media. *'irāḳin* or *'irāḳain*, the two *'Irāḳs*, the cities of Baṣra and Kūfa. *a.*

عراقي *'irāḳī*, produced in or belonging to *'Irāḳ* (especially applied to the breed of horses from that country); m. a Parthian. *a.*

عرائض *'arā,iẓ*, f. (pl. of عريضه) letters, petitions, representations. *a.*

عرب *'arab*, m. Arabia; an Arabian. *a.*

عرباني *'arbānī*, a kind of musicians. *d.*

عربده *'arbada*, m. a conflict, dispute, battle, antipathy. *a.*

عربستان *'arabistān*, the land of the Arabs, also a province of Persia so called. *p.*

عربي *'arabī*, m. } of or belonging to Arabia;
عربيه *'arabīya*, f, } the Arabic language, &c. *a.*

عرس *'urs*, m. oblations, offerings to a saint; a marriage feast. *'irs*, m. a spouse. *a.*

عرش *'arsh*, m. a roof; a throne; the ninth heaven, where the throne of God is. *'arsh se le farsh tak*, from the highest of the heavens to the earth (lit. to the carpet under foot). *a.*

عرصه *'arṣa*, m. a plain; an area, a court; a chessboard; space of time (as *do gharī ke 'arṣe meṅ*, in the space of two *gharīs*); time, while, interval. *is 'arṣe meṅ*, in this interval, in the mean time. *a.*

عرض *'arẓ*, f. a petition, request; breadth; a military muster. *'arẓ-dāsht*, f. a written petition. *'arẓ-begī*, the person who presents all petitions either written or by word of mouth. *'arẓ-dār*, broad. *'araẓ*, f. an accident, any thing that befals one, disease, sickness; a muster of troops. *a.*

عرضاً *'arẓan*, in breadth. *'araẓan*, accidentally; by chance. *a.*

عرضي *'urẓī*, f. a petition, memorial, request, representation, letter (from an inferior). *a.*

عرف *'urf*, known (the name by which a person or thing is generally called or known); equivalent to our terms, "commonly called," "*alias*" &c., as *shahri shāh-jahān-ābād 'urf Dihlī*, "the city of *shāh-jahān-ābād*, commonly called *Dihlī* or *Dillī*." *a.*

عرفا *'urafā*, (pl. of عارف) the ingenious, the intelligent; judges, magistrates. *a.*

عرفات *'arafāt*, name of a sacred hill, some twelve miles from Mecca, where the pilgrims halt. *a.*

عرفان *'irfān*, wisdom, knowledge. *a.*

عرفه *'arafa*, a vigil, a wake (of a festival). *'irfa*, diligent inquiry, knowledge. *a.*

عرفي *'urfī*, notorious, public; name of a Persian poet. *a.*

عرق *'araḳ*, m. juice, essence, spirit, sap (hence our word "arrack"); the root of any thing; sweat; *'araḳ-gīr*, a skullcap; part of a *ḥuḳḳa* (same as *chilamchī*, q. v.) *a.*

عروج *'urūj*, m. ascent, rising. *a.*

عروس *'arūs*, f. m. bride, a spouse in general. *a.*

عروسانه *'arūsāna*, like a bride. *a.*

عروسي *'arūsī*, nuptial; f. a marriage feast. *a.*

عروض *'arūẓ*, f. versification; m. Mecca and Medina, with their adjacent territory. *a.*

عري *'urī*, } naked, stripped, bare, deprived
عريان *'uryān*, } or void of. *a.*

عرياني *'uryānī*, f. nakedness, nudity. *a.*

عريض *'arīẓ*, large, wise, expanded. *a.*

عريضه *'arīẓa*, a petition, memorial. *a.*

عز *'izz*, m. glory, dignity, grandeur; adj. rare, excellent, glorious. *a.*

عز *'azza*, (lit.) "he or it was or is glorious," or "may he be glorified," used only in Arabic phrases, as *'azza wa jalla*, He is honoured and glorified, *i.e.* God, the Almighty. *'azza-smuhu* (for *'azza-ismuhu*), glorious is His name. *a.*

عزا *'azā*, condolence, lamenting. *'azā-dār*, one who is in mourning. *'azā-khāna*, the house of mourning. *a.*

عزازيل *'azāzīl*, name of a devil or fallen angel; a kind of bird so called. *a.*

عزب *'azab*, an unmarried person. *a.*

عزت *'izzat*, f. grandeur, power, honour, respect, glory. *a.*

عزراعيل *'izrā,īl* or *'izrā,il*, the name of the angel of death. *a.*

عزل *'azl*, m. removal from office. *a.*

عزلت *uzlat*, f. retirement (from office, &c.), dismissal, discharge. *a.*

عزلتي *'uzlatī*, m. a hermit, a recluse. *a. p.*

عزلي *'azlī*, f. retirement, abdication. *a.*

عزم *'azm*, m. design, intention, purpose, resolution, undertaking. *a.*

عزمت *'azmat*, f. design, the decree of God. *a.*

عزيز *'azīz*, dear, excellent, beloved, precious; m. a worthy or pious personage; a great man, a saint; a title of the king of Egypt. *a.*

عزيزي *'azīzī*, f. greatness, sanctity, friendship, respect. *a.* [&c. *a.*

عزيمت *'azīmat*, f. (v. عزم) design, purpose,

عساكر *'asākir* (pl. of عسكر), armies, troops. *a.*

عسر *'asar* or *'asir*, difficult, used only in Arabic phrases, as *'asaru-l-'ubūr*, difficult to cross or pass over. *a.*

عسرت *'usrat*, f. difficulty, distress. *a.*

عسس *'asas* (pl. of عاس), the patrol, the night watch. *a.*

عسكر *'askar*, m. an army, force, troop. *a.*

عسكري *'askarī*, m. a soldier; adj. military, of or relating to an army. *a.*

عسل *'asal*, m. honey (of bees or of dates). *a.*

عشا *'ishā*, f. the first watch of the night; the prayers said when going to rest. *'ishā-namāz* or *-ṣalāt*, evening prayers. *'ashā*, m. supping, supper, treating with a supper. *a.*

عشاق *'ushshāḳ* (pl. of عاشق), lovers. *a.*

عشبة *'ushba*, m. sarsaparilla. *a.*

عشر *'ushr*, the tenth part, a tithe. *'ushri shar'ī*, the tenths or tithes prescribed by divine law. *'ushri 'ashīr*, the tenth of a tenth, used indefinitely to denote a very small part. *a.*

عشر *'ashar* or عشرة *'ashara*, ten. *a.*

عشرات *'asharāt* (pl. of عشر), tens. *a.*

عشرت *'ishrat* or *'ashrat*, f. society, pleasant and familiar conversation; pleasure, delight, enjoyment. *'ishrat-fazā*, one who increases mirth or enjoyment. *a.*

عشرتخانه *'ishrat-khāna*, m. } a house of pleasure or entertainment. *a. p.*
عشرتگاه *'ishrat-gāh*, f. }

عشرة *'ashara*, m. a decade, the name of the first ten days of the *Muḥarram* (v. *dahā*). *a.*

عشق *'ishḳ*, m. love. *'ishḳ-bāz*, a man of gallantry. *'ishḳ-bāzī*, f. amorous toying, love-making. *'ishḳ-pechā*, m. the name of a flower (*Ipomœa quamoclit*), American jasmine. *'ishḳ-pechān*, ivy. *'ishḳ hai*, an exclamation of praise; excellent! well done! bravo! *a*

عشقي *'ishḳī*, relating to love, a lover. *a.*

عشورة *'ashūra*, m. the first ten days of the *Muḥarram*. *a.*

عشوة *'ishwa*, *'ashwa*, or *'ushwa*, m. an obscure, concealed, dangerous affair; the beginning of darkness at night; a fire seen from a distance at night; (met. but most used in Persian and Hindī), coquetry, ogling, blandishments, amourous playfulness. *'ishwa-gar*, a coquette. *'ishwa-garī*, coquetry. *a.*

عشير *'ashīr*, the tenth part. *a.*

عصا *'aṣā*, m. a club, stick, staff, mace. *a.*

عصابردار *'aṣā-bardār*, m. a mace-bearer. *a. p.*

عصار *'aṣṣār*, m. an oil-maker or presser *a.*

عصارة *'uṣāra*, m. expressed juice; dregs after the juice is expressed. *a.*

عصافير *'aṣāfīr* (pl. of عصفور), sparrows. *a.*

عصب *'aṣab*, m. a tendon, a nerve, a ligament. *a.*

عصر *'aṣr* or *'uṣr*, m. time, age. *'aṣar* or *'aṣr*, the time of prayer before sunset. *a.*

عصفر *'uṣfur*, m. saffron in the flower (*Carthamus tinctorius*). *a.*

عصفور *'uṣfūr*, m. a sparrow. *a.*

عصمت *'iṣmat* (properly *'aṣmat*), f. defence, protection (especially from sin), hence chastity, honour, integrity, continence. *a.*

عصه *'aṣa*, a handkerchief tied round the head (by women) when going to bed. *d.*

عصيان *'iṣyān*, m. sin, transgression, rebellion, opposition. *a.*

عضد *'aẓd* or *'aẓad*, the arm (from the shoulder to the elbow). *'aẓadu-d-daula*, the arm of the state; a man's name. *a.*

عضله *'aẓala*, m. a tendon, a muscle. *a.*

عضو *'aẓo*, or *'aẓv*, or *'iẓw*, m. a member, a joint. *a.*

عطا *'aṭā*, f. a gift, present, favour. *'aṭā-bakhsh*, liberal. *'aṭā-k.*, to bestow freely. *a.*

عطار *'aṭṭār*, m. a perfumer or druggist; name of a celebrated Persian poet. *a.*

عطارد *'uṭārid*, the planet Mercury; quicksilver. *a.*

عطاري *'aṭṭārī*, relating to a druggist; f. the business of perfumer or druggist. *a.*

عطر *'aṭr* or *'iṭr*, m. perfume, fragrance, essence, ottar (of roses, &c.). *'aṭr-dān*, a perfume-box. *aṭr-mālī*, f. the act of rubbing or applying perfume. *a.*

عطريات *'iṭriyāt*, pl. perfumes, scents. *a.*

عطريت *'aṭriyat* or *'iṭriyat*, fragrance, odour, perfume. *a.*

عطسان *'aṭsān*, } m. sneezing, a sneeze. *a.*
عطسه *'aṭsa*, }

عطش *'aṭash*, f. thirst. *'aṭish*, thirsty. *a.*

عطشان *'aṭshān*, m. } very thirsty, burning with thirst or desire. *a.*
عطشي *'aṭshā*, f. }

عطف *'aṭf*, m. favour, affection, kindness, a present, bounty; connecting, joining. *ḥarfi 'aṭf*, a copulative conjunction. *a.*

عطوفت *'uṭūfat*, inclination; affection, favour, kindness. *a.*

عظام *'iẓām* (pl. of عظم), bones; (pl. of *'aẓīm*) the great. *uẓām* or *'uẓẓām*, adj. great. *a.*

عظم *'aẓm*, m. a bone. *'iẓm* or *'uẓm*, greatness, magnificence; pomp, pride. *a.*

عظمت *'aẓamat* or *'aẓmat*, f. greatness, magnificence, magnitude, aggrandizement. *a.*

عظمىٰ *'aẓmā*, supreme, the very greatest. *wizārati 'uẓmā*, the dignity of grand *wazīr*, or prime minister. *a.*

عظيم *'aẓīm*, great, high in dignity, large. *'aẓīmu-sh-shān*, of high station, rank, or dignity. *a.*

عفاريت *'afārīt* (pl. of عفريت), horrible demons or giants. *a.*

عفاف *'afāf*, abstaining; chastity, continence. *a.*

عفت *'iffat*, f. purity, chastity, continence, virtue, abstinence, modesty. *a.*

عفريت *'ifrīt*, m. any thing frightful or horrible; a giant, demon, spectre, ogre. *a.*

عفص *'afṣ*, m. gall (both the tree and the nut). *a.*

عف عف *'af-'af* or *'uf-'uf*, the barking of a dog; an imitative sound like our *bow-wow*. *a.*

عفو *'afū*, m. absolution, forgiveness. *a.*

عفوپيشه *'afū-pesha*, forgiving, merciful. *a.p.*

عفوصت *'ufūṣat*, astringency, constipation; bitterness. *a.*

عفونت *'ufūnat*, f. corruption, infection, stink (especially of a dead carcase). *a.*

عفي *'afā*, (used benedictively) as *'afa-l-lāhu-'an-hu*, may God have had mercy upon him! *a.*

عفيف *'afīf*, temperate, abstinent. *a.*

عفيفه *'afīfa*, a chaste, modest woman. *a.*

عقاب *'uḳāb*, m. an eagle. *'iḳāb*, m. chastisement. *a.*

عقائد *'aḳā,id* (pl. of عقيده), articles of faith, religious tenets. *a.*

عقب *'aḳab*, behind, after, in the rear, in pursuit; m. the rear, the heel. *'aḳab-k.*, a. to follow. *a.*

عقبىٰ *'uḳbā*, m. end, conclusion, accomplishment; the future or next world. *a.*

عقد *'aḳd*, m. a knot; the marriage knot, marriage; a compact, agreement; a collar, a necklace; a bulse, a string (of pearls, &c.). *'aḳd-bandī*, the concluding of any contract, more especially the tying of the marriage-knot. *a.*

عقده *'uḳda*, m. a knot, matrimony; an excrescence (especially at the joints, or where bones have been broken); a node; an impediment in speech; perplexed affairs, entangled things, confused words. *'uḳda-kushā*, one who solves difficulties. *a.*

عقر *'aḳr*, a marriage portion or dower. *a.*

عقرب *'aḳrab*, m. a scorpion; the sign Scorpio; (met.) a quarrelsome person; (in Dakh.) the hand of a watch. *a.*

عقرقرحا *'aḳarḳarḥā*, m. the name of a medicine, the herb pellitory. *a.*

عقل *'aḳl*, f. wisdom, opinion, sense, understanding. *'aḳl-thijnā*, to be astonished. *'aḳl kharachnā*, to act wisely, lit to expend one's wisdom. *'aḳl daurānā* a. to consider, to think. *a.*

عقلا *'uḳalā* (pl. of عاقل), the wise, the prudent. *'aḳlan*, adv. reasonably, prudently. *a.*

عقلمند *'aḳl-mand*, wise, sensible, intelligent. *a.p.*

عقلمندي *'aḳlmandī*, f. wisdom, sound sense. *a.p.*

عقلونت *'aḳl-want* or *'aḳl-wantā*, wise. *d.*

عقلي *'aḳlī*, reasonable, rational, judicious. *a.*

عقوبت *'aḳūbat*, f. punishment, torment, chastisement, torture. *'aḳūbati dozakh*, damnation. *a.*

عقول *'aḳūl*, wise, sagacious. *'uḳūl* (pl. of عقل), sciences, minds, understandings. *a.*

عقيده *'aḳīda* or *'aḳīdat*, m. faith, belief, a fundamental article of religion; fidelity. *'aḳīdat-mand*, faithful. *a.*

عقيق *'aḳīḳ*, m. a cornelian, a red gem. *a.*

عقيق البحر *'aḳīḳu-l-baḥr*, Mocha stone. *a.*

عقيقه *'aḳīḳa*, m. the hair upon new-born infants; the sixth day after childbirth, or a feast given on that day. *a.*

عقيم *'aḳīm*, m. barren, having no children. *a.*

عقيمه *'aḳīma*, f. barren, a woman past child-bearing. *a.*

عكس *'aks*, m. reflection; inversion; a shadow or reflected image; the contrary, opposite; spite, opposition. *a.*

علا *'alā*, m. glory, sublimity, exaltation, superiority; adj. most high or glorious. *a.*

علاج *'ilāj*, m. a remedy, cure, medicine. *a.*

علاحده *'alāḥida* (for *'alaiḥida*), separate, apart. *a.*

علاقگي *'alāḳagī*, connection, attachment. *a.p.*

علاقه *'alāḳa* or *'ilāḳa*, m. relation, connection, interest; pretension, right; commerce, correspondence, communication. *'alāḳa-band* or *'ilāḳa-band*, a lace-maker, a tape-maker. *'ilāḳa-bandī*, the business of lace-making; also lace-work in general. *'alāḳa-dār*, the person who becomes responsible for the payment of village rates, &c. *'alāḳa-mand*, connected, dependent, responsible. *a.*

علام *'allām*, omniscient, God. *'allāmu-l-ghuyūb*, acquainted with things invisible; an epithet of the Almighty. *a.*

علامت *'alāmat*, a mark, badge, sign, token, emblem, device, a coat of arms. *'alāmati dast-khaṭṭ*, a mark in place of a signature. *a.*

علامه *'allāma*, wise, learned. *'allāma,e 'aṣr*, the most learned of the time. *a.*

علامه *'alāma* (same as *'alāmat*), a mark, &c. *a.*

علانيه *'alāniya*, openly, publicly. *a.*

علاوه *'alāwa*, besides, in addition. *a.*

علت *'illat*, f. cause, pretence; filth, dirt; disease, weakness. *ḥarfi 'illat*, the interchangeable letters, *alif*, *wāw*, and *ye*; all material substances are said to have four causes; *'illati ṣūrī*, formal cause, *i. e.* that form in which its essence consists; *'illati ghā,ī*, final cause, or purpose for which it was made; *'illati fā'ilī*, efficient cause (as the maker, if the work of man); *'illati māddī*, material cause, or the matter of which the thing is made. *a.*

علف *'alaf*, m. grass, hay, food for cattle. *a.*

علفزار *'alaf-zār*, pasturage, a meadow. *a. p.*

علفه *'ulafa* (for *'ulūfa*), salary, daily pay. *d.*

علق *'alaḳ*, m. hanging, suspending, adhering,

علقت *'alaḳat*, suspension. *a.*

علل *'ilal* (pl. of علت), infirmities, pretences, &c. *a.*

علم *'ilm*, m. science, knowledge. *'ilmi asmā*, the knowledge of the names, *i. e.* of the attributes of God. *'ilmi ilāhī*, theology. *'ilmu-l-yaḳīn*, certain knowledge, demonstration. *'ilmi taṣawwuf*, the mystic or contemplative science; the doctrines of the *ṣūfīs* *'ilmi tashrīḥ*, anatomy. *'ilmi tawārīkh*, history, chronology. *'ilmi ḥikmat*, philosophy, physics. *'ilmi raḳam*, or *-ghubār*, or *-ḥisāb*, arithmetic. *'ilmi riyāẓī*, the mathematical sciences. *'ilmi siḥar*, magic. *'ilmi shi'r*, poetry, versification, scansion. *'ilmi ṭabī'ī*, natural philosophy. *'ilmi 'arūẓ*, poetry, versification. *'ilmi fiḳh*, jurisprudence. *'ilmi kalām*, scholastic theology. *'ilmi-bayān*, or *-balāghat*, or *-ma'ānī*, the explanatory science, *i. e.* rhetoric, oratory, eloquence. *'ilmi kīmiyā*, alchemy. *'ilmi mūsīḳī*, music. *'ilmi nujūm*, astronomy, astrology. *'ilmi handasa*, geometry. *'ilm o faẓl*, knowledge and virtue. *a.*

علم *'alam*, m. a spear; standard, banner, ensign; sign, mark; (in gram.) a proper name. *a.*

علما *'ulamā* (pl. of عالم), the learned. *a.*

علمبردار *'alam-bardār*, a standard-bearer. *a. p.*

علمخوان *'ilm-khwān*, a student, studious. *a. p.*

علمدار *'alam-dār*, a standard-bearer. *a. p.*

علمدان *'ilm-dān*, learned, wise. *a. p.*

علمي *'ilmī*, scientific, doctrinal. *a.*

علو *'ulū* or *'alw*, m. an eminence, height, sublimity. *a.*

علوفه *'ulūfa*, m. stipend, salary, daily pay, [subsistence money. *a.*

علوم *'ulūm* (pl. of علم), sciences. *a.*

علوي *'ulwī*, lofty, sublime; celestial. *a.*

علوي *'alawī*, a descendant or follower of *'Alī* the son-in-law of *Muḥammad*. *a.*

علي *'alī*, a man's name; the name of *Muḥammad's* son-in-law: he was, according to the *Sunnīs*, the fourth *khalīfa* or successor of *Muḥammad*, but the *Shī'as* make him the direct successor, not acknowledging the other three caliphs. *'alī kī kamān*, lit. the bow of 'Alī; the rainbow. *a.*

علي *'alā*, on, upon, above, about: this word is used only in Arabic phrases, as *'alā-l-aṣar*, instantly; *'alā-t-taḥḳīḳ*, according to truth, verily; *'alā-l-khuṣūṣ*, in particular; *alā-d-dawām*, perpetually; *'alā-ṣ-saḥar*, or *'alā-ṣ-ṣubāḥ*, in the morning. *'alā hāẕa-l-ḳiyās*, in like manner, in a similar way. *a.*

عليحده *'alāḥida* or *'alaiḥida*, separate, apart. *a.*

عليل *'alīl*, weak, sick, indisposed. *a.*

عليم *'alīm*, wise, learned, knowing. *a.*

عليه *'alaihi*, on him, } used in Arabic
عليهم *'alaihim*, on them, } phrases, as *'alaihi-s-salām*, on him be peace, may he rest in peace. *a.*

عليون *'illiyūn*, the seventh heaven; adj. high, sublime. *a.*

عم *'amm*, m. an uncle, father's brother *'amm-zāda*, paternal uncle's son. *a.*

عماد *'imād*, a prop, a pillar, support. *'imādu-d-daula*, the support of the state; a man's name. *a.*

عمارات *'imārāt* (pl. of عمارت), buildings. *a.*

عمارت *'imārat*, a public edifice, a building; a habitation; a fortification. *a.*

عماري *'amārī*, f. the litter in which people sit on an elephant: when it has no canopy it is called a *hauda*. *a.*

عمال *'ummāl* (pl. of عامل), agents, &c. *a.*

عمامه *'imāma* or *'amāma*, a turban, a tiara. *a.*

عمان *'umān*, the southern coast of Arabia. *baḥri 'umān*, the sea between Ethiopia and India. *umān*, the high sea, the main ocean: "I think this must be a mistake: *baḥri 'umān* is the common name of the Persian Gulf. I never heard it applied to the southern Indian ocean; *'umān* generally signifies the coast of the Persian gulf."—(Binning.) *a.*

عمد *'amd*, wilful, a legal term analogous to the "malicium" of Roman law: thus, *ḳatl*, "slaughter, bloodshed;" *ḳatli 'amd*, "wilful murder."—(Binning.) *a.*

عمدًا *'amdan*, deliberately, purposely. *a.*

عمدانه *'umdāna*, like a noble or grandee. *a p.*

عمدت *'umdat*, a support, pillar, prop. *'umdatu-l-khawāṣṣ*, a prime minister. *'umdatu-l-mulk*, the pillar of the state, a title bestowed on officers of high rank. *a.*

عمدگي *'umdagī*, f. greatness, &c.; sumptuousness. *a.*

عمده *'umda*, great, noble; m. a grandee, a support, a pillar, a prop, confidence, reliance, trust. *a.*

عمر *'umr*, f. age, lifetime, period of life. *'umar*, the name of the second in succession from *Muḥammad*. *'umr-darāz*, of long life. *a.*

عمرو زيد *'umar wa zaid*, Umar and Zaid, two celebrated gentlemen of straw, like our "John Nokes and Thomas Styles," who figure largely in Muhammadan legal and scholastic discussions. *a.*

عمره *'umra*, m. pilgrimage to Mecca; visiting a wife while in the house of her parents. *a.*

عمق *'umuḳ*, m. depth, profundity. *a.*

عمل *'amal*, m. action, operation, work, practice, effect, dominion, territory. *'amal-dār*, m. one who has command; a collector. *'amal-dārī*, a collectorship. *'amal-nāma*, an order, a warrant; a code of instructions. *amal meṅ lānā*, to carry into effect. *'amal-k.* to act or operate *a.*

عملاً *'amalan*, in fact, indeed, truly. *a.*

عمل پتّہ *'amal-patta*, عمل دستك *'amal-dastak*, عمل سند *'amal-sanad*, عمل نامہ *'amal-nāma*, } m. a deed granting authority to collect rents or revenue dues. *a.p.h.*

عمل گذار *'amal-guzār*, a collector of revenue. *a.p.*

عمله *'amala* (pl. of عامل), agents, officers, subordinates. *'imla*, work; wages, hire. *a.*

عملي *'amalī*, artificial, practical. *ḥikmati 'amalī*, natural or practical philosophy; f. payment of revenue in kind. *a.*

عملية *'amalīyat*, practice (pl. *'amalīyāt*). *a.*

عمو *'ammū*, m. a paternal uncle. *a.*

عمود *'amūd*, m. a perpendicular (in geometry). *'amūdu-ṣ-ṣubḥ*, the spreading light of the dawn. *a.*

عموداً *'amūdan*, perpendicularly. *a.*

عموم *'amūm*, common, general, universal. *a.*

عموماً *'amūman*, commonly, generally. *a.*

عميق *'amīḳ*, deep, profound. *a.*

عميم *'amīm*, full, complete; universal. *a.*

عن *'an*, from, with, afte., on, concerning, above, before. *'an-ḳarībi-z-zamān*, in a little time, soon *a.*

عنا *'anā*, f. distress, labour, trouble. *a.*

عناب *'unnāb*, the jujube tree and fruit. *a. p.*

عنابي *'unnābī*, of a carnation colour. *a. p.*

عناد *'inād*, m. obstinacy, peverseness, resistance, stubbornness. *a.*

عناصر *'anāṣir* (pl. of عنصر), elements. *a.*

عنان *'inān*, f. reins, a bridle. *a.*

عنايات *'ināyāt* (pl of عنايت), favours, gifts, presents. *a.*

عنايت *'ināyat*, f. favour, gift, present. *a.*

عنب *'inab*, the grape. *bintu-l-'inab*, the daughter of the grape—wine. *'inabu-ṣ-ṣa'lab*, black, nightshade. *a.*

عنبر *'ambar*, m. ambergris, a rich perfume. *a.*

عنبربار *'ambar-bār*, odoriferous, fragrant. *a.p.*

عنبرچه *'ambarcha*, an ornament for the neck full of *'ambar*; a smelling-bottle. *a.p.*

عنبري *'ambarī*, عنبرين *'ambarīn*, } of or resembling ambergris (as to smell or colour). *a.p.*

عنبرينه *'ambarīna*, a kind of perfume. *a. p.*

عنتر *'antar*, a famous Arabian hero, whose exploits form the theme of a well-known Arabic romance. *a.*

عند *'ind*, near, before, with, about, in, according to, &c. *'inda-l-ba'ẓ*, according to some. *'inda-t-taḥḳīḳ*, in truth, certainly. *'inda-l-lāh*, with or before God. *'inda-l-wuṣūl*, on the arrival, when it happens, in such an event. *'inda-l-waḳt*, in time, in the critical juncture. *a.*

عندليب *'andalīb*, f. a nightingale. *c*

عنديات *'indiyāt* (pl. of عنديه), opinions, tenets, absurdities, fables. *a.*

عنديه *'indiya*, m. one's peculiar opinion or trust. *a.*

عنصر *'unṣur* or *'unṣar*, a primary element. *a.*

عنصري *'unṣurī*, elementary; name of a Persian poet cotemporary with Firdausī. *a.*

عنسل *'unsal* or *'unsul*, a sea leek, a squill. *a.*

عنفوان *'unfuwān*, m. the beginning (of any thing); vigour; the flower of youth. *a.*

عنقا *'anḳā*, m. the phœnix, a fabulous bird, called by the Persians *simurgh*, q. v.; adj. (met.) rare, wonderful, curious. *a.*

عنقريب *'an-ḳarīb*, near, soon, shortly, nearly. *a.*

عنكبوت *'ankabūt*, f. a spider. *a.*

عنوان *'unwān* or *'inwān* (vulg. *'anwān*), m. the ornamented title-page of a book; that whereby any thing is known; that which is understood by any thing; mode, manner. *a.*

عنين *'innīn*, impotent, weak, frail. *a.*

عواقب *'awāḳib* (pl. of عاقبت), ends, consequences; posterity. *a.*

عوام *'awāmm* (pl. of عامّه), the vulgar, the populace. *'awāmm wa khawāṣṣ*, plebeians and nobles, the people at large. *'awāmmu-n-nās*, the common people, the populace at large. *a.*

عوامل *'awāmil* (pl. of عامله), (in gram.) words which govern others. *a.*

عوائب *'awā,ib* (pl. of عائبه), blemishes, defects; faults, vices. *a.*

عود *'ūd*, m. wood, timber; a staff, a stick; the wood aloes. "In the Dakhanī dialect this word usually signifies 'gum benzoin;' while 'lignum aloes' is commonly called *agar*."—(Binning). *a.*

عود *'aud*, m. returning; a man of abilities, experience, and prudence. *a.*

عودسوز *'ūd-soz*, a censer in which they burn aloes wood. *a. p.*

عودي *'ūdī*, relating to aloes wood. *'ūdī-takht*, heaven. *a. p.*

عوذ *'auz*, m. refuge, asylum, fleeing to God for protection. *a.*

عور *'ūr*, naked, monocular, one-eyed. *a.*

عورات *'aurāt* (pl. of عورت), in Hind., women; in Arab., pudenda. *a. p. h.*

عورت *'aurat*, f. this word in Hind. denotes simply a woman or a wife; but in Arabic and Persian it denotes the particular parts of man or woman which are concealed through modesty. "Are the words *'aurat* and *'aurāt* ever used in Persian in the sense of 'women?' I think not. In the corrupt and vitiated Persian of India they are so, but I do not think any native of Persia would use the words, except in the Arabic sense."—(Binning). *a.*

عورتانه *'auratāna*, like a woman. *a. h.*

عوض *'iwaz*, m. reward, retribution, return, any thing substituted for another, exchange, ready money, hard cash, recompense; adv. instead, for. *a.*

عون *'aun*, m. aid, assistance; a defender, an aider. *a.*

عهد *'ahd*, m. contract, compact, obligation, promise, treaty; time, season, conjuncture, reign (of a king, prince, &c); an oath, a vow; a mandate, will, or testament; lifetime. *a.*

عهددار *'ahd-dār*, an officer who engages to collect the revenue of a district for a small percentage. *a. p.*

عهدشکن *'ahd-shikan*, a promise breaker. *a. p.*

عهدشکني *'ahd-shikanī*, f. a breach of contract, breach of faith. *a.*

عهدنامه *'ahd-nāma*, m. a letter of agreement; articles of peace or capitulation; a diploma. *a. p.*

عهده *'uhda*, m. a commission, an obligation, an agreement; business, office, post (vul. *hudda*). *'uhda-barā*, one who acquits himself of any task or commission. *'uhda-barā-h.*, to acquit one's self of an obligation. *'uhda-barā,ī*, f. completing an agreement, being able to perform any work. *'uhda-bandī*, f. an agreement to pay a debt by regular instalments. *'uhda-dār* or *'uhde-dār*, intrusted with a business, holding a commission, an officer. *a.*

عيادت *'iyādat*, f. visiting (of the sick). *a.*

عياذا بالله *'iyāzan-bi-l-lāh*, interj. may God avert or forbid. *a.*

عيار *'ayār* or *'iyār*, m. a mark, proof, test, standard, assay, touch. *'iyāri dānish*, the criterion of knowledge; name of the Persian version of Pilpay's fables made by *Abu-l-fazl*, translated into Hindūstānī under the title of *Khirad Afroz*. *a.*

عيار *'aiyār*, cunning, sly, shrewd; m. a knave. *a.*

عيارپنا *'aiyār-panā*, m. } slyness, knavery. *a. h. p.*
عيارگي *'aiyāragī*, f. }

عيارني *'aiyārnī*, f. a cunning or artful woman. *a. h.*

عياره *'aiyāra*, f. a sly or cunning woman. *a.*

عياري *'aiyārī*, f. cunningness, artfulness; an artful woman. *a.*

عياش *'aiyāsh*, jovial, luxurious. *a.*

عياشي *'aiyāshī*, f. joviality, luxuriousness. *a.*

عيال *'iyāl*, m. family, children, domestics. *'iyāl-dār*, a man who is burdened with a large family.

عيان *'ayān*, clear, manifest, public, conspicuous, visible. *a.*

عيب *'aib*, m. fault, defect, a vice, blemish, sin, disgrace, infamy. *'aib-jo*, one who seeks for faults. *'aib-chīn*, one who carefully collects trifling errors. *'aib-chīnī*, culling of errors, what is vulgarly called criticism. *'aib-go*, a slanderer, a calumniator. *'aib-gīr*, one who seizes upon another's faults. *'aib-lagānā*, to defame. *a.*

عيبي *'aibī*, vicious, faulty, infamous. *a.*

عيد *'īd*, f. a solemnity, festival, holy day; Easter. *'īdi-azhā* or *'īdi ḳurbān*, a festival held in commemoration of Abraham's offering up his son Isaac (or Ishmael according to the Muḥammadans). *a.*

عيدي *'īdī*, a present, which it is usual to make on the day of *'īd*, an Easter gift. *a.*

عيسیٰ *'īsā*, Jesus, our Lord. *a.*

عيسوي *'īsawī* (also *'īsa,ī*), Christian. *a.*

عيش *'aish*, m. pleasure, delight. *'aish-gāh* or *-maḥall*, place or house of enjoyment. *'aish-o-jaish*, joy and delight, excessive pleasure. *a.*

عين *'ain*, m. the eye, sight; the very essence or best part of a thing; a fountain; the sun; money, gold, &c.; adj. very, exact, intrinsic, real, just. *'ainu-l-ḳaṭr*, brimstone. *'ain waḳt par*, in the very nick of time, at the precise moment. *a.*

عينك *'ainak*, f. spectacles, glasses to assist the sight. *a.*

عينين *'ainain* (du. of عين), the two eyes. *a.*

عينيه *'ainīya*, relating to the eye. *a.*

عيوب *'uyūb* (pl. of عيب), vices, defects, &c. *a.*

عيوق *'aiyūḳ*, the bright star Capella. *a.*

غ

غ *ghain*, called *ghaini mu'jama* or *ghaini manḳūṭa*, the nineteenth letter of the Arabic alphabet, the twenty-second Persian, and the twenty-fifth Hindūstānī. This letter is Arabic or Persian, but has no corresponding sound or character in the Sanskrit or any of the native dialects of India. It is one of the guttural letters, its sound being that of an aspirated *g* resembling the Northumberland *r*. The Musalmāns of India generally sound this letter correctly; but by most of the Hindūs, especially in Bengal, it is sounded like *g* hard in *go*, as *gulām* for *ghulām*, a slave. In reckoning by *abjad* it stands for 1000.

غابر *ghābir*, left, lasting, remaining. *a.*

غاته *ghāṭa*, m. a slave. *h.*

غادر *ghādir*, m. a cheat; adj. deceitful. *a.*

غار *ghār*, m. a cavern, a pit; a deep gash or wound. *yāri ghār*, a companion in a cave or prison, *i. e.* an intimate friend. *gharr*, m. a deceiver. *a.*

غارت *ghārat*, rapine, plunder, devastation. *ghārat-k.*, to plunder, devastate, lay waste. *ghārat-ghol*, m. sudden loss or destruction; suddenly or unexpectedly lost. *ghārat-gar*, a plunderer, an oppressor. *a.*

غارم *ghārim*, a debtor so helpless as to be the subject of *zakāt*, or alms. *a.*

غاريقون *ghārīḳūn*, m. agaric (Gr. αγαρικον). *g.*

غازه *ghāza*, m. red colour with which women paint their face. *p.*

غازي *ghāzī*, m. a conqueror, a hero, particularly so if he has fought against and slain one or more infidels. *ghāzī mard*, a hero; (met.) a horse. *ghāzī miyān*, name of a saint, who, according to some authorities, was nephew of *Sulṭān Maḥmūd ghaznawī*: a festival is held in commemoration of him at the beginning of May. *a.*

غازيانه ghāziyāna, bravely, heroically. *a.*
غاشيه ghāshiya, a saddle-cloth or cover; a porter's burden. *a. p.*
غافر ghāfir, one who pardons. *a.*
غافل ghāfil, senseless, stupid, apathetic, negligent, indolent, imprudent, careless, thoughtless, not on one's guard. *ghāfil-gīr*, attacking unawares. *a.*
غافلاً ghāfilan, imprudently, carelessly. *a.*
غافلي ghāfilī, f. inattention, negligence. *a.*
غال ghāl, (in comp.) rolling, wallowing; a cavern in which they keep cattle; a bee hive. *p.*
غالب ghālib, overcoming, excelling. *ghālib honā*, n. to overcome. *a.*
غالبًا ghāliban, chiefly, principally, apparently, probably, most likely, upon the whole. *a.*
غالي ghālī, dear, precious; f. a carpet, tapestry. *a. p.*
غاليچه ghālīcha, m. a small carpet. *p.*
غامض ghāmiẓ, abstruse, difficult, obscure. *a.*
غانٹا ghānṭā, imperious, forward. *a.*
غاني ghānī, rich, wealthy, independent. *a.*
غاور ghāwir, powerful; considerate. *a.*
غاي ghāy (pl. of غايت), ends, extremities. *a.*
غائب ghā,ib, absent, concealed, invisible, vanished; the third person (in gram.). *ghā,ib-bāz*, m. a conjuror. *a.*
غائبانه ghā,ibāna, in absence, invisibly. *a*
غايت ghāyat, adv. very, extremely, chiefly; f. the end, extremity, excess; a standard, flag; ordure. *'ilmi ghāyat*, mathematics. *a.*
غائط ghā,iṭ, m. excrement, dung. *a.*
غب ghibb, f. a tertian ague, visiting every alternate day. *a.* [day. *a.*
غبًا ghibban, seldom, rarely; every second
غبار ghubār, f. dust; vapour; clouds of dust, impurity, foulness; (met.) vexation, affliction, perplexity. *ghubār-ālūda* or *-ālūd*, covered with dust. *ghubāri khāṭir*, affliction, disturbance in mind. *a.*
غباره ghubāra, m. a bomb, a shell, or mortar for throwing shells. *p.*
غباوت ghabāwat, f. inadvertency, stupidity. *a.*
غبغب ghabghab, m. a dewlap, a double chin. *chāhi ghabghab*, a pit in the chin. *p.*
غبن ghabn, m. fraud, deceit; loss (of money, &c.). *ghabni fāḥish*, a gross fraud, applied especially to the forced sale of a property far below its value. *ghaban*, m. weakness in mind, mistake, forgetfulness; adj. weak in mind, liable to deception. *a.*
غبي ghabī, weak in mind, forgetful, negligent, imprudent. *a.* [ging, boasting. *a.*
غپ ghap, the sound made by a blow; brag-
غپاغپ ghapāghap, *sonum congressus in coitu*. *h.*

غپ چپ ghap-chup, silent, noiseless. *d.*
غپكا ghaphā (v. ghap), noise of a blow. *d.*
غٹ ghaṭ, the noise of gulping or swallowing; a troop, band, or gang. *d.*
غٹا ghaṭṭā, a corn on the foot; a cork or stopper of a bottle. *d.*
غٹ پٹ ghaṭ-paṭ, hand to hand, congression, shock, conflict, encountering, *congressus*. *h.*
غٹكنا ghaṭaknā, to coo (as doves). *h.*
غچ ghach, غچا ghachā, غچاغچ ghachāghach, غچاكا ghachākā, } m. slapping, clapping; *sonum congressus in coitu*; the sound of walking in mire; the sound of striking with a spear or sword. *h.*
غچ پچ بولنا ghichpich bolnā, n. to speak thick. *h.*
غچو ghachū, m. غچي ghachī, f. } a hole made in the ground by boys for playing at tip-cat. *ghachū-pāra*, m. name of a game, tipcat. *h.*
غد ghad, a thump, blow. *d.*
غدار ghadār, a cavern, a pit. *d.*
غدار ghaddār, fraudulent, sly; a cheat. *a.*
غداغد ghad-ā-ghad, thumping; a succession of blows. *d.*
غدد ghudud, m. a hard lump formed in the flesh, a glandular swelling. *a.*
غدر ghadr, m. perfidy, fraud, villany, ingratitude; noise, bustle. *a.*
غدير ghadīr, fraudulent, perfidious; name of a festival celebrated by the *Shī'as* (v. Wilson's Gl.). *a.*
غذا ghizā, f. aliment, diet, provision, food (pl. *aghziya*). *a.*
غذايت ghizāyat, f. aliment, provision. *a.*
غرا gharrā, white, bright, splendid, illustrious, noble. *a.* [sun. *p.*
غرا ghurā (for ghurra), white, bright; the
غراب ghurāb, a crow, raven, rook, or jackdaw; a kind of Arab ship vulgarly called a *grab*. *a.*
غراره gharāra, m. a large sack. *a.*
غراز ghurrāz, frowning, haughty, brave. *a.*
غرازي gharrāzī, f. haughtiness, bravery. *a.*
غرازيل gharāzīl, the devil, Satan. *a.*
غرامت gharāmat, debt; a mulct, a fine. *a.*
غران gharān or gharrān, rapacious, fierce. *p.*
غرانا ghurrānā, n. to frown. *h.*
غرائب gharā,ib, غرائبات gharā,ibāt, } (pl. of غريبه) rare or wonderful events, strange things. *a.*

غرب *gharb*, m. the setting of the sun, the west. *a.*

غربا *ghurabā* (pl of غريب), the poor, or the strangers. *a.*

غربال *ghirbāl*, f. a sieve; a riddle. *a.*

غربت *ghurbat*, f. travelling, being far from one's country and friends, exile; wretchedness. *a.*

غربي *gharbī*, western, occidental. *a.*

غرزنگ *ghurzang*, m. a bound, jump. *p.*

غرش *gharsh*, غرشا *gharshā*, غرشي *gharshī*, indignation, anger, rage, passion (also *ghurrish*). *p.*

غرض *gharaẓ*, f. design, view, wish, intention, end, business, meaning, need, occasion, use, want, interestedness, selfishness, hatred, spite; adv. in short, in a word, in fine. *gharaẓ-āshnā*, interested. *gharaẓ-ālūd* or *-āmez*, selfish, interested, designing. *gharaẓ-bāwlā*, a slave to one's passions. *gharaẓ-mand*, self-interested, desirous, wishing for. *gharaẓ-mandī*, f. desire, selfishness. *a.*

غرضانه *gharaẓāna*, selfishly, malevolently. *a.p.*

غرضي *gharaẓī*, selfish, interested, designing. *a.h.*

غرغر *ghurghur*, noise, uproar, tumult; (a man) muttering with rage. *p.*

غرغره *gharghara*, m. gargling. *a.*

غرفش *ghurfish*, f. reproof, intimidation, threatening, bullying (particularly that of a coward who affects bravery). *p.*

غرفه *ghurfa*, an upper apartment, a window, a parlour. *p.*

غرق *gharḳ*, m. drowning, sinking; adj. drowned, immersed, sunk. *a.*

غرقاب *gharḳ-āb*, deep water, a whirlpool. *a. p.*

غرقي *gharḳī*, f. flooded lands, inundation. *a.*

غرکانا *ghurkānā*, a. to frighten, to terrify. *d.*

غرکنا *ghuraknā*, n. to be afraid, frightened. *d.*

غرکي *ghurkī*, fear, dread, aversion. *d.*

غرنده *gharanda*, *ghuranda*, or *ghurranda*, roaring, fierce, rapacious. *p.*

غروب *ghurūb*, m. setting (of the sun, &c.); the west. *ghurūb honā*, n. to be set (the sun or moon, &c.). *a.*

غرور *ghurūr* or *gharūr*, m. pride, haughtiness, vain-glory, vanity. *a.*

غروري *ghurūrī*, f. haughtiness, pride. *a. h.*

غره *gharra*, haughty, proud; misled, deceived; cross; m. pride. *a.*

غره *ghurra*, m. the first day of the moon; a fast, fasting; whiteness, brightness; a white spot in the forehead of a horse; the forehead. *a.*

غريب *gharīb*, m. a foreigner, a stranger; adj. poor; mild, humble; rare, wonderful, strange. *gharīb-parwar*, cherisher of the poor. *gharīb-mār*, f. oppression of the poor. *gharīb-nawāz*, courteous to strangers, kind to the poor, hospitable. *a.*

غريبانه *gharībāna*, fit for the poor, humbly. *a.*

غريبه *gharība*, f. of غريب, q. v. *a.*

غريبي *gharībī*, f. humility, wretchedness, poverty. *a.*

غرير *gharīz*, nature; meekness, gentleness. *a. p.*

غريزي *gharīzī*, innate, natural. *a.*

غريق *gharīḳ*, m. a drowning person; adj. immersed, drowned. *gharīḳ-āb*, deep, out of man's depth. *gharīḳi raḥmat*, overwhelmed with mercy, drowned in the grace of God. *a.*

غرين *gharīn*, a wood, forest, or thicket, frequented by lions. *p.*

غريو *gharew* or *ghirīw*, m. noise, tumult; a mob; a gurgling noise in the throat, growling. *p.*

غريوان *gharīwān*, a present, a gift. *ghirīwān*, one who laments or exclaims. *p.*

غڑپ کرنا *gharap-karnā*, to cause to sink, to immerse. *d.*

غڑپ هونا *gharap-honā*, to sink, to be drowned. *d.*

غڑچه *gharachcha* (explained by داٹ), a thicket, clump, &c. *d.*

غزا *ghazā*, m. making war (against infidels). *ghazā-ṣafā*, war, plunder, devastation. *a.*

غزال *ghizāl* or *ghazāl*, m. a young deer, a fawn, a gazelle; the sun; a delicate young person. *a.*

غزاله *ghizāla*, or *ghazāla*, m. a young deer, a fawn. *a.*

غزل *ghazal*, f. an ode, a short poem or amatory sonnet. *ghazal-khwān*, a repeater of odes. *a.*

غسال *ghassāl*, m. one whose business it is to wash the bodies of the dead. *a.*

غساله *ghasāla*, m. dirty water with which any thing has been washed; bathing. *a.*

غسل *ghusl*, m. bathing, ablution. *ghusl-khāna*, m. a bath, bagnio. *a.*

غش *ghash*, m. stupor, fainting. *ghash-ānā*, or *ghash-paṛnā*, to faint. *a.*

غشمشم *ghashamsham*, intrepid, headstrong. *a.*

غشي *ghashī*, fainting, being stupefied. *a.*

غشيت *ghashyat*, a swoon, a fainting-fit. *a.*

غصب *ghaṣab*, m. violence, injustice, force, oppression, ravishing, plunder. *a.*

غصون *ghuṣūn* (pl. of غصن), young branches. *a.*

غصه *ghuṣṣa*, m. strangulation, suffocation; (met.) anxiety, grief; (in Hind.) anger, passion. *ghuṣṣe*, in anger, angry. *ghuṣṣe se bhūt hojānā*, to rage like a fiend. *ghuṣṣa-nāk* or *ghuṣṣa-war*, passionate. *a.*

غضب *ghaẓab*, m. violence, oppression, injustice, compulsion, passion, rage, vengeance, anger; adj. angry. *ghaẓab-ālūda*, oppressive; full of rage. *a.*

غضبًا *ghaẓaban*, angrily, in a rage. *a.*

غضبان *ghaẓabān*, angry, enraged. *a.*

غضبي *ghazabī*, f. violence, anger; adj. angry. *a.*

غضروف *ghuzrūf*, m. gristle. *a.*

غضنفر *ghazanfar*, a lion, a champion, a hero. *a.*

غفار *ghaffār*, forgiving (the Deity). *a.*

غفر *ghafar*, غفران *ghufrān*, } m. pardon, remission of sins, forgiveness. *a.*

غفس *ghafs*, thick, close (as cloth), substantial. *a.*

غفل *ghafal*, m. غفلت *ghaflat*, f. } carelessness, negligence, inadvertency, neglect. *ghaflat-zada*, struck with carelessness. *khwābi ghaflat* or *ghaflat kā khwāb*, sheer apathy or indifference. *a.*

غفور *ghafūr*, clement, forgiving, merciful. *a.*

غفير *ghafīr*, all, many, numerous. *a.*

غل *ghul*, m. noise, tumult. *ghul-ghupāra*, m. clamour, disturbance. *ghul-ghadr*, noise and tumult. *p.*

غل *ghill*, m. hatred, malice, perfidy, fraud, trick, envy. *ghil o ghish*, f. apprehension, objection. *be ghil o ghish*, without hesitation, boldly, frankly. *a.*

غلاظت *ghilāzat*, f. thickness, spissitude, coarseness, hardness, roughness; roughness of manners; (in Hind.) filth. *a.*

غلاف *ghilāf*, m. a case, a cover, a sheath; the prepuce. *a.*

غلاله *ghilāla*, m. an under waistcoat. *a.*

غلام *ghulām*, m. (in Pers. and Hind.) a male slave; (in Arab.) a boy or youth; a young man at maturity. *ghulām-pāra, puerorum amoribus deditus*; *ghulām-gardish*, m. a shed for servants to sit under. *a.*

غلامي *ghulāmī*, f. slavery, servitude. *a.*

غلبه *ghalaba*, m. superiority, conquest, assault, strength; prevalency, predominancy. *a.*

غلتان *ghaltān* (same as غلطان, q. v.).

غلچگي *ghalchagī*, a strolling life. *p.*

غلچه *ghalcha*, a vagabond, a strolling fellow; a rustic, a villager. *a.*

غلط *ghalat*, m. an error, a mistake; adj. wrong, erroneous. *ghalatu-l-'āmm*, m. a popular mistake, a vulgar error. *ghalat-kār*, delusive. *ghalat-kārī*, f. deception. *ghalat-go*, a false relater. *ghalat-go,ī*, f. relating falsehoods. *ghalat-navīs*, an erroneous writer. *a.*

غلطان *ghaltān*, rolling, wallowing. *ghaltān-pechān*, wallowing, rolling, floundering. *p.*

غلطاني *ghaltānī*, f. act of rolling, weltering, wallowing, floundering. *p.*

غلطه *ghalta*, m. a leathern sheath over a scabbard. *a.*

غلطي *ghalatī*, f. a mistake, error. *a.*

غلطيدن *ghaltīdan*, to roll, to wallow. *p.*

غلظت *ghilzat*, f. filthiness, grossness, rudeness. *a.*

غلغله *ghulghula*, m. noise, tumult; a kind of dish. *p.*

غلمان *ghilmān*, m. (pl. of غلام) boys who attend on the virtuous in Paradise. *a.*

غلو *ghulū*, transgressing; excess, rebellion. *a.*

غلوله *ghalūla*, a small ball, a pellet. *p.*

غله *ghalla*, m. the produce of the earth; grain, corn. *ghalla-dān*, m. a granary. *ghalla-farosh*, a grain-merchant, a monopolist of grain. *ghalla-faroshī*, monopoly of grain. *a.*

غليان *ghalayān*, boiling over, fermenting. *a.*

غليطه *ghaleta*, m. a blow, a thump. *d.*

غليظ *ghalīz*, dirty, filthy, gross, rude. *a.*

غليل *ghulel*, f. a pellet-bow. *ghulel-bāz*, m. a pelleter (with a bow). *ghulel-bāzī*, f. pelleting. *p.*

غليلا *ghulelā*, غليله *ghulela*, } m. a pellet. *p.*

غليلچي *ghulelchī*, m. a pelleter. *p.*

غليواج *ghalewāj* (also *ghalewāz* and *ghalewāzh*), a species of bird, a kite. *p.*

غم *gham*, m. grief. *gham-ālūda*, grieved. *gham-khwār*, devouring sorrow, *i. e.* afflicted, sad; condoling, pitying; an intimate friend. *gham-khwāragī* or *gham-khwārī*, f. affliction; real friendship; commiseration, sympathy. *gham-khurak*, a heron. *gham-dīda*, one who has felt sorrow. *gham-rasīda*, one to whom sorrow has come. *gham-zada*, grieved. *gham-zadagī*, f. grief. *gham-kash*, one who endureth sorrow. *gham karnā*, to bemoan, to sorrow. *gham khānā*, to suffer grief; also to devour one's grief, *i. e.* to have patience. *gham-nāk*, and *gham-gīn*, disconsolate, sorrowful. *a.*

غماز *ghammāz*, m. an informer, a talebearer. *a.*

غمازي *ghammāzī*, f. talebearing. *a.*

غمزه *ghamza*, m. a wink, an amorous glance, coquetry, ogling. *p. a.*

غمي *ghamī*, غمين *ghamīn*, } sad, sorrowful. *p.*

غن *ghan*, m. a heavy stone for pressing oil, &c.; (in Hindī) dead drunk. *p.*

غنا *ghanā*, f. riches, wealth. *ghinā*, f. a song. *a.*

غنائم *ghanā,im* (pl. of غنيمت) spoils, prey, plunder; enemies, plunderers. *a.*

غنج *ghunj*, a wink, an amorous glance or gesture. *p.*

غنچه *ghuncha*, m. a bud. *ghuncha-dahan*, with a mouth like a rosebud, a mistress. *p.*

غنڈه *ghunda*, m. a fop, a ridiculous fellow. *p.*

غنغنانا *ghunghunānā*, n. to mutter, to grumble; to buzz, to hum. *a.*

غنم *ghanm*, *ghanam*, or *ghunm*, carrying off (as plunder). *ghanam*, sheep, cattle, a flock: this term corresponds to the old Gaelic word *creach*, which denotes either the act of carrying off cattle, or the cattle carried off. The Americans seem to use the word plunder in the sense of stock or property. *a.*

غنه *ghunna*, m. a sound through the nose, the buzzing of flies; quiescent, nasal (the letter *nūn*). *a*

غني *ghanī*, independent; rich, wealthy, opulent. *a.*

غنيم *ghanīm*, m. an enemy, a plunderer. *a.*

غنيمت *ghanīmat*, f. plunder; abundance, good fortune, affluence. *a.*

غواص *ghawwāṣ*, m. a diver (for pearls, &c.) *a.*

غواصي *ghawwāṣī*, f. diving for pearls. *a.*

غوامض *ghawāmiẓ* (pl. of غامضه), intricate questions. *a.*

غوت غات *ghot-ghāt*, puzzled, confounded. *h.*

غوث *ghauṡ*, m. a title of *Muḥammadan* saints, whose ardour of devotion, according to vulgar tradition, is such, that in the act of worship their head and limbs fall asunder. *a.*

غوثيت *ghauṡiyat*, saintship, devoteeism. *a.*

غوچ *ghūch*, a horned ram used to fight. *p.*

غور *ghaur*, m. reflection, consideration, meditation. *ghaur-pardākht*, f. attendance on. *a.*

غوره *ghūra*, m. unripe grapes, or dates; a colour in pigeons. *p.*

غوري *ghorī*, f. a kind of porcelain, which breaks the moment poison is put into it. *p.*

غوزه *ghoza* (also *ghozha*), a pod of cotton. *p.*

غوط *ghoṭ*, m. immersion, dive; consideration. *ghoṭ mārnā*, to disappear. *ghoṭ meṅ ānā*, to faint. *a.*

غوطم غاته *ghoṭam-ghāta*, m. a game in which swimmers dip one another under the water. *a. p.*

غوطه *ghoṭa*, m. dipping, diving; a dip, a dive. *ghoṭa-bāz*, a diver. *ghoṭa-khor*, a diver, any thing that dips, or is dipped; a sort of firework so called. *ghoṭa-khorī*, f. dipping, being dipped. *ghoṭa-denā*, a. to dip, to plunge under water. *ghoṭa-khānā*, to be dipped; to dive; to be deceived; to travel in a miry road; to stray, to wander, to lose one's way. *a.*

غوغا *ghaughā*, m. noise, disturbance, uproar, clamour. *p.*

غوغاي *ghaughā,ī*, noisy; m. a disturber. *p.*

غوك *ghūk*, m. a frog, a toad; a butt for archers. *p.*

غول *ghūl* (vulg. *ghol*), m. an imaginary species of sylvan demons, of different shapes and colours, supposed to devour men and animals (from which our European loup-garou, or man-wolf, seems to be borrowed). *ghūli-bayābānī*, a demon that haunts the woods or deserts. *a.*

غول *ghol*, m. a crowd, a troop, a gang. *ghol kā ghol*, a dense crowd. *h.*

غولدنگ *gholidang*, } turbulent, seditious,
غولەدنگ *gholadang*, } vicious; stout, fat, round. *p.*

غونچي *ghaunchī*, f. a hole in a path (such as those made by the feet of animals). *h.*

غياث *ghiyāṡ*, listening to complaints, redressing wrongs, assistance, redress, succours. *ghiyāṡu-l-islām*, the succourer of the faith. *a.*

غيار *ghiyār*, providing for one's dependants, any piece of dress which distinguishes a class, as a soldier's uniform, &c. *a.*

غياص *ghiyāṣ*, diving, studying deeply. *a.*

غيب *ghaib*, latent, concealed, absent, invisible, mysterious. *'alami ghaib*, the other world. *ghaib-dān*, skilled in discovering mysteries, a prophet, diviner, omniscient. *a.*

غيبانه *ghaibāna*, invisibly, in one's absence. *a. p.*

غيباني *ghaibānī*, f. a strumpet, an impudent woman. *a. p.*

غيبت *ghaibat*, f. being invisible, absence. *ghībat*, slander, detraction, any thing secretly whispered of an absent person; parts of a district or tract of country, away from the station where the chief authority resides, in contradistinction to *ḥuẓūr*, q. v. *a.*

غيب غليله هونا *ghaib ghalela honā*, to be lost. *d.*

غيبي *ghaibī*, absent, invisible, &c., heavenly, divine. *a.*

غير *ghair*, other, different; foreign; (sub.) a stranger; adv. except, unless; in comp. it denotes negation or the absence of a thing, as *ghair-ḥāẓir*, absent; *ghair-ḥāẓirī*, f. absence; *ghair-ẕālik*, besides. *ghair-mu'aiyan*, unstable; *ghair-ābād*, devoid of cultivation; *ghair band o bast*, unsettled; *ghair-dasta*, exempt from imposts; *ghair-jam'*, rent-free; *ghair-ḳabūl*, not agreeing to; *ghair-kharch*, extra or miscellaneous, expenses; *ghair-khirāj*, rent-free lands; *ghair-wāḳi'*, a false statement. *ghair-mashrūṭ*, unconditional (v. Wilson's Glossary). *a.*

غيراز *ghair-az*, except, besides, other than. *p.*

غيرت *ghairat*, f. modesty, bashfulness, honour, courage; jealousy, enmity, emulation, a nice sense of honour. *ghairat-mand*, emulous, jealous. *a.*

غيره *ghairu-hu*, } more, besides that, or
غيرها *ghairu-hā*, } those; in addition to
غيرهم *ghairu-hum*, } that, &c.; *wa-ghairu-hu* (generally pronounced *wa-ghaira*, et cetera, and so forth. *a.*

غيريت *ghairīyat*, jealousy, strangeness. *a.*

غيور *ghayūr*, jealons in point of honour or of love; an epithet of the Diety. *a.*

غيوري *ghayūrī*, f. jealousy. *a.*

ف

ف *fe* or *fā*, the twentieth letter of the Arabic alphabet, the twenty-third in the Persian, and the twenty-sixth in the Hindūstānī. This letter exists not in Sanskrit, nor in any of the modern dialects of India thence derived; and in words from the Persian or Arabic the Indians frequently change *f* into *p* or *ph*, as *pālez* for *fālez*, a field of melons. Prefixed to Arabic words (with the short *a* as *fa*) it denotes, and, then, afterwards, as *fa-ḳaṭ*, and that is all, merely, only. Its sound is precisely that of the English *f*. In reckoning by *abjad* it stands for eighty.

فاتح *fātiḥ*, one who opens, a conqueror. *a.*

فاتحه *fātiḥa*, f. commencement, exordium; the first chapter of the *ḳur,ān*, which being repeated when praying for the souls of the dead, the word comes to mean prayers offered up in the name of saints, &c., and, vulgarly, oblations made to saints, &c. *khair kī fātiḥa*, at prayer offered up for the welfare of an, one. *a.*

فاجر *fājir*, m. } a fornicator, an adulterer, a
فاجره *fājira*, f. } sinner; adj. sinful, unchaste. *a.*

فاحش *fāḥish*, obscene, indecent, impudent, shameful, enormous, gross. *a.*

فاحشه *fāḥisha*, f. a harlot; any thing abominable. *a.*

فاخته *fākhta*, f. a dove; name of a colour. *fākhta-ur-jānā*, n. to be confounded, to faint. *wuh din gaye jo khalīl khān fākhta urāte the*, the days of *khalīl khān's* prosperity (or splendour) are gone. *p.*

فاختئي *fākhta,ī*, f. dove-colour. *p.*

فاخر *fākhir*, excellent, precious, honourable; m. a boaster, an egotist. *a.*

فاخرت *fākhirat*, } excellent. *khil'ati fākhira*,
فاخره *fākhira*, } a splendid robe of honour. *a.*

فادزهر *fād-zahr*, the bezoar stone. *p.*

فاذا *fa,iẕā*, verily then, in that case. *a.*

فار *fār*, a rat, a mouse. *a.*

فارخطي *fār-khaṭṭī* (for *fārigh-khaṭṭī*, q.v.). *a. h.*

فارس *fārs* or *pārs*, one of the southern provinces of Persia, ancient Parthia. *p.*

فارس *fāris*, m. a horseman, a rider, a cavalier. *a.*

فارسي *fārsī* also *fārsīyat*, and *fārsīya*, f. the Persian language; adj. Persian. *p.*

فارغ *fārigh*, free, at leisure, ceasing from labour; absolved, discharged; contented. *fārighu-l-bāl* or *fārighu-l-ḥāl*, independent, contented. *fārigh honā*, to have done with any thing, to be at leisure. *a.*

فارغ خطانه *fārigh-khaṭṭāna*, m. a fee given for writing a *fārigh-khaṭṭī*. *a. p.*

فارغ خطي *fārigh-khaṭṭī*, f. a written deed of release, or full acquittance. *a.*

فاروق *fārūḳ* (or *tiryākī fārūḳ*), the best sort of treacle or theriaca. *a.*

فازهر *fāzahr*, (v. *fād-zahr*) bezoar. *p.*

فاسد *fāsid*, m. } vicious, perverse, depraved,
فاسده *fāsida*, f. } corrupt. *a.*

فاسق *fāsiḳ*, m. } a fornicator, an adulterer or
فاسقه *fāsiḳa*, f. } adultress; a. sinner, a worthless fellow; an unchaste woman, one unworthy of credit as a witness in a court of law. *p.*

فاش *fāsh*, apparent, manifest, known. *a.*

فاشرا *fāsharā*, a species of ivy; m. bryony. *a.*

فاصله *fāṣila*, m. separation; space, intermediate space. *a.*

فاضل *fāẓil*, excellent, learned, virtuous; abundant. *fāẓiltar*, more excellent. *a.*

فاطمه *fāṭima*, f. the daughter of the prophet *Muḥammad*, and the wife of the caliph *'Alī*. *a.*

فاطميت *fāṭimīyat*, f. the *Fāṭimite* dynasty, which reigned in Egypt from A.D. 908 to 1171. *a.*

فاعل *fā'il*, making, doing, acting; m. an agent; the participle active; the nominative. *fā'ili ḥaḳīḳī*, the true agent, God. *fā'ili mukhtār*, master of one's own actions; a free agent. *a.*

فاعلي *fā'ilī*, m. } effective, efficient. *a.*
فاعليه *fā'ilīya* f. }

فاعليت *fā'ilīyat*, f. agency; the quality or nature of agent, or noun of agency. *a.*

فاق *fāḳ*, f. the notch of an arrow, arrow. *a.*

فاقه *fāḳa*, m. poverty, necessity, want; (in Pers. and in Hindī) a fast, fasting (from want, not as a religious duty). *fāḳa-kash*, one who fasts, a faster; famished. *fāḳa khainchnā* or *fāḳoṅ marnā*, to starve. *fāḳa-mast*, one who is starving, but conceals his distress. *a.*

فاكهه *fākiha* (also *fākihat*), fruit. *a.*

فال *fāl*, f. an omen, augury, presage; enchantment. *a.*

فالتو *fāltū*, spare, surplus, remainder. *h.*

فالج *fālij*, m. the palsy (particularly *hemiplegia*). *a.*

فالز *fāliz* (for *falez*, q. v.). *p. d.*

فالسه *fālsa* (in Urdū پهالسا), a shrub bearing a berry, when ripe, of a dark purple colour, containing two or three small stones (*Grewia asiatica*). *h. d.*

فالوده *fālūda* (or *pālūda*), smooth, clear; a kind of flummery or sweetmeat. *p.*

فاليز *fālez* (or *pālez*), f. a field of melons. *p.*

فام *fām*, joined to nouns of colour, implies a tendency to such colour; as *siyah-fām*, blackish. *p.*

فانوس *fānūs*, f. a shade (to keep the wind from a candle), a lantern. *fānūsi khiyāl* or *fānūsi khiyālī*, or *charkhī fānūs*, a lantern which revolves by the smoke of the candle within, and has on the side of it figures of various animals; a magic lantern. *a.*

فاني *fānī*, frail, transitory, inconstant, perishable. *jahāni fānī*, this transitory world. *a.*

فائده *fā,ida*, m. profit, gain, advantage, utility. *fā,ida-mand*, profitable, gratified, edified. *a.*

فائز *fā,iz*, overtaking, reaching, obtaining. *a.*

فائق *fā,iḳ*, superior, paramount. *a.*

فبها *fa-bihā*, interj. excellent! bravo! very well, so be it. *a.*

فتا *fatā*, m. a youth; young (animals). *a.*

فتادگي *futādagī*, f. a fall, act of falling. *p*

فتادن *futādan* (for *uftādan*), to fall, &c. *p.*

فتاده *futāda*, fallen, prostrate. *p.*

فتح **fatḥ**, f. an aperture, opening; victory, triumph, conquest. *fatḥ-pech*, a mode of tying the turban. *fatḥ-mand*, victorious. *fatḥ-nāma*, m. despatches announcing victory; a bulletin. *fatḥ-nishān*, a victorious standard (opened only in battle). *fatḥ-naṣīb*, victorious, of victorious fortune. *fatḥ-yāb*, victorious. *a.*

فتحه **fatḥa**, m. the vowel point *zabar*, or short *a* (so called by the Arabs); the beard. *a.*

فتراك **fitrāk**, m. cords fastened to a saddle behind, meant for hanging game to; saddle straps. *p.*

فتق **fatak**, m. a rupture, or hernia. *a.*

فتقا **fatkā**, f. *patentiore rima (mulier)*. *a.*

فتنه **fitna**, m. calamity; sedition; perfidy; sin; temptation, seduction. *fitna-angez*, a fomenter of disturbances, &c. *fitna-angezī*, f. causing disturbances, &c. *fitna-jo*, quarrelsome, seditious. *guli fitna*, a species of mimosa or acacia, bearing flowers and having a powerful scent. *a.*

فتني **fitnī**, a dish of rice and milk of a thicker consistency than *khīr*, q. v. *d.*

فتوت **fatūwat**, f. liberality, generosity. *a.*

فتوح **futūḥ**, f. (pl. of فتح), victories; (met.) abundance, easy circumstances, income received gratuitously. *a.*

فتوحات **futūḥāt**, (barbarous pl. of فتح) victories. *a.*

فتوحي **fatūḥī**, f. a kind of jacket without [sleeves. *a.*

فتور **futūr** (commonly *fitūr*), m. weakness, infirmity; (Hind.) quarrelling, mutiny, insubordination, rebellion. *a.*

فتوري **fitūrī**, a rebel, a mutineer. *a. h.*

فتوريا **fatūriyā**, dispersed, ruined, undone; (Hind.) exciting quarrels. *a.*

فتوي **fatwā**, m. a judicial decree, judgment, sentence delivered by a *ḳāẓī*. *a.*

فتيله **fatīla**, m. a match, a wick. *fatīla-soz*, m. a candlestick. *a.*

فجر **fajar** or **fajr**, f. morning, dawn of day, early. *baṛī fajar*, very early, "multo mane." *a.*

فجل **fujul**, m. a radish; the heel; adj. thick. *a.*

فجور **fajūr**, adulterous, wicked. *fujūr*, wickedness, lust, adultery. *a.*

فحاش **faḥḥāsh**, salacious, obscene, talking [indecently. *a.*

فحاشي **faḥḥāshī**, f. } obscenity (in word or
فحش **fuḥsh**, m. } deed); ribaldry, bawdry. *a.*

فحوا **faḥwā**, m. style, contents, signification, sense, meaning. *faḥwā,e kalām*, signification, sense, scope, meaning, spirit (of a speech or composition). *a.*

فخ **fakh**, a noose, snare; the chase. *p.*

فخ **fakhkh**, snoring; weakness in the legs. *a.*

فخر **fakhr**, m. glory, nobility, ornament, grace; boasting, egotism, pride, ostentation. *fakhru t-tujjār*, the chief of the merchants; a title given to an eminent merchant or banker. *a.*

فخري **fakhrī**, f. a kind of grape so called. *a.*

فخريه **fakhrīya**, m. boasting, vain glory. *a.*

فدا **fidā**, f. sacrifice, consecration, redemption, devoting one's self to save another, ransom, exchange, cartel. *a.*

فداءي **fidā,ī**, courageous, valiant; a volunteer in any desperate undertaking. *a.*

فدك **fadak**, name of a town near Khaibar. *a.*

فدوي **fidwī**, devoted, a devoted servant, subject or vassal. *a.*

فدويت **fidwīyat**, devotedness, allegiance. *a.*

فر **far** or **farr**, m. state, pomp, dignity, splendour, glory, lustre, beauty, grace. *p.*

فرا **farā**, back, behind, again, above, on, over, towards. *p.*

فرات **furāt**, the river Euphrates. *a.*

فراخ **farākh**, ample, abundant, large, cheap, wide, plentiful; (in Dakh.) a joke, a jest, pleasantry. *farākh-rū*, cheerful, merry. *p. a.*

فراخور **farākhur**, fit, corresponding, quad-[rating. *p.*

فراخي **farākhī**, f. abundance, cheapness; prosperity, happiness; a girth. *p.*

فراده **furāda** } (pl. of فرد), alone, single, soli-
فرادي **furādā** } tary, one by one. *a.*

فرار **firār**, flight, running away. *a.*

فراري **firārī**, a person who has absconded. *a.*

فراز **farāz**, m. ascent, acclivity; adj. high, aloft, exalted; (in comp.) exalting, elevating. *farāz-k.*, to open (a door). *p.*

فرازي **farāzī**, f. highness, exaltation. *p.*

فراس **farās**, a species of the date tree. *a.*

فراست **firāsat**, f. physiognomy; penetration, sagacity, understanding, acuteness. *a.*

فراش **farrāsh**, m. a servant whose business it is to spread the carpets, &c., a sweeper. *firāsh*, spreading. *firāsh-khāna* or *farāsh-khāna*, m. the room where carpets, &c. are kept. *a.*

فراشي **farrāshī**, f. the spreading of carpets, &c. the business of a *farrāsh*. *a.*

فراغ **firāgh**, cessation from labour, repose, rest, leisure; happiness, competency. *a.*

فراغت **farāghat**, f. leisure, repose; abundance, ease, happiness, competency. *a.*

فراق **firāḳ**, m. distance, separation, distinction, absence. *firāḳ-zada*, absent, separated, one doomed to absence. *a.*

فراقي **firāḳī**, separated, absent. *a.*

فرامرز **farāmarz**, the keeper of a citadel. *p.*

فرامش *farāmush*, } forgotten. *farāmosh-kār*
فراموش *farāmosh*, } or *-gār*, unmindful, forgetful. *p.*

فراموشي *farāmoshī*, f. forgetfulness. *p.*

فرامين *farāmīn* (Arab. pl. of فرمان), orders, commands, mandates, precepts. *p.*

فرانا *farrānā*, n. to snort or sneeze (a horse); to come quickly. *h.*

فراوان *firāwān*, much, abundant, copious, sufficient, opulent. *p.*

فراواني *firāwānī*, f. abundance, opulence. *p.*

فراهم *farāham*, m. collection; contraction; adj. collected, gathered. *p.*

فرائض *farā,iẓ* (pl. of فريضة), the knowledge of dividing inheritances agreeably to law. *a.*

فربه *farbih*, fat, stout, corpulent. *p.*

فربهي *farbihī*, f. fatness, strength. *p.*

فرتوت *fartūt*, old and decrepid. *p.*

فرج *faraj*, f. cheerfulness, delight, pleasure, joy. *farj*, f. *pudendum tum maris tum feminæ*. *a.*

فرجام *farjām*, m. end, conclusion, issue; happiness, prosperity; utility. *p.*

فرح *faraḥ*, joyful, pleased, satisfied, cheerful. *a.*

فرحاً *faraḥan*, gladly, cheerfully. *a.*

فرحان *furḥān*, joyful, glad, happy. *a.*

فرحت *farḥat*, f. delight, pleasure, cheerfulness, joy, amusement. *farḥat-āṡār*, pleasant, happy. *farḥ-tu-l-liḳā*, pleasant to look at; the name of a kite, the Pondicherry eagle (*Falco ponticerianus*). *a.*

فرخ *farrukh*, happy, fortunate. *p.*

فرخسير *farrukh-siyar*, name of one of the emperors of Delhī, A.D. 1713, &c. *p.*

فرخنده *farkhunda*, happy, fortunate. *farkhunda-ṭāli'*, fortunate; of happy destiny. *p.*

فرد *fard*, f. a sheet (of paper), a statement, list, roll, verse, piece; an individual; one; single; odd. *fardi-kāsht*, a statement of the peasant's cultivation. *fardi tashkhīṣ*, a settlement record. *a.*

فردا *fardā*, to-morrow; (met.) the day of resurrection (to express the rapidity and certainty of its approach). *fardā,e ḳiyāmat*, f. the great day of judgment. *p.*

فرد حقيقت *fardi-ḥaḳīḳat*, a manifesto or memorial. *a.*

فردسوال *fard-sawāl*, a petition or application. *a.*

فردوس *firdaus*, m. a garden, paradise. *a.*

فردوسي *firdausī*, n. name of a celebrated poet of Tūs, in Persia, about A.D. 1000. *p.*

فردي *fardī*, f. a roll, catalogue. *a.*

فرديات *fardiyāt* (pl. of فرد or فردي), catalogues, statements, details. *a.*

فرزانگي *farzānagī*, f. wisdom, science, excellence. *p.*

فرزانه *farzāna*, wise, intelligent, excellent, distinguished; applied to a pawn at chess, that which has reached the last square on the board, and thereby become promoted to the rank of *farzīn*, q. v. *p.*

فرزند *farzand*, m. a child, son, or daughter. *farzandi rashīd*, a good, intelligent child. *p.*

فرزندي *farzandī*, f. childhood, the rank or condition of a child. *p.*

فرزي *farzī*, } f. the wazīr or minister (which
فرزين *farzīn*, } we in Europe call queen) at chess. *farzīn-band*, m. a term used at chess for which we have no equivalent. *p.*

فرس *faras*, m. a horse; the knight in chess. *furs*, Persia, the Persians. *a.*

فرستادن *firistādan*, to send. *firistāda*, one sent; an ambassador, a legate, an envoy. *p.*

فرسخ *farsakh*, } m. a parasang (or measure
فرسنگ *farsang*, } of about 18,000 feet), a league. *p.*

فرسوده *farsūda*, worn out, obliterated. *p.*

فرش *farsh*, m. spreading, carpeting, bedding; a cushion, mat, carpet, &c. *farsh-furūsh*, the carpets. *a.*

فرشتگان *firishtagān*, angels, &c. *p.*

فرشته *firishta*, m. an angel, an apostle, prophet, missionary. *p.*

فرشي *farshī*, f. a kind of *ḥuḳḳa*; "a large *ḥuḳḳa* which stands on the ground, in contradistinction to smaller implements which may be carried in the hand."—(Binning.) *a.*

فرصت *furṣat*, f. leisure, freedom, ease, convenience, opportunity, relief, rest. *a.*

فرض *farẓ*, m. a divine command, a duty, the omission of which is considered as a mortal sin; an obligation. *farẓ-k.*, a. to consider as a positive indispensable duty, to grant, to admit, to suppose for argument's sake. *farẓ-h.*, to be incumbent or essential. *a.*

فرضاً *farẓan*, hypothetically; for instance. *a.*

فرضول *farẓūl*, m. the hammer of a flint-lock (Gilchrist calls this an Arabic or Persian word, but I never met with an Arab or Persian who understood it. In the former language this part of a gun-lock is termed *misht*, and in Persian *ḳāshluḳ*).—(Binning.) *h.*

فرضي *farẓī*, hypothetically assumed. *a.*

فرضيت *farẓiyat*, hypothesis, assumption. *a.*

فرط *farṭ*, superfluity, abundance; a hill top. *a.*

فرع *far'*, f. a bough, a branch (of a tree, particularly the top branches). *a.*

فرعون *fir'aun*, Pharaoh, a title common to the kings of Egypt about the time of Moses, as that of Ptolemy was in the time of the Romans; (met.) any cruel tyrant. *a.*

فرعوني *fir'aunī*, f. haughtiness, tyranny. *a.*

فرغول *farghūl*, f. a wrapper, a great coat, cloak. *p.*

فرفراد *farfarānā*, to snort (as a horse or other animal). *h.*

فرق *farḳ*, m. difference, distance, distinction, dispersion; the head, the top of any thing, summit; adj. distant, separate, distinct; interj. away! aside! *a.*

فرقان *furḳān*, m. the *ḳur,ān* (as distinguishing or separating truth from falsehood.) *a.*

فرقت *furḳat*, f. distance, separation, distinction; bereavement, absence. *a.*

فرقدان *farḳadān*, m. two stars near the pole, in the constellation of the lesser bear. *a.*

فرقه *firḳa*, m. a religious or philosophic sect; a tribe, troop, company, society. *a.*

فرمے *farmā* (also *farmā,e*), (in comp.) commanding, performing. *p.*

فرمان *farmān*, m. a mandate, command, order; a royal patent: according to Gladwin it denotes a grant, decree, patent, or command of the emperor; a royal commission, or mandate. In Bengal the term is used for a patent to trade duty free. By way of eminence it means the charter which the Company obtained from the emperor *Farru<u>kh</u>-siyar*, granting them a liberty of trading, and other privileges. *farmān-bardār*, subject to orders, obedient. *farmān-bardārī*, f. obedience, subjection. *farmān-dih*, one who issues orders; a king, a ruler. *farmān-dihī*, f. authority, sovereign power. *farmān-rawā*, a king, a sovereign. *farmān-rawā,ī*, f. kingly power, sovereignty. *p.*

فرمانا *farmānā*, a. to order, to command; when put in the mouth of kings and superiors, it may signify to say, to do, to accomplish. *p.*

فرمائش *farmā,ish*, f. an order (particularly for goods, &c.), commission, any thing commissioned, pleasure, will, commands. *p.*

فرمائشي *farmā,ishī*, particularly ordered or bespoken (any thing); excellent. *p.*

فرمودن *farmūdan* (r. *farmā,e*), to order. *p.*

فرنگ *farang*, Europe, the country of the Franks. *p.*

فرنگي *farangī*, m. (from Fr. *franc*) a Frank, a European in general; adj. European. *p.*

فرنگستان *farangistān*, m. Europe. *p.*

فرني *firnī*, f. a dish resembling hasty pudding made of ground rice and milk. *p.*

فرو *faro* (before a word beginning with a vowel, *farod*), down, below, under. *faro-tan*, humble, depressed. *faro-tanī*, f. humility, submissiveness. *p.*

فروتر *farotar*, lower down. *p.*

فروخت *faro<u>kh</u>t*, f. sale. *faro<u>kh</u>t-k.*, a. to sell. *<u>kh</u>arīd-faro<u>kh</u>t*, buying and selling, traffic. *p.*

فروختن *faro<u>kh</u>tan* (r. *farosh*), to sell; (r. *faroz*), to inflame, to kindle, to illumine. *p.*

فروخته *faro<u>kh</u>ta*, sold; kindled, illuminated. *p.*

فرود *farod*, m. descending, alighting, stopping; adv. down, beneath. *farod-gāh*, f. a halting-place. *p.*

فروز *faroz*, (in comp.) kindling, inflaming. *p.*

فروزان *farozān*, luminous, resplendent. *p.*

فروش *farosh*, (in comp.) selling, as *ḥalwā-farosh*, a seller of sweetmeats, &c. *p.*

فروش *furūsh* (pl. of فرش), carpets. *a.*

فروشنده *faroshanda*, selling, one who sells. *p.*

فروشي *faroshī*, f. (v. *farosh*) selling. *p.*

فروع *furū'* (pl. of فرع), heads, tops; branches; chiefs of tribes or families. *a.*

فروغ *farogh*, m. illumination, light, splendour. *p.*

فروگذاشتن *faro-guzāshtan*, to pretermit, to neglect. *p.*

فروماندگي *faro-māndagī* (also *faro-mānī*), f. helplessness, weakness, dejection. *p.*

فروماندن *faro-māndan*, to lag behind, to be exhausted. *p.*

فرومانده *faromānda*, dejected, tired, depressed, fatigued, weak, helpless. *p.*

فرومايه *faro-māya*, worthless, low, sordid, mean, ignoble. *p.*

فرهاد *farhād*, name of a celebrated Persian statuary, who, to please his mistress *Shīrīn*, dug through an immense mountain. *p.*

فرهنگ *farhang*, f. wisdom, understanding; a dictionary, a vocabulary, a glossary. *p.*

فرياد *faryād*, f. complaint, exclamation, lamentation, cry for help. *faryād-ras*, one who attends to a complaint, a defender. *faryād-rasī*, f. redress of grievances. *p.*

فريادي *faryādī*, m. a complainant, a plaintiff, one who sues for justice. *p.*

فريب *fareb*, f. deceit, trick, deception, fraud. *fareb-āmez* or *fareb-kār*, fraudulent, deceitful. *fareb-<u>kh</u>urda*, deceived, imposed upon; (in comp.) cheating deceiving, alluring; as, *mardum-fareb*, betraying men. *fareb-khānā*, to be imposed upon. *fareb-d.*, to impose upon another. *p.*

فريبا *farebā*, فريبنده *farebanda*, } a deceiver; adj. fallacious, deceitful. *p.*

فريبندگي *farebandagī*, f. fraud, deceitfulness. *p.*

فريبي *farebī*, m. a cheat, an impostor; f. (in comp.) deceiving. *p.*

فريدبوٹي *farīd-būṭī*, f. a kind of medicinal herb (*Menispermum hirsutum*). *h.*

فريدون *farīdūn*, name of an ancient king of Persia, famed for his virtues. *p.*

فريضه *farīẓa*, a divine positive command. *a.*

فريفتن *fareftan* (r. *fareb*), to deceive. *p.*

فريفته *farefta*, deceived; enamoured. *p.*

فريق *farīḳ*, m. a troop, squadron, corps. *farīḳain*, du. both parties. *farīḳi awwal*, the first party. *farīḳi s̤ānī*, the defendant party in a law suit. *a.*

فزا *fazā*, (in comp.) increasing, augmenting, as *jān-fazā*, increasing one's life or spirit. *p.*

فزود *fazūd* (for *afzūd*), increase, &c. *p.*

فزول *fizūl*, m. the hammer of a flint lock. *d.*

فزون *fazūn* (v. *afzūn*), increasing, &c. *p.*

فساد *fasād*, m. depravity, iniquity, wickedness, violence, war, horror, mutiny, sedition, rebellion. *a.*

فسادي *fasādī*, quarrelsome, vicious, mutinous; m. an incendiary; a rebel. *a. p.*

فسان *fisān* or *fasān*, a whetstone. *p.*

فسانه *fasāna*, tale, fiction, narrative. *p.*

فسح *fash*, Easter, the passover. *a.*

فسحت *fusḥat*, liberty, satisfaction; (lit.) width, room, space. *a.*

فسخ *faskh*, m. violation (as of an agreement), dissolving (a marriage); dislocation. *a.*

فسردگي *fasurdagī*, f. congelation. *p.*

فسرده *fasurda* or *fisurda*, congealed. *fasurda-dil*, cold-hearted. *fasurda-bayān*, one whose words are destitute of force or meaning. *p.*

فسق *fisḳ*, m. adultery, obscenity, impudence, iniquity, sin, falsehood. *a.*

فسوس *fasos* (for *afsos*), interj. alas! pity it is! *p.*

فسون *fusūn*, incantation; fraud, deceit. *p.*

فسونا *fusūnā*, an enchanter, a deceiver. *p.*

فشار *fashār*, scattering. *fishār*, compressing, piercing. *p.*

فشان *fishān*, (in comp.) strewing, scattering, shedding; as *ātash-fishān*, scattering fire. *p.*

فشانده *fishānda*, strewed, scattered. *p.*

فشاني *fishānī*, f. (in comp.) strewing, &c. *p.*

فشرده *fishurda*, squeezed, compressed. *p.*

فصاحت *faṣāḥat*, f. eloquence, pure language, elegance of style. *a.*

فصاد *faṣṣād*, m. a surgeon, phlebotomist. *a.*

فصادي *faṣṣādī*, f. surgery, phlebotomy. *a.*

فصد *faṣd*, f. opening a vein, bleeding, phlebotomy. *faṣd kholnā*, a. to bleed. *a.*

فصل *faṣl*, f. a section, article, chapter; time, season, crop, harvest. *a.*

فصل خريف *faṣli kharīf*, the autumnal harvest of rice, millet, &c. *a.*

فصل ربيع *faṣli rabī'*, (lit.) the season of spring: it also denotes the first or early harvest of the year. *a.*

فصلي *faṣlī*, name of an æra instituted some three hundred years ago by the emperor Akbar. It then agreed with the Hijra; but as the Faṣlī years are solar, it falls behind the latter æra at the rate of three years per century. *a.*

فصلي سال *faṣlī sāl*, the revenue year: of this there are different epochs in various parts of India. *a.p.*

فصيح *faṣīḥ*, eloquent, sweet or pure (in language or writings). *a.*

فصيحي *faṣīḥī*, f. eloquence, purity of style. *a.*

فصيل *faṣīl*, f. breastworks, entrenchment, ramparts (vulg. *ṣafīl*). *a.*

فضا *faẓā*, an open space, an extensive open field, arena, area. *pur-faẓā*, spacious. *a.*

فضاله *fuẓāla*, m. remains, remainder. *a.*

فضائل *faẓā,il* (pl. of فضيلت), virtues, excellencies, learning, merits. *a.*

فضل *faẓl*, m. excellence, virtue; increase, gain; gift, reward, favour. *a.*

فضلا *fuẓalā* (pl. of فاضل), learned and good men. *a.*

فضله *fuẓla*, m. remainder, redundancy; leaving, refuse. *a.*

فضول *faẓūl*, exuberant, excessive, redundant; a busy-body, a mischief-maker. *faẓūl kharch*, extravagant, profuse. *faẓūl-go*, a prolix speaker, one who talks much; a boaster, an egotist. *a.*

فضولي *faẓūlī*, f. exuberance, redundance, mischief-making; m. an intermeddler, one who acts as agent without any authority. *faẓūlī bai'*, the sale of another's property without consent. *a.*

فضيح *faẓīḥ*, ignominious, infamous. *a.*

فضيحت *faẓīḥat*, f. disgrace, ignominy, infamy. *faẓīḥat-k.*, to disgrace, defame. *a.*

فضيحتي *faẓīḥatī*, disgraceful, infamous. *a.*

فضيلت *faẓīlat*, f. excellence, perfection; virtue, knowledge, learning. *a.*

فطر *fuṭr* or *fiṭr*, m. breaking (a fast); commencing, broaching; the festival held on breaking Lent, which is also called *'īdu-l-fiṭr*. *a.*

فطرت *fiṭrat*, f. } wisdom, sagacity; nature,
فطره *fiṭra*, m. } creation, form; deceit, trick; alms given on the *'īdu-l-fiṭr*. *fiṭrat laṛānā*, a. (vulg.) to practise tricks or stratagems. *a.*

فطرتي *fiṭratī*, sagacious, cunning. *a.*

فطنت *fiṭnat*, understanding, sagacity. *a.*

فعال *fi'āl* (pl. of فعل), works, actions, doings. *a.*

فعل *fi'l*, m. action, work, operation; a verb. *fi'li 'abaṡ*, lost labour, an absurd undertaking. *fi'li lāzimī*, a verb neuter. *fi'li muta'addī*, a verb active or causal. *bi-l-fi'l*, in fact, in reality, actually, presently. *a.*

فعلاً *fi'lan*, in fact, indeed. *fi'lan wa ḳaulan*, in deed and word. *a.*

فعله *fa'ala* (pl. of فاعل), agents, &c. *fi'la*, a single deed or action. *a.*

فغان *fighān*, m. lamentation, clamour, complaint; interj. alas! *p.*

فغفور *faghfūr*, m. the emperor of China. *p.*

فق *faḳ*, astonished, dismayed. *h.*

فقدان *fiḳdān*, loss, want, deprivation. *a*

فقر *faḳr* or *fuḳr*, m. poverty; a life of poverty with resignation and content. *a.*

فقرا *fuḳarā* (pl. of فقير), the poor; religious mendicants, darweshes. *a.*

فقره *fiḳra*, m. a line, a sentence. *fiḳra-bandī*, f. arrangement, eloquence. *a.*

فقط *faḳaṭ* (properly *fa-ḳaṭṭ* or *fa-ḳaṭ*), merely, simply, only, solely, no more. *a.*

فقه *fiḳh*, f. knowledge of religion and law; theology, jurisprudence. *a.*

فقير *faḳīr*, m. a beggar, a dervise; a man who leads what is called a holy life: there is a great variety of them: they are always in the character of persons collecting alms, and are frequently known to subject themselves voluntarily to extreme torture, in the hopes of appeasing an offended deity. They are in general a worthless set of villains, who, to obtain money from the credulous natives, put on the appearance of extreme sanctity, under the cloak of which they commit the greatest excesses; adj. poor, indigent. *a.*

فقيران *faḳīrān*, land bestowed on *faḳīrs*. *a. p.*

فقيرانه *faḳīrāna*, in the manner of a *faḳīr*. *a. p.*

فقيرني *faḳīrnī*, } f. a poor woman, a female
فقيره *faḳīra*, } devotee. *a. h.*

فقيري *faḳīrī*, f. devoteeism, poverty, humility. *a.*

فقيه *faḳīh*, a man conversant with religion and law; a theologian, a lawyer. *a.*

فك *fakk*, the under and upper jaw. *a.*

فكر *fikr*, f. and m. thought, reflection, consideration, counsel, advice; solicitude. *a.*

فكرت *fikrat*, thought; the subject of thought or care. *a.*

فكرمند *fikr-mand*, } thoughtful, sorrowful,
فكري *fikrī*, } pensive, anxious. *a. p.*

فكندن *fikandan*, to cast down, to throw away. *fikandanī*, fit to be thrown away. *fikanda*, cast or thrown down. *p.*

فگار *figār*, lame, crippled, wounded; afflicted, confused, distracted. *dil-figār*, heart-afflicting. *p.*

فگن *figan* (v. *afgan*), overthrowing. *p.*

فلاح *falāḥ*, f. prosperity, happiness, safety, refuge. *a.*

فلاخن *falākhan* or *falākhun* (also *falākhān*), f. a sling for throwing stones. *p.* [phera. *a.*

فلاسفة *falāsifat* (pl. of فيلسوف), philoso-

فلاطون *falāṭūn* (πλατων), Plato. *a.*

فلاكت *falākat*, f. an evil, a disgrace; a misfortune, adversity. *falākati-falak*, the frowns of fortune; the evils of destiny. *a.*

فلاكتي *falākatī*, unfortunate. *a.*

فلان *fulān*, m. such a one or thing. *falān* or *falānī*, f. (met.) *pudendum muliebre*. *a.*

فلانه *fulāna*, m. such a one, &c. *falāna*, m. *penis virilis*. *a.*

فلز *filizz*, m. ore, metal; dross, scoria. *a.*

فلزات *filizzāt*, mines, ores, metals. *a.*

فلس *fals* or *fils*, a small coin, an obolus. *falas*, indigence, want. *a.*

فلسفت *filsafat*, f. philosophy. *a.*

فلسفي *falsafī*, a philosopher. *a.*

فلفل *filfil*, f. pepper. *a.*

فلك *falak*, m. the heavens, the sky, the firmament; fate, fortune. *falak ko khabar na honī kisī ke* (lit. a thing being unknown to one's stars), implies great inattention and ignorance. *falaku-l-aflāk*, the primum mobile, empyrean heaven. *falak-zada*, oppressed by fate or fortune, planet-struck. *falak-sair*, extremely swift. *a.*

فلكي *falakī*, heavenly, relating to fate or fortune. *a.*

فلم *falam*, m. a small silver coin current in Southern India, and called by Europeans "a fanam:" twelve fanams make a rupee, and from 40 to 45 fanams, a pagoda or *hūn*. *d.*

فلوس *fulūs*, m. (pl. of فلس) small coins, a *paisā*: money in a general sense. *a.*

فليته *falīta*, m. (per met. for *fatīla*) match torch, wick; a wick composed of paper inscribed with mystic words, by inhaling the smoke of which demons are expelled from those possessed; a cord of twisted thread sewn between the two folds of the hem of a garment to strengthen it. *falīta-dār*, a matchlock; any thing that has a match or wick; cloth hemmed with a cord or *falīta*. *a.*

فم *fam*, m. the mouth. *fami mi'da*, the orifice of the stomach. *a.*

فن *fann* (also *fan*), m. science; skill, sagacity, stratagem, art. *fan-fareb*, m. art and cunning. *fan-farebī*, artful, cunning. *a.*

فنا *fanā*, f. mortality, frailty, death. *a.*

فنجان *finjān*, m. a porcelain dish; a coffee-cup, such as the Arabs, Persians, and Turks use. It is very small, being scarcely larger than half an egg-shell, and, instead of a saucer, rests in a small case of silver or other metal called *ẓarf*.—(Binning). *p.*

فند *fand*, fraud, deceit, trifles, vain words. *p.*

فندق *funduḳ*, f. a filbert nut; a ball or bullet; a finger tip. *funduḳ band*, staining the tips of the fingers so as to resemble the filbert-nut. *a.*

فندي *fandī*, fraudulent, deceitful. *p.*

فنون *funūn* (pl. of فن), arts, sciences. *a.*

فو *fū*, m. valerian; the mouth. *a.*

فواد *fuwād*, m. the heart. *a.*

فواره *fawwāra*, m. a fountain, a jet, drain, a spring. *a.*

فواكه *fawākih*, m. (pl. of فاكهه) fruits. *a.*

فوائد *fawā,id* (pl. of فائده), gains, advantages, profits, benefits. *a.* [be interred. *a.*

فوت *faut*, f. death. *faut-honā*, n. to die; to

فوته *fūta* or *fota*, a cloth which they wrap round the middle when going to bathe. *fota* is sometimes used improperly for *foṭa*, q.v. *p.*

فوتي *fautī*, adj. dead; property of one who dies intestate and without legal heirs (which escheats to the sovereign). *fautī firārī*, adj. killed and missing; property of persons dying intestate or absconding. *fautī-nāma*, a list of the killed; annual bills of mortality. *a.*

فوج *fauj*, f. an army, a multitude. *a.*

فوجدار *fauj-dār*, an officer of the police so called, a magistrate. *a. p.*

فوجداري *fauj-dārī*, the office of *fauj-dār*. *fauj-dārī 'adālat*, chief criminal court. *a. p.*

فور *fūr*, name of a *rāja* of *ḳanūj*, slain by Alexander the Great, Porus. *p.*

فور *faur*, m. celerity, haste. *fi-l-faur*, immediately, instantly. *a.*

فورًا *fauran*, quickly, suddenly, instantly, directly. *a.*

فوز *fauz*, victory, advantage, fruition. *a.*

فوطه *foṭa*, m. a bag; the testicle; tax, revenue, a purse. *foṭa-dār* (vulg. *pota-dār*), a banker; a person who inspects the different coins, and determines their rate of exchange. *foṭa-dārī*, f. bankership, banking, the office of *foṭa-dār*. *foṭe bahādurī ke*, the testicles. *p.*

فوفل *fawful* or *fūfal*, the betel-nut. *a.*

فوق *fauḳ*, m. superiority, excellence, altitude, loftiness; prep. over, above. *a.*

فوقاني *fauḳānī*, superior; dotted above, as some letters are, such as *te*, &c. *a.*

فوقيت *fauḳīyat*, f. preference, pre-eminence, superiority, excellence. *a.*

فولاد *fūlād*, f. (same as *pūlād*), steel. *p.*

فولادي *fūlādī*, made of steel; f. a pikestaff. *p.*

فهرست *fihrist*, f. an inventory, list, index, table of contents, schedule, &c. *p.*

فهم *fahm*, m. understanding, intellect, comprehension. *fahm-dār*, acute, intelligent; (in comp.) perceiving, discerning, &c., *tez-fahm*, of a quick capacity. *sukhan-fahm*, understanding a speech or discourse. *a. p.*

فهمايش *fahmāyish*, f. causing to understand, instruction, explanation. *p.*

فهميد *fahmīd*, f. understanding. *p.*

فهميدگي *fahmīdagī*, f. comprehension. *p.*

فهميدن *fahmīdan*, to understand. *p.*

فهميده *fahmīda*, understood. *p.*

فهيم *fahīm*, learned, intelligent. *a.*

في *fī*, in, into, among, of, to, with, for, by, concerning; each (or for each), per; as *fī man*, per maund, &c. *fi-l-badīha*, readily, quickly, extempore. *fi-l-jumla*, upon the whole. *fi-l-ḥāl*, now, immediately, on the spot or instant, directly. *fi-l-ḥaḳīḳat*, really, truly, in effect, in fact. *fi-l-faur*, now, in short, immediately, directly. *fi-l-masal*, allegorically. *fi-n-nāri wa-s-saḳari*, in hell flames. *fi-l-wāḳi'*, in reality, in fact. *a.*

فياض *faiyāẓ*, liberal, generous, profuse, copious, munificent, benevolent. *a.*

فياضي *faiyāẓī*, f. liberality, benevolence. *a.*

فيته *fīta*, m. ribbon, tape (Port. *fita*). *Port.*

فيرني *fīrnī* (Dakh. for فرني), a kind of pudding. *d.*

فيروز *fīroz*, victorious, happy, fortunate. *fīroz-asar fīroz-bakht*, also *fīroz-mand*, victorious, conquering, prosperous. *fīroz-mandī*, f. victory, prosperity. *p.*

فيروزه *fīroza*, m. a turquoise stone, used as a talisman for bringing the wearer good luck. *p.*

فيروزي *fīrozī*, f. victory, good fortune. *p.*

فيصل *faiṣal*, m. decision, decree, determination; division, separation. *faiṣal-k.*, a. to settle, to decide, to adjust. *a.*

فيصل نامه *faiṣal-nāma*, a decree, an award; an instrument denoting that a cause has been finally settled. *a. p.*

فيصله *faiṣala*, m. a decree, settlement. *a.*

فيض *faiẓ*, m. plenty, abundance; grace, favour, bounty. *faiẓi 'āmm*, m. general abundance; adj. liberal, profuse. *faiẓ-bakhsh* or *faiẓ-rasān*, one who bestows favours; liberal, munificent. *a.*

فيضان *fayaẓān*, overflowing, redundancy. *a.*

فيل *fīl*, m. an elephant. *fīl-bān*, m. an elephant-driver (or -feeder). *fīl-khāna*, a place for elephants, an elephant stable. *fīl-dandān*, m. ivory. *fīl-murgh*, m. a turkey. *fīl-nishīn*, one who rides on an elephant. In chess *fīl* originally denoted the rook; at present it is applied to the piece which we absurdly call the bishop. *a. p.*

فيلپا *fīl-pā*, having a swelling in one's leg, having elephantiasis. *p.*

فيلپايه *fīl-pāya*, m. a pillar, a prop; the upright post over the mouth of a well. *p.*

فيلپاءي *fīl-pā,ī*, f. elephantiasis. *p.*

فيلخانه *fīl-khāna*, m. elephant stables. *p.*

فيلسوف *failsūf*, f. (Gr. φιλοσοφος) a philosopher; intelligent, knowing; (met.) in Hind. cunning, artful. *g.*

فيلفوس *failfūs*, فيلقوس *failḳūs*, } Philip, the king of Macedon, father of Alexander. *a.*

فيلي *fīlī*, belonging to an elephant. *a.*

فيما *fī-mā*, in that which, as to what. *fī-mā-ba'd*, as to the future, henceforth. *fī-mā-bain*, as to what there is between (us, &c.). *a.*

فيول *fuyūl* (pl. of فيل), elephants. *a.*

فيه *fī-hi*, in him, it, or that. *a.*

فيها *fī-hā*, in her, it, or that. *a.*

فيهم *fī-him*, in or among them. *a.*

ق

ق *ḳāf*, called *ḳāfi ḳarashat*, the twenty-first letter of the Arabic alphabet, the twenty-fourth Persian, and twenty-seventh Hindūstānī: its sound is harder than that of *kāf* (the following letter), being formed deep in the throat, by the pressure of the root of the tongue against it, and has been compared to the cawing of a raven: in reckoning by *abjad* it stands for one hundred. "The people of Southern India generally sound this letter erroneously like *kh*; the Persians confound it with *gh*, sounding either letter as *ḳ* or *gh* indiscriminately."—(Binning.) *a.*

قا *ḳā*, the cawing of a rook or crow. *ḳā-ḳā-k.*, the caw like a crow. *a.*

قاآن *ḳā-ān*, a title among the Tartars, equivalent to Emperor or supreme ruler: it is sometimes applied to the emperor of China: it must not be confounded with the inferior title *khān*, as is generally done by our writers on Tartary, &c. *p.*

قاب *ḳāb*, f. a large dish used for kneading dough and other purposes; m. a measure of length, viz. the distance from the middle to the extremities of a bow. *ḳāb i ḳausain*, two cubits' length. *a.*

قاب *ḳāb*, the case of a watch. *d.*

قابض *ḳābiẓ*, seizing, taking; m. an astringent; a receiver, possessor; occupant. *ḳābiẓu-l-arwāḥ*, the seizer of souls, the angel of death. *a.*

قابل *ḳābil*, possible, capable, skilful, sufficient, able, worthy, clever. *a.*

قابله *ḳābila*, f. a skilful woman, a midwife. *a.*

قابلي *ḳābilī*, } **قابليت *ḳābilīyat***, } f. possibility, skill, sufficiency, capability, fitness. *a.*

قابو *ḳābū*, m. power, command, authority, opportunity, possession, will. *ḳābū-pānā*, to get the opportunity. *ḳābū-parast*, tyrannical. *ḳābū-parastī*, f. tyranny. *ḳābū-chalānā*, a. to exercise one's power. *t.*

قابوچي *ḳābūchī*, despotic, tyrannical. *t.*

قابيل *ḳābīl*, Cain, the eldest-born of Eve (properly *ḳā,īn*, q. v.). *ḳābīl wa hābīl*, Cain and Abel. *a.*

قاتل *ḳātil*, killing, mortal, deadly; m. a murderer; homicide. *a.*

قادر *ḳādir*, potent, powerful, capable, skilful; [the Omnipotent. *a.*

قاذف *ḳāẕif*, a false accuser, a slanderer. *a.*

قاروره *ḳārūra*, m. a flask, glass; a urinal (sent to physicians for inspection). *a.*

قارون *ḳārūn*, supposed to be the same as *Korah*, whom the *Muḥammadans* describe as the cousin of Moses: on account of his riches and avarice his name is proverbially applied to all misers: they add that it was on account of his refusal to pay Moses a tithe of his possessions for the public use, the earth opened and swallowed him up. *a.*

قاري *ḳārī*, m. a reader, especially of the [*ḳur,ān*. *a.*

قاز *ḳāz*, m. a duck or goose. *t*

قازه *ḳāza*, a long rein for leading horses. *ḳāza-dār*, a groom. *d.*

قاسم *ḳāsim*, dividing; m. a distributor. *ḳāsimu-l-arzāḳ*, distributor of daily bread, *i. e.* God. *a.*

قاش *ḳāsh*, f. the eyebrow; a bit, a slice (of melon, &c.), a piece. *t.*

قاصد *ḳāṣid*, m. a courier, an express, a messenger, a postman (Anglo-Indian, *cossid*); adj. resolved on, bound to. *a.*

قاصدي *ḳāṣidī*, f. situation of courier, &c.; adj. of or relating to a courier. *a.*

قاصر *ḳāṣir*, insufficient, defective, impotent deficient, failing. *ḳāṣiru-l-bayān*, whose meaning is defective, inexplicable. *a.*

قاضي *ḳāẓī*, m. a Muḥammadan judge, civil, criminal, and ecclesiastic. *ḳāẓiyu-l-ḳuẓāt*, the supreme judge. *a.*

قاطبة *ḳāṭibat* (or *ḳāṭiba*), all, every one. *a.*

قاطبةً *ḳāṭibatan*, generally, universally. *a.*

قاطر *ḳāṭir*, a mule. *t.*

قاطع *ḳāṭiʻ*, cutting, rescinding; adj. peremptory, decisive, explicit. *ḳāṭi'u-ṭ-ṭarīḳ*, a robber, a highwayman. *a.*

قاع *ḳāʻ*, a plain, a desert; level ground. *ḳā'i* [*basīṭ*, the vast desert. *a.*

قاعده *ḳā'ida*, m. basis, groundwork; rule, custom, institution; the rules of grammar. *a.*

قاف *ḳāf*, m. or *kohi ḳāf*, the mountain of *ḳāf*, supposed to surround the world, and bound the extreme horizon: it rests on the stone *ṣakhrat*, an entire emerald, the reflection from which occasions the azure colour of the sky, according to the poets: the *kohi ḳāf* is the abode of the *devs* and *jinn* (or genii), and also of the *paris* or fairies; the famous *sīmurgh*, or great griffin, is also an inhabitant of the same interesting region. *a.*

قافله *ḳāfila*, m. a body of travellers, a caravan. *ḳāfila-bāshī* or *ḳāfila-sālār*, m. the leader or chief of a caravan. It may be observed that the term *bāshī* is Turkish, and denotes chief, head, as *ar-bāshī*, chief of the troops, &c.: *ḳāfila-bāshī*, therefore, does not denote the abstract feminine noun, viz. "chieftainship of a caravan," as we have seen it stated in some dictionary. *a.*

قافيه *ḳāfiya*, m. rhyme, cadence, metre, the last letter in a verse, to which all the other distichs rhyme: in poems which terminate in a double rhyme, the penult syllable is *ḳāfiya*, the last being called *radīf*. *ḳāfiya tang honā*, to be very poor or distressed. *a.*

قاق *ḳāḳ*, dry, lean, thin, feeble; disproportionately tall. *a.*

قاقا *ḳā-ḳā*, the note of a crow; an imitative sound, like our word cuckoo. *a.*

قاقله *ḳāḳula*, m. cardamoms. *a.*

قاقم *ḳāḳum*, m. a fine kind of ermine. *a.*

قال *ḳāl*, m. a word, a saying; loquaciousness; boasting, egotism. *ḳāl mārnā*, to be very loquacious; to rebuke, to reproach. *ḳāl maḳāl*, m. altercation, wrangling. *ḳāla-llāhu ta'ālā*, "God the Most High hath said," a phrase generally prefixed to quotations from the *ḳur,ān*. *a.*

قالب *ḳālib*, m. a mould, model, form; bust, figure; the body. *a.*

قالبي *ḳālibī*, cast in a mould, made on a mould, moulded. *a.*

قالي *ḳālī*, f. a carpet, tapestry. *p.*

قاليچه *ḳālīcha*, m. a small carpet. *p.*

قالين *ḳālīn*, f. a carpet, tapestry. *p.*

قامت *ḳāmat*, f. stature, shape, form, figure, body. *ḳadd o ḳāmat*, f. stature and size, general appearance. *a.* [Arabic lexicon. *a.*

قاموس *ḳāmūs*, m. the ocean; the name of an

قان *ḳāṅ*, the sound uttered by a duck. *ḳāṅ-ḳāṅ-k.*, to quack as a duck. *h.*

قانت *ḳānit*, obedient to God, devout; silent. *a.*

قانع *ḳāni'*, contented, satisfied. *a.*

قانون *ḳānūn*, m. rule, regulation, statute, canon; a dulcimer or harp. *ḳānūn-go*, m. an officer in each district, acquainted with its customs, the nature of the tenures of the land, &c. *ḳānūn-go,ī*, f. the office of a *ḳānūn-go*. *g.*

قاهر *ḳāhir*, oppressive; subduing, triumphing. *a.*

قاهره *ḳāhira*, f. a conqueress, victrix. *al ḳāhira*, grand Cairo, q. d. Augusta or Victoria. *a.*

قائد *ḳā,id*, m. a leader, a general; the star in the tail of the Lesser Bear. *a.*

قائزه كرنا *ḳā,iza karnā*, a. to tie up a horse's head by passing the bridle to his tail, to prevent his biting, &c. while being rubbed down. *a. p.*

قائزي *ḳā,izī*, f. a bridle used whilst cleaning a horse, a bit. *a.*

قائل *ḳā,il*, acquiescing, agreeing, giving up a point; adj. subdued, confuted. *ḳā,il-k.*, to confute, to convince, to convict. *ḳā,il honā*, n. to acquiesce, to acknowledge, to yield. *a.*

قائم *ḳā,im*, erect, perpendicular; firm, fixed, durable; attentive, persevering. *ḳā,imu-n-nār*, fixed quicksilver (*i. e.* fixed by fire). *ḳā,im-mizāj*, of a settled temper. *ḳā,im-maḳām*, a viceroy, lieutenant, vicegerent. *a.*

قائمه *ḳā,ima*, erect, perpendicular; m. a perpendicular line; a right angle. *a.*

قائمي *ḳā,imī*, firmness, durability. *a.*

قائين *ḳā,īn* (v. قابيل), Cain, the first-born of Eve: the Arabs have changed the word into *ḳābīl*, probably because it rhymes with *hābīl*, Abel; or the change may have resulted from the ignorance of a copyist; for if the diacritical points, as often happens, be omitted, the two forms *ḳā,īn* and *ḳābīl* become nearly the same. *a.*

قب *ḳabb*, m. the sound of a falling sword. *a.*

قبا *ḳabā*, f. a garment (quilted), a jacket; a kind of long gown. *ḳabā*, name of a village near *Madīna*, in Arabia; the earth, ground, soil. *ḳabā,e postīn*, a fur cloak. *p. a.*

قباحت *ḳabāḥat*, f. villany, deformity, dishonesty, baseness, evil, ill, wrong, inconvenience. *a.*

قباله *ḳabāla*, m. a deed, writing; a bond, written agreement, contract, a bill of sale. *a.*

قبائل *ḳabā,il* (pl. of قبيله), family (wife and children, &c.); tribes. *a.*

قبح *ḳubh* or *ḳabḥ*, baseness, deformity. *a.*

قبر *ḳabar*, f. a grave, a tomb. *ḳabar-kan*, a gravedigger. *a.*

قبرستان *ḳabaristān*, } f. a burying-ground, a
قبرگاه *ḳabar-gāh*, } cemetery. *a. p.*

قبس *ḳabs* or *ḳabas*, m. lighting or getting fire from another, striking, or asking fire; learning, teaching; a firebrand, a match, any thing for kindling fire with; adj. quick, expeditious. *a.*

قبض *ḳabẓ*, f. contraction; costiveness; a receipt; tax, tribute. *ḳabẓu-l-wuṣūl*, f. a receipt, acknowledgment. *a.*

قبضه *ḳabẓa*, m. a grasp; a handle; the gripe of a sword. *a.*

قبضيت *ḳabẓīyat*, f. seizure, costiveness. *a.*

قبل *ḳabl*, m. the anterior part, the front; adj. first, anterior; adv. before. *ḳabl az ān-ki*, before that, *anteaquam*. *ḳabl az īn*, before now, heretofore. *a.*

قبل *ḳibal*, power; plenty; presence; on the part of, in respect of. *ḳubl* or *ḳubul*, *pudendum viri vel fœminæ*; (pl. of *ḳabīl*), tribes, &c. *a.*

قبله *ḳibla*, m. any thing opposite; that part to which *Musalmāns* turn their face when at prayer; hence the word means Mecca, an altar, temple; worship; father. *ḳibla,e kaunain*, the *ḳibla* of both worlds (applied to *Muḥammad*). *ḳibla-gāh*, the place turned to when at prayer; generally means a father; a patron or protector. *ḳibla,e 'ālam* (*ḳibla* of the world), a title applied to oriental monarchs. *ḳibla-numā*, lit. that which shews where the *ḳibla* is situated; a complex mathematical instrument, wrongly supposed to be the mariners' compass; but in reality it is an astrolabe which was used for finding the bearing of Mecca before the compass was known to the Arabs: of course the term is now applied to the European compass. *a.*

قبور *ḳubūr* (pl. of قبر), tombs. *a.*

قبور *ḳubūr*, } holsters for pistols. *a.*
قبوره *ḳabūra*, }

قبول *ḳabūl* or *ḳubūl*, m. consent, favourable reception, concession, approbation, assent; adj. approved, consented. *ḳabūl-ṣūrat*, of a pleasant figure, handsome, well-favoured. *ḳabūl-k.*, a. to assent, allow, confess, consent, to own, to promise. *ḳabūl honā*, to be acceptable; to be agreed on. *a.*

قبولنا *ḳabūlnā*, a. to agree, to consent, to assent, to accept, to choose. *a. h.*

قبولي *ḳabūlī*, f. a kind of food, rice and pulse boiled together. *a.*

قبوليت *ḳabūliyat*, f. a written agreement. *a.*

قبه *ḳubba*, m. a vault, an arch, a dome; a small ornament shaped like a pine-apple on the top of a flagstaff or spire. *a.* [ugly, shameful. *a.*

قبيح *ḳabīḥ*, vile, detestable, deformed, bad,

قبيل *ḳabīl*, m. a species, kind; family, tribe, kindred, progeny. *a.* [a wife. *a.*

قبيله *ḳabīla* (also *ḳabīlā*), m. a family, a tribe;

قتال *ḳitāl*, battle, slaughter, fighting. *ḳattāl*, a slayer, a murderer. *ḳuttāl* (pl. of *ḳātil*), murderers. *a.*

قتل *ḳatl*, m. slaughter, homicide, murder. *ḳatli 'āmm*, m. a general massacre. *ḳatli 'amd*, wilful murder. *ḳatli-khaṭā*, killing by mistake. *ḳatl-k.*, a. to kill, to execute; to murder. *ḳatl-gāh*, place of execution or of slaughter. *a.*

قتلا *ḳatlā*, قتله *ḳatla*, } m. a slice, fragment. *h.*

قتيل *ḳatīl*, m. قتيله *ḳatīla*, f. } killed, murdered, or beheaded. *a.*

قحبگي *ḳaḥbagī*, f. whoredom, fornication. *a.*

قحبه *ḳaḥba*, m. a cough; f. an old woman (subject to coughing); a whore, a prostitute (accustomed to notify her profession by coughing, Gol.); adj. unchaste. *a.*

قحط *ḳaḥt*, m. famine, dearth. *ḳaḥṭ-zada*, afflicted or visited with famine. *ḳaḥṭ-sāl* or *-sālī*, a season of dearth or famine. *a.*

قد *ḳadd*, m. stature. *ḳadd-āwar ḳadd-dār*, or *ḳadd-kash*, tall, of commanding stature. *ḳadd-kham-k.*, a. to bow down. *a.*

قدامت *ḳadāmat*, f. priority, excellence, precedence. *a.*

قدح *ḳadaḥ*, m. a goblet, glass, bowl; a satire or lampoon. *a.*

قدر *ḳadr* or *ḳadar*, f. worth, value, price; quantity; destiny, fate. *ḳadr-bakhsh*, source of dignity. *ḳadr-dān*, a just appreciator, knowing the worth of (a person). *ḳadr-dānī*, f. appreciation of another's merit; patronage. *ḳadr-shinās*, knowing the worth of (a person). *a.*

قدرت *ḳudrat*, f. power, authority; omnipotence. *a.*

قدرتي *ḳudratī*, adj. divine, not made or produced by man; f. a mushroom; a toadstool. *ḳudratī rang*, white; natural colour (not stained or dyed). *a.*

قدس *ḳuds*, m. holiness, sanctity; Jerusalem; the angel Gabriel; adj. holy, pure. *a.*

قدس سره *ḳaddasa sirra-hu*, may he (the Almighty) sanctify his sepulchre! (a phrase added when speaking of a holy or great man deceased.) As these words are generally written without vowels, it is uncertain whether they are not to be read in a passive sense, as *ḳuddisa sirru-hu*, may his tomb be sanctified; the latter reading, however, is very doubtful. *a.*

قدسي *ḳudsī*, holy; m. the angel Gabriel. *a.*

قدسيه *ḳudsiya*, celestial, holy. *a.*

قدغن *ḳadaghan*, care, injunction, prohibition. *p.*

قدم *ḳadam*, m. a pace, a step, a footstep; the sole of the foot. *ḳadam-bāz*, fleet. *ḳadam ba-ḳadam*, step by step, gently. *ḳadam-bos*, one who kisses the feet of a superior; one who pays respect. *ḳadam-bosī*, f. kissing the feet, obeisance. *ḳadam-chūmnā*, a. to kiss the feet; to leave the company of another, to bid adieu. *ḳadam-chhūne*, to touch or embrace one's feet. *ḳadam-ranja-farmānā* or *-karnā*, to take the trouble of visiting (another), to condescend to visit or wait upon (spoken of a superior towards an inferior). *ḳadam-lagnā*, to take protection; to walk well (a horse). *ḳadam-lene*, to acknowledge the superiority of another (either in good or evil qualities: most frequently in the latter). *a.*

قدم *ḳidam*, m. a man excelling in virtue; eternity (Gol.). *a.*

قدما *ḳudamā* (pl. of قديم), the ancients. *a.*

قدوس *ḳuddūs* or *ḳaddūs*, pure, holy, blessed. *a.*

قدوم *ḳudūm*, m. arrival, coming near. *a.*

قدير *ḳadīr*, powerful; the Almighty. *a.*

قديم *ḳadīm*, ancient, old. *ḳadīmu-l-aiyām*, ancient of days; times of old; adv. from time immemorial. *a.*

قديمي *ḳadīmī*, old, aged, former, ancient. *ḳadīmī ra'īyat*, an occupant of land by hereditary descent. *a.*

قذف *ḳazf*, accusing one falsely of unnatural crimes or adultery. *a.*

قرابادين *ḳarābādīn*, قرابازين *ḳarābāzīn*, } f. an antidote, a panacea, an effectual remedy (a term used in medicine). *a.*

قرابت *ḳarābat*, f. kin, vicinity, relationship, affinity, propinquity. *a.*

قرابتي *ḳarābatī*, related, relative. *a.*

قرابه *ḳarāba*, m. a flagon. *a.*

قرابين *ḳarābīn*, f. a carbine; a weapon something between a pistol and a blunderbuss, having a short, wide, bell mouthed barrel. It is used with one hand, like a pistol, and is a favourite firearm among the Turkish and Arab horsemen and irregular cavalry. The Turks originally borrowed the weapon, as well as its name, from the Genoese.

قراءت *ḳirā,at*, f. pronunciation, reading (more especially of the *ḳur,ān*). *a.*

قراد *ḳarrād*, a monkey-keeper. *a.*

قرار *ḳarār*, m. rest, tranquillity, quietness; firmness, stability; ratification, agreement, engagement; waiting, patience. *ḳarār-dād*, an engagement, contract, agreement. *ḳarār-wāḳi'ī*, accurately, positively. *a.*

قراري *ḳarārī*, firm, stable; ratified, agreed to. *a.*

قراضه *ḳurāẓa*, a small particle (of gold or silver); what falls off in filing. *a.*

قراط *ḳirrāṭ*, a carat, the twenty-fourth part of an ounce, or, according to Gladwin, the one-twentieth of an ounce. *a.*

قراف *ḳirāf*, "*rem habere cum conjuge.*" *a.*

قراقر *ḳarāḳar*, grumbling of the guts. *borborygmi.* *a.*

قران *ḳirān*, m. conjunction of the planets; propinquity, contiguity; a period of 10, 20, 30, 40, 80, or 120 years. *ḳirān-k.*, to accomplish something wonderful. *ḳirānu-s-sa'dain*, the conjunction of the two fortunate planets Jupiter and Venus; the name of a celebrated poem by Amīr Khusrū, of Dihlī. *ṣāḥibi ḳirān*, prosperous, mighty (lit. one who has been born under a fortunate junction of two or more planets; a title of honour). *a.*

قرآن *ḳur,ān*, m. the book containing the precepts, &c. of *Muḥammad*. *kur,ān uṭhānā* (lit. to raise up the *ḳur,ān*), to swear. *kur,ān par hāth dharnā*, to lay the hand on the *ḳur,ān*, to swear. *ḳur,ān kā jāma pahannā*, to swear excessively. *a.*

قراني *ḳur,ānī*, of or relating to the *ḳur,ān*. *āyāti ḳur,ānī*, verses quoted from the *ḳur,ān*. *ḳur,ānī-mullā*, a Muḥammadan officer who administers oaths taken on the *ḳur,ān*. *a.*

قراول ḳarāwal, m. the advanced guard of an army; a sentinel, a picquet; a gamekeeper. t.

قراولي ḳarāwalī, f. skirmishing (of outposts), a running fight. t.

قرائن ḳarā,in (pl of قرينه), connections, circumstances. a.

قرب ḳurb, m. propinquity, kindred. a.

قربان ḳurbān, m. a sacrifice, victim, oblation; a quiver. a.

قرباني ḳurbānī, devoted, sacrificed. a.

قربت ḳurbat, } f. nearness, proximity; relationship, affinity. a.
قربي ḳurbā, }

قربجوار ḳurb-jawār, near neighbourhood. a.

قرت ḳurrat, joy, gladness. ḳurratu-l-'ain, a coldness (i. e. a lustre or cheerfulness) of the eye. a.

قرحه ḳarḥa, m. a wound, a pimple, sore, ulcer. a.

قرص ḳurṣ, m. an orb, a pellet, a ball of paste, a disc (of the sun or moon), a round loaf of bread. a.

قرض ḳarẓ, m. a loan, debt, money borrowed at interest. ḳarẓi ḥasana, money lent without interest, and repaid at the pleasure of the borrower. ḳarẓ-khwāh, a dun, a creditor. ḳarẓ-dār, a debtor. ḳarẓ-dārī, f. being in debt. ḳarẓ denā, a. to lend. ḳarẓ rakhnā, a. to owe. ḳarẓ lenā. a. to borrow. a.

قرضه ḳarẓa (v. قرض), a loan, debt, &c. a.

قرضي ḳarẓī, m. a debtor, a borrower; adj. borrowed, got as a loan. a.

قرط ḳurṭ m. cutting; amputation; a piece, a little, a mouthful; an ear-ring. a.

قرطاس ḳirṭās, m. paper (Gr. χάρτης, Lat. charta). g.

قرعه ḳur'a, m. a lot (which among the Arabs was drawn by shooting arrows); a wager, wagering, drawing lots, seeking one's fortune by opening a book, &c. ḳur'a-andāz, a caster or drawer of a lot. a.

قرق ḳurḳ, m. an embargo; confiscation, the act of seizing, attacking, seizure; inclosure, hindrance, prevention of access; "an order issued to the inhabitants of a place to keep themselves within doors, while the wives and female establishment of a prince or grandee travel through that part of the country."—(Binning). h.

قرقرا ḳarḳarā, m. the name of a bird (*Ardea virgo*), the demoiselle crane. a.

قرقي ḳurḳī, confiscated. ḳurḳī parwāna, a warrant issued to sequester a property. h.

قرمز ḳirmiz, m. crimson; kermes. ḳirmizi farangī, cochineal (hence Chermes or Kermes). a.

قرمزي ḳirmizī, of a scarlet or crimson colour; f. scarlet cloth. a. [cuckold, &c. u.

قرمساق ḳurram-sāḳ, a term of abuse, pimp,

قرن ḳarn, m. conjunction of the planets; a space of ten years, or any multiple thereof up to 120; a horn. a.

قرنا ḳarnā, a kind of French horn. a.

قرناءي ḳarnā,ī, f. a trumpet (of horn). a.

قرنبيق ḳarambīḳ, an alembic, a still. a.

قرنفل ḳaranful, m. (Gr. καρυόφυλλος), a clove. g. [a coral. t.

قرول ḳaraul, m. (for ḳarāwal, q. v.). ḳurūl,

قرولي ḳaraulī, f. a picquet, grand guard; hunting. t.

قريب ḳarīb, near, neighbouring, nigh, almost, about, akin; a relative or near relation. a.

قريبا ḳarībā or ḳarīban, near, close upon. a.

قريبه ḳarība or ḳarībat, f. a near female relative. a.

قريش ḳuraish, a noble tribe of Arabs, of whom Muḥammad's grandfather was chief. a.

قريشي ḳuraishī, of or relating to the ḳuraish tribe. a.

قرين ḳarīn, conjoined, contiguous, connected; (in comp.) joined by, or possessed of, as 'izzat-ḳarīn, honourable, possessed of honour. a.

قرينه ḳarīna, m. similarity, likeness; symmetry; cause, context, connection, tenour. a.

قريه ḳarya, m. a village or parish. a.

قز ḳaz, m. silk (particularly raw silk). p.

قزلباشي ḳazal-bāshī or ḳizil-bāshī, m. a kind of *Mughal* soldier: the ḳazal-bāshīs are considered to be the descendants of the captives given to *Shaikh Haidar* by *Tamerlane*: they wore the red caps assumed by those captives as a mark of distinction and are considered as the best troops of the Persian armies. t. [oath. a.

قسامت ḳisāmat, f. the administration of an

قساوت ḳasāwat, f. hardness of heart, grief, anguish, pain, chagrin. a. [revenge. a.

قسر ḳasar, m. violence, compulsion, retaliation,

قسط ḳisṭ, f. portion, instalment; tax. ḳisṭ-bandī, f. an agreement for a stated payment of a sum of money, to be discharged at several times; settlement of the revenues or taxes by instalment. ḳusṭ, name of a plant (*Costus arabicus*). a.

قسم ḳism or ḳasm, f. kind, species, sort; part, division; in law it denotes the equal partition of cohabitation which a husband is required by law to make among his wives when he has a plurality of them. a.

قسم ḳasam, f. an oath. ḳasam-dilānā or -khilānā, a. to administer an oath. ḳasam khānā, a. to take an oath, to swear. a.

قسمت ḳismat, f. fate, fortune, lot; share, distribution, portion; a division, particularly of inheritance: when any part of the pargana is transferred from one zamīndār to another, each part is called a ḳismat pargana. a.

قسمي ḳasamī, sworn. ḳasamī honā, n. to be sworn, to be upon oath. a.

قسميه ḳasamīya, upon oath; swearing. a.

قسيس *ḳasīs* or *ḳissīs*, a presbyter, a priest. *a.*

قسيم *ḳasīm*, beautiful, handsome. *a.*

قشر *ḳashr* or *ḳishr*, m. peel, skin, bark, husk, shell, crust. *a.*

قشعريرة *ḳusha'rīra*, the hair standing on end (from horror). *a.*

قشقة *ḳashḳa*, m. a mark made by the Hindūs on the forehead, with sandal, &c. *h.*

قشمش *ḳishmish*, dried grapes or currants. *p.*

قشون *ḳashūn*, a body of troops, a brigade, a division, an army. *t.*

قصا *ḳiṣṣā* (for قصة), a tale, a story, &c. *a.*

قصاب *ḳaṣṣāb*, m. a butcher. *a.*

قصابة *ḳaṣāba*, m. a handkerchief tied round the head (worn by women principally). *a.*

قصابي *ḳaṣṣābī*, f. the trade of a butcher. *a.*

قصاص *ḳaṣāṣ* or *ḳiṣāṣ*, m. the law of retaliation, as an eye for an eye, &c.: this word is used in contradistinction to *diyat*, q. v. *a.*

قصاءي *ḳaṣā,ī*, m. a butcher; adj. cruel, hard-hearted. *a.*

قصائد *ḳaṣā,id*, قصائدات *ḳaṣā,idāt*, (pl. of قصيدة) odes of greater length than the *ghazal*. *a.*

قصائني *ḳaṣā,inī*, a butcher's wife. *a. h.*

قصب *ḳaṣab*, a town, a large village; a *ḳalam* or reed; a fine species of linen cloth made in Egypt; a woman's head-gear. *a.*

قصبات *ḳaṣbāt* (pl. of *ḳaṣba*), small towns. *a.*

قصبة *ḳaṣba*, m. a small town (particularly when inhabited by decent people or families of some rank); a township, including both the town and all the lands attached to it. *a.*

قصد *ḳaṣd*, m. desire, wish, inclination, machination, conspiracy, project, purpose. *ḳaṣdi muṣammam*, fixed resolution, firm intention. *a.*

قصدا *ḳaṣdā* or *ḳaṣdan*, voluntarily, intentionally, purposely, expressly. *a.*

قصر *ḳaṣr*, m. diminution, defect; evening twilight (q. d. defect of light); an edifice, a palace, a building, an elegant villa. *a.*

قصص *ḳiṣaṣ* (pl. of قصة), tales, stories, &c. *a.*

قصف *ḳaṣf*, m. the wind breaking, dashing to pieces (a ship); blowing with a loud noise (wind), thundering. *ḳaṣif*, adj. weak, broken, split. *a.*

قصور *ḳuṣūr*, m. error, sin, fault, defect, omission, want, failure; the allowance or premium on the exchange of *rupīs*, in contradistinction to *baṭṭā*, or discount. *a.*

قصوري *ḳuṣūrī*, defect, error, failure. *a. h.*

قصة *ḳiṣṣa*, m. a tale, a story, narration; (met. in Hind.) a quarrel, a dispute. *ḳiṣṣa-khwān*, a story-teller. *ḳiṣṣa-kotāh*, or *ḳiṣṣa mukhtaṣar*, or *al-ḳiṣṣa*, in one word; to cut short a long story. *ḳiṣṣa kotāh-karnā*, to settle a dispute. *a.*

قصيدة *ḳaṣīda*, m. a poem, a long ode, exceeding a hundred couplets, or rather more. *a.*

قضا *ḳaẓā*, f. fate, destiny; death, fatality praying at the appointed time; administration of justice, jurisdiction, mandate, judgment, decree; saying a prayer after the time appointed for it is passed. *ḳaẓā o ḳadar*, f. fate, predestination. *ḳaẓā,e ḥājat*, attending to the calls of nature. *ḳaẓā,e 'umrī*, repeating the prayers to make up for having omitted prayers in the former part of one's life. *ḳaẓārā* or *ḳaẓā-kār*, accidentally, by chance, providentially. *ḳaẓā-k.*, to make up for a former omission of a religious duty; as, for example, to fast after the *Ramaẓān* on account of not having fasted then. *a.*

قضات *ḳuẓāt* (pl. of قاضي), judges, justices. *ḳaẓāt*, f. vice, disgrace, stain. *a.*

قضارا *ḳaẓārā*, accidentally, by chance. *a. p.*

قضاق *ḳazzāḳ*, قضاك *ḳazzāk*, m. a robber, a ruffian, a brigand, Cossack. *t.*

قضاقي *ḳazzāḳī*, robbery, brigandage. *t.*

قضاكار *ḳaẓā-kār*, by chance, accidentally. *a. p.*

قضاوت *ḳaẓāwat*, the office of judge. *a. d.*

قضايا *ḳaẓāyā* (pl. of قضية), disputes, quarrels. *a.*

قضبان *ḳuẓbān* (pl. of قضيب), long and slender branches. *a.*

قضيب *ḳaẓīb*, m. a rod, a long slender branch; a small sword; *penis*. *a.*

قضية *ḳaẓīya* or *ḳaẓiya*, m. declaration, proposition, determination; history, narrative; death; *natura fœminæ, vulva*; a syllogism (in logic); (in Hin. and Per.) a quarrel, wrangle. *ḳaẓiya-dallāl*, one who excites quarrel. *ḳaẓiya mol-lenā*, to take on one's self the quarrel of another, to interfere without cause in the disputes of others. *a.*

قط *ḳaṭ* or *ḳaṭṭ*, m. cutting transversely, making a pen; adj. sufficient. *fa-ḳaṭṭ* or *fa-ḳaṭ*, only, merely, alone, &c. *ḳaṭ-zan*, m. a stamp; a pin or peg on which pens are cut. *ḳaṭ-lagānā*, a. to mend a pen. *a.*

قطار *ḳaṭār* or *ḳiṭār*, f. a line, string (of animals, as of camels, &c.), rank, order, series, row. *a.*

قطاع *ḳuṭṭā'* (pl. of قاطع), robbers, &c. *a.*

قطامة *ḳuṭṭāma*, f. a strumpet, an adulteress. *a.*

قطب *ḳuṭb*, m. the iron spindle or axis on which a millstone turns; the polar star, the north pole. *ḳuṭbi janūbī*, the antarctic or south pole. *ḳuṭbi shimālī*, the arctic or north pole; a prince, chief; a title or degree of rank among religious mendicants. *ḳuṭb numā*, a mariner's compass. *ḳuṭbi samā* the axis of heaven. *a.*

قطر *ḳuṭr*, m. a diameter of a circle. *ḳaṭr*, dropping, falling in. *a.*

قطرات *ḳaṭrāt* (pl. of قطرة), drops. *ḳaṭrāti shabnam*, dew-drops. *a.*

قطران *ḳiṭrān* or *ḳaṭrān*, m. (Gr. κεδρία or κέδριον) tar, liquid pitch (for wheels). *a. g.*

قطرة *ḳaṭra*, m. a drop. *ḳaṭra-zan* or *ḳaṭra zanān*, trotting about; running to and fro hastily. *a.*

قطع *ḳaṭ'*, f. shape, form, cut (of a coat, &c); segment, portion, section, division. *ḳaṭ'i rāh*, getting over a journey. *ḳaṭ'i riḥm*, breaking off all connexion with one's relatives. *ḳaṭ'i ṭarīḳ*, highway robbery. *ḳaṭ'i naẓar*, independent of, disregarding, besides, laying out of the question. *ḳaṭ' karnā*, to pass or traverse (a road, &c.). *ḳaṭ' honā*, to be passed or performed (a journey, &c.). *a.*

قطعى *ḳaṭ'ā* or *ḳaṭ'an*, never, not at all. *a.*

قطعه *ḳiṭ'a*, m. a section, division; a strophe. *ḳiṭ'a-band*, a kind of verse, in which the meaning of the first verse of each stanza is completed in the last. *a.*

قطعه *ḳaṭ'a* or *ḳuṭ'a*, a plot of ground. *a.*

قطعي *ḳaṭ'ī*, verily, truly; f. a tailor's measure. *a.*

قطمير *ḳiṭmīr*, m. the thin pellicle on a date-stone; name of the dog which accompanied the seven sleepers. *naḳīr o ḳiṭmīr*, minutely, exactly, to the point. *a.*

قطن *ḳuṭn*, *ḳuṭun* or *ḳuṭṭun*, cotton. *a.*

قطني *ḳuṭnī*, made of cotton. *a.*

قعب *ḳa'b*, m. a cavern, a pit, a furrow, a cup; a hidden meaning of a speech. *a.*

قعر *ḳa'r*, m. a gulf, an abyss, the bottom of a well, &c.). *ḳa'ri daryā*, the depth of a river; the sea. *a.*

قعود *ḳu'ūd*, sitting down; remaining in one place. *a.*

قفا *ḳafā*, f. the back of the head, nape of the neck; adv. secretly, behind one's back. *a.*

قفتان *ḳaftān*, m. a robe of honour. *t.*

قفس *ḳafas*, قفص *ḳafaṣ*, m. a cage, a lattice, net-work. *a.*

قفل *ḳufl* (vulg. *ḳulaf*), m. a lock, a bolt. *a.*

ققنس *ḳuḳnus*, ققنوس *ḳuḳnūs*, the phœnix, an imaginary bird. *a.*

قفيز *ḳafīz*, a measure of about 64lbs.; also a measure of surface of about 144 cubits square. *a.*

قل *ḳul*, m. reading of the *sūra* or chapter of the *ḳur,ān* entitled *ḳul huwa-l-lāh*, which is done by way of benediction over fruits and sweetmeats presented to the guests at the conclusion of the religious annual feasts held in commemoration of ancestors and other relatives. Hence it comes to signify conclusion. *ḳul ho-chukā*, it is all over. *ḳul huwa-l-lāh paṛhnā*, to grumble (the guts); to be excessively hungry (v. under *antṛī*). *a.*

قلاب *ḳullāb*, m. the hood put on a hawk to blind him; drawing and relaxing the string of a bow repeatedly before discharging the arrow. *a.*

قلابه *ḳulāba*, m. a staple, hinge, link, hook. *a.*

قلاچ *ḳallāch*, قلاش *ḳallāsh*, shrewd, malicious; wretched, friendless; cunning; addicted to drinking, a drunkard. *t.*

قلب *ḳalb*, m. the heart, mind, soul, understanding; kernel, marrow; adj. inverted; adulterated. *ḳalb-k.*, a. to turn over, to invert, to turn. *a.*

قلبه *ḳalba*, m. a plough. *ḳalba-rānī*, f. ploughing, driving the plough. *a.*

قلبي *ḳalabī*, cordial, hearty, sincere. *a.*

قلت *ḳillat*, f. littleness, penury, scarcity, want, indigence, paucity. *a.*

قلتبان *ḳaltabān*, m. a pimp, a wittol, a mean scoundrel; a contented or conniving cuckold. *a.*

قلتباني *ḳaltabānī*, the state or conduct of a pimp. *a. p.*

قلتين *ḳullatain*, a public warm-bath; hence, adj. common to all, hackneyed; a (cup) used by every one who comes; a common woman or prostitute. *Mīr Ḥasan* says, *na dījo wuh piyāla jo ho ḳullatain*, Give me not that cup which is hackneyed among the multitude. *a.*

قلزم *ḳulzum*, m. a sea; the Red Sea or Arabian Gulf: it strictly denotes the town of Clysma in Egypt, near the head of the Arabian Gulf.

قلعجات *ḳil'ajāt* (barbarous pl. of قلعه, q. v.). *a. p.*

قلعچه *ḳil'acha*, m. a small fort; a redoubt. *a. p.*

قلعه *ḳil'a* (properly *ḳal'a*), m. a fort, a palace or royal residence. *ḳil'a-dār*, commandant of a garrison. *ḳil'a-dārī*, f. the command of a garrison; the office, emoluments, &c. of a *ḳil'a-dār*. *a.*

قلعي *ḳala'ī*, f. tin. *ḳala'ī,i kushta*, calx of tin, putty. *ḳala'ī khulnā*, n. the removal of one's disguise, so that his real qualities appear. *ḳala'ī-gar*, a tinner of pots. *ḳala'ī-garī*, f. the business of tinning pots. *a.*

قلفي *ḳulfī*, f. a small *ḥuḳḳa* snake; a cup with a cover (pec. in which ice is moulded). *a.*

قلق *ḳalaḳ*, m. disquietude, commotion, anxiety. *a.* [of an elephant. *h.*

قلقاري *ḳilḳārī*, f. shrieking, roaring; the voice

قلقل *ḳulḳul*, f. the noise made by water in the neck of a bottle, when pouring out, gurgling. *ḳilḳil*, a species of plant producing a grain that is hard black, and odoriferous. *a.*

قلقله *ḳulḳula*, m. a kind of *ḥuḳḳa*. *a.*

قلم *ḳalam*, m. (by Hindūs f.) a reed; a pen; a mode of writing characters, handwriting; f. a section or paragraph of a chapter in a book; cuttings of trees, &c. for planting; a kind of fireworks. *ḳalam-band-k.*, a. to take down, to write. *ḳalam-bandī*, f. signature, signing an agreement. *ḳalam-tarāsh*, m. a penknife. *ḳalam jārī honā*, levying of forces. *ḳalam dān*, m. an inkstand. *ḳalam-rau*, m. empire, sovereignty, jurisdiction. *ḳalam-kār*, an engraver. *ḳalam-kārī*, f. workmanship; a species of flowered calico or chintz. *ḳalam-k.*, to cut. *ḳalam-kashī*, f. writing. *ḳalam-lagānā*, to plant slips or cuttings. *ek-ḳalam* or *yak-ḳalam*, utterly, entirely, altogether. *a.*

قلماق *ḳalmāḳ*, a Calmuc Tartar. *p.*

قلماقني *ḳalmāḳanī*, a female Calmuc: sometimes these are armed, and serve as a body-guard to princesses. *p.*

قلمان *ḳalmān*, the upper part of the beard or moustaches trimmed on each side so as to resemble pencils *a. d.*

قلمون *ḳalamūn* (v. *bū-ḳalamūn*), a chameleon. *g.*

قلمه *ḳulma*, m. sausage, or any food stuffed into the intestines of animals, haggis, black pudding. *a.*

قلمي *ḳalamī*, written, committed to writing; tapering (like a *ḳalam*). *ḳalamī-k.*, to write (a letter); crystallized (saltpetre, &c.). *a.*

قلنج *ḳulinj* (properly *kolinj*), the cholic. *a.g.*

قلندر *ḳalandar*, m. a kind of monk, who deserts the world, wife, friends, &c., and travels about with shaven head and beard; the fly of a tent. *a.*

قلندرا *ḳalandarā*, m. a kind of silk cloth; the fly of a tent. *a.*

قلندري *ḳalandarī*, f. a kind of tent (having a fly to it), life or profession of a *ḳalandar*. *a.*

قلوب *ḳulūb* (pl. of قلب), hearts, kernels. *a.*

قله *ḳulla*, the summit of a mountain. *a.*

قلي *ḳulī*, m. a slave, a labourer, porter, a cooley. *t.*

قليان *ḳaliyān*, m. (Dakh. *ḳiliyān*) a small and simple kind of *ḥukka* or tobacco-pipe for smoking through water: the Persians pronounce it *ḳaliyūn*. *p.*

قليل *ḳalīl*, little, small, moderate, a few, rare. *ḳalīl o kas̤īr*, small and great. *a.*

قليه *ḳaliya*, m. the name of a dish of broiled flesh, &c.; also a kind of soap ashes. *a.*

قمار *ḳimār*, m. dice or any game of hazard. *ḳimār-bāz* or *ḳimārī*, a gambler. *ḳimār-bāzī*, f. gambling. *a.*

قماري *ḳamārī* (pl. of قمري), female turtle-doves. *a.*

قماش *ḳamāsh*, m. breeding, manners; trifles. household furniture. *ḳimāsh*, name of a suit at cards (v. *tāj*). *a.*

قمچي *ḳamchī*, f. a horsewhip; a bamboo twig. *t.*

قمر *ḳamar*, m. the moon. *a.*

قمري *ḳumrī*, f. ring-dove. *ḳamarī*, lunar, relating to the moon. *a.*

قمقمه *ḳumḳuma*, m. a jug, a pitcher; a scent-bottle; a vessel in which the red mixture is contained with which they play at the *holī* festival; a round shade or lantern. *a.*

قميص *ḳamīṣ*, m. a shirt; hence, Fr. *chemise*, It. *camicia*, Port. *camisa*, Hind. and Beng. *kamīj*. *a.*

قنات *ḳanāt*, f. the walls of a tent, or canvas inclosure, with which a sort of court-yard is formed in camp, a screen. *a.*

قناديل *ḳanādīl* (pl. of قنديل), candles, lampa. *a.*

قناره *ḳannāra*, a slaughter-house, shambles; a row of iron hooks on which a butcher suspends his joints of meat. *a.*

قناعت *ḳinā'at* or *ḳanā'at*, f. contentment, tranquillity; abstinence. *a.*

قنب *ḳinnab* or *ḳannab*, hemp, cannabis. *a.*

قنبر *ḳumbur*, قنبرا *ḳumburā*, a lark; a crest on a bird's head. *a.*

قند *ḳand*, m. sugar, sugar-candy. *a.*

قندهار *ḳandhār*, name of a country to the west of the Indus. *p.*

قنديل *ḳandīl*, f. a candle; lamp, lantern, chandelier, shade. *a.*

قنوت *ḳunūt*, f. devotion, piety. *a.*

قنوج *ḳanūj*, *ḳanoj*, or *ḳanauj*, name of a celebrated ancient city of India, situated on the Ganges. *p.*

قنوط *ḳunūṭ*, f. despair, despairing. *a.*

قواعد *ḳawā,id* (pl. of قاعده), rules, military exercise. *ḳawā'id-gāh*, parade, place for drill, &c. *a.*

قوال *ḳawwāl*, m. a kind of musician, a singer; a story-teller; adj. speaking, conversing. *a.*

قوالي *ḳawwālnī*, a female singer, &c. *a. h.*

قوام *ḳawām*, m. justice, equity. *ḳiwām*, that on which any thing rests or in which it consists, essence, syrup. *a.*

قوامي *ḳiwāmī*, ropy, syrupy, thick. *a.*

قوانين *ḳawānīn* (pl. of قانون), rules, regulations, ordinances, statutes. *a.*

قوت *ḳūt*, f. food, aliment, livelihood, subsistence, victuals. *a.*

قوت *ḳuwwat*, f. power, virtue, authority, faculty, strength, vigour. *ḳuwwati ākhiẕa*, strength of mind. *ḳuwwati bāṣira*, sight. *ḳuwwati bāh*, lust. *ḳuwwati jāẕiba*, power of attraction, allurement. *ḳuwwati ḥāfiẓa*, memory. *ḳuwwati dāfi,a*, power of expulsion. *ḳuwwati dil*, strength of mind. *ḳuwwati ẕātiya*, natural virtue or power. *ḳuwwati sāmi'a*, hearing. *ḳuwwati shāmma*, smelling. *ḳuwwati māsika*, power of retention. *ḳuwwati mi'da*, strength of stomach. *ḳuwwati mumaiyiza*, distributive power, discrimination. *ḳuwwati hāẓima*, digestion. *a.*

قوتي *ḳūṭī*, f. a small box, a snuff-box, a pill-box. *h.*

قوج *ḳoj*, also *ḳoch*, a horned fighing ram. *p.*

قور *ḳor*, f. a new rope of fine cotton; a chain of elephants; edging, twist, tape. *ḳor-khāna*, an armory, a wardrobe. *a.*

قورچي *ḳorchī*, m. a keeper of a wardrobe. *a.*

قورما *ḳormā*, قورمه *ḳorma*, m. a kind of dish, a savoury stew. *u.*

قوس *ḳaus*, f. a bow; m. the sign of the Archer (*Sagittarius*). *ḳausi ḳuzaḥ*, f. the rainbow. *a.*

قوش *ḳūsh*, a word used in checking or intimidating dogs; a bird, more especially a hawk or falcon. *ḳūsh bāz*, a sportsman, a fowler. *ḳūsh-khāna*, an aviary. *ḳūsh-begī*, the chief falconer or keeper of hawks. *t.*

قوقنوس *ḳūḳnūs* (*ḳūḳnus*, *ḳuḳnus*, or *ḳuḳnūs*), m. the name of a bird, phœnix. *p.*

قول *ḳaul*, m. a word, saying; agreement, promise, consent, contract; a kind of song. *ḳaul-bīṛā*, the betel of contract, a ceremony gone through as a ratification of an agreement. *ḳaul-nāma*, m. a written agreement. *ḳaul o fi'l*, m. word and deed. *ḳaul-ḳarār* or *ḳaul o ḳarār*, m. an agreement. *a.*

قولنج **ḳolinj, ḳūlinj,** or **ḳūlunj,** the cholic, a griping pain in the bowels. *a. g.*

قولي **ḳaulī,** of or relating to an agreement; land held under a *ḳaul* or stipulated tenure. *a.*

قوم **ḳaum,** f. tribe, sect, caste, a people, nation, family. *ḳaum o khwesh,* pl. m. friends and relatives. *a.* [same tribe, &c. *a.*

قوميت **ḳaumīyat,** f. connection, being of the

قوي **ḳawī,** strong, solid, powerful, vigorous. *ḳawī-bāzū* or *ḳawī-bāl,* strong armed. *ḳawī-pai,* sinewy. *ḳawī-jussa* or *ḳawī-haikal,* robust, strong-bodied. *a.*

قوءيماق **ḳo,emāḳ,** a kind of bread made of flour, white of eggs, and onions fried in *ghī.* *d.*

قهار **ḳahhār,** very powerful, a conqueror, a subduer, an avenger; adj. imperious, avenging. *a.*

قهر **ḳahr,** m. severity, chastisement, rage, indignation, vengeance, judgment. *ḳahri ḳiyāmat,* is applied both in panegyric and satire to denote great disturbance. "*ḳahri darwesh bar jāni darwesh,*" the rage of the poor man affects only himself, *i.e.* no one regards it. *a.*

قهقرا **ḳahḳarā,**
قهقرة **ḳahḳara,**
قهقري **ḳahḳarā,**
} retiring, retreating back, retrograde motion. *a.*

قهقها **ḳahḳahā,**
قهقهه **ḳahḳaha,**
} laughing loudly and indecently. *ḳahḳahā-marnā,* to laugh heartily. *a.* [pot. *a.*

قهوه **ḳahwa,** m. coffee. *ḳahwa-dān,* a coffee-

قي **ḳai,** f. vomiting, a frequent vomiting. *ḳai jullāb,* the cholera morbus. *ḳai lāne-wālā,* (in medicine) an emetic. *a.*

قياس **ḳiyās,** m. measuring, comparing; judgment, opinion; supposition, thought, guess, theory, a syllogism. *ḳiyās-k.,* to guess, to estimate *a.*

قياساً **ḳiyāsan,** by guess, hypothetically. *a.*

قياسي **ḳiyāsī,** analogical, regular; imaginary, conjectural. *a.*

قيافه **ḳiyāfa,** m. appearance, likeness, air, manner, mode, representation. *ḳiyāfa-shinās,* a physiognomist. *ḳiyāfa-shināsī,* the science of physiognomy. *a.*

قيام **ḳiyām,** m. standing erect, resurrection; stability; attention; residence, settlement. *a.*

قيامت **ḳiyāmat,** f. the general resurrection, the last day; (met.) calamity; excessively great. *ḳiyāmat-k.,* a. to oppress; to do any thing wonderful. *a.*

قيامي **ḳiyāmī,** f. stability, steadiness. *a.*

قيتار **ḳītār,** a guitar (Gr. κιθάρα). *g.*

قيد **ḳaid,** f. a fetter, imprisonment; an obligation, compact; an obstacle. *ḳaid-khāna,* m. a prison. *ḳaid-k.,* to imprison. *ḳaid-h.* or *-rahnā,* to be imprisoned. *a.*

قيدي **ḳaidī,** m. a prisoner, a captive. *a.*

قير **ḳīr,** m. a pitch, a kind of bitumen flowing from some mountains. *ḳīr-dār,* besmeared with pitch. *ḳīr-gūn,* of the colour of pitch. *a.*

قيس **ḳais** (commonly called *ḳaisi majnūn*), name of a famous lover. *a.*

قيراط **ḳīrāt,** m. a carat, the twenty-fourth part of an ounce, a weight of four grains; four barleycorns. *a.*

قيصر **ḳaiṣar,** m. Cæsar, an emperor; the general name for the Greek or Turkish emperor. *l.*

قيصوم **ḳaiṣūm,** m. southernwood (*Artemisia abrotanum*). *a.*

قيف **ḳīf,** a funnel.

قيفال **ḳīfāl,**
قيفل **ḳīfal,**
} the cephalic vein. *g.*

قيل **ḳīl,** m. a word, speech, saying. *ḳīl o ḳāl,* m. conversation, controversy, altercation. *a.*

قيلوله **ḳailūla,** m. sleeping at mid-day, a meridian nap. *a.* [ture. *a.*

قيم **ḳaiyim,** true; standing, erect; m. na-

قيمت **ḳīmat,** f. price, value, worth. *a.*

قيمتي **ḳīmatī,** valuable, high-priced, costly. *a.*

قيمه **ḳīma,** m. minced meat. *ḳīma-pulāw,* a kind of dish. *a.*

قينچي **ḳainchī,** f. scissars; an oblique or St. Andrew's cross; the cross beams of the roof of a cottage. *ḳainchī-k.,* to prune trees, or cut the hair. *ḳainchī bāndhnā,* to bind or fasten an unskilful rider on his horse. *u.*

قيود **ḳuyūd** (pl. of قيد), fetters, &c. *ḳaid-kuyūd-k.,* to imprison. *a.*

قيوم **ḳaiyūm,** permanent, stable, lasting; eternal, an epithet of the Deity. *a.*

قيوميت **ḳaiyumīyat,** permanency, stability. *a.*

ك

ك **kāf,** called *kāfi tāzī* or *kāfi 'arabī,* the Arabian *kāf* (in contradistinction to the letter *gāf,* called *kāfi 'ajamī,* i.e. Persian *kāf*). It is the twenty-second letter of the Arabic alphabet, the twenty-fifth Persian, and twenty-eighth Hindūstānī. It is sounded like our *k* or *c* hard, and corresponds to the *ka* of the Sanskrit. In reckoning by *abjad* it counts twenty. Affixed to the end of Persian words it forms diminutives or expressions of contempt; as, *mardak,* a little man, or one of no value; *ṭiflak,* a little child: this also is an expression of endearment; as, *māmak,* dear little mother.

ك क **ka,** the corresponding letter in the Devanāgarī alphabet. Added as a termination to Sanskrit words it denotes agency; as, *janak,* a father, from *jan,* producing. *s.*

ك **ka,** prefixed to Arabic words denotes like, resembling; as, *ka-l-naḳsh fi-l-ḥajar,* like an engraving on stone.

ك क *ka*, कु *ku*, or का *kā*, prefixed to Sanskrit words denotes bad, vile, little, or contemptible; as, *ka-putr*, a bad son; *ku-path* (lit. a bad road), aberration, heresy; *kā-purush*, a vile man, a coward. *s.*

کا का *kā*, postpos. sign of the genitive case; of, belonging to; an adjective termination, as *kāṭh-kā ghorā*, a wooden horse, from *kāṭh*, wood. *h.*

کا का *kā* (*bhākhā*), whom, what, which? *h.*

کابر *kābir*, great, grand, illustrious. *a.*

کابر काबर *kābar*, a mixed soil of clay and sand, suitable to any crop except rice. *h.*

کابس काबिस *kābis*, } f. an earth with which
کابش काबिष *kābish*, } earthenware is varnished. *h.*

کابک *kābuk*, f. a pigeon-house. *p.*

کابل *kābul*, the capital of *Afghānistān*, formerly a province of the Mogul empire. *p.*

کابلی *kābulī*, f. a kind of pea (that came from Kābul). *kābulī miṭṭī*, f. Armenian bole. *p.*

کابوس *kābūs*, m. the nightmare; *modus cercus coeundi*. *a.*

کابوک *kābūk*, a pigeon-house. *p.*

کابیری काबेरी *kāberī*, name of a river, the Cavery. *s.*

کابین *kābīn*, a marriage portion, or settlement which a husband must pay his wife if he divorces her on insufficient grounds. *p.* [course. *s.*

کاپتھ कापथ *kā-path*, m. a wrong road, bad

کاپتھیہ कापथ्य *kā-paṭhya*, m. vice, fraud, dishonesty. *s.*

کاپرش कापुरुष *kā-purush*, m. a coward, a mean wretch, contemptible man. *s.*

کاپنا *kāpnā* (v. *kāmpnā*), to tremble, &c. *d.*

کاپور *kāpūr* (v. *kāfūr*), camphor. *d.*

کاپھل कापल *kāphal*, m. a bitter seed. *s.*

کات *kāt* (for *kāṭ*), the spur of a cock. *d.*

کاتب *kātib*, m. an amanuensis, a copier, a writer, a clerk. *a.*

کاتبی *kātibī*, f. a kind of short-sleeved garment; name of a Persian poet. *kātibī samūr* an honorary furred robe. *a.*

کاتر कातर *kātar*, timid, gentle, cowardly; irresolute, confused, distressed, perplexed; m. a large kind of fish (*Cyprinus catla*); timidity, agitation. *s.*

کاتک कातिक *kātik* (also *kārtik*), m. name of the seventh Hindū month (Oct.-Nov.), the full moon of which is near *krittikā*, or the Pleiades. *s.*

کاتنا कातना *kātnā*, a. to spin, to wrap round. *s.*

کاٹ काट *kāṭ*, f. a cut, incision, execution; spur of a cock; scum; virulence. *kāṭ-k.*, a. to wound, to cut. *kāṭ-kūṭ*, f. clippings, chips, scraps. *kāṭ-kūṭ-k.*, a. to clip, to cut out; to deduct. *kāṭ-khānā*, a. to bite. *s.*

کاٹک *kāṭak*, hard, severe, difficult. *d.*

کاٹ‌کوٹ काटकूट *kāṭ-kūṭ*, f. clippings, chips (v. *kāṭ*). *s.* [&c. *h.*

کاٹن काटन *kāṭan*, act of cutting or clipping,

کاٹنا काटना *kāṭnā*, a. to cut, to clip; to bite; to reap; to saw; to stop, to stay; to waste, to spend, to pass away (the time); to pass (a road); to interrupt, to intercept; to shame, to make ashamed. *kāṭ-ḍālnā*, to cut off, to amputate. *s.*

کاٹو काटू *kāṭū*, m. cutter; adj. corrosive. *s.*

کاٹھ काठ *kāṭh*, m. wood, timber, stock; a scabbard. *kāṭh-putlī*, f. a puppet, a toy. *kāṭh-chabānā*, a. (lit. to chew wood) to fare hardly. *kāṭh kā ullū*, m. a sad blockhead; adj. impenetrable, stupid. *kāṭh-kabār*, wooden articles. *kāṭh kī bhambo*, f. a sad blockhead (woman). *kāṭh-kīṛā*, a bug. *kāṭh men pāṅw denā*, to be imprisoned, to be in the stocks. *kāṭh-men-ḍak*, a toad. *kāṭh honā*, a. to pine away; to be petrified with astonishment. *s.*

کاٹھڑا काठड़ा *kaṭhṛā*, m. a wooden pot. *s.*

کاٹھنیہ काठिन्य *kāṭhinya*, m. difficulty, hardness, cruelty. *s.*

کاٹھی काठी *kāṭhī*, f. body; scabbard; shape; wood, timber; appearance, person; a saddle. *s.*

کاٹیری *kāṭerī*, name of Satan's wife. *d.*

کاج काज *kāj*, } m. business, occupation, a
کاجا काजा *kājā*, } work, an action, affair. *s.*

کاجل काजल *kājal*, m. lamp-black (with which the eyelids are painted). *kājal kī koṭhrī*, a place from going into which, or an affair the being engaged in which, brings disgrace or suspicion on one's character. *s.*

کاجن *kājan*, m. (v. *kāran*) account, cause. *s.*

کاجو *kājū*, m. the cashew nut. *d.*

کاجی काजी *kājī*, busy, employed. *kāje*, by reason of, for the sake of. *h.*

کاچ काच *kāch*, m. glass, alkaline ashes, any salt of potash or soda in a glassy or crystalline state; crystal, ornaments of crystal, quartz; a disease of the eyes. *kāch-lavan*, m. black salt, a medicinal salt, prepared by calcining fossil salt and the fruit of the emblic myrobalan together, and used as a tonic aperient. *kāch-mal*, m. black salt or soda. *kāch-mani*, m. crystal, quartz. *s.*

کاچا काचा *kāchā*, unripe, raw; simple, unknowing, uninstructed. *h.*

کاچھ काछ *kāchh*, m. a cloth worn round the hips, passing between the legs and tucked in behind; the upper part of the thigh. *s.*

کاچھا *kāchhā* (the same as *kāchh*, q. v.). *d.*

کاچھن काछन *kāchhan*, f. a female gardener. *s.*

کاچھنا काछना *kāchhnā*, to bind or tie up the *kāchh*, to cover the nakedness. *s.*

کاچھنا काछना *kāchhnā*, a. to skim, to gather. *h.*

کاچھنی काछनी *kāchhnī*, f. (v. *kāchh*) a cloth, &c. *s.* [cultivates and sells potherbs. *s.*

کاچھی काछी *kāchhī*, m. a gardener. who

کاچي *kāchī*, f. milk pottage. *p.*

کاخ *kā<u>kh</u>*, m. an upper story, a gallery, balcony, tower, battlements, a palace, a villa. *p.*

کادا कादा *kādā*, m. slime, mud, mire, alluvial deposit. *s.*

کادر कादर *kādar*, timid, timorous, agitated, distressed, irresolute. *s.*

کادراءي कादराई *kādarā,ī*, } f. timidity, timorousness. *s.*
کادري कादरी *kādarī*,

کادو कादौ *kādau*, m. slime, mud, mire. *s.*

کاذب *kāẕib*, false; (sub.) a liar. *a.*

کار *kār*, m. business, an action, affair, work, profession, labour, &c. *kār-āzmūda*, experienced in affairs, practised. *kār-āmad*, *kār-āmada* or *kār-āmadanī*, useful, profitable, what may be turned to account. *kār-bār*, m. business, avocation. *kār-bārī*, a trader; a transactor of business, a manager or officer. *kār-bardārī*, undertaking a business. *kār-pardāz*, a manager, one who carries on the business. *kār-pardāzī*, f. completing a business. *kār-chob*, m. embroidery; an embroiderer. *kār-chobī*, embroidered. *kār-<u>kh</u>āna*, m. a workshop, manufactory; an arsenal, dockyard, or any place where public works are carried on; (met.) a great work; *vulva*. *kār-<u>kh</u>āna-dār*, a steward, butler. *kār-dār*, an agent, especially of government. *kār-dān*, versed, skilled, expert. *kār-dānī*, experience, skill. *kār-dīda*, one who has seen service, expert. *kār-rawā*, useful, fit for use. *kār-rawā,ī*, f. usefulness; carrying on of a business, occupation, management, conduct. *kār-zār*, f. battle, war, conflict. *kār-sāz*, m. the Deity. *kār-farmā*, an emperor, minister, commander, superintendant. *kār-kun*, a director, manager, an officer whose business it is to keep records. *kār-gāh* or *-gah*, a workshop, manufactory. *kār-nāma*, a record of affairs, history. *kār-gar*, effectual, active (as a medicine). *p.*

کارو कारु *kāru*, m. an artisan, a mechanic. *s.*

کارا *kārā*, name of a tree (*Webera Tetrandra*). *d.*

کارا कारा *kārā*, m. a black snake; adj. black. *kārī-nūn*, black salt; muriate of soda. *s.*

کاراگار कारागार *kārāgār*, m. a gaol, a prison. *s.*

کارت‌بيريه कार्तवीर्य *kārta-bīrya*, m. a king, also called Arjun, a celebrated hero distinct from the Pandu prince; one of the *Jain Chakravartis*, or rulers of the world. *s.*

کارپاس कार्पास *kārpās*, f. the cotton plant (*Gossypeum*); cotton cloth, &c. *kārpāsī*, made of cotton. *s.*

کارپنيه कार्पण्य *kārpanya*, m. poverty, indigence. *s.*

کارتك कार्तिक *kārtik* (v. *kātik*), a Hindū month, corresponding to our October or November. *s.*

کارتکوتسو कार्तिकोत्सव *kārtikotsav*, m. the day of full moon in the month Kārtik, a festival. *s.*

کارتوس *kārtūs*, m. (corrup. of cartouch) a cartridge. *e.*

کارج कार्य or कारज *kārj* or *kāraj*, m. an action, an affair, work, business, profession, cause, origin, motive, object. *kārj-chintā*, f. caution, prudence, consideration. *kārj-siddhi*, f. accomplishment, success, attainment of an object. *s.*

کارخانجات *kār-<u>kh</u>ānajāt*, pl. workshops, &c. *p.*

کارد *kārd*, f. a knife. *kārd dar ustu<u>kh</u>wān rasīd*, the knife has reached the bone, *i.e.* he is reduced to the last extremity. *p.*

کارستان *kāristān*, the seat of action. *p.*

کارستاني *kāristānī*, f. workmanship. *p. d.*

کارشاپن कार्षापण *kārshāpan*, m. a weight of silver equal to sixteen pans of *kauṛīs*; a weight of copper equal to eighty rattis; a weight of shells equal to eighty *kauṛīs*; a husbandman. *s.*

کارشك कार्षक *kārshak*, m. a husbandman. *kārshik*, m. a husbandman; a weight. *s.*

کارك कारक *kārak*, an agent; acting, doing; m. action (especially in grammar); case (in gram.). *s.*

کارکر कारुकर *kārukar*, m. an artist, an artificer; an agent. *s.*

کارمك कार्मिक *kārmik*, worked, embroidered. *kārmuk*, m. a bow. *s.*

کارن कारण *kāran*, m. cause, motive, principle, account, reason, occasion, action, agency, means. *s.*

کارنجا *kāranjā*, m. the cock or spout of a cistern, barrel, &c.; mouth of a water channel. *d.*

کارنده *kāranda* or *kārinda*, adj. laborious; working; m. a manager, an agent or officer. *p.*

کارنك कारुणिक *kārunik*, compassionate, tender, kind. *s.*

کاروان *kārwān*, m. a caravan, a large body of travellers, merchants, or pilgrims, united for mutual protection on the journey. *kārwān-sarā* or *-sarā,e*, a caravanserai, a public building for the reception of caravans. *p.*

کاروان‌باشي *kārawān-bāshī*, m. the chief of a caravan. *p. t.*

کاروانك *kārawānak*, a crane, a heron. *p.*

کارواني *kārawānī*, of or belonging to a caravan; one of those forming a caravan. *p.*

کاروبار *kār o bār*, } business, occupation, profession. *p.*
کاروکرد *kār o kard*,

کاره *kārih*, hating, detesting, loathing. *a.*

کاري *kārī*, effectual. *kārī zak<u>h</u>m* or *za<u>kh</u>mi kārī*, a deep wound, a mortal wound. *p.*

کاري कारी *kārī*, as a termination, denotes agency, as *adhi-kārī*, a ruler. *s.*

کاري कारी *kārī*, f. the dish called curry. (This word is perhaps borrowed from the English name of the dish, as that name is said to be a corruption of *ḳaliya*, a kind of stew, in some respects different from a curry.—B.). *h.*

کاريز *kārez*, a canal, an aqueduct. *p.*

کاريزي *kārezī*, of or belonging to a canal; (land) irrigated from a canal. *p.*

کاريگر *kārī-gar*, m. a workman; a good workman. *p.*

کاريگري *kārī-garī*, f. masterly work, workmanship. *p.*

کاريه कार्य *kārya*, m. cause, business (v. *kārj*). *s.*

کاڑا काड़ा *kāṛā*, m. a young buffalo; (in Dakh.) a decoction, a sick man's beverage. *h.*

کاڑنا *kāṛnā*, a. to extract, to bring out (v. *kāṛhnā*). *d.*

کاڑھ काढ़ *kāṛh*, m. *membrum virile*. *h.*

کاڑھا काढ़ा *kāṛhā*, m. a decoction (v. *kāṛā*). *h.*

کاڑھنا काढ़ना *kāṛhnā*, n. to draw forth (as a sword), to draw, to draw off, to skin, to take out, to extricate; to draw lines or figures, to delineate, to work flowers on cloth. *h.*

کاڑي *kāṛī*, f. a single straw, a blade of grass. *d.*

کاڑي‌کسپٹ *kāṛī-kaspaṭ*, clay (v. *kachrā*). *d.*

کاس कास *kās*, f. a kind of grass of which rope is made (*Saccharum spontaneum*); m. a cough. *kās-swās*, m. asthma. *s.*

کاس *kās*, m. a cup, a goblet, a bowl. *a.*

کاس *kās*, m. a very small copper coin (called by Europeans "cash"), current, until within late years, in Southern India. Eighty kās (or "cash") made one fanam, and twelve fanams a rupee. *d.*

کاسال कासालु *kāsālu*, m. an esculent root, a sort of yam. *s.*

کاسب *kāsib*, m. an artist, a tradesman. *a.*

کاسبي कासबी *kāsbī* or *kāsibī*, m. a weaver. *a. h.*

کاست *kāst*, f. diminution, loss, damage. *be kam o kāst*, without loss or damage. *p.*

کاست कास्त *kāst*, m. name of a plant, *Chara* (Bruce, M.S.). *h.*

کاستن *kastan* (r. *kāh.*), to lessen, diminish. *p.*

کاستني *kāstanī*, f. diminution, loss, damage; a plant. *p.*

کاستیا कास्त्या *kāstyā*, a sickle. *h.*

کاسد *kāsid*, worthless, deficient in quantity or quality, not selling or passing current. *a.*

کاسرالحجر *kāsiru-l-ḥajar*, m. (lit.) the stone-breaker, the plant saxifrage. *a.*

کاسگهن कासघ्न *kāsa-ghna*, removing cough, pectoral. *kāsa-ghnī*, f. a sort of prickly nightshade (*Solanum jacquini*). *s.*

کاسمرد कासमर्द *kās-mard*, m. a plant (*Cassia* or *Senna esculenta*). *s.*

کاسناشني कासनाशिनी *kās-nāshinī*, f. a thorny plant used as a remedy for the cough. *s.*

کاسني *kāsnī*, f. endive (*Cichorium endivia*). *p.*

کاسه *kāsa*, m. a cup, a goblet, a plate, bowl. *kāsa,e chīnī*, porcelain, chinaware. *kāsa rabāb kā*, the chest or body of a fiddle, &c. *kāsa,e sar*, the skull. *kāsa-les*, m. a sycophant, a lickspittle. *kāsa-lesī*, sycophancy. *a.*

کاسي *kāsī* (for *kāshī*), the city of Benares. *s.*

کاسیس कासीस *kāsīs*, m. green vitriol, green sulphate of iron. *s.*

کاش *kāsh* or *kāsh-ki*, int. would to God [that! *p.*

کاش काश *kāsh*, f. cough; m. a kind of grass (v. *kās*). *s.*

کاشانه *kāshāna*, m. a house, dwelling. *p.*

کاشاني *kāshānī*, of or relating to the city of *Kāshān*; a fine kind of velvet. *p.*

کاشتن *kāshtan* (r. *kār*), to sow, to cultivate. *p.*

کاشٹھ काष्ठ *kāshṭha*, m. wood, timber. *kāshṭha-kuṭṭ*, m. the woodpecker. *kāshṭha-kīṭ*, m. an insect or worm found in decayed wood. *s.*

کاشٹھک काष्ठक *kāshṭhak*, m. aloe wood or agallochum. *s.*

کاشٹھي काष्ठी *kāshṭhī*, of wood, wooden. *s.*

کاشغر *kāshghar*, a city of Chinese Tartary. *p.*

کاشف *kāshif*, m. a detector, a discoverer. *a.*

کاشکي *kāshke* or *kāshkī*, may it happen! God send! would that! *p.*

کاشي काशी *kāshī*, f. Benares, the sacred city of the Hindūs. *s.*

کاظم *kāẓim*, m. one who restrains. *kāẓimu-l-ghaiẓ*, one who restrains his anger. *a.*

کاغذ *kāghaz*, m. paper; letter; charter. *kāghaz-bahā*, office allowance for stationery. *p.*

کاغذي *kāghazī*, f. a kind of lime; a paper case; m. a stationer or vender of paper; a paper manufacturer; a writer; adj. delicate, soft, thin. *p.*

کاغذین *kāghazīn*, made of paper. *p.*

کافر *kāfir*, m. an infidel, one who denies the existence of a God; (met.) a mistress, sweetheart. *a.*

کافرانه *kāfirāna*, like an infidel. *a.*

کافري *kāfirī*, of or relating to an infidel; a negro; an African Caffre or Coffery; f. infidelity; unbelief. *kāfirī mirch*, a kind of pepper. *kāfirī wālā*, a term applied to negroes in general. *a.*

کافل *kāfil*, a sponsor, a surety or bail. *a.*

کافور *kāfūr*, m. camphor. *kāfūr honā*, to run away, to disappear, to scamper off, to vanish. *a.*

کافوري *kāfūrī*, camphorated, pure, white. *sham'i kāfūrī*, a candle made of camphorated wax. *a.*

کافه *kāffa* or *kāfa*, m. the whole; a tribe, a multitude. *kāfa,e anām*, all mankind. *a.*

کافي *kāfī*, sufficient, sufficing, enough. *a.*

کاك *kāk*, m. biscuit; bran; the pupil of the eye; adj. small, minute. *p.*

کاك काक *kāk*, m. a crow. *kāk-pachh* or *kāk-paksh*, m. feather of a crow; tresses. *s.*

کاکا काका *kākā*, m. (in Pers.) elder brother; a slave (belonging to one's father); (in Hind.) a paternal uncle. *p. h.*

کاکبندهیا काकवन्ध्या *kāk-bandhyā*, f. a woman that bears only one child. *s.*

کاکپیل काकपीलु *kāk-pīlu*, m. a kind of ebony. *s.*

كاكاتوا *hākātū,ā,* } the cockatoo, a species of
كاكاطوا *hākāṭū,ā,* } large parrot well known in India. *h.*

كاكڈسنگي *hākadsingī,* flowers of the ink nut. *d.*

كاكريز *kāhrez,* m. the name of a colour, approaching to purple. *p.*

كاكريزي *kāhrezī,* purple-coloured. *p.*

كاكڑا काकड़ा *kāhṛa,* m. a kind of leather. *h.*

كاكڑاسنگي काकड़ासिंगी *kākṛā-singī,* f. name of a medicine. *s.*

كاكل *kākul,* f. a curl, lock, ringlet; a tuft of hair left on the top of the head. *p.*

كاكلوت *kāklūt,* desire, avarice, avidity. *d.*

كاكلوتي *kāklūtī,* avaricious, greedy. *d.*

كاكمدگ काकमद्गु *kāk-madgu,* m. a water-hen, a gallinule. *s.*

كاكمرد काकमर्द *kāk-mard,* m. the colocynth or bitter apple. *s.* [plant. *d.*

كاكمري *kāk-marī,* the cocculus indicus or its

كاكن काकरा *kākan,* m. a leprosy with black and red spots, considered incurable. *s.*

كاكني काकिणी *kākinī,* five gandas, or twenty cowries. *h.*

كاكول काकोल *kākol,* m. a poisonous substance of a black colour, possibly the berry of the cocculus indicus; a division of hell. *s.*

كاكولي काकोली *kākolī,* f. a sweet and cooling drug used for allaying fever, removing phlegm, &c.: it is said to be a root brought from Nepal or Morang. *s.*

كاكونجكي काकूंजकी *kākūnjkī,* f. a ranunculus. *h.*

كاكھ काख *kākh,* f. the armpit. *kākh-alā,ī,* f. a painful suppurating tumour in the armpit (v. *kānkh*). *s.*

كاكي काकी *kākī,* f. a maternal aunt. *p. h.*

كاگ काग *kāg* or كاگا कागा *kāgā,* m. a crow. *s.*

كاگد *kāgad,* m. (corrup. for *kāghaẕ*) paper. *p.*

كال काल *kāl,* m. time; a name of *Yama* or *Jam,* the regent of the dead; death, angel of death; season, age; dearth, famine, calamity; (met.) a snake. *kāl-bitānā, -kāṭnā,* or *-gaṁwānā,* a. to waste one's time, to spend time. *kāl bas hona,* to be in the hands of death; to be seized by fate. *kāl-paṛnā,* the coming on of a famine. *kāl-dharm,* m. death, dying. *kāl-prabhāt,* m. the sultry season, autumn. *kāl-kshep,* m. the spending, of time, the enduring of suffering. *s.*

كال काल *kāl* (for *kal*), to-morrow (*bhāshā*). *s.*

كالا काला *kālā,* black, dark; name of a snake; m. time; name of *Krishṇa.* *kālā bāl,* m. the lower part of the belly, the pubes. *kālā bāl apnā samajhnā,* to despise one exceedingly. *kālā chor,* an unknown person. *kālā dāna,* name of a purgative seed (*Convolvulus nil?*). *kālā zīra* or *kālā-jīrā,* m. seeds of the *Nigella Indica, Roxb.* *kālā muṉh karnā,* to break off all connection with another; to disgrace; to copulate; to expel. *kālā namak,* m. a kind of rock-salt impregnated with sulphur and bitumen, which leaves an hepatic flavour in the mouth: it is much used medicinally. *kāle-baran,* of the colour of a snake. *kāle-bāl,* m. the pubes. *kāle-kos,* a great distance. *s.*

كالا *kālā,* m. silk cloths, and, in general, any kind of household furniture. *kālā,e bad ba-rīshi khāwind,* let bad things be returned to their proprietor. *p.*

كالاپتي कालापत्ती *kālāpattī,* f. the act of calking a ship or boat. *h.*

كالاپن कालापन *kālāpan,* m. blackness. *s.*

كالاگر कालागुरु *kālā-guru,* m. a black kind of aloe wood or agallochum. *s.*

كالانتر कालान्तर *kālāntar,* m. interval, process of time. *s.* [used as a purgative. *s.*

كالانجني कालाञ्जनी *kālānjanī,* f. a small shrub

كالبد *kālbud,* m. the human body; the heart, a model, figure, form. *p.*

كالپنك काल्पनिक *kālpnik,* feigned, forged, factitious; m. a hypocrite. *kālpniktā,* f. hypocrisy. *s.*

كالچكر कालचक्र *kāl-chakra,* m. a cycle, a period. *s.*

كالداس कालिदास *kālidās,* one of the nine poets or gems of Vikramāditya's court, and author of Sacuntalā, Raghuvansa, Nalodaya, &c. *s.*

كال راتر कालरात्रि *kāl-rātri,* m. a particular night, the 7th of the 7th month of the 77th year, after which a man is considered exempt from attention to the usual ordinances. *s.*

كالسار कालसार *kāl-sār,* m. the black antelope. *s.*

كالسرپ कालसर्प *kāl-sarp,* m. the black and most deadly variety of the cobra (*Coluber naga*). *s.*

كالسوتر कालसूत्र *kāl-sūtr,* m. one of the twenty-one hells. *s.*

كالك कालक *kālak,* f. blackness; one of the expressions of quantity (corresponding to our *a, b, x, y,* &c) in Bija Ganita or algebra; freckle, mark, spot. *s.*

كالك कालिक *kālik,* m. blackness, lampblack, the soot which collects under pots, &c., a fault or flaw in gold; ink, blacking; a line of hair extending to the navel; a small bird commonly called *Syām,* the curlew. *kāluk,* dark. *s. d.*

كالكا कालिका *kālikā,* f. the goddess *Kālī,* q. v. adj. periodical. *kālikā vriddhi,* periodical interest. *s.*

كالكشيپ कालक्षेप *kāla-kshep,* m. misspending of time; passing one's days in sorrow. *s.*

كالكوت कालकूट *kālkūṭ,* m. the poison of a snake. *s.*

كالكھ कालख *kālakh,* m. freckle, mark, spot. *s.*

كالكيل कालकील *kālkīl,* a confused sound, a tumult (v. *kālkil*). *h.*

كالگندھ कालगन्ध *kāl-gandh,* m. a kind of cobra di capello. *s.* [and purgative salt. *s.*

كال لون काललवण *kāl-lavan,* m. a factitious

كال نرياس कालनिर्यास *kāl-niryās,* m. a fragrant and resinous substance. *s.*

كالما कालमा *kālmā,* m. suspicion, calumny. *h.*

کالمیشکا कालमेषिका *kāl-meshikā* f. Bengal madder; black *Teorī*. *s.*

کالمیشي कालमेषी *kāl-meshī*, f. a plant (*Serratula* or *Conyza anthelmintica*); Bengal madder (*Rubia manjeth*). *s.*

کالنجر कालञ्जर *kālanjar*, m. a name of *Shiva*; a rock in Bandelkhand, the modern Callinger, or the adjacent country; an assembly of religious mendicants, Callinger being one of their meeting places. *s.*

کالندي कालिन्दी *kālindī*, f. a name of the river Jamunā (properly, *kālī-nadī*). *s.*

کالوا *kālwā*, a river, watercourse, channel or canal. *d.*

کالي काली *kālī*, f. black; the Hecate of the Hindūs, and wife of Shiva, to whom human sacrifices are offered; the Nile; ink. *kālī būṇ*, m. the name of a plant. *kālī tulsī*, f. basil (*Ocymum sanctum* or *basilicum*). *kālī zīrī* or *kālī miṭṭī*, f. black lead. *kalī mirich*, f. black pepper. *s.*

کالي काली *kāli*, } m. the name of a serpent
کالیا कालिया *kāliyā*, } with a hundred and ten hoods, which was vanquished and killed by *Krishṇa*; adj. black (complexion). *s.*

کالیبهومي कालीभूमी *kālī-bhūmī*, f. a rich black soil, vegetable mould. *s.*

کالي‌ده कालीदह *kālī-dah*, m. the name of a whirlpool in the river Jamunā in which the serpent *Kālī* lived. *s.*

کالیسر कालेसर *kālesar*, } m. name of a
کالیشور कालेश्वर *kāleshwar*, } drug. *s.*

کالین कालीन *kālīn*, timely, seasonable. *s.*

کالیهر कालीहर *kālīhar*, f. a buck, a stag. *h.*

کام काम *kām*, m. desire, wish, intention; the god of love, Cupid; (for *karm*) business, action, deed, work, employment; packet, mail, post-bag. *kām ānā*, n. to come into use, to be wanted, to be of service; to be smitten, to be slain in the field. *kām tamām-k.*, a. to accomplish, to finish; to kill, to make away with. *kām tamām h.*, to be finished, killed, made away with. *kām chalānā*, a. to carry on business. *kām rakhnā*, to make use of. *kām-kāj*, business, occupation. *kām-kājī*, laborious, active, alert; a manager or superintendant. *kām-kel*, f. amorous dalliance, coition. *kām meṇ lānā*, to employ, to use. *kām nikālnā*, a. to carry into effect, to accomplish one's desire. *s.*

کام *kām*, m. the palate; desire. *p.*

کاماتر कामातुर *kāmātur*, libidinous, lustful, distracted with lust. *s.*

کاماٹي *kāmāṭī*, a mason, a builder. *d.*

کامار कामारि *kāmāri*, m. a mineral substance used in medicine, a kind of pyrites. *s.*

کامارت कामार्त *kāmārt*, lustful, lovesick, lascivious. *s.*

کامارتهي कामार्थी *kāmārthī*, a person who carries baskets filled with Ganges water to distant places. *s.*

کماندھ कामान्ध *kāmāndh*, blind by lust, lustful. *s.*

کامبوج काम्बोज *kāmboj*, m. a country in the north of India, Camboge, Cambay, or Kambāch; a horse of the Camboge breed. *s.*

کامپنا काम्पना *kāmpnā*, to tremble (v. کانپنا). *s.*

کامدار *kām-dār*, a man of business, an agent, a steward, manager. *h p.*

کامداري *kām-dārī*, f. stewardship, agency. *h.p.*

کام‌دهین कामधेनु *kām-dhenu*, name of a cow, belonging to Indra, that grants every thing requested of her; a cow that gives much milk. *s.*

کامدیو कामदेव *kāmdew* (for *kāma-deva*), the Hindū Cupid. He was son of *Vishṇu* and *Rukmiṇī*, and husband of *Rati* (or Venus). Having offended *Mahādeva*, he was destroyed by the flame from the eyes of the angry deity. He was, however, born again as *Pradyumna*, son of *Krishṇa*, but was immediately seized by *Sambara* (whom it had been foretold he would destroy), and thrown into the ocean, where he was swallowed by a fish, which, being caught, was presented to *Sambara*, and happened to be given to *Rati* to clean. *Rati* took out the infant and reared him till he was able to destroy *Sambara* (v. under *rati*). *s.*

کامراج कामराज *kāmrāj*, m. *sonchus*. *h.*

کامران *kām-rān*, fortunate, successful. *p.*

کامراني *kām-rānī*, f. fortune, prosperity, felicity, success. *p.*

کامروپ कामरूप *kāmrūp*, m. a district lying east of Bengal, now part of Assam; adj. pleasing, beautiful; assuming every shape at will. *kāmrūpī* or *kāmrūpin*, pleasing, beautiful; a native of Kāmrūp. *s.*

کامري कामरी *kāmarī* or *kāmrī*, f. a blanket. *s.*

کامك कामुक *kāmuk*, cupidinous, desirous, lustful. *s.*

کامکاج कामकाज *kām-kāj*, work, business in general. *s.*

کامکار *kām-kār*, } one who accomplishes what-
کامگار *kām-gār*, } ever he wishes; powerful, an absolute monarch; a hunting-bird which infallibly secures its prey. *p.*

کامکي कामुकी *kāmukī*, a libidinous woman. *s.*

کامکیل कामकेलि *kām-keli*, f. amorous dalliance, coition. *s.*

کامل *kāmil*, perfect, complete; learned, accomplished, entire. *kāmil-'aiyār*, of perfect standard or assay (a coin). *a.*

کاملا कामला *kāmalā*, f. jaundice, excess or obstruction of bile. *s.*

کاملة *kāmila* (fem. of *kāmil*), perfect, &c. *a.*

کاملي *kāmilī*, } f. perfection, complete-
کاملیت *kāmilīyat*, } ness. *a.*

کامن कामिन *kāmin*, an amorous man, an uxorious husband; a woman, a beautiful woman; the ruddy goose; a pigeon, a sparrow; a boy dressed in female attire, who dances in the season of the *holī*. *s.*

کامنا कामना *kāmnā*, f. desire, wish, inclination. *s.*

کامني कामिनी *kāminī*, a lovely and beautiful woman; libidinous, lustful. *s.*

کامود कामोद *kāmod*, m. } name of a musical
کامودا कामोदा *kāmodā*, f. } mode or *rāginī*, sung in the night. *s.*

كامودك कामोदक *kāmodak*, m. oblation of water to deceased friends, &c., exclusive of those for whom it is directed by law. *s.*

كامون *kāmūn* (v. *kammūn*), cumin seed. *d.*

كامي कामी *kāmī*, libidinous, lustful, impassioned, fond; busy. *s.*

كامي कामी *kāmī*, f. a lump of gold, a nugget. *h.*

كامياب *kām-yāb*, prosperous, happy, successful, one who attains what he wishes. *p.*

كاميابي *kām-yābī*, f. prosperity, happiness. *p.*

كاميتر कामयितृ *kāmayitṛi*, libidinous, lustful, desirous. *s.*

كاميه काम्य *kāmya*, agreeable, desirable, amiable. *kāmya-dān*, an acceptable or desirable gift. *kāmya-karm*, m. a supererogatory work. *s.*

كان कान *kān*, m. the ear; one blind of an eye. *kān ameṭnā*, to pull the ears, to chastise. *kān bharnā* or *kān bhar-denā*, to excite dissension by tale-bearing. *kān bhar ke sunnā* (Dakh.), to hear attentively. *kān par jūṇ na chalnā*, to be very negligent. *kān par rakhnā*, a. to remember; n. to abstain. *kān par hāth dharnā*, to refuse, to deny. *kān pakaṛnā*, to confess inferiority. *kān phūṭnā*, n. to be deaf. *kān phoṛnā*, to make a noise. *kān phūnknā*, a. to tell tales, to excite quarrels; to tutor. *kān-jhukānā*, a. to desire to hear. *kān dharnā*, a. to hear, to attend; n. to be attentive. *kān dabākar chale jānā*, to run away. *kān dabānā* or *buchiyānā*, to turn back the ears, as a horse does when preparing to bite. *kān de sunnā*, a. to hear attentively. *kān denā*, give ear, to hear, to be attentive. *kān-salā,ī*, f. name of an insect. *kān kā parda*, the tympanum. *kān kāṭnā*, to get the better of, to surpass, to overcome, to outwit. *kān khirolnī* (Dakh.), to scratch the ear. *kān khaṛe honā*, to be alarmed. *kān kholnā* or *kān khol denā*, (lit. to open one's ears) to inform; to make acquainted with, to warn, to caution. *kān-lagnā*, to get into one's confidence. *kān malnā*, to admonish, to punish, to chastise. *kān meṭnā* (for *kān ameṭnā*), to pull the ears, &c. *kān-mail*, m. ear-wax. *kān-mail-wālā*, a person whose employment is to pick or clean the ears. *kān meṅ unglī de-rahnā*, to stop one's ears, to turn a deaf ear to what is said. *kān meṅ bāt mārnā*, to pretend not to hear. *kān meṅ paṛnā*, n. to be heard (a speech). *kān meṅ tel ḍālnā*, to pretend not to hear. *kān meṅ tel ḍālke so rahnā*, to be inattentive or negligent. *kān meṅ ḍālnā* or *kahnā*, to whisper, to tell. *kān na hilānā*, to be silent. *kānoṅ-kān kahnā*, a. to whisper. *kān hilānā*, n. to acquiesce in. *kān hone*, to understand, comprehend, to be warned, or take example. *s.*

كان *kān*, f. a mine or quarry; (for *hi-ān*) since that, for that. *kān-kan*, a mine-digger. *p.*

كان कान *kān*, f. modesty, shame, respect. *kān-k.*, a. to shame; to be ashamed. *kān chhoṛnā*, a. to act impudently. *kān na mānnā* or *na-k.*, to treat with disrespect; m. a husband. *h.*

كان *kāṅ* (for *kahāṅ*), where? whither? *d.*

كان कां *kāṅ*, the sound or cry made by a crow. *kāṅ-kāṅ-k.*, to make a noise like the crows. *h.*

كانا काणा *kānā*, blind of one eye, one-eyed; (fruit, nuts, &c.) whose kernel is rotten, or which has no kernel; foolish, stupid. *kānā-bātī-k.*, to consult, to advise, to whisper. *kānā phūsī*, f. whispering. *kānā ṭirī*, f. the name of a grass. *kānā-kānī-k.*, to whisper. *kānī kauṛī*, a cowry with a hole in it. *s.*

كانپ *kāmp*, misfortune or evil luck. *kāmp-mārnā*, evil luck to befall or happen. *d.*

كانپ कांप *kāmp*, mud thrown up and deposited by watercourses or rivers. *h.*

كانپنا कांपना *kāmpnā*, n. to shiver, to tremble, to quake, to shake. *s.* [(v. *kā,e-phal*). *s.*

كانپهل कानफल *kān-phal*, m. name of a fruit

كانت कान्त *kānt*, pleasing, agreeable, beautiful; m. a husband. *kānti*, f. splendour, decoration. *s.*

كانتا कान्ता *kāntā*, f. wife, beloved, a lovely woman; beauty, splendour, light. *s.*

كانٹا कांटा *kāṅṭā*, m. a thorn, spine; a fork; the pricker of a musket; small (goldsmiths') scales; a spur; a type; a fishing-hook; a fish-bone; the tongue of a balance; a kind of firework (v. *hāthī kāṅṭā*). *kāṅṭā sā nikal jānā*, to be freed from distress or injury. *kāṅṭon par ghasiṭnā* (lit. to drag upon thorns), to extol or exalt one above his merits (used by a person who from humility disclaims the praises bestowed on him). *kāṅṭe bone*, to prepare distress or misfortune for one's self. *kāṅṭā-muḥarrir*, a clerk employed to note and register weighments. *s.*

كانٹها कांठा *kāṅṭhā*, near, proximate. *s.*

كانجي कांजी *kāṅjī*, f. a kind of pickle (or vinegar) made by steeping rice in water and letting the liquor ferment, which is kept for use sometimes twenty years. *s.*

كانچ कांच *kāṅch*, raw; m. a disorder in which the intestinum rectum is prolapsed; a prolapsus ani. *kāṅch nikālnā*, *ani procidentia*. *h.*

كانچ कांच *kāṅch*, m. glass (v. *kāch*). *s.*

كانچا कांचा *kāṅchā*, raw (v. *kāchā*). *h.*

كانچكوري *kāṅch-kūrī*, f. cowage (*Dolichos pruriens*). *d.*

كانچن काञ्चन *kāñchan*, m. gold; adj. (also *kāñchan-may*) golden, made of gold. *s.*

كانچها *kāṅchhā*, f. desire, wish, inclination. *s.*

كانچي *kāṅchī*, a kind of marriage ceremony. *d.*

كاند *kāṅd*, a wall, an embankment. *d.*

كاندا कांदा *kāṅdā*, m. an onion. *s.*

كاندو कांदो *kāṅdo*, m. mud, slime. *s.*

كاندو कांदू *kāṅdū*, m. a sugar-boiler; a tribe whose business it is to fry corn, prepare sweetmeats, &c. *s.*

كاندها कांधा *kāṅdhā*, m. the shoulder. *kāṅdhā hilānā*, to shrug up the shoulders. *kāṅdhā denā*, a. to assist; to carry away the dead. *s.* [tect. *s.*

كاندهنا कांधना *kāṅdhnā*, a. to assist, to pro-

كانڈ कांड *kāṅḍ*, m. a section, part, division; sport, exhibition. *s.*

كانڈلي कांडली *kāṅḍlī*, f. purslain (*Portulaca*). *h.*

كانڈور *kāṅḍūr*, a coward; pusillanimous. *d.*

كانڈي कांडी *kāṅḍī*, f. a rafter; a sentence of the Vedas; yoke of a plough or vehicle. *s.*

كانڑنا कांड़ना *kāṅṛnā*, a. to tread, to trample. *h.*

كانس कांस *kāṅs*, m. f. a species of grass (*Saccharum spontaneum*); also bell-metal, &c. (v. *kāṅsā*). *s.*

کانسا कांसा *kānsā*, m. bell-metal, white copper or brass, queen's metal, any amalgum of zinc and copper. *s.*

کانسه कांसः *kānsa*, m. a cup, bowl, glass, goblet; bell-metal. *kānsa-gar*, one who makes cups, bowls, &c. *kānsa-garī*, f. the business of cup-making. *s.*

کانسیه कांस्य *kānsya*, m. bell-metal (v. *kānsā*). *kānsya-kār*, m. a brazier, a pewterer, a worker in white or bell-metal. *kānsya-nīl*, m. blue vitriol, considered as collyrium. *s.*

کانکر कांकर *kānkar*, m. a nodule of limestone. *s.*

کانکشا कांक्षा *kānkshā*, f. desire, wish, inclination. *s.*

کانکه *kān-ki* (for *ki-ān-ki*), for he who. *p.*

کانکه कांख *kānkh*, f. the armpit. *s.*

کانکها कांखा *kānkhā*, m. straining (when at stool, &c.). *h.*

کانکهنا कांखना *kānkhnā*, a. to grunt. *h.*

کانگري कांगरी *kāngrī*, f. a chafing-dish. *h.*

کانگن कांगन *kāngan*, m. } name of a plant or
کانگني कांगनी *kāngnī*, f. } its seed (*Panicum Italicum*). *s.*

کانن कानन *kānan*, m. a forest, desert, wood. *s.*

کانه कान्ह *kānh*, m. one of the names of *Krishna*; a husband. *h.*

کانه *ka-anna-hu*, as if he (or it) was, as it were. *a.*

کانهر कान्हर *kānhar*, one of the names of [*Krishna*. *h.*

کانهڑا कान्हड़ा *kānhṛā*, m. name of a musical mode or *rāginī*; a kind of nightingale. *h.*

کاني *kānī*, mineral, relating to mines. *p.*

کاني काणी *kānī*, f. a woman blind of one eye. *s.*

کاني *kānī* (for *kahānī*), a story, a tale. *d.*

کاني कानी *kānī*, f. resentment, spite. *h.*

کانیکبج कान्यकुब्ज *kānyakubj*, m. the ancient name of *Kanauj*. *s.*

کاو *kāw*, digging, excavating, investigating. *p.*

کاوادینا कावादेना *kāwā-denā*, a. to ring or lounge (a horse); to trick, to sham. *h.*

کاواك *kāwāk*, long, awkward; hollow, empty; cracked, useless. *p.*

کاواکي *kāwākī*, f. length; hollowness. *p.*

کاور कावर *kāwar* f. the baskets in which the Hindūs carry about the Ganges water. *h.*

کاوڑ *kāwaṛ*, a stick or bamboo carried on the shoulder, to the ends of which are suspended boxes, baskets, &c., called in Urdū *bahangī*, q. v. *kāwaṛ wālā*, the person who carries baggage, &c., in this manner, commonly called by Europeans in the Carnatic "a cowry-cooley," in Urdū *bahangī-wālā* or *bahangī-bardār*.—Binning. *d.*

کاوش *kāwish*, f. digging, research; meditating, reflecting, menacing. *p.*

کاوکاو *kāw-kāw*, diligent investigation, strict research, scrutiny, pains, toil. *p.*

کاول *kāwal*, } (v. *gasht*) surrounding, per-
کاولي *kāwalī*, } ambulating, patrolling; fees paid for protection of property; black mail. *d.*

کاولگر *kāwal-gār*, } a patrol, a sentinel. *d.*
کاولیگار *kāwalī-gār*, }

کاول پٹي *kāwal paṭṭī*, a commitment to jail. *d.*

کاوي *kāwī*, f. digging, excavating, investigation (from *kāwīdan*). *p.*

کاویٹ *kāwīṭ* (v. کویٹ), wood-apple, &c. *d.*

کاویه काव्य *kāvya*, m. a poem, a poetical composition. *kāvya-chaur*, m. a plagiarist. *s.*

کاه *kāh*, f. grass, straw. *kāh-gil*, straw and mud mixed to plaster walls with. *p.*

کاهربا *kāh-rubā*, yellow amber. *p.*

کاهش *kāhish*, f. diminution, emaciation, care, anxiety. *p.*

کاهکشان *kāhkashān*, the milky way. *p.*

کاهل *kāhil*, slow, indolent, lazy, languid, sick, tardy. *kāhil-mizāj*, indolent. *a.*

کاهل काहल *kāhla*, mischievous. *s.*

کاهلا *kāhilā*, ailing, sick, indisposed. *a.*

کاهلاپشپ काहलापुष्प *kāhlā-pushp*, m. thorn apple (*Datura metel*). *s.*

کاهلاگي *kāhilāgī*, indolence, &c. (v. *kāhilī*). *d.*

کاهلانه *kāhilāna*, slowly, lazily. *a.*

کاهلپنا *kāhilpanā*, m. } indolence, languor,
کاهلي *kāhilī*, f. } sloth, sickness, tardiness. *a.*

کاهن काहण *kāhan*, m. an aggregate number consisting of sixteen pans, or 1280 *kaurīs*. *s.*

کاهن *kāhin*, m. prophet, priest; a soothsayer, conjuror, sorcerer, augur, an astrologer. *a.*

کاهو *kāhū*, m. the name of a vegetable, the seed of which is good for a cold, a lettuce (*Lactuca sativa*). *p.*

کاهو काहू *kāhū* (in the Braj dialect, infl. of *ko,ū*), any one, some one or something. *h.*

کاهي *kāhī*, f. greenness, name of a dish; adj. of or relating to straw or grass. *p.*

کاهي काहे *kāhe* (infl. of *kyā*), why, what. *kāhe ko*, why, wherefore. *h.*

کاهیده *kāhīda*, diminished, wasted. *kāhīdan*, to waste, diminish. *p.*

کائي काई f. the green scum on the surface of stagnant pools, or the green mould that sticks to walls and pavements, scum, fur, paste; (in Dakh.) green, raw, or unripe fruit. *h.* [sou. *s.*

کایا काया *kāyā*, f. the body, appearance, per-

كاياپوتي कायापूती *kāyā-pūtī*, f. the cajeput, from whence is prepared the well-known oil. The word is originally Malay.

كائپهل कायफल or काइफल *kā,ephal*, m. name of a medicine, an aromatic bark (*Fragaria vesca*) (As. Res. vol. vi. p. 380). *s.*

كايتهه कायथ *kāyath*, m. name of a tribe of Hindūs, proceeding from a Kshatriya father and a Sūdra mother, and generally employed as clerks or copyists. *s.*

كاير कायर *kāyar*, timid, timorous, a coward. *s.*

كائر *kā,ir*, name of a bird, the Indian thrush, also called *sāt b,hā,ī*. *h.*

كايستهه कायस्थ *kāyasth*, m. the Supreme Being; a caste of Hindūs (same as *kāyath*). *s.*

كايك कायक *kāyak*, bodily, personal. *s.*

كائلا *kā,ilā* (for *kāhilā*), sick, ailing. *d.*

كائنات *kā,ināt* (pl. of كائنة), all things existing; f. the world, universe, beings, creatures. *a.*

كايه काय *kāya*, m. the body (v. *kāyā*). *s.*

كب कब *kab*, when? *kab-tak*, *-talak*, *-lag*, or *-ta,īṅ*, till when? how long? *kab-se*, since what time? *kab-kab*, when? *kab-kā*, *-ke*, or *-kī*, of what time? *kab-lo*, till when? how long? *s.*

كب कवि *kabi* or *kab*, m. (for *kavi*) a poet. *kub*, a hump (on the back). *s.*

كبّا कुब्बा *kubbā*, hump-backed. *s.*

كباب *kabāb*, m. a roast, meat cut into slices and then roasted or fried on skewers. *kabāb-k.*, a. to burn, to roast. *kabāb honā*, to burn; to be enraged; (met.) to be desperately in love. *p.*

كباب‌چيني *kabāb-chīnī*, f. cubebs (*Piper cubeba*); jungle cloves. *p.*

كبابه *kabāba*, m. cubebs (*Piper cubeba*). *a.*

كبابي *kabābī*, fit to be roasted; roasting; m. one who roasts; a vendor of *kabābs*. *p.*

كباده *kabāda*, m. a bow, not very strong, for practising with. *p.*

كبار *kibār* (pl. of كبير), grandees, nobles, men distinguished for wealth, knowledge, or sanctity. *kabbār* or *kubbār*, very great. *a.*

كباڙ कबाड़ *kabāṛ* or *kibāṛ*, m. a door, a gate. *s.*

كبت कवित *kabit*, m. } a sort of verse used by
كبتا कविता *kabitā*, f. } the Hindūs, poetry,
a poem (applied to compositions in the Hindī or Braj dialects). *s.*

كبتائي कविताई *kabitā,ī*, f. poetry, &c. *s.*

كبٹ *kabaṭ*, a kind of delicate dish. *d.*

كبجا कुब्जा *kubjā*, hump-backed, crooked. *s.*

كبد *kabid*, m. the liver, the heart. *a.*

كبڈّي कबड्डी *kabaḍḍī*, f. a game among boys, who divide themselves into two parties, one of which takes its station on one side of a line or ridge called *pālā*, made on the ground, and the other on the other: one boy, shouting *kabaḍḍī*, *kabaḍḍī*, passes the line and endeavours to touch one of those on the opposite side: if he is able to do this and to return to his own party, the boy that was so touched is supposed to be slain, that is, he retires from the game; but if the boy who made the assault be seized and unable to return, he dies, or retires in the same manner: the assault is thus made from the two sides alternately, and that party is victorious of which some remain after all their opponents are slain. *h.*

كبر *kibr* or *kubr*, m. grandeur, pride, dignity. *kabar*, capers (fruit or berry). *a.*

كبرا कबरा *kabrā*, grey, dirty white, variegated. *s.*

كبرا *kubarā* (pl. of كبير), the great, grandees, &c. *a.*

كبرى *kubrā*, m. the major of a syllogism. *a.*

كبريا *kibriyā*, m. grandeur, magnificence; pride; a name of God. *a.*

كبريت *kibrīt*, m. sulphur; fine gold or silver. *kibrīti aḥmar*, the philosopher's stone. *a.*

كبريتي *kibrītī*, of or relating to sulphur. *a.*

كبڙ कुबड़ *kubaṛ*, m. a hump (on the back). *s.*

كبڑا कुबड़ा *kubṛā*, hump-backed, crooked. *s.*

كبك *kabk*, m. name of a bird of the partridge kind. *kabki darī*, m. a beautiful species of partridge. *kabk-raftār*, moving gracefully. *p.*

كبل *kubal*, difficult, severe. *d.*

كبندهه कबन्ध *kabandh*, m. a headless trunk (still retaining a little life, so as to have the power of moving). *s.*

كبوتر *kabūtar*, m. a pigeon. *kabūtar-bāz* or *kabūtar-bān*, a pigeon-fancier; one who rears pigeons and bets upon their flight, &c. *kabūtar-bacha*, m. a young pigeon; an unripe poppy-head wrapped up in pease-meal and fried in butter or oil. *kabūtar-jhar*, name of a plant (*Justicia nasuta*). *p.*

كبوترخانه *kabūtar-khāna*, m. a pigeon-house. *p.*

كبود *kabūd*, m. azure, blue; a kind of willow; a sort of blue sheepskin: a heron. *p.*

كبودي *kabūdī*, blue, azure, cerulean. *kabūdī-rang*, azure-coloured. *p.*

كبهارجا कुभार्जा *ku-bhārjā* (for *ku-bhāryā*), f. [a bad wife. *s.*

كبهاو कुभाव *ku-bhāw*, m. ill-treatment, ill-temper, evil disposition. *s.*

كبهو कभू *kabhū*, } ever, some time or other.
كبهون कभूं *kabhūṅ*, } *kabhī kabhī*, sometimes,
كبهي कभी *kabhī*, } now and then, at times.
kabhī ke, of some time, some time ago. *kabhī na kabhī*, some time or other. *h.*

كبير *kabīr*, large, immense, great, full-grown, senior; name of a famous *faḳīr* and saint, who flourished about the close of the fifteenth century. *kabīr panthī*, m. the followers of *Kabīr*. *kabīr kā ulṭā*, transposition. *a.*

كبير कुबेर *kuber*, the God of wealth (v. *kuver*).

کبيسر कबीसर *kabīsar*, } (for *kavīshwar*), a
کبيسور कबीश्वर *kabīswar*, } first-rate poet, lit. prince of poets: the Arabs and Persians have a similar term, *maliku-sh-shu'arā*. *s.*

کبيسة *kabīsa*, m. intercalary. *sāli kabīsa*, leap-year. *a.*

کبيشور कबीश्वर *kabīshwar* or *kabīshar*, m. (for *kavīshwar*), an eminent poet (v. *kabīsar*). *s.*

کبيکج *kabīkaj*, a kind of wild parsley, and a deadly poison. *p.*

کبين *kabīn* (for *kabhīn*), at any time. *d.*

کپ कपि *kapi*, m. an ape, a monkey. *s.*

کپا कुप्पा *kuppā*, m. a large leathern vessel for holding oil, *ghī*, &c. *kuppā luṛhnā*, the decease of a king, &c. *kuppā honā*, to become very fat. *s.*

کپاتر कुपात्र *ku-pātr*, unfit, incapable. *s.*

کپاٹ कपाट *kapāṭ*, m. a shutter, a door, the panel of a door. *s.*

کپاٹي لگام *kapāṭī-lagām*, a snaffle bridle. *h. p.*

کپار कपार *kapār*, m. (v. *kapāl*) skull, cranium; fate, destiny. *s.*

کپاري कपारी *kapārī*, shrewd, sly; m. a caste in Bengal who sell greens, &c. *h.*

کپاري कपारी *kapārī*, a title of *Shiva*, who carries a skull in his hand and a chain of them round his neck; a cavesson or noseband for a horse. *ardh kapārī*, pain of half the head (*hemicrania*); an areca nut having two kernels, or rather one of those kernels which are convex on one side and flat on the other, where it was in contact with its fellow: these nuts, from the doctrine of signatures, are said to be a remedy for the *hemicrania*. *s.*

کپاس कपास *kapās*, f. cotton (undressed); the cotton plant (*Gossypium herbaceum*). *s.*

کپاسي *kapāsī*, made of cotton (a garment). *s.*

کپال कपाल *kapāl*, m. the head, forehead; a skull or cranium; fate, destiny. *kapāl phuṭnā*, to be unfortunate. *kapāl khulnā*, to have a favourable turn of fortune. *s.*

کپالي कपाली *kapālī*, a title of *Shiva* (v. *kapārī*). *kapālī āsan*, an attitude of *faķīrs* in worship, standing on their heads. *kapālī kriyā*, a ceremony among Hindūs: when a dead body is burning and nearly reduced to ashes, the nearest relative breaks the skull with the stroke of a bamboo and pours melted butter into the cavity: hence *kapālī kriyā-k.*, to think intensely, to beat or cudgel one's brains. *s.*

کپالي कपाली *kapālī*, m. name of a caste (in Beng.) (v. *kapārī*). *h.*

کپت कुपित *kupit*, incensed, angry. *s.*

کپتر कपुत्र *kaputr* or कुपुत्र *kuputr*, m. a bad, undutiful, and wicked son. *s.*

کپتھ कुपथ *ku-path*, (lit. bad road, or the wrong way) deviation, aberration, heresy. *kupathgāmī*, wicked, going in a bad or wrong road. *s.*

کپتھ कपित्थ *kapitth*, m. the elephant or wood apple (*Feronia elephantium* or *Cratæva valanga*). *s.*

کپٹ कपट *kapaṭ*, designing, insincere; f. spite, adulteration, trick, deceit, subterfuge. *kapaṭtā*, f. deceitfulness. *kapaṭ-rūpdhārī*, a hypocrite. *kapaṭ-lekhya*, m. a forged document. *kapaṭ-vesh*, m. disguise. *kapaṭ-veshī*, disguised: m. a hypocrite. *s.*

کپٹي कपटी *kapaṭī*, insincere, false, hypocritic, adulterated. *s.*

کپچا कपचा *kapchā*, m. a kind of jacket. *h.*

کپر कपर *kapar*, m. (v. *kapaṛ*) cloth, &c. *s.*

کپرامرش कुपरामर्श *ku-parāmarsh*, m. bad advice. *s.*

کپردھول कपरधूल *kapar-dhūl*, m. a kind of gauze. *h.*

کپرش कुपुरुष *ku-purush*, m. a vile man, a poltroon. *s.*

کپرکوٹ कपरकूट *kapar-kūṭ*, pounded up with rags (clay for making crucibles, &c.). *s.*

کپڑ कपड़ *kapaṛ* or *kapar*, m. cloth. *kapaṛ-chhān-k.*, a. to strain. *kapaṛ chhan*, impalpable (powder); deep (consultation); thoroughly sifted (intelligence, &c.). *s.*

کپڑا कपड़ा *kapṛā*, m. cloth; clothes, dress, habit. *kapṛā-oṛhnā* or *-pahannā*, to put on clothes. *kapṛoṅ se honā*, n. to have the menses. *kapṛe*, pl. dress apparel. *kapṛe rangnā*, to become a *faķīr*. *kapṛe ko jhol denā*, to give an alarm.—(*Gilch.*) *kapṛe-wapṛe* clothes. *s.*

کپڑپھول *kapaṛ-phūl*, a silk cloth worked with gold and silver flowers, worn as a head-dress by females. *d.*

کپڑدھول कपड़धूल *kapaṛdhūl*, m. gauze. *h.*

کپڑکوٹھا कपड़कोठा *kapaṛ-kothā*, m. a tent. *s.*

کپ کپي कपकपी *kap-kapī*, f. shivering, trembling, quaking, perturbation. *s.*

کپل कपिल *kapil*, m. name of a Hindū sage. *s.*

کپلا कपिला *kapilā*, f. a brown-coloured cow. *s.*

کپنا कपना *kapnā*, n. to shiver, to tremble, to quake; adj. trembling. *s.*

کپوت कपोत *kapot*, m. a pigeon or dove, especially the spotted-necked pigeon. *s.*

کپوت कपूत *kapūt* or कुपूत *kupūt*, m. a degenerate or villainous son. *s.*

کپوتي कपूती *kapūtī*, f. degeneracy (in a son). *s.*

کپور कपूर *kapūr*, m. camphor; also name of a flower. *s.*

کپورکچري कपूरकचरी *kapūr-kacharī*, f. name of a medicine. *h.*

کپوري कपूरी *kapūrī*, m. a kind of betel-leaf so called. *s.*

کپول कपोल *kapol*, m. the cheek. *kapol-genduā*, a small circular pillow to rest the cheek upon. *s*

کپھ कफ **kaph**, m. phlegm; watery froth or foam. *kaph-nāshan*, anti-phlegmatic. *kaphī*, phlegmatic. *s.*

کپي कपी **kapī**, m. a monkey; a pulley or block. *kuppī*, f. a vial, a skin, a leather bottle. *s.*

کت कत **kat** or **kit**, where? whither? why? how? how many? how much? *s.*

کتا कुत्ता **kuttā**, m. a dog; the scear of a gun-lock, the part which is acted upon by the trigger; a hand-vice. *kuttā mūtyā*, a toadstool or fungus. *tāzī kuttā*, a greyhound. *h.*

کتا कित्ता **kittā**, how many? how much? what quantity? *s.*

کتاب **kitāb**, f. a book, writing, despatches, scripture, a letter. *kitābi ilāhī* or *kitābi majīd*, the holy book, the *ḳur,ān*. *kitāb-farosh*, a bookseller. As *the* book, το βιβλίον, it is applied to the Old Testament of the Jews, the New Testament of the Christians, and the *ḳur,ān* of the *Muhammadans*: hence Jews and Christians, as well as *Muhammadans*, are styled "*ahli kitāb*" "the people of the book," the rest of mankind being classed as pagans. *a.*

کتابت **kitābat**, f. } writing, inscription, a
کتابه **kitāba**, m. } motto; title-page; in law, a written engagement whereby a slave is entitled to emancipate himself either by labour or money; an epitaph. *a.*

کتابي **kitābī**, of or belonging to a book; hence a Jew or Christian (v. *kitāb*), for *Muhammadans* admit that these are possessed of scriptural authority, though inferior to the *ḳur,ān*; of the shape of a book, *i.e.* rectangular or oblong. *kitābī chaprā*, a long or oval face. *a.*

کتارا कतारा **katārā**, m. a kind of sugar-cane. *h.*

کتان **kattān**, m. a kind of cloth, linen (it is said to be rent by exposure to the moonlight, and hence is represented by oriental poets as enamoured of the moon. *katān*, linseed. *a.*

کتان कत्तान **kattān**, m. a knife, a dagger (Beng.). *s.*

کتانا कताना **katānā**, a. to get spun, to cause to spin. *s.*

کتاعي कताई **katā,ī**, m. spinning; the price paid for spinning. *s.*

کتب **kutub** (pl. of کتاب), books. *kutub-khāna*, a library. *a.*

کتبيا **kitabiyā**, f. a small book. *a.*

کتپ कुतप **kutap** or कुतुप **kutup**, m. the eighth hour or portion of the day, about noon. *s.*

کتخدا **kat-khudā**, m. (for *kad-khudā*) master of a family, a married man; a viceroy or locum tenens. *p.*

کتخداعي **kat-khudā,ī**, f. marriage; office of viceroy. *kat-khudā,ī-k.*, to marry. *p.*

کتر कुतरु **kutru**, m. a puppy. *katru*, m. a cutter. *s.*

کترا कतरा **katrā**, m. parings, clippings. *s.*

کتراپ कुत्रापि **kutrāpi**, somewhere or other. *s.*

کترانا कतराना **katrānā**, a. to cause to clip, to cut out; to leave the high road, stealing away by by-paths, to go round about, to shrink, to go sideways. *katrākar chalnā*, to desert one's companion. *s.*

کتراعي कतराई **katrā,ī**, f. price paid for cutting out; adv. sideways. *s.*

کتربهيد **katar-bhed**, fraud, guile, deceit. *d.*

کتربيونت कतरबेयोंत **katar-be,ont**, m. cutting out; (met.) meditation, consultation, anxiety. *s.*

کترن कतरन **katran**, f. parings, clippings. *kutran*, that which is gnawed or bitten off by the teeth. *s.*

کترنا कतरना **katarnā**, a. to clip, to cut (as with scissors), to cut out, to pare. *kutarnā*, a. to cut with the teeth. *s.*

کترني कतरनी **katarnī**, f. scissors. *s.*

کترو कुतरू **kutrū**, m. a puppy (in Bengal, from the custom of calling dogs by this sound). *h.*

کترو कुतरू **kutrū**, m. one who cuts or bites. *s.*

کتسا कुत्सा **kutsā**, f. reproach, contempt, censure. *s.*

کتست कुत्सित **kutsit**, despicable, contemptible. *s.*

کتف **katif** or **kitf**, m. the shoulder-blades. *a.*

کتك **kitak**, some, several, a few. *d.*

کتك **kutak** (for *kūtak*, q. v.), a pestle, &c. *p.*

کتکا कुतका **kuthā**, m. a short stick with which *bhang* is ground. *h.*

کتل कतल **kattal**, f. a lump of stone, brick, or earth. *h.*

کتلا कतला **katlā**, m. a slice; adj. rank, rancid, musty, flabby. *s. h.*

کتمان **kitmān**, concealment, concealing. *a.*

کتنا कितना **kitnā**, how many? how much? what number? *kitne-ek*, a few, some. *kitnā-hī*, how many (or much) soever. *s.*

کتنا कतना **katnā**, n. to be spun. *s.*

کتنئي कतनई **katna,ī**, f. spinning. *s.*

کتوال **kutwāl**, m. a kind of police-officer; a minor sort of magistrate (v. *kotwāl*). *p.*

کتوالي **kutwālī**, f. the office of *kutwāl*. *p.*

کتونك कुतूनक **kutūnak**, m. weakness of the eyes in infants. *s.*

کتوهل कुतूहल **kutūhal**, m. f. eagerness, desire, curiosity; show, spectacle, entertainment, sport, pastime, festivity. *kutūhalī*, sportive, fond of sport. *s.*

کتهه कथ **kath**, m. the astringent vegetable extract which the natives eat with betel-leaf. It is the produce of a species of *mimosa* (*chadira*), *Catechu*, *Terra japonica*. *h.*

کتها कथा **kathā**, f. a story, tale, fable, relation, narrative. *s.*

کتهت कथित **kathit**, told, related. *s.*

کتھک कथक *kathak* or *katthak* (also *kathik*), m. a story-teller; a kind of singer; one who reads the Purānas in public. *s.*

کتھن कथन *kathan*, m. the act of saying or telling. *s.*

کتھنا कथना *kathnā*, a. to tell, to say, to [relate. *s.*

کتھوپکتھن कथोपकथन *kathopakathan*, m. conversation, dialogue, narration. *s.*

کتي *kate* (probably an abbrev. of کہتي "they say"), an expletive, answering to "so, thus, that," &c., much used in the Dakhani dialect. *d.*

کتي कुत्ती *kuttī*, f. (fem. of *kuttā*) a bitch. *h.*

کتیا कुतिया *kutiyā* or *kuttiyā*, f. a little bitch. *h.*

کتیرا कतीरा *katīrā*, m. a gum resembling tragacanth, obtained from the *Sterculia urens* of Dr. Roxb.: the name is also given to the real gum tragacanth, obtained from the *Astragalus verus*. *h.*

کتیك *kit-ek* (for *kitne-ek*), some, few. *d.*

کتئیں *ki-ta,iṅ* (for *ke-ta,iṅ*), to, up to, &c. *d.*

کٹ कुट *kuṭ*, m. name of a medicine (*Costus Arabicus*). *s.*

کٹ कटि *kaṭi* or *kaṭ*, f. the reins, the loins, the waist. *kaṭi-keharī* or *kaṭ-kehrī*, having a waist elegant as the lion's (epithet of a handsome woman). *s.*

کٹ कट *kaṭ*, m. black colour to mark chintz with. *kiṭṭ*, m. a kind of sour dish; excrement, dirt. *h.*

کٹ कटु *kaṭu*, m. pungency, pungent taste; a flower (*Michelia champaca*); adj. pungent, fierce, hot, impetuous. *s.*

کٹا कट्टा *kaṭṭā*, robust, able-bodied; m. a large [louse. *h.*

کٹا कटा *kaṭā*, f. killing, slaughter. *kaṭā-k.*, to slaughter. *s.*

کٹا *kaṭṭā*, a bundle, a file of papers, a bunch, a handful, a faggot or bundle of sticks, a parcel. *d.*

کٹاچھ *kaṭāchh*, m. (for *kaṭāksh*, q.v.) ogling, a leer, glance, or side look. *s.*

کٹار कटार *kaṭār*, m. a dagger having a broad straight blade; the hilt comes up on either side of the wrist, while it is grasped by a crossbar in the centre; a polecat. *h.*

کٹار कुटार *kuṭār*, m. an impatient little [horse. *s. h.*

کٹار कुट्टार *kuṭṭār*, m. copulation. *s.*

کٹارا कटारा *kaṭārā*, m. name of a medicinal plant (globe thistle, *Echinops echinatus, Roxb.*). *h.*

کٹارا *kaṭārā*, the aloe plant. *d.*

کٹاري कटारी *kaṭārī*, f. a small dagger (v. *kaṭār*). *h.*

کٹاریا कटारिया *kaṭāriyā*, m. a kind of silk cloth, with stripes in the form of daggers. *h.*

کٹاسا कटासा *kaṭāsā*, inclined to bite. *s.*

کٹاسخت *kuṭā-sakht*, m. a very dog. *h. p.*

کٹاکش कटाक्ष *kaṭāksh*, m. ogling, a leer, a glance, a side look. *s.*

کٹال कटाल *kaṭāl*, flood, spring tide (Beng.). *h.*

کٹانا कटाना *kaṭānā*, to cause to cut, or bite. *s.*

کٹاو कटाव *kaṭāw*, m. a kind of flowering on cloths; cutting, reaping, harvest. *h.*

کٹاہ कटाह *kaṭāh*, m. a shallow boiler for oil or butter, &c. *s.*

کٹائي कटाई *kaṭā,ī*, f. harvest. *h.*

کٹایا कुटाया *kuṭāyā*, m. *Solanum jacquini*, (*Willd.*). *h.*

کٹبندھن कटबंधन *kaṭ-bandhan*, m. a wooden clog or ring with which an elephant is fastened. *s.*

کٹپھل कटफल *kaṭ-phal*, m. a small tree found in the north-west of Hindūstān, the bark and seeds of which are used in medicine and as aromatics: the fruit is also eaten: the common name is *kāyaphal*. *s.*

کٹت काटित *kaṭit*, m. vent, sale. *h.*

کٹتا कटुता *kaṭutā*, f. pungency, sharpness; testiness, irritability. *s.*

کٹج कुटज *kuṭaj*, m. a medicinal plant (*Echites antidysenterica*): the seeds are used as a vermifuge. *s.*

کٹر कट्टर *kaṭṭar*, inclined or addicted to bite (a [horse). *h.*

کٹر कटर *kaṭar*, cruel, relentless; (sub.) a caitiff. *s.*

کٹر कुटिर *kuṭir*, m. a cottage, a hut. *s.*

کٹرا कटरा *kaṭrā*, also *kaṭra*, m. a market, suburbs, the market-town belonging to a fort. *h.*

کٹرنا *kaṭarnā*, m. a species of fish. *d.*

کٹ رہنا कटरहना *kaṭ-rahnā*, n. to be cut, to be cut off, intercepted, divided, separated, or stopped up (as a road by being infested with thieves, &c.). *h.*

کٹري कट्टरी *kaṭṭrī*, the horizontal beam to which the bullocks are attached in a sugar-mill: it also denotes land recovered from large rivers. *h.*

کٹك कटक *kaṭak*, m. f. an army. *s.*

کٹکا *kaṭkā*, a peck or seizure with the beak. *kaṭkā bharnā*, to peck with the beak, to bite with the teeth. *d.*

کٹکٹ कुटकुट *kuṭkuṭ*, m. nibbling, itching, scratching (in Dakh.) *kaṭ-kaṭ*, an imitative sound, a click, a tick, or tick-tick. *h.*

کٹکٹانا *kaṭ-kaṭānā*, to gnash or grind the [teeth. *d.*

کٹکٹي کھانا *kaṭaḥṭī-khānā*, to experience grief, trouble, or vexation. *d.*

کٹکر कटकर *kaṭhar*, } m. railings, balus-
کٹکرا कटकरा *kaṭharā*, } trade, palings, enclosure (for *kaṭh-gharā*, q. v.). *h.*

کتکرنج कटकरंज *kaṭharanj*, کتکلیجی कटकलेजी *kaṭhaleji*, } f. the febifrnge nut (*Guilandina bonduccella, Lin.*; *Cæsalpinia bonduccella, Roxb.*). *s.*

کتکنا कटकना *kaṭkanā*, m. a picture (on wood); plan, scheme, sketch; adj. shrewd, cunning. *h.*

کتکھانا कटखाना *kaṭkhānā*, a. to bite. *h.*

کتکھنا कटखना *kaṭhkhanā*, inclined to bite. *h.*

کتکی कुटकी *kuṭkī*, f. a gnat; estrangement from, or desertion of, friends. *h.*

کتکی कुटकी *kuṭkī*, f. name of a medicine. *s.*

کتکینہ कटकीनः *kaṭkīna*, a sub-lease, or under-farm. *kaṭkīna-dār*, an under-farmer of revenue, a sub-tenant (Glad.). *h.*

کتگھرا कटघरा *kaṭ-gharā*, کتگر कटगर *kaṭgar*, } m. a wooden cage or railing, a balustrade. *s.*

کتل कुटिल *kuṭil*, crooked, bent, perverse, dishonest; cruel, ruthless. *kuṭil-tā*, f. crookedness; guile, dishonesty. *s.*

کتم कुटम *kuṭum*, کتمب कुटुम्ब *kuṭumb*, } m. kin, family, tribe, caste, relatives. *s.*

کتمبن कुटुम्बिन *kuṭumbin*, کتمبی कुटुम्बी *kuṭumbī*, کتمی कुटुमी *kuṭumī*, } m. householder, paterfamilias. *kuṭumbinī*, f. the wife of a householder, a matron. *s.*

کتمرم *kaṭmaram*, m. a raft, a float, commonly called a "catamaran." The word is originally Tamul, and signifies in that language "tied logs." *d.*

کتمست *kaṭmastā* (v. *kaṭh mastā*), strong-bodied, very powerful and lusty. *d.*

کتن कुट्टन *kuṭṭan*, کتنا कुटना *kuṭnā*, } m. a pimp, a pander, a mischief-maker. *s.*

کتنا कटना *kaṭnā*, n. to be cut; to pass or be spent (as time); to be bashful, abashed, to be interrupted; to die of wounds. *s.*

کتناپا कुटनापा *kuṭnāpā*, m. pimping. *s.*

کتناس कटनास *kuṭnās*, m. the name of a bird (*Coracias*). *h.*

کتنانا कुटनाना *kuṭnānā*, a. to entice, to seduce, to inveigle, to wheedle, to coax. *s.*

کتنائی कुटनाई *kuṭnā,ī*, f. the wages of a pimp. *s.*

کتنب कुटुम्ब *kuṭumb*, m. tribe, family, kindred. *s.*

کتنٹ कुटन्नट *kuṭannaṭ*, m. a plant (*Bignonia indica*). *s.*

کتنی कटनी *kaṭnī*, f. the season for cutting the grain, harvest. *s.*

کتنی कुटनी *kuṭnī* or *kuṭṭanī*, f. a bawd, a procuress, a go-between. *s.* [to be cut. *s.*

کتوانا कटवाना *kaṭwānā* (v. *kaṭānā*), to cause

کتورا कटोरा *kaṭorā*, کتورہ कटोरः *kaṭora*, } m. a brass bowl, a cup, goblet, &c. of metal. *h.*

کتوری कटोरी *kaṭorī*, f. a small bowl or cup of metal. *h.*

کتوسی कटूसी *kaṭūsī*, f. smut, obscenity. *h.*

کتول कटोल *kaṭol*, m. a man of a degraded tribe, a *Chanḍāl*: a plant (perhaps cowage, *Dolichos pruriens*). *s.*

کتھ कठ *kaṭh*, m. (contraction of *kāṭh*, wood). *kaṭh-bandhan* or *-bandan*, m. a wooden ring with which the feet of elephants are fastened. *kaṭh-birūkī*, f. a toad. *kaṭh-bel*, the wood-apple (*Feronia elephantum*). *kaṭh-belā*, m. name of a flower (*Jasminum multiflorum*). *kaṭh-phorā*, a woodpecker (*Picus*). *kaṭh-gulāb*, m. a kind of rose (*Rosa chinensis*). *kaṭh-mastā*, very stout and lusty. *kaṭh-hańsī*, affected or forced smiles (with internal displeasure). *s.*

کتھا कट्ठा *kaṭṭhā*, m. a land-measure (the twentieth part of a *bīghā*); a corn-measure, containing five *sers*. *h.*

کتھا कटहा *kaṭahā*, snapping, inclined to bite. *s.*

کتھار कुठार *kuṭhār*, m. an axe; (in Dakh.) *kaṭhār* (for *kaṭār*), a dagger. *s.*

کتھاری कुठारी *kuṭhārī*, کتھالی कुठाली *kuṭhālī*, } f. an earthen vase prepared for melting gold, silver, &c.; a crucible. *h.*

کتھاک कुठाकु *kuṭhāku*, m. a bird, the woodpecker. *s.*

کتھر कटहर *kaṭhar*, m. a wooden cage in which wild beasts are kept; also a kind of fruit (v. *kaṭhal*); adj. hard. *s.*

کتھر कुठर *kuṭhar*, m. the post round which the string of the churning-stick winds. *s.*

کتھرا कटहरा *kaṭharā*, m. a wooden cage; a railing, a palisade. *s.*

کتھرا कठरा *kaṭhrā*, کتھڑا कठड़ा *kaṭhṛā*, } m. a tub, a tray, a plate, a trough; a young male buffalo. *s.*

کتھری कठरी *kaṭhrī*, f. a small tub, trough. *s.*

کتھگھرا कठघरा *kaṭhgharā*, m. a wooden cage; a railing, a palisade. *s.*

کتھل कटहल *kaṭhal*, m. name of a fruit and tree; the jack-tree and fruit (*Artocarpus integrifolia, Roxb.*). *s.*

کتھل कठिल्ल *kaṭhill*, m. *Momordica charantias*. *s.*

کتھلا कठला *kaṭhlā*, m. a wooden ornament, or a charm put on a child's neck. *s.*

کتھن कठिन *kaṭhin*, difficulty, obscure, painful, troublesome; acute; hard, solid; unkind, severe. *kaṭhintā*, f. hardness, severity, difficulty *kaṭhin-hṛiday* or *kaṭhināntahkaran*, hard-hearted. *s.*

کتھنجر कठिञ्जर *kaṭhinjar*, m. a plant worshipped by the Hindūs, commonly called Tulsī (*Ocymum sanctum*, or sacred basil). *s.*

كٹهندر कठंदर *kaṭhandar*, m. dropsy, tympany, hardness of the stomach. *s.* [with). *s.*

كٹهني कठिनी *kaṭhinī*, f. chalk (for writing

كٹهوتي कठौती *kaṭhautī*, f. a tub, a plate, a trencher, platter. *s.*

كٹهور कुठौर *ku-ṭhaur*, wrong place, misplaced. *s.*

كٹهور कठोर *kaṭhor*, } cruel, relentless, severe,
كٹهول कठोल *kaṭhol*, } callous; hard, solid. *s.*

كٹهورتا कठोरता *kaṭhoratā*, f. hardness, firmness; cruelty, relentlessness. *s.*

كٹهيا कठिया *kaṭhiyā*, m. a trencher, a platter; a snare, a trap, trepan. *s.*

كٹي कुटी *kuṭī*, f. a cottage. *kaṭī*, f. (v. *kaṭi*) the reins, loins, &c. *s.*

كٹيا कटिया *kaṭiyā*, f. a fishing-hook. *kaṭaiyā*, coarse grass growing on fields left fallow. *h.*

كٹير कुटीर *kuṭīr*, m. a small house, a hovel. *s.*

كٹيرا *kaṭerā*, railings, palings; a balustrade. *d.*

كٹيرا कटीरा *kaṭīrā*, } thorny; active, brave (a
كٹيلا कटीला *kaṭīlā*, } soldier); a kind of plant. *s.*

كٹيو कटेव *kaṭe,o* or कुटेव *kuṭe,o*, f. a bad habit. *h.*

كثافت *kas̤āfat*, f. density, fulness, repletion. *a.*

كثرت *kas̤rat*, f. abundance, excess; practice. *ba-kas̤rat* or *kas̤rat-se*, in plenty, abundantly, numerously. *kas̤rat-k.*, to practise, to exercise one's self. *a.*

كثرتي *kas̤ratī*, usual, practised, familiar. *a. d.*

كثف *kas̤f*, m. a crowd, multitude. *a.*

كثير *kas̤īr*, many, much, abundant, fruitful, copious, numerous, excessive. *kas̤īru-l-'iyāl*, having a numerous family. *a.*

كثيف *kas̤īf*, thick, dense, opaque. *kas̤īfu-l-auḳāt*, bad times, dirty weather; miserable. *a.*

كج कुज *kuj*, the planet Mars; Tuesday. *s.*

كج *kaj*, crooked, wry; (met.) perverse, cross. *kaj-āghand*, *-āghanda*, *-āgand*, or *-āganda*, a cuirass quilted with silk. *kaj-bāz*, one who plays false, fraudulent. *kāj-bahs̤*, one who reasons absurdly. *kaj-bahs̤ī*, f. absurd reasoning. *kaj-chashm*, squint-eyed. *kaj-khulḳ*, ill-tempered. *kaj-dān marez*, evasion, subterfuge, putting off. *kaj-raw*, one who walks obliquely; unprincipled. *kaj-rawī*, walking obliquely; unprincipled conduct, depravity. *kaj-ṭab'*, cross-tempered. *kaj-fahm*, stupid, misunderstanding, perverting a meaning. *kaj-kulah*, a beau (lit. wearing the cap awry). *kaj-mizāj*, cross, ill-tempered; stupid. *kaj-nagar*, envious, malignant looks. *kaj-nihād*, of a crooked disposition, perverse. *kaj-nazar*, scowling ("lumine torvo"); met. envious, malignant. *p.*

كجا *kujā*, where? whither? how? *az-kujā*, whence? *har-kujā*, everywhere. *p.*

كجات कुजाति *ku-jāti* or *ku-jāt*, base, of mean extraction or bad caste; one who has lost his caste. *s.*

كجاچت *kajāchit*, perhaps, should, sometime or other. *s.*

كجانا *kujānā*, a. to cause to rot, to waste. *d.*

كجاوه *kajāwa*, m. a camel's saddle; a kind of camel's litter in which females travel. *p.*

كجرا कजरा *kajrā*, m. lampblack used for painting the eyes. *s.*

كجرارا कजरारा *kajrārā*, black (eyes) without painting. *s.* [black. &c. *s.*

كجروا कजरवा *kajarwā*, m. (v. *kajrā*) lamp-

كجك *kajak*, f. the iron instrument used in driving elephants. *p.*

كجل कज्जल *kajjal*, } m. lampblack, soot, col-
كجلا कजला *kajlā*, } lyrium prepared from soot. *s.*

كجلوٹي कजलौटी *kajlauṭī*, f. a pot for keeping *kajjal*; an iron instrument like snuffers, used to receive smoke, prepare and keep lampblack. *s.*

كجليبن कुजलीबन *kujlī-ban*, m. a forest frequented by elephants. *s.*

كجنا *kujnā*, n. to be rotten or putrescent; to wear out, to decay. *d.*

كجي *kajī*, f. crookedness, crossness. *p.*

كچ कच *kach*, m. rawness, simplicity; water in which rice has been washed. *h.*

كچ कुच *kuch*, m. and f. bosom, breasts, bubbies. *kach*, m. hairs. *s.*

كچا कचा *kachchā*, unripe, crude; raw, unbaked; silly, unknowing, green, inexperienced, false; clay-built, slight. *kachā-pan*, m. rawness, crudity. *h.*

كچار कचार *kachār* (v. *kachhār*) moist land, &c. *h.*

كچاكچ *kachā-kach*, debate, altercation. *d.*

كچاكهانا *kachchā khānā*, to become angry. *d.*

كچاگر कुचाग्र *kuchāgra*, m. a nipple. *s.*

كچال कुचाल *ku-chāl*, f. misbehaviour, misconduct. *s.* [root (*Arum colocasia*). *h.*

كچالو कचालू *kachālū*, m. name of an esculent

كچالي कुचाली *ku-chālī*, of ill-behaviour. *s.*

كچائي कचाई *kachchā,ī*, f. rawness; indigestion, surfeit. *h.*

كچبچ कचबच *kach-bach*, m. pl. breed, offspring, family, brats, children. *h.*

كچپچ कचपच *kach-pach*, f. crowd; infants, brats. *kich-pich*, f. mud, mire, &c.; adj. close, thick, stuffed together. *h.* [iades. *h.*

كچپچيا कचपचिया *kach-pachiyā*, m. the Ple-

كچپن कचपन *hach-pan*, m. rawness; simplicity, want of experience. *h.*

كچر कुचर *kuchar*, censorious, detracting. *s.*

كچرا कचरा *hachrā*, m. the raw *kharbūza* or musk-melon; clay. *kichrā* (v. *kichṛā*). *h.*

كچرا *kachrā*, m. rubbish, dirt, sweepings. *d.*

كچرپچرهونا किचरपिचर होना *kichar-pichar honā*, to be very wet. *h.*

كچري कचरी *hacharī*, } m. name of a fruit
كچريا कचरिया *hachariyā*, } (*Cucumis maduraspatanus*). *h.*

كچڙا किचड़ा *hichṛā*, m. the gummy substance that oozes from the eye. *kachṛā*, an unripe melon of a very small size. *s.*

كچڙانا किचड़ाना *kichṛānā*, n. to have a gummy running at the eyes, to be blear-eyed. *s.*

كچك कचक *kachak*, f. pain (of a wound); limp. *h.* [sprain, to twist. *h.*

كچكانا कचकाना *hachkānā*, a. to strain, to

كچكچ कसकच *hachhach*, m. debate, altercation. *h.*

كچكچانا किचकिचाना *hichhichānā*, a. to grind (or gnash) the teeth. *kachkachānā*, n. to swarm, to be very abundant; to be gritty. *h.*

كچكچاهٹ कचकचाहट *hachhachāhat*, f. the act of debating, &c. *h.*

كچكڙا कचकड़ा *hachhaṛā*, m. tortoise-shell. *s.*

كچكنا कचकना *kachahnā*, n. to strain, to sprain, to twist; to limp; to pain, to ache. *h.*

كچكول *hachhol*, f. a cup or bowl (generally a beggar's); a wallet; a miscellany, an olla podrida, a commonplace book. *p.*

كچ كهانا *hach-khānā*, to suffer grief or vexation. *d.*

كچكيلا कचकेला *kachhelā*, m. a kind of plantain which is eaten boiled, as a vegetable. *s.*

كچلا कुचला *kuchlā*, m. a vomic nut (*Strychnos nux vomica*). *kachlā*, m. clay. *h.*

كچل دينا कुचलदेना *kuchal-denā*, } a. to
كچل ڈالنا कुचलडालना *huchal-ḍālnā*, } bruise, &c.; to overlay. *h.* [crush. *h.*

كچلنا कुचलना *huchalnā*, a. to bruise, to

كچلون कचलोन *kachlon*, a kind of salt, said to promote digestion. *h.*

كچلوهو कचलोहू *kach-lohū*, m. bloody ichor discharged along with purulent matter. *h.*

كچلوهي कचलोही *kach-lohī*, } untemper-
كچلوهيا कचलोहिया *kach-lohiyā*, f. } ed iron. *s.*

كچلي *hachlī* (for *kenchlī*), the slough or skin of a snake. *d.*

كچلي कुचली *kuchlī*, f. the canine teeth. *h.*

كچمچ कचमच *hach-mach*, gibberish, babble, nonsense, unintelligible language. *h.*

كچمر कचुमर *kachumar*, m. a kind of pickle. *kachumar kar ḍālnā*, to cut to pieces.

كچنار कचनार *hachnār*, } f. a tree, the flowers
كچنال कचनाल *hachnāl*, } of which are a delicate vegetable (*Bauhinia variegata*). *s.*

كچندن कुचन्दन *ku-chandan*, m. red sanders (*Pterocarpus santalinus*); saffron or logwood. *s.*

كچو कचु *kachchū* (also *kachū*) m. name of a plant (*Arum colocasia*). *h.*

كچواٹ *hachwāṭ*, vexation, abhorrence, dislike. *d.* [*gata*. *s.*

كچوءار कचुआर *hachu,ār*, m. *Bauhinia varie-*

كچوانا *hachwānā*, to be grieved or vexed, to be tired or disgusted with (a person). *d.*

كچوانسي कचवांसी *kachwāṅsī*, a minute division of surface in land measure. *h.*

كچور कचूर *kachūr*, m. the name of a drug (*Curcuma reclinata* or *zerumbet*, *Roxb.*). *s.*

كچوري कचौरी *kachaurī*, f. a dish made of wheaten flour and pulse. *h.*

كچومر कचूमर *kachūmar*, m. a kind of pickles. *kachūmar kar-ḍālnā*, to cut to pieces. *h.*

كچه *kacha* (v. *kachā*). *hacha āmdanī*, gross import, the payment made by a *zamīndār* of his rent to government. *h. p.*

كچھ कछ *hachh* (also *kachhu*), m. a tortoise; the privities (Gilch.). *s.*

كچھ कुछ *kuchh* (in Braj. *kachhu*), any, some, something, little, whatever. *kuchh aur*, something else. *kuchh aur gānā*, to give a false explanation. *kuchh ek*, some few or little. *kuchh tum ne parā pāyā*, have you found a treasure? (lit. have you found any thing that has been dropped?) an expression addressed to one who seems inordinately pleased without apparent cause. *kuchh tum ne khwāb dekhā*, what! have you dreamt this, or seen a vision? (an expression used to a person who relates improbabilities; also to depict the astonishment of the speaker at any unexpected act of another). *kuchh se kuchh*, from one state to another, from this to that. *kuchh se kuchh honā*, to be entirely changed. *kuchh i. se, kuchh us se*, what with this, what with that. *kuchh kā kuchh*, something besides, in a different manner, on the contrary; progression, advancement. *kuchh na kuchh*, some at least, some thing or other. *kuchh nahīn*, it is nothing. *kuchh ho*, whatever may happen, come what may. *bahut kuchh*, a great deal. *h.*

كچهار कछार *hachhār*, moist and low land by a river; alluvial formation. *h.*

کچھارن कछारना *kachhārnā*, a. to wash, to rinse. *s.*

کچھپ कच्छप *kachchhap*, m. a tortoise, a turtle. *s.*

کچہري कचहरी *kachahrī* or *kachharī* (vul. *cutcherry*), f. a hall of justice, town-house, court, a public office for the receipt of the revenue, &c. *h.*

کچھ‌لنپٹ कछलंपट *kachh-lampaṭ*, m. a libertine; adj. lewd, dissolute, lecherous. *h.*

کچھنا कछना *kachhnā*, n. to be washed or rinsed. *h.*

کچھنا कछना *kachhnā*, m. a kind of breeches, which cover very little of the thigh. *s.*

کچھني कछनी *kachhnī*, f. a smaller kind of breeches (than the preceding). *s.*

کچھو कछू *kachhū* (v. *kuchh*), any, some, &c. *h.*

کچھوا कछवा *kachhwā*, low land. *h.*

کچھوءا कछूआ *kachhū,ā*, m. a tortoise, a turtle. *kachhū,ā-ḍābar*, uneven-bottomed (a river deep and shallow alternately). *s.*

کچھوارہ कछवारा *kachhwāra*, ground cultivated by gardeners or *kāchhīs*, q. v. *h.*

کچھواها कछवाहा *kachhwāhā* or *kachwāha*, m. a tribe of *rāj-pūts*, claiming descent from *Kus*, the son of *Rāmachandra*: the *rājās* of *Jainagar* are of this family. *h.*

کچھوٹي कछौटी *kachhauṭī*, f. a cloth worn between the legs to conceal the privities. *s.*

کچھي कच्छी *kachchhī*, m. a horse (with a hollow back) from the province of *Kachh*, on the banks of the Sind or Indus river. *h.*

کچهيري *kachherī* (for *kachahrī*), an office, &c. *d.*

کچي *kachī* or *kachchī* (v. *kach*), raw, &c. *kachchī-khurūj*, the raw or tumid itch. *d.*

کچيا कुचिया *kuchiyā*, m. the lobe of the ear (*Gil.*). *kachiyā*, m. a reaping-hook or sickle. *h.*

کچيانا कचियाना *kachiyānā*, n. to be frightened, to draw back, to shrink. *h.*

کچياهٹ कचियाहट *kachiyāhaṭ*, f. abhorrence. *h.*

کچيرا कचेरा *kacherā*, m. the name of a tribe. *h.*

کچيري *kacherī* (v. *kachahrī*), an office. *d.*

کچيلا कुचेला *kuchelā*, *kachelā*, or *kachailā*, ill-clad; old, dirty, or tattered (clothes). *s.*

كحال *kaḥḥāl*, m. an oculist. *kaḥāl*, a collyrium. *a.*

كحل *kuḥl*, m. a collyrium or antimony reduced to a fine powder. *a.*

کد कद *kad*, when? at what time? *s.*

كد *kad*, m. a house, a retreat, a den. *p.*

كد *kadd*, f. examination, search, inquiry, trouble, labour, endeavour. *kadd o kāwish*, f. search, inquiry, examination, application. *a.*

کدا कदा *kadā*, when? at what time? *s.*

کداپ कदापि *kadāpi*, } at some time or other; peradventure. *s.*
کداچت कदाचित *kadāchit*, }

کداچار कदाचार *kad-āchār*, wicked, profligate. *s.*

کدار कुदार *kudār*, m. a pickaxe, mattock, spade, hoe. *s.*

کدارا किदारा *kidārā*, m. name of a musical mode or *rāginī*, sung in the midnight of summer. *s.*

کداربسنت किदारबसन्त *kidār-basant*, m. name of a musical mode. *s.*

کداري कुदारी *kudārī*, f. (v. *kudālī*), a small hoe. *s.*

کداکار कदाकार *kad-ākār*, ill-shaped, ugly. *s.*

کدال कुदाल *kudāl* or *kuddāl*, m. a hoe, a pickaxe, a spade. *kuddāl*, m. mountain ebony (*Bauhinia variegata*). *s.*

کدالي कुदाली *kudālī*, f. a small mattock; a pickaxe. *s.*

کدام *kudām*, which (of the two)? who? what? of what kind or sort? *p.*

کدانا कुदाना *kudānā*, a. to dandle; to cause to leap; (met.) to provoke. *s.*

کدايا कुदाया *kudāyā*, m. a kind of dove. *h.*

کدبانو *kad-bānū*, f. the mistress of a family. *p.*

کدخدا *kad-khudā*, m. the father of a family, a married man. *p.*

کدخداءي *kad-khudā,ī*, f. establishing a family; marriage. *kad-khudā,ī-k.*, to marry. *p.*

کدر *kadr* or *kadir*, muddy, obscure. *kadar*, being turbid or muddy (water); (met.) being distressed or perplexed in mind. *a.*

کدر कदर *kadar*, m. a white sort of *mimosa*. *s.*

کدرا कुदरा *kudrā*, m. a pickaxe. *s.*

کدرانا कुदराना *kudrānā*, n. to frisk, to leap, to caper. *h.*

کدرشٹ कुदृष्टि *ku-drishṭi*, f. weak sight, evil eye. *s.*

کدريه कदर्य *kadarya*, avaricious, miserly. *s.*

کدکنا कुदकना *kudaknā*, n. to frisk, to leap, to bound, to hop on one foot. *h.*

کدل कुद्दल *kuddal*, m. mountain ebony. *s.*

کدل कदल *kadal*, m. f. } the plantain or banana (tree or leaf) (*Musa sapientum*). *s.*
کدلک कदलक *kadlak*, m. }
کدلي कदली *kadlī*, f. }

کدم कदम *kadam*, کدمب कदंब *kadamb*, } m. the name of a tree (*Nauclea orientalis*). *kadamb-pushpī*, f. a plant, the flowers of which resemble those of the *kadamb*, commonly called *mundīrī*. *s.*

کدن कदन *kadan*, m. a killer, destroyer; the act of killing, destroying. *s.*

کدن *kudan*, side, direction; adv. towards. *d.*

کدو *kadū* or *kaddū*, m. a pumpkin or pumpion (*Cucurbita lagenaria*); *membrum virile*. *p.*

کدوانا कुदवाना *kudwānā*, a. to cause to dandle. *s.*

کدودانہ *kadū-dāna*, m. the name of a disease, in which the body is covered with pustules like the seeds of the *kadū* plant; intestinal worms (*Tænia cucurbitina*). *p.*

کدورت *kadūrat*, f. foulness, impurity (in water, &c.); (met.) perturbation, depression of spirits, affliction, resentment. *a.*

کدوکش *kaddū-kash*, m. a kind of instrument for cutting and cleaning pumpkins, &c. *p.*

کده *kada*, m. (in comp.) a place, a house, &c.; as *ātash-kada*, a fire-temple; *mai-kada*, a tavern. *p.*

کدھر किधर *kidhar*, where? whither? in what direction? *kidhar-se*, whence? from what quarter? *h.*

کدھن *kudhan*, side, direction; adv. towards. *d.*

کدھو कधू *kadhū*, کدھي कधी *kadhī*, } ever, some time or other: the forms *kadhūṅ* and *kadhīṅ* also occur. *s.*

کديما कदीमा *kadīmā*, m. an iron crow; a pumpkin (*Cucurbita pepo*). *h.*

کديور *kadewar*, m. a gardener. *p.*

کڈھب कुढब *ku-ḍhab*, ill-shaped, ill-mannered. *h.*

کڈھنگ कुढंग *ku-ḍhang*, unmannerly, ill-bred. *kuḍhangī*, f. rudeness. *h.*

کذاب *kazzāb*, m. an enormous liar. *a.*

کذالك *ka-zālik*, like that, in that manner. *a.*

کذب *kazb* or *kizb*, m. lying; a lie. *a.*

کر कर *kar*, m. the hand; m. f. tribute, duty, custom, fee, tax. *s.*

کر कुरु *kuru*, name of an ancient sovereign of northern India, also the name of his territory. *kuru* or *uttara-kuru*, the most northerly of the four *mahādwīpas*, or principal divisions of the known world. *kuru-bansī*, of the race of Kuru. *kuru-kshetra*, the country near Delhī, where the great battle was fought between the *Kauravas* and the *Pāṇḍavas*. *s.*

کر *kar*, deaf; m. purpose; power, strength; felicity. *kar o far*, or *karr o farr*, pomp and pride. *p.*

کرا करा *karā* or करा *karrā*, hard, adulterated, bad (as coin). *s.*

کرا *kirā* (dat. and acc. of *ki*), whom? to whom? *p.*

كرات *karrāt* (pl. of كرة), times, &c. *karrāt-marrāt*, repeatedly, many times and oft. *a.*

کرات किरात *kirāt*, m. a savage, a tribe of mountaineers or highlanders living by the chase; the Cirrhadæ of the ancients. *s.*

کرار *karrār*, attacking violently; reiterated assault. *a.*

کرارا करारा *karārā*, hard, stiff, rigid. *s.*

کراڑا *karāṛā*, m. the shore, coast. *d.*

کراکل कराकुल *karākul*, the name of a bird; a kind of heron or curlew. *s.*

کرال कराल *karāl*, m. resin, pitch; adj. great, large, lofty, formidable. *s.*

کرام *kirām* (pl of كريم), noble, &c. *kurām*, great, high in rank or authority, venerable; m. magnitude, dignity, authority. *a.*

کرامات *karāmāt* (pl. of كرامت), miracles; deeds of excellence (v. *mu'jizāt*). *a.*

کرامت *karāmat*, f. generosity, magnificence; nobleness, excellence; a miracle performed by pious individuals not prophetically inspired: a miracle wrought by a prophet is termed *mu'jiza*, q. v. *a.*

کرام کاتبين *kirāmuṉ kātibīn*, recording angels. *a.*

کران *karān* (per metath. for *kanār*), m. a shore, coast, margin, bank, side, boundary. *p.*

کرانا करीना *karrānā*, n. to be hard or stiff. *karānā*, a. to cause to be done or made, to actuate, to effect. *s.*

کرانا किराना *kirānā*, m. grocery; a. to adjust; to sift, to separate by turning round in a winnowing fan (differing from *phaṭaknā*). *s.*

کرانت करांत *karānt*, m. a saw. *s.*

کرانت क्रान्ति *krānti* or *krānt*, f. ascending, surmounting; declination of a heavenly body; the sun's course on the ecliptic; the ecliptic, or the space of the heavens included within the tropics (also *krānti-manḍal*); the torrid zone; lustre, splendour. *s.*

کرانتي करांती *karāntī*, m. a sawyer. *s.*

کرانجنا *karānjnā*, کرانسنا *karāṅsnā*, } (v. *karāhnā*) to sigh, to groan from pain. *d.*

کرانہ *karāna*, m. (for *kanāra*, v. *karān*). *p.*

کراني क्रानी *krānī*, m. a clerk, a writer: the term is generally applied to native clerks, or those of mixed breed, in the service of Europeans. *h.*

کراو किराव *kirāw*, m. a small pea (*Pisum arvense*). *s.*

کراو कराव *karā,o*, a term applied by some inferior tribes to concubinage generally, but more especially to the marriage of a widow with the brother of a deceased husband. *h.*

کراهت *karāhat*, f. dislike, disgust, aversion. *a.*

کراهتاً *karāhatan*, unwillingly, with aversion. *a.*

کراهنا कराहना *karāhnā*, n. to sigh, to utter ah! (from pain); to groan. *h.*

کراهي कराही *karāhī*, f. a flat vessel of iron, brass, or earth, in which food is boiled or fried. *karāhī chāṭnā*, to lick the pot (from indigence or extreme avarice), hence *usne karāhī chāṭī*, applied as a reproach to a bridegroom if it rain on his wedding procession. *karāhī-lenā*, a species of ordeal, in which oil is made boiling hot in the vessel above described; a small piece of gold, as a ring, is put in it, and the suspected person is to take it out: if he do this without injury to his hand, he is pronounced innocent. *s.*

کراهيت *karāhiyat*, f. disagreeableness, disgust, abhorrence, aversion, hatred, abomination. *a.*

کراءيچا *karā,ejā*, m. the oval-leafed rosebay (*Nerium antidysentericum*), a plant whose seeds are used in medicine as a tonic or febrifuge. In Urdū it is called *indra-jau*, q. v. *d.*

کرايل करायल *karāyal*, m. rosin or resin. *h.*

کرايه *kirāya*, m. hire, fare, rent. *kirāya chalānā*, to let any thing the use of which is in moving, as a horse, cart, &c. *kirāya-dār*, a tenant, one who hires any thing. *kirāya-k*, to let. *kirāya lenā*, to hire, to rent. *a.*

کرب *karb* or *karab*, vexation, affliction. *a.*

کربا कुबा *kurbā*, hump-backed, crooked; (in Dakh.) a kind of sheep having much wool. *s.*

کربت *kurbat*, f. affliction, distress, grief. *a.*

کربدار कर्बुदार *karbudār*, m. mountain ebony; blue barleria. *s.*

کربرا कर्बुरा *karburā*, f. trumpet-flower (*Bignonia suaveolens*); a sort of basil (*Ocymum gratissimum*). *s.*

کربلا *karbalā*, name of a place in *'Irāḳ*, where *Husain* the son of *'Alī* suffered martyrdom, and where his tomb is still visited by pilgrims. *a.*

کربلاءي *karbalā,ī*, of or relating to Karbalā.

کربورك कर्बूरक *karbūrak*, m. zedoary (v. *karpūrak*).

کربي करबी *karbī*, f. the stalk of *juwār* or *bājrā* (*Holcus sorgum* and *spicatus*). *h.*

کرپا कृपा *kṛipā* or *kirpā*, f. favour, kindness, pity, compassion. *kṛipā-sindhu*, ocean of grace or mercy *kṛipā-may*, compassionate. *kṛipā-nidhān*, the abode of mercy or kindness. *kṛipā-hīn*, unfeeling. *s.*

کرپاس कर्पास *karpās*, m. cotton. *karpāsī*, f. the cotton tree. *s.*

کرپال कृपालु *kṛipālu* or *kirpāl*, compassionate, liberal, obliging, kind, benevolent, propitious. *s.*

کرپان कृपाण *kṛipān*, m. a sword, a scimitar, a sacrificial knife. *s.*

کرپان *karpān*, m. an eruptive cutaneous disorder to which children are subject. *d.*

کرپن कृपण *kṛipan* or *kirpan*, miserly. *kṛipantā*, f. stinginess. *s.*

کرپور कर्पूर *karpūr*, m. camphor. *karpūr-tail*, m. camphor liniment. *karpūr-mani*, m. a white mineral used medicinally. *s.*

کرپورك कर्पूरक *kapūrak*, m. zedoary (*Curcuma zerumbet*). *s.*

کرت कृत *krit* or *kṛita*, made, done, composed, perfect; f. fruit, consequence; the *Sat-jug*, or golden age. *s.*

کرت *karrat*, f. one time, one assault. *do karrat*, twice; *si karrat*, thrice. *a.*

کرتا *kurtā*, m. a large tunic, upper garment, frock, shirt. *p.*

کرتا कर्ता *kartā*,
کرتار कर्तार *kartār*, } m. an author, doer, creator; nominative (in gram.); a proprietor, master, a husband. *s.*

کرتارته कृतार्थ *kṛitārth*, m. the granting of a supplication, the fulfilment of one's wishes; adj. successful, having obtained one's purpose, or accomplished one's designs. *kritārthatā*, f. success. *s.*

کرتال करताल *kartāl*,
کرتالي करताली, *kartālī*, } f. the name of a musical instrument, a kind of small cymbal: the word may also mean beating time with the hands. *s.*

کرتب कर्तब *kartab*, m. action, business; skill. *s.*

کرتر कर्तृ *kartṛi*, a doer, a maker, an agent. *s.*

کرترم कृत्रिम *kṛitrim*, made, factitious, artificial. *kṛitrim-putr*, m. an adopted son. *kṛitrim-mitr*, an acquired friend. *s.*

کرتري कर्तरी *hartarī*, f. a pair of scissors or shears. *s.*

کرتکا कृत्तिका *kirttikā* or *kṛittikā*, f. the third mansion of the moon; the Pleiades. *s.*

کرتگهن कृतघ्न *kṛitaghna*
کرتگهني कृतघ्नी *kṛitaghnī*, } ungrateful, neglectful of favours, an ingrate. *s.*

کرتگهنتاءي कृतघ्नताई *kṛitaghnatā,ī*, f. ingratitude. *s.*

کرتگي कृतज्ञ *kritagya*, grateful, mindful of favours. *s.*

کرتگيتا कृतज्ञता *kritagyatā*, f. gratitude. *s.*

کرتل करतल *kar-tal*, m. the palm of the hand. *s.*

کرتني *kurtanī*, a kind of shirt or short jacket. *d.*

کرتوت करतूत *kartūt* or *kirtūt*, f. action business. *s.*

کرتويه कर्तव्य *kartavya*, proper to be done, necessary, practicable. *kartavyatā*, f. practicability, propriety. *s.*

کرته *kurta*, m. a kind of tunic, waistcoat, or jacket. *p.*

کرتهي कुरथी *kurthī*, f. a kind of vetch (*Dolichos biflorus.*) *s.*

کرتي *kurtī*, f. a waistcoat for women or jacket for soldiers. *p.*

کرتي करती *kartī*, f. the skin of a calf stuffed and placed near the mother, to make her give milk. *h.*

کرتيا किरतिया *kirtiyā*, m. a dancer, a singing-boy. [golden age. *s.*

کرت‌یگ कृतयुग *kṛit-yug*, m. the first or

کرج *kuruj*, the moulting of fowls. *d.*

کرچ किर्च *kirch* or *kirich*, f. a sword, especially a straight one to thrust with; a splinter. *malay.*

کرچور कचूर *karchūr*, m. a plant (*Curcuma reclinata*). *s.*

کرچورك कचूरक *karchūrak*, m. zedoary (*Curcuma zerumbet*). *s.* [ladle. *h.*

کرچها कछा *karchhā*, m. a large spoon, a

کرچهال कछाल *karchhāl* or कुछाल *kurchhāl*, f. a bound, spring, jump. *h.*

کرچهل कछुल *karchhul*, f. an iron spoon; a sword made of soft iron. *h.*

کرچهني कछनी *karchhanī*, f. an iron skimmer. *h.*

کرچهي कछी *karchhī*, f. a spoon; a skein (a ringlet). *h.*

کرچهيتر कुरुक्षेत्र *kuru-chhetra*, m. the country near Dihli, the scene of the great battle fought between the *Kauravas* and *Pāndavas*. *s.*

کرخت *karakht*, austere, rigid, insensible, of no feeling. *p.*

کرختگي *karakhtagī*, } f. dryness, austerity. *p.*
کرختي *karakhtī*, }

کرد कर्द *kard*, m. mud, mire, clay. *s.*

کردا करदा *kardā*, m. exchange, balance made to make up a deficiency in coin, or the difference between the price of new things and old given in exchange. *h.*

کردار *kirdār* or *kardār*, m. action, labour, deed, art, business, manner, conduct. *p.* [ize. *h.*

کردکهلانا करदिखलाना *kar-dikhlānā*, a. to real-

کردگار *kirdgār* or *kirdigār*, m. God the creator, Providence. *p.*

کردم कर्दम *kardam*, m. mud, mire, clay. *s.*

کردن कर्दन *kardan*, m. grumbling of the bowels, borborygmi. *s.* [form. *p.*

کردن *kardan* (r. *kun*), to do, to act, to per-

کردنت कृदन्त *kṛidant*, m. derivative from a verb; name of a treatise on syntax. *s.*

کردني *kardanī*, fit to be done, practicable, feasible. *p.*

کردورا *kardorā*, a string tied round the waist, to which a *langoṭī* is fastened; a kind of chain of gold or silver worn round the waist by men. *d.*

کردهـ क्रुध *krudha*, f. anger, passion. *kruddha*, angry. *s.*

کرده *karda*, done, accomplished; m. a deed, action, fact; in comp. it means one who has done, as *kār-karda*, one who has done business; experienced. *p.*

کردهمري करधमरी *kardhamrī*, } f. a girdle,
کردهني करधनी *kardhanī*, } zone, cordon. *s.*

کرڑا कड़ा *karṛā*, stiff, hard, harsh. *s.*

کرس कुरस *ku-ras*, bad-juiced, of bad essence; m. bad taste; spirituous or vinous liquors. *s.*

کرسان کا پتي *kursān kā paṭṭī* (explained by *kamar-sār* or *kamar-sāl*, q. v.). *d.*

کرست कुरसत *kursat*, m. a kind of coarse sugar. *h.*

کرستا कृसता *kṛisatā*, f. (for *krishatā*), smallness, thinness, leanness. *s.*

کرسف *kursuf*, } m. cotton, &c. put into an
کرسوف *kursūf*, } inkstand; a cloth used by menstruous women; a pessary. *a.*

کرسي *kursī*, f. a chair, a stool, a seat; a throne; the eighth heaven, the throne of God; the name of a place within about fourteen miles of Lakhnau, the inhabitants of which are said to be foolish or mad. *kursī kā hai*, he is from *kursī*, *i. e.* he is mad or foolish (this is precisely what the ancient Greeks used to say with regard to the Thracian Abdera and its citizens). *kursī-nāma*, a genealogical tree. *kursī-nishīn*, established in office, enthroned. *a.*

کرسي करसी *karsī*, f. small lumps of cow-dung dried for fuel. *s.*

کرش कृषि *kṛishi*, f. husbandry, agriculture. *s.*

کرش कृश *kṛish*, small, thin, minute. *s.*

کرشان कृषाण *kṛishān*, m. a husbandman, a ploughman. *s.* [a slender shape. *s.*

کرشانگي कृशाङ्गी *kṛishāngī*, f. a woman with

کرشپهل कर्षफल *karsh-phal*, m. beleric myrobalan (*Terminalia belerica*). *s.*

کرشتا कृशता *kṛishatā*, f. slenderness, thinness. *s.*

کرشك कर्षक *karshak* or कृषक *kṛishak*, m. a cultivator of the soil. *s.*

کرشمه *kirishma*, m. ogling, an amorous look or gesture, blandishment, a wink, a glance. *p.*

کرشن कृष्ण *kṛishṇ* or *kṛishṇa*, black; dark blue; m. name of a Hindū incarnation (v. *kishan*). *kṛishṇ-pachh* or *-paksh*, m. the dark half of the lunar month, darkness. *kṛishna-phal*, m. a fruit, the *Corinda*. *kṛishna-tā*, f. blackness. *kṛishna-tāmar*, m. a kind of sandal wood of a dusky copper hue. *kṛishna-jaṭā*, f. the Indian spikenard. *kṛishna-jīrak*, m. *Calonji*, a plant with a small black seed (*Nigella indica*). *kṛishna-charan*, m. name of a plant (*Poinciana pulcherrima*). *kṛishna-shār* or *-sārang*, m. the black antelope. *kṛishna-lavan*, m. a factitious salt, a muriate of soda. *kṛishna-loh*, m. the loadstone. *s.*

کرشن कर्षण *karshan*, m. ploughing, tilling; drawing attracting. *s.* [*Krishṇa*. *s.*

کرشناشرت कृष्णाश्रित *kṛishnāshrit*, devoted to

کرشن‌ندي कृष्णानदी *krishnā-nadī*, f. name of a river, possibly the Kistna in Deccan. *s.*

کرشناواس कृष्णावास *krishnāvās*, m. the holy fig-tree. *s.*

کرشناوتار कृष्णावतार *krishnāvatār*, m. the incarnation of the god *Vishnu* in the form of *Krishna*. *s.*

کرشني कर्षिणी *karshinī*, f. a medicinal sort of moon-plant; the bit of a bridle. *s.*

کرشوتھ करशोथ *kar-shoth*, m. œdematous swelling of the hands. *s.*

کرک कर्क *kark*, m. a crab; the sign Cancer. *s.*

کرکا कर्का *karkā*, m. a pæan, a war-song. *h.*

کرکانا करकाना *karkānā*, a. to strain, to sprain, to break. *h.*

کرکٹ कुरकुट *kurkuṭ*, f. sweepings, rubbish. *h.*

کرکٹ कर्कट *karkaṭ*, m. a crab; the sign Cancer; a kind of bird (the Numidian crane). *s.*

کرکٹي किरकिटी *kirkiṭī*, f. a mote, or particle of dust, fallen into the eye. *h.*

کرکچ करकच *karkach*, m. a kind of salt, sea salt made by evaporation. *h.*

کرکر *karkar*, (properly the past conj. part. of *karnā*, "to do," and signifying "having done.") It is much employed in the Dakhanī dialect in the sense of "as, that, because;" and also "named or called;" and sometimes as a mere conjunctive expletive, having no particular meaning. With the infinitive of a verb it will give the sense of "intentionally," the verb being afterwards repeated in its proper mood or tense: for example, *main ise phoṛnā-karkar nain phoṛā*, "I did not break this intentionally; so, *main us kutte ko chhoṛnā-karkar chhoṛ-diyā*, "I purposely did let that dog loose."—(Binning).

کرکرا करकरा *karkarā*, m. bad coin; name of a bird (Numidian crane). *kirkirā*, gritty, sandy. *s.*

کرکرانا किरकिराना *kirkirānā*, n. to be gritty, to grate. *h.* [f. cracking. *h.*

کرکراهٹ करकराहट *kirkirāhaṭ* or *karkarāhaṭ*,

کرکري कुरकुरी *kurkurī*, f. belly fretting, gripes in a horse. *h.*

کرکره *karkara*, m. laughing immoderately. *a.*

کرکس करकस *karkas*, piercing, harsh, obdurate, violent, sharp. *s.*

کرکسا करकसा *karkasā*, f. a termagant, a scold. *s.*

کرکش कर्कश *karkash*, violent, hard, harsh, unkind, unfeeling, miserly. *s.* [*tra*).

کرکشيتر कुरुक्षेत्र *kuru-kshetra* (v. *kuru-chhe-*

کرکناتھ करकनाथ *karak-nāth*, a kind of fowl, the bones of which are said to be black. *h.*

کرکو *kar-ko* (for *kar-kar*), having done, or made (conj. part. of *karnā*). *d.* [&c. *h.*

کرکھ करखा *karkhā*, m. (v. *kaṛkhā*) war-song,

کرکيتر कर्केतर *karketar*, m. a kind of gem

کرگ *karg*, m. a rhinoceros. *p.*

کرگدا करगदा *kargadā*, m. a string worn round the waist. *h.*

کرگدن *kargadan*, m. a rhinoceros. *p.*

کرگس *kargas*, m. a vulture, a kind of arrow. *p.*

کرگه *kargah*, m. a weaver's shop; the hole in the ground in which his feet play. *p.*

کرگهن करगहन *kargahan*, m. protection. *s.*

کرل करिल *karil*, m. a sprout, a shoot. *h.*

کرل कुरुल *kurul*, m. a curl or lock of hair, especially on the forehead. *s.*

کرلگوا करलगूआ *karlagū,ā*, uxorious. *s.*

کرلانا करलाना *kar-lānā*, a. to effect, to settle; (cor. of *killānā* or *chillānā*) to shriek. *h.*

کرم कूर्म *kurm* or *kurma*, m. tortoise, a turtle; the name of the second Hindū incarnation. *s.*

کرم क्रम *kram*, m. order, method, progress. *s.*

کرم कर्म *karm*, *karam*, or *karma*, m. business, action, proceeding; fortune, fate, destiny. *karam-bhog*, m. fulfilling of destiny; suffering the consequences of actions, whether good or bad; accusative case; Hindū worship, devotion; name of a bird. *karm-chyut*, dismissed from office. *karm-dushṭ*, immoral, disreputable. *karm-siddhi*, f. success, accomplishment. *karm-shuddh*, m. approved occupation. *karm-shūr* or *karm-shīl*, assiduous, laborious, persevering. *karm-kār*, a worker; a blacksmith. *karm-kārak*, a worker; the accusative case. *karm-kāṇḍ*, m. the body of religious ceremonies commanded by Hindū law or custom. *karm-vipāk*, m. the consequences of actions. *karm-yug*, m. the *kali* or present age of the world. *s.*

کرم कृमि *kṛimi* or क्रमि *krami*, m. a worm, an insect; lac, the red dye. *kṛimi-dantak*, m. tooth-ache from decay. *kṛimi-ghna*, vermifuge; m. a shrub, commonly called Bairang (*Ericybe paniculata*). *kṛimi-har*, vermifuge. *s.* [silkworm. *p.*

کرم *kirm*, m. a worm. *kirmi pīla*, m. the

کرم *karam* or *kurm*, m. liberality, kindness, graciousness, benignity, excellence. *a.*

کرم *karam* or *karam kī bhājī*, a cabbage (v. *karamb*). *p.*

کرمادهرمي कर्माधर्मी *karmā-dharmī*, devout, virtuous; fortunate; accidental. *s.*

کرماني گندم *kirmānī gandum*, m. vermicelli (*Gilch.*). *p.*

کرمب *karamb*, m. a cabbage, cauliflower. *p.*

کرمج कृमिज *kṛimij*, m. agallochum. *kṛimijā*, f. lac, a red dye. *s.*

کرمچاري करमचारी *karamchārī*, m. an inferior officer to collect the revenue from a certain division of a village; the village accountant. *s.*

کرمشٹھ कर्मिष्ठ *karmishṭha*, active, diligent. *s.*

كرمك *kirmak*, m. the fire-fly; (dim. of *kirm*) a small fly. *p.*

كرمكارك कर्मकारक *karm-kārak*, m. the accusative case. *s.*

كرم كلا *karam-kallā*, m. a cabbage, a cauliflower. *p.*

كرمل कृमिल *krimil*, having worms, wormy. *krimilā*, f. a fruitful woman. *s.*

كرمي कृमी *krimī*, affected with worms. *s.*

كرمي क्रिमी *krimī*, m. worm, insect; lac. *s.*

كرمي कर्मी *karmī*, relating to work, doing works; fortunate. *s.*

كرمي किर्मी *kirmī*, f. the palās tree. *s.*

كرمي कुर्मी *kurmī*, m. a tribe of husbandmen; also *kumbī*. *h.*

كرميندريه कर्मेन्द्रिय *karmendriya*, m. an organ of action: five are reckoned, hand, foot, larynx, organ of generation, and anus. *s.*

كرميوه करमेवा *karmewa*, m. name of a vegetable. *h.*

كرن करन *karaṇ*, m. making, doing; cause, instrument; accomplishing an action; an astrological division of time, of which there are eleven, seven moveable and four fixed, and two of them are equal to a lunar day; the hypothenuse of a triangle; the diameter or diagonal of a square, parallelogram, &c., a secant. *s.*

كرن किरण *kiraṇ*, f. the sunbeams, the rays of the sun. *kiran-may*, radiant, bright. *s.*

كرن कर्ण *karṇ* or *karṇa*, m. the ear; helm of a ship or boat. *karṇ-pāk*, m. inflammation of the outer ear. *karṇ-pālī*, f. a garland or string of jewels pendent from the ear. *karṇ-pratināh*, m. a disease of the ear, suppression of the excretion of wax. *karn-phūl* or *karan-phūl*, m. a kind of earring. *karṇ-jalūkā* or *karṇ-kīṭī*, f. a small centipede (*Julus cornifex*). *karn-darpan*, m. an earring. *karn-srāv*, m. discharge of ichorous matter through the ear. *karṇ-shūl*, m. earache. *karṇ-gūth*, m. ear-wax. *karn-latikā*, f. the lobe of the ear. *karṇ-madgur*, m. a sort of sheat-fish (*Silurus unitus*). *karṇ-mukuṭ*, m. an earring. *karṇ-mal*, m. ear-wax. *karṇ-mūl*, a parotis, or swelling near the ear. *s.*

كرن करन *karan*, m. lace cut into small pieces and put on a cap. *s.*

كرنا करना *karnā*, a. to do, to make, to perform, to effect, to act, to avail, to set, thrust, use, coire. *s.*

كرنا करना *karnā*, m. name of a kind of citron (*Citrus*). *h.*

كرنا करुणा *karuṇā*, f. tenderness, compassion, mercy. *karuṇā-nidhān*, the asylum or abode of mercy (an epithet of God). *karuṇātmak* or *karuṇā-may*, compassionate, tender. *s.*

كرنا *karnā*, a kind of trumpet. *p.*

كرنات कर्णाट *karnāṭ*, } the country called
كرناتك कर्णाटक *karnāṭak*, } the Carnatic, in the south of India: the name was anciently applied to the central districts of the Peninsula, including Mysore. *s.*

كرناتي कर्णाटी *karnāṭī*, f. name of a rāginī. *s.*

كرنالنكار कर्णालङ्कार *karnālankār*, m. an earring. *s.*

كرنب *haramb*, cabbage, cauliflower. *p.*

كرنبا *karambā*, a dish prepared of cabbage. *p.*

كرنبيدهن कर्णवेधन *karṇa-bedhan* or *-vedhan*, m. the act of piercing or boring the ears. *karṇa-vedhanī*, f. an instrument for piercing the ear. *s.*

كرنپر कर्णपुर *karn-pur*, m. the capital of Karna, the ancient Bhaugalpore. *s.*

كرن پهل कर्णफल *karn-phal*, m. a kind of fish (*Ophiocephalus kurrawey*). *s.*

كرنج करञ्ज *karanj*, m. a plant (*Galedupa arborea*). *s.*

كرنجا *karanjā*, m. name of a tree (*Dalbergia arborea*). *d.*

كرندن क्रन्दन *krandan*, m. weeping, lamenting. *s.*

كرن دهار कर्णधार *karan-dhār* or *karn-dhār*, m. a supercargo, pilot, or helmsman. *s.*

كرنڈ कुरण्ड *kuranḍ*, m. corundum stone (*Adamantinus corundum*). *h.*

كرنگ कुरङ्ग *kurang*, m. a species of deer. *s.*

كرنم *karnam*, m. a village accountant (v. *kamchārī*). *d.*

كرنهار करनहार *karanhār*, doer, maker. *s.*

كرني कर्णिनी *karninī*, f. a disease of the uterus, prolapsus or polypus uteri. *s.*

كرني करणी *karnī*, f. action, business; a trowel; (in arith.) a surd or irrational quantity; m. one of the seven mountains which divide the universe. *s.*

كرني والا करनेवाला *karne-wālā*, m. maker, doer. *s.*

كرو किरौ *kirau*, m. a hollow tooth; endive; adj. broken, rugged, tattered. *h.*

كرو *kurū* (v. كر *kuru*), name of an ancient king of Delhi. *s.*

كروا करुआ *karū,ā*, m. an earthen pipkin. a pot with a spout. *karū,ā chauth*, the name of a Hindū holy day, celebrated in the month of *Kārtik*. *s.*

كروا *karwā* (for *karwā*, q. v.), bitter, &c. *d.*

كروارا करवारा *karwārā*, } m. a paddle, a rud-
كروال करवाल *karwāl*, } der. *h.*

كرواره *karwāra*, the bucket for raising water from a well. *h.*

كروان किरवान *kirwān*, f. a sword. *s.*

كروانا करवाना *karwānā*, to cause to make, &c. *s.*

كروانسي *karwānsī*, the twentieth part of a *biswānsī*, q. v. *h.*

كروانك *karwānak*, m. name of a bird, commonly called the stone curlew, or bastard floriken. *s.*

کروبیان karrūbiyān, } a rank of angels, the
کروبین karūbīn, } cherubim. *a.*

کروپ कुरूप *ku-rūp*, deformed, misshapen; m. (or *kurūp-tā*, f.) ugliness. *ku-rūpi*, ill-shaped, ugly. *s.*

کروت करोत *karot*, m. a saw. *s.*

کروت किरवत *kirwat*, f. action, deed, doing. *s.*

کروٹ करवट *karwaṭ*, f. sideways, sleeping on the side. *karwaṭ lenā*, to turn (in bed). *karwaṭ-k.*, to turn over. *s.*

کرودھ क्रोध *krodh*, m. anger, passion, resentment. *krodh-may*, angry, passionate. *krodh-varjit*, free from anger, mild. *krodh-vas*, passionate, violent. *s.*

کرودھن क्रोधन *krodhan*, } angry, passionate, wrathful; also *krodhin*. *krodhanā*, f. a passionate woman, a vixen. *s.*
کرودھوان क्रोधवान *krodhwān*,
کرودھي क्रोधी *krodhī*,

کرور क्रूर *krūr*, cruel, pitiless, hard-hearted, savage, terrible. *krūratā*, f. cruelty. *krūr-drish*, evil-eyed, mischievous. *krūr-karmā*, fierce, cruel. *krūr-koshṭh*, torpid or costive bowels. *s.*

کرور करोर *karor*, } name of an aggregate number amounting to one hundred *lāks*, or ten millions, vulgarly called *crore*. *karor-pati*, possessor of a *karor* (of *rupīs*). *karor khukh*, m. a liar. *s.*
کروڑ करोड़ *karoṛ*,

کروڑا करोड़ा *karoṛā*, } m. a tax-gatherer, an inspector, an overseer. *h.*
کروڑي करोड़ी *karoṛī*,

کروش क्रोश *krosh*, m. a measure of distance, a *kos*, q. v.

کروك कुरुवक *kuruvak*, m. the crimson amaranth; a purple species of Barleria: also a yellow kind. *s.*

کرول कुरुविल *kuru-vill*, } m. a ruby. *s.*
کرولو कुरुविल्व *kuru-vilv*,

کرولنا *kirolnā* or *kirūlnā*, a. to scrape. *d.*

کرونچ क्रौंच *kraunch*, m. one of the Dwipas or divisions of the world. *s.*

کروند कुरुविन्द *kuru-vind*, m. a ruby. *s.*

کروندا करौंदा *karaūndā* or *karondā*, m. name of a fruit, the Corinda (*Carissa carandas*). *s.*

کروني करोनी *karonī*, f. milk that sticks to the bottom of a pot after boiling. *h.*

کروه *karoh*, m. a *kos*, a measure of distance nearly equal to two miles, but varying in every part of the country. *p.*

کرویر करवीर *karavīr* or *karwīr*, m. the name of a flower (*Oleander* or *Nerium odorum*). *s.*

کره *karh* and *kurh*, f. aversion, abomination, detestation, abhorrence; trouble, molestation. *a.*

کره कुरह *kurh* or *kurah*, a circular inclosure. *h.*

کره *kurra*, m. a colt, a young camel. *karra*, a time or turn, as *yak-karra*, once; *do-karra*, twice, &c. *p. a.*

کره *kura*, m. a globe, any thing spherical. *kura,i ātash*, the region of fire; *kura,i āb*, of water. *kura,i arẓ*, the terrestrial globe. *kura,i bād*, region of wind. *kura,i khāk*, the globe of earth. *a. p.*

کرهاً *karhan* or *kurhan*, with difficulty, reluctantly, unwillingly. *a.*

کرها करहा *karhā*, } f. the loins. *h.*
کرهانه करहानः *karhāna*,

کري क्रय *kray*, m. buying, purchase. *kray-bikray*, m. buying and selling, traffic. *s.*

کري कुर्री *kurrī*, f. gristle, cartilage. *h.*

کرئي *kura,ī*, spherical, globular. *a.*

کریا क्रिया *kriyā*, f. deed, an act, a religious act, obsequies; a verb; (also *kiriyā*) an oath. *s.*

کریات *kiryāt*, f. a plant (*Justicia paniculata*) used in medicine, &c., forming the basis of the well-known tincture called the *Drogue amere*. *d.*

کریاکرم क्रियाकर्म *kriyā-karm*, m. performance of obsequies. *s.*

کریال कुर्याल *kuryāl*, f. the state of a bird sitting at ease and in security, trimming its wings with its beak: hence, ease, security, hope, confidence of success. *kuryāl men ghulelā lagnā*, to be disappointed, or fall into misfortune, in the moment of security, or when sure of success. *h.*

کریپاك *karīpāk*, name of a plant, the leaves of which are used in cookery. *h.*

کریت क्रीत *krīt*, bought, purchased. *s.*

کریت कुरीति *ku-rīti* or *ku-rīt*, m. misconduct, bad manners. *s.*

کریت *kret*, f. a furrow. *d.*

کریت करैत *karait*, } m. a snake (of a very venomous kind). *h.*
کریتا करैता *karaitā*,

کریتا क्रीता *krītā*, } m. a son bought from his parents and adopted. *s.*
کریتك क्रीतक *krītak*,

کریٹ किरीट *kirīṭ*, m. a crest, a diadem. *s.*

کریر करीर *karīr*, m. the shoot of a bamboo; a thorny plant growing in deserts and fed upon by camels (*Capparis aphylla*). *s.*

کریرا करेरा *karerā*, hard, stiff, vehement. *s.*

کریڑا क्रीड़ा *krīṛā*, f. play, game, sport, pastime. *krīṛā-ratn*, m. copulation. *krīṛā-wat*, sportive. *s.*

کریز *kurīz*, the moulting of birds. *kurīz-k.*, to moult. *p.*

کریکر करेकर *karekar*, abreast, even with. *h.*

کریل करील *karīl*, m. the name of a plant (*Capparis*). *s.*

كريلا करेला *karelā*, m. the name of a vegetable (*Momordica charantia*); (Dakh.) a kind of firework. *s.*

كريلنا कुरेलना *kurelnā*, a. to poke, to thrust. *h.*

كريم *karīm*, bountiful, magnificent, benevolent, gracious, liberal. *karīmu-n-nafs*, generous of disposition. *a.*

كريما *karīmā* (voc. poetic.), O gracious (God). *karīmaṉ*, adv. kindly, graciously. *a. p.*

كريمج क्रीमिज *krīmij*, m. the *aguru*, or aloe wood. *s.*

كريمي *karīmī*, f. grace, bounty, &c. *a. p.*

كريه *karīh*, detestable, abominable, filthy, dirty. *karīh-manzar*, ugly, of detestable aspect. *karīhu-ṣ-ṣaut*, possessed of an execrable voice. *a.*

كريندريه क्रियेन्द्रिय *kriyendriya*, m. an organ of action, v. *karmendriya*. *s.*

كڑ कड़ *kaṛ*, f. the seed of safflower (*Carthamus tinctorius*. *h.*

كڑ किड़ *kiṛ*, m. a worm. *kiṛ-khāyā*, worm-eaten; marked with small-pox, pitted, spotted. *h.*

كڑا कड़ा *kaṛā*, hard, stiff; arch, sly, knowing, penetrating, harsh, sharp, cruel, obdurate; m. a ring worn on the wrists, ankles, &c., a ringlet, bracelet; the handle of a door, or any thing in form of a ring. *s.*

كڑاپا *kuṛāpā*, m. anguish, grief, pain. *d.*

كڑاپن *kaṛāpan*, hardness, stiffness. *d.*

كڑاڑا कड़ाड़ा *kaṛāṛā*, m. the perpendicular bank of a river, &c, a precipice, declivity. *h.*

كڑاري *kuṛārī*, f. an axe, a bill-hook. *d.*

كڑاقا *kaṛāḳā* (v. *kaṛākā*), a crash, &c. *d.*

كڑاكا कड़ाका *kaṛākā*, m. the crash made by breaking any thing; a rigid fast (in which nothing of food or drink has entered the mouth). *h.*

كڑاكڑ कड़ाकड़ *kaṛākaṛ*, m. successive crashes. *h.*

كڑاوا *kaṛāwā*, care, charge, trust. *d.*

كڑاه कड़ाह *kaṛāh*, m. a shallow iron boiler (in which sugar, &c. is boiled). *s.*

كڑاهي कड़ाही *kaṛāhī*, f. a small boiler, a frying pan. *s.*

كڑته *kuṛta*, m. (for *kurta*) a coat, a jacket. *d.*

كڑتي *kuṛtī*, a trough or vessel for animals to drink out of. *d.*

كڑربون कड़रबून *kaṛarbūn*, m. name of a plant. *h.*

كڑك कड़क *kaṛak*, f. a crash, a crack; thunder: agility. *kaṛak dauṛnā*, to gallop, to go at full speed (a horse). *kuṛuk*, f. clucking (a hen). *h.*

كڑكا कड़का *kaṛkā*, m. pæan, song of triumph. *h.*

كڑكا *karkā*, m. bank of a river, shore, precipice, steep bank. *d.*

كڑكڑا कड़कड़ा *kaṛkaṛā*, hard, stiff, strong. *s.*

كڑكڑانا कुड़कुड़ाना *kuṛkuṛānā*, to cluck (a laying hen); to speak angrily, to murmur. *kiṛkirānā*, to gnash the teeth from rage. *kaṛkaṛānā*, to give such a sound as oil or butter when boiling. *h.*

كڑكنا कड़कना *kaṛaknā*, n. to crack, to crackle; to thunder. *kuṛaknā* (same as *kuṛkuṛānā*, q. v) *h.*

كڑكها कड़खा *kaṛkhā*, m. commemoration, mention; encouraging the soldiers in time of battle, by pointing out the good effects of steadiness and valour, extolling the actions of former heroes, &c.; war-song. *h.*

كڑكهيت कड़खैत *kaṛkhait*, m. a kind of bard, an officer in Indian armies whose business it is to encourage the soldiers by the exhortations called *kaṛkhā*; a species of Indian Tyrtæus. *h.*

كڑما कुड़मा *kuṛmā*, m. tribe, caste, family, race. *s.*

كڑمچودي कुड़ुमचोदी *kuṛum-chodī*, f. incest. *s.*

كڑنا कड़ना *kaṛnā*, a. to perforate, to pierce. *h.*

كڑنا *kuṛnā* (v. *kuṛhnā*), to grieve, &c. *d.*

كڑوا कड़वा *kaṛwā*, bitter; strong, virulent; hard-hearted; brave. *kaṛwā tel*, oil made from sesamum-seed, bitter oil. *kaṛwā-k.*, to give or expend unwillingly. *kaṛwā-honā*, to be enraged. *kaṛwe kasele din*, hard and cruel times. *s.*

كڑواهٹ कड़वाहट *kaṛwāhaṭ*, f. pungency, bitterness; (in Dakh.) are used the forms *kaṛwāt*, *kaṛwās*, and *kaṛwāgī*, bitterness, &c. *s.*

كڑوڑ कड़ोड़ *kaṛoṛ* (v. *karoṛ*), ten millions; also *karor*. *s.*

كڑوڑا *kaṛoṛā* (v. *karoṛā*), a tax-gatherer, &c. *s.*

كڑوي कड़वी *kaṛwī*, f. stubble. *h.*

كڑها किड़हा *kiṛhā*, worm-eaten; weevil-eaten. *s.*

كڑهاپا *kuṛhāpā* (also *kuṛhāpan*), vexation, grief. *d.*

كڑهانا कुढ़ाना *kuṛhānā*, a. to vex, to afflict, to grieve, to trouble, to anger. *s.*

كڑهك कुढ़क *kuṛhak*, } f. grief, sorrow, lamentation. *s.*
كڑهن कुढ़न *kuṛhan*, }

كڑهنا कुढ़ना *kuṛhnā*, n. to grieve, to mourn, to lament, to pine. *s.*

كڑهنا कढ़ना *kaṛhnā*, n. to be extracted, drawn, pulled out; to escape, rise, slip, issue, spring; to be drawn or painted. *h.*

كڑهوا कढ़ुआ *kaṛhū,ā*, m. a loan, a debt; a premium on a loan; a deduction from the sum lent. *h.*

كڑهي कढ़ी *kaṛhī*, f. a dish consisting of the meal of pulse (*Chanā* or *Cicer arietinum*), dressed with sour milk. *h.*

كڑي कड़ी *kaṛī*, f. a rafter, a beam, a fetter, a ring, a staple. *h.*

كز *kaz* (for *ki-az*), since from, as from. *p.*

كزاك *kazāk* (for *ḳazzāḳ*, q. v.) a robber, &c. *a*

كزاكي *kazākī*, f. highway robbery. *d.*

كزك *kazak* (for *kazhak*), an iron kook. *p.d.*

كژ *kazh*, crooked (same as *kuj*, q. v.). *p.*

كژدم *kazh-dum*, m. a scorpion, a dragon; (lit. of a crooked tail). *p.*

كژك *kazhak*, kind of hook or crook, an iron hook with which they regulate the motions of an elephant. *p.*

كس किस *kis*, inter. pron. inflect. whom? which? what? *kis-ṭaraḥ*, what manner? how? *kis-ḳadar*, how much? to what degree or extent? *kis-kis*, which (used interrogatively, and expressive of much, many, various). *kis-liye*, why? wherefore? *s.*

كس कस *kas*, m. strength, power; assay; the decoction of a colouring substance. *s.*

كس *kas*, m. a man, a person, one, any one. *kas o kob*, family, dependants (Gilc.). *kas o nākas*, everybody, noble and plebeian, gentle and simple. *p.*

كس *kus*, m. (Gr. κύσος) *vulva*. *kus marānā*, to play the strumpet. *p.*

كسا कसा *kasā*, tight, straitened. *h.*

كساد *kasād*, not current, not in demand or use, flat sale or bad market, penury, indigence. *a.*

كسار कसार *kasār*, m. a kind of sweetmeat. *h.*

كسار *kasār*, a brazier, maker of brass pots and utensils. *d.*

كساري किसारी *kisārī*, f. a kind of pulse (*Lathyrus sativus*). *h.*

كسافت *kasāfat*, f. sediment; obscuration, an eclipse. *a.*

كسالا *kasālā*, astringent, bitter. *d.*

كسالا *kasālā* (for *kasālā̤*), sick, indisposed. *a.*

كساله *kasāla*, m. heaviness, slowness; sickness, grief, affliction, distress. *a.*

كسان किसान *kisān*, m. a husbandman, ploughman, peasant, farmer. *kasān* (pl. of *kas*), persons, &c. *s.p.*

كسانا कसाना *kasānā*, a. to cause to try, prove, or assay; to cause to tighten; n. to be spoiled (curds, &c.) by standing in a metal vessel. *s.*

كساو कसाव *kasa,o*, m. astringency. *h.*

كساوا *kasāwā*, a handkerchief tied round the head on going to bed. *d.*

كساوٹ कसावट *kasāwaṭ*, } f. proving, tightening, astringency;
كساهٹ कसाहट *kasāhaṭ*, } an astringent. *h.*

كسايا कसाया *kasāyā*, ready, tied up. *h.*

كساي कसाई *kasā,ī*, m. a butcher; adj. cruel, hard-hearted (for *ḳaṣā,ī*, q.v.). *a. h.*

كسب *kasb* or *kasab*, m. trade, profession, employment; gain, acquisition (by labour). *a.*

كسبت *kisbat*, f. the case (or bag) barbers, surgeons, &c. keep their tools in; a piece of leather worn by a *bhishtī* or water-man on his left hip, on which he rests the bag containing water. *kisbat-nāma*, m. a book containing the histories of barbers, surgeons, &c., and directions for their practice. The *bhishtīs* have also such a book. *a. p.*

كسبني *kasbinnī*, } f. a kept mistress, a strumpet, a harlot. *d.*
كسبين *kasbīn*, }

كسبهرا *kas-bharā*, m. a worker in bell-metal. *h.*

كسبي *kasbī*, m. an artisan, a craftsman; f. a prostitute, an artiste. *a.*

كستوان *kastuwān*, a kind of horse-cloth. *p.*

كستورا कस्तूरा *kastūrā*, f. an oyster. *h.*

كستوري कस्तूरी *kastūrī*, f. musk (the animal substance so called); also a kind of plant. *s.*

كسٹ *kasṭ* (v. *kashṭ*), m. want, penury, &c. *s.*

كسر *kasar* or *kasr*, m. loss, affliction, breach; the short vowel *i*; rout, putting to flight. *kasri shān*, loss of honour. *a.*

كسرا *kisrā*, Chosroes (v. كسرىٰ). *a. p.*

كسرات *kasarāt* (pl. of كسره), losses, &c. *a.*

كسرات कुसरात *kusarāt*, f. health, welfare. *s.*

كسره *kasra* or *kasrat* (v. *kasar*), affliction, flight or rout (of an enemy); the short vowel *i*. *a.*

كسرىٰ *kasrā̤*, the title of the king of Persia (hence the Greek forms Cyrus, Chosroes); an emperor. *kisrā̤* or *kisrī* seems to have the same signification, but generally applied to *Naushīrwān* the Just, who lived in the time of Justinian. *p.*

كسسته *kusista*, broken, abrupt. *kusistagī*, breach, interruption. *p.*

كسطرح *kis-ṭaraḥ*, how? in what manner? *h.a.*

كسطرف *kis-ṭaraf*, whither? in what direction? *h. a.*

كسك कसक *kasak*, f. pain, stitch, affliction. *h.*

كسكت कसकुट *kaskut*, m. bell-metal. *s.*

كسكسا कसकसा *kaskasā*, gritty, sandy (bread). *h.*

كسكساي कसकसाए *kaskasā,e*, tied up, ready. *h.*

كسكنا कसकना *kasaknā*, n. to suffer pain, to be painful. *h.*

كسگر *kasgar*, m. a plasterer; potter, *a. p.*

كسل कुसल *kusal* (for *kushal*), f. health and prosperity, safety; weal, happy. *s.*

كسل *kasal*, m. laxness, slowness, indolence; cowardice; sickness, relaxation; *non emittere in coitu*. *kasil*, cowardly, slothful. *a.*

كسلات *kusalāt* (v. *kusaltā*), health, &c. *s.*

كسلان *kaslān*, } lazy, languid, sick, relaxed, cowardly, slothful, impotent. *a. p.*
كسلمند *kasal-mand*, }
كسلناك *kasal-nāk*, }

كسلتا कुशलता *kusaltā*, f. health and prosperity, welfare in general. *s.*

كسم कुसुम *kusum*, m. a flower with which cloths are dyed red, bastard saffron, safflower (*Carthamus tinctorius*); the menstrual discharge; ophthalmia. *s.*

كسمانجن कुसुमाञ्जन *kusumānjan*, m. calx of brass, used as collyrium. *s.*

كسمراني *kus-marānī*, a strumpet, a harlot. *p.h.*

كسمسانا कसमसाना *kasmasānā*, to move, to shake. *h.*

كسن कसन *kasan*, m. rack, torment, torture. *h.*

كسنا कसना *kasnā*, a. to tighten, to tie; to assay, to try, to prove, examine; to fry in melted butter; m. a bundle, a wallet. *h.*

كسنبه कुसुम्भ *kusumbh* (v. *kusum*), a flower, &c. *s.*

كسنبها कुसुम्भा *kusumbhā*, m. the dye of safflower (*Carthamus tinctorius*); met. an infusion of bhang (*Cannabis sativa*) used for intoxication. *s.*

كسنبهي कुसुम्भी *kusumbhī*, cloths dyed with safflower. *s.*

كسند *kasand*, a species of bell-metal. *d.*

كسنگ कुसङ्ग *ku-sang*, m. bad company. *s.*

كسنئي किसनई *kisna,ī*, f. husbandry, agriculture. *s.*

كسو किसू *kisū* (inflec. of *ko,ī* or *kuchh*), any, some. *h.*

كسواسطي *kis-wāsṯe*, on what account? why? for what cause or reason? *h. a.*

كسوانا कसवाना *kaswānā*, a. (from *kasānā*) to cause to be tightened. *s.*

كسوپن कुस्वप्न *ku-swapna*, m. a bad dream, nightmare, unsound sleep. *s.*

كسوت *kiswat*, f. dress, appearance, robe, habit; met. figure, form, manner. *a.*

كسوٹي कसौटी *kasauṭī*, f. a touchstone, assay, proof. *s.*

كسور *kusūr*, m. (pl. of كسر) fractions (in arithmetic). *a.*

كسوف *kusūf*, m. an eclipse of the sun. *a.*

كسوندي कसौंदी *kasaundī*, f. a kind of pickle; name of a plant (*Cassia sophera*). *h.*

كسي किसे *kise*, whom? to whom? (dat. or acc. of *kaun*). *kisī* (inflec. of *ko,ī*), any, some. *s.*

كسي *kase*, some one, any one. *kase-ki*, that person who, whosoever. *p.* [terest. *s.*

كسيد कुसीद *ku-sīd*, m. usury, loan with interest. *s.*

كسيدا कुसीदा *kusīdā*, m. a money-lender (also *kusīdik*). *s.*

كسيرا कसेरा *kaserā*, m. a brazier or pewterer. *s.*

كسيرو कसेरु *kaserū*, m. a root so called (*Cyperus tuberosus, Willd.*). *s.*

كسيس कसीस *kasīs*, m. martial vitriol (*Sulphas ferri*). *h.*

كسيف *kasīf*, impure; thick, dreary, unpleasant. *kasīfu-l-auḳāt*, miserable, having dreary times of it. *a.* [strong, vigorous. *s.*

كسيلا कसेला *kaselā*, astringent. कसीला *kasīlā*,

كش *kash*, (in comp.) drawing, pulling, carrying, bearing, enduring, as *miḥnat-kash*, one who endureth affliction. *p.*

كش *kush*, (in comp.) destroying, subduing, killing, as *dev-kush*, the giant-killer. *p.*

كش कष *kash*, m. the touchstone; assay; the decoction of a colouring substance. *s.*

كش कुश *kush* or *kusha*, m. the name of a grass deemed highly sacred among the Hindūs (*Poa cynosuroides*). *s.*

كشا *kushā*, (in comp.) opening, displaying, expanding, solving, loosening, conquering, as *dil-kushā*, expanding the heart; *kishwar-kushā*, conquering kingdoms or dominions. *p.*

كشاد *kushād*, opening, loosening or untying, expansion; cheerfulness. *p.*

كشادگي *kushādagī*, f. an aperture, expansion, opening of heart, joy, latitude. *p.*

كشاده *kushāda*, opened, uncovered, expanded, loosened; wide, ample, extensive, displayed, revealed, free; cheerful, frank. *kushāda-peshānī*, of an open countenance, gay, cheerful. *kushāda-dil*, open-hearted, generous. *kushāda-rū,e*, of an open countenance, gay, cheerful. *kushāda-rau*, epithet of a horse that walks wide or straddles behind. *p.*

كشار क्षार *kshār*, m. a salt, black salt; ashes; borax, borate of soda, alkali; a cautery. *kshār-ras*, m. a salt or alkaline flavour. *kshār-karm*, m. applying caustic alkali to proud flesh, &c. *kshār-mṛittikā*, f. saline soil, impure sulphate of soda. *kshār-vṛiksh*, m. any tree yielding potash, as the plantain, &c. *s.*

كشاسن कुशासन *kushāsan*, m. a mat made of the *kusha* grass. *s.*

كشاف *kashshāf*, m. a discoverer, solver, explainer; adj. very clear or explicit. *a.*

كشاكش *kashā-kash* (also *kashā-kashī*), f. attraction, allurement; contention, struggle, difficulty, distraction, perplexity, crowding, mutual pulling, penury, distress. *p.*

كشان *kashān*, drawing, bearing, enduring. *p.*

كشانت क्षान्त *kshānt*, patient, enduring. *kshānti*, f. patience, forbearance. *s.*

كشاوٹ कषावट *kashāwaṭ*, f. an astringent. *s.*

كشايش *kushāyish*, f. aperture, opening, clearness, serenity. *p.*

كشايه कषाय *kashāya*, m. astringency. *s.*

كشت *kusht*, killing, slaughter. *p.*

كشت *kisht*, f. check (a well-known term at chess); m. a sown field, growing crop. *p.*

كشت क्षिति *kshiti*, f. the earth; loss, destruction; the end of the world. *kshiti-pāl*, m. a king. *s.*

كشتري क्षत्री *kshatrī* (for *kshatriya*), a man of the second or military caste. *s.*

كشتزار *kisht-zār*, a sown field beginning to look green. *kisht-zār-i dīv*, the devil's cornfield, *i.e.* this present wicked world. *p.*

كشتكار *kisht-kār*, a peasant, husbandman. *p.*

كشتكاري *kisht-kārī*, f. husbandry, agriculture. *p.*

كشتگان *kushtagān*, the killed or slain, applied poetically to those desperately in love. *p.*

كشتن *kishtan*, (r. *kār*) to sow, to till, to cultivate. *p.*

كشتن *kushtan*, (r. *kush*), to slay, to kill; m. slaying, killing. *p.*

كشتني *kushtanī*, worthy of death. *p.*

كشت وكار *kisht-o-kār*, sowing, tillage. *p.*

كشته *kushta*, killed, slain; a preparation of mercury. *p.*

كشتي *kushtī*, f. wrestling. *kushtī-bāz* or *-gar*, or *-gīr*, a wrestler. *p.*

كشتي *kishtī*, f. a ship, vessel, bark, boat; a tray; a beggar's plate or pot. *p.*

كشتيبان *kishtī-bān*, m. the master of a vessel, familiarly called, the skipper; a pilot. *p.*

كشٹ कष्ट *kashṭ*, m. want, penury, affliction, vehemence, violence, acuteness (of pain), agony. *kashṭi*, f. test, trial; pain, trouble. *kashṭ-kar*, giving pain or trouble; (in Dakh.) *kusht* (for *kushṭh*), m. leprosy. *s.*

كشٹھ कुष्ठ *kushṭh*, m. leprosy; a plant (*Costus speciosus*). *kushṭh-nāshan*, m. white mustard; a sort of yam. *kushṭh-nāshinī*, f. a plant (*Psoralia corylifolia*). *s.*

كشٹھي कुष्ठी *kushṭhī*, leprous; a leper. *s.*

كشٹي कष्टी *kashṭī*, suffering a painful and tedious labour (a woman), afflicted. *s.*

كشدر क्षुद्र *kshudr*, small, little, mean, low, poor, avaricious. *kshudratā*, f. smallness, meanness. *kshudr-buddhi*, simple, silly. *kshudr-rog*, m. a minor disease. *s.*

كشدھا क्षुधा *kshudhā*, f. hunger. *kshudhārt* or *kshudhit*, hungry. *s.*

كشر क्षुर *kshur*, m. a razor; a horse's hoof. *s.*

كشرات *kusharāt*, f. (v. *kushal*) health, welfare, happiness. *s.*

كشري क्षुरी *kshurī*, f. a knife. *s.*

كشش *kashish*, f. attraction, allurement; difficulty, contention, dispute; a sweep or dash in writing, a stroke of the pen. *kushish*, killing, manslaughter, sacrifice. *p.*

كشف *kashaf*, m. a tortoise, the sign Cancer. *p.*

كشف *kashf*, m. an opening, a manifestation, revelation, declaration, solution, explanation. *a.*

كشفي *kashfī*, revealed, expounded. *a.*

كشك *kushk*, a palace, mansion. *kashak*, a line or stripe. *p.*

كشك *kashk*, barley broth; a kind of dish made of wheat, butter, and meat, all stewed together. *a. d.*

كشكچي باشي *kashakchī-bāshī*, m. a watchman, guard, porter. *t.*

كشكول *kashkūl* or *kashkol*, a beggar, a beggar's cup or wallet (v. *kachkol*). *p.*

كشل कुशल *kushal*, m.
كشلات कुशलात *kushalāt*, f.
كشلتا कुशलता *kushaltā*, f.
كشلچھم कुशलछेम *kushal-chhem*, f.
} health, happiness, welfare, prosperity, safety. *s.*

كشلا कुशला *kushalā*, happy, well, right. *s.*

كشلي कुशली *kushalī*, auspicious, happy. *s.*

كشم क्षम *ksham*, able, fit; m. fitness. *s.*

كشما क्षमा *kshamā*, f. patience, forbearance. *kshamā-wān* or *-jukt*, patient, enduring. *s.*

كشما क्ष्मा *kshmā*, f. the earth. *kshmā-bhṛit* or *-pati*, m. a king. *kshmā-tal*, m. the surface of the earth. *s.*

كشمانڈ कुष्माण्ड *kushmāṇḍ*, m. a pumpkin, a gourd; a drug; a certain rite performed as penance. *s.*

كشمش *kishmish*, f. raisins, a small kind of stoneless raisin, commonly called by Europeans the Sultana raisin. *p.*

كشمكش *kashmakash*, f. want, penury, distress. *p.*

كشمنا क्षमना *kshamnā*, a. to pardon, to forgive. *s.*

كشمير कश्मीर *kashmīr*, the country or valley of Cashmere, to the north of India. *p.*

كشميرن *kashmīrin*,
كشميرني *kashmīrnī*,
} f. a Cashmerian woman, a dancing-girl. *p. h.*

كشميري *kashmīrī*, of or belonging to Cashmere, a Cashmerian; the language of Cashmere. *p.*

كشن किशन *kishan*, the Hindū god *Kṛishṇa*. He is considered as the eighth avatār or incarnation of the deity. He was the younger brother of the the third *Rāma* (or *Balarāma*), and an incarnation of *Vishṇu*. His parents were *Vasudeva* and *Devakī*, but he was brought up in the house of *Nanda* and *Yasodā*, to conceal him from the tyrant *Kaṅsa*, to whom it had been predicted that the eighth-born child of this family would destroy him. In the family of *Nanda* he passed his life among the *gopas* and *gopīs*. During his childhood he slew the serpent *Kāliya*, and many giants and monsters. Afterward he put the tyrant *Kansa* to death, protected *Yudhishthira*, and kindled the war described in the *Mahābhārata*. He is the Apollo of the Hindūs, and is supposed by Captain Wilford to have lived about 1300 years before Christ. *s.*

كشن क्षण *kshan*, m. an instant, a measure of time equal to four minutes. *kshanāntar*, a moment afterwards. *kshan-mātr*, momentary, but for a moment. *s.*

كشن कषण *kashan*, m. touch or test of gold [by the touchstone. *s.*

كشن *kashan*, *kashn*, or *kashin*, large, copious, ample, much, numerous. *p.*

كشنده *kushanda*, a slayer, a murderer. *p.*

كشنك क्षणिक *kshanik*, } momentary, transient. *s.*
كشني क्षणी *kshanī*, }

كشنيز *kishnīz*, m. coriander (*Coriandrum sativum*). *p.*

كشوٹي कषौटी *kashautī*, f. a touchstone. *s.*

كشود *kushūd*, opening, openness. *p.*

كشودر क्षौद्र *kshaudr*, m. honey; a flower (*Michelia champaca*). *s.*

كشودن *kushūdan* (r. *kushā,e*), to open; to reduce (a fortress), to subdue or conquer. *p.*

كشور किशोर *kishor*, m. a child, a son; a youth, a lad under fifteen, a minor. *s.*

كشور क्षौर *kshaur*, m. the shaving of the head or beard. *s.*

كشور *kishwar*, m. a climate, country, region. *kishwar-kushā*, a subduer of regions. *p.*

كشورا किशोरा *kishorā*, young, infantine. *s.*

كشورك क्षौरिक *kshaurik*, m. a barber. *s.*

كشوري क्षौरी *kshaurī*, f. a razor. *s.*

كشون क्षौणि *kshauni*, f. the earth. *s.*

كشوكا क्षविका *kshavikā*, f. a kind of rice. *s.*

كشي क्षय *kshay*, m. loss, waste, destruction; consumption, decay; (in alg.) negative quantity. *kshay-rog*, m. consumption. *kshay-rogī* (fem. *kshay-roginī*), consumptive. *kshay-sampad*, f. total loss, ruin. *kshay-kās*, m. a consumptive cough. *kshay-kāl*, m. the end of the world. *kshay-nāshinī*, f. a plant (*Celtis orientalis*). *kshay-vāyu*, m. a wind that is to blow at the end of the world. *s.*

كشي *kushī* or *kashī* (in comp.), (v. *kush* and [*kash*). *p.*

كشيپ कश्यप *kashyapa*, m. a deified sage, the son of Marichi, and father of the immortals; a kind of deer. *s.*

كشيپ क्षेप *kshep*, m. throwing, casting; (in arithm.) addendum. *s.*

كشيپن क्षेपण *kshepan*, m. throwing, casting. *s.*

كشيتر क्षेत्र *kshetr*, m. a field; a sacred spot, a place of pilgrimage; a wife; a plane figure (in geom.), a diagram. *kshetr-sīmā*, f. the boundaries of a field. *s.*

كشيترگ क्षेत्रज्ञ *kshetrag* or *kshetragya*, clever, skilful; a husbandman; the soul, the emanation of the divinity residing in the body. *s.*

كشيد खेद *khed*, m. sorrowing, moaning. *s.*

كشيدگي *kashīdagī*, f. displeasure. *p.*

كشيدن *kashīdan*, to draw, extend, prolong. *p.*

كشيده *kashīda*, m. a kind of needle-work; adj. reserved, sullen, supercilious. *kashīda-abrū*, having long eyebrows. *kashīda-khātir*, displeased, distressed, or distracted in mind. *kashīda-rū*, having a long or wrinkled face. *kashīda-bālā*, *kashīda-kadd*, or *kashīda-kāmat*, of a tall stature, tall. *p.*

كشير क्षीर *kshīr*, m. water; milk. *kshīr-sphatik*, m. a milky crystal, opal. *kshīr-kakolikā*, f. a root from the Himālaya used as a drug. *s.*

كشيرو कशेरु *kasherū*, m. a kind of grass (*Scirpus kysoor*); a root (*Cyperus tuberosus*); one of the divisions of *Jambu-dwīpa*. *s.*

كشيرود क्षीरोद *kshīrod*, m. the sea of milk, one of the seven seas surrounding the world. *s.*

كشيري क्षीरी *kshīrī*, milky, yielding milk; m. a sort of *mimusops*. *s.*

كشيل कुशील *ku-shīl*, ill-behaved, wicked. *kushīlitā*, f. misconduct, bad disposition. *s.*

كشيم क्षेम *kshem*, happy, well, prosperous; m. welfare, eternal happiness; term of civil address to a Vaisya. *kshem-kar*, propitious, conferring happiness. *kshem-wān*, happy, prosperous. *s.*

كشين क्षीण *kshīn*, thin, feeble, slender, wasted, destroyed, poor. *kshīntā*, f. slenderness, thinness, decay. *kshīn-shakti*, feeble, impotent. *kshīn-wān*, wasted, decayed. *s.*

كشيي क्षयी *kshayī*, wasting, decaying, consumptive. *s.*

كعب *ka'b*, m. the heel, the ankle; a cube. *a.*

كعبت *ka'bat*, f. a cube, a die or play-bone; any kind of square building, hence the temple of Mecca. *a.*

كعبتين *ka'batain*, du. the two sacred temples, Mecca and Jerusalem; any game with two dice. *a.*

كعبه *ka'ba*, m. a square building, the temple of Mecca. *a.*

كف *kuf* (v. *kufū*), family, caste, tribe. *a.*

كف *kaf*, f. foam, froth, spittle, scum. *p.*

كف *kaff*, f. the hand, the palm, *kaffi pā*, the sole of the foot. *kaffi dast*, the palm of the hand; met. a level and desert plain. *a.*

كفاءت *kafā,at*, resemblance; similarity of condition in persons about to be married. *a.*

كفار *kuffār* (pl. of كافر), infidels, idolaters. *a.*

كفارت *kafārat*, f. } penitence, penance, atonement, expiation for sin. *a.*
كفاره *kafāra*, m. }

كفاف ***kafāf***, m. pittance, daily bread; adj. equal, adequate. *a.*

كفالت ***kafālat***, f. pledge, pawn, security, responsibility. *kafālat-nāma*, a bail-bond. *a.*

كفايت ***kifāyat***, f. sufficiency, enough, abundance, plenty, surplus; economy, thrift. *kifāyat-shiʻār*, economical, thrifty. *kifāyat-karna*, a. to save, to answer, to serve, to do, to content one's self. *a.*

كفايتي ***kifāyatī***, f. abundance, plenty, sufficiency; adj. thrifty; cheap, purchased for less than its value. *a.*

كفايه ***kifāya*** (v. *kifāyat*), sufficiency, &c. *a.*

كفت ***kaft***, a rupture, a split; *kuft*, a sprain, bruise. *p.* [cracked. *p.*

كفته ***kufta***, sprained, bruised. *kafta*, split,

كفتار ***kaftār***, a hyena, an animal between the wolf and the dog, common in Syria. *p.* [snake. *p.*

كفچه ***kafcha***, m. a spoon; the hood of a

كفچه ***kafcha***, a kind of jacket. *d.*

كفر ***kufr***, m, paganism, infidelity, incredulity, ingratitude. *kufr-go*, a blasphemer. *kufr-go,ī*, blasphemy. *a.*

كفران ***kufrān***, ingratitude, being ungrateful to one's benefactor. *kufrāni ni'mat*, unthankfulness for past favours or benefits. *a.*

كفرستان ***kufristān***, the country of infidels, a mountainous region to the north-east of Kābul. *a. p.*

كفري ***kufrī***, a pagan, a Caffre, generally applied to a barbarous race inhabiting the south-east coast of Africa. *a. p.*

كفش ***kafsh***, f. a shoe, a slipper (high-heeled and shod with iron). *kafsh-dos* or *kafsh-gar*, a shoemaker. *p.*

كفك ***kafh*** or ***kafak***, froth, scum, spittle stained part (of the palm of the hand). *p.*

كفگير ***kaf-gīr***, m. a skimmer, a spoon, a ladle (generally perforated like a colander). *p.*

كفل ***kafal***, the buttocks, the haunches, the crupper of a horse, a kind of cloth used instead of a saddle. *p.*

كفن ***kafan***, m. a shroud (coffin). *kafan phāṛke bolnā* expresses the impossibility of remaining silent on the sight of something wonderful. *kafan-dafan*, burial, funeral. *a.*

كفنانا ***kafnānā***, a. to shroud, to dress for the grave. *a. h.*

كفن چور ***kafan-chor***, (lit. a shroud-stealer) a caitiff, ruffian, villain, miscreant. *p. h.*

كفني ***kaʻnī***, f. a dress worn by *faķīrs* (for a full description of which v. *Qanoon Islam*, p. 80, Glossary). *a.*

كفو ***kufū***, m. tribe, caste, family, brotherhood; adj. alike, equal, resembling. *a.*

كفور ***kafūr***, an infidel. *kufūr*, infidelity. *a.*

كفه ***kaffa***, smuggling (especially of opium). *a.*

كفيل ***kafīl***, m. a security, ransomer, surety, hostage, bail (meaning the person). *a.*

كك किकि ***kiki***, m. the blue jay. *s.*

ككا काका ***kakā***, m. a paternal uncle. *h.*

ككٹ कुक्कुट ***kukkuṭ***, m. a cock, any male bird. *kukkuṭ-vrat*, m. a religious observance (worship of Shiva) held by women in Bhādoṅ for the sake of obtaining offspring. *s.*

ككٹي कुक्कुटी ***kukkuṭī***, f. a hen. *s.*

ككر कुक्कुर ***kukur***, ***kukkur***, or ***kukar***, m. a dog; a *kshatriya*. *s.*

ككرم कुकर्म ***ku-karm*** or ***ku-karma***, m. wickedness, sin, depravity, misconduct. *ku-karm-kārī*, wicked, depraved. *s.*

ككرمتا कुकुरमुत्ता ***kukur-mutā***, m. a mushroom, a toadstool. *s.* [ly, a malefactor. *s.*

ككرمي कुकर्मी ***ku-karmī***, one who acts wicked-

ككروندا ककरौन्दा ***kakrondā*** or कुकरौन्दा ***kukrondā***, m. name of a plant and fruit (*Celsia*). *s.*

ككري कुक्कुरी ***kukkurī***, f. a bitch. *s.*

ككري ककरी ***kakrī***, f. (v. *kakhrī*) the armpit. *s.*

ككريا कुक्रिया ***ku-kriyā***, f. a crime, a sin. *s.*

ككڑا कुकड़ा ***kukṛā***, m. a cock, a male bird. *s.*

ككڑي ककड़ी ***kakṛī***, f. a kind of cucumber (*Cucumis utilissimus, Roxb.*). *s.*

ككڑي कुकड़ी ***kukṛī***, f. a hen, a female bird. *s.*

ككش कक्ष ***kaksh***, m. the armpit, the side or flank. *s.*

ككش कुक्षि ***kukshi***, m. the belly, the abdomen. *s.*

ككشا कक्षा ***kakshā***, f. the end of the lower garment, which, after the cloth is carried round the body, is brought up behind and tucked into the waistband; a woman's girdle. *s.*

ككنا ककना ***kaknā***, m. } a ring worn on the
ككني ककनी ***kaknī***, f. } wrist, a bracelet. *s.*

ككورنا ककोरना ***kakornā***, a. to scrape (the earth as fowls do), to hollow, to excavate. *h.*

ككونك कुकूणक ***kukūnak***, m. weakness of the eyes in infants. *s.*

ككهرا ककहरा ***ka-kahrā***, m. the alphabet. *s.*

ككهري ककरी ***kakhrī***, f. the armpit; soreness of the armpit. *s.*

ککهوري कखौरी *kakhaurī*, } f. a painful sup-
ککهولي कखौली *kakhaulī*, } purating tumour in the armpit. *s.* [infamy. *s.*

ککهيات कुख्याति *ku-khyāti*, f. evil report,

ککهئالي कखिआली *kakhi,ālī*, f. a bundle of sheaves of corn given as perquisites to reapers and village servants. *h.*

ککيانا किकियाना *kikiyānā*, n. to shriek, to scream. *h.* [corner, architrave. *h.*

کگر कगर *kagar* or *kaggar*, m. the edge, border,

کل *kal*, scald-headed, bald. *p.*

کل *kull*, all, universal; m. sum, amount, totality. *kull-jam'* or *-kāmil*, sum total, the full amount. *kull-rakba*, the whole contents or area of a village and its lands. *a.*

کل कुल *kul* or *kula*, m. family, pedigree, race, relations, household. *kula-devī*, f. the family goddess; any female deity worshipped in particular by a family through successive generations. *s.*

کل कल *kal*, m. to-morrow, yesterday. *kal-kī bāt*, news of yesterday, something that happened very lately. "In the Dakhanī dialect *kal* is used only in the sense of yesterday. To morrow is expressed by *ṣabāh* or *ṣubāh*."—(Binning). *s.*

کل कल *kal*, f. ease, tranquillity, peace, relief, quiet, rest; a trap, a machine, a lock; the trigger of a gun; for (*kalī*), a bud, an unblown flower blossom. *kal kā ādmī*, an automaton, a puppet; (met.) a very weak person, an upstart. *kal kā ghorā*, a very well-trained and obedient horse. *kal-makal*, trouble, uneasiness. *s.* [bly. *s.*

کل किल *kil*, certainly, indeed, verily, proba-

کل कलि *kali* or *kal*, m. the name of the fourth period of the Hindūs (v. *kalijug*); f. a bud; quicklime. *s.*

کلا *kallā*, m. a cabbage; the head. *kallā pā,cha*, m. name of a dish, the head and feet. *kallā-khushk*, lantern-jawed; (met.) treacherous, cunning, malicious; noise, tumult. *kallā-kār*, noisy, tumultuous. *kallā-thallā*, pomp and splendour. *p.*

کلا कला *kalā*, f. the sixteenth part of the moon, a digit; a minute, the sixtieth part of a degree; part, portion; art, trick, craft. *kalā-bāzī*, f. turning over head and heels, tumbling, juggling. *kalā na badnā*, a. to disobey, to decline, not to succeed. *kalā na lagnā*, not to have an advantage, not to avail. *s.*

کلا कुल्ला *kullā*, m. gargling, rinsing the mouth. *h.*

کلا *kullā* (v. *kulāh*), a cap, hat, &c. *p. d.*

کلاب *kilāb* (pl. of کلب), dogs. *kullāb*, a pot-hook. *kallāb*, a keeper of dogs. *a.*

کلابتن कलाबत्तुन *kalābattun*, } m. gold
کلابتون कलाबत्तून *kalābattūn*, } thread, a silver thread. *h.*

کلابه *kalāba*, m. a clew, a hank, skein, a reel, a wheel (for winding thread on). *p.*

کلاپ कलाप *kalāp*, m. assemblage, multi-

کلاپروار कल्लापरवार *kallā-parwār*, m. a kind of sweetmeat. *h.*

کلاچار कुलाचार *kulāchār*, m. practice or observance peculiar to a family. *s.*

کلاح *kulāḥ*, smiling bitterly, grinning. *a.*

کلاخ *kulākh* (for *kulāḥ*), surly, grinning, sulky. *a.*

کلار कलार *kalār*, m. a distiller; a seller of spirituous liquors, a tavern-keeper; a toddy-drawer; a man who extracts the juice of the palmyra and date trees. *h.* [of *kalār*. *h.*

کلارن कलारिन *kalārin* or *kalārnī*, f. female

کلاري कलारी *kalārī*, m. a tavern-keeper. *h.*

کلاسه *kalāsa*, a well where travellers drink (more especially pilgrims to Mecca). *p.*

کلاغ *kalāgh* or *kulāgh*, a crow, rook, raven. *p.*

کلاغ پيشه *kalāgh-pesha*, m. a jackdaw. *p.*

کلاغچه *kalāghcha*, m. a little rook, a magpie. *p.*

کلال कुलाल *kulāl*, m. a potter. *p. s.*

کلال *kalāl*, m. (v. *kalār*), a distiller, &c. *kalāl-jam'*, duty on spirituous liquors. *kalāl-khāna*, a liquor-shop or distillery. *d.*

کلالي *kalālī*, m. a vintner, tavern-keeper. *d.*

کلام *kalām*, m. a word, speech, discourse, talk, conversation. *kalāmu-l-lāh*, the word of God, which among Musalmāns means of course the *Ḳur,ān*. *a.*

کلان *kalān*, large, great, big, elder. *p.*

کلانا *kalānā*, to mix together, to be confused. *d.*

کلانا कल्लाना *kallānā*, n. to burn, to be inflamed (as the skin by rubbing pepper, &c. on it). *kilānā*, a. to winnow; to strike with the fist. *kalānā*, a. to parch grain. *h.*

کلانت क्लान्त *klānt*, wearied, exhausted, depressed. *klānt-manā*, low-spirited, languid. *klānti*, f. fatigue, weariness. *s.*

کلانتر *kalān-tar*, the elder, the greater. *p.*

کلانچ कुलांच *kulānch*, f. a bound, spring, leap, jump, bounce. *kulānch mārnā*, to bound, to skip. *h.*

کلاني *kalānī*, f. greatness, seniority. *p.*

کلانوت कलांवत *kalāṅwat*, } m. a minstrel, a
کلاونت कलावन्त *kalāwant*, } kind of singer or musician. *h.* [well-born. *s.*

کلاونت कुलावन्त *kulāwant*, of a noble race,

کلاوه *kalāwa*, m. a ball of thread; the stirrups on the neck of an elephant; the elephant's neck. *p.*

کلاه *kulāh*, m. a cap, hat, tiara, crown. *p.*

کلاهك कलाहक *kalāhak*, m. a musical instrument. *s.* [&c. *s.*

کلاهل

كلاءي कलाई *kalā,ī*, f. the wrist. *h.*

كلاءي कलाई *kalā,ī*, f. pulse, leguminous seeds in general. *s.*

كلايه कलाया *kalāya*, a kind of long bean, very nutritious, used as food for horses. *h.*

كلب *kalb*, m. a dog, a hound. *a.*

كل بدهو कुलवधू *kul-badhū*, f. a virtuous woman of a noble family. *s.*

كلبلا कुलबुला *kulbulā*, vermicular, peristaltic. *h.*

كلبلانا कुलबुलाना *kulbulānā*, n. to itch; to fidget, to writhe (as a worm or snake under torture); to grumble or rumble (the bowels). *h.*

كلبلاهٹ कुलबुलाहट *kulbulāhaṭ*, f. peristaltic or vermicular motion. *s.*

كل بوڙ कुलबोड़ *kul-boṛ*, one who disgraces his family. *s.*

كلبوڙنا कुलबोड़ना *kul-boṛnā*, a. to disgrace [one's family. *s.*

كلبه *kulba*, m. a house, hut, closet, cottage. *kulba,e iḥzān*, an afflicted or distressed family. *p.*

كلپ कलप *kalap*, m. a kind of dye for the hair; a kind of starch called *mānḍī*, q. v. *h.*

كلپ कल्प *kalpa*, m. a *shāstra* or sacred work, one of the six *vedāngas*; a day and night of Brahmā, amounting to a period of 4,320,000,000 solar years of mortals (this period, according to the Hindūs, measures the duration of the present world, and a period of equal duration will pass during its annihilation): the word *kalpa* also denotes the destruction of the world; propriety, fitness; alternative, doubt; resolution, purpose; one of the trees of *swarga*, or Indra's paradise. *kalpa-kshaya* or *kalpānta*, m. the end of the world. *s.*

كلپال कुलपालि *kul-pāli*, f. a chaste woman. *s.*

كلپالك कुलपालक *kul-pālak*, nourishing a family. *s.*

كلپانا कलपाना *kalpānā*, a. to grieve, to distress. *s.*

كلپبرچهه कल्पवृक्ष *kalpa-bṛichḥ*, كلپتر कल्पतरु *kalpa-taru*, كلپوركش कल्पवृक्ष *kalpa-vṛiksha*, } m. one of the fabulous trees of Indra's heaven, or *swarga*, said to yield whatever may be desired. *s.*

كلپت कल्पित *kalpit*, made, arranged, artificial. *s.*

كلپت कुलपति *kul-pati*, m. head of a family. *s.*

كلپنا कलपना *kalapnā*, n. to be grieved or vexed. *h.*

كلپنا कल्पना *kalpnā*, m. a scheme, a contrivance; a forgery, an imitation. *s.*

كلپوج कुलपूज्य *kul-pūj* (for *kul-pūjya*), m. a family priest; object of adoration or reverence in a family (a household god). *s.*

كلتارن कुलतारण *kultāran*, m. a youth who is a credit to his family. *s.*

كلتر कलत्र *kalatr*, f. a wife. *s.*

كلتن *kulattan*, evil, bad, wicked. *d.*

كلتها कुलत्था *kulatthā*, f. a blue stone used as collyrium and astringent. *s.*

كلتهي कुलथी *kulthī*, f. name of a grain, Madras horse-gram (*Dolichos biflorus*). *s.*

كلٹا कुलटा *kulṭā*, f. an unchaste woman, a prostitute. *s.*

كلٹي कुलटी *kulṭī*, f. red arsenic. *s.*

كل جبها कलजिभा *kal-jibhā*, malignant, ill-omened, one whose curses prevail. *s.*

كلجگ कलियुग *kali-jug* (for *kali-yuga*), m. the name of one of the four Hindū periods or ages (v. *yuga*); the fourth, or present period, which is the worst of all, like the iron age of the classical writers. The celebrated French astronomer, Mr. Bailly, supposes the *kali-jug* to have commenced 3102 years before Christ, the number of its years is 432,000; at the expiration of which the world is to be destroyed. *s.*

كلجهوان कलजहवाँ *kaljahwān*, tawny, sallow complexioned. *h.*

كلجيبي *kaljībī* (for *kaljibhā*, q. v.) malignant, &c. *d.*

كلچا कुलचा *kulchā* or *kulcha*, m. capital, principal, stock in trade. *h.*

كلچه *kulcha*, m. (v. *kulīcha*) a kind of bread. *p.*

كلچهن कुलच्छण *ku-lachchḥan*, m. misconduct, bad temper; an ugly visage. *s.*

كلچهنا कुलच्छणा *kulachchḥanā*, ill-tempered, ill-favoured, ill-omened. *s.*

كلدروهي कुलद्रोही *kula-drohī*, m. one who brings disgrace or reproach on his family. *s.*

كلدهرم कुलधर्म *kul-dharm*, m. observance peculiar to a family. *s.*

كلديوي कुलदेवी *kul-devī*, f. the family goddess. *s.*

كلر कलर *kalar*, a kind of fullers' earth. *h.*

كلر कल्लर *kallar*, barren, sterile (land); salt (as food). *h.*

كلس कलश *kalas* or *kalash*, m. a dome, cupola, spire, or the ornament on the top of a dome, a pinnacle; a water-pot. *kalas-sthāpan-k.*, a. to make an offering of a jar of water to any deity; five twigs of the following sacred trees are previously placed in it, viz. the *ashwattha* (*ficus religiosa*), the *vaṭa* (*ficus Indica*), the *udumbar* (*ficus glomerata*), the *shamī* (*mimosa albida*), and the *āmra* or mango tree. *s.*

كلسا कलशा *kalsā*, m. a pinnacle (v. *kalas*). *s.*

كلسرا *kalsirā*, depraved, vicious; m. an enemy. *s.*

كلسي कलसी *kalsī*, f. a water-pot or jar, usually made of baked clay. *s.*

كلش कलश *kalash*, m. a dome, &c. (v. *kalas*).

كلشت क्लिशित *klishit*, كلشٹ क्लिष्ट *klishṭ* } afflicted, distressed, wearied. *s.*

كلشرا कलशिरा *kalshirā*, black-headed; m. man. *s.*

كلغي *kalghī*, f. an ornament on the turban. *t.*

كلف *kalaf*, m. a padlock; attention; a pimple or spot on the face. *a.*

كلفت *kulfat*, f. trouble, vexation, distress. *a.*

كلك *kilk*, f. a reed, a pen. *p.*

كلك किलक *kilak*, f. splendour, lustre (of a gem). *h.*

كلك कलिक *kalik*, m. a curlew. *s.*

كلك कल्क *kalk*, m. sediment, dregs, dirt, filth, ear-wax; sin, fraud; the beleric myrobalan; adj. sinful, wicked. *s.*

كلكار مارنا *kilkār-mārnā*, to make a loud noise. *d.*

كلكاري किलकारी *kilkārī*, f. chattering, snarling, grinning; a shout of joy. *kilkārī mārnā*, n. to express pleasure by any sound or cry. *s.*

كلكشن कुलक्षण *ku-lakshan*, m. same as *ku-lachchhan*, q. v.

كلكل कलकल *kalkal*, m. wrangling, quarrelling, the buz of a crowd. *h.*

كلكلا किलकिला *kilkilā*, m. the kingfisher (*Halcyon*): peevishness, fretfulness, anger; f. a sound expressing joy. *kulkulā*, m. gargling. *h.*

كلكلان *kulkullān*, m. one entrusted with the whole ceremony of a house; a factotum or major domo. *a.*

كلكلانا किलकिलाना *kilkilānā*, n. to be fretful, to snap, to snarl, to be peevish, to squabble. *s.*

كلكل كانٹا किलकिलकांटा *kilkil-kānṭā*, m. a game among boys. One boy, having drawn several lines upon a stone, hides it, and the others repeating the words *kilkil-kānṭā*, run about searching for it. Whoever finds the stone has a right to strike the boy who hid it three times with his fingers on the back of the hand. *h.*

كلكلي कुलकुली *kulkulī*, f. itch; (in Dakh.) violent laughter. *h.*

كلكم *kalkam*, lamp-black (applied medicinally to the eyes). *d.*

كلكنچت किलकिञ्चित *kil-kinchit*, m. wanton or amorous pastime, or gestures. *s.*

كلكي *kalkī*, a kind of instrument for smoking with. *d.*

كلكي कलकी *kalkī*, m. the name of the tenth Hindū incarnation which is yet to come. The deity will assume the appearance of a Brāhman, who is to be born in the town of Sambal, and in the family of *Vishṇu Sharmā*. He will ride on horseback, and put to death all the wicked. *s.*

كلگا कलगा *kalgā*, m. the name of a flower, cockscomb (*Amaranthus*); prince's feather. *h.*

كلگٹ *kalgaṭ*, an axe, a pickaxe. *d.*

كلگي *kalgī* (for *kalghī*, q.v.), an ornament, &c. *d.*

كلما कुलमा *kulmā*, m. a sausage. *h.*

كلمت *kalimat*, f. (v *kalima*). *a.*

كل مكل कलमकल *kal-makal*, f. trouble, uneasiness. *h.*

كلملانا कलमलाना *kalmalānā*, n. to fidget, to writhe. *h.*

كلمه *kalima* (vulg. *kalma*), m. a word, speech saying; part of speech; the *Muhammadan* confession of faith. *kalme kī unglī*, f. the fore-finger. *kalima paṛhnā*, to repeat the *Muhammadan* confession of faith. *kalima-e ḥakk*, the speaking of the truth (in evidence, &c.). *a.*

كلمي कलमी *kalmī*, f. *Convolvolus repens*, used as an esculent vegetable. *s.*

كلنا *kilnā*, n. to groan, to lament. *d.*

كلناش कुलनाश *kul-nāsh*, m. a reprobate, an outcast. *s.*

كلنج कलञ्ज *kalanj*, an animal struck with a poisoned weapon. *s.*

كلنج कुलञ्ज *kulanj*, cutting behind in walking (a horse). *h.*

كلنجن कुलञ्जन *kulanjan*, m. a plant (*Alpinia galanga* or *Galanga major*); a seed (*Nigella sativa*). *s.*

كلنك कलङ्क *kalank*, m. calumny, accusation, reflection, suspicion, scandal, spot, obloquy. *s.*

كلنكت कलङ्कित *kalankit*, calumniated, defamed. *s.*

كلنكي कलङ्की *kalankī* (fem. *kalankinī*), stained, blemished, disgraced; liable to reproach; (also cor. of *kalkī*, q. v.). *s.*

كلنگ *kulang*, m. a fowl of a large breed, a crane, a heron. *p.*

كلنگ कलिङ्ग *kaling*, m. the febrifuge nut-plant (*Cæsalpinia* or *Guilandina bonducella*); the name of a country, especially applied to a district on the Coromandel coast between Cuttack and Madras. *s.*

كلنگا कलिङ्गा *kalingā*, f. a plant, commonly called *teorī*, the bark of which is used a purgative. *s.*

كلنگان مچھي *kalingān-machhī*, the whiting (fish). *d.*

كلنگڑا *kalangṛā*, a water-melon. *d.*

كلني किलनी *kilnī*, f. a tick (insect that pesters dogs, &c.). *h.*

كلوار कलवार *kalwār*, m. a distiller, a vender of spirituous liquors (v. *kalār*). *s.*

كلوار *kull-wār*, with or according to the whole (assessment, &c.). *a. h.*

كلوان कुलवान *kulwān*, nobly born, of a good family. *s.*

كلواي किलवाई *kilwā,ī*, a small rake used for gathering grass together into a cocklet. *h.*

كلوٹا कलूटा *kalūṭā*, of black complexion; tawny. *s.*

كلور कलोर *kalor*, m. and f. a heifer. *h.*

كلوخ *kulūkh*, m. a clod of earth. *kulūkh-andāz*, a slinger. *kulūkh-kūb*, a mallet for breaking clods. *p.*

كلول कलोल *kalol*, f. wantonness, friskiness, play, gambol. *kallol*, m. joy, happiness, pleasure. *s.*

كلول कलवल *kalwal*, f. misfortune, calamity. *s.*

كلونت कुलवन्त *kulawant*, also *kulawantā*, pure, of noble descent, of a good family. *s.*

كلونتي कुलवन्ती *kulawantī*, f. chaste, of pure or noble descent. *s.*

كلونجي कलौंजी *kalaunjī*, f. the name of a small blackish pyramid-shaped seed, used medicinally (*Nigella Indica, Roxb.*). *h.*

كلونڈا *kalaundā*, diffident, bashful. *d.*

كلويٹ *kalweṭ*, a stag, a male antelope. *d.*

كله *kalla*, m. the head; the jaws or cheeks. *kalla-pur-bād*, an empty head (lit. full of wind). *kalla-zan*, a boaster. *kalla-zanī*, f. boasting. *p.*

كلہ कलह *kalah*, m. quarrel, strife. *kalah-kār* or *-kārī*, quarrelsome (a man). *kalah-kāriṇī* or *kalah-kārī*, a quarrelsome woman, a scold or termagant. *s.*

كله *kulah* (v. *kulāh*), a cap, tiara, &c. *kulah-dār*, an absolute sovereign. *kulah-dārī*, f. sovereignty. *kulah-shajra*, succession to the property of a religious person (from *kulah*, the cap worn by *faķīrs*). *p.*

كلہ काल्ह *kalh* (v. *kal*), to-morow, yesterday. *s.*

كلهارا कलहारा *kalahārā*, quarrelsome, violent. *s.*

كلهاڑا कुल्हाड़ा *kulhāṛā*, m. } an axe, a hatchet;
كلهاڑي कुल्हाड़ी *kulhāṛī*, f. } a kind of land tenure (v. Wilson). *s.* [firework. *h.*

كلهڑ कुलहड़ *kulhaṛ* or *kullhaṛ*, m. a kind of

كلهڑا कुलहड़ा *kulhaṛā*, m. a kind of cup or earthen vessel larger than *kulhiyā*, q. v. *h.*

كلهشجرا *kulah-shajarā*, succession and property of a saint, *faķīr*, &c. *p. a.*

كلهم *kullu-hum*, all of them, the whole. *a.*

كلهي कलही *kalahī*, f. a scold, a termagant. *s.*

كلهيا कुल्हिया *kulhiyā*, f. a cup, a small round vessel. *kulhiyā meṅ guṛ phoṛnā*, lit. to break sugar in a small cup, to do a work with few hands which requires many. *kulhiyā lagānā*, cupping. *s.*

كلي किल्ली *killī*, f. a key, a bolt. *kullī*, f. gargling or rinsing the mouth, washing the mouth. *h.*

كلي *kullī*, f. total sum, the whole; adj. universal, total, all, every. *a.*

كلي कली *kalī*, f. a bud, an unblown flower, blossom; quicklime; the *kal-yug* or *kal-jug*, q. v., the fourth age of the Hindūs. *s.*

كليات *kulliyāt* (pl. of كليت), every thing; the whole (poetic) works of an author; as, *kulliyāti Saudā*, the whole of the poems, &c. of *Saudā*. *a.*

كليان कल्याण *kalyāṇ*, m. welfare, prosperity; name of a *rāg* sung at night; a leguminous shrub (*Glycine debilis*); adj. happy, fortunate. *kalyān-vachan*, m. good wishes. *s.*

كليانا कलियाना *kaliyānā*, n. to blossom, to bloom. *s.* [picious. *s.*

كلياني कल्याणी *kalyānī*, happy, prosperous, aus-

كليت *kullīyat*, all; universality, totality, the whole. *a.*

كليجا कलेजा *kalejā*, m. the liver (v. *kaleja*).

كليجن कुलीजन *kulījan*, m. the name of a drug (the root of *Piper betel*). *s.*

كليجن *kulījan*, galangale (Gladwin). *h.*

كليجه कलेजा *kaleja*, m. the liver; (met.) courage, spirit, magnanimity. *kaleja ulaṭnā*, to be fatigued with excessive vomiting. *kaleja phaṭnā*, to be disturbed with grief or jealousy. *kaleja ṭhanḍhā-k.*, to obtain one's wish, to get ease. *kaleja ṭhanḍhā honā*, to be quite at ease. *kaleja jalnā kisī-kā*, to suffer sorrow, to mourn. *kaleja kāmpnā*, to be afraid, to suffer cold. *kaleje par sāmp phirnā*, to suffer jealousy or envy. *kaleje se lagā-rakhnā*, or *-lenā*, to caress, embrace, love exceedingly. *kaleje meṅ ḍāl-rakhnā*, to love or esteem exceedingly. *h.*

كليچه *kulīcha*, a kind of bread, biscuit. *p.*

كليد क्लेद *kled*, m. wetness, moisture. *s.*

كليد *kalīd* or *kilīd*, f. a key. *p.*

كلي دراز *kalle-darāz*, talkative, abusive. *kalle-darāzī*, f. abuse; reviling. *d.*

كليس कलेस *kales* (for *klesha*), m. sickness, pain, trouble, vexation, affliction, torment; (Hind.) quarrel, contention. *s.* [church. *g.*

كليسه *kalīsa*, m. (Gr. ἐκκλησια) a Christian

كليش क्लेश *klesh*, m. pain, affliction, anguish; care, trouble. *s.*

كليشت क्लेशित *kleshit*, pained, distressed. *s.*

كليم *kalīm*, one who speaks to another, a familiar. *mūsā kalīmu-l-lāh*, Moses the speaker with God. *a.*

كلين कुलीन *kulīn*, noble, of respectable descent, well born, gentle. *s.*

كلينا कुलीना *kulīnā*, m. a kind of pickles. *h.*

كليناءي कुलीनाई *kulīnā,ī*, } f. nobility, respect-
كلينتا कुलीनता *kulīntā*, } ability of descent, gentility. *s.*

كليو क्लीव *klīv*, m. the neuter gender; an eunuch; adj. weak, impotent; idle, slothful. *s.*

كليئو कलेऊ *kale,ū*, m. a light morning meal, also the same as *kalewā*. *s.*

كليوا कलेवा *kalewā*, m. cold meat, stale victuals, a luncheon. *s.*

كليور कलेवर *kalewar*, m. the body. *s.*

كليويه क्लैव्य *klaivya*, m. impotence, unmanliness; the neuter gender. *s.*

كليه कल्य *kalya*, m. the dawn or break of day; adv. yesterday, to-morrow; adj. healthy, recovered from sickness; deaf and dumb. *s.*

كليه *kullīya* (v. *kullīyat*), totality; adj. general, universal. *a.*

كم किम *kim*, what? which? how? *s.*

كم **kam**, how much? how many? *a.*

كم **kam**, deficient, less, little; (this word is much used as first member of a compound, generally denoting negation or inferiority). *kam-ikhtilāt*, unsocial. *kam-āzār*, of little injury. *kam-asbāb* or *kam-biẓā'at*, of few goods or means, poor. *kam-aṣl*, low bred, vile. *kam-bakht*, unfortunate (reproachfully), a rascal, villain, wretch. *kam-bakhtī*, f. unfortunateness, adversity, misfortune. *kam-bar*, a division of the suits at cards (v. *tāj*). *kam-bahā*, of little value. *kam-besh*, more or less. *kam-pā*, of short duration. *kam-pāya*, in a mean condition, of low degree. *kam-jur,at*, cowardly. *kam-chal*, slow paced (a horse). *kam-chor* (for *kām-chor*), a skulker. *kam-ḥarakat*, indolent, lazy. *kam-ḥauṣila*, unaspiring, unambitious, poor-spirited. *kam-kharch*, parsimonious, stingy. *kam-kharch bālā-nishin*, applied to things of good quality purchased cheaply. *kam-kharchī*, parsimony. *kam-kharchī meṅ ūṭā gīlā*, expresses an expense being unavoidably incurred by a person who is already in poverty (if too much water be mixed inadvertently with flour of which bread is to be made, the paste becomes so thin as to render it necessary to add more flour. The phrase supposes this accident to happen to a person who has not the means of procuring more). *kam-khirad*, unwise, ignorant. *kam-khor* or *kam-khur*, abstemious, eating little (particularly applied to a horse). *kam-khorāk* or *kam-khurāk*, abstemious, eating little. *kam-ẕāt*, low bred, of low caste. *kam-ẕihn*, forgetful; without abilities. *kam-rāh*, slow, without bottom (a horse). *kam-rang*, of a pale or faint colour. *kam-rau*, slow paced (a horse). *kam-zadanī-k.*, to affect extraordinary humility. *kam-zor*, weak, powerless. *kam-ziyād*, more or less. *kam-sāl*, young, of tender years. *kam-sufra*, one whose table is scantily furnished. *kam se kam*, very little. *kam-shān*, humble, mild, affable, unassuming *kam-sharr*, well disposed, of good dispositions. *kam-sharḥ*, low wages. *kam-shauḳ*, indifferent, *kam-ẓarf*, ignoble, vile, stupid, silly, witless. *kam-'aḳl* stupid, ignorant. *kam-'iyār*, below standard, a base coin. *kam-fahm*, stupid. *kam-ḳadar*, worthless. *kam-ḳadam*, slow-paced. *kam-ḳuwwat*, feeble powerless. *kam-ḳīmat*, low-priced. *kam-kār*, unexperienced in business. *kam-kāsht*, decrease in a ryot's cultivation compared with the preceding season. *kam-k.*, a. to diminish; to depreciate. *kam-kam*, a little. *kam-guftār* or *kam-go*, taciturn, of few words. *kam-māyagī*, smallness of capital. *kam-māya*, ill-provided. *kam-naẓar*, dim-sighted, weak-sighted. *kam-o besh*, less or more. *kam-o beshī*, less or more-ness. *kam o kāst*, loss, deficiency. *kam-himmat*, spiritless. *kam-yāb*, scarce, rare, unprocurable. *kam-yābī*, f. rarity. *p.*

كما **kamā**, like, such as, like that which. *kamā fi-l-awwal*, as (it was) originally. *kamā ḥakkuhu*, as it ought; in a proper manner. *kamā-yambaghī*, as it suits. *a.*

كما **kammā**, m. a document written on the leaf of a palmyra tree rolled up into a ball; proceedings; intelligence. *d.*

كمابيش **kam-ā-besh**, less or more. *p.*

كماچ कुमाच **kumāch**, a kind of unleavened bread. *kumāch sā muṅh*, a broad face; a jolly, moonlike countenance. *h.*

كماد **kimād**, hot cloth or any fomentation applied to an afflicted part. *a.*

كمار कुमार **kumār**, m. a boy, son, a prince. *s.*

كماركا कुमारिका **kumārikā**, f. a daughter, damsel, a princess. *s.*

كمارگ कुमार्ग **ku-mārg**, m. (v. *ku-path*) wrong road, &c. *s.*

كماري कुमारी **kumārī**, f. a daughter, &c. (v. *kumārikā*). *s.*

كماست कमासुत **kamāsut**, m. a journeyman, a servant, a workman, earner. *h.*

كمال **kamāl**, m. perfection, excellence; completion, conclusion; punctuality. *a.*

كمالات **kamālāt**, (pl.) perfections, excellencies. *a.*

كمالت **kamālat**, } perfection, &c. (v. *kamāl*). *a. d.*
كماليت **kamāliyat**, }

كمان **kamān**, f. a bow; a spring. *kamān-abrū*, with arched eyebrows (epithet of a mistress). *kamān chaṛhnā*, to be strung or drawn tight (a bow); (Dakh.) to be victorious. *kamān-dār*, an archer, one armed with a bow. *kamān-dān*, a bow case. *kamān-sāz*, a bow maker, an archer. *kamān-kash*, an archer; adj dealing destruction, as *abrū,e kamān-kash*, eyebrows (shooting the arrows of love). *kamāni kaiyānī*, the Kaianian bow, *i. e.* a strong bow, such as the Persians used under the Kaianian dynasty. *kamān-gar*, one who makes holes. *p.*

كمانا कमाना **kamānā**, a. to earn; to work, to perform, to perpetrate, to commit; to clean (leather, or a privy). *h.*

كمانا **kamānā**, a. to lessen, to abate. *p. h.*

كمانچه **kamāncha**, m. a little bow; the bow of a fiddle; a steel spring. *p.*

كمانه **kamāna**, the plectrum, or bow, of any musical instrument. *p.*

كماني **kamānī**, bowed, bent, curved; a steel spring. *baṛī kamānī*, the mainspring of a gun-lock. *chhoṭī kamānī*, the feather spring. *p.*

كماءو कमाऊ **kamā,ū**, laborious, industrious. *h.*

كماهي **kamā-hiya** or **kamā-hī**, as things are, as the affair stands; f. nature or real state (of a thing). *a.*

كماءي कमाई **kamā,ī**, f. earning, gain; work, performance. *kamā,ī-pūt*, or *kamā,ī kā beṭā*, a grown-up son. *h.*

كمائش **kamā,ish**, f. business in general. *p. d.*

كمبا कुम्बा **kumbā**, m. tribe, family, caste. *s.*

كمبه कुम्भ **kumbh** (v. كنبه), m. a water-pot; the sign Aquarius. *s.*

كمبي कुम्बी **kumbī**, m. a peasant, a cultivator. *h.*

كم پاءيري **kam-pā,irī**, mean, base. *d.*

كمپرش किम्पुरुष **kim-purush**, m. one of the nine parts of the world, between the Himāchal and Himakūṭ mountains: a despicable man. *s.*

كمت कुमत **ku-mat** or कुमति **ku-mati**, f. stupidity, folly; adj. foolish, deficient in prudence, indiscreet; wicked, vicious. *s.*

كمتر **kamtar**, less, least, smaller. *p.*

كمترين **kamtarīn**, least, very small. *p.*

كمتي **kamtī**, f. deficiency. *p.*

كمٹھ कमठ *hamaṭh*, m. a tortoise, a turtle. *s.*

كمٹھا कमठा *kamṭhā*, a bow (made of bamboo). *h.*

كم خواب *ham-k͟hwāb* or *kim-k͟hwāb* (vulg. "kincob"), silk worked with gold and silver flowers; brocade. *p.*

كمد कुमद *humad* or कुमुद *kumud*, m. a white esculent lotus, that expands its petals during the night, and closes them during the day-time (*Nymphæa esculenta*). *s.*

كمدني कुमुदिनी *kumudinī*, f. a place abounding [in lotus. *s.*

كمر *kamar*, f. the loins; a girdle, a belt, zone; an arch; the flank (of an army). *kamar bāndhnā*, to get ready, to resolve. *kamar-basta*, ready prepared; an attendant. *kamar-band*, m. a girdle, a zone; a long piece of cloth girt round the loins; adj. alert, ready for battle, prepared, armed. *kamar-bandī*, f. arming, preparation for battle, &c. *kamar-baiṭhnā*, to be helpless. *kamar-paṭṭā*, a kind of ring or zone encircling the waists of women (this kind of girdle is composed of many flat pieces of silver or gold, embossed and ornamented, linked together). *kamar-pakaṛke uṭhnā*, to be weak. *kamar pakaṛnā*, to urge a claim against one. *kamar ṭūṭnā*, to be hopeless; to be deserted by one's friends; (lit.) to become weak in the loins (an incurable disease, to which horses in many parts of India are liable). *kamar toṛnā*, to take away one's hopes; to draw over one's friends or adherents to the side of his enemies. *kamar-dār*, a servant, a serving-man. *kamar-dawāl*, a leathern belt. *kamar rah-jānā*, to have a pain in the loins (from long standing. *kamar sīdhī karnī*, to lie down. *kamar kas bāndhnā*, to be determined on an undertaking. *kamar-kash*, a hero, a brave man. *kamar-kushā,ī*, f. ungirding the loins, a species of oriental exaction made by officials placed as guards over any one in restraint, for permission to pull off his clothes, and perform the necessary functions of life. *kamar-koṭā*, a parapet. *kamar-koṭhā*, a part of a beam passing through the wall and appearing outside. *kamar-kholnā*, to quit service. *kamar khol-baiṭhnā*, to sit at ease. *kamar mārnā*, to strike sideways; to attack an army in flank. *kamar mazbūt-k.*, to undertake a work of expense. *kamar hilānā*, to endeavour; to copulate. *p.*

كمرا *kamarā*, m. (Lat. *camera*) a chamber, a room, cabin of a ship. *e.*

كمرسار *kamar-sār*, } a kind of ornament worn
كمرسال *kamar-sāl*, } round women's waists. *d.*

كمركهہ कमरख *kamrakh*, m. the name of a fruit (*Averrhoa carambola*). *s.*

كمري *kamrī* or *kamarī*, of or relating to the waist or loins; weak in the loins (a horse). *kamarī-angarkhā*, m. a short jacket or waistcoat, a spencer. *p.*

كمڑها कमढ़ा *kamṛhā*, m. name of a gourd (*Cucurbita pepo*). *h.*

كم صلا *kam ṣalā*, m. a method of transmuting words, so as to form, in writing, a cypher, and in speech a gibberish or cant language, unintelligible to all who do not possess the key. The plan is simply to interchanged mutually one letter for another at the pleasure of the writer, and communicate the key to the person to whom the epistle is sent. For example, the Persian alphabet consists of thirty-two letters: take any sixteen of these you please, and make them mutually change places, according to your own will and pleasure, with the remaining sixteen; you will for some time baffle the curiosity of those who are not in the secret. *a.p.*

كمك *kumak*, f. aid, assistance. *p.*

كمكا *kamkā*, left, what remains. *d.*

كم كم कुमकुम *hum-kum* (also *kun-kum*), m saffron. *s.*

كمكما *kumkumā*, lukewarm. *d.*

كمكماٹ *kumkumāṭ*, lukewarmness. *d.*

كمكي *kumakī*, auxiliary, an ally. *p.*

كمل कम्मल *kammal*, m. a blanket. *s.*

كمل कमल *kamal*, m. the lotus (*Nelumbium speciosum, Willd.; Nymphæa nelumbo, Lin.*) *s.*

كمل *kammal*, a kind of earring; a long strip of palm leaf rolled up and inserted in the aperture bored in the lobe of the ears. *d.*

كملا कमला *kamalā*, m. name of the caterpillar or larva of a brown moth, covered with fine bristles, which on handling it adhere to the skin and excite itching: it is destructive to trees; the palmer worm; f. a name of the goddess Lakshmī; an excellent woman. *s.*

كملانا कुमलाना *kumlānā*, n. to wither, to fade. *h.*

كمل باءي कमलबाइ *kamal-bā,e*, m. name of a disorder; jaundice. *s.*

كملني कमलिनी *kamlinī*, f. a place abounding in lotus flowers. *s.*

كملي कमली *kamlī*, f. a small blanket. *kamlī kīṛā*, a palmer worm, or hairy caterpillar. *s.*

كمن कमन *kaman*, libidinous, desirous; beautiful, desirable. *s.* [intrigue. *s.*

كمنترنا कुमन्त्रणा *ku-mantranā*, m. bad counsel,

كمند *kamand*, f. a kind of scaling ladder, made of cord, and chiefly used by thieves; a halter; a noose, a snare, a lasso. *p.*

كمنڈل कमण्डल *kamandal*, m. an earthen or wooden water-pot, used by the ascetic and religious student. *s.*

كمنيت *kamnait*, m. an archer, a bowman. *p.*

كمنيتي *kamnaitī*, f. archery, use of the bow. *p.*

كمنيه कमनीय *kamanīya*, pleasing, desirable. *s.*

كموانا कमवाना *kamwānā*, a. to cause to work, to earn. *s.*

كمود कमूद *hamūd*, m. the name of a drug used for dyeing, being the dust from the outside of the capsules of *Rottlera tinctoria*; said to be also a purgative medicine and aphrodisiac. *h.*

كمودني कमोदिनी *kamodinī*, f. a sort of water-lily described as expanding its petals during the night, and closing them during the day (*Menyanthes Indica* or *cristata*). *s.*

كموري कमोरी *kamorī*, f. a small earthen pot. *h.*

كمون *kammūn*, m. cummin seed. *a.*

كموني *kammūnī*, f. a medicine in which cummin seed is mixed. *a.*

كمهار कुम्हार *kumhār*, m. a potter, a manufacturer of earthen vessels. *kumhārnī*, f. a potter's wife. *s.*

كمهاري कुम्हारी *kumhārī*, f. a creature like a wasp, which forms its abode of clay. *h.*

كمهلانا कुम्हलाना *kumhlānā*, n. to wither, to blast, to droop, to blight. *s.*

كمهير कुम्हीर *kumhīr* (for *kumbhīr*), an alligator. *s.*

كمي *kamī*, f. deficiency, loss, abatement, *p.*

كميا कमिया *kamiyā*, an agricultural labourer. *h.*

كميت *kumait*, m. bay (colour of a horse). *kamīyat* or *kamiyat*, f. quantity. *a.*

كميڈيا कुमेडया *kumeḍyā* (also *kumeṅḍyā* or *kumeṅḍhyā*), m. a small elephant. *h.*

كمير कुमेरु *kumeru*, m. the southern hemisphere or pole. *s.*

كميرا कमेरा *kamerā*, m. a workman, a journeyman, an assistant. *h.*

كميلا कमीला *kamīlā*, m. the name of a drug (v. *kamūd*). *h.*

كمين *kamīn*, f. an ambush. *kamīn-gāh*, f. an ambuscade or place of ambush. *a. p.*

كمين *kamīn*, defective, mean; m. a kind of village serf. *p.*

كمينڈهيا कमेंढया *kumeṅḍhyā*, } a small species of
كمينڈيا कमेंडया *kumeṅḍyā*, } the elephant. *s.*

كمينه *kamīna*, mean, base, abject, defective. *p.*

كن किन *kin* (infl. pl. of *kaun*), whom? what? *h.*

كن कन *kan*, appreciating, valuing (a field); a weevil. *kan-k.*, a. to value. *kan-kūt*, appraisement of a crop on the field, valuation. *h.*

كن कण *kan*, m. grain, corn; a grain, a minute particle, an eye of corn, a spark or facet of a gem. *s.*

كن *kan*, (in comp.) digging, as *khār-kan*, a digger of thorns. *kun*, (in comp.) making or acting, as *ham-kun*, a companion, one who acts along with another. *p.*

كن *kun*, be (thou). *kun fa kān* or *kun fa yakūn*, be and it was, or be and it is, these phrases are used as epithets of Omnipotence. *a.*

كن *kan* (for *kane*), near, close by. *d.*

كنا *kanā* (for *kahnā*), to speak, tell. *d.*

كنا कणा *kaṇā* (v. *kaṇikā*), fine sand, &c.; also the dark lunar fortnight of *āsin*. *s.*

كنا कन्ना *kannā*, m. the notches on the two sides of the upper leather of a shoe; the part of a paper kite to which the string is tied. *h.*

كنادار कन्नादार *kannā-dār*, m. a kind of shoe or slipper (v. *kannā*). *h. p.*

كنار *kinār*, m. bosom, embrace; side, edge, margin. *kinār khainchnā*, a. to give up, to quit, to leave. *kinār o bos*, kissing and embracing. *p.*

كنارا *kinārā*, } m. side, margin, part, limit,
كناره *kināra*, } boundary, edge. *kinārā-k.*, a. to abstain, to refrain. *kināre hojānā*, to retire, to withdraw. *kināre*, aside, ashore. *p.*

كنارنا *kanārnā* (v. *karāhnā*), to groan. *d.*

كناري किनारी *kinārī*, f. (gold or silver) lace; edge, border. *kinārī-bāf*, a lace-maker. *h.*

كناس *kannās*, m. a sweeper: (met.) an avaricious ill-tempered person. *a.*

كناكچو कनाकचू *kanā-kachū*, m. the name of a vegetable, a species of arum. *h.*

كناگت कनागत *kanāgat*, f. a *srāddhā* or religious ceremony, performed daily by Hindūs during the dark half of the month *āsin*, in honour of deceased ancestors or *pitris*. Hence that fortnight is called *kanā*. *s.*

كنان *kunān* (in comp. v. *kun*), doing, acting; (pl. of *kun*) doers, actors. *p.*

كن آنكهي कनांखी *kan-ānkhī*, f. a side glance, a sly wink (on the part of a female). *s.*

كنايت *kināyat*, f. } a wink, nod, sign, hint,
كنايه *kināya*, m. } allusion, metaphor; an ironical expression. *a.*

كنبا कुंबा *kuṅbā* or *kumbā*, m. tribe, caste, family, brotherhood. *s.*

كنبٹ *kumbaṭ*, agricultural labour, farming. *d.*

كنبل कम्बल *kambal*, m. (v. *kammal*) a blanket. *s.*

كنبوج कम्बोज *kamboj*, m. a country in the north of India, Camboge or Cambay. *s.*

كنبه कुंभ *kumbh*, m. a water-pot; Aquarius. *kumbh kā melā*, the twelfth year fair at Hardwār, a celebrated Hindū pilgrimage. *kumbhnī*, the sixth-year fair. *s.*

كنبهار कुंभार *kumbhār*, } m. a potter. *s.*
كنبهكار कुंभकार *kumbh-kār*, }

كنبهكا कुंभिका *kumbhikā*, f. a disease of the eyes, a stye. *s.*

كنبهكاملا कुंभकामला *kumbh-kāmlā*, f. a sort of jaundice.

كنبهلا कुंभला *kumbhlā*, f. a plant with flowers like those of the *Nauclea cadamba*. *s.*

كنبهيپاك कुंभीपाक *kumbhī-pāk*, m. a hell in which the wicked are supposed to be baked like potters' vessels. *s.*

كنبهير कुंभीर *kumbhīr*, m. an alligator. *s.*

كنبي *kumbī*, a peasant, a husbandman, a cultivator. *kumbī-log*, the peasantry. *s.*

كنپ कम्प *kamp*, m. shivering, tremor.

كنپانا कम्पाना *kampānā*, a. to cause to tremble, to agitate. *s.*

كنپاه कम्पाहा *kampāhā*, } tremulous, trembling, fearful. *s.*
كنپت कम्पित *kampit*, }

كنپٹي कनपटी *kanpaṭī*, f. the upper part of the side of the face, between the temples and the ears. *s.*

كنپمان कम्पमान *kampmān*, adj. trembling. *s.*

كنپن कम्पन *kampan*, m. trembling, quivering. *s.*

كنپنا कम्पना *kampnā*, n. to tremble, to shake. *s.*

كنپھٹا कनफटा *kan-phaṭā*, m. a Jogī with slit ears. *s.*

كنت कंत *kant*, m. a husband, a sweetheart. *s*

كنت किन्तु *kintu*, conj. but, again. *s.*

كنتگھن किन्तुघ्न *kintughna*, m. one of the eleven Karans, or astronomical periods. *s.*

كنتل कुन्तल *kuntal*, hair. *s.*

كنتھا कंथा *kanthā*, m. an apparatus or band round the neck of a Jogī to carry things on; a beggar's wallet. *s.*

كنتھ *kanthā*, a story, tale, narrative. *kanthe sānā*, to narrate circumstances or affairs. *d.*

كنتي कुन्ती *kuntī*, f. the wife of *Pāṇḍu* and mother of the five *Pāṇḍava* princes by as many gods. *s.*

كنٹار कंटार *kanṭār*, prickly, thorny. *s.*

كنٹر कंटर *kanṭar*, miserly, niggardly. *h.*

كنٹك कंटक *kanṭak*, m. a thorn; a bad man; a mean enemy. *s.*

كنٹكاري कंटकारी *kanṭakārī*, f. a sort of prickly nightshade (*Solanum jacquini*); the silk-cotton tree (*Bombax heptaphyllum*). *s.*

كنٹكي कंटकी *kanṭakī*, thorny, vexatious. *s.*

كنٹھ कंठ *kanṭh*, m. wind-pipe, or the lump on the wind-pipe, the larynx, Adam's apple; the bosom, voice; adj. by heart, committed to memory. *kanṭhā-rūndhan*, strangulation. *kanṭh-bhūshā*, f. a collar or short necklace. *kanṭh phūṭnā*, n. to be broken (the voice of a boy), becoming hoarse as he approaches to puberty. *kanṭh-mālā*, f. a kind of necklace of gold and jewels; the bronchocele or goitre; scrofula. *kanṭh-k.*, a. to get by heart. *kanṭh-mani*, m. a jewel worn on the throat. *s.*

كنٹھا कंठा *kanṭhā*, m. a necklace or rosary of large beads made of silver, crystal or the earth of *Karbalā*. *s.*

كنٹھابھرن कंठाभरण *kanṭhābharan*, the ornaments of the neck. *s.*

كنٹھاگر कंठाग्र *kanṭhāgra*, by rote, by memory. *s.*

كنٹھت कुण्ठित *kunṭhit*, ashamed.

كنٹھستھ कंठस्थ *kanṭhastha*, by heart, by rote. *s.*

كنٹھلا कंठला *kanṭhlā*, m. a necklace composed of pieces of gold and silver, put on children to avert evil. *s*

كنٹھي कंठी *kanṭhī*, f. a short necklace. *s.*

كنٹيا कंटिया *kanṭiyā*, f. a fishing-hook; a vessel for keeping oil. *h.*

كنج कंज *kanj*, m. the lotus. *s.*

كنج कुंज *kunj*, m. an arbour, a bower. *s.*

كنج *kunj*, m. a corner, a confined place, a grove. *p.*

كنجا कंजा *kanjā*, blue-eyed. *h.*

كنجال *kanjāl* or *kunjāl*, the green scum formed on stagnant water. *d.* [&c. *d.*

كنجايش *kunjā,ish* (for *gunjā,ish*), capacity.

كنجد *kunjud*, the grain sesame. *p.*

كنجر कंजर *kanjar*, m. name of a low caste of people, generally employed in selling strings, &c.; they also catch and eat snakes. *h.*

كنجر कुंजर *kunjar*, } m. (also *kunjal*), an elephant. *s.*
كنجڑ कुंजड़ *kunjaṛ*, }

كنجڑا कुंजड़ा *kunjṛā*, m. name of a caste whose business it is to sell vegetables, fruits, &c.; a fruiterer. *h.*

كنجڑن कुंजड़न *kunjṛan*, } f. the female of *kunjṛā*. *h.*
كنجڑي कुंजड़ी *kunjṛī*, }

كنجشك *kunjashk* or *kunjishk*, f. a sparrow. *p.*

كنجل कुंजल *kunjal*, m. an elephant: (according to the author of the *Arā,ish i Mahfil*) *kunjal* denotes the large species of elephant, the smaller species being called *kumendyā*. *s.*

كنجوس कंजूस *kanjūs*, m. a miser, a niggard. *h.*

كنجوسي कंजूसी *kanjūsī*, f. stinginess, meanness, penuriousness. *h.*

كنجي कुंजी *kunjī*, f. a key. *s.*

كنجيا कंजिया *kanjiyā*, f. a small stithe, a stye. *h*

كنچت किञ्चित *kinchit*, a little, something. *s.*

كنچ कंचु *kanchu*, } a bodice or jacket (also *kunchkī*). *s.*
كنچكي कंचुकी *kanchukī*, }

كنچلي किंचली *kinchlī* (also *kanchlī*), f. the slough (of a snake, &c.). *s.*

كنچن कंचन *kanchan*, m. gold. *kanchan-khachit*, inlaid with gold. *s.*

كنچن कंचन *kanchan*, m. a kind of caste or tribe, somewhat akin to our gypsies, the females being generally dancers, &c. *kanchan-bān*, a real or genuine *kanchan*, by birth. *s.*

كنچني कंचनी *kanchanī*, f. a female of the *kanchan* tribe; a dancing girl, a strumpet. *s.*

كند कंद *kand*, m. a bulbous or tuberous root one of an esculent sort (*Arum campanulatum*); garlic; an affection of the feminine organ. *s.*

كند *kund*, blunt; slow, obtuse. *p.*

كند कुंद *kund*, m. name of a flower (*Jasminum grandiflorum*). *s.*

كندا कंदा *kandā*, m. a squill (*Erythronium Indicum*); (for *kanda*) engraved. *kandā-k.*, to engrave (as seals, &c.). *kandā-kār*, m. an engraver. *h. p.*

كندا कुंदा *kundā*, m. the shoulder. *s.*

كنداسا कंदासा *kandāsā*, m. a priapus, obelisk, the lingam. *h.*

كندر कुन्दुरु *kunduru*, f. the resin of the *Boswelia thurifera*, gum olibanum, or frankincense. *s.*

كندر कंदर *kandar*, m. f. } an artificial or natural cave; a chasm
كندرا कंदरा *kandarā*, m. } in a mountain. *s.* [*dā*]. *s.*

كندرا कंद्रा *kandrā*, m. a squill (same as *kandā*).

كندرا कुंदरा *kundrā*, } m. a stack, a rick. *h.*
كندڑا कुंदड़ा *kundṛā*, }

كندركوٹ कुंदरकूट *kundar-kūṭ*, m. name of a medicine (*Olibanum*). *s.*

كندس *kandas*, m. sneeze-wort. *kundus*, a kind of poisonous weed. *p.*

كندسار कंदसार *kandsār*, m. a stag, buck, deer. *s.*

كندل कंदल *kandal*, m. the name of a gum (*Sagapenum*). *s.*

كندل कुंदल *kundal*, m. the finest gold. *s.*

كندلا कंदला *kandalā*, m. a précipice; a cave; a kind of silver thread. *h.*

كندلا कुंदला *kundlā*, a kind of tent. *h.*

كندن कुंदन *kundan*, m. very fine gold. *kundan-kūṭ*, m. a medicine (*Olibanum*). *s.*

كندن *kandan*, to dig, to erase, extirpate; m. digging, extirpating, giving up; (in comp.) as *jān-kandan* or *jān-kandanī*, giving up the ghost; agonies of death. *p.*

كندوري *kandūrī*, f. a linen (or leather) table-cloth: a feast or ceremony observed in honour of holy personages, at which prayers are offered up in their behalf, and food distributed. When this feast is celebrated in honour of *Fāṭima*, only women (and those the most virtuous) can partake: no male is ever permitted to see the food dressed on this occasion and set apart for an offering to the prophet's daughter; name of a gourd (v. *bimb*). *p.*

كنده *kunda*, m. a block; the stock of a gun; a billet of wood. *kunda-chaṛhānā* or *-lagānā*, to stock a gun. *kanda*, dug up, engraved. *kanda-kār*, an engraver, *kanda-kārī*, f. the art of engraving. *kanda-k.*, to engrave (as seals, &c.). *p.*

كنده कुंदः *kunda*, m. the shoulder. *kunda jhāṛnā*, to prepare to fly (a bird). *s.*

كندھ कंध *kandh*, } m. the shoulder. *kandhā*
كندھا कंधा *kandhā*, } *denā*, to carry a dead body. *s.*

كندھيانا कंधियाना *kandhiyānā*, a. to shoulder, to place on the shoulder. *s.*

كندھيلي कंधेली *kandhelī*, f. a kind of pannel or pack-saddle. *h.*

كندي *kundī*, f. obtuseness, stupidity. *p.*

كندي कुंदी *kundī*, f. the act of calendering (cloth). *kundī-k.*, to calender (cloth); to beat, to cudgel. *kundī-gar*, m. a calenderer. *h.*

كنڈ कुंड *kunḍ*, m. an abyss, pool, spring, a pit, a hole for sacrifice or fire. *s.*

كنڈا कंडा *kanḍā*, m. dry cow-dung, picked up in the fields, &c., used for fuel. *h.*

كنڈا कंडा *kanḍā*, m. a reed, a bush. *s.*

كنڈاري कंडारी *kanḍārī*, m. a helmsman, steersman. *s.*

كنڈال कंडाल *kanḍāl*, m. a kind of hautboy. *h.*

كنڈالا *kunḍālā*, m. a large flat vessel, in which bottles of water, wine, &c., are cooled by means of ice or saltpetre; an earthenware pan, in which clothes are washed. *d.*

كنڈرانا कंडराना *kanḍrānā*, n. to bristle; to dislike or abhor. *h.*

كنڈري कंडरी *kanḍarī*, m. or f. name of a vegetable, a kind of mustard. *h.*

كنڈل कुंडल *kunḍal*, m. a large ring worn in the ears; a circle; a halo round the sun or moon. *kunḍal mārnā*, to form a coil. *s.*

كنڈلي कुंडली *kunḍlī* or *kunḍalī*, f. a coil, ring, curl; a serpent, a snake. *kunḍalī banānā*, to curl. *s.*

كنڈليا कुंडलिया *kunḍaliyā*, m. a species of Hindī stanza, which invariably ends with the word with which it began: it is hence compared to a circle or the coil of a snake, the opposite ends of which unite. *s.*

كنڈھ *kunḍh* (v. *kunḍ*), a tank, a pool, &c. *h.*

كنڈي कंडी *kanḍī*, f. cakes of dried cow-dung, used as fuel. *s.*

كنڈي कुंडी *kunḍī*, f. a chain or iron catch to fasten a door, a hasp or staple. *h.*

كنڈيرا कंडेरा *kanḍerā*, m. a cleaner of cotton. *h.*

كنر किन्नर *kinnar*, m. a kind of singers or choristers in the court of Indra; a demigod attached to the service of Kuvera, the god of riches. *s.*

كنرس कणरस *kan-ras*, m. taking a pleasure in hearing (music, &c.). *h.*

كنرسيا कणरसिया *kanrasiyā*, m. a lover of music, an amateur. *s.*

كنڑبوجي कुंड़बोजी *kunṛ-bojī*, } the name given by
كنڑمنڈلا कुंड़मुंडला *kunṛ-munḍlā*, } husbandmen to the day on which sowing is concluded. *h.*

کنڑي कनड़ी *kanṛī*, f. name of a musical mode or *rāginī*. *h.*

کنز *kanz*, m. a treasure, store. *a.*

کنس कंस *kaṅs* or *kaṅsa*, the name of a wicked tyrant whom *Krishṇa* was born to destroy. *s.*

کنسلائي कनशलाई *kan-salā,ī* or *-shalā,ī*, f. a kind of scolopendra or julus, which is said to get into the brain through the ears, and by its bite occasion excessive pain, and even death. *s.*

کنش *kanish*, m. a miser, a niggard. *d.*

کنست *kanist*, } m. Christian church, a Jewish synagogue, a temple of idolaters. *p.*
کنشت *kanisht*, }

کنشٹھ कनिष्ठ *kanishṭh*, adj. little, least, smallest; m. a younger brother. *s.*

کنشٹھا कनिष्ठा *kanishṭhā*, } f. the little finger. *s.*
کنشٹھکا कनिष्ठिका *kanishṭhikā*, }

کنعان *kan'ān*, the country of Canaan. *a.*

کنعاني *kan'ānī*, of or relating to Canaan, a Canaanite. *a.*

کنف *kanaf*, side, shore; a wing. *a.*

کنک कनक *kanak*, m. gold; the plant *Datura*, or thorn-apple (*Datura metel*). *kanik*, m. wheaten flour. *s.*

کنک कणिक *kanki*, f. ground rice, or the scraps that fly off in pounding rice to separate it from the husk. *s.*

کنکا कणिका *kanikā*, f. fine sand (particularly grittiness or sand in bread); an atom, a particle, a grain; a kind of rice. *s.*

کنکاج *kinkāj*, } advice, council, consideration. *p.*
کنکاش *kinkāsh*, }

کنکالن कंकालिन *kankālin*, f. a kind of witch, hag, or sorceress. *s.*

کنکٹا कनकटा *kankaṭā*, ear-cropt, earless. *s.*

کنکٹي कनकटी *kankaṭī*, f. a disorder in the ears. *s.*

کنکر किङ्कर *kinkar*, m. a slave, a bondsman. *s.*

کنکر कंकर *kankar*, m. a nodule of limestone; stone, gravel. *s.*

کنکرا कंकरा *kankarā*, m. a stone ball with which boys play, a marble, pebble. *s.*

کنکرول कंकरोल *kankrol*, m. a kind of gourd (*Momordica mixta, Roxb.*). *s.* [marble. *s.*

کنکري कंकरी *kankarī*, f. a small stone ball or

کنکرول कंक्रोल *kānkrol*, m. a kind of gourd (*Momordica mixta*). *s.*

کنکريلا कंक्रेला *kankrelā*, abounding in gravel. *s.*

کنکلاٹ *kankalāṭ*, a sort of stiff sandy loam. *h.*

کنکم कुङ्कुम *kunkum*, m. saffron (*Crocus sativus*). *s.*

کنکما कुङ्कुमा *kunkumā*, m. a vessel in which the red mixture is contained with which they play at the Holī. *s.* [ornament for the wrist. *s.*

کنکن कंकण or कङ्कण *kankan*, m. a bracelet, or

کنکنا *kunkunā*, lukewarm. *d.*

کنکني किङ्किणी *kinkiṇī*, f. a kind of girdle with small bells or any tinkling ornament (for women and children). *s.*

کن کوا *kan-kauwā*, a species of flying kite. *d.*

کنکوت *kan-kūt*, estimated valuation of the crop while standing in the field. *h.*

کنکھ कुनख *kunakh*, m. a disease of the nails. *kunakhī*, having diseased nails. *s.*

کنکھجورا कंखजूरा *kankhajūrā*, m. centipede (*Scolopendra*); (v. *kan-salā,ī*). *s.*

کنکھي कंखी *kankhī*, } f. a side glance, a squint, a sly look, ogle. *kankhiyā dekhnā*, to ogle, to look with side glance, to leer. *s.*
کنکھيا कंखिया *kankhiyā*, }

کنکي कणकी *kankī*, f. ground rice, or the scraps that fly off in pounding rice to separate it from the husk. *s.*

کنکائي *kankā,ī*, of or relating to *kankā*, a place famous for its breed of horses. *p.*

کنگاش *kingāsh*, counsel, deliberation. *p.*

کنگال कंगाल *kangāl*, poor, friendless, miserly. *kangāl-bānkā*, poor and proud. *s.* [tion. *s.*

کنگالتا कंगालता *kangālatā*, f. poverty, destitu-

کنگالٹر कंगालटर *kangālṭar*, vain-glorious. *s.*

کنگالن कंगालिन *kangālin*, f. a witch, a sorceress. *s.*

کنگايش *kingā,ish*, parsimony (v. *kangāl*). *s. h.*

کنگروڑ कंगरोड़ *kangroṛ*, m. the ridge of the back, the spine; name of a bird (water fowl). *h.*

کنگره *kangura*, m. a niched battlement of a castle, &c.; a port-hole, a vidette; a pinnacle, a turret; a parapet wall; plumes upon helmets, or ornaments upon crowns. *kangura-dār*, spired, having a turret, parapet, &c. *p.*

کنگري किङ्गरी *kingrī*, f. a musical instrument something like the *bīn* or *vīna*, having only two steel strings and three or four pumpkins or calabashes as sounding boards: it is somewhat smaller than the *vīnā*. *h.* [letic. *h.*

کنگڑا कुंगड़ा *kungṛā*, able-bodied, robust, ath-

کنگڑائي कुंगड़ाई *kungṛā,ī*, f. strength, robustness. *h.*

کنگلتا कुंगलता *kangaltā*, f. penury, poverty. *s.*

كنگن कंगन *kangan*, m. an ornament worn on the wrists by Hindū women. *s.*

كنگنا कंगना *kangnā*, m. a thread tied round a bridegroom's wrist. *s.*

كنگني कंगनी *kangnī*, f. a cornice; a small grain, millet (*Panicum italicum*). *s.*

كنگوره *kangūra*, m. (v. *kangura*). *p.*

كنگوڑي कङ्गूड़ी *kangūṛī*, f. the lobe of the ear. *h.*

كنگها कङ्घा *kanghā*, m. } a comb, (in Dakh.) كنگهي कङ्घी *kanghī*, f. } *kango,ī*. *kanghī sañwārnā*, to adjust the hair which has been disordered in sleep. *kanghī-k.*, to comb the hair. *s.*

كنگهوءا *kanghū,ā*, m. a kind of rake or harrow. *d.*

كنگي *kangī*, f. a large jar or vessel in which grain is kept: it is made of split cane or wicker-work plastered with clay. *d.*

كننده *kunanda*, a maker, a factor, an agent. *kananda*, a digger, an instrument for digging. *p.*

كنوار *kanwār*, m. a small species of the aloe from which the medicinal drug is obtained. *d.*

كنوار कुँवार *kuṅwār*, } (v. *kumār*, &c.) a كنوارا कुँवारा *kuṅwārā*, } son, a boy, an unmarried youth; a prince, an heir apparent. *s.*

كنواري कुँवारी *kuṅwārī*, f. a daughter, an unmarried girl; a princess. *s.*

كنوان *kuṅwāṅ* (for *kū,ā*, q. v.), a well. *h.*

كنواءي कनवाई *kanwā,ī*, f. boring the ears. *s.*

كنوٹها कनौठा *kanauṭhā* or *kanoṭhā*, m. any situation in an apartment close to an angle of the wall. *s.*

كنوٹي *kanoṭī*, the ear (of a horse). *d.*

كنوج कनोज *kanoj* or *kanauj*, an ancient city and kingdom of India, where Porus is supposed to have reigned. *s.*

كنوجيا कनौजिया *kanaujiyā*, } a native of the كنوجيه कनौजियः *kanaujiya*, } city or kingdom of Kanoj; also the designation of various tribes, originally from that ancient kingdom. *s.*

كنور कुँवर *kuṅwar*, m. a boy, a son, a child; the son of a *rājā*, a prince. *s.*

كنوڑا कनौड़ा *kanauṛā* (v. *kanauṅḍā*). *kanauṛā-k.*, a. to gain ascendancy over another, or make him stand in awe. *h.*

كنول कँवल *kaṅwal*, m. the lotus (*Nymphæa nelumbo*); a shade for a candle, made of coloured silk or paper, ornamented. *kaṅwal-bād*, the jaundice. *kaṅwal-dah*, very deep water abounding with lotuses. *kaṅwal-nain*, having eyes like the flowers of the lotus. *s.*

كنون *kunūn* (v. *aknūn*), now, presently. *p.*

كنونڈ कनौंड *kanaunḍ*, m. diffidence, bashfulness. *h.*

كنونڈا कनौंडा *kanaunḍā*, diffident, bashful, standing in awe of, or afraid to meet another. *h.*

كنوه कनवः *kanwa*, a measure of capacity, the twentieth part of a ser. *h*

كنوءي कनवई *kanwa,ī*, a kind of clayey soil. *h.*

كنويا किनवैया *kinwaiyā*, m. a purchaser, a buyer. *s.*

كنه *kunh*, substance, quantity, measure, space, whole, total, extreme. *a.*

كنها कनहा *kanhā*, m. an officer employed by government to value the crops on the field. *kanihā*, revengeful malevolent. *h*

كنهاءي कनहाई *kanhā,ī*, f. valuation of crops of grain; m. a name of *Krishṇa* (*Bhāshā*). *h.*

كنهر कनहर *kanhar*, a rudder, a helm. *h.*

كنهرا कनहरा *kanharā*, m. attention, listening. *h.*

كنهريلا कनहरीला *kanharīlā*, m. a steersman. *h.*

كنهيا कन्हैया *kanhaiyā*, a name of *Krishṇa*. *h.*

كني कन्नी *kannī*, f. a spark of a diamond or of any other gem; bran. *kannī kāṭnā*, to undermine a person, or effect his ruin by clandestine means. *s.*

كني कने *kane*, near, close by, with, &c. *h.*

كنيا कन्या *kanyā*, f. an unmarried girl, a daughter; a virgin; the sign Virgo. *kanyā-putra* or *-suta*, the son of an unmarried girl. *kanyā-dān*, giving a girl in marriage; a gift to a girl upon her marriage a dowry. *s.*

كنيا कनैया *kanaiyā*, f. the ceremony of boring [the ears. *s.*

كنيانا कनियाना *kaniyānā*, a. to go to one side, to avoid one, to dodge, to shun. *h.*

كنياهٹ कनियाहट *kaniyāhaṭ*, f. shyness, coyness, timidity. *h.*

كنيت कुनीति *kunīti*, f. bad behaviour, ill manners; bad policy. *s.*

كنيت *kinyat* or *kunyat*, f. a metaphor, a name taken from the father, mother, &c. of the person signified, such as Arabian names beginning with *Ibn* or *Bin*, son, or the Celtic appellations beginning with *Mac*. *a.*

كنيٹي कनेटी *kaneṭī*, f. pulling the ears. *h.*

كنير कनेर *kaner*, m. a tree (*Cascaria ovata*). *kaner* or *kanel*, f. the name of a flower, the oleander (*Nerium odorum*): this flowering shrub grows wild in the beds of rivers and other moist places in most parts of Asia. Its Persian name is *khar-zahra*, and Arabic *difla*. *h.*

كنيرا कनीरा *kanīrā*, m. name of a caste of people, generally arrow-makers. *a.*

كنيز *kanīz*, } f. a female servant, a hand- كنيزك *kanīzak*, } maid, a slave girl. *p.*

كنيزي *kanīzī* (or *kanīzakī*), servitude. *p.*

كنيكا कन्यका *kanyakā*, f. a girl, a maiden; the Socotrine aloe (*Aloe perfoliata*). *s.*

كنيل *kanel* (v. *kaner*), f. name of a flower. *h.*

كنيه *kanaiya*, m. the ceremony of boring the ears. *s.*

كو को *ko*, post. (sign of the dative, and sometimes of the accusative) to, for. *kau* (in the Braj dialect) for *kā*, of. *ko* for *ko,ī*, any one; also for *kaun*, who? *ko* for *ki-o* (rel. pr.), who, which; (lit. that he, &c.). *h.*

كو *kū*, a broad street, square, market-place; residence or abode. *kū ba kū*, from street to street; from place to place. *p.*

كو *ko* (same as *kar*, &c.), the sign of the conjunctive participle. *kau* (same as *kab*), when? *d.*

كو कवि *kavi*, m. a poet. *s.*

كوءا कूआ *kū,ā*, m. a well; slice, division (of the jack fruit); cocoon (of the silk worm). *ko,ā*, angle (of the eye). *s.*

كوا कौवा *kawwā*, m. a crow. *kawwā-ṭhenṭhī*, f. name of a flower (*Clitoria ternatea*); (v. *aparājitā*). *kawwe kā nishāsta*, (lit. "crow's starch") a kind of arrowroot. *h.*

كوءار कूआर *kū,ār*, m. name of the sixth Hindū month, otherwise called *āsin*. *s.*

كوءارا कूआरा *kū,ārā*, m. an unmarried person, a bachelor. *kū,ārī*, an unmarried girl. *s.*

كوارپنه कूआरपना *kū,ārpanā*, m. the unmarried state. *s.*

كواري कूआरी *kū,ārī*, f. a maid, a damsel. *s.*

كواڑ किवाड़ *kiwāṛ*, | كواڑا किवाड़ा *kiwāṛā*, } m. a door, gate of a city, entrance. *h.*

كوافر *kawāfir* (pl. of كافر), infidels. *a.*

كواكب *kawākib* (pl. of كوكب), stars, constellations. *a.*

كوءان कूआं *kū,āṅ* (v. *kū,ā*), a well, a pit. *s.*

كوانچ किवांच *kiwāṅch*, name of a plant, cowach, a vermifuge (*Dolichos pruriens*). *h.*

كوءانر कूआंर *kū,āṅr* (v. *kū,ār*), m. the month [*āsin*. *s.*

كوب *kob*, | كوبان *kobān*, } (in comp.) beating, pounding, bruising. *p.*

كوبڑ कूबड़ *kūbaṛ*, m. a hump. *h.*

كوبڑا कूबड़ा *kūbṛā*, hump-backed. *h.*

كوبه *koba*, m. a wooden instrument for beating terraces, &c. with. *koba-kārī*, f. thumping, beating. *p.*

كوبي कोबी *kobī*, f. a cabbage, cauliflower. *h.*

كوپ कूप *kūp*, m. a well, a hole. *s.*

كوپ कोप *kop*, m. rage, passion, anger. *kop-jwalit* or *kop-dīpt*, incensed, enraged. *kop-wān*, passionate, angry. *kop-vej*, m. violence, impetuosity of passion. *s.*

كوپاكل कोपाकुल *kopākul*, furious, enraged. *s.*

كوپانوت कोपान्वित *kopānwit*, full of resentment. *s.*

كوپن कोपन *kopan*, wrathful, passionate. *s.*

كوپنا कोपना *kopnā*, n. to be angry; to be enraged; f. a passionate woman. *s.*

كوپني कोपिनी *kopinī*, f. | كوپي कोपी *kopī*, m. } passionate, rageful, wrathful. *s.*

كوپي कूपी *kūpī*, f. a small well. *s.*

كوپيرا कूपैरा *kūpairā*, unlucky, inauspicious. *h.*

كوپين कोपीन *kopīn* or कौपीन *kaupīn*, f. a cloth worn (round the waist) between the legs, commonly called a *langoṭī*, q. v.; a privy part. *s.*

كوت कूत *kūt*, m. survey, a task, guess, appraisement; rough estimate or valuation. *h.*

كوت कूत *kūt*, m. the base of a right-angled triangle. *s.*

كوتا कविता *kavitā*, | كوتائي कविताई *kavitā,ī*, } f. poetry, a poem. *s.*

كوتاه *kotāh*, small, little, short; mean. *kotāh-andesh*, improvident. *kotāh-bīn*, one who sees a short way; dim-sighted. *kotāh-pāe* or *kotāh-pācha*, short-footed; name of a kind of quadruped with a spotted back and horns like a deer: the term is applied sometimes to a hare, and hence (met.) to a very short, sneaking, little man. *kotāh-ḳadd*, of short stature. *kotāh-nazar*, short-sighted. *p.*

كوتاهي *kotāhī*, f. smallness, shortness; meanness, littleness; deficiency. *p.*

كوتك *kūtak*, m. a club, a short stick with which *bhang* is ground, a pestle. *kūtak-mārnā*, to cudgel, to thrash with a stick. *kūtak-khānā*, to receive a cudgelling or beating. *p.*

كوتك कौतुक *kautuk*, m. joy, pleasure, diversion, play, show, pastime, scene. *kūtak*, one of the rules in arithmetic or algebra. *s.*

كوتكي कौतुकी *kautukī*, m. a tumbler, a dancer, one who contributes to divert by exhibitions, &c.; adj. sportive. *s.*

كوتل कोतल *kotal*, m. a led horse. *kotal-kash*, m. a surcingle, particularly for fastening body cloths. *h.*

كوت‌مير कोतमीर *kot-mīr*, f. a kind of greens, coriander (v. *kothmīr*). *h.*

كوتنا कूतना *kūtnā*, a. to value, to appraise. *h.*

كوتوال *kotwāl*, m. the chief officer of the police for a city or town; a superintendant of the market. *p.*

كوتوالي *kotwālī*, f. the office of a *kotwāl*. *kotwālī chabūtara*, a place or hall for the office of a *kotwāl*. *p.*

كوتهه कोथ *koth*, m. inflammation and ulceration of the angles of the eyelids; gangrene. *s.*

كوته *kotah* (v. *kotāh*), short, little, mean. *kotah-andesh*, short-sighted, imprudent, improvident, indiscreet, wanting foresight. *kotah-ḳadd*, of short stature. *kotah-gardan*, short-necked; (met.) wicked, deceitful. *s.*

كوتهمير कोथमीर *kothmīr*, m. the coriander-plant; the seed is called *dhaniyā*, q. v. *s.*

كوتهي *kotahī*, f. (v. *kotāhī*), smallness, &c. *p.*

كوٹ कोट *koṭ* or कोट्ट *koṭṭ*, m. a fort, redoubt, castle; much, many. *kūṭ*, paper used to make paste-board. *koṭ-bāndh-baiṭhnā*, to sit with the legs crossed like the Asiatics, to sit (as they fancy) at one's ease. *h.*

كوٹ कोटि *koṭi*, a crore, or ten millions. *s.*

كوٹ कूट *kūṭ*, f. mimicry, buffoonery; fraud, trick. *kūṭ-tā*, f. falsehood, fraud. *s.*

كوٹاپلي *koṭāpalī*, f. a mallet. *d.*

كوٹارتھ-بهاشتا कूटार्थभाषिता *kūṭārtha-bhāshitā*, f. a tale, a fiction. *s.*

كوٹر कोटर *koṭar*, m. a kind of greens; holes made by birds in trees. *h.* [beaten, &c. *d.*

كوٹگا *koṭgā* (explained by *lat-khor*), kicked,

كوٹلي कोठली *koṭlī*, a division in a granary for different sorts of grain. *h.*

كوٹنا कूटना *kūṭnā*, to pound, to beat, to macerate; to cudgel. *h.* [worm. *s.*

كوٹھ कोठ *koṭh*, m. a species of leprosy; ring-

كوٹھا कोठा *koṭhā*, m. a house built of burnt bricks or stone; a story, a floor; a barn or storehouse. *h.*

كوٹھري कोठरी *koṭhrī*, f. a room, a chamber. *h.*

كوٹھمير کا كيڑا *koṭhmīr-kā kīṛā*, a winged bug. *d.*

كوٹھور कोठौर *koṭhaur* or *kūṭhaur*, out of place, improper. *h.*

كوٹھي कोठी *koṭhī*, f. a small (*pakkā*) house, a warehouse; granary, dwelling, mansion, barrack, chamber, bank, chest, factory; a banking house; the chamber of a gun; the womb; the ferrule or mounting at the end of a scabbard. *koṭhī-wāl*, a wholesale merchant, a warehouse-keeper. *h.* [grain. *h.*

كوٹي कोटी *koṭī*, an earthen reservoir for

كوثر *kausar*, m. the name of a well in paradise, from which flows a river of nectar; (met.) a beneficent prince or chief. *a.*

كوجاگر कोजागर *ko-jāgar*, (who is awake?) m. a night spent in festivity in the full moon of Aswin, in honour of Lakshmī. *s.*

كوچ *kūch*, m. marching, decamping. *kūch-k.*, n. to march, to depart. *p.*

كوچ कवच *kavach*, m. armour, a coat of mail; a drum used in battle, a kettle-drum; a tree (*Hibiscus populneoides*); an amulet, a charm. *kavach-patr*, m. a tree commonly called *Bhojpatr*, the bark of which, inscribed with mystical verses, serves as amulet. *ku-vach*, abusive, detracting. *s.*

كوچك *kūchak*, small, little, diminutive. *p.*

كوچكا कूचिका *kūchikā*, f. a small brush, a hair pencil. *s.* [lour, purple. *p.*

كوچكي *kūchakī*, f. smallness; name of a co-

كوچه *kūcha*, m. a lane, a street, a narrow passage, a row. *kucha-gadā*, a street beggar. *kūcha-gard*, one who perambulates the streets, a vagrant. *kūcha-gardī*, f. perambulation of the streets, wandering about in a city. *p.*

كوچها कूछा *kūchhā*, m. a tuft, cluster. *s.*

كوچي कूची *kūchī* (also *kūṅchī*), f. a brush. *s.*

كوچيا कूचिया *kūchiyā*, a small tamarind; part of the ear, the lobe. *h.*

كود कूद *kūd*, f. } a spring, jump, leap,
كودا कूदा *kūdā*, m. } bound. *kūdā bighā*, a bighā measured by so many leaps. *s.*

كودرو कोद्रव *kodrav*, m. a small grain, same as *kodo* q. v.

كودك *kodak*, m. a youth, a youngster, a boy. *p.*

كودگر *kodgar*, m. a digger, an excavator. *p.*

كودن *kaudan*, m. a horse of little value used to carry burthens; adj. weak in mind, dull. *a.*

كودنا कूदना *kūdnā*, n. to leap, to bound, to jump; (met.) to rejoice; to boast. *kūdnā-phāndnā*, n. to jump, to leap (about, as for joy). *s.*

كودو कोदो *kodo*, } m. name of a small grain,
كودرو कोद्रो *kodro*, } sown early during the rainy seasons (*Paspalum frumentaceum*, *Kan.*, *MS.*). *s.*

كور *kor* or *kūr*, blind. *kor-bakht*, unfortunate. *kor-bakhtī*, f. misfortune, calamity. *p.*

كور कोर *kor*, f. edge, border, margin, side; point; a crore, or ten millions. *h.*

كور कूर *kūr*, m. a violator; adj. cruel, savage. *kaur*, a mouthful. *h.* [*kuṅdr*). *h.*

كور *kuṅvar*, m. a son, a prince (v. *kuṅwar* or

كورا कोरा *korā*, new, unhandled, unused, fresh (applied only to clothes and earthen vessels; hence it is the mercantile name for plain silk cloth undyed). *kore-rahnā*, to be disappointed. *korā kāghaz*, white paper, i. e. paper not written upon. *h.*

كوراپن *korāpan*, newness, freshness; met. virginity of a girl. *h.*

كورپنڈ कौरपण्डु *kaur-paṇḍu*, the *Kauravas* and *Pāṇḍavas*, the patronymics of two ancient families of Delhi. *s.* [unblown flower. *h.*

كورك कोरक *korak*, m. a bud, blossom, an

كورم कूर्म *kūrm*, m. a tortoise (v. *kurm*). *s.*

كورنش *kornish*, f. a kind of salutation, which consists in raising the hand to the forehead and bending the head and shoulders forwards; adoration. *p.*

كورنگي कोरङ्गी *korangī*, f. small cardamums. *s.*

كورني कूरनी *kūrnī*, f. a scoop. *h.*

كورو कौरव *kaurava* or *kaurū*, a descendant of *Kuru*. *s.*

كورو कोरो *koro*, m. a rafter, a transverse beam. *h.*

كوري कोरी *korī*, f. a virgin, a damsel; (same as *koṛī*) a score, twenty. *h.*

كوري *korī* or *kūrī*, f. blindness. *p.*

كوري آنكهه سي ديكهنا *korī āṅkh se dekhnā*, to look from the corner of the eye. *d.*

كوڑ कोढ़ *koṛ*, m. the leprosy. *kūṛ* (v. *kūṛh*), foolish, stupid, &c. *s.*

كوڑا कोड़ा *koṛā*, m. a whip. *koṛā-h.*, a. to whip; to reduce to obedience; to put a horse to his speed by whipping. *koṛā mārnā*, a. to flog, to apply the lash. *kauṛā*, m. a shell of a large kind. *kūṛā*, sweepings, dirt, rubbish. *h.*

كوڑبالا कोड़बाला *koṛ-bālā*, m. the name of a bird; also the name of a snake; and lastly, the name of a flower. *h.* [excavate. *h.*

كوڑنا कोड़ना *koṛnā*, a. to dig out, to scoop,

كوڑه कूढ़ *kūṛh*, foolish, stupid, a sloven, a simpleton. *s.*

كوڑه कोढ़ *koṛh*, m. the leprosy; the white leprosy, causing a discolouring of the skin. This is the disease in a mild form: it is often curable. The black leprosy, which is incurable, and in which the fingers and toes, &c. rot and drop off, is called *juẕām*. *koṛh meṅ khāj nikalnā*, the itch to break out in leprosy, or in leprosy to catch the itch; (met.) to have one misfortune added to another. *s.*

كوڑهنا कोढ़ना *koṛhnā*, a. to vex, to afflict, to grieve. *h.* [leprosy. *h.*

كوڑهي कोढ़ी *koṛhī*, a leper, one affected by

كوڑي कोड़ी *koṛī*, f. a score, twenty (probably a corruption of the English word); (in Dakh.) a sloping pavement of stonework at one end of a tank, to let the water off when the tank is too full. *h.*

كوڑي कौड़ी *kauṛī*, f. a small shell used as coin (*Cypræa moneta*); money, fare, hire; a gland; the point of the sternum, or ensiform cartilage. *phuṭī kauṛī* or *kānī kauṛī*, a bit of money of the lowest value. *kauṛī-būk*, venal. *h.*

كوڑيالا कौड़ियाला *kauṛiyālā* or *kauṛiyāla*, m. a kind of snake; a rich person; name of a bird, the kingfisher. *h.*

كوز *kūz*, m. a hump. *kūz-pusht*, hump-backed. *kūz-pushtī*, hump-backedness. *p.*

كوزه *kūza*, m. a gugglet or goglet, a long-necked earthen pot for water; a jug or mug; a kind of rose; a lump of sugar which has been crystallized in an earthen pot. *p.*

كوس कोश *kos*, m. a measure of about two miles, but varying in different parts of India; a piece added to the end of a sleeve, a cuff. *s.*

كوس *kūs*, m. a kettledrum, drum. *p.*

كوسا कोसा *kosā*, a curse, malediction. *d.*

كوستبهه कौस्तुभ *kaustubh*, m. the jewel on *Krishṇa's* breast. *s.* [*rāj-pūts*. *h.*

كوسك कौसिक *kausik*, name of a tribe of

كوسكي *kausikī* (v. *kaushikī*) *s.*

كوسلي कोसली *koslī*, m. new leaves just sprouting. *h.*

كوسنا कोशना *kosnā*, a. to curse. *s.*

كوسنبهه कौसुम्भ *kausumbh*, dyed with safflower. *s.* [comp.) striving, exerting. *p.*

كوش *kaush*, a kind of slipper. *kosh*, (in

كوش कोश *kosh* or कोष *kosha*, m. a sheath, a scabbard; a judicial trial by oath or ordeal; a dictionary; a testicle; a nutmeg; (same as *kos*, q. v.) *kosh-bṛiddhi*, f. swelling of the testicle. *s.*

كوش कौश *kaush*, m. the city of Kanyākubja or Kanauj. *s.*

كوشٿهه कोष्ठ *koshṭh*, m. a granary; an apartment; any of the viscera, as heart, lungs, &c. *koshṭhāgni*, m. the digestive faculty, the gastric juice. *s.*

كوشش *koshish*, endeavour, effort, attempt, application, study. *koshishi behūda*, a vain attempt. *koshish-k.*, to attempt, to endeavour. *p.*

كوشك *kūshk*, m. a palace, a villa. *p.*

كوشكي कौशिकी *kaushikī*, f. name of a river in the province of Bahār. *s.*

كوشل कोशल *koshal*, m. f. or *koshalā*, f. a name of the city of Ayodhya (Oude) or neighbouring district. *kaushal*, m. happiness, welfare. *s.*

كوشلي कौशली *kaushalī*, f. greeting, friendly inquiry, respectful present. *kaushalya*, m. good fortune, well-being. *s.*

كوشنا कोशना *koshnā*, a. to curse. *s.*

كوشيدن *koshīdan*, to strive, to make efforts. *p.*

كوشيه कौशेय or कौषेय *kausheya*, silken. *s.*

كوفت *koft*, f. vexation, grief, anguish; inlaying of gold on steel or any other metal. *koft-kob*, beating. *koft-gar*, m. a gilder. *p.*

كوفتن *koftan* (r. *kob*), to pound, to beat, to hash (meat, &c.). *p.* [of dish. *p.*

كوفته *kofta*, pounded, beaten (meat); a kind

كوفه *kūfa*, a town on the Euphrates, near Baṣra. *a.* [to cry, to sob. *s.*

كوك कूक *kūk*, f. sobbing, crying. *kūk-mārnā*,

كوك कोक *kok*, m. *scientia modorum diversorum coeundi; a quodam Kok paṇḍit explicata unde nomen;* the ruddy goose (*Anas cascara*). *h.*

كوك कवक *kawak*, m. same as *kawal*, q. v.

كوكا कोका *kokā*, m. a foster-brother, nurse's son; a small nail, a tack; a kind of lotus. *h.*

كوكب *kaukab*, m. a star, a constellation. *a.*

كوكبه *kaukaba*, m. stars made of gold, silver, tinsel, &c., as ornaments or insignia of rank. *s.*

كوكر कूकर *kūkar*, m. a dog. *kūkar-chal*, f. a trot. *kūkar-mutā*, m. a mushroom (growing on wood), a toadstool. *s.*

كوكري कूकरी *kūkrī*, f. a bundle of thread; maize, Indian corn (*Zea mais*); the gripes. *h.*

كوكڑيانا कूकड़ियाना *kūkaṛiyānā*, a. to cover, to overlay. *h.*

كوكشاستر कोकशास्त्र *koh-shāstr*, m. the name of a treatise by *Kok-panḍit* (v. *kok*). *s.*

كوكل कोकिल *kokil*, } f. the name of a bird;
كوكلا कोकिला *kokilā*, } a black cuckoo (*Cuculus*). *kokil-baini*, speaking like the *kokil*, eloquent as the *kokil*. *s.*

كوكنا कूकना *kūknā*, n. to sob, to cry, to scream; to sound (as the *kokil*); to wind up a watch. *h.*

كوكنار *kūknār*, m. the poppy plant. *p.*

كوكني कोकिनी *kokinī*, short, abbreviated. *h.*

كوكو कूकू *kūkū*, m. the cooing of a dove; an omelette (also the dish called *kūkū pulāw*). *h.*

كوكه कोख *kokh*, } m. f. the womb, the ab-
كوكها कोखा *kokha*, } domen, *hypochondrium*. *kokh-bandh*, barren. *s.*

كول कोल *kol*, m. a creek, a bay; any long narrow passage, a lane; name of a tribe of mountaineers between Benares and Bundelcund; a country, *Calinga*, on the sea-coast from Cuttack to Madras. *h.*

كول कवल *kaval* or कौल *kaul*, m. a mouthful; a kind of fish; an astringent wash for the mouth, a gargle; adj. well-born, of a good family. *kūl*, bank of a river; a heap, a mound; a pond or pool. *s.*

كولا कौला *kaulā*, m. (corner of a room, &c.) an armful; embrace; a sheaf or armful of corn (v. *kauliyā*). *h.*

كولا कौला *kaulā*, m. a kind of orange. *h.*

كولا कूला *kūlā*, m. the hip, the buttock. *h.*

كولا कोला *kolā*, m. a jackal. *kolon ko daghā denā*, to cheat the jackals, *i. e.* to escape death, to rob the gallows. *h.*

كولاهل कोलाहल *kolāhal*, m. noise, uproar, tumult; quarrelling. *s.*

كولٹي *kūlṭī*, a wooden poker, or stake burnt [at one end. *d.*

كولڈا कोलड़ा *kolḍā* (v. *koṛā*), a whip, &c. *h.*

كولسا *kolsā*, m. charcoal (in Urdū *ko,elā*). *d.*

كولك कौलिक *kaulik*, ancestral. *s.*

كولو कोलू *kolū*, m. an oilman, name of a caste whose business it is to sell oil. *h.*

كولو कौलव *kaulav*, m. one of the astronomical periods called *karans*. *s.*

كولهو कोल्हू *kolhū*, m. a sugar-mill; an oilman's press. *kolhū meṅ paṛwā denā*, to macerate in a press; an expression signifying to destroy utterly, to crush to atoms. *h.*

كولي कोली *kolī*, m. a weaver. *kūlī* (for *ḳulī*), a labourer, porter, a cooley. *h.* [arms.

كولي कौली *kaulī*, f. embrace, grasp of the

كولي कोले *kole*, lap, bosom, embrace. *h.*

كوليا कौलिया *kauliyā*, m. a lane, a narrow street. *kauliyā*, a bundle of sheaves of corn given as perquisites to reapers and village servants. *h.*

كوليا कौलिया *kauliyā*, f. a small mouthful. *s.*

كوليانا कोलियाना *koliyānā* or *kauliyānā*, a. to take in the lap, to embrace. *h.*

كومار कौमार *kaumār*, m. youth, childhood. *kaumārī*, adj. maiden, virgin. *s.* [bread. *h.*

كومانچه कूमांछ *kūmāṅchh*, m. f. a kind of

كومد कौमुद *kaumud*, m. the month Kārtik. *s.*

كومدي कौमुदी *kaumudī*, f. moonlight. *s.*

كومل कोमल *komal*, soft, placid, tender. *s.*

كوملتا कोमलता *komaltā*, } or *komalatā*,
كوملتائي कोमलताई *komaltā,ī*, } f. softness, placidity. *s.*

كومهل कूम्हल *kūmhal*, burglary. *kūmhal-denā*, to break into (a house) through the wall. *h.*

كون कौन *kaun*, pron. who? which? what? *h.*

كون कौं *kauṅ*, postpos. for *ko*, dat. and acc. *h.*

كون *kaun*, that which exists; the universe. *kaun wa makān*, the whole creation. *a.*

كون कोण *koṇ*, m. a corner, an angle. कोणि *koṇi*, having a crooked arm. *s.*

كون *kūn*, f. podex, the backside. *p.*

كونا कोणा *koṇā*, m. corner, side, an angle. *koṇā-dār*, having corners or angles. *s.*

كوناكتهرا कोणाकुथरा *koṇā-kuthrā*, m. house, room, hole and corner, every corner, &c. *s.*

كوناءي कूनाई *kunā,ī*, f. a scrap. *s.*

كونبهل *kombhal* (v. *komhal*), burglary, &c. *h.*

كونپل कोंपल *kompal*, m. f. a young shoot, a bud. *s.*

كونپلي *kompalī*, f. (v. *kompal*) a bud, &c. *d.*

كونت कोन्त *kont*, f. a spear. *s.*

كونت कूंत *kūnt*, m. conjecture, guess.

كونج कूंज *kūṅj* (also *kūṅjā*), m. the name of a bird, perhaps the crane.

كونچ कूंच *kūṅch*, m. the little red seed that goldsmiths use for weights (*Abrus precatorius*). *s.*

كونچلي konchlī, a long tooth; the tusk of a boar. d. [to pierce, to stab, to gore. h.

كونچنا कोंचना koṅchnā or kūṅchnā, a. to thrust,

كونچي कूंची kūṅchī, f. (also kūchī) a brush. h.

كوندا कौंधा kaundā, m. (v. kaundhā). h.

كوندار कोणदार kona-dār, cornered, angled. s.

كوندلا कूंदला kūndlā, m. a kind of tent. h.

كوندنا कौंदना kauṅdna, n. to glare, flash, lighten. h. [flash (as of lightning). h.

كوندھ कौंध kauṅdh, f. splendour, brightness,

كوندھا कौंधा kauṅdhā, m. lightning. h.

كوندھنا कौंधना kaundhnā, n. to lighten, to flash (as lightning). h.

كونڈا कूंडा kūṇḍā, m. a vessel for kneading bread in, a platter; the chaff or coarse part of rice. *kūṇḍā kārlnā*, to prosper. *kūṇḍā-k., dicitur cum plures viri, unus post alterum, mulierum violant.* h.

كونڈبار konḍ-bār, straight, tight, narrow. d.

كونڈنا konḍnā, a. to imprison, to confine. d.

كونڈھا कोंढा konḍhā, m. name of a gourd (*Cucurbita pepo*). s.

كونڈي कूंडी kūṇḍī, f. an instrument or vessel in which snuff and bhang, &c. are ground. h.

كونسا कौनसा kaun-sā, what like? of what kind or sort? h.

كونكن कोङ्कण konkan, m. the name of a country in the southern peninsula (vulg. *concan*). s.

كونلا कौंला kauṅlā, m. a species of orange; a corner; adj. raw, unripe; young, of few years. *kauṅlī haḍḍī*, gristle. d.

كون مكان kaun-makān, } the world, the
كون ومكان kaun o makān, } universe, all created beings. a.

كونه कोण konā, m. a corner, an angle (v. konā). h.

كوني kaunī, worldly, material. a.

كوني kūnī, m. a catamite, a sodomite. p.

كونيري कोनेरी konerī, f. (v. konā) an angle. s.h.

كوني konī, f. (for kohnī) the elbow. d.

كونين kaunain, the two worlds, *i.e.* the present and future, or the world of mortals and that of immortals. a.

كوءو कोऊ ko,ū (Braj for ko,ī), any, some. h.

كوودار कोविदार kovidār, m. a species of ebony (*Bauhinia variegata*). s.

كوورا कूबरा kūvrā, m. a humpbacked man. s.

كوه koh, m. mountain, a hill, hillock. *kohi akhẓar*, the green or emerald mountain, *i.e.* the mountain *ḳāf*. *koh-paikar*, like a mountain, huge, gigantic, "instar montis." *kohi rawān* or *kohi rawanda*, the moving mountain, *i.e.* the elephant. p.

كوها कूहा kūhā, f. fog, mist, vapour. h.

كوهان kauhān, m. the hump of a bullock or camel. p.

كوهچه kohcha, a small mountain, a hill. p.

كوهخر koh-khar, the oneager or wild ass. p.

كوهر कोहर kohar, m. a fog; name of a fruit. h.

كوهرا कूहरा kūhrā, m. fog, mist. h.

كوهڑ कोहड़ kohaṛ, the frame of the mouth of a well. h. [try. p.

كوهسار koh-sār, mountainous, a hilly coun-

كوهستان kohistān, m. a forest; a mountainous country; *'Irāḳ* or ancient Parthia. p.

كوهني कोहनी kohnī, f. the elbow. s.

كوهه kauha, m. the hump of an ox or camel. p.

كوهي kohī, of or relating to the mountains; m. a mountaineer, a highlander. p.

كوهي कोही kohī, f. a species of hawk (*Falco cristatellus, B.*). h.

كوءي कोई ko,ī, any, anybody, one, a or an, somebody. *ko,ī dam meṅ*, in a few moments, speedily. *ko,ī-sā*, certain, somebody, something. *ko,ī na ko,ī*, some one or other. *ko,ī nahīṅ*, nobody. *ko,ī hai?* is there any one (in attendance)? a phrase used in India for calling servants, hence the well-known nickname "*qui hy*," applied to old Indians. s.

كوي कोई ko,ī, f. the water lily (*Nymphæa lotus*). h. [(*Artocarpus integrifolia*). h.

كوي कोई ko,ī, f. the pulp of the jack fruit

كوءي kū,e or kū, m. a street, a lane. p.

كوءيتا ko,etā, m. billhook, a cutting instrument used by toddy-drawers (called in Urdū *dāw*). d.

كويت kawit (same as kāwit), the wood-apple (called in Urdū *kaṭh-bel*, q. v.). d.

كوير कूबेर kuver or kuvera, m. the Hindū Plutus, the god of riches. s.

كوءيري kū,īrī, f. a ring worn as an ornament round the toe. d.

كويڑي कोएड़ी ko,eṛī, m. a planter, a husband man, a gardener; name of a Hindū caste whose profession is husbandry. h.

كويل कोयल koyal or कोइल ko,il or ko,el, f. name of a bird, the Indian cuckoo (*Cuculus*); a flower (*Clitoria tornatea*). s.

كوءيلا कोयला koyalā or कोएला ko,elā, m. charcoal. s. [*ius coboius*). s.

كويي कवयी kavayī, f. a kind of flat-fish (*Co-*

كويلو kawelū, m. a tile. d.

كوين कोयण koyaṇ, m. a corner. s.

كه ख kh, the aspirate form of क; the sky, ether. s.

كه *ki*; this word is used in various ways; 1st, as a rel. pron. who, which, that; 2nd, as a conj. that, since, for, 3rd, it is frequently employed in the sense of the Greek ὅτι, denoting thus, as follows saying, &c. *p.*

كه *kih.* small, little, slender, mean. *p.*

كها कहा *kahā*, m. order, leave, saying, confession, affirmation, advice. *s.*

كهابڑ खाबड़ *khābaṛ*, uneven (used in conjunction with *aubaṛ*). *h.* [stead. *h.*

كهات खात *khāt*, f. manure; (Dakh.) a bed-

كهات खात *khāt*, m. a pit; a subterraneous granary (in Hind. generally changed into *khāḍ*). *s.*

كهاتا खाता *khātā*, m. the act of eating; daily account, day-book. *khātā-bāṛī*, f. a storehouse. *h.*

كهاتابندي खाताबंदी *khātā-bandī*, f. an abstract of individual accounts. *h.*

كهاتاوني खाताधनी *khātāwanī*, f. a ledger. *h.*

كهاتگي *khātagī*, f. food, eating. *d.*

كهاتي खाती *khātī*, f. name of a caste generally employed as cartwrights. *h.*

كهاٹ खाट *khāṭ*, f. (also *khawāṭ*) a bedstead, a bier, a cot on which dead bodies are conveyed to the pile. *s.*

كهاج खाज *khāj*, m. f. the itch. *s.*

كهاجا खाजा *khājā*, m. name of a sweetmeat like pie-crust. *s.* [vour. *s.*

كهاجانا खाजाना *khā-jānā*, to eat up, to de-

كهاد खाद *khād*, f. (v. *khāt*) dung, manure; the expense incurred by the cultivators in preparing their ploughing apparatus. *s. h.*

كهاڈ खाद *khāḍ*, m. (v. *khāt*) a pit, &c. *s.*

كهادر खादर *khādar*, low or alluvial lands fit for rice cultivation. *h.* [rower, a user. *s.*

كهادك खादक *khādak*, lit. an eater; a bor-

كهادي *khādī*, a kind of coarse cotton stuff. *d.*

كهاديه खाद्य *khādya*, edible; m. victuals. *s.*

كهار खार *khār*, m. alkali, potash, impure carbonate of potash or soda. *s.*

كهار कहार *kahār*, m. name of a tribe of Sudras in Bahar, employed in cities as palankeen bearers. *s.*

كهارا खारा *khārā*, salt, brackish. *s.*

كهارا खारा *khārā*, m. a net (in which straw is tied). *h.*

كهارج खारज *khārj*, f. the bass in music. *h.*

كهاروءا खारूआ *khārū,ā*, m. a coarse kind of red cloth of cotton. *h.*

كهاروا खारवा *khārwā*, m. a sailor (a term much used on the western coasts of India). *h.*

كهارواماٹي खारवामाटी *kharwā-māṭī*, alkaline soil. *h.*

كهاري खारी *khārī*, salt, brackish; f. a creek, an inlet or backwater. *khārī shor*, very brackish and saline. *s.*

كهاڑو *khāṛū*, a decrepit old man. *d.*

كهاسا कुहासा *kuhāsā*, m. a fog, a mist, a vapour. *s.*

كهاسني कहासुनी *kahā-sunī*, } f. discussion,
كهاكهي कहाकही *kahā-kahī*, } altercation, conversation. *s.*

كهاگ खाग *khāg*, m. the horn of a rhinoceros; a pillar or mound marking the boundaries of a village. *s.*

كهال *kuhhāl*, m. an oculist. *kihāl* (pl. of *kahl*), men of full age, from 30 to 50; men beginning to turn grey. *a.*

كهال खाल *khāl*, an inlet of the sea or of a large river, a creek. *h.*

كهال खाल *khāl*, } f. skin, hide; bellows; a
كهالا खाला *khālā*, } rivulet, river, canal. *khāl khainchnā*, to take the skin off, to flay. *s.*

كهالت *kahālat*, f. indolence, inactivity, sloth. *a.*

كهام *khām*, m. a post or pillar; tentpole; mast of a ship; column. *d.*

كهان खान *khān* or खानि *khāni*, f. a mine; (met.) a nest, a heap, abundance, receptacle. *p. s.*

كهان कहां *kahāṅ*, where? whither? *kahāṅ tak*, how far? how long? to what degree? *kahāṅ se*, whence? *kahāṅ kā kahāṅ*, to what degree? extremely, immensely. *h.*

كهانا खाना *khānā*, a. to eat, to suffer, sustain, or experience; to embezzle; (met.) to hold, to contain; to get. *ḳasam khānā*, to make oath, to swear. *khā-jāna*, to eat up. *khā,e ghar ke bhāṅse ginnā*, or *khā,e bhāle meṅ chhed bhānā* (Dakh.), to act treacherously, to prove ungrateful. *s.*

كهانا खाना *khānā*, m. food, dinner, eating. *khānā-pīnā*, food and drink, livelihood. *s.*

كهانا कहाना *kahānā*, a. to cause to speak: it also signifies, in a neuter sense, "to be called or named." *h.*

كهانت *kihānat*, office of priest; divination, soothsaying. *a.*

كهانچ खांच *khāṅch*, m. slime, mud. *h.*

كهانچا खांचा *khāṅchā*, m. a tray, a basket, a pannier; a cage, a hencoop; a marsh, a quagmire; muddy or marshy soil. *h.*

كهاندا *khāndā* (for *kāndhā*), m. the shoulder. *d.*

كهانڈ खांड *khāṅḍ*, m. sugar (coarse). *s.*

كهانڈا खांडा *khāṅḍā*, m. a sword, cutlass; a cleaver (butcher's); a flake or slice (of fish). *khāṅḍe ke dhar par chalnā*, to arbitrate, to decide. *s.*

کهانڈنا खांडना *khāndnā*, a. to excavate, to pound. *h.* [of coughing. *s.*

کهانسنا खांसना *khāṅsnā*, n. to cough; m. act

کهانسي खांसी *khāṅsī*, f. a cough. *s.*

کهانکهر खानखर *khānkhar*, m. a pit, a shaft (of a mine); any thing very dry. *h.*

کهانگ खांग *khāṅg*, m. a tusk. *h.*

کهانهارا खान्हारा *khānhārā*, m. eater, devourer. *s.*

کهاني कहानी *kahānī*, f. a tale, story, fable. *s.*

کهاو खाव *khāw*, f. manure. *khā,ū*, m. a glutton. *h.* [ing, an adage. *s.*

کهاوت कहावत *kahāwat*, f. a proverb, a say-

کهاء وميت *khā,ū-mīt*, avaricious, greedy. *d.*

کهاون कहावन *kahāwan*, m. (v. *kāhan*) an aggregate number of 1280 *kauris*. *s.*

کهاءي खाई *khā,ī*, f. a ditch, trench, a moat, especially as a boundary between two estates. *s.*

کهب *khab*, a wrinkle, a fold, a notch, a groove. *d.*

کهبا खब्बा *khabbā*, left-handed. *h.*

کهبسا खबसा *khabsā*, m. slime, mud. *h.*

کهبنا खुबना *khubnā*, } a. to affect, to pene-
کهبهنا खुभना *khubhnā*, } trate, to stick into; to adorn. *h.*

کهپاچ खपाच *khapāch*, f. a piece torn off from a bamboo, a splinter; a very lean person. *h.*

کهپانا खपाना *khapānā*, a. to dry up, to destroy, to waste, to make away with (a thing). *h.*

کهپت खपत *khapat*, expended; f. vent, sale. *h.*

کهپتي खपती *khaptī*, f. vent, sale, expense; request; a lunatic. *h.* [of mango. *s.*

کهپٹا खपटा *khapṭā*, m. a broken tile; a slice

کهپر खपुर *khapur*, m. the betel tree (*Areca fanfel or catechu*).

کهپر खप्पर *khappar*, m. the skull, the cranium; a chafing-dish; an earthen cup used by *jogis*. *s.*

کهپرا खपरा *khaprā*, m. a tile for roofing. *s.*

کهپرا खपरा *khaprā*, m. an arrow with a broad point. *h.*

کهپري खपरी *khaprī*, f. a small tile; the skull. *s.*

کهپريا खपरिया *khapariyā*, a heavier sort of plough for stiff soil. *h.*

کهپريل खपरैल *khaprail*, f. a tiled house; (in Dakh.) *khaprel*, a tile. *khaprel kī jālī*, a window built of semicircular tiles. *s.*

کهپکهپاٹ *khupkhupāṭ*, envy, spite. *d.*

کهپکهپانا *khupkhupānā*, to pierce, to envy, become enraged. *d.*

کهپلا *khiplā*, m. a fish scale; crust or scab. *d.*

کهپنا खपना *khapnā*, n. to be dried up; to sell, to go off; to remain, to join, to mix with, to enter, to penetrate; m. a company (of travellers, &c.). *h.*

کهتا *khattā*, a kind of liniment for inflamed eyes. *d.* [is kept. *h.*

کهتا खत्ता *khattā*, m. a cavity in which grain

کهتر *kih-tar*, less, very small, junior, mean, low. *p.* [caste of *khatrī*. *s.*

کهتراني खतरानी *khatrānī*, f. a female of the

کهتري *kihtarī*, f. littleness, smallness, &c. *p.*

کهتري खत्री *khatrī*, m. the second of the four grand Hindū castes, being that of the military order. *s.*

کهترين *kihtarīn*, very small, the least. *p.*

کهتوارا खतवारा *khatwārā*, m. a dunghill.

کهٹي खुत्ती *khuttī*, f. a purse, a small bag. *h.*

کهٹ खट *khaṭ* (for *shaṭ*), six. *khaṭ-pad*, m. (six-legged) a species of large black bee (v. *alī*). *khaṭ ras*, the six tastes (which are enumerated under *ras*, q. v.). *khaṭ-shāstr*, the six philosophical schools or sects of the Hindūs (called otherwise *khaṭ-darshan*, or *shaṭ-darshan*, or *shan-darshana*), viz.: 1. the *nyāya* or logic, taught by the sage *Gotama*; 2. the *vaisheshika*, taught by *Kaṇāda* or *Kaṅrāda*. It agrees with *nyāya* in some points and differs in others; 3. the *mīmāṅsā*, taught by *Jaimani*. It consists of rules for the construction and right interpretation of the *vedās*; 4. the *vedānta*, taught by *Vyāsadeva*. This constitutes the science of theology; 5. the *sānkhyā*, taught by *Kapila*. The followers of this sect disbelieve in a creator, saying that the universe is from all eternity; 6. the *pātanjal*, introduced by *Sheshanāga*. It agrees in every point with the *sānkhyā*, excepting that these make God to be the creator. *s.*

کهٹ खट *khaṭ* (v. *khāṭ*), f. a bedstead. *s.*

کهٹ *khiṭ*, filth, impurity. *khiṭ-jamnā*, filth to collect, or gather. *d.*

کهٹا खट्टा *khaṭṭā*, acid, sour. *khaṭṭā-sā*, sourish. *h.*

کهٹاپا *khuṭā-pā*, malice, spite, rancour. *d.*

کهٹاپٹي खटापटी *khaṭāpaṭī*, f. wrangling, quarrelling. *h.*

کهٹاپن खटापन *khaṭāpan*, } m. acidity, sour-
کهٹاپنا खटापना *khaṭāpanā*, } ness, moroseness. *h.*

کهٹاس खटास *khaṭās* or *khaṭṭās*, m. a pole cat; the cibet or zibet cat (*Viverra zibetha*). *h.*

کهٹاساگ खट्टासाग *khaṭṭā-sāg*, m. the herb sorrel. *h.*

کهٹاکا खटाका *khaṭākā*, m. a crash. *h.*

کهٹال खटाल *khaṭāl*, m. spring tide. *h.*

کھٹاو खटाव *khaṭāw*, m. a pin with which a boat is fastened. *h.*

کھٹائي खटाई *khaṭā,ī*, f. acidity, sourness; an acid. *khuṭā,ī*, f. perfidy, malice. *h.*

کھٹ پٹ खटपट *khaṭ-paṭ*, f. wrangling, contention, strife, clashing of weapons. *h.*

کھٹپٹ *khaṭ-paṭ* (v. *ghaṭ-paṭ*), conflict, wrangling, contention, quarrelling. *d.*

کھٹپچرا *khuṭ-pachṛā*, m. a spiteful malicious [person. *h.*

کھٹپورا खटपूरा *khaṭ-pūrā*, a kind of rake worked by hoemen for breaking up the soil into small beds. *h.*

کھٹچھپر खटछप्पर *khaṭ-chhappar* (v. *chhappar-khaṭ*), m. a bedstead with curtains. *s. h.*

کھٹ راگ खटराग *khaṭ-rāg*, m. wrangling; singing discordantly. *s.*

کھٹریا खटरिया *khaṭriyā*, m. name of an in- [sect. *h.*

کھٹک खट्टिक *khaṭṭik*, a hunter, one who lives by killing and selling game. *s.*

کھٹک खटक *khaṭak*, } or *khuṭkā*, m. apprehension, scruple, suspicion, doubt, suspense; sound of footsteps. *h.*
کھٹکا खटका *khaṭkā*, }

کھٹکانا खटकाना *khaṭkānā*, m. rapping, thumping, rattling (of a door, &c.). *h.*

کھٹکنا खटकना *khaṭaknā*, n. to wrangle, to offend, to rankle; to pierce (as a thorn); (sub.) doubt, hesitation, disgust. *khuṭaknā*, a. to nibble; to doubt. *h.*

کھٹ کھٹ *khaṭ-khaṭ*, noise, voice, sound; toil, trouble, difficulty; quarrelling, wrangling. *d.*

کھٹکھٹانا खटखटाना *khaṭkhaṭānā*, (v. *ṭhak-ṭhakānā*), to rap, tap, &c. *h.*

کھٹکھٹي *khiṭkhiṭī*, f. the sound of laughter, [giggling. *d.*

کھٹگیر खटगीर *khaṭgīr*, m. a bug. *s. p.*

کھٹمتوا खटमुत्वा *khaṭ-mutwā*, m. a piss-a-bed. *h.*

کھٹمل खटमल *khaṭmal*, m. a bug; the bed pollutor. *s.*

کھٹمیٹھا खटमीठा *khaṭ-mīṭhā*, m. a mixed taste of sour and sweet, agreeable. *h. s.*

کھٹنا खटना *khaṭnā*, a. to last (Beng.). *h.*

کھٹو खट्टू *khaṭṭū*, m. a labourer (Beng.). *h.*

کھٹو *khuṭṭū*, ashamed, abashed. *d.*

کھٹوا खटवा *khaṭwā*, f. a bedstead. *s.*

کھٹوات *khaṭwāṭ*, } confinement to bed from sickness (v. *aṭwāṭ*).
کھٹواتي *khaṭwāṭī*, }

کھٹوارا खटवारा *khaṭwārā*, m. a dunghill. *h.*

کھٹولا खटोला *khaṭolā*, m. a small bedstead. *s.*

کھٹولنا *khaṭolnā*, a bedstead, a kind of net or snare *d.*

کھٹي खुट्टी *khuṭṭī*, f. a treasure, hoard, store, a gnat. *h.*

کھٹیا खटिया *khaṭiyā*, f. a bedstead; a bier. *khudā kare uskā khaṭiyā nikle*, God grant his bier may be carried out, or may he die, (a common form of cursing). *s.*

کھٹیال *khaṭyāl*, soiled, filthy, impure. *d.*

کھٹیک खटीक *khaṭīk*, m. a hunter or fowler one who lives by killing and selling game. *s.*

کہج कहज *kahaj*, m. the strawberry. *h.*

کھجانا खिजाना *khijānā*, a. to vex, to tease, to irritate, to trouble, to disturb. *h.*

کھجانا खुजाना *khujānā*, a. to scratch, to rub gently with the nails, to titillate or tickle. *s.*

کھجلا खुजला *khujlā*, m. a kind of sweetmeat. *s.*

کھجلاپن खुजलापन *khujlāpan*, m. itching, titillation. *s.*

کھجلانا खुजलाना *khujlānā*, n. to itch, to [scratch, to tickle. *s.*

کھجلانا खिजलाना *khijlānā*, a. to vex, tease, irritate, disturb; n. to get angry. *h.*

کھجلاهٹ खुजलाहट *khujlāhaṭ*, f. titillating, itching. *s.*

کھجلنا खुजलना *khujalnā* (v. *khujhlānā*), n. to [itch, &c. *s.*

کھجلي खुजली *khujlī*, f. the itch, scab, herpes. *s.*

کھجور खजूर *khajūr*, m. a date, or date tree (*Phœnix dactylifera*); wild date (*Elate silvestris, Lin., Phœnix sylvestris, Roxb.*); a kind of sweetmeat. *khajūr-chhaṛī*, a kind of silk cloth stained with waving marks like the traces of the old leaves on the trunk of the date tree. *s.*

کھجورا खजूरा *khajūrā*, m. the ridge of a thatched roof; adj. plaited (as locks of hair). *h.*

کھجوریا खजूरिया *khajūriyā*, m. a little date or date tree. *s.*

کھجھ खिझ *khijh*, f. fretfulness, vexation, [teasing. *s.*

کھجھانا खिझाना *khijhānā*, to fret, to be vexed. *s.*

کھجھراها खुझराहा *khujhrāhā*, stringy, ropy. *h.*

کھجھلانا खिझलाना *khijhlānā*, } n. to be vexed, teased, irritated.
کھجھنا खिझना *khijhnā*, }

کھچا खिचा *khichā*, tense, tight; fine, slen- [der. *h.*

کھچاو खिचाव *khichāw*, m. drag, pull, draught; tenseness, tightness. *h.*

کھچا खचा *khachā*, } set (as a jewel), studded, inlaid. *s.*
کھچت खचित *khachit*, }

کھچر खचर *khachar*, m. a cloud. *s.*

کھچڑا *khichṛā* (v. *khichṛī*), a kind of dish. *d*

کهچڑي खिचड़ी *hhichṛī*, f. a dish made of pulse and rice boiled together; the flower of the ber tree (*Zizyphus jujuba*); earnest to dancing women when they are engaged for an entertainment; a mixed heap of gold and silver coin; a barbarous mixture of two languages, a *lingua franca* or jargon. *s.*

کهچنا खचना *hhachnā*, n. to be set (as a jewel). *s.*

کهچنا खिचना *hhichnā*, n. to be pulled, to be drawn; to be extracted, to be tightened, to be endured. *h.*

کهچوانا खिचवाना *hhichwānā* (v. *hhiṅchwānā*), a. to cause to draw. *h.*

کهدا *hhaddā*, m. a hole dug in the ground. *d.*

کهدانا खुदाना *hhudānā*, a. to cause to dig or to engrave. *s.*

کهدبدانا खदबदाना *hhadbadānā*, } n. to simmer, to make a boiling noise. *h.*
کهدکهدانا खदखदाना *hhadkhadānā*, }

کهدر खदिर *hhadir*, m. a tree, the resin of which is used in medicine, *kutthā* or catechu (*Mimosa catechu*). *khadiropam*, m. the Bābul (*Acacia Arabica*). *s.*

کهدڑنا *hhidaṛnā*, a. to pursue, to chase. *hhidaṛ-denā*, to drive, to propel. *d.*

کهدنا खुदना *hhudnā*, n. to be dug, hollowed, delved, or engraved. *s.*

کهدني खुदनी *hhudnī*, f. searching; a spade. *s.*

کهدوانا खुदवाना *hhudwānā*, a. to cause to be dug, delved, or engraved. *s.*

کهدها खुधा *hhudhā*, f. hunger, appetite. *s.*

کهدهارت खुधार्त *hhudhārt*, hungry. *s.*

کهدواعي खुधवाई *hhudwā,ī*, f. act of digging, &c., wages of digging, &c. *s.*

کهدي खदी *hhadī*, f. the name of a grass that grows in ponds. *h.*

کهدي खुद्दे *hhudde*, f. the spaces in a necessary between the little brick partitions; the space from which a tooth has fallen out or been extracted. *h.*

کهديڑ खदेड़ *hhader*, f. pursuit, chase. *h.*

کهديڑنا खदेड़ना *hhaderṇā*, a. to pursue, to hunt, to give chase. *h.*

کهڈّا *hhaḍḍā*, m. the kneepan. *d.*

کهر खुर *hhur*, m. a (cloven) hoof, a horse's hoof. *s.*

کهر खर *hhar* (v. *hhaṛ*), f. grass straw, grass and trees. *h.*

کهر *hhar*, m. (in Persian *khar*) an ass. *h.*

کهرا खरा *hharā*, pure, prime, best sort, genuine, honest, candid, sincere. *s.*

کهرا खर्रा *hharrā*, m. the rough draft of a letter or any writing; an iron instrument to rub horses with, a currycomb; an ulcer with hardness of the skin on the back of the foot. *h.*

کهرا कुहरा *kuhrā*, m. fog, vapour, mist. *s.*

کهراٹا खर्राटा *hharrāṭā*, m. snoring. *s.*

کهرارا *hharārā*, a currycomb. *d.*

کهراکا खराका *hharākā*, m. a crashing noise. *h.*

کهرام कुहराम *kuhrām*, m. weeping, lamentation. *h.*

کهرانا कहराना *kahrānā* (v. *karāhnā*), to groan (as a sick person). *h.*

کهرانت खुरांट *hhurāṅṭ*, very old. *h.*

کهراهند खराहन्द *hharāhand*, f. the stalk of burnt grass. *h.*

کهراعي खराई *hharā,ī*, f. purity, excellence, probity, trustiness, honesty. *h.*

کهرب खर्ब *hharb*, m. an aggregate number of 100 *arbs*; a billion, a dwarf, short, low. *s.*

کهربا *kah-rubā*, m. (lit. straw-attracting) amber; *Oriental anime* (gum resin from the *Vateria Indica*). *p.*

کهربايي *kah-rubā,ī*, f. the quality of amber; adj. of or relating to amber. *p.*

کهربر खरबर *hharbar*, f. sound of a horse's feet in galloping; hurry, bustle, commotion, tumult. *h.*

کهرپا खरपा *hharpā*, m. a sandal; the seam of a garment which extends from the armpit down the side. *khurpā*, an instrument for scraping grass for horses; the knee-pan, patella. *h.*

کهرپي खुरपी *hhurpī*, f. a scraper, a weeding-knife, the tool with which grass is scraped up for horses; a shovel for cleaning out a bird cage. *h.*

کهرج खर्ज *hharj* (for *khārj*), the bass (in music). *h.*

کهرجور खजूर *hharjūr*, m. date, date tree. *harjūr-ras*, m. the juice of the wild date, tārī, used to leaven the bread, and as an intoxicating drink. *s.*

کهرچن खुरचन *hhurchan*, f. pot-scrapings. *h.*

کهرچنا खुरचना *hhurachnā*, a. to scrape. *h.*

کهرچني खुरचनी *hhurachnī*, f. a scraper, a scoop or shovel. *h.*

کهرچهرا खरछरा *hharchharā*, rough. *h.*

کهرسا खिरसा *hhirsā*, m. a dish made with biestings, or the milk of a cow just calved. *s.*

کهرسمبل *hharsambal*, a large kind of kidney-bean, the *Duffin* bean (*Dolichos lunatus*). *d.*

کهرک खरक *hharak*, f. a cow-house, a cow-shed. *h.*

کهرك *hhark*, a sword (v. *hhaṛg*). *d.*

کهرکانا खरकाना *hharkānā*, a. to thump, to shake; to frighten away, to put to flight; to sell. *h.*

کهرکن खिरकिन *hhirkin*, f. a window. *h.*

کهرکهرا खरखरा *hharhharā*, m. a currycomb. *khurkhurā*, rough. *s.*

کهرکهريا खरखरिया *hharkhariyā*, f. a chair, a litter.

کهرل खरल *kharal*, m. a stone for grinding medicine on, a mortar. *s.*

کهرلي *hhurlī*, f. stall or manger in a stable. *d.*

کهرما खुरमा *hhurmā*, m. a kind of sweetmeat.

کهرن खिरन *khiran*, f. a black ring painted on a tambourine. *h.*

کهرنا कहरना *kaharnā*, n. (for *karāhnā*) to groan. *h.*

کهرنجا खरंजा *kharanjā*, m. pavement. *h.*

کهرنڈ खुरण्ड *khurand*, m. a scab. *s.*

کهرنکهه खरंख *kharanhh*, dry, dried up.

کهرني खिरनी *khirnī*, f. name of a tree and its fruit (*Mimusops kauki*). *s.*

کهروٹنا खरोटना *kharoṭnā*, a. to scratch. *h.*

کهروج *kharoj*, scratching, scraping. *d.*

کهروچنا खरोचना *kharochnā*, a. to scrape, to scratch. *h.*

کهرونٹ खरौंट *kharoṅṭ*, f. a scratch with the nail. *kharoṅṭnā*, to scratch. *h.*

کهره खहे *kharh*, f. straw. *h.*

کهرها खरहा *kharhā*, m. a hare, a rabbit. *h.*

کهرهارنا खरहारना *kharhārnā*, a. to sweep. *h.*

کهرهرا खरहरा *hharharā*, m. a currycomb. *h.*

کهرهك खरहक *kharhak*, a portion of grain given at the end of harvest to village servants. *h.*

کهرهي खरही *hharhī*, f. a stack, a rick; a kind of grass. *h.*

کهري खुरी *hhurī*, f. a (cloven) hoof; a horse's hoof. *p.*

کهری खरी *kharī*, oil-cake; chalk. *s.*

کهريا खुरिया *khuriyā*, m. the knee-pan; an instrument like a cup, formed of a cocoa-nut shell or other material with which clothes are marked with stripes. *h.*

کهريرنا खुरेरना *khurernā*, a. to run after, to persecute, to catch, to enclose. *h.*

کهريشٹ ख्रीष्ट *hhrīshṭ*, Jesus Christ. *hhrīsh-ṭiān*, m. a Christian. *g.*

کهڑ खड़ *khaṛ*, f. grass, straw. *h.*

کهڑا खड़ा *khaṛā*, erect, upright, standing up, steep, high, aground, ready, ripe, perpendicular; (fig.) honest, all right; payable on demand. *khaṛā karnā*, a. to raise, to station, to place, to stick up, to place erect, to procure a fictitious person for some purpose. *khaṛā honā*, n. to stand up, to be erect, to rise. *h.*

کهڑارا *hhuṛārā*, an aviary, a hen-house or place of any kind where birds are kept. *d.*

کهڑاکا खड़ाका *khaṛākā*, m. a crash, noise made in breaking. *h.*

کهڑانو खड़ांव *khaṛāṅw*, کهڑاون खड़ाऊं *khaṛā,ūṅ*, } m. pattens. *khaṛāṅw-dār*, a kind of shoes fastened to pattens; (in Dakh.) *khaṛāwāṅ*. *h.*

کهڑاي *hhaṛā,ī*, f. erectness, steepness. *h. d.*

کهڑبڑ *kharber*, clang of metals. *d.*

کهڑبڑاهٹ खड़बड़ाहट *hharbaṛāhaṭ*, کهڑبڑي खड़बड़ी *kharbaṛī*, } f. hurry, bustle, tumult, uproar; noise of horse's feet; griping on going to stool. *h.*

کهڑتل *hhaṛtal*, spoiled, bad, destroyed. *d.*

کهڑجانا खिड़जाना *hhiṛ-jānā*, n. to be dashed out (the brains). *h.*

کهڑسان खड़सान *kharsān*, m a whetstone, a grindstone. *h.*

کهڑك खड़क *kharak*, f. an imitative sound. *kharak jānā*, to take warning, to be apprised. *h.*

کهڑك खड़क *kharak*, f. a cow-house, a cow-shed. *h.*

کهڑکا खड़का *kharhā*, m. (prop. *khaṭkā*) doubt, apprehension; a tooth-pick. *h.*

کهڑکٹ खड़कट *khaṛkaṭ*, chalk for writing. *h.*

کهڑکنا खड़कना *khaṛahnā*, n. to crash, to tinkle, to clang (as metal). *h.*

کهڑکهڑانا खड़खड़ाना *khaṛkhaṛānā*, a. to creak, to clatter, to rattle, to jar; to grind the teeth; to snore. *h.*

کهڑکهڑاهٹ खड़खड़ाहट *khaṛkhaṛāhaṭ*, f. creaking, jarring (as a door), rattling, snoring. *h.*

کهڑکي खिड़की *hhaṛkī* or *khiṛkī*, f. a window, a gate, back door, sally port. *h.*

کهڑگ खड़ग *khaṛag* or *khaṛg*, m. f. a sword, a scimitar. *h.*

کهڑل खड़िल *khaṛil*, f. a mortar.

کهڑلا खुड़ला *khuṛlā*, adj. rough; m. a hen-house. *h.*

کهڑمنڈل खड़मंडल *khaṛ-mandal*, wrangling. *h.*

کهڑنکهه खड़ंख *khaṛanhh*, dry, arid, parched. *h.*

کهڑوا खड़ूआ *khaṛū,ā*, m. an ornament worn on the wrist, a bracelet. *h.*

کهڑه खढ़ *hharh*, f. straw.

کهڑي खड़ी *khaṛī* or *kharī miṭṭī*, f. chalk. *rām-khaṛī* or *kaṭ-khaṛī*, f. a species of steatites, with which children learn to write, and used in giving a polish to stucco. *s.*

کهڑي بند खड़ेबंद *khaṛe-band*, a day-book, a journal; an account drawn out on a loose bit of paper. *h.*

کهڑي پتهر *khaṛe patthar*, a slab of stone placed under a pillar or post, the plinth of a column, a flat stone having a hole bored in it, in which a pole is set upright. *d.*

کھڑي کھڑي खड़ेखड़े *khaṛe khaṛe*, soon, immediately, instantly, presently, quickly. *h.*

کھڑیا खड़िया *khaṛiyā*, f. chalk, a mark. *s.*

کھس खिस *khis*, grinning, shewing the teeth; a tooth (v. *khis*). *h.*

کہسار *kuh-sār*, m. a mountainous country. *p.*

کھساري खिसारी *khisārī*, f. (v. *kisārī*) a kind of pulse. *h.*

کھسانا खसाना *khasānā*, a. to ruin; n. to fall in, to sink; to open, to loosen (Beng.). *h.*

کھسانا खिसाना *khisānā* or *khisā,e rahnā*, n. to flinch, to draw back, to be abashed. *h.*

کھسپھٹك खस्फटिक *khasphaṭik*, m. crystal, the sun gem, the moon gem. *s.*

کہستان *kuhistān*, Persian *Irāḳ*, a mountainous region (v. *kohistān*). *p.*

کھسرا खसरा *khasrā* (also *khasrā-bahī* f.) m. a day-book, field-book, waste-book, rough drawings; a scab; a kind of eruptive disease. *h.*

کھسرپھسر खुसरफुसर *khusar-phusar*, m. whispering. *h.*

کھسریر खसरीर *kha-ṣarīr*, m. a celestial body. *s.*

کھسکانا खसकाना *khaskānā* or खिसकाना *khiskānā*, a. to remove, to shove out of the way, to slide away. *h.*

کھسك جانا खिसकजाना *khisāk-jānā*, n. to slip away, to steal away, to slide. *h.*

کھسکنا खिसकना *khisaknā*, n. to stir, to slip, to slip away, to sheer off. *h.*

کھسکنت खसकन्त *khaskant*, f. separation, running away. *h.*

کھسکھس खसखस *khashkhas*, f. the poppy-head, the scented root of a grass (*Andropogon muricata*) used for door-screens. *khaskhas-ras*, m. poppy-juice, opium. *s.*

کھسکھسا खसखसा *khaskhasā*, m. grinding the teeth. *h.*

کھسکھسانا खसखसाना *khaskhasānā*, to grind the teeth. *h.*

کھسلانا खिसलाना *khislānā*, a. to cause to slip. *h.*

کھسلاو खिसलाव *khislāw*, m. causing to slip, slipping, slipperiness. *h.*

کھسلاهٹ खिसलाहट *khislāhaṭ*, f. sliding, slipperiness. *h.*

کھسلنا खिसलना *khisalnā*, n. to slip; adj. slippery. *h.*

کھسلها खिसलहा *khislahā*, slippery. *h.*

کھسنا खिसना *khisnā*, n. to fall, to sink (as a terrace); to drop off; to become old, decline in years. *h.*

کھسوٹنا खसोटना *khasoṭnā*, a. to pull, to pluck, to pull the hair, to scratch, to tear, to cause the hair to stand on end. *h.*

کھسیانا खिसियाना *khisiyānā*, n. to grin; adj. fretful, peevish, bashful, abashed. *h.*

کھسیانپت खिसियानपत *khisiyānpat*, f.; کھسیانپن खिसियानपन *khisiyānpan*, m.; کھسیاهٹ खिसियाहट *khisiyāhaṭ*, f. } vexation, fretfulness. *h.*

کھشانا *khishānā* (v. *khisiyānā*), to grin. *d.*

کہف *kahf*, a cave, a large cavern, a grotto. *aṣḥābi kahf*, the companions of the cave, otherwise known as the seven sleepers of Ephesus. *a.*

کہك कुहुक *kuhuk*, f. the notes of the *koyal*, q.v. *s.*

کھکھا *khakhā*, old, ancient, long elapsed. *d.*

کھکسا *khiksā*, m. N. B. The meaning of this word is not given in Hunter: he merely refers us to another word (*gagrol* or *kakrol*) nowhere to be found. It is probably the same as *kheksā*, spot, mark. *h.*

کہکشان *kahkashān*, m. the milky way, galaxy. *p.*

کہکنا कुहुकना *kuhuknā*, n. to sound (as the *koyals* do). *s.*

کھکورنا *khikornā*, to scrape, to scratch. *d.*

کھکھ खुख *khukh*, poor, miserable. *h.*

کھکھورنا खखोरना *khakhorna*, a. to scrape, to scoop. *h.*

کھکیڑنا खकेड़ना *khaheṛnā* or *khakheṛnā*, a. to hurry. *h.*

کھگ खग *khag*, m. a general term for a bird; air, wind (lit. what moves in the sky). *s.*

کہگل *kah-gil*, prepared mud or plaster for building; grass and mud mixed together to plaster walls with. *p.*

کھگول खगोल *khagol*, m. the vault or circle of the heavens, the planisphere. *khagol-vidyā*, f. astronomy. *s.*

کھگیس खगेश *khages* or *khagesh*, m. a species of gigantic crane, well known in India as "the adjutant." *s.*

کھل खल *khal*, low, vile, base, wicked; m. a worthless person, a malicious person; an oil-cake; a pit. *khall*, m. sediment of oil, oil-cake. *khalī*, m. a mill, a stone or vessel for grinding. *s.*

کہل *kahal*, sloth, languor, indolence. *a.*

کھلا खुला *khulā*, open, wide, naked, loose, unconfined; clear, fair (as the sky). *khule bandoṅ*, at large, free, without restraint. *s.*

کھلا खल्ला *khallā*, m. a shoe (in Dakh.) a threshing-floor, place where grain is trodden out by oxen. *h.*

کہلا بھیجنا कहलाभेजना *kahlā-bhejnā*, a. to send a message, to cause to be announced verbally. *h.*

کهلار खलार *khalār*, m. hollow, bottom. *khilār*, playsome. *h.*

کهلاڑ खिलाड़ *khilāṛ*, } playsome, funny; کهلاڑي खिलाड़ी *khilāṛī*, } mischievous, full of tricks; a gambler, one addicted to gaming. *s.*

کهلاڑي खलाड़ी *khalāṛī*, f. the place in which salt is boiled; (in Beng.). *h.*

کهلال *khalāl*, quite wet, weltering. *d.*

کهلالا *khalālā*, m. a fountain, jet d'eau. *d.*

کهلانا खिलाना *khilānā*, a. to feed; to cause to swear; to administer an oath; to cause to suffer, as *mar-khilānā*, to cause to be beaten; to amuse, to play with, to dandle; to make to blossom. *s.*

کهلانا खुलाना *khulānā*, a. to cause to be opened. *s*

کہلانا कहलाना *kahlānā*, a. to cause to say, to call; n. to be called or named; to parch, to wither; to become weak, to be lazy. *s. a.*

کهلاؤ खिलाऊ *khilā,ū*, m. giving to eat, feeder; adj. causing to bloom. *s.*

کهلاءي खिलाई *khilā,ī* (*dā,ī*), a dry nurse. *khilā,ī-pilā,ī*, charge of maintenance. *s.*

کهلبل खलबल *khalbal*, f. hurry, bustle, agitation, alarm; tumult. *h.*

کهل بلانا खलबलाना *khalbalānā*, n. to boil; (met.) to be agitated, to be in commotion. *h.*

کهل بلي *khalbalī*, f. hurry (v. *khalbal*). *h.*

کهلتا खलता *khalatā*, f. malice, worthlessness. *s.*

کهلت खल्लिट *khalliṭ*, bald. *s.*

کهل جانا खिलजाना *khil-jānā*, n. to blossom, to bloom; to laugh, to be delighted. *h.*

کهل جانا खुलजाना *khul-jānā*, to be opened, to be revealed or unravelled; to be let loose; to clear up (as the weather) from foul to fair; to smile, to shine. *s.*

کهلڑا खलड़ा *khalṛā*. m. the skin, the hide. *s.*

کهلڑي खलड़ी *khalṛī*, f. skin, hide, membrane; the prepuce. *s.* [vexed, or displeased. *h.*

کهلسانا खुलसाना *khulsānā*, n. to be angry,

کهلکهل खिलखिल *khilkhil*, the sound of laughter, tittering, giggling. *h.*

کهل کهلانا खिलखिलाना *khilkhilānā*, n. to laugh loudly and heartily; to giggle, to titter. *h.*

کهل کهلانا खलखलाना *khalkhalānā*, n. to rumble, to grumble (the bowels). *h.*

کهل کهيلنا खुलखेलना *khul-khelnā*, a. to indulge openly in vices which were formerly practised in secret. *h.*

کهلگا *khulgā*, m. a buffalo, a bison. *d.*

کهلنا खुलना *khulnā*, n. to be opened, to be revealed; to be dispersed, to be unravelled; to be laid aside (restraint); to clear up (the sky), to smile, shine, expand. *h.*

کهلنا खिलना *khilnā*, n. to blow (as a flower); to be delighted; to laugh. *h.* [wither. *h.*

کہلنا कहलना *kahalnā*, to be parched, to

کهلنگا खलंगा *khalangā*, m. a park. *s.*

کهلو खिल्लू *khillū* or *khillo*, humorous, playsome, funny. *s.*

کهلواڑ खिलवाड़ *khilwāṛ*, humorous, playful, funny, pleasant, entertaining. *s.*

کهلوانا खिलवाना *khilwānā*, a. to cause to play, to amuse, or entertain (in play). *khulwānā*, to cause to be opened, to get opened. *s.*

کهلوڑ खिलौड़ *khalauṛ*, playful; addicted to gaming. *s.* [guage. *s.*

کهلوکت खलोक्ति *khalokti*, f. abuse, low lan-

کهلونا खिलौना *khilaunā*, m. a toy, any kind of plaything, bauble, gewgaw. *s.*

کهليهان खलिहान *khalihān*, m. a threshing-floor (v. *khaliyān*). *s.* [grain. *d.*

کهله *khalla*, m. a granary, a heap or store of

کهلي खली *khalī* or *khallī*, f. the dregs of mustard-seed, &c. after the oil is pressed out; oil-cakes. *s.*

کهلي खिल्ली *khillī*, f. jest, joke, humour. *khillī-bāz*, humorous, playsome, funny. *khillī-bāzī*, f. humour, fun, play. *khallī*, oil-cakes, &c. (v. *khalī*). *s.*

کهليان खलियान *khaliyān*, m. a granary, a barn, a threshingfloor. *s.*

کهليانا खलियाना *khaliyānā*, a. to skin, to flay. *s.*

کهلي بندون खुलेबंदों *khule-bandoṅ*, unceremonious, free, unrestrained. *h.*

کهليش खलेश *khalesh* or *khalīsh*, m. a fish (*Trichopodus colisa*). *s.*

کهليل खलेल *khalel*, m. scented oil; a hole made by children for playing at trap-ball or marbles. *p.*

کهليهان खलीहान *khalīhān*, m. a threshing-floor. *s.*

کهم खम *kham*, m. a pillar, stake, post. *kham thoṅknā*, to strike the hands against the arms preparatory to wrestling, &c.; to challenge. *s.*

کهماچ खमाच *khamāch*, f. name of a *rāginī*. *h.*

کهمبا खंबा *khambā*, } m. a post, a pillar, a کهمبه खंभ *khambh*, } stake. *h.*

کهمس खमस *khamas*, sultry, the hot weather. *h.*

کهمساءي खमसाई *khāmsā,ī*, f. sultriness, heat. *h.*

کهميلن खमीलन *khamīlan*, m. lassitude, weariness, sleepiness. *s.*

کہن *kuhan*, old, ancient. *kuhan-sāl*, aged, advanced in years. *kuhan-sālī*, f. old age. *p.*

کہن खन *khan*, m. a division of a house, a storey, a flight of rooms; a mine; a certain day of the fortnight, as the full, change, &c. of the moon. *khan*, the sky, the air; the hold of a ship. *s.*

کہن कहन *kahan*, m. a saying, a bye-word. *s.*

کہن खिन्न *khinn*, distressed, suffering, wearied. *s.*

کہنا कहना *kahnā*, a. to tell, to speak, to say, to bid, to order, to call; to affirm, to acquaint, to advise; to compose, to repeat, to read or quote; m. saying, advice, order. *kah-denā*, to tell, to bid, to order. *s.*

کہناوت कहनावत *kahnāwat*, f. a proverb, a saying; style. *s.*

کھنبا खंबा *khambā*, کھنبھ खंभ *khambh*, کھنبھا खंभा *khambhā*, } m. a pillar, a post, a stake. *h.*

کھنتي खंती *khantī*, f. a paddle for digging the ground. *s.*

کھنج खञ्ज *khanj*, lame, crippled, limping. *s.*

کھنجا खञ्जा *khanjā*, f. a species of metre, a stanza of two lines, one of thirty-two the other of thirty feet. *s.*

کھنجري खंजरी *khanjarī*, f. a small tambourine, a timbrel. *h.*

کھنجریٹ खंजरीट *khanjrīṭ*, کھنجن खंजन *khanjan*, } m. name of a small bird, a species of wagtail. *s.*

کھنچ खिंच *khinch*. f. pulling, a pull. *s.*

کھنچانا खिंचाना *khinchānā*, a. to pull, to draw, to tighten, to delineate; to cause to draw or to endure. *s.* [tightening. *s.*

کھنچاوٹ खिंचावट *khinchāwaṭ*, f. drawing,

کھنچنا खिंचना *khinchnā*, n. to be drawn, tightened, delineated; to be borne or suffered. *s.*

کھنچوانا खिंचवाना *khinchwānā*, a. to cause to be pulled, drawn, tightened, or delineated. *s.*

کھند खंद *khand*, a piece, a portion, a district, a province, as *Bandel-khand* (vulg. *Bundlecund*). *h.*

کھنداںا खंदाना *'khandānā*, m. a pit from which earth has been dug to make bricks or pottery; a notch in a log of wood. *h.*

کھندڑي खिंदड़ी *khindṛī*, f. a pallet, a beggar's bedding. *h.*

کھندل *khandal*, a field, an open plain. *d.*

کھندلات *khandalāt*, act of trampling under foot. *d.* [press under the feet. *d.*

کھندلنا खुंदलना *khundalnā*, a. to trample or

کھنڈ खंड *khanḍ*, m. side, portion, piece, part of the world, division of a house, part, apartment chapter, section; a flaw in a jewel; sugar; the songs of Padmāwat. *s.*

کھنڈ *khinḍ*, a hole, perforation, a mine. *d.*

کھنڈانا खिंडाना *khinḍānā*, a. to scatter. *h.*

کھنڈتا खंडिता *khanḍitā*, f. a woman who provoked at the infidelities of her husband or lover is rather abusive, speaks her mind freely, but retains no malice in her breast. *s.*

کھنڈت کرنا खंडितकरना *khanḍit-karnā*, a. to prevent, to interrupt, to refute. *s.*

کھنڈر खंडर *khanḍar*, desolated, spoiled, destroyed; m. a broken-down building, ruins of a village, &c. *h.* [small bird, a wagtail. *s.*

کھنڈریچ खंडरीच *khanḍrīch*, m. name of a

کھنڈلا खंडला *khanḍlā*, m. a flake, a slice (especially of fish), a division or piece (of land). *s.*

کھنڈلا खुंडला *khunḍlā*, m. the hollow of a tree. *h.*

کھنڈن खंडन *khanḍan*, m. act of reducing any thing to pieces, breaking, dividing, rescinding, thwarting; refuting, &c. *khanḍan karnā*, to cut up, to refute. *s.*

کھنڈنا खंडना *khanḍnā*, a. to refute, to interrupt, prevent; to cut, to divide; to demolish. *s.*

کھنڈنا खिंडना *khinḍnā*, n. to be scattered. *h.*

کھنڈھ खंढ *khanḍh*, m. district, province, division, section or subdivision of a book, poem, &c. *s.*

کھنڈھور खंढोर *khanḍhor*, m. turbid. *h.*

کھنڈیر *khanḍer* (v. *khanḍar*), desolated, &c. *d.*

کھنس खुंस *khuns*, m. animosity, spite, rancour; malice, anger. *h.* [years. *p.*

کہن‌سال *kuhan-sāl*, old, aged, advanced in

کھنسانا खुनसाना or खुंसाना *khunsānā*, n. to be angry. *h.*

کھنسي खुनसी *khunsī*, angry, wrathful. *h.*

کھنک *khank*, feeble, frail, weak. *d.*

کھنکلي खंकली *khankalī*, f. the name of a plant, polypody, a kind of moss. *h.*

کھنکنا खनकना *khanaknā*, also *khanakhnā*, n. to jingle, to ring; to clink (as metal bowls). *h.*

کھنکھ खंख *khankh*, land that requires to be left fallow for a year or two. *h.*

کھنکھارنا खंखारना *khankhārnā*, a. to cough, to make a noise of coughing. *h.*

کھنکھڑ खंखड़ *khankhaṛ*, dry and crackling. *h.*

کھنگال ڈالنا खंगालडालना *khangāl-ḍālnā*, to murder privately. *h.* [rinse. *h.*

کھنگالنا खंगालना *khangālnā*, a. to wash, to

کهنگر खंगर *khangar* or *khangaṛ*, m. semi-vitrified bricks. *h.*

کهنگل खंगल *khangal*, } tusked. *h.*
کهنگيل खंगेल *khangail*, }

کهنگهارنا खंगारना *khanghārnā*, a. to hawk, [to hem. *h.*

کهنگي *kuhnagī*, f. old age, oldness. *p.*

کهنه *kuhna*, old, ancient, faded (as a garment). *p.*

کهني खनी *khanī*, a pit or hole in which rice in the husks is kept. *h.*

کهني कुहनी *kuhnī*, f. the elbow. *s.*

کهو *khhau*, a subterraneous vault for storing grain, &c. *d.*

کهوءا खोआ *kho,ā*, m. plaster; coarse brick-dust; milk inpissated by boiling. *h.*

کهوا खवा *khavā*, m. the shoulder. *s.*

کهوانا कहवाना *kahwānā*, a. to cause to speak.

کهوانا खोआना *kho,ānā*, a. to cause to lose.

کهوبار खोबार *khobār*, m. a hog-sty. *s.*

کهوپ खोप *khop*, f. a cave, a corner; a rent, a fissure (Beng.). *h.*

کهوپا खोपा *khopā*, m. the hair of the head braided and tied up on the top of the head.

کهوپرا खोपरा *khoprā*, m. the kernel of a cocoa-nut, the dried interior pulp. *h.*

کهوپري खोपरी *khoprī*, f. the skull, a shell, pate. *khoprī khā-jānā*, a. to spend or lavish another's property. *s.*

کهوتهي खूथी *khūthī*, f. (also *khūṭhī*) a scab. *h.*

کهوٹ खोट *khoṭ*, f. a blunder, vice, blemish, defect. *h.*

کهوٹ *khūṭ*, side, direction; towards. *d.*

کهوٹا खोटा *khoṭā*, m. perfidious, impious, false; faulty, defective; base (as coin); forged (a bank note); spiteful, malicious. *h.*

کهوٹاءي खोटाई *khoṭā,ī*, f. perfidy, impiety; faultiness, spitefulness, malice; forgery. *h.*

کهوٹاءيگي *khoṭā,egī*, f. (v. *khoṭā,ī*) perfidy. *d.*

کهوٹنا खूटना *khūṭnā*, a. to pluck, to pick the leaves, &c. of vegetables. *h.*

کهوٹهي खूठी *khūṭhī*, f. (likewise *khūthī*) scab. *h.*

کهوج खोज *khoj*, m. search, inquiry, trace, mark. *khoj-meṅ rahnā*, to try to find fault with one, to endeavour to pick a hole in another's coat. *h.*

کهوجانا खोजाना *kho-jānā*, n. to be lost. *h.*

کهوج کهاج खोजखाज *khoj-khāj*, f. vexation; inquiry, investigation. *h.*

کهوجنا खोजना *khojnā*, a. to search for, to inquire after, to explore. *h.*

کهوجه खोझ *khojh*, f. search, inquiring after. *h.*

کهوجها खूझा *khūjhā*, m. sediment, dregs, mouldiness of vinegar, &c. *h.*

کهوجيا खूजिया *khujiyā* or खोजिया *khojiyā*, a searcher, inquirer, investigator. *h.*

کهود खोद *khod*, m. a push, a thrust, a pass. *khūd*, f. refuse. *h.*

کهودبيواد खोदबेवाद *khod-bewād*, m. search, inquiry. *h.*

کهودر खूद्र *khūdr* (for *kshūdra*), small, mean, vile. *s.*

کهودر खोदर *khodar*, m. name of a certain pace (of a horse). *h.*

کهودرا खोदरा *khodrā*, pock-marked. *h.*

کهودرانا खूद्राना *khūdrānā*, n. to trot. *h.*

کهودنا खोदना *khodnā*, a. to dig, to delve, to hollow; to search for. *s.*

کهودني खोदनी *khodnī*, f. searching; a spade. *khodnī-k.*, a. to investigate, to search, to find out. *h.*

کهودو *khaudau* (v. *khodnī*), searching. *d.*

کهودي खोदी *khodī*, f. digging, culture of land. *h.*

کهور खोर *khor*, f. an alley; a covering; the rage or curse of a god. *h.*

کهورا खौरा *khaurā*, m. (cor. from *khorā*) the rot (among sheep), the falling off of the hairs. *p.*

کهورا *khorā*, a cavity, pit, den. *d.*

کهورانٹ खूरांट *khūrānṭ*, old soil, soil trodden down by the hoofs of cattle. *h.*

کهورو *khaurū*, the roaring or bellowing of a bull. *h.*

کهوري खोरी *khorī*, f. an alley. *h.*

کهوڑ खूड़ *khūṛ*, m. a furrow.

کهوڑ खौड़ *khauṛ*, f. the *tilak* or mark which the Hindūs make on the forehead. *s.*

کهوڑ *khoṛ* (explained by *kanak*), gold? &c. *d.*

کهوڑ *khoṛ*, a largeish piece of sandal. *d.*

کهوڑا *khoṛā*, m. stocks, wooden manacles in which the hands are secured. *d.*

کهوڑکا *khoṛkā*, a dry or withered shrub. *d.*

کهوڑل *khoṛil*, worthy of blame; disgraceful. *d.*

کهوسا खोसा *khosā*, having little or no beard (a man) (for the Persian *kosa*, q. v.). *p.*

کهوسا खोसा *khosā*, m. rind, peel, skin, shell (Beng.); name of a marauding tribe on the borders of Sind. *h.*

کهوسنا खोसना *khosnā*, a. to take or snatch away; to pull out hairs. *h.*

کهوکها खोखा *khokhā*, m. a boy (Beng.); a bill of exchange, the amount of which has been paid, remaining in the hand of him who has paid it, by way of voucher. *h.*

کهوکهلا खोखला *khokhlā*, hollow, excavated (as a tooth or a tree, &c.). *s.*

کهوکهي खूखी *khūkhī* or *khokhī*, f. (Beng.) a little girl. *h.*

کهول खोल *khol*, f. m. a case, sheath; hollow (as of a tree, &c.), a cavity. *s.*

کهول بندي खोलबन्दी *khol-bandī*, f. the changing of a horse's shoe. *h.*

کهولاماںجا *kholā-mānjā*, a porcupine, a hedgehog. *d.*

کهوڑ खोलड़ *kholaṛ*, کهوڑا खोलड़ा *kholṛā*, m. a hollow (as of a tree, &c.). *s.*

کهولنا खोलना *kholnā*, a. to open, to loosen, to shine, to expand, to unravel; to set sail or unmoor (a ship). *s.*

کهولنا खौलना *khaulnā*, n. to boil, to be agitated by heat. *h.*

کهومنا खूमना *khūmnā*, n. to wax old. *h.*

کهوں कहूं *kahūn* (v. *kahīn*), anywhere, somewhere, &c. *h.*

کهونا खोना *khonā*, a. to lose; to part with, to get rid of, to do away with; m. a leaf which contains a parcel of betel or flowers, &c. *h.*

کهونپا खोंपा *khonpā*, m. (Beng.) the hair of the head braided or tied up on the top of the head. *h.*

کهونتا खोंता *khontā*, m. a bird's nest. *h.*

کهونٹ खूंट *khūnṭ*, m. a corner, an angle; ear-wax; station, portion, pivot or central point. *khonṭ*, m. blemish, defect, flaw, deception. *h.*

کهونٹا खोंटा *khonṭā*, deficient, adulterated, bad (as coin), false, deceitful; m. a tent-pin, a pin, a peg, nail; protection. *khonṭe ke bal kūdnā*, to become insolent, relying on protection. The idea seems to be taken from a person using freedoms with an animal, which, being fastened by a rope to a pin is unable to get at him (as in the case of that very amiable personage Mr. Quilp and the dog), so that *khonṭā* is only indirectly a protection by restraining the adversary. *h.*

کهونٹا खूंटा *khūnṭā*, m. a wooden stake. *s.*

کهونٹلا खूंटला *khūnṭlā*, m. name of a drug. *h.*

کهونٹي खूंटी *khūnṭī*, f. a small stake, a peg. *s.*

کهونچ खूंच *khūnch*, m. the tendo Achillis. *khūnch-mārnā*, to hamstring. *h.*

کهونچ खोंच *khonch*, f. a cut or rent in cloth, &c. *h.*

کهونچا खोंचा *khonchā*, m. a thrust, stuffing. *h.*

کهونچاکهانچي खोंचाखांची *khonchākhānchī*, f. thrusting, stuffing; mutual wrangling or quarrelling. *h.*

کهونچالنا *khūnchālnā*, کهونچ مارنا *khūnch mārnā*, to prick, to puncture. *d.*

کهونچنا खोंचना *khonchnā*, a. to thrust, to stuff. *h.*

کهونچي खोंची *khonchī*, f. any thing stuffed into another, as grass into thatch; trifling purchases; part of grain which is to be parched taken as pay by the person who parches it; something paid by those who draw water at a well to the *bhihishti*, who attends there with his bucket, for the use of it. *h.*

کهوندنا खूंदना *khūndnā*, a. to paw or dig up the earth (as a bull when angry). *h.*

کهوندها खोंधा *khondhā*, m. a bird's nest. *h.*

کهونڈر खोंडर *khonḍar*, gleanings or leavings on the threshing-floor after the grain has been removed. *h.*

کهونڈکل खोंडकल *khonḍkal*, m. a hollow. *s.*

کهونڈلا खोंडला *khonḍlā*, toothless, hollow. *s.*

کهونسنا खोंसना *khonsnā*, a. to stuff, to thrust in, to cram. *h.*

کهونکهنا खोंखना *khonkhnā*, n. to cough. *s.*

کهونکهي खोंखी *khonkhī*, f. a cough. *s.*

کهوه खोह *khoh*, m. a cavern, abyss, a pit. *h.*

کهوئي खोई *kho,ī*, f. the dry part of sugar-cane after expressing the juice; clothes folded up and put on the head as a defence against rain. *h.*

کهويا खोया *khoyā*, m. refuse; that which is destroyed or thrown away. *h.*

کهي कही *kahī*, f. a foraging party; also forage, supplies. *h.*

کهي कुही *kuhī*, f. a species of hawk.

کهيات ख्यात *khyāt* or *khyāta*, celebrated, renowned; styled or called. *s.*

کهياتي ख्याति *khyāti*, f. fame, celebrity, title. *s.*

کهياتياپن ख्यात्यापन्न *khyātyāpanna*, famous, possessed of honour and renown. *s.*

کهيارا *khiyārā*, sly, artful, deceitful. *d.*

کهيال खैआल *khai,āl* or ख्याल *khyāl*, m. sport, play, amusement. *s.*

کهيانا खियाना *khiyānā*, n. to be worn, to be abraded. *s.*

کهيپ खेप *khep*, f. a trip, voyage; a piece of base metal inserted in coin, or cracked coin; a term in algebra; something added to a sum; an apartment. *khep hārnā*, n. to sustain a loss. *s.*

کهيپا खेपा *khepā*, an idiot, a madman, a fool (Beng.). *s.*

کهيپنا खेपना *khepnā*, a. to pass the time. *s.*

کهيپيا खेपिया *khepiyā*, m. a voyager. *s.*

کهيت खेत *khet*, m. a field, a field of battle; ground; a holy place. *khet-ānā*, to become helpless. *khet chhoṛnā*, a. to fly from the battle. *khet-rahnā*, n. to remain on the field (of battle) to be killed. *khet-bānṭ*, allotment of land to villagers. *khet-chiṭṭhā*, a rough field-book. *khet-dār*, the occupant or owner of a field. *khet-khaṭṭ*, mortgage of a field. *s.*

كهيتوار खेतवार *khetwār*, field by field. *khetwār jam'-bandī*, amount of revenue assessed upon each field. *h.*

كهيتي खेती *khetī*, f. husbandry; crop, produce; adj. arable. *khetī-bārī*, f. husbandry, agriculture. *khetī-paṭārī*, agricultural labour. *khetī-har*, m. a peasant, a husbandman. *s.*

كهيتك खेतक *kheṭak*, sport, chase, hunting; f. a weapon, the club of Balarām. *s.*

كهيتكي खेटकी *kheṭkī*, m. a sportsman, a hunter. *s.*

كهيج खीज *khīj*, f. anger, vexation. *s.*

كهيجنا खीजना *khījnā*, n. to be angry, to be vexed. *s.*

كهيچ खीच *khīch*, m. reluctance, repugnance. *h.*

كهيچر खेचर *khechar*, m. a planet; a bird; a *vidyādhar*, or kind of demigod; genii. *s.*

كهيچنا खीचना *khīchnā* (v. *khīṅchnā*), to draw, to pull. *h.*

كهيد खेद *khed*, m. sorrow, grief, pain. *s.*

كهيدا खेदा *khedā*, m. the trap or inclosure in which elephants are caught. *h.*

كهيداءي खेदाई *khedā,ī*, of or relating to a trap, &c. *khedā-i afyāl*, expenses incurred in catching wild elephants; a cess levied for that purpose. *h.*

كهيدت खेदित *khedit*, sorrowful, afflicted. *s.*

كهيدنا खेदना *khednā*, a. to run after, to persecute, to pursue. *h.*

كهير खीर *khīr*, f. rice-milk, a dish of rice and milk. *s.*

كهير खैर *khair*, كهيرا खैरा *khairā*, } m. a tree (***Mimosa catechu***). *s.*

كهيرا खैरा *khairā*, m. a sprat (or a kind of fish very like one); adj. brown. *h.*

كهيرا खीरा *khīrā*, m. a cucumber. *h.*

كهيري खीरी *khīrī* (for *kshīrī*), f. an udder. *s.*

كهيري खेरी *kherī*, f. after-birth. *h.*

كهيڑا खेड़ा *kheṛā*, f. a village, a hamlet, the land immediately adjacent to a village. *h.*

كهيڑهي खेढ़ी *kheṛhī*, f. membranes in which the fœtus is enveloped, secundines. *h.*

كهيڑهي खेढ़ी *kheṛhī*, كهيڑي खेड़ी *kheṛī*, } f. a kind of iron or steel, a sort of country-made steel. *h.*

كهيڑيالو *kheṛyālū*, m. a peasant, a husbandman, a villager. *d.*

كهيس खीस *khīs*, m. a kind of cloth, diaper, damask, a sheet or wrapper of such cloth. *h.*

كهيس खीस *khīs*, f. loss; grin, shrug; biestings. *khīs nikālnā*, a. to grin. *h.*

كهيسا खीसा *khīsā*, m. a rubber, a hair glove (used in baths). *h.* [pocket. *p.*

كهيسا *khīsā*, m. (for *kīsa* or *hesa*, q. v.) a

كهيسڑا खेसड़ा *khesṛā*, m. a kind of cloth. *h.*

كهيسنا खीसना *khīsnā*, n. to grin, to shew the teeth. *h.*

كهيش खेश *khesh*, m. a kind of cloth, diaper, damask; a sheet of such cloth.

كهيكتا *khekṭā*, hardship, severity, distress. *d.*

كهيكسا खेकसा *kheksā*, m. a mark, a spot, a sign. *h.*

كهيل खील *khīl*, f. parched grain, inflated or puffed out by heat so as to appear like froth. *a.*

كهيل खेल *khel*, m. play, game, sport, fun, pastime. *s.*

كهيلا खैला *khailā*, m. a young bullock, a steer. *h.*

كهيلت खेलत *khelat*, part. pres. playing, sporting. *s.*

كهيل كهلاڑي खेलखिलाड़ी *khel-khilāṛī*, playsome, wanton; an unchaste (woman), an adulteress, strumpet. *s.*

كهيلنا खेलना *khelnā*, a. to play, to frisk, to sport; to romp about (as children). *s.*

كهيلي खीली *khīlī*, f. betel-leaf made up with the different ingredients. *h.*

كهيم كسل खेमकुशल *kẖem-kusal* (for *kshem-kushal*), f. health, welfare, prosperity, both bodily health and worldly affairs. *s.*

كهين *kihīn*, كهينه *kihīna*, } young, little, small, the youngest. *p.*

كهين कहीं *kahīn*, somewhere, anywhere, wheresoever, whithersoever. *aur kahīn*, anywhere else. *jahān-kahīn*, in whatever place or quarter. *kahīn-kā kahīn*, here and there. *kahīn na kahīn*, somewhere or other. *kahīn kā*, queer, strange. *kahīn nahīn*, nowhere. *har kahīn* everywhere. *h.*

كهينچ खैंच *khaiṅch*, f. pulling; scarcity. *h.*

كهينچاكهينچ खैंचाखैंच *khaiṅchā-kaiṅch*, كهينچاكهينچي खैंचाखैंची *khaiṅchā-khaiṅchī*, } f. pulling and hauling. *h.*

كهينچ كهميت *khaiṅch-khameṭ*, struggle, contention. *d.*

كهينچنا खैंचना *khaiṅchnā*, *khīṅchnā*, or *kheṅchnā*, a. to pull, to draw, to tighten; to draw or delineate (a picture); to endure, to suffer, to feel. *h.*

كهيوا खेवा *khewā*, m. fare, ferry-money, price of passage in a boat, passage-money; crossing over a river. *s.*

كهيوٹ खेवट *khewaṭ*, } m. a rower, a
كهيوٹيا खेवटिया *khewaṭiyā*, } boatman, a ferryman. *s.* [man. *s.*

كهيوك खेवक *khewak*, m. a rower, a boatman. *s.*

كهئونا खेना *khe-onā*, a. to row, to punt, to paddle; to suffer or endure (pain, calamity, &c.). *s.*

كهيه खीह *khīh*, f. an alkaline earth, fossil alkali. *h.*

كي कै *kai*, how many? several, sundry. *kai ek*, some few; conj. or, either. *s.*

كي *kai*, a great king (especially the kings of Persia of the Kyānian dynasty); when? how many? *p.*

كي के *ke*, post. mas. (inflect. of *kā*, m.) of, to. *ke-pās*, near, close by, with. *ke-se*, from. *kī* (fem. of *kā*), of, belonging to. *kai*, conj. or, either. *h.*

كي *kī*, why? wherefore? what? *d.*

كئي कई *ka,ī*, several, some, sundry. *ka,ī ek*, several, sundry. *s.*

كيا क्या *kyā*, pron. what? how? why? whether. *kiyā* or *kīyā*, done, made (past of *karnā*); doings, a deed. *kyā kahe to*, for example, thus. *h.*

كياري कियारी *kiyārī* or क्यारी *kyārī*, f. a bed (of a garden); a frame. *s.*

كياست *kiyāsat*, f. ingenuity, quickness of parts (or great vivacity), cunning. *ṣāḥib-kiyāsat*, ingenious, sagacious. *a.*

كيال *kayyāl*, m. a weigher, a measurer of grain in a village. *a.*

كيالي *kayyālī*, f. a weighman's fee or perquisites for weighing or measuring grain. *a.*

كيان *kyān*, near, at the house of. *d.*

كيت केतु *ketu* or *ket*, m. the dragon's tail or descending node; a demon; a falling star (also *ketu-tārā*); a comet. *kait*, m. name of a tree (*Feronia elephantum*). *s.*

كيتا केता *ketā*, how much? how many? *h.*

كيت رتن केतुरत्न *ketu-ratn*, m. *Lapis lazuli*. *s.*

كيتك केतिक *ketik*, somewhat, a little, a few. *h.*

كيتكي केतकी *ketkī*, f. name of a flower (*Pandanus odoratissimus, Roxb.*). *s.*

كيتمال केतुमाल *ketu-mal*, m. one of the nine divisions of the known world, the western portion of Jambu-dwīpa. *s.*

كيتها कैथा *kaithā*, m. an intoxicating drink made from the fruit of the *kait*; name of a tree (v. *kait*). *s.*

كيتهي कैथी *kaithī*, f. or *kaithī-nāgarī*, a character used chiefly by Kāyaths about Patna. *s.*

كيتئين केताईं *ke-ta,īn* (also *ke-tā,īn*, *ke-tain*, or *ke-ten*), a termination or postposition of nearly the same import as *ko* (v. *ta,īn*). *h.*

كيٹ कीट *kīṭ*, m. an insect, a worm, a reptile; the dregs of oil in a lamp, or that collected in a *hukka* snake. *s.*

كيچ कीच *kīch*, } f. dirt, mud, slime. *h.*
كيچڑ कीचड़ *kīchaṛ*, }

كيچوك केचूक *kechūk*, m. an esculent root (*Arum colocasia*). *s.* [Persia. *p.*

كيخسرو *kai-khusrū*, Cyrus the Great, king of Persia. *p.*

كيد *kaid*, m. deceit, fraud, treachery; adapting, adjusting; vomiting, casting forth; menstruous (a woman); war; the croaking of a raven. *a.*

كيدار केदार *kedar*, m. a field, a mountain; a part of the Himālaya range of mountains. *s.*

كيدهر कीधर *kīdhar*, whither? which way? *h.*

كير कैर *kair*, m. name of a shrub (v. *karīl*). *h.*

كير *ker* or *kīr*, m. *penis, sive membrum virile*. *p.*

كير कीर *kīr*, m. a parrot. *s.* [poison. *s.*

كيراٹك कैराटक *kairāṭak*, m. a species of poison. *s.*

كيرت कीरत *kīrat* or कीर्ति *kīrti*, f. praise, renown. *kīrat-wān* or *kīrti-man*, m. renowned. *kīrit*, f. virtue. *s.*

كيرتن कीर्त्तन *kīrttan*, m. speech, words; shouting for joy, singing aloud, celebrating, praising. *s.*

كيرتنا कीर्त्तना *kīrtanā*, f. fame, glory. *s.*

كيرك कीरक *kīrak*, m. a parrot, paroquet. *s.*

كيرها कीरहा *kīrhā*, m. wormy or wormeaten. *s.*

كيري कैरी *kairī*, f. a small unripe mango. *kairī ānkh*, a wall eye, an eye the pupil of which is grey. *h.*

كيڑ *kīṛ*, m. a worm, an insect (same as *kīṛā*); mildew, rot. *kīṛ-khāyā mūn̐*, (lit. a wormeaten face), i. e. freckled, pock-marked. *d.*

كيڑا कीड़ा *kīṛā*, m. a worm, an insect, a reptile, a maggot, a snake, a leech. *s.*

كيڑا केड़ा *keṛā*, m. a sapling, a slender twig. *h.*

كيڑها कीड़हा *kīṛhā*, wormy, wormeaten. *s.*

كيس केश *kes*, f. the hair of the head; a cock's comb. *s.*

كيسا कैसा *kaisā*, pron. what like? what sort or kind? how? adv. in what manner? *kaisā-hī*, howsoever, how much soever. *h.*

كيستي *kīstī* (for *ki astī*), who art thou? *p.*

كيسر केसर *kesar*, f. saffron, yellow colour. *s.*

كيسري केसरी *kesarī*, m. a lion. *s.*

كيسريا केसरिया *kesariyā*, of a saffron colour, yellow. *kesariyā-bānā*, m. dressed in yellow, saffron coloured. *s.*

كيسو कैसो *kaiso*, *kaisau*, } (Braj for *kaisā*)
كيسوں कैसौं *kaisaun̐*, } how? in what manner? what like? what sort of? *h.*

كيسه *kīsa* or *kesa*, m. a purse. *kīsa-bur*, a cut-purse. *kīsa,i kamar*, a girdle buckled round the waist, to which are attached all the apparatus of a hunter or musketeer, viz. a large powder-horn for loading, a small ditto for priming, pouches for bullets, flint, steel, and tinder, &c. *p.*

كيسي कैसे *kaise* (v. *kaisā*), how? what like? *h.*

كيش *kesh*, f. faith, religion, manner, quality. *kāfir-kesh*, prone to infidelity; (met.) a mistress, sweetheart. *kish*, an island at the mouth of the Persian Gulf. *p.*

كيش केश *kesh*, m. the hair of the head; a cock's comb. *keshākeshī*, f. pulling the hair mutually. *s.*

كيشر केशर *keshar*, m. a plant, also called *nāgeshar* (*Mesua ferrea*); a shrub used in dyeing (*Rottleria tinctoria*). *s.*

كيشرن केशरिन *kesharin*, }
كيشري केशरी *kesharī*, } m. a lion. *s.*

كيشويش केशवेश *kesh-vesh*, m. a tress or fillet of hair. *s.*

كيشي केशी *keshī*, f. a lock of hair on the crown of the head. *s.*

كيف *kaif*, how, in what manner; (met.) intoxication; an intoxicating drug. *a.*

كيفي *kaifī*, intoxicated, a drunkard, a sot. *a.*

كيفيت *kaifīyat*, f. story, statement, account, relation, state, circumstances, quality, mode. *a.*

كيك *kaik*, a flea. *kaik shalwār men̈ honā*, to be fidgety or uneasy. *p.*

كيكا केका *kekā*, f. the cry of a peacock. *s.*

كيكاوس *kai-kā,ūs* or *kai-kāvus*, just, noble; name of a king of Persia. *p.*

كيكر केकर *kekar*, squint-eyed. *h.*

كيكڑ कीकड़ *kīkaṛ*, m. the acacia tree (v. *babūl*). *h.*

كيكڑا केकड़ा *kekṛā*, m. a crab, the sign Cancer. *s.*

كيكي केकी *kekī*, m. a peacock. *s.*

كيل केल *kel* or केलि *keli*, f. amorous dalliance, coition. *s.*

كيل कैल *kail*, f. a sprout, a shoot; (in Arab.) a measure of grain and dry goods. *h.*

كيل कील *kīl*, f. a small nail, peg, tack, pin, bolt, wedge; the core of a boil. *kīl-kān̈ṭā*, tools, apparatus; (in Dakh.) tar, pitch. *s.*

كيلا कीला *kīlā*, f. a small nail, a tack, peg. *kelā*, m. a plantain, a banana. *s.*

كيلاس कैलास *kailās*, m. the name of a mountain placed by the Hindūs amongst the Himālaya or snowy range to the north of Hindustān: it is the fabulous residence of Kuvera, and the favourite haunt of Shiva. *s.*

كيلن केलन *kelan*, f. a daughter-in-law. *h.*

كيلنا कीलना *kīlnā*, a. to charm a snake, so as to prevent his biting. *s.*

كيلي केली *kelī*, f. play, sport, dalliance. *s.*

كيلي *kīlī*, a key; a peg, a screw-nail. *d.*

كيمخت *kīmukht*, m. the leather of a horse or ass, shagreen. *p.*

كيمختي *kīmukhtī*, made of *kīmukht*. *p.*

كيمخواب *kīmkhwāb*, m. (same as *kimkhwāb*, q. v.) silk, &c. *p.*

كيميا *kīmiyā*, m. (Gr. χημια) alchymy. *kīmiyā-k.*, a. (fig.) to do any thing very well, to work miracles. *kīmiyā-gar*, m. a chemist, alchymist. *kīmiyā-garī*, f. alchymy. *g.*

كين कैन *kain*, f. a bamboo twig. *h.*

كين *kain* (for *kahīn*, q. v.) somewhere, anywhere. *d.*

كين *kīn*, m. (v. *kīna*) hatred, enmity, rancour, malice. *kīn-toz*, one who foments dissensions and lawsuits; adj. malevolent. *p.*

كينا कीना *kīnā*, a. to make (v. *karnā*); also past tense, done, made: the verb *karnā* borrows its past participle, and the tenses thence formed, from *kīnā*. *s.*

كينا कीना *kīnnā*, }
كيننا कीना *kinnā*, } a. to purchase, to buy. *s.*

كينچل केंचुल *kain̈chul*, }
كينچلي केंचली *kain̈chlī*, } f. the slough of a snake. *s.*

كينچوا केंचवा *ken̈chwā*, m. an earthworm. *s.*

كيند केन्दु *kendu*, m. a sort of ebony (*Diospyros tomentosa*). *s.*

كيندر केन्द्र *kendra*, m. centre of a circle, pole. *s.*

كيندك केन्दुक *kenduk*, m. a resinous sort of ebony (*Diospyros glutinosa*). *s.*

كينكڑا केंकड़ा *ken̈kṛā* (v. *kekṛā*), m. a crab. *s.*

كينور *kīnwar*, rancorous, malevolent. *p.*

كينويا कीनवैया *kīnwaiyā*, a purchaser. *s.*

كينه *kīna*, m. malice, spite, rancour, hatred. *kīna-war*, *kīna-kash*, *kīnā-jo*, or *kīna-khwāh*, malicious, spiteful, rancorous, inimical, vindictive, malevolent. *p.*

كيني कीनी *kīnī* (Braj), 3rd pers. sing. fem. past tense of *karnaun*, to do or make. *h.*

كيواڑ केवाड़ *kewāṛ*, m. the shutter of a door, a door. *s.*

كيوان *kaiwān*, m. the planet Saturn. *p.*

كيوانچ केवांच *kewān̈ch*, f. cowitch (*Dolichos pruriens*). *s.*

كيواني *kaiwānī*, of or relating to Saturn. *p.*

كيوٹ केवट *kevaṭ*, }
كيورت केवर्त *kevart*, } m. a fisherman (also *kaivart*).

کیئوڑا केओड़ा *ke,oṛā* or केवड़ा *kevṛā*, m. name of a flower (*Pandanus odoratissimus, Roxb.*). *s.*

کیول केवल *kewal* or *keval*, only, alone; all, entire; completely, peculiarly, only, merely, simply; m. a species of knowledge, probably that of the unity of God. *s.*

کیولي केवली *kevlī*, f. horoscope, nativity. *s.*

کیولیه कैवल्य *kaivalya*, m. eternal emancipation; release of the soul from further transmigration. *s.*

کیون क्यूं *kyūṅ* or क्यों *kyoṅ*, why? wherefore? how? well? what then? *kyūṅ-ki*, because, since. *kyūṅ-kar*, how? *kyūṅ na ho*, why not? what for no? *h.*

کیون क्यौं *kyauṅ*, same as *kyūṅ* (also same compounds). *b.*

کیونکه *kyuṅ-ki*, since, because that. *h. p.*

کیهر केहर *kehar*, } m. a lion. *s.*
کیهري केहरी *keharī*, }

کیهون कैहौं *kaihaūṅ*, 1st pers. sing. aorist (Braj.) of *karnauṅ*, I may do or make. *h.*

کئي *ka,ī*, some, a few. *ka,i ek*, some, several. *h.*

کیيور केयूर *keyūr*, m. a bracelet worn on the upper arm.

گ

گ *gāf*, called *kāf-i-'ajamī* (the Persian *kāf*, it being unknown in the Arabic), the twenty-sixth letter of the Persian alphabet, and the twenty-ninth Hindūstānī. Its sound is that of *g* hard, as in the words *go*, *give*, never like that of *g* in the words *gem*, *gentle*. In reckoning by *abjad* it counts 20, the same as *kāf* (the preceding letter). The Arabs sometimes substitute *jīm* for *gāf*, as *lajām* for *lagām*, a bridle. The people of India, on the other hand, often substitute *gāf* for *ghain*, as *kāgaz* or *kāgaj* for *kāghaz*, paper. *p. h.*

گ ग *ga*, is the corresponding letter in the Devanāgarī alphabet. As a termination, in Sanskrit words, it denotes motion, as *bhujang*, a serpent, (lit.) what goes in a curve, or, as the Americans would say, "a spiralizer." *s. h.*

گاب गाब *gāb*, m. name of a tree, the fruit of which contains a glutinous astringent juice, with which the bottoms of boats are smeared, and in which nets are soaked (*Diospyros glutinosa, Kœn. MS; Embryopteris glutinifera, Roxb. Pl. Cor.* 70). *h.*

گابه गाभ *gābh*, m. pregnancy; (in Dakh) *gāb*. *s.*

گابها गाभा *gābhā*, m. a new leaf springing from the centre of a plantain-tree; (in Dakh.) *gābā*. *s.*

گابهن गाभिन *gābhin*, pregnant, with young; (in Dakh.) *gābin*. *s.*

گابهنا गाभना *gābhnā*, a. to snub, to chide. *h.*

گات गात f. the body; apparel. *s.*

گات गातु *gātu*, m. a celestial chorister. *s.*

گاتا गाता *gātā*, m. pasteboard. *h.*

گاتر गात्र *gātra*, m. the body, a limb, a member. *s.* [metre, rhythm. *s*

گاتها गाथा *gāthā*, f. a stanza, song, chaunt,

گاتهك गाथक *gāthak*, m. a singer, a musician, a chaunter of the Purānas. *s.*

گاتي गाती *gātī*, f. a plaid, a mantle. *s.*

گاٹا गाटा *gāṭā*, } the yoking of bullocks toge-
گاٹه गाठ *gāṭa*, } ther for the purpose of treading out grain: it also denotes a plot or piece of land, a division of a village. *h.*

گاٹهبندي गाठःबन्दी *gāṭa-bandī*, f. the division of a village by *gāṭas*. *h.* [q. v.) *h.*

گاٹیوار गाटेवार *gāṭewār* (same as *gāṭa-bandī*,

گاج गाज *gāj*, f. scum, froth; a thunderbolt. *gāj-mārā*, thunderstruck; afflicted, unfortunate. *h.*

گاج *gāj*, bangles or bracelets made of glass. *d.*

گاجا गाजा *gājā*, a term signifying the first or early rice-sowing in the districts at the foot of the hills. *h.*

گاجاباجا गाजाबाजा *gājā-bājā*, m. the sound or clangour of various musical instruments. *h.*

گاجر गाजर *gājar* or *gājir*, f. a carrot (*Daucus carota*). *s.*

گاجل *gājal*, a seller of glass bangles. *d.*

گاجن गाजन *gājan*, m. sounding, roaring. *s.*

گاجنا गाजना *gājnā*, n. to thunder; to roar as a lion or other wild beast; to be pleased, happy, cheerful, delighted. *s.*

گاچه गाछ *gāchh*, m. a tree. *gāchh-mirch*, Cayenne pepper (*Capsicum*); (in Dakh.) *gāch*.

گاچهي गाछी *gāchhī*, a pad put over the back of a beast of burden. *h.*

گاد गाद *gād*, f. sediment (of dirty water). *h.*

گادر गादर *gādar*, half-ripe (grain or fruit); m. (Beng.) a heap, stock, rick. *h.*

گادنا गादना *gādnā*, a. to ram down. *h.*

گادي गादी *gādī*, f. (v. *gaddī*) a cushion, a throne, &c. *h.*

گاڈر गाडर *gāḍar*, f. a sheep, an ewe. *h.*

گاڈرو गाडरू *gāḍrū*, m. a charm against venom. *h.*

گاذر *gāẕur*, m. a washerman, a bleacher. *p.*

گار गार *gār*, f. (v. *gālī*) abuse, insulting language; (in Dakh.) m. hail, frost. *s.*

گار *gār*, (in comp.) a doer or agent, as *khidmat-gār*, an attendant, from *khidmat*. *p.*

گار *gār*, m. hail, frost. *d.*

گارا गारा *gārā*, m. mud kneaded or prepared for making pottery; name of a *rāginī* or musical mode. *h.*

گارنا गारना *gārnā*, a. to strain; to squeeze; to milk. *s.*

گاره गारा *gāra*, low land on which the water [does not lie long. *s.*

گارلا *gārlā*, gray, light blue. *d.*

گاري गारी *gārī*, f. (v. *gālī*) abuse. *s.*

گاري *gārī*, f. (in comp.) abstract form of *gār*, as *khidmat-gārī*, f. attendance, service, waiting upon a person. *p.*

گاڑا गाड़ा *gāṛā*, m. a ditch, pit, cavern; an ambuscade. *gāṛe baiṭhnā*, n. to be concealed, to lie in ambush. *s.*

گاڑا गाड़ा *gāṛā*, m. a cart, a carriage. *s.*

گاڑتهوپ गाड़थोप *gāṛ-thop*, f. burying, burial. *s.*

گاڑنا गाड़ना *gāṛnā*, a. to bury, to set, to drive in, to fix, to sink. *s.*

گاڑوڑي *gāṛūṛī*, m. a juggler, a buffoon. *d.*

گاڑه गाढ़ *gāṛh*, f. a difficulty. *s.*

گاڑه *gāṛa*, low lands on which water does not lie long; (in Dakh.) a species of cloth. *h.*

گاڑها गाढ़ा *gāṛhā*, thick, close, dense; sly, shrewd, knowing, wise; strong or potent (as an infusion of tea-leaves, &c.); turbid, muddy. *s.*

گاڑهنا गाढ़ना *gāṛhnā*, a. to malleate; to form by hammering; to drive down, to sink, to bury. *h.*

گاڑي गाड़ी *gāṛī*, f. a cart, a carriage. *gāṛī-wān* or *gāṛī-bān*, m. a carter, a coachman. *s.*

گازر *gāzir* or *gāzur*, m. a washerman, a fuller, a bleacher (commonly *gāzir*, *gāzur*). *gāzir-mahall*, a tax formerly levied on washermen in Bengal. *p.*

گاكر गाकर *gākar* (v. *gāṅkar*), coarse bread. *h.*

گاگر गागर *gāgar*, } f. a pot for holding
گاگري गागरी *gāgrī*, } water, a guglet. *s.*

گرگرا गागरा *gāgrā*, name of a low caste of sweepers (v. *bhangī*). *h.*

گال गाल *gāl*, m. a cheek; a species of tobacco. *s.h.*

گال गालि *gāli*, m. curse, imprecation (v. *gālī*).

گالا गाला *gālā*, } m. a pod of cotton; a ball
گاله गालः *gāla*, } of carded cotton (known also by the name of *goḍhā*). *h.*

گالي गाली *gālī*, f. abuse. *gālī-galūj*, f. reciprocal abuse; brawling, quarrelling. *gālī-denā*, a. to abuse, to revile. *s.*

گاليان गालियां *gāliyāṅ*, (pl.) abusive words; a species of indecent nuptial songs. *s.*

گام *gām*, m. a pace, step. *p.*

گام गाम *gām*, m. (for *grām*, usually *gāṅw*) a village. *s.*

گامبهري गाम्भीर्य *gāmbhirya*, m. depth, pro- [fundity. *s.*

گامك गामुक *gāmuk*, going, moving. *s.*

گامني गामिनी *gāminī*, (in comp.) going, moving. *s.*

گان गान *gān*, m. a song, singing. *s.*

گانا गाना *gānā*, a. to sing, to celebrate. *s.*

گانتهنا गांथना *gānthnā*, a. to lay bricks in mortar; to string, to thread, to arrange. *s.*

گانٹھ गांठ *gāṅṭh*; m. f. } a knot, a knob, a
گانٹھا गांठा *gāṅṭhā*, m, } joint; a bundle.
گانٹھي गांठी *gāṅṭhī*, f. } *gāṅṭh ukhaṛnā*, dislocation. *gāṅṭh paṛnā*, is applied to the fixing of enmity towards any one in the breast. *gāṅṭh-joṛā*, joining, splicing. *gāṅṭh-dār*, knotted. *gāṅṭh kā pūrā*, wealthy, rich. *gāṅṭh kā khonā*, to act to one's own prejudice. *gāṅṭh kholnā*, the untying of a knot; prodigality, expense; removal of prejudice. *gāṅṭh-gaṭhīlā*, knotty (as a stick), compact (as a man). *s.*

گانٹھنا गांठना *gāṅṭhnā*, a. to tie, to join, to make adhere, to stitch; to reduce to obedience or subjection. *s.*

گانٹھي‌دار *gāṅṭhī-dār*, an occupant of lands by heritable tenure. *h.p.*

گانجا गांजा *gāṅjā*, m. (v. *gāṅjhā*) the hemp [plant, &c. *s.*

گانجر गांजर *gāṅjar*, f. a kind of grass or verdure. *h.*

گانجنا गांजना *gāṅjnā*, a. to store, to hoard; to stir, to agitate; to churn. *p.h.*

گانجها गांझा *gāṅjhā*, m. the hemp plant (*Cannabis sativa*); the fructification, when nearly ripe, is bruised and smoked for intoxication. The leaves dried are ground in water and drunk for the same purpose. In this state it is called *bhang* and *sabzī*. *gāṅjhā wālā*, a seller of *bhang*. *s.*

گاندهار गान्धार *gāndhār*, m. one of the seven notes of music; a country, Candahar. *s.*

گاندهاري गान्धारी *gāndhārī*, f. one of the female deities of the Jains. *s.*

گاندهرب गान्धर्व *gāndharb*, m. a heavenly chorister, song, singing; a form of marriage, that which requires only mutual and amorous agreement. *s.*

گاندهك गान्धिक *gāndhik*, m. a perfumer; a kind of worm having a strong fetid smell. *s.*

گانڈ गांड *gāṅḍ*, f. the anus, privities. *gāṅḍ-ghalat*, dead, stupid. *gāṅḍ-marā,o*, a sodomite. *s.*

گانڈا गांडा *gāṅḍā*, m. sugar-cane ready for cutting. *h.*

گانڈر गांडर *gāṅḍar*, } f. a kind of grass used
گانڈل गांडल *gāṅḍal*, } for thatching: it grows in land subject to inundation, and its root yields the *khas* or *khas-khas*, of which *ṭaṭṭīs* are made (*Andropogon muricatum*, *Retz*). *h.*

گانڈو गांडू *gāṅḍū*, m. a catamite; a sodomite (*cinædus*). *h.*

گانڈيو गांडीव *gāṅḍīva*, m. the name of the bow [of Arjuna. *s.*

گانڑ गांड़ *gāṅṛ*, f. (v. *gāṅḍ*) the anus. *h.*

گانسنا गांसना *gāṅsnā*, a. to pierce, to transfix; to spit (a fowl, &c.). *h.*

گانسي गांसी *gāṅsī*, f. the iron point of an [arrow. *h.*

گانکر गांकर *gānkar*, name of an inferior kind of bread made of *arhar*. *h.* [order. *h.*

گانگن गांगन *gāngan*, m. the name of a dis-

گانه *gāna*, (as an affix in Pers.) time or fold, e.s *panj-gāna*, fivefold. *p.*

گانو गांव *gānw*, گانون गांओं *gānon*, گاءون गाओं *gā,on*, } m. a village, a town, a district. *s.*

گانونو गांवना *gān,onā*, a. to sing. *s.*

گاو *gāw*, f. a cow; (in Pers.) a bull, an ox. *gāw-palang*, a cameleopard. *gāw-dosh*, a milking-pail, a churn. *gāw-dīda*, a kind of bread. *gāw-zabān*, name of a kind of bread; bugloss. *gāw-zorī*, f. violence, brute force. *gāwi 'ambar*, the sea cow, from which the Persians suppose ambergris to come. *gāw-mesh*, a buffalo. *s. p.*

گاواره *gāwāra*, m. a cradle (v. *gahwāra*). *p.*

گاواگوشت *gāwā-gosht*, beef. *s. p.*

گاواگهي गावाघी *gāwā-ghī*, m. cow's clarified butter. *s.*

گاوتكيه *gāw-tahiya*, m. a kind of pillow or bolster; a large bolster which supports the back when seated. *p.*

گاوچراي *gāw-charā,ī*, f. grazing (of cattle); a tax levied on pasture lands. *p. h.*

گاوخانه *gāw-khāna*, a house or stall for cattle. *p.*

گاودم *gāw-dum*, گاودمبل *gāw-dumbāl*, } thick at one end and thin at the other; acclivity, descent; f. a trumpet, a tube. *p.*

گاودي गावदी *gāwdī*, a simpleton, blockhead. *h.*

گاوسار *gāw-sār*, like an ox; name of Farīdūn's mace. *p.*

گاوشماري *gāw-shumārī*, an enumeration or census of cattle; a tax upon cattle. *p.*

گاوشير *gāw-shīr*, f. name of a medicinal gum or gum resin, opoponax. *p.* [fice. *h*

گاوگهپ गावघप *gāo-ghap*, fraud, deceit, arti-

گاوگهپو गावघपू *gā,o-ghapū*, deceitful, alluring. *h.*

گاولي गावली *gā,olī* or *gāwalī*, m. a cowherd. *h.*

گاءون गाओं *gā,on*, m. (v. *gānw*) a village. *s.*

گاءونبٹ गाओंबट *gā,on-bat*, a subdivision of a district into several villages. *s.*

گاءونٹي गाओंटी *gā,ontī*, of or belonging to a village. *s.*

گاءون خرچه *gā,on-kharcha*, m. expenses or charges incurred in the municipal administration of a village. *s. p.*

گاونگر *gāwangar*, m. a singer, a musician. *d.*

گاه *gāh*, f. time; place. *shikār-gāh*, a place proper for hunting. *'ibādat-gāh*, a place of worship; mosque, church. *nā-gāh*, suddenly. *gāh-be-gāh* or *gāh o be-gāh*, occasionally, frequently, at all seasons, in season and out of season. *gāh-gāh*, repeatedly, again and again. *p.*

گاه गाह *gāh*, m. an alligator, a shark. *s.*

گاهك गाहक *gāhak*, m. a chapman, purchaser. *gun-gāhak*, an appreciator of another's merits. *jān kā gāhak*, the pursuer of one's life. *s*

گاهگاه गाहिगाहि *gāhi gāhi*, adv. with much inquiry or research. *h.* [times. *p.*

گاهگاهي *gāh-gāhe*, some time or other, at

گاهن गाहन *gāhan*, m. a kind of harrow (with teeth) for eradicating grass from ploughed land. *h.*

گاهنا गाहना *gāhnā*, a. to caulk, to thrash, to tread out corn; to inquire, to search, to investigate. *h.*

گاهي *gāhe*, at one time, some time. *p.*

گاهي गाही *gāhī*, f. five (an aggregate made up of five parts). *h.*

گاءي गाए *gā,e* or *gā,ī*, f. a cow. *s.*

گايترن गायत्रिन *gāyatrin*, m. a tree that yields the resin formerly called terra japonica (*Mimosa catechu*). *s.*

گايتري गायत्री *gāyatrī*, f. a Vedic metre, a stanza of four lines of six syllables each; a sacred verse from the Rig Veda to be recited mentally: it is personified and considered as a goddess, the mother of the first three castes. *s.* [*congredi. p.*

گاءيدن *gā,īdan*, to embrace; *cum muliere*

گاءيده *gā,īda*, a woman who has lost her virginity; *vel quæ cum viro concubuit. p.*

گاءي رون *gā,e ron*, a calculus or hard substance found in the gall-bladder of oxen, and which is used in medicine. *d.*

گايك गायक *gāyak*, m. a singer, a celebrator. *s.*

گاين गायन *gāyan*, a singer (male or female). *s.*

گاءين गाईं *gā,īn*, name of a small clan of *rāj-pūts* in the district of Kopa-cheet.—Ell. Gl. *h.*

گبر *gabr*, m. a fire-worshipper, a follower of Zoroaster, an infidel, one who does not believe in the *Muhammadan* faith. *p.*

گبر *gabbar*, wealthy, rich, prosperous. *d.*

گبرو गबरू *gabrū*, a clown, a young man, an unformed youth, a johnie raw; a bridegroom. *h.*

گبروتا गुबरौता *gubrautā* or *gabrautā*, m. a beetle found in dunghills or old cow-dung (*Scarabæus stercorarius, Lin.; copris, Geoff.*). The forms *gabraundā* and *gabraurā* are also in use. *h.*

گبهانا गुभाना *gubhānā*, گبهونا गुभोना *gubhonā*, } a. to thrust, stick into. *h.*

گبهرو गभरू *gabhrū*, m. (v. *gabrū*) a clown, &c. *h.*

گبهست गभस्ति *gabhasti*, f. a ray of light, a sun or moonbeam. *s.* [grave. *s.*

گبهير गभीर *gabhīr*, deep, dense, profound,

گبهيلا गुभीला *gubhīlā*, m. hard lumps in the intestines produced by costiveness; *scybala. h.*

گپ गप *gap*, f. prattle, tattling. *gap-mārnā*, a. to prattle, to tattle. *h.*

گپال गुपाल **gupāl**, m. (v. *gopāl*) a cowherd; a name of *Krishṇa*; a man's name frequently used among Hindūs. *s.*

گپت गुप्त **gupt** or **gupta**, preserved, protected, hidden; invisible; adv. privately, secretly: as second member of a compound proper name it belongs especially to men of the Vaisya caste. *gupti*, f. concealment, protection. *gupta-gati*, m. a spy, a secret emissary. *s.*

گپتدان गुप्तदान **gupta-dān**, m. a mode of giving alms in secret to Brāhmans. *s.*

گپتي गुप्ती **guptī**, f. a hidden sword, a sword stick. *s.*

گپسا गपसा **gapsā**, hard soil of a whitish appearance. *h.*

گپ‌شپ गपशप **gap-shap**, f. prattle, tattling, chit-chat, small talk. *h.*

گپکنا गपकना **gapaknā**, a. to swallow, to gulp. *h.*

گپها गुफा **guphā**, f. a cave, a vault, a den. *s.*

گپي गप्पी **gappī**, m. a tattler, a prattler. *h.*

گت गत **gat** or गति **gati**, f. going, march, procedure; state, condition, course of events, fate; an air or tune; funeral rites; custom, habit, gait, way; appearance; pace, gait, salvation. *gati-k.*, to perform the funeral rites. *s.*

گت गत **gat** or **gata**, gone, reached, attained; the past. *s.*

گتّ **guttā**, m. rent, lease of land, farm. *d.*

گتارتھ गतार्थ **gatārth**, according to the past; inferring from the past, inferred, understood. *s.*

گتانا **gutānā**, to cause to appoint, &c. *d.*

گتکل गतकुल **gat-kul**, unclaimed inheritance, lands, &c., of which the legal owners are extinct. *s.*

گتنا **gutnā**, a. to appoint, to determine; n. to be occupied or employed. *d.*

گتھنا गुथना **guthnā**, n. to be strung or threaded, as pearls; to be arrayed. *s.*

گتھواں गुथवां **guthwāṅ**, that which has been strung, &c. *s.*

گتي गती **gatī**, f. (v. *gati*), state, condition, &c. *s.*

گتي गते **gate**, gently, softly, by degrees. *s.*

گٹ **gaṭ** or گٹّي **gaṭṭī**, f. bank of a river or tank, &c. *d.*

گٹا गट्टा **gaṭṭā**, m. the part of a *hukka* pipe which fixes into the top of the metal part or bottle; the ankle; a row of gems, &c. *h.*

گٹبینگن गुटबेंगन **guṭ-bengan** (v. *bhaṭ-kaṭaiyā*), m. name of a prickly plant. *h.*

گٹ‌پٹ गटपट **gaṭ-paṭ**, f. higgledy-piggledy. *h.*

گٹرمل गटड़मल्ल **gaṭarmal** (also **gaṭarmal**), m. a nickname for a monkey. *h.*

گٹکا गुटका **guṭkā** or गुटिका **guṭikā**, m. a ball prepared by devotees, by putting which in their mouths they are supposed to become invisible; a sweetmeat swallowed as a bolus without chewing; a small book worn as an amulet. *s.*

گٹکاري गिटकारी **giṭkārī** (also **giṭkarī**), f. a particular vocal sound in singing; quavering? warbling? *h.*

گٹکنا गुटकना **guṭaknā**, n. to coo as a dove; to swallow. *h.*

گٹکوري गिटकौरी **giṭkaurī**, f. a pebble. *h.*

گٹگٹ **gaṭ-gaṭ**, the noise made by a liquid poured from a bottle or guglet. *d.*

گٹوارا गटवारा **gaṭwārā**, } m. (also **ganṭhwārā**)
گٹوارہ गटवारः **gaṭwāra**, } name of a tribe of *jāṭs*.

گٹها गट्ठा **gaṭṭhā**, m. a bundle, pack; root of onion, turmeric, &c., a clove of garlic. *s.*

گٹها गट्ठा **gaṭṭhā**, m. the twentieth part of a *jarīb* (v. *jarīb*, a land measure). *h.*

گٹهانا गठाना **gaṭhānā**, a. to attach, connect, join. *s.*

گٹهاني गठानी **gaṭhānī**, f. a species of tax levied by *zamīndārs*, on the cultivators of the soil. *h.*

گٹهاو गठाव **gaṭhā,o**, m. connection, junction, contrivance. *gaṭhā,o-gāṅṭhnā*, a. to contrive well, to manage one's cards well. *s.*

گٹهبندهن गठबंधन **gaṭh-bandhan**, m. conjunction, binding together; a Hindū marriage ceremony, whereby the bride's and the bridegroom's clothes are fastened together: after which a procession takes place to a river or piece of water. *s.*

گٹهجوڑا गठजोड़ा **gaṭh-joṛā** (v. *gaṭh-bandan*). *s.*

گٹهر गठर **gaṭhar**, m. a large bundle, a bale. *s.*

گٹهري गठरी **gaṭhrī**, f. a bundle, packet, parcel; total, amount, a sum of money sealed up in a bag; crew, pack. *gaṭhrī bāndhnā*, a. to pack up, to gather (money, &c.). *gaṭhrī-k.*, a. to add (figures). *s.*

گٹهکٹا गठकटा **gaṭh-kaṭā**, m. a cut-purse. *s.*

گٹهکٹائي गठकटाई **gaṭh-kaṭā,ī**, } f. purse-cut-
گٹهکٹي गठकटी **gaṭh-kaṭī**, } ting, pilfering, theft. *s.*

گٹهلا गुठला **guṭhlā**, being set on edge (the teeth). *h.*

گٹهلي गुठली **guṭhlī**, f. a kernel, stone, seed. *h.*

گٹهنا गठना **gaṭhnā** (also **guṭhnā**), n. to be joined or connected, to be tied or knotted together, to unite, collude. *h.*

گٹهوءا गठूआ **gaṭhū,ā**, m. knots in cloth, also a marriage ceremony (v. *gaṭh-bandan*). *h.*

گٹهوانا गठवाना **gaṭhwānā**, a. to cause to join or to adhere. *h.*

گٹهوانسي गठवांसी **gaṭhwāṅsī**, the twentieth part of a *gaṭhā*, q. v. *h.*

گٹهوند गठौंद **gaṭhaund**, a deposit or trust bound up in a bag. *s.*

گٹهي गठी **gaṭhī**, f. a ball; pack, a pad put on the back of a beast of burden. *h.*

گٹهيا गठिया **gaṭhiyā**, f. a bump; pains in the joints; a bag, sack; bundle, pannier. *s.*

گٹھیاباۓو गठियाबाव *gaṭhiyā-bāw*, f. rheumatism. *gaṭhiyā-bā,ī*, anthritis, gout in the joints. *s.*

گٹھیلا गठीला *gaṭhīlā*, knotty; robust. *h.*

گٹیا गटिया *gaṭiyā*, f. a small bundle. *h.*

گج गज *gaj*, m. an elephant; a yard (for *gaz*). *s.*

گجا गजा *gajā*, m. part of a cart; a kind of sweetmeat. *h.*

گجانا गजाना *gajānā*, n. to work, to ferment. *h.*

گجپاتل गजपाटल *gaj-pāṭal*, m. (v. *kajjal*) lampblack, with which the eyelids are painted. *s.*

گجپال गजपाल *gaj-pāl*, m. an elephant-keeper. *s.*

گجپت गजपति *gaj-pati*, the title of a *rājā*, master of elephants. *s.*

گجدنت गजदन्त *gaj-dant*, m. (elephant tooth), ivory; a name of *Ganesha*. *s.*

گجر गजर *gajar*, the chimes rung at the expiration of a watch or *pahar* of the day or night; but sometimes restricted to those at the close of the fourth watch, the word *pahar* being more commonly used for the middle chimes (Gilch.): according to the author of the *Arā,ish i Maḥfil*, the term *gajar* is applied to the morning and evening chimes, when, on the conclusion of the fourth *pahar* they strike "eight bells" four times over (v. *pahar*). *h.*

گجر गज्जर *gajjar*, swampy ground. *h.*

گجرا गजरा *gajrā*, m. the leaf of the carrot; a kind of jewels, ornament for the wrist, bracelet; the waving lines on *mashrū* (a kind of silk cloth). *h.*

گجرات गुजरात *gujarāt*, the province of Guzerat. *p.* [Guzerat. *p.*

گجراتي गुजराती *gujarātī*, of or belonging to

گجراج गजराज *gaj-rāj*, m. a large elephant. *s.*

گجراهار गजराहार *gajrāhār*, m. a wreath or necklace of flowers; a gold ornament of the same form. *h.*

گجربهت गजरभत्त *gajar-bhatt*, m. a dish of boiled carrots. *h.*

گجرني गुजरनी *gujarnī*, a female of the *gūjar* tribe of *rāj-pūts* (v. *gūjar*). *h.*

گجري गुजरी *gūjrī* (for *gugrī*), f. the square or market-place of a city (v. *chauk*). *h.*

گجگاه गजगाह *gaj-gāh*, m. a string composed of several tassels made of the hair of a species of ox, and suspended as an ornament from an elephant's neck, or fastened to a horse's ears, extending on both sides to the saddle. *s.*

گجگمني गजगमनी *gaj-gamanī*, } walking (state
گجگوني गजगौनी *gaj-gaunī*, } ly) like an elephant; an epithet made use of to express a graceful gait in a female. *s*

گجمنه गजमनिह *gaj-manih*, } m. an elephant
گجموتي गजमोती *gaj-motī*, } gem, or an elephant pearl: it is a popular idea among the Hindūs that the finest gems and pearls are to be found in the heads of elephants and serpents. *s.*

گجنال गजनाल *gaj-nāl*, m. a large gun or cannon. *s.*

گجني गजनी *gajnī*, f. bole, earth. *h.*

گجها गझा *gajhā*, m. winning, gaining. *h.*

گجهن गझिन *gajhin*, thick, dense (as trees). *h.*

گجهن गुझन *gujhan*, thickly, closely, densely. *h.*

گجيا गुजिया *gujiyā*, f. an earring, a kind of sweetmeat. *h.*

گچ गच *gach*, m. mortar, cement, old mortar knocked off walls, &c.; the floor. *h.*

گچ गच *gach*, thick, close, dense (as trees). *h.*

گچ پچ गचपच *gach-pach*, crowded, stuffed together, close, thick. *h.* [ades. *h.*

گچ پچيا गिचपिचिया *gich-pichiyā*, m. the Plei-

گچکاري *gach-kārī*, building with *gach* or cement. *h. p.* [son). *h.*

گچگينا गचगीना *gach-gīnā*, short and fat (per-

گچها गुच्छा *guchchhā*, dapper, neat, compact. *s.*

گچها गुच्छा *guchchhā* or *guchchha*, m. a bunch, a cluster (of fruit); ear of corn; a tassel *h.*

گچهيدار गुच्छेदार *guchhe-dār*, f. a kind of turban. *h.*

گچي *guchī*, a parcel of betel leaves amounting to one hundred in number. *gachī*, cemented. *d.*

گد *gud*, the brain; marrow; kernel. *d.*

گد गुद *gud*, m. } the anus. *s.*
گدا गुदा *gudā*, f. }

گدا गुड्डा *guddā*, m. a baby, doll; a wind-gall; a bough, a branch. *h.*

گدا गदा *gadā*, f. a club, a mace. *gadū-dhar* (mace-bearing), a name of *Vishnu*. *s.*

گدا *gadā*, m. a beggar, a mendicant; adj. poor, indigent. *p.* [solve. *p.*

گداختن *gudākhtan* (r. *gudāz*), to melt, dis-

گداخته *gudākhta*, melted, dissolved. *p.*

گداز *gudāz*, melting, mild, gentle, affable; (in comp.) melting, or melter; (met.) exterminating as *zulm-gudāz*, the exterminator of oppression. *p.*

گدازان *gudāzān* (v. *gudāz*), melting, &c.; pl. melters or refiners of gold. *p.*

گدانکر गुदाङ्कुर *gudānkur*, m. piles. *s*

گدالا *gadālā*, m. an elephant's saddle. *d.*

گداي *gadā,ī*, f. } poverty, beggary, mendi-
گدايه *gadāya*, m. } city, want. *p.*

گدبدا गदबदा *gadbadā*, corpulent, fat. *h.*

گدر गदर *gadar*, } (also *gaddar*), half-ripe
گدرا गदरा *gadrā*, } fruit or corn. *h.*

گدڑي गुदड़ी *gudṛī*, f. a pallet, a beggar's bedding, quilts, &c.; the garment of a darwesh; a daily market. *h.*

گدڑيا गुदड़िया *gudaṛiyā*, clothed in patched garments or in rags; one who lets quilts for hire. *gudariyā pīr*, a tree near a town or village on which people tie up rags in the manner of votive tablets, which they believe to be efficacious for the accomplishment of their wishes. *h.*

گدكا गदका *gadkā*, m. a foil for fencing with; a mace, club; (in Dakh.) *gadgā*. *s.*

گدكيلك गुदकीलक *gud-kīlak*, m. piles. *s.*

گدگد गदगद *gadgad*, rejoicing, joyful. *s.*

گدگدا गदगदा *gadgadā*, m. a grain (*Guilandina bonducella*).

گدگدا गुदगुदा *gudgudā*, soft, plump. *h.*

گدگدانا गुदगुदाना *gudgudānā*, a. to tickle, to titillate. *s.*

گدگداهٹ गुदगुदाहट *gudgudāhaṭ*, } f. tittilation, pruri-
گدگداءي गुदगुदाई *gudgudā,ī*, } ence, tick-
گدگدي गुदगुदी *gud-gudī*, } ling. *h.*

گدگرا गदगरा *gadgarā*, abounding in moisture [(a soil). *h.*

گدگره गुदग्रह *gud-grah*, m. constipation, flatulence, &c. *s.*

گدگڑا *gadgaṛā*, dark, obscure, muddy; turbid. *d.*

گدگول गदगोल *gad-gol*, m. thick and muddy water. *h.*

گدل *gadal*, m. a large species of bat, commonly called the "flying fox or vampyre." *d.*

گدلا गदला *gadlā*, turbid, muddy, dull, dirty. *h.*

گدلاءي गदलाई *gadlā,ī*, f. turbidness, muddiness, dulness. *h.*

گدھ गिद्ध *giddh*, m. a vulture. *s.*

گدھا गधा *gadhā*, m. an ass, a donkey. *gadhe par chaṛhānā*, (lit. to mount one upon a jackass) applies to a mode of punishment common in the East. The culprit has his face blackened, he is then seated on a donkey with his face towards its tail, having old shoes rags, &c. fastened round his neck, and thus he is paraded through the city. *gadhā-pūrnā*, m. *Boerhavia diffusa*. *gadhe kā hal*, a donkey's plough. Formerly it was not uncommon in the East to yoke donkeys in a plough, and drive them over the ruins of a captured town or fort, as a mode of insulting a vanquished enemy. *s.*

گدھري गद्दरी *gaddharī*, f. the unripe pod of the gram plant, or *Cicer arietinum*. *h.*

گدھي गधी *gadhī* (v. *gadhā*), a she ass. *s*

گدي गद्दी *gaddī*, f. a cushion, pad, pack-saddle, bedding, or any thing stuffed; a seat; a sovereign's throne. *gaddī-nishīn*, one who sits on the *gaddī*, a prince, principal or president. *h.*

گدي गुद्दी *guddī*, f. the nape of the neck. *h.*

گديچت गदीचत *gadīchat*, a kind of grass resembling *dūb*, but about thrice as large: it is much used as fodder. *h.*

گديگم كرنا *guddīgam-k.*, a. to beat thoroughly. *d.*

گديل गदेल *gadel*, m. a child. *h.*

گديلا गदेला *gādelā*, m. a thick bedding. *h.*

گديه गद्य *gadya*, m. prose. *s.*

گڈ गुड *guḍ* same as *guṛ*, q. v. *s.*

گڈ गड *gaḍ*, a boundary-mark, a landmark. *h.*

گڈا *giḍḍā*, of short or small stature. *d.*

گڈبڈ गडबड *gaḍbaḍ*, higgledy-piggledy. *h.*

گڈريا गडरिया *gaḍariyā*, m. a sheperd; a caste of Hindūs so named, of which there are several subdivisions (v. Ell. Glos.). *s.*

گڈه *gaḍḍa*, m. a bulbous root. *d.*

گڈھ गढ *gaḍh*, m. a fortress, a castle, a citadel. *s.*

گڈھي गढी *gaḍhī*, f. a small fortress, &c. (v. *gaṛh* and *gaṛhī*). *s.*

گڈي गुड्डी *guḍḍī*, f. a child's kite; a pinion. *gaḍḍī*, f. a bundle of paper containing ten quires. *h.*

گذار *guẕār*, m. a ferry, a passage; passing; performing, executing, paying; (in comp.) forwarding, paying, executing, as *māl-guẕār*, a tenant, *i.e.* one who forwards or pays rent. *p.*

گذارا *guẕārā*, m. a ferry; a ferryboat; a passage, passing. *p.*

گذارت *guẕārat*, through the medium of, by the hands of (an individual making payments). *p.*

گذارش *guẕārish*, f. payment; a petition, request; representation, explanation. *p.*

گذارنا *guẕārnā*, a. to cause to pass, to forward. *p.h.*

گذاره *guẕāra*, m. passage, passing; a ferry, [a ferryboat. *p.*

گذاري *guẕārī*, f. (abst. of *guẕār*) forwarding, &c. *p.*

گذاشتن *guẕāshtan*, a. (r. *guẕār*), to quit, to abandon; to dismiss, to perform; to pay, to permit. *p.*

گذاف *guẕāf*, f. boasting, a falsehood, a lie, an inconsiderate word, vain, rash (speech). *p.*

گذر *guẕar*, f. a passage, a ferry, a ford; passing, elapsing. *guẕar-jānā*, n. to pass by, to elapse *guẕar-k.*, to cross over. *p.*

گذران *guẕrān*, f. life, passing; employment, livelihood. *guẕrān-k.*, to pass one's life, to enjoy one's self. *p.*

گذراننا *guẕarānnā*, a. to present, to offer. *p.h*

گذربان *guẕar-bān*, f. a ferryman, an officer who collects the customs at ferries; a guardian at any pass; a road-watch. *p.*

گذرگاه *guzar-gāh*, f. ferry, ford, passage. *p.*

گذرنا *guzarnā*, n. to pass, to go, to pass by or over; to omit, to abstain from, to decline; to terminate; to die. *p. h.*

گذري *guzrī*, f. a market, especially one held in the afternoon by the roadside. *p.*

گذشتن *guzashtan*, n. (r. *guzar*) to pass, to cross over (a river, &c.); to elapse. *p.*

گذشته *guzashtā*, m. past, elapsed. *p.*

گر गर *gar*, m. sickness, disease; poison, antidote. *s.*

گر गिरि *giri* or *gir*, m. a hill, mountain; adj. [venerable, worshipful. *s.*

گر गुरु *guru* (or contr. *gur*), m. a spiritual parent or director from whom the youth receives the initiation, a religious teacher; a father, or any venerable male relative; the planet Jupiter; adj. great, weighty; respectable, eminent, best; arduous, difficult. *guru-pāk*, difficult of digestion. *guru-tar*, more important or weighty. *guru-jan*, an elder, a venerable person. *guru-daiwat*, m. the eighth lunar constellation. *guru-ratu*, m. a topaz. *guru-kārya*, m. a momentous affair; the office of spiritual teacher. *guru-laksh*, m. knowledge which can be acquired from a living instructor only. *guru-mukh honā*, to receive from a guru the initiatory prayer, to become a scholar. *guru-wār*, m. Thursday. *h.*

گر *gar*, excoriation or scratching of a horse. *d.*

گر *gar*, (in comp.) a maker or workman, as *zar-gar*, a worker in gold, a goldsmith; conj. (contr. from *agar*) if. *p.*

گرا गर्रा *garrā*, bayish (colour in a horse or [pigeon). *h.*

گرا गरा *garā* (for *galā*), m. the throat, the neck. *h.*

گرارا गरारा *garārā*, m. a sack (for holding the walls of a tent, &c.). *h.*

گراري गरारी *garārī*, f. an instrument for twisting thread or string; the block over which a well-rope traverses. *h.*

گراز *gurāz*, a hog, a boar; a harrow. *p.*

گراس ग्रास *grās* or *girās*, m. a mouthful; fodder for cattle. *h.*

گراسي गरासी *garāsī*, an implement for cutting *jawār* stalks, thorn-bushes, &c. *a.*

گرام ग्राम *grām*, *garām*, or *girām*, a village; a musical scale, an octave. *grām-vāsī*, m. a villager. *grām-yājak* or *grām-purohit*, m. the village priest. *grāmādhikārī* or *grāmādhipati*, the headman of a village. *s.*

گرامك ग्रामिक *grāmik*, rustic, rude. *s.*

گرامني ग्रामणी *grāmanī*, m. a barber; f. a whore, a harlot; a female villager *s.*

گرامي *girāmī* or *garāmī*, dear, precions, elegant, revered, great, excellent. *p.*

گرامياسوه ग्राम्याश्व *grāmyāswa*, m. (village horse) an ass. *s.*

گرامين ग्रामीण *grāmin*, m. a villager, a peasant; adj. rustic, rude. *s.*

گراميه ग्राम्य *grāmya*, m. rustic speech, the *Prākrit*; adj. village-born, rustic. *grāmya-dharm*, m. copulation. *s.*

گران *girān* or *garān*, heavy, important; precious, dear. *girān-bār*, heavily burdened, prolific; (met.) wealthy. *girān-pā,e*, slow in motion, heavy-paced. *girān-pusht*, strong, sturdy; a porter. *girān-jān* or *-khātir*, oppressed in mind, tremulous from old age. *girān-māya*, precious, of noble birth, of great worth. *p.*

گرانا गिराना *girānā*, a. to fell, to overturn, to abase, to throw down; to spill, to drop; to strike. *girā-denā*, to throw, to beat, to cast down. *h.*

گرانون गरांवन *garāṅwan*, m. a tether. *h.*

گراني *girānī*, f. scarcity, dearth, dearness of provisions, &c.; grief, vexation or heaviness of spirit, weight, importance; m. a heavy, dull person. *p.*

گراءو गुराव *gurā,o*, m. a stock or collection of sheaves; an instrument for cutting *jawār* stalks, &c. for fodder. *h.*

گراوا गरावा *garāwā*, a light, poor soil. *h.*

گراه ग्राह *grāh*, m. taking, seizure; an alligator, a crocodile, a shark. *s.* [cepts. *s.*

گراهك ग्राहक *grāhak*, one who takes or ac-

گراهيه ग्राह्य *grāhya*, worthy of acceptance. *s.*

گرائي गुराई *gurā,ī*, f. fairness, whiteness; yellowness; pale redness, ruddiness. *h.*

گرائدن *girā,īdan*, to have an affection or inclination towards. *p.* [conceit. *s.*

گرب गर्व *garb* or *garab*, m. vanity, pride,

گرب गुरब *gurab*, name of an agricultural process by which the ground is broken and pulverized. *h.*

گربتا गर्वता *garbatā* or *garabtā*, f. pride; a proud woman. *s.*

گربز *gurbuz*, } artful, fawning, flattering, se-
گرپز *gurpuz*, } ductive. *p.*

گربونتي गर्ववन्ती *garb-wantī*, a proud woman. *s*

گربه गर्भ *garbha* or *garbh*, m. pregnancy; fœtus, embryo; the belly, the inside; the bed of the Ganges when the river is fullest. *s.*

گربه *gurba*, m. a cat. *gurba,e miskīn*, (met.) a wicked rogue (lit. poor puss). *s.*

گربهادهان गर्भाधान *garbhādhān*, m. a ceremony supposed to procure conception. *s.*

گربهاءي *gur-bhā,ī*, m. a fellow-disciple. *s.*

گربه‌پاتك गर्भपातक *garbh-pātak*, m. a red kind of *morunga* supposed to produce abortion. *s.*

گربهدا गर्भदा *garbhdā*, f. a shrub so called. *s.*

گربهداس गर्भदास *garbh-dās*, m. son of a slave-girl. *s.*

گربه‌روپ गर्भरूप *garbh-rūp*, m. (for *garbh-rūpī*) a child, an infant. *s.* [miscarriage. *s.*

گربه‌شراو गर्भस्राव *garbh-shrāv*, m. abortion,

گربهي गर्भिणी *garbhinī*, گربهوتي गर्भवती *garbhwatī*, گربهونتي गर्भवन्ती *garbhwantī*, } f. pregnant, with child, teeming. *s.*

گرپرنا गिरपड़ना *gir-parnā*, n. to fall down. *h.*

گرت गर्त *gart*, m. a hole, a cavity. *s.*

گرتهاپن गिरथापन *girthāpan*, m. economy. *s.*

گرتهت ग्रथित *grathit*, strung, tied together or in order. *s.*

گرتي *gartī*, a modest or chaste woman. *d.*

گرج गर्ज *garj*, f. bellowing, roaring; thunder, rumbling of clouds. *garji*, m. distant thunder. *gurj*, snarling. *s.*

گرجا गिरिजा *girijā*, f. a name of the goddess *Pārvatī*, as daughter of the personified Himālaya mountain. *s.*

گرجاٹ *garjāṭ*, the noise of thunder. *d.*

گرجاننت गिरिजानन्त *girijānant*, گرجانند गिरिजानन्द *girijānand*, } m. a name of *Ganesha*. *s.*

گرجر गुर्जर *gurjar*, m. a district in the south-west, Gujarāt; the people of Gujarāt.

گرجري गुर्जरी *gurjarī*, f. name of a *rāginī*. *s.*

گرجن गर्जन *garjan*, m. sound, noise; passion, wrath; bellowing, roaring, sound of thunder. *guru-jan*, m. an elder (v. *guru*). *s.*

گرجنا गरजना *garajnā*, n. to thunder, to roar, to bellow. *gurajnā*, to snarl. *s.*

گرجه *girja* or *girija*, m. a church (Portug. *igreja*, from ἐκκλησία). *p.*

گرجي *gurjī*, m. a Georgian; a servant-boy; a hut; a kind of dog. *p.*

گرچ गुर्च *gurch*, f. name of a creeping plant (*Menispermum glabrum*). *s.*

گرچه *garchi* (for *agarchi*), although. *p.*

گرد *gard*, f. dust; the globe, fortune. *gard-ālūda*, loaded or defiled with dust; (in comp.) traversing, encircling, or travelling over, as *jahān-gard*, one who has travelled around or over the world. *p.*

گرد *gird*, m. round, a circle, environs, parts adjacent; postpos. near, about. *gurd*, strong, valiant, a hero. *p.*

گردا *girdā*, m. a circle, a ring, a hoop; the hair cut in a circular form; a round carpet spread under a *ḥuḳḳa*; adj. round, circular. *p.*

گردا गुरदा *gurdā* (v. *kothū*), a sugar-mill. *h.*

گرداب *girdāb*, m. a whirlpool, an abyss, a gulf, a vortex. *p.*

گرداگرد *girdāgird*, m. all round, round about, on every side. *p.*

گردان *gardān*, f. revolving, revolution, turning, winding; (in gram.) inflection, declension, conjugation. *p.*

گردانا *gardānnā*, a. to conjugate, to inflect, to turn. *h.*

گردانك *gardānak*, f. the pointers (two stars in the Great Bear). *p.*

گردانیدن *gardānīdan*, a. to cause to revolve, to avert, turn away. *p.*

گرداوا *girdāwā*, m. a patrol, a watch. *p.*

گرداور *girdāwar*, adv. all around, round; m. a patrol (v. *girdwār*). *p.*

گرداوري *girdāwarī*, f. patroling, inspecting, going the rounds; collecting, bringing together, amassing. *p.*

گردباد *girdbād* or *gardbād*, f. a whirlwind, a devil. *p.*

گردبالش *gird-bālish*, m. a small round pillow, laid under the cheek; a large cylindrical pillow. *p.*

گردبگرد *gird-ba-gird*, گردپیش *gird-pesh*, } m. all around, all about. *p.*

گردبه गर्दभ *gardabh*, m. the white lotus; an ass. *s.*

گردبهي गर्दभी *gardabhī*, f. an insect, a kind of beetle springing from cow dung. *s.*

گردچهنا *gur-dachhinā*, rent-free land given to a spiritual teacher; a present made to a *guru* by his disciple on completing his education, or receiving his initiation. *s.*

گردش *gardish*, f. turning round, revolution, vicissitude; reversion, circulation. *gardishi āsmān*, the revolution of the spheres. *p.*

گردگار *girdigār*, m. God, the Creator. *p.*

گردگان *girdgān*, m. a walnut; the ball of a pellet-bow, a pellet. *p.*

گردن *gardan*, f. the neck. *gardan-band*, m. a collar, a necklace. *gardan kāṭnā*, a. to behead. *gardan kā ḍorā* (*ḍorā*). *gardan-kash*, proud, haughty, vain, insolent, refractory, stubborn. *gardan-kashī*, insolence, rebellion. *gardan-kashī-k.*, a. to rebel. *gardan-mārnā*, a. to behead, to kill, to put to death by decapitation. *p.*

گردنا *gardanā*, m. the neck (v. *gardan*). *p.*

گردنواح *gird-nawāḥ*, f. environs, vicinity. *p.*

گردني *gardanī*, f. a blow on the neck; a horse-cloth. *gardanī denā*, a. to drive a man by the neck. *p.*

گردوار *girdwār*, a patrol, a watch, a guard; a superintendant or inspector of police or customs. *p.*

گردواري *girdwārī*, the office or duty of a *girdwār*. *p.*

گردوڑا गदोड़ा *gardoṛā*, m. a small pit. *h.*

گردون *gardūn*, m. a wheel; an engine for pulling up trees by the roots; the firmament, the heavens; fortune, chance; a chariot, a child's go-cart. *p.*

گرده *gurda*, m. a kidney; (met.) courage. *girda*, a shield; a round pillow; a kind of round cake but not thin. *garda*, a kind of powder. *p.*

گردهاري गिरिधारी *giri-dhārī*, m. (lit. the upholder of the mountains) a name of *Krishṇa*. *s.*

گردهارن गिरिधारण *giri-dhāran*, m. the upholding of a mountain. *giridhāran-k.*, to uphold or support a mountain. *s.*

گردهر गृध्र *gṛidhr*, m. a vulture. *s.*

گردهر गृध्रु *gṛidhru*, } covetous, greedy. *gṛidhru-tā*, f. greediness. *s.*
گردهرا गृध्रा *gṛidhrā*, }

گردي *gardī*, f. (in comp.) separation; misfortune, affliction. *pādshāh-gardī*, the dethroning of a king. *ashrāf-gardī*, a calamity on all the nobility. *paṭhān-gardī*, the invasion of the *Paṭhāns* under *Aḥmad shāh Durrānī*. *p.*

گرديدن *gardīdan*, n. to become, to change, to revolve. *p.*

گرديده *gardīda*, converted, turned, estranged. *p.*

گرديزي *gardezī*, name of a tribe of *saiyids* in the district of Muzaffarpūr. *h.*

گرديوت गुरुदैवत *guru-daiwat*, m. the eighth lunar mansion. *s.*

گرڈ गरुड *garuḍa* (v.*garuṛ*), m. the bird and vehicle of *Vishṇu*: he is generally represented as a being something between a man and a bird, and considered as sovereign of the feathered race. *s.*

گرر गिरिर *girir*, m. a hyena. *h.*

گرراج गिरिराज *giri-rāj*, m. a name of the hill of Govardhan, the Parnassus of the Hindūs; a name of *Krishṇa*. *s.*

گررتن गुरुरत्न *guru-ratn*, m. a topaz. *s.*

گرڑ गरुड़ *garuṛ*, m. a large kind of heron (*Ardea argala*), known to Anglo-Indians as "the adjutant." "I incline to think this a mistake: *garur*, wherever I have heard the word used, invariably signifies the sacred kite, commonly called 'Brahminy kite,' said to be the vehicle of *Vishṇu*. I do not think it ever signifies the adjutant.—Consult Moor's Pantheon or other works on Hindū mythology. The 'Brahminy kite,' a bird about the size of a large hawk, having reddish wings and back, and a white head and breast, is called in Southern India *garuṛ*, or, in the Indian dialects, *garuḍa* or *garuṛa pakshī*: this, I think, must be the bird to which the name properly applies. The 'adjutant' is but little known in Southern India, and the only name for it I have ever heard is *haṛ gilā*."—Binning. In Hindū mythology, the regent of birds; a large vulture. *s.*

گرز *gurz*, m. a mace, a club, a battle-axe. *gurz-bardār*, a macebearer. *gurz-mār*, a *Muḥammadan faḳīr*, who carries a club armed with spikes by which he wounds himself in order to extort alms from the very pious or very foolish people. *p.*

گرسار गिरिसार *giri-sār*, m. the Malaya mountain in the south of India. *s.*

گرست ग्रस्त *grast*, inacurately pronounced, slurred. *s.*

گرسنگي *gursanagī* or *gursinagī*, f. hunger. *p.*

گرسنه *gursana* or *gursina*, hungry. *p.*

گرسي *gursī*, f. a cottage, a hut, a shed. *d.*

گرش ग्रिष *grish*, f. the name of the fourth of the six seasons, including from 15th *Baisāk* to 15th *Asāṛh*; summer; heat, or hot season. *s.*

گرفت *girift*, f. taking, capture, seizure; a handle, catch, clutch; an objection, criticism. *p.*

گرفتار *giriftār*, m. a captive, a prisoner; adj. involved or overwhelmed (in trouble, &c.). *p.*

گرفتاري *giriftārī*, f. bondage, captivity, imprisonment; embarrassment. *p.*

گرفتگي *giriftagī*, f. capture, detention, catching. *giriftagī e āwāz*, f. hoarseness. *p.*

گرفتن *giriftan* (r. *gir*), to take, to seize; to begin or betake one's self to. *p.*

گرفته *girifta*, seized, caught, taken; used in comp. both as first and last member, as *ajal-girifta*, seized by fate; at the point of death; *girifta-khāṭir* or *-dil*, afflicted at heart. *p.*

گركهئي गुरखई *gurkhā,ī*, a kind of mortgage. *h.*

گرگ *gurg*, m. a wolf. *gurg-zāda*, a young wolf, a wolf's cub. *p.*

گرگ गर्ग *garg*, one of the ten principal Munis or saints; name of a sect of Brāhmans. *garg-bansī*, a clan of *rāj-pūts*. *s.*

گرگا गुर्गा *gurgā*, m. a servant-boy, a brat; a vagabond; the knee joint. *a.*

گرگابي गुर्गाबी *gurgābī*, f. a kind of shoe or slipper. *h.*

گرگٹ गिरगिट *girgiṭ* or *girguṭ*, m. a lizard; a chameleon; the tree lizard, often called by Europeans "the blood-sucker." *h.*

گرگج गर्गज *gargaj*, m. a scaffold; a tower, a bastion; a cavalier. *h.*

گرگر *gargar*, one of the names of God. *girgir*, a species of bean or pea. *p.*

گرگرانا गरगराना *gargarānā*, n. to gurgle; to thunder; to roll; to roar (as a tiger), to rumble. *h.*

گرگري गुर्गुरी *gurgurī*, f. ague, the cold fit of a fever, a quotidian fever. *h.*

گرگري गर्गरी *gargarī*, f. a water vessel, a guglet. *s.*

گرگوا गरगवा *gargawā*, a kind of grass which grows in low grounds during the rains. *h.*

گرگي गुरगी *gurgī*, f. a wench; a slave-girl; knee-breeches. *h.*

گرگيا गरगया *gargayā*, f. a sparrow. *h.*

گرل गरल *garal*, m. venom. *garli*, venomous. *s.*

گرم *garm*, hot, warm; ardent, active, zealous, fiery, choleric, virulent; throng (as a market). *garm-ikhtilāṭ*, of warm affection. *garm-ikhtilāṭī*, f. warmth of affection. *garm-bāzār* or *-bāzārī*, (lit.) a warm or crowded market; (met.) great demand, high value. *garm bolnā*, to speak readily and to the purpose. *garm-joshī*, warmth of affection. *garm-rav* or *-rah*, going at a quick pace. *garm-sukhan*, speaking forcibly. *garm-shitāb*, hastening. *garm-k.*, to warm. *garm nagāra*, looking keenly or eagerly. *garm honā*, to be angry. *p.*

گرما *garmā*, m. summer. *garmāgarm*, hot and hot. *p.*

گرما गरिमा *garimā*, f. importance, self-importance, vanity, boast. *s.*

گرمابه *garmāba*, m. a warm or hot bath. *p.*

گرمان *garmānā*, n. to be angry; to enliven. *p.*

گرمکه गुरुमुख *guru-mukh* (v. *guru*).

گرمي *garmī*, f. warmth, heat; the venereal disease. *garmī-k.*, to affect fondness. *p.*

گرميدار *garmī-dār*, feverish, diseased. *p.*

گرنا गिरना *girnā*, n. to fall, to drop, to sink, to be spit. *girte-parte*, (lit. repeatedly falling) with much toil or with great difficulty; (Pers.) *uftān o khezan*, q. v. *a.*

گرنته ग्रन्थ *granth*, f. a code, a book, particularly the book of the Sikh religion, composed by *Nānak Shāh*. *granthi*, a knot, a joint, a tie. *s.*

گرنته‌كار ग्रन्थकार *granth-kār*, m. an author, bookmaker, writer, the founder of a system or sect. *s.*

گرنتهم *grantham*, m. a character in which Sanskrit is written and printed in Southern India, where the Nagarī character is unknown. *d.*

گرنجن गृञ्जन *gṛinjan*, m. poisoned flesh; garlic. *s.*

گرو *giro*, *girw*, or *giraw*, m. a wager, bet; pledge, pawn, a mortgage. *p.*

گرو गुरू *gurū*, m. a spiritual guide, tutor, pastor, teacher. *garv*, m. pride, arrogance. *s.*

گروا गरवा *garwā*, heavy; important; respectable, demure. *garwāpan*, m. respectability. *s.*

گروار गुरुवार *guru-wār*, m. Thursday. *s.*

گروانا गिरवाना *girwānā*, a. (c. of *girānā*) to cause to be felled or thrown down. *h.*

گروائن गुरुवाइन *guruwā,in*, f. the wife of a guru. *s.*

گروبار गुरूबार *gurū-bār*, m. Thursday. *s.*

گروت गर्वित *garvit*,
گرور गर्वर *garvar* } proud, haughty, arrogant. *s.*

گرور गिरिवर *giriwar*, m. a mountain, a hill. *s.*

گروني गुर्विणी *gurvinī*,
گروي गुर्वी *gurvī*, } f. a pregnant woman. *s.*

گروه *guroh*, m. a band, troop, levy of people, company, crew. *p.*

گروي *girwī*, any thing pledged or pawned; f. an insect mischievous to standing corn. *p. h.*

گرويدار *girwī-dār*, the holder of a pledge or mortgage. *p.*

گرويدگي *girwīdagī*, f. admiring, following; adoring, adherence, attachment. *p.*

گرويدن *girwīdan*, to follow; to admire, &c. *p.*

گرويده *girwīda*, attracted, attached to, admiring, captivated, a believer. *p.*

گروي‌نامه *girwī-nāma*, m. a deed of mortgage. *p.*

گره गृह *gṛih* or ग्रह *grah* (for *gṛiha*), m. a house, dwelling. *gṛih-pati*, m. a householder. *gṛih-bhūmi*, f. the site of a house. *gṛih-taṭī*, f. a terrace in front of a house. *gṛih-kapotak*, m. the domestic pigeon. *gṛih-nāshan*, m. a pigeon. *gṛih-vāṭikā*, f. a garden or grove near a house. *s.*

گره ग्रह *grah* or *graha*, m. a planet. *grah-pūjā*, f. worship of the planets. *grah-pīṛā*, f. the influence of an unpropitious planet. *grah rāj*, m. the sun, the moon, the planet Jupiter. *grah-patra*, a horoscope. *s.*

گره *girih*, f. a knot; knuckle, joint, articulation; a division of a *gaz*, three finger-breadths; prejudice, misunderstanding. *girih-bur*, a cut-purse. *girih-paṛnā*, dissension arising between two people. *girih khulnā*, n. denotes restoration of friendship. *p.*

گرها गर्हा *garhā*, f. abuse, censure, reproach. *s.*

گرهادهار ग्रहाधार *grahādhār*, m. the polar star. *s.*

گرهادهين ग्रहाधीन *grahādīn*, subject to planetary influence. *s.*

گرهامي ग्रहामय *grahāmay*, m. epilepsy, convulsions, demoniacal possession. *s.*

گرهچه *girihcha*, a small knot or joint. *p.*

گرهست गिरहस्त *girhast* or *girhist* (for गृहस्थ *gṛikastha*), a householder, a peasant, a husbandman. *s.*

گرهستهاپن ग्रहस्थापन *graha-sthāpan*, m. invoking the presence of the nine planets. *s.*

گرهستهاسرم गृहस्थाश्रम *gṛihasth-āshram* or *girhast-āshram*, the profession or condition of a householder or married man. *s.*

گرهستهي गृहस्थी *gṛihasthī* or गिरहस्ती *girhastī*, f. husbandry, housewifery, household; adj. of or relating to a householder. *s.*

گرهن ग्रहण *grahan*, m. taking, seizure; acceptance, assent; an eclipse. *s.* [proach. *s.*

گرهن गर्हण *garhan*, m. censuring, blame, re-

گرهني गृहिणी *gṛihinī*, f. a wife. *s.*

گرهني ग्रहणी *grahanī*, f. diarrhœa, dysentery. *s.*

گرهور गुड़हौर *guṛhaur*, stacks of cow-dung. *h.*

گرهيت गृहीत *gṛihīt*, taken, seized, caught. *s.*

گرهيتا ग्रहीता *grahītā*, taking, disposed to take. *s.*

گرهيه गृह्य *gṛihya*, a partisan, belonging to a party, to be taken or seized; domestic; a ritual book. *s.*

گرهيه गर्ह्य *garhya*, low, vile, contemptible. *s.*

گري गुर्री *gurrī*, f. parched barley. *h.*

گري गरी *garī*, f. the kernel of a cocoa-nut. *h.*

گرّي गर्री *garrī*, f. an instrument for twisting a thread or string; the term is also applied to a haystack, a rick, a stack of thatched grain. *h.*

گري *garī*, f. (abst. of *gar* in comp.) denotes action, business, &c., as *zar-garī*, the business of a goldsmith. *p.*

گريا गुरिया *guriyā*, f. a bead (of a rosary, &c.). *s.*

گريار गरियार *gariyār*, a bullock that lies down in the midst of his work. *h.*

گريان *giryān*, weeping; one who weeps. *p.*

گرياني *giryānī*, weeping, shedding of tears. *p.*

گريبان *girebān*, m. a collar, cap; pocket; (fig.) the neck. *girebān-gīr*, an accuser, a plaintiff, complainant. *girebān men munh ḍālnā*, to confess and be ashamed of one's faults. *p.*

گريختن *gurekhtan* (r. *gurez*) to run away, to flee, to escape. *p.*

گريز *gurez*, f. flight, deviation, abhorrence, aversion, abstinence, fasting, regression, fugitive. *p.*

گريزان *gurezān*, running away, shunning. *p.*

گريستن *girīstan* (r. *giriy*), to weep, to lament. *p.*

گريشم ग्रीष्म *grīshm*, m. } hot season, extending from 15th *Baisāk* to 15th *Ashāṛh*, summer; heat; adj. hot, warm. *graishm*, belonging to the hot season. *s.*
گريكهم *girekham*, f. }

گريشمي ग्रैष्मी *graishmī*, f. double jasmine. *s.*

گريو ग्रैव *graiv*, m. a necklace, a collar. *s.*

گريوا ग्रीवा *grīvā*, f. the neck, the back part of the neck. *s.*

گريوا *girewā*, } a low hill, an acclivity, ravine, steep pass. *p. s.*
گريوه *girewa*, }

گريوان *girewān* (v. *girebān*), a collar, &c. *d.*

گريه गेह *greh*, m. a house, mansion, abode. *s.*

گريه *girya*, m. crying, lamentation, plaint. *girya o zārī*, f. bewailing, weeping and lamentation. *girya-k.*, a. to weep, to cry, to lament. *p.*

گڑ गुड़ *guṛ*, m. molasses, treacle. *guṛ-ambā*, mangoes boiled with meal and sugar. *s.*

گڑا गड़ा *gaṛā*, m. name given to a large sheaf. *h.*

گڑابٹاءي गड़ाबटाई *gaṛā-baṭā,ī*, division of produce in the sheaf without threshing. *h.*

گڑاسي गड़ासी *gaṛāsī*, f. an instrument for cutting sugar-cane. *h.*

گڑاكو *guṛākū*, tobacco prepared for the *hukka*. *d.*

گڑانا गुड़ाना *guṛānā*, a. to dig; to cause to be dug. *h.*

گڑانا गड़ाना *gaṛānā*, a. to thrust in; to cause to enter. *s.*

گڑانبه गुड़ांब *guṛāmba*, mangoes boiled with meal and sugar, resembling mango fool. *s.*

گڑاءو गड़ाव *gaṛā,o*, an instrument for cutting *jawār* stalks. *h.*

گڑبڑ गड़बड़ *gaṛbaṛ*, m. higgledy-piggledy, confused. *h.*

گڑبڑا गड़बड़ा *gaṛbaṛā*, m. bustle, confusion; motion of the bowels (*Borborygmi*). *h.*

گڑبڑانا गड़बड़ाना *gaṛbaṛānā*, n. to be confounded, to fear. *h.*

گڑبڑاهٹ गड़बड़ाहट *gaṛbaṛāhaṭ*, f. confusion, fright, alarm, bustle. *h.*

گڑبڑي *gaṛbaṛī*, f. confusion, fright, alarm. *d.*

گڑپشپ गुड़पुष्प *guṛ-pushp*, } m. *Bassia latifolia*, from the flowers of which a spirituous liquor is distilled, and the nuts of which afford oil. *s.*
گڑپهول गुड़फूल *guṛ-phūl*, }

گڑتي *gaṛtī*, a friend, a companion *d.*

گڑچ गुड़च *guṛach*, m. name of a medicine (*Menispermum glabrum*). *s.*

گڑچا *gaṛachchā*, } (v. *ḍāṭ*) threatening, snubbing, browbeating. *d.*
گڑد *gaṛad*, }

گڑري गुड़री *guṛarī* (v. *jūṛā*), a kind of rope. *h.*

گڑريا गड़रिया *gaṛariyā*, m. a shepherd or goatherd (v. *gaḍariyā*). *h.*

گڑسي *guṛsī*, f. a cottage, hut, shed. *d.*

گڑك गड़क *gaṛak*, m. a fish, a kind of gilthead. *s.*

گڑگا गुड़गा *guṛgā*, the knee. *guṛge po munḍī jhukānā*, to ponder, meditate, reflect. *h.*

گڑگڑانا गड़गड़ाना *gaṛgaṛānā*, n. to thunder, to roll, to roar (as a tiger), to rumble, to gurgle. *guṛguṛānā*, n. to rumble (the bowels). *giṛgiṛānā*, a. to beseech, to implore earnestly and humbly. *h.*

گڑگڑي गुड़गुड़ी *guṛguṛī*, f. a small *hukka*, vulgarly called the hubble-bubble, generally made of a cocoa-nut shell, and having a straight inflexible tube. *h.*

گڑگودر गड़गूदड़ *guṛgūdar*, m. old and tattered garments. *h.*

گڑگي गुड़गी *guṛgī*, f. knee-breeches. *h.*

گڑلون गड़लवण *gaṛ-lavan*, m. rock or fossile salt, especially that found in the district of Sāmbhar. *s.*

گڑن गड़न *gaṛan*, f. a swamp, a morass. *h.*

گڑنا गड़ना *gaṛnā*, n. to penetrate, to enter, to lie, to be sunk or buried (in the earth), to be driven into the earth. *h.*

گڑنته गड़ंथ *gaṛanth*, m. name of a game, tip-cat; a mode of an incantation performed for the destruction of any person (*māran*); to secure his affection (*mohan*); to subject him to obedience (*basīkaran*); to imprison him, or deprive him of the power of action or speech (*stambhan*); to drive him away (*uchchāṭan*); or to call him (*ākarshan*). Certain words are pronounced over an effigy of the person or his name in writing, which is afterwards buried. *h.*

گڑنگ *gaṛang* (also *gaḍang*), a magazine. *d.*

گڑوا गड़वा *gaṛwa* or गड़ुवा *gaṛuwā*, m. a kind of waterpot; a flowerpot carried about by musicians and dancing-women at the feast of *Basant-panchamī*, as an offering to people of rank, from whom they receive presents in return. *h.*

گڑوات *gaṛwāṭ*, f. burying, perforating. *d.*

گڑوانا गड़वाना *gaṛwānā*, a. to cause to enter, to perforate, to stick into, to cause to be buried or driven into the earth. *h.*

گڑونا गड़ोना *gaṛonā*, a. to pierce, to perforate, to bore, to stick into. *h.*

گڑھ गढ़ *gaṛh*, m. a castle, a hill, fort. *h.*

گڑھا गढ़ा *gaṛhā*, m. a cavity, a hole, a pit, abyss. *s.*

گڑھانا गढ़ाना *gaṛhānā* (v. *gaṛhnā*), to malleate, or cause to form by hammering, to bury, &c. *h.*

گڑھائي गढ़ाई *gaṛhā,ī*, f. price of malleating or making jewellery, burying. *h.*

گڑھت गढ़त *gaṛhat* or गढ़ट *gaṛhaṭ*, f. form, shape, fashion, make. *h.*

گڑھل गुढ़ल *guṛhal*, m. *Hibiscus Syriacus*, commonly called by Europeans "the shoe-flower" *h.*

گڑھنا गढ़ना *gaṛhnā*, a. (v. *ṭhonknā*) to drive in, as a stake; n. to be driven in. *s.*

گڑھنا गढ़ना *gaṛhnā*, a. to malleate, to form by hammering; to make, to form; n. to be made, fashioned. *h.*

گڑھوار गढ़वार *gaṛhwār*, fat, coarse, thick. *h.*

گڑھي गढ़ी *gaṛhī*, f. a small fort, a castle, a village fortification of mud, flanked with towers. Under former governments there was scarcely a village in India without its *gaṛhī*; now the word is nearly unknown. *gaṛhī-band*, a favourable tenure of land in Bundelkand, to those of the inhabitants who obstinately defended their forts against the Marhattas. *h.*

گڑھئی गढ़ई *gaṛha,ī*, } f. a small pond or
گڑھيا गढ़िया *gaṛhiyā*, } tank. *h.*

گڑھيا गढ़िया *gaṛhiyā*, f. a pike, javelin, spear. *h.*

گڑھيا गढ़ैया *gaṛhaiyā*, f. a small tank or pond; m. a burier. *h.*

گڑھيبند गढ़ीबन्द *gaṛhī-band*, name of a species of tenure by which lands are held (v. *gaṛhī*). *h.*

گڑھيلا गढ़ेला *gaṛhelā*, m. a cavity, a pit, an abyss. *h.* [fortress. *d.*

گڑي *gaṛī*, a friend, a companion; f. a small

گڑيا गुड़िया *guṛiyā*, m. one whose business is to sell *guṛ*, q. v. *s.*

گڑيا गुड़िया *guṛiyā*, f. a doll, a child's puppet. *h.*

گڑيار गड़ियार *gaṛiyār*, stout-hearted, stiff-necked, stubborn, obstinate. *h.*

گڑياري गड़ियारी *gaṛiyārī*, f. obstinacy, &c. *h.*

گڑيرن गड़ेरन *gaṛeran*, the receptacle for the sugar-cane before it is cut up. *h.*

گڑيري गड़ेरी *gaṛerī*, f. a joint or piece of the sugar-cane. the portion between two knots. *h.*

گڑيريا गड़ेरिया *gaṛeriyā*, m. a shepherd. *h.*

گز *gaz*, m. an instrument for measuring with; a yard; a ramrod. *ilāhī-gaz*, the standard measure of distance established by Akbar: it is very nearly thirty-three inches English. *p.*

گزا *gazā*, biting, hurtful; harm, loss. *p.*

گزار *guzār*, a pass, passage, transit. *p.*

گزارش *guzārish*, f. utterance, explanation; interpretation of dreams. *p.*

گزاف *guzāf* or *gizāf*, vanity, idle or foolish words and deeds; adj. foolish, vain, idle. *p.*

گزان *guzān*, choosing, selecting. *gazān*, stinging, biting, injuring. *p.* [a devil. *p.*

گزك *gazāk*, f. a relish (eaten with wine, &c.);

گزند *gazand*, f. misfortune, calamity, loss, injury, mischief, harm. *p.*

گزنه *gazna*, a kind of nettle. *p.*

گزنده *gazanda*, stinging, biting, venomous or noxious (animals or vermin). *p.* [ton). *p.*

گزي *gazī*, f. a coarse kind of cloth (of cot-

گزيدن *gazīdan*, to bite, to sting, to injure. *p.*

گزيدن *guzīdan* (r. *guzīn*), to choose, select. *p.*

گزيدني *guzīdanī*, worthy of being chosen. *p.*

گزيده *guzīda*, chosen, selected, excellent. *gazīda*, injured, bitten, alarmed. *p.*

گزير *guzīr*, aid, remedy. *gazīr* or *gizīr*, the superintendant of collectors of the revenue, a manager or head agent; a commander; the night watch. *p.*

گزين *guzīn*, (in comp.) choosing, preferring, electing. *khalwat-guzīn*, fond of retirement, a hermit. *p.*

گزينه *gazīna*, m. a thick (or close) and rather coarse kind of cotton cloth. *p.*

گسار *gusār*, (in comp.) removing, dissipating, assuaging; as *gham-gusār*, the dissipator of sorrow, *i. e.* a sincere friend. *p.*

گسائن *gusā,īn* (for *gosā,īn*, q. v.). *d.*

گستاخ *gustākh*, arrogant, presumptuous, uncivil, cruel, rude. *p.*

گستاخانه *gustākhāna*, impudently, rudely. *p.*

گستاخ‌دست *gustākh-dast*, dexterous, clever-handed. *p.*

گستاخي *gustākhī*, f. arrogance, presumption, rudeness, cruelty. *gustākhī mu'āf*, pardon my rudeness. *p.* [woman. *h.*

گستان गस्तान *gastān*, f. a foolish, dissolute

گستانگر गस्तानगर *gastāngar*, m. a clown; adj. ignorant, foolish, uninformed. *h.*

گستر *gustar*, (in comp.) spreading, strewing, scattering, diffusing; as, *'adālat-gustar*, one who diffuses or dispenses justice. *p.*

گسترانيدن *gustarānīdan*, } to spread, to dif-
گستردن *gustardan*, } fuse. *p.*

گسترده *gustarda*, spread (a bed); a foundation. *p.*

گستري *gusturī*, f. (abst. of *gustar* in comp.) spreading, &c.; as, *'adālat-gustarī*, the promoting of justice. *p.*

گسستن *gusistan* (also *gusilīdan* and *gusekhtan*), r. *gusil*, to break, to destroy. *p.*

گسل *gusil*, (in comp.) breaking, destroying; as, *jān-gusil*, soul-breaking or life-destroying. *p.*

گسیاں *gusiyyāṅ* or *gusaiyāṅ* (v. *gosaiyāṅ*, &c.), the deity. *s.*

گشاد *gushād*, } (v. *kushād* and *kushāda*)
گشادہ *gushāda*, } opening, opened, &c. *p.*

گشادن *gushādan* (v. *kushādan*), to open, &c. *p.*

گشت *gasht*, f. surrounding, going round (especially guards patroling); walk, walking, perambulation, strolling. *p.*

گشت‌سلامي *gasht-salāmī*, f. a tax levied by *ḥākis* when on a circuit. *p.*

گشتمحال *gasht-maḥāll*, a toll or transit duty levied on boats for passing through a *zamīndārī*. *p.*

گشتن *gashtan* (r. *gard*), to become, &c. (v. *gardīdan*). *p.*

گشته *gashta*, returned, become, formed. *p.*

گشتي *-gashtī*, watch, sentinel, patrol; f. a present made to a revenue officer on making his tour through his district. *p.*

گشتيا *gashtiyā*, m. a watchman, a patrol; a collector of market dues. *p.* [a patrol. *d.*

گشتي‌بان *gashtī-bān*, a watchman, a sentinel,

گشٹ गुष्ट *gushṭ*, m. cabal; an assembly. *s.*

گفت *guft*, a word, saying, speech, discourse (generally used in compounds). *p.*

گفتار *guftār*, speech, mode of speaking. *p.*

گفت‌شنيد *guft-shanīd* (v. *guft o shanīd*). *p.*

گفتگو *guft-go* or *guft-gū*, f. conversation, discourse, chitchat. *p.*

گفتن *guftan* (r. *go* or *gū*), to say, to speak.

گفتني *guftanī*, fit to be told or spoken. *p.*

گفت‌وشنيد *guft o shanīd* or *guft o shanūd*, f. conversation, dialogue; contention, debate, controversy. *p.*

گفت‌وگو *guft o go* (v. *guft-go*), discourse, &c. *p.*

گفته *gufta*, spoken, told; an order or command. *p.*

گگر गगर *gagar*, } f. a waterpot. *s.*
گگري गगरी *gagrī*, }

گگل गुग्गुल *guggul*, m. name of a tree or gum (*Amyris agallocha*): bdellium.

گگن गगण *gagan*, m. sky, firmament. *gagan-kī bachche-wālī murghī*, the group of stars called the Pleiades. *s.*

گگن‌بهيڑ गगणभेड़ *gagan-bheṛ*, m. a pelican (*Pelecanus onocrotalus*). *s.*

گگندهول गगणधूल *gagandhūl*, f. dust of the *Pandanus odoratissimus*. *s.*

گل *gul*, m. a rose, a flower; the snuff of a candle; the albugo; a seton, an issue, a mark made by burning; balls of charcoal, used for burning the tobacco in a *ḥuḳḳa*; the *caput mortuum* of tobacco left on the tile of a *ḥuḳḳa* after smoking. *gul-āchīn*, m. the name of a flower (*Plumeria*). *guli ashrafī*, *Calendula* (*Bruce, MS.*); *Linum trigynum, Roxb.* *gul-afshān* (v. *gul-fishān*). *gul anās kī jaṛ*, m. salep. *gul-andām*, slender, delicate. *gul i aurang*, m. name of a flower. *gul bāndhnā*, to char the end of the match of a gun. *gul-barg*, m. a roseleaf; (met.) a mistress. *gulbarga*, name of a city (called by Europeans Calburgah or Kulberga), formerly the capital of the Bahmanī Sultans of the Deccan. *guli bakāwali*, name of a charming little romance in the Hindūstānī language by *Nihāl Chand Lahorī*. *gul-piyāda*, m. a species of rose without smell. *guli ja'farī*, *Tagetes patula*. *guli jawānī*, the venereal disease. *gul jharnā*, to drop the charred part (a match). *guli chāndnī*, f. the name of a flower. *gul-chashm*, labouring under albugo. *gul-chihra*, rosy-faced. *gul charre uṛānā*, to be addicted to pleasure, to live expensively. *gul-chīn*, m. a gardener. *guli chīnī*, name of a flower (*Chrysanthemum Indicum*). *gul-khāl*, m. spotted. *guli-khaṭmī*, the common hollyhock. *guli khairā* or *guli khairū*, m. Chinese and Persian hollyhock (*Alcea rosea, Lin.*; *Althea rosea, Roxb.*). *gul-dār*, spotted. *gul dān*, m. a flowerpot. *guli-dā,ūdī*, *Chrysanthemum Indicum*. *gul-dasta*, m. a nosegay. *gul-denā*, to scar, to make an issue. *gul-rukh* or *gul-rukhsār*, rosy-cheeked. *gul-rukhān* (pl.), the rosy-cheeked ones, the fair ones. *guli-ra'nā*, m. a beautiful delicate scented rose. *gul-rang*, rose-coloured, red. *gul-rū*, rosy, ruddy; (used sub.) a mistress, a sweetheart. *gul-rez*, a kind of silken stuff; adj. shedding flowers. *gul-zār*, m. a garden (or bed) of roses. *guli sūranjān*, m. flower of the hermodactyl plant (*Colchicum Illyrium*). *guli sūrī*, f. a Persian rose very fragrant. *guli sosan*, f. a lily. *guli shab-bo*, f. tuberose (*Polianthes tuberosa*). *gul-shakar* or *gul-shakarī*, f. conserve of roses. *gul i ṣad barg*, m. (same as *ṣad barg*) (met.) the sun. *guli ṭurra*, *Poinciana pulcherrima*. *guli 'abbās*, m. the name of a plant, marvel of Peru (*Mirabilis jalapa*). *guli 'ajā,ib*, m. the name of a flower (*Hibiscus mutabilis*). *gul-'izār* or *'uẕār*, rosy-cheeked. *gul-fām*, like the rose, a mistress. *guli farang*, m. the name of a flower (*Vinca rosea*). *gul-fishān*, scattering roses, agreeable, pleasant. *gul-ḳand*, m. conserve of roses. *gul-kāṭnā*, a. to snuff a candle. *gul-kārī*, f. flowering; painting flowers. *gul-katarnā*, to snuff a candle; to calumniate. *gul-k.*, to extinguish (a candle or lamp); to flash in the pan, and miss fire (a gun). *gul-khānā*, to be cauterized or to cauterize one's self; a practice among lovers, who burn themselves with heated pieces of coin, to recommend themselves by their fortitude to the notice of their mistresses. *gul-khandā*, m. a bell. *gul-kesh*, m. the cockscomb flower (*Amaranthus cruentus*). *gul-gasht*, m. walking in the garden; a pleasant place for walking and recreation, especially if blooming with roses and other flowers. *gulgashti muṣallā*, the bower of *Muṣallā*, the name of an enchanting spot near Shīrāz in Persia, the favourite haunt of the poet *Ḥāfiẓ* when he lived, and where his ashes still repose. *gul-lahana*, m. cauliflower. *gul-lagānā*, a. to brand, to mark. *gul lenā*, to snuff a candle. *guli makhmal*, f. globe amaranth (*Gomphrena globosa*). *guli mukarrar*, m. syrup of roses. *gul mihindī*, f. name of a flower (*Impatiens balsamina*). *gul-mekh*, f. a stud, a tack, a nail. *guli mekhakī*, the pink. *guli nishāt*, (lit.) flower of joy, grape-wine. *gul honā*, to be extinguished or go out (a candle). *guli yūsuf*, the anemone. *p.*

گل *gil*, f. earth, clay. *gili armanī*, f. Armenian bole. *gil-andāzī*, f. an enbankment of earth, with a ditch, for confining water on the lands, and to serve as a reservoir. *gili ḥikmat*, f. lute, cement. *gil dar gil-k.*, (lit. to throw earth on earth) said when, in burying the dead, earth is thrown immediately on the corpse; whereas the usual custom is, after depositing it in the grave, to lay planks over it and then fill up the remaining cavity with earth. *p.*

گل गल *gal*, m. the neck, the throat. *gal bahiyāṅ ḍālnā*, a. to throw one's arms round another's neck. *gal-denā*, to throttle, to choke, to hang. *s.*

گل *gul* the fire-ball of a *huḳḳa*; (in comp. for *gol*) a bullet. *gul-chalā*, a rifleman, a musqueteer. *s.*

گل *gal*, m. a noose, a snare, a fish-hook, the gallows. *gal-denā*, to hang a criminal. *d.*

گلا गला *galā*, m. the throat, neck; voice; a funnel, a syphon or tube; adj. rotten, dissolved, melted, wasted. *galā uṭhānā*, (lit. to lift up the throat) to apply acrid substances, such as pepper, &c. to the *uvula* of a child, when it becomes hoarse or loses its voice from the relaxation of that part. *galā bandhānā*, to ensnare one's self, especially in the bonds of love. *galā-baiṭhā*, hoarse. *galā baiṭhnā* or *paṛnā*, n. to be hoarse, *galā phānsnā*, a. to hang, to choke. *galā dabānā*, a. to strangle. *galā denā*, to waste. *galā-kāṭnā*, to cut the throat. *galā ghonṭnā*, a. to throttle, to choke. *gale paṛnā*, to seek the friendship of one who is averse from it. *gale paṛī bajā,e sidh*, we should make a virtue of necessity. *gale kā hār honā*, to seek and persist in a quarrel or dispute, to tease, to importune; to seek with ardour the friendship or affection of any one; to persecute with kindness or attention. *gale lagnā*, to embrace. *gale manḍhnā*, to importune. *s.*

گلا गुल्ला *gullā*, m. a pellet shot from a pellet-bow. *h.*

گلا *gillā*, moist, damp, wet. *d.*

گلاب *gulāb*, (in Per.) rose water; (in Hind.) the rose. *gulāb-pāsh*, m. a bottle from which rose-water is sprinkled. *gulāb-pāshī*, f. the sprinkling of rose-water. *gulāb-pānī*, rose-water. *gulāb-chashm*, meek, soft, or gentle-eyed. *gulāb kā phūl*, the rose. *p.*

گلاب جامن *gulāb-jāman*, f. the rose-apple (*Eugenia jambos, Roxb.*). *p.*

گلابي *gulābī*, rosy; rose-colour, damask; f. a vial, bottle, flagon; a kind of sweetmeat, a pear. *gulabī jāṛā*, m. the season of spring. *p. h.*

گلار गलार *galār*, m. the name of a bird. *h.*

گلال गुलाल *gulāl*, m. a farinaceous powder dyed red, which the Hindūs throw on each others' clothes, in the *holī* saturnalia. *gulāl-chashm*, reddish eye. *gulāl-bāṛī*, f. a royal pavilion, a tent. *gulālī*, of the colour of *gulāl*, or stained with it. *h.*

گلالا गल्लाला *gallālā*, m. gargarism. *h.*

گلاماٹي गलामाटी *galāmaṭī*, rich free mould. *h.*

گلان ग्लान *glān*, wearied, languid. *glāni*, f. languor. *s.*

گلانا गलाना *galānā* or *galā-denā*, a. to melt, to dissolve; to soften; to waste or squander away. *galāne-wālā*, m. a menstruum; a solvent. *s.*

گلاءو गलाऊ *galā,ū*, soluble, sceptical, weakening; dissolver. *galā,o*, m. solution. *s.*

گلاوا *gillāwā*, m. prepared clay, dirt, mud. *p.*

گلاوٹ गलावट *galāwaṭ*, f. solution, act of melting or dissolving. *s.*

گلاءي गलाई *gulā,ī*, f. roundness, globularity. *s.*

گلبانگ *gul-bāng*, f. warbling; fame, rumour; sound; the war-cry; the cry of *Allāh, Allāh*, when rushing to battle; glad tidings. *p.*

گلباه गलबाह *gal-bāh*, گلباهي गलबाही *gal-bāhī*, گلبهي गलबही *gal-bahī*, } f. embrace, embracing, caressing by throwing the arms over the neck. *s.*

گلبدن *gul-badan*, m. a kind of silk cloth; adj. with a body or person beautiful as the rose (epithet of a mistress). *p.*

گلبن *gul-bun*, m. a rose-tree, a rose-bush. *p.*

گلبهي गलबही *gal-bahī*, f. throwing the arms round the neck. *s.*

گلبيل *gul-bel*, m. name of a creeper plant (*Menispermum cordefolium*). *d.*

گلپه गुल्फ *gulph*, m. the ankle. *h.*

گل پهٹاکي गलफटाकी *gal-phaṭākī*, f. scolding; bragging, boasting. *gal phaṭākī-k.*, a. to scold; to utter falsehoods, to brag. *h.*

گلپهڑا गलफड़ा *galphaṛā*, m. the jaws; the angle of the mouth. *h.*

گلپهننا गुलफुनना *gulphunanā*, name of an herb which grows in fields sown with *ḵharīf* grains. *h.*

گلپهوٹ गलफूट *gal-phūṭ*, f. vaunt, vaunting. *h.*

گل پهولا गलफूला *galphūlā*, chubby. *h.*

گلت गलित *galit*, fallen, dropped, sunk. *s.*

گلتا *galtā*, m. a sheath, a scabbard. *p.*

گلتاڑ गलताड़ *galtāṛ*, the name given to the inner pegs of a yoke. *h.*

گلتراش *gul-tarāsh*, m. snuffers. *p.*

گل تکيه *gal-takiya*, m. a kind of pillow or bolster (for the neck). *h. p.*

گلتنس गलतंस *galtans*, dying without issue. *h.*

گلتني गलतनी *galtanī*, f. part of the headstall of a bridle. *h.*

گلٹ गिलट *gilaṭ*, m. } a protuberance, a hard
گلٹي गिलटी *gilṭī*, f. } swelling, a gland, a knot, a tumour. *h.*

گل جندڑا गलजन्दड़ा *gal-jandṛā*, m. a handkerchief used as a sling for the arm, also called *galgandā*. *h.*

گلجهڑي गुलझड़ी *gul-jhaṛī*, f. conglomeration. *gul-jhaṛī dil kī*, grief, displeasure, mental uneasiness. *h.*

گل چکان *gul chakān*, m. the flowers of the *mahū,ā* (*Bassia latifolia, Roxb.*). *p.*

گل چلا गुलचला *gul-chalā*, m. a musketeer, a cannoneer, a rifleman. *s.*

گلخار *gul-ḵhār*, the flower or blossom of the *bhaṭ-katiyā*, a kind of herb, q. v. *p.*

گل خن *gul-ḵhan*, m. a stove, a furnace. *p.*

گلخور *galḵhor*, m. a horse's halter. *p.*

گلدم *guldum*, a nightingale. *p. h.*

گلدينا *gal-denā*, a. to throttle, to choke, to put to death by hanging. *h.*

گلزار *gul-zār*, a garden of roses; name of a musical note. *p.*

گلستان *gulistān*, m. a rose-garden; the name of a well-known book written by *Muṣliḥu-d-dīn shaiḵh Sa'dī* of *Shīrāz*. *p.*

گلسري galsarī, f. an ornament worn round the neck by married women. d.

گلشن gul-shan, m. a rose-garden; a delightful spot, place of enjoyment; adj. cheerful. p.

گلکا गलका galkā, f. a boil, swelling, tumour. h.

گلکهور gal-khor (for gal-<u>kh</u>or), a horse's halter. d.

گلگل गलगल galgal, m. a citron; name of a bird; a mixture of lime and linseed-oil, forming a kind of mortar impenetrable to water. h.

گلگلا गुलगुला gulgulā, m. sweet cakes fried in butter; adj. soft. h. [mollify. s.

گلگلانا गुलगुलाना gulgulānā, a. to soften, to

گلگلاهٹ गुलगुलाहट gulgulāhaṭ, f. act of softening; softness. s.

گلگلي gulgulī, f. a kind of dish; swollen rice mixed with molasses, formed into balls. d.

گلگنڈ गलगण्ड galgaṇḍ, m. inflammation or enlargement of the glands of the neck. h.

گلگوتهنا गुलगूथना gulgūthnā, plump, handsome, chubby. h.

گلگون gul-gūn, rose-coloured; name of a horse of Shīrīn, the mistress of Farhād. p.

گل‌گونه gul-gūna, m. cosmetic. p.

گلگير gul-gīr, m. snuffers. p.

گلم गुल्म gulm, m. a division of an army, consisting of 9 platoons, each amounting to 9 elephants, 9 chariots, 27 horse, and 45 foot; the spleen, a disease of the spleen. s.

گلنا गलना galnā or gal-jānā, n. to melt, to be dissolved, to be wasted away. s.

گلنار gul-nār or guli anār, m. the flower of the pomegranate; scarlet (colour). p.

گلناري gulnārī, of or relating to the flower of the pomegranate. p. [lour. p.

گلناري رنگ gul-nārī rang, m. carnation co-

گلندا गलन्दा galandā, abusive, scurrilous. h.

گلنڈا गलण्डा galanḍā, stentorophonic, having a tremendously loud voice. h.

گلني गलनी galnī, f. wasting, consumption. h.

گلو gulū, m. the gullet, the throat, the windpipe. gulū-gīr, that which fastens on the throat, as acrid food, &c.; met. an accuser. gulū-band, m. neckcloth. p.

گلو गिलौ gilau, m. Menispermum glabrum. gulū, the pod of the Bassia latifolia, which yields a very useful oil. h.

گلو गुलू gulū, the pod of the mahwā tree, which yields a useful oil. h.

گلواه गलबाह galvāh, f. an embrace, throwing the arms on the neck. s.

گلوري गिलौरी gilaurī, f. betel-leaf prepared and folded up. h.

گلوگا गुलूगा gulūgā, m. a monkey's pouch. u.

گلوندا गिलौंदा gilaundā, m. the flower of the mahū,ā (Bassia latifolia) after it has fallen off. h.

گله gila, m. complaint, lamentation, reproach, blame. gala or galla, m. a flock, a herd. galla-bān pastor, shepherd; (Hind.) a vessel in which shopkeepers put money received for things sold in the course of the day; a tile. p.

گل‌هار गलहार galhār, soluble, corruptible. h.

گلهتي गुलहत्ती gulhattī, f. rice-gruel, or rice and water boiled together and seasoned with salt. h.

گلهر गलहर galhar or गलहड़ galhaṛ, m. the goitre, swelling in the neck. s.

گلهري गिलहरी galahrī, f. a squirrel. h.

گلهي गलही galhī, f. the forecastle (of a boat, &c.), prow. h. [swain. h.

گلهيا गलहैया galhaiyā, m. forecastle-man, boat-

گلهينڈا गलहेण्डा galhenḍā, abusive, scurrilous. h.

گلي गिल्ली gillī, f. a span (measure of circumference, i. e. the circle formed by joining the ends of the thumb and fore-finger); an ear of Indian corn (Zea mays) from which the seeds have been taken out; the short stick in the game of tip-cat, which is struck by the longer one called ḍanḍā. gillī or gullī ḍanḍā khelnā, to play at tip-cat. gullī, a kind of pigeon. h.

گلي गली galī (also gallī), f. a lane, a narrow pass between mountains. galī ba galī or galī-galī, from lane to lane. galī-kūcha, m. a narrow lane. gulī, f. a pill, a bolus; a disease. gullī, f. a whetstone, a polishing stone. h.

گلي gullī, f. a species of red coral. d.

گلي गुल्ली gullī, m. a kind of pigeon. h.

گلي gilī, earthen, made of clay. p.

گليا गल्या galyā, m. a bullock that lies down in the midst of its work. h.

گليارا गलियारा galiyārā, m.
گلياره गलियारः galiyāra, m.
گلياري गलियारी galiyārī, f.
} a lane, street, passage, abode. h.

گليانا गलियाना galiyānā, a. to abuse; to cram (a horse, &c.). to force food or medicine down the throat. h.

گلي‌باز gale-bāz, a sweet singer. s. p.

گلير गिलियर giliyar, lazy, indolent. h.

گليري gilerī, f. a squirrel. d.

گليگنڈ गलेगण्ड galegaṇḍ, m. a species of bird, the adjutant or Ardea argalla. s.

گليل गुलैल gulail or गुलेल gulel, f. a pellet-bow. h.

گليم gilīm, a blanket; a garment of goats' hair. p. [tree. h.

گليندا गुलेन्दा gulendā, the pod of the mahwā

گم gum, lost, wanting, missing; distracted. gum-shuda or gum-gashta, lost. gum-k., a. to lose; n. to be proud. gum-nām, ignoble, nameless, unknown to fame, consigned to oblivion. gum-ho. get off! away! make yourself scarce. p.

گماشتگي *gumāshtagī*, f. office of *gumāshta*; commision, charge, agency. *p.*

گماشتن *gumāshtan* (r. *gumār*), to send, to depute; to entrust one with full powers. *p.*

گماشته *gumāshta*, an agent, a factor; an envoy with full powers. *p.*

گمان *gumān*, m. doubt, suspicion, opinion, fancy, supposition, imagination. *gumān-lānā* or *-karnā*, to suppose, to imagine, to suspect. *p.*

گمانا *gumānā*, a. to lose, to let a thing be lost. *p. h.*

گمانا गमाना *gamānā*, a. to pass one's time. *h.*

گماني *gumānī*, jealous; doubtful; a suspicious character. *p. d.*

گمبهير गम्भीर *gambhīr*, deep (applied to soil); serious, sedate. *s.*

گمبهيرتا गम्भीरता *gambhīratā*, f. depth; seriousness. *s.*

گمت गमत *gamat*, m. a road, path. *ek-gamat*, together, on one road, in one body. *s.*

گمت *gammat*, employment, occupation; rejoicings merry-makings, pleasure. *d.*

گمٹ गुम्मट *gummaṭ*, m. }
گمٹي गुमटी *gumṭī*, f. } a tower, bastion (perhaps from *gumbad*, q. v.). *h.*

گمٹا गुमटा *gumṭā*, m. a swelling or tumour resulting from a blow, a bruise. *d.*

گمچي *gumchī*, f. a species of wild liquorice (*Abrus precatorius*). Its seed is a small scarlet pea, used as weights by druggists, and called *ratī*: women string them together for necklaces and other ornaments. It is called in Urdū *gunj* and *ghungchī*.—(Binning). *d.*

گمراه *gumrāh*, erring, wandering, on the wrong road; abandoned, depraved. *s.*

گمراهي *gumrāhī*, f. deviation, depravity. *p.*

گمره *gumrah* (v. *gumrāh*), erring, &c. *p.*

گمرهي *gumrahī* (v. *gumrāhī*), error, &c. *p.*

گمري गुमरी *gumrī*, f. vertigo, giddiness. *h.*

گمڑا गुमड़ा *gumṛā*, m. protuberance, a swelling. *h.*

گمسا गुमसा *gumsā*, musty, mouldy. *h.*

گمك गमक *gamak*, f. the sound of a kettle-drum; a beat or march; a shake or clash in music. *h.*

گمکا गुमका *gumkā*, the separation of the corn from the husks. *h.*

گمکيلا गमकीला *gamkīlā*, spicy, fragrant, odoriferous. *h.*

گمن गमन *gaman* or *gamana*, m. act of going. *gamin*, a passenger. *s.*

گمنا *gamnā*, n. to pass or elapse, to be spent (as time); to put off or procrastinate. *d.*

گمناگمن गमनागमन *gamanāgaman*, m. going and coming, passing and repassing, intercourse. *s.*

گمهوش *gum-hosh*, without sensation; stupified. *p.*

گميتا गम्यता *gamyatā*, f. accessibility, perceptibility. *s.*

گميه गम्य *gamya*, attainable, accessible. *s.*

گن गुण *gun* (for *guna*), m. skill, cleverness, sense, understanding; quality, mode, method, manner; virtue, merit; a string; a rope, a favour, a kindness; a quality, an attribute or property in general (but especially of excellence); a principle or property incident to humanity, of which three are enumerated (v. *rajo-gun*). *gun-bhransh*, m. loss of all good qualities. *gun-chhāndnā*, to pass over a person's good qualities. *gun-sāgar* (ocean of excellence), endowed with all virtues. *gun-stuti*, f. panegyric, eucomium. *gun kā palṭā denā*, to repay a benefit. *gun-k.*, to benefit. *gun-gāhak*, a patron of merit. *gun-mānnā*, to acknowledge a favour. *gun-may*, *gun-wān*, possessed of merit accomplished. *gun-hīn*, void of merit. *s.*

گن गण *gaṇ*, m. a troop, a flock, a multitude; a body of troops equal to 29 chariots, 81 horse, and 135 foot; troops of inferior deities, considered as Shiva's attendants, and under the especial superintendence of Ganesha. *s.*

گنا गुणा *gunā*, (in comp.) fold, turn, time; as *do-gunā*, twofold. *s.*

گنا गन्ना *gannā*, m. the sugar-cane (especially when ready for cutting). *h.*

گنا गिणना *ginnā* or गणना *gannā*, a. to count, to reckon, to number. *s.*

گناه *gunāh*, m. a fault, error, crime, sin. *p.*

گناهگار *gunāh-gār*, m. a sinner, a criminal. *p.*

گناهگاري *gunāh-gārī*, f. sinfulness, criminality. *p.*

گنبد *gumbad*, }
گنبذ *gumbaz*, } m. a vault, an arch, cupola, dome, tower; a vaulted building. *p.*

گنبذي *gumbazī*, dome-shaped, vaulted. *p.*

گنبهير गंभीर *gambhīr*, }
گنبهيرا गंभीरा *gambhīrā*, } adj. deep; serious, thoughtful, grave: this term is also applied to a soil which is of a rich quality, and attains more than usual depth before the subsoil is reached. *gambhīratā*, f. depth (of water), sound thought. *s.*

گنپت गणपति *gaṇ-pati* (v. *ganesh*), m. lord of hosts; a name of *Gaṇesha*, q. v. *s.*

گنت गणित *ganit*, m. calculation, enumeration, arithmetic; adj. counted, reckoned. *ganit-kār*, m. an astrologer, an arithmetician. *s.*

گنتا गणता *gantā*, f. arithmetic. *s.*

گنتا गुणता *guntā*, f. excellence, multiplication. *s.*

گنتهوانا गुंथवाना *gunthwānā*, a. to cause to string, &c.

گنتي गिणती or गिन्ती *gintī*, f. number, reckoning, account; the first day of the month; a muster or specimen. *s.*

گنٹا *gunṭā*, m. a tank, a pool. *d.*

گنتم *ganṭam*, m. an iron style for writing upon palm leaves. *d.*

گنٹھ गंठ *ganṭh*, f. (v. *gānṭh*) a knot, bundle, &c. *s.*

گنٹھا गंठा *ganṭhā*, a fractional part of a *jarīb* (v. *gaṭṭhā*). *h.*

گنٹھجوڑا गंठजोड़ा *ganṭh-joṛā*, m. uniting, splicing. *ganṭh-joṛā bāndhnā*, to tie together the skirts of the mantles of bride and bridegroom; a ceremony attending marriage performed by the *purohit* or officiating family priest. *s.*

گنٹھکٹا गंठकटा *ganṭh-kaṭā* or *-kaṭṭā*, m. a robber, a cutpurse. *h.*

گنٹھوارا गंठवारा *ganṭhwārā*, name of a tribe of [*jāṭs*. *h.*

گنج *ganj*, m. a granary, heap, treasury; a village or town where grain is kept; market, mart; a case. *ganji ilāhī*, the Divine treasury, *i.e.* the word of God. *ganj-bakhsh*, generous, liberal, profuse, extravagant. *ganji-ḳārūn*, the wealth of *ḳārūn*, applied to vast riches in general. *ganji-gāw*, or *-gāwān*, or *-gāwmesh*, the treasure of *Jamshīd*, dug up in the reign of *Bahrām* and distributed among the poor. *p.*

گنج गुंज *gunj*, f. echo, buzzing, hollow sound. *s.*

گنج गंज *ganj*, m. a scald head (*Tinea capitis*). *h.*

گنج गुंज *gunj*, | m. the seed of *Abrus precatorius*, or the shrub itself. *p.*
گنجا गुंजा *gunjā*, |

گنجا गंजा *ganjā*, scald-headed; bald. *h.*

گنجان गुंजान *gunjān*, thick, close together, dense. *h.* [(of trees). *h.*

گنجاني गुंजानी *gunjānī*, f. thickness, closeness

گنجاعي गिंजाई or गिनजाई *ginjā,ī*, f. name of an insect (v. *kanslā,ī*). *h.*

گنجائش *gunjā,ish*, | capacity, containing, holding, room; profit, gain;
گنجاعي *gunjā,ī*, |
capability (of a village respecting revenue). *p.*

گنجائشي *gunjā,ishī*, roomy; profitable. *p.*

گنجت गुंजत *gunjat*, adj. buzzing, humming.

گنجدار *ganj-dār*, m. a treasurer, a possessor of a treasure. *p.*

گنجرنا गुंजरना *gunjarnā*, n. to roar, to growl. *h.*

گنجشك *gunjishk*, a sparrow, or any small bird. *p.*

گنجني گهاس *ganjnī ghās*, a kind of sweet smelling grass, used for a variety of purposes. *d.*

گنجور *ganjwar*, a treasurer. *ganjūr*, a treasure. *p.*

گنجها गुंझा *gunjhā*, grave, venerable. *h.*

گنجهار गुंजहार *gunjhār*, m. a necklace composed of the *gunj* seed. *h.*

گنجهيل गंजैल *ganjhail*, addicted to the use of *gānjhā*, q. v. *h.*

گنجي *ganjī*, rue gruel, conjee. *d.*

گنجيا गंजिया *ganjiyā*, f. a wallet, a bag (in which grass-cutters keep their sickle, &c.). *s.*

گنجيدن *ganjīdan* or *gunjīdan*, to be contained (in a place); to have room. *p.*

گنجيفه *ganjīfa*, m. a pack of cards; a game of cards: the pack consists of ninety-six cards divided into eight suits. *p.*

گنجيلي *ganjelī* (v. *bhangelā*), a sack, &c. *h.*

گنجينه *ganjīna*, a magazine, a treasury. *p.*

گند गंद *gand*, f. stink, filth, odour, smell. *s.*

گندا गंदा *gandā*, stinking, filthy, foul, nasty. *s.*

گندر गिंदर *gindar*, a kind of insect very destructive to growing grain. *h.*

گندروالا गंदरवाला *gandarwālā* or *gandaṛwālā*, the receptacle for the sugar-cane at the mill before it is cut up. *h.*

گندروپين गन्दरूपिन *gandrūpīn*, a Hindū dancing girl. *h.*

گندرويه गणद्रव्य *gaṇ-dravya*, m. public property. *s.*

گندري गिंदुरी *gindurī*, a circular twist of straw or grass for supporting a vessel with a round bottom. *h.*

گندك गंदक *gandak* (v. *gandhak*), f. brimstone, sulphur, gunpowder. *gandak kā 'aṭr*, sulphuric acid. *p. s.* [coarseness, thickness. *p.*

گندگي *gandagī*, f. filth, stink. *gundagī*, f.

گندم *gandum*, m. wheat. *gandum i kirmānī*, vermicelli. *gandum-gūn*, wheat-colour, *i.e.* brown, swarthy. *p.* [*rum*). *h.*

گندنا गंदना *gandnā*, f. a leek (*Allium por-*

گندھ गंध *gandh*, f. smell, perfume, odour, scent. *s.*

گنده *ganda*, fetid, stinking. *ganda-bahār*, f. rain which falls in the cold weather. *ganda-dahan*, stinking breath. *ganda-fīroza* or *ganda-bīroza*, m. the name of a drug (*Olibanum*); a kind of turpentine. *p.*

گنده *gunda*, coarse, thick, strong. *p.*

گندهار गंधार *gandhār*, m. the name of a *rāg* or musical mode. *s.* [ing. *h.*

گندهاوٹ गुंधावट *gundāwat*, f. plaiting, braid-

گندهبروزه *gandh-biroza*, frankincense. *h.*

گندهراج गंधराज *gandhrāj*, m. (*Gardenia florida*) sandal; any sweet-smelling flower. *s.*

گندهرب गंधर्व *gandharb* or *gandharv*, m. an aërial minstrel, a kind of celestial musician, a class of demigods who inhabit Indra's heaven, and form the orchestra at all the banquets of the principal deities; a kind of deer. *gandharb byāh*, m. a kind of marriage, like that which still holds good in Scotland, being merely a mutual pledge between the man and woman either before witnesses or in writing. *gandharb-gīt*, m. a cherub's song or singing. *s.*

گندهرس गन्धरस *gandh-ras*, m. myrrh, frankincense. *s* [wood. *s.*

گندهسار गन्धसार *gandh-sār*, m. sandal, sandal-

گندهك गंधक *gandhak*, f. brimstone, sulphur. *gandhak kā tel*, oil of vitriol, vitriolic acid. *gandhak kā 'aṭr*, sulphuric acid; (also termed *rūḥi a'ẓam*, and *araḳi gūgard*. *s*.

گندهكاشٹھ गन्धकाष्ठ *gandh-kāshṭh*, m. a fragrant wood, as sandal, aloe-wood. *s*.

گندهمادن गन्धमादन *gandh-mādan*, m. name of a mountain; sulphur. *s*.

گندهنا गुंधना *gundhnā*, n. to be kneaded, or to be plaited. *h*. [adj. fragment. *s*.

گندهوه गन्धवह *gandh-vah*, m. wind, zephyr;

گندهي गंधी *gandhī*, m. a person who sells rose-water, essences, and scents; a perfumer; a green bug *s*.

گندهيل गंधेल *gandhel*, m. name of a species of sweet smelling grass. *s*.

گندهيلا गंधीला *gandhīlā*, having a smell (good or bad); stinking, fetid; odorous, scented. *s*.

گنديدن *gandīdan*, to stink, to have a foul smell. *p. h*.

گنديري गंदेरी *ganderī*, f. a joint or piece of the sugar-cane. *h*. [grub. *h*.

گنديلا गंदैला *gandailā*, name of a destructive

گنديلا गुंदेला *gundelā*, producing gum (a tree). *s*.

گنڈ गराड *ganḍ*, m. a cheek; a boil, a pimple; a spot; a rhinoceros. *ganḍi*, the goitre or bronchocele. *gunḍ*, a furrow. *h*.

گنڈا गंडा *ganḍā*, m. a ring, a circle; a kind of horse-collar; a knotted string tied round the neck of a child, &c. as a charm or talisman. *ganḍā* (for *ganḍak*) denotes the number four, an aggregate of four *kauṛīs* or *paisas*, fastened round the neck of a child to serve as a talisman. *s*. [fellow. *d*.

گنڈا *gunḍā*, m. (v. *ghunḍa*), a fop, a dissolute

گنڈاسا गंडासा *ganḍāsā*, m. a sort of axe, a pole-axe, a sickle in general. *h*.

گنڈاسي गंडासी *ganḍāsī*, f. an instrument for cutting sugar-cane, a sickle. *h*.

گنڈري गिंडुरी *ginḍurī*, a kind of rope (v. *jūṛā*). *h*.

گنڈك गराडक *ganḍak*, m. a rhinoceros. *h*.

گنڈكي गराडकी *ganḍakī*, f. a river in the north of India. *s*.

گنڈلي गुराडली *gunḍlī*, coiling (of a snake). *h*.

گنڈم *ganḍam*, calamity, a misfortune. *d*.

گنڈمالا गराडमाला *ganḍ-mālā*, f. inflammation of the glands of the neck. *h*.

گنڈه *ganḍa* (v. *ganḍā*), four cowries. *h*.

گنڈهو गंढू *ganḍhū* (v. *jāṭ*), name of a tribe. *h*.

گنڈهيلا गंढीला *ganḍhīlā*, name of a vagrant tribe. *h*.

گنڈي गंडी *ganḍī*, a circle, particularly that which *Rāmachandra* drew round *Sītā* to protect her from *Rāwan* (v. *rāmachandra*). *s*.

گنڈي *gunḍī*, f. a stud, knob; a button. *d*.

گنڈيا *ganḍiyā* (v. *gānḍū*), m. a catamite. *d*.

گنڈيري गंडेरी *ganḍerī*, f. a joint or portion of the sugar-cane, a segment. *s*.

گنك गणक *ganak*, m. an arithmetician, astrologer, one who casts nativities. *gunak*, the multiplier (in arithmetic). *s*.

گنكا गणिका *ganikā*, f. a courtesan, a harlot. *s*.

گنكاٹا गनकाटा *gan-kāṭā*, } m. a man employed
گنكٹا गनकटा *ganhaṭā*, } to cut the sugar-canes into lengths of about six inches, for feeding the mill. *h*.

گنكهان गुणखान *gun-khān* (mine of merit) very worthy. *s*. [ger. *s*.

گنكي गणकी *ganakī*, f. the wife of an astrolo-

گنگ गंग *gang*, m. a river in general, a stream; the Ganges. *gang-barār* or *gang-barāmad*, alluvial land recovered from a river, epecially from the Ganges. *do-gang*, in two streams (a river). *gang-shikast*, encroachment of the Ganges (or any river) by diluvion. *s.p*.

گنگ *gung*, } dumb, mute, speechless. *p*.
گنگا *gungā*, }

گنگا गंगा *gangā*, f. the river (Ganges) in particular; a river in general. *s*.

گنگاپار गंगापार *gangā-pār*, m. the further bank of the Ganges. *s*.

گنگاپتر गंगापुत्र *gangā-putr*, (lit. the son of the Ganges) a man of low caste employed to remove dead bodies; a Brāhman who conducts the ceremonies of pilgrimage on the Ganges. *s*.

گنگاتير गंगातीर *gangā-tīr*, m. the bank of the Ganges. *s*. [to the Ganges. *s*.

گنگاجاترا गंगायात्रा *gangā-jātrā*, f. pilgrimage

گنگاجل गंगाजल *gangā-jal*, m. the water of the Ganges. *s*.

گنگاجمني गंगाजमनी *gangā-jamnī*, f. a kind of ear-ring; a species of precious metal. *h*.

گنگادهر गंगाधर *gangādhar*, m. an epithet of *Shiva*. *s*.

گنگادوار गंगाद्वार *gangā-dwār*, m. the place where the Ganges enters the plains; Haridwār. *s*.

گنگاكشيتر गंगाक्षेत्र *gangā-kshetr*, m. the land extending for about two *cos* on either side of the Ganges. *s*.

گنگاله गंगालः *gangāla*, lands subject to inundation of the Ganges. *s*.

گنگان गुणगान *gun-gān*, m. panegyric, praise. *gun-gān k.*, to sing, to celebrate; to prattle (as infants).

گنگاهك गुणग्राहक *guṇ-gāhak*, m. a discerner of merit, a patron of learning. *s*.

گنگنا गुंगुना *gungunā*, milk-warm; snuffling, snuffler. *gungunā*, m. tepidity. *h.*

گنگنانا गुंगुनाना *gungunānā*, n. to be milk-warm; to snuffle; to sing slowly or with a low voice; to mutter, to grumble. *h.*

گنگنه गुंगुनः *gunguna*, milk-warm; snuffling. *h.*

گنگودك गंगोदक *gangodak*, water of the Ganges, or any holy river. *s.*

گنمان *guṇmān* (v. *guṇ-wān*), skilful, &c. *s.*

گنن गुणिन *gunin*, endowed with good qualities, skilful. *s.*

گنن गणन *gaṇan*, m. } counting, reckoning,
گننا गणना *gaṇanā*, f. } enumeration, calculation. *s.*

گننا गणना *gannā*. a. to count, to reckon up. *s.*

گننيي गणनीय *gananīya*, numerable, countable. *s.*

گنوار गंवार *gaṅwār*, m. a countryman, a villager, a clown; adj. stupid, boorish. *s.*

گنوان गुणवान *guṇ-wān*, talented, virtuous, accomplished, skilful, meritorious. *s.*

گنوانا गंवाना *gaṅwānā*, a. to lose, to throw away, to spend in vain, to waste, to squander, to pass, to trifle. *h.*

گنوانا गिणवाना *ginwānā*, a. to cause to count. *s.*

گنواو गंवाऊ *gaṅwā,ū*, one who squanders, a prodigal. *h.*

گنوري गनौरी *ganaurī*, f. a bulrush. *h.*

گنونت गुणवन्त *guṇ-want* (v. *guṇ-wān*), skilful. *s.* [&c. *s.*

گنوي गंवी *gaṅwī*, of or relating to a village,

گنوي گانو गंवीगांव *gaṅwī-gāṅw*, rustic hamlets or villages. *s.*

گنه *gunah*, m. (v. *gunāh*) a crime, a sin. *gunah-kār* or *-gār*, a criminal, a sinner. *gunah-kārī* or *-gārī*, f. criminality, sinfulness; a fine for crimes and misdemeanors; revenue derived from judicial fines. *h.*

گني गुणी *guṇī*, skilful, virtuous, possessed of any quality or art; a snake-catcher, one who charms the snakes; a sorcerer. *s.*

گني गनी *ganī*, a kind of coarse bag. *h.*

گني गण्य *gaṇyā*, that which may be numbered. *s.*

گنيس गणेस *ganes*, } the name of a Hindū di-
گنيش गणेश *ganesh*, } vinity; the Janus of the Hindūs; the god of wisdom, represented with an elephant's head, and attended by a rat: he was the son of *Mahādeva* by a daughter of the mountain *Himālaya*; and, in consequence of his being the remover of obstacles or difficulties, he is invoked at the commencement of every affair of consequence. Most Hindū books commence with the phrase *śri-ganeshāya namah*, reverence be to the divine Ganesha (similar to the *b-ismi-'-lāh*, of the Musalmāns). *s.*

گنيشور गुणेश्वर *guneshwar*, m. name of a mountain in Bandelkand. *s.*

گني کا تهل *ganne kā thal*, plantation of sugar-cane. [grass used in thatching. *h.*

گنيل गनेल *ganel* or *gannel*, a species of long

گنين गुणियन *guṇiyan*, meritorious, virtuous. *s.*

گو गो *go*, गौ *gau*, or *gav*, f. a cow, or animal of the cow kind. *s.*

گو *gau* or *gaw*, m. a measure of four *kos*, or about eight miles (called in Hindī *jojan* or *yojan*, q. v.). *d.*

گو *go* or *gū*, speak, suppose. *go-ki*, although, even if; (in comp.) speaking, as *bad-go*, speaking evil, slanderous. *p.*

گو गू *gū*, f. human excrement.

گوءا गूआ *gū,ā*, f. betel-nut. *s.*

گواچه गवाच्छ *gawāchh*, m. a skylight, a bull's-eye; a hole to admit light, a lattice window. *s.*

گوار *gawār*, a race of gypsies in India. *guwār*, a thing easy of digestion. *khush-guwār*, sweet, agreeable, easy of digestion. *p.*

گوارا *gawārā*, } agreeable, pleasant; digest-
گواران *guwārān*, } ing, digestible, digestion;
گواره *guwāra*, } bearing, enduring, submitting to. *gawārā-k.*, to digest; to endure or submit to a necessity. *p.*

گواري गवारी *gawārī*, f. a dwelling-house, a family, a cowhouse. *h.*

گواك गुवाक *guwāk*, m. the betel-nut tree (*Areca faufel* or *catechu*).

گواکه गवाख *gawākh*, m. (for गवाक्ष *gavākshẖ*) a bull's-eye; the light that is admitted by a window; a skylight, an air-hole, a loop-hole. *s.*

گوال गवाल *gawāl* (v. *gayāl*), unclaimed land. *h.*

گوال ग्वाल *gwāl*, } m. a cowherd; name of
گوالا ग्वाला *gwālā*, } a Hindū caste whose occupation is the tending of cattle. *s.*

گوالن ग्वालिन *gwālin*, f. a female cowherd, a woman of the *gwālā* caste. *s.*

گوانا गवाना *gawānā*, a. to cause to sing. *h.*

گواه *gawāh*, m. a witness, one who gives evidence (pl. *gawāhān*). *p.*

گواهي *gawāhī*, f. evidence, testimony. *p.*

گوبا *gobā*, a vessel for receiving the *sendhī* or palm-juice. *d.*

گوبر गोबर *gobar*, cow-dung dried and used as fuel. *gobar-khānā*, a. to do penance (by eating cow-dung). *h.*

گوبرگنيس गोबरगनेश *gobar-ganes*, fat, sleek, corpulent; m. a fool, a simpleton. *s.*

گوبروندا गोबरौंदा *gobrondā*, m. the name of a beetle found in cow-dung (*Scarabæus*). *s.*

گوبري गोबरी *gobrī*, f. plaster made with cow-dung; name of a tribe in Rohilcund. *s.*

گوبري *gobri*, f. the measles; cowdung. *d.*

گوبند गोबिन्द *gobind*, a name of *Krishna*. *s.*

گوبهي गोभी *gobhī*, f. name of a medicinal herb (*Hieracium, Bruce, MS.*) *sufaid gobhī, Cacalia sonchifolia;* a term in card-playing. *s.*

گوپ गोप *gop* or *gopa*, m. name of a Hindū caste, a cowherd (v. *gwālā*). *s.*

گوپ गोप *gop*, f. a gold necklace. *h.*

گوپال *gūpāl*, an iron mace, an iron throne. *p.*

گوپال गोपाल *gopāl*, گوپالك गोपालक *gopālah*, } m. a cowherd; one of the names of *Krishna;* a protector, a king. *s.*

گوپرس गोपरस *gop-ras*, m. gum, myrrh. *h.*

گوپشٹمي गोपष्टमी *gopashtamī*, the eighth day of *Kārtik* (*shukla-paksha*). *s.*

گوپمحال *gop-mahall*, pasture grounds. *h. a.*

گوپن गोपन *gopan*, m. concealment. *gopan-k.*, a. to conceal, to hide. *s.*

گوپنيه गोपनीय *gopanīya*, fit to be concealed. *s.*

گوپهن गोफन *gophan*, m. گوپهنا गोफना *gophnā*, f. گوپهني गोफनी *gophnī*, f. گوپهيا गोफिया *gophiyā*, f. } a sling (for throwing with); a sling used by persons stationed on the *dāmcha*, or platform for watching the crops. *h.*

گوپي गोपी *gopī*, f. the female of *gopa*, q. v. *s*

گوپي چندن गोपीचन्दन *gopī-chandan*, m. a species of white clay. *s.*

گوت गोत *got*, گوتا गोता *gotā*, گوتر गोत्र *gotra*, گوترا गोत्रा *gotrā*, گوتره गोत्रः *gotra*, } m. parentage, lineage, pedigree, stock of a family; genus, species; a caste collectively; a branch or subdivision of a tribe or caste. *s.*

گوتا गोता *gotā*, the mustard-seed. *h.*

گوترج गोत्रज *gotraj*, m. a relation, one born in the family, applied to the members of a family who are connected by common ancestral rites, and bearing the same name; a clansman. *s.*

گوترهتيا गोत्रहत्या *gotra-hatyā*, striking or killing a person of the same *gotra*. *s.*

گوتم गोतम *gotam* or *gotama*, the name of a *munī* or saint, famous in Hindū mythology: he was the author of the Nyāya or logic, and his doctrines corresponded with those of Aristotle. *Gotama* and his wife *Ahalyā* lived in a retired forest, where *Indra*, happening to pass, was struck with the beauty of the latter, and, assuming the appearance of *Gotama*, he deceived the *munī's* wife and slept with her, which, being discovered, *Gotama* cursed them both: to *Indra* he said, "May your testicles fall to the ground!" which accordingly took place; but *Brahmā* advised the *munī* to restore to *Indra* the aforesaid indispensable articles, together with those of a ram, cut out for that purpose: hence *Indra* is called *meshānda-kosha* (ram-testicled); the saint then caused his wife *Ahalyā* to be turned into stone, in which state she remained till *Rāmachandra* (son of *Dasharatha*) passing that way with his brother *Lachhman*, relieved her, and restored her to her original form, and being thus purified by *Rāma's* mercy, she was again received by her husband. *s.*

گوتم راجپوت गौतमराजपूत *gautam-rājpūt*, گوتميان गौतमियान *gautamiyān*, } name of a numerous tribe of *rāj-pūts* about *Azīm-garh* and *Gorakpūr*. *s.*

گوتهه गूथ *gūth*, m. a round ball of cotton, &c. *h.*

گوتهان गोथान *gothān*, m. place for assembling the cattle of a village. *s.*

گوتهنا गूथना *gūthnā*, a. to thread, to string; to plait, to braid, to stitch; to spit, or put on a spit. *s.*

گوتي गोती *gotī*, m. a kinsman, relative, connection; adj. of or belonging to the same race, lineage, &c. *s.*

گوٹ गोट *got*, a counter, piece, or man at backgammon, chess, &c. *s.*

گوٹ गोट *got*, f. the hem of a garment. *h.*

گوٹا गोटा *gotā*, m. (gold or silver) lace, or edging (rather narrow). *h.*

گوٹارا गोटारा *gotārā*, the rich lands immediately adjacent to a village. *h.*

گوٹبستي गोटबस्ती *gotabastī*, the chief or first assemblage of houses erected on the settlement of a village; those subsequently built being called *tholā* or *pattī*. *h.*

گوٹي गोटी *gotī*, f. the small-pox, a pock. *h.*

گوٹيكا गौटीका *gautikā*, the head manager of a village. *h.*

گوجاگرك गोजागरिक *gojāgarik*, happy, fortunate, auspicious. *s.*

گوجر गोजर *gojar*, m. a centipede (*Scolopendra*). *s.*

گوجر गूजर *gūjar*, m. name of a caste among *rāj-pūts*, originally from Gujrāt, formerly notorious for their thieving propensities. *s.*

گوجرا गोजरा *gojarā*, m. barley and *chanā* sown together. *h.*

گوجري गूजरी *gūjrī* (also *gūjarnī*), f. the female of the *gūjar* tribe; name of an ornament worn on the wrists and feet; an earthen image representing a milkmaid. *s.*

گوجري गूजरी *gūjrī*, f. name of a *rāg* or musical mode. *s.*

گوجري गोजरी *gojarī*, wheat and barley sown together in the same field. *h.*

گوجها गोझा *gojhā*, m. a species of thorny grass which springs up during the rains. *h.*

گوجي गूजी *gūjī*, f. a stick, a club. *s.*

گوجئي गोजई *goja,ī*, f. wheat and barley sown together in the same field. *h.*

گوچر गोचर *gochar*, m. perception, information adj. known, perceived. *s.*

گوچري गोचरी *gocharī*, visible, seen, perceived. *s.*

گوچنا गोचना *gochnā*, a. to catch, to seize. *gauchanā*, m. a field of wheat and *chanā* sown together. *s*

گوچهي गौछी *gauchhī*, } f a hole or pit.
گوچي गौची *gauchī*,

گوچهئي गौछई *gauchha,ī*, f. a sprout, a shoot. *h.*

گود गोद *god*, f. the lap, bosom; the elephantiasis. *god pasārnā*, to ask, to beg. *god-k.*, to embrace. *god-lenā*, to adopt. *h.*

گودا गूदा *gūdā*, m. brain, marrow, kernel, pith, crumb. *s.*

گودارا गोदारा *godārā*, a subdivision of the *jāṭ* [tribe. *h.*

گودام गूदाम *gūdām*, (vulg. *godown*) a warehouse; (*unde derivatur?*)

گودان गौदान *gau-dān*, m. the presenting or giving of a cow (especially to a Brāhman). *s.*

گوداوري गोदावरी *godāvarī*, f. the river Godavery, in the Deccan. *s.*

گودر गूदर *gūdar*, fat, plump. *h.*

گودري गोदरी *godarī*, a circular twist of grass or twine for supporting the bottom of a round vessel. *h.*

گودڑ गूदड़ *gūdaṛ*, m. a quilt; a bundle of old clothes; any old tattered clothes; a kind of silk stuff. *gūdaṛ-khail* (applied only to females), foolish, unmannerly, rude. *gūdaṛ sīnā*, to stitch together. *gūdaṛ kā lāl* or *gūdaṛ meṅ gandaurā nikalnā*, good proceeding from evil. *h.*

گودڑي गूदड़ी *gūdṛī*, f. a quilt (particularly that of a *faḳīr*); a bundle. *h.*

گودنا गोदना *godnā* or *gūdnā*, a. to prick, to puncture, to tattoo, to brand as a criminal; m. marks of tattooing. *h.*

گودنت गोदन्त *godant*, m. yellow orpiment; a cow's tooth; a fossil substance of a white colour, apparently an earthy salt. *s.*

گودوهني गोदोहनी *go-dohnī*, f. a milkpail. *s.*

گودها गोधा *godhā*, f. a leathern fence worn by archers on the left arm to protect it from the bowstring. *s.*

گودهڑ गोधड़ *godhaṛ*, the weeds, &c. collected from a ploughed field by a harrow. *h.*

گودهڑا गोधड़ा *godhṛā*, m. } a bough, a branch. *h.*
گودهڑي गोधड़ी *godhṛī*, f. }

گودهڑي गूधड़ी *gūdhṛī*, f. (v. *gūdṛī*) a quilt, a bundle. *h.*

گودهم गोधुम *godhum*, m. wheat. *s.*

گودهنا गूधना *gūdhnā* (also *gūṅdhnā*), a. to knead (flour, &c.) *h.*

گودهورا गोधौरा *godhaurā*, m. } evening, twilight. *s.*
گودهولي गोधूली *godhūlī*, }

گودهوم गोधूम *godhūm*, m. wheat. *s.*

گودهينو गोधेनु *go-dhenū*, f. a milch-cow. *s.*

گودي गोदी *godī*, f. lap, embrace, bosom (v. *god*). *h.*

گوديا गूदिया *gūdiyā*, desirous, wishing. *h.*

گوڈري गोडरी *goḍarī* (v. *gīnḍurī* or *jūṛā*). *h.*

گوڈهڑ गोढड़ *goḍhaṛ*, name given to weeds and grasses collected from a ploughed field. *h.*

گور *gor*, f. tomb, grave; the wild ass. *gor par gor karnī*, to seek an employment, office, or place which is already occupied. *gori gharībān*, a burial-ground for strangers. *gor-kan*, a gravedigger. *p.*

گور *gaur*, a pagan, an infidel, a fire-worshipper: the term is generally applied by Musalmāns to those who believe not in *Muḥammad*. *p.*

گور गौर *gaur*, fair-complexioned; a name of the goddess *Pārvatī*. *s.*

گورا गोरा *gorā*, white, fair, or fair-complexioned, a European in general. N.B. When applied to horned cattle it signifies red.—Ell. Gl. *s.*

گورا गौरा *gaurā*, a male sparrow; a name of the goddess *Pārvatī*; name of a tribe of *Ahīrs*. *h.*

گوراگمتا *gorā-gumtā*, red and white. *d.*

گوراهر गौराहर *gaurāhar*, an obscure tribe of *rāj-pūts* on the borders of *Aligaṛh*. *h.*

گوراءي गोराई *gorā,ī*, a clan of *rāj-pūts* in the Agra district. *h.*

گورخر *gor-khar*, m. the onager or wild ass. *p.*

گورڑو *goraṛū* (v. *darrāj*), a partridge. *d.*

گورس गोरस *goras*, m. milk, buttermilk, curdled milk. *s.*

گورستان *gor-istān*, m. a burying-ground. *p.*

گورسها गोरसहा *goras-hā*, (a child) reared with the milk of cattle; m. a sodomite. *s.*

گورسي गोरसी *gorasī*, f. a vessel for holding milk, &c., a milkpail. *s.*

گورگاري गोरगारी *gorgārī*, a curious method of settling boundary disputes in Chota Nāgpūr (v. Wilson). *h.*

گورگ دهندا *gorag-dhandā*, life, existence; affliction, annoyance; a Chinese puzzle, consisting of a number of pins passed through holes in an oblong plate, these pins having rings at one end, through which an oblong ring is passed. *d.*

گورو गुरु *gūrū*, m. (for *guru*) a saint, a holy man, a spiritual director. *gūrū-lachh*, knowledge which can only be acquired from a living instructor; adj. heavy, hard of digestion. *s.*

گورو गौरव *gaurav*, m. reputation, respectability, consequence, or weight. *s*

گورو गोरु *goru*, } m. an ox; f. a cow.
گوروءا गोरुआ *gorū,ā*, } *gorū,ā ḍhukān*, m. twilight (the time of bringing home the cows). *gorū,ārī berā*, f. evening. *s.*

گوروارى بيرا गोरुवारीबेरा *goruwārī-berā*, twilight time of bringing home the cows. *h.*

گوروت गोरुत *go-rūt*, m. a measure of distance equal to two *cos*. *s.*

گوروت गौरवित *gauravit*, venerable. *s.*

گوروچنہ गोरोचना *go-rochnā* or *go-rūchnā*, f. a bright yellow pigment used in dyeing. *s.*

گوروہ गौरुवः *gauruwa*, name of an inferior *rāj-pūt* tribe in Agra and Mathura. *h.*

گوري गौरी *gaurī*, f. the name of a *rāginī* or musical mode; one of the names of *Pārvatī*. *s.*

گوريا गौरया *gauriyā*, f. a sparrow. *h.*

گوريٹ गोरेट *goreṭ* or गोरैट *gorait*, a watchman, a village messenger. *h.*

گوڑ गौड़ *gauṛ*, m. name of a division of the central part of Bengal; an ancient city, formerly the capital of Bengal; inhabitant of *Gauṛ* (a Brāhman). *gauṛ-brāhman*, one of the ten tribes of Brāhmans. *gauṛ-ṭhākur*, a tribe of *rāj-pūts* in *Furrakhābād*. *gauṛ-kāyath*, one of the twelve subdivisions of the Kāyath caste. *gauṛ-rāj-pūt*, one of the classes of *rāj-pūts*. *gauṛ-tagā*, name of an important tribe of Brāhmanical descent in the north-west of India (v. Ell. Gl. p. 355). *s.*

گوڑ गोड़ *goṛ*, m. the leg, the foot. *h.*

گوڑا गौड़ा *gauṛā*, m. name of a caste in *Uṛesā* or Orissa, who are generally palki carriers: they also serve in the domestic capacity of what the Anglo-Indians call "bearers," whose duties are limited to take charge of the wardrobe, bedding, &c.; name of a *rāginī* or musical mode. *h.*

گوڑنا गोड़ना *goṛnā*, a. to dig, to scrape; m. a hoe for digging up sugar-cane, &c.

گوڑھ गूढ़ *gūṛh*, abstruse, difficult, abstracted; secret, mysterious. *gūṛh-baktā*, m. a pedagogue, a pedant. *s.*

گوڑھا गोढ़ा *goṛhā*, fields near a village homestead. *h.*

گوڑھارتھ गूढ़ार्थ *gūṛh-ārth*, of obscure or hidden meaning. *s.*

گوڑھپات गूढ़पात *gūṛh-pāt*, m. a snake. *s.*

گوڑھپرش गूढ़पुरुष *gūṛh-purush*, m. a spy, a secret emissary, a disguised agent, a scout. *s.*

گوڑھتا गूढ़ता *gūṛhtā*, f. abstruseness, secrecy. *s.*

گوڑھج गूढ़ज *gūṛhaj*, a son whose father is not ascertained. *s.*

گوڑھمارگ गूढ़मार्ग *gūṛh-mārg*, m. a subterraneous passage, a defile, a by-road or secret way. *s.*

گوڑھيا गोढ़िया *goṛhiyā*, the homestead, fields near a village. *h.*

گوڑي गोड़ी *goṛī*, f. taking away. *goṛī-k.*, to take away, to steal, to walk off with. *h.*

گوڑي गौड़ी *gauṛī*, f. rum or spirit distilled from *guṛ*; one of the *rāginīs* or musical modes. *h.*

گوڑيا गुड़िया *gūṛiyā*, m. a doll, a puppet. *h.*

گوڑيا गौड़िया *gauṛiyā*, m. inhabitant of *Gauṛ*; hence the followers of *Chaitanya* of *Nadiyā* are so called. The philosopher flourished about the year 1407 of *Sālivāhana*: he was by birth a Brāhman, and having become a Sanyāsī, maintained that the doctrines of the Vedās had been hitherto misunderstood, and explained them in a manner peculiar to himself. His sect is a branch of the *Vaishnava*, or worshippers of *Vishṇu*. His disciples in various parts of India are said to amount to five millions. His followers believe him to have been an incarnation of the Deity. *s.*

گوڑيت गोड़ैत *goṛait*, a village watchman, an intelligencer. *s.*

گوز *goz*, m. a fart. *gauz* or *gūz*, a walnut. *p.*

گوز *gauz*, گوزن *gawazn*, } m. an elk, a deer, a roe. *p.*

گوسالا गौसाला *gau-sālā* (also *go-sālā*), a cow-house, a cowshed. *s.*

گوسالہ *gosāla*, m. a calf; (met.) a dolt, a blockhead. *p.*

گوساعين गोसाईं *gosā,īn*, m. the Deity; a saint, a holy person; the descendants of the disciples of *Chaitanya* of *Nadiyā*. *gosā,īn-ṭākī*, a small cess formerly levied in Birbhūm for the support of holy persons. *s.*

گوسپند *gospand*, گوسفند *gosfand*, } f. a sheep, a goat. *p.*

گوستن गोस्तन *gostan*, m. a cluster of blossoms, a nosegay. *h.*

گوستني गोस्तनी *gostanī*, f. a grape. *h.*

گوستهان गोस्थान *go-sthān*, m. a cowpen, a place for cattle. *s.*

گوسو गोसव *go-sav*, m. the sacrifice of a cow; one of the grand sacrifices of the Hindūs in former times, but for a long period past not permitted. *s.*

گوسوامي गोस्वामी *goswāmī*, a religious mendicant in general: as a special name it is applied to very different classes of Hindū ascetics (v. Wilson). *s.*

گوسيان गोसैयां *gosaiyān*, گوسينيا गोसैंया *gosainyā*, } m. the Deity. *s.*

گوش *gosh*, m. the ear. *gosh-pech* or *gosh-pīch*, an ornament worn in the turban. *gosh-dār*, a guardian, keeper. *gosh-zad*, which strikes the ear; hearsay. *gosh-guzār*, heard, reported; a hearer. *gosh-māl*, pulling (or rubbing or boxing) the ears, rebuking. *gosh-mālī*, f. rebuke, punishment. *gosh-wār* or *-wāra*, an ear-ring. *p.*

گوش *gosh* (for *gosht*), flesh, &c. *d.*

گوشال गोशाल *go-shāl*, گوشالا गौशाला *gau-shālā*, } m. a cowhouse, a shed for cattle. *s.*

گوشپيچ *goshpech*, m. a shawl worn round the head, a kind of turban. *p.*

گوشپد गोष्पद *gosh-pad*, m. a kind of measure, as much as a cow's footstep will hold; a cow's foot or its mark. *s.*

گوشت *gosht*, m. meat, flesh. *gosht-i-nākhun honā* expresses intimate friendship. *p.*

گوشتاب *gosht-āb*, gravy, soup. *p.*

گوشتابہ *goshtāba*, soup made of minced meat. *p.*

گوشتاوا *goshtāwā*, m. pounded or minced meat, also soup or gravy thereof. *p.*

گوشتين *goshtīn*, fleshy (an epithet chiefly applied to the tongue, as in this phrase) *zabāni goshtīn ast teghi āhanīn*, the tongue, though of flesh, is yet a sword of steel. *p.*

گوشٹ गोष्ठ *goshṭ*, f. plot, cabal, conspiracy. *s.*

گوشٹھ गोष्ठ *goshṭh*, m. a cowpen, a fold for cattle. *s.*

گوشٹھي गोष्ठी *goshṭhī*, f. an assembly, a meeting; conversation, discourse; family connections. *s.*

گوشچي *goshchī*, a listener, a spy, an emissary, a sentinel, an informer. *p.*

گوشوارہ *goshwāra*, m. an ear-ring; an embroidered cloth worn as an ornament over the sides of a turban; the abstract of an account; a summary, an index; boring the ears (of female children). *p.*

گوشہ *gosha*, m. a corner, the horn or pointed extremity of a bow: a closet, retirement, privacy; side. *goshe-dār*, angular. *gosha-guzīn* or *gosha-gīr*, retired; (sub.) a hermit. *gosha-girī*, f. withdrawal from worldly affairs; retirement, seclusion. *gosha-nishīn*, retired (sitting in a corner), a hermit, solitary. *kamān ke goshe meṅ pakaṛnā*, to seize with facility (lit. to catch with the bow without shooting). *p.*

گوکرن गोकर्ण *go-karṇ*, m. a span; a kind of deer; also a mule. *s.*

گوکشر गोक्षुर *go-kshur*, m. a plant (*Ruellia longifolia* and *Tribulus languinosus*). *s.*

گوکل गोकुल *gokul*, m. the country round Brindāvan where *Krishṇa* was born and passed his boyhood; a herd of cattle; a cowhouse or station. *s.*

گوکہ *goki*, although, notwithstanding that. *p.*

گوکھ गौख *gaukh*, m. a threshold, a portico. *h.*

گوکھرو गोखरू *gokhrū*, m. name of an ornament (bells tied round the ankles); a joint; name of a plant (*Tribulus lanuginosus*, also *Ruellia longifolia*). *baṛā gokhrū*, *Pedalium murex*. *s.*

گوگا गोगा *gogā*, name of a *pīr* or saint held in much veneration in Delhī and the upper Du'āb. *h.*

گوگرد *gūgird*, sulphur, brimstone. *gūgirdi aḥmar*, red sulphur; the philosopher's stone. *p.*

گوگل गूगल *gūgal*, m. name of a tree or gum (*Amyris agallocha, Roxb.*, cor. pl. vol. iii.); *bdellium*. *s.*

گوگلي गूगली *gūglī*, f. a cockle-shell (Beng.). *h.*

گول गोल *gol*, m. a circle, a ball, any thing round, a jar; adj. round, circular. *gol-phal*, m. the testicle. *gol-sā*, roundish. *gol-gol*, round. *s.*

گول गोल *gol*, a party from another village sojourning with their cattle, for pasture. *gūl*, a channel cut for conveying water to a field; a road, a path; a bunch of unripe Indian corn. *h.*

گول *gol*, m. a blockhead, an idiot. *p.*

گولا गोला *golā*, m. a granary, store-room; a jackal. *golā-dār*, a wholesale grain merchant. *h.*

گولا गोला *golā*, m. a cannon-ball; a large beam of wood; a kind of pigeon; the kernel of a cocoanut; f. a globe, a sphere; a large water-jar. *golā ḍaṇḍā*, m. name of a game, tipcat. *golā laṭhī-k.*, to tie up the hands and feet. *s*

گولادھيايہ गोलाध्याय *gol-ādhyāya*, m. the section of the *Sūrya-siddhānta* (and other astronomical works) devoted to the doctrine of the sphere. *s.*

گولاو गोलार *golār*, m. roundness; f. a globe, a sphere; rotundity. *s.*

گولارا गोलारा *golārā*, round, globular. *s.*

گولاکار गोलाकार *golākār*, spheric. *s.*

گولائي गोलाई *golāī*, } f. roundness, sphericity. *s.*
گولتا गोलता *golatā*, }

گولر गूलर *gūlar*, f. a wild fig (*Ficus glomerata, Roxb.*); also cotton-pods which have not yet burst. *h.* [a drawer. *p.*

گولك *golak*, f. the *kotwāl's* treasure-pot, a till,

گولك गोलक *golak*, m. } a bastard child by
گولکا गोलिका *golikā*, f. } illegitimate connection with a widow. *s.*

گول‌مرچ गोलमिर्च *gol-mirch*, f. black pepper (*Piper nigrum*).

گولنداز *gol-andāz*, m. a cannoneer, gunner, bombardier, a marksman. *p.*

گولندازي *gol-andāzī*, f. gunnery, ball practice. *p.*

گولوك गोलोक *golok*, m. name of the heaven of *Vishṇu*. *s.*

گولہ *gola*, m. a cannon-ball (v. *golā*). *p.*

گولي गोली *golī*, m. any small ball, a bullet, a musket-ball; a pill; a jar. *golī mārnā*, to shoot at with a bullet. *s.*

گولي *gaulī*, m. a grazier, a cowherd. *d.*

گوم *gom*, m. a kind of centipede. *d.*

گوما *gūmā*, m. a name of a plant used as a tonic, and cure for the ear-ache, ague, &c. (*Pharnaceum mollugo*). *p.*

گومڑا गूमड़ा *gūmṛā*, m. a bump, swelling. *h.*

گومکھ गोमुख *go-mukh*, m. a breach in a wall. *h.*

گومکھي गोमुखी *go-mukhī*, f. a cloth bag containing a rosary: the hand being thrust in counts the beads; the chasm in the Himālaya mountains through which the Ganges issues. *s.*

گوموتر गोमूत्र *go-mūtr*, m. the cow's urine. *s.*

گومي गोमय *gomay*, m. cowdung. *s.*

گوميدسنبھ गोमेदसन्निभ *gomed-sannibh*, m. chalcedony or opal. *s.*

گوميدك गोमेदक *go medak*, m. a kind of gem or precious stone from the Himālaya mountains. *s.*

گوميدھ गोमेध *go-medh*, m. the sacrifice of a cow. *s.*

گون गोण *gon*, f. sack, a bag (of coarse cloth) fastened on the side of a beast of burden to carry grain in. *s.*

گون गौं *gauṅ*, f. opportunity, advantage. *gauṅ-gīr*, controller, uncontrolled, ruler, invested with authority. *gauṅ ghāt*, f. power, opportunity. *h.*

گون गवन *gawan*, m. going, moving. *s.*

گون *gūn*, (in comp.) implies similitude of colour, as *gul-gūn*, rosy-colour, red. *p.*

گونا गौना *gaunā*, m, bringing home a wife. *s.*

گوناگون *gūnāgūn*, of different colours or kinds, various, manifold. *p.*

گونتهنا गुंथना *gūṅthnā*, a. (v. *gūṅṭhnā*) to [thread. *s.*

گونٹا गौंटा *gaunṭā*, village expenses. *h.*

گونٹهه गोंठ *goṅṭh*, m. a kind of wide stitch or sewing; lands assigned rent-free for religious purposes; the endowment of a temple. *h.*

گونٹها गोंठा *goṅṭhā*, m. dried cowdung for fuel. *s.*

گونٹهنا गूंथना *gūṅṭhnā*, a. to thread, to string; to stitch; to spit, or put on a spit. *gūṅthwānā*, a. to cause to string, &c. *s.*

گونٹيا गोंटिया *goṅṭiyā*, m. the chief manager of a village. *gauṅṭiyā*, f. a small hamlet. *h.*

گونج गूंज *gūṅj*, f. echo, buzzing, resounding, hollow sound, roar. *s.*

گونجنا गूंजना *gūṅjnā*, n. to resound, to hum, to buzz, to roar, to growl. *s.*

گونجها गूंझा *gūṅjhā*, m. a kind of sweetmeat. *h.*

گونچري *gonchrī*, a tick, an insect which annoys cattle. *d.*

گوند गोंद *gond* or गूंद *gūnd*. f. gum. *gond-dānī*, a vessel in which gum is kept to seal letters with. *gond-kash*, an instrument for spreading gum with (in sealing letters). *s.*

گوند गोंद *gond*, name of a rush which grows in marshy ground, and is much used in making mats and baskets; (Dakh.) a kind of sweetmeat. *h.*

گوندا गोंदा *goṅdā*, m. a thin dough or pap made of the flour of *Cicer arietinum*, for feeding birds. *h.*

گوندلا गूंदला *gūṅdlā*, round, circular; m. a ring, a circle. *h.* [&c. *h.*

گوندنا गूंदना *gūṅdnā*, a. (v. *gūndhnā*) to knead,

گوندني गोंदनी *gondnī*, f. a reed, of the leaves of which coarse mats are made (*Typha*). *gūndnī*, f. a tree yielding a gummy fruit. *h.*

گوندهن गूंधन *gūndhan*, m. dough, act of kneading, plaiting, braid. *h.*

گوندهنا गूंधना *gūndhnā*, a. to knead; to plait, to braid, to plat, to weave. *h.*

گوندي गोंदी *gondī*, f. name of a tree (*Cordia*). *h.*

گونڈ गोंड *gonḍ*, name of the aboriginal inhabitants of the Saugor territory. *h.*

گونڈا गोंडा *gonḍā* (v. *ahīr*), a caste of cowherds; a suburb, field near a village. *h.*

گونڈلي गोंडली *gonḍlī*, f. name of a tree. *h.*

گونرا गोंरा *goṅrā*, m. a kind of reservoir (for water). *h.*

گونڑا गूंड़ा *guṅṛā*, m. a beam (of a ship), the cross timbers (of a boat). *h.*

گونس गोनस *gonas*, m. a large serpent, a boa.

گونگا गूंगा *gūngā*, dumb, speechless, mute. *h.*

گونگان کرنا गुनगानकरना *gūngān-karnā*, a. to sing, to celebrate, to prattle (or crow) as infants. *h.*

گونگائي गूंगाई *gūngā,ī*, f. dumbness. *h.*

گون گهات गौंघात *gauṅ-ghat*, f. power, opportunity. *h.* [mode, manner, kind. *p.*

گونه *gūna*, m. colour, form, species, figure.

گونهار गौन्हार *gaunhār*, m. the company who attend the bride when being brought home. *s.*

گوني *gaunī* (v. *gaun*), opportunity, &c. *d.*

گووا गोवा *gowā*, manure, cow-dung. *h.*

گوواري गोवारी *gowārī*, a dwelling-house, a family, a cowhouse; a cowherd. *h.*

گووردهن गोवर्द्धन *gowardhan*, m. a hill near Mathura which was upheld by *Krishṇa* to shelter the cowherds from a storm. *s.*

گوونا गोवना *gowanā*, a. to hide, to conceal. *s.*

گوه गोह *goh*, m. a lizard, iguana; a Gangetic alligator. *gūh*, f. human excrement. *s.*

گوه गौह *gauh*, f. perseverance, diligence. *h.*

گوهار गोहार *gohār*, m. tumult, uproar. *h.*

گوهاري गोहारी *gohārī*, f. rich and highly-cultivated land. *h.*

گوهان गौहान *gauhān*, a village made over to any person on a permanent assessment. *h.*

گوهاني गौहानी *gauhānī*, f. lands situated close round a village; the village itself; fields on which cattle graze. *h.* [grain by bullocks. *s.*

گوهائي गोहाई *gohā,ī*, f. the treading out of

گوهتيا गोहत्या *go-hatyā*, f. the killing of a cow, among Hindūs a most heinous crime. *s.*

گوهر *gauhar* or *gohar*, m. a pearl, a gem, a jewel; lustre of a gem, or sword; essence, disposition, substance, form; offspring; intellect, wisdom. *gauhar-afshān*, *-bār*, or *nigār*, showering or scattering gems; (met.) an eloquent discourse or composition. *gauhar-sanj*, one who weighs or examines gems; a critic. *p.* [cattle. *h.*

گوهر गोहर *gohar*, m. a broad pathway for

گوهرا गोहरा *goharā*, m. cakes of dried cowdung; an ally, a succourer, an assistant. *s.*

گوهرها गोहरहा *goharhā*, m. an ally, succourer, an assistant. *h.*

گوهري गोहरी *goharī*, f. demurrage. *h.*

گوهڑيا गुहड़िया *gūhaṛiyā*, m. a dunghill, a place where excrement is thrown. *s.*

گوهوان गोहूअन *gohū,an*, m. a snake, the boa. *s.*

گوهون गोहूं *gohūṅ*, m. (v. *gehūṅ*) wheat. *h.*

گوهونا गोहूना *gohūnā*, } m. name of a kind of
گوهونه गोहूनः *gohūna*, } snake; the boa. *s.*

گوهي गूही *gūhī*, defiled (*cacatus*). *h.*

گوي *go,e*, m. a ball; (in comp.) same as *go*, as *'aib-go,e*, satirical or censorius. *go,ī*, f. speech, eloquence. *p.*

گوي *gawwī*, a den (of a wild beast); a pit, a hole, an excavation. *d.*

گويا गुवैया *guwaiyā*, f. a gossip; a woman's female friend; adj. eloquent, conversable. *p. h.*

گويا गवैया *gawaiyā*, m. a singer, a minstrel. *s.*

گويا *goyā*, adj. speaking or endowed with speech; adv. thus, in this manner, as you would say, as if one would say. *p.*

گوياك *goyāk*, } talkative, loquacious, conversing. *p.*
گويان *goyān*, }

گوئيان गुइयां *gū,iyān*, m. a partner (at any game). *h.*

گوياءي *goyā,ī*, f. conversation, talk. *p.*

گويرك गवेरुक *gaveruk*, m. red chalk.

گوءين गोईं *go,īn*, a pair of plough oxen, sometimes called *do-gāwā*. *h.*

گوينڈ ग्वैंड *gwainḍ* or *gwainḍe*, adv. near. *h.*

گويند ग्वैंड *go,enḍ* or *gwenḍ*, } m. a suburb, vicinage, fields near a village, homestead. *h.*
گوينڈا ग्वैंडा *gwainḍā*, }

گويندگي *goyandagī*, f. a dialect, speech. *p.*

گوينده *goyanda*, m. an orator, a speaker; (in Dakh.) an informer, a spy, a criminal admitted as king's evidence; an approver. *p.*

گويه गव्य *gavya*, of or belonging to a cow. *s.*

گه घ *gha* the aspirate of ग *ga*. *s. h.*

گه गह *gah*, f. a handle. *guh*, f. human excrement. *s.*

گه *gah*, f. (v. *gāh*) time, place. *gah-gah*, sometimes, from time to time. *p.*

گها गुहा *guhā*, f. a cave, cavern. *s.*

گهابرا घाबरा *ghābrā*, confused, confounded. *h.*

گهات घात *ghāt*, f. aim, design, snare; ambuscade. *ghāt-k.*, to waylay, to lie in ambush. *ghāt taknā*, to watch an opportunity. *h.*

گهات घात *ghāt*, f. killing, slaughter; a bruise, a blow; product of a multiplication. *s.*

گهاتا घाता *ghātā*, m. name of a plaything. *h.*

گهاتك घातक *ghātak*, m. an enemy, a murderer. *ghātuk*, mischievous, murderous, cruel. *s*

گهاتن घातन *ghātan*, m. killing, slaughter, murder. *s.*

گهاتو *ghātū*, m. a deceiver. *d.*

گهاتي घाती *ghātī*, murderous, felonious; insidious, wily. *s. h.*

گهاٹ घाट *ghāṭ*, m. f. a landing-place, a quay, wharf, ford, pass; bathing-place on a river side; an entrance into a country over mountains, or through any difficult pass; also a public ferry over any river, or a landing-place where customs are usually collected. *ghāṭ-mār*, m. a smuggler. *ghāṭ-mārnā*, a. to smuggle. *ghāṭ-kaptān*, a harbour-master, master attendant at a seaport. *ghāṭ-mānjhī*, a ferryman *s.*

گهاٹ घाट *ghāṭ*, m. mode, manner, shape; offence, deficiency; want, abatement; adj. abated, less. *h.*

گهاٹا घाटा *ghaṭā*, m. acclivity, ascent; deficiency, abatement, reduction. *h.*

گهاٹاني घाटानी *ghāṭānī*, } f. a toll levied on crossing rivers or hill-passes. *h.*
گهاٹباري घाटबारी *ghāṭ-bārī*, }

گهاٹمارا घाटमारा *ghāṭ-mārā*, m. a smuggler; smuggling in general. *h.*

گهاٹوال घाटवाल *ghāṭ-wāl*, } m. a ferryman, a person in charge of a landing place or of a mountain pass. *h.*
گهاٹوالا घाटवाला *ghāṭ-wālā*, }

گهاٹي घाटी *ghāṭī*, f. a strait, a pass (in a mountain, &c.). *h.*

گهاٹيا घाटिया *ghāṭiyā*, m. a Brāhman who sits in a *ghāṭ* of the Ganges to keep the clothes, &c. of those that resort to make ablution. *s.*

گهار घार *ghār*, a kind of clay soil. *ghār hojānā* is applied to land worn away by running water. *h.*

گهار गुहार *guhār*, f. m. an assistant, aid; bawling, tumult, alarm. *h.*

گهاري घारी *ghārī*, f. a valley or ravine; cattle-sheds. *h.*

گهاس घास *ghās*, f. grass, fodder, straw, meadow, pasture. *ghās-pāt*, sweepings, rubbish. *s.*

گهاسكاٹا घासकाटा *ghās-kāṭā*, } m. a man whose office is to cut and procure fresh grass daily for the horses of his employer. *h.*
گهاسكٹا घासकटा *ghās-kaṭā*, }

گهاگر *ghāgar*, the rope tied to the foot of an elephant. *d.*

گهاگراگول *ghāgrā-gol*, perplexed, bewildered, distracted. *d.*

گهاگس घागस *ghāgas*, m. a large kind of fowl. *h.*

گهاگه घाघ *ghāgh*, old, aged, experienced; sly, wily, shrewd. *h.*

گهاگهرا घाघरा *ghāghrā*, m. a petticoat; name of a river, *Gogra*; name of a plant (*Xanthium Indicum*, *Kœn. M.S.*). *ghāghrā-gol*, perplexed. *s.*

گهال घाल *ghāl*, f. mischief, distraction, ruin. *h.*

گهال गुहाल *guhāl* (v. *gau-sālā*), a cowhouse. *h.*

گهالا *ghālā*, calamity, evil, misfortune. *d.*

گهالك घालक *ghālak*, m. a ruler, destroyer, desolater. *h.*

گهالميل घालमेल *ghāl-mel*, jumbled. *h.*

گهالنا घालना *ghālnā*, a. to desolate, to ruin; to thrust in. *h.*

گهام घाम *ghām*, f. sunbeams, sunshine; sweat (Beng). *s.*

گهامڑ घामड़ *ghāmaṛ*, simple, artless; a blockhead. *h.*

گهان घान *ghān*, f. as much as is thrown in at one time into a mill, or a mortar, &c. *h.*

گهانا घाना *ghānā*, m. (v. *ghānī*), a sugar-cane press, an oil-mill. *h.*

كهانتي घांटी *ghānṭī*, f. Adam's apple, the larynx. *s.*

كهانتي *ghānṭī*, f. strips of different-coloured cloths tied round the ankles by *Muḥarram faḳīrs*. *d.*

كهانجني गुहांजनी *guhānjanī*, f. a stithe (in the eye). *h.*

كهانس *ghāṅs*, grass, green turf. *ghāṅs kā chakkā*, a sod of turf, a square-cut piece of turf. *d.*

كهانسي *ghāṅsī*, a kind of covering. *d.*

كهانگراگهول *ghāṅgrā-ghol* (v. *ghāgrā-gol*). *d.*

كهاني घानी *ghānī*, f. an oil-mill (or press); a sugar-mill. *h.*

كهاءو घाव *ghā,o* or *ghāw*, m. a wound, a sore. *h.*

كهاءوكهپ घाउघप *ghā,ū-ghap* or घावघप *ghā,o-ghap*, living from hand to mouth, improvident; m. a spendthrift. *h.*

كهاءي गुहाई *guhā,ī*, f. meconium (of infants). *gahā,ī*, the process of treading sheaves of corn by bullocks, for separating the grain from the ears and stalks. *h.*

كهاءي घाई *ghā,ī*, f. cudgelling; stratagem, fraud, a decoy; number five (in reckoning); the interval between the fingers or toes, the junction of the fingers, the space at the root where the fingers separate; the angle formed by a branch with the trunk of a tree, or space at the root of the branch; a cut or stroke with the broadsword or cudgel (of these there are twelve). *h.*

كهايل घायल *ghāyal*, घाइल *ghā,el* or *ghā,il*, wounded. *h.*

كهاءين घाइन *ghā,in*, (one) time, turn. *h.*

كهبرات *ghabrāt* (for *ghabrāhaṭ*, q. v.). *d.*

كهبرانا घबराना *ghabrānā*, n. to be confused, confounded, alarmed, perplexed, agitated, embarrassed, terrified. *h.*

كهبراهٹ घबराहट *ghabrāhaṭ*, f. confusion, perplexity, agitation, perturbation, alarm. *h.*

كهپ घुप *ghup*, dark, hidden, obscure. *h.*

كهپچي घपची *ghapchī*, f. grasp, embrace. *h.*

كهت गुहत *guhat*, covered, concealed, plaiting the hair. *s.*

كهتر *ghatar*, daybreak, the morning. *d.*

كهتيا घतिया *ghatiyā*, m. a murderer. *s.*

كهٹ घट *ghaṭ*, m. a water-pot; body. *ghaṭṭ*, a landing-place, a quay, steps leading to the water's edge. *s.*

كهٹ घट *ghaṭ*, f. mind, heart, thought, soul. *h.*

كهٹ *ghaṭ*, fast, firm, tight, strong, thick, hard, compact. *d.*

كهٹا घटा *ghaṭā*, f. cloudiness, gathering of the clouds; clouds, crowds. *s.*

كهٹا घट्टा *ghaṭṭā*, m. a corn of the feet, a cork, a plug. *h.*

كهٹاٹوپ घटाटोप *ghaṭāṭop*, m. a covering of a *pālkī* or carriage. *h.*

كهٹانا घटाना *ghaṭānā*, a. to lessen, to decrease, to diminish. *ghuṭānā*, a. to shave clean, to polish. *h.*

كهٹاو घटाव *ghaṭāw*, m. deficiency, reduction, falling (as a river, or price of any thing), depreciation. *h.*

كهٹاونا घटावना *ghaṭāwnā*, a. to reduce, to cause to subside or decrease. *h.*

كهٹاءي घुटाई *ghuṭā,ī*, f. perfidy, villany. *h.*

كهٹتي घटती *ghaṭtī*, f. deficiency, diminution, decrease. *h.*

كهٹداسي घटदासी *ghaṭ-dāsī*, f. a bawd or procuress. *s.*

كهٹك घटक *ghaṭak*, m. a mediator, go-between, an ambassador, attorney, messenger; one who adjusts a marriage (Beng.). *s.*

كهٹكا घटिका *ghaṭikā*, f. the ankle; a portion of the day or night (v. *muhūrt*); a *danḍ*, or period of 24 minutes. *s.*

كهٹن घटन *ghaṭan*, m. occurring, happening. *s.*

كهٹنا घटना *ghaṭnā*, n. to abate, to decrease, to subside, to sink, to fall. *h.*

كهٹنا घुटना *ghuṭnā*, n. to be rubbed, to be suffocated or stifled; to spread (as smoke); m. the knee. *ghuṭnoṅ chalnā* or *ghuṭnī chalnā*, to crawl about on the knees as a child. *h.*

كهٹنت घटन्त *ghaṭant*, f. diminution, decrease. *h.*

كهٹنيه घटनीय *ghaṭnīya*, liable to abatement, or decrease, or diminution. *s.*

كهٹوار घटवार *ghaṭwār*, } m. a wharfinger, one
كهٹوال घटवाल *ghaṭwāl*, } who has the care of a *ghāṭ*. *s.*

كهٹها घटहा *ghaṭhā*, m. an offender, transgressor. *h.*

كهٹي घटी *ghaṭī*, f. the *ghaṛī* or Indian clock, a plate of metal on which the hours are struck. *s.*

كهٹي घुट्टी *ghuṭṭī*, f. (v. *ghūṅṭī*) a kind of medicine for children. *h.*

كهٹي घटी *ghaṭī* or *ghaṭṭī*, f. deficiency, loss, diminution, abatement. *ghaṭṭī*, a small or inferior landing-place. *s.*

كهٹيا घटिया *ghaṭiyā*, low-priced, cheap. *h.*

كهچاكهچ घचाघच *ghachāghach*, thick. *h.*

كهچپچ घिचपिच *ghich-pich*, thick, confused, muddy. *ghich-pich-baknā* or *-bolnā*, to speak thick. *h.*

كهر घर *ghar*, m. house, dwelling, apartment, drawer, compartment, groove. *ghar-basā*, one who is at home or keeps to the house; indolent, inactive. *ghar ba-ghar*, to or in every house, from house to house. *ghar baiṭhnā* or *ghar baiṭh-jānā* (lit.) to rest at home, to go home; (idiomatically) to be ruined. *ghar chalānā*, a. to provide for one's household expenses (Beng.). *ghar-dwārī*, f. a kind of tax, poll-tax, hearth-money. *ghar ḍubonā*, to ruin one's self and family. *ghar ḍūbnā*, to be ruined. *ghar kā dhelānā rahnā* (Dakh.), to be desolated or destroyed. *ghar karnā*, a. to fix, to settle, to establish a family. *ghar khokar tamāshā dekhnā*, to ruin one's self and spend the time in idle pleasures. *ghar-ghālnā*, to ruin or utterly destroy. *ghar honā* expresses affection and unanimity between husband and wife. *h.*

گهر *guhar*, m. a gem; essence; race, family; nature, disposition. *bad-guhar*, of a bad disposition (v. *gohar*). *p.*

گهرا घर्रा *gharrā*, m. a rattling noise in the throat, which dying people are afflicted with, pain, agony, pang. *h.* [lour. *s.*

گهرا गहरा *gahrā*, deep. *gahrā-rang*, deep co-

گهراپا गहरापा *gahrāpā*, } m. depth, pro-
گهراپن गहरापन *gahrāpan*, } fundity. *s.*

گهرات घ्रात *ghrāt* or *ghrāta*, smelt, inhaled. *s.*

گهراٹا घर्राटा *gharrāṭā*, m. snoring, snorting. *s.*

گهرامي घरामी *gharāmī*, m. a thatcher. *s.*

گهران घ्राण *ghrāṇ*, m. the nose, smell; smelling. *s.*

گهرانا घराना *gharānā*, m. family, household. *s.*

گهرانا घिराना *ghirānā*, a. to cause to surround or inclose. *h.* [a. to assist. *h.*

گهرانا गुहराना *guhrānā*, n. to call out, to bawl;

گهران ترپن घ्राणतर्पन *ghrāṇ-tarpan*, m. fragrance, odour, a fragrance, a perfume. *s.*

گهراند घिरांद *ghirānd*, f. stink (particularly that of urine). *s.*

گهرانيندريه घ्राणेन्द्रिय *ghrāṇendriya*, f. the nose, the sense of smelling. *s.*

گهراو गहराओ *gahrā,o*, m. } depth, profundity;
گهراي गहराई *gahrā,ī*, f. } a pit or cavity. *s.*

گهربار घरबार *ghar-bār*, m. family, household concerns or household goods. *ghar-bār basānā*, to consummate a marriage. *ghar-bār honā*, to undergo the consummation of a marriage. *s.*

گهرباري घरबारी *ghar-bārī*, f. housewifery, domestic concerns; m. a householder. *s.*

گهربراو घरबराव *ghar-barāw*, m. household furniture, &c. *s.* [house. *h.p.*

گهربندي *ghar-bandī*, a slave born in the

گهربهاڑا *ghar-bhāṛā*, m. house-rent. *h.*

گهرپتي घरपत्ती *ghar-pattī*, a kind of house-tax (now abolished). *s.h.*

گهرپهانت घरफांत *ghar-phānt*, an arrangement entered into for paying the government revenue. *s.h.*

گهرت घरत *gharat*, f. make, form. *ghurat*, a pen for cattle. *h.*

گهرت घृत *ghṛit*, m. *ghī* or clarified butter. *s.*

گهرتکماري घृतकुमारी *ghṛit-kumārī*, f. the aloe-plant. *s.*

گهرتکوار घृतकुवार *ghṛitakuwār*, m. (v. *ghīkuwār*), a kind of plant. *s.*

گهردواري घरद्वारी *ghar-dwārī*, f. a house-tax; also a kind of illegal cess from shopkeepers and householders. *s.*

گهرڑ घरड़ *gharaṛ*, the dry moth-plant cut and given as fodder to cattle. *h.*

گهرسبيل *ghar-sabīl*, advances to peasants in order to enable them to build their cottages. *h.a.*

گهرشن घर्षण *gharshan*, m. grinding, pounding. *s.*

گهرشني घर्षणी *gharshanī*, f. turmeric. *s.*

گهرکا *ghirkā*, a kind of children's game. *d.*

گهرکنا घुरकना *ghuraknā*, a. to browbeat, to reprimand, to frown at, to rebuke, to growl, to snarl. *h.*

گهرکي घुरकी *ghurkī*, f. rebuff, browbeating, rebuke, frowning at. *h.* [(*Silurus*). *s.*

گهرگهٹ घर्घट *ghar-ghaṭ*, m. a kind of fish

گهرگهر घर्घर *gharghar*, m. the river Gogra; gurgling, rumbling. *h.*

گهرگهرا घुरघुरा *ghur-ghurā*, m. the mole-cricket (*Gryllus gryllotalpa*); a phagedenic ulcer, or *Herpes exedens* (so named from digging in the flesh as the mole-cricket does in earth or sand). *h.*

گهرم घर्म *gharm*, m. heat, the hot season; sunshine; sweat, perspiration. *s.*

گهرنا घरना *gharnā*, a. to fashion or shape (as metal with a hammer). *h.*

گهرنا घिरना *ghirnā*, n. to be surrounded, inclosed; to be collected around; to gather (as the clouds). *h.*

گهرنا घृणा *ghṛiṇā*, f. abhorrence, disgust, blame, censure, pity, shame, bashfulness. *s.*

گهرنانا घुरनाना *ghurnānā*, n. to snore. *h.*

گهرنس घुरनस *ghurnas*, m. the tendo Achillis. *h.*

گهرني घिरनी *ghirnī*, f. a pulley; an instrument for twisting ropes; a kind of pigeon, the tumbler pigeon. *ghirnī khānā*, to go round. *s.*

گهرني घुरनी *ghurnī*, f. a vertigo, swimming of the head; rolling. *gharnī*, f. a wife. *s.*

گهرنئي घरनई *gharna,ī*, f. a raft made with pots, a float (of pots). *s.*

گهرو घरऊ *ghara,ū*, domestic, household. *s.*

گهروا घरूआ *gharū,ā*, } m. a small house
گهروندا घरौंदा *gharaundā*, } which children make to play in. *s.* [*rāj-pūts*. *h.*

گهروار गहरवार *gaharwār*, name of a tribe of

گهروارا घरवारा *gharwārā*, } name of a district
گهرواره घरवारः *gharwāra*, } in Bundelcund, said to have been bestowed rent-free on Brāhmans by Rājā Rām Baghel. *h.*

گهروالا घरवाला *ghar-wālā*, m. husband, householder. *s.* [a house; housekeeping. *s.*

گهروالي घरवाली *ghar-wālī*, f. a wife, mistress of

گهري गहरी *gahrī*, low swampy ground fit for rice cultivation. *h.*

گهري घरी *gharī* (for *ghaṛī*, q.v.), an hour, &c.; a fold, a plait, folded up, gathered or tucked up. *h.*

گھریلا घरेला *gharelā*, domestic; tame. *s.*

گھڑ घुड़ *ghuṛ*, m. a horse. *ghuṛ-chaṛh*, horse-riding. *ghuṛ-chaṛhā*, a horseman, a rider, a trooper. *ghuṛ-chaṛhī*, f. riding; a female rider. *ghuṛ-dauṛ*, a race-course. *ghuṛ-sār* or *-sāl*, m. a stable. *ghuṛ-muṅhā*, horse-faced. *s.*

گھڑا घड़ा *ghaṛā*, m. an earthen water-pot; a jar, a pitcher. *s.*

گھڑبہل घुड़बहल *ghuṛ-bahal*, f. a four-wheeled carriage for riding in, drawn by horses. *s.*

گھڑت घड़त *ghaṛat*, shaped or manufactured by being beaten or hammered, in contradistinction to being cast or run (metal articles). *h.*

گھڑسنا घुड़सना *ghuṛasnā*, n. to curl, to become curled. *h.*

گھڑکنا घुड़कना *ghuṛaknā*, a. to frown, to browbeat, to reprimand. *h.*

گھڑکی घुड़की *ghuṛkī*, f. frowning, browbeating, rebuke. *h.* [to thunder. *h.*

گھڑگھڑانا घड़घड़ाना *ghaṛghaṛānā*, n. to growl,

گھڑنا घड़ना *ghaṛnā*, a. to fashion, form, shape; to forge, to work (metals); to knock, to hammer. *h.*

گھڑنا *ghaṛnā*, n. to happen (a calamity). *d.*

گھڑولا घड़ोला *ghaṛolā*, m. a pot, a pitcher, a jug, a mug. *s.*

گھڑونچا घड़ोंचा *ghaṛonchā*, m. } a stand for wa-
گھڑونچی घड़ोंची *ghaṛonchī*, f. } ter-pots, &c. *s.*

گھڑی घड़ी *ghaṛī*, f. a portion of time, the space of twenty-four minutes, but applied generally to the European hour of sixty minutes; an instrument for measuring time, a clock, watch, &c. *ghāṛī meṅ tolā ghaṛī meṅ māshā*, at one time an ounce, at another a grain (expressing a person of a changeable disposition): as a revenue term the word *ghaṛī* denotes the subdivision of a village; a fold, a plait. *p. s.*

گھڑی घड़ी *ghaṛī* (dim. of *ghaṛā*), a small pot. *s.*

گھڑیا घड़िया *ghaṛiyā*, f. a crucible; a honeycomb; the womb. *h.*

گھڑیال घड़ियाल *ghaṛiyāl*, m. a plate of brass or bell-metal for sounding the *ghaṛis* of each *pahar* or watch of the day and night; a gong; a crocodile; (in Dakh.) a watch, a clock. *ghaṛī-yāl kā shīsha*, an hour-glass. *s.*

گھڑیالا घड़ियाला *ghaṛiyālā*, } m. the person
گھڑیالی घड़ियाली *ghaṛiyālī*, } who attends the *ghaṛī*, and strikes the hours. *s.*

گھس घुस *ghus*, m. f. entering, penetrating; creeping. *h.*

گھسانا घुसाना *ghusānā*, a. to thrust in, to stuff in, to cram, to cause to penetrate, to force in. *h.*

گھسانا घिसाना *ghisānā*, a. to cause to rub. *s.*

گھساو घिसाव *ghisaw*, m. } attrition, rub-
گھساوٹ घिसावट *ghisāwaṭ*, f. } bing, friction, abrasion. *s.* [trance. *h.*

گھس پیٹھ घुसपैठ *ghus-paiṭh*, f. access, en-

گھسٹنا घसिटना *ghasiṭnā* (also *ghisaṭnā*), n. to be dragged, to be trailed along. *s.*

گھسرا घसरा *ghasrā*, mischievous, hurtful. *s.*

گھسراند घुसरांद *ghusrānd*, a kind of creeping grass with a yellow flower. *h.*

گھسڑنا घुसिड़ना *ghusiṛnā*, n. to be thrust in. *h.*

گھسمر घस्मर *ghasmar*, gluttonous, voracious. *s.*

گھسن घसन *ghasan*, f. the act of rubbing. *s.*

گھسنا घुसना *ghusnā*, n. to enter, to be thrust in, or forced in. *h.*

گھسنا घसना *ghasnā* or घिसना *ghisnā*, n. to be rubbed, to be abraded, to fret, to wear; a. to rub, to whet; to beat; adj. apt to be worn by rubbing. *s.*

گھسنی घिसनी *ghisnī*, by rubbing; as *gaṅr ghisnī karnā* or *ghisnī chalnā*, to move along, rubbing on the ground, as a child on his buttocks before he is able to walk. *s.* [grass-cutter. *s.*

گھسیارا घसियारा *ghasiyārā* or *ghasiyāṛā*, m. a

گھسیارن घसियारिन *ghasiyārin*, f. the wife of a *ghasiyārā*. *s.* [drag. *s.*

گھسیانا घिसियाना *ghisiyānā*, a. to trail, to

گھسیٹنا घसीटना *ghasīṭnā*, a. to drag, to pull, to trail. *s.*

گھسیڑنا घुसेड़ना *ghuseṛnā*, a. to thrust, to stuff, to cram, to force in, to pierce, to insinuate. *h.*

گھسیلا घसीला *ghasīlā*, grassy, abounding in grass. *s.* [cation. *h.*

گہک गहक *gahak*, f. the emotion of intoxi-

گہکنا गहकना *gahaknā*, n. to be agitated by intoxication. *h.*

گہکی गहकी *gahkī*, f. purchase; m. a purchaser. *s.*

گھگری *ghagrī*, f. a kind of musical instrument (v. *Qanoon i Islam*); a hollow metallic ring, having some small shot within, so as to rattle when shaken. *d.*

گہگہانا गहगहाना *gahgahānā*, n. to quiver, to shake or undulate. *h.*

گھگھرا घघरा *ghaghrā*, m. } a petticoat, &c. (v.
گھگھری घघरी *ghaghrī*, f. } *ghāgrā*). *s.*

گھگھی घिघी *ghighī*, f. faltering in speech. *ghighī bandh jānā*, to falter, to be unable to speak. *h.*

گھگھیانا घिघियाना *ghighiyānā*, n. to falter, to be unable to speak (from fear, joy, &c.); to coax, to wheedle, to fawn, to beseech. *h.*

گہگیر *gahgīr*, unbroken (a horse). *p.*

گہل गहल *gahal*, f. (v. *ghaud*) a bunch of grapes, &c. *h.*

گھلانا *ghulānā*, a. to deceive, to trick. *d.*

گھلانا घुलाना *ghulānā*, a. to melt, to dissolve. *h.*

گھلاؤ घुलाऊ *ghulāū*, adj. melting. *h.*

گھلاوٹ घुलावट *ghulāwaṭ*, f. act of melting or dissolving. *h.*

گهل‌مل घुलमिल *ghul-mil*, dissolved, mixed; melted in kindness. *h. s.*

گهلنا घुलना *ghulnā*, n. to melt, to be dissolved, to be mellowed, to rot (as fruit); to become lean, to waste. *h.*

گهلوا घलूआ *ghalū,ā* or *ghalwā* (also घुल्वा *ghulwā*), to boot, over and above; m. a small quantity given above the purchase. *h.*

گهلوانا घुलवाना *ghulwānā*, a. to cause to mix with a liquid, to dissolve. *h.*

گهلوت गहलोत *gahlot*, name of a tribe of *rāj*-[pūts. *h.*

گهماسان घमासान *ghamāsān* (v. *ghamsān*), battle, &c. *h.*

گهماگهم घमाघम *ghamāgham*, or گهماگهم गहमागहम *gahmāgaham*, } thick, crowded, dense (as the population of a city, trees of a forest, &c.). *h.*

گهمانا घमाना *ghamānā*, to sun, to bask in the sun. *s.*

گهمانا घुमाना *ghumānā*, a. to revolve, to circulate, to whirl, to roll, to brandish, to encircle; to beguile, to delude. *ghumānā phirānā*, a. to prevaricate. *h.*

گهماو घुमाव *ghumā,o*, m. as much land as can be ploughed in a day by a single pair of bullocks. *h.*

گهمبير घंबीर *ghambīr* (v. *mutaḥammil*), affable, patient, enduring. *d.*

گهمرا घुमरा *ghumrā*, m. the name of a plant (*Phlomis*); name of an insect. *h.*

گهمرول घमरौल *ghamraul*, f. crowd, confusion in a general engagement. *h.*

گهمري घुमरी *ghumrī*, f. the vertigo, swimming of the head. *s.*

گهمڑانا घुमड़ाना *ghumṛānā*, n. (v. *ghūmnā*) to [roll, &c. *h.*

گهمس घमस *ghamas*, f. heat, closeness. *s.*

گهمسان घमसान *ghamsān*, m. battle, engagement. *s.*

گهمگهما घुमघुमा *ghumghumā*, m. revolution, going round; subterfuge, evasion, prevarication; doubt, suspense, hesitation. *h.*

گهمگمانا घुमघुमाना *ghumghumānā*, a. to revolve; to prevaricate. *h.*

گهمنڈ घमण्ड *ghamanḍ*, m. pride, haughtiness, arrogance. *ghumanḍ*, gathering of the clouds. *h.*

گهمنڈي घमण्डी *ghamanḍī*, haughty, a proud man. *h.*

گهمنا *ghumnā*, n. to resound, re-echo, reverberate; to go round, to turn, to roll. *d.*

گهموري घमोरी *ghamorī*, f. the prickly heat. *s.*

گهموءي घमूई *ghamū,ī*, f. name of a plant. *h.*

گهن घन *ghan*, m. an assemblage, a number, quantity; (in arithmetic) cube of a number; (in geometry) a solid; adj. material, solid, gross, compact, hard, firm, impenetrable; very, much. *s.*

گهن घन *ghan*, m. gathering of the clouds; clouds; an anvil, a sledge-hammer. *s.*

گهن घिण *ghiṇ*, f. disgust; shame, bashfulness. *ghiṇ denā*, a. to reproach, to abash. *ghin khānā*, to be disgusted, sick. *s.*

گهن घुण *ghun*, m. name of an insect destructive to wood and meal, grain and flour; a weevil; rancour. *h.*

گهن गहण *gahan*, m. an eclipse; wood, forest. *s.*

گهنا गहना *gahnā*, m. jewels, ornaments; any thing in pledge, a pawned article, a mortage. *h.*

گهنا गहना *gahnā*, a. to lay hold of, to handle, to seize, to catch; to blush. *s.*

گهنا घना *ghanā*, thick, close, confused, numerous, much, many; m. a sporting preserve (same as *ramnā*, q. v.). *h.*

گهنا घुणा *ghunā*, (wood, grain, flour, &c.) destroyed by the insect *ghun*, weevil-eaten. *s.*

گهنا घुणा *ghunā*, malicious, spiteful, revengeful, bearing malice, rancorous, cautious, designing. *h.*

گهنا गहिना *gahinā*, a heavy plank or flat piece of wood on which a man stands while it is dragged by oxen over a ploughed field to level the ground. *h.*

گهنانا घिणाना *ghinānā*, n. to be disgusted; adj. disgusting. *s.*

گهنبير *ghambīr*, affable, patient, enduring. *d.*

گهنپهل घनफल *ghan-phal*, m. the contents of a solid (in geom.). *s.*

گهنتا घनता *ghantā*, f. firmness, compactness. *s.*

گهن‌تن‌برن घनतनबरन *ghan-tan-baran* or *-varan*, an epithet of *Krishṇa*; (lit.) having the body of the colour of the clouds. *s.*

گهنٹ घंटु *ghanṭu*, m. a string of bells tied on an elephant's chest by way of ornament. *s.*

گهنٹا घंटा *ghanṭā*, m. a bell, clock, hour. *s.*

گهنٹاشبد घंटाशब्द *ghanṭā-shabd*, m. bell-metal. *s.*

گهنٹالي घंटाली *ghanṭālī*, f. a small bell. *s.*

گهنٹكا घंटिका *ghanṭikā*, f. the uvula or soft palate. *s.*

گهنجوالا घनज्वाला *ghanjwālā*, f. lightning. *s.*

گهنچ घंच *ghanch*, m. the neck. *h.*

گهن‌چڑي *ghan chiṛī*, f. the hornbill, a bird (*Buceros*). *d.*

گهند घंद *ghand*, a subdivision of the *jāṭs*. *h.*

گهوندي घूंदी *ghūndī*, or گهنڈي घुंडी *ghunḍī*, } f. a button; name of an herb which grows in rice-fields after the crop is cut. *h.*

گهنسار घनसार *ghansār*, m. camphor; mercury, or some form of it. *s.*

گهنسي घुंसी *ghunsī*, malicious; a receiver of [bribes. *h.*

گهنسيام घनश्याम *ghan-syām*, m. black as a cloud; one of the names of *Kṛishṇa*: it may also denote black clouds. *s.*

گهنگچي घुंगची *ghungchī*, f. a little red seed (*Abrus precatorius*). *h.*

گهنگرج घनगरज *ghan-garaj*, m. the roar of the cloud, thunder, any loud noise; adj. loud-sounding. *s.*

گهنگري *ghungrī*, f. a cloak or mantle of hairy coarse woollen stuff; a caterpillar or palmer worm. *d.*

گهنگول घंगोल *ghangol*, the name of the water-lily which produces the celebrated *nīlūfar* flower. *h.*

گهنگونا घुनगौना or घुंगौना *ghuṅgaunā*, m. a plaything, a child's rattle. *h.*

گهنگهانا घिंघाना *ghingānā*, n. to be hoarse. *h.*

گهنگهچي घुंघची *ghunghchī*, same as *ghungchī*, q. v.

گهنگرو घुंगरू *ghuṅgrū*, } m. morris bells, worn
گهنگهرو घुंघरू *ghunghrū*, } on the ankles by dancing-girls; a small bell in general. *h.*

گهنگهس घंघस *ghanghas*, a subdivision of the *jāṭs*. *s.*

گهنگهن घनघन *ghanghan*, f. an imitative sound. *h.*

گهنگهنا घिनघिना *ghinghinā*, disgusting, loathsome, odious. *s.*

گهنگهنانا घनघनाना *ghangnanānā*, n. to jingle, to ring, to tinkle, to sound like a wheel in revolution. *h.*

گهنگهور घनघोर *ghan-ghor*, m. cloudiness, gathering of the clouds; roar of the clouds, *i.e.* thunder; adj. cloudy, overcast. *s.*

گهنگهورنا घंघोरना *ghaṅghornā*, } a. to rinse; to
گهنگهولنا घंघोलना *gangholnā*, } mix any liquid by stirring it about. *h.*

گهنگهيرا घनघेरा *ghangherā*, } m. a petticoat. *s.*
گهنگيرا घनगेरा *ghangerā*, }

گهنمول घनमूल *ghan-mūl*, m. cube root (in arithmetic). *s.*

گهنون गुहनौं *guhnauṅ*, (Braj) to thread, to string; to plait, to braid. *h.*

گهنونا घिणौना *ghinaunā*, disgusting, abominable, loathsome. *s.*

گهني गहनी *gahnī*, f. oakum; act of caulking; pledged. *gahnī dharnā*, a. to pawn, to pledge. *h.*

گهنيا घुनिया *ghuniyā*, spiteful, rancorous, bearing malice, malicious. *h.*

گهنيانا घिणियाना *ghiniyānā*, n. to be disgusted. *s.*

گهنيرا घनेरा *ghanerā*, much, many. *h.*

گهنيس घनेस *ghanes*, m. name of a bird (*Buceros Malabaricus*). *s.*

گهوا घुआ *ghuā*, m. a coarse kind of cotton. *h.*

گهوءا *ghū,ā*, m. the carpenter beetle, an insect which perforates wood. *d.*

گهوا गहवा *gahwā*, m. pincers, forceps. *h.*

گهواره *gahwāra*, m. a swing, a cradle. *p.*

گهوپا घोपा *ghopā*, m. a sort of hooded cloak or loose mantle for rainy or cold weather. *h.*

گهوٹ घोट *ghoṭ*, f. polish. *ghūṭ*, m. a gulp, draught. *h.*

گهوٹا घोटा *ghoṭā*, m. a wooden rubber. *h.*

گهوٹک घोटक *ghoṭak*, m. a horse. *h.*

گهوٹنا घूटना *ghūṭnā*, a. to gulp, to drink, to guzzle. *ghoṭnā*, a. to plod; to shave, to polish, to calendar. *h.*

گهوٹني घोटनी *ghoṭnī* or *ghūṭnī*, f. a rubber. *h.*

گهوٹو घोटू *ghoṭū*, polished, smooth (words). *h.*

گهوٹي घोटी *ghoṭī*, f. land which has been under a rice crop. *h.*

گهوٹي घूटी *ghūṭī*, f. the ankle-joint. *s.*

گهوٹي घूटी *ghūṭī* (v. *ghūṅṭī*), a medicine, &c. *h.*

گهوڈ घौद *ghaud*, } f. a bunch or cluster of
گهور घौर *ghaur*, } grapes, dates, or plantains. *h.*

گهوڈا घोडा *ghoḍā*, m. a horse. *h.*

گهور घूर *ghūr*, m. staring; a dunghill; name of a kind of sandy soil. *h.*

گهور घोर *ghor*, m. trepidation, horror, dread. *ghor ghūṅṭnā*, to be inwardly displeased, to conceal one's dislike or indignation; the sound of a drum; adj. frightful, awful; deep (colour of a horse). *ghor-ākṛiti*, *ghor-darshan*, *ghor-rūp*, or *ghor-rūpī*, of frightful aspect, terrific, hideous. *ghor-nidrā*, deep sleep. *s.*

گهورا घूरा *ghūrā*, m. soil, manure, sweepings; a dunghill. *h.*

گهوربرار घूरबरार *ghūr-barār*, a species of dues or tax. *h. p.*

گهورت घूरत *ghūrat*, cattle-pens. *h.*

گهورچڑها *ghor-chaṛhā* (v. *ghuṛ-chaṛhā*). *h.*

گهورچي घूरची *ghūrchī*, f. a twist in thread, entanglement. *h.*

گهورنا घूरना *ghūrnā*, a. to stare at, to fix the eyes on; to look at angrily. *h.*

گهوري गहूरी *gahūrī*, demurrage. *h.*

گهوريا घूरिया *ghūriyā*, s. a dunghill. *h.*

گهوڑ घौड़ *ghauṛ*, f. a bunch (of plantains). *h.*

گهوڑا घोड़ा *ghoṛā*, m. a horse; a cock (of a gun); the knight at chess. *ghoṛā chaṛhānā*, to cock a gun. *s.*

گهوڑپهوڑ *ghoṛ-phoṛ*, the guana lizard. *d.*

گهوڑي घोड़ी *ghoṛī*, a mare. *h.*

گهوس घूस *ghūs*, m. a bandicote rat (*Mus Malabaricus, Shaw; Mus giganteus, Lin. Trans.* vol. vii.); (for *ghūsh*) a bribe. *h.*

گهوس घोष *ghos*, name of a caste; a cowherd. *s.*

گهوسا घूसा *ghūsā*, m. a thump, a blow of the fist, buffet; a large kind of rat, bandicote. *h.*

گهوست घूसत *ghūsat*, m. a young owl. *h.*

گهوسم گهوسا घूसमघूसा *ghūsam-ghūsā*, m. thumping and pulling, boxing. *h.*

گهوسي घोसी *ghosī*, m. a Musalmān milkman or cowherd, said to be converted from the Hindū *ahīr* caste. *s.*

گهوش घोष *ghoṣh*, m. a station of herdsmen; a caste of milkmen; a cowherd. *s.*

گهوشنا घोषणा *ghoṣhṇā*, } a. to repeat, to reiterate, to speak aloud;
گهوکهنا घोखना *ghokhṇā*, } f. speaking aloud, making a great noise, crying, proclaiming. *s.*

گهوگهو घूघू *ghūghū*, m. the ring-necked dove, an owl. *h.*

گهوگهوا घूघूआ *ghūghū,ā*, an owl, a blockhead. *h.*

گهوگهي घोघी *ghoghī*, f. a pocket, pouch, wallet; a turtle-dove. *h.*

گهول घोल *ghol*, m. buttermilk. *s.*

گهولا घोला *gholā*, m. an intoxicating potion made of *bhang*, or opium, a solution; name of a fish. *ghole meṅ ḍālnā*, a. to involve in difficulty. *h.*

گهولانا *ghūlānā*, a. to deceive, to outwit. *d.*

گهولگهماو घोलघुमाव *ghol-ghumāw*, m. evasion, subterfuge. *h.*

گهول ميل घोलमेल *ghol-mel*, m. mixture, mixing. *h.*

گهولنا घोलना *gholnā*, m. to mix with a liquid, to dissolve. *h.*

گهوم घूम *ghūm*, back, round, about. *s.*

گهوم *ghūm*, a kind of children's game. *d.*

گهوماءو घूमाओ *ghūmā,o*, as much land as can be ploughed in one day by a pair of bullocks. *h.*

گهوم گهمالا घूमघुमाला *ghūm-ghumālā* or *-ghūmālā*, loose (as a robe), full. *s.*

گهوم گهميلا घूमघुमेला *ghūm-ghumelā* or *-ghūmelā*, revolving, circling, round. *s.*

گهومنا घूमना *ghūmnā*, n. to go round, to turn, to roll, to wheel. *sir ghūmnā*, n. to be giddy. *s.*

گهون घून *ghūn*, m. rancour, malice, spite. *h.*

گهونا घूना *ghūnā*, secret, cautious; designing, malicious, spiteful, rancorous. *h.*

گهونت घूंत *ghūnt*, rent-free lands assigned as endowments of religious establishments. *h.*

گهونٹ घूंट *ghūṅṭ*, m. or घोंट *ghoṅṭ*, f. a gulp, a draught, pull. *h.*

گهونٹنا घूंटना *ghūṅṭnā*, a. to gulp, to drink, to swallow. *ghoṅṭnā*, a. to polish by rubbing; (met.) to investigate; to strangle; m. a stone, &c. with which any thing is polished; the knee. *h.*

گهونٹي घूंटी *ghūṅṭī*, f. a medicine consisting of aloes, spices, and borax, given to new-born infants to clear out the meconium (in Urdū *ghuṭṭī*). *h.*

گهونس घूंस *ghūṅs*, m. (v. *ghūs*) a rat, &c. also the clenched fist. *h.*

گهونسا घूंसा *ghūṅsā*, m. (v. *ghūsā*) a thump, &c. *h.*

گهونسلا घोंसला *ghoṅslā*, m. a (bird's) nest. *h.*

گونهگا घोंगा *ghongā*, m. a cockle or cockle-shell, a snail (*Cochlea helix*); also called *ā,inthā* (v. *shāmuk*). *h.*

گهونگچي घूंगची *ghūngchī* (v. *ghungchī*), a small seed, &c. *s.*

گهونگر घूंगर *ghūngar*, m. a curl. *ghūngar-wāle bāl* or *ghungaryāle-bāl*, curled hair. *h.*

گهونگرو घूंगरू *ghūngrū*, m. name of an ornament worn round the ankles, with bells fastened to it; a bell. *h.*

گهونگني घूंगनी *ghūngnī*, f. a sort of stirabout, or grain of any kind (pulse or wheat, &c.) boiled whole. *h.*

گهونگهٹ घूंघट *ghūnghaṭ*, f. a veil; concealing the face with a veil, &c. *ghūnghaṭ kāṛhnā*, to draw a veil over the face. *ghūnghaṭ karnā*, a. to veil; to draw back his neck (a horse). *ghūnghaṭ khānā*, n. to be broken or defeated (an army). *h.*

گهونگهچي घूंघची *ghūnghchī*, f. a small red and black seed (*Abrus precatorius*). &c. *h.*

گهونگهر घूंघर *ghūnghar* (v. *ghūngar*), a curl, &c. *h.*

گهونگهرو घूंघरू *ghūnghrū* (v. *ghūngrū*), a small bell, a kind of ornament, &c. *h.*

گهونگهي घूंघी *ghūnghī*, } f. cloths folded up
گهونگي घूंगी *ghūngī*, } and put on the head as a defence against the rain; a cockle or snail, a small *ghūngā*. *h.*

گهونگي घूंगी *ghūngī*, f. (v. *gindar*) name of an insect. *h.*

گهوءي घूई *ghū,ī*, f. name of an herb which grows during the rains on high grounds. *h.*

گهويان घोयां *ghoyāṅ*, f. name of an esculent root (*Arum colocasia*). *h.*

گههر घहर *ghahar*, f. thunder. *h.*

گهہرانا घहराना *ghahrānā*, } n. to thunder; to
گهہرنا घहरना *ghaharnā*, } roar, to bawl. *h.*

گهي घी *ghī*, m. clarified butter. *s.*

گهي गुही *guhī*, defiled with excrement. *s.*

گهي *gahe*, once, one time, any time, some time. *p.*

گهئي घई *gha,ī*, f. (v. *chullī*) staddles, &c. *h.*

گهيا घिया *ghiyā*, m. name of a vegetable, a pompion (*Cucurbita lagenaria*). *ghiyā tora,ī*, *Luffa pentandra*, *Roxb.* *h.*

گهيپنا घेपना *ghepnā*, a. to mix, to mingle, to unite into a paste, as flour and water. *h.*

گهيتلا घेतला *ghetlā*, m. a kind of shoe. *h.*

گهيٹنا *gheṭnā*, to mix, to knead together. *d.*

گهير घेर *gher*, round, surrounding, inclosing; loose (as a robe), full; winding, meandering; m. circumference; calumny, reproach, complaint. *gher-dār*, full, loose (a robe), circular, extensive. *gher-ghār-karnā*, to surround, to stop or hinder. *h.*

گهيرا घेरा *gherā*, round, surrounded; m. a circle; a siege or blockade, a fence; vertigo. *gherā ḍālnā*, to surround, to lay a siege. *ghere meṅ paṛnā*, to be surrounded. *h.*

گهيرا *ghairā* (for گهرا), deep. *h. d.*

گهيرنا घेरना *ghernā*, a. to surround, to encircle, hem in, blockade. *ghernā-ghārnā*, *gher-denā*, or *gher-lenā*, to surround, to besiege. *h.*

گهيرني घेरनी *ghernī*, f. a handle for turning a spinning-wheel, a winch. *s.*

گهيك गुह्यक *guhyak*, m. a kind of demigod attendant upon Kuvera. *s.*

گهيكوار घीकुवार *ghīkuwār*, m. name of a medicinal plant (*Aloe perfoliata*). *s.*

گهيگا घेगा *ghegā*, m. } the bronchocele, the
گهيگها घेघा *gheghā*, } goitre, or Derbyshire neck. *h.*

گهيگرا घेगरा *ghegarā* also *ghegharā*, m. the unripe pod of *gram*; also the unripe bole of cotton before it bursts. *h.*

گهيلا घीला *ghīlā*, m. the name of a very large wild creeper. *h.*

گهيلوني घेलौनी *ghelaunī*, a gratuity allowed a purchaser in addition to the article purchased, such as our baker's dozen, *i. e.* thirteen instead of twelve. *h.*

گهينٹا घेंटा *gheṅṭā*, m. } a pig; the unripe pod
گهينٹي घेंटी *gheṅṭī*, f. } of *gram* and other pulses. *h.*

گهينچنا घेंचना *ghenchnā* (v. *khaiṅchnā*), to pull. *h.*

گهينگا घेंगा *ghengā*, a wen, a tumour. *h.*

گهيور घेवर *ghewar*, f. a kind of sweetmeat. *h.*

گهيؤن *ghe,ūṅ* (for گيهون), m. wheat. *d.*

گهيه गुह्य *guhyā*, concealable, requiring concealment; f. the anus, the privy parts. *s.*

گيا गया *gayā* or गैया *gaiyā*, f. a cow. *gayā* (past. part. of *jānā*), gone, been. *gayā-guzariyā*, useless, past and gone. *s.*

گيا गया *gayā*, f. the name of a city in the province of Bihār, and a celebrated place of pilgrimage. *s.*

گياپت ज्ञापित *gyāpit*, notified, revealed. *s.*

گياپك ज्ञापक *gyāpak*, adj. making known, proclaiming; m. an informer. *s.*

گياپن ज्ञापन *gyāpan*, m. the act of making known, apprising. *s.*

گيات ज्ञात *gyāt*, known, understood. *gyāt-siddhānt*, m. a man completely versed in a science. *s.*

گيات ज्ञाति *gyāti*, m. a father; a distant kinsman. *s.*

گياتا ज्ञाता *gyātā*, m. one acquainted with any thing. *gyātā-purush*, a learned man. *s.*

گياتانوي ज्ञातान्वय *gyātānway*, m. name of *Varddhamān*, the last Jin or Jain Pontiff. *s.*

گياتر ज्ञातृ *gyātṛi*, knowing, wise. *s.*

گياتييه ज्ञातेय *gyāteya*, m. relationship, affinity. *s.*

گياره ग्यारह *gyārah* (com. *igārah*), eleven. *h.*

گيارهوان ग्यारहवाँ *gyārahwāṅ*, m. } the ele-
گيارهوين ग्यारहवीं *gyārahwīṅ*, f. } venth. *h.*

گياري गयारी *gayārī*, } f. the land of deceased
گيالي गयाली *gayālī*, } *biswa-dārs*, or tenants, lying unclaimed. *h.*

گيالي गयाली *gayālī*, a class of Gayā Brahmāns, who officiate in certain religious ceremonies performed by pilgrims at that place. *s.*

گيان ज्ञान *gyān*, m. knowledge, understanding, intelligence, intellect, knowing; knowledge of a specific and religious kind which tends to exempt the soul from further transmigration. *gyān daurānā*, to meditate deeply. *s.*

گيان‌درپن ज्ञानदर्पण *gyān-darpan*, m. one of the Jain saints. *s.*

گيانن ज्ञानिन *gyānin*, m. an astrologer, a fortune teller; a sage. *gyāninī*, wise, intelligent. *s.*

گيانوان ज्ञानवान *gyānwān*, } intelligent, know-
گياني ज्ञानी *gyānī*, } ing, sagacious, judicious, one possessing religious wisdom. *s.*

گيانيندريه ज्ञानेन्द्रिय *gyānendriyā*, m. an organ of perception or consciousness. *s.*

گياه *giyāh*, f. grass, straw, green herbage. *p.*

گيبر गेबर *gebar*, m. name of a bird. *h.*

گيپا गेपा *gepā*, m. a nipple. *h.*

گيپا *gīpā*, m. a sheep or goat's ventricle stuffed with minced meat and rice, a pudding. *p.*

گيپاءي *gīpā,ī*, m. a seller of puddings. *p.*

گيپت ज्ञपित *gyapit*, taught, made known. *s.*

گيپت ज्ञप्ति *gyapti*, f. understanding, comprehension. *s.*

گيت गीत *gīt*, m. a song. *gīt-gānā*, to sing. *s.*

گيتا गीता *gītā*, f. a rhapsody or episode, as the *Bhāgavad-gītā*, an episode of the *Mahābhārata*. *s.*

گيتي *gītī* or *getī*, f. the world, the universe. *gītī-afroz* or *gītī-faroz*, world-illumining, an epithet of the sun. *gītī-ārā,e*, world-adorning. *gītī-sitān*, emperor or conqueror of the world. *gītī-naward*, one who has traversed the world, an epithet of Alexander. *p.*

گيتم गीटम *gīṭam*, m. a coarse kind of carpet not coloured. *h.*

گيدا गदा *geaā*, m. a young unfledged bird; (met.) an infant. *h.*

گيدرا गेदरा *gedrā*, simple, ignorant, silly. *h.*

گيدڑ गीदड़ *gīdaṛ*, m. a jackal (*Canis aureus*). *h.*

گيدڑبهبکي गीदड़भभकी *gīdaṛ-bhabkī*, f. bullying, bluster, bravado. *h.*

گيدهه गीध *gīdh*, m. (v. *gidh*) a vulture. *s.*

گيدي *gīdī*, adj. stupid; m. a blockhead. *p.*

گير *gīr*, (in comp.) taking, seizing, holding; as *'ālam-gīr* or *jahān-gīr*, seizing or conquering the world. *p.*

گيرا गैरा *gairā*, m. a sheaf of corn, such as will yield a ser and a quarter of grain, given to village servants in harvest. *h.*

گيراماٹي गेरामाटी *gerā-māṭī*, loam of fine clay. *h.*

گيرا *gīrā*, گيراءي *gīrā,e*, (in comp.) one who holds or takes; detention, captivity. *mīras-gīrā*, one who takes an inheritance, the heir-at-law to an estate. *p.*

گيردار *gīr-dār*, also *gīr o dār*, (lit. take and hold) the confused clamour of combatants; battle or contest; absolute authority or dominion. *p.*

گيرزا *gerzā*, a kind of quail. *d.*

گيرك गैरिक *gairik*, گيرو गेरू *gerū*, m. a kind of red earth or ochre, soil of a red colour. *s.* [ochre. *s.*

گيروءا गेरुआ *gerū,ā*, red, of the colour of

گيروءي गेरुई *gerū,ī*, f. smut, mildew; adj. of the colour of *gerū*. *s.*

گيري *gīrī*, f. (abst. of *gīr*) seizing, &c. *p.*

گيري गेरी *gerī*, گيڑي गेड़ी *geṛī*, f. name of a game, knocking a stick over a line by throwing another stick at it. *h.*

گيسو *gesū*, m. a curl, sidelock, ringlet; pl. *gesū,ān*, curls, ringlets, &c. *p.*

گيشن गेष्ण *geshn*, گيشنو गेष्णु *geshnu*, m. a professional singer, an actor, a mimic, a chaunter of the *Sāma Veda*. *s.*

گيگٹا गेगटा *gegṭā*, m. a crab. *h.*

گيگلي गेगली *geglī*, f. a trollop, a slattern. *h.*

گيل गील *gīl* or गैल *gail*, f. a road, a path. *h.*

گيلا गेला *gelā*, simple. गीला *gīlā*, moist, damp, wet; m. name of a wild creeper (*Mimosa scandens*). *h.*

گيلان *gīlān*, name of a country lying to the south of the Caspian sea and north of *'Irāḳ*, between *Māzanderān*, and *Āzur-bā,ījān*. *p.*

گيلاني *gīlānī*, a native of Gīlān. *p.*

گين *gīn*, (in comp.) denotes abounding with, full of, affected by (generally in an unfavourable sense); as *gham-gīn*, sorrowful; *andoh-gīn*, affected by grief. *p.*

گينا गैना *gainā*, m. a bush; a small species of bullock. *h.*

گينت गैंत *gaint*, گينتي गैंटी *gaintī*, f. a pickaxe. *h.*

گينٹهه गेंठ *genṭh*, f. name of a fish. *h.*

گينج गींज *gīnj*, f. a dish generally used in the festival of the *Muḥarram*. *h.*

گينجنا गींजना *gīnjnā*, n. to crumple. *h.*

گيند गेंद *gend*, m. an elephant. *h.*

گيند गेंद *gend*, f. a ball to play with. *gend-tarī khelna*, n. to play at striking a ball. *s.*

گيندا गेंदा *gendā*, m. marigold; a ball. *s.*

گيندگهوارا *gend-gahwārā*, flowers formed like the scale of a balance tied on to images. *d.*

گيندوا *gendwā*, m. the tapeworm, a worm in the intestines. *d.*

گيندي गेंदी *gendī*, f. a ball (to play with). *s.*

گينڈ गेंड *genḍu*, m. a ball (for playing with). *s.*

گينڈا गैंडा *gainḍā* (also गेंडा *genḍā*), m. a rhinoceros. *s.*

گينڈك गेंडक *genḍak*, m. marigold. *h.*

گينڈو गेंडू *genḍū*, m. a ball for playing with. *h.*

گينگلا *gainglā* (v. *dīwāna*), mad, insane. *d.*

گيني गैनी *gainī*, f. a kind of small chariot drawn by *gainā* bullocks (in Guzerat). *h.*

گيهه गेह *geh*, m. a house, mansion, dwelling. *s.*

گيه *giyah*, گيها *giyahā*, fresh grass, grass in general. *p.*

گيهان *gaihān*, m. the world, time, fortune. *p.*

گيهري गैहरी *gaihrī*, f. demurrage. *h.*

گيهوان गेहूआं *gehū,ān*, m. the colour of wheat; name of a grass; adj. of the colour of wheat. *s.*

گيهون गेहूं *gehūn*, m. wheat. *s.*

ل

ل *lām*, the twenty-third letter of the Arabic alphabet, the twenty-seventh in Persian, and the thirtieth in Hindūstānī. Its sound is that of the English *l* in *live*, *long*. In reckoning by *abjad* it stands for 30. In Persian and Hindūstānī it is frequently permuted into *re*, and *vice versâ*, as *zarrū* for *zallū*, a leech; *bār* for *bāl*, hair; *dīwāl* for *dīwār*, a wall; *talwār* for *tarwār*, a sword.

ل ल *la*, the corresponding letter in the Devanāgarī alphabet.

لا *lā*, a negative or privative particle denoting in Arabic phrases no, not, not at all, by no means, without, as *lā ilāha illa-l-lāh*, there is no God but God. In composition with other nouns it has the effect of our prefixed particles un-, in, as *lā ubālī*, fearing nothing, insolent, licentious, petulant; *lā-budd* or *lā-buddu*, necessarily, infallibly, assuredly, doubtless; adj. unavoidable; *lā-tu'add*, innumerable; *lā-sānī*, (lit.) without a second, "*cui nullus est secundus*," incomparable; *lā-jaram*, necessarily, undoubtedly, indispensably; *lā-jawāb*, incapable of answering, silenced, speechless, disconcerted; *lā-chār* or *-chāra* (pl *lā-chā* *ragān*), without remedy, helpless; destitute, forlorn, poor. *lā-chāragī* or *lā-chārī*, f. forlornness, helplessness. *la-ḥāṣil*, unproductive, profitless. *lā-ḥall*, difficult, not to be solved, abtruse, indissoluble. *lā ḥaul wa lā ḳūwata illā bi-l-lāhi*, there is no power nor virtue but in God, *i.e.* there is no striving against fate or the decrees of Providence. This phrase is repeated by good Musalmāns in the way of condolence on the occurrence of any astounding calamity. It is said also with a view to drive away evil spirits. *lā-kharāj* or *-kharājī*, rent-free, exempt from assessment. *lā-da'wā* or *lā-da'wī*, (lit. no claim) a deed of release, an acquittance in full. *lā-dawā*, incurable, irremediable. *lā-raib*, doubtless, unquestionable. *lā-zāla*, (in prayer) may it never fail. *lā-zabān*, silent, speechless; abuse. *lā-zawāl*, unperishable, eternal. *lā-sukhan*, silent, taciturn; m. abuse, improper talk. *lā-sharīk*, without any partner or associate. *lā-shakk*, doubtless. *lā-'ilāj*, beyond cure, without remedy. *lā-kalām*, taciturn, undisputed. *lā-kalām bāḳī*, an undisputed balance or remainder. *lā makān*, without place, invisible, God. *lā-maut*, immortal, imperishable. *la-nihāyat*, endless, interminable. *lā-wāris*, without heirs. *lā-wāris māl*, property to which there is no heir; hence it escheats to the state. *lā-wārisī*, the condition of being without an heir. *lā-walad*, without offspring, childless. *lā-yajūz*, not allowed, illegal. *lā-yazāl* or *lā-yazal*, the Eternal. *lā'ya'nī*, absurd, obscene, abusive. *lā-yufham*, not to be understood, unintelligible. *lā-yamūt*, immortal, deathless. *a.*

لابہ *lāba*, m. a supplication, request; ridicule, irony, a jest, any thing facetious; flattery. *p.*

لابھ लाभ *lābh*, m. profit, produce, acquisition. *lābh-k.*, to attain, to gain, to acquire. *s.*

لابھالابھ लाभालाभ *lābhālābh*, m. profit and loss. *s.*

لاپھنا लाफना *lāphnā*, n. to jump. *h.*

لات *lāt*, name of an idol worshipped by the pagan Arabians. *a.*

لات लात *lāt*, f. a kick. *lāt mārnā*, to kick. *h.*

لاٹ लाट *lāṭ*, f. an obelisk, a steeple, a minaret, a pillar; a club, a staff; adj. dirty, soiled (as cloth by keeping). *h.*

لاٹا लाटा *lāṭā*, m. a kind of food eaten by the poor (*mahūā* pounded with grain). *h.*

لاٹھ लाठ *lāṭh*, f. an obelisk, pillar, steeple, minaret; club, staff; the vertical part of an oil-mill. *s.*

لاٹھا *lāṭhā*, m. a large club or stick. *d.*

لاٹھي लाठी *lāṭhī*, f. a club, stick, crutch. *lāṭhī-paṭhī*, cudgelling, beating with sticks. *s.*

لاج लाज *lāj*, f. bashfulness, modesty, shame. *s.*

لاجا लाजा *lājā*, fried grain. *s.*

لاجنا *lājnā*, to feel ashamed or abashed. *d.*

لاجورد *lājaward*, m. azure; *Lapis lazuli*. *p.*

لاجوردي *lājawardī*, made of or consisting of *Lapis lazuli*. *p.*

لاجونت लाजवन्त *lāj-want*, modest, bashful, chaste decent. *s.* [tenacity. *p.*

لاجها लाझा *lājhā*, m. viscosity, glutinousness,

لاحق *lāḥiḳ*, touching, adhering, joining; adjoining; an appendage; a dependant. *a.*

لاد लाद *lād*, f. load; bowel. *lād-phānd*, f. loading and packing. *h.*

لادن *lādan*, m. (Gr. Λαδανον) *Ladanum*, a resinous substance exuding from the leaves and branchlets of the *Cistus creticus*. *a. p.*

لادنا लादना *lādnā*, a. to load, to lade. *h.*

لادو लादू *lādū*, fit to carry a load. *lādū-k.*, to mount a horse or colt for the first time. *h.*

لادي लादी *lādī*, f. a small load (particularly a washerman's). *h.*

لاديا लादिया *lādiyā*, m. a loader. *h.*

لاڈ लाड *lāḍ*, m. (v. *lāṛ*) lovingness, &c. *s.*

لاڈلا लाडला *lāḍlā* (v. *lāṛlā*), darling, &c. *s.*

لاڈو लाडु *lāḍū* (v. *laḍḍū*), a kind of sweetmeat. *h.*

لار लार *lār*, m. saliva, spittle. *s.*

لاڑ लाड़ *lāṛ*, m. lovingness, coaxing, the playfulness of a child. *lāṛ-laṛānā*, to fondle a child. *s.*

لاڑکپور लाड़कपूर *lāṛ-kapūr*, *Lāṛ* and *Kapūr*, names of two celebrated and merry minstrels who lived at the court of Akbar. *h.* [*lāṛilā*. *s.*

لاڑلا लाड़ला *lāṛlā*, darling, dear; (in Dakh.)

لازب *lāzib*, firm, solid, adhesive. *a.*

لازم *lāzim*, necessary, urgent, suitable, proper, important, inseparable. *lāzim malzūm*, intimate friendship. *a.*

لازمہ *lāzima*, m. any thing requisite or necessary; whatever is fit and proper. *a.*

لازمي *lāzimī*, f. necessity, urgency. *p.*

لاژورد *lāzhuward* (v. *lājaward*), lapis lazuli. *p.*

لاسا लासा *lāsā*, m. any thing clammy or glutinous; the milk of plants; size, birdlime. *h.*

لاش *lāsh*, } f. a dead body, a corpse, a carcass. *lāsh-paṭṭī*, statement of
لاشہ *lāsha*, } an inquest held on a dead body. *p. h.*

لاشا *lāshā*, m. (for *lāsā*) birdlime. *d.*

لاغر *lāghar*, lean, thin. *p.*

لاغري *lāgharī*, f. leanness. *p.*

لاف *lāf*, f. boasting, vanity, self-praise. *lāf-zan*, a boaster. *lāf-zanī*, f. boasting. *lāf-guzāf*, boasting, gasconading. *lāf-mārnā* or *-zadan*, to boast, to brag. *p.*

لاك *lāk*, m. a kneading-trough; a tortoise, which is also called *lāk-pusht*. *p.*

لاكشا लाक्षा *lākshā*, f. lac, a red dye, or the insect from which it is prepared; its nest is formed of a resinous substance, which is used as sealing wax. *lākshā-bṛiksh* or *lākshā-taru*, m. the palās tree (*Butea frondosa*). *lākshā-prasādan*, m. the red Lodh, the bark of which is used in dyeing as an astringent. *s.*

لاكن *lākin*, but; (more commonly *lekin*, q. v.). *a.*

لاكھ लाख *lakh*, m. gum lac, a kind of wax formed by the *Coccus lacca*; sealing-wax. *lākh-kī battī*, a stick of sealing wax. *lākh lagānā*, to shut up or conceal. *s.*

لاكھ *lākh* (for *laksha*), one hundred thousand. *s.*

لاكهنا लखना *lākhnā*, a. to apply lac. *s.*

لاكهوان *lakhwāṅ*, the hundredth thousand. *s.h.*

لاكهي लाखी *lākhī*, f. a red colour procured from lac. *s.*

لاگ लाग *lāg*, f. striking, hitting, fixing, a stroke; enmity, rancour, spite; affection, love; cost, expenditure; a secret; approach. *lāg lagnā*, to fall in love. *s.*

لاگت लागत *lāgat*, f. expense, cost. *s.*

لاگنا लागना *lāgnā*, n. (v. *lagnā*) to apply, to begin, &c. *s.*

لاگو लागू *lāgū*, desirous, adhering to. *s.*

لاگوٹ *lāguṭ*, love, affection, attachment. *d.*

لاگهو लाघव *lāghav*, m. health, lightness, delicacy, meanness, insignificance, frivolity. *s.*

لاگي लागी *lāgī*, f. a mark, butt; affection, love. *s.*

لال *lāl*, red; dumb; inflamed; m. a ruby. *lāl-sāg*, m. name of a vegetable (*Amaranthus gangeticus, Willd.*). *p.*

لال लाल *lāl*, dear, beloved; m. an infant son, a boy; spittle, saliva; the name of a bird (the male of *Fringilla amandava*). *s.*

لالا लाला *lālā*, m. sir, master; a schoolmaster; a writer, clerk or copyist: it may also denote a slave; f. saliva, spittle. *h.*

لالا *lālā*, m. a head-servant, a major-domo, a babbler, a prating fellow. *p.*

لالاجي लालाजी *lālā-jī*, sir, master; a mode of address used towards a respectable man not of high rank. *h.*

لالاٹك लालाटिक *lālāṭik*, relating to fate or destiny. *s.*

لالاميهہ लालामेह *lālāmeh*, passing mucous urine. *s.*

لال بجهكڑ लालबुझक्कड़ *lāl bujhakkaṛ*, an intelligent person; one who comprehends quickly, or who readily divines what has happened or is to happen from certain symptoms. As a proper name or epithet it is generally used ironically for a wiseacre, an ignorant fool who pretends to more sense than his neighbours: as in the following answer given by a person of this description, when consulted respecting the marks of an elephant's feet in mire, by people who had never seen such an animal: *yih to būjhe Lāl-Bujhakkaṛ aur na būjhe ko,e; pāyan chakkī bāndhkar mat harnā kūdā ho,e.* "Surely *Lāl-Bujhakkaṛ* and none else can understand this: may not an antelope with a millstone tied to his feet have bounded here?" This gentleman is evidently of the same family with the Wise Men of Gotham. Some twenty or thirty years ago there was a very popular little book current in Scotland, attributed to the pen of the celebrated Adam Smith, entitled "The History of Wise Willie and Witty Eppy." Wise Willie is undoubtedly the full brother of *Lāl-Bujhakkaṛ*, for once upon a time the folk of Fife brought him a horseshoe which they had picked up, and he sagely assured them that it was the new moon, only it puzzled him sorely to account for its having fallen in Fife, as he had seen it the night before far to the south-west over a very remote part of the country. *h.s.*

لالت ललित *lālit*, loved, desired, cherished, treated tenderly, coaxed, seduced. *s.*

لالتيه लालित्य *lālitya*, m. beauty, gracefulness, gaiety. *s.*

لالچ लालच *lālach*, m. longing, covetousness, greediness, selfishness, avarice; occasion, view, want. *s.*

لالچي लालची *lālchī*, covetous, greedy, avaricious, interested, selfish. *s.*

لالري लालरी *lālrī* or लालड़ी *lālṛī*, f. a kind of ruby; a false stone resembling a ruby. *h.*

لالسا लालसा *lālsā* or *lālasā*, f. ardent desire, regret, sorrow, longing, asking; the longing of a pregnant woman. *s.*

لال كدو लालकद्दू *lāl-kaddū*, a kind of pumpkin. *h. p.*

لالن लालन *lālan*, adj. wheedling, coaxing; f. a mistress, a sweetheart. *lālin*, m. a seducer. *s.*

لالني लालिनी *lālinī*, f. a wanton woman. *s.*

لاله *lāla*, m. a tulip. *lāla-rukh*, *-rukhsār*, or *-'izār*, having cheeks of the hue of the tulip, vermilion cheeked. *lālā-zār*, a bed or garden of tulips. *lāla-rang*, *-fām*, or *-gūn*, of a tulip colour. *lāla-wash*, tulip-like. *p.*

لالي लाली *lālī*, m. a seducer, deceiver. *s.*

لالي *lālī*, f. redness, blood-colour. *p.*

لآلي *la,ālī* (pl. of لولو), pearls. *a.*

لالي پڑنا लालेपड़ना *lālo parnā*, to be extremely desirous and unable fully to express one's wish. *s. h*

لام *lām*, m. a ringlet; adj. (from the figure of the letter) crooked, curled. *lām kāf kahnā*, to abuse, to give abuse. *a. p.*

لامسه *lāmisa*, m. feeling, touching, the sense of feeling. *a.*

لامع *lāmi'*, splendid, shining, bright. *a.*

لامي *lāmī*, لاميه *lāmīya*, } (lit. of or relating to the letter *lām*) a term used in grammar, equivalent to "the final letter of a verbal root." The idea originates from *lām* being the last letter of the root *f'il*, used in Arabic grammar as a model for inflection and conjugation; a species of poem, of which every couplet ends with the letter *lām*. *a.*

لانا लाना *lānā* (for *le-ānā*), a. to bring; to breed, to produce, to make; to induce, to persuade. *lānā-bandī*, assessment of land according to the number of ploughs employed on it. *h.*

لانپ लांप *lāmp*, f. bound, leap, spring. *h.*

لانچ *lānch*, a bribe. *lānch-khor*, one who is bribed, one who takes suborning fees. *d.*

لانڈا लांडा *lānḍā* (v. *landūṛā*), tailless, &c. *h.*

لانڈگا *lānḍgā*, m. a wolf. *lānḍgī*, a she-wolf. *h.*

لانڑ लांड़ *lāṅṛ*, the *penis* or *membrum virile*. *jum'e-rāt kā lāṅṛ*, a term applied to any thing used up, or unfit for service. *h.*

لانك लाँक *lāṅk*, f. quantity, measure; the loins: bird-lime; chaff. *h.*

لانگل लाङ्गल *lāngal*, m. a plough; the *penis*. *s.*

لانگلك लाङ्गलिक *lāngalik*, m. a kind of poison. *s.*

لانگول लाङ्गूल *lāngūl*, m. a hairy tail; the *penis*. *s.*

لانگهنا लाँघना *lāṅghnā*, a. (v. *phāṅdnā*) to leap or jump over, &c. *s.*

لاو लाव *lāw*, m. a rope for raising water from a well; the cable of a boat; adj. cutting down. *lā,ū*, one who brings. *h.*

لاوا लावा *lāwā*, m. parched grain; f. a sort of quail (*Perdix chinensis*). *s.*

لاوالترا लावालुत्रा *lāwā-lutrā*, m. a talebearer. *h.*

لاوچرس लावचरस *lāw-charas*, irrigation by water raised from wells in the leather bag or bucket called *charas*. *h.*

لاوساو लावसाव *lāwsāw*, m. profit, advantage. *s.*

لاولاو लावलाव *lā,o-lā,o*, m. covetousness, avarice (lit. "bring, bring"). *h.*

لاولشكر *lā,o-lashkar*, an army. *d.*

لاونا लावना *lāwanā* (v. *lānā*), to bring, &c. *h.*

لاونعم *lā wa na'am*, yea and nay, or, more stictly speaking, "nay and yea;" "no and *yes*." *a.*

لاونكي लावणिकी *lāvaṇikī*, } f. beautiful,
لاونيوتي लावण्यवती *lāvanyavatī*, } lovely (woman); a female's name. *s.*

لاونيه लावण्य *lāvaṇya*, m. saltness, beauty, elegance, grace. *s.*

لاوو लावू *lāvū*, f. a pumpkin, a gourd (*Cucurbita lagenaria*). *s.*

لاوه *lāwa*, a jest, joke; game of tipcat. *p.*

لاه लाह *lāh*, m. a kind of cloth resembling gauze. *h.*

لاه लाह *lāh*, m. advantage, welfare; lac. *s.*

لاها लाहा *lāhā*, m. advantage, profit. *s.*

لاهوت *lāhūt*, the Divinity, the Divine Being. *a.*

لاهور *lāhaur* or *lāhor*, the city and kingdom of Lahore. *p. h.*

لاهوري *lāhaurī* or *lāhorī*, of or relating to Lahore. *lāhorī namak*, rock salt from Lahore. *h. p.*

لاهي लाही *lāhī*, f. name of a plant. *h.*

لاءي लाई *lā,ī*, f. sweetmeat, parched rice mixed with sugar. *h.*

لاءي *lā,e*, black mud, sediment; a fold or ply. *p.*

لائح *lā,iḥ*, evident, clear, manifest. *a.*

لائحت *lā,iḥat* or *lā,iḥa*, f. any thing clear or manifest; proof, clearness, demonstration. *a.*

لائق *lā,iḳ*, } worthy, adapted, proper, suit-
لائقه *lā,iḳa*, } able, fit, able, capable, qualified. *a.*

لائقي *lā,iḳī*, f. fitness, capability. *a.*

لايك लायक *lāyak*, (in comp.) bringing, getting, procuring. *s. h.*

لائم *lā,im*, a slanderer, an accuser. *a.*

لب *lubb*, m. the essence of any thing; the heart; the soul. the mind; a kernel. *a.*

لب *lab*, m. lip; brim, edge; shore, coast, bank, margin (of a lake, &c.). *lab-basta*, having closed lips, silent. *lab-bastagī*, f. silence. *lab-k͟hā*, fastidious, fretful; (sub.) a prig. *labi dāryā*, the sea-shore, river-side. *lab o lahja*, m. conversation. *lab-rez*, brimful, overflowing. *lab-rezī*, f. brimfulness, abundance. *p.*

لباب *libāb* (pl. of لبيب), the wise, the prudent. *a.*

لبا लिब्बा *libbā*, m. a slap, blow, buffet. *h.*

لباد *labbād*, a felt manufacturer. *a.*

لباده *lubāda* (also *labāda*), m. a wrapper, great coat, an outer garment. *a.*

لبار लबार *labār*, m. a liar, a talker, a babbler. *h.*

لباڑ *labāṛ*, plunder, spoil. *d.*

لباڑنا *labāṛnā*, a. to plunder, to spoil. *d.*

لباڑي *labāṛī*, f. a plunderer, a ravager. *d.*

لباس *libās*, m. apparel, garments, clothes, dress; a veil; forgery. *a.*

لباسي *libāsī*, false, forged, counterfeit. *a.*

لبالب *lab-ā-lab*, brimful, running over. *p.*

لبان *lubān*, frankincense, *olibanum*; resin of the *Boswellia serrata, Roxb.* See *As. Res.*, vol. ix.; (at least in India) Benzoin. *a.*

لبخا *lab-k͟hā*, m. a fop, a prig, a beau. *lab-k͟hā-pak͟hnā*, a thorough fop, a regular exquisite. *p.*

لبد *libd*, felt-cloth. *lubad* or *lubbad*, much wealth.

لبدار लबदार *labdār*, mud, thick mud formed by water flooding a stiff soil. *h.*

لبده लब्ध *labdh*, gained, acquired, attained got. *lubdh*, covetous, greedy, desirous; m. a lecher a libertine. *s.*

لبدهپتر लब्धपुत्र *labdha-putr*, an adopted son. *s.*

لبدهچيتا लब्धचेता *labdh-chetā*, recovered, restored to one's senses; come to a right mind. *s.*

لبدهداس लब्धदास *labhda-dās*, a slave received as a gift or transfer.

لبدهك लुब्धक *lubdhak*, m. a hunter, a libertine, a rake, a whoremonger, a covetous or greedy man. *s.*

لبدي लुबदी *lubdī*, f. a poultice, a cataplasm. *h.*

لبرا लबरा *labrā*, } m. a liar, a tattler; adj
لبڑا लबड़ा *labṛā*, } left-handed. *h.*

لبرچٹاءي लबरचटाई *labar-chaṭā,ī* or *labaṛ-chaṭā,ī*, f. giving the breast to a child when it contains no milk. *h.*

لبرسبر लबरसबर *labar-sabar* or *labaṛ-sabaṛ*, m. tittle-tattle, nonsense. *h.*

لبڑخندا *labaṛ-khandā*, } a mischievous child
لبڑخندي *labāṛ-khandī*, } (also *labaṛ-khandā*). *h.*

لبرغٹا *labar-ghaṭṭā*, } लबरघट्टा { fastidious,
لبرگھٹا *labar-ghattā*, } { fretful, touchy. *h.*

لبڑنا *labaṛnā*, to act or talk foolishly. *d.*

لبڑو लबड़ो *labṛo*, f. false and talkative (a woman). *h.*

لبلب लबलब *lablab*, m. grit, sand, gravel. *h.*

لبلب *lublub*, kind, benevolent to inferiors. *a.*

لبلبا लबलबा *lablabā*, clammy, glutinous. *lablabā* or *liblibā*, m. the pancreas. *h.*

لبلبه *lablaba* or *libliba*, m. the pancreas. *h.*

لب‌لوس लबलोस *lab-los*, naked, shapeless; f. flattery. *h.*

لبنان *lubnān*, Mount Libanus. *a.*

لبنه *libna*, a brick or tile; a mural quadrant. *a.*

لبني लबनी *labnī*, f. the pot in which *tāṛī* is collected from the tree. *h.*

لبوب *lubūb* (pl. of لب), essences, &c. *a.*

لبهاذ लुभाना *lubhānā*, a. (v. *lalchānā*) to allure, &c. *s.*

لبهيه लभ्य *labhya*, attainable, procurable. *s.*

لبي *lābe* (for *labbaik*, q. v.), yes, sir; hey! *p.*

لبي लबी *labī*, f. the juice of the sugar-cane when boiling into sugar. *h.*

لبيدا लबेदा *labedā*, m. a club, a cudgel. *h.*

لبيرا लबेरा *laberā*, m. name of a fruit (*Cordia myxa*). *h.*

لبيك *labbaik*, what do you want with me? here I am; what would you have? *labbaiki ijābat bolnā*, to depart this life (used in a serious and respectful manner). *a.*

لپ लप *lap*, f. a handful, the space in the palm of the hand closed so as to hold water. *h.*

لپ लिपि *lipi*, f. writing, a written paper. *s.*

لپا लप्पा *lappā*, m. brocade, gold or silver cloth. *h.*

لپاٹي लपाटी *lapāṭī*, f. lying, tattling. *h.*

لپاٹيا लपाटिया *lapāṭiyā*, m. a tattler, a liar. *h.*

لپانا लिपाना *lipānā*, a. to cause to smear or plaster. *s.*

لپانك लपानक *lapānah*, slender, thin. *h.*

لپاءي लिपाई *lipā,ī*, f. smearing, plastering. *s.*

لپت लिप्त *lipt*, besmeared, anointed; contaminated; embraced, united. *lupt*, gone, lost. *luptatā*, f. disappearance. *s.*

لپٹ लपट *lapaṭ*, f. odour; warmth, glow. *h.*

لپٹا लपटा *lapṭā*, m. a kind of molasses; relation, connection; name of a grass (*Panicum verticillatum*); (v. *lapṭī*). *h.*

لپٹانا लिपटाना *lipṭānā*, } n. to cling, to stick,
لپٹنا लिपटना *lipaṭnā*, } to adhere (also *lapṭānā*, *lapaṭnā*). *h.*

لپٹاو लिपटाव *lipṭā,o*, m. adhesion. *h.*

لپٹي लपटी *lapṭī*, f. pap, any glutinous liquid food. *h.*

لپ‌جهپ लपझप *lap-jhap*, nimble, quick, [fast. *h.*

لپچي लपची *lapchī*, f. a skate (the fish). *h.*

لپري लुपरी *luprī*, f. pap. *h.*

لپڑي लिपड़ी *lipṛī*, f. an old ragged turban. *h.*

لپسي लपसी *lapsī*, f. a glutinous kind of food, pottage, pap, spoonmeat. *s.*

لپك लपक *lapak*, f. a flash (of lightning, &c.); the spring (of a tiger, &c.); a bounce, a snatch. *h.*

لپكا लपका *lapkā*, m. a snatch; nimbleness; a bad custom or habit. *h.*

لپيكار लिपिकार *lipi-kār*, } m. a scribe, a
لپيكر लिपिकर *lipi-kar*, } writer. *s.*

لپكانا लपकाना *lapkānā*, a. to snatch, to seize. *h.*

لپكنا लपकना *lapaknā*, n. to flash (as lightning); to rush, pounce, or spring on a prey (as the tiger, &c.); a. to snatch or seize suddenly. *h.*

لپكي लपकी *lapkī*, f. a stitch; (in Dakh.) *lupkī*, fear. *h.*

لپ‌لپ लुपलुप *lup-lup*, m. lapping (as a dog drinking). *lap-lap*, nimble, quick. *lap-lap khānā*, to eat quickly. *h.*

لپنا लिपना *lipnā*, n. to be plastered, smeared, or washed over. *s.* [&c. *s*

لپوانا लिपवाना *lipwānā*, a. to cause to plaster,

لپي लिपी *lipī*, f. writing, a written paper. *s.*

لپيٹ लपेट *lapeṭ*, m. f. a fold, a ply, envelope, twist bandage, fillet. *lapeṭ-jhapeṭ* or *-sapeṭ*, f. evasion, subterfuge. *h.*

لپيٹا *lapeṭā* (v. *lapeṭ*), a fold, a ply, &c. *d.*

لپيٹن लपेटन *lepeṭan*, f. a roller on which cloth is wound in the loom; a button, &c. *h.*

لپيٹنا लपेटना *lapeṭnā*, a. to wrap up, to fold, to enclose, to pack, to roll, to spread. *h.*

لپيٹوان लपेटवाँ *lapeṭwāṅ*, twisted, ornamented with gold or silver thread wound round it. *h.*

لت लत *lat*, f. bad habits, whim, whimsey; (for *lāt*) a kick. *lat-khorā*, kicked, beaten; contemptible, mean; (sub.) a slave; a threshold. *lat-zada*, of bad habits, vicious. *lat-kob*, beating, cudgelling. *lat-kundan*, ignominious treatment. *lat-mardan-k.*, to trample or tread on. *lat-mardan meṅ paṛnā*, n. to be trampled under foot or disgraced. *h.*

لت लत *lat*, f. the hanging branch of a creeper. *s.*

لتا लता *latā*, f. a creeper, vine; the musk-creeper, said to grow in the Deccan. *s.*

لتا लत्ता *lattā*, m. a rag, tatter. *p. h.*

لتادرم लताद्रुम *latā-drum*, m. a timber-tree (*Shorea robusta*). *s.*

لتاڑ लताड़ *latāṛ*, f. calamity, misfortune, labour. *h. d.*

لتاڑنا लताड़ना *latāṛnā*, a. to work, to cause to toil, to exhaust by labour, to bring down, to affront, to insult, to irritate. *h.*

لتاکام लताकाम *latā-kām*, name of a most famous woman, a heroine of romance (properly *kāma-latā*). *s.*

لتپتا *lutputa*, savoury, delicious. *d.*

لتر लतर *latar*, f. an old shoe. *h.*

لترا लुतरा *lutrā*, m. a sycophant, a tell-tale, a babbler, a tattler, a backbiter. *h.*

لترپتر *latar-patar*, wet, soaked through. *d.*

لترہ *latra*, a part, a fragment; a man rendered lazy by fat; adj. rent, torn; old, base, vile. *lutra*, a tell-tale; adj. expelled, driven off. *p.*

لتري लतरी *latrī*, f. an old shoe; a kind of vetch. *h.*

لتکا लतिका *latikā*, f. a twining plant, a creeper. *s.*

لتھاڑنا लिथाड़ना *lithāṛnā*, a. to draggle. *h.*

لتھر लथर *lathar*, } stiff, rigid. *lathaṛ-pathaṛ*,
لتھڑ लथड़ *lathaṛ*, } besmeared with mud, &c. so as to walk with difficulty. *h.*

لتھڑنا लथड़ना *latharnā* or लिथड़ना *litharnā*, n. to be draggled. *h.*

لتھیڑنا लथेड़ना *latheṛnā*, a. to draggle or besmear with dirt. *h.*

لتي लत्ती *lattī*, f. the string of a child's top; a cloth tied to the end of a pole to direct the flight of pigeons; a kick when swimming. *lattī-k.*, to run away. *h.*

لتيا लतिया *latiyā*, a person of bad habits. *h.*

لتيانا लतियाना *latiyānā*, a. to kick; to beat. *h.*

لٹ लट *laṭ*, f. tangled hair, a clotted lock; a tadpole; m. a blockhead, a fool; fault, defect. *laṭ-jānā*, to become entangled. *liṭ*, a kind of bread. *h.*

لٹا लटा *laṭā*, reduced (by sickness, &c.), lean, emaciated. *h.*

لٹا लट्टा *laṭṭā*, a measuring rod or pole: twenty square *laṭṭās* make a *bighā*.

لٹاپٹا लटापटा *laṭā-paṭā*, m. baggage, furniture, effects. *h.*

لٹارا *luṭārā*, m. a thief, a robber, a plunderer, freebooter. *d.*

لٹانا लिटाना *liṭānā*, a. to cause to lie, to lay down, to place. *h.*

لٹانا लुटाना *luṭānā*, a. to squander; to cause to plunder or be plundered, from *loṭnā*, to cause to wallow or roll about. *luṭā-luṭā kar mārnā*. to beat severely. *h.*

لٹارنا लिटारना *liṭārnā*, a. (v. *liṭānā*) to lay, &c. *h.*

لٹاءي लटाई *laṭā,ī*, f. a kind of roller on which the string of a kite is wound. *h.*

لٹ پٹ लटपट *laṭ-paṭ*, staggering; tripping, stammering (from fear); folded, tangled. *h.*

لٹ پٹا लटपटा *laṭ-paṭā*, playful, innocent, wanton, frisky, humorous; irregularly folded (a turban). *h.*

لٹ پٹانا लटपटाना *laṭpaṭānā*, n. to stagger, to trip. *h.*

لٹ پٹي लटपटी *laṭpaṭī*, f. stumbling, staggering, swaggering. *h.*

لٹس लुटस *luṭas* or *luṭṭas*, m. ruin, devastation, plunder. *s.*

لٹک लटक *laṭak*, f. resemblance; adj. hanging, dangling; an affected motion in blandishment or coquetry. *laṭak-chāl*, f. affected gait, coquetry. *h.*

لٹکا लटका *laṭkā*, m. incantation, conjuring-rod, a philtre, a quack medicine or nostrum. *h.*

لٹکانا लटकाना *laṭkānā*, a. to hang, to make dangle, to suspend. *h.*

لٹکاو लटकाव *laṭkāw* or *laṭkā,o*, m. hanging, suspension. *h.*

لٹکن लटकन *laṭkan*, m. any thing hanging; drops (worn in the ear); a fruit with which clothes are dyed yellow; name of a handsome green bird which often remains hanging by the feet; a stand for waterpots; the drops of a crystal lustre. *h.*

لٹکنا लटकना *laṭaknā*, n. to hang, to dangle, to be suspended. *h.*

لٹن लटन *laṭan*, crop early sown, that is sown during the cold season. *h.*

لٹنا लुटना *luṭnā*, n. to be sacked or plundered. *s.*

لٹو लट्टू *laṭṭū* or *luṭṭū*, m. a child's top. *laṭṭū honā*, n. to fall in love. *h.*

لٹوانا लुटवाना *luṭwānā* (also *luṭwā-lenā*), to cause to be sacked or given up to plunder. *s.*

لٹورا लटोरा *laṭorā*, } m. name of a bird, the
لٹوڑا लटोड़ा *laṭoṛā*, } butcher bird (*Lanius*). *h.*

لٹوري लटूरी *laṭūrī*, } f. a small curl, lock, ring-
لٹوڑي लटूड़ी *laṭūṛī*, } let. *laṭūriyān*, tangled short hair. *h.*

لٹویا लुटवैया *luṭwaiyā*, m. a plunderer, a spendthrift. *s.*

لٹھ लठ *laṭh*, m. a stick, club. *laṭh-bāz*, a cudgel player. *laṭh-bāzī*, f. cudgelling. *h.*

لٹھا लट्ठा *laṭṭhā*, m. a beam, timber. *h.*

لٹھالٹھم लठालठम *laṭhā-laṭham*, m. } mutual
لٹھالٹھي लठालठी *laṭhā-laṭhī*, f. } beating with cudgels. *h.*

لٹھ پٹھ लठपठ *laṭh-paṭh*, wet, soaked through. *h.*

لٹھر लट्ठर *latthar*, f. slack, remiss, lazy. *h.*

لٹھي *lathī* or *latthī*, f. a staff, a cudgel. *h.*

لٹھیوالا लठीवला *lathī-wālā*, a man armed with a bludgeon: many such are employed by zamīndārs, indigo planters, and others, with a view to settle all disputes respecting lands and boundaries. *h.*

لٹھیانا लठियाना *lathiyānā*, a. to belabour, to cudgel. *h.*

لٹي लिट्टी *litti*, f. balls or thick cakes of paste baked on coals. *s.*

لٹیا लुटिया *lutiyā*, f. a small pot. *h.*

لٹیر लुटेरु *luteru*, لٹیرا लुटेरा *luterā*, m. a squanderer, a prodigal, spendthrift. *s.*

لثات *lisāt* (pl. of لثت *lisat*), the gums. *a.*

لج *lujj*, the main ocean, an abyss *a.*

لجا लज्जा *lajjā*, f. (v. *lāj*) modesty, bashfulness. *lajjā-bān*, ashamed, abashed. *lajjā-rahit*, shameless, void of shame. *lajjā-shīl*, bashful, of a modest disposition. *lajjā-hīn*, shameless, impudent. *s.*

لجاجت *lajājat*, f. importunity, adulation. *a.*

لجاکار लज्जाकार *lajjā-kār*, لجاکاري लज्जाकारी *lajjā-kārī*, shameful, causing or occasioning shame (also *lajjā-kar*). *s.*

لجالو लजालू *lajālū*, m. the name of a sensitive plant (*Mimosa natans* or *pudica*); adj. bashful. *s.*

لجام *lajām*, m. (v. *lagām*) a bridle. *a. p.*

لجامان लज्जामान *lajjā-mān*, abashed, ashamed. *s.*

لجانا लजाना *lajānā*, n. to be ashamed or abashed, to blush. *s.*

لجانوت लज्जान्वित *lajjānwit*, لجاوان लज्जावान *lajjāwān*, لجاوتي लज्जावती *lajjāwatī*, ashamed, abashed, modest, bashful. *s.*

لجاونتي लजावन्ती *lajā-wantī*, f. the sensitive plant (v. *lajālū*). *s.*

لجت लज्जित *lajjit* or लिज्जत *lajjat*, abashed, ashamed. *s.*

لجکارکا लजकारिका *laj-kārikā*, f. the sensitive plant (*Mimosa pudica*). *s.*

لجلاج लजलाज *laj-lāj*, name of the inventor of chess (according to the Arabs); an instructor in gambling. *s.*

لجلجا लुजलुजा *lujlujā* or लजलजा *lajlajā*, clammy, viscous, glutinous. *h.*

لجلجانا लजलजाना *lajlajānā*, n. to become softened; a. to soften. *h.*

لجمان लज्जमान *lajjamān*, being ashamed. *s.*

لجوانا लजवाना *lajwānā*, a. to make one ashamed, to cause one to blush, to shame or put to shame. *s.*

لجونتي लजवन्ती *lajwantī*, f. (v. *lajālū*) bashful, &c. *s.*

لجه *lujja*, m. deep water, the middle of the sea, an abyss. *a.*

لجهڑي लिजड़ी *lijhṛī*, f. after-birth, placenta. *h.*

لجیا लज्या *lajyā*, f. modesty, bashfulness. *s.*

لجیانا लजियाना *lajiyānā*, n. to blush, to be ashamed. *s.*

لجیلا लजीला *lajīlā*, bashful, modest. *s.*

لچ लुच *luch*, pure, mere, stark naked. *luch-bahādur*, a vagabond. *luch-pan*, m. libertinism, rakishness. *h.*

لچا लुच्चा *luchchā*, m. a vagabond, a libertine, a rake, a profligate, a bankrupt; adj. low, mean. *h.*

لچا *lachchā*, a kind of ornament for the neck worn by women. *h.*

لچامي लुचामी *luchchāmī*, f. libertinism. *h.*

لچانا लचाना *lachānā*, a. to bend, to bow, to crook. *h.*

لچپن लुचपन *luch-pan*, m. profligacy, libertinism. *h.*

لچر लचर *lachar*, m. a simpleton a ninny, a noodle, a foolish fellow. *h.*

لچرا लुचरा *luchrā*, m. a spider; (in Dakh.) a sycophant, &c. (same as *lutrā*, q. v.). *h.*

لچك लचक *lachak*, f. spring, elasticity; (in Dakh.) *lichik*, m. a sprain, a bruise. *h.*

لچکا लचका *lachkā*, m. jolt; a barge, a kind of boat; part. bent. *h.*

لچکانا लचकाना *lachkānā*, n. to jolt, to strain. *h.*

لچکتا लचकता *lachaktā*, elastic, springy. *h.*

لچکنا लचकना *lachaknā*, n. to spring, to bend. *h.*

لچلچ *lach-lach*, the sound made by a dog when drinking. *d.*

لچلچانا लचलचाना *lachlachānā*, n. to be clammy or glutinous; to be elastic; to lick up. *h.*

لچنا लचना *lachnā*, n. to bend, to be bent. *h.*

لچو लिचू *lichū*, a kind of fruit something like a plum, but much sweeter. *h.*

لچها लच्छा *lachchhā*, m. a bundle (of thread), a ball or skein of thread, &c.; a necklace fitting closely round the neck. *h.*

لچهمن लक्ष्मण *lachhman*, m. the name of the son of *Dasharatha* by *Sumitrā* (the half-brother of *Rāmachandra*, q. v.). *s.*

لچهمي लक्ष्मी *lachhmī*, f. prosperity, wealth; splendour, beauty. In Hindū mythology, the goddess of abundance, the daughter of the ocean and wife of *Vishnu*. She is also called *Padmā*, *Kamalā*, and *Shrī*, and is supposed to be the Ceres of the ancients. *s.*

لچهن लच्छन *lachchhan*, m. (for *lakshan*) sign, mark, symptom, feature. *s.*

لچهنا लछना *lachhnā*, m. a species of grain (*Cynosurus coracanus*), called by Europeans "Natchenny." *h.*

لچهي लछी *lachhī*, blood and water mixing. *h.*

لچي लिची *lichī* (v. *lichū*), a kind of fruit. *h.*

لچيلا लचीला *lachīlā*, elastic, flexible. *h.*

لچئي लुचई *lucha,ī*, a species of cake. *h.*

لحاظ *liḥāẓ*, m. a look, a glance, view, sense, respect, observing attentively. *liḥāẓ-k.*, to observe, to notice; to mind, to regard. *a.*

لحاف *liḥāf*, m. a coverlet, a quilt, a counterpane; a quilted upper garment; (met.) a wife. *a.*

لحد *laḥad*, f. a niche in the side of a sepulchre in which dead bodies are deposited; (in Hindūstān) a place where the dead are washed. *a.*

لحظ *laḥẓ*, looking through half-shut eyes. *a.*

لحظه *laḥẓa*, m. a moment, the twinkling of an eye; a look, a glance. *a.*

لحم *laḥm*, m. flesh, meat; solder; adj. carnivorous. *a.*

لحن *laḥn*, f. a sound, a note; melody, modulation. *a.*

لحيت *liḥyat* or *liḥya*, beard, moustaches. *liḥyatu-t-tais*, goat's beard, the name of a certain herb (*Hypœstes*). *a.*

لخ *lukh*, a flag, a reed. *p.*

لخت *lakht*, m. a piece, bit, part, portion, some, a little, somewhat. *lakhti jigar*, a piece of one's liver (generally applied as an expression of endearment to a child). *p.*

لخلخ *lakhlakh*, weak, lean, feeble. *s.*

لخلخا *lakhlakhā*, } odour, perfume; a cephalic
لخلخه *lakhlakha*, } medicine; a censer in which to burn odours. *p.*

لخلخانا *lakhlakhānā*, n. to be starved, to be so reduced by hunger as to be unable to move. *d.*

لدانا लदाना *ladānā*, a. to load. *h.*

لداو लदाव *ladāw*, m. a load; an arched roof or terrace. *h.*

لدپهندا लदफन्दा *lad phandā*, m. packing and loading. *h.*

لدغ *ladgh*, } sting of a scorpion, bite of a
لدغه *ladgha*, } snake. *a.*

لدنا लदना *ladnā*, n. to be loaded, to be laden. *lad-lenā*, to load one's self, to mount (a horse, &c.). *h.*

لدو लड्डू *laddū*, m. (also *laḍḍū*) a kind of sweetmeat, made of sugar with cocoa-nut kernel rasped, and cream, and formed into balls. *man ke laḍḍū khānā*, to build castles in the air. *ṭhag ke laḍḍū khā baiṭhnā*, to be distracted, foolish, or intoxicated (spoken of one who talks or acts absurdly in opposition to his usual good sense. The allusion is taken from the notorious *ṭhags*, who join a party of travellers, and having got into their confidence, entertain them with sweetmeats impregnated with *datura* or other intoxicating drug, that they may murder and rob them with impunity while under its stupifying influence). *h.*

لدوانا लदवाना *ladwānā*, to cause to load. *h.*

لڈك लड्डुक *laḍḍuk*, m. a kind of sweetmeat, a ball of flour fried with oil or ghī, and mixed with sugar and spices. *h.*

لڈو लड्डू *laḍḍū*, m. (same as *laddū*, q. v.). *h.*

لذات *lazzāt* (pl. لذت), enjoyments, &c. *a.*

لذت *lazzat*, f. pleasure, enjoyment, delight, flavour, deliciousness, taste, savour, sweetness. *lazzat-yāb*, obtaining pleasure. *a.*

لذيذ *lazīz*, delicious, pleasant, delightful sweet, savoury, luscious. *a.*

لرچها लर्छा *larchhā*, m. a skein. *h.*

لر लर *lar*, a measuring rod for the measurement of land; 400 square *lars* make a *bīghā*. *h.*

لرز *larz*, } trembling, fear, terror. *p.*
لرزا *larzā*, }

لرزان *larzān*, trembling, fearing. *p.*

لرزانا *larzānā*, a. to cause to shake, quiver, &c. *p.*

لرزش *larzish* f. shivering, quaking, trembling, quivering. *p.*

لرزنا *laraznā*, n. to shake, to quiver, to tremble. *p. h.*

لرزه *larza*, m. shaking, shivering; an earthquake; tremor. *p.*

لرزي *larzī*, f. an ague, the cold fit of an ague. *p.*

لرزيدن *larzīdan*, n. to tremble, to shiver. *p.*

لروا लिरवा *lirwā* or *liru,ā*, rice straw (especially such as is fit for fodder). *h.*

لڑ लड़ *laṛ*, f. a string (of pearls, &c.), a thread, a row; a strand of a rope or cord; a party. *laṛ meṅ rahnā*, to be in one's party. *h.*

لڑا लड़ा *laṛā*, (in comp. with a numeral) string or thread, as *ek-laṛā*, of one string; *do-laṛā*, of two, &c. *h.*

لڑاك लड़ाक *laṛāk*, } quarrelsome, contentious,
لڑاكا लड़ाका *laṛākā*, } pugnacious; a good fighter; (in Dakh.) *laṛākh*. *s.*

لڑالڑي लड़ालड़ी *laṛā-laṛī*, mutual quarrelling. *s. h.*

لڑانا लड़ाना *laṛānā*, a. to make fight, to fight, to bait, to play. *s.*

لڑانكا लड़ांका *laṛaṅkā*, quarrelsome, contentious. *s.*

لڑائي लड़ाई *laṛā,ī*, f. battle, quarrel, war, fight. *laṛā,ī-k.*, to war, to fight. *s.*

لڑباولا लड़बावला *laṛbāwlā*, mad, foolish. *h.*

لڑبڑ लड़बड़ *laṛbaṛ*, stammering; reeling. *h.*

لڑبڑا लुड़बुड़ा *luṛbuṛā*, rash, inconsiderate; meddlesome, intrusive. *h.*

لڑبڑانا लड़बड़ाना *laṛbaṛānā*, n. to stutter, to stammer; to reel, to stagger. *h.*

لڑت *laṛat*, quarrelling, strife, contest. *d.*

لڑکا लुड़का *luṛkā*, m. a Hindū ornament worn in the ears. *h.*

لڑکا लड़का *laṛkā*, m. a boy, child, infant, babe. *laṛkā-bālā*, m. a child. *laṛkā-laṛkī*, boys and girls, children. *s.*

لڑکاپن लड़कापन *laṛkā-pan*, m. childhood. *s.*

لڑکاکول *laṛ-kākul*, name of a mountain tribe in Chattisghar. *h.*

لڑکائي लड़काई *laṛkā,ī*, f. childhood, boyhood; the being of a child or boy. *s.*

لڑک بدھ लड़कबुद्धि *laṛak-buddhi*, f. childishness, the wisdom of a child. *s.*

لڑک پن लड़कपन *laṛak-pan*, m. childhood. *s.*

لڑکھرانا लड़खराना *laṛkharānā*, } to stutter, to
لڑکھڑانا लड़खड़ाना *laṛkhaṛānā*, } stammer; to stagger, to trip. *h.*

لڑکھڑي लुड़खुड़ी *luṛ-khuṛī*, f. rolling; flattery, coaxing, wheedling. *h.*

لڑکھنا लुड़खना *luṛakhnā*, n. to roll, to fall (or roll) off, to slip, to slide. *h.*

لڑکي लड़की *laṛkī*, f. a girl, a damsel, a daughter. *s.* [fighting, battling. *s.*

لڑنا लड़ना *laṛnā*, n. to fight, to quarrel; m.

لڑنا *luṛnā* (also *liṛnā*), to wallow, welter, grovel (v. *luṛhnā*). *d.*

لڑنت लड़न्त *laṛant*, contentious, quarrelling; f. fighting, contending. *s.*

لڑويا *laṛwaiyā*, one who seeks combat, a quarrelsome, combative person. *d.*

لڑھا लढ़ा *laṛhā*, m. a cart. *h.*

لڑھانا लुढ़ाना *luṛhānā*, a. to roll over, to upset. *s.*

لڑھکنا लुढ़कना *luṛhaknā*, } n. to roll, to be
لڑھنا लुढ़ना *luṛhnā*, } tossed about, to be upset. *s.*

لڑھي लढ़ी *laṛhī*, } f. a small cart, a sled or
لڑھيا लढ़िया *laṛhiyā*, } sledge. *h.*

لڑھيا लुढ़िया *luṛhiyā*, f. (v. *loṛhā*) a pestle, &c. *h.*

لڑھيانا लुढ़ियाना *luṛhiyānā*, also लढ़ियाना *laṛhiyānā*, a. to double hem a garment. *h.*

لڑي लड़ी *laṛī*, f. a string (of pearls, &c.). *h.*

لڑيانا लड़ियाना *laṛiyānā*, a. to thread, to string. *h.*

لزج *lazij*, adhesive, tenacious. *a.*

لزوجت *lazūjat*, f. tenacity, adhesiveness. *a.*

لزوم *luzūm*, m. expediency, necessity, behoving, what is requisite. *a.*

لس लस *las*, m. tenacity, viscosity, glutinousness. *las-dār*, viscous, glutinous, clammy. *las-dārī*, f. tenacity, viscosity, glutinousness. *s.*

لساع *lassā'*, stinging (as a scorpion, &c.). *a.*

لسان *lisān*, f. the tongue, language, idiom, dialect. *lisānu-s-saur*, bugloss, borage. *lisānu-l-ḥamal*, plantain. *lisānu-l-'aṣāfīr*, the seed of the ash-tree. *lisānu-l-kalb*, the herb dog's tongue (*Cynoglossum*). *lassān*, very eloquent. *a.*

لساني *lassānī*, } f. eloquence, elocu-
لسانيت *lassāniyat*, } tion. *a.*

لست लसित *lasit*, seen, evident, obvious. *s.*

لسکنا लसकना *lasaknā*, n. to become viscous, to become moist (or stiff) as a field. *h.*

لس لسا लसलसा *las-lasā*, viscous, clammy, adhesive. *s.*

لسلسات *laslasāt*, clamminess, viscosity. *d.*

لس لسانا लसलसाना *laslasānā*, n. to be clammy or glutinous, to agglutinate. *a.*

لسماماٹي *lasmāmāṭī* (v. *lashmāmāṭī*). *h.*

لسنا लसना *lasnā*, n. to become, to befit; to shine. *Bihārī Lāl says: Sakhī sohat gopāl ke ur gunjan kī māl; bāhar lasat hiye mano dābānal kī jwāl*; "Oh my friend! that necklace of the seeds of *abrus* adorns the breast of *Gopāl*; it appears opposite to his heart like the flame of a fire which consumes the forest." (A speech of *Rādhā*, in the *Satsa,ī*, on seeing *Krishna* wear such a necklace, the work of her rival. She compares it to fire, both from the colour and the effect which the sight of it has on her bosom). *s.*

لسوڑا लसोड़ा *lasoṛā* or लिसौड़ा *lisauṛā*, m. name of a glutinous fruit (*Cordia myxa*). *baṛā lasoṛā* (*Cordia latifolia, Roxb.*). *s.*

لسي लस्सी *lassī*, milk and water. *h.*

لسيانا लसियाना *lasiyānā*, a. to be viscous, to be clammy. *s.*

لشٹم پشٹم लशटम पशटम *lashṭam pashṭam*, topsy-turvy, with difficulty, with much ado. *h.*

لشکر *lashkar*, m. an army. *lashkar khalāṣ*, a trull, a strumpet. *lashkar-gāh*, f. a camp. *pesh-lashkar*, the advance guard, the van. *pas lashkar*, the rear. In India the word has gradually come to signify a native sailor, vulgarly called a "lascar," or, per metathesin, a "rascal:" it is also applied to tent-pitchers, inferior artillerymen, and coolies, or camp followers, &c. *a.*

لشکرکش *lashkar-kash*, the leader of an army, a general. *lashkar-kashī*, f. generalship, the leading forth of an army. *p.*

لشکري *lashkarī*, m. a soldier, any thing belonging to an army; adj. military. *p.*

لشماماٹي लशमामाटी *lashmāmāṭī*, adhesive clay land. *h.* [a freckle. *h.*

لشن लशुन *lashun*, m. garlic (*Allium sativum*)

لطافت *laṭāfat*, f. pleasantness, facetiousness, wit. *a.* [witticisms. *a.*

لطائف *laṭā,if* (pl. of لطيفه), pleasantries,

لطف *luṭf*, m. courtesy, kindness, benignity, graciousness, gentleness; wit, pleasantry. *a.*

لطفي *luṭfī*, f. an adopted child, or child brought up in the family. *a.*

لطم *laṭm*, also *laṭma*, m. a blow, slap, box. *a.*

لطيف *laṭīf*, kind, courteous, benevolent, elegant; witty, facetious. *laṭīf-ṭab'* or *laṭīfu-ṭ-ṭab'*, of gentle dispositions, &c. *a.*

لطيفاً *laṭīfan*, pleasantly, delicately. *a.*

لطيفه *laṭīfa*, m. a pleasantry, jest, joke, raillery. *laṭīfa-go*, a facetious person, a jester; adj. witty. *a.*

لظي *laẓẓā*, m. a blazing flame; name of the second mansion of hell, to which the followers of the prophet of Mecca have charitably consigned all Christians.—(B.) *a.*

لعاب *lu'āb*, m. viscosity, sliminess, spittle, snot, mucus, saliva. *a.*

لعابي *lu'ābī*, viscous, slimy. *a.*

لعان *li'ān*, imprecation, cursing; in the language of the law it signifies testimonies confirmed by oath on the part of a husband and wife (whose testimony is strengthened by an imprecation of the curse of God on the part of the husband, and the wrath of God on the wife), in case of the former accusing the latter of adultery. *a.*

لعب *la'b*, m. playing, a play, a game, sport. *lab' o laghw*, play and trifling. *a.*

لعبت *la'bat* or *lu'bat*, f. a puppet, a doll, a plaything. *la'bat-bāz*, a player of puppets. *la'bat-bāzī*, f puppet-playing; any theatrical entertainment. *a.*

لعل *la'l*, m. a ruby; any bright gem; (met.) the lips of a mistress. *p.*

لعلي *la'lī*, } of a ruby colour, set with rubies;
لعلين *la'līn*, } a kind of flower. *p.*

لعن *lā'n*, f. cursing, imprecating. *la'n ṭa'n*, f. cursing and taunting. *a.*

لعنت *la'nat*, f. an imprecation, curse. *la'nat ba-heck*, (lit. nothing to swear at) so so, better than bad. *la'nat karnā*, to curse.

لعنتي *la'natī*, cursed, one under a ban. *a.*

لعوق *la'ūḳ*, an electuary, any medicine to be licked or sucked. *a.*

لعين *la'īn*, accursed, execrable, detested. *shaiṭāni la'īn*, the execrable Satan; the arch-fiend. *a*

لغا *laghā*, blundering, committing mistakes in speech, &c. *a.*

لغات *lughāt* (pl. of لغت, q. v.), languages,

لغام *laghām*, f. (v. *lagām*), a bridle, &c. *p.*

لغت *lughat*, f. tongue, speech, dialect, language; dictionary, glossary; a word. *a.*

لغز *laghz*, a slip, a stumble, a fall. *p.*

لغز *lughaz* or *lughz*, m. any ambiguous phrase, an enigma, a riddle. *a.*

لغزان *laghzān*, slipping, stumbling. *p.*

لغزش *laghzish*, f. a slip, a stumble, an error. *p.*

لغزيدن *laghzīdan*, to slip, to stumble. *p.*

لغو *laghw* or *lagho*, preposterous, contemptible, absurd, false. *a.*

لغوي *lughawī*, linguistic. *lughawī ma'nī*, the verbal or literal sense of a passage. *a.*

لغويات *laghwiyāt* (pl. of لغوي), inconsiderate or vain words, nonsense. *a.*

لغي *laghī*, any thing rashly spoken, an absurdity, nonsense. *a.*

لغيات *laghiyāt* (pl. of لغي), vain words, foolish speeches, absurdities. *a.*

لف *laff*, m. involving, folding, twisting, complicating, joining, assembling, mixing. *a.*

لفاظ *laffāẓ*, extremely eloquent. *a.*

لفاظي *laffāẓī*, f. eloquence, oratory. *a.*

لفافه *lifāfa*, m. a cover, envelope, enclosure, a wrapper, outward case. *lifāfa-k.*, to wrap up, to enclose. *s.*

لفظ *lafẓ*, m. a word, a saying, a phrase, an expression. *a.*

لفظاً *lafẓan*, literally, explicitly, distinctly. *a.*

لفظي *lafẓī*, of or relating to a word or pronunciation; verbal. *a.*

لفيف *lafīf*, a promiscuous multitude, a friend or acquaintance; adj. collected indiscriminately from all parts. *a.*

لقا *likā*, f. act of meeting, seeing or fighting with any one; (met.) death; the face, form, visage, countenance. *lukā*, a roguish fellow; adj. vain. *lakkā*, m. a kind of pigeon. *a.*

لقات *laḳāt*, lean, infirm (Pers. لكات). *a.*

لقب *laḳab*, m. a title, surname or epithet (either honourable or opprobrious). *a.*

لقصان *luḳṣān*, a vulgar but common corruption of *nuḳṣān*, q. v. *d.*

لقطه *luḳṭa*, m. treasure trove, waifs and strays. *a.*

لقلق *laḳlaḳ*, m. a stork (also *laglag*). *a.*

لقلقه *laḳlaḳa*, m. the voice of a stork; a continual motion of the jaw or of the tongue (in serpents); eloquence, pronunciation. *a.*

لقمان *luḳmān*, a famous eastern fabulist (supposed to be the same as Æsop). *a.*

لقمه *luḳma*, m. a morsel, mouthful, sop. *a.*

لقمه‌پرهيزي *luḳma-parhezī*, f. a bigoted or superstitious prejudice, real or affected, against certain common articles of food, entertained by some as a token of great piety and devotion: this absurd affectation is sneered at by Hafiz, in one of his odes. St. Paul condemns this piece of bigotry (1 Timothy iv. 3); and Hudibras has a fling at the *luḳma-parhez* gentry of his times, who, as he sayeth,

"Quarrel with mince-pyes and disparage
Their best and dearest friend plum-porridge,
Fat pig and goose itself oppose,
And blaspheme custard thro' the nose."—(B.) *a.p.*

لقنتي *luknatī*, m. a stutterer, one who stammers. *a.*

لقندرا *lukandrā*, m. a scamp, profligate, cheat. *h.*

لق ودق *lakk o dakk*, waste, dreary; a desert. *a.*

لقوه *lakwa*, m. a spasmodic distortion of the face. *a.*

لقيط *lakīt*, a foundling child. *a.*

لك लुक *luk*, m. a falling star, a meteor. *s.*

لك लुक *luk*, m. varnish. *a. h.*

لك लख *lak*, a hundred thousand. *p. s.*

لکا लिक्खा *likkhā*, f. a nit, a young louse. *lakhā*, a piece, a lump. *h.*

لکا लुका *lukā*, hidden, concealed. *h.*

لکانا लुकाना *lukānā*, a. to hide, to conceal. *h.*

لکانجن लुकाञ्जन *lukānjan*, an ointment, by applying which to a man's eyes he is said to become invisible. *s.*

لکاونا लुकावना *lukāwanā*, a. to conceal. *h.*

لکپتي *lak-patī*, rich; a millionaire. *d.*

لکتالگت *laktā-lagat*, successively, one after another. *d.*

لکتي लकती *laktī*, the total rent of a property or an estate (v. *jam'-bandī*). *h.*

لکٹ लकुट *lakuṭ*, m. a staff, stick, club. *h.*

لکچ लकच *lakach* or लकुच *lakuch*, m. a species of the bread-fruit tree (*Artocarpus lacucha*); also *likuch*. *h.*

لکد *lakad*, f. a kick, a cuff, a blow. *p.*

لکڑ लकड़ *lakaṛ*, m. wood, a cudgel, beam, bar. *lakaṛ-bāz*, a cudgel-player. *lakaṛ-bāzī*, f. cudgel-playing, fencing. *lakaṛ-hārā*, a wood-cutter, or seller of wood. *h.*

لکڑا लकड़ा *lakṛā*, m. a hyena; a large beam, wood. *lakṛā lagnā*, affliction to happen. *h.*

لکڑپھور लकड़फोर *lakaṛ-phor*, m. a woodpecker. *h.*

لکڑکوٹ लकड़कोट *lakaṛ-koṭ*, m. a stockade. *h.*

لکڑي लकड़ी *lakṛī*, f. wood, a staff; (met.) adj. stiff. *h.*

لکش लक्ष *laksh*, m. a *lak*, one hundred thousand. *s.*

لکشت लक्षित *lakshit*, seen, marked. *s.*

لکشمن लक्ष्मण *lakshman*, the son of *Dasharath*, the half brother and faithful companion of *Rāma*. *s.*

لکشمي लक्ष्मी *lakshmī*, f. (v. *lachhmī*) fortune, &c. *lakshmī-wān*, prosperous, beautiful. *s.*

لکشن लक्षण *lakshan*, m. (v. *lachhan*) a mark, &c. *s.*

لکشيه लक्ष्य *lakshya*, to be seen or noted; m. a mark, a sign, a butt; a *lak*. *s.*

للك كرنا *lak karnā*, a. to cleanse, to purify. *d.*

للك للك كرنا *lak-lak-karnā*, to shine, to glitter, to twinkle. *d.*

لکلکانا *laklakānā*, n. to gasp or pant (with heat or thirst). *d.*

لکلوٹ *lakloṭ* (v. *lakh-luṭ*), extravagant, wasteful. *d.*

لکنا लुकना *luknā*, n. to lie hid, to be concealed. *h.*

لکنت *luknat*, speaking a barbarous language; stuttering. *a.*

لکندرا लुकन्द्रा *lukandrā*, m. a rake, a profligate. *h.*

لکھا लिखा *likhā*, m. f. that which is written (on the forehead); fate, predestination, destiny; any thing written. *s.*

لکھا लखा (Pers. pl. of لك), hundreds of thousands. *p.*

لکھابسوا *lakhā-beswā*, name of a cunning courtesan mentioned in the Gul. Bakāwalī. *h.*

لکھانا लिखाना *likhānā*, a. to get written, to cause to be written; to teach to write. *s.*

لکھاو लखाउ *lakhā,ū*, significant, perceptible. *lakhā,o* or *lakhāw*, m. act of seeing or perceiving. *s.*

لکھاو लिखाव *likhāw*, m. } act of writ-
لکھاوٹ लिखावट *likhāwaṭ*, f. } ing *s.*

لکھاءي लिखाई *likhā,ī*, f. the wages of writing; the labour of writing; the art or business of writing. *s.*

لکھپت लखपति *lakh-pati*, } m. rich, prosper-
لکھپتي लखपती *lakh-patī*, } ous, master of a *lakh*, or, as we say, "worth a plum;" "a millionaire." *s.*

لکھت लिखत *likhat*, m. f. a letter, missive writing; scripture, any thing written. *s.*

لکھت लिखित *likhit*, written, delineated. *s.*

لکھ تنگ लिखतं *likh-tang*, m. writing, paper, a deed or document. *s.*

لکھ لٹ लखलुट *lakh-luṭ*, extravagant, a spendthrift (lit. squanderer of a *lakh*). *s.*

لکھ لکھانا लखलखाना *lakhlakhānā*, n. to gasp, or pant with heat or thirst (as birds). *h.*

لکھ لينا लिखलेना *likh-lenā*, a. to copy, to write out. *h.*

لکھن लिखन *likhan*, m. f. writing in general, any written document; scripture; fate, destiny. *s.*

لکھنا लिखना *likhnā*, a. to write, to paint or delineate. *lakhnā*, a. to see, to look at; to understand; n. to disappear. *s.*

لکھن लखन *lakhan*, m. (for *lakshan*) a mark; destiny. *s.*

لکھنت लिखन्त *likhant*, m. predestination, fate. *s.*

لکھنو लखनौ *lakhnau*, the capital of Oude. *h.*

لکھنوتي लखनौती *lakhnautī*, name of an ancient city in the north of Bengal, now in ruins. *h.*

لکھني लिखनी *likhnī*, f. a pen; also used as a declinable passive participle, as *jo chiṭhī likhnī thī*, the letter which was to have been written, "quæ epistola scribenda erat." *likhnī-dās*, a writer, amanuensis, copyist, quill-driver. *s.*

لکھوانا लिखवाना *likhwānā*, a. to cause to be delineated or written out; to cause (one's picture) to be drawn. *s.*

لکھوٹا लखौटा *lakhauṭā*, besmeared with lack. *lakhanṭā-k.*, to smear with lack, to glaze. *s.*

لکھیا लखिया *lakhiyā*, m. one who sees, a spectator. *s.*

لکھیرا लखेरा *lakherā*, m. a varnisher. *h.*

لکیر लकीर *lakīr*, f. a line, lineament, streak. *h.*

لگ लग *lag*, to, as far as, near, till, until, whilst, during. *s.*

لگا लग्गा *laggā*, m. affection, attachment; interest or influence with a person; applying or comparing one thing with another; a pole with which a boat is impelled. *laggā na khānā*, to bear no comparison with; to be incompatible or inconsistent with. *s.*

لگاتار लगातार *lagātār*, successive, incessant, repeatedly. *h.*

لگالگ *lagālag*, close together; uninterruptedly, incessantly. *a.*

لگام *lagām*, f. a bridle, a bit (v. *lajām*). *p.*

لگان लगान *lagān*, m. stopping or making fast (a boat, &c.); a place for halting a boat. *s.*

لگانا लगाना *lagānā*, a. to apply, to close, to attach, to place, to join, to add, to shut, to spread, to fasten, to fix, to plant, to plaster, to put to work, to use, to impute, to lay, to reserve, to report any thing in the way of scandal. *lagānā bujhānā*, to excite quarrels. *lagā-lenā*, to attach to one's self, to conciliate, to win. *lagā-mārnā*, a. to calumniate. *s.*

لگاو लगाव *lagāw*, m. series, relation, symmetry, application, connection; contact, adherence; access. *be-lagāw*, impregnable, inaccessible. *s.*

لگاوت लगावट *lagāwat*, f. union, attachment, application. *s.*

لگاعي लुगाई *lugā,ī*, f. woman (v. *logā,ī*). *lagā,ī*, the rent or revenue charged on a field or estate. *h.*

لگ بھگ लगभग *lag-bhag*, close, near, about, almost, by, thereabout. *h.*

لگت *lagat*, at that very instant. *d.*

لگت लगित *lagit*, connected with, attached to. *s.*

لگتا लगता *lagtā*, m. also *lagtī*, f. assessment or stipulated rent of land. *h.*

لگتاتار लगतातार *lagtātār*, continual, successive, without intermission. *h. p.*

لگتالگت *lagtā-lagat*, repeatedly, in succession, one after another. *d.*

لگٹي *lugṭī* (v. *lūkaṭī*), a poker. *d.*

لگ چلنا लगचलना *lag-chalnā*, to follow closely; to court one's friendship. *h.*

لگر लगुर *lagur*, } m. a staff, stick; an iron
لگڑ लगुड़ *laguṛ*, } club, or one bound with iron. *lagur-hast*, armed with a stick. *h.*

لگڑ लगड़ *lagaṛ*, a species of hawk. *h.*

لگڑانا *lagṛānā*, to cause to rub. *d.*

لگڑنا *lagaṛnā*, to rub. *lagaṛ-kar mārnā*, to give a violent beating. *d.*

لگلگ लगलग *laglag* (same as *laḳlaḳ*) a stork. *h.*

لگن लगन *lagan* or लग्न *lagna*, m. f. a moment; the rising of a sign of the zodiac or the sun's entrance into it; friendship, love; espousal, appointing the day of marriage; m. a large flat copper basin; adj. attached to, joined to, intent on. *lagan-kundalī*, a circle for a horoscope; (in Dakh.) same as *tak* or *lag*, up to. *s.*

لگنا लगना *lagnā*, n. to be applied, fixed, attached, to be close to, to touch, to come in contact with, to attain, to reach, to join; to be, to belong, to become, to suit; to begin (when accompanied with the inflected infinitive of another verb); to happen, to befall, to seem, to taste; to be connected with, to regard. *lag-raknā*, to continue without interruption, to continue fixed. *lagā-rahna*, to be occupied or busy in. *s.*

لگنا लग्ना *lagnā*, m. a bard, a panegyrist. *s.*

لگوءا लगूआ *lagū,ā*, m. a paramour. *s.*

لگوانا लगवाना *lagwānā*, a. to cause to be attached, applied, fixed, or fastened; to cause to be laid out or planted (an orchard). *s.*

لگون *lagūn*, (same as *lag*) up to, as far as. *d.*

لگھ लघु *laghu*, light, not heavy, small, mean, low, short (as a vowel). *laghu-bele*, adv. shortly. *laghutā*, f. lightness, meanness. *laghu-chetā*, low-minded, frivolous. *laghu-dīṭh*, short-sighted. *laghu-dundubhī*, m. a small kettledrum. *laghu-garg*, m. a kind of fish (*Pimelodus?*) *laghu-māṅs*, m. the francoline partridge. *laghu-mitr*, m. a friend of little value. *laghu-mūl*, (in alg.) the least root with reference to the additive quantities. *s.*

لگونهان लगुंहां *lagūṅhān*, thickly set, continuous; pleasing, beautiful, delightful, alluring. *s.*

لگھو लघू *laghū*, short. *laghū-bele*, shortly. *laghū-dīṭh*, short-sighted. *laghū-karan*, m. reducing in weight or consequence; thinking little of. *s.*

لگھواهار लघ्वाहार *laghwāhār*, temperate in eating. *h.*

لگي लग्गी *laggī*, f. a pole, a staff, gibstaff. *h.*

لگي هات *lage-hāt*, together with, just after, immediately upon. *d.*

للا लला *lalā*, m. a boy. *h.*

للاٹ ललाट *lalāṭ*, } m. the forehead; fate, des-
للاڑ *lalāṛ*, } tiny, fortune (also *lilāṭ*, *lilāṛ*). *s.*

للاٹریکھا ललाटरेखा *lalāṭ-rekhā*, f. a line on the forehead, supposed to indicate long life, a coloured sectorial mark on the forehead. *s.*

للاٹکا ललाटिका *lalāṭikā*, f. an ornament worn on the forehead, a mark made with sandal on the forehead. *s.*

للانا लिलाना *lilānā*, n. to long for. *h.*

لله الحمد والمنة *li-lāhi-l-ḥamd wa-l-minna*, to God be praise and thanksgiving. *a.*

للت ललित *lalit*, f. a name of a *rāginī* or musical mode; adj. beautiful, lovely. *a.*

للتا ललिता *lalitā*, f. a woman in general; a wanton. *s.*

للچانا ललचाना *lalchānā*, n. to be tantalized, to long for, to covet; a. to excite desire, to tantalize. *h.*

للدمبو ललदंबू *lal-dambū*, m. a flower (*Nerium odorum*). *s.*

للك ललक *lalak*, f. a sudden gush of water, &c.; (met.) whim, fancy, caprice. *h.*

للكار ललकार *lalkār*, bawling, calling. *h.*

للكارنا ललकारना *lalkārnā*, a. to call, to bawl after, to halloo after, to challenge, to set up the war whoop, to bawl out insultingly. *h.*

للكانا ललकाना *lalkānā*, n. to excite to quarrel, to set on to fight. *h.* [upon. *h.*

للكنا ललकना *lalaknā*, n. to attack, to fall

للگنڈا ललगंडा *lal-gaṇḍā*, m. a species of monkey; a kind of mango fruit. *h.*

للگنڈي ललगंडी *lal-gaṇḍī* (f. of *lal-gaṇḍā*), a female monkey. *s.*

للن ललन *lalan*, m. pleasure, sport, pastime. *s.*

للنا ललना *lalanā*, f. a woman addicted to pleasure, a wanton woman. *s.*

للوپتو ललोपत्तो *lallo-patto*, m. wheedling, coaxing, flattering, adulation. *h.*

للي लली *lalī*, f. a girl; adj. impotent. *h.*

للیانا ललियाना *laliyānā*, a. to coax, to wheedle, to beg earnestly; to redden. *h.*

لم लिम *lim*, f. unjust censure, calumny; indication, trace. *h.*

لمبا लंबा *lambā*, long, tall. *lambā-k.*, to lengthen, to extend; to beat, to drub. *s.*

لمبارا *lambārā*, a wandering tribe who deal in grain, salt, &c. (v. *banjārā*). *h.*

لمبان लंबान *lambān*, m. length. *s.*

لمبانا लंबाना *lambānā*, a. to lengthen. *s.*

لمبائي लंबाई *lambā,ī*, f. length. *lambā,ī chaurā,ī*, f. size, length and breadth; (met.) pomp. *s.*

لمبت लंबित *lambit*, suspended, hanging. *s.*

لمبر लंबर *lambar*, fox (v. *lomṛī*). *h.*

لمبكا लंबिका *lambikā*, f. the uvula. *s.*

لمبو लंबू *lambū* (v. *lambā*), long, tall, &c. *s.*

لمبوت *lambot*, m. a longboat, ship's boat. *e.*

لمبها लंभा *lambhā*, m. hare, a rabbit; f. a sort of chain enclosure or fence. *h.*

لمبي लंबी *lambī*, f. long, tall; a kind of bounding pace in a horse. *lambī sāns bharnī* (lit. to fetch a long sigh), to regret, to lament. *lambī-k.*, a. to make a horse capriole, or throw out his forelegs. *s.*

لمبیان کرنا लंबियांकरना *lambiyān-k.*, n. to prance. *s.* [monger. *s.*

لمپٹ लिम्पट *limpaṭ*, m. a lecher, a whore-

لمپٹ लम्पट *lampaṭ*, false, lying; dissolute, reprobate; m. a libertine, a lecher. *kachh lampaṭ*, incontinent, dissolute, lewd. *s.*

لمپٹتا लम्पटता *lampaṭtā*, f. libertinism, dissoluteness. *s.*

لمترانگ *lamtarāng* (v. *lambā*), long, &c. *d.*

لمتنگا *lam-ṭangā*, long-legged, spindle-shanks. *h.* [musket. *h.*

لم چھڑ लमछड़ *lam-chhaṛ*, f. a long kind of

لم چھڑا लमछड़ा *lam-chhaṛā*, tall, long. *h.*

لمحه *lamḥa*, m. a moment, minute, glance, or twinkling of an eye. *lamḥa-lamḥa*, every moment constantly, perpetually. *h.*

لمڈور *lam-ḍor*, strings or cords used in fishing. *d.*

لمس *lams*, m. the touch, feeling, handling; the sense of feeling. *s.*

لمعات *lam'āt* (pl. of لمعه), rays of the sun. *a.*

لمعه *lam'a*, m. splendour, brilliancy; shining, glaring; the glare of the sun. *a.*

لمکانا लमकाना *lamkānā*, n. to stretch out the hands to take any thing; a hare, a rabbit. *h.*

لمکنا लमकना *lamkanā*, }
لمها लम्हा *lamhā*, } m. a hare, a rabbit. *s.*
لنبها लंभा *lambhā*, }

لمن *li-man*, to whomsoever, to whom. *li-man al-mulk*, he to whom is (or belongs) the kingdom. *a.*

لمهر लमहर *lamhar*, a tree that has sprung up of itself in a cultivated field, and which the cultivator may legally cut down. *h.*

لنبا लंबा *lambā*, long, tall (v. لمبا). *s.*

لنبان लंबान *lambān*, length, tallness. *s.*

لنبوت *lambot* (v. لمبوت) a longboat. *e.*

لن ترانی *lan-tarā-nī*, f. (for *la-an tarā-nī*, lit. egad! if you saw me!) boasting, gasconading. *lan-tarānī-wālā*, m. a braggart, a boaster. *a. h.*

لنٹك लुंटक *lunṭak*, m. a kind of potherb (*Chironia centauroides*). *h.*

لنج लुंज *lunj*, }
لنجا लुंजा *lunjā*, } lame, crippled, without hands or feet. *lunj-munj*, utterly lame. *p. h.*
لنجه लुंजः *lunja*, }

لنڈ लंड *land*, m. (also *lanṛ*) *penis* (v. *lānṛ*). *s.*

لنڈا लुंडा *lunḍā*, tailless, tailcropt; (in Dakh.) m. a mass, a lump. *h.*

لنڈورا लंडूरा *lanḍūrā*, tailless; (a person) without friends, forlorn. *h.*

لنڈهنا लुंढना *lunḍhnā* (for *luṛhnā*), to roll, &c. *h.*

لنڈیانا लुंडियाना *lunḍiyānā*, n. to roll. *h.*

لنڑ लंड़ *lanṛ*, m. (same as *lanḍ*) the penis.

لنک लङ्क *lanh*, f. the reins, the loins; m. a heap, abundance. *h.*

لنکا लङ्का *lanhā*, f. the capital of Rāvana, in Ceylon; the name is also applied to that island. *s.*

لنکاستهایي लङ्कास्थायी *lanhā-sthāyi*, m. a plant (*Euphorbia tirucalli*). *s.*

لنکایکا लङ्कायिका *lankāyikā*, } f. a plant (*Trigonella corniculata*). *s.*
لنکوپکا लङ्कोपिका *lankopikā*, }

لنگ *lung*, m. a cloth worn between the legs. *lung mārnā*, to tie on the *lung*. *lang*. lame; m. limping, lameness. *p.*

لنگ लिङ्ग *ling* or *linga*, m. a sign, a token; *membrum virile*, a *priapus*; the emblem of *Mahādeva*; the phallus; (in gram.) gender of nouns. *s.*

لنگارچن लिङ्गार्चन *lingārchchan*, m. worship of the *linga*. *s.*

لنگر लंगर *langar*, m. the *raphe* of the perineum. *h.*

لنگر *langar*, m. an anchor; a stay or rope for supporting a tent; an almshouse; the plaits of a robe; adj. worthless, mean. *langar uṭhānā*, to weigh anchor; to feed the poor, or raise an almshouse to give a feast to the poor. *langar par honā*, to be at anchor. *langar-khāna*, an almshouse, an asylum for the poor and destitute. *langar-kharch*, provisions or expenses for the support of the poor. *langar-ḍālnā* or *-karnā*, (in Pers.) *-nihādan*, to cast anchor. *p.*

لنگرائي लंगराई *langrā,ī*, f. worthlessness. *h.*

لنگرخانه *langar-khāna*, m. an hospital, an almshouse, an asylum for the poor. *p.*

لنگري लङ्गरी *langrī*, f. a large shallow pan, made of metal, and generally used to knead bread in, or for serving rice. *h.*

لنگري *langarī*, m. provisions distributed to the poor. *p.*

لنگڑا लङ्गड़ा *langṛā*, lame, one who limps. *p. h.*

لنگڑانا लङ्गड़ाना *langṛānā*, n. to limp, to walk lame. *p. h.*

لنگڑاهٹ लंगड़ाहट *langṛāhaṭ*, } f. state of limping, or being lame. *p. h.*
لنگڑائي लंगड़ाई *langṛā,ī*, }

لنگڑنا *langaṛnā*, n. (same as *langṛānā*). *d.*

لنگن लिङ्गन *lingan*, m. embracing, caressing. *s.*

لنگناش लिङ्गनाश *ling-nāsh*, m. the loss or destruction of the *penis*. *s.*

لنگوٹ लङ्गोट *langoṭ*, m. (v. *langoṭī*). *langoṭ-band*, a bandage to which the *langoṭ* is fastened; one devoted to celibacy. *p. h.*

لنگوٹا लङ्गोटा *langoṭā*, m. } a narrow slip of cloth passed between the thighs, and tucked into a waistbelt before and behind to conceal the privy parts. *p. h.*
لنگوٹي लङ्गोटी *langoṭī*, f. }

لنگوٹیا लङ्गोटिया *langoṭiyā*, f. (dim. of *langoṭī*). *langoṭiyā-yār*, an old friend (from childhood), a very intimate friend. *p. h.*

لنگوچا लङ्गूचा *langūchā*, m. a sausage. *h.*

لنگور लङ्गूर *langūr*, m. a baboon, a monkey. *s.*

لنگهن लङ्घन *langhan*, m. fast, fasting, abstinence; act of jumping over or springing over; going by leaps and jumps; exceeding, transgressing, disregarding propriety. *langhan paṛnā*, to catch (as a disorder). *s.*

لنگهنا लङ्घना *langhnā*, a. to jump over; n. to be jumped over, to pass over, to pass. *s.*

لنگهي लङ्घनी *langhnī*, f. fast, fasting. *s.*

لنگي *lungī*, f. (v. *lung* or *langoṭā*) a narrow slip of cloth, &c. *p.*

لنگي लिङ्गी *lingī*, m. a worshipper of *Shiva* (in the phallic type). *linghi-vesh*, m. the dress of a worshipper of *Shiva*, the insignia of a religious student, the skin, staff, bowl, &c. *s.*

لو लो *lo*, take, hold; interj. lo! look, see, there now; (in Dakh. the form *le,o* is used). *h.*

لو लू *lū*, f. a hot wind (same as *lūh*). *h.*

لو लौ *lau*, f. the flame of a candle, any pointed flame (Scotch, *low*). *lau lagnī*, the frequent and long-continued repetition of any saying (particularly a lover calling on his mistress, or a dying man on God). *lau-lagānī* denotes intense praying or untiring meditation on God. *s.*

لو लव *lava*, m. reaping, cutting corn; the sixtieth part of the twinkling of an eye; applied also to a larger division of time, thirty-six twinklings of an eye; the numerator of a fraction. *s.*

لوا *liwā*, m. a standard, a banner. *a.*

لوا लवा *lawā*, m. a kind of quail (*Perdix chinensis*). *s.*

لوءاٹ लूआट *lū,āṭ* or लूआत *lū,āt*, m. (v. *lū-kaṭ*) half burnt (wood), a brand. *h.*

لواحق *lawāhiḳ* (pl. of لاحق), servants, domestics, followers, dependants, family. *a.*

لوازم *lawāzim*, } (pl. of لازمه), necessary things, requisites, essentials. *a.*
لوازمه *lawāzima*, }

لواک लवाक *lavāk*, m. a sickle, a reaping-hook. *s.*

لوالانا लिवालाना *liwā-lānā*, a. to bring, to procure. *h.*

لوانا लिवाना *liwānā*, a. to cause (one), to take or receive. *s.*

لوانک लवाणक *lavānak*, m. a sickle, a reaping-hook. *s.*

لوبا *lobā*, a kind of bean. *p.*

لوبان लोबान *lobān* (for *lubān*), m. a kind of gum, incense, benzoin. *a. h.*

لوباني *lobānī*, milk-white. *lobānī 'ūd*, the whitest sort of benzoin. *a. h.*

لوبه लोभ *lobh*, m. avarice, covetousness; temptation. *lobh-mohit*, deluded by avarice. *lobh-virah*, free from cupidity. *s.*

لوبهنا लोभना *lobhnā*, n. to be enamoured. *s.*

لوبهي लोभी *lobhī*, covetous, avaricious. *arth-lobhī*, greedy of gain; a name given to a jackal in one of the fables in the *Akhlāḳi Hindī*. *s.*

لوبيا लोबिया *lobiyā*, m. a kind of bean (*Dolichos sinensis*). *p.*

لوپ लोप *lop*, m. rejection, cutting off in general: a term in grammar for dropping letters or syllables; disappearance, erasure. *s.*

لوپڑي लोपड़ी *lopṛī*, f. a lump of any thing moist; a poultice composed of flour, turmeric, and oil or clarified butter. *h.*

لوتا लूता *lūtā*, f. a spider; local inflammation produced by the urine of a spider. *s.*

لوتھ लोथ *loth* or *lūth*, f. a corpse, a dead body. *h.*

لوتھا लोथा *lothā*, m. a bag, a sack, a stupe. *h.*

لوتھرا लोथरा *lothrā*, m. } a lump of flesh (also
لوتھري लोथरी *lothrī*, f. } *lothṛā* and *lothṛī*). *s.*

لوتھي लोथी *lothī*, f. a staff, club (knotted). *h.*

لوٹ लौट *lauṭ*, m. turning over, inverting; returning. *h.*

لوٹ लूट *lūṭ*, f. plunder, pillage, booty. *lūṭ-bāz*, a plunderer, murderer. *lūṭ-pāṭ*, f. plunder and sacking. *lūṭ-kaūṭ*, f. plundering and ravaging. *s.*

لوٹ लोट *loṭ*, } m. a pot, a pipkin, a water-
لوٹا लोटा *loṭā*, } ing-pot. *h.*

لوٹاسجي लोटासजी *loṭā-sajī*, f. a kind of earth containing fossil alkali. *h.*

لوٹالاٹي लूटालाटी *lūṭā-lāṭī*, } f. plundering,
لوٹالوٹ लूटालूट *lūṭā-lūṭ*, } sacking, pil-
لوٹالوٹي लूटालूटी *lūṭā-lūṭī*, } laging. *s.*

لوٹانا लौटाना *lauṭānā*, a. to turn over, to invert; to turn back, to return, to give back, to reject. *h.*

لوٹاءي लूटाई *lūṭā,ī*, f. plunder, pillage, booty. *h.*

لوٹ‌پاٹ *lūṭ-pāṭ*, plundering, pillaging. *d.*

لوٹ‌پوٹ लोटपोट *loṭ-poṭ*, wallowing, tumbling and tossing, restless. *loṭ-poṭ honā*, n. to be in love. *loṭ-poṭ rahnā*, to toss about, to continue restless. *h.*

لوٹ‌پوٹيا लोटपूटिया *loṭ-pūṭiyā*, m. water-cresses. *h.*

لوٹن लोटन *loṭan*, m. tumbling, tossing about; a kind of pigeon, tumbler; a bush. *s.*

لوٹنا लोटना *loṭnā*, n. to wallow, to roll about, to sprawl. *loṭnā-poṭnā*, n. to wallow, to turn or roll over. *lauṭnā*, to turn over; to turn back, to return. *h.*

لوٹنا लूटना *lūṭnā*, a. to plunder; to squander. *s.*

لوٹھا *lauṭhā*, m. a young man. *d.*

لوٹي लूटी *lūṭī*, } m. a plunderer, a mounted
لوٹيا लूटिया *lūṭiyā*, } robber, a *pindhārī*. *lūṭī-wālā*, a man who lives by robbery. *h*

لوث *laus*, m. contamination, pollution, defilement, impurity: in law it denotes blood-stains, &c., so as to constitute circumstantial evidence against a suspected murderer. *a.*

لوچ *lūch*, squint-eyed; naked (Fr. "louche?"). *p.*

لوچا लोचा *lochā*, } m. (v. *lothrā*) a lump
لوچك लोचक *lochak*, } of flesh, a ball of meat; stibium, or lamp-black. *h.*

لوچن लोचन *lochan*, m. the eye. *s.*

لوچن *lochan* or *lochun*, m. filings, powder. *h*

لوچنا लोचना *lochanā*, m. a lump of flesh (v *lochak*).

لوچنامي लोचनामय *lochanāmay*, m. diseased affection of the eye, ophthalmia. *s.*

لوچن‌كركٹ लोचनककेट *lochan-harkaṭ*, } m. name of
لوچن‌مستك लोचनमस्तक *lochan-* [*mastak*, } a flower *Celesia cristata*). *s.*

لوح *lauḥ*, m. a plank, a table, a board or tablet on which any thing is written. *lauḥ ḳalam*, the tablet and pen on and with which the decrees of the deity are written. *lauḥi maḥfūẓ*, the eternal or preserved tablets, on which, according to the Musalmāns, God has recorded from the beginning all the actions of the human race. *a.*

لودھ लोध *lodh*, } m. a kind of medicine; a
لودھر लोध्र *lodhr*, } tree the bark of which is used in dyeing (*Symplocos racemosa*). *s.*

لودھا लोधा *lodhā*, } m. name of a caste or
لودھي लोधी *lodhī*, } tribe whose occupa-
لودھيا लोधिया *lodhiyā*, } tion is agriculture; a husbandman. *h.*

لودي लोदी *lodī*, m. name of a tribe among the *Paṭhāns*. *s.*

لور लोर *lor*, m. (v. *lolak*) an earring; a tear. *s.*

لوري लूरी *lūrī*, f. a kind of parrot (v. *nūri*). *h.*

لوريان *lūriyān*, name of a mountainous tribe in Persia. *p.*

لوڑا लौड़ा *lauṛā*, m. *membrum virile*. *s.*

لوڑھا लोढ़ा *loṛhā*, m. a stone pestle with which materials are triturated on a stone. *s.*

لوز *lauz*, m. an almond; a kind of sweetmeat. *s.*

لوزيات *lauziyāt*, sweetmeats in which almonds are mixed. *s.*

لوس *laus*, m. taste, tasting. *s.*

لوشٹ लोष्ट *loshṭ* or लोष्टु *loshṭu*, m. a clod, a lump of earth; rust of iron or iron-filings. *loshṭ-may*, made of a clod, or of earth.

لوط *lūṭ* the patriarch Lot. *lauṭ*, m. any thing agreeable to the heart, an inclination, affection; a cloak; a man expert and expeditious in business; joining, bringing together (friends, &c.). *a.*

لوطي *lūṭī*, m. an inhabitant of Sodom; adj. *præposteræ veneri addictus.* *s.*

لوك लूक *lūk*, f. (v. *lūh*) a hot wind. *h.*

لوك लोक *lok*, m. people, mankind; a world or division of the universe; a region, country. *tīn lok*, three regions, or *tīnoṅ lok*, the three regions (par excellence), viz. 1st, *swarg-lok* or *swarga-lok*, the heaven; 2nd, *mart-lok* or *martya-lok*, the earth, the region under the sun; 3rd, *pātāl*, the region under the earth. *lok-pāl*, m. a king; a protector of the world, applied to the divinities who are supposed to protect the regions, viz. sun, moon, fire, wind, Indra, Yama, Varuna, Kuvera. *lok-jit*, a conqueror of the world. *lok-rāchchhas*, a demon (the spirit of a wicked man converted into a demon). *lok-krit*, m. the creator, Brahma. *lok-nāth*, m. a sovereign of the universe. *s.*

لوك लवक *lavak*, who or what cuts, reaps, &c. *s.*

لوكا लूका *lūkā*, m. pieces of burning matter thrown out from a conflagration. *lūkā lagānā*, to inflame, or excite quarrels, &c. *s*

لوكا लौका *laukā*, m. a kind of pumpkin (*Cucurbita lagenaria*); lightning, flash, glitter. *s.*

لوكاچاري *lokāchārī*, f. way of the world. *d.*

لوكالوك लोकालोक *lokālok*, m. a chain of mountains surrounding the world (v. As. Res. vol. viii. p. 283). *s.*

لوكانتر लोकान्तर *lokāntar*, m. the other world. *s.*

لوكايتك लौकायतिक *laukāyatik*, m. an atheist, a materialist, a Bauddh. *s.*

لوكپرسدھ लोकप्रसिद्ध *lok-prasiddh*, notorious, well-known, of world-wide renown. *s.*

لوكتري लोकत्रय *lokatray*, m. the three worlds (v. *lok*), the whole universe. *s.*

لوكٹ लूकट *lūkaṭ*, half-burnt (wood). *h.*

لوكٹي लूकटी *lūkṭī*, f. a wooden poker or stake burnt at one end; a fox. *h.*

لوكجيت लोकजीत *lok-jīt*, m. a conqueror of the world. *s.*

لوك چلانا लूकचलाना *lūk chalānā* (v. *lūkh chalānā*), a. to charm, to fascinate. *h.*

لوكرا लोकरा *lokrā*, m. tatters, torn clothes. *h.*

لوكرنجن लोकरञ्जन *lok-ranjan*, m. popularity, gaining public confidence. *s.*

لوكڑي लोकड़ी *lokṛī*, f. (v. *lūkṭī*) a wooden poker, &c. *h.*

لوكك लौकिक *laukik*, mundane, worldly, human; ceremonial, ceremonious. *laukiktā*, f. worldliness, worldly currency or custom. *s.*

لوكنا लोकना *lokná*, a. to catch. *lūknā*, n. to be scorched by the sun or hot wind; to have a *coup de soleil.* *h.*

لوكن लूकना *lūknā* (also *lauknā*), a. to see, to behold. *s.*

لوكنا लौकना *lauknā*, n. to shine, to glitter, to flash, to lighten. *s.*

لوكنيه लोकनीय *lokanīya*, visible, to be seen. *s.*

لوكواءي लूकवाई *lūkwā,ī*, f. conflagration. *h.*

لوكھ लूख *lūkh*, f. a flame. *lūkh chalānā*, a. to charm, to fascinate. *s.*

لوكھر लोखर *lokhar*, m. tools, old iron pots, pans, hardware. *s.*

لوكي लौकी *laukī*, f. a kind of pumpkin. *h.*

لوگ लोग *log*, m. people, mankind. *s.*

لوگاءي लोगाई *logā,ī*, f. a female, a woman. *s.*

لول लोल *lol*, m. tears, the fluid in which the eyes appear sometimes to be overwhelmed, undulation, glimmer; adj. shaking, trembling, waving. *s.*

لولا लोला *lolā*, m. a suppository, a kind of solid clyster. *h.*

لولا लूला *lūlā*, lame-handed, maimed; m. a roll of paper. *h.*

لولپ लोलुप *lolup*, very desirous, longing, greedy. *s.*

لولك लोलक *lolak*, m. an ear-ring, drop, pendant. *s.*

لولكا लोलिका *lolikā*, f. a sort of dock or sorrel (*Rumex vesicarius*). *s.*

لولكي लोलकी *lolkī*, f. the lobe of the ear. *s.*

لولو *lūlū*, m. a pearl (pl. *la,ālī*). *a.*

لولو *lūlū*, m. a people in Persia, called also *kārājī*; a goblin to frighten children (*Boorh. Qat.*). *p.*

لولوا लूलूआ *lūlū,ā*, m. a paw. *h.*

لولوءي *lūlū,ī*, of or relating to pearls. *a.*

لولي *lūlī*, f. a prostitute, a harlot. *lūlī,e falak*, the planet Venus. *p.*

لوم लोम *lom* or लूम *lūm*, m. hair, a tail, a hairy tail; the base of a triangle, &c.; a picket, outpost, sentry. *s.*

لوم *laum*, m. blame, accusation, reprehension, reproach. *a.*

لومڑي लोमड़ी *lomṛī*, f. a fox (also *lombṛī*). *s*

لومس लोमस *lomas*, hairy; name of a *rishi* or saint. *s.*

لومسار लोमसार *lomsār*, m. the emerald. *s.*

لومش लोमश *lomash*, hairy, covered with or made of hair. *lomash-parninī*, f. name of a plant (*Glycene debilis*). *lomash-mārjār*, m. the polecat. *s.*

لومشا लोमशा *lomshā*, f. name of a plant (*Leea hirta*); Indian spikenard (*Valeriana jatamansi*); cowach (*Carpopogon pruriens*); green vitriol, orris root. *s.*

لومكرن लोमकर्ण *lom-karn*, m. a hare. *s.*

لومكوپ लोमकूप *lom-kūp*, m. a pore of the skin. *s.*

لوموش लोमविष *lom-vish*, m. an animal whose hair is supposed to be poisonous, as the tiger. *s.*

لومهرشن लोमहर्षण *lom-harshan*, m. horripilation, erection of the hair of the body. *s.*

لون लोन *lon*, लवण *lavan*, or लून *lūn*, m. salt; adj. salt, saline. *s.*

لون लवन *lavan*, m. the process of reaping. *s.*

لون *laun*, m. colour, external form; species, genus. *s.*

لون लौं *loṅ* or लौं *lauṅ*, till, to, up to; (for [*lūh*, q. v.) a hot wind. *h.*

لونا लौना *launā*, m. balancing, making scales equal; a. to reap. *lonā*, m. name of a fruit (*Annona reticulata*). *h.*

لونا लोणा or लोना *lonā*, salt, brackish; barren or salt (land); m. purslain (*Portulaca oleracea*); the salt that effloresces from walls, &c. *lonā-pan*, m. saltness. *s.*

لونا लवना *lavanā*, f. a small river in Tirhut.

لونار लोनार *lonār*, m. salt lands; a place where salt is produced, a saltpit. *s.*

لوناكر लवणाकर *lavanākar*, m. a salt mine. *s.*

لونانب लवणाम्बु *lavanāmbu*, m. the sea, salt water. *s.*

لوند लौन्द *laund*, m. an intercalary month. *h.*

لوند *lawind*, free, independent; having no fixed residence; ignorant, unlearned, foolish; poor: scarce of provisions; uxorious; (sub.) a soldier, a volunteer, an adventurer; a rake. *p.*

لوندا लोंदा *londā*, m. a lump of clay, clod. *h.*

لونڈا लौंडा *launḍā*, m. a boy, a slave boy, a brat. *launḍā-bāz*, a sodomite. *launḍā-bāzī*, f. sodomy. *h.*

لونڈي लौंडी *launḍī*, } f. a girl, a slave girl,
لونڈيا लौंडिया *launḍiyā*, } a servant girl. *h.*

لون سمدر लवणसमुद्र *lavan-samudr*, m. the sea of salt water. *s.*

لون كهان लवणखानि *lavan-khāni*, m. a salt mine, especially that of Sāmbhar in Ajmīr. *s.*

لونگ लौंग *laung*, लवङ्ग *lavang*, or लोंग *long*, m. the clove tree (*Myristica caryophyllata*); f. a clove (*Caryophyllus aromaticus*). *laung-charā*, m. a kind of dish prepared from peasemeal. *s.*

لونگرا लूणग्रा *lūngrā*, salt, brackish. *laungrā*, m. name of a medicine. *h.*

لونوتم लवणोत्तम *lavanottam*, m. nitre; rock or river salt (lit. the finest salt). *s.*

لوني लौनी *launī* or *lavanī*, f. wages paid in kind to reapers in harvest time. *h. s.*

لوني लूणी or लूनी *lūnī*, f. the salt that effloresces from walls, &c.; butter. *s.*

لونيا लूनिया *lūniyā*, salt, brackish; m. purslain (*Portulaca oleracea*). *s.*

لونيا लूनिया *lūniyā*, m. a pioneer; a maker of salt; name of a tribe or caste of *baniyās*. *a.*

لوه लूह *lūh*, f. a hot wind. *h.*

لوه लोह *loh*, m. iron, steel; aloe wood or agallochum. *lauh*, made of iron; m. iron. *low-lāth*, m. an iron mace or club. *loh-may*, made of iron. *s.*

لوها लोहा *lohā*, m. iron. *lohā-bajānā*, to fight with swords. *lohā-maḥall*, the iron department; revenue derived from iron mines. *s.*

لوهابهسار लोहाभिसार *lohābhisār*, m. lustration of arms, a ceremony performed on the ninth of the light half of the month Aswin. *s.*

لوهار लोहार *lohār*, m. a blacksmith. *lohār khāna*, a blacksmith's forge or shop, a smithy. *h.*

لوهار लौहार *lauhār*, m. a trance. *h.*

لوهارن लोहारन *lohāran* or लोहारिन *lohārin*, f. a blacksmith's wife. *s.*

لوهان लोहान *lohān*, adj. bloody. *s.*

لوهاني लोहानी *lohānī*, m. name of a tribe among the *Paṭhāns* or *Afghāns*. *h.*

لوهت लोहित *lohit*, red; m. blood. *lohit ānan*, red-faced; m. an ichneumon. *s.*

لوهتك लोहितक *lohitak*, m. a ruby; calx of brass. *s.*

لوهج लोहज *lohaj*, m. bell-metal; rust of iron, iron filings. *s.*

لوهجت लोहजित *loh-jit*, m. the diamond. *s.*

لوه چور लोहचूर *loh-chūr*, }
لوه چورن लोहचूर्ण *loh-chūrn*, } m. iron filings. *s.*
لوه چون लोहचून *loh-chūn*, }

لوه دراوي लोहद्रावी *loh-drāvī*, m. borax (as fusing metal). *s.*

لوهسار लोहसार *loh-sār*, f. an iron mine. *s.*

لوهكار लोहकार *loh-kār*, m. a blacksmith. *s.*

لوهكانت लोहकान्त *loh-kānt*, m. the loadstone. *s.*

لوهكٹ लोहकिट्ट *loh-kiṭṭ*, m. rust of iron, iron filings. *s.* [shrub. *s.*

لوكنٹك लोहकण्टक *loh-kanṭak*, m. a thorny

لوهمارك लोहमारक *loh-mārak*, m. a plant (*Achyranthes triandra*). *s.*

لوهنڈا लोहण्डा *lohanḍā*, m. an iron pot. *s.*

لوهو लोहू *lohū*, m. blood. *lohū-baiṭhnā*, to pass blood by stool. *lohū phaṭnā*, to have leprosy. *lohū ḍālnā*, to spit blood. *lohū-luhān*, covered with blood. *s.*

لوهي लोही *lohī*, f. a lump, a mouthful; a kind of silk cloth; dawn just before sunrise. *h.*

لوهيا लोहिया *lohiyā*, made of iron. *s.*

لوءي लोई *loī*, f. blanket, flannel; splendour of the countenance, honour. *lūī*, f. a poultice, a round lump of dough prepared for making into bread or cakes. *s.* [takes. *h.*

لويا लिवैया *liwaiyā*, m. (v. *lewaiya*) one who

لوين लोयन *loyan*, m. the eye. *s.*

له *lahu*, to him, or, to it. *la-hā*, to her. *a.*

لهاب *luhāb*, m. blazing, flame without smoke, burning. *a.*

لهار लुहार *luhār*, m. a blacksmith. *s.*

لهارن लुहारिन *luhārin*, f. the female of *luhār*, a blacksmith's wife. *s.*

لہاڑا लिहाड़ा *lihāṛā*, vile, base, mean, contemptible. *h.* [with blood. *s.*

لہان लुहान *luhān*, bloody, covered or smeared

لہانگي लुहाङ्गी *luhāngī*, f. a staff armed with iron. *s.* [with blood. *s.*

لہانہ लुहानः *luhāna*, bloody, smeared or stained

لہاءي लिहाई *lihā,ī*, f. a kind of paste or glue made from tamarind stones pounded and boiled to a jelly, used by bookbinders, &c. *h.*

لہب *lahab*, m. flame; flying or ascending (as dust). *a.*

لہبر लहबर *lahbar*, m. a kind of parroquet. *h.*

لہبیرا लहबेरा *lahberā*, m. name of a plant. *h.*

لہجہ *lahja*, m. the tongue, voice, sound, tune, accent. *a.* [fore, consequently. *a.*

لہذا *lihāzā*, on that account; because, there-

لہر लहर *lahar*, f. a wave; whim, fancy, vision; the effect of the poison of a snake, intoxication; a waving pattern in embroidery; emotion, excitement. *s.*

لہرا लहरा *lahrā*, m. a quaver, shake, trill (in music); evasion. *h.*

لہرا लुहरा *luhrā*, m. a younger, junior. *h.*

لہرا लहर्रा *laharrā*, m. name of a grain (*bājrā*, *Holcus spicatus*). *h.*

لہرالگانا लहरालगाना *lahrā lagānā*, to evade, to avoid performing an agreement. *h.*

لہرانا लहराना *lahrānā*, n. to tantalize; to undulate; to play loosely, to put off. *s.*

لہربہر लहरबहर *lahar-bahar*, f. prosperity. *h.*

لہرنا लहरना *laharnā*, n. to undulate; to play as waves. *h.*

لہري लहरी *lahrī*, inconstant, capricious; unsteady as the waves. *s.* [ing or painting. *s.*

لہریا लहरिया *lahriyā*, waved, a mode of dye-

لہسن लहसन *lahsan*, m. garlic; a freckle. *s.*

لہسنیا लहसनिया *lahsaniyā*, m. name of a precious stone; (in Dakh.) garlic; adj. savouring or smelling of garlic. *h.*

لہسوڑا लहसोड़ा *lahsoṛā*, m. name of a fruit (*Cordia myxa* or *latifolia*). *h.*

لہک लहक *lahak*, f. glitter, flash, glare. *h.*

لہکارنا लहकारना *lahkārnā*, a. to fondle, to pat and encourage a horse, &c. *h.*

لہکانا लहकाना *lahkānā*, a. to warble, to quaver; to cause to shine or glitter; to blow up a fire. *h.* [flashing. *h.*

لہکاوٹ लहकावट *lahkāwaṭ*, f. glittering,

لہکنا लहकना *lahaknā*, n. to warble, to quaver; to wave; to be kindled, to rise up into a flame; to glitter to shine. *h*

لہکور लहकौवर *lahkauwar*, m. rice milk eaten by a bride and bridegroom. *h.*

لہکیلا लहकीला *lahkīlā* or *lahkelā*, glittering flashing. *h.* [paying. *h.*

لہلوٹ लहलोट *lahloṭ*, borrowing and never

لہلہا लहलहा *lahlahā*, blooming, flourishing. *h.*

لہلہانا लहलहाना *lahlahānā*, n. to bloom, to be verdant, to flourish. *h.* [stiff mud. *h.*

لہلہي लहलही *lahlahī* or *lahlhī*, mud, thick or

لہنا लहना *lahnā*, n. to answer, to avail, to boot, to signify; a. to find, to get, to experience m. outstanding debt; fate, destiny. *h.*

لہنج *lahanj*, a stone on which washermen beat their linen; a whetstone; concord, harmony. *p*

لہنجہ *lahanja*, misfortune, calamity. *d.*

لہنڈا लुहण्डा *luhanḍā*, m. an iron pot. *s.*

لہنگا लहंगा *lahangā*, m. a petticoat. *h.*

لہو *lahv* or *lahw*, m. playing, amusing one's self, unbending the mind; play, any thing ludicrous or jocular. *lahv o la'b*, m. play, sport, mirth, amusement, game, fun. *a.*

لہو लहू *lahū* or *luhū*, (Dakh. *lhau*) m. (v. *lohū*) blood. *lahū-luhān*, covered or besmeared with blood. *lhau anṭānā*, to experience sorrow (lit. to make the blood boil). *lhau ghūṅṭnā*, to suffer with patience. *s.*

لہوا लहूआ *lahū,ā*, m. name of a plant. *h.*

لہوا *lahauwā* or *lhauwā*, m. (v. *lohā*) iron. *d.*

لہواٹي *lahauwāṭī* (v. *lūhṭī*), f. a poker. *d.*

لہواچابنا *lhauwā chabnā*, (lit. to chew iron) to act boldly or perform prodigies of valour. *d.*

لہوار *lahwār*, a blacksmith. *lahwār khāne meṅ sūiyāṅ bechnā*, a. to make an absurd or improper boast. *d.*

لہیندي लिहैंडी *lihainḍī*, the act of throwing up water for irrigation from a pond or river, with a kind of basket worked by two men. *h.*

لي लय *lai*, f. voice, sound, tone, melody, modulation, symphony, singing in tune; ardent affection or desire, immersion, absorption. *s.*

لي ले *le*, till, to, from; (part. of *lenā*) having taken; imper. take; interj. come! well! *h.*

لئي *la,ī*, much, very, excessively. *d.*

لئي लिए *li,e*, for, on account of; with, taking or having, as *wuh talwār hāth meṅ li,e shahr meṅ gayā* he went to the city with a sword in his hand. *h.*

لیا लीआ *lī,ā*, land which is annually flooded. *h.*

لیاري लयारी *layārī* or ल्यारी *lyārī*, m. a wolf. *h.*

لیاقت *liyāḳat*, f. worth, merit, skill, abilities, dignity, knack. *a.*

لیانا लेआना *le-ānā*, a. to bring: in the Deccan this comp. verb is never contracted into *lānā*, as it is generally in the north. *d.* [with. *h.*

لي بہاگنا लेभागना *le-bhāgnā*, to run away

لیبڑ लीबड़ *lībaṛ*, m. rheum (of the eyes). *h.*

لیپ लेप *lep*, m. plaster, ointment; plastering, smearing; mortar, *chunām*. *s.*

لی پالك लेपालक *le-pālak*, m. an adopted child; adopted. *s.*

لی پالنا लेपालना *le-pālnā*, a. to adopt, to rear, to bring up, to father (a child). *s.*

لیپالیپ लेपालेप *lepā-lep*, m. complete plastering. *s.*

لی پڑنا लेपड़ना *leparnā*, a. to lie with, *coire*; to involve another in one's disgrace. *h.*

لیپڑی लीपड़ी *līpṛī*, f. a rag; a small turban. *h.*

لیپك लेपक *lepak*, m. a plasterer, a bricklayer. *s.*

لیپن लेपन *lepan*, m. act of plastering, plastering. *s.*

لیپنا लेपना *lepnā* or लीपना *līpnā*, a. to plaster or smear over. *s.*

لیپی लेपी *lepī*, m. a plasterer, a bricklayer. *s.*

لیپیه लेप्य *lepya*, m. plastering, smearing. *s.*

لیت लेत *let*, m. plaster, paste, batter. *h.*

لیترا लीतरा *lītrā*, m. an old shoe. *h.*

لیت ولعل *lait o la'all*, evasion, prevarication, subterfuge, procrastination. *a.*

لیٹ लेट *leṭ*, m. mortar, plaster, *chunām*. *s.*

لیٹنا लेटना *leṭnā*, n. to repose, to lie down, to lie, to rest. *h.*

لیجانا लेजाना *le-jānā*, a. to take away, to carry, to run away with, to submit, to win. *h.*

لیجهی लीझी *lījhī*, f. dregs (of a dye, or of any thing that has been chewed), sediment. *h.*

لیچ جانا लीचजाना *līch-jānā*, n. to submit, to succumb, to subside. *h.*

لیچڑ लीचड़ *līchaṛ*, stingy, niggardly. *h.*

لیچی लीची *līchī*, f. name of a fruit (*Scytalia Litchi, Roxb.*). *chin.*

لید लीद *līd*, f. the dung of horses or elephants. *h.*

لیر लीर *līr*, f. a strip or slip of cloth. *h.*

لی رکهنا लेरखना *le-rakhnā*, a. to provide, to keep ready, to procure, to preserve. *h.*

لیرو लेरू *lerū*,
لیروا लेरूआ *lerū,ā*, } m. a calf. *h.*

لی رهنا लेरहना *le-rahnā*, n. to cheat, to pilfer. *h.*

لیزم *lezam*, f. a kind of bow with an iron chain instead of a string, which the natives use in their gymnastic exercises. *p.*

لیس लैस *lais*, ready, brought; m. a kind of vinegar; a practising arrow; a spring. *h.*

لیس लेश *les*, m. mark, sign, effect; a little. *s.*

لیس *les*, (in comp.) licking, as *kāsa-les*, a plate-licker, a glutton. *p.*

لیسالیس लेसालेस *lesā-les*, m. plastering.

لیسنا लेसना *lesnā*, a. to plaster, to spread, to daub; to kindle, to foment (a quarrel). *h.*

لیش लेश *lesh*, m. (v. *les*) mark, sign, &c.; adj. small, little; m. smallness, a little. *h.*

لیك लीक *līk*, f. the marks of a carriage wheel, path, track, trace; stain, ignominy, disgrace. *h.*

لیك *lek*,
لیکن *lekin*, } but, moreover, yet, notwithstanding. *a. h.*

لیکه लेख *lekh*, m. a letter, an epistle. *s.*

لیکه लीख *līkh*, f. a nit, the egg of a louse. *h.*

لیکها लेखा *lekhā*, m. account, reckoning. *lekhā-bahī*, an account-book, a day-book; book-keeping. *s. h.*

لیکهك लेखक *lekhak*, m. a writer, amanuensis, accountant. *s.*

لیکهکی लेखकी *lekhakī*, f. the business of a writer. *s.*

لیکهن लेखन *lekhan*, m. writing, scripture; the bark of the *bhoj* tree, used for writing on. *s.*

لیکهنی लेखनी *lekhnī*, f. a pen, a reed. *s.*

لیکهنی लेखनी *lekhanī*, a pen (v. *likhnī*). *s.*

لیکیه लेख्य *lek ya*, a writing, a manuscript, a letter, an epistle. *s.*

لیکهیه लेख्य *lekhya*, m. a letter. *lekhya-patr*, m. a written paper, a letter. *lekhya-sthān*, m. an office, a country-house. *s.*

لیگر *legar* (v. *regar*), m. black alluvial soil cotton ground. *h.*

لیل लील *līl* (for *nīl*), f. indigo; adj. blue. *s.*

لیل *lail*, f. night. *lail o nahār*, night and day. *a.*

لیلا लेला *lelā*, m. a lamb. *s.*

لیلا लीला *līlā*, blue, of indigo colour. *s.*

لیلا लीला *līlā*, f. play, sport, diversion amorous sport. *s.*

لیلاوتی लीलावती *līlāvatī*, f. a wanton or sportful woman; name of a Sanskrit work on arithmetic, algebra, and mensuration. *s.*

لیل کنٹه लीलकण्ठ *līl-kanṭh*, m. name of a bird, the jay bird (*Coracias Bengalensis*). *s.*

لیلنا लीलना *līlnā*, a. to swallow, to gulp. *h.*

لیلوٹ लेलूट *lelūṭ*, borrowing and never paying. *h.*

لیلت *lailat*, f.
لیله *laila*, m. } night, one night. *lailatu-l-ḳadr*, the night of power (v. *ḳadr*). *lailatu-l-mirāj*, the night of *Muhammad's* ascent to heaven on the winged beast *burāḳ*, q. v. *lailatu-l-waḥshat* (night of desolation) or *lailatu-l-waḥdat* (night of solitude), the first night after burial, when the soul is supposed still to remain with the body. *a.*

لیلی *lailī* (also *lailā*), name of the celebrated mistress of *Majnūn*; a mistress or beloved woman in general: *lailī* may also denote nocturnal; one who works in the night. *a.*

لي لينا लिलेना *le-lenā*, a. to take, to receive, to accept of, to take by force, to extort. *h.*

ليم लीम *līm*, m. concord, peace. *h.*

لئيم *la,īm*, reprehensible; miserly, sordid. *a.*

لي مرنا लेमरना *le-marnā*, n. to calumniate. *s.*

ليمو लीमू *lemū* or *līmū*, m. a lime (*Citrus medica*); (in Dakh.) *līmūn.* *s.*

لين लेन *len*, the act of taking. *h.*

لين लीन *līn* or *līna*, embraced, clung or adhered to; melted, dissolved; absorbed, immersed. *s.*

لينا लेना *lenā*, a. to take, to accept, to get, to hold, to pick, to win, to receive. *le-ānā*, to bring, to fetch. *le-jānā*, to take away, to carry. *h.*

ليناديئا लेनादेना *lenā-denā* (lit. taking and giving), m. traffic, trade (v. contracted form *len-den*). *h.*

لينت *līnat*, f. softness. *a.*

لين دين लेनदेन *len-den*, m. traffic, trade, barter, buying and selling; borrowing and lending. *h.*

ليندها लेंढा *lendhā*, m. smut, mildew; a flock of goats or sheep; a pack of dogs. *h.*

ليندي लेंडी *lendī*, f. goats' dung; a cur, a country dog; adj. impotent. *h.*

لينه *līna*, m. a kind of palm. *a.*

ليو लेव *lew*, m. plaster falling from a wall. *h.*

ليوا लेवा *lewā*, m. one who takes; plaster; that which is spread on the outside of a new pot; udder. *h.*

ليواديئي लेवादेई *lewā-de,ī*, f. (also *lewā-dewī*, and *lewe-dewe*) lending and borrowing, traffic, trade. *h.*

ليولر लेवार *lewār*, m. mud (to plaster a wall with). *h.*

ليواس लेवास *lewās*, m. plaster. *h.*

ليويا लेवैया *lewaiyā*, m. a taker, one who takes. *h.*

ليهن लेहन *lehan*, m. licking, tasting with the tongue. *lehin*, m. borax. *s.*

ليهنا लेहना *lehnā*, m. pasture, provender. *h.*

ليهيه लेह्य *lehya*, m. food or beverage of the gods, nectar, ambrosia; adj. fit for being licked. *s.*

ليي लिये *liye*, for the sake of, on account of. *s.*

ليئي लेई *le,ī*, f. paste. *h.*

م

mīm, the twenty-fourth letter of the Arabic alphabet, the twenty-eighth Persian, and the thirty-first Hindūstānī. It is one of the labial letters, its sound being that of the English *m*. In reckoning by *abjad* it stands for 40.

م म *ma*, the corresponding letter in the Devanāgarī alphabet.

ما *mā*, which, what, that which, whatsoever, as far as; why, wherefore; no, not; how; somewhat, something. *mā-ba'd*, that which follows, the sequel. *mā-baḳa*, *mā-bā-baḳī*, or *mā-bāḳī*, the rest, the remainder, arrears, balance. *mā bihi-l-iḥtiyāj*, whatever is necessary. *mā ḥaṣal*, any thing collected, the harvest, produce of fruit trees, &c., profit or income. *mā ḥaẓar*, that which is present or ready. *mā bi-ḳalbi*, or *mā fi-ẓ-ẓamīr*, secret, what is in the mind. *ma shā Allāh*, what God wills. *mā ṣadḳ*, that which is true. *mā-fauḳ*, what is above or superior. *mā ḳabl*, what is before. *mā lā-kalām*, what is unutterable, indescribable. *mā marra*, or *mā-maẓā*, that which passed or occurred. *mā lā-yulāḳ*, what is beyond endurance, intolerable. *mā lā-yanḥall*, what cannot be solved, inextricable. *mā warā* what is beyond. *mā yuḥtaj*, what is necessary. *mā ya,ūl*, that which may come about or return. *a.*

ما *mā*, m. water, juice; *semen*; splendour, lustre, temper. *mā,u-l-jubn*, whey (of goats' milk). *mā,u-l-ḥaiyāt*, water of life. *mā,u-l-'a sal*, metheglin. *mā,u-l-luḥm*, distilled water from kids' flesh with spices. *mā,u-l-ḳara'*, the juice of the pumpkin. *mā,u-l-ward*, rose-water. *a.*

ما *mā*, (pl. of 1st pers. pron.) we, us, our. *p.*

ما मा *mā*, f. a mother; a name of the goddess *Lachhmī*. *s.*

مآب *ma,āb*, a receptacle, repository. *'izzat ma,āb*, the seat of grandeur. *a.*

ماباپ माबाप *mā-bāp*, m. mother and father: parents. *s.*

مابون *mābūn*, m. a catamite; adj. infamous, despicable. *a.*

مابين *mā-bain*, meanwhile, interim; adj. intermediate. *a.*

ماپ माप *māp*, } m. measure, the act of
ماپن मापन *māpan*, } measuring. *s.*

ماپتول मापतूल *māp-tūl*, a system of measures and weights. *s.*

ماپنا मापना *māpnā*, a. to measure. *māpā shorbā aur ginī daliyāṅ* is applied to express scarcity of provisions, also penurious economy. *s.*

ماپهل *mā-phal* (v. *mājū-phal*). *h.*

مات मात *māt*, f. an accent, a vowel; (for *mātā*) a mother. *s.*

مات *māt*, f. (in chess) mate, or what we call checkmate, which last phrase is a corruption of *shāh māt*, "the king is dead, or done for;" adj. astonished, confounded. *māt-k.*, to win, to give checkmate, to overcome in any contest. *p.*

ماتا माता *mātā*, f. mother; the small-pox; adj. drunk, intoxicated. *mātā pitrī*, mother and father, parents. *s.*

ماتامهه मातामहः *mātāmaha*, a maternal grandfather. *mātāmahī*, f. a maternal grandmother. *s.*

ماتر मात्र *mātr*, only, solely, merely. मातृ *mātri*, (used only in comp.) a mother; as *mātri-bandhu*, a mother's relative; *mātri-datta*, what is given by a mother to a bride at her marriage. *s.*

ماترا मात्रा *mātrā*, f. a vowel; a dose. *s.*

ماترك मात्रक *mātrak*, merely, only, solely. *s.*

ماترگهاتك मातृघातुक *mātri-ghātuk*, m. a matricide. *s.* [another's prosperity. *s.*

ماتسر मात्सर *mātsar*, envious, or impatient of

ماتسرج मात्सर्य *mātsarj* (for *mātsarya*), m. envy, malice. *s.*

مات کي بهاجي *māt kī bhājī*, f. the edible amaranth (*Amaranthus oleraceus*). *h.*

ماتل मातुल *mātul*, m. a maternal uncle. *mātul-putrak*, the son of a maternal uncle (a cousin). *s.*

ماتلا मातुला *mātulā*, ماتلاني मातुलानी *mātulānī*, ماتلي मातुली *mātulī*, f. an aunt, the wife of a maternal uncle. *s.*

ماتم *mātam*, m. grief, mourning, especially public mourning, as that which is held for a prince, or at the *Muḥarram*. *mātam-dār*, a mourner. *mātam-pursī*, f. oblations, funeral obsequies, condolence. *mātam khāna*, the house of mourning. *p.*

ماتمداري *mātam-dārī*, f. pompous or public mourning. *p.*

ماتمزده *mātam-zada*, a mourner; melancholy. *p.*

ماتمسرا *mātam-sarā*, ماتمکده *mātam-kuda*, m. the house of mourning. *p.*

ماتمي *mātamī*, relating to mourning, dressed in mourning. *mātamī libās*, mourning apparel. *p.*

ماتنا मातना *mātnā*, n. to be intoxicated. *s*

ماتنگ मातङ्ग *mātang*, m. an elephant. *s.*

ماتها माथा *māthā*, m. the forehead; the ridge of thatch; prov. *māthā ṭhanaknā*, (lit. denotes ringing or throbbing of the forehead) implies a presentiment of the conclusion from certain marks observed in the commencement of an affair. It is generally understood to indicate an unfortunate termination. *māthā ragaṛnā*, (lit. to rub the forehead, viz. on the ground) to implore humbly (of the Deity, a saint, or a king). *mātha par chaṛhnā*, to tyrannize, to oppress. *s.*

ماتهر माथुर *māthur*, m. an inhabitant of Mathurā; name of a sect among *kāyaths*; also a caste or sect of Brāhmans. *s.*

ماتهي لينا माथीलेना *māthī lenā*, a. to make even (particularly a thatch). *h.*

ماٹ *māṭ*, m. a vat or boiler; pan for the manufacture of indigo, &c.; a large vessel or jar. *d.*

ماٹها माठा *māṭhā*, perverse, lazy, obstinate; m. (v. *maṭṭhā*) buttermilk. *h.*

ماٹهو माठू *māṭhū*, m. a buffoon (a term of reproach). *h.* [to envy. *h.*

ماٹي माटी *māṭī*, f. earth, dust. *māṭī-phaknā*,

مآثر *ma,āsir* (pl. of مأثرة), m. signs, marks, memorials, worthy or illustrious actions; histories, traditions; memoirs, biographies. *a.*

ماجائي माजाई *mā-jā,ī*, f. a full sister, born of the same mother. *s.*

ماجايا माजाया *mā-jāyā*, m. a brother, born of the same mother. *mājā,e bhā,ī*, uterine brothers. *s.*

ماجرا *mājarā*, ماجرى *mā-jarā*, m. state, condition, circumstances; an event, incident, occurrence, adventure. *a.* [apple. *s.*

ماجوپهل माजूफल *mājū-phal*, a gall-nut, oak-

ماجهدهار माझधार *mājh-dhār* (also *manjh-dhār*), f. the middle of the stream or current. *s.*

ماچا माचा *māchā*, m. a large bedstead or platform; a frame or stage on which they sit to drive away birds, &c. from cornfields. *māchā-toṛ*, a lazy person who never stirs from his bed; a kind of soldier among the *rāj-pūts*, very indolent, and much addicted to opium, but active and brave when roused. *s.*

ماچه‌خر *mācha-khar*, m. a dolt, a stupid fellow. *p.* [*char*). *s.*

ماچهر माछर *māchhar*, m. a mosquito (v. *mach-*

ماچهي माछी *māchhī*, f. a fly (v. *makhkhī*). *s.*

ماچي माची *māchī*, f. a harrow; a small bedstead; (in Dakh.) a fly. *s.*

ماچين *māchīn*, m. name of a country; China or Chinese Tartary. *p. s.*

ماخذ *mākhaz*, m. a source, origin, receptacle whence any thing is taken. *a.*

ماخڑا *mākharā*, m. a dolt, a lubber. *h.*

ماخوذ *mākhūz*, taken out, borrowed, adopted. *a.*

ماخوليا *mākhūliyā* (Gr. μελαγχολία), madness, insanity, melancholy. *g.*

مادام *mādām*, whilst, until, as long as. *a.*

مأدب *mu,addab*, civil, respectful; civilly, respectfully, reverentially. *a.* [comiast. *a.*

مادح *mādiḥ*, m. one who praises, an en-

مادر *mādar*, f. a mother. *mādar-zād*, naked as born of the mother; innate. *mādari mādar*, a maternal grandmother. *p.*

مادري *mādarī*, motherly, maternal; (Dakh.) a sample, specimen, model, pattern. *p.*

مادك मादक *mādak*, intoxicating, maddening. *s.* [tion. *s.*

مادکتا मादकता *mādkatā*, f. state of intoxica-

مادوان *mādwān* (for *mādiyān*), a mare, &c. *h.*

ماده *māda*, female, feminine; (sub.) a female. *māda-gāw*, a cow. *p.*

مادّه *ma,adda* or *mādda*, m. a matter, subject, article, affair, clause. *a.*

مادهريه माधुर्य *mādhurya*, m. sweetness. *s.*

مادهو माधो *mādho* or माधव *mādhava*, a name of *Krishna*. *s.*

مادهولتا माधोलता *mādholatā*, a large species of creeper with white fragrant flowers (*Gærtnera racemosa*). *s.*

مادهوي माधवी *mādhavī*, f. a large kind of creeper (*Gærtnera racemosa*). *s.*

ماذهوي माधवी *mādhvī*, f. } spirituous
مادهويك माध्वीक *mādhwīk*, m. } liquor distilled from the *bassia latifolia*; wine. *s.*

مادي *mādī* (v. *mādīn*), a female. *d.*

مادّي *māddī*, material, relating to matter. *a.*

ماديان *mādiyān*, m. a mare, a she-ass. *p.*

ماديت *ma,addiyat*, f. substantialness, materiality (pl. *ma'addīyāt*). *a.*

مادين *mādīn*, f. a female. *p.*

ماذون *māzūn*, a licensed slave, *i. e.* one permitted by his owner to trade, &c., as is done to serfs in Russia. *a.*

مار मार *mār*, f. beating; battle; a blow (in comp.) killing, killer; m. plague, epidemy. *mār parnā*, n. to be beatnn. *mār-pīṭ*, f. drubbing, assault and battery. *mār-dhār*, f. thumping and beating severely. *mār-denā*, a. to smite, to beat; to dismiss a suit, to quash a complaint. *mār-ḍālnā*, a. to kill, to smite, to slay outright. *mār-saknā*, n. to be able to beat. *mār-kuṭā,ī*, f. beating and bruising. *mār-khānā*, a. to get a drubbing. *mār-girānā*, a. to knock down. *mār-lānā*, a. to rob, to take by robbery. *mār-lenā*, a. to smite, to overcome, to conquer. *mār-marnā*, to commit suicide; to fall in battle after killing some of the enemy. *mār-hārnā*, to beat severely. *mār-haṭānā*, a. to overcome, to beat and drive back. *mār*, m. a name of *Kāmadeva*. *s.*

مار मार *mār*, a stiff clay or loamy soil with some sand or vegetable mould; a black loam. *h.*

مار *mār*, m. a snake. *mār-pech*, circumvolution. *mār-pech kī rāh*, a crooked or winding path. *mār-gīr*, m. a snake-catcher. *p.*

مارا मारा *mārā*, soil that is productive only during the rainy season. *h.*

مارا मारा *mārā*, beaten, slain; foundered or overturned (a boat, &c.); m. a victim. *mārā parnā*, n. to be killed or slain. *mārā kūṭī karnā*, to blot paper in writing, to spoil a letter or document. *mārā-mārī*, mutual beating; *preposteræ veneris usus reciprocus*. *mārā mārā phirnā*, to wander. *s.*

ماراتمك मारात्मक *mārātmāk*, murderous. *s.*

ماراجانا माराजाना *mārā-jānā*, n. to be slain; to be overcome; to be overturned or sunk (as a boat); to be cut off (a caravan, detachment, &c.). *s.*

مارب *ma,arab* or *mārab*, m. the time or place of any necessary business; (pl. of *mārabat*) necessary things, necessity. *a.*

مارپيٹ मारपीट *mār-pīṭ*, f. beating, thumping; assault and battery. *s.*

مارت मारित *mārit*, killed, slain, slaughtered.

مارتنڈ मार्तण्ड *mārtanḍ*, the sun. *s.*

مارتول *mārtol*, m. (Port. *martello*) a hammer, (in Dakh.) a turnscrew. *port.*

مارجار मार्जार *mārjār*, m. or *mārjārī*, f. the common-cat, the wild or pole-cat. *s.*

مارجن मार्जन *mārjan*, m. cleaning, wiping, rubbing the body with oil, &c., sprinkling with water for purification before the performance of religious ceremonies. *s.*

مارد *mārid*, m. an evil genie, one of those who, as Moslems say, rebelled against Solomon. *a.*

مارك मारक *mārak*, m. plague, epidemic. *s.*

ماركت मारकत *mārkat*, of the colour of emerald. *s.*

مارگ मारग *mārag*, मार्ग *mārg*, or *mārga*, m. a road, a path, a way. *rājā-mārg*, a royal road, a principal main road or highway; doctrine, creed, belief. *s.*

مارگپال मार्गपाल *mārg-pāl*, a watchman, a patrol, a guardian of the road, "custos viarum" *s.*

مارگي मार्गी *mārgī*, a traveller, a follower; one who goes the road literally or spiritually. *s.*

مارگشر मार्गशिर *mārgshir*, m. the month *Agrahāyan* (Nov.-Dec.). *s.*

مارن मारण *māran*, m. killing, slaughter. *māranhārā*, m. smiter, slayer. *s.*

مارنا मारना *mārnā*, m. to smite, beat, drive, punish, cast, mar, ruin, conquer, crack, destroy, fine, take, set, smother, stamp, sting, stop, throw, toss, quench, run. *s.*

مارو मारू *mārū*, m. name of a warlike musical instrument, a kettledrum; name of a deadly weapon composed of two antelope horns pointed with stell; (in comp.) smiting, killing, killer. *h.*

مارو मारू *mārū*, } fatal, deadly, warlike,
ماروا मारवा *mārwā*, } m. name of a *rāg* or musical mode. *h.*

ماروت *mārūt*, name of an angel; adj. great. *a.*

ماروش *mārūsh* or *ma,arūsh*, made, formed, created. *a.*

ماري मारी *mārī*, f. plague, epidemic. *s.*

ماري मारे *māre*, for, by, from, through, because of, by reason of, on account of, in consequence of. *h.*

مارڑني माड़नी *māṛnī*, f. paste. *h.*

مارڑواڑ माड़वाड़ *māṛwāṛ*, name of a country to the west of Jainagar. *s.*

مارڑيا माड़िया *māṛiyā*, lean, thin. *h.*

مازو *māzū*, m. the oak-apple or gall. *p.*

ماس मास *mās*, m. a month; flesh, meat. *māsānt*, f. the last day of the solar or lunar month. *mās-vriddhi*, monthly interest. *s.*

ماسا मासा *māsā*, m. a small weight (v. *māsha*). *s.*

ماسانت मासान्त *māsānt*, m. day of new moon. *s.*

ماسا मासा *māsa*, a land measure, three-fourths of a *bighā*, q. v. *h.*

ماسك मासिक *māsik*, monthly; m. an obsequial rite performed every day of the new moon. *s.*

ماس كبار मासकबार *mās-kabār* (cor. from Port. *mes*, a month, and *acabar*, to end, to terminate), the last day of a month. *port.*

ماسن मासन *māsan*, m. a medicinal seed (*Serratula anthelmintica*).

ماسوا *mā-siwā*, besides, moreover, save, except; whatever else. *a.*

ماسي मासी *māsī*, f. mother's sister, maternal aunt (v. *mānsī*). *s.* [old. *s.*

ماسين मासीन *māsīn*, of a month, a month

ماش माष *māsh*, m. a kind of vetch or kidney-bean (*Phaseolus max* or *radiatus*). *s.* [*sha*).

ماشا माषा *māshā*, m. a small weight (v. *mā-*

ماشپرني माषपर्णी *māsh-parnī*, f. a leguminous shrub (*Glycine debilis*). *s.*

ماشه माषः *māsha*, m. name of a small weight consisting of eight *rattīs*, q. v. *s.*

ماضي *māẓī*, past (time); m. (in gram.) the preterite or indefinite past tense. *a.*

ماکند माकन्द *mākand*, m. the mango. *s.*

ماکندي माकन्दी *mākandī*, f. emblic myrobalan. *s.*

ماکهن माखन *mākhan*, m. (v. *makkhan*) butter. *s.*

ماکهو *mākhū*, m. a weaver's shuttle. *d.*

ماکیان *mākiyan*, f. a fowl, a hen. *p.*

ماگده मागध *māgadh*, m. a bard, a minstrel whose duty it is to recite the praises of sovereigns, their genealogy, and the deeds of their ancestors, in their presence; and to attend on the march of an army and animate the soldiers by martial songs: the minstrel forms a particular caste, said to spring from a *Vaishya* father and *Kshatriya* mother; in mythology they are said to have been created at once by the will of *Shiva*: under the name of *bhāṭs* they are still numerous in some parts of India, especially Gujerāt, where they are a privileged tribe (v. *bhāṭ*); *māgadh*, as an adjective, denotes "belonging to, or produced in, the province of Magadha or South Bihār." *s.*

ماگدهي मागधी *māgadhī*, f. a kind of jasmine (*Jasminum auriculatum*); long-pepper (*Piper longum*); a sort of cardamums; a *Prākrit* dialect.

ماگنا मागना *māgnā*, a. to ask for. *h.*

ماگه माघ *māgh*, m. name of the tenth Hindū month, the full moon of which is near *maghā* or *a Leonis* (*Regulus*) (Jan.-Feb.). *s.*

ماگهات माघात *māghāt*, land broken up in *māgh* for next year's crop. *māghāt-kī-phasal* (for *faṣl*), the crops sown in or immediately after *māgh*. *h.*

ماگهي माघी *māghī*, f. a potherb (*Hingsta repens*). *s.*

مال *māl*, m. property, wealth, merchandise, goods; the public revenue of a state; a prize (in a lottery, &c.). *māl-khāwind*, a proprietor. *māl-dār*, wealthy, rich. *māl-dārī*, f. wealthiness. *māl-zāda*, a son of a whore, a pimp or pander. *māl-zādī*, f. a bawd, a whore. *māl-ẓāmin*, a security (for property or money, in opposition to *ḥāẓir-ẓāmin*, q. v.). *māli murdum-khor*, a consumer of the property of others, one who borrows and never pays. *māl-wājib*, revenue or rents due to government. *a.*

مال माल्ल *māl*, m. a prize-fighter, a champion, a wrestler; f. a necklace, a garland. *s.*

مال *ma,āl*, m. end, termination, issue, tendency. *khair ma,āl*, a happy issue or tendency. *ma,āl-andesh*, one who looks to the issue of things. *ma,āl-andeshī*, consideration of the end or consequence. *a. p.*

مال *māl*, (in comp.) rubbing, polishing as *rū-māl*, a towel, face-rubber. *p.*

مالا माला *mālā*, f. a Hindū rosary, a necklace, a garland; a book. *mālā-phal*, m. the seed of the Eleocarpus, of which rosaries are made. *s.*

مالاکار मालाकार *mālākār*, m. a flower-seller, a gardener. *s.*

مالامال *mālāmāl*, full, replete, abundant. *p.*

مالپوا मालपूआ *mālpū,ā*, m. a kind of sweetmeat, a pancake. *h.*

مالتي मालती *māltī*, f. a bud, a blossom; name given to different flowers—1. *Echites caryophyllata*, *Roxb.*; 2. *Jasminum grandiflorum*; 3. (or *māltīlatā*) *Gærtnera racemosa*, *Roxb.*, or *Banisteria Bengalensis*, *Lin.*; 4. *Bignonia suaveolens*. *s.*

مالخانه *māl-khāna*, a treasury, a storehouse. *a. p.*

مالدهني *māl-dhanī*, m. a possessor of property, especially of land. *p. s.*

مالسري मालश्री *mālsrī*, f. name of a *rāg* or musical mode. *s.*

مالش *mālish*, rubbing, polishing, furbishing. *mālish-k.*, to rub, &c.; to thresh or trample corn by the feet of oxen. *p.*

مالك *mālik*, m. master, lord, possessor, proprietor, owner. *māliku-l-ḥazīn*, name of a certain waterfowl. *māliku-l-mulk*, a title addressed to sovereign princes, prime ministers, &c. *a.*

مالکا मालका *mālakā*, f. a garland. *s.*

مالکانه *mālikāna*, like a master or owner; in the manner of an owner; m. an annual or monthly allowance paid to a *zamīndār* by the person who occupies his lands, whether the state or a *jāgīrdār*. *s.*

مال کنگني मालकङ्गनी *mālkangnī*, f. *Celastrus*. *h.*

مالکوس मालकोस *mālkos*, m. name of a *rāg*. *s.*

مالکي *mālikī*, royal, princely, lordly. *a.*

مالکیت *mālikiyat*, f. possession, property, patronage; ownership, proprietorship. *a.*

مالگذار *māl-guzār*, m. a tenant, a subject, a landholder. *p.*

مالگذاري *māl-guzārī*, f. rent, the paying of rents or revenues; land paying revenue, in contradistinction to *lā-khirāj*, q. v. *p.*

مالمفت *māl-muft* or *māli muft*, property acquired without cost or labour; property given away without requital or benefit. *a. p.*

مالمست *māl-mast*, purse-proud, intoxicated with wealth. *p.*

مالمستي *māl-mastī*, pride of wealth. *p.*

مالن मालिन *mālin*, } f. a gardener's wife,
مالني मालिनी *mālinī*, } female gardener or flower-seller. *s.* [of Malwa. *s.*

مالو मालव *mālawa*, m. the province or people

مالور *māl-war*, rich, opulent. *p.*

مالوف *mālūf*, familiar, accustomed to live in friendship, ordinary, customary. *a.*

مالي *mālī*, f. (in comp.) abst. of *māl*, q.v. *p.*

مالي *mālī*, relating to wealth or revenue. *mālī-peshkār*, a revenue accountant. *a.*

مالي माली *mālī*, m. a gardener, a florist. *s.*

ماليت *māliyat*, f. wealth, wealthiness. *a.*

ماليخوليا *mālīkhūlīyā* (μελαγχολια), melancholy; twaddle, or wretched and tedious talk. *g.*

ماليدن *mālīdan*, to rub, anoint. *p.*

ماليده *mālīda*, m. bread or cakes made with flour, milk, butter, sugar, &c. *p.*

مالیوان माल्यवान *mālyawān*, ماليوت माल्यवत *mālyawat*, } m. a mountainous range lying eastward of Mount Meru. *s.*

ماليه माल्य *mālya*, m. a garland, a chaplet. *s.*

مام *mām*, ماما *māmā*, } f. mother (old women in general are so called). *māmi nāf*, a midwife. *p.* [*māmū*, q. v. *s.*

ماما मामा *māmā*, m. a maternal uncle (also

ماماءي *māmā,ī*, f. midwifery. *p.*

مامك मामक *māmak*, selfish; m. a miser, a niggard *s.*

مامك *māmak*, a dear little mother. *p.*

مامن *māman*, m. place of security. *a.*

مامو मामू *māmū*, also *māmūṅ*, m. an uncle, mother's brother; a snake; (phrase used at night, when it is deemed unlucky to call a serpent by its proper name). *s.*

مامور *māmūr*, ordered, commanded; fixed; appointed to a situation; determined, defined; (sub.) usage, established custom. *a.*

مامول *māmūl*, m. hope, expectation; adj. hoped for, expected. *a.*

مامون *māmūn*, rendered secure, preserved, exempted; firm, constant. *a.* [wife. *s.*

مامي मामी *māmī*, f. an aunt, maternal uncle's

مامي پينا मामीपीना *māmī pīnā*, a. to shew partiality. *h.* [in. *s.*

مان माँ *māṅ*, f. (v. *mā*) a mother; postpos.

مان मान *mān*, m. character, dignity, honour; ceremony; arrogance, pride; measure in general; blandishment; adv. suppose, grant. *mān-gumān* or *mān-mahat*, m. dignity, state, honour. *mān-gaun*, m. respect. *s.*

مانا *mānā*, alike, equal, resembling. *p.*

مانا मानना *mānnā*, a. to respect, believe, accept, acknowledge, receive, agree, allow, confess, consent, grant, take, trust, yield, submit, suppose, obey, own, permit, regard, mind, attend to. *s.*

مانپان *mān-pān*, respecting, honouring. *d.*

مانت *mānat*, likeness, resemblance; purpose, vow, resolution. *d.* [f. pride, dignity. *s.*

مانتا मानता *māntā*, f. vow, promise. *mānitā*,

مانج मांज *māṅj*, pus, matter, serum. *s.*

مانجشتھ माञ्जिष्ठ *māṅjishṭh*, m. of a red colour. *s.*

مانجنا मांजना *māṅjnā*, a. to scour, to scrub, to clean. *s.*

مانجھ मांझ *māṅjh*, m. name of a *rāginī*, or musical mode; the middle; a kind of verse. *māṅjh-dhār*, f. the middle of the stream. *h.*

مانجھا मांझा *māṅjhā*, m. a paste mixed with pounded glass, and applied to the string of a kite to cut that of another with; a feast given by a bride-groom previous to the wedding; the trunk of a tree. *h.*

مانجھت मांझत *māṅjhat*, f. state, dignity. *h.*

مانجھي मांझी *māṅjhī*, m. master of a vessel; a boatman, sailor, a steersman. *h.*

مانچيو *mānachyu* or *mānchyu*, name of a tribe of Tartars (commonly *Manchoo*). *t.*

ماند मांद *māṅd*, f. faded, a dull colour; a dunghill; the den of a wild beast. *h.*

ماندا *māndā* (for *mānda*, q. v.), tired, &c. *p. h.*

ماندگي *māndagī*, f. fatigue, weariness. *p.*

ماندن *māndan*, to remain; to be fatigued or worn out. *p.*

مانده *mānda*, tired, weary, fatigued. *p.*

مانڈ मांड *mānḍ*, m. rice-water, rice-gruel, starch, paste. *s.*

مانڈا मांडा *mānḍā*, m. film, speck (on the eye); a kind of bread. *h.*

مانڈنا मांडना *mānḍnā*, a. to rub; to tread or trample down, to knead; to make, to stir, to commit; to starch. *s.* [porary building, &c. *s.*

مانڈھا मांढा *mānḍhā*, m. (v. *maḍhā*) a tem-

مانڈي मांडी *mānḍī*, f. starch made of rice-flour. *s.*

مانس मानस *mānas*, mental; m. the mind; a lake in the Himālaya mountains. *s.*

مانس मानुष *mānus*, m. a human being, a man. *s.*

مانس मांस *māṅs*, m. flesh, meat. *māṅs-bhaksh* or *māṅs-ād*, carnivorous. *s.*

مانسنوان मानसनवान *mān-sanwān*, m. welcome. *s.* [*leriana jatamansi*). *s.*

مانسي मांसी *māṅsī*, f. Indian spikenard (*Va-*

مانش मानुष *mānush*, مانشي मानुष्य *mānushya*, } m. a man, a human being. *mānushyā*, m. humanity. *mānushī*, f. a woman. *s.*

مانع *mānī'*, m. an obstacle, impediment; a forbidder, preventer. *mānī' honā*, to prevent, to forbid, to prohibit. *kyā mānī'*, what binders? quid obstat? *a.* [terruption. *a.*

موانعات *mānī'āt* (pl. of مانع), obstacles, in-

مانعت *māni'at*, f. prohibition, obstacle. *a.*

مانك मानिक *mānik*, m. a kind of gem, ruby. *lid kā mānik*, a horse. *mānak*, m. a plant, the root of which is eaten (*Arum indicum*). *s.*

مانك جوڑ मानिकजोड़ *mānik-jor*, m. name of a bird (*Ardea leucocephala*). *h.*

مانكهہ मानुष *mānukh*, m. (for *mānush*), a man, a human being. *s.*

مانكيه माणिक्य *mānikya*, m. a ruby. *s.*

مانگ मांग *māng*, f. a line on the top of the head where hair is parted; division; prow; a betrothed damsel. *māng nikālnā*, to divide the hair in a straight line on the top of the head. *h.*

مانگ چكني मांगचिकनी *māng-chiknī*, f. name of a bird. *h.*

مانگ دينا मांगदेना *māng-denā*, a. to borrow for another, to ask for and give to another. *h.*

مانگلك माङ्गलिक *māngalik*, propitious. *s.*

مانگ لينا मांगलेना *māng-lenā*, a. to borrow. *h.*

مانگليه माङ्गल्य *māngalya*, m. happiness. *s.*

مانگنا मांगना *māngnā*, a. to ask for, to require, to demand, to beg, to pray, to want, to desire, to seek, to will. *māng tāng karnā*, to ask for. *h.*

مانگني मांगनी *māngnī*, f. asking or betrothing in marriage.

مانگي मांगी *māngī*, f. a loan, what is borrowed; betrothed (a woman). *h.*

ماننا मानना *mānnā*, a. to admit, to agree to, to receive favourably, to mind, to attend to, to take (v. *mānnā*). *burā mānnā*, to take amiss, to take as an affront. *bhalā mānnā*, to take in good part. *burā mānnā yā bhalā*, to take ill or well. *s.*

مانند *mānand* or *mānind*, f. and m. like, resembling, resemblance. On the application of this word as a preposition v. Hind. Gr. p. 99. *p.*

مانني माननी *māninī*, proud, haughty. *s.*

مانني‌ه माननीय *mānanīya*, adj. to be respected. *s.*

مانو मानव *mānav*, m. a man, a manikin; a child. *s.* [cat. *s.*

مانو मानो *māno*, suppose, grant, as if; m. a

مانوت मानवत *mānwat* (fem. *mānwatī*), proud, haughty. *s.* [lowly. *s.*

مان ورجت मानवर्जित *mān-varjit*, humble,

مانوس *mānūs*, m. a companion, associate, friend. *a.* [kin. *s.*

مانوك माणवक *mānavak*, m. a boy, a mani-

مانوي मानवी *mānavī*, f. a woman. *s.*

مانہ मांह *mānh*, postpos. in; (same as *men*). *s.*

مانہاني मानहानि *māna-hāni*, loss of character or reputation. *s.*

مانہو मानहू *mānhū* (v. *māno*), suppose, grant; like, resembling. *s.*

مانہين मनहीन *māna-hīn*, disreputable, vile. *s.*

ماني मानी *mānī*, proud, haughty. *s.*

مانيه मान्य *mānya*, respectable, venerable. *s.*

ماوا मावा *māwa*, f. substance; starch; the yolk of an egg: leaven; milk inspissated by boiling. *h.*

ماوا *māwā*, f. dwelling, abode, habitation. *a.*

ماوس मावस *māwas*, f. the conjunction of the sun and moon; the change of the moon. *s.*

ماولي *māwalī*, f. a mother. *d.*

ماه *māh*, m. the moon; a month. *māhi kan'ānī* (moon of *kan'ān*), Joseph, the son of Jacob. *māh-ba-māh* or *māh-māh*, monthly. *p.*

ماهاتمك माहात्मिक *māhātmik*, magnanimous, majestic, of great sanctity. *s.*

ماهاتميه माहात्म्य *māhātmya*, m. majesty, greatness; the peculiar efficacy or virtue of a divinity, of a sacred shrine, &c.; a work giving an account of the merits of a holy place or object. *s.*

ماهاجنك माहाजनिक *māhājanik*, fit for great persons. *s.* [kingly. *s.*

ماهاراجك माहाराजिक *māhārājik*, imperial,

ماهاكل माहाकुल *māhākul*, of a great family. *s.*

ماهپار *māh-pār*, / ماهپاره *māh-pāra*, (lit.) a piece of the moon; a handsome person. *p.*

ماهتاب *māhtāb*, m. the moon; moonlight, moonshine. *p.*

ماهتابي *māhtābī*, f. a kind of firework, blue-light; a kind of figured cloth. *p.*

ماهر *māhir*, acute, ingenious, sagacious, skilful, clever, proficient. *a.*

ماهر माहुर *māhur*, m. poison, venom. *h.*

ماهرو *mah-rū*, having a face beautiful as the moon; charming, elegant. *p.*

ماهن माहिं *māhin*, in (same as *men*). *h.*

ماهو माहू *māhū*, m. (v. *kan-salā,ī*). *h.*

ماهوار *māhwār*, / ماهواري *māhwārī*, monthly, per month, monthly wages. *p.*

ماهي *māhī*, f. a fish. *māhī-tawa*, m. a frying-pan. *māhī-dandān*, m. a fish's tooth, of which the hilts of swords, &c. are made; ivory of the walrus (imported from Russia, and which the Persians and Indians suppose to be the tooth of a large fish). *māhī-farosh*, m. a fishmonger. *māhī-gīr*, m. a fisherman. an otter (*Lutra lutreola, Shaw*). *māhī marātib*, m. certain honours, of which the privilege is especially conferred on princes and great nobles; they are denoted by the figure of a fish, with other insignia (two balls) carried as ensigns upon elephants. *p.*

ماهيانه *māhiyāna*, m. monthly salary. *p.*

ماهيت *māhiyat*, f. state, condition, circumstances, quality, value, essence, intrinsic worth. *a.*

ماهيچه *māhīcha*, small threads of paste boiled with soup, vermicelli. *p.*

ماهي خوار *māhī-khwār*, a heron. *p.*

ماهيدان **mähī-dān**, a fishpond, a preserve-pond. *p.*

ماءي माई **mā,e** or **mā,ī**, f. a mother. *s.*

ماءي **mā,ī**, of or relating to water, watery. *a.*

مايا माया **māyā**, f. kindness, pity, sympathy, compassion, mercy, feeling, affection; idealism, illusion; prosperity, riches, opulence; a deception depending on the power of the Deity, whereby mankind believe in the existence of external objects which are in fact nothing but idea. *māyā-paṭu*, delusive, expert in deceiving. *māyā-may*, deceptive. *s.*

مايا **māyā** (for **māya**, q. v.) wealth, &c. *p.*

ماياپاتر मायापात्र **māyā-pātra**, rich, opulent, wealthy. *s.*

ماياوي मायावी **māyāvī**, m. a juggler, a conjuror. *s.*

مائك मायिक **māyik**, illusory, deceptive. *s.*

مائكا मायका **mā,ekā**, m. the maternal mansion (applied only to a woman). *s.*

مائل **mā,il**, inclined towards, taking delight in, affectionate, having a propensity, inclination, or partiality; addicted, apt. *a.*

مائن माईं **mā,īn**, f. aunt (v. *māmī*). *h.*

مايوس **māyūs**, desperate, hopeless. *a.*

مايوسي **māyūsī**, f. hopelessness, desperation. *a.*

مايه **māya**, m. wealth, stock, money; root, origin, principle; a capital in trade, stock or store; measure, quantity, value. *girān-māya*, of great value, costly. *faro-māya*, base, despicable. *p.*

مباح **mubāḥ**, m. any indifferent action, which incurs neither praise nor blame; lawful pleasure. *a.*

مباحثه **mubāḥaṣa**, m. a dispute, contest, debate, investigation, argumentation. *a.*

مباد **ma-bād**, مبادا **ma-bādā**, } by no means, God forbid, lest, let it not so happen. *p.*

مبادرت **mubādarat**, f. haste, expedition; labouring. *a.*

مبادله **mabādala**, m. exchange, barter, retaliation, recompense. *a.*

مبادي **mabādī**, f. beginnings, origins. *a.*

مبارات **mubārāt**, dissolution of marriage, partnership, &c., by mutual consent. *a.*

مبارز **mubāriz**, m. a hero, a warrior; adj. prepared or ready for war. *p.*

مبارك **mubārak**, happy, fortunate, blessed, august, sacred, holy, welcome, well, auspicious. *a.*

مبارك‌باد **mubārak-bād**, (lit.) may he be blessed or fortunate; blessing, congratulation. *a. p.*

مباركبادي **mubārak-bādī**, f. congratulation, benediction. *a. p.*

مباركي **mubārakī**, f. blessing, auspiciousness. *a.*

مباشر **mubāshir**, a superintendant, an agent; (in law) the doer of any thing; a culprit, a criminal. *a.*

مباشرت **mubāsharat**, f. commencement or undertaking of any affair; having carnal knowledge of a woman. *a.*

مباف **mu-bāf** (for **mū-bāf**), a braid of hair, a hair ribbon. *p.*

مبالغ **mabāligh** (pl. of مبلغ), sums of money. *mubāligh*, one who exaggerates or goes to extremes. *a.*

مبالغه **mubālagha**, m. exaggeration, hyperbole; diligence, endeavour; dwelling on a subject. *a.*

مباهات **mubāhāt**, boasting, glorying, pride, arrogance; glory, honour. *a.*

مباهي **mubāhī**, glorious, exalted; presuming, arrogant, proud. *a.*

مبايعت **mubāya'at**, entering into a contract of purchase or sale. *a.*

مبتدا **mubtadā**, f. commencement, principle, or subject of a proposition; substantive noun in the nominative case. *mubtadā o khabar*, f. the subject and predicate or substantive and adjective (in syntax). *a.*

مبتدي **mubtadī**, m. beginning, a young scholar, a disciple just commencing to learn, a tyro; a founder, commencer. *a.*

مبتذل **mubtazal**, contemptible, base. *a.*

مبتسم **mubtasim**, smiling, laughing. *a.*

مبتلا **mubtalā**, مبتلي **mubtalī**, } afflicted, unfortunate, involved in trouble, tried with affliction, inured to distress. *a.*

مبحث **mabḥas**, time and place for disputation, disputation. *a.*

مبخر **mubakhkhar**, perfumed, odorous. *a.*

مبدا **mabdā**, the beginning, origin, source, principle. *a.*

مبدع **mabda'**, an invention, discovery, fiction, *mubdi'*, a creator, author, inventor, founder; one who feigns or tells a lie. *a.*

مبدل **mubaddal**, changed, altered. *a.*

مبذر **mubazzir**, prodigal, lavish. *a.*

مبذري **mubazzirī**, prodigality, waste. *a.*

مبذول **mabzūl**, expended, bestowed. *a.*

مبر **mubirr**, superior to one's companions. *a.*

مبرا **mubarrā**, free, absolved, exempted, far removed from. *mubarrā-k.*, to acquit, to absolve, to exempt, to free. *a.*

مبرات **mabarrāt** (pl. of مبرت), good deeds, works of beneficence. *a.*

مبرت **mabarrat**, f. doing good, beneficence; a public work (as a caravanseral, &c.) built by pious Musulmāns. *a.*

مبرم **mubram**, twisted of two threads twined together; firm, strong, urgent. *ḳazā,e mubram*, irresistible fate.

مبرهن **mubarhan**, demonstrative, evident, manifest. *a.*

مبسوط **mabsūṭ**, spread out, expanded, *a.*

مبشر *mubashshir*, m. a bearer of glad tidings, an evangelist. *a.*

مبصر *mubaṣṣir*, one who can see; provident, penetrating; clear, conspicuous. *mubṣir*, seeing; clear. *a.*

مبطل *mubṭal* or *mubaṭṭal*, abolished, annihilated. *mubṭil* or *mubaṭṭil*, abolishing, defacing, or destroying; an abolisher. *a.*

مبغوض *mabghūẓ*, hated, detested, odious, viewed as an enemy. *a.*

مبلغ *mablagh*, m. the place of arrival; amount, sum, ready money; much, many. *mablagh-bandī*, adjusted balance of an account. *a.*

مبني *mabnī*, also *mabnā*, m. a foundation. *mabnī-i fasād*, an aggressor, the origin of strife. *a.*

مبهم *mubham*, occult, unknown, keeping concealed; ambiguous, equivocal. *a.*

مبهوت *mabhūt*, stupified, astonished, struck dumb with astonishment, confounded. *a.*

مبهي *mubahhī*, *aphrodisiaca*, provocative; that which excites venery.

مبيت *mabīt*, passing the night; doing any thing in the night-time, abiding; a bedchamber, or any place wherein to pass the night. *a.*

مبيعي *mubī'ī*, sold, bought; venal. *a.*

مبين *mubīn*, manifest, clear. *mubaiyan*, explained, illustrated. *a.*

ميان मपान *mapān*, m. measuring, measure. *s.*

ميانا मपाना *mapānā*, a. to cause to be measured. *s.* [sure. *s.*

ميت كهپت मपतखपत *mapat-khapat*, f. mea-

مپنا मपना *mapnā*, n. to be measured. *s.*

مپوانا मपवाना *mapwānā*, a. to have measured, or get measured, or cause to be measured. *s.*

مت मत *mat*, m. purpose, wish, intent; knowledge, doctrine, belief; f. manner, method, way, mode, system; wisdom, opinion, understanding, parts. *mat-hīn*, void of understanding. *mati*, f. understanding, intellect; wish, desire. *s.*

مت मत *mat*, neg. par. (used with the imperative), don't, as *mat jā,o*, don't go. *h.*

مت मत्त *matt*, intoxicated, drunk. *s.*

مت मित *mit*, measured. *miti*, f. measuring, measure, proof, evidence; date, interest. *pakkā miti*, interest allowed by bankers on money received, dated from the day following receipt. *kachchā-miti*, interest charged on money advanced, dated from the day before the transaction. *s.*

متا मता *mata*, m. counsel, advice, opinion. *s.*

متابعت *mutāba'at*, f. obsequiousness; following, understanding, or imitating one another, submitting, obeying; doing any thing solidly and certainly, doing in the same manner after another. *a.*

متاثر *muta,aṣṣir*, touched, impressed, affected, affective, efficacious. *a.*

متاخرين *muta,akhkhirīn*, modern, late. *a.*

متادب *muta,addab*, well-bred, learned, polite. *a.* [ing. *a.*

متادي *muta,addī*, prepared, ready, perform-

متاذي *muta,azzī*, afflicted, troubled, grieved. *a.*

متارا *matārā*, wealth, substance. *d.*

متاس मुतास *mutās*, f. desire or inclination to piss. *s.*

متاسا मुतासा *mutāsā*, desirous of pissing. *s.*

متاسف *muta,assif*, sorrowful, afflicted, anxious, oppressed with grief. *a.*

متاشن मिताशन *mitāshan*, moderate in diet. *s.*

متاع *matā'*, f. merchandise, goods, chattels, furniture, effects, &c., valuables. *a.*

متالف *muta,allif*, m. one who cultivates the acquaintance, or conciliates the goodwill of another. *a.*

متالم *muta,allim*, grieved, sad, afflicted, pained, discontented. *a.*

متامل *muta,ammil*, contemplative, considering, examining attentively. *a.*

متانا मुताना *mutānā*, to cause to make water. *mutāne wālā*, (in medicine) a diuretic. *h.*

متانت *matānat*, f. firmness, solidity; a fortification, a castle; obstinacy. *a.*

متانتر मतान्तर *matāntar*, another method, tenet, or opinion. *s.*

متانتراچار मतान्तराचार *matāntarāchār*, the observance of another method or tenet. *s.*

متانسار मतानुसार *matānusār*, conformity to usage, opinion, or tenet. *s.*

متاولمبي मतावलम्बी *matāvalambī*, a sectary, one attached to a certain sect, tenet, or opinion. *s.*

متاهل *mutāhil*, a married man. *a.*

متبحر *mutabaḥḥir*, profound, especially in learning. *a.* [ternately. *a.*

متبدل *mutabaddil*, inverting, changing al-

متبدي *mutabaddī*, m. a commencer, a beginner. *a.*

متبذل *mutabaẓẓil*, despised, not cared for. *a.*

متبرك *mutabarrak*, fortunate, august, blessed, holy. *a.*

متبسم *mutabassim*, smiling, laughing, risible. *a.*

متبنگي *mutabannagī*, the adopting of a son or child. *a. h.*

متبني *mutabannā*, adopted (son or child). *a.*

متبهرم मतिभ्रम *mati-bhram*, m. } error,
متبهرانت मतिभ्रान्ति *mati-bhrānti*, f. } mistake, misapprehension. *s.*

متتبع *mutatabbi'*, imitative; (sub. m.) an imitator. *a.* [emissary. *a.*

متجسس *mutajassis*, m. a spy, a scout, an

متجلي *mutajallā*, splendid, illuminated. *a.*

متحد *muttaḥid*, united, made one. *a.*

متحرفه *mutaḥarrifa*, m. professional tax, duties levied on certain trades and occupations. *a.*

متحرك *mutaḥarrik*, moved, moving one's self, moveable; accented with short vowels. *ghair mutaḥarrik*, immoveable; not having a vowel. *a.*

متحرم *mutaḥarrim*, revered, respected, prohibited, unlawful. *a.*

متحقق *mutaḥakkik*, a verifier. *mutaḥakkak*, verified. *a.*

متحمد *mutaḥammid*, praised, praiseworthy. *a.*

متحمل *mutaḥammil*, affable, considerate; enduring, patient, suffering, bearing a burthen. *a.*

متحير *mutaḥaiyir*, astonished, wondering, confounded. *a.*

متخاصمين *mutakhāṣimain*, the two contending [parties in a law-suit. *a.*

متخلص *mutakhalliṣ*, pure; surnamed; safe, delivered from evil. *a.*

متخيل *mutakhaiyil*, imagining, suspecting, fancying (good or evil). *mutakhaiyila*, imagination fancy. *a.*

متداول *mutadāwal*, } common, customary,
متداوله *mutadāwala*, } usual. *a.*

متدين *mutadaiyin*, orthodox, religious. *a.*

متر मित्र *mitr* or *mitra*, m. a friend, friendship. *mitra-bhed*, breach of friendship. *mitra-druh*, a false or treacherous friend. *mitra-lābh*, acquisition of a friend, forming friendship. *s.*

متراءي मित्राई *mitrā,ī*, f. friendship, friendly intercourse. *s.*

مترادف *mutarādif*, continued, successive; synonymous. *a.*

مترادف [condensed. *a.*

متراكم *mutarākim*, accumulated, heaped up,

مترانا मतराना *matrānā*, to persuade. *s.*

مترتا मित्रता *mitratā*, f. friendship, friendly intercourse. *s.*

مترتب *mutarattib*, arranged. *s.*

مترجم *mutarjim*, m. an interpreter; a translator. *mutarjam*, translated. *a.*

مترحم *mutaraḥḥim*, compassionate, merciful, tender, affectionate. *a.*

متردد *mutaraddid*, rejected; adverse; wandering; irresolute, perplexed, ambiguous, hesitating. *a.*

متردروهي मित्रद्रोही *mitra-drohī*, a false or treacherous friend. *s.*

مترسل *mutarassil*, one who sends, the writer or sender of a letter. *a.*

مترصد *mutaraṣṣid*, expecting, watching, exploring; contemplating, gazing at. *a.*

مترضي *mutaraẓẓī*, contenting, satisfying. *a.*

مترقب *mutarakkib*, expecting, watching, observing, desiring. *a.*

متركب *mutarakkib*, composing, compound-[ing. *a.*

متروك *matrūk*, abolished, obsolete, rejected, relinquished. *māl matrūk*, estate of a person deceased. *matrūku-l-isti'māl*, unusual, not practised, disused, obsolete. *a.*

متروكه *matrūka* (pl. *matrūkāt*), estate, goods, or property of a person deceased, to which his heirs are legally entitled. *a.*

متزائد *mutazā,id*, increasing, multiplying. *a.*

متزلزل *mutazalzal*, shaken, convulsed (as the earth by an earthquake). *a.*

متساوي *mutasāwī*, equal, parallel, right, straight. *a.*

متسر मत्सर *matsar*, envious, niggardly, co-[vetous. *a.*

متسرا मत्सरा *matsarā*, f. envy, anger, passion; a gnat, a musquito. *s.*

متسري मत्सरी *matsarī* (fem. *matsarinī*), envious, wicked. *s.*

متسع *muttasi'*, broad, large, diffused. *mutsi'* or *mutassa'*, making up the number nine. *a.*

متسلط *mutasalliṭ*, despotic (command), absolute (dominion). *a.*

متسلم *mutasallim*, receiving any thing in charge, keeping in possession. *mutasallam* (part. pas.), delivered, consigned. *a.*

متسلي *mutasallī*, consoled, satisfied, comforted, condoled. *a.*

متسيه मत्स्य *matsya*, m. a fish; the fish-avatār of *Vishṇu*, the Purāna in which it is related; a country (Dinajpoor and Rungpoor). *matsya-rāj*, m. the fish called *Rohi* (*Cyprinus rohita*). *s.*

متشابه *mutashābih*, like, resembling; (sub.) an allegory, a simile, metaphor. *a.*

متشرع *mutasharri'*, orthodox, observing the *Shar'* or Divine law. *a.*

متشكل *mutashakkil*, like, resembling. *a.*

متشكي *mutashakkī*, complaining, a complainer. *a.*

متصدع *mutaṣaddi'*, importuning, troubling, [plaguing. *a.*

متصدي *mutaṣaddī*, m. an accountant, a writer, a clerk; turning away the face, opposing; attempting, daring, intent on. *a.*

متصرف *mutaṣarrif*, profuse, extravagant; possessing, occupying; embezzling. *a.*

متصل *muttaṣil*, near, contiguous, adjoining. *a.*

متصور *mutaṣawwir*, considering, reflecting, considerate, imagining, conceiving. *mutaṣawwar*, imagined, considered. *a.*

متصوف *mutaṣauwif*, mystical, obscure, meta-[physical. *a.*

متضبط *mutaẓabbiṭ*, seizing forcibly. *a.*

متضرب *mutaẓarrib*, agitated, disturbed, uneasy, beaten. *a.*

متضعف *mutaẓa''af*, weak, contemptible. *a.*
متضمن *mutaẓammin*, including, comprehending. *a.*
متظلم *mutaẓallim*, obscured, darkened, oppressed, injured. *a.*
متع *mat'*, f. enjoying, reaping the advantage of; advancing (as the day). *a.*
متعارف *muta'āraf*, known, acknowledged, well known to each other. *a.*
متعاقب *muta'āḳib*, successive, following, pursuing; adv. afterwards. *a.*
متعال *muta'āl*, } high, sublime, lofty. *a.*
متعالي *muta'ālī*, }
متعبد *muta'abbid*, devout, religious; refractory, stubborn (a camel). *a.*
متعجب *muta'ajjib*, wonderful, admiring, wondering, astonished. *a.*
متعدد *muta'addid*, many, various; ready, prepared; (sub.) a number exceeding 10,000. *a.*
متعدم *muta'addam*, wanting, deficient. *a.*
متعدي *muta'addī*, a transgressor, a wicked wretch; (in gram.) an active, transitive, or causal verb. *a.*
متعذر *muta'azzir*, making an apology; deserving pardon; difficult, impossible; stained; defaced. *a.*
متعرا *mata'rā*, wealth, substance. *d.*
متعرض *muta'arriẓ*, m. opposing, resisting, giving pain or trouble. *a.*
متعسر *muta'assir*, difficult, impossible. *a.*
متعصب *muta'aṣṣib*, bigoted, partial, prejudiced. *a.*
متعفن *muta'affin*, putrid, corrupted, rotten, stinking. *a.*
متعقد *muta'aḳḳid*, consolidated, fastened together. *a.*
متعلق *muta'alliḳ*, hanging, suspended; belonging to, concerning; connected with, attached to, addicted; m. a relation or kinsman. *a.*
متعلقات *muta'alliḳāt*, } pl. domestics, children, family. *a.*
متعلقان *muta'alliḳān*, }
متعلم *muta'allam*, being taught, learning; (sub.) a scholar, disciple. *muta'allim*, teaching, a teacher. *a.*
متعند *muta'annid*, an enemy, one who seeks another's ruin and destruction. *a.*
متعه *mut'a*, use, profit, conveniency, marrying *pro tempore*, an easy kind of marriage permitted to good Musulmāns when absent from home: the Sunnis, however, consider it illegal and immoral. *a.*
متعين *muta'aiyin*, appointed to, fixed, constituted, deputed, determined. *a.*
متعينه *muta'aiyana*, m. a station, post, command; an appointment, establishment. *a.*

متغلب *mutaghallib*, victorious, overcoming. *a.*
متغير *mutaghaiyir*, changed, inconsistent, disturbed, stupified perplexed, estranged. *a.*
متفاوت *mutafāwit*, diverse, different. *a.*
متفحص *mutafaḥḥiṣ*, an inquirer, examiner, investigator. *mutafaḥḥaṣ*, examined. *a.*
متفرق *mutafarriḳ*, separate, distinct, dispersed, scattered. *a.*
متفرقات *mutifarriḳāt*, pl. various and scattered things, items of an account, sundries. *a.*
متفرقة *mutifarriḳat* or *mutifarriḳa*, various, sundry; horseguards, spearmen, or archers, attending a monarch when he travels. *a.*
متفق *muttafiḳ*, united, agreeing, unanimous, consenting; m. an accomplice, an associate. *a.*
متفكر *mutafakkir*, contemplative, considering, serious, thoughtful, pensive, grave. *a.*
متفني *mutafannī*, vicious, worthless, faulty. *a.*
متقاضي *mutaḳāẓī*, exacting or receiving (payment of a debt); a dun. *a.*
متقدم *mutaḳaddim*, ancient, anterior, antique, preceding; (sub.) a chief, president, guardian. *a.*
متقدمان *mutaḳaddimān*, } pl. the ancients, predecessors. *a.*
متقدمين *mutaḳaddimīn*, }
متقرب *mutakarrib*, approaching, having access; (sub.) a royal relative or favourite. *a.*
متقرر *mutakarrir*, made fast, confirmed, established. *a.*
متقي *muttaḳī*, abstinent, refraining, abstemious, sober, temperate. *a.*
متكا *muttakā*, a cushion, couch, pillow. *a.*
متكبر *mutakabbir*, proud, haughty, arrogant, disdainful. *a.*
متكبرانه *mutakabbirāna*, arrogantly, haughtily. *a.*
متكفل *mutakaffil*, a bail, a surety; (in revenue language) an officer who examines accounts and puts his seal on them when passed in the subordinate *kachahrīs*, before they are sent to court. *a.*
متكلم *mutakallim*, speaking; (sub.) a speaker, declaimer; (in gram.) the first person. *a.*
متكي *muttakī*, one who leans or reclines. *a.*
متلاشي *mutalāshī*, m. an inquirer, searcher. *a.*
متلاطش *mutalāṭiṣ*, } dashed together, agitated (as the waves). *a.*
متلاطم *mutalāṭim*, }
متلاناجيكا मतलानाजीका *matlānā jī kā*, n. to be sick at the stomach, to feel nausea. *h.*
متلاهث मतलाहट *matlāhaṭ*, } f. sickness at the stomach, nausea. *h.*
متلاءي मतलाई *matlā,ī*, }
متلذذ *mutalazziz*, one who relishes or takes delight (in a thing). *a.*

متلف *mutlif*, consuming, ruining; (sub.) a consumer, prodigal. *a.*

متلون *mutalawwin*, changeable, various. *a.*

متلي मतली *matlī*, f. nausea, sickness. *h.*

متمادي *mutamādī*, persevering, continuing, prolonging. *a.*

متمان मतिमान *mati-mān*, sensible, intelligent. *s.*

متمان मतिमान *matimān*, wise, intelligent. *s.*

متمتع *mutamatti'*, enjoying, relishing. *a.*

متمرد *mutamarrid*, vicious, stubborn, disobedient, refractory. *a.* [law). *a.*

متمشي *mutamashshī*, going on, practised (in

متمشية *mutamashshīya*, acted upon, bearing upon (as laws). *a.*

متمكن *mutamakkin*, powerful; residing; (sub.) an inhabitant. *mutamakkan*, m. (in gram.) a diptote, or noun of two cases. *a.*

متمني *mutamannī*, wishing, desiring, hoping; the optative mood (in gram.). *a.*

متمول *mutamawwil*, enriched, wealthy. *a.*

متن *matan* or *matn*, m. the text of a book, the middle. *a.*

متنا मतना *matnā*, m. a kind of sugar-cane. *h.*

متنا मुतना *mutnā*, one who pisses much, a piss-a-bed. *s.*

متنا मतना *matnā*, a. to knead, to squeeze. *h.*

متنازع *mutanāza'*, disputed, contested (in law). *a.*

متناسب *mutanāsib*, similar, proportionate. *a.*

متناقض *mutanāķiz̤*, discordant, contradictory. *a.*

متناهي *mutanāhī*, finished, determined, terminated, arrived at the utmost extreme. *a.*

متنبه *mutanabbih*, circumspect, diligent. *a.*

متنبي *mutanabbī*, one who calls himself a prophet; name of a celebrated Arabian poet. *a.*

متنجم *mutanajjim*, a star-gazer, an astrologer. *a.*

متنجن *mutanjan*, m. a kind of dish, a *pulā,o.* *p.*

متنجن گوسپندي *mutanjan gospandī*, a kind of dish (*pulā,o*) made of goat's flesh, or of mutton. *p.*

متنعم *mutana''im*, affluent, opulent, enjoying all the comforts of life. *a.*

متنفر *mutanaffir*, averse, disgusted, abhorring, detesting. *a.*

متنفس *mutanaffis*, solitary, single. *a.*

متنگ मतङ्ग *matang*, m. an elephant. *s.*

متنكي *matnagī*, proof, documents; what may be relied on as evidence in a law-suit. *a. p.*

متو मतौ *matau*, m. (Braj) counsel, advice. *s.*

متواتر *mutawātir*, } successive, or succes-
متوارد *mutawārid*, } sively. *a.*

متواچ मितवाच *mit-vāch*, prudent or measured in speech. *s.* [complaisant. *a.*

متواضع *mutawāẕi'*, complimenting, humbling,

متوالا मतवाला *matwālā*, intoxicated. *nīnd se matwālā*, one overpowered with sleep from the effects of opium. *s h.*

متوالي *mutawālī*, successive. *a.*

متوت मतवत *mattavat*, like one drunk, in the manner of a drunkard. *s.*

متوجه *mutawajjih*, turning, facing, travelling towards; attending to, favouring. *a.*

متوحش *mutawaḥḥish*, terrified, scared away. *a.*

متوسط *mutawassiṭ*, intermediate, middling. *a.*

متوسل *mutawassil*, adjoining, conjoining; trusting in God. *a.*

متوصل *mutawaṣṣil*, connected, related, joined to, depending on, arriving; (sub.) a dependant, connection. *a.*

متوطن *mutawaṭṭin*, inhabitant, native, inhabiting, residing. *a.*

متوع *matū'* (quere مطوع), (in law) a person of incompetent understanding, v. Wilson's Glossary. *a.*

متوفر *mutawaffir*, many, numerous, plentiful, copious. *a.* [funct. *a.*

متوفي *mutawaffī* or *mutawaffā*, dead, de-

متوقع *mutawaķķi'*, expecting, an expectant. *a.*

متوقف *mutawaķķif*, slow, tardy, delaying, waiting for, expecting. *a.*

متوكل *mutawakkil*, resigned to the will of God, trusting another, resigned to one's fate. *a.*

متولد *mutawallid*, born, generated. *a.*

متولي *mutawallī*, a superintendant (or treasurer of a mosque); a kinsman. *a.*

متونا मतौना *mataunā*, the grain called *kodo*, q. v. *h.* [&c. *d.*

متها मथा *mathā*, m. (v. *māthā*) the forehead,

متهاني मथानी *mathānī*, f. a churning vessel. *s.*

متهاون *mutahāwin*, one who neglects, despises, or holds cheap. *a.*

متهت मथित *mathit*, m. buttermilk without any watery admixture. *s.*

متهر मुतिहर *mutihar*, m. straw, &c. mixed with horses' urine. *s.*

متهرا मथुरा *mathurā*, f. name of a city in the province of Agra, the birthplace of *Krishṇa*. *s.*

متهرني मथुर्नी *mathurnī*, f. the female of *mathuriyā*, q. v. *s.*

متهري मुतिहरी *mutihrī*, f. a hole in which the dirt of a stable (particularly urine) is collected. *s.*

متهريا मथुरिया *mathuriyā*, m. name of a caste of Brāhmans of Mathurā. *s.*

متهس मिथस *mithas*, mutually, reciprocally. *s.*

متهم *muttaham*, suspected, accused, arraigned. *muttahim*, one who suspects. *a.*

متهن मिथुन *mithun*, m. a couple, a pair; copulation; the constellation Gemini; a pair; hence the Bengalese represented the constellation by a man and woman. *s.*

متهن मथन *mathan*, m. act of churning. *mathin*, m. a churning-stick. *s.*

متهنا मथना *mathna*, a. to churn; to knead, to work; m. a churn-staff. *s.*

متهني मथनी *mathnī*, f. a churn-staff. *s.*

متهني بهاو मिथुनीभाव *mithunī bhā,o*, m. amorous inclination. *s.*

متهنيا मथनिया *mathniyā*, f. a churning-vessel. *s.*

متهوٹ मथौट *mathauṭ*, m. contribution, subscription, capitation. *s.*

متهورا मथौरा *mathaurā*, m. a parasol, parapluie, umbrella. *s.*

متهيا मिथ्या *mithyā*, adj. false, counterfeit; m. falsehood, untruth; adv. falsely. *s.*

متهياپرتگيه मिथ्याप्रतिज्ञ *mithyā-pratigya*, treacherous, guilty of a breach of promise. *s.*

متهياچار मिथ्याचार *mithyā-chār*, acting falsely. *s.*

متهيادرشٹ मिथ्यादृष्टि *mithyā-drishṭi*, f. atheism; heresy. *s.*

متهيامت मिथ्यामति *mithyā-mati*, f. error, ignorance, mistake. *s.*

متهياوادي मिथ्यावादी *mithiyā-vādī*, one who utters falsehood, a liar. *s.*

متهين मतहीन *mat-hīn* or *mati-hīn*, stupid, ignorant. *s.*

متي मिती *mitī*, f. date; interest (m. *mitī*). *s.*

متين *matīn*, strong, firm, solid; obstinate; sententious. *a.*

متّا *maṭṭā* (v. *chaugān*), a bat or club, &c. *d.*

متاپا मुटापा *muṭāpā*, f. fatness, grossness. *h.*

متانا मिटाना *miṭānā*, a. to efface, to erase, to obliterate, to abolish. *h.*

متاي मुटाई *muṭā,ī*, f. fatness, bigness. *h.*

متر मटर *maṭar*, m. a pea (*Pisum sativum*). *h.*

مترا मटरा *maṭrā*, m. a kind of pea; name of a kind of silk cloth. *h.*

متري मटरी *maṭrī*, f. a kind of pea. *h.*

متريلا मटरीला *maṭrīlā*, mixed with peas. *h.*

متك मटक *maṭak*, f. coquetry, ogling. *maṭuk* (for *mukuṭ*), a crown. *h.*

متكا मटका *maṭkā*, m. a large earthen jar. *h.*

متكانا मटकाना *maṭkānā*, a. to wink, to ogle, to twinkle. *h.*

متكلا मटकुला *maṭhulā*, a kind of dumpling. *h.*

متكن मटकन *maṭkan*, m. f. coquetry, ogling. *h.*

متكنا मटकना *maṭaknā*, n. to wink, to ogle, to coquet. *maṭkanā*, m. a small vessel for taking water out of a larger. *h.*

متكوتها मटकोठा *maṭkothā*, m. a house of earth. *h.*

متكي मटकी *maṭkī*, f. a child's coral, or plaything which infants suck; a small jar; a churn, a vessel in which milk is churned; a wink, a twinkle, closing of the eyes. *h.*

متنا मिटना *miṭnā*, n. to expire, to be effaced, to cease existing. *h.*

متهه मठ *maṭh*, m. a Hindū college or convent, a pagan temple, a devotee's abode. *s.*

متهه मुठ *muṭh*, m. f. grasp, clutch; the fist; a blow with the fist. *muṭh-mard*, m. a robber, a ruffian. *s.*

متها मट्ठा *maṭṭhā*, m. buttermilk. *s.*

متها मठा *maṭhā* or *maṭṭhā*, slow, lazy, indolent. *miṭṭhā*, m. a kiss; adj. sweet. *h.*

متها *muṭṭhā*, m. the handle of a plough. *d.*

متهاس मिठास *miṭhās*, f. } sweetness. *s.*
متهانس मिठांस *miṭhāns*, m. }

متهالا मिठाला *miṭhālā*, a productive moisture inherent in a soil. *h.*

متهاي मिठाई *miṭhā,ī*, f. a sweetmeat; sweetness. *s.*

متهڑي मठड़ी *maṭhṛī*, } f. a kind of sweetmeat. *s.*
متهري मिठरी *miṭhrī*, }

متهوٹ मठौट *muṭhauṭ*, poll-tax, impost. *h.*

متهور मठोर *maṭhor*, } f. a jar. *h.*
متهوري मठौरी *maṭhaurī*, }

متهولي मठोली *maṭholī* or *muṭholī*, f. onanism. *h.*

متهوليا मुठोलिया *muṭholiyā*, m. one who commits onanism. *h.*

متهي मुट्ठी *muṭṭhī*, f. a handful, grasp; fist. *s.*

متهي मिट्ठी *miṭṭhī*, f. a kiss. *h.*

متهيا मुठिया *muṭhiyā*, m. a handful. *s*

متي मिट्टी *miṭṭī* or मट्टी *maṭṭī*, f. earth. *miṭṭī par laṛnā*, to dispute about land. *miṭṭī pakaṛnā*, to bite the ground; to be overcome or overturned; to be perverse or obstinate, to resist. *miṭṭī denā*, to bury. *miṭṭī ḍālnā*, to conceal the crime or fault of another. *miṭṭī karnā*, to ruin or destroy. *miṭṭī men milnā*, to be ruined or disgraced *miṭṭī khānā*, to eat flesh. *miṭṭī honā*, to become weak or faint, to be ruined. *miṭṭī kā tel*, petroleum, a kind of bitumen, supposed to possess marvellous salutary qualities. *s.*

متيا मिटिया *miṭiyā*, f. an earthen pot. *muṭiyā* (for *moṭiyā*), a porter, carrier. *s.*

متيا मट्टिया *maṭṭiyā*, a well without a frame, merely excavated. *h.*

متيارا मटियारा *maṭiyārā*, m. arable land, rich soil. *s.*

متيانا मटियाना *maṭiyānā*, n. to wink at, to connive; to suffer, to tolerate. *h.*

متياو मटियाव *matiyāw*, m. sufferance, toleration. *h.*

مثابه *maṣāba* or *maṣābat*, a step, a degree, a station; a place where people assemble. *a.*

مثال *miṣāl*, f. simile, likeness, similitude. *a.*

مثالي *miṣālī*, like, resembling. *a. h.*

مثانه *maṣāna*, the bladder, the place which holds the fœtus. *a.*

مثبت *muṣbit*, one who confirms, proves, or establishes. *muṣabbat*, established, ratified. *a.*

مثبوت *maṣbūt*, firm, fixed, established. *a.*

مثقال *maṣḳāl* or *miṣḳāl*, m. a weight containing 4 *māshas* and 3½ *ratis*. *a.*

مثل *maṣal*, f. a fable, allegory, simile, metaphor, proverb; post, station, department, an example. *miṣl*, f. similitude, likeness; (in law) a suit or plea. *miṣlī dīwānī*, a civil suit. *miṣlī faujdārī*, a criminal suit. *a.* [stance. *a.*

مثلاً *miṣlan* or *maṣalan*, for example, for instance.

مثلث *muṣallaṣ*, three-cornered, triple. *muṣallaṣ maṣlā*, an allegorical fable. *a.*

مثله *muṣla* or *maṣula*, a question, proposition, precept, example; punishment by way of example. *a.*

مثلي *miṣlī*, like, equal; (in law) an article which, being lent or sold, is to be replaced by another quite similar. *a.*

مثمر *muṣmir*, fruitful. *muṣammar*, fruit ripe for gathering; fruit-bearing. *a.*

مثمن *muṣamman*, consisting of eight, octangular, eight-fold. *a.*

مثنوي *maṣnawī*, f. the sort of verse in which the couplets rhyme regularly, as in English heroic verse. The term is applied, *par excellence*, to a moral work in this kind of metre by Maulavī Rūmī. *a.*

مثني *muṣannā*, m. a copy, the second. *a.*

مج मज *maj*, ripe, mellow. *h.*

مجا मज्जा *majjā*, m. marrow, pith, kernel. *s.*

مجادل *mujādil*, contentious, disputant, quarrelsome. *a.*

مجادله *mujādala*, m. contention, dispute, altercation; a conflict, scuffle. *a.*

مجاري *mujārī*, current; in force (a law). *a.*

مجاز *majāz*, lawful, convenient; superficial, insincere, feigned; metaphorical. *a.*

مجازاً *majāzan*, by way of metaphor. *a.*

مجازي *majāzī*, superficially; adj. metaphoric, hyperbolical. *a.*

مجال *majāl*, f. power, ability, strength. *a.*

مجالس *majālis* (pl. of مجلس), conferences, assemblies, convivial conversations, sederunts. *a.*

مجالست *mujālasat*, f. sitting together, an assembly. *a.*

مجامع *majāmiʻ* (pl. of مجمع), congregations. *a.*

مجامعت *mujāmaʻat*, f. carnal connection, coition, *coitus*. *a.*

مجانبت *mujānabat*, being near or at the side of a person; also retiring, withdrawing. *a.*

مجانست *mujānasat*, f. being akin, or homogeneous. *a.*

مجاور *mujāwir*, m. a neighbour; a sweeper of a mosque (devoutly employed or fixed to the mosque). *a.*

مجاورت *mujāwarat*, } f. neighbourhood, intimacy, familiarity. *a.*
مجاوري *mujāwirī*, }

مجاوز *mujāwiz*, transgressing, exceeding, bounding. *a.*

مجاهد *mujāhid*, one who labours or endeavours; a warrior (especially in the defence of the true faith). *a.*

مجاهدت *mujāhadat* or *mujāhada*, f. a holy war, fighting in defence of religion. *a.*

مجبور *majbūr*, constrained, forced, restricted. *a.*

مجبوري *majbūrī*, f. constraint, restriction. *a.*

مجتبي *mujtabā*, elected, chosen, elect. *a.*

مجترم *mujtarim*, guilty, arraigned. *a.*

مجتمع *mujtamiʻ*, assembled, convened; agreeing in the same opinion; (a man) arriving at full strength. *a.*

مجتهد *mujtahid*, one who wages war against infidels; a title conferred on the heads of the law and religion, a doctor (in law). *a.*

مجحر *majḥar*, m. an asylum, a biding-place. *a.*

مجد *majd*, m. glory, grandeur, splendour, the honour derived from ancestors. *gu-l-majd*, glorious, right honourable. *a.*

مجدد *mujaddad*, new, recent, modern. *a.*

مجذوب *majẕūb*, attracted, abstracted; a religious fanatic. *a.*

مجذور *majẕūr*, m. square (in arithmetic). *a.*

مجذوم *majẕūm*, leprous. *a.*

مجرا *mujrā*, m. (in Pers. and Hind.) allowance, premium, deduction; (in Hind.) obeisance, respects, visit, audience. *mujre-gāh*, place of audience for the reception of visitors. *mujrā-k.*, a. to visit. *a.*

مجراعي *mujrā,ī*, m. one who pays his respects *i. e.* servants, ministers, &c. *a.*

مجرب *mujarrib*, trying, proving. *mujarrab*, adj. expert, skilful, experienced. *a.*

مجرد *mujarrad*, solitary, alone, unmarried. *a.*

مجرداً *mujarradan*, singly, solely, only. *a.*

مجردات *mujarradāt*, pl. incorporeal beings. *a.*

مجردي *mujarradī*, f. solitude, solitariness, celibacy. *a.*

مجرم *mujrim*, criminal; (sub.) a sinner. *a.*

مجروح *maj'rūḥ*, wounded, lacerated. *a.*

مجرىٰ *mujrā* (v. *mujrā*) allowing, &c. *a.*

مجزا *mujazzā*, divided into several parts. *a.*

مجسم *mujassam*, having a body, embodied, corpulent, incorporated, incarnate. *a.*

مجصوص *majṣūṣ*, plastered, besmeared. *a.*

مجعد *muja''ad*, curled (as the hair). *a.*

مجلا *mujallā*, polished, furbished, illustrated, manifested, decked, adorned. *a.*

مجلد *mujallid*, m. a bookbinder. *mujallad*, bound (a volume). *a.*

مجلس *majlis*, f. an assembly, a company, congregation, convention. *a.*

مجلسي *majlisī*, a person assisting at an assembly. *a.*

مجلىٰ *mujallā* (v. *mujallā*) adorned, &c. *a.*

مجمد *mujammad*, congealed. *a.*

مجمر *majmir*, m. a chafing-dish; a censer for incense; perfume. *a.*

مجمع *majma'* or مجمعة *majma'a*, m. an assembly, meeting, a collection. *majma'u-l-baḥrain*, the meeting of the two seas, the title of a Persian historical work. *a.*

مجمل *mujmal*, m. a summary, compendium, abridgment. *mujmil*, one who sums up. *a.*

مجملاً *mujmalan*, summarily, in short. *a.*

مجموع *majmū'*, مجموعة *majmū'a*, } m. a crowd, assembly; a large tray or salver; a compound perfume; a collection, magazine, compendium; a form (in printing); adj. collected, assembled, contained, all, the whole. *majmū'a-dār* (record-keeper), a title given to the servants of a *ḳānūn-go*. *a.*

مجموعي *majmū,ī*, aggregate, collected. *a.*

مجنس *mujannas*, a mongrel, of mixed breed; adj. composed of different kinds. *a.*

مجنون *majnūn*, insane, in love; m. the name of a celebrated lover, whose amours with *Lailā* are the subject of poems by several eminent hands, such as *Nizāmī*, *Amīr Khusrū*, and *Jāmī*, &c. *a.*

مجنونيت *majnūnīyat*, f. insanity, love-madness. *a.*

مجور मजूर *majūr*, مجورا मजूरा *majūrā*, } m. (said to be a corruption of *mazdūr*) a labourer, a carrier. *p. h.*

مجوري *majūrī* (for *mazdūrī*) labour. *p.*

مجوز *mujawwiz*, holding or proving to be lawful; permitting or allowing to pass; urging, pressing. *a.*

مجوس *majūs*, m. a guebre, or follower of Zoroaster, a magian, a fire-worshipper, a magician. *p.a.*

مجوسى *majūsī*, of or relating to the magi. *p.*

مجوف *mujawwaf*, hollow, concave, vaulted. *majūf*, thick, large-bellied. *a.*

مجھ मुझ *mujh*, inflex. of 1st pers. pron. me. *h.*

مجھار मझार *majhār*, m. (v. *mānjh*) the middle, the centre, in the middle. *s.*

مجھاري मझारी *majhārī*, in the midst. *s.*

مجھلا मझला *majhlā*, middling, intermediate. *s.*

مجهلة *majhala*, m. wrangling. *a.*

مجهود *majhūd*, oppressed with labour, or vexation; (sub.) care, trouble, endeavour, diligence. *a.*

مجهول *majhūl*, little known; (sub.) passive voice; (in gram.) applied to the letters *wāw* and *yā* when the former has the sound of *o* in *mole*, and the latter that of *ē* in *fête*. *majhūlī muṭlaḳ*, very indolent or useless. *a.*

مجھولا मझोला *majholā*, middling, intermediate. *s.*

مجھولي मझोली *majholī*, f. a small cart on two wheels. *h.*

مجهولي *majhūlī*, f. ignorance, apathy. *a.*

مجھے मुझे *mujhe*, (acc. or dat.) pron. me, to me. *h.*

مجھيلي मझेली *majhelī*, f. a small cart. *h.*

مجي *muje* (v. *mujhe*), me, to me. *d.*

مجيب *mujīb*, listening to, granting, consenting, taking well. *a.*

مجيت मजीत *majīt*, cheap, that which is sold at an underprice; bought at second hand. *h.*

مجيٹھ मजीठ *majīṭh*, f. name of a drug used for dyeing red (*Rubia munjit*, *Roxb.*). *s.*

مجيد *majīd*, glorious, honourable, noble. *a.*

مجيرا मजीरा *majīrā*, m. small cymbals. *s.*

مچ *mach*, drowsiness, apathy; a standard for gold. *d.*

مچا मुचा *muchchā*, m. a large lump of flesh or meat. *machā* (v. *machān*), a platform. *h.*

مچالا *machālā*, m. a platform, &c. (v. *machān*). *d.*

مچامچ मचामच *machāmach*, chokeful, stuffed. *h.*

مچان मचान *machān*, m. a stage, a frame, a bench, platform, raised seat. *s.*

مچانا मचाना *machānā*, a. to make, to stir, to commit, to produce, to excite, commit. *h.*

مچرانا मिचराना *michrānā*, a. to eat without an appetite. *h.*

مچرمچر मिचरमिचर *michar-michar*, eating without an appetite. *h.*

مچك मचक *machak*, f. pain in the joints. *h.*

مچكارنا मिचकारना *michkārnā*, a. to rinse. *h.*

مچكانا मचकाना *machkānā*, a. to wink. *h.*

مچكنا मचकना *machaknā*, n. to have pain in the joints; to creak (as a bedstead, &c.). *h.*

مچل मचल *machal*, } perverse, refractory, dis-
مچلا मचला *machlā*, } obedient, cross, obstinate, pert. *h.*

مچلاپن मचलापन *machlāpan*, m. stubbornness. *h.*

مچلانا मचलाना *machlānā*, n. to feel nausea, to be sick at the stomach; to pretend ignorance. *h.*

مچلاها मचलाहा *machlāhā*, squeamish, stubborn. *h.*

مچلاهٹ मचलाहट *machlāhaṭ*, f. stubbornness. *h.*

مچلائي मचलाई *machlā,ī*, f. } pertness, per-
مچلپن मचलपन *machal-pan*, m. } verseness, obstinacy. *h.*

مچلکه *muchalka* or *muchalkā*, m. a bond, a note of hand, an agreement. *t.*

مچلنا मचलना *machalnā*, n. to be perverse, refractory, disobedient, &c. *h.*

مچمچ मचमच *mach-mach*, an imitative sound. *h.*

مچمچانا मचमचाना *machmachānā*, n. to creak (as a bedstead heavily laden) (v. *machkanā*). *h.*

مچنا मिचना *michnā*, a. to shut, to close. *h.*

مچنا मचना *machnā*, n. to be made, committed, stirred up, perpetrated, produced. *h.*

مچنگ *muchang*, f. harp; name of a musical instrument, a Jew's harp. *p.*

مچوا मचवा *machwā*, m. a boat. *h.*

مچوانا मचवाना *machwānā*, to cause to make, &c. *h.*

مچوڑنا मचोड़ना *machoṛnā*, a. to twist, to break by twisting. *h.*

مچولنا मिचौलना *michaulnā*, a. to shut the eyes. *h.*

مچھ मच्छ *machchh* or मछ *machh*, m. a fish; the name of the first *avatār*, or incarnation, when *Vishṇu* appeared in the shape of the small fish *sapharī* to *Satyabratā* or *Hayagrīva*, to warn him of the general deluge, and desire him to place the four *Vedas* in the boat, which he (*Vishṇu*) would preserve. The fish was first taken up by *Hayagrīva* in his hands when bathing; it was then of the size of a *Pūṭhī*, but afterwards grew too large for being contained in a tank, river, &c., and was carried to the sea; where afterwards it supported the ark with its horn. *Satyabratā* lived about 3000 years before Christ. *s.*

مچھر मच्छर *machchhar*, } m. a gnat, a musquito.
مچھڑ मच्छड़ *machchhaṛ*, } *machchhar kī jhūl kā chor*, one who would steal the minutest thing, a mean, petty pilferer. *s.*

مچھرک *muchharak* (v. *masen*), the down upon the lips. *d.*

مچھرنگا मछरंगा *machhrangā*, m. name of a bird, a species of kingfisher. *h.*

مچھري मछरी *machhrī*, } f. a fish. *machhlī*
مچھلي मछली *machhlī*, } *bandar*, the port of
مچھي मच्छी *machchhī*, } Masulipatam. *s.*

مچھندر मछन्दर *machhandar*, m. a rat; (met.) adj. stupid. *h.*

مچھندر मछन्दर *machhandar*, name of a *jogī*. *s.*

مچھوا मछवा *machhwā* or *machhuwā*, m. a fisherman. *s.*

مچھي मच्छी *machchhī*, f. a kiss; a fish (v. *machhlī*. *machchhiyāṅ lenā*, to kiss. *h.*

مچيا मचिया *machiyā*, m. a stool, a chair. *s.*

مچياو मचियाव *machiyāw*, m. honey. *h.*

محابا *muḥābā*, m. repect, regard, friendship, affection. *be muḥābā*, without respect (of persons or circumstances). *a.*

محاذي *muḥāẕī*, opposite, parallel. *a.*

محارب *muḥārib*, m. a warrior, a combatant. *a.*

محاربت *muḥārabat*, } battle, combat, war,
محاربه *muḥāraba*, } fight. *a.*

محاسب *muḥāsib*, m. an accountant, one who keeps accounts; calculating, an examiner, an auditor of accounts. *a.*

محاسبه *muḥāsaba*, m. computation, calculation, account. *muḥāsaba-dār*, an accountant, one who has accounts to settle. *muḥāsaba-ṭalab*, demanding a settlement of accounts. *a.*

محاسن *maḥāsin* (pl. irreg.), the beard and mustaches; virtues, laudable actions. *a.*

محاش *maḥāsh*, m. goods, effects, wealth. *a.*

محاصر *muḥāṣir*, a besieger, one who surrounds or blockades (a fort, &c.). *a.*

محاصره *muḥāṣara*, surrounding, besieging, investing, blockading, sitting down before a fort, &c. *a.*

محاصل *maḥāṣil* (pl. of محصول), profits, gains, &c. *a.*

محاصلات *maḥāṣilāt*, (barbarous pl. of the preceding). *a.*

محاضر *muḥāẓir*, present, in attendance (in court). *a.*

محاضرت *muḥāẓarat*, f. appearing before or against another. *a.*

محافظ *muḥāfiẓ*, a defender, commander. *muḥāfiẓ i daftar*, keeper of the records. *a.*

محافظت *muḥāfaẓat*, f. preservation, protection, guardianship, custody; keeping in mind or memory. *a.*

محافه *muḥāfa*, m. (properly *miḥaffa*), a *pālkī*, a kind of litter in which women travel. *a.*

محاقله *muḥāḳala*, sale of corn in the ear before it is ripe. *a.*

محال *maḥāll*, m. (pl. of محل or محله), streets, squares, courts, places, houses, districts, departments, lands, or any public funds producing revenue to government. *a.*

محال *muḥāl*, impossible, absurd. *muḥāli muṭlaḳ*, very difficult, absolutely impossible, quite absurd. *maḥāl*, art, deception. *a.*

محالات *muhālāt*, pl. absurdities, impossibilities. *a.*

محامد *mahāmid* (pl. of محمدة), praiseworthy actions. *a.*

محاورات *muhāwarāt* (pl. of محاورة), dialogues, idioms, &c. *a.*

محاورت *muhāwarat*, f. } idiom, usage, current
محاورة *muhāwara*, m. } speech, phraseology, dialogue, conversation, conference. *a.*

محايت *mahāyat*, partition of usufruct. *a.*

محب *muhibb*, m. a friend, a lover. *a.*

محبت *mahabbat*, f. friendship, love, affection, attachment, charity, or goodwill to all men. *a.*

محبس *mahbas*, m. a prison. *mihbas*, bed furniture. *muhbas*, imprisoned. *a.*

محبوب *mahbūb*, beloved, (sub.) a sweetheart. *mahbūbu-l ḳulūb*, cordially beloved. *a.*

محبوبانه *mahbūbāna*, lit. a sweetheart. *a. p.*

محبوبه *mahbūba*, f. beloved, a sweetheart, a mistress, a lovely woman. *a.*

محبوبي *mahbūbī*, f. loveliness, amiability. *a.*

محبوس *mahbūs*, imprisoned, confined, a prisoner. *mahbūs-khāna*, a jail, a prison. *mahbūs-sanad*, a warrant of committal, or, as our law hath it, a mittimus. *a.*

محتاج *muhtāj*, necessitous, needy, indigent; a mendicant. *a.*

محتاجي *muhtājī*, f. state of indigence. *a.*

محتاط *muhtāt*, guarded, circumspect. *a.*

محتال *muhtāl*, insidious, deceptive; a deceiver; (in law) a person who accepts the responsibility of one person for his claim upon another. *muhtāl 'alaihi*, the person who has become responsible. *a.*

محترز *muhtariz*, cautious, careful, wary; abstemious. *a.*

محترف *muhtarif*, an artist, an artisan. *a.*

محترفه *muhtarifa*, a tax on trade; duties levied on certain trades and occupations. *a.*

محترم *muhtarim*, honoured, respected, sacred, revered, venerable. *a.*

محتسب *muhtasib*, m. a censor; a superintendant of the police, appointed by the Muhammadans to superintend the morals of the people, to regulate the weights and measures, and to prevent unlawful games, drinking, and other disorders. *a.*

محتسبي *muhtasibī*, the office of *muhtasib*, q. v. *a.*

محتشم *muhtashim*, having many followers, powerful, great. *a.*

محتكر *muhtakir*, a forestaller. *a.*

محتلم *muhtalim*, a dreamer, one arrived at the age of puberty; adj. polluted. *a.*

محتمل *muhtamal* or *muhtamil*, suspected, conjectured; suspicious, doubtful, possible, probable, suffering patiently. *a.*

محجوب *mahjūb*, veiled; modest, bashful.

محجوبي *mahjūbī*, f. modesty, bashfulness. *a.*

محجور *mahjūr*, forbidden, prohibited. *a.*

محدب *muhaddab*, convex. *a.*

محدث *muhaddis*, a narrator, a relater. *a.*

محدود *mahdūd*, limited, bounded. *a.*

محذوف *mahzūf*, omitted, cut off (as a particle in Arabic Syntax). *a*

محراب *mihrāb*, f. the principal place in a mosque, where the priest prays to the people with his face turned towards Mecca; the royal closet or chamber. *a.*

محرابي *mihrābī*, arched; of or like the *mihrāb*. *a.*

محرر *muharrir*, m. a writer, a clerk. *muharrar*, written, inscribed. *a.*

محرف *muharraf*, inverted, transposed. *a.*

محرق *muharriḳ*, inflamed, burning (a fever). *muhriḳ*, incentive, giving warmth. *muhriḳan*, in a burning state. *a.*

محرك *muharrik*, moving, putting in motion; (sub.) a mover, persuader, executer. *a.*

محرم *muharram*, sacred, forbidden; (sub.) the name of the first *Muhammadan* month, held sacred on account of the death of *Husain*, son of *'Alī*, who was killed by *Yazīd*, near *Kūfa*. *a.*

محرم *mahram*, a sponse, an intimate friend; any one who is admitted into the women's apartments; boddice, the part of the dress in which the breasts are confined. *muhrim*, a prohibitor, interdictor. *a.*

محرمات *muharramāt*, things forbidden. *a.*

محرميت *mahramīyat*, f. the state of being a confidant. *a.*

محروس *mahrūs*, guarded, preserved. *a.*

محروسه *mahrūsa*, m. a garrisoned or fortified place; well governed or protected territory, as those subject to established sovereign power. *mamāliki mahrūsa*, the countries occupied by any sovereign. *a.*

محروق *mahrūḳ*, torrid, scorched. *a.*

محروقه *mahrūḳa*, fuel, combustibles. *a.*

محروم *mahrūm*, prohibited, excluded; unfortunate, wretched, plundered, deprived of the support of life, disappointed. *a.*

محرومي *mahrūmī*, } f. exclusion, prohi-
محروميت *mahrūmīyat*, } bition, disappointment. *a.*

محزون *mahzūn*, grieved, vexed, afflicted. *a.*

محسن *muhsin*, benefitting, obliging. *a.*

محسوب *mahsūb*, computed, numbered, carried to account. *a.*

محسود *mahsūd*, envied, hated. *a.*

محسوس *mahsūs*, perceived, felt known for certain; pl. *mahsūsāt*, things felt, things perceptible to the senses. *a.*

محشر *maḥshar*, m. a place of assembly, the last judgment. *a.*

محشور *maḥshūr*, raised from the dead. *a.*

محشي *muḥashshā*, illustrated (a book, &c.) by marginal notes. *a.*

محصل *muḥaṣṣil*, m. a tax-gatherer, a bailiff, a dun; adj. collecting, gathering, inquiring. *a.*

محصلانه *muḥaṣṣilāna*, m. } the fees of the bailiff or tax-gatherer. *a.*
محصلي *muḥaṣṣilī*, f.

محصلي *muḥaṣṣilī*, f. office of tax collector. *a.*

محصن *muḥṣan* or *muḥṣana*, chaste, continent. *a.*

محصور *maḥṣūr*, besieged, surrounded, detained, restrained. *a.*

محصول *maḥṣūl*, m. tax, duty, excise, custom, postage, produce of any thing, public revenue from any source. *maḥṣūl-dār*, yielding or having a profit; a collector or receiver of taxes. *a.*

محصولي *maḥṣūlī*, of or relating to taxes, &c. *a.*

محض *maḥẓ*, pure, unmixed; adv. merely, entirely, wholly, purely. *a.*

محضر *maḥẓar*, m. royal presence, appearance, a general application or petition; nature, temper, disposition. *maḥẓar-khāna*, a police station or court. *maḥẓar-nāma*, m. a muster-roll, list of those who are present. *a.*

محظور *maḥẓūr*, forbidden, unlawful. *a.*

محظورات *maḥẓūrāt*, pl. unlawful things. *a.*

محظوظ *maḥẓūẓ*, glad, cheerful, contented, delighted, pleased. *a.*

محظي *muḥẓī*, preferring, favouring. *a.*

محفل *maḥfil*, f. the place or time of meeting, assembly, congregation, congress. *a.*

محفوظ *maḥfūẓ*, guarded, protected, preserved; committed to memory. *a.*

محفه *miḥaffa*, m. a covered chair or *palkī* for women. *a.*

محق *muḥiḳḳ*, acting properly, doing justice, knowing for certain. *maḥḳ*, cancelling; burning; having a right. *a.*

محقر *muḥaḳḳar*, despised, contemptible. *a.*

محقق *muḥaḳḳaḳ*, confirmed, certified, authenticated, verified, known for truth. *muḥaḳḳiḳ*, (part. act.) verifying, affirming. *a.*

محققانه *muḥaḳḳiḳāna*, truly, accurately. *a.*

محك *miḥak* or *miḥakk*, f. touchstone, test. *a.*

محكم *muḥkam*, strengthened, firm, fortified, strong; adv. strenuously, firmly. *a.*

محكمات *maḥkamāt* (pl. of محكمه), tribunals, &c. *a.*

محكمه *maḥkama*, m. a tribunal, court of justice, judgment-seat. *maḥkama-auḳāf*, local agency; a court of trust. *a.*

محكمي *muḥkamī*, strength, firmness. *a.*

محكوم *maḥkūm*, subjected, under command; invested with supreme power; sentenced, condemned. *a.*

محكومي *maḥkūmī*, state of subjection. *a.*

محل *maḥall*, m. a place, building, house, mansion, seraglio, district, quarter, abode, time, opportunity. *maḥall-sarā*, the inner or female apartments (of a mansion). *maḥalli mujrā*, the place of obeisance; clearing of accounts. *a.*

محلات *maḥallāt*, pl. houses, places, &c. *a.*

محلل *muḥallil*, one who makes lawful that which was illegal; (in med.) dissolvent. *muḥallal*, made lawful. *a.*

محللات *muḥallilāt*, discutientia, or medicines which dissolve morbid fluids. *a.*

محلوف *maḥlūf*, sworn, having had the oath administered. *maḥlūf-alaihi*, the thing or circumstance sworn to. *a.*

محله *maḥalla*, a quarter (or part of a town), district, division, ward. *maḥalla-dār*, an officer in charge of a ward; an alderman. *a.*

محلي *maḥallī*, an attendant on the seraglio; a eunuch. *a.*

محمد *muḥammad*, adj. praised, praiseworthy; m. name of the Arabian prophet. *a.*

محمده *maḥmida*, a laudable action; fame. *a.*

محمدي *muḥammadī*, *Muḥammadan*; a follower of or believer in *Muḥammad*. *a.*

محمل *maḥmil*, m. that by which any thing is supported; a camel's saddle, or that which fastens the two parts of a camel's load; a litter carried on a camel. *a.*

محمود *maḥmūd*, worthy, laudable; m. a man's name; a king of *Ghaznī*, son of *Sabaktagīn*. *a.*

محموده *maḥmūda*, scammony. *a.*

محمودي *maḥmūdī*, f. a kind of fine muslin; a silver coin, worth about eightpence of our money; name of an *Afghān* tribe. *a.*

محن *miḥan* (pl. of محنت), toils, troubles, &c. *a.*

محنت *miḥnat*, f. labour, trouble, misfortune, difficulty, calamity, affliction, trial, temptation, perplexity, sorrow. *miḥnat-zada*, struck with affliction. *miḥnat-kash*, one who endures affliction. *miḥnat ko pīnā*, (Dakh.) to suffer patiently under affliction. *a.*

محنتانه *miḥnatāna*, pay of labour, wages. *a.*

محنتي *miḥnatī*, m. a labourer; adj. laborious, painstaking, difficult, unfortunate. *a.*

محو *maḥv*, *maḥw*, or *maḥo*, effaced, forgotten, erased, obliterated. *a.*

محور *miḥwar*, m. an axis. *a.*

محوط *muḥauwaṭ*, surrounded by a wall. *a.*

محوطه *muḥauwaṭa*, m. an enclosure, area. *muḥauwiṭa*, the wall, &c. forming an enclosure. *a.*

محويت *maḥwiyat*, effacement, obliteration. *a.*

محيط *muḥīṭ*, containing, surrounding, encircling; comprehending, knowing. *baḥri muḥīṭ*, the main ocean. *muḥīṭi dā,ira*, the circumference of a circle. *a.*

محيطه *muhīta*, land within the supply of a well, &c. (v. *chak*). *a.*

محيل *muhīl*, m. a cheat, deceiver, knave, prevaricator. *a.*

مخا *mu<u>kh</u>ā*, Moka, a seaport town of Arabia, on the Red Sea. *a.*

مخادم *ma<u>kh</u>ādim* (pl. of مخدم), servants, domestics, ministers. *a.*

مخارج *ma<u>kh</u>ārij* (pl. of مخرج), expenses, disbursements. *a.*

مخاصمت *mu<u>kh</u>āṣamat*, opposition, hostility, altercation, quarrelling. *a.*

مخاطب *mu<u>kh</u>āṭib*, m. a speaker, the person who addresses another. *mu<u>kh</u>āṭab*, the person addressed; (in gram.) the second person. *a.*

مخاطبين *mu<u>kh</u>āṭibīn*, pl. those who speak to or address others. *a.*

مخاطره *mu<u>kh</u>āṭara*, m. danger, peril, hazard. *a.*

مخافت *mu<u>kh</u>āfat*, dread, danger; pl. *mu<u>kh</u>āfāt*, dangers, &c. *a.*

مخالطت *mu<u>kh</u>ālaṭat*, f. associating, conversing, mixing together in society. *a.*

مخالف *mu<u>kh</u>ālif*, opposite, adverse, contrary, dissentient; (sub.) an enemy, an opponent. *a*

مخالفت *mu<u>kh</u>ālafat*, f. opposition, adversity, repugnance, variance, enmity. *a.*

مخبر *mu<u>kh</u>bir*, announcing news, signifying, certifying, telling news. *mu<u>kh</u>biri ṣādiḳ*, the bringer of certain intelligence. *a.*

مخبط *mu<u>kh</u>abbaṭ*, disordered in the intellect. *a.*

مختار *mu<u>kh</u>tār*, chosen, selected; absolute, independent, invested with power and authority; (sub.) a free agent; an agent acting with full power for another. *mu<u>kh</u>tāri kār*, a superintendant, a director of affairs. *mu<u>kh</u>tār-nāma*, a power of attorney. *mu<u>kh</u>tāran*, as an agent. *a.*

مختاري *mu<u>kh</u>tārī*, f. independence, power, authority, free agency; office of *mu<u>kh</u>tār*. *a.*

مختاله *mu<u>kh</u>tāla*, an impostor, a deceiver. *a.*

مخترع *mu<u>kh</u>tari'*, m. an inventor, author, founder; commencing. *mu<u>kh</u>tara'*, invented, discovered, contrived. *a.*

مختص *mu<u>kh</u>taṣṣ*, appropriated, peculiar; chosen, elected; private, domestic. *a.*

مختصر *mu<u>kh</u>taṣar*, abbreviated, abridged; (sub.) a compendium, an epitome. *a.*

مختفي *mu<u>kh</u>tafī*, hidden, concealed; also hiding, lurking. *a.*

مختل *mu<u>kh</u>tall*, confused, confounded, disturbed, corrupted; emaciated. *a.*

مختلط *mu<u>kh</u>taliṭ*, confused, perplexed, mixed, jumbled together. *a.*

مختلف *mu<u>kh</u>talif*, مختلفه *mu<u>kh</u>talifa*, } diverse, discordant, different, various *a.*

مختوم *ma<u>kh</u>tūm*, sealed, signed, concluded, name of a flower. *a.*

مختون *ma<u>kh</u>tūn*, circumcised. *a.*

مخجل *mu<u>kh</u>ajjal*, confounded, bashful, ashamed. *a.*

مخدر *mu<u>kh</u>addar*, concealed (under a veil). *a.*

مخدرات *mu<u>kh</u>dirāt*, (in medicine) narcotics. *a.*

مخدوم *ma<u>kh</u>dūm*, served; (hence) m. a master; f. *ma<u>kh</u>dūma*, a mistress. *a.*

مخدوميت *ma<u>kh</u>dūmiyat*, f. mastership. *a.*

مخذول *ma<u>kh</u>zūl*, contemned, despised. *a.*

مخرج *ma<u>kh</u>raj*, m. utterance, pronunciation. *mu<u>kh</u>raj*, any thing given out, expenditure. *a.*

مخروط *ma<u>kh</u>rūṭ*, مخروطه *ma<u>kh</u>rūṭa*, } a cone, a cylinder; adj. conical, cylindrical. *a.*

مخروطات *ma<u>kh</u>rūṭāt*, pl. conic sections. *a.*

مخزن *ma<u>kh</u>zan*, m. a magazine, storehouse, granary; (hence Span. *almazen*, Port. *almazem*, Ital. *magazzino*, Fr. *magazin*, Eng. *magazine*). *a.*

مخصور *ma<u>kh</u>ṣūr*, injured, damaged. *a.*

مخصوص *ma<u>kh</u>ṣūṣ*, peculiar, particular. *ma<u>kh</u>ṣūṣ-k.*, to impute, ascribe. *a.*

مخضر *mu<u>kh</u>azzar*, verdant, flourishing. *a.*

مخطط *mu<u>kh</u>aṭṭaṭ*, marked with lines; having incipient beard or down on the face (a youth). *a.*

مخطوب *ma<u>kh</u>ṭūb*, affianced, betrothed. *a.*

مخطور *ma<u>kh</u>ṭūr*, thought, imagined, conceived, supposed. *a.*

مخفف *mu<u>kh</u>affaf*, alleviated; light; contemptible; (a consonant) having a short for a long vowel. *a.*

مخفوض *ma<u>kh</u>fūẓ*, depressed, submissive. *a.*

مخفي *ma<u>kh</u>fī*, concealed, secret, clandestine, occult, private. *a.*

مخل *mu<u>kh</u>ill*, disturbing, spoiling, ruining; (sub.) a disturber, interrupter. *a.*

مخلا *mu<u>kh</u>allā*, empty; dismissed, set at liberty, repudiated, set free. *mu<u>kh</u>allā bi-ṭ-ṭab'*, unceremonious. *a.*

مخلد *mu<u>kh</u>allad*, eternal, durable, permanent. *a.*

مخلص *mu<u>kh</u>liṣ*, m. a friend; a bachelor (q.d. a free man); adj. sincere, pure, true. *ma<u>kh</u>laṣ*, an asylum. *a.*

مخلصانه *mu<u>kh</u>liṣāna*, sincere, friendly, candid; like a friend. *a.*

مخلصي *ma<u>kh</u>laṣī*, f. escape, release, shelter, asylum, deliverance, liberation. *a.*

مخلع *mu<u>kh</u>alla'*, dressed or presented with a <u>kh</u>il'at, q. v. *a.*

مخلوط *ma<u>kh</u>lūṭ*, mixed, blended, confused *a.*

مخلوق *ma<u>kh</u>lūḳ*, created, formed, produced. *a.*

مخلوقات *ma<u>kh</u>lūḳāt*, pl. creatures, created things. *a.*

مخلوقيت *ma<u>kh</u>lūḳīyat*, f. the creation. *a.*

مخمر *mu<u>kh</u>mir*, fermented, leavened. *mu<u>kh</u>ammir*, leavening. *a.*

مخمس *mu<u>kh</u>ammas*, m. a kind of verse containing five lines; a pentagon or five-sided figure; adj. quintuple, pentangular. *a.*

مخمسات *mu<u>kh</u>ammasāt*; pl. verses or stanzas of five lines; five-sided figures. *a.*

مخمصه *ma<u>kh</u>maṣa*, m. hunger, wretchedness. *a.*

مخمل *ma<u>kh</u>mal*, m. velvet. *a.*

مخملي *ma<u>kh</u>malī*, made of velvet. *a.*

مخمور *ma<u>kh</u>mūr*, intoxicated, completely drunk. *a.*

مخنث *mu<u>kh</u>annaṡ*, effeminate, abject, infamous; (sub.) an hermaphrodite; *exoletus, qui corpus prostituit cinædis.* *a.*

مخنوق *ma<u>kh</u>nūḳ*, suffocated, strangled. *a.*

مخوف *ma<u>kh</u>ūf*, dangerous, dreadful. *mu<u>kh</u>awwif*, terrifying. *mu<u>kh</u>awwaf*, terrified. *a.*

مخيانا *mi<u>kh</u>iyānā*, a. to beat, to subdue, to overcome. *p. h.*

مخير *mu<u>kh</u>aiyir*, bountiful, charitable, liberal, left to free choice, indifferent, giving an option of two things. *mu<u>kh</u>aiyar*, possessed of free choice. *a.*

مخيل *mu<u>kh</u>aiyil*, imagining, fancying, doubting, being deceived, conjecturing from physiognomy. *a.*

مخيله *ma<u>kh</u>īla*, m. imagination, conception, thought, opinion, suspicion. *a.*

مخيم *mu<u>kh</u>īm*, pitching a tent. *mu<u>kh</u>aiyam*, m. an encampment. *a.*

مد *madd*, f. extension, production, lengthening; the flux of the sea; the mark (ٓ) placed sometimes over *alif*, which gives it a long broad sound; a peculiar mode of writing certain words in accounts. *madd o jazr*, tide, the flux and reflux of the sea. *maddi naẓar*, f. kind looks, encouragement; extensive view *mudd*, a kind of dry measure varying from one to two *raṭl*, q. v. *a.*

مد मद *mad*, m. wine, spirits, any intoxicating beverage; inebriety, intoxication; (met.) pride, haughtiness, arrogance, conceit. *mad-khor*, a drunkard. *a.*

مد *mad*, having a bad smell. *d.*

مد मुद *mud*, } f. pleasure, delight, joy. *s.*
مدا मुदा *mudā*, }

مداح *maddāḥ*, m. an encomiast, eulogist, panegyrist. *a.*

مداحي *maddāḥī*, f. act of praising, eulogy. *a.*

مداخل *madā<u>kh</u>il* (pl. of مدخل), incomes, revenues. *madā<u>kh</u>i-ma<u>kh</u>ārij*, additions and diminutions, income and expenditure. *a.*

مداخلت *mudā<u>kh</u>alat* (also *mudā<u>kh</u>ala*), f. access; entering into, intermeddling. *a.*

مدار *madār*, m. a circumference; a centre; a place of turning or returning; a place where one stops or stands, a station, a seat. *'izzat-madār*, the seat of glory. *madāru-l-mahāmm*, m. the minister, *i.e.* the centre of affairs. *madār i kār*, the principal of affairs, the issue or result of an action. *shāh-madār*, name of a celebrated Musalmān saint. *a.*

مدار मदार *madār*, m. f. name of a plant (*Asclepias gigantea*). *s.*

مدارا *mudārā*, m. } humility, humanity,
مدارات *mudārāt*, f. } politeness, affability, courtesy; deceit, circumvention, dissimulation. *a.*

مدارج *madārij* (pl. of مدرج), steps, degrees, ascents, ways. *a.*

مدارس *madāris* (pl. of مدرسه), colleges. *a.*

مداري मदारी *madārī*, m. a juggler. *h.*

مداري *madārī*, of or relating to *madār*. *a.*

مداريا मदारिया *madāriyā*, m. the followers of the saint *Madār*, q. v. *p. h.*

مدافعت *mudāfa'at*, repulsion, warding off. *a.*

مدام *mudām*, always; permanent, lasting, fixed; continually; f. wine, spirits. *a.*

مدامي *mudāmī*, adj. eternal, perpetual. *a.*

مداوا *mudāwā*, } curing a disease, aiding,
مداوات *mudāwāt*, } assisting, remedying *a.*

مداوتي *madāwatnī*, a female go-between, whose business is to look out for eligible wives or concubines for the benefit of single gentlemen. *d.*

مداوره *mudāwara*, m. going about, surrounding, encircling, encompassing, adjusting (a business). *a.*

مداومت *mudāwamat*, f. eternity, continuance, perpetuity; assiduity. *a.*

مدائح *madā,iḥ* (pl. of مدحه), laudable actions. *a.*

مداين *mudāyin*, a debtor; a creditor. *a.*

مداينت *mudāyanat*, mutual credit, dealings as debtor and creditor on both sides. *a.*

مدباس *mad-bās*, m. smell of the jack fruit. *d.*

مدبر *mudabbir*, adj. disposing in order, governing; prudent, ingenious; m. a manager, counsellor, director. *mudbir*, retiring, bashful, modest *mudabbar*, (in law) a slave to whom emancipation has been promised. *a.*

مدبري *mudabbirī*, act of managing, &c. *mudbirī*, adversity, bad luck. *a.*

مدت *muddat*, f. a space of time, a long time, antiquity. *muddatu-l-'umr*, during life. *muddati madīd*, a long space of time. *a.*

مدت मुदित *mudit*, rejoiced, pleased, delighted; m. pleasure, happiness. *s.*

مدح *madḥ*, f. praise, eulogium, commendation. *madḥ-khwān*, a bard, a panegyrist. *a.*

مدحرج *mudaḥrij*, what revolves. *a.*

مدحه *midḥa*, also *midḥat*, a praiseworthy action. *a.*

مدخل mudkhil, entering, penetrating. mudkhal, entered, inserted. madkhal, income, revenue. a.

مدخن madkhan, a place where smoke issues. a.

مدخول madkhūl, entered, put in, inserted. a.

مدخوله madkhūla, f. a concubine. a.

مدد madad, f. assistance, help, succour. madad-khwāh, one who asks assistance. madad-khwāhī, f. entreaty, imploring for aid. madad-kharch, charitable distributions, sums paid to help others. madad-ma'āsh, a grant of means of subsistence; assessment of revenue for the support of religious houses. a.

مدد मदद madad, a mixture of betel-leaf and opium used for smoking. h.

مددگار madad-gār, an assister, protector, ally. a. p. [tection. p.

مددگاري madad-gārī, f. aid, assistance, pro-

مدر mudirr, causing to flow, diuretic. a.

مدرا मदिरा madirā, f. spirits, wine. s.

مدرا मुद्रा mudrā, f. a sign, a signet-ring; a silver coin; an attitude or gesture; a ring worn by jogis in their ears. s.

مدرات mudirrāt, (in med.) stimulants. a.

مدرانکت मुद्राङ्कित mudrānkit, } sealed, stamped. s.
مدرت मुद्रित mudrit, }

مدرس mudarris, m. a professor, a head of a college. mudarras, a student. a.

مدرسانه madrasāna, academical, scholastic. a. p.

مدرسه madrasa, m. a university, a college, a school for the diffusion of Muḥammadan learning. a.

مدرسي mudarrisī, f. professorship. a.

مدرك mudrik, comprehending, understanding; one who comprehends. a.

مدركه mudrika, m. strength of understanding, intellectual powers, genius. a.

مدعا mudda'ā, m. desire, wish, meaning, suit, view, object, scope, intention. a. [jects. a.

مدعات mudda'āt, pl. desires, views, ob-

مدعي mudda'ī, m. a plaintiff, suitor, claimant, prosecutor; an enemy. mudda'ī 'alaihi (properly mudda'ā 'alaihi), a defendant (in law); criminal. "In the courts of Southern India, mudda'ī is erroneously used in the sense of 'defendant,' while the plaintiff is termed faryādī."—(B.) a.

مدعيت mudda'īyat, a plaint, a charge; the act of making a claim or suit in law; a female plaintiff. a.

مدعيه mudda'iya, f. a female plaintiff. a.

مدغم mudghim, inserting (a letter), joining two letters by tashdīd. mudgham doubled by tashdīd (a letter). a.

مدفن madfan, } m. a place for interment, a tomb. a.
مدفنه madfana, }

مدفون madfūn, buried, concealed, interred. a

مدقق mudaḳḳiḳ, examining minutely. a.

مدقوق madḳūḳ, hectic; pounded. a.

مدك मदिक madik, proud, intoxicated with wealth, purse-proud. madak, a pellet of opium or other drug for smoking. s.

مدگ मुद्ग mudg, m. a sort of kidney-bean (Phaseolus mungo). s.

مدگر मुद्गर mudgar, m. a mallet, a mace, a hammer; a kind of jasmine. s.

مدگرسي मद्गुरसी madgursī, f. a sort of fish. s.

مدل mudul, capital, stock, store. d.

مدلل mudallil, wheedling, a wheedler. a.

مدماتا मदमाता mad-mātā, also madmāṅtī and (in Dakh.) madmatā, drunk, intoxicated. s.

مدمغ mudammigh, proud, fastidious, foolish. h.

مدن mudun (pl. of مدينه), cities, towns. a.

مدن मदन madan, m. love, lust; a name of Kāmadeva; name of a medicinal plant, datura; the plant called main-phal (Gardenia dumetorum, Kæn. Vangueria spinosa, Roxb.). madan-vash, subdued by love, in love. s. [flower. s.

مدن بان मदनबान madan-bān, name of a

مدور mudawwar, round, circular. a.

مدھ मद्ध maddh, amidst, amid; m. temperament. s.

مدھ मधु madhu, m. honey, ardent spirit; the nectar or honey of flowers; the season of spring; the month of Chaitra; name of a demon slain by Kṛishṇa. a.

مده madda, m. the long vowels, or alif, wāw, and ye, when quiescent, and preceded by a letter which has their homogeneous short vowel; as in the words māl, wealth; sūd, gain; and pīl, an elephant. a.

مدھبن मधुबन madhu-ban, m. a name of Mathurā, q. v. s. [a bee. s.

مدھپ मधुप madhup, m. lit. honey-drinking,

مدھپر मधुपुर madhu-pur, m. a name of Mathurā, q. v. s. [fruit. s.

مدھپرس मधुपरस madhu-paras, m. ripe, juicy

مدھپرك मधुपर्क madhu-park, m. a dish of curds (ghī and honey) to be offered to a respectable guest. s. [Mathurā, q. v. s.

مدھپري मधुपुरी mudhu-purī, f. a name of

مدھترن मधुतृण madhu-tṛin, m. sugar-cane. s.

مدھر मधुर madhur, m. } sweet, pleasant to the ears, as music. s.
مدھري मधुरी madhurī, f. }

مدھرس मधुरस madhu-ras, m. sweetness (in flavour or in speech). s. [an arbitrator. s.

مدھست मद्धस्त maddhast or maddhasta, m.

مدھسودن मधुसूदन madhu-sūdan, a name of Kṛishṇa, who slew a demon called Madhu, q. v. s.

مدهكر मधुकर *madhukar*, m. the honey-maker, a bee; name of *Udhav*, a relative of *Krishna*; a plant (*Achyranthes aspera*); a fruit, the round sweet lime. *s.*

مدهكري मधुकरी *madhukrī*, f. a kind of bread baked on live coals (used among the ascetics or *jogīs*); victuals given in alms to pilgrims. *s.*

مدهكوش मधुकोष *madhu-kosh*, m. the honey-comb, or hive. *s.*

مدهم मद्धम *maddham*, middling, temperate. *s.*

مدهمات मधुमात *madhu-māt*, m. name of a *rāginī* or musical mode. *s.*

مدهماتا मधमाता *madh-mātā* or मधुमाता *madhu-mātā*, intoxicated, drunk. *s.*

مدهماس मधुमास *madhu-mās*, m. the month of *Chaitra*. *s.*

مدهماكهي मधुमाखी *madhu-mākhī*, f. a honey-bee. *s.*

مدهمي मधुमय *madhu-may*, sweet, luscious. *s.*

مدهوش *madhūsh*, astonished, confounded; inebriated. *a.*

مدهوكري मधूकरी *madhūkrī* (v. *madhukrī*), a kind of bread. *s.*

مدهولك मधूलक *madhūlak*, m. a sort of bassia growing in watery or mountainous situations; sweetness. *s.*

مدهيانه मध्याह्न *madhyānh* or *madhyāhna*, m. midday, noon. *s.*

مدهيم मध्यम *madhyam*, middle, intermediate, middling; m. the fifth note of the gamut. *madhyamā*, f. the middle finger. *madhyam-lok*, m. the middle world, the earth. *s.*

مدهيه मध्य *madhya*, middle, intermediate; m. the middle. *madhya-bhāg*, m. the centre. *madhya-desh*, m. the middle region, a part of India, comprising the modern province of Allahabad, Agra, Delhi, Oude, &c. *madhya-stha*, centrical, middle; m. a middleman, an umpire, a mediator. *madhya-sthatā*, f. middle state or character. *madhya-lok*, the middle world, the earth. *madhya-vartī*, central, being amidst; m. a mediator. *s.*

مديح *madīh*, a praiseworthy action. *a.*

مديد *madīd*, long, extensive. *a.*

مديرا मदेरा *maderā*, f. spirituous liquor. *s. h.*

مدينه *madīna*, m. a city, a state; name of a city in Arabia, Medina, famed as the burying-place of *Muhammad*. *a.*

مديون *madyūn*, a debtor, one involved in debt. *a.*

مديه मद्य *madya*, m. wine, spirituous liquor. *madya-pīt* or *madya-pa*, drunk, a drunkard. *s.*

مڈها मढा *maḍhā*, m. a temporary building, an open shed or hall, adorned with flowers, and erected on festive occasions, as at marriages, &c. *s.*

مڈهيا मढैया *maḍhaiyā*, m. a cottage, a hut. *s.*

مڈي *maḍḍī*, f. dregs, sediment. *d.*

مذاب *muẕāb*, liquid, melted. *la'li muẕāb*, a liquid ruby, red wine. *a.*

مذاق *maẕāḳ*, m. taste, tasting; the palate. *a.*

مذاكره *maẕākira* (pl. of مذكره), things worthy of being remembered. *muẕākara*, conference, conversation. *a.*

مذاهب *maẕāhib* (pl. of مذهب), forms of religion, sects, modes. *a.*

مذبح *maẕbiḥ*, m. a place of sacrifice, an altar. *a.*

مذبذب *muẕabẕib*, doubtful, wavering, hesitating, fluctuating, suspended. *a.*

مذبوح *maẕbūḥ*, killed, slain, sacrificed. *a.*

مذبوحات *maẕbūḥat*, pl. victims, animals sacrificed. *a.*

مذبوحي *maẕbūḥī*, f. state of being sacrificed. *a.*

مذبور *maẕbūr* (for مزبور), written, above-written. *a.*

مذكر *muẕẕakhar*, (in gram.) masculine. *a.*

مذكره *maẕkara*, m. mentioning, relating. *a.*

مذكور *maẕkūr*, before mentioned, remembered; (sub. m.) mention, discourse. *a.*

مذكورات *maẕkūrāt*, pl. discourses, relations, matters mentioned, things aforesaid; items. *a.*

مذلت *maẕallat*, baseness, contempt. *a.*

مذمت *maẕammat*, f. satire, abuse, scorn, contempt. *a.*

مذموم *maẕmūm*, scorned, contemptible, despised. *a.*

مذنب *muẕnib*, a sinner, a criminal. *a.*

مذهب *maẕhab*, m. religion, sect, mode, manner. *muẕahhab*, illuminated, (as a fine manuscript, letter, &c.).

مر *mur* or *murr*, m. myrrh, bitterness; adj. bitter. *a.*

مر मुर *mur*, the name of a *daitya* or demon killed by *Vishnu*. *s.*

مر मरु *maru*, m. a region destitute of water, a desert, sands; the province of Marwar. *maru-bhūmi*, dry, sterile, or sandy land. *maru-des*, or *-sthal*, a desert country; the region between Rājputāna and the Indus. *s.*

مرا मुर्रा *murrā*, m. a squib. *h.*

مرا मरा *marā* or *marā hū,ā*, dead. *s.*

مرا मुरा *murā*, a species of small fish. *h.*

مرابحت *murābaḥat*, legal profit on the sale of any article. *a.*

مرآت *mir,āt*, f. a mirror, speculum. *marrāt*, (pl. of *marra* or *marrat*) times, turns. *a.*

مراتب *marātib* (pl. of مرتبه), dignities; times; affairs; (barbarous pl. *marātibāt*). *a.*

مراجعت *murāja'at*, f. return, recourse; repeating. *a.*

مراحل *marāḥil*, journeys, stages, day's journeys. *a.*

مراحم *marāḥim*, favours, kindnesses, gifts. *a.*

مراد *murād*, f. desire, wish, intention, design, inclination. *a.*

مرادات *murādāt*, pl. things desired, designs. *a.*

مرادبخش *murād-bakhsh*, the giver of one's desire, a man's name. *a.*

مرادف *murādif*, synonymous. *a.*

مرادمند *murād-mand*, } desirous, longing
مرادونتا *murād-wantā*, } for; needy, necessitous. *a. p. h.*

مرادي *murādī*, favourably, agreeably to one's wish; f. change, small money. *a.*

مراديات *murādiyāt*, obtaining one's wishes, desirables. *a.*

مرار मुरारि *murāri*, } m. q. d. the foe of *mur*;
مراري मुरारी *murārī*, } an epithet of *Krishṇa*. *s.*

مراسلت *murāsalat*, epistolary correspondence. *a.*

مراسم *marāsim* (pl. of مرسم or مرسومه), marks, signs, vestiges; laws, usages, customs, conventions, observances. *a.*

مراعات *murā'āt*, f. looking back upon, considering, reflecting, viewing attentively through half-eyes; attending to, listening; taking care of, preserving, guarding. *a.*

مراغبت *murāghabat*, desire, propensity. *a.*

مرافعت *murāfa'at*, citing before a judge, a lawsuit. *a.* [company. *a.*

مرافقت *murāfakat*, association, travelling in

مراقب *murākib*, an observer, inspector. *a.*

مراقبه *murākaba*, m. observation, contemplation; fearing God. *a.*

مرال मराल *marāl*, m. a duck, a sort of goose with red legs and bill. *s.* [kill. *h.*

مرانا मराना *marānā*, a. to cause to strike or

مراءو *marā,o* (also *marā,onī*), fatal, deadly. *d.*

مراءو मुराऊ *murā,ū*, m. (v. *murā,ī*) a vegetable merchant. *h.*

مراهق *murāhik*, a lad near the age of puberty. *a.*

مراءي मुराई *murā,ī*, m. one whose business it is to grow and sell vegetables. *h.*

مراءي *murā,ī*, a hypocrite, a seeming saint. *a.*

مرايا *marāyā* (pl. of مرآت), mirrors, &c. *a.*

مرايات *murāyāt*, f. acting hypocritically, hypocrisy. *a.* [fection. *a.*

مربا *murabbā* (v. مربه), m. a preserve, con-

مرباساز *murabbā-sāz*, m. a confectioner. *a. p.*

مربع *murabba'*, being four in number; square, quadrangular, quadrilateral; sitting cross-legged (like a tailor); having a quartan ague. *a.*

مربوط *marbūṭ*, bound, fastened; arranged, construed, grammatical. *a.*

مربه *murabba*, pickled, preserved; m. a confection, jam. *a.*

مربهكها मरभूक्खा *marbhukkhā*, } starved to
مربهوكها मरभूखा *marbhūkhā*, } death, voracious, greedy. *s.* [war. *s.*

مربهو मरुभू *marubhū*, m. the province of Mar-

مربي *murabbī*, a tutor, guardian, protector, patron. *murabbā*, a confection. *a.*

مرپچ मरपच *mar-pach*, rotten, fermented, macerated. *a.*

مرپچنا मरपचना *mar-pachnā*, n. to suffer pain or sorrow; to labour excessively. *a.*

مرت मृत *mṛit* or *mṛita*, dead, deceased. *s.*

مرت मिर्त *mirt* (for *mṛityu*), f. death, dying. *s.*

مرتاض *murtāẓ*, exercised, disciplined. *a.*

مرتال मृताल *mṛitāl*, m. a fragrant earth, called also *Surat* earth. *s.*

مرتب *murattab*, arranged, regulated, prepared. *murtib*, wearisome, tedious. *murattib*, one who arranges. *murattab-k.*, to arrange. *a.*

مرتبان *martabān*, m. a jar for keeping preserves in, a vessel of the finest China porcelain which poison cannot penetrate. *a.*

مرتبه *martaba*, m. (also *martabat*, f.) a step, degree, dignity, office, employment, charge, rank of honour. *a.*

مرتد *murtadd*, an apostate, a renegade; one who has seceded from the Musalmān faith, and is (or was) consequently an outlaw. *a.*

مرتسنان मृतस्नान *mṛit-snān*, funeral ablution, bathing after mourning. *a.*

مرتضي *murtaẓā*, chosen, approved; one of the titles of *'Alī*. *s.*

مرتعش *murta'ish*, trembling, frightened. *a.*

مرتفع *murtafa'*, elevated, exalted, high, sublime, aggrandized. *a.*

مرتك मृतक *mṛitak*, m. a dead body, a corpse. *s.*

مرتكا मृत्तिका *mṛittikā*, f. earth, clay, soil. *s.*

مرتكب *murtakib*, mounted, carried, riding; perpetrating, committing. *a.*

مرتكرا मृत्किरा *mṛit-kirā*, f. an earthworm. *s.*

مرتكلپ मृतकल्प *mṛit-kalp*, insensible, fainted. *s.*

مرتول *martūl* (v. *mārtūl*), a turnscrew. *martol*, a hammer. *d.*

مرتويه मर्तव्य *martavya*, mortal, what is to die. *s.*

مرتها मिथ्या *mirthā*, false, lying, untrue. *s.*

مرتهن *murtahan*, pledged, pawned. *murtahin*, a pawnbroker, mortgagee. *a.*

مرتي मृत्यु *mṛityu*, f. death, dying. *s.*

مرتيلوك मर्त्यलोक *martya-lok*, m. the earth, the world of mortals (v. *lok*). *s.*

مرتينجي मृत्युञ्जय *mṛityun-jay*, the conqueror of death; a name of *Shiva*. *s.*

مرتيه मर्त्य **martya**, m. a man, a mortal. *s.*

مرثيه **marsiya**, m. an elegy, a funeral eulogium, particularly one sung during the *Muharram* in commemoration of the descendants of *'Alī.* *marsiya khwān*, a repeater of the *marsiya.* *marsiya khwānī*, act of repeating or singing the *marsiya.* *a.*

مرجاد मर्याद **marjād**, مرجادا मर्यादा **marjādā**, } f. station, rank, dignity, respect, honour, steadiness, rectitude, propriety of conduct. *s.*

مرجادك मर्यादिक **marjādik**, respectable, honourable. *s*

مرجان **marjān**, m. coral, a small pearl. *p.*

مرجانا मरजाना **mar-janā**, n. to die, to expire. *s.*

مرجاني **marjānī**, of or relating to coral. *p.*

مرجع **marja'**, m. time or place of return, asylum, refuge, repetition. *a.*

مرجوع **marjū'**, returned, referred; brought into court (a suit); fem. *marjū'a.* *a.*

مرجهانا मुरझाना **murjhānā**, n. to wither, to fade, to pine, to droop. *h.*

مرجهن मुरझन **murjhan**, m. pining, fading. *h.*

مرجي **murjī'**, m. one who delays doing what he promises; one of the sect called *murji,at* or *murjiyat*, who procrastinate the practice of good works as altogether unnecessary, and who deem faith sufficient for attaining salvation. *a.*

مرجيا मरजीया **marjiyā**, a diver (for pearls). *s.*

مرچ मिर्च **mirch** or मरिच **marich**, f. pepper. *gol-mirch*, black pepper. *lāl-mirch*, capsicum, Cayenne pepper; (in Dakh.) *mirchā, mirchānī*, or *mirchī.* *s.*

مرچا मिर्चा **mirchā**, مرچاءي मिर्चाई **mirchā,ī**, } m. Chili pepper (*Capsicum frutescens*). *s.*

مرچنگ मुरचङ्ग **mur-chang**, f. a jew's-harp. *p.h.*

مرچها **murchhā** (v. *mūrchhā*), swoon, fainting. *h.*

مرحب **marhab**, m. amplitude; adj. large, spacious, wide. *a.*

مرحبا **marhabā**, interj. (lit. may you enjoy a spacious abode!) hail! welcome! God bless you! *a.*

مرحله **marhala**, m. a day's journey, a stage, the time or place of travelling; an inn; a battery, the bastion of a fort. *a.*

مرحمت **marhamat**, f. pity, compassion, mercy, clemency, favour; a present. *a.*

مرحوم **marhūm**, one who has found mercy, *i.e.* one deceased, the late; as *nawwābī marhūm*, the late *nawwāb.* *a.* [city of Medina. *a.*

مرحومة **marhūmat**, f. defunct, deceased; the

مرخص **murakhkhas**, permitted or allowed (to depart), dismissed. *a.*

مرد **marad**, obstinacy, perverseness. *a.*

مرد **mard**, m. a male, a man, a hero (*vir*). *mardi ādmī*, a gentleman. *mardi ādmiyat*, gentlemanly conduct. *mard-bāz*, a lascivious woman, adultress, strumpet. *mard-bāzī*, f. adultery. *mard-bachcha*, the son of a brave man. *p.* [mild. *s.*

مرد मृदु **mridu**, soft; blunt, not sharp; gentle,

مرداد **murdād**, name of a Persian month corresponding with our July. *p.*

مردار **murdār**, polluted, impure, squalid, ugly, profane; (sub.) carrion. *murdār-khwār*, a species of eagle or crow that feeds filthily, a vulture. *p.*

مردارسنگ **murdār-sang**, also **murdā-sang** or *murda-sang*, m. litharge. *p.*

مردان **mardān**, pl. men, heroes, warriors. *p.*

مردانگي **mardānagī**, f. manliness, bravery. *p.*

مردانه **mardāna**, manly, brave; male or relating to males; propria quæ maribus; (as male apartments, &c.). *p.*

مرداني **mardānī**, f. a masculine (woman). *p.*

مردت मर्दित **mardit**, rubbed, anointed. *s.*

مردتا मृदुता **mridutā**, f. softness. *s.*

مردد **muraddad**, reprobated, ruined, perplexed. *muraddid*, one who drives to and fro; a repeller. *a.*

مردك **mardah**, m. a little man, a manikin; a low fellow, a puppy, a rascal. *p.*

مردكار **mard-kār**, one who acts manfully, a hero; adj. heroic, valiant. *p.*

مردم **mardum**, m. man in general, a polite man; the pupil of the eye; adj. civil, humane. *mardum-āzār*, an oppressor. *mardum-āzārī*, f. oppression, tyranny, robbery and murder. *mardum i chashm*, the pupil of the eye. *mardum-khwār*, man-devouring, cruel. *mardum-khez*, producing good men. *mardum-dar*, man-rending, ferocious. *mardum-kush*, a manslayer, a murderer. *mardum-kushī*, manslaughter, murder. *mardum-gazā*, man-stinging, injurious. *p.*

مردمان **mardumān**, pl. people, men and women in general. *p.*

مردمانا **mardamānā**, m. (same as *mard*) a man. *d.* [eyes. *p.*

مردمك **mardumak**, f. the pupil of the

مردمي **mardumī**, f. manliness, bravery, civility, humanity (in Dakh. *mardumgī*). *p.*

مردن मर्दन **mardan**, m. rubbing the body, bruising, trampling. *s.*

مردن **murdan**, (r. *mīr*) to die, to perish. *p.*

مردنگ मृदङ्ग **mridang** or मिर्दङ्ग **mirdang**, f. a kind of drum, a long drum, broader in the middle than at the ends. *s.*

مردنگي मिर्दङ्गी **mirdangī**, مردنگيا मिर्दङ्गिया **mirdangiyā**, } m. a beater of the *mirdang.* *s.*

مردني मर्दनी **mardanī**, m. one who anoints. *mardaniyān*, m. pl. attendants who rub oil, perfumed paste, &c., over the body. *s.*

مردني *murdanī*, worthy of death. *p.*

مردوا *mardū,ā*, m. a man, a fellow (a term of contempt). *p.*

مردود *mardūd*, rejected, excluded, reprobated, repulsed, confuted; m. an apostate. *a.*

مردودي *mardūdī*, f. apostacy; rejection. *a.*

مرده *murda*, dead; m. a corpse. *murda-sho*, one who washes the dead. *murda-farosh*, a name of a caste whose business it is to carry the dead. *p.*

مردها मिर्धा *mirdhā*, m. an officer employed by government in villages, an overseer, exciseman. *h.*

مردي *mardī*, manliness, manhood, virility. *marde-ādmī*, a gentleman. *p.*

مررهنا मररहना *mar-rahnā*, n. to be dead; (met.) to be deeply in love. *s.*

مرز *marz*, m. region, district. *marz o kishwar*, empire, territory. *p.*

مرزا *mirzā*, m. a prince; a title of *Musalmāns*. *mirzā-mizāj*, nice; fastidious. *mirzā-manish*, genteel, respectable. *p.*

مرزاءي *mirzā,ī*, f. gentility, pride, arrogance. *p.*

مرزبان *marz-bān*, m. a governor of the frontier, a prince. *p.*

مرزبوم *marz-būm*, also *marz o būm*, m. region, district, empire, territory. *h.*

مرزبه *marzaba*, m. a way, mode; regimen, government. *a.* [mode, manner. *a.*

مرس *maras* (pl. of مرسه), ropes. *maris*, way,

مرسا मसा *marsā* or *marshā*, m. name of a potherb (*Amaranthus oleraceus*). *s.*

مرسان *marsān*, f. a small whetstone. *a.*

مرستهل मरुस्थल *marusthal*, barren, dry, without water, desert. *s.*

مرسل *mursal*, m. a messenger, a divine messenger, a prophet, an apostle; of which class the *Muḥammadans* reckon 313; the whole number of prophets (*ambiyā*) are reckoned by the most moderate to amount to 124,000; pl. *mursalīn*. *a.*

مرسله *mursala*, m. an epistle, a missive; a necklace. *a.*

مرسوم *marsūm*, accustomed, notified, prescribed; persuaded, a mandate. *a.*

مرشا मरषा *marshā*, m. a potherb (*Amaranthus oleraceus*). *s.*

مرشا मृषा *mṛishā*, falsely; in vain. *s.*

مرشد *murshid*, m. an instructor, a director, guide (to salvation), a teacher, a monitor. *a.*

مرشدي *murshidī*, f. instruction in matters of religion. *a.*

مرصع *muraṣṣa'*, covered with gold, set or studded with jewels, cloth so ornamented. *a.*

مرض *maraẓ*, m. sickness, disease. *a.*

مرضعه *murẓi'a* or *murẓi'at*, a wet nurse. *a*

مرضي *marẓī*, agreeable, acceptable; taking favourably; f. will, assent, pleasure. *a.*

مرضيات *marẓiyāt*, pl. things, agreeable. *a.*

مرضيةً *marẓiyatan*, willingly. *a.*

مرطب *murṭib*, humid, moist; verdant. *muraṭṭib*, making moist. *a.*

مرطبان *marṭabān*, m. a glazed vessel, a jar. *a.*

مرطوب *marṭūb*, wet, damp, moist, full of humours. *a.*

مرعوب *mar'ūb*, terrified, overawed. *a.*

مرغ *murgh*, m. a fowl, bird, cock (particularly house fowl). *murghi aiwān*, the sparrow. *murghi biriyān*, a broiled fowl. *margh*, a species of grass, pasture. *p.*

مرغا *murghā*, m. a cock, any male bird. *p.*

مرغابي *murghābī*, f. a waterfowl. *p.*

مرغان *murghān*, pl. birds. *murghāni chaman*, birds of the grove, nightingales. *p*

مرغباز *murgh-bāz*, a cock-fighter; one who feeds cocks. *p.*

مرغزار *margh-zār*, m. a place abounding in verdure or in pasture, a meadow. *p.*

مرغك *murghak*, a little bird, a small fowl. *p.*

مرغوب *marghūb*, desirable, amiable, lovely, beautiful, estimable. *a.*

مرغول *marghūl*, } m. locks, twisted or plaited;
مرغولا *margholā*, } quavering (in singing). *p.*

مرغولنا *margholnā*, n. to warble (as a bird). *d.*

مرغي *murghī*, f. a hen. *murghī-wālā*, m. a poulterer *p.* [both ends). *p.*

مرفا *marfā*, m a kind of drum (beaten at

مرفق *mirfaḳ*, m. the elbow; a cubit. *a.*

مرفوع *marfū'*, exalted; marked with the vowel *pesh*, or short *u*. *a.*

مرفه *marfa* (v. *marfā*), a drum, &c. *p.*

مرفه *muraffah*, quiet, tranquil, contented, happy, prosperous; comfortable. *a.*

مرقب *marḳab*, m. a place of observation. *a.*

مرقت *maraḳat*, a kind of broth. *a.*

مرقد *marḳad*, f. a bed; a grave, a sepulchre, tomb; a medicine promoting sleep. *a.*

مرقع *muraḳḳa'*, clothed in rags, patched, mended; m. a scrap-book; fine penmanship. *a.*

مرقوم *marḳūm*, written, described, inscribed, above-mentioned. *a.*

مرك मरक *marak*, m. epidemy, pestilence. *s.*

مركانا मुरकाना *murkānā*, n. to twist, to writhe. *h.*

مركب **markab**, m. a horse, ship, camel, or any thing in or on which a person is carried. *a.*

مركب *murakkab*, compounded, composed, combined, mixed. *a.*

مركبات *murakkabāt*, pl. compound medicines; name given to a species of stanza in poetry. *a.*

مركت मरकत *markat*, m. an emerald. *s.*

مركٹ मरकट *markaṭ*, m. a monkey, an ape. *markaṭī*, f. a small or female monkey. *s.*

مركتيند मर्कटेन्दु *markaṭendu*, m. a sort of ebony. *s.* [house. *h.*

مركچا मरकचा *markachā*, m. the ridge of a

مركر मरकर *markar*, having been dead; (met.) with difficulty. *h.*

مركز *markaz*, m. a centre, the centre of a circle; a halting-place; an upper part of a letter, as *kāf kā markaz*, the upper or bent part of the letter *kāf*. *a.* [wish, desire. *a.*

مركوز *markūz*, fixed; hid, concealed; (sub.)

مركونڈي *murkūṅḍī*, prostrate, lying down. *murkūṅḍī mārnā*, to confine one's self to bed; to lie down and cover one's self up as when going to sleep. *d.*

مركها मरकहा *markahā*, }
مركهاها मरखाहा *markhāhā*, } addicted to beating, striking, or butting (a man
مركهنا मरखना *markhanā*, }
or animal). *h.*

مركهپنا मरखपना *mar-khapnā*, n. to die. *h.*

مركهنا मरखना *markhanā*, addicted to beating, &c. (v. *markahā*). *h.*

مركي मुरकी *murkī*, f. an ornament worn in the ear; the *tragus* of the ear. *h.*

مرگ मृग *mṛig* or *mirg*, m. a deer. *mirg-tṛishṇā*, m. (v. *sarāb*) a mirage, &c. *mirg-chiṛā*, m. name of a small bird. *mirg-chhālā*, the skin of a deer worn and used as beds by devotees. *mirg-sālā*, a deer park. *mirg-mad*, m. musk. *mirg-nābhi*, m. musk, a bag of musk. *mirg-nainī*, *-nayanī*, *-netrī*, or *-lochanī*, deer-eyed (an epithet of a mistress). *s.*

مرگ *marg*, f. death; *margi mufājāt*, sudden death. *p.* [*mis colocynthida*). *s.*

مرگادني मृगादनी *mṛigādanī*, colocynth (*Cucu-*

مرگ بهوجني मृगभोजनी *mṛig-bhojanī*, f. bitter apple or colocynth. *s.* [rage. *s.*

مرگترش मृगतृष *mṛig-tṛish*, f. (v. *sarāb*) mi-

مرگ راج मृगराज *mṛig-rāj*, m. the king of beasts, a lion. *s.*

مرگ سرا मृगशिरा *mṛig-sirā* or *mṛig-shirā*, f. the fifth mansion of the moon; λ *Orionis*. *s.*

مرگل मरगल *margal*, fried (fish). *h.*

مرگهٹ मरघट *marghaṭ*, m. the place where Hindūs burn their dead; a crematory. *s.*

مرگي मृगी *mṛigī*, f. a doe, a female deer. *s.*

مرگي मिर्गी *mirgī*, f. the epilepsy. *h.*

مرگيوالا मुरगीवाला *murgī-wālā*, m. a poulterer (for *murghī-wālā*, q. v.). *p. h.*

مرگيا मृगया *mṛigyā*, f. hunting (of the deer). *s.*

مرگيندر मृगेन्द्र *mṛigendra*, m. the lion. *s.*

مرگيها मिर्गीहा *mirgīhā*, m. one afflicted with the epilepsy. *h.*

مرلا मुरला *murlā*, toothless; m. a peacock. *h.*

مرلي मुरली *murlī*, f. a fife, flute, pipe. *murlī-dhar*, a name of *Krishṇa*. *s.*

مرم मरम *maram* or मर्म *marma*, m. situation, circumstances, occurrences; news or account of what has happened to a person, &c.; a secret; secret meaning or purpose; secrecy, confidence; knowledge; margin. *s.*

مرم मुरम *muram*, a kind of gravelly soil. *h.*

مرمت *marammat*, f. mending, repairing. *a.*

مرمر *marmar*, m. (Gr. μάρμαρον from μαρμαίρω, to shine) marble. *g.*

مرمر मरमर *marmar*, m. sound made by treading upon dry leaves, &c. *s*

مرمرا मुरमुरा *murmurā*, m. a kind of food, rice pressed flat and eaten raw (so named in imitation of the sound which it gives in chewing). *h.*

مرمرانا मरमराना *marmarānā*, n. to creak as a new shoe (an imitative sound). *s.*

مرمري मर्मरी *marmarī*, f. a sort of pine (*Pinus devadaru*). *s.*

مرمستهان मर्मस्थान *marma-sthān*, any part of the body where a wound would be fatal; one's weak side, raw, or sore part. *s.*

مرمگيه मर्मज्ञ *marma-gya*, }
مرمويدي मर्मवेदी *marma-vedī*, } a learned or intelligent man. *s.*

مرن मरण *maran*, m. death, dying moments. *s.*

مرنا मरना *marnā*, n. to die, to expire, to cease; (met.) to desire vehemently, to set one's heart upon any thing; m. dying. *s.*

مرنڈ मुरण्ड *muranḍ*, a country on the north-west of Hindūstān, now called Lamgan. *s.*

مرنڈاكرنا मुरण्डाकरना *muranḍā karnā*, a. to tie, to captivate. *muranḍā-kar-ḍālnā*, to entrance, to enchant, to captivate. *h.*

مروا मरुआ *maru,ā* or *marū,ā*, name of a strong-scented plant (*Artemisia vulgaris*; *Ocymum pilosum*, *Roxb.*). *s.*

مرواريد *marwārīd*, m. a pearl; (met.) a son. *p.*

مروانا मरवाना *marwānā*, a. to cause to be beaten or killed. *marwā-ḍālnā*, to dismiss a charge or complaint. *s.* [passionate. *h.*

مرواهي मरवाही *marwāhī*, affectionate, com-

مروت *murūwat*, f. manliness, virility, fortitude; affection, humanity, generosity. *murūwat torna*, to cease behaving affectionately. *a.*

مروتي *murūwatī*, humane, generous. *a.*

مروج *murawwaj*, selling (merchandise), current, saleable, usual. *a.*

مروحت *mirwaḥat*, a fan, a ventilator. *a.*

مرور *murūr*, m. passing, elapsing, a passage, pass, transition, avenue. *a.*

مرور मरोर *maror*, } f. twist, flexion, turn,
مروڑ मरोड़ *maroṛ*, } writhe, convolution. *maroṛ-bāz*, an affected person. *h.*

مروڑا मरोड़ा *maroṛā*, m. a twisting of the bowels, pain in the bowels, flux, gripes. *h.*

مروڑپهلي मरोड़फली *maroṛ-phalī*, f. name of a plant (*Helicteres Isora*), the fruit of which is used in medicine. *h.*

مروڑنا मरोड़ना *maroṛnā*, a. to twist, to writhe, to contort, to distort, to gripe, to yearn. *h.*

مروڑي मरोड़ी *maroṛī*, f. twisting, contortion, writhing; a screw. *h.*

مرول मरोलि *maroli*, } m. (v. *makar*) a kind
مرولي मरोली *marolī*, } of marine monster. *h.*

مرونا *mironā*, n. to perambulate, to keep watch (as the patrol). *d.*

مروه मरोह *maroh*, f. affection, kindness, humanity, compassion, mercy, pity. *h.*

مروه *marwa*, m. a mountain near Mecca. *a.*

مروهي मरोही *marohī* (also *marwāhī*), affectionate, merciful, compassionate. *h.*

مروي *marwī*, related, alleged, told. *a.*

مرويه मरवैया *marwaiyā*, one dying, one at the point of death. *s.*

مره *marra* or *marrat*, one time or turn, once. *marratan*, once upon a time. *a.*

مرها मुरहा *murhā*, m. an orphan; a peacock. *s.*

مرهه मुरहा *murhā*, m. convolution; adj. twisted. *h.*

مرهٹّا मरहट्टा *marhaṭṭā* or *marhaṭṭa*, m. a Marhatta. *s.*

مرهم *marham*, m. a plaster, ointment, salve. *marham-nih*, he who lays on a salve or plaster. *marham-paṭṭi*, a plaster, ointment or salve spread upon a piece of cloth or leather. *a.*

مرهوب *marhūb*, terrible, dreadful. *a.*

مرهون *marhūn*, pawned, pledged. *marhūni minnat*, bound in gratitude. *a.*

مرهي मुरही *murhī*, f. a twist, contortion, writhe, convolution. *h.*

مري मरी *marī* or *marrī*, f. the plague, pestilence, the cholera morbus. *s.*

مرئي *mar,ī*, visible, perceptible. *a.*

مرئي मुरई *mura,ī*, f. (v. *mūlī*) a radish. *h.*

مرياد *maryād*, limit, &c. (v. *marjād*, &c.). *s.*

مريٹها मरैठा *maraiṭhā*, twisted, wound up, bound round. *h.*

مريچ मरीच *marīch*, the name of a demon employed by *Rāvana* to entice away *Sītā*; f. pepper (*Piper nigrum*). *s.*

مريچ मरीचि *marīchi*, } f. a ray, a sunbeam;
مريچي मरीची *marīchī*, } m. name of a saint, son of Brahmā; one of the seven *rikhis*, represented by the seven stars in Ursa Major (η *Urs. Maj.*); a niggard, a miser. *s.*

مريچكا मरीचिका *marīchikā*, f. the vapour called mirage. *s.*

مريخ *mirrīkh*, m. Mars, called also *jallādi* [*falak*. *a.*

مريد *murīd*, desirous, willing; m. a disciple, a scholar, a follower. *a.*

مريد *marīd*, rebellious, obstinate, perverse, [stubborn. *a.*

مريدي *murīdī*, f. scholarship, the state or period of being a disciple. *a.*

مريض *marīẓ*, sick, diseased. *a.*

مريل मरियल *mariyal*, lean, emaciated, much reduced by sickness. *s.*

مريلا मरेला *murelā*, m. a pea-chick. *s.*

مڑكونڈي *muṛhūndī*, inverted, topsy-turvy. *d.*

مڑنا मुड़ना *muṛnā*, n. to be twisted, to be bent, turned. *h.*

مڑوڑ मड़ोड़ *maroṛ*, f. twist, turn, contortion. *maroṛ-bāz*, an affected person. *h.*

مڑوڑا मड़ोड़ा *maroṛā*, m. a twisting of the bowels, gripes. *h.*

مڑوڑنا मड़ोड़ना *maroṛnā*, a. to twist, to writhe, [to contort. *h.*

مڑوڑي मड़ोड़ी *maroṛī*, twisting, convolution; a screw or spiral. *maroṛī mekh*, a screw nail. *h.*

مڑه मुढ़ *muṛh*, m. a head man, a chief. *s.*

مڑها मढ़ा *maṛhā*, lined, headed, covered or topped (as a drum with parchment). *h.*

مڑهن मढ़न *maṛhan*, f. lining, heading (of a drum, &c.). *h.*

مڑهنا मढ़ना *maṛhnā*, a. to cover (as a book with leather, or a drum with parchment), to gild, to case. *h.*

مڑهي मढ़ी *maṛhī*, } f. a cottage, a tem-
مڑهيا मढ़ैया *maṛhaiyā*, } ple. *h.*

مڑهيانا मुढ़ियाना *muṛhiyānā*, n. to be twisted, to be writhed. *h.*

مڑي *maṛī*, f. a border, bank or division between garden beds or plats in a field; a bed or plat; section of a rice field; a parterre. *d.*

مڑيانا मड़ियाना *maṛiyānā*, a. to paste. *s.*

مزا *mazā*, m. (for *maza*, q.v.) taste, flavour. *p.*

مزابنت *muzābanat*, sale of corn in the field as it stands, without weighing or measuring. *a.*

مزاج *mizāj*, m. temperament, constitution, complexion, habit of body; temper, disposition. *mizāj-dān*, knowing the temperament. *mizāj-sharīf*, a very respectful term of inquiry respecting a person's health, q. d., "How is your noble or precious temperament?" *mizāj-go*, a flatterer. *mizāj-go,ī*, f. flattery. *mizāj-gīr*, agreeable, suited to the temper or taste. *a.*

مزاجي *mizājī*, habitual, constitutional; nice, dainty, squeamish. *a. p.*

مزاح *muzāḥ* (also *muzāḥat*), m. a jest, a joke. *mizāḥ*, jesting (with another person). *a.*

مزاحم *muzāḥim*, forbidding, hindering; m. an obstacle, a preventive, a preventer; adj. inconvenient. *a.*

مزاحمت *muzāḥamat*, f. prevention, hindrance, impediment. *a.*

مزاخ *mazākh*, m. jest, a joke, pleasantry. *a.*

مزار *mazār*, m. and f. a place of visitation, hence a sepulchre, tomb, grave, shrine. *a.*

مزارع *mazāri'* (pl. of مزرع), sown fields, &c. *muzāri'*, a husbandman. *a.*

مزارعت *mazāra'at*, cultivated lands. *a.*

مزامير *mazāmīr* (pl. of مزمور), psalms, &c. *a.*

مزاولت *muzāwalat*, f. remedying, curing; seizing or watching for (prey); entering into or managing affairs. *a.*

مزبله *mazbala*, m. a privy, a necessary, a dunghill, any place where filth is thrown. *a.*

مزبور *mazbūr*, written, above-mentioned, before-mentioned. *a.*

مزجات *muzjāt*, a trifle, a matter of little value. *a.*

مزخرف *muzakhraf*, ornamented, varnished, deceitful. *muzakhrif*, a deceiver, a cheat, a liar. *a.*

مزخرفات *muzakhrafāt*, pl. idle tales; lying vanities. *a.*

مزد *muzd*, m. a reward, premium, salary, wages, recompense. *p.*

مزدور *mazdūr*, m. a day labourer, a labourer in general. *mazdūr-paṭṭī*, a tax (formerly levied) on day labourers. *p.*

مزدوري *mazdūrī*, f. pay, hire, fare, wages; the price of labour. *p.*

مزرا *mazrā* (cor. of مزرع, q. v.). *h.*

مزرع *mazra'*, } a field sown or prepared for
مزرعه *mazra'a*, } sowing, a corn-field. *a.*

مزروع *mazrū'*, sown, cultivated. *a.*

مزعفر *muza'far*, m. a kind of dish, a saffroned pulāw. *a.*

مزكي *muzakkā*, purified, cleaned, justified. *muzakkī*, a purifier, a purgator. *a.*

مزگان *mizgān* (v. *mizhgān*), the eyelash. *p.*

مزمار *mizmār*, a pipe, a flute. *a.*

مزمزه *mazmaza*, shaking to and fro. *a.*

مزمن *muzmin*, chronic, permanent, of long continuance, obstinate (as a disease). *a.*

مزمور *mazmūr* (pl. مزامير *mazāmīr*), m. a psalm, a hymn. *a.*

مزواد *mizwād*, a traveller's provision bag. *a.*

مزور *muzawwir*, m. a knave, a cheat, a liar. *muzawwar*, a lie, a falsehood. *a.*

مزور *mazūr*, m. (for *mazdūr*) a labourer. *p.*

مزه *maza*, m. taste, flavour, any thing agreeable to the palate or mind, &c., a tit-bit or *bon mot*. *maza-dār*, also *maze-dār*, savoury, possessed of flavour. *maza-dārī*, f. savouriness. *p.*

مزيت *maziyat*, excellence; excess. *a.*

مزيد *mazīd*, m. increase, augmentation, advantage. *mazīd-k.*, to take away the dinner, table-cloth, &c. *a.* [&c. *p. h.*

مزيدار *maze-dār* (v. *maza-dār*), savoury,

مزير *mazīr*, intrepid, bold, stout-hearted. *a.*

مزين *muzaiyan*, adorned. *a.*

مژده *muzhda*, m. joyful tidings. *p.*

مژگان *mizhgān* or *muzhgān*, f. the eyelashes *p.*

مژه *mizha*, f. the eyelash. *p.*

مس *mis*, m. copper. *mis i zar-andūd*, (lit. gilded copper) insincerity. *p.*

مس मुस *mus*, land along the high banks of rivers. *h.*

مس *mass*, m. touch. *mass-k.*, to feel. *a.*

مس मिस *mis*, m. pretence, fraud, trick (v. *mish*). *masi*, m. f. ink. *s.*

مسا *masā*, f. evening. *masā-l-khair*, good evening. *ṣubḥ wa masā*, morning and evening. *a.*

مسا मसा *masā* or मस्सा *massā*, m. a wart, a fleshy excrescence. *s.*

مساجد *masājid* (pl. of مسجد), mosques. *a.*

مساح *massāḥ*, a measurer, a geometrician. *a.*

مساحت *masāḥat*, f. measurement, geometry, land surveying. *a.*

مساحقه *masāḥika*, m. *mulier quæ aliæ mulieri se pro viro gerit, quæ confrictu libidinem alterius explet*. *a.*

مساحي *masāḥī*, land surveying. *a.*

مسار मसार *masār*, m. an emerald. *h.*

مساس *masās*, m. mutual contact; *coitus*. *a.*

مساعد *musā'id*, assisting, aiding. *a.*

مساعده *musā'ada*, m. favour, assistance; mutual aid. *a.*

مسافت *masāfat*, f. distance, space, interval. *a.*

مسافحت *musāfaḥat*, f. adultery, whoring, debauchery. *a.*

مسافر *musāfir*, a traveller, passenger, stranger. *musāfir-parwar* or *-nawāz*, one who cherishes travellers, adj. hospitable. *musāfar*, travelled. *a.*

مسافرانه *musāfirāna*, like a traveller. *a. p.*

مسافرت *musāfarat*, f. travelling (in a body); journeying; being a stranger. *a.*

مسافرخانه *musāfir-khāna*, m. a house for the reception of travellers, a caravanseral. *a. p.*

مسافري *musāfirī*, state of travelling. *a.*

مساکت *masākat*, f. avarice, stinginess. *a*

مساکن *masākin* (pl. of مسکن), habitations, mansions. *a.*

مساکين *masākīn* (pl. of مسکين), the poor. *a.*

مسالك *masālik* (pl. of مسلك), ways, paths. *a.*

مسام *masām* or *masāmm*, m. a pore (of the skin), ducts or canals of the body. *a.*

مسامات *masāmāt*, pl. pores of the skin. *a.*

مسامحة *musāmaḥat* (also *musāmaḥa*), m. treating any one gently, pardoning; negligence. *a.*

مسان मसान *masān*, m. a place where dead bodies are burnt; an evil spirit, a demon. *s.*

مسان मुसाना *musānā*, a. to cause to steal. *s.*

مسانڈ *musānḍ*, an effort, attempt; assault, attack. *d.*

مساحت *masāḥat*, measuring, measurement. *a.*

مساوات *musāwāt*, f. equation, evenness, equality. *a.*

مساودت *musāwadat*, f. contending for superiority, dominion. *a.*

مساوي *musāwī*, equal, parallel, equivalent; neutral, impartial; suitable, convenient. *a.*

مساهله *musāhala*, negligence, carelessness. *a.*

مسائل *masā,il* (pl. of مسئله), questions; the precepts of *Muḥammad*; demands, propositions. *a.*

مسبب *musabbib*, m. the first cause. *musabbibu-l-asbāb*, the causer of causes, *i. e.* God. *musabbibi ḥaḳīḳī*, the true cause, God the Almighty. *a.*

مسبتات *musabbitāt*, f. hypnotics; opiate medicines. *a.*

مسبرد मसबिर्द *masbird*, m. a wart, a fleshy excrescence or swelling. *s.*

مسبع *musabba'* heptagonal, composed of or relating to the number seven. *a.*

مست *mast*, drunk, intoxicated; lustful, wanton, proud. *p.*

مستاجر *mustājir*, m. a tenant, one who rents a house, a contractor, a renter, a farmer. *a.*

مستاجري *mustājirī*, f. renting, farming, holding or settlement in a farm. *a.*

مستاصل *mutāṣal*, extirpated, ruined. *a.*

مستامن *mustāmin*, one who seeks protection. *a.*

مستانه *mastāna*, intoxicated; like a man intoxicated. *p.*

مستاني *mastānī*, f. intoxicated; lustful, lecherous, salacious (woman). *p.*

مستبد *mustabidd*, solitary, acting alone. *a.*

مستتر *mustatir*, veiled, concealed, hidden. *a.*

مستثني *mustasnā*, excellent, extraordinary, praised, laudable, selected, excepted from any common rule. *a.*

مستجاب *mustajāb*, acceptable, agreeable. *mustajābu-d-da'wāt*, one whose prayers are accepted. *a.*

مستجمع *mustajmi'* met together. *a.*

مستحب *mustaḥibb*, loving, affectionate. *a.*

مستحسن *mustaḥsan*, virtuous, approved, laudable, beautiful. *a.*

مستحضر *mustaḥẓir*, one who is present, or one who wishes to be present. *a.*

مستحق *mustaḥiḳḳ* or *mustaḥaḳḳ*, worthy, deserving, having a right to. *a.*

مستحکم *mustaḥkim* or *mustaḥkam*, firm, fast, established, strong. *a.*

مستحيل *mustaḥīl*, changed, transmuted. *a.*

مستخرج *mustakhraj*, drawn out, extracted. *a.*

مستخلص *mustakhliṣ*, free, liberated. *a.*

مستدام *mustadām*, perpetual, immemorial, assiduous, constant in any thing. *a.*

مستدعي *mustad'ī*, petitioner, suitor, claimant. *a.*

مستدير *mustadīr*, round, spherical. *khatti mustadir*, the circumference (of a circle). *a.*

مسترد *mustaradd*, returned, restored. *a.*

مستري *mistarī*, a master artificer, as a mason, &c., probably from the English "master."

مستزاد *mustazād*, increased; m. the name of a kind of verse in which every line has a shorter one annexed to it. *a.*

مستسقي *mustasḳī*, affected with dropsy, one who is craving drink. *a.*

مستطاب *mustaṭāb*, good, agreeable, excellent, pure. *a.*

مستطيل *mustaṭīl*, m. a parallelogram. *a.*

مستظهر *mustaẓhir*, one who cries for help. *mustaẓhar*, aided, assisted. *a.*

مستعار *musta'ār*, any thing borrowed. *a.*

مستعجل *musta'jil*, one who hastens. *a.*

مستعد *musta'idd*, prepared, ready, capable, able, fit, proper, worthy. *musta'iddi 'ilm*, learned. *a.*

مستعرب *musta'rib*, one who becomes or affects to be an Arab. *a.*

مستعصي *musta'ṣī*, rebellious, stubborn, sinful. *a.*

مستعفي *musta'fī*, one who seeks to be excused or relieved (from duty); one who resigns (an office). *a.*

مستعمل *musta'mal*, used, applied, accustomed; second-hand. *a.*

مستغاث *mustaghāṡ*, one who is applied to for aid or redress. *a.*

مستغاث عليه *mutaghāṡ'alaihi*, a defendant. *a.*

مستغرق *mustaghriḳ* or *mustaghraḳ*, drowned, immersed (literally or metaphorically). *a.*

مستغفر *mustaghfir*, one who asks pardon, penitent. *a.*

مستغني *mustaghnī*, rich, independent, satisfied, contented, purse-proud. *a.*

مستغنيانه *mustaghniyāna*, proudly, superciliously, independently. *a.* [tiff. *a.*

مستغيث *mustghīṡ*, m. a complainant, plain-

مستفاد *mustafād*, received, acquired, benefited. *a.* [gating. *a.*

مستفسر *mustafsir*, interrogating, investi-

مستفيد *mustafīd*, gaining, profiting, acquiring, edified, benefited. *a.*

مستفيض *mustafīẓ*, diffused, divulged; favoured, obliged. *a.*

مستقبح *mustaḳbaḥ*, hateful, detestable. *a.*

مستقبل *mustaḳbil*, m. future, the future tense (in gram.). *mustaḳbal*, a front view (of a figure). *a.*

مستقبليات *mustaḳbiliyāt*, pl. future events, things to come. *a.*

مستقر *mustaḳirr*, remaining firm, constant, firm, stable. *mustaḳarr*, fixed, firmly settled, a fixed abode. *a.*

مستقل *mustaḳill*, stable, firm, durable; absolute, independent, despotic. *a.*

مستقيم *mustaḳīm*, right, straight, standing erect, faithful, loyal, resolute. *a.*

مستك मुस्तक *mustak*, m. a kind of fragrant grass (*Cyperus rotundus*); a sort of poison. *s.*

مستك मस्तक *mastak*, m. and f. the head, the skull; the forehead (particularly of an elephant); the top of any thing. *s.*

مستكي मस्तकी *mastakī*, of or relating to the head. *s.* [ciliated. *a.*

مستمال *mustamāl*, soothed, persuaded, con-

مستمد *mustamidd*, asking assistance. *a.*

مستمر *mustamirr*, firm, constant, durable, persevering. *a.* [perform any thing). *a.*

مستمسك *mustamsak*, bound or pledged (to

مستمع *mustami'*, a listener, a hearer. *a.*

مستمند *mustamand*, poor, wretched, afflicted; a complainant; an accuser. *p.*

مستمندانه *mustamandāna*, wretchedly, like a poor unhappy individual. *p.*

مستند *mustanad*, supported (by any thing). *mustanid*, one who leans on, and supports himself (by any thing). *a.* [gigantic. *d.*

مستنڈہ *mustanḍa*, strong-bodied; powerful,

مستوجب *mustaujib*, worthy, fitting, deserving, meriting; m. an author, cause. *a.*

مستور *mastūr*, covered, concealed, veiled. *a.*

مستورات *mastūrāt*, women (of the *ḥaram*). *a.*

مستورة *mastūra*, f. a chaste woman. *a.*

مستوري *mastūrī*, f. privacy, retirement. *a.*

مستوفي *mustaufī*, paying or receiving in full (a debt); m. a head clerk, an auditor. *mustaufī-garī*, f. clerkship, audit. *a.*

مستول मस्तूल *mastūl*, m. mast of a ship. *e.*

مستولي *mastaulī*, overcoming, subduing, taking possession of, surmounting. *a.*

مستوي *mustawī*, equal, straight, direct. *a.*

مستهلك *mustahlik*, ruinous, destructive. *a.*

مستي *mastī*, f. drunkenness, intoxication; lust, wantonness. *p.*

مستيسا *mastīsā*, half-caste; the offspring of a European father and Indian mother (the word is Portuguese).

مستيمن *mustaimin*, prosperous, secure. *a.*

مسجد *masjid* or *masjad*, f. a mosque, a temple. *a.*

مسجدي *masjidī*, relating to a mosque. *a.*

مسجع *musajja'*, rhythmical (speech); harmonious or measured (periods). *a.*

مسجل *musajjal*, proved, authenticated and sealed by a judge. *a.*

مسجود *masjūd*, adored, worshipped. *a.*

مسح *masḥ*, m. wiping, washing, cleaning; anointing; perambulating, travelling. *a.*

مسحور *masḥūr*, fascinated, enchanted. *a.*

مسحوق *masḥūḳ*, worn, brayed, bruised. *a.*

مسخ *maskh*, m. changing, metamorphosing from a superior to an inferior shape. *maskh honā*, n. to be changed, to be metamorphosed into an inferior shape, as from man to beast. *a.*

مسخر *musakhkhar*, taken, subdued. *a.*

مسخراپن *maskharāpan*, m. }
مسخرگي *maskharagī*, f. } jesting, buffoonery, drollery. *a. h.*
مسخري *maskharī*, f. }

مسخرة *maskhara*, m. a droll, a jester, a buffoon, a fool, a laughing-stock. *a.*

مسدس *musaddas*, composed of six; m. a kind of verse consisting of six lines; a hexagon. *a.*

مسدود *masdūd*, shut, obstructed, closed. *a.*

مسدهان मसिधान *masi-dhān*, m. } m. an ink-
مسدهاني मसिधानी *masi-dhānī*, f. } stand. *s.*

مسرت *misrit*, mixed, mingled. *s.*

مسرت *masarrat*, f. gladness, cheerfulness, joy. *a.* [as reverence, excellence, &c. *s.*

مسرجي *misrajī*, a title given to Brāhmans,

مسرف *musrif*, prodigal, extravagant. *a.*

مسرنگي मसरंगी *masrangī*, f. a kind of pulse fried. *s.*

مسرور *masrūr*, glad, cheerful, exulting, gay, delighted, pleased. *masrūrī*, gladness, &c. *a.*

مسروق *masrūḳ*, stolen, robbed, surreptitious (fem. *masrūḳa*). *a.* [plain. *a.*

مسطح *musaṭṭaḥ*, level, even; (sub.) an open

مسطر *misṭar*, f. a board ruled with threads for marking paper preparatory to writing; a ruler; a line. *a.*

مسطور *masṭūr*, written, expressed, before-mentioned, delineated, above-specified. *a.*

مسطورات *masṭūrāt*, things aforesaid, &c. *a.*

مسعد *mus'ad*, } happy, fortunate, propitious,
مسعود *mas'ūd*, } august. *a.*

مسقط *masḳaṭ*, place of falling. *masḳaṭu-r-rās*, one's birthplace, native country. *a.*

مسقف *musaḳḳaf*, roofed, ceiled in. *a.*

مسك मसक *masak*, m. a gnat. *s.*

مسكا *musakkā*, m. muzzle used to prevent oxen from eating grain. *a.*

مسكان मुसकान *muskān*, f. a smile or grin, a kind of laugh without opening the mouth. *h.*

مسكانا मुसकाना *muskānā*, n. to smile, to grin. *maskānā*, a. to tear, rend, split, burst. *h.*

مسكتي *muskuṭī*, grinning, smiling. *d.*

مسكر *muskir*, inebriating, intoxicating. *a.*

مسكرات *muskurāṭ*, grinning, smiling. *d.*

مسكرانا मुसकुराना *muskurānā*, n. to smile, to grin, to smirk. *h.*

مسكراهت मुसकुराहट *muskurāhaṭ*, } f. smiling,
مسكراءي मुसकुराई *muskurā,ī*, } grinning, smirking, laughing. *h.*

مس كرنا *mass-karnā*, a. to touch. *a. h.*

مسكن *maskan*, m. a dwelling, habitation. *musakkin*, anodyne. *a.* [rent, burst. *h.*

مسكنا मसकना *masaknā*, n. to be torn, split,

مسكنات *musakkināt*, f. anodynes or sedatives, medicines alleviating pain. *a.*

مسكنت *maskanat*, f. humility, poverty, misery. *a.*

مسكون *maskūn*, inhabited, habitable. *a.*

مسكه *maska*, m. butter (especially fresh). *p.*

مسكين *miskīn*, poor, miserable, humble, wretched, indigent; name of a Hindūstānī poet (of Delhī). *a.*

مسكيني *miskīnī*, f. poverty, indigence. *a.*

مسگر *misgar*, a coppersmith, a brazier. *p.*

مسل मुसल *musal*, m. a wooden pestle, a club. *musal dhār barasnā*, to rain very heavily, or as we say in the vulgate, "to rain cats and dogs." *s.*

مسئلت *mas,alat*, a question, proposition, an action, a thing. *a.* [mour. *a.*

مسلح *musallaḥ*, armed for war, clad in ar-

مسلخ *maslakh*, a slaughter-house, shambles. *a.*

مسلسل *musalsal*, concatenated, successive, linked, chained. *a.*

مسلط *musallaṭ*, conquered, subdued; conquest. *musalliṭ*, m. a governor, ruler. *a.*

مسلك *maslak*, m. a way, path, track, an institution, regulation, rule of conduct. *a.*

مسلم *muslim*, a Musalmān, a believer in and follower of the *Muḥammadan* faith; name of a famous martyr, the nephew of *'Alī* the son-in-law and fourth successor of *Muḥammad*. "The deaths of *Muslim* and his sons *Muḥammad* and *Ibrāhīm* form the subject of a very beautiful elegy by *Miskīn* of Delhī, one of the best specimens of poetry in the Hindūstānī language."—(Binning). *musallam*, keeping safe, preserving in liberty; complete, sound, safe, entire, whole; free, exempted from. *a.*

مسلمان *musalmān* (v. *muslim*), m. a true believer, a *Muḥammadan*. "Dr. Gilchrist expresses his doubts regarding the legitimacy of this word, and inclines to deem it an Indian fabrication. This is not the case. The word is not properly Arabic, nor is it known to the Arabs; but it is generally used by Persians and Turks, and may be met with in some of the best Persian authors, Sa'dī, Kashifī, &c."—(Binning). *a.*

مسلماني *musalmānī*, f. the *Muḥammadan* religion: (vulg.) circumcision; (in India) a female Musalmān; adj. of or relating to the religion of *Muḥammad*. *a.*

مسلنا मसलना *masalnā*, a. to bruise, to crush. *s.*

مسلوب *maslūb*, seized, snatched away; spoiled, stripped. *a.*

مسلوك *maslūk*, beaten; trodden; inserted. *a.*

مسلول *maslūl*, consumptive. *a.*

مسله *masla* (properly *mas,ala*), m. question, proposition, a precept of *Muḥammad*; a point of law. *a.*

مسما *musammā*, called, denominated. *a.*

مسمات *musammāt*, f. (v. *musammā*).

مسمار *mismār*, m. destruction, ruin; mischief to crops committed by cattle; a nail, peg, pin. *mismār karnā*, a. to raze, to destroy. *mismār ho-jānā*, to fall into ruin. *a.*

مسماري *mismārī*, ruination, destruction. *a. h.*

مسمسانا मसमसाना *masmasānā*, n. to suppress one's sentiments from fear, to be mealy mouthed; (in Dakh.) *musmusānā*, to breathe hard. *h.*

مسمن *musamman*, made fat, fattened. *a.*

مسموع *masmū'*, heard, audible. *a.*

مسموم *masmūm*, poisoned; injured or infected by poison (meat). *a.*

مسمّى *musammā*, named, denominated, entitled; above-mentioned. *a.*

مسنّ *musinn*, old, aged, advanced in years. *a.*

مسن मसन *masan*, m. a medicinal fruit (*Serratula anthelmintica*). *s.*

مسن मिसन *misan*, a soil mixed of clay and sand. *h.*

مسنا मिसना *misnā*, n. to be ground or pulverized. *h.*

مسند *masnad*, f. a throne, a large cushion, a prop, a chair. *masnad-nishīn*, a reigning prince. *a.*

مسندآرا *manad-ārā*, adorning the throne, *i.e.* a king. *a. p.*

مسندي *masnadī*, of or relating to the *masnad*. *a. h.*

مسنون *masnūn*, legal, adopted into use; meritorious; circumcised. *a.*

مسنوي *masnawī* (for مثنوي, q. v.), a poem, &c. *a.*

مسواك *miswāk*, f. a stick used by the natives, a tooth-brush. *a.*

مسوده *musawwada* or *maswada*, m. a sketch or rough draft of a letter, &c. *a.*

مسور मसूर *masūr*, f. a kind of pulse (*Ervum hirsutum* or *Cicer lens*). *s.*

مسوري मसूरी *masūrī*, } f. a kind of small-pox. *s.*
مسوريا मसूरिया *masūriyā*, }

مسوڑا मसूड़ा *masūṛā*, m. the gums (of the teeth). *h.*

مسوسا मसोसा *masosā*, twisted; grieved, afflicted; m. affliction, remorse, regret. *h.*

مسوسنا मसोसना *masosnā*, a. to twist; to squeeze, wring; n. to be grieved or vexed. *h.*

مسهري मसहरी *masahrī* or *masihrī*, f. curtains (of a bed) made of very fine gauze, generally green, and commonly called "mosquito curtains," their sole use being to keep out the mosquitoes during the night. *s.*

مسهل *mushil*, aperient, purgative, laxative. *a.*

مسي *misī*, made of copper. *p.*

مسي मिसी *misī* or मिस्सी *missī*, f. a powder with which they tinge the teeth of a black colour (made of vitriol, &c.); adj. f. made of vetches. *misī-dān*, a box of gold, &c. for holding *misī*. *misī*, f. fennel, &c. (v. *mishī*) *h.*

مسي मसी *masī*, f. ink. *s.*

مسيادهار मस्याधार *masyādhār*, an inkstand. *s.*

مسيح *masīḥ*, } the Messiah, Christ our Lord. *a.*
مسيحا *masīḥā*, }

مسيحاءي *masīḥā,ī*, } Christ-like, of or relating to the Messiah, Christian; f. office or works of the Messiah. *a.*
مسيحي *masīḥī*, }

مسيدان मिसीदान *misī-dān*, a box of gold or silver, &c. for holding *misī*. *h. p.*

مسير *masīr*, going, walking, proceeding on a journey. *a.*

مسين मसें *masen*, f. pl. hair or down on the upper lip which appears in early youth. *h.*

مسين मसीन *masīn* or *misīn*, m. a vetch, pulse *h.*

مسينا मसीना *māsīnā* or *misīna*, f. linseed (*Linum utilatissimum*). *h.*

مش मिष *mish*, m. fraud, trick, deception, pretence, sham; stratagem; envy. *s.*

مش मश *mash*, m. a mosquito. *s.*

مشابه *mushābih*, resemblance, picture, similitude; probability; like. *mushābih bihi*, compared with it. *a.*

مشابهت *mushābahat*, f. } similitude, likeness, conformity, resemblance; probability. *a.*
مشابهه *mushābaha*, m. }

مشاتمت *mushātamat*, f. reproaching, abusing, reviling. *a.*

مشار *mushār*, signified, indicated. *mushārun ilaihi*, abovementioned, aforesaid. *a.*

مشارك *mushārik*, m. a comrade, an associate, a partner, partaker. *a.*

مشاركت *mushārakat*, f. community, society, association, partnership. *a.*

مشاطگي *mashāṭagī*, f. the business of a *mashāṭa*, or tirewoman, &c. *a.*

مشاطه *mashāṭa*, f. a waiting maid, a woman who combs hair, a bride dresser; a woman who makes or concerts marriages, a go-between. *a.*

مشاعره *mushā'ara*, m. contending, or excelling in poetry; lying or sleeping together under one coverlid; a meeting of poets. *a.*

مشافهه *mushāfaha*, oral communication, conversation. *a.*

مشاق *mashshāḳ*, m. a practiser, a proficient; adj. well-versed or -practised. *a.*

مشاقي *mashshāḳī*, through practice. *a. h.*

مشام *mashām*, m. the smell, the sensorium of smell, sense of smelling. *a.*

مشاورت *mushāwarat*, f. counsel, deliberation, consultation. *a.*

مشاهده *mushāhada*, m. sight, vision; ocular demonstration. *mushāhada-k.*, a. to look at, to contemplate, to view. *a.*

مشاهره *mushāhara*, m. bargaining, settling or hiring by the month; monthly salary, pay, wages. *a.*

مشاهير *mashāhīr* (pl. of مشهور), those who are renowned or distinguished. *a.*

مشائخ *mashā,ikh* (pl. irreg. of شيخ), old men; holy persons, dervises, adorers. *a.*

مشائخانه *mashā,ikhāna*, in the manner of holy men. *a. p.* [piety. *a.*

مشائخي *mashā,ikhī*, f. holiness, sanctity,

مشايعت *mushāya'at*, the following of some guide or leader in religious matters. *a.*

مشائعت *mushā,i'at*, f. the ceremony of accompanying a visitor, on his departure, to the door of the house; a mark of respect shewn only to one of superior rank. *a.* [forated. *a.*

مشبك *mushabbak*, latticed, grated, per-

مشبه *mushabbah*, assimilated, like. *a.*

مشت *musht*, f. the fist, a blow with the fist, a handful. *p.*

مشت मुषित *mushit*, stolen, robbed, pilfered. *s.*

مشتاق *mushtāḳ*, full of desire, desirous, wishing, longing (to see a person). *a.*

مشتاقانه *mushtāḳāna*, with a great desire (of seeing one). *a.*

مشتبه *mushtabih*, obscure, ambiguous. *a.*

مشترك *mushtarik*, m. a partner, an associate, an accomplice. *mushtarak*, held in common. *a.*

مشتري *mushtarī*, f. buying; m. a purchaser; the planet Jupiter. *a.* [pugilist. *p.*

مشتزن *musht-zan*, m. a boxer, a bruiser, a

مشتزني *musht-zanī*, f. boxing, the pugilistic art. *p.* [fire. *mushta'il*, grey-haired. *a.*

مشتعل *mushta'al*, inflamed, kindled, set on

مشتق *mushtaḳḳ*, derived (as one word from another; derivative. *a.*

مشتمل *mushtamil*, comprehending, containing, comprising. *a.*

مشتهر *mushtahir*, a proclaimer. *mushtahar*, proclaimed, celebrated, famous. *a.*

مشتهي *mushtahī*, longing, desiring, wishing. *a.*

مشتهيات *mushtahiyāt*, f. provocations, *aphrodisiaca*. *a.*

مشتي *mushtī*, fine silk cloth, or a garment made thereof; a handful, a small number or quantity. *mushtī,e khāk*, a handful of dust. *p.*

مشٹ मुष्ट *mushṭ*, m. theft, robbery. *h.*

مشٹ मष्ट *mashṭ*, f. silence. *mashṭ mārnā*, to remain silent. *h.*

مشٹ मिष्ट *mishṭ*, sweet, sugary. *s.*

مشٹامشٹي मुष्टामुष्टी *mushṭā-mushṭī*, f. or *-mushṭi*, m. thumping and pulling, boxing, fisticuffs. *s.*

مشٹان मिष्टान्न *mishṭānn*, m. sauce, seasoning, gravy; a mixture of sugar and acids eaten with rice, &c. *s.*

مشٹمار मुष्टमार *mushṭmār*, m. a pilferer, a robber. *mushṭmār kar baiṭhnā*, to sit with the knees held up by clasping the arms round them. *s.*

مشٹي मुष्टी *mushṭī*, f. the fist, the closed hand; stealing, pilfering. *s.*

مشٹيبندھ मुष्टीबन्ध *mushṭī-bandh*, m. one who clenches the fist. *s. p.* [boxing. *s.*

مشٹيپات मुष्टीपात *mushṭī-pāt*, m. pummelling,

مشٹيمشٹ मुष्टिमुष्टि *mushṭī-mushṭi*, fist to fist, fisticuffs. *s.*

مشجر *mushajjar*, m. a kind of silk cloth. *mushjir*, abounding in trees. *a.*

مشخص *mushakhkhas*, certain, ascertained, stipulated; a fine, an amercement. *a.*

مشدد *mushaddad*, strengthened; (applied to a letter that is doubled or marked with the symbol *tashdīd*). *a.*

مشر मिश्र *mishr* or *mishar*, adj. mixed, blended, mingled; m. mixing, mixture; a title of Brāhmans, who were brought to India from *Shākadwīp* by *Krishṇa* in order to cure the leprosy of his son *Shāmba*; also a title of Brāhmans from *Maithal*, &c.; a Hindū physician; a respectable person. *s.*

مشرب *mashrab*, m. place of drinking; imbibing; sect, religion; nature, temper, humour. *a.*

مشربه *mashraba*, a dining-room, a parlour. *a.*

مشرت मिश्रित *mishrit*, mixed, mingled, added; respected, respectable. *s.*

مشرح *musharraḥ*, explained, commented upon; meat cut into small pieces. *a.*

مشرف *musharraf*, exalted, ennobled; ornamented. *mushrif*, an examiner, inspector, observer; near, approaching, impending. *a.*

مشرق *mashriḳ*, m. the east. *mashriḳain*, (du.) the east and west. *bu'du-l-mashriḳain* or *dūrī,e mashriḳain*, as far as east is from west. *a.*

مشرقي *mashriḳī*, eastern, oriental. *a.*

مشرك *mushrik*, m. an infidel, an idolater, a polytheist. *musharrak*, common (to many). *a.*

مشرن मिश्रण *mishraṇ*, m. mixing, uniting; addition. *s.* [fried. *s*

مشرنگي मषरङ्गी *mash-rangī*, f. a kind of pulse

مشرو *mashrū*, m. a kind of silk cloth (v. *mashrū'*). *a.*

مشروب *mashrūb*, drunk, imbibed, potable. *a.*

مشروح *mashrūḥ*, explained, illustrated, commented upon; above-mentioned. *a.*

مشروحا *mashrūḥan*, agreeably to the explanation, circumstantially. *a.*

مشروط *mashrūṭ*, } agreed upon, stipulated;
مشروطي *mashrūṭī*, } (sub.) a settled revenue of ten per cent. allowed to the *zamīndārs*. *a.*

مشروع *mashrū'*, initiated, begun, commenced; legal, just, prescribed by law; m. a kind of cloth made of silk and cotton mixed (dressed in which it is lawful for Musalmāns to pray, that not being allowed in cloth entirely of silk). *a.*

مشاع *mush'ā*, mixed, as common property, so that the shares cannot be distinguished. *a.*

مشعبد *musha'bid*, } m. a conjurer, a juggler. *a.*
مشعبذ *musha'biz*, }

مشعر *mush'ir*, signifying, denoting, indicating, bearing the marks of. *mash'ar* or *mish'ar*, any one of the five senses. *a.*

مشعره *mash'ara*, m. a place where poets meet to read their verses, &c. *a.*

مشعل *mash'al*, f. } m. a torch, flambeau, lanthern. *mash'ala-dār*, torchbearer. *a.*
مشعله *mash'ala*, m. }

مشعلچي *mash'alchī*, m. a torchbearer. *a. t.*

مشغل *mushghal*, busied, employed. *a.*

مشغله *mashghala*, m. employment, pastime; a tumult, a crowd. *a.*

مشغول *mashghūl*, employed, occupied, busy, diligent, anxious. *a.*

مشغوله *mashghūla*, m. employment, occupation, pastime, business. *a.*

مشغولي *mashghūlī*, f. the being employed, the state of being in office. *a.*

مشفق *mushfiḳ*, kind, shewing favour, condoling, merciful. *a.*

مشفقانه *mushfiḳāna*, favourably, kindly. *a.*

مشق *mashḳ*, f. piercing suddenly with a spear; striking with velocity; beating, lashing, tearing; combing; drawing (a garment, thing, &c.) every way in order to stretch it; eating of the best parts (of forage, &c.); (a man) galled between the thighs; tall, slender (girl); (met.) an example, copy to write after, exercise, practice, usage, use. *a.*

مشقاب *mushḳāb*, f. a large shallow vessel, in which bread is kneaded. *t.*

مشقت *mashaḳḳat*, m. trouble, labour, pains, toil. *a.*

مشقي *mashḳī*, acquired by practice. *a.*

مشك *mashk*, f. a leather bag, especially for carrying water, a water-bag; the Eastern bagpipe: this instrument has no drone, but simply a goat-skin bag with a mouthpiece and chanter: the latter is sometimes composed of two pipes joined together like a double flageolet. This instrument seems to be known all over the East: the Persians call it *nai-ambāna*, and the Arabs *zummāra bil-ḳirba*. *mushk* (in Arabic *misk*), m. musk. *mushk-bār*, diffusing musk, scented like musk; (met.) a mistress's lock. *mushk billī* or *mishk bilā,o*, a civet-cat, the animal from which is obtained the perfume called *zubād*, or, vulgo, *jawād* *mushk-fām*, musk-coloured; (met.) the locks of a mistress. *p.*

مشك मशक *mashak*, m. a gnat, a mosquito. *s.*

مشك मुष्क *mushk*, m. scrotum, testicle. *s.*

مشكل *mushkil*, difficult, intricate, hard, painful; a difficulty. *mushkil-pasand*, one who delights in difficulties. *mushkil-kushā*, a disperser of difficulties *mushkil-guzar* or *-guzār*, difficult to pass. *a*

مشكّل *mushakkal*, well-shaped, handsome. *a.*

مشكلات *mushkilāt*, pl. things difficult. *a.*

مشكور *mashkūr*, praised, laudable, agreeable, rewarded, thanked. *a.*

مشكوري *mashkūrī*, f. reward, thanking. *a.*

مشكوك *mashkūk*, doubtful, uncertain, problematical. *a.*

مشكي *mushkī*, dark bay approaching to black (colour of a horse). *p.*

مشكيزه *mashkīza*, m. a small leather bottle. *p.*

مشكين *mushkīn*, musky, dark, of a sable hue. *p.*

مشكين چڙهانا मुश्कें चढ़ाना *mushken-chaṛhānā* or *-bāndhnā*, a. to pinion, to tie the hands behind the back. *h.*

مشل मुषल *mushal*, m. a club, a mace, a pestle. *s.*

مشلول *mashlūl*, paralytic. *a.*

مشمول *mashmūl*, comprehended, contained, surrounded. *a.*

مشموم *mashmūm*, sweet-smelling, odoriferous, fragrant, perfumed. *a.*

مشورت *mashwarat*, f. } counsel, consultation, advice. *a.*
مشوره *mashwara*, m. }

مشوش *mushawwash*, disturbed, confused, intricate; distressed, uneasy, perplexed. *a.*

مشهد *mashhad*, a burying-place, especially for martyrs; name of a Persian city, formerly Tūs. *a.*

مشهري मशहरी *mash-harī* or *mashahrī*, f. mosquito curtains. *s.*

مشهود *mashhūd*, attested, proved, evinced, clear, manifest. *a.*

مشهور *mashhūr*, } celebrated, published, divulged, conspicuous, famous. *mashhūr hai*, it is related, it is a current report. *mashhūra,e āfāḳ*, (a person or thing) celebrated throughout the world. *a.*
مشهوره *mashhūra*, }

مشي मिशी or मिषी *mishī*, f. spikenard (*Valeriana jatamansi*); a sort of fennel (*Anethum pannorium*); common anise. *s.*

مشي मषी *mashī*, f. ink; the stalk of the *Nyctanthes tristis*. *s.*

مشي *mashī*, m. walking, going. *a.*

مشيت *mashīyat* or *mashī,at*, f. power or will, pleasure; the will of God, fate, strength. *a.*

مشيخت *mashīkhat* or *mashyakhat*, seniors, elders, old men; princes, presidents; doctors, high priests: this is an irregular or redundant plural of *shaikh*, like *mashā,ikh*. *a.*

مشير *mushīr*, m. a counsellor, a senator. *mushīr i khāṣṣ*, a privy counsellor. *a.*

مشين *mushīn*, villainous, worthless. *mushaiyan*, stately, dignified. *a.*

مصابرت *muṣābarat*, patient, or enduring with patience. *a.*

مصاحب *muṣāḥib*, m. a companion, friend, favourite, aide-de-camp, courtier. *a.*

مصاحبت *muṣāḥabat*, } f. companionship, society, familiar intercourse, communion. *a.*
مصاحبي *muṣāḥibī*, }

مصاحف *maṣāḥif* (pl. of مصحف), books, volumes, &c. *a.*

مصادرت *muṣādarat*, oppression, spoliation. *a.*

مصارعت *muṣāra'at*, wrestling; a contest. *a.*

مصارف *maṣārif* (pl. of مصرف), expenses, disbursements; changes, vicissitudes. *a.*

مصاف *maṣāff*, f. a field of battle, the ranks of an army. *a.*

مصافحه *muṣāfaha*, m. shaking hands. *a.*

مصالح *maṣāliḥ*, m. (pl. of مصلحت) affairs; honour, glory, employments; materials. *maṣālaḥ* (in Hind.) condiments, drugs, spices, seasoning. *maṣālaḥ d* or *-ḍālnā*, to season. *a.*

مصالحت *muṣālaḥat*, f. } reconciliation, pacification. *muṣālaḥa-k.*, to reconcile. *a.*
مصالحه *muṣālaḥa*, m. }

مصائب *maṣā,ib* (pl. of مصيبت), afflictions, calamities. *a.*

مصباح *miṣbāḥ*, f. a lamp, a torch, a lantern. *a*

مصبر *muṣabbar*, aloes (the drug merely). *z.*

مصحف *maṣḥaf*, *miṣḥaf*, or *muṣḥaf*, m. a volume, a book, a page; the *Ḳurān*, as "the book," par excellence. *a.*

مصحوب *maṣḥūb*, accompanied, accompanying. *a.*

مصداق *miṣdāḳ*, a proof of veracity. *a.*

مصدر *maṣdar*, m. source, origin, spring, theme; the infinitive or noun of action; a place. *a.*

مصدري *maṣdarī*, of or relating to the source, or to the infinitive (in gram.). *a.*

مصدع *muṣaddi'*, troublesome, annoying. *a.*

مصدق *muṣaddiḳ*, a verifier, an affirmer. *muṣaddaḳ*, verified, substantiated, attested. *a.*

مصدور *maṣdūr*, } issued, derived, derivative. *a.*
مصدوره *maṣdūra*, }

مصر *miṣr*, m. Egypt, also Cairo, the capital of Egypt, any large city. *a.*

مصر *muṣirr*, one who perseveres or insists; adj. obstinate, unflinching. *a.*

مصراع *miṣrā'*, } m. a hemistich, a line (in poetry); leaf of a folding-door. *a.*
مصرع *muṣarra'*, }
مصرعه *miṣra'a*, }

مصرف *muṣrif*, prodigal. *maṣraf*, m. expense, disbursement, cost, charge. *a.*

مصروع *maṣrū'* prostrated; epileptic, or seized with epilepsy. *a.*

مصروف *maṣrūf*, expended, employed; turned, changed, declinable. *a.*

مصري *miṣrī*, adj. of or relating to Egypt; f. sugar-candy; m. an Egyptian. *a.*

مصطبه *maṣṭaba*, an inn or caravanserai for the reception of strangers. *a.*

مصطفى *muṣṭafa*, chosen, selected; m. one of the titles of *Muḥammad*. *a.*

مصطكي *maṣṭakī*, f. (Gr. μαστίχη) mastiche (the resin of the *Pistacia lentiscus*). *g.*

مصطلح *muṣṭalaḥ*, idiomatic, metaphoric; an idiom, a phrase. *a.*

مصطلحات *muṣṭalaḥāt*, pl. idiomatic expressions, &c. *a.*

مصفا *muṣaffā*, clean, pure, transparent; justified. *a.*

مصقل *miṣḳal*, any thing used in polishing. *a.*

مصقلا *miṣḳalā*, } a polisher, any instrument with which a thing is polished. *a.*
مصقله *miṣḳala*, }

مصقول *maṣḳūl*, polished, furbished. *a.*

مصلا *muṣallā*, m. a carpet to pray on. *a.*

مصلح *muṣliḥ*, m. one who rectifies, a mediator, pacifier, adviser, reformer. *a.*

مصلحت *maṣlaḥat*, f. an action, occupation, expediency, the best thing to be done; counsel, advice. *maṣlaḥat-k.*, a. to consult, to combine. *a.*

مصلحتا *maṣlaḥatā* or *maṣlaḥatan*, advisedly, wisely. *a.*

مصلوب *maṣlūb*, crucified, suspended. *a.*

مصلي *muṣallī*, holy, righteous. *muṣallā*, a spot near Shīrāz, celebrated by *Ḥāfiz* for its rosy bowers. *a.*

مصمم *muṣammam*, fixed, concluded, determined. *a.*

مصنع *muṣanna'*, factitious, artificial. *a.*

مصنف *muṣannif*, m. a composer, an author. *muṣannaf*, composed; a composition. *a.*

مصنفات *muṣannafāt*, books, works, compositions. *a.*

مصنوع *maṣnū'*, formed, created, made, prepared; artificial; an invention, contrivance. *a.*

مصنوعات *maṣnū'āt*, pl. inventions, contrivances, works of skill. *a.*

مصنوعي *maṣnū'ī*, artificial, fictitious. *a.*

مصور *muṣawwir*, m. a painter, sculptor; forming, figuring. *muṣawwar*, a painting, a picture. *a.*

مصوري *muṣawwirī*, f. the art of painting. *a.*

مصون *maṣūn*, guarded, kept in safety. *a.*

مصيبت *muṣībat*, f. a misfortune, disaster, affliction, adversity, evil, misery, ill. *muṣībat i nāgahānī*, an unlooked-for disaster or affliction. *muṣībat-zada*, struck with misfortune, &c. *a.*

مضادت *muẓāddat*, opposition, antipathy. *a.*

مضارب *muẓārib*, a factor, a manager. *a.*

مضاربه **muẓāraba**, m. a battle, conflict, combat; a partnership of stock on the one hand, and labour or management on the other. h.

مضارع **muẓāri'**, m. the aorist (in gram); adj. resembling, similar to. a.

مضاعف **muẓā'af**, doubled, increased, multiplied. a.

مضاف **muẓāf**, annexed, added; related; (sub.) a noun placed in construction; one who is joined to others with whom he has no natural connection. *muẓāf ilaihi*, the noun governed. a.

مضافات **muẓāfāt**, pl. things annexed, appendages. a.

مضامين **maẓāmīn** (pl. of مضمون), the contents of a book (epistle, &c.). a.

مضايقه **muẓāyaḳa**, m. penury, necessity, distress, poverty; moment, consequence, significance. *kuchh muẓāyaḳa nahīṅ*, it is of no consequence. a.

مضبوط **maẓbūṭ**, strong; possessed, occupied, restrained, moderated. a.

مضبوطي **maẓbūṭī**, f. strength, firmness, durability. a.

مضحاك **miẓḥāk**, laughing, merry, facetious. a.

مضحك **muẓḥik**, ridiculous, droll, laughable. a.

مضحكات **muẓḥikāt**, pl. jests, jokes, funny sayings or doings. a.

مضحكه **maẓḥuka**, m. humour, fun, drollery, a pun, *bon mot*. a.

مضر **muẓirr**, pernicious, hurtful. a.

مضراب **miẓrāb**, a musical plectrum or bow. a.

مضرت **maẓarrat**, f. detriment, damage, injury. a.

مضطر **muẓṭarr**, rendered desperate, afflicted. a.

مضطرب **muẓṭarib**, agitated, disturbed, afflicted, chagrined, anxious, uneasy. a.

مضطربانه **muẓṭaribāna**, in a state of agitation or anxiety; confusedly. a.

مضغه **muẓgha**, m. a lump of flesh; a glutton, an ill-bred person. a.

مضمار **miẓmār**, a large plain or place for exercise, a race-course, downs. a.

مضمحل **muẓmaḥill**, disappearing, vanished. a.

مضمر **muẓmir**, conceiving, imagining. *muẓmar*, concealed, imagined, conceived in the mind; (in gram.) the antecedent. a.

مضمضه **maẓmaẓa**, m. washing or rinsing out the mouth. a.

مضمن **muẓamman**, contained, inserted, a kind of poem. a.

مضموم **maẓmūm**, added, joined, accumulated; (a letter) marked with the vowel-point *ẓamma* or *pesh* i. e. the short u). a.

مضمون **maẓmūn**, m. sense, signification, purport; contents (of a letter or book). a.

مضور **maẓūr**, becoming acrid, pricking the tongue (wine or milk). a.

مضي **maẓā**, lit. "it is past." *maẓā mā maẓā*. "let bygones be bygones;" (in Hind.) "*jo hū,ā so hū,ā*." a.

مطا **maṭā**, m. favour, protection. a.

مطابق **muṭābiḳ**, conformable, equal, corresponding, suitable, agreeable to. a.

مطابقت **muṭābaḳat**, f. conformity, equality. a.

مطاع **muṭā'**, obedient; obeyed. a.

مطالب **maṭālib** (pl. of مطلب), demands, requisitions, desiderata. a.

مطالبه **muṭālaba**, a demand, asking, exacting. a.

مطالعه **muṭāla'a**, m. contemplation, consideration; reading, study. *muṭāla'a k.*, to read, study peruse. a.

مطاهره **muṭāhara**, purifying, cleansing, ablution. a.

مطايبه **muṭāyaba**, sport, joking, pleasantry. a.

مطبخ **maṭbakh**, m. a place for cooking; a kitchen. *miṭbakh*, a cooking utensil. a.

مطبخي **maṭbakhī**, culinary; s. a cook. s.

مطبع **maṭba'**, a printing-office. a.

مطبق **muṭabbaḳ**, multiplied, doubled. a.

مطبوخ **maṭbūkh**, cooked, dressed. a.

مطبوع **maṭbū'**, agreeable, acceptable, worthy, laudable; natural, innate. a.

مطرب **muṭrib**, a musician, singer, minstrel. a.

مطربي **muṭribī**, f. the life or art of a musician; minstrelsy, music, singing. a.

مطرد **muṭṭarid**, flowing, current; prosperous. *muṭṭarad*, universal; to be constantly observed (as a rule or law). a.

مطرود **maṭrūd**, rejected, dejected, abjected; (sub.) an infidel. a.

مطروحات **maṭrūḥāt**, pl. things rejected. a.

مطعوم **maṭ'ūm**, food, any thing eatable. a.

مطعومات **maṭ'ūmāt**, pl. things eatable. a.

مطعون **maṭ'ūn**, reproached; accursed. a.

مطلا **muṭallā**, gilt, gilded, covered with gold. a.

مطلب **maṭlab**, m. a question, petition, intention, wish, desire; purpose, meaning, an object of pursuit; substance or purport of any writing, &c.; stricken with pestilence. a.

مطلع **maṭla'**, m. the place of rising, the east; the first couplet of a *ghazal* or ode. a.

مطلع **muṭṭali'**, rising, perceiving, informed. *muṭṭali'-k.*, (or in Pers.) *-gardānīdan* to inform, to acquaint. *muṭṭali'-h.* (in Pers.) *-shudan*, to be informed. a

مطلق **muṭlaḳ**, absolute, universal, principal, supreme; wholly, at all at all; not in the least, never, entirely, altogether. *muṭlaḳu-l-'inān*, free, giving the reins. a.

مطلقاً *muṭlaḳan*, absolutely, not at all. *a.*

مطلقه *muṭallaḳa*, f. a divorced woman. *a.*

مطلوب *maṭlūb*, demanded, required, necessary, wanted. *a.*

مطمح *muṭmaḥ*, a butt for archers. *a.*

مطمع *muṭma'*, a thing desired or wished for. *a.*

مطمئن *muṭma,inn*, quiet, secure, tranquil. *a.*

مطنجن *muṭanjan* (v. *mutanjan*), a *pulā,o*. *a.*

مطوق *muṭawwaḳ*, ornamented with a collar or chain (round the neck). *a.*

مطول *maṭūl*, one who delays payment of a debt, or the performance of a promise. *miṭwal*, gentle, soft, easy. *muṭawwal*, extended, prolonged, tall. *a.*

مطهر *muṭahhir*, a purifier, a cleanser. *muṭahhar*, pure, holy, purified. *maṭhar*, a place for purification, purgatory. *a.*

مطهره *maṭhara*, a vessel from which they pour holy water in ablution. *a.*

مطيب *muṭaiyab*, aromatic, perfumed. *a.*

مطير *maṭīr*, dropping, raining. *a.*

مطيع *muṭī'*, abject, obedient, submissive, obsequious. *a.* [theatrical spectacles. *a.*

مظاهر *maẓāhir* (pl. of مظهر), objects of show,

مظاهرت *muẓāharat*, a formula of divorce. *a.*

مظفر *muẓaffar*, victorious, a conqueror. *muẓaffar wa manṣūr*, victorious and supported (for on high). *a.*

مظلل *muẓallal*, shaded (from the sun). *a.*

مظلم *muẓlim*, dark (night); one who walks in darkness. *a.* [cruelty. *a.*

مظلمه *maẓlama*, oppression, tyranny, injustice,

مظلوم *maẓlūm*, injured, oppressed; mild, gentle, modest, submissive. *a.*

مظلومي *maẓlūmī*, مظلوميت *maẓlūmīyat*, } f. modesty, meekness; the state of being oppressed. *a.* [nion. *a.*

مظنه *maẓinna*, m. suspicion, conjecture, opi-

مظهر *maẓhar*, m. a place where any spectacle is represented, a theatre, stage. *muẓhir*, one who exhibits, displays, &c., an informer; a claimant, a prosecutor. *muẓhar 'alai-hi*, the defendant, the one complained against. *a.*

مع *ma'*, with, together, along with. *a.*

معا *ma'an*, along with, at the same time. *mi'ā*, a gut, the intestines. *a.*

معابد *ma'ābid* (pl. of عبد and معبد, q.v.), servants (of God); sacred places, temples. *a.*

معاتب *mu'ātib*, one who chides or blames. *mu'ātab*, reprehended, blamed. *a.*

معاتبت *mu'ātabat*, reproof, reprehension. *a.*

معاد *ma'ād*, the place or state to which one returns; the next world. *a.*

معادن *ma'ādin* (pl. of معدن), mines, quarries. *a.*

معاذ *ma'āẕ*, taking refuge, flying to God. *ma'āẕu-l-lāh*, God be our refuge! may God forbid. *a.*

معارض *mu'āriẓ*, m. an adversary, opponent, competitor. *a.* [tion. *a.*

معارضه *mu'āraẓa*, m. contradiction, opposi-

معارف *ma'ārif* (pl. of معرفه), sciences, acquirements. *a.*

معاش *ma'āsh* f. means of living, livelihood, subsistence; also place of living. *bad-ma'āsh*, a disreputable person. *a.*

معاشرت *mu'āsharat*, associating, conversation, living and eating together. *a.*

معاصر *mu'āṣir*, contemporary; pl. *mu'āṣirīn*, coevals, contemporaries. *a.*

معاصي *ma'āṣī* (pl. of معصيه), sins, crimes. *mu'āṣī*, rebellious, criminal. *a.*

معاف *mu'āf*, absolved, exempted, dispensed with, forgiven. *a.*

معافي *mu'āfī*, f. immunity, exemption; adj. forgiven, remitted: in revenue language it denotes lands the rents of which, previously payable to government, are remitted in perpetuity to the holder. *mu'āfī chiṭṭhī*, an order to pass free of toll or tax. *mu'āfī-dār*, one holding any thing free of tax. *mu'āfī zamīn*, land revenue-free. *mu'āfī ma'mūlī*, established or customary remissions. *mu'āfī-rawāna* or *-nāma*, an order of exemption from duty or tax. *mu'āfī sāl*, a year of exemption from assessment on some special account. *a.*

معاقبت *mu'āḳabat*, chastisement, penalty. *a.*

معاقل *ma'āḳil* (pl. of معقلة, q. v.). *a.*

معاقلت *mu'āḳalat*, a fine of atonement for bloodshed. *a.*

معالج *mu'ālij*, m. a physician, a doctor. *a.*

معالجه *mu'ālaja*, m. curing, healing; a remedy, adjustment (of any affair). *a.*

معالم *ma'ālim*, signs, vestiges, banners. *a.*

معالي *ma'ālī* (pl. of معلاة, q. v.), highnesses, eminences. *a.*

معاملات *mu'āmalāt*, pl. affairs, transactions. *a.*

معامله *mu'āmala* (also *mu'āmalat*), affair, business, negociation, transaction. *a.*

معاند *mu'ānid*, a rebel; an obstinate person. *a.*

معانقه *mu'ānaḳa*, m. throwing the arms round another's neck, embracing. *a.* [senses. *a.*

معاني *ma'ānī* (pl. of معني), significations,

معاودت *mu'āwadat*, f. returning (to a former habitation), coming or going. *a.*

معاوضت *mu'āwaẓat* or *mu'āwaẓa*, f. retaliating, returning like for like. *mu'āwaza-k.*, to barter to swap. *a.*

معاون *mu'āwin*, m. assisting, an assistant. *a*

معاونت *mu'āwanat*, f. assistance. *a.*

معاهده *mu'āhada*, confederacy, alliance. *a.*

معائب *ma'ā,ib* (pl. of معاب), vices, blemishes. *a.*

معاينه *mu'āyana*, m. beholding. *a.*

معبد *ma'bid*, m. a place of worship, temple, mosque, church. *mu'abbid*, m. an adorer, a worshipper. *a.*

معبر *mu'abbir*, m. an interpreter of dreams. *a.*

معبر *ma'bar*, m. a pass, ferry, ford. *mi'bar*, a ferry-boat. *a.*

معبود *ma'būd*, adored, worshipped; God. *a.*

معتاد *mu'tād*, m. custom, habit, use; size, weight, bulk; adj. accustomed, wont. *a.*

معتبر *mu'tabar*, confidential, respectable, worthy of confidence, reputable, trustworthy. *a.*

معتبري *mu'tabarī*, trustworthiness, respectability. *a.*

معتد *mu'tadd*, numbered, reckoned. *a.*

معتدل *mu'tadil*, temperate, tolerable. *a.*

معترض *mu'tariẓ*, opposing, hindering, interposing. *a.*

معترف *mu'tarif*, acknowledging, confessing; one who acknowledges. *a.*

معتزل *mu'tazil*, one who secedes or separates (especially in religious matters). *a.*

معتزلي *mu'tazilī*, an atheist, an infidel. *a.*

متعصم *mu'taṣim*, a servant, attendant · adj. preserved, secure. *a.*

معتق *mu'taḳ*, manumitted, liberated, emancipated (a slave). *mu'tiḳ*, one who liberates a slave. *a.*

معتقد *mu'taḳid*, m. a believer, a faithful friend or servant, a supporter. *a.*

معتكف *mu'takif*, assiduous in prayer, religious, devout. *a.*

معتمد *mu'tamad*, trustworthy, confided in. *mu'tamad 'alaihi*, one in whom confidence is placed. *a.*

معجب *mu'jib*, a vain fop, a man who has a very high opinion of himself not shared in by other people. *a.*

معجز *mu'jiz*, } a miracle. *a.*
معجزه *mu'jiza*, }

معجزات *mu'jizāt* (pl. of معجز), miracles. "The term *mu'jizāt* is applied only to those miracles which are performed by first-rate prophets: those wrought by inferior personages are termed *karāmāt*."—(B.) *a.*

معجل *mu'ajjal*, prompt, done without delay. *a.*

معجوم *ma'jūm*, } f. an electuary, medicine, confection; an aphrodisiac. *a.*
معجون *ma'jūn*, }

معدلت *ma'dalat*, f. justice, equity. *a.*

معدن *ma'dan*, m. and f. a mine, a quarry. *a.*

معدني *ma'danī*, mineral, metallic; f. metal, produce of the mine. *a.*

معدود *ma'dūd*, numbered, computed. *a.*

معدوله *ma'dūla*, avoided, passed over (as a letter in a word, which, though written, is not pronounced). *a.*

معدوم *ma'dūm*, non-existent, abolished, annihilated, extinguished. *a.* [chondrium. *a.*

معده *mi'da*, m. the stomach; (lit.) hypo-

معدي *ma'dā*, pass transit; a passage. *a.*

معذب *mu'azzab*, hindered; punished, tortured. *a.*

معذرت *ma'zarat*, an excuse, apology. *a.*

معذور *ma'zūr*, excused, excusable; disappointed. *a.*

معرا *mu'arrā*, bare, naked, bald; pure. *a.*

معراج *mi'rāj*, m. a ladder, stair, any thing by which one ascends; ascent, ascension. *a.*

معرض *ma'riẓ*, m. an occasion, a contingency, an occurrence; a place of meeting. *a.*

معرف *mu'arrif*, describing, defining, praising. *a.*

معرفت *ma'rifat* or *ma'rifa*, f. knowledge; account, cause, reason; deposit, trust; prep. by means of, through the means of, by the hands of. *a.*

معركه *ma'raka* or *ma'rika*, m. a field of battle. *ma'rikai-jihād* or *-kārzar*, a field of contest, an amphitheatre. *ma'rika-gīr*, a rope-dancer. *a.*

معروض *ma'rūẓ*, presented, offered, submitted; (sub.) a representation, a petition. *a.*

معروف *ma'rūf*, known; active voice of a verb; the letters *wao* and *ye* are said to be *ma'rūf* when the former has the sound of *oo* in *mood* or of *u* in *rule*, and the latter of *ee* in *feel* or *i* in *machine*; as in the words *nūr*, splendour, and *fīl*, an elephant. *a.*

معزز *mu'azzaz*, honoured, revered, esteemed, honourable, exalted. *a.*

معزول *ma'zūl*, deposed, displaced, dismissed from office, degraded, disposted. *a.*

معزولي *ma'zūlī*, f. dismissal from office, state of not being employed, being in disgrace. *a.*

معسور *ma'sūr*, difficult, arduous. *a.*

معشر *ma'shar*, m. a company, a troop, a society. *mu'ashshar*, a decagon, or any thing made up of or relating to the number ten. *a.*

معشوق *ma'shūḳ*, m. } a beloved object, a loved one, a mistress. *a.*
معشوقه *ma'shūḳa*, f. }

معشوقانه *ma'shūḳāna*, like a beloved one. *a.p.*

معشوقي *ma'shūḳī*, } f. loveliness, amiability, being beloved. *a.*
معشوقيت *ma'shūḳiyat*, }

[saffron (*Carthamus tinctorius*). *a.*

معصفر *mu'aṣfar*, m. safflower or bastard

معصم *mi'ṣam*, the wrist, the bracelet place. *a.*

معصوم *ma'ṣūm*, defended, preserved; innocent, simple; (sub.) an infant. *a.*

معصومي *ma'sūmī*, } f. innocence, simplicity; infancy. *a.*
معصوميت *ma'sūmiyat*, }

معصيت *ma'ṣiyat*, disobedience, sin, rebellion. *a.*

معضلات *mu'zilāt*, difficulties, troubles, arduous affairs; perplexing questions. *a.*

معطر *mu'aṭṭar*, perfumed, fragrant. *a.*

معطل *mu'aṭṭal*, idle, vacant, unemployed (applied especially to an official who has been suspended or dismissed), neglected, destitute, out of use, idle, fallow land. *a.*

معطلي *mu'aṭṭalī*, f. being out of employment. *a.*

معطوف *ma'ṭūf*, turned, twisted; conjoined, coupled. *a.*

معظم *mu'aẓẓam*, honoured, great, respected. *mu'ẓam*, the superior, the greater. *a.*

معقلة *ma'kalat*, fine for bloodshed; homicide for which atonement has been made. *a.*

معقول *ma'ḳūl*, reasonable, probable, just, pertinent, proper. *a.*

معقولات *ma'ḳūlāt*, probabilities, words or things consistent with reason. *a.*

معقولي *ma'ḳūlī*, } f. reasonableness, probability. *a.*
معقوليت *ma'ḳūliyat*, }

معك *ma'ak* or *ma'aka*, with thee. *allāhu ma ak*, may God be with thee. *a.*

معكوس *ma'kūs*, inverted, backwards. *ma'kūs parhnā*, "to read (the *ḳur.ān*) backwards," a ceremony performed while concocting certain incantations, as to say one's prayers backwards was, with us, considered an appropriate step to be taken when about to invoke the aid of the powers of darkness.—(B.) *a.*

معلا *mu'allā*, sublime, elevated, exalted. *a.*

معلاة *ma'lāt*, highness, nobility, rank, grandeur, eminence. *a.*

معلق *mu'allaḳ*, suspended, pendulous, hanging; (in law) pending, undecided. *a.*

معلقات *mu'allaḳāt*, pl. things suspended; generally applied to certain celebrated Arabian poems, that had the honour of being suspended in the temple of Mecca. *a.*

معلم *mu'allim*, m. an instructor, a preceptor, a pilot. *mu'allam*, taught, instructed. *mu'lam*, notable, distinguished by a particular mark or badge. *a.*

معلمي *mu'allimī*, f. instruction, pilotage. *a.*

معلوف *ma'lūf*, fed, fattened (as cattle or camels); pastures. *a.* [tempered. *a.*

معلول *ma'lūl*, indisposed, sick, diseased, distempered.

معلوم *ma'lūm*, known, distinguished, notorious, evident, apparent, obvious; (sub.) the active voice of a verb. *a.*

معلومات *ma'lūmāt*, things known, sciences. *a.*

معلي *mu'allā*, exalted, high, elevated, eminent, sublime. *a.*

معما *mu'ammā*, m. an enigma, an acrostic; a verse of mysterious meaning, a riddle, rebus, or charade. *a.*

معمات *mu'ammāt*, pl. enigmas, dark sayings. *a.*

معمار *mi'mār*, m. a builder, an architect, a mason. *a.*

معماري *mi'mārī*, f. architecture, art of building, masonry. *a.*

معمر *mu'ammar*, aged, blessed with long life. *a.*

معمل *mu'mil* or *mu'ammil*, causing to be done or performed. *a.*

معموديه *ma'mūdiyya*, m. baptism. *a.*

معمور *ma'mūr*, full, abounding in, stocked with; cultivated, happy, delightful, closed. *a.*

معموره *ma'mūra*, m. a cultivated or inhabited spot. *a.*

معمول *ma'mūl*, made, prepared; established, customary, practised; m. custom, habit. *a.*

معمي *mu'ammā* (v. *mu'ammā*), a riddle, an enigma, &c. *a.*

معن *ma'n*, name of an Arab who was a very liberal man. *a.*

معنا *ma'nā*, m. sense, meaning, signification. *a.*

معناوي *ma'nāwī*, significant, real, true. *a.*

معنبر *mu'ambar*, perfumed with amber. *a.*

معنقه *ma'naḳa*, m. a collar, or any thing similar, round the neck. *a.*

معنوي *ma'nawī*, essential, intrinsic, real; significant. *a.*

معني *ma'nī*, f. }
معني *ma'ne*, m. } meaning, sense, signification, reality. *a.*
معني *ma'nā*, m. }

معود *mu'auwad*, exercised, trained, accustomed, familiar. *a.*

معول *ma'ūl*, overcome exhausted. *a.*

معون *ma'ūn*, m. aid, assistance, favour. *a.*

معونت *ma'ūnat*, f. assistance, protection. *a.*

معه *ma'a* or *ma'ahu*, with, together with, along with. *a.*

معهذا *ma'a hāẕā*, along with that, in addition to that, nevertheless. *a.*

معهود *ma'hūd*, agreed, established, fixed, appointed, determined, promised. *a.*

معيار *mi'yār*, m. a touchstone; the mark or standard of money, weight, or measure. *a.*

معيت *ma'iyat*, being together, co-existence. *a.*

معيشت *ma'ishat*, f. food and other necessaries of life, subsistence. *a.*

معين *mu'aiyan*, established, ascertained, certified. *mu'aiyan ẓābiṭa*, established rule or custom. *mu'īn*, an assistant. *a.*

معيوب *ma'yūb*, wicked, vicious, defective, opprobrious, infamous. *a.*

معيوبي *ma'yūbī*, f. vice, wickedness. *a.*

مغ *mugh*, m. a tavern-keeper; also one of the magi, a worshipper of fire. *mugh-bacha*, the son of a tavern-keeper, or worshipper of fire. *p.*

مغاره *maghāra*, a den, a cavern. *a.*

مغاك *mughāk*, m. a pit. *p.*

مغالطه *mughālaṭa*, m. leading into error, mutual misunderstanding. *a.*

مغاير *mughāyir*, contrary, different, repugnant. *a.*

مغايرت *mughāyarat*, f. barter; disagreement, repugnance. *a.*

مغتنم *mughtanim*, enriched, possessed of, enjoying. *a.*

مغچه *mughcha*, m. soreness under the arms. *p.*

مغرب *maghrab* or *maghrib*, m. the west, the western regions, generally applied to the north coast of Africa. *p.*

مغربي *maghrabī*, western, occidental; of or relating to north Africa. *a*

مغرق *mughraḳ*, gilded, covered with or immersed in gold or silver. *mugharraḳ*, immersed, plunged in water, also gilded or covered with gold. *a.*

مغروت *maghrūt*, m. } any thing seized by main force, plundered. *a. h.*
مغروته *maghrūta*, f. }

مغرور *maghrūr*, proud, arrogant, haughty, fastidious; deceived, taken in; (in law) a man who marries a woman under a misconception. *a.*

مغروري *maghrūrī*, f. pride, arrogance. *a.*

مغز *maghz*, m. the brain, marrow, kernel, pith; (met.) pride, arrogance. *maghz bhinnānā*, to have a buzzing in the ears. *maghz pachānā* or *phirānā*, to tease, to distract. *maghz khālī-k.*, to distract, to talk much and foolishly. *maghz-dār*, full of marrow, kernel, pith, brain. *maghz khānā*, to tease, to distract. *p.*

مغزي *maghzī*, f. edging, border. *p.*

مغزا *maghzā*, m. a field of battle. *a.*

مغفر *mighfar*, m. a helmet. *a.*

مغفرت *maghfirat*, f. absolution, remission, pardon. *a.*

مغفور *maghfūr*, pardoned; met. applied to one who is dead, in the sense of the late, the deceased, &c. (v. *marḥūm*). *a.*

مغل *mughal*, m. a Mogul, a native of Turtary or Tūrān. In India the term is erroneously applied to Persians, and in the Deccan to Musalmāns in general. *p.*

مغلاني *mughlānī*, f. a Mogul female. *p.*

مغلائي *mughalā,ī*, adv. in Mogul or Muhammadan fashion. "à la Mogul." *d.*

مغل پٹھان *mughal-paṭhān*, *i.e.* "the *Mughuls* and *Paṭhāns*," a kind of game resembling draughts, or rather a sad corruption of the more noble game of chess (v. *Qanoon e islam*). *h.*

مغلطه *mughlaṭa*, an improper question, an error in speech. *a.*

مغلظ *mughallaẓ*, m. } severe or heavy (applied to a fine or mulct for blood). *a.*
مغلظه *mughallaẓa*, f. }

مغلق *mughlaḳ*, abstruse. *a.*

مغلم *mughlim*, libidinous; (sub.) a pæderast. *a.*

مغلوب *maghlūb*, conquered, overcome, subdued. *a.*

مغلوبيت *maghlūbīyat*, subjugation, subjection. *a.*

مغموم *maghmūm*, grieved, sorrowful, sad. *a.*

مغناطيس *mighnāṭīs* (μαγνῆτις), m. the magnet or loadstone. *g.*

مغني *mughannī*, m. a singer, a musician. *a.*

مغول *mighwal*, a long small sword; a man's name. *a.*

مغيب *mughaiyab*, concealed, hidden. *a.*

مغير *mughaiyar*, changed, altered. *a.*

مغيلان *mughīlān*, the acacia tree, the Egyptian or Arabian thorn. *a.*

مفاجات *mufājāt* (for *mufāja'at*), f. sudden death. *a.*

مفاخرت *mufākharat*, f. boasting, glorying, arrogance. *a.*

مفارقت *mufāraḳat*, f. separation, alienation, absence. *a.*

مفاسد *mafāsid* (pl. of مفسدت), evils. *a*

مفاصل *mafāṣil* (pl. of مفصل), the joints. *a.*

مفاصله *mufāṣala*, distance, space, interval. *a.*

مفاوضه *mufāwaẓa*, company, association. *a.*

مفايشه *mufāyasha*, m. boasting, vaunting, contending for superiority. *a.*

مفت *muft*, gratuitously, gratis, for nothing. *muft-khor*, a parasite. *p.*

مفتاح *miftāḥ*, a key or any instrument by which a door is opened. *a.*

مفتتات *mufattitāt*, f. *lithontriptica* (in medicine), drugs, &c. which tend to dissolve a calculus in the bladder. *a.*

مفتح *mufattih*, that which opens. *mufattaḥ*, opened, taken or conquered (a town). *a.*

مفتحات *mufattiḥāt*, f. *deobstruentia* (in medicine). *a.*

مفتخر *muftakhir*, boasting, gasconading. *a.*

مفتر *muftar*, weak, languid, enfeebled. *a.*

مفتري *muftarī*, m. a slanderer, liar, calumniator. *a.*

مفتقر *muftaḳir*, reduced to poverty. *a.*

مفتن *mufattan*, seduced into evil; charmed, bewitched, bereft of reason. *mufattin*, a seducer, &c. *a.*

مفتوح *maftūḥ*, opened; taken, subdued (as a town, &c.); (in gram.) having the short vowel *fatḥa* (َ). *a.*

مفتون *maftūn*, tried (as gold by the fire); insane, fascinated, mad with love. *a.*

مفتي *muftī*, m. a lawgiver. Among the Turks the *mufti* is the supreme head of the law. *a.*

مفخر *mufakhkhar*, glorious, held in high honour. *a.*

مفر *mafarr*, an asylum, a refuge. *a.*

مفرح *mufarriḥ*, exhilarating; an exhilarating medicine, in which rubies are an ingredient. *a.*

مفرد *mufrad*, solitary, alone, single, singular number. *a.*

مفردات *mufradāt*, simples, things uncompounded (in medicine). This is the title of various works on Oriental Materia Medica, as *mufradāti sikandarī*, *mufradatī Ghanī Muḥammad*, &c. *a.*

مفرط *mufriṭ*, vast, excessive. *a.*

مفرق *mafriḳ*, m. the crown of the head. *a.*

مفروح *mafrūḥ*, glad (tidings). *a.*

مفرور *mafrūr*, fled, run away, absconded. *a.*

مفروض *mafrūẓ*, required as a sacred duty, indispensable. *a.*

مفروغ *mafrūgh*, at leisure, disengaged. *a.*

مفروق *mafrūḳ*, separated, divided, dispersed. *a.*

مفسد *mufsid*, a seditious person, author of evil. *a.*

مفسدپن *mufsid-pan*, m. litigiousness, seditiousness. *a.h.*

مفسدي *mufsidī*, seditious, litigious (person); f. seditiousness, strife, litigation. *a.*

مفسر *mufassar*, explained, commented on, declared. *mufassir*, m. an interpreter. *a.*

مفشيات *mufashshiyāt*, f. carminatives. *a.*

مفصل *mufaṣṣal*, distinct, full, ample, detailed (account of circumstances); adv. particularly, diffusively, distinctly, fully. In Bengal the term *mufaṣṣal* or *mufaṣṣil*, is used to denote the country or upper provinces in opposition to Calcutta the metropolis. *mufaṣṣal-'adālat*, a provincial court of justice. *mufaṣṣal-kharch*, charges of collection in the provinces. *mufaṣṣal-ḳānūn-go*, a district or provincial accountant and registrar. *a.*

مفصلي *mufaṣṣalī*, a Mufassalite, a person from the country; adj. of or relating to the country. *a.h.*

مفعول *maf'ūl*, that which is governed or acted upon; the accusative case; the participle passive; (met.) a catamite. *a.*

مفعوليت *maf'ūliyat*, the state of being acted upon. *a.*

مفقود *mafḳūd*, not to be found, missing, wanting; (in law) a person of whom it is not known whether he be alive or dead. *a.*

مفلس *muflis*, poor, wretched; a bankrupt; a childless man; a bachelor. *a.*

مفلسي *muflisī*, f. poverty, destitution, bankruptcy. *a.*

مفلوج *maflūj*, palsied, paralytic. *a.*

مفلوك *maflūk*, unfortunate; poor, needy. *a.*

مفوض *mufawwaẓ*, resigned, delivered over, committed to the care of. *a.*

مفهوم *mafhūm*, comprehended, understood. *a.*

مفيد *mufīd*, profitable, useful, salutary. *a.*

مقابا *muḳābā* (for *muḳawwā*), a dressing-case or box. *a.*

مقابر *maḳābir* (pl. of مقبرة), tombs, sepulchres. *a.*

مقابل *muḳābil*, opposite, confronting, collecting. *a.*

مقابله *muḳābala*, m. or *muḳābalat*, f. comparison, collation, confronting, presence. *a.*

مقابه *muḳāba* (for *muḳawwā*), m. a dressing-box. *a.*

مقاتله *muḳātala*, m. slaughter, carnage, battle. *a.*

مقاربت *muḳārabat*, f. drawing near, proximity. *a.*

مقارض *muḳāriẓ*, the managing or acting partner in a concern. *a.*

مقارضه *muḳāraẓa*, entering into partnership. *a.*

مقارنت *muḳāranat*, f. conjunction, connection. *a.*

مقاسمه *muḳāsama*, m. division of lands or crops, &c. *a.*

مقاصد *maḳāṣid* (pl. of مقصد), designs, enterprises, attempts. *a.*

مقاعد *muḳā'id*, m whatever comes behind another; a guardian, keeper. *a.*

مقال *maḳāl*, } m. speech, discourse, saying,
مقاله *maḳāla*, } sentence, a word. *a.*

مقام *maḳām*, m. dwelling, mansion, a place of residence or encamping; halting of an army. *a.*

مقامات *maḳāmāt*, pl. sittings; conversations or discourses. *a.*

مقامر *muḳāmir*, a dice-player, a gambler. *a.*

مقامي *maḳāmī*, residing, a resident. *a.*

مقاومت *muḳāwamat*, f. opposition, resistance, competition. *a.*

مقبر *maḳbar*, } m. a burying-place, a tomb,
مقبرة *maḳbara*, } sepulchre, monument. *a.*

مقبل *muḳbil*, prosperous, fortunate, favouring, propitious. *a.*

مقبوض *maḳbūẓ*, taken, seized, occupied, possessed, imprisoned. *a.*

مقبوضا *maḳbūẓā*, occupied, tenanted (as the lands of a village). *a.*

مقبول *maḳbūl*, agreeable, acceptable, taking in good part, agreed on; one of the faithful; (sub.) a mistress. *a.*

مقبولي *maḳbūlī*, f. agreeability, agreeableness. *a.*

مقبوليت *maḳbūlīyat*, f. agreement, agreeableness; orthodoxy. *a.*

مقتبس *muḳtabis*, m. one who quotes, a quoter; receiving, acquiring, borrowing from another. *muḳtabas* (part. pass.), quoted. *a.*

مقتدا *muḳtadā*, followed, initiated, imitable. *a.*

مقتدر *muḳtadir*, powerful, strong. *a.*

مقتدي *muḳtadī*, m. an imitator, a follower. *a.*

مقترب *muḳtarab*, brought near, approximated. *a.*

مقتصر *muḳtaṣar*, summary, abstract. *a.*

مقتضا *muḳtaẓā*, } exacted, required; (sub.)
مقتضا *muḳtaẓā*, } exigence, necessity, expediency; adj. comformable. *a.*

مقتضي *muḳtaẓī*, one who exacts or demands. *a.*

مقتل *maḳtal*, m. a place of slaughter; the place of death, *i.e.* any diseased or wounded part of the body that causes death. *a.*

مقتول *maḳtūl*, killed, slain, slaughtered. *a.*

مقتولي *maḳtūlī*, state of being killed. *a. h.*

مقدار *miḳdār*, m. quantity, measure, space, number. *a.*

مقدر *muḳaddar*, predestined; understood, not expressed; (sub.) fate, destiny. *muḳaddir*, the Deity (as predestinator). *a.*

مقدس *muḳaddas*, holy, consecrated. *baitu-l-muḳaddas*, Jerusalem. *maḳdis*, a holy place, a sanctuary. *a.*

مقدسه *muḳaddasa*, f. a holy woman. *a.*

مقدم *muḳaddam*, antecedent, prior; (sub.) the headman of a village; the advanced guard. *muḳdim*, m. arrival. *a.*

مقدمات *muḳaddamāt* (pl. of مقدمه), premises, prefaces, &c. *a.*

مقدمه *muḳaddama* or *muḳaddamat*, m. the first part, preface, preamble; cause (in law); business; subject, affair, matter. *muḳaddamatu-l-jaish*, the advanced guard of an army. *a.*

مقدمي *muḳaddamī*, of or relating to a *muḳaddam*; f. office, dues, or rights of a *muḳaddam*. *a.*

مقدور *maḳdūr*, predestined, possible; m. power, ability, possibility, fate. *tā maḳdūr* or *maḳdūr-bhar*, to the best of one's ability. *a.*

مقدورات *maḳdūrāt*, things predestined or possible. *a.*

مقدوري *maḳdūrī*, f. power, predestination. *a.*

مقذوف *maḳẕūf*, m. } falsely accused of adul-
مقذوفه *muḳẕūfa*, f. } tery (man or woman). *a.*

مقر *maḳarr*, m. a residence, station, place of rest. *muḳirr*, establishing, conforming, settling (affairs); confessing, professing (in law) one who admits a claim or confesses a crime. *muḳirr bi-hi*, the claim which is admitted, or the crime confessed. *muḳirr la-hu*, the person in whose favour a claim is admitted. *a.*

مقراض *miḳrāẓ*, f. scissors, shears. *a.*

مقرب *muḳarrab*, approximated, admitted; (sub.) relatives. *muḳarrabu-l-ḥaẓrat*, the king's relatives, blood royal. *muḳarrabu-l-khidmat*, confidential servants. *a.*

مقرحات *muḳarrihāt*, (in medicine) vesicatoria. *a.*

مقرر *muḳarrar*, certain, infallible, established, unquestionable; adv. assuredly, unquestionably. *a.*

مقرري *muḳarrarī*, f. an appointment; a fixed tenure in perpetuity. *muḳarrarī-dār*, m. the holder of a *muḳarrarī* tenure. *a.*

مقرض *muḳarraẓ*, cut, clipped with scissors. *a*

مقروض *maḳrūẓ*, lent, a loan. *a.*

مقروضي *maḳrūẓī*, m. one who is in debt. *a.*

مقروق *maḳrūḳ*, m. } seized, sequestered, con-
مقروقه *maḳrūḳa*, f. } fiscated (as goods or effects). *a.*

مقرون *maḳrūn*, near, conjoined, connected, related. *a.*

مقري *muḳrī*, one who causes or orders to read; the reader of a mosque. *a.*

مقسم *maḳsam*, a part, a portion. *maḳsim*, time or place of partition. *muḳsim*, swearing (by God). *muḳsam*, m. an oath; a place where they swear. *muḳassim*, dividing, distributing, dispersing. *muḳassam*, divided; having a beautiful face; beautified. *a.*

مقسوم *maḳsūm*, distributed, divided; the quotient, an allotment, a portion. *a.*

مقشر *muḳashshar*, barked, skinned, peeled. *a.*

مقصد *maḳṣad*, m. intention, design, meaning, purpose, desire, wish, object, scope. *a.*

مقصر *muḳaṣṣar*, deficient, defective. *a.*

مقصود *maḳṣūd*, m. intention, wish; adj. intended, aimed at. *a.*

مقصور *maḳṣūr*, } abridged, diminished;
مقصوره *maḳṣūra*, f. } insufficient, defective. *a.*

مقط *miḳaṯṯ*, a small piece of ivory, bone, &c. on which oriental penmen nib their writing reeds or *ḳalams*. *a.*

مقطر *muḳaṯṯir*, distilling, dropping. *muḳaṯṯar*, distilled. *a.*

مقطع *maḳṯa'*, m. the last verse of a poem; cutting, amputating. *miḳṯa'*, m. shears for cutting cloth, silver, &c.; a cutting instrument in general. *muḳaṯṯa'*, adj. cut, cut out, shaped; well-dressed, well-shaped, beautiful; fixed rate of assessment. *a.*

مقطعات *muḳaṯṯa'āt*, pl. small kinds of garments; a species of short poems. *a.*

مقعد *maḳ'ad*, f. a place to sit on; the hips; the anus, podex.

مقعر *muḳa''ar*, excavated, hollowed out; concave; profound, deep. *a.*

مقفا *muḳaffā*, measured (prose); (sub.) an oration rhythmically composed. *a.*

مقفل *muḳaffal*, locked, bolted (a door). *a.*

مقل *muḳl*, bdellium; a fragrant kind of gum tree. *a.*

مقلب *muḳallib*, he who converts or turns. *muḳallibu-l ḳulūb*, the converter of hearts, God. *a.*

مقلد *muḳallad*, counterfeited, imitated. *a.*

مقلوب *maḳlūb*, turned, inverted, converted. *maḳlūb mustawī*, a word or sentence which may be read backward or forward, as *darad* (or in English, madam), a palindrome. *a.*

مقناطيس *miḳnāṭīs*, the magnet or loadstone. *a.*

مقنع *maḳna'*, مقنعه *maḳna'a*, } a veil of muslin or cloth, worn over the head and reaching to the ground (chiefly applied to a bride's veil). *a.*

مقود *miḳwad*, reins, bridle; a rope, a hawser. *a.*

مقوله *maḳūla*, said, repeated over and over again. *a.*

مقوم *muḳauwim*, adjusting, fixing a price. *a.*

مقوي *muḳawwī*, strengthening. *muḳawwī,i dil*, cardiac. *muḳawwī,i dimāgh*, cephalic. *muḳawwī,i kabid*, hepatic. *muḳawwī,i mi'da*, tonic. *a.*

مقهور *maḳhūr*, conquered, subdued, disturbed, oppressed, vexed. *a.*

مقي *muḳī*, an emetic. *maḳā*, cleaning (the teeth). *a.*

مقياس *miḳyās*, m. the stile of a dial; the hand of a watch, &c.; the nilometer in Egypt. *a.*

مقيت *muḳīt*, powerful; a guardian, keeper, feeder or nourisher. *a.*

مقيد *muḳaiyad*, bound, fettered, confined; diligent, attentive, fixed, dedicated to; noted, signed, registered. *a.*

مقيش *mukḳaish* or *muḳaiyash*, m. brocade (properly *muḳaiyas*). *a.*

مقيشي *mukḳaishī*, brocaded, embroidered. *a.*

مقيم *muḳīm*, m. a resident, a dweller, an inhabitant; adj. assiduous, fixed, constant. *a.*

مقيم *maḳīm*, m. a broker, an appraiser. *p.*

مقيمي *maḳīmī*, f. brokerage, valuation. *p.*

مقيي *muḳaiyī*, emetic (in medicine). *a.*

مكا मुक्का *mukkā*, m. a thump, a blow with the fist; (in Dakh.) adj. dumb, mute. *s.*

مكابره *mukābara*, haughtiness, contention. *a.*

مكاتب *mukātib*, m. مكاتبه *mukātiba*, f. } a slave who has worked out his or her emancipation according to a *kitābat* or written agreement. *a.*

مكاتبت *mukātabat*, f. correspondence (by letters); emancipation of a slave effected by his own earnings, by his master's leave. *a.*

مكاتبات *mukātabāt*, pl. letters, epistolary correspondence. *a.*

مكاتيب *makātib* (pl. of مكتوب), writings, letters. *a.*

مكار *makkār*, m. مكاره *makkāra*, f. } a cheat, a knave, impostor. *a.*

مكارم *makārim*, laudable actions or qualities. *a.*

مكاره *makārih* (pl. of مكروه), things detestable or abominable. *a.*

مكاري *makkārī*, f. fraud, imposture, cheating, roguery. *a.*

مكاشفه *mukāshafa*, f. acting openly, displaying any thing, revelation. *a.*

مكافات *mukāfāt*, f. recompense, retribution, retaliation, requital. *a.*

مكالمت *mukālamat*, conversation, discourse. *a.*

مكان *makān*, m. a place, station, dwelling. *makān-dār*, the owner of a place; (vul.) the *faḳīr* who occupies any particular station; a watchman. *a.*

مكانات *makānāt*, pl. stations, dwellings. *a.*

مكانت *makānat*, مكانه *makāna*, } place, &c. (same as *makān*, q. v.).

مكاي मकाई *makā,ī*, maize, Indian corn. *h.*

مكائد *makā,id* (pl. of مكيده), frauds, stratagems. *a.*

مكبيرا *mukbīrā*, m. a kind of wild rue. *d.*

مكت मुक्त *mukt* or *mukta*, m. a pearl. *s.*

مكت मुक्त *mukt* or मुक्ति *mukti*, f. pardon, absolution, salvation, exemption from transmigration; the imaginary reabsorption of the emancipated spirit into its great primary source; identification with the Supreme Being; liberation, setting free or loose. *s.*

مكت मुक्त *mukt* or *mukta*, adj. absolved, freed, exempt from all further transmigration; (sub.) m. the spirit released from mundane existence, and reintegrated with its divine original. *s.*

مكتا मुक्ता *muktā*, much, many. *h.*

مكتا मुक्ता *muktā*, مكتاپهل मुक्ताफल *muktā-phal*, } m. a pearl. *s.*

مكتاولي मुक्तावली *muktāwalī*, f. a pearl necklace. *s.*

مكتب *maktab*, m. a school; a place for writing. *maktab-khāna*, a school-house. *a.*

مكتداتا मुक्तिदाता *mukti-dātā*, a saviour. *s.*

مكتسب *muktasib*, (in law) one who makes profit, a gainer, an acquirer. *a.*

مكتفي *muktafī*, turning down (a vessel); content, having enough. *a.*

مكتوب *maktūb*, written; m. a letter, any thing written, an epistle. *a.*

مكتوبات *maktūbāt*, pl. writings, letters. *a.*

مكتوبي *maktūbī*, epistolary, delivered in writing. *a.*

مكتوم *maktūm*, hidden concealed. *a.*

مكٹ मुकुट *mukuṭ* or मकुट *makuṭ*, a crown, a diadem, a crest, a tiara. *s.*

مكث *maks̤*, *miks̤*, or *muks̤*, delay. *a.*

مكحال *mikḥāl*, مكحل *mikḥal*, } the instrument with which they apply collyrium to the eyes. *a.*

مكحول *makḥūl*, anointed with collyrium. *a.*

مكدا *mukdā*, مكدها *mukdhā*, } dumb, mute; stupid; a simpleton. *d.*

مكدر *mukaddar*, sullied, afflicted, disturbed, vexed, anxious. *a.*

مكر *makr*, m. fraud, deceit, evasion, imposture. *makr-chakar*, m. fraud and subterfuge. *a.*

مكر मुकुर *mukur*, m. a mirror, a looking-glass. *a.*

مكر मकर *makar*, m. a fabulous marine monster, a shark or alligator; name of the tenth zodiacal sign, the sign Capricorn, represented by a water animal with the body and tail of a fish and the neck and head of an antelope. *makar-ākrit*, shaped like the *makar*. *a.*

مكرر *mukarrar*, repeated. *mukarrar-k.*, a. to repeat, to say over a second time. *a.*

مكرم *mukarram*, venerable, noble, illustrious, respected, revered. *a.*

مكرمت *makramat*, f. honour, glory, dignity, nobility, liberality, generosity, grace, goodness, bounty. *a.*

مكرنا मुकरना *makarnā*, a. to deny. *h.*

مكرند मकरन्द *makarand*, m. the nectar or honey of a flower; the *kokila* or Indian cuckoo; a fragrant kind of mango; a species of jasmine (*Jasminum pubescens*). *h.*

مكرندوتي मकरन्दवती *makarand-watī*, f. the trumpet-flower (*Bignonia suaveolens*). *h.*

مكرونا मकरोना *makronā*, a. to wet (slightly). *h.*

مكروه *makrūh*, hated, odious, abominable, disgusting, obscene, any act or thing not absolutely forbidden by *Muhammadan* law, but from which it is advisable to abstain. *a.*

مكروهات *makrūhāt*, things abominable or disgusting. *a.*

مكرهائيا *mahar-hā,iyā*, fraudulent, deceitful; f. *makar-hā,ī*, a deceitful or cunning woman. *a. h.*

مكري मुकरी *mukrī*, f. a kind of short poem of frequent use in the Braj dialect, the peculiarities of which are these: it consists of four lines, each composed of four trochees. In the three first the speaker, a female, appears to talk of her lover; but, on the question being put by a friend, applies the whole to some other object. Hence the name from *mukarnā*, to deny. Thus, *Bāṭ chalat miro anchrā gahe; merī sune na apnī kahe. Nā kachhu mo son jhagrā jhānṭā; kyūn sakhī, sajjan? nā sakhī, kānṭā*, "As I went along the road, he seized my robe, neither heard what I said, nor made any reply. In short, we had not the smallest dispute. Who, friend, your lover? No, friend, a thorn. *h.*

مكري *makarī*, fraudulent, deceitful. *a. h.*

مكڑ मकड़ *makaṛ*, مكڑا मकड़ा *makṛā*, } m. a kind of grain; a spider. *s.*

مكڑانا मकड़ाना *makṛānā*, to fidget, to waver, to be averse, to counteract, to move crookedly, to wind about. *a.*

مكڑي मकड़ी *makṛī*, f. a spider. *makṛī kā jālā*, a spider's web, hence (met.) any thing very fine and slender. *s.*

مكس *maks*, offering a price, bidding at a sale; cheapening, lowering the price. *a.*

مكسب *maksab*, gain, acquisition, earnings, the means of getting a livelihood. *a.*

مكسر *mukassar*, broken, smashed. *a.*

مكسور *maksūr*, مكسوره *maksūra*, } a letter marked with the vowel *kasra*; broken, cut; a fraction (in arithmetic). *a.*

مكشكا मक्षिका *makshikā*, f. a bee, a fly. *s.*

مكشوف *makshūf*, revealed, disclosed, open, detected, discovered. *a.*

مكفول *makfūl*, locked; clenched or secured (by bond, &c.), pledged. *a.*

مكل मुकुल *mukul*, m. an opening bud. *s.*

مكلت मुकुलित *mukulit*, half-closed, half-shut, blinking, winking. *s.*

مكلف *mukallaf*, carefully executed, well-made, elegant, elaborate, costly. *mukallif*, troublesome, ceremonious; one who incommodes. *a.*

مكلل *mukallal*, crowned, ornamented with jewels. *mukallil*, careful, diligent. *a.*

مكمكات *makmakāt*, fragrance. *d.*

مكمكانا *makmakānā* (v. *mahaknā*), to emit a pleasant odour. *d.*

مكمل *mukammal*, perfect, complete, accomplished. *a.*

مكنت *miknat* or *muknat*, power, might. *a.*

مكند मुकुन्द *mukund*, m. gum olibanum, a precious gem; quicksilver; a name of *Vishṇu*. *s.*

مكنون *maknūn*, concealed, secret, hidden. *durri maknūn*, a pearl (large and valuable). *a.*

مكو मको *mako*, m. name of a species of *Solanum* (*nigrum*?). *h.*

مكوڑا मकोड़ा *makoṛā*, m. a large ant. *h.*

مكوك *makkūk*, name of a measure. *d.*

مكوئي मकोइ *mako,e*, m. sarsaparilla (also same as *mako*, q. v.). *h.*

مكه मख *makh*, f. sacrifice, oblation. *s.*

مكه मुख *mukh*, m. the mouth, the face; adj. first, initial, chief. *s.*

مكه *makka*, m. the city of Mecca in Arabia, where *Muhammad* was born, and to which his followers are enjoined to make a pilgrimage at least once during life. *makke kā sabza*, balm of Mecca (*Melissa officinalis*). *a.*

مكهاگن मुखाग्नि *mukhāgni*, m. fire put into the mouth of the corpse at the time of lighting the funeral pile; a sacrificial fire. *s.*

مكهانا मखाना *makhānā*, m. name of a plant, (*Euryale ferox*). *s.*

مكهبهيڑ *mukh-bheṛ*, opposite, confronting. *d.*

مكهپورن मुखपूरण *mukh-pūran*, m. a mouthful. *s.*

مكهڑا मुखड़ा *mukhṛā*, m. the mouth, the face. *s.*

مكهن मक्खन *makkhan* or मखन *makhan*, m. butter. *h.*

مكهنا मखना *makhnā*, m. a kind of elephant which has no tusks; a cock without spurs. *h.*

مكهنڈ *mukhanḍ*, strong, able, powerful. *d.*

مكهنڈاگي *mukhanḍāgī*, f. power, strength. *d.*

مكهنيا मखनिया *makhaniyā*, m. a man who deals in butter. *h.*

مكهورا मखूरा *makhūrā*, a large black ant. *h.*

مكهون *makhūn*, m. a flea, a bug. *d.*

مكهي मक्खी *makkhī* or मखी *makhī*, f. a fly; the sight of a gun. *makkhī uṛānā*, to flatter or perform servile offices for any one; to have ulcers on the body (so as to be constantly employed in driving away the flies from them); to be a good marksman (so as to hit a fly with a ball or arrow). *makkhī jhalnā*, to have veneral ulcers. *makkhī-chūs*, a miser, a niggard; a skin-flint. *makkhī mārnā*, to be idle, to be unemployed, to trifle. *s.*

مكهي *mukhhī*, a thump or blow with the fist. *d.*

مكهيا मुखिया *mukhiyā*, } chief, primary, principal, superior. *s.*
مكهيه मुख्य *mukhya*, }

مكهيتا मुख्यता *mukhyatā*, f. pre-eminence, being best, being chief or superior. *s.*

مكي मुक्की *mukkī*, f. a thump, a blow. *s.*

مكئي मकई *maka,ī*, *h.* } maize, Indian corn (*Zea mays*).
مكي جاري *makī jārī*, *d.* }

مكيدت *makīdat*, f. deceiving, defrauding, ensnaring. *a.*

مكيده *makīda*, having sucked, sucked. *p.*

مكير *muker*, a flour-merchant. *d.*

مكين *makīn*, m. master of the house, inhabitant; adj. fixed. *a.*

مگ मग *mag*, m. a road, a path, way. *mag dekhnā*, to expect, to look out for. *s.*

مگانا मगाना *magānā*, a. to send for. *h.*

مگاهي मगाही *magāhī*, a tribe of agriculturists in Behar. *h.*

مگدر मुगदर *mugdar*, a kind of heavy wooden mallet, used for exercise in strengthening the muscles, like our dumb-bells. *s.*

مگده मगध *magadh*, m. name of a country, South Behar, including Patna, Gayā, &c.; a family bard or minstrel. *s.*

مگده मुग्ध *mugdh*, lovely, beautiful; stupid, ignorant; simple, silly; an idiot, a fool. *s.*

مگدها मुग्धा *mugdhā*, f. a virgin, a young and lovely woman. *s.*

مگدهتا मुग्धता *mugdhatā*, f. loveliness; ignorance, simplicity. *s.*

مگر *magar*, unless, perhaps, except, only, if it is not, moreover. *p.*

مگر मगर *magar*, m. an alligator, a crocodile. *s*

مگرا मगरा *magrā*, proud, haughty, presuming, fastidious, arrogant, cross, obstinate, impatient. *h.*

مگراپن मगरापन *magrāpan*, m. } arrogance, pride, haughtiness, stubborness. *h.*
مگراهي मगराही *magrāhī*, f. }
مگرائي मगराई *magrā,ī*, f. }

مگرمچهه मगरमच्छ *magar-machh*, m. (same as [*magar*) an alligator. *s.*

مگري मगुरी *magurī*, f. name of a fish, a species of *silurus* (*Silurus pelorius*). *s.*

مگري *magrī*, f. the flat roof of a house. *d.*

مگريلا मगरेला *magrelā*, a small blackish triangular pyramidical-shaped seed of a very pungent smell (*Nigella Indica*). *s.*

مگس *magas*, f. a fly; a kind of Indian corn; a freckle. *magas-rān*, a flapper for driving away flies. *magas-rānī*, act of driving away flies. *p.*

مگسر मगसिर *magasir* (v. *mangasir* or *mārgashir*), m. name of the eighth Hindū month. *s.*

مگسگير *magas-gīr*, (lit. the flycatcher) m. a spider; a spider's web. *p.*

مگسي *magasī*, flea-bitten (colour of a horse), [freckled. *p.*

مگن मगन *magan* or मग्न *magna*, plunged, immersed, drowned; cheerful, delighted, pleased, glad, happy, immersed in joy. *s.*

مگنتا मगनता *magantā*, f. transport, cheerfulness, delight. *s.*

مگه मघ *magh*, m. one of the *dwīpas* or divisions of the world; name of a drug; the country of Arracan: the name, under the corrupted forms "mug" or "mugg," is applied generally to natives of Arracan. *s.*

مگو *ma-go* or *-gū*, say not, tell not. *p.*

مگها मघा *maghā*, m. name of the tenth mansion of the moon, *a Leonis, Regulus*. *s.*

مگهن मघन *maghan*, odoriferous, fragrant. *h.*

مكهي मघी *maghī* or मगही *magahī*, belonging to *Magadh* (a thing); f. a sort of grain. *s.*

مكهيا मगहैया *maghaiyā* or मघया *maghayā*, m. inhabitant of *Magadh*; name of a caste of Brāhmans. *s.*

مل *mul*, m. wine. *p.*

مل मल *mal*, m. dirt; any excretion of the body, as serum, semen, blood, urine, fæces, earwax, &c.; dreg, sediment, rust. *s.*

مل मल्ल *mall*, strong, athletic; m. a hero, a wrestler, a warrior. *mall-juddh* or *-yuddh*, wrestling. *mallu*, m. a bear. *s.*

ملا *malā*, time, either of day or night; a desert. *a.*

ملا *mullā*, m a Muhammadan lawyer, a doctor, a schoolmaster; a decoy bird; adj. learned. *mullā,e ḳur,ānī*, the law-officer in the Anglo-Indian courts appointed for taking the oaths of such witnesses as are Musalmāns, by swearing them on the *Ḳur,ān*. *a.*

ملاء *malā,a*, an assembly, a crowd of people. *a.*

ملابست *mulābasat*, the confounding or falsifying of an account, &c.; dissimulation. *a.*

ملاپ मिलाप *milāp*, f. agreement, reconciliation, concord, understanding, union, adjustment, visit. *s.*

ملاپي मिलापी *milāpī*, civil, affable, sociable, friendly, familiar, intimate, convivial. *s.*

ملا جلا मिलाजुला *milā-julā*, social, sociable. *h.*

ملاح *mallāḥ*, m. a boatman, a sailor, a mariner; a manufacturer of salt. *a.*

ملاحت *malāḥat*, f. being salt; elegancy; beauty, excellence. *a.*

ملاحد *mulāḥid*, impious, heretical; pl. *mulāḥidin*, heretics, unbelievers. *a.*

ملاحظه *mulāḥaẓa*, m. looking at, contemplating, consideration (often used for reading), notice, view, regard. *mulāḥaẓa shud*, it has been seen or inspected, a phrase written on documents by the proper officers, like the "visé" of a passport; (in Dakh.) kindness, an obliging disposition. *mulāḥaẓe-wālā*, an obliging, civil person. *a.*

ملاحي *mallāḥī*, f. the business of a *mallāḥ*, q. v.; seamanship, &c. *a.*

ملاذ *malāẕ*, m. an asylum, refuge, protection. *a.*

ملار मल्लार *mallār* or *malār*,
ملاري मल्लारी *mallārī*, } f. name of a *rāginī* or musical mode sung during the rains. *s.*

ملازم *mulāzim*, assiduous, diligent, attentive, attached to; (sub.) a servant, attendant. *a.*

ملازمت *mulāzamat*, f. assiduity, diligence; service; (met.) paying respects to a superior. *a.*

ملازمي *mulāzimī*, f. service, attendance. *a.*

ملاطفه *mulāṭafa*, m. (also *mulāṭafat*) courtesy, kindness, politeness, favour; a letter or epistle. *a.*

ملاطيه *malāṭiya*, name of a town on the Euphrates, capital of Armenia Minor. *a.*

ملاعبت *mulā'abat*, playing, sporting. *a.*

ملاقات *mulāḳāt*, f. interview, meeting, a visit, conversation, encountering. *a.*

ملاقي *mulāḳī*, meeting. *mūlāḳī honā*, to have interview with, to encounter. *a.*

ملاگر मलागिर *malāgir* or *malāgiri*, m. the name of a mountain where much sandal-wood is produced (v. *malay*.) *s.*

ملاگري *mullā-garī*, f. the office or rank of *mullā*, q. v. *a. p.*

ملاگيري मलागीरी *malāgīrī*, m. the colour of sandal-wood. *s.*

ملال *malāl*, m. sadness, grief, anguish, languor, vexation. *a.*

ملالت *malālat*, f. affliction, sadness. *a.*

ملام *malām*, m. reproach, reprehension, rebuke, blame, accusation, reviling. *a.*

ملامت *malāmat*, f. reproach, rebuke. *a.*

ملامتي *malāmatī*, reproached, reprehensible. *a.*

ملان मिलान *milān*, causing a mixture, making parties agree, adjustment of quarrels. *h.*

ملان म्लान *mlān*, foul, dirty; languid, weary, faded, withered. *mlānī*, f. languor, decay, foulness. *s.*

ملانا मलाना *malānā*, a. to cause to rub, grind, or scour. *h.*

ملانا मिलाना *milānā*, a. to mix; to join, to adjust, to apply, to cement, to close, to compare, to reconcile, agree, find, get, meet, to visit. *mulānā*, a. to appraise. *s.*

ملاني मिलानी *milānī*, f. meeting, mingling. *s.*

ملاني *mullānī*, f. the wife of a *mullā*; a learned woman, a schoolmistress. *a.*

ملاو मिलाव *milā,o* or *milāw*, (in Dakh.) *milāwā*, adjustment, arbitration; m. union, mixture, reconciliation. *h.*

ملاءي मलाई *malā,ī*, f. cream, buttermilk. *h.*

ملاءي मुलाई *mulā,ī*, f. appraisement, valuation. *s.*

ملاءي *mullā,ī*, f. office of *mullā*, q. v. *a. h.*

ملائك *malā,ik*,
ملايكه *malā,ika*, } (pl. of ملك) angels, the angelic host. *a.*

ملائم *mulā,im*, soft, tender, gentle, mild, affable. *a.*

ملايمت *mulāyamat*, f. softness, tenderness. *a.*

ملبا मलबा *malbā*, m. rubbish, refuse. *malbā-ḳharch*, village expenses, &c. (v. Wilson's Glossary.) *h.*

ملبب *mulabbab*, brimful, abundant. *a.*

ملبس *mulabbas*, clothed, dressed, confused, mixed, embroiled. *a.*

ملبوس *malbūs*, clothed; (sub.) clothes (which have been worn). *a.*

ملبوسات *malbūsāt*, pl. old worn-out garments. *a.*

ملبوسي *malbūsī*, habitually worn (clothes). *a. h.*

ملبهو मल्लभू *mall-bhū*, f. an arena for wrestlers; the site of any field of battle. *s.*

ملت *millat*, f. religion, faith, a religious sect or creed; a nation, a people. *a.*

ملت मिलित *milit*, mixed, united, combined or connected with; found, met with, encountered. *s.*

ملت मलत *malat*, m. a worn rupee (or other coin). *h.*

ملتاني मुलतानी *multānī*, of or relating to Multān; a Multanian; f. name of a *rāginī* or musical mode. *multānī maṭṭī*, f. Armenian bole. *h.*

ملتجا *multajā*, m. an asylum, a protector. *a.*

ملتجي *multajī*, flying to or taking refuge with one. *a.*

ملتزم *multazim*, constrained, compelled, necessarily following, convicted; m. a tenant or hirer; a farmer or collector of tolls or customs. *a.*

ملتفت *multafit*, one who shews regard, courteous. *multafat*, esteemed, attended to. *a.*

ملتقط *multaḳiṭ*, one who finds and rears a deserted child; one who finds a treasure, &c. *a.*

ملتمس *multamis*, begging, praying, supplicating. *a.*

ملتوي *nultavī*, delayed, postponed, spinning out, protracted; pending (a lawsuit). *a.*

ملتويات *multaviyāt*, pl. lawsuits still pending or undecided. *a.*

ملٹهي *mulaṭṭhī*, f. liquorice. *d.*

ملجا *maljā*, m. an asylum, retreat, place of refuge, security, support. *a.*

ملجاترا मल्लयात्रा *mal-jātrā*, f. a match of wrestling or boxing. *s.* [ing. *s.*

ملجدهـ मल्लयुद्ध *mall-judh*, m. wrestling, box-

ملچهـ मलिछ *malichh*, an unclean race, those who make no distinction between clean and unclean food, a barbarian: in this class the Hindūs reckon all people whose religion differs from their own. *s.*

ملح *milḥ*, salt; (met.) beauty, science. *a.*

ملحد *mulḥid*, m. a heretic, an unbeliever, one who denies the resurrection, a deist. *a.*

ملحق *mulḥaḳ*, joined, added, annexed, adhering. *a.*

ملحوظ *malḥūẓ*, contemplated, thought of. *a.*

ملحوظات *malḥūẓāt*, thoughts, meditations, agitations of mind. *a.*

ملخ *malakh*, m. a locust; a cricket. *p.*

ملدل मलदल *mal-dal*, rubbing, grinding. *s.*

ملذذ *mulazzaz*, delicious. *a.*

ملزم *mulzam*, convicted, convinced; conjoined, annexed, inseparable. *a.*

ملزوم *malzūm*, inseparable, affixed to, belonging to. *a.*

ملسوت *malsūt*, f. a vice; a screw, a worm or spiral. *malsūtī*, cut spirally, wormed; a screwnail. *malsūtī pul*, a drawbridge. *d.*

ملشٹهـ मलिष्ठ *malishṭh*, m. } very foul or unclean; very wicked; f. a woman during menstruation. *s.*
ملشٹها मलिष्ठा *malishṭhā*, f. }

ملطفات *mulaṭṭifāt*, f. attenuantia (in physic). *a.*

ملعون *mal'ūn*, cursed, excommunicated, execrated, driven out of society. *a.*

ملغوبا *malghobā*, m. emitting saliva; name of a dish (*māsh* mixed with *dahī*). *h. p.*

ملفوظ *malfūẓ*, a thing spoken or expressed, annals. *a.*

ملفوظات *malfūẓāt*, pl. sayings; annals. *a.*

ملفوف *malfūf*, wrapped up, involved, inclosed; collected, gathered. *a.*

ملقب *mulaḳḳab*, surnamed, nicknamed. *a.*

ملك *mulk*, m. a country. *mulk-dārī*, *-rānī*, *-sitānī*, or *-gīrī*, f. dominion, empire, government, sovereignty, political affairs; conquest. *a.*

ملك *malak*, m. an angel. *malaku-l-maut*, the angel of death, *'Azrā,il*. *a.* [*amlāk*). *a.*

ملك *milk*, m. possession, property, right (pl.

ملك *malik*, a king; a title of honour conferred by the sovereigns of Egypt on prime ministers and generals. *maliku-t-tujjār*, king of merchants, a title given to the chief merchant in a city. *maliku-l-khawāṣṣ*, the chief of the nobles. *malik-zāda*, a king's son, a prince. *a.*

ملك *malk*, doubt, suspicion, apprehension. *d.*

ملكا मल्लिका *mallikā*, f. Arabian jessamine (*Jasminum zambac*). *h.* [ments. *d.*

ملكات *malkāt* (pl. of ملكه), qualities, endow-

ملكاٹ *malkāṭ*, bile, excess of bile. *d.*

ملكت *milkat*, f. property, possession. *mulkat*, f. kingdom, sovereignty. *a.*

ملكنا मलकना *malaknā*, n. to walk like a chairman, &c. (trotting and raising the shoulders); (Dakh.) to feel a nausea. *h.*

ملكوت *malakūt*, f. spirits, angels, the angelic world; empire, dominion. *a.*

ملكه *malika*, f. a queen; quickness of perception, strength of intellect. *a.*

ملكهم मलखम *malkham*, the upright post in a sugar-mill. *h.*

ملكي *milkī*, m. a farmer. *mulkī*, adj. civil, political; relating to the country or empire, or to land and revenue affairs. *malakī* (f. *malakīya*), angelic. *a.*

ملكيت *milkīyat*, f. property, possession. *a.*

ملگندھ मल्लिगन्धि *malli-ganahi* or *malli-gandhī*, m. aloe-wood. *h.*

ملل *milal* (pl. of ملت), religious sects, &c. *malal*, wearied, languid, vexed. *a.*

ملماس मलमास *malmās*, m. an intercalary month. *s.*

ملمع *mulamma'*, plated, covered with gold or silver; a species of poem, the distichs of which are written in Persian and Arabic alternately. *a.*

ململ मलमल *malmal*, f. muslin. *h.*

ململا मलमला *malmalā*, brackish (as water). *h.*

ملميٹ मलमेट *malmeṭ*, adj. ruined; decided (a dispute). *malmeṭ honā*, to perish. *malmeṭ karnā*, a. to destroy, raze. *h.*

ملن मलन *malan*, m. a path; act of rubbing or grinding. *h.*

ملن मिलन *milan*, m. mixing with, associating with, meeting, agreement. *s.*

ملن मलिन *malin*, m. } opaque; dirty, foul,
ملنا मलिना *malinā*, f. } filthy, vile; (met.) soiled with crime or vice, sinful, depraved. *s.*

ملنا मलना *malnā*, a. to rub, to anoint; to trample on; to thresh grain by treading it out (by the feet of oxen) in the oriental fashion. *h.*

ملنا मिलना *milnā*, n. to be mixed, confounded; to meet, to join; to be met with; to be got; to occur, to come (into one's possession); to associate, to agree, to suit, to coalesce. *milnā julnā* or *milnā jhulnā*, to meet cordially, to have unrestricted intercourse. *mile jule rahnā*, to live together in great harmony. *milnā hilnā*, to act together, to coalesce, to join. *s.*

ملنتا मलिनता *malintā*, f. filth, impurity, vileness. *s.*

ملنسار मिलनसार *milansār*, civil, affable, sociable. *s.*

ملنساري मिलनसारी *milansārī*, f. civility, affability. *s.*

ملنگ मलङ्ग *malang*, m. a kind of Muhammadan dervise or ascetic, who lets his hair grow loose and uncombed; name of a bird. *h.*

ملنگي मलङ्गी *malangī*, m. a salt-maker. *h.*

ملنمکھ मलिनमुख *malin-mukh*, cruel, fierce, savage; vile, wicked. *s.*

ملني मलिनी *malinī*, f. a woman during menstruation. *s.*

ملو मल्लू *mallū*, m. a bear; a monkey. *h.*

ملوانا मिलवाना *milwānā*, a. to cause to mix, &c. *s.*

ملواءي मलवाई *malwā,ī*, f. price of scouring (rubbing, &c.). *h.*

ملوث *mulauwas*, polluted, defiled. *a.*

ملوك मलूक *malūk*, m. a kind of worm. *h.*

ملوك *mulūk* (pl. of ملك *malik*), kings. *a.*

ملوكانه *mulūkāna*, royal, princely. *a. p.*

ملول *malūl*, sad, dejected, grieved, melancholy, fatigued, languid. *a.*

ملولا *malolā*, m. vexation, grief, affliction, sadness, melancholy, regret. *a.*

ملوم *malūm*, blamed, reproached. *a.*

ملون *mulawwan*, variegated, distinguished by many colours. *a.*

ملوني मिलौनी *milaunī*, f. alloy, adulteration, mixture. *h*

ملويا मलवैया *malwaiyā*, m. one who rubs. *s.*

ملە *milla* (v. *millat*), religion, &c. *a.*

ملهتي मलहती *malhatī*, } f. name of a medi-
ملهٹي मुलहट्ठी *mulhaṭṭī*, } cinal root, liquorice. *p. h.*

ملهم *mulham*, inspired. *a.*

ملهم *mulhim*, m. inspiring, one who inspires.

ملهم *malham*, m. (for *marham*), salve, plaster. *a. p.*

ملهي *mulhī*, m. a mimic, a buffoon. *a.*

ملي मलय *malay* or *malaya*, } m. name of
مليا मलैया *malayā* or *malaiyā*, } a mountain, the western Ghats in the peninsula; the neighbouring country Malayalim or Malabar. *s.*

مليا मलया *malayā*, f. a plant commonly called teori (*Convolvulus turpethum*). *s.*

مليا मलिया *maliyā*, m. a small vessel of wood or of the shell of a cocoa-nut, for holding the oil used in inunction. *h.*

مليا چل मलयाचल *malayāchal*, m. the mountain Malay. *s.*

مليا گير मलयागीर *malayā-gīr*, m. (v. *malāgir*) name of a mountain. *malayā-gīrī*, m. the colour of sandal-wood. *s.*

ملي پنج मलेपञ्ज *male-panj*, aged above ten years (a horse). *h.*

مليج मलयज *malayaj*, m. sandal-wood. *s.*

مليچه मलेच्छ *malechh* or म्लेच्छ *mlechchha*, m. a term applied to an unclean race, those who make no distinction between clean and unclean food, a barbarian, or one speaking any language but Sanskrit, and not subject to the usual Hindū institutions. *mlechh-bhojan*, m. wheat. *mlechh-jāti*, m. a barbarian, a man of an outcast race. *mlechh-desh*, m. the countries bordering on India, or inhabited by barbarians. *mlechh-vāk*, adj. speaking a barbarous dialect. *s.*

مليچهت म्लेच्छित *mlechhit*, spoken barbarously, m. barbarous language, ungrammatical speech. *s.*

مليح *malīḥ*, agreeable, sweet, charming, beautiful. *a.*

مليك *malīk*, m. a king, a pirate. *a.*

ملي ميدان *male maidān*, apparent, public. *p.*

ملين *mulaiyin*, softening, emollient. *mulaiyan*, softened, soothed, pacified. *a.*

ملين मलीन *malīn*, filthy; vexed, indisposed. *s.*

مليوار मलेवार *malewār*, the country of Malabar. *h.*

مم मम *mam* or *mama*, my, mine. *s.*

ممات *mamāt*, place or time of death; death. *mumāt*, mortal; obsolete. *a.*

مماس *mumāss*, tangent, touching, contiguous. *a.*

مماست *mumāssat*, f. touch, contact; coition. *a.*

مماطلت *mumāṭalat*, f. putting off, deferring (the payment of a debt). *a.*

مماكهي मुमाखी *mumākhī*, f. a honey-bee. *s.*

ممالك *mamālik* (pl. of مملكت), kingdoms, provinces, states. *a.*

ممانعت *mumāna'at*, f. hindrance, prohibition. *a.*

مماني मुमानी *mumānī*, f. an aunt; the wife of a mother's brother. *s.*

ممتا ममता *mamtā*, f. pride, arrogance, self-sufficiency; affection; the interest or affection entertained for other objects from considering them as belonging to or connected with one's self. *s.*

ممتاجكت ममतायुक्त *mamtā-jukt*, selfish; m. a miser, a niggard. *s.*

ممتاز *mumtāz*, chosen, illustrious, exalted, eminent. *a.*

ممتحن *mumtaḥin*, one who examines or tries, an examiner. *mumtaḥan*, one who has passed trial or examination; hence, experienced, skilful. *a.*

ممتد *mumtadd*, extended, prolonged. *a.*

ممتلي *mumtalī*, replete, filled up. *a.*

ممتنع *mumtana'*, prohibited, impossible. *a.*

ممتو ममत्व *mamatwa* (v. *mamtā*). *s.*

ممتوعه *mamtū'a*, f. a woman who has been temporarily married (v. *mut'a*). *a.*

ممد *mumidd*, m. an assistant; an extender, protracter. *a.*

ممدوح *mamdūḥ*, praised, celebrated, laudable (pl. *mamdūḥīn*). *a.*

ممدود *mamdūd*, extended, lengthened, or protracted; f. *mamdūda*. *a.*

ممر *mumirr*, m. passage, pass, transit, ford; account, cause. *a.*

ممريز *mamrīz* (cor. of مهميز *mihmez*), a spur. *d.*

ممزوج *mamzūj*, tempered, mixed, diluted. *sharābi mamzūj*, wine mixed with water. *a.*

ممسك *mumsik*, m. a miser, a niggard; retaining; adj. parsimonious, stingy. *a.*

ممسكي *mumsikī*, avarice, stinginess. *a. p.*

ممسوخ *mamsūkh*, metamorphosed. *a.*

ممسوس *mamsūs*, tangible, touched; furious. *a.*

ممقوت *mamḳūt*, hated, held as an enemy. *a.*

ممكن *mumkin*, possible. *mumkinu-d-dukhūl*, accessible. *a.*

ممكنات *mumkināt*, pl. possibilities. *a.*

مملكت *mamlukat*, f. sovereignty, dominion, empire, kingdom; grandeur. *a.*

مملو *mamlū*, replete, filled up. *a.*

مملوك *mamlūk*, possessed, in one's power; m. a purchased slave or a captive. *a.*

ممنوع *mamnū'*, prohibited; hindered, forbidden. *a.*

ممنون *mamnūn*, obliged, pleased, satisfied, gratified; receiving a favour, favoured. *a.*

ممنوني *mamnūnī*, f. obligation, favour. *a.*

ممورش मुमूर्षु *mumūrshu*, m. a man at the point of death, a dying man. *s.*

مموڑا ममोड़ा *mamoṛā*, m. twist, wreath; ache, pain (particularly in the bowels). *h.*

ممولا *mamolā*, m. a wagtail (*Motacilla*). *a*

ممولا *mamūlā* or *mamolā*, nice, squeamish, thin-skinned, easily offended. *d.*

ممياساس ममियासास *mamiyā-sās*, f. husband's or wife's maternal aunt. *s.*

ممياسسر ममियाससुर *mamiyā-sasur*, m. husband's or wife's maternal uncle. *s.*

ممیانا *mamiyānā*, to bleat (a sheep). *h.*

مميرا ममेरा *mamerā*, relating to the maternal uncle; as, *mamerā bhā,ī*, mother's brother's son; *mamerī bahin*, mother's brother's daughter. *s.*

مميز *mumaiyiz*, judicious, discriminating. *mumaiyaz*, discriminated, discerned. *a.*

مميزي *mumaiyizī*, f. judiciousness, &c. *a. h.*

من मन *man*, m. mind, heart, soul, spirit, inclination. *man-bhānā*, n. to please the mind; adj. grateful to the mind; (sub.) a sweetheart, mistress. *man-bhānā munḍiyā hilānā*, to pretend to refuse that which a person secretly desires. *man-bhāwan*, acceptable, agreeable to the mind. *man-pūran*, confidence, satisfaction of mind. *man-chor*, heart-stealer. *man-darāwardī*, fanciful, invented (speech or story). *man-kāmnā*, desire, wish. *man-lānā*, to fix the mind upon, to apply to. *man-lagan*, heart-attachment, heart-engaging. *man mār rahnā*, to suffer pain with patience. *man-mān*, m. heart's desire, choice. *man-mānā* or *man māntā*, agreeable, conformable to one's wish or inclination, pleasing, soothing (to the soul); a mistress, sweetheart. *man-māne*, as the mind may desire. *man-mauj*, m. self-conceit. *man-maujī*, self-conceited. *s.*

من मुनि *muni* or *mun*, m. a sage, a saint. *s.*

من मणि *maṇi* or *maṇ*, m. f. a gem, a jewel, a precious stone. *s.*

من *man*, (in Pers. the 1st pers. pron.) I, me; m. the name of a weight (forty sers) (v. Wils. Gl.). *p.*

من *min*, from, in, by. *min-ba'd*, afterwards, for the future. *a.*

من मनु *manu*, *Manu*, the saint and legislator, the son of Brahmā; a man in general. *s.*

منا मन्ना *mannā*, n. to be soothed, propitiated. *s.*

منابر *manābir* (pl. of منبر), pulpits. *a.*

منات *manāt*, one of the three chief idols of the pagan Arabs previous to *Muḥammad*. *a.*

مناجات *munājāt*, f. prayers, recommendations, &c. *a.*

مناجاتي *munājātī*, m. or f. one who prays,

منادمت *munādamat*, society, intimacy, familliarity *a.*

منادي *manādī*, m. proclamation. *munādī*, a proclaimer, a herald; a small drum. *a.*

منار *manār*, مَنارا *manārā*, منارہ *manāra*, } m. a minaret, a lofty turret adjoining a *Muḥammadan* mosque, from the summit of which the *mu,azzin* (q. v.) calls the faithful to prayers. *a.*

منارتھ मनार्थ *manārth*, m. purpose, design, intention. *s.*

منازعت *munāza'at*, f. contest, controversy, litigation, altercation. *a.*

منازل *manāzil* (pl. of منزل), mansions, stages, &c. *manāzili-mutabāyina*, separate or distinct tenements or apartments, in opposition to *manāzili-mulāzima*, contiguous or adjoining tenements. *a.*

مناسب *munāsib*, proper, convenient, fit, pertinent, congruous. *a.*

مناسبت *munāsabat*, مناسبي *munāsibī*, } f. suitableness, proportion, connection, relation, comparison. *a.*

مناصحت *munāṣaḥat*, advice, admonition. *a.*

مناظرہ *munāẓara*, f. disputation, contest. *a.*

منافع *manāfi'*, m. (pl. of منفعت) profits, advantages, gains, benefits. *a.*

منافق *munāfiḳ*, m. a hypocrite, an atheist, an enemy. *a.*

مناقب *manāḳib* (pl. of منقبہ), virtues, abilities. *a.*

مناقبت *munāḳabat*, f. virtue, ability, praise. *a.*

مناقشہ *munāḳasha*, dispute, contention. *a.*

مناقض *munāḳiẓ*, contrary, repugnant. *a.*

مناکحت *munākaḥat*, marriage, nuptials. *a.*

منال *manāl*, substance, wealth, profit, mode, mauna. *a.*

منانا मनाना *manānā*, a. to persuade, to conciliate, to soothe, to coax, to assuage, to appease, to put in mind, to propitiate; to do, to act, to perform, to make. *manānā-danānā*, to appease, to conciliate. *s*

مناونا मनावना *manāwnā*, a. (v. *manānā*) to persuade, &c. *h.*

مناهي *manāhī* (pl. of منهي), prohibited or forbidden things; crimes, transgressions; fem. prohibition. *a.*

منبت *munabbat*, inlaid; mosaic work. *munabbat-kār*, one who inlays. *munabbat-kārī*, inlaying. *munabbatī*, inlaid. *a.*

منبر *mimbar*, m. a pulpit, a reading-desk. *a.*

منبسط *mumbasiṭ*, dilated, extended, rejoicing, exulting *a.*

منبع *mambu'*, m. a fountain, jet d'eau. *a.*

منبهاون मनभावन *man-bhāwan*, منبهاونا मनभावना *man-bhāwanā*, } acceptable, agreeable, pleasant, amusing, charming. *s*

منت *minnat*, f. an obligation, favour, humble and earnest supplication. *minnat-dār* or *minnat-kash*, under obligation, obliged. *minnat-shinās*, grateful, one who is sensible of obligations. *a.*

منت मनत *manat* or मन्नत *mannat*, f. acknowledgment; a vow, a promise; desire, intention. *s.*

منتج *muntaj*, result, consequence; deduced, inferred. *chi muntaj*, what is the inference *a.*

منتخب *muntaḵẖab*, chosen, selected; (sub.) a selection; pl. *muntaḵẖabāt*. *a.*

منتر मन्त्र *mantra* or *mantar*, m. a division of the Vedas, a sacred formula; a charm, spell, philtre incantation, fascination; secret consultation or advice. *mantr-jantr*, incantation, exorcism. *mantr-gupti*, f. secret counsel. *s.*

منترنا मन्त्रणा *mantranā*, f. advice, counsel. *s.*

منتري मन्त्री *mantrī*, m. a counsellor, prime minister; an adviser; a viceroy; an enchanter. *s.*

منتشر *muntashar*, published, divulged, explained, diffused, dispersed. *a.*

منتصب *muntaṣib*, erected, set up. *a.*

منتظر *muntaẓir*, expecting with impatience, tarrying for. *a.*

منتظم *muntaẓam*, ordered, arranged, disposed, adjusted. *a.*

منتفع *muntafi'*, m. a gainer, one who uses, enjoys, or has the advantage of a thing. *a.*

منتفي *muntafī*, rejected, dissipated, destroyed. *a.*

منتقش *muntaḳish*, carved, engraved; painted. *a.*

منتقل *muntaḳal*, transported, carried. *a.*

منتقم *muntaḳim*, taking revenge, avenging. *a.*

منتھ मन्थ *manth*, m. a churning-stick; a dish made of barley-meal with *ghī* and water; a sort of gruel or porridge; a disease of the eyes, cataract or opacity, rheum, excretion of the eyes. *s.*

منتھت मन्थित *manthit*, adj. churned; (sub. buttermilk. *s.*

منتھن मन्थन *manthan*, m. agitating, stirring, churning. *s.*

منتھني मन्थनी *manthanī*, f. a churning-vessel. *s.*

منتهى *muntahā*, m. the end, conclusion, boundary, extremity; adj. finished, concluded. *muntahī*, learned (*i. e.* one who has finished his studies). *a.*

منتي मिन्ती *mintī*, f. an apology, submission, solicitation. *h.*

منتها *manthā*, extinct, non-existent. *d.*

منج मंजु *manju*, beautiful, pleasant. *s.*

منج मनुज *manuj*, m. man in general. *s.*

منج मुञ्ज *munj*, منجا मुञ्जा *munjā*, } m. a sort of grass from the fibres of which a string is prepared, of which a Brāhman's girdle is made, the sacred cord. *s.*

منجا मनुजा *manujā*, f. a woman, wife. *s.*

منجا मञ्जा *manjā*, m. a bedstead, a throne. *s.*

منجا *manjā*, any high place where one may escape from an inundation. *a.*

منجا मंजा *manjā*, a kind of religious ceremony, anointing the body with turmeric on some special festive occasions. *h.*

منجار मञ्जार *manjār*, m. a cat. *s.*

منجر मञ्जर *manjar*, m. f. the blossom (of a tree). *s.*

منجر *munjirr*, drawn, brought back. *a.*

منجري मञ्जरी *manjarī* (v. *manjar*), a cluster of flowers; name of a musical mode. *s.*

منجل मंजुल *manjul*, beautiful, pleasant. *s.*

منجل *munjal*, m. the fruit of the palmyra tree (called in Urdū, *tarkul*, q. v.). *d.*

منجلاب *manjalāb*, polluted water, more especially that in which any thing impure, such as a dog or carrion has been thrown. *p.*

منجلي *munjalī*, conspicuous, apparent. *a.*

منجم *munajjim*, m. an astronomer, an astrologer, an almanack maker. *a.*

منجمد *munjamid*, congealed, concreted. *a.*

منجمله *min-jumla*, upon the whole. *a.*

منجن मंजन *manjan*, m. tooth-powder, dentifrice; rubbing the body over with unguents. *s.*

منجنا मंजना *manjnā*, n. to be polished, to be smoothed, to be cleaned. *s.*

منجنيق *manjanīk*, a huge warlike engine for flinging stones, a ballista. *g.*

منجوشا मञ्जूषा *manjūshā*, a large basket. *s.*

منجهه *munjh*, inflec. (of *main*; v. *mujh*) me, to me. *d.*

منجهلا मंझला *manjhlā*, middle, second (of three). *h.*

منجهولا मंझोला *manjholā*, middle, second, middlemost. *s.*

منجهولي मंझोली *manjholī*, f. (v. *majholī*) a small cart or carriage on two wheels drawn by bullocks. *s.*

منجيث मंजीठ *manjīṭ*, f. (v. *majīṭh*) a kind of drug. *s.*

منجي خانه *manje-khāna*, the room in which a young person, about to be married, is seated for a certain number of days. *d.*

منجيرا मंजीरा *manjīrā*, m. name of a musical instrument, a kind of cymbals: it consists of two small cups tied together with a string and played upon by striking one against the other. *s.*

منچ मंच *manch*, m. a high place, alcove, altar, a bed, a bedstead, a platform, a scaffold; an elevated shed in the fields where a watchman is stationed; a throne, a dais. *s.*

منچا *manchā*, m. a platform, a stage, scaffolding. *d.*

منچلا मनचला *man-chalā*, assiduous, active, bold. *s.*

منچلي मनचली *man-chalī*, f. assiduity, zeal. *s.*

منحرف *munḥarif*, change, inverted, declining or turning from; (sub.) a trapezium (in geometry). *a.*

منحرفي *munḥarifī*, apostatism, backsliding, the being a renegade. *a.*

منحصر *munḥasir*, surrounded, besieged, restricted; applicable to, peculiar to. *a.*

منحني *munḥanī*, lean, thin, flexible, bent, crooked, decrepit. *a.*

منحوس *manḥūs*, unfortunate, unlucky. *a.*

منخر *minkhar* or *mankhir*, the nostril. *a.*

منخرين *minkharain*, (dual) the two nostrils. *a.*

مند *mand*, a possessive particle, which, added to nouns, implies endowed with, or having, or possessed of; as, *'akl-mand*, sensible; *daulat-mand*, rich. *p.*

مند मन्द *mand*, abated, slow, tedious; dull, foolish; bad, ill; low (as a tone); Saturday; the planet Saturn. *mand mand*, gently, softly. *mand-gati*, slow-paced, softly, gently. *s.*

مندا मन्दा *mandā*, gentle, mild, affable, cheap, abated, allayed; slow; a little. *s.*

منداتما मन्दात्मा *mand-ātmā*, slow of apprehension, dull. *s.*

مندادر मन्दादर *mandādar*, disregarding, neglecting, disrespectful. *s.*

مندار मन्दार *mandār*, m. the name of a mountain, famous in India, with which the ocean was churned; one of the five trees of *Swarga*; name of a plant, swallow-wort (*Asclepias gigantea*); the coral tree (*Erythrina fulgens*). *s.*

مندايمان मन्दायमान *mandāyamān*, delaying, going tardily. *s.*

مندبدهه मन्दबुद्धि *mand-buddhi*, stupid, foolish. *s.*

مندبهاگيه मन्दभाग्य *mand-bhāgya*, unhappy, unfortunate. &c. *s.*

مندتا मन्दता *mandatā*, f. slowness, mildness, &c. *s.*

مندر मन्दिर *mandir*, m. a house, mansion, palace, dwelling, temple. *s.*

مندر मन्दर *mandar*, m. the mountain *mandar* with which the ocean is said to have been churned by the Asuras; one of the trees of paradise; *Swarg*, or paradise; adj. large, bulky. *s.*

مندرا मन्दरा *mandarā*, m. squat, dapper. *h.*

مندرا मुन्द्रा *mundrā*, m. a collar, a ring. *s.*

مندرج *mundarij* or *mundaraj*, contained, inserted, included; comprehending, containing. *a.*

مندرجه *mundarija*, m. contents, that which is included or contained. *a.*

مندرس *mundaris*, obliterated, cancelled. *a.*

مندري मुन्द्री *mundrī*, f. a ring, a collar; a finger-ring. *s.*

مندككر *mandi-kukur*, f. a sort of fish so named. *s.*

مندل मँदल *mandal*, f. a kind of drum made of wood and beaten with the fingers. *h.*

مندل *mandal*, f. a fountain, a jet d'eau; (cor. of *bandar*) a port, harbour. *h.*

مندمت मन्दमति *mand-mati*, dull, stupid, slow of apprehension. *s.*

مندنا मुन्दना *mundnā*, n. to be shut, closed. *s.*

مندهاسيه मन्दहास्य *manda-hāsya*, m. a gentle laugh, a smile. *s.*

منديل *mindīl*, f. a tablecloth; a towel; a species of high turban. *a.*

منديمان मन्दयमान *mandyamān*, slow, tardy. *s.*

منڈ मुण्ड *muṇḍ*, shaved, bald; low, mean; m. the head; a bald pate; the trunk of a lopped tree; a head man. *manḍ*, m. scum, froth; pith, essence; rice-water, rice-gruel (v. *mānḍ*). *s.*

منڈ *muṇḍ*, blunt, dull. *d.*

منڈا *muṇḍā*, m. the shoulder. *d.*

منڈا मण्डा *manḍā*, m. name of a sweetmeat. *s.*

منڈا मुण्डा *muṇḍā*, the head; the head of a paper kite; Bengal madder (*Rubia manjeth*); adj. shaven, bald, uncovered; a kind of uncovered *palkī*. *s.*

منڈاسا मुण्डासा *muṇḍāsā*, m. a kind of small turban. *h.*

منڈاسبند *muṇḍās-band*, m. a man. *d.*

منڈان *manḍān*, the world, the universe. *d.*

منڈانا मुण्डाना *muṇḍānā*, a. to shave, to cause to be shaved. *s.*

منڈپ मण्डप *manḍap*, m. a temporary building, an open shed erected on festive occasions; a house; a temple. *s.*

منڈت मण्डित *manḍit*, ornamented, overlaid, covered; (met.) accomplished. *muṇḍit*, bald, shorn, shaven. *s.* [shaven-headed. *s.*

منڈتشرا मुण्डितशिरा *muṇḍit-shirā*, bald-pated,

منڈک मुण्डक *muṇḍak*, m. a barber. *s.*

منڈکاري مارنا मुण्डकारीमारना *muṇḍhārī mārnā*, to lie round with the knees to the belly. *s.*

منڈل मण्डल *manḍal*, m. a circle, orb, sphere, disc; the heavens, sky, firmament; a round tent; an officer employed in villages, an exciseman; a ringleader; a district; the country over which the twelve princes called *chakra-vartis* are supposed to have ruled. *s.*

منڈلا मुण्डला *muṇḍlā*, shaved. *s.*

منڈلاکار मण्डलाकार *manḍal-ākār*, circular, round. *s.*

منڈلانا मण्डलाना *manḍlānā*, a. to make a circuit, to hover (as birds); to be enveloped. *h.*

منڈلي मण्डली *manḍalī*, f. an assembly, congregation. *s.* [pigeon. *h.*

منڈليا मण्डलिया *manḍaliyā*, m. a tumbler

منڈمال मुण्डमाल *muṇḍmāl*, a necklace of human heads. *s*

منڈن मुण्डन *muṇḍan*, m. the first shaving of a child (a religious ceremony among the Hindūs). *manḍan*, m. an ornament, jewels, trinkets. *s.*

منڈنا मुण्डना *muṇḍnā*, a. to be shaved. *s.*

منڈو मुण्डू *muṇḍū*, m. a devotee, a monk; a *sanyāsī*, a *gosain*. *h.*

منڈوا मण्डूआ *manḍū,ā* or मण्डवा *manḍwā*, m. an alcove, arbour; "a shade thown out in front of the veranda of a house, generally constructed of bamboo posts with a thatch of palmyra leaves or grass, called by Europeans in the Carnatic "a pandaul." *h.*

منڈوانا मुण्डवाना *muṇḍwānā*, a. to get shaved, to cause to be shaved. *h.* [(*Bignonia Indica*). *s.*

منڈوک मण्डूक *manḍūk*, m. a frog; a flower

منڈوکي मण्डूकी *manḍūkī*, f. a female or small frog; a plant (*Siphonanthus Indica* or *Hydrocotyle Asiatica*). *s.*

منڈوي मँडवी *manḍwī*, f. a kind of food. *h.*

منڈھ *muṇḍh*, shameless, impudent. *d.*

منڈھا मण्ढा *manḍhā*, m. an open shed or hall adorned with flowers for the bride and bridegroom. *s.*

منڈھايا मण्ढाया *manḍhāyā*, starched. *s.*

منڈھپ मण्ढप *manḍhap*, m. (v. *manḍap*) a shed, a temple. *s.* [cover, &c. *s.*

منڈھنا मण्ढना *manḍhnā*, a. (v. *maṛhnā*) to

منڈھوانا मण्ढवाना *manḍhwānā*, to cause to cover, &c. *s.* [a *jogī's* hut. *s.*

منڈھي मण्ढी *manḍhī*, f. a cottage, a temple,

منڈھيانا मण्ढियाना *manḍhiyānā*, a. (v. *manḍiyānā*) to starch. *s.*

منڈي मुण्डी *muṇḍī*, m. a barber; f. name of a medicinal plant (*Sphæranthus Indicus*). *s.*

منڈي मण्डी *manḍī*, f. a market (v. *hāṭ*); (in Dakh.) a shop or storehouse for the sale of goods on commission or by auction; a shop for the sale of grain, having a storehouse attached. *h.* [mit. *s.*

منڈيا मुण्डिया *muṇḍiyā*, m. the head, the sum-

منڈيانا मण्डियाना *manḍiyānā*, a. to apply starch or dye (to the hair). *s.* [face. *d.*

منڈي توڑنا *muṇḍī toṛnā*, to turn away one's

منڈير मुण्डेर *muṇḍer*, मुण्डेरी منڈيري *muṇḍerī*, } f. the coping of a wall, the roof. *h.*

منڈيري मुण्डीरी *muṇḍīrī*, f. a creeper bearing a red and yellow flower. *s.*

منڑوا मँड़ुआ *manṛu,ā*, m. منڑوي मँडुई *manṛu,ī*, f. } name of a grain (on the coast called *rāgī*), *Cynosurus coracanus*. *h.*

منزل *manzil*, f. a day's journey; rank, dignity; a stage, an inn, a caravanserai; habitation, dwelling; boundary, limit, goal; a story or floor (of a house); deck (of a ship); mansion of the moon (in astrology). *munzil*, one who causes to alight, one who receives a stranger hospitably; *emittens semen*. *munzal*, that which is sent down, an angel. *manzil kāṭnā*, to accomplish a journey. *h.*

منزلت *manzilat*, f. dignity, station, condition, rank, post of honour; a house of accommodation for travellers. *a.*

منزلخانه *manzil-khāna*, } a post-house, a halting-place after a day's journey, an inn. *a.p.*
منزلگاه *manzil-gāh*, }

منزله *manzila* (v. *manzilat*), dignity, &c. *a.*

منزول *munzawil*, perishing, decaying, failing. *a.*

منزوي *munzawī*, m. a solitary man, a hermit; adj. lonely, solitary. *a.*

منزه *munazzah*, pure, blameless, holy; exempted from, free. *a.*

منس मनस *manas*, m. the mind, the heart, the intellect, the understanding. *s.*

منس *muns* or *manus*, m. a man, a male. *d.*

منسا मनसा *mansā*, f. wish, desire, intention, design, purport, purpose. *mansā* or *mansā-devī*, f. the goddess of the serpent race, and the particular protectress against their venom. *s.*

منستاپ मनस्ताप *manas-tāp*, m. mental distress. *s.*

منستهان मुनिस्थान *muni-sthān*, m. a hermitage, the abode or retirement of holy sages. *s.*

منسج *mansij*, m. a weaver's shop. *minsaj*, the instrument by which the web is stretched when working; the part of a horse about the fore shoulder and under the mane. *a.*

منسج मनसिज *manasij*, m. the Hindū cupid, *Kāmadeva*. *mansij*, mental intellectual. *s.*

منسروا मनसर्वा *mansarwā*, m. a man, male. *h.*

منسك मनस्क *manask*, mental, intellectual. *s.*

منسكار मनस्कार *manas-kār*, m. the attention of the mind to its own sensations, consciousness of pleasure or pain. *s.*

منسلك *munsalik*, joined, connected, united together. *a.*

من سلوی *mann salwā*, manna and quails (wherewith the Israelites where fed in the wilderness). *a.*

منسوب *mansūb*, related, addicted to, belonging to, depending on. *mansūb-k.*, to connect with, to attribute to. *a.*

منسوخ *mansūkh*, cancelled, obliterated, abolished, broken. *a.*

منسيرو मनसेरू *manserū*, m. a man, a male. *s.*

منش मनुष *manush*, a man, a person, a human being (v. *manukh*). *s.*

منش *manish*, f. magnanimity, dignity, gravity; temperament, disposition, content, cheerfulness; pride, arrogance; desire. *p.*

منشا *manshā*, m. allusion, origin, principle, source, beginning. *munshā*, intention, inclination. *a.*

منشات *munshāt*, writings, compositions. *a.*

منشار *minshār*, m. a saw, hand-saw; a fan, a ventilator. *a.*

منشور *manshūr*, divulged, published; m. a royal mandate, diploma, patent. *a.*

منشي *munshī*, m. a writer, a clerk, a secretary; (commonly means) a tutor, a teacher of languages, more particularly of Hindūstānī, Persian, and Arabic. *munshi-garī*, f. the business of a *munshī*. *a.*

منشي मनुषी *manushī*, f. a woman, a female. *s.*

منشيانه *munshiyāna*, clerk-like. *a. p.*

منشيه मनुष्य *manushya*, m. a man, a mortal. *s.*

منشيتوه मनुष्यत्व *manushyatwa*, m. the state or condition of man, manhood, humanity. *s.*

منصب *manṣab*, m. dignity, office, ministry, magistracy. *manṣab-dār*, an officer (military); a magistrate, a person who holds an appointment under government. *manṣabi ḳaẓā*, the office of *kāẓī* or judge. *a.*

منصرف *munṣarif*, departing, receding. *munṣarif-k.*, depart, set out. *a.*

منصف *munṣif*, equitable, just; (sub.) a distributor of justice; a judge, an arbitrator. *a.*

منصفا *munṣifan*, equitably, justly. *a.*

منصفانه *munṣifāna*, candidly, equitably. *a.*

منصفي *munṣifī*, f. office of *munṣif*; judgment, arbitration, just criticism. *a.*

منصوب *manṣūb*, constituted, excited; marked with the vowel point *fatḥa* (َ); fixed, established, appointed, named for. *a.*

منصوبه *manṣūba*, m. contrivance, project. *manṣūba-bāz*, considerate, foreseeing, prudent, sagacious, ingenious. *a.*

منصور *manṣūr*, aided, protected, defended, victorious, conquering, triumphant. *a.*

منصوص *manṣūṣ*, manifested, clear. *a.*

منصه *manaṣṣa* or *minaṣṣa*, the chamber or tent of a bride. *a.*

منضج *munẓij* (pl. *munẓijāt*), suppurantia (in medicine). *a.*

منطبع *munṭabi'*, tame, trained, obedient, tractable, yielding. *a.*

منطفي *munṭafī*, extinguished, extinct. *a.*

منطق *manṭiḳ*, oration, logic, eloquence. *a.*

منطقه *minṭaḳa*, m. } m. a girdle, zone, belt. *minṭaḳatu-l-burūj*, the celestial girdle, *i. e.* the zodiac. *minṭaḳa,e mabrūda*, the frigid zone. *minṭaḳa,e, maḥrūḳa*, the torrid zone. *minṭaḳa,e mu'tadila*, the temperate zone. *a.*
منطقت *minṭaḳat*, f. }

منطقي *manṭiḳī*, logical, dialetic; m. a logician, an eloquent and sound disputant. *a.*

منظر *manẓar*, m. countenance, face, visage, aspect; a spectacle, theatre. *a.*

منظور *manẓūr*, seen, looked at, admired, visible, chosen, approved of, agreeable, acceptable. *manẓūri naẓar*, chosen, agreeable to the sight, beloved; (sub.) a mistress. *a.*

منظوري *manẓūrī*, f. approval, admiration. *a.*

منظوم *manẓūm*, منظومه *manẓūma*, } joined, threaded, arranged in order; metrical, versified, poetic. *a.*

منع *man'*, m. prohibition, forbidding, refusal, hindrance. *man' karnā*, to forbid, to prohibit. *a.*

منعدم *mun'adim*, destroyed, annihilated, annulled, ruined, extinct, lost. *a.*

منعقد *mun'aḳid*, tied, bound; agreed on, concluded (a treaty, marriage, &c.). *a.*

منعكس *mun'akis*, inverse, inverted, topsy-turvy, turned head downwards. *a.*

منعم *mun'im*, m. a benefactor; adj. liberal. *a.*

منعم *muna''am*, rich, affluent. *a.*

منغص *munagh ghaṣ*, miserable, melancholy. *a.*

منفخ *minfakh*, m. a pair of bellows. *a.*

منفذ *manfaẕ*, a passage; an orifice. *a.*

منفرج *munfarij*, open, separate; tranquil, contented, happy. *a.*

منفرجه *munfarija*, m. an obtuse (angle). *a.*

منفرد *munfarid*, single, separate, solitary. *a.*

منفسد *munfasid*, corrupted, depraved. *a.*

منفصد *manfaṣid*, flowing, fluent. *a.*

منفصل *munfaṣil*, m. منفصله *munfaṣila*, f. } disjoined, distinct, dissected, separated. *a.*

منفعت *manfa'at*, f. emolument, profit, gain, advantage. *a.*

منفعل *munfa'il*, disturbed, afflicted; bashful, abashed, ashamed. *a.*

منفك *munfakk*, separated, disjoined. *a.*

منفي *manfī*, negative; repulsed, rejected, banished. *a.*

منقا *munaḳḳā*, Cape raisins, currants. *a.*

منقاد *munḳād*, obedient, tractable. *a.*

منقار *minḳār*, f. a bird's bill, a beak. *a.*

منقاش *minḳāsh*, tweezers, pincers. *a.*

منقب *minḳab*, m. an instrument with which they tap for the dropsy, a trochar. *a.*

منقبت *manḳabat*, f. praise; virtue; natural talent or abilities. *a.*

منقبض *munḳabiẓ*, constituted, contracted. *a.*

منقتل *munḳatil*, slain, killed. *a.*

منقح *munaḳḳaḥ*, rendered clear or manifest; cleared of weak words (a verse). *a.*

منقسم *munḳasim*, divided into parts. *a.*

منقش *munaḳḳash*, painted, embroidered. *minḳash*, pincers, tweezers. *a.*

منقضي *munḳaẓī*, elapsed, past, expired. *a.*

منقطع *munḳaṭi'*, terminated, finished, broken off, exterminated, disjoined. *munḳaṭi' honā*, *a.* to be cut off, to be finished, or settled, or terminated. *a.*

منقل *manḳal*, a chafing dish. *a.*

منقله *manḳala*, a day's journey, or the space travelled; a halting place; a way through mountains. *a.*

منقوش *manḳūsh*, painted, engraved, carved, embroidered. *a.*

منقوط *manḳūṭ*, spotted, having dots; a species of composition in which all the letters employed have dots. *a.* [translated. *a.*

منقول *manḳūl*, transcribed, copied; narrated,

منقولات *manḳūlāt*, pl. things transferable; personal property. *a.*

منقوله *manḳūla*, moveable or personal property in opposition to *ghair-manḳūla*, real property. *a.*

منقي *munaḳḳā*, m. cleaned, purged, purified; a species of raisin. *a.* [cies of raisin. *a. h.*

منكا मुनक्का *munakkā* (for *munaḳḳā*), m. a spe-

منكا मनका *mankā*, m. a rosary, a bead, beads of gold, silver, &c. (beads of glass are called *pot*); the vertebræ of the neck. *mankā ḍhalaknā*, (lit.) the bending of the neck; to be at the point of death. *h.*

منكامنا मनकामना *mankāmnā*, f. desire, wish. *s.*

منكدر *munkadir*, quick, hastening. *a.*

منكر *munkir*, denying, rejecting; *Munkir Nakīr*, the names of two angels, who, agreeably to the *Muhammadan* creed, are supposed to examine the spirits of the departed in the tomb. *munkir honā*, to deny. *a.*

منكر *munkar*, denied. *a.* [played. *a.*

منكشف *munkashif*, discovered, revealed, dis-

منكوحه *mankūḥa*, f. a married woman, a lawful wife; adj. married. *a.*

منكه मनुष *manukh*, m. a man, individually or collectively, man, mankind. *s.*

منكيان كاهار *mankiyān kā hār*, a necklace of pearls. *d.* [stark naked. *d.*

منگا *mungā*, naked, bare. *nanga-mungā*,

منگابهیجنا मङ्गाभेजना *mangā-bhejnā*, منگانا मङ्गाना *mangānā*, } *a.* to send for, to procure. *h.*

منگت मङ्गत *mangat*, منگتا मङ्गता *mangtā*, } m. a beggar, a borrower. *h.*

منگتي *mangtī*, f. asking, a request. *mangtī lagānā*, to act as *sazāwāl*, q. v. *d.*

منگرا मङ्गरा *mangrā*, the ridge of a house. *h.*

منگڑا मनगड़ा *man-gaṛā*, powerful. *h.*

منگسر मङ्गसिर *mangasir*, m. the eighth solar month (Nov.-Dec.); according to some systems it is reckoned the first month. *s.*

منگل मङ्गल **mangal**, adj. auspicious, beautiful, pleasing; m. health, welfare, pleasure: Tuesday; the planet Mars; the Tuesc of the Saxons, *unde, mangal-bār,* Dies Martis, "Tuesc's day or Tuesday." *mangal-āchār* or *-chār*, a song of congratulation, a marriage tidings, epithalamium; festivity. *mangal-samāchār*, glad song or the Gospels. *s.*

منگلاچرن मंगलाचरण **mangal-ācharan**, worship or salutation to Ganesha at the commencement of an undertaking. *s.*

منگلامکهی मङ्गलामुखी **mangalā-mukhī**, m. f. [a musician, minstrel. *s.*

منگلسوتر मङ्गलसूत्र **mangala-sūtra**, lit. the lucky thread, used in the marriage ceremony, v. Wilson. *s.*

منگلکوٹ मङ्गलकोट **mangal-koṭ**, name of a place. *mangal-koṭī*, f. a kind of carpet so named. *h.*

منگلوار मङ्गलवार **mangal-wār**, m. Tuesday. *s.*

منگلی मङ्गली **mangalī**, triumphant, joyous. *mangalī-log*, people employed on rejoicings. *s.*

منگن मङ्गन **mangan**, f. debt, dunning. *s.*

منگنا मंगना **mangnā** (v. *māngnā*), to ask, &c. *h.*

منگنی मङ्गनी **mangnī**, f. betrothing, asking in marriage; a loan. *mangnī denā*, to lend. *h.*

منگنی मिङ्गनी **mingnī**, goat's or sheep's dung. *h.*

منگوانا मङ्गवाना **mangwānā**, a. to send for, to procure. *s.*

منگوس **mangūs**, a weasel, a mongoose, a ferret (v. *newalā*) *d.*

منگولا मङ्गूला **mangūlā**, m. a small tassel. *h.*

منگهٹا मनघटा **manghaṭā**, m. the raised masonry round the mouth of a well. *h.*

منگیتر मङ्गेतर **mangetar**, m. and f. one to whom a man or woman is betrothed. *h.*

من‌مارنا मनमारना **man-mārnā**, a. to resist one's own inclination, to be grieved or troubled in mind. *s.*

منمالا मणिमाला **mani-mālā**, f. a necklace of gems. *s.* [love. *s.*

منمتھ मन्मथ **manmath**, m. Cupid, *Kāmadeva*;

من‌من मुनमुन **munmun**, puss, puss! a mode of calling a cat. *h.* [*maujī*, conceited. *s.*

منموج मनमौज **man-mauj**, self-conceit. *man-*

منموهن मनमोहन **man-mohan**, m. f. heart-ravishing; a sweetheart, a mistress; a name of *Krishna*. *s.*

منمی मणिमय **mani-may**, made of gems. *s.*

منن मनन **manan**, m. minding, understanding. *s.*

منّا मना **mannā**, n. to be conciliated, soothed, tranquillized. *s.*

منو मनू **manū** (for *manu*), name of a celebrated sage and legislator; a monkey. *s.*

منو मनो **mano**, like, as if. *s.*

منوءا मनूआ **manū,ā**, f. a kind of cotton; m. puss (a cat). *h.*

منوءا मनूआ **monū,ā**, m. mind, soul, life. *a.*

منوال **minwāl**, m. mode, manner, rule, form. *a.*

منوان मन्वान **manwān**, m. thinking, conceiving, minding, regarding. *s.*

منوتی मनौती **manautī**, f. bail, security; a person referred to to pay the debt, &c. of another; surety, assurance, acknowledgment *manautī-dār*, a person who becomes surety for another for a handsome *consideration*. *s. p.*

منور **munawwar**, illustrated, explained, illuminated, clear, splendid, brilliant. *a.*

منورتھ मनोरथ **manorath**, desire, wish, design, intention. *s.* [pleasing. *s.*

منورم मनोरम **manoram**, beautiful, lovely,

منوگپت मनोगुप्त **mano-gupt**, thought on or pondered over secretly. *s.*

منوگت मनोगत **mano-gat**, seated in the mind. *s.*

منوگیه मनोज्ञ **mano-gya**, beautiful, lovely, handsome, pleasing, agreeable. *s.*

منولولیه मनोलौल्य **mano-laulya**, m. fancy, caprice, whim. *s.*

منونتر मन्वन्तर **manwantara** (vulg. *manwantar*), m. the reign of *Manu*, a period equal to seventy-one ages of the gods, or 306,720,000 years of mortals, or with its *sandhi*, or interval of universal deluge, 308,448,000 years; fourteen *manwantras* constitute a *kalpa*, or period of 4,320,000,000 years. According to Hindū cosmogony, there have been innumerable *man wantras* since the first creation of the universe. *s.*

منونیت मनोनीत **mano-nīt**, chosen, preferred. *s.*

منوهاری मनोहारी **manohārī**, m. } beautiful,
منوهارنی मनोहारिणी **manohārinī**, f. } pleasing, agreeable, lovely. *s.* [ful, pleasant. *s.*

منوهر मनोहर **manohar**, heart-ravishing, beauti-

منهه मुंह **munh**, m. mouth, face, countenance, presence, orifice; respect, complaisance; (met.) power, fitness, qualification, ability. *munh utar-jānā*, to have the face shrunk or withered by weakness and emaciation. *munh akhrī*, verbal, by word of mouth. *munh-ā-munh*, brimful. *munh-ānā*, v. n. to be salivated. *munh-andherā* or *munh-paknā*, twilight; evening; dusk, obscure. *munh bārnā*, to refrain. *munh-bānā*, to open the mouth, to gape. *munh bigārnā*, to frown, to make faces. *munh bigarnā*, to be displeased; to have the taste blunted or depraved. *munh banānā*, to make faces. *munh-band*, a muzzle. *munh band karnā*, to hold one's tongue. *munh bolā bhā,ī*, an intimate friend (lit. one called a brother). *munh bharī*, f. a bribe, a sop. *munh pānā*, to get into one's good graces; to presume on the favour of another. *munh-paṭṭā*, a horse's headstall. *munh par fākhta uṛ jānā*, to change colour. *munh par garm honā*, to behave disrespectfully in the presence of a superior. *munh par lānā*, to tell, to relate. *munh par hawā,ī-uṛnī*, or *-phirnī*, or *chhuṭnī* (lit. to have a squib or rocket discharged against one's face), to change colour. *munh pasārnā*, to gape with surprise, &c. *munh phirnā*, to turn away from, to be displeased with, to be disgusted. *munh phernā*, to abstain from. *munh phailānā*, to presume, to desire much, to gape. *munh-pīṭh-k.*, to speak in anger or bitterness. *munh taknā*, to be astonished or afflicted. *munh topā*, m. bribe. *munh to dekho*, look at his face (applied to a person who pretends or aspires to something beyond his power or capacity). *munh tornā*, to harass. *munh thuthānā*, to make faces. *munh thaṭhānā*, to slap one's face, to box the ears. *munh ṭeṛhā karnā*, to make wry faces. *muṅh chiṛānā*, to make mouths. *muṅh chaṛhnā*, to become intimate with, to attach one's self to. *muṅh chalānā*, to bite, or being inclined to bite (as a horse). *muṅh-chor*, shamfaced, bashful, timid, sheepish. *muṅh chorī*, bashfulness. *muṅh chhipānā*, to hide one's face (from bashfulness). *muṅh dikhānā*, to shew one's face, to appear with confidence and satisfaction (generally, as in English, joined with a negative). *muṅh dikhā,ī*, f. a present given by the friends of the family and the women of the neighbourhood on their first visit to a bride. *muṅh dekh rakhnā*, to stare at with surprise. *muṅh dekh-kar bāt karnā*, to flatter, to speak what one supposes will be agreeable to his hearers. *muṅh dekhnā*, to look up to (for aid, &c.); to have a regard for one; to be astonished or helpless. *muṅh dekhe kī ulfat* or *prīt*, apparent friendship or affection. *muṅh denā*, to make familiarized. *muṅh ḍālnā*, to beg, to request; (a horse) to bite. *muṅh rakhnā*, to keep on good terms with. *muṅh zabānī*, verbal (message or evidence), *vivâ voce*. *muṅh-zor*, headstrong, obstinate. *muṅh sukaṛnā*, to change colour. *muṅh se phūl jhaṛne*, to abuse, to reproach. *muṅh fak̤ hojānā*, to change colour (especially from fear). *muṅh kālā karnā* (lit. to blacken the the face), to incur disgrace; to punish, to disgrace. *muṅh kā phūhar*, abusive. *muṅh kā niwālā*, any thing easily attained. *muṅh karnā*, to confront, to compare; to give abuse; to burst or open (as an abscess); to make the first attempt at seizing game (a young hound or other animal used in hunting); to turn one's face, or direct one's steps towards any particular object or place. *muṅh kholnā*, to abuse. *muṅh ke kawwe uṛ jāne*, to look blank on any occasion. *muṅh kī lo,ī utarnī* or *jānī*, to lose the sense of shame. *muṅh laṭkānā*, to be down in the mouth, to make a long face. *muṅh lagānā*, to familiarize, to be intimate with inferiors. *muṅh lagnā*, to have the mouth burned by any pungent substance; to become intimate, to be familiarized, to become a favourite. *muṅh leke rah jānā*, to be silent from shame. *muṅh mārnā* or *sīnā*, to stop one's mouth, to put one to silence; to feed; to bite. *muṅh māṅgī*, that which is demanded. *muṅh moṛnā*, to turn away, to abstain from any thing. *muṅh meṅ pānī ānā*, to desire with eagerness. *apnā sā muṅh leke phir jānā*, or *-ānā*, to return disappointed from any enterprise. *s.*

منه मिंह *miṅh*, m. rain (v. *meṅh*). *s.*

منه मनहु *manahu*, suppose, as if, like. *s.*

منه मिंह *miṅh* (for *meṅh*), rain. *s.*

منها *minhā*, m. } (lit. from that) deduction, subtraction; re-
منهاءي *minhā,ī*, f. } mission of rent or revenue. *a.*

منهاج *minhāj*, highway or road; a wide street. *a.*

منهار मणिहार *manihār*, m. a person who makes or sells (*chūṛīs*) the glass bracelets which the women wear on their wrists. *h.*

منهار मनुहार *manuhār*, f. fascinating, beautiful. *s.*

منهاري मनहारी *manhārī* or मनुहारी *manuhārī*, heart-ravishing, charming, fascinating. *s.*

منهاري मणिहारी *mani-hārī*, f. the trade in jewels. *s.*

منهان मुंहां *muṅhāṅ*, thrush, salivation. *s.*

منهاءي *manhā,ī*, f. forbidding, prohibition. *minhā,ī*, adj. (lit. from that) subtracted, deducted. *minhā,ī-dār*, a holder of land exempted from revenue payment. *a.*

منهايگي *minhāyagī*, f. deduction from an assessment for some special reason. *a. p.*

منهدم *munhadim*, demolished, destroyed. *a.*

منهدي *minhdī*, f. (v. *meṅhdī*) name of a plant. *s.*

منهرن मनहरण *man-haran*, m. heart-stealing. *s.*

منهزم *munhazim*, put to flight, discomfited. *a.*

منهل *manhal*, place of drinking; a tomb; profuse liberality. *a.*

منهنال मुंहनाल *muṅh-nāl*, m. f. the mouthpiece of a pipe or *ḥuḳḳa* tube. *s.*

منهو मनहू *manahū*, adv. suppose, as if, like. *s.*

منهي *manhī*, forbidden, prohibited. *a.*

منهيات *manhiyāt*, (pl.) unlawful things. *a.*

مني *manī*, f. death, fate; *sperma genitale viri aut mulieris*. *a.*

مني मुनी *munī*, m. a holy man, a saint, a sage. *manī*, m. a gem. *s.*

مني *manī*, presumption, boasting, egotism. *p.*

منيا मुनिया *muniyā*, f. the female of the little birds called *amadavats* (or lal. *Fringilla amandava*). *s.*

منيار *maniyār*, m. (v. *manihār*). *h.*

منيب *munīb*, m. a patron, a manager, a master, a principal; a client, constituent. *munīb-gumāshta*, a head clerk or manager of a bank, &c. *a.*

منيبانه *munībāna*, the fee or perquisite of a manager. *a. p.*

منيت *munīyat*, f. a wish, desire, hope. *a.*

مني تهني मनीथनी *manī thanī*, m. name of a blemish in horses. *h.*

منير *munīr*, shining, splendid, illuminating, illustrious. *a.*

منيش मुनीश *munīsh* or *munīs*, m. a saint; the chief of the saints or sages. *s.*

منيع *manī'*, inaccessible, impregnable. *a.*

منيف *munīf*, eminent, exalted, noble, sublime. *a.*

مو मौ *mau*, m. honey. *mo* (for *maiṅ* or *mujh*), I, me. *mohi* or *mokauṅ*, to me. *s.*

مو *mū*, m. the hair. *mū-bāf*, a hair ribbon. *mū-bāfī*, f. the making of hair ribbons. *mū ba mū*, hair by hair, minutely, circumstantially. *mū-shigāf*, one who splits hairs, a critic, a subtle reasoner. *mū-shigāfī*, f. criticism, or rather minute details of small errors in which small men delight. *mū-ḳalam*, a hair pencil. *mau*, mewing (as a cat). *p.*

موا मूआ *mū,ā*, dead, lifeless, dull; impotent (a common term of abuse). *mū,ā bādal*, m. sponge. *mū,ā-sho*, m. a washer of dead bodies. *h.*

موات *muwāt*, f. waste land. *a.*

مواج *mawwāj*, waving, boisterous. *a.*

مواجب *mawājib*, salaries, wages, pensions. *a.*

مواجهه *muwājaha*, m. presence, confronting, appearance, face to face. *a.*

مواحنت *muwāḥanat*, f. hatred, dislike, enmity. *a.*

مواخذ *muwākhaz*, taken, chastised. *a.*

مواخذه *muwākhaza*, m. taking satisfaction, retaliating, chastising, calling to a severe account. *a.*

مواد *mawādd* (pl. of مادّه), articles, matters, arguments, points; females; humours of the body. *a.*

موازنه *muwāzina*, list or statement of all the land belonging to a village, also called *raḳba-bandī*, q. v. *a.*

موازي *muwāzī*, parallel, being exactly opposite to, and resembling one another. *a.*

مواس मवास *mawās*, m. protection, refuge, asylum. *h.*

مواسا *muwāsā*, society, fellowship; good or fortunate action; condoling with. *a.*

مواشي *mawāshī* (pl. of ماشية), quadrupeds, cattle, more especially domestic beasts, as cows, buffaloes, sheep, and goats. *a.*

مواصلت *muwāṣalat*, f. conjunction, adhesion, interview. *a.*

مواضع *mawāẓi'* (pl. of موضع), places. *a.*

مواضعت *muwāẓa'at*, a sale by which loss is incurred. *a.*

مواظبت *mawāẓabat*, assiduity, perseverance. *a.*

موافق *muwāfiḳ*, conformable with, proportional to, consonant, congruous, apt, like, agreeing, suiting, favourable, propitious. *a.*

موافقت *muwāfaḳat*, f. conformity. *muwāfaḳat-k.*, to enter into friendship, to conform, &c. *a.*

موالات *muwālāt*, f. friendship, affection, pursuing a business steadily or without intermission. *a.*

موالي *mawālī* (pl. of مولىٰ), lords, masters; friends; servants, slaves. *muwālī*, one who aids or assists. *a.*

مواليد *mawālīd* (pl. of مولود), sons. *mawālīdi salāsa*, m. the three kingdoms of nature (viz. animal, vegetable, and mineral). *a.*

موانست *muwānasat* or *mu,ānasat*, f. companionship, fellowship, society, familiarity, intimacy. *a.*

موانع *mawāni'*, n. (pl. of مانع), impediments, obstacles. *a.*

مواهبت *muwāhabat*, f. contending with another in liberality or munificence. *a.*

موبد *mūbad* or *mūbid*, m. a doctor, a philosopher, a counsellor of state; a worshipper of the sun, a priest of the *pārsīs*, or fire-worshippers. *p.*

موت *maut*, f. death, resting, reposing. *a.*

موت मूत *mūt*, m. urine, piss. *mūt-aṭaknā*, to labour under a total suppression of urine. *s.*

موتاد *mautād* (for *mu'tād*), f. quantity. *a.*

موتا *mautā*, the dead (v. *mautā*). *a.*

موتر मूत्र *mūtr* or *mūtra*, m. piss, urine. *s.*

موترا मोत्रा *motrā*, m. spavin. *h.*

موتراتيت मूत्रातीत *mūtrātīt*, m. difficult or slow passage of urine. *s.*

موتراگهات मूत्राघात *mūtrāghāt*, m. suppression of urine. *s.*

موتردوس मूत्रदोष *mūtr-dos*, m. gonorrhœa, considered as a urinary complaint. *s.*

موترشك मूत्रशुक *mūtr-shuk*, m. white urinary sediment. *s.*

موتركرچهر मूत्रकृच्छ्र *mūtr-kṛichhra*, m. strangury. *s.*

موترمارگ मूत्रमार्ग *mūtr-mārg*, m. the urethra. *s.*

موتنا मूतना *mūtnā*, to piss, (or, as nice people have it) to make water. *s.*

موتها मोथा *mothā*, m. a kind of grass the root of which is used in medicine (*Cyperus rotundus*). *s.*

موتهرا मोथरा *mothrā*, m. name of a disease in horses, splint, spavin. *h.*

موتي मोती *motī*, m. a pearl. *motī pirone*, to string pearls; (met.) to speak eloquently; to weep (the tears being compared to pearls). *motī kūṭ kar bharne*, to be very bright (applied to an eye). *motī kī sī āb utarnī*, to be disgraced. *s.*

موتىٰ *mautā* (pl. of ميت), the dead. *a.*

موتيا मोतिया *motiyā*, m. the name of a flower (*Jasminum zambac*, var. β *Roxb.*); (in Dakh.) a pearl; adj. of the colour of pearls. *h.*

موتيابند मोतियाबिन्द *motiyā-bind*, m. the name of a kind of blindness; *gutta serena*. *s.*

موتي‌چور मोतीचूर *motī-chūr*, m. a kind of sweetmeat; a certain description of eye among pigeons. *h.*

موٹ मोट *moṭ*, m. f. (v. *moṭh*) a bundle, package, &c. *moṭ-kā moṭ bechnā*, to sell wholesale. *h.*

موٹا मोटा *moṭā*, fat, corpulent, thick, coarse, great, large. *h.*

موٹاپا मोटापा *moṭāpā*, m.
موٹاپن मोटापन *moṭāpan*, m.
موٹائي मोटाई *moṭā,ī*, f.
} fatness, corpulency, thickness, coarseness (in Dakh. *moṭāgī*). *h.*

موٹرا मोटरा *moṭrā*, m. a bundle, package, load. *h.*

موٹري मोटरी *moṭrī*, f. a small bundle, a parcel, knapsack. *h.*

موٹكي मोटकी *moṭkī*, f. a mattock, a pickaxe; a fat woman; a *rāginī*. *h.*

موٹلا मोटला *moṭlā*, fat, gross, coarse. *h.*

موٹه मोठ *moṭh*, m. f. a bundle, package, bale, a load; amount, total; a leather bucket for raising water; a kind of grain, lentils, vetches. *h.*

موٹه मूठ *mūṭh*, f. handle, hilt; fist, handful; name of a game. *mūṭh kī mūṭh*, handful after handful, numerous handfuls. *s.*

موٹها मूठा *mūṭhā*, m. a handle. *s.*

موٹهرا मूठरा *mūṭhrā*, a kind of printing, consisting of spots on cloth, leather, &c. *h.*

موٹھي मूठी *mūṭhī*, f. the fist, hand, handful. *s.*

موٹھيا मूठिया *mūṭhiyā*, m. a handful. *s.*

موٹھيا मोठिया *moṭhiyā*, } m. a porter, bearer,
موٹيا मोटिया *moṭiyā*, } carrier of burdens, a labourer. *h.*

موثر *muwassir* or *mu,assir*, penetrating, making an impression, efficacious. *mu,assar*, impressed upon, affected by. *a.*

موج *mauj*, f. a wave; whim, caprice. *mauj ā-jānī*, an imagination coming into the mind. *mauj-khez*, stormy, boisterous. *mauj raknā*, to be proud. *mauj-zan*, waving, boisterous, billowy, tumultuous. *mauj mārnā*, a. to fluctuate, to waver; (met.) is applied to express self-enjoyment without restraint. *mauji nasīm*, a cooling squall. *a.*

موج मूज *mūj* (for *mūnj*, q. v.), a species of grass. *s.* [count. *a.*

موجب *mūjib*, m. cause, motive, reason, ac-

موجبه *mūjiba*, m. a thing of importance (whether good or bad); the rewards or punishments of eternity; (in logic) an affirmative proposition (opposed to *sāliba*, q. v.). *a.*

موجد *mūjid*, m. an author, causer; corroborating, reinstating (after sickness or poverty). *a.*

موجر *mūjir*, hiring, letting to farm, renting. *a.*

موجز *mūjaz*, m. a summary, compendium, epitome. *a.* [debt). *a.*

موجل *muwajjal*, deferred (as payment of a

موجود *maujūd*, found, present, existing, standing before, at hand. *a.*

موجودات *maujūdāt*, pl. f. creatures, existences, created beings; a review or muster of troops. *a.*

موجه *mauja*, m. a wave, a small billow. *a.*

موجه *muwajjah*, agreeable, acceptable. *a.*

موچ मोच *moch*, m. strain, twist; a tree (*Hyperanthera morunga*). *h.*

موچا मोचा *mochā*, m. a large lump of flesh; crops beaten down by wind and rain. *h.*

موچا मोचा *mochā*, m. a plantain tree (*Musa sapientum*). *s.* [(*Nigella Indica*). *s.*

موچاٹ मोचाट *mochāṭ*, m. a pungent seed

موچرس मोचरस *moch-ras*, m. gum of the semul (or silk-cotton tree) (*Bombax heptaphyllum*). *s.*

موچك मोचक *mochak*, m. the silk-cotton tree (*Bombyx heptaphyllum*); the plantain (*Musa sapientum*); a liberator. *s.*

موچكانا मूचकाना *mūchkānā*, a. to sprain. *h.*

موچن मोचन *mochan* (from मूष), m. theft, robbery. *h.* [wife. *h.*

موچن मोचन *mochan* (also *mochnī*), a cobbler's

موچن मोचन *mochan*, } m. release, acquit-
موچنا मोचना *mochnā*, } tal. *s.*

موچنا मोचना *mochnā*, a. to let go, to set free, to shed, to put off, to extinguish. *s.*

موچنا मूचना *mūchnā*, m. pincers, tweezers; a. to pinch; to shut, to close. *s.* [shade. *s.*

موچني मोचिनी *mochinī*, f. a prickly night-

موچھ मोक्ष *mochh* or *moksh*, m. release, liberation, deliverance, absolution, salvation, beatitude, final and eternal happiness, the liberation of the soul from the body, and its exemption from further transmigration. *s.*

موچھ मूछ *mūchh*, f. whiskers, moustaches. *mūchh marorā roṭī torā*, one who is proud of eating the bread of idleness. *h.*

موچھاکڑي मूछाकड़े *mūchh-ākṛe*, } m. stiff and
موچھکڑي मूछकड़े *mūchh-akṛe*, } bushy whiskers. *h.* [kers. *h.*

موچھيل मूछैल *mūchhail*, having large whis-

موچي मोची *mochī*, m. a saddler, cobbler, shoemaker, a worker in leather. "In Southern India the *mochī* does not make shoes or saddles, but binds books and manufactures a variety of ornamental wares."—(Binning). *h.*

موچينه *mū-chīna*, tweezers, pincers. *p.*

موحد *muwaḥḥid*, one who believes in one God; a unitarian; adj. orthodox. *mauḥid* or *mauḥad*, single. *a.* [in one God. *a. p.*

موحدانه *muwaḥḥidāna*, like one who believes

موحش *mūḥish*, desolate, wild; famished; terrible.

موخذ *muwakhkhaẕ*, taken, seized, retaliated upon, called to account. *a.*

موخر *muwakhkhir*, posterior, consequent; delayed, procrastinated. *a.*

مود मोद *mod*, m. delight, pleasure. *s.*

مودب *mu,addub*, respectful, civil, polite, courteous, well-trained or disciplined (also used adverbially). *a.* [tion. *a.*

مودت *mawaddat*, f. friendship, love, affec-

مودت मोदित *modit*, pleased, delighted. *s.*

مودري मूद्री *mūdrī*, f. a finger-ring. *s.*

مودع *mūda'*, a trustee, one to whom property is entrusted. *mūdi'*, a depositor, one who leaves any thing in trust with another. *a.*

مودك मोदक *modak*, delighting, rejoicing, causing happiness or delight; m. name of a sweetmeat. *s.* [foolish. *h.*

مودھو मोधू *modhū*, guileless, artless, simple,

مودى *muwaddā*, performed, paid. *muwaddī*, f. a cause, a motive; causing; paying, performing what is due. *a.*

مودي मोदी *modī*, m. a merchant, a shopkeeper, a grain-merchant, steward, providore. *modīkhāna*, a pantry. *h.*

موڈ मूड *mūḍ* (for *mūṇḍ*), the head. *s.*

موذن *muwazzin* or *mu,azzin*, m. a public crier to prayers (among *Muḥammadans*). *a.*

موذي *mūẕī*, noxious, troublesome, importunate, vexatious, pernicious. *mūẕī-garī*, f. troublesomeness. *a.*

مور *mor*, m. an ant. *mor-malakh*, innumerable (as the ants and locusts). *p.*

مور मोर *mor*, m. a peacock. *mor-pankhī*, f. a kind of pleasure-boat, barge. *mor-mukuṭ*, a peacock's crest. *maur*, m. the blossom of a tree (especially of the mango). *s.*

مور मोर *mor*, m. twist, turn. *maur*, the shoulder; a chaplet worn by Hindūs at the time of marriage. *h.*

مور मोर *mor*,
مورا मोरा *morā*, } possessive pron. mine, my. *h.*

مورانا मौराना *maurānā*, n. to blossom, flourish (particularly the mango tree). *s.*

مورت मूर्ति *mūrti*, f. body, figure, form, image. *mūrat* (for *mūrti*), f. a statue, an idol; a person (term used by Bairāgīs). *s.*

مورتمان मूर्तिमान *mūrtimān*, also *mūrtimanta*, material, substantial, having shape or substance, incarnate. *s.*

مورث *mūris̤*, m. a cause, an author; the person from whom an inheritance is derived. *mūris̤i 'ālī*, a remote progenitor. *a.*

مورچال *morchāl*, f. lines of intrenchment, trenches (in a fort). *p.*

مورچنگ मोरचङ्ग *morchang*, f. a jew's harp. *h.*

مورچه *morcha*, m. rust; a battery; (dim. of *mor*) a little ant. *p.*

مورچها मूर्च्छा *mūrchhā*, f. a swoon, stupefaction. *mūrchhā-ānā* or *-khānā*, to swoon. *s.*

مورچهاگت मूर्च्छागत *mūrchhāgat*, a state of swoon or stupefaction; astonishment. *s.*

مورچهت मूर्च्छित *mūrchhit*, faint, entranced, fainted, in a swoon, insensible. *s.*

مورچهل मोरछल *morchhal*, m. a fan for driving away flies, a brush. *h.*

مورچهن मूर्च्छन *mūrchhan*, adj. fainting; syncope, swoon. *s.*

مورخ *muwarrikh*, m. an annalist, a historian, a chronologer, biographer. *muwarrakh*, dated. *a.*

مورد *mūrd*, m. the myrtle. *p.*

مورد *maurid*, m. the place of arrival; descending, alighting, appearing. *a.*

موردها मूर्द्धा *mūrddhā*, m. the head, the summit. *s.*

مورکه मूरख *mūrakh* or मूर्ख *mūrhh*, ignorant. *mūrakh gānṭh*, the insisting of an ignorant fellow upon what he says, stubbornness. *s.*

مورکهپنا मूरखपना *mūrakh-panā*, m.
مورکهتا मूरखता *mūrakhtā*, f.
مورکهتاءي मूरखताई *mūrkhatā,ī*, f.
مورکهيه मौरख्य *maurkhya*, m. } ignorance, stupidity, folly, barbarism. *s.*

مورني मोरनी *mornī*, f. a peahen; (Dakh.) a kind of ornament worn on the top of the ear (by women). *h.*

موروث *maurūs̤*, hereditary, inherited. *a.*

موروثي *maurūs̤ī*, hereditary, by succession. *maurūs̤ī ijāra*, a hereditary farm. *a.*

موري मोरी *morī*, f. a pipe or subterraneous passage (for water). *h.*

موريانه *moriyāna*, rust, more especially that which cannot be polished. *p.*

موڑ मूड़ *mūṛ*, m. the head. *mauṛ*, m. a high crowned hat worn by the bridegroom at the wedding. *s.*

موڑ मोड़ *moṛ*, m. a turn, twist, convolution, writhe, sprain, fistula. *h.*

موڑ *moṛ*,
موڑکا *moṛkā*, } m. young shoots of a tree or plant. *d.*

موڑنا मोड़ना *moṛnā*, a. to twist, to bend, to screw; n. to turn away. (Dakh.) *moṛ-denā*, to defeat, put to flight. *moṛ-khānā*, to be defeated, routed. *h.*

موڑه मूढ़ *mūṛh*, stupid, brutal; m. a fool, a simpleton. *mūṛh-man*, stupid, of dull mind. *s.*

موڑها मोढ़ा *moṛhā*, m. a low stool or seat; the shoulder. *h.*

موڑهاتما मूढ़ात्मा *mūṛhātmā*, foolish, a fool,

موڑهتا मूढ़ता *mūṛhtā*, f.
موڑهيه मौढ्य *mauṛhya*, m. } folly, silliness. *s.*

موز *mauz*, m. a plantain. *mauz machhī*, a whiting. *a.*

موزون *mauzūn*, weighed, well-adjusted, well-measured (verse). *a.*

موزه *moza*, m. a stocking, boot. *moza-gīr*, a horse that bites his rider. *p.*

موزي ساز *moze-sāz*, m. a bootmaker. *p.*

موس *mūs*, a crucible. *d.*

موسا मूसा *mūsā*, m. a mouse, a rat. *s.*

موسا मौसा *mausā*, m. an uncle, mother's sister's husband. *s.*

موساءي *mūsā,ī*, f. Judaism, following of the religion and laws of Moses. *a.*

موسرا मूसरा *mūsrā*, m. a rat, a mouse. *s.*

موسري मूसरी *mūsrī*, f. a mouse, a female rat. *s.*

موسقي *mūsīkī*, f. (Gr. μουσική) music. *g.*

موسل मूसल *mūsal*, m. a wooden pestle, especially the large one used for beating grain in a mortar; (Dakh.) *mūslāṅ soṅ ḍhol bajānā*, to make merriment. *s.*

موسلا मूसला *mūslā*, m. a tap-root; the fusiform receptacle of a many-seeded fruit (as the *Artocarpus*, *Annona*, &c.). *mūslā-dhār*, raining very heavily. *s.*

موسم *mausim*, also *mausam*, m. season, time. *mausimi-bahār* or *-bahārī*, the vernal season, the spring. *a.*

موسمي *mausimī*, seasonable, in season. *a.*

موسنا मूसना *mūsnā* or *mosnā*, a. to pilfer, to steal, to defraud, to snatch or seize by force. *s.*

موسوم *mausūm*, marked, signed, impressed, named, called, aforesaid, above-mentioned. *a.*

موسوي *mūsawī*, of or relating to Moses. *a.*

موسي मौसी *mausī*, f. an aunt, mother's sister. *s.*

موسيٰ *mūsā* or *mūsī*, Moses the Jewish legislator. *a.*

موسيچه *mūsīcha*, m. name of a bird. *p.*

موسيرا मौसेरा *mauserā*, m. belonging or related to the mother's sister's husband, as *mauserā bhā,ī*, a cousin, son of a mother's sister. *mauserī bahin*, daughter of a mother's sister. *s.*

موسيقار *mūsīḳār*, music; a musician; a kind of musical instrument. *p.*

موسيقي *mūsīḳī*, f. (Gr. μουσική) music. *g.*

موش मूष *mosh* or *mūsh*, m. a rat, a mouse. *mosh-dān*, a mouse-trap. *moshi dashtī*, m. a mole. *moshgīr*, the mouse-taker, a sparrowhawk. *s. p.*

موشا मोषा *moshā*, f. stealing, theft. *s.*

موشت मूषित *mūshit*, stolen. *s.*

موشح *muwashshaḥ*, ornamented, decorated. *a.*

موشك *mūshak*, a bat, vesper-fly. *p.*

موشك मूषक *mūshak* or मूषिक *mūshik*, m. a rat, a mouse; a plunderer, a thief (also *moshak*). *s.*

موشكور *mūshi-kor*, a mole, a musk rat. *p.*

موشن मूषण *mūshan* or *moshan*, m. stealing, pilfering. *s.*

موصل *mūṣil*, m. a carrier, a bearer. *muwaṣṣal*, arrived, joined. *mauṣil* (vulg. *mūṣal*), name of a city, Mossul. *a.*

موصوف *mauṣūf*, described, celebrated, praised; before-mentioned; (sub.) a noun substantive qualified by an adjective. *a.*

موصول *mauṣūl*, joined, coupled, arrived; m. tax collection; a relative pronoun. *a.*

موصي *mūṣī* or *muwaṣṣī*, m. making a will, a testator. *a.*

موصيٰ *mūṣā* or *muwaṣṣā*, devised by will. *mūṣā bi-hi*, a legacy, a bequest. *mūṣā la-hu*, a legatee.

موصيه *mūṣiya* or *muwaṣṣiya*, f. a testatrix. *a.*

موضع *mauẓa'*, m. a village, district, place; occurrence, conjecture. *mauẓa' aṣlī*, the chief village or that originally settled. *mauẓa'-dāḵẖilī*, the part of a village superadded to the original. *mauẓa'-wār*, by villages (applied to the assessment). *a.*

موضوع *mauẓū'*, m. a subject, object; adj. established, placed, situated; conventional. *a.*

موضينا *mauẓīnā*, a village registrator. *a. h.*

موطن *mauṭin*, m. birthplace, dwelling, home. *a.*

موظف *muwaẓẓaf*, fixed, limited, allowed. *a.*

موعد *mau'id*, m. a promise; predicting, foretelling. *a.*

موعظت *mau'iẓat*, f. advice, admonition. *a.*

موعود *mau'ūd*, promised, predicted, predestined. *a.*

موفق *muwaffaḳ*, favoured, assisted. *a.*

موفور *maufūr*, copious, full, numerous, abundant, many, plentiful. *a.*

موقت *muwaḳḳat*, fixed or restricted to a certain definite time. *a.*

موقر *muwaḳḳar*, honoured, revered, respected; grave, solemn, austere. *a.*

موقع *mauḳa'*, proper, fit, suitable; m. a place where any thing happens, a contingency. *a.*

موقف *mauḳif*, m. a station, post, place. *a.*

موقوف *mauḳūf*, deferred, postponed, relinquished, delayed, dependent on. *mauḳūf karnā*, to cease, to leave off, to abolish. *a.*

موقوفي *mauḳūfī*, f. stopping, arrest of judgment (in law); setting aside. *a.*

موك मूक *mūk*, mute, dumb, speechless. *s.*

موكا मूका *mūkā*, m. the fist; a thump, blow; a spy-hole. *s.*

موكب *mauhib*, m. an army, forces, a choice body of troops. *a.*

موكد *muwakkad*, confirmed, corroborated, efficacious. *a.*

موكش मोक्ष *moksh* or *mokshạ*, m. (v. *mochh*) deliverance. *mokshit*, liberated. *mokshak*, m. a deliverer. *s.*

موكل *muwakkal*, m. one who is appointed guardian; a superintendant, vicegerent. *muwakkil*, a constituent, one who delegates power. *a.*

موكلا *moklā*, opened, extended; m. a plant, a vegetable. *moklā-rūp*, a plant, a young shoot. *d.*

موكه मोख *mokh*, } m. a small hole in a wall
موكها मोखा *mokhā*, } for admitting light and air, an air-hole, an aperture. *s.*

موكها मूखा *mūhhā*, m. the ridge of a thatch, the topping or coping of a wall. *h.*

موكهي मूखी *mūkhī*, m. a kind of pigeon. *h.*

موكهي मूखी *mūkhī*, } f. a thump, a blow with
موكي मूकी *mūkī*, } the fist. *s.*

موكهيه मौख्य *maukhya*, m. pre-eminence. *s.*

موگدھ मौग्ध *maugdha*, m. simplicity, silliness. *s.*

موگرا मोगरा *mogrā*, m. a mallet, a pounder, a ramrod; the dog-head nail of the cock of a flint lock; name of a flower, great double Arabian or Tuscan jasmine (*Jasminum zambac*, var. γ *Roxb.*; *Mogorium*, *Lamarck*). *s.*

موگري मुगरी *mūgrī* or मोगरी *mogrī*, f. a mallet for beating cloths with, &c. *s.*

موگھ मोघ *mogh*, vain, useless, fruitless; f. trumpet-flower (*Bignonia suaveolens*). *s.*

موگھاس मोघाश *moghās*, indulging vain hopes. *s.*

موگھگیان मोघज्ञान *mogha-gyān*, m. cultivating worldly or vain knowledge, or any sort of knowledge that is not religious. *s.*

مول मूल *mūl*, m. origin, root, race, generation; text (of a book, opposed to notes); name of the nineteenth lunar mansion (ν or υ *Scorpionis*); adj. real. *s.*

مول मोल *mol*, m. purchase; price. *mol-lenā*, a. to buy, purchase. *mol-baṛhānā*, a. to enhance. *mol-tol*, fixing a price; traffic, purchasing. *mol-ṭhahrānā*, to appraise, to estimate, to value. *s.*

مولا *maulā* (for *maulạ*), m. a master, a lord; judge, magistrate; a slave. *maulā,e a'lā*, a patron, one who makes or promises a bequest. *maulā,e asfal*, a client; one in whose favour a bequest is made. *a.*

مولا *mūlā*, an angle, a corner. *d.*

مولانا *maulānā*, (lit. our Lord, &c.), m. a title given to persons respected for learning, a doctor. *a.*

مولاٸي *maulā,ī*, f. judgeship, lordship. *a.*

مولد *maulid*, m. nativity, birth; native land, birthplace. *muwallad*, begotten: the term is applied in India to Arabs born in that country, whether pure or half-caste. *a.*

مولسري मौलसरी *maulsarī*, f. name of a tree (*Mimusops elengi*). *h.*

مولع *mūla'*, addicted to, passionately fond of. *a.*

مولف *muwallif* or *mu,allif*, a compiler, a composer, author, editor. *mu,allaf*, composed, edited (a book). *a.*

مولفات *mu,allafāt*, pl. writings, compositions, compilations. *a.*

مولك मौलिक *maulik*, of inferior rank or caste among *Kāyasths*. *s.*

مولم *mūlam* (*bawāsīr*), emeroids, piles. *d.*

مولمي *mūlamī* (*siṛī*), mad, insane. *d.*

مولنا मौलना *maulnā*, n. to bloom, to bud, to blossom (the mango tree); to intoxicate (as *bhang*, &c.). *h.*

مولود *maulūd*, born, generated; a son; birthday, nativity; an elegiac chant, funeral service. *a.*

مولودي *maulūdī*, m. a mourner, one who chants the *maulūd*. *a.*

موله *mūlah* or *muwallah*, disturbed, struck, distracted with love, grief, or fear. *a.*

مولوي *maulavī*, m. a learned man, a doctor. *a.*

مولىٰ *maulạ* (v. *maulā*), lord, master. *a.*

مولي मूली *mūlī*, f. a radish. *s.*

مولي मौली *maulī*, f. a lock of hair on the crown of the head; a diadem, a tiara; the head. *s.*

موليا मूलिया *mūliyā*, born while the moon is in *mūl* (ν or υ *Scorpionis*), which is considered unlucky. *s.*

موليرا *maulerā* (*bhā,ī*), mother's brother's son. *d.*

موليري *maulerī* (*bahin*), mother's brother's daughter. *d.*

موليه मूल्य *mūlya*, m. price. *s.*

موم *mom*, m. wax. *mom-battī*, a wax candle. *mom-jāma*, m. wax-cloth. *mom-dil*, tender-hearted. *mom-raughan*, wax and oil mixed together. *mom kī nāk*, a person of a fickle disposition. *p.*

موماكهي मौमाखी *maumākhī*, f. a honey-bee. *s.*

مومن *mūmin*, orthodox, faithful, believing; m. a Musalmān weaver. *a.*

مومنين *mūminīn*, pl. the faithful. *amīru-l-mūminīn*, commander of the faithful, a title adopted by the caliph Omar and retained by his successors. *a.*

مومي *momī*, waxen; of the colour of wax; (applied to chintz), prepared after stamping, by covering the flowers with wax to prevent their being spoiled by other colours afterwards applied. *p.*

موميٰ *mūmạ*, hinted at, mentioned, agreed on. *mūmạ-ilaihi*, aforesaid, above-mentioned. *a.*

موميا *momiyā*, m. a mummy. *p.*

مومياٸي *momiyā,ī*, f. name of a medicine; adj. of or resembling a mummy. *p.*

مون मौन *maun*, m. silent (as devotees who have made a vow not to speak); taciturnity. *s.*

مون *mūn* or *mon*, mouth, face. *mūn-ger*, headstrong. *d.*

مونا मौना *maunā*, m. a large jar; a basket. *h.*

مونا मूना *mūnā*, n. to die. *s.*

مونتا मौनता *maunatā*, f. taciturnity, silence. *s.*

مونت *maunat* or *ma,unat*, f. provisions, daily food; a wallet; saddle-bags. *a.*

مونث *muwannas*, feminine, effeminate. *a.*

مونج मूंज *mūnj*, } m. the name of a grass of
مونجا मूंजा *mūnjā*, } which ropes are made (*Saccharum munja*). *s.*

مونجي मौञ्जी *maunjī* or *mūnjī*, f. the girdle of a Brāhman made of three strings of *munj* grass. *maunjī bandhan*, m. investiture with the sacrificial cord. *s.*

مونچ मूंच *mūnch*, } f. moustaches, the hair
مونچھ मूंछ *mūnchh*, } on the upper lip. *s.*

مونڌري मूंदरी *mūndrī*, f. a finger-ring. *s.*

مونڌنا मूंदना *mūndnā*, a. to shut, to cover, to close, to imprison, to involve. *s.*

مونڈ मूंड़ *mūṅḍ*, m. the head. *mūṅḍ-bherā*, butting (as rams). *mūṅḍ pānā*, a. to coax, to wheedle. *s.*

مونڈچورا मूंड़चूरा *mūṅḍ-chūrā*, m. a kind of pillar. *h.*

مونڈلا मूंड़ला *mūṅḍlā*, shaved, cropped. *s.*

مونڈنا मूंड़ना *mūṅḍnā*, a. to shave; to instruct, convert or make a disciple of; to wheedle out of any thing. *ulṭe usture se mūṅḍnā*, to cheat one. *s.*

مونڈھا मूंढ़ा *mūṅḍhā* or मोंढा *moṅḍhā*, m. the shoulder, a hump; a footstool; shoots of the sugar-cane. *h.*

مونڈي मूंड़ी *mūṅḍī*, f. the head, the summit. *s.*

مونڑ मूंड़ *mūṅṛ*, m. the head, the top. *s.*

مونڑلا मूंड़ला *mūṅṛlā*, head-shaven. *s.*

مونڑنا मूंड़ना *mūṅṛnā*, a. to shave. *s.*

مونس *mūnis* or *mu,nis*, m. a companion, an intimate friend; soliciting; Thursday. *a.*

مونسل मूंसल *mūṅsal* (for *mūsal*, q. v.), a wooden pestle. *s.*

مونسلا *mūṅslā* (v. *mūslā*), a tap-root, &c. *s.*

مونکي मूंकी *mūṅkī*, f. a blow with the fist. *h.*

مونگ मूंग *mūṅg*, f. name of a kind of pulse commonly called black gram (*Phaseolus mungo*). *mūṅg-phalī*, f. the name of the ground-nut, or pig-nut of the West Indies (*Arachis hypogæa*). *s.*

مونگا *mūṅgā*, m. the morunga or horse-radish tree (called in Urdū *sahajnā* or *sanjhnā*). *d.*

مونگا मूंगा *mūṅgā*, m. coral. *h.*

مونگچي मूंगची *mūṅgchī*, } f. name of a dish
مونگري मूंगरी *mūṅgrī*, } made with *mūṅg*. *s.*

مونگيا मूंगिया *mūṅgiyā*. m. name of a colour (red coral coloured). *h.*

مونو मूनू *mūnū*, little, of small quantity. *h.*

مونه मूंह *mūṅh* or *moṅh*, m. the mouth, the face (v. *muṅh*). *s.*

مونهاں मूंहां *mūṅhāṅ*, m. soreness in the mouth, the aphthæ or thrush, salivation. *mūṅhāṅ-mūṅh*, *tête-à-tête*, face to face; brimful, topful. *mūṅhāṅ-mūṅhī*, f. altercation, squabble, wrangle. *s.*

مونهري मोंहरी *moṅhrī*, f. a kennel, a drain. *s.p.*

موني मौनी *maunī*, f. a small round basket, a work-basket. *monī*, f. point, end. *h.*

موني मौनी *maunī*, silent, tacit; m. a class of mendicants who make a vow to observe perpetual silence, like Paul the Silentiary. *s.*

موه मोह *moh*, f. fainting, senselessness, ignorance, folly, spiritual ignorance, error, bewilderment; pity, compassion, sympathy, kindness, affection, allurement, fascination. *moh-lenā*, a. to attach, to allure, to fascinate. *moh meṅ ānā*, to faint, as at the sudden appearance of a friend or mistress. *s.*

موه मोहि *mohi*, pron. to me, me. *h.*

موها *mohā*, m. (in Urdū *mahu,ā*) name of a tree. *d.*

موهانا मोहाना *mohānā*, m. the mouth (of river), inlet, outlet. *s.*

موهب *mauhib*, m. a present, a gift. *mūhab*, any thing presented, unbought. *mūhib*, one who accepts a present, the person to whom any thing is given. *a.*

موهت मोहित *mohit*, faint, senseless; allured, fascinated, charmed. *s.*

موهن मोहन *mohan*, adj. fascinating, stupefying, m. seduction, the overpowering of reason by sensual allurements; copulation; a sweetheart, a mistress; a name of *Krishṇa*. *mohan-bhog*, a kind of sweetmeat. *mohan-mālā*, name of an ornament, a string or necklace composed of gold, beads, and corals. *s.*

موهنا मोहना *mohnā*, a. to allure, to charm, or steal. *mohanā*, winning, captivating, charming. *s.*

موهني मोहनी *mohnī* or *mohinī*, f. an enchantress, a courtesan; a philter. *mohinī*, f. a kind of jasmine, called also *tripurā-mālī*. *s.*

موهوب *mauhūb*, given, granted. *mauhūb ilaihi*, (in law) a legatee. *a.*

موهوم *mauhūm*, imagined, imaginary. *a.*

موهي मोही *mohī* (fem. *mohinī*), illusion, beguiling. *s.*

موي موی *mū,e*, m. hair. *mū,e nihānī* or *mū,e zihār*, or *mū,e 'āna*, hair (*Circa pubes*). *p.*

مويد *mu,aiyad*, confirmed, fortified. *a.*

مويز *mawez* or *mawīz*, m. a raisin; dried grapes. *p.*

مويشي *maweshī* (corrup. of *mawāshī*), f. a herd or drove of oxen. *a.*

مويه *moya*, weeping, lamentation. *p.*

مه *mih*, great, chief, principal. *mah*, m. the moon; a month. *mah-pāra*, a mistress. *p.*

مه महि *mahi*, f. the earth. *s.*

مها महा *mahā*, great, illustrious; very, extremely. *mahā-brāhman* or *-pātr*, a Brāhman who officiates at funerals, and is first fed after the mourning for a dead person. *mahā-pāp*, atrocity, great sin. *mahā-pāpī*, atrocious, great sinner. *mahā-pātak*, great crime, mortal sin, as killing a Brāhman, &c. *mahā-pātakī*, a great offender. *mahā-prabhu*, m. a holy man, a king. *mahā-purush*, a holy man. *mahā-prasād*, the meat which is offered to the Deity (especially to *Jagannāth*), and afterwards distributed. *mahā-jāl*, a seine, a large fishing-net. *mahā-rāj*, great king, excellency. *mahā-rājā*, a Hindū emperor. *mahārājā-dhirāj*, a paramount sovereign, an emperor. *mahā-rānī*, f. an empress. *mahā-sankh*, the skull of a dead body. *mahā-mārī*, the plague, pestilence, or any epidemical disease. *mahāmāṅs*, human flesh (one who takes money on giving his daughter in marriage is said to sell [*mahāmāṅs*] human flesh). *s.*

مهابت *mahābat*, f. majesty, greatness, reverence, fear, dread, awe. *a.*

مهابلي महाबली *mahā-balī*, of great power or strength. *s.*

مهابهارت महाभारत *mahā-bhārat*, f. the great war of the descendants of *Bhārata*; the name of the grand epic poem of the Hindūs by *Vyāsadeva*, containing an account of the dissensions and wars of the *Kurus* and *Pāṇḍus*. two great collateral branches of the house of *Bhārata*, so called from *Bharata*, its founder. *s.*

مہابھاگ महाभाग *mahā-bhāg*, pure, holy, virtuous in a high degree; eminent, exalted. *s.*

مہابھاگتا महाभागता *mahā-bhāgtā*, possession of the eight cardinal virtues; exalted station or merit. *s.* [sillanimous, cowardly. *s.*

مہابھیت महाभीत *mahā-bhīt*, very timid, pu-

مہابھیتا महाभीता *mahā-bhītā*, f. a sort of sentive plant (*Mimosa pudica*). *s.*

مہاپات महापात *mahā-pāt*, } m. a heinous
مہاپاتك महापातक *mahā-pātak*, } crime, such as the murder of a Brāhman. *s.*

مہاپاسك महापासक *mahā-pāsak*, m. a religious mendicant. *s.*

مہاپتھ महापथ *mahā-path*, m. the main road, the principal path or entrance; the way of all flesh. *s.*

مہاپرساد महाप्रसाद *mahā-prasād*, m. an offering of food, &c., to an idol. *s.*

مہاپرش महापुरुष *mahā-purush*, m. a great man, applied especially to religious ascetics. *s.*

مہاپرلی महाप्रलय *mahā-pralaya*, m. a destruction of the world, occurring after every period of 4,320,000,000 years; a total destruction of the universe, happening after a period commensurate with the life of Brahmā, or 100 years, each day of which is equal to the period above stated, and each night of which is of similar duration: at the expiration of this term the seven *lokas* or divisions of the universe, with the saints, gods, and Brahmā himself, are annihilated. *s.* [(*Clitoria ternatea*). *s.*

مہاپشپا महापुष्पा *mahā-pushpā*, f. a flower

مہاپکشی महापक्षी *mahā-pakshī*, f. an owl. *s.*

مہاتکت महातिक्त *mahātikt*, very bitter; m. the large *nīm* tree (*Melia sempervirens*). *s.*

مہاتل महातल *mahātal*, m. the fifth in descending of the seven *pātāls* or regions under the earth; said to be inhabited by various races of evil beings, such as the *nāgas*, the *asurs*, the *daityas*, &c. *s.*

مہاتم महातम *mahātam*, m. greatness, grandeur, rank, dignity; the benefit derived from any good work. *s.* [mous. *s*

مہاتما महात्मा *mahātmā*, liberal, magnani-

مہاتمپربھا महातमप्रभा *mahātam-prabhā*, f. the very lowest division of *nāraka* or hell. *s.*

مہاتیجا महातेजा *mahā-tejā*, very bright, very energetic or vigorous. *s.*

مہاتیشن महातीक्ष्ण *mahā-tīshṇ*, very sharp (literally or figuratively). *s.*

مہاجان महाज्ञान *mahā-jān*, of great knowledge, very wise. *s.*

مہاجر *muhājir*, one who abandons or quits (his native country). *a.*

مہاجرت *muhājarat*, m. separation, distance, desertion, flight, abandoning (a country). *a.*

مہاجشا महायशा *mahā-jashā*, illustrious. *s.*

مہاجگ महायुग *mahā-jug*, m. v *mahā-yug*. *s.*

مہاجگیہ महायज्ञ *mahā-jagya*, m. an essential sacrifice, a sacrament. *s.*

مہاجن महाजन *mahā-jan*, m. a banker, a money-dealer, merchant; a good or trustworthy person. *s.*

مہاجنتر महायन्त्र *mahā-jantr*, m. any great mechanical work, a lock, a dyke. *s.*

مہاجنی महाजनी *mahājanī*, f. the business of a *mahājan*; interest, commission. *s.*

مہاد *mihād*, m. a throne, sofa, bed, chair. *a.*

مہادنت महादन्त *mahā-dant*, of large tusks; m. an elephant. *s.*

مہادھات महाधातु *mahā-dhātu*, m. gold; the great metal (*par excellence*). *s.*

مہادیو महादेव *mahādev* or *mahā-deva*, m. a name of *Shiva*. *s.*

مہاڈول महाडोल *mahā-ḍol*, m. a state *pālkī* for princes and great personages. *s.*

مہار *mahār*, f. reins, a bridle; a piece of wood put through a perforation in the nose of a camel to guide him by. *p.*

مہارا म्हारा *mhārā*, pos. pron. my, mine. *h.*

مہاراتر महारात्र *mahā-rātr*, m. midnight. *s.*

مہاراج महाराज *mahā-rāj*, m. a sovereign, an emperor; excellency. *s.*

مہارانی महारानी *mahā-rānī*, f. a queen in her own right. *s.* [excellence. *a.*

مہارت *mahārat*, f. subtlety, acuteness, genius,

مہاڑی *mhāṛī*, a house, mansion, palace, the upper story of a house. *d.* [in youth). *s.*

مہاسا मुहासा *muhāsā*, m. a pimple (on the face

مہاسانتپن महासान्तपन *mahā-sāntapan*, m. sort of ridiculous and disgusting penance. *s.*

مہاساهس महासाहस *mahā-sāhas*, m. excessive violence, brutal assault. *s.*

مہاستوہ महासत्त्व *mahā-satwa*, good, virtuous, just. *s.* [lation. *s.*

مہاسکھ महासुख *mahā-sukh*, m. coition, copu-

مہاسوچھم महासूक्ष्म *mahā-sūchhma* or *mahā-sūkshma*, subtile, fine, minute. *s.*

مہاشٹمی महाष्टमी *mahāshṭamī*, (lit. the great eighth); the eighth (day or night) of the bright fortnight of *āsin*. *s.*

مہاشنکھ महाशङ्ख *mahā-shankh*, m. a thousand millions. *s.* [nanimous, liberal. *s.*

مہاشی महाशय *mahā-shay* or *mahāshaya*, mag-

مہاکال महाकाल *mahā-kāl* or *mahākāla*, a name or rather a form of *Shiva* as identified with Time, in his character of the destroying deity, being then represented of a black colour, and of an aspect more or less terrific: *Shiva* or *Mahākāla* may be considered as a personification of time, that destroys all things. *s.*

مهاكالي महाकाली *mahā-kālī*, f. the wife of *Shiva*, and one of the terrific forms of *Durgā*. *s.*

مهاكايه महाकाय *mahā-kāya*, large-bodied, bulky, stout. *s.*

مهاكل महाकुल *mahā-kul*, } eminent by
مهاكلين महाकुलीन *mahākulīn*, } birth, of good family or extraction. *s.*

مهاكند महाकन्द *mahā-kand*, m. garlic, a very large esculent root, a sort of yam. *s.*

مهاكوپ महाकूप *mahā-kūp*, m. a large or deep well. *s.*

مهاكوڙه महाकोढ़ *mahā-koṛh*, m. a species of leprosy. *s.*

مهاكول महाकूल *mahā-kūl*, of a good family. *s.*

مهاكهال महाखाल *mahā-khāl*, m. a rush of the sea upon a contiguous flat region. *s.*

مهال *mahāl*, formidable, dreadful (places). *a.*

مهالوه महालोह *mahā-loh*, m. the loadstone, magnet. *s.*

مهالي महालय *mahā-lay*, m. God, the Supreme Being; a place of refuge, a sanctuary, an asylum. *s.*

مهام *mahāmm* (pl. of مهمه), serious affairs, important transactions. *a.*

مهاماش महामाष *mahā-māsh*, m. a kind of bean (*Dolichos catjang*). *s.*

مهامانس *mahā-māṅs*, m. human flesh. *s.*

مهامايا महामाया *mahā-māyā*, f. the goddess *Durgā*; worldly illusion or unreality. *s.*

مهامولیه महामूल्य *mahā-mūlya*, costly, precious; m. a ruby. *s.*

مهاموه महामोह *mahāmoh*, very ignorant. *s.*

مهاميد महामेद *mahā-med*, m. the coral tree; a drug so named, described as a tonic and stimulant. *s.*

مهانا मुहाना *muhānā*, m. the mouth of a river; channel or bed of a river; an estuary, the conflux of two rivers. *s.*

مهانا मिहाना *mihānā*, n. to grow damp. *h.*

مهانبهاو महानुभाष *mahānubhā,o*, magnanimous, liberal; m. a gentleman. *s.*

مهاندرا महानिद्रा *mahā-nidrā*, f. (long sleep) death. *s.*

مهانرك महानरक *mahā-narak*, m. a division of hell. *s.*

مهانشا महानिशा *mahā-nishā*, f. midnight. *s.*

مهانمب महानिम्ब *mahā-nimb*, m. a large kind of nimb tree (*Melia sempervirens*). *s.*

مهانند महानन्द *mahānand*, m. eternal beatitude. *s.*

مهانومي महानवमी *mahānavamī*, f. the ninth day of the bright fortnight of *āsin*. *s.*

مهاني *mihānī*, मिहानी f. a churn. *h.*

مهانيل महानील *mahā-nīl*, m. the emerald. *s.*

مهاوت महावत *mahāwat*, } m. an elephant
مهاوته महावथ *mahāwath*, } driver or keeper (commonly written *mahout*). *s.*

مهاوتني *mahāwatnī*, } f. wife of a *mahāwat*. *s.*
مهاوتي *mahāwatī*, }

مهاوٹه महावठ *mahāwaṭh*, m. rain which falls in the month of *Māgh*. *s.*

مهاور महावर *mahāwar*, m. the red colour extracted from lac insects. *h.*

مهاوش महाविष *mahā-vish*, m. a small snake highly venomous (supposed to be two-headed). *s.*

مهاوشو महाविषुव *mahā-vishuv*, m. the moment of the vernal equinox. *s.*

مهاون महावन *mahā-van*, m. a large forest. *s.*

مهاويچ महावीचि *mahā-vīchi*, f. one of the divisions of the infernal regions. *s.*

مهاهاس महाहास *mahā-hās*, m. a boisterous laugh. *s.*

مهايشا महायशा *mahā-yashā*, illustrious, celebrated. *s.*

مهايگ महायुग *mahā-yug*, m. the agregate of the four *yugas* or ages, being 4,320,000,000 years. *s.*

مهايگي महायज्ञ *mahā-yagya*, m. an essential sacrifice, a kind of sacrament of the Hindū religion. *s.*

مهاينتر महायन्त्र *mahā-yantra*, m. any great mechanical work, as a lock or dyke. *s.*

مهب *mahabb*, m. a vent; a place whence or whither the wind blows. *muhibb*, waking, rousing; *libidine actus et in fœmellam insiliens admissarius*. *a.*

مهت महत *mahat*, great, glorious, large, bulky; excellent; f. greatness, grandeur, dignity. *s.*

مهتا महता *mahtā*, m. a scribe, a clerk; an agent or man of business. *s.*

مهتاب *mahtāb*, m. the moon; moonshine; a kind of fireworks. *p.*

مهتابي *mahtābī*, f. a kind of fireworks; an open high terrace; adj. of or belonging to the moon; ornamented with gold, tinsel, &c. *p.*

مهتادي महतादी *mahtādi*, m. a head village peon; a village bailiff or constable. *s.*

مهتاري महतारी *mahtārī*, f. a mother. *s.*

مهتدي *muhtadī*, directed, guided, steered (to the right or left). *a.*

مهتر *mihtar*, greater; m. a prince; a chief; a sweeper. *p.*

مهتراني *mihtarānī*, f. female of *mihtar*; also a female innkeeper. *p.*

مهتراعي *mihtarā,ī*, f. chiefship. *p.*

مهتم *muhtamm* or *muhtimm*, solicitous, anxious, concerned (for another). *a.*

مهتمم *muhtamim*, thoughtful, anxious; a superintendant, factor. *muhtamim band o bast*, a government officer who settles the revenue of villages, districts, &c. *a.*

مهتو महतो *mahto*, m. the headman of a village; a person employed by the landholder to collect the rent from a village; a land bailiff. *s.*

مهتول *muhtawil*, terrified, trembling. *a.*

مهتوہ महत्त्व *mahattwa*, m. greatness (in bulk, in rank, or in merit). *s.*

مهجالا *mahjālā* (for *mahā-jālā*), a large net. *d.*

مهجور *mahjūr*, separated, cut off, left, forsaken (especially by one's beloved). *a.*

مهجوري *mahjūrī*, f. absence, separation. *a.*

مهچه *mahcha*, m. a little moon, the ornament or emblem on the top of an ensign staff, the crescent (of the Saracens). *p*

مهد *mahad* or *mahd*, m. a swing, a cradle. *a.*

مهداسري महदाश्रय *mahad-āsray*, dependent upon, or attached to the great. *s.*

مهدوم *mahdūm*, destroyed, totally ruined. *a.*

مهدي *mahdī*, a guide or convoy; the name of the twelfth and last Imām, according to the doctrines of the Shī'ahs, who is said to be still living, but invisible, and will appear at the approach of the day of judgment.—(B.) *a.* [plant. *s.*

مهدي मिहदी *mihdī*, f. (v. *meṅhdī*) name of a

مهر *mahar*, m. a marriage portion or gift settled upon the wife before marriage; contracting by writing for such settlement. *mahari misl*, the marriage portion settled and determined by the mother or female relatives of the bride, according to her rank, and equal to the portions of her married friends of the same station. *mahr-nāma*, a deed of settlement (of dowry). *a.*

مهر *muhr* or *muhur*, f. a seal; a gold coin; virginity, maidenhead; the gold *muhr* is sixteen *rupīs*, or nearly a guinea and a half of our money, at Calcutta, and fifteen *rupis* at Madras and Bombay. *p.*

مهر *mihr*, m. love, friendship, affection, kindness; the sun; the name of a Persian month in which falls the autumnal equinox. *p.*

مهر महर *mahar*, m. a chief. *mahar* or *mahri*, f. a wife, a woman. *h.*

مهر *muhr*, m. a peacock. *d.*

مهرا महरा *mahrā*, m. a *pālkī* bearer. *mihrā*, a man who appears in the habit of a woman. *muhrā*, m. van, vanguard. *h.*

مهرا *muharrā*, pounded, comminuted. *a.*

مهرارو मिहरारू *mihrārū*, f. a woman. *h.*

مهرانہ *mahrāna*, a fee paid to the *ḳāẓī* at a wedding. *a. p.*

مهراءي महराई *mahrā,ī* or *mihrā,ī*, f. the business of a *pālkī* bearer; a kind of song among the cow herds. *h.*

مهربان *mihr-bān*, friendly, kind, affectionate. *p.*

مهربانگي *mihr-bāngī*, } f. friendliness, kindness, favour. *mihr-bānī-k.*, to favour, to have the goodness (to do any thing). *p.*
مهرباني *mihr-bānī*,

مهرت मुहुरत *muhurt* (for *muhūrat*, q. v.). *s.*

مهردار *muhr-dār*, keeper of the seal. *p.*

مهرگل *muhri gul*, a species of cloth. *p.*

مهركن *muhr-kan*, a seal-engraver. *muhr-kanī*, the art of seal engraving. *p.*

مهركوا *muhr kawwā*, the crow-pheasant (*Cuculus castaneus*), also called *mahokhā*, q. v. *d.*

مهرلوك महर्लोक *maharlok*, m. a division of the universe destined for the reception of saints. *s.*

مهرمهو मुहुर्मुहु *muhur-muhu*, again and again. *s.*

مهرو *mah-rū* (v. *māh-rū*), moon-faced, beautiful. *p.*

مهروا मिहरवा *mihrwā*, f. a woman. *h.*

مهرورزي *mihr-warzī*, f. kindness, acting friendly. *p.*

مهروش *mihr-wash*, like the sun. *p.*

مهرونتا *mihr-wantā*, affectionate, kind. *p. h.*

مهره *muhra*, m. a shell; a rubber; a chessman, a counter for playing at any game, as chess, draughts, &c.; a charmed stone said to be found in the head of a serpent. *p.*

مهره‌دار *muhra-dār*, polished, glazed. *p*

مهري *muhrī*, f. a drain, a gutter; adj. sealed, stamped. *p.*

مهري मुहरी *muhrī*, f. the cuff of the sleeve of a jacket, or the extremity of the leg of a pair of trousers; the bore (of a gun). *h.*

مهري मिहरी *mihrī*, } f. a woman. *h.*
مهريا मिहरिया *mihriyā*,

مهش महिष *mahiṣh*, m. a male buffalo. *s.*

مهشاكش महिषाक्ष *mahiṣh-ākṣh*, m. name of a plant, the bdellium tree. *s.*

مهشي महिषी *mahiṣhī*, f. the female buffalo. *s.*

مهك महक *mahak*, f. odour, perfume, fragrance. *mahakk*, m. diffusive fragrance. *h.*

مهكانا महकाना *mahkānā*, a. to exhale (agreeable scent); to diffuse perfume, to regale. *h.*

مهكنا महकना *mahaknā*, n. to exhale agreeable smells, to emit odour, to be perfumed. *h.*

مهكيلا महकीला *mahkīlā*, odoriferous, spicy, aromatic. *h.*

مهلت *muhlat*, f. retarding, deferring; laziness, indolence; respite, time, leisure. *a.*

مهلك महल्लक *mahallak*, m. (v. *maḥallī*) a eunuch. *a. h.* [deadly. *a.*

مهلك *muhlik*, destroying, killing, fatal,

مهلكه *mahlaka*, m. a dangerous place, a desert, a place of slaughter. *a.*

مهم *muhimm*, f. important, urgent, momentous business. *a.*

مهما महिमा *mahimā*, f. grandeur, greatness. *s.*

مهمات *muhimmāt*, pl. important affairs, subjects of great moment; expeditions. *a.*

مهمان *mihmān*, m. a stranger; a guest; a son-in-law. *mihmān-dār*, an entertainer, host; an officer appointed to receive and entertain an ambassador. *mihmān-dārī*, f. hospitality; situation of *mihmān-dār*. *p.*

مهمان‌پرور *mihmān-parwar*, hospitable. *p.*

مهمان‌خانه *mihmān-khāna*, مهمان‌سراي *mihmān-sarā,e*, } m. a house for the entertainment of guests or strangers, a hospitable mansion. *p.*

مهماني *mihmānī*, f. entertainment, hospitality; adj. relating to a guest, &c. *p.*

مهمل *muhmil*, negligent, careless, indolent. *muhmal*, obsolete; m. a buffoon. *a.*

مهملات *muhmalāt*, absurdities. *a.*

مهمله *muhmala*, without points (letter). *a.*

مهموز *mahmūz*, having the symbol *hamza* (applied to the letters *alif* or *wāo* or *ye* marked with *hamza*, shewing it to be a radical letter). *a.*

مهميز *mihmīz*, a spur. *mihmīz-khur*, a horse that will bear the spur. *p.*

مهنا महना *mahnā*, a. to churn. *s.*

مهنا मिहना *mihnā*, m. sarcasm. *mihnā phenknā*, to sneer. *h.*

مهنت महन्त *mahant*, m. a monk, an abbot, a religious superior, a chief of the *fakirs*. *s.*

مهنتاءي महन्ताई *mahantā,ī*, مهنتي महन्ती *mahantī*, } f. the rank or office of a *mahant*. *s.*

مهندس *muhandis*, m. a geometrician. *a.*

مهندسي *muhandisī*, f. geometry. *a.*

مهندي *mihindī* or *mihndī*, f. (v. *menhdī* or *mihdī*). *s.*

مهنگا महङ्गा *mahangā*, m. dear, high-priced, [expensive. *s.*

مهنگي महङ्गी *mahangī*, f. a dearth, scarcity, famine; adj. f. dear, high-priced. *s.*

مهوءا महुआ *mahu,ā* or महूआ *mahū,ā* (also *mahwā*), m. name of a tree (*Bassia latifolia*) bearing flowers which are sweet, and from which a spirituous liquor is distilled commonly called Parsee brandy. The tree appears to be the same as the Shea-tree of Africa described in the travels of Mungo Park and others. The nuts afford an oil used instead of butter. *s.*

مهوار *mahwār*, m. مهوارا *mahwārā*, m. مهواري *mahwārī*, f. } monthly pay or salary; a deed settling the payment of revenue by monthly instalments. *p.*

مهوتساه महोत्साह *mahotsāh*, persevering, diligent; m. diligence, effort, exertion. *s.*

مهوتسو महोत्सव *mahotsav*, m. a great festival. *s.*

مهوچھ महोच्छ *mahochh*, m. an ox; a blockhead. *s.*

مهوچها महोछा *mahochhā*, m. a funeral feast among *fakirs*. *s.*

مهودار महोदार *mahodār*, mighty, powerful. *s.*

مهودي महोदय *mahoday*, m. Kanauj (both the ancient city and district); final beatitude (v *mukti*); prosperity, elevation. *s.*

مهوديم महोद्यम *mahodyam*, diligent, persevering; m. great effort, energy, exertion. *s.*

مهور *muhūr* (pl. of مهر), marriage portions. *a.*

مهور *mhūr*, m. (v. *muhr*) a peacock. *d.*

مهورت मुहूर्त *muhūrt*, *mahūrt* or *mahūrat*, f. a time consisting of two *gharīs* or forty-eight minutes; a moment, especially a lucky moment (in astrology). *s.*

مهوري *mhūrī*, f. a water channel, drain, pipe. *d.*

مهوس *muhauwas*, very desirous, distractedly in love. *muhauwis*, m. an alchemist. *a.*

مهوسا महोसा *mahosā*, مهوسه *mahosa*. } m. a freckle, a spot. *h.*

مهوسي *muhauwisī*, f. alchymy. *a. h.*

مهوش *mah-wash*, moon-like; (met.) a sweetheart, a beautiful and lovely woman. *p.*

مهوشدھ महौषध *mahaushadh*, m. garlic, long pepper. *mahaushadhī*, f. *dūb* grass; a kind of sensitive plant (*Mimosa pudica*). *s.*

مهوشدھي महौषधी *mahaushadhī*, f. dry ginger a potherb (*Hingsta repens*). *s.*

مهوکش महोक्ष *mahoksh*, m. a large bull or ox. *s.*

مهوکها महोखा *mahokhā*, m. the name of a bird commonly called the crow pheasant (*Cuculus castaneus*, *Buch.*). *h.*

مهي मही *mahī*, f. the earth; butter-milk; name of a river. *mahī-pat* or *mahī-pati*, m. lord of the earth. *mahī-may*, earthen, made of earth. *s.*

مهيا *muhaiyā*, prepared, ready, arranged. *a.*

مهيب *muhīb*, formidable, awful, severe, grave, revered. *a.*

مهيپ महीप *mahīp*, مهيپال महीपाल *mahīpāl*, مهيپت महीपति *mahīpati*, } m. lord of the earth, sovereign, prince, king, ruler. *s.* [earth. *s.*

مهيتل महीतल *mahī-tal*, m. the surface of the

مهير महेर *maher*, m. مهيري महेरी *maherī*, f. } the name of a dish consisting of rice or other grain, boiled in sour milk. *h.*

مهيره महीरुह *mahī-ruh*, m. a tree. *s.*

مهيس महेस *mahes*, مهيش महेश *mahesh*, مهيشور महेश्वर *maheshwar*, } m. a name of *Mahādeva* or *Shiva*; a worshipper or follower of *Shiva*. *s.*

مهيلا महेला *mahelā*, m. a food given to horses, consisting of boiled kidney beans (*Phaseolus max.*); a mash. *s.*

مهيلتا महीलता *mahī-latā*, f. an earth-worm. *s.*

مهين *mihīn*, fine, subtile, thin (not coarse). *mihīn-doz*, a tailor, a person who performs any fine needlework. *p.*

مهين *mihīn* (for *mihtarīn*), greatest, eldest [born. *p.*

مهينا *mahīnā*, m. a month; monthly pay. *mahīnā charhnā*, to be in arrears. *mahīnā-dār*, a monthly servant. *p.*

مهيندا *mhendā*, m. } the plant called Egyptian privet (*Lawsonia*
مهيندي *mhendī*, f. } *inermis*), from the leaves of which a red dye is extracted with which natives of the East stain their hands and feet. *d.*

مهيندر महेन्द्र *mahendr*, m. *Indra*, the ruler of *Swarga*; name of a range of mountains. *s.*

مهيو महौ *mahyau*, m. buttermilk. *h.*

مي *mai*, f. wine, spirituous liquor. *mai-khor*, or *-khwāra*, or *-gusār*, a sot, a winebibber, a drunkard. *mai-kada* or *-khāna*, a tavern. *mai-gūn*, auburn, fair, wine-coloured. *mai nāb*, pure wine. *mai-nosh*, a winebibber. *mai-noshī*, wine-drinking. *s.*

مي मय *may* or *maya*, (in comp.) made or composed of, as, *mahi-may*, made of earth. *s.*

ميا मया *mayā*, f. kindness, pity, sympathy, compassion, mercy, feeling, affection (v. *māyā*). *s.*

ميا मैया *maiyā*, f. (same as *mā*) a mother. *s.*

ميان मियाँ *miyāṅ* or *myāṅ*, m. sir, master, an address expressive of respect, especially to an elderly person; a schoolmaster; a title by which eunuchs are addressed. *miyāṅ ādmī*, a respectable person. *miyāṅ-jī*, the respected master, especially applied to a schoolmaster. *h.*

ميان *miyān*, f. a scabbard; the loins, the waist, the middle. *miyān-basta*, ready, prepared (for action), loin-girded. *miyān-tahī*, f. the middle fold of any garment which consists of three. *miyāṅ-jī*, m. a mediator, an arbitrator, a broker, a go-between. *p.*

ميانگي *miyānagī*, f. mediation. *p.*

ميانه *miyāna*, middling; (in Hind.) m. a kind of sedan or *pālkī*. *miyāna-ḳadd*, of middling stature. *p.*

مياني *miyānī*, f. a codpiece. *p.*

ميبها मैभा *maibhā*, f. stepmother. *s.*

مئت *mi,at*, a hundred. *a.*

ميت *maiyit* or *mait*, a dead body. *a.*

ميت मीत *mīt*, m. a friend, a lover. *s.*

ميت मीत *mīt*, } m. a pitcher; a porringer;
ميتا मीता *mītā*, } a cup. *h.*

ميتا मीता *mītā*, m. a namesake. *s.*

ميتر मैत्र *maitr* or *maitra*, friendly, amicable. *s.*

ميتري मैत्री *maitrī*, f. friendship; the seventeenth lunar asterism. *s.* [friend. *s.*

ميتن मीतन *mītan*, f. a female namesake or

ميتهل मैथिल *maithil* or *maithal*, inhabitant of Mithilā or Tirhūt. *s.*

ميتهن मैथुन *maithun*, m. venery, coition, union, marriage. *s.*

ميتهي मेथी *methī*, f. the plant fenugreek (*Trigonella fenugræcum*). *s.* [*gifera*). *s.*

ميٹلا मेटुला *meṭulā*, f. a tree (*Spondias man-*

ميٹنا मेटना *meṭnā*, a. to efface, to blot out, to atone for, to wipe out, to annihilate; to thwart. *h.*

ميٹها मीठा *mīṭhā*, sweet; slow; m. a very active vegetable poison; name of a fruit; an impotent man. *s.*

ميٹهاس मीठास *mīṭhās*, } f. sweetness, sweet-
ميٹهاءي मीठाई *mīṭhā,ī*, } meat in general. *mīṭhā,ī-wālā*, a maker or vender of sweetmeats, a confectioner. *s.*

ميٹهي मीठी *mīṭhī*, f. } a kiss. *h.*
ميٹهيا मीठिया *mīṭhiyā*, m. }

ميٹهي لكڑي *mīṭhī-lakṛī*, f. liquorice root. *h.*

ميٹي كدو *mīṭī kaddū*, f. red pumpkin. *d.*

ميثاق *mīsāḳ*, m. an agreement, a promise, compact, bargain, alliance, confederacy, league. *s.*

ميجنا मीजना *mījnā*, a. to rub with the hands. *s.*

ميجو मीजू *mīju*, m. lentil (v. *masūr*). *h.*

ميچ मीच *mīch*, f. death, extinction. *h.*

ميچك मेचक *mechak*, m. sulphuret of antimony. *s.*

ميچنا मीचना *mīchnā*, } a. to close the eyes, to
ميچهنا मीछना *mīchhnā*, } shut, to wink. *h.*

ميخ *mekh*, f. a nail, a tentpin, a hook, a tenter. *mekh ṭhonknā*, to nail. *mekh-chū*, f. a mallet, a hammer. *mekh mārnā*, to overcome. *p.*

ميخي *mekhī*, adulterated, plugged (as a coin). *mekhī rūpaiya*, a rupee which has been hollowed, and then filled with lead, copper, &c. *p.*

ميد मेद *med*, m. sacrifice, offering oblation; marrow; fat, excessive corpulency. *s.*

ميدا मेदा *medā*, f. a kind of drug; a sort of root resembling ginger. *s.*

ميدا *maidā* (for *maida*, q. v.), flour, &c. *p.*

ميدان *maidān*, m. a plain, an open field; a field of battle; parade ground. *p.*

ميداني *maidānī*, m. a person who precedes a general or *wazīr* and proclaims his titles; a kind of *ḥuḳḳa* used by *faḳīrs*; flour made into dough for the preparation of sweetmeats. *p.*

ميدسوي मेदस्वी *medaswī*, robust, stout, strong; fat, corpulent. *s.*

ميدني मेदिनी *medinī* or *mednī*, f. the earth; a body of pilgrims going to visit the tomb of a saint (in Dakh.) income, probably a corruption of *āmadnī*. *s.*

ميدوبردھ मेदोवृद्धि *medobriddhi*, f. corpulency, enlargement of the scrotum. *s.*

ميدودھرا मेदोधरा *medodhrā*, m. the omentum. *s.*

ميده *maida*, m. flour of the finest kind; also fine bread. *p.*

ميدھ मेध *medh*, m. (v. *med*) a sacrifice, &c. *s.*

ميدھ मेधि *medhi*, f. a post fixed in the centre of a threshing-floor, to which the cattle are attached as they turn round to tread out the corn. *h.*

ميدھ मेधा *medhā*, f. apprehension, understanding, sagacity, genius. *s.*

ميدھاوي मेधावी *medhāwī*, } intelligent, of ready compre-
ميدھر मेधिर *medhir*, } hension. *s.*

ميڈا मेडा *maiḍā* or मेड़ा *maiṛā*, a platform or scaffold in a corn-field where a person is stationed for watching the crop. *h.*

ميڈك *meḍak* (for *meṅḍak*, q. v.), a frog. *s. h.*

ميڈھ मेढ *meḍh*, gleanings of corn left on the field. *h.*

ميڈھا मेढा *meḍhā*, m. a ram. *s.*

ميذنه *mīzana* or *maizana*, the steeple of a mosque, from the top of which people are summoned to prayer. *a.*

مير *mīr*, a chief, leader; a title by which *saiyids* are addressed. *mīri ātish*, the chief of the fireworks, or artillery, master of the ordnance. *mīr-ātishī*, f. the office of *mīri ātish*. *mīr-ākhur*, master of the horse. *mīr-baḥr*, a collector of port duty. *mīr baḥrī*, harbour dues. *mīr-bakhshī*, paymaster-general. *mīr-sāmān*, head steward. *mīr shikār*, a birdcatcher; (met.) a pimp. *mīri 'adl*, a person who pronounced judgment on the offender, according to the sentence of the *ḳāẓī*. This office resembled that of the "doomster" in our Scottish courts in former days. *mīri majlis*, the master of the ceremonies. *mīri manzil*, quartermaster-general. *mīri-bandar*, m. superintendant of a sea-port. *mīr-bandarī*, f. situation of *mīri bandar*. *mīr-maḥalla*, inspector of police. *mīr-munshī*, chief secretary. *mīr-pesh-kār*, accountant-general. *mīr-tuzuk*, chief marshal, an officer whose duty it is to preserve order in a march or procession. *a. p.*

مير मेरु *meru*, m. name of an imaginary but very sacred mountain, which, according to the Hindūs, attains the very respectable elevation of 84,000 *yojanas*, or something near 672,000 English miles. *s.*

ميرا मेरा *merā*, (pron. progressive) my, mine. *h.*

ميراث *mīrāṡ*, f. heritage, patrimony, inherited property or right. *mīrāṡ-dār*, the holder of hereditary lands or offices. *a.*

ميراثن *mīrāṡan*, f. a singing-girl (of a caste who sing only before women). *a.*

ميراثي *mīrāṡī*, hereditary, inherited; m. a singer (of a caste who follow their profession from generation to generation). *mīrāṡī-ra'īyat*, a hereditary cultivator. *a.*

ميران *mīrān*, m. a portion paid to the head of a department out of the fees received by the inferior officers. *p.*

ميربخشي *mīr-bakhshī*, m. a generalissimo, paymaster-general. *p.*

ميردا *mīrdā*, a caste of migratory shepherds in the south of India, or an individual of that caste. *d.*

ميرزا *mīrzā*, m. (v. *mirzā*) a prince, grandee, noble. *mīrzā-manish*, of princely or noble rank, respectable: when this term is prefixed to a name it denotes "secretary," or "civilian" in general, as *Mīrzā-Ibrāhīm*; when it follows a name it denotes "prince," as *'Abbās-Mīrzā*. *p.*

ميرك मेरुक *meruk*, m. fragrant resin; incense. *h.*

ميرو मेरु *merū*, m. an axis. *s.*

ميرو मेरो *mero* or *merau*, pron. my, mine. *h.*

ميري *mīrī*, m. a winner at play (among schoolboys) he that comes first to the schoolmaster to say his lesson. *p.*

ميڑا *maiṛā*, a platform, a scaffold (v. *maiḍā*). *h.*

ميڑھ मेढ़ *meṛh* or मेढ़ा *meṛhā*, m. a ram. *s*

ميڑھشرنگي मेढ़शृङ्गी *meṛh-shṛingī*, f. a kind of milky plant, the fruit of which is crooked like a ram's horn (*Asclepias geminata*). *s.*

ميز *mez*, f. a table. *mez bichhānā*, a. to lay the cloth; (in Dakh.) *mez-lenā*, to take one's measure for a suit of clothes (probably a corruption of the English expression). *p.*

ميزان *mīzān*, f. a balance, a pair of scales, the sign *Libra*: measure, metre, rhyme, verse, prosody; the regulator of a watch; addition (in arithmetic). *mīzān denā* or *lagānā*, to add, to cast up. *a.*

ميزبان *mezbān*, } m. an entertainer, a host. *p.*
ميزمان *mez-mān*, }

ميزباني *mezbānī* or *mezmānī*, f. hospitality, housekeeping. *p.*

ميسر *muyassar*, attained, attainable, procurable, obtainable; facilitated, easy, favourable, practicable, possible. *a.*

ميسره *maisara* or *maisarat*, opulence, prosperity; the left wing of an army. *a.*

ميسنا मीसना *mīsnā*, a. to grind, pulverize, to tweak, to rumple, to crumple. *h.*

ميسور *maisūr*, facilitated, made easy, prosperous, going on successfully; the kingdom of Mysore. *a.*

ميسورات *maisūrāt*, prosperous affairs, good fortune. *a.*

ميسي *mesī*, f. goat or sheepskin leather uncoloured. *d.*

ميش मेष *mesh*, m. a sheep, a ram; the sign *Aries*. *mesh-chashm*, sheepish, sheep-eyed; (met.) a blockhead. *p. s.*

ميشوم *maishūm*, unfortunate, unlucky, disagreeable. *a.*

ميشي मेषी *meshī*, f. a ewe, a sheep. *s.*

ميشي मीशी *mīshī*, f. a kind of leather, shamois. *s.*

ميعات *mai'āt* (pl. of ميعة q. v.). *a.*

ميعاد *mī'ād*, m. the time or place of a promise; size, dimension, length and breadth. *a.*

ميعادي *mī'ādī*, limited as to time, &c. *mī'ādī ijārā*, a farm let for a limited time. *a. h.*

ميعة *mai'at*, the beginning of day, or of youth. *a.*

ميغ *megh*, m. a cloud; a mist, a fog. *p.*

ميفروش *mai-farosh*, a wine-seller or -dealer. *p.*

ميكا मैका *maikā*, m. kindred, relatives, mother's family. *s.*

ميكال *mīkāl*, ميكائيل *mīkā,īl*, } m. the archangel Michael. *a.*

ميكڈمبر *mehḍambar*, a canopy over the *hauda* or saddle of an elephant. *d.*

ميكهه मेख *mekh*, m. a ram; the sign *Aries* (v. *mesh*); a pin, peg, nail (for *mekh*). *s. p.*

ميكهلا मेखला *mekhlā*, f. a woman's girdle or zone; a Brāhman's sacrificial string. *h.*

ميكهلي मेखली *mekhlī*, f. a sackcloth. *h.*

ميگم *megam*, the white leprosy. *d.*

ميگهه मेघ *megh*, m. a cloud; name of a *rāg* or musical mode appropriated to the wet season and last watch of the night before the first dawn of day, and said to have proceeded from the head of Brahmā, or else from the sky; a fragrant grass (*Cyperus rotundus*). *megh-baran*, of the colour of the clouds. *megh-pati* or *megh-rāj*, lord of the clouds, the thunderer. *megh-jyotis*, m. a flash of lightning. *s.*

ميگهاگم मेघागम *megh-āgam*, m. the rainy season. *s.*

ميگهتمر मेघतिमिर *megh-timir*, m. cloudiness, cloudy weather. *s.*

ميگهدوار मेघद्वार *megh-dwār*, m. sky, heaven, ether. *s.*

ميگهديپ मेघदीप *megh-dīp*, m. a flash of lightning. *s.*

ميگهراج मेघराज *megh-rāj*, m. the thunderer. *s.*

ميگهراگ मेघराग *megh-rāg*, m. one of the six modes of music. *s.*

ميگهکال मेघकाल *megh-kāl*, m. the rainy season. *s.*

ميگهگرجن मेघगर्जन *megh-garjan*, m. thunder. *s.*

ميگهمالا मेघमाला *megh-mālā*, f. a gathering or succession of clouds. *s.*

ميگهناد मेघनाद *megh-nād*, m. the noise or grumbling of the clouds; the palās tree (*Butea frondosa*); a sort of amaranth (*Amaranthus polygamus*). *s.*

ميل *mīl*, f. a needle, skewer, or wire instrument, used to apply a collyrium to the eyes, and, when heated, to put out the eyes, or blind people by drawing it hot before the eye; the barrel of a gun. *p.*

ميل मेल *mel*, m. connection, relationship, agreement, combination, concord, reconciliation, union, mixture, mixing, meeting, assemblage, a fair, a court of justice. *s.*

ميل मैल *mail*, m. dirt, scum. *mail-baiṭhnā*, to gather a crust. *mail chhāṅṭnā*, to refine, strain, purify. *mail-khora*, an under vestment (as under petticoat, &c.); a saddle-cloth. *mail kāṭnā*, to refine to purify. *s.*

ميل *mīl*, m. a mile, *mail*, inclination, wish, desire; affection, regard, partiality, fondness, aptitude. *mail rakhnā*, to associate with *mail karnā*, to close in with. *a.*

ميلا मेला *melā*, m. a fair, a great concourse of people met for the purpose of worshipping a particular deity, having at the same time a view to the worshipping of mammon. *melā milnā*, to meet full in the face. *melā-ṭhelā*, crowding and pushing, a crowd. *s.*

ميلا मैला *mailā*, dirty, foul, defiled. *mailā-k.*, to dirty. *mailā-kuchīlā*, dirty. *mailā hojānā*, to tarnish, to become turbid, to be dirty. *s.*

ميلان *mayalān*, or *mailān*, m. inclination, affection, respect, regard; loving; Pers. name of a certain philosopher. *a.*

ميلن मीलन *mīlan*, m. twinkling, blinking, winking. *h.*

ميلنا मेलना *melnā*, a. to thrust in, to stuff in, to cram, to penetrate, to force in. *h.*

ميلي मेली *melī*, m. a partaker; adj. friendly. *s.*

ميمانسا मीमांसा *mīmāṅsā*, f. one of the philosophical systems of the Hindūs. *s.*

ميمانسك मीमांसक *mīmāṅsak*, m. a follower of the *mīmāṅsā* philosophy. *s.*

ميمنا मेमना *memnā*, m. a kid. *h.*

ميمنت *maimanat*, f. fortune, prosperity, happiness. *a.*

ميمنة *maimana*, the right wing of an army. *a.*

ميمون *maimūn*, fortunate, auspicious, prosperous; m. a baboon, monkey; *membrum virile*. *a.*

ميمياانا मीमियाना *mīmiyānā*, to bleat (a kid). *h.*

مين में *meṅ*, post. in, into, among, on, at. *maiṅ*, pron. I. *maiṅ khush merā khudā khush* is used to express high satisfaction with any circumstance or proposition. *h.*

مين मैन *main*, a common short grass growing on rich and inundated land, and choking the crops. *h.*

مين मीन *mīn*, m. f. a fish; the sign *Pisces*; the name of the first incarnation of *Vishṇu*. *main*, Cupid or *Kāmadeva*. *s.*

مينا *mīnā*, m. a goblet, a glass, a decanter; a blue colour; enamel; heaven, the azure vault, paradise; the blue stone, blue vitriol, caustic. *mīnā-kār*, an enameller. *mīnā-kārī*, enamelling. *p.*

مينا मैना *mainā*, f. name of a bird, a kind of starling (*Coracias Indica*). *mīnā*, a caste of Hindūs, professedly thieves. *h.*

مينار *mīnār*, m. minaret, obelisk, steeple. *a.*

ميناگهاتي मीनाघाती *mīnā-ghātī*, m. a crane; a fisherman. *s.*

مينانڈ मीनाण्ड *mīnāṇḍ*, m. fish spawn, roe, milt. *s.*

ميناءي *mīnā,ī*, f. enamel. *p.*

مين پهل मैनफल *main-phal*, m. name of a fruit used in medicine (*Vanguera spinosa, Roxb.*); the emetic nut. *s.*

مينجنا मींजना *mīṅjnā*, a. to rub, to scour. *s.*

مینڌهي मन्धी *mendhī*, f. a plant (same as *meṅhdī*, q. v.). *h.*

مینڈ मेंड *menḍ*, f. a bank (raised to separate fields), a border; a dam or dyke. *menḍ parnā*, the rising of waves in the sea. *h.* [a well. *h.*

مینڈا मेंडा *menḍā*, m. the brim or parapet of

مینڈک मेंडक *menḍak*, m. } a frog; the rump
مینڈکي मेंडकी *menḍkī*, f. } of a horse. *menḍkī ko zukām honā*, (lit.) a frog having caught cold, expresses pride or consequential airs assumed by worthless persons. *s.*

میندہ मेंढ *maiṅḍh*, gleanings, corn left on the field in small quantity. *h.*

مینڈها मेंढा *menḍhā*, m. a ram; the swell of the tide called the boar. *s.*

مینڈهل मेंढल *menḍhal* or *maiṅḍhal*, m. a fruit so called (*Guilandina bonducella*); a kind of firework which bursts with an explosion. *h.*

مینڈي मेंडी *meṅḍī* (v. *meṅhdī*). *h.*

مینڈیانا मेंडियाना *menḍiyānā*, n. to skirt, to inclose with a bank. *h.*

مینرنگا मीनरङ्गा *mīn-rangā*, m. a kingfisher. *s.*

مینسل मैनसिल *mainsil*, m. red arsenic (*Realgar*). *s.* [sheep, camels, &c. *h.*

مینگني मेंगनी *mengnī*, f. the dung of goats,

مینگي मींगी *mīngī*, f. marrow, pith, essence. *h.*

مینو *mīnū*, heaven, paradise. *p.*

مینہ मेंह *meṅh*, m. rain. *meṅh barasnā*, n. to rain. *meṅh chhūṭnā*, to rain hard. *s.*

مینہدي मेंहदी *meṅhdī*, f. the name of a plant, from the leaves of which a red dye is prepared with which the natives stain their hands and feet; the henna plant or flower, called by the Arabs *ḥinā* (*Lawsonia inermis*). *h.*

میو मेव *mew*, } m. a tribe inhabiting
میواتي मेवाती *mewātī*, } the mountainous pro-
میوڑا मेवड़ा *mewṛā*, } vince of Mewāt, much addicted to robbing. *h.*

میوا मीवा *mīwā*, f. the worm of the intestines. *h.*

میوا *mewā* (for *mewa*, q. v.), fruit, &c. *p.*

میوجات *mewajāt*, pl. fruits (v. *mewa*). *p.*

میور मयूर *mayūr*, m. a peacock; a flower so called, the cockscomb (*Celosia cristata*), a plant (*Achyranthes aspera*). *s.*

میورار मयूरारि *mayūrāri* or *mayurārī*, m. a chameleon, a lizard. *s.*

میورچوڑا मयूरचूड़ा *mayūr-chūṛā* or *-chūrā*, f. cockscomb (*Celosia cristata*). *s.*

میوري मयूरी *mayūrī*, f. a peahen. *s.*

میوڑا मेवड़ा *mevṛā*, m. (v. *mev*) a tribe, &c. *h.*

میوکه मयूख *mayūkh*, m. the gnomon of a sundial. *s.*

میون म्यूँ *myūṅ*, an imitative sound, the cry of the cat. *myūṅ-k.*, to mew or cry as a cat. *h.*

میوہ *mewa*, m. fruit. *mewa-dār*, fruit-bearing, fruitful. *mewa-farosh*, a fruiterer. *p.*

میوها *mewahā*, } pl. fruits. *mewahā,e*
میوہجات *mewa-jāt*, } *gūn-ā-gūn*, fruits of many kinds. *p.* [gonorrhœa, &c. *s.*

میہ मेह *meh*, m. urine, piss; urinary disease,

میہتر मेहतर *mehtar*, m. a sweeper (v. *mihtar*). *p. h.*

میہتراني मेहतरानी *mehtarānī*, f. female of *mehtar*; a female sweeper or innkeeper. *p.*

میہکا मैहिका *maihikā*, m. a male buffalo. *s.*

میہکي मैहिकी *maihikī*, f. a female buffalo. *s.*

میہمان *mehmān* or *mīhmān*, m. a guest. *p.*

میہنا मेहना *mehnā*, m. a taunt. *mehnā mārnā*, a. to taunt. *h.*

میہنہا मेहन्हा *mehanhā*, m. a taunter. *h.*

میہون *mehūṅ* (corrup. of *meṅh*), rain. *d.*

مئي *ma,ī* (also मयी *mayī*), f. a harrow; a ladder. *h.*

ن

ن *nūn*, the twenty-fifth letter of the Arabic alphabet, the twenty-ninth of the Persian, and the thirty-second Hindūstānī: it is one of the dental letters, and has the sound of the English *n*, with the following exceptions: the letter *nūn* has a very soft nasal sound in plural terminations in *āṅ*, *eṅ*, *īṅ*, and *oṅ*, and in the terminations in *ūṅ* and *eṅ* of the aorist and imperative of verbs; it has also this nasal sound in the middle of some words, as *muṅh*, the face, *haṅsnā*, to smile, &c., for which no rule can be laid down: in this dictionary the nasal sound of *n* is always indicated by *ṅ*: when *nūn* precedes *be* or *pe* it has the sound of *m*, as *minbar*, a pulpit (for *minbar*), *sampat*, prosperity, for *sanpat*, (as is the case in Greek and Latin). In reckoning by *abjad*, the letter *nūn* stands for 50; in almanacks it expresses the conjunct aspect of the stars; finally, the letter *nūn* with the short *a* (as *na*) prefixed to verbs renders the sense negative, as *bolā*, he spoke, *na-bolā*, he did not speak.

ن न *na*, or ण *ṇa*, the corresponding letters in the Devanāgarī alphabet. *s. h.*

ن नि *ni*, a Sanskrit prefix denoting "within," "below," "under," &c.; as *ni-patan*, falling down; sometimes it is a contraction of *nir*, q. v.; as *ni-ḍar*, fearless. *s. h.*

نا *nā*, no, not, a negative particle prefixed to nouns, participles, and affirmative adjectives simple or compound, has the same meaning as the English prefixes in-, un-, dis-, &c.; as, *nā-āshnā*, unacquainted, unknown. *nā-āshnā,ī*, f. shyness, acting the stranger, reservedness. *nā-umed*, or *-ummaid*, hopeless, despairing. *nā-i'timād*, not to be trusted. *nā-i'timādī*, trustworthlessness. *na-umedī*, f. despair, hopelessness. *nā-andesh*, evident, requiring no thought. *nā-inṣāf*, unjust, inequitable. *nā-ahl*, unworthy, unfit. *nā-bā-*

lig͟h, not arrived at the age of puberty. *nā-bālig͟hī*, nonage, minority. *nā-ba-k͟hirad*, unwise, unwisely. *nā-ba-kār*, useless. *nā-ba-kārī*, uselessness. *nā-būd*, that never existed, annihilated, vanished. *nā-bīnā*, blind. *nā-bīnā,ī*, f. blindness. *nā-bīnī*, weak-sighted, seeing imperfectly. *nā-pāk*, polluted, dirty, unclean, filthy, impure, defiled. *nā-pākī*, uncleanness, pollutedness, defilement, impurity. *nā-pā,edār*, unstable, frail, unsteady, fickle, transitory. *nā-padīd*, invisible, not to be found, unconspicuous, private, concealed. *nā-parwā*, intrepid, fearless, careless. *nā-parhezgār*, unchaste, sinful. *nā-pasand* or *nā-pasandīda*, unchosen, disapproved of. *nā paid* or *nā-paidā*, unborn, that has never existed, not to be found. *nā-tāb*, weak, infirm. *nā-tarāsh*, also *nā-tarāshīda*, unshaved; unpolite, unlicked. *nā-tarbiyat*, uneducated. *nā-tars*, severe, hard-hearted, pitiless, fearless. *nā-tamām*, unfinished, imperfect, deficient. *nā-tamāmī*, deficiency, imperfectness. *nā-tawān* or *nā-tawānā*, powerless, weak, infirm, impotent. *nā-tawānī* or *nā-tawānā,ī*, weakness, impotence. *nā-jā,iz*, unsuitable, unlawful. *nā-jins*, of no family, ignoble; strange. *nā-chār*, remediless, helpless, forlorn, distressed, constrained. *nā-chārī*, helplessness, impotence. *nā-chāḳ*, unsound, out of order. *nā-chāḳī*, f. laziness, coolness, lukewarmness, displeasure, disagreement. *nā-chīz*, of no consequence, trifling, insignificant. *nā-chīzī*, f. insignificance, nullity. *nā-ḥaḳḳ*, unjust, untrue; unjustly. *nā-ḥaḳḳ-shinās*, inequitable, ungrateful, having no notions of justice. *nā-k͟hudā*, an atheist, an impious man; (for *nāo-k͟hudā*), captain of a vessel. *nā-k͟hudā-tars*, not fearing God. *nā-k͟halaf*, wicked, vicious (boy). *nā k͟hwānda*, unread, unlearned. *nā-k͟hwāh*, unwilling, constrained; unwillingly, constrainedly. *nā-k͟hūb*, bad *nā-k͟hush*, displeased, unpleasant. *nā-k͟hushī*, f. displeasure. *nā k͟hush-āwāz*, having a disagreeable voice (a singer). *nā-dār*, poor, without possession, insolvent. *nā-dārī*, f. poverty, insolvency. *nā-dihand* or *-dihanda* not paying what is due; stingy, close-fisted. *nā-dīdagī*, f. poverty, bankruptcy. *nā-dīdanī*, not to be seen. *nā-dīda*, unseen; a person who has seen little. *nā-rāẓ*, dissatisfied. *nā-rasā*, unworthy, unfit; ill-bred, unmannerly. *nā-rasā,ī*, f. unworthiness, unfitness; unmannerliness, unskilfulness. *nā-rasīda*, not yet arrived. *nā-rafta*, not gone. *nā-rawā*, not current or passable, "no go." *nā-zād*, a barren woman. *nā-zā,īda*, a woman who has not yet produced children. *nā-zor*, weak. *nā-zorī*, f. weakness. *nā-zeb*, ugly, ill-shaped, inelegant. *nā-zebā,ish* or *nā-zebā,ī*, f. ugliness, deformity, ungracefulness, plainness. *nā-sāz*, discordant, dissonant, discrepant; obscene, rude, uncivil. *nā-sāzkār* or *-sāzgār*, discordant, unfavourable. *nā-sāzgārī* or *kārī*, f. discordance, absurdity, dissension. *nā-sāzī*, f. discordance, dissension. *nā-sipās*, ungrateful, disagreeable, unthankful. *nā-sipāsī*, f. ungratefulness. *nā-sazā*, unmerited, unworthy, indecent, impertinent, foolish. *nā-sufta*, unbored. *nā-sufta bih*, a cunning person. *nā-samajh*, unintelligent. *nā-samjhī*, f. ignorance. *nā-shād*, cheerless, low-spirited, dull, dissatisfied, hippish. *nā-shādī*, f. dulness, melancholy, displeasure, dissatisfaction. *nā-shāyasta*, unworthy, improper, indecent. *nā-shudanī*, one from whom no good is to be expected; unfit to live; absurd, impracticable; ill-fated. *nā-shusta*, unwashed. *nā-shukr*, ungrateful. *nā-shukrī karnā*, to act ungratefully. *nā shakīb* or *nā-shakībā*, impatient, unsteady. *nā-shakībī* or *nā-shakībā,ī*, f. impatience, non-endurance. *nā-shob*, unwashed. *nā-ṣabr*, impatient. *nā-ṣawāb*, not right, sinful, bad, unwholesome. *nā-ṭāḳat*, weak, infirm. *nā-ṭāḳatī*, f. weakness. *nā-farmān*, disobedient; name of a flower of a purple colour. *nā-fahm*, stupid, unintelligent. *nā-ḳābil*, unfit. *nā-ḳabūl*, unacceptable; rejecting, refusing, disgusting. *nā-ḳuwwat*, weak. *nā-ḳuwwatī*, f. weakness. *na-kārī*, inutility, incompetency. *nā-kāragī*, f. idleness, laziness. *nā-kāra*, useless, bad. *nā-kām*, unwilling, disappointed, discontented. *nā-kāmī*, f. disappointment, discontent. *nā-kas*, a person of light character, or of no consequence. *nā-kasī*, f. worthlessness. *nā-kand*, m. a colt. *nā-guzīr*, necessary, indispensable. *nā-gawār*, unarranged; indigested; unacceptable, unpalatable, unwholesome. *nā-lā,iḳ*, unfit, unworthy. *nā-mutanāhī*, infinite, divine. *nā-maḥram*, a stranger, one who is not permitted to enter the women's apartment. *nā-murād*, dissatisfied, disappointed. *nā-murādī*, dissatisfaction, disappointment, despair, despondency. *nā-mard*, *nā-mardāna*, or *nā-mardum*, unmanly, a coward; impotent. *nā-mardī*, unmanliness, cowardice, impotence. *nā-maṭbū'*, unacceptable, disagreeable, unpleasant; unnatural. *nā-ma'ḳūl*, improper. *nā-mulā,im*, hard. *nā-munāsib*, improper, not to the purpose. *nā-mauzūn*, discordant (melody). *nā-nihāda*, not allotted. *nā-waḳt*, out of season, untimely. *nā-wāriṡ*, friendless, patronless, without a master or protector. *nā-wāḳif*, unskilled, unacquainted with, ignorant, inexperienced. *nā-wāḳifīyat*, f. inexperiencedness, *naumed* (for *nā-umed*, q.v.). *nāhamtā*, incomparable. *nā-hamwār*, uneven, irregular, capricious. *nā-hamwārī*, f. inequality. *nā-yāb*, scarce, unprocurable. *nā-yaksān*, unequal, dissimilar. *p.*

نا ***nā***, an expletive much used in the Dakhanī dialect. It has no meaning in particular, but may be supposed to convey some emphasis.—(B.) *d.*

ناب ***nāb***, m. a groove or channel; fluting. *nābdār*, grooved, fluted, indented. *d.*

ناب ***nāb***, pure, genuine. *p.*

ناب ***nāb***, m. a canine tooth, a tusk. *a.*

نابدان ***nābdān*** (v. *nāwdān*), m. a gutter. *p.*

نابر ***nābar***, m. one who denies. *d.*

نابھ नाभि ***nābhi***, f. the navel; a centre. *s.*

نابھک नाभक ***nābhak***, m. a myrobalan (*Terminalia chebula*). *s.*

نابھچھیدن नाभिछेदन ***nābhichhedan***, m. division of the umbilical cord. *s.*

نابھگولک नाभिगोलक ***nābhigolak***, m. a prominent or ruptured navel. *s.*

نابھناڑي नाभिनाड़ी ***nābhināṛī***, نابھنالا नाभिनाला ***nābhinālā***, } f. the umbilical cord. *s.*

نابھي नाभी ***nābhī***, f. the navel. *s.*

ناپ नाप ***nāp***, f. measure. *nāp-jokh*, measuring and weighing. *s.*

ناپت नापित ***nāpit***, m. a barber, a shaver, a surgeon. *s.*

ناپتشالا नापितशाला ***nāpit-shālā***, f. a barber's shop. *s.*

ناپگار ***nāpigār***, filthy, vile. *p.*

ناپنا नापना ***nāpnā***, a. to measure, to weigh. *s.*

نات ***nāt*** (for *nāth*, q. v.), master, &c. *d.*

ناتا नाता ***nātā***, m. relationship, kin, alliance. *h.*

ناتر नातर ***nātar***, if not, then, otherwise, else. *s*

ناتن नातिन ***nātin***, ناتني नातिनी ***nātinī***, } f. granddaughter, daughter's daughter. *s.*

ناتھ नाथ ***nāth***, m. a master, a husband; often used as an affix to the names of *jogīs*, as *Gorakhnāth*; f. the string in a bullock's nose; a seton. *s.*

ناتھا ***nāthā*** (v. *nātā*), relationship, &c. *d.*

ناتھت नाथित ***nāthit*** having the nose pierced (a bullock). *s.*

ناتهنا नाथना *nāthnā*, a. to bore a bullock's nose, and put a string in it to guide him by. *s.*

ناتهوت नाथवत *nāthwat*, dependent, subservient, subject. *s.*

ناتي नाती *nātī*, m. grandson, daughter's son; f. a granddaughter. *s.*

ناتيدار नातेदार *nātedār*, a relative, a kinsman. *h. p.*

ناٹ नाट *nāṭ*, a pillar, obelisk; the Carnatic [country. *h.*

ناٹا नाटा *nāṭā*, dwarf, dapper, short. *h.*

ناٹاپن नाटापन *nāṭāpan*, m. lowness of stature. *h.*

ناٹك नाटक *nāṭak*, m. the business of a *naṭ*; a kind of Sanskrit composition, a comedy; an actor. *s.*

ناٹكا नाटिका *nāṭikā*, f. a short or light comedy. *s.*

ناٹكسال *nāṭak-sāl*, m. an actor, player, mimic. *d.*

ناٹكيه नाटकीय *nāṭakīya*, comic, dramatic. *s.*

ناٹمگار *nāṭamgār* (v. *mahājan*), a great merchant, &c. *d.*

ناٹهه नाठ *nāṭh*, m. non-existence. *s.*

ناٹيه नाट्य *nāṭya*, m. the science or art of dancing or acting; the union of song, dance, and instrumental music. *s.*

ناٹيشالا नाट्यशाला *nāṭya-shālā*, f. a theatre, a building for dramatic exhibitions. *s.*

ناج नाज *nāj*, m. (contr. of *anāj*) grain, provision. *h.*

ناجي *nājī*, free, liberated; excused, escaped, saved (fem. *nājiya*). *a.*

ناچ नाच *nāch*, m. dance; an entertainment given by rich Hindūs. *nāch-nachānā*, to make to dance, to tease, or as we say "to lead one a dance." *s.*

ناچخ *nāchakh*, a halbert; a battle-axe; a two-pointed spear; a short javeline. *p.*

ناچنا नाचना *nāchnā*, n. to dance. *h.*

ناحيه *nāḥiya*, m. territory, country, district, a tract, coast, shore. *a.*

ناخدا *nākhudā* (for *nāo-khudā*), m. master or commander of a ship, captain or supercargo; (in Anglo-Hindi) "*nay-quiddie.*" *p.*

ناخداءي *nā-khudā,ī*, f. office of a commander of a ship; seamanship, navigation. *p.*

ناخن *nākhun*, m. nail (of the fingers), claw (of a beast), or talon (of a bird). *nākhun-gīr* or *-tarāsh*. m. an instrument for cutting the nails with. *nākhun lenā*, to pare the nails; to trip or stumble (a horse). *p.*

ناخنه *nākhuna*, m. an instrument used to strike the strings of a guitar with, a *plectrum*; a haw or web in the eye (*unguis*). *p.*

ناد नाद *nād*, m. sound; a song; a semicircle used as an abbreviation, &c. *nād-k.*, to roar (as a tiger); to sing. *s.*

ناد *nād* (v. *sarīkhā*), like, &c. *d.*

نادان *nā-dān*, ignorant, simple. *p.*

ناداني *nā-dānī*, f. ignorance, simplicity. *p.*

ناداها नादाहा *nādāhā*, m. a spout, a canal. *h.*

نادر *nādir*, rare, wonderful, choice. *nādir i rozgār*, the wonder of the age. *a.*

نادرات *nādirāt*, wonderful events. *a.*

نادرشاه *nādir-shāh*, name of a famous depredator of India who sacked Delhi in A.D. 1739. *nādir-shāhī*, of or relating to Nādir Shāh; the invasion of India by that adventurer. *a. p.*

نادره *nādira* (fem. of *nādir*, q. v.). *a.*

نادري *nādirī*, f. a rarity; adj. of or relating to Nādir, or Nādir Shāh. *a.*

نادلي *nādalī*, a kind of charm or talisman, a stone inscribed with words from the *ḳur,ān*, and hung as a preserving amulet round children's necks. *d.*

نادم *nādim*, bashful, penitent, repenting, abashed, ashamed. *a.*

نادنا नादना *nādnā*, a. to begin. *h.*

نادهنا नाधना *nādhnā*, a. to yoke. *h.*

ناديي नादेयी *nādeyī*, f. name of a kind of reed (*Calamus fasciculatus*); a plant (*Pranna herbacea*; the China rose. *s.*

ناڈكا नाडिका *nāḍikā*, f. a *gharī*, q. v.; the space of twenty-four minutes. *s.*

نار *nār*, f. fire, hell; the mind. *a.*

نار *nār*, m. a pomegranate (*Punica granatum*). *p.*

نار नार *nār*, f. a woman; m. the stalk of the lotus; a herd, drove; barrel of a gun; counsel, advice; the fibre of which rope is made; the neck. *h.*

نارا नारा *nārā*, m. red thread; fibres of the cocoa-nut or palm, commonly called "coir," of which ropes, &c. are made. *h.*

ناراين नारायण *nārāyaṇ* or *nārāyaṇa*, m. a Hindū name for the deity; a name of *Vishṇu*. *s.*

نارائنتيل नारायणतैल *nārāyaṇ-tail*, m. an oil of great reputed efficacy in many complaints: it is extracted from a variety of plants. *s.*

نارائنكشيتر नारायणक्षेत्र *nārāyaṇ-kshetra*, m. four cubits of the soil on either side of the stream of the Ganges. *s.*

نارايني नारायणी *nārāyaṇī*, f. the wife of *Nārāyaṇa* or *Vishṇu*; a plant (*Asparagus racemosa*); adj. relating to *Nārāyaṇ*. *s.*

ناربوار नारबिवार *nārbiwār*, m. the membrane in which the *fœtus* is enveloped; *secundines*. *h.*

نارجيل *nārjīl*, m. a cocoa-nut; the cocoa-nut tree (*Cocos nucifera*). *p.*

نارد नारद *nārad*, m. the name of a Hindū saint, son of *Brahmā*; (met.) a disputant, one fond of altercation. *s.*

نارد *nārd*, m. the tike or dog-louse; a miser. *p.*

نارك नारक *nārak*, m. hell, the infernal regions; adj. infernal. *s.* [ble. *s.*

ناركي नारकी *nārakī*, infernal, hellish, damna-

ناركيل नारिकेल *nārikel*, m. the cocoa-nut. *s.*

نارنج *nāranj*, m. an orange. *p.*

نارنجي *nāranjī*, orange-coloured. *p.*

نارنگي नारङ्गी *nārangī*, f. an orange. *s.*

نارو नारू *nārū*, m. the guinea-worm. *h.*

ناروان *nārwān*, } m. a species of elm. *p.*
نارون *nārwan*, }

ناري नारी *nārī*, f. a woman; the pulse; the umbilical cord; a kind of greens; an artery. *s.*

ناري *nārī*, fiery; hellish. *a.*

ناريا नारिया *nāriyā*, m. a person who feels the pulse. *s.* [tinism, lechery. *s.*

نارپرسنگ नारीप्रसङ्ग *nārī-prasang*, m. liber-

نارچ नारीच *nārich*, m. an esculent root (*Arum colocasia*). *s.*

ناريدوشن नारीदूषण *nārī-dūshan*, a vice or breach of duty in a woman, such as drinking spirits, keeping bad company, &c. *s.*

ناریر नारियर *nāriyar*, } m. a cocoa-nut; a
ناريل नारियल *nāriyal*, } *hukka* made of a cocoa-nut. *s.*

ناريل کي روئي *nāriyal kī rū,ī*, f. a soft downy substance of a light brown colour, found on the exterior of the lower part of the leaves or branches of the cocoa-nut: it is used as a styptic, and also for tinder. *h.*

ناريلي नारियली *nāriyalī*, m. a *hukka* made of a cocoa-nut; a cup made of cocoa-nut shell; sap or liquor extracted from the cocoa-nut tree, commonly called "toddy" by Europeans. *s.* [*nāṛī*). *s.*

ناڑ नाड़ *nāṛ* or नाड़ि *nāṛi*, the pulse, &c. (v.

ناڑا *nāṛā*, m. tape. *d.*

ناڑپتر नाड़िपत्र *nāṛi-patr*, m. an esculent root (*Arum colocasia*). *s.*

ناڑکا नाड़िका *nāṛikā*, f. an Indian hour, or twenty-four minutes. *s.* [tial equator. *s.*

ناڑمنڈل नाड़िमण्डल *nāṛi-mandal*, m. the celes-

ناڑي नाड़ी *nāṛī*, f. any tubular organ of the body, artery, vein, gut, &c.; the pulse; a fistula; an hour of twenty-four minutes; (in Dakh.) *nāṛī-dekhnā*, to beat, strike. *s.* [(*Arum colocasia*). *s.*

ناڑيچ नाड़ीच *nāṛīch*, m. an esculent root

ناڑي نکشتر नाड़ीनक्षत्र *nāṛī-nakshatr*, m. the planet of a person's nativity. *s.*

ناڑي ورن नाड़ीव्रण *nāṛī-vran*, m. an ulcer. *s.*

ناز *nāz*, m. blandishments; coquetry, playfulness, gracefulness, elegance, soothing, fondling, amorous playfulness, softness; pride, consequential airs. *nāz uṭhānā*, a. to bear with the airs or whims of another. *nāz-bardār*, one who bears the whims of another, a flatterer. *nāz-bardārī*, f. flattery. *nāz-parwarda*, delicately brought up, a spoiled child. *nāz-pesha*, a coquette. *nāz-nakhrā*, m. coquetry. *nāz e niyāz*, toying, amorous play. *s.*

نازان *nāzān*, sporting, toying (as lovers); boasting, glorying. *p.*

نازبو *nāzbo*, m. name of an herb (*Ocymum pilosum, Roxb.*). *p.*

نازك *nāzuk*, thin, light, subtile, delicate, tender, elegant; facetious, gracious, genteel. *nāzuk-adā*, the nightingale. *nāzuk-andām*, delicately formed in every limb. *nāzuk-badan*, delicate (epithet of a mistress); a species of jujube (*Zizyphus jujuba*). *nāzuk-mizāj*, of a delicate complexion. *nāzuk-wujūd*, delicate of body. *p.*

نازكي *nāzukī*, f. delicacy, softness, tenderness. *p.*

نازل *nāzil*, descending; dismounting; alighting. *nāzil-honā* or *-shudan*, to descend, to alight. *a.*

نازله *nāzila*, m. a misfortune, disorder, calamity. *a.* [a mistress, a lovely woman. *p.*

نازنين *nāznīn*, delicate, beautiful, charming;

نازيدن *nāzīdan*, to coquet, to coy it, to assume a cold and haughty look. *p.*

ناس *nās*, pl. mankind, human beings. *a.*

ناس नास *nās*, f. snuff; m. (for *nāsha*) non-existence, annihilation, loss, destruction. *nās-dān*, m. a snuff-box. *s.*

ناسا नासा *nāsā*, m. the nose; a disease of the nose, called also *nākṛā*, q. v. *s.*

ناسادكشناورت नासादक्षिणावर्त *nāsā-dakshinā-vart*, m. wearing the nose-ring in the right nostril by women who have money and children. *s.*

ناساشوكه नासाशोख *nāsā-shokh*, m. drying of the nostrils. *s.*

ناسانا नासाना *nāsānā*, a. to annihilate, to spoil, to destroy. *s.*

ناساوامـاورت नासावामावर्त *nāsā-vāmāvart*, n. wearing the nose-ring in the left nostril, a mark of sorrow. *s.* [of the nose. *s.*

ناساونش नासावंश *nāsā-vansh*, m. the bridge

ناسپال नासपाल *nāspāl*, m. the rind of an unripe pomegranate (used in dyeing). *h.*

ناسپالي नासपाली *nāspālī*, of or relating to *nāspāl*. *nāspālī rang*, the colour extracted from *nāspāl*. *h.*

ناست नास्ति *nāsti* or *nāst*, f. nonentity, annihilation; adv. no, not so. *s.*

ناستتوه नास्तित्व *nāstitwa*, m. non-existence. *s.*

ناستك नास्तिक *nāstik*, } m. an atheist, one
ناستكي नास्तिकी *nāstikī*, } who denies a future state of rewards and punishment; or, in general, one who denies the divine authority of the Vedas, or who entertains doubts as to the authenticity of the Purānas. *s.* [lief, heresy. *s.*

ناستكتا नास्तिकता *nāstiktā*, f. atheism, unbe-

ناستكيه नास्तिक्य *nastikya*, m. unbelief in the creed of the Hindūs, infidelity. *s.*

ناسج *nāsij*, m. a composer, making an oration. *a.*

ناسخ *nāsikh*, m. a copier of a book, an amanuensis; erasing, abolishing. *a.*

ناسك *nāsik*, devoted to God. *a.*

ناسك नासक *nāsak*, m. a destroyer, an exterminator. *s.* [the mucus of the nose. *s.*

ناسكا नासिका *nāsikā*, f. the nose. *nāsikā-mal*,

ناسمجهه नासमझ *nā-samajh*, unintelligent. *s.*

ناسمجهي नासमझी *nā-samjhī*, f. ignorance. *s.*

ناسن नासन *nāsan*, m. destruction, perishing. *s.*

ناسنا नासना *nāsnā*, n. to flee, to run away; a. to destroy, to exterminate. *s.*

ناسوت *nāsūt*, human nature, humanity. *a.*

ناسور *nāsūr*, m. a fistula, an ulcer. *a.*

ناسيه नास्य *nāsya*, m. the rein of an ox passed through the nostril. *s.*

ناش नाश *nāsh*, m. loss, destruction. *s.*

ناشپاتي *nāshpātī*, f. a pear (*Pyrus communis*). *p.*

ناشت नाशित *nāshit*, destroyed, lost. *s.*

ناشتا *nāshtā*, / ناشته *nāshta*, } m. breakfast, luncheon, refreshment; adj. hungry. *nāshtā-k.*, to breakfast. *p.*

ناشك नाशक *nāshak*, m. a destroyer, spoiler. *s.*

ناشن नाशन *nāshan*, m. destruction, ruination. *s.*

ناشني नाशिनी *nāshinī*, f. / ناشي नाशी *nāshī*, m. } destructive, destroying, a destroyer. *s.*

ناشين नाशयन *nāshyan*, m. destroying, annihilating. *s.*

ناصب *nāṣib*, erecting, fixing, placing. *a.*

ناصح *nāṣiḥ*, m. an adviser, a monitor, a sincere friend or counsellor; adj. faithful. *a.*

ناصر *nāṣir*, m. a defender, an assistant. *a.*

ناصيت *nāṣiyat* or *nāṣiya*, the forehead, the fore locks over the forehead. *a.*

ناطق *nāṭiḳ*, m. speaking, a speaker; a rational or human being. *a.*

ناطقه *nāṭiḳa*, m. the faculty of speech. *a.*

ناظر *nāẓir*, seeing, observing, inspecting; m. a spectator, an inspector, a superintendent, a guard, keeper, supervisor; an officer employed in a judicial court, superior to all peons, bailiffs, &c., a sheriff. *nāẓiri-jam'dār*, the head police-officer. *nāẓir-khāna*, the sheriff's office. *a.*

ناظره *nāẓira*, m. the eye, sight, vision; reading, studying. *nāẓira-khwānī*, reading (in opposition to repeating by heart). *a.*

ناظري *nāẓirī*, f. office of an inspector, act of inspecting, &c. *a.*

ناظم *nāẓim*, m. a composer, arranger, adjuster; a poet, composer of verses; a governor, a ruler. *a.*

ناظمي *nāẓimī*, f. office of a *nāẓim*, q. v. *a.*

ناغاني *nāghānī* (for *nā-gahānī*), sudden, &c. *d.*

ناغه *nāgha*, vacant, void, nought, unemployed; m. adjournment, respite. *bilā-nāgha*, without fail, forthwith. *t.*

ناف *nāf*, f. the navel; centre or middle. *p.*

نافذ *nāfiẓ*, penetrating, passing, getting through, having effect, obeyed (an order). *a.*

نافع *nāfi'*, salutary, profitable, advantageous useful. *a.*

نافله *nāfila*, a work of supererogation. *a.*

نافه *nāfa* or *nāfa,i mushk*, m. a pod of musk. *p.*

ناقد *nāḳid*, m. a person whose business it is to examine coin and ascertain its goodness, an assayer, a critic, a connoisseur. *a.*

ناقص *nāḳiṣ*, imperfect, unfinished, deficient, mutilated, inexpert. *nāḳiṣi 'aḳl*, deficient in sense, dull, stupid. *nāḳiṣ honā*, to waut. *a.*

ناقل *nāḳil*, m. a painter, delineator; a relater, narrator, reporter. *a.*

ناقوس *nāḳūs*, m. a bell, or rather a thin oblong piece of wood suspended by two strings, by the eastern Christians, to summon the congregation to divine service; a sort of conch for calling people to prayers. *a.*

ناقه *nāḳa*, f. a she-camel. *a.*

ناك नाक *nāk*, m. the heavens, paradise, æther, sky, the atmosphere. *s.*

ناك नाक *nāk*, f. the nose. *nāk chaṛhānā*, to turn up one's nose, to be angry or displeased. *nāk rakhnā*, to preserve one's honour. *nāk sakoṛnā*, to turn up one's nose, to be displeased. *nāk kaṭānā*, to lose one's honour. *nāk kaṭī honā*, to lose one's honour. *s.*

ناك *nāk*, (as an affix) full, affected with, &c., as *gham-nāk*, affected with grief. *p.*

ناكا नाका *nākā*, m. the extremity of a road; the eye of a needle; an alley, avenue, lane. *nākebandī*, shutting up a road; collecting of transit duties. *nāke-dār*, the receiver of customs or transit duties. *h.*

ناكا नाका *nākā*, m. an alligator, a crocodile. *s.*

ناكتخدا *nā-kat-khudā*, / ناكدخدا *nā-kad-khudā*, } unmarried, a bachelor. *nā-kat-khudā,ī* or *nā-kad-khudā,ī*, the unmarried state, or state of single blessedness. *p.*

ناكڑا नाकड़ा *nākṛā*, m. an inflammation in the nose; polypus. *s.*

ناكشتر नाक्षत्र *nākshatr*, m. a month computed by the moon's passage through the twenty-seven mansions. *s.* [the lunar asterisms. *s.*

ناكشترك नाक्षत्रिक *nākshatrik*, belonging to

ناكشتركي नाक्षत्रिकी *nākshatrikī*, f. stellar influence. *s.*

ناكل नाकुल *nākul*, belonging or relating to [an ichneumon. *s.*

ناكلي नाकुली *nākulī*, f. name of a plant; the ichneumon plant, believed to furnish the mongoose with an antidote when bitten by a snake. *s.*

ناكي नाकी *nākī*, of or relating to nose. *s.*

ناگ नाग *nāg*, m. a snake, an elephant; the hooded snake, commonly called, cobra di capello, and which the Hindūs consider a sacred reptile. The word is also applied to the fabulous serpents with human faces, who are supposed to inhabit the lower regions; a small tree (*Mesua ferrea*); a sort of grass (*Cyperus pertenuis*); a tree (*Rottleria tinctoria*); one of the astronomical periods called *Karans*; lead; poison. *nāg-bhāshā*, a *prākṛit* language said to be used by the serpentine race who inhabit *Pātāl*. *nāg-panchamī*, name of a Hindū holiday, the 5th of *Shrāvan*, *shukl puksh*, on which day they worship a snake to procure blessings on their children. *nāg-kanyā*, a race of females said to inhabit *Pātāl* or the regions under the earth, and to be of serpentine extraction, but very beautiful. *nāg-lok*, the regions under the earth, *Pātāl*; not being accessible to the sun, it is illuminated by very resplendent jewels. *s.*

ناگا नागा *nāgā*, m. a caste of Hindū mendicants who go naked: sometimes they are armed, and serve as mercenaries to native princes. *s.*

ناگابها नागाभा *nāgābhā*, m. the ancient city of *Hastināpūr*. *s.*

ناگانچلا नागाञ्चला *nāgānchalā*, m. a boring-rod. *s.* [ancient Delhi. *s.*

ناگانگ नागाङ्ग *nāgāng*, m. *Hastināpūr*, or

ناگاه *nā-gāh*, in no time, suddenly, unexpectedly, all at once, unawares. *p.*

ناگبلا नागबला *nāg-balā*, f. a creeping plant (*Hedysarum lagopodioides*). *s.* [tree. *s.*

ناگبندھ नागबन्धु *nāg-bandhu*, m. the holy fig-

ناگبھد नागभिद् *nāg-bhid*, m. a sort of snake (*Amphisbæna*). *s.*

ناگبیل नागबेल *nāg-bel*, m. the betel plant. *s.*

ناگپاس नागपास *nāg-pās*, m. a running noose of a rope; name of a country, the same as *nāgaur* *s.*

ناگپتني नागपत्नी *nāg-patnī*, f. a female of the serpent race. *s.*

ناگپشپ नागपुष्प *nāg-pushp*, m. a tree used in dyeing (*Rottleria tinctoria*) a small tree (*Mesua ferrea*), a flower (*Michelia champaca*). *s.*

ناگ پھانس नागफांस *nāg-phāṅs*, f. a noose used to seize an enemy in battle, resembling the arms of the *Retiarii* among the Roman gladiators. *h.*

ناگپھني नागफनी *nāg-phanī*, f. a hedge-plant so called, the prickly pear (*Cactus ficus Indica*). *s.*

ناگجیون नागजीवन *nāg-jīvan*, m. tin. *s.*

ناگجوها नागजिह्वा *nāg-jivhā*, f. a plant (*Asclepias pseudosarsa*). *s*

ناگجوهكا नागजिह्विका *nāg-jivhikā*, f. red arsenic. *s.* [ivory. *s.*

ناگدنت नागदन्त *nāg-dant*, m. elephant's tooth,

ناگدنتي नागदन्ती *nāg-dantī*, f. a sort of sunflower (*Heliotropium Indicum*). *s.*

ناگدون नागदौन *nāg daun*, m. a kind of wood, by touching which it is said that fetters spontaneously fall off; the plant asparagus. *s.*

ناگ دونا नागदौना *nāg-daunā*, m. name of a plant (*Artemisia vulgaris*). *s.*

ناگر नागर *nāgar*, adj. town-born or bred, clever, sharp, knowing; name of a tribe of Gujrātī Brāhmans; a cunning or expert person; a sort of grass (*Cyperus pertenuis*); a form of writing, the *Deva-nāgarī*). *s.* [*perus*). *s.*

ناگرمستا नागरमुस्ता *nāgar-mustā*, f. a grass (*Cy-*

ناگرموتها नागरमोथा *nāgar-mothā*, m. name of a sweet-smelling grass (*Cyperus pertenuis*, &c. *Roxb.*). *s.*

ناگرنگ नागरङ्ग *nāgrang*, m. the orange, especially the Silhet orange (*Citrus aurantium*). *s.*

ناگري नागरी *nāgarī*, the character in which the Sanskrit language is generally written and printed in Northern India (called also *Deva-nāgarī*); f. an artful or clever woman; a sort of euphorbia. *s.*

ناگ كيسر नागकेशर *nāg-kesar* or *-keshar*, m. name of a tree (*Mesua ferrea*). *s.*

ناگل नागल *nāgal*, m. a plough. *s.*

ناگماتر नागमातृ *nāg-mātṛi*. f. name of the goddess *Manasā*, supposed to preside over snakes; red arsenic. *s.*

ناگن नागन *nāgan* or *nāgin*, } f. a female serpent. *s.*
ناگني नागिनी *nāginī*, }

ناگود नागोद *nāgod*, } m. armour for the front or the belly,
ناگودر नागोदर *nāgodar*, } a breastplate, a cuirass. *s.*

ناگور नागौर *nāgaur*, m. name of a country near *Mārwāṛ*. *s.*

ناگورا नागौरा *nāgaurā*, of or belonging to *Nagaur*; a fine breed of bullocks so called. *s.*

ناگهان *nāgahān*, } sudden, suddenly. *p.*
ناگهاني *nāgahānī*, }

ناگیسر नागेशर *nāgesar* or *nāgeshar*, f. name of a flower (*Mesua ferrea*); Indian rose chestnut. *s.*

ناگیسري नागेशरी *nāgesarī*, of the colour of the *nāgesar*, yellow. *s.*

نال नाल *nāl*, along with, accompanying; near. *soch bhai bharī kharī sakhī lakhi nāl kī*, her accompanying friends, seeing this, were filled with extreme anxiety and terror. *h.*

نال नाल *nāl*, m. a tube; barrel of a gun; the navel-string; stalk of the lotus. *s.*

نالا नाला *nālā*, m. a ravine, a rivulet, canal, gutter, furrow (vulg. "nullah"). *h.*

نالان *nālāṇ*, lamenting, lamentable. *p.*

نالتا नालिता *nālitā*, f. a kind of potherb (*Hibiscus cannabinus*). *s.*

نالش *nālish*, f. complaint, lamentation, exclamation, a groan; accusation in a law court. *p.*

نالشي *nālishī*, m. a plaintiff, a complainant. *p.*

نالكا नालिका *nālikā*, f. name of an esculent root (*Arum colocasia*). *h.*

نالكي नालकी *nālkī*, f. a sort of sedan or litter, generally used by people of rank. *h.*

نالگي *nālagī*, f. weeping, lamentation. *p.*

نالنا *nālnā*, to weep, to lament. *p. h.*

ناله *nāla*, m. lamentation, weeping; a small river, a canal. *p.*

نالي नाली f. a drain; a straw, a stalk; a tubular vessel of the body; a tubulated tile; a sinuous ulcer or fistula. *s.*

ناليدن *nālīdan*, to mourn, lament, weep; to [complain. *p.*

ناليورن नालीव्रण *nālīvran*, m. a fistulous or sinuous sore. *s.*

نام नाम *nām*, m. name, character, fame, reputation, honour. *nām-dār*, famous, celebrated. *nām-dārī*, celebrity. *nām-dharnā*, *s.* to name, to fix a name on (particularly a bad name). *nām dharwānā*, to be defamed; to give name to a child. *nām-denā*, to give a name to, to make conspicuous. *nām ḍabonā*, to lose one's honour or reputation. *nām rakhnā*, to name. *nām karnā*, to establish a name, to become famous. *shi'r un ne k͟hūb kahe, āfāḳ meṅ apnā nām kiyā*, he has composed elegant verses, and extended his fame in the world. *nām-lenā*, to praise; to repeat the name of God. *nām lekar māṅg khānā*, to beg alms in the name of another. *nām nikālnā*, to become celebrated; to investigate the perpetrator of any crime. *nām honā*, to be conspicuous, famous, or renowned. *nām o nishān*, name and vestige, or address. *s. p.*

نامبرده *nām-burda*, the above-named, the afore-mentioned or said. *p.*

نامزد *nām-zad*, destined, declared, named, appointed; notorious. *p.*

نامشيش नामशेष *nām-shesh*, dead, deceased. *s.*

نامكرن नामकरण *nām-karan*, m. the act of naming a child first after birth. *s.*

نامم नामम *nāmam*, the mark made on the forehead by the Hindūs. *h.*

نامنا नामना *nāmnā*, a. to name, to praise, to panegyrise. *s. p.*

نامور *nām-war*, celebrated, famous. *p.*

ناموري *nām-warī*, f. celebrity, renown, fame. *p.*

ناموس *nāmūs*, f. reputation, fame, renown; disgrace; the female part of a family. *a.*

ناموسي *nāmūsī*, of or relating to the female part of a family. *a.*

نامه *nāma*, m. a letter, book, writing; (in comp.) history, account, as *shāh-nāma*, the account of the kings, an epic poem by Firdausī. *p.*

نامي *nāmī*, illustrious, celebrated. *nāmī honā*, to be celebrated. *nāme*, adv. by name. *p.*

نامي *nāmī*, growing, increasing. *a.*

نامية *nāmiya*, m. a creature; a stem, stalk of grapes. *ḳuwwati nāmiya*, power of growth or of increasing. *a.*

نان *nān*, f. bread. *nāni ābī*, bread which has been kneaded with water. *nān-bā,ī*, *nān-bā,ī'*, or *nān-paz*, a baker. *nān-pazī*, f. the trade of a baker, baking. *nāni tikī*, dry bread. *nān-k͟hatā,ī*, f. a kind of sweetmeat. *nāni-ribāṭ*, bread given in monasteries to travellers, mendicants, &c. *nāni raug͟hanī*, bread mixed with boiled butter. *nāni ni'mat*, a kind of bread. *nāni nihārī*, breakfast *nāni wakf*, bread bestowed in charity. *p.*

نانا नाना *nānā*, m. maternal grandfather. *h.*

نانا नाना *nānā*, various, several, sundry. *nānā-vidh*, or *nānā-bhānti*, or *nānā-rūp*, or *nānā-prakār*, in various ways or modes, multiform, of many sorts or kinds. *s.*

نانا नाना *nānā*, a. to bend, to bow down. *s.*

ناناورن नानावर्ण *nānā-varṇ*, many-coloured. *s.*

ناند नान्द *nānd*, f. a large earthen pan. *h.*

ناندنا नान्दना *nāndnā*, to live; to be domesticated; to associate with; also for *nāndhnā*, q. v. *h.*

ناندهنا नान्धना *nāndhnā*, a. to begin. *h.*

نانديا नान्दिया *nāndiyā*, m. the bull, and vehicle of *Shiva*. *s.*

نانديمكه नान्दीमुख *nandī-mukh*, m. a species of ceremony performed on festive occasions to the manes of deceased ancestors *s.*

نانڈيا नाडिया *nāṇḍiyā*, } (v. *nāndiyā*), the
نانڑيا नाड़िया *nāṅṛiyā*, } bull, &c. of the god *Shiva*. *s.*

نانك नानक *nānak*, name of a saint, founder of the sect of Sikhs. *nānak-panthī* or *-shāhī*, or *nānak-matā*, m. a Sikh or follower of *Nānak*. *h.*

نانكار *nānkār*, m. an allowance of money or land to *zamīndārs*, *ḳānūngos*, &c. for subsistence; land granted to servants for their maintenance. *p.*

نانكاري *nānkārī*, of or belonging to the allowance, &c. called *nānkār*, q. v. *nānkārī-zamīn*, land assigned rent-free to *zamīndārs*. *s.*

نانكمتا नानकमता *nānak-matā*, a follower of [*Nānak*. *h.*

نانگهنا नाङ्घना *nānghnā*, a. to step across, to jump over, to pass, to leap over. *s.*

نانو नांव *nāṅw*, } m. (cor. of *nām*) a name,
نانون नाओं *nāṅ,on*, } a noun. *s. p.*

نانو *nānū*, a simple song or story which mothers repeat when rocking a child *p.*

نانه नांह *nāṅh*, no, not, nay. *s. h.*

نانهيال नान्हियाल *nānhiyāl*, f. maternal grand-father's family. *h.*

ناني नानी *nānī*, f. maternal grandmother. *h.*

ناو नाव *nāw*, f. a boat, ship, vessel. *s.*

ناءو नाऊ *nā,ū*, m. a barber. *s.*

ناودان *nāw-dān*, m. a dock, an aqueduct, a gutter. *p.*

ناوك *nāwak*, f. an arrow; a tube, canal; a bee's sting; the tube through which an arrow is projected. *nāwak-andāz*, an archer. *p.*

ناوك नाविक *nāvik*, } belonging to a vessel;
ناوكي नावकी *nāoki*, } m. helmsman, pilot, sailor. *s.*

ناءون नाऊँ *nā,oṅ*, m. a name, a noun. *s. p.*

ناونا नावना *nāonā*, a. to bend downwards, to bow, to cause to stoop. *s.*

ناونوش *nāw-nosh* (for *nā,e,wa nosh*), carousing, banqueting, &c. *p.*

ناه नाहि *nāhi*, no, not, nay. *s.*

ناهر नाहर *nāhar* or *nāhir*, m. a tiger. *h.*

ناهيد *nāhid*, m. the planet Venus. *p.*

ناهين नाहीं *nāhīṅ*, no, not, nay, no indeed. *nāhīṅ-nāhīṅ*, not at all. *s.*

ناءي नाई *nā,ī*, m. a barber. *s.*

ناءي *nā,e* or *nā,ī*, a reed, a pipe, a flageolet, a flute, a fife. *p.*

نائب *nā,ib*, m. a deputy, vicegerent, lieutenant, substitute. *nā,ib-dīwān*, the deputy treasurer or accountant. *nā,ib-ḳāẓī*, the deputy judge. *nā,ib-nāẓim* or *-ṣūba-dār*, the deputy governor of a *ṣūba* or province. *a.*

نائبي *nā,ibī*, deputyship, lieutenancy. *a.*

ناءيچه *nā,īcha* or *naicha*, m. a small reed, a *ḥuḳḳa* snake. *p.*

ناير *nāyar*, } a name of a tribe of Hindūs in
نايڑ *nāyaṛ*, } Southern India, commonly called "Nairs." *d.*

نائره *nā,ira* or *nā,irat*, fire, heat, inflammation, flame, enmity, hatred. *a.*

نايزه *nāyaza*, } m. a canal, a tube; the
نايژه *nāyazha*, } *urethra*. *p.*

نايك नायक *nāyak*, m. a chief, a leader, a man, a youth; a native officer of the lowest rank, corresponding to corporal in our corps; a person well conversant in dancing, singing, &c. *s.*

نايكا नायिका *nāyikā*, f. female of *nāyak*; the mistress of a house (particularly of a brothel). *s.*

نايكوار *nayahwār*, under a *nāyak* (a village, &c.). *s. p.*

ناين नायन *nāyan* or नाइन *nā,in*, (fem. of [*nā,ī*) a barber's wife. *s.*

ناي‌نوش *nā,e-nosh*, piping and drinking; carousing, banqueting. *p.*

نبات *nabāt*, f. vegetation; an herb, vegetable, grass. *'ilmi nabāt*, botany. *a.*

نبات *nabāt*, f. sugar; sweetmeats. *p.*

نباتات *nabātāt*, pl. vegetables, plants. *a.*

نباتي *nabātī*, made or consisting of vegetables (a dish) *a.*

نبارن निबारन *nibāran*, m. (also *nivāran*) hindering, prevention, stoppage, forbidding. *s.*

نبارنا निबारना *nibārnā*, a. to forbid. *s.*

نباڑا *nibāṛā*, passing, transit, passage. *d.*

نباڑن निबाड़न *nibāṛan*, m. spending, separating. *h.*

نباڑنا निबाड़ना *nibāṛnā*, a. to keep one's engagements, &c., to accomplish, to perform; to spend, to end; separate. *h.*

نباش *nabbāsh*, a grave-digger; a plunderer of the dead; one who strips the dead of their grave-clothes. *a.*

نباض *nabbāẓ*, m. one who feels the pulse, a physician. *a.* [pulse. *a.*

نباضي *nabbāẓī*, the science of examining the

نباءو *nibā,o* (for *nibāhū*, q.v.), lasting, &c. *d.*

نباه निबाह *nibāh*, m. accomplishment, maintenance, supply, sufficiency, keeping. *s.*

نباهنا निबाहना *nibāhnā*, a. to accomplish; to protect, to guard, to take care of; to keep one's faith; to behave; to afford; to conduct, to perform; to wear, to last or endure for a long time. *s.*

نباهو निबाहू *nibāhū*, lasting, permanent, sufficient for one's purpose. *s.* [ment. *h.*

نبٹيرا निबटेरा *nibṭerā*, m. determination, settle-

نبخته *ni-bakhta*, unfortunate. *s. p.*

نبسه *nabasa*, a daughter's child. *p*

نبرد *nabard*, m. battle, engagement, war. *p.*

نبڑنا निबड़ना *nibaṛnā*, n. to be settled, to be decided, to be finished or spent. *h.*

نبشتن *nabishtan* (for *nawishtan*), to write. *p.*

نبض *nabẓ*, f. the pulse. *nabz dekhnā*, to feel the pulse. *a.*

نبل निबल *nibal* (for *nir-bal*), weak, without power or strength; fem. *nibalā*, a woman. *s.*

نبلائي निबलाई *nibalā,ī*, f. weakness. *s.*

نبندھ निबन्ध *nibandh*, affixed, ascertained; m. binding, confinement, constipation. *s.*

نبوت *nubūwat*, f. prophecy. *a.*

نبوي *nabawī*, of or relating to the prophet (*Muḥammad*); prophetical. *a.*

نبهه नभः *nabha*, m. the sky, the air, the firmament. *s.*

نبهاڑنا *nibhāṛnā*, a. (v. *nibāṛnā*), to finish. *d.*

نبهاگا निभागा *ni-bhāgā*, } (for *nir-bhāgya*),
نبهاگي निभागी *ni-bhāgī*, } unfortunate. *s*

نبهانا निभाना *nibhānā*, a (v. *nibāhnā*), to accomplish, &c. *s.*

نبهو निभाओ *nibhā,o*, permanence, lasting quality, durability. *s.*

نبهچر नभचर *nabha-char*, that which soars in the air, a bird, a cloud, wind. *s.*

نبهرما *nibhramā*, without respect, worthless. *d.*

نبهستهت नभस्थित *nabha-sthit*, situated in the sky; also m. name of one of the infernal regions. *s.*

نبهنا निभना *nibhnā*, n. to serve, to succeed, pass, live; to be accomplished, performed; a. to preserve, to take care of, to afford, to conduct, to perform. *s.*

نبي *nabī*, m. a prophet. *a.*

نبيدن निवेदन *nibedan*, m. an address, petition, representation to a superior. *s.*

نبيره *nabīra*, m. a grandson, son's son. *nabīrī*, a son's daughter. *p.*

نبيڑا निबेड़ा *niberā*, m. (v. *nibṭerā*) settlement, end, finishing. *s.*

نبيڑنا निबेड़ना *nibeṛnā*, a. to spend, to end, to perform. *s.*

نبيڑو निबेरू *niberū*, performing, finishing. *s.*

نبيسه *nabīsa*, m. a grandson. *p.*

نبيسي *nabīsī*, f. a granddaughter. *p.*

نبين नवीन *nabīn* (for *navīn*), new, fresh. *s.*

نپ निप *nip*, m. the kadamb tree. *s.*

نپات निपात *nipāt*, m. death, dying, falling. *s.*

نپان निपान *nipān*, m. a trough, a reservoir of water. *s.*

نپاٹنا निपाटना *nipāṭnā*, a. (same as *nipṭānā*, [q. v.). *h.*

نپتت निपतित *nipatit*, fallen. *s.*

نپتن निपतन *nipatan*, m. falling. *s.*

نپٹ निपट *nipaṭ*, very, exceedingly. *h.*

نپٹارا निपटारा *nipṭārā*, m. end, finishing. *h.*

نپٹارو निपटारू *nipṭārū*, m. who finishes, terminates. *h.*

نپٹانا निपटाना *nipṭānā*, a. to settle, to decide, to conclude, to terminate, [&c. *h.*

نپٹنا निपटना *nipaṭnā*, n. to be settled, finished, &c. *h.*

نپن निपुण *nipuṇ*, distinguished, clever, skilful. *s.*

نپنسك नपुंसक *napunsak*, m. (in gram.) neuter gender; an hermaphrodite, a eunuch; adj. impotent, imbecile, cowardly. *s.*

نپوتا निपूता *nipūtā*, without a son, childless. *s.*

نپهل निःफल *niphal* (f. *niphalā*), fruitless. *s.*

نت नित *nit*, always, continually, ever; the base of an obtuse-angled triangle. *nit-nit*, perpetually. *s.*

نت नत *nat* or *nata*, m. the zenith distance of a planet, &c. *nati*, f. bending, curvature. *s.*

نتا नित्ता *nittā*, f. (for *nityatā*) perpetuity. *s.*

نتانت नितान्त *nitānt*, much, excessive; excessively. *s.*

نتانش नतांश *natānsh*, m. zenith distance. *s.*

نتانگ नतांग *natāng*, bent, stooping. *natāngī*, f. a woman. *s.*

نتپرت नितप्रीत *nit-prati*, } always, perpetually,
نتٹهه नितउठ *nit-uṭh*, } without interval. *s.*

نتائج *natā,ij* (pl. of نتيجه), births, results, conclusions, consequences. *a.*

نترام नितराम *nit-rām*, always, eternally. *s.*

نت گلا *nat gullā*, m. a cockle or mussel, small shell-fish. *d.*

نتل नितल *nital*, m. a division of hell.

نتمكه नतमुख *nat-mukh*, down-faced, looking down. *s.*

نتنب नितम्ब *nitamb*, m. the buttocks, posteriors of a woman. *s.*

نتني नतिनी *natinī*, f. a daughter's daughter. *h.*

نته नथ *nath*, m. a large ring worn in the nose; a rope passed through the nose of an ox. *s.*

نتهارنا निथारना *nithārnā*, a. to pour, to purify water or other liquid by letting the feculent matter subside, and pouring off the clear; to milk a cow. *h.*

نتهرا निथरा *nithrā*, clear (water whose impurity has subsided). *h.*

نتهنا नथना *nathnā*, m. a nostril; a ring for the nose; n. to have the nose pierced (a bullock). *h.*

نتهني नथनी *nathnī*, f. a small ring worn in the nose; a ring inserted in the hilt of a sword; a cord tied round a bullock's nose, by which the animal is guided. *h.*

نتهي नथी *nathī*, f. a file or bundle of official papers tied up together (more especially those relating to a law-suit). *h.*

نتي नित्य *nitya* (v. *nit*), constantly, ever. *nitya-pralay*, m. the constant loss of living beings. *nitya-yukt*, always busy. *nitya-yauvan*, ever young. *s.*

نتي नित्ती *nittī*, f. (cor. of *niktī*) small scales, such as goldsmiths use. *h.*

نتيانتيا नित्यानित्य *nityānityā*, eternal and perishable. *s.*

نتياندهياي नित्यानध्याय *nityānadhyāya*, m. a period when the perusal of the Vedas is entirely prohibited, as the day of full moon, &c. *s.*

نتيت नतैत *natait*, m. a relative, kinsman. *h.*

نتيتا नित्यता *nityatā*, f. perpetuity, constancy. *s.*

نتيجه *natīja*, m. result, consequence, issue, what necessarily follows, retribution, reward; a fœtus, offspring, birth. *a.*

نتيدا नित्यदा *nityadā*, always, constantly, eternally. *s.*

نتيدان नित्यदान *nitya-dān*, m. daily alms. *s.*

نتيكرم नित्यकर्म *nitya-karma*, m. the constant or daily ceremonies of religion, those religious duties which are of constant recurrence. *s.*

نتيه नित्य *nitya*, eternal, everlasting, continual, fixed, invariable; adv. always, eternally. *s.*

نٹ नट *naṭ*, m. a tumbler, a dancer; the name of a tribe, who are generally jugglers, rope-dancers, &c.; a sort of reed (*Aruno tibialis*); a mode of music. *s.* [*bonduccella*). *h.*

نٹا नटा *naṭā*, f. name of a shrub (*Cæsalpinia*

نٹارا निटारा *niṭārā*, m. (cor. of *nibṭerā*) determination, final settlement, decree. *h.*

نٹبر नटबर *naṭbar*, m. (v. *naṭwā*) a tumbler. *h.*

نٹپترکا नटपत्रिका *naṭ-patrikā*, m. the egg-plant (*Solanum melongena*). *h.*

نٹر निटर *niṭar*, poor, worn out (applied to land that is over-cultivated). *h.*

نٹ کھٹ नटखट *naṭ-khaṭ*, roguish, waggish, artful, trickish, shrewd; m. a cheat, a rogue; naughty or fretful (as a child). *h.*

نٹکھٹی नटखटी *naṭ-khaṭī*, f. roguery, trickery, artfulness; fretfulness. *h.* [ment. *h.*

نٹمنڈن नटमण्डन *naṭmanḍan*, m. yellow orpi-

نٹن नटन *naṭan* or नटिन *naṭin*, the female of *naṭ*, q. v. *naṭan*, m. the art of dancing. *s.*

نٹن नटन *naṭan*, f. denial, negation. *h.*

نٹنا नटना *naṭnā*, a. to deny. *h.*

نٹناراین नटनारायण *naṭnārāyan*, m. name of a musical mode. *s.* [q. v. *h.*

نٹني नटिनी *naṭinī* or *naṭnī*, female of *naṭ*,

نٹوا नटवा *naṭwā*, m. a tumbler, juggler, gipsy. *h.* [sly, cunning, shrewd. *s.*

نٹھر निठुर *niṭhur*, obdurate, relentless, cruel;

نٹھرائی निठुराई *niṭhurā,ī*, } f. cruelty, obdu-
نٹھرتا निठुरता *niṭhurtā*, } racy. *s.*

نٹھلا निठल्ला *niṭhallā*, m. idleness; adj. idle. *h.*

نٹي नटी *naṭī*, f. a medicinal plant; a whore; an actress, a dancing-girl; red arsenic. *s.*

نثار *nis̤ār*, m. scattering, throwing, strewing; money which is thrown among the people on festive occasions; largesse; sacrifice. *a.*

نثاري *nis̤ārī*, of or relating to *nis̤ār*, q. v. *a.*

نثر *nas̤r*, f. prose. *nas̤r o naz̤m*, prose and verse. *a.*

نج निज *nij*, self, own, particular, individual, personal. *nij-tij-se*, properly, as it ought to be. *nij-kā*, of or belonging to self, own, peculiar. *s.*

نجابت *najābat*, f. nobleness, generosity. *a.*

نجات *najāt*, f. freedom, pardon, salvation, absolution, deliverance; escape, flight. *a.*

نجار *najjār*, m. a carpenter. *s.*

نجاري *najjārī*, f. the business of a carpenter. *a.*

نجاست *najāsat*, f. filth, dirt, nastiness, impurity. *a.*

نجبا *nujabā* (pl. of نجیب), nobles, heroes. *a.*

نجت नियुत *nijut* (also *niyut*), a million. *s.*

نجد *najd* or *najad*, a portion of central Arabia. *a.*

نجس *najis*, m. dirty, filthy, nasty. *najas*, dirtiness, filthiness, dung. *a.* [place. *s.*

نجستهان निजस्थान *nija-sthān*, m. one's own

نجسي *nijassī*, unlucky, of evil omen. *d.*

نجش *najsh*, enhancing the price of an article at a sale. *a.*

نجف *najaf*, m. high ground to which water does not reach; name of a place in which is the tomb of *'Alī*. *a.*

نجك *najik*, near, close by (this seems to be another corruption of *nazdīk*, q. v.). *d.*

نجم *najm*, m. a star, a planet; fortune; a horoscope, calculation of nativity. *a.*

نجوت निजजोत *nij-jot*, lands cultivated by the proprietors or revenue-payers for their own benefit. *s.*

نجوم *nujūm* (pl. of نجم), stars. *'ilmi nujūm*, astrology. *a.*

نجومي *nujūmī*, m. an astrologer; fem. the astrological art or science. *a.*

نجهانا निझाना *nijhānā*, a. to spy, to pry into. *h.*

نجھ تجھ निझतिझ *nijh-tijh*, f. correctness, propriety. *h.*

نجھوٹنا निझोटना *nijhoṭnā*, a. to twitch. *h.*

نجھول निझोल *nijhol*, steady, easy-paced, walking or running smoothly, without agitation (epithet applied to an elephant). *s.*

نجیب *najīb*, excellent, noble, generous, praiseworthy; (sub.) a hero, a volunteer; a certain class of Indian soldiers who are distinguished by a peculiar dress. *najību-ṭ-ṭarfain*, noble on both sides (father and mother). *a. p.*

نجیبزاده *najīb-zāda*, m. noble by birth, a young nobleman. *a.*

نجیبزادي *najīb-zādī*, f. daughter of a noble. *a. p.*

نجیبي *najībī*, f. nobility, &c. (v. *najābat*). *a.*

نچانا नचाना *nachānā*, a. to cause to dance. *s.*

نچمچانا नचमचाना *nach-machānā*, a. to lead a dance; to tease. *s.*

نچنت निचिन्त *nichint* or *nichant*, free from thought, anxiety, or care, unconcerned, careless, at leisure. *s.*

نچنتائي निचिन्ताई *nichintā,ī* or *nichantā,ī*, f. carelessness, fearlessness, thoughtlessness, unconcern, leisure. *s.* [dance. *s.*

نچوانا नचवाना *nachwānā*, a. to cause to

نچوانا नुचवाना *nuchwānā*, to cause to pluck out, to cause to pinch. *h.*

نچوڑ निचोड़ *nichoṛ*, m. the end or termination of any affair; the burthen, or that on which any thing depends. *h.* [&c. *h.*

نچوڑانا निचोड़ाना *nichoṛānā*, to cause to wring,

نچوڑنا निचोड़ना *nichoṛnā*, a. to wring, to squeeze, to strain, to extort. *h.*

نچوڑو निचोड़ू *nichoṛū*, نچوڑوا निचोड़वा *nichoṛwā*, } rapacious, extortionate; m. an extortioner. *a.*

نچوڑوانا *nichoṛwānā* (v. *nichoṛānā*, &c.). *h.*

نچویا नचवैया *nachwaiyā*, m. a dancer. *s.*

نچھاور निछावर *nichhāwar*, f. sacrifice, victim. *h.*

نچھتر नछत्तर *nachhattar* (for *nakshatra*), a lunar mansion, or constellation in the moon's path, a star or asterism; the Hindūs, besides the common division of the zodiac into twelve signs, divide it into twenty-seven *nakshatras*, two and a quarter of which are included in each sign: each *nakshatra* has its appropriate name. *s.*

نچھتری नछत्री *nachhatrī* or *nachhattarī*, born under a fortunate planet; fortunate. *s.*

نچھکا *nichhakkā*, pure, genuine, innocent of, untainted with, free from. *d.*

نچھل *nichhal*, clean, pure, clear. *d.*

نچے निचय *nichay*, m. certainty. *s.*

نچیت *nichīt*, without thought or anxiety. *d.*

نحافت *nuḥāfat*, f. being emaciated, leanness, emaciation. *a.*

نحر *naḥr*, a sacrifice. *yaumu-n-naḥr*, the day of sacrifice, being the tenth of *zu-l-ḥijja*, when the pilgrims assemble at Mecca. *a.*

نحس *naḥs*, unlucky, bad, inauspicious; m. an evil omen, bad luck. *a.*

نحسیت *naḥsiyat*, f. inauspiciousness. *a.*

نحو *naḥw*, f. (in gram.) syntax; way, path, track, manner, mode. *a.*

نحوست *naḥūsat*, f. a bad presage, a misfortune, evil omen, abomination. *a.*

نحوي *naḥwī*, grammatical; m. a grammarian, one skilled in syntax. *a.*

نحویت *naḥwiyat*, f. the art grammatical. *a.*

نحیف *naḥīf*, lean, meagre, weak, slender. *a.*

نخ *nakh*, a thread in general; a rank (of soldiers); a kind of carpet; a little, a few. *p.*

نخاس *nakhkhās*, m. a cattle or slave market; one who deals in cattle or slaves. *a.*

نخالص *nikhālaṣ* (v. *khulāṣa*), essence, &c. *a.*

نخچیر *nakhchīr*, m. the chase, game, prey, hunting. *nakhchīr-gāh*, hunting-ground. *p.*

نخرا *nakhrā*, نخره *nakhra*, } m. trick, artifice, joke, waggery, coquetry, deceit, shame, pretence. *nakhra-tillā*, blandishments. *nakhra-bāz*, affected, coquetish. *nakhra-bāzī*, coquetry, &c. *p.*

نخست *nukhust* (properly *nakhust*), m. the beginning, the first; adv. at first. *nukhust-zād*, the eldest son. *nukhust-zādī*, primogeniture. *p.*

نخستگي *nukhustagī*, f. first-fruits, priority. *p.*

نخستین *nukhustīn*, the first, the very first. *p.*

نخشاره *nakhshāra*, the cheek, the face. *d.*

نخشب *nakhshab*, the full moon; name of a city in *Turkestan*, famous for a celebrated well called *chāhi nakhshab*. *p.*

نخل *nakhl*, m. a date-tree, a palm-tree (and often used for a young tree of any kind), a plant. *nakhl-band*, m. a gardener, a maker of artificial flowers. *nakhl-bandī*, a plantation. *nakhli-maḥmūd*, name of a stage or resting-place for pilgrims from Persia on their way to or from Mecca, three days' journey from Kūfa. *a.*

نخلستان *nakhlistān*, نخله *nakhla*, } m. a palm plantation. *p.*

نخوت *nakhwat*, f. pride, haughtiness, pomp, magnificence. *a.*

نخود *nukhud* or *nukhūd*, m. a kind of pulse (*Cicer arietinum*). *nukhud-āb*, a kind of food given after physic has been taken: it consists of pulse and meat boiled together for a long time. *p.*

ند नद *nad*, m. a river (commonly *nadī*). *s.*

ندا *nidā*, f. sound, voice, calling. *a.*

نداگھکال निदाघकाल *nidāgh-kāl*, m. the hot season, two months previous to the rains. *s.*

نداف *naddāf*, m. a cotton dresser, also a dealer in cotton. *a.*

ندافي *naddāfī*, f. dressing of cotton, the trade of a *naddāf*. *a.*

ندامت *nadāmat*, f. repentance, penitence, contrition, regret. *a.*

ندان निदान *nidān*, at last, at length, lastly, after all, altogether; f. (in medicine) knowledge of the symptoms of diseases (*diagnosis*). *s.*

ندرا निद्रा *nidrā*, f. sleep, sleepiness. *nidrā-yamān*, sleeping. *nidrālu*, sleepy; f. a sort of perfume. *s.*

ندرت निद्रित *nidrit*, sleepy, drowsy. *s.*

ندرت *nudrat*, f. oddness, singularity, rareness. *a.*

ندرشن निदर्शन *nidarshan*, m. example, precept. *s.*

ندشٹ निदिष्ट *nidishṭ*, ordered, advised, explained. *s.*

ندگدھکا निदिग्धिका *nidigdhikā*, f. a sort of prickly nightshade (*Solanum jacquini*). *s.*

ندما *nudamā* (pl. of نديم), courtiers. *a.*

ندولا नदोला *nadolā*, m. a large earthen pan. *h.*

ندھ निधि *nidhi*, m. one of *Kuvera's* divine treasures, a receptacle. *s.*

ندھان निधान *nidhān*, m. a place, house, a receptacle, a vessel; a treasure (v. *nidhi*). *s.*

ندھڑک निधड़क *nidhaṛak*, abruptly, without fear or reflection. *h.*

ندھن निधन *nidhan*, poor, indigent. *nidhantā*, f. poverty. *s.*

ندي नदी *nadī* or *naddī*, f. a river. *s.*

نديا नदिया *nadiyā*, m. a river; a small stream. *s.*

نديتير नदीतीर *nadī-tīr*, m. bank of a river. *s.*

نديج नदीज *nadīj*, m. the marshy date-tree, another tree (*Pentaptera arjuna*); adj. aquatic, produced in the river. *s.*

نديسرج नदीसर्ज *nadī-sarj*, m. a tree (*Pentaptera arjuna*). *s.*

نديش निदेश *nidesh*, m. order, direction. *nideshī*, directing, pointing out. *s.*

نديكانت नदीकान्त *nadī-kānt*, m. name of a small tree (*Vitex negundo*); another tree (*Barringtonia acutangula*). *s.*

نديكانتا नदीकान्ता *nadī-kāntā*, f. the rose-apple (*Eugenia jambu*); a kind of shrub (*Leea hirta*). *a.*

نديكول नदीकूल *nadī-kūl*, m. the bank or shore of a river. *nadī-kūl-priya*, a sort of reed (*Calamus rotang*). *s.*

نديم *nadīm*, m. a companion, an intimate friend, a courtier. *a.*

نديبي नदेयी *nadeyī*, f. name of a plant (*Premna herbacea*). *s.*

نڈر निडर *niḍar*, fearless, without fear. *s.*

نڈھال निढाल *niḍhāl*, } still, motionless. *h.*
نڈھول निढोल *niḍhol*, }

نذر *nazr*, f. a vow; a present or gift (offered to a superior). any thing dedicated; (met.) an interview which is generally preceded by a present. *nazri dargāh*, an assignment of revenue to a shrine or religious establishment. *nazri 'īd*, presents made at religious festivals. *nazri imāmān* or *-pīrān*, gifts to holy men. *nazr o niyāz*, vows and oblations. *a.*

نذرامام *nazri-imām*, presents given at the *Muḥammadan* places of worship, in memory of the *imāms Ḥasan* and *Ḥusain*. *nazri a,imma*, a gift of lands for the support of priests; charity lands. *a.*

نذرانه *nazrāna*, m. gifts, &c. offered or received when people of rank meet or pay their respects to a prince; a kind of tribute; fees paid to government as an acknowledgment for a grant of land or any public office. *a. p.*

نذردرگاه *nazri-dargāh*, land given as an endowment to places of religious worship among the *Muḥammadans*, the produce of which is supposed to be applied to the expenses of the establishment, such as the subsistence of the attendants, illuminations, repairs. *a. p.*

نذرونياز *nazr o niyāz*, f. vows and oblations made voluntarily, not observed on any particular days or occasions.—(B.). *a. p.*

نذور *nuzūr* or نذورات *nuzūrāt* (pl. of نذر), vows, gifts, &c. *a.*

نر नर *nar*, m. a male, a man; adj. masculine, male. *p. s.*

نر निर *nir*, without, deprived of; a privative prep. much used before Sanskrit words, similar in signification to the Persian *be*, as *nir-gandh*, scentless. *s.*

نر निरा *nira*, mere, pure, only, unalloyed, single, simple. *h.*

نراپد निरापद *nir-āpad*, prosperous, fortunate. *s.*

نرادر निरादर *nir-ādar*, of bad dispositions, disrespectful, uncourteous. *s.*

نرادهار निराधार *nir-ādhār*, without support.

نرادهم नराधम *narādham*, m. a vile man, a wretch. *s.*

نراس निराश *nir-ās* or *nir-āsh*, hopeless, desperate. *s.*

نراشري निराश्रय *nir-āshray*, without refuge, destitute. *s.*

نراشس निराशिस *nir-āshis*, without blessing. *s.*

نراشي निराशी *nir-āshī*, f. despair. *s.*

نراکار निराकार *nir-ākār*, without form or figure; incorporeal. *s.*

نراکانکشي निराकाङ्क्षी *nir-ākānkshī*, content, without desire. *s.*

نرالا निराला *nir-ālā*, pure, mere, simple, unmixed, unalloyed; rare, strange, odd. *h.*

نرالسيه निरालस्य *nir-ālasya*, not slothful, active. *s.*

نرالي निराले *nirāle*, aside, apart. *h.*

نرامال निरामालु *nirāmālu*, m. the wood-apple. *s.*

نرامشي निरामिषी *nir-āmishī*, living without eating flesh, free from sensual desires. *s.*

نرامي निरामय *nir-āmay*, m. the wild goat; a boar. *s.*

نرانا निराना *nir-ānā*, a. to reap (a harvest). *h.*

نراهار निराहार *nir-āhār*, without food, fasting. *s.*

نراياس निरायास *nir-āyās*, easy, ready, without trouble. *s.*

نرايده निरायुध *nir-āyudh*, unarmed, defenceless. *s.*

نربده निर्बुद्धि *nir-buddhi*, senseless, unintelligent. *s.*

نربس निर्बश *nir-bas* or *nir-bash*, without strength, powerless. *s.*

نربسي निर्बिसी *nir-bisī*, f. zedoary, a spicy plant somewhat like ginger in its leaves, but of a sweet scent (*Amomum zedoaria*, *Willd.*; *Curcuma zedoaria*, *Roxb.*). *s.*

نربل निर्बल *nir-bal*, weak, strengthless. *s.*

نربلتا निर्बलता *nir-baltā*, f. weakness, impotence. *s.*

نربنده निर्बन्धु *nir-bandhu*, friendless, without relatives. *s.*

نربنس निर्बंश *nir-bańs* or *nir-bańsh*, without race, childless; extinct (a race or family). *s.*

نربوجه निर्बूझ *nir-būjh*, not to be understood, incomprehensible. *s.*

نربهو नरभू *nar-bhū*, f. the land of men, India. *s.*

نربهي निर्भय *nir-bhai*, fearless, undaunted. *s.*

نربيج निर्बीज *nir-bīj*, without seed, childless; extinct (a race or family). *s.*

نربير निर्बैर *nir-bair*, free from hatred or enmity. *s*

نرپ नृप *nṛip* or *nṛipa*,
نرپت नरपति *nar-pati*,
نرپت नृपति *nṛi-pati*, } m. a king, a prince. *s.*

نرپابهیر नृपाभीर *nṛipābhīr*, m. music played at the royal meals. *s.*

نرپاسن नृपासन *nṛipāsan*, m. a throne. *s.*

نرپامي नृपामय *nṛipāmay*, m. consumption. *s.*

نرپانش नृपांश *nṛipānsh*, m. royal portion or revenue. *s.*

نرپاورت नृपावर्त *nṛipāvart*, m. a kind of gem. *s.*

نرپ‌پریه नृपप्रिय *nṛip-priya*, m. the thorny bamboo (*Bambusa spinosa*). *s.*

نرپت नृपति *nṛi-pati*, m. a king (v. *nṛip*). *s.*

نرپچهـ निर्पेछ *nir-pachh* or निर्पक्ष *nir-paksh*, helpless, of no party, friendless. *s.*

نرپدرم नृपद्रुम *nṛip-drum*, m. a tree (*Cassia fistula*). *s.*

نرپر नरपुर *nar-pur*, m. one of the three *lokas* or regions of the universe; the abode of man, the earth. *s.*

نرپرادهـ निरपराध *nir-aparādh*, faultless, blameless (also *niraparādhī*). *s.*

نرپریه नरप्रिय *nar-priya*, friendly to mankind. *s.*

نرپم निरुपम *nir-upam*, unequalled, having no likeness. *s.*

نرپنیت नृपनीति *nṛip-nīti*, f. royal policy. *s.*

نرپوچت नृपोचित *nṛipochit*, kingly, fit for a king. *s.*

نرپهل निर्फल *nir-phal*, fruitless, of no avail. *s.*

نرپیکش निरपेक्ष *nirapeksh*, independent of, regardless, careless. *s.*

نرت नित्त *nirt* (for *nṛitya*), m. dance (also *nṛiti*, f.). *s.*

نرتانا नित्ताना *nirtānā*, a. to make dance; to make pure, to clean. *s.*

نرتر निरुत्तर *nir-uttar*, silenced, without an answer. *s.*

نرتک नर्तक *nartak*, m.
نرتکي नर्तकी *nartakī*, f. } (also *nirtak*) an actor, a mimic, a player of any description, a dancer, a juggler. *nartak*, a reed (*Arundo karka*). *s.*

نرتن नर्तन *nartan*, m. dancing, acting. *s.*

نرتو नृतू *nṛitū*, m. a dancer, a mimic. *s.*

نرتنا नितना *nirtnā*, n. to dance, to jump about playfully. *s.*

نرتیک नृत्यक *nṛityak*,
نرتیکاري नृत्यकारी *nṛitya-kārī*, f. } a dancer, an actor, mimic, juggler. *s.*

نرتیه नृत्य *nṛitya*, m. dancing, acting, pantomime. *s.*

نرجا नरजा *narjā*, m. small scales. *h.*

نرجت निर्जित *nir-jit*, conquered, subdued. *s.*

نرجر निर्जर *nir-jar*, immortal, undecaying; m. nectar, ambrosia, the food of the gods. *s.*

نرجل निर्जल *nir-jal*, dry, desert, without water; m. a desert, a waste. *s.*

نرجن निर्जन *nir-jan*, solitary, deserted, without a soul. *s.*

نرجه नरजः *narja*, m. small scales. *h.*

نرجهر निर्झर *nir-jhar*, m. a cascade or torrent. *s.*

نرجیو निर्जीव *nir-jīv*, inanimate, without life. *s.*

نرچا निचा *nirchā*, m. a kind of greens (*Corchorus capsularis*). *h.*

نرچهل निछल *nir-chhal*, simple, guileless. *s.*

نرخ *nirkh*, m. price (fixed by the officers of police), price current, tariff, assize. *nirkh-bandī*, a document in which prices are recorded. *nirkh-dārogha*, a clerk of the market. *p.*

نرخڑا *narkharā*, m.
نرخڑي *narkharī*, f. } the throat, the throttle. *h.*

نرخنامه *nirkh-nāma*, m. an account or bill of current or settled market prices. *p.*

نرخي *nirkhī*, m. the person who fixes the price current, an appraiser, assizer. *p.*

نرد *nard*, f. a counter, chessman, &c.; draughts, &c., any game played with counters, backgammon. *p.*

نردبان *nardbān* or *nardubān*, m. a staircase, steps, a ladder, especially a scaling-ladder. *p.*

نردشت निर्दिष्ट *nir-disht*, described, pointed out, ascertained. *s.*

نردوتک नर्दटक *nardwaṭak*, m. a stanza of four parts, of seventeen syllables each. *s.*

نردوش निर्दोष *nir-dosh*,
نردوشي निर्दोषी *nir-doshī*,
نردوکهـ निर्दोख *nir-dokh*, } faultless, blameless, without defect or blemish. *s.*

نردوند निर्द्वन्द *nir-dwand*, not double; without dispute or quarrel, peaceably. *s.*

نردهار निर्धार *nir-dhār*,
نردهارن निर्धारण *nir-dhāran*, } m. ascertaining, settling or fixing with accuracy, certainty. *s.*

نردهارت निर्धारित *nir-dhārit*, ascertained, determined. *s.*

نردهرم निर्धर्म *nir-dharm*, impious, immoral. *nṛi-dharm*, m. manly property or duty. *s.*

نردهکاري निरधिकारी *nir-adhikārī*, one acting without right or authority. *s.*

نردهن निर्धन *nir-dhan*, indigent, without wealth. *s.*

نردهن निर्दहन *nir-dahan*, m. marking-nut. *s.*

نردهني निर्दहनी *nir-dahanī*, f. a sort of creeper, from the fibres of which bowstrings are made (*Sanseveria zeylanica*). *s.*

نردئي निर्दई *nir-da,ī*, निर्दय *nir-day*, or निर्दयी *nir-dayī*, cruel, merciless, hardhearted. *s.*

نرديش निर्देश *nir-desh*, m. order, command, description, pointing out, depicting or exhibiting. *s.*

نرديو नृदेव *nṛi-dev*, m. a king. *s.*

نررتهك निरर्थक *nir-arthak*, negligent, careless, indolent; obsolete, of no signification, vain, fruitless. *s.*

نرروپ नररूप *nar-rūp*, m. the human form; adj. (also *nar-rūpī*) having the human form. *s.*

نرس निरस *niras*, worse, inferior; dry, tasteless, insipid, unsavoury; m. dryness, insipidity. *s.*

نرست निरस्त *nirast*, expelled, abandoned. *s.*

نرستر निरस्त्र *nir-astr*, unarmed, without weapons. *s.*

نرسنگا नरसिंगा *nar-singā*, m. a horn, wind [instrument. *s.*

نرسنگه नरसिंह *nar-singh* or नृसिंह *nṛi-singh*, the name of the fourth *avatār* or incarnation of *Vishṇū*, which happened in *Satya-yuga*, upon the following occasion. *Hiranya-kashipu*, an impious prince, was enraged at his son *Prahlād* for worshipping the Almighty, and tried every means of destroying him, by poison, by throwing him into fire, into the ocean, &c., yet *Prahlād* lived. "If your God is present everywhere," says *Hiranya-kashipu*, "let him come from an alabaster pillar," on which *Narsingha* appeared, with the lower part of a man and the upper part of a lion, destroyed the father, and set the son on the throne, &c.; a chief, a great man. *s.*

نرسنگيا नरसिंगिया *nar-singiyā*, m. one who plays on the horn. *s*

نرسون नरसों *narson*, the fourth day past or to come, some days ago or hence. *s.*

نرغا *narghā*, m. surrounding; a kind of long drum. *narghā karnā*, to surround. *a.*

نرقل *narḳal*, m. a kind of reed of which mats are made (v. *narkaṭ*). *s.*

نرك नरक *narak*, m. hell. *narak-kuṇḍ*, a well or pit in hell. *s.*

نركت निरुक्त *nirukt*, obscure, obsolete; m. a glossary of Vedic terms (also *nirukti*, f.).

نركٹ नरकट *narkaṭ*, m. a reed of which mats are made (*Arundo tibialis, Roxb.*). *s.*

نركس नरकस *narkas*, m. the windpipe. *h.*

نركستها नरकस्था *narkasthā*, f. the river of hell. *s.*

نركش निरक्ष *niraksh*, having no latitude; m. the equator. *niraksh-desh*, the equatorial region; Lankā or Ceylon. *s.*

نركل नरकल *narkal*, a reed (v. *narkaṭ*). *s.*

نركهڑا नरखड़ा *narkhaṛā*, m. } the throat, the
نركهڑي नरखड़ी *narkhaṛī*, f. } throttle. *h.*

نركهنا निरखना *nirakhnā*, a. to look behind one, to look at. *s.*

نرگ *nargā* (for *narghā*), a kind of drum. *d.*

نرگاو *nar-gāw*, m. a bull. *p.*

نرگت निर्गत *nirgat*, gone out, departed. *s.*

نرگس *nargis*, f. a narcissus; (met.) the eye of a mistress. *nargisi makhmūr*, an epithet applied to a mistress's eyes (intoxicated Narcissus). *p.*

نرگستان *nargistān*, } m. a bed of narcissus
نرگسدان *nargis-dān*, } flowers; a phial into which they put a narcissus. *p.*

نرگسي *nargisī*, of or relating to the narcissus; name of a species of cloth. *p.*

نرگم निर्गम *nir-gam*, m. going forth, exit. *s.*

نرگن निर्गुण *nir-guṇ*, unstrung (as a bow, necklace, &c.); without passions or human qualities (an epithet of God); without estimable qualities, worthless, unskilful. *nirguna-twa*, m. the state of being free from all qualities. *s.*

نرگنٹهي निर्गुण्ठी *nir-gunṭhī*, f. a shrub (*Vitex negundo*); the root of the lotus. *s.*

نرگنده निर्गन्ध *nirgandh*, inodorous. *nirgandh-pushpī*, f. the Simal or silk-cotton tree. *s.*

نرگهن निर्घिन *nir-ghin*, not odious, not to be detested. *s.*

نرگهنٹ निर्घण्ट *nirghanṭ*, m. a vocabulary, [an index. *s.*

نرليپت निर्लिप्त *nir-lipt*, unsmeared, undefiled; a name of *Krishṇa*. *s.*

نرلج निर्लज्ज *nir-lajj*, shameless, impudent. *s.*

نرلوبه निर्लोभ *nir-lobh*, } disinterested, free
نرلوبهي निर्लोभी *nir-lobhī*, } from avarice. *s.*

نرم *narm*, soft; defective (coin); easy, gentle, silly. *p.*

نرماده *narmāda*, m. a hinge; a joint. *p.*

نرماگي *narmāgī*, } softness, tenderness. *p. d.*
نرمائي *narmā,ī*, }

نرماليه निर्माल्य *nir-mālya*, m. purity, clearness, cleanness; the remains of an offering presented to a deity. *s.*

نرمان निर्माण *nirmān*, m. make, manufacture, construction; pith, marrow, essence. *s.*

نرمانا *narmānā*, a. to soften, to render mild. *p. h.*

نرمت निर्मित *nir-mit*, made, fabricated, artificial. *s.*

نرمد निर्मद *nir-mad*, sober, quiet; m. an elephant out of rut. *s.*

نرمدا नर्मदा *narmadā*, f. the Nerbudda river. *s.*

نرمل निर्मल *nir-mal*, } pure, limpid, clean,
نرملا निर्मला *nir-malā*, } transparent, spotless. *s.*

ناملتا निर्मलता *nir-malatā*, f. } pureness,
نرملتوه निर्मलत्व *nir-malatwa*, m. } limpidness, pellucidness, cleanness, clearness, transparency. *s.*

نرملي निर्मली *nir-malī*, f. name of a seed with which water is cleared (*Strychnos potatorum*); the clearing nut. *s.*

نرمم निर्मम *nir-mam*, disinterested, unselfish. *s*

نرممت निर्ममता *nir-mamtā*, f. } disregard of
نرممتوہ निर्ममत्व *nir-mamtwa*, m. } self, dis-
interestedness. *s.* [serted. *s.*

نرمنش निर्मनुष *nir-manush*, uninhabited, de-

نرمول निर्मूल *nir-mūl*, baseless, unfounded, eradicated. *s.*

نرموهي निर्मोही *nir-mohī*, unkind, cold-blooded, void of affection or attachment; a stoic. *s.*

نرمه *narma*, soft. *narma i gosh*, the lobe of the ear. *p.*

نرمي *narmī*, } f. softness, tenderness,
نرميت *narmīyat*, } sweetness, delicacy; simplicity, silliness. *p.*

نرميدھ नरमेध *nar-medh*, m. a human sacrifice. *s.*

نرناتھ निर्नाथ *nir-nāth*, having no master or protector. *nirnāthtā*, f. widowhood. *s.*

نرنتر निरन्तर *nir-antar*, incessant, without interval. *nirantarābhyās*, m. private study, diligent pursuit. *s.*

نرنجن निरञ्जन *nir-anjan*, unstained; void of passion; m. the Supreme Being. *s.*

نرنجنا निरञ्जना *nir-anjanā*, f. the day of full moon. *s.* [lated. *s.*

نرندریه निरिन्द्रिय *nir-indriya*, maimed, muti-

نرنکار निरङ्कार *nir-ankār*, } without form (the
نرنکال निरङ्काल *nir-ankāl*, } Deity). *s.*

نرنکش निरङ्कुश *nir-ankush*, unchecked, uncontrolled. *s.* [teous. *s.*

نرنمسکار निर्नमस्कार *nir-namaskār*, uncour-

نرنی निर्णय *nirnai*, fixed, established, certain, appointed; m. ascertainment, certainty. *s.*

نرنیت निर्णीत *nirnīt*, ascertained, determined, decreed. *s.* [not windy. *s.*

نروات निर्वात *nir-vāt*, m. a calm; adj. still,

نروان निर्वाण *nir-vāṇ*, extinguished, extinct; m. beatitude, emancipation from matter and reunion with the Deity. *s.*

نرواہ निर्वाह *nir-vāh*, m. accomplishment, completion, end; maintaining, providing means, sufficiency. *s.*

نروپ निरूप *ni-rūp*, without form (the Deity); incorporeal. *s.* [pointed. *s.*

نروپت निरूपित *nirūpit*, ascertained, ap-

نروپن निरूपण *nirūpan*, m. ascertaining, determining *s.* [tion of *Vishṇu*. *s.*

نروراہ नृवराह *nṛi-varāh*, m. the boar incarna-

نرورت निर्वृत *nir-vṛit*, ended, emancipated, content. *nir-vṛitti*, f. completion, rest, final emancipation. *s.* [*zedoarda*). *s.*

نروشي निर्विषी *nirvishī*, f. a plant (*Curcuma*

نروکار निर्विकार *nir-vikār*, unchanged, unaltered, uniform. *s.*

نروکھ नरूख *narūkh*, male, masculine. *h.*

نروگ निरोग *nirog*, } in high health and
نروگي निरोगी *nirogī*, } spirits; free from sickness. *s.*

نروگھن *nir-vighna*, unobstructed, freely. *s.*

نرون निर्वन *nir-van*, bare, open (a country). *s.*

نروندھیا निर्विन्ध्या *nir-vindhyā*, f. a river that rises in the Vindhya mountains. *s.*

نرویك निर्विवेक *nir-vivek*, foolish, indiscriminating. *s.*

نروج निर्वीज *nir-vīj*, seedless, impotent. *s.*

نرویرج निर्वीर्य *nir-vīrj*, tame, emasculated. *s.*

نروید निर्वेद *nir-ved*, not having the Vedas; infidel, unscriptural. *s.* [mity. *s.*

نروير निर्वैर *nir-vair*, friendly, free from en-

نره नरः *nara* or *narra*, m. a male; adj. rough, rude, ugly. *s.*

نرهڑ नरहड़ *narhaṛ*, m. a shank, a leg. *h.*

نرهس निर्हस *nir-has*, dull, grave, averse to laughter. *s.* [from pride. *s.*

نرهنکار निरहङ्कार *nir-ahankār*, humble, free

نري नरी *narī*, f. a kind of leather, skin; goat or sheepskin leather coloured or dyed; a weaver's shuttle. *h.*

نریا नरिया *nariyā*, f. a tile. *h.*

نریاس निर्यास *nir-yās*, m. extract, decoction; exudation. *s.*

نریٹ नरेट *nareṭ*, m. } throat, windpipe. *na-*
نریٹا नरेटा *nareṭā*, m. } *reṭī dabānā*, to
نریٹي नरेटी *nareṭī*, f. } throttle. *h.*

نریچھا निरीछा *nirīchā*, f. looking at, hope, expectation. *s.*

نریس नरेस *nares*, } m. lord of men,
نریش नरेश *naresh*, } ruler, king, a
نریشور नरेश्वर *nareshwar*, } sovereign. *s.*

نریش निरीश *nirīsh*, m. the body of a plough. *s.*

نریکشن निरीक्षण *nirīkshan*, looking at, seeing, expecting. *nirīkshit*, beheld, expected. *nirīkshmān*, adj. looking, expecting. *s.* [spy. *s.*

نریکھنا निरेखना *nirekhnā*, a. to behold, to

نریندر नरेन्द्र *narendra*, m. a king, a sovereign. *s.*

نرینه *narīna*, a male, masculine. *p.*

نڑ नड़ *naṛ*, m. a reed (*Arundo tibialis*); a tribe whose employment is making glass bracelets. *s.*

نڑڑا *naṛaṛā*, } the throat, the windpipe, the
نڑڑي *naṛaṛī*, } weasand (v. *nareṭ*). *d.*

نزكيه नड़कीय *naṛkīya*, abounding in reeds. *s.*

نزلا *naṛlā*, the throat, the windpipe (v. *naṛeṛ*). *d.*

نزمين नड़मीन *naṛ-mīn*, m. a small fish haunting reedy places. *s.* [reeds. *s*

نزوان नड़वान *naṛ-wān*, reedy, abounding in

نزي *naṛī*, a kind of fireworks. *d.*

نز *nazz*, brisk, active; ground from which water flows. *a.*

نزاد *nazād*, نزاده *nazāda*, (v. *nizhād*) origin, root, family, &c. *p.*

نزار *nizār*, thin, slender, subtile. *p.*

نزاري *nizārī*, f. thinness, slenderness. *p.*

نزاع *nizā'*, m. contention, litigation, dispute, controversy. *a.* [ness. *a.*

نزاكت *nazākat*, f. elegance, politeness, soft-

نزاهت *nazāhat*, f. purity, exemption or remoteness from sin. *a.*

نزد *nizd* or *nazd*, نزديك *nazdīk*, near, hard by, close to, neighbouring, contiguous, almost, about; the word *nazdīk* has somehow been doomed to undergo several corruptions; the Hindūs of the north change it into *nagīch*, and the people of the Deccan into *nazik*, *najik*, *nazik*, &c. *p.*

نزديكي *nazdīkī*, f. propinquity, vicinity, nearness, neighbourhood. *p.*

نزع *naz'*, m. the last breath, gasping in the agonies of death. *a.*

نزك *nazik* (for *nazdīk*, q. v.), near, &c. *p.d.*

نزله *nazla* (also *nuzla*), m. a defluction of humours, a catarrh. *a.*

نزول *nuzūl*, m. descent, alighting, sojourning; a cataract (in the eye). *nuzūli āb*, a swelling of the testicle, which (excepting the case of a blow, or of *hernia*) is universally ascribed to the descent of water; it therefore comprehends *hydrocele, hernia humoralis,* and *scirrhus*: in revenue language, escheated property that has lapsed to the state from want of legal claimants. *a.*

نزهت *nuzhat*, f. verdure, freshness; pleasure, delight, cheerfulness; distance; integrity; ornament. *a.*

نزيك *nazīk* (for *nazdīk*, q. v.), near, &c. *nazikī*, nearness, neighbourhood. *p. d.*

نژاد *nizhād* or *nazhād*, m. origin, root, seed, family, descent, extraction. *p.*

نژند *nizhand* or *nazhand*, formidable; astonished, sad, angry; m. a learned preceptor. *p.*

نس *nas*, f. a vein; a sinew. *nas-dār*, sinewy, full of veins. *a.*

نس *nus*, m. the environs of the mouth; understanding. *p.* [*nir*) without, &c. *s*

نس *nis*, a privative particle used in comp. (v.

نس निस *nis* or निसि *nisi*, نسا निसा *nisā*, f. night. *nisā-char*, a demon; a robber, a thief; a nocturnal animal, an animal that watches and feeds by night. *nisā-kār* or *-nāth*, the moon. *s.*

نسا नसा *nasā*, f. the nose. *s.*

نسا *nisā*, f. pl. women, ladies; the female sex. *a.*

نسار निःसार *ni-sār*, sapless, pithless; vain; m. a plant (*Trophis aspera*). *s.*

نساس निसास *nisās*, m. breath, respiration. *s.*

نساج *nassāj*, m. a weaver; an inventor. *a.*

نسانا नसाना *nasānā*, a. to spoil, to destroy, to squander, to annihilate; n. to be destroyed, &c. *s.*

نسائم *nasā,im* (pl. of نسيم), breezes, &c. *a.*

نسب *nasab*, m. genealogy, lineage, family, caste. *nasab-nāma*, m. pedigree, account of descent, genealogical tree. *a.*

نسبت *nisbat*, f. relation, affinity, betrothal or betrothed; attribute, reference; (past pos.) respecting, regarding. *a.*

نسبتي *nisbatī*, related, having reference to; m. a wife's brother. *a.* [the moon. *s.*

نسپت निसपति *nis-pati*, m. the lord of night,

نسپره निस्पृह *ni-spṛih* or *ni-spṛiha*, content, free from envy, indifferent. *s.*

نسپرها निस्पृहा *ni-spṛihā*, f. a plant (*Gloriosa superba*). *s.* [able. *s.*

نسپند निस्पन्द *nispand*, still, steady, immove-

نسپريه निस्प्रीह *nisprīh* (for *nispṛih*, q. v.), exempt from desires. *s.* [nose. *h.*

نست नस्त *nast*, m. a snuff, sternutatory; the

نستا नस्ता *nastā*, f. a hole bored in the septum of the nose. *h.*

نستار निस्तार *nistār*, m. acquittal, release, rescue; security; final beatitude. *s.*

نستارا निस्तारा *nistārā*, m. definitive settlement, decision, decree, adjustment; blessing. *s.*

نستارنا निस्तारना *nistārnā*, a. to release, to acquit, to exempt the soul from further transmigration. *s.*

نستاربيج निस्तारबीज *nistār-vīj*, m. the cause of salvation, faith in any deity. *s.*

نسترن *nastaran*, m. the white rose of India (*Rosa glandulifera, Roxb.*); name of a kind of cloth. *p.*

نستعليق *nasta'līk* (for *naskh-ta'līk*), m. a kind of Persian writing (or character). *a.*

نستوك निस्तोक *nistok*, m. definitive settlement, decision, decree, adjustment. *s.*

نستيج निस्तेज *nis-tej*, نستيجس निस्तेजस *nis-tejas*, dull, obscure, impotent. *s.*

نستيه निःसत्य *ni-satya*, false, untrue. *ni-satyatā*, f. falsehood. *s.*

نسج *nasj*, m. act of weaving. *a.*

نسچت निश्चित *nischit*, sure, undoubted. *s.*

نسچر निसचर *nis-char*, } m. a man or animal
نسچرا निसचरा *nis-charā*, } that prowls about in the night; a demon, a robber, a thief. *s.*

نسچرائي निसचराई *nis-charā,ī*, f. prowling about. *nischarā,ī k.*, to prowl in the night. *s.*

نسچي निश्चय *nischai*, indubitable, certain, inevitable, positive, sure, questionless. *s.*

نسخ *naskh*, m. abolition; transcribing; a kind of Arabic character. *a.*

نسخجات *nuskhajāt* (barbarous pl. of نسخه), recipes, books, copious, volumes. *a.*

نسخه *nuskha*, m. a recipe, prescription of ingredients for any composition; an exemplar, prototype, a copy or model; a writing, a book, a letter. *nuskha-navisī*, recipe-writing, copies, &c. *h.*

نسر *nasr*, m. a vulture, an eagle. *nasru-ṭ-ṭā,ir*, the constellation of the Eagle. *nasru-l-wāḳi'*, the constellation Lyra. *s.*

نسرن निःसरण *ni-saran*, m. death; exit, going forth; expedient; final beatitude. *s.*

نسرنا निसरना *nisarnā*, n. to move out, to come forth; to issue. *s.*

نسرين *nasrīn*, m. a wild rose; the sweet briar or eglantine. *p.*

نسرين *nasrain* (du. the two *nasrs*, q. v.), the constellations of the Eagle and the Lyra. *a.*

نسق *nasaḳ*, m. order, series, arrangement; usage, manner, style; manner of writing. *a.*

نسقچي *nasaḳ-chī*, an arranger (of an army); a chamberlain, an orderly officer; an executioner. *nasaḳchī-bāshī*, chief chamberlain or orderly. *a. t.*

نسكپٹ निस्कपट *nis-kapaṭ*, without fraud or deceit; open, artless, honest, sincere. *s.*

نسكهه निःसुख *ni-sukh*, disagreeable, unhappy. *s.*

نسل *nasl*, f. race, pedigree, genealogy, descent, breed, caste, origin, family. *a.*

نسلاً *naslan*, by descent. *naslan-bi-naslin*, in regular descent; or succession. *a.*

نسلي *naslī*, of or relating to family. *a.*

نسناس *nasnās* or *nisnās*, m. an imaginary monster; a monstrous race of men or demons who have only one leg and thigh, and move by leaping; a satyr, a fawn; a kind of ape, the marmoset, an ourang-outang. *a.* [*nasnās*). *a.*

نسناسي *nasnāsī*, monstrous, diabolical (v.

نسنٹهه निसठ *nisanṭh*, ill-omened. *h.*

نسندهه निसन्धि *nisandhi*, solid, tight, not leaky. *s.*

نسندهه निसिन्धु *ni-sindhu*, m. a shrub (*Vitex negundo*). *s.* [compactness. *s.*

نسندهائي निसन्धाई *nisandhā,ī*, f. solidity,

نسنديهه निस्सन्देह *nis-sandeh*, undoubted, beyond suspicion, undoubtedly. *s.*

نسنك निसङ्क *ni-sank*, without fear, fearlessly; free from doubt or suspicion. *s.*

نسنكٹ निसङ्कट *ni-sankaṭ*, without trouble or difficulty, easily. *s.*

نسنكوچ निसङ्कोच *ni-sankoch*, without contracting; without shame or reserve. *s.*

نسنگ निःसङ्ग *ni-sang*, separated, unconnected. *s.*

نسنيها निःस्नेहा *ni-snehā*, f. linseed. *s.*

نسواد निःस्वादु *ni-swādu*, insipid, tasteless. *s.*

نسواس निस्वास *niswās*, m. breath. *s.*

نسوه निःस्व *ni-swa*, poor, indigent. *s.*

نسه निःसह *ni-saha*, unbearable, irresistible. *ni-sahatwa*, n. inability to bear, impatience. *s.*

نسها *nasahā*, veiny, veined. *a. h.*

نسي नसी *nasī*, f. a coulter, a ploughshare. *nasya*, nasal, relating to the nose. *h. s.*

نسيان *nisyān*, m. forgetting, oblivion. *a.*

نسيٹهه नसीठ *nasīṭh*, ill-omened. *h.*

نسيلا *nasīlā*, veined; of good breed. *a. h.*

نسيج *nasīj*, a garment of fine texture. *a.*

نسيم *nasīm*, f. a gentle zephyr, fragrant air, a breeze. *nasīmi saḥar*, the morning breeze. *a.*

نسيني निसैनी *nisainī* or निसेनी *nisenī*, f. a wooden ladder. *s.*

نسيه *nasiya* or *nisiya*, a thing not worth while; any thing forgotten; extended credit: money promised. *a. p.*

نسيه नस्य *nasya*, nasal; m. snuff. *s.*

نسيها नसीहा *nasīhā*, a light plough used in tender soils. *h.*

نش निश *nish*, } f. night: *nish*, as a prefix,
نشا निशा *nishā*, } denotes without, deprived of, as *nish-chhidr*, without flaw or hole. *s.*

نشا *nashā*, m. intoxication, a headache or crop sickness (from over drinking). *nashā-khor*, a person who takes intoxicating drugs, &c., a drunkard. *a.* [water-lily. *s.*

نشاپشپ निशापुष्प *nishā-pushp*, m. the white

نشات *nashāt*, f. a creature; any thing produced or growing; appearing, growing. *a.*

نشاچر निशाचर *nishā-char*, walking at night; m. a *Rākshas* or goblin, a thief; an animal that feeds by night. *s.*

نشاچري निशाचरी *nishā-charī*, f. a harlot, a whore, a night-walker, a female fiend; a sort of perfume. *s.*

نشاد निषाद *nishād*, m. the first musical note; a man of degraded caste. *s.*

نشاسته *nishāsta*, m. starch. *p.*

نشاط *nashāṭ*, m. gladness, joy, pleasure. *nishāt*, brisk, cheerful, lively. *a.*

نشاك नशाक *nashāk*, m. a bird, a sort of crow. *s.*

نشاكر निशाकर *nishā-kar*, m. the moon. *s.*

نشاكرنا निशाकरना *nishā karnā*, a. to be responsible. *yih kām tumhāre gimme hai, agar bigregā to is kā nishā tum ko karnā hogā*, this affair is committed to your charge; should it be spoiled, you must be responsible for it (or make it good). *h.*

نشان *nishān*, m. a mark, sign, signal; a scar; a butt; family arms, armorial bearings; an ensign, flag, standard, colours. *nishān-bardār*, a standard-bearer. *nishān-paṭṭī*, a descriptive list or roll (of fugitive slaves, deserters, &c). *nishān-dār*, a standard-bearer; adj. marked, signed; possessing armorial bearings. *nishān-d.*, to point out. *p.*

نشاناتھ निशानाथ *nishnā-nāth*, m. the moon, ruler of night. *s.*

نشانت निशान्त *nishānt*, quiet, tranquil, patient; m. a house, dwelling; end of night, break of day. *s.*

نشانتناري निशान्तनारी *nishānt-nārī*, f. a housewife. *s.*

نشاندن *nishāndan*, to cause to sit; to place; to quench or smother a fire. *p.*

نشاندھ निशान्ध *nishāndh*, blind at night. *s.*

نشانه *nishāna*, m. a mark, a butt. *nishāna-andāz*, unerring. *p.*

نشاني *nishānī*, f. a mark, sign, token; a token of remembrance, keepsake. *p.*

نشائت *nashā,iyat*, intoxication. *a.*

نشبد निःशब्द *ni-shabd*, silent, voiceless. *s.*

نشپاپ निष्पाप *nish-pāp*, sinless (also *nish-pāpī*). *s.*

نشپادن निष्पादन *nishpādan*, doing, accomplishing, producing. *nishpādit*, effected, produced. *s.*

نشپت निष्पत्ति *nishpatti*, f. completion, consummation. *s.*

نشپتر निष्पुत्र *nish-putr*, sonless. *s.*

نشپراکرم निष्पराक्रम *nish-parākram*, weak, powerless. *s.* [a coward. *s.*

نشپرش निष्पुरुष *nish-purush*, m. a eunuch,

نشپره निष्पृह *nish-pṛih*, contented, free from envy. *s.* [groundless. *s.*

نشپربوجن निष्प्रयोजन *nish-prayojan*, causeless,

نشپشپا निशिपुष्पा *nishi-pushpā*, f. name of a flower (*Nyctanthes tristis*). *s.*

نشپن निष्पन्न *nishpann*, done, concluded. *s.*

نشپھل निष्फल *nish-phal*, barren, fruitless, impotent. *nishphalā* or *nishphalī*, f. a woman past child-bearing. *s.*

نشتر *nashtar*, f. a lancet, a fleam. *nashtar lagānā*, to bleed, to phlebotomize. *p.*

نشٹ नष्ट *nashṭ*, lost, destroyed. *nashṭtā*, f. destruction. *nashṭ-chandr*, m. the moon on the fourth lunation of either half of Bhadr. *nashṭ-chetan*, fainted, insensible. *s.*

نشٹا नष्टा *nashṭā*, f. an adulteress. *s.*

نشٹھا निष्ठा *nishṭhā*, f. confirmation, belief. *s.*

نشٹھان निष्ठान *nishṭhān*, m. sauce, condiment. *s.*

نشٹھر निष्ठुर *nishṭhur*, hard, harsh. *nishṭhurtā*, f. harshness. *s.* [m. certainty. *s.*

نشچت निश्चित *nish-chit*, certain, determined;

نشچر निश्चर *nish-char* (v. *nis-char*), a prowler. *s.*

نشچراي निश्चराई *nish-charā,ī*, f. prowling in the night. *s.*

نشچکن निश्चुक्कण *nishchukkan*, m. a tooth-powder prepared of sulphate of iron. *s.*

نشچل निश्चल *nish-chal*, still, fixed, immoveable. *s.* [posed immoveable). *s.*

نشچلا निश्चला *nish-chalā*, f. the earth (sup-

نشچلانگ निश्चलाङ्ग *nish-chalāng*, m. a kind of crane (*Ardea nivea*); a mountain, a rock. *s.*

نشچنت निश्चिन्त *nish-chint*, thoughtless, inconsiderate. *s.*

نشچھدر निश्छिद्र *nish-chhidr*, without flaw or defect; having no hole or rent. *s.*

نشچي निश्चय *nish-chai*, m. certainty, trust, belief, faith; adj. actual, real, ascertained; actually, undoubtedly. *s.*

نشچیشٹ निश्चेष्ट *nish-cheshṭ*, powerless, incapable of effort. *s.*

نشدھ निषध *nishadh*, m. a mountainous range north of the Himālaya; a country in the south-east of India. *nishiddh*, prohibited. *nishiddhatā*, f. prohibition. *s.*

نشر *nashr*, m. spreading (as a carpet); diffusing, publishing (news); life; penetrating or sinking into. *nashr-k.*, to sink or blot (as ink on bad paper). *a.* [tude. *s.*

نشريس निःश्रेयस *nishreyas*, m. final beati-

نشست *nishast*, f. sitting. *nishast-barkhāst*, f. good breeding, etiquette, politeness. *nishast-gāh*, f. a place where people meet to sit and talk. *p.*

نشستن *nishastan* (r. *nishīn*), to sit, to settle down or cease. *p.* [less. *s.*

نشكارن निष्कारन *nish-kāran*, causeless, ground-

نشكام निष्काम *nish-kām*, free from wish; unwillingly. *s.* [cere. *s.*

نشكپت निष्कपट *nish-kapaṭ*, guileless, sin-

نشكرش निष्कर्ष *nish-harsh*, m. certainty, ascertainment. *s.*

نشكرمن निष्क्रमण *nish-kraman*, m. going forth; taking a child for the first time out of the house. *s.*

نشكنٿك निष्कण्टक *nish-kanṭak*, without thorns, free from trouble. *s.*

نشكنٿه निष्कण्ठ *nish-kanṭh*, m. a plant (*Capparis trifoliata*). *s.*

نشنسي निःसंशय *ni-shansay*, undoubted. *s.*

نشنك निशङ्क *ni-shank* (also *nishankā*), fearless; boldly. *s.*

نشنك निषण्णक *nishannak*, m. a potherb (*Marsilea dentata*). *s.*

نشنگ निषङ्ग *nishang*, m. union, meeting. *s.*

نشو *nasho* or *nashw*, m. vegetation. *nashw o namā*, growing up. *a.*

نشواس निःश्वास *nishwās*, m. breath expired. *s.*

نشور *nushūr*, rising from the dead, resurrection. *a.*

نشور नश्वर *nashwar*, m. } mischievous, destructive. *s.*
نشورا नश्वरा *nashwarā*, f. }

نشوة *nashwa*, drunkenness, exhilaration from wine. *a.*

نشيب *nasheb*, descent, declivity, hollow, low. *nasheb-farāz*, (lit.) down and up (our idiom is up and down); the ups and downs of life; profit and loss, the advantages and disadvantages of any affair. *p.*

نشيت निशैत *nishait*, m. a crane (*Andea nivea*). *s.*

نشيتهه निशीथ *nishīth*, m. midnight, night. *s.*

نشيده निषेध *nishedh*, m. } prohibition, negation, prevention. *s.*
نشيدهتا निषेधता *nishedhatā*, f. }

نشيش निःशेष *ni-shesh*, complete, entire. *s.*

نشيلا निशेला *nishelā*, *nashelā*, or *nashīlā*, intoxicating. *a. h.*

نشيم *nishīm*, m. a bird's nest, a resting-place. *p.*

نشيمان *nishīmān*, } m. a seat, a bench, a mansion. *p.*
نشيمن *nishīman*, }

نشين *nishīn*, (in comp.) seated on, dwelling in, &c., as *takht-nishīn*, seated on the throne, a reigning monarch. *p.*

نشين नश्यन *nashyan*, perishing, decaying. *s.*

نشيني *nishīnī*, f. (abstr. of *nishīn*) sitting, &c. *p.*

نص *nass*, shewing forth, manifesting; proof, demonstration; m. a text, a clear and express dictum of law which cannot be set aside. *a.*

نصاب *niṣāb*, f. a root, origin, principle; dignity, fortune; capital, principal, property; a certain estate, or number of cattle for which a tax is paid. *niṣābu-ṣ-ṣibyān* (lit. the capital stock of children), the title of an Arabic vocabulary with Persian translation in rhyme. *a.*

نصارىٰ *naṣārā*, m. Nazareth, the name of a city; (in a plural or collective sense) Nazarenes, Christians. *a.*

نصائح *naṣā,iḥ* (pl. of نصيحت), counsels, advices, admonitions. *a.*

نصب *naṣb*, m. fixing, erecting, planting, an establishment. *naṣb-k.*, to establish, to appoint. *naṣb-h.*, to be fixed. *a.*

نصر *naṣr*, m. assistance, victory. *a.*

نصراني *naṣrānī*, m. a Christian, the Christian religion (pl. *naṣārā*, q. v.). *a.*

نصرانيت *naṣrānīyat*, f. a Christian woman, the Christian religion. *a.*

نصرت *nuṣrat*, f. victory, assistance, defence. *a.*

نصف *niṣf*, half; middle-aged. *niṣfu-n-nahār*, midday. *a.*

نصفانصف *niṣfā-niṣf*, } half, dividing into two, cutting through the middle, being in the middle, half and half. *a.*
نصفانصفي *niṣfā-niṣfi*, }

نصيب *naṣīb*, m. fortune, lot, chance, portion, part, fate, destiny (in Hindūstānī it is always construed as a plural). *naṣīb larne*, to be competitor for any thing; (lit. fortune fighting for any one) the commencement of prosperity. *naṣīb jagnā*, to be fortunate. *a.*

نصيبه *naṣība*, m. a lot, fortune. *naṣība-war*, fortunate. *a.*

نصيحت *naṣīḥat*, f. advice, counsel, admonition. *naṣīḥat-āmez*, fraught with good counsel. *naṣīḥat-gar* or *-go*, an adviser, a monitor. *naṣīḥat karnā* or *denā*, (met.) to reprove, to reprimand, to chastise. *a.*

نصير *naṣīr*, m. an assistant, a defender, a friend. *a.*

نصيري *nuṣairī*, a Musalmān who believes in the divinity of *'Alī*; name of a tribe inhabiting various parts of Syria and Asia Minor. They are supposed to be descendants of the Assassins or followers of the *shaikh-ul-jabal* "old man of the mountain," a sect nearly exterminated in the thirteenth century by Hūlākū Khān. *a.*

نضارت *naẓārat*, f. freshness, beauty, verdure, pleasingness, lustre, brightness, floridness. *a.*

نضج *naẓij*, ripe, mature, soft. *naẓj* or *nuẓj*, ripening, suppuration. *a.*

نطع *niṭ'* or *niṭa'*, *naṭ'* or *naṭa'*, a piece of dressed leather which they spread as a table or table-cloth; also one on which they play at draughts or chess. *a.*

نطفه *nuṭfa*, m. seed; *sperma hominis*; the sea; clear water. *nuṭfa bintu-l-'inab*, (lit.) "the seed of the daughter of the grape," *i. e.* a bastard begotten in a fit of intoxication; a term of abuse. *a.*

نطق *nuṭk*, speech, diction, utterance, articulation. *a.*

نظارگي *naẓāragī* or *naẓẓāragī*, f. seeing, looking at observation. *a.*

نظاره *naẓāra* or *naẓẓāra*, m. the sight, vision; m. a spectator. *naẓāra-bāz* or *-kun*, a gazer. *a.*

نظافت *naẓāfat*, purity, cleanness, neatness. *a.*

نظام *nizām*, m. order, disposition, arrangement; custom, habit; a string of pearls; a composer, arranger; a ruler or sovereign prince; basis, foundation, constitution. *nizāmu-l-mulk*, the administrator of the empire. *a.*

نظام *nazzām* for *nuzzām* (pl. of ناظم), a governor, ruler; a prince or lord; the title of the prince of Hyderabad in the Deccan.—(Binning). I would with due deference suggest that the words *nazzām* and *nawwāb*, are not plurals and never were intended as such by the people of India. They are merely that derived form of the root called by the Arabs "*ismi-mubālaghatin*," or "noun of excess," such as *ḥajjām*, *jallād*, &c.—(D. F.). *a.*

نظامت *nizāmat*, f. arrangement, government; the administration of criminal justice. *nizāmat-'adālat*, the chief criminal court of the British government in Bengal: it was originally established at *Murshid-ābād*, and removed to Calcutta in 1790. *a.*

نظائر *nazā,ir* (pl. of نظيرة), those who are looked upon or revered above others, eminent or distinguished men, nobles, grandees. *a.*

نظر *nazar*, f. the sight, vision, look, a glance; doubt, perplexity. *nazar-andāz*, rejected. *nazar-andāzī*, estimate of a crop, &c. by inspection without measurement. *nazar-bāz*, an ogler; a juggler. *nazar-bāzī*, f. ogling. *nazar-band*, m. fascination (of conjurors); the art of causing non-existent things to appear to the person influenced by this species of magic, or altering the appearance of persons and things in his eyes; causing a deception of sight (Scottice "glamour"); strictly watched (without being imprisoned). *nazar-bandī*, f. confinement, arrest. *nazari sānī*, a review or second examination of recruits, at which they are finally passed; revisal of a writing or book. *nazar-gāh*, theatre, amphitheatre. *nazar milānā*, to compare. *nazroṅ se girānā*, to disgrace. *nazroṅ se girnā*, to sink into disgrace. *nazar lagnā*, to cast the evil eye, to bewitch with a glance (pl. *nazarāt*). *a.*

نظران *nazarān*, vision, sight, seeing. *a.*

نظري *nazrī*, f. visible, visual. *a.*

نظم *nazm*, f. poetry, verse; order, arrangement; a string. *nazm o nasaq*, order and arrangement. *a.*

نظمي *nazmī*, m. a composer, arranger, adjuster; a poet, a versifier. *a.*

نظورة *nazūrat*, the first line or van of an army. *a.*

نظير *nazīr*, m. example, instance, parallel; adj. alike, resembling, equal to. *nazīru-s-samt*, the Nadir (in astronomy). *a.*

نظيرة *nazīrat*, one who is looked upon or revered above others; comparison, example, specimen. *a.*

نظيف *nazīf* (fem. *nazīfa*), pure, clean. *a.*

نعال *ni'āl* (pl. of نعل), shoes, &c. *a.*

نعت *na't*, f. praise (especially of *Muḥammad*), eulogium; an epithet; an adjective noun. *a.*

نعرة *na'ra*, m. a shout, clamour, noise. *na'ra-kash* or *-zan*, one who shouts out. *na'ra-kashī* or *-zanī*, f. shouting. *a.*

نعش *na'sh*, a bier, a coffin; a litter on which a sick person is carried. *banātu-n-na'sh*, the constellation of the Bear. *a.*

نعل *na'l*, m. shoe (of a horse or man); a horse-shoe; the ferrule at the end of a scabbard; a hoof; a wife. *na'l-band*, a blacksmith who shoes horses, a farrier. *na'l-bandī*, f. giving a horse new shoes, in opposition to *khol-bandī*, which means changing a horse's shoes; a light tribute, horse-shoe money. *s.*

نعلين *na'alain*, du. a pair of shoes of a particular kind, *i. e.* with wooden soles. *a.*

نعم *ni'am* (pl. of نعمت), favours; pleasures, comforts, or blessings (of life). *ni'ma*, an expression of approval or praise. *ni'ma-l-badal*, change for the better. *a.*

نعما *na'mā*, } f. favour, graciousness, benefit; delight, joy; affluence,
نعمت *ni'mat*, } ease, wealth. *ni'mat-khur* or *-khwār*, enjoying ease or affluence. *a.*

نعنا *na'nā*, } m. plant, spearmint, mint
نعناع *na'nā'*, } (*Mentha sativa*). *a.*

نعوذ *na'ūzu*, (lit.) let us seek refuge. *na'ūzu bi-l-lāhi*, let us flee to God (from any thing wicked). *a.*

نعوظ *nu'ūz*, m. *surrectus et intensus* (*penis*). *a.*

نعيب *na'īb*, the croaking of a raven, &c. *a.*

نعيم *na'īm*, m. beneficent, bountiful, God; quiet, repose, tranquillity. *jannatu-n-na'īm* or *jannati na'īm*, the paradise of repose, the delights of paradise. *a.*

نغارة *naghāra* (for *naḳāra*), a kettle-drum. *naghārchī*, a drummer. *t. d.*

نغد *naghd* (for *naḳd*), cash, ready money. *d.*

نغز *naghz*, beautiful, good, excellent; any thing rare or wonderful; sincere, swift, nimble. *naghzak*, (dim. form) good, pretty; the mango. *p.*

نغم *nagham*, } m. melody, song, modulation; a musical note; a sweet
نغمة *naghma*, } voice. *naghma-sarā,ī*, or *-sanjī*, music, melody. *a.*

نفاذ *nafāz*, m. penetrating, pervading, piercing; escape from an enemy; adj. obeyed (an order). *a.*

نفاس *nafās* or *nifās*, m. child-birth, labour, bringing forth; a woman for forty days after child-birth, puerperal period. *a.*

نفاست *nafāsat*, f. exquisiteness, deeming a thing of high value. *a.*

نفاط *nafāṭ*, m. naphtha, bitumen, or a place where it is found in plenty; lamp-oil. *a.*

نفاق *nifāḳ*, m. hypocrisy, fallacy, prevarication; (in Pers. and Hind.) disagreement, enmity. *a.*

نفت *naft* or *nift*, naphtha, any combustible matter. *p.*

نفخ *nafkh*, m. blowing (with the mouth), sounding (a horn, &c.); inspiring, breathing into; swelling. *a.*

نفذ *nafz*, m. penetrating, piercing, pervading. *a.*

نفر *nafar*, m, a groom, a servant; an individual or person, as *tīn nafar*, three persons. *nafar gaṭṭī faiṣala*, settlement of land revenue, taxes, &c., made with the individual cultivators themselves, independent of any landholder; also called *ra'iyat-wārī faiṣala*, q. v. *a.*

نفراگي *nafarāgi* or *nafarā,i*, f. service, &c. (v. *nafarī*). *d.*

نفراني *nafrānī*, f. (fem. of *nafar*) female servants, &c. *a.*

نفرت *nafrat*, f. abomination, aversion; flight, terror. *nafrat-angez*, exciting aversion. *a.*

نفري *nafarī*, f. service, profession, trade (particularly of a groom); a giant, demon. *a.*

نفرين *nafrīn*, f. detestation, abhorrence; an imprecation, curse, opprobrious words; flight, terror. *p.*

نفس *nafas*, m. the breath, respiration; the voice or sound from the breast; a minute, an instant. *nafasi bāz-pasīn*, the last breath. *nafas-gīr*, suffocated. *a.*

نفس *nafs*, the soul, spirit, essence, substance; concupiscence, sensuality; sperm; desire; gravity; pride; envy; vice; the *penis*. *nafsu-l-amr*, the essence, soul, or foundation of a thing. *nafsi-ammāra* or *-bahīmī*, inordinate appetites, concupiscence, beastly propensities. *nafs-parast*, a sensualist. *nafsi-sab'ī* or *-lawwāma*, irascibility or promptitude to the vindictive passions. *nafs-kush*, one who controls his passions. *nafs-kushī*, self-denial. *nafsi-muṭma,inna* or *-malakī*, benevolence. *nafsi mulhima*, the inspiring breath or spirit. *a.*

نفساني *nafsānī*, luxurious, carnal, sensual. *a.*

نفسانيت *nafsānīyat*, f. luxury, sensuality, carnality; pride, pomp, stateliness. *a.*

نفسي *nafsī*, carnal, sensual, animal or beastly. *nafase*, for an instant, one moment. *a.*

نفط *nafṭ*, | نفطة *nafṭa*, } naphtha, bitumen, lamp-oil. *nafṭa-andāzī*, an exhibition of fireworks. *a.*

نفع *naf'*, | نفعة *naf'a*, } m. profit, advantage, interest. *naf'-k.*, to benefit. *naf'-h.*, to be benefitted. *naf'a-nuḳṣān*, profit and loss. *s.*

نفقة *nafḳa*, m. the necessary expenses for living; in the language of the law it signifies all those things which are necessary to the support of life, such as food, clothes, and lodging: many confine it solely to food. *a.*

نفل *nafl*, m. a voluntary act of devotion which may be omitted innocently, as not being prescribed by law; a work of supererogation. *nafal*, plunder (from infidels). *a.*

نفوذ *nafūẕ*, m. penetrating, piercing, pervading. *s.*

نفور *nafūr*, frightened, fleeing from; abhorring, hating. *nufūr*, excelling, conquering. *a.*

نفوس *nufūs* (pl. of نفس *nafs*), souls, spirits, individuals, persons. *a.*

نفي *nafī*, m. forbidding, prohibition; rejecting, refusing; negative; refuse, filth, refusal; annihilation, non-existence; (in law) the denial of a child's paternity, and its consequent rejection, on the part of a man. *a.*

نفير *nafīr*, f. a brazen trumpet. *p.*

نفيري *nafīrī*, f. a kind of trumpet. *p.*

نفيس *nafīs*, precious, delicate, exquisite. *a.*

نقا *naḳā*, f. purity, cleanness; pure, clean; good, virtuous, exemption. *a.*

نقاب *niḳāb*, m. a veil, a hood for the face. *niḳāb-dār* or *-posh*, one who wears a veil; adj. veiled. *a.*

نقاد *naḳḳād*, m. a person whose business it is to examine money and ascertain its goodness, an assayer; an adept. *a.*

نقارچي *naḳār-chī*, m. one who beats the kettle-drum. *a. t.*

نقارخانه *naḳār-ḵẖāna*, the place at the porch of a palace where the drums are beaten at stated intervals. *a.*

نقارة *naḳāra* or *naḳḳāra*, m. a kettle-drum. *naḳāra bajāte phirnā*, to make a proclamation by beat of drum. *a.*

نقاري *naḳārī*, m. one who beats the kettle-drum. *a.*

نقاش *naḳḳāsh*, m. a painter, a draftsman, a carver, a sculptor, an embroiderer. *a.*

نقاشي *naḳḳāshī*, f. drawing, painting, sculpture, embroidery, statuary. *a.*

نقال *naḳḳāl*, m. a mimic, an actor, a player; fem. *naḳḳālin*, an actress, &c. *a.*

نقالي *naḳḳālī*, f. acting, mimicking. *a.*

نقاوت *naḳāwat*, f. purity, cleanness. *a.*

نقاهت *naḳāhat*, f. recovering from disease, convalescence; imbecility, feebleness, languidness. *a.*

نقب *naḳb*, m. a rabbit's burrow, a subterraneous excavation, a mine, a gallery; an instrument used by miners, thieves, &c. for piercing walls; digging through a wall. *a.*

نقبا *nuḳabā* (pl. of نقيب), chiefs, leaders, &c. *a.*

نقبزن *naḳab-zan*, m. a burglar. *a. p.*

نقبزني *naḳab-zanī*, f. burglary. *a. p.*

نقد *naḳd*, | نقدة *naḳda*, } m. ready money, cash. *naḳd-ā-naḳd*, prompt payment. *naḳd o jins*, money and commodities. *a.*

نقدة *naḳda*, cash, &c. (v. *naḳd*). *naḳde kā joṛā*, a bangle for the wrist. *a. d.*

نقدي *naḳdī*, monied, abounding in cash; payable in cash or ready money (goods). *naḳdī-chiṭṭhī*, cash receipt. *naḳdī-gumāshta*, a cash-keeper. *a.*

نقرس *niḳris* or *naḳris*, the gout. *a.*

نقرة *nuḳra*, m. silver; a white colour (in horses). *nuḳra,e ḵẖām*, virgin silver. *a.*

نقرئي *nuḳra,ī*, made of silver; inlaying of silver or other metal upon wood, &c. *a.*

نقش *naḳsh*, f. painting, embroidering, a picture, drawing, map, portrait. *naḳsh-band*, m. a painter, an embroiderer. *naḳsh-bandī*, f. painting, embroidery; a kind of religious ceremony of the Persian monks.

nakṣh-bandiyā, m. a kind of Musalmān *faḳīr* or mendicant (v. Wilsons Glossary). *naḳshi dīwār*, thunderstruck, confounded so as to appear like a picture on the wall. *naḳsh ka-l-ḥajar*, or more properly *ka-n-naḳsh fi-l-ḥajar*, (lit.) like an engraving in stone, indelible. *naḳsh o nigār*, painting and ornamenting. *a.*

نقشه *naḳsha*, m. a portrait, &c., model, pattern; a map, plan, chart, delineation. *a.*

نقشي *naḳshī*, painted, engraved. *a.*

نقص *nuḳṣ*, m. want, defect, blemish. *a.*

نقصان *nuḳṣān*, m. loss, defect, deficiency, detriment, injury, prejudice, mischief. *a.*

نقض *naḳẓ*, rupture, violation of a contract. *a.*

نقط *nuḳṭ*, a drop. *nuḳaṭ* (pl. of نقطه), drops. *yak-nuḳṭ*, a single drop. *a. p.*

نقطه *nuḳṭa*, m. a point, a dot, a spot, a stain, a vowel; a geometrical point; centre of a circle. *nuḳṭa lagānā*, to vilify; to attach blame, to accuse. *a.*

نقل *naḳl*, f. a history, narrative, tale, story; copying, mimicking, acting; transcribing; imitating, a copy. *naḳli makān*, the first stage of a journey, or halting-place at a very little distance, where they remain some time to collect what may have been forgotten of the requisites for travelling; this first stage is often made long before they really mean to set off, for the sake of seizing a lucky moment to commence a journey in; transmigration; change of place, removal. *naḳl-band*, a compiler of narratives. *naḳl-navīsī*, f. copying. *nuḳl*, sweetmeats, dessert. *naḳl-k.*, to remove, to transfer, to copy. *a.*

نقلا *naḳlā*, a subordinate village belonging to an estate. *a.*

نقلدان *nuḳl-dān*, m. a plate for holding fruit, sweetmeats, &c. *a. p.*

نقلي *naḳlī*, m. a narrator, story-teller; buffoon; adj. handed down, copied, traditional. *naḳlī wa 'aḳlī*, traditional and rational. *h.*

نقليات *naḳliyāt*, anecdotes, tales, stories. *a.*

نقمت *niḳmat*, f. punishment, revenge, hatred. *a.*

نقوش *naḳūsh*, a sort of shrub. *nuḳūsh* (pl. of *naḳsh*), pictures, inscriptions, dots on dice. *a.*

نقوع *naḳū'*, m. an infusion (a term used in medicine). *a.*

نقول *nuḳūl* (pl. of نقل), narratives, tales, anecdotes; copies. *a.*

نقي *naḳī*, pure, clean, excellent. *a.*

نقيب *naḳīb*, m. a chief, a leader; an intelligent person; a servant or herald whose business it is to proclaim the titles of his master, and to introduce those who pay their respects to him; an aide-de-camp or adjutant. *a.*

نقير *naḳīr*, m. a trough of a hollowed palm-tree, in which they make a strong wine from dates; adj. small, little, few. *naḳīr o ḳiṭmīr*, every particle, all the minutiæ. *a.*

نقيض *naḳīẓ*, adverse, contrary, opposite; m. an enemy, an opponent. *a.*

نقيه *naḳīh*, faint, feeble, weak. *a.*

نك नक *nak*, f. (used in comp.) the nose. *nak-ghisnī*, rubbing the nose on the earth in prostration or as a punishment. *s.*

نكا नक्का *nakkā*, m. the ace at cards or on dice. *nakkā dū,ā*, a kind of game at dice. *h.*

نكات *nikāt* (pl. of نكته), points, conceits, witticisms. *a.*

نكاح *nikāḥ*, m. matrimony, marriage; it denotes the most honourable kind of marriage, though in Bengal the term is only applicable to a left-handed marriage, such as that of a widow, which is considered disreputable. *nikāḥi mut'at* or *nikāḥi muwaḳḳat*, a temporary marriage, very common among Musalmāns, especially when detained from home: it is celebrated with certain forms, and not considered disreputable, but it is null and void in law. *a.*

نكاحي *nikāḥī*, married (a woman). *a.*

نكار नकार *nakār*, m. refusal, denial. *s.*

نكارا *nakārā* (for *nā-kāra*), useless. *p.*

نكارن निःकारण *nikāran*, causeless. *s.*

نكارنا नकारना *nakārnā*, a. to refuse, to deny. *s*

نكاره *nakāra*, worthless, useless, invalid. *p.*

نكاس निकास *nikās*, m. skirts, suburbs, outer boundary of land attached to a town, &c.; issue, outlet, vent, source, origin, spring; adjustment of accounts, accomplishment; (corrup. of *nakhkhās*) a daily fair for cattle. *s.*

نكاسپتر निकासपत्र *nikās-patra*, m. statement of adjusted accounts. *s.*

نكاستا निकास्ता *nikāstā*, m. a prop, a pillar. *h.*

نكاسنا निकासना *nikāsnā*, a. to take out, to extract (v. *nikālnā*). *s.*

نكاسنويس *nikās-nawīs*, m. an officer in the *zamīndārī kachahrī*, who takes and examines the account of the collections in the *mufaṣṣil*. *s. p.*

نكاسي निकासी *nikāsī*, f. taxes collected on goods passing out of a town, export duties, &c. *nikāsī kī chiṭṭhī*, f. a permit, a passport. *s.*

نكال निकाल *nikāl*, m. contrivance, outlet, projection. *nikāl-denā*, to cashier, to banish, to expel. *nikāl-ḍālnā*, to deduct, to strike out. *nikāl-lānā*, to bring off. *nikāl-lenā*, to dig up, to take out. *s.*

نكال *nakāl*, m. an exemplary punishment, a preventive, restraint. *a.*

نكالا *nakālā*, m. an eruption on the skin. *d.*

نكالنا निकालना *nikālnā*, a. to take out, to turn out, to send out, to exclude, to pull, to do, to perform, to pick, to invent. *s.*

نكام निकाम *nikām*, voluntarily, willingly. *s.*

نكاما *nikāmā*, نكامه *nikāma*, نكامي *nikāmī*, } useless, base, worthless, good for nothing. *d.*

نكانا निकाना *nikānā*, a. to weed. *h.*

نكاءي निकाई *nikā,ī*, f. the price paid for weeding a field; the act of weeding. *h.*

نکائي *nikā,ī*, f. goodness, welfare, prosperity, beauty. *p.* [tune. *a.*

نکبت *nakbat*, f. adversity, calamity, misfor-

نکپٹ निकपट *ni-kapaṭ*, sincere, candid. *s.*

نکپوڑا *nakpoṛā*, m. } the nose, the nostrils. *d.*
نکپوڑي *nakpūṛī*, f. }

نکتمال नक्तमाल *nakt-māl*, m. a tree (*Galedupa arborea*). *s.* [roguish. *s.*

نکتوڑا नकतोड़ा *nak-toṛā*, droll, waggish,

نکته *nukta*, m. a subtle or quaint conceit, a mystical signification. *nukta-bīn* or *-chīn*, a caviller, a carper. *nukta-pardāz*, acute, subtle. *nukta-pardāzī*, f. acuteness. *nukta-dān*, *-shinās*, or *-ras*, acute, conversant with subtleties, or whatever is mysterious. *a.*

نکتي निकती *niktī*, f. a balance, small scales. *h.*

نکٹ निकट *nikaṭ*, near, close by, about, in possession of. *nakuṭ*, m. the nose. *s.*

نکٹا नकटा *nakṭā*, m. nose-clipt, noseless; m. a rogue. *s.* [comb duck. *h.*

نکٹا नकटा *nakṭā*, m. the name of a bird, the

نکٹورتي निकटवर्ती *nikaṭ-vartī*, one who is or lives near, a neighbour. *s.*

نک‌چڑھا नकचढ़ा *nak-chaṛhā*, angry, fretful, ill-tempered, warm, passionate. *s.*

نکچھکني नकछिकनी *nak-chhiknī*, f. name of a sternutatory plant. *s.*

نکح *nikaḥ* (for *nikāḥ*, q. v.), marriage. *a. d.*

نکر *nakir*, sagacious, penetrating, ingenious. *nukar*, ignorant. *a.*

نکر निकर *nikar*, m. a flock, a multitude; a heap, a bundle; pith, sap, essence. *h.*

نکر नक्र *nakr*, m. an alligator; the nose. *s.*

نکرت निकृत *nikṛit*, dishonest, wicked, low; vile. *nikṛiti*, f. wickedness, dishonesty. *s.*

نکرراج नक्रराज *nakr-rāj*, the royal alligator, a shark. *s* [low, vile. *s.*

نکرشٹ निकृष्ट *nikṛishṭ*, outcast, despised,

نکرنا निकरना *nikarnā*, n. to go forth, to issue. *s.*

نکره *nakra* or *nakira*, undetermined, unrestricted, indefinite or generic (noun). *a.*

نکڑا नकड़ा *nakṛā*, m. an inflammation in the nose, the polypus (v. *nākṛā*). *s.*

نکس *nakas* (v. *nā-kas*), vile, abject. *p.*

نکس *naks*, inclining downward, inverting, placing topsy-turvy. *a.*

نکسنا निकसना *nikasnā*, n. to go out, to issue. *s.*

نکسور *naksūr*, the nostrils. *d.*

نکسیر नकसीर *naksīr*, the veins of the nose. *naksīr phūṭnā*, to bleed at the nose. *s.*

نکشتر नक्षत्र *nakshatra*, a star, an asterism (v. *nachhattar*). *nakshatra-chakra*, m. a diagram for astrological purposes. *nakshatra-mālā*, f. a necklace of twenty-seven pearls; the table of lunar asterisms. *s.*

نکشتري नक्षत्री *nakshatrī*, born under an auspicious planet. *s.*

نکشپت निःक्षिप्त *ni-kshipt*, rejected, abandoned, forgone, given or thrown away; pledged, left, deposited. *s.* [pledge, a deposit. *s.*

نکشیپ निक्षेप *nikshep*, m. what is left, a

نکل नकुल *nakul*, m. the Bengal mongoose. *s.*

نکل‌بھاگنا निकलभागना *nikal-bhāgnā*, to run away. *h.*

نکل‌پڑنا निकलपड़ना *nikal-paṛnā*, n. to come out, to be drawn forth. *h.* [go away. *h.*

نکل‌جانا निकलजाना *nikal-jānā*, to escape, to

نکل‌چلنا निकलचलना *nikal-chalnā*, to escape; (met.) to surpass another, to be advanced or promoted; to speak much or display one's talent (spoken of a person who from the modesty of a stranger had formerly been silent). *h.*

نکلنا निकलना *nikalnā*, n. to be extracted, drawn, or pulled out; to be taken off, to begin, to be invented, to escape, to rise, slip, issue, spring. *s.*

نکلوانا निकलवाना *nikalwānā*, a. to cause to go out, to drive out. *nikalwā denā*, to expel, to banish. *s.*

نکلیشٹا नकुलेष्टा *nakuleshṭā*, } f. name of a
نکلیشٹکا नकुलेष्टका *nakuleshṭkā*, } plant said to be used by the mongoose as an antidote (*Croton polyandrum*). *s.*

نکما निकम्मा *nikammā*, useless, good for nothing. *s.* [*polyandrum*). *s.*

نکنبھ निकुम्भ *nikumbh*, m. a plant (*Croton*

نکنٹک निकंटक *nikanṭak*, plain, easy; happy, without enmity. *s.*

نکنج निकुञ्ज *nikunj*, m. an arbour, a bower, a place overgrown with creepers. *s.*

نکند निकंद *ni-kand*, without root, torn up, extirpated. *s.*

نکو नक्कू *nakkū*, infamous, vile, wicked. *h.*

نکو *niko* or *nikū*, good, beautiful, fair. *p.*

نکو *nako*, do not, not (negative particle equivalent to *mat* in Urdū). *d.*

نکوا नकुआ *nakū,ā*, m. the nose; the point of any thing. *s.* [(of the nose). *s.*

نکواسا नकवासा *nakwāsā*, m. name of a disease

نکوچک निकोचक *nikochak*, m. a tree (*Allangium hexapetalum*). *s.* [turvy. *p.*

نکوسار *nikū-sār*, head downwards, topsy-

نکوسنا निकोसना *nikosnā*, n. to grin. *h.*

نکوسیر *nikū-siyar*, } of good conduct, of
نکوسیرت *nikū-sīrat*, } amiable qualities. *p.a.*

نکوکار *nikū-kār*, m. a well-doer. *nikū-kārī*, f. beneficence. *p.*

نکوهش *nakohish* or *nikohish*, f. spurning, rejecting, despising. *p.*

نکوئی *nikū,ī*, f. goodness, beauty, virtue. *p.*

نکوئیان *nikū,iyān*, pl. virtues, good or noble qualities. *p.*

نکهه नख *nakh*, m. a finger-nail. *nakh-sikh* or *nakh-se sikh-talak*, from top to toe. *s.*

نکهه *nakh*, m. (for *nakh*) the string of a paper kite. *p.*

نکهاد निषाद *nikhād*, m. one of the seven notes in music; name of a Hindū inferior caste; a *chandāl*, q. v. *s.*

نکهارنا निखारना *nikhārnā*, a. to strain, to bleach, to purify. *h.*

نکهانك नखांक *nakhānk*, m. the mark left by the nails in scratching. *s.*

نکهپد नखपद *nakh-pad*, m. a scratch, mark of a finger-nail. *s.*

نکهت नखत *nakhat*, m. a star, a constellation. *s.*

نکهت *nakhat*, f. perfume, odour, any thing odoriferous. *a.*

نکهتري नखत्री *nakhatrī*, born under an auspicious planet. *s.*

نکهٹر *nikhaṭar*, spiteful, implacable. *nikaṭar-panā*, implacability. *d.*

نکهٹو निखट्टू *nikhaṭṭū*, idle, thriftless. *h.*

نکهد निखद *nikhad*, ominous, pernicious. *h.*

نکهدا निखदा *nikhdā*, m. perniciousness. *h.*

نکهر नखर *nakhar*, m. nail (of the finger, &c.). *s.*

نکهرانا निखराना *nikhrānā*, a. to settle, to purify. *h.*

نکهرب निखर्ब *nikharb*, m. } a dwarf; a billion;
نکهربا निखर्बा *nikharbā*, f. } adj. dwarfish. *s.*

نکهرنا निखरना *nikharnā*, n. to be peeled, skinned; to be cleaned, cleared, or settled. *h.*

نکهریکه नखरेख *nakh-rekh*, } f. the marks
نکهریکها नखरेखा *nakh rekhā*, } left by the nails, a scratch. *s.*

نکهکهادي नखखादी *nakh-khādī*, who or what eats with nails or talons. *s.*

نکهل निखिल *nikhil*, all, entire, complete. *s.*

نکهلیکها नखलेखा *nakh-lekhā*, f. (v. *nakh-rekh*). *s.*

نکهنڈ निखण्ड *nikhanḍ*, half, mid, midway. *s.*

نکهنگ निखङ्ग *nikhang*, f. a quiver. *s.*

نکهوٹ निखोट *nikhoṭ*, m. plain dealer; any thing without blemish. *h.*

نکهورا *nikhorā*, inhuman, pitiless. *nikhorāgī*, f. inhumanity. *d.*

نکهورنا निखोरना *nikhornā*, } a. to peel, to skin,
نکهوڑنا निखोड़ना *nikhoṛnā*, } to clean. *h.*

نکهوسنا निखोसना *nikhosnā*, a. to grin. *h.*

نکهي नखी *nakhī*, nailed, clawed, having nails or talons; f. a kind of perfume; a dried substance of the shape of a nail. *s.*

نکهیانا नखियाना *nakhiyānā*, } a. to claw, to
نکیانا नकियाना *nakiyānā*, } scratch. *s.*

نکي नक्की *nakkī*, f. speaking through the nose, a nasal sound. *s.*

نکیر *nakīr*, m. the name of an angel (v. *munkir*). *a.*

نکیل नकेल *nakel*, f. the wooden or iron instrument fixed to a camel's nose, and to which the string by which he is led is fastened; a cavezon (or cavesson). *s.*

نکیلا नुकीला *nukīlā*, pointed, sharp at top. *h.*

نکي مونٹهه नक्कीमूंठ *nakkī-mūṅṭh*, f. name of a game. *h.*

نگ नग *nag*, m. the stone of a ring, or a stone on which a name, &c. is cut; a mountain. *s.*

نگار *nigār*, m. a picture, portrait, effigy, idol; a beautiful woman, mistress; adj. brilliant, bright; (in comp.) beautifying. *nigār-khāna*, a house for pictures. *nigār-istān*, a picture-gallery, name of several works in the Persian language. *p.*

نگاري *nigārī*, f. (abst. of *nigār*) painting. *p.*

نگارین *nigārīn*, embellished, beautified, decorated; a beloved object. *p.*

نگاشري नगाश्रय *nagāshray*, living in mountains. *s.*

نگالي निगाली *nigālī*, f. a small *ḥukka* snake, the wooden pipe of a *ḥukka* snake. *p.*

نگاه *nigāh*, f. a look, glance, the aspect; observation, watching; custody, care. *p.*

نگاهبان *nigāh-bān*, m. a guard, a keeper. *p.*

نگاهباني *nigāh-bānī*, f. custody, guardianship. *p.*

نگاهدار *nigāh-dār*, } m. a guard, keeper;
نگاهداره *nigāh-dāra*, } interj. look out! have a care! *p.*

نگاهداشت *nigāh-dāsht*, looking after, enlisting. *nigāh-dāsht-k.*, to enlist. *p.*

نگاهداشتن *nigāh-dāshtan*, to keep; to watch or look out; to preserve with care. *p.*

نگبهد नगभिद *nag-bhid*, m. a plant (*Plectanthus scuttellaroides*). *s.*

نگبهو नगभू *nag-bhū*, of a mountain; a mountaineer. *s.*

نگپت नगपति *nag-pati*, m. the lord of mountains, the Himālaya. *s.*

نگت निगत *nigat*, naked. *h.*

نگج नगज *nagaj*, mountain-born, mountaineer. *s.*

نگچانا नगचाना *nagchānā*, n. to approach. *h.*

نگچاهٹ नगचाहट *nagchāhaṭ*, } f. approaching, arriving. *h.*
نگچاءي नगचाई *nagchā,ī*,

نگدونا नगदौना *nagdaunā*, m. (v. *nāgdaunā*) wormwood. *s.*

نگر नगर *nagar*, m. a city, a town. *nagar-jan*, town's folks. *nagar-nārī*, a courtesan, a woman of the town. *nagar-koṭ*, name of a town in the Panjāb, also called Kāngrā. *nagar-vartī*, one who dwells in a city. *s.*

نگر निगर *nigar*, m. eating, swallowing. *s.*

نگر निग्गर *niggar* or *nigar*, solid. *h.*

نگران *nigrān*, m. looking, beholding, expecting. *p.*

نگرستن *nigaristan* (r. *nigar*), to look, to behold. *p.*

نگرسوروپني नगरस्वरूपिणी *nagar-swarūpinī*, a species of metre. *s.*

نگروپانت नगरोपान्त *nagaropānt*, m. suburb. *s.*

نگره निग्रह *nigrah*, m. aversion, disfavour, discouragement, dislike. *s.*

نگري नगरी *nagarī*, f. a town, a village; adj. of or belonging to a city. *s.*

نگڑ निगड़ *nigaṛ*, m. an iron chain for the feet (especially of an elephant); fetters; the stocks. *s.*

نگڑگهٹ *nigaṛ-ghaṭ*, impudent, bold. *d.*

نگلنا निगलना *nigalnā*, a. to swallow, to gulp down. *s.*

نگم निगम *nigam*, scripture, holy writ; the Vedas; certainty, assurance. *s.*

نگمن निगमन *nigaman*, m. logical conclusion, winding up of a syllogism. *s.*

نگم نواسي निगमनिवासी *nigam-niwāsī*, dwelling in the Vedas, a name of *Brahmā*. *s.*

نگن नगन *nagan* or नग्न *nagna*, naked (f. *nagnā*). *s.*

نگنا नगणा *nagnā*, heart-pea (*Cardiospermum halicacabum*). *s.*

نگناٹ नग्नाट *nagnāṭ*, m. a naked mendicant. *s.*

نگنتو नग्नत्व *nagnatwa*, m. nudity, nakedness. *s.*

نگندا निगन्दा *nigandā*, m. } quilting. *h.*
نگنداءي निगन्दाई *nigandā,ī*, f.

نگندنا निगन्दना *nigandnā*, a. to quilt. *h.*

نگنکا नग्निका *nagnikā*, f. a girl before menstruation.

نگنهو नग्नहू *nagn-hū*, m. ferment, a drug used to throw the mixture for spirituous liquors into fermentation. *s.*

نگنيکرن नग्नीकरण *nagnī-karan*, m. stripping, undressing. *nagnī-kṛit*, stripped. *s.*

نگوڑا निगोड़ा *nigoṛā*, m. (lit. without feet) a wretch, wight; adj. ill-tempered, cross-grained. *h.*

نگوڑه निगूढ़ *nigūṛh*, profound, obscure, hidden, concealed. *s.*

نگوڑهارتھ निगूढ़ार्थ *nigūṛhārth*, having a hidden sense or purpose. *s.*

نگون *nigūn*, hanging downward, upside down. *nigūn-bakht*, helpless, unfortunate. *nigūn-sār*, hanging the head from shame, inverted, upside down topsy-turvy. *p.*

نگه *nigah* (v. *nigāh*), sight, &c. *p.*

نگهات निघाति *nighāti*, f. an iron mace or club. *s.*

نگهبان *nigah-bān*, m. watchman, keeper. *p.*

نگهباني *nigah-bānī*, f. watching, taking care of. *p.*

نگهدار *nigah-dār*, } m. a guardian, keeper, an observer. *p.*
نگهداره *nigah-dāra*,

نگهداري *nigah-dārī*, f. keeping (a secret); observation, watching. *p.*

نگهداشت *nigah-dāsht*, watching; enlisting. *p.*

نگهن निघ्न *nighn* or *nighna*, docile, subservient, dependent. *s.*

نگهنٹ निघण्टु *nighanṭu*, m. a vocabulary, a collection of words or names. *s.*

نگياني *nigyānī*, weak in mind, silly, ignorant. *d.*

نگيچ नगीच *nagīch*, near, close by (a corruption of *nazdīk*, q. v.) *h.*

نگين *nagīn*, } m. a ring, especially the signet-ring of a prince; the stone or bezel of a ring. *p.*
نگينه *nagīna*,

نل नल *nal*, m. the name of a celebrated king and hero; a reed (*Arundo karka*); a tube, spout, joint of bamboo, or other hollow wood; a measuring rod consisting of three *ilāhī gaz* or yards of Akbar (v. *ilāhī*); the bamboo which fowlers use to entangle game by applying birdlime to the top of it. *nal chalānā*, (lit. setting the bamboos in motion)-expresses a magical practice adopted for the discovery of theft. Two pieces of split bamboo, of equal lengths, are applied to one another side by side, and held by two men, one at each end. It is said that any persons taken at random may be employed for this purpose. Then the magician pronounces certain incantations, the efficacy of which is pretended to be such, that the bamboos spontaneously move towards the place where the thief or the stolen goods are, and drag the men along with them. *nal dar nal*, one tube within another. *s.*

نلا नला *nalā*, m. the ureters, urinary ducts. *āhanī nalā*, *bhū,īṅ nalā*, *dam-nalā*, and *hath-nalā*, names of various kinds of fireworks (v. *Qanoon i islām*, p. 58, app.). *s.*

نلاهٹ निलाहट *nilāhaṭ*, f. blueness. *s.*

نلج निलज्ज *nilajj*, نلجا निलज्जा *ni-lajjā*, } shameless, bold, rude. *s.*

نلڈا *naldā*, نلڈي *naldī*, } the windpipe, the throat, the weasand (also *nalṛā* and *nalṛī*). *d.*

نلکا नलिका *nalikā*, f. a perfume so called. *s.*

نلن नलिन *nalin*, f. a lotus or water-lily; the Indian crane. *s.*

نلني नलिनी *nalinī*, f. an assemblage of lotus flowers, a place abounding with the lotus. *s.*

نلو नल्व *nalw*, m. a furlong, a space measured by four hundred cubits. *h.*

نلوءا नलुआ *nalū,ā*, m. a tube, a joint of bamboo to convey letters in; straw. *s.*

نلي नली *nalī*, f. a tube, spout; the windpipe, ureter, &c.; a gun barrel; *morbus plerumque a manustupratione ortus, in quo membrum virile exile fit nec erigi potest*; the bone of the leg, the *tibia*; a weaver's shuttle, or the little tube within the shuttle on which the woof is wound. *s.*

نليا नलिया *naliyā*, m. name of a caste whose employment is to catch birds by means of limed *nals* (v. *nal*). *s.*

نم नम *nam* (for *nān*), no, not. *s.*

نم *nam*, moist, damp, wet. *nam-khurda*, destroyed by moisture. *nam-dīda*, having the eyes moist, weeping. *p.*

نما *namā* (also *numā*), increase, augmenting. *a.*

نما *numā* or *numā,e*, (in comp.) shewing, exhibiting, pointing out; an index, a guide. *p.*

نماز *namāz*, f. prayer, those especially prescribed by the *Muhammadan* law, which are offered up five times a day. *namāz-guzār*, praying, attending divine service; one who prays. *namāzi janāza*, the funeral service of the *Muhammadans*. *namāz-gāh*, the place in a mosque where prayers are read. *p.*

نمازي *namāzī*, m. a person who prays; adj. relating to prayers; devout, or in the constant habit of praying. *p.*

نماشام *namā-shām* (for *namāzi-shām*), time of evening prayer, soon after sunset. *namā-shām utarnā*, to be degraded. *p.*

نمام *nammām*, m. a calumniator, an accuser. *a.*

نمانا निमाना *nimānā*, simple, without guile; singular, unlike to all others, sheepish. *h.*

نماءي *numā,e* (in comp. v. *numā*). *numā,ī*, f. display, exhibiting. *p.*

نمايان *numāyān*, apparent, evident, bold (as a picture), prominent. *p.*

نمايش *numā,ish* or *numāyish*, f. appearance, form, figure, face, vision, sight, spectacle, affection. *p.*

نمايندہ *numāyanda*, shewing; an exhibitor. *p.*

نمب निम्ब *nimb*, m. name of a tree (*Melia azad-dirachta*). *s.*

نمبتر निम्बतरु *nimb-taru*, m. the coral-tree, one of the trees of paradise. *s.*

نمبکوڑي निम्बकौड़ी *nimb-kauṛī*, f. the fruit of the nimb-tree. *s.*

نمبو निम्बू *nimbū*, m. the common lime-tree. *s.*

نمبولي निम्बोली *nimbolī*, of or relating to the nimb-tree. *s. d.*

نمت निमित्त *nimitt*, m. cause, motive, instrument; (met.) fortune; for the sake of, by reason of. *namat*, bending, stooping, bowed. *s*

نمتمان निमित्तमान *nimitt-mān*, نمتي निमित्ती *nimittī*, } prosperous, fortunate. *s.*

نمد *namad*, نمدا *namdā*, } m. a coarse woollen garment; *membrum virile*. *namad-posh*, clothed in woollen. *namadi zīn*, a coarse woollen saddle-cloth. *p.*

نمر नम्र *namr*, bending; (met.) courteous. *s.*

نمر *nimr* or *namir*, a panther, a leopard. *a.*

نمرتا नम्रता *namrtā*, f. condescension, courtesy. *s.*

نمرمکھ नम्रमुख *namr-mukh*, نمرمکھي नम्रमुखी *namr-mukhī*, } having the head bent, looking down. *s.*

نمرود *namrūd*, Nimrod (the mighty hunter of [old). *a.*

نمست नमसित *namasit*, reverenced, respected, worshipped. *s.*

نمسکار नमस्कार *namaskār*, m. salutation, [adoration. *s.*

نمسکاري नमस्कारी *namaskārī*, f. a kind of sensitive plant. *s.*

نمسيت नमस्यित *namasyit*, نمسيہ नमस्य *namasya*, } venerable, reverenced, entitled to respect. *s.*

نمش नमश्च *namsh*, m. a kind of food or dish made of milk, whipt cream. *s.*

نمش निमिष *nimish*, m. the twinkling of an eye, an instant of time. *s.*

نمط *namat*, f. likeness, a mode, manner, way, [custom. *a.*

نمك *namak* or *nimak*, m. salt; (met.) spirit, animation; bread, subsistence. *namak-parwarda*, a domestic slave, one fed on the salt. *namaki angūr*, cream of tartar. *namak-chashī*, the first feeding of a child about six months of age, which is attended with certain ceremonies. *namak-harām*, disloyal, wicked, evil, disobedient, perfidious, ungrateful. *namak-halāl*, loyal, submissive, faithful, grateful. *namak-dān*, a saltcellar. *namak-sār*, saline, a salt-pit. *kaṭe par namak lagānā*, (lit. to put salt upon a wound) to add one grief or vexation to another. *namak-kā tezāb*, muriatic acid. *namak-mahāll*, revenue derived from salt. *p.*

نمکوڑي निमकौड़ी *nim-kauṛī*, f. the berry of the nim tree. *s.*

نمکھ निमिख *nimikh*, m. a moment (of time), [a twinkling of the eye. *s.*

نمکي निमकी *nimkī*, نمکين नमकीन *namkīn*, } f. pickled lemons. *p. h.*

نمكين **namkīn**, salt, salted, brackish; witty, poignant, sarcastic; handsome, beautiful. *namkīn pānī*, brine, pickle. *p.*

نمكيني **namkīnī**, f. saltnesss, sweetness, agreeableness. *p.*

نمگيرا **nam-gīrā**, / نمگيره **nam-gīra**, } m. a canopy, an awning. *p.*

نمل **namil**, brisk, handy, nimble, ready. *numal* or *numul*, an ant. *a.*

نمن नमन **naman**, like, resembling. *niman*, stout, strong, tight, good; (Dakh.) in that way, like that. *h.*

نمن नमन **naman**, bending, stooping, bowed. *nimn*, deep, profound, low (ground), stooping. *s.*

نمناك **nam-nāk**, moist, wet, fresh. *p.*

نمناكي **nam-nākī**, f. moistness, freshness. *p.*

نمنانا निमनाना **nimnānā**, a. to strengthen, to ameliorate. *h.*

نمنائي निमनाई **nimnā,ī**, f. strength, stoutness. *h*

نمنتا निम्नता **nimnatā**, f. depth, profundity. *s.*

نمو **namw** or **numū**, m. vegetation growth, increase. *a.*

نمود **namūd**, f. index, guide, appearance; adj. apparent, public, shewn, exhibited, famous, prominent. *numūd honā*, to appear, to be celebrated. *p.*

نمودار **namūdār**, m. an index, exemplar, proof, symbol, specimen, imitation, model; adj. noted, famed, conspicuous. *p.*

نموداري **namūdārī**, f. publicity; in revenue language it denotes a compensation given by the *ryot*, for not having the extent of his lands ascertained by an actual measurement. *p.*

نمودن **namūdan** (r. *numā,e*), a. to shew; to do or occasion; n. to appear, to seem. *p.*

نمونه **namūna**, m. an example, muster; model, type, specimen, pattern. *p.*

نمه नमः **namah**, m. reverence, salutation. *s.*

نمي **namī**, f. coolness, moistness, &c. *p.*

نمير नमेरु **nameru** or **namerū**, m. the seed of the elocarpus. *s.*

نميش निमेष **nimesh** (v. *nimish*). *s.*

نميگر नमेगुरु **nameguru** or **namegurū**, m. a spiritual teacher. *s.*

نميلن निमीलन **nimīlan**, m. shutting of the eyelids, winking; death, dying. *s.*

نناد निनाद **ninād**, m. sound, noise. *s.*

نناںوا निनांवा **ninānwā**, / ننانوان निनांवां **ninānwān**, } m. the thrush, aphthæ. *h.*

ننانوي निन्नान्वे **ninnānwe** or **ninānawe** (also *ninānawwe*), ninety-nine. *ninānawe ke pher meṅ paṛnā*, to be entirely absorbed in the acquisition of wealth; to be involved in difficulties. *s.*

ننايا निनाया **nināyā**, m. a bug. *h.*

نند नन्द **nand** or ननद **nanad**, f. a sister-in-law, husband's sister. *nanda*, m. name of the foster-father of *Krishna*. *nanda-lāl*, the beloved of *Nanda*, that is, *Krishna*. *ninad*, m. sound in general. *s.*

نندا निन्दा **nindā**, f. accusation, scorn, defamation. *s.*

نندااس निन्दास **nindās**, f. drowsiness, inclination to sleep. *s.*

ننداسا निन्दासा **nindāsā**, sleepy, drowsy. *s.*

نندااستت निन्दास्तुति **nindāstuti**, f. irony, ironical praise. *s.*

نندت निन्दित **nindit**, blamed, reproached; low, vile, despicable. *s.*

نندك निन्दक **nindak**, m. a calumniator; adj. censorious, querulous. *nandik*, m. toon, a tree the wood of which resembles mahogany (*Cedrella tuna*). *s.*

نندكائي निन्दकाई **nindakā,ī**, f. querulousness, censoriousness. *s.*

نندن निन्दन **nindan**, m. reproach, censure, blame; adj. abusing, blaming. *s.*

نندن नन्दन **nandan**, m. a son; the garden of *Indra*; the paradise of the Hindūs; adj. delighting. *s.*

نندنا निन्दना **nindnā**, a. to vilify, to defame. *s.*

نندني नन्दिनी **nandinī**, f. wife's sister. *s.*

ننددركش नन्दिवृक्ष **nandi-vṛiksh**, m. a tree (same as *nandik*). *s.*

نندوسي नंदोसी **nandosī**, / نندوئي नंदोई **nando,ī**, } m. husband's sister's husband. *s.*

نندولا नंदोला **nandolā**, m. a large earthen vessel, a trough for animals to feed from. *s.*

نندهنا नंधना **nandhnā**, a. to begin. *h.*

نندي नन्दी **nandī**, m. the bull of *Shiva*; f. a benedictive verse eulogising a king or deity. *s.*

نندي ननदी **nandī**, / نندیا ननदिया **nandiyā**, } f. (v. *nand*) a sister-in-law. *s.*

نندیه निन्द्य **nindya**, bad, vile, reprehensible. *s.*

ننكا नंका **nankā**, m. a little child, a son (an expression of endearment). *h.*

ننگ **nang**, f. honour, reputation, esteem; (contra) disgrace, infamy. *nang o nāmūs*, honour; shame, disgrace. *p.*

ننگ नंग **nang**, / ننگا नंगा **nangā**, } naked; shameless. *nangā-jhūrī*, f. searching, examining (as people leaving a workshop, to prevent pilfering). *nangā-sir*, bareheaded. *nangā-k.*, to bare, to uncover. *nangā-mādar-zād*, stark naked as from the womb. *nangā mungā* or *mnangā*, utterly naked. *nange-pairoṅ* or *-pā,oṅ*, barefooted. *nange pā,oṅ honā*, (Dakh.) to be prepared or resolute to fight. *nangī talwār*, a naked sword. *nangī shamsher*, a drawn sword; one who speaks his mind freely and without reserve. *s.*

ننگٹا नंगटा **nangṭā**, naked. *h.*

ننگدھڑنگ नंगधड़ंग **nang-dhaṛang**, stark naked. *h.*

ننگیالینا नङ्गियालेना *nangiyā-lenā*, a. to take and strip. *s.*

ننها नन्हा *nanhā*, } small, diminutive,
ننهاں नन्हां *nannhāṅ*, } neat, natty, tidy. *h.*

ننهال ननिहाल *nanihāl*, f. maternal grandfather's family. *h.*

نو *nau*, new, young, fresh, raw. *nau-ābād*, newly settled, peopled, colonised, or cultivated. *nau-āmoz*, one who learns any thing new, a novice, inexperienced. *nau-bāwa*, a young tree. *nau-bā,ī*, a new custom. *nau-baṛhiyā*, an upstart. *nau-bahār*, the spring. *nau-jawān*, a lad, a youth just arrived at adolescence. *nau-jawānī*, prime of life, youth. *nau-khāsta*, new-risen (a youth). *nau-khez*, new-risen, fresh, tender. *nau-khezī*, f. freshness (of vegetation). *nau-daulat*, an upstart, one who has newly attained wealth. *nau-sikh* or *nau-sikhiyā*, a novice, a student. *nau-mulāzim*, a new servant, a recruit, a novice. *nau-mulāzimī*, f. novitiate. *p.*

نو नौ *nau*, नव *nav*, or *nava*, nine; new, fresh, raw. *nava-bālā* or *nava-jauvanā*, f. a girl just grown up to puberty. *nava-baddhu* or *nava-phalikā*, f. a bride, a newly-married woman; a girl in whom menstruation has commenced. *nava-dwār*, having nine doors or outlets, as the human body. *nava-rātr*, a period of nine nights, devoted to the worship of *Durgā*. *nau-ratan* or *nava-ratna*, a bracelet. *nava sūtikā*, f. a woman recently delivered. *nava-shāyak*, m. a name given to the inferior castes, such as cowherds, gardeners, &c. *nava shrāddh*, m. the first of the series of sacrifices to the manes of a deceased relative. *nava-varikā*, f. a newly-married woman. *nava-vastra*, m. new clothes. *nava-yauvanā*, f. a young woman. *s.*

نوا *nawā*, f. voice, sound, modulation, song; opulence, wealth, subsistence. *p.*

نوا नवा *nawā*, new, fresh, recent. *s.*

نواب *nuwwāb* (pl. of نائب), vicegerents, lieutenants, deputies, governors. *nawwāb*, (vulgarly) a nabob, a governor of a town or district (v. *naẓẓām*). *s.*

نوابي *nawwābī*, f. deputyship; situation or office of *nawwāb*; a kind of cloth; adj. relating to a *nawwāb*. *a.*

نواح *nawāḥ*, environs, district, tract, coast, shore. *nuwāḥ*, m. act of lamenting, bewailing, complaining. *a.*

نواحي *nawāḥī* (pl. of ناحيه), territories, environs. *a.*

نواختن *nawākhtan* (r. *nawāz*), to rear, protect; to cherish, to soothe. *p.*

نواخته *nawākhta*, protected, reared, cherished, caressed. *p.*

نوادر *nawādir* (pl. of نادره), rare things, wonderful occurrences. *a.*

نوار निवार *niwār*, m. hindering, opposition; f. tape (of a coarse kind). *niwār-bāf*, a tape-weaver. *s.h.*

نوارت निवारित *niwārit*, hindered, opposed. *s.*

نوارن निवारण *niwāran*, m. hindering, impediment. *s.*

نوارنا नवारना *nawārnā*, n. to travel, to walk, to wander, to stray; to go round, to surround. *h.*

نوارنا निवारना *niwārnā* or *nivārnā*, a. to prevent. *s.*

نواره *nawāra*, a large boat, a barge. *p. h.*

نواري नवारी *nawārī* or निवारी *niwārī*, f. name of a flower, sort of jasmine. *s.*

نواڑ *niwāṛ*, f. (v. *niwār*) tape, &c. *h.*

نواڑا नवाड़ा *niwāṛā* or *nawāṛā*, m. a boat; a particular kind of boat. *h.*

نواز *nawāz*, (in comp.) cherishing, caressing, soothing; playing, performing. *banda-nawāz*, cherisher of servants. *barbuṭ-nawāz*, a player on the harp. *p.*

نوازش *nawāzish*, f. caressing, blandishment, kindness, politeness (pl. *nawāzishāt*). *p.*

نوازنا *nawāznā*, a. to cherish, to caress, to favour. *p.h.*

نوازنده *navāzanda*, m. a cherisher. *p.*

نوازي *nawāzī* (abst. of *nawāz*, q. v.). *p.*

نواس निवास *nivās* or *niwās*, m. dwelling, residence. *s.*

نواسا *nawāsā*, } m. a grandson, more espe-
نواسه *nawāsa*, } cially, a daughter's son. *p.*

نواسي *nawāsī*, f. a granddaughter, a daughter's daughter. *p.*

نواسي नवासी *nawāsī* or *nawwāsī*, eighty-nine. *h.*

نواسي निवासी *niwāsī*, m. } dwelling, abiding
نواسني निवासिनी *niwāsinī*, f. } in, inhabiting; an inhabitant (chiefly used in composition). *s.*

نواسير *nawāsir* (pl. of ناسور), running sores. *a.*

نوافل *nawāfil* (pl. of نافلة), acts of supererogation. *a.*

نواقل *nawākil* (pl. of ناقله), things copied or related; histories, traditions. *a.*

نوال *nawāl*, a benefit; mode, dimension. *a.*

نواله *nawāla* or *niwāla*, m. a morsel, a mouthful; the wadding of a gun. *a.*

نوالي *nawālī*, f. a tidbit, a small morsel. *a.*

نوان निवान *niwān*, low (ground), level. *s.*

نوان नव्वां *nawwāṅ* or *nau,āṅ*, the ninth. *s.*

نوان नवान्न *nawānn*, m. new rice or grain; a ceremony observed on first eating the rice, &c. of the preceding harvest. *s.*

نوانا नवाना *nawānā* or } a. to bend down-
निवाना *niwānā*, } wards; to double,
نواونا निवावना *niwāonā*, } to fold; to cause to submit to, to cause to stoop. *h.*

نوانبر नवाम्बर *navāmbar*, new unbleached cloth. *s.*

نوانش नवांश *navānsh*, m. a ninth, the ninth part. *s.*

نوائب *nawāi,b* (pl. of نائبة), accidents, vicissitudes. *a.*

نوبالا नवबाला *nava-bālā*, f. a girl just grown up to puberty. *s.*

نوبت *naubat*, f. a period, time, turn; relieving guard, keeping watch; an accident; oportunity, occasion, vicissitude, degree, pitch, weight; drums beating at the gate of a great man at certain intervals. *naubat-ṭalabī*, f. applying to be heard in one's turn (in a law court). *a.*

نوبت‌خانه *naubat-khāna*, m. the royal orchestra, generally a large room over the outer gate of the palace, for martial music. *a.p.*

نوبدهو नववधू *nava-badhū*, f. a bride or newly married woman. *s.*

نوبرار *nau-barār*, land recently made subject to assessment. *p.*

نوبهار *nau-bahār*, early spring, or as Virgil hath it "novum ver." *p.*

نوپر नूपुर *nūpur*, m. a ring or ornament for the ankles or toes. *s.*

نوپهلکا नवफलिका *nava-phalikā*, f. a bride, a woman in whom menstruation has just begun. *s.*

نوتا नौता *nautā*, m. a portico; adj. stooping, bending down. *navatā*, f. novelty. *s.*

نوتا नौता *nautā* or *notā*, m. an invitation. *s.*

نوتن नूतन *nūtan*, new, recent, fresh. *nūtan twa*, m. novelty. *s.*

نوتنا नौतना *nautnā*, a. to invite. *s.*

نوجوبنا नौजौबना *nau-jaubanā*, } f. a girl just
نوجوونا नवजोवना *nava-jovanā*, } grown up to puberty. *s.*

نوچ नोच *noch*, a pinch, a gripe, a scratch. *nochā-nāchī*, pinching and scratching mutually. *h.*

نوچنا नोचना *nochnā* or *nauchnā*, a. to pinch, to gripe, to scratch, to claw. *h.*

نوچندي नौचन्दी *nauchandī*, of or relating to the new moon. *s.*

نوچهاتر *nava-chhātr*, m. a young student, a novice. *s.*

نوچهاور नौछावर *nauchhāwar*, m. a propitiatory offering, sacrifice, victim. *h.*

نوچي नौची *nauchī*, f. a young girl kept by a bawd. *h.*

نوح *nūḥ*, the patriarch Noah. *heb.*

نوحه *nauḥa*, m. lamentation, moaning, mourning over the dead. *nauḥa-gar*, a lamenter, mourner. *a.*

نود नूद *nūd*, m. the mulberry tree (*Morus Indica*). *s.*

نود *nawad* or *nuwad*, ninety. *nawad-bār*, ninety times. *p.*

نودوار नवद्वार *nava-dwār*, having nine doors or outlets (an epithet applied to the body). *s.*

نودهه नौध *naudha*, m. a young plant, or fresh shoot or branch of a plant. *h.*

نودها नूधा *nūdhā*, m. a species of tobacco. *h.*

نور *nūr*, m. light, splendour. *nūr-afzā*, *nūr-afshān*, light-increasing, light-diffusing. *nūr jānā munh kā*, paleness of the face. *nūri-chashm* or *nūri 'ainain*, or *nūri dīda*, m. (light of the eyes) a son. *a.*

نورا *nūrā*, m. depilatory. *a.*

نورا निवरा *nivarā*, f. an unmarried girl. *s.*

نوراتر नवरात्र *nava-rātr*, m. the first nine nights of Aswin, devoted to *Durgā*. *s.*

نوراني *nūrānī*, serene, light, clear; f. brightness, serenity. *a.*

نورباف *nūr-bāf*, m. a weaver. *nūr-bāfī*, weaving. *p.*

نورت निवृत्ति *nivritti*, f. rest, final emancipation. *s.*

نورتن नौरतन *nau-ratan* or नवरत्न *nava-ratna*, m. nine kinds of gems; nine poets at the court of Vikramāditya; f. name of an ornament worn on the arm and wrist, and consisting of nine different gems. *s.*

نورد *naward*, f. a ply, a fold; (in comp.) traversing, &c.; to overlook or lose sight of. *p.*

نوردن *nawardan* (also *nawardīdan*), to omit. *p.*

نورس *nau-ras*, } young, fresh, tender,
نورسته *nau-rusta*, } recent, newly arrived
نورسيده *nau-rasīda*, } or come forth. *p.*

نوروز *nau-roz*, m. new year's day according to the Persian calendar, being that on which the sun enters *Aries*; this is called *'āmma*, or general, and the sixth of the same month is called *khāṣṣa*, or particular: both are celebrated by feasts, the liberation of prisoners, &c. *p.*

نوروزي *nau-rozī*, of or relating to new year's day; f. the festival of the new year. *p.*

نوري नूरी *nūrī*, f. name of a bird of the parrot kind, commonly called *lūrī* (*psittacus*). *h.*

نوري *nūrī*, splendid, bright, clear. *a.*

نوڑانا *niwaṛānā*, a. to cause to bend or stoop, to turn or direct. *d.*

نوڑنا *niwaṛnā*, n. to bend, stoop or incline. *d.*

نوڑهانا नौढ़ाना *nauṛhānā*, a. to bend, to bow. *s.*

نوڑهنا नौढ़ना *nauṛhnā*, n. to bend, to incline downwards; to be obedient, to stoop. *s.*

نوسات *nau-sāt*, (lit. "nine and seven") a division of the crop whereby the *zamindār* takes nine parts and the cultivator the remaining seven parts out of sixteen. *h.*

نوسادر नौसादर *nausādar*, m. *sal ammoniac*. *s.*

نوسر *nausir*, new, recent. *nausir tālāw*, a newly excavated tank. *d.*

نوسکه नौसिख *nau-sikh*, a novice, a young student or disciple. *s.*

نوسوتکا नवसूतिका *nava-sūtikā*, a newly married woman. *s.*

نوش *nosh*, m. a drink, a draught; a present; honey; a reward; (in comp.) drinking, as *mai-nosh* or *bāda-nosh*, a wine-drinker. *noshi jān farmānā*, to eat, to drink (applied to a king or superior). *nosh karnā*, to drink, to devour, to swallow, to sup, to sip. *p.*

نوشاد *nau-shād*, name of a city famous for the beauty of its inhabitants, more especially that of the damsels thereof. *p.*

نوشادر नौसादर *naushādar*, m. *sal ammoniac. s.*

نوشانوش *nosh-ā-nosh*, drinking with full cups, in repeated bumpers. *p.*

نوشايك नवशायक *nava-shāyak*, m. a name given to nine inferior classes, cowherd, gardener, oilman, &c. *s.*

نوشتخواند *navisht-khwānd*, f. epistolary correspondence, reading and writing. *p.*

نوشتن *nawishtan* (r. *nawīs*), to write. *p.*

نوشتني *nawishtanī*, fit to be written. *p.*

نوشته *nawishta*, m. a writing, any thing written. *p.*

نوشدارو *nosh-dārū*, an antidote; treacle, an electuary. *p.*

نوشرادھ नवश्राद्ध *nava-shrāddh*, m. a series of nine funeral offerings. *s.*

نوشكست *nau-shikast*, waste alluvial land newly cultivated. *p.*

نوشكھ नौशिख *nau-shikh*, m. a student, a novice. *s.*

نوشو *nau-shaw*, new, recent, fresh; a newly-married man, a bridegroom.

نوشه *naushah*, m. a young king; a bridegroom. *nosha*, fortunate, happy, prosperous, sweet, cheerful. *p.*

نوشهانه *nau-shahāna*, in the manner of a young king or bridegroom. *p.*

نوشي *noshī*, f. abst. of *nosh* (in comp.) as *mai-noshī*, wine-drinking. *p.*

نوشيروان *noshīrwān* or *naushīrwān*, a celebrated king of Persia, famed for his justice: he was contemporary with Justinian. *p.*

نوشين *noshīn*, sweet, pleasant. *p.*

نوع *nau'*, m. kind, species, sort, manner, mode. *nau'ī*, specific. *a.*

نوعيت *nau'iyat*, f. specification, speciality. *a.*

نوك *nok*, f. a bill, a beak; end, point, angle. *nok-jhok*, f. pulling and hauling. *nok-chok*, f. talking by inuendoes. *nok-dār*, pointed. *noki zabān*, by heart, on the tip of the tongue. *p.*

نوكا नौका *naukā*, f. a boat. *s.*

نوكالكا नवकालिका *nava-kālikā*, f. a woman who has just attained the period of menstruation; a bride. *s.*

نوكر *naukar*, m. a servant. *naukar-chākar*, domestics in general. *p.*

نوكراني *naukarānī*, } f. a female servant, a
نوكرني *naukarnī*, } waiting-woman. *p. h.*

نوكري *naukarī*, f. service, attendance. *naukarī-pesha*, one who lives on employments. *p.*

نوكھنڈ नौखंड *nau-khanḍ*, m. (lit.) the nine sections or portions. *nau-khanḍ prithwī kā*, the nine climes or divisions of the earth: they are usually denominated the nine *dwīpas* (islands) or *varshas* (countries) which constitute *jambu-dwīpa*, the central portion of the world, or the known world. *s.*

نوكيلا नोकीला *nokīlā*, sharp-pointed. *p. h.*

نوگرها नवग्रहा *nava-grahā*, m. (pl.) the nine planets, *i. e.* the seven planets and the ascending and descending nodes. *s.*

نوگري नौगरी *naugarī*, f. a female ornament worn on the wrist. *s.*

نول *nol*, f. beak, bill (of a bird); the spout or neck of a decanter or teapot. *p.*

نول नवल *nawal*, beautiful; m. sapling. *h.*

نول *naul*, m. freight, fare, hire. *a.*

نولا नवला *navalā* or *naulā*, f. a young woman. *s.*

نولاسي नौलासी *naulāsī*, tender, soft, delicate. *h.*

نوليوا नौलेवा *nau-lewā*, alluvial deposit by an inundation. *h.*

نوم नवम *navam* or *navama*, the ninth. *s.*

نوم *naum*, f. sleep, rest, stillness. *a.*

نوماسا नौमासा *nau-māsā*, m. name of a feast given in the ninth month of pregnancy. *s.*

نومالكا नवमालिका *nava-mālikā*, f. double jasmine (*Jasminum zambac*). *s.*

نوم توم *naum-taum*, dull, sing-song (speech). *a. h.*

نومي नौमी *naumī* or नवमी *navamī*, f. the ninth day of a lunar fortnight. *s.*

نوميد *naumed*, hopeless, desperate. *naumedī*, f. despair, desperate condition. *p.*

نومين नौमीं *naumīṅ* or नवमीं *navamīṅ*, f. ninth day of the moon. *s.*

نون नोन *non* or नून *nūn*, m. salt (v. *lon*). *h.*

نونا नौना *naunā*, n. to bend; to incline downwards; to be obedient, to stoop. *s.*

نونا नोना *nonā*, a. to tie the feet of a cow when milking. *h.*

نونا नोना *nonā*, salt. *nonā-pānī*, m. salt-water. *h.*

نونا नोना *nonā*, m. a kind of custard apple (*Annona reticulata*). *h.*

نونتنا नौंतना *nauṅtnā*, a. to invite (v. *notnā*). *s.*

نوندھ नवनिधि *nava-nidhi*, f. the nine treasures of Kuvera. *s.*

نونچا नोन्चा *nonchā*, land abounding with saline matter. *h.*

نونچي नोन्चै *nonchai*, a kind of factitious salt. *h.*

نوني नूनी *nūnī*, m. *penis puerilis*. *h.*

نوني नोनी *nonī*, f. efflorescence of salt on a wall. *s.*

نوني नवनी *navanī*, f. } fresh butter. *s.*
نونيت नवनीत *navanīt*, m. }

نونيا नोनिया *noniyā* or नूनिया *nūniyā*, m. purslain (*Portulaca oleracea*); a maker of or dealer in salt, a saltpetre-maker. *s.*

نونير नोनेर *noner*, saline (as soil). *h.*

نوورکا नववरिका *nava-varikā*, f. a newly married woman. *s.*

نووستر नववस्त्र *nava-vastr*, m. new cloth. *s.*

نوي नव्वे *navwe*, ninety. *navya*, new, recent, young. *s.*

نوي नवी *navī* or *nave*, f. the string with which a cow's feet are tied when milking, a tether. *s.*

نويبهوت नवीभूत *navībhūt*, renewed, revived. *s.*

نويد *navīd*, m. glad tidings. *p.*

نويدن निवेदन *nivedan*, m. petition, representation. *s.*

نويس *nawīs*, (in comp.) writing, as *khush-nawīs*, one who writes beautifully. *p.*

نويسنده *navīsanda*, m. a writer, a clerk, an accountant, a transcriber. *p.*

نويکرت नवीकृत *navīkṛit*, renewed, revived. *s.*

نوءين *no,īn* or *nūyīn*, a prince, a grandee (a commander of ten thousand). *p.*

نوين नवीन *nawīn*, new, youthful, recent. *s.*

نوينتا नवीनता *nawīnatā*, f. newness, youthfulness. *s.*

نويوونا नवयौवना *nava-yauvanā*, f. a young woman. *s.*

نويه नव्य *navya*, new, recent, young. *s.*

نه न *na*, neg. part. no, not, neither. *s. p.*

نه *nuh*, nine. *nih*, (in comp.) placing, as *marham-nih*, one who applies plaster (to a wound). *p.*

نه नुह *nuh* or नह *nah*, nail, talon. *nuh-* or *nah-lenā*, to trip, to stumble. *nih*, a prefix like *nir*, &c., as *nih-kāran*, without cause. *nahi*, nay, no, not. *s.*

نهاٹنا *nhāṭnā*, n. to run away, to flee. *d.*

نهاٹو *nhāṭū*, a fugitive, a deserter. *d.*

نهاد *nihād*, m. nature, form, habit, stature, quality, disposition, mind, heart; family, race. *bad-nihād*, wicked, cruel. *p.*

نهادن *nihādan* (r. *nih*), to place, lay down. *p.*

نهار *nahār*, m. the day, diffusion of light. *a.*

نهارمنه नहारमुंह *nahār-munh*, (in Dakh.) *nahar mūh*, without eating (as a person is in the morning before breakfast). *s.*

نهارنا निहारना *nihārnā*, } a. to look at,
نهارنون निहारनौं *nihārnaun*, } to watch, to look after, to spy, to see. *h.*

نهاروا नहारुआ *nahārū,ā*, m. a guinea-worm (*Filaria medinensis*). *h.*

نهاري *nahārī*, f. breakfast; a kind of bit or bridle. *p.*

نهاکا निहाका *nihākā*, f. an iguana, or the Gangetic alligator. *s.*

نهال *nihāl*, m. a young plant, a shoot, a sucker, a sapling. *p.*

نهال निहाल *nihāl*, exalted, pleased, happy. *h.*

نهالچه *nihālcha*, m. a quilt, wrapper, coverlet, &c., mattress. *p.*

نهالي *nihālī*, f. a young plant; a kind of quilt, small carpet, a cushion. *p.*

نهان नहान *nahān*, m. bathing, ablution. *h.*

نهان *nihān*, latent, hid, concealed, clandestine. *nihān-r.* or *-dāshtan*, to keep secret. *p.*

نهانا नहाना *nahānā* or *nhānā*, n. to bathe, to wash. *h.*

نهانٹنا *nhānṭnā*, n. to run away, to flee. *d.*

نهاني *nihānī*, f. concealment; adv. secretly, in private. *andāmi nihānī*, the private parts. *p.*

نهاني नहानी *nahānī* or निहानी *nihānī*, f. menstruation. *h.*

نهاءي निहाई *nihā,ī*, f. an anvil. *h.*

نهايا नहाया *nahāyā*, bathed, bathing. *h.*

نهايت *nihāyat*, f. the extremity, boundary; excess; adj. very much, extreme, excessive; remarkable; adv. at the utmost, extremely. *a.*

نهب *nahb*, m. rapine, plunder, spoil. *a.*

نهتها निहत्था *nihatthā*, unarmed. *s.*

نهٹا नहट्टा *nahaṭṭā* or नुहट्टा *nuhaṭṭā*, m. a scratch with the nail or talon. *h.*

نهج *nahaj*, m. a road, way, path, manner; prescribing, giving instructions. *a.*

نهچي निहचै *nihchai* (v. *nishchai*), indubitable, certain, &c. *s.*

نهر *nahr*, f. a stream, rivulet, a canal (of running water). *a.*

نهرانا निहुराना *nihurānā*, a. to cause to crook, bend, bow. *h.*

نهرنا निहुरना *nihurnā*, } n. to condescend, to
نهڑنا निहुड़ना *nihuṛnā*, } incline or bend downward, to stoop. *h.*

نهرني नहरनी *naharnī*, f. an instrument with which the nails are pared, a shoemaker's awl. *s.*

نهضت *nuhẓat*, f. marching, departure, rising up. *nuhẓat-k.*, to march, to depart, &c. *a.*

نهفتگي *nihuftagī*, f. concealment, obscurity. *p.*

نهفتن *nihuftan*, to hide, to conceal. *p.*

نهفته *nihufta* or *nahufta*, concealed, hidden, private. *p.*

نهك नहक *nahak*, meagre, lean. *h.*

نهل निहल *nihal*, alluvial land recovered from water courses. *h.*

نهلانا नहलाना *nahlānā*, a. to cause to bathe. *h.*

نهلوانا नहलवाना *nahalwānā*, a. to cause to be bathed. *h.*

نهم *nuhum* (also *nuhumīn*), the ninth. *p.*

نهن नहिं *nahin* (for *nahīn*), no, not. *h.*

نهنا *nhannā*, small, little, young. *d.*

نهنگ *nihang*, m. a crocodile; a water dragon, or other similar monster; (met.) a pen. *p.*

نهنگ निहङ्ग *nihang*, naked; free from care. *nihang lārlā*, a careless child or person. *h.*

نهنواد *nhanwād*, m. and f. a child. *d.*

نهني नहनी *nahanī*, f. an instrument for cutting the nails; a kind of chisel used in polishing and turning brass, &c. *s.*

نهورا निहोरा *nihorā*, m. favour, obligation, kindness; begging, requesting humbly, coaxing. *h.*

نهورنا निहूरना *nihūrnā*, } a. to incline, to bend
نهوڑنا निहूड़ना *nihūṛnā*, } downwards, to stoop. *h.*

نهي *nahī*, f. prohibition, an interdict. *a.*

نهي नही *nahī* (for *nahīn*), no, not. *h.*

نهيب *nahīb* or *nihīb*, m. fear, terror; grief, anguish, anxiety; expedition, haste. *a.*

نهير नहियर *nahiyar*, f. a wife's family. *h.*

نهين नहीं *nahīn*, no, not, nay. *nahīn-to*, otherwise, else. *s.*

ني *nai*, f. a reed, tube, cane; pipe, fife, flute. *ne* or *nī*, no, not, nay. *p.*

ني ने *ne*, a postposition used in Hindūstānī to denote the agent of a transitive verb in any of the tenses formed by the past participle (v. Hind. Gram. p. 103). *h.*

نيا नया *nayā*, new. *naye sir se*, anew, afresh; *naiyā*, m. a boatman, ferryman. *s.*

نيابت *niyābat*, f. deputyship, vicegerency, lieutenancy, &c. (v. *nā,ib*). *a.*

نيابتا *niyābatan*, virtually, really. *a.*

نيات न्याति *nyāti*, caste, kind, sort. *s. h.*

نيار न्यार *nyār* or नियार *niyār*, m. forage, fodder, food of cattle. *h.*

نيارا न्यारा *nyārā* or नियारा *niyārā*, adj. apart, aloof, distinct, different, separate, extraordinary, uncommon; m. the scoriæ left after refining gold, silver, or other metals, from which a minute portion of those metals is obtainable. *niyāre*, adv. apart, separately, independently. *a.*

نياريا न्यारिया *nyāriya*, m. one who extracts metals from their scoriæ; adj. prudent, cautious, not easily imposed on. *h.*

نياز *niyāz*, f. petition, supplication, prayer; indigence, poverty; a thing dedicated. *niyāz-k.*, a. to dedicate, to consecrate. *niyāz-ṣinat* or *-mand*, indigent, humble, a petitioner. *niyāzi rasūl*, offerings of food, &c. in the name of the prophet *Muḥammad*. *p.*

نيازمند *niyāz-mand*, indigent; m. a suppliant. *p.*

نيازمندي *niyāz-mandī*, f. indigence, supplication. *p.*

نيازي *niyazī*, a lover, a friend; name of a tribe of Afghāns. *p.*

نياس न्यास *nyās*, a pledge, a deposit. *s.*

نيام *niyām*, m. a sheath, scabbard; a bandage for a broken limb; the plough-tail or handle. *p.*

نيامڑ न्यामड़ *nyāmaṛ*, a tree which has sprung up of itself in a cultivated field, and which the cultivator may legally cut down. *h.*

نيامك नियामक *niyāmak*, m. a boatman, a sailor, a steersman, a helmsman, a pilot; a charioteer. *s.*

نياو न्याव *nyāw*, m. justice, equity. *nyāw-k.*, to judge, to administer justice. *s.*

نياءي न्याई *nyā,ī* or *niyāyī*, m. a distributor of justice; a logician. *s.*

نياي न्याय *nyā,e*, *nyāya*, or नियाय *niyāya*, m. justice; reason, argument, disputation, sophistry. *nyā,e-shāstr*, m. logic. *niyāya-k.*, to administer justice, to decide. *s.*

نياياچار न्यायाचार *nyāyāchār*, } m. a virtuous
نيايادهار न्यायाधार *nyāyādhār*, } man, an example of propriety. *s.*

نيايتا न्यायता *nyāyatā*, f. fitness, propriety. *s.*

نيايش *niyā,ish* or *niyāyish*, f. blessing, benediction, praise. *p.*

نيايك न्यायक *niyāyak* or नियायक *niyāyak*, m. a judge. *nyāyik* or *naiyāyik*, a reasoner, arguer, logician, sophist. *s.*

نيايه न्याय्य *nyāya*, right, proper. *s.*

نيايي न्यायी *nyāyī* or नियायी *niyāyī*, m. an administrator of justice; a logician. *s.*

نيبو नीबू *nībū* (v. *nīmbū*), m. lemon, lime-[tree. *s.*

نيبيد नैबेद *naibed*, m. food consecrated to a deity, an oblation. *s.*

نيبيدن नीबेदन *nībedan*, m. a petition, representation (properly *nivedan*). *s.*

نيپ नीप *nīp*, m. the *hadamb* tree (*Nauclea kadamba*); a species of Ixora (*Ixora bandhuca*); a sort of Asoka. *s.*

نيپال नेपाल *nepāl*, name of a country, Nepal. *s.*

نيپال नैपाल *naipāl*, } produced in Ne-
نيپالك नैपालिक *naipālik*, } pal, or belonging to that country. *s.*

نيپالكا नेपालिका *nepālikā*, f. arsenic. *s.*

نيپالي नैपाली *naipālī*, f. double jasmine, red arsenic (*Nyctanthes tristis*). *s.*

نيپر नेपुर *nepur*, f. an ornament worn on the [ankles. *s.*

نيپن नैपुण *naipuṇ*, } m. skill, cleverness,
نيپنيه नैपुण्य *naipuṇya*, } dexterity. *s.*

نيپنج *nay,e-panj*, m. a horse under five years old. *p.*

نیپور नीपूर *nīpūr, penis, membrum virile. h.*

نیپیچ *nai-pīch* or *-pech*, f. the snake tube of a *ḥuḳḳa*. *p.*

نیت *niyat*, f. wish, intention, design, will, purpose, desire, aim, object. *a.*

نیت नियत *niyat*, self-governed, ruled, restrained. *niyat-ātmā*, self-regulated, self-controlled or restrained. *niyat-āhār*, abstemious. *niyat-endriya*, of restrained or subdued passions. *s.*

نیت नीति *nīti* or *nīt*, f. guidance, moral conduct, polity, political science, treating especially of the administration of government, and the morality, both public and private, of king and people. *nīti shāstr* or *nīti-vidyā*, the science or code of ethics, moral philosophy, or polity. *s.*

نیت नियुत *niyut*, a million, ten hundred thousand. *s.*

نیتر नेत्र *netr*, m. the eye; the string of a churning-rope. *s.*

نیترامبو नेत्राम्बु *netr-āmbū*, m. a tear. *s.*

نیترپنڈ नेत्रपिण्ड *netr-pinḍ*, m. the eyeball. *s.*

نیتررنجن नेत्ररञ्जन *netr-ranjan*, m. collyrium. *s.*

نیترروگ नेत्ररोग *netr-rog*, m. any disease of the eye. *s.*

نیترلوت नेत्रलोत *netralot*, m. a prisoner. *h.*

نیتروتسو नेत्रोत्सव *netrotsav*, m. any pleasing or beautiful object. *s.*

نیتروشدھ नेत्रौषध *netraushadh*, m. collyrium in general, green sulphate of iron. *s.*

نیتروشدھی नेत्रौषधी *netraushadhī*, f. name of a drug. *s.*

نیتکتھا नीतिकथा *nīti-kathā*, f. any work or treatise on polity or good government. *s.*

نیتگیہ नीतिज्ञ *nītigya*, m. a statesman, politician. *s.*

نیتمت नीतिमत *nītimat*, moral, eminent for royal duties. *s.*

نیتودیا नीतिविद्या *nīti-vidyā*, f. political science. *s.*

نیتی नेती *netī*, f. a cord used to whirl round the churn-staff with. *s.*

نیتی *niyatī*, intentional, designedly. *a.*

نیٹ *nīṭ*, straight, upright. *d.*

نیٹا नेटा *neṭā*, m. snot, snivel; (Beng.) left-handed. *h.*

نیج नैज *naij*, own, proper. *s.*

نیجانا नैजाना *naijānā*, n. to stoop, to bend down. *h.*

نیچ नीच *nīch*, low, mean, vulgar, base; below, beneath, under, down. *nīch-ūṅch*, f. inequality; the ups and downs of life. *nīch-sonār*, a jeweller of low caste. *nīch-nhāwī*, an inferior sort of barber. *s.*

نیچا नीचा *nīchā*, below, down. *nīchā-ūṅchā*, up and down, uneven ground. *nīche suroṅ se bolnā*, to sing with a low voice, or hum a tune (*jocosè autem, crepitus ventris hâcce voce subintelligitur*); *kalāṅwatnī tire gāne se diḳḳ hūṅ; bahut nīche suroṅ se boltī hai*, "songstress, I am tired of your lays, you sing too low," which latter phrase may be taken in *two* senses. *s.*

نیچان *nīchān*, m. low lands, a valley. *d.*

نیچائی नीचाई *nīchā,ī*, f. inferiority, vileness. *s.*

نیچگامی नीचगामी *nīcha-gāmī*, water (lit. that which goes downwards). *s.*

نیچو नीचू *nīchū* (v. *nīche*), below, &c. *s.*

نیچہ *naicha*, m. a *ḥuḳḳa* snake or tube. *naicha-band*, a person who makes *ḥuḳḳa* snakes. *naicha-bandī*, the trade of a *naicha-band*. *p.*

نیچے नीचे *nīche*, below, beneath, under, down. *nīche ūpar*, upside down. *nīche jānā*, n. to descend, to submit, to subside, to succumb. *nīche girānā*, to knock a person down. *s.*

نیخوا *neḵẖwā* (for *neh-ḵẖwāh*, q. v.). a well-wisher. *neḵẖwe-panā*, m. goodwill, benevolence. *d.*

نید नीद *nīd*, f. sleep, slumber, repose. *s.*

نیدشٹھ नेदिष्ठ *nedishṭh*, m. a tree (*Alangium hexapetalum*). *s.*

نیدنا *nīdnā*, n. to sleep, to repose. *s.*

نیدھ नियुद्ध *niyuddh*, m. close fight, personal struggle. *s.*

نیر *naiyir*, m. the sun; the moon; adj. bright, clear, shining. *naiyiri a'ẓam*, the sun. *naiyirain*, the two luminaries, *i. e.* the sun and moon. *a.*

نیر नियर *niyar*, near, beside, close by. *s.*

نیر नीर *nīr*, } m. water, sap, juice. *s.*
نیرا नीरा *nīrā*, }

نیراشیہ नैराश्य *nairāshya*, m. hopelessness, despair. *s.*

نیرائی नियराई *niyarā,ī*, f. nearness, contiguity. *s.*

نیرت नैरित or नैऋत *nairit*, m. the ruler of the south-west quarter. *s.*

نیرتھ नीरथ *nīrath* (for *nir-arth*), fruitless, profitless. *s.*

نیرتی नैरिती or नैऋती *nairitī*, f. the south-west quarter. *s.*

نیرج नीरज *nīraj*, aquatic; m. a sort of costus (*Costus speciosus*), a lotus in general; an otter. *s.*

نیرجس नीरजस *nīrajas*, having no pollen (as a flower); f. a woman not menstruating. *s.*

نیرس नीरस *nīras*, dry, withered, insipid, void of taste (morally or physically). *s.*

نیرکت नैरुक्त *nairukt*, obsolete, uncommon, belonging to the glossary of the *Veda*. *s.*

نیرگن नैर्गुण *nairgun*, m. absence of good qualities or properties. *s.*

نیرملیہ नैर्मल्य *nairmalya*, m. cleanness, purity. *s.*

نیرنگ *nairang*, m. deceit, trick, pretence, evasion, incantation, magic, sorcery; a miracle, any thing new. *nairang-sāz*, a magician, sorcerer. *p.*

نيرنگي *nairangī*, f. magic, deception. *p.*

نيرو *nerū* or *nīrū*, m. strength, power. *p.*

نيرو नेरौ *nerau*, near, beside, close by. *s.*

نيروءا नेरूआ *nerū,ā*, m. straw. *h.*

نيروگ नीरोग *nīrog*, healthy, free from sickness. *s.*

نيروگتا नीरोगता *nīrogtā*, f. health, freedom from sickness. *s.*

نيري नेरे *nere*, beside, near, close by. *h.*

نيڑنا नेड़ना *neṛnā*, a. to care for, to look after. *h.*

نيڑي *neṛe*, in the shelter of, near, beside. *d.*

نيز *nīz*, also, likewise, again, at the same time, moreover. *p.*

نيزه *neza* or *naiza*, m. a spear, lance, javelin, dart, pike; a piece of reed from which pens are made. *neza-bāz*, a spearman. *neza-bāzī*, f. throwing the spear. *neze-bardār* or *neze-dār*, a spearman, or one armed with a spear. *p.*

نيسان *naisān*, m. name of the seventh Syrian month, corresponding to the Persian *Farwardīn*, the Hind. *Baisākh*, and our April. *abri naisān*, the vernal cloud, April showers; the rain which falls while the moon is in the mansion *Swātī*, and of which, if it drop into a shell, pearls are formed, but which turns to poison if it happens to fall into the mouth of a serpent (v. *swāti*). *p.*

نيست *nest* or *nīst*, (lit.) it is not; nought. *nest-k.*, a. to abolish, to annihilate, to ruin, to destroy. *nest-nābūd-k.* or *nest o nābūd-k.*, to demolish, to annihilate, to ruin. *nest-nābūd honā*, n. to perish, to be annihilated, ruined, &c. *p.*

نيست न्यस्त *nyast*, deposited, delivered. *s.*

نيستان *naistān*, m. a sugar-plantation, field of sugar-cane; a place where canes or reeds grow. *p.*

نيستي *nestī* or *nīstī*, f. non-existence, nullity, annihilation. *p.*

نيسرنا नीसरना *nīsarnā*, n. (v. *nisarnā*) to go out, to issue forth (in Braj. *nīsarnaui*). *s.*

نيش *nesh*, m. sting (of a venomous animal); a puncture; a lancet. *nesh-zan*, what inflicts a sting; (met.) an incendiary, one who inflames disputes, a tell-tale. *nesh-zanī*, f. exciting quarrels. &c. *p.*

نيشتر *neshtar*, m. a lancet. *p.*

نيشكر *naishakar*, f. sugar-cane. *p.*

نيفا *nefā* or *nīfā*, }
نيفه *nefa* or *nīfa*, } m. a breeches-belt, the part of the drawers through which the string runs to tie them round the loins with. *p.*

نيك *neh*, good, lucky; (sub.) any thing good. *nek-akhtar*, of a good star. *nek-andesh*, a well-wisher, benevolent, friendly, affectionate; fortunate. *nek bāz*, just, virtuous, of good actions, of fair play. *nek-bakhi*, fortunate (commonly means of good dispositions). *nek bakhtī*, f. good fortune, goodness of conduct. *nek-pāk*, virtuous. *nek-tan*, sleek-skinned (a horse). *nek-khaṣlat*, or *-kho*, or *-kir ār*, of good dispositions or habits. *nek-khwāh*, well-wishing, faithful, grateful. *nek-diyānat*, having a clear conscience. *nek-zāt* or *-ṭinat*, of good disposition. *nek-raw*, good-paced (horse). *nek-raftagān*, those who have died and left behind them a good name. *nek-fāl*, of happy omen. *nek-farjām*, of happy end. *nek-goe*, one who speaks well, eloquent. *nek-ḳāl*, well-spoken. *nek-mard*, a good man. *nek-mangar*, handsome, comely, elegant. *nek-nām*, good name, celebrity; of good character, renowned. *nek-nāmī*, good character. *nek-nihād*, of good dispositions. *nek-nīyat*, well-meaning. *p.*

نيك नेक *nek*, नेकु *neku*, or *naik*, little, a little. *naik*, many, various. *naik-bhed*, various, manifold. *naik-rūp*, multiform. *h. s.*

نيكا *nīkā* or *nekā*, good (v. *neho*). *p.*

نيكار न्यक्कार *nyakkār*, m. contempt, disrespect. *s.*

نيكت नियुक्त *niyukt*, engaged in, applied or attached to; authorised, called upon, appointed. *s.*

نيكٹيه नैकट्य *naikaṭya*, m. proximity. *s.*

نيكو *neko* (in Hind. *nīko* or *nīkau*), good, beautiful, elegant. *neko-kār*, of good actions, a beneficent person. N.B.—*neko* or *nīkū* may be compounded with other words, like *nek*, and with the same signification. *p.*

نيكي *nekī*, f. goodness, piety, virtue, probity. *p.*

نيگ नेग *neg*, f. marriage presents made to relatives, and to particular servants, and considered by them as perquisites which they are entitled to. *h.*

نيگرودھ न्यग्रोध *nyagrodh*, m. the Indian fig-tree. *nyagrodhī*, f. a plant (*Salvinia cucullata*). *s.*

نيگم नैगम *naigam*, m. an Upanishad. *s.*

نيگي नेगी *negī*, m. a village servant; any public servant who claims a fee or present on particular occasions. *negī jogī*, tenants aud dependants, to whom it is customary to give the *neg*, q. v. *h.*

نيل नील *nīl*, blue; m. indigo, blue; the blue mountain, one of the nine ranges which divide the world; one of the nine treasures of Kuvera; a gem, the sapphire; the blue Maina; blue vitriol. *nīl* or *nīl kā māṭh bigaṛnā*, (lit.) a vat of indigo being spoiled; (met.) employed to express the persecutions of fortune: the phrase is also used on hearing something very wonderful and incredible (said to originate from a notion entertained by dyers, that when their dye, through any accident, has been spoiled, it may be restored by telling some miraculous story). *nīl-koṭhī*, an indigo-factory. *nīl-wālā*, an indigo-planter or dealer. *nīl-gāw*, f. an animal (known by the name of *līlgā,ī* and *rojh*), the white-footed antelope of Pennant and *Antilope picta* of Pallas. *nīl-gūn*, cerulean. *p. s.*

نيل *nail*, m. obtaining, acquiring. *nīl*, the river Nile. *a.*

نيلا नीला *nīlā*, blue, black, or dark blue. *nīlā pīlā karnā*, to render blue and yellow (the eyes); to be greatly enraged. *nīlā thothā*, blue vitriol; sulphate of copper. *p. s.*

نيلاب *nīl-āb*, the river Attock or Indus. *p.*

نيلاشمن नीलाश्मन *nīlāshman*, m. a blue stone, a sapphire. *s.*

نيلام नीलाम *nīlām* (for *leilām*, Port.), m. auction, a public sale, or, as the Anglo-Bengālīs say, "an outcry." *h. port.*

نيلامي *nīlāmī*, saleable by auction. *port.*

نيلامبر नीलाम्बर *nīlāmbar*, dresses in dark blue clothes; m. dark blue garments. *s.*

نیلامچی *nīlāmchī*, m. an auctioneer. *s.*

نیلامدار *nīlām-dār*, one who holds an estate purchased at a public sale. *h. p.*

نیلانجن नीलाञ्जन *nīlānjan*, m. blue vitriol. *s.*

نیلانگ नीलाङ्ग *nīlāng*, m. the Indian crane, the blue jay. *s.* [colour. *s.*

نیلائی नीलाई *nīlā,ī*, f. blueness, dark blue

نیل بڑی नीलबड़ी *nīl-baṛī*, f. a lump of indigo. *s.*

نیلپاچن नीलपाचन *nīl-pāchan*, m. steeping or maceration of indigo. *nīl-pāchan-bhānd*, m. an indigo vat. *s.*

نیلپچھ नीलपिच्छ *nīl-pichh*, m. a falcon. *s.*

نیلپدم नीलपद्म *nīl-padma*, m. the blue lotus. *s.*

نیلپرشٹھ नीलपृष्ठ *nīl-pṛishṭh*, m. a kind of fish, the *rohi* (*Cyprinus denticulatus*). *s.*

نیلپشپکا नीलपुष्पिका *nīl-pushpikā*, f. the indigo-plant. *s.*

نیلج नीलज *nīlaj*, m. blue steel. *s.*

نیلجھنٹی नीलझिण्टी *nīl-jhinṭī*, f. blue barleria. *s.*

نیلک नीलक *nīlak*, blue (stained or dyed); m. one of the terms used in *bīja ganita* or algebra (as we use the letters *a, b*, or *x, y*). *s. p.*

نیلکا नीलिका *nīlikā*, f. the *Nyctanthes tristis* (a species of it with blue flowers); the indigo-plant. *s.*

نیلکرنٹک नीलकुरुण्टक *nīl-kuruṇṭak*, m. blue barleria. *s.*

نیلکرونچ नीलक्रौञ्च *nīl-krauñch*, m. a sort of curlew or heron. *s.* [lotus. *s.*

نیلکمل नीलकमल *nīl-kamal*, m. the blue

نیلکنٹھ नीलकण्ठ *nīl-kanṭh*, blue-neck, name of a bird, the jay (*Coracias Bengalensis*), a kind of peacock; a name of *Mahādeva* (he is called by this name because his throat was stained blue by swallowing the poison produced by overchurning the ocean with the mountain *Mandara* by the *Surs* and *Asurs*, to procure the *amrita*); a gallinule, a sparrow, a wagtail, a peacock; *Hyperanthera morunga*. *s.*

نیلکنٹھاکش नीलकण्ठाक्ष *nīl-kanṭhāksh*, the *elæocarpus* seed. *s.*

نیل گندن *nīlgandan*, a bruise. *d.*

نیللوہ नीललोह *nīl-loh*, m. blue steel. *s.*

نیللوہت नीललोहित *nīl-lohit*, purple, of a purple colour; m. a mixture of red and blue. *s.*

نیلم नीलम *nīlam*, m. (v. *nīl-mani*). *s.*

نیلمرتکا नीलमृत्तिका *nīl-mṛittikā*, f. iron pyrites; black mould. *s.*

نیل من नीलमणि *nīl-mani*, m. name of a precious stone, a sapphire. *s.* [ment. *s.*

نیلنبر नीलम्बर *nīlambar*, m. a dark blue gar-

نیلنی नीलिनी *nīlinī*, f. indigo (*Indigofera tinctoria*). *s.* [pis lazuli). *s.*

نیلوپل नीलोपल *nīlopal*, m. a blue stone (*La-*

نیلورن नीलवर्ण *nīl-varṇ*, blue, of a blue colour. *s.* [lotus). *p.*

نیلوفر *nīlūfar*, m. the lotus nilufer (*Nymphæa*

نیلوفری *nīlūfarī*, of or relating to the lotus. *p.*

نیلہ *nīla*, the sediment of indigo. *p.*

نیلی *nīlī*, blue, of indigo colour. *p.*

نیم *nīm*, half, the middle. *nīmā nīm*, half-and-half. *nīm-bursh*, a poached egg (half-boiled or half-fried, &c.). *nīm-pukht*, half-cooked, half-ripe, parboiled. *nīm-tar*, middling. *nīm-jān*, half-dead (with fear, &c.). *nīm-josh*, coddled. *nīm-josh k.*, to coddle. *nīm-khwāb*, dosing. *nīm-khurda*, half-eaten, the remains of victuals. *nīm-rāẓī*, half-satisfied. *nīm-sāl*, half a year; *nīm-sālī*, half-yearly. *nīm-lāl*, a class of pilgrims to Jagannāth so called. *p. s.*

نیم नेम *nem* (also नियम *niyam*), a vow, compact, agreement, assent, promise; stability, fixedness, forbearance; any religious observance in general, such as fasting, watching, pilgrimage, praying; piety rule, precept, usage, practice. *nem-dharm*, m. abstinence, good conduct. *s.* [*dirachta*). *s.*

نیم नीम *nīm*, m. name of a tree (*Melia azad-*

نیمانند नीमानन्द *nīmānand*, m. name of a Hindū saint and founder of a sect. *s.*

نیماوت नीमावत *nīmāwat*, f. the system of the followers of *Nīmānand*. *s.*

نیمب *nīmb*, m. (v. *nīm*) the tree. *s.*

نیمبو नींबू *nīmbū*, m. lemon, lime. *s.*

نیمبولی *nīmbolī*, f. a kind of necklace worn by married women. *d.*

نیمت नियमित *niyamit*, regulated, prescribed. *s.*

نیمچکر नेमिचक्र *nemi-chakra*, a prince descended from *Parīkshit* who removed the capital of India from Hastināpur to Kausāmbi. *s.*

نیمچہ *nīmcha*, m. a small scimitar or sword, or bow; a dagger, a hanger. *p.*

نیم چہرہ *nīm-chihra*, m. an imaginary being having half a face, one arm, &c. It is male and female, the male having the right hand, the female the left; when united, they resemble a human being; when separate, they are supposed to move with amazing velocity on one foot, and are considered as very dangerous and cruel. *p.*

نیمروز *nīm-roz*, m. midday; name of a portion of Persia, comprising the provinces of Segistān, or Sīstān, and Mikrān. *p.*

نیمشارنیہ नैमिषारण्य *naimishāranya*, m. the forest in which the *Mahābhārat* was recited to the Rishis by Sauti. *s.*

نیمک नैयमिक *naiyamik*, regular, prescribed. *s.*

نیمن नीमन *nīman*, strong; well-finished; solid. *h.* [ing, checking. *s.*

نیمن नियमन *niyaman*, m. binding, restrain-

نیمہ *nīma*, m. a garment like a *jāma*, but not so full at the breast. *nīma-āstīn*, half-sleeved, a particular kind of jacket. *nīma-shām*, evening. *p.*

نيمي नेमी *nemī*, conscientious, abstemious, continent, chaste; f. a tree (*Dalbergia ujainensis*). *nemi-chakra*, name of a prince descended from *Parikshit*, who is said to have removed the capital of India from Hastināpur to Kausāmbi. *s.*

نين नैन *nain* or नयन *nayan* (also *nainā*), m. the eye. *s.*

نين *nain* (v. *nahīn*), no, not, nay. *nen* (for *ne*, q. v.), by, through. *d.*

نين नैन *nain*, } m. a tether, a rope fastened
نينا नैना *nainā*, } round the neck or foot of a bullock, &c. *h.* [of the eye. *s.*

نينا नैना *nainā* or नयना *nayanā*, f. the pupil

نينتا नियन्ता *niyantā*, m. a charioteer, a coachman; a ruler, a governor, a master. *s.*

نيند नींद *nīnd*, m. sleep. *nīnd uchāt-honā*, to be unable to sleep, or to have sleep broken. *nīnd-bhar sonā*, to sleep sound; to be at ease. *nīnd-bhar*, having had abundance of sleep. *s.*

نيندنا नींदना *nīndnā*, a. to deny; to blame, to censure; n. to sleep, to repose. *s.*

نيندو नींदू *nīndū*, m. a sleeper. *s.*

نيندي नींदी *nīndī*, sleepy, drowsy. *s. h.*

نينسکھ नैनसुख *nain-sukh*, m. name of a flower. *s.*

نينوپانت नयनोपान्त *nayanopānt* or *nainopānt*, m the outer angle or canthus of the eye. *s.*

نينوتسو नयनोत्सव *nayanotsav* or *nainotsav*, m. a lamp; any lovely or desired object. *s.*

نينوشدھ नयनौषध *nayan-aushadh* or *nainaushadh*, m. green sulphate of iron. *s.*

نيو नेव *new* or *nīw*, f. the foundation (of a house, &c.). *new ḍālnā*, to found, to lay the foundation. *h.*

نيو नीवा *nīwā*, m. stillness, calmness. *s.*

نيوار नेवार *newār*, f. tape (v. *niwār*). *h.*

نيوارنا नेवारना *newārnā*, a. to shut out, to exclude. *s.* [down. *h.*

نيوانا नेवाना *newānā*, a. to bend, to bow

نيوتا नेवता *neotā*, or न्योता *nyotā*, m. an invitation, or the presents sent along with it. *h.*

نيوتانا नेवताना *neotānā* or न्योताना *nyotānā*, نيوتنا नेवतना *neotnā* or न्योतना *nyotnā*, } a. to invite (more especially to an entertainment). *s.*

نيوجت नियोजित *niyojit*, intrusted with, appointed to, directed, ordered. *s.*

نيوجن नियोजन *niyojan*, m. ordering, commanding, directing, appointing. *s.*

نيور नेवर *newar*, f. a sore in the feet of a horse. *h.*

نيوڑانا *nyoṛānā*, a. to bend, to bow. *d. h.*

نيوڑنا *nyoṛnā*, } n. to bend, to bow, to
نيوڑھنا *nyoṛhnā*, } stoop. *d.*

نيوش *niyūsh*, (in comp.) hearing. *p.*

نيوشيدن *niyūshīdan*, to listen. *p.*

نيوشنده *niyūshanda*, hearing, a hearer. *p.*

نيوگ नियोग *niyog*, m. an order or command, authority, appointment. *s.*

نيوگي नियोगी *niyogī*, m. a minister, deputy, agent; adj. appointed (v. *niyukt*). *s.*

نيول नेवल *neval*, } m. a weasel, a ferret
نيولا नेवला *newalā*, } (*Viverra mungo*); also *nyolā*. *s.*

نيول नेवल *newal* (same as *newar*, q. v.). *h.*

نيئون नेऊन *ne,ūn*, m. butter. *s.*

نيون न्यून *nyūn*, blameable, vile, wicked, despicable; less, deficient, defective. *s.*

نيونا नेवना *newnā*, n. to stoop, to bow or bend. *s.*

نيونادھك न्यूनाधिक *nyūnādhik*, unequal, more or less. *s.* [imperfect. *s.*

نيونانگ न्यूनाङ्ग *nyūnāng*, maimed, mutilated,

نيونتا न्यूनता *nyūnatā*, f. deficiency, inferiority. *s.*

نيونجي नेवञ्जी *newanjī*, f. name of a flower. *s.*

نيونيندريه न्यूनेन्द्रिय *nyūn-endriya*, deficient in some organ, as blind, deaf, &c. *s.*

نيويديه नैवेद्य *naivedya*, m. food consecrated to a deity, an oblation. *s.* [Dakh.) *nehā*. *s.*

نيه नेह *neh*, f. friendship, affection; oil; (in

نيه *nīya* (v. *nīyat*, intention, &c.). *a.*

نيهار नीहार *nīhār*, m. frost, hoar frost; heavy dew. *s.*

نيهر नैहर *naihar*, f. a wife's mother's family. *h.*

نيهي नेही *nehī*, m. a friend, a lover. *s.*

نيئين *nai,īn* or *na,īn*, made of reeds. *p.*

نيين नैयन *naiyan* (for *nayan*, q.v.), the eye. *s.*

و

و *wāw*, the twenty-sixth letter of the Arabic alphabet, the thirtieth Persian, and the thirty-third Hindūstānī. At the beginning of a word or syllable it generally corresponds in sound to our *w*. In reckoning by *abjad* it stands for six. In ephemerides it represents Friday and the sign *Libra*. *Wāw* not beginning a word or syllable contributes to form the long vocal sounds *o*, *ū*, and *au*, fully explained in my Persian and Hindūstānī Grammars.

و व *va* or *wa*, the corresponding letter in the Devanāgarī alphabet. In words purely Sanskrit it has the sound of our *v*. Again, the Sanskrit *v* is frequently changed into *b* in the modern Hindūstānī and Bengālī; hence a Hindī word not found under this letter should be looked for under *b*.

و *wa*, a copulative conjunction equivalent to our "and, with, but, now;" it is used in connecting words and phrases from the Arabic and Persian. When it merely connects two words it is sounded *o*, *shab o roz*, night and day. *a. p.*

و वि *vi*, a particle and prefix, generally denoting separation, disjunction, ascertainment, progress, privation; and nearly equal to our English prefixes, *a-*, *di-*, *dis-*, *e-*, *ex-*, *in-*, *un-*, &c., as *vi-rakt*, averse, indifferent. *s.*

وا *wā*, open (as a door, &c.); adv. again; back, behind; prep. (for *bā*) with, as *wā o guftam* for *bā o guftam*, I spoke with him; interj. an expression of pain, alas! *wā-mānda*, tired, fatigued; remaining behind. *p.*

وا वा *wā*, inflec. sing. of the third pers. pron. him, her, it, that. *vā*, conj. or, either. *h. s.*

واست *wā-bast* (v. *wā-basta*), bound, &c. *p.*

واستگان *wā-bastagān*, m. pl. connections, relatives, adherents, dependants. *p.*

وابستگي *wā-bastagī*, f. dependence, adherence. *p.*

وابسته *wā-basta*, bound, related, connected with, depending on; (sub.) an adherent, relative, or dependant. *p.*

واپس *wāpas*, behind, afterward, then, again, back, returning. *wāpas-denā* or *-karnā*, to return, to give back. *wāpas rakhnā*, to detain, to retard. *p.*

واپسين *wāpasīn*, last, posterior, hindmost. *p.*

واپل वापल *vāpal*, m. a kind of holy basil; the black species of *tulsī* grass. *s.*

واپي वापी *vāpī*, f. a tank, pond, lake, pool. *s.*

وات वात *vāt*, m. air, wind; rheumatism, gout, inflammation of the joints; wind, as one of the humours of the body. *vāt-pitt*, m. rheumatism attended with fever. *vāt-phull*, inflated, puffed up with wind. *vāt-jwar*, fever arising from vitiated wind. *vāt-rakt*, m. acute gout or rheumatism. *vāt-rog*, m. rheumatism, gout. *vāt-rogī*, rheumatic, gouty. *vāt-shūl*, cholic with flatulence. *vāt-vairī*, m. the castor-oil tree. *vāt-vriddhi*, swelled testicle. *vāt-vyādhi*, f. any disease attributed to a disorder of the wind. *s.*

واتار वातारि *vātāri*, f. the castor-oil tree; a plant (*Asparagus racemosus*). *s.*

واتسليه वात्सल्य *vātsalya*, m. tenderness, affection. *s.*

واتك वातक *vātak*, m. a plant (*Marsilia quadrifolia*). *s.*

واتكي वातकी *vātakī*, rheumatic, gouty. *s.*

واتل वातुल *vātul*, gouty, rheumatic; m. a whirlwind, a hurricane. *s.*

واتييه वातीय *vātīya*, windy, relating to wind. *s.*

واٹ वाट *vāṭ* (v. *bāṭ*), f. a road, a path. *s.*

واٹكا वाटिका *vāṭikā*, f. the site of a house or building. *s.*

واٹي वाटी *vāṭī*, f. a house, a building, a garden, an orchard, a plantation. *s.*

واثق *wāsiḳ*, strong, robust; firm, secure, confiding, depending upon. *man wāsiḳ bi-l-lāhi*, "he who placeth his trust in God" (the Sultan of Maskat's motto). "The prince of Maskat has been styled *Imām* by Europeans, for what reason it would be difficult to say, as it is a title he has never assumed. He is always by his own people entitled Sultan."—(B.) *a.*

واجب *wājib*, necessary, expedient, worthy, proper, convenient, just, reasonable. *wājibu-l-adā*, necessary to be discharged (duties, &c.). *wājibu-t-ta'zīr* punishable. *wājibu-t-ta'ẓīm*, worthy of respect and attention. *wājibu-l-'arẓ*, fit to be represented; a written representation or petition. *wājibu-l-ḳatl*, deserving of death. *wājibu r-ri'āyat*, deserving to be honoured or obeyed. *wājibu-l-wujūd*, God (whose existence is necessary). *a.*

واجبات *wājibāt*, pl. things requisite, proper, or expedient to be done. *a.*

واجبي *wājibī*, f. expediency; a salary, a stipend; adj. expedient, proper, &c. *s.*

واجپرشٹھ वाजिपृष्ठ *vājiprishṭh*, m. globe amaranth. *s.*

واجپييه वाजपेय *vāj-peya*, m. a particular sacrifice. *s.*

واجپييي वाजपेयी *vāj-peyī*, m. one who performs the sacrifice last named. *s.*

واجي वाजी *vājī*, m. a plant (*Justicia adhenatoda*); a horse (v. *bājī*). *s.*

واجيكر वाजीकर *vājī-kar*, adj. aphrodisiac. *s.*

واجيكرن वाजीकरण *vājī-karan*, m. excitement of amorous desires by means of aphrodisiacs. *s.*

واچ वाच *vāch*, } f. speech, speaking; a
واچا वाचा *vāchā*, } phrase, a proverb or adage. *s.*

واچاٹ वाचाट *vāchāṭ*, } talkative, gabbling,
واچال वाचाल *vāchāl*, } chattering, talking much and idly or blameably. *s.*

واچك वाचक *vāchak*, m. a word, a speaker. *vāchik*, verbal; m. news, tidings, intelligence. *s.*

واچكپتر वाचिकपत्र *vāchik-patr*, m. a despatch, news-letter, a gazette. *s.*

واچنك वाचनिक *vāchnik*, verbal. *s.*

واچھڑي वाछिड़े *wāchhiṛe*, m. pl. praising, applauding. *h.*

واچيه वाच्य *vāchya*, m. a speech, a sentence; adj. fit to be spoken. *s.*

واحد *wāḥid*, one, sole, individual, single, singular. *wāḥidu-l-'ain*, one-eyed. *wāḥid shāhid*. God is my witness; (met.) giving, bestowing. *a.*

واحديت *wāḥidīyat*, unity; name of a sect of *Muhammadans*. *a.*

واخي *wākhe*, trouble, ceremony. *d.*

واد वाद *vād*, m. discourse, dispute, assertion, discussion; a complaint, accusation. *s.*

وادانواد वादानुवाद *vādānuvād*, m. attack and rejoinder; plaint and reply. *s*

وادسادهن वादसाधन *vād-sādhan*, m. argument, maintaining a controversy. *s.*

واده *wāda*, origin, source, essence (of any thing). *p.*

وادي वादी *vādī*, speaking, discoursing, telling, uttering; m. a sage, an expounder of the laws; an accuser or plaintiff in a law-suit. *s.*

وادي *wādī*, f. a valley, any low ground; low land through which a river flows, what in North Britain is called "a strath;" the channel of a river; a desert. *a.*

واديده वादयुद्ध *vād-yuddh*, m. controversy, dispute. *s.*

واديه वाद्य *vādya*, m. any musical instrument. *vādya-bhāṇḍ*, m. a multitude of musical instruments. *vādya-kar*, a player on a musical instrument. *s.*

وار वार *wār*, m. a blow, a wound, gash; an assault; the near bank of a river, on this side. *h.*

وار वार *vār* or *wār*, m. a day of the week; a multitude, a heap; f. time, leisure, delay, waiting, patience. *s.*

وار *wār*, (in comp. means) like, resembling; worthy of; having, possessing, endowed with, as *shāh-wār*, worthy of a king. *ummaid-wār*, hopeful. *p.*

وار वारि *vāri* m. water. *vāri-pravāh*, m. a cascade, a current of water *s.*

وارا वारा *wārā*, m. cheapness, thrift; benefit, gain; a victim; adj. cheap. *h.*

وارايار वारापार *wārāpār* (v. *wār-pār*). *s.*

وارانسي वाराणसी *vārāṇasī*, f. the holy city of Benares. *s.*

واريرني वारिपर्णी *vāri-parnī*, f. name of an aquatic plant (v. *vāri-mūlī*). *s.*

واريار वारपार *wār-pār*, on both sides, through and through; m. bounds. *s.*

وارت वारित *vārit*, hindered, prevented, impeded. *s.*

وارتا वार्ता *vārtā*, f. tidings, news, intelligence; rumour, report, word. *s.*

وارتك वार्तिक *vārtik*, relating to news, commentary, explanatory; m. a gloss, a commentary, a supplementary explanation. *s.*

وارث *wāriṡ*, m. an heir, master, lord, owner. *wāriṡ-h.*, to inherit. *a.*

وارثي *wāriṡī*, heritage, inheritance. *a.*

وارج वारिज *vārij*, (lit. water-born) aquatic; m. a conch shell, any bivalve shell; the lotus; salt. *s.*

وارچر वारिचर *vārichar*, aquatic, living or moving in the water; m. a fish. *s.*

وارد *wārid*, coming, arriving, approaching; adj. being present. *wārid o ṣādir*, a guest, a traveller; comer and goer. *a.*

وارد वारिद *vārid*, m. (lit. water-giver) a cloud; adj. productive of water. *s.*

واردات *wāridāt*, pl. f. events, accidents. *a.*

واردهه वारिधि *vāridhi*, f. the sea, the ocean. *s.*

واردهك वार्द्धक *vārddhak*, } m. old age, infirmity of old age. *s.*
واردهكيه वार्द्धक्य *vārddhakya*, }

وارتهه वारिरथ *vāri-rath*, m. a raft, a float. *s.*

وارستگان *wā-rastagān*, pl. the saved, those delivered. *p.*

وارستگي *wā-rastagī*, f. salvation, deliverance. *p.*

وارسته *wā-rasta*, delivered, saved. *p.*

وارسك वार्षिक *vārsik* or *vārshik*, yearly, annual; of or belonging to the rainy season. *s.*

وارشه वार्ष *vārsha*, annual, relating to one year; also relating to the rainy season. *s.*

وارفتگان *wā-raftagān*, pl. the lost ones. *p.*

وارفته *wā-rafta*, lost, wandered astray. *p.*

وارك वारक *vārak*, opposing, obstructing, an obstacle or agent of resistance. *s.*

واركرپور वारिकर्पूर *vāri-karpūr*, m. the Ilis or Hilsa fish (*Cluponodon Ilisha*). *s.*

واركنٹك वारिकण्टक *vāri-kanṭak*, m. an aquatic plant (*Pistia stratioites*); another plant (*Trapa spinosa*). *s.*

وارمولي वारिमूली *vāri-mūlī*, f. an aquatic plant (*Pistea stratoites*). *s.*

وارن वारन *wāran*, m. offerings, oblations, sacrifices. *h.*

وارن वारण *vāraṇ*, m. prohibition, hindering; guarding, defending. *s.*

وارنا वारना *wārnā*, a. to surround, to encircle, to go round; to offer (in sacrifice, &c.); to devote one's self. *h.*

وارندهه वारिनिधि *vārinidhi*, f. the sea, the ocean. *s.*

وارني वारुणी *vāruṇī*, f. spirituous liquor; the west; the twenty-fifth lunar mansion. *s.*

واردن वारिवदन *vāri-vadan*, m. a fruit (*Flacourtia cataphracta*). *s.*

وارهت वार्हत *vārhat*, m. the fruit of the *Solanum Jacquini*. *s.*

واري پهيري वारीफेरी *wārī-pherī*, a kind of religious or superstitious ceremony. *wārī-pherī-h.*, to be devoted to one; to be transported with joy. *h.*

واڑ वाड़ *vāṛ* or *wāṛ*, (in comp.) inclosure, place; as, *satī-wāṛ*, the place where a Hindū widow is sacrificed. *s.*

واڑا वाड़ा *wāṛā*, a quarter of a town, &c. where people of the same caste or trade dwell. *h.*

واڑي वाड़ी *vāṛī* or *wāṛī*, f. an inclosure, a court-yard, an orchard; adj. indiscreet, *s.*

واز *wāz* (for *bāz*, q. v.), open, &c. *p.*

وازون *wāzūn*, } inverted; preposterous, unfortunate. *p.*
واژون *wāzhūn*, }
واژگون *wāzhgūn*, }

واس वास *vās*, m. a house, dwelling, habitation. *s.*

واس वासु *vāsu*, m. a name of *Vishṇu*, the soul or the supreme being, considered as the soul of the universe. *s.*

واسا वासा *wāsā* or *vāsā*, abode, &c. (v. *basā*). *s.*

واست वासित or वाशित *vāsit*, perfumed, scented; clothed; peopled, flourishing (a country). *s.*

واست वास्तु *vāstu*, the site or foundation of a house. *s.*

واستو वास्तव *vāstav*, determined, fixed, substantial. *s.*

واستوك वास्तूक *vāstūk*, m. a kind of potherb (*Chenopodium album, &c.*). *s.*

واستويه वास्तव्य *vāstavya*, to be abided in, habitable. *s.*

واسديو वासुदेव *vāsudev*, m. *Krishṇa*, the son of *Vasudeva*. *s.*

واسر वासर *vāsar*, m. a day. *s.*

واسط *wāsiṭ*, a mediator; medium, means; name of a city on the Tigris, between Kūfa and Baṣra. *a.*

واسطه *wāsṭa*, m. (properly *wāsiṭa*) account, sake, cause, reason, medium, means. *a.*

واسطي *wāsṭe*, on account of, for. *wāsṭī* or *wāsiṭī*, f. a reed, a pen. *a.*

واسع *wāsi'*, ample, capacious, wide. *a.*

واسن वासन *vāsan*, m. cloth, clothes; abode. *s.*

واسنت वासन्त *vāsant*, vernal, belonging to the spring. *s.*

واسوخت *wā-sokht*, f. an impassioned style in poetry. *wā-sokhta*, inflamed, impassioned. *p.*

واسوز *wā-soz*, ardour, burning. *p.*

واسي वासी *vāsī*, abiding, dwelling; a dweller. *s.*

واسيه वास्य *vāsya*, m. vapours, tears. *s.*

واشا वाशा *vashā*, f. name of a plant (*Justitia ganderussa*). *s.*

واشت वाशित *vāshit*, perfumed, scented. *s.*

واشد *wā-shud*, opening, expansion. *p.*

واشدن *wā-shudan*, to be opened or expanded. *p.*

واشده *wā-shuda*, opened, expanded. *p.*

واششٹهي वाशिष्ठी *vāshishṭhī*, f. the Gūmti river, in the kingdom of Oude. *s.*

واصف *wāṣif*, one who praises (God). *a.*

واصل *wāṣil*, joined, connected, coupled, arrived, met; money paid; realisation of revenues, rents, &c. *wāṣil bāķī*, collections and balances, payments made and outstanding dues. *wāṣil bāķī karnā*, to state an account. *a.*

واصلات *wāṣilāt*, pl. accounts of collected money, the total collected. *a.*

واضح *wāẓiḥ*, evident, apparent, manifest, clear, obvious. *a.*

واضع *wāẓi'*, placing, establishing; m. an inventor, founder, an establisher. *a.*

واعظ *wā'iẓ*, m. a monitor, a preacher, an admonisher, an adviser. *a.*

وافر *wāfir*, abundant, plentiful, copious, much, many, opulent, ample. *a.*

وافي *wāfī*, sincere, honourable; entire, complete; plentiful, numerous (fem. *wāfiya*). *a.*

واق *wāķ*, m. name of a bird of the crane or heron species. *a.*

واقع *wāķi'*, befalling, happening, occurring, arriving, appearing. *fil wāķi'* or *wāķi' men*, very true, very right, certainly, in fact, in reality. *a.*

واقعات *wāķi'āt*, f. (pl. of واقعه) accidents, events, occurrences, intelligence. *a.*

واقعه *wāķi'a*, m. an occurrence, event; intelligence news; death. *wāķi'a-dīda*, a man of experience. *wāķi'a-navīs* or *-nigār*, an intelligencer, newswriter. *a.*

واقعي *wāķi'ī*, right, true, proper; adv. verily, truly, of a surety. *a.*

واقف *wāķif*, experienced, intelligent, knowing, learned, sensible. *wāķif-ḥāl* or *-kār*, experienced, intelligent, a connoisseur. *wāķif-kārī*, experience, intelligence, knowledge. *a.*

واقفيت *wāķifiyat*, experience, knowledge, intelligence. *a.*

واك वाक *vāk*, m. word, language, speech. *vāk paṭu*, eloquent, able in speech. *vāk-paṭutā*, f. eloquence. *vāk-chāpalya*, m. gossipping, idle talk. *vāk-chapal*, frivolous (in speech). *vāk-chhal*, m. prevarication, equivocation. *s.*

واكيارتهه वाक्यार्थ *vākyārth*, the meaning or purport of a speech or sentence. *s.*

واكيه वाक्य *vākya*, m. a sentence, aphorism, word, speech. *vākya-khaṇḍan*, m. refuting or criticising an assertion. *s.*

واگ वाग *vāg* (v. *vāk*). *vāg-jāl*, a collection of sentences. *vāg-dāna*, a promise; betrothment *vāg-datt*, promised, pledged. *vāg-dattā*, f. a virgin betrothed. *vāg-dosh*, m. speaking evil, defamation, abuse. *s.*

واگذاشته *wā-guzāshta*, released, remitted. *p.*

واگهري वाघरी *vāgharī*, name of a caste (or individual of it) whose occupation is the snaring and catching of wild beasts. *s.*

وال वाल *wāl*, m. revenge. *h.*

وال *wāl*, superior, high, eminent. *d.*

وال वाल *wāl*, } m. a particle; (in comp.)
والا वाला *wālā*, } signifies keeper, man, inhabitant, master, as *rakh-wāl* or *-wālā*, a keeper; *nāw-wālā*, boatman; *dillī-wāl* or *-wālā*, inhabitant of Dillī; *ghar-wālā*, master or keeper of a house. Added to an inflected infinitive it denotes the agent, as *bolne-wālā*, speaker; *likhne-wālā*, writer, &c. *h.*

والا *wālā*, exalted in dignity, sublime, high. *wālā-jāh*, of exalted rank or station. *wālā-shān*, of exalted dignity. *wālā-ķadar*, of high worth or dignity. *p.*

والا *wa,illā*, and if not, but yet, still, howsoever. *a.*

والد *wālid*, m. a father. *a.*

والده *wālida*, m. a mother. *a.*

والدين *wālidain*, m. the two parents. *a.*

والميك वाल्मीकि *vālmīki* or *vālmīk*, m. the author of the *Rāmāyana*. *s.*

واله *wāla* (for *wāl* or *wālā*, q. v.).

واله *wālih*, distracted, mad with love; stupified, astonished. *a.*

والي वाली *wālī* (f. of *wāl* or *wālā*, q.v.). *h.*

والي *wālī*, m. a prince, sovereign, ruler; a chief, superior, master. *a.*

واليه वल्या *vālya*, m. childhood. *s.*

وام वाम *wām*, m. debt, credit, lending, borrowing; (for *fām*) colour. *wām-dār*, a debtor; a creditor. *p.*

وام वाम *vām*, left, not right; vile, base, wicked. *s.*

واما वामा *vāmā*, f. a woman. *s.*

واماچار वामाचार *vāmāchār*, m. the doctrine of the *tantras*, according to one system; the left-hand ritual, use of flesh, spirits, &c. *s.*

واماچاري वामाचारी *vāmāchārī*, m. a follower of the left-hand portions of the *tantras*. *s.*

وامتا वामता *vāmtā*, f. perverseness, contrariety, wickedness. *s.*

واماندگان *wā-māndagān*, pl. those left behind, those who are fatigued. *p.*

واماندگي *wā-māndagī*, f. weariness, fatigue, falling behind from weariness. *p.*

وامق *wāmiḳ*, a lover; name of a most famous lover of *'azrā*. *a.*

وامن वामन *vāman*, m. a dwarf, one of the incarnations of *Vishṇu*; adj. short, vile, low, base. *s.*

وامني वामनी *vāmanī*, f. a female dwarf. *s.*

وان वान *wān* or *vān*, a particle; (in comp.) possessing, endowed with, &c., as *dhan-wān*, possessing wealth, rich; for the Persian *bān* it signifies agent, &c., as *dar-wān*, door-keeper. *s.*

وان वाण *vāṇ*, m. an arrow; a sharp-pointed missile. *s.*

وان वान *vān*, m. the rolling of the water from wind, a heavy sea, the high tide, commonly called the bore or boar; a ship, a boat (a term used only in Western India). *s.*

وان वाँ *wāṅ* (for *wahāṅ*), there, in that place. *h.*

وانپرستھ वानप्रस्थ *vān-prasth*, m. a Brāhman, Kshatriya, or Vaishya of the third grade or order, who has passed through the conditions of student and householder, and has betaken himself to the forest for divine meditation. *s.*

وانجيه वाणिज्य *vāṇijya*, m. trade, traffic. *s.*

وانچھا वाञ्छा *vānchhā*, f. wish, desire. *s.*

وانچھت वाञ्छित *vānchhit*, wished, desired, longed for. *s.*

وانچھن वाञ्छन *vānchhan*, m. wishing, desiring. *s.*

وانچھني वाञ्छिनी *vānchhinī*, f. a wanton woman. *s.*

وانچھي वाञ्छी *vānchhī*, wishing, desirous. *s.*

وانر वानर *vānar*, m. } an ape, a monkey. *s.*
وانري वानरी *vānarī*, f. }

وانسي वांशी *vāṅsī*, f. the manna of the bamboo. *s.*

وانگميه वांङ्मय *vāngmaya*, eloquent. *s.*

واني वाणी *vāṇī*, f. speech, sound, voice. *s.*

واودوك वावदूक *vāvadūk*, talking much, gabbling, prattling; m. a great talker. *s.*

واودوكتا वावदूकता *vāvadūktā*, f. garrulousness, loquaciousness. *s.*

واويلا *wāwailā*, m. lamentation, bewailing. *a.*

واه *wāh*, f. interj. (of admiration) bravo! &c., admirable. *wāh wā* or *wāh wāh*, f. bravo! bravo! *p.*

واهه वाहि *wāhi*, (dat. of third pron.) to him, to her, &c. *h.*

واهب *wāhib*, m. a giver; (in law) one who executes a deed of gift; adj. liberal, generous. *wāhibu-l-'aṭāyāt* or *wāhibu-l-'aṭāyā*, the giver of gifts (*par excellence*), i. e. God. *wāhibi be minnat*, disinterestedly liberal (the Deity). *a.*

واهك वाहक *vāhak*, m. a horseman, a porter, a carrier, a bearer. *s.*

واهم *wāhim*, thinking, imagining, being of opinion. *a.*

واهمه *wahima*, m. imagination, fancy. *a.*

واهن वाहन *vāhan*, m. a vehicle, a conveyance of any kind, as a horse, elephant, carriage, boat, &c. *s.*

واهني वाहिनी *vāhinī*, f. an army, a body of forces, consisting of 81 elephants, 81 cars, 243 horse, and 405 foot; a cohort, a battalion. *vāhini-pati*, a commander of a *vāhinī*, a general. *s.*

واهي *wāhī*, weak, ill-founded (premises, &c.). *wāhī tabāhī*, absurdity, unmeaning chatter. *a.*

واهيات *wāhiyāt*, absurdities, fiddle-faddle. *a.*

واهيه वाह्य *vāhya*, outer, external. *s.*

واي *wā,e*, interj. alas! fie! woe to you! (in Dakh.) rheumatism. *a.*

واي वायु *vāyu*, m. air, wind, or its personified deification; the air of the body; morbid affection of the windy humours. *vāyu-bhakshan*, m. fasting, living on air. *vāyu-sam*, like wind, swift, unsubstantial. *vāyu-kon*, m. the north-west. *vāyu-grast*, affected by wind, flatulent, epileptic. *vāyu-gulm*, m. a whirlpool, a hurricane. *vāyu-gand*, m. flatulence, indigestion. *vāyu-nivritti*, f. calm, lull; cure of windy disorders. *s.*

وايگولا वायगोला *wā,e-golā*, cholic, flatulency. *s.*

واين वायन *vāyan*, m. sweetmeats or cakes forming a light refreshment, allowed to be taken during a religious fast. *s.*

وايو वायव *vāyav*, windy, relating to the wind. *vāyū* (for *vāyu*, q. v.), air, wind, &c. *s.*

وايوي वायवी *vāyavī*, f. the region of the wind, the north-west. *s.*

وبا *wabā*, f. the plague, or any pestilential disorder, pestilence. *a.*

وبال *wabāl*, m. an unhealthy climate or atmosphere; a crime, fault; punishment for crime; pest, plague; vexation, misfortune; a curse; adj. painful, vexatious. *a.*

وبهو विभु *vibhu*, omnipresent, all-pervading; always, eternal. *s.*

وبهاگ विभाग *vi-bhāg*, m. part, portion, share; partition of an inheritance; the numerator of a fraction (in arithmetic). *jīvad-vibhāg*, partition made (of an estate, &c.) during the life of a father. *a-jīvad-vibhāg*, partition made after the father's decease. *prakāsh-vibhāg*, public partition in the presence of witnesses. *rahasya-vibhāg*, private partition. *anyonya-vibhāg*, mutual partition. *sama-vibhāg*, equal division of a father's property among his sons. *vibhāg-patrikā*, a deed of partition. *s.*

وبهتا विभुता *vibhutā*, f. power, supremacy. *s.*

وبهرانت विभ्रान्ति *vi-bhrānti*, f. } error, confu-
وبهرم विभ्रम *vi-bhram*, m. } sion, doubt, apprehension. *s.*

وبهكت विभक्त *vi-bhakt*, divided, portioned, separated. *vi-bhakti*, f. part, portion, a division; inflexion of nouns, a declension. *s.*

وبهو विभव *vibhau*, m. substance, thing, property, wealth; supreme or superhuman power. *s.*

وبهوت विभूति *vibhūti*, m. superhuman power; dignity, dominion. *vibhūti-mān*, endowed with supreme power. *s.*

وبهوشت विभूषित *vibhūshit*, decorated, adorned. *s.* [coration. *s.*

وبهوشن विभूषण *vibhūshan*, m. ornament, de-

وبهيشن विभीषण *vibhīshan*, fearful. formidable, terrific, horrible. *s.*

وپاشا विपाशा *vipāshā*, f. the Vipāsā or Beya river in Panjāb. *s.*

وپاك विपाक *vipāk*, m. cooking, dressing. *s.*

وپت विपत or विपत्ति *vipat* or *vipatti*, f. adversity, calamity, misfortune. *vipatti-jukt*, unfortunate. *vipatti-rahit*, prosperous. *vipat-sāgar*, m. a heavy calamity. *vipat-kāl*, m. time of adversity. *s.*

وپتا वप्ता *vaptā*, m. a sower, a planter, &c.; a father. *s.* [course. *s.*

وپتهه विपथ *vipath*, m. a bad road, wrong

وپد विपद *vipad*, } f. calamity, &c. (v. *vi-*
وپدا विपदा *vipadā*, } *pat*). *vipad-uddhār*, m. extrication from misfortune. *vipad-rahit*, prosperous. *vipad-grast*, involved in calamity. *vipad-yukt*, unfortunate. *s.*

وپر विप्र *vipr* or *vipra*, m. a Brāhman. *s.*

وپريت विपरीत *viparīt*, reversed, inversed, opposite, contrary. *s.*

واپريتتا विपरीतता *viparītatā*, f. } contrariety;
وپريية विपर्यय *viparyaya*, m. } reversion of condition. *s.*

وپكش विपक्ष *vipaksh*, opposed, adverse; m. an enemy, adversary. *s.* [impartial. *s.*

وپكشپات विपक्षपात *vipaksha-pāt*, indifferent,

وپكشتا विपक्षता *vipakshatā*, f. hostility, opposition; contradiction in argument. *s.*

وپل विपल *vipal*, m. a moment, a simple breathing. *vipul*, large, broad, deep. *s.*

وپلتا विपुलता *vipultā*, f. magnitude, extent. *s.*

وپن वपन *vapan*, m. sowing seed; shaving; *semen virile*. *vipin*, m. wood, forest. *s.*

وپهل विफल *viphal*, vain, unmeaning, fruitless. *s.* [fruitlessness. *s.*

وپهلتا विफलता *viphaltā*, f. unprofitableness,

وت वित्त *vitt* or *vitta*, m. wealth, property, thing, substance. *vitta-wān*, rich. *vitta-hīn*, poor, indigent. *s.*

وت वत *vat*, an affix denoting similitude, as *pashu-vat*, like a beast. *s.*

وتان वितान *vitān*, m. an awning, a canopy. *s.*

وتد *watid* or *watad*, a peg, a pin. *watidu-l-arz*, the antipodes. *a.* [Panjāb. *s.*

وتدر वितद्रु *vitadru*, name of a river in the

وترشن वितृष्ण *vitrishn*, content, satisfied, free from desire. *s.*

وترشنتا वितृष्णता *vitrishnatā*, f. satisfaction, contentment. *s.* [sion. *s.*

وترك वितर्क *vitark*, m. reasoning, discus-

وترن वितरण *vitaran*, m. abandoning, quitting; a gift, donation; crossing. *s.*

وتس वत्स *vats* (properly *vatsya*), m. a calf, the young of any animal; a year; the breast. chest. *s*

وتست वितस्ति *vitasti*, f. a long span measured by the extended thumb and little finger, considered equal to twelve fingers. *s.*

وتستر वत्सतर *vatstar*, m. a steer. *s.*

وتستري वत्सतरी *vatstarī*, f. a she-calf. *s.*

وتسر वत्सर *vatsar*, m. a year; a young bullock. *s.*

وتسرية वत्सरीय *vatsarīya*, yearly, annual. *vatsarīya gaman*, the sun's annual course through all the signs of the zodiac. *s.*

وتسك वत्सक *vatsak*, m. a child; a calf; a medicinal plant (*Wrightea antidysenterica*). *s.*

وتسل वत्सल *vatsal*, m. affection, kindness; adj. kind, affectionate. *s.* [tion. *s.*

وتسلتا वत्सलता *vatsaltā*, f. tenderness, affec-

وتسنابھ वत्सनाभ *vatsnābh*, m. a kind of active poison, the root of the *aconite ferox*. *s.*

وتل वितल *vital*, m. one of the seven divisions of *Pātāl*, the second division of it. *s*

وتنا वुतना *wutnā* or वितना *witnā*, that much. *h.*

وتنڈا वितण्डा *vitaṇḍā*, f. controversy, argument, refutation, criticism. *s.*

وتيرة *watīra*, m. a path, way; manner, habit, custom. *nek-watīra*, of good disposition. *a.*

وٹ वट *vaṭ*, m. the large Indian fig-tree. *s.*

وٹ वटु *vaṭu*, m. a lad, a youth, a religious student, or *Brahmachārī*; name of a flower. *s.*

وٹپ विटप *viṭap*, m. a new shoot, a branch. *s.*

وٹسارکا विटसारिका *viṭsārikā*, f. a sort of thrush, a variety of the bird usually called (in Beng.) *mainā*. *s.*

وٹک वटुक *vaṭuk* (v. *vaṭu*), m. a lad, a young man in general. *s.*

وٹکا वटिका *vaṭikā*, f. a kind of dish. *s.*

وٹوٹ *waṭwaṭ*, twaddle, nonsense. *d.*

وٹوٹانا *waṭwaṭānā*, to talk nonsense. *d.*

وٹوٹي *waṭwaṭī*, a chatterer, a babbler. *d.*

وٹورا विटौरा *viṭaurā* (v. *biṭaurā*), a heap of cakes made of cow-dung and dried for fuel. *s.*

وثاق *wis̤āḳ*, stipulating, pledging one's faith, entering into a confederacy. *a.*

وثق *was̤ḳ*, m. confidence, trusting in. *a.*

وثوق *wus̤ūḳ*, m. strength, firmness, steadfastness, confiding in, trusting to. *a.*

وثيق *was̤īḳ*, firm, steady, strong; confiding or putting trust (in God). *a.*

وثيقت *was̤īḳat*, f. } وثيقه *was̤īḳa*, m. } firmness, solidity, confidence, faith; a bond, obligation, written agreement (Pers. pl. *was̤īḳajāt*). *a.*

وج *waj* (properly *wajj*), galangal. *a. p.*

وجات विजाति *vi-jāti*, f. a different species, tribe, or caste. *s.*

وجاهت *wajāhat*, f. respect, appearance, position, personal respectability; credit. *a.*

وجب *wajab* or *wujab*, m. a span, a measure of nine inches in length. *p.*

وجت विजित *vijit*, subdued, defeated. *vijitendriya*, of subdued organs or passions. *s.*

وجد *wajd*, m. ecstacy, excessive love. *wijd* or *wujd*, opulence; discovering, procuring, finding. *a.*

وجدان *wajdān* or *wijdān*, rapture, ecstacy. *a.*

وجر वज्र *vajr* or *vajra*, m. a thunderbolt in general, the thunderbolt of *Indra* in particular; the diamond; adj. hard, impenetrable. *vajr-āghāt*, m. a thunderbolt, a sudden and astounding calamity. *vajr-ābhyās*, m. cross multiplication. *vajr-badh*, m. death by lightning; cross multiplication. *vajr-pāt*, m. a stroke of lightning. *vajr-pushp*, m. the blossom of the sesamum. *vajr-may*, hard, adamantine. *vajr-valli*, f. a species of sunflower. *s.*

وجڑي वजड़ी *wajṛī*, the bowels, intestines. *wajṛī-baṭī*, the contents of the abdomen. *h.*

وجع *waja'*, m. disease, pain, affliction; complaint, mourning. *waja' i mafāṣil*, rheumatism. *a.*

وجن विज्ञ *vijna* (v. *vigya*), skilful, learned. *s.*

وجن विजन *vi-jan*, private, lonely, solitary. *s.*

وجناپن विज्ञापन *vijnāpan*, m. teaching, instructing, informing. *s.*

وجوب *wujūb*, being necessary, necessity, obligation, duty, debt. *a.*

وجود *wujūd*, m. invention; existence, body, essence, substance; *penis*. *bā-wujūd*, notwithstanding *bā wujūde ki*, notwithstanding that. *a.*

وجور विज्वर *vijwar*, exempt from decay, free from fever. *s.*

وجوه *wujūh* (pl. of وجه *wajh*), faces, aspects; chiefs (of a country, &c.). *a.*

وجوهات *wujūhāt*, superfluous or additional pl. of *wujūh*, faces, &c. *a.*

وجه *wajh*, f. cause, motive; mode, manner, way; face, visage, appearance, semblance; (in Pers. and Hind.) wages, salary, money. *wajhi tasmiya*, the cause of giving any particular name, the etymology of words. *wajhi ḥāl*, mode of living, state of circumstances. *a.*

وجها *wajhā*, m. allowance, pension, salary. *a.*

وجي विजय *vijay*, m. victory, triumph, conquest. *vijay-mān* or *vijayī*, victorious, triumphant. *s.*

وجيا विजया *vijayā*, f. hemp, or the tops of the plant, used as narcotic. *s.*

وجيز *wajīz*, } وجيزة *wajīza*, } abridged, short, epitomized. *a.*

وجيه *wajīh*, m. a prince, a chief; adj. of a noble presence, handsome, specious. *a.*

وجيي विजयी *vijayī*, victorious, triumphant, conquering. *s.*

وچ वच *vach*, m. } وچا वचा *vachā*, f. } orris root (*Acorus calamus*). *s.*

وچار विचार *vichār*, m. the exercise of judgment or reason, consideration, deliberation. *s.*

وچارت विचारित *vichārit*, judged, discussed, determined, decided. *s.*

وچارک विचारक *vichārak*, } وچارکرتا विचारकर्ता *vichār-kartā*, } m. a judge, an investigator. *s.*

وچاريه विचार्य *vichārya*, that which is proper to be discussed, &c. *s.*

وچال विचल *vichāl*, intervening, intermediate. *s.*

وچتر विचित्र *vichitr*, variegated, spotted. *s.*

وچکشن विचक्षण *vichakshan*, clever, able; sensible, wise; skilful, proficient. *s.*

وچل विचल *vichal*, unsteady, unfixed. *s.*

وچلن विचलन *vichalan*, m. fickleness, unsteadiness. *s.*

وچن वचन *vachan*, m. speech, sentence, rule; a dictum in law; a text from a work of authority. *vachan-kar*, obedient; m. author of a precept. *vachan-kram*, m. discourse, order of speech. *vachan-grāhī*, conformable, compliant. *vachan-mātr*, m. mere words, assertion unsupported by facts. *s.*

وچوچ *wachwach* (v. *waṭwaṭ*), babble, nonsense, &c. *wachwachānā*, to babble. *wachwachī*, a babbler, a tweedler. *d.*

وچهيد विच्छेद *vichhed*, m. separation, prevention. *s.*

وحدانيت *waḥdānīyat*, f. believing in the unity of the deity; unity, singularity. *a.*

وحدت *waḥdat*, f. unity, oneness (as that of the deity). *a.*

وحش *waḥsh*, a wild beast, beast of prey. *a.*

وحشت *waḥshat*, f. fright, fear; a desert, a solitude, a dreary place. *waḥshat-angez* or *waḥshat-nāk*, frightful, exciting horror. *a.*

وحشي *waḥshī*, wild (man or beast), savage, fierce; name of a Persian poet. *waḥshī-panā*, m. wildness, ferocity, the savage state. *a.*

وحل *waḥal*, m. slime, ooze, mud, clay. *a.*

وحوش *wuḥūsh* (pl. of وحش), wild beasts. *a.*

وحي *waḥī*, f. divine revelation, inspiration, a voice from heaven. *a.*

وحيد *waḥīd*, alone, unique, singular. *waḥī-du-l-'aṣr*, the nonpareil of the age. *a.*

ود *wadd*, m. love, friendship, affection. *a.*

ودا विदा *vidā* (probably for وداع, q. v.), f. dismission, taking leave, farewell, adieu. *h.*

وداد *widād*, m. love, friendship. *a.*

ودارن विदारण *vidāran*, m. tearing, breaking, splitting, severing, dividing. *s.*

ودارنا विदारना *vidārnā*, n. to tear, to rend. *s.*

وداع *widā'*, m. farewell, adieu; a benediction. *widā'-k.*, to bid adieu, to dismiss. *a.*

وداعي *widā'ī*, m. one who is taking his leave; f. a present made at parting. *a.*

ودال वदाल *vadāl*, m. a sheat (a kind of fish) (*Solurus boalis*). *s.*

ودت विदित *vidit*, known, perceived, understood. *s.*

ودر विदर *vidar*, m. the Indian prickly pear (*Cactus Indicus*). *s.*

ودر *wadar* or *wadarāt*, babble, prattle. *d.*

ودرم विद्रुम *vidrum*, m. coral. *s.*

ودرنا *wadarnā*, to babble, to jabber. *d.*

ودش विदिश *vidish*, ودشا विदिशा *vidishā*, ودك विदिक *vidik*, f. an intermediate point of the compass. *s.*

ودگدھ विदग्ध *vidagdh*, clever, shrewd; m. a libertine; an intriguer; a scholar, a pandit. *vidag-dhatā*, f. sharpness, cleverness. *s.*

ودن वदन *vadan*, m. the mouth, the face. *s.*

ودوان विद्वान *vidwān*, learned, intelligent. *s.*

ودود *wadūd*, loving, friendly, affectionate. *a.*

ودورج विदूरज *vidūraj*, m. the *lapis lazuli*. *s.*

ودويش विद्वेष *vidwesh*, m. enmity, hatred. *s.*

ودويشي विद्वेषी *vidweshī*, m. an enemy; adj. hostile, inimical. *s.*

ودھ वधु *vadhu*, f. a son's wife; a wife in general. *vidhi*, m. a sacred precept, an act or rule prescribed by the *veda*; rule, formula. *s.*

ودھان विधान *vidhān*, m. act, action, religious rites and ceremonies; rule, precept, ordinance, injunction; form, mode, manner. *s.*

ودھايك विधायक *vidhāyak*, one who entrusts or deposits. *s.*

ودھر विधुर *vidhur*, m. separation, agitation of mind. *s.*

ودھرم विधर्म *vi-dharm*, a religion different from one's own, heterodoxy. *s.*

ودھوا विधवा *vidhwā*, f. a widow. *vidhwā-vedan*, m. marrying a widow. *s.*

ودھونس विध्वंस *vidhwaṅs*, m. aversion, dislike, enmity, disrespect; destruction. *s.*

ودھونسي विध्वंसी *vidhwaṅsī*, hostile, adverse, pernicious, destructive. *s.*

ودھييه विधेय *vidheya*, compliant, tractable, fit or proper to be done or recomended. *s.*

وديا विद्या *vidyā*, f. knowledge, learning, science, sacred or profane. *s.*

وديابهياس विद्याभ्यास *vidyābhyās*, m. study, diligent application. *s.*

ودياپراپت विद्याप्राप्ति *vidyā-prāpti*, f. acquirement of knowledge, sound learning. *s.*

وديادان विद्यादान *vidyā-dān*, diffusing knowledge or science. *s.*

وديادھر विद्याधर *vidyādhar* (v. *bidyādhar*), a kind of demigod. *s.*

وديادھن विद्याधन *vidyā-dhan*, m. money acquired by teaching. *s.*

وديارتھي विद्यार्थी *vidyārthī*, m. a student, pupil, disciple. *s.*

وديالابھ विद्यालाभ *vidyā-lābh*, m. acquisition of learning. *s.*

وديالي विद्यालय *vidyālay*, m. a school, college. *s.*

وديావان विद्यावान *vidyāvān*, learned, scientific. *s.*

ودياهين **विद्याहीन** *vidyā-hīn*, ignorant, uninstructed. *s.*

وديت **विद्युत** *vidyut*, f. the lightning. *s.*

وديرن **विदीर्ण** *vidīrna*, torn, rent, split. *s.*

وديش **विदेश** *videsh*, m. a foreign country, abroad, any place away from home. *videsh-gaman*, m. travelling, going abroad. *s.*

وديشج **विदेशज** *videshaj*, } m. a foreigner; adj.
وديشي **विदेशी** *videshī*, } foreign, exotic. *s.*

وديعت *wadī'at*, f. deposit, trust. *wadī'ati ḥayāt*, death, depositing of life. *a.*

وديمان **विद्यमान** *vidyamān*, m. being, existence, being present. *s.*

وديه **विदेह** *videh*, incorporeal, without body. *s.*

وڈا **वडा** *vaḍā*, m. pulse ground and fried with oil or butter. *s.*

وڈنبت **विडम्बित** *viḍambit*, low, abject, distressed. *s.*

وڈنبنا **विडम्बना** *viḍambnā*, afflicting, distressing. *s.*

وڈورج **विडूरज** *viḍūraj*, m. *lapis lazuli*. *s.*

ور *war* (for *wa agar*), and if, but. Added to nouns it implies possession, as *jān-war*, an animal, a beast, a bird (lit. life-possessor). *p.*

ور **वर** *var*, m. a boon, a blessing; a bridegroom; adj. best, excellent. *var-pradān*, m. conferring a boon. *s.*

ورا **वरा** *warā*, situated on this side (of a river, &c.), near, close by. *h.*

ورا *warā* (properly *warā,a*), beyond, on the further side, behind; besides, except. *a.*

وراتيه **व्रात्य** *vrātya*, m. a man of the three first classes who has not received the investiture. *vrātyā*, f. the female of a *vrātya*. *s.*

وراٹ **विराट** *virāṭ*, m. name of a country (now Berar). *s.*

وراٹج **विराटज** *virāṭaj*, m. an inferior kind of diamond from Berar. *s.*

وراٹك **वराटक** *varāṭak*, m. the small shell called a cowrie (used as money). *s.*

وراثت *wirāsat*, f. heritage, inheritance. *a.*

وراثتًا *wirāsatan*, by way of inheritance. *a.*

وراجت **विराजत** *virājat*, } splendid, hand-
وراجمان **विराजमान** *virājmān*, } some, shining. *s.*

وراجنا **विराजना** *virājnā* (v. *birājnā*), to be splendid, &c. *s.*

وراد *warrad*, m. a gardener, a flower-man. *a.*

وراگ **विराग** *virāg*, m. the absence of desire or passions; indifference to all earthly matters. *s.*

وراگي **विरागी** *virāgī*, void of passion or desire, stoical. *s.*

ورال **विराल** *virāl* (for *viṛāl*), m. a cat. *s.*

ورام **विराम** *virām*, m. cessation, pause; the mark used under a letter in Devanāgarī shewing that it is not followed by a vowel. *s.*

ورانسي **वराणसी** *varāṇasī*, f. Benares, the sacred city of the Hindūs. *s.*

وراه **वराह** *varāh* or *varāha*, m. a hog, a boar; the third incarnation of *Vishṇu* (in the form of a boar); one of the eighteen smaller *dwipas* or divisions of the universe. *s.*

ورپاش *warpāsh*, act of rubbing the hands together. *d.*

ورپاشنا *warpāshnā*, to rub the hands together. *d.*

وربردان **वरप्रदान** *var-pradān*, m. conferring a boon. *s.*

ورت **व्रत** *vrat* or *vrata*, m. any meritorious act of devotion, such as a vow, penance, &c. *s.*

ورت **वृत्ति** *vṛitti* or *vṛitt*, m. f. livelihood, profession, means of gaining a livelihood; a circle. *vṛitt-khanḍ*, m. sector or segment of a circle. *s.*

ورت **वर्त्ति** *vartti*, f. the wick of a lamp. *s.*

ورت **विरत** *virat*, stopped, ceased, rested. *virati*, f. stop, cessation, pause, rest. *s.*

ورتا **वर्त्ता** *varttā*, m. a wooden pencil for writing on a board. *h.*

ورتانت **वृत्तान्त** *vṛittānt*, m. tidings, rumour, intelligence: a tale, a story. *s.*

ورتك **वर्तक** *wartak*, m. one who earns a maintenance; a merchant, a trader; (in Dakh.) a bearer, porter, carrier. *s. d.*

ورتكا **वर्त्तिका** *varttikā*, f. a quail; the wick of a lamp. *s.*

ورتل **वर्तुल** *vartul*, round, circular, spherical, globular. *s.*

ورتمان **वर्तमान** *vartamān*, being, existing, dwelling; present (tense in gram.). *s.*

ورتن **वर्तन** *vartan*, m. livelihood, means of subsistence, income, profit. *s.*

ورتها **वृथा** *vṛithā*, uselessly, fruitlessly, in vain. *vṛithā-dān*, an improper gift, and one that may be annulled. *s.*

ورتي **वर्त्ती** *varttī*, f. the wick of a lamp. *s.*

ورتي **व्रती** *vratī*, observing a vow; m. an ascetic, a devotee. *s.*

ورث *wirs*, becoming an heir, receiving (any thing) by inheritance or bequest. *a.*

ورثه *warsa*, m. heritage, an inheritance. *a.*

ورج **वृजि** *vṛiji*, f. name of a country, now called Braj. *s.*

ورجا **विरजा** *virjā* or *virajā*, f. a species of grass, *dūb*. *s.*

ورجت **वर्जित** *varjit*, abandoned, avoided, excluded, excepted. *s.*

ورجن **वर्जन** *varjan*, quitting, shunning, avoiding. *s.*

ورجنيه **वर्जनीय** *varjanīya*, improper, censurable, wicked, what ought to be avoided. *s.*

ورچت विरचित *virachit*, made, prepared, effected; written, composed. *s.*

ورخرچ *war-kharch*, profuse, lavish. *p.*

ورخرچي *war-kharchī*, f. profusion, prodigality, extravagance. *p.*

ورد *ward*, m. a rose, a flower; the leaf or petal of a flower. *wird*, daily use, practice, task, a section of the *ḳur,ān*; access, approach; continual motion or employment; a halting-place, stage. *wird karnā*, to repeat. *wird waẓīfa paṛhnā*, to perform one's daily tasks of devotion. *a.*

ورد वरद *varad*, adj. granting a boon or prayer; propitious, favourable. *s.*

وردان वरदान *var-dān*, m. the granting of a boon. *s.*

وردھ वृद्ध *vṛiddh*, old, aged; m. an old man. *vriddh-sevā*, f. reverence of old age. *vṛiddhi*, f. increase, prosperity, success, rise; increase of the moon; enlargement of the scrotum; interest, usury. *vṛiddhi-shrāddh*, m. a sacrifice to the manes of progenitors on any prosperous occasion. *vṛiddhi-mān* or *varddh-mān*, prosperous, increasing in wealth, &c. *s.*

وردھ विरुद्ध *viruddh*, opposed, hindered; reverse, contrary, hostile. *s.*

وردھا वर्द्धा *warddhā*, m. a bull, a bullock. *s.*

وردھا वृद्धा *vṛiddhā*, f. an old woman. *s.*

وردھاوستھا वृद्धावस्था *vṛiddhāvasthā*, f. the condition of old age. *s.*

وردھت वर्द्धित *varddhit*, grown, expanded, increased, thriven. *s.*

وردھتا. विरुद्धता *viruddhatā*, f. opposition, enmity, incongruity. *vṛiddhatā*, f. old age. *s.*

وردھمان वर्द्धमान *varddhmān*, } growing, thriv-
وردھن वर्द्धन *varddhan*, } ing; *varddhan*, m. growth, increase. *s.*

وررهنا वररहना *war-rahnā*, n. to be victorious. *h.*

ورزش *warzish*, f. abstinence, sobriety; custom, habit; gain; labour, exertion, exercise. *p.*

ورزيدن *warzīdan*, to practice, to perform, to evince. *p.*

ورس विरस *viras*, insipid, tasteless. *s.*

ورسا *warsā*, m. parade, drill, military exercise; a parade ground or place where soldiers are exercised. *d.*

ورش वृष *vṛish*, m. a bull, the sign *Taurus*. *s.*

ورش वर्ष *varsh*, m. a year; a division of the earth; the rainy season (v. *varshā*, &c.). *varsh-parvat*, m. a mountainous range dividing two *varsh* or parts of the world. *varsh-shat*, m. a century. *varsh-sahasra*, m. a thousand years. *varsh-āyut*, ten thousand years. *s.*

ورشا वर्षा *varshā*, } m.pl. the rains,
ورشاكال वर्षाकाल *varshā-kāl*, } or rainy season. *s.*

ورشاوسان वर्षावसान *varshāvasān*, m. autumn. *s.*

ورشت वर्षत *varshat*, raining, sprinkling, showering. *s.*

ورشٹ वृष्टि *vṛishṭi*, f. rain. *vṛishṭi-kā*, m. the rainy season. *s.*

ورشٹھ वरिष्ठ *varishṭh*, best, dearest. *s.*

ورشچك वृश्चिक *vṛishchik*, m. a scorpion; the sign *Scorpio*. *s.*

ورشن वर्षण *varshan*, m. raining, rain. *s.*

ورشوتسرگ वृषोत्सर्ग *vṛishotsarga*, the letting loose of a bull at certain ceremonies, as at marriages, obsequies, &c.: the bull is thenceforth considered sacred, and wanders about unmolested and unappropriated; he is called "a brāhminī bull;" a vicious brute he generally turns out. *s.*

ورشيك वर्षैक *varshaik* or *varshyan*, yearly, annual. *s.*

ورطه *warta*, m. a labyrinth, a whirlpool, embarrassment, any situation of danger and difficulty. *a.*

ورع *wara'*, m. timidity, apprehensive of doing wrong, temperance, continence. *a.*

ورغلانا *warghalānā* or *warghalānnā*, a. to deceive, to decoy, to inveigle. *p.*

ورق *waraḳ*, m. a leaf (of a tree, book, &c.); a card, a slice. *waraḳ utārnā*, to page and line (a book). *waraḳ tarāshnā*, to cut cards. *waraḳu-l-khiyāl*, m. name of an intoxicating drug (*Cannabis sativus*). *waraḳ-dāghī*, written paper. *waraḳ-dāghī karnā*, to page (a book). *a.*

ورقي *waraḳī*, of or relating to a leaf. *a.*

ورك वृक *vṛik* or *vṛika*, m. a wolf. *s.*

وركت विरक्त *virakt*, averse, indifferent, stoical. *virakti*, f. aversion, indifference. *virakt-bhāo*, disinclined, disliking. *s.*

وركش वृक्ष *vṛiksh*, m. tree. *vṛiksh-char*, m. a monkey. *vṛiksh-chhāyā*, f. the shade of trees, grove. *vṛiksh-dhūp*, m. turpentine. *vṛiksh-ropan*, m. planting trees. *vṛiksh-may*, abounding with trees. *vṛiksh-nāth*, m. the Indian fig-tree. *s.*

وركھ वृष *vṛikh*, m. a bull, *Taurus* (v. *vṛish*). *s.*

ورگ वर्ग *varg*, m. class, tribe; a class of letters; a chapter, a section; a square number. *varg-ghan*, the square of a cube. *varg-mūl*, square root. *s.*

ورل वरल *varal*, m. a wasp. *viral* or *virlā*, fine, delicate, thin; loose, apart. *s.*

ورلا वरला *warlā*, on this side of a river, &c. *h.*

ورم *waram*, m. a swelling, tumour; adj. inflated; enraged. *waram-karnā*, to swell (any part of the body). *waram-honā*, to be inflated, to be enraged. *a.*

ورما वर्मा *warmā* (v. *barmā*), a gimlet, &c. *h.*

ورن वर्ण *varn* or *varnā*, m. a class, caste; an order, colour, hue; a letter of the alphabet; a coefficient. *varn-āsram*, the class and state of a person. *varn-dharm*, the particular duty of each caste. *varn-rekhā*, f. a kind of white fossil. *varn sreshṭh*, of a good tribe or caste; a Brāhman. *varn-sankar*, mixture or confusion of castes. *varn-kram*, order of the Hindū castes; the alphabet. *varn-gat*, algebraic. *varn-mālā*, f. the alphabet. *varn-hīn*, an outcast. *s.*

ورن वरुण *varun*, m. the god of the waters and regent of the west. *s*

ورن व्रण *vran*, m. a tumour, boil, ulcer. *s.*

ورن विरण *viran*, m. a fragrant grass (*Andropogon schœnantum*). *s.*

ورنا वरणा *varnā*, f. the Barnā, a rivulet near Benares. *s.*

ورنت वर्णित *varnit*, described, explained. *s.*

ورند वृन्द *vṛind*, m. a multitude, a heap. *s.*

ورندا वृन्दा *vṛindā*, f. the holy basil (*Ocymum sanctum*). *s.*

ورنڈال वरण्डालु *varanḍālu*, m. the castor-oil tree. *s.*

ورنن वर्णन *varnan*, m. describing, expatiating, pointing out qualities or excellences. *s.*

ورننا वर्णना *varnanā*, f. praise, panegyric. *s.*

ورنه *warna* (for *wa, gar, na*), and if not. *p.*

وروپ विरूप *virūp*, ورویک विरूपक *virūpak*, } deformed, monstrous, misshapen, hideous. *s.*

وروٹي वर्वटी *varvaṭī*, f. a sort of bean (*Dolichos catjang*). *s.*

ورود *warūd*, m. arrival, coming, appearing, approaching, descending, alighting. *a.*

ورودھ विरोध *virodh*, m. enmity, opposition. *s.*

ورودھي विरोधी *virodhī*, adverse, hostile, opposing; m. an enemy. *s.*

ورہ विरह *virah*, m. separation, absence. *s.*

ورہت विरहित *virahit*, void, free from. *s.*

ورہت वृहत *vṛihat*, great, large. *s.*

ورہجن वृहज्जन *vṛihajjan*, m. a great man. *s.*

ورہدگہ वृहद्गुह *vṛihadguh*, m. a country lying behind the Vindhya near Malwa. *s.*

ورہسپت वृहस्पति *vṛihaspati*, m. the planet Jupiter or its regent. *vṛihaspati-chakr*, m. a cycle of 60 years. *vṛihaspati-wār*, m. Thursday. *s.*

ورہني विरहिणी *virahinī*, f. ورہي विरही *virahī*, m. } separate, absent; f. a woman separated from her lover. *s.*

ورهي वर्ही *varhī*, m. a peacock. *s.*

وري वरे *ware*, on this side, near. *ware girnā*, to fall short, *h.*

وريڑا व्रीड़ा *vrīṛā*, f. shame, bashfulness. *s.*

وريہ व्रीहि *vrīhi*, m. rice. *s.*

وريڑت व्रीड़ित *vrīṛit*, ashamed, modest. *s.*

وريک विरेक *virek*, m. a purgative. *s.*

ورييان वरीयान *variyān*, m. the eighteenth *yuga* or period. *s.*

وڑال विड़ाल *viṛāl*, m. a cat. *s.*

وڑشي वड़िशी *vaṛishī*, f. a fish-hook. *s.*

وزارت *wizārat*, f. the dignity of *wazīr*; the office of prime minister or grand visir. *a.*

وزان *wazzān*, one who weighs; one who versifies. *wazān*, blowing (wind). *a. p.*

وزر *wazr* or *wizr*, m. a crime, sin, fault; arms; a burden, a load. *a.*

وزرا *wuzarā* (pl. of وزير), ministers, &c. *a.*

وزن *wazn*, m. weight, measure; metre, rhyme, verse; reputation, esteem, honour; examination. *wazn-dār* or *-kash*, a weighman. *wazn-kashī*, the office, or perquisites of a weighman. *a.*

وزني *waznī*, heavy, weighty. *a.*

وزيده *wazīda*, blown, (from *wazīdan* to blow). *p.*

وزير *wazīr*, m. a minister of state; the queen at chess; the knave at cards. *wazīru-l-mamālik*, the grand *wazīr*. *a.*

وزيري *wazīrī*, f. the office of a minister of state. *a.*

وس *vas* (for *vash*, q. v.), authority, &c. *s.*

وس वसु *vasu*, m. wealth, thing, substance. *vasu-mān*, rich, wealthy. *s.*

وس विस *wis* (infl. of *wuh*), him, her, &c. *h.*

وس *was*, children, progeny, offspring. *d.*

وسارا *wasārā*, m. the veranda or porch of a house, an awning, shed, or thatch. *d.*

وساطت *wasāṭat*, f. mediation, intercession, medium. *a.*

وساکها विसाखा *visākhā*, the sixteenth mansion of the moon. *s.*

وسال विसाल *visāl*, large, extensive. *s.*

وسالت *wasālat*, f. mediation, channel, medium, means. *a.*

وسپشٹ विस्पष्ट *vispashṭ*, apparent, manifest; open, plain, intelligible. *s.*

وسپهوٹ विस्फोट *visphoṭ*, m. وسپهوٹا विस्फोटा *visphoṭā*, f. وسپهوٹک विस्फोटक *visphoṭak*, m. } a boil, a pustule; small-pox. *s.*

وست वस्तु *vastu*, m. thing, matter, substance. *vastu-bhāv*, f. chattels, things, baggage. *vastu-tas*, in fine, in fact, substantially. *vastu-mātr*, an outline of any subject. *vastu-hāni*, f. loss of substance or property. *s.*

وستار विस्तार *vistār*, spreading, extension. *s.*

وستر विस्तर *vistar* (Pers. *bistar*). m. a bed. *s.*

وستر वस्त्र *vastr* or *vastra*, m. raiment, apparel, clothes. *vastr-ānchal*, m. hem of a garment. *vastr-bhedī*, m. a tailor. *s.*

وسترا *wastarā* (corrupt. of *ustura*, q. v.), a razor. *d.*

وسترت विस्तृत *vistṛit*, spread, diffused. *vistriti*, f. the diameter of a circle. *s.*

وستي वसती *vasatī*, f. a house, dwelling, abode, residence. *s.*

وستيرن विस्तीर्ण *vistīrn*, spread out, expanded. *s*

وسدا वसुदा *vasudā* or *vasudhā*, f. the earth. *s.*

وسديو वसुदेव *vasudev*, m. the name of the father of *Krishna*. *s.*

وسرام *visrām*, وسرانت *visrānt*, } (v. *vishrām*), &c. *s.*

وسرجن विसर्जन *visarjan*, m. gift, donation; quitting, dismissing; setting a bull at liberty (v. *vrishotsarga*). *s.*

وسرگ विसर्ग *visarg* or *visarga*, m. the soft aspirate marked by two dots (in the *Devanāgarī* character) being a substitute for the letters *sa* or *ra*. *s.*

وسط *wasaṭ*, m. the middle, the centre; adj. middling (sort, &c.); central; suitable, just, proper, excellent, great, magnificent. *a.*

وسطي *wasaṭī*, middling, neither long nor short (pronunciation). *a.*

وسعت *wus'at*, f. latitude, amplitude, space; leisure, convenience, opportunity, ease. *a.*

وسق *wasḳ* or *wisḳ*, a load of corn, a horse or or camel load. *a.*

وسك वसुक *vasuk*, m. *sāmbhar* salt. *s.*

وسليش विश्लेष *vislesh*, m. disunion, separation. *s.*

وسمان वसुमान *vasu-mān*, wealthy, rich. *s.*

وسمت विस्मित *vismit*, astonished, dismayed. *s.*

وسمتي वसुमती *vasumatī*, f. the earth. *s.*

وسمرت विस्मृत *vismrit*, forgotten. *vismriti*, f. forgetting, forgetfulness. *s.*

وسمه *wasma*, m. the leaves of woad, or indigo (with an extract from which the natives stain their beards, cloths, &c.). *wasma-posh*, dressed in cloths stained with *wasma*. *wasma-dār*, stained with *wasma*. *a.*

وسمي विस्मय *vismay*, m. wonder, astonishment. *s.*

وسميي विस्मयी *vismayī*, surprised, astonished. *s.*

وسن वस्त्र *vasn* or वसन *vasan*, m. cloth, clothes. *s.*

وسنت वसन्त *vasant*, m. the season of spring; dysentery, diarrhœa; small-pox. *vasant-otsav*, the celebration on the return of spring. *vasant-kusum*, name of a tree (*Cordia myxa* and *latifolia*). *s.*

وسنتي वसन्ती *vasantī*, of or relating to spring. *s.*

وسو विस्व *viswa* (v. *vishwa*), the world. *s.*

وسواد विस्वाद *viswād*, tasteless, insipid. *s.*

وسواس *waswās*, m. the temptations of the devil, distraction of mind; doubt, suspense, hesitation, apprehension, perplexity, superstition, scrupulousness. *a.*

وسواسي *waswāsī*, doubtful, causing suspense, distracting, apprehensive. *a.*

وسور विस्वर *viswar*, discordant, inharmonious. *s.*

وسوسه *waswasa*, m. temptation. *a.*

وسوك वसूक *vasūk*, m. *sāmbhar* salt. *s.*

وسي विसे *wise* (inflect. of *wuh*), him, her, it, to him, to her, to it, or to that. *h.*

وسيت वसीत *wasīt*, وسيٹھ वसीठ *wasīṭh*, } m. an agent, ambassador (for *wasīṭ*, Arab.). *h.*

وسيع *wasī'*, extensive, spacious. *a.*

وسيله *wasīla*, m. affinity, propinquity; cause, conjuncture; support, prop; means (of effecting any thing); patronage. *wasīla-dār*, a client, dependant. *wasīla-dārī*, clientship, dependence. *a.*

وسيم *wasīm*, beautiful, elegant, comely. *a.*

وش *wash*, (in comp.) like, resembling, as *mah-wash*, moon-like, beautiful. *p.*

وش वश *vash*, humbled, sudued, tamed; fascinated, enchanted; m. authority, mastership, subjection. *s.*

وش विष *vish*, m. poison, venom. *vish-āpah*, antidotic, an antidote. *vish-āpahā*, f. a kind of birth wort (*Aristolochia Indica*). *vish-ālū*, venomous, poisonous. *vish-bhakshan*, m. taking poison. *vish-bhujang*, m. a poisonous snake. *vish-dhar*, venomous. *vish-sūchak*, the Greek partridge. *vish-ghātī*, antidotic, an antidote; m. a tree (*Mimosa sirisa*). *vish-mantr*, a snake-catcher, a charm for curing snake bites. *vish-nāshan* or *-nāshī*, m. an antidote; a tree (*Mimosa sirisa*). *vish-vidyā*, f. the administration of antidotes, the art of curing poisons. *vish-vaidya*, m. a dealer in antidotes, one who cures the bite of a snake, &c. *vish-har*, m. an antidote. *vish-hirday* or *-hridaya*, malicious, malignant. *s.*

وشاد विषाद *vishād*, m. lassitude, dejection, want of energy, lowness of spirits. *s.*

وشادي विषादी *vishādī*, dejected, disconsolate, sorrowful. *s.*

وشاكار विशाकार *vishākār*, m. name of a plant (*Euphorbia*). *s.*

وشاكها विशाखा *vishākhā*, f. the sixteenth lunar asterism. *s.*

وشال विशाल *vishāl*, great, large, eminent, illustrious. *s.*

وشالتا विशालता *vishālatā*, f. greatness, eminence, distinction. *s.*

وشان विषाण *vishān*, m. the horn of an animal, tusks of an elephant, boar, &c. *s.*

وشاني विषाणी *vishānī*, m. an animal with horns or tusks. *s.*

وشتا वशिता *vashitā*, f. fascination, bewitching; holding in subjection. *s.*

وشٹ विष्टि *vishṭi*, f. name of an astronomical period; labour without pay. *s.*

وشٹر विष्टर *vishṭar*, m. a seat, stool, chair; Brāhman's seat. *s.*

وشٹمبھ विष्टम्भ *vishṭambh*, m. constipation, obstruction (of urine); paralysis. *s.*

وشٹھا विष्ठा *vishṭhā*, f. fæces, ordure. *s.*

وشٹي विष्टी *vishṭī*, forced or unpaid labour. *s.*

وشد विशद *vishad*, white, clear, stainless. *s.*

وشدھر विषधर *vish-dhar*, m. a snake; adj. venomous. *s.*

وشرام विश्राम *vishrām*, m. rest, repose; pause, cessation; composure. *s.*

وشرانت विश्रान्त *vishrānt*, rested, calm, tranquil. *vishrānti*, f. rest, tranquillity. *s.*

وششتر विशस्त्र *vishastr*, unarmed, without weapons. *s.*

وششٹ विशिष्ट *vishisht*, endowed with, possessed of, having, inherent. *s.*

وششٹھ वशिष्ठ *vashishth*, m. a *rishi* or divine sage of the first order; one of the seven stars of *Ursa Major*. *s.*

وشم विषम *visham*, difficult of access, rough, uneven; difficult of comprehension, as an obscure book, &c.; odd (in numbers); fearful, frightful. *visham-jwar*, an intermittent fever. *visham-sāhas*, m. temerity, daring. *s.*

وشن विष्णु *vishnu*, m. one of the three principal Hindū deities, and the preserver of the universe. *vishnu-bhakta*, a worshipper of *Vishnu*. *vishnu-priti* or *vishnūttara*, a grant of rent-free land to Brāhmans in honour of *Vishnu*, or to maintain his worship. *vishnu-pad*, m. the sky, the firmament. *vishnu-padī*, f. one of the twelve *sankrāntis* or periods when the sun enters a sign of the zodiac, especially the first after the equinox. *vishnu-krāntā*, name of a flower (*Clitorea ternatea*). *vishnu-vallabhā*, name of a small fragrant plant so called (*Echites caryophyllata*); a fragrant shrub (*Ocymum sanctum*). *s.*

وشن विषणि *vishani*, m. a sort of snake. *s.*

وشنپران विष्णुपुराण *vishnu-purāna*, m. one of the sacred and poetical works of the Hindūs, supposed to have been compiled and composed by the poet *Vyāsa*, and comprising the whole body of Hindū theology: a *purāna* in general treats of five peculiar topics, the creation, the destruction and renovation of worlds, the genealogy of gods and heroes, the reigns of the *manus*, and the transactions of their descendants: there are eighteen acknowledged *purānas*: 1. *Brāhma*; 2. *Padma*, or the lotus; 3. *Brahmānda*, or the egg of *Brahmā*; 4. *Agni*, or fire; 5. *Vishnu*; 6. *Garuda*, his bird or vehicle; 7. *Brahma-vaivarta*, or transformations of *Brahmā*; 8. *Shiva*; 9. *Linga*; 10. *Nārada*, son of *Brahmā*; 11. *Skanda*, son of *Shiva*; 12. *Mārkandeya*, so called from a sage of that name; 13. *Bhavishyat*, or prophetic; 14. *Matsya*, or the fish; 15. *Varāha*, or boar; 16. *Kurma*, or tortoise; 17. *Vāmana*, or dwarf; and 18. the *Bhāgavat*, or life of *Krishna*, which last is by some considered as a spurious and modern work: the *purānas* are reckoned to contain four-hundred thousand stanzas; there are also eighteen *upa-purānas*, or similar poems of inferior sanctity and different appellations: the whole constitute the popular or poetical creed of the Hindūs, and some of them, or particular parts of them, are very generally read and studied. *s.*

وشنک विशङ्क *vishank*, fearless, undaunted. *s.*

وشو विषुव *vishuv*, } m. the equinox.
وشوت विषुवत *vishuvat*, } *vishuv-chhāyā*, f. the shadow of the gnomon at noon when the sun is on the equinox. *vishuv-din* or *-kāl*, m. the day of the equinox. *vishuvat-rekhā*, the equinoctial line. *s.*

وشوا विश्वा *vishwā*, f. a tree whose bark is used in dyeing red, commonly called *atis* (*Betula*). *s.*

وشواتم विश्वात्म *vishwātma*, m. the universal spirit. *s.*

وشواس विश्वास *vishwās*, m. trust, faith, confidence. *vishwās-bhang*, m. breach of confidence. *vishwās-pātr*, one who is trustworthy. *vishwās-krit*, inspiring confidence. *vishwās-ghāt*, m. violation of trust. *vishwās-ghātak*, m a traitor, one who betrays confidence. *s.*

وشواسي विश्वासी *vishwāsī*, trusting or confiding in; trusty, honest. *s.*

وشوامتر विश्वामित्र *vishwāmitra*, m. a Muni of the military caste, the preceptor of *Rāma*. *s.*

وشوک विशोक *vishok*, without grief, happy. *s.*

وشوکا विश्वका *vishwakā*, f. a gull (*Larus ridibundus*). *s.*

وشونبھر विश्वंभर *vishwambhar*, all-sustaining. *s.*

وشوه विश्व *vishwa*, all, entire, whole, universal; m. the world, the universe; a deity of a particular class, worshipped in the funeral rites. *vishwa-jit*, all-subduing. *vishwa-jan*, all men, mankind. *vishwa-devā*, m. name of a plant (*Hedysarum lagopodioides*). *vishwa-dhārī*, all-sustaining. *vishwa-rāj*, m. a universal sovereign. *vishwa-rūp*, multiform, universal, omnipresent, *Vishnu*. *vishwa-rochan*, an esculent root so called (*Arum colocasia*). *vishwa-sārak*, the prickly pear (*Costus Indicus*). *vishwa-srishtā*, God, the creator of all. *vishwa-krit*, the maker of all. *vishwa-karma*, the son of *Brahmā* and artist of the gods. *vishwa-vyāpti*, f. universal diffusion. *vishwa-vyāpak* or *-vyāpī*, all-pervading, every where diffused. *s.*

وشويشور विश्वेश्वर *vishweshwar*, m. lord of the universe, a form of *Shiva* especially worshipped at Benares. *s.*

وشي विषय *vishay*, m. any object of sense; an object, pursuit, affair. *s.*

وشي वशी *vashī*, subdued; m. a sage with subdued passions. *vashī-bhūt*, subjugated to another's will. *vashī-krit*, fascinated, subjected. *vashī-karan*, m. subduing (by drugs, charms, &c.), enchanting. *s.*

وشياتما वश्यात्मा *vashyātmā*, of a subdued mind. *s.*

وشيتا वश्यता *vashyatā*, f. humility, subjection. *s.*

وشير वशीर *vashīr*, m. a pungent fruit, (*Pothos officinalis*). *s.*

وشيش विशेष *vishesh*, m. sort, kind; excellence. *s.*

وشيشن विशेषण *visheshan*, discriminative. *s.*

وشيشيه विशेष्य *visheshya*, principal, chief; a substantive. *s.*

وشيه वश्य *vashya*, tame, humbled. *s.*

وشيي विषयी *vishayī*, m. a sensualist, materialist, man of the world. *s.*

وصال *wisāl*, m. union, meeting, interview; death; society, confederacy. *a.*

وصايا *wasāyā* (pl. of وصيت), wills, testaments; precepts, injunctions. *a.*

وصايت *wisāyat* (v. *wasiyat*), testament, &c. *a.*

وصف *wasf*, m. praise, encomium, description, description of qualities, merit, virtue, worth. *a.*

وصفيت *wasfiyat*, act or state of eulogy. *a.*

وصل *wasl*, m. meeting, union, conjunction. *wasl-k.*, to unite, to paste, to conjoin, to annex. *s.*

وصلت *wuslat*, f. } joining, conjunction; a
وصله *wusla*, m. } vinculum; a symbol used in Arabic orthography (v. Gram.). *wasla* (corruptly used for *fasla*), a section. *a.*

وصلچه *waṣalcha*, m. a shred, a fragment. *a. p.*

وصلي *waṣalī*, f. a piece of wood, plank, paste-board, slate, parchment, &c., on which children learn to write; adj. copulative, conjunctive. *a.*

وصمت *waṣmat*, f. reproach, disgrace; crime, sin, fault; torpor, languor. *a.*

وصول *wuṣūl*, m. arrival, conjunction; acquisition or enjoyment of any thing desired; realization of revenue. *wuṣūl-k.*, to collect. *wuṣūl honā*, to get, to be arrived. *a.*

وصولي *wuṣūlī*, recoverable (a debt, &c.). *a.*

وصي *waṣī*, m. an executor, administrator, a guardian. *a.*

وصيت *waṣīyat*, f. a last will and testament; precept, mandate; making a will. *waṣīyat-nāma*, a last will or testament. *waṣīyat-k.*, to leave by will, to devise, to bequeath. *a.*

وصيد *waṣīd*, a threshold, a portion or space before a door. *a.*

وضاحت *waẓāḥat*, clearness, purity. *a.*

وضاعت *waẓā'at*, f. humility, humiliation. *a.*

وضع *waẓ'*, f. situation, state, condition, manner, mode, procedure, position, conduct. *waẓ'i ḥamal*, abortion, miscarriage. *waẓ'-k.*, to deduct, to subtract; to invent or found (an art, &c.). *a.*

وضعي *waẓ'ī*, of or relating to situation. *a.*

وضو *waẓū* or *wuẓū*, m. ablution (performed before prayer, and consists in washing first the hands, then the mouth inside, then throwing water on the forehead, washing the whole face, arms, and lastly the feet). *a.*

وضوح *wuẓūḥ*, m. evidence, proof. *a.*

وضيع *waẓī'*, ignoble, base, plebeian, low; m. a deposit, a trust, any thing committed to the care of another. *sharīf o waẓī'*, nobles and plebeians. *a.*

وضيعت *waẓī'at*, trust, deposit; a deduction. *a.*

وطد *waṭid*, firm, steady, strengthened, solid; confirmed, corroborated. *a.*

وطر *waṭar*, m. any thing necessary; necessity, use; any thing that lies at heart. *a.*

وطن *waṭan*, m. native country, residence, abode, home, birthplace. *waṭan-dushman*, a traitor. *waṭan-dost*, a patriot. *a.*

وطني *waṭanī*, belonging to one's country. *a.*

وطي *waṭī*, f. *subigens mulierum*, coition; kicking, treading under foot. *a.*

وظائف *waẓā,if* (pl. of وظيفه), pensions, stipulated salaries, daily tasks or duties. *a.*

وظيفه *waẓīfa*, m. a pension, stipend, salary, stipulated allowance of provision (per day, month, or year); any thing agreed on; daily task, religious duty. *waẓīfa-dār*, the holder of a pension. *a.*

وظيفي *waẓīfī*, m. a stipendiary, pensioner; adj. of or relating to a salary, duty, &c. *a.*

وعده *wa'da*, m. a promise, vow; agreement, bargain. *wa'da-bandī*, f. an agreement. *wa'da-dār*, one who is bound by engagement. *wa'da khilāf*, a false contract; a person who does not keep his promise. *wa'da-shikan*, a promise-breaker. *wa'da-shikanī*, f. breach of promise. *wa'da-farāmosh*, forgetful of one's promise. *wa'da-wa'īd*, evading a promise. *wa'da-wafā*, observing one's promise. *a.*

وعظ *wa'ẓ*, m. advice, admonition, exhortation respecting future rewards and punishments, a sermon. *a.*

وعيد *wa'īd*, threatening or predicting any thing bad; promising any thing good. *a.*

وغا *waghā*, war, battle, tumult; a tiger. *p.*

وغيره *wa-ghaira*, et cetera, and so forth. *a.*

وفا *wafā*, f. performing a promise, observation of faith, sincerity, fidelity, sufficiency. *wafā-parast*, faithful, sincere *wafā-begāna*, faithless. *wafā-dār*, faithful, sincere. *wafā-dārī*, f. sincerity, fidelity. *wafā-k.*, to fulfil, to suffice, to prove effective. *a.*

وفات *wafāt*, f. death, decease. *wafāt yāftan*, to die. *a.*

وفاق *wifāḳ*, m. concord, harmony, good understanding, unanimity. *a.*

وفاءي *wafā,ī*, f. fidelity, sincerity. *a.*

وفر *wafr*, full, complete, entire, numerous, copious, abundant. *a.*

وفق *wafḳ*, m. a sufficiency; agreement, concord, congruity; just proportion. *a.*

وفور *wufūr*, m. multitude, plenty, abundance; adj. full, complete, copious. *a.*

وقاحت *waḳāḥat*, impudence; impudent. *a.*

وقار *waḳār*, m. dignity, estimation; steadiness, constancy; modesty, mildness, honour, reputation. *a.*

وقاع *wiḳā'*, rushing upon the enemy, battle, encounter; *coitus*. *a.*

وقائع *waḳā,i'* (pl. of وقيعه), news, events. *waḳā,i'-nigār*, an intelligencer. *waḳā,i'-nigārī*, f. the office of an intelligencer. *waḳā,i'-navīs*, a court secretary, whose duty it is to write down and chronicle all the acts and deeds, public and private, of the prince, the occurrences and news of the court, state affairs, &c. *a.*

وقت *waḳt*, m. time, season, opportunity; (met.) adversity. *waḳt ba waḳt*, from time to time. *waḳt be waḳt*, constantly, perpetually. *waḳt parnā*, to suffer misfortunes, to be distressed. *waḳt kāṭnā*, to pass away the time. *waḳti nāzuk*, delicate times. *waḳt nā waḳt*, occasionally, without any stated time. *waḳt-yāb*, finding an opportunity. *waḳti gurg o mesh* (lit.) "the time of the wolf and sheep," the dusk of evening or grey of the morning, when the light is insufficient to enable one to distinguish a wolf from a sheep. The French have a precisely similar phrase. "Entre chien et loup."—(Binning). *a.*

وقتيت *waḳtīyat*, f. seasonableness. *a.*

وقتيه *waḳtīya*, timely, seasonable. *a.*

وقر *waḳr*, m. dignity, honour, character; adj. mild, modest, sedate. *a.*

وقف *waḳf*, m. tranquillity; firmness, constancy; a legacy for pious uses; lands, &c. belonging to mosques, colleges, and charitable institutions, for their support and maintenance. *waḳf-nāma*, a written deed of endowment. *a.*

وقفه *wakfa*, m. pause, delay; choking, stopping, retarding, respite; vacancy. *a.*

وقفيت *wakfiyat*, f. the book in which legacies for pious uses are registered. *a.*

وقوع *waḳūʻ*, m. a contingency, accident, event, occurrence. *a.*

وقوف *wuḳūf*, m. experience, information, sense, understanding, wisdom. *wuḳūf-dār*, informed of, experienced. *a.*

وقوفي *wuḳūfī*, sensible, intelligent. *a.*

وقيه *waḳīyah*, a weight of two and a quarter pounds. *wuḳiyat*, a weight of seven *misḳāls* and forty *dirhams*. *a.*

وك वक *vak* or *vaka*, m. a crane (*Ardea nivea*); also a tree so called (*Sesbana grandiflora*). *s.*

وکار विकार *vikār*, m. change of form or nature; sickness, disease. *s.*

وکاش विकाश *vikāsh*, m. } display, manifestation; appearance, publicity. *s.*
وکاشتا विकाशता *vikāshtā*, f. }

وکاشن विकाशन *vikāshan*, m. act of displaying. *s.*

وکال विकाल *vikāl*, m. twilight. *s.*

وکالت *wakālat*, f. agency, embassy, deputation; office of *wakīl*. *wakālatan*, by deputy. *a.*

وکپشپ वकपुष्प *vak-pushp*, m. name of a tree (*Æschynomene grandiflora*). *s.*

وکتا वक्ता *vaktā* (v. *baktā*), m. a speaker. *s.*

وکتر वक्त्र *vaktra*, m. the face, the mouth. *s.*

وکتويه वक्तव्य *vaktavya*, fit to be spoken. *s.*

وکٹ विकट *vikaṭ*, great, large, formidable, frightful, hideous, horrible. *s.*

وکر वक्र *vakr*, crooked, curved; indirect, evasive. *vakr-pushp*, m. the *Sesbana grandiflora*. *vakr-gāmī*, who or what goes tortuously; fraudulent, dishonest, evasive. *vakr-gati*, crooked gait; foppishness. *s.*

وکرانت विक्रान्त *vikrānt*, valiant, mighty, victorious; a hero, a warrior. *s.*

وکرت विकृत *vikṛit*, averse, estranged; m. digust, aversion. *vikrit-ākār*, changed in aspect or form. *s.*

وکرتا वक्रता *vakratā*, f. crookedness, knavery, craft, cunning; evasive or jesuitical speech. *s.*

وکرتي विकृती *vikṛitī*, f. change of any kind, as of purpose, mind, form, nature; sickness, disease. *s.*

وکرم विक्रम *vikram*, m. heroism, prowess, heroic valour, great power or strength; overcoming, subduing. *s.*

وکرم विकर्म *vi-karm*, misdoing. *vikarm-kriyā*, f. an illegal or immoral act. *s.*

وکرماجيت विक्रमाजीत *vikramājīt*, } m. the name
وکرمادتيه विक्रमादित्य *vikramāditya*, }
of a celebrated prince, the sovereign of *Ujjain*, and the reputed founder of an era among the Hindūs, still in use, commencing 56 years before the Christian era. *s.*

وکرمي विक्रमी *vikramī*, m. a lion; a hero. *s.*

وکرنك विकर्णिक *vikarnik*, m. the district Sāraswat, in the north-west of Hindūstān. *s.*

وکروکت वक्रोक्ति *vakrokti*, f. equivoque, evasion; pun, covert expression, hint, sarcasm. *s.*

وکري वक्री *vakrī*, crooked, dishonest. *vakrī-bhā,o*, m. curvature; fraudulent disposition. *s.*

وکري विक्रय *vikray*, m. sale, selling, vending. *vikrayī*, a seller, vendor. *s.*

وکريت विक्रीत *vikrīt*. sold, vended. *s.*

وکريتا विक्रेता *vikretā*, } m. a vendor, seller
وکريي विक्रयी *vikrayī*, }

وکست विकसित *vikasit*, blown, as a flower, [budded. *s.*

وکشه वक्षः *vaksha*, m. the breast, the bosom. *s.*

وکشپت विक्षिप्त *vikshipt*, thrown, cast; bewildered, foolish. *s.*

وکشيپ विक्षेप *vikshep*, m. casting, throwing; perplexity; celestial latitude. *s.*

وکل विकल *vikal*, confused, confounded; one-sixtieth of a *kalā*, the sixtieth part of a degree. *vakul*, m. name of plant (*Mimosa elengi*). *s.*

وکلا *wukalā* (pl. of وکيل), agents, ambassadors. *a.*

وکلپ विकल्प *vikalp*, m. error, doubt, indecision; (in gram.) admitting of more than one rule; (in rhetoric) antithesis. *s.*

وکمپت विकम्पित *vikampit*, trembling, agitated; palpitating, heaving. *s.*

وکنٹك विकण्टक *vikanṭak*, m. name of a herbaceous plant (*Hedysarum alhagi*). *s.*

وکهالنا *wakhālnā*, a. to spew, to vomit. *d.*

وکهياپن विख्यापन *vikhyāpan*, m. explaining, expounding. *s.*

وکهيات विख्यात *vikhyāt*, known, notorious, famous. *vikhyāti*, f. fame, celebrity, renown, notoriety. *s.*

وکيل *wakīl*, m. an agent, ambassador, representative, counsellor (at law). *wakīl muṭlaḳ*, a plenipotentiary, a vicegerent invested with full powers. *a.*

وکيلي *wakīlī*, f. office of *wakīl*, agency, embassy. *a.*

وگر *wagar*, (conj. for *wa* and *gar*), and if, [but. *wa-gar-na*, and if not. *p.*

وگره विग्रह *vigrah*, m. the body; extension diffusion war, battle, opposition, encounter. *s.*

وگن विगुण *vigun*, bad, worthless. *s.*

وگوڑھ विगूढ़ *vigūṛh*, concealed, hidden. *s.*

وگھات विघात *vighāt*, } m. obstacle, impediment.
وگھن विघ्न *vighn*, } *vighn-siddhi*, f. removal of obstacles. *vighn-kārī*, impeding, obstructing. *vighn-nāshak*, removing difficulties. *vighn-nāshan*, m. or *vighn-siddhi*, f. the removing of obstacles. *s.*

وگھنت विघ्नित *vighnit*, stopped, prevented, obstructed, impeded. *s.*

وگي विज्ञ *vigya*, skilful, clever, learned. *s.*

وگياپن विज्ञापन *vigyāpan*, m. teaching, informing. *s.*

وگيات विज्ञात *vigyāt*, known, famous. *s.*

وگيان विज्ञान *vigyān*, m. knowledge, science. *s.*

وگيتا विज्ञता *vigyatā*, f. wisdom, learning. *s.*

ول विल *vil* or विल्ल *vill*, m. a pit hole, cavity; a chasm, cavern. *s.*

ولا *wilā* or *walā*, f. friendship, affinity; a kingdom, authority, power. *willā*, conj. and if not; otherwise. *a.*

ولا *wilā*, m. time, season. *a. p.*

ولا वला *walā*, near, hither, on this side. *h.*

ولاپ विलाप *vilāp*, m. lamentation, sound of grief or distress. *s.*

ولاد *wilād*, nativity, child-birth; procreation. *a.*

ولادت *wilādat*, f. nativity, birth, generation. *a.*

ولاس विलास *vilās*, m. sport, play, wantonness. *s.*

ولاسني विलासिनी *vilāsinī*, a wanton woman, [a whore, a harlot. *s.*

ولاسي विलासी *vilāsī*, m. a sensualist; adj. sportive. wanton. *s.*

ولاكا वलाका *valākā*, f. a small kind of crane, a row or line of cranes. *s.*

ولايت *wilāyat*, f. an inhabited country, dominion, district; a foreign country; possession, being master of any thing; by the natives of India this term is used to denote any country except their own, but more especially Persia, Arabia, and Great Britain. *a.*

ولايتي *wilāyatī*, European, foreign. *wilāyatī khaṭṭ*, a kind of *Nasta'līk* character. *wilāyatī sem*, beans. *wilāyatī pānī*, soda-water. *wilāyatī baingan*, the tomata or love-apple. *wilāyatī mako,e*, the fruit called Cape gooseberry, or Brazil cherry. *tāza wilāyatī*, a new comer to India; in Anglo-Indian phraseology "a griffin," or more colloquially a "griff." *a.*

ولبھ वल्लभ *vallabh*, beloved, desired, dear; m. a lover, husband, friend; a superintendant. *s.*

ولتھي *walthī*, } the caves of a house. *d.*
ولتي *waltī*, }

ولج विलज्ज *vilajj*, shameless, impudent, unabashed. *s.*

ولد *walad*, m. a son, offspring. *waladu-z-zinā*, a son of a whore, a bastard; an earth-worm. *a.*

ولسن विलसन *vilasan*, m. sporting, dallying. *s.*

ولكل वल्कल *valkal*, m. the bark of a tree. *s.*

ولگ विलग *vilag*, separate, apart. *s.*

ولمب विलम्ब *vilamb*, m. slowness, tardiness, delay. *s.*

ولمبنا विलम्बना *vilambnā*, m. delaying, retarding. *s.*

ولميك वल्मीक *valmīk*, m. the celebrated poet, *Vālmīki*, author of the Rāmāyana. *s.*

ولو विल्व *vilv*, m. a fruit tree commonly called *bel* (*Ægle marmelos*). *s.*

ولوبھن विलोभन *vilobhan*, m. allurement, temptation. *s.*

ولوٹك विलोटक *viloṭak*, m. name of a kind of fish (*Cuprea cultrata*). *s.*

ولوچن विलोचन *vilochan*, m. the eye. *vilochan-pāt*, a glance of the eye. *s.*

ولوڑنا विलोड़ना *viloṛnā*, a. to shake, to churn. *s.*

ولوكت विलोकित *vilokit*, seen, beheld. *s.*

ولوكن विलोकन *vilokan*, m. sight, seeing, looking. *s.*

ولوكنا विलोकना *viloknā*, a. to see, to behold, to look, to view. *s.*

ولوكنيه विलोकनीय *vilokanīya*, agreeable, beautiful. *s.*

ولوله *walwala*, m. howling, lamenting; a tumult, noise, uproar. *a.*

ولوم विलोम *vilom*, reverse, opposite, contrary, backwards. *vilom-trairāsik*, rule of three inverse. *vilom-kriyā* or *-vidhi*, rule of inversion. *s.*

ولوونا विलोवना *vilovnā*, a. to churn, to agitate. *s.*

ولي विलय *vilay*, m. dissolution, destruction of the world. *s.*

ولي *walī*, m. a holy man, a favourite (of God); a prince, lord, master; a guardian; a servant, a slave. *walī-'ahd*, an heir, a *locum tenens*, vicegerent. *walī-'ahdī*, heritage, the state of being an heir apparent; deputyship. *walī-khangar*, m. an assistant, protector. *walī-ni'mat*, a benefactor, a patron, a title of respect by which a father is addressed. *a.*

ولي *wa-le*, }
وليك *wa-leh*, } but then, and further, and nevertheless. *a. p.*
وليكن *wa-lekin*, }

وليمه *walīma*, a banquet, a marriage feast. *a.*

ولين विलयन *vilayan*, m. destroying, corroding, liquefying, attenuating. *s.*

وماتا विमाता *vimātā*, } f. a stepmother, a father's wife. *s.*
وماتر विमातृ *vimātṛi*, }

وامارگ विमार्ग *vimārg*, m. a bad road, a wrong path, evil conduct. *s.*

ومان विमान *vimān*, m. a car or chariot of the gods, sometimes serving as a seat or throne, and sometimes carrying them through the skies, self-moving. *s.*

ومب विम्ब *vimb*, m. the disc of the sun, image, shadow; the gourd of the *Momordica monadelpha*. *s.*

ومرش विमर्श *vimarsh*, m. investigation, trial. *s.*

ومكت विमुक्त *vimukt*, loosed, liberated. *vimukti*, f. liberation; final release. *s.*

ومكهه विमुख *vimukh*, averted, having the face cast down; opposed. *s.* [opposition. *s.*

ومكهتا विमुखता *vimukhtā*, f. turning away,

ومكهي विमुखी *vimukhī*, averted, turned away; hostile, averse to or from. *s.*

ومل विमल *vimal*, pure, clean. *vimal-ātmā*, pure in spirit, undefiled. *vimal-mani*, m. chrystal. *s.*

وملان विम्लान *vimlān*, fresh, pure from decay. *s.*

ومن वमन *vaman*, m. vomiting, an emetic. *s.*

وموچت विमोचित *vimochit*, liberated, set free. *s.*

وموچن विमोचन *vimochan*, m. act of liberating. *s.* [mind, foolish. *s.*

وموڑهاتما विमूढ़ात्मा *vimūṛh-ātmā*, deluded in

وموكش विमोक्ष *vimoksh*, m. liberation, freedom. *s.* [guiled. *s.*

وموهت विमोहित *vimohit*, fascinated, be-

وموهن विमोहन *vimohan*, m. the act of seducing, tempting, confounding the mind and exciting the passions. *s.*

وموهني विमोहनी *vimohanī*, fascinating, bewitching, tempting. *s.* [to vomit. *s.*

ومي वमी *vamī*, f. vomiting; adj. sick, inclined

ون विन *win* (inflect. pl. of *wuh*), them, those. *h.*

ون वन *van*, m. a forest, wood, grove; *van-āsray*, m. a dwelling in a forest. *van-ānt*, the skirts of a wood. *van-chārī*, savage; m. a forester. *van-char*, an ape, a monkey. *van-rāj*, m. a lion, king of the forest. *van-sthāyī*, being or abiding in a wood; m. a hermit, an anchoret. *van-sthit*, situated in a forest. *van-kachu*, a species of *arum* (*Arum calocasia*). *van-vās* or *-vāsī*, an anchoret, a hermit. *van-virāl*, a wild cat (*Felis caracal*). *s.*

ونا विना *vinā*, without, except. *s.*

ونانهه विनाथ *vināth*, deserted, unowned. *s.*

وناش विनाश *vināsh*, m. disappearance, destruction, loss, annihilation. *s.*

وناشت विनाशित *vināshit*, destroyed, effaced. *s.*

وناشك विनाशक *vināshak*, } m. a destroyer;
وناشي विनाशी *vināshī*, } adj. destructive.
vināshī, perishing, being destroyed. *s.*

ونانت वनान्त *vanānt*, m. the skirts of a wood. *s.*

ونپات विनिपात *vinipāt*, m. falling; a calamity. *vinipāt-shansī*, portentous. *s.*

ونت विनत *vinat*, bent, stooping; humble, modest. *vinati*, f. bending, modesty. *s.*

ونتا वनिता *vanitā*, f. a woman in general, a beloved woman, a wife, a mistress. *s.*

ونٹك वण्टक *vanṭak*, m. a part, a portion. *s.*

ونٹن वण्टन *vanṭan*, m. portioning, dividing. *s.*

ونچت वञ्चित *vanchit*, tricked, deceived. *s.*

ونچك वञ्चक *vanchak* or वञ्चुक *vanchuk*, fraudulent, crafty: m. a jackal, a rogue, cheat. *s.*

ونچن वञ्चन *vanchan*, m. } cheating, fraud,
ونچنا वञ्चना *vanchanā*, f. } deception. *s.*

وند विन्दु *vindu*, m. a drop of liquid; a spot, dot, mark. *s.* [*drum tesselatum*, &c.). *s.*

وندا वन्दा *vandā*, f. a parasite plant (*Epiden-*

وندن वन्दन *vandan*, m. obeisance to a Brāhman, &c. by touching the feet. *s.*

وندنا वन्दना *vandnā*, f. praise, praising, especially the gods or great men. *s.*

وندني वन्दनी *vandnī*, f. reverence, worship, adoring. *s.* [to be adored. *s.*

وندنيه वन्दनीय *vandanīya*, praiseworthy, fit

وندهي विन्ध्य *vindhya*, } the
وندهياچل विन्ध्याचल *vindhyāchal*, } Vindhya
range of mountains, which divide Hindūstān proper from the Deccan. *vindhyāṭavī*, f. the great Vindhya forest. *vindhya-vāsinī*, f. a name of *Durgā*, a shrine of *Durgā*, near *Mirzāpūr*. *s.*

وندي वन्दी *vandī*, a captive, prisoner; a panegyrist, bard, herald; a flatterer. *s.*

ونديه वन्द्य *vandya*, fit to be praised, commendable, laudable. *s.*

ونس वंश *vans* (for *vansha*), m. race, lineage, family. *vans-bhojya*, m. hereditary estate. *vans-paramparā*, f. descent, lineage. *vans-charitr*, m. genealogy, history of the race. *vans-samāchār*, m. family usage. *vans-vriddhi*, f. prosperity of a family. *s.*

ونساولي वंशावली *vansāvalī*, f. a pedigree, genealogy. *s.*

ونسپت वनस्पति *vanaspati*, m. a tree that bears fruit but no apparent blossoms. *s.*

ونس روچنا वंशरोचना *vans-rochanā*, } f. an
ونس لوچن वंशलोचन *vans-lochan*, } earthy
white concretion in the hollow of the bamboo. *s.*

ونسك वंशिक *vansik*, belonging to a family, a bamboo, &c. *vansak*, m. a small fish (*Cynoglosus lingua*). *s.*

ونسي वंशी *vansī*, f. a pipe, a flute. *vansī-dhar*, m. a piper; a name of *Krishna*. *s.*

ونشت विंशति *vinshati*, twenty. *vinshatitam*, the twentieth. *s.*

ونشٹ विनष्ट *vinashṭ*, destroyed, lost. *vinashṭi*, f. disappearance, destruction. *s.*

ونك वङ्क *vank*, m. the bend of a river; crookedness. *s.*

ونگ बङ्ग *vang*, m. Bengal. *s.*

وني विनिमय *vinimay*, m. barter, exchange. *s.*

ونود विनोद *vinod*, eagerness, sport, pleasure. *s.*

ونهين विन्हें *winhen*, (oblique pl.) them, to them or those. *h.*

ونهين वुहीं *wuñhīn*, that very (time, place, &c.), immediately, on the spot, in that very manner. *h.*

وني विनय *vinay*, m. affability, modesty, reverence, decency. *s.*

ونيا वन्या *vanyā*, f. a multitude of groves; a quantity of water, a flood, a deluge; name of a plant (*Physalis flexuosa*). *s.*

ونياس विन्यास *vinyās*, m. assemblage, collection; site, receptacle. *s.*

ونياك विन्याक *vinyāk*, m. name of a tree (*Echites scholaris*). *s.*

ونيت विनीत *vinīt*, modest, humble. *vinīt-ātmā*, well-behaved; humble. *s.*

ونيلا वनेला *vanelā*, savage, wild. *s.*

ونيه वन्य *vanya*, savage, wild; of the forest, produced in the wood. *s.*

ونيي विनयी *vinayī*, courteous, affable. *s.*

وو वो *wo*, (third pers. pr. pl.) those, they. *h.*

وواد विवाद *vivād*, m. contest, contention. *s.*

ووادي विवादी *vivādī*, disputing; m. a litigant. *s.*

وواس विवास *vivās*, | ووासन विवासन *vivāsan*, } m. exile, banishment, expulsion from house and home. *s.*

وواه विवाह *vivāh*, m. marriage, of which eight forms are enumerated by Manu (v. Wilson's Glossary). *s.*

وواهت विवाहित *vivāhit*, m. | وواهتا विवाहिता *vivāhitā*, f. } married. *s.*

ووद वोद *wod*, wet, moist. *s.*

ووदال वोदाल *wodāl*, m. a sheat fish (*Silurus boalis*). *s.*

وودھ विविध *vividh*, various, of many sorts or forms. *s.*

وور विवर *vivar*, m. a hole, a chasm; fault, defect. *s.*

وورجت विवर्जित *vivarjit*, left, abandoned; avoided, shunned. *s.*

وورجن विवर्जन *vivarjan*, m. abandoning, leaving; shunning. *s.*

وورن विवरण *vivaraṇ*, m. explanation, gloss, comment, description. *s.*

وورن विवर्ण *vivarṇ* or *vivarṇa*, a man of low caste, an outcast. *s.*

ووس विवश *vivas*, independent; sedate, at the point of death. *s.*

ووستر विवस्त्र *vivastr*, naked, unclothed. *s.*

ووشاؤن वोशाञोन *woshā,on*, the winnowing of grain. *h.*

ووکشا विवक्षा *vivakṣhā*, f. wish, desire. *s.*

ووکشت विवक्षित *vivakṣhit*, wished, desired. *s.*

ووکشتا विवक्षिता *vivakṣhitā*, f. purpose, wish. *s.*

وول वोल *wol* or *vol*, m. gum, myrrh. *s.*

وون वूं *wūn* or वों *won*, so, in that manner. *won-hī* or *won-hīn*, also *wohī* or *wohīn*, in that very manner, that instant. *won kā wohī*, exactly the same as before. *h.*

وويچك विवेचक *vivechak*, m. a judge, one who discriminates truth from falsehood. *s.*

وويچن विवेचन *vivechan*, m. | وويچنا विवेचना *vivechanā*, f. | وويك विवेक *vivek*, m. | وويكتا विवेकता *vivekatā*, f. } discrimination, judgment, distinguishing truth from falsehood. *s.*

وويكي विवेकी *vivekī*, m. a judge, sage, philosopher; adj. judicious, discriminative. *s.*

وه वुह *wuh* or वह *wah*, pron. he, she, it, that sometimes for *we*, they, those. *h.*

وهابي *wahhābī*, a follower of the doctrines of Shaikh 'Abdu-l-wahhāb, an Arabian reformer of the last century: in India the term is equivalent to "infidel" or "unbeliever," just as we good Protestants are called "heretics," and doomed in due time to a certain warm berth, &c., by our very charitable fellow-worms of the Romish persuasion. *a.*

وهار विहार *vihār*, m. play, sport, pastime. *s.*

وهاري विहारी *vihārī*, playful, sportive. *s.*

وهان वहां *wahān* or वुहां *wuhān*, there, thither, yonder. *wahān kā wahān*, in that very place. *h.*

وهب *wahb*, m. giving, bestowing. *a.*

وهبي *wahbī*, given or bestowed. *a.*

وهر वहिर *vahir*, out, without. *vahir-des*, m. a foreign land. *vahir-bhūt*, expelled, excluded. *s.*

وهرن विहरण *viharan*, m. taking off or away; going about for pleasure. *s.*

وهسنا विहसना *vihasnā*, n. to smile, to laugh. *s.*

وهلا वहला *vahlā* or *wahla*, m. an attack, assault. *h.*

وهم *wahm*, m. imagination, idea, fancy; (in law) suspension, doubt; anxiety, apprehension. *a.*

وهمه *wahma*, a whim, a fancy; an idea. *a.*

وهمي *wahmī*, imaginary, conjectural. *a.*

وهن वह्नि *vahni*, m. fire, or its deity, Agni. *s.*

وهنگ विहङ्ग *vihang*, | وهنگم विहङ्गम *vihangam*, } m. a bird, that which soars in the sky. *s.*

وهي वही *wahī* or *wuhī*, pron. he himself, that very. *h.*

وهئي वहई *vaha,ī*, f. side, quarter, way. *s.*

وهين वुहीं *wuhīn*, that very time or place, immediately, on the spot. *h.*

وهين विहीन *vihīn*, abandoned, left, deserted, deprived of. *s.*

وي वे *we*, (pron. pl.) they, those. *h.*

وي *wai*, fie! ho! *wai-ka*, fie upon thee! *a. p.*

وياپ व्याप *vyāp*, } m. occupation, business, trade; practice. *s.*
وياپار व्यापार *vyāpār*, }

وياپاري व्यापारी *vyāpārī*, busy, occupied; m. a trader, a dealer, a man of business. *s.*

وياپت व्याप्त *vyāpta*, pervaded, penetrated by, filled with. *vyāpti*, f. pervading, inherence, universal permeation, omnipresence. *vyāpti-mān*, diffusive, pervading. *s.*

وياپك व्यापक *vyāpak*, diffusive, comprehensive, extending. *s.*

وياپكتا व्यापकता *vyāpaktā*, f. diffusion, pervadence. *s.*

وياپنا व्यापना *vyāpnā*, a. n. to spread through, to penetrate, to pervade, to affect or influence. *s.*

وياپي व्यापी *vyāpī*, diffusive, comprehensive. *s.*

وياپيتا व्याप्यता *vyāpyatā*, f. penetrability. *s.*

وياج व्याज *vyāj*, m. interest, usury; deceit, fraud, guile; disguise, wickedness. *s.*

وياجو व्याजू *vyājū*, m. the principal or capital sum put out at interest. *s.*

وياجي व्याजी *vyājī*, m. one who takes interest; money that bears interest, or which is lent or borrowed at interest. *s.*

ويادھ व्याध *vyādh*, } m. a hunter, a low or wicked man. *s.*
ويادھا व्याधा *vyādhā*, }

ويادھ व्याधि *vyādhi*, f. sickness, disease in general. *vyādhi-rahit*, free from disease, in good health. *s.*

ويادھت व्याधित *vyādhit*, } sick, ill, diseased. *s.*
ويادھي व्याधी *vyādhi*, }

وياس व्यास *vyās* or *vyāsa*, m. a celebrated sage and author, the reputed compiler of the *Vedas* and *Purāṇas*; also the founder of the *Vedānta* philosophy; diffusion, extension; the diameter of a circle. *s.*

وياكرن व्याकरण *vyākaran*, m. grammar, exposition. *vaiyākaran*, grammatical; m. a grammarian. *s.*

وياكرني व्याकरणी *vyākaranī*, m. a grammarian. *s.*

وياكل व्याकुल *vyākul*, } or *vyākul-manā*, confounded, bewildered, perplexed, overcome with fear. *vyākultā*, f. perplexity, alarm. *s.*
وياكلت व्याकुलित *vyākulit*, }

وياكھيا व्याख्या *vyākhyā*, f. exposition, explanation, gloss, comment. *s.*

وياكھيان व्याख्यान *vyākhyān*, m, explaining, expounding. *s.*

وياگھات व्याघात *vyāghāt*, m. obstacle, impediment. *s.*

وياگھاتي व्याघाती *vyāghātī*, obstructive, whatever resists, opposes, &c. *s.*

وياگھر व्याघ्र *vyāghra*, m. a tiger. *vyāghra-nakhī*, f. a tiger's claw; a sort of perfume; a scratch of the finger nails. *s.*

ويام व्याम *vyām*, m. a fathom, or the space between the tips of the fingers of either hand when the arms are extended. *s.*

وياموه व्यामोह *vyāmoh*, pain, perplexity. *s.*

ويان व्यान *vyān*, m. one of the five vital airs, that which is diffused throughout the body. *s.*

وياوهارك व्यावहारिक *vyāvahārik*, m. a counsellor, a minister. *s.*

وياوهاري व्यवहारी *vyāvahārī*, usual, customary, judicial, legal; m. a counsellor, a minister. *s.*

ويايام व्यायाम *vyāyām*, m. fatigue, labour; exercise, gymnastics. *s.*

ويبھچار، व्यभिचार *vyabhichār*, following improper courses, doing what is wrong or prohibited. *s.*

ويبھچارني، व्यभिचारिणी *vyabhichārinī*, f. a wanton woman, an unchaste wife. *s.*

ويبھچاري، व्यभिचारी *vyabhichārī*, m. an adulterer; one who follows what is improper; going astray. *s.*

ويبھو वैभव *vaibhava*, m. grandeur, wealth. *s.*

ويتا वेता *wetā*, so much, that much. *h.*

ويتا वेत्ता *vettā*, m. a sage, one who knows the nature of the soul and of God; adj. knowing, conversant with. *s.*

ويتاگ *waitāg*, m. disgust, weariness. *waitāg lena*, to be tired or disgusted with any person or thing. *d.*

ويتاگي *waitāgī*, wearied, disgusted. *d.*

ويتال वेताल *vetāl*, m. a spirit, a goblin, especially one supposed to haunt cemeteries, and believed to have the power of reanimating dead bodies. *s.*

ويتپت व्युत्पत्ति *vyut-patti*, f. science, learning, etymology. *s.*

ويتپن व्युत्पन्न *vyutpann*, learned, proficient; derived, generated, begotten. *s.*

ويتر वेत्र *vetr*, m. a reed, a cane, a ratan. *vetr-wati*, the name of the Betwa river in Malwa. *s.*

ويتركت व्यतिरिक्त *vyatirikt*, different, distinct. *s.*

ويترني वैतरणी *vaitaranī*, f. a river of hell. *s.*

ويتريك व्यतिरेक *vyatirek*, m. difference, separating; prep. without, deprived of. *s.*

ويتس वेतस *vetas*, m. the common ratan. *s.*

ويتكرم व्यतिक्रम *vyatikram* (also व्युत्क्रम *vyut-kram*), inverted order, reverse, opposition, irregular arrangement. *s.*

ويتن वेतन *vetan*, m. hire, wages. *vetan-ādāna*, non-payment of wages. *s.*

ويتنا वेतना *wetnā*, that much, or that many. *h.*

ويتها व्यथा *vyathā*, f. pain in general (bodily or mental). *vyathā-rahit*, free from pain. *vyathā-kar*, causing pain, excruciating. *s.*

ويتيپات व्यतीपात *vyatī-pāt*, m. a great and portentous calamity, an evil omen or portent. *s.*

ويتيت व्यतीत *vyatīt*, past, gone, elapsed. *s*

ويتيي व्यत्यय *vyatyay*, m. contrariety. *s.*

ويٹكا वीटिका *vīṭikā*, f. the betel plant, betel, *pān*, q. v. *s.*

ويج बीज *vīj*, m. seed (of plants), cause, origin in general; *semen virile*. *vīj-kosh*, m. any seed vessel. *vīj-koshī*, f. a pod, a legume. *vīj-ganit*, m. (lit. enumeration of seeds) algebra, analysis. *s.*

ويجن बीजन *vījan* or व्यजन *vyajan*, m. a fan, ventilator. *s.*

ويجي बीजी *vījī*, m. a sower, a progenitor. *s.*

ويد वेद *ved* or *veda*, m. the *Veda* or the *Vedas* in the aggregate; the original *Veda* is believed by the Hindūs to have been revealed by *Brahmā*, and to have been preserved by tradition until it was arranged in its present order by a sage, who thence obtained the surname of *Vyāsa* or *Vedavyāsa*, that is, compiler of the *Vedas*. He distributed the Indian scripture into four parts, which are severally entiled *Rig*, *Yajush*, *Sāma* and *Atharva*, and each of which bears the common denomination of *Veda*. In addition to the sacred *Vedas*, there are the *Upaveda*, a division of Hindū science deduced immediately from the *Vedas*. Four works are included under this denomination, and severally entitled *Ayush*, *Gandharva*, *Dhanush*, add *Sthāpatya*. The first was delivered to mankind by *Brahmā*, *Indra*, *Dhanwantari*, and five other deities, and comprises the theory of disorders and medicines, with the practical methods of curing diseases; the second, or music, was invented and explained by *Bharata*; the third *Upaveda* was composed by *Viswāmitra*, on the fabrication and use of arms and implements handled in war by the tribe of *Kshatriyas*; and *Vishwakarmā* revealed the fourth in various treatises on sixty-four mechanical arts, for the improvement of such as exercise them. *ved-punya*, m. the sanctity of the *Vedas*. *s.*

ويدابهياس वेदाभ्यास *vedābhyās*, m. study of the *Veda*; the repetition of the mystical syllable *om*. *s.*

ويدانت वेदान्त *vedānta*, m. the theological part of the *Veda*, as contained in the *Upanishads*; a a system of philosophy so called. *s.*

ويدانتي वेदान्ती *vedāntī*, m. a follower of the *Vedānta* *s.*

ويدانگ वेदाङ्ग *vedāng*, m. a sacred science subordinate to and in some sense part of the *Vedas*, such as grammar, prosody, astronomy, criticism. *s.*

ويدك वैदिक *vaidik*, scriptural, derived from the *Veda*; a Brāhman conversant with the *Vedas*. *s.*

ويدكا वेदिका *vedikā*, f. a kind of altar; a quadrangular space of ground prepared for sacrificial ceremonies, &c. *s.*

ويدكرم वेदकर्म *veda-karma*, m. }
ويدكريا वेदक्रिया *veda-kriya*, f. } any religious ceremony regulated according to the *Vedas*. *s.*

ويدگيه वेदज्ञ *veda-gya*, m. a Brāhman who knows the *Veda*. *s.*

ويدماتا वेदमाता *ved-mātā*, f. a sort of mystical prayer; *Gāyatrī*, personified as the mother of the *Vedas*. *s.*

ويدن वेदन *vedan*, m. }
ويدنا वेदना *vednā*, f. } pain, smart, agony. *s.*

ويدورج वैदूर्य *vaidūrj* or *vaidūrya*, m. the *lapis lazuli*. *s.*

ويدوكت वेदोक्त *vedokt*, scriptural, taught or declared in the Veda. *s.*

ويدوياس वेदव्यास *ved-vyās*, m. the Muni Vyāsa, the compiler of the Vedas. *s.*

ويده वेध *vedh*, m. perforation, piercing, depth (in measurement). *s.*

ويدهت वेधित *vedhit*, pierced, perforated. *s.*

ويدهك वेधक *vedhak*, sharp, piercing, a perforator. *s.*

ويدهنا वेधना *vedhnā*, a. to pierce, perforate. *s.*

ويدهني वेधनी *vedhnī*, f. a small gimlet. *s.*

ويدهي वेधी *vedhī*, piercing, perforating. *s.*

ويدي वेदी *vedī*, f. a kind of altar; m. a pandit, a learned Brāhman, a teacher. *s.*

ويديشك वैदेशिक *vaideshik*, foreign, strange; m. a stranger, a foreigner. *s.*

ويديه वैद्य *vaidya*, m. a doctor, a physician. *vaidya-nāth*, the head physician in *Indra's* court. *s.*

وير वीर *vīr*, m. a hero, a warrior, a champion; adj. heroic, mighty. *vīr-bhadr*, m. a distinguished warrior. *s.*

وير वैर *vair*, m. enmity, hostility. *ver* (v. *ber*), the egg-plant. *s.*

ويراگ वैराग *vairāg*, m. absence or suppression of worldly passions and affections. *s.*

ويراگي वैरागी *vairāgī*, m. an ascetic, a devotee. *s.*

ويراگيه वैराग्य *vairāgya*, m. absence of worldly desires; total subjection of the passions. *s.*

ويران *wairān* or *wīrān*, desolated, laid waste, depopulated, ruined; a village under the headman of another village. *wairān-kherā*, deserted site of a village. *p h.*

ويرانه *wīrāna*, m. a solitude, a deserted or desolated place. *p.*

ويراني *wairānī* or *wīrānī*, f. desolation, depopulation, destruction; a desert country. *p.*

ويرتا वीरता *vīratā*, f. (also *vīratwa*, m.) heroism, valour. *vairitā*, f. enmity, hatred. *s.*

ويرته व्यर्थ *vyarth*, useless, vain; unmeaning. *s.*

ويرتهتا व्यर्थता *vyarthatā*, f. inutility; nonsense, want of meaning. *s.* [(v. *virya*). *s.*

ويرج वीर्ज्य *vīrj* or *vīrjya*, m. strength, vigour

ويرني वैरिणी *vairinī*, f. } an enemy, a foe; adj.
ويري वैरी *vairī*, m. } hostile, inimical, rancorous. *s.*

ويريه वीर्य *vīrya*, m. strength, vigour, power, heroism, valour; *semen virile*; seed (of plants). *vīrya-wān* or *-vishisht*, strong, vigorous, courageous. *vīrya-virahit* or *-hīn*, devoid of power, cowardly, seedless, impotent. *vīrya-hāni*, f. loss of vigour or courage, impotence. *s.* [Hindūs. *s.*

ويس वैस *vais* (v. *vaishya*), the third class of

وبس वयस *vayas*, m. age, time of life. *s.*

ويسا वैसा *waisā*, like that, in that manner, so, that much. *waisā kā waisā*, such as before. *waisā-hī*, in that same way, even like that, such as that. *h.*

ويساكهه वैसाख *vaisākh* (v. *baisākh*), the name of a month. *s.* [month *vaisākh*. *s.*

ويساكهي वैसाखी *vaisākhī*, relating to the

ويساهي वैसाही *waisā-hī*, in that very manner, just such as that, even so. *h.*

ويست व्यस्त *vyast*, confounded, bewildered; spread, pervaded, penetrated. *s.* [rence. *s.*

ويستتا व्यस्तता *vyastatā*, f. agitation, inhe-

ويسر वेसर *vesar*, m. (also *veshar*), a mule. *s.*

ويسك वयस्क *vayask*, relating to age, aged. *s.*

ويسن व्यसन *vyasan*, m. vice, profligacy. *s.*

ويسين वैसें *vaiseṅ* or *waiseṅ*, freely, without cost. *s.*

ويسيه वयस्य *vyasya*, relating to age, aged; m. a contemporary, an associate. *s.*

ويسيه वैस्य *vaisya* (v. *vaishya*). *s*

ويش वेश *vesh* or वेष *veṣh*, m. ornament, dress, decoration. *s.*

ويشاكهه वैशाख *vaishākh*, m. the first month of the Hindū calendar (April-May). *s*

ويشاكهي वैशाखी *vaishākhī*, the day of the full moon in the month of *vaishākh*. *s.*

ويشتت वेष्टित *veshṭit*, surrounded, encompassed, wrapped up. *s.* [passing. *s.*

ويشتن वेष्टन *veshṭan*, m. surrounding, encom-

ويشدان वेशदान *veshdān*, m. the sunflower. *s.*

ويشدهاري वेशधारी *vesh-dhārī*, m. a hypocrite, a false devotee. *s.*

ويشر वेशर *veshar*, m. (also *vesar*) a mule. *s.*

ويشميه वैषम्य *vaishamya*, m. inequality, unevenness; solitariness, singleness. *s.*

ويشنو वैष्णव *vaishnav*, m. a follower of *Vishṇu*; adj. of or relating to *Vishṇu*. *s.*

ويشنوي वैष्णवी *vaishnavī*, f. name of a flower (*Clitoria tornatea*); sacred basil (*Ocymum sanctum*). *s.*

ويشي वैश्य *vaishya*, m. a Hindū of the third class, generally employed in trade and agriculture. *vaishya-kriyā*, f. the occupation, &c. of a *Vaishya*, commerce, agriculture. *s.*

ويشيني वैश्यनी *vaishyanī*, f. a woman of the *Vaishya* caste. *s.*

ويشيا वेश्या *veshyā*, f. a harlot, a whore; a plant (*Cissampelos hexandra*). *s.*

ويكال वैकाल *vaikāl*, m. evening, afternoon. *s.*

ويكانت वैकान्त *vaikānt*, m. a kind of gem said to resemble a diamond. *s.*

ويكت व्यक्त *vyakt*, wise, learned, evident, clear, specific. *vyakti*, f. individuality, appearance, person; manifestation; case, inflexion. *s.*

ويكت वेकट *vekaṭ*, m. a sort of a fish (perhaps the common *Bhekti*). *s.* [sion. *s.*

ويكليه वैकुल्य *vaikulya*, m. perplexity, confu-

ويكنته वैकुण्ठ *vaikunṭh*, m. name of *Vishṇu*; also the paradise of *Vishṇu* (v. *baikunṭh*). *s.*

ويگ वेग *veg*, m. speed, velocity; adj. or adv. quick, quickly. *s.*

ويگتا वेगिता *vegitā*, f. speed, quickness, rapidity. *s.* [tracted. *s.*

ويگر व्यग्र *vyagr*, bewildered, perplexed, dis-

ويگرتا व्यग्रता *vyagratā*, f. perplexity, anxiety. *s.*

ويگوان वेगवान *vegwān*, } swift, fleet, rapid;
ويگي वेगी *vegī*, } quickly, rapidly, speedily. *s.*

ويل *wail*, m. reprisal, revenge, retaliation. *wail-kash*, vindictive. *wail-kashī*, f. retaliating. *s.*

ويلا वेला *velā*, f. time, tide (v. *belā*). *s.*

ويلكشن वैलक्षन *vailakshan*, m. indifference, contrariety. *s.*

وين वेणु *veṇu*, m. a flute, a pipe. *veṇu-vād*, a flute-player. *s.*

وينا वीणा *vīṇā*, f. the Indian lute, a kind of guitar, usually having seven strings, and a large gourd at each end of the finger-board. *s.*

وينا वीना *wīnā*, m. a bundle of thread, a skein. *h.* [symbol. *s.*

وينجك व्यञ्जक *vyanjak*, m. a sign, mark,

وينجن व्यञ्जन *vyanjan*, m. sauce, condiment; a consonant. *s.*

وينچنا वैंचना *wainchnā* or *vainchnā*, } a. to
وينچهنا वैंछना *vainchhnā*, } skin. *h.*

وينك वैणिक *vainik*, m. lutist, a player on the *vinā*. *s.* [digit or *angul*. *s.*

وينگل व्यङ्गुल *vyangul*, m. the sixtieth part of

ويني वेणी *veni*, f. unornamented and braided hair; confluence of rivers. *s.*

ويو व्यव *vyava* or *vyav* (for *vi ava*), a compound particle denoting separation, division, &c., as *vyavachhed*, m. dividing, separating. *s.*

ويودهان व्यवधान *vyavadhān*, m. intervening, intervention, intermediate space. *s.*

ويودهايك व्यवधायक *vyavadhāyak*, adj. intervening, intermediate. *s.*

ويوسايه व्यवसाय *vyavasāya*, m. effort, exertion; industry, perseverance; plan, trick. *s.*

ويوسايي व्यवसायी *vyavasāyī*, active, energetic, engaged in business. *s.*

ويوستها व्यवस्था *vyavasthā*, f. separating; a decree; an engagement, a contract. *vyavasthā-patra*, a written extract from the codes of law, given as a decision by the Hindū law officers. *s.*

ويوستهاپك व्यवस्थापक *vyavasthāpak*, m. one who decrees or decides (in law). *s.*

ويوستهت व्यवस्थित *vyavasthit*, decreed, divided. *s.*

ويوكلن व्यवकलन *vyava-kalan*, m. subtraction. *s.*

ويوگ वियोग *viyog*, m. absence, separation. *s.*

ويوگي वियोगी *viyogī*, separated, absent; m. the ruddy goose. *s.*

ويوه व्यूह *vyūh*, m. military array, the arrangement of troops in various positions. *s.*

ويوهار व्यवहार *vyavahār*, m. usage, custom; business; practice of the courts, judicial procedure, law-suit. *s.*

ويوهارك व्यवहारिक *vyavahārik*, } customary,
ويوهاري व्यवहारी *vyavahārī*, } usual; litigant, being party to a suit; following one's ordinary pursuits. *s.*

ويوهاريه व्यवहार्य *vyavahārya*, to be observed or practised, customary, usual. *s.*

ويوهت व्यवहित *vyavahit*, placed near, intervening; concealed. *s.*

ويه *waih*, interj. well! bravo! *h.*

ويي व्यय *vyay* or *vyaya*, m. expenditure, expending; destruction, disappearance; the twentieth year of the Hindū cycle. *s.*

ه

ه *hā*, called *hā,i hawwaz*, and *hā,ī mudawwara*, the twenty-seventh letter of the Arabic alphabet, the thirty-first of the Persian, and thirty-fourth Hindūstānī; in reckoning by *abjad*, it counts five; in almanacks, it denotes Thursday and the sign *Virgo*, also the planet *Venus* and the moon.

ه ह *ha*, the corresponding letter in the Devanāgarī.

ه हि *hi*, (in Braj) a termination denoting the dative or accusative case; to, for; it is sometimes a contraction of the particle *hī*, q. v. denoting very, indeed, &c. *h.*

ها हा *hā*, an interjection of weariness, sorrow, pleasure, reproach, &c. *s.*

هابل *hābil*, } Abel, the son of Adam, and
هابيل *hābīl*, } brother of Cain. *a.*

هاپر हापर *hāpar*, f. a seed-bed (or rather nursery) for sugar-cane. *h.*

هاپنا *hāpnā* (for *hāmpnā*, q.v.), to pant, &c. *d.*

هات हात *hāt* (for *hāth*, q. v.), m. the hand. *hāt sūn jānā*, to be without choice, or helpless. *hāt kāṭnā*, to express regret, to grieve. *hāt men lapāt men dhar chāṭnā*, to squander, to lavish. *hāt mūn kā*, means, capital, stock. *s. d.*

هاتف *hātif*, crying, exclaiming; m. an angel; an encomiast; a voice from heaven, or from an invisible speaker. *a.*

هاته हाथ *hāth*, m. the hand; a cubit; possession, power. *hāth ānā*, to come into one's possession or power, to be obtained. *hāth uṭhānā*, to leave off, to refrain from, to desist; to salute by raising the hand to the head; both these meanings are alluded to in the following example: *hāth uṭhā jaur aur jafā se tū; yihī goyā salām hai terā*, restrain thy hands from violence and injustice; this is thy salutation; to beat; to give alms. *hāth oṭ lenā*, a. to receive with both hands open and stretched out together. *hāth-bāndhnā*, a. to join hands in a supplicating posture. *hāth baṛhānā*, to endeavour to get any thing; to gain possession of the property of others. *hāth band honā*, to be much engaged in business, to have no leisure; to be poor or indigent. *hāth bharnā*, to have the hands wearied or fatigued. *hāth baiṭhnā*, to acquire perfection in any art by practice. *hāth pāṅw phūl jāne*, to be distressed or confounded. *harek gul se wuh ṣūrat dekhī maḳbūl; ki mere hāth pāṅwoṅ sab gaye phūl*, from the sight of that countenance, more beautiful than any rose, all my senses were confounded (lit. my hands and feet were swelled). *hāth pāṅw phailānā*, to extend one's business or schemes. *hāth-pāṅw* or *-pair mārnā*, to strive, to endeavour, to strain, toil, to struggle; to be agitated; to sprawl. *hāth patthar tale dabnā*, to be helpless. *hāth par dharā rahnā ek chīz kā*, to be in readiness (spoken of things). *hāth paṛnā*, to come into one's possession. *hāth pasārnā*, to ask, to beg. *hāth pakṛe lejānā*, to hand a person. *hāth phūl*, m. name of a plant (*Pothos*). *hāth phernā*, to stroke, to caress, to coax. *hāth phenknā*, to fence. *hāth joṛnā*, to supplicate, to entreat earnestly. *hāth jhāṛnā*, to give, to bestow. *hāth jhūṭā honā*, to have the hands defiled; to lose the power of the hands. *hāth chāṭnā*, to relish any food exceedingly, to lick one's lips. *hāth-chālākī*, f. expertness. *hāth dhonā*, to be disappointed, to be hopeless. *hāth denā*, to concern one's self in or about; to make a bargain by taking hold of the hands of the other party under a cloth (a practice chiefly used in settling the price of horses and jewels). *hāth ḍālnā*, to interfere in; to encroach. *hāth roknā*, to prevent. *hāth-sameṭnā*, to refrain from giving, &c. *hāth ṣāf karnā*, to learn, practice, or exercise any art; to slay; to discharge from office. *hāth kānoṅ par rakhnā*, to be astonished; to deny vehemently. *hāth-karnā*, to subdue, to have possession. *hāth kamar par rakhnā*, to be very feeble. *hāth khainchnā*, to refrain, to desist, to abstain. *hāth lagānā*, to reprove, to punish, to torment; to be employed in any business. *hāth lagnā*, to be got, obtained, acquired. *hāth mārnā*, to promise; to acquire, to plunder; to wound with a sword. *hāth milānā*, to claim equality; to prepare to wrestle. *hāth mālnā*, to regret, to repent, to lament. *hāth meṅ rakhnā*, to possess, to hold in subjection. *hāthoṅ hāth*, out of hand, over hand, quick, expeditious. *hāthoṅ hāth lejānā*, to carry away quickly. *hāthī-hāth karnā*, to act in concord, to pull together. *s.* [power. *s.*

هاتها हाथा *hāthā*, m. the hand, possession,

هاتها بانهي हाथाबांही *hātha-bāṅhī*, } f. mutual
هاتها پاءي हाथापाई *hāthā-pā,ī*, } beating, fisticuffs. *hāthā-pā,ī-k.*, to box or beat mutually. *s.*

هاتهاپهچي हाथाफची *hātha-phachī*, f. name of a game. *s.*

هاتهاجوڙي हाथाजोड़ी *hātha-joṛī*, f. name of a plant (*Lycopodium imbricatnm*). *s.*

هاتهچٹهي *hāth-chiṭṭhī*, a letter or note written by the sender's own hand. *h.*

هاتهي हाथी *hāthī*, m. an elephant; the thirteenth lunar mansion. *hāthī-khāna*, an elephant stable. *hāthī-hangām*, remission (of rent, &c.) for losses arising from depredations by wild elephants. *hāthī-dāṅt*, m. ivory. *hāthī-wān*, an elephant-driver; the thirteenth mansion of the moon. *hāthī pāṅw*, elephantiasis, Barbadoes leg. *hāthī sūṇḍ kā pānī*, a waterspout at sea. *s.*

هاتهي چك हाथीचक *hāthī-chak*, name of a kind of grass, artichoke. *s.*

هاتي *hātī* (for هاتهي *hāthī*), an elephant. *d.*

هاتي هات *hāte-hāt* (for *hāthī-hāth*, q.v.), acting in concord. *d.*

هاٹ हाट *hāṭ*, } m. f. a market, a shop; a
هاٹه हाठ *hāṭh*, } fair, or moveable market. *s.*

هاٹو हाटू *hāṭū*, m. a market-man. *s.*

هاجي *hājī*, m. a satirical poet. *a.*

هادي *hādī*, m. a director, leader, guide. *a.*

هار हार *hār*, (in comp. means), the performer of any act, corresponding to the English terminations *er* or *ing*; thus, *bahār āyī na dekhan-hār āyā*; *anār āyā, na chākhan-hār āyā*, the spring is arrived, but no one is come to behold it; the pomegranates are ready, but there is no one to taste them. *h.*

هار हार *hār*, m. a necklace, a wreath, a chaplet; a flock (of cattle); pasturage; the cultivated space immediately round a village; a village common; (in arith.) a divisor, the denominator of a fraction; f. loss, forfeiture, discomfiture; being overcome. *hār-mānnā* or *mān-lenā*, to give up a dispute, to acknowledge all lost. *hār-jīt*, gambling, hazard. *hār-jīt-k.*, to gamble. *p. s.*

هارا हारा *hārā*, (in comp.) the performer of any act, or dealer in any article. It is often represented in English by the word *man*, as *lakaṛ-hārā*, a woodman, a woodcutter, a dealer in wood. *h.*

هارا हारा *hārā*, m. a necklace, wreath, chaplet. *s.*

هارج हार्ज *hārj*, m. *Beleric myrobalan*. *s.*

هارجيت हारजीत *hār-jīt*, m. gambling, hazard. *s.*

هارد हार्द *hārdd*, m. affection, kindness. *s.*

هارسنگار हारसिंगार *hārsingār*, m. the weeping nyctanthes. *s.*

هارك हारक *hārak*, m. a plunderer, a thief, a cheat, a rogue, a gambler; a tree (*Trophis aspera*); (in arith.) divisor. *s.* [pigeon. *s.*

هارل हारल *hāral*, m. (v. *hāriyal*) a kind of

هارنا हारना *hārnā*, n. to be overcome, to lose (in play). *hār-denā*, a. to squander, to gamble away. *s.*

هارو हारू *hārū*, m. a loser (in play). *s.*

هاروت *hārūt*, the name of an angel, who, together with another named *Mārūt*, having severely censured mankind before the throne of God, was sent down to earth to judge of the temptations to which man was subject. They could not withstand them: they were seduced by the planet Venus in form of a woman, for which they were suspended by the feet in a well in Babylon, where they are to remain in great torment until the day of judgment (v. *ḳur,ān*, chap. 2). *a.*

هارون *hārūn*, m. (for *ḥarūn*) wicked, refractory, roguish. *a.*

هارون *hārūn*, Aaron, the brother of Moses. *hārūn ar-rashīd*, the fifth *khalīfa* of the house of *'Abbās*, and twenty-sixth from *Muḥammad*. *heb.*

هاريل हारियल *hāriyal*, m. a name of a pigeon (*Columba hurriala*, *Buch.*); adj. of a green colour. *s.*

هاريه हार्य *hārya*, m. *Beleric myrobalan*; (participle) to be snatched away. *s.*

هاڙ हाड़ *hāṛ*, m. a bone. *hāṛ-joṛā*, m. name of a plant (*Cisus quadrangularis*). *hāṛ-lenā*, to examine the correctness of a pair of scales, or of weights and measures. *h.*

هاڙا हाड़ा *hāṛā*, a tribe of *rāj-pūts* so called. *h.*

هاس हास *hās*, f. laughing, laughter. *hās-har*, causing laughter, ridiculous. *s.*

هاستن हास्तिन *hāstin*, elephantine. *hāstin-pur* (also *hastināpur*), ancient Delhi. *s.*

هاسكا हासिका *hāsikā*, f. laughter, mirth. *s.*

هاسي हासी *hāsī*, laughing, smiling. *s.*

هاسيه हास्य *hāsya*, laughable; m. laughter. *s.*

هاضم *hāẓim*, loose, languid, relaxed; soft, gentle; digestive. *a.*

هاضمه *hāẓima*, (f. of *hāẓim*) digestive. *ḳu-wati hāẓima*, the digestive powers. *a.*

هال हाल *hāl*, m. a plough; adj. quick. *hāli*, f. a helm, a rudder. *s. h.*

هالا हाला *hālā*, f. wine, vinous or spirituous liquor. *h.* [earthquake. *s.*

هالاڈولا हालाडोला *hālā-ḍolā*, m. shaking; an

هالاهل हालाहल *hālāhal*, m. a sort of strong poison. *hālāhal-dhar*, m. a small black and highly venomous snake. *s.* [liquor. *s.*

هالاهلي हालाहली *hālāhalī*, f. wine, spirituous

هالك *hālik*, in a dying state; destructive, deadly. *a.*

هالگرا हालगरा *hālgarā*, land that retains moisture. *h.*

هالم हालिम *hālim*, m. cress, cresses (*Lepidium sativum*). *h.*

هالنا हालना *hālnā*, n. to shake, to be agitated. *h.*

هاله *hāla*, m. a halo or circle round the moon. *p.*

هالي हाली *hālī*, m. an agricultural labourer, a man employed for the duties of ploughing. *s.*

هامان *hāmān*, name of Abraham's brother; name of Pharaoh's *wazīr*. *a.*

هامن *hāmun*, هامون *hāmūn*, m. a desert, a plain, a level ground. *hāmūn-naward*, a traveller or wanderer of the desert. *p.*

هامي بهرنا *hāmī-bharnā* (corruptly for *ḥāmī-*, &c., q. v.), to consent, &c. *a. h.*

هان हान *hān* or हानि *hāni*, f. loss, deficiency, injury, slaughter. *s.*

هان हाँ *hāṅ*, interj. make haste! know! have a care! let it not be! far from it! *p.*

هان हाँ *hāṅ*, yes, verily, truly. *hāṅ kahnā*, to agree; contr. (of *yahāṅ*) here, hither, &c. *h.*

هانپنا हांपना *hampnā*, هانپهنا हांफना *hāmphnā*, n. to pant, to be out of breath. *h.*

هانڈا हांडा *hāṇḍā*, m. a cooking-pot. whether of clay or metal. *h.*

هانڈنا हायडना *hāṇḍnā*, n. to wander, to ramble. *h.*

هانڈي हांडी *hāṇḍī*, هانڑي हांड़ी *hāṇṛī*, f. a pot, a small cauldron. *s.*

هانس हांस *hāṅs*, m. a duck, a goose, a swan. *s.*

هانس *hāṅs*, m. the neck; the collar-bone: in old English and modern Scotch, "the halse or hauss." *s.*

هانسي हांसी *hāṅsī*, f. laughing, joking, ridicule. *s.*

هانك हांक *hāṅk*, f. cry, bawling, calling to (loud); driving. *hāṅk-pukār*, f. uproar, outcry. *hāṅk mārnā*, to bawl after, to call to. *h.*

هانكاهانك हांकाहांक *hāṅkā-hāṅk*, m. driving. *h.*

هانكنا हांकना *hāṅknā*, a. to drive: to bawl to. *h.*

هانكي हांकी *hāṅkī*, f. a vessel on which they make *siwa,iṅ* or vermicelli; a sieve. *h.*

هانگر हांगर *hāṅgar*, m. a shark. *h.*

هانهي हांही *hāṅ-hī*, هانهين हांहीं *hāṅ-hīṅ*, yes, yea, indeed, verily. *h.*

هاني हानी *hānī*, occasioning loss. *s.*

هاو हाव *hāw*, m. coquetry, blandishment, dalliance, airs. *hāw-bhāw*, m. charm, attraction, welcome, hospitality. *s.*

هاون *hāwan*, m. a mortar. *hāwan-kob*, m. one who pounds in a mortar. *p.*

ها‌ها हाहा *hāhā*, m. flattery; importunity, earnest request, supplication. *hāhā khānā*, to flatter, to wheedle, to entreat. *h.*

ها‌ها *hāhā*, m. laughing, ha ha! *hāhā-hīhī*, f. laughing. *hāhā-hīhī-k.*, to laugh. *hāhā jigī jigī*, an expression of approbation, also of earnest request. *h.*

ها‌ها हाहा *hāhā*, interj. alas! ah! *s.*

هاهاكار हाहाकार *hāhā-kār*, m. consternation; lamentation; the noise of battle. *s.*

هاي हाय *hā,e* or हायहाय *hā,e-hā,e*, interj. alas! alas! f. a sigh. *hā,e mārnā*, to sigh. *s.*

هائل *hā,il*, terrible, horrible, awful. *a.*

هائلات *hā,ilāt*, pl. things terrible, &c. *a.*

هاين हायन *hāyan*, m. year; a sort of rice. *s.*

هايه *hāya* (same as *hā,e*), alas! *d.*

هباڈبا हब्बाडब्बा *habbā-ḍabbā*, the whooping-cough. *h.*

هبڑا हबड़ा *habṛā*, ill-shaped, clumsy. *h.*

هبط *habṭ*, decrease (of price or bulk, &c.), falling. *a.*

هبل *hubal*, name of an ancient idol at Mecca, worshipped by the Arabs before the time of *Muḥammad*. *a.*

هبنق *habannaḳ*, m. a dwarf; a weak, silly person. *a.*

هبوب *habūb*, a furious wind. *a.*

هبوط *hubūṭ*, decreasing, &c. (v. *habṭ*). *a.*

هبه *hiba*, m. a gift. *hiba-nāma*, a deed of gift. *hiba-dār*, the receiver of a gift. *a.*

هپ हप *hap*, m. act of suddenly snatching with the mouth and swallowing. *hap-jhap*, quick. *hap-jhap khānā*, to eat quickly and voraciously. *h.*

هپهہپهانا हफहफाना *haph-haphānā*, n. to pant, to be out of breath. *h.*

هت हत *hat*, interj. begone! fie! m. multiplication. *h.*

هت हित *hit*, m. love, friendship, affection, benevolence, benefit; adj. suitable, proper, fit friendly, benevolent. *s.*

هت हुत *hut*, offered with fire; m. oblation. *s.*

هت *hat*, the hand (v. *hath* and its compounds). *d.*

هتك *hatk*, m. levity, affront, disrespect. *hatk denā*, to insult or affront a person by joking with him in an irritating manner, such as in England is vulgarly termed "chaffing." *a.*

هتكار हितकार *hit-kār*, هتكاري हितकारी *hit-kārī*, هتكر हितकर *hit-kar*, m. a friend; adj. kind, benevolent; benefactor. *s.*

هتكاري हितकारी *hit-kārī*, f. friendship, benevolence. *s.*

هتن हतन *hatan*, m. act of slaying. *s.*

هتنا हतना *hatnā*, a. to kill, to slaughter. *s.*

هتو हितू *hitū*, m. a friend, a benefactor. *s.*

هتو हुतो *huto* or हुतौ *hutau*, (Braj) was. *h.*

هتوان हितवान *hitwān*, friendly, beneficent. *s.*

هتوپديش हितोपदेश *hitopadesh*, m. friendly or salutary advice. *s.*

هتوٹي *hatoṭī*, f. } a hammer, an anvil, a
هتوڑا *hatoṛā*, m. } sledge hammer. *d.*
هتوڑي *hatoṛī*, f. }

هتهه हथ *hath*, m. (contr. of *hāth*, q. v.) hand, &c. *hathā-bāṅhen*, f. a set-to at fisticuffs. *hath-balī*, f. strength of hand, force; dishonesty. *hath-phūl*, m. a kind of firework. *hath-pher*, m. sleight of hand, especially a trick played by fraudulent dealers, who by sleight of hand substitute bad money for good when they receive it, and insist upon returning it to the payer.—N.B. The trick is most neatly done by a Frenchwoman who sells tobacco, &c. in this neighbourhood; borrowing. *hath pher-lenā*, to borrow. *hath-jholā*, m. a hand-barrow. *hath-chapū,ā*, m. snack, share. *hath-chhūṭ*, a beater. *hath-kaṭī*, f. name of a cut with the sword which is intended to take off or disable the adversary's hand. *hath-kaṛī*, f. a handcuff, fetter, manacle. *hath-tewā*, m. a ceremony in marriage among the Hindūs (the hands of the bride and bridegroom are joined palm to palm with some flour put between them, and tied with a red thread). *hath-nāl*, f. a small cannon carried on elephants, &c. *s.*

هتها हथा *hatthā*, m. a handle; a shovel, a baker's peel; a sleeve. *s.*

هتهرس हथरस *hathras*, m. amorous dalliance, toying; self-pollution, onanism *s.*

هتهري हथरी *hatharī*, f. a handle, a winch (of a spinning-wheel). *s.*

هتهکڑا हथकड़ा *hath-kaṛā*, m. manacle, handcuff. *h.* [custom, knack. *s.*

هتهکهنڈا हथखण्डा *hath-khanḍā*, m. habit,

هتهل हथल *hathal*, a handle of brass, &c. *h.*

هتهني हथनी *hathnī*, f. a she-elephant. *s.*

هتهوٹي हथौटी *hathauṭī*, f. dexterity, art, skill. *s.* [hammer. *s.*

هتهوڑا हथौड़ा *hathauṛā* or *hathoṛā*, m. a sledge-

هتهوڑي हथौड़ी *hathauṛī*, f. a small hammer. *h.*

هتهي हथी *hathī*, f. a brush for rubbing down horses with, or rather a hair glove; a rubber. *h.*

هتهيا हथिया *hathiyā*, m. the thirteenth mansion of the moon, *Corvus*; the breaking up of the rains. *hathiyā kī rāh*, the milky way. *s.*

هتهيار हथियार *hathiyār*, m. f. a tool, arms, implements, apparatus. *hathiyār-band*, armed. *hathiyār bāndhnā*, a. to arm. *s.* [hands on. *s.*

هتهيانا हथियाना *hathiyānā*, a. to seize, to lay

هتهياءي हथ्याई *hathyā,ī*, f. murder, slaughter. *s.*

هتهيلا हथेला *hathelā*, m. a thief, robber. *s.*

هتهيلي हथेली *hathelī*, f. the palm of the hand, or an impression of it. *hathīlī*, the handle of a plough. *s.*

هتيا हत्या *hatyā*, f. murder, slaughter. *s.*

هتيارا हत्यारा *hatyārā*, m. } a murderer, an as-
هتياري हत्यारी *hatyārī*, f. } sassin, a wretch,
a villain; adj. inhuman, bloodthirsty. *s.*

هتياءي हत्याई *hatyā,ī*, f. murder. *s.*

هتيشي हितैषी *hitaishī*, seeking another's welfare. *s.*

هٹ हट *haṭ*, f. insisting upon, obstinacy, perverseness. *haṭ-k.*, to insist upon; (in Dakh.) to be cross (as a child). *s.*

هٹ हट्ट *haṭṭ*, m. a market, a fair. *h.*

هٹا हट्टा *haṭṭā*, a large wooden shovel or ladle for watering the fields from acqueducts. *h.*

هٹاکٹا हटाकटा *haṭā-kaṭā* or *haṭṭā-kaṭṭā*, stout and active. *h.* [wards, to back. *h.*

هٹانا हटाना *haṭānā*, a. to repel, to drive back-

هٹتال हटताल *haṭtāl*, f. shutting up all the shops in a market (on account of oppression, &c.). *s.*

هٹاو *haṭā,o*, retreating, falling back. *d.*

هٹکانا हटकाना *haṭkānā*, a. to stop. *h.*

هٹکاهٹکي हटकाहटकी *haṭkā-haṭkī*, f. driving back; struggling. *h.*

هٹکنا हटकना *haṭaknā*, n. to be repulsed, to be driven back, to move, to stop. *h.*

هٹنا हटना *haṭnā*, n. to go back, to be driven back, to retire, to move, to shrink, to be defeated. *h.*

هٹوا हटवा *haṭwā*, m. a person employed in a market to measure rice, grain, &c. *s.*

هٹواءي हटवाई *haṭwā,ī*, f. the office of a *haṭwā*, q. v. *s.*

هٹهه हठ *haṭh*, m. violence, oppression, rapine; f. teasing; allegation; obstinacy, peverseness. *haṭh-dharmī*, perverseness, obstinacy. *haṭh-k.* or *haṭh kī tek par h.*, to resist or disobey obstinately, to be perverse or peevish. *s.* [ately. *s.*

هٹهات हठात *haṭhāt*, by chance; immedi-

هٹهر हट्ठर *haṭṭhar*, m. hurry, impatience. *h.*

هٹهرنا हठरना *haṭharnā*, n. to hurry, to be impatient. *h.* [or pettish. *s.*

هٹهنا हठना *haṭhnā*, n. to be peevish, perverse,

هٹهي हठी *haṭhī*, peevish, obstinate, perverse. *s.*

هٹهيلا हठीला *haṭhīlā*, teasing (child), pettish, perverse, peevish. *haṭhīle*, a class of reputed saints, one of whom is buried at Barech. *s.*

هٹي हट्टी *haṭṭī*, f. a petty market or fair (in Dakh.); a flock, a herd; a sheepfold, place where sheep or cattle are confined at night, a pound for cattle. *d.*

هتيا हटिया *haṭiyā*, f. market (v. *hāṭ*). *s.*

هجر *hajr*, m. } m. separation, disjunction, de-
هجران *hijrān*, } sertion of country or friends. *a.*

هجده *hajdah* (for *hazhdah*), eighteen. *hajdahum*, the eighteenth. *p.*

هجرت *hijrat*, f. } separation, departure from
هجره *hijra*, m. } one's country and friends; flight; the flight of *Muhammad* from Mecca to Madina (whence the *Muhammadan* era commences), which happened on the 16th of July, A.D. 622. *hajrat*, one year (*Gol.*). *a.*

هجري *hijrī*, of or belonging to the *hijrat*, q.v. *a.*

هجڑا हिजड़ा *hijṛā*, m. an hermaphrodite, a eunuch. *h.*

هجم *hajim*, m. driving in; repulsing; attacking suddenly; extirpation. *a.*

هجو *hajo* or *hajw*, f. satire, a lampoon, a pasquinade. *hajo maliḥ*, f. apparent praise but real satire, irony. *a.*

هجوم *hujūm*, m. a crowd, an assault, attack, impetuosity. *hujūm-k.*, to rush upon. *a.*

هجي *hajī* (also *hije*), m. spelling. *a.*

هچرمچر हचरमचर *hachar-machar*, m. dispute, cavil, excuse. *h.*

هچکا हचका *hachkā*, m. a jolt, shock. *h.*

هچکارا *hichkārā*, useless, bad. *p.*

هچکانا हिचकाना *hichkānā*, a. to jolt. *h.*

هچکچانا हिचकिचाना *hichkichānā*, n. to doubt, to hesitate, to be in suspense, to falter. *h.*

هچکچي हिचकिची *hichkichī*, f. hesitation. *hichkichī bāndhnā*, to gnash the teeth. *h.*

هچکنا हिचकना *hichaknā*, n. to draw back from, to decline, to shrink, to waver. *h.*

هچکولا हचकोला *hachkolā*, m. a jolt (of a carriage, &c.). *h.*

هچکي हिचकी *hichkī*, f. the hiccough; sobbing. *hichkiyān lenā*, to sob bitterly. *h.*

هد *hadd*, m. breaking, demolishing, ruining. *hidd*, liberal, a generous man. *a.*

هدا تدي کرنا हुद्दातुद्दीकरना *huddā-tuddī karnā*, a. to threaten mutually. *h.*

هدايا *hadāyā* (pl. of هديه, q. v.), presents, &c. *a.*

هدايت *hidāyat*, f. a guide or direction in the road to salvation. *a.*

هدف *hadaf*, m. a mark, a butt (for archers, &c.). *hadaf mārnā*, to strike the mark, to hit the nail on the head. *a.*

هدل *hudal*, a quagmire, a slough. *d.*

هدم *hadm*, m. ruin, destruction. *hadim*, a destroyer. *a.*

هده *huda*, a statement of estates to be sold by auction (Wilson's Gloss.).

هدهد *hudhud*, m. name of a bird (*hoopoe*). *a.*

هدى *hudā*, m. pointing out the right way. *hadī*, f. cattle carried to Mecca to be sacrificed; given as an offering; a bride; a captive. *a.*

هديارو हद्यारू *hadyārū*, a ring on the thumb. *h.*

هديانا हदियाना *hadiyānā*, n. to hesitate; to be alarmed, or apprehensive, to shrink. *h.*

هدياها हदियाहा *hadiyāhā*, sheepish, shamefaced, timid, bashful, scrupulous. *h.*

هدياهٹ हदियाहट *hadiyāhaṭ*, f. scrupulousness, sheepishness, shyness. *h.*

هديه *hadiya*, m. a present (particularly to superiors); the price of a *ḳur,ān*. *a.*

هڈ *haḍ* (v. *haṛ*), a bone. *haḍ-phūṭnā*, to make progress. *haḍ-jor* (v. *haṛ-joṛā*) name of a plant. *d.*

هڈا हड्डा *haḍḍā*, m. a wasp; a bone; spavin. *haḍḍe mothre nikālnā*, (lit.) to break out in spavins and œdematous swellings; (met.) to adopt an evil conduct. *s. h.*

هڈ پهوٹنا *haḍ phūṭnā*, to advance, to be promoted. *d.*

هڈي हड्डी *haḍḍī*, f. a bone; the hard part in the centre of a carrot or other similar root. *s.*

هڈيلا हड्डीला *haḍḍīlā*, bony, full of bones. *s.*

هذا *hāẕā* (for هاذا), this. *a.*

هذر *hazar*, m. nonsense, frivolous talk. *a.*

هذيان *hazyān*, m. raving, vain useless words. *a.*

هر *har*, every, any. *har ān*, constantly; whenever. *har ek*, each, every one. *har bāb*, every chapter, all sciences, every circumstance. *har-bābī*, master of knowledge of every kind. *har bār*, every time. *har-jā,ī*, a vagabond, a stroller. *har ḥāl*, howsoever. *har dil 'azīz*, beloved by every one, popular. *har dam*, every moment. *har dam khiyālī*, whimsical, capricious; *har degī chamcha*, a sponger, one who hangs on others for a maintenance. *har zamān*, every time. *har sāl*, every year, annually. *har gāh*, whenever; wherever. *har waḳt*, at all times, frequently, continually. *har yak*, every one. *p.*

هر हर *har*, m. a rogue, a wag; (for *hal*), a plough; a divisor, division. *har-bhog*, m. anarchy, confusion, uproar. *har-bhūm kā rāj* (also *har-bong kā rāj*), a country or place in which injustice prevails (v. Roebuck's Orient. Prov. part II. p. 187). *s.*

هر हर *har* or *hara*, a name of *Mahādeva*. *s.*

هر हरि *hari*, m. a name of *Vishṇu*. *hari-bhajan*, m. adoration of *Vishṇu*. *hari-bhakt*, a *Vaishnava*, or worshipper of *Vishṇu*. *hari-pairī*, f. a *ghāṭ*, or landing-place dedicated to *Vishṇu*. *s.*

هر *hirr*, m. a male cat. *a.*

هرا हुर्रा *hurrā*, m. dispersion (of an army, an assembly, &c.). general jail delivery. *harrā*, a sound, a voice, a shout. *h.*

هرا हर्रा *harrā*, m. name of an astringent nut, myrobalan (*Terminalia citrina*). *s.*

هرا हरा *harā*, green, fresh, verdant. *s.*

هراتر हरातर *harātar*, a place where the ploughs are working for the day. *h.*

هراتي हराती *harātī*, belonging to a plough. *h.*

هراج *harrāj* or *harāj*, running fast (a horse); m. a public sale by outcry, an auction. *harrāj-k.*, to sell by auction. *d.*

هرار हिरार *hirār*, raw, rare, fresh. *h.*

هراس *hirās*, m. fear, terror, dread. *p.*

هراسان *hirāsān*, frightened, frightening. *p.*

هراسيدن *hirāsīdan*, to fear; to frighten. *p.*

هرانا हराना *harānā*, a. to win, to overcome, to beat (at cards), to weary, to tire. *hirānā*, a. to lose, to mislay. *h.*

هرانكه *har-ān-ki*, who or whatsoever. *p.*

هراو *harā,o*, defeat (at cards, &c.). *d.*

هراول *harāwal* or *hirāwal*, m. the advanced guard of an army. *t.*

هراي हराई *hirā,ī* (for *halā,ī*), f. ploughing; the portion of land included within one circuit of a plough. *h.*

هراي हराई *harā,ī*, f. greenness, freshness, [verdure. *s.*

هراينه *har-āyina* or *har-ā,īna*, necessarily, undoubtedly, at all events. *p.*

هربرا हरबरा *harbarā*, m. the chick-pea. *h.*

هربونگ हरबोंग *har-bong*, same as *har-bhong*, q. v.

هربهجن हरिभजन *hari-bhajan*, m. adoration [of *Vishṇu*. *s.*

هربهكت हरिभक्त *hari-bhakt*, m. a worshipper of *Vishṇu*. *s.*

هربهوگ हरभोग *har-bhog*,
هربهوم हरभूम *har-bhūm*,
هربهونگ हरभोंग *har-bhong*, } m. the name of a very foolish *rājā*, or king noodle, said to have flourished once upon a time at Jhoonsee (also called *harbhong-pūr*), near Allahabad; he is proverbial for his stupidity and misrule, hence the expression "*harbaong-kā rāj*," or "*har-bhog-kā rāj*," is applied to signify civil disorder and maladministration in general, anarchy, confusion. For an entertaining account of the sayings and doings of *Harbhong*, v. Elliott's Glossary, p. 391. *s.*

هرپوجي हरपूजी *har-pūjī*, f. the worship of the plough, a ceremony held on the day when ploughing closes: the plough is washed and decorated with garlands, and to use it or lend it after this day is deemed unlucky. *s.*

هرپهاريوڑي हरफारेवड़ी *harphārewṛī*,
هرپهروري हरफरौरी *harpharaurī*, } f. name of a sour fruit, commonly called the "Indian gooseberry," although it bears no resemblance whatever to a gooseberry (*Averrhoa acida, Lin.*; *Cicca disticha Gmel.*, *Phyllanthus cheramela, Roxb.*). *s.*

هرت हरित *harit*, verdant, green, fresh; of a green colour. *s.*

هرتا हर्ता *hartā*, m. a thief, a depredator, [a spoiler. *s.*

هرتاشمن हरिताश्मन *haritāshman*, m. blue vitriol, a turquoise, an emerald. *s.*

هرتال हरताल *hartāl* or हरिताल *haritāl*, f. orpiment, yellow arsenic. *s.*

هرٹ हरट *haraṭ*, a Persian wheel for drawing water from a well. *h.*

هرٹكل हरटकुल *haraṭ-kul*, m. one of the subdivisions of *Gaur* Brāhmans. *h.*

هرج *harj*, m. tumult, sedition, confusion, loss, injury, harm; interruption. *harj-marj*, tumult, agitation, sedition. *a.*

هرجنس *har-jins*, grain of all sorts. *p. a.*

هرچند *harchand*, whensoever, howsoever, as often as, although. *p.* [although. *p.*

هرچندكه *harchandki*, notwithstanding that,

هرچندن हरिचन्दन *hari-chandan*, m. a yellow sort of sandal-wood. *s.* [happen. *p.*

هرچه بادا باد *harchi bādā bād*, let what will

هرحاصلي *har-ḥāsilī*, land bearing crops. *s. a.*

هرد हर्द *hard*, f. turmeric (*Curcuma longa*). *s.*

هرد ह्रद *hrad*, m. a pond, a tank, a lake. *s.*

هرد हृद *hṛid* or *hird* or हिरद *hirad*,
هردا हृदा *hṛidā* or हिरदा *hirdā*, } m. heart, mind, soul, life; the seat of thought and feeling, knowledge. *s.*

هردا हरदा *hardā*, m. mildew, smut (in corn). *h.*

هرداول हिरदावल *hirdāwal*, m. name of a defect (in horses). It is a feather or curling lock of hair on the breast, which is reckoned unlucky for the rider). *s.*

هردرا हरिद्रा *haridrā*, f. turmeric. *s.*

هردو *har-do*, each of the two, both. *p.*

هردوار हरिद्वार *haridwār*, m. a celebrated place of pilgrimage in the north of India, where the Ganges issues from the mountains (vulg. Hurdwar). *s.*

هردواس हरदुवास *harduwās*, a clan of *rāj-pūts* so called. *h.* [mound. *h.*

هردور हरिदौर *haridaur*, a kind of oblong

هردي हृदय *hṛidaya*, m. (v. *hṛid*) the heart. *s.*

هرديو हरिदेव *haridev*, m. name of an asterism; *srāvana*. *s.* [Hindūs. *h.*

هرديها हरदेहा *hardehā*, name of a tribe of

هرڈا हड़ा *harḍā*,
هرڑا हड़ा *harṛā*, } m. an astringent nut, myrobalan (*Terminalia chebula* or *citrina*). *s.*

هرزگي *harzagī*, f. nonsense, absurdity. *p.*

هرزه *harza*, absurd, nonsensical, frivolous, m. trifles, bagatelles. *harza-kār* or *harza-gard*, a foolish gossiping person, one who busies himself in trifles. *harza-go*, one who talks nonsense, an idle talker. *harza-gardī* or *-go,ī*, f. gossip, nonsensical chat. *p.*

هرس हरिस *haris* or *haras*, the tail of a plough; the beam of a plough. *s.*

هرسا हुर्सा *hursā*, m. a stone on which sandal-wood is ground. *s.*

هرسجا हरसज्जा *har-sajjā*, m. a sharer in a plough; reciprocal aid in ploughing a field. *h.*

هرسنگار हरसिंगार *harsingār*, m. the weeping nyctanthes (*Nyctanthes arbor tristis*). *s.*

هرسو ह्रस्व *hrasva*, short, low in stature; m. a dwarf; a short vowel. *s.*

هرسوت हरसोत *harsot*, the first furrow ploughed; the first ploughing of the season. *h.*

هرش हर्ष *harsh*, m joy, mirth, pleasure. *s.*

هرشت हर्षित *harshit*, } pleased, delighted,
هرشٹ हृष्ट *hrisht*, } happy. *hrisht-pusht*, well-conditioned, well fed and happy. *s.*

هرشنا हर्षना *harshnā*, n. to blow (as a flower); to be delighted. *s.*

هرشودي हर्षोदय *harshoday*, m. appearance or occurrence of joy or happiness. *s.*

هرفاليوري *harfāle,orī*, f. (see هرپهاريوڙي). *d.*

هرك हरक *harak*, m. a divisor, division. *s.*

هركا हरका *harkā*, m. crying, whining. *h.*

هركاره *har-kāra*, m. a running footman; a spy; messenger; a factotum. *p.*

هركانا हरकाना *harkānā*, a. to stop, forbid, prevent; (from the Arab. *harq*) to scorch. *h. a.*

هركٹ हरकट *harkat*, cutting rice while green and unripe. *h.*

هركجا *har-kujā*, everywhere; wherever. *p.*

هركدام *har-kudām*, whosoever, whichever. *p.*

هركنا हरकना *haraknā*, n. to stop; (for *haraknā*) to be scorched. *h.*

هركني हुरुकनी *huruknī*, f. a dancing-girl, a whore, a courtesan, a harlot. *h.*

هركه हरख *harakh* (for *harsh*), m. blowing, blooming; joy, delight, happiness, pleasure. *s.*

هركهت हरखित *harkhit*, }
هركهٹ हरखिट *harkhit*, } pleased, delighted. *s.*

هركهنا हरखना *harakhnā* or *harkhnā*, n. to blow (as a flower); to be delighted. *s.*

هركي हिरकी *hirkī*, f. shift, contrivance. *h.*

هركيا हरकिया *harkiyā*, snappish, peevish. *h.*

هرگاه *har-gāh*, whenever, wherever. *p.*

هرگز *hargiz*, ever, at any time, on any account. *p.*

هرگنڈا हुरगुण्डा *hurgundā*, m. name of a vegetable. *h.*

هرگني हरगुणी *har-gunī*, }
هرگوني हरगूनी *har-gūnī*, } skilful, clever. *p. s.*

هرگه *har-gah* (for *har-gāh*), whenever. *p.*

هرگهسيٹ हरघसीट *har-ghasīt*, all the cultivated land of a village. *h.*

هرگيلا हरगीला *har-gīlā*, m. a crane, called by Europeans "the adjutant bird" (v. *har-gilā*). *s.*

هرلا हरला *harlā*, *Terminalia chebula*. *h.*

هرلا हुरला *hurlā*, running away in terror. *h.*

هرم *harim*, old, decrepit; m. mind, understanding, intellect. *a.*

هرمز *hurmuz*, the isle of Ormuz in the Persian Gulf; name of several kings of Persia who reigned between A. D. 272 and the conquest of the kingdom by the *Muhammadans* in the seventh century. *p.*

هرمزي *hirmizī*, f. name of a red earth. *a.*

هرمشٹا हरमुष्टा *harmushtā*, stout, robust, active. *h.*

هرمشٹي हरमुष्टी *harmushtī*, f. robustness; thick-headedness. *h.*

هرن हरन *haran*, हरिन *harin*, or हिरन *hiran*, m. a deer (properly an antelope). *s.*

هرن हरण *haran*, m. abstraction, subtraction; plunder, sack; seizing, carrying off; the hand; *semen virile*; (in arithm.) division. *haran-dukh*, taking away or dissipating grief, anguish, or trouble. *s.*

هرنا हरना *harnā*, m. a stag, a buck, a male antelope; a. to seize on, to take forcibly; to steal, to spoil, to plunder. *s.*

هرنا हरना *harnā*, m. a pommel (of a saddle). *hurnā*, a. to beat down (as paviors). *h.*

هرنباڑي *haran-bārī*, f. (lit. fold or enclosure for antelopes) a house of correction, penitentiary. *d.*

هرنمن हरिन्मणि *harinmani*, m. an emerald. *s.*

هرنوٹا हरनौटा *harnautā* or *hirnautā*, m. a fawn. *s.*

هرني हरनी *harnī* or हरिणी *harinī*, f. a doe, a hind; a class of women, the same as *chatrinī*. *s.*

هرواها हरवाहा *harwāhā*, m. a ploughman, an agricultural bondsman. *h.*

هروتا हरौता *harautā*, the beginning of the ploughing season. *s.*

هروٹي हरौटी *harautī*, f. a cane, staff. *h.*

هروري हरौरी *haraurī*, f. the occupation of ploughing. *haraurī par jā,o*, go and put your hand to the plough. *harorī*, money lent by a cultivator to a ploughman. *h.*

هرول हरवल *harwal*, advances (without interest) made to ploughmen. *h.*

هره *hirra*, f. a she-cat. *a.*

هرها हरहा *harhā*, stray (an ox); unbroken and vicious cattle; plough-bullocks. *h.*

هرهر हुरहुर *hurhur* also *hurhura*, m. name of a plant (*Cleome viscosa*). *h.*

هرهفت *har-haft*, adorned, dressed; m. a narcissus. *p.*

هرهميش *har-hamesh*, perpetuity, for ever and ever. *p. h.*

هري हरी *harī*, m. (v. *harī*), a name of *Vishṇu*. *s.*

هري हरी *harī*, contribution of assistance by villagers in ploughing the fields of zamīndārs. *h.*

هريا *haryā* (v. *harā*), green, verdant. *d.*

هريا हरिया *hariyā*, m. a ploughman; a worshipper, a devotee. *h.*

هريالا हरियाला *hariyālā*, verdant, green, grassy; a small green bird commonly called the "flycatcher" (*Merops viridis*). *s.*

هريالي हरियाली *hariyālī*, f. verdure, greenness, name of a kind of grass called in Urdū *dūb*, q. v. *d.*

هريانا हरियाना *hariyānā*, n. to become green, to wax green; a. to stop, to prevent. *s.*

هريانو हरियांव *hariyānw*, a kind of division of the crop. *h.* [ness. *s.*

هرياول हरियावल *hariyāwal*, f. verdure, fresh-

هريتا हरीता *harītā*, } the first commencement
هريته हरीतः *harīta*, } of ploughing in the rainy season. *h.* [(*Terminalia chebula*). *s.*

هريتكي हरीतकी *harītkī*, f. yellow myrobalan

هرير हरियर *hariyar*, close of the sowing season. *h.* [verdant. *harīrā* (v. *harīlā*). *s.*

هريرا हरेरा *harerā*, m. a vegetable; verdure,

هريسه *harīsa*, m. a kind of thick pottage, made of bruised wheat boiled to a consistency; to which they add meat, butter, cinnamon, and aromatic herbs. *p.*

هريل हरियल *hariyal*, m. a green pigeon (*Columba hurriala, Buch.*). *h.* [a runaway. *s.*

هريلا हरीला *harīlā*, verdant, green; a coward,

هريوا हरीवा *harīwā*, m. a kind of parroquet. *h.*

هڑ हड़ *haṛ*, f. name of a nut (myrobalan); an ornament resembling that fruit; m. bilboes, the stocks. *h.* [the bones. *s.*

هڑ हड़ *haṛ*, m. a bone. *haṛ-phūṭan*, pains in

هڑ *huṛ*, ignorant; m. a fool, a simpleton. *d.*

هڑا हड़ा *haṛā*, m. a skyrocket. *h.*

هڑا *haṛṛā* (for *harrā*, q. v.). *huṛṛā*, raw or uncooked grain. *d.*

هڑاهڑي हड़ाहड़ी *haṛāhaṛī*, f. the twang of a bow. *huṛā-huṛī*, haste, precipitation. *h.*

هڑبڑانا हड़बड़ाना *haṛbaṛānā*, n. to be confused, to hurry. *h.* [riot. *h.*

هڑبڑي हड़बड़ी *haṛbaṛī*, f. hurry, alarm, uproar,

هڑبڑيا हड़बड़िया *haṛbaṛiyā*, easily agitated, irritable. *h.* [bones. *s.*

هڑپهوٹن हड़फूटन *haṛ-phūṭan*, m. pains in the

هڑجوڑا हड़जोड़ा *haṛ-joṛā*, m. name of a medicinal plant (*Cissus quadrangularis*). *h.*

هڑدنگا हुड़दङ्गा *huṛ-dangā*, turbulent. *h.*

هڑدنگي हुड़दङ्गी *huṛ-dangī*, f. turbulence. *h.*

هڑك हुड़क *huṛuk*, m. a kind of drum in form like a sand-glass (generally played on by bearers). *s.*

هڑكا हुड़का *huṛkā*, m. pining (particularly applied to children separated from parents); the bar of a door. *h.*

هڑكت हड़कत *haṛkat*, m. *Acanthus ilicifolius*. *h.*

هڑكيلا हड़गीला *haṛ-gīlā*, m. name of a bird, the gigantic crane (*Ardea argala*), commonly called the adjutant by Europeans in Bengal. *s.*

هڑنگا *haṛangā*, ruination, destruction. *d.*

هڑوار हड़वार *haṛwār*, } m. a place where bones
هڑواڑ हड़वाड़ *haṛwāṛ*, } are laid. *h. s.*

هڑهڑانا हड़हड़ाना *haṛhaṛānā* (also *hiṛhiṛānā*), n. to shudder, to shiver; to crash, to rattle. *h.*

هڑهڑاهت हड़हड़ाहत *haṛhaṛāhat*, f. a crack. sound. *h.*

هڑهڑي हड़हड़ी *haṛhaṛī* or हुड़हुड़ी *huṛhuṛī*, f. the twang of a bow. *h.*

هزار *hazār*, thousand. *hazār-chashma*, m. a cancer (disease). *hazār-dāstān*, a kind of nightingale, so called from the immense variety of its notes. *hazār-gā,īda* or *-mekhī*, a common strumpet. *p.*

هزارا *hazārā*, } a double flower; the balsam
هزاره *hazāra*, } flower; a divided stream or jet-d'eau (like that of a watering-pan). *p.*

هزاران *hazārān*, thousands; a nightingale; a term used at the game of *nard*. *p.*

هزارپا *hazār-pā*, a millipede or scolopendra. *p.*

هزاروان *hazārwān*, the one thousandth. *p. h.*

هزارها *hazārhā*, pl. (Pers.) thousands. *p.*

هزاري *hazārī*, m. the commander of a thousand; adj. relating to a thousand (used in comp.), as *yak-hazārī*, one who receives 1000 rupīs per month; a commander of one thousand. *hazārī-bazārī*, people at large, military and civil. *p.*

هزاريان *hazāriyān*, pl. regiments of a thousand men each, employed in the Northern Circars. *p.*

هزال *hazzāl*, m. a droll, a jester. *a.*

هزبر *hizbar*, m. a lion; adj. thick, strong, hard. *hizbar-jang*, the lion in fight, a man's name or title. *p.*

هزل *hazl*, m. a jest, a joke; (in law), a sham contract, in which the parties give a mutual pledge that it shall be of no effect. *hazl-go*, an idle talker. *a.*

هزليات *hazliyāt*, jests; nonsensical talk. *a.*

هزم *hazm*, flying, rout or flight (of an army). *a.*

هزيمت *hazīmat*, f. flight, rout, defeat. *hazīmat khānā*, to be defeated. *a.*

هژدهاتي *hazhdhātī* (v. *azhdhātī*). *s. p.*

هژده *hazhdah* (for *hasht-dah*), eighteen. *hazhdah hazār 'ālam*, the eighteen thousand living species, believed by the *Muḥammadans* to be the whole number of existing varieties of animals. *p.*

هس हस *has*, m. a consonant; (for *hañs*), a swan. *s.*

هس *has*, } (for *hañs*, *hañsā*) laughter. *d.*
هسا *hasā*, }

هسانا हसाना *hasānā* (prop. *hañsānā*), a. to make (one) laugh, to cause to laugh. *s.*

هساءي हसाई *hasā,ī*, f. (prop. *hañsā,ī*) ridiculing, laughing. *s.*

هست *hast*, f. being, existence; n. is, exists. *p.*

هست हस्त *hast*, m. the hand; a cubit. *s.*

هست हसत *hasat*, adj. laughing, smiling. *s.*

هست हस्ति *hasti*, m. an elephant. *hasti-dant*, m. ivory. *s.*

هست हस्त *hast*, } m. name of the thirteenth
هستا हस्ता *hastā*, } mansion of the moon, *Corvus.* *s.*

هستپال हस्तिपाल *hastipāl*, an elephant-keeper [or driver. *s.*

هستدنت हस्तिदन्त *hasti-dant*, m. elephant's tooth, ivory. *s.*

هستمد हस्तिमद *hasti-mad*, m. the juice that exudes from an elephant's temple when in rut. *s.*

هستنابود *hast-nābūd*, a remission of revenues for lands deficient in produce. *p.*

هستناپر हस्तिनापुर *hastinā-pur*, m. the name of the ancient capital of *Yudhishṭhira* and his brethren, the remains of which still exist about fifty-seven miles N. E. of the modern city of Dihlī, on the banks of the old channel of the Ganges. *s.*

هستني हस्तिनी *hastinī*, f. a female elephant (v. *padminī*) a description of women, the worst of the four classes. *s.*

هست و بود *hast o būd*, the present state of revenues, &c. compared with that of former years. *hast o būdī*, land which has been assessed on a comparative valuation. *p.*

هستي *hastī*, m. existence, entity; the world. *p.*

هستي हस्ती *hastī*, m. an elephant. *s.*

هسكا हिसका *hiskā*, m. imitation, copying; contention, rivalry, emulation. *h.*

هسكاهسكي हिसका हिसकी *hiskā-hiskī*, f. mutual emulation. *h.*

هسلي हसुी *haslī*, m. the collar-bone, clavicle; a collar (of gold or silver, &c.) worn round the neck as an ornament. *h.*

هسمكه *hasmukh*, cheerful, of a smiling countenance. *d.*

هسن हसन *hasan*, m. laughter, laughing. *hasnā*, to laugh, to smile. *s.*

هسي *hasī* (v. *hañsī*), sport, fun, &c. *d.*

هسيا हसिया *hasiyā*, m. a reaping-hook, a sickle. *h.*

هش *hush*, m. (for *hosh*, q. v.) understanding, care, attention, study. *h.*

هشت *hisht*, m. a hiss, &c.; interj. pish! [avaunt! *h.*

هشت *hasht*, eight. *hasht-bāgh*, the eight gardens, *i. e.* the eight heavens. *p.*

هشتاد *hashtād*, eighty. *hashtād-sāla*, a person eighty years old, an octogenarian. *p.*

هشتپهلو *hasht-pahlū*, } m. an octagon; adj.
هشتگوشه *hasht-gosha*, } of eight sides or angles. *p.*

هشتم *hashtum*, the eighth. *p.*

هشت‌مشت *husht-musht* (also *husht o musht*), f. wrestling and boxing. *p.*

هشت‌منظر *hasht-manẓar*, the eight heavens; the zodiac along with the planetary orbits. *p.*

هشتمي *hashtumī* or *hashtumīn*, the eighth (day or night). *p.*

هشتن *hishtan* (r. *hil*), to leave, to quit, to overlook. *p.*

هشدار *hush-dār*, have a care, look out. *p.*

هشيار *hushyār*, intelligent, prudent, cautious, abstinent, sober. *p.*

هشياري *hushyārī*, f. prudence, alertness. *p.*

هضم *haẓm*. m. digestion. *haẓm-āwar*, digestive. *haẓm-k.*, (met.) to embezzle. *a.*

هضميت *haẓmīyat*, digestiveness. *a.*

هفت *haft*, seven. *haft-iḳlīm*, the seven climes, *i. e.* the whole habitable world. *haft-andām*, the name of the great vein that runs through the arm. *haft-khwān*, the seven feasts given by *Rustam* on his way to *Māzandarān* (v. *shāhnāma*). *haft-rangī*, of seven colours; capricious, artful, cunning. *haft-ḳalam* seven sorts of Persian handwriting. *haft-ḳalamī*, one who writes the seven handwritings aforesaid. *haft-kishwar*, the seven regions, the world. *haft-hazārī*, m. a commander of seven thousand; f. the command of seven thousand. *haft-hasht*, abuse, idle talk, &c. *p.*

هفتاد *haftād*, seventy. *haftādum*, seventieth. *p.*

هفتدهم *haft-dahum* or *-dahumīn*, the seventeenth. *s.*

هفتم *haftum* or *haftumīn*, the seventh. *p.*

هفتگانه *haft-gāna*, seven times or sevenfold; adv. in or by sevens. *p.*

هفته *hafta*, m. a week. *hafta-dost*, slight acquaintance, an inconstant friend. *hafte-kā din*, Saturday. *p.*

هفئي *hafa,ī*, active, clever, alert. *h.*

هكا हिक्का *hikkā*, f. hiccough. *h.*

هكابكا हक्काबक्का *hakkā-bakkā*, confused (when any thing is to be done); aghast. *h.*

هكارنا हकारना *hakārnā*, a. to drive oxen or other cattle in a circle, as when treading out grain. *h.*

هكالنا हकालना *hakālnā*, a. (v. *hakārnā*) to drive, &c. *d.*

هكبكانا हकबकाना *hakbakānā*, n. to be confused or irresolute, to be aghast. *h.*

هكري हिकरी *hikrī*, cultivated reeds grown on low marshy grounds. *h.*

هكلا हकला *haklā*, stuttering, stammering. *h.*

هكلانا हकलाना *haklānā*, n. to stammer, to stutter, to falter. *h.*

هكلاها हकलाहा *haklāhā*, m. a stammerer. *h.*

هك‌هك كرونا हुकहुककररोना *huk-huk-kar ronā*, to burst repeatedly into tears. *h.*

هگاس हगास *hagās*, f. inclination to go to stool, tenesmus. *hagāsī baṭṭakh*, a restless, fidgetting person. *h.*

هگانا हगाना *hagānā*, a. to cause to go to stool. *h.*

هگ‌بهرنا हगभरना *hag-bharnā*, n. to be defiled (by fæces). *h.*

هگنا हगना *hagnā*, n. to go to stool. *h.*

هگنڈا हगण्डा *hagaṇḍā*, defiled with excrement. *h.*

هگنيٹي हगनेटी *hagneṭī*, f. a field to which people repair to ease themselves; *podex. h.*

هگوان *hagwān*, m. a diarrhœa, purging. *d.*

هل हल *hal*, m. a plough. *hal-jotā*, a tiller, a ploughman. *s.*

هل हल *hal*, m. the after-birth. *h.*

هلا हिला *hilā*, mud; a quagmire; moist ground trodden soft by cattle; adj. domesticated, tame. *hilā-milā*, amicable, attached. *h.*

هلا हल्ला *hallā*, m. uproar, tumult; assault. *hallā* (for *harrā*), the yellow myrobalan. *h.*

هلاس हुलास *hulās*, m. alacrity, joy, gladness. *s.*

هلاس हुलास *hulās*, f. snuff. *h.*

هلاك *halāk*, m. perdition, ruin, slaughter, death; adj. lost, fatigued, killed, dead. *halāk karnā*, to destroy, to overwhelm, to drive to destruction, to distress, to fatigue, to kill. *halāk honā*, to be killed, to be fatigued, to be tired. *a.*

هلاكت *halākat*, f. death, destruction; (in law) homicide, manslaughter. *a.*

هلاكلا हल्लाकल्ला *hallā-kallā*, m. loquacity, foolish talking. *h.*

هلاكو *halākū*, deadly; m. a destroyer. *a. h.*

هلاكي *halākī*, f. destruction, ruination. *a.*

هلال *hilāl*, m. the new moon, the first and last two or three days of the moon. *hilāl-daur*, a kind of bow. *a.*

هلالي *hilālī*, f. a kind of arrow; a segment of a circle; m. name of a Persian poet; adj. of or relating to the new moon. *s.*

هلانا हिलाना *hilānā*, a. to move, to agitate; to familiarize, to tame; to cause to swim. *h.*

هلاهل हलाहल *halāhal*, m. poison, especially deadly poison. *s. p.*

هلاوا हलावा *halāwā*, agitation, &c. *h.*

هلاءي हलाई *halā,ī*, f. ploughing. *s.*

هلاءيتا हलायता *halā,etā*, the first ploughing of the season, generally preceded by the taking of omens and other superstitious ceremonies. *s.*

هلبرار *hal-barār*, assessment according to the number of ploughs. *s. p.*

هلبل हलबल *halbal*, hurry, confusion. *h.*

هلبلانا हलबलाना *halbalānā*, n. to hurry, to be confused. *h.*

هلبلاهٹ हलबलाहट *halbalāhaṭ*, f. hurry, confusion (the effect of hurry). *h.*

هلبندي *halbandī* (v. *halbarār*), assessment according to the number of ploughs. *s. p.*

هلپنا हलपना *halapnā*, n. to toss, to tumble about, to shudder in a fever. *h.*

هل‌پهل हलफल *hal-phal*, f. affability; hurry, perturbation. *h.* [man. *s.*

هلجوتا हलजोता *hal-jotā*, m. a tiller, a plough-

هلتڈّي हलतड्डी *haltaḍḍī*, f. a drill plough. *h.*

هل‌چل हलचल *hal-chal*, f. fright, perturbation, hubbub, tumult, anarchy. *h.*

هلدا हलदा *haldā*, a disease of the *cerealia*, by which the plant withers and assumes a yellow tinge. *s.*

هلدار *hal-dār*, the possessor of a plough. *s. p.*

هلدهر हलधर *hala-dhar* or *hal-dhar*, m. a name of *Balarāma*, the elder brother of *Krishṇa*. *s.*

هلدي हलदी *haldī*, f. turmeric (*Curcuma longa*); a marriage ceremony of anointing the parties with turmeric. *s.*

هلديا हलदिया *haldiyā*, m. a kind of poison; the jaundice; a class of merchants; adj. yellow. *s.*

هلرا हलरा *halrā*, m. a wave or billow. *h.*

هلراونا हलरावना *halrāwnā*, a. to amuse, to play with, to dandle. *h.*

هلڑ हुल्लड़ *hullaṛ*, m. alarm, tumult, uproar, commotion, bustle, disturbance. *h.*

هلس हलस *halas*, the beam of a plough. *h.*

هلسا हिलसा *hilsā*, f. name of a fish (*Clupea alosa*). *s.*

هلساري हलसारी *halsārī*, f. (v. *halbarār*). *s.*

هلسانا हुलसाना *hulsānā*, a. to cheer, to rejoice. *s.*

هلسنا हुलसना *hulasnā*, n. to be rejoiced, pleased, delighted. *s.*

هلكا हलका *halkā*, light (in weight or character), debased, mean; silly, easy, soft, cheap. *halkā-pan*, m. lightness, levity (of conduct); vanity, despicableness. *halkā jānnā*, to disdain, to disesteem. *halkā karnā*, to lighten, to assuage; to abase, to affront. *h.*

هلكارنا हुलकारना *hulkārnā*, a. to set on (as a dog on a bull), to instigate, to halloo on. *h.*

هلكان *halkān*, confounded, confused, tired, wearied. *a.*

هلكانا हलकाना *halkānā*, a. to abet, to lighten. *h*

هلكاءي हलकाई *halkā,ī*, f. lightness, levity. *h.*

هلك رهنا हिलकरहना *hilak-rahnā*, to cling to. *h.*

هلكنا हिलकना *hilaknā*, n. to writhe or suffer contortions (from affliction or pain, chiefly applied to children); (in Dakh.) *hulaknā*, to rush on, to attack, to charge. *h.* [billow. *s.*

هلكور हिलकोर *hilkor*, f. agitation; a wave,

هلكورا हिलकोरा *hilkorā*, m. a wave, billow. *s.*

هلكورنا हलकोरना *halkornā* or हिलकोरना *hilkornā*, a. to gather, to collect; to billow, to wave. *hilkornā*, n. to agitate, to shake, to disturb, to perplex; n. to fluctuate, to waver. *s.*

هلكوره *hilkora* (v. *hilkorā*), m. a wave, billow. *s.* [pend. *h.*

هلگانا हिलगाना *hilgānā*, a. to hang, to sus-

هلگنا हिलगना *hilagnā*, n. to be hung on, to be entangled, to adhere, to stick to; to be constant. *h.*

هلگي हलगी *halgī*, gently, softly; (in Dakh.) f. a small kind of drum. *h.*

هلمل جانا हिलमिलजाना *hil-mil jānā*, n. to be mixed; n. to be intimate; to be jumbled together. *h.*

هلموچكا हिलमोचिका *hilmochikā*, } f. a potherb
هلموچي हिलमोची *hilmochī*, } (*Hingtsha repens*). *s.*

هلن हिलन *hilan*, m. motion, agitation; (in Dakh.) *halan*. *h.*

هلنا हिलना *hilnā*, n. to shake, to be moved; to be familiarized, to be tamed. *hil-milnā*, to meet together. *h.*

هلو *hallū*, slowly, easily, gently. *d.*

هلوءا हलुआ *halū,ā*, battered (as a whore). *h.*

هلواها हलवाहा *halwāhā*, m. a ploughman. *s.*

هلواهي हलवाही *halwāhī*, f. tillage, agriculture. *s.* [wave, billow. *s.*

هلورا हलोरा *halorā* or हिलोरा *hilorā*, m. a

هلورنا हलोनेा *halornā*, a. to collect, to gather. *h.*

هلورنا हिलोरना *hilornā*, n. to billow, to wave. *s.*

هلوري مارنا हिलोरी मारना *hilorī mārnā*, a. to heave, to rise (as the sea). *h.* [roar. *a.*

هله *halla* (for *ḥamla*), m. an assault; an up-

هله *halla*, a kind of necklace. *d.*

هلهل हुलहुल *hulhul*, m. name of a plant (v. *hurhur*); snow. *h. s.* [poison. *p. s.*

هلهل हलहल *halhal* or *halhil*, m. a mortal

هلهلا हलहला *halhalā*, m. poison, venom. *p.s.*

هلهلاٹ हलहलाट *halhalāṭ*, m. trembling through fever or fear. *h.*

هلهلانا हलहलाना *halhalānā*, a. to shake (from the effect of an ague, &c.), to tremble; a. to shake, to cause to tremble. *h.* [ague. *h.*

هلهلي हलहली *halhalī*, f. sickness, disease; an

هلهليا हलहिलया *halhaliyā*, m. poison. *s.*

هلي हली *halī*, a ploughman. *s.*

هليا हलिया *haliyā*, m. a herd (of oxen), drove, flock (of cows). *h.*

هلياك हलियाक *haliyāk*, also *haliyāg*, wages of ploughmen. *s.*

هليانا हलियाना *haliyānā*, n. to nauseate. *h.*

هليدن *hilīdan*, to quit; to leave alone; to omit. *p.*

هليسه *halīsa*, m. an oar. *p.* [(v. *harrā*). *a. p.*

هليله *halela*, m. name of an astringent nut

هليون *halyūn* or *haliyūn*, asparagus. *p.*

هم हम *ham*, pron. first pers. plur. we. *s.*

هم *hamm*, m. grief, care, solicitude; turning a thing anxiously in the mind. *hum* (Arab.), affixed pron. 3rd pers. pl. them, of them. *a.*

هم *ham*, also, even, likewise, in the same manner, equally; (in comp.) together with, the same as, mutual, as *ham-āshyān*, of the same nest, intimate, birds of a feather. *ham-āghosh*, embracing, locked in each other's arms. *ham-āghoshī*, f. embrace. *ham-āwāz*, concordant, harmonious. *ham-āwez*, an equal, a rival. *ham-āhang*, harmonious, concordant. *ham-bazm*, of the same society, associating together. *ham-bistar*, sleeping together, lying on the same bed. *ham-pā*, a companion, an attendant. *ham-palla* or *-pahlū*, a partisan, peer, partner. *ham-piyāla*, pot companion. *ham-pesha*, of the same trade. *ham-tarāzū*, of equal weight, fairly matched. *ham-ta'līm*, a fellow student. *ham-jalīs*, an intimate companion. *ham-jins*, congener, of the same species. *ham-jamb*, sitting together, a friend. *ham-jāt*, of the same caste or tribe. *ham-jawār*, a townsman, a neighbour. *ham jolī*, equal, peer, coeval. *ham-chashm*, equal. *ham-chashmī*, f. equality, rivalry. *ham-chashmī-k.*, to contend. *ham-khāna*, a fellow-lodger, a companion, a spouse. *ham-khwāba*, a bedfellow, a spouse. *ham-dāstān*, being in the same story. *ham-dabistān*, a schoolfellow. *ham-dard*, a partner in adversity, sympathetical. *ham-digar*, together. *ham-dil*, loving, of the same inclination, a friend. *ham-dam*, a friend, a companion. *ham-rāz*, acquainted wth one another's secrets. *ham-rāe*, of one purpose; an accomplice, or confederate. *ham-zād*, of the same age, a playfellow; a *jin*, which is said to be produced at the moment of the birth of every child, and to accompany him through life. *ham-zānū*, sitting together, a companion. *ham-zulf*, a wife's sister's husband (v. *sāṛhū*). *ham-sāya*, a neighbour, neighbouring. *ham-sabaḳ*, a class-fellow. *ham-sarī*, equality, evenness. *ham-safra*, a fellow-traveller. *ham-sang*, of the same weight, fairly matched *ham-sinn*, of equal age, a playfellow. *ham-shakl*, of the same appearance, alike, resembling. *ham-shahr* or *ham-shahrī*, a townsman. *ham-shīra*, a sister. *ham-ṭabaḳ*, a messmate. *ham-'inān*, a companion, associate, peer, equal. *ham-'akd*, coeval, contemporary. *ham-ḳadd*, of equal stature. *ham-ḳadam*, a companion, attendant, footman. *ham-ḳaum*, of the same tribe. *ham-kāsa*, a cup companion. *ham-kufū*, of the same family. *ham-kinār*, embracing. *ham-gap*, a gossip. *ham-maghab*, of the same religion. *ham-maṣlaḥat*, confederated. *ham-maktab*, a schoolfellow. *ham-nām*, a namesake. *ham-nidā*, singing together, singing in concord. *ham-nasl*, of the same breed. *ham-nishīn*, a companion. *ham-namak* or *ham-niwāla*, a messmate. *ham-nawā,ī*, a fellow songster. *ham wazn*, of equal weight. *ham-waṭan*, a compatriot. *p*

هم हिम *him*, m. frost, snow, cold; name of the fifth or cold season. *him-kar* or *him-wat*, frigorific, cold, chill, frosty. *s.*

هما हुम्मा *hummā*, m. the sudden influx of the tide at new and full moon in the river Hoogly, called by Europeans "the *bore*" (why? I know not). *h.*

هما *humā*, m. an eagle, a phœnix, a bird of paradise; a fabulous bird of happy omen peculiar to the East. It is supposed that every head it overshadows will wear a crown (v. *'anḳā*). *p.*

هماتم *hamātam*, } equality, rivalry, competition. *d.*
هماتمي *hamātamī*, }

همارا हमारा *hamārā*, pron. (gen. pl. of *main*) ours, our. *h.*

همارو हमारौ *hamārau*, (Braj) our, of us. *h.*

هماشما *hamā-shumā*, we two, we both. *h. p.*

همال *hamāl* or *humāl*, alike, equal, resembling; a peer, a companion; a friend, a confidant. *p.*

هماليه हिमालय *himālaya* or *himālay*, m. (lit. the abode of snow), the name of the snowy range of mountains which bounds India to the north-east. *s.*

همان *ham-ān*, even this, or that. *p.*

همانا *hamānā*, m. the opinion, imagination; adj. like, resembling; immediately, suddenly; ditto, the same thing repeated, as before, again. *p.*

هماندم *ham-ān-dam*, } that instant, at that very moment. *p.*
همانگاه *ham-ān-gāh*, }

هماوتي हिमावती *himāwatī*, f. a sort of moon-plant. *s.*

همائي *humā,e*, m. (v. *humā*) queen Humā,ī (grandmother to Dārāb II.). *humā,ī*, of or relating to the *humā*; fortunate, auspicious. *p.*

همايون *humāyūn*, fortunate, august, sacred, royal, imperial. *humāyūn-fāl*, of auspicious omen. *humāyūn-gāh*, the royal residence. *hamāyūn-nāma*, name of a version of Pilpay's fables in the Turkish language. *p.*

همت *himmat*, f. spirit, inclination, resolution, bravery, liberality, courage, purpose, design; auspices, favour. *himmat khwāstan*, to ask a blessing. *a.*

همتا *hamtā*, equal, alike; m. a fellow, match or equal. *p.*

همتائي *hamtā,ī*, f. likeness, equality. *p.*

همتي *himmatī*, bold, daring, courageous. *a.*

همچنان *ham-chun-ān*, in that manner. *p.*

همچنين *ham-chun-īn*, in this manner. *p.*

همچو *ham-chū*, even as, like, such as. *p.*

همدان *hamadān*, name of a town of Persian Irāḳ, north-west of Ispahān. *p.*

همدست *ham-dast*, in hand. *ham-dast-k.*, to procure, to get, to obtain. *ham-dast-h.*, to be found, got, or procured. *p. h.*

همراه *hamrāh*, m. a fellow-traveller; prep. with, together with, along with. *p.*

همراهي *hamrāhī*, f. companionship in travelling; a travelling companion. *p.* [&c. *s.*

همره *hamrah* (v. *ham-rāh*), a fellow-traveller,

همزت *hamzat*, } the symbol *hamza* (v. Hind. or Pers. gram.). *a.*
همزه *hamza*, }

همكر हिमकर *himkar*, frigorific, cold. *s.*

همكن *ham-kun*, a companion, colleague. *p.*

همكنا हुमकना *humaknā*, n. to assault, to stretch forward. *h.*

همگي *hamagī*, f. totality; the whole, all. *p.*

همن हमन *haman*, } we, us, to us. *s. h.*
همنا हमना *hamnā*, }

هموار *hamwār*, plain, equal, level; proper, suitable, fit; gentle, easy, docile. *p.*

همواره *hamwāra*, always, continually. *p.*

همواري *hamwārī*, f. (abst. of *hamwār*, in comp.) *p.*

هموت हिमवत *himwat*, cold, frosty. *s.*

همه *hama*, all, the whole, every one. *hama-dān*, knowing everything, experienced, wise. *p.*

هميانى *hamyānī*, f. a purse. *p.*

هميدون *hamīdūn*, now; always; in this manner, at this moment. *p.*

هميشگي *hameshagī*, f. perpetuity, eternity. *p.*

هميشه *hamesha*, always, ever, continually, perpetually. *p.*

همين हमें *hamen*, us, to us. *hamīn*, we ourselves, even we. *h.*

همين *hamīn*, this very, even this, even so. *p.*

هميني हिमेनी *himenī*, f. (v. *hamiyānī*) a purse. *d.*

هميو हमेव *hame,o*, m. vanity, egotism, arrogance, pride. *s.*

هن हुन *hun*, f. name of a coin; a pagoda. *h.*

هنا हनना *hannā*, a. to kill, to give a blow. *s.*

هنا *hannā*, m. the pommel of a saddle. *d.*

هنپهنا हंफना *hamphnā*, n. to be out of breath, to pant. *h.*

هنپهيل हंफैल *hamphail*, short-winded. *h.*

هنتا हन्ता *hantā*, m. a murderer, a slayer. *s.*

هنتال हिन्ताल *hintāl*, m. the marshy date-tree (*Phœnia paludosa*). *s.*

هنجار *hanjār*, m. a straight road, a true method; a mason's rule, a plumb-line, a level, &c. *nā-hanjār* astray, wicked, unfortunate, rude, unpolite. *p.*

هند *hind*, m. India, an Indian. *a. p.*

هندبا *hindbā*, *hindibā*, and *hindubā*, m. name of a white seed, endive (*Cichorium endivia*). *p.*

هندسان *hindsān*, } (for *hindūstān*), India. *p.*
هتدستان *hindustān*, }

هندسه *handasa*, m. the science of geometry. *hindasa*, numeration by the letters of the alphabet, arithmetic. *a.*

هندني हिन्दनी *hindnī* or *hindanī*, f. an Indian female. *h. p.*

هندو *hindū*, m. a negro; a black Arabian, Indian, or Ethiopian; a Gentoo; an infidel; (met.) a mole or lock (of a mistress). *a. p.*

هندوان हिन्दुवान *hinduwān*, a species of fruit. *h.*

هندوانه *hindwāna* or *hinduwāna*, m. a water-melon, a kind of pumpkin. *p.*

هندورنا हिंदोरना *hindornā*, a. to puddle. *h.*

هندوستان *hindūstān*, m. India (particularly applied to the Upper Provinces). *p.*

هندوستاني *hindūstānī*, of or relating to India, the language of that country; a native of India. *p.*

هندول हिन्दोल *hindol*, m. a swing; a musical mode. *s.*

هندوي *hinduwī*, of or relating to the blacks, Indian, Hindū; an old Indian dialect. *hunduwī*, a bill of exchange. *p. h.*

هندي *hindī*, Indian, relating to India; the dialect of the Hindūs so called. *p.*

هنڈا हण्डा *hanḍā*, m. a caldron. *hanḍā phoṛnā*, (lit. to break the pot), to disclose a secret, to let the cat out of the bag. *s.*

هنڈا हण्डा *hanḍā*, a species of grass. *h.*

هنڈابھاڑا हुण्डाभाड़ा *hunḍā-bhāṛā*, m. contract for transportation of goods, including the payment of duties. *h.*

هنڈار हुण्डार *hunḍār*, m. a wolf. *h.*

هنڈانا हण्डाना *hanḍānā*, a. to banish, to expel, to drive out of a city, to disgrace (by public punishment); to move round. *h.*

هنڈاون हुण्डावन *hunḍāwan*, m. exchange, or price paid for a bill of exchange. *s.*

هنڈکا हण्डिका *hanḍikā*, f. an earthen pot. *s.*

هنڈن हिण्डन *hinḍan*, m. wandering, roaming; copulation. *s.*

هنڈول हिंडोल *hinḍol*, m. name of a *rāg* or musical mode, sung in the morning of spring. *s.*

هنڈولا हिंडोला *hindolā* or *handolā*, m. a swing, a cradle; a song describing the swing, and sung during that exercise. *s.*

هنڈوي हुण्डवी *hunḍawī*, } f. a bill of exchange,
هنڈي हुण्डी *hunḍī*, } a money-order. *hunḍī-darsanī*, a bill payable at sight. *hunḍī mi'ādī*, a bill payable after a stipulated interval. *hunḍī-wāl*, an exchange-merchant. *s.*

هنڈھ हुंढ *hunḍh*, mutual assistance in tillage. *h.*

هنڈي हण्डी *hanḍī*, f. an earthen pot or boiler. *s.*

هنڈيان हुण्डियान *hunḍiyān*, m. exchange, or price paid for a bill of exchange. *s.*

هنڈير हिण्डीर *hinḍīr*, m. cuttle-fish bone; a tonic, a stomachic. *s.*

هنڈيوال हुण्डीवाल *hunḍīwāl*, m. an exchange-merchant. *s.*

هنر *hunar*, m. skill, ingenuity, virtue; an art or handicraft. *hunar-band*, *-dār*, *-mand*, or *-war*, f. clever, skilful. *hunar-mandī*, &c., skilfulness, dexterity, accomplishments. *p.*

هنرمندانه *hunar-mandāna*, skilfully, cleverly. *p.*

هنري *hunarī*, clever, skilful. *p.*

هنس हंस *hans*, m. a swan, a goose, a duck; (met.) life. *s.*

هنس हनस *hanas*, the beam of a plough. *h.*

هنسا हंसा *hansā*, m. laughing, laughter. *s.*

هنسا हिंसा *hinsā*, f. injury, mischief, slaughter. *s.*

هنسال हिंसालु *hinsālu*, mischievous, hurtful. *s.*

هنسانا हंसाना *hansānā*, a. to cause to laugh, to tickle. *s.*

هنساءي हंसाई *hansā,ī*, f. laughter, derision. *s.*

هنسر हिंस्र *hinsr*, hurtful, murderous, savage. *s.*

هنسراج हंसराज *hansrāj*, a kind of herb so named, used medicinally; a species of rice. *s.*

هنسرك हिंस्रक *hinsrak*, m. a beast of prey. *s.*

هنسك हंसक *hansak*, m. the flaminga. *hinsak*, mischievous, ferocious; m. a beast of prey: an enemy. *s.*

هنسگامني हंसगामिनी *hans-gāminī*, } walking
هنسگمني हंसगमनी *hans-gamanī*, } gracefully as a swan (a woman). *s.*

هنسلي हंसली *hanslī*, f. the collar-bone; a collar (of gold or silver, &c.) worn round the neck as an ornament. *h.*

هنسمكھ हंसमुख *hans-mukh*, cheerful, merry, laughing, facetious, jolly. *s.*

هنسن हिंसन *hinsan*, injuring, hurting. *s.*

هنسنا हंसना *hansnā*, n. to laugh, to smile. *s.*

هنسوءا हंसुआ *hansu,ā*, m. a sickle. *h.*

هنسوڑ हंसोड़ *hansoṛ*, facetious, merry, cheerful; (sub.) a wag. *hansoṛ-pan*, m. facetiousness. *s.*

هنسي हंसी *hansī*, f. sport, fun, laughter, mirth, ridicule. *s.*

هنسيا हंसिया *hansiyā*, m. sickle, a reaping-hook. *h.*

هنكاٹا *hankāṭā*, m. a shout, a noise. *d.*

هنكار हुङ्कार *hunkār*, m. uttering a menacing sound, roaring, bellowing. *s.*

هنكار हंकार *hankār*, } m. cry, outcry,
هنكارا हंकारा *hankārā*, } alarm. *s.*

هنكارنا हंकारना *hankārnā*, a. to drive away, to expel; to bawl to, to call; to hoist (sails, &c.). *h.*

هنکاري हंकारी *hankārī*, proud, egotistical. *s.*

هنکالنا *hankālnā*, } a. to drive, &c. (v.
هنکانا हंकाना *hankānā*, } *hānknā*). *d.*

هنگ *hang*, m. the understanding, wisdom. *p.*

هنگ हिङ्गु *hingu*, m. assafœtida. *s.*

هنگام *hangām*, m. season, time, period. *p.*

هنگامه *hangāma*, m. an assembly, a crowd; tumult, uproar, riot; assault. *hangāma-karnā* or *machānā*, to raise a disturbance. *hangāma-gīr*, tumultuous. *p.*

هنگامي *hangāmī*, extra, temporary; a deputy, a person employed to act temporarily for another. *p.*

هنگفت *hanguft*, thick, dense; cloth of a firm texture. *p.*

هنگل हिङ्गुल *hingul*, m. vermilion. *s.*

هنگلاج हिंगलाज *hinglāj*, m. a temple of *Devī*, a place of pilgrimage. *s.*

هنگن *hingan*, m. a kind of firework. *d.*

هنمان हनुमान *hanumān*, m. (v. *hanūmān*), a baboon, &c. *s.*

هنمت *hanamat* (v. *hanūmān*). *hanamat kī dum honā*, to be long or lengthy (as the tail of *Hanūmān*). *d.*

هنن हनन *hanan*, m. killing, injuring; multiplication. *s.*

هننا हनना *hannā*, a. to kill, to smite. *s.*

هنوتا हिनौता *hinautā*, m. supplication, humility. *s.*

هنود *hunūd* (pl. of هند or هندو), the Hindūs. *a.*

هنوز *hanoz*, yet, hitherto, still. *hanoz dillī dūr hai* ("it is a far cry to Loch Awe") is used to express that the conclusion of an affair is far distant. *p. h.*

هنومان हनुमान *hanūmān*, m. a monkey; the name of the monkey who headed *Rāma's* forces against *Rāvana*. *s.*

هنوماني हनुमानी *hanūmānī*, of or relating to *hanūmān*. *s.*

هنهنات हिनहिनाट *hinhināṭ*, neighing. *h.*

هنهنانا हिनहिनाना *hinhinānā*, a. to neigh. *h.*

هني *hanī*, agreeable; easily obtained; inestimable. *a.*

هو *hū*, pron. (lit. He, He is) God. *hū kā'ālam*, a desert plain (q. d. "where no being but God exists"). *huwa huwa* or *hū-ba-hū*, exactly. *a.*

هو हो *ho*, a vocative particle. *hū*, an emphatic affix (v. *hī*), even, indeed. *s.*

هوا *hawā*, f. wind, air, atmosphere; lust, desire; love, affection. *hawā bāndh-kar jānā*, to beat to windward. *hawā-batānā*, to reject one's petition, to disappoint; *hawā bandhnā*, to appear. *hawā bandī karnā*, to build castles in the air; to calumniate. *hawā-parast*, vain, fickle, giddy, volatile; a sensualist. *hawā phirnī*, to change condition. *hawā chhuṛānā*, to break wind. *hawā-khwāh*, a friend. *hawā-ḥirṣ*, covetousness, envy, greediness. *hawā-dār*, airy. *hawā denā*, to blow the coal, to foment a quarrel. *hawā-zadagī*, a disease so called, cold, catarrh. *hawā se bāt karnā*, to rival the wind in speed. *hawā se laṛnā*, implies a readiness to quarrel. *hawā karnā*, to fan; to broach, to divulge, to disclose, to publish. *hawā khānā*, to take the air; to walk about idly. *hawā ke babūle phornā* or *hawā men pulā,o pakānā*, to build castles in the air. *hawā-gīr*, a rocket-maker. *hawā o hawas*, lust, concupiscence, sensuality, luxury, vanity, ambition. *hawā ho jānā*, to scamper off, to vanish, to disappear. *a.*

هوا हूआ *hū,ā*, been, become; ago, elapsed. *h.*

هوا हौवा *hauwā*, m. a bugbear, an ogre. *h.*

هوام *hawamm*, m. (pl. of هامه) reptiles, insects, serpents. *a.*

هوان *hawān* m. (for *hāwan*), m. a mortar. *p.*

هوان *hawān*, contempt, misery, distress. *a.*

هوآنا होआना *ho-ānā*, n. to have gone to and returned. *h.*

هواو हिवाव *hivā,o* or *hivāw*, m. energy, manhood, courage. *s.*

هواي *hawā,ī*, f. a sky-rocket; adj. of or relating to the air, aerial, windy; vain, ideal. *a. p.*

هوبهو *hū-ba-hū*, quite, perfectly. *a.*

هوپاهپ हूपाहप *hūpāhap*, secretly, silently. *h.*

هوت होत *hot*, m. f. } wealth, means, ability;
هوتا होता *hotā*, m. } adj. being, becoming. *hotā-jātā*, coming and going. *h.*

هوتا होता *hotā*, } the priest who officiates at
هوتر होतृ *hotṛi*, } the *hom* sacrifice (v. *hom*). *s.*

هوتارهيگا होतारहेगा *hotā-rahegā*, an expression used in reply to terms of abuse, implying that "what you said of me is applicable to yourself;" "tu quoque." *h.*

هوتب होतब *hotab*, m. predestination, fate. *s.*

هوتبيتا होतब्यता *hotabyatā*, f. (v. *hotavyatā*). *s.*

هوتو होतव *hotav*, m. predestination, destiny. *s.*

هوتويتا होतव्यता *hotavyatā*, f. fate, destiny; that which is preordained to happen. *s.*

هوته *hoth*, interj. ho! hallo! *bhā,ī hoth*, hark ye, friend! hallo there! *d.*

هوتي होते *hote*, during, while, in the presence of; *hote hote*, gradually. *makān se hote*, near the house, or just out of it. *h.*

هوٹھ होठ *hoṭh*, m. (v. *honṭh*) the lip. *s.*

هوجانا होजाना *ho-jānā*, n. to have happened, to become. *h.*

هوچکنا होचुकना *ho-chuknā*, n. to be finished, to be expired, to have elapsed. *h.*

هوچنا हूचना *hūchnā*, a. to miss, to err, to mistake. *h.*

هودج *haudaj*, } m. a litter (used on an ele-
هوده *hauda*, } phant or camel, in which Arabian ladies travel). *a.*

هوده *hūda*, truth, wisdom; adj. true, just; old. *p.*

هور *haur*, conj. (v. *aur*) and; but. *d.*

هورهنا होरहना *ho-rahnā*, n. to be, become. *h.*

هوري होरी *horī* (v. *holī*), name of a festival, &c. *s.*

هوريا हूरिया *hūriyā*, a small clan of *rāj-pūts*. *h.*

هوڙ होड़ *hoṛ*, f. a wager, an agreement, a bargain. *hoṛ bāndhnā*, a. to bargain, &c. *hoṛ-badnā*, a. to wager, to bet, &c. *hoṛ lagānā*, a. to wager; to make an agreement; n. to be positive, obstinate, or perverse. *hoṛ hārnā*, a. to lose a wager, &c. *hūṛ*, f. wrangling. *h.*

هوڙ *hūṛ*, ignorant, foolish. *d.*

هوڑاهوڑي हूड़ाहूड़ी *hūṛā-hūṛī*, f. striving, wrangling. *h.*

هوڙل होड़ल *hoṛal*, m. talc, mica. *h.*

هوس *havas*, m. desire, lust, concupiscence; ambition, curiosity; inordinate desire. *hawas-bāz*, indulging inclination. *hawas pakānā*, to form an inordinate desire. *hawas-dār*, or *-kash*, desirous. *a.*

هوسكنا होसकना *ho-sahnā*, n. to be possible. *h.*

هوسناك *hawas-nāk*, هوسي *hawasī*, } desirous, wilful, curious, ambitious. *p.a.*

هوش *hosh*, m. understanding, judgment, sense; mind, soul. *hosh pakaṛnā*, to recollect. *hosh men ānā*, to come into one's senses; to recover from a swoon, &c. *p.* [to baulk. *h.*

هوشكارنا होशकारना *hoshkārnā*, a. to disappoint,

هوشمند *hosh-mand*, intelligent, wary. *p.*

هوشمندي *hoshmandī*, f. understanding, prudence. *p.*

هوشنگ *hoshang*, name of the second king of Persia, of the *Peshdādiyān* dynasty. *p.*

هوشي *hoshī*, sensible, intelligent. *p.*

هوشيار *hoshyār*, intelligent, attentive, careful, clever, sensible. *p.*

هوشياري *hoshyārī*, f. sobriety, carefulness. *p.*

هوشيه हविष्य *havishya*, m. rice mixed with *ghī* or clarified butter. *s.*

هوك हूक *hūk*, f. pain, stitch, ache, shooting pain, twitch. *hūk-hūk-kar ronā*, to sob and cry. *h.*

هوكا हौका *haukā*, هوكها हौखा *haukhā*, } m. ambition, cupidity, covetousness. *h.*

هوكهه हविख *havikh* (for *havishya*), m. *ghī*, rice mixed with *ghī*. *havikh-firnī*, rice and milk. *s.*

هوكي होके *hoke*, through, by, proceeding from. *h.*

هوگلا हूगला *hūglā*, m. a kind of reed commonly called "elephant grass." *h.*

هول हूल *hūl*, f. a thrust, an attack. *hūl-d.*, to goad, thrust, drive, urge. *h.*

هول *haul*, m. terror. *haul-dil*, terrified; hypochondriac affection, melancholy. *haul-nāk*, frightful, terrible. *a.* [parched in the pod. *s.*

هولا होला *holā*, m. the chick pea having been

هولا होला *holā*, m. name of a kind of boat (large and flat-bottomed). *h.*

هولڙ हूलड़ *hūlaṛ*, m. tumult, uproar, alarm, disturbance. *h.* [&c. *s.*

هولكا होलिका *holikā* (v. *holī*), a festival,

هولنا हूलना *hūlnā*, a. to goad, to thrust, to push. *h.*

هولي होली *holī*, f. the great festival held at the approach of the vernal equinox; the song which is sung during the festival. *s.*

هولي हौले *haule*, gently, slowly, easily. *h.*

هولي हौली *haulī*, f. a liquor-shop. *h.*

هوليتا होलेना *ho-lenā*, n. to be completed. *h.*

هوم होम *hom*, m. a kind of fire-worship; oblation, sacrifice, a kind of burnt-offering, the casting of clarified butter, &c. into the sacred fire as an offering to the gods, accompanied with prayers and invocations, according to the object of the sacrifice. *hom-karne-wālā*, a fire-worshipper; a performer of the *hom*. *s.*

هومنا होमना *homnā* or *hom-k.*, a. to offer up the *hom* sacrifice. *s.*

هومي होमी *homī*, the offerer of an oblation. *s.*

هون हून *hūn*, m. a coin, called also a *pagoda*, valued at from 3½ to 3¾ rupees. *h.*

هون हूं *hūṅ*, too, also, yes, well, exactly; m. a magical or mystical monosyllable. *s.*

هون हूं *hūṅ*, I am. *hoṅ*, they or we may be. (Braj.) *hauṅ*, I am or may be. *h.*

هون हवन *havan*, m. sacrifice, offering. *s.*

هونا होना *honā*, n. to be, to exist, to become, to belong, to have, to serve, to answer, to come, t do, to stand. *ho-ānā*, to have gone to and returned .

هونٹ *hoṅṭ*, the lip. *hoṅṭ chābnā*, to chew the lip; to be afraid; to be mortified or penitent. *d.*

هونٹا होंटा *hoṅṭā*, three and a half (a term in use among surveyors). *h.*

هونٹهه होंठ *hoṅṭh*, m. the lip. *s.*

هونٹهي होंठी *hoṅṭhī*, m. the bit of a bridle. *s.*

هونڈار हुंडार *huṅḍār*, a wolf. *h.*

هونس हौंस *hauṅs* (corrup. of *hawas*, q.v.), f. desire, wish. *hauṅs karnā*, to desire. *h.*

هونسا *hauṅsā*, envy, jealousy. *d.*

هونسنا *hauṅsnā*, to be envious or jealous. *d.*

هونسي *hauṅsī*, desirous, emulous. *d.*

هونكرنا हूंकरना *hūṅ-karnā*, to make the sound *hūṅ*, in anger, from fear, or as an incantation, &c. *s.*

هونكنا होंकना *hoṅknā*, n. to plant, to puff. *h.*

هونهار होन्हार *honhār*, possible; what is to happen. *h.*

هون‌هان हूंहां *hūṅ-hāṅ*, m. uproar, tumult. *h.*

هونيوالا होनेवाला *honewālā*, هونيهارا होनेहारा *honehārā*, being, about to be; practicable, possible. *h.*

هوها हूहा *hūhā*, m. report, rumour, popular fame; a storm; pageantry, ostentation. *h.*

هوي ह्वै *hwai*, having been; through, by. *hwai-hai*, will be or become. *b.*

هوىٰ *hawā*, f. desire, love, inclination, will, wish (v. *hawā*). *a.*

هويت *huwīyat*, divinity, the divine essence. *a.*

هويدا *hawaidā* or *huwaidā*, clear, manifest, evident, open. *p.*

هويه हव्य *havya*, m. an offering to the gods. *s.*

هي *hai*, interj. alas! strange! wonderful! *hai hai*, alas! &c. *p.*

هي हे *he*, a vocative particle. *s.*

هي हय *hay*, m. a horse; the yak. *s.*

هي ही *hī*, an emphatic affix of frequent occurrence; very, even, indeed, only; altogether. *hai*, is, art. *h.*

هي ही *hī*, هيا हिया *hiyā*, m. heart, breast, mind, soul, life. *s.*

هيأت *hai,at*, f. astronomy, the aspect of the heavens; face, visage, countenance, aspect. *hai,ati majmū'ī*, collectively. *a.*

هياسا *hayāsā*, a girth, a surcingle. *p.*

هياشنا हयाश्ना *hayāshnā*, f. the gum olibanum tree. *s.*

هيان *hiyān*, grief or regret at one's absence. *d.*

هياو हियाव *hiyāv* or *hiyā,o*, m. courage, spirit, valour. *s.*

هيبت *haibat*, f. fright, perturbation, awe. *haibat dikhlānā*, to appal, to terrify. *haibat-zada*, aghast, appalled. *haibat-nāk*, frightful, terrific. *a.*

هيت हेत *het* or हेतु *hetu*, m. meaning, object, intention, theme, cause, reason, account. *s.*

هئت *hiat*, هيئت *hai,at*, the outward form of the heavens; astronomy. *a.*

هيٹھ हेठ *heṭh*, below, down, under. *h.*

هيٹھا हेठा *heṭhā* (also *heṭā*), indolent, pusillanimous, cowardly. *heṭhā-pan*, m. cowardice. *h.*

هيٹھا हीठा *hīṭhā*, m. a person appointed to take care of the standing crops. *h.*

هيجا *hījā*, battle, combat, conflict. *a.*

هيجان *hayajān*, vehemence, disturbance. *a.*

هيجڑا हीजड़ा *hījṛā*, m. a eunuch, hermaphrodite. *h.*

هيچ *hech*, any, any thing; nothing; worthless, good for nothing. *hech-madān*, ignorant, simple, an ignoramus. *hech pūch*, trifles, things of no account. *p.*

هير हीर *hīr*, m. essence; pith, energy, vigour; essential, pure. *s.*

هير हीर *hīr*, Hero, the celebrated mistress of Leander, called by the Indians *Rānjhā*, q. v. *h.*

هيرا हीरा *hīrā*, m. a diamond; adamant. *s.*

هيراپهيري *herā-pherī*, f. strolling about. *d.*

هيرامن हीरामन *hīrāman*, m. a kind of parroquet (*Psittacus*). *h.*

هيرانا हीराना *hīrānā*, the manuring of a field by penning cattle or sheep on it. *h.*

هيراول हीरावल *hīrāval* or हीरावलि *hīrāvali*, m. a kind of chequered blanket worn by *faḳīrs*. *s.*

هيراولي हीरावली *hīrāvalī*, a string of diamonds. *s.*

هيرك हीरक *hīrak*, m. a diamond; adamant. *s.*

هيرن हीरण *hīran*, m. (for *hiranya*) gold. *s.*

هيرنا हेरना *hernā*, a. to look after; to search for, to hunt, to chase, to pursue, to catch, stop. *h.*

هيري हेरी *herī*, name of a tribe of Musalmān *rāj-pūts* in *Jaipūr*, a *pargana* of *Murādābād*. *s. h.*

هيڑا *hīṛā*, flesh, bulk, body. *d.*

هيز *hīz*, pusillanimous, impotent, effeminate; m. an hermaphrodite. *p.*

هيزم *hezum*, f. firewood. *hezum-farosh*, a wood-merchant. *hezum-kash*, a woodman or cutter. *p.*

هيژده *hīzhdah* or *hezhdah*, eighteen. *hezhdah hazār 'ālam*, the 18,000 created beings (v. *hazhdah*). *p.*

هيضه *haiẓa*, m. the cholera morbus, a flux and vomit, the cholic. *a.*

هيك हैक *haik*, m. a horse. *hīk*, sickness at the stomach, qualm, disgust. *h.*

هيكل *haikal*, f. a figure, face, form, stature or shape of body, appearance, person; any great building, a palace, a temple; an ornament worn round the neck (of man and beast). *a.*

هيگا हैगा *haigā* (the same as *hai*), is, may be; (an expression of consent), probably, suppose so, doubtless. *h.*

هيگر *haigīr* or *haigar*, a brown horse with a black mane or tail. *p.*

هيگريو हयग्रीव *hay-grīv*, m. a demon who stole the Vedas and was slain by *Vishnu* in his fish *Avatār*. *s.*

هيگندها हयगन्धा *hay-gandhā*, f. a plant (*Physalis flexuosa*).

هيل हील *hīl*, هيلا हीला *hīlā*, m. mud, slime, ooze. *h.*

هيلا हेला *helā* (v. *bhangī*), a low caste. *h.*

هيلا हेला *helā*, f. wanton dalliance, lascivious endearment; disrespect, contempt. *s.*

هيلاج *hailāj*, m. the time of labour or birth; (in astrology) a mark by which the duration of life is foretold: (it is said to signify a wife, and to be derived from a Greek word of that meaning, perhaps ἄλοχος). *p.*

هيلا مارنا हेलामारना *helā mārnā*, a. to shove, to launch, to dash through water. *h.*

هيلنا हेलना *helnā*, n. to swim. *h.*

هيلي हेले *hele*, a subdivision of the *jāṭ* tribe (so called). *h.* [the six seasons. *s.*

هيم हेम *hem*, m. gold. *him*, m. snow; one of

هيماچل हेमाचल *hemāchal*, m. name of a mountain, called also *Sumeru*. *s.*

هيمتار हेमतार *hem-tār*, m. blue vitriol. *s.*

هيمتر हेमतरु *hem-taru*, m. the thorn-apple. *s.*

هيمكشيري हेमक्षीरी *hem-kshīrī*, f. a medicinal sort of moon-plant. *s.*

هيمكوٹ हेमकूट *hem-kūṭ*, m. one of the ranges of mountains dividing the known continent into nine *varshas* or regions. *s.*

هيمنت हेमन्त *hemant*, f. name of the fifth season of the Hindūs, the months *Agrahāyan* and *Paush* (Nov.-Dec.). *s.*

هيمه *hīma*, m. wood, firewood. *p.*

هين हीन *hīn*, deficient, little, abated; left, quitted; wasted, worn; void of, free from. *s.*

هين हीं *hīṅ*, an emphatical particle. *hīṅ-hān bharnā*, to concede. *h.*

هينبينا हेनबेना *henbenā*, spoilt, ruined. *h.*

هينتا हीनता *hīntā*, f. abatement, alleviation. *s.*

هينجات हीनजाति *hīn-jāti*, outcast, vile, degraded. *s.*

هينچ *hīnch*, an emphatic particle (v. *hīṅ*). *d.*

هيندرا *hendrā*, ill-bred, stupid, clownish. *hendrā-panā* or *hendrāgī*, clownishness. *d.*

هينسنا हींसना *hīṅsnā*, n. to neigh, to scream or make a noise, as a horse when kicking. *h.*

هينكارنا हींकारना *hīnkārnā*, a. to low. *h.*

هينگ हींग *hīng*, m. *assafœtida*. *hīng hagnā*, to void by stool involuntarily; (met.) to pine. *s.*

هينگا हेंगा *hengā* or हैंगा *haingā*, m. a harrow. *h.*

هينگي हैंगे *hainge*, we or they are. *h.*

هينگو हींगू *hingū* (v. *hing*), assafœtida. *s.*

هينورن हीनवर्ण *hīn-varṇ*, of a low caste, degraded. *s.*

هيؤ हीओ *hī,o* or हियो *hiyo*, the sound made when calling cattle. *h.* [soul. *s.*

هيؤ हीओ *hī,o* or हियौ *hiyau*, m. heart, mind,

هيوانت हेवान्त *hevānt*, m. the name of a season (v. *hemant*). *s.*

هيوبنس हयोबंस *hayo-bans*, name of a tribe of *rāj-pūts* in the province of Benares. *h.*

هيولا *hayūlā* (also *haiyūlā*), m. matter, origin, first principle; appearance; the first sketch of a picture. *a.*

هيولاني *haiyūlānī*, material, relating to matter or first principles. *a.*

هيونت हेवन्त *hewant*, f. (for *hemant*, q.v.) name of the fifth or cold season *s.*

هيهات *haihāt*, interj. alas! begone! subst. bewailing, lamentation. *a.* [of laughter. *h.*

هي هي हीही *hī-hī*, an interjection of surprise,

ي

ي *yā*, called *yā,e ḥuṭṭī* or *yā,e musannāt i taḥtānī*, the twenty-eighth letter of the Arabic alphabet, the thirty-second Persian, and thirty-fifth Hindūstānī: in reckoning by *abjad* it stands for ten; in the almanacks it is the character of *Jupiter*, and of the sign *Aquarius*.

ي य *ya*, the corresponding letter in the Devanāgarī alphabet: in words of Sanskrit origin it is frequently changed into *jīm*, as *judh* or *juddh* for *yuddh*, battle, contest.

يا *yā*, interj. or voc. particle O! *a.*

يا या *yā*, pron. this; (in comp) a dealer in any act, as *kapriyā*, a cloth-merchant, *baṭohiyā*, a traveller, &c. *h.*

يا *yā*, conj. either, or, whether. *yā takht yā takhta*, "either a throne or a bier," said when a man is resolved to conquer or die. Nelson said, "a Peerage or Westminster Abbey." *p.*

ياب *yāb*, (in comp.) obtaining, finding, as *kām-yāb*, one who obtains his wish. *p.*

يابسات *yabisāt*, f. epulotica, medicines tending to dry up and heal ulcers and sores. *a.*

يابنده *yābanda*, a finder; finding, discovering. *p.*

يابو याबू *yābū*, m. a pony, Galloway nag. *h.*

يابي *yābī*, f. (in comp) attainment, as *kām-yābī*, the attainment of one's desires. *p.*

ياپن यापन *yāpan*, m. spending or passing away time. *s.* [going, transmigration. *s.*

ياتايات यातायात *yātāyāt*, m. coming and

ياتر यात्रु *yātru*, ياترك यात्रिक *yātrik*, ياتري यात्री *yātrī*, } m. a pilgrim, a traveller. *s.*

ياترا यात्रा *yātrā*, f. pilgrimage; departure, march, journey; festival, procession. *yātrā-karan*, m. setting forth on a journey or march. *s.*

ياتنا यातना *yātnā*, f. pain, agony, sharp or acute pain; the pains of hell. *s.*

ياتهارتهك याथार्थिक *yāthārthik*, just, true, right. *s.* [titude. *s.*

ياتهارتهي याथार्थ्य *yāthārthya*, m. truth, rec-

ياجك याजक *yājak*, m. an officiating priest, a Brāhman who conducts any part of a sacrifice. *s.*

یاجن याजन *yājan*, m. conducting a sacrifice, or causing its performance. *s.*

یاجوج ماجوج *yājūj mājūj*, Gog and Magog. *a.*

یاجیہ याज्य *yājya*, m. property or presents derived from officiating at sacrifices. *s.*

یاچت याचित *yāchit*, asked, begged, solicited. *yāchita* or *yāchitaka*, a particular form of deposit, whereby the holder is allowed (by law) the use of the article deposited. *s.* [cant. *s.*

یاچك याचक *yāchak*, m. a beggar, a mendi-

یاچنا याचना *yāchnā*, f. asking, begging. *s.*

یاد *yād*, f. memory, recollection. *yād-āwarī*, f. remembrance, calling to mind. *yād-būd*, a keepsake. *yād-dāsht*, f. a memorandum. *yād-ash-ba-khair*, blessed be his memory! an expression used when mentioning an absent friend. *yād-farāmosh*, name of a game. *yād dilānā*, to remind. *yād-gār*, any thing given as a memorial, a valuable present to a mistress or friend; a monument, any thing memorable, worthy of remembrance, or which recalls a person or thing to memory. *yād-gārī*, f. a keepsake, a token. *p.*

یادو यादव *yādav*, m. a descendant of *Yadu*, an epithet of *Kṛishṇa*. *s.*

یار *yār*, m. a friend, a lover; an assistant. *yār-bāz*, a wanton woman, a whore; adj. wanton. *yār-bāzī*, fornication. *yār-bāsh*, voluptuous, sensual. *yār-bāshī*, sensuality, &c. *yār i ghār*, a sincere friend, like one of the seven sleepers (v. *aṣḥāb* or *kahf*), or like *Abū Bakr*, the faithful friend and companion of *Muḥammad*. *yār i wafā-dār*, a faithful friend. *p.*

یارا *yārā*, m. power, strength, boldness. *p.*

یارانہ *yār-āna*, friendly, like a friend. *p.*

یارنی *yārnī*, a female friend, a sweetheart, a mistress. *p. h.*

یارہ *yāra*, m. a broad bracelet; the wrist; a wound; power, strength; a shrewd man; friendship; necessity; tax, toll, revenue. *p.*

یاری *yārī*, f. friendship, love; assistance; (commonly means) intriguing. *p.*

یازدہ *yāzdah*, eleven. *yāzdahum*, the eleventh. *p.* [yawning. *p.*

یازہ *yāza*, yawning, or stretching the arms in

یاس *yās*, m. despair; fear, terror. *a.*

یاسم *yāsim*, } m. jasmine or jessamine.
یاسمن *yāsmin*, } *yāsmin-bo* or *-bū*, redolent
یاسمون *yāsmūn*, } of jasmine. *p.*
یاسمین *yāsmīn*, }

یافت *yāft*, f. perquisite, earnings; fees, bribes, and douceurs extorted by official persons: a native official commonly speaks of a situation being worth so much in *darmāhā*, or regular salary, and so much in *yāft*. *p.*

یافتن *yāftan* (r. *yāb*), to find, to obtain. *p.*

یافہ *yāfa*, vain, futile; ribaldry. *yāfa-dārī*, idle talk. *yāfa-darā,ī*, idle boasting, loquacity. *p.*

یاقوت *yāḳūt*, m. a ruby, a precious stone. *yāḳūti kabūd* the sapphire. *yāḳūti zard*, the topaz. *a.*

یاقوتی *yāḳūtī*, of or relating to a ruby, ruby-coloured; a kind of ornamental handwriting. *a.*

یاگ याग *yāg*, m. a sacrifice, any ceremony in which offerings and oblations are presented. *s.*

یاگیك याज्ञिक *yāgyik*, m. an institutor of a sacrifice. *s.*

یاگییہ याज्ञिय *yāgyiya*, fit for sacrifice. *s.*

یال *yāl*, f. a horse's mane. *p.*

یام *yam*, m. season, time, weather. *a.*

یام याम *yām*, a watch, or one-eighth of a natural day (same as *pahar*, q. v.). *s.*

یامنی यामनी *yāmnī*, Musalmān, foreign, not Hindū. *yāminī*, f. a night. *s.*

یامنی بھاشا यामनीभाषा *yāmnī-bhāshā*, f. the language of the *Yavans* (q. v.). *s.*

یان यान *yān*, m. any vehicle or form of conveyance, as a carriage, horse, litter, &c. *s.*

یاں यां *yāṅ* (for *yahāṅ*), here. *s.*

یاوت यावत *yāvat*, as much as, as far as, as long as. *s.*

یاوجیو यावज्जीव *yāvajjīv*, } during life,
یاوجیون यावज्जीवन *yāvajjīvan*, } as long as life. *s.* [friend, companion. *p.*

یاور *yāwar*, m. an assistant, coadjutor; a

یاوری *yāwarī*, f. aid, assistance, *p.*

یاوك यावक *yāvak*, m. the red colour procured from the lac insect. *s.*

یاون यावन *yāvan*, m. } of or relating to a Ya-
یاونی यावनी *yāvanī*, f. } van or Musulmān. *s.*

یاوہ *yāwa*, absurd, vain, futile; lost, ruined. *yāwa-go*, an absurd talker. *p.*

یاہی याही *yāhī*, (pron. dat. and accus.) this, to this. [chase). *p.*

یایا *yāyā*, a call (used in calling birds of

یبوسۃ *yabūsat* or *yabūsa*, dryness, aridity. *a.*

یت युत *yut*, (in comp.) connected with, possessed of, as *dharma-yut*, virtuous. *shrī-yut*, prosperous. *s.*

یت यति *yati*, m. a sage whose passions are completely under subjection; a religious mendicant, especially one of the Jain sect. *s.*

یتا *yatā*, so much, this much or many. *d.*

یتر यत्र *yatr* or *yatra*, where, wheresoever; in whatever place. *p.*

یتشخانہ *yatash-khāna*, m. an antechamber, a hall of audience. *s.*

یتن यत्न *yatn* or *yatna*, m. effort, exertion, energy, carefulness, remedy. *s.*

يتنوان यत्नवान *yatnavān*, يتنوت यत्नवत *yatnavat*, يتني यत्नी *yatnī*, } persevering, diligent, making an effort or exertion. *s.*

يتنييه यतनीय *yatanīya*, to be exerted or persevered in, an effort to be made. *s.*

يتورت यतव्रत *yatvrat*, firm to an engagement or vow. *s.*

يتها यथा *yathā*, as, like, such, according to. *yathā-jog*, *-jogya*, *-yog*, or *-yogya*, as is proper, "comme il faut." *s.*

يتهابهمت यथाभिमत *yathābhimat*, according to one's wish or purpose. *s.*

يتهاتتها यथातथा *yathā-tathā*, in any way, any how. *s.*

يتهارتهه यथार्थ *yathārth*, right, proper, according to the sense; adv. properly, suitably. *s.*

يتهارتهتا यथार्थता *yathārthatā*, f. rectitude, propriety, fitness. *s.*

يتهاستهت यथास्थित *yathāsthit*, circumstantially. *s.*

يتهاسكت यथासक्ति *yathā-sakti*, as far as possible. *s.*

يتهاسكهه यथासुख *yathā-sukh*, happily. *s.*

يتهاسمبهو यथासम्भव *yathā-sambhav*, suitable, according to circumstances. *s.*

يتهاشاستر यथाशास्त्र *yathā-shāstr*, according to the *Shāstras*; agreeably to holy writ. *s.*

يتهاشكت यथाशक्ति *yathā-shakti*, as much as possible; to the extent of one's ability. *s.*

يتهاكال यथाकाल *yathā-kāl*, opportunely, timely. *s.*

يتهاكام यथाकाम *yathā-kām*, at pleasure. *s.*

يتهاكامي यथाकामी *yathā-kāmī*, wilful, independent. *s.*

يتهاكتهنچت यथाकथंचित *yathā-kathaṅ-chit*, in some way or other, any how. *s.*

يتهاكرتويه यथाकर्तव्य *yathā-kartavya*, what is right or proper to be done. *s.*

يتهاكرم यथाक्रम *yathā-kram*, in order, methodically. *s.*

يتهاكلپ यथाकल्प *yathā-kalp*, as designed. *s.*

يتهامكهين यथामुखीन *yathā-mukhīn*, like, resembling, of a similar appearance. *s.*

يتهاوت यथावत *yathā-vat*, truly, exactly, as it was, according to usage. *s.*

يتهاودهه यथाविधि *yathā-vidhi*, according to rule. *s.*

يتهاوسر यथावसर *yathāvasar*, يتهاوكاش यथावकाश *yathāvakāsh*, } according to opportunity, as occasion offers. *s.*

يتهوچت यथोचित *yathochit*, as it is best, proper, suitable. *s.*

يتهوكت यथोक्त *yathokt*, true, as it has been stated. *s.*

يتهيچها यथेच्छा *yathechchhā*, according to one's desire. *s.*

يتهيشتهه यथेष्ट *yatheshtha*, as it is wished or commanded. *s.*

يتي यती *yatī*, m. a sage with subdued passions. *s.*

يتيم *yatīm*, m. an orphan, pupil, ward; a valuable jewel. *durrī yatīm*, a large and precious pearl which is found alone in the shell. *a.*

يتيمي *yatīmī*, f. state of orphancy; adj. of or relating to an orphan. *a.*

يتيندريه यतेंद्रिय *yatendriya*, chaste, pure, of subdued passions. *s.*

يثرب *yasrib*, a name of the sacred city of Medina in Arabia. *a.*

يجرويد यजुर्वेद *yajur-ved*, يجس यजुस *yajus*, } the second of the four *Vedas*, or scriptural authorities of the Hindūs. *s.*

يجمان यजमान *yajmān*, m. one who employs Brāhmans for the performance of a sacrifice (v. *jajman*). *s.*

يچهه *yachh*, m. (v. *yahsha*). *s.*

يحيا *yahyā*, St. John the Baptist. *a.*

يخ *yakh*, m. ice. *yakh-basta*, frozen, icebound. *p.*

يخني *yakhnī*, f. gravy (prepared to dress *pulāw* in), sauce, stew. *yakhnī-pulāw*, a kind of *pulāw*, prepared with gravy. *p.*

يد *yad*, m. a hand; a handle; aid, assistance; power, vigour; benefit, service. *a.*

يد यदि *yadi*, conj. when, since, if. *s.*

يد यदु *yadu*, m. the name of an ancient king, the ancestor of *Krishna*; also the name of the country over which *Yadu* ruled. *yadu-bans*, m. the tribe of *Yadu*. *yadu-bansī*, m. a descendant of *Yadu*. *s.*

يدا यदा *yadā*, when, at what time. *s.*

يدناته यदुनाथ *yadu-nāth*, m. the lord of Yadu, *Krishna*. *s.*

يداتدوا यदातदवा *yadā-tadwā*, somehow or other. *s.*

يدودهه यदवधि *yadavadhi*, since when. *s.*

يدهه युद्ध *yuddh*, m. battle, war, fight. *s.*

يدهشتهر युधिष्ठिर *yudhishthir*, m. the elder of the five Pandava princes. *s.*

يدهمان युधमान *yudhmān*, fighting, pugnacious. *s.*

يدي *yade* (same as *yih*), he, she, it, or they. *d.*

يديپ यद्यपि *yadyapi*, if, even if, when. *s.*

يراق *yarāk*, arms, accoutrements, weapons. *t.*

يرغا *yarghā*, m. an amble (pace of a horse); name of a bird. *yarghā chalānā*, to amble. *p.*

يرغمال *yarghamāl*, m. a hostage. *p.*

يرغه *yargha* (v. *yarghā*), an amble, &c. *p.*

يرقان *yarkān*, m. the yellow jaundice. *a.*

يرو *yarū*, m. manure, dung. *d.*

يزد *yazd*, God; the name of a city in the eastern part of Fārs or Persia proper. *yazd-parast*, a worshipper of God. *p.*

يزدان *yazdān*, m. God, the Almighty. *p.*

يزداني *yazdānī*, divine. *p.*

يزدي *yazdī*, of or relating to the city of Yazd; a species of cloth manufactured at Yazd. *p.*

يزيد *yazīd*, m. name of an arch heretic among the *Muhammadans*; the son of Moaviyah, the first caliph (*khalīfa*) of the Ommiade dynasty; wicked, cruel, execrable. *a.*

يزيدي *yazīdī*, of the sect of *Yazīd*. *a.*

يسار *yasār*, m. left, the left side; plenty, opulence, affluence. *yasār o yamīn*, left and right. *dasti yasār*, the left hand. *a.*

يسار *yasār*, m. an unlucky person. *p.*

يساول *yasāwal*, m. a servant of parade carrying a silver or gold staff; a state messenger; a horseman attendant on a man of rank. *p.*

يسر *yasr*, m. facility, lenity; prosperity, wealth. *yasar*, easy, soft, gentle, humane: ready, prepared. *a.*

يسير *yasīr*, motherless (a child). *a.*

يش यश *yash* or यशः *yasha*, m. fame, reputation, renown, glory. *yash-apayash*, m. good or bad name. *yash-pat* or *-pati*, reputable, renowned. *yash-kām*, ambitious, emulative, desirous of fame or glory. *yash-kar*, rendering famous, conferring celebrity. *s.*

يشب *yashb* or *yasht*, m. a species of jasper found on Mount Imaus. *a. p.*

يشٹ यष्टि *yashṭi*, m. a staff, a stick, a staff armed with iron, &c., used as a weapon, a club, a mace. *s.*

يشٹك यष्टिक *yashṭik*, m. a bird, the lapwing. *s.*

يشٹمدھ यष्टिमधु *yashṭimadhu*, m. liquorice root. *s.*

يشٹي यष्टी *yashṭī*, f. (v. *yashṭi*) a staff, &c. *s.*

يشسوان यशस्वान् *yashaswān*, } famed, renowned, celebrated. *s.*
يشسوي यशस्वी *yashaswī*, }

يشم *yashm* or *yashim*, m. a sort of jasper or agate, more particularly that which comes from China, supposed to be an infallible charm against lightning. *p.*

يشمي *yashmī*, of or relating to jasper. *p.*

يعبوب *ya'būb*, m. a swift horse. *a.*

يعسوب *ya'sūb*, m. the king or queen of the bees; a prince or chief of a nation. *a.*

يعقوب *ya'kūb*, Jacob, James. *a.*

يعني *ya'ne* or *ya'nī*, videlicet, that is to say, namely; for, because. *a.*

يغما *yaghmā*, } m. plunder, prey, booty, spoil, pillage, rapine. *p.*
يغمان *yaghmān*, }
يغمه *yaghma*, }

يقين *yakīn*, m. certainty, truth; name of a Hindūstānī poet; adj. true. *yakīn-k.*, to ascertain. *yakīn lānā*, to believe. *yakīn honā*, to become certain. *a.*

يقيناً *yakīnan*, verily, certainly, assuredly. *a.*

يقيني *yakīnī*, f. certainty, infallibility, truth; adj. true, indisputable. *a.*

يك *yak*, one, a, an. *yak-ād* or *-ādh*, a few. *yak-ā-yak*, all at once. *yak-bār* or *-bāra*, once, one time. *yak-bārgī* or *-bārī*, all at once, once. *yak-bar-yak* or *yak-ba-yak*, successively. *yak-bagghā*, a horse striving always to go on one side, pressing on one rein. *yakaṭ*, *yakṭhā*, *yakṭhār*, or *yak-ṭhān*, collected, assembled together. *yak-ja*, together. *yak-jān*, of one soul, a friend. *yak-jaddī*, of the same stock, descended from the same ancestors. *yak-jihat*, of one accord, unanimous; a friend. *yak-jihtī*, f. unanimity, friendship. *yak-chashmī*, one-eyed. *yak-chand* or *-chandī*, somewhat, a little. *yak-choba*, one-poled (a tent). *yak-dāna*, an incomparable gem. *yak-dast*, even, entire, homogenous. *yak-dastī*, one-handed. *yak-dil*, of one heart, unanimous, resolute. *yak-dilī*, concord, unanimity. *yak-ẕāt*, of the same caste or tribe. *yak-rāh*, going on (the same road). *yak-rukhī*, a kind of bow. *yak-rū*, unanimous. *yak-rū,ī*, unanimity, friendship. *yak-rah* or *-rāh*, once, of the same path. *yak-zabān*, of one speech, unanimous. *yak-sān* or *-sār*, equal, alike, even, the same, ditto, conformable, plain, level, parallel, *yak-sānī*, uniformity, identity, parity. *yak-kalam*, consistent (a writer); all, total, all at once. *yak-lakht*, all at once *yak-lautā*, single, solitary; a single child (without brother or sister). *yāk-lohī*, a sword blade made of one piece of steel. *yak-musht*, or *-muṭṭhī*, or *muṭh*, a handful; (met.) all at once, prompt payment, *yak-munh*, talking consistently. *yak-manī*, unanimity, friendship. *yak-na-yak*, one or other. *yak-hī*, the same, equal, alike. *p.*

يكا *yakkā*, single, solitary; m. the ace (at cards); a one-horse chaise; a trooper who serves alone; unique, unequalled. *yakkā-tāz*, one who singly assaults the enemy, a brave hero. *yakkā sipāhī* a single soldier. *p.*

يكاون *yakāwan* (for *ikāwan*), fifty-one. *d.*

يكائي *yakā,ī*, f. unit, uniqueness. *p.*

يكايك *yak-āyak*, all at once, suddenly. *p.*

يكباچھي *yak-bāchhī*, distribution of one sum or cess levied equably upon all lands. *p. h.*

يكت युक्त *yukt*, joined, united; fixed, fit, proper, possessed, endowed with; project. *s.*

يكت युक्ति *yukti*, f. union, fitness; skill, dexterity, contrivance, wit, art; project; usage, custom; purport or meaning of a passage, &c. *s.*

يكتا *yaktā*, single, simple, unique; a garment without a lining. *p.*

يكتاره *yaktāra*, a kind of guitar with one string. *d.*

يكتاليس *yaktālīs* (for *iktālīs*), forty-one. *d*

يكتائي *yaktā,ī*, f. singleness, singularity, uniqueness. *p.*

یکترا यकत्रा *yakatrā*, the sum total or amount; the numeral 101; interest at the rate of one per cent per month. *p. s.*

یکترسا युक्तरसा *yukt-rasā*, f. a plant (*Mimosa octandra*). *s.*

یکدگر *yak-digar*, یکدیگر *yak-dīgar*, } one another, mutually. *p.*

یکس *yakas* (same as *yak*), one. *d.*

یکش यक्ष *yaksh* or *yaksha*, m. a species of demigod, attendant especially on *Kuvera*, and employed in the care of his gardens and treasures. *s.*

یکشما यक्ष्मा *yakshmā*, m. pulmonary consumption. *s.*

یکشني यक्षिणी *yakshinī* or *yakshanī*, f. a female *yaksha*, or fairy. *s.*

یکشنبه *yak-shamba*, Sunday. *p.*

یکفردي *yak-fardī*, یکفصلي *yak-faṣlī*, } land producing only one crop in the year. *p.*

یکل *yakal*, single, solitary. *yakal-pan*, solitude. *d.*

یکلاءي *yaklā,ī*, f. a veil (or cloak, or sheet, worn over the head and shoulders) of one breadth without a seam.

یکلو *yaklū*, simple, single (thread). *p.*

یکلوتا *yaklautā*, a single child (without brother or sister). *p. h.*

یکنگ *yakang*, alone, lonely, solitary. *d.*

یکوترا यकोत्रा *yakotrā* (v. *yakatrā*), sum total, &c. *s.*

یکون *yakūn*, it will be, it is; the sum total of an account. *a. p.*

یکه *yaka*, one, singular, unique; at once, together. *p.*

یکیلا *yakelā*, solitary, alone, singular. *d.*

یگ युग *yug* or *yuga*, m. an age of the world or great period; a pair, a couple, a brace, a term used in the game of *Chausar* (the opposite of a blot, two or more men standing on the same square). *yug-yug*, perpetually, eternally. *yug phornā*, to cause difference between friends. *yug-ān-yug*, ages of ages, for ages. The Hindūs reckon four *yugas* or ages since the creation of the present world, viz.: 1. the *Krita-yug* or *Satya-yug*, which lasted 1,728,000 solar years; 2. the *Treta-yug*, of 1,296,000 years; 3. the *Dwāpar-yug*, of 864,000 years; and lastly, the *Kali-yug*, whose duration is 432,000 years, and of which nearly 5000 years have already elapsed. These four ages bear a marked affinity to the gold, silver, brazen, and iron ages of the Greeks and Romans, in all of which mankind are supposed to undergo a progressive deterioration. *s.*

یگان *yagān*, singly, unique. *yagān yagān*, one by one, one after another. *p.*

یگانت युगान्त *yugānt*, m. the end of the four *yugas* or ages, when, according to the Hindūs, a total destruction of the universe takes place. *yugānt-bandhu*, a permanent and steady friend. *s.*

یگانگت *yagānagat*, f. singularity; unity, concord, unanimity, conjunction, union. *p.*

یگانگي *yagānagī*, f. singularity, excellence; concord, unanimity. *p.*

یگانه *yagāna*, m. kindred; adj. single, sole, singular, incomparable; agreed, unanimous. *p.*

یگانیت *yagāniyat*, f. solitariness; kindred. *p.*

یگپت युगपत *yugapat*, at one time. *s.*

یگل युगल *yugal*, m. a pair, a brace, couple. *s.*

یگن यज्ञ *yagna*, m. a sacrifice, or religious ceremony in which oblations are presented. *yagna-bhūmi*, f. a place prepared for a sacrifice. *yagna-pātr*, m. a sacrificial vessel. *yagna-purush*, m. a name of *Vishnu*. *yagna-pashu*, a victim, any animal offered in sacrifice. *yagna-sthān*, m. a place of sacrifice. *yagna-siddhi*, f. performance of sacrifice, obtaining the objects of a sacrifice. *yagna-sūtr*, m. the characteristic thread worn by the three principal classes of Hindūs. *yagna-shālā*, f. a temple, a shrine, a place of sacrifice. *s.*

یگنوپویت यज्ञोपवीत *yagnopavīt*, m. the sacrificial thread or cord originally worn by the three first classes of Hindūs over the left shoulder and under the right (it is now worn only by Brāhmans); the term also signifies the ceremony of investiture. *s.*

یگنوپویتي यज्ञोपवीती *yagnopavītī*, a Brāhman, &c. invested with the sacred thread. *s.*

یگنیه यज्ञिय *yagniya*, suitable for a sacrifice. *yagniya-desh*, the country of the Hindūs, those countries in which the ritual and institutes of the Hindū system are enforced. *s.*

یل *yal*, m. a hero, a champion, a brave man; adj. corpulent, robust. *p.*

یلاپهیلا यलाफैला *yalā-phailā*, unconfined, extended, spread; adv. at ease. *h.*

یلدا *yaldā*, the longest night of winter, a long and dreary night. *p.*

یله *yala*, m. liberation, release; adj. free, released; crooked; vain, absurd; alone, single, solitary; subst. fem. a bad woman or prostitute. *p.*

یلغار *yalghār*, یلغر *yalghar*, } the sudden incursion of an army into a country. *t.*

یلیل *yalīl*, contempt, disgust, aversion. *d.*

یم यम *yam*, m. the angel of death, the regent of the realms of death. *s.*

یم *yam*, m. the sea, the main ocean, the vast deep, without any shore in sight. *a.*

یمدوت यमदूत *yam-dūt*, m. an infernal sprite, the messenger or minister of *yama*, death. *s.*

یمک यमक *yamak*, twin, fellow, one of a pair. *s.*

یمل यमल *yamal*, m. a pair, a brace. *s*

یمن *yumn*, m. felicity, prosperity. *yaman*, the right hand or side; name of a country, Arabia Felix. *a.*

یمن यमन *yaman*, m. name of a *rāginī* or musical mode. *h.*

یمن यमन *yaman* (v. *yavan*), an Ionian, &c. *s.*

يمنا **यमुना** *yamunā*, f. the *yamunā* or *jamunā* river; in mythology, the personified river is considered as the daughter of *Sūrya*, or the sun, and sister of *Yama*. *s.*

يمني *yamanī*, m. a cornelian; adj. of or belonging to *yaman* or Arabia Felix. *a.*

يمين *yamīn*, m. an oath: in its primitive sense it means strength or power, also the right hand; in the language of the law it signifies an obligation, by means of which the resolution of the vower is strengthened in the performance, or the avoidance of any thing. *yamīni ghamūs*, a false oath, wilful perjury. *yamīni lighū*, (lit. a nugatory oath) is an oath taken concerning an incident or transaction already past, when the swearer believes that the matter to which he thus bears testimony accords with what he swears, and it should happen to be actually otherwise. *yamīni-ma'kūd* or *-mun'akid*, an oath respecting some future matter which must be kept, unless it be absolutely sinful, in which case it may be broken, subject, however, to expiation. *yamīni faur*, a sudden oath or vow made on an emergency. *a.*

ينتر **यन्त्र** *yantra*, m. (v. *jantra*) a diagram of a mystical nature or astrological character; a machine in general; any instrument or apparatus; a musical instrument. *s.*

ينترنا **यन्त्रणा** *yantranā*, m. pain, anguish. *s.*

ينتري **यन्त्री** *yantrī*, m. a conjurer, wizard; an instrument for drawing wire. *s.*

يو *yo* (for *yih*), he, she, &c. *d.*

يو **यव** *yau* or *yava*, m. barley, more especially the measure of one barley-corn. *s.*

يو **युवा** *yuvā*, m. (v. *juvā*) a young man. *s.*

يواس **यवास** *yavās*, m. name of a flower (*Hedysarum alhagī*). *s.*

يواني **यवानी** *yavānī*, f. a plant (*Ligusticum ajwaen*. *s.*

يوپ **यूप** *yūp*, m. a sacrificial post, a trophy, a column erected in honour of a victory. *s.*

يوپهل **यवफल** *yau-phal*, name of a medicinal plant. *s.* [*tīkh*). *s.*

يوتش **योतिष** *yotish*, astrology, &c. (v. *jo-*

يوتشي **योतिषी** *yotishī*, m. an astrologer. *s.*

يوتك **यौतक** *yautak*, m. a nuptial present. *yautik* or *yautikh*, astrology. *s.*

يوته **यूथ** *yūth*, m. a multitude of birds or beasts, a herd, a flock. *s.*

يوتهي **यूथी** *yūthī*, f. a sort of jasmine. *s.*

يوتي **युवती** *yuvatī*, f. a young woman. *s.*

يوجن **योजन** *yojan*, a measure of distance equal to four *kos*. *s.*

يوجنا **योजना** *yojanā*, f. joining, meeting. *s.*

يودها **योद्धा** *yoddhā*, m. a warrior, a soldier, a combatant. *yodhā-pan*, m. heroism, pugnacity. *s.*

يودهن **योधन** *yodhan* m. fighting, battle. *s.*

يودهي **योधी** *yodhī*, m. a warrior, a combatant. *s.*

يوراج **युवराज** *yuva-rāj*, also *yuva-rājā*, m. a young prince, the heir-apparent. *s.*

يوراجيه **युवराज्य** *yuva-rājya*, m. state or dignity of heir-apparent. *s.*

يورش *yūrish*, m. assault, storm, invasion. *p.*

يوز *yūz*, m. a panther, pard, or lynx; the *chīta* or hunting leopard. *p.*

يوس **यूष** *yūs* (also *yūsh*), m. pea-soup, pease-porridge; a sort of broth. *s.*

يوسف *yūsuf*, the patriarch Joseph. *a.*

يوشت **योषित** *yoshit*, f. a woman in general, also a wife (like the French "femme"). *s.*

يوكا **यूका** *yūkā*, f. a louse, vermin. *s*

يوكشار **यवक्षार** *yavakshār*, } m. saltpetre, nitre;
يوكهار **यवखार** *yavakhār*, } nitrate of potash. *s.*

يوگ **योग** *yog* or *yoga*, m. junction, joining, union; a fortunate moment; opportunity; penance, devotion; adj. possible, capable. *yog-āsan*, m. a kind of religious posture. *yog-pat*, a part of a devotee's dress. *yog-sevā*, practising religious abstractions. *yoga-kshema*, property, possessions; especially property assigned for charitable deeds. *yog-nāvik*, a kind of fish. *yog-nidrā*, light sleep, wakefulness. *yog-vahī*, alkali, quicksilver; a medium for mixing medicines. *s.*

يوگني **योगिनी** *yoginī*, f. a female fiend or sprite attendant on, and created by *Durgā*; in some places eight *yoginīs* are enumerated by name. *s.*

يوگي **योगी** *yogī*, m. a devotee, an ascetic; a magician. *yogya*, fit, proper; clever. *s.*

يوگيتا **योग्यता** *yogyatā*, f. fitness, capability, ability. *s.*

يوگيشور **योगेश्वर** *yogeshwar*, m. a principal sage; a deity; a magician, the object of devout contemplation. *s.*

يوگيه **योग्य** *yogya*, clever, accomplished; able, powerful; fit, proper. *s.*

يوم *yaum*, m. (corruptly *yom*) a day. *yaumu-l-ḥisāb*, or *yaumu-l-ḥashr*, or *yaumu-l-ḳiyāmat*, the day of the resurrection; the day of rendering one's account. *yaumu-l-fiṭr*, the day of breaking fast, viz. the day following the fast of the *Ramaẓān*. *a.*

يوماً *yauman*, one day; daily. *a.*

يوميه *yaumiya* (or *yomiya*), daily; m. daily sustenance or allowance to pensioners of any kind. *yaumiya-dār*, a pensioner. *a.*

يون **यवन** *yavan*, m. name of a country, supposed to be that inhabited by the Greeks: by late Hindū writers the term is usually applied to Arabia, or in general to those countries inhabited by Musalmāns; this name formerly meant an Ionian or a Greek, but now is applied to both the Muḥammadan and European invaders of India, and is often used as a general term for any foreign or barbarous race. *yavan-āchārya*, an astronomical writer frequently alluded to by ancient Hindū astronomers, supposed to be Ptolemy. *yavan-āl*, a kind of grass. *s.*

یوں यूँ yūn̐, योँ yon̐, or यौँ yaun, thus, in this manner. *yūn̐ na yūn̐*, one way or other. *yūn̐-hīn̐*, in this very manner, thus, accidentally, by chance, causelessly, easily. *h.*

یوناچارج यवनाचार्य yavanāchārj, m. an astro- nomical writer frequently quoted, perhaps Ptolemy. *s.*

یونال यवनाल yavanāl, m. a sort of grass, the grain of which is eaten (*Andropogon* or *Holcus bicolor*). *s.*

یونان yūnān, Ionia, Ancient Greece, so called till subdued by the Romans, after which the term *Rūm* has been generally applied to the Eastern Roman Empire at large. *a.*

یونانی yūnānī, m. an Ionian, a Grecian. *a.*

یونانیان yūnāniyān, the Ionians, the Greeks. *a.*

یونس yūnas, m. the prophet Jonah or Jonas. *a.*

یونی योनी yonī, f. the womb, the vulva yaunī, relating to the womb, uterine. *yavanī*, f. a female *yavan.* *s.*

یوون यौवन yauvan, m. youth, manhood. *yauvan-dashā*, f. adolescence. *yauvan-darp*, m. pride of youth, rashness. *s.*

یوونوان यौवनवान yauvan-wān, m. } young,
یوونوتی यौवनवती yauvan-watī, f. } youth-
ful. *s.*

یہ यिह yih or यह yah, pron. this, he, she, i*t*, the. *h.*

یہاں यहाँ yahān̐, here, hither; as a masc preposition it denotes at, or in possession of, like the French *chez*, as *mere yahān̐*, in my house, or in my possession, "chez moi." *yahān̐-tak*, or *-talak*, or *-lag*, thus far, to such a degree. *yahān̐-se*, hence. *yahān̐ kā yahīn̐*, in this very place, exactly here. *yahān̐ kahīn̐*, here or hereabouts. *s.*

یہود yahūd, m. a Jew, a Hebrew. *a.*

یہودا yahūdā, Judah, Judas, Jude. *a*

یہودانہ yahūdāna, adv. after the Jewish man- ner; m. a strip of yellow cloth which Jews are obliged to wear as a badge of distinction in some *Muham madan* countries. *a. p.*

یہودی yahūdī (v. yahūd), a Jew. *a.*

یہودیہ yahūdīya, the land of Judea. *a.*

یہوں yhūn̐ (for yūn̐), thus, so. *d.*

یہی यिही yihī यही or yahī, the same, itself, this very (person or thing). *h.*

یہیں यहीं yahīn̐, even here. *yahīn̐-se*, hence, on this very account. *h.*

یے ये ye (pl. of yih), these, they. *ye-hī* or *ye,ī*, these very (persons, &c.). *h.*

ییلم yelam, m. (v. ایلم elam) an auction, a [sale. *d.*